Traveling With Your Pet
The AAA PetBook®

The AAA guide to more than 12,000
pet-friendly, AAA-RATED® lodgings
and 400 campgrounds
across the United States and Canada

7th Edition

AAA PUBLISHING

President & CEO	**Robert Darbelnet**
Executive Vice President, Publishing & Administration	**Rick Rinner**
Managing Director, Travel Information	**Bob Hopkins**
Director, Product Development & Sales	**Bill Wood**
Director, Publishing Marketing	**Patty Wight**
Director, Manufacturing & Quality	**Susan Sears**
Director, Tourism Information Development (TID)	**Michael Petrone**
Director, Publishing Operations/Travel Information	**Jeff Zimmerman**
Director, Publishing/GIS Systems & Development	**Ramin Kalhor**
Director, GIS/Cartography	**Jan Coyne**
Director, Purchasing & Corporate Services	**Becky Barrett**
Director, Business Development	**Gary Sisco**
Product Manager	**Lisa Spence**
Manager, Business Line Publicity	**Justin McNaull**
Print Buyer	**Bob Bailes**
TID Regional Managers	**Lisa Brenneman, Todd Cronson, Michel Mousseau, Stacy Brunick, Patrick Schardin**
TID Field Operations Manager	**Laurie DiMinico**
Manager, Travel Information Operations	**Brenda Daniels**
Publishing Business Manager	**Linda Indolfi**
Manager, Electronic Media Design	**Mike McCrary**
Manager, Pre-Press/Photo Services & Product Support	**Tim Johnson**
Manager, Graphic Communication Services	**Yvonne Macklin**
Manager, Application Development	**Scott Chrisien**
Development Editor	**Greg Weekes**
Art Director and Cover Design	**Barbra Natali**
Photo Research	**Denise Campbell**
Quality Services	**Andrea Payne-Lecky**
Paginator	**Christine Carter**
Technical Specialist	**Roland Levett**
System Analyst	**Samuel Allen**
Programmer	**James Cothrine**
Data Processors	**Janice Bruno, Dawn Garrison, Kelly Giewont, Jennifer Lopresti, Andrea Tlumacki**
Proofreader	**Janet D'Amico**

AAA wishes to acknowledge the following for their assistance: Dogpark.com®

Cover Photos

Couple walking on dock	**Benelux Press/Index Stock/PictureQuest**
Kutya and owner in park	**AAA Photo Contest winner Edua Wilde**
Mr. Henry	**AAA Photo Contest winner Amy Sauer**

Published by AAA Publishing
1000 AAA Drive, Heathrow, Florida 32746

Seventh Edition Copyright © 2005 AAA Publishing. All rights reserved.
ISBN 1-59508-041-4 Stock Number 552205
Printed in the USA by Dickinson Press

Traveling with Your Pet Photo Contest Entry Form

The next time you go on vacation with your pet, be sure to take along your camera.

The winning entry in AAA's PetBook Photo Contest will appear on the cover of the 8th edition of **Traveling With Your Pet: The AAA PetBook®**. The winner also will receive $100, five complimentary copies of the book as well as a year's supply of Milk-bone dog snacks.

MILK·BONE

Please print

Name: _____

Address: _____

City: _____ **State:** _____ **Zip code:** _____

Daytime phone: _____ **Evening phone:** _____

Pet's name: _____ **Animal breed:** _____

Please answer the following questions:

*1. Why do you travel with your pet? _____

_____

*2. What is your favorite place or city to take your pet, and why? _____

_____

3. Tell us about an adventure you had while traveling with your pet. _____

_____

*Required answer

Official Rules

1. Email digital photos to Petbookcontest@national.aaa.com. Please send the photo as a .jpeg file attachment no larger than 2 MB, and include the information requested on the entry form in the body of the email. The digital photo must have a minimum resolution of 1200 pixels by 1600 pixels. The entry form information (name, address, phone, pet's name, animal breed and answers to questions) must be included in the email for contest consideration. Minor digital enhancement for cropping, red-eye removal, filters and correction functions are permitted, but images that are determined to be significantly altered will be disqualified. Photographers are not permitted to place borders or frames around their image or to place a watermark, signature, date or copyright notices on the image.

2. Send printed photos that are in focus, color and no larger than 8" x 10" unmounted along with the completed entry form to:

> **PetBook Photo Contest**
> **AAA**
> **1000 AAA Drive, MS 64**
> **Heathrow, FL 32746**

Official Rules *continued*

3. Photos must be postmarked by Nov. 22, 2005, and received by Nov. 30, 2005, to be eligible for the contest.

4. Photos must feature at least one pet and have a travel theme.

5. The entrant must be the person who took the photo and who has full rights to the photo.

6. The entrant must obtain full consent from all models or persons appearing in the photo for full use of the photo, including use and publishing in this contest and the other uses stated herein.

7. More than one photo may be entered, but a separate, completed entry form must accompany each photo. (This includes photos sent digitally.)

8. The photos become the property of AAA and will not be returned. The prize-winning photo, including all rights of every kind therein, will become the sole and exclusive property of AAA.

9. A panel of judges will choose the winning photo based on the following qualities: impact, lighting, composition and effectively conveying the idea that *Traveling With Your Pet: The AAA PetBook*® is about traveling on vacation with your pet. Posed or studio photographs are not preferred.

10. The winner will be notified **by mail** by Dec. 19, 2005.

Disclaimer

By participating, entrants agree that: (i) these rules and the decisions of AAA shall be final in all respects, and (ii) AAA may put the winner's photo on the front or back cover or spine of the 8th edition of Traveling With Your Pet: The AAA PetBook®. The winner grants AAA the right to use his or her name, likeness, portrait, picture, photo, answers on entry form and/or prize information for advertising, publicity and promotional purposes relating to the book, *Traveling With Your Pet: The AAA PetBook*, and the contest without compensation or permission (unless prohibited by law). The winner agrees to hold harmless and release AAA from any injuries, losses or damages of any kind that may result from taking a photo intended to be submitted. The pet travel accessories prize will be selected at the sole discretion of AAA. The winner agrees to hold harmless and release AAA from use of the pet travel accessories. AAA is not responsible for late, lost or misdirected entries or mail; for technical, hardware or software malfunctions, lost or unavailable network connections, or failed, incorrect, inaccurate, incomplete, garbled or delayed electronic communications, whether caused by the sender or by any of the equipment or programming associated with or utilized in this promotion, or by any human error that may occur in the processing of entries; or for loss of or damage to any entries. AAA retains the right to not award the prize should no acceptable photos be received.

Eligibility

No purchase is necessary to enter the contest or claim the prize. Open to U.S. or Canadian residents 18 years or older except for employees of AAA, CAA and their clubs.

By submitting an entry I agree that I have read the Contest Rules, assent thereto, and submit the enclosed picture in accordance therewith; I attest thatI own all rights to the picture and it has not been published or accepted for publication in any medium; and if the picture portrays any living person or persons, I have secured a model release or releases. I further agree that should my entry be chosen as the winning entry I will execute all necessary paperwork/releases as requested by AAA.

ABOUT THIS BOOK

Welcome to the 7th edition of *Traveling With Your Pet — The AAA PetBook*®. *Traveling With Your Pet* is a must for the traveler who's also an animal lover. This comprehensive book provides all the information you need to know about taking a four-legged friend on the road. Will Spot be a good car passenger? Is it safe to take Snowball on a plane? What are the important rules of pet etiquette? Is pet insurance a good idea? *Traveling With Your Pet* answers all of these questions and more. Here are just some of the features covered:

- Dog parks where you and your furry friends can play, exercise or just relax.

- An extensive listing of animal clinics compiled by the Veterinary Emergency & Critical Care Society. Names, addresses and phone numbers provide valuable information for unexpected or emergency situations, both en route and at your destination.

- A roundup of pet-friendly attractions.

- National public lands in the United States and Canada that allow pets, along with recreation information.

- Border crossing procedures and tips for travelers — both entering Canada from the United States and vice versa.

- Policies pertaining to service animals.

Traveling With Your Pet lists more than 12,000 AAA-RATED® lodgings. And the listings show AAA's trustworthy diamond ratings, the traveler's assurance of quality. Other handy features include:

- Informative highway directions.

- Specific information about lodgings' pet policies: deposits and fees (rounded to the nearest dollar), housekeeping service, designated rooms and other stipulations relating to travelers with pets.

- Additional details about the lodgings themselves, including icons for amenities, recreation, dining and accessibility.

- Icons designating AAA's member discount programs.

- Listings for AAA's highest rated campgrounds, including rate and pet policy information and service/amenity icons.

All of this valuable information is packaged in a contemporary, easy-to-read format, making *Traveling With Your Pet — The AAA PetBook* as indispensable an on-the-road companion as Spot's water dish or Snowball's litter box. Don't leave home without it, and remember: It always pays to *Travel With Someone You Trust*®.

TABLE OF CONTENTS

Traveling With Pets

Many people view their pets as full-fledged members of the family. Spot and Snowball often have their own beds, premium-quality foods, a basketful of toys and a special place in their humans' hearts.

Until it's time to go on vacation, that is. Then the family dog or cat is consigned to "watching the fort" at home while everyone else experiences the joy of traveling. Many pet lovers hesitate to take their animals with them because they don't think they'll be able to find accommodations that accept four-legged guests. Others aren't sure how — or if — their furry friends will adapt.

The truth is, including a pet in the family vacation is fairly easy, so long as you plan ahead. Most pets respond well to travel, a fact that isn't lost on the tourism industry. More than 12,000 AAA-RATED® hotels and motels from coast to coast are pet-friendly, and airline bookings for pet passengers are on the rise. Great companions at home, pets are earning their stripes on the road, too.

So if you've been longing to hit the trail with a canine or feline companion, read the tips on the following pages. You may find that a getaway can be far more enjoyable with than without your pet.

Should Your Pet Travel?

Before you make reservations, determine if your pet is able to travel. Most animals can and do make the most of the experience, but a small percentage simply are not cut out for traveling. Illness, physical condition and temperament are important factors, as is your pet's ability to adjust to such stresses as changes to his environment and routine. When in doubt, check with your veterinarian. If you feel your pet isn't up to the trip, it's better for everyone if he stays home.

❀ Rule 1: Pets who are very young, very old, pregnant, sick, injured, prone to biting or excessive vocalizing, or who cannot follow basic obedience commands should not travel.

Even if Spot and Snowball are seasoned travelers, take into account the type of vacation and activities you have planned. No pet is going to be happy (or safe) cooped up in a car or hotel room. Likewise, the family dog may love camping and hiking, but the family cat may not. Putting a little thought toward your animal's needs and safety will pay off in a more enjoyable vacation for everyone.

❀ Rule 2: If your pet can't actively participate in the trip, she should stay home.

Most of the information in this book pertains to cats and dogs. If you own a bird, hamster, pig, ferret, lizard or other exotic creature, remember that unusual animals are not always accepted as readily as more conventional pets. Always specify the type of pet you have when making arrangements.

Also check states' animal policies. **Hawaii** imposes 5-, 30- and 120-day quarantines for all imported carnivorous animals to prevent the importation of rabies. Guide dogs and other service animals are exempt from the quarantine provided they have a standard health certificate and a current rabies vaccination with documentation of the product name, lot or serial number and the lot expiration date. Upon arrival they still must be examined for external parasites and undergo serum antibody testing and microchip identification. For additional details, obtain the brochure Animal Quarantine Station Rabies Information from the Hawaii Department of Agriculture, Animal Quarantine Station, 99-951 Halawa Valley St., Aiea, HI 96701-5602; phone (808) 483-7151, fax (808) 483-7161. The Web site address is www.hawaiiag.org/hdoa/ai_aqs_info.htm.

North Carolina has stringent restrictions regarding pets in lodgings. Make certain you understand an accommodation's specific policies before making reservations.

❀ Rule 3: Be specific when making travel plans that include your pet. Nobody wants unpleasant surprises on vacation.

If Spot and Snowball stay behind, leave them in good hands while you're gone. **Family, friends and neighbors** make good sitters (provided they're willing), especially if they know your pet and can care for him in your home. Provide detailed instructions for feeding, exercise and medication, as well as phone numbers for your destination, your veterinarian and your local animal emergency clinic.

Professional pet sitters offer a range of services, from feeding and walking your pet daily to full-time house sitting while you are gone. Interview several candidates, and always check credentials and references. For additional information, contact the National Association of Professional Pet Sitters or Pet Sitters International. *(See sidebars on p. 8 and p. 9.)*

Kennels board many animals simultaneously and generally are run by professionals who will provide food and exercise according to your instructions. Pets usually are kept in a run (dogs) or cage (cats and small dogs) and may not get the same level of human interaction as at home. **Veterinary clinics** also board pets and may be the best choice if yours is sick, injured or needs special medical care. For further information on how to select a kennel, contact the American Boarding Kennels Association.

Veterinarians, fellow pet owners and professional associations are a good source of referrals for sitters and kennels.

❀ Rule 4: Never leave your pet with someone you don't trust.

Travelers Who Have Disabilities

Individuals with disabilities who own service animals to assist them with everyday activities undoubtedly face challenges, but traveling should not be one of them. Service animals (the accepted term for animals trained to help people with disabilities) are not pets and thus are not subject to many of the laws or policies pertaining to pets.

The Americans With Disabilities Act (ADA) defines a service animal as "any guide dog, signal dog or other animal individually trained to provide assistance to an individual with a disability." ADA regulations stipulate that public accommodations are required to modify policies, practices and procedures to permit the use of a service animal by an individual with a disability.

The purpose of these regulations is to provide equal access opportunities for people with disabilities and to ensure that they are not separated from their service animals. A tow truck operator, for example, must allow a service animal to ride in the truck with her owner rather than in the towed vehicle.

Public accommodations may charge a fee or deposit to an individual who has a disability — provided that fee or deposit is required of all customers — but no fees or deposits may be charged for the service animal, even those normally charged for pets.

The handler (the animal's owner) is responsible for her care and behavior; if she creates an altercation or poses a direct threat, the handler may be required to remove the animal from the premises and pay for any resulting damages.

Choosing a Pet Sitter

Before hiring a pet sitter, ask:

- Is he or she insured (for commercial liability) and bonded?
- What is included in the fee?
- Does the sitter require that your pet have a current vaccination?
- What kind of animals does the sitter typically care for?
- How will a medical, weather or home emergency be handled?
- Does he or she fully understand your pet's medical or dietary needs?
- How much time will be spent with your pet?

The pet sitter should:

- Have a polished, professional attitude.
- Provide references.
- Have a standard contract outlining terms of service.
- Have experience in caring for animals.
- Insist on current vaccinations.
- Ask about your pet's health, temperament, schedule and needs.
- Visit and interact with your pet before you leave.
- Devote time and attention to your pet.
- Be affiliated with pet care organizations.

Be sure you:

- Explain your pet's personality — favorite toys, good and bad habits, hiding spots, general health, etc.
- Leave care instructions, keys, food and water dishes, extra supplies (food, medication, etc.), and phone numbers for your veterinarian and an emergency contact.
- Bring pets inside before leaving.

Choosing a Kennel

Before reserving a kennel, ask:

- What is included in the fee?
- Are current vaccinations required?
- What kind of animals do they board?
- How will a medical or weather emergency be handled?
- Will your pet be kept in a cage or run?
- Will your pet receive daily exercise?
- Does the kennel fully understand your pet's medical or dietary needs?
- How and how often will staff interact with your pet?

The kennel should:

- Require proof of current vaccinations.
- Be clean, well-ventilated and offer adequate protection from the elements.
- Have separate areas for dogs, cats and other animals, with secure fencing and caging.
- Clean and disinfect facilities daily.
- Give your pet his regular food on his regular schedule.
- Provide soft bedding in runs/cages.
- Understand your pet's medical needs.
- Provide or obtain veterinary care if necessary.
- Offer sufficient supervision.
- Have a friendly, animal-loving staff.

Be sure you:

- Notify staff of behavior quirks (dislike of other animals, children, etc.).
- Provide food and medication.
- Leave a familiar object with your pet.
- Leave phone numbers for your veterinarian and an emergency contact.
- Spend time with your pet before boarding him.

The **Delta Society,** an organization devoted to companion and service animals, has information about laws that affect people and service animals in public accommodations. Phone (425) 226-7357 for a catalog, or visit www.deltasociety.org.

Preparing Your Pet for Travel

Happily, many vacations can be planned to include fun activities for pets. Trips to parks, nature trails, the ocean or lakes offer exposure to the world beyond the window or fence at home, as well as the chance to explore new sights and sounds. Even the streets of an unfamiliar city can provide a smorgasbord of discoveries for your animal friend to enjoy.

Once you decide Spot and Snowball are ready to hit the road, plan accordingly:

❧ **Get a clean bill of health from the veterinarian.** Update your pet's vaccinations, check his general physical condition and obtain a health certificate showing proof of up-to-date inoculations, particularly rabies, distemper and kennel cough. Such documentation will be necessary if you cross state or country lines, and also may come in handy in the unlikely event your pet gets lost and must be retrieved from the local shelter. Don't forget to ask the doctor about potential health risks at your destination (Lyme disease, heartworm infection) and the necessary preventive measures.

If your pet is taking prescribed medicine pack a sufficient supply, plus a few days' extra. Also take the prescription in case you need a refill. Be prepared for emergencies by getting the names and numbers of clinics or doctors at your destination from your veterinarian or the American Animal Hospital Association. **Hint:** Obtain these references before you leave and keep them handy throughout the trip.

Make sure your pet is in good physical shape overall, especially if you are planning an active vacation. If your animal is primarily sedentary or overweight, he may not be up to lengthy hikes through the woods.

Note: Some owners believe a sedated animal will travel more easily than one that is fully aware, but this is rarely the case. In fact, tranquilizing an animal can make travel much more stressful. Always consult a veterinarian about what is best for your pet, and administer sedatives only under the doctor's direction. In addition, never give an animal medication that is specifically prescribed for humans. The dosage may be too high for an animal's much smaller body mass, or may cause dangerous side effects.

❧ **Acclimate your pet to car travel.** Even if you're flying, your pet will have to ride in the car to get to the airport or terminal, and you don't want any unpleasant surprises before departure.

CONTACT INFORMATION

The following organizations offer information, tips, brochures and other travel materials designed to help you and your pet enjoy a happy and safe vacation.

American Animal Hospital Association
12575 W. Bayaud Ave., Lakewood, CO 80228
(303) 986-2800 — www.healthypet.com

American Boarding Kennels Association
1702 East Pikes Peak Ave.
Colorado Springs, CO 80909
(719) 667-1600 — www.abka.com

American Society for the Prevention of Cruelty to Animals
424 E. 92nd St., New York, NY 10128-6804
(212) 876-7700 — www.aspca.org

American Veterinary Medical Association
1931 N. Meacham Rd., Suite 100
Schaumburg, IL 60173
(847) 925-8070 — www.avma.org

Dogpark.com®
716 Fourth St., San Rafael, CA 94901
www.dogpark.com

Humane Society of the United States
2100 L St. NW, Washington, DC 20037
(202) 452-1100 — www.hsus.org

National Association of Professional Pet Sitters
15000 Commerce Pkwy., Suite C
Mt. Laurel, NJ 08054
(856) 439-0324 — www.petsitters.org

PetGroomer.com
P.O. Box 2489
Yelm, WA 98597
(360) 446-5348 — www.petgroomer.com

Pet Sitters International
201 E. King St., King, NC 27021
(336) 983-9222 — www.petsit.com

USDA-APHIS
Deputy Administrator
USDA-APHIS-Animal Care
4700 River Rd., Unit 84
Riverdale, MD 20737
(301) 734-7833 — www.aphis.usda.gov/ac

Some animals are used to riding in the car and even enjoy it. But most associate the inside of the carrier or the car with one thing only: the annual visit to the V-E-T. Considering that these visits usually end with a jab from a sharp needle, it's no wonder that some pets forget their training and act up in the car. If this is your situation, you will have to re-train your animal to view a drive as a reward, not a punishment.

Begin by allowing your pet to become used to the car without actually going anywhere. Then take short trips to places that are fun for animals, such as the park or the drive-through window at a fast-food restaurant. (Keep those indulgent snacks to a minimum!) Be sure to praise her for good behavior with words, petting and healthy treats. It shouldn't take long before you and your furry friend are enjoying leisurely drives without incident. *(See Traveling by Car, p. 12.)*

🐾 **Brush up on behavior.** Will Snowball make a good travel companion? Or will he be an absolute terror on the road? Don't wait until the vacation is already under way to find out; review general behavioral guidelines with respect to your animal, keeping in mind that the unfamiliarity of travel situations may test the temperament of even the most well-behaved pet.

It's a good idea to socialize Spot by exposing her to other people and animals (especially if she normally stays inside). You're likely to encounter both on your trip, and it is important that she learns to behave properly in the company of strangers. Make her introduction to the outside world gradual, such as a walk in a new neighborhood or taking her along while you run errands. Exposure to new situations will help reduce fear of the unknown and result in more socially acceptable behavior.

Is your pet housebroken? How is he around children? Does he obey vocal commands? Be honest about your animal's ability to cope in unfamiliar surroundings. Depending on the length and nature of the trip and your pet's level of command response, an obedience refresher course might be a good idea.

🐾 **Learn about your destination.** Check into quarantines or other restrictions well in advance, and make follow-up calls as your departure date approaches. Find out what types of documentation will be required — not just en route, but on the way home as well.

Be aware of potential safety or health risks where you're going, and plan accordingly. For example, the southeastern United States — particularly Florida — is home to alligators and heartworm-carrying mosquitoes, and many mountainous and wooded areas may harbor ticks that transmit Lyme disease.

Confirm all travel plans within a few days of your departure, especially with lodgings and airlines; their policies may have changed after you made the reservations. If you plan to visit state parks or attractions that accept pets on the premises, obtain their animal regulations in advance.

🐾 **Determine the best mode of transportation.** Most people traveling with pets drive. Many airlines do accept animals in the passenger cabin or cargo hold, and as more

WHAT TO TAKE

❑ Carrier or crate. *(See Selecting a Carrier or Crate, p. 11, for specifications.)*

❑ Nylon or leather collar or harness, license tag, ID tag(s) and leash. All should be sturdy and should fit your pet properly.

❑ Food and water dishes.

❑ Can opener and spoon (for canned food).

❑ An ample supply of food, plus a few days' extra.

❑ Bottled water from home. (Many animals are finicky about their drinking water.)

❑ Cooler with ice.

❑ Healthy treats.

❑ Medications, if necessary.

❑ Health certificate and other required documents.

❑ A blanket or other bedding. (If your pet is used to sleeping on the furniture, bring an old blanket or sheet to place on top of the hotel's bedding.)

❑ Litter supplies (for cats or other small animals), a scooper and plastic bags (for dogs).

❑ Favorite toys.

❑ Carpet deodorizer.

❑ Chewing preventative.

❑ A recent photograph and a written description including name, breed, gender, height, weight, coloring and distinctive markings.

❑ Grooming supplies:
comb/brush
nail clippers
shampoo
cloth and paper towels
cotton balls/tissues

❑ First-aid kit:
gauze, bandages and adhesive tape
hydrogen peroxide
rubbing alcohol
ointment
muzzle
scissors
tweezers (for removing ticks, burrs, splinters, etc.)
local emergency phone numbers
first-aid guide (such as *Pet First Aid: Cats & Dogs*, published by The Humane Society of the United States and the American Red Cross)

people choose to fly with their pet airlines are becoming more pet-conscious. Restrictions vary as to the type and number of pets an airline will carry, however, so inquire about animal shipping and welfare policies before making reservations. If your pet must travel in the cargo hold, heed the cautionary advice in the Traveling by Air section. *(See p. 12.)*

Flying is really the only major option to car travel. Amtrak, as well as Greyhound and other interstate bus lines, do not accept pets. **Note:** Seeing-eye dogs and other service animals are exempt from the regulations prohibiting pets on Amtrak and interstate bus lines. Local rail and bus companies may allow pets in small carriers, but this is an exception rather than a rule.

The only cruise ship that currently permits pets is the Cunard Line's *Queen Elizabeth 2* (on trans-Atlantic crossings); kennels are provided, but animals are accepted on a very limited basis. Some charter and sightseeing boat companies permit pets onboard, however.

A word of advice: Never try to sneak your pet onto any mode of public transportation where she is not permitted. You may face legal action or fines, and the animal may be confiscated if discovered.

🐾 **Pack as carefully for your pet as you do for yourself.** *(See checklist, below.)* Make sure she has a collar with a license tag and ID tag(s) listing her name and yours, along with your address and phone number. As an added precaution, some owners outfit their dog with a second tag listing the name and number of a contact person at home. Popular backup identification methods are to have your animal tattooed with an ID number (usually a social security number) or to implant a microchip under her skin.

If your pet requires medication, make sure that is specified on his tag. This helps others understand your animal's needs and also may prevent people from keeping a found pet or from stealing one to sell.

Note: Choke chains, collars that tighten when they are pulled, may be useful during training sessions, but they do not make good full-time collars. If the chain catches on something, your pet could choke herself trying to pull free. For regular wear, use a harness or a conventional collar made of nylon or leather.

Selecting a Carrier or Crate

This is one of the most important steps in ensuring your pet's safety when traveling. A good-quality carrier not only contains your pet during transit, it also gives him a safe, reassuring place to stay when confinement is necessary at your destination. Acclimate the animal before the trip so he views the crate as a cozy den, not a place of exile.

If you plan to travel by car, a carrier will confine your pet en route, and also may come in handy if Spot or Snowball must stay in the room unsupervised. A secured crate will prevent your pet from escaping from the room when the cleaning staff arrives, or at night if camping in the open. *(See At Your Destination, p. 15.)*

Some airlines allow small pets to travel in the passenger cabin as carry-on luggage. There are no laws dictating the type of carrier to use, but remember that it must be small enough to fit under a standard airplane seat, usually **13 by 9 by 23 inches or 10 by 16 by 24 inches.** If your pet will be flying in the cargo hold, you must use a carrier that meets U.S. Department of Agriculture Animal and Plant Health Inspection Service (USDA-APHIS) specifications. *(See Traveling by Air, p. 12.)*

Crates are available at pet supply stores; some airlines also sell carriers. Soft-sided travel bags are handy for flyers with small pets. The Sherpa Bags sold by Sherpa's Pet Trading Co. are approved by most major airlines and are available in three sizes for animals weighing up to 6, 16 and 22 pounds; phone (800) 743-7723 for information, or visit their Web site: www.sherpapet.com.

Even if you never take to the skies, these common-sense guidelines provide a good rule of thumb in selecting a crate for other uses. USDA-APHIS rules stipulate the following:

🐾 The crate must be enclosed, but with ventilation openings occupying at least 14 percent of total wall space, at least one-third of which must be located on the top half of the kennel. A three-quarter-inch lip or rim must surround the exterior to prevent air holes from being blocked.

🐾 The crate must open easily, but must be sufficiently strong to hold up during normal cargo transit procedures (loading, unloading, etc.).

🐾 The floor must be solid and leakproof, and must be covered with an absorbent lining or material (such as an old towel or litter).

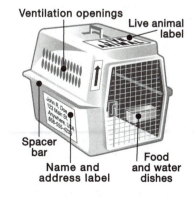

Ventilation openings

Live animal label

Spacer bar

Name and address label

Food and water dishes

❧ The crate must be just large enough to allow the animal to turn freely while standing, and to have a full range of normal movement while standing or lying down.

❧ The crate must offer exterior grips or handles so that handlers do not have to place their hands or fingers inside.

❧ If the carrier has wheels, they must be removed or immobilized prior to loading.

❧ One-inch lettering stating "Live Animal" or "Wild Animal" must be placed visibly on the exterior, and must be accompanied by directional arrows showing the crate's proper orientation. It also is a good idea to label the crate with your name, home address and home phone number, as well as an address and phone number where you can be reached during the trip. (Hint: Use an adhesive label or an indelible marker and write directly on the crate, as paper may be ripped off accidentally in transit.)

❧ Attach a list of care instructions (feeding, watering, etc.) for a 24-hour period to the exterior of the carrier. This will help airport workers care for your pet if he is sent to the wrong destination.

❧ If you are traveling with multiple pets, note that crates may contain only one animal whose weight exceeds 20 pounds. Smaller animals may travel together under the following guidelines: one species to a crate, except compatible dogs and cats of similar size; two puppies or kittens under 6 months of age; 15 guinea pigs or rabbits; 50 hamsters. **Note:** These are federal limits; airlines may impose more stringent regulations.

Traveling by Car

The first step in ensuring your pet's well-being during a vacation is to train her to ride in the car. For safety reasons, pets should be confined to the back seat, either in a carrier or a harness attached to the car's seat belt. This keeps the animal from interfering with or distracting the driver, and also may save her life in the event of an accident. And a restrained animal will not be able to break free and run away the second the car door is opened.

To help prevent car sickness, feed your pet a light meal four to six hours before departing. Do not give an animal food or water in a moving vehicle.

Never allow your pet to ride in the bed of a pickup truck. It's illegal in some states; he also can jump out or be thrown, endangering himself and others on the road. Harnessing or leashing him to the truck bed is not advisable either: If he tries to jump out, he could be dragged along the road or the restraint could become a noose. Avoid placing animals in campers or trailers as well. **If your pet cannot ride in the car with you, leave him at home.**

Don't let your dog stick her head out the window, no matter how enjoyable it seems. Road debris and other flying objects can injure delicate eyes and ears, and the animal is at greater risk for severe injury if the vehicle should stop suddenly or be struck. If it is hot outside, run the air conditioner instead of opening the windows, and be sure that the air flow is reaching your pet.

AAA recommends that drivers stop every two hours to stretch their legs and take a quick break from driving. Your pet will appreciate the same break. Plan to visit a rest stop every four hours or so to let him have a drink and a chance to answer the call of nature. (Cat owners should bring along a litter box; dog owners should clean up afterward.)

Be sure your pet is leashed before opening the car door. This is not merely a courtesy to fellow travelers; it will prevent her from unexpectedly breaking free and running away. Keep in mind that even the most obedient pet may become disoriented during travel or in strange places and set off for home. **Hint:** If your pet is not used to traveling, use a harness instead of a collar; it is more difficult for an animal to wriggle out of a harness.

NEVER leave an animal in a parked car, even if the windows are partially open. Even on pleasant days the temperature inside a car can soar to well over 100 degrees in less than 10 minutes, placing your pet at risk for heatstroke and possibly death. On very cold days, hypothermia is a risk. Also, animals left unattended in parked cars frequently are stolen.

Traveling by Air

(Service animals are normally exempt from most of the regulations and fees specified in this section. Check policies with the airline when making reservations.)

Opinion is divided as to whether air travel is truly safe for pets. Statistically, it is less dangerous than being a passenger in a car, but some experts warn of potentially deadly conditions for animals. The truth lies somewhere in between: Most pets arrive at their destination in fine condition, but death or injury is always a possibility. Before you decide to fly, know the risk factors and the necessary precautions to keep your pet safe.

❧ **Determine whether your pet is fit to fly.** The Animal Welfare Act (AWA), administered by USDA-APHIS, specifies that dogs and cats must be at least eight weeks old and weaned at least five days before air travel. Animals that are very young, very old, pregnant, ill or injured should not fly at all. Cats, snub-nosed dogs (pugs, boxers, etc.) and long-nosed dogs (shelties, collies, etc.) are prone to severe respiratory difficulties in an airplane's poorly ventilated cargo hold and should travel only in the passenger cabin (if size allows) with their owner.

❧ **Decide where your pet will fly.** Most animals fly in the hold as checked baggage when traveling with their owners, or as cargo when they are unaccompanied. The AWA was enacted to ensure animals traveling in this manner are treated humanely and are not subjected to dangerous or life-threatening conditions. For specific requirements pertaining to your animal, check with the airline in advance, as policies vary. Some airlines will not ship dogs as checked baggage, and United Airlines will only accept dogs shipped as cargo from "known shippers"; i.e., commercial shippers or licensed pet breeders.

Items classified as "dangerous goods" (dry ice or toxic chemicals, for example) must be transported in a different part of the hold from where live animals are carried. Some planes are designed to have separate hold areas, but so-called "people mover" airlines that are primarily interested in getting human passengers from one point to another as quickly as possible may not give priority to this feature. Check your airline's specific baggage policies so you know exactly where in the hold your pet will be traveling.

Small pets may be taken into the passenger cabin with you as carry-on luggage. This places the animal's welfare squarely in your hands but is feasible only if he is very well-behaved and fits comfortably in a container that meets standard carry-on regulations. *(See Selecting a Carrier or Crate, p. 11.)* Keep in mind that the carrier — with the animal inside — must be kept under the seat in front of you throughout the flight. **Note:** AWA regulations do not apply to animals traveling in the cabin.

❧ **Do your homework.** Investigate the airline's animal transport and welfare policies, especially if you are flying with a small or commuter airline. All airlines are subject to basic AWA regulations, but specific standards of care vary greatly from one company to another. Do your research well in advance and confirm the information 24-48 hours before departing.

The more information an airline provides, the better care your pet is likely to receive. Beware of companies that have vague animal welfare guidelines, or none at all. All major airlines provide information about pet transport on their websites. Also talk to fellow travelers and pet owners about their experiences. Finally, keep in mind that airlines are not required to transport live animals and can refuse to carry them for any reason.

❧ **Protect your investment.** Most people think of their pets as part of the family, but the legal system assigns them the same value as a piece of luggage. Inquire about insurance — an airline that won't insure animals in its care may not be the right one for your pet. (Always read the fine print before purchasing any insurance policy.) Also ask if the airline's workers are trained to handle animals. Few are, but it doesn't hurt to check. Remember, it's up to you to choose an airline that values pets and will treat yours with care.

HEATSTROKE AND HYPOTHERMIA

The best way to treat heatstroke or hypothermia is to prevent it. Do not leave pets unattended in a car, even if only for a few minutes. Also heed airlines' restrictions on pet travel, and carefully investigate animal welfare policies to make certain the airline has safeguards to protect your pet from both conditions.

Other preventive measures are to avoid strenuous exercise — including such activities as hiking and "fetch" — when the sun is strongest (10 a.m.-2 p.m.), and to provide your pet access to clean, fresh drinking water at all times.

Following are the warning signs and basic first aid for heatstroke and hypothermia. Always be alert to your pet's physical condition and watch for symptoms — immediate attention to the situation may mean the difference between life and death. If your pet is struck with either disorder, take him to an animal hospital or veterinarian as fast as safely possible.

HEATSTROKE

Symptoms
- rapid, shallow breathing
- excessive salivation
- heavy panting
- hot to the touch
- glazed eyes
- unsteadiness, dizziness
- deep red or purple tongue or gums
- vomiting
- body temperature of 104 F or higher

First Aid
- place pet in the shade
- quickly dampen with cool water, especially on the head and neck
- give small amounts of water

HYPOTHERMIA

Symptoms
- shivering
- weakness
- lethargy
- cold to the touch
- body temperature of 95 F or lower

First Aid
- place in a warm area
- wrap in towels or a blanket
- quickly warm by gently massaging the head, chest and extremities

❀ **Understand the potential hazards.** Because a plane's cargo hold is neither cooled nor heated until take off, the most dangerous time for your pet is that spent on the ground in this unventilated compartment. In summer the space absorbs heat while the plane sits on the tarmac; the reverse is true in winter, when it is no warmer inside the hold than outside. Both instances expose pets to the possibility of serious injury or death from heatstroke or hypothermia. **Note:** The latter also may be a concern during flight if the hold's heater is disabled or turned off, allowing the temperature to drop to near-freezing levels.

To minimize these risks, USDA-APHIS rules prohibit animals from being kept in the hold or on the tarmac for more than 45 minutes when temperatures are above 85 F or below 45 F. Some airlines impose even tighter temperature restrictions and may not permit animals to fly on planes going to cities where the ground temperatures may exceed these limits. American and Delta, for example, do not carry animals in their cargo holds May 15 through Sept. 15. (Exceptions may be made for animals whose veterinarians certify they are acclimated to colder temperatures, but never warmer.)

❀ **Make stress-free travel arrangements.** Once you decide to fly, reserve space for Spot or Snowball when you arrange your own tickets, preferably well in advance of your travel date. Airlines accept only a limited number of animals per flight — usually two to four in the passenger cabin and one pet per passenger — on a first-come, first-served basis. More animals are generally allowed in the cargo hold.

Prepare to pay an additional fee, about $75-$100 each way; the cost is often greater for large animals traveling on a flight without their owner. (Unfortunately, pets are not eligible for frequent flyer miles.) Always reconfirm your reservations and flight information 24-48 hours before departure.

If your pet will be flying in the hold, travel on the same plane and reserve a nonstop flight. This not only reduces the danger of heatstroke or hypothermia during layovers, it also eliminates the possibility that she will be placed on the wrong connecting flight. In summer, fly during the early morning or late evening when temperatures are cooler. Because of large crowds and the chance of heavy air traffic causing delays, avoid holiday travel whenever possible.

Additional precautions may be necessary when traveling outside the United States and Canada. Other countries may impose lengthy quarantines, and airline workers outside North America may not be bound by animal welfare laws. *(See International Travel, p. 17.)*

❀ **Play an active role in your pet's well-being.** Flying safely with your pet requires careful planning and attention to its welfare. See the veterinarian within 10 days of departure for a health certificate (required by most airlines) and a pre-flight check-up.

Address any concerns you have about your pet traveling by air, especially if you are considering tranquilization. Sedation usually is not recommended for cats and dogs, regardless of whether they fly in the cabin or in the hold. Exposure to increased altitude pressure can create respiratory and cardiovascular problems; animals with short, wide heads are particularly susceptible to disorientation and possible injury. Sedation should never be administered without your veterinarian's approval.

Obtain an airline-approved carrier and acclimate your pet to its presence by leaving it open with a familiar object inside. A sturdy, well-ventilated crate adds an additional measure of protection.

Because animals are classified as luggage, they may be loaded on the plane via conveyor belt. If the crate falls off the belt, your pet could be injured or released. Ask that she be hand-carried on and off the plane, and that

AIRLINE CONTACT INFORMATION

Following is a list of the major North American airlines and their toll-free reservation numbers.

Website addresses have been given for those airline websites that include information about flying with animals. Hint: Look under links for baggage, cargo or programs and services, or do a site search for "pets."

Air Canada . . . . (888) 247-2262
www.aircanada.ca

Alaska Airlines . . . . (800) 252-7522
www.alaskaair.com

America West Airlines . . . . . . (800) 327-7810
www.americawest.com

American Airlines . . . . (800) 433-7300
www.americanair.com

Continental Airlines . . . . (800) 523-3273
www.continental.com

Delta Airlines. . . . . (800) 221-1212
www.delta.com

Northwest Airlines . . . . (800) 225-2525
www.nwa.com

Southwest Airlines . . . . (800) 435-9792
www.iflyswa.com

(Accepts service animals only.)

United Airlines . . . . (800) 864-8331
www.ual.com

US Airways . . . . (800) 428-4322
www.usair.com

you be permitted to watch both procedures. Also ask about "counter-to-counter" shipping, in which the animal is loaded immediately before departure and unloaded immediately after arrival. There usually is an additional fee for this service.

Make sure you will have access to your pet if there is a lengthy layover or delay. Think twice about flying on an airline that won't allow you to check on your animal under such circumstances.

❧ **Prepare for the flight.** Keep in mind that traveling with an animal will require additional pre-flight time and preparation on your part. Exercise your pet before the flight, and arrive at least two but not more than four hours before departure. If he is traveling as carry-on luggage, check-in is normally at the passenger terminal; if he is traveling as checked baggage or as cargo in the cargo hold, proceed to the airline's cargo terminal, which is often in a different location. Find this out when making reservations and again when confirming flight information.

Make sure your animal's crate is properly labeled and secured, but do not lock it in case airline personnel have to provide emergency care. Include an ice pack for extra comfort on a hot day or a hot water bottle on a cold day. **Hint:** Wrap in a towel to prevent leaking.

Do not feed your pet less than four hours before departure, but provide water up until boarding. **Hint:** Freeze water in the bowl so that it melts throughout the trip, providing a constant drinking source.

Spot or Snowball should wear a sturdy collar (breakaway collars are recommended for cats) and two identification tags marked with your name, home address and phone number, and travel address and phone number. It's also a good idea to clip your pet's nails before departure so they won't accidentally get caught on any part of the carrier.

Note: You may be required to take your pet out of the carrier as you pass through security on your way to the gate. Make sure the animal is wearing a collar and leash or harness.

Attach food and water dishes inside the carrier so that airline workers can reach them without opening the door. If the trip will take longer than 12 hours, also attach a plastic bag with at least one meal's worth of dry food. Animals under 16 weeks of age must be fed every 12 hours, adult animals every 24 hours. Water must be provided at least every 12 hours, regardless of the animal's age.

Allow your pet to answer the call of nature before boarding, but do not take her out of the carrier while in the terminal. As a courtesy, wait until you are outside and away from fellow travelers. Keep her leash with you — do not leave it inside or attached to the kennel.

If your pet is traveling as carry-on luggage, let the passenger sitting next to you know. Someone with allergies may want to change seats.

Perhaps the most important precaution is to alert the flight crew and the captain that your pet is aboard. The pilot must activate the heater for the cargo hold; make sure this is done once you are in the air. If there are layovers or delays, ask the flight crew to be sure your pet has adequate shelter and/or ventilation; better yet, ask them to allow you to check in person.

If you have arranged to watch your pet being unloaded, ask a flight attendant to call the baggage handlers and let them know you are on the way. Above all, do not hesitate to voice any concerns you have for your pet's welfare — it is your responsibility to do so.

❧ **Be prepared for emergencies.** In the unlikely event your pet gets lost en route, contact the airline, local humane shelters, animal control agencies or USDA-APHIS. Many airlines can trace a pet that was transferred to the wrong airport. If your pet is injured in transit, proceed to the nearest animal hospital; register any complaints with USDA-APHIS. **Hint:** Carry a list of emergency contact numbers and a current photograph of your pet in your wallet or purse, just in case.

At Your Destination

How well you and your companion behave on the road directly affects the way future furry travelers will be treated. Always clean up after your pet and keep him under your control. This is not only a courtesy to fellow human travelers; it's the surest way to enjoy a safe and happy vacation.

Inquire about pet policies before making lodging reservations. Properties may impose restrictions on the type or size of pet allowed, or they may designate only certain rooms, such as smoking rooms, for travelers with animals. If you have a dog, get a room on the first floor with direct access outside, preferably near a walking area; keep her leashed on any excursion.

Lodgings may have supervision policies requiring that pets be crated when unattended or that they may not be left alone at all. Allow your pet only in designated exercise or animal-approved areas; never take him into such off-limits places as the lobby, pool area, patio or restaurant. Prepare to receive limited housekeeping service, or none at all.

Expect to pay some type of additional charge, which may be per room or per pet and may include any of the following: refundable deposit, non-refundable deposit, daily fee, weekly fee.

If staying with friends or relatives, make certain your pet is a welcome guest. Know and respect their "house rules," especially if they have small children or pets of their own.

Once in the room, check for such hazards as chemically treated toilet water, hiding spaces and electrical cords before freeing your pet. Give her time to adjust to her new surroundings under your supervision.

Above all, practice good "petiquette":

🐾 Try not to leave your pet alone, but if you must, crate or otherwise confine her.

🐾 Crate at night as well.

🐾 To keep your pet and the housekeeper from having an unexpected encounter, leave the "Do Not Disturb" sign on the door when you go out without him.

🐾 Barking dogs make poor hotel neighbors — keep your pet quiet.

🐾 Don't allow your pet on the furniture. If she insists on sleeping on the bed, bring a bedspread or sheet from home and place that on top of the hotel bedding.

🐾 Clean up after your pet immediately — inside the room and out — and leave no trace of him behind when checking out.

🐾 Dispose of litter and other "accidents" properly — check with housekeeping.

🐾 Notify the management immediately if something is damaged, and be ready to pay for repairs.

🐾 Add a little extra to the housekeeping tip.

🐾 When you take your pet out of the room, keep her leashed, especially in wilderness areas and around small children. No matter how obedient she is at home, new stimuli and distractions may cause her to forget or ignore vocal commands. Know and obey animal policies at parks, beaches and other public areas. Check before arriving to make certain animals still are welcome, even if you've been there before — the rules may have changed.

🐾 Look for outdoor cafes when selecting restaurants. For health reasons, pets are not permitted inside eating establishments, but many restaurants allow animals to sit quietly with their owners at outdoor tables. Drive-through restaurants are another alternative.

In Case of Emergency

Be prepared for any turn of events by knowing how to get to the nearest animal hospital. *(See Animal Clinics, p. 48.)* Also have the name and number of a local animal shelter and a local veterinarian handy — ask your veterinarian for a recommendation. Take first-aid supplies with you and know how to use them. An animal in pain may become aggressive, so exercise caution at all times.

Emergency evacuation shelters do not accept pets, and domesticated animals do not fare well if left to weather an emergency on their own, especially when far from home. Avert a potential tragedy by planning in advance where you will go with your pet in case of evacuation. Use the listings in this book to find other lodgings willing to take you and your pet. Above all, don't wait for disaster to strike. Leave as soon as the evacuation order is announced, and take your animal with you.

The Great Outdoors

Travelers planning an active or camping vacation should make some additional preparations. Check in advance to be sure your pet is permitted at campgrounds, parks, beaches, trails and anywhere else you will be visiting. If there are restrictions — and there usually are — follow them. Remember that pets other than service animals usually are not allowed in public buildings.

Note: It is not advisable to take animals other than dogs into wilderness areas. For example, bringing a pet is not recommended at some national parks in Alaska. Also keep in mind that rural areas often have few veterinarians and even fewer boarding kennels.

Use common sense. Clean up after your pet, do not allow excessive vocalizing and keep her under your control. If the property requires your pet to be leashed or crated at all times, do so. Few parks or natural areas will allow a pet to be unattended, even when chained — the risk of disagreeable encounters with other travelers or wildlife is too great. The National Park Service may confiscate pets that harm wildlife or other visitors.

If camping, crate your pet at night to protect him from the elements and predators. (Chaining confines the animal but won't keep him from becoming a midnight snack.)

When hiking, stick to the trail and keep your pet on a short leash. It is all too easy for an unleashed pet to wander off and get lost or fall prey to a larger animal. Keep an eye out for such wildlife as alligators, bears, big cats, porcupines and skunks, and avoid other dogs and small children. Be aware of indigenous poisonous plants, such as English ivy and oleander, or those causing physical injury, such as cactus, poison ivy or stinging nettle. Your veterinarian or local poison control center should be able to give you a full list of hazardous flora.

Before setting out on the trail, make sure both of you are in good physical shape. An animal that rarely exercises at home will not suddenly be ready for a 10-mile trek across uneven terrain. Plan a hike well within the limits of your pet's endurance, and don't push — remember, if Spot gets too tired to make it back on her own, you'll have to carry her.

Carry basic first-aid supplies, including a first-aid guide. *(See What to Take, p. 10.)* Also carry fresh drinking water for both of you — "found" water may contain harmful germs or toxins. Drink often, not just when thirst strikes, and have your pet do the same. Watch for signs of dehydration, leg or foot injuries, heat exhaustion or heatstroke. Stop immediately and return home or to camp if any of these occur.

Note: Dogs can carry their own backpacks (check your local pet store for specially designed packs), but should never carry more than one-third of their body weight. Train the dog to accept the pack beforehand, and only use it with a strong, healthy animal in excellent physical condition.

No matter where or how you spend your vacation, visit the veterinarian when you return home to check for injuries, parasites and general health.

Note: Most campgrounds accept pets. The AAA CampBook guides are an excellent source for obtaining detailed information regarding pet policies, restrictions and extra charges for campgrounds in the United States and Canada. AAA members may obtain complimentary copies of the CampBook guides at their local AAA club.

Traveling Between the U.S. and Canada

Traveling across the international border with your pet — either from the United States into Canada or from Canada into the United States — should prove largely hassle-free, although some basic regulations need to be kept in mind.

Passports to enter Canada or return to the United States are not required for native-born citizens of either country. Proof of citizenship is required; a birth or baptismal certificate and a photo ID (a driver's license, which also establishes proof of residence) normally are sufficient. Naturalized citizens should carry their naturalization certificate, and U.S. resident aliens must have an Alien Registration Receipt Card (Green Card).

U.S. Customs grants returning U.S. citizens who stay in Canada more than 48 hours an individual $800 exemption (if not used within the prior 30 days). Any amount over the $800 exemption is subject to duty.

The exemption is based on fair retail value and applies to goods acquired for personal or household use or as gifts but not intended for sale. All items for which the exemption is claimed must accompany you upon return. A $200 exemption is granted for stays of less than 48 hours.

A 7 percent Goods and Service Tax (GST) is levied on most items sold and most services rendered in Canada. In Nova Scotia, New Brunswick and Newfoundland, a Harmonized Sales Tax (HST) of 15 percent (which includes the GST) is charged on goods and services. Rebates can be claimed on some items. Brochures that explain the GST and contain a rebate form are available at tourist information centers, customs offices and duty free shops at the border and in airports.

U.S. citizens taking pet cats and dogs three months of age and older into Canada must carry a health certificate signed by a licensed veterinarian that describes the animal and provides proof of rabies vaccination within the past 12 or 36 months, depending on the type of vaccine. Collar tags are not sufficient proof of immunization. The certificate also is

needed to bring a pet back into the United States; make sure the vaccination doesn't expire while you're in Canada.

Service animals are exempt from these rules. Also exempt are up to two puppies or kittens under three months old; obtain a certificate of health from your veterinarian indicating that the animal is too young to vaccinate. **Note:** Pets entering Canada through Newfoundland require a certificate and entry permit, which must be obtained in advance. For details, contact the Canadian Embassy; 501 Pennsylvania Ave. N.W., Washington, DC 20001; phone (202) 682-1740. The Web site address is www.canadianembassy.org.

The Canadian Food Inspection Agency (CFIA) provides additional pet information; phone (613) 225-2342. If you need assistance while in Canada, contact the U.S. Embassy, 490 Sussex Dr., Ottawa, ON, Canada K1N 1G8; phone (613) 238-5335.

Canadian Customs allows Canadian citizens to bring back from the United States, duty and tax free, goods valued up to $200 any number of times per year, provided the visit is 48 hours or more. A $50 exemption, excluding alcoholic beverages and tobacco products, may be claimed if the visit is 24 hours or more and no other exemption is being used. If returning from a visit of seven days or more (not counting the day of departure from Canada), the exemption goes up to $750.

Canadian travelers may take pet cats and dogs into the United States with no restrictions, but U.S. Customs requires that dogs have proof of rabies vaccination no less than 30 days before arrival. For additional information on U.S. regulations, contact the Animal and Veterinary Services department of the USDA-APHIS National Center for Import and Export, (301) 734-3277.

International Travel

If you plan to travel abroad with Spot or Snowball, prepare for a lengthy flight and at least a short quarantine period. Be aware that airline and animal workers in other countries may not be bound by the same animal welfare laws that exist in the United States and Canada. Contact the embassy or consulate at your destination for information about documentation and quarantine requirements, animal control laws and animal welfare regulations.

As with any trip, have your pet checked by your regular veterinarian within 10 days of departure to obtain a health certificate showing proof of rabies and other inoculations. If you are traveling with an animal other than a domesticated dog or cat, check with USDA-APHIS for restrictions or additional documentation required.

The booklet "Pets and Wildlife" has general information about traveling abroad with animals; write U.S. Customs & Border Protection, 1300 Pennsylvania Ave. NW, Room 34A, Washington, D.C. 20229; phone (202) 354-1000.

Note: Many island nations, such as Australia and the United Kingdom, are rabies-free and impose a quarantine on animals brought in from the United States and Canada. Hawaii imposes 5-, 30- and 120-day quarantines for all imported animals except guide dogs.

Loss Prevention Tips

Searching the woods or an unfamiliar town for a missing pet is easily prevented by following these helpful tips:

* Have your pet wear a sturdy nylon or leather collar with current ID and rabies tags firmly attached. Be sure the ID tag includes the phone number of an emergency contact.

* Keep your pet on a leash or harness. Even trained animals can become agitated or disoriented in unfamiliar surroundings and fail to obey vocal commands.

* Attach the leash or harness while your pet is still inside the closed car or crate.

* Do not leave your pet unattended at any time, anywhere. A stolen pet is extremely difficult to recover.

* Escape-proof your hotel room by crating your pet and asking hotel management to make certain no one enters your room while you are gone. (Inform the property that you're traveling with an animal when making reservations.)

* Take along a recent picture and a detailed written description of your pet.

If your pet gets lost these steps will improve your chances of recovery:

* If your pet is lost in transit, contact the airline immediately. Ask to trace the animal via the airline's automated baggage tracking system.

* Contact local police, animal control, animal shelters, humane organizations and veterinary clinics with a description and a recent photograph. Stay in contact until your pet is found, and provide your home and destination phone numbers.

* Post signs and place an ad in the local newspaper so that anyone who comes across your pet knows she is lost and how to reach you.

The Last Word

You are ultimately responsible for your pet's welfare and behavior while traveling. Since animals cannot speak for themselves, it is up to you to focus on your pet's well-being every step of the way. It also is important to make sure he conducts himself properly so that other pets will be welcome visitors in the future. Following the common-sense information in this book will help ensure that both you and your animal companion have a safe and happy trip.

PET-FRIENDLY PLACES

IN THE U.S. AND CANADA

Dog Parks
Attractions
National Public Lands
Animal Clinics

Dog Parks

A dog park is a place where people and their dogs can play together. These places offer dogs an area to play, exercise and socialize with other dogs while their owners enjoy the park-like setting. Dog park size and features vary greatly from location to location, from several hundred square feet in urban areas to several hundred acres in the suburbs and rural locations. Dog owners should remember to always keep their animal leashed until they reach the dog park entrance, to maintain voice control of their animal at all times, to bring their own supply of bags for picking up after their pet (and to be diligent in doing so), and to always have fresh water available for their dog. Please observe all dog park rules.

This list of dog parks in the United States and Canada is provided by Dogpark.com®. Dogpark.com is all about dogs — all breeds, all mixes of breeds, and all shapes, sizes and dispositions. It provides articles and information about dogs and their care, health and play. Online, visit www.dogpark.com.

The dog parks listed here welcome people who travel with their dogs; private parks or parks requiring local residency are not included. **Note:** Fence types and heights vary, and some areas have no fencing at all, requiring that the dog be under firm voice control.

United States

ARIZONA

Chaparral Park - Scottsdale
5401 N. Hayden Rd, (at the southeast corner of McDonald Drive and Hayden Road)
Daily sunrise-9 p.m.
2.2 acres, fenced, separate small and large dog areas, shade, water, benches, restroom.

Horizon Park - Scottsdale
15444 N. 100th St. (Thompson Peak Parkway and 100th Street, east of SR 101 off Frank Lloyd Wright Boulevard)
Daily sunrise-10:30 p.m.
Fenced, benches, tables, disposal bags, parking, phones, restrooms, lighted, trash cans, bring your own water, little shade.

Vista del Camino Park - Scottsdale
7700 East Pierce St.; take Pierce Street heading west from Hayden Road
Daily sunrise-10:30 p.m.
Drinking fountains (one for people and one for pooches), benches, mutt mitt stations, lighted. The fenced-in area is all turf and just under an acre in size. Restroom facilities nearby.

Creamery Park - Tempe
tempe.gov/pkrec/parkfacil/offleash.htm
8th Street and Una Avenue (just south of University near Rural)
Daily 6 a.m.-midnight
Fenced, benches, disposal bags, parking, lighted, water, trash cans.

Jaycee Park - Tempe
tempe.gov/pkrec/parkfacil/offleash.htm
5th Street and Hardy Drive
Daily 6 a.m.-midnight
Fenced, benches, disposal bags, trees, parking, lighted, water, trash cans. Access for the disabled.

Mitchell Park - Tempe
tempe.gov/pkrec/parkfacil/offleash.htm
Mitchell Drive and 9th Street
Daily 6 a.m.-midnight
Fenced, benches, disposal bags, trees, parking, lighted, water, trash cans. Access for the disabled.

Papago Park - Tempe
tempe.gov/pkrec/parkfacil/offleash.htm
Curry Road and College Avenue
Daily 6 a.m.-midnight
Fenced, disposal bags, trees, parking, lighted, water, trash cans.

Tempe Sports Complex (opening fall 2005) - Tempe
tempe.gov/pkrec/parkfacil/offleash.htm
Warner Road and Hardy Drive
Daily 6 a.m.-midnight
Fenced, disposal bags, trees, parking, lighted, water, trash cans.

CALIFORNIA

Calabasas Bark Park - Calabasas
cityofcalabasas.com/recreation/barkpark.html
4232 Las Virgenes Rd., south of the Las Virgenes Municipal Water District (approximately 2 miles west of US 101 on the south side)
Daily 5 a.m.-9 p.m.
Fenced, benches, trees, parking, lighted, water, trash cans, scoops, doggie drinking fountain.

Costa Mesa Bark Park - Costa Mesa
cmbarkpark.org, hotline (949) 733-4101
Arlington Drive and Newport Boulevard, across from the Orange County Fairgrounds Equestrian Center
Wed.-Mon. dawn-dusk; phone ahead in rainy conditions
Fenced, benches, tables, disposal bags, trees, parking, restrooms, water, trash cans, grass surface, 2.1 acres. Access for the disabled.

Elizabeth Anne Perrone Dog Park - Glen Ellen
sonoma-county.org/PARKS/foundation/
perrone_dog_park.htm
13630 Sonoma Hwy. in Sonoma Valley Regional Park (SR 12 between Arnold Drive and Madrone Road)
Daily sunrise-sunset
Fully fenced, 1 acre, double-gated entry, doggy drinking fountain.

CALIFORNIA (CONT'D)

Huntington Dog Beach - Huntington Beach
dogbeach.org
Pacific Coast Highway between 21st and Seapoint streets
Daily 5 a.m.-10 p.m.; parking lot closes at 8 p.m.
Benches and tables on the bluffs above the beach, disposal bags, metered parking, restrooms, trash cans. Dogs may be off leash anywhere on the beach while under an owner's supervision. Access for the disabled to the sand.

Laguna Niguel Pooch Park - Laguna Niguel
ci.laguna-niguel.ca.us/index.asp?SID=481
31461 Golden Lantern near Chapparosa Park
Tues.-Thurs. and Sat. 7 a.m.-dusk, Sun. 8 a.m.-dusk, Mon. and Fri. noon-dusk
Fenced, landscaped, water source, 1.1 acres.

Long Beach Recreation Dog Park - Long Beach
geocities.com/lbdogpark
5201 East 7th St. at Park
Daily sunrise-10 p.m.
Fenced, benches, tables, disposal bags, trees, parking, lighted, water, trash cans, separate fenced area for small dogs, crushed-granite ground cover. Access for the disabled.

Palm Springs Dog Park - Palm Springs
ci.palm-springs.ca.us/dogpark.html
222 Civic Dr. North, behind City Hall
Daily dawn-10 p.m.
Fenced, benches, tables, disposal bags, trees, parking, phones, lighted, water, trash cans, shelter. Beautiful fence designed and built by sculptor Phill Evans; dual-level drinking fountains, large and small dog areas, antique fire hydrants. Access for the disabled.

Rancho Cucamonga Dog Park - Rancho Cucamonga
North end of East Avenue north of Summit Avenue; the dog park is part of Etiwanda Creek Park
Daily dawn-dusk
Fences, trees, parking, phones, restrooms, water, dog washing facility, puppy/small dog area.

Redondo Beach Dog Park - Redondo Beach
rbdogpark.com
Located on the southeast corner of 190th Street and Flagler Lane
Daily dawn-dusk.; closed Wed. dawn-noon for maintenance
Fences, benches, disposal bags, trees, parking, phones, water, trash cans, separate fenced small dog area. Access for the disabled.

Bannon Creek Dog Park - Sacramento
cityofsacramento.org/parksandrecreation/parks/dogpark1.htm
In Bannon Creek Park on Bannon Creek Drive, off of Azevedo Drive (near West El Camino)
Daily sunrise-10 p.m. Well-fenced, about a half-acre, bench, water spigot for dogs, trash cans, disposal bags. Access for the disabled.

Granite Dog Park - Sacramento
cityofsacramento.org/parksandrecreation/parks/dogpark1.htm
On Ramona Avenue off Power Inn Road (in Granite Regional Park)
Daily sunrise-10 p.m.
Fenced, 2 acres, bench, water spigot for dogs, trash cans, disposal bags. Access for the disabled.

Partner Park - Sacramento
cityofsacramento.org/parksandrecreation/parks/dogpark1.htm
5699 South Land Park Dr. (at Fruitridge Road), behind Belle Cooledge Community Center
Daily sunrise-10 p.m.
Fenced, lighted, over 2 acres, landscaped with turf and mature trees, bench, water spigot for dogs, trash cans, disposal bags. Access for the disabled.

Balboa Park - San Diego
sandiego.gov/park-and-recreation/general-info/dogs.shtml
There are two off-leash areas within Balboa Park: Nate's Point at El Prado, on the southwest side of Cabrillo Bridge; and Morley Field, northwest of the tennis courts.
Daily 24 hours
Large field.

Cadman Community Park - San Diego
sandiego.gov/park-and-recreation/general-info/dogs.shtml
4280 Avati Dr.
Phone (858) 581-9929 for specific hours
Unfenced.

Capeheart Park (Pacific Beach) - San Diego
sandiego.gov/park-and-recreation/general-info/dogs.shtml
Soledad Mountain Road and Feldspar Street
Daily 24 hours
Two fenced pens on turfed areas, one for small dogs and one for other breeds, areas to provide water for dogs, drinking fountain, picnic tables and benches, parking.

Dog Beach - San Diego
sandiego.gov/park-and-recreation/general-info/dogs.shtml
Beach area is located in Ocean Beach at the west end of Voltaire Street; enter the parking lot at the west end of Voltaire Street.
Daily 24 hours
Disposal bags, trash cans, water, restrooms nearby. Access for the disabled.

Fiesta Island - San Diego
sandiego.gov/park-and-recreation/general-info/dogs.shtml
This island in Mission Bay Park allows dogs anywhere outside the fenced areas.
Daily 6 a.m.-10 p.m.

Grape Street Park - San Diego
sandiego.gov/park-and-recreation/general-info/dogs.shtml
Grape Street and Granada Avenue
Mon.-Fri. 7:30-10 a.m. and 4-9 p.m., Sat.-Sun. and holidays 9-11 a.m. and 4-9 p.m.
Benches, tables, trees, parking, restrooms, lighted, water, trash cans.

CALIFORNIA (CONT'D)

Alamo Square Park - San Francisco
sfgov.org/site/recpark_index.asp?id=1448
Western half of the park, along Scott Street between
Hayes and Fulton streets
Daily 6 a.m.-10 p.m.
Unfenced; dogs must be under firm voice control.

Alta Plaza Park - San Francisco
sfgov.org/site/recpark_index.asp?id=1448
Second terrace of park, on Clay Street between Scott and
Steiner streets
Daily 6 a.m.-10 p.m.
Unfenced; dogs must be under firm voice control.

Bernal Heights - San Francisco
sfgov.org/site/recpark_index.asp?id=1448
Top of the hill (the entire section bounded by Bernal
Heights Boulevard)
Daily 6 a.m.-10 p.m.
Unfenced; dogs must be under firm voice control.

Buena Vista Park - San Francisco
sfgov.org/site/recpark_index.asp?id=1448
Buena Vista West at Central Avenue
Daily 6 a.m.-10 p.m.
Unfenced; dogs must be under firm voice control.

Corona Heights - San Francisco
sfgov.org/site/recpark_index.asp?id=1448
Field area next to Randall Museum at Roosevelt Way and
Museum Way
Daily 6 a.m.-10 p.m.
Fenced area.

Crocker Amazon Playground - San Francisco
sfgov.org/site/recpark_index.asp?id=1448
Northern portion of park between LaGrande and Dublin
streets, adjacent to community garden
Daily 6 a.m.-10 p.m.
Unfenced; dogs must be under firm voice control.

Dolores Park - San Francisco
sfgov.org/site/recpark_index.asp?id=1448
Central area of the park delineated with hedges and
designated by signs
Daily 6 a.m.-10 p.m.
Unfenced; dogs must be under firm voice control.

Douglass Park - San Francisco
sfgov.org/site/recpark_index.asp?id=1448
Upper field at 27th and Douglass streets
Daily 6 a.m.-10 p.m.
Unfenced; dogs must be under firm voice control.

Eureka Valley Recreation Center - San Francisco
sfgov.org/site/recpark_index.asp?id=1448
On Collingwood side of park, adjacent to the tennis courts.
Daily 6 a.m.-10 p.m.
Fenced area.

Golden Gate Park - San Francisco
sfgov.org/site/recpark_index.asp?id=1448
Southeast section bounded by Lincoln Way, King Drive
and 2nd and 7th avenues
Northeast section at Stanyan and Grove streets
South-central area bounded by Martin Luther King Jr.
Drive, Middle Drive and 34th and 38th avenues
Fenced dog training area near 38th Avenue and Fulton
Street.

Lafayette Park - San Francisco
sfgov.org/site/recpark_index.asp?id=1448
Near Sacramento Street, between Octavia and Gough
streets
Daily 6 a.m.-10 p.m.
Unfenced; dogs must be under firm voice control.

Lake Merced - San Francisco
sfgov.org/site/recpark_index.asp?id=1448
Northern lake area at Lake Merced Boulevard and
Middlefield Drive
Daily 6 a.m.-10 p.m.
Unfenced area; dogs must be under firm voice control.

McKinley Square - San Francisco
sfgov.org/site/recpark_index.asp?id=1448
San Bruno Avenue and 20th Street, on the west slope
Daily 6 a.m.-10 p.m.
Unfenced area; dogs must be under firm voice control.

McLaren Park - San Francisco
sfgov.org/site/recpark_index.asp?id=1448
The area bounded by Shelly Drive and Mansell Avenue at
the top of the hill
Daily 6 a.m.-10 p.m.
Unfenced area; dogs must be under firm voice control.

Mountain Lake Park - San Francisco
sfgov.org/site/recpark_index.asp?id=1448
East end of park, north of Lake Street at 8th Avenue
Daily 6 a.m.-10 p.m.
Unfenced area; dogs must be under firm voice control.

Pine Lake Park - San Francisco
sfgov.org/site/recpark_index.asp?id=1448
West of and contiguous to Stern Grove and adjacent to
the parking lot entered via Crestlake and Vale streets
Daily 6 a.m.-10 p.m.
Unfenced area; dogs must be under firm voice control.

Potrero Hill Mini Park - San Francisco
sfgov.org/site/recpark_index.asp?id=1448
22nd Street between Arkansas and Connecticut streets
Daily 6 a.m.-10 p.m.
Unfenced area; dogs must be under firm voice control.

Stern Grove - San Francisco
sfgov.org/site/recpark_index.asp?id=1448
North side, along Wawona Street between 21st and 23rd
avenues
Daily 6 a.m.-10 p.m.
Unfenced area; dogs must be under firm voice control.

St. Mary's Recreation Center - San Francisco
sfgov.org/site/recpark_index.asp?id=1448
Lower terrace of park (enter at Justin and Benton streets)
Daily 6 a.m.-10 p.m.
Fenced area.

Upper Noe Recreation Center - San Francisco
sfgov.org/site/recpark_index.asp?id=1448
30th Street between Church and Sanchez streets, behind
and along the baseball field
Daily 6 a.m.-10 p.m.
Fenced area.

CALIFORNIA (CONT'D)

Field of Dogs - San Rafael
fieldofdogs.org
3540 Civic Center Dr. near the intersection of US 101 and North San Pedro Road
Daily sunrise-sunset
Fenced, double-gated entry, parking, benches, tables, disposal bags, trees, parking, water, trash cans, shelter. Access for the disabled.

DeTurk Roundbarn Park - Santa Rosa
ci.santa-rosa.ca.us/rp/
819 Donahue St. between West 8th and 9th streets
Daily during daylight hours
Fenced, water. This is a small neighborhood park.

Doyle Park Dog Park - Santa Rosa
ci.santa-rosa.ca.us/rp/
700 Hoen Ave. within Doyle Park (Enter via Hoen Avenue, go west on Sonoma, turn left on Hoen and then turn right into the parking lot. The fenced dog park is behind the stadium.)
Daily during daylight hours
Approximately 3/4 acre, fully fenced, bench, water, disposal bags.

Galvin Dog Park - Santa Rosa
ci.santa-rosa.ca.us/rp/
3330 Yulupa Ave. (within Don Galvin Park, next to Bennet Valley Golf Course)
Daily during daylight hours
Fenced, trees, parking, water, trash cans. Has double gate at main entrance for easier coming and going with your dog. Access for the disabled.

Northwest Community Dog Park - Santa Rosa
ci.santa-rosa.ca.us/rp/
Part of Northwest Community Park (Go west on Gurneville Road, turn right on Marlow and then turn right into the park's parking lot, at the first traffic light. Walk east along the path; the dog park is on the left.)
Daily during daylight hours
Approximately 1 acre, fenced, separate small dog park adjacent, benches, bathrooms nearby, trash cans, disposal bags, water.

Rincon Valley Dog Park - Santa Rosa
ci.santa-rosa.ca.us/rp/
5108 Badger Rd. (within Rincon Valley Community Park)
Daily during daylight hours
Approximately 1/2 acre, fenced, benches, tables, access for the disabled, disposal bags, trees, parking, phones, restrooms, water, trash cans, fenced pond area for dogs, separate fenced large and small pond areas. Large dog area closes during the winter; pond and small dog exercise area are open year-round. Monitors are present during peak hours to enforce rules.

Off-leash, unfenced, under voice control areas:

Doyle Park - Santa Rosa
ci.santa-rosa.ca.us/rp/
Mon.-Fri. 6-9 a.m.
Dogs may be off leash within the park, but must be kept on leash from the parking lot to the park entrance.

700 Doyle Park Drive - Santa Rosa
ci.santa-rosa.ca.us/rp/
Enter on Hoen Avenue, go west on Sonoma, turn left on Hoen and then turn right into the parking lot. There is an unfenced, off-leash area to the right of the fenced dog park.
Daily 6-9 a.m., early Apr.-late Oct.

Franklin Park - Santa Rosa
ci.santa-rosa.ca.us/rp/
2095 Franklin Ave.
Daily 6-8 a.m.

Southwest Community - Santa Rosa
ci.santa-rosa.ca.us/rp/
1698 Hearn Ave.
Daily 6-8 a.m.

Youth Community - Santa Rosa
ci.santa-rosa.ca.us/rp/
1725 Fulton Rd.
Daily 6-8 a.m.

Remington Dog Park - Sausalito
dogpark-sausalito.com
Ebbtide at Bridgeway
Mon.-Fri. 7-7, Sat.-Sun. 8-7
Fully fenced with safety gated entrance, water, tents for shelter, parking, scoops and scooper cleaning station, trash cans, lighted, tennis balls and racquets provided, picnic tables and benches.

Sierra Madre Dog Park - Sierra Madre
ci.sierra-madre.ca.us/departments/administrative_services/licenses_detail.asp?ID=279
611 East Sierra Madre Blvd., south of the tennis courts in Sierra Vista Park
Daily 6 a.m.-10 p.m. A pass must be obtained in order to use the park. Either daily or calendar year passes are available; a daily pass is $5. Passes can be purchased at City Hall; the Sierra Madre Police Department, 242 W. Sierra Madre Blvd.; or the Sierra Madre Community Recreation Center, 611 E. Sierra Madre Blvd.
Fenced, double-gated entry, benches, disposal bags, trees, parking, phones, restrooms, lighted, water, trash cans, separate fenced areas for large/active dogs and "special needs" dogs. Access for the disabled.

COLORADO

Grandview Off-Leash Dog Park - Aurora
For additional information phone (303) 739-7160
17900 E. Quincy Ave. (west of Quincy Reservoir and just east of Pitkin Street)
Daily dawn-dusk
Fenced, parking, water, trash cans.

East Boulder Community - Boulder City
ci.boulder.co.us/parks-recreation/PARKS/dog_parks_main.htm
5660 Sioux Dr.
Daily dawn-dusk
Fenced, disposal bags, parking, water, trash cans, fenced-off swimming area. Access for the disabled.

COLORADO (CONT'D)

Foothills Community Park - Boulder City
*ci.boulder.co.us/parks-recreation/PARKS/
dog_parks_main.htm*
West of Broadway between Locust Avenue and Lee Hill
Road
Daily dawn-dusk
Fenced, disposal bags, parking, trash cans, water. Access
for the disabled.

Howard H. Hueston Park - Boulder City
*ci.boulder.co.us/parks-recreation/PARKS/
dog_parks_main.htm*
34th Street near O'Neal Parkway
Daily dawn-dusk
Non-fenced area; dogs must be under voice and sight
control. Benches, tables, trees, parking, trash cans. Access
for the disabled.

Valmont Dog Park - Boulder City
*ci.boulder.co.us/parks-recreation/PARKS/
dog_parks_main.htm*
Valmont and Airport roads
Daily dawn-dusk
Fenced, disposal bags, parking, trash cans, water. Access
for the disabled.

Palmer Park - Colorado Springs
ci.colospgs.co.us/Page.asp?NavID=2723
At Maizeland Road and Academy Boulevard
Daily 5 a.m.-11 p.m., May-Oct.; 5 a.m.-9 p.m., rest of year
Fenced, benches, tables, parking, water, trash cans,
disposal bags, restrooms. Access for the disabled.

Rampart Dog Park - Colorado Springs
ci.colospgs.co.us/Page.asp?NavID=2723
8270 Lexington Dr. (from the intersection of Lexington
Drive and N. Union Boulevard, go north on Lexington,
then turn left into the park entrance)
Daily 5 a.m.-11 p.m., May-Oct.; 5 a.m.-9 p.m., rest of year
Fenced, benches, trees, parking, disposal bags, water,
trash cans. Access for the disabled.

Denver Off-Leash Dog Park - Denver
*denvergov.org or email kelledl@ci.denver.co.us for
additional information*
678 South Jason St. (the large area directly behind the
Denver Municipal Animal Shelter)
Daily sunrise-sunset
Fenced, parking, grass, toys. Access for the disabled.

FLORIDA

Happy Tails Canine Park - Bradenton
51st Street West at G.T. Bray Park, about halfway
between Manatee Avenue and Cortez Road
Daily dawn-dusk
Approximately 3 acres, 8-foot fence, benches, tables,
parking (including handicapped spaces), disposal bags,
trees, restrooms (a short walk outside the park), water,
trash cans.

Dr. Paul's Pet Care Center Dog Park - Coral Springs
TopPetCare.com
Off Sportsplex Drive in the Sportsplex Regional Park
Complex (park off Sportsplex Drive at the west pedestrian
entrance)
Daily dawn-9:30 p.m.
Enclosed, separate small and large dog areas, paved
running path, watering area, lights, dog shower, dog
statues, dog and people water fountains, landscaping,
disposal bag dispensers, trash barrels, picnic table,
weatherproof dog agility equipment, gazebo, trees, shaded
area, restroom and snack vending machine adjacent.

The Dog Park in Lake Ida Park - Delray Beach
co.palm-beach.fl.us/parks
2929 Lake Ida Rd. (take the Atlantic Avenue West exit off
I-95, proceed west to Congress Avenue, go north on
Congress for 1 mile, turn right onto Lake Ida Road,
proceed east under I-95, park entrance is on the left)
Daily sunrise-sunset; closed Thurs. noon-3 for
maintenance
2.5 acres, separate fenced areas for large and small dogs,
two canine drinking stations, dog washing area, eight
shaded sitting areas, partial paved pathway, dispensers
and receptacles for disposal bags, restrooms and parking
areas nearby, information kiosk.

Pooch Pines Dog Park at Okeeheelee Park - Delray Beach
co.palm-Beach.fl.us/parks
7715 Forest Hill Blvd. (Take the Forest Hill Blvd. West exit
off I-95 and proceed west to the main Okeeheelee Park
entrance on the north side of the road. Follow the park
road to the Pooch Pines sign and turn right; the dog park
is at the top of the hill.)
Daily sunrise-sunset; closed Wed. noon-3 for maintenance
Approximately 5 acres, separate fenced areas for small
and large dogs, canine drinking stations, dog washing
area, shaded sitting areas, paved pathways, dispensers
and receptacles for disposable bags, restroom and parking
nearby.

Bark Park at Snyder Park - Fort Lauderdale
ci.fort-lauderdale.fl.us/cityparks/snyder/barkpark
3299 S.W. 4th Ave. (dogs must remain in the car until
arrival at the Bark Park and are not permitted in the
remainder of Snyder Park)
Daily 7 a.m.-7:30 p.m., Apr.-Sept.; 7-6:30, rest of year.
Closed Jan. 1 and Dec. 25
Fee Mon.-Fri. $2; senior citizens and ages 6-12, $1.50.
Fee Sat.-Sun. and holidays $2.50; senior citizens and
ages 6-12, $1.50.
Fenced, benches, trees, disposal bags, parking, restrooms,
water, trash cans, agility equipment, separate small dog
area, two hose stations, drinking fountains, two open-air
pavilions, small nature area with more than 20 labeled
native trees. Freshwater dog swim Sat.-Sun. and holidays
10-5, first weekend in Mar.-first Sun. in Dec.; fee $1.
Access for the disabled.

FLORIDA (CONT'D)

Dog Wood Off-Leash Park - Gainesville
dogwoodpark.com
5505 S.W. Archer Rd., 1 mile west of I-75
Sat.-Sun. noon-5 (may stay until dusk once in the park)
Fee $9 plus tax for the first dog, $1 plus tax for each
additional dog per family (otherwise $2.50 plus tax for
each additional dog in the group)
Approximately 15 acres, 6-foot-high chain link fence,
double-gated entrances and exits, jogging trail, hammocks,
picnic tables, lounge chairs, swinging benches, regular
benches, two huge dog swimming ponds, wading pools,
fountain, gazebo, agility course, sunny and shady small
dog areas, dog shower, indoor restrooms, soft drinks for
sale, free bottled water, agility equipment, park-provided
tennis balls, multiple clean-up stations with disposal bags.
Dog Wood Park also offers a do-it-yourself dog wash, a
doggie boutique, dog day care, a dog photography studio,
and agility and obedience training. Some breeds must be
neutered in order to enter the park; phone (352) 335-1919
for details.

Paw Park of Historic Sanford - Sanford
pawparksanford.org
427 French Ave. (US 17/92) in Sanford's Historic District.
From I-4, take the SR 46 exit (exit 101C, Sanford/Mount
Dora), proceed east on SR 46 approximately 4 miles to
French Avenue, turn right (southbound) and get into the
left-thru lane; the Paw Park is on the left just past the
Burger King.
Daily 7:30 a.m.-8 p.m.
Fenced, double-gated entrance, paved walkway, benches,
tables, self-watering bowls, water misting station, dog
showers, small dog area, disposal bag dispensers,
parking, community bulletin board, historic lighting, parking,
nicely shaded with mature oak trees, 20 minutes north of
downtown Orlando. Access for the disabled.

17th Street Park & Paw Park - Sarasota
cgov.net
4570 17th St.
Daily dawn-dusk
Approximately 6 acres, 6-foot fence, lighted, benches,
tables, disposal bags, trees, parking, restrooms, water,
trash cans, dog shower, small dog area, double-gated
entrance, community bulletin board.

Lakeview Park - Sarasota
scgov.net
7150 Lago St.
Daily dawn-midnight
Six-foot fence, benches, tables, disposal bags, many trees,
parking, restrooms, water, trash cans, dog shower,
community bulletin board, small dog area, double-gated
entrance. Access for the disabled.

Brohard Beach & Paw Park - Venice
scgov.net
1600 Harbor Dr. South
Daily dawn-midnight
Boardwalk to beach, 6-foot fence, benches, tables, shelter,
disposal bags, trees, water, trash cans, small dog area,
dog shower, community bulletin board, parking. Access for
the disabled.

Woodmere Park & Woodmore Paw Park - Venice
scgov.net
3951 Woodmere Park Blvd. (at Alligator Creek near
Jacaranda)
Daily dawn-dusk
Fenced, double-gated entrance, benches, tables, disposal
bags, trees, parking, restrooms, water, trash cans,
double-gated small dog section near the front gate, dog
shower, community bulletin board. Access for the disabled.

MICHIGAN

Orion Oaks Bark Park - Lake Orion
co.oakland.mi.us/parksrec/ppark/lyon.html
Off Joslyn Road, south of Clarkston Road (park at the
north Joslyn Road entrance and follow the signs)
Daily half an hour before sunrise-half an hour after sunset
A park pass is required. A daily pass is available at the
Lake Orion Township office (open Mon.-Fri.), located on
Joslyn Road south of the park; or at Independence Oaks
County Park (open daily), located on Sashabaw Road 2
1/2 miles north of I-75. Resident fee $5 per day, $28 for
an annual pass. Non-resident fee $10 per vehicle for daily
entry, $49 for an annual pass; over 62, $3 per vehicle for
daily entry, $23 for an annual pass. Fenced, 7 acres,
benches, tables, disposal bags, trees, water source,
parking, Portajohns, trash cans. Access for the disabled. A
portion of Lake Sixteen is reserved for canine swimmers.

Lyon Oaks Bark Park - Lyon Township
co.oakland.mi.us/parksrec/ppark/orion.html
Pontiac Trail, between Wixom and Old Plank roads
Daily half an hour before sunrise-half an hour after sunset
A park pass is required; daily and annual passes are
available at the park. Resident fee $5 per day, $28 for an
annual pass. Non-resident fee $10 per vehicle for daily
entry, $49 for an annual pass; over 62, $3 per vehicle for
daily entry, $23 for an annual pass. 13 acres, fenced,
benches, tables, disposal bags, parking, restrooms, trash
cans, open fields, water pump available spring 2004.

MINNESOTA

Note: In the greater Minneapolis area there are nine
off-leash sites located within a 15-minute drive of
downtown Minneapolis/St. Paul. There are an additional 10
sites located in rural/suburban areas of the seven-county
metropolitan area. Some sites require permits for off-leash
use and/or parking; others have no permit requirements.
Please read descriptions carefully.

Minneapolis dog parks: All Minneapolis dog parks
require a permit for use. The Minnehaha site also requires
a permit for parking. For Minneapolis dog park permit
information phone (612) 348-4250. Nearby dog parks in
St. Paul, Maplewood, Shoreview and Roseville do not
require a permit for use.

MINNESOTA (CONT'D)

Alimagnet Dog Park - Burnsville (south metro suburb)
alimagnetdogpark.org
1200 Alimagnet Pkwy. (Cross street is County Road 11; from central St. Paul, proceed south on I-35E to the County Road 42 exit. Proceed east to County Road 11, then go north on County Road 11 to Alimagnet Parkway and turn right. The dog park will be on the right.)
Daily 5 a.m.-10 p.m.
7 acres, fenced, benches, tables, disposal bags, trees, water, phones, restrooms, parking, trash cans, pond, wooded areas, open field, mowed prairie grass trail, double-gated entrance. A permit is required; phone the Recreation Department at (952) 895-4500.

Coates (south metro rural)
Located in the center of Dakota County near Coates, on Blaine Avenue south of Country Road 46 (160th Street E.)
Daily 5 a.m.-10 p.m.
The 16-acre fenced site has both wooded and open space with a walking trail loop. There is no surface water. Parking, portable toilets, tables, bag dispensers and waster containers are available on site. Be sure to bring drinking water for your dog! A permit is required.

Elm Creek Park Reserve - Dayton (northwest metro rural)
threeriversparkdistrict.org/trails/trails_pet.cfm
Daily 5 a.m.-sunset
Fenced, tables, trees, parking, restrooms, trash cans. Over 30 acres with mowed trail through area. Use is by permit only; day permits are available at the site. For an annual special use permit phone Park Guest Services at (763) 559-9000.

Battle Creek Off-Leash Site - Maplewood (east central metro)
co.ramsey.mn.us/parks/parks/offleash.asp
Lower Afton and McKnight
Daily sunrise-sunset
12 acres, partially fenced, tables, parking, trash cans. No permit required.

Columbia Park - Minneapolis
dogromp.org
St. Anthony Parkway off Central Avenue
Daily 6 a.m.-10 p.m.
Approximately 2 acres, double-gated entry at the east and west ends of the park, fully fenced, parking, disposal bag dispensers, bench.

Franklin Terrace - Minneapolis
dogromp.org
Franklin Terrace and 30th Avenue S.
Daily 6 a.m.-10 p.m.
2.6 acres, fully fenced, double-gated entry at the east and west ends of the site, disposal bag dispensers, bench, on-street parking.

Lake of the Isles Park - Minneapolis
dogromp.org
Lake of the Isles Parkway and W. 28th Street
Daily 6 a.m.-10 p.m.
2.6 acres, fully fenced, two double-gated entry vestibules at the northern end of the site, lighted at the southern end, disposal bag dispensers, benches.

Minnehaha Park - Minneapolis
dogromp.org
Minnehaha Avenue and E. 54th Street
Daily 6 a.m.-10 p.m.
Approximately 4.2 acres along the Mississippi River (where dogs can swim), partially fenced, disposal bag dispensers, lighted parking area (permit required), Portajohn in parking area.

Egan Park's Off-Leash Area - Plymouth
http://www2.ci.plymouth.mn.us, Parks & Recreation Dept. phone (763) 509-5200
Located in northwest Plymouth on the south side of County Road 47, about two blocks west of Dunkirk Lane
Daily sunrise-sunset
10 acres, unfenced area, trash cans, bring your own water. No permit required.

Cleary Lake Regional Park - Prior Lake (south metro rural)
threeriversparkdistrict.org/trails/trails_pet.cfm
Daily 5 a.m.-sunset
35 acres with pond, fenced, tables, parking, restrooms, trash cans. Trails are mowed in summer, packed in winter. Annual pet exercise area permit or daily use fee required; day permits are available at the site. For an annual special use permit phone Park Guest Services at (763) 559-9000.

Lake Sarah Regional Park - Rockford (west metro rural)
threeriversparkdistrict.org/trails/trails_pet.cfm
Approximately 30 miles west of Minneapolis and east of County Road 92 (Take US 55 west to County Road 92, proceed south to Lake Sarah Drive, turn left and then turn left again onto the first gravel road; the parking lot for the off-leash area is on the left-hand side.)
Daily 5 a.m.-sunset
Trees, parking, restrooms, trash cans. Over 30 acres with mowed parking area. Use is by permit only; day permits are available at the site. For an annual special use permit phone Park Guest Services at (763) 559-9000.

Crow-Hassan Park Reserve - Rogers (northwest metro rural)
threeriversparkdistrict.org/trails/trails_pet.fmc
West of Rogers on Sylvan Lake Road (From I-94, take the Rogers exit and go south through town to the T intersection. Turn right on County Road 116 and proceed to County Road 203. Turn left and follow County Road 203 to the park entrance.)
Daily 5 a.m.-sunset
Fenced, tables, trees, parking, restrooms, trash cans. Over 30 acres with a mowed trail through the area. Use is by permit only; day permits are available at the site. For an annual special use permit phone Park Guest Services at (763) 559-9000.

Woodview Dog Park - Roseville (central)
co.ramsey.mn.us/parks/parks/offleash.asp
Located off Larpenteur Avenue, just east of Dale Street (access gate to main off-leash area is about 100 yards down the bike trail)
Daily sunrise-sunset
Partially fenced (along bike trail only), 3 acres, disposal bags, trees, water, tables, parking, trash cans. Small dog area (fenced). Access for the disabled. No permit required.

MINNESOTA (CONT'D)

Rice Creek Off-Leash Site - Shoreview (northeast metro)
co.ramsey.mn.us/parks/parks/offleash.asp
Located just south of County Road J on Lexington Avenue
Daily sunrise-sunset
12 acres, not fenced, tables, parking, trash cans, flat with prairie vegetation, small pond. No permit required.

Bass Lake/Belt Line - St. Louis Park (west central)
stlouispark.org/PermitsForms/2005Off-LeashApp.pdf
Interim site is located at the Bass Lake Preserve on West 36th Street and Belt Line Boulevard (east of the tennis courts)
Daily sunrise-sunset
Fenced, 1.5 acres. Bring drinking water for your dog! A permit is required (see pdf link above).

Arlington-Arkwright (ArlArk) Dog Park - St. Paul
dogromp.org
Located on Arkwright Street at Arlington Avenue (From I-35E, take the Maryland Avenue exit east to Arkwright Street, then go north; the park is on the right-hand side.)
Daily sunrise-9 p.m.
Fenced, 4.5-acre site with trails and woods, disposal bags, tables, parking, trash cans. There are multiple entrances, and park users sometimes leave the gates open; be sure you have voice control of your dog to prevent escapes. No permit required.

Otter Lake Dog Park - White Bear Township (northeast suburban)
dogromp.org
Take I-35E to the County Road J exit, then County Road J east to Otter Lake Road. Take Otter Lake Road south to the dog park; the entrance is next to the boat launch.
Daily sunrise-sunset
10+ acres of partially fenced rolling hills with both wooded and open prairie vegetation. The site is fenced adjacent to Otter Lake Road and along most of the south boundary; it is bounded on the east by a large wetland and on the north by Otter Lake. Although not fully fenced, it shouldn't present a problem for most dogs. There also is a separate 1-acre, fully fenced small dog area. No permit required.

NEVADA

Desert Breeze Park - Las Vegas
accessclarkcounty.com, (702) 455-8200
8425 W. Spring Mountain Rd. (at Durango)
Daily 6 a.m.-11 p.m.
Two dog runs, one for large and one for small dogs. Runs are fenced and include benches, lights and water.

Desert Inn Dog Park - Las Vegas
accessclarkcounty.com, (702) 455-8200
3570 Vista del Monte
Daily 6 a.m.-11 p.m.
Fenced, water, benches.

Dog Fancier's Park - Las Vegas
accessclarkcounty.com, (702) 455-8200
5800 E. Flamingo Rd. (cross streets are E. Flamingo and Jimmy Durante)
Daily 6 a.m.-11 p.m.
12-acre park used for dog shows and training. There is a separate fenced dog run area.
Groups often reserve the park for dog shows and related activities including canine trials, agility training and club meetings. For information on upcoming events, phone the 24-hour Dog Fancier's hotline at (702) 564-3647. To reserve the park for a canine-related event, phone (702) 367-6796.

Molasky Park Dog Run - Las Vegas
accessclarkcounty.com, (702) 455-8200
1065 E. Twain, west of Maryland Parkway
Daily 6 a.m.-11 p.m.
This 10-acre park has three dog runs located off Katie Road. Two runs are open at a time to rest the grass. Sitting areas, waste receptacles, water taps.

Shadow Rock Dog Park - Las Vegas
accessclarkcounty.com, (702) 455-8200
2650 Los Feliz (cross streets Lake Mead past Hollywood)
Daily dawn-dusk
Fenced dog run is located east of the park area. Benches, trash cans, water.

Shadow Rock Dog Park - Las Vegas
accessclarkcounty.com, (702) 455-8200
2650 Los Feliz (cross streets Lake Mead past Hollywood)
Daily dawn-dusk
Fenced dog run is located east of the park area. Benches, trash cans, water.

Silverado Ranch Park Dog Park (Central SE) - Las Vegas
accessclarkcounty.com, (702) 455-8200
9855 S. Gillespie
Daily 6 a.m.-11 p.m.
Dog runs are fenced and include benches, lights and water. Two runs are available, one for dogs under 30 pounds and the other for dogs over 30 pounds.

Sunset Park (SE) - Las Vegas
accessclarkcounty.com, (702) 455-8200
2601 E. Sunset Rd.
Daily 6 a.m.-11 p.m.
Two dog runs for large and small breeds. Fenced, benches, tables, nearby restrooms, lights, water. The closest parking to the dog park is off Eastern between Sunset Road and Warm Springs Road.

NEW YORK

New York City (Manhattan & boroughs)
urbanhound.com
nycgovparks.org/sub_things_to_do/facilities/ af_dog_runs.html

Ewen Park ("John's Run"), Riverdale - Bronx
Riverdale to Johnson avenues, south of West 232nd Street and down the steps in the clearing on the right
Daily dawn-dusk
Plastic lawn furniture, scenic views.

NEW YORK (CONT'D)

Seton Park, Riverdale - Bronx
West 235th Street and Independence Avenue (west of
Independence on 235th Street, near the Spuyten Duyvil
Library)
Daily dawn-dusk

Canine Court, Van Cortlandt Park - Bronx
West 252nd Street and Broadway (enter on the path on
252nd and follow it about 100 feet to the left)
Daily dawn-dusk
Two huge runs, a basic dog run and a canine agility
playground with a teeter-totter, hurdles, a ladder, three
chutes and a hanging tire.

Owl's Head Park, Bay Ridge - Brooklyn
68th Street and Shore Road
Disposal bags, tree, grass surface.

Hillside Park, Brooklyn Heights - Brooklyn
Columbia Heights and Middagh Street
Daily 24 hours
Fenced.

Palmetto Playground, Brooklyn Heights - Brooklyn
Columbia Place and State Street (in a corner by the BQE)
Daily 24 hours
Water supply, four benches, one park light.

Prospect Park - Brooklyn
fidobrooklyn.org, 888-604-3422
Grand Army Plaza and Flatbush; off-leash areas may be
accessed from all park entrances
Off-leash times: daily 9 p.m.-9 a.m., Apr.-Oct.; 5 p.m.-9
a.m., rest of year (in the 80-acre Long Meadow and
6-acre Peninsula Meadow). Dogs may be off-leash in the
15-acre Nethermead Mon.-Fri. 5 p.m -9 a.m. year-round
(except holidays). On holidays and weekends, the hours
above apply to Nethermead as well. At **all** other times,
dogs must be on a leash; minimum fine for
non-compliance is $100. There are no fenced or small dog
areas. There is a small swimming area in the Long
Meadow near the 9th Street entrance. Trees, restrooms
(at Long Meadow only; may not be available early in the
morning), water (some fountains equipped with troughs for
dogs). **Note:** Use of the area is at the dog owner's risk.
Dogs may be off-leash with appropriate supervision in
three large meadows at the hours specified above; please
observe all off-leash rules. Rules are posted at park
entrances and at www.fidobrooklyn.org. Dogs must be on
a leash at **all** other places and times.

Carl Shurz Park, Upper East Side - Manhattan
East 86th Street at East End Avenue
Daily dawn-1 a.m.
Benches, scoops, pea gravel surface. Past the main run,
toward the East River, is a second run for small dogs that
has a superb view of the river and the 59th Street Bridge.

Fishbridge Park, Lower East Side - Manhattan
Dover Street at Pearl Street, just south of the Brooklyn
Bridge
Daily dawn-dusk
Water hose, wading pool (summer only), benches, lockbox
for toys, lockbox with newspapers for picking up after your
dog.

**J. Hood Wright Park, Inwood/Ft. George/Washington
Heights - Manhattan**
West 173rd Street between Fort Washington Avenue and
Haven Avenue

**Madison Square Park, Gramercy/Flatiron/Union Square
- Manhattan**
East 24th Street at Fifth Avenue
Daily 6 a.m.-midnight
Disposal bags, water supply, benches, trees.

Peter Detmold Park, Midtown East - Manhattan
East 49th Street at FDR Drive (behind Beeckman Place)
Daily dawn-9 p.m., June-Sept.; dawn-8 p.m., Mar.-May
and Oct.-Nov.; dawn-7 p.m., rest of year
Benches, disposal bags, trees, historical lamps.

**Riverside Park at 72nd Street, Upper West Side/
Morningside Heights - Manhattan**
West 72nd Street
Daily 6 a.m.-1 a.m.
Bench, disposal bags, scoopers, hanging flowerpots.

**Riverside Park at 87th Street, Upper West Side/
Morningside Heights - Manhattan**
West 87th Street
Daily dawn-dusk
Separate large and small dog areas, fountain and hose.

**Riverside Park at 105th Street, Upper West Side/
Morningside Heights - Manhattan**
riversidedog.org
West 105th Street, Riverside Park Central Promenade
Daily dawn-dusk
Water fountain for dogs, small dog area, disposal bag
dispensers, benches, trees, crushed granite surface.

**Theodore Roosevelt Park, Upper West Side/
Morningside Heights - Manhattan**
West 81st Street at Columbus Avenue
Daily 8 a.m.-10 p.m.
Water faucets for dogs, a water fountain for humans,
many benches, a separate run for small dogs, shade
trees.

Thomas Jefferson Park, Harlem - Manhattan
East 112th Street at First Avenue
Daily 24 hours
Benches, wood chips.

Tompkins Square Park, East Village - Manhattan
East 9th Street at Avenue B
Daily 6 a.m.-midnight
Benches, picnic tables, water, a dog memorial.

Washington Square Park, West Village - Manhattan
West 4th Street at Thompson Street
Daily 6 a.m.-midnight
Benches, trees, water hose, water bowls, scoopers, pea
gravel surface.

Doughboy Plaza, Woodside - Queens
Windmuller Park
Woodside Avenue from 54th to 56th streets (also south of
Woodside at 56th Street)
Daily dawn-dusk
Fenced, trash can.

OHIO

Mt. Airy Dog Park - Cincinnati
cincinnati-oh.gov/cityparks/pages/-4327-/
Located within Mt. Airy Forest's Highpoint Picnic Area on Westwood Northern Boulevard, between Montana Avenue and North Bend Road
Daily dawn-dusk
Fenced, benches, tables, trees, parking, restrooms, water, trash cans, shelter. Access for the disabled.

OREGON

Alton Baker Park - Eugene
ci.eugene.or.us/parks/maps/dog_parks.htm
South of Leo Harris Parkway
Daily 6 a.m.-11 p.m.
Fenced, parking, water, disposal bag receptacles, benches and/or tables and simple shelters for protection from sun/rain. Park in the lot south of Autzen Stadium and cross the pedestrian bridge to the dog park.

Amazon Park - Eugene
ci.eugene.or.us/parks/maps/dog_parks.htm
East of 29th Street and Amazon Parkway
Daily 6 a.m.-11 p.m.
Fenced, water, disposal bag receptacles, benches and/or tables and simple shelters for protection from sun/rain, parking nearby.

Morse Ranch - Eugene
ci.eugene.or.us/parks/maps/dog_parks.htm
Crest Drive and Lincoln Street (park in the main parking area at 595 Crest Dr. and take the trail east)
Daily 6 a.m.-11 p.m.
Fenced, water, disposal bag receptacles, benches and/or tables and simple shelters for protection from sun/rain.

Chimney Park - Portland
parks.ci.portland.or.us/OffLeash/sites.htm
9360 N. Columbia Blvd.
6 acres of off-leash meadow and trails. Not fenced; dogs should be under excellent voice command.

East Delta Park - Portland
parks.ci.portland.or.us/OffLeash/sites.htm
N. Denver and Martin Luther King Jr. Boulevard
5-acre, fenced field with trees and benches is located off I-5 exit 307 on I-5 across from the East Delta Sports Complex. Water is not available. Open during dry season only, May-October. Dogs are not allowed on the sports fields.

Gabriel Park - Portland
parks.ci.portland.or.us/OffLeash/sites.htm
S.W. 45th Street and Vermont
The 1.5-acre, fenced, off-leash area has trees, picnic tables and water. Open during dry season only, May-October. Dogs must remain leashed when not in the off-leash area.

West Delta Park - Portland
parks.ci.portland.or.us/OffLeash/sites.htm
North Expo and Broadacre roads (located just north of Portland International Raceway)
Off-leash site, large open field, not fenced; dogs should be under excellent voice command.

TEXAS

White Rock Lake Dog Park - Dallas
dallasdogparks.org
Mockingbird Point within White Rock Lake Park
Tues.-Sun. 5 a.m.-midnight
Approximately 2 1/2 acres, fenced, benches, disposal bags, trees, parking, restrooms, trash cans, water fountains. Three separate areas are fenced - 3/4 acre for small dogs, 1 3/4 acres for large dogs and an area for dogs swimming in White Rock Lake.

VIRGINIA

Note: Disposal bag receptacles are provided at Alexandria parks; patrons must provide their own bags.

Ben Brenman Park - Alexandria
ci.alexandria.va.us/recreation/parks/dogpark.html#fenced
Along Backlick Creek
Daily 6 a.m.-10 p.m.
Fenced, trash bins, parking, disposal bag receptacles.

Dog Park - Alexandria
ci.alexandria.va.us/recreation/parks/dogpark.html#fenced
5000 block of Duke Street east of the Charles E. Beatley, Jr. Library
Daily 6 a.m.-10 p.m.
Fenced, trash bins, parking, disposal bag receptacles.

Montgomery Park - Alexandria
ci.alexandria.va.us/recreation/parks/dogpark.html#fenced
At the corner of Fairfax and 1st streets
Daily 6 a.m.-10 p.m.
Fenced, trash bins, parking, disposal bag receptacles.

Simpson Stadium Park - Alexandria
ci.alexandria.va.us/recreation/parks/dogpark.html#fenced
At Monroe Avenue
Daily 6 a.m.-10 p.m.
Fenced, trash bins, parking, disposal bag receptacles, dog-accessible water fountains.

Off-leash, unfenced, under voice control areas:

Chinquapin Park - Alexandria
ci.alexandria.va.us/recreation/parks/dogpark.html#unfenced
At the east end of the loop road
Daily 6 a.m.-10 p.m.
Unfenced site.

Hooff's Run - Alexandria
ci.alexandria.va.us/recreation/parks/dogpark.html#unfenced
East of Commonwealth Avenue between Oak and Chapman streets
Daily 6 a.m.-10 p.m.
Unfenced site. Please note area is marked by bollards.

Monticello Park - Alexandria
ci.alexandria.va.us/recreation/parks/dogpark.html#unfenced
Area to the east of the entrance
Daily 6 a.m.-10 p.m.
Unfenced 50-foot by 200-foot site. Please note area is marked by bollards.

VIRGINIA (CONT'D)

Tarleton Park - Alexandria
ci.alexandria.va.us/recreation/parks/dogpark.html#unfenced
Along Old Mill Run west of Gordon Street
Daily 6 a.m.-10 p.m.
Unfenced site.

WindMill Hill Park - Alexandria
ci.alexandria.va.us/recreation/parks/dogpark.html#unfenced
Gibbon and Union streets
Daily 6 a.m.-10 p.m.
Unfenced site.

Dog exercise area - Alexandria
ci.alexandria.va.us/recreation/parks/dogpark.html#unfenced
Northeast corner of Founders Park (at Oronoco Street and the Potomac River)
Daily 6 a.m.-10 p.m.
Unfenced 100-foot by 100-foot site. Please note area is marked by bollards.

Dog exercise area - Alexandria
ci.alexandria.va.us/recreation/parks/dogpark.html#unfenced
Southeast corner of Braddock Road and Commonwealth Avenue
Daily 6 a.m.-10 p.m.
Unfenced site.

Dog exercise area - Alexandria
ci.alexandria.va.us/recreation/parks/dogpark.html#unfenced
Area between Ft. Williams and New Ft. Williams Parkway
Daily 6 a.m.-10 p.m.
Unfenced site. Please note area is marked by bollards.

Dog exercise area - Alexandria
ci.alexandria.va.us/recreation/parks/dogpark.html#unfenced
Southeast corner of Armistead and Beauregard streets
Daily 6 a.m.-10 p.m.
Unfenced site.

Dog exercise area - Alexandria
ci.alexandria.va.us/recreation/parks/dogpark.html#unfenced
Along Chambliss Street, south of the tennis courts at Grigsby Avenue
Daily 6 a.m.-10 p.m.
Unfenced site. Please note area is marked by bollards.

Dog exercise area - Alexandria
ci.alexandria.va.us/recreation/parks/dogpark.html#unfenced
East side of entrance to Fort Ward Park
Daily 6 a.m.-10 p.m.
Unfenced 100-foot by 100-foot site. Please note area is marked by bollards.

Dog exercise area - Alexandria
ci.alexandria.va.us/recreation/parks/dogpark.html#unfenced
From Median to Timberbranch Parkway between Braddock Road and Oakley Place
Daily 6 a.m.-10 p.m.
Unfenced site. Please note area is marked by bollards.

Dog exercise area - Alexandria
ci.alexandria.va.us/recreation/parks/dogpark.html#unfenced
Area west of the Edison Street cul-de-sac, between the bike trail and Berkey Photo Processing
Daily 6 a.m.-10 p.m.
Unfenced site. Please note area is marked by bollards.

Dog exercise area - Alexandria
ci.alexandria.va.us/recreation/parks/dogpark.html#unfenced
200 feet of the W&OD Railroad right-of-way located south of Raymond Avenue
Daily 6 a.m.-10 p.m.
Unfenced site. Please note area is marked by bollards.

Benjamin Banneker Park - Arlington County
arlingtondogs.org
1600 block of North Sycamore Street (Take I-66 west to Sycamore Street/exit 69. Turn left on Sycamore and proceed past the East Falls Church Metro Station. Turn right onto North 16th Street and take the first right, which dead-ends at the dog exercise area.)
Daily sunrise to a half-hour after sunset
Fully fenced, water source, picnic table and benches.

Fort Barnard Park - Arlington County
arlingtondogs.org
Corner of South Pollard Street and South Walter Reed Drive (From Route 50, take Glebe Road south. Turn right on South Walter Reed Drive and proceed to Pollard Street; the park is on the right-hand side.)
Daily sunrise to a half-hour after sunset
Fully fenced, water source, picnic table and benches.

Glencarlyn Park - Arlington County
arlingtondogs.org
301 South Harrison St. (From Route 50, head west to the Carlin Springs Road exit. Exit right and then turn left at the stop sign. Pass under Route 50 and follow Carlin Springs to 4th Street. Turn left on 4th Street and proceed five blocks until the road ends at the Glencarlyn Park sign. Follow the park road until it ends. Park and walk over a small bridge and stream to the exercise area.)
Daily sunrise to a half-hour after sunset
Unfenced area located near a creek and woods, picnic table and benches.

Madison Community Center - Arlington County
arlingtondogs.org
3829 North Stafford St. (From Lee Highway/US 29 northbound or southbound, turn onto Military Road and follow it to the end. Turn left onto Old Glebe Road; the exercise area is on the left. Drive past and turn left into the Community Center entrance. Park in the center's front lot and walk to the left of the building to enter the area.)
Daily sunrise to a half-hour after sunset
Fully fenced.

Shirlington Park - Arlington County
arlingtondogs.org
2601 S. Arlington Mill Dr. (The dog area is located along the bicycle path behind a storage facility that borders South Four Mile Run, between Shirlington Road and South Walter Reed Drive; it is close to but not in Jennie Dean Park. Heading east on South Four Mile Run, take a right on Nelson; if heading west on South Four Mile Run, take a left. Proceed on Nelson and park behind the storage facility. The dog area is between the facility and the water; there is no signage indicating its location.)
Daily sunrise to a half-hour after sunset
Partially fenced, water source, picnic table and benches.

VIRGINIA (CONT'D)

Utah Park - Arlington County
arlingtondogs.org
3308 S. Stafford St. (From I-395 North or South, take the Shirlington exit and follow signs to Quaker Lane. From Quaker Lane, take the first right onto 32nd Road S. Take the next right onto S. Stafford Street and follow the curve to the yield sign. At the sign, turn left onto 32nd Street. Park at the bottom of the hill or along the street. The dog exercise area is on the far side of the softball diamond from the parking lot.)
Daily sunrise to a half-hour after sunset
Fully fenced, water source, picnic table and benches.

Red Wing Park - Virginia Beach
vbgov.com/e-gov/vbcsg/faqinfo/0,1172,5353,00.html
1398 General Booth Blvd.
Daily 7:30 a.m.-sunset; closed Jan. 1, Martin Luther King Day, Veterans Day, Thanksgiving and Dec. 25
Fenced, benches, disposal bags, parking, restrooms, water. Access for the disabled.
Annual fee $5 for first-time visitors, who must register at the park office, show proof of their pet's rabies shot and vaccines, and obtain a city dog license.

Woodstock Community Park - Virginia Beach
vbgov.com/e-gov/vbcsg/faqinfo/0,1172,5353,00.html
5709 Providence Rd.
Daily 7:30 a.m.-sunset; closed Jan. 1, Martin Luther King Day, Veterans Day, Thanksgiving and Dec. 25
Fenced, benches, disposal bags, parking, restrooms. Access for the disabled.
Annual fee $3 for first-time visitors, who must register at the park office, show proof of their pet's rabies shot and vaccines, and obtain a city dog license.

WASHINGTON

Dr. Jose Rizal Park - Seattle
coladog.org
1008 12th Ave. South, on North Beacon Hill (off-leash area is in the lower portion of the park)
Daily 6 a.m.-11 p.m.
4 acres, fenced, double-gated entry, parking, beautiful view of downtown, doggie drinking fountain.

Genesee Park - Seattle
coladog.org
46th Avenue South and South Genesee Street
Daily 6 a.m.-11 p.m.
Fenced, double-gated entry, doggie drinking fountain, parking.

Golden Gardens Park - Seattle
coladog.org
8498 Seaview Pl. N.W. in Ballard
Daily 6 a.m.-11 p.m.
Fenced, lighted, parking, doggie drinking fountain. The off-leash area is located in the upper (eastern) portion of the park, not in the lower beach area. Please note that dogs are not allowed on the beach.

I-90 "Blue Dog Pond" - Seattle
coladog.org
Martin Luther King Jr. Way and South Massachusetts Street, on the northwest corner
Daily 6 a.m.-11 p.m.
Fenced, parking, sculpture of large blue dog, doggie drinking fountain. Note: There are no off-leash areas in I-90 Lid Park, located just east of Blue Dog Pond.

Magnuson Park - Seattle
coladog.org
6500 Sandpoint Way N.E. (enter the park at 74th Street and drive to the end of the road)
Daily 6 a.m.-11 p.m.
9 acres, fenced, small dog area, beach access, parking, shelter, double-gated entry, doggie drinking fountain.

Northacres Park - Seattle
coladog.org
West of I-5 at North 130th Street
Daily 6 a.m.-11 p.m.
Fenced, double-gated entry, parking, doggie drinking fountain. The off-leash area is in the northeast corner of the park at 12530 Third Ave. N.E., north of the ball field. Parking is available on the west side of the park along 1st Street N.E. and on the south side along North 125th Street.

Regrade Park
coladog.org
Downtown at 3rd Avenue and Bell Street
13,000 square feet, fenced, double-gated entry, doggie drinking fountain.

Westcrest Park - Seattle
coladog.org
8806 8th Ave. S.W. in West Seattle
Daily 6 a.m.-11 p.m.
Fenced, parking, doggie drinking fountain. The off-leash area is located along the east side of the reservoir.

Woodland Park - Seattle
coladog.org
West of the tennis courts on West Green Lake Way North
Daily 6 a.m.-11 p.m.
Fenced, double-gated entry, doggie drinking fountain, parking.

Canada

ALBERTA

91 Street Right of Way - Edmonton
gov.edmonton.ab.ca (780) 496-1475
Berm east of 91 Street, starting at 10 Avenue and extending north to Whitemud Freeway and east to 76 Street
Unfenced site.

Buena Vista Great Meadow - Edmonton
gov.edmonton.ab.ca (780) 496-1475
North of Laurier Park and Buena Vista Drive and south of Melton Ravine (in the vicinity of 88 Avenue)
Unfenced site. Does not include the pedestrian bridge access trail, Yorath property or the trail north to McKenzie Ravine. This is a hot-air balloon site, so please leash your dog when balloons launch.

Hermitage Park North - Edmonton
gov.edmonton.ab.ca (780) 496-1475
129 Avenue to 137 Avenue, also 22 Street along the riverbank where signs designate an off-leash area.
Unfenced site. This is a multi-use area in the valley north of the park's fishing pond and picnic area.

Jackie Parker Park - Edmonton
gov.edmonton.ab.ca (780) 496-1475
Whitemud Freeway and 50th Street
Unfenced site. Includes the area south of the 44 Avenue entrance. Does not include golf course.

Keehewin Blackmud - Edmonton
gov.edmonton.ab.ca (780) 496-1475
Pipeline corridor, 104 Street and 20 Avenue to the south end of 109 Street (excludes Bearspaw Drive West and Blackmud Creek and Ravine)
Unfenced site.

Kennedale - Edmonton
gov.edmonton.ab.ca (780) 496-1475
Ravine west of the 40 Street loop, west to 47 Street and the top of the bank
Unfenced site.

Lauderdale - Edmonton
gov.edmonton.ab.ca (780) 496-1475
South end of Grand Trunk Park, from 127 to 129 Avenue and 113A to 109 Street
Unfenced site.

Mill Creek Ravine - Edmonton
gov.edmonton.ab.ca (780) 496-1475
Access is from 68 Avenue and 93 Street (west side of Argyll Park) or from the north side of Argyll Park
Unfenced site. A granular trail along the bottom of the ravine leads to the Whyte (82) Avenue overpass.

Terwillegar Park - Edmonton
gov.edmonton.ab.ca (780) 496-1475
Park access via Rabbit Hill Road
Unfenced site. This is a multi-use area.

MANITOBA

Bourkevale Park - Winnipeg
winnipeg.ca/publicworks/parks/fieldsforfido.asp
Area south of the dike, along the riverbank
Daily 6 a.m.-10 p.m.
Unfenced site, trash cans, parking, bring your own disposal bags.

Juba Park & Pioneer Avenue - Winnipeg
winnipeg.ca/publicworks/parks/fieldsforfido.asp
All vacant land west of the walkway to Juba Park
Daily 6 a.m.-10 p.m.
Unfenced site, trash cans, parking, bring your own disposal bags.

Kil-Cona Park - Winnipeg
winnipeg.ca/publicworks/parks/fieldsforfido.asp
The area north of the west parking lot
Daily 6 a.m.-10 p.m.
Unfenced site, trash cans, parking, bring your own disposal bags.

King's Park - Winnipeg
winnipeg.ca/publicworks/parks/fieldsforfido.asp
South end of park, south of the lake
Daily 6 a.m.-10 p.m.
Unfenced site, trash cans, parking, bring your own disposal bags.

Maple Grove Park - Winnipeg
winnipeg.ca/publicworks/parks/fieldsforfido.asp
North area of park
Daily 6 a.m.-10 p.m.
Unfenced site, trash cans, parking, bring your own disposal bags.

Westview Park - Winnipeg
winnipeg.ca/publicworks/parks/fieldsforfido.asp
Entire park is an off-leash area
Daily 6 a.m.-10 p.m.
Unfenced site, trash cans, parking, bring your own disposal bags.

United States

CALIFORNIA

Disneyland® Resort

(714) 781-4565, 1313 S. Harbor Blvd. via I-5 Disneyland Drive and Disney Way exits, Anaheim
Disneyland® Resort consists of two family-oriented theme parks — Disneyland Park and Disney's California Adventure Park — and the shops, restaurants and entertainment of Downtown Disney®. Indoor kennel facilities $10. Mon.-Fri. 10-8, Sat. 9 a.m.-midnight, Sun. 9 a.m.-10 p.m. Extended hours in summer; phone ahead to confirm. Admission to either park $53; over 60, $51; ages 3-9, $43. Parking fee. disneyland.disney.go.com

SeaWorld Adventure Park

(619) 226-3901 or (800) 257-4268, 500 SeaWorld Dr., San Diego
SeaWorld offers four major animal shows, rides and playgrounds, a marina and exhibits featuring marine creatures from around the world. Pet facility provided for a nominal charge on a first-come, first-serve basis. Opens daily at 9, mid-June through Labor Day; at 10, rest of year. Closing times vary. Admission $50; ages 3-9, $40. Parking fee.
www.seaworld.com/ca

Universal Studios Hollywood

(800) 864-8377, 100 Universal City Plaza, Universal City
In addition to thrill rides and arcade games, Universal Studios gives visitors a behind-the-scenes look at the workings of a major film and TV studio. Complimentary kennel service. Daily 9-9 in summer, 10-6 rest of year. Box office closes at 5 in summer, at 4 rest of year. Hours may vary; phone ahead to confirm. Closed Thanksgiving and Dec. 25. Admission $53; over 59, $51; under 48 inches tall $43. Parking fee.
themeparks.universalstudios.com

DISTRICT OF COLUMBIA

Washington Monument

(202) 426-6841, 15th Street and Constitution Avenue N.W., Washington, D.C.
This instantly recognizable 555-foot marble obelisk commemorates our nation's first president and is surrounded by expansive grounds. Pets on leash. Daily 9-5; closed Dec. 25. Free. www.nps.gov/wamo

FLORIDA

Busch Gardens Tampa Bay

(866) 353-8622 or (888) 800-5447, 3000 E. Busch Blvd., Tampa
This African-themed family entertainment park and outstanding zoological facility features all kinds of thrill rides and numerous opportunities for animal observation. Outdoor kennel facilities. Generally open daily at 9 a.m.; closing times vary. Phone ahead to confirm hours. Admission $55; ages 3-9, $45. Parking fee.
www.buschgardens.com

SeaWorld Orlando

(407) 351-3600 or (800) 327-2424, 7007 SeaWorld Dr. at I-4 and SR 528 (Bee Line Expressway), Orlando
A research facility as well as a theme park, SeaWorld Orlando presents crowd-pleasing animal shows starring a family of performing killer whales. Air-conditioned kennels ($8). Generally opens daily at 9; closing times vary. Phone ahead to confirm hours. Admission $59; ages 3-9, $48. Parking fee. www.seaworld.com

Universal Orlando Resort

(407) 363-8000, off I-4 exit 75A (eastbound) or 74B (westbound) following signs, Orlando
At Universal Orlando you can "ride the movies" at the Universal Studios theme park, cavort with superheroes and cartoon characters at the Islands of Adventure theme park, or visit the specialty shops, celebrity-themed restaurants and entertainment venues at CityWalk. Air-conditioned and outdoor kennels. Theme parks open daily at 9 a.m.; closing times vary by season. Phone ahead to confirm hours. CityWalk open daily 11 a.m.-2 a.m. Admission to both theme parks $59.75; ages 3-9, $48. Individual CityWalk venue charges vary. Parking fee $9.
themeparks.universalstudios.com

Walt Disney World® Resort

(407) 824-4321, theme parks accessible from US 192, Osceola Parkway and several I-4 exits, Lake Buena Vista
Walt Disney World has — count 'em — four theme parks: Magic Kingdom® Park, Epcot®, Disney's Animal Kingdom® Theme Park and Disney-MGM Studios, plus shopping, dining and entertainment at the Downtown Disney® Area. Air-conditioned and outside kennels. Theme parks generally open daily at 9 a.m.; closing times vary. One-day, one-park admission $59.75; ages 3-9, $48. Parking fee. disneyworld.disney.go.com

GEORGIA

Six Flags Over Georgia

(770) 948-9290, 275 Riverside Pkwy. (off I-20), Austell
Six Flags offers more than 100 rides, attractions and shows, a 12,000-seat concert amphitheater, Broadway-style musical shows and a July 4 fireworks display. Kennel facilities (water provided, but no food). Open daily at 10 a.m., late May to mid-Aug.; Sat.-Sun. at 10, mid-Mar. to late May and mid-Aug. to late Oct. Closing times vary. Admission $43.99, over 54 and under 49 inches tall $26.99, under 2 free. Parking fee.
www.sixflags.com

ILLINOIS

 Six Flags Great America

(847) 249-4636 or (847) 249-1776, 542 N. Route 21, Gurnee
Batman the Ride, Iron Wolf and Raging Bull are among the thrill rides at this family theme park, which also has a section of rides and attractions for children under 54 inches tall. Kennel facilities. Open daily at 10 a.m., late Apr. to mid-Sept.; Sat.-Sun. at 10, mid-Sept. to late Oct. Closing times vary; phone ahead to confirm hours. Admission $44.99, over 60 and under 55 inches tall $29.99, under 3 free. Parking fee. www.sixflags.com

IOWA

 Pella Historical Village

(641) 628-2409 or 628-4311, 507 Franklin St., Pella
A country store, log cabin, grist mill, windmill, smithy and other buildings (including Wyatt Earp's boyhood home) are reminders of this town's Dutch Heritage. Pets on leash (grounds only). Mon.-Sat. 9-5, Mar.-Dec.; Thurs.-Sat. 9-5, rest of year. Admission $8; ages 5-18, $2.

MASSACHUSETTS

 Bunker Hill Monument

(617) 242-5641, in Monument Square on Breed's Hill, Charlestown
Part of Boston National Historical Park, this 221-foot-tall granite obelisk commemorates the site of the Battle of Bunker Hill on June 17, 1775. Pets on leash (grounds only); must pick up after pet. Visitor lodge and exhibits daily 9-5. Free. www.nps.gov/bost/Bunker_Hill/htm

MISSISSIPPI

 Vicksburg National Military Park

(601) 636-0583, 3201 Clay St. (entered on the eastern edge off US 80)
More than 1,260 memorials, monuments, statues and markers honor the Union and Confederate troops who engaged in the siege of Vicksburg in 1863. Pets on leash. Grounds open daily dawn-dusk; visitor center daily 8-5. Admission $8 per private vehicle. www.nps.gov/vick

MISSOURI

 The Gateway Arch

(877) 982-1410, Memorial Drive and Market Street, St. Louis
This curved, stainless steel monument soars 630 feet high and symbolizes the gateway to the West. A tram ride takes visitors to an observation deck. Pets on leash (grounds only). Tram ticket center open daily 8 a.m.-10 p.m., Memorial Day-Labor Day; 9-6, rest of year. Closed Jan. 1, Thanksgiving and Dec. 25. Tram ride $8; ages 13-16, $7; ages 3-12, $3. www.gatewayarch.com

NORTH CAROLINA

 Paramount's Carowinds Theme Park

(704) 588-2600 in N.C., (803) 548-5300 or (800) 888-4386, 10 miles south on I-77 to exit 90, Charlotte
Themed areas at this park depict the past and present of the Carolinas, and offer roller coasters and water rides, children's play areas and other family entertainment. Air-conditioned kennels. Open daily, Jun.-Jul.; various times from late Mar. through May 31 and Aug. 1 to early Oct. Hours vary seasonally; phone ahead. Admission $44.99; over 55 and ages 3-6 or under 48 inches tall, $27.99. Parking fee. www.carowinds.com

OHIO

 Paramount's Kings Island

(513) 754-5700 or (800) 288-0808, Kings Island Drive (off I-71 exits 24 and 25), Kings Mills
Kings Island is a family entertainment park featuring 12 hair-raising roller coasters; WaterWorks, a water recreation playground; costumed cartoon characters; and a variety of live shows. Outdoor kennel facilities (fee). Open daily at 9 a.m., late May-Labor Day weekend; Sat.-Sun. at 9 a.m., early Apr. to mid-May. Phone ahead to confirm hours. Admission $44.99; over 59, ages 3-6 or under 48 inches tall, $26.99. Parking fee. www.pki.com

PENNSYLVANIA

 Hersheypark

(800) 437-7439, 100 W. Hersheypark Dr. (just off SR 743 and US 422), Hershey
The emphasis is on thrill rides at Hersheypark, plus live entertainment that includes a marine mammal show, song and dance reviews and big-name performers. Air-conditioned kennels. Open daily at 10 a.m., mid-May to late Sept.; Fri.-Sun. at 10, selected weekends in May. Closing times vary; phone ahead to confirm hours. Admission $39.95; over 54 and ages 3-8, $22.95; 70 and over $16.95.
Parking fee. www.hersheypark.com

TEXAS

 SeaWorld San Antonio

(210) 523-3611 or (800) 722-2762, 10500 Sea World Dr. (off SR 151 at the junction of Westover Hills Boulevard and Ellison Drive), San Antonio
Killer and beluga whales, sea lions, otters, walruses and dolphins perform at this marine life park, which also has shark exhibits, a penguin habitat and a children's playground. Outdoor kennel facilities (owner must provide food and water containers). Open daily at 10 a.m., early Mar.-Nov. 30; closing times vary. Admission $43.99; ages 3-9, $33.99 (phone to confirm times and admission). Parking fee. www.buschgardens.com/seaworld/tx

 Six Flags Over Texas

(817) 530-6000, 2201 Road to Six Flags (at the junction of I-30 and SR 360 exit 30), Arlington
Themed areas, each featuring thrill rides, food and entertainment, depict Texas under six different flags: Spain, France, Mexico, the Republic of Texas, the Confederate States of America and the United States. Air-conditioned kennels. Open daily, June 1 to mid-Aug.; Sat.-Sun (also Labor Day), late Mar. through May 31, mid-Aug. through Oct. 31 and early to mid-Dec. Hours vary; phone ahead to confirm schedule. Admission $41.99; over 54, the physically impaired and under 48 inches tall, $26.99; under 3 free. Parking fee. www.sixflags.com

VIRGINIA

 Busch Gardens Williamsburg

(800) 343-7946, 3 miles east on US 60 or off I-64 exit 242A, Williamsburg[<]This European-themed adventure park offers something for the entire family, from thrill rides to dance and music shows to villages representing England, Germany, France and other nations. Outdoor kennel facilities (England parking lot); fee $4 per pet per day. Open daily at 10 a.m., early May-Labor Day; closing times vary. Open at 10, late Mar.-early May and day after Labor Day-late Oct.; days and closing times vary. Admission $49.95; ages 3-6, $42.95. Parking fee. www.buschgardens.com

 Paramount's Kings Dominion

(804) 876-5000, 16000 Theme Park Dr. (on SR 30 1/2 mile east off I-95 exit 98), Doswell
Eight themed areas make up Kings Dominion, a full-scale theme park with thrill rides, kiddie play areas, costumed characters, live shows and specialty shopping.
Air-conditioned and outside kennels (fee); water provided, but not food. Park open daily, Memorial Day-Labor Day; Sat.-Sun., mid-Mar. to day before Memorial Day and first Sat. after Labor Day to mid-Oct. Hours vary seasonally; phone ahead. Admission $45.99; over 54, $39.99; ages 3-6, $31.99. Parking fee. www.kingsdominion.com

WASHINGTON

 Hovander Homestead

(360) 384-3444, 1 mile south via Hovander Road, Ferndale
This restored house, dating from 1903 and furnished with antiques, is within a large park encompassing gardens, picnic sites and a children's farm zoo. Pets on leash (grounds only). Grounds open daily 8 a.m.-dusk; house open Thurs.-Sun. noon-4:30, June 1-Labor Day. Grounds $4 per private vehicle. House $1; ages 5-12, 50 cents. www.co.whatcom.wa.us/parks/hovander/hovander.jsp

Canada

ONTARIO

Upper Canada Village

(613) 543-4328 or (800) 437-2233, 7 miles (11 kilometers) east on CR 2 off Hwy. 401, Morrisburg
Upper Canada Village re-creates life during the 1860s through a working community of artisans and costumed interpreters who perform chores typical of the era. Pets on leash (grounds only). Daily 9:30-5, Victoria Day weekend-Oct. 9. Village admission $16.95; over 65, $15.95; students with ID $10.50; ages 5-12, $7.50. www.uppercanadavillage.com

Paramount Canada's Wonderland

(905) 832-7000 or 832-8131, off Hwy. 400 (Rutherford Road exit northbound or Major Mackenzie Drive E. exit southbound) at 9580 Jane St., Vaughan
Thrill rides at this theme park include the Top Gun coaster and Drop Zone, a free-fall plunge, while Scooby Doo's Haunted Mansion and Hanna-Barbera Land will entertain little ones. Air-conditioned kennels (fee). Open daily at 10 a.m., late May-Labour Day; some weekends early to late May and day after Labour Day-second Sun. in Oct. Closing times vary. Grounds admission $24.99. Grounds and rides passport $49.99; over 59 and ages 3-6, $24.99. Parking fee. www.canadas-wonderland.com

NATIONAL PUBLIC LANDS

The National Public Lands listed below permit pets on a leash. Keep in mind that animals may be prohibited from entering public buildings and even some areas outdoors, particularly those that are ecologically sensitive. Specific pet policies vary from park to park and are subject to change. Always check in advance regarding any applicable regulations and to confirm that pets are still permitted where you are going.

Never leave your pet unattended. Keep him leashed or crated at all times. Follow park guidelines faithfully, and monitor your pet's behavior; the National Park Service may confiscate pets that harm wildlife or other visitors. *For additional information on outdoor vacations, see The Great Outdoors, p. 16.*

United States

ALABAMA

Conecuh National Forest
On the Alabama-Florida border.
(334) 222-2555
🚴 ⛺ 🥾 🏕 🏊

Horseshoe Bend National Military Park
12 mi. north of Dadeville on SR 49.
(256) 234-7111
🥾 🏕 🏊 🏠

Talladega National Forest
In central Alabama.
(256) 362-2909
⛺ 🥾 🏕 🏊

Tuskegee National Forest
Northeast of Tuskegee.
(334) 727-2652
⛺ 🥾 🏕

William B. Bankhead National Forest
In northwestern Alabama.
(205) 489-5111
🚴 ⛺ 🥾 🏕 🏊

ALASKA

Chugach National Forest
Along the Gulf of Alaska from Cape Suckling to Seward.
(907) 743-9500
⛺ 🥾 🏕 🏠

Denali National Park and Preserve
In south-central Alaska.
(907) 683-2294
⛺ 🥾 🏕 🏠 🍽

Glacier Bay National Park and Preserve
North of Cross Sound to the Canadian border.
(907) 697-2230
⛺ 🥾 🏠 🍽

Kenai Fjords National Park
Southeastern side of the Kenai Peninsula.
(907) 224-3175 or 224-2132
⛺ 🥾 🏕 🏠

Lake Clark National Park and Preserve
In southern Alaska.
(907) 228-6220
⛺ 🥾 🏠

Tongass National Forest
In southeastern Alaska.
(907) 586-8751 or 228-6220
⛺ 🥾 🏕 🏠

Wrangell-St. Elias National Park and Preserve
In southeastern Alaska, northwest of Tongass National Forest.
(907) 822-5234
⛺ 🥾 🏕 🏠 🍽

ARIZONA

Apache-Sitgreaves National Forests
In east-central Arizona.
(928) 333-4301
🚴 ⛺ 🥾 🏕 🏠 🍽

Coconino National Forest
In north-central Arizona.
(928) 527-3600
⛺ 🥾 🏕 🏊 🍽

Coronado National Forest
In southeastern Arizona and southwestern New Mexico.
(520) 388-8300
🚴 ⛺ 🥾 🏕 🏠

Glen Canyon National Recreation Area
In north-central Arizona.
(928) 608-6404 or 608-6200
⛺ 🥾 🏕 🏊 🏠 🍽

Grand Canyon National Park
In northwestern Arizona.
(928) 638-7888
⛺ 🥾 🏕 🏠 🍽

Kaibab National Forest
In north-central Arizona.
(928) 635-4061 or (800) 863-0546
⛺ 🥾 🏕 🏠 🍽

🚴 Bicycling   ⛺ Camping   🥾 Hiking   🏕 Picnicking
🏊 Swimming   🏠 Visitor center   🍽 Food service

Lake Mead National Recreation Area
In northwestern Arizona.
(702) 293-8906

Petrified Forest National Park
In east-central Arizona, east of Holbrook.
(928) 524-6228

Prescott National Forest
In central Arizona.
(928) 443-8000 or TDD (928) 443-8001

Saguaro National Park
Two districts, 15 mi. east and west of Tucson.
(520) 733-5153

Tonto National Forest
In central Arizona.
(602) 225-5200

ARKANSAS

Buffalo National River
In northwestern Arkansas.
(870) 741-5443

Felsenthal National Wildlife Refuge
7 mi. west of Crossett on US 82.
(870) 364-3167

Hot Springs National Park
In western Arkansas.
(501) 624-3383

Ouachita National Forest
In west-central Arkansas and southeastern Oklahoma.
(501) 321-5202

Ozark National Forest
In northwestern Arkansas.
(479) 968-2354

St. Francis National Forest
In east-central Arkansas.
(870) 295-5278

CALIFORNIA

Angeles National Forest
In southern California.
(626) 574-5200

Cleveland National Forest
In southwestern California.
(858) 673-6180

Death Valley National Park
Along the Nevada border in east-central California.
(760) 786-2331

Eldorado National Forest
In central California.
(530) 644-6048

Golden Gate National Recreation Area
North of the Golden Gate Bridge and in northern and western San Francisco.
(415) 561-4700

Inyo National Forest
In central California.
(760) 873-2400

Joshua Tree National Park
East of Desert Hot Springs.
(760) 367-5500

Klamath National Forest
In northern California.
(530) 842-6131

Lassen National Forest
In northeastern California.
(530) 257-2151

Lassen Volcanic National Park
In northeastern California.
(530) 595-4444

Los Padres National Forest
In southern California.
(805) 968-6640 or TDD (805) 968-6790

Mendocino National Forest
In northwestern California.
(530) 934-2350 or 934-3316, or TDD (530) 934-7724

Modoc National Forest
In northeastern California.
(530) 233-5811

Mojave National Preserve
Between I-15 and I-40 in southeastern California.
(760) 733-4040

Plumas National Forest
In northern California.
(530) 283-2050
🚵 🔺 🥾 ⛱ 🏊 👥 🍽

Point Reyes National Seashore
Along the California coast just north of San Francisco.
(415) 464-5100
🚵 🔺 🥾 ⛱ 👥

Redwood National Park
On the northern California coast.
(707) 464-6101, ext. 5064 or 5265
🚵 🔺 🥾 ⛱ 🏊 👥 🍽

San Bernardino National Forest
In southern California.
(909) 382-2600
🚵 🔺 🥾 ⛱ 🏊 👥 🍽

Santa Monica Mountains National Recreation Area
West from Griffith Park in Los Angeles to the Ventura County line.
(805) 370-2301 or 370-2300 in Calif.
🚵 🔺 🥾 ⛱ 👥 🍽

Sequoia and Kings Canyon National Parks
In east-central California.
(559) 565-3341
🔺 🥾 ⛱ 👥 🍽

Sequoia National Forest
In south-central California.
(559) 784-1500
🚵 🔺 🥾 ⛱ 🏊 👥 🍽

Shasta-Trinity National Forests
In northern California.
(530) 226-2500
🔺 🥾 ⛱ 🏊 👥 🍽

Sierra National Forest
In central California.
(559) 297-0706
🚵 🔺 🥾 ⛱ 🏊 👥 🍽

Six Rivers National Forest
In northwestern California.
(707) 441-3523 or (707) 442-1721
🚵 🔺 🥾 ⛱ 🏊 👥 🍽

Smith River National Recreation Area
Within Six Rivers National Forest in northwestern California.
(707) 457-3131
🚵 🔺 🥾 ⛱ 🏊

Stanislaus National Forest
In central California.
(209) 532-3671
🚵 🔺 🥾 ⛱ 🏊 🍽

Tahoe National Forest
In north-central California.
(530) 265-4531
🔺 🥾 ⛱ 🏊 👥 🍽

Whiskeytown-Shasta-Trinity National Recreation Area
North and west of Redding.
(530) 242-3400
🚵 🔺 🥾 ⛱ 🏊 👥

Yosemite National Park
In central California.
(209) 372-0200
🚵 🔺 🥾 ⛱ 🏊 👥 🍽

COLORADO

Arapaho and Roosevelt National Forests
In north-central Colorado.
(970) 498-2770 or TDD 498-2707
🚵 🔺 🥾 ⛱ 🏊 👥 🍽

Arapaho National Recreation Area
In north-central Colorado.
(970) 887-4100 or TDD 887-4101
🚵 🔺 🥾 ⛱ 🏊

Black Canyon of the Gunnison National Park
In western Colorado.
(970) 641-2337
🔺 🥾 ⛱ 👥 🍽

Curecanti National Recreation Area
In south-central Colorado between Gunnison and Montrose, paralleling US 50.
(970) 641-2337
🔺 🥾 ⛱ 🏊 👥 🍽

Grand Mesa-Uncompahgre-Gunnison National Forests
In west-central Colorado.
(970) 874-6600
🚵 🔺 🥾 ⛱ 🍽

Mesa Verde National Park
In southwestern Colorado.
(970) 529-4465
🔺 🥾 ⛱ 👥 🍽

Pike National Forest
In central Colorado.
(719) 553-1400
🚵 🔺 🥾 ⛱ 👥

Rio Grande National Forest
In south-central Colorado.
(719) 852-5941
🚵 🔺 🥾 ⛱ 👥

Rocky Mountain National Park
In north-central Colorado.
(970) 586-1206 or 586-1333
🔺 🥾 ⛱ 👥 🍽

🚵 Bicycling   🔺 Camping   🥾 Hiking   ⛱ Picnicking
🏊 Swimming   👥 Visitor center   🍽 Food service

Routt National Forest
In northwestern Colorado.
(970) 879-1870
⬚⬚⬚⬚⬚⬚

San Isabel National Forest
In south-central Colorado.
(719) 553-1400
⬚⬚⬚⬚

San Juan National Forest
In southwestern Colorado.
(970) 247-4874
⬚⬚⬚⬚⬚⬚⬚

White River National Forest
In west-central Colorado.
(970) 945-2521
⬚⬚⬚⬚⬚⬚

FLORIDA

Ocala National Forest
In north-central Florida.
(352) 236-0288
⬚⬚⬚⬚⬚⬚⬚

GEORGIA

Chattahoochee and Oconee National Forests
In central and northern Georgia.
(770) 297-3000
⬚⬚⬚⬚⬚

Chattahoochee River National Recreation Area
North of Atlanta.
(678) 538-1200
⬚⬚⬚

IDAHO

Boise National Forest
In southwestern Idaho.
(208) 373-4007
⬚⬚⬚⬚⬚⬚⬚

Caribou National Forest
In southeastern Idaho.
(208) 524-7500
⬚⬚⬚⬚

Clearwater National Forest
In northeastern Idaho.
(208) 476-4541
⬚⬚⬚⬚⬚

Hells Canyon National Recreation Area
In western Idaho and northeastern Oregon.
(509) 758-0616 or 758-1957
⬚⬚⬚⬚⬚

Idaho Panhandle National Forests
In northern and northwestern Idaho.
(208) 765-7223
⬚⬚⬚⬚⬚

Nez Perce National Forest
In northwestern Idaho.
(208) 983-1950
⬚⬚⬚⬚⬚⬚

Payette National Forest
In west-central Idaho.
(208) 634-0700
⬚⬚⬚⬚⬚⬚

Salmon-Challis National Forest
In east-central Idaho.
(208) 756-5100
⬚⬚⬚⬚⬚

Sawtooth National Forest
In south-central Idaho.
(208) 737-3200 or TDD (208) 737-3235
⬚⬚⬚⬚⬚⬚⬚

Sawtooth National Recreation Area
In south-central Idaho.
(208) 727-5013 or (800) 260-5970
⬚⬚⬚⬚⬚⬚⬚

Targhee National Forest
In southeastern Idaho.
(208) 624-3151
⬚⬚⬚⬚⬚

ILLINOIS

Shawnee National Forest
In southern Illinois.
(618) 253-7114 or (800) 699-6637
⬚⬚⬚⬚

INDIANA

Hoosier National Forest
In southern Indiana.
(812) 275-5987
⬚⬚⬚⬚⬚

Indiana Dunes National Lakeshore
On the southern shore of Lake Michigan.
(219) 926-7561, ext. 225
⬚⬚⬚⬚⬚⬚

KENTUCKY

Big South Fork National River and Recreation Area
In southeastern Kentucky and northeastern Tennessee.
(423) 286-7275 or (606) 376-5073
⬚⬚⬚⬚⬚⬚

Daniel Boone National Forest
In eastern Kentucky.
(859) 745-3100
⬚⬚⬚⬚⬚

Daniel Boone National Forest (Laurel River Lake)
In southeastern Kentucky west of Corbin.
(859) 745-3100
⬚⬚⬚⬚

Daniel Boone National Forest (Rockcastle)
In southeastern Kentucky 22 mi. southwest of London via SR 192/3497.
(859) 745-3100
△ 🕵 ⛱ 🏊

Land Between the Lakes National Recreation Area
In western Kentucky and Tennessee.
(270) 924-2000 or (800) 525-7077
🚲 △ 🕵 ⛱ 🏊 🏠

Mammoth Cave National Park
In south-central Kentucky 10 mi. west of Cave City.
(270) 758-2180
🚲 △ 🕵 ⛱ 🏠 🍴

LOUISIANA
Bayou Sauvage National Wildlife Refuge
Within the New Orleans city limits.
(985) 882-2000
🕵 ⛱

Kisatchie National Forest
In central and northern Louisiana.
(318) 473-7160
△ 🕵 ⛱ 🏊

Sabine National Wildlife Refuge
8 mi. south of Hackberry on SR 27.
(337) 762-3816
🕵 🏠

MAINE
Acadia National Park
Along the Atlantic coast southeast of Bangor.
(207) 288-3338
🚲 △ 🕵 ⛱ 🏊 🏠 🍴

MARYLAND
Assateague Island National Seashore
In southeastern Maryland south of Ocean City.
(410) 641-1441 or 641-3030
🚲 △ 🕵 ⛱ 🏊 🏠

MICHIGAN
Hiawatha National Forest
In Michigan's Upper Peninsula.
(906) 786-4062
🚲 △ 🕵 ⛱ 🏊 🏠

Huron-Manistee National Forests
In the northern part of the Lower Peninsula.
(231) 775-2421 or (800) 821-6263
🚲 △ 🕵 ⛱ 🏊 🏠

Ottawa National Forest
In Michigan's Upper Peninsula.
(906) 932-1330
🚲 △ 🕵 ⛱ 🏊 🏠

Pictured Rocks National Lakeshore
Along Lake Superior in Michigan's Upper Peninsula.
(906) 387-2607
△ 🕵 ⛱ 🏊 🏠

Sleeping Bear Dunes National Lakeshore
Along Lake Michigan in the northwestern part of the Lower Peninsula.
(231) 326-5134
△ 🕵 ⛱ 🏊 🏠

MINNESOTA
Chippewa National Forest
In north-central Minnesota.
(218) 335-8600 or TDD (218) 335-8632
🚲 △ 🕵 ⛱ 🏊 🏠 🍴

Superior National Forest
In northeastern Minnesota.
(218) 626-4300
🚲 △ 🕵 ⛱ 🏊 🏠 🍴

MISSISSIPPI
Bienville National Forest
In central Mississippi.
(601) 469-3811
△ 🕵 ⛱ 🏊 🏠

Gulf Islands National Seashore
Along the Gulf of Mexico in southern Mississippi.
(228) 875-9057
△ ⛱ 🏊 🏠

MISSOURI
Mark Twain National Forest
In southern Missouri.
(573) 364-4621
🚲 △ 🕵 ⛱ 🏊

Mark Twain National Forest (Big Bay)
1 mi. southeast of Shell Knob on SR 39, then 3 mi. southeast on CR YY.
(573) 364-4621
△ ⛱ 🏊

Mark Twain National Forest (Crane Lake)
12 mi. south of Ironton off SR 49 and CR E.
(573) 364-4621
🚲 🕵 ⛱

Mark Twain National Forest (Fourche Lake)
18 mi. west of Doniphan on SR 160.
(573) 364-4621
🕵 ⛱

🚲 Bicycling   △ Camping   🕵 Hiking   ⛱ Picnicking
🏊 Swimming   🏠 Visitor center   🍴 Food service

Mark Twain National Forest (Noblett Lake)
8 mi. west of Willow Springs on SR 76, then 1.5 mi. south on SR 181, 3 mi. southeast on CR AP and 1 mi. southwest on FR 857.
(573) 364-4621

Mark Twain National Forest (Pinewoods Lake)
2 mi. west of Ellsinore on SR 60.
(573) 364-4621

Mark Twain National Forest (Red Bluff)
1 mi. east of Davisville on CR V, then 1 mi. north on FR 2011.
(573) 364-4621

Ozark National Scenic Riverways
In southeastern Missouri.
(573) 323-4236

MONTANA

Beaverhead-Deerlodge National Forest
In southwestern Montana.
(406) 683-3900

Bighorn Canyon National Recreation Area
In southern Montana and northern Wyoming.
(406) 666-2412

Bitterroot National Forest
In western Montana.
(406) 363-7161

Custer National Forest/Dakota Prairie Grasslands
In southeastern Montana.
(406) 657-6200

Flathead National Forest
In northwestern Montana.
(406) 758-5204

Gallatin National Forest
In south-central Montana.
(406) 522-2520

Glacier National Park
In northwestern Montana.
(406) 888-7800

Helena National Forest
In west-central Montana.
(406) 449-5201

Kootenai National Forest
In northwestern Montana.
(406) 293-6211

Lewis and Clark National Forest
In central Montana.
(406) 791-7700

NEBRASKA

Nebraska National Forest
In central and northwestern Nebraska.
(308) 432-0300 or TDD (308) 432-0304

Oglala National Grassland
In northwestern Nebraska, 6 mi. north of Crawford via SR 2.
(308) 432-4475 or 665-3900

NEVADA

Great Basin National Park
In central Nevada, 5 mi. west of Baker near the Nevada-Utah border.
(775) 234-7331

Lake Mead National Recreation Area
In southeastern Nevada.
(702) 293-8906

Humboldt-Toiyabe National Forest
In central, western, northern and southern Nevada and eastern California.
(775) 331-6444

NEW HAMPSHIRE

White Mountain National Forest
In northern New Hampshire.
(603) 528-8721 or TDD (603) 528-8722

NEW JERSEY

Gateway National Recreation Area
In northeastern New Jersey (Sandy Hook Unit).
(732) 872-5970

NEW MEXICO

Carson National Forest
In north-central New Mexico.
(505) 758-6200

Chaco Culture National Historical Park
In northwestern New Mexico.
(505) 786-7014

Cibola National Forest
In central New Mexico.
(505) 346-3900
⟦🚴⟧ ⟦🏕⟧ ⟦🥾⟧ ⟦🌳⟧ ⟦🏊⟧ ⟦🏛⟧ ⟦🍽⟧

Gila National Forest
In southwestern New Mexico.
(505) 388-8201
⟦🏕⟧ ⟦🥾⟧ ⟦🌳⟧ ⟦🏊⟧ ⟦🏛⟧

Lincoln National Forest
In south-central New Mexico.
(505) 434-7200 or TTY (505) 434-7296
⟦🚴⟧ ⟦🏕⟧ ⟦🥾⟧ ⟦🌳⟧ ⟦🍽⟧

Santa Fe National Forest
In north-central New Mexico between the San Pedro
Mountains and the Sangre de Cristo Mountains.
(505) 438-7840
⟦🚴⟧ ⟦🏕⟧ ⟦🥾⟧ ⟦🌳⟧ ⟦🏛⟧

NEW YORK

Finger Lakes National Forest
In south-central New York on a ridge between Seneca and
Cayuga lakes, via I-90, I-81 and SR 17.
(607) 546-4470
⟦🏕⟧ ⟦🥾⟧ ⟦🌳⟧

Fire Island National Seashore
In southeastern New York on Fire Island, off the south
shore of Long Island.
(631) 289-4810
⟦🏕⟧ ⟦🥾⟧ ⟦🌳⟧ ⟦🏊⟧ ⟦🏛⟧ ⟦🍽⟧

Gateway National Recreation Area (Jamaica Bay District)
On Brooklyn and Queens boroughs in New York City.
(718) 354-4606
⟦🚴⟧ ⟦🥾⟧ ⟦🌳⟧ ⟦🏊⟧ ⟦🏛⟧ ⟦🍽⟧

Gateway National Recreation Area (Staten Island Unit)
On Staten Island borough in New York City.
(718) 354-4606
⟦🚴⟧ ⟦🥾⟧ ⟦🌳⟧ ⟦🏊⟧ ⟦🏛⟧ ⟦🍽⟧

NORTH CAROLINA

Cape Hatteras National Seashore
In eastern North Carolina along the Outer Banks.
(252) 473-2111 or 441-5711
⟦🏕⟧ ⟦🥾⟧ ⟦🌳⟧ ⟦🏊⟧ ⟦🏛⟧

Croatan National Forest
In southeastern North Carolina.
(252) 638-5628
⟦🏕⟧ ⟦🥾⟧ ⟦🌳⟧ ⟦🏊⟧

Great Smoky Mountains National Park
In western North Carolina and eastern Tennessee.
(865) 436-1200
⟦🏕⟧ ⟦🥾⟧ ⟦🌳⟧ ⟦🏊⟧ ⟦🏛⟧

Nantahala National Forest
At North Carolina's southwestern tip.
(828) 257-4200 or 526-3765
⟦🚴⟧ ⟦🏕⟧ ⟦🥾⟧ ⟦🌳⟧ ⟦🏊⟧

Nantahala National Forest (Hanging Dog)
5 mi. northwest of Murphy on SR 1326.
(828) 257-4200 or 526-3765
⟦🏕⟧ ⟦🥾⟧

Nantahala National Forest (Jackrabbit Mountain)
10 mi. northeast of Hayesville via US 64, SR 175 and SR
1155.
(828) 257-4200 or 526-3765
⟦🏕⟧ ⟦🥾⟧ ⟦🌳⟧ ⟦🏊⟧

Nantahala National Forest (Standing Indian Mountain)
9 mi. west of Franklin on US 64, then 2 mi. east on old
US 64 and 2 mi. south on FR 67.
(828) 257-4200 or 526-3765
⟦🏕⟧ ⟦🥾⟧ ⟦🌳⟧

Pisgah National Forest
In western North Carolina.
(828) 257-4200
⟦🚴⟧ ⟦🏕⟧ ⟦🥾⟧ ⟦🌳⟧ ⟦🏊⟧ ⟦🏛⟧ ⟦🍽⟧

Pisgah National Forest (Lake Powhatan)
7 mi. southwest of Asheville on SR 191 and FR 3807.
(828) 257-4200
⟦🚴⟧ ⟦🏕⟧ ⟦🥾⟧ ⟦🌳⟧ ⟦🏊⟧

Pisgah National Forest (Rocky Bluff)
3 mi. south of Hot Springs on SR 209.
(828) 257-4200
⟦🏕⟧ ⟦🥾⟧ ⟦🌳⟧

Uwharrie National Forest
In central North Carolina.
(910) 576-6391
⟦🏕⟧ ⟦🥾⟧ ⟦🌳⟧ ⟦🏊⟧

NORTH DAKOTA

Theodore Roosevelt National Park (North Unit)
In western North Dakota.
(701) 623-4466
⟦🏕⟧ ⟦🥾⟧ ⟦🌳⟧ ⟦🏛⟧

Theodore Roosevelt National Park (South Unit)
In western North Dakota.
(701) 623-4466
⟦🏕⟧ ⟦🥾⟧ ⟦🌳⟧ ⟦🏛⟧

Note: Leashed pets allowed in front country only;
some restrictions apply.

OHIO

Cuyahoga Valley National Park
In northeastern Ohio.
(216) 524-1497
⟦🚴⟧ ⟦🥾⟧ ⟦🌳⟧ ⟦🏛⟧ ⟦🍽⟧

🚴 Bicycling   🏕 Camping   🥾 Hiking   🌳 Picnicking
🏊 Swimming   🏛 Visitor center   🍽 Food service

OKLAHOMA

Chickasaw National Recreation Area
In south-central Oklahoma.
(580) 622-3165

Ouachita National Forest
In southeastern Oklahoma and west-central Arkansas.
(501) 321-5202

OREGON

Crater Lake National Park
On the crest of the Cascade Range off SR 62.
(541) 594-3100

Deschutes National Forest
In central Oregon 6 mi. south of Bend via US 97.
(541) 383-5300

Fremont-Winema National Forests
In south-central Oregon.
(541) 947-2151

Hells Canyon National Recreation Area
In northeastern Oregon and western Idaho.
(541) 523-3356 or (800) 523-1235

Malheur National Forest
In eastern Oregon.
(541) 575-3000

Mount Hood National Forest
In northwestern Oregon.
(888) 622-4822

Ochoco National Forest
In central Oregon off US 26.
(541) 416-6500

Oregon Dunes National Recreation Area
Between North Bend and Florence.
(541) 271-3611

Rogue River-Siskiyou National Forest
In southwestern Oregon off I-5 from Medford.
(541) 858-2200

Siuslaw National Forest
In western Oregon.
(541) 750-7000

Umatilla National Forest
In northeastern Oregon.
(541) 278-3716

Umpqua National Forest
In southwestern Oregon 33 mi. east of Roseburg on SR 138.
(541) 672-6601 or TDD (541) 957-3459

Wallowa-Whitman National Forest
In northeastern Oregon.
(541) 523-6391

Willamette National Forest
In western Oregon.
(541) 465-6521

PENNSYLVANIA

Allegheny National Forest
In northwestern Pennsylvania.
(814) 723-5150 or TDD (814) 726-2710

Delaware Water Gap National Recreation Area
In eastern Pennsylvania and northwestern New Jersey.
(570) 588-2451 or (570) 588-7044

SOUTH CAROLINA

Francis Marion National Forest
On the Coastal Plain north of Charleston.
(803) 561-4000

Sumter National Forest
In western South Carolina.
(803) 561-4000

SOUTH DAKOTA

Badlands National Park
In southwestern South Dakota.
(605) 433-5361, ext. 100

Black Hills National Forest
In southwestern South Dakota.
(605) 673-9200 or TDD (605) 673-4954

Custer National Forest
In northwestern South Dakota and southeastern Montana.
(605) 797-4432

Wind Cave National Park
In southwestern South Dakota.
(605) 745-4600

TENNESSEE

Big South Fork National River National Recreation Area
In northeastern Tennessee and southeastern Kentucky.
(423) 286-7275 or (606) 376-5073
🚲 ⛺ 🥾 ⛱ 🏊 👥

Cherokee National Forest
In eastern Tennessee.
(423) 476-9700
🚲 ⛺ 🥾 ⛱ 🏊 👥

Great Smoky Mountains National Park
In eastern Tennessee.
(865) 436-1200
⛺ 🥾 ⛱ 🏊 👥

Land Between the Lakes National Recreation Area
In western Kentucky and Tennessee.
(270) 924-2000 or (800) 525-7077
🚲 ⛺ 🥾 ⛱ 🏊 👥 🍴

TEXAS

Amistad National Recreation Area
Northwest of Del Rio via US 90.
(830) 775-7491
⛺ 🥾 ⛱ 🏊 👥

Angelina National Forest
In east Texas.
(936) 897-1068
⛺ 🥾 ⛱ 🏊 🍴

Big Bend National Park
Southeast of Alpine on SR 118 and US 385.
(432) 477-2251
⛺ 🥾 ⛱ 👥 🍴

Davy Crockett National Forest
In east Texas.
(936) 655-2299
⛺ 🥾 ⛱ 🏊 🍴

Guadalupe Mountains National Park
110 mi. east of El Paso on US 62/180.
(915) 828-3251
⛺ 🥾 ⛱ 👥

Lake Meredith National Recreation Area
45 mi. northeast of Amarillo and 9 mi. west of Borger via SR 136.
(806) 857-3151
⛺ ⛱ 🏊 🍴

Padre Island National Seashore
On Padre Island paralleling the Texas coast between Port Isabel and Corpus Christi.
(361) 949-8068
⛺ 🥾 ⛱ 🏊 👥 🍴

Sabine National Forest
In east Texas.
(409) 787-3870
⛺ 🥾 ⛱ 🏊

Sam Houston National Forest
40 mi. north of Houston in east Texas.
(936) 344-6205 or (888) 361-6908
🚲 ⛺ 🥾 ⛱ 🏊 🍴

UTAH

Arches National Park
5 mi. northwest of Moab on US 191.
(435) 719-2100 or TTY (435) 259-5279
⛺ 🥾 ⛱ 👥

Ashley National Forest
In northeastern Utah.
(435) 789-1181
🚲 ⛺ 🥾 ⛱ 🏊 👥 🍴

Bryce Canyon National Park
26 mi. southeast of Panguitch via US 89 and SRs 12 and 63.
(435) 834-5322
⛺ 🥾 ⛱ 👥 🍴

Canyonlands National Park
In southeastern Utah.
(435) 259-7164
⛺ 🥾 ⛱ 👥

Capitol Reef National Park
5 mi. east of Torrey on SR 24.
(435) 425-3791
🚲 ⛺ 🥾 ⛱ 👥

Dixie National Forest
In southwestern Utah.
(435) 865-3700
🚲 ⛺ 🥾 ⛱ 🏊 👥 🍴

Fishlake National Forest
In south-central Utah.
(435) 896-9233
🚲 ⛺ 🥾 ⛱ 👥 🍴

Flaming Gorge National Recreation Area
In northeastern Utah.
(435) 784-3445
🚲 ⛺ 🥾 ⛱ 🏊 👥 🍴

Glen Canyon National Recreation Area
In south-central Utah.
(928) 608-6404 or 608-6200
⛺ 🥾 ⛱ 🏊 👥 🍴

Manti-La Sal National Forest
In southeastern Utah.
(435) 637-2817
⛺ 🥾 ⛱ 🍴

🚲 Bicycling   ⛺ Camping   🥾 Hiking   ⛱ Picnicking
🏊 Swimming   👥 Visitor center   🍴 Food service

Uinta National Forest
In central Utah.
(801) 377-5780

Wasatch-Cache National Forest
In north-central and northeastern Utah.
(801) 236-3400

Zion National Park
In southwestern Utah.
(435) 772-3256

VERMONT

Green Mountain National Forest
In south-central Vermont.
(802) 747-6700

VIRGINIA

George Washington and Jefferson National Forests
In western Virginia and the eastern edge of West Virginia.
(888) 265-0019

Mount Rogers National Recreation Area
In southwestern Virginia.
(276) 783-5196 or (800) 628-7202

Shenandoah National Park
In northwestern Virginia.
(540) 999-3500

WASHINGTON

Gifford Pinchot National Forest
In southwestern Washington.
(360) 891-5000

Lake Roosevelt National Recreation Area
In northeastern Washington.
(509) 633-9441

Mount Baker-Snoqualmie National Forest (Douglas Fir)
2 mi. east of Glacier on SR 542.
(425) 775-9702 or (800) 627-0062, ext. 0

Mount Baker-Snoqualmie National Forest (Horseshoe Cove)
14 mi. north of Concrete on Baker Lake.
(425) 775-9702 or (800) 627-0062, ext. 0

Mount Baker-Snoqualmie National Forest (Shannon Creek)
24 mi. north of Concrete on Baker Lake.
(425) 775-9702 or (800) 627-0062, ext. 0

Olympic National Forest
In northwestern Washington.
(360) 956-2400

WEST VIRGINIA

Monongahela National Forest
In eastern West Virginia.
(304) 636-1800 (voice and TDD)

New River Gorge National River
Between Fayetteville and Hinton.
(304) 465-0508

Spruce Knob-Seneca Rocks National Recreation Area
In east-central West Virginia.
(304) 257-4488

WISCONSIN

Apostle Islands National Lakeshore
Off northern Wisconsin's Bayfield Peninsula in Lake Superior.
(715) 779-3397

Chequamegon-Nicolet National Forest
In north-central and northeastern Wisconsin.
(715) 762-2461 or TTY (715) 762-5701 (Chequamegon),
(715) 362-1300 or TTY (715) 362-1383 (Nicolet)

St. Croix National Scenic Riverway
Running 252 mi. from Cable to Prescott.
(715) 483-3284

WYOMING

Bighorn Canyon National Recreation Area
In Montana and northern Wyoming.
(307) 548-2251

Bighorn National Forest
In north-central Wyoming.
(307) 674-2600

Devils Tower National Monument
Between Sundance and Hulett.
(307) 467-5283

Flaming Gorge National Recreation Area
On the Wyoming-Utah border.
(435) 784-3445

Fossil Butte National Monument
14 mi. west of Kemmerer on US 30.
(307) 877-4455
[symbols]

Grand Teton National Park
In northwestern Wyoming.
(307) 739-3300
[symbols]

Medicine Bow National Forest
In southeastern Wyoming.
(307) 745-2300
[symbols]

Shoshone National Forest
In northwestern Wyoming.
(307) 527-6241
[symbols]

Yellowstone National Park
In northwestern Wyoming.
(307) 344-7311
[symbols]

Canada

ALBERTA

Elk Island National Park
In central Alberta, east of Edmonton.
(780) 992-2950
[symbols]

Jasper National Park
In west-central Alberta along the British Columbia border.
(780) 852-6161
[symbols]

Waterton Lakes National Park
In Alberta's southwestern corner.
(403) 859-5133, or 859-2224 during the winter
[symbols]

BRITISH COLUMBIA

Glacier National Park
In southeastern British Columbia.
(250) 837-7500
[symbols]

Kootenay National Park
In southeastern British Columbia.
(250) 347-9615 or (800) 748-7275
[symbols]

Mount Revelstoke National Park
In southeastern British Columbia.
(250) 837-7500
[symbols]

Pacific Rim National Park Reserve
On the southwestern coast of Vancouver Island.
(250) 726-7721 or 726-4212, Jun. 1 to mid-Sept.
[symbols]

Yoho National Park
On the British Columbia-Alberta border.
(250) 343-6783
[symbols]

MANITOBA

Riding Mountain National Park
In southwestern Manitoba.
(204) 848-7275 or (800) 707-8480
[symbols]

NEW BRUNSWICK

Fundy National Park
On Hwy. 114, 130 km. southwest of Moncton.
(506) 887-6000
[symbols]

Kouchibouguac National Park
On Hwy. 134, north of Moncton.
(506) 876-2443 or TDD (506) 876-4205
[symbols]

NEWFOUNDLAND

Gros Morne National Park
On Newfoundland's western coast.
(709) 458-2417, 458-2066 or TDD (709) 772-4564
[symbols]

Terra Nova National Park
In eastern Newfoundland.
(709) 533-2801
[symbols]

NORTHWEST TERRITORIES

Nahanni National Park Reserve
145 km. west of Fort Simpson in southwestern Northwest Territories.
(867) 695-3151
[symbols]

 Bicycling   Camping   Hiking   Picnicking
 Swimming   Visitor center   Food service

Wood Buffalo National Park
On the Northwest Territories-Alberta border.
(867) 872-7960
▲ 🥾 ⛲ ⛵ 🏕

NOVA SCOTIA

Cape Breton Highlands National Park
5 km. northeast of Chéticamp on Cabot Tr.
(902) 224-2306 or (888) 773-8888
▲ 🥾 ⛲ ⛵ 🏕 📷

Kejimkujik National Park and National Historic Site
In southwestern Nova Scotia off Hwy. 8 at Maitland
Bridge.
(902) 682-2772
▲ 🥾 ⛲ ⛵ 🏕 📷

ONTARIO

Bruce Peninsula National Park
In southwestern Ontario.
(519) 596-2233 or 596-2263
▲ 🥾 ⛲ ⛵

PRINCE EDWARD ISLAND

Prince Edward Island National Park
Along the island's northern shore.
(902) 566-7050
♿ ▲ 🥾 ⛲ ⛵ 🏕 📷

QUEBEC

Forillon National Park of Canada
20 km. northeast of Gaspé via Hwy. 132.
(418) 368-5505 or (800) 463-6769
♿ ▲ 🥾 ⛲ ⛵ 🏕 📷

La Mauricie National Park of Canada
North of Trois-Rivières via Hwy. 55.
(819) 538-3232 or (800) 463-6769
♿ ▲ 🥾 ⛲ ⛵ 🏕 📷

SASKATCHEWAN

Grasslands National Park of Canada
Between Val Marie and Killdeer in southern
Saskatchewan.
(306) 298-2257
▲ 🥾 ⛲ 🏕

Prince Albert National Park
In central Saskatchewan.
(306) 663-4522
♿ ▲ 🥾 ⛲ ⛵ 🏕 📷

ANIMAL CLINICS

This list of animal clinics in the United States and Canada is provided by the Veterinary Emergency & Critical Care Society as a service to the community for information purposes only. This is not to be construed as a certification or an endorsement of any clinic listed. For further information, contact the society at (210) 698-5575 or online at www.veccs.org. Note: Hours frequently change, and not all clinics are open 24 hours or in the evening. In addition, not all facilities listed here are emergency clinics. In non-emergency situations, it's best to call first.

If you are traveling to an area not covered in this list, be prepared for an emergency by asking your regular veterinarian to recommend a clinic or veterinarian at your destination. The American Animal Hospital Association also provides a veterinary locator service to clinics that meet the association's high standards for veterinary care. Contact the association at (303) 986-2800 or online at www.healthypet.com.

United States

ALABAMA
Village Veterinary Clinic
403 Opelika Rd., Auburn
(334) 821-7730

Emergency and Specialty Animal Medical Center
2864 Acton Rd., Birmingham
(205) 967-7389

Lakeview Pet Wellness Center
3222 6th Ave. S., Birmingham
(205) 323-1536

Emergency Clinic of North Alabama
2112 S. Memorial Pkwy., Huntsville
(256) 533-7600

Rehm Animal Clinic
951 Hillcrest Rd., Mobile
(251) 639-9120

Carriage Hills Animal Clinic
3200 E. Bypass, Montgomery
(334) 277-2867

ALASKA
Pet Emergency Treatment
3315 Fairbanks St., Anchorage
(907) 274-5636

ARIZONA
Emergency Animal Clinic
86 W. Juniper Ave., Gilbert
(480) 497-0222

Franklin Veterinary Hospital
1721 E. University Dr., Mesa
(480) 890-8283

Mesa Veterinary Hospital
858 N. Country Club Dr., Mesa
(480) 833-7330

Emergency Animal Clinic
9875 W. Peoria Ave., Peoria
(623) 974-1520

Emergency Animal Clinic
2260 West Glendale Ave., Phoenix
(602) 995-3757

Palo Verde Animal Hospital
1215 E. Northern Ave., Phoenix
(602) 944-9661

Emergency Animal Clinic
14202 N. Scottsdale Rd., Suite 163, Scottsdale
(480) 949-8001

Paradise Valley Emergency Animal Clinic
6969 E. Shea Blvd., #225, Scottsdale
(480) 991-1845

Animal Emergency Service
4832 E. Speedway St., Tucson
(520) 327-5624

Grant Road Small Animal Hospital
1675 West Grant Rd., Tucson
(520) 792-1858

ARKANSAS
Animal Emergency Clinic
8735 Sheltie Dr., Maumelle
(501) 224-3784

CALIFORNIA
Animal Hospital of Antioch
2204 A St., Antioch
(925) 754-6700

Antioch Veterinary Hospital
1432 West 10th St., Antioch
(925) 757-2233

Central Coast Pet Emergency Clinic
1558 W. Branch St., Arroyo Grande
(805) 489-6573

Animal Emergency and Urgent Care
4300 Easton Dr., #1, Bakersfield
(661) 322-6019

Pet Emergency Treatment Service Inc.
1048 University Ave., Berkeley
(510) 548-6684

United Emergency Animal Clinic
1657 S. Bascom Ave., Campbell
(408) 371-6252

Acacia Veterinary Hospital
479 East Ave., Chico
(530) 345-1338

Contra Costa Veterinary Emergency Center
1410 Monument Blvd., Concord
(925) 798-2900

Solano Pet Emergency Clinic
4437 Central Pl., Cordelia
(707) 864-1444

East Valley Emergency Pet Clinic
938 N. Diamond Bar Blvd., Diamond Bar
(909) 861-5737

Dublin Veterinary Hospital
7410 Amador Valley Blvd., #D, Dublin
(925) 828-5520

Emergency Pet Clinic of San Gabriel Valley
3254 Santa Anita Ave., El Monte
(626) 579-4550

Greenback Veterinary Hospital
8311 Greenback Ln., Fair Oaks
(916) 725-1541

All Care Animal Referral Center
18440 E. Amistad St., Fountain Valley
(714) 963-0909

Central Veterinary Hospital & Emergency Service
5245 Central Ave., Fremont
(510) 797-7387

Veterinary Emergency Services
1639 N. Fresno St., Fresno
(559) 486-0520

Orange County Emergency Pet Clinic
12750 Garden Grove Blvd., Garden Grove
(714) 537-3032

Pet Medical Center Chatoak
17659 Chatsworth St., Granada Hills
(818) 363-7444

Animal Emergency Clinic
12022 La Crosse Ave., Grand Terrace
(909) 825-9350

North Orange County Emergency Pet Clinic
1474 S. Harbor Blvd., La Habra
(714) 441-2925

Pet Emergency & Specialty Center
5232 Jackson Dr., #105, La Mesa
(619) 462-4800

Loomis Basin Veterinary Clinic
3901 Sierra College Blvd., Loomis
(916) 652-5816

Adobe Animal Hospital
396 First St., Los Altos
(650) 948-9661

Animal Emergency Facility
1535 South Sepulveda Blvd., Los Angeles
(310) 473-1561

Eagle Rock Emergency Pet Clinic
4254 Eagle Rock Blvd., Los Angeles
(323) 254-7382

VCA/West Los Angeles Animal Hospital
1818 South Sepulveda Blvd., Los Angeles
(310) 473-2951

Animal Urgent Care
28085 Hillcrest, Mission Viejo
(949) 364-6228

Monterey Animal Hospital Inc.
725 Foam St., Monterey
(831) 373-0711

Crossroads Animal Emergency & Referral Center
11057 E. Rosecrans Ave., Norwalk
(562) 863-2522

South Peninsula Veterinary Emergency Clinic
3045 Middlefield Rd., Palo Alto
(650) 494-1461

Animal Emergency Clinic of Pasadena
2121 Foothill Blvd., Pasadena
(626) 564-0704

McClave Veterinary Hospital
6950 Reseda Blvd., Reseda
(818) 881-5102

Rimforest Animal Hospital
1299 Bear Springs Rd., Rimforest
(909) 337-8589

Animal Care Center of Sonoma County
6470 Redwood Dr., Rohnert Park
(707) 584-4343

Emergency Animal Clinic of Sacramento
9700 Business Park Dr., #404, Sacramento
(916) 362-3111

Sacramento Emergency Veterinary Clinic
2201 El Camino Ave., Sacramento
(916) 922-3425

San Clemente Veterinary Hospital
1833 South El Camino Real, San Clemente
(949) 492-5777

VCA Hillcrest Animal Center
246 W. Washington St., San Diego
(619) 299-7387

Emergency Animal Hospital & Referral Center
2317 Hotel Cir. South, San Diego
(619) 299-2400

All Animals Emergency Hospital
1333 9th Ave., San Francisco
(415) 566-0531

Mission Pet Hospital
720 Valencia St., San Francisco
(415) 552-1969

Pets Unlimited
2343 Fillmore St., San Francisco
(415) 563-6700

South Bay Veterinary Specialists
5440 Thornwood Dr., #H, San Jose
(408) 363-8066

Bay Area Veterinary Medical Group
14790 Washington Ave., San Leandro
(510) 352-6080

California Veterinary Specialist
100 N. Rancho Santa Fe Rd., Ste. #133, San Marcos
(760) 734-4433

North Peninsula Veterinary Emergency Clinic
227 N. Amphlett Blvd., San Mateo
(650) 348-2575

Santa Cruz Veterinary Hospital
2585 Soquel Dr., Santa Cruz
(831) 475-5400

Pet Care Veterinary Hospital
1370 Fulton Rd., Santa Rosa
(707) 579-5900

Beverly Oaks Animal Hospital
14302 Ventura Blvd., Sherman Oaks
(818) 788-2022

American Veterinary Hospital
2109 Tapo St., #3, Simi Valley
(805) 581-9111

Rancho Sequoia Veterinary Hospital
3380 Los Angeles Ave., Simi Valley
(805) 522-7476

Animal Emergency Center
11740 Ventura Blvd., Studio City
(818) 760-3882

Emergency Pet Clinic of Temecula
27443 Jefferson Ave., Temecula
(951) 695-5044

Pet Emergency Clinic of Thousand Oaks
2967 North Moorpark Rd., Thousand Oaks
(805) 492-2436

Animal Emergency Clinic of the Desert
72-374 Ramon Rd., Thousand Palms
(760) 343-3438

Emergency Pet Clinic of South Bay
2325 Torrance Blvd., Torrance
(310) 320-8300

Central Animal Hospital
281 North Central Ave., Upland
(909) 981-2855

Pet Emergency Clinic of Ventura
2301 S. Victoria Ave., Ventura
(805) 642-8562

Washington Blvd. Animal Hospital
12116 East Washington Blvd., Whittier
(562) 693-8233

COLORADO

All Pets Veterinary Clinic
5290 Manhattan Cir., Boulder
(303) 499-5335

Boulder Emergency Pet Clinic
1658 30th St., Boulder
(303) 440-7722

Animal Emergency Care Center North
5752 North Academy Blvd., Colorado Springs
(719) 260-7141

Animal Emergency Care Center South
3775 Airport Rd., Colorado Springs
(719) 578-9300

Alameda East Veterinary Hospital
9770 E. Alameda Ave., Denver
(303) 366-2639

Colorado State University Veterinary Teaching Hospital
300 W. Drake Rd., Fort Collins
(970) 221-4535

Centennial Veterinary Clinic
5151 S. Federal Blvd., Ste. #H-6, Littleton
(303) 795-0130

Wheat Ridge Animal Hospital
3695 Kipling St., Wheat Ridge
(303) 424-3325

CONNECTICUT

East of the River Veterinary Emergency Clinic
222 Boston Tpk., Bolton
(860) 646-6134

Shoreline Animal Emergency Clinic
7365 Main St., Stratford
(203) 375-6500

Connecticut Veterinary Center
470 Oakwood Ave., West Hartford
(860) 233-8564

FLORIDA

Veterinary Emergency Clinic of Central Florida
195 Concord Dr., Casselberry
(407) 644-4449

Volusia Animal Emergency Clinic
US 92, Daytona Beach
(386) 252-4300

American Animal Emergency
103 N. Powerline Rd., Deerfield Beach
(954) 428-9888

Animal Emergency and Referral Center
3984 S. US 1, Fort Pierce
(772) 466-3441

Affiliated Pet Emergency
7520 W. University Ave., Gainesville
(352) 373-4444

Chasewood Animal Hospital
6390 W. Indiantown Rd., #16, Jupiter
(561) 745-4944

Veterinary Emergency Clinic
3609 Hwy. 98 S., Lakeland
(863) 665-3199

Lantana Animal Clinic
3530 Lantana Rd., Lantana
(561) 439-0694

Promenade Animal Hospital
4424 N. University Dr., Lauderhill
(954) 748-9600

Veterinary Emergency Clinic of Central Florida
33040 Professional Dr., Leesburg
(352) 728-4440

Animal Emergency Clinic South
8429 S.W. 132nd St., Miami
(305) 251-2096

Knowles Emergency Clinic
1000 N.W. 27th Ave., Miami
(305) 649-1234

Knowles Snapper Creek Animal Clinic
9933 Sunset Dr., Miami
(305) 279-2323

Emergency Veterinary Clinic Okaloosa/Walton
210 A Government Ave., Niceville
(850) 729-3335

Veterinary Emergency Clinic of Central Florida
2080 Principal Row, Orlando
(407) 438-4449

Pet Emergency of Palm Beach County
3816 Northlake Blvd., Palm Beach Gardens
(561) 691-9999

Emergency Animal Clinic
6602 Pines Blvd., Pembroke Pines
(954) 962-0300

Animal Hospital
8560 N. Davis Hwy., Pensacola
(850) 479-9484

Animal Emergency Clinic of Pasco
8740 US Hwy. 19 N., Port Richey
(727) 841-6575

Emergency Veterinary Clinic of Sarasota
7517 S. Tamiami Tr., #107, Sarasota
(941) 923-7260

Animal Emergency of Hernando
3496 Deltona Blvd., Spring Hill
(352) 666-0904

Animal Emergency Clinic of St. Petersburg
3165 22nd Ave. N., St. Petersburg
(727) 323-1311

Allied Veterinary Emergency Hospital
401 East 9th Ave., Tallahassee
(850) 222-0123

Northwood Animal Hospital
1881-B North Martin Luther King Jr. Blvd., Tallahassee
(850) 385-8181

Murphy Animal Hospital
6845 N. Dale Mabry, Tampa
(813) 879-6090

American Animal Emergency Clinic
3425 Forest Hill Blvd., West Palm Beach
(561) 433-2244

Summit Boulevard Animal Hospital
1000 S. Military Tr., #B and C, West Palm Beach
(561) 439-7900

GEORGIA

Animal Emergency Clinic of Sandy Springs
228 Sandy Springs Pl., Atlanta
(404) 252-7881

Augusta Animal Emergency
208 Hudson Trace, Augusta
(706) 733-7458

Animal Emergency Care
2009 Mercer University Dr., Macon
(478) 750-0911

Cobb Emergency Veterinary Clinic
630 Cobb Pkwy. N., Ste. C, Marietta
(770) 424-9157

Peachtree Corners Animal Clinic
4020 Holcomb Bridge Rd., Norcross
(770) 448-0700

Animal Emergency Center of North Fulton
900 Mansell Rd., #19, Roswell
(770) 594-2266

Chattahoochee Animal Clinic
1176 Alpharetta St., Roswell
(770) 993-6329

Savannah Veterinary Emergency and Specialty Referral Center
317 Eisenhower Dr., Savannah
(912) 355-6113

ILLINOIS

Animal Emergency Center
2005 Mall St., Collinsville
(618) 346-1843

Emergency Veterinary Care South
13715 S. Cicero Ave., Crestwood
(708) 388-3771

Animal Emergency and Treatment Center
1810 Belvidere Rd., Grayslake
(847) 548-5300

Emergency Veterinary Services
820 Ogden Ave., Lisle
(630) 960-2900

Animal Emergency and Critical Care Center
1810 Frontage Rd., Northbrook
(847) 564-5775

Emergency Veterinary Services of St. Charles
530 Dunham Rd., St. Charles
(630) 584-7447

INDIANA

All Pet Emergency Clinic
104B South Heidelbach, Evansville
(812) 422-3300

Northeast Indiana Veterinary Emergency & Specialty Hospital
5818 Maplecrest Rd., Fort Wayne
(260) 426-1062

Indianapolis Veterinary Emergency and Medical Center
5245 Victory Dr., Indianapolis
(317) 782-4418

Veterinary Centers of America
4030 W. 86th St., Indianapolis
(317) 872-0200

New Carlisle Animal Clinic
8935 East US 20, New Carlisle
(574) 654-3129

Calumet Emergency Veterinary Clinic
216 W. Lincoln Hwy., Schererville
(219) 865-0970

Arbor View Animal Hospital
244 W. US Hwy. 6, Valparaiso
(219) 762-6586

IOWA

Animal Emergency Clinic & Referral Center of Central Iowa
6110 Crescent Ave., Des Moines
(515) 280-3051

KANSAS

Mission Medvet
5914 Johnson Dr., Mission
(913) 722-5566

Veterinary Specialty & Emergency Center
11950 W. 110th St., Overland Park
(913) 642-9563

Wichita Emergency Veterinary Clinic
727 S. Washington, Wichita
(316) 262-5321

KENTUCKY

Colonial Animal Clinic
1601 Argillite Rd., Flatwoods
(606) 836-8112

Hagyard Davidson McGee Veterinarians
4250 Ironworks Pike, Lexington
(859) 255-8741

Jefferson Animal Hospital & Emergency Center
4504 Outer Loop, Louisville
(502) 966-4104

LOUISIANA

Buccaneer Villa Veterinary Hospital
8220 W. Judge Perez Dr., Chalmette
(504) 271-1234

Westbank Pet Emergency Clinic, Inc.
403 Lapalco Blvd., Gretna
(504) 392-1932

Animal Emergency Clinic
1955 Veterans Memorial Blvd., Metairie
(504) 835-8508

Gentilly Veterinary Hospital
7006 Read Ln., New Orleans
(504) 242-4200

MAINE

Animal Emergency Clinic of Mid Maine
37 Strawberry Ave., Lewiston
(207) 777-1110

Norway Veterinary Hospital
Route 26, 10 Main St., Norway
(207) 743-6384

Animal Emergency Clinic
352 Warren Ave., Portland
(207) 878-3121

MARYLAND

Anne Arundel Veterinary Emergency Clinic, Inc.
808 Bestgate Rd., Annapolis
(410) 224-0331

Emergency Veterinary Clinic
32 Mellor Ave., Catonsville
(410) 788-7040

Veterinary Referral Associates, Inc.
15021 Dufief Mill Rd., Gaithersburg
(301) 340-3224

Beltway Emergency Animal Hospital
11660 Annapolis Rd., Glenn Dale
(301) 464-3737

Emergency Animal Center, Inc.
1896 Urbana Pike, #23, Hyattstown
(301) 831-1088

Metropolitan Emergency Animal Clinic
12106 Nebel St., Rockville
(301) 770-5225

Animal Emergency Center and Chesapeake Veterinary Referral
1209 Cromwell Bridge Rd., Towson
(410) 252-8387

Southern Maryland Veterinary Referral Center and Emergency
3485 Rockefeller Ct., Waldorf
(301) 638-0988

Westminster Veterinary Hospital-Emergency Trauma Center
269 W. Main St., Westminster
(410) 848-3363

MASSACHUSETTS

Angell Animal Center
350 S. Huntington Ave., Boston
(617) 522-7282

Roberts Animal Hospital
516 Washington St., Hanover
(781) 826-2306

Holyoke Animal Hospital
320 Easthampton Rd., Holyoke
(413) 538-8700

Animal Health Care Associates
Martha's Vineyard Airport, Martha's Vineyard
(508) 693-6515

Highland Animal Hospital
31 Wellesley Ave., Needham
(781) 433-0467

Tufts University School Of Veterinary Medicine
200 Westboro Rd., North Grafton
(508) 839-5395

South Deerfield Veterinary Clinic
Elm Street and Route 5 & 10, South Deerfield
(413) 665-3626

Veterinary Associates of Cape Cod
16 Commonwealth Ave., South Yarmouth
(508) 394-3566

Angell Animal Medical Center
171 Union St., Springfield
(413) 785-1221

VCA/Wakefield Animal Hospital
19 Main St., Wakefield
(781) 245-0045

MICHIGAN

Affiliated Veterinary Emergency Services
3412 E. Walton Rd., Auburn Hills
(248) 371-3713

Lansing Veterinary Urgent Care
5133 S. Martin Luther King Jr. Blvd., Lansing
(517) 393-9200

Veterinary Medical Center
243 N. Jebavy Dr., Ludington
(231) 843-9073

Veterinary Emergency Service & Critical Care
28223 John R Rd., Madison Heights
(248) 547-4677

Veterinary Emergency Service West
40850 Ann Arbor Rd., Plymouth
(734) 207-8500

Michigan Veterinary Specialists
21600 West Eleven Mile Rd., Southfield
(248) 354-6660

Affiliated Veterinary Emergency Services
14085 Northline Rd., Southgate
(734) 284-1700

Union Lake Veterinary Hospital
6545 Cooley Lake Rd., Waterford
(248) 363-1508

MINNESOTA

South Metro Animal Emergency Care Clinic
14690 Pennock Ave., Apple Valley
(952) 953-3737

Emergency Veterinary Service
1615 Coon Rapids Blvd., Coon Rapids
(763) 754-9434

Emergency Veterinary Service
4708 Olson Memorial Hwy., Golden Valley
(763) 529-6560

Animal Emergency Clinic
301 University Ave., St. Paul
(651) 293-1800

MISSISSIPPI

Bienville Animal Medical Center
1524 Bienville Blvd., Ocean Springs
(228) 872-1231

MISSOURI

Animal Emergency Clinic
12501 Natural Bridge Rd., Bridgeton
(314) 739-1500

Animal Emergency Clinic
9937 Big Bend Blvd., St. Louis
(314) 822-7600

MONTANA

Animal Medical Clinic
5100 9th Ave. South, Great Falls
(406) 761-8183

NEBRASKA

VCA-Rohrig Animal Hospital
8022 W. Dodge Rd., Omaha
(402) 399-8100

NEVADA

Carson Tahoe Veterinary Hospital
3389 S. Carson St., Carson City
(775) 883-8238

Animal Emergency Center
1914 E. Sahara Ave., Las Vegas
(702) 457-8050

Painted Desert Animal Hospital
4601 N. Rancho Dr., Las Vegas
(702) 645-2543

Animal Emergency Center
6425 S. Virginia St., Reno
(775) 851-3600

NEW HAMPSHIRE

Animal Emergency Clinic of Southern New Hampshire
2626 Brown Ave., Pine Island Plaza, Manchester
(603) 666-6677

State Line Veterinary Hospital
325 S. Daniel Webster Hwy., Nashua
(603) 888-2751

Animal Medical Center
1550 Woodbury Ave., Portsmouth
(603) 436-4922

NEW JERSEY

Ocean County Veterinary Hospital
838 River Ave., Lakewood
(732) 363-7202

Oradell Animal Hospital
580 Winters Ave., Paramus
(201) 262-0010

Alliance Emergency Veterinary Clinic
540 Route 10 West, Randolph
(973) 328-2844

NEW MEXICO

Albuquerque Animal Emergency Clinic
5005 Prospect Ave. N.E., Albuquerque
(505) 884-3433

Great Plains Veterinary Clinic
2720 Lovington Hwy., Hobbs
(505) 392-5513

Ruidoso Animal Clinic
160 Sudderth, Ruidoso
(505) 257-4027

Emergency Veterinary Clinic of Santa Fe
1311 Calle Nava, Santa Fe
(505) 984-0625

NEW YORK

Central Veterinary Hospital
388 Central Ave., Albany
(518) 434-2115

Greater Buffalo Veterinary Services
4949 Main St., Amherst
(716) 839-4043

Bayside Animal Clinic
36-43 Bell Blvd., Bayside
(718) 224-4451

Bellerose Animal Hospital
242-01 Jamaica Ave., Bellerose
(718) 347-1057

Brooklyn Veterinary Emergency Service
453 Bay Bridge Ave., Brooklyn
(718) 748-5180

Far Rockaway Animal Hospital
1833 Cornaga Ave., Far Rockaway
(718) 327-0256

Boulevard Animal Clinic
112-49 Queens Blvd., Forest Hills
(718) 261-1231

Terrace Animal Clinic
501 Great Neck Rd., Great Neck
(516) 466-9191

Homer Animal Clinic
66 S. West St., Homer
(607) 749-7223

Animal Emergency Center of Queens P.C.
187-11 Hillside Ave., Jamaica
(718) 454-4141

Animal Emergency Clinic of Kingston
1112 Morton Blvd., Kingston
(845) 336-0713

Hilton Hospital for Animals
120 Merrick Rd., Lynbrook
(516) 887-2914

Animal Medical Center/Bobst Hospital
510 East 62nd St., New York
(212) 838-8100

VCA/Manhattan Veterinary Group
240 East 80th St., New York
(212) 988-1000

Riverside Animal Hospital
250 West 108th St., New York
(212) 865-2224

Orchard Park Veterinary Medical Center
3507 Orchard Park Rd., Orchard Park
(716) 662-6660

Animal Emergency Clinic of Hudson Valley
84 Patrick Ln., Poughkeepsie
(845) 471-8242

Animal Hospital
640 Willowbrook Rd., Staten Island
(718) 494-0050

Veterinary Emergency Center
1293 Clove Rd., Staten Island
(718) 720-4211

The Veterinary Medical Center
2612 Erie Blvd. East, Syracuse
(315) 446-7933

Valley Cottage Animal Hospital
202 Route 303, Valley Cottage
(845) 268-9263

Central Veterinary Associates
73 W. Merrick Rd., Valley Stream
(516) 825-3066

Animal Care Hospital
4535 Old Vestal Rd., Vestal
(607) 770-9999

Schroon River Animal Hospital
150 Schroon River Rd., Warrensburg
(518) 623-3181

Nassau Animal Emergency Clinic
740 Old Country Rd., Westbury
(516) 333-6262

NORTH CAROLINA

Freedom Animal Hospital
3055 Freedom Dr., Charlotte
(704) 399-6534

Triangle Pet Emergency Treatment Service
3319 Chapel Hill Blvd., Durham
(919) 489-0615

Veterinary Emergency Clinic of Gaston County
728 E. Franklin Blvd., Gastonia
(704) 866-7918

Cabarrus Emergency Veterinary Clinic
1317 S. Cannon Blvd., Kannapolis
(704) 932-1182

Emergency Veterinary Clinic
2440 Plantation Center Dr., Matthews
(704) 844-6440

After Hours Small Animal Emergency Clinic
409 Vick Ave., Raleigh
(919) 781-5145

Ansede Animal Hospital
3535 South Wilmington St., #107, Raleigh
(919) 661-1515

Wilmington Animal Emergency Clinic
5333 Oleander Dr., Wilmington
(910) 791-7387

Forsyth After Hours Veterinary Emergency Clinic
7781 Northpoint Blvd., Winston-Salem
(336) 896-0902

OHIO

Animal Emergency & Specialty Clinic
5320 West 140th St., Brookpark
(216) 362-6000

Dayton Emergency Veterinary Clinic
2714 Springboro West, Dayton
(937) 293-2714

Animal Medical & Emergency Hospital
2527 West Dublin-Granville Rd., Dublin
(614) 889-2556

Lorain County Animal Emergency Center
1909 North Ridge Rd., Lorain
(440) 240-1400

County Animal Hospital
1185 Reading Rd., Mason
(513) 398-8000

Aaron Animal Clinic and Emergency Hospital
7640 Broadview Rd., Parma
(216) 901-9980

Columbus Veterinary Emergency Service
300 E. Wilson Bridge Rd., Worthington
(614) 846-5800

OKLAHOMA
Midtown Animal Hospital
1101 S.W. Park Ave., Lawton
(580) 353-3438

Veterinary Emergency and Critical Care Hospital
1800 W. Memorial Rd., Oklahoma City
(405) 749-6989

Animal Emergency Center
7220 E. 41st St., Tulsa
(918) 665-0508

OREGON
Willamette Veterinary Clinic
650 S.W. Third St., Corvallis
(541) 753-5750

Dove Lewis Emergency Animal Hospital
1984 N.W. Pettygrove St., Portland
(503) 228-7281

Salem Veterinary Emergency Clinic
3215 Market St. N.E., Salem
(503) 588-8082

Emergency Veterinary Clinic of Tualatin
19314 S.W. Mohave Ct., Tualatin
(503) 691-7922

PENNSYLVANIA
Providence Veterinary Hospital
24th and Providence Ave., Chester
(610) 872-4000

Animal Emergency & Critical Care Service
2010 Cabot Blvd., Langhorne
(215) 750-2774

Metropolitan Veterinary Center
560 McNeilly Rd., Pittsburgh
(412) 344-6888

Allegheny Veterinary Emergency Associates
1810 Rte. 286, Pittsburgh
(724) 325-1881

Castle Shannon VCA
3610 Library Rd., Pittsburgh
(412) 885-2500

Tri-County Veterinary Emergency Service
2250 Old Bethlehem Pike, North Quakertown
(215) 536-6245

Valley Central Emergency Veterinary Hospital
210 Fullerton Ave., Whitehall
(610) 435-5588

Animal Emergency Clinic
3256 Susquehanna Tr., York
(717) 767-5355

RHODE ISLAND
North Kingstown Animal Hospital
3736 Quaker Ln., North Kingstown
(401) 295-9777

Warwick Animal Hospital
1950 Elmwood Ave., Warwick
(401) 785-2222

SOUTH CAROLINA
South Carolina Veterinary Emergency Care Center
132 Stonemark Ln., Columbia
(803) 798-3837

Animal Hospital of North Myrtle Beach
2501 Hwy. 17 S., North Myrtle Beach
(843) 272-8121

Veterinary Emergency Clinic of Spartanburg
1291 Ashville Hwy., Spartanburg
(864) 591-1923

TENNESSEE
Keith Street Animal Clinic
1990 Keith St., Cleveland
(423) 476-1804

After Hours Pet Emergency Clinic
215 Center Park Dr., Knoxville
(865) 966-3888

TEXAS
I-20 Animal Medical Center
5820 I-20 West, Arlington
(817) 478-9238

Animal Emergency Hospital of Austin
4106 N. Lamar Blvd., Austin
(512) 459-4336

Emergency Animal Hospital of N.W. Austin
4434 Frontier Tr., Austin
(512) 899-0955

Emergency Animal Clinic of Northwest Austin
12034 Research Blvd., #8, Austin
(512) 331-6121

North Texas Emergency Pet Clinic
1712 W. Frankford Rd., Carrollton
(972) 323-1310

Emergency Animal Clinic
12101 Greenville Ave., #118, Dallas
(972) 994-9110

Whiterock Animal Hospital
11414 East Northwest Hwy., Dallas
(214) 328-3255

El Paso Animal Emergency Center
2101 Texas Ave., El Paso
(915) 545-1148

Airport Freeway Animal Emergency Clinic
411 N. Main St., Euless
(817) 571-2088

Fort Worth Animal Medical Center
8331 W. Freeway, Fort Worth
(817) 560-8387

Animal Emergency Clinic
8921 Katy Frwy., Houston
(713) 932-9589

Animal Emergency Clinic Caldera Road
1100 Gulf Frwy. S., #104, League City
(281) 332-1678

Lake Olympia Animal Hospital
3603 Glenn Lakes, Missouri City
(281) 499-7242

Permian Basin Emergency Veterinary Clinic
13528 W. US Hwy. 80, Odessa
(432) 561-8301

Emergency Pet Clinic
8503 Broadway, #105, San Antonio
(210) 822-2873

Emergency Pet Clinic
503 E. Sonterra Blvd., San Antonio
(210) 404-2873

Southwest Freeway Animal Hospital & Emergency Center
15575 Southwest Frwy., Sugar Land
(281) 491-8387

UTAH

Animal Medical Services
469 W. Center St., Orem
(801) 225-3346

Central Emergency Animal Clinic
55 E. Miller Ave., Salt Lake City
(801) 487-1325

VERMONT

Lamoille Valley Veterinary Services
278 Vermont Route #15 East, Hyde Park
(802) 888-7911

VIRGINIA

Alexandria Animal Hospital
2660 Duke St., Alexandria
(703) 823-3601

Albemarle Veterinary Hospital
445 Westfield Rd., Charlottesville
(434) 973-6146

Animal Emergency Clinic of Fredericksburg
1210 Snowden St., Fredericksburg
(540) 371-0554

Animal Emergency Hospital & Referral Center
2 Cardinal Park Dr., #101B, Leesburg
(703) 777-5755

Animal Emergency Clinic of Central Virginia
1000 Miller Park Sq., Lynchburg
(434) 846-1504

Veterinary Internal Medicine Practice
8610 Centreville Rd., Manassas
(703) 631-1030 (referrals only)

Veterinary Emergency Center
3312 W. Cary St., Richmond
(804) 353-9000

Springfield Emergency Veterinary Hospital
6651-F Backlick Rd., Springfield
(703) 451-8900

Silver Spring Veterinary Hospital
241 Garber Ln., Winchester
(540) 662-2301

WASHINGTON

After Hours Animal Emergency
718 Auburn Way N., Auburn
(253) 939-6272

Aerowood Animal Hospital
2975 156th Ave. S.E., Bellevue
(425) 746-6557

Snoqualmie Valley Animal Hospital
32020 S.E. 40th St., Fall City
(425) 222-7220

Vista Veterinary Hospital
5603 W. Canal Dr., Kennewick
(509) 783-2131

Veterinary Specialty Center
20115 44th Ave. W., Lynnwood
(425) 697-6106

Animal Emergency and Trauma Center
19494 7th Ave. N.E., #F, Poulsbo
(360) 697-7771

Emerald City Emergency Clinic
4102 Stone Way N., Seattle
(206) 634-9000

Five Corners Veterinary Hospital
15707 1st Ave. S., Seattle
(206) 243-2982

Pet Emergency Clinic
21 E. Mission Ave., Spokane
(509) 326-6670

Animal Emergency Clinic
5608 South Durango, Tacoma
(253) 474-0791

Emergency Veterinary Service
6818 E. 4th Plain Blvd., Vancouver
(360) 694-3007

WEST VIRGINIA

Middletown Animal Clinic
1615 Bobbeck Ln., Fairmont
(304) 366-6130

Kanawha Valley Animal Emergency Clinic
5304 MacCorkle Ave. S.W., South Charleston
(304) 768-2911

WISCONSIN

Fox Valley Animal Referral Center
4706 New Horizons Blvd., Appleton
(920) 993-9193

Animal Emergency Center
2100 W. Silver Spring Dr., Glendale
(414) 540-6710

Emergency Clinic for Animals
229 W. Beltline Hwy., Madison
(608) 274-7772

Animal Clinic
2734 Calumet Dr., Sheboygan
(920) 458-3636

Emergency Veterinary Service
360 Bluemound Rd., Waukesha
(262) 542-3241

Canada

BRITISH COLUMBIA

Animal Emergency Clinic
#103-6337 198th St., Langley
(604) 514-1711

Vancouver Animal Emergency Clinic, Ltd.
1590 West 4th Ave., Vancouver
(604) 734-5104

ONTARIO

Park Animal Hospital
1958 Burnham Thorpe Rd. E., Mississauga
(905) 625-5222

Niagara Veterinary Emergency Clinic
2F Tremont Dr., #1, St. Catharines
(905) 641-3185

PET-FRIENDLY LODGINGS

How to Use the Listings
U.S. Lodgings
Canadian Lodgings
Campground Listings

Some 12,000 AAA-RATED® properties across North America accept traveling pets. This guide provides listings for those lodgings in the United States and Canada that roll out the welcome mat for pets as well as the people who love them.

For the purpose of this book, "pets" are domestic cats or dogs. If you are planning to travel with any other kind of animal — particularly such exotic pets as birds or reptiles — check with the property before making definite plans. If you are taking a nontraditional pet, expect to keep her crated at all times.

Note: Always inform the management that you are traveling with an animal; you may be fined if you do not declare your pet. Many properties require guests with pets to sign a waiver or release form and to pay for the room with a credit card. Of course, whether you pay in cash or by credit card, you will be held liable for any damages caused by your pet, even if the property does not charge a deposit or pet fee. It is not a good idea to leave your pet unattended in the room, but if you must, crate him and notify the management. When in public areas, keep your pet leashed and do not allow him to disturb other guests.

About the Listings

Geographic listings are used for accuracy and consistency; lodgings are listed under the city or town in which they physically are located — or in some cases under the nearest recognized city or town. For a complete list of all cities within a state or province, see the comprehensive City Index at the beginning of the corresponding section.

U.S. properties are shown first, followed by Canadian properties. Most listings are alphabetically organized by state or province, city and establishment name. Reflecting contemporary travel patterns, properties in some cities or towns may instead be listed within destination cities or areas. Such "vicinity cities" and their listings will be shown alphabetically in the destination city or area, and the vicinity city also will appear in alphabetical order in the City Index, along with the page number on which the listings begin.

Each listing provides the following information (see sample listing, next page):

❶ Symbol denoting Official Appointment (OA) properties. The OA program permits properties to display and advertise the 🆎 or 🆎 logo. OAs have a special interest in serving AAA/CAA members. Ask if they offer special member amenities such as free breakfast, early check-in/late check-out, free room upgrade, free local phone calls, etc.

❷ Diamond rating. See next page.

❸ Property name.

❹ Lodging classification. See p. 62.

❺ Special amenities offered. These properties provide an additional benefit to pets, such as treats, toys or gifts, pet sitting and/or walking, a pet menu, food/water dishes, pet sheets or pillows, pet beds or other extras.

❻ Telephone number.

❼ Two-person (2P) rate year-round, and cancellation notice validity period (if more than 48 hours). Rates listed are usually daily, but weekly rates also may be listed. **Note:** Most properties accept any or all of the major credit cards, including American Express, MasterCard and VISA. If a property accepts only cash, the phrase "(no credit cards)" follows the rates.

❽ Physical address and highway location. If no physical address was available, the phrase "call for directions" appears.

❾ Exterior or interior corridors.

❿ Pet policies. If the phrase "pets accepted" appears, the property does accept pets but specific information was unavailable at press time. Otherwise, pet-specific policies are denoted as follows:

Size. "Very small" denotes pets weighing up to 10 pounds; "small," up to 25 pounds; "medium," up to 50 pounds; and "large," up to 100 pounds. If no size is specified, the property accepts pets of all sizes.

Species. "Other" indicates the property accepts animals other than dogs and cats. Always call ahead and specify the type of pet you plan to bring.

Deposits and fees. Includes the dollar amount, the type of charge (refundable deposit or nonrefundable fee), the frequency of the charge and whether the charge is per pet or per room.

Designated rooms. Guests with pets are placed in certain rooms, often smoking rooms or those on the ground floor.

Housekeeping service. The phrase "service with restrictions" denotes properties that require the pet to be crated, removed or attended by the owner during housekeeping service.

Supervision. The pet is required to be supervised at all times.

Crate. The pet must be crated when the owner is not present. If this policy applies only to cats, the phrase "(cats only)" will follow.

⓫ Property discounts and amenities:

🆂🅰🆅🅴 Minimum 10% discount.

🅰🆂🅺 May offer discount.

🆂🅳 Senior discount.

❌ Non-smoking rooms.

♿ Semi-accessible or ♿ fully accessible.

📧 Hearing impaired.

🚿 Roll-in showers.

- 🔋 Refrigerator.
- ▣ Coffee maker.
- ⑪ Restaurant on premises.
- ➥ Pool.
- ⊠ Recreational activities.
- 𝕂 No air conditioning.
- 𝕎 No TV.
- ☎ No telephones.

Please note: Some in-room amenities represented by the icons in the listings may be available only in selected rooms, and may incur an extra fee. Please inquire when making your reservations.

It is important to remember that animal policies do change; always confirm policies, restrictions and fees with the lodging when making reservations and again 1-2 days before departure.

Listing information is subject to change. All listing information was accurate at press time. However, lodging rates and policies change and the publisher cannot be held liable for changes occurring after publication.

AAA Diamond Ratings

Before a property is listed by AAA, it must satisfy a set of minimum standards regarding basic lodging needs as identified by AAA members. If a property meets those requirements, it is assigned a diamond rating reflecting the overall quality of the establishment.

AAA ratings range from one to five diamonds and indicate the property's physical and service standards as measured against the standards of each diamond level. The rating process takes into account the property's classification; i.e., its physical structure and style of operation.

♦ These establishments typically appeal to the budget-minded traveler. They provide essential, no-frills accommodations. They meet the basic requirements pertaining to comfort, cleanliness, and hospitality.

♦♦ These establishments appeal to the traveler seeking more than the basic accommodations. There are modest enhancements to the overall physical attributes, design elements, and amenities of the facility typically at a modest price.

♦♦♦ These establishments appeal to the traveler with comprehensive needs. Properties are multifaceted with a distinguished style, including marked upgrades in the quality of physical attributes, amenities and level of comfort provided.

♦♦♦♦ These establishments are upscale in all areas. Accommodations are progressively more refined and stylish. The physical attributes reflect an obvious enhanced level of quality throughout. The fundamental hallmarks at this level include an extensive array of amenities combined with a high degree of hospitality, service, and attention to detail.

♦♦♦♦♦ These establishments reflect the characteristics of the ultimate in luxury and sophistication. Accommodations are first-class. The physical attributes are extraordinary in every manner. The fundamental hallmarks at this level are to meticulously serve and exceed all guest expectations while maintaining an impeccable standard of excellence. Many personalized services and amenities enhance an unmatched level of comfort.

Lodging Classifications

🅱🅱 **Bed & Breakfast:** Usually smaller establishments emphasizing a more personal relationship between operators and guests, leading to an "at home" feeling. Guest units tend to be individually decorated. Rooms may not include some modern amenities such as televisions and telephones, and may have a shared bathroom. Usually owner-operated, with a common room or parlor separate from the innkeeper's living quarters, where guests and operators can interact during evening and breakfast hours. Evening office closures are normal. A continental or full, hot breakfast is served and is included in the room rate.

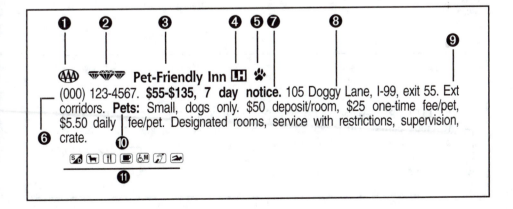

CA Cabin/Cottage: Vacation-oriented, small-scale, free-standing houses or cabins. Units vary in design and decor and often contain one or more bedrooms, living room, kitchen, dining area and bathroom. Studio-type models combine the sleeping and living areas into one room. Typically, basic cleaning supplies, kitchen utensils, and complete bed and bath linens are supplied. The guest registration area may be located off-site.

CI Country Inn: Although similar in definition to a bed and breakfast, country inns are usually larger in size, provide more spacious public areas and offer a dining facility that serves at least breakfast and dinner. May be located in a rural setting or downtown area.

CO Condominium: Establishments that primarily offer guest accommodations that are privately owned by individuals and available for rent. These can include apartment-style units or homes. A variety of room styles and decor treatments are offered, and limited housekeeping service is typical. May have off-site registration.

LH Large-scale Hotel: A multistory establishment with interior room entrances. A variety of guest unit styles are offered. Public areas are spacious and include a variety of facilities such as a restaurant, shops, fitness center, spa, business center or meeting rooms.

M Motel: Low-rise or multistory establishment offering limited public and recreational facilities.

RA Ranch: Often offers rustic decor treatments and food and beverage facilities. Entertainment and recreational activities are geared to a Western-style adventure vacation. May provide some meeting facilities.

SH Small-scale Hotel: A multistory establishment typically with interior room entrances. A variety of guest unit styles are offered. Public areas are limited in size and/or the variety of facilities available.

VH Vacation Home: Vacation-oriented or extended-stay, large-scale, freestanding houses that are routinely available for rent through a management company. Houses vary in design and décor and often contain two or more bedrooms, living room, full kitchen, dining room and multiple bathrooms. Typically, basic cleaning supplies, kitchen utensils, and complete bed and bath linens are supplied. The guest registration area may be located off-site.

Campground Listings

Geographic listings are used for accuracy and consistency. Campgrounds are listed under the city or town in which they physically are located — or in some cases under the nearest recognized city or town. Not all listings include physical addresses. U.S. campgrounds are given first, followed by Canadian campgrounds. Listings are alphabetically organized by state or province, city and campground name.

Note: Call first before taking your pet on a camping trip, as campground policies regarding pets may change.

Each listing provides the following information (see sample listing):

❶ Location.

❷ Campground name.

❸ Symbol denoting Official Appointment (OA) campgrounds. The OA program permits privately operated campgrounds to display and advertise the AAA or CAA logo. OAs have a special interest in serving AAA/CAA members.

❹ Telephone number.

❺ Fee range for a specified number of persons, including the fee for an extra person (XP) staying at the campground.

❻ Most campgrounds accept any or all of the major credit cards, including American Express, MasterCard and Visa. If a campground accepts only cash, the sentence "(no credit cards)." appears.

❼ Physical address (if available), highway location and mailing address (if available).

❽ Pet policies (as applicable). Size designations are "very small" (pets weighing up to 10 pounds); "small," up to 25 pounds; "medium," up to 50 pounds; and "large," up to 100 pounds. If no size is specified, the campground accepts pets of all sizes.

❾ Campground discounts and amenities:

    🆂 10% senior discount for members over 59

    🚫 No Tents.

    ➥ Pool.

    ⊠ Recreational activities.

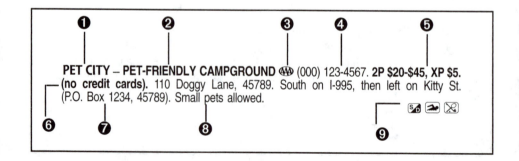

United States

ALABAMA

CITY INDEX

ABBEVILLE

◆◆ **Best Western-Abbeville Inn** [SH]
(334) 585-5060. **$55.** 1237 US 431. Jct SR 27. Ext corridors. **Pets:** $10 daily fee/pet. Service with restrictions, supervision.
[SD] ⊠ ▮ 🖥 🏊

ALBERTVILLE

◆◆ **Jameson Inn** [SH]
(256) 891-2600. **$49-$104.** 315 Martling Rd. On US 431, just e of SR 75. Ext corridors. **Pets:** Very small, other species. $10 daily fee/room. Service with restrictions, supervision.
[A$K] ⊠ ♿ ▮ 🖥 🏊

ALEXANDER CITY

◆◆ **Jameson Inn** [SH]
(256) 234-7099. **$49-$104.** 4335 US Hwy 280. US 280, just s of jct SR 22; just w of jct SR 63. Ext corridors. **Pets:** Very small, other species. $10 daily fee/room. No service, supervision.
[A$K] ⊠ ♿ ▮ 🖥 🏊

ANDALUSIA

◆◆ **Days Inn** [SH]
(334) 427-0050. **$53-$59.** 1604 Dr. MLK Jr Expwy. Just e on US 84 Bypass. Ext corridors. **Pets:** Accepted.
[A$K] [SD] ⊠ ▮ 🖥 🏊

[AAA] ◆◆ **Scottish Inn** [M]
(334) 222-7511. **$28-$50.** 1421 Hwy 84 E. Just e on US 84 Bypass. Ext corridors. **Pets:** $4 daily fee/pet. Service with restrictions, supervision.
[SAVE] [SD] ⊠ ▮ 🏊

ARAB

◆◆ **Jameson Inn** [SH]
(256) 586-5777. **$49-$104.** 706 N Brindlee Mountain Pkwy. On US 231, 0.5 mi n of jct SR 69. Ext corridors. **Pets:** Very small, other species. $10 daily fee/room. Service with restrictions, supervision.
[A$K] ⊠ ♿ ▮ 🖥 🏊

ARDMORE

[AAA] ◆◆ **Budget Inn** [M]
(256) 423-6699. **$40-$70.** I-65 & Hwy 53. I-65, exit 365, just se. Ext corridors. **Pets:** Accepted.
[SAVE] [SD] ⊠ ▮

ATHENS

[AAA] ◆◆ **Best Western Athens Inn** [SH]
(256) 233-4030. **$59-$99.** 1329 Hwy 72. I-65, exit 351, just w. Ext corridors. **Pets:** Small. $10 daily fee/pet. Service with restrictions, crate.
[SAVE] [SD] ⊠ ▮ 🖥 🏊

◆◆ **Country Hearth Inn** [SH]
(256) 232-1520. **$54-$99.** 1500 Hwy 72 E. I-65, exit 351, just e on US 72. Ext corridors. **Pets:** Medium. $10 daily fee/room, $10 one-time fee/room. Service with restrictions, supervision.
[A$K] [SD] ⊠ ▮ 🖥 🏊

◆◆ **Days Inn Athens** [SH]
(256) 233-7500. **Call for rates.** 1322 Hwy 72 E. I-65, exit 351, just nw. Ext corridors. **Pets:** Accepted.
⊠ ▮ 🖥 🏊

◆◆◆ **Hampton Inn Athens** [SH]
(256) 232-0030. **$70-$85.** 1488 Thrasher Blvd. I-65, exit 351, just ne. Ext corridors. **Pets:** Small. $25 one-time fee/room. Service with restrictions, supervision.
[A$K] ⊠ ▮ 🖥 🏊

◆◆ **Sleep Inn Athens** [SH]
(256) 232-4700. **$49-$89.** 1115 Audubon Ln. I-65, exit 351, just nw. Int corridors. **Pets:** Large. $10 daily fee/pet. Designated rooms, service with restrictions, supervision.
[A$K] [SD] ⊠ ♿ 🖥 🏊

◆◆ **Super 8** [SH]
(256) 233-1446. **$49-$69.** 1325 Hwy 72. I-65, exit 351, just w. Int corridors. **Pets:** Other species. $5 daily fee/pet. Service with restrictions, supervision.
[A$K] [SD] ⊠ ▮ 🖥

ATTALLA

[AAA] ◆◆ **Econo Lodge** [SH]
(256) 538-9925. **$49-$64.** 507 Cherry St. I-59, exit 183, just w. Int corridors. **Pets:** Small, dogs only. $25 deposit/pet. Service with restrictions, supervision.
[SAVE] [SD] ⊠ ▮ 🖥 🍴 🏊

[AAA] ◆◆◆ **Holiday Inn Express Gadsden/Attalla** [SH] 🐾
(256) 538-7861. **$56.** 801 Cleveland Ave. I-59, exit 183 northbound, just e; exit southbound, through first set of lights, then just e. Ext corridors. **Pets:** Other species. $25 one-time fee/pet. Service with restrictions, supervision.
[SAVE] [SD] ⊠ ♿ ▮ 🖥 🏊

AUBURN

[AAA] ◆◆◆ **Auburn University Hotel & Dixon Conference Center** [LH]
(334) 821-8200. **$89-$205.** 241 S College St. I-85, exit 51, 3.5 mi w. Int corridors. **Pets:** Other species. Service with restrictions.
[SAVE] [SD] ⊠ ♿[M] 👂 ▮ 🖥 🍴 🏊

[AAA] ◆◆ **Best Western University Convention Center** [SH]
(334) 821-7001. **$99, 7 day notice.** 1577 S College St. I-85, exit 51, 1.4 mi w. Ext corridors. **Pets:** Other species. Service with restrictions.
[SAVE] ⊠ ▮ 🖥 🍴 🏊

Excite Your Dog On the Go... with MILK-BONE® Doggie-Delicious Treats!

You love the excitement of treating your dog at home. Don't forget to share the same excitement with your dog on the road... by giving him the delicious, meaty **Milk-Bone®** dog snacks that he loves!

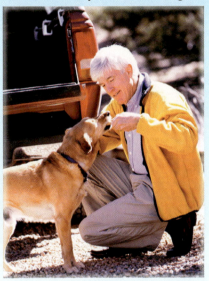

Before your next trip, buy a pack of Milk-Bone® biscuits or chewy treats and save 75¢!

▼▼▼ **Econo Lodge** **M**
(334) 826-8900. **$70-$160.** 2145 S College St. I-85, exit 51, just n. Ext corridors. **Pets:** Accepted.
(ASK) (Sᴅ) (✕) (🛏) (▯)

▼▼▼ **Jameson Inn** **SH**
(334) 502-5020. **$49-$104.** 1212 Mall Pkwy. I-85, exit 58, 1.5 mi w on US 280, then 2.9 mi sw on US 29/SR 14. Ext corridors. **Pets:** Very small, other species. $10 daily fee/room. Service with restrictions, supervision.
(ASK) (✕) (🛏) (▯) (≈)

BIRMINGHAM METROPOLITAN AREA

BESSEMER

▲▲▲ ▼▼▼▼ **Best Western Hotel & Suites** **SH**
(205) 481-1950. **$59-$200.** 5041 Academy Ln. I-20/59, exit 108, just sw. Int corridors. **Pets:** Other species. $10 daily fee/pet. Service with restrictions, supervision.
(SAVE) (Sᴅ) (✕) (🎾) (🛏) (▯) (≈)

▼▼▼▼ **Comfort Inn** **SH**
(205) 428-3999. **$70-$120.** 5051 Academy Ln. I-20/59, exit 108, just sw. Int corridors. **Pets:** Other species. Service with restrictions.
(ASK) (Sᴅ) (✕) (🎾) (🛏) (▯) (≈)

▼▼ **Jameson Inn** **SH**
(205) 428-3194. **$49-$104.** 5021 Academy Ln. I-20/59, exit 108, just sw. Ext corridors. **Pets:** Very small, other species. $10 daily fee/room. Service with restrictions, supervision.
(ASK) (✕) (⅙M) (🔌) (🎾) (🛏) (▯) (≈)

▼ **Motel 6 #426** **M**
(205) 426-9646. **$43-$53.** 1000 Shiloh Ln. I-20/59, exit 108, 1 mi ne on US 11. Ext corridors. **Pets:** Accepted.
(Sᴅ) (✕) (🎾) (≈)

BIRMINGHAM

▲▲▲ ▼▼▼▼ **AmeriSuites (Birmingham/Inverness)** **SH**
(205) 995-9242. **$99-$129.** 4686 Hwy 280 E. I-459, exit 19 (US 280), 1.7 mi e. Int corridors. **Pets:** Accepted.
(SAVE) (Sᴅ) (✕) (⅙M) (🎾) (🛏) (▯) (≈)

▲▲▲ ▼▼▼ **Baymont Inn & Suites Birmingham** **SH**
(205) 995-9990. **$59-$64.** 513 Cahaba Park Cir. I-459, exit 19 (US 280), 1.2 mi e. Int corridors. **Pets:** Accepted.
(SAVE) (Sᴅ) (✕) (🛏) (▯)

▼▼ **Best Inn & Suites** **SH**
(205) 836-5400. **$55-$65.** 9225 Parkway E. I-59, exit 134, just w, then just s on US 11. Ext corridors. **Pets:** Other species. $25 deposit/room. Designated rooms, service with restrictions, supervision.
(ASK) (Sᴅ) (✕) (🛏) (▯)

▲▲▲ ▼▼▼▼ **Best Western Mountain Brook** **SH**
(205) 991-9977. **$70-$200.** 4627 Hwy 280 E. I-459, exit 19 (US 280), 1.4 mi e. Ext corridors. **Pets:** Small. $20 one-time fee/room. Service with restrictions, supervision.
(SAVE) (Sᴅ) (✕) (▯) (≈) (✕)

▼▼▼▼ **Drury Inn & Suites-Birmingham Southeast** **SH**
(205) 967-2450. **$62-$102.** 3510 Grandview Pkwy. I-459, exit 19 (US 280), southeast corner. Int corridors. **Pets:** Large, other species. Service with restrictions, supervision.
(ASK) (✕) (🎾) (🛏) (▯) (≈)

▼▼▼▼ **Holiday Inn-Airport** **SH**
(205) 591-6900. **$75-$90.** 5000 Richard Arrington Blvd. I-20/59, exit 129, just s. Int corridors. **Pets:** Accepted.
(ASK) (Sᴅ) (✕) (▯) (🍴) (≈)

▼▼ **Homestead Studio Suites Hotel-Birmingham/Perimeter Park South** **SH**
(205) 967-3800. **$54-$64.** 12 Perimeter Park S. I-459, exit 19 (US 280), 0.5 mi e, then just s. Ext corridors. **Pets:** Accepted.
(ASK) (Sᴅ) (✕) (⅙M) (🔌) (🎾) (🛏) (▯)

▲▲▲ ▼▼▼▼ **Pickwick Hotel** **SH**
(205) 933-9555. **$97.** 1023 20th St S. 1.5 mi s of downtown (Five Points area). Int corridors. **Pets:** Accepted.
(SAVE) (Sᴅ) (✕) (🛏) (▯)

▼▼▼▼ **Residence Inn By Marriott** **SH** 🐾
(205) 991-8686. **$115-$125.** 3 Green Hill Pkwy. I-459, exit 19 (US 280), 2 mi e. Ext corridors. **Pets:** Other species. $75 one-time fee/room. Service with restrictions, crate.
(ASK) (✕) (🎾) (▯) (≈) (✕)

▲▲▲ ▼▼▼▼ **The Tutwiler-A Wyndham Historic Hotel** **LH**
(205) 322-2100. **$99-$169.** 2021 Park Pl N. Downtown. Int corridors. **Pets:** Accepted.
(SAVE) (✕) (🔌) (🛏) (▯) (🍴)

CALERA

▼▼▼ **Holiday Inn Express** **SH**
(205) 668-3641. **$63-$89.** 357 Hwy 304. I-65, exit 231, just se. Ext corridors. **Pets:** Accepted.
(ASK) (Sᴅ) (✕) (🎾) (🛏) (▯) (≈)

HOMEWOOD

▲▲▲ ▼▼▼▼ **La Quinta Inn & Suites Birmingham (Homewood)** **SH**
(205) 290-0150. **$79-$120.** 60 State Farm Pkwy. I-65, exit 255, 0.9 mi on northwest frontage road. Int corridors. **Pets:** Service with restrictions, supervision.
(SAVE) (✕) (🎾) (🛏) (▯) (≈)

▼▼▼ **Microtel** **SH**
(205) 945-5550. **$35-$45.** 251 Summit Pkwy. I-65, exit 256 northbound; exit 256A southbound, just w. Int corridors. **Pets:** Other species. $10 daily fee/room. Service with restrictions, supervision.
(ASK) (Sᴅ) (✕) (🎾)

▲▲▲ ▼▼▼▼ **Ramada Inn** **SH**
(205) 916-0464. **$65-$149.** 226 Summit Pkwy. I-65, exit 256 northbound; exit 256A southbound, just w. Int corridors. **Pets:** Very small, other species. $25 one-time fee/pet. Service with restrictions, crate.
(SAVE) (Sᴅ) (✕) (🛏) (▯) (≈)

▼▼ **Red Roof Inn** **M**
(205) 942-9414. **$42-$59.** 151 Vulcan Rd. I-65, exit 256 northbound; exit 256A southbound, just nw. Ext corridors. **Pets:** Accepted.
(✕)

▼▼▼ **Residence Inn by Marriott** **SH** 🐾
(205) 943-0044. **Call for rates.** 50 State Farm Pkwy. I-65, exit 255, 1 mi on northwest frontage road. Int corridors. **Pets:** Large, other species. $75 one-time fee/pet. Service with restrictions, crate.
(Sᴅ) (✕) (🎾) (🛏) (▯) (≈) (✕)

▲▲▲ ▼▼▼ **Super 8 Motel** **SH**
(205) 945-9888. **$47-$53.** 140 Vulcan Rd. I-65, exit 256 northbound; exit 256A southbound, just nw. Int corridors. **Pets:** Small, other species. $5 daily fee/pet. Service with restrictions.
(SAVE) (Sᴅ) (✕) (🛏) (▯)

▼▼▼ TownePlace Suites by Marriott **SH**
(205) 943-0114. **$75-$119.** 500 Wildwood Cir. I-65, exit 255, 0.6 mi w, then just n. Int corridors. **Pets:** Accepted.
(ASK) (S❄) (X) (Ġ.M) (Ġ.) (❚) (💻) (≈)

HOOVER

◆◆◆ ▼▼▼ AmeriSuites (Birmingham/Riverchase) **SH**
(205) 988-8444. **$99-$129.** 2980 John Hawkins Pkwy. I-459, exit 13, 0.5 mi s on US 31, then 0.8 mi w on SR 150. Int corridors. **Pets:** Accepted.
(SAVE) (S❄) (X) (Ġ.) (❚) (💻) (≈)

◆◆◆ ▼▼▼ La Quinta Inn & Suites Birmingham
(Hoover/Riverchase) **SH**
(205) 403-0096. **$66-$110.** 120 Riverchase Pkwy E. I-65, exit 247 (Valleydale Rd), just w. Int corridors. **Pets:** Small, other species. Service with restrictions, crate.
(SAVE) (X) (Ġ.) (❚) (💻) (≈)

IRONDALE

◆◆◆ ▼▼▼ Best Western Rime Garden Inn & Suites **SH**
(205) 951-1200. **$99, 7 day notice.** 5320 Beacon Dr. I-20, exit 133 westbound, just sw. Ext corridors. **Pets:** Small. $25 one-time fee/pet. Service with restrictions, crate.
(SAVE) (S❄) (X) (❚) (💻) (¶) (≈)

LEEDS

◆◆◆ ▼▼▼ Days Inn of Leeds **M**
(205) 699-9833. **$54-$60.** 1835 Ashville Rd. I-20, exit 144B eastbound; exit 144A westbound, just s. Ext corridors. **Pets:** $7 daily fee/pet. Service with restrictions, supervision.
(SAVE) (S❄) (X) (❚) (≈)

MOODY

▼▼ Super 8 Motel **M**
(205) 640-7091. **$56-$62.** 2451 Moody Pkwy. I-20, exit 144, 1 mi n on US 411. Ext corridors. **Pets:** Accepted.
(ASK) (S❄) (X) (❚)

ONEONTA

◆◆◆ ▼▼▼ Best Western Colonial Inn **SH**
(205) 274-2200. **$65-$70.** 293 Valley Rd. On SR 75, 0.5 mi n of jct US 231. Ext corridors. **Pets:** Accepted.
(SAVE) (S❄) (X) (Ġ.) (❚) (💻) (≈)

PELHAM

◆◆◆ ▼▼▼ Best Western at Oak Mountain **SH**
(205) 982-1113. **$69-$79.** 100 Bishop Cir. I-65, exit 246, just sw, then just s on State Park Rd. Int corridors. **Pets:** Small, other species. Designated rooms, service with restrictions, supervision.
(SAVE) (S❄) (X) (Ġ.) (❚) (💻) (≈)

◆◆◆ ▼▼▼ Comfort Inn **SH**
(205) 444-9200. **$69-$130, 10 day notice.** 110 Cahaba Valley Pkwy. I-65, exit 246, just nw. Ext corridors. **Pets:** Very small. $10 daily fee/ room. Designated rooms, no service, supervision.
(SAVE) (S❄) (X) (❚) (💻) (≈)

TRUSSVILLE

▼▼ Jameson Inn **SH**
(205) 661-9323. **$49-$104.** 4730 Norrell Dr. I-59, exit 141, just e on Chalkville Rd, then just n. Ext corridors. **Pets:** Very small, other species. $10 daily fee/room. Service with restrictions, supervision.
(ASK) (X) (Ġ.) (❚) (💻) (≈)

VESTAVIA HILLS

◆◆◆ ▼▼▼ Hampton Inn South **SH**
(205) 822-2224. **$84-$104.** 1466 Montgomery Hwy. I-65, exit 252 (US 31), 0.5 mi e. Ext corridors. **Pets:** Accepted.
(SAVE) (S❄) (X) (💻) (≈)

END METROPOLITAN AREA

BOAZ

▼▼ Key West Inn **SH**
(256) 593-0800. **$48-$85.** 10535 SR 168. 0.5 mi w of jct US 431. Ext corridors. **Pets:** $5 daily fee/pet. Service with restrictions, crate.
(ASK) (S❄) (X) (❚) (💻)

CLANTON

◆◆◆ ▼▼▼ Best Western Inn **SH**
(205) 280-1006. **$75-$85, 5 day notice.** 801 Bradberry Ln. I-65, exit 205, 0.5 mi e. Ext corridors. **Pets:** Small. $8 daily fee/pet. Service with restrictions, supervision.
(SAVE) (X) (Ġ.) (❚) (💻) (≈)

◆◆◆ ▼▼▼ GuestHouse International Inn **SH** 🐾
(205) 280-0306. **$54-$58.** 946 Lake Mitchell Rd. I-65, exit 208, just w. Ext corridors. **Pets:** Other species. $20 deposit/pet. Service with restrictions, supervision.
(SAVE) (S❄) (X) (💻) (≈)

CULLMAN

◆◆◆ ▼▼▼ Best Western Fairwinds Inn **SH**
(256) 737-5009. **$49-$98.** 1917 Commerce Ave NW. I-65, exit 310, just e. Ext corridors. **Pets:** Other species. $9 daily fee/room. Service with restrictions, crate.
(SAVE) (S❄) (X) (❚) (💻) (≈)

▼▼ Comfort Inn **SH**
(256) 734-1240. **Call for rates.** 5917 Alabama Hwy 157 NW. I-65, exit 310, just e. Ext corridors. **Pets:** Accepted.
(X) (❚) (💻) (≈)

▼▼ Days Inn **SH**
(256) 739-3800. **$53.** 1841 4th St SW. I-65, exit 308, just e. Ext corridors. **Pets:** Other species. $5 daily fee/room. Service with restrictions, supervision.
(ASK) (S❄) (X) (❚) (≈)

DALEVILLE

▼▼ The Lodge **M**
(334) 598-6304. **$43-$45.** 444 N Daleville Ave. 1 mi n of jct US 84 and SR 85. Ext corridors. **Pets:** Accepted.
(ASK) (S❄) (X) (❚) (💻) (≈)

DECATUR

▼▼▼ Comfort Inn **SH**
(256) 355-1037. **$79-$125.** 3239 Point Mallard Pkwy. I-65, exit 334, just w. Int corridors. **Pets:** Small, other species. $10 daily fee/room. Service with restrictions, supervision.
(ASK) (S❄) (X) (📷) (Ġ.) (❚) (💻) (≈)

▼▼▼▼ **Comfort Inn & Suites** SH
(256) 355-1999. **$70-$90.** 2212 Danville Rd SW. SR 67, jct Beltline Rd SW. Int corridors. **Pets:** Other species. $35 deposit/pet, $10 daily fee/pet. Service with restrictions, supervision.

ASK SÒ ✕ 丛 🛢 🖵 ➰

▼▼▼ **Jameson Inn** SH
(256) 355-2229. **$49-$104.** 2120 Jameson Pl SW. SR 67, 1.6 mi s of jct US 72A, 3.9 mi n of jct US 31. Ext corridors. **Pets:** Very small, other species. $10 daily fee/room. Service with restrictions, supervision.

ASK ✕ 丛 🛢 🖵 ➰

▼▼▼ **Microtel Inn & Suites** SH
(256) 301-9995. **$55-$81.** 2226 Beltline Rd SW. On SR 67, 4 mi w of jct US 31. Int corridors. **Pets:** Small. $15 one-time fee/room. Service with restrictions, crate.

ASK SÒ ✕ 丛 🕭 丛 🛢 🖵

▼▼▼▼ **Ramada Limited** SH
(256) 353-0333. **$47-$57.** 1317 Hwy 67 E. I-65, exit 334, 4 mi w; 0.4 mi se of jct US 31. Ext corridors. **Pets:** Other species. $10 one-time fee/pet. Service with restrictions, crate.

✕ 🛢 🖵 ➰

DEMOPOLIS

▼▼ **Riverview Inn** M
(334) 289-0690. **$50.** 110 Yacht Basin Dr. 1.8 mi n on S Walnut from US 80. Ext corridors. **Pets:** Small. $15 one-time fee/pet. Service with restrictions, supervision.

ASK SÒ ✕ 🛢 🖵 🍴

DOTHAN

🔺 ▼▼▼ **Best Value Inn & Suites** SH
(334) 793-5200. **$45.** 2901 Ross Clark Cir. On US 231 Bypass. Ext corridors. **Pets:** Medium. $50 deposit/room. Designated rooms.

SAVE SÒ ✕ 🛢 🖵 ➰

🔺 ▼▼▼▼ **Comfort Inn** SH
(334) 793-9090. **$78-$99.** 3593 Ross Clark Cir. Just sw of jct US 231 N. Int corridors. **Pets:** Small. $10 daily fee/pet. Service with restrictions, supervision.

SAVE SÒ ✕ 丛 🕭 🛢 🖵 ➰

▼▼ **Days Inn** SH
(334) 793-2550. **$40-$46, 7 day notice.** 2841 Ross Clark Cir. 2 mi sw on US 231 Bypass. Ext corridors. **Pets:** $5 daily fee/pet. Service with restrictions, supervision.

ASK SÒ ✕ 🛢 🖵 ➰

🔺 ▼▼▼▼ **Holiday Inn Express** SH
(334) 671-3700. **$55-$98.** 3071 Ross Clark Cir. US 231 Bypass at jct US 84 W. Ext corridors. **Pets:** Other species. $15 one-time fee/pet. Service with restrictions, crate.

SAVE SÒ ✕ 丛 🕭 🛢 🖵

🔺 ▼▼▼▼ **Holiday Inn-South** SH
(334) 794-8711. **$70-$90, 10 day notice.** 2195 Ross Clark Cir SE. 2 mi s on US 231 Bypass at jct US 84 W. Ext corridors. **Pets:** Accepted.

SAVE SÒ ✕ 丛 丛 🛢 🖵 🍴 ➰

▼▼▼▼ **Howard Johnson Express Inn** SH
(334) 792-3339. **$59-$69.** 2244 Ross Clark Cir. On US 231 Bypass. Ext corridors. **Pets:** Accepted.

ASK SÒ ✕ 🛢 🖵 🚫

▼ **Motel 6 #1233** M
(334) 793-6013. **$35-$47.** 2907 Ross Clark Cir SW. On US 231, 0.7 mi s of jct US 84. Ext corridors. **Pets:** Accepted.

SÒ ✕ 丛 🛢 🖵 ➰

🔺 ▼▼▼▼ **Quality Hotel** SH
(334) 794-6601. **$49-$69.** 3053 Ross Clark Cir. 2 mi w on US 231 Bypass; just s of jct US 84 W. Ext corridors. **Pets:** Accepted.

SAVE SÒ ✕ 丛 🕭 丛 🛢 🖵 🍴 ➰

▼▼ **Ramada Inn** SH
(334) 792-0031. **$55-$89.** 3011 Ross Clark Cir. US 231 Bypass at jct US 84 W. Ext/int corridors. **Pets:** Accepted.

ASK SÒ ✕ 🛢 🖵 🍴 ➰

ENTERPRISE

▼▼▼ **Comfort Inn** SH
(334) 393-2304. **$69-$79.** 615 Boll Weevil Cir. On SR 167, 0.5 mi s of jct US 84/SR 248. Ext corridors. **Pets:** Accepted.

ASK SÒ ✕ 🕭 🛢 🖵 ➰

EUFAULA

▼▼▼▼ **Eufaula Comfort Suites** SH
(334) 616-0114. **Call for rates.** 12 Paul Lee Pkwy. Jct US 431 and Paul Lee Pkwy, 2.5 mi s of downtown. Int corridors. **Pets:** Other species. $25 one-time fee/room. Service with restrictions, crate.

✕ 丛 🕭 丛 🛢 🖵 ➰ 🚫

▼▼▼ **Jameson Inn** SH
(334) 687-7747. **$49-$104.** 136 Towne Center Blvd. On US 431, 1.1 mi s of US 82. Ext corridors. **Pets:** Very small, other species. $10 daily fee/room. Service with restrictions, supervision.

ASK ✕ 🛢 🖵 ➰

▼▼ **Ramada Inn** SH
(334) 687-2021. **$55.** 631 E Barbour St. On US 82, 0.5 mi e of jct US 431. Ext corridors. **Pets:** Medium. $5 daily fee/pet. Service with restrictions, crate.

ASK SÒ ✕ 🛢 🖵 🍴 ➰

EVERGREEN

🔺 ▼▼ **Comfort Inn** SH
(251) 578-4701. **$63-$68.** 198 Ted Bates Rd. I-65, exit 96 (SR 83), on southwest service road. Ext corridors. **Pets:** $5 daily fee/pet. Service with restrictions.

SAVE SÒ ✕ 丛 🛢 🖵 ➰

▼▼ **Days Inn of Evergreen** M
(251) 578-2100. **$55-$61.** Rt 2. I-65, exit 96 (SR 83), just w. Ext corridors. **Pets:** $10 daily fee/pet. Service with restrictions, supervision.

ASK ✕ 🛢 🖵

FAIRHOPE

▼▼ **Key West Inn** M
(251) 990-7373. **$50-$150.** 231 S Greeno Rd (Hwy 98). I-10, exit 35A, 9.7 mi s on US 98, on the east side. Ext corridors. **Pets:** Accepted.

ASK SÒ ✕ 丛 🛢 🖵 ➰

FLORENCE

▼▼ **Days Inn-Florence** M
(256) 766-2620. **$50-$70.** 1915 Florence Blvd. On US 72. Ext corridors. **Pets:** Very small, other species. $20 one-time fee/room. No service, supervision.

ASK SÒ ✕ 🛢 ➰

▼▼ **Jameson Inn** SH
(256) 764-5326. **$49-$104.** 115 Ana Dr. On US 43/72, just nw of jct SR 133 (Cox Creek Pkwy). Ext corridors. **Pets:** Very small, other species. $10 daily fee/room. Service with restrictions, supervision.

ASK ✕ 丛 🛢 🖵 ➰

Super 8 Motel **M** 🐾
(256) 757-2167. **$46-$86.** 101 Hwy 72 & 43 E. 3.8 mi e on US 43/72 from jct SR 133 (Cox Creek Pkwy). Ext corridors. **Pets:** Medium. $25 deposit/pet, $7 daily fee/pet. Designated rooms, service with restrictions, supervision.

FOLEY

Holiday Inn Express **SH**
(251) 943-9100. **$68-$143.** 2682 S McKenzie St. SR 59, 1.9 mi s of jct US 98. Ext corridors. **Pets:** Accepted.

Key West Inn **SH**
(251) 943-1241. **$59-$139.** 2520 S McKenzie St. SR 59, 1.8 mi s of jct US 98. Ext corridors. **Pets:** Medium. $15 daily fee/pet. Designated rooms, service with restrictions, crate.

FORT PAYNE

Econo Lodge **SH**
(256) 845-4013. **$55-$65.** 1412 Glenn Blvd SW. I-59, exit 218, just w. Ext corridors. **Pets:** Medium. $10 daily fee/room. Designated rooms, service with restrictions, supervision.

GADSDEN

Days Inn Gadsden **SH**
(256) 442-7913. **$55-$160, 14 day notice.** 1612 W Grand Ave. I-59, exit 181, 0.6 mi e on SR 77. Ext corridors. **Pets:** Accepted.

Motel 6 **SH**
(256) 543-1105. **$41-$45.** 1600 Rainbow Dr. I-759, exit 4A, 0.8 mi s on US 411. Ext corridors. **Pets:** Accepted.

GREENVILLE

Best Western Inn **SH**
(334) 382-9200. **$55-$80.** 56 Cahaba Rd. I-65, exit 130, just w on SR 185. Ext corridors. **Pets:** Small. $5 daily fee/pet. Service with restrictions, supervision.

Comfort Inn **SH**
(334) 383-9595. **$60-$80.** 1029 Fort Dale Rd. I-65, exit 130, just w. Int corridors. **Pets:** Small. $5 daily fee/pet. Service with restrictions, supervision.

Econo Lodge **M**
(334) 382-3118. **$49-$70, 7 day notice.** 946 Fort Dale Rd. I-65, exit 130, just ne on SR 185. Ext corridors. **Pets:** $10 daily fee/pet. Service with restrictions, supervision.

Jameson Inn **SH**
(334) 382-6300. **$49-$104.** 71 Jameson Ln. I-65, exit 130, just n on SR 185. Ext corridors. **Pets:** Other species. $10 daily fee/room. Service with restrictions, supervision.

GUNTERSVILLE

Super 8 Motel-Guntersville **M**
(256) 582-8444. **$44-$49.** 14341 Hwy 431 S. On US 431, 2 mi s of jct SR 69. Ext corridors. **Pets:** Accepted.

HAMILTON

Days Inn **SH**
(205) 921-1790. **$59.** 1849 Military St S. US 78, exit 14, 1 mi n, then 1 mi w on US 43. Ext corridors. **Pets:** $10 daily fee/pet. Service with restrictions.

HUNTSVILLE

Baymont Inn & Suites Huntsville **SH**
(256) 830-8999. **$59-$79.** 4890 University Dr. I-565, exit 14B, 2.6 mi n on Research Park Blvd, then 1 mi e on US 72. Int corridors. **Pets:** Accepted.

Best Inns **M**
(256) 539-9671. **$45-$90.** 1304 N Memorial Pkwy. I-565, exit 19B, 0.5 mi n on US 231/431, east side service road. Ext corridors. **Pets:** Small. Service with restrictions, supervision.

GuestHouse Suites Plus **SH**
(256) 837-8907. **$65-$105.** 4020 Independence Dr. I-565, exit 17A, 1.1 mi n on SR 53 (Jordan Ln), just w on US 72, then just n. Ext corridors. **Pets:** Accepted.

Hilton Huntsville **LH**
(256) 533-1400. **$84-$158.** 401 Williams Ave. Just w of Church St; downtown. Int corridors. **Pets:** Accepted.

La Quinta Inn Huntsville (Research Park) **SH**
(256) 830-2070. **$66-$91.** 4870 University Dr. I-565, exit 14B, 2.6 mi n on Research Park Blvd, then 1 mi e on US 72. Ext corridors. **Pets:** Accepted.

La Quinta Inn Huntsville (Space Center) **SH**
(256) 533-0756. **$66-$86.** 3141 University Dr. I-565, exit 17A, 1.1 mi n on SR 53 (Jordan Ln), then 0.6 mi e on US 72. Ext corridors. **Pets:** Other species. Service with restrictions.

JASPER

Jameson Inn **SH**
(205) 387-7710. **$49-$104.** 1100 Hwy 118. SR 118, 1.8 mi w of jct SR 69. Ext corridors. **Pets:** Very small, other species. $10 daily fee/room. Service with restrictions, supervision.

MADISON

Motel 6–1087 **M**
(256) 772-7479. **$41-$51.** 8995 Madison Blvd. I-565, exit 8, just n on Wall Triana Hwy, then just w. Ext corridors. **Pets:** Medium, other species. Service with restrictions, supervision.

MOBILE

Ashbury Hotel and Suites **SH**
(251) 344-8030. **$59-$99.** 600 S Beltline Hwy. I-65, exit 4, 0.7 mi sw on west service road. Ext/int corridors. **Pets:** Accepted.

Drury Inn **SH**
(251) 344-7700. **$60-$100.** 824 W I-65 Service Rd S. I-65, exit 3 (Airport Blvd), just sw on service road. Int corridors. **Pets:** Large, other species. Service with restrictions, supervision.

▽▽ **Econo Lodge Mobile** 🆂🅷
(251) 343-4911. **$52-$62.** 156 Beltline Hwy S. I-65, exit 4, 0.5 mi s on west frontage road. Int corridors. **Pets:** Accepted.
🅰🅢🅚 🆂🔟 ✖ 💺 🎛 💻 🏊

▽▽▽ **Holiday Inn-Bellingrath Gardens** 🆂🅷
(251) 666-5600. **$60-$80.** 5465 Hwy 90 W. I-10, exit 15B, just ne. Int corridors. **Pets:** Accepted.
🅰🅢🅚 🆂🔟 ✖ 🎿 💺 🎛 💻 🍴 🏊

🅐🅐🅐 ▽▽▽ **La Quinta Inn Mobile** 🆂🅷
(251) 343-4051. **$66-$95.** 816 W I-65 Service Rd S. I-65, exit 3 (Airport Blvd), just s on west service road. Ext corridors. **Pets:** Other species. No service, supervision.
🆂🅰🆅🅴 ✖ 🎛 💻 🏊

▽ **Motel 6** 🅼
(251) 660-1483. **$34-$42.** 5488 Inn Rd. I-10, exit 15B, just nw on N Frontage Rd. Ext corridors. **Pets:** Small. Service with restrictions, supervision.
🅰🅢🅚 ✖ 💺 🎛 🏊

🅐🅐🅐 ▽ **Olsson's Motel** 🅼
(251) 661-5331. **$45-$55, 20 day notice.** 4137 Government Blvd. I-65, exit 1B, 2 mi w on US 90. Ext corridors. **Pets:** Small, dogs only. $15 deposit/pet. Service with restrictions, supervision.
🆂🅰🆅🅴 ✖ 🎛

▽▽ **Ramada Inn & Suites** 🆂🅷
(251) 660-1520. **$69-$93, 3 day notice.** 5472A Inn Rd. I-10, exit 15B, just nw on service road. Ext corridors. **Pets:** Accepted.
🅰🅢🅚 🆂🔟 ✖ 🎛 💻 🏊

▽▽ **Ramada Inn-I-65** 🆂🅷
(251) 342-3220. **$65-$85.** 850 W I-65 Service Rd S. I-65, exit 3 (Airport Blvd), 0.5 mi sw on west service road. Ext corridors. **Pets:** Accepted.
🅰🅢🅚 🆂🔟 ✖ 💻 🍴 🏊

▽▽ **Red Roof Inn-North** 🆂🅷
(251) 476-2004. **$41-$61.** 33 I-65 Service Rd E. I-65, exit 4, just s on east service road. Ext corridors. **Pets:** Large, other species. Service with restrictions, crate.
✖

▽▽ **Red Roof Inn-South** 🆂🅷
(251) 666-1044. **$42-$60.** 5450 Coca Cola Rd. I-10, exit 15B, just ne on service road. Ext corridors. **Pets:** Accepted.
✖ 🎿 💺

▽▽▽▽ **Residence Inn by Marriott Mobile** 🆂🅷
(251) 304-0570. **Call for rates.** 950 W I-65 Service Rd S. I-65, exit 3 (Airport Blvd), 0.5 mi s on west service road. Int corridors. **Pets:** Accepted.
✖ 🅼 💺 🎛 💻 🏊 🗙

▽▽▽▽ **TownePlace Suites by Marriott** 🆂🅷
(251) 345-9588. **$79-$119.** 1075 Montlimar Dr. I-65, exit 3 (Airport Blvd), 0.5 mi w, then 0.5 mi s. Int corridors. **Pets:** Medium, other species. $75 one-time fee/room. Service with restrictions, crate.
🅰🅢🅚 🆂🔟 ✖ 🎛 💻

MONROEVILLE
▽▽ **Days Inn of Monroeville** 🆂🅷
(251) 743-3297. **$56-$69.** 4389 S Alabama Ave. Jct US 84 and SR 21, 0.5 mi n. Ext corridors. **Pets:** Accepted.
🅰🅢🅚 🆂🔟 ✖ 🎛 💻 🏊

MONTGOMERY
🅐🅐🅐 ▽▽▽▽ **Baymont Inn & Suites Montgomery** 🆂🅷
(334) 277-6000. **$64-$79.** 5225 Carmichael Rd. I-85, exit 6, just sw. Int corridors. **Pets:** Accepted.
🆂🅰🆅🅴 🆂🔟 ✖ 🅼 🎿 🎛 💻 🏊

🅐🅐 ▽▽ **Best Inn and Suites** 🆂🅷
(334) 288-5740. **$45-$48, 5 day notice.** 977 W South Blvd. I-65, exit 168, just e. Ext corridors. **Pets:** $10 daily fee/pet. Service with restrictions.
🆂🅰🆅🅴 🆂🔟 ✖ 🎛 💻 🏊

▽▽ **Best Inns of America-Montgomery** 🆂🅷
(334) 270-9199. **$69-$99.** 5135 Carmichael Rd. I-85, exit 6, just sw. Int corridors. **Pets:** Other species. Service with restrictions, crate.
🅰🅢🅚 🆂🔟 ✖ 🎿 💺 🎛 💻 🏊

🅐🅐🅐 ▽▽▽ **Best Western Monticello Inn** 🆂🅷
(334) 277-4442. **$60-$70.** 5837 Monticello Dr. I-85, exit 6, just ne. Ext corridors. **Pets:** Accepted.
🆂🅰🆅🅴 🆂🔟 ✖ 🎛 💻 🏊

🅐🅐 ▽▽▽ **Days Inn-Midtown** 🆂🅷
(334) 269-9611. **$79.** 2625 Zelda Rd. I-85, exit 3 (Ann St), just sw. Ext corridors. **Pets:** Medium. $5 daily fee/pet. Service with restrictions, supervision.
🆂🅰🆅🅴 🆂🔟 🎛 🏊

▽▽▽▽ **Holiday Inn-East** 🆂🅷
(334) 272-0370. **Call for rates.** 1185 Eastern Bypass. I-85, exit 6, just ne. Ext/int corridors. **Pets:** Accepted.
✖ 🅼 🎿 💺 🎛 💻 🍴 🏊 🗙

🅐🅐🅐 ▽▽▽▽ **La Quinta Inn Montgomery** 🆂🅷
(334) 271-1620. **$66-$90.** 1280 East Blvd. I-85, exit 6, just sw. Int corridors. **Pets:** Accepted.
🆂🅰🆅🅴 ✖ 💻 🏊

▽ **Motel 6 #149** 🅼
(334) 277-6748. **$43-$55.** 1051 Eastern Blvd. I-85, exit 6, just n. Ext corridors. **Pets:** Accepted.
🆂🔟 ✖ 🏊

▽▽▽▽ **Residence Inn by Marriott** 🆂🅷
(334) 270-3300. **$121-$145.** 1200 Hilmar Ct. I-85, exit 6, 0.4 mi se on Carmichael Rd. Ext/int corridors. **Pets:** Accepted.
🅰🅢🅚 🆂🔟 ✖ 🎿 💺 🎛 💻 🏊 🗙

▽▽▽▽ **TownePlace Suites by Marriott** 🆂🅷
(334) 396-5505. **$94-$119.** 5047 Townplace Dr. I-85, exit 6, just sw, off Carmichael Rd. Int corridors. **Pets:** Accepted.
✖ 🅼 🎿 💺 🎛 💻

OPELIKA
▽▽ **Days Inn Opelika** 🆂🅷
(334) 749-4701. **$55-$125, 3 day notice.** 1014 Anand Ave. I-85, exit 62, just s. Ext corridors. **Pets:** $7 daily fee/pet. Designated rooms, service with restrictions, supervision.
🅰🅢🅚 🆂🔟 ✖ 🎛 💻

▽▽ **Travelodge** 🅼
(334) 749-1461. **Call for rates.** 1002 Columbus Pkwy. I-85, exit 62, just w. Ext corridors. **Pets:** Accepted.
✖ 🎛 💻 🏊

OPP
▽▽ **Executive Inn** 🆂🅷
(334) 493-6399. **$55.** 812 Florala Hwy 331 S. On US 331, 0.9 mi s of jct US 84. Ext corridors. **Pets:** Accepted.
🅰🅢🅚 🆂🔟 ✖ 🎛 💻 🏊

OXFORD
🅐🅐🅐 ▽▽▽▽ **Best Western-Anniston/Oxford** 🆂🅷
(256) 831-3410. **$49-$89.** US 78 & SR 21. I-20, exit 185, just n. Ext corridors. **Pets:** Accepted.
🆂🅰🆅🅴 🆂🔟 ✖ 🎛 💻 🏊 🗙

Jameson Inn Oxford SH
(256) 835-2170. **$49-$104.** 161 Colonial Dr. I-20, exit 188, just nw. Ext corridors. **Pets:** Very small, other species. $10 daily fee/room. Service with restrictions, supervision.

ASK ⊠ ⌕ ⊞ 💻 ⇌

Motel 6 #542 M
(256) 831-5463. **$41-$51.** 202 Grace St. I-20, exit 185, just s. Ext corridors. **Pets:** Accepted.

S⊘ ⊠ ⌕ ⊞ ⇌

OZARK

All American Ozark Inn M ❀
(334) 774-5166. **$53-$58.** Deese Rd, US 231 S. 0.5 mi s of jct SR 249. Ext corridors. **Pets:** Medium, other species. Service with restrictions.

SAVE S⊘ ⊠ ⊞ 💻 ⇌

Jameson Inn SH
(334) 774-0233. **$49-$104.** 1360 S US Hwy 231. 0.4 mi s of jct SR 249. Ext corridors. **Pets:** Very small, other species. $10 daily fee/room. Service with restrictions, supervision.

ASK ⊠ ⌕M ⊞ 💻 ⇌

Quality Inn & Suites-Ozark/Ft Rucker SH
(334) 774-7300. **$70.** 151 Hwy 231 N. US 231, 0.3 mi n of jct SR 249. Ext corridors. **Pets:** Accepted.

ASK S⊘ ⊠ ⊞ 💻 ⑪ ⇌

PHENIX CITY

Holiday Inn Express SH
(334) 298-9321. **$60-$70.** 1700 E US 280 Bypass. US 280/431 Bypass. Ext corridors. **Pets:** Medium. Service with restrictions, supervision.

SAVE S⊘ ⊠ ⊞ 💻 ⇌

PRATTVILLE

Jameson Inn SH
(334) 361-6463. **$49-$104.** 104 Jameson Ct. I-65, exit 179, 1 mi w. Ext corridors. **Pets:** Very small, other species. $10 daily fee/room. Service with restrictions, supervision.

ASK ⊠ ⌀ ⌕ ⊞ 💻 ⇌

PRICEVILLE

Days Inn SH
(256) 355-3297. **$59-$99.** 63 Marco Dr. I-65, exit 334, just e. Ext corridors. **Pets:** Small. $10 daily fee/pet. Service with restrictions, crate.

ASK S⊘ ⊠ ⌕ ⊞ 💻 ⇌

SCOTTSBORO

Best Western Scottsboro SH
(256) 259-4300. **Call for rates.** 46 Micah Way. On US 72, just s of jct SR 35. Ext corridors. **Pets:** Small, other species. $10 daily fee/pet. Service with restrictions, supervision.

⊠ ⊞ 💻 ⇌

Jameson Inn SH
(256) 574-6666. **$49-$104.** 208 Micah Way. On US 72, just s of jct SR 35. Ext corridors. **Pets:** Very small. $10 daily fee/room. Service with restrictions, supervision.

ASK ⊠ ⌕ ⊞ 💻 ⇌

SELMA

Comfort Inn SH
(334) 875-5700. **$60-$70.** 1812 Hwy 14 E. Jct SR 14 and US 80 Bypass. Int corridors. **Pets:** Accepted.

ASK S⊘ ⊠ ⊞ 💻 ⇌

Holiday Inn SH
(334) 872-0461. **$60-$65.** 1710 W Highland Ave. 2.3 mi w on US 80. Ext corridors. **Pets:** Accepted.

ASK S⊘ ⊠ ⌀ ⊞ 💻 ⑪ ⇌

Jameson Inn SH
(334) 874-8600. **$49-$104.** 2420 Broad St. SR 22, just n of jct US 80. Ext corridors. **Pets:** Very small, other species. $10 daily fee/room. Service with restrictions, supervision.

ASK ⊠ ⌕ ⊞ 💻 ⇌

SHEFFIELD

Holiday Inn Sheffield/Florence SH
(256) 381-4710. **$99-$125.** 4900 Hatch Blvd. 4 mi n on US 43 from jct US 72. Int corridors. **Pets:** Accepted.

SAVE S⊘ ⊠ ⊞ 💻 ⑪ ⇌ ⊠

STEVENSON

Budget Host Inn M
(256) 437-2215. **$45-$55, 3 day notice.** 42973 US Hwy 72. On US 72, just s of CR 85. Ext corridors. **Pets:** Very small. $5 daily fee/pet. Service with restrictions, supervision.

SAVE S⊘ ⊠ ⊞ 💻

TROY

Holiday Inn Express SH
(334) 670-0012. **$59-$62.** Hwy 231 at US 29. On US 231, just n of jct US 29. Ext corridors. **Pets:** Accepted.

ASK S⊘ ⊠ ⊞ 💻 ⇌

Holiday Inn-of Troy SH
(334) 566-1150. **$78, 3 day notice.** Hwy 231 at US 29. On US 231, just n of jct US 29. Ext corridors. **Pets:** Medium, other species. $5 daily fee/pet. Service with restrictions, supervision.

ASK S⊘ ⊠ ⊞ 💻 ⑪ ⇌

TUSCALOOSA

Best Value Inn SH
(205) 556-7950. **$49-$150.** 3501 McFarland Blvd. I-59/20, exit 73, just ne on US 82. Ext corridors. **Pets:** Accepted.

ASK S⊘ ⊠ ⊞ 💻 ⇌

Jameson Inn SH
(205) 345-5018. **$49-$104.** 5021 Oscar Baxter Rd. I-59/20, exit 71A, just s. Ext corridors. **Pets:** Very small, other species. $10 daily fee/room. Service with restrictions, supervision.

ASK ⊠ ⌕ ⊞ 💻 ⇌

La Quinta Inn Tuscaloosa SH
(205) 349-3270. **$58-$81.** 4122 McFarland Blvd E. I-59/20, exit 73, just sw on US 82. Ext corridors. **Pets:** Service with restrictions, supervision.

SAVE ⊠ ⊞ 💻 ⇌

Masters Inn M
(205) 556-2010. **$43-$103.** 3600 McFarland Blvd. I-59/20, exit 73, just nw on US 82. Ext corridors. **Pets:** Accepted.

SAVE S⊘ ⊠ ⇌

Motel 6 #432 M
(205) 759-4942. **$41-$53.** 4700 McFarland Blvd E. I-59/20, exit 73, just se on US 82. Ext corridors. **Pets:** Accepted.

S⊘ ⊠ ⌕ ⊞ ⇌

VANCE

Wellesley Inn & Suites SH
(205) 556-3606. **$79-$109.** 11170 Will Walker Rd/Daimler Benz Blvd. I-59/20, exit 89 southbound, just s; exit northbound, 0.8 mi n on Mercedes Dr, 0.3 mi w, then just s. Int corridors. **Pets:** Small, other species. $15 one-time fee/pet. Designated rooms, service with restrictions, supervision.

SAVE S⊘ ⊠ ⌕M ⌕ ⊞ 💻

YORK

Days Inn-York SH
(205) 392-9675. **$44.** 17700 SR 17. I-59/20, exit 8, just s. Ext corridors. **Pets:** Accepted.

ASK S⊘ ⊠ ⌕M ⊞ 💻

ALASKA

ANCHORAGE

◆◆◆ ▼▼ Best Western Barratt Inn 🆂🅷 🌼
(907) 243-3131. **$69-$180.** 4616 Spenard Rd. International Airport Rd, just ne of jct Jewel Lake and Spenard rds. Ext/int corridors. **Pets:** $50 deposit/room, $10 daily fee/room. Designated rooms, service with restrictions, crate.

[SAVE] [S⬤] [✕] [と] [🌙] [📶] [🅗] [🖥] [💲] [ℍ]

◆◆◆ ▼▼▼ Comfort Inn Ship Creek 🆂🅷
(907) 277-6887. **$79-$239.** 111 W Ship Creek Ave. At 3rd and E sts, 0.3 mi n on E St, across the railway, just e on Ship Creek Ave (formerly Warehouse Ave); downtown. Int corridors. **Pets:** Medium. $10 daily fee/pet. Designated rooms, service with restrictions, supervision.

[SAVE] [S⬤] [✕] [と] [🌙] [🖥] [🅗] [🖥] [💲] [≈] [⊗]

◆◆◆ ▼▼ Days Inn Downtown 🆂🅷
(907) 276-7226. **$69-$250.** 321 E 5th Ave. At Cordova and E 5th Ave; downtown. Ext/int corridors. **Pets:** Other species. $25 deposit/pet. Designated rooms, service with restrictions, crate.

[SAVE] [✕] [と] [🌙] [🖥] [🅗] [🖥] [💲]

◆◆◆ ▼▼ Long House Alaskan Hotel 🆂🅷
(907) 243-2133. **$62-$139.** 4335 Wisconsin St. International Airport Rd, 1.5 mi ne on Spenard Rd, nw on Wisconsin St at 43rd Ave, then just e. Int corridors. **Pets:** Accepted.

[SAVE] [S⬤] [✕] [と] [🖥] [🅗] [🖥] [💲] [ℍ]

◆◆◆ ▼▼ Merrill Field Inn 🅼
(907) 276-4547. **$65-$136.** 420 Sitka St. 1 mi e via US 1 (Glenn Hwy). Ext corridors. **Pets:** Other species. $7 daily fee/pet. Service with restrictions, supervision.

[SAVE] [S⬤] [✕] [🅗] [💲] [ℍ]

◆◆◆ ▼▼▼ Microtel Inn & Suites 🆂🅷
(907) 245-5002. **$69-$149.** 5205 Northwood Dr. 1.7 mi e of airport. Int corridors. **Pets:** Other species. $10 daily fee/room. Designated rooms, service with restrictions, supervision.

[SAVE] [S⬤] [✕] [と] [🌙] [🖥] [🅗] [💲]

◆◆◆ ▼▼▼ Millennium Alaskan Hotel Anchorage 🅻🅷
(907) 243-2300. **$160-$290.** 4800 Spenard Rd. International Airport Rd, just ne from jct Jewel Lake and Spenard rds. Int corridors. **Pets:** Other species. $50 deposit/room.

[SAVE] [S⬤] [✕] [と] [🌙] [🖥] [🅗] [🖥] [💲] [ℍ] [⊗]

◆◆◆ ▼▼ Motel 6–4216 🅼
(907) 677-8000. **$64-$149.** 5000 A St. Jct C St and International Airport Rd. Int corridors. **Pets:** Medium. Designated rooms, service with restrictions, supervision.

[SAVE] [S⬤] [✕] [と] [🖥]

▼▼▼ Ramada Inn Anchorage Downtown 🆂🅷
(907) 272-7561. **$79-$239.** 115 E 3rd Ave. Jct Barrow St; downtown. Ext/int corridors. **Pets:** Accepted.

[ASK] [S⬤] [✕] [🅗] [💲] [ℍ]

▼▼▼▼ Residence Inn by Marriott 🆂🅷 🌼
(907) 563-9844. **$129-$344.** 1025 E 35th Ave. Corner of US 1 (New Seward Hwy) and 36th Ave. Int corridors. **Pets:** Large, other species. $10 daily fee/pet, $85 one-time fee/room. No service, supervision.

[ASK] [S⬤] [✕] [🌙] [🖥] [🅗] [🖥] [💲] [≈] [⊗]

▼▼▼ Sheraton Anchorage Hotel 🅻🅷 🌼
(907) 276-8700. **$169-$279.** 401 E 6th Ave. 6th Ave and Denali St. Int corridors. **Pets:** Medium, dogs only. Designated rooms, supervision.

[ASK] [S⬤] [✕] [と] [🌙] [🖥] [🅗] [🖥] [💲] [ℍ] [⊗]

◆◆◆ ▼▼▼ Super 8 Motel-Anchorage 🆂🅷
(907) 276-8884. **$70-$150.** 3501 Minnesota Dr. At 36th Ave, just n of Spenard Rd. Int corridors. **Pets:** Accepted.

[ASK] [S⬤] [✕] [🌙] [🖥] [🅗] [💲]

◆◆◆ ▼▼▼ Westmark Anchorage Hotel 🅻🅷
(907) 276-7676. **$109-$219.** 720 W 5th Ave. At G St and W 5th Ave; downtown. Int corridors. **Pets:** Accepted.

[SAVE] [✕] [🌙] [🖥] [🅗] [🖥] [💲] [ℍ]

CANTWELL

◆◆◆ ▼▼ Backwoods Lodge 🅼
(907) 768-2232. **$90-$130, 10 day notice.** Denali Hwy MM 133.8. Parks Hwy, (Milepost 210), just e on Denali Hwy. Ext corridors. **Pets:** Medium. Designated rooms, service with restrictions, supervision.

[SAVE] [S⬤] [✕] [🅗] [💲] [ℍ]

EAGLE RIVER

▼▼ Eagle River Inn & Suites 🆂🅷 🌼
(907) 622-3232. **$59-$139.** 13049 Old Glenn Hwy. Jct Glenn Hwy (SR 1), Eagle River exit, just e, just s. Int corridors. **Pets:** Large, other species. $10 daily fee/pet. Designated rooms, service with restrictions, crate.

[ASK] [S⬤] [✕] [🅗] [💲] [ℍ]

◆◆◆ ▼▼ Eagle River Motel 🅼
(907) 694-5000. **$54-$94, 3 day notice.** 11111 Old Eagle River Rd. Glenn Hwy, exit Eagle River, just e; center. Ext corridors. **Pets:** $7 daily fee/pet. Designated rooms, service with restrictions, crate.

[SAVE] [✕] [🅗] [💲] [ℍ]

FAIRBANKS

▼▼ Best Western Fairbanks Inn 🆂🅷
(907) 456-6602. **$59-$179 (no credit cards).** 1521 S Cushman St. Just s of Airport Way. Int corridors. **Pets:** Small, other species. $10 daily fee/pet. Designated rooms, service with restrictions, supervision.

[ASK] [S⬤] [✕] [と] [🅗] [💲] [ℍ]

◆◆◆ ▼▼▼ Comfort Inn-Chena River 🆂🅷
(907) 479-8080. **$79-$169.** 1908 Chena Landings Loop. Airport Way, just n on Peger Rd, then just e on Phillips Field Rd, follow signs in wooded area south of road. Int corridors. **Pets:** Accepted.

[SAVE] [✕] [と] [🅗] [💲] [≈]

◆◆◆ ▼▼▼ Pike's Waterfront Lodge 🆂🅷
(907) 456-4500. **$99-$235.** 1850 Hoselton Rd. Jct Airport and Hoselton rds. Ext/int corridors. **Pets:** $10 daily fee/room. Designated rooms, crate.

[SAVE] [S⬤] [✕] [🅗] [💲] [ℍ] [⊗]

▼▼ Regency Fairbanks Hotel 🆂🅷
(907) 452-3200. **$99-$169.** 95 10th Ave. Just w of SR 2 (Steese Expwy); center. Int corridors. **Pets:** Accepted.

[ASK] [✕] [🅗] [💲] [ℍ]

▼▼ **Super 8 Motel** M
(907) 451-8888. **$79-$139.** 1909 Airport Way. Airport Way at Wilbur St. Int corridors. **Pets:** Accepted.
A$K S▒ ⊠ 🖥

GUSTAVUS

▼▼◆ **Glacier Bay's Bear Track Inn** M
(907) 697-3017. **$704, 60 day notice.** 255 Rink Creek Rd. 7 mi e of airport; at the end of Rink Creek Rd. Int corridors. **Pets:** Medium, dogs only. $50 one-time fee/pet. Service with restrictions, supervision.
A$K S▒ ⊠ 🍴 ⊠ 🐾 ᄑ ☎

HAINES

▲▲▲ ▼ **Captain's Choice Inc Motel** M
(907) 766-3111. **$82-$117.** 108 2nd Ave N. Jct 2nd Ave and Dalton St. Ext corridors. **Pets:** Other species. $10 one-time fee/room. Service with restrictions, supervision.
SAVE ⊠ 🖥 🖵 🐾

HOMER

▲▲▲ ▼▼ **Best Western Bidarka Inn** M
(907) 235-8148. **$89-$143.** 575 Sterling Hwy. 0.3 mi n on Sterling Hwy (SR 1). Ext/int corridors. **Pets:** Other species. $10 daily fee/room. Service with restrictions, supervision.
SAVE S▒ ⊠ 🖥 🖵 🍴 🐾

JUNEAU

▼▼ **Best Western Country Lane Inn** M
(907) 789-5005. **$100-$130.** 9300 Glacier Hwy. Just e off Egan Dr. Ext corridors. **Pets:** Accepted.
A$K S▒ ⊠ 🖥 🖵

▲▲▲ ▼▼ **Frontier Suites Airport Hotel** SH
(907) 790-6600. **$90-$144.** 9400 Glacier Hwy. At Juneau International Airport. Ext/int corridors. **Pets:** Small, dogs only. Service with restrictions, crate.
SAVE S▒ ⊠ ᇎ 🖥 🖵 🍴 ⊠ 🐾

▼ **Juneau Super 8** SH
(907) 789-4858. **$80-$114.** 2295 Trout St. At airport, just nw to Glacier Hwy, just e. Int corridors. **Pets:** Accepted.
S▒ ⊠ 🐾

▲▲▲ ▼▼ **Westmark Baranof** SH
(907) 586-2660. **$139-$159.** 127 N Franklin St. At 2nd and Franklin sts; downtown. Int corridors. **Pets:** Accepted.
SAVE ⊠ 🖉 🖥 🖵 🍴 🐾

KETCHIKAN

▲▲▲ ▼▼▼ **Best Western Landing** SH
(907) 225-5166. **$129-$185.** 3434 Tongass Ave. Across from the Alaska Marine Hwy ferry terminal. Ext/int corridors. **Pets:** Other species. $50 deposit/pet, $10 daily fee/pet. Designated rooms, service with restrictions, crate.
SAVE ⊠ 🖥 🖵 🍴

▼ **Ketchikan Super 8 Motel** SH
(907) 225-9088. **$97-$135.** 2151 Sea Level Dr. From Alaska Marine Hwy ferry terminal, 0.9 mi se to Washington St, then just s; from airport ferry terminal, 1.3 mi se. Int corridors. **Pets:** Accepted.
A$K S▒ ⊠ 🖥 🐾

KODIAK

▲▲▲ ▼▼ **Best Western Kodiak Inn** SH
(907) 486-5712. **$89-$129, 30 day notice.** 236 W Rezanof Dr. 0.3 mi w of ferry terminal; center. Ext/int corridors. **Pets:** Accepted.
SAVE S▒ ⊠ 🖉 🖥 🖵 🍴 🐾

MOOSE PASS

▲▲▲ ▼ **Trail Lake Lodge** M
(907) 288-3101. **$59-$105, 7 day notice.** MM 29.5 Seward Hwy. US 9 (Seward Hwy) at MM 29.5. Ext corridors. **Pets:** Medium. Designated rooms, service with restrictions, supervision.
SAVE S▒ ⊠ 🍴 🐾

SITKA

▼▼ **Super 8 Motel-Sitka** SH
(907) 747-8804. **$100-$129.** 404 Sawmill Creek Rd. Just e from corner of Lake St and Halibut Point/Sawmill Creek rds; center. Int corridors. **Pets:** $6.50 one-time fee/room. Service with restrictions, supervision.
A$K S▒ ⊠ 🖉 🐾

SKAGWAY

▼ **Westmark Inn Skagway** SH
(907) 983-6000. **$121.** 3rd & Spring St. Downtown. Ext/int corridors. **Pets:** Accepted.
A$K ⊠ &M 🖥 🖵 🍴 🐾

TOK

▲▲▲ ▼▼◆ **Cleft of the Rock Bed & Breakfast** CA
(907) 883-4219. **$65-$135, 3 day notice.** MM 0.5 Sundog Tr. Jct SR 1 and 2 (Alaskan Hwy), 3 mi w on SR 2 (Alaskan Hwy) to Sundog Tr, then 0.5 mi n. Ext/int corridors. **Pets:** Other species. $5 daily fee/pet. Service with restrictions, supervision.
SAVE ⊠ 🖥 🖵 ⊠ 🐾

▲▲▲ ▼▼▼ **Westmark Inn Tok** M
(907) 883-5174. **$129.** Jct Alaska Hwy & Glenn Hwy. On SR 1; jct SR 2 (Alaskan Hwy). Ext corridors. **Pets:** Other species. Designated rooms, supervision.
SAVE ⊠ 🖵 🍴 🐾

TRAPPER CREEK

▼▼ **Gate Creek Cabins** CA
(907) 733-1393. **$90-$125, 7 day notice.** Mile 10.5 Petersville Rd. From MM 114 (Parks Hwy), 10.5 mi w at Petersville Rd. Ext corridors. **Pets:** Accepted.
A$K ⊠ 🖥 🖵 ⊠ 🐾 ☎

VALDEZ

▲▲▲ ▼▼ **Best Western Valdez Harbor Inn** SH
(907) 835-3434. **$89-$179.** 100 Harbor Dr. Just s at Meals Dr. Int corridors. **Pets:** Medium. $50 deposit/pet, $25 one-time fee/pet. Designated rooms, service with restrictions, supervision.
SAVE S▒ ⊠ 🖏 🖥 🖵 🍴 🐾

WASILLA

▲▲▲ ▼▼ **Best Western Lake Lucille Inn** SH
(907) 373-1776. **$89-$219.** 1300 W Lake Lucille Dr. George Parks Hwy (SR 3), just w on Hallea Ln; center. Int corridors. **Pets:** Accepted.
SAVE S▒ ⊠ 🖉 🖥 🖵 🍴 ⊠ 🐾

▼▼ **Pioneer Ridge B & B Inn** BB
(907) 376-7472. **$79-$155, 7 day notice.** 2221 Yukon Cir. Jct George Parks Hwy (SR 3), 1.5 mi s on Fairview Loop Rd, follow signs onto Lin-Lu Rd and onto Yukon. Int corridors. **Pets:** Accepted.
⊠ 🖥 🖵 ⊠ 🐾 ᄑ

WILLOW

▼▼ **Alaskan Host Bed & Breakfast** BB
(907) 495-6800. **$90-$115, 14 day notice.** Milepost 66.5 Old Parks Hwy. Parks Hwy, Milepost 66, 1 mi e at Old Parks Hwy. Ext/int corridors. **Pets:** Small, dogs only. Designated rooms, supervision.
⊠ 🖥 ⊠ 🐾 ☎

ARIZONA

AJO

💎 La Siesta Motel Ⓜ
(520) 387-6569. **Call for rates.** 2561 N Ajo-Gila Bend Hwy. On SR 85, 1.8 mi n of town plaza. Ext corridors. **Pets:** Accepted.

🅰🅰🅰 💎 Marine Motel Ⓜ
(520) 387-7626. **$40-$65.** 1966 N 2nd Ave. On SR 85, 1 mi n of town plaza. Ext corridors. **Pets:** Accepted.
[SAVE] [S🅱] [✕] [🛏] [💻] [🏊]

BELLEMONT

🅰🅰🅰 💎💎 Bellemont Microtel Inn 🆂🅷
(928) 556-9599. **$49-$99.** 12380 W Interstate Hwy 40. I-40, exit 185, just n. Int corridors. **Pets:** $15 daily fee/pet. Service with restrictions, supervision.
[SAVE] [S🅱] [✕] [🔬M] [🔒] [🎾] [🛏] [💻]

BENSON

🅰🅰🅰 💎💎 Best Western Quail Hollow Inn Ⓜ
(520) 586-3646. **$60-$80.** 699 N Ocotillo Ave. I-10, exit 304, just s. Ext corridors. **Pets:** Medium. $10 daily fee/pet. Designated rooms, service with restrictions, supervision.
[SAVE] [S🅱] [✕] [🎾] [🛏] [💻] [🏊]

💎💎 Motel 6 Benson #4036 🆂🅷
(520) 586-0066. **$41-$77.** 637 S Whetstone Commerce Dr. I-10, exit 302, just s to Frontage Rd, then just e. Int corridors. **Pets:** Accepted.
[✕] [🔬M] [🛏] [🏊]

💎💎 Super 8 Motel Ⓜ
(520) 586-1530. **$55-$120.** 855 N Ocotillo Ave. I-10, exit 304, just n. Ext corridors. **Pets:** Accepted.
[A$K] [S🅱] [✕] [🛏] [🏊]

BISBEE

🅰🅰🅰 💎💎💎 Audrey's Inn 🄲🄾
(520) 227-6120. **$95-$455.** 20 Brewery Ave. In historic district; corner of Howell Ave. Int corridors. **Pets:** Other species. No service.
[SAVE] [✕] [🛏] [💻]

🅰🅰🅰 💎💎 San Jose Lodge Ⓜ
(520) 432-5761. **$65-$105, 3 day notice.** 1002 Naco Hwy. 1.5 mi s from jct SR 92. Ext corridors. **Pets:** Dogs only. $10 daily fee/pet. Designated rooms, service with restrictions, supervision.
[SAVE] [✕] [🛏] [🍴] [🏊]

BULLHEAD CITY

🅰🅰🅰 💎💎💎 Best Western Bullhead City Inn 🆂🅷
(928) 754-3000. **$49-$99.** 1126 Hwy 95. 1.8 mi s of Laughlin Bridge. Ext corridors. **Pets:** Medium. $20 one-time fee/room. Service with restrictions, supervision.
[SAVE] [S🅱] [✕] [🎾] [🛏] [🏊]

CAMERON

🅰🅰🅰 💎💎💎 Cameron Trading Post Motel, Restaurant & Gift Shop 🆂🅷
(928) 679-2231. **$49-$119.** US 89. 1 mi from the east gate turn off. Ext corridors. **Pets:** Accepted.
[SAVE] [✕] [🛏] [💻] [🍴]

CAMP VERDE

🅰🅰🅰 💎💎💎 Comfort Inn 🆂🅷
(928) 567-9000. **$59-$139.** 340 Goswick Way. I-17, exit 287, just e, then just s. Int corridors. **Pets:** Medium. $15 one-time fee/room. Designated rooms, service with restrictions, supervision.
[SAVE] [S🅱] [✕] [🎾] [🔒] [🛏] [💻] [🏊]

🅰🅰🅰 💎💎 Days Inn & Suites of Camp Verde 🆂🅷
(928) 567-3700. **$54-$99.** 1640 W Hwy 260. I-17, exit 287, just e, then just n. Int corridors. **Pets:** Other species. $10 one-time fee/pet. Designated rooms, service with restrictions, supervision.
[SAVE] [✕] [🎾] [🔒] [🛏] [💻] [🏊]

CASA GRANDE

💎💎💎 Best Western Casa Grande 🆂🅷
(520) 836-1600. **$59-$130.** 665 Via Del Cielo. I-10, exit 194 (SR 287), 1 mi w. Ext corridors. **Pets:** Other species. $10 one-time fee/pet. Service with restrictions, supervision.
[A$K] [S🅱] [✕] [🔬M] [🎾] [🛏] [💻] [🏊] [✕]

🅰🅰🅰 💎💎💎 Holiday Inn Casa Grande 🆂🅷
(520) 426-3500. **$69-$99.** 777 N Pinal Ave. I-10, exit 194 (SR 287), 3.9 mi w. Int corridors. **Pets:** Other species. Service with restrictions, supervision.
[SAVE] [S🅱] [✕] [🎾] [🛏] [💻] [🍴] [🏊]

💎 Motel 6-1263 Ⓜ
(520) 836-3323. **$38-$61.** 4965 N Sunland Gin Rd. I-10, exit 200. Ext corridors. **Pets:** Other species. Service with restrictions, supervision.
[S🅱] [✕] [🔒] [🛏] [🏊]

🅰🅰🅰 💎💎💎 Super 8 Motel 🆂🅷
(520) 836-8800. **$49-$129.** 2066 E Florence Blvd. I-10, exit 194 (SR 287), 0.6 mi w on SR 187. Int corridors. **Pets:** $10 daily fee/pet. Service with restrictions, supervision.
[SAVE] [S🅱] [✕] [🔒] [🛏] [🏊]

CHAMBERS

AAA **WWW** Chieftain Inn **M**
(928) 688-2754. **$75-$150.** I-40 & 191 Interchange. I-40, exit 333, just n at jct US 191. Ext corridors. **Pets:** Accepted.
SAVE 🛏 ✕ 🖉 🖥 🍴 🌊

CHINLE

AAA **WWWW** Best Western Canyon de Chelly Inn **M**
(928) 674-5875. **$79-$119.** 100 Main St, Rt 7. US 191, just e. Ext corridors. **Pets:** Medium. $5 daily fee/pet. Service with restrictions, crate.
SAVE 🛏 ✕ 🖥 🖥 🍴 🌊

COTTONWOOD

AAA **WWWW** Best Western Cottonwood Inn **M**
(928) 634-5575. **$71-$99.** 993 S Main St. On SR 89A, at SR 260. Ext corridors. **Pets:** Very small, dogs only. $10 daily fee/pet. Designated rooms, service with restrictions, supervision.
SAVE 🛏 ✕ 🖥 🖥 🌊

AAA **WWW** Budget Inn & Suites **M**
(928) 634-3678. **$52-$105.** 1089 Hwy 260. On SR 260, just e of jct SR 89A. Ext corridors. **Pets:** Small. $10 daily fee/pet. Designated rooms, service with restrictions, supervision.
SAVE 🛏 ✕ 🖥 🖥

AAA **WW** Little Daisy Motel **M**
(928) 634-7865. **$48-$52.** 34 S Main St. On SR 89A, just n. Ext corridors. **Pets:** Other species. $20 deposit/room. Service with restrictions, crate.
SAVE 🛏 ✕ 🖥

AAA **WWW** Pines Motel **M** ❀
(928) 634-9975. **$44-$79.** 920 S Camino Real. Jct SR 260, just nw on SR 89A, then just s. Ext corridors. **Pets:** $10 one-time fee/room. Service with restrictions.
SAVE 🛏 ✕ 🖥 🖥 🌊

AAA **WWW** Quality Inn **M**
(928) 634-4207. **$59-$109.** 301 W Hwy 89A. On SR 89A, 1.8 mi s of jct SR 260. Ext corridors. **Pets:** Medium. $20 one-time fee/pet. Designated rooms, service with restrictions, supervision.
SAVE 🛏 ✕ 🖥 🖥 🍴 🌊

AAA **WW** The View Motel **M**
(928) 634-7581. **$48-$58.** 818 S Main St. On SR 89A, 0.4 mi nw of jct SR 260. Ext corridors. **Pets:** Dogs only. $5 daily fee/pet. Service with restrictions, supervision.
SAVE ✕ 🖥 🌊

EAGAR

AAA **WWW** Best Western Sunrise Inn **M**
(928) 333-2540. **$70-$84.** 128 N Main St. From jct SR 260, just n; from jct US 60, 1.5 mi s. Ext corridors. **Pets:** Small. $10 one-time fee/pet. Service with restrictions, supervision.
SAVE 🛏 ✕ 🖉 🖥 🖥

EHRENBERG

AAA **WWW** Best Western Flying J Motel **SH**
(928) 923-9711. **$69-$199.** S Frontage Rd. I-10, exit 1, just s; 0.5 mi e of the Colorado River. Int corridors. **Pets:** Accepted.
SAVE 🛏 ✕ 🖥 🖥 🌊

ELOY

WW Super 8 Motel **M**
(520) 466-7804. **$49-$99, 7 day notice.** 3945 W Houser Rd. I-10, exit 203 (Toltec Rd), just e, then just s. Ext corridors. **Pets:** Accepted.
ASK 🛏 ✕ 🖥 🌊

FLAGSTAFF

AAA **WWW** AmeriSuites (Flagstaff/Interstate Crossroads) **SH**
(928) 774-8042. **$74-$94.** 2455 S Beulah Blvd. I-40, exit 195, just n to Forest Meadows St, just w, then just s. Int corridors. **Pets:** Medium, other species. Service with restrictions, supervision.
SAVE 🛏 ✕ 🖉 🖥 🖥 🖥 🌊

AAA **WWW** Best Western Kings House Motel **M**
(928) 774-7186. **$45-$119.** 1560 E Route 66. I-40, exit 198 (Butler Ave), just w, just n on Enterprise, then just w. Ext corridors. **Pets:** Medium. $10 daily fee/pet. Service with restrictions, supervision.
SAVE 🛏 ✕ 🖥 🌊

AAA **WWW** Budget Host Saga Motel **M**
(928) 779-3631. **$28-$46.** 820 W Route 66. I-40, exit 195, 1.5 mi n on SR 89A (Milton Rd), then just w; exit 191 eastbound, just n. Ext corridors. **Pets:** $6 daily fee/pet. Designated rooms, supervision.
SAVE 🛏 ✕ 🖥 🖥

AAA **WWW** Canyon Inn **M**
(928) 774-7301. **$34-$125.** 501 S Milton Rd. I-40, exit 195, 1.5 mi n. Ext corridors. **Pets:** Accepted.
SAVE 🛏 ✕ 🖥 🖥

AAA **WWWW** Comfort Inn I-17/I-40 **SH**
(928) 774-2225. **$59-$139.** 2355 S Beulah Blvd. I-40, exit 195, just n to Forest Meadows St, then 1 blk w. Int corridors. **Pets:** Large. $5 daily fee/room. Service with restrictions, supervision.
SAVE 🛏 ✕ 🖉 🖥 🖥 🌊

AAA **WWW** Days Inn East **SH**
(928) 527-1477. **$39-$169, 3 day notice.** 3601 E Lockett Rd. I-40, exit 201, just n, 0.5 mi w on I-40 business loop, then just n. Int corridors. **Pets:** Accepted.
SAVE 🛏 ✕ 🖥 🖥 🌊

AAA **WWW** Days Inn Route 66 **M** 🐾
(928) 774-5221. **$39-$129.** 1000 W Route 66. I-40, exit 195, 1.5 n on Milton Rd, then just w. Ext corridors. **Pets:** $10 daily fee/room. Designated rooms, service with restrictions, supervision.
SAVE 🛏 ✕ 🖉 🖥 🌊

AAA **WWW** Econo Lodge **SH**
(928) 774-7701. **$50-$109.** 2480 E Lucky Ln. I-40, exit 198 (Butler Ave), just n, then just e. Int corridors. **Pets:** Very small, dogs only. $10 daily fee/pet. Designated rooms, service with restrictions, supervision.
SAVE 🛏 ✕ 🖥 🖥 🌊

AAA **WWW** Econo Lodge-University **M**
(928) 774-7326. **$43-$99.** 914 S Milton Rd. I-40, exit 195, 1.2 mi n. Ext corridors. **Pets:** Medium. Designated rooms, service with restrictions, supervision.
SAVE 🛏 ✕ 🖥 🖥 🌊

AAA **WWWW** Holiday Inn Flagstaff/Grand Canyon **SH**
(928) 714-1000. **$59-$199.** 2320 E Lucky Ln. I-40, exit 198 (Butler Ave), just n, then just e. Int corridors. **Pets:** Other species. $25 one-time fee/room. Service with restrictions, supervision.
SAVE 🛏 ✕ 🖉 🖥 🖥 🖥 🍴 🌊 🖫

AAA **WWW** Howard Johnson Inn **M**
(928) 526-1826. **$39-$109.** 3300 E Route 66. I-40, exit 201, just n, then 0.6 mi w. Ext corridors. **Pets:** Other species. $7 daily fee/pet. Service with restrictions, supervision.
SAVE 🛏 ✕ 🖥 🖥 🍴

△△△ ▽▽▽ InnSuites Hotel & Suites Flagstaff/Grand Canyon SH ☙
(928) 774-7356. **$44-$119.** 1008 E Route 66. I-40, exit 198 (Butler Ave), just w, just n on Enterprise, then 0.5 mi w. Ext corridors. **Pets:** Medium, other species. $25 one-time fee/pet. Designated rooms, service with restrictions, crate.
[SAVE] [S♦] [✕] [🛏] [▦] [≈]

▽▽▽ La Quinta Inn & Suites SH
(928) 556-8666. **$65-$125.** 2015 S Beulah Blvd. I-40, exit 195, just n to Forest Meadow St, then just w. Int corridors. **Pets:** Medium, other species. Service with restrictions, supervision.
[ASK] [✕] [🗗] [🖥] [🛏] [▦] [≈]

▽ Motel 6 Flagstaff-Butler Ave #301 M
(928) 774-1801. **$40-$55.** 2010 E Butler Ave. I-40, exit 198 (Butler Ave), just n. Ext corridors. **Pets:** Accepted.
[S♦] [✕]

▽ Motel 6-Flagstaff West #1000 M ☙
(928) 779-3757. **$40-$55.** 2745 S Woodlands Village. I-40, exit 195, just n to Forest Meadows St, w to Beulah Blvd, just s, then just w. Ext corridors. **Pets:** Medium, other species. Service with restrictions, supervision.
[S♦] [✕] [🖥] [🗗] [🛏] [≈]

△△△ ▽ Parkside Family Inn & Suites M
(928) 774-8820. **$18-$139.** 121 S Milton Rd. I-40, exit 195B, 2.5 mi n. Ext corridors. **Pets:** Small. $7 daily fee/pet. Supervision.
[SAVE] [S♦] [✕] [🛏]

△△△ ▽▽▽▽ Quality Inn I-40/I-17 SH
(928) 774-8771. **$34-$99.** 2000 S Milton Rd. I-40, exit 195, just n to Forest Meadows, then right. Int corridors. **Pets:** Other species. $10 daily fee/pet. Service with restrictions, supervision.
[SAVE] [S♦] [✕] [🗗] [🖥] [▦] [≈]

△△△ ▽▽▽ Quality Inn-Lucky Lane M
(928) 226-7111. **$44-$69.** 2500 E Lucky Ln. I-40, exit 198 (Butler Ave), just n, then just e. Ext corridors. **Pets:** Medium, other species. $5 daily fee/room. Service with restrictions, supervision.
[SAVE] [S♦] [✕] [🗗] [🛏] [▦] [≈]

△△△ ▽▽▽▽ Radisson Woodlands Hotel Flagstaff LH
(928) 773-8888. **$69-$179.** 1175 W Route 66. I-40, exit 195, 1.5 mi n on Milton Rd, then 0.5 mi w. Int corridors. **Pets:** Medium, dogs only. $25 one-time fee/room. Designated rooms, service with restrictions, supervision.
[SAVE] [S♦] [✕] [🗗] [🖥] [🛏] [▦] [🍽] [≈] [✕]

△△△ ▽▽▽ Ramada Limited-Lucky Lane M
(928) 779-3614. **$49-$69.** 2350 E Lucky Ln. I-40, exit 198 (Butler Ave), just n, then just e. Ext corridors. **Pets:** Medium, other species. $5 daily fee/room. Service with restrictions, supervision.
[SAVE] [S♦] [✕] [🗗] [🛏] [▦] [≈]

△△△ ▽▽▽ Ramada Limited West SH
(928) 773-1111. **$49-$144.** 2755 S Woodlands Village Blvd. I-40, exit 195, just n to Forest Meadows St, w to Beulah Blvd, just s, then w. Ext corridors. **Pets:** Medium. $10 one-time fee/room. Designated rooms, service with restrictions, supervision.
[SAVE] [S♦] [✕] [🗗] [🛏] [▦] [≈] [✕]

△△△ ▽▽▽ Red Roof Inn M
(928) 779-5121. **$39-$69.** I-40, exit 198 (Butler Ave), just n, then just e. Ext corridors. **Pets:** Medium, other species. $5 daily fee/room. Service with restrictions, supervision.
[SAVE] [S♦] [✕] [🗗] [🛏] [▦] [≈]

▽▽▽▽ Residence Inn by Marriott Flagstaff M
(928) 526-5555. **$60-$175.** 3440 N Country Club Dr. I-40, exit 201, just s. Ext corridors. **Pets:** Accepted.
[ASK] [S♦] [✕] [🗗] [🖥] [🛏] [▦] [≈] [✕]

△△△ ▽▽▽ Rodeway Inn East SH ☙
(928) 526-2200. **$39-$99.** 2650 E Route 66. I-40, exit 201, 0.5 mi n, then 2.5 mi w. Ext corridors. **Pets:** Small. $10 one-time fee/pet. Service with restrictions, supervision.
[SAVE] [S♦] [✕] [▦]

△△△ ▽▽▽ Sleep Inn M
(928) 556-3000. **$80-$100.** 2765 S Woodlands Village Blvd. I-40, exit 195, just n to Forest Meadows St, w to Beaulah Rd, just s, then just w. Int corridors. **Pets:** Accepted.
[SAVE] [S♦] [✕] [🖥] [🗗] [🖥] [🛏] [▦] [≈]

△△△ ▽▽▽ Super 8 Motel M
(928) 774-4581. **$45-$125.** 602 W Route 66. I-40, exit 195, 1.5 mi n on SR 89A, then just w. Ext corridors. **Pets:** $10 daily fee/pet. Service with restrictions, supervision.
[SAVE] [S♦] [✕] [🛏] [▦] [≈]

△△△ ▽▽▽ Travel Inn M
(928) 774-3381. **$36-$70.** 801 W Route 66. I-40, exit 191, 2 mi e. Ext corridors. **Pets:** $10 daily fee/pet. Service with restrictions, crate.
[SAVE] [✕] [🗗] [🛏]

△△△ ▽▽▽▽ Travelodge-Grand Canyon/Flagstaff M ☙
(928) 526-1399. **$25-$99.** 2610 E Route 66. I-40, exit 201, just n, then 1.7 mi w on I-40 business loop. Ext corridors. **Pets:** Other species. $10 daily fee/pet. Service with restrictions, supervision.
[SAVE] [S♦] [✕] [🛏] [▦] [🍽] [≈]

△△△ ▽▽▽ Travelodge Hotel SH
(928) 779-6944. **$34-$120.** 2200 E Butler Ave. I-40, exit 198 (Butler Ave), just n. Int corridors. **Pets:** Other species. $10 daily fee/pet. Service with restrictions, supervision.
[SAVE] [S♦] [✕] [🛏] [▦] [🍽] [≈]

FOREST LAKES

△△△ ▽▽▽ Forest Lakes Lodge M
(928) 535-4727. **$55-$74.** 876 AZ Hwy 260. On SR 260. Ext corridors. **Pets:** Small, dogs only. $10 one-time fee/pet. Supervision.
[SAVE] [S♦] [✕] [🛏] [Ⓐ]

GILA BEND

▽ America's Choice Inn & Suites M
(928) 683-6311. **$65.** 2888 Butterfield Tr. I-8, exit 119, just nw. Int corridors. **Pets:** Accepted.
[ASK] [S♦] [✕] [🛏] [≈]

△△△ ▽▽▽ Best Western Space Age Lodge M
(928) 683-2273. **$69-$109.** 401 E Pima St. Center. Ext corridors. **Pets:** Service with restrictions.
[SAVE] [S♦] [✕] [🛏] [▦] [🍽] [≈]

GLOBE

▽▽▽ Comfort Inn M
(928) 425-7575. **$64-$159.** 1515 South St. On US 60, 1 mi e of town. Ext corridors. **Pets:** Accepted.
[ASK] [S♦] [✕] [🛏] [▦] [≈]

▽▽▽ Motel 6 #4223 M
(928) 425-5741. **$49-$99.** 1699 E Ash St. On US 60, 1.3 mi e of town. Ext/int corridors. **Pets:** Accepted.
[ASK] [S♦] [✕] [🗗] [🛏] [≈]

GRAND CANYON NATIONAL PARK (SOUTH RIM)

▽▽▽ Grand Hotel SH ☙
(928) 638-3333. **$99-$149, 3 day notice.** Hwy 64. On SR 64; 2 mi s of South Rim entrance. Int corridors. **Pets:** $50 deposit/pet. Designated rooms, service with restrictions, supervision.
[✕] [🗗] [🛏] [▦] [🍽] [≈]

ⒶⒶⒶ ▼▼▼ Rodeway Inn-Red Feather Lodge 🆂🅷
(928) 638-2414. **$49-$139.** Hwy 64. On SR 64; 2 mi s of South Rim entrance. Ext/int corridors. **Pets:** Other species. $50 deposit/room, $10 daily fee/pet. Designated rooms, service with restrictions, supervision.
ⓈⒶⓋⒺ ⑯ ⊗ ⌑ ⌨ ▣ ⑪ ⇌

HEBER

ⒶⒶⒶ ▼▼▼ Best Western Sawmill Inn 🆂🅷
(928) 535-5053. **$59-$99.** 1877 Hwy 260. 0.5 mi e of center. Ext corridors. **Pets:** Other species. $10 daily fee/pet. Service with restrictions, supervision.
ⓈⒶⓋⒺ ⑯ ⊗ ⌑ ⌨ ▣ ▣

HOLBROOK

ⒶⒶⒶ ▼▼▼ Best Inn Ⓜ
(928) 524-2654. **$43.** 2211 E Navajo Blvd. I-40, exit 289, 1 mi w. Ext corridors. **Pets:** Accepted.
ⓈⒶⓋⒺ ⑯ ⊗ ▣ ▣

ⒶⒶⒶ ▼▼▼ Best Western Adobe Inn Ⓜ
(928) 524-3948. **$40-$75.** 615 W Hopi Dr. I-40, exit 285, 1 mi e on US 180. Ext corridors. **Pets:** Small. $10 daily fee/pet. Service with restrictions, supervision.
ⓈⒶⓋⒺ ⑯ ⊗ ▣ ▣ ⇌

ⒶⒶⒶ ▼▼▼ Best Western Arizonian Inn 🆂🅷 🐾
(928) 524-2611. **$61-$84.** 2508 Navajo Blvd. I-40, exit 289, 0.5 mi w. Ext corridors. **Pets:** Other species. $30 deposit/room. Supervision.
ⓈⒶⓋⒺ ⑯ ⊗ ▣ ▣ ⇌

▼▼ Comfort Inn 🆂🅷
(928) 524-6131. **$59-$75.** 2602 E Navajo Blvd. I-40, exit 289, just w. Ext corridors. **Pets:** Accepted.
ⒶⓈ🅚 ⑯ ⊗ ▣ ▣

▼▼ Econo Lodge 🆂🅷
(928) 524-1448. **$40-$50.** 2596 E Navajo Blvd. I-40, exit 289, just w. Ext corridors. **Pets:** Accepted.
ⒶⓈ🅚 ⑯ ⊗ ▣ ▣ ⇌

▼▼▼▼ Holbrook Holiday Inn Express Ⓜ
(928) 524-1466. **$74-$89.** 1308 E Navajo Blvd. I-40, exit 286, just e. Int corridors. **Pets:** Medium. $10 one-time fee/room. Service with restrictions, supervision.
ⒶⓈ🅚 ⑯ ⊗ ▣ ▣ ⇌

ⒶⒶⒶ ▼ Holbrook Inn Ⓜ
(928) 524-3809. **$26-$30.** 235 W Hopi Dr. I-40, exit 285, 1.5 mi e on US 180. Ext corridors. **Pets:** Accepted.
ⓈⒶⓋⒺ ⑯ ⊗ ▣ ▣

ⒶⒶⒶ ▼ Relax Inn Ⓜ
(928) 524-6815. **$35.** 2418 E Navajo Blvd. I-40, exit 289, 0.4 mi w. Ext corridors. **Pets:** Accepted.
ⓈⒶⓋⒺ ⊗ ▣

JEROME

▼▼▼▼ Connor Hotel of Jerome 🆂🅷
(928) 634-5006. **$85-$135, 3 day notice.** 164 Main St. Center. Int corridors. **Pets:** Other species. Service with restrictions, supervision.
⊗ ▣ ▣

KAYENTA

▼▼▼ Hampton Inn of Kayenta 🆂🅷
(928) 697-3170. **$59-$104.** Hwy 160. On US 160, just w. Int corridors. **Pets:** Accepted.
ⒶⓈ🅚 ⑯ ⊗ ⌨ ▣ ▣ ⑪ ⇌

KINGMAN

ⒶⒶⒶ ▼▼▼ Best Western A Wayfarer's Inn 🆂🅷
(928) 753-6271. **$75-$92.** 2815 E Route 66. I-40, exit 53, 0.5 mi w on Route 66. Ext corridors. **Pets:** Accepted.
ⓈⒶⓋⒺ ⑯ ⊗ ⌑ ▣ ▣

ⒶⒶⒶ ▼▼▼ Best Western King's Inn & Suites 🆂🅷
(928) 753-6101. **$75-$92.** 2930 E Route 66. I-40, exit 53, just w. Ext corridors. **Pets:** $8 one-time fee/room. Designated rooms, service with restrictions, supervision.
ⓈⒶⓋⒺ ⑯ ⊗ ⌑ ⌨ ▣ ▣

ⒶⒶⒶ ▼▼▼ Brunswick Hotel 🆂🅷
(928) 718-1800. **$35-$150.** 315 E Andy Devine Ave. On Route 66; downtown. Int corridors. **Pets:** Medium. $10 one-time fee/room. No service.
ⓈⒶⓋⒺ ⑯ ⊗ ⌨ ▣ ⑪

ⒶⒶⒶ ▼▼▼ Days Inn West Ⓜ
(928) 753-7500. **$39-$89.** 3023 E Andy Devine Ave. I-40, exit 53, just w on Route 66. Ext corridors. **Pets:** Other species. $10 daily fee/pet. Supervision.
ⓈⒶⓋⒺ ⑯ ⊗ ▣ ⇌

ⒶⒶⒶ ▼ Hill Top Motel Ⓜ
(928) 753-2198. **$34-$78, 5 day notice.** 1901 E Andy Devine Ave. I-40, exit 53, 2 mi w on Route 66. Ext corridors. **Pets:** Accepted.
ⓈⒶⓋⒺ ⑯ ⊗ ▣ ⇌

▼ Motel 6–1114 Ⓜ
(928) 753-9222. **$37-$51.** 424 W Beale St. I-40, exit 48, just se on Business Loop I-40/US 93. Ext corridors. **Pets:** Accepted.
⑯ ⊗ ⌑ ⌨ ⇌

▼ Motel 6–1366 Ⓜ
(928) 757-7151. **$37-$47.** 3351 E Andy Devine Ave. I-40, exit 53, just e on Route 66. Ext corridors. **Pets:** Medium, other species. Service with restrictions, supervision.
⑯ ⊗ ⌨ ⇌

ⒶⒶⒶ ▼▼▼ Quality Inn Ⓜ
(928) 753-4747. **$59-$89.** 1400 E Andy Devine Ave. I-40, exit 48, 2 mi e on Route 66. Ext corridors. **Pets:** Accepted.
ⓈⒶⓋⒺ ⑯ ⊗ ⌑ ▣ ▣ ⇌ ⊗

ⒶⒶⒶ ▼▼▼ Super 8 Motel 🆂🅷
(928) 757-4808. **$39-$59.** 3401 E Andy Devine Ave. I-40, exit 53, just e on Route 66. Int corridors. **Pets:** $10 daily fee/pet. Designated rooms, service with restrictions, supervision.
ⓈⒶⓋⒺ ⑯ ⊗ ▣

LAKE HAVASU CITY

ⒶⒶⒶ ▼▼▼ Best Western Lake Place Inn 🆂🅷
(928) 855-2146. **$65-$285.** 31 Wing's Loop. 1 mi e of SR 95 via Swanson Ave; downtown. Ext corridors. **Pets:** Medium. $5 daily fee/pet. Service with restrictions, supervision.
ⓈⒶⓋⒺ ⊗ ▣ ▣ ⇌

▼▼▼▼ Hampton Inn Lake Havasu 🆂🅷
(928) 855-4071. **$79-$119.** 245 London Bridge Rd. 0.5 mi n of London Bridge. Int corridors. **Pets:** Other species. $10 daily fee/room. Designated rooms, service with restrictions, supervision.
ⒶⓈ🅚 ⑯ ⊗ ⌑ ⌨ ▣ ▣ ⇌

ⒶⒶⒶ ▼▼▼ Island Inn Hotel 🆂🅷
(928) 680-0606. **$55-$315.** 1300 W McCulloch Blvd. 0.7 mi w of London Bridge/SR 95. Int corridors. **Pets:** Large. $10 one-time fee/pet. Service with restrictions, supervision.
ⓈⒶⓋⒺ ⊗ ▣ ⑪ ⇌

◈ ◇◇ **Island Suites** 🆂🅷
(928) 855-7333. **$50-$95, 7 day notice.** 236 S Lake Havasu Ave. Just s of jct McCulloch Blvd. Int corridors. **Pets:** Medium. $10 one-time fee/pet. Service with restrictions, supervision.
🆂🅰🆅🅴 🆂🏠 ✖️ 🛢️ 💻 🏊

◇ **Lake Havasu City Super 8** Ⓜ
(928) 855-8844. **$48-$129.** 305 London Bridge Rd. Just w of SR 95, exit Palo Verde; 0.5 mi n of London Bridge. Int corridors. **Pets:** Medium. $7 one-time fee/room. Designated rooms, service with restrictions, supervision.
🅰🆂🅺 🆂🏠 ✖️ 🏊

◈ ◇ **Motel 6 Lake Havasu** Ⓜ
(928) 855-3200. **$41-$205.** 111 London Bridge Rd. 0.3 mi n of London Bridge. Int corridors. **Pets:** Medium. Service with restrictions, supervision.
🆂🅰🆅🅴 ✖️

◇ ◇ **Ramada Inn** Ⓜ
(928) 855-1111. **$83-$115.** 271 S Lake Havasu Ave. SR 95, just e on Swanson Ave, just s. Ext corridors. **Pets:** Medium. $20 one-time fee/room. Designated rooms, service with restrictions, supervision.
🅰🆂🅺 🆂🏠 ✖️ 🍳 🅿️ 🛢️ 💻 🍴 🏊

MUNDS PARK

◈ ◇ ◇ **Motel In The Pines** Ⓜ
(928) 286-9699. **$35-$89.** 80 W Pinewood Rd. I-17, exit 322, just e. Ext corridors. **Pets:** Accepted.
🆂🅰🆅🅴 🆂🏠 ✖️ 🛢️ 💻

NOGALES

◈ ◇ ◇ **Best Western Siesta Motel** Ⓜ
(520) 287-4671. **$70-$75.** 673 N Grand Ave. On Business Loop I-19, 1 mi n of International border. Ext corridors. **Pets:** Small. $10 daily fee/pet. Designated rooms, service with restrictions, supervision.
🆂🅰🆅🅴 🆂🏠 ✖️ 🛢️ 💻 🏊

◇ **Motel 6 Nogales #71** Ⓜ
(520) 281-2951. **$41-$55.** 141 W Mariposa Rd. I-19, exit 4, 0.9 mi e. Ext corridors. **Pets:** Accepted.
🆂🏠 ✖️ 🅿️ 🛢️ 🏊

PAGE

◈ ◇ ◇ ◇ **Best Western Arizona Inn** 🆂🅷
(928) 645-2466. **$43-$83.** 716 Rimview Dr. 0.7 mi e of US 89 via SR 89L. Int corridors. **Pets:** Medium. $10 daily fee/pet. Service with restrictions, supervision.
🆂🅰🆅🅴 🆂🏠 ✖️ 🍳 🛢️ 💻 🏊

◈ ◇ **Budget Host Economy Inn** Ⓜ
(928) 645-2488. **$35-$64, 3 day notice.** 121 S Lake Powell Blvd. 1.3 mi e of US 89/SR 89L. Ext corridors. **Pets:** Medium. $10 one-time fee/pet. Designated rooms, service with restrictions, supervision.
🆂🅰🆅🅴 🆂🏠 ✖️ 🏊

◈ ◇ ◇ **Lake Powell Days Inn** 🆂🅷
(928) 645-2800. **$59-$109.** 961 N Hwy 89. Just s. Int corridors. **Pets:** Other species. $10 daily fee/pet. Service with restrictions, supervision.
🆂🅰🆅🅴 🆂🏠 ✖️ 🍳 🅿️ 🛢️ 🏊

◈ ◇ ◇ ◇ **Lake Powell Resort and Marina** 🅻🅷
(928) 645-2433. **$59-$139.** 100 Lakeshore Dr. 4 mi n of Glen Canyon Dam via US 89. Int corridors. **Pets:** Accepted.
🆂🅰🆅🅴 🆂🏠 ✖️ 🍳 🛢️ 💻 🍴 🏊 ✖️

◇ ◇ **Linda's Lake Powell Condos** 🅲🅾
(928) 353-4591. **$88-$114, 3 day notice.** 1019 Tower Butte. 6 mi n on US 89. Ext corridors. **Pets:** Accepted.
🅰🆂🅺 ✖️ 🛢️ 💻

◈ ◇ ◇ **Motel 6-Page/Lake Powell #4013** 🆂🅷
(928) 645-5888. **$39-$69, 3 day notice.** 637 S Lake Powell Blvd. On Business Loop SR 89L, just e of US 89. Int corridors. **Pets:** Small. Designated rooms, service with restrictions, supervision.
🆂🅰🆅🅴 🆂🏠 ✖️ 🍳 🏊

◈ ◇ ◇ **Quality Inn, At Lake Powell** 🆂🅷 🐾
(928) 645-8851. **$39-$109.** 287 N Lake Powell Blvd. 0.8 mi e of US 89/SR 89L. Int corridors. **Pets:** Large, other species. $20 daily fee/pet. Designated rooms, service with restrictions.
🆂🅰🆅🅴 🆂🏠 ✖️ 🍳 🛢️ 💻 🏊

PARKER

◈ ◇ ◇ **Best Western Parker Inn** 🆂🅷
(928) 669-6060. **$89.** 1012 Geronimo Ave. SR 95, just e. Int corridors. **Pets:** Small, other species. Designated rooms, service with restrictions.
🆂🅰🆅🅴 🆂🏠 ✖️ 🍳 🛢️ 💻 🏊

PAYSON

◈ ◇ **Best Value Inn** Ⓜ
(928) 474-2283. **$50-$90.** 811 S Beeline Hwy. On SR 87, 0.7 mi s of SR 260. Ext/int corridors. **Pets:** Accepted.
🆂🅰🆅🅴 🆂🏠 ✖️ 🛢️ 💻

◈ ◇ ◇ **Best Western Payson Inn** 🆂🅷
(928) 474-3241. **$69-$149.** 801 N Beeline Hwy. On SR 87, 0.6 mi n of SR 260. Ext corridors. **Pets:** Dogs only. $10 daily fee/room. Service with restrictions, supervision.
🆂🅰🆅🅴 🆂🏠 ✖️ 🍳 🛢️ 💻 🏊

◈ ◇ ◇ **Comfort Inn** Ⓜ
(928) 474-5241. **$50-$180.** 809 E Hwy 260. On SR 260, 0.8 mi e of SR 87. Ext corridors. **Pets:** Medium, dogs only. $25 one-time fee/pet. Designated rooms, service with restrictions, supervision.
🆂🅰🆅🅴 🆂🏠 ✖️ 🛢️ 💻 🏊

◈ ◇ ◇ **Days Inn & Suites** 🆂🅷
(928) 474-9800. **$59-$129.** 301-A S Beeline Hwy. On SR 87, just s of SR 260. Int corridors. **Pets:** Small, other species. $10 daily fee/pet. Designated rooms, service with restrictions, supervision.
🆂🅰🆅🅴 🆂🏠 ✖️ 🍳 🛢️ 💻 🏊

◇ ◇ ◇ **Majestic Mountain Inn** 🆂🅷
(928) 474-0185. **$65-$150.** 602 E Hwy 260. On SR 260, 0.5 mi e of SR 87. Ext corridors. **Pets:** Dogs only. $10 daily fee/pet. Service with restrictions, supervision.
✖️ 🛢️ 💻 🏊

◇ **Motel 6 #4201** Ⓜ
(928) 474-4526. **$45-$79.** 101 W Phoenix St. On SR 87, 1.1 mi s of SR 260. Int corridors. **Pets:** Accepted.
🆂🏠 ✖️ 🛢️

◈ ◇ ◇ ◇ **Paysonglo Lodge** 🆂🅷
(928) 474-2382. **$55-$135.** 1005 S Beeline Hwy. On SR 87, 0.9 mi s of SR 260. Ext corridors. **Pets:** Small, dogs only. Designated rooms, service with restrictions, supervision.
🆂🅰🆅🅴 🆂🏠 ✖️ 🛢️ 💻 🏊

PHOENIX METROPOLITAN AREA

APACHE JUNCTION

Apache Junction Motel M ❖
(480) 982-7702. **$38-$66, 3 day notice.** 1680 W Apache Tr. US 60, exit 195, 2 mi n, then just w. Ext corridors. **Pets:** Small, dogs only. $15 one-time fee/pet. Designated rooms, service with restrictions, supervision.

Apache Junction Super 8 SH
(480) 288-8888. **$59-$114.** 251 E 29th Ave. US 60, exit 196 (Idaho Rd/SR 8 E), just n. Ext/int corridors. **Pets:** Small, dogs only. $50 deposit/pet, $10 daily fee/pet. Service with restrictions, supervision.

Gold Canyon Golf Resort LH
(480) 982-9090. **$135-$310, 3 day notice.** 6100 S Kings Ranch Rd. US 60, exit Kings Ranch Rd, 1 mi n. Ext corridors. **Pets:** Medium. $75 one-time fee/room. Service with restrictions, supervision.

BUCKEYE

Days Inn-Buckeye SH
(623) 386-5400. **$70-$200.** 25205 W Yuma Rd. I-10, exit 114 (Miller Rd), just sw. Ext corridors. **Pets:** Accepted.

CAREFREE

The Boulders Resort & Golden Door Spa-A Wyndham Luxury Resort LH
(480) 488-9009. **$169-$525, 21 day notice.** 34631 N Tom Darlington Dr. Scottsdale Rd, 11 mi n of Bell Rd. Ext corridors. **Pets:** Accepted.

Carefree Resort & Villas LH ❖
(480) 488-5300. **$69-$229.** 37220 Mule Train Rd. SR 101, exit 36 (Pima Rd), 12.2 mi n to Cave Creek Rd, 1 mi w, then 0.4 mi n. Ext/int corridors. **Pets:** $50 one-time fee/room. Designated rooms, supervision.

CAVE CREEK

Cave Creek Tumbleweed Hotel M
(480) 488-3668. **$99-$199, 14 day notice.** 6333 E Cave Creek Rd. Jct Scottsdale Rd/Tom Darlington Rd, 1.3 mi w. Ext corridors. **Pets:** $75 deposit/room. Service with restrictions, supervision.

CHANDLER

Chandler Super 8 SH
(480) 961-3888. **$51-$73.** 7171 W Chandler Blvd. I-10, exit 160 (Chandler Blvd), just e. Int corridors. **Pets:** Other species. $5 daily fee/pet. Service with restrictions, supervision.

Comfort Inn SH ❖
(480) 705-8882. **$59-$119.** 255 N Kyrene Rd. I-10, exit 160 (Chandler Blvd), 1.5 mi e, then just n. Int corridors. **Pets:** Small. Designated rooms, service with restrictions, supervision.

Hawthorn Suites Chandler SH
(480) 705-8881. **$89-$179.** 5858 W Chandler Blvd. I-10, exit 160 (Chandler Blvd), 1.5 mi e. Int corridors. **Pets:** Other species. $25 one-time fee/pet. Service with restrictions, crate.

Homewood Suites by Hilton SH
(480) 753-6200. **$69-$139.** 7373 W Detroit St. I-10, exit 160 (Chandler Blvd), 0.4 mi e, n on 54th St. Int corridors. **Pets:** Accepted.

Prime Hotel & Suites Phoenix/Chandler SH
(480) 961-4444. **$72-$126.** 7475 W Chandler Blvd. I-10, exit 16 (Chandler Blvd), just e, then just s on Southgate Dr. Int corridors. **Pets:** Accepted.

Red Roof Inn-Chandler SH
(480) 857-4969. **$50-$68.** 7400 W Boston St. I-10, exit 160 (Chandler Blvd), just e, then s on Southgate Dr. Int corridors. **Pets:** Accepted.

Residence Inn-Chandler Fashion Center SH
(480) 782-1551. **$95-$150, 14 day notice.** 200 N Federal St. I-10, exit 160 (Chandler Blvd), 4.2 mi e, just n on N Metro Blvd, then just e. Int corridors. **Pets:** Accepted.

San Marcos Resort and Conference Center LH
(480) 812-0900. **$79-$129, 3 day notice.** 1 San Marcos Pl. Just s on Arizona Ave from jct Chandler Blvd, just w on Buffalo St; in historic downtown. Ext corridors. **Pets:** Accepted.

Southgate Motel M
(480) 940-0308. **$45-$80.** 7445 W Chandler Blvd. I-10, exit 160 (Chandler Blvd), just e, then just s on Southgate Dr. Ext corridors. **Pets:** Accepted.

Windmill Suites of Chandler SH ❖
(480) 812-9600. **$79-$139.** 3535 W Chandler Blvd. I-10, exit 160 (Chandler Blvd), 4 mi e. Int corridors. **Pets:** Other species. Service with restrictions, supervision.

GLENDALE

Best Western Phoenix-Glendale SH
(623) 939-9431. **$59-$119.** 7116 N 59th Ave. I-17, exit 205 (Glendale Ave), 4.3 mi w, then just n. Ext corridors. **Pets:** Other species. $10 daily fee/pet. Service with restrictions.

Ramada Limited SH
(623) 412-2000. **$59-$139.** 7885 W Arrowhead Towne Ctr Dr. Loop 101, exit 14 (Bell Rd), 0.3 mi e, then just n on 79th Ave. Ext corridors. **Pets:** Other species. $10 daily fee/pet. Designated rooms, service with restrictions, crate.

GOODYEAR

Best Western Phoenix Goodyear Inn M
(623) 932-3210. **$62-$85, 7 day notice.** 55 N Litchfield Rd. I-10, exit 128, 0.8 mi s. Ext/int corridors. **Pets:** Accepted.

Hampton Inn & Suites SH
(623) 536-1313. **$89-$189.** 2000 N Litchfield Rd. I-10, exit 128, 0.5 mi n. Int corridors. **Pets:** Small, other species. $25 deposit/room. Service with restrictions, supervision.

▼▼▼ **Holiday Inn Express** SH
(623) 535-1313. **$89-$189.** 1313 N Litchfield Rd. I-10, exit 128, just n.
Int corridors. **Pets:** Large, other species. Service with restrictions.
[ASK] [S6] [X] [&] [8] [D] [≈]

▼▼▼ **Wingate Inn & Suites** SH ❀
(623) 547-1313. **$99-$169.** 1188 N Dysart Rd. I-10, exit 129 (Dysart
Rd), just n. Int corridors. **Pets:** Small, other species. $25 deposit/room.
Service with restrictions, supervision.
[ASK] [S6] [X] [&] [8] [D] [≈]

LITCHFIELD PARK

△△△ ▼▼▼ ▼▼▼ **The Wigwam Resort** LH
(623) 935-3811. **$205-$489, 7 day notice.** 300 Wigwam Blvd. I-10, exit
128 (Litchfield Rd), 2.4 mi n, then 0.4 mi e. Ext corridors.
Pets: Accepted.
[SAVE] [S6] [X] [&] [8] [D] [¶¶] [≈] [X]

MESA

△△△ ▼▼▼ **Arizona Golf Resort & Conference**
Center LH ❀
(480) 832-3202. **$129-$189.** 425 S Power Rd. 1.3 mi n of US 60
(Superstition Frwy), exit 188 (Power Rd); southeast corner of Broad-
way and Power rds; entrance on Broadway Rd. Ext corridors.
Pets: Large, other species. Service with restrictions.
[SAVE] [X] [&] [8] [D] [¶¶] [≈] [X]

△△△ ▼▼ **Best Western Dobson Ranch Inn**
Resort SH ❀
(480) 831-7000. **$60-$135.** 1666 S Dobson Rd. Just s of US 60 (Superstition Frwy), exit 177 (Dobson Rd). Ext/int corridors. **Pets:** Small, dogs
only. Designated rooms, service with restrictions, crate.
[SAVE] [S6] [X] [8] [D] [¶¶] [≈]

△△△ ▼▼ **Best Western Mesa Inn** SH
(480) 964-8000. **$60-$100.** 1625 E Main St. 2 mi n of US 60 (Superstition Frwy), exit Stapley Dr, 0.5 mi e. Ext corridors. **Pets:** Other
species. $10 one-time fee/pet. Service with restrictions, supervision.
[SAVE] [S6] [X] [8] [D] [≈]

△△△ ▼▼ **Best Western Mezona Inn** SH
(480) 834-9233. **$49-$149.** 250 W Main St. Just e of Country Club Dr;
downtown. Ext corridors. **Pets:** Medium, other species. Designated
rooms, service with restrictions, crate.
[SAVE] [S6] [X] [8] [D] [≈]

△△△ ▼▼ **Best Western Superstition Springs Inn &**
Suites SH
(480) 641-1164. **$59-$139.** 1342 S Power Rd. Just n of US 60 (Superstition Frwy), exit 188 (Power Rd), on northwest corner of Power Rd
and Hampton Ave. Ext corridors. **Pets:** Accepted.
[SAVE] [S6] [X] [&] [8] [D] [≈]

△△△ ▼▼ **Days Inn** SH
(480) 844-8900. **$49-$99.** 333 W Juanita. US 60 (Superstition Frwy),
exit 179 (Country Club Dr), just s, then just e. Int corridors.
Pets: Accepted.
[SAVE] [S6] [X] [&] [8] [D] [≈] [X]

△△△ ▼▼▼ **Holiday Inn Hotel & Suites** LH ❀
(480) 964-7000. **$109-$169.** 1600 S Country Club Dr. US 60 (Superstition Frwy), exit 179, just s. Ext/int corridors. **Pets:** Medium. $20 one-time
fee/room. Service with restrictions, crate.
[SAVE] [S6] [X] [&] [8] [D] [≈] [X]

▽▽ **Homestead Studio Suites Hotel-Phoenix**
East/Mesa SH
(480) 752-2266. **$47-$76.** 1920 W Isabella. Just s of US 60 (Superstition Frwy), exit 177 (Dobson Rd). Ext corridors. **Pets:** Other species.
$25 one-time fee/pet. Service with restrictions.
[ASK] [S6] [X] [&] [8] [D]

▼▼▼ **La Quinta Inn & Suites Phoenix (Mesa East)** SH
(480) 654-1970. **$85-$135.** 6530 E Superstition Springs Blvd. US 60
(Superstition Frwy), exit 187 (Superstition Springs Blvd) eastbound,
just se; exit 188 (Power Rd) westbound, just sw. Int corridors.
Pets: Accepted.
[ASK] [X] [&M] [7] [&] [8] [D] [≈] [X]

▼▼▼ **La Quinta Inn & Suites Phoenix (Mesa West)** SH
(480) 844-8747. **$75-$145.** 902 W Grove Ave. US 60 (Superstition
Frwy), exit 178 (Alma School Rd), just n, then just e. Int corridors.
Pets: Accepted.
[ASK] [X] [7] [&] [8] [D] [≈]

▼▼ **Motel 6-Mesa North #378** M
(480) 844-8899. **$44-$61.** 336 W Hampton Ave. US 60 (Superstition
Frwy), exit 179 (Country Club Dr), just n, then just e. Ext corridors.
Pets: Accepted.
[S6] [X] [&] [8] [≈]

▼▼ **Motel 6-Mesa South #1030** M
(480) 834-0066. **$43-$61.** 1511 S Country Club Dr. US 60 (Superstition
Frwy), exit 179 (Country Club Dr), northeast corner. Ext corridors.
Pets: Accepted.
[S6] [X] [&] [8] [≈]

▼▼▼ **Phoenix Marriott Mesa** LH
(480) 898-8300. **$89-$189.** 200 N Centennial Way. US 60 (Superstition
Frwy), exit 180 (Mesa Dr), 2 mi n, just w on Main St, then just n. Int
corridors. **Pets:** Accepted.
[ASK] [S6] [X] [&] [8] [D] [¶¶] [≈] [X]

▼▼▼ **Residence Inn by Marriott Mesa** SH
(480) 610-0100. **$69-$169.** 941 W Grove Ave. US 60 (Superstition
Frwy), exit 178 (Alma School Rd), just n, then just e. Int corridors.
Pets: Large, other species. $75 one-time fee/room. Service with restrictions.
[X] [&M] [7] [&] [8] [D] [≈] [X]

▼▼ **Sleep Inn of Mesa** SH
(480) 807-7760. **$59-$109.** 6347 E Southern Ave. US 60 (Superstition
Frwy), exit 188 (Power Rd), 0.8 mi n, then 0.4 mi w to mall entrance.
Int corridors. **Pets:** Small, other species. $25 deposit/pet. Designated
rooms, service with restrictions, supervision.
[ASK] [S6] [X] [&] [8] [D] [≈]

△△△ ▼▼▼ **Super 8 Motel-Mesa/Gilbert Rd** SH
(480) 545-0888. **$49-$69.** 1550 S Gilbert Rd. US 60 (Superstition
Frwy), exit 182 (Gilbert Rd), 1 blk n. Int corridors. **Pets:** Accepted.
[SAVE] [S6] [X] [&] [8] [≈]

▼▼ **Travelodge Suites Mesa** SH
(480) 832-5961. **$39-$79.** 4244 E Main St. US 60 Superstition Frwy),
exit 185 (Greenfield Rd), 2 mi n, then just w. Ext corridors.
Pets: Medium. $10 daily fee/pet. Service with restrictions, supervision.
[ASK] [S6] [X] [&] [8] [D] [≈]

△△△ ▼▼▼ **Windemere Hotel and Conference Center** SH
(480) 985-3600. **$69-$139.** 5750 E Main St. 0.7 mi e of Higley Rd. Ext
corridors. **Pets:** Medium. Designated rooms, service with restrictions,
supervision.
[SAVE] [S6] [X] [8] [D] [¶¶] [≈]

PARADISE VALLEY

▼▼▼ **Hermosa Inn** SH
(602) 955-8614. **$115-$690, 7 day notice.** 5532 N Palo Cristi Rd. 1 mi
s of Lincoln Dr, corner of Stanford Dr. Ext corridors. **Pets:** Accepted.
[ASK] [S6] [X] [D] [¶¶] [≈] [X]

△△△ ▼▼▼ ▼▼▼ **Sanctuary on Camelback Mountain** LH
(480) 948-2100. **$155-$625, 7 day notice.** 5700 E McDonald Dr. US
101, exit McDonald Dr, 3.9 mi w. Ext corridors. **Pets:** Medium. Service
with restrictions.
[SAVE] [S6] [X] [&] [D] [¶¶] [≈] [X]

PEORIA

▼▼▼ Comfort Suites by Choice Hotels Sports Complex SH ❀
(623) 334-3993. **$49-$159.** 8473 W Paradise Ln. Loop 101, exit 14 (Bell Rd), just e to 83rd Ave, then just s. Int corridors. **Pets:** Small. $50 one-time fee/room. Designated rooms, service with restrictions, supervision.

A$K 🛏 ✕ 🛗 🛎 🖥 ⊗

▼▼▼ Holiday Inn Express Hotel & Suites SH
(623) 853-1313. **$89-$169.** 16771 N 84th Ave. Loop 101, exit 14 (Bell Rd), just w, then just s. Int corridors. **Pets:** Small, other species. $25 deposit/room. Service with restrictions, supervision.

A$K 🛏 ✕ 🛗 🛎 🖥

▼▼▼ La Quinta Inn & Suites Phoenix (West/Peoria) SH
(623) 487-1900. **$85-$185.** 16321 N 83 Ave. Loop 101, exit 14 (Bell Rd), just e, then just s. Int corridors. **Pets:** Other species. Service with restrictions, crate.

A$K ✕ 🛗 🛎 🖥 ⊗

▼▼▼ Residence Inn by Marriott SH
(623) 979-2074. **$72-$199.** 8435 W Paradise Ln. Loop 101, exit 14 (Bell Rd), just e, just s on 83rd Ave, then just w. Int corridors. **Pets:** Accepted.

✕ 🛗 🛎 🖥 ⊗

PHOENIX

⬥⬥⬥ ▼▼▼ AmeriSuites (Phoenix/Metro Center) SH
(602) 997-8800. **$79-$139.** 10838 N 25th Ave. I-17, exit 208 (Peoria Ave), just e, then 0.3 mi n. Int corridors. **Pets:** Accepted.

SAVE 🛏 ✕ 🛗 🛎 🖥

⬥⬥⬥ ▼▼▼▼ Arizona Biltmore Resort & Spa LH ❀
(602) 955-6600. **$195-$625, 7 day notice.** 2400 E Missouri. Jct Camelback Rd, 0.5 mi n on 24th St, then 0.4 mi w. Ext/int corridors. **Pets:** Medium. $50 one-time fee/room. Designated rooms, supervision.

SAVE ✕ 🛗 🖥 🍽 ⊗

▼▼▼ Best Western SH
(602) 864-6233. **$59-$89.** 8101 N Black Canyon Hwy. I-17, exit 206 (Northern Ave), just e, then just n; on east side of freeway. Ext corridors. **Pets:** Accepted.

A$K 🛏 ✕ 🛗 🛎 🖥

⬥⬥⬥ ▼▼▼ Best Western Airport Inn SH
(602) 273-7251. **$75-$199.** 2425 S 24th St. I-10, exit 150B westbound, just s; exit 151 (University Dr) eastbound, just n to I-10 westbound, 1 mi w to exit 150B (24th St), then just s. Ext/int corridors. **Pets:** Small. $10 one-time fee/pet. Designated rooms, service with restrictions, supervision.

SAVE 🛏 ✕ 🛗 🛎 🖥 🍽

⬥⬥⬥ ▼▼▼ Best Western Bell Hotel SH
(602) 993-8300. **$49-$109.** 17211 N Black Canyon Hwy. I-17, exit 212, just e, then just n. Ext corridors. **Pets:** Accepted.

SAVE 🛏 ✕ 🛗 🛎 🖥

⬥⬥⬥ ▼▼▼▼ Best Western InnSuites Hotel Phoenix Northern/Airport SH
(602) 997-6285. **$59-$129.** 1615 W Northern Ave. Loop 51, 0.3 mi w. Ext corridors. **Pets:** Medium, other species. $25 one-time fee/room. Designated rooms, service with restrictions, crate.

SAVE 🛏 ✕ 🛗 🛗 🛎 🖥 🍽 ⊗

▼▼▼ Candlewood Suites SH
(602) 861-4900. **$49-$109.** 11411 N Black Canyon Hwy. I-17, exit 208 (Peoria Ave), just e, then 0.4 mi n. Int corridors. **Pets:** Large, other species. $50 one-time fee/room. Supervision.

A$K 🛏 ✕ 🛗 🛎 🖥

⬥⬥⬥ ▼▼▼ Clarion Hotel @ Phoenix Tech Center SH ❀
(480) 893-3900. **$54-$134.** 5121 E La Puente Ave. I-10, exit 157 (Elliot Rd), just w, just n on 51st St, then just e. Ext corridors. **Pets:** Medium, other species. $25 one-time fee/room. Designated rooms, service with restrictions, supervision.

SAVE 🛏 ✕ 🛗 🖥 🍽 ⊗

⬥⬥⬥ ▼▼▼ Comfort Inn Black Canyon SH
(602) 242-8011. **$59-$129.** 5050 N Black Canyon Hwy. I-17, exit 203 (Camelback Rd), just w, then just n on west side of freeway. Ext corridors. **Pets:** Accepted.

SAVE 🛏 ✕ 🛗 🛎 🖥

▼▼▼ Comfort Inn North SH
(602) 866-2089. **$59-$79.** 1711 W Bell Rd. I-17, exit 212 (Bell Rd), 1 mi e. Ext corridors. **Pets:** Accepted.

A$K 🛏 ✕ 🛗 🛎 🖥

▼▼▼ Comfort Suites by Choice Hotels SH
(602) 861-3900. **$49-$129.** 10210 N 26th Dr. I-17, exit 208 (Peoria Ave), just e, just s on 25th Ave, then 0.3 mi w on W Beryl Ave. Int corridors. **Pets:** Medium, other species. $50 one-time fee/pet. Service with restrictions.

A$K 🛏 ✕ 🛗 🛗 🛎 🖥

⬥⬥⬥ ▼▼▼ Comfort Suites Conference Center SH
(602) 279-3211. **$62-$143.** 3210 NW Grand Ave. I-17, exit 201 (Thomas Rd), just w to 27th Ave, just n, then 0.7 mi nw. Ext corridors. **Pets:** Small, other species. $25 one-time fee/room. Service with restrictions, supervision.

SAVE 🛏 ✕ 🛗 🛎 🖥

⬥⬥⬥ ▼▼▼ Crowne Plaza Phoenix SH
(602) 943-2341. **$59-$129.** 2532 W Peoria Ave. I-17, exit 208 (Peoria Ave), just e, then just n on 25th ave. Int corridors. **Pets:** $25 one-time fee/room. Service with restrictions, crate.

SAVE 🛏 ✕ 🛗 🛗 🛎 🖥 🍽

⬥⬥⬥ ▼▼▼ Days Inn-Airport M
(602) 244-8244. **$45-$99.** 3333 E Van Buren St. Loop 202, exit 1C (32nd St), 0.6 mi s, then just e. Ext/int corridors. **Pets:** Large, other species. $20 one-time fee/pet. Service with restrictions, supervision.

SAVE 🛏 ✕ 🛗 🛎 🖥 🍽

⬥⬥⬥ ▼▼▼ Econo Lodge Inn & Suites-Downtown SH ❀
(602) 528-9100. **$59-$119.** 202 E McDowell Rd. Just e of Central Ave. Int corridors. **Pets:** Small, other species. $50 deposit/room. Service with restrictions, supervision.

SAVE 🛏 ✕ 🛎 🖥

▼▼▼ Embassy Suites Phoenix Airport at 24th St SH
(602) 957-1910. **$69-$189.** 2333 E Thomas Rd. SR 51, exit 2, just e. Ext corridors. **Pets:** Medium. $15 daily fee/pet. Service with restrictions, supervision.

A$K 🛏 ✕ 🛗 🛎 🖥 🍽

⬥⬥⬥ ▼▼▼ Embassy Suites Phoenix-Biltmore SH
(602) 955-3992. **$89-$289.** 2630 E Camelback Rd. Just n of Camelback Rd, on 26th St. Int corridors. **Pets:** Small. $25 one-time fee/pet. Service with restrictions.

🛏 ✕ 🛗 🛎 🖥 🍽

⬥⬥⬥ ▼▼▼ Embassy Suites Phoenix North LH
(602) 375-1777. **$129-$232.** 2577 W Greenway Rd. I-17, exit 211, just e. Ext corridors. **Pets:** Accepted.

SAVE 🛏 ✕ 🛗 🛗 🛎 🖥 🍽 ⊗

⬥⬥⬥ ▼▼▼ Hilton Suites-Phoenix LH
(602) 222-1111. **$79-$239.** 10 E Thomas Rd. Just e of Central Ave; in Phoenix Plaza. Int corridors. **Pets:** Medium, dogs only. $50 deposit/pet, $50 one-time fee/pet. Service with restrictions, crate.

SAVE 🛏 ✕ 🛗 🛗 🛎 🖥 🍽 ⊗

Holiday Inn Express Hotel & Suites SH
(480) 785-8500. **$79-$109.** 15221 S 50th St. I-10, exit 160 (Chandler Blvd), just w. Int corridors. **Pets:** Medium. Designated rooms, service with restrictions.

Holiday Inn Express Hotel & Suites SH
(602) 453-9900. **$69-$119.** 3401 E University Dr. I-10, exit 151 (University Dr), just n. Int corridors. **Pets:** Accepted.

Holiday Inn West SH
(602) 484-9009. **$69-$125.** 1500 N 51st Ave. I-10, exit 139 (51st Ave), just n. Int corridors. **Pets:** Medium. $25 one-time fee/pet. Service with restrictions, supervision.

Homestead Studio Suites Hotel-Phoenix North/Metro M
(602) 944-7828. **$47-$76.** 2102 W Dunlap Ave. I-17, exit 207, 0.7 mi e. Ext corridors. **Pets:** Accepted.

Homewood Suites by Hilton SH
(602) 508-0937. **$129-$169, 15 day notice.** 2001 E Highland Ave. Just e of 20th St. Int corridors. **Pets:** Accepted.

Homewood Suites Hotel SH
(602) 674-8900. **$79-$149.** 2536 W Beryl Ave. I-17, exit 208 (Peoria Ave), just e, just s on 25th Ave, then just w. Int corridors. **Pets:** Other species. $200 deposit/room, $50 one-time fee/room. Service with restrictions, supervision.

Howard Johnson Phoenix Airport M
(602) 220-0044. **Call for rates.** 124 S 24th St. I-10, exit 150B (24th St) westbound, 1.5 mi n; exit 151 (University Dr) eastbound, 1 mi w to 24th St, then 1.7 mi n. Ext corridors. **Pets:** Accepted.

La Quinta Inn & Suites Phoenix (Chandler) SH
(480) 961-7700. **$95-$125.** 15241 S 50th St. I-10, exit 160 (Chandler Blvd), just w, then just n. Int corridors. **Pets:** Accepted.

La Quinta Inn Phoenix SH
(602) 956-6500. **$65-$120.** 4727 E Thomas Rd. Just w of 48th St. Ext/int corridors. **Pets:** Medium. $50 deposit/room. Service with restrictions, supervision.

La Quinta Inn Phoenix (North) SH
(602) 993-0800. **$75-$125.** 2510 W Greenway Rd. I-17, exit 211, just e. Ext corridors. **Pets:** Medium. Service with restrictions, supervision.

La Quinta Inn Phoenix (Thomas Road) M
(602) 258-6271. **$65-$115.** 2725 N Black Canyon Hwy. I-17, exit 201 (Thomas Rd), just e, then just s on east side of freeway. Ext corridors. **Pets:** Accepted.

Motel 6 Phoenix-Black Canyon #1304 M
(602) 277-5501. **$35-$61.** 4130 N Black Canyon Hwy. I-17, exit 202 (Indian School Rd), just w. Ext corridors. **Pets:** Accepted.

Motel 6 Phoenix East M
(602) 267-8555. **Call for rates.** 5315 E Van Buren St. Loop 202 eastbound, exit 4 (52nd/Van Buren sts) just s, then just e. Ext corridors. **Pets:** Accepted.

Motel 6 Phoenix-North #344 M
(602) 993-2353. **Call for rates.** 2330 W Bell Rd. I-17, exit 212A, just e. Ext corridors. **Pets:** Accepted.

Motel 6 Phoenix-Northern Ave #1185 M
(602) 995-7592. **$35-$61.** 8152 N Black Canyon Hwy. I-17, exit 206, just w, then just s. Ext corridors. **Pets:** Medium. Service with restrictions, supervision.

Motel 6 Phoenix West #696 M
(602) 272-0220. **$43-$65.** 1530 N 52nd Dr. I-10, exit 139, just n to McDowell, just w, then just s. Ext corridors. **Pets:** Accepted.

Premier Inns M
(602) 943-2371. **$39-$109.** 10402 N Black Canyon Hwy. I-17, exit 208 (Peoria Ave), 0.3 mi w to 28th Dr, just s, just e on Metro Pkwy E, then just n on 27th Ave. Ext corridors. **Pets:** Accepted.

Prime Hotel & Suites Phoenix Airport SH
(602) 220-4400. **$101-$147.** 427 N 44th St. Loop 202, exit 2 (44th St), 0.5 mi s. Int corridors. **Pets:** Small. Service with restrictions, supervision.

Ramada Plaza Hotel and Suites-Phoenix at Metro Center SH ❖
(602) 866-7000. **$59-$149.** 12027 N 28th Dr. I-17, exit 209 (Cactus Rd), just w, then just s. Int corridors. **Pets:** $25 daily fee/room. Designated rooms, service with restrictions, crate.

Red Roof Inn SH
(602) 233-8004. **$50-$68.** 5215 W Willetta. I-10, exit 139 (51st Ave), just n, just e on McDowell Rd, then just s. Int corridors. **Pets:** Medium. Service with restrictions, supervision.

Red Roof Inn-Camelback SH
(602) 264-9290. **$89-$125.** 502 W Camelback Rd. I-17, exit 203 (Camelback Rd), 1.8 mi e. Int corridors. **Pets:** Accepted.

Red Roof Inn-Phoenix SH
(602) 866-1049. **$49-$72.** 17222 N Black Canyon Hwy. I-17, exit 212, just w, then just n. Int corridors. **Pets:** Accepted.

Residence Inn by Marriott SH ❖
(602) 864-1900. **$59-$137.** 8242 N Black Canyon Hwy. I-17, exit 207 (Dunlap Ave), just w, then 0.8 mi s. Ext/int corridors. **Pets:** $75 one-time fee/pet. Service with restrictions, supervision.

Residence Inn by Marriott Phoenix Airport SH ❖
(602) 273-9220. **$59-$189.** 801 N 44th St. Loop 202, exit 152 (40th and 44th sts) eastbound; exit 152 (44th) westbound, just s. Int corridors. **Pets:** Large, other species. $75 one-time fee/room. Service with restrictions, crate.

Royal Palms Resort and Spa LH ❖
(602) 840-3610. **$179-$525, 7 day notice.** 5200 E Camelback Rd. Just e of 52nd St. Ext/int corridors. **Pets:** Small, other species. $200 deposit/ room, $100 one-time fee/room. Designated rooms, service with restrictions, crate.

▼▼▼▼ Sheraton Crescent Hotel 🄻🄷
(602) 943-8200. **$89-$279.** 2620 W Dunlap Ave. I-17, exit 207 (Dunlap Ave), just e. Int corridors. **Pets:** Medium, other species. Service with restrictions, crate.
ⒶⓈⓀ 🔊 ✕ 🖐 📷 🖊 🛏 💻 🍴 🏊 ⊠

Ⓐ ▼▼▼▼ Sheraton Wild Horse Pass Resort & Spa 🄻🄷 ❀
(602) 225-0100. **$189-$575, 7 day notice.** 5594 W Wild Horse Pass Blvd. I-10, exit 162, 2.4 mi w. Int corridors. **Pets:** Medium, dogs only. Designated rooms, service with restrictions, supervision.
ⓈⒶⓋⒺ 🔊 ✕ 🖊 🛏 🍴 🏊 ⊠

Ⓐ ▼▼▼ Sleep Inn Phoenix North 🅂🄷
(602) 504-1200. **$40-$120.** 18235 N 27th Ave. I-17, exit 214A, just w, then just s. Int corridors. **Pets:** Small. $50 deposit/room, $15 daily fee/pet. Designated rooms, service with restrictions.
 ⓈⒶⓋⒺ 🔊 ✕ 🖐 🖊 🛏 💻 🏊

Ⓐ ▼▼▼ Sleep Inn Sky Harbor Airport 🅂🄷
(480) 967-7100. **$55-$109.** 2621 S 47th Pl. I-10, exit 151 (University Dr), 2 mi n, then just w. Int corridors. **Pets:** Medium. $25 one-time fee/room. Designated rooms, service with restrictions, supervision.
ⓈⒶⓋⒺ 🔊 ✕ 🖊 🛏 💻 🏊

▼▼ Studio 6 Phoenix-Deer Valley #6030 🅂🄷
(602) 843-1151. **$49-$73.** 18405 N 27th Ave. I-17, exit 214A (Union Hills Dr), just w, then just s. Ext corridors. **Pets:** Other species. $10 daily fee/room. Service with restrictions, supervision.
🔊 ✕ 🖊 🛏 💻

▼▼ Sunshine Hotel & Suites 🅂🄷
(602) 604-4900. **$59-$89.** 3600 N 2nd Ave. Just n of Osborn Rd, 0.5 mi s of Indian School; downtown. Ext/int corridors. **Pets:** Accepted.
ⒶⓈⓀ 🔊 ✕ 🖊 🛏 💻 🍴 🏊 ⊠

▼▼ Super 8 Motel-Phoenix 🅂🄷
(602) 415-0888. **$70-$100.** 1242 N 53rd Ave. I-10, exit 139 (51st Ave), just s to Latham Rd, then just w. Int corridors. **Pets:** Accepted.
ⒶⓈⓀ 🔊 ✕ 🛏

▼▼▼ TownePlace Suites by Marriott 🅂🄷
(602) 943-9510. **$39-$100.** 9425 N Black Canyon Hwy. I-17, exit 207, just e, then 0.3 mi n. Int corridors. **Pets:** Accepted.
ⒶⓈⓀ 🔊 ✕ 🖊 🛏 💻 🏊

Ⓐ ▼▼ Travelers Inn 🅂🄷
(602) 233-1988. **$47-$72.** 5102 W Latham St. I-10, exit 139 (51st Ave), just sw. Ext corridors. **Pets:** Other species. Service with restrictions, supervision.
ⓈⒶⓋⒺ 🔊 ✕ 🛏 💻 🏊

Ⓐ ▼▼▼ Wellesley Inn & Suites (Phoenix/Chandler) 🅂🄷
(480) 753-6700. **$79-$109.** 5035 E Chandler Blvd. I-10, exit 160 (Chandler Blvd), just w. Ext corridors. **Pets:** Other species. $25 daily fee/room. Service with restrictions, supervision.
ⓈⒶⓋⒺ 🔊 ✕ 🖊 🛏 💻 🏊

Ⓐ ▼▼▼▼ Wellesley Inn & Suites Phoenix/Metro Center 🅂🄷
(602) 870-2999. **$49-$89.** 11211 N Black Canyon Hwy. I-17, exit 208 (Peoria Ave), just e, then 0.3 mi n on east side of freeway. Ext corridors. **Pets:** Accepted.
ⓈⒶⓋⒺ 🔊 ✕ 🖊 🛏 💻 🏊 ⊠

Ⓐ ▼▼▼▼ Wellesley Inn & Suites (Phoenix/Midtown) 🅂🄷
(602) 279-9000. **$89-$149.** 217 W Osborn Rd. Just w of Central Ave; between Indian School and Thomas rds. Int corridors. **Pets:** Accepted.
ⓈⒶⓋⒺ 🔊 ✕ 🖐 📷 🛏 💻 🏊

Ⓐ ▼▼▼ Wellesley Inns & Suites (Phoenix/Airport) 🅂🄷
(602) 225-2998. **$49-$109.** 4357 E Oak St. Loop 202, exit 2 (44th St), 1 mi n. Ext corridors. **Pets:** Accepted.
ⓈⒶⓋⒺ ✕ 🖐 🛏 💻 🏊

Ⓐ ▼▼▼ Wingate Inn Phoenix 🅂🄷
(602) 716-9900. **$69-$149.** 2520 N Central Ave. I-10, exit 145 (7th St), just n to McDowell Rd, 0.4 mi w, then 0.7 mi n. Int corridors. **Pets:** Accepted.
ⓈⒶⓋⒺ 🔊 ✕ 🖊 🛏 💻 🏊

SCOTTSDALE

Ⓐ ▼▼▼▼ AmeriSuites (Scottsdale/Old Town) 🅂🄷
(480) 423-9944. **$79-$159.** 7300 E 3rd Ave. Just e of Scottsdale Rd. Int corridors. **Pets:** Medium, other species. $25 one-time fee/pet. Service with restrictions, crate.
ⓈⒶⓋⒺ 🔊 ✕ 🖐 🖊 🛏 💻 🏊

Ⓐ ▼▼▼ Best Western Papago Inn & Resort 🅂🄷
(480) 947-7335. **$59-$149.** 7017 E McDowell Rd. From Scottsdale Rd, just w. Ext corridors. **Pets:** Accepted.
ⓈⒶⓋⒺ 🔊 ✕ 🛏 💻 🏊

Ⓐ ▼▼▼▼ Camelback Inn, A JW Marriott Resort & Spa 🄻🄷
(480) 948-1700. **$129-$449, 14 day notice.** 5402 E Lincoln Dr. 0.5 mi e of Tatum Blvd, on north side of Lincoln Dr. Ext corridors. **Pets:** Service with restrictions, crate.
ⓈⒶⓋⒺ 🔊 ✕ 🖐 📷 🖊 🛏 💻 🍴 🏊 ⊠

Ⓐ ▼▼▼▼ Chaparral Suites Resort 🅂🄷
(480) 949-1414. **$99-$219.** 5001 N Scottsdale Rd. At Chaparral Rd. Ext corridors. **Pets:** Medium, dogs only. $25 one-time fee/pet. Service with restrictions, supervision.
ⓈⒶⓋⒺ 🔊 ✕ 📷 🖊 🛏 💻 🍴 🏊

▼▼ Comfort Suites by Choice Hotels-Old Town 🅂🄷
(480) 946-1111. **$49-$149.** 3275 N Drinkwater Blvd. N of Thomas Rd; just e of Scottsdale Rd. Int corridors. **Pets:** Accepted.
ⒶⓈⓀ 🔊 ✕ 🖐 🖊 🛏 💻

▼▼▼ Country Inn & Suites By Carlson 🅂🄷
(480) 314-1200. **$62-$120.** 10801 N 89th Pl. Loop 101, exit 41, just e on Shea Blvd, then just n. Int corridors. **Pets:** Small. $50 one-time fee/room. Designated rooms, service with restrictions, supervision.
ⒶⓈⓀ 🔊 ✕ 📷 🖊 🛏 💻 🏊

Ⓐ ▼▼▼▼ The Fairmont Scottsdale Princess 🄻🄷 ❀
(480) 585-4848. **$169-$549, 14 day notice.** 7575 E Princess Dr. 0.6 mi n of Bell Rd, 0.5 mi e of Scottsdale Rd, on south side of Princess Dr. Ext/int corridors. **Pets:** Small. $30 daily fee/room. Service with restrictions, supervision.
ⓈⒶⓋⒺ 🔊 ✕ 🖐 📷 🖊 🛏 💻 🍴 🏊 ⊠

Ⓐ ▼▼▼▼ Four Seasons Resort Scottsdale at Troon North 🄻🄷 ❀
(480) 515-5700. **$205-$4000, 7 day notice.** 10600 E Crescent Moon Dr. SR 101, exit 36 (Pima Rd), 4.7 mi n, 2 mi e on Happy Valley, then 1.5 mi n on Alma School Rd. Ext corridors. **Pets:** Very small, other species. Service with restrictions, supervision.
ⓈⒶⓋⒺ ✕ 🖐 📷 🖊 🛏 💻 🍴 🏊 ⊠

▼▼▼ Hampton Inn-Oldtown/Fashion Square Scottsdale 🅂🄷
(480) 941-9400. **$59-$169.** 4415 N Civic Center Plaza. Scottsdale Rd, just e on Camelback Rd, then just s on 75th St. Ext/int corridors. **Pets:** $50 one-time fee/room. Service with restrictions.
ⒶⓈⓀ 🔊 ✕ 🖐 📷 🖊 🛏 💻 🏊

Ⓐ ▼▼▼▼ Hilton Scottsdale Resort & Villas 🄻🄷 ❀
(480) 948-7750. **$69-$269, 3 day notice.** 6333 N Scottsdale Rd. Loop 101, exit 45, 2.1 mi w on McDonald Dr, then 0.3 mi n. Int corridors. **Pets:** Medium, dogs only. $50 deposit/room, $50 one-time fee/room. Designated rooms, service with restrictions, supervision.
ⓈⒶⓋⒺ 🔊 ✕ 🖐 📷 🖊 🛏 💻 🍴 🏊 ⊠

⚠⚠⚠ Holiday Inn Express Hotel & Suites-Scottsdale SH
(480) 675-7665. **$59-$209.** 3131 N Scottsdale Rd. Northeast corner of Scottsdale Rd and Earll Dr. Int corridors. **Pets:** Accepted.
`SAVE` `S` `✕` `&M` `·` `📶` `💻` `≈`

⚠⚠ Homestead Studio Suites Hotel-Scottsdale SH
(480) 994-0297. **$52-$90.** 3560 N Marshall Way. Just w of Scottsdale Rd on Goldwater, then just s. Ext corridors. **Pets:** Accepted.
`ASK` `S` `✕` `&M` `·` `📶` `💻` `≈`

⚠⚠⚠ Hospitality Suite Resort SH
(480) 949-5115. **$49-$119.** 409 N Scottsdale Rd. Just n of McKellips Rd; on east side of Scottsdale Rd. Ext corridors. **Pets:** Small, dogs only. Designated rooms, service with restrictions, supervision.
`SAVE` `S` `✕` `📶` `💻` `🍽` `≈` `✕`

⚠⚠⚠ The Inn at Pima, A Condominium Suite Hotel CO
(480) 948-3800. **$59-$189.** 7330 N Pima Rd. 0.4 mi n of Indian Bend Rd, on west side of Pima Rd. Ext/int corridors. **Pets:** $10 daily fee/pet. Designated rooms, service with restrictions, supervision.
`SAVE` `S` `✕` `·` `📶` `💻` `≈` `✕`

⚠⚠⚠⚠ La Quinta Inn & Suites Phoenix (Scottsdale) SH
(480) 614-5300. **$75-$155.** 8888 E Shea Blvd. Loop 101, exit Shea Blvd, northeast corner. Int corridors. **Pets:** Accepted.
`SAVE` `✕` `&M` `🌀` `·` `📶` `💻` `≈`

⚠⚠⚠⚠ Millennium Resort Scottsdale, McCormick Ranch LH
(480) 948-5050. **$69-$299, 3 day notice.** 7401 N Scottsdale Rd. 0.8 mi n of Indian Bend Rd. Int corridors. **Pets:** Accepted.
`SAVE` `S` `✕` `🌀` `💻` `🍽` `≈` `✕`

⚠ Motel 6 Scottsdale #29 M
(480) 946-2280. **$45-$77.** 6848 E Camelback Rd.. Just w of Scottsdale Rd. Ext corridors. **Pets:** Medium, other species. Service with restrictions, supervision.
`S` `✕` `·` `🍽` `≈`

⚠⚠ The Phoenician LH
(480) 941-8200. **$275-$725, 7 day notice.** 6000 E Camelback Rd. 0.5 mi w of 64th St. Ext/int corridors. **Pets:** Small. $50 one-time fee/pet. Designated rooms, service with restrictions, supervision.
`SAVE` `S` `✕` `🌀` `·` `📶` `💻` `🍽` `≈` `✕`

⚠⚠⚠⚠ Renaissance Scottsdale Resort LH
(480) 991-1414. **$89-$296.** 6160 N Scottsdale Rd. Just n of McDonald Dr, on west side of Scottsdale Rd. Ext corridors. **Pets:** Accepted.
`SAVE` `S` `✕` `&M` `🌀` `·` `📶` `💻` `🍽` `≈` `✕`

⚠⚠⚠ Residence Inn by Marriott SH
(480) 948-8666. **$99-$199.** 6040 N Scottsdale Rd. Just n of McDonald Dr. Ext/int corridors. **Pets:** Other species. $75 one-time fee/room. Service with restrictions.
`SAVE` `✕` `&M` `🌀` `·` `📶` `💻` `≈` `✕`

⚠⚠⚠ Residence Inn Scottsdale North SH 🐾
(480) 563-4120. **$99-$299.** 17011 N Scottsdale Rd. SR 101, exit 34 (Scottsdale Rd), 1.1 mi s, then just e on 17050 N. Int corridors. **Pets:** Small. $75 one-time fee/room. Designated rooms, service with restrictions, crate.
`ASK` `S` `✕` `·` `📶` `💻` `≈` `✕`

⚠⚠⚠ Rodeway Inn of Scottsdale M 🐾
(480) 946-3456. **$44-$109.** 7110 E Indian School Rd. Just w of Scottsdale Rd, on north side of Indian School Rd. Ext corridors. **Pets:** Medium. $10 daily fee/room. Service with restrictions, supervision.
`SAVE` `S` `✕` `🌀` `·` `📶` `💻` `≈`

⚠⚠⚠ Scottsdale Marriott at McDowell Mountains SH
(480) 502-3836. **$259-$299.** 16770 N Perimeter Dr. Loop 101, exit 36 (Princess Dr), just w to N Perimeter Dr, then 0.6 mi s. Int corridors. **Pets:** Accepted.
`SAVE` `S` `✕` `&M` `🌀` `·` `📶` `💻` `🍽` `≈` `✕`

⚠⚠⚠ Scottsdale Park Suites M
(480) 949-8637. **$60-$119.** 1251 N Miller Rd. 0.5 mi e of Scottsdale Rd, on McDowell Rd, then just s. Ext corridors. **Pets:** Small. $10 daily fee/room. Designated rooms, service with restrictions.
`SAVE` `S` `✕` `📶` `💻` `≈` `✕`

⚠⚠⚠ Sleep Inn SH
(480) 998-9211. **$54-$139.** 16630 N Scottsdale Rd. Just s of Bell Rd. Int corridors. **Pets:** Accepted.
`SAVE` `S` `✕` `&M` `📶` `💻` `≈`

⚠⚠⚠ Summerfield Suites by Wyndham-Scottsdale SH
(480) 946-7700. **$89-$219.** 4245 N Drinkwater Blvd. 0.3 mi e of Scottsdale Rd. Ext corridors. **Pets:** Small. $200 one-time fee/room. Service with restrictions.
`ASK` `✕` `·` `📶` `💻` `≈` `✕`

⚠⚠ TownePlace Suites by Marriott SH 🐾
(480) 551-1100. **$59-$139.** 10740 N 90th St. Loop 101, exit Shea Blvd, just e to 90th St, then just n. Int corridors. **Pets:** $75 one-time fee/room. Service with restrictions.
`ASK` `✕` `&M` `🌀` `·` `📶` `💻` `≈`

⚠⚠⚠⚠ The Westin Kierland Resort & Spa LH 🐾
(480) 624-1000. **$139-$550, 7 day notice.** 6902 E Greenway Pkwy. 0.5 mi w of Scottsdale Rd. Int corridors. **Pets:** Designated rooms, service with restrictions.
`SAVE` `S` `✕` `·` `💻` `🍽` `≈` `✕`

SURPRISE

⚠⚠⚠ Days Inn & Suites SH
(623) 933-4000. **$49-$129.** 12477 W Bell Rd. US 60 (Grand Ave), 1.1 mi e, then just s on Greasewood St. Int corridors. **Pets:** Medium. $50 deposit/room, $10 one-time fee/pet. Service with restrictions, supervision.
`SAVE` `S` `✕` `·` `📶` `💻` `≈`

⚠⚠⚠ Windmill Suites at Sun City West SH 🐾
(623) 583-0133. **$69-$159.** 12545 W Bell Rd. US 60 (Grand Ave), 1 mi e. Int corridors. **Pets:** Large. Designated rooms, service with restrictions, supervision.
`SAVE` `S` `✕` `🌀` `·` `📶` `≈` `✕`

TEMPE

⚠⚠⚠ AmeriSuites (Tempe/Arizona Mills) SH
(480) 831-9800. **$79-$149.** 1520 W Baseline Rd. I-10, exit 155 (Baseline Rd), 0.4 mi e. Int corridors. **Pets:** Medium, other species. $10 daily fee/room. Service with restrictions, supervision.
`SAVE` `S` `✕` `·` `📶` `💻` `≈`

⚠⚠⚠ AmeriSuites (Tempe/Phoenix Airport) SH
(480) 804-9544. **$99-$139.** 1413 W Rio Salado Pkwy. Just w of Priest Dr. Int corridors. **Pets:** Accepted.
`SAVE` `S` `✕` `·` `📶` `💻` `≈`

⚠⚠⚠ Best Western Inn of Tempe SH
(480) 784-2233. **$59-$119.** 670 N Scottsdale Rd. SR 202 Loop (Red Mountain Frwy), exit 7, just s. Int corridors. **Pets:** Small. $25 deposit/room. Designated rooms, service with restrictions, supervision.
`SAVE` `S` `✕` `·` `📶` `💻` `≈`

▼▼▼▼ **Candlewood Suites** SH
(480) 777-0440. **$59-$123.** 1335 W Baseline Rd. I-10, exit 155 (Baseline Rd), 0.5 mi e; just e of Priest Dr. Int corridors. **Pets:** Medium. $75 one-time fee/room. Service with restrictions, supervision.

ASK 🔊 ✕ 🖼 🛏 💻 ⊇ ✕

AAA ▼▼▼▼ **Comfort Inn/Tempe ASU/Airport** SH
(480) 966-7202. **$49-$129.** 1031 E Apache Blvd. SR 202 Loop (Red Mountain Frwy), exit 7 (Rural Rd S), 1.5 mi s, then just e. Int corridors. **Pets:** Other species. $50 deposit/room.

SAVE 🔊 ✕ 🐾 🖼 🛏 💻 ⊇ ✕

▼▼▼▼ **Country Inn & Suites By Carlson** SH
(480) 345-8585. **$69-$110.** 1660 W Elliot Rd. I-10, exit 157, just e. Ext corridors. **Pets:** Other species. $250 deposit/room.

ASK 🔊 ✕ 🛏 💻 ⊇

AAA ▼▼▼▼ **Fiesta Inn Resort** LH
(480) 967-1441. **$69-$135.** 2100 S Priest Dr. I-10, exit 153 (Broadway Rd), 0.5 mi e. Ext corridors. **Pets:** Service with restrictions, crate.

SAVE 🔊 ✕ 🐾 🖼 🛏 💻 🍴 ⊇ ✕

AAA ▼▼▼▼ **Hampton Inn & Suites** SH
(480) 675-9799. **$80-$134.** 1429 N Scottsdale Rd. SR 202 Loop (Red Mountain Frwy), exit 7, 0.5 mi n. Ext corridors. **Pets:** Accepted.

SAVE 🔊 ✕ 🐾 🖼 🛏 💻 ⊇ ✕

▼▼▼ **Hawthorn Suites Ltd** SH 🐾
(480) 633-2744. **$59-$99.** 2301 E Southern Ave. Loop 101, exit Southern Ave/Baseline Rd; at southeast corner. Int corridors. **Pets:** Large, other species. $25 one-time fee/room. Service with restrictions, supervision.

ASK 🔊 ✕ 🖼 🐾 🛏 💻 ⊇

▼▼ ▼ **Holiday Inn Express/Tempe** SH
(480) 820-7500. **$49-$99.** 5300 S Priest Dr. I-10, exit 155 (Baseline Rd), 0.4 mi e, then just s. Int corridors. **Pets:** Small. $20 daily fee/pet. Designated rooms, service with restrictions, crate.

ASK 🔊 ✕ 🛏 💻 ⊇

▼▼▼▼ **Homestead Studio Suites**
Hotel-Phoenix/Airport/Tempe SH
(480) 557-8880. **$61-$95.** 2165 W 15th St. I-10, exit 153 (Broadway Rd), 0.3 mi ne, just nw on S 52nd St, then just w. Int corridors. **Pets:** Other species. $25 daily fee/room. Service with restrictions.

ASK 🔊 ✕ 🖼 🛏 💻 ⊇

AAA ▼▼▼▼ **InnSuites Hotels & Suites Tempe/Phoenix**
Airport SH
(480) 897-7900. **$59-$129.** 1651 W Baseline Rd. I-10, exit 155 (Baseline Rd), just e. Ext corridors. **Pets:** Medium, other species. $25 one-time fee/pet. Designated rooms, service with restrictions, crate.

SAVE 🔊 ✕ 🛏 💻 🍴 ⊇ ✕

▼▼▼▼ **La Quinta Inn Phoenix (Sky Harbor South)** SH
(480) 967-4465. **$75-$125.** 911 S 48th St. I-10, exit 153 (Broadway Rd) eastbound; exit 153A (University Dr) westbound, 0.8 mi n; on south side of University Dr and east side of SR 143 (Hohokam Expwy). Ext corridors. **Pets:** Accepted.

ASK ✕ 🐾 🖼 🛏 💻 ⊇

▼ **Motel 6 #1315** M
(480) 945-9506. **Call for rates.** 1612 N Scottsdale Rd. Loop 202, exit 7, 0.6 mi n. Ext corridors. **Pets:** Large, other species. No service, supervision.

✕ ⊇

AAA ▼▼▼ **Quality Inn Airport/ASU** SH
(480) 774-2500. **$69-$129.** 1375 E University Dr. 0.5 mi e of Rural Rd. Int corridors. **Pets:** Accepted.

SAVE 🔊 ✕ 🖼 🛏 💻 ⊇

AAA ▼▼▼ **Ramada Limited** SH
(480) 413-1188. **$50-$94.** 1701 W Baseline Rd. I-10, exit 155 (Baseline Rd), just e. Ext corridors. **Pets:** Accepted.

SAVE ✕ 🐾 🖼 🛏 💻 ⊇

AAA ▼▼▼ **Ramada Limited Tempe-ASU** M
(480) 736-1700. **$55-$129.** 1915 E Apache Blvd. US 60 (Superstition Frwy), exit 175, 1.9 mi n on McClintock Dr, then 0.3 mi e. Ext corridors. **Pets:** Medium. $50 deposit/room. Service with restrictions, supervision.

SAVE 🔊 ✕ 🛏 💻 ⊇

▼▼▼ **Red Roof Inn Phoenix Airport** SH
(480) 449-3205. **$52-$72.** 2135 W 15th St. I-10, exit 153 (Broadway Rd), just nw on S 52nd St, then just w. Int corridors. **Pets:** Accepted.

✕ 🖼 ⊇

AAA ▼▼▼▼ **Residence Inn by Marriott** SH 🐾
(480) 756-2122. **$89-$199, 3 day notice.** 5075 S Priest Dr. I-10, exit 155 (Baseline Rd), 0.4 mi e, then just n. Ext/int corridors. **Pets:** Other species. $75 one-time fee/room.

SAVE 🔊 ✕ 🐾 🖼 🛏 💻 ⊇ ✕

▼▼▼ **Rodeway Inn Tempe Airport East** M
(480) 967-3000. **Call for rates.** 1550 S 52nd St. I-10, exit 153 (Broadway Rd), 0.3 mi ne. Ext corridors. **Pets:** Accepted.

✕ 🐾 🛏 💻 ⊇

AAA ▼▼▼▼ **Sheraton Phoenix Airport Hotel** LH 🐾
(480) 967-6600. **$119-$229.** 1600 S 52nd St. I-10, exit 153 (Broadway Rd), 0.3 mi ne. Int corridors. **Pets:** Medium. $50 deposit/room. Service with restrictions, supervision.

SAVE 🔊 ✕ 🐾 🖼 🛏 💻 🍴 ⊇ ✕

▼▼▼ **Studio 6 Extended Stay #6031** SH
(602) 414-4470. **$55-$65.** 4909 S Wendler Dr. I-10, exit 155 (Baseline Rd), just w, then 0.4 mi n. Ext corridors. **Pets:** Accepted.

🔊 ✕ 🖼 🛏 💻 ⊇

AAA ▼▼▼ **Tempe Mission Palms Hotel** SH
(480) 894-1400. **$105-$209.** 60 E 5th St. Just e of Mill Ave, 0.3 mi n of University Dr; downtown. Int corridors. **Pets:** Accepted.

SAVE 🔊 ✕ 🐾 🖼 🛏 💻 🍴 ⊇ ✕

▼▼ ▼ **Tempe Super 8** M
(480) 967-8891. **$34-$109.** 1020 E Apache Blvd. Just e of Rural Rd. Ext corridors. **Pets:** Medium, other species. $15 one-time fee/room. Designated rooms, service with restrictions, crate.

ASK ✕ 🛏 ⊇

AAA ▼▼▼▼ **Wyndham Buttes Resort** SH
(602) 225-9000. **$99-$219.** 2000 Westcourt Way. I-10, exit 153 (Broadway Rd) westbound, 0.8 mi w to 48th St, then 0.3 mi s; exit 48th St eastbound, 0.5 mi s. Int corridors. **Pets:** Small. $25 one-time fee/pet. Service with restrictions.

SAVE ✕ 🐾 💻 🍴 ⊇ ✕

YOUNGTOWN

AAA ▼▼▼▼ **Best Western Inn & Suites of Sun City** SH
(623) 933-8211. **$60-$130.** 11201 Grand Ave. On US 60, just se of 113th Ave. Ext/int corridors. **Pets:** Medium, other species. Designated rooms, service with restrictions, supervision.

SAVE 🔊 ✕ 🐾 🖼 🛏 💻 ⊇

END METROPOLITAN AREA

PINETOP-LAKESIDE

♦♦♦ ♦♦♦ Bear Mountain Inn & Suites SH
(928) 368-6600. **$49-$85.** 1637 W White Mountain Blvd. On SR 260.
Int corridors. **Pets:** Accepted.
SAVE SÓ ✕ ☎ ▣

♦♦♦ ♦♦♦ Best Western Inn of Pinetop M ❀
(928) 367-6667. **$79-$109.** 404 E White Mountain Blvd. On SR 260.
Ext corridors. **Pets:** Medium. $15 daily fee/pet. Service with restrictions,
supervision.
SAVE SÓ ✕ ☎ ▣

♦♦♦ ♦♦♦♦ Holiday Inn Express SH
(928) 367-6077. **$69-$119.** 431 E White Mountain Blvd. On SR 260. Int
corridors. **Pets:** Accepted.
SAVE SÓ ✕ ☎ ▣ ⊠

♦♦♦ Lazy Oaks Resort CA ❀
(928) 368-6203. **$69-$85 (no credit cards), 21 day notice.** 1075 Larson Rd. Jct SR 260, 0.8 mi s on Rainbow Lake Dr, then 0.6 mi w. Ext
corridors. **Pets:** Medium. Supervision.
☎ ▣ ⊠ 🗶 ☒

♦♦♦♦ Northwoods Resort CA
(928) 367-2966. **$79-$149, 14 day notice.** 165 E White Mountain Blvd.
On SR 260. Ext corridors. **Pets:** Other species. $12 daily fee/pet. No
service, supervision.
✕ ☎ ▣ ⊠ 🗶 ☒

♦♦♦ ♦♦♦ Super 8 Motel SH
(928) 367-3161. **$65-$75.** 1202 E White Mountain Blvd. On SR 260,
east end of town. Int corridors. **Pets:** Accepted.
SAVE SÓ ✕ ☎ ⊸

♦♦♦ ♦♦♦ Woodland Inn & Suites M
(928) 367-3636. **$69-$139, 3 day notice.** 458 E White Mountain Blvd.
On SR 260. Ext corridors. **Pets:** Medium, other species. $10 daily fee/pet.
Service with restrictions, supervision.
SAVE SÓ ✕ ☎ ▣

PRESCOTT

♦♦♦♦ Arizona Vacation Lodging CA
(928) 778-9573. **$479-$1050 (weekly), 14 day notice.** 5555 Onyx Dr.
Jct SR 89, 5 mi e on SR 69, 0.4 mi s on dirt/gravel road. Ext corridors.
Pets: Other species. $10 daily fee/pet. No service, crate.
✕ ☎ ▣ ⊠

♦♦♦ ♦♦♦ Best Western Prescottonian Motel M
(928) 445-3096. **$89-$109.** 1317 E Gurley St. On SR 89, just s of jct
SR 69. Ext corridors. **Pets:** Other species. Service with restrictions, supervision.
ASK SÓ ✕ ☎ ☎ ▣ ⊸

♦♦♦ ♦♦♦ Comfort Inn of Prescott M
(928) 778-5770. **$59-$169.** 1290 White Spar Rd. On SR 89, 1.5 mi s of
town center. Ext corridors. **Pets:** Medium, dogs only. $10 daily fee/pet.
Designated rooms, service with restrictions, supervision.
SAVE SÓ ✕ ☎ ☎ ▣

♦♦♦ ♦♦♦ Lynx Creek Farm Bed & Breakfast BB
(928) 778-9573. **$75-$170, 14 day notice.** 5555 Onyx Dr. Jct SR 89, 5
mi e on SR 69, 0.4 mi s on dirt/gravel road. Ext corridors. **Pets:** Other
species. $10 daily fee/pet. No service, crate.
✕ ☎ ▣ ⊸ ⊠ 🅦 ☒

♦♦♦ Motel 6 #0166 M
(928) 776-0160. **$45-$65.** 1111 E Sheldon St. 0.4 mi e of jct SR 89;
center. Ext corridors. **Pets:** Other species. Supervision.
SÓ ✕ ☎ ☎ ⊸

♦♦♦ ♦♦♦ Prescott Super 8 Motel M
(928) 776-1282. **$45-$75.** 1105 E Sheldon St. 0.4 mi e of jct SR 89. Int
corridors. **Pets:** Dogs only. $10 one-time fee/room. Service with restric-
tions, supervision.
ASK SÓ ✕ 🞪 ☎ ▣ ⊸

♦♦♦ ♦♦♦♦ Quality Inn & Suites and Conference
Center SH
(928) 777-0770. **$89-$209.** 4499 Hwy 69. On SR 69, 3.6 mi e of jct SR
89. Int corridors. **Pets:** Small, dogs only. $25 one-time fee/pet. Service
with restrictions, supervision.
SAVE SÓ ✕ ☎ ☎ ▣ ⑪ ⊸ ☒

PRESCOTT VALLEY

♦♦♦ ♦♦♦ Days Inn/Prescott Valley M
(928) 772-8600. **$79-$109.** 7875 E Hwy 69. On SR 69, corner of
Windsong Rd. Ext corridors. **Pets:** Other species. $50 deposit/room.
Service with restrictions.
SAVE SÓ ✕ ☎ ▣ ⊸

QUARTZSITE

♦♦♦ Super 8 Motel-Quartzsite M
(928) 927-8080. **$69-$134, 14 day notice.** 2050 W Dome Rock Rd.
I-10, exit 17, just s to Frontage Rd, then 0.6 mi w. Int corridors.
Pets: Accepted.
ASK ✕ ☎

RIO RICO

♦♦♦ ♦♦♦♦ Esplendor Resort at Rio Rico LH
(520) 281-1901. **$99-$159.** 1069 Camino Caralampi. I-19, exit 17 (Rio
Rico Dr), 0.5 mi w. Ext corridors. **Pets:** Other species. $25 one-time
fee/room. Service with restrictions.
SAVE SÓ ✕ ☾M 🞪 ☎ ▣ ⑪ ⊸ ☒

SAFFORD

♦♦♦ ♦♦♦ Best Western Desert Inn M
(928) 428-0521. **$65-$75.** 1391 W Thatcher Blvd. US 191, 1 mi w on
US 70. Ext corridors. **Pets:** Accepted.
SAVE SÓ ✕ ☎ ▣ ⊸

♦♦♦ ♦♦♦ Comfort Inn M
(928) 428-5851. **$67-$74.** 1578 W Thatcher Blvd. US 191, 1.3 mi w on
US 70. Ext corridors. **Pets:** Small. $10 daily fee/pet. Service with restric-
tions, supervision.
ASK SÓ ✕ ☎ ▣ ⊸

♦♦♦ ♦♦♦ Days Inn M
(928) 428-5000. **$69.** 520 E Hwy 70. US 191, 0.5 mi e. Ext corridors.
Pets: $10 daily fee/room. Service with restrictions, supervision.
SAVE SÓ ✕ ☾M 🞪 🞪 ☎ ▣ ⊸ ☒

♦♦♦ Econo Lodge M
(928) 348-0011. **$42-$46.** 225 E Hwy 70. Just e of jct US 191 and 70.
Ext corridors. **Pets:** Accepted.
ASK SÓ ✕ ☎ ⊸

♦♦♦ ♦♦♦ Quality Inn & Suites SH
(928) 428-3200. **$114-$184.** 420 E Hwy 70. US 191, 0.5 mi e. Ext/int
corridors. **Pets:** Medium. $10 daily fee/room. Service with restrictions,
crate.
ASK SÓ ✕ 🞪 ☎ ▣ ⊸ ☒

ST. JOHNS

♦♦♦ Days Inn M
(928) 337-4422. **Call for rates.** 125 E Commercial St. Center. Ext
corridors. **Pets:** Accepted.
✕ ☎

SEDONA

Best Western Inn of Sedona SH
(928) 282-3072. **$105-$179.** 1200 W Hwy 89A. Jct SR 179, 1.2 mi w. Ext corridors. **Pets:** Other species. $10 daily fee/room. Designated rooms, service with restrictions.

Desert Quail Inn M
(928) 284-1433. **$69-$139.** 6626 Hwy 179. On SR 179, 6.9 mi s of jct SR 89A. Ext corridors. **Pets:** Accepted.

El Portal Sedona BB
(928) 203-9405. **$225-$495.** 95 Portal Ln. Jct SR 89A, just s on SR 179, then just w. Ext/int corridors. **Pets:** Other species. Designated rooms, service with restrictions, supervision.

Hilton Sedona Resort & Spa LH
(928) 284-4040. **$209-$489, 3 day notice.** 90 Ridge Trail Dr. Jct SR 89A, 7.3 mi s on SR 179. Int corridors. **Pets:** Accepted.

Iris Garden Inn M
(928) 282-2552. **$79-$99, 3 day notice.** 390 Jordan Rd. Jct SR 179, 0.3 mi n on SR 89A, just w. Ext corridors. **Pets:** Accepted.

L'Auberge de Sedona Resort SH
(928) 282-1661. **$179-$479, 14 day notice.** 301 L'Auberge Ln. Jct SR 89A and 179, just n to L'Auberge Ln (east side of SR 89A), just n down the hill. Ext/int corridors. **Pets:** Other species. $75 one-time fee/room. Designated rooms, service with restrictions.

The Lodge at Sedona BB 🐾
(928) 204-1942. **$160-$325, 14 day notice.** 125 Kallof Pl. SR 179, 1.8 mi w on SR 89A, then just s. Ext/int corridors. **Pets:** Dogs only. $200 deposit/room, $35 daily fee/room. Designated rooms, service with restrictions, supervision.

Matterhorn Lodge M 🐾
(928) 282-7176. **$69-$129.** 230 Apple Ave. SR 89A, just w; uptown. Ext corridors. **Pets:** Large, other species. $10 daily fee/room. Designated rooms, service with restrictions, crate.

Red Rock Inn M
(928) 284-2487. **$59-$135.** 65 E Cortez Dr. 6.9 mi s on SR 179, from jct SR 89A, just e. Ext corridors. **Pets:** Accepted.

Sedona Real Inn SH 🐾
(928) 282-1414. **$99-$319.** 95 Arroyo Pinon. On SR 89A, 3 mi w of jct SR 179. Ext corridors. **Pets:** Small, other species. $20 one-time fee/pet. Designated rooms, service with restrictions, crate.

Sedona Super 8 SH
(928) 282-1533. **$69-$109.** 2545 W Hwy 89A. On SR 89A, 2.4 mi w of jct SR 179. Int corridors. **Pets:** Medium. $25 one-time fee/room. Service with restrictions, supervision.

Sky Ranch Lodge M
(928) 282-6400. **$75-$159.** Airport Rd. SR 179, 1 mi w on SR 89A, then 1 mi s on west side. Ext corridors. **Pets:** Other species. $10 daily fee/pet. Service with restrictions, supervision.

Village Lodge M
(928) 284-3626. **$49-$59.** 78 Bell Rock Blvd. Jct SR 89A, 6 mi s on SR 179, then just w; in Village of Oak Creek. Ext/int corridors. **Pets:** Medium, other species. Supervision.

SELIGMAN

Canyon Lodge M
(928) 422-3255. **$44-$47.** 114 E Chino Ave. I-40, exit 121, 1 mi n, then 1 mi e on Route 66. Ext corridors. **Pets:** Designated rooms, supervision.

SHOW LOW

Best Western Paint Pony Lodge M
(928) 537-5773. **$67-$140.** 581 W Deuce of Clubs Ave. On US 60 and SR 260. Ext corridors. **Pets:** Accepted.

Days Inn M
(928) 537-4356. **$71-$91.** 480 W Deuce of Clubs Ave. On US 60 and SR 260. Ext/int corridors. **Pets:** Medium. $10 one-time fee/room. Service with restrictions, supervision.

Kiva Motel M
(928) 537-4542. **$48-$58, 3 day notice.** 261 E Deuce of Clubs Ave. On US 60 and SR 260. Ext corridors. **Pets:** Medium, dogs only. $5 one-time fee/pet. Service with restrictions, supervision.

Motel 6 #4102 M
(928) 537-7694. **$50-$60.** 1941 E Deuce of Clubs Ave. Just e of jct SR 260. Ext corridors. **Pets:** Accepted.

Sleep Inn SH
(928) 532-7323. **$62-$89.** 1751 W Deuce of Clubs Ave. On SR 260, 0.5 mi w of US 60. Int corridors. **Pets:** Other species. $10 daily fee/room. Service with restrictions, supervision.

SIERRA VISTA

Best Western Mission Inn M
(520) 458-8500. **$72-$79.** 3460 E Fry Blvd. Just w of jct SR 90 and 92. Ext corridors. **Pets:** Medium, other species. $5 daily fee/pet. Service with restrictions, supervision.

Quality Inn SH
(520) 458-7900. **$69-$74.** 1631 S Hwy 92. On SR 92, 1 mi s of jct SR 90. Int corridors. **Pets:** $10 daily fee/pet. Designated rooms, service with restrictions.

Sierra Suites SH
(520) 459-4221. **$84-$104.** 391 E Fry Blvd. Jct SR 90 and 92, 2.2 mi w. Ext corridors. **Pets:** Small. $25 one-time fee/pet. Designated rooms, service with restrictions, supervision.

Super 8 Motel M
(520) 459-5380. **$45-$70.** 100 Fab Ave. Jct Business SR 90 and Fry Blvd, then just e of main gate to Fort Huachuca. Ext corridors. **Pets:** Dogs only. $10 one-time fee/room. Service with restrictions, supervision.

Windemere Hotel & Conference Center SH
(520) 459-5900. **$89-$109, 3 day notice.** 2047 S Hwy 92. 1.5 mi s of jct SR 90. Int corridors. **Pets:** Large. $50 deposit/pet. Service with restrictions, crate.

TAYLOR

🔺🔺 ▽▽▽ Silver Creek Inn M
(928) 536-2600. **$53-$69.** 825 N Main St. On SR 77. Ext corridors. **Pets:** Other species. $50 deposit/room, $10 daily fee/room. Service with restrictions, supervision.
[SAVE] [S♦] [✕] [🛏] [🖵]

TOMBSTONE

🔺🔺 ▽▽▽ Best Western Lookout Lodge SH ❀
(520) 457-2223. **$80-$106.** 801 US Hwy 80 W. On SR 80, 1 mi n. Ext corridors. **Pets:** Large. $20 daily fee/pet. Designated rooms, service with restrictions, crate.
[SAVE] [S♦] [✕] [🛏] [🖵] [🍴] [⊃]

🔺🔺 ▽▽▽▽ Holiday Inn Express Tombstone SH
(520) 457-9507. **$79-$129.** 1001 N Hwy 80. On SR 80, 1 mi n. Int corridors. **Pets:** Small. $20 one-time fee/pet. Service with restrictions, supervision.
[SAVE] [S♦] [✕] [⅊M] [🛏] [🖵] [⊃]

🔺🔺 ▽▽▽ Tombstone Motel M
(520) 457-3478. **$80-$100.** 502 E Fremont St. On SR 80; between 5th and 6th sts. Ext corridors. **Pets:** Small. $50 deposit/pet. Designated rooms, no service, crate.
[SAVE] [S♦] [✕] [🛏]

🔺🔺 ▽▽▽ Trail Riders Inn M
(520) 457-3573. **$55.** 13 N 7th St. Just e; center. Ext corridors. **Pets:** Dogs only. $6 daily fee/pet. Supervision.
[SAVE] [✕] [⊃]

TUBA CITY

🔺🔺 ▽▽▽ Quality Inn SH
(928) 283-4545. **$85-$110.** Main St & Moenave Rd. 1 mi n of US 160. Int corridors. **Pets:** Medium. $10 one-time fee/room. Service with restrictions, supervision.
[SAVE] [S♦] [✕] [🛏] [🖵] [🍴]

TUCSON METROPOLITAN AREA

CATALINA

▽▽ ▽▽ Super 8 Motel-Tucson/Catalina M
(520) 818-9500. **$51-$75.** 15691 N Oracle Rd. 4.6 mi n of Tangerine Rd. Ext/int corridors. **Pets:** Accepted.
[A$K] [S♦] [✕] [⅊] [🛏] [⊃]

GREEN VALLEY

🔺🔺 ▽▽▽▽ Baymont Inn & Suites SH
(520) 399-3736. **$62-$139.** 90 W Esperanza Blvd. I-19, exit 65, just w. Int corridors. **Pets:** Small, dogs only. $50 deposit/room. Designated rooms, service with restrictions, supervision.
[SAVE] [S♦] [✕] [⅊] [⅊] [🛏] [🖵] [⊃]

🔺🔺 ▽▽▽▽ Best Western Green Valley SH
(520) 625-2250. **$65-$124.** 111 S La Canada Dr. I-19, exit 65, just w, then just s. Int corridors. **Pets:** Small, dogs only. $10 daily fee/pet. Designated rooms, service with restrictions, supervision.
[SAVE] [S♦] [✕] [🛏] [🖵] [🍴] [⊃]

▽▽ ▽▽ Holiday Inn Express SH
(520) 625-0900. **$70-$135.** 19200 S I-19 Frontage Rd. I-19, exit 69 (Duval Mine Rd), west side of interstate, then just s. Int corridors. **Pets:** Designated rooms, supervision.
[A$K] [S♦] [✕] [⅊] [⅊] [🛏] [🖵] [⊃] [⊠]

MARANA

▽▽ ▽▽ Comfort Inn I-10 & Ina SH
(520) 579-7202. **$49-$159.** 4930 W Ina Rd. I-10, exit 248 (Ina Rd), just w. Int corridors. **Pets:** Accepted.
[A$K] [S♦] [✕] [⅊] [🛏] [🖵] [⊃]

▽▽ ▽▽ Park Inn SH
(520) 744-3382. **$39-$159.** 4910 W Ina Rd. I-10, exit 248 (Ina Rd), just w. Ext corridors. **Pets:** Accepted.
[A$K] [S♦] [✕] [⅊] [🛏] [🖵] [⊃]

🔺🔺 ▽▽▽▽ Ramada Limited & Suites SH
(520) 572-4235. **$59-$199.** 6020 W Hospitality Rd. I-10, exit 246 (Cortaro Rd), just w, then just n. Int corridors. **Pets:** Very small, dogs only. $10 daily fee/pet. Designated rooms, no service, supervision.
[SAVE] [S♦] [✕] [⅊M] [⅊] [🛏] [🖵] [⊃]

▽▽ ▽▽ Red Roof Inn Tucson North SH
(520) 744-8199. **$45-$72.** 4940 W Ina Rd. I-10, exit 248 (Ina Rd), just w. Int corridors. **Pets:** Small, other species. No service, supervision.
[✕] [⅊] [🛏] [⊃]

🔺🔺 ▽▽▽ Super 8 Motel SH
(520) 572-0300. **$59-$110.** 8351 N Cracker Barrel Rd. I-10, exit 246 (Cortaro Rd), just w. Int corridors. **Pets:** Accepted.
[SAVE] [S♦] [✕] [⅊] [🛏] [⊃]

ORO VALLEY

🔺🔺 ▽▽▽▽ Hilton Tucson El Conquistador Golf & Tennis Resort LH
(520) 544-5000. **$79-$269, 3 day notice.** 10000 N Oracle Rd. I-10, exit 248 (Ina Rd), 5.4 mi e, then 4.4 mi n. Ext/int corridors. **Pets:** Medium. $50 one-time fee/room. Designated rooms, service with restrictions, supervision.
[SAVE] [✕] [⅊M] [⅊] [🛏] [🖵] [🍴] [⊃] [⊠]

TUCSON

🔺🔺 ▽▽▽▽ AmeriSuites (Tucson/Airport) SH
(520) 295-0405. **$69-$179.** 6885 S Tucson Blvd. Just n of Tucson International Airport. Int corridors. **Pets:** Large. Service with restrictions.
[SAVE] [S♦] [✕] [⅊M] [⅊] [🛏] [🖵] [⊃]

▽▽ ▽▽ Arizona Plaza Hotel SH
(520) 740-0123. **$49-$99.** 1601 N Oracle Rd. I-10, exit 256 (Grant Rd), 0.8 mi e, then 0.6 mi s. Ext/int corridors. **Pets:** Accepted.
[A$K] [S♦] [✕] [⅊] [🖵] [⊃]

🔺🔺 ▽▽ Best Value Inn-Tucson M
(520) 884-5800. **$50-$120.** 810 E Benson Hwy. I-10, exit 262, just s. Ext corridors. **Pets:** $25 deposit/room. Service with restrictions, supervision.
[SAVE] [S♦] [✕] [🛏] [⊃]

🔺🔺 ▽▽▽ Best Western Executive Inn SH
(520) 791-7551. **$45-$139.** 333 W Drachman St. I-10, exit 257 (Speedway Blvd), 0.4 mi e to Main St, then 0.3 mi n. Int corridors. **Pets:** Other species. $35 one-time fee/room.
[SAVE] [S♦] [✕] [⅊] [🛏] [🖵] [🍴] [⊃]

🔺🔺 ▽▽▽▽ Best Western InnSuites Hotel & Suites Tucson-Catalina Foothills SH ❀
(520) 297-8111. **$59-$139.** 6201 N Oracle Rd. I-10, exit 250 (Orange Grove Rd), 4 mi e, then just s. Ext corridors. **Pets:** Medium, other species. $25 one-time fee/pet. Designated rooms, service with restrictions, crate.
[SAVE] [S♦] [✕] [🛏] [🖵] [⊃] [⊠]

♦♦ Clarion Hotel-Randolph Park SH
(520) 795-0330. **$73-$126.** 102 N Alvernon. Jct Campbell Rd, 2.2 mi e on Broadway, then just n. Ext/int corridors. **Pets:** $25 one-time fee/room. Designated rooms, service with restrictions, supervision.

♦♦♦ Clarion Santa Rita Hotel & Suites SH
(520) 622-4000. **Call for rates.** 88 E Broadway Blvd. I-10, exit 258 (Broadway Blvd/Congress St), 0.6 mi e. Ext/int corridors. **Pets:** Accepted.

♦♦♦ Comfort Suites SH
(520) 295-4400. **$79-$119.** 6935 S Tucson Blvd. Just n of Tucson International Airport. Int corridors. **Pets:** Medium. $25 one-time fee/room. Crate.

♦♦ Comfort Suites at Tucson Mall SH ♣
(520) 888-6676. **$69-$149, 30 day notice.** 515 W Auto Mall Dr. I-10, exit 254 (Prince Rd), 1.9 mi e, then 1.2 mi n. Int corridors. **Pets:** Other species. $10 one-time fee/pet. Service with restrictions, crate.

♦♦♦ Comfort Suites Tanque Verde/Sabino Canyon SH
(520) 298-2300. **$79-$179.** 7007 E Tanque Verde Rd. Jct Grand Rd, 0.4 mi ne. Ext corridors. **Pets:** Small. $25 one-time fee/pet. Service with restrictions, supervision.

♦♦♦ Country Inn & Suites By Carlson SH
(520) 575-9255. **$59-$139.** 7411 N Oracle Rd. SR 77 (Oracle Rd), just n of Ina Rd. Ext corridors. **Pets:** Accepted.

♦♦ Doubletree Hotel at Reid Park LH
(520) 881-4200. **$119-$289.** 445 S Alvernon Way. I-10, exit 259 (22nd St), 4 mi e, then just n. Ext/int corridors. **Pets:** Accepted.

♦♦ Econo Lodge M
(520) 622-6714. **$49-$109.** 1136 N Stone Ave. I-10, exit 257 (St Mary Speedway) eastbound, just e, then just n. Ext corridors. **Pets:** Dogs only. $10 deposit/pet, $10 one-time fee/room. Designated rooms, service with restrictions, supervision.

♦♦ Embassy Suites Hotel @ Tucson International Airport SH
(520) 573-0700. **$109-$229.** 7051 S Tucson Blvd. At entrance to Tucson International Airport. Ext corridors. **Pets:** Accepted.

♦♦ Ghost Ranch Lodge M ♣
(520) 791-7565. **$46-$130.** 801 W Miracle Mile. I-10, exit 255 (Miracle Mile), 1 mi e, just w of Oracle Rd (SR 77). Ext corridors. **Pets:** Medium, other species. Designated rooms, service with restrictions, supervision.

♦♦♦ Hampton Inn North SH
(520) 206-0602. **$79-$149.** 1375 W Grant Rd. I-10, exit 256 (Grant Rd), just w. Int corridors. **Pets:** Medium. Designated rooms, service with restrictions, supervision.

♦♦ Holiday Inn Express Hotel & Suites Tucson Airport SH
(520) 889-6600. **$79-$149.** 2548 E Medina Rd. 0.5 mi n of entrance to Tucson International Airport. Int corridors. **Pets:** Small. $50 deposit/pet. Service with restrictions, supervision.

♦♦ InnSuites Hotels & Suites Tucson City Center SH ♣
(520) 622-3000. **$59-$139.** 475 N Granada Ave. I-10, exit 258 (Broadway Blvd/Congress St), just e, then 0.4 mi n. Ext/int corridors. **Pets:** Medium, other species. $25 one-time fee/pet. Designated rooms, service with restrictions, crate.

♦♦♦ La Posada Lodge & Casitas SH
(520) 887-4800. **$79-$189.** 5900 N Oracle Rd. 0.5 mi s of Orange Grove Rd. Ext corridors. **Pets:** Accepted.

♦♦♦ La Quinta Inn & Suites Tucson Airport SH
(520) 573-3333. **$75-$165.** 7001 S Tucson Blvd. Just n of Tucson International Airport. Int corridors. **Pets:** Accepted.

♦♦♦ La Quinta Inn Downtown SH
(520) 624-4455. **$49-$109.** 750 Starr Pass Blvd. I-10, exit 259 (Starr Pass Blvd), just w. Int corridors. **Pets:** Other species. Designated rooms, service with restrictions, supervision.

♦♦♦ La Quinta Inn Tucson (East) SH
(520) 747-1414. **$75-$135.** 6404 E Broadway. Just e of Wilmot Rd. Ext corridors. **Pets:** Accepted.

♦♦♦ The Lodge At Ventana Canyon LH
(520) 577-4000. **$95-$497, 21 day notice.** 6200 N Clubhouse Ln. I-10, exit 256 (Grant Rd), 8.6 mi e to Tanque Verde Rd, 0.6 mi e to Sabino Canyon Rd, 2 mi n, then 3.2 mi n on Kolb Rd. Ext/int corridors. **Pets:** Accepted.

♦♦ Lodge on the Desert SH ♣
(520) 325-3366. **$89-$219.** 306 N Alvernon Way. I-10, exit 258 (Broadway Blvd/Congress St), 4 mi e, then just n. Ext corridors. **Pets:** $15 daily fee/room. Service with restrictions, supervision.

♦♦♦♦ Loews Ventana Canyon Resort LH ♣
(520) 299-2020. **$145-$445, 7 day notice.** 7000 N Resort Dr. I-10, exit 256 (Grant Rd), 8.6 mi e, 0.6 mi ne on Tanque Verde Rd, 2 mi n on Sabino Canyon Rd, then 3.5 mi n on Kolb Rd. Ext/int corridors. **Pets:** Other species. Designated rooms, service with restrictions, supervision.

♦ Motel 6 Tucson-22nd Street #1196 M
(520) 624-2516. **$41-$85.** 1222 S Freeway Rd. I-10, exit 259 (Starr Pass Blvd), just w, then just s on frontage road. Ext corridors. **Pets:** Accepted.

♦ Motel 6 Tucson-Congress Street #50 M
(520) 628-1339. **$41-$85.** 960 S Freeway. I-10, exit 258 (Broadway Blvd/Congress St), 0.7 mi s on west side of interstate. Ext corridors. **Pets:** Accepted.

♦ Motel 6 Tucson North #1127 M
(520) 744-9300. **$42-$85.** 4630 W Ina Rd. I-10, exit 248 (Ina Rd), just e to Camino de Oeste, then just n. Int corridors. **Pets:** Accepted.

♦♦ Park Inn Tucson Airport SH
(520) 294-2500. **$59-$119.** 2803 E Valencia Rd. 1 mi ne of Tucson International Airport; just e of Tucson Blvd. Ext/int corridors. **Pets:** Accepted.

▼▼▼▼ Radisson Hotel City Center LH
(520) 624-8711. **$71-$219.** 181 W Broadway. I-10, exit 258 (Broadway Blvd/Congress St), just e. Int corridors. **Pets:** Medium, other species. $25 one-time fee/room. Designated rooms, service with restrictions, supervision.
[ASK] [S6] [X] [🏠] [💻] [🍴] [≈]

⬧ ▼▼▼▼ Radisson Suites Tucson LH
(520) 721-7100. **$59-$149.** 6555 E Speedway Blvd. Just e of Wilmot Rd. Ext corridors. **Pets:** Medium. $50 one-time fee/room. Designated rooms, service with restrictions, supervision.
[SAVE] [S6] [X] [🏠] [💻] [🍴] [≈] [X]

⬧ ▼▼◆ Ramada Inn & Suites Foothills Resort SH
(520) 886-9595. **$49-$199.** 6944 E Tanque Verde Rd. Jct Campbell Ave, 5.5 mi e on Grant Rd, then just ne. Ext corridors. **Pets:** Small, other species. $25 one-time fee/pet. Service with restrictions, crate.
[SAVE] [S6] [X] [🏠] [💻] [≈] [X]

⬧ ▼▼◆ Ramada Limited Tucson West M 🐾
(520) 622-6491. **$66-$115.** 665 N Freeway. I-10, exit 257 (St. Mary's Rd/Speedway Blvd), just s. Ext corridors. **Pets:** Large, other species. Service with restrictions.
[SAVE] [S6] [X] [🏠] [💻] [≈]

▼ Red Roof Inn-Tucson South M
(520) 571-1400. **$62-$72.** 3704 E Irvington Rd. I-10, exit 264 westbound; exit 264B eastbound. Ext corridors. **Pets:** Accepted.
[X] [🏠] [💻] [≈]

⬧ ▼▼▼▼ Residence Inn by Marriott SH
(520) 721-0991. **$89-$209, 10 day notice.** 6477 E Speedway Blvd. Just e of Wilmot Rd. Ext corridors. **Pets:** Accepted.
[SAVE] [X] [🏠] [🏠] [💻] [≈] [X]

⬧ ▼▼▼▼ Riverpark Inn SH
(520) 622-6611. **$59-$149.** 350 S Freeway. I-10, exit 258 (Broadway Blvd/Congress St), just w, then 0.4 mi s. Ext/int corridors. **Pets:** Accepted.
[SAVE] [S6] [X] [🏠] [💻] [🍴] [≈]

⬧ ▼▼▼ Rodeway Inn I-10 & Grant Rd M
(520) 622-7791. **$59-$139, 3 day notice.** 1365 W Grant Rd. I-10, exit 256 (Grant Rd), just w. Ext corridors. **Pets:** Accepted.
[SAVE] [S6] [X] [🏠] [🏠] [💻] [🍴] [≈]

▼▼▼▼ Sheraton Tucson Hotel & Suites SH
(520) 323-6262. **$149-$279.** 5151 E Grant Rd. Jct Campbell Ave, 3.6 mi e. Ext/int corridors. **Pets:** Medium, dogs only. Service with restrictions, supervision.
[ASK] [S6] [X] [&M] [🏠] [🏠] [🏠] [💻] [🍴] [≈] [X]

▼▼ Studio 6 Extended Stay #6002 M
(520) 746-0030. **$48-$73.** 4950 S Outlet Center Dr. I-10, exit 264A eastbound; exit 264B westbound, just s, then just nw on Julian Dr. Ext corridors. **Pets:** Accepted.
[S6] [X] [🏠] [🏠] [💻] [≈]

⬧ ▼ Super 8 Central East M
(520) 790-6021. **$54-$110, 3 day notice.** 1990 S Craycroft Rd. I-10, exit 265 (Alvernon Way), 4 mi n to Golflinks Rd, 2 mi e, then just n. Ext corridors. **Pets:** Very small. $5 daily fee/pet, $25 one-time fee/pet. Designated rooms, service with restrictions, supervision.
[SAVE] [S6] [X] [🏠] [≈]

⬧ ▼▼▼▼ TownePlace Suites by Marriott SH
(520) 292-9697. **$89-$159.** 405 W Rudasill Rd. Jct Orange Grove Rd, 0.5 mi s on Oracle Rd, then just e. Int corridors. **Pets:** Large, other species. $75 one-time fee/pet. Service with restrictions, crate.
[SAVE] [S6] [X] [🏠] [🏠] [💻] [≈]

⬧ ▼▼▼▼ The Westin La Paloma Resort & Spa LH 🐾
(520) 742-6000. **$99-$469, 7 day notice.** 3800 E Sunrise Dr. From SR 77 (Oracle Rd), 4.6 mi e on Ina Rd via Skyline and Sunrise drs, just s on Via Palomita. Ext corridors. **Pets:** Medium, other species. Service with restrictions, crate.
[SAVE] [S6] [X] [🏠] [🏠] [💻] [🍴] [≈] [X]

⬧ ▼▼▼ Westward Look Resort LH
(520) 297-1151. **$79-$319, 3 day notice.** 245 E Ina Rd. I-10, exit 248 (Ina Rd), 6 mi e, then just n on Westward Look Dr. Ext corridors. **Pets:** Accepted.
[SAVE] [S6] [X] [🏠] [🏠] [🏠] [💻] [🍴] [≈] [X]

⬧ ▼▼▼ Windmill Suites at St. Philip's Plaza SH
(520) 577-0007. **$79-$179.** 4250 N Campbell Ave. I-10, exit 254 (Prince Rd), 4 mi e, then 1 mi n. Int corridors. **Pets:** Accepted.
[SAVE] [S6] [X] [🏠] [🏠] [≈] [X]

END METROPOLITAN AREA

WICKENBURG

▼▼ AmericInn SH
(928) 684-5461. **$66-$92, 10 day notice.** 850 E Wickenburg Way. 1.3 mi se on US 60. Int corridors. **Pets:** Small. $6 daily fee/pet. Service with restrictions, supervision.
[ASK] [S6] [X] [🏠] [🏠] [💻] [🍴] [≈]

⬧ ▼▼▼▼ Best Western Rancho Grande SH 🐾
(928) 684-5445. **$64-$111.** 293 E Wickenburg Way. On US 60; center. Ext corridors. **Pets:** Other species. $8 daily fee/room. Service with restrictions.
[SAVE] [S6] [X] [🏠] [🏠] [💻] [≈] [X]

▼▼ Super 8 Motel M
(928) 684-0808. **$70-$75.** 975 N Tegner Rd. 1 mi n of US 60 and 93. Ext/int corridors. **Pets:** Accepted.
[ASK] [S6] [X] [🏠] [🏠] [💻]

WILLCOX

⬧ ▼▼ Best Western Plaza Inn SH
(520) 384-3556. **$70.** 1100 W Rex Allen Dr. I-10, exit 340, just s. Ext corridors. **Pets:** Medium. $15 daily fee/pet. Service with restrictions, supervision.
[SAVE] [S6] [X] [🏠] [🏠] [💻] [🍴] [≈]

⬧ ▼▼▼ Days Inn M
(520) 384-4222. **$48-$60.** 724 N Bisbee Ave. I-10, exit 340, just s. Ext corridors. **Pets:** Large. $5 daily fee/pet. No service, supervision.
[SAVE] [S6] [X] [🏠] [≈]

▼ Motel 6 Willcox #410 M
(520) 384-2201. **$35-$45.** 921 N Bisbee Ave. I-10, exit 340, just s. Ext corridors. **Pets:** Accepted.
[S6] [X] [🏠] [≈]

WILLIAMS

⬧ ▼ A Westerner Motel M 🐾
(928) 635-4312. **$24-$52.** 530 W Route 66. I-40, exit 161, 1.3 mi e. Ext corridors. **Pets:** Medium, other species. $5 daily fee/pet. Service with restrictions.
[SAVE] [S6] [X] [🏠]

Budget Host Inn M
(928) 635-4415. **$20-$48.** 620 W Route 66. I-40, exit 161, 1.3 mi e. Ext corridors. **Pets:** Medium. $10 daily fee/pet. Designated rooms, no service, supervision.
[SAVE] [S6] [X] [B]

The Canyon Motel M ❧
(928) 635-9371. **$40-$90, 7 day notice.** 1900 E Rodeo Rd/Route 66. I-40, exit 165 (Grand Canyon), 1 mi s on Business Loop 40, then just w. Ext corridors. **Pets:** Dogs only. $7 daily fee/pet. Designated rooms, service with restrictions, crate.
[SAVE] [X] [B] [D] [≈] [X] [☎]

Days Inn M
(928) 635-4051. **$46-$108.** 2488 W Route 66. I-40, exit 161, just e. Int corridors. **Pets:** Accepted.
[SAVE] [S6] [X] [∅] [B] [≈]

El Rancho Motel M ❧
(928) 635-2552. **$32-$68.** 617 E Route 66. I-40, exit 163, 0.5 mi s, then 0.4 mi e. Ext corridors. **Pets:** $5 daily fee/pet. Designated rooms, service with restrictions, supervision.
[SAVE] [S6] [X] [B] [D] [≈]

Highlander Motel M
(928) 635-2541. **$25-$48.** 533 W Route 66. I-40, exit 161, 1.3 mi e. Ext corridors. **Pets:** Small. $5 one-time fee/pet. Service with restrictions, supervision.
[SAVE] [S6] [X]

Holiday Inn Williams SH
(928) 635-4114. **$69-$139.** 950 N Grand Canyon Blvd. I-40, exit 163, just s. Int corridors. **Pets:** Other species. No service.
[SAVE] [X] [&M] [∅] [≈] [B] [D] [†1] [≈]

Motel 6-4122 M
(928) 635-9000. **$32-$60.** 831 W Route 66. I-40, exit 161, 1 mi e. Int corridors. **Pets:** Medium, other species. Service with restrictions, supervision.
[SAVE] [S6] [X] [B] [≈]

Mountainside Inn SH
(928) 635-4431. **$49-$99.** 642 E Route 66. I-40, exit 163, 0.6 mi s, then just e. Ext corridors. **Pets:** Accepted.
[SAVE] [S6] [X] [∅] [B] [D] [†1] [≈]

Quality Inn Mountain Ranch Resort SH
(928) 635-2693. **$59-$119.** 6701 E Mountain Ranch Rd. I-40, exit 171 (Deer Farm Rd), just s. Ext corridors. **Pets:** $25 one-time fee/room. Service with restrictions, supervision.
[SAVE] [S6] [X] [B] [D] [†1] [≈] [X]

Rodeway Inn M
(928) 635-1412. **$39-$79.** 750 N Grand Canyon Blvd. I-40, exit 163, just s. Int corridors. **Pets:** Very small. $10 daily fee/pet. No service, supervision.
[SAVE] [S6] [X] [B]

Travelodge Williams M
(928) 635-2651. **$35-$69.** 430 E Route 66. I-40, exit 163, 0.5 mi s, then just e. Ext corridors. **Pets:** Dogs only. $7.50 one-time fee/pet. Service with restrictions, supervision.
[SAVE] [S6] [X] [B] [D] [≈]

WINDOW ROCK

Quality Inn Navajo Nation Capital SH
(928) 871-4108. **$75-$80.** 48 W Hwy 264. Center. Ext corridors. **Pets:** $50 deposit/pet. Service with restrictions, supervision.
[SAVE] [S6] [X] [B] [D] [†1]

WINSLOW

Best Western Adobe Inn SH
(928) 289-4638. **$67-$95.** 1701 N Park Dr. I-40, exit 253. Int corridors. **Pets:** Small, other species. $10 daily fee/pet. Service with restrictions, supervision.
[SAVE] [S6] [X] [&] [B] [D] [†1] [≈]

Days Inn SH
(928) 289-1010. **$50-$80.** 2035 W Hwy 66. I-40, exit 252, just s. Int corridors. **Pets:** Accepted.
[SAVE] [X] [&] [B] [≈]

Econo Lodge SH
(928) 289-4687. **$49-$89.** 1706 North Park Dr. I-40, exit 253. Ext corridors. **Pets:** Small, other species. $5 one-time fee/room. Service with restrictions, crate.
[SAVE] [S6] [X] [∅] [B] [D] [≈]

Holiday Inn Express-Winslow SH
(928) 289-2960. **$99.** 816 Transcon Ln. I-40, exit 255, just n. Int corridors. **Pets:** Accepted.
[ASK] [X] [&] [B] [D] [≈]

La Posada Hotel SH ❧
(928) 289-4366. **$89-$129, 3 day notice.** 303 E 2nd St. I-40, exit 252, s to Route 66, then 0.5 mi e; downtown. Int corridors. **Pets:** Other species. $10 one-time fee/room. Designated rooms, service with restrictions, supervision.
[ASK] [S6] [X] [†1] [☎]

Motel 6 Winslow #4012 M
(928) 289-9581. **$39-$57.** 520 W Desmond St. I-40, exit 253, just w on North Park Dr. Int corridors. **Pets:** Accepted.
[SAVE] [S6] [X] [&] [B] [≈]

Super 8 Motel M
(928) 289-4606. **$48-$78.** 1916 W Third St. I-40, exit 252, just e. Int corridors. **Pets:** Accepted.
[SAVE] [S6] [X] [B]

Travelodge Townhouse of Winslow M
(928) 289-4611. **$50-$95.** 1914 W Third St. I-40, exit 252, 0.5 mi e. Ext corridors. **Pets:** Accepted.
[SAVE] [S6] [X] [B] [D] [≈]

YUMA

Best Western Coronado Motor Hotel M
(928) 783-4453. **$69-$129.** 233 4th Ave. I-8, exit 4th Ave eastbound, 0.5 mi s; exit 1 (Giss Pkwy) westbound, 0.5 mi w. Ext corridors. **Pets:** Accepted.
[SAVE] [S6] [X] [B] [D] [†1] [≈]

Best Western InnSuites Hotel & Suites Yuma SH ❧
(928) 783-8341. **$59-$109.** 1450 Castle Dome Ave. I-8, exit 2 (16th St/US 95), just ne. Ext corridors. **Pets:** Medium, other species. $25 one-time fee/pet. Designated rooms, service with restrictions, crate.
[SAVE] [S6] [X] [∅] [B] [D] [†1] [≈] [X]

Clarion Suites SH
(928) 726-4830. **$93-$149.** 2600 S 4th Ave. I-8, exit 2 (16 St/US 95) eastbound, 1 mi w, then 1.3 mi s; exit 3 (SR 280) westbound, 0.5 mi s, then 2 mi w. Ext corridors. **Pets:** Accepted.
[ASK] [S6] [X] [&] [B] [D] [≈]

Comfort Inn SH
(928) 782-1200. **$89-$129.** 1691 S Riley Ave. I-8, exit 2 (16th St/US 95), just w. Int corridors. **Pets:** $10 daily fee/room. Service with restrictions, supervision.
[ASK] [S6] [X] [&M] [&] [B] [D] [≈]

ⒶⒶⒶ ♦♦ Howard Johnson Inn 🆂🅷
(928) 344-1420. **$70-$91.** 3181 S 4th Ave. I-8, exit 3E (SR 280 S), 1 mi s to 32nd St, then 2 mi w. Ext corridors. **Pets:** Accepted.
SAVE ✖ 🔧 🖥 ➿

♦♦ Microtel Inn & Suites 🆂🅷
(928) 345-1777. **Call for rates.** 11274 S Fortuna Rd, Suite H. I-8, exit 12 (Fortuna Rd), just s, then w on Frontage Rd. Int corridors. **Pets:** Accepted.
✖ 🔧 🖥 ➿

♦ Motel 6 Yuma East #1031 🅼
(928) 782-9521. **$37-$63.** 1445 E 16th St. I-8, exit 2 (16th St/US 95), just e. Ext corridors. **Pets:** Accepted.
✖ ➿

♦♦ Oak Tree Inn 🆂🅷
(928) 539-9000. **Call for rates.** 1730 Sunridge Dr. I-8, exit 2 (16th St/US 95), just e, then just s. Int corridors. **Pets:** $10 daily fee/pet. Service with restrictions, supervision.
✖ 🔧 🖥 ➿

ⒶⒶⒶ ♦♦ Quality Inn Airport 🆂🅷
(928) 726-4721. **$64-$154.** 711 E 32nd St. I-8, exit 3E (SR 280), 1.2 mi s, then 1.9 mi w. Ext corridors. **Pets:** Small. $25 one-time fee/pet. Service with restrictions, crate.
SAVE ✖ 🔧 🖥 🍽 ➿

ⒶⒶⒶ ♦♦ Ramada Inn Chilton Conference Center 🆂🅷
(928) 344-1050. **$94-$119.** 300 E 32nd St. I-8 business loop, 2.3 mi s of jct US 95. Ext corridors. **Pets:** Accepted.
SAVE ✖ 🔧 🖥 🍽 ➿

♦♦ Shilo Inn Hotel-Yuma 🆂🅷
(928) 782-9511. **$134-$168.** 1550 S Castle Dome Rd. I-8, exit 2 (16th St/US 95), just ne. Int corridors. **Pets:** Large, other species. $10 daily fee/pet. Service with restrictions, crate.
ASK ✖ 🔧 🖥 🍽 ➿ ✖

ⒶⒶⒶ ♦♦ Yuma Cabana Motel 🅼
(928) 783-8311. **$42-$69.** 2151 S 4th Ave. I-8, exit 2 (16th St/US 95), 1 mi w, then 0.5 mi s. Int corridors. **Pets:** Accepted.
SAVE ✖ 🔧 ➿

♦♦ Yuma Super 8 Motel 🆂🅷
(928) 782-2000. **$59-$109.** 1688 S Riley Ave. I-8, exit 2 (16th St/US 95), just w. Int corridors. **Pets:** $10 daily fee/room. Service with restrictions, supervision.
ASK ✖ 🔧 🖥 ➿

ARKANSAS

ALMA

▽▽▽ **Alma Inn and Suites** SH
(479) 632-4141. **$49-$70.** 439 Hwy 71 N. I-40, exit 13, just n. Ext/int corridors. **Pets:** Other species. Designated rooms, service with restrictions, supervision.
[ASK] [S⌀] [✕] [🛏] [🖵]

ARKADELPHIA

◆◆◆ ▽▽▽ **Best Western-Continental Inn** SH
(870) 246-5592. **$54-$99.** 136 Valley St. I-30, exit 78, just e. Ext corridors. **Pets:** Accepted.
[SAVE] [S⌀] [✕] [🔥] [🛏] [🖵] [≈]

▽▽▽ **Comfort Inn** SH
(870) 246-3800. **$63-$80.** 100 Crystal Palace Dr. I-30, exit 78, just sw. Int corridors. **Pets:** Accepted.
[ASK] [S⌀] [✕] [🛏] [🖵] [≈]

◆◆◆ ▽▽▽ **Super 8 Motel** SH
(870) 246-8585. **$61-$65.** 118 Valley St. I-30, exit 78, just e. Ext corridors. **Pets:** $5 daily fee/pet. Service with restrictions, supervision.
[SAVE] [S⌀] [✕] [🛏] [≈]

BATESVILLE

▽▽▽ **Ramada Inn of Batesville** SH
(870) 698-1800. **$74-$79.** 1325 N St Louis St. 1 mi n on US 167. Ext corridors. **Pets:** Medium. Service with restrictions, crate.
[ASK] [S⌀] [✕] [🔊] [🛏] [🖵] [🍴] [≈]

BEEBE

▽▽▽ **Days Inn** SH
(501) 882-2008. **$59-$99, 3 day notice.** 100 Tammy Ln. US 67/167, exit 28, just e. Ext corridors. **Pets:** Small, dogs only. $10 daily fee/pet. Service with restrictions, supervision.
[ASK] [S⌀] [✕] [🔥] [🛏] [🖵] [≈]

BENTON

◆◆◆ ▽▽▽ **Best Inn of Benton** SH
(501) 776-1515. **$40-$55.** 1221 Hot Springs Rd. I-30, exit 117. Int corridors. **Pets:** $5 daily fee/pet. Designated rooms, service with restrictions, supervision.
[SAVE] [S⌀] [✕] [🛏]

▽▽▽ **Days Inn** SH
(501) 776-3200. **$41-$55, 10 day notice.** 17701 I-30. I-30, exit 118, on eastbound service road. Ext corridors. **Pets:** Accepted.
[ASK] [S⌀] [✕] [🔊] [🛏] [≈]

BENTONVILLE

▽▽▽▽ **TownePlace Suites by Marriott Bentonville/Rogers** SH 🐾
(479) 621-0202. **$59-$169.** 3100 SE 14th St. I-540, exit 86, just e. Int corridors. **Pets:** Other species. $75 one-time fee/room.
[ASK] [S⌀] [✕] [▬M] [🔊] [🔥] [🛏] [🖵] [≈]

BLYTHEVILLE

▽▽▽ **Comfort Inn of Blytheville** SH
(870) 763-7081. **$55-$75.** 1520 E Main. I-55, exit 67, just w. Ext corridors. **Pets:** Accepted.
[ASK] [S⌀] [✕] [🛏] [🖵] [🍴] [≈]

▽▽▽ **Hampton Inn** SH
(870) 763-5220. **$67-$74.** 301 N Access Rd. I-55, exit 67, just nw. Ext corridors. **Pets:** Small, other species. $10 one-time fee/pet. Designated rooms, no service.
[✕] [🖵] [🍴] [≈]

▽▽▽ **Holiday Inn** SH
(870) 763-5800. **$79-$109.** 1121 E Main. I-55, exit 67, just w. Ext/int corridors. **Pets:** Medium, other species. $25 one-time fee/room. Designated rooms, service with restrictions, supervision.
[✕] [🛏] [🖵] [🍴] [≈] [✕]

▽▽▽ **Pear Tree Inn By Drury** SH
(870) 763-2300. **$50-$74.** 239 N Service Rd. I-55, exit 67, just nw. Int corridors. **Pets:** Large, other species. Service with restrictions, supervision.
[ASK] [✕] [🔊] [🛏] [🖵]

BRYANT

▽▽▽ **Best Value Inn & Suites** M
(501) 653-7800. **$49-$59.** 407 W Commerce St. I-30, exit 123, just sw. Ext corridors. **Pets:** Medium, dogs only. $6 daily fee/pet. Designated rooms, service with restrictions, supervision.
[ASK] [S⌀] [✕] [🛏] [🖵]

▽▽▽ **Super 8 Motel** M
(501) 847-7888. **$52-$57.** 201 Dell Dr. I-30, exit 123, just e. Ext corridors. **Pets:** $20 deposit/pet. Service with restrictions, supervision.
[ASK] [S⌀] [✕] [🛏]

CABOT

▽▽▽ **Days Inn of Cabot** M
(501) 843-0145. **$56-$61.** 1114 W Main St. US 67/167, exit 19 (SR 89), just e. Ext corridors. **Pets:** $5 daily fee/pet. Designated rooms, service with restrictions, crate.
[ASK] [S⌀] [✕] [🛏] [≈]

▽▽▽ **Super 8 of Cabot** M
(501) 941-3748. **$56-$61.** 15 Ryeland Dr. US 67/167, exit 19 (SR 89), just e. Ext corridors. **Pets:** $5 daily fee/pet. Service with restrictions, crate.
[ASK] [S⌀] [✕] [🛏] [≈]

CAMDEN

▽▽▽ **Holiday Inn Express** SH 🐾
(870) 836-8100. **$75-$99.** 1450 Hwy 278 SW. 1 mi w of jct US 79 and 278. Int corridors. **Pets:** Medium. Designated rooms, service with restrictions, supervision.
[ASK] [S⌀] [✕] [▬M] [🔊] [🛏] [🖵] [≈]

CARLISLE

△△△ ▽▽▽ Best Western Carlisle 🆂🅷
(870) 552-7566. **$59-$79, 14 day notice.** 1505 Bankhead Dr. I-40, exit 183, just s. Ext corridors. **Pets:** Accepted.
🆂🅰🆅🅴 🆂🅾 ⊠ 💻 ⚓

CLARKSVILLE

△△△ ▽▽▽ Best Western Sherwood Inn 🆂🅷
(479) 754-7900. **$39-$59, 10 day notice.** 1203 S Rogers Ave. I-40, exit 58, just n. Ext corridors. **Pets:** Other species. Service with restrictions, supervision.
🆂🅰🆅🅴 🆂🅾 ⊠ 🖬 💻 ⚓

△△△ ▽▽▽ Comfort Inn 🆂🅷
(479) 754-3000. **$60-$130.** 1167 S Rogers Ave. I-40, exit 58, just n. Ext corridors. **Pets:** Medium. $20 daily fee/room. Designated rooms, service with restrictions, supervision.
🆂🅰🆅🅴 🆂🅾 ⊠ 🖬 💻 ⚓

CONWAY

△△△ ▽▽▽ Comfort Inn 🆂🅷
(501) 329-0300. **$60-$84.** 150 Hwy 65 N. I-40, exit 125, just n. Ext corridors. **Pets:** Medium. $20 one-time fee/room. Service with restrictions, supervision.
🆂🅰🆅🅴 🆂🅾 ⊠ 🖉 🖬 💻 ⚓

△△△ ▽▽▽ Days Inn 🆂🅷
(501) 329-0300. **$49-$60, 14 day notice.** 1002 E Oak St. I-40, exit 127, just n. Ext corridors. **Pets:** Small, other species. $20 one-time fee/room. Service with restrictions.
🆂🅰🆅🅴 🆂🅾 ⊠ 🖬 💻 ⚓

▽▽ Motel 6 #260 🅼
(501) 327-6623. **$39-$49.** 1105 Hwy 65 N. I-40, exit 125, just se. Ext corridors. **Pets:** Service with restrictions, supervision.
🆂🅾 ⊠ 🖉 🖘 ⚓

△△△ ▽▽▽ Ramada Inn 🆂🅷
(501) 329-8392. **$49-$65, 14 day notice.** 815 E Oak St. I-40, exit 127. Ext corridors. **Pets:** Medium. $20 one-time fee/room. Service with restrictions, crate.
🆂🅰🆅🅴 🆂🅾 ⊠ 🖉 🖬 💻 🍴 ⚓

EL DORADO

▽▽▽▽ La Quinta Inn El Dorado 🆂🅷
(870) 863-6677. **$65-$70.** 2303 Junction City Rd. Just e of jct US 167 and 82B. Ext/int corridors. **Pets:** Accepted.
🅰🆂🅺 ⊠ 🖉 🖬 💻 ⚓

EUREKA SPRINGS

△△△ ▽▽▽▽ 1886 Crescent Hotel & Spa 🆂🅷
(479) 253-9766. **$99-$179, 3 day notice.** 75 Prospect Ave. 1.3 mi n of jct SR 23 on US 62B Historic Loop. Int corridors. **Pets:** Medium. Service with restrictions, crate.
🆂🅰🆅🅴 🆂🅾 ⊠ 🖬 💻 🍴 ⚓ ⊠

△△△ ▽▽▽ Basin Park Hotel 🆂🅷
(479) 253-7837. **$89-$149, 3 day notice.** 12 Spring St. 0.7 mi n of jct US 62 via SR 23 N; downtown. Int corridors. **Pets:** Small. Service with restrictions, crate.
🆂🅰🆅🅴 🆂🅾 ⊠ 🖬 💻 🍴

△△△ ▽▽▽▽ Best Western Inn of the Ozarks 🆂🅷
(479) 253-9768. **$49-$99.** 207 W Van Buren St. On US 62, 0.5 mi w of jct SR 23. Ext corridors. **Pets:** Accepted.
🆂🅰🆅🅴 🆂🅾 ⊠ 🖉 🖘 🖬 💻 🍴 ⚓ ⊠

△△△ ▽▽▽ Colonial Mansion Inn 🆂🅷
(479) 253-7300. **$38-$98, 3 day notice.** 154 Huntsville Rd. Just s of jct US 62 and SR 23. Ext/int corridors. **Pets:** Small. Designated rooms, crate.
🆂🅰🆅🅴 ⊠ 🖬 💻 ⚓

▽▽ Days Inn 🅼
(479) 253-8863. **$49-$109, 3 day notice.** 120 W Van Buren St. On US 62, just w of jct SR 23 N. Ext corridors. **Pets:** Small, dogs only. $15 daily fee/room. Service with restrictions, supervision.
🅰🆂🅺 🆂🅾 ⊠ 🖬 💻 ⚓

△△△ ▽▽▽ Howard Johnson Express 🆂🅷
(479) 253-6665. **$49-$110.** 4042 E Van Buren St. 1.8 mi e of jct US 62 and SR 23. Ext corridors. **Pets:** Accepted.
🆂🅰🆅🅴 🆂🅾 ⊠ 💻 ⚓

▽▽ The Joy Motel 🅼
(479) 253-9568. **$39-$93, 3 day notice.** 216 W Van Buren St. 0.5 mi w of jct US 62 and SR 23. Ext corridors. **Pets:** Accepted.
🅰🆂🅺 🆂🅾 🖬 💻 ⚓

▽▽▽▽ Lazee Daze Log Cabin Resort 🅲🅰
(479) 253-7026. **Call for rates.** 5432 Hwy 23 S. 6.1 mi s of jct US 62 and SR 23. Ext corridors. **Pets:** Dogs only. $50 one-time fee/room. No service, crate.
⊠ 🖬 💻 🈂

▽▽ Road Runner Inn 🅼
(479) 253-8166. **$49-$70, 7 day notice.** 3034 Mundell Rd. On US 62, 4.3 mi w, 3.9 mi s on SR 187, then 3 mi se. Ext corridors. **Pets:** Accepted.
🅰🆂🅺 🖬 💻 🈂

▽▽ Travelers Inn 🅼
(479) 253-8386. **$32-$58, 3 day notice.** 2044 E Van Buren St. On US 62, just e of jct US 62 and SR 23. Ext corridors. **Pets:** Small, dogs only. Service with restrictions, crate.
⊠ 🖬 ⚓

△△△ ▽▽▽ Travelodge 🆂🅷
(479) 253-8992. **$38-$120.** 110 Huntsville Dr. Jct US 62 and SR 23. Ext corridors. **Pets:** Accepted.
🆂🅰🆅🅴 🆂🅾 ⊠ 💻 ⚓

FAYETTEVILLE

△△△ ▽▽▽ Best Western Windsor Suites 🆂🅷
(479) 587-1400. **$54-$164.** 1122 S Futrall Dr. I-540, exit 62, just se. Ext corridors. **Pets:** Small, other species. $10 one-time fee/pet. Designated rooms, service with restrictions.
🆂🅰🆅🅴 🆂🅾 ⊠ 🖬 💻 ⚓

△△△ ▽▽▽ Days Inn 🆂🅷
(479) 443-4323. **$65-$100.** 2402 N College Ave. I-540, exit 67, 1.6 mi e, then 1.9 mi s on US 71 business route. Ext corridors. **Pets:** Accepted.
🆂🅰🆅🅴 🆂🅾 ⊠ 🖬 💻 ⚓

△△△ ▽▽▽ Holiday Inn Express-University of Arkansas Area 🆂🅷
(479) 444-6006. **$80.** 1251 N Shiloh Dr. I-540, exit 64, just nw. Int corridors. **Pets:** Accepted.
🆂🅰🆅🅴 🆂🅾 ⊠ 🖉 🖘 🖬 💻 ⊠

▽▽ Motel 6 Fayetteville #552 🅼
(479) 443-4351. **$43-$55.** 2980 N College Ave. I-540, exit 67, 1.6 mi e, then 0.9 mi s on US 71B. Ext corridors. **Pets:** Small. Service with restrictions, crate.
🆂🅾 ⊠ 🖘 ⚓

▼▼ **Quality Inn** SH
(479) 444-9800. **$68-$100.** 523 S Shiloh Dr. I-540, exit 62, just w. Ext corridors. **Pets:** Very small. $15 one-time fee/room. Designated rooms, no service, supervision.

ASK S✿ ✕ ❚ ▣ ⚓

♦♦♦ ▼▼▼▼ **Radisson Hotel Fayetteville** LH
(479) 442-5555. **$69-$135.** 70 N East Ave. Just w of US 71B and SR 471; downtown. Int corridors. **Pets:** Small. $50 deposit/room, $5 one-time fee/room. Service with restrictions, supervision.

SAVE S✿ ✕ ﬗ ❚ ▣ ¶¶ ⚓

▼▼ **Sleep Inn by Choice Hotels** SH
(479) 587-8700. **$84-$124.** 728 Millsap Rd. I-540, exit 67, 1.6 mi e, then just s on US 71B. Int corridors. **Pets:** Accepted.

ASK S✿ ✕ ﬗ ❚ ▣

▼ **Super 8 Motel-Fayetteville** SH
(479) 521-8866. **$49-$75.** 1075 S Shiloh Dr. I-540, exit 62, just w. Int corridors. **Pets:** Accepted.

ASK S✿ ✕ ❚

FORREST CITY

▼▼ **Days Inn** SH
(870) 633-0777. **$63, 14 day notice.** 350 Barrow Hill Rd. I-40, exit 241B, just n. Ext corridors. **Pets:** Medium. $5 one-time fee/pet. Service with restrictions, supervision.

ASK S✿ ✕ ﬗ ❚ ▣ ⚓

▼▼▼ **Holiday Inn** SH
(870) 633-6300. **$70-$90.** 200 Holiday Dr. I-40, exit 241B, just n. Ext corridors. **Pets:** Accepted.

ASK S✿ ✕ ❚ ▣ ¶¶ ⚓

FORT SMITH

▼▼▼ **Aspen Hotel & Suites** SH
(479) 452-9000. **$94-$120.** 2900 S 68th St. I-540, exit 8B (Rogers Ave), just e. Int corridors. **Pets:** Accepted.

ASK S✿ ✕ ❚ ▣ ⚓

▼▼ **Baymont Inn & Suites Fort Smith** SH
(479) 484-5770. **$54-$74.** 2123 Burnham Rd. I-540, exit 8A (Rogers Ave), just w. Int corridors. **Pets:** Other species. $25 deposit/room. Service with restrictions, supervision.

ASK S✿ ✕ ﬗ ✇ ❚ ▣ ⚓

♦♦♦ ▼▼ **Best Western Kings Row Inn & Suites** SH
(479) 452-4200. **$55-$70.** 5801 Rogers Ave. I-540, exit 8A (Rogers Ave), just w. Ext corridors. **Pets:** Large, other species. $20 deposit/room. Service with restrictions.

SAVE S✿ ✕ ✇ ❚ ▣ ⚓

▼▼ **Comfort Inn** SH
(479) 484-0227. **$149.** 2120 Burnham Rd. I-540, exit 8A (Rogers Ave), just w. Int corridors. **Pets:** Accepted.

ASK ✕ ✇ ❚ ▣ ⚓ ✕

▼▼▼▼ **Holiday Inn Express** SH
(479) 452-7500. **Call for rates.** 6813 Phoenix Ave. I-540, exit 8A (Rogers Ave), 0.6 mi e, then 0.5 mi s. Int corridors. **Pets:** Medium. $20 one-time fee/pet. Designated rooms, service with restrictions, supervision.

✕ ﬗ ✇ ❚ ▣ ⚓ ✕

▼▼▼▼ **Holiday Inn Fort Smith City Center** LH ✿
(479) 783-1000. **$109.** 700 Rogers Ave. Just s of US 64 (Garrison Ave); downtown. Int corridors. **Pets:** Medium, other species. $25 one-time fee/room. Designated rooms, service with restrictions.

✕ ✇ ✇ ❚ ▣ ¶¶ ⚓ ✕

▼ **Motel 6 Fort Smith #0133** M
(479) 484-0576. **$42-$53.** 6001 Rogers Ave. I-540, exit 8B (Rogers Ave), just w. Ext corridors. **Pets:** Medium, other species. Service with restrictions, supervision.

S✿ ✕ ﬗ ⚓

▼▼▼▼ **Residence Inn by Marriott** SH
(479) 478-8300. **$99-$139.** 3005 S 74th. I-540, exit 8A (Rogers Ave), 0.8 mi e. Int corridors. **Pets:** Accepted.

ASK ✕ ✇ ﬗ ❚ ▣ ⚓ ✕

▼ **Super 8 Motel** M
(479) 646-3411. **$55-$60, 7 day notice.** 3810 Towson Ave. 2 mi s of SR 22. Ext corridors. **Pets:** Very small, dogs only. $5 one-time fee/pet. Designated rooms, service with restrictions, supervision.

ASK S✿ ✕ ✇ ❚ ▣ ⚓

GAMALIEL

▼ **Twin Gables Resort** CA
(870) 467-5686. **$55-$67, 7 day notice.** 3166 Hwy 101. Jct CR 806. Ext corridors. **Pets:** Accepted.

ASK S✿ ✕ ❚ ⚓ ✕ ✇

GENTRY

▼▼▼▼ **Apple Crest Inn Bed & Breakfast** BB
(479) 736-8201. **$100-$165, 7 day notice.** 12758 S Hwy 59. On SR 59, 1 mi s. Int corridors. **Pets:** Other species. $25 one-time fee/room. Designated rooms, crate.

ASK S✿ ✕

GLENWOOD

▼▼ **Riverwood Inn** M
(870) 356-4567. **$60-$70.** 363 Hwy 70 E. On US 70, 0.5 mi e. Ext corridors. **Pets:** Small. $5 daily fee/room. Designated rooms, service with restrictions, crate.

ASK ✕ ⚓

HARRISON

▼▼ **Comfort Inn** SH
(870) 741-7676. **$62-$89.** 1210 Hwy 62/65 N. 1 mi n on US 62/65/412. Ext/int corridors. **Pets:** Accepted.

ASK S✿ ✕ ✇ ❚ ▣ ⚓

♦♦♦ ▼ **Family Budget Inn** M ✿
(870) 743-1000. **$37-$40.** 401 S Main (Hwy 65B S). 0.7 mi s of jct SR 7. Ext corridors. **Pets:** Small. $50 deposit/room, $3 daily fee/room. Designated rooms, no service, supervision.

SAVE S✿ ✕ ❚ ▣ ⚓

▼▼▼▼ **Holiday Inn Express Hotel & Suites** SH
(870) 741-3636. **$62-$86.** 117 Hwy 43 E. Just e from jct US 62/65/412 and SR 43. Int corridors. **Pets:** Small. $25 one-time fee/pet. Supervision.

ASK S✿ ✕ ﬗ ❚ ▣ ⚓ ✕

HAZEN

▼▼ **Super 8 Motel** SH
(870) 255-2888. **$50-$65, 4 day notice.** 2809 Hwy 63. I-40, exit 193, just s. Ext corridors. **Pets:** Accepted.

ASK S✿ ✕ ❚ ▣ ⚓

HOPE

♦♦♦ ▼▼ **Best Western** SH
(870) 777-9222. **$55-$59.** 1800 Holiday Dr. I-30, exit 30, just nw. Ext corridors. **Pets:** Other species. Service with restrictions.

SAVE S✿ ✕ ❚ ▣ ⚓

HOT SPRINGS

♦♦♦ ▼▼▼▼ **Clarion Resort** SH
(501) 525-1391. **$75-$159.** 4813 Central Ave. 5.5 mi s of jct US 270 and SR 7. Int corridors. **Pets:** Medium. $10 daily fee/room. Service with restrictions, crate.

SAVE S✿ ✕ ✇ ❚ ▣ ¶¶ ⚓ ✕

Embassy Suites Hot Springs 🄻🄷
(501) 624-9200. **$149-$199.** 400 Convention Blvd. Just w of jct US 70. Int corridors. **Pets:** Small. $25 daily fee/room. Service with restrictions, supervision.
(SAVE) ⊠ 🄼 🔲 🔲 🔲 🔲 🔲 🔲 ⊠

Lake Hamilton Resort 🄷
(501) 767-8606. **$84-$160.** 2803 Albert Pike Rd. 5 mi w on US 270. Int corridors. **Pets:** Accepted.
(SAVE) 🄼 ⊠ 🔲 🔲 🔲 🔲 ⊠

Margarete Motel 🄼
(501) 623-1192. **$65-$120.** 217 Fountain St. Just e of jct SR 7. Ext corridors. **Pets:** Other species. $20 deposit/room. Designated rooms.
(SAVE) ⊠ 🔲 🔲

Travelier Inn 🄼
(501) 624-4681. **$48-$62.** 1045 E Grand Ave. 1 mi e of jct US 270B and 70. Ext corridors. **Pets:** Other species. $5 one-time fee/room. Service with restrictions.
(SAVE) 🄼 ⊠ 🔲 🔲

Velda Rose Resort Hotel & Spa 🄻🄷
(501) 623-3311. **$85.** 217 Park Ave. On US 70B and SR 7; center. Int corridors. **Pets:** Accepted.
(SAVE) 🄼 ⊠ 🔲 🔲 🔲 🔲

JACKSONVILLE

Days Inn 🄼
(501) 982-1543. **$55-$65, 3 day notice.** 1414 John Harden Dr. US 67/167, exit 10B southbound; exit 11 northbound. Ext corridors. **Pets:** Medium. $6 daily fee/pet. Designated rooms, service with restrictions, supervision.
(ASK) 🄼 ⊠ 🔲 🔲

JONESBORO

Comfort Inn & Suites 🄷
(870) 972-9000. **$65-$114.** 2911 Gilmore Dr. US 63, exit Stadium Blvd/Caraway Rd, just n. Int corridors. **Pets:** Accepted.
(ASK) 🄼 ⊠ 🔲 🔲 🔲 🔲

Holiday Inn Express 🄷
(870) 932-5554. **$74-$80.** 2407 Phillips Dr. US 63, exit Stadium Blvd/Caraway Rd, just n. Int corridors. **Pets:** Accepted.
(ASK) 🄼 ⊠ 🔲 🔲 🔲

Motel 6–0187 🄼
(870) 932-1050. **$33-$37.** 2300 S Caraway Rd. US 63, exit Stadium Blvd/Caraway Rd, 0.6 mi n. Ext corridors. **Pets:** Other species. Service with restrictions, supervision.
⊠ 🔲

LITTLE ROCK

AmeriSuites (Little Rock/Financial Center) 🄷
(501) 225-1075. **$85.** 10920 Financial Center Pkwy. Jct I-430 and 630, exit Shackleford Rd. Int corridors. **Pets:** Accepted.
(SAVE) 🄼 ⊠ 🔲 🔲 🔲

Baymont Inn & Suites Little Rock West 🄷
(501) 225-7007. **$53-$61.** 1010 Breckenridge Rd. I-430, exit 8, just e to Breckenridge Rd, then just s. Int corridors. **Pets:** Other species. Service with restrictions, supervision.
(ASK) 🄼 ⊠ 🔲 🔲 🔲

Comfort Inn & Suites, Downtown Little Rock @ The Clinton Library 🄷
(501) 687-7700. **$62-$98.** 707 I-30. I-30, exit 140A, just e. Int corridors. **Pets:** Medium. $25 one-time fee/room. Service with restrictions.
(SAVE) 🄼 ⊠ 🄼 🔲 🔲 🔲

Embassy Suites Hotel Little Rock 🄻🄷
(501) 312-9000. **$109-$199.** 11301 Financial Center Pkwy. Jct I-430 and 630, just w. Int corridors. **Pets:** Accepted.
(SAVE) ⊠ 🄼 🔲 🔲 🔲 🔲 🔲 🔲 ⊠

Hampton Inn Little Rock I-30 🄷
(501) 562-6667. **$74.** 6100 Mitchell Dr. I-30, exit 133. Int corridors. **Pets:** Other species. $25 daily fee/pet. Service with restrictions, supervision.
(SAVE) 🄼 ⊠ 🔲 🔲

Holiday Inn Select 🄷
(501) 223-3000. **$99-$114.** 201 S Shackleford Rd. Jct I-430 and 630. Ext/int corridors. **Pets:** Accepted.
(ASK) ⊠ 🔲 🔲 🔲 🔲 🔲

La Quinta Inn Litle Rock (West) 🄷
(501) 224-0900. **$68-$81.** 200 S Shackleford Rd. I-430, exit 6; I-630, exit Shackleford Rd N; jct I-430 and 630. Ext corridors. **Pets:** Accepted.
(SAVE) ⊠ 🔲 🔲 🔲

La Quinta Inn Little Rock (Medical Center Area) 🄷
(501) 664-7000. **$66-$91.** 901 Fair Park Blvd. I-630, exit 4, just s. Ext corridors. **Pets:** Accepted.
(ASK) ⊠ 🄼 🔲 🔲 🔲

La Quinta Inn Little Rock (Otter Creek Area) 🄷
(501) 455-2300. **$65-$85.** 11701 I-30. I-30, exit 128, just e. Ext corridors. **Pets:** Accepted.
(SAVE) ⊠ 🔲 🔲 🔲

Residence Inn by Marriott 🄷
(501) 312-0200. **$89-$150.** 1401 S Shackleford Rd. I-430, exit 5, just n. Int corridors. **Pets:** Accepted.
(SAVE) ⊠ 🄼 🔲 🔲 🔲 🔲 🔲 ⊠

LONOKE

Days Inn 🄷
(501) 676-5138. **$65-$70.** 105 Dee Dee Ln. I-40, exit 175, just n. Ext corridors. **Pets:** Accepted.
(SAVE) 🄼 ⊠ 🔲 🔲 🔲

Super 8 Motel 🄷
(501) 676-8880. **$59-$69.** 102 Dee Dee Ln. I-40, exit 175, just n. Int corridors. **Pets:** Medium. $10 daily fee/pet. Service with restrictions, supervision.
(SAVE) 🄼 ⊠ 🔲 🔲 🔲

MAGNOLIA

Best Western-Coachman's Inn 🄷
(870) 234-6122. **$72.** 420 E Main St. 1.3 mi w of jct US 79 and 82B. Ext corridors. **Pets:** Small. $20 deposit/room. Service with restrictions, supervision.
(ASK) 🄼 ⊠ 🔲 🔲 🔲 🔲

MARION

Best Western-Regency Motor Inn 🄷
(870) 739-3278. **$65-$75, 7 day notice.** 3635 I-55. I-55, exit 10, just nw. Ext corridors. **Pets:** Small, other species. Service with restrictions, supervision.
(ASK) 🄼 ⊠ 🔲 🔲 🔲 🔲

MAUMELLE

Comfort Suites 🄷
(501) 851-8444. **$74-$149.** 14322 Frontier Dr. I-40, exit 142, just sw. Int corridors. **Pets:** Accepted.
(ASK) 🄼 ⊠ 🔲 🔲 🔲 🔲

▼▼ Quality Inn of Maumelle 🆂🅷
(501) 851-3500. **$59-$79.** 14325 Frontier Dr. I-40, exit 142, just sw. Ext corridors. **Pets:** Medium. $10 one-time fee/room. Designated rooms, service with restrictions, supervision.
🅰🅂🅺 ⬛ ✖ 🅸 ⤳

MOUNTAIN HOME

▼▼ Best Western Carriage Inn 🆂🅷
(870) 425-6001. **$51-$71.** 963 Hwy 62 E. 1.3 mi e on US 62B. Ext corridors. **Pets:** Small, other species. $10 deposit/room. Designated rooms, service with restrictions, supervision.
🅰🅂🅺 ⬛ ✖ ⬜ ⤳

▲▲▲ ▼▼▼ Teal Point Resort 🅲🅰
(870) 492-5145. **$67-$126, 45 day notice.** 715 Teal Point Rd. 7 mi e on US 62, 0.6 mi n on CR 406, follow signs. Ext corridors. **Pets:** Other species. $7 daily fee/pet. Designated rooms, service with restrictions, supervision.
🆂🅰🆅🅴 🅸 ⤳ ✖ 🆉

MOUNTAIN VIEW

▼▼ Best Western Fiddlers Inn 🅼
(870) 269-2828. **$56-$95.** 601 Sylomore. 1 mi n on SR 5, 9 and 14. Ext corridors. **Pets:** Accepted.
🅰🅂🅺 ⬛ ✖ 🅸 ⬜ ⤳

NEWPORT

▲▲▲ ▼▼▼ Park Inn 🅼
(870) 523-5851. **$63-$68.** 901 Hwy 367 N. US 67, exit 83, 1 mi w, then 0.3 mi n. Ext corridors. **Pets:** Other species. $10 one-time fee/pet. Crate.
🆂🅰🆅🅴 ⬛ ✖ 🅸 ⬜ ⤳

NORTH LITTLE ROCK

▼▼ Baymont Inn & Suites North Little Rock 🆂🅷
(501) 758-8888. **$59-$79.** 4311 Warden Rd. US 67/167, exit 1B northbound; exit 1 southbound. Int corridors. **Pets:** Accepted.
🅰🅂🅺 ⬛ ✖ 🈁 🅻 🅸 ⬜ ⤳

▼▼ Days Inn 🅼
(501) 945-4100. **$50-$70.** 5800 Pritchard Dr. I-40, exit 157. Ext corridors. **Pets:** Accepted.
🅰🅂🅺 ⬛ ✖ 🅸

▼▼ Days Inn 🆂🅷
(501) 851-3297. **$59.** 7200 Bicentennial Rd. I-40, exit 142. Ext corridors. **Pets:** Accepted.
🅰🅂🅺 ⬛ ✖ 🈁 🅸

▼▼▼ Hampton Inn 🆂🅷
(501) 771-2090. **$69-$74.** 500 W 29th St. I-40, exit 152. Int corridors. **Pets:** Very small. $35 one-time fee/pet. Designated rooms, service with restrictions, supervision.
🅰🅂🅺 ⬛ ✖ 🈁 🅸 ⬜ ⤳

▲▲▲ ▼▼▼ La Quinta Little Rock (North) 🆂🅷
(501) 945-0808. **$68-$85.** 4100 E McCain Blvd. Jct US 67/167, exit 1A northbound; exit 1 southbound. Ext corridors. **Pets:** Accepted.
🆂🅰🆅🅴 ✖ 🈁 🅸

▼▼ Red Roof Inn 🆂🅷
(501) 945-0080. **$55-$60.** 5711 Pritchard Dr. I-40, exit 157, just s. Int corridors. **Pets:** Accepted.
🅰🅂🅺 ✖ 🅸 ⤳

▼▼▼ Residence Inn by Marriott-North 🆂🅷
(501) 945-7777. **$114-$150, 14 day notice.** 4110 Healthcare Dr. I-40, exit 156. Int corridors. **Pets:** Other species. $75 one-time fee/room. Service with restrictions, supervision.
🅰🅂🅺 ⬛ ✖ 🅻 🅸 ⬜ ⤳ ✖

▼▼ Super 8 North Little Rock 🅼
(501) 945-0141. **$48-$51, 3 day notice.** 1 Gray Rd. I-40, exit 157, just n. Ext/int corridors. **Pets:** $5 daily fee/pet. No service, supervision.
🅰🅂🅺 ⬛ ✖ ⤳

▲▲▲ ▼▼▼ Travelodge 🅼
(501) 758-8110. **$50-$60.** 3100 N Main. I-40, exit 153A eastbound, just n; exit SR 107 westbound, just w. Ext corridors. **Pets:** Accepted.
🆂🅰🆅🅴 ⬛ ✖ 🅸 ⬜ ⤳

OZARK

▼▼ Oxford Inn 🅼
(479) 667-1131. **$45.** 305 N 18th St. I-40, exit 35, 3 mi s on SR 23. Ext corridors. **Pets:** Other species. $10 daily fee/pet. Service with restrictions, crate.
🅰🅂🅺 ⬛ ✖ 🅸 ⤳

PARAGOULD

▼▼ Ramada Inn 🆂🅷
(870) 239-2121. **$84-$88.** 2310 W Kingshighway. 0.8 mi w of jct US 412 and 49. Ext/int corridors. **Pets:** Other species. $20 daily fee/pet. Service with restrictions, supervision.
🅰🅂🅺 ✖ 🅸 ⬜ 🍴 ⤳

PINE BLUFF

▼▼▼ Hampton Inn Pine Bluff 🆂🅷 🐾
(870) 850-0444. **$80.** 3103 E Market St. I-530, exit 46, just n. Int corridors. **Pets:** Small, other species. Service with restrictions, crate.
🅰🅂🅺 ⬛ ✖ 🈁 🅰 🅻 🅸 ⬜ ⤳

▼▼▼ Holiday Inn Express Hotel & Suites 🆂🅷
(870) 879-3800. **$80.** 3620 Camden Rd. I-530, exit 39, just sw. Int corridors. **Pets:** Small, other species. $25 one-time fee/room. Service with restrictions, supervision.
🅰🅂🅺 ✖ 🈁 🅻 🅸 🅸 ⤳

POCAHONTAS

▼▼ Days Inn & Suites 🆂🅷
(870) 892-9500. **$75.** 2805 Hwy 67 S. 1.7 mi s. Int corridors. **Pets:** Small. $25 deposit/pet, $10 daily fee/pet. Designated rooms, service with restrictions, supervision.
🅰🅂🅺 ⬛ ✖ 🅸 ⬜ ⤳

ROGERS

▲▲▲ ▼▼▼ AmeriSuites (Rogers/Bentonville) 🆂🅷
(479) 633-8555. **$129-$139.** 4610 W Walnut. I-540, exit 85, just e. Int corridors. **Pets:** Other species. Supervision.
🆂🅰🆅🅴 ⬛ ✖ 🈁 🅰 🅻 🅸 ⬜ ⤳

▲▲▲ ▼▼▼ Embassy Suites Northwest Arkansas 🅻🅷
(479) 254-8400. **$89-$289.** 3303 Pinnacle Hills Pkwy. I-540, exit 83, just w, then 0.6 mi s. Int corridors. **Pets:** Medium. $50 one-time fee/room. Service with restrictions, crate.
🆂🅰🆅🅴 ⬛ ✖ 🈁 🅰 🅻 🅸 ⬜ 🍴 ⤳ ✖

▼▼▼ Residence Inn by Marriott 🆂🅷
(479) 636-5900. **$129-$159.** 4611 W Locust St.. I-540, exit 85, 0.4 mi n on 46th St. Int corridors. **Pets:** Small, other species. $75 one-time fee/pet. Service with restrictions, crate.
🅰🅂🅺 ⬛ ✖ 🈁 🅻 🅸 ⬜ ⤳ ✖

RUSSELLVILLE

▼▼ Comfort Inn 🅼
(479) 967-7500. **$59-$69.** 3019 E Parkway Dr. I-40, exit 84, just s. Ext corridors. **Pets:** Accepted.
🅰🅂🅺 ⬛ ✖ 🅸 ⬜ ⤳

(AAA) ▼▼▼ Holiday Inn SH ❀
(479) 968-4300. **$59.** 2407 N Arkansas Ave. I-40, exit 81, just s. Ext corridors. **Pets:** Other species. Service with restrictions.
[SAVE] [S∂] [✕] [⬛] [▣] [¶] [≥]

▼ Motel 6 Russellville #265 M
(479) 968-3666. **$37-$47.** 215 W Birch St. I-40, exit 81, just n. Ext corridors. **Pets:** Other species. Service with restrictions, supervision.
[S∂] [✕] [⬚] [⬛] [≥]

▼ Park Motel M
(479) 968-4862. **$30-$44.** 2615 W Main St. I-40, exit 81, 2 mi s on SR 7, 1.6 mi w on US 64. Ext corridors. **Pets:** Other species. Service with restrictions, supervision.
[ASK] [S∂] [✕] [⬛] [≥]

▼▼ Super 8 Motel-Russellville SH
(479) 968-8898. **$46-$56.** 2404 N Arkansas Ave. I-40, exit 81, just s. Int corridors. **Pets:** Small. $10 daily fee/pet. Service with restrictions, supervision.
[ASK] [S∂] [✕] [⬚] [⬛]

SEARCY

▼▼▼ Hampton Inn SH
(501) 268-0654. **$77-$87.** 3204 E Race Ave. US 67, exit 46, just w. Ext/int corridors. **Pets:** Small. $20 daily fee/pet. Designated rooms, service with restrictions, crate.
[ASK] [✕] [⬚] [⬛] [▣] [≥] [✕]

(AAA) ▼ Royal Inn M
(501) 268-3511. **$49-$59.** 2203 E Race Ave. US 67, exit 46, 1.1 mi w. Ext corridors. **Pets:** Small, dogs only. $5 daily fee/pet. Designated rooms, service with restrictions, supervision.
[SAVE] [S∂] [✕] [⬛] [▣]

SILOAM SPRINGS

▼▼ Super 8 Motel M
(479) 524-8898. **$55.** 1800 Hwy 412 W. Center. Ext corridors. **Pets:** Very small. Service with restrictions, supervision.
[ASK] [S∂] [✕] [⬚] [⬛] [▣] [≥]

SPRINGDALE

▼▼▼ Baymont Inn & Suites Springdale SH
(479) 751-2626. **$75-$105.** 1300 S 48th St. I-540, exit 72, just e on US 412. Int corridors. **Pets:** Large, other species. Service with restrictions, crate.
[ASK] [S∂] [✕] [⬚M] [⬚] [⬚] [⬛] [▣] [≥]

(AAA) ▼▼▼ Comfort Suites SH
(479) 725-1777. **$80-$85.** 1099 Rieff St. I-540, exit 72, just w. Int corridors. **Pets:** Accepted.
[SAVE] [S∂] [✕] [⬚] [⬛] [▣] [≥] [✕]

(AAA) ▼▼▼ Hampton Inn & Suites SH
(479) 756-3500. **$119-$179.** 1700 S 48th St. I-540, exit 72, just e. Int corridors. **Pets:** Accepted.
[SAVE] [S∂] [✕] [⬚M] [⬚] [⬚] [⬛] [▣] [≥]

(AAA) ▼▼▼ Holiday Inn Northwest AR Hotel & Convention Center LH
(479) 751-8300. **$159-$199.** 1500 S 48th St. I-540, exit 72, just e on US 412. Int corridors. **Pets:** Medium, dogs only. $75 deposit/room. Designated rooms, service with restrictions.
[SAVE] [S∂] [✕] [⬚] [⬚] [⬚] [⬛] [▣] [¶] [≥] [✕]

▼▼▼ Residence Inn by Marriott SH
(479) 872-9100. **$119-$149.** 1740 S 48th St. I-540, exit 72, e to 48th St, then 0.5 mi s. Int corridors. **Pets:** Other species. $75 one-time fee/room. Service with restrictions, crate.
[ASK] [S∂] [✕] [⬚] [⬛] [▣] [≥] [✕]

STAR CITY

▼▼ Super 8 Motel-Star City SH
(870) 628-6883. **$69.** 1308 N Lincoln St. Just n on US 425. Int corridors. **Pets:** Accepted.
[ASK] [✕] [⬛] [▣] [≥]

STUTTGART

▼▼ Holiday Inn Express SH
(870) 673-3616. **$69-$124.** 708 W Michigan. Just w on US 63/79. Ext corridors. **Pets:** Large, other species. $5 daily fee/pet. Designated rooms, service with restrictions, supervision.
[ASK] [S∂] [✕] [⬛] [▣] [≥]

TEXARKANA

▼▼ Baymont Inn & Suites Texarkana SH
(870) 773-1000. **$49-$69.** 5102 N State Line Ave. I-30, exit 223B, just n. Int corridors. **Pets:** $25 deposit/room. Service with restrictions, supervision.
[ASK] [S∂] [✕] [⬚] [⬛] [▣] [≥]

(AAA) ▼▼▼ Best Western Kings Row Inn & Suites M
(870) 774-3851. **$64-$70.** 4200 N State Line Ave. I-30, exit 223A, just s. Ext/int corridors. **Pets:** Accepted.
[SAVE] [✕] [⬛] [▣] [¶] [≥]

(AAA) ▼▼▼ Holiday Inn Texarkana SH
(870) 774-3521. **$79.** 5100 N State Line Ave. I-30, exit 223B, just n. Int corridors. **Pets:** Accepted.
[SAVE] [S∂] [✕] [⬚] [⬛] [▣] [¶] [≥] [✕]

(AAA) ▼▼▼ Quality Inn SH
(870) 772-0070. **$70-$90.** 5210 N State Line Ave. I-30, exit 223B, just n. Ext corridors. **Pets:** Accepted.
[SAVE] [S∂] [✕] [⬛] [▣] [≥]

VAN BUREN

▼▼ Comfort Inn SH
(479) 474-2223. **$59-$79.** 3131 Cloverleaf. I-540, exit 2A, just s. Int corridors. **Pets:** Medium, dogs only. $15 one-time fee/pet. Service with restrictions, supervision.
[ASK] [S∂] [✕] [⬛] [▣] [≥]

▼▼ Holiday Inn Express SH
(479) 474-8100. **$68.** 1903 N 6th St. I-40, exit 5, just n. Ext corridors. **Pets:** $20 daily fee/pet. Designated rooms, no service, supervision.
[✕] [▣] [≥]

▼ Motel 6 Van Buren #1264 M
(479) 474-8001. **$35-$52.** 1716 Fayetteville Rd. I-40, exit 5, just s. Ext corridors. **Pets:** Accepted.
[S∂] [✕] [⬚] [≥]

▼▼ Super 8 Motel SH
(479) 471-8888. **$49-$69.** 106 North Plaza Ct. I-40, exit 5, just s. Ext/int corridors. **Pets:** Medium, dogs only. $25 one-time fee/pet. Service with restrictions, supervision.
[ASK] [S∂] [✕] [⬛] [▣] [≥]

CALIFORNIA

CITY INDEX

ALTURAS

AAA ▼▼/▼ Best Western Trailside Inn **M**
(530) 233-4111. **$75-$80.** 343 N Main St. On US 395. Ext corridors.
Pets: Small, dogs only. $10 one-time fee/pet. Designated rooms, service with restrictions, supervision.
SAVE $ⅮX🄷💷🌊

ANAHEIM

AAA ▼▼/▼ Anaheim Marriott Hotel **LH**
(714) 750-8000. **$109-$199.** 700 W Convention Way. I-5, exit Katella Ave, 0.6 mi w to Harbor Blvd, 0.3 mi s, then just w. Int corridors.
Pets: Other species. $50 one-time fee/room.
SAVE X🄶🄼⊘🄵🄷💷🍽🌊🄌

AAA ▼▼/▼ Anaheim Plaza Hotel & Suites **SH**
(714) 772-5900. **$99-$119.** 1700 S Harbor Blvd. I-5, exit Katella Ave, 0.5 mi w, then just n. Ext corridors. **Pets:** Medium. $50 deposit/room. Designated rooms, service with restrictions, supervision.
SAVE $ⅮX🄷💷🍽🌊

Anaheim Quality Inn Maingate M ❀
(714) 750-5211. **$65-$119.** 2200 S Harbor Blvd. I-5, exit Chapman Ave, 1.5 mi w, then just n. Ext corridors. **Pets:** Medium, dogs only. $100 deposit/room, $25 one-time fee/pet. Service with restrictions.
SAVE S❺ ✕ 🛏 🖵 ≈

Anaheim TownePlace Suites By Marriott M
(714) 939-9700. **$89-$149.** 1730 S State College Blvd. I-5, exit Katella Ave, 0.5 mi e, then just n. Int corridors. **Pets:** Small. $75 one-time fee/room. Service with restrictions, supervision.
SAVE S❺ ✕ 🛏 🖵 ≈

Anaheim Vagabond Inn Executive M
(714) 971-5556. **$59-$109.** 2145 S Harbor Blvd. I-5, exit Katella Ave, 0.6 mi w, then 0.6 mi s. Ext corridors. **Pets:** Accepted.
SAVE S❺ ✕ 🛏 🖵 ≈

Best Western Anaheim Stardust M
(714) 774-7600. **$59-$119.** 1057 W Ball Rd. I-5, exit Ball Rd, just w. Ext corridors. **Pets:** Accepted.
SAVE S❺ ✕ 🛏 🖵 ≈

Clarion Hotel Anaheim Resort LH
(714) 750-3131. **$69-$199, 3 day notice.** 616 Convention Way. I-5, exit Katella Ave, 0.6 mi w to Harbor Blvd, then 0.3 mi s. Int corridors. **Pets:** Medium. $10 daily fee/room, $25 one-time fee/room. Designated rooms, service with restrictions, supervision.
SAVE S❺ ✕ 🛏 🖵 🍴 ≈

Coast Anaheim Hotel LH ❀
(714) 750-1811. **$69-$199, 3 day notice.** 1855 S Harbor Blvd. I-5, exit Katella Ave, 0.6 mi w, then just s. Int corridors. **Pets:** Medium, dogs only. Designated rooms, service with restrictions, crate.
SAVE S❺ ✕ 🛏 🖵 🍴 ≈ ✕

Embassy Suites Hotel Anaheim-North Near Disneyland Resort LH
(714) 632-1221. **$109-$204.** 3100 E Frontera St. SR 91, exit Glassell St, just se. Int corridors. **Pets:** Medium. $50 one-time fee/pet. Supervision.
SAVE ✕ 🛏 🖵 🍴 ≈ ✕

Hilton Anaheim LH
(714) 750-4321. **$79-$299, 7 day notice.** 777 Convention Way. I-5, exit Katella Ave, just w to Harbor Blvd, just s, then just w. Int corridors. **Pets:** Accepted.
✕ ⚙M 🐾 🖵 🛏 🖵 🍴 ≈ ✕

La Quinta Inn and Suites SH
(714) 635-5000. **$75-$139.** 1752 S Clementine St. I-5, exit Katella Ave, just n. Int corridors. **Pets:** Medium. Supervision.
A$K S❺ ✕ 🛏 🖵 ≈

Red Roof Inn Anaheim-Maingate M
(714) 520-9696. **$64-$71.** 100 Disney Way. I-5, exit Disney Way. Ext corridors. **Pets:** Small. No service, supervision.
✕ 🛏 ≈

Residence Inn By Marriott SH
(714) 533-3555. **$119-$269.** 1700 S Clementine St. I-5, exit Katella Ave, just w, then just n. Ext corridors. **Pets:** Accepted.
SAVE S❺ ✕ 🛏 🖵 ≈ ✕

Sheraton Anaheim Hotel LH ❀
(714) 778-1700. **$85-$105.** 900 S Disneyland Dr. I-5, exit Ball Rd. Int corridors. **Pets:** Small, dogs only. $25 one-time fee/room. Service with restrictions, supervision.
A$K S❺ ✕ 🐾 🛏 🖵 🍴 ≈ ✕

Staybridge Suites by Holiday Inn-Anaheim Resort SH
(714) 748-7700. **$109-$259.** 1855 S Manchester Ave. I-5, exit Katella Ave, just s, adjacent to west side of freeway. Int corridors. **Pets:** Medium. $150 one-time fee/room. Service with restrictions, supervision.
SAVE S❺ ✕ 🛏 🖵 ≈ ✕

ANAHEIM HILLS

Best Western Anaheim Hills M
(714) 779-0252. **$64-$79.** 5710 E La Palma Ave. SR 91, exit Imperial Hwy, 0.3 mi n. Ext/int corridors. **Pets:** Accepted.
A$K S❺ ✕ 🛏 🖵 ≈ ✕

ANDERSON

AmeriHost Inn-Anderson M
(530) 365-6100. **Call for rates.** 2040 Factory Outlet Dr. I-5, exit Factory Outlet Dr, just w. Int corridors. **Pets:** Small, other species. $10 daily fee/pet. Supervision.
S❺ ✕ ⚙M 🐾 🛏 🖵 ≈ ✕

Best Western Knights Inn M
(530) 365-2753. **$80.** 2688 Gateway Dr. I-5, exit Central Anderson eastbound; exit Lassen Park westbound, just e. Ext corridors. **Pets:** Accepted.
SAVE S❺ ✕ 🛏 🖵 ≈

ANGELS CAMP

Angels Hacienda BB
(209) 785-8533. **Call for rates.** 7 mi on SR 4, then 5 mi. Int corridors. **Pets:** Accepted.
S❺ ✕ 🛏 ≈ 🐾

Angels Inn Motel M 🐾
(209) 736-4242. **$75-$105.** 600 N Main St. SR 49, north end of town. Ext corridors. **Pets:** Other species. $40 deposit/room. Designated rooms, service with restrictions, supervision.
SAVE S❺ ✕ 🛏 🖵

Best Western Cedar Inn & Suites M
(209) 736-4000. **$89-$169.** 444 S Main St. On SR 49; center of town. Ext/int corridors. **Pets:** Dogs only. $10 daily fee/pet. Designated rooms, service with restrictions, supervision.
SAVE S❺ ✕ ⚙M 🐾 🛏 🖵 ≈ ✕

Jumping Frog Motel M
(209) 736-2191. **$60-$150.** 330 Murphys Grade Rd. SR 49, n of Angels Camp Center, just left. Ext corridors. **Pets:** Accepted.
SAVE S❺ ✕ 🖵

ARCATA

Arcata Super 8 SH
(707) 822-8888. **$45-$90.** 4887 Valley West Blvd. US 101, exit Guintoli Ln, 2 mi n. Int corridors. **Pets:** $50 deposit/room, $5 daily fee/pet. Service with restrictions, supervision.
SAVE S❺ ✕ 🛏

Best Western Arcata Inn M
(707) 826-0313. **$62-$125.** 4827 Valley West Blvd. US 101, exit Guintoli Ln, 2 mi n. Ext corridors. **Pets:** Dogs only. $10 one-time fee/pet. Designated rooms, service with restrictions, supervision.
SAVE S❺ ✕ 🐾 🐾 🛏 🖵 ≈

Comfort Inn M
(707) 826-2827. **$65-$150.** 4701 Valley West Blvd. US 101, exit Guintoli Ln, 2 mi n. Ext corridors. **Pets:** Medium, dogs only. $10 daily fee/pet. Designated rooms, service with restrictions, supervision.
SAVE S❺ ✕ ⚙M 🐾 🛏 🖵 ≈

AAA WWW Hotel Arcata SH
(707) 826-0217. **$120-$200.** 708 9th St. At Central Plaza. Int corridors. **Pets:** Other species. $50 deposit/pet, $5 daily fee/pet. Service with restrictions, supervision.
[SAVE] [S&] [X] [◻] [♨] [⚿]

AAA WWWW Quality Inn-Arcata SH
(707) 822-0409. **$59-$139.** 3535 Janes Rd. US 101, exit Guintoli Ln/Janes Rd, 2 mi n. Int corridors. **Pets:** $10 daily fee/pet. Service with restrictions, supervision.
[SAVE] [S&] [X] [◻] [◻] [≈] [⊗]

ARROYO GRANDE

AAA WW Premier Inns M
(805) 481-4774. **$44-$119.** 555 Camino Mercado. US 101, exit Oak Park Rd, just e, then 0.3 mi s. Ext corridors. **Pets:** Small. Service with restrictions, supervision.
[SAVE] [S&] [X] [◻] [≈]

AUBURN

AAA WWWW Best Western Golden Key M
(530) 885-8611. **$75-$115.** 13450 Lincoln Way. I-80, exit Foresthill Rd. Ext corridors. **Pets:** Accepted.
[SAVE] [S&] [X] [&M] [◻] [◻] [≈]

AAA WW Foothills Motel M
(530) 885-8444. **$65-$105.** 13431 Bowman Rd. I-80, exit Foresthill Rd. Ext corridors. **Pets:** Accepted.
[SAVE] [S&] [X] [&M] [◻] [≈]

WWWW Holiday Inn-Auburn M
(530) 887-8787. **$109-$149.** 120 Grass Valley Hwy. Jct I-80 and SR 49. Int corridors. **Pets:** Small, dogs only. $20 one-time fee/pet. Designated rooms, service with restrictions, supervision.
[ASK] [X] [&M] [◻] [◻]

AAA WWW Travelodge M
(530) 885-7025. **$60-$85.** 13490 Lincoln Way. I-80, exit Foresthill Rd. Ext/int corridors. **Pets:** Medium. $10 daily fee/pet. Designated rooms, service with restrictions, supervision.
[SAVE] [S&] [X] [&M] [◻] [◻] [≈]

BAKERSFIELD

AAA WWWW Bakersfield Red Lion Hotel SH
(661) 327-0681. **$59-$179.** 2400 Camino Del Rio Ct. SR 99, exit SR 58 (Rosedale Hwy), just s. Ext/int corridors. **Pets:** $10 daily fee/pet. Service with restrictions.
[SAVE] [S&] [X] [◻] [◻] [♨] [≈] [⊗]

AAA WWW Best Inn M
(661) 764-5221. **$54-$64.** 200 Trask St. I-5, exit Stockdale Hwy, just e. Ext corridors. **Pets:** Medium, other species. $5 daily fee/pet. Designated rooms, service with restrictions, supervision.
[SAVE] [S&] [X] [◻] [◻]

AAA WWW Best Western Crystal Palace Inn & Suites SH
(661) 327-9651. **$69-$129, 3 day notice.** 2620 Buck Owens Blvd. SR 99, exit Buck Owens Blvd northbound; exit Rosedale Hwy southbound. Int corridors. **Pets:** Accepted.
[SAVE] [S&] [X] [⊘] [◻] [◻] [◻] [♨] [≈] [⊗]

AAA WWWW Best Western Heritage Inn M
(661) 764-6268. **$70-$109.** 253 Trask St. I-5, exit Stockdale Hwy, just e. Ext corridors. **Pets:** Medium. $10 one-time fee/pet. Service with restrictions, supervision.
[SAVE] [S&] [X] [&] [◻] [◻] [≈]

AAA WWWW Best Western Hill House SH ☼
(661) 327-4064. **$59-$99, 3 day notice.** 700 Truxtun Ave. SR 99, exit California Ave, just e, just n on Oak St, then 1.5 mi e. Int corridors. **Pets:** Medium. $10 daily fee/pet. Service with restrictions, supervision.
[SAVE] [S&] [X] [◻] [◻] [♨] [≈]

WWW Days Inn M
(661) 324-5555. **$69-$89, 3 day notice.** 4500 Buck Owens Blvd. SR 99, exit SR 58 (Rosedale Hwy) southbound, just e to Pierce Rd, then 0.7 mi n; exit Airport Dr northbound to Buck Owens Blvd, then just s. Ext corridors. **Pets:** Small. $20 one-time fee/room. No service, supervision.
[ASK] [S&] [X] [◻] [◻] [≈]

WWWW Doubletree Hotel LH ☼
(661) 323-7111. **$79-$139.** 3100 Camino Del Rio Ct. SR 99, exit SR 58 (Rosedale Hwy), just w. Int corridors. **Pets:** Other species. $15 one-time fee/room.
[X] [&M] [⊘] [&] [◻] [◻] [♨] [≈] [⊗]

AAA WWWW Holiday Inn Select Convention Center LH
(661) 323-1900. **$80-$99.** 801 Truxtun Ave. SR 99, exit California Ave, 1.2 mi e, 0.4 mi n on Chester Ave, then just e. Int corridors. **Pets:** Accepted.
[SAVE] [S&] [X] [&M] [⊘] [&] [◻] [◻] [♨] [≈] [⊗]

WWW Howard Johnson Express Inn M
(661) 396-1425. **$65.** 2700 White Ln. SR 99, exit White Ln, then just e. Ext corridors. **Pets:** Medium, dogs only. Service with restrictions, supervision.
[ASK] [S&] [X] [◻] [◻] [≈]

AAA WWWW La Quinta Inn Bakersfield M 🐾
(661) 325-7400. **$95-$119.** 3232 Riverside Dr. SR 99, exit SR 58 (Rosedale Hwy) southbound; exit Buck Owens Blvd northbound, just n of Rosedale Hwy. Ext corridors. **Pets:** Medium. Service with restrictions, supervision.
[SAVE] [X] [&M] [⊘] [◻] [◻] [≈]

AAA WW Liberty Inn Motel M
(661) 366-1630. **$50-$57.** 8230 E Brundage Ln. SR 99, 7 mi e on SR 58, exit SR 284 (Weed Patch Hwy), just n, then just e. Ext/int corridors. **Pets:** Small, other species. $5 one-time fee/pet. Service with restrictions, supervision.
[SAVE] [S&] [X] [◻] [≈]

AAA WWWW Quality Inn M
(661) 325-0772. **$72-$135.** 1011 Oak St. SR 99, exit California Ave, just e, then just s. Ext/int corridors. **Pets:** Medium, other species. $10 daily fee/pet. Designated rooms, service with restrictions, supervision.
[SAVE] [S&] [X] [◻] [◻] [≈]

AAA WWW Ramada Limited-Central M ☼
(661) 831-1922. **$70-$100.** 830 Wible Rd. SR 99, exit Ming Ave, 0.8 mi ne. Ext corridors. **Pets:** Medium, other species. $5 daily fee/pet. Service with restrictions, supervision.
[SAVE] [S&] [X] [&] [◻] [◻] [≈]

WWWW Residence Inn by Marriott SH ☼
(661) 321-9800. **$129.** 4241 Chester Ln. SR 99, exit California Ave, 0.5 mi w, then just n. Ext corridors. **Pets:** Other species. $75 one-time fee/room. Service with restrictions, supervision.
[ASK] [S&] [X] [&M] [⊘] [&] [◻] [◻] [≈] [⊗]

WWW Rio Bravo Resort LH
(661) 872-5000. **$85-$129, 3 day notice.** 11200 Lake Ming Rd. SR 99, exit SR 178, 12 mi e, then 2.5 mi n on Alfred Harrell Hwy. Int corridors. **Pets:** Accepted.
[ASK] [S&] [X] [◻] [◻] [♨] [⊗]

AAA WW Super 8 Motel Bakersfield M
(661) 322-1012. **$59-$79.** 901 Real Rd. SR 99, exit California Ave, just w, then just s. Ext corridors. **Pets:** Small. $10 daily fee/pet. Service with restrictions, supervision.
[SAVE] [S&] [X] [◻] [≈]

AAA WW Vagabond Inn North M
(661) 392-1800. **$45-$55.** 6100 Knudsen Dr. SR 99, exit Olive Dr, west side. Ext corridors. **Pets:** Accepted.
[SAVE] [S&] [X] [◻] [◻] [≈]

(AAA) ▼▼ Vagabond Inn South M
(661) 831-9200. **$49-$55.** 6501 Colony St. SR 99, exit Panama Ln, just e, then just s. Ext corridors. **Pets:** Accepted.
[SAVE] [S❄] [✕] [🛏] [💻] [≋]

BANNING

(AAA) ▼▼ Banning Travelodge M
(951) 849-1000. **$69-$89.** 1700 W Ramsey St. I-10, exit 22nd St, 0.5 mi e, then just n. Ext corridors. **Pets:** Medium. $5 daily fee/pet. Designated rooms, service with restrictions, supervision.
[SAVE] [S❄] [✕] [🛏] [💻] [≋]

▼▼◆ Days Inn M
(951) 849-0092. **$57-$140.** 2320 W Ramsey St. I-10, exit 22nd St, just n, then just w. Ext corridors. **Pets:** Medium. $10 daily fee/pet. Designated rooms, service with restrictions, supervision.
[ASK] [S❄] [✕] [🛏] [💻] [≋]

(AAA) ▼ Super 8 Motel M
(951) 849-8888. **$57-$199.** 1690 W Ramsey St. I-10, exit 22nd St, just n, then 0.4 mi e. Int corridors. **Pets:** Medium. $5 daily fee/pet. Designated rooms, service with restrictions, supervision.
[SAVE] [S❄] [✕] [🛏] [💻] [≋]

BARSTOW

(AAA) ▼▼ Barstow-Super 8 Motel M
(760) 256-8443. **$58-$75.** 170 Coolwater Ln. I-15/40, exit E Main St, 0.3 mi w, then just s. Ext corridors. **Pets:** Other species. $5 daily fee/pet. Service with restrictions, crate.
[SAVE] [S❄] [✕] [🛏] [💻] [≋]

(AAA) ▼▼◆ Best Western Desert Villa Inn M
(760) 256-1781. **$69-$139, 3 day notice.** 1984 E Main St. I-15/40, exit Main St westbound; exit Montara eastbound, 0.5 mi e of I-15. Ext corridors. **Pets:** Medium, other species. $15 one-time fee/room. Service with restrictions, supervision.
[SAVE] [✕] [👤M] [🐾] [🖼] [🛏] [💻] [🍴] [≋]

(AAA) ▼▼ Days Inn M
(760) 256-1737. **$49-$59.** 1590 Coolwater Ln. I-15/40, exit E Main St, just w, then just s on Roberta St. Ext corridors. **Pets:** Accepted.
[SAVE] [S❄] [✕] [🛏] [≋]

(AAA) ▼ Executive Inn M
(760) 256-7581. **$35.** 1261 E Main St. I-15/40, exit E Main St, 0.8 mi w. Ext corridors. **Pets:** Other species. $5 one-time fee/pet. Service with restrictions, supervision.
[SAVE] [S❄] [✕] [🛏] [≋]

(AAA) ▼ Gateway Motel M
(760) 256-8931. **$42-$72.** 1630 E Main St. I-15/40, exit E Main St, just e. Ext corridors. **Pets:** Accepted.
[SAVE] [S❄] [✕] [🛏] [≋]

▼▼◆ Holiday Inn Express, Barstow-Historic Route 66 SH
(760) 256-1300. **$89-$99.** 1861 W Main St. I-15/40, exit W Main St, 0.8 mi ne. Int corridors. **Pets:** Other species. $25 deposit/room. Service with restrictions, supervision.
[ASK] [S❄] [✕] [🛏] [≋]

▼▼◆ Holiday Inn Express Hotel & Suites SH
(760) 253-9200. **$79-$219.** 2700 Lenwood Rd. I-15/40, exit Lenwood Rd, just e, then 0.5 mi s. **Pets:** Other species. $25 deposit/room. Service with restrictions, supervision.
[ASK] [S❄] [✕] [👤M] [🐾] [🖼] [🛏] [≋]

◆ Motel 6 Barstow #1355 M
(760) 256-1752. **$40-$51.** 150 N Yucca Ave. I-15/40, exit E Main St, 0.5 mi w, then just s. Ext corridors. **Pets:** Accepted.
[S❄] [✕] [≋]

(AAA) ▼▼ Quality Inn M
(760) 256-6891. **$49-$99.** 1520 E Main St. I-15/40, exit E Main St, 0.3 mi w. Ext corridors. **Pets:** Small. $10 one-time fee/room. Designated rooms, service with restrictions, supervision.
[SAVE] [S❄] [✕] [🛏] [💻] [🍴] [≋]

▼▼ Ramada Inn SH
(760) 256-5673. **$79-$99.** 1511 E Main St. I-15/40, exit E Main St, 0.3 mi w. Int corridors. **Pets:** Medium. $20 one-time fee/pet. Service with restrictions, supervision.
[ASK] [S❄] [✕] [👤M] [🛏] [💻] [🍴] [≋]

(AAA) ▼ Stardust Inn M
(760) 256-7116. **$35-$38.** 901 E Main St. I-15/40, exit Barstow Rd, 0.8 mi n, then 0.4 mi e. Ext corridors. **Pets:** Accepted.
[SAVE] [S❄] [✕] [🛏] [≋]

BEAUMONT

(AAA) ▼ Best Value Inn M
(951) 845-2185. **$65-$129.** 625 E 5th St. I-10, exit SR 79 (Beaumont Ave), just n. Ext corridors. **Pets:** Small. $5 daily fee/pet. Service with restrictions, supervision.
[SAVE] [S❄] [✕] [🛏] [≋]

(AAA) ▼▼◆ Best Western El Rancho Motor Inn M
(951) 845-2176. **$75-$170.** 480 E 5th St. I-10, exit SR 79 (Beaumont Ave), just n, then just e. Ext corridors. **Pets:** Very small. $15 daily fee/pet. Designated rooms, service with restrictions, supervision.
[SAVE] [S❄] [✕] [🛏] [💻] [🍴] [≋]

BENICIA

(AAA) ▼▼◆ Best Western Heritage Inn SH
(707) 746-0401. **$80-$109.** 1955 E 2nd St. I-780, exit Central Benicia/E 2nd St, just e. Int corridors. **Pets:** Medium. $25 one-time fee/pet. Service with restrictions, crate.
[SAVE] [S❄] [✕] [🛏] [💻] [≋]

BEN LOMOND

(AAA) ▼▼ Econo Lodge M
(831) 336-2292. **$69-$169, 7 day notice.** 9733 Hwy 9. SR 9, 0.3 mi n; on San Lorenzo River. Ext corridors. **Pets:** Accepted.
[SAVE] [S❄] [✕] [🛏] [💻] [≋]

BERKELEY

(AAA) ▼▼ Best Value Golden Bear Inn SH
(510) 525-6770. **$69-$89.** 1620 San Pablo Ave. I-80, exit Gilman E, just 2 mi s. Ext corridors. **Pets:** $15 daily fee/pet. Service with restrictions, supervision.
[SAVE] [S❄] [✕] [🛏]

BERRY CREEK

▼▼▼ Lake Oroville Bed & Breakfast BB
(530) 589-0700. **$125-$175, 5 day notice.** 240 Sunday Dr. SR 162, exit SR 70, 15 mi e on SR 162 to Bell Ranch Rd, 0.5 mi w. Int corridors. **Pets:** Other species. $10 daily fee/pet. Service with restrictions, supervision.
[ASK] [S❄] [✕] [👤M] [🐾] [🛏]

BIG BEAR LAKE

▼▼◆ Alpine Village Suites Lodge M
(909) 866-5460. **$89-$189, 3 day notice.** 546 Pine Knot Ave. SR 18 business route; in the village. Ext/int corridors. **Pets:** Accepted.
[ASK] [S❄] [✕] [🛏] [💻] [≋]

▼▼◆ Best Western Big Bear Chateau SH 🐾
(909) 866-6666. **$79-$299, 3 day notice.** 42200 Moonridge Rd. SR 18, 1.5 mi e of Pine Knot Ave, then 0.5 mi s. Int corridors. **Pets:** Dogs only. $30 daily fee/room. Service with restrictions, crate.
[ASK] [S❄] [✕] [🛏] [💻] [🍴] [≋] [✕]

Big Bear Lakefront Lodge M
(909) 866-8271. **$45-$199, 3 day notice.** 40360 Lakeview Dr. SR 18, 0.5 mi w of Pine Knot Ave, 0.5 mi nw. Ext/int corridors. **Pets:** Accepted.

Cozy Hollow Lodge CA
(909) 866-9694. **$49-$279, 15 day notice.** 40409 Big Bear Blvd. SR 18, 0.8 mi w. Ext corridors. **Pets:** Medium, dogs only. $100 deposit/room, $10 daily fee/pet, $25 one-time fee/room. Designated rooms, service with restrictions, supervision.

Eagle's Nest Bed & Breakfast BB
(909) 866-6465. **$75-$165, 5 day notice.** 41675 Big Bear Blvd. SR 18, 1 mi e of Pine Knot Ave. Ext/int corridors. **Pets:** Other species. $10 daily fee/pet. Designated rooms, service with restrictions, supervision.

Golden Bear Cottages CA
(909) 866-2010. **$79-$119, 30 day notice.** 39367 Big Bear Blvd. SR 18, 2 mi w of village. Ext corridors. **Pets:** Other species. $10 daily fee/pet. Designated rooms, service with restrictions, crate.

Grey Squirrel Resort CA
(909) 866-4335. **$94-$187, 14 day notice.** 39372 Big Bear Blvd. SR 18, 2.5 mi w of village. Ext corridors. **Pets:** $10 daily fee/pet. No service, crate.

Honey Bear Lodge M
(909) 866-7825. **$39-$229, 7 day notice.** 40994 Pennsylvania Ave. SR 18 business route (Pine Knot Ave), just e. Ext corridors. **Pets:** Dogs only. $200 deposit/room, $10 daily fee/pet. Designated rooms, service with restrictions, supervision.

Majestic Moose Lodge CA
(909) 866-2435. **$69-$249, 7 day notice.** 39328 Big Bear Blvd. SR 18, 2.5 mi w of village. Ext/int corridors. **Pets:** Accepted.

Pine Knot Guest Ranch CA
(909) 866-6500. **$79-$189.** 908 Pine Knot Ave. Just s of SR 18 business route and downtown area. Ext corridors. **Pets:** Other species. $10 daily fee/pet. Designated rooms, service with restrictions.

Shore Acres Lodge CA
(909) 866-8200. **$105-$295, 14 day notice.** 40090 Lakeview Dr. SR 18, 0.5 mi w of Pine Knot Ave, then 0.7 mi nw. Ext corridors. **Pets:** Accepted.

Sleepy Forest Cottages CA
(909) 866-7444. **$65-$249, 15 day notice.** 426 Eureka Dr. SR 18, 0.7 mi e of Pine Knot Ave, then just n. Ext corridors. **Pets:** Dogs only. $100 deposit/room, $25 daily fee/pet. Designated rooms, service with restrictions, supervision.

Stage Coach Lodge CA
(909) 878-3008. **$103-$165, 14 day notice.** 652 Jeffries Rd. SR 18, 0.5 mi e of Pine Knot Ave, then 0.3 mi s. Ext corridors. **Pets:** Other species. $10 daily fee/pet. Designated rooms, service with restrictions, supervision.

Timber Haven Lodge CA
(909) 866-7207. **$99-$250, 14 day notice.** 877 Tulip Ln. SR 18, 1.8 mi w of Pine Knot Ave, 0.4 mi s. Ext corridors. **Pets:** Dogs only. $10 daily fee/pet. Designated rooms, service with restrictions, supervision.

The Timberline Lodge CA
(909) 866-4141. **$118-$200.** 39921 Big Bear Blvd. SR 18, 1.5 mi w of Pine Knot Ave. Ext corridors. **Pets:** $10 daily fee/pet.

BIG PINE

Big Pine Motel M
(760) 938-2282. **$45.** 370 S Main. On US 395. Ext corridors. **Pets:** Accepted.

Bristlecone Motel M
(760) 938-2067. **$44-$68.** 101 N Main St. On US 395. Ext corridors. **Pets:** Other species. $4 one-time fee/pet. Service with restrictions, crate.

BISHOP

Best Western Bishop Holiday Spa Lodge M
(760) 873-3543. **$79-$119.** 1025 N Main St. On US 395. Ext corridors. **Pets:** Medium, other species. $10 daily fee/pet. Designated rooms, service with restrictions, supervision.

Comfort Inn M
(760) 873-4284. **$79-$108.** 805 N Main St. On US 395. Ext corridors. **Pets:** Medium. $5 daily fee/pet. Designated rooms, service with restrictions, supervision.

Holiday Inn Express Hotel & Suites SH
(760) 872-2423. **$99-$159.** 636 N Main St. On US 395. Int corridors. **Pets:** Small, dogs only. $20 daily fee/pet. Designated rooms, service with restrictions, supervision.

Motel 6–4094 M
(760) 873-8426. **$49-$89.** 1005 N Main St. On US 395. Ext corridors. **Pets:** Small. Service with restrictions, supervision.

Ramada Limited M
(760) 872-1771. **$69-$99.** 155 E Elm St. On US 395, just e. Ext corridors. **Pets:** Large, other species. $10 daily fee/pet. Designated rooms, service with restrictions, supervision.

Thunderbird Motel M
(760) 873-4215. **$50-$109.** 190 W Pine St. Just w of US 395. Ext corridors. **Pets:** Accepted.

Vagabond Inn M
(760) 873-6351. **$79-$99.** 1030 N Main St. On US 395. Ext corridors. **Pets:** Medium, other species. $5 daily fee/pet. Service with restrictions.

BLYTHE

Best Western Sahara Motel M
(760) 922-7105. **$69-$149.** 825 W Hobsonway. I-10, exit Lovekin Blvd, just n, then just w. Ext corridors. **Pets:** Accepted.

Comfort Suites M
(760) 922-9209. **$50-$149.** 545 E Hobsonway. I-10, exit 7th St, just n, then just w. Ext corridors. **Pets:** Medium, other species. $10 daily fee/pet. Service with restrictions, supervision.

🅰🅰🅰 ❤❤❤❤ Holiday Inn Express Ⓜ
(760) 921-2300. **$89-$159, 7 day notice.** 600 W Donlon St. I-10, exit Lovekin Blvd, just e. Ext corridors. **Pets:** Medium. $20 daily fee/pet. Designated rooms, service with restrictions, supervision.
🆂🅰🆅🅴 🆂🔒 ❌ 🍴 💻 🏊

🅰🅰🅰 ❤❤❤ Super 8 Motel Ⓜ
(760) 922-8881. **$45-$140, 3 day notice.** 550 W Donlon St. I-10, exit Lovekin Blvd, just s. Int corridors. **Pets:** Small. $5 one-time fee/pet. Service with restrictions, supervision.
🆂🅰🆅🅴 🆂🔒 ❌ 🍴 🏊

🅰🅰🅰 ❤❤❤ Travelers Inn Express Ⓜ
(760) 922-3334. **$69-$139.** 1781 E Hobsonway. I-10, exit Intake Blvd, just n, then just w. Ext corridors. **Pets:** Medium, other species. Designated rooms, service with restrictions, supervision.
🆂🅰🆅🅴 🆂🔒 ❌ 🍴 💻 🏊

BORREGO SPRINGS

🅰🅰🅰 ❤❤❤❤ Borrego Springs Resort Hotel 🆂🅷
(760) 767-5700. **$94-$135.** 1112 Tilting T Dr. SR 22, 1.5 mi s on Borrego Valley Rd, just w. Int corridors. **Pets:** Very small. $50 deposit/pet. Designated rooms, service with restrictions, crate.
🆂🅰🆅🅴 🆂🔒 ❌ 🏋 🍴 💻 🍴 🏊 🚫

BRAWLEY

🅰🅰🅰 ❤❤❤❤ Brawley Inn Ⓜ
(760) 344-1199. **$60-$120.** 575 W Main St. On SR 86 and 78. Ext/int corridors. **Pets:** Accepted.
🆂🅰🆅🅴 🆂🔒 ❌ 🍴 💻 🏊

BREA

❤❤ ❤❤ Homestead Studio Suites Hotel-Brea/Anaheim Ⓜ
(714) 528-2500. **$78-$93.** 3050 E Imperial Hwy. SR 57, exit Imperial Hwy, 1.4 mi e. Ext corridors. **Pets:** Small. $25 daily fee/pet. Supervision.
🅰🆂🅺 🆂🔒 ❌ 🍴 💻

🅰🅰🅰 ❤❤ Hyland Motel Ⓜ
(714) 990-6867. **$55-$60, 3 day notice.** 727 S Brea Blvd. SR 57, exit Imperial Hwy, 1 mi w, then 0.7 mi s. Ext corridors. **Pets:** Very small, dogs only. Designated rooms, service with restrictions, supervision.
🆂🅰🆅🅴 ❌ 🍴 💻

🅰🅰🅰 ❤❤❤ Woodfin Suite Hotel Ⓜ
(714) 579-3200. **$129.** 3100 E Imperial Hwy. SR 57, exit Imperial Hwy, 1.5 mi e. Ext corridors. **Pets:** Other species. $150 deposit/pet, $5 daily fee/pet. Service with restrictions, crate.
🆂🅰🆅🅴 🆂🔒 ❌ 🍴 💻 🏊

BRIDGEPORT

🅰🅰🅰 ❤❤ Best Western Ruby Inn Ⓜ
(760) 932-7241. **$95-$155.** 333 Main St. On US 395; center. Ext corridors. **Pets:** Medium. Designated rooms, service with restrictions, supervision.
🆂🅰🆅🅴 🆂🔒 ❌ 🍴 💻

🅰🅰🅰 ❤ Redwood Motel Ⓜ 🐾
(760) 932-7060. **$55-$149.** 425 Main St. On US 395; on the north side of town. **Pets:** Dogs only. $10 daily fee/pet. Designated rooms, service with restrictions, supervision.
🆂🅰🆅🅴 🆂🔒 ❌ 🏋 🍴 💻

🅰🅰🅰 ❤❤ Silver Maple Inn Ⓜ
(760) 932-7383. **$75-$95.** 310 Main St. On US 395; center. Ext corridors. **Pets:** Other species. Service with restrictions, supervision.
🆂🅰🆅🅴 🆂🔒 ❌ 🍴 💻 🏧

🅰🅰🅰 ❤❤❤ Walker River Lodge Ⓜ
(760) 932-7021. **$55-$200.** 100 Main St. On US 395; at south end of town. Ext corridors. **Pets:** Service with restrictions, supervision.
🆂🅰🆅🅴 🆂🔒 ❌ 📷 🍴 💻 🏊 🚫

BUELLTON

🅰🅰🅰 ❤❤❤ Quality Inn Solvang/Buellton Ⓜ 🐾
(805) 688-0022. **$70-$130.** 630 Ave of Flags. US 101, exit first Buellton southbound; exit Frontage Rd northbound, just w over freeway. Ext/int corridors. **Pets:** Medium. $25 one-time fee/room. Service with restrictions, supervision.
🆂🅰🆅🅴 ❌ 🍴

❤❤❤❤ Rancho Santa Barbara Marriott 🆂🅷 🐾
(805) 688-1000. **$129-$249.** 555 McMurray Rd. US 101, exit SR 246, just e, then just n. Int corridors. **Pets:** Other species. $50 one-time fee/room. Designated rooms, service with restrictions, supervision.
🅰🆂🅺 🆂🔒 ❌ 🍴 💻 🍴 🏊 🚫

BURNEY

🅰🅰🅰 ❤❤ Burney Motel Ⓜ
(530) 335-4500. **$45-$69, 3 day notice.** 37448 Main St. 0.8 mi e on SR 299. Ext corridors. **Pets:** Accepted.
🆂🅰🆅🅴 ❌ 🍴 💻 🚫

🅰🅰🅰 ❤ Charm Motel Ⓜ
(530) 335-2254. **$44-$89, 3 day notice.** 37363 Main St. 0.8 mi e on SR 299. Ext corridors. **Pets:** Dogs only. $5 daily fee/pet. Service with restrictions, supervision.
🆂🅰🆅🅴 🆂🔒 ❌ 🍴 💻

🅰🅰🅰 ❤ Green Gables Motel Ⓜ 🐾
(530) 335-2264. **$50-$82, 3 day notice.** 37385 Main St. 0.8 mi e on SR 299. Ext corridors. **Pets:** Other species. $5 daily fee/pet. Service with restrictions, supervision.
🆂🅰🆅🅴 🆂🔒 ❌ 🍴 💻 🏊 🚫

🅰🅰🅰 ❤❤ Shasta Pines Motel Ⓜ
(530) 335-2201. **$49-$116, 7 day notice.** 37386 Main St. 0.8 mi e on SR 299. Ext corridors. **Pets:** Very small, other species. $20 deposit/pet, $7 daily fee/pet. Designated rooms, service with restrictions, supervision.
🆂🅰🆅🅴 🆂🔒 ❌ 🔳 🍴 💻 🏊 🚫

BUTTONWILLOW

🅰🅰🅰 ❤❤❤ Super 8 Motel Ⓜ
(661) 764-5117. **$47-$49.** 20681 Tracy Ave. I-5, exit SR 58, just e. Ext corridors. **Pets:** Small, dogs only. Designated rooms, service with restrictions, supervision.
🆂🅰🆅🅴 🆂🔒 ❌ 🏋 🍴 🏊

CALIMESA

🅰🅰🅰 ❤❤❤ Calimesa Inn Motel Ⓜ
(909) 795-2536. **$65-$75.** 1205 Calimesa Blvd. I-10, exit Calimesa Blvd, just ne. Ext corridors. **Pets:** Small. $10 daily fee/pet. Designated rooms, service with restrictions, supervision.
🆂🅰🆅🅴 🆂🔒 ❌ 🍴 🏊

CALIPATRIA

🅰🅰🅰 ❤❤❤ Calipatria Inn & Suites Ⓜ 🐾
(760) 348-7348. **$80-$205.** 700 N Sorenson. On SR 111. Ext corridors. **Pets:** Other species. $15 deposit/room, $5 one-time fee/room. Service with restrictions, supervision.
🆂🅰🆅🅴 🆂🔒 ❌ 🍴 💻 🍴 🏊

CAMBRIA

❤❤ Cambria Shores Inn Ⓜ 🐾
(805) 927-8644. **$105-$180, 7 day notice.** 6276 Moonstone Beach Dr. SR 1, exit Moonstone Beach Dr, just w, then 0.8 mi s. Ext corridors. **Pets:** Dogs only. $10 daily fee/pet. Supervision.
❌ 🍴 💻 🏧

▽▽▽▽ Fog Catcher Inn **M** ❖
(805) 927-1400. **$119-$359.** 6400 Moonstone Beach Dr. SR 1, exit Moonstone Beach Dr, just w, then 0.7 mi s. Ext corridors. **Pets:** Large. $27.25 one-time fee/room. Designated rooms, service with restrictions, supervision.
(ASK) (S⊘) (X) (▭) (⤳) (⌀)

▲▲▲ ▽▽▽ Mariners Inn by the Sea **M**
(805) 927-4624. **$79-$169, 3 day notice.** 6180 Moonstone Beach Dr. SR 1, exit Moonstone Beach Dr, just w, then 1 mi s. Ext corridors. **Pets:** Accepted.
(SAVE) (X) (🖥) (⌀)

▽▽▽▽ Sea Otter Inn **M**
(805) 927-5888. **$79-$269, 3 day notice.** 6656 Moonstone Beach Dr. SR 1, exit Moonstone Beach Dr, just w, then 0.5 mi s. Ext corridors. **Pets:** Accepted.
(ASK) (S⊘) (X) (🖥) (▭) (⤳) (⌀)

CAMERON PARK

▽▽▽▽ Best Western Cameron Park Inn **M**
(530) 677-2203. **Call for rates.** 3361 Coach Ln. 12 mi w of Placerville on US 50, exit Cameron Park Dr. Ext corridors. **Pets:** Accepted.
(S⊘) (X) (♿M) (🖥) (▭) (⤳)

CAMINO

▽▽▽ Camino Hotel-Seven Mile House **BB**
(530) 644-7740. **$86-$119, 7 day notice.** 4103 Carson Rd. US 50, exit at Camino, just n. Int corridors. **Pets:** Accepted.
(ASK) (S⊘) (X) (♿M) (⌀) (W) (☎)

CAMPBELL

▲▲▲ ▽▽▽▽ Campbell Inn **M**
(408) 374-4300. **$109.** 675 E Campbell Ave. SR 17, exit Hamilton Ave E, 0.3 mi to Bascom Ave, 0.3 mi s, then 0.3 mi w. Ext corridors. **Pets:** Dogs only. $50 one-time fee/room. Service with restrictions, supervision.
(SAVE) (S⊘) (X) (🖥) (▭) (⤳) (X)

▲▲▲ ▽▽▽▽ Residence Inn By Marriott-San Jose **M**
(408) 559-1551. **$149-$179.** 2761 S Bascom Ave. SR 17, exit Camden Ave E, just n. Ext corridors. **Pets:** Medium, other species. $75 one-time fee/room. Service with restrictions.
(ASK) (S⊘) (X) (▭) (⤳)

CAPITOLA

▲▲▲ ▽▽▽▽ Best Western Capitola By-the-Sea Inn & Suites **SH**
(831) 477-0607. **$79-$219.** 1435 41st Ave. SR 1, exit 41st Ave, 4 blks w. Int corridors. **Pets:** Accepted.
(SAVE) (S⊘) (X) (♿M) (♿) (🖥) (▭) (⤳)

▲▲▲ ▽▽▽ Capitola Inn **M**
(831) 462-3004. **$85-$160.** 822 Bay Ave. SR 1, exit Bay Ave, just w. Ext/int corridors. **Pets:** Small, dogs only. $20 one-time fee/pet. Designated rooms, service with restrictions, supervision.
(SAVE) (S⊘) (X) (🖥) (⤳)

CARLSBAD

▲▲▲ ▽▽▽▽▽ Four Seasons Resort Aviara **LH** ❖
(760) 603-6800. **$405-$530, 3 day notice.** 7100 Four Seasons Point. I-5, exit Poinsettia Ln/Aviara Pkwy, 1 mi e on Poinsettia Ln, then 1 mi s on Aviara Pkwy. Int corridors. **Pets:** Very small. Crate.
(SAVE) (X) (▭) (🍴) (⤳) (X)

▲▲▲ ▽▽▽ Inns of America **M** ❖
(760) 931-1185. **$89-$129.** 751 Raintree Dr. I-5, exit Poinsettia Ln, just w to Ave Encinas, then just n. Ext corridors. **Pets:** Medium, other species. $10 daily fee/room. Service with restrictions, supervision.
(SAVE) (S⊘) (X) (🖥) (🍴) (⤳)

▽▽▽ Motel 6–1021 **M**
(760) 434-7135. **$49-$69.** 1006 Carlsbad Village Dr. I-5, exit Carlsbad Village Dr, just w. Ext corridors. **Pets:** Accepted.
(S⊘) (X)

CARPINTERIA

▲▲▲ ▽▽▽▽ Holiday Inn Express **SH**
(805) 566-9499. **$89-$199.** 5606 Carpinteria Ave. US 101, exit Casitas Pass Rd, just s, then just e. Int corridors. **Pets:** Medium. $10 daily fee/room. Designated rooms, service with restrictions, supervision.
(SAVE) (S⊘) (X) (♿M) (🎧) (♿) (🖥) (▭) (⤳)

CASTAIC

▲▲▲ ▽▽▽ Comfort Inn **M**
(661) 295-1100. **$59-$89.** 31558 Castaic Rd. I-5, exit Parker Rd northbound, 0.3 mi ne; exit Lake Hughes Rd southbound, 0.5 mi se. Ext corridors. **Pets:** Accepted.
(SAVE) (S⊘) (X) (🎧) (🖥) (▭) (⤳)

CASTRO VALLEY

▽▽▽ Holiday Inn Express **SH**
(510) 538-9501. **$105.** 2532 Castro Valley Blvd. I-580, exit Castro Valley Blvd, 0.3 mi n. Int corridors. **Pets:** Small. $20 daily fee/pet. Service with restrictions, supervision.
(ASK) (S⊘) (X) (🖥) (▭) (⤳)

CATHEDRAL CITY

▽▽▽ Comfort Suites **M**
(760) 324-5939. **$49-$169.** 69-151 E Palm Canyon Dr. I-10, exit Date Palm Dr, 5 mi s, then just e. Ext corridors. **Pets:** Small. $10 daily fee/pet. Service with restrictions, supervision.
(ASK) (S⊘) (X) (🖥) (▭) (⤳)

▲▲▲ ▽▽▽▽ Doral Desert Princess Resort, Palm Springs **LH**
(760) 322-7000. **$69-$135, 3 day notice.** 67-967 Vista Chino. I-10, exit Date Palm Dr, 0.5 mi s, then 1 mi w. Int corridors. **Pets:** Medium. $50 one-time fee/pet. Designated rooms, service with restrictions.
(SAVE) (S⊘) (X) (🖥) (▭) (🍴) (⤳) (X)

CAYUCOS

▽▽▽ Cayucos Beach Inn **M** ❖
(805) 995-2828. **$85-$135, 3 day notice.** 333 S Ocean Ave. On SR 1 business route. Ext corridors. **Pets:** Other species. $10 one-time fee/room. Service with restrictions, crate.
(X) (🖥) (▭)

▲▲▲ ▽▽ Cypress Tree Motel **M** ❖
(805) 995-3917. **$45-$110.** 125 S Ocean Ave. On SR 1 business route. Ext corridors. **Pets:** Other species. $10 daily fee/pet. Service with restrictions, supervision.
(SAVE) (S⊘) (X) (🖥) (▭) (⌀)

▲▲▲ ▽▽ Dolphin Inn **M**
(805) 995-3810. **$49-$199, 3 day notice.** 399 S Ocean Ave. On SR 1 business route. Ext corridors. **Pets:** Dogs only. $10 one-time fee/pet. Service with restrictions, supervision.
(SAVE) (S⊘) (X) (🖥) (▭) (⌀)

▲▲▲ ▽▽ Estero Bay Motel **M**
(805) 995-3614. **$49-$145, 6 day notice.** 25 S Ocean Ave. On SR 1 business route. Ext corridors. **Pets:** Small. $10 one-time fee/pet. Service with restrictions, supervision.
(SAVE) (S⊘) (X) (🖥) (▭) (⌀)

▲▲▲ ▽▽ Shoreline Inn **M** ❖
(805) 995-3681. **$99-$165.** 1 N Ocean Ave. On SR 1 business route. Ext corridors. **Pets:** Other species. $10 one-time fee/room. Service with restrictions, supervision.
(SAVE) (S⊘) (X) (🖥) (▭) (⌀)

CEDARVILLE

 Sunrise Motel **M**
(530) 279-2161. **$60-$65, 4 day notice.** 54889 Hwy 299. 0.5 mi w on SR 299. Ext corridors. **Pets:** Medium. $25 deposit/pet, $10 daily fee/pet. Designated rooms, service with restrictions, supervision.

CHESTER

Chester Manor Motel **M**
(530) 258-2441. **$95-$105.** 306 Main St. On SR 36. Ext corridors. **Pets:** Accepted.

CHICO

Budget Inn of Chico **SH**
(530) 342-9472. **$55-$95.** 1717 Park Ave. SR 99, exit 20th E, then right. Ext corridors. **Pets:** Accepted.

Deluxe Inn **M**
(530) 342-8386. **$45-$89.** 2507 Esplanade. 2 mi n on SR 99 business route. Ext corridors. **Pets:** Small. $4 daily fee/pet. Designated rooms, service with restrictions, supervision.

The Esplanade Bed & Breakfast **BB**
(530) 345-8084. **$75-$120.** 620 Esplanade. 0.3 mi n; downtown. Int corridors. **Pets:** Accepted.

Heritage Inn Express **M**
(530) 343-4527. **$80, 30 day notice.** 725 Broadway. SR 32, exit SR 99, 1 mi w. Ext corridors. **Pets:** Accepted.

Holiday Inn of Chico **M**
(530) 345-2491. **$109-$200.** 685 Manzanita Ct. Just w of SR 99, via Cohasset Rd. Int corridors. **Pets:** Large, other species. $25 one-time fee/room. Service with restrictions, supervision.

Music Express Inn **BB**
(530) 345-8376. **$76-$125.** 1145 El Monte Ave. SR 99, exit SR 32, 1 mi e to El Monte Ave, then just n. Ext/int corridors. **Pets:** $10 daily fee/room. Service with restrictions, supervision.

Oxford Suites **SH**
(530) 899-9090. **$95.** 2035 Business Ln. SR 99, exit 20th St E. Int corridors. **Pets:** Medium. $25 one-time fee/pet. Service with restrictions, supervision.

Safari Garden Motel **M**
(530) 343-3201. **$50-$55.** 2352 Esplanade. 2 mi n on SR 99 business route. Ext corridors. **Pets:** Small, dogs only. $15 one-time fee/room. Designated rooms, service with restrictions, supervision.

Super 8 Motel **M**
(530) 345-2533. **$70-$150.** 655 Manzanita Ct. Just w of SR 99, via Cohasset Rd. Int corridors. **Pets:** $4 daily fee/pet. No service, supervision.

CHOWCHILLA

Days Inn **M**
(559) 665-4821. **$58-$68.** 220 E Robertson Blvd. SR 99, exit Robertson Blvd W. Ext corridors. **Pets:** Accepted.

CLIO

Molly's Bed & Breakfast **BB**
(530) 836-4436. **$90-$110, 7 day notice.** 276 Lower Main St. Just e of SR 89. Int corridors. **Pets:** Dogs only. $10 daily fee/pet. Designated rooms, service with restrictions, supervision.

COALINGA

Best Western Big Country Inn **M**
(559) 935-0866. **$69-$109.** 25020 W Dorris Ave. I-5, exit SR 198/ Hanford-Lemoore, just w. Ext corridors. **Pets:** Medium. $10 daily fee/pet. Designated rooms, service with restrictions, supervision.

The Inn at Harris Ranch **SH**
(559) 935-0717. **$119-$131.** 24505 W Dorris Ave. I-5, exit SR 198, just e; at Hanford-Lemoore off-ramp. Ext/int corridors. **Pets:** Accepted.

COLTON

Hampton Inn & Suites **SH**
(909) 370-2424. **$89-$179.** 250 N 9th St. I-10, exit 9th St, just n. Int corridors. **Pets:** Small. $25 daily fee/pet. Designated rooms, service with restrictions, supervision.

COLUMBIA

Columbia Gem Motel **CA**
(209) 532-4508. **$69-$158, 7 day notice.** 22131 Parrotts Ferry Rd. 3 mi n of Sonora; 1 mi from Columbia State Historic Park. Ext corridors. **Pets:** Dogs only. Supervision.

CONCORD

Best Western Heritage Inn **M**
(925) 686-4466. **$69-$109.** 4600 Clayton Rd. 3 mi e at Wharton Way. Ext corridors. **Pets:** Medium. $100 deposit/pet. Service with restrictions, supervision.

Holiday Inn Concord **SH**
(925) 687-5500. **$79-$149.** 1050 Burnett Ave. I-680, exit E Concord Ave, just e. Ext/int corridors. **Pets:** Medium. $25 one-time fee/pet. Service with restrictions.

Premier Inns **M**
(925) 674-0888. **$54-$74.** 1581 Concord Ave. SR 242, exit Clayton Rd northbound; exit Concord Ave southbound, just e. Ext corridors. **Pets:** Small, other species. Service with restrictions, supervision.

Sheraton Concord Hotel **SH**
(925) 825-7700. **$89-$179.** 45 John Glenn Dr. I-680, exit Concord Ave, just e. Int corridors. **Pets:** Accepted.

CORNING

Best Western Inn Corning **M**
(530) 824-2468. **$69-$99.** 2165 Solano St. I-5 E, exit Corning, 1 blk e. Ext corridors. **Pets:** Small. $10 daily fee/pet. Designated rooms, service with restrictions, supervision.

Comfort Inn **M**
(530) 824-5200. **$69-$109.** 910 Hwy 99 W. I-5, exit Corning Rd, just e. Int corridors. **Pets:** $10 daily fee/pet. Service with restrictions, supervision.

△△△ ▽▽▽▽ Days Inn M
(530) 824-2000. **$55-$145.** 3475 Hwy 99 W. I-5, exit South Ave, 0.3 mi s. Int corridors. **Pets:** Other species. $50 deposit/room, $5 daily fee/pet. Designated rooms, service with restrictions, supervision.
SAVE Sb X GM (S) 8 2a

CORONA

△△△ ▽▽▽▽ Dynasty Suites Corona M
(951) 371-7185. **$70-$82.** 1805 W 6th St. SR 91, exit 6th St eastbound; exit Maple St westbound, just s. Ext corridors. **Pets:** Small. $10 daily fee/pet. Supervision.
SAVE Sb X 8 2a

COSTA MESA

△△△ ▽▽▽▽ Comfort Inn of Costa Mesa M
(949) 631-7840. **$69-$109.** 2430 Newport Blvd. SR 55, exit 22nd St, just n, on east side of freeway. Ext corridors. **Pets:** Small. $10 daily fee/pet. Designated rooms, service with restrictions, supervision.
SAVE Sb X 8 2a

▽▽▽▽ Hilton Costa Mesa LH
(714) 540-7000. **$89-$269, 3 day notice.** 3050 Bristol St. I-405, exit Bristol St, just s. Int corridors. **Pets:** Accepted.
ASK Sb X 8 TI 2a X

△△△ ▽▽▽▽ La Quinta Inn Costa Mesa (John Wayne/Orange Co. Airport) M
(714) 957-5841. **$89-$109.** 1515 S Coast Dr. I-405, exit Harbor Blvd, just n, then just w. Ext corridors. **Pets:** Small. Designated rooms, service with restrictions, supervision.
SAVE X 8 2a

△△△ ▽▽▽▽ Ramada Limited & Suites SH
(949) 645-2221. **$98-$128.** 1680 Superior Ave. Just w of SR 55 (Newport Blvd) at 17th St. Ext corridors. **Pets:** Small. $50 deposit/pet. Designated rooms, service with restrictions, supervision.
SAVE Sb X 8 2a

▽▽▽▽ Residence Inn by Marriott SH ☙
(714) 241-8800. **$109-$159.** 881 W Baker St. SR 73, exit Bear St; SR 55, exit Baker St. Ext corridors. **Pets:** Other species. $75 one-time fee/room. Supervision.
X 8 2a X

△△△ ▽▽▽ Vagabond Inn M ☙
(714) 557-8360. **$54-$99.** 3205 Harbor Blvd. I-405, exit Harbor Blvd, just s; entrance from Gisler Ave, just w of Harbor. Ext corridors. **Pets:** Small. $5 daily fee/pet. Service with restrictions, supervision.
SAVE Sb X 8 2a

▽▽▽▽ The Westin South Coast Plaza Hotel LH
(714) 540-2500. **$185-$340.** 686 Anton Blvd. I-405, exit Bristol St, just n, then just e. Int corridors. **Pets:** Accepted.
X TI 2a X

△△△ ▽▽▽▽ Wyndham Orange County Airport LH
(714) 751-5100. **$109-$159.** 3350 Ave of the Arts. I-405, exit Bristol St, n to Anton Blvd, just e, then just n. Int corridors. **Pets:** Large. $150 one-time fee/room. Designated rooms, service with restrictions, crate.
SAVE X TI 2a

CRESCENT CITY

▽▽▽▽ Best Value Inn M
(707) 464-4141. **$59-$72.** 440 Hwy 101 N. On US 101. Ext corridors. **Pets:** Large, dogs only. $7 daily fee/pet. Designated rooms, service with restrictions, supervision.
ASK Sb X 8 X

△△△ ▽▽▽▽ Hampton Inn & Suites-Crescent City SH
(707) 465-5400. **$119-$139.** 100 A St. US 101, exit Front St, just w. Int corridors. **Pets:** Accepted.
SAVE Sb X 8 2a

△△△ ▽▽▽ Super 8 M ☙
(707) 464-4111. **$45-$100.** 685 Hwy 101 S. E of US 101 S. Ext corridors. **Pets:** Small, dogs only. $10 daily fee/pet. Designated rooms, service with restrictions, supervision.
SAVE Sb X X K

CROMBERG

▽▽▽ Long Valley Resort CA ☙
(530) 836-0754. **$75-$85, 14 day notice.** 59532 Hwy 70. SR 70. Ext corridors. **Pets:** Other species. $7 daily fee/pet. Designated rooms, no service, supervision.
X GM (S) 8 TI X Z

CUPERTINO

△△△ ▽▽▽▽ Cypress Hotel LH ☙
(408) 253-8900. **$189-$279.** 10050 S De Anza Blvd. SR 85, exit Stevens Creek Blvd E, just s. Int corridors. **Pets:** Service with restrictions.
SAVE Sb X 8 TI

CYPRESS

▽▽▽ Homestead Studio Suites Hotel-Cypress/Long Beach SH
(714) 761-2766. **$84-$99.** 5990 Corporate Ave. I-605, exit Katella Ave, 3 mi e, 0.4 mi n on Valley View Ave, then just w. Int corridors. **Pets:** Small. $25 daily fee/pet. Supervision.
ASK Sb X 8

△△△ ▽▽▽▽ Woodfin Suite Hotel-Cypress SH
(714) 828-4000. **$129.** 5905 Corporate Ave. I-605, exit Katella Ave, 3 mi e, 0.4 mi n on Valley View Ave, then just w. Int corridors. **Pets:** Accepted.
SAVE Sb X 8 2a

DANA POINT

△△△ ▽▽▽▽ Laguna Cliffs Marriott Resort & Spa LH
(949) 661-5000. **$189-$369, 3 day notice.** 25135 Park Lantern. I-5, exit Pacific Coast Hwy, just w on Harbor Dr. Int corridors. **Pets:** Designated rooms, service with restrictions, supervision.
SAVE Sb X 8 TI 2a X

△△△ ▽▽▽▽▽ The St. Regis Monarch Beach Resort & Spa LH ☙
(949) 234-3200. **$485-$5500.** One Monarch Beach Resort. I-5, exit Pacific Coast Hwy northbound, 3 mi n; exit Crown Valley Pkwy southbound, 3 mi w, 1 mi s on Pacific Coast Hwy, then 0.5 mi e on Niguel Rd. Int corridors. **Pets:** Small. $75 one-time fee/pet. Designated rooms, service with restrictions, supervision.
SAVE Sb X GM (S) TI 2a X

DAVIS

△△△ ▽▽▽ Best Western University Lodge M
(530) 756-7890. **$75-$105.** 123 B St. Just e of University of California Campus. Ext corridors. **Pets:** Other species. $20 daily fee/pet. Service with restrictions, supervision.
SAVE Sb X GM 8 X

△△△ ▽▽▽▽ Howard Johnson Hotel M
(530) 792-0800. **$89-$169.** 4100 Chiles Rd. I-80, exit Mace Blvd, just s, then 0.3 mi w. Int corridors. **Pets:** Accepted.
SAVE Sb X GM (S) 8 TI 2a

DEATH VALLEY NATIONAL PARK

▽ Stovepipe Wells Village M
(760) 786-2387. **$79-$99.** SR 190. On SR 190; 24 mi nw of visitor center. Ext corridors. **Pets:** Medium. $50 deposit/room. Service with restrictions, supervision.
X (S) 8 TI 2a Z

DELANO

[AAA] ◆◆ **Comfort Inn** [M]
(661) 725-1022. **$57-$70.** 2211 Girard St. SR 99, exit County Line Rd, just e. Ext corridors. **Pets:** Small. $10 daily fee/room. Service with restrictions, supervision.
[SAVE] [SD] ☒ ▣ ☕ 🏊

DINUBA

◆◆◆ **Reedley Country Inn** [BB]
(559) 638-2585. **$85-$95, 3 day notice.** SR 99, exit Manning Ave, 10 mi e, then 1 mi s on Rd 52 (Reed Ave). Ext/int corridors. **Pets:** Accepted.
☒

DIXON

[AAA] ◆◆◆ **Best Western Inn Dixon** [M]
(707) 678-1400. **$90-$135.** 1345 Commercial Way. I-80, exit Pitt School Rd, 8 mi w of University of California Davis Campus. Ext/int corridors. **Pets:** $50 deposit/room, $10 one-time fee/room. Designated rooms, service with restrictions, supervision.
[SAVE] [SD] ☒ ♿ 🚿 ▣ ☕ 🏊

DOWNIEVILLE

◆◆ **Riverside Inn** [M]
(530) 289-1000. **$70-$79, 3 day notice.** 206 Commercial St. SR 49; center. Ext corridors. **Pets:** Other species. $10 one-time fee/room. Service with restrictions, supervision.
[A$K] [SD] ☒ ▣ ☕ 🏋 [AC] ☎

DUBLIN

[AAA] ◆◆◆ **AmeriSuites (San Francisco/Dublin)** [SH]
(925) 828-9006. **$109.** 4950 Hacienda Dr. I-580, exit Hacienda Dr, then n. Int corridors. **Pets:** Accepted.
[SAVE] [SD] ☒ ♿ 🚿 ▣ ☕ 🏊

DUNNIGAN

◆◆ **Best Value Inn** [M] 🐾
(530) 724-3333. **$59-$99.** 3930 Road 89. I-5, exit Dunnigan. Int corridors. **Pets:** Medium, other species. $10 daily fee/pet. Service with restrictions, supervision.
[A$K] [SD] ☒ ♿ ▣ 🏊

[AAA] ◆◆◆ **Best Western Country** [M] 🐾
(530) 724-3471. **$65-$159.** 3930 Road 89. I-5, exit Dunnigan. Ext corridors. **Pets:** Medium, other species. $10 daily fee/pet. Service with restrictions, supervision.
[SAVE] [SD] ☒ ♿ ▣ ☕ 🏊

[AAA] ◆ **Budget 8 Motel** [M]
(530) 724-3411. **$55-$65.** 4930 CR 99 W. I-5, exit CR 8, just e. Ext corridors. **Pets:** Medium. $5 daily fee/pet. Service with restrictions, supervision.
[SAVE] [SD] ♿ ▣

DUNSMUIR

[AAA] ◆◆◆ **Caboose Motel-Railroad Park Resort** [M] 🐾
(530) 235-4440. **$90-$115.** 100 Railroad Park Rd. I-5, exit 728 (Railroad Park Rd), 1 mi s. **Pets:** Large. $10 daily fee/pet. Service with restrictions, supervision.
[SAVE] ☒ ▣ ☕ 🍴 🏊

[AAA] ◆◆ **Cedar Lodge Motel** [M]
(530) 235-4331. **$55-$125, 4 day notice.** 4201 Dunsmuir Ave. I-5, exit 730 (Dunsmuir/Siskiyou), 0.5 mi w. Ext corridors. **Pets:** Medium, dogs only. $10 daily fee/pet. Designated rooms, service with restrictions, supervision.
[SAVE] [SD] ☒ ▣ ☕

EL CENTRO

◆◆ **Barbara Worth Golf Resort and Convention Center** [SH]
(760) 356-2806. **$93-$99.** 2050 Country Club Dr. I-8, exit Bowker Rd, 2 mi n, then 3 mi e on CR S-80; 9 mi e of SR 86. Ext/int corridors. **Pets:** Accepted.
[A$K] [SD] ☒ ▣ ☕ 🍴 🏊 🏋

◆◆ **Brunner's** [M]
(760) 352-6431. **$79-$149, 3 day notice.** 215 N Imperial Ave. I-8, exit Imperial Ave, 1 mi n. Ext corridors. **Pets:** Accepted.
[A$K] [SD] ☒ ▣ ☕ 🍴 🏊

◆◆ **Days Inn** [M]
(760) 352-5511. **$49-$69.** 1425 Adams Ave. I-8, exit Imperial Ave, 1.4 mi n, then just w on SR 86 and I-8 business loop. Ext corridors. **Pets:** Accepted.
[A$K] [SD] ☒ ▣ 🏊

[AAA] ◆◆ **Ramada Inn El Centro** [M]
(760) 352-5152. **$87-$97.** 1455 Ocotillo Dr. I-8, exit Imperial Ave, just n, then just e. Ext corridors. **Pets:** Accepted.
[SAVE] [SD] ☒ ▣ ☕ 🍴 🏊

◆◆ **Vacation Inn** [M]
(760) 352-9700. **$55-$75, 3 day notice.** 2015 Cottonwood Cir. I-8, exit Imperial Ave, just n, then just w. Ext corridors. **Pets:** Accepted.
[A$K] [SD] ☒ ▣ ☕ 🍴 🏊

EL PORTAL

[AAA] ◆◆◆ **Yosemite View Lodge** [M]
(209) 379-2681. **$85-$269, 7 day notice.** 11136 Hwy 140. Just w of Yosemite National Park West Gate. Ext corridors. **Pets:** Accepted.
[SAVE] ☒ ♿ 👂 🚿 ▣ ☕ 🏊 🏋

EMERYVILLE

[AAA] ◆◆◆ **Woodfin Suite Hotel San Francisco Bay Bridge** [LH]
(510) 601-5880. **$149.** 5800 Shellmound St. I-80, exit Powell St. Int corridors. **Pets:** Other species. $150 deposit/pet, $5 daily fee/pet. Service with restrictions.
[SAVE] [SD] ☒ ▣ ☕ 🏊 🏋

ENCINITAS

[AAA] ◆◆◆ **Best Western Encinitas Inn & Suites at Moonlight Beach** [M]
(760) 942-7455. **$109-$190, 3 day notice.** 85 Encinitas Blvd. I-5, exit Encinitas Blvd, just w. Ext corridors. **Pets:** Medium, other species. $50 one-time fee/room. Service with restrictions, supervision.
[SAVE] [SD] ☒ ▣ ☕ 🍴 🏊

ESCONDIDO

[AAA] ◆◆◆ **Best Western Escondido** [SH]
(760) 740-1700. **$79-$119, 3 day notice.** 1700 Seven Oaks Rd. I-15, exit El Norte Pkwy, just e. Int corridors. **Pets:** Small, other species. $25 one-time fee/pet. Service with restrictions, crate.
[SAVE] [SD] ☒ ▣ ☕ 🏊

[AAA] ◆◆ **Comfort Inn Escondido** [SH]
(760) 489-1010. **$79-$129.** 1290 W Valley Pkwy. I-15, exit Valley Pkwy, just w. Int corridors. **Pets:** Accepted.
[SAVE] [SD] ☒ ▣ ☕ 🏊

[AAA] ◆ **Rodeway Inn** [M]
(760) 746-0441. **$54-$149.** 250 W El Norte Pkwy. I-15, exit El Norte Pkwy, 1 mi e. Ext corridors. **Pets:** Accepted.
[SAVE] [SD] ☒ ▣ ☕

ETNA

▼ Motel Etna M
(530) 467-5330. **$44.** 317 Collier Way. Just w of SR 3. Ext corridors.
Pets: Accepted.
⊠ ⊟

EUREKA

▼◆ Bayview Motel M
(707) 442-1673. **$75-$150.** 2844 Fairfield St. E of US 101, exit Henderson, at top of hill, just n. Ext corridors. **Pets:** Small. $5 daily fee/room. Designated rooms, supervision.
A$K S⊿ ⊠ ⬅ ⊟ ⬜ ♨

▲ ▼◆▼ Best Western Bayshore Inn M
(707) 268-8005. **$88-$149.** 3500 Broadway. US 101, s of Bayshore Mall. Ext corridors. **Pets:** Dogs only. $20 one-time fee/pet. Designated rooms, service with restrictions, supervision.
SAVE S⊿ ⊠ ⬅ ⊟ ⬜ ⏸ ≈ ⊠

▲ ▼◆▼ Eureka Ramada Limited M
(707) 443-2206. **$69-$90.** 270 5th St. On US 101 northbound. Int corridors. **Pets:** Medium. $10 daily fee/pet. Service with restrictions, supervision.
SAVE S⊿ ⊠ ⊟ ⬜ ♨

▲ ▼◆▼ Eureka Town House Motel M
(707) 443-4536. **$50-$125.** 933 4th St. US 101 southbound; corner of 4th and K sts. Ext corridors. **Pets:** Medium, dogs only. $10 daily fee/pet. Designated rooms, service with restrictions, supervision.
SAVE S⊿ ⊠ ⊟ ⬜ ♨

▼ Eureka Travelodge M
(707) 443-6345. **$75-$175.** 4 4th St. On US 101; corner of 4th and B sts. Ext corridors. **Pets:** Accepted.
A$K S⊿ ⊠ ⊟ ⬜ ≈ ♨

▼◆ Quality Inn Eureka M
(707) 443-1601. **$75-$200.** 1209 4th St. US 101 southbound; between M and N sts. Ext corridors. **Pets:** Accepted.
A$K S⊿ ⊠ ⊟ ⬜ ≈ ♨

▲ ▼◆▼ Red Lion Hotel Eureka M
(707) 445-0844. **$119-$129.** 1929 4th St. US 101 northbound; between T and V sts. Int corridors. **Pets:** Accepted.
SAVE S⊿ ⊠ ⬅ ⊟ ⬜ ⏸ ≈

▲ ▼◆▼ Sunrise Inn & Suites M
(707) 443-9751. **$45-$85.** 129 4th St. US 101, exit C St southbound; exit C St W northbound; downtown. Ext corridors. **Pets:** $6 daily fee/pet. Service with restrictions, supervision.
SAVE S⊿ ⊠ ⊟ ♨

FAIRFIELD

▲ ▼ Econo Lodge Inn & Suites M
(707) 864-2426. **$54-$99.** 4625 Central Way. I-80, exit Suisun Valley Rd, just e. Ext corridors. **Pets:** Medium. $5 daily fee/room. Service with restrictions, supervision.
SAVE S⊿ ⊠ ⬅M ⊟ ⬜

FALLBROOK

▲ ▼◆▼ Best Western Franciscan Inn M
(760) 728-6174. **$67-$95.** 1635 S Mission Rd. I-15, exit CR S-13, 6.5 mi sw. Ext corridors. **Pets:** Medium. $15 one-time fee/pet. Designated rooms, service with restrictions, supervision.
SAVE S⊿ ⊠ ⊟ ⬜ ≈

FALL RIVER MILLS

▲ ▼ ◆ Hi-Mont Motel M ❀
(530) 336-5541. **$61-$96, 3 day notice.** 43021 Bridge St. 1 mi w on SR 299. Ext corridors. **Pets:** Other species. $5 daily fee/pet. Service with restrictions, supervision.
SAVE S⊿ ⊠ ⬅ ⊟ ⬜

▼◆▼ Pit River Lodge [CI]
(530) 336-5005. **Call for rates.** 24500 Pit One PowerHouse Rd. I-299 E, exit Pit One PowerHouse Rd. Int corridors. **Pets:** Accepted.
S⊿ ⊠ ⊟ ⬜ ⏸ ♨

FERNDALE

▼◆▼ Collingwood Inn Bed & Breakfast [BB] ❀
(707) 786-9219. **$99-$203, 14 day notice.** 831 Main St. US 101, exit Ferndale, 5 mi w. Int corridors. **Pets:** Other species. $25 daily fee/pet.
A$K S⊿ ⊠ ♨ ♨

▲ ▼◆▼ Shaw House Bed & Breakfast Inn [BB]
(707) 786-9958. **$115-$275, 15 day notice.** 703 Main St. US 101, exit Main St W. Int corridors. **Pets:** Small, other species. $30 daily fee/pet. Designated rooms, service with restrictions, supervision.
SAVE ⊠ ♨ ♨

FIREBAUGH

▲ ▼◆▼ Best Western Apricot Inn M
(559) 659-1444. **$69-$109.** 46290 W Panoche Rd. I-5, exit W Panoche Rd, just w. Ext corridors. **Pets:** Large. $5 daily fee/pet. Service with restrictions, supervision.
SAVE S⊿ ⊠ ⬜ ≈

FISH CAMP

▼◆▼ Apple Tree Inn [CA]
(559) 683-5111. **$99-$209.** 1110 Hwy 41. 2 mi from South Gate to Yosemite National Park. Ext corridors. **Pets:** Other species. $50 one-time fee/pet. Designated rooms, service with restrictions, supervision.
A$K S⊿ ⊠ ⬅M 🖨 ≈ ⊠ ♨

▼◆▼ The Narrow Gauge Inn M 🐾
(559) 683-7720. **$79-$195, 4 day notice.** 48571 Hwy 41. 4 mi from South Gate to Yosemite National Park. Ext corridors. **Pets:** Large, other species. $25 one-time fee/pet. Designated rooms, service with restrictions, supervision.
⊠ ⊟ ⬜ ⏸ ≈

FOLSOM

▼◆▼ Residence Inn by Marriott [SH] ❀
(916) 983-7289. **$144-$175, 14 day notice.** 2555 Iron Point Rd. US 50, exit Bidwell St, just n. Int corridors. **Pets:** Medium, other species. $75 one-time fee/pet. Service with restrictions.
A$K S⊿ ⊠ ⬅M ⬅ ⬜ ≈ ⊠

FORTUNA

▲ ▼◆▼ Best Western Country Inn M
(707) 725-6822. **$105-$130.** 2025 Riverwalk Dr. US 101, exit Kenmar Rd/Riverwalk Dr, just w. Ext corridors. **Pets:** Medium, dogs only. $10 one-time fee/room. Designated rooms, service with restrictions, supervision.
SAVE S⊿ ⊠ ⬅M 🖨 ⊟ ⬜ ≈

▲ ▼◆▼ Fortuna Super 8 M
(707) 725-2888. **$60-$105.** 1805 Alamar Way. US 101, exit Kenmar Rd/Riverwalk Dr, just w. Ext corridors. **Pets:** Medium, dogs only. $10 daily fee/pet. Designated rooms, service with restrictions, supervision.
SAVE S⊿ ⊠ ⬅ ⊟ ⬜

▲ ▼◆▼ Holiday Inn Express M 🐾
(707) 725-5500. **$75-$169.** 1859 Alamar Way. US 101, exit Kenmar Rd/Riverwalk Dr, just w. Ext corridors. **Pets:** Small. $20 deposit/pet, $10 daily fee/pet. Designated rooms, service with restrictions, supervision.
A$K S⊿ ⊠ ⊟ ⬜ ≈ ⊠

▲▲▲ ▽▽▽ Travel Inn SH
(707) 725-6993. **$59-$89, 3 day notice.** 275 12th St. Hwy 101, exit 12th St, 1 mi w. Ext corridors. **Pets:** Very small, dogs only. $10 daily fee/pet. Designated rooms, no service, supervision.
SAVE S6 X 📧

FOUNTAIN VALLEY

▲▲▲ ▽▽▽ Ramada Limited-Huntington Beach/Fountain Valley M
(714) 847-3388. **$89-$109.** 9125 Recreation Cir. I-405, exit Warner Ave W northbound; exit Magnolia southbound, just w. Ext corridors. **Pets:** Small. $25 deposit/room, $10 daily fee/pet. Designated rooms, service with restrictions, supervision.
SAVE S6 X 📧 ▦

▽▽▽ Residence Inn by Marriott SH
(714) 965-8000. **$119-$169.** 9930 Slater Ave. I-405, exit Brookhurst St, just n, then just w. Ext corridors. **Pets:** Medium. $75 one-time fee/pet.
X 📧 ▦ ⊠

FREMONT

▲▲▲ ▽▽▽▽ AmeriSuites (Silicon Valley/Fremont) SH ❀
(510) 623-6000. **$94.** 3101 W Warren Ave. I-880, exit Warren Ave/ Mission Blvd, just w. Int corridors. **Pets:** Medium, other species. $10 daily fee/pet. Designated rooms, service with restrictions, supervision.
SAVE S6 X 📧 ▦

▲▲▲ ▽▽▽ Best Western Garden Court Inn SH
(510) 792-4300. **$59-$110.** 5400 Mowry Ave. I-880, exit Mowry Ave, just e. Int corridors. **Pets:** Medium. $10 daily fee/pet. Designated rooms, service with restrictions, supervision.
SAVE S6 X 📧 ▦

▲▲▲ ▽▽▽ Fremont Marriott LH
(510) 413-3700. **$74-$139.** 46100 Landing Pkwy. I-880, exit Fremont Blvd/Cushing Pkwy, then w. Int corridors. **Pets:** Accepted.
SAVE X ▦ 🍴 ▦

▽▽ ▽▽ Homestead Studio Suites Hotel-Fremont SH
(510) 353-1664. **$72-$87.** 46080 Fremont Blvd. I-880, exit Fremont Blvd/Cushing Pkwy, just w. Int corridors. **Pets:** Accepted.
ASK S6 X ▦

▽▽▽▽ La Quinta Inn & Suites Fremont SH ❀
(510) 445-0808. **$99-$119.** 46200 Landing Pkwy. I-880, exit Fremont Blvd/Cushing Pkwy, just w. Int corridors. **Pets:** Service with restrictions.
ASK X ▦ 📧 ▦

▽▽ ▽▽ Residence Inn By Marriott M
(510) 794-5900. **Call for rates.** 5400 Farwell Pl. I-880, exit Mowry Ave, just e. Ext corridors. **Pets:** Accepted.
S6 X 📧 ▦ ⊠

FRESNO

▲▲▲ ▽▽▽ Comfort Inn M
(559) 275-2374. **$69-$150.** 5455 W Shaw Ave. SR 99, exit Shaw Ave. Int corridors. **Pets:** Small, other species. $75 deposit/room, $25 daily fee/ pet. Designated rooms, service with restrictions, supervision.
SAVE S6 X ▦ 📧 ▦

▲▲▲ ▽▽ ▽ Days Inn-Parkway M
(559) 268-6211. **$56-$84.** 1101 N Parkway Dr. SR 99, exit Olive St, just w. Ext corridors. **Pets:** Accepted.
SAVE S6 X ▦ ▦

▲▲▲ ▽▽▽▽ Holiday Inn Express-Barcus M
(559) 277-5700. **$99-$119.** 5046 N Barcus. SR 99, exit Shaw Ave, just e. Int corridors. **Pets:** Medium. $20 one-time fee/room. Service with restrictions, supervision.
SAVE S6 X ▦ ▦ 📧 ▦

▽▽▽▽ La Quinta Inn Fresno/Yosemite M
(559) 442-1110. **$80-$99.** 2926 Tulare St. SR 99, exit Fresno St, 2 mi e. Ext corridors. **Pets:** Service with restrictions, supervision.
ASK X ▦ ▦ ▦ 📧 ▦

▲▲▲ ▽▽▽ Red Roof Inn M
(559) 431-3557. **$50-$70.** 6730 N Blackstone Ave. SR 41, exit Herndon Ave, then w. Ext corridors. **Pets:** Accepted.
SAVE S6 X ▦ ▦

▲▲▲ ▽▽▽ Red Roof Inn M ❀
(559) 276-1910. **$52-$73.** 5021 N Barcus Ave. SR 99, exit Shaw Ave. Ext corridors. **Pets:** Medium. Service with restrictions, supervision.
SAVE S6 X ▦ ▦

▽▽▽ Residence Inn by Marriott M
(559) 222-8900. **$84-$159.** 5322 N Diana Ave. SR 41, exit Shaw Ave, 0.3 mi w, n on Blackstone Ave, then e on Barstow Ave. Int corridors. **Pets:** Accepted.
ASK S6 X ▦ ▦ ▦ ▦ 📧 ▦ ⊠

▲▲▲ ▽▽▽▽ Super 8-Parkway M
(559) 268-0741. **$59-$89.** 1087 N Parkway Dr. SR 99, exit Olive Ave, just w. Ext corridors. **Pets:** Medium. $10 daily fee/pet. Service with restrictions, supervision.
SAVE S6 X ▦ 📧 ▦

▲▲▲ ▽▽▽▽ TownePlace Suites by Marriott M ❀
(559) 435-4600. **$69-$129.** 7127 N Fresno St. SR 41, exit Herndon Ave E. Int corridors. **Pets:** Other species. $75 one-time fee/room. Service with restrictions, supervision.
SAVE S6 X ▦ ▦ ▦ 📧 ▦

▽▽ University Inn M
(559) 294-0224. **$52-$85.** 2655 E Shaw Ave. SR 41, exit Shaw Ave, 1.5 mi e. Ext corridors. **Pets:** Accepted.
ASK S6 X ▦ ▦

▲▲▲ ▽▽ Valley Inn M
(559) 233-3913. **$35-$45.** 933 N Parkway Dr. SR 99, exit Olive Ave, then w. Ext corridors. **Pets:** Small, dogs only. $10 daily fee/room. Service with restrictions, supervision.
SAVE X ▦

FULLERTON

▽▽▽▽ Four Points by Sheraton Fullerton/Anaheim SH
(714) 635-9000. **$85-$115.** 1500 S Raymond Ave. SR 91, exit Harbor Blvd, just n to Orangethorpe Ave, 1 mi e, then just s. Ext/int corridors. **Pets:** Accepted.
ASK S6 X ▦ 📧 🍴 ▦ ⊠

▲▲▲ ▽▽▽ Fullerton Inn M
(714) 773-4900. **$65-$75, 3 day notice.** 2601 W Orangethorpe Ave. SR 91, exit Magnolia Ave, just n, then just e. Ext corridors. **Pets:** Very small. $10 daily fee/pet. Designated rooms, service with restrictions, supervision.
SAVE S6 X ▦ ▦

▽▽▽▽ Fullerton Marriott Hotel at California State Univ SH
(714) 738-7800. **$99-$179.** 2701 E Nutwood Ave. SR 57, exit Nutwood Ave, just w. Int corridors. **Pets:** Accepted.
ASK X ▦ ▦ 📧 🍴 ▦ ⊠

GALT

▲▲▲ ▽▽ Royal Delta Inn M
(209) 745-9181. **$49-$53.** 1040 N Lincoln Way. SR 99, exit Pringle Ave. Ext corridors. **Pets:** Accepted.
SAVE X ▦ ▦

GARBERVILLE

(AAA) ▼▼▼▼ Best Western Humboldt House Inn M
(707) 923-2771. **$79-$119.** 701 Redwood Dr. US 101, 1st exit. Ext corridors. **Pets:** Accepted.
[SAVE] [S₀] [✕] [⚷] [🛏] [⊲]

(AAA) ▼▼▼ Motel Garberville M
(707) 923-2422. **$49-$79.** 948 Redwood Dr. On US 101 business route. Ext corridors. **Pets:** Small, dogs only. $5 daily fee/pet. Designated rooms, service with restrictions, supervision.
[SAVE] [S₀] [✕] [🛏] [⊡]

(AAA) ▼▼▼ Sherwood Forest Motel M
(707) 923-2721. **$60-$100.** 814 Redwood Dr. On US 101 business route. Ext corridors. **Pets:** Medium, other species. Designated rooms, no service, supervision.
[SAVE] [S₀] [✕] [🛏] [⊡] [⊲]

GARDEN GROVE

▼▼▼▼ Anaheim Marriott Suites SH 🐾
(714) 750-1000. **$109-$209.** 12015 Harbor Blvd. I-5, exit Chapman Ave, 1.5 mi w, then just s. Int corridors. **Pets:** Other species. $15 daily fee/pet. Designated rooms, service with restrictions, supervision.
[ASK] [✕] [🛏] [⊡] [🍴] [⊲] [✕]

▼▼▼ Candlewood Suites Anaheim-South SH
(714) 539-4200. **$71.** 12901 Garden Grove Blvd. SR 22, exit Haster St westbound, just w; exit Fairview St eastbound, just nw. Int corridors. **Pets:** Large. Service with restrictions, supervision.
[ASK] [S₀] [✕] [🛏] [⊡]

▼▼▼ Holiday Inn Express Hotel & Suites Garden Grove SH
(714) 539-3535. **$89, 3 day notice.** 12867 Garden Grove Blvd. SR 22, exit Haster St westbound, just s, then just w; exit Fairview St eastbound, just n, then just w. Int corridors. **Pets:** Accepted.
[ASK] [S₀] [✕] [🛏] [⊡] [⊲]

▼▼▼ Homewood Suites by Hilton-Anaheim/Maingate SH
(714) 740-1800. **$139.** 12005 Harbor Blvd. I-5, exit Chapman Ave, 1.4 mi w, then just n. Int corridors. **Pets:** Accepted.
[ASK] [S₀] [✕] [🛏] [⊡] [⊲]

(AAA) ▼▼▼▼ Residence Inn Anaheim Resort Area SH
(714) 591-4000. **$129-$369, 3 day notice.** 11931 Harbor Blvd. I-5, exit The City Dr/Chapman Ave, 1 mi w on Chapman Ave, then just n. Int corridors. **Pets:** Medium. $75 one-time fee/room. Service with restrictions, supervision.
[SAVE] [S₀] [✕] [⚷ᴹ] [⏰] [♿] [🛏] [⊡] [⊲] [✕]

GILROY

(AAA) ▼▼▼ Leavesley Inn M
(408) 847-5500. **$68-$75.** 8430 Murray Ave. US 101, exit Leavesley Rd, just w. Ext corridors. **Pets:** Medium. $20 one-time fee/pet. Service with restrictions, supervision.
[SAVE] [S₀] [✕] [🛏] [⊲]

GLENNVILLE

▼▼ The Bunkhouse Motel M
(661) 536-9100. **$65-$85.** 12044 Hwy 155 S. On SR 155 at Granite Rd. Ext corridors. **Pets:** Accepted.
[ASK] [S₀] [✕] [🛏] [⊡] [🍴]

GRASS VALLEY

(AAA) ▼▼▼ Alta Sierra Village Inn M
(530) 273-9102. **$69-$190, 10 day notice.** 11858 Tammy Way. 6 mi s, 1.1 mi e on Alta Sierra Dr, 0.8 mi w on Norlene, then 0.5 mi e on Tammy, follow signs to Alta Sierra Country Club. Ext corridors. **Pets:** Dogs only. $10 one-time fee/room. Service with restrictions, supervision.
[SAVE] [✕] [⚷ᴹ] [🛏] [⊡] [⊠]

(AAA) ▼▼▼ Best Western Gold Country Inn M
(530) 273-1393. **$70-$120.** 11972 Sutton Way. SR 20 and 49, exit Brunswick Rd, just e; midway between Grass Valley and Nevada City. Ext corridors. **Pets:** Medium, other species. $15 one-time fee/pet. Service with restrictions, supervision.
[SAVE] [S₀] [✕] [⚷ᴹ] [🛏] [⊡] [⊲]

(AAA) ▼▼ Coach N' Four Motel M
(530) 273-8009. **$62-$124, 3 day notice.** 628 S Auburn St. SR 49, exit E Empire St, 0.3 mi e, then just s. Ext corridors. **Pets:** Medium, other species. $10 daily fee/pet. Designated rooms, service with restrictions, supervision.
[SAVE] [S₀] [✕] [⚷ᴹ] [🛏]

(AAA) ▼▼▼ Golden Chain Resort Motel M
(530) 273-7279. **$62-$102.** 13413 SR 49. On SR 49, 2.5 mi s. Ext corridors. **Pets:** Medium. $10 deposit/pet. Service with restrictions, supervision.
[SAVE] [S₀] [✕] [⚷ᴹ] [🛏] [⊲]

▼▼▼ Grass Valley Courtyard Suites SH 🐾
(530) 272-7696. **$125-$290, 3 day notice.** 210 N Auburn St. SR 49, exit Central Grass Valley. Ext corridors. **Pets:** Medium, dogs only. $25 one-time fee/pet. Service with restrictions, supervision.
[ASK] [S₀] [✕] [⚷ᴹ] [⚷] [🛏] [⊡] [⊲] [✕]

(AAA) ▼▼ Stagecoach Motel M
(530) 272-3701. **$55-$110.** 405 S Auburn St. SR 49, exit Colfax Ave, 0.4 mi s. Ext corridors. **Pets:** Other species. $10 one-time fee/pet. Designated rooms, no service, supervision.
[SAVE] [S₀] [✕] [🛏] [⊡]

GRIDLEY

(AAA) ▼▼▼ Gridley Inn M 🐾
(530) 846-4520. **$69.** 1490 Hwy 99, Suite A. On SR 99, 1 mi s. Ext corridors. **Pets:** Medium. $10 daily fee/pet. Service with restrictions, supervision.
[SAVE] [S₀] [✕] [🛏] [⊡] [⊲]

(AAA) ▼▼▼ Pacific Motel M
(530) 846-4580. **$55-$65.** 1308 Hwy 99. On SR 99, 1 mi s. Ext corridors. **Pets:** Accepted.
[SAVE] [S₀] [✕] [🛏] [⊡] [⊲]

GROVELAND

(AAA) ▼▼▼ Best Value Yosemite Westgate BuckMeadows Lodge M
(209) 962-5281. **$69-$179, 3 day notice.** 7633/7647 Hwy 120. On SR 120, 12 mi e. Ext corridors. **Pets:** Large, other species. $10 daily fee/room. Designated rooms, service with restrictions, supervision.
[SAVE] [S₀] [✕] [🛏] [⊡] [⊲]

(AAA) ▼▼▼▼ Groveland Hotel at Yosemite National Park CI 🐾
(209) 962-4000. **$145-$185.** 18767 Main St. Center. Int corridors. **Pets:** $10 daily fee/pet. Service with restrictions, crate.
[SAVE] [✕] [⊡] [🍴]

HANFORD

(AAA) ▼▼▼▼ Sequoia Inn SH
(559) 582-0338. **$65-$109.** 1655 Mall Dr. SR 198, exit 12th Ave, then n. Int corridors. **Pets:** Large, other species. $100 deposit/room, $10 daily fee/room. Designated rooms, service with restrictions, supervision.
[SAVE] [S₀] [✕] [🛏] [⊡] [⊲]

HAYWARD

Comfort Inn
(510) 538-4466. **$79-$150.** 24997 Mission Blvd. 1.8 mi e of I-880, exit SR 92 (Jackson St), 0.5 mi s on SR 238 (Mission Blvd). Ext corridors. **Pets:** Small, other species. $100 deposit/room. Service with restrictions.

La Quinta Inn & Suites Hayward/Oakland Airport SH
(510) 732-6300. **$84-$103.** 20777 Hesperian Blvd. I-880, exit A St, 0.5 mi w. Int corridors. **Pets:** Accepted.

MainStay Suites SH
(510) 731-3571. **$69-$129.** 835 West A St. I-880, exit A St, just w. Int corridors. **Pets:** Medium, other species. $100 deposit/room, $15 daily fee/pet. Service with restrictions, supervision.

HEMET

Best Western Inn of Hemet M
(951) 925-6605. **$82-$134.** 2625 W Florida Ave. 2.4 mi w of SR 79 N (San Jacinto St) on SR 74/79. Ext corridors. **Pets:** Small. $10 one-time fee/room. Designated rooms, service with restrictions, supervision.

Coach Light Motel M
(951) 658-3237. **$60-$75.** 1640 W Florida Ave. 1.7 mi w of SR 74 N (San Jacinto St) on SR 74/79. Ext corridors. **Pets:** Dogs only. $10 daily fee/pet. Service with restrictions, supervision.

HESPERIA

Days Inn Suites-Hesperia/Victorville M
(760) 948-0600. **$69-$79.** 14865 Bear Valley Rd. I-15, exit Bear Valley Rd, 0.5 mi e of Victor Valley Mall. Ext corridors. **Pets:** Accepted.

La Quinta Inn & Suites Victorville SH
(760) 949-9900. **$90-$150.** 12000 Mariposa Rd. I-15, exit Bear Valley Rd, just e, then just s. Int corridors. **Pets:** Small. $50 deposit/pet. Designated rooms, service with restrictions, supervision.

Super 8 Motel M
(760) 949-3231. **$49-$89.** 12033 Oakwood Ave. I-15, exit Bear Valley Rd, just se. Ext corridors. **Pets:** Accepted.

HUNTINGTON BEACH

Hilton Waterfront Beach Resort LH
(714) 845-8000. **$189-$229, 3 day notice.** 21100 Pacific Coast Hwy. I-405, exit Beach Blvd, 6 mi s, then just w. Int corridors. **Pets:** Very small. $100 deposit/room. Service with restrictions, supervision.

IDYLLWILD

Fireside Inn CA
(951) 659-2966. **$65-$130 (no credit cards), 10 day notice.** 54540 N Circle Dr. From SR 243 and town center, 0.3 mi ne. Ext corridors. **Pets:** Small, dogs only. $20 one-time fee/room. Designated rooms, no service, supervision.

IMPERIAL

Imperial Valley Inn M
(760) 355-4500. **$59-$89.** 1093 Airport Blvd. On SR 86. Ext corridors. **Pets:** Accepted.

INDEPENDENCE

Ray's Den Motel M
(760) 878-2122. **$49-$74.** 405 N Edwards. On US 395. Ext corridors. **Pets:** Dogs only. $6 daily fee/room. Service with restrictions, supervision.

INDIO

Best Western Date Tree Hotel M
(760) 347-3421. **$49-$189.** 81-909 Indio Blvd. I-10, exit Monroe St westbound, 0.5 mi s; exit Indio Blvd eastbound, 2.4 mi s. Int corridors. **Pets:** Accepted.

Indian Palms Country Club & Resort SH
(760) 775-4444. **$84-$169.** 48-630 Monroe St. I-10, exit Monroe St, 2 mi s. Ext corridors. **Pets:** Medium, dogs only. $30 daily fee/room. Designated rooms, service with restrictions.

Palm Shadow Inn M
(760) 347-3476. **$59-$144.** 80-761 Hwy 111. I-10, exit Jefferson Ave, 2.5 mi s, then 0.7 mi e. Ext corridors. **Pets:** Accepted.

Quality Inn M
(760) 347-4044. **$65-$131.** 43505 Monroe St. I-10, exit Monroe St, 0.5 mi s. Int corridors. **Pets:** $50 deposit/pet. Service with restrictions, supervision.

Royal Plaza Inn SH
(760) 347-0911. **$49-$129, 3 day notice.** 82-347 Hwy 111. I-10, exit Monroe St, 1.8 mi s, then 0.4 mi e. Int corridors. **Pets:** Dogs only. $5 daily fee/pet. Service with restrictions, supervision.

Super 8 Motel M
(760) 342-0264. **$59-$169.** 81753 Hwy 111. I-10, exit Monroe St, 1.8 mi s, then 0.5 mi w. Ext corridors. **Pets:** Small. $50 deposit/pet, $15 daily fee/pet. Designated rooms, service with restrictions, supervision.

IRVINE

Candlewood Suites-Irvine Spectrum SH
(949) 788-0500. **$109-$139.** 16150 Sand Canyon Ave. I-5, exit Sand Canyon Ave, 1.4 mi w to Hospital Rd, then 0.3 mi s. Int corridors. **Pets:** Medium. $75 one-time fee/room. Designated rooms, service with restrictions, supervision.

Hilton Irvine/Orange County Airport LH
(949) 833-9999. **$89-$219.** 18800 MacArthur Blvd. I-405, exit MacArthur Blvd, 0.5 mi s. Int corridors. **Pets:** $50 one-time fee/room. Designated rooms, service with restrictions.

La Quinta Inn Irvine Spectrum (Old Historic Site) M
(949) 551-0909. **$95-$125.** 14972 Sand Canyon Ave. I-5, exit Sand Canyon Ave, just w. Ext/int corridors. **Pets:** Accepted.

Residence Inn by Marriott-Irvine Spectrum SH
(949) 380-3000. **$109-$169.** 10 Morgan. I-5, exit Alton Pkwy, 2 mi e. Ext corridors. **Pets:** Other species. $75 one-time fee/room. Service with restrictions.

JACKSON

Amador Motel M
(209) 223-0970. **$54-$69, 5 day notice.** 12408 Kennedy Flat Rd. 1.5 mi n at jct SR 49 and 88 on Frontage Rd. Ext corridors. **Pets:** $10 one-time fee/pet. Service with restrictions, supervision.

Best Western Amador Inn SH
(209) 223-0211. **$75-$105.** 200 S Hwy 49. On SR 49. Int corridors. **Pets:** Accepted.

JAMESTOWN

1859 Historic National Hotel, A Country Inn CI
(209) 984-3446. **$95-$150, 3 day notice.** 18183 Main St. Downtown. Int corridors. **Pets:** Medium, other species. $15 daily fee/pet. Service with restrictions, supervision.

Country Inn Sonora M
(209) 984-0315. **$59-$179.** 18730 Hwy 108. On SR 108 and 49, 1 mi e of town. Ext corridors. **Pets:** Medium. $10 daily fee/pet. Designated rooms, service with restrictions, supervision.

JUNE LAKE

Double Eagle Resort/Spa, Inc CA
(760) 648-7004. **$215-$240, 30 day notice.** 5587 Hwy 158. On SR 158; 3 mi w of village. Ext corridors. **Pets:** Large, other species. $20 one-time fee/room. Service with restrictions, supervision.

Gull Lake Lodge M
(760) 648-7516. **$60-$165, 14 day notice.** 132 Leonard Ave. Just n of SR 158; via Knoll and Bruce sts. Ext corridors. **Pets:** Other species. Designated rooms, service with restrictions, supervision.

KERNVILLE

River View Lodge M
(760) 376-6019. **$79-$119, 3 day notice.** 2 Sirretta St. On Kernville Rd, at the bridge; center. Ext corridors. **Pets:** Other species. $20 daily fee/pet. Supervision.

KETTLEMAN CITY

Best Western Kettleman Inn and Suites M
(559) 386-0804. **$79-$169.** 33410 Powers Dr. E of and adjacent to I-5, exit SR 41 N, 0.3 mi to Bernard, then 0.3 mi n. Ext corridors. **Pets:** Medium, other species. $5 daily fee/pet. Designated rooms, service with restrictions, supervision.

Super 8 M
(559) 386-9530. **$49-$79.** 33415 Powers Dr. E of and adjacent to I-5, exit SR 41 N, 0.3 mi to Bernard, then 0.3 mi n. Ext corridors. **Pets:** Small, other species. $40 deposit/room, $10 one-time fee/pet. Service with restrictions, supervision.

KING CITY

Courtesy Inn M
(831) 385-4646. **$54-$130.** 4 Broadway Cir. US 101, exit Broadway, just w. Ext corridors. **Pets:** Small. $10 one-time fee/pet. Designated rooms, service with restrictions, supervision.

KINGSBURG

Swedish Inn M
(559) 897-1022. **$58-$129.** 401 Conejo St. SR 99, exit Conejo St, just w. Ext corridors. **Pets:** Accepted.

KLAMATH

Motel Trees M
(707) 482-3152. **$48-$86.** 15495 Hwy 101 N. 4 mi n on US 101. Ext corridors. **Pets:** $35 daily fee/pet. Service with restrictions, supervision.

KYBURZ

Kyburz Resort Motel M
(530) 293-3382. **$49-$99.** 13668 Hwy 50. On US 50; halfway between Placerville and South Lake Tahoe. Ext corridors. **Pets:** Accepted.

LAGUNA BEACH

Best Western Laguna Brisas Spa Hotel M
(949) 497-7272. **$109-$289.** 1600 S Coast Hwy. SR 133, 1 mi s on SR 1. Ext/int corridors. **Pets:** Small, dogs only. $50 daily fee/pet. Designated rooms.

The Carriage House-Bed & Breakfast BB
(949) 494-8945. **$140-$175, 3 day notice.** 1322 Catalina St. SR 133, 1 mi s on S Coast Hwy to Cress St, then just e. Ext corridors. **Pets:** $10 daily fee/pet. Supervision.

Casa Laguna Inn BB
(949) 494-2996. **$135-$325, 5 day notice.** 2510 S Coast Hwy. SR 133, 1.3 mi s on SR 1. Ext corridors. **Pets:** Other species. $25 daily fee/pet. Service with restrictions, supervision.

LAKE ARROWHEAD

Arrowhead Saddleback Inn CI
(909) 336-3571. **$98-$178, 7 day notice.** On SR 173, jct SR 189; across from entrance to Lake Arrowhead Village. Ext/int corridors. **Pets:** Other species. $8 daily fee/pet. Designated rooms, service with restrictions, supervision.

Lake Arrowhead Resort LH
(909) 336-1511. **$129-$209, 7 day notice.** 27984 Hwy 189. Just w of SR 173; in Lake Arrowhead Village. Int corridors. **Pets:** Other species. $15 daily fee/room. Supervision.

Storybook Inn BB
(909) 337-0011. **$89-$109, 7 day notice.** 28717 SR 18. SR 18, 1.1 mi e of jct SR 173. Ext/int corridors. **Pets:** Other species. Designated rooms, service with restrictions.

LAKE FOREST

Candlewood Suites-Irvine East SH
(949) 598-9105. **$89-$119.** 3 S Pointe Dr. I-5, exit Bake Pkwy, 2.6 mi e, then just s. Int corridors. **Pets:** Accepted.

LAKE TAHOE AREA

KINGS BEACH

◆◆◆ ▼ Stevenson's Holliday Inn Ⓜ
(530) 546-2269. **$79-$129, 7 day notice.** 8742 N Lake Blvd. SR 28, 1 mi e of SR 267. Ext corridors. **Pets:** Other species. $5 one-time fee/room. No service, supervision.
SAVE Ⓢ ✖ Ⓜ 🖪 ➤ 🗲

SOUTH LAKE TAHOE

◆◆◆ ▼▼▼ Alder Inn Ⓜ
(530) 544-4485. **$48-$180, 14 day notice.** 1072 Ski Run Blvd. 2.5 blks s off US 50 on Ski Run Blvd; 0.8 mi below Heavenly Valley Ski Lift Terminal. Ext corridors. **Pets:** Accepted.
SAVE Ⓢ ✖ 🖪 📺 ➤ 🗲

◆◆◆ ▼▼▼ Alpenrose Inn Ⓜ
(530) 544-2985. **$50-$140, 7 day notice.** 4074 Pine Blvd. 0.3 mi n of US 50 via Park Ave. Ext corridors. **Pets:** Accepted.
SAVE ✖ 🖪 📺

◆◆◆ ▼▼▼ Ambassador Motor Lodge Ⓜ
(530) 544-6461. **$55-$110.** 4130 Manzanita Ave. Just s of US 50 on Stateline Ave. Ext corridors. **Pets:** Accepted.
SAVE ✖ 🖪 📺 ➤ 🗲

◆◆◆ ▼▼▼▼ Best Western Timber Cove Lodge Ⓜ
(530) 541-6722. **$79-$209.** 3411 Lake Tahoe Blvd. 1.5 mi w of casino center, 0.5 mi w of Ski Run Blvd. Ext corridors. **Pets:** Other species. $100 deposit/pet, $25 daily fee/pet. Designated rooms, service with restrictions, supervision.
SAVE Ⓢ ✖ Ⓜ 🖪 🍽 ➤ 🗲

◆◆◆ ▼▼▼ Blue Jay Lodge Ⓜ
(530) 544-5232. **$79-$139.** 4133 Cedar Ave. 2 blks from casino center. Ext corridors. **Pets:** $10 daily fee/pet. Designated rooms, service with restrictions.
SAVE Ⓢ ✖ Ⓜ 🖪 📺 ➤

◆◆◆ ▼ Budget Inn Ⓜ
(530) 544-2834. **$32-$150, 3 day notice.** 3496 Lake Tahoe Blvd. On US 50, 1.5 mi w of casino center. Ext corridors. **Pets:** Dogs only. $5 one-time fee/pet. Service with restrictions, supervision.
SAVE Ⓢ ✖ 🖪 ➤ 🗲

◆◆◆ ▼ Cal Va Rado Motel Ⓜ
(530) 541-3900. **$39-$85.** 988 Stateline Ave. Just n of US 50; near casino center. Ext corridors. **Pets:** Medium, other species. Designated rooms, service with restrictions.
SAVE Ⓢ ✖ 🖪 🗲

◆◆◆ ▼ Capri Motel Ⓜ
(530) 544-3665. **$55-$110.** 932 Stateline Ave. Just s of US 50. Ext corridors. **Pets:** Accepted.
SAVE ✖ 🖪 📺 ➤ 🗲

◆◆◆ ▼ Cedar Inn & Suites Ⓜ
(530) 543-0159. **$35-$69.** 890 Stateline Ave. US 50, 2 blks n, at Stateline and Manzanita aves. Ext corridors. **Pets:** $10 daily fee/pet. Designated rooms, no service.
SAVE Ⓢ ✖ 🖪 📺 ➤

◆◆◆ ▼▼▼ Cedar Lodge Ⓜ 🐾
(530) 544-6453. **$40-$340.** 4069 Cedar Ave. N off US 50, toward the lake; at Cedar and Friday aves; 3 blks from the casino center. Ext corridors. **Pets:** Medium, dogs only. $20 one-time fee/pet. Designated rooms, service with restrictions, supervision.
SAVE ✖ 🖪 📺 ➤

◆◆◆ ▼▼▼ Days Inn-Casino Area/South Lake Tahoe Ⓜ
(530) 541-4800. **$42-$275.** 968 Park Ave. 3 blks w of casino center, 1 blk n off US 50 toward lake at Park and Cedar aves. Int corridors. **Pets:** Medium. $10 daily fee/pet. Designated rooms, service with restrictions, supervision.
SAVE Ⓢ ✖ 📺 ➤

▼▼ Fireside Lodge B & B 🅱🅱 🐾
(530) 542-1717. **$69-$155, 30 day notice.** 515 Emerald Bay Rd. SR 89, 1 mi n of US 50. Ext corridors. **Pets:** Dogs only. $100 deposit/room, $20 daily fee/pet. Service with restrictions, crate.
A$K Ⓢ ✖ 🖪 📺 🗲 🗲

◆◆◆ ▼▼▼ High Country Lodge Ⓜ
(530) 541-0508. **$35-$150.** 1227 Emerald Bay Rd. US 50, 0.5 mi n of airport. Ext corridors. **Pets:** Small. $5 daily fee/pet. Designated rooms, service with restrictions, supervision.
SAVE Ⓢ ✖ 🖪 📺 🗲

◆◆◆ ▼▼◆ Inn By The Lake Ⓜ 🐾
(530) 542-0330. **$98-$238.** 3300 Lake Tahoe Blvd. US 50, 2 mi s of casino center. Int corridors. **Pets:** Small, dogs only. $22 daily fee/pet. Designated rooms, service with restrictions, supervision.
SAVE Ⓢ ✖ Ⓜ 🗲 🖪 📺 ➤ 🗲

◆◆◆ ▼ Pistantes Coyote Den Ⓜ
(530) 541-2282. **$35-$195, 4 day notice.** 1211 Emerald Bay Rd. US 50, 0.5 mi n of airport. Ext corridors. **Pets:** Accepted.
SAVE Ⓢ ✖ 🖪 🗲

◆◆◆ ▼ Ridgewood Inn Ⓜ
(530) 541-8589. **$49-$135, 3 day notice.** 1341 Emerald Bay Rd. US 50, 0.5 mi n of airport. Ext corridors. **Pets:** Other species. $5 daily fee/room. Designated rooms, service with restrictions, supervision.
SAVE Ⓢ ✖ 🖪 📺 🗲

▼ Stateline Lodge Ⓜ 🐾
(530) 544-3075. **Call for rates.** 913 Friday Ave. 0.3 mi w of casino center. Ext corridors. **Pets:** Medium. $10 one-time fee/pet. Designated rooms, no service.
Ⓢ ✖ 🖪 🍽 ➤ 🗲

◆◆◆ ▼ Tahoe Colony Inn Ⓜ 🐾
(530) 544-6481. **$45-$110.** 3794 Montreal Rd. Just s of US 50. Int corridors. **Pets:** Large, other species. $40 deposit/pet. Service with restrictions, supervision.
SAVE Ⓢ ✖ 🖪 ➤ 🗲

◆◆◆ ▼▼◆▼ Tahoe Keys Resort 🅲🅾 🐾
(530) 544-5397. **$150-$1500.** 599 Tahoe Keys Blvd. US 50, exit Tahoe Keys Blvd, 1 mi w. Ext corridors. **Pets:** Other species. $100 deposit/pet, $25 one-time fee/pet. Designated rooms, service with restrictions, supervision.
SAVE Ⓢ ✖ 🖪 📺 ➤ 🗲 🗲

◆◆◆ ▼▼▼ Tahoe Valley Lodge Ⓜ
(530) 541-0353. **$75-$395, 7 day notice.** 2241 Lake Tahoe Blvd. 0.5 mi e of jct US 50 and SR 89, at Tahoe Keys Blvd. Ext corridors. **Pets:** Very small, dogs only. $10 daily fee/pet. Designated rooms, service with restrictions, supervision.
SAVE Ⓢ ✖ 🖪 📺 ➤

TAHOE VISTA

▼▼ Holiday House Ⓜ 🐾
(530) 546-2369. **$125-$225, 14 day notice.** 7276 N Lake Blvd. SR 28, 1 mi w of SR 267. Ext corridors. **Pets:** Other species. $10 daily fee/pet, $30 one-time fee/pet. Service with restrictions, supervision.
✖ Ⓜ 📺 🗲

TRUCKEE

▼▼ **Alpine Country Lodge** M
(530) 587-3801. **Call for rates.** 12260 Deerfield Dr. I-80, exit Donner Pass Rd, just s. Ext corridors. **Pets:** Medium. $10 daily fee/pet. Designated rooms, service with restrictions, supervision.
[SO] [X] [&M] [🔒] [💻] [📶]

▼▼ **The Inn at Truckee** M
(530) 587-8888. **Call for rates.** 11506 Deerfield Dr. I-80, exit SR 89, just s. Int corridors. **Pets:** Accepted.
[SO] [X] [&M] [🔒] [💻]

END AREA

LANCASTER

◈◈◈ ▼▼▼ **Best Western Antelope Valley Inn** M
(661) 948-4651. **$104-$109.** 44055 N Sierra Hwy. SR 14, exit Ave K, 2.3 mi e. Ext/int corridors. **Pets:** Accepted.
[SAVE] [SO] [X] [🔒] [💻] [🍴] [📶]

◈◈◈ ▼▼▼ **Desert Inn Hotel** M
(661) 942-8401. **$82-$112.** 44219 N Sierra Hwy. SR 14, exit Ave K, 1.4 mi e, then just n. Ext corridors. **Pets:** Accepted.
[SAVE] [SO] [X] [🔒] [💻] [🍴] [📶] [X]

▼▼▼ **Oxford Inn & Suites** M 🐾
(661) 949-3423. **$89-$169.** 1651 W Ave K. SR 14, exit Ave K, just w. Int corridors. **Pets:** $50 one-time fee/pet. Service with restrictions, crate.
[ASK] [X] [&M] [🌀] [📺] [🔒] [💻] [📶]

LA PALMA

▼▼▼ **La Quinta Inn & Suites Orange County (Buena Park)** SH
(714) 670-1400. **$95-$130.** 3 Center Pointe Dr. SR 91, exit Orangethorpe Ave/Valley View St, just n. Int corridors. **Pets:** Other species. Service with restrictions, supervision.
[ASK] [X] [🌀] [🔒] [💻] [📶]

LATHROP

▼▼▼ **Days Inn** M
(209) 982-1959. **$86-$90.** 14750 S Harlan Rd. I-5, exit Lathrop Rd. Int corridors. **Pets:** Small. $10 daily fee/pet. Service with restrictions, supervision.
[ASK] [SO] [X] [&M] [🔒] [📶]

LEBEC

▼▼ **Best Rest Inn** M 🐾
(661) 248-2700. **$49-$89.** 51541 N Peace Valley Rd. I-5, exit Frazier Park, just w. Int corridors. **Pets:** Other species. $10 daily fee/pet. Designated rooms, service with restrictions.
[ASK] [SO] [X] [&M] [🔒] [🍴] [📶]

◈◈◈ ▼▼▼▼ **Ramada Limited Grapevine** M
(661) 248-1530. **$67-$95.** 9000 Country Side Ct. I-5, exit Grapevine, just w. Ext corridors. **Pets:** Medium. $5 daily fee/pet. Designated rooms, service with restrictions, supervision.
[SAVE] [SO] [X] [&M] [📺] [🔒] [💻] [📶]

LEE VINING

◈◈◈ ▼▼▼ **Murphey's Motel** M
(760) 647-6316. **$53-$108.** 51493 Hwy 395. On US 395; in town. Ext corridors. **Pets:** Small. $5 daily fee/room. Service with restrictions, supervision.
[SAVE] [X] [🔒] [💻]

LEMOORE

◈◈◈ ▼▼▼ **Best Western Vineyard Inn** M 🐾
(559) 924-1261. **$82.** 877 E "D" St. SR 198, exit Houston St, 0.8 ni nw. Ext corridors. **Pets:** Other species. $50 deposit/room. Service with restrictions, supervision.
[SAVE] [X] [&M] [🔒] [💻] [📶]

LINDSAY

◈◈◈ ▼▼ **Super 8 Motel** M 🐾
(559) 562-5188. **$59-$85.** 390 N Hwy 65. On SR 65. Ext corridors. **Pets:** Small. $10 daily fee/room. Designated rooms, no service, supervision.
[SAVE] [SO] [X] [🔒] [📶]

LIVERMORE

▼▼▼ **Ramada Limited** SH
(925) 456-5422. **$79-$169.** 7600 Southfront Rd. I-580, exit N Greenville Rd, just s. Int corridors. **Pets:** Other species. $25 daily fee/room, $100 one-time fee/room. Service with restrictions, crate.
[ASK] [SO] [X] [&M] [🔒] [💻] [📶]

▼▼▼ **Residence Inn By Marriott** M
(925) 373-1800. **$149-$194.** 1000 Airway Blvd. I-580, Airway Blvd, Collier Canyon Rd, just n. Ext corridors. **Pets:** Accepted.
[ASK] [SO] [X] [💻] [📶] [X]

LODI

◈◈◈ ▼▼ **El Rancho Motel** M 🐾
(209) 368-0651. **$55-$60.** 603 N Cherokee Ln. SR 99, exit Turner Rd, just s. Ext corridors. **Pets:** Very small. $25 deposit/pet. Service with restrictions, supervision.
[SAVE] [SO] [X] [&M] [🔒] [📶]

LOMPOC

◈◈◈ ▼▼▼ **Best Value Inn** M
(805) 735-3737. **$49-$199.** 1200 N H St. SR 1, 1.3 mi n. Ext corridors. **Pets:** Accepted.
[SAVE] [SO] [X] [🔒] [🍴]

◈◈◈ ▼▼ **Days Inn** M 🐾
(805) 733-5000. **$85.** 3955 Apollo Way. SR 1, exit Constellation Blvd, just e; 3.5 mi n of Ocean Ave. Ext/int corridors. **Pets:** Medium, dogs only. $10 daily fee/pet. Designated rooms, service with restrictions, supervision.
[SAVE] [SO] [X] [🔒] [💻] [🍴] [📶] [X]

▼▼ **Quality Inn & Executive Suites** SH
(805) 735-8555. **$79-$109.** 1621 N H St. On SR 1, 1.8 mi n. Int corridors. **Pets:** Other species. $25 one-time fee/pet. Designated rooms, service with restrictions, crate.
[ASK] [SO] [X] [🔒] [💻] [📶] [X]

◈◈◈ ▼▼ **Vagabond Inn** M
(805) 735-7744. **$69-$129.** 1122 N H St. SR 1, 1.2 mi n. Ext/int corridors. **Pets:** Large, other species. $25 one-time fee/room. Designated rooms, service with restrictions, crate.
[SAVE] [SO] [X] [🔒] [💻] [📶]

LONE PINE

◈◈◈ ▼▼▼ **Best Western Frontier Motel** M
(760) 876-5571. **$64-$109.** 1008 S Main St. On US 395; at south end of town. Ext corridors. **Pets:** Accepted.
[SAVE] [SO] [X] [&M] [🌀] [📺] [🔒] [💻] [📶]

△△△ ▽▽▽▽ Dow Villa Motel M
(760) 876-5521. **$62-$96.** 310 S Main St. On US 395. Ext corridors.
Pets: Large. $50 deposit/room. Designated rooms, service with restrictions,
supervision.
[SAVE] [S○] [✕] [⟲] [⅍] [🛏] [💻] [⇌]

△△△ ▽ Lone Pine Budget Inn Motel M
(760) 876-5655. **$45-$99, 3 day notice.** 138 W Willow St. US 395, just
w. Ext corridors. **Pets:** Accepted.
[SAVE] [S○] [✕] [🛏] [💻]

△△△ ▽▽ ▽ National 9 Trails Motel M
(760) 876-5555. **$45-$99, 3 day notice.** 633 S Main St. On US 395.
Ext corridors. **Pets:** Small, dogs only. $10 daily fee/pet. Designated rooms,
service with restrictions, supervision.
[SAVE] [✕] [🛏] [💻] [⇌]

LOS ALAMITOS

▽▽▽▽ Residence Inn by Marriott-Cypress/Orange
County SH
(714) 484-5700. **$129-$149.** 4931 Katella Ave. I-605, exit Katella Ave,
1.5 mi e. Int corridors. **Pets:** Accepted.
[ASK] [✕] [🛏] [💻] [⇌] [✕]

LOS ALTOS

▽▽▽▽ Marriott Residence Inn-Palo Alto/Los Altos M
(650) 559-7890. **Call for rates.** 4460 El Camino Real. US 101, exit San
Antonio Rd, 2 mi w to SR 82, then just n. Int corridors. **Pets:** Accepted.
[S○] [✕] [ᴹ] [⅍] [💻] [⇌] [✕]

LOS ANGELES METROPOLITAN AREA

ARCADIA

▽▽▽▽ Residence Inn by Marriott SH
(626) 446-6500. **$154-$199.** 321 E Huntington Dr. I-210, exit Huntington
Dr, 0.5 mi w, then just n on Gateway Dr. Ext corridors. **Pets:** Accepted.
[ASK] [S○] [✕] [ᴹ] [⟲] [⅍] [🛏] [💻] [⇌] [✕]

BEVERLY HILLS

▽▽▽▽ Avalon Hotel SH
(310) 277-5221. **$195-$395.** 9400 W Olympic Blvd. I-10, exit Robertson
Blvd, 1.7 mi n, then 0.8 mi w. Ext/int corridors. **Pets:** Accepted.
[ASK] [S○] [✕] [💻] [¶¶] [⇌]

△△△ ▽▽▽▽ The Beverly Hills Hotel and
Bungalows LH ❀
(310) 276-2251. **$430-$530.** 9641 Sunset Blvd. I-405, exit Sunset Blvd,
3.7 mi e. Int corridors. **Pets:** Small, dogs only. $200 one-time fee/pet.
Designated rooms.
[SAVE] [✕] [ᴹ] [⟲] [⅍] [¶¶] [⇌] [✕]

△△△ ▽▽▽▽ Luxe Hotel Rodeo Drive SH
(310) 273-0300. **$375.** 360 N Rodeo Dr. I-405, exit Wilshire Blvd, 4.4 mi
e, then just n. Int corridors. **Pets:** Medium, other species. $250 deposit/
room, $10 daily fee/room, $200 one-time fee/room. Service with restrictions.
[SAVE] [S○] [✕] [🛏] [💻] [¶¶] [✕]

△△△ ▽▽▽▽ The Mosaic Hotel SH
(310) 278-0303. **$209-$229.** 125 S Spalding Dr. I-405, exit Wilshire
Blvd, 2.2 mi e, then just s. Ext/int corridors. **Pets:** Accepted.
[SAVE] [S○] [✕] [🛏] [💻] [¶¶] [⇌]

△△△ ▽▽▽▽▽ The Peninsula Beverly Hills SH ❀
(310) 551-2888. **$425-$3500.** 9882 S Santa Monica Blvd. I-405, exit
Santa Monica Blvd, 2.2 mi e at Wilshire Blvd. Int corridors. **Pets:** Other
species. $35 daily fee/pet. Service with restrictions.
[SAVE] [✕] [💻] [¶¶] [⇌] [✕]

△△△ ▽▽▽▽▽ Raffles L'Ermitage Beverly Hills SH ❀
(310) 278-3344. **$418-$448.** 9291 Burton Way. I-10, exit Robertson
Blvd, 3.1 mi n, then just w. Int corridors. **Pets:** Small. $150 one-time
fee/pet. Supervision.
[SAVE] [✕] [ᴹ] [⟲] [💻] [¶¶] [⇌] [✕]

▽▽ ▽▽ Regent Beverly Wilshire LH ❀
(310) 275-5200. **$405-$7500.** 9500 Wilshire Blvd. I-405, exit Wilshire
Blvd, 4.5 mi e. Int corridors. **Pets:** Very small. Service with restrictions,
supervision.
[✕] [ᴹ] [⟲] [⅍] [¶¶] [⇌] [✕]

BURBANK

▽▽▽▽ Burbank Airport Hilton & Convention Center LH
(818) 843-6000. **$89-$209.** 2500 Hollywood Way. I-5, exit Hollywood
Way, 1 mi s. Int corridors. **Pets:** Medium, other species. $25 daily fee/
room. Service with restrictions, supervision.
[✕] [🛏] [💻] [¶¶] [⇌]

▽▽▽▽ The Graciela Burbank SH ❀
(818) 842-8887. **$215-$1000.** 322 N Pass Ave. SR 134, exit Hollywood
Way westbound, just w on Alameda Ave, then 0.5 mi n on Pass Ave;
exit Pass Ave eastbound, 0.5 mi n. Ext corridors. **Pets:** Small. $150
one-time fee/room. Service with restrictions, supervision.
[ASK] [S○] [✕] [🛏] [💻] [¶¶] [✕]

△△△ ▽▽▽▽ Safari Inn, A Coast Hotel M
(818) 845-8586. **$83-$152.** 1911 W Olive Ave. I-5, exit Olive Ave, 1.3 mi
sw. Ext corridors. **Pets:** Other species. $25 one-time fee/pet. Designated
rooms, supervision.
[SAVE] [S○] [✕] [⟲] [⅍] [🛏] [💻] [¶¶] [⇌]

CERRITOS

▽▽▽▽ Sheraton Cerritos Hotel at Towne Center SH ❀
(562) 809-1500. **$279-$550.** 12725 Center Court Dr. SR 91, exit
Artesia/Bloomfield Dr, just s. Int corridors. **Pets:** Small, dogs only. Service with restrictions, supervision.
[ASK] [S○] [✕] [ᴹ] [💻] [¶¶] [⇌] [✕]

CHATSWORTH

▽▽ ▽▽ Ramada Inn SH
(818) 998-5289. **$83-$98.** 21340 Devonshire St. SR 118, exit De Soto
Ave, 1.5 mi s, then 0.5 mi w. Int corridors. **Pets:** Small. $50 deposit/
room, $10 daily fee/pet. Designated rooms, service with restrictions, super-
vision.
[ASK] [S○] [✕] [ᴹ] [⟲] [🛏] [💻] [¶¶] [⇌]

▽▽▽▽ Staybridge Suites SH ❀
(818) 773-0707. **$133-$178.** 21902 Lassen St. SR 118, exit Topanga
Canyon Blvd, 2 mi s, then just e. Ext corridors. **Pets:** Medium, other
species. $150 one-time fee/room. Service with restrictions.
[ASK] [✕] [ᴹ] [⟲] [🛏] [💻] [⇌] [✕]

CULVER CITY

▽▽▽▽ Four Points by Sheraton Culver City LH
(310) 641-7740. **$89-$109.** 5990 Green Valley Cir. I-405, exit
Sepulveda Blvd, just n, then just e. Int corridors. **Pets:** $25 one-time
fee/pet. Designated rooms, service with restrictions.
[ASK] [S○] [✕] [🛏] [💻] [¶¶] [⇌]

ⓐ ▽▽▽▽ **Radisson Hotel-LA Westside** ⒧Ⓗ
(310) 649-1776. **$89-$149.** 6161 W Centinela Ave. I-405, exit Jefferson
Blvd, just s, then just nw. Int corridors. **Pets:** Accepted.
[SAVE] [S🐾] [✕] [🛏] [📺] [🍴] [🏊]

DOWNEY

ⓐ ▽▽▽▽ **Embassy Suites Hotel** ⒧Ⓗ
(562) 861-1900. **$167-$197.** 8425 Firestone Blvd. I-605, exit Firestone
Blvd, 2 mi w. Int corridors. **Pets:** Accepted.
[SAVE] [✕] [🛏] [📺] [🍴] [🏊] [✕]

EL SEGUNDO

▽▽▽▽ **Embassy Suites-LAX South** ⒧Ⓗ
(310) 640-3600. **$124-$219.** 1440 E Imperial Ave. I-405, exit Imperial
Hwy, 1.6 mi w. Int corridors. **Pets:** Small, other species. $25 daily fee/pet.
Service with restrictions.
[✕] [🛏] [📺] [🍴] [🏊]

▽▽▽▽ **Homestead Studio Suites Hotel-LAX/El**
Segundo Ⓜ
(310) 607-4000. **$89-$104.** 1910 E Mariposa Ave. I-105, exit Sepulveda
Blvd, 1 mi s. Ext corridors. **Pets:** Accepted.
[ASK] [S🐾] [✕] [🛏M] [🕐] [🔯] [🛏] [📺]

▽▽▽▽ **Summerfield Suites by Wyndham-El Segundo** Ⓜ
(310) 725-0100. **$89-$149.** 810 S Douglas St. I-405, exit Rosecrans
Ave, 0.5 mi e, then just n. Ext/int corridors. **Pets:** Accepted.
[ASK] [✕] [🛏M] [🕐] [🔯] [🛏] [📺] [🏊] [✕]

GLENDALE

▽▽▽▽ **Homestead Studio Suites**
Hotel-Glendale/Burbank ⓈⒽ ❀
(818) 956-6665. **$99-$114.** 1377 W Glenoaks Blvd. I-5, exit Western
Ave, 0.4 mi e, then 0.6 mi s. Int corridors. **Pets:** Medium. $25 daily
fee/pet. Service with restrictions, supervision.
[ASK] [S🐾] [✕] [🛏M] [🕐] [🔯] [🛏] [📺]

▽▽▽ **Los Angeles Days Inn-Glendale** ⓈⒽ
(818) 956-0202. **$114, 3 day notice.** 450 W Pioneer Dr. SR 134, exit
Pacific Ave, just s, then just e. Ext corridors. **Pets:** Small, other species.
$50 deposit/room. Designated rooms, service with restrictions, supervision.
[ASK] [S🐾] [✕] [🛏] [📺] [🍴] [🏊]

ⓐ ▽▽▽ **Vagabond Inn Glendale** Ⓜ
(818) 240-1700. **$89-$99.** 120 W Colorado St. SR 134, exit Brand Blvd,
1 mi s, then just w. Ext corridors. **Pets:** Medium. $10 daily fee/pet.
Designated rooms, service with restrictions, crate.
[SAVE] [S🐾] [✕] [🛏] [📺] [🏊]

HAWTHORNE

▽▽▽ **TownePlace Suites by Marriott** Ⓜ ❀
(310) 725-9696. **$79-$119.** 14400 Aviation Blvd. I-405, exit Rosecrans
Ave, 0.4 mi w. Int corridors. **Pets:** Large, other species. $75 one-time
fee/room. Supervision.
[ASK] [S🐾] [✕] [🛏] [📺] [🏊]

HOLLYWOOD

ⓐ ▽▽▽▽ **Ramada Inn and Conference Center-Hollywood**
Near Universal Studios ⓈⒽ ❀
(323) 315-1800. **$89-$109.** 1160 N Vermont Ave. US 101, exit Vermont
Ave, 0.5 mi n. Int corridors. **Pets:** $25 daily fee/room. Designated rooms,
service with restrictions, crate.
[SAVE] [S🐾] [✕] [🛏] [📺] [🍴] [🏊] [✕]

INDUSTRY

▽▽▽▽ **Pacific Palms Conference Resort** ⒧Ⓗ
(626) 810-4455. **$159-$1050.** One Industry Hills Pkwy. SR 60, exit
Azusa Ave, 1.3 mi n, 0.5 mi w. Int corridors. **Pets:** Accepted.
[ASK] [S🐾] [✕] [📺] [🍴] [🏊] [✕]

LA MIRADA

▽▽▽▽ **Residence Inn by Marriott** ⓈⒽ
(714) 523-2800. **$149-$189.** 14419 Firestone Blvd. I-5, exit Valley View,
just n, then 0.5 mi e. Ext corridors. **Pets:** Medium, other species. $75
one-time fee/room. Crate.
[ASK] [S🐾] [✕] [🛏] [📺] [🏊] [✕]

LONG BEACH

ⓐ ▽▽▽▽ **The Coast Long Beach Hotel** ⓈⒽ
(562) 435-7676. **$105-$135.** 700 Queensway Dr. I-710, exit Harbor
Scenic Dr (Queen Mary), 1 mi s. Ext corridors. **Pets:** Accepted.
[SAVE] [✕] [🛏] [📺] [🍴] [🏊] [✕]

ⓐ ▽▽▽ **Days Inn-City Center** Ⓜ
(562) 591-0088. **$75.** 1500 E Pacific Coast Hwy. I-710, exit SR 1
(Pacific Coast Hwy), 2 mi e. Ext corridors. **Pets:** Accepted.
[SAVE] [S🐾] [✕] [🛏M] [🛏] [📺]

ⓐ ▽▽▽▽ **GuestHouse Hotel Long Beach** Ⓜ
(562) 597-1341. **$89-$109.** 5325 E Pacific Coast Hwy. I-405, exit SR 22
(Long Beach) northbound, 2 mi nw; exit Lakewood Blvd southbound, 2
mi se on SR 1. Ext corridors. **Pets:** $10 daily fee/room. Designated
rooms, service with restrictions, crate.
[SAVE] [S🐾] [✕] [🕐] [🔯] [🛏] [📺] [🏊]

ⓐ ▽▽▽▽ **Holiday Inn-Long Beach Airport** ⒧Ⓗ
(562) 597-4401. **$95-$125.** 2640 Lakewood Blvd. I-405, exit Lakewood
Blvd, just s. Ext/int corridors. **Pets:** Accepted.
[SAVE] [S🐾] [✕] [🛏] [📺] [🍴] [🏊]

▽▽▽▽ **Renaissance Long Beach Hotel** ⒧Ⓗ
(562) 437-5900. **$94-$219.** 111 E Ocean Blvd. I-710, exit Broadway/
Downtown, 0.8 mi e to Long Beach Blvd, just s, then just w. Int
corridors. **Pets:** Medium. $75 one-time fee/room. Service with restrictions,
supervision.
[✕] [📺] [🍴] [🏊] [✕]

▽▽▽▽ **The Westin Long Beach** ⒧Ⓗ ❀
(562) 436-3000. **$299-$460.** 333 E Ocean Blvd. I-710, exit Broadway/
Downtown, 0.8 mi e to Long Beach Blvd, then just s. **Pets:** Medium.
$75 one-time fee/room. Service with restrictions, crate.
[ASK] [S🐾] [✕] [📺] [🍴] [🏊] [✕]

LOS ANGELES

ⓐ ◆ **Beverly Laurel Motor Hotel** Ⓜ
(323) 651-2441. **$94-$109.** 8018 Beverly Blvd. I-10, exit Fairfax Ave,
2.8 mi n, then just w. Ext corridors. **Pets:** Medium. $25 daily fee/pet.
Service with restrictions, supervision.
[SAVE] [S🐾] [✕] [🛏] [📺] [🍴]

ⓐ ▽▽▽▽ **Four Points by Sheraton LAX** ⒧Ⓗ ❀
(310) 645-4600. **$99.** 9750 Airport Blvd. I-405, exit Century Blvd, 1.5 mi
w, then just n. Ext/int corridors. **Pets:** Medium. $10 daily fee/pet. Desig-
nated rooms, service with restrictions, supervision.
[SAVE] [✕] [🛏] [📺] [🍴] [🏊]

ⓐ ▽▽▽▽ **Four Seasons Hotel Los Angeles at Beverly**
Hills ⒧Ⓗ
(310) 273-2222. **$340-$470.** 300 S Doheny Dr. I-10, exit Robertson
Blvd, 3 mi n to Burton Way, then just w. Int corridors. **Pets:** Accepted.
[SAVE] [✕] [🛏] [📺] [🍴] [🏊] [✕]

▽▽▽▽ **Furama Hotel Los Angeles** ⒧Ⓗ
(310) 670-8111. **$66-$90.** 8601 Lincoln Blvd. I-405, exit La Tijera Blvd,
1.2 mi sw, then 1.6 mi w. Int corridors. **Pets:** Accepted.
[ASK] [✕] [🛏] [📺] [🍴] [🏊]

ⓐ ▽▽▽▽ **Holiday Inn Brentwood/Bel-Air** ⒧Ⓗ
(310) 476-6411. **$99-$189.** 170 N Church Ln. I-405, exit Sunset Blvd,
just w, then just n. Int corridors. **Pets:** Medium, other species. $50
one-time fee/room. Service with restrictions, supervision.
[SAVE] [S🐾] [✕] [🛏] [📺] [🍴]

◆◆◆◆ **Hotel Bel-Air** [SH]
(310) 472-1211. **$385-$575, 3 day notice.** 701 Stone Canyon Rd. I-405, exit Sunset Blvd, 2 mi e, then 0.8 mi n. Ext corridors. **Pets:** Accepted.
🚭 ▣ 🍴 🏊

◆◆◆ **Le Meridien at Beverly Hills** [LH]
(310) 247-0400. **$159-$299.** 465 S La Cienega Blvd. I-10, exit La Cienega Blvd, 2.5 mi n. Ext corridors. **Pets:** Accepted.
🚭 ♿M 🦻 ♿ ☕ 🍴 🏊 🏋

◆◆◆ **Los Angeles Airport Hilton & Towers** [LH]
(310) 410-4000. **$109-$229.** 5711 W Century Blvd. I-405, exit Century Blvd, 0.8 mi w. Int corridors. **Pets:** Accepted.
[A$K] 🚭 ▣ ☕ 🍴 🏊 🏋

◆◆◆ **Los Angeles Airport Marriott Hotel** [LH]
(310) 641-5700. **$99-$259.** 5855 W Century Blvd. I-405, exit Century Blvd, 1 mi w. Int corridors. **Pets:** Accepted.
[A$K] [S/D] 🚭 🦻 ♿ ▣ 🍴 🏊 🏋

[AAA] ◆◆◆ **Luxe Hotel Sunset Boulevard** [SH]
(310) 476-6571. **$250, 3 day notice.** 11461 Sunset Blvd. I-405, exit Sunset Blvd, just w. Int corridors. **Pets:** $250 deposit/room, $200 one-time fee/room. Designated rooms, service with restrictions, supervision.
[SAVE] 🚭 ▣ ☕ 🍴 🏊 🏋

[AAA] ◆◆◆◆ **Omni Los Angeles Hotel** [LH]
(213) 617-3300. **$110-$199.** 251 S Olive St. SR 110, exit 4th St southbound; exit 6th St northbound, just e, then just n. Int corridors. **Pets:** Small, other species. $50 one-time fee/room. Service with restrictions, supervision.
[SAVE] [S/D] 🚭 ♿M 🦻 ▣ ☕ 🍴 🏊 🏋

[AAA] ◆◆◆ **Radisson Hotel at Los Angeles Airport** [LH]
(310) 670-9000. **$79-$210.** 6225 W Century Blvd at Sepulveda Blvd. I-405, exit Century Blvd, 1.6 mi w. Int corridors. **Pets:** Small. $150 deposit/room. Service with restrictions, supervision.
[SAVE] [S/D] 🚭 ☕ 🍴 🏊 🏋

◆◆◆ **Residence Inn by Marriott-Beverly Hills** [SH] 🐾
(310) 277-4427. **$171-$260.** 1177 S Beverly Dr. I-10, exit Robertson Blvd, 1.6 mi n to Pico Blvd, then 0.6 mi w. Int corridors. **Pets:** Medium, dogs only. $10 daily fee/pet, $80 one-time fee/room. Service with restrictions.
[A$K] [S/D] 🚭 ▣ ☕

[AAA] ◆◆◆◆ **St Regis Hotel Los Angeles** [LH]
(310) 277-6111. **$485-$535.** 2055 Avenue of the Stars. I-10, exit Robertson Blvd, 2.7 mi n to Olympic Blvd, 1.9 mi w, then just n. Int corridors. **Pets:** Accepted.
[SAVE] 🚭 ♿M 🦻 ☕ 🍴 🏊 🏋

◆◆◆ **Sheraton Gateway Hotel, Los Angeles Airport** [LH]
(310) 642-1111. **$269-$500.** 6101 W Century Blvd. I-405, exit Century Blvd, 1.3 mi w. Int corridors. **Pets:** Accepted.
[A$K] [S/D] 🚭 ☕ 🍴 🏊

[AAA] ◆◆ **Travelodge Hotel at Lax** [SH] 🐾
(310) 649-4000. **$54-$89.** 5547 W Century Blvd. I-405, exit Century Blvd, 0.5 mi w. Ext/int corridors. **Pets:** Other species. Designated rooms, service with restrictions, crate.
[SAVE] [S/D] 🚭 ▣ ☕ 🍴 🏊

[AAA] ◆◆ **Vagabond Inn Los Angeles-USC** [M] 🐾
(213) 746-1531. **$89-$99.** 3101 S Figueroa St. SR 110, exit Adams Blvd, 0.5 mi s. Ext corridors. **Pets:** Small. $10 daily fee/pet. Designated rooms, service with restrictions, supervision.
[SAVE] [S/D] 🚭 ▣ ☕ 🏊

[AAA] ◆◆◆◆ **The Westin Century Plaza Hotel and Spa** [LH] 🐾
(310) 277-2000. **$409-$429.** 2025 Avenue of the Stars. I-10, exit Robertson Blvd, 2.7 mi n to Olympic Blvd, 1.9 mi w, then just n. Int corridors. **Pets:** Small, other species. $20 daily fee/room. Service with restrictions, supervision.
[SAVE] 🚭 ♿M 🦻 ♿ ☕ 🍴 🏊 🏋

◆◆◆ **The Westin Hotel-Los Angeles Airport** [LH]
(310) 216-5858. **$89-$169, 3 day notice.** 5400 W Century Blvd. I-405, exit Century Blvd, just w. Int corridors. **Pets:** Accepted.
[S/D] 🚭 ☕ 🍴 🏊 🏋

MANHATTAN BEACH

◆◆◆ **Residence Inn by Marriott** [SH]
(310) 421-3100. **$189.** 1700 N Sepulveda Blvd. I-405, exit Rosecrans Ave, 1.5 mi w, then 1 mi s on SR 1. Ext corridors. **Pets:** Accepted.
[A$K] [S/D] 🚭 ▣ ☕ 🏊 🏋

MISSION HILLS

[AAA] ◆◆ **Mission Hills Inn** [M]
(818) 891-1771. **$83.** 10621 Sepulveda Blvd. I-405, exit Devonshire St, just e, then just n; SR 118 (Simi Valley Frwy), just s. Ext/int corridors. **Pets:** Very small. $20 daily fee/pet. Designated rooms, service with restrictions, supervision.
[SAVE] [S/D] 🚭 🦻 ▣ ☕ 🏊

MONROVIA

◆◆◆ **Homestead Studio Suites Hotel-Monrovia/Pasadena** [SH] 🐾
(626) 256-6999. **$89-$104.** 930 S Fifth Ave. I-210, exit Huntington Dr, just w, then just n. Int corridors. **Pets:** Medium, other species. $75 one-time fee/room. Designated rooms, service with restrictions, supervision.
[A$K] [S/D] 🚭 ♿M ♿ ▣ ☕

PASADENA

[AAA] ◆◆ **Quality Inn Pasadena** [M]
(626) 796-9291. **$69-$99.** 3321 E Colorado Blvd. I-210, exit Madre St, just s, then 0.3 mi e. Ext corridors. **Pets:** Other species. $15 daily fee/room. Designated rooms, service with restrictions, supervision.
[SAVE] [S/D] 🚭 ▣ ☕ 🏊

[AAA] ◆◆◆◆ **The Ritz-Carlton, Huntington Hotel & Spa** [LH]
(626) 568-3900. **$275-$3000.** 1401 S Oak Knoll Ave. I-210, exit Lake Ave, 2 mi s. Ext/int corridors. **Pets:** Dogs only. $125 deposit/room. Service with restrictions, supervision.
[SAVE] 🚭 ▣ ☕ 🍴 🏊 🏋

◆◆◆ **Sheraton Pasadena Hotel** [LH]
(626) 449-4000. **$129-$209.** 303 E Cordova St. I-210, exit Los Robles Ave, 0.7 mi s, then just w. Int corridors. **Pets:** Accepted.
[A$K] [S/D] 🚭 ♿M ▣ ☕ 🍴 🏊 🏋

[AAA] ◆ **Super 8** [M]
(626) 449-3020. **$59-$99.** 2863 E Colorado Blvd. I-210, exit San Gabriel Blvd, 0.3 mi s, then just e. Ext corridors. **Pets:** Accepted.
[SAVE] [S/D] 🚭 ▣ 🏊

[AAA] ◆◆ **Vagabond Inn** [M]
(626) 449-3170. **$68-$99.** 1203 E Colorado Blvd. I-210, exit Hill St, just s, then just w. Ext/int corridors. **Pets:** Accepted.
[SAVE] [S/D] 🚭 ▣ ☕ 🏊

[AAA] ◆◆ **Westway Inn** [M]
(626) 304-9678. **$75-$350, 30 day notice.** 1599 E Colorado Blvd. I-210, exit Allen Ave westbound; exit Hill Ave eastbound, 0.8 mi s. Ext corridors. **Pets:** Medium. $10 daily fee/pet. Designated rooms, service with restrictions, crate.
[SAVE] 🚭 ▣ ☕ 🏊

POMONA

◆◆ **Sheraton Suites Fairplex** LH
(909) 622-2220. **$229-$249.** 601 W McKinley Ave. I-10, exit White Ave eastbound, 0.5 mi n, then just w; exit Fairplex Dr westbound, 1 mi n, then 0.7 mi e. Int corridors. **Pets:** Accepted.
[ASK] [S6] [✕] [🔒] [▢] [🍴] [⇌] [✕]

◆◆ **Shilo Inn Pomona Hotel** SH 🐾
(909) 598-0073. **$96-$157.** 3200 Temple Ave. SR 57, exit Temple Ave, just w. Int corridors. **Pets:** Other species. $10 daily fee/pet. Service with restrictions, crate.
[ASK] [S6] [✕] [🔒] [▢] [🍴] [⇌] [✕]

SAN DIMAS

◆◆ **Red Roof Inn** M
(909) 599-2362. **$54-$99.** 204 N Village Ct. I-210, exit Arrow Hwy, just e. Ext corridors. **Pets:** Accepted.
[✕] [⅙M] [🐾] [🔒] [⇌]

SAN PEDRO

◆◆◆ **Holiday Inn San Pedro-LA Harbor** SH
(310) 514-1414. **$99-$119.** 111 S Gaffey St. I-110, exit Gaffey St, just s. Int corridors. **Pets:** Accepted.
[ASK] [S6] [✕] [🔒] [▢] [🍴] [⇌]

◆◆◆ **Marina Hotel San Pedro** LH
(310) 514-3344. **$99-$199.** 2800 Via Cabrillo Marina. I-110, exit Gaffey St, 1.5 mi s, then 0.5 mi e on 22nd St. Int corridors. **Pets:** Small. $50 deposit/room. Service with restrictions, supervision.
[ASK] [S6] [✕] [🔒] [▢] [🍴] [⇌] [✕]

◆◆◆ **Vagabond Inn** M
(310) 831-8911. **$60-$75.** 215 S Gaffey St. I-110, exit Gaffey St, just s of terminus. Ext corridors. **Pets:** Accepted.
[SAVE] [S6] [✕] [🔒] [▢] [⇌]

SANTA CLARITA

◆◆◆◆ **Residence Inn by Marriott** SH
(661) 290-2800. **$129-$159.** 25320 The Old Rd. I-5, exit Lyons Ave, just w. Int corridors. **Pets:** Accepted.
[ASK] [✕] [⅙M] [🐾] [🐾] [🔒] [▢] [⇌] [✕]

SANTA MONICA

◆◆◆ **The Fairmont Miramar Hotel Santa Monica** LH 🐾
(310) 576-7777. **$249-$1399.** 101 Wilshire Blvd. I-10, exit Lincoln Blvd, 0.6 mi n, then 0.6 mi w. Ext/int corridors. **Pets:** Small, other species. $125 deposit/pet. Service with restrictions, supervision.
[SAVE] [✕] [▢] [🍴] [⇌] [✕]

◆◆◆ **The Georgian** SH 🐾
(310) 395-9945. **$159-$194.** 1415 Ocean Ave. I-10, exit Lincoln Blvd, just n, then 0.5 mi w on Broadway. Int corridors. **Pets:** Medium. $100 one-time fee/pet.
[ASK] [✕] [🔒] [▢] [🍴]

◆◆◆◆ **Le Merigot–A JW Marriott Hotel & Spa** LH 🐾
(310) 395-9700. **$249-$499.** 1740 Ocean Ave. I-10, exit Lincoln Blvd, 0.3 mi s, 0.6 mi w on Pico Blvd, then just n. Int corridors. **Pets:** $150 deposit/room, $35 one-time fee/room. Service with restrictions.
[SAVE] [S6] [✕] [🍴] [⇌] [✕]

◆◆◆◆ **Loews Santa Monica Beach Hotel** LH
(310) 458-6700. **$210-$350.** 1700 Ocean Ave. I-10, exit Lincoln Blvd, 0.3 mi s, 0.6 mi w on Pico Blvd, then just n. Int corridors. **Pets:** Accepted.
[SAVE] [✕] [♿] [🐾] [🐾] [🍴] [⇌] [✕]

◆◆ **Travelodge-Santa Monica/Pico Blvd** M
(310) 450-5766. **$79-$149.** 3102 W Pico Blvd. I-10, exit Centinela Ave, just n, then just w. Ext corridors. **Pets:** Small. $100 deposit/room. Designated rooms, service with restrictions, crate.
[ASK] [S6] [✕] [🔒] [▢]

SHERMAN OAKS

◆◆◆ ◆◆◆ **Best Western Carriage Inn** M
(818) 787-2300. **$93-$137.** 5525 Sepulveda Blvd. I-405, exit Burbank Blvd, just e, then just s. Ext/int corridors. **Pets:** Accepted.
[SAVE] [S6] [✕] [🐾] [🔒] [▢] [🍴] [⇌]

TARZANA

◆◆ **St. George Motor Inn** M
(818) 345-6911. **$74-$89.** 19454 Ventura Blvd. US 101, exit Tampa Ave, just s, then just w. Ext corridors. **Pets:** Accepted.
[ASK] [S6] [✕] [🔒] [▢] [⇌]

TORRANCE

◆◆ **Homestead Studio Suites Hotel-Torrance/Redondo Beach** SH
(310) 543-0048. **$84-$99.** 3995 Carson St. I-405, exit Hawthorne Blvd, 3.6 mi s; I-110, exit Carson St, 4.5 mi w. Int corridors. **Pets:** Small, dogs only. $75 one-time fee/pet. Service with restrictions, supervision.
[ASK] [S6] [✕] [⅙M] [🐾] [🐾] [🔒] [▢]

◆◆◆ **Residence Inn by Marriott** SH 🐾
(310) 543-4566. **$85-$169.** 3701 Torrance Blvd. I-405, exit Hawthorne Blvd, 3.2 mi s, then just e. Ext corridors. **Pets:** Medium. $75 one-time fee/room. Service with restrictions, crate.
[ASK] [✕] [🔒] [▢] [⇌] [✕]

◆◆◆ **Staybridge Suites** M
(310) 371-8525. **$169.** 19901 Prairie Ave. I-405, exit Crenshaw Blvd, just s to 190th St, 1 mi w, then just s. Ext/int corridors. **Pets:** Accepted.
[SAVE] [S6] [✕] [🔒] [▢] [⇌] [✕]

WEST COVINA

◆◆◆ **Hampton Inn** SH
(626) 967-5800. **$89.** 3145 E Garvey Ave N. I-10, exit Barranca St, just n, then just e. Int corridors. **Pets:** Accepted.
[SAVE] [S6] [✕] [⅙M] [🐾] [🔒] [▢] [⇌]

WEST HOLLYWOOD

◆◆◆ **The Grafton on Sunset** SH
(323) 654-4600. **$175-$450.** 8462 Sunset Blvd. I-10, exit La Cienega Blvd, 4.4 mi n, then just e. Int corridors. **Pets:** Medium. $100 one-time fee/room. Supervision.
[ASK] [✕] [⅙M] [🐾] [🐾] [🔒] [🍴] [⇌]

◆◆◆ **Le Montrose Suite Hotel** SH 🐾
(310) 855-1115. **$175-$225.** 900 Hammond St at Cynthia St. I-10, exit La Cienega Blvd, 2.6 mi n to San Vicento Blvd, 1.3 mi nw, then just w on Cynthia St. Int corridors. **Pets:** Medium, other species. $100 one-time fee/room. Service with restrictions.
[ASK] [S6] [✕] [🔒] [▢] [🍴] [⇌] [✕]

◆◆◆ **Le Parc Suite Hotel** LH
(310) 855-8888. **$355-$465.** 733 N West Knoll Dr. I-10, exit La Cienega Blvd, 3.5 mi n, just w on Melrose Ave, then just n. Int corridors. **Pets:** Accepted.
[ASK] [S6] [✕] [🔒] [▢] [🍴] [⇌] [✕]

AAA ▼▼▼▼ **Wyndham Bel Age** 🄻🄷 ❀
(310) 854-1111. **$189-$209.** 1020 N San Vicente Blvd. I-10, exit La Cienega Blvd, 2.6 mi n, then 1.5 mi nw. Int corridors. **Pets:** Medium. $100 deposit/room, $50 one-time fee/room. Service with restrictions, supervision.
⟦SAVE⟧ ⟦✕⟧ ⟦💻⟧ ⟦🍴⟧ ⟦≈⟧

WHITTIER

AAA ▼▼▼ **Vagabond Inn** 🄼
(562) 698-9701. **$60-$80.** 14125 E Whittier Blvd. I-605, exit Whittier Blvd, 3.5 mi e. Ext corridors. **Pets:** Accepted.
⟦SAVE⟧ ⟦S🐾⟧ ⟦✕⟧ 🛏 ⟦💻⟧ ⟦≈⟧

END METROPOLITAN AREA

LOS BANOS

AAA ▼▼▼ **Best Western Executive Inn** 🅂🄷
(209) 827-0954. **$71-$82.** 301 W Pacheco Blvd. On SR 152. Int corridors. **Pets:** Dogs only. $10 daily fee/pet. Service with restrictions, supervision.
⟦SAVE⟧ ⟦S🐾⟧ ⟦✕⟧ ⟦&M⟧ ⟦♿⟧ 🛏 ⟦💻⟧ ⟦≈⟧ ⟦✕⟧

AAA ▼▼ **Regency Inn** 🄼
(209) 826-3871. **$49-$55.** 349 W Pacheco Blvd. On SR 152; center. Ext corridors. **Pets:** Medium. $20 deposit/pet, $5 daily fee/pet. Service with restrictions, supervision.
⟦SAVE⟧ ⟦S🐾⟧ ⟦✕⟧ 🛏 ⟦💻⟧ ⟦≈⟧

LOS GATOS

AAA ▼▼▼▼ **Los Gatos Lodge** 🄼
(408) 354-3300. **$99-$159.** 50 Saratoga Los Gatos Rd. SR 17, exit E Los Gatos, just e. Ext/int corridors. **Pets:** Medium. Service with restrictions, supervision.
⟦SAVE⟧ ⟦S🐾⟧ ⟦✕⟧ ⟦&M⟧ ⟦♿⟧ 🛏 ⟦💻⟧ ⟦🍴⟧ ⟦≈⟧ ⟦✕⟧

LOS OSOS

AAA ▼▼▼ **Sea Pines Golf Resort** 🄼
(805) 528-5252. **$99-$139.** 1945 Solano St. SR 1, exit Los Osos/Baywood Park, 4 mi s on S Bay Blvd, 1.6 mi w on Los Osos Valley Rd, 0.3 mi n on Pecho Rd, then just w on Skyline Dr. Ext corridors. **Pets:** Small. $15 one-time fee/pet. Designated rooms, service with restrictions, crate.
⟦SAVE⟧ ⟦S🐾⟧ ⟦✕⟧ 🛏 ⟦💻⟧ ⟦🍴⟧ ⟦✕⟧

LOST HILLS

▼▼ **Days Inn of Lost Hills** 🄼
(661) 797-2371. **$40-$90.** 14684 Aloma St. I-5, exit SR 46, just w. Ext corridors. **Pets:** Other species. $6 one-time fee/pet. Supervision.
⟦ASK⟧ ⟦S🐾⟧ ⟦✕⟧ 🛏 ⟦💻⟧ ⟦≈⟧

MADERA

AAA ▼▼▼▼ **Best Western Madera Valley Inn** 🄼 🐾
(559) 664-0100. **$89-$149.** 317 North G St. SR 99, exit Central Madera, just e. Int corridors. **Pets:** Medium. $25 one-time fee/pet. Supervision.
⟦SAVE⟧ ⟦S🐾⟧ ⟦✕⟧ 🛏 ⟦💻⟧ ⟦🍴⟧ ⟦≈⟧

AAA ▼▼▼ **Motel 6 #4247** 🄼
(559) 675-8697. **$54-$85, 3 day notice.** 22683 Ave 18 1/2. SR 99, exit Ave 18 1/2, just w. Int corridors. **Pets:** Supervision.
⟦SAVE⟧ ⟦S🐾⟧ ⟦✕⟧ ⟦♿⟧ 🛏 ⟦≈⟧ ⟦✕⟧

▼▼ **Super 8** 🄼
(559) 661-1131. **$70-$80.** 1855 W Cleveland Ave. SR 99, exit Cleveland Ave, just w. Ext corridors. **Pets:** $5 daily fee/pet. Service with restrictions, supervision.
⟦ASK⟧ ⟦S🐾⟧ ⟦✕⟧ 🛏 ⟦💻⟧ ⟦≈⟧

MAMMOTH LAKES

AAA ▼▼▼▼ **Discovery 4 Condominiums** 🄲🄾
(760) 934-6410. **$132-$308, 30 day notice.** 25 Lee Rd. Old Mammoth Rd, 1.5 mi w on SR 203 (Main St) and Lake Mary Rd, just nw on Davidson Rd, then just s. Ext corridors. **Pets:** Large, other species. $20 daily fee/pet. Designated rooms, supervision.
⟦SAVE⟧ ⟦✕⟧ ⟦💻⟧ ⟦≈⟧ ⟦✕⟧

AAA ▼▼▼ **Econo Lodge Wildwood Inn** 🄼
(760) 934-6855. **$69-$149, 7 day notice.** 3626 Main St. SR 203 (Main St), 0.7 mi w of Old Mammoth Rd. Ext corridors. **Pets:** Medium. $10 daily fee/pet. Service with restrictions, supervision.
⟦SAVE⟧ ⟦S🐾⟧ ⟦✕⟧ 🛏 ⟦💻⟧ ⟦≈⟧ ⟦AC⟧

▼▼▼ **Mammoth Ski & Racquet Club** 🄲🄾
(760) 934-7368. **$122-$205, 28 day notice.** 248 Mammoth Slopes Dr. From Old Mammoth Rd, take SR 203, 1 mi w; SR 203, just n, Canyon Blvd, 0.8 mi w, then just s. Int corridors. **Pets:** Dogs only. $20 daily fee/pet. Designated rooms, no service.
⟦ASK⟧ ⟦S🐾⟧ ⟦✕⟧ 🛏 ⟦💻⟧ ⟦≈⟧ ⟦✕⟧ ⟦AC⟧

▼▼▼ **Shilo Inn** 🅂🄷 ❀
(760) 934-4500. **$99-$219.** 2963 Main St. SR 203, just e of Old Mammoth Rd. Int corridors. **Pets:** Other species. $15 daily fee/room. Service with restrictions, supervision.
⟦ASK⟧ ⟦S🐾⟧ ⟦✕⟧ ⟦&M⟧ ⟦🌊⟧ 🛏 ⟦💻⟧ ⟦≈⟧ ⟦✕⟧

AAA ▼▼▼ **Sierra Lodge** 🅂🄷
(760) 934-8881. **$69-$199.** 3540 Main St. SR 203, 0.6 mi w of Old Mammoth Rd. Int corridors. **Pets:** Other species. $10 daily fee/pet. Designated rooms, service with restrictions.
⟦SAVE⟧ ⟦S🐾⟧ ⟦✕⟧ 🛏 ⟦AC⟧

AAA ▼▼▼ **Sierra Nevada Rodeway Inn** 🅂🄷
(760) 934-2515. **$99-$569, 7 day notice.** 164 Old Mammoth Rd. Just s of SR 203. Ext/int corridors. **Pets:** Medium. Designated rooms, service with restrictions, crate.
⟦SAVE⟧ ⟦S🐾⟧ ⟦✕⟧ 🛏 ⟦💻⟧ ⟦≈⟧ ⟦✕⟧ ⟦AC⟧

▼▼ **Swiss Chalet Motel** 🄼
(760) 934-2403. **$60-$120, 7 day notice.** 3776 Viewpoint Rd. 0.7 mi w of Old Mammoth Rd; adjacent to SR 203. Ext corridors. **Pets:** Accepted.
⟦ASK⟧ ⟦S🐾⟧ ⟦✕⟧ 🛏 ⟦AC⟧

MANTECA

AAA ▼▼▼▼ **Best Western Executive Inn & Suites** 🄼
(209) 825-1415. **$73-$85.** 1415 E Yosemite Ave. Jct SR 99 and 120, exit Yosemite Ave. Ext corridors. **Pets:** Accepted.
⟦SAVE⟧ ⟦S🐾⟧ ⟦✕⟧ ⟦&M⟧ 🛏 ⟦💻⟧ ⟦≈⟧

MARIPOSA

AAA ▼▼▼ **Best Value Mariposa Lodge** 🄼
(209) 966-3607. **$59-$89.** 5052 Hwy 140. Center. Ext corridors. **Pets:** $10 daily fee/pet. Service with restrictions, supervision.
⟦SAVE⟧ ⟦S🐾⟧ ⟦✕⟧ 🛏 ⟦💻⟧ ⟦≈⟧

AAA ▼▼▼ **Best Western Yosemite Way Station Motel** 🄼
(209) 966-7545. **$44-$96.** 4999 Hwy 140. SR 140 at SR 49 S. Ext corridors. **Pets:** Accepted.
⟦SAVE⟧ ⟦✕⟧ ⟦&M⟧ ⟦♿⟧ ⟦💻⟧ ⟦≈⟧

AAA ▼▼▼ **Miners Inn** 🄼
(209) 742-7777. **$59-$130.** 5181 Hwy 49 N. On SR 49, n at SR 140. Ext/int corridors. **Pets:** Medium, dogs only. $10 one-time fee/pet. Designated rooms, service with restrictions, supervision.
⟦ASK⟧ ⟦✕⟧ 🛏 ⟦💻⟧ ⟦🍴⟧ ⟦≈⟧

MARYSVILLE

△△△ ▽▽▽ Best Value Inn M
(530) 743-1531. **$50-$80.** 904 E St. Jct SR 70 and 20. Ext corridors. **Pets:** Medium, dogs only. $5 daily fee/pet. Service with restrictions, supervision.
[SAVE] [S&] [✕] [&M] [🖶]

MERCED

△△△ ▽▽▽ Merced-Yosemite Travelodge M
(209) 722-6224. **$45-$75.** 1260 Yosemite Pkwy. SR 99, exit SR 140, just e. Ext corridors. **Pets:** Small. $10 daily fee/pet. Designated rooms, service with restrictions, supervision.
[SAVE] [S&] [✕] [&M] [&*] [🖶] [💻] [≈]

MILPITAS

△△△ ▽▽▽ Best Western Brookside Inn M
(408) 263-5566. **$69-$119.** 400 Valley Way. I-880, exit Calaveras Blvd (SR 237/N Abbott Ave), just e. Ext/int corridors. **Pets:** Accepted.
[SAVE] [S&] [✕] [&*] [🖶] [💻] [≈] [✕]

▽▽▽▽ Embassy Suites Milpitas/Silicon Valley LH
(408) 942-0400. **$129-$199.** 901 E Calaveras Blvd. I-680, exit Calaveras Blvd W (SR 237). Int corridors. **Pets:** Medium. $50 one-time fee/room. Service with restrictions, supervision.
[ASK] [✕] [🖶] [💻] [¶¶] [≈] [✕]

▽▽ Homestead Studio Suites Hotel-Milpitas/Silicon Valley M
(408) 433-9700. **$84-$99.** 330 Cypress Dr. SR 237, exit McCarthy S. Ext/int corridors. **Pets:** Accepted.
[ASK] [S&] [✕] [&*] [💻]

△△△ ▽▽▽ Inns of America M ❀
(408) 946-8889. **$79.** 270 S Abbott Ave. I-880, exit Calaveras Blvd (SR 237), just e. Ext corridors. **Pets:** Other species. $10 one-time fee/room. Service with restrictions, supervision.
[SAVE] [S&] [✕] [🖶] [💻] [≈]

▽▽▽▽ Residence Inn By Marriott SH
(408) 941-9222. **$89-$159.** 1501 California Cir. I-880, exit Dixon Landing Rd E, just s. Int corridors. **Pets:** Accepted.
[ASK] [S&] [✕] [&*] [💻] [≈] [✕]

△△△ ▽▽▽▽ ▽▽▽ Sheraton San Jose At Silicon Valley LH
(408) 943-0600. **$59-$189.** 1801 Barber Ln. 4 mi n of San Jose Airport; 0.3 mi nw of I-880 and Montague Expwy. Ext/int corridors. **Pets:** Accepted.
[SAVE] [S&] [✕] [🖶] [💻] [¶¶] [≈] [✕]

▽▽▽▽ TownePlace Suites by Marriott SH
(408) 719-1959. **$59-$129.** 1428 Falcon Dr. I-680, exit Montague Expwy, just w, then just n. Int corridors. **Pets:** Medium. $75 one-time fee/pet. Service with restrictions, supervision.
[ASK] [✕] [💻] [≈]

MIRANDA

△△△ ▽▽▽▽ Miranda Gardens Resort CO
(707) 943-3011. **$95-$225, 7 day notice.** 6766 Avenue of the Giants. US 101, exit Miranda E. **Pets:** Accepted.
[SAVE] [S&] [✕] [🖶] [💻] [≈] [🎿] [✆]

MI-WUK VILLAGE

▽▽▽ Mi-Wuk Village Inn & Resort M ❀
(209) 586-3031. **$109-$145.** 24680 SR 108. 15 mi e of Sonora. Ext corridors. **Pets:** Dogs only. $20 daily fee/pet. Designated rooms, service with restrictions, supervision.
[ASK] [S&] [✕] [🖶] [💻] [≈]

MODESTO

△△△ ▽▽▽ Best Western Town House Lodge M
(209) 524-7261. **$78-$85.** 909 16th St. SR 99, exit Central Modesto at I St, 1 mi e. Ext corridors. **Pets:** Accepted.
[SAVE] [S&] [✕] [&M] [🖶] [💻] [≈]

▽▽▽▽ DoubleTree LH
(209) 526-6000. **$69-$169.** 1150 9th St. SR 99, exit Central Modesto northbound; exit Maze Blvd southbound. Int corridors. **Pets:** Medium, dogs only. $20 one-time fee/pet. Designated rooms, service with restrictions, supervision.
[S&] [✕] [&M] [🏊] [&*] [🖶] [💻] [¶¶] [≈]

△△△ ▽▽▽ Howard Johnson Express Inn M
(209) 537-4821. **$65-$90.** 1672 Herndon Rd. SR 99, exit Hatch Rd, then s. Ext corridors. **Pets:** Small, other species. $50 deposit/pet. Designated rooms, service with restrictions, supervision.
[SAVE] [S&] [✕] [&M] [🖶] [💻] [≈]

▽▽▽ Microtel Inn & Suites M
(209) 538-6466. **$79-$99.** 1760 Herndon Rd. SR 99, exit Hatch Rd E, just s. Int corridors. **Pets:** Small, other species. $75 deposit/pet. Designated rooms, service with restrictions, supervision.
[ASK] [S&] [✕] [&*] [🖶] [💻] [≈]

▽▽▽ Red Lion Hotel Modesto SH
(209) 521-1612. **Call for rates.** 1612 Sisk Rd. SR 99, exit Briggsmore Ave. Int corridors. **Pets:** Accepted.
[S&] [✕] [&M] [🖶] [💻] [¶¶] [≈] [✕]

△△△ ▽▽ Travelodge M
(209) 524-3251. **$45-$70.** 722 Kansas Ave. SR 99, exit Kansas Ave, then w. Ext corridors. **Pets:** Accepted.
[SAVE] [S&] [✕] [&M] [🖶] [💻] [≈]

MOJAVE

△△△ ▽▽▽ Best Value Inn M
(661) 824-9317. **$60-$80.** 16352 Sierra Hwy. On SR 14 and 58. Ext corridors. **Pets:** Large, other species. $8 daily fee/pet. Service with restrictions, supervision.
[SAVE] [S&] [✕] [🖶] [💻] [≈]

△△△ ▽▽▽▽ Best Western Desert Winds M
(661) 824-3601. **$70-$75.** 16200 Sierra Hwy. On SR 14 and 58. Ext corridors. **Pets:** Medium, other species. $10 daily fee/room. Service with restrictions, supervision.
[SAVE] [S&] [✕] [🖶] [💻] [≈]

△△△ ▽▽▽ Desert Inn M
(661) 824-2518. **$49-$54.** 1954 Hwy 58. Just e of SR 14. Ext corridors. **Pets:** Service with restrictions, crate.
[SAVE] [S&] [✕] [🖶] [💻]

△△△ ▽▽▽ Econo Lodge M
(661) 824-2463. **$39-$69.** 2145 Hwy 58. Just e of SR 14. Ext corridors. **Pets:** $6 daily fee/pet. Supervision.
[SAVE] [✕] [🖶] [💻] [≈]

△△△ ▽▽▽▽ Mariah Country Inn & Suites SH
(661) 824-4980. **$95.** 1385 Hwy 58. 1.5 mi e of SR 14. Int corridors. **Pets:** Medium, other species. $10 daily fee/room. Service with restrictions, supervision.
[SAVE] [S&] [✕] [&M] [🏊] [&*] [🖶] [💻] [¶¶] [≈]

MONTEREY PENINSULA AREA

CARMEL-BY-THE-SEA

Best Western Carmel Mission Inn SH ❖
(831) 624-1841. **$69-$439.** 3665 Rio Rd. 1 mi s on SR 1. Ext/int corridors. **Pets:** Other species. $35 one-time fee/pet. Designated rooms, service with restrictions, supervision.
SAVE S⬛ ✕ 🛏 💻 🍴 ≈

Briarwood Inn BB
(831) 626-9056. **$110-$235, 7 day notice.** 3 blks n off Ocean Ave at San Carlos St and 4th Ave. Ext corridors. **Pets:** Small, dogs only. $25 daily fee/pet. Service with restrictions, supervision.
SAVE S⬛ ✕ 🛏 💻 🅺

Carmel Country Inn BB ❖
(831) 625-3263. **$165-$325, 7 day notice.** 4 blks n of Ocean Ave at Dolores St and 3rd Ave. Ext corridors. **Pets:** Other species. $20 daily fee/pet. Designated rooms, supervision.
✕ 🛏 💻 🅺

Carmel Fireplace Inn Bed & Breakfast M
(831) 624-4862. **$99-$285, 7 day notice.** 3 blks n off Ocean Ave at San Carlos St and 4th Ave. Ext corridors. **Pets:** Small, dogs only. $25 daily fee/pet. Service with restrictions, supervision.
SAVE S⬛ ✕ 🛏 💻 🅺

Carmel Garden Court BB
(831) 624-6926. **$150-$245, 7 day notice.** 3 blks n off Ocean Ave, at 4th Ave and Torres St. Ext corridors. **Pets:** Medium. $50 one-time fee/room. Service with restrictions, supervision.
SAVE ✕ 🛏 💻 🅺

Carmel River Inn M ❖
(831) 624-1575. **$63-$135, 3 day notice.** 1 mi s on SR 1, n of Carmel River Bridge at Oliver Rd. Ext corridors. **Pets:** Other species. $10 daily fee/pet. Designated rooms, service with restrictions.
ASK S⬛ ✕ 🛏 💻 ≈ 🅺

Carmel Tradewinds Inn M
(831) 624-2776. **$195-$575, 3 day notice.** 4 blks n off Ocean Ave; at Mission St and 3rd Ave. Ext corridors. **Pets:** Accepted.
ASK S⬛ ✕ 🛏 💻 🅺

Coachman's Inn M
(831) 624-6421. **$135-$425, 3 day notice.** Just s of Ocean Ave on San Carlos St; between 7th and 8th aves. Ext corridors. **Pets:** Small, dogs only. $20 daily fee/pet. Designated rooms, service with restrictions, supervision.
SAVE S⬛ ✕ ⬛M 🛏 💻 🅺

Cypress Inn SH ❖
(831) 624-3871. **$125-$550, 3 day notice.** Just s off Ocean Ave at Lincoln St and 7th Ave. Ext/int corridors. **Pets:** $25 daily fee/pet. Designated rooms, service with restrictions, supervision.
✕ 🅺

Wayside Inn M ❖
(831) 624-5336. **$99-$305, 7 day notice.** 1 blk s off Ocean Ave, at Mission St and 7th Ave. Ext corridors. **Pets:** Other species. Designated rooms, service with restrictions, supervision.
SAVE S⬛ ✕ 🛏 💻 🅺

CARMEL VALLEY

Carmel Valley Lodge M ❖
(831) 659-2261. **$149-$219, 7 day notice.** 8 Ford Rd. 11.5 mi e of SR 1; at Carmel Valley and Ford rds. Ext corridors. **Pets:** Dogs only. $10 daily fee/pet. Service with restrictions, supervision.
SAVE S⬛ ✕ 🏊 💻 ≈ ✕ 🅺

Los Laureles Lodge M
(831) 659-2233. **$85-$595, 3 day notice.** 313 W Carmel Valley Rd. 10.5 mi e of SR 1. Ext corridors. **Pets:** Accepted.
SAVE S⬛ ✕ 🛏 💻 🍴 ≈ 🅺

MARINA

Heritage Marina Days Inn M
(831) 384-9784. **Call for rates.** 416 Reservation Rd. SR 1, exit Reservation Rd, 1.8 mi e. Ext corridors. **Pets:** Accepted.
✕ 🛏 💻

MONTEREY

Bay Park Hotel SH ❖
(831) 649-1020. **$79-$259.** 1425 Munras Ave. SR 1, exit Munras Ave, just w. Int corridors. **Pets:** Small, other species. $20 daily fee/room. Designated rooms, service with restrictions, supervision.
SAVE S⬛ ✕ ⬛M 🏊 🔆 🛏 💻 🍴 ≈

Best Western The Beach Resort SH ❖
(831) 394-3321. **$99-$389.** 2600 Sand Dunes Dr. SR 1, exit Del Rey Oaks, just w. Ext corridors. **Pets:** Large, other species. $25 daily fee/room. Designated rooms, service with restrictions, crate.
SAVE S⬛ ✕ 💻 🍴 ≈

Best Western Victorian Inn M ❖
(831) 373-8000. **$129-$369.** 487 Foam St. SR 1, exit Monterey, 3.4 mi w. Ext/int corridors. **Pets:** Other species. $100 deposit/room, $35 one-time fee/room. Designated rooms, service with restrictions.
SAVE S⬛ ✕ ⬛M 🏊 🔆 🛏 💻 🅺

El Adobe Inn M ❖
(831) 372-5409. **$49-$199, 3 day notice.** 936 Munras Ave. SR 1, exit Munras Ave, 0.6 mi w. Ext corridors. **Pets:** Medium, dogs only. $10 daily fee/pet. Designated rooms, service with restrictions, supervision.
SAVE ✕ 🏊 🛏 💻 🅺

Hyatt Regency-Monterey Resort & Conference Center LH
(831) 372-1234. **$139-$249, 3 day notice.** 1 Old Golf Course Rd. SR 1, exit Aguajito northbound; exit Monterey southbound, just e. Int corridors. **Pets:** Accepted.
SAVE ✕ ⬛M 🏊 🔆 🛏 💻 🍴 ≈ ✕ 🅺

Monterey Bay Lodge M ❖
(831) 372-8057. **$89-$319.** 55 Camino Aguajito. SR 1, exit Aguajito Rd, just w. Ext corridors. **Pets:** Medium, dogs only. $100 deposit/pet, $15 daily fee/pet. Designated rooms, service with restrictions, supervision.
SAVE ✕ 🛏 💻 🍴 ≈

Monterey Fireside Lodge M
(831) 373-4172. **$65-$309, 3 day notice.** 1131 10th St. SR 1, exit Aguajito Rd or Monterey, just w. Ext corridors. **Pets:** Large, other species. $20 daily fee/pet. Designated rooms, service with restrictions, supervision.
SAVE ✕ 🛏 🅺

PACIFIC GROVE

Bide-A-Wee Inn & Cottages M
(831) 372-2330. **$69-$169, 3 day notice.** 221 Asilomar Ave. 1 mi n of SR 68. Ext corridors. **Pets:** Large, dogs only. $15 daily fee/pet. Designated rooms, service with restrictions, supervision.
SAVE S⬛ ✕ 🛏 💻 🅺

The Gatehouse Inn BB ❖
(831) 649-8436. **$125-$220, 3 day notice.** 225 Central Ave. Center. Ext/int corridors. **Pets:** Medium, dogs only. $25 daily fee/pet. Designated rooms, service with restrictions, supervision.
SAVE S⬛ ✕ 🅺

AAA ▼▼▼ Olympia Motor Lodge **M**
(831) 373-2777. **$110-$180, 3 day notice.** 1140 Lighthouse Ave. 1 mi w. Ext corridors. **Pets:** Accepted.
SAVE ✕ 🛗 🏊 🗗

▼▼ Sea Breeze Inn and Cottages **M** 🐾
(831) 372-7771. **$69-$179.** 1100 Lighthouse Ave. Just w of Seventeen Mile Dr; Lighthouse and Grove Acre. Ext/int corridors. **Pets:** $5 daily fee/pet, $25 one-time fee/pet. Designated rooms, service with restrictions, supervision.
A$K S✕ ✕ 🛗 🖳 🗗

▼ Sea Breeze Lodge **M** 🐾
(831) 372-3431. **$59-$159.** 1101 Lighthouse Ave. Just w of Seventeen Mile Dr. Ext corridors. **Pets:** $5 daily fee/pet, $25 one-time fee/pet. Designated rooms, service with restrictions, supervision.
✕ 🛗 🖳 🏊 🗗

PEBBLE BEACH

▼▼▼▼ The Lodge at Pebble Beach **LH** 🐾
(831) 624-3811. **$555-$935, 3 day notice.** Seventeen Mile Dr. Off SR 1. Ext/int corridors. **Pets:** Medium, dogs only.
✕ S✕ 🎱 🖳 🍴 🏊 ✕ 🗗

SEASIDE

AAA ▼▼▼ Econo Lodge Bay Breeze **M**
(831) 899-7111. **$49-$260.** 2049 Fremont Blvd. SR 1, exit Sand City/Seaside, just e. Ext/int corridors. **Pets:** Small. Service with restrictions, supervision.
SAVE S✕ ✕ 🛗 🖳 🗗

END AREA

MORGAN HILL

AAA ▼▼▼ Best Western Country Inn **SH**
(408) 779-0447. **$65-$110.** 16525 Condit Rd. US 101, exit Tennant Ave or E Dunne Ave, just e. Int corridors. **Pets:** Accepted.
SAVE S✕ ✕ 🛗 🖳 🏊

▼▼▼ Residence Inn by Marriott **SH**
(408) 782-8311. **$119-$149.** 18620 Madrone Pkwy. US 101, exit Cochrane W, just n. Int corridors. **Pets:** Accepted.
A$K S✕ ✕ 🛗 🖳 🏊

MORRO BAY

AAA ▼▼▼ Best Western El Rancho **M**
(805) 772-2212. **$79-$179.** 2460 Main St. SR 1, exit SR 41, 0.5 mi n. Ext corridors. **Pets:** Other species. $10 one-time fee/pet. Service with restrictions, supervision.
SAVE S✕ ✕ 🛗 🖳 🏊 🗗

AAA ▼▼▼ Morro Bay Sandpiper/Keystone Inn **M**
(805) 772-7503. **$60-$149, 3 day notice.** 540 Main St. SR 1, exit Morro Bay Blvd, 0.7 mi w, then 0.4 mi s. Ext corridors. **Pets:** Medium, dogs only. $10 daily fee/pet. Designated rooms, no service, supervision.
SAVE S✕ ✕ 🛗 🖳 🗗

MOUNTAIN VIEW

▼▼ Homestead Studio Suites Hotel-Mountain View/Silicon Valley **M**
(650) 962-1500. **$84-$99.** 190 E El Camino Real. On SR 82, just w of SR 85. Ext corridors. **Pets:** Medium, other species. $75 one-time fee/pet. Service with restrictions.
A$K S✕ ✕ 🛗M 🛗 🖳

AAA ▼▼▼ Tropicana Lodge **M**
(650) 961-0220. **$75-$105.** 1720 El Camino Real W. US 101, exit Shoreline Blvd, 2 mi to SR 82, just n. Ext/int corridors. **Pets:** Other species. Designated rooms, service with restrictions, crate.
SAVE S✕ ✕ 🛗M 🛗 🖳 🏊

MOUNT SHASTA

AAA ▼▼▼ A-1 Choice Inn **M**
(530) 926-4811. **$69-$99, 3 day notice.** 1340 S Mt Shasta Blvd. I-5, exit McCloud/SR 89, just n at first left, then 1 mi. Ext corridors. **Pets:** Very small, dogs only. $10 daily fee/pet. Designated rooms, service with restrictions, supervision.
SAVE S✕ ✕ 🛗 🖳 🏊

AAA ▼▼▼ Best Western Tree House Motor Inn **M** 🐾
(530) 926-3101. **$98-$170.** 111 Morgan Way. I-5, exit Central Mt Shasta (2nd exit), just e. Ext/int corridors. **Pets:** Medium. $10 daily fee/pet. Service with restrictions, supervision.
SAVE S✕ ✕ 🎱 🛗 🖳 🍴 🏊

AAA ▼▼▼ Econo Lodge **M**
(530) 926-3145. **$69-$79.** 908 S Mt Shasta Blvd. I-5, exit Central, 0.5 mi e, then 0.5 mi s. Ext corridors. **Pets:** Medium. $5 daily fee/pet. Service with restrictions, supervision.
SAVE S✕ ✕ 🛗 🖳 🏊

▼▼ Mt Shasta Ranch Bed & Breakfast **BB**
(430) 926-3870. **$70-$125, 3 day notice.** 1008 W A Barr Rd. I-5, exit Central Mt Shasta, 1.5 mi w. Ext/int corridors. **Pets:** Large, other species. $10 one-time fee/pet. Service with restrictions, supervision.
A$K S✕ ✕ 🛗 🖳 ✕

AAA ▼▼▼ Swiss Holiday Lodge **M** 🐾
(530) 926-3446. **$50-$80.** 2400 S Mt Shasta Blvd. I-5, exit McCloud/SR 89, just n at first left. Ext corridors. **Pets:** Small, other species. $8 daily fee/pet. Service with restrictions, supervision.
SAVE S✕ ✕ 🛗 🖳

NEEDLES

AAA ▼▼▼▼ Best Western Colorado River Inn **M**
(760) 326-4552. **$55-$75, 7 day notice.** 2371 W Broadway. I-40, exit W Broadway/River Rd, 0.3 mi e; on Business Loop I-40. Ext corridors. **Pets:** Small. $25 deposit/room. Designated rooms, service with restrictions, supervision.
SAVE S✕ ✕ 🛗 🖳 🏊

AAA ▼▼▼ Best Western Royal Inn **M**
(760) 326-5660. **$55-$75, 7 day notice.** 1111 Pashard St. I-40, exit W Broadway. Ext corridors. **Pets:** Small. $25 deposit/room. Designated rooms, service with restrictions, supervision.
SAVE S✕ ✕ 🛗 🖳 🏊

AAA ▼▼▼ Days Inn & Suites **M**
(760) 326-5836. **$60-$110.** 1215 Hospitality Ln. I-40, exit J St, just se. Ext corridors. **Pets:** Other species. $10 daily fee/pet. No service, supervision.
SAVE S✕ ✕ 🖍 🛗 🗗

▼▼ Super 8 Motel of Needles **M**
(760) 326-4501. **$59-$69.** 1102 E Broadway. I-40, exit US 95 (E Broadway), just sw. Ext corridors. **Pets:** Accepted.
A$K S✕ ✕ 🛗 🗗

AAA ◈◈◈ Travelers Inn **M**
(760) 326-4900. **$40-$65, 3 day notice.** 1195 3rd St Hill. I-40, exit J St, just e, then just s. Ext corridors. **Pets:** Small, other species. $25 deposit/room. Designated rooms, service with restrictions, supervision.
[SAVE] [S☐] [✕] [∅] [✦] [▥] [≈]

NEVADA CITY

AAA ◈◈ Nevada City Inn **M**
(530) 265-2253. **$69-$99.** 760 Zion St. SR 20 and 49, exit Gold Flat/Ridge Rd, 0.3 mi w, then 0.3 mi n. Ext corridors. **Pets:** $10 daily fee/pet. Designated rooms, service with restrictions, crate.
[SAVE] [S☐] [✕] [✦M] [▥] [▥]

NEWARK

◈◈◈ Homewood Suites by Hilton **SH**
(510) 791-7700. **$109.** 39270 Cedar Blvd. I-880, exit Mowry Ave, w to Cedar Blvd, then 0.3 mi s. Int corridors. **Pets:** Accepted.
[ASK] [S☐] [✕] [✦] [▥] [▥] [≈] [✕]

◈◈◈ Residence Inn by Marriott Newark/Silicon
    Valley **SH** ✿
(510) 739-6000. **$99-$199.** 34566 Dumbarton Ct. SR 84, exit Newark Blvd, just s. Int corridors. **Pets:** Other species. $10 daily fee/pet, $75 one-time fee/room. Service with restrictions.
[ASK] [✕] [✦M] [✦] [▥] [≈]

◈◈◈ TownePlace Suites Newark **SH**
(510) 657-4600. **$59-$99.** 39802 Cedar Blvd. I-880, exit Mowry Ave, just w to Cedar Blvd, then s. Int corridors. **Pets:** Accepted.
[ASK] [✕] [▥] [≈]

AAA ◈◈◈ Woodfin Suites **M**
(510) 795-1200. **$89-$129.** 39150 Cedar Blvd. I-880, exit Mowry Ave, just w, then 0.3 mi s. Ext corridors. **Pets:** Accepted.
[SAVE] [S☐] [✕] [✦] [▥] [≈]

NEWPORT BEACH

AAA ◈◈◈◈ Four Seasons Hotel Newport Beach **LH**
(949) 759-0808. **$400-$550.** 690 Newport Center Dr. SR 73, exit Mac-Arthur Blvd northbound, 3 mi s to San Joaquin Hills Rd, then 0.5 mi w; exit Jamboree Rd southbound, 2.5 mi s to San Joaquin Hills Rd, then 0.5 mi e. Int corridors. **Pets:** Accepted.
[SAVE] [✕] [✦M] [∅] [▥] [▥] [¶] [≈] [✕]

AAA ◈◈◈ The Sutton Place Hotel **LH**
(949) 476-2001. **$99-$229.** 4500 MacArthur Blvd. I-405, exit MacArthur Blvd, 1 mi s. Int corridors. **Pets:** Accepted.
[SAVE] [S☐] [✕] [▥] [¶] [≈] [✕]

NIPOMO

◈◈ Kaleidoscope Inn & Gardens B&B **BB**
(805) 929-5444. **$125, 7 day notice.** 130 E Dana St. US 101, exit Tefft St, 0.7 mi e, just s on Thompson Rd, then just e. Ext/int corridors. **Pets:** Large, other species. Designated rooms, service with restrictions, crate.
[ASK] [S☐] [✕] [✗] [▥] [✗]

NOVATO

AAA ◈◈◈◈ Inn Marin **M** ✿
(415) 883-5952. **$99-$149.** 250 Entrada Dr. US 101, exit Ignacio Blvd, just w, then just n on Enfrente Rd. Ext corridors. **Pets:** Other species. $20 one-time fee/pet. Service with restrictions, crate.
[SAVE] [S☐] [✕] [✦M] [✦] [▥] [▥] [¶] [≈]

AAA ◈◈◈ Novato Days Inn **M**
(415) 897-7111. **$64-$159.** 8141 Redwood Blvd. US 101, exit San Marin Dr, 1 mi n. Ext corridors. **Pets:** Medium, dogs only. $10 daily fee/room. Service with restrictions, supervision.
[SAVE] [S☐] [✕] [✦M] [▥] [▥] [¶] [≈]

AAA ◈ Novato Travelodge **M**
(415) 892-7500. **$69-$94.** 7600 Redwood Blvd. US 101, exit San Marin Dr, just w. Ext corridors. **Pets:** Small. $10 daily fee/pet. Designated rooms, service with restrictions, supervision.
[SAVE] [S☐] [✕] [✦M] [▥] [▥] [≈]

OAKHURST

AAA ◈◈◈ Best Western Yosemite Gateway Inn **M**
(559) 683-2378. **$49-$104.** 40530 Hwy 41. SR 49, 0.8 mi n of jct SR 49. Ext corridors. **Pets:** Accepted.
[SAVE] [S☐] [✕] [✦M] [∅] [✦] [▥] [▥] [≈] [✕]

AAA ◈◈ Comfort Inn-Oakhurst **M**
(559) 683-8282. **$49-$109.** 40489 Hwy 41. SR 49, 0.5 mi n. Ext corridors. **Pets:** Other species. $10 daily fee/pet. Service with restrictions, supervision.
[SAVE] [S☐] [✕] [∅] [▥] [▥] [≈]

OAKLAND

AAA ◈◈◈ Best Western Inn at the Square **SH**
(510) 452-4565. **$99-$159.** 233 Broadway. I-880, exit Broadway northbound, 0.3 mi w; exit 12th westbound, w to 7th St, s to Broadway. Int corridors. **Pets:** Small. $100 deposit/room. Designated rooms, service with restrictions, crate.
[SAVE] [S☐] [✕] [▥] [▥] [≈]

◈◈◈ Hilton Oakland Airport **LH**
(510) 635-5000. **$69-$199.** 1 Hegenberger Rd. I-880, exit Hegenberger Rd, 1 mi w, 1.3 mi e of Oakland Airport. Int corridors. **Pets:** Accepted.
[✕] [✦] [▥] [▥] [¶] [≈]

◈◈◈ Homewood Suites **SH**
(510) 663-2700. **$99-$269.** 1103 Embarcadero. I-880, exit 5th/Embarcadero southbound; exit 16th/Embarcadero northbound. Int corridors. **Pets:** Other species. $300 deposit/room, $50 one-time fee/room. Service with restrictions, crate.
[ASK] [✕] [▥] [▥] [≈]

OCEANSIDE

AAA ◈◈◈ La Quinta Inn **SH** ✿
(760) 450-0730. **$71-$125.** 937 N Coast Hwy. I-5, exit Coast Hwy, just w. Int corridors. **Pets:** Other species. $50 deposit/room. Designated rooms, service with restrictions, supervision.
[SAVE] [S☐] [✕] [✦M] [∅] [▥] [▥]

AAA ◈◈ Motel 6 #4208 **M**
(760) 721-1543. **$65-$85.** 909 N Coast Hwy. I-5, exit Coast Hwy, just w. Int corridors. **Pets:** Medium, other species. Supervision.
[SAVE] [S☐] [✕] [✦M] [∅] [✦] [▥] [≈]

OJAI

AAA ◈◈ Best Western Casa Ojai **M**
(805) 646-8175. **$77-$125.** 1302 E Ojai Ave. 0.8 mi e on SR 150. Ext corridors. **Pets:** Medium, dogs only. $15 daily fee/pet. Designated rooms, service with restrictions, supervision.
[SAVE] [S☐] [✕] [▥] [▥] [≈]

◈◈◈◈ Blue Iguana Inn **M** ✿
(805) 646-5277. **$95-$145, 7 day notice.** 11794 N Ventura Ave. 2.5 mi w of town on SR 33. Ext corridors. **Pets:** Medium, dogs only. $20 daily fee/pet. Designated rooms, service with restrictions, supervision.
[ASK] [S☐] [✕] [▥] [▥] [≈] [✕]

AAA ◈◈ Oakridge Inn **M**
(805) 649-4018. **$80-$130.** 780 N Ventura Ave. In Oak View; 4 mi s on SR 33; 2 mi e of Lake Casitas. Ext corridors. **Pets:** Small, dogs only. $50 deposit/pet, $15 daily fee/pet. Service with restrictions, supervision.
[SAVE] [S☐] [✕] [▥] [▥]

△△△ ▽▽▽ ▽▽▽ Ojai Valley Inn & Spa **LH** ❀
(805) 646-1111. **$400-$2000, 3 day notice.** 905 Country Club Rd. 1 mi w on SR 150, 0.3 mi s. Ext/int corridors. **Pets:** Medium, dogs only. $50 daily fee/pet. Designated rooms, service with restrictions.
SAVE ⊠ 🔊ᴹ 🔲 🔲 🔲 🔲 🔲 🔲 ⊠

ONTARIO

△△△ ▽▽▽▽ AmeriSuites (Los Angeles/Ontario Mills) **SH**
(909) 980-2200. **$79-$169.** 4760 E Mills Cir. I-10, exit Milliken Ave, just n, then 0.5 mi e on Ontario Mills Dr. Int corridors. **Pets:** Small, other species. $50 one-time fee/room. Service with restrictions, crate.
SAVE ⊠ 🔊ᴹ 🔲 🔲

▽▽▽▽ Baymont Inn & Suites **SH**
(909) 987-5940. **$90-$150.** 4395 E Ontario Mills Pkwy. I-10, exit Milliken Ave, just n, then just e. Int corridors. **Pets:** Accepted.
ASK 🔊 🔲 🔲 🔲

△△△ ▽▽▽▽ Country Inn & Suites by Carlson **M**
(909) 937-6000. **$124.** 231 N Vineyard Ave. I-10, exit Vineyard Ave, just s. Ext corridors. **Pets:** Accepted.
SAVE 🔊 ⊠ 🔲 🔲 🔲 🔲

△△△ ▽▽▽▽ Doubletree Hotel Ontario **LH**
(909) 937-0900. **$89-$219.** 222 N Vineyard Ave. I-10, exit Vineyard Ave, 0.4 mi s. Int corridors. **Pets:** Accepted.
SAVE ⊠ 🔊ᴹ 🔲 🔲 🔲 🔲 🔲

△△△ ▽▽▽▽ Hilton Ontario Airport **LH**
(909) 980-0400. **$75-$219.** 700 N Haven Ave. I-10, exit Haven Ave, just n. Int corridors. **Pets:** Accepted.
SAVE ⊠ 🔊ᴹ 🔲 🔲 🔲 🔲 🔲 ⊠

▽▽▽▽ Holiday Inn Hotel & Suites Airport Ontario **SH** ❀
(909) 466-9600. **$79-$129.** 3400 Shelby St. I-10, exit Haven Ave, just n to Inland Empire Blvd, w to Lotus Ave, then just s. Ext/int corridors. **Pets:** Medium, other species. $25 one-time fee/pet. Designated rooms, service with restrictions, crate.
ASK 🔊 ⊠ 🔲 🔲 🔲 🔲 🔲 ⊠

▽▽▽▽ La Quinta Inn & Suites Ontario (Airport) **SH** ❀
(909) 476-1112. **$99-$129.** 3555 Inland Empire Blvd. I-10, exit Haven Ave, just n, then just e. Int corridors. **Pets:** Small. Service with restrictions, crate.
ASK ⊠ 🔊ᴹ 🔲 🔲 🔲 🔲

▽▽▽▽ Residence Inn by Marriott **SH** ❀
(909) 937-6788. **$159-$179.** 2025 Convention Center Way. I-10, exit Vineyard Ave, just s, then 1 blk e. Ext corridors. **Pets:** Small, other species. $10 daily fee/room, $150 one-time fee/room. Service with restrictions, crate.
ASK 🔊 ⊠ 🔲 🔲 🔲 🔲 ⊠

ORANGE

△△△ ▽▽▽▽ Hilton Suites Anaheim/Orange **SH**
(714) 938-1111. **$95-$225, 3 day notice.** 400 N State College Blvd. I-5, exit State College Blvd, just s. Int corridors. **Pets:** Small. $25 deposit/pet. Service with restrictions, supervision.
SAVE 🔊 ⊠ 🔲 🔲 🔲 🔲 🔲 ⊠

ORLAND

△△△ ▽▽▽ Amber Light Inn Motel **M** ❀
(530) 865-7655. **$50-$58.** 828 Newville Rd. I-5, exit Chico (SR 32), 0.3 mi e. Ext corridors. **Pets:** Small. $7 one-time fee/pet. Service with restrictions, supervision.
SAVE 🔊 ⊠ 🔲 🔲

△△△ ▽▽▽ Orland Inn **M**
(530) 865-7632. **$55-$61.** 1052 South St. I-5, exit South St, 0.5 mi s; northbound exit I-5 E via Orland-Fairgrounds; southbound exit I-5 E via CR 16; in Stony Creek Shopping Center. Ext corridors. **Pets:** Other species. $5 one-time fee/pet. Service with restrictions, crate.
SAVE 🔊 ⊠ 🔊ᴹ 🔲 🔲

OROVILLE

△△△ ▽▽▽ Best Value Inn **M** ❀
(530) 533-7070. **$65-$110.** 580 Oro Dam Blvd. SR 70, exit Oroville Dam Blvd, 0.3 mi e. Ext corridors. **Pets:** Other species. $20 deposit/room, $6 daily fee/pet. Designated rooms, service with restrictions, crate.
SAVE 🔊 ⊠ 🔲 🔲

△△△ ▽▽▽ Days Inn-Oroville **M**
(530) 533-3297. **$70-$80.** 1745 Feather River Blvd. SR 70, exit E Montgomery St, just e to Feather River Blvd, then 0.5 mi s. Ext corridors. **Pets:** Medium. $10 daily fee/pet. Service with restrictions, supervision.
SAVE 🔊 ⊠ 🔲 🔲 🔲

△△△ ▽▽▽ Sunset Inn **M**
(530) 533-8201. **$47-$150.** 1835 Feather River Blvd. SR 70, exit E Montgomery St, 0.5 mi s. Ext corridors. **Pets:** Accepted.
SAVE 🔊 ⊠ 🔲 🔲 🔲

OXNARD

△△△ ▽▽▽▽ Best Western Oxnard Inn **M**
(805) 483-9581. **$99-$109.** 1156 S Oxnard Blvd. US 101, exit Rose Ave northbound, 3 mi s, then 1 mi se; exit Oxnard Blvd southbound, 3.5 mi s. Ext corridors. **Pets:** Medium. $20 one-time fee/room. Supervision.
SAVE 🔊 ⊠ 🔊ᴹ 🔲 🔲 🔲 🔲

▽▽▽▽ Residence Inn At River Ridge **SH**
(805) 278-2200. **$129-$179.** 2101 W Vineyard Ave. US 101, exit Vineyard Ave, 1.8 mi w. Ext corridors. **Pets:** $75 one-time fee/pet. Service with restrictions, supervision.
ASK 🔊 ⊠ 🔊ᴹ 🔲 🔲 🔲 🔲 🔲 ⊠

△△△ ▽▽▽ Vagabond Inn Oxnard **M**
(805) 983-0251. **$71-$94.** 1245 N Oxnard Blvd. US 101, exit Vineyard Ave northbound; exit Oxnard Blvd southbound, 1.5 mi s. Ext corridors. **Pets:** Accepted.
SAVE 🔊 ⊠ 🔊ᴹ 🔲 🔲 🔲 🔲 🔲

PALMDALE

▽▽▽▽ Residence Inn by Marriott **SH**
(661) 947-4204. **$120-$150, 14 day notice.** 514 W Ave P. SR 14, exit Ave P, just w. Int corridors. **Pets:** Other species. Designated rooms, supervision.
ASK 🔊 ⊠ 🔊ᴹ 🔲 🔲 🔲 🔲 🔲 ⊠

PALM DESERT

△△△ ▽▽▽▽ Best Western Palm Desert Resort **M**
(760) 340-4441. **$79-$229.** 74-695 Hwy 111. I-10, exit Cook St, 4.4 mi s, then 0.3 mi w. Ext corridors. **Pets:** Medium. $50 deposit/room. Designated rooms, service with restrictions, crate.
SAVE 🔊 ⊠ 🔲 🔲 🔲 ⊠

△△△ ▽▽▽▽ Comfort Suites **M**
(760) 360-3337. **$79-$199.** 39-585 Washington St. I-10, exit Washington St, just n. Int corridors. **Pets:** Medium, other species. $100 deposit/room, $15 one-time fee/room. Service with restrictions, supervision.
SAVE 🔊 ⊠ 🔲 🔲 🔲 ⊠

▽▽ Desert Patch Inn **M**
(760) 346-9161. **$57-$149, 7 day notice.** 73758 Shadow Mountain Dr. I-10, exit Cook St, 4.4 mi s to SR 111, 1.2 mi w to San Luis Rey Ave, just s, then just e. Ext corridors. **Pets:** Accepted.
⊠ 🔲 🔲 🔲

△△△ ▽▽ ▽▽ The Inn at Deep Canyon M
(760) 346-8061. **$47-$127, 3 day notice.** 74470 Abronia Tr. I-10, exit Cook St, 4.4 mi s to SR 111, 0.5 mi w, then just s on Deep Canyon Rd. Ext corridors. **Pets:** Large, other species. $10 daily fee/pet. Designated rooms, service with restrictions.

[SAVE] [S✕] [✕] [🛏] [💻] [🏊] [✕]

▽▽▽ Residence Inn by Marriott SH
(760) 776-0050. **$89-$269.** 38-305 Cook St. I-10, exit Cook St, 0.8 mi s. Ext corridors. **Pets:** Small, other species. $75 one-time fee/room. Designated rooms, service with restrictions, supervision.

[ASK] [✕] [🛏] [💻] [🏊] [✕]

PALM SPRINGS

△△△ ▽▽ ▽▽ A Place In The Sun M ☙
(760) 325-0254. **$79-$149, 7 day notice.** 754 San Lorenzo Rd. Just e of Palm Canyon Dr via Mesquite Ave and Random Rd. Ext corridors. **Pets:** Other species. $15 daily fee/pet. Service with restrictions, supervision.

[SAVE] [S✕] [✕] [🛏] [💻] [🏊] [✕]

▽▽ ▽▽ Casa Cody Country Inn M
(760) 320-9346. **$69-$259, 3 day notice.** 175 S Cahuilla Rd. SR 111, just w on Tahquitz Canyon Way, then just s. Ext corridors. **Pets:** Other species. $15 daily fee/pet. Service with restrictions, supervision.

[🛏] [💻] [🏊]

▽▽ ▽▽ ▽▽ Hilton Palm Springs Resort LH
(760) 320-6868. **$118-$178, 3 day notice.** 400 E Tahquitz Canyon Way. Just e of Indian Canyon Dr. Int corridors. **Pets:** Accepted.

[✕] [🛏] [💻] [🍴] [🏊] [✕]

▽▽ ▽▽ ▽▽ La Mancha Private Villas & Spa Resort SH
(760) 323-1773. **$99-$699, 3 day notice.** 444 N Avenida Caballeros. 0.6 mi e of Palm Canyon Dr, on Tahquitz Canyon Way, then 0.5 mi n. Ext corridors. **Pets:** Accepted.

[ASK] [S✕] [✕] [🛏] [💻] [🍴] [🏊] [✕]

▽▽ ▽▽ ▽▽ Palm Springs Riviera Resort LH
(760) 327-8311. **$69-$219.** 1600 N Indian Canyon Dr. 1.5 mi n of Tahquitz Canyon Way. Int corridors. **Pets:** Accepted.

[SAVE] [S✕] [✕] [🛏] [💻] [🍴] [🏊] [✕]

▽▽ ▽▽ Quality Inn Resort M
(760) 323-2775. **$59-$169.** 1269 E Palm Canyon Dr. 2.3 mi se of Tahquitz Canyon Way. Ext corridors. **Pets:** Medium, dogs only. $50 deposit/room. Service with restrictions.

[ASK] [S✕] [✕] [🛏] [💻] [🍴] [🏊]

△△△ ▽▽ ▽▽ Ramada Resort Inn & Conference Center SH
(760) 323-1711. **$59-$179.** 1800 E Palm Canyon Dr. 2.7 mi se of Tahquitz Canyon Way. Ext/int corridors. **Pets:** $20 daily fee/pet. Designated rooms, service with restrictions, supervision.

[SAVE] [S✕] [✕] [🛏] [💻] [🍴] [🏊] [✕]

▽▽ Super 8 Lodge M
(760) 322-3757. **$42-$72.** 1900 N Palm Canyon Dr. 1.4 mi n of Tahquitz Canyon Way. Ext corridors. **Pets:** Dogs only. $10 one-time fee/room. Service with restrictions, crate.

[ASK] [S✕] [✕] [🛏] [💻] [🏊]

△△△ ▽▽ ▽▽ Vagabond Inn Palm Springs M ☙
(760) 325-7211. **$59-$129.** 1699 S Palm Canyon Dr. 1.5 mi s of Tahquitz Canyon Way. Ext corridors. **Pets:** Small. $10 daily fee/pet. Designated rooms, no service, supervision.

[SAVE] [S✕] [✕] [🛏] [💻] [🍴] [🏊]

△△△ ▽▽ ▽▽ ▽▽ Wyndham Palm Springs LH
(760) 322-6000. **$99-$189, 3 day notice.** 888 Tahquitz Canyon Way. 0.4 mi e of Indian Canyon Dr. Int corridors. **Pets:** Small, dogs only. $150 deposit/pet, $35 one-time fee/pet. Designated rooms, service with restrictions, supervision.

[SAVE] [✕] [🛏] [💻] [🍴] [🏊] [✕]

PALO ALTO

▽▽ ▽▽ ▽▽ Crowne Plaza Cabana Hotel SH ☙
(650) 857-0787. **$189-$219.** 4290 El Camino Real. US 101, exit San Antonio Rd, 0.4 mi n. Ext/int corridors. **Pets:** Small. $100 deposit/room, $25 one-time fee/room. Designated rooms, supervision.

[ASK] [✕] [S✕] [🚗] [🛏] [🛏] [💻] [🍴] [🏊] [✕]

▽▽ ▽▽ ▽▽ Sheraton Palo Alto Hotel SH
(650) 328-2800. **Call for rates.** 625 El Camino Real. US 101, exit Embarcadero W to SR 82, then 0.5 mi n. **Pets:** Accepted.

[S✕] [✕] [S✕] [🛏] [💻] [🍴] [🏊]

▽▽ ▽▽ ▽▽ The Westin Palo Alto LH
(650) 321-4422. **Call for rates.** 675 El Camino Real. US 101, exit to Embarcadero, right on El Camino Real, then just n. Int corridors. **Pets:** Accepted.

[✕] [S✕] [🛏] [💻] [🍴] [🏊]

PARADISE

△△△ ▽▽ ▽▽ ▽▽ Comfort Inn M
(530) 876-0191. **$69-$94.** 5475 Clark Rd. SR 191, 0.5 mi s of Pearson Rd. Int corridors. **Pets:** Large, other species. $100 deposit/room, $10 daily fee/room. Designated rooms, service with restrictions, supervision.

[SAVE] [S✕] [✕] [S✕] [🛏] [💻] [🏊]

△△△ ▽▽ ▽▽ Lantern Inn M
(530) 877-5553. **$60-$90.** 5799 Wildwood Ln. 1 blk w off Skyway. Ext corridors. **Pets:** Medium, dogs only. $10 daily fee/pet. Service with restrictions, supervision.

[SAVE] [S✕] [✕] [🛏] [💻] [🏊]

△△△ ▽▽ ▽▽ Paradise Inn M
(530) 877-2127. **$59-$99.** 5423 Skyway. 1.5 mi w. Ext corridors. **Pets:** Small, dogs only. $10 daily fee/pet. Designated rooms, service with restrictions, supervision.

[SAVE] [S✕] [✕] [🛏] [💻] [🏊]

△△△ ▽▽ ▽▽ ▽▽ Ponderosa Gardens Motel M
(530) 872-9094. **$75-$95.** 7010 Skyway. 2 blks e; center. Ext corridors. **Pets:** Other species. $6 deposit/pet. No service, supervision.

[SAVE] [✕] [S✕] [🛏] [💻] [🏊]

PASO ROBLES

△△△ ▽▽ ▽▽ ▽▽ Hampton Inn & Suites SH
(805) 226-9988. **$95-$165.** 212 Alexa Ct. US 101, exit SR 46 W, just sw. Int corridors. **Pets:** Small. Service with restrictions, supervision.

[SAVE] [S✕] [✕] [S✕] [🚗] [🛏] [💻] [🏊]

PHELAN

△△△ ▽▽ ▽▽ Best Western Cajon Pass M
(760) 249-6777. **$65-$149.** 8317 Hwy 138. I-15, exit Silver Lake/US 138, just w. Ext corridors. **Pets:** Accepted.

[SAVE] [S✕] [✕] [🛏] [💻] [🏊]

PIRU

▽▽ ▽▽ ▽▽ Heritage Valley Inn CI
(805) 521-0700. **$135-$195, 3 day notice.** 691 N Main St. SR 126, 0.7 mi n. Int corridors. **Pets:** Other species. $100 deposit/room. Supervision.

[ASK] [S✕] [✕] [🍴]

PISMO BEACH

▽▽ ▽▽ ▽▽ Cliffs Resort SH ☙
(805) 773-5000. **$209-$299, 3 day notice.** 2757 Shell Beach Rd. US 101, exit Spyglass Dr northbound; exit Shell Beach Rd southbound, just w, then just n. Int corridors. **Pets:** Dogs only. Designated rooms, service with restrictions.

[ASK] [S✕] [✕] [S✕] [🛏] [💻] [🍴] [🏊] [✕]

▼▼▼ **Cottage Inn by the Sea** Ⓜ
(805) 773-4617. **$89-$249.** 2351 Price St. US 101, exit Shell Beach Rd northbound, just w, 0.5 mi s; exit Price St southbound, just w, then just s. Ext corridors. **Pets:** Accepted.

ⒶⓈⓀ ⓈⒹ ✕ ⓉⓂ ⦸ Ⓖ 🖥 💻 ⇌ Ⓚ

ⒶⒶ ▼▼▼▼ **Oxford Suites Resort** ⓈⒽ ✿
(805) 773-3773. **$99-$189.** 651 Five Cities Dr. US 101, exit 4th St, just w, then just n. Ext corridors. **Pets:** Medium. $10 daily fee/pet. Designated rooms, service with restrictions, supervision.

ⓈⒶⓋⒺ ⓈⒹ ✕ ⓉⓂ ⦸ 🖥 💻 ⇌

▼▼▼ **Sandcastle Inn** Ⓜ
(805) 773-2422. **$99-$329.** 100 Stimson Ave. US 101, exit Price St northbound, 0.3 mi s, then just w; exit Hinds Ave southbound, just w, then just s. Ext/int corridors. **Pets:** $10 daily fee/pet. Designated rooms, no service, supervision.

ⒶⓈⓀ ⓈⒹ ✕ ⓉⓂ ⦸ Ⓖ 🖥 💻

▼▼ **Sea Gypsy Motel** ⒸⓄ
(805) 773-1801. **$55-$165.** 1020 Cypress St. US 101, exit Price St northbound, 0.5 mi n to Pismo Ave, then just w; exit Hines Ave southbound, 0.3 mi w, then just n. Ext/int corridors. **Pets:** Other species. $15 daily fee/pet. Service with restrictions, supervision.

✕ 🖥 💻 ⇌ Ⓚ

ⒶⒶ ▼▼ **Shell Beach Motel** Ⓜ
(805) 773-4373. **$71-$154.** 653 Shell Beach Rd. US 101, exit Shell Beach Rd northbound, just w, then 1.2 mi s; exit Price St southbound, just w, then 1 mi n. Ext corridors. **Pets:** $15 daily fee/pet. Service with restrictions, supervision.

ⓈⒶⓋⒺ ✕ 🖥 💻 ⇌ Ⓚ

▼▼▼ **Spyglass Inn** ⓈⒽ
(805) 773-4855. **$99-$279.** 2705 Spyglass Dr. US 101, exit Spyglass Dr northbound; exit Shell Beach Rd southbound, just w, then just n. Ext corridors. **Pets:** Medium. $10 daily fee/pet. Designated rooms, service with restrictions, supervision.

ⒶⓈⓀ ⓈⒹ ✕ ⓉⓂ ⦸ 🖥 💻 🍴 ⇌ Ⓚ

PLACENTIA

▼▼▼ **Residence Inn by Marriott** ⓈⒽ ✿
(714) 996-0555. **$89-$139.** 700 W Kimberly Ave. SR 57, exit Orangethorpe Ave, just w, just n on Placentia Ave, then just e. Ext corridors. **Pets:** Medium, other species. $75 one-time fee/pet. Service with restrictions.

ⒶⓈⓀ ✕ 🖥 💻 ⇌ ✕

PLACERVILLE

ⒶⒶ ▼▼ **Mother Lode Motel** Ⓜ
(530) 622-0895. **$52-$78.** 1940 Broadway. 2 mi e; adjacent to US 50, exit Point View Dr. Ext corridors. **Pets:** Small. $10 daily fee/pet. Designated rooms, no service, supervision.

ⓈⒶⓋⒺ ⓈⒹ ✕ ⓉⓂ Ⓖ 🖥 💻 ⇌

PLEASANT HILL

▼▼▼ **Residence Inn By Marriott-Pleasant Hill** Ⓜ ✿
(925) 689-1010. **$179-$209.** 700 Ellinwood Way. I-680, exit Willow Pass Rd to Taylor W; S Contra Costa Blvd, e on Ellinwood Dr, then n. Ext/int corridors. **Pets:** Large. $75 one-time fee/room. Supervision.

ⒶⓈⓀ ✕ 💻 ⇌ ✕

▼▼▼ **Summerfield Suites by Wyndham-Pleasant Hill** ⓈⒽ
(925) 934-3343. **$99-$179.** 2611 Contra Costa Blvd. I-680, exit Contra Costa Blvd, then w. Int corridors. **Pets:** Medium, other species. $200 one-time fee/room. Service with restrictions.

ⒶⓈⓀ ✕ ⓉⓂ Ⓖ 💻 ⇌ ✕

PLEASANTON

ⒶⒶ ▼▼▼ **Crowne Plaza Hotel Pleasanton** ⓁⒽ ✿
(925) 847-6000. **$69-$149.** 11950 Dublin Canyon Rd. I-580, exit Foothill Rd, 0.3 mi s. Int corridors. **Pets:** Small. $25 one-time fee/pet. Designated rooms, service with restrictions, crate.

ⓈⒶⓋⒺ ⓈⒹ ✕ Ⓖ 🖥 💻 🍴 ⇌

▼▼ **Ramada Inn** Ⓜ
(925) 463-1300. **$75-$95.** 5375 Owens Ct. I-580, exit Hopyard Rd, just s. Ext corridors. **Pets:** Accepted.

ⒶⓈⓀ ⓈⒹ ✕ 🖥 💻 ⇌

ⒶⒶ ▼▼▼ **Residence Inn by Marriott** ⓈⒽ
(925) 227-0500. **$79-$159.** 11920 Dublin Canyon Rd. I-580, exit Foothill Blvd S, then w. Int corridors. **Pets:** Accepted.

ⓈⒶⓋⒺ ⓈⒹ ✕ ⓉⓂ Ⓖ 💻 ⇌ ✕

▼▼▼ **Summerfield Suites by Wyndham-Pleasanton** Ⓜ
(925) 730-0070. **$89-$174.** 4545 Chabot Dr. I-580, exit Hopyard Rd, 1 mi s, e on Stoneridge Dr, then s. Ext corridors. **Pets:** Medium, other species. $10 daily fee/room, $150 one-time fee/room. Service with restrictions.

ⒶⓈⓀ ✕ ⓉⓂ Ⓖ 💻 ⇌ ✕

POLLOCK PINES

ⒶⒶ ▼▼▼ **Best Value Westhaven Inn** Ⓜ
(530) 644-7800. **$80-$90.** 5658 Pony Express Tr. US 50, exit Pollock Pines, just n. Ext corridors. **Pets:** Medium. $10 daily fee/pet. Service with restrictions, supervision.

ⓈⒶⓋⒺ ⓈⒹ ✕ ⓉⓂ 🖥 💻

ⒶⒶ ▼▼▼ **Best Western Stagecoach Inn** Ⓜ
(530) 644-2029. **$99-$119.** 5940 Pony Express Tr. US 50, exit Pollock Pines eastbound, 1 mi e; exit Sly Park westbound; 12 mi e of Placerville. **Pets:** Accepted.

ⓈⒶⓋⒺ ⓈⒹ ⓉⓂ 💻 ⇌

PORTOLA

▼▼ **Sleepy Pines Motel** Ⓜ
(530) 832-4291. **$61-$91.** 74631 Hwy 70. On SR 70. Ext corridors. **Pets:** Dogs only. Service with restrictions, supervision.

✕ 🖥 💻 Ⓚ

QUINCY

ⒶⒶ ▼▼ **Pine Hill Motel** Ⓜ ✿
(530) 283-1670. **$70-$80.** 42075 Hwy 70. 1 mi s. Ext corridors. **Pets:** Medium. $5 daily fee/pet. Service with restrictions, supervision.

ⓈⒶⓋⒺ ✕ 🖥 ✕

RANCHO CORDOVA

ⒶⒶ ▼▼▼ **AmeriSuites (Sacramento/Rancho Cordova)** ⓈⒽ ✿
(916) 635-4799. **$79-$129, 3 day notice.** 10744 Gold Center Dr. US 50, exit Zinfandel Dr, just s. Int corridors. **Pets:** Service with restrictions, crate.

ⓈⒶⓋⒺ ⓈⒹ ✕ ⓉⓂ Ⓖ 🖥 💻 ⇌

ⒶⒶ ▼▼▼ **Best Western Heritage Inn** Ⓜ
(916) 635-4040. **$69-$99.** 11269 Point East Dr. US 50, exit Sunrise Blvd S; 12 mi e of Sacramento. Int corridors. **Pets:** Accepted.

ⓈⒶⓋⒺ ⓈⒹ ✕ ⓉⓂ 🖥 💻 🍴 ⇌

ⒶⒶ ▼▼ **Inns of America** Ⓜ
(916) 351-1213. **$79-$99.** 12249 Folsom Blvd. US 50, exit Hazel Ave, just s. Ext corridors. **Pets:** Accepted.

ⓈⒶⓋⒺ ⓈⒹ ✕ ⓉⓂ 🖥 💻 ⇌

▼▼▼ **Residence Inn by Marriott** Ⓜ
(916) 851-1550. **$121-$149.** 2779 Prospect Park Dr. US 50, exit Zinfandel Dr. Int corridors. **Pets:** Accepted.
Ⓐ🆂🄺 🆂🛏 ✖ 🛗 🖼 🖥 🏊 ⊗

🆁🆁🆁 ▼▼▼▼ **Wingate Inn** 🆂🅷 ✿
(916) 858-8680. **$69-$109.** 10745 Gold Center Dr. US 50, exit Zinfandel Dr, just s. Int corridors. **Pets:** Other species. Service with restrictions, supervision.
🆂🄰🆅🄴 🆂🛏 ✖ 🛗 🛏 🖥 🏊

RANCHO MIRAGE

🆁🆁🆁 ▼▼▼ ▼▼▼ **The Westin Mission Hills Resort** 🅻🅷 ✿
(760) 328-5955. **$89-$450, 7 day notice.** 71-333 Dinah Shore Dr. I-10, exit Bob Hope Dr/Ramon Rd, 0.3 mi w on Ramon Rd, 1 mi s on Bob Hope Dr, then 0.6 mi w. Ext corridors. **Pets:** Small, dogs only. Designated rooms, service with restrictions, supervision.
🆂🄰🆅🄴 🆂🛏 ✖ 🖥 🍴 🏊 ⊗

RED BLUFF

🆁🆁🆁 ▼▼ **Best Value Inn & Suites** Ⓜ ✿
(530) 529-2028. **$55-$90.** 30 Gilmore Rd. I-5, exit SR 36 W (Central District), just s. Ext corridors. **Pets:** Medium. $7 daily fee/pet. Designated rooms, service with restrictions, supervision.
🆂🄰🆅🄴 🆂🛏 ✖ 🛗 🖼 🛏 🖥 🏊

▼▼ **Days Inn & Suites** Ⓜ ✿
(530) 527-6130. **$60-$66.** 5 John Sutter St. I-5, exit S Main St southbound, just right; exit S Main St northbound, cross over bridge, then just right. Ext corridors. **Pets:** Medium. $25 deposit/pet, $10 daily fee/pet. Service with restrictions, supervision.
Ⓐ🆂🄺 🆂🛏 ✖ 🛏 🏊

▼▼ **Econo Lodge** Ⓜ
(530) 528-8890. **$50-$100.** 1142 N Main St. I-5, exit 351 northbound, just s; exit Antelope Blvd southbound, 0.5 mi w, then just n. Ext corridors. **Pets:** Accepted.
Ⓐ🆂🄺 🆂🛏 ✖ 🛏 🖥 🏊

🆁🆁🆁 ▼▼▼ **Lamplighter Lodge** Ⓜ
(530) 527-1150. **$60-$85, 7 day notice.** 210 S Main St. I-5, exit via business loop. Ext corridors. **Pets:** Small. $5 daily fee/pet. Designated rooms, service with restrictions, supervision.
🆂🄰🆅🄴 🆂🛏 ✖ 🛏 🏊

🆁🆁🆁 ▼ **Sportsman Lodge** Ⓜ
(530) 527-2888. **$55-$110.** 768 Antelope Blvd. I-5, exit 36 W (Central District), 1.5 mi e. Ext corridors. **Pets:** $7 daily fee/pet. Service with restrictions, supervision.
🆂🄰🆅🄴 🆂🛏 ✖ 🛏 🖥 🏊

🆁🆁🆁 ▼▼▼ **Super 8 Motel** Ⓜ
(530) 527-8882. **$60-$100.** 203 Antelope Blvd. I-5, exit 36W (Central District). Int corridors. **Pets:** Other species. $7 daily fee/pet. Service with restrictions, supervision.
🆂🄰🆅🄴 🆂🛏 ✖ 🛏 🏊

🆁🆁🆁 ▼▼ **Travelodge Red Bluff** Ⓜ ✿
(530) 527-6020. **$60-$90.** 38 Antelope Blvd. I-5, exit 36 W (Central District), just w. Ext corridors. **Pets:** Medium. $7 daily fee/pet. Designated rooms, service with restrictions, supervision.
🆂🄰🆅🄴 ✖ 🛏 🖥 🏊

REDCREST

🆁🆁🆁 ▼ **Redcrest Resort** 🅲🅰 ✿
(707) 722-4208. **$50-$140, 14 day notice.** 26459 Avenue of the Giants. US 101, exit Redcrest, just n. Ext corridors. **Pets:** $7 daily fee/pet. Designated rooms, no service, supervision.
🆂🄰🆅🄴 ✖ 🛏 🖥 ⊗ 🄺 🄵

REDDING

🆁🆁🆁 ▼▼▼ **Best Western Hospitality House** Ⓜ
(530) 241-6464. **$55-$89.** 532 N Market St. I-5, exit Lake Blvd northbound, just w, 0.5 mi to Market St, then 0.5 mi s; exit Market St southbound, then 2 mi s. Ext corridors. **Pets:** Small, dogs only. $10 daily fee/pet. Designated rooms, service with restrictions, supervision.
🆂🄰🆅🄴 🆂🛏 ✖ 🛏 🖥 🍴 🏊

🆁🆁🆁 ▼▼▼ **Best Western Ponderosa Inn** Ⓜ
(530) 241-6300. **$69.** 2220 Pine St. I-5, exit Cypress Ave, 1.5 mi w. Ext corridors. **Pets:** Accepted.
🆂🄰🆅🄴 🆂🛏 ✖ 🛏 🖥 🏊

🆁🆁🆁 ▼▼▼ **Comfort Inn** Ⓜ
(530) 221-6530. **$78-$199.** 2059 Hilltop Dr. I-5, exit Cypress Ave E, 0.3 mi n. Ext corridors. **Pets:** Other species. $15 one-time fee/room. Service with restrictions, crate.
🆂🄰🆅🄴 🆂🛏 ✖ 🛏 🖥 🏊

🆁🆁🆁 ▼▼▼▼ **Grand Manor Inn & Suites** Ⓜ
(530) 221-4472. **$78-$117.** 850 Mistletoe Ln. I-5, exit Cypress Ave E, 0.8 mi n on Hilltop Dr. Int corridors. **Pets:** Accepted.
🆂🄰🆅🄴 🆂🛏 ✖ 🖼 🛏 🖥 🏊

🆁🆁🆁 ▼▼▼▼ **Holiday Inn Express** Ⓜ
(530) 241-5500. **$94-$99.** 1080 Twin View Blvd. I-5, exit Twin View Blvd, just w. Int corridors. **Pets:** Other species. $30 one-time fee/room. Designated rooms, service with restrictions, supervision.
🆂🄰🆅🄴 🆂🛏 ✖ 🛗 🛏 🖥 🏊

🆁🆁🆁 ▼▼▼▼ **La Quinta Inn Redding** Ⓜ ✿
(530) 221-8200. **$100-$119.** 2180 Hilltop Dr. I-5, exit Cypress Ave E, 0.5 mi n. Int corridors. **Pets:** Other species. Service with restrictions, supervision.
🆂🄰🆅🄴 ✖ 🖼 🛏 🖥 🏊

▼▼▼ **Oxford Suites** Ⓜ ✿
(530) 221-0100. **$85-$105.** 1967 Hilltop Dr. I-5, exit Cypress Ave E, 0.5 mi n. Ext/int corridors. **Pets:** Small. $25 one-time fee/pet. Service with restrictions, supervision.
Ⓐ🆂🄺 🆂🛏 ✖ 🛏 🖥 🏊

🆁🆁🆁 ▼▼▼▼ **Ramada Limited** Ⓜ
(530) 246-2222. **$74-$96.** 1286 Twin View Blvd. I-5, exit Twin View Blvd E, just n. Int corridors. **Pets:** Medium, other species. $15 one-time fee/room. Designated rooms, service with restrictions, supervision.
🆂🄰🆅🄴 🆂🛏 ✖ 🛗 🖼 🛏 🖥 🏊

🆁🆁🆁 ▼▼▼ **Redding Travelodge** Ⓜ
(530) 243-5291. **$70-$99.** 540 N Market St. I-5, exit Lake Blvd northbound, just w, 0.5 mi to Market St, then 0.5 mi s; exit Market St southbound, then 2 mi s. Ext corridors. **Pets:** Accepted.
🆂🄰🆅🄴 🆂🛏 ✖ 🖼 🛏 🖥 🏊

🆁🆁🆁 ▼▼▼▼ **Red Lion Hotel Redding** Ⓜ
(530) 221-8700. **$80-$107.** 1830 Hilltop Dr. I-5, exit SR 44 and 299 (Hilltop Dr). Int corridors. **Pets:** Medium, other species. $50 deposit/pet. Designated rooms, service with restrictions, supervision.
🆂🄰🆅🄴 🆂🛏 ✖ 🖼 🛏 🖥 🍴 🏊 ⊗

🆁🆁🆁 ▼▼▼ **River Inn** Ⓜ
(530) 241-9500. **$65-$85.** 1835 Park Marina Dr. I-5, exit SR 44 W; 1 mi w, exit Park Marina Dr. Ext corridors. **Pets:** Accepted.
🆂🄰🆅🄴 🆂🛏 ✖ 🛏 🖥 🏊

REDLANDS

🆁🆁🆁 ▼▼▼ **Best Western Sandman Motel** Ⓜ
(909) 793-2001. **$59-$125.** 1120 W Colton Ave. I-10, exit Tennessee St, just s, then just e. Ext corridors. **Pets:** $50 deposit/pet. Designated rooms, service with restrictions, supervision.
🆂🄰🆅🄴 🆂🛏 ✖ 🛏 🖥 🏊

△△△ ▽▽▽ Dynasty Suites-Redlands M
(909) 793-6648. **$72-$90.** 1235 W Colton Ave. I-10, exit Tennessee St, just s, then just w. Ext corridors. **Pets:** Very small. $10 daily fee/pet. Designated rooms, service with restrictions, supervision.
SAVE ⊠ ⊟ ▣ ⇝

REDWAY

△△△ ▽▽▽ Dean Creek Resort M
(707) 923-2555. **$58-$135, 3 day notice.** 4112 Redwood Dr. US 101, exit Redwood Dr northbound; exit Redway/Shelter Cove southbound, just w. Ext corridors. **Pets:** $100 deposit/pet. Service with restrictions, supervision.
SAVE ⊠ ⊟ ▣ ⇝

REDWOOD CITY

▽▽▽ ▽▽▽ Hotel Sofitel San Francisco Bay At Redwood Shores LH
(650) 598-9000. **$249-$279.** 223 Twin Dolphin Dr. US 101, exit Marine World Pkwy E, 0.5 mi s. Int corridors. **Pets:** Accepted.
ASK SⓄ ⊠ Ⓜ ⌨ ▣ ⅱ ⇝

▽▽▽ TownePlace Suites by Marriott M
(650) 593-4100. **Call for rates.** 1000 Twin Dolphin Dr. US 101, exit Redwood Shores Pkwy, 0.3 mi e, then just s. Int corridors. **Pets:** Very small. $75 one-time fee/pet. Service with restrictions, crate.
SⓄ ⊠ Ⓜ ⌨ ▣

REEDLEY

△△△ ▽▽▽ Edgewater Inn M
(559) 637-7777. **$79-$89.** 1977 W Manning Ave. 12 mi e of SR 99 via Manning Ave. Ext corridors. **Pets:** Medium, dogs only. $8 daily fee/pet. Designated rooms, service with restrictions, supervision.
SAVE SⓄ ⊠ ⊟ ▣ ⇝

RIALTO

△△△ ▽▽▽ Best Western Empire Inn M ❀
(909) 877-0690. **$79-$149, 3 day notice.** 475 W Valley Blvd. I-10, exit Riverside Ave, just n, then 0.5 mi w. Ext corridors. **Pets:** Medium. $30 deposit/room, $10 one-time fee/pet. Designated rooms, service with restrictions, supervision.
SAVE SⓄ ⊠ ⊟ ▣ ⅱ ⇝

RIDGECREST

△△△ ▽▽▽ Best Western China Lake Inn M
(760) 371-2300. **$89.** 400 S China Lake Blvd. On US 395 business route. Ext corridors. **Pets:** Small. $10 one-time fee/pet. Service with restrictions, supervision.
SAVE SⓄ ⊠ ⊟ ▣ ⇝

△△△ ▽▽▽ Carriage Inn M ❀
(760) 446-7910. **$85-$143.** 901 N China Lake Blvd. On SR 178 and US 395 business route. Ext corridors. **Pets:** Large. $25 one-time fee/room. Designated rooms, service with restrictions.
SAVE SⓄ ⊠ Ⓜ ⌨ ⊟ ▣ ⅱ ⇝ ⊠

△△△ ▽▽▽ Econo Lodge M
(760) 446-2551. **$53-$90.** 201 Inyokern Rd. On SR 178 and US 395 business route, just w of China Lake Blvd. Ext corridors. **Pets:** Small, dogs only. Service with restrictions, supervision.
SAVE ⊠ ⊟ ▣ ⇝

△△△ ▽▽▽ Heritage Inn & Suites SH
(760) 446-7951. **$75-$88.** 1050 N Norma. On US 395 business route, just w. Int corridors. **Pets:** $100 deposit/room. Service with restrictions, crate.
SAVE SⓄ ⊠ ⊟ ▣ ⅱ ⇝

△△△ ▽▽▽ Quality Inn M
(760) 375-9731. **$89.** 507 S China Lake Blvd. On US 395 business route. Ext corridors. **Pets:** Small. $10 one-time fee/pet. Service with restrictions, supervision.
SAVE SⓄ ⊠ ⊟ ▣ ⇝

△△△ ▽▽▽ Vagabond Inn M
(760) 375-2220. **$70.** 426 China Lake Blvd. On US 395 business route. Ext corridors. **Pets:** Small. $10 one-time fee/pet. Service with restrictions, supervision.
SAVE SⓄ ⊠ ⊟ ▣

RIO DELL

△△△ ▽▽ Humboldt Gables Motel M
(707) 764-5609. **$50-$80.** 40 W Davis St. US 101, exit Rio Dell/Davis St W. Ext corridors. **Pets:** Accepted.
SAVE SⓄ ⊠ Ⓜ ⊟ ▣ Ⓚ

RIVERSIDE

△△△ ▽▽▽ Best Western of Riverside M
(951) 359-0770. **$85-$170.** 10518 Magnolia Ave. SR 91, exit Tyler St, 0.5 mi nw, then 0.3 mi sw. Ext corridors. **Pets:** Accepted.
SAVE SⓄ ⊠ ⊟ ▣ ⇝

△△△ ▽▽▽ Dynasty Suites Riverside M
(951) 369-8200. **$71-$83.** 3735 Iowa Ave. I-215 and SR 60, exit University Ave, just w, then just n. Ext corridors. **Pets:** Small. $10 daily fee/pet. Designated rooms, service with restrictions, supervision.
SAVE SⓄ ⊠ ⊟ ▣ ⇝

ROCKLIN

△△△ ▽▽▽▽ Howard Johnson Hotel M
(916) 624-4500. **$99-$169.** 4420 Rocklin Rd. I-80 E, exit Rocklin Rd. Int corridors. **Pets:** Small, other species. $100 deposit/room, $20 one-time fee/room. Designated rooms, service with restrictions, supervision.
SAVE SⓄ ⊠ Ⓜ ⌀ ⌨ ⊟ ▣ ⇝

▽▽ ▽▽ Ramada Limited M
(916) 632-3366. **$59-$119.** 4480 Rocklin Rd. I-80, exit Rocklin Rd. Int corridors. **Pets:** Accepted.
ASK SⓄ ⊠ Ⓜ ⌨ ⊟ ▣ ⇝

ROSEVILLE

△△△ ▽▽▽ Best Western Roseville Inn M
(916) 782-4434. **$72.** 220 Harding Blvd. I-80, exit Douglas Blvd, just w, then just n. Ext corridors. **Pets:** $10 daily fee/pet. Designated rooms, service with restrictions, supervision.
SAVE SⓄ ⊠ Ⓜ ⊟ ▣ ⇝

▽▽▽▽ Oxford Suites M ❀
(916) 784-2222. **$89-$129.** 130 N Sunrise Ave. I-80, exit Douglas Blvd, just e, then 0.3 mi n. Ext/int corridors. **Pets:** $25 one-time fee/room. Service with restrictions, supervision.
ASK SⓄ ⊠ Ⓜ ⌨ ⊟ ▣ ⇝

▽▽▽ Residence Inn by Marriott SH
(916) 772-5500. **$119-$199, 14 day notice.** 1930 Taylor Rd. I-80, exit Eureka-Taylor Rd, just s. Int corridors. **Pets:** Accepted.
ASK SⓄ ⊠ Ⓜ ⌨ ▣ ⇝ ⊠

SACRAMENTO

△△△ ▽▽▽ Best Western Expo Inn M
(916) 922-9833. **$85-$150.** 1413 Howe Ave. Jct SR 16 and US 50, exit Howe Ave, 2.5 mi n. Int corridors. **Pets:** Medium. $50 deposit/room. Designated rooms, service with restrictions, crate.
SAVE ⊠ Ⓜ ⊟ ▣ ⇝

AAA ▽▽▽▽ **Best Western Harbor Inn & Suites** **M**
(916) 371-2100. **$69-$169.** 1250 Halyard Dr. 4 mi w; exit Business Rt 80 via Harbor Blvd. Ext/int corridors. **Pets:** Accepted.
[SAVE] [S&] [✕] [&M] [📶] [🖵] [⊃]

AAA ▽▽▽▽ **Candlewood Suites** **SH**
(916) 646-1212. **$89-$124.** 555 Howe Ave. US 50, exit Howe Ave, 1.5 mi n. Int corridors. **Pets:** Accepted.
[SAVE] [✕] [&M] [&⍓] [📶] [🖵]

▽▽ ▽▽ **Canterbury Inn** **M**
(916) 927-0927. **$59-$89.** 1900 Canterbury Rd. Business Rt 80, exit Exposition Blvd, 0.4 mi w to Leisure Ln, then just n of SR 160. Ext corridors. **Pets:** Accepted.
[✕] [&M] [🖵] [⊃]

AAA ▽▽▽▽ **Clarion Hotel Near Calexpo** **SH**
(916) 487-7600. **$79-$179.** 2600 Auburn Blvd. Business Rt 80, exit Fulton Ave. Int corridors. **Pets:** Accepted.
[SAVE] [S&] [✕] [&M] [📶] [🖵] [❚❚] [⊃]

▽▽▽▽ **Doubletree Hotel** **LH**
(916) 929-8855. **$90-$210.** 2001 Point West Way. 1 blk off Business Rt 80, exit via Arden Way. Int corridors. **Pets:** Small, other species. $50 one-time fee/room. Service with restrictions, supervision.
[ASK] [S&] [✕] [&M] [&⍓] [📶] [🖵] [❚❚] [⊃]

AAA ▽▽▽▽ **Econo Lodge** **M**
(916) 443-6631. **$49-$109.** 711 16th St. Business Rt 80, exit 15th St eastbound; exit 16th St westbound; I-5, exit J St. Ext corridors. **Pets:** Other species. $10 daily fee/pet. Designated rooms, service with restrictions.
[SAVE] [S&] [✕] [&M] [📶]

▽▽ ▽▽ **Homestead Studio Suites Hotel-Sacramento** **M**
(916) 564-7500. **$75-$89.** 2810 Gateway Oaks Dr. I-5, exit W El Camino Ave, just w, then 0.4 mi n. Ext corridors. **Pets:** Accepted.
[ASK] [S&] [✕] [&M] [&⍓]

▽▽ ▽▽ **Host Airport Hotel** **M**
(916) 922-8071. **$90-$150.** 6945 Airport Blvd. 11 mi nw of state capitol; 6 mi nw of I-80, off I-5. Ext corridors. **Pets:** Accepted.
[ASK] [S&] [✕] [&M] [🖵]

▽▽▽▽ **La Quinta Inn Sacramento (Downtown)** **M**
(916) 448-8100. **$105-$129.** 200 Jibboom St. I-5, exit Richards Blvd W, 2.3 mi nw of Business Loop 80. Ext corridors. **Pets:** Accepted.
[ASK] [✕] [&M] [📶] [🖵] [⊃]

▽▽▽▽ **La Quinta Inn Sacramento (North)** **M**
(916) 348-0900. **$100-$125.** 4604 Madison Ave. I-80, exit Madison Ave, 0.3 mi e. Ext corridors. **Pets:** Service with restrictions.
[ASK] [✕] [&M] [🖵] [⊃]

▽▽▽▽ **Marriott Residence Inn** **M**
(916) 920-9111. **$89-$179.** 1530 Howe Ave. 2.5 mi n of jct SR 16 and US 50, exit Howe Ave. Ext corridors. **Pets:** Medium, other species. $75 one-time fee/room. Service with restrictions, crate.
[ASK] [S&] [✕] [&M] [⌖] [📶] [🖵] [⊃]

AAA ▽▽▽▽ **Radisson Hotel** **SH**
(916) 922-2020. **$109-$189.** 500 Leisure Ln. Business Rt 80, exit Exposition Blvd, 0.4 mi w. Ext corridors. **Pets:** Medium, dogs only. $50 deposit/room, $50 one-time fee/room. Service with restrictions, supervision.
[SAVE] [S&] [✕] [&M] [⌖] [&⍓] [🖵] [⊃] [✕⊃]

▽▽▽▽ **Red Lion Hotel Sacramento** **M**
(916) 922-8041. **$89-$119.** 1401 Arden Way. I-80, via Arden Way; in Arden Fair Shopping Plaza. Ext/int corridors. **Pets:** Accepted.
[ASK] [S&] [✕] [&M] [📶] [🖵] [❚❚] [⊃] [✕⊃]

▽▽▽▽ **Red Roof Inn** **M**
(916) 927-7117. **$57-$87.** 3796 Northgate Blvd. I-80, exit Northgate Blvd, just s. Ext corridors. **Pets:** Medium. Designated rooms, service with restrictions, supervision.
[ASK] [S&] [✕] [&M] [⊃]

▽▽▽▽ **Residence Inn by Marriott** **M**
(916) 649-1300. **$99-$154.** 2410 W El Camino Ave. I-5, exit W El Camino Ave. Ext corridors. **Pets:** Other species. $75 one-time fee/room.
[ASK] [S&] [✕] [&M] [📶] [🖵] [⊃]

AAA ▽▽▽▽ **Vagabond Executive Inn Old Town** **M**
(916) 446-1481. **$79-$119.** 909 3rd St. I-5, exit J St (Old Sacramento), 8 blks w of the state capitol. Ext corridors. **Pets:** Small, dogs only. $10 daily fee/room. Designated rooms, service with restrictions, supervision.
[SAVE] [S&] [✕] [&M] [🖉] [📶] [🖵] [⊃]

SALINAS

AAA ▽▽ ▽▽ **Ramada Limited** **M**
(831) 424-4801. **$59-$149.** 109 John St. US 101, exit John St, 0.7 mi w. Ext corridors. **Pets:** Small, other species. $25 deposit/pet. Service with restrictions, supervision.
[SAVE] [S&] [✕] [&⍓] [📶] [🖵]

▽▽▽▽ **Residence Inn by Marriott-Salinas** **SH** 🐾
(831) 775-0410. **$109-$139, 14 day notice.** 17215 El Rancho Way. US 101, exit Laurel Ave, just w. Int corridors. **Pets:** Other species. $135 one-time fee/room. Service with restrictions.
[ASK] [S&] [✕] [&M] [&⍓] [🖵] [⊃] [✕⊃]

AAA ▽▽ **Vagabond Inn** **M**
(831) 758-4693. **$60-$180.** 131 Kern St. US 101, exit Market St, just e. Ext corridors. **Pets:** $5 daily fee/pet. Service with restrictions.
[SAVE] [S&] [✕] [&M] [🖵] [⊃]

SAN ANDREAS

▽▽▽▽ **The Robins Nest** **BB** 🐾
(209) 754-1076. **$90-$155, 7 day notice.** 247 W St. Charles St. SR 49; north end of town. Int corridors. **Pets:** Large, other species. Designated rooms, service with restrictions, supervision.
[ASK] [S&] [✕] [📶] [🖵]

SAN BERNARDINO

▽▽▽▽ **La Quinta Inn San Bernardino** **M**
(909) 888-7571. **$109-$125.** 205 E Hospitality Ln. I-10, exit Waterman Ave, just n, then 0.3 mi w. Ext corridors. **Pets:** Accepted.
[ASK] [✕] [&M] [🖉] [📶] [🖵] [⊃]

SAN CLEMENTE

▽▽▽▽ **Holiday Inn-San Clemente Resort** **SH**
(949) 361-3000. **$139-$159.** 111 S Avenida de la Estrella. I-5, exit Avenida Palizada southbound; exit Avenida Presidio northbound, just s, then just w. Int corridors. **Pets:** Accepted.
[ASK] [✕] [📶] [🖵] [❚❚] [⊃]

SAN DIEGO METROPOLITAN AREA

CHULA VISTA

▽▽▽▽▽ La Quinta Inn San Diego (Chula Vista) **M**
(619) 691-1211. **$115-$159.** 150 Bonita Rd. I-805, exit E St/Bonita Rd, just w. Ext corridors. **Pets:** Small. Service with restrictions, supervision.

A$K ⊠ ▣ ➾

▽ Motel 6 San Diego-Chula Vista #1037 **M**
(619) 422-4200. **$47-$68.** 745 E St. I-5, exit E St, just e. Ext corridors. **Pets:** Accepted.

S⬧ ⊠ ➾

CORONADO

▽▽▽▽▽ Coronado Island Marriott Resort **LH**
(619) 435-3000. **$229-$299.** 2000 2nd St. I-5, exit Coronado Bridge, 1.5 mi w to Glorietta Blvd, then just ne. Ext corridors. **Pets:** Other species. $75 one-time fee/room.

A$K ⊠ ▤ ▣ ⫟ ➾ ⊠

▽▽ Crown City Inn **M** ❀
(619) 435-3116. **$99-$179.** 520 Orange Ave. I-5, exit Coronado Bridge, 1.5 mi w, then just s. Ext corridors. **Pets:** Large, other species. $8 daily fee/pet. Designated rooms, service with restrictions, supervision.

⊠ ⫶ᴹ ⫸ ▤ ▣ ⫟

▵▵▵ ▽▽▽▽▽ Loews Coronado Bay Resort **LH** ❀
(619) 424-4000. **$210-$350.** 4000 Coronado Bay Rd. I-5, exit Coronado Bridge, 1.7 mi w to Orange Ave, 1 mi sw to Silver Strand Blvd, then 4.5 mi s to Coronado Cays. Ext/int corridors. **Pets:** Other species.

SAVE ⊠ ▤ ▣ ⫟ ➾ ⊠

DEL MAR

▵▵▵ ▽▽▽▽▽ Del Mar Inn, A Clarion Carriage House **SH** ❀
(858) 755-9765. **$79-$199.** 720 Camino Del Mar. I-5, exit Del Mar Heights Rd, 1 mi w, then 0.3 mi n. Int corridors. **Pets:** Small. $25 one-time fee/room. Designated rooms, service with restrictions, crate.

SAVE S⬧ ⊠ ➾

▽▽▽ Doubletree Hotel Del Mar **LH**
(858) 481-5900. **$99-$249.** 11915 El Camino Real. I-5, exit Carmel Valley Rd, 0.3 mi e. Int corridors. **Pets:** Medium. $50 deposit/room, $30 daily fee/pet. Designated rooms, service with restrictions, crate.

A$K S⬧ ⊠ ▤ ▣ ⫟ ➾

LA JOLLA

▵▵▵ ▽▽▽▽ La Jolla Cove Suites **SH** ❀
(858) 459-2621. **$239-$599.** 1155 Coast Blvd. I-5, exit La Jolla Village Dr, 1 mi w to Torrey Pines Rd, 2.5 mi to Prospect St, 0.5 mi s to Girard Ave, then just w. Ext corridors. **Pets:** Small. $15 daily fee/pet. Designated rooms, service with restrictions, supervision.

SAVE S⬧ ⊠ ▤ ▣ ➾ ⊠ 🅺

▵▵▵ ▽ La Jolla Village Lodge **M**
(858) 551-2001. **$70-$220.** 1141 Silverado St. I-5, exit La Jolla Pkwy northbound, 1.5 mi w to Torrey Pines Rd, 1 mi w, then 0.8 mi sw; exit La Jolla Village Dr southbound, 1 mi w to Torrey Pines Rd, then 3.6 mi sw. Ext corridors. **Pets:** Other species. $20 one-time fee/pet. Designated rooms, service with restrictions, supervision.

SAVE S⬧ ⊠ ▤ ▣

▽▽▽ ▽▽ La Valencia Hotel **LH**
(858) 454-0771. **$300-$2000.** 1132 Prospect St. I-5, exit La Jolla Pkwy northbound, 1.5 mi w to Torrey Pines Rd, 1 mi w, then 0.6 mi sw; exit La Jolla Village Dr southbound, 1 mi w to Torrey Pines Rd, 2.7 mi sw, then 0.6 mi sw. Ext/int corridors. **Pets:** Accepted.

⊠ ▤ ▣ ⫟ ➾ ⊠

Residence Inn by Marriott La Jolla

▽▽▽▽ Residence Inn by Marriott La Jolla **SH** ❀
(858) 587-1770. **$110-$159.** 8901 Gilman Dr. I-5, exit Gilman Dr, 1.5 mi nw. Ext corridors. **Pets:** $75 one-time fee/pet. Designated rooms, service with restrictions.

A$K ⊠ ▣ ➾ ⊠

▽▽▽▽ San Diego Marriott La Jolla **LH**
(858) 587-1414. **$125-$179.** 4240 La Jolla Village Dr. I-5, exit La Jolla Village Dr, 0.5 mi e. Int corridors. **Pets:** Medium. $50 one-time fee/room. Designated rooms, service with restrictions, supervision.

A$K ⊠ ⫶ᴹ ⫸ ⫷ ⫶ ▤ ▣ ⫟ ➾ ⊠

LA MESA

▽ Motel 6 San Diego-La Mesa #1319 **M**
(619) 464-7151. **$49-$61.** 7621 Alvarado Rd. I-8, exit Fletcher Pkwy, just s, then just w. **Pets:** Accepted.

S⬧ ⊠

POWAY

▵▵▵ ▽▽▽▽ Best Western Country Inn **M** ❀
(858) 748-6320. **$75-$129.** 13845 Poway Rd. I-15, exit Poway Rd, 4 mi e. Ext corridors. **Pets:** Small. $15 daily fee/room. Designated rooms, service with restrictions, supervision.

SAVE S⬧ ⊠ ⫶ᴹ ⫸ ⫷ ▤ ▣ ➾ ⊠

▵▵▵ ▽▽ Ramada Limited **M**
(858) 748-7311. **$69-$109.** 12448 Poway Rd. I-15, exit Poway Rd, 3 mi e. Ext corridors. **Pets:** Small, other species. $10 daily fee/pet. Service with restrictions, supervision.

SAVE ⊠ ▤ ▣ ➾

RANCHO BERNARDO

▵▵▵ ▽▽▽▽ Four Points By Sheraton Rancho Bernardo **SH**
(858) 485-9250. **$159-$239.** 11611 Bernardo Plaza Ct. I-15, exit Rancho Bernardo Rd, just e to Bernardo Center Dr, then just s. Int corridors. **Pets:** Accepted.

SAVE S⬧ ⊠ ⫶ᴹ ⫷ ▤ ▣ ⫟ ➾

▵▵▵ ▽▽▽▽ La Quinta Inn San Diego (Rancho Penasquitos) **SH**
(858) 484-8800. **$105-$119.** 10185 Paseo Montril. I-15, exit Rancho Penasquitos Blvd, just w. Ext corridors. **Pets:** Medium, other species. Service with restrictions.

SAVE ⊠ ⫶ᴹ ▤ ▣ ➾

▵▵▵ ▽▽▽ ▽▽ Rancho Bernardo Inn **SH**
(858) 487-1611. **$179, 3 day notice.** 17550 Bernardo Oaks Dr. I-15, exit Rancho Bernardo Rd, 1 mi e, then 1 mi n. Ext/int corridors. **Pets:** Dogs only. $100 one-time fee/room. Designated rooms, service with restrictions, supervision.

SAVE ⊠ ⫶ᴹ ⫷ ⫶ ▣ ⫟ ➾ ⊠

▽▽ Rancho Bernardo Travelodge **M**
(858) 487-0445. **$77-$90.** 16929 W Bernardo Dr. I-15, exit Rancho Bernardo Rd, just w, then just s. Ext corridors. **Pets:** Accepted.

A$K S⬧ ⊠ ▤ ▣ ➾

▽▽▽▽ Residence Inn San Diego Rancho Bernardo/Carmel Mountain Ranch **SH** ❀
(858) 673-1900. **$139-$219.** 11002 Rancho Carmel Dr. I-15, exit Carmel Mountain Rd, just e. Ext/int corridors. **Pets:** Medium, other species. $75 one-time fee/room. Service with restrictions, supervision.

⊠ ▤ ▣ ➾ ⊠

▼▼▼▼ Staybridge Suites Carmel Mountain SH
(848) 487-0900. **$155-$199.** 11855 Ave of Industry. I-15, exit Carmel Mountain Rd, 1 mi ne to second Rancho Carmel Dr, just w to Innovation Dr, just n, then just e. Int corridors. **Pets:** Medium, other species. $150 one-time fee/room.

ASK ✕ ﹠M ⟨ ⬚ 🛏 💻 ⇌ ✕

RANCHO SANTA FE

▼▼▼▼ The Inn at Rancho Santa Fe SH
(858) 756-1131. **$195-$230, 3 day notice.** 5951 Linea del Cielo. I-5, exit Lomas Sante Fe Dr, 4 mi e on CR S-8. Ext/int corridors. **Pets:** Accepted.

ASK ﹠ ✕ 🛏 💻 ⇌ 🍽 ⇌ ✕

SAN DIEGO

▲▲▲ ▼▼▼ Best Western Lamplighter Inn & Suites M
(619) 582-3088. **$75-$130.** 6474 El Cajon Blvd. I-8, exit 70th St, 0.5 mi s, then 1 mi w. Ext corridors. **Pets:** $10 daily fee/pet. Service with restrictions, supervision.

SAVE ﹠ ✕ 🛏 💻 ⇌

▲▲▲ ▼▼▼▼ The Bristol LH
(619) 232-6141. **$119-$129.** 1055 First Ave. I-5, exit Front St, 0.5 mi s at C St; downtown. Int corridors. **Pets:** Dogs only. $50 deposit/room. Service with restrictions, supervision.

SAVE ﹠ ✕ 🛏 💻 🍽

▼▼ ▼▼ Crown Point View Suite-Hotel SH
(858) 272-0676. **$105-$205, 7 day notice.** 4088 Crown Point Dr. I-5, exit Garnet Ave, 1 mi e to Morrell St, then 0.5 mi s. Ext corridors. **Pets:** Accepted.

ASK 🛏 💻 ✕

▲▲▲ ▼▼▼▼ Doubletree Club Hotel San Diego Zoo/SeaWorld
        Area LH
(619) 881-6900. **$109-$199, 3 day notice.** 1515 Hotel Cir S. I-8, exit Hotel Cir, south side. Int corridors. **Pets:** Accepted.

SAVE ✕ 🛏 ﹠M ⟨ ⬚ 🛏 💻 🍽 ⇌ ✕

▲▲▲ ▼▼▼▼ Doubletree Hotel San Diego-Mission
        Valley LH ❀
(619) 297-5466. **$139-$239.** 7450 Hazard Center Dr. SR 163, exit Friars Rd, 0.3 mi e to Frazee Rd, then just s. Int corridors. **Pets:** Medium, other species. $50 one-time fee/room. Supervision.

SAVE ✕ 🛏 💻 🍽 ⇌ ✕

▼▼▼▼ Hampton Inn SeaWorld/Airport SH
(619) 299-6633. **$116-$145.** 3888 Greenwood St. I-8, exit Sports Arena Blvd, 0.5 mi s, 0.3 mi e on Hancock St, then 0.4 mi s on Kurtz St. Int corridors. **Pets:** Accepted.

ASK ﹠ ✕ 🛏 💻 ⇌

▲▲▲ ▼▼▼▼ Holiday Inn on the Bay LH ❀
(619) 232-3861. **$119-$179.** 1355 N Harbor Dr at Ash St. I-5, exit B St northbound, 1.8 mi w to Ash St, just n to Ash St, then just w; exit Front Ave southbound, 0.5 mi s to Ash St, then just w. Int corridors. **Pets:** Other species. $75 deposit/room, $25 one-time fee/room. Service with restrictions, supervision.

SAVE ﹠ ✕ 🛏 💻 🍽 ⇌

▼▼ ▼▼ Homestead Studio Suites Hotel-San Diego/Mission
        Valley M
(619) 299-2292. **$84-$99.** 7444 Mission Valley Rd. SR 163, exit Friars Rd, 1 mi ne via Mission Center Dr. Ext corridors. **Pets:** Accepted.

ASK ﹠ ✕ ﹠M ⟨ ⬚ 🛏 💻

▼▼ ▼▼ Homestead Studio Suites Hotel-San Diego/Sorrento
        Mesa M
(858) 623-0100. **$99-$114.** 9880 Pacific Heights Blvd. I-805, exit Mira Mesa Blvd, 1 mi e. Ext corridors. **Pets:** Accepted.

ASK ﹠ ✕ ﹠M ⟨ ⬚ 🛏 💻

▼▼▼▼ Horton Grand Hotel SH
(619) 544-1886. **$169-$279.** 311 Island Ave. I-5, exit Front St southbound, 1.2 mi s, then just e; exit J St northbound, 1 mi w, just n on 3rd Ave, then just e. Int corridors. **Pets:** Accepted.

ASK ﹠ ✕ 🛏 💻 🍽

◆ Motel 6 San Diego-Downtown #1419 M
(619) 236-9292. **$55-$81.** 1546 2nd Ave. I-5, exit 6th Ave northbound, 0.3 mi w, then just s; exit 2nd Ave southbound, just s. Int corridors. **Pets:** Accepted.

﹠ ✕

◆ Motel 6 San Diego North #1020 M
(858) 268-9758. **$55-$69.** 5592 Clairemont Mesa Blvd. I-805, exit Clairemont Mesa Blvd, just w. Ext corridors. **Pets:** Accepted.

﹠ ✕

▲▲▲ ▼▼▼ Ocean Villa Inn M 🐾
(619) 224-3481. **$89-$189.** 5142 W Point Loma Blvd. I-8, exit Sunset Cliff Blvd, 1.5 mi sw. Ext corridors. **Pets:** Medium, other species. $100 deposit/room, $25 one-time fee/room. Designated rooms, service with restrictions, supervision.

SAVE ﹠ ✕ 🛏 💻 ⇌

▲▲▲ ▼▼▼ Old Town Inn M
(619) 260-8024. **$60-$140.** 4444 Pacific Hwy. I-5, exit SeaWorld Dr, just w, then 1 mi s. Ext corridors. **Pets:** $10 daily fee/pet. Service with restrictions, supervision.

SAVE ﹠ ✕ ﹠M ⟨ ⬚ 🛏 💻 ⇌

▲▲▲ ▼▼▼ Pacific Shores Inn M
(858) 483-6300. **$59-$159, 3 day notice.** 4802 Mission Blvd. I-5, exit Garnet Ave, 2.5 mi w, then 0.3 mi n. Ext corridors. **Pets:** Small, dogs only. $25 one-time fee/room. Designated rooms, service with restrictions, crate.

SAVE ﹠ ✕ 🛏 💻 ⇌

▲▲▲ ▼▼▼ Premier Inn M
(619) 291-8252. **$49-$129.** 2484 Hotel Circle Pl. I-8, exit Taylor St, just n. Ext corridors. **Pets:** Medium. $20 deposit/pet. Service with restrictions, supervision.

SAVE ﹠ ✕ 🛏 ⇌

▲▲▲ ▼▼ Premier Inn M
(619) 223-9500. **$55-$170.** 3333 Channel Way. I-5/8, exit Rosecrans St, 0.5 mi s, 1 mi nw on Sports Arena Blvd, then just e. Ext corridors. **Pets:** Accepted.

SAVE ﹠ ✕ ﹠M 🛏 💻 ⇌

▼▼▼▼ Red Lion Hanalei Hotel LH
(619) 297-1101. **$95-$134.** 2270 Hotel Cir S. I-8, exit Tayor St, just n, then just e. Ext corridors. **Pets:** Medium, other species. $75 deposit/pet. Designated rooms, service with restrictions, supervision.

✕ ﹠M ⟨ ⬚ 💻 ⇌ ✕

▼▼▼▼ Residence Inn by Marriott San Diego
        Downtown SH ❀
(619) 338-8200. **$119-$229.** 1747 Pacific Hwy. I-5, exit Front St southbound, just s to Grape St, 0.3 mi w, then just n; exit Hawthorn St northbound, 0.4 mi w, then just s. Int corridors. **Pets:** Medium, other species. $75 one-time fee/room. Service with restrictions.

ASK ﹠ ✕ 🛏 💻 ⇌

▲▲▲ ▼▼▼▼ Residence Inn San Diego/Mission Valley/
        SeaWorld Area SH ❀
(619) 881-3600. **$139-$359, 3 day notice.** 1865 Hotel Cir S. I-8, exit Hotel Cir, south side. Int corridors. **Pets:** Medium, other species. $75 one-time fee/room. Service with restrictions.

SAVE ﹠ ✕ ﹠M ⟨ ⬚ 🛏 💻 ⇌ ✕

▼▼▼ **Residence Inn San Diego Ranch Bernardo/Scripps Poway** SH
(858) 635-5724. **$109-$189.** 12011 Scripps Highland Dr. I-805, exit Mercy Rd/Scripps Poway Pkwy, just e, then just n. Int corridors. **Pets:** Accepted.
ASK 🏠 ✕ ♿ 🅿 🐾 💻 🐕 ➾ ✕

▼▼▼ **Residence Inn San Diego-Sorrento Mesa** SH
(858) 552-9100. **$159-$259.** 5995 Pacific Mesa Ct. I-805, exit Mira Mesa Blvd, 1.5 mi e. Int corridors. **Pets:** Other species. $75 one-time fee/room. Service with restrictions, supervision.
🏠 ✕ 🅿 💻 ➾ ✕

▼▼▼ **San Diego Marriott Hotel & Marina** LH
(619) 234-1500. **$405-$425.** 333 W Harbor Dr. I-5, exit Front St, 1.3 mi s, then just w. Int corridors. **Pets:** Other species. $75 deposit/room. Service with restrictions.
ASK ✕ 🅿 💻 🍴 ➾ ✕

▼▼▼ **San Diego Marriott Mission Valley** LH
(619) 692-3800. **Call for rates.** 8757 Rio San Diego Dr. I-8, exit Qualcomm Way, just n. Int corridors. **Pets:** Small. $75 one-time fee/room. Designated rooms, service with restrictions, supervision.
✕ 💻 🍴 ➾ ✕

▼▼▼ **Shelter Pointe Hotel & Marina** SH
(619) 221-8000. **$139-$219.** 1551 Shelter Island Dr. I-5, exit Rosecrans St southbound, 3 mi sw; exit Hawthorn St northbound, 3 mi nw on Harbor Dr to Scott Rd, then 0.5 mi w. Ext/int corridors. **Pets:** Small. $100 one-time fee/room. Service with restrictions, supervision.
ASK 🏠 ✕ 🅿 💻 🍴 ➾ ✕

▼▼▼ **Sheraton San Diego Hotel and Marina** LH 🐾
(619) 291-2900. **$169, 3 day notice.** 1380 Harbor Island Dr. I-5, exit Hawthorn St northbound, just e to Harbor Dr, 1.5 mi w, then just s; exit Kettern/Hancock southbound, just s to Laurel St, just w to Harbor Dr, 1.5 mi w, then just s. Ext/int corridors. **Pets:** Medium, dogs only. Service with restrictions, supervision.
ASK 🏠 ✕ 💻 🍴 ➾ ✕

AAA ▼▼▼ **Sheraton San Diego Hotel Mission Valley** LH 🐾
(619) 260-0111. **$209-$219.** 1433 Camino del Rio S. I-8, exit Mission Center Rd, south side. Int corridors. **Pets:** Dogs only. $50 one-time fee/room. Service with restrictions, supervision.
SAVE 🏠 ✕ 🅿 💻 🍴 ➾

AAA ▼▼▼ **Sheraton Suites San Diego** LH ❀
(619) 696-9800. **$369.** 701 A St/7th Ave. I-5, exit Front St, 0.5 mi s. Int corridors. **Pets:** Other species. Service with restrictions, supervision.
SAVE 🏠 ✕ ♿ 🅿 🐾 💻 🍴 ➾

▼▼▼ **Sommerset Suites Hotel** SH
(619) 692-5200. **$79-$279.** 606 Washington St. SR 163, just w. Ext/int corridors. **Pets:** Medium, other species. $35 one-time fee/room. Service with restrictions, crate.
ASK 🏠 ✕ ➾

▼▼▼ **Staybridge Suites by Holiday Inn-Sorrento Mesa** SH
(858) 453-5343. **$129-$199.** 6639 Mira Mesa Blvd. I-805, exit Mira Mesa Blvd, 2.3 mi e. Int corridors. **Pets:** Accepted.
ASK 🏠 ✕ ♿ 🐾 🐕 🅿 💻 ➾

▼▼▼ **Staybridge Suites Riviera-San Diego Downtown** SH
(619) 795-4000. **$169-$229.** 1110 A St. SR 163, exit Ash St, just e. Int corridors. **Pets:** Accepted.
ASK ✕ ♿ 🐾 🐕 🅿 💻

AAA ▼ **Vagabond Inn-Point Loma** M
(619) 224-3371. **$64-$164.** 1325 Scott St. I-8, exit Nimintz Blvd, 2 mi s to Rosecrans St, just w to Jarvis St, then just s; in Point Loma area. Ext corridors. **Pets:** Medium. $10 daily fee/pet. Service with restrictions, supervision.
SAVE 🏠 ✕ 🅿 💻 ➾

▼▼▼ **The Westin Horton Plaza** LH
(619) 239-2200. **$209-$409.** 910 Broadway Cir. I-5, exit Front St southbound, 0.9 mi s to Broadway, just e, then just s; exit 6th Ave northbound, 0.6 mi s, just w, then just s. Int corridors. **Pets:** Accepted.
ASK 🏠 ✕ ♿ 🐾 🐕 🅿 💻 🍴 ➾ ✕

SAN FRANCISCO METROPOLITAN AREA

BELMONT

▼▼▼ **Summerfield Suites by Wyndham-Belmont/Redwood Shores** M
(650) 591-8600. **$79-$129.** 400 Concourse Dr. US 101, exit Marine World Pkwy, just e, then just n on Oracle Pkwy. Ext corridors. **Pets:** Medium, other species. $200 one-time fee/room. Service with restrictions, crate.
ASK ✕ ♿ 🐕 💻 ➾

BRISBANE

▼▼▼ **Homewood Suites** SH
(650) 589-1600. **$119-$189.** 2000 Shoreline Ct. US 101, exit Sierra Point Pkwy, just e. Int corridors. **Pets:** Accepted.
ASK 🏠 ✕ ♿ 🐾 🐕 🅿 💻 ➾

BURLINGAME

AAA ▼▼▼ **Crowne Plaza** LH ❀
(650) 342-9200. **$79-$150.** 1177 Airport Blvd. US 101, exit Broadway-Burlingame or Old Bayshore, just e. Int corridors. **Pets:** Other species. $100 deposit/room. Service with restrictions, supervision.
SAVE 🏠 ✕ ♿ 🐕 🅿 💻 🍴 ➾

AAA ▼▼▼ **Doubletree Hotel-San Francisco Airport** LH ❀
(650) 344-5500. **$79-$179.** 835 Airport Blvd. US 101, exit Broadway-Burlingame or Anza Blvd, just e. Int corridors. **Pets:** Medium, other species. $20 one-time fee/room. Designated rooms, service with restrictions.
SAVE ✕ ♿ 🐾 🐕 🅿 💻 🍴

Embassy Suites-SFO Burlingame 🏨
(650) 342-4600. **$134-$194.** 150 Anza Blvd. US 101, exit Broadway-Burlingame or Anza Blvd, just e. Int corridors. **Pets:** Small, other species. $50 deposit/room. Service with restrictions, supervision.

Red Roof Inn Ⓜ 🐾
(650) 342-7772. **$54-$64.** 777 Airport Blvd. US 101, exit Broadway-Burlingame or E Anza Blvd; just s of airport. Ext corridors. **Pets:** Other species. Service with restrictions, crate.

San Francisco Airport Marriott 🏨
(650) 692-9100. **$99-$219.** 1800 Old Bayshore Hwy. US 101, exit Millbrae Ave, just e. Int corridors. **Pets:** Medium. $75 one-time fee/room. Service with restrictions.

Sheraton Gateway Hotel-San Francisco International Airport 🏨 🐾
(650) 340-8500. **$189.** 600 Airport Blvd. US 101, exit Broadway-Burlingame or Anza Blvd, 0.3 mi e. **Pets:** Small, dogs only. Designated rooms, service with restrictions, supervision.

Vagabond Inn-SFO Ⓜ
(650) 692-4040. **$69-$99.** 1640 Bayshore Hwy. US 101, exit Millbrae Ave, just e. Ext corridors. **Pets:** Large. $10 daily fee/pet. Designated rooms, service with restrictions, supervision.

CORTE MADERA

Marin Suites Hotel Ⓜ
(415) 924-3608. **$154-$204.** 45 Tamal Vista Blvd. US 101, exit Tamalpais Rd/Paradise Dr. Ext corridors. **Pets:** Other species. $10 daily fee/pet. Designated rooms, service with restrictions, supervision.

HALF MOON BAY

Harbor View Inn Ⓜ
(650) 726-2329. **$86-$186.** 51 Ave Alhambra. 4 mi n of jct SR 92 and 1; e of SR 1. Ext corridors. **Pets:** Accepted.

Holiday Inn Express Ⓜ
(650) 726-3400. **$99-$149.** 230 S Cabrillo Hwy. On SR 1, just s of SR 92. Ext corridors. **Pets:** Large, other species. $10 daily fee/pet. Designated rooms, service with restrictions, supervision.

Miramar Lodge & Conference Center Ⓜ
(650) 712-1999. **$79-$159.** 2930 N Cabrillo Hwy. On SR 1. Ext corridors. **Pets:** Large. $20 daily fee/pet. Service with restrictions, supervision.

Ramada Limited Ⓜ
(650) 726-9700. **Call for rates.** 3020 N Cabrillo Hwy. 2 mi n of jct SR 92 and 1, w of SR 1. Ext corridors. **Pets:** Accepted.

The Ritz-Carlton, Half Moon Bay 🏨
(650) 712-7000. **$295-$395, 7 day notice.** 1 Miramontes Point Rd. 3 mi s of jct SR 92 and 1, w of SR 1 at Miramontes Point Rd. Ext/int corridors. **Pets:** Accepted.

MILLBRAE

Clarion Hotel-San Francisco Airport 🏨
(650) 692-6363. **$79-$99.** 401 E Millbrae Ave. US 101, exit Millbrae Ave, just e. Int corridors. **Pets:** Accepted.

The Westin Hotel-San Francisco Airport 🏨 🐾
(650) 692-3500. **$189.** 1 Old Bayshore Hwy. Just e of US 101, exit Millbrae Ave. Int corridors. **Pets:** Medium, dogs only. Service with restrictions, supervision.

SAN BRUNO

Regency Inn Ⓜ
(650) 589-7535. **$69-$75.** 411 E San Bruno Ave. US 101, exit San Bruno Ave, 0.4 mi w. Ext corridors. **Pets:** Other species. $15 daily fee/pet. Designated rooms, service with restrictions, supervision.

Staybridge Suites Ⓜ
(650) 588-0770. **$89-$159.** 1350 Huntington Ave. I-380, exit El Camino Real N, e on Sneath Ln. Ext corridors. **Pets:** $50 one-time fee/room.

SAN CARLOS

Homestead Studio Suites Hotel-San Carlos/Redwood Shores Ⓜ
(650) 368-2600. **$94-$109.** 3 Circle Star Way. US 101, exit Whipple Ave, w to Industrial, then just n. Int corridors. **Pets:** Medium. $75 one-time fee/pet. Service with restrictions.

SAN FRANCISCO

Argonaut Hotel 🏨 🐾
(415) 563-0800. **$129-$269.** 495 Jefferson St. Fisherman's Wharf; adjacent The Cannery. Int corridors. **Pets:** Designated rooms, service with restrictions, supervision.

Beresford Arms 🅂🄷
(415) 673-2600. **$92-$109.** 701 Post St. 3 blks w of Union Square. Int corridors. **Pets:** Accepted.

Best Western Civic Center Motor Inn Ⓜ
(415) 621-2826. **$89-$149.** 364 9th St. Just n off freeway; exit civic center, at Harrison St. Ext corridors. **Pets:** Accepted.

Best Western Tuscan Inn at Fisherman's Wharf 🅂🄷 🐾
(415) 561-1100. **$139-$249.** 425 Northpoint St. Just s of Fisherman's Wharf at Mason St. Int corridors. **Pets:** Other species. Service with restrictions, crate.

Campton Place Hotel 🅂🄷 🐾
(415) 781-5555. **$335-$470.** 340 Stockton St. Just n of Union Square. Int corridors. **Pets:** Medium. $35 daily fee/room. Service with restrictions.

Cartwright Hotel 🅂🄷 🐾
(415) 421-2865. **$119-$219.** 524 Sutter St. Union Square at Powell St. Int corridors. **Pets:** Medium, other species. Service with restrictions, supervision.

Clarion Hotel Cosmo 🅂🄷
(415) 673-6040. **$89-$159.** 761 Post St. 3 1/2 blks w of Union Square. Int corridors. **Pets:** Accepted.

Crowne Plaza Union Square 🏨
(415) 398-8900. **$119-$299.** 480 Sutter St. Just n off Union Square; corner of Powell St. Int corridors. **Pets:** Small. $100 deposit/room. Service with restrictions, supervision.

▼▼▼▼ **Diva Hotel** SH
(415) 885-0200. **$130.** 440 Geary St. Just w of Union Square. Int corridors. **Pets:** Medium, other species. $50 one-time fee/room. Service with restrictions, supervision.
[ASK] [S⌀] [✕] [▯]

AAA ▼▼▼▼ **Executive Hotel Vintage Court** SH
(415) 392-4666. **$139-$199.** 650 Bush St. 2 blks n of Union Square. Int corridors. **Pets:** Accepted.
[SAVE] [S⌀] [✕] [&M]

▼▼▼ ▼▼▼ **The Fairmont San Francisco** LH
(415) 772-5000. **$189-$379.** 950 Mason St. Atop Nob Hill at California St. Int corridors. **Pets:** Accepted.
[ASK] [✕] [&M] [⌀] [⌀] [▯]

▼▼▼ ▼▼▼ **Four Seasons San Francisco** LH
(415) 633-3000. **$469-$600.** 757 Market St. Between 3rd and 4th sts. Int corridors. **Pets:** Accepted.
[ASK] [✕] [&M] [⌀] [▯] [⇌] [✕]

AAA ▼▼▼ **Harbor Court Hotel** SH 🐾
(415) 882-1300. **$189-$249.** 165 Steuart St. On Embarcadero; between Howard and Mission sts. Int corridors. **Pets:** Service with restrictions, crate.
[SAVE] [S⌀] [✕] [&M] [▯] [⇌]

AAA ▼▼▼ **Holiday Inn Civic Center** LH
(415) 626-6103. **$85-$199.** 50 8th St. 2 blks from civic auditorium; just s of Market St and BART Station. Int corridors. **Pets:** Accepted.
[SAVE] [✕] [&M] [⌀] [⌀] [⬛] [▭] [▯] [⇌]

AAA ▼▼▼ **Holiday Inn Select & Spa Downtown** LH
(415) 433-6600. **$259.** 750 Kearny St. Adjacent to North Beach. Int corridors. **Pets:** Dogs only. $100 deposit/room. Service with restrictions, crate.
[SAVE] [✕] [&M] [⌀] [⌀] [⬛] [▭] [▯] [⇌]

▼▼ ▼▼ **Hotel Beresford** SH
(415) 673-9900. **$92-$104.** 635 Sutter St. 1 blk nw of Union Square at Mason St. Int corridors. **Pets:** Accepted.
[ASK] [S⌀] [✕] [&M] [▯] [✕]

▼▼ ▼▼ **Hotel Metropolis** SH
(415) 775-4600. **$95.** 25 Mason St. US 101 (Van Ness Ave), exit Market St, just w. Int corridors. **Pets:** Accepted.
[ASK] [S⌀] [✕] [⬛] [✕]

AAA ▼▼▼ ▼▼▼ **Hotel Monaco** LH 🐾
(415) 292-0100. **$179-$399.** 501 Geary St. Just w of Union Square at Taylor St. Int corridors. **Pets:** Other species. Designated rooms, service with restrictions, supervision.
[SAVE] [S⌀] [✕] [&M] [⌀] [▭] [▯] [✕]

AAA ▼▼▼ ▼▼▼ **Hotel Nikko San Francisco** LH
(415) 394-1111. **$185.** 222 Mason St. 3 blks w of Union Square. Int corridors. **Pets:** Accepted.
[SAVE] [S⌀] [✕] [&M] [⌀] [▭] [▯] [⇌] [✕]

AAA ▼▼▼ ▼▼▼ **Hotel Palomar** SH 🐾
(415) 348-1111. **$179-$369.** 12 Fourth St. At Market St; downtown. Int corridors. **Pets:** Other species. Designated rooms, service with restrictions, crate.
[SAVE] [S⌀] [✕] [&M] [⌀] [⬛] [▯]

AAA ▼▼▼ ▼▼▼ **Hotel Triton** SH 🐾
(415) 394-0500. **$129-$199.** 342 Grant Ave. Near Union Square at Bush St. Int corridors. **Pets:** Dogs only. Designated rooms, service with restrictions, crate.
[SAVE] [S⌀] [✕] [&M] [▭]

▼▼▼ **Hotel Union Square** SH
(415) 397-3000. **$105.** 114 Powell St. US 101, exit Market E to Powell St, just n of cable car turnaround. Int corridors. **Pets:** Accepted.
[ASK] [S⌀] [✕] [✕]

▼▼▼ ▼▼ **Kensington Park Hotel** SH 🐾
(415) 788-6400. **$125.** 450 Post St. US 101 (Van Ness Ave), exit 5th St, right to Ellis St, right on Taylor St. Int corridors. **Pets:** Medium, other species. $50 one-time fee/room. Designated rooms, service with restrictions, crate.
[ASK] [S⌀] [✕] [⬛] [▯] [✕]

▼▼▼ ▼▼▼ **La Quinta Inn & Suites** SH
(415) 673-4711. **$79-$119.** 1050 Van Ness Ave. On US 101 (Van Ness Ave). Int corridors. **Pets:** Accepted.
[ASK] [S⌀] [✕] [▭]

AAA ▼▼▼ ▼▼▼ **The Laurel Inn** M 🐾
(415) 567-8467. **$175.** 444 Presidio Ave. 1 mi w of US 101 (Van Ness Ave), 1 mi e of Park Presidio Blvd (SR 1) at California St. Int corridors. **Pets:** Service with restrictions, supervision.
[SAVE] [✕] [&M] [⌀] [⬛] [▭] [✕]

▼▼▼ ▼▼▼ **Mandarin Oriental, San Francisco** LH 🐾
(415) 276-9888. **$495-$775.** 222 Sansome St. US 101, s on Lombard St, e on Bush, then s. Int corridors. **Pets:** Small, dogs only. $29 daily fee/pet. Service with restrictions, supervision.
[ASK] [S⌀] [✕] [⌀] [▭] [▯] [✕]

AAA ▼▼▼ ▼▼▼ **Monticello Inn** SH 🐾
(415) 392-8800. **$129-$199.** 127 Ellis St. Just w of Union Square. Int corridors. **Pets:** $200 deposit/room. Designated rooms, service with restrictions, supervision.
[SAVE] [S⌀] [✕] [▭] [▯]

▼▼▼ ▼▼▼ **Omni San Francisco Hotel** LH 🐾
(415) 677-9494. **$329-$379.** 500 California St. At Montgomery St; downtown financial district. Int corridors. **Pets:** Small. $50 one-time fee/room. Service with restrictions, crate.
[ASK] [S⌀] [✕] [▭]

AAA ▼▼▼ ▼▼ **Pacific Heights Inn** M
(415) 776-3310. **$79-$150.** 1555 Union St. Just w of US 101 (Van Ness Ave). Ext corridors. **Pets:** Accepted.
[SAVE] [S⌀] [✕] [&M] [⌀] [⬛] [▭] [✕]

▼▼▼ ▼▼▼ **Palace Hotel** LH
(415) 512-1111. **$199-$539.** 2 New Montgomery St. Just e of Union Square at Market St. Int corridors. **Pets:** Accepted.
[ASK] [S⌀] [✕] [&M] [⌀] [⌀] [▯] [⇌] [✕]

AAA ▼▼▼ ▼▼▼ **Pan Pacific Hotel San Francisco** LH
(415) 771-8600. **$360-$670.** 500 Post St. Just w of Union Square at Mason St. Int corridors. **Pets:** Accepted.
[SAVE] [S⌀] [✕] [&M] [⌀] [▯]

AAA ▼▼▼ ▼▼▼ **The Prescott Hotel** SH 🐾
(415) 563-0303. **$139-$1200.** 545 Post St. Just w of Union Square. Int corridors. **Pets:** Small. Designated rooms, service with restrictions, supervision.
[SAVE] [S⌀] [✕] [▯]

AAA ▼▼▼ **San Francisco Marriott Fisherman's Wharf** LH 🐾
(415) 775-7555. **$109-$219.** 1250 Columbus Ave. Just s of Fisherman's Wharf at Bay St. Int corridors. **Pets:** Large. $100 one-time fee/room. Service with restrictions, crate.
[SAVE] [S⌀] [✕] [&M] [⌀] [⌀] [⬛] [▭] [▯]

AAA ▼▼▼ ▼▼▼ **Serrano Hotel** SH 🐾
(415) 885-2500. **$139-$239.** 405 Taylor St. Just w of Union Square. Int corridors. **Pets:** Other species. Service with restrictions, supervision.
[SAVE] [✕] [&M] [⌀] [▯] [✕]

⚑ ▽▽ ▽▽ Sheraton Fisherman's Wharf LH ❀
(415) 362-5500. **$139-$279.** 2500 Mason St. Just se of Fisherman's Wharf at Beach St. Int corridors. **Pets:** Large, dogs only. Service with restrictions, supervision.
[SAVE] [S🐾] [✕] [🕭M] [🐾] [🛅] [📁] [💻] [🍴] [🏊]

⚑ ▽▽▽ Sir Francis Drake Hotel LH
(415) 392-7755. **$129-$239.** 450 Powell St. Just off Union Square at Sutter St. Int corridors. **Pets:** Accepted.
[SAVE] [S🐾] [✕] [🛅] [📁] [🍴]

⚑ ▽▽ Travelodge By The Bay M ❀
(415) 673-0691. **$71-$109.** 1450 Lombard St. On US 101 (Van Ness Ave). Ext corridors. **Pets:** Small. $20 daily fee/pet. Designated rooms, service with restrictions, crate.
[SAVE] [✕] [🕭M] [🐾] [💻]

⚑ ▽▽ ▽▽ Villa Florence Hotel SH
(415) 397-7700. **$139-$209.** 225 Powell St. Just s of Union Square. Int corridors. **Pets:** Accepted.
[SAVE] [S🐾] [✕] [🐾] [🛅] [💻] [🍴]

⚑ ▽▽▽ ▽▽▽ The Westin St. Francis LH ❀
(415) 397-7000. **$129-$599.** 335 Powell St. On Union Square. **Pets:** Small, dogs only. $75 one-time fee/room. Supervision.
[SAVE] [S🐾] [✕] [🐾] [💻] [🍴] [🏊]

SAN MATEO

▽▽ ▽▽ Homestead Studio Suites Hotel-San Mateo/SFO M
(650) 574-1744. **$79-$94.** 1830 Gateway Dr. SR 92, exit Edgewater Blvd, se of jct US 101 and SR 92. Ext corridors. **Pets:** Small. $75 one-time fee/pet. Service with restrictions.
[ASK] [S🐾] [✕] [🕭M] [🐾] [🛅] [💻]

⚑ ▽▽▽ ▽▽▽ Radisson Villa Hotel SH
(650) 341-0966. **$129-$289.** 4000 S El Camino Real. 8 mi s of San Francisco International Airport; US 101, exit W Hillsdale Blvd, 0.5 mi s on SR 82. Ext/int corridors. **Pets:** Accepted.
[SAVE] [S🐾] [✕] [🕭M] [🐾] [🛅] [💻] [🍴] [🏊]

▽▽▽ ▽▽▽ Residence Inn by Marriott M
(650) 574-4700. **Call for rates.** 2000 Winward Way. 0.8 mi se from jct US 101 and SR 92; exit SR 92 via Edgewater Blvd. Ext corridors. **Pets:** Accepted.
[S🐾] [✕] [🕭M] [🐾] [🛅] [💻] [🏊] [✕🐾]

SAN RAFAEL

▽▽ ◆ Villa Inn M
(415) 456-4975. **$75-$95.** 1600 Lincoln Ave. Off US 101 at Lincoln Ave off-ramp; exit Central San Rafael northbound, 0.3 mi w on Fourth St, then 0.5 mi n. Ext corridors. **Pets:** Medium, dogs only. $20 deposit/room. Designated rooms, service with restrictions, supervision.
[✕] [🕭M] [🐾] [🛅] [💻] [🏊]

SOUTH SAN FRANCISCO

⚑ ▽▽ ◆ Howard Johnson Express Inn M
(650) 589-9055. **$49-$159.** 222 S Airport Blvd. US 101, exit S Airport Blvd, just e. Ext corridors. **Pets:** Accepted.
[SAVE] [S🐾] [✕] [🕭M] [🛅] [💻]

⚑ ▽▽▽ ▽▽▽ La Quinta Inn San Francisco (Airport) M ❀
(650) 583-2223. **$109-$129.** 20 S Airport Blvd. US 101, exit S Airport Blvd, just w. Int corridors. **Pets:** Large, other species. Service with restrictions, crate.
[SAVE] [✕] [🕭M] [🐾] [🛅] [💻] [🏊]

END METROPOLITAN AREA

SAN JOSE

⚑ ▽▽▽ ▽▽▽ Best Western Gateway Inn SH
(408) 435-8800. **$99-$109.** 2585 Seaboard Ave. US 101, exit Trimble Rd E; 1 mi ne of San Jose International Airport. Int corridors. **Pets:** Small. $100 deposit/pet. Service with restrictions, supervision.
[SAVE] [S🐾] [✕] [🛅] [💻] [🏊]

▽▽▽ ▽▽▽ Comfort Inn SH
(408) 287-9380. **$69-$109.** 875 N 13th St. US 101, exit 13th St/Old Oakland Rd, just w. Int corridors. **Pets:** Accepted.
[ASK] [S🐾] [✕] [🛅] [🍴]

⚑ ▽▽▽ ▽▽▽ Doubletree Hotel San Jose LH ❀
(408) 453-4000. **$89-$229.** 2050 Gateway Pl. 0.3 mi e of San Jose International Airport via Airport Blvd; w of US 101, exit N 1st St; US 101 northbound, exit Brokaw Rd. Int corridors. **Pets:** Medium, other species. $50 deposit/pet. Service with restrictions, supervision.
[SAVE] [✕] [🛅] [💻] [🍴] [🏊]

▽▽▽ ▽▽▽ The Fairmont San Jose LH ❀
(408) 998-1900. **$119-$250.** 170 S Market St. At Fairmont Plaza. Int corridors. **Pets:** Small. $25 daily fee/room. Supervision.
[✕] [🍴] [🏊] [✕🐾]

⚑ ▽▽▽ ▽▽▽ Hilton San Jose & Towers LH
(408) 287-2100. **$89-$269.** 300 Almaden Blvd. Downtown. Int corridors. **Pets:** Accepted.
[SAVE] [S🐾] [✕] [🕭M] [🛅] [💻] [🍴] [🏊]

▽▽ ▽▽ Homestead Studio Suites Hotel-San Jose SH
(408) 573-0648. **$84-$99.** 1560 N 1st St. 1 mi e of San Jose International Airport; US 101, exit N 1st St, then s. Int corridors. **Pets:** Accepted.
[ASK] [S🐾] [✕] [💻]

▽▽▽ ▽▽▽ Homewood Suites by Hilton M
(408) 428-9900. **$149-$179.** 10 W Trimble Rd. 2 mi ne of San Jose International Airport; US 101, exit Trimble Rd, 1.3 mi e. Ext/int corridors. **Pets:** Small, dogs only. $50 one-time fee/room. Designated rooms, service with restrictions, crate.
[ASK] [✕] [🕭M] [🐾] [💻] [🏊] [✕🐾]

⚑ ▽▽▽ ▽▽▽ Hotel De Anza LH
(408) 286-1000. **$109-$399.** 233 W Santa Clara St. Downtown. Int corridors. **Pets:** Small. $30 one-time fee/pet. Service with restrictions, supervision.
[SAVE] [✕] [💻] [🍴]

⚑ ▽▽▽ ▽▽▽ Howard Johnson M
(408) 280-5300. **$79-$169.** 1215 S 1st St. Jct I-280 and SR 82, 0.8 mi s. Ext corridors. **Pets:** Accepted.
[SAVE] [S🐾] [✕] [🛅] [💻]

▽▽▽ ▽▽▽ Sierra Suites SH
(408) 453-3000. **$79-$199.** 55 E Brokaw Rd. US 101, exit First St/Brokaw Rd, just e. Int corridors. **Pets:** Medium, other species. $5 daily fee/pet, $100 one-time fee/pet. Service with restrictions, crate.
[ASK] [S🐾] [✕] [🐾] [💻] [🏊]

⚑ ▽▽▽ ▽▽▽ Staybridge Suites by Holiday Inn M
(408) 436-1600. **$62-$125.** 1602 Crane Ct. US 101, exit Brokaw Rd E, 0.4 mi to Bering S, then 0.5 mi. Ext corridors. **Pets:** Accepted.
[SAVE] [S🐾] [✕] [🛅] [💻] [🏊]

▽▽▽ ▽▽▽ TownePlace Suites by Marriott San Jose/Cupertino SH
(408) 984-5903. **Call for rates.** 440 Saratoga Ave. I-280, exit Saratoga Ave, just n. Int corridors. **Pets:** Accepted.
[✕] [💻] [🏊]

Vagabond Inn San Jose M ☙
(408) 453-8822. **$69-$99.** 1488 N 1st St. I-880, exit N 1st St, then w. Ext corridors. **Pets:** Large, other species. $10 daily fee/pet. Service with restrictions, supervision.
[SAVE] [S&] [✕] [🛢] [▭] [⤳]

SAN JUAN BAUTISTA

San Juan Inn M
(831) 623-4380. **$79-$99.** 410 The Alameda. Jct SR 156. Ext corridors. **Pets:** Other species. $15 daily fee/pet.
[SAVE] [S&] [✕] [🛢] [▭] [⤳]

SAN JUAN CAPISTRANO

Best Western Capistrano Inn M
(949) 493-5661. **$79-$179, 3 day notice.** 27174 Ortega Hwy. I-5, exit SR 74 (Ortega Hwy), just e. Ext corridors. **Pets:** Other species. $25 one-time fee/room. Service with restrictions.
[SAVE] [S&] [✕] [🛢] [▭] [⤳]

SAN LUIS OBISPO

Best Western Royal Oak Hotel M
(805) 544-4410. **$79-$150.** 214 Madonna Rd. US 101, exit Madonna Rd, just s. Ext/int corridors. **Pets:** Medium. $10 one-time fee/pet. Service with restrictions, supervision.
[SAVE] [S&] [✕] [&M] [🖊] [&] [🛢] [▭] [⤳]

Days Inn M
(805) 549-9911. **$59-$199.** 2050 Garfield St. US 101, exit Monterey St, just sw. Ext corridors. **Pets:** Medium, dogs only. $10 daily fee/pet. Designated rooms, service with restrictions, supervision.
[SAVE] [S&] [✕] [&M] [🖊] [&] [🛢] [▭] [⤳]

Heritage Inn Bed & Breakfast BB ☙
(805) 544-7440. **$85-$200, 7 day notice.** 978 Olive St. US 101, exit SR 1/Morro Bay northbound, just w on Santa Rosa St, then just s; exit Santa Rosa St southbound, just ne. Int corridors. **Pets:** Medium, other species. $100 deposit/room, $25 one-time fee/pet. No service, supervision.
[ASK] [S&] [✕] [K] [W] [☎]

Holiday Inn Express SH
(805) 544-8600. **$99-$229.** 1800 Monterey St. US 101, exit Monterey St, just w. Int corridors. **Pets:** Medium, dogs only. $25 one-time fee/room. Service with restrictions, supervision.
[ASK] [S&] [✕] [🛢] [▭] [🍴] [⤳]

Ramada Inn Olive Tree M
(805) 544-2800. **$79-$249.** 1000 Olive St. US 101, exit Morro Bay northbound, just w on Santa Rosa St, then just s; exit Santa Rosa St southbound, just ne. Ext corridors. **Pets:** Accepted.
[SAVE] [S&] [✕] [&M] [🖊] [🛢] [▭] [⤳]

Sands Suites & Motel M
(805) 544-0500. **$59-$219.** 1930 Monterey St. US 101, exit Monterey St, just sw. Ext corridors. **Pets:** Other species. $10 one-time fee/pet. Service with restrictions, supervision.
[SAVE] [S&] [✕] [🛢] [▭] [⤳]

San Luis Creek Lodge SH ☙
(805) 541-1122. **$109-$249.** 1941 Monterey St. US 101, exit Monterey St, just e. Ext/int corridors. **Pets:** Medium. $25 one-time fee/pet. Supervision.
[ASK] [S&] [✕] [🛢] [▭]

Super 8 Motel M
(805) 544-6888. **$49-$119.** 1951 Monterey St. US 101, exit Monterey St, just e. Ext corridors. **Pets:** Medium, dogs only. $10 daily fee/pet. Designated rooms, service with restrictions, supervision.
[SAVE] [S&] [✕] [&M] [🖊] [🛢] [▭] [⤳]

SAN MARCOS

Lake San Marcos Resort SH
(760) 744-0120. **$139-$179.** 1025 La Bonita Dr. SR 78, exit Rancho Santa Fe Rd, 2 mi s, 0.5 mi e via Lake San Marcos Dr and San Marino Dr; at Lake San Marcos. Ext/int corridors. **Pets:** Medium. $10 daily fee/pet. Service with restrictions, supervision.
[ASK] [S&] [✕] [🛢] [▭] [🍴] [⤳] [⤨]

SAN RAMON

Homestead Studio Suites Hotel-San Ramon M
(925) 277-0833. **$94-$109.** 18000 San Ramon Valley Blvd. I-680, exit Bollinger Canyon Rd E, just n. Ext corridors. **Pets:** Accepted.
[ASK] [S&] [✕] [&] [🛢] [▭]

Residence Inn by Marriott M
(925) 277-9292. **$89-$209.** 1071 Market Pl. I-680, exit Bollinger Canyon Rd E, 0.5 mi e. Ext corridors. **Pets:** $75 one-time fee/room. Supervision.
[ASK] [✕] [&] [▭] [⤳] [⤨]

San Ramon Marriott at Bishop Ranch LH
(925) 867-9200. **$79-$209.** 2600 Bishop Dr. I-680, exit Bollinger Canyon E, n on Sunset, then just w. Int corridors. **Pets:** Accepted.
[ASK] [✕] [🛢] [▭] [🍴] [⤳] [⤨]

SAN SIMEON

Motel 6 Premiere–1212 SH
(805) 927-8691. **$45-$67.** 9070 Castillo Dr. Just e of SR 1. Int corridors. **Pets:** Accepted.
[S&] [✕] [🛢] [🍴] [⤳]

Silver Surf Motel M ☙
(805) 927-4661. **$39-$186.** 9390 Castillo Dr. Just e of SR 1. Ext corridors. **Pets:** $10 daily fee/pet. Designated rooms, service with restrictions, supervision.
[SAVE] [S&] [✕] [🛢] [▭] [⤳] [K]

SANTA ANA

Motel 6 #738 M
(714) 558-0500. **$45-$61.** 1623 E 1st St. I-5, exit 4th St, just s on Mabury St, then just w. Ext corridors. **Pets:** Other species. Service with restrictions, supervision.
[S&] [✕] [🛢]

Quality Suites-Orange County Airport M
(714) 957-9200. **$10-$119.** 2701 Hotel Terrace Dr. SR 55, exit Dyer Rd W, just w. Ext corridors. **Pets:** Accepted.
[SAVE] [S&] [✕] [🛢] [▭] [⤳]

Red Roof Inn M
(714) 542-0311. **$60-$70.** 2600 N Main St. I-5, exit Main St, 0.3 mi n. Ext/int corridors. **Pets:** Medium, other species. Designated rooms, service with restrictions, supervision.
[ASK] [S&] [✕] [⤳]

SANTA BARBARA

Best Western Beachside Inn M
(805) 965-6556. **$145-$289.** 336 W Cabrillo Blvd. US 101, exit Bath St northbound, just w on Haley St to Castillo St, then 0.4 mi s; exit Castillo St southbound, 0.3 mi s. Ext corridors. **Pets:** Large, other species. $20 daily fee/pet. Service with restrictions, supervision.
[SAVE] [S&] [✕] [🛢] [▭] [⤳]

Blue Sands Motel M
(805) 965-1624. **$85-$209, 3 day notice.** 421 S Milpas St. US 101, exit Milpas St, 0.3 mi s. Ext corridors. **Pets:** Medium. $5 daily fee/pet. Designated rooms, service with restrictions, supervision.
[SAVE] [S&] [✕] [🛢] [▭] [⤳] [K]

▽▽▽ **Fess Parker's Doubletree Resort** LH ❀
(805) 564-4333. **$160-$415, 3 day notice.** 633 E Cabrillo Blvd. US 101, exit Milpas St, just s, then just w. Ext/int corridors. **Pets:** Other species. Designated rooms, service with restrictions, supervision.
⊠ 🛅 💻 🍴 🏊 ⊠

▽▽▽ ▽▽▽ **Four Seasons Biltmore Santa Barbara** LH ❀
(805) 969-2261. **$500-$1225, 3 day notice.** 1260 Channel Dr. US 101, exit Olive Mill Rd, 0.3 mi s. Ext/int corridors. **Pets:** Small, other species. Designated rooms, service with restrictions, supervision.
ASK ⊠ 🛅 💻 🍴 🏊 ⊠

AAA ▽▽▽ **Harbor House Inn** M
(805) 962-9745. **$99-$275.** 104 Bath St. US 101, exit Cabrillo Blvd (left hand exit), 3 mi n, then just e; exit Castillo St southbound, 0.4 mi w, just s on Cabrillo Blvd, then just e. Ext corridors. **Pets:** Medium. $15 daily fee/pet. Designated rooms, service with restrictions, supervision.
SAVE S🐾 ⊠ 🛅 💻 📶

▽▽▽ **Marina Beach Motel** M
(805) 963-9311. **$79-$269.** 21 Bath St. US 101, exit Haley St northbound, just w to Castillo St, 0.3 mi s to Natoma St, just e, then just s; exit Castillo St southbound, 0.3 mi s to Natoma St, just e, then just s. Ext corridors. **Pets:** Small. $15 daily fee/pet. Designated rooms, service with restrictions, supervision.
ASK S🐾 ⊠ 🛅 💻

▽▽▽ **Pacifica Suites** SH
(805) 683-6722. **$119-$259.** 5490 Hollister Ave. US 101, exit Patterson Ave, 0.5 mi s, then 0.5 mi w. Ext/int corridors. **Pets:** Other species. $10 daily fee/pet. Designated rooms, service with restrictions, supervision.
ASK S🐾 ⊠ 🔬M 🚭 ♿ 🛅 💻 🏊

SANTA CATALINA ISLAND

AAA ▽▽▽ **Best Western Catalina Canyon Hotel & Spa** M
(310) 510-0325. **$89-$279, 3 day notice.** 888 Country Club Dr. 0.5 mi from the harbor via Sumner Ave. Ext corridors. **Pets:** Medium. $50 one-time fee/room. Designated rooms, service with restrictions, crate.
SAVE S🐾 ⊠ 💻 🍴 🏊 ⊠

SANTA CLARA

AAA ▽▽▽ **GuestHouse International Inn & Suites-Silicon Valley** M
(408) 241-3010. **$65-$95.** 2930 El Camino Real. SR 82, 0.5 mi w of San Tomas Expwy; US 101, exit S Bowers Ave. Ext corridors. **Pets:** Other species. $10 daily fee/pet.
SAVE S🐾 ⊠ 🔬M 🛅 💻 🏊

AAA ▽▽▽ **Santa Clara Marriott Hotel** LH
(408) 988-1500. **$169-$199.** 2700 Mission College Blvd. 0.5 mi e off US 101, exit Great America Pkwy; 0.8 mi s of Great America Theme Park. Int corridors. **Pets:** Accepted.
SAVE S🐾 ⊠ 🛅 💻 🍴 🏊 ⊠

AAA ▽▽▽ **The Vagabond Inn** M
(408) 241-0771. **$49-$139.** 3580 El Camino Real. On SR 82, southeast corner of Lawrence Expwy cloverleaf. Ext corridors. **Pets:** Other species. $10 daily fee/pet. Service with restrictions, crate.
SAVE S🐾 ⊠ 🛅 💻 🏊

AAA ▽▽ **Wellesley Inn (Santa Clara)** SH
(408) 257-8600. **$74-$89.** 5405 Stevens Creek Blvd. I-280 and Lawrence Expwy, exit Stevens Creek Blvd, just w. Int corridors. **Pets:** Small. $50 one-time fee/room. Service with restrictions, supervision.
SAVE S🐾 ⊠ 🛅 💻

▽▽▽ ▽▽▽ **The Westin Hotel-Santa Clara** LH 🐾
(408) 986-0700. **$99-$259.** 5101 Great America Pkwy. 0.8 mi e off US 101, exit Great America Pkwy. Int corridors. **Pets:** Medium. Service with restrictions.
ASK ⊠ 🔬M 🚭 🛅 💻 🍴 🏊 ⊠

SANTA CRUZ

AAA ▽▽▽ **Bay Front Inn** M
(831) 423-8564. **$48-$185.** 325 Pacific Ave. 6 blks se of SR 1. Ext corridors. **Pets:** Other species. $10 daily fee/pet. Service with restrictions, supervision.
SAVE ⊠ 🛅 🏊

AAA ▽▽▽ **Coast Santa Cruz Hotel** SH
(831) 426-4330. **$149-$349.** 175 W Cliff Dr. At the Wharf. Int corridors. **Pets:** Accepted.
SAVE S🐾 ⊠ 🛅 💻 🍴

AAA ▽▽▽ **Continental Inn** M
(831) 429-1221. **$75-$260, 7 day notice.** 414 Ocean St. 5 blks from beach; between Broadway and Soquel aves. Ext corridors. **Pets:** Accepted.
SAVE S🐾 ⊠ 🛅 💻 🏊

AAA ▽▽▽ **GuestHouse International Pacific Inn** M
(831) 425-3722. **$69-$189, 3 day notice.** 330 Ocean St. 1 mi from jct SR 1 and 17. Int corridors. **Pets:** $15 daily fee/pet. Service with restrictions, supervision.
SAVE S🐾 ⊠ 🛅 💻 🏊

AAA ▽▽▽ **Ocean Pacific Lodge** M
(831) 457-1234. **$77-$160.** 301 Pacific Ave. SR 1 and 17, exit w via Ocean St, 1 mi w to Broadway, turn right, left on Front St to Pacific Ave, then just right. Ext corridors. **Pets:** Accepted.
SAVE S🐾 ⊠ 🛅 🏊

SANTA MARIA

AAA ▽▽▽ **Best Western Big America** M
(805) 922-5200. **$89-$149.** 1725 N Broadway. US 101, exit Broadway, 0.5 mi w. Ext corridors. **Pets:** Medium. Service with restrictions, supervision.
SAVE S🐾 ⊠ 🛅 💻 🏊

▽▽▽ **Historic Santa Maria Inn** LH
(805) 928-7777. **$129-$159.** 801 S Broadway. US 101, exit Main St, 1 mi w, then 0.5 mi s. Int corridors. **Pets:** Medium. $50 one-time fee/pet. Service with restrictions, supervision.
ASK S🐾 ⊠ 🛅 💻 🍴 🏊 ⊠

AAA ▽▽▽ **Holiday Inn Hotel & Suites** LH ❀
(805) 928-6000. **$120-$145.** 2100 N Broadway. US 101, exit Broadway, just w. Int corridors. **Pets:** Medium, other species. $10 daily fee/pet. Service with restrictions, supervision.
SAVE S🐾 ⊠ 🔬M 🚭 🛅 💻 🍴 🏊 ⊠

SANTA NELLA

AAA ▽▽▽ **Comfort Inn** M ❀
(209) 827-8700. **$75-$80.** 28821 W Gonzaga Rd. 3 mi w of I-5; SR 152, exit Gonzaga Rd, just s. Ext corridors. **Pets:** Large. $10 one-time fee/pet. Service with restrictions, crate.
SAVE S🐾 ⊠ 🛅 💻 🏊

AAA ▽▽▽ **Holiday Inn Express** M
(209) 826-8282. **$75-$95.** 28976 W Plaza Dr. I-5, exit SR 33, just e. Ext corridors. **Pets:** Accepted.
SAVE S🐾 ⊠ 🛅 💻 🏊

▽▽ **Ramada Inn Mission de Oro** SH
(209) 826-4444. **$75-$109, 3 day notice.** 13070 Hwy 33 S. I-5, exit SR 33, just w. Ext/int corridors. **Pets:** Medium. $10 one-time fee/pet. Service with restrictions, supervision.
ASK S🐾 ⊠ 🛅 💻 🍴 🏊

SCOTTS VALLEY

Hilton Santa Cruz/Scotts Valley SH
(831) 440-1000. **$119-$249.** 6001 La Madrona Dr. SR 17, exit Mt
Hermon Rd. Int corridors. **Pets:** Medium, dogs only. $25 daily fee/pet.
Designated rooms, service with restrictions, supervision.

SELMA

Super 8 Motel SH
(559) 896-2800. **$64-$82.** 3142 S Highland Ave. SR 99, exit Floral Ave.
Int corridors. **Pets:** Accepted.

SHASTA LAKE

Bridge Bay Resort M
(530) 275-3021. **$78-$103, 3 day notice.** I-5, exit 690, e of I-5, exit
Bridge Bay Rd; 12 mi n of Redding. Ext corridors. **Pets:** $50 deposit/
pet, $10 one-time fee/pet. Designated rooms, service with restrictions,
supervision.

Fawndale Lodge & RV Resort M
(530) 275-8000. **$59-$91, 10 day notice.** I-5, exit 689, 1 mi s of Shasta
Lake; e of I-5, exit Fawndale Rd; 10 mi n of Redding. Ext corridors.
Pets: Other species. Supervision.

SHELTER COVE

Inn of the Lost Coast M
(707) 986-7521. **$105-$135.** 205 Wave Dr. 23 mi w of US 101 via
Shelter Cove Rd, 1 mi n on Upper Pacific Rd, w on Lower Pacific Rd.
Ext corridors. **Pets:** $10 daily fee/pet. Designated rooms, service with
restrictions, supervision.

SIERRA CITY

Herrington's Sierra Pines M
(530) 862-1151. **$69-$125, 7 day notice.** 104 Main St. 0.5 mi w on SR
49; 12 mi n of Downieville Center. Ext corridors. **Pets:** Other species.
Supervision.

SMITH RIVER

Ship Ashore Motel M
(707) 487-3141. **$60-$140.** 12370 Hwy 101. 2.8 mi n on US 101; 3 mi
s of OR-CA state line. Ext corridors. **Pets:** Accepted.

SOLEDAD

Best Western Valley Harvest Inn M
(831) 678-3833. **$79-$170.** 1155 Front St. US 101, exit Soledad, just e.
Ext/int corridors. **Pets:** Small, dogs only. $10 daily fee/pet. Designated
rooms, service with restrictions, supervision.

SOLVANG

Meadowlark Inn M
(805) 688-4631. **$110-$225, 7 day notice.** 2644 Mission Dr. On SR
246, 1.6 mi e. Ext corridors. **Pets:** Accepted.

Royal Copenhagen Inn M
(805) 688-5561. **$71-$189, 3 day notice.** 1579 Mission Dr. On SR 246.
Ext/int corridors. **Pets:** Other species. Designated rooms, service with
restrictions, supervision.

SONORA

Aladdin Motor Inn M
(209) 533-4971. **$79-$112.** 14260 Mono Way (Hwy 108). On SR 108,
3.5 mi e. Ext/int corridors. **Pets:** $5 one-time fee/pet. Designated rooms,
service with restrictions, supervision.

Best Western Sonora Oaks M
(209) 533-4400. **$94-$116.** 19551 Hess Ave. 3.5 mi e on SR 108.
Ext/int corridors. **Pets:** Medium. $20 daily fee/room. Designated rooms,
service with restrictions, supervision.

Miners Motel M
(209) 532-7850. **$59-$75, 3 day notice.** 18740 SR 108. On SR 108
and 49, 1 mi e of Jamestown. Ext corridors. **Pets:** Medium, dogs only.
$5 daily fee/pet. Service with restrictions, supervision.

Sonora Days Inn M
(209) 532-2400. **$75-$95.** 160 S Washington St. Downtown. Ext/int
corridors. **Pets:** Medium. $10 one-time fee/pet. Designated rooms, service
with restrictions, supervision.

Sonora Gold Lodge M
(209) 532-3952. **$39-$99.** 480 Stockton St. 0.5 mi sw on SR 108
business route and 49. Ext corridors. **Pets:** Other species. $20 one-time
fee/pet. Designated rooms, service with restrictions, supervision.

STOCKTON

Best Value Inn M
(209) 466-7777. **$58.** 1707 W Fremont St. I-5, exit Fremont St, just w.
Ext corridors. **Pets:** Medium. $25 deposit/room. Designated rooms, service
with restrictions, supervision.

Comfort Inn & Suites M
(209) 478-4300. **$64-$135.** 2654 W March Ln. I-5, exit March Ln, just e.
Ext corridors. **Pets:** Other species. $25 deposit/room. Service with restric-
tions, supervision.

Econo Lodge of Stockton M
(209) 466-5741. **$55-$62.** 2210 S Manthey Rd. I-5, exit 8th St, 0.3 mi s
of jct SR 4. Int corridors. **Pets:** Very small, dogs only. $10 one-time
fee/pet. Designated rooms, service with restrictions, supervision.

Howard Johnson Express Inn-Marina M
(209) 948-6151. **$80-$100.** 33 N Center St. 1 blk n; w off El Dorado St
via Weber; SR 99 southbound, exit Wilson Way; SR 99 northbound, w
via Mariposa Rd to Charter Way; I-5, exit downtown. Ext corridors.
Pets: Medium, dogs only. $10 daily fee/pet. Designated rooms, service with
restrictions, supervision.

La Quinta Inn Stockton M
(209) 952-7800. **$99-$112.** 2710 W March Ln. I-5, exit March Ln, just w.
Ext corridors. **Pets:** Accepted.

Residence Inn by Marriott SH
(209) 472-9800. **$89-$139.** 3240 W March Ln. I-5, exit March Ln, 0.5 mi
w. Int corridors. **Pets:** Large, other species. $75 one-time fee/room. Serv-
ice with restrictions, crate.

SUNNYVALE

Four Points by Sheraton Sunnyvale 🆂🅷 ❀
(408) 738-4888. **$129.** 1250 Lakeside Dr. US 101, exit Lawrence Expwy S, e on Oakmead. Int corridors. **Pets:** Supervision.
[SAVE] [S🐾] [✕] [🛏] [▭] [📺] [🛁] [☒]

Homestead Studio Suites Hotel-Sunnyvale/Santa Clara 🅼
(408) 734-3431. **$74-$89.** 1255 Orleans Dr. N of SR 237, exit Mathilda Ave, then e on Moffett Park Dr. Ext corridors. **Pets:** Accepted.
[ASK] [S🐾] [✕] [▭]

Maple Tree Inn 🆂🅷 ❀
(408) 720-9700. **$109-$185.** 711 E El Camino Real. SR 82; between Fair Oaks and Wolfe Rd; 2.5 mi w of US 101. Int corridors. **Pets:** Medium. $10 daily fee/pet. Designated rooms, service with restrictions, supervision.
[SAVE] [S🐾] [✕] [🖊] [🛏] [🛁]

Quality Inn-Sunnyvale 🆂🅷
(408) 744-1100. **$65-$165.** 1280 Persian Dr. US 101, exit Lawrence Expwy N, 1 mi n to Persian Dr, then 0.3 mi w. Int corridors. **Pets:** Accepted.
[ASK] [S🐾] [✕] [🛏] [▭] [🛁]

Residence Inn by Marriott 🅼
(408) 720-1000. **Call for rates.** 750 Lakeway Dr. US 101, exit Lawrence Expwy S, then e on Oakmead. Ext corridors. **Pets:** Accepted.
[✕] [▭] [🛁] [☒]

Residence Inn by Marriott 🅼
(408) 720-8893. **Call for rates.** 1080 Stewart Dr. US 101, exit Lawrence Expwy S, w on Duane Ave W. Ext corridors. **Pets:** Accepted.
[S🐾] [✕] [🛏] [▭] [🛁]

Staybridge Suites 🅼 ❀
(408) 745-1515. **$75-$174.** 900 Hamlin Ct. SR 237, exit Mathilda Ave S, w on Ross. Ext corridors. **Pets:** Medium. $150 one-time fee/pet. Service with restrictions, supervision.
[ASK] [S🐾] [✕] [🛏] [▭] [🛁] [☒]

TownePlace Suites by Marriott Sunnyvale/Mountain View 🆂🅷
(408) 733-4200. **$69-$149.** 606 S Bernardo Ave. SR 85, exit El Camino Real (SR 82), 0.5 mi s. Int corridors. **Pets:** Accepted.
[ASK] [S🐾] [✕] [▭]

Vagabond Inn 🅼
(408) 734-4607. **$69-$209.** 816 Ahwanee Ave. US 101, exit Mathilda Ave S, then s. Ext corridors. **Pets:** $10 daily fee/pet. Service with restrictions, supervision.
[SAVE] [S🐾] [✕] [🛏] [▭] [🛁]

Wild Palms Hotel 🅼
(408) 738-0500. **$169.** 910 E Fremont Ave. I-280, exit Wolfe Rd, just e. Ext corridors. **Pets:** Accepted.
[✕] [🛏] [🛁]

Woodfin Suites 🅼
(408) 738-1700. **Call for rates.** 635 E El Camino Real. US 101, exit Fair Oaks, 2.5 mi w to SR 82 E. Ext corridors. **Pets:** Accepted.
[S🐾] [✕] [🛏] [▭] [🛁]

SUSANVILLE

America's Best Inns 🅼
(530) 257-4522. **Call for rates.** 2705 Main St. 1.5 mi e on SR 36. Ext corridors. **Pets:** Accepted.
[S🐾] [✕] [🛏]

River Inn 🅼
(530) 257-6051. **$50-$60.** 1710 Main St. 0.8 mi e on SR 36. Ext corridors. **Pets:** Dogs only. $10 daily fee/pet. Designated rooms, service with restrictions, supervision.
[SAVE] [S🐾] [✕] [🛏] [🛁]

Super 8 Motel 🅼
(530) 257-2782. **$56-$68.** 2975 Johnstonville Rd. SR 36, 1.8 mi e. Ext corridors. **Pets:** Small, other species. $5 daily fee/pet. Designated rooms, service with restrictions, supervision.
[SAVE] [✕] [🛏] [🛁]

TEHACHAPI

Best Western Mountain Inn 🅼
(661) 822-5591. **$76-$89.** 418 W Tehachapi Blvd. SR 58, exit SR 202, 1 mi e. Ext corridors. **Pets:** Accepted.
[SAVE] [S🐾] [✕] [🛏] [▭] [🛁]

Tehachapi Summit Travelodge 🅼
(661) 823-8000. **$72-$85.** 500 Steuber Rd. SR 58, exit Monolith eastbound; exit Tehachapi Blvd westbound. Int corridors. **Pets:** Other species. $7 one-time fee/room. Designated rooms, service with restrictions, supervision.
[SAVE] [S🐾] [✕] [🛏] [▭] [🛁]

THOUSAND OAKS

Motel 6 #1360 Thousand Oaks 🅼
(805) 499-0711. **$47-$59.** 1516 Newbury Rd. US 101, exit Ventu Park Rd, just w, then just n. Ext corridors. **Pets:** Accepted.
[S🐾] [✕] [🛁]

Premier Inns 🅼
(805) 499-0755. **$49-$69.** 2434 W Hillcrest Dr. US 101, exit Borchard Rd, just e, then just n. Ext corridors. **Pets:** Medium. Service with restrictions, supervision.
[SAVE] [S🐾] [✕] [Ⓜ] [🛏] [🛁]

Thousand Oaks Inn 🆂🅷 ❀
(805) 497-3701. **$90-$115.** 75 W Thousand Oaks Blvd. US 101, exit Moorpark Rd, just n, then just w. Ext corridors. **Pets:** Small. $75 one-time fee/room. Designated rooms, service with restrictions, supervision.
[ASK] [S🐾] [✕] [🛏] [▭]

THOUSAND PALMS

Red Roof Inn 🅼
(760) 343-1381. **$52-$79.** 72-215 Varner Rd. I-10, exit Ramon Rd, just n, then just w. Ext corridors. **Pets:** Accepted.
[SAVE] [S🐾] [✕] [🛏] [▭] [🛁]

THREE RIVERS

Buckeye Tree Lodge 🅼 ❀
(559) 561-5900. **$68-$124, 3 day notice.** 46000 Sierra Dr. SR 198, 6 mi ne of town center; 0.5 mi sw of entrance to Sequoia National Park. Ext corridors. **Pets:** Medium. $7 daily fee/pet. No service, supervision.
[SAVE] [S🐾] [✕] [🛏] [▭] [🛁]

Gateway Lodge 🅼
(559) 561-4133. **$79-$125, 7 day notice.** 45978 Sierra Dr. SR 198, 6 mi ne of town center; 0.5 mi sw of entrance to Sequoia National Park. Ext corridors. **Pets:** Accepted.
[SAVE] [S🐾] [✕] [🛏] [▭] [📺] [☒]

Lazy J Ranch Motel 🅼 ❀
(559) 561-4449. **$85-$119, 3 day notice.** 39625 Sierra Dr. SR 198, 2.5 mi sw of town center. Ext corridors. **Pets:** $5 one-time fee/pet. Service with restrictions, supervision.
[SAVE] [S🐾] [✕] [🛏] [▭] [🛁] [☒]

(AAA) ▼▼▼ Sequoia Village Inn 🄲🄰
(559) 561-3652. **$69-$259, 14 day notice.** 45971 Sierra Dr. SR 198, 6 mi ne of town center; 0.5 mi sw of entrance to Sequoia National Park. Ext corridors. **Pets:** $5 daily fee/pet. Service with restrictions, supervision.
[SAVE] [✕] [🛏] [▭] [⇘] [⊘]

(AAA) ▼▼▼ Sierra Lodge 🅼
(559) 561-3681. **$50-$112, 7 day notice.** 43175 Sierra Dr. SR 198, 1 mi se of town center; 3 mi sw of entrance to Sequoia National Park. Ext corridors. **Pets:** Other species. $20 deposit/room, $5 daily fee/pet. Designated rooms, service with restrictions, supervision.
[SAVE] [S🔊] [✕] [🛏] [▭] [≋]

TRACY

(AAA) ▼▼♦ Best Western Luxury Inn 🅼
(209) 832-0271. **$59-$79, 3 day notice.** 811 W Clover Rd. I-205, exit Central Tracy. Int corridors. **Pets:** Very small. $50 deposit/pet, $20 daily fee/pet. Designated rooms, service with restrictions, supervision.
[SAVE] [S🔊] [✕] [&M] [🖼] [🛏] [▭] [⇘] [✕]

TRINIDAD

(AAA) ▼▼♦ Bishop Pine Lodge 🄲🄰
(707) 677-3314. **$80-$90, 7 day notice.** 1481 Patricks Point Dr. Just w on US 101, exit Trinidad northbound, 2 mi n; exit Seawood southbound, 1 mi s. Ext corridors. **Pets:** $10 daily fee/pet. No service, supervision.
[SAVE] [S🔊] [✕] [🛏] [▭] [🐾]

(AAA) ▼▼ Trinidad Inn 🅼
(707) 677-3349. **$90-$150.** 1170 Patricks Point Dr. US 101, exit Trinidad northbound, 1.5 mi w; exit Seawood southbound, 1.5 mi s. Ext corridors. **Pets:** Accepted.
[SAVE] [✕] [🛏] [▭] [🐾]

TULARE

(AAA) ▼▼♦▼ Best Western Town & Country Lodge 🅼
(559) 688-7537. **$73-$150.** 1051 N Blackstone St. SR 99, exit Prosperity Ave, just w. Int corridors. **Pets:** Medium. $20 one-time fee/room. Service with restrictions, supervision.
[SAVE] [S🔊] [✕] [🖼] [🛏] [▭] [⇘]

(AAA) ▼▼♦▼ Charter Inn 🆂🅷
(559) 685-9500. **$69-$119.** 1016 E Prosperity Ave. SR 99, just e. Int corridors. **Pets:** Small. $100 deposit/room, $5 daily fee/pet. Service with restrictions, supervision.
[SAVE] [S🔊] [✕] [&M] [🌀] [🖼] [🛏] [▭] [⇘] [✕]

(AAA) ▼▼ Days Inn 🅼
(559) 686-0985. **$70-$75.** 1183 N Blackstone St. SR 99, exit Prosperity Ave, just w. Ext corridors. **Pets:** Medium. $5 daily fee/pet. Service with restrictions, supervision.
[SAVE] [S🔊] [✕] [🛏] [⇘]

(AAA) ▼▼ Quality Inn 🅼
(559) 686-3432. **$69-$75.** 1010 E Prosperity Ave. SR 99, exit Prosperity Ave, just e. Int corridors. **Pets:** Small, dogs only. $10 daily fee/pet. Designated rooms, service with restrictions, supervision.
[SAVE] [S🔊] [✕] [🖼] [🛏] [▭] [⇘] [✕]

TURLOCK

(AAA) ▼▼♦ Travelodge 🅼
(209) 668-3400. **$75-$90.** 201 W Glenwood Ave. SR 99, exit Lander. Ext corridors. **Pets:** Small, dogs only. $25 deposit/room. Designated rooms, service with restrictions, supervision.
[SAVE] [S🔊] [✕] [&M] [🖼] [🛏] [▭] [≋]

TWENTYNINE PALMS

(AAA) ▼▼♦ Best Western Gardens Inn & Suites 🅼 🐾
(760) 367-9141. **$79-$112.** 71487 Twentynine Palms Hwy. On SR 62; 1.8 mi w of town center. Ext/int corridors. **Pets:** Medium, other species. $100 deposit/room, $10 daily fee/pet. Designated rooms, service with restrictions, supervision.
[SAVE] [S🔊] [✕] [🛏] [▭] [⇘]

▼▼ Circle C Lodge 🅼
(760) 367-7615. **$84-$91.** 6340 El Rey Ave. On SR 62, just n; 1.5 mi w of town center. Ext corridors. **Pets:** Accepted.
[ASK] [S🔊] [✕] [🛏] [▭] [⇘]

▼▼ Sunnyvale Garden Suites Hotel 🄲🄾
(760) 361-3939. **$89-$119.** 73843 Sunnyvale Dr. SR 62, 0.7 mi n on Adobe Rd, just e on S Slope, just n on Ocotillo, then just e. Ext corridors. **Pets:** Accepted.
[ASK] [S🔊] [✕] [🛏] [▭] [✕]

VACAVILLE

(AAA) ▼▼♦ Best Western Heritage Inn 🅼
(707) 448-8453. **$79-$90.** 1420 E Monte Vista Ave. I-80, exit Monte Vista Ave, just n. Ext corridors. **Pets:** Medium, other species. Designated rooms, service with restrictions, supervision.
[SAVE] [S🔊] [✕] [🛏] [▭] [⇘]

▼▼♦▼ Residence Inn by Marriott 🆂🅷
(707) 469-0300. **$129-$169.** 360 Orange Dr. I-80, exit Orange Dr eastbound, 0.5 mi; exit Monte Vista westbound, freeway overpass to E Nut Tree Pkwy. Int corridors. **Pets:** Accepted.
[ASK] [S🔊] [✕] [&M] [🖼] [🛏] [▭] [⇘] [✕]

▼▼♦▼ Vacaville Super 8 🅼
(707) 449-8884. **$69-$89.** 101 Allison Ct. I-80, exit Monte Vista Ave, just n. Int corridors. **Pets:** Dogs only. $10 one-time fee/room. Service with restrictions, supervision.
[ASK] [S🔊] [✕] [&M] [▭] [⇘]

VALLEJO

(AAA) ▼▼♦▼ Holiday Inn at Napa Gateway 🆂🅷
(707) 644-1200. **$84-$119.** 1000 Fairgrounds Dr. I-80, exit Marine World Pkwy (SR 37), 0.3 mi n. Int corridors. **Pets:** Other species. $25 one-time fee/room. Service with restrictions, crate.
[SAVE] [S🔊] [✕] [&M] [🖼] [🛏] [▭] [🍴] [⇘]

▼▼ Ramada Inn 🅼
(707) 643-2700. **$109-$119.** 1000 Admiral Callaghan Ln. I-80 S, exit Columbus Pkwy, 0.5 mi w. Ext corridors. **Pets:** Accepted.
[ASK] [S🔊] [✕] [🛏] [▭] [⇘]

VENTURA

(AAA) ▼▼♦▼ La Quinta Inn Ventura 🅼
(805) 658-6200. **$96-$112.** 5818 Valentine Rd. US 101, exit Victoria Ave, just s, then just n. Ext/int corridors. **Pets:** Accepted.
[SAVE] [✕] [&M] [🌀] [🛏] [▭] [⇘]

▼▼♦▼ Marriott Ventura Beach Hotel 🅻🅷
(805) 643-6000. **$149-$379.** 2055 Harbor Blvd. US 101, exit Seaward Ave, just w, then 0.5 mi n. Int corridors. **Pets:** Medium, other species. $75 one-time fee/room. Service with restrictions.
[ASK] [S🔊] [✕] [&M] [🌀] [🖼] [🛏] [▭] [🍴] [⇘]

(AAA) ▼▼♦ Vagabond Inn Ventura 🅼
(805) 648-5371. **$69-$159.** 756 E Thompson Blvd. US 101, exit California St northbound, just n, then just e; exit Ventura Ave southbound, 0.6 mi e. Ext corridors. **Pets:** Accepted.
[SAVE] [S🔊] [✕] [🛏] [▭] [🍴] [⇘]

VICTORVILLE

▲▲▲ ❖❖❖ Best Western Green Tree Inn & Suites 🅂🄷
(760) 245-3461. **$84-$94.** 14173 Green Tree Blvd. I-15, exit SR 18 W (Palmdale Rd), just e. Ext corridors. **Pets:** Small. $25 one-time fee/pet. Service with restrictions, supervision.
🆂🅰🆅🄴 💲 ✖ 👤 📶 📺 🍽 ⇋

▲▲▲ ❖❖❖ Comfort Suites Hotel 🅂🄷
(760) 245-6777. **$89-$119.** 12281 Mariposa Rd. I-15, exit Bear Valley Rd, just e, then just n. Int corridors. **Pets:** Dogs only. $50 deposit/room. Service with restrictions, crate.
🆂🅰🆅🄴 💲 ✖ 👤 📺 ⇋

❖❖ Ramada Inn 🅂🄷
(760) 245-6565. **$85.** 15494 Palmdale Rd. I-15, exit SR 18 W (Palmdale Rd), just w. Int corridors. **Pets:** Accepted.
🄰🅂🄺 ✖ 👤 📺 🍽 ⇋

❖❖ Red Roof Inn 🄼
(760) 241-1577. **$59-$99.** 13409 Mariposa Rd. I-15, exit Bear Valley Rd northbound, just e, then 1.5 mi n; exit Green Tree Blvd southbound, just e, then 1.5 mi s. Ext corridors. **Pets:** Large. Service with restrictions.
✖ 👤 📺 ⇋

▲▲▲ ❖❖❖ Travelodge Victorville 🄼
(760) 241-7200. **$54-$74.** 12175 Mariposa Rd. I-15, exit Bear Valley Rd, just e, then just n. Int corridors. **Pets:** Small, dogs only. $20 deposit/room, $8 one-time fee/room. Service with restrictions, supervision.
🆂🅰🆅🄴 💲 ✖ 👤 ⇋

VISALIA

▲▲▲ ❖❖❖ Best Western Visalia Inn 🄼
(559) 732-4561. **$88-$94.** 623 W Main St. SR 198, exit SR 63 S (Mooney Blvd), just n, then 0.9 mi e. Ext corridors. **Pets:** Small, dogs only. $10 one-time fee/pet. Service with restrictions, supervision.
🆂🅰🆅🄴 💲 ✖ 👤 📺 ⇋

▲▲▲ ❖❖❖ Lamp Liter Inn 🄼
(559) 732-4511. **$69-$109.** 3300 W Mineral King Ave. SR 198, exit SR 63 S (Mooney Blvd), 0.5 mi w. Ext corridors. **Pets:** Accepted.
🆂🅰🆅🄴 💲 ✖ 👤 📺 ⇋

▲▲▲ ❖ Super 8 🄼
(559) 627-2885. **$55-$95.** 4801 W Noble Ave. SR 198, exit Akers St, just s, then 0.5 mi e on frontage road. Ext corridors. **Pets:** Other species. $5 daily fee/pet. Service with restrictions, supervision.
🆂🅰🆅🄴 💲 ✖ 👤 ⇋

▲▲▲ ❖❖❖ Visalia Holiday Inn Hotel & Conference Center 🄻🄷
(559) 651-5000. **$109-$169.** 9000 W Airport Dr. SR 99, exit SR 198, just e to Plaza Dr, then just s. Int corridors. **Pets:** Large. $25 one-time fee/room. Service with restrictions, supervision.
🆂🅰🆅🄴 💲 ✖ 👤 📺 🍽 ⇋ ✕

VISTA

❖❖❖ La Quinta Inn San Diego (Vista) 🄼
(760) 727-8180. **$105-$125.** 630 Sycamore Ave at Thibodo Rd. SR 78, exit Sycamore Ave, just sw. Ext/int corridors. **Pets:** Accepted.
🄰🅂🄺 ✖ 👤 📺 ⇋

WALNUT CREEK

▲▲▲ ❖❖❖ Embassy Suites Hotel 🄻🄷
(925) 934-2500. **$129-$229.** 1345 Treat Blvd. I-680, exit Treat Blvd northbound; exit Oak Park Blvd southbound, then e; at Pleasant Hill Bart Station. Int corridors. **Pets:** Accepted.
🆂🅰🆅🄴 💲 ✖ 👤 👤 📺 🍽 ⇋ ✕

▲▲▲ ❖❖❖ Holiday Inn Walnut Creek 🅂🄷
(925) 932-3332. **$79-$199.** 2730 N Main St. I-680, exit N Main St, just n. Int corridors. **Pets:** Medium. $100 deposit/pet, $25 one-time fee/pet. Service with restrictions, supervision.
🆂🅰🆅🄴 💲 ✖ 👤 📺 🍽 ⇋

WATSONVILLE

▲▲▲ ❖❖ Best Western Rose Garden Inn 🄼
(831) 724-3367. **$59-$159.** 740 Freedom Blvd. On SR 152. Ext corridors. **Pets:** Accepted.
🆂🅰🆅🄴 💲 ✖ 👤 📺 ⇋

❖❖ Red Roof Inn 🅂🄷
(831) 740-4520. **$54-$84.** 1620 W Beach St. SR 1, exit Riverside Dr (SR 129), just w. Int corridors. **Pets:** Accepted.
🄰🅂🄺 ✖ 👤 📺 ⇋

WEAVERVILLE

▲▲▲ ❖❖ 49er Motel 🄼
(530) 623-4937. **$55-$140, 7 day notice.** 718 Main St. On SR 299. Ext corridors. **Pets:** Medium, other species. $10 one-time fee/room. Service with restrictions, supervision.
🆂🅰🆅🄴 ✖ 👤 📺 ⇋

▲▲▲ ❖❖❖ Best Western Weaverville Victorian Inn 🄼
(530) 623-4432. **$65-$198.** 1709 Main St. On SR 299. Ext corridors. **Pets:** Accepted.
🆂🅰🆅🄴 💲 ✖ 🖊 👤 📺 🍽 ⇋

▲▲▲ ❖ Motel Trinity 🄼
(530) 623-2129. **$45-$80, 3 day notice.** 1112 Main St. Ext corridors. **Pets:** Other species. $5 daily fee/pet. Service with restrictions, supervision.
🆂🅰🆅🄴 💲 ✖ 👤 📺 ⇋

❖ Red Hill Motel 🄲🄰
(530) 623-4331. **$38-$78.** Red Hill Rd. SR 299, just w of SR 3. Ext corridors. **Pets:** Medium. $5 one-time fee/pet. Service with restrictions, supervision.
👤 📺

WEED

▲▲▲ ❖❖❖ Comfort Inn 🄼
(530) 938-1982. **$69-$99.** 1844 Shastina Dr. I-5, exit S Weed, just e. Int corridors. **Pets:** Large, other species. $100 deposit/room, $10 daily fee/room. Designated rooms, service with restrictions, supervision.
🆂🅰🆅🄴 💲 ✖ 👥 👤 📺 ⇋

▲▲▲ ❖❖❖ Holiday Inn Express 🄼
(530) 938-1308. **$69-$120.** 1830 Black Butte Dr. Just e of I-5, in town. Int corridors. **Pets:** Other species. $10 one-time fee/pet. Service with restrictions, supervision.
🆂🅰🆅🄴 💲 ✖ 👤

▲▲▲ ❖❖ Sis-Q-Inn Motel 🄼 🐾
(530) 938-4194. **$50-$120.** 1825 Shastina Dr. I-5, exit S Weed. Int corridors. **Pets:** Small, other species. $8 one-time fee/pet. Service with restrictions, supervision.
🆂🅰🆅🄴 💲 ✖ 👤

WESTLEY

▲▲▲ ❖❖❖ Econo Lodge 🄼
(209) 894-3900. **$65-$90, 3 day notice.** 7100 McCracken Rd. I-5, exit Westley, then e. Ext corridors. **Pets:** $10 daily fee/pet. No service, supervision.
🆂🅰🆅🄴 💲 ✖ 👤 📺 ⇋

WESTMORLAND

ᐯᐯ ᐯᐯ Super 8 Motel M
(760) 351-7100. **$70-$75.** 351 W Main St. On SR 86. Int corridors. **Pets:** Dogs only. $10 daily fee/pet. Designated rooms, no service, supervision.
(A$K) (S⚡) (✕) (🛏) (🏊)

WILLIAMS

ᐯᐯᐯ ᐯᐯ Comfort Inn M
(530) 473-2381. **$70-$85.** 400 C St. I-5, exit Williams, just w on E St, then just n on 4th St. Ext corridors. **Pets:** Accepted.
(SAVE) (S⚡) (✕) (🛏) (🛏) (🖥) (🏊)

ᐯᐯᐯ ᐯᐯᐯ Granzella's Inn M
(530) 473-3310. **$80-$110.** 391 6th St. I-5, exit Williams, 0.5 mi w. Int corridors. **Pets:** Other species. $10 one-time fee/room. Designated rooms, service with restrictions, supervision.
(SAVE) (S⚡) (✕) (🛏) (🛁) (🛏) (🖥) (🍴) (🏊)

ᐯᐯᐯ ᐯᐯ Stage Stop Inn M
(530) 473-2281. **$45-$50.** 300 N 7th St. I-5, exit SR 20 business route, 3 blks w. Ext corridors. **Pets:** Accepted.
(SAVE) (S⚡) (✕) (🛏) (🏊)

WILLOW CREEK

ᐯᐯᐯ ᐯᐯ Bigfoot Motel M
(530) 629-2142. **$55-$125.** 39039 Hwy 299. SR 299; center of town. Ext corridors. **Pets:** Accepted.
(SAVE) (✕) (🛏) (🏊)

WILLOWS

ᐯᐯᐯ ᐯᐯᐯ Best Western Golden Pheasant Inn M
(530) 934-4603. **$69-$89.** 249 N Humboldt Ave. I-5, exit Willow-Elk Creek-Glenn Rd, just e. Ext corridors. **Pets:** Accepted.
(SAVE) (S⚡) (✕) (🛏) (🛏) (🖥) (🍴) (🏊)

ᐯᐯᐯ ᐯᐯ Days Inn M
(530) 934-4444. **$69-$119.** 475 N Humboldt Ave. I-5, exit Willow-Elk Creek-Glenn Rd, just e. Ext corridors. **Pets:** Accepted.
(SAVE) (S⚡) (✕) (🛏) (🛏) (🖥) (🏊)

ᐯᐯᐯ ᐯᐯ Economy Inn M
(530) 934-4224. **$50-$70.** 435 N Tehama St. I-5, exit SR 162, (Willow-Elk Creek-Glenn Rd), 1 mi e. Ext corridors. **Pets:** Small. $5 one-time fee/pet. Designated rooms, service with restrictions, supervision.
(SAVE) (S⚡) (✕) (🛏)

ᐯᐯ ᐯᐯ Motel 6 M
(530) 934-7026. **$37-$68.** 452 N Humboldt Ave. I-5, exit Willow-Elk Creek-Glenn Rd, just e. Ext corridors. **Pets:** Medium, other species. $7 daily fee/pet. Service with restrictions, supervision.
(A$K) (S⚡) (✕) (🛏) (🖥) (🏊)

ᐯᐯ ᐯᐯ Super 8 Motel of Willows M
(530) 934-2871. **$39-$70.** 457 Humboldt Ave. I-5, exit Willow-Elk Creek-Glenn Rd. Int corridors. **Pets:** Medium. $20 deposit/pet, $10 daily fee/pet. Designated rooms, service with restrictions, supervision.
(A$K) (S⚡) (✕) (🛏) (🏊)

WINE COUNTRY AREA

BODEGA BAY

ᐯᐯᐯ ᐯᐯᐯ Bodega Coast Inn M
(707) 875-2217. **$129-$299.** 521 SR 1 N. 2 blks s. Ext corridors. **Pets:** Medium, other species. $30 daily fee/pet. Designated rooms, service with restrictions, crate.
(SAVE) (S⚡) (✕) (🛏) (🛏) (🖥) (AC)

CALISTOGA

ᐯᐯ ᐯᐯ Washington Street Lodging CA
(707) 942-6968. **$95-$140 (no credit cards), 3 day notice.** 1605 Washington St. On SR 29. Ext corridors. **Pets:** Other species. $15 one-time fee/pet. Service with restrictions.
(✕) (🛏) (🛏) (🖥) (🌀)

CLOVERDALE

ᐯᐯ Cloverdale Oaks Inn M
(707) 894-2404. **$65-$129.** 123 S Cloverdale Blvd. US 101, exit Citrus Fair Dr, 0.4 mi w to S Cloverdale Blvd, then just n. Ext corridors. **Pets:** Accepted.
(A$K) (S⚡) (✕) (🛏) (🛏) (🖥)

FORT BRAGG

ᐯᐯᐯ ᐯᐯᐯ Beachcomber Motel M 🐾
(707) 964-2402. **$59-$250.** 1111 N Main St. Ext corridors. **Pets:** Other species. $10 daily fee/pet. Designated rooms, service with restrictions, supervision.
(SAVE) (S⚡) (✕) (🛏) (🖥) (AC)

ᐯᐯᐯ ᐯᐯ Beach House Inn M
(707) 961-1700. **$89-$175, 3 day notice.** 100 Pudding Creek Rd. 0.7 mi n on SR 1. Int corridors. **Pets:** Medium, dogs only. $25 daily fee/pet. Designated rooms, service with restrictions, supervision.
(SAVE) (S⚡) (✕) (🛏) (🖥) (AC)

GUALALA

ᐯᐯ ᐯᐯ Cleone Gardens Inn M
(707) 964-2788. **$86-$140, 3 day notice.** 24600 N Hwy 1. On SR 1, 3 mi n. Ext corridors. **Pets:** Dogs only. Designated rooms, service with restrictions, supervision.
(✕) (🛏) (🖥) (AC)

ᐯᐯᐯ ᐯᐯᐯ The Emerald Dolphin Inn M 🐾
(707) 964-6699. **$55-$180, 3 day notice.** 1211 S Main St. On SR 1. Ext corridors. **Pets:** Dogs only. $10 daily fee/room. Designated rooms, service with restrictions, supervision.
(A$K) (S⚡) (✕) (🛏) (🖥) (AC)

ᐯᐯᐯ ᐯᐯᐯ Seabird Lodge M
(707) 964-4731. **$76-$118.** 191 South St. 0.8 mi n of Noyo River Bridge; 1 blk e off SR 1. Ext corridors. **Pets:** Small. $8 daily fee/pet. Designated rooms, service with restrictions, supervision.
(SAVE) (S⚡) (✕) (🛏) (🖥) (🏊) (AC)

ᐯᐯᐯ ᐯᐯᐯ Tradewinds Lodge M
(707) 964-4761. **$59-$150.** 400 S Main St. 6 blks s on SR 1. Ext corridors. **Pets:** Other species. $10 daily fee/room. Designated rooms, service with restrictions, supervision.
(SAVE) (S⚡) (✕) (🛏) (🖥) (🍴) (🏊) (✕) (AC)

GUALALA

ᐯᐯ ᐯᐯ Gualala Country Inn M
(707) 884-4343. **$95-$165, 3 day notice.** 47955 Center St. East side of SR 1. Ext/int corridors. **Pets:** Other species. $10 one-time fee/pet. Service with restrictions, supervision.
(✕) (🛏) (🖥) (AC)

ᐯᐯ ᐯᐯ Surf Motel M
(707) 884-3571. **$95-$179.** 39170 S Hwy 1. West side of SR 1. Ext corridors. **Pets:** Other species. $10 one-time fee/pet. Service with restrictions, supervision.
(✕) (🛏) (🖥) (AC)

GUERNEVILLE

AAA ▽▽▽ Ferngrove Cottages 🅒🅐 ❀
(707) 869-8105. **$89-$239, 3 day notice.** 16650 Hwy 116. On SR 116. Ext corridors. **Pets:** Large, other species. $15 daily fee/pet. Designated rooms, service with restrictions, supervision.
[SAVE] [S🐾] [✕] [🚻M] 🖼 🔲 💻 ➿ ✕ 🅐 🗷

HEALDSBURG

AAA ▽▽▽▽ Best Western Dry Creek Inn Ⓜ
(707) 433-0300. **$195-$250, 3 day notice.** 198 Dry Creek Rd. US 101, exit Dry Creek Rd, just e. Ext corridors. **Pets:** $25 daily fee/pet. Service with restrictions.
[SAVE] [S🐾] [✕] [🚻M] 🖼 🔲 💻 ➿

▽▽▽▽ Duchamp 🅒🅐
(707) 431-1300. **$275-$450, 14 day notice.** 421 Foss St. US 101, exit Central Healdsburg. Ext corridors. **Pets:** Medium, dogs only. $500 deposit/room, $50 daily fee/room. Designated rooms, service with restrictions, supervision.
[ASK] [✕] [🚻M] 🔲 ➿

AAA ▽▽▽ Fairview Motel Ⓜ
(707) 433-5548. **$59-$139, 3 day notice.** 74 Healdsburg Ave. US 101, exit Central Healdsburg, just e; exit N Guernville/Westside Rd. Ext corridors. **Pets:** Accepted.
[SAVE] [S🐾] [✕] [🚻M] 🔲 💻 ➿

JENNER

▽▽▽ Jenner Inn 🅒🅘 ❀
(707) 865-2377. **$98-$278, 10 day notice.** 10400 Hwy 1. On SR 1 at jct SR 116. Ext corridors. **Pets:** Other species. $35 daily fee/room. Designated rooms, service with restrictions, supervision.
[ASK] [S🐾] [✕] [🚻M] 🔲 💻 🍽 🅐 🗷

LITTLE RIVER

AAA ▽▽▽▽ Auberge–Seaside Cottages 🅱🅱
(707) 937-0088. **$109-$325, 14 day notice.** 8200 N Hwy 1. 2 mi s of Mendocino, w of SR 1. Ext/int corridors. **Pets:** Accepted.
[SAVE] [S🐾] [✕] [🚾] 🔲 💻 ✕ 🅐

AAA ▽▽▽▽ The Inn at Schoolhouse Creek 🅱🅱
(707) 937-5525. **$105-$275, 14 day notice.** 7051 N Hwy 1. 3 mi s of Mendocino; e of Coast Hwy. Ext corridors. **Pets:** Accepted.
[SAVE] [S🐾] [✕] 🔲 💻 🅐

MENDOCINO

▽▽▽▽ Abigail's Bed & Breakfast 🅱🅱 ❀
(707) 937-0934. **$99-$299, 14 day notice.** 951 Ukiah St. Center. Int corridors. **Pets:** Medium. $25 one-time fee/pet. Service with restrictions, supervision.
[ASK] [S🐾] [✕] 🔲 💻 🅐 🗷

AAA ▽▽▽▽ Blackberry Inn Ⓜ ❀
(707) 937-5281. **$105-$215, 5 day notice.** 44951 Larkin Rd. SR 1, exit Larkin Rd, just e. Designated rooms, service with restrictions, supervision. **Pets:** Small, other species. $10 daily fee/pet.
[SAVE] [S🐾] [✕] 🔲 💻 🅐

▽▽▽▽ Hill House Inn 🅒🅘 ❀
(707) 937-0554. **$121-$250, 5 day notice.** 10701 Pallette Dr. SR 1, exit Little Lake St, just w to stop sign, right to entrance. Ext/int corridors. **Pets:** Medium, other species. $15 one-time fee/pet. Designated rooms, service with restrictions, supervision.
[ASK] [S🐾] [✕] 🔲 💻 🍽 🅐

▽▽▽▽ MacCallum House Inn 🅱🅱 ❀
(707) 937-0289. **$120-$325, 7 day notice.** 45020 Albion St. Center. Ext/int corridors. **Pets:** Other species. $25 daily fee/pet. Designated rooms.
[ASK] [S🐾] [✕] 🔲 💻 🍽

▽▽▽ McElroy's Inn 🅱🅱
(707) 937-1734. **$85-$115, 7 day notice.** 998 Main St. SR 1, exit Main St, just w. Int corridors. **Pets:** Accepted.
[S🐾] [✕] 🔲 🅐 🎬 🗷

AAA ▽▽▽▽ Mendocino Seaside Cottages 🅱🅱 ❀
(707) 485-0239. **$145-$391 (no credit cards), 14 day notice.** 10940 Lansing St. SR 1, exit Little Lake Rd; exit Lansing St, 0.6 mi nw. Ext/int corridors. **Pets:** $80 deposit/room. No service, supervision.
[SAVE] [S🐾] [✕] 🔲 💻 🅐

AAA ▽▽▽▽ Stanford Inn by the Sea & Spa-Big River Lodge 🅒🅘 ❀
(707) 937-5615. **$235-$475, 7 day notice.** SR 1, exit Comptche-Ukiah Rd, 0.5 mi e. Ext corridors. **Pets:** Other species. $25 one-time fee/pet. Supervision.
[SAVE] [S🐾] [✕] [🚻M] [🚾] 🔲 💻 🍽 ➿ ✕ 🅐

NAPA

AAA ▽▽▽▽ The Napa Inn 🅱🅱
(707) 257-1444. **$120-$295, 10 day notice.** 1137 Warren St. SR 29, exit 1st St, 0.5 mi e, 0.3 mi n. Int corridors. **Pets:** Accepted.
[SAVE] [✕] [🚻M] 🔲 💻

▽▽▽▽ Napa River Inn Ⓜ ❀
(707) 251-8500. **$159-$499.** 500 Main St. Downtown. Int corridors. **Pets:** Medium. $25 daily fee/pet. Service with restrictions, supervision.
[ASK] [S🐾] [✕] [🚻M] [🚾] 🔲 💻

AAA ▽▽▽ Napa Valley Redwood Inn Ⓜ
(707) 257-6111. **$67-$150.** 3380 Solano Ave. Just w off SR 29 via Redwood Rd, then just s. Ext corridors. **Pets:** Other species. $10 one-time fee/room. Service with restrictions, supervision.
[SAVE] [S🐾] [✕] [🚻M] [🚾] 🔲 💻 ➿

OCCIDENTAL

AAA ▽▽▽ Occidental Lodge Ⓜ
(707) 874-3623. **$64-$119.** 3610 Bohemian Hwy. In the village. Ext corridors. **Pets:** Medium. $8 daily fee/pet. Service with restrictions, supervision.
[SAVE] [S🐾] [✕] [🚻M] 🔲 💻 ➿

PETALUMA

AAA ▽▽▽▽ Quality Inn-Petaluma Ⓜ
(707) 664-1155. **$90-$180.** 5100 Montero Way. US 101, exit Old Redwood Hwy-Penngrove northbound; exit Petaluma Blvd N-Penngrove southbound (east side). Ext/int corridors. **Pets:** Other species. $15 daily fee/room. Service with restrictions, crate.
[SAVE] [S🐾] [✕] [🚻M] [🚾] 🔲 💻 ➿ ✕

ROHNERT PARK

AAA ▽▽▽▽ Best Western Inn Ⓜ
(707) 584-7435. **$78-$125, 3 day notice.** 6500 Redwood Dr. US 101, exit Rohnert Park Expwy, just w. Ext corridors. **Pets:** Service with restrictions, supervision.
[SAVE] [S🐾] [✕] [🚻M] 🔲 💻 ➿

ST. HELENA

▽▽▽▽ El Bonita Motel Ⓜ
(707) 963-3216. **$89-$289, 3 day notice.** 195 Main St. 0.8 mi s on SR 29. Ext corridors. **Pets:** Medium, other species. $5 daily fee/pet. Service with restrictions.
[✕] [🚻M] [🚾] 🔲 💻 ➿

AAA ▽▽▽▽ Harvest Inn 🅢🅗 ❀
(707) 963-9463. **$255-$675, 7 day notice.** One Main St. 1.5 mi s on SR 29. Ext corridors. **Pets:** Medium, other species. $75 one-time fee/room. Designated rooms.
[SAVE] [S🐾] [✕] [🚻M] [🚾] 🔲 💻 ➿

SANTA ROSA

Best Western Garden Inn M
(707) 546-4031. **$75-$129.** 1500 Santa Rosa Ave. US 101, exit Baker Ave northbound; exit Corby Ave southbound. Ext corridors. **Pets:** Accepted.

Santa Rosa Motor Inn M
(707) 523-3480. **$65-$90.** 1800 Santa Rosa Ave. US 101, northbound exit Baker Ave; southbound exit Corby Ave. Ext corridors. **Pets:** $50 deposit/room, $3 daily fee/pet, $10 one-time fee/pet. Service with restrictions, crate.

Travelodge M
(707) 542-3472. **$50-$109.** 1815 Santa Rosa Ave. 1.5 mi s on US 101 business route; exit US 101 via Baker Ave northbound; exit Santa Rosa Ave-Corby southbound. Ext corridors. **Pets:** $20 daily fee/pet. Service with restrictions, supervision.

SONOMA

Best Western Sonoma Valley Inn M
(707) 938-9200. **$143-$314, 3 day notice.** 550 2nd St W. 1 blk w of town plaza. Ext corridors. **Pets:** Accepted.

UKIAH

Best Value Inn Ukiah M
(707) 468-9167. **$49-$89.** 693 S Orchard Ave. US 101, exit Gobbi St W. Ext corridors. **Pets:** Medium, other species. $5 daily fee/pet. Designated rooms, service with restrictions, supervision.

Days Inn M
(707) 462-7584. **$60-$129.** 950 N State St. US 101, exit N State St, 0.5 mi s. Ext corridors. **Pets:** Other species. $10 daily fee/pet. Designated rooms, service with restrictions, supervision.

Rodeway Inn M
(707) 462-2906. **$65-$89.** 1050 S State St. US 101, exit Talmage Rd off-ramp, 0.5 mi w. Ext corridors. **Pets:** Accepted.

Super 8 Motel M
(707) 462-6657. **$49-$99, 7 day notice.** 1070 S State St. US 101, exit Talmage Rd, 1 mi w. Ext corridors. **Pets:** $10 daily fee/pet. No service, supervision.

WESTPORT

De Haven Valley Farm BB
(707) 961-1660. **$94-$151, 3 day notice.** 39247 N Hwy 1. SR 1, 18 mi n of jct SR 20, just n of Branscomb Rd. Ext/int corridors. **Pets:** Accepted.

WILLITS

Baechtel Creek Inn & Spa M
(707) 459-9063. **$69-$160.** 101 Gregory Ln. US 101, just w. Ext corridors. **Pets:** Small, dogs only. $15 one-time fee/pet. Designated rooms, service with restrictions, supervision.

YOUNTVILLE

Vintage Inn SH
(707) 944-1112. **$215-$550, 7 day notice.** 6541 Washington St. SR 29, exit Yountville; center. Ext corridors. **Pets:** $30 one-time fee/room. Service with restrictions.

END AREA

WOODLAND

Days Inn M
(530) 666-3800. **$69-$95, 3 day notice.** 1524 E Main St. I-5, exit Main St (Woodland) northbound; exit SR 113 (Davis) southbound. Int corridors. **Pets:** Small. $10 daily fee/pet. No service, supervision.

YERMO

Oak Tree Inn SH
(760) 254-1148. **$82.** 35450 Yermo Rd. I-15/40, exit Ghost Town Rd, just e, then just s. Int corridors. **Pets:** Accepted.

YOSEMITE NATIONAL PARK

The Redwoods In Yosemite VH
(209) 375-6666. **$121-$672, 10 day notice.** 8038 Chilnualna Falls Rd. 6 mi inside the southern entrance via SR 41 and Chilnualna Falls Rd. Ext corridors. **Pets:** Other species. $10 daily fee/pet. Designated rooms, no service, supervision.

YREKA

AmeriHost Inn-Yreka M
(530) 841-1300. **$79-$95.** 148 Moonlit Oaks Ave. I-5, exit SR 3 (Fort Jones Rd). Int corridors. **Pets:** Medium. $10 one-time fee/pet. Service with restrictions, supervision.

Best Western Miner's Inn M
(530) 842-4355. **$72-$99.** 122 E Miner St. I-5, exit Central Yreka, just w. Ext corridors. **Pets:** $10 daily fee/room. Designated rooms, supervision.

Comfort Inn M
(530) 842-1612. **$65-$99.** 1804-B Fort Jones Rd. I-5, exit SR 3 (Fort Jones Rd). Int corridors. **Pets:** Medium. $20 deposit/pet, $7 one-time fee/pet. Designated rooms, service with restrictions, supervision.

Econo Lodge M
(530) 842-4404. **$55-$75.** 526 S Main St. I-5, exit Central Yreka, 0.3 mi s. Ext corridors. **Pets:** Medium. $20 deposit/pet, $10 one-time fee/pet. Service with restrictions, supervision.

Super 8-Yreka M

(530) 842-5781. **$52-$68.** 136 Montague Rd. I-5, exit Montague Rd, just w. Ext corridors. **Pets:** $25 deposit/room, $5 one-time fee/pet. Designated rooms, service with restrictions, supervision.

YUBA CITY

Comfort Inn M

(530) 674-1592. **$55-$80.** 730 Palora Ave. SR 99, exit Bridge St, 0.5 mi s of jct SR 20. Int corridors. **Pets:** Accepted.

Days Inn & Suites M

(530) 674-0201. **$62-$69.** 4228 S Hwy 99. SR 99, 4.5 mi s of SR 20. Ext corridors. **Pets:** $10 daily fee/pet. Designated rooms, service with restrictions, supervision.

Days Inn-Downtown-Yuba City M

(530) 674-1711. **$45-$80.** 700 N Palora Ave. SR 99, exit Bridge St, 0.5 mi s of SR 20. Ext corridors. **Pets:** Accepted.

YUCCA VALLEY

Oasis of Eden Inn & Suites M

(760) 365-6321. **$70-$139.** 56377 Twentynine Palms Hwy. 1 mi w of jct SR 62 and 247. Ext corridors. **Pets:** Small. $75 deposit/room, $10 daily fee/pet. Designated rooms, service with restrictions, supervision.

Super 8 Motel M

(760) 228-1773. **$64-$119.** 57096 Twentynine Palms Hwy. On SR 62, 0.3 mi w of jct SR 247. Int corridors. **Pets:** $20 deposit/pet. Service with restrictions, crate.

Yucca Inn & Suites M

(760) 365-3311. **$59-$139.** 7500 Camino Del Cielo. Just n of SR 62. Ext corridors. **Pets:** Accepted.

COLORADO

ALAMOSA

△△△ ▽◆▽ Best Western Alamosa Inn 🅂🄷 ❀
(719) 589-2567. **$70-$100.** 2005 Main St. 1 mi w on US 160 and 285. Ext corridors. **Pets:** Medium. $15 one-time fee/pet. Service with restrictions, supervision.
🆂🅰🆅🅴 🆂 ✕ 🄷 🖵 🛁

△△△ ▽◆▽ Clarion Hotel of the Rio Grande 🅂🄷
(719) 589-5833. **$80-$100.** 333 Sante Fe Ave. Just e of jct SR 17 on US 160. Int corridors. **Pets:** $25 deposit/room. Service with restrictions, supervision.
🆂🅰🆅🅴 🆂 ✕ ⚙ 🖉 🄷 🖵 🍽 🛁 🚫

△△△ ▽◆▽ Comfort Inn of Alamosa 🅂🄷
(719) 587-9000. **$65-$110, 14 day notice.** 6301 Rd 107 S. 2.3 mi w on US 160. Int corridors. **Pets:** $15 one-time fee/room. Service with restrictions, supervision.
🆂🅰🆅🅴 🆂 ✕ ⚙ 🄷 🖵 🛁

▽◆▽ Days Inn 🅂🄷
(719) 589-9037. **$35-$65, 5 day notice.** 224 O'Keefe Pkwy. Just e of jct SR 17 and US 160. Int corridors. **Pets:** Accepted.
🄰🅂🄺 🆂 ✕

ASPEN

▽◆▽ Aspen Meadows Resort A Dolce Conference Destination 🄻🄷
(970) 925-4240. **$215-$549, 14 day notice.** 845 Meadows Rd. 3 blks e of SR 82 via 7th Ave. Ext/int corridors. **Pets:** $100 deposit/room. Service with restrictions.
🄰🅂🄺 ✕ ⚙ 🄷 🖵 🍽 🛁 🚫 🎾

△△△ ▽◆▽ Aspen Mountain Lodge 🅂🄷 ❀
(970) 925-7650. **$89-$359.** 311 W Main St. Just w on SR 82; between 2nd and 3rd sts. Int corridors. **Pets:** $20 daily fee/room. Service with restrictions, supervision.
🆂🅰🆅🅴 🆂 ✕ 🄷 🖵 🛁

▽◆▽ Hotel Aspen 🅂🄷
(970) 925-3441. **$99-$405, 3 day notice.** 110 W Main St. On SR 82, just w. Ext/int corridors. **Pets:** Accepted.
🄰🅂🄺 🆂 ✕ 🄷 🖵 🛁

△△△ ▽◆▽ ▽◆▽ Hotel Jerome 🅂🄷 ❀
(970) 920-1000. **$255-$1445, 30 day notice.** 330 E Main St. On SR 82; downtown. Int corridors. **Pets:** $75 one-time fee/room. Service with restrictions, supervision.
🆂🅰🆅🅴 🆂 ✕ 🍽 🛁 🚫

▽◆▽ ▽◆▽ Hotel Lenado 🄱🄱 ❀
(970) 925-6246. **$125-$395, 30 day notice.** 200 S Aspen St. Just s of SR 82 via Aspen St at jct of Hopkins St. Ext/int corridors. **Pets:** Accepted.
🄰🅂🄺 🆂 ✕ 🄷 🖵

△△△ ▽◆▽ Limelite Lodge 🄼 ❀
(970) 925-3025. **$69-$290, 14 day notice.** 228 E Cooper St. Just s of SR 82, at Monarch and Cooper sts. Ext corridors. **Pets:** Other species. $10 daily fee/pet. Designated rooms, service with restrictions, crate.
🆂🅰🆅🅴 ✕ ⚙ 🄷 🖵 🛁

△△△ ▽◆▽ ▽◆▽ The Little Nell 🄻🄷 ❀
(970) 920-4600. **$270-$4600, 30 day notice.** 675 E Durant Ave. Beside the gondola at the base of Aspen Mountain. Int corridors. **Pets:** Other species. Service with restrictions, supervision.
🆂 🄷 🖵 🍽 🛁 🚫

▽◆▽ ▽◆▽ St. Regis Aspen 🄻🄷
(970) 920-3300. **$435-$1675, 14 day notice.** 315 E Dean St. SR 82, s on Monarch St, then just e. Int corridors. **Pets:** Accepted.
🄰🅂🄺 🆂 ✕ 🖉 🍽 🛁 🚫

△△△ ▽◆▽ ▽◆▽ Sky Hotel 🄻🄷 ❀
(970) 925-6760. **$169-$319, 14 day notice.** 709 E Durant Ave. At base of Aspen Mountain. Ext/int corridors. **Pets:** Medium, dogs only. Service with restrictions, supervision.
🆂🅰🆅🅴 🆂 ✕ ⚙ 🖵 🍽 🛁 🚫

BEAVER CREEK

▽◆▽ ▽◆▽ Comfort Inn-Vail/Beaver Creek 🅂🄷
(970) 949-5511. **$59-$179.** 161 W Beaver Creek Blvd. I-70, exit 167, just s, then w. Int corridors. **Pets:** Large, other species. $40 one-time fee/room. Designated rooms, service with restrictions, supervision.
🄰🅂🄺 🆂 ✕ 🖉 🄷 🖵 🛁

▽◆▽ ▽◆▽ The Ritz-Carlton, Bachelor Gulch 🄻🄷
(970) 748-6200. **$195-$1050, 60 day notice.** 0130 Daybreak Ridge. I-70, exit 167, s on Avon and Village rds (beyond gatehouse), w on Prater Rd, follow signs to Bachelor Gulch. Int corridors. **Pets:** Accepted.
✕ ⚙ 🖉 🖵 🍽 🛁 🚫

BOULDER

△△△ ▽◆▽ Best Western Boulder Inn 🅂🄷
(303) 449-3800. **$84-$114.** 770 28th St. US 36 at Baseline Rd. Int corridors. **Pets:** Medium. $100 deposit/room. Designated rooms, supervision.
🆂🅰🆅🅴 🆂 ✕ 🄷 🖵 🍽 🛁 🚫

Boulder Broker Inn SH
(303) 444-3330. **$109-$149.** 555 30th St. US 36 (28th St), exit Baseline Rd, 0.3 mi e to 30th St, then just s. Int corridors. **Pets:** Accepted.

Boulder Outlook Hotel & Suites SH ❖
(303) 443-3322. **$100-$120.** 800 28th St. US 36 (28th St), exit Baseline Rd via Frontage Rd. Ext/int corridors. **Pets:** Dogs only. $10 daily fee/room. Designated rooms, service with restrictions, crate.

Boulder University Inn M ❖
(303) 417-1700. **$60-$119.** 1632 Broadway. From US 36, exit Baseline (CO 93), 0.3 mi s, then 3 mi nw. Ext corridors. **Pets:** $100 deposit/room, $15 daily fee/room. Service with restrictions, supervision.

Foot of The Mountain Motel M
(303) 442-5688. **$70-$85.** 200 Arapahoe Ave. 1.8 mi w of US 36 (28th St). Ext corridors. **Pets:** Accepted.

Homewood Suites by Hilton SH ❖
(303) 499-9922. **$109-$265.** 4950 Baseline Rd. 0.3 mi e of US 36; SR 157 (Foothills Pkwy), exit Baseline Rd, just w; entry off Baseline Rd. Ext/int corridors. **Pets:** Other species. $50 one-time fee/room.

Millennium Harvest House Boulder LH
(303) 442-3850. **$109-$139.** 1345 28th St. Just s of jct Arapahoe Rd and 28th St (US 36). Int corridors. **Pets:** Accepted.

Quality Inn & Suites Boulder Creek SH ❖
(303) 449-7550. **$79-$149.** 2020 Arapahoe Ave. US 36 (28th St), 0.5 mi w. Ext/int corridors. **Pets:** Large. $100 deposit/room, $15 daily fee/room. Service with restrictions, supervision.

Residence Inn by Marriott SH ❖
(303) 449-5545. **$99-$179.** 3030 Center Green Dr. 0.5 mi e of US 36 (28th St); e on Valmont Rd at corner of Foothills Pkwy. Ext corridors. **Pets:** Other species. $75 one-time fee/room.

Super 8 of Boulder M
(303) 443-7800. **$55-$130.** 970 28th St. On US 36 (28th St). Ext corridors. **Pets:** Other species. $5 daily fee/pet. Service with restrictions, supervision.

BRECKENRIDGE

The Hunt Placer Inn BB ❖
(970) 453-7573. **$149-$270, 14 day notice.** 275 Ski Hill Rd. SR 9 (Main St), just w toward Peak 8. Int corridors. **Pets:** Medium, dogs only. $25 daily fee/room. Designated rooms, service with restrictions, supervision.

Wildwood Suites CO
(970) 453-0232. **$75-$395, 30 day notice.** 120 Sawmill Rd. From SR 9, just w on Ski Hill Rd, then just s. Int corridors. **Pets:** Large, dogs only. $75 one-time fee/pet. Designated rooms, supervision.

BROOMFIELD

Omni Interlocken Resort LH ❖
(303) 438-6600. **$109-$239.** 500 Interlocken Blvd. US 36 (Boulder Tpke), exit Interlocken Loop, then w, just s via signs. Int corridors. **Pets:** Small, dogs only. $50 one-time fee/room. Service with restrictions, supervision.

TownePlace Suites by Marriott Boulder/Broomfield SH ❖
(303) 466-2200. **$89-$159.** 480 Flatiron Blvd. US 36 W (Boulder Tpke), Interlocken Loop, to first traffic light, w on Interlocken Blvd, then s. Int corridors. **Pets:** Large, other species. $25 daily fee/room. Service with restrictions.

BRUSH

Best Value Inn Brush SH
(970) 842-5146. **$35-$72.** 1208 N Colorado Ave. I-76, exit 90B, just n. Ext/int corridors. **Pets:** $10 daily fee/pet. Designated rooms, no service, supervision.

Microtel Inn SH
(970) 842-4241. **$52-$72.** 975 N Colorado Ave. I-76, exit 90A, just s. Int corridors. **Pets:** Large, dogs only. $15 daily fee/pet. Designated rooms, service with restrictions, supervision.

BUENA VISTA

Alpine Lodge M
(719) 395-2415. **$45-$65, 15 day notice.** 12845 Hwy 24 & 285. 2 mi s on US 24, 0.5 mi e on US 24 and 285. Ext corridors. **Pets:** Accepted.

Best Western Vista Inn M ❖
(719) 395-8009. **$69-$139.** 733 US Hwy 24 N. 0.5 mi n. Int corridors. **Pets:** Large, dogs only. $50 deposit/room, $7 daily fee/pet. Designated rooms, service with restrictions, supervision.

BURLINGTON

Burlington Comfort Inn SH
(719) 346-7676. **$59-$120, 14 day notice.** 282 S Lincoln St. I-70, exit 437, just n on US 385. Int corridors. **Pets:** Large. $50 deposit/room, $10 daily fee/room. Designated rooms, service with restrictions, supervision.

Chaparral Motor Inn M
(719) 346-5361. **$45-$59.** 405 S Lincoln St. I-70, exit 437, just n on jct US 385. Ext corridors. **Pets:** Small, other species. $7 daily fee/pet. Service with restrictions, supervision.

Sloans Motel M
(719) 346-5333. **$40-$60, 7 day notice.** 1901 Rose Ave. I-70, exit 437, 0.5 mi n on US 385, just e on US 24; exit 438 westbound, 1 mi w on US 24. Ext corridors. **Pets:** Accepted.

CANON CITY

Best Western Royal Gorge Motel M
(719) 275-3377. **$50-$110.** 1925 Fremont Dr. 0.8 mi e on US 50. Ext/int corridors. **Pets:** Other species. $15 one-time fee/room. Designated rooms, no service, supervision.

Comfort Inn SH
(719) 276-6900. **$59-$99.** 311 Royal Gorge Blvd. On US 50, just w of downtown. Int corridors. **Pets:** Accepted.

Holiday Inn Express SH
(719) 275-2400. **$79-$125.** 110 Latigo Ln. 2.5 mi e of SR 115 on US 50. Int corridors. **Pets:** Small, other species. $10 daily fee/pet. Designated rooms, service with restrictions, supervision.

** AAA ♦♦♦ Quality Inn & Suites M**
(719) 275-8676. **$79-$189.** 3075 E Hwy 50. 2 mi e of jct SR 115 and US 50; center. Int corridors. **Pets:** Other species. Designated rooms, service with restrictions, supervision.

SAVE 🛇 ⊠ 🛅 🖵 🍴 🏊

AAA ♦♦♦ Royal Gorge Inn M
(719) 269-1100. **$55-$99.** 217 N Raynolds Ave. 1 mi e on US 50, just n. Int corridors. **Pets:** Accepted.

SAVE 🛇 ⊠ 🛅 🏊

CARBONDALE

AAA ♦♦♦♦ Comfort Inn & Suites SH ☙
(970) 963-8880. **$79-$169.** 920 Cowen Dr. Jct of SR 82 and 133, just s via signs. Int corridors. **Pets:** Other species. $10 daily fee/pet. Designated rooms, service with restrictions, supervision.

SAVE 🛇 ⊠ 🗲 🛅 🖵 🏊 ⊠

AAA ♦♦♦ Days Inn-Carbondale SH
(970) 963-9111. **$69-$119, 3 day notice.** 950 Cowen Dr. Jct SR 82 and 133. Int corridors. **Pets:** Accepted.

SAVE 🛇 ⊠ 🗲 🏊 ⊠

AAA ♦ Thunder River Lodge M ☙
(970) 963-2543. **$46-$85.** 179 Hwy 133. Just s on SR 133, from jct SR 82. Ext corridors. **Pets:** Other species. $25 deposit/room, $5 daily fee/pet. Designated rooms, service with restrictions, supervision.

SAVE ⊠

CASTLE ROCK

AAA ♦♦♦♦ Best Western Inn & Suites of Castle Rock SH ☙
(303) 814-8800. **$79-$119.** 595 Genoa Way. I-25, exit 184 (Meadows Pkwy), just w to Castleton Way, just s, then e on Genoa Way. Int corridors. **Pets:** Medium. $15 daily fee/pet. Designated rooms, service with restrictions, supervision.

SAVE 🛇 ⊠ 🗲 🗲 🛅 🖵 🏊

♦♦♦♦ Comfort Suites SH ☙
(303) 814-9999. **$59-$109.** 4755 Castleton Way. I-25, exit 184 (Meadows Pkwy), w to Castleton Way; entry on eastside. Int corridors. **Pets:** Other species. $10 daily fee/room. No service, supervision.

ASK 🛇 ⊠ 🗲M 🗲 🗲 🛅 🖵 🏊

♦♦♦ Holiday Inn Express SH
(303) 660-9733. **$79-$109.** 884 Park St. I-25, exit 182, just w. Int corridors. **Pets:** Accepted.

ASK 🛇 ⊠ 🗲 🛅 🖵 🏊

CEDAREDGE

AAA ♦♦♦♦ Howard Johnson Express Inn M
(970) 856-7824. **$69-$109, 14 day notice.** 530 S Grand Mesa Dr. Just s on SR 65. Int corridors. **Pets:** Accepted.

SAVE 🛇 ⊠ 🗲 🛅 🖵 🏊

COLORADO SPRINGS METROPOLITAN AREA

COLORADO SPRINGS

AAA ♦♦♦ Airport Value Inn & Suites SH
(719) 596-5588. **$54-$99.** 6875 Space Village Ave. US 24, 6 mi e; adjacent to Peterson Air Force Base. Ext/int corridors. **Pets:** Accepted.

SAVE 🛇 ⊠ 🗲M 🛅 🖵

AAA ♦♦♦♦ AmeriSuites (Colorado Springs/Garden of the Gods) SH
(719) 265-9385. **$79-$139.** 503 W Garden of the Gods Rd. I-25, exit 146, just w. Int corridors. **Pets:** Medium, other species. $10 daily fee/pet. Service with restrictions, crate.

SAVE 🛇 ⊠ 🗲 🛅 🖵 🏊

AAA ♦♦♦ Apollo Park Executive Suites CO
(719) 634-0286. **$55-$75, 7 day notice.** 805 S Circle Dr, 2-B. I-25, exit 138, 2.5 mi e. Int corridors. **Pets:** Accepted.

SAVE 🛇 ⊠ 🛅 🖵 🏊

AAA ♦♦♦ Best Western Airport Inn SH
(719) 574-7707. **$69-$99.** 1780 Aeroplaza Dr. I-25, exit 139 (US 24 Bypass), 4 mi e on Fountain Blvd. Int corridors. **Pets:** Small. $10 daily fee/pet. Designated rooms, supervision.

SAVE ⊠ 🗲M 🛅 🖵 🏊 ⊠

AAA ♦♦♦♦ Best Western Executive Inn & Suites SH
(719) 576-2371. **$65-$159.** 1440 Harrison Rd. I-25, exit 138, just w; on northwest corner of interchange; entry through restaurant. Int corridors. **Pets:** Accepted.

SAVE 🛇 ⊠ 🗲M 🗲 🛅 🖵 🏊

AAA ♦♦♦♦♦ The Broadmoor LH ☙
(719) 634-7711. **$230-$470, 7 day notice.** 1 Lake Ave. I-25, exit 138, 3 mi w on Circle Dr which becomes Lake Ave. Int corridors. **Pets:** Other species. $35 daily fee/pet. Designated rooms.

SAVE ⊠ 🗲M 🗲 🗲 🛅 🖵 🍴 🏊 ⊠

AAA ♦ Chief Motel M ☙
(719) 473-5228. **$35-$65.** 1624 S Nevada Ave. I-25, exit 140. Ext corridors. **Pets:** Other species. $20 deposit/room, $5 daily fee/pet, $5 one-time fee/pet. Service with restrictions, supervision.

SAVE 🛇 ⊠ 🛅

AAA ♦♦♦♦ Comfort Inn North SH
(719) 262-9000. **$49-$119.** 6450 Corporate Dr. I-25, exit 149 (Woodmen Rd), just w to 2nd light, then 0.3 mi s. Int corridors. **Pets:** Medium. $10 daily fee/pet. Service with restrictions, supervision.

SAVE 🛇 ⊠ 🗲M 🗲 🗲 🛅 🖵 🏊 ⊠

AAA ♦♦♦ Comfort Suites SH
(719) 536-0731. **$59-$129.** 1055 Kelly Johnson Blvd. I-25, exit 150, just s on Academy Blvd to Kelly Johnson Blvd, then w. Int corridors. **Pets:** Other species. $10 daily fee/pet. Designated rooms, service with restrictions, crate.

SAVE 🛇 ⊠ 🗲M 🗲 🛅 🖵 🏊 ⊠

AAA ♦♦♦ Days Inn-Air Force Academy SH
(719) 266-1317. **$49-$94.** 8350 Razorback Rd. I-25, exit 150, just s, then e. Int corridors. **Pets:** Accepted.

SAVE 🛇 ⊠ 🗲M 🛅 🖵 🏊

♦♦♦ Doubletree Hotel Colorado Springs, World Arena SH ☙
(719) 576-8900. **$99-$199.** 1775 E Cheyenne Mountain Blvd. I-25, exit 138, just w. Int corridors. **Pets:** Medium, other species. $10 daily fee/room. Service with restrictions, supervision.

⊠ 🗲M 🗲 🗲 🖵 🍴 🏊 ⊠

♦♦♦ Drury Inn-Pikes Peak SH
(719) 598-2500. **$55-$125.** 8155 N Academy Blvd. I-25, exit 150, just s, then e. Int corridors. **Pets:** Large, other species. Service with restrictions, supervision.

ASK ⊠ 🗲 🛅 🖵 🏊

Econo Lodge Inn & Suites World Arena SH 🐾
(719) 632-6651. **$45-$80.** 1623 S Nevada Ave. I-25, exit 140, just s. Ext corridors. **Pets:** Other species. $10 deposit/pet, $10 one-time fee/pet. Service with restrictions, crate.
(SAVE) (S🐾) (✕) (👓) (🔒) (💻) (🏊)

Homewood Suites by Hilton SH
(719) 265-6600. **$109-$209.** 9130 Explorer Dr. I-25, exit 151, 0.8 mi e; across from Focus on the Family. Int corridors. **Pets:** Medium, other species. $25 one-time fee/pet. Service with restrictions, crate.
(✕) (🖥) (🍴) (👓) (🔒) (💻) (🏊)

Homewood Suites by Hilton Colorado Springs Airport SH
(719) 574-3700. 2875 Zeppelin Rd. I-25, exit 139, 4 mi e on US 24 Bypass (Fountain Blvd) to Powers Rd, then s. Int corridors. **Pets:** Medium. $50 one-time fee/pet. Designated rooms, service with restrictions, supervision.
(ASK) (S🐾) (✕) (🏊) (👓) (🔒) (💻) (🏊) (✕)

La Quinta Inn & Suites Colorado Springs (South/Airport) SH
(719) 527-4788. **$79-$119.** 2750 Geyser Dr. I-25, exit 138 (Circle Dr), just w to Cheyenne Mountain Blvd, then just s. Int corridors. **Pets:** Accepted.
(SAVE) (✕) (🏊) (🍴) (👓) (🔒) (💻) (🏊)

La Quinta Inn Colorado Springs (Garden of the Gods) SH
(719) 528-5060. **$69-$109.** 4385 Sinton Rd. I-25, exit 146, just e. Ext/int corridors. **Pets:** Accepted.
(SAVE) (✕) (🍴) (🔒) (💻) (🏊)

Le Baron Hotel, Downtown Colorado Springs SH
(719) 471-8680. **$69-$109.** 314 W Bijou St. I-25, exit 142, northwest corner. Int corridors. **Pets:** Other species. $50 deposit/room. Service with restrictions, supervision.
(ASK) (S🐾) (✕) (🍴) (🔒) (💻) (🍽) (🏊)

Marriott TownePlace Suites Colorado Springs SH
(719) 594-4447. **$139-$149.** 4760 Centennial Blvd. I-25, exit 146 (Garden of the Gods Rd), 1 mi w, n on Centennial Blvd, then first left. Int corridors. **Pets:** Accepted.
(✕) (🏊) (👓) (🔒) (💻) (🏊)

Quality Inn-Garden of the Gods SH 🐾
(719) 593-9119. **$39-$129.** 555 W Garden of the Gods Rd. I-25, exit 146, just w. Int corridors. **Pets:** Other species. $50 deposit/room. Designated rooms, service with restrictions.
(ASK) (S🐾) (✕) (🍴) (🔒) (💻) (🏊)

Radisson Inn & Suites LH
(719) 597-7000. **$89-$109.** 1645 N Newport Rd. I-25, exit 139, 4 mi e on US 24 Bypass (Fountain Blvd). Int corridors. **Pets:** Medium, other species. $100 deposit/pet, $25 one-time fee/room. Service with restrictions, crate.
(SAVE) (S🐾) (✕) (🏊) (🍴) (👓) (🔒) (💻) (🍽) (🏊) (✕)

Radisson Inn Colorado Springs North LH
(719) 598-5770. **$79-$169.** 8110 N Academy Blvd. I-25, exit 150, just s. Int corridors. **Pets:** Medium, other species. $50 deposit/room. Service with restrictions.
(SAVE) (S🐾) (✕) (🏊) (🍴) (👓) (🔒) (💻) (🍽) (🏊) (✕)

Rainbow Lodge and Inn M
(719) 632-4551. **$55-$95, 7 day notice.** 3709 W Colorado Ave. I-25, exit 141, 2.5 mi w on US 24, just n on 31st, then 0.7 mi w. Ext corridors. **Pets:** Small, other species. $25 deposit/room. Service with restrictions, supervision.
(SAVE) (S🐾) (✕) (🔒) (🏊)

Ramada Limited East-Airport SH
(719) 596-7660. **$59-$89.** 520 N Murray Blvd. I-25, exit 141, e to Wahsatch, n to Platte, 3.8 mi e to Murray Blvd, then just n. Ext/int corridors. **Pets:** Other species. $25 deposit/room. Service with restrictions, supervision.
(ASK) (S🐾) (✕) (👓) (🔒) (💻) (🏊)

Residence Inn by Marriott-Central SH 🐾
(719) 574-0370. **$69-$129.** 3880 N Academy Blvd. I-25, exit 146, 6 mi e on Austin Bluffs Pkwy to Academy Blvd (SR 83), 0.3 mi s. Ext corridors. **Pets:** Other species. $75 one-time fee/room. No service.
(ASK) (S🐾) (✕) (🏊) (👓) (🔒) (💻) (🏊) (✕)

Residence Inn by Marriott Colorado Springs North at Interguest Pkwy SH
(719) 388-9300. **$89-$279.** 9805 Federal Dr. I-25, exit 153, just e, then s. Int corridors. **Pets:** Medium. $75 one-time fee/pet. Designated rooms, service with restrictions.
(ASK) (S🐾) (✕) (🏊) (👓) (🔒) (💻) (🏊) (✕)

Residence Inn by Marriott-Colorado Springs South SH
(719) 576-0101. **$109-$209.** 2765 Geyser Dr. I-25, exit 138, just w to E Cheyenne Mountain Blvd, then just s. Int corridors. **Pets:** Other species. $75 one-time fee/room.
(ASK) (S🐾) (✕) (🏊) (👓) (🔒) (💻) (🏊) (✕)

Rodeway Inn SH
(719) 471-0990. **$50-$60.** 2409 E Pikes Peak Ave. I-25, exit 143, e on Uintah to Union, s to Pikes Peak, then e; exit 138, ne on Circle Dr to Pikes Peak Ave, then w. Ext corridors. **Pets:** Accepted.
(S🐾) (✕) (🔒) (💻) (🏊)

Sheraton Colorado Springs Hotel LH 🐾
(719) 576-5900. **$159-$199.** 2886 S Circle Dr. I-25, exit 138, just e. Int corridors. **Pets:** Service with restrictions, supervision.
(SAVE) (S🐾) (✕) (🏊) (👓) (🔒) (💻) (🏊) (✕)

Sleep Inn SH
(719) 260-6969. **$39-$99.** 1075 Kelly Johnson Blvd. I-25, exit 150, just s on Academy Blvd to Kelly Johnson Blvd, then w. Int corridors. **Pets:** Other species. $10 daily fee/pet. Designated rooms, service with restrictions, crate.
(ASK) (S🐾) (✕) (🏊) (👓) (💻)

Stagecoach Motel M 🐾
(719) 633-3894. **$39-$69.** 1647 S Nevada Ave. I-25, exit 140, just s. Ext corridors. **Pets:** Small, other species. $5 daily fee/pet. Service with restrictions.
(SAVE) (S🐾) (✕) (🔒)

Staybridge Suites-Air Force Academy SH
(719) 590-7829. **$79-$149.** 7130 Commerce Center Dr. I-25, exit 149, just w, then n. Int corridors. **Pets:** Accepted.
(SAVE) (S🐾) (✕) (🏊) (🏊) (👓) (🔒) (💻) (🏊) (✕)

Travel Inn M 🐾
(719) 636-3986. **$35-$65.** 512 S Nevada Ave. I-25, exit 141, just e to Nevada Ave, then just s. Ext/int corridors. **Pets:** Other species. $20 deposit/room, $5 daily fee/pet, $5 one-time fee/pet. Service with restrictions, supervision.
(SAVE) (S🐾) (✕) (🔒)

Travelodge SH
(719) 632-4600. **$35-$90, 5 day notice.** 2625 Ore Mill Rd. I-25, exit 141, 2.3 mi nw on US 24; entry via 26th St. Int corridors. **Pets:** Other species. $20 one-time fee/room. Service with restrictions, supervision.
(SAVE) (S🐾) (✕) (🔒) (💻)

Wyndham Colorado Springs LH
(719) 260-1800. **$65-$85.** 5580 Tech Center Dr. I-25, exit 147 (Rockrimmon Blvd), 0.5 mi w. Int corridors. **Pets:** Accepted.
(SAVE) (✕) (🏊) (🔒) (💻) (🍴) (🏊) (✕)

MANITOU SPRINGS

AAA **W** **W** **Park Row Lodge** **M**
(719) 685-5216. **$39-$69.** 54 Manitou Ave. I-25, exit 141, 4 mi nw on US 24, exit Manitou Ave, then just se. Ext corridors. **Pets:** Small. $10 one-time fee/room. Service with restrictions, crate.

SAVE S6 X 8

AAA **W** **Red Wing Motel** **M**
(719) 685-5656. **$40-$120.** 56 El Paso Blvd. I-25, exit 141, 4 mi w on US 24, just e to Beckers Ln, then n. Ext corridors. **Pets:** Medium, other species. $7 one-time fee/room. Service with restrictions.

SAVE S6 X 8 P

W **Santa Fe Motel** **SH**
(719) 475-8185. **Call for rates.** 3 Manitou Ave. I-25, exit 141, 2.5 mi w on US 24, just n on 31st St, then 0.9 mi w on Colorado Ave. **Pets:** Accepted.

X 8 P

AAA **W** **W** **Silver Saddle Motel** **M** 🐾
(719) 685-5611. **$64-$85, 7 day notice.** 215 Manitou Ave. I-25, exit 141, 4 mi w on US 24 to Manitou Ave, then just e on US 24 business route. Ext corridors. **Pets:** Other species. Service with restrictions, supervision.

SAVE S6 X P 2

AAA **W** **W** **Ute Pass Motel** **M**
(719) 685-5171. **$40-$200, 14 day notice.** 1132 Manitou Ave. I-25, exit 141, 4 mi w, then just w on US 24 business route. Ext corridors. **Pets:** Other species. $50 deposit/room, $10 daily fee/pet. Service with restrictions, crate.

SAVE S6 X 8 P X

END METROPOLITAN AREA

COPPER MOUNTAIN

AAA **W** **W** **Copper Mountain Resort** **CO**
(970) 968-2882. **$134-$269.** 0509 Copper Rd. I-70, exit 195. Int corridors. **Pets:** Accepted.

SAVE X 8 P 🍴 2 X AC

CORTEZ

AAA **W** **W** **Anasazi Motor Inn** **M**
(970) 565-3773. **$55-$71.** 640 S Broadway. 0.5 mi sw on US 160 and 491. Ext corridors. **Pets:** Medium, other species. $50 deposit/room. Designated rooms, service with restrictions, supervision.

SAVE S6 X 8 🍴 2 X

AAA **W** **W** **Best Western Turquoise Inn &**
Suites **SH** 🐾
(970) 565-3778. **$69-$149.** 535 E Main St. On US 160. Ext corridors. **Pets:** $15 one-time fee/room. Designated rooms, service with restrictions, supervision.

SAVE S6 X 8 P 2

AAA **W** **W** **Budget Host Inn** **M**
(970) 565-3738. **$38-$78.** 2040 E Main St. 1.3 mi e on US 160, w of jct SR 145. Ext corridors. **Pets:** Medium. $5 daily fee/pet. Designated rooms, service with restrictions, supervision.

SAVE S6 X 8 P 2

AAA **W** **W** **CareFree Inn Sands** **M**
(970) 565-3761. **$46-$76.** 1120 E Main St. 0.3 mi e on US 160. Ext/int corridors. **Pets:** Accepted.

SAVE S6 X 8 P 2

AAA **W** **W** **Comfort Inn** **SH**
(970) 565-3400. **$59-$104.** 2321 E Main St. 1.3 mi e on US 160. Ext/int corridors. **Pets:** Other species. $10 one-time fee/room. Service with restrictions, supervision.

SAVE S6 X 8 P 2

AAA **W** **W** **Days Inn** **SH**
(970) 565-8577. **$49-$99.** US Hwy 160 at State 145. 1.5 mi e on US 160, at jct SR 145. Ext/int corridors. **Pets:** Other species. $10 one-time fee/room. Service with restrictions, supervision.

SAVE S6 X 8 P 🍴 2

W **W** **Econo Lodge** **M**
(970) 565-3474. **$42-$89.** 2020 E Main St. 1.3 mi e on US 160. Ext corridors. **Pets:** Other species. Designated rooms, service with restrictions, crate.

ASK S6 X 8 P 2

AAA **W** **W** **Holiday Inn Express** **SH**
(970) 565-6000. **$89-$149.** 2121 E Main St. 1.3 mi e on US 160. Int corridors. **Pets:** Other species. Designated rooms, supervision.

SAVE S6 X 🏊 8 2 X

AAA **W** **W** **Tomahawk Lodge** **M**
(970) 565-8521. **$37-$75.** 728 S Broadway. 1 mi sw on US 160 and 491. Ext corridors. **Pets:** Dogs only. $25 deposit/pet. Designated rooms, service with restrictions, supervision.

SAVE S6 X P 2

W **W** **Travelodge** **M**
(970) 565-7778. **$40-$79.** 440 S Broadway. 0.8 mi sw on US 160 and 491. Ext corridors. **Pets:** Other species. $5 daily fee/pet. Service with restrictions, crate.

ASK S6 X 8 P 2

CRAIG

AAA **W** **W** **Black Nugget Motel** **M**
(970) 824-8161. **$40-$65.** 2855 W Victory Way. 1.5 mi w on US 40, 0.3 mi w of jct SR 13. Ext corridors. **Pets:** Other species. $4 daily fee/pet. Supervision.

SAVE S6 X 8 X

W **W** **W** **Craig Holiday Inn** **SH**
(970) 824-4000. **$79-$99.** 300 S Hwy 13. 0.3 mi s on SR 13, from jct US 40. Int corridors. **Pets:** Accepted.

ASK S6 X 🏊 8 P 🍴 2 X

AAA **W** **W** **Deer Park Inn and Suites** **SH**
(970) 824-9282. **$79-$139.** 262 Commerce St (Hwy 13). Jct US 40, just 0.3 mi s on SR 13. Int corridors. **Pets:** Medium, other species. $50 deposit/room. Service with restrictions, supervision.

SAVE S6 X 6M 🏊 8 2

CRESTED BUTTE

W **W** **W** **Grand Lodge Crested Butte** **LH**
(970) 349-8000. **$69-$289, 3 day notice.** 6 Emmons Loop. 2.5 mi n on SR 135. Int corridors. **Pets:** Large, other species. $30 daily fee/room. Designated rooms, service with restrictions, supervision.

ASK S6 X 8 P 🍴 2 X

W **W** **Old Town Inn** **SH**
(970) 349-6184. **$59-$98, 14 day notice.** 708 6th St. Se on SR 135. Int corridors. **Pets:** Accepted.

ASK S6 X

CRIPPLE CREEK

▼▼▼▼ **Double Eagle Hotel/Casino** 🆂🅷
(719) 689-5000. **Call for rates.** 442 E Bennett Ave. On SR 67; at northwest entry to town diagonal from Cripple Creek Museum. Int corridors. **Pets:** Accepted.
❌ 🐾 🛏 🖥 🍴

DELTA

🅰🅰🅰 ▼▼▼ **Best Western Sundance** 🅼
(970) 874-9781. **$85.** 903 Main St. 0.5 mi s on US 50. Ext corridors. **Pets:** $10 daily fee/pet. Service with restrictions, crate.
🆂🅰🆅🅴 🆂 ❌ 🛏 🖥 🍴 ➥ ❌

▼▼▼▼ **Comfort Inn** 🅼
(970) 874-1000. **$80-$100.** 180 Gunnison River Dr. Just n, w of jct US 50 and 92. Int corridors. **Pets:** $10 daily fee/pet. Supervision.
🅰🆂🅺 🆂 ❌ 🛏 🖥

🅰🅰🅰 ▼▼▼ **South Gate Inns** 🅼
(970) 874-9726. **$45-$80.** 2124 S Main St. 1.5 mi s on US 50. Ext corridors. **Pets:** Medium, dogs only. $5 one-time fee/pet. Designated rooms, no service, supervision.
🆂🅰🆅🅴 🆂 ❌ 🛏 🖥 ➥

DENVER METROPOLITAN AREA

AURORA

🅰🅰🅰 ▼▼▼▼ **AmeriSuites (Denver/Airport)** 🆂🅷
(303) 371-0700. **$109-$134.** 16250 E 40th Ave. I-70, exit 283 (Chambers Rd), just n, then 0.5 mi e. Int corridors. **Pets:** Other species. Service with restrictions, crate.
🆂🅰🆅🅴 🆂 ❌ 🐾 🅼 🅿 🐾 🛏 🖥 ➥

🅰🅰🅰 ▼▼▼▼ **Best Western Gateway Inn & Suites** 🆂🅷
(720) 748-4800. **$69-$129.** 800 S Abilene St. I-225, exit 7 (Mississippi Ave), e to Abilene St, then 3 blks n. Int corridors. **Pets:** Accepted.
🆂🅰🆅🅴 🆂 ❌ 🐾 🅼 🐾 🛏 🖥 ➥

🅰🅰🅰 ▼▼▼ **Comfort Inn Denver Southeast** 🆂🅷
(303) 755-8000. **$49-$89.** 14071 E Iliff Ave. I-225, exit 5, just e. Int corridors. **Pets:** Medium. $20 one-time fee/pet. Service with restrictions, supervision.
🆂🅰🆅🅴 🆂 ❌ 🐾 🅼 🐾 🐾 🛏 🖥

▼▼▼ **The Hearthside TSS** 🆂🅷
(303) 481-0379. **$59-$99.** 14090 E Evans. I-225, exit 5 (E Iliff Ave), e to Blackhawk St, then 0.4 mi nw. Int corridors. **Pets:** Small, other species. $10 daily fee/pet. Designated rooms, service with restrictions, supervision.
🅰🆂🅺 🆂 ❌ 🐾 🛏 🖥

🅰🅰🅰 ▼▼▼▼ **Holiday Inn DIA** 🅻🅷
(303) 371-9494. **$85-$119.** 15500 E 40th Ave. I-70, exit 283 (Chambers Rd), just n, then just e. Int corridors. **Pets:** $25 one-time fee/room. Service with restrictions, supervision.
🆂🅰🆅🅴 🆂 ❌ 🐾 🅼 🐾 🐾 🛏 🖥 🍴 ➥ ❌

▼▼▼▼ **Homestead Studio Suites Hotel-Denver/Aurora** 🅼
(303) 750-9116. **$52-$62.** 13941 E Harvard Ave. I-225, exit 5, just e on E Iliff Ave to Blackhawk St, then just s. Ext corridors. **Pets:** Small. $25 daily fee/room. Service with restrictions, crate.
🅰🆂🅺 🆂 ❌ 🐾 🅼 🐾 🛏 🖥

🅰🅰🅰 ▼▼▼▼ **La Quinta Inn Denver (Aurora)** 🅼
(303) 337-0206. **$69-$89.** 1011 S Abilene St. I-225, exit 7, just e, then n. Ext corridors. **Pets:** Medium, other species. Service with restrictions, supervision.
🆂🅰🆅🅴 ❌ 🐾 🅼 🐾 🖥 ➥

🅰🅰🅰 ▼▼▼ **Sleep Inn Denver International Airport** 🆂🅷
(303) 373-1616. **$59-$99.** 15900 E 40th Ave. I-70, exit 283; from airport, Pena Blvd S to 40th Ave W. Int corridors. **Pets:** Accepted.
🆂🅰🆅🅴 🆂 ❌ 🐾 🅼 🐾 🐾 🛏 🖥 ➥

🅰🅰🅰 ▼▼▼ **Wellesley Inn & Suites (Denver/Aurora)** 🆂🅷
(303) 337-7000. **$69-$89.** 14095 E Evans Ave. I-225, exit 5 (E Iliff Ave), just e to Blackhawk St, then just n. Int corridors. **Pets:** Accepted.
🆂🅰🆅🅴 🆂 ❌ 🐾 🅼 🐾 🐾 🛏 🖥 ➥

CENTENNIAL

🅰🅰🅰 ▼▼▼▼ **Embassy Suites Denver Tech Center** 🆂🅷 🐾
(303) 792-0433. **$79-$199.** 10250 E Costilla Ave. I-25, exit 197, 1 mi e on Arapahoe Rd, 0.3 mi s on Havana St, then w. Int corridors. **Pets:** Medium. $75 one-time fee/room. Designated rooms, service with restrictions, crate.
🆂🅰🆅🅴 ❌ 🐾 🅼 🐾 🐾 🛏 🖥 🍴 ➥

DENVER

▼▼▼ **Best Western Central Denver** 🆂🅷
(303) 296-4000. **$45-$115.** 200 W 48th Ave. I-25, exit 215 northbound; exit 214B southbound. Int corridors. **Pets:** Medium. $10 daily fee/room. Service with restrictions, supervision.
🅰🆂🅺 🆂 ❌ 🛏 🖥 🍴 ➥

🅰🅰🅰 ▼▼▼▼ **Brown Palace Hotel** 🅻🅷 🐾
(303) 297-3111. **$199.** 321 17th St, Tremont & Broadway. I-25, exit 210 (E Colfax Ave) to Lincoln St, n to Tremont, then just w. Int corridors. **Pets:** Small, dogs only. $60 deposit/room. Service with restrictions.
🆂🅰🆅🅴 ❌ 🐾 🐾 🛏 🍴 ❌

🅰🅰🅰 ▼▼ **Cameron Motel** 🅼
(303) 757-2100. **$52-$65.** 4500 E Evans Ave. I-25, exit 203, then w. Ext corridors. **Pets:** Medium. $5 daily fee/pet. Designated rooms, service with restrictions, supervision.
🆂🅰🆅🅴 🆂 ❌ 🛏

🅰🅰🅰 ▼▼▼▼ **Comfort Inn Downtown Denver** 🆂🅷
(303) 296-0400. **$89-$139.** 401 17th St. I-25, exit 210 (E Colfax Ave) to Lincoln St, n to Tremont, then just w; opposite Brown Palace Hotel. Int corridors. **Pets:** Small, dogs only. $100 deposit/room. Service with restrictions.
🆂🅰🆅🅴 ❌ 🐾 🖥 🍴

▼▼▼▼ **Denver Marriott Hotel City Center** 🅻🅷
(303) 297-1300. **$189-$269.** 1701 California St at 17th St. I-25, exit 210 (E Colfax Ave) to Welton St, 0.5 mi ne, nw on 18th, then 1 blk. Int corridors. **Pets:** Accepted.
❌ 🐾 🐾 🛏 🖥 🍴 ➥ ❌

▼▼▼ **Denver Marriott Tech Center** 🅻🅷
(303) 779-1100. **$165, 3 day notice.** 4900 S Syracuse St. I-25, exit 199, exit Bellview e to Syracuse St, then just n. Int corridors. **Pets:** Medium, other species. $50 one-time fee/room. Service with restrictions.
❌ 🅼 🐾 🐾 🛏 🖥 🍴 ➥

▼▼▼▼ **DoubleTree Hotel Denver** 🅻🅷
(303) 321-3333. **$89-$179.** 3203 Quebec St. I-70, exit 278, 0.5 mi s; I-270, exit 4. Int corridors. **Pets:** $20 one-time fee/room. Service with restrictions, crate.
❌ 🐾 🐾 🛏 🖥 🍴 ➥ ❌

▼▼▼▼ **Drury Inn-Denver East** SH
(303) 373-1983. **$55-$95.** 4380 E Peoria St. I-70, exit 281, just n. Int corridors. **Pets:** Large, other species. Service with restrictions, supervision.

[ASK] [✕] [☷] [▤] [▥] [⊇]

AAA ▼▼▼▼ **Embassy Suites Aurora-Denver** LH
(303) 375-0400. **$89-$199.** 4444 N Havana St. I-70, exit 280, just n. Int corridors. **Pets:** Accepted.

[SAVE] [✕] [&M] [☷] [▤] [▥] [▦] [¶] [⊇] [✕]

AAA ▼▼▼▼ **Four Points by Sheraton at Denver University-a Barcelo Hotel** SH
(303) 757-8797. **$139-$199.** 1475 S Colorado Blvd. I-25, exit 204, 0.5 mi n; entry on Arkansas St. Int corridors. **Pets:** Accepted.

[SAVE] [S☷] [✕] [&M] [☷] [▥] [▤] [▥] [▦] [¶] [⊇]

▼▼▼▼ **The Four Points by Sheraton Denver Southeast** LH
(303) 758-7000. **$199.** 6363 E Hampden Ave. I-25, exit 201, just e. Ext/int corridors. **Pets:** Accepted.

[ASK] [S☷] [✕] [▤] [▥] [▦] [¶] [⊇] [✕]

AAA ▼▼ **Guesthouse Hotel Denver Stapleton** SH
(303) 388-6161. **$65-$150.** 3737 Quebec St. I-70, exit 278, just s. Int corridors. **Pets:** Other species. $20 one-time fee/room. Service with restrictions, supervision.

[SAVE] [S☷] [✕] [▤] [▥] [¶] [⊇]

▼▼▼ **Hampton Inn & Suites Denver Tech Center** SH ❖
(303) 804-9900. **$59-$119.** 5001 S Ulster St. I-25, exit 199, e to Ulster St, then just n. Int corridors. **Pets:** Medium. Service with restrictions, supervision.

[ASK] [S☷] [✕] [&M] [☷] [▥] [▤] [▥] [⊇]

AAA ▼▼▼▼ **Hampton Inn DIA** SH
(303) 371-0200. **$90-$100.** 6290 Tower Rd. I-70, exit 186 (Tower Rd), 3.5 mi n. Int corridors. **Pets:** Accepted.

[SAVE] [S☷] [✕] [☷] [▥] [▤] [▥]

AAA ▼▼▼▼ **Holiday Chalet A Victorian Bed & Breakfast** BB ❖
(303) 437-8245. **$94-$160.** 1820 E Colfax Ave. I-25, exit 210, 1.3 mi e on US 40. Int corridors. **Pets:** $5 daily fee/room.

[SAVE] [S☷] [✕] [▤] [▥]

▼▼▼▼ **Holiday Inn-Denver Central** LH
(303) 292-9500. **$99-$159.** 4849 Bannock St. I-25, 215 northbound; exit 214B southbound, 1 mi s. Ext/int corridors. **Pets:** Medium. $250 deposit/room. Designated rooms, service with restrictions, supervision.

[ASK] [S☷] [✕] [☷] [▥] [▤] [▥] [¶] [⊇]

▼ **Homestead Studio Suites Hotel-Denver/Tech Center-North** SH
(303) 689-9443. **$64-$74.** 4885 S Quebec St. I-25, exit 199, just w to Quebec St, then just n; next to Mountain View Golf Course. Ext corridors. **Pets:** Accepted.

[ASK] [S☷] [✕] [&M] [☷] [▥] [▤] [▥] [✕]

AAA ▼▼▼ ▼▼▼ **Hotel Monaco Denver** SH ❖
(303) 296-1717. **$169-$285.** 1717 Champa St. I-25, exit 212A (Speer Blvd S), s to Curtis St, w to 19th St, 1 blk s to Champa St, then 2 blks w. Int corridors. **Pets:** Large, other species. Service with restrictions, supervision.

[SAVE] [S☷] [✕] [&M] [☷] [▥] [▤] [▥] [¶] [✕]

AAA ▼▼▼▼ **Hotel Teatro** SH ❖
(303) 228-1100. **$225-$395.** 1100 14th St. I-25, exit 212 (Speer Blvd), just ne on Lawrence St, then e to 14th St; exit Auraria Pkwy northbound. Int corridors. **Pets:** Dogs only.

[SAVE] [S☷] [✕] [☷] [▥] [▤] [▥] [¶] [✕]

AAA ▼▼▼▼ **J W Marriott Denver At Cherry Creek** SH
(303) 316-2700. **$209-$241.** 150 Clayton Ln. I-25, exit 5 (University Blvd), 2.4 mi n to 1st Ave, just e, then just n. Int corridors. **Pets:** Large, dogs only. Service with restrictions, supervision.

[ASK] [S☷] [✕] [&M] [☷] [▥] [▤] [¶]

▼▼▼▼ **La Quinta Inn & Suites Denver (Airport/DIA)** SH
(303) 371-0888. **$79-$99.** 6801 Tower Rd. I-70, exit 286, 4.2 mi n; 0.8 mi s of Pena Blvd. Int corridors. **Pets:** Other species. Service with restrictions.

[✕] [&M] [☷] [▥] [▤] [▥] [⊇] [✕]

▼▼▼▼ **La Quinta Inn Denver (Central)** SH
(303) 458-1222. **$69-$99.** 3500 Park Ave W. I-25, exit 213, take 38th Ave, just s, left at Fox St, left on Park to 2nd light, then U-turn. Ext/int corridors. **Pets:** Accepted.

[ASK] [✕] [☷] [▥] [▤] [▥] [⊇]

AAA ▼▼▼▼ **La Quinta Inn Denver (Cherry Creek)** SH ❖
(303) 758-8886. **$69-$99.** 1975 S Colorado Blvd. I-25, exit 204, just s. Ext corridors. **Pets:** Small. Service with restrictions, supervision.

[SAVE] [✕] [☷] [▥] [⊇]

▼▼▼ **Magnolia Hotel-Downtown** SH
(303) 607-9000. **$250-$280.** 818 17th St. I-25, exit 212A (Speer Blvd S) to Market St, e to 17th St, then s to jct 17th and Stout sts. Int corridors. **Pets:** $10 daily fee/pet. Service with restrictions, supervision.

[ASK] [S☷] [✕] [&M] [☷] [▥] [▤] [▥]

AAA ▼▼▼ **Quality Inn Denver East** SH
(303) 371-5640. **$49-$89.** 3975 Peoria Way. I-70, exit 281 eastbound; exit 282 westbound, just s. Ext corridors. **Pets:** Accepted.

[SAVE] [S☷] [✕] [▤] [▥] [⊇]

AAA ▼▼▼▼ **Radisson Hotel Denver Stapleton Plaza** LH
(303) 321-3500. **$69-$95.** 3333 Quebec St. I-70, exit 278, 0.3 mi s; I-270, exit 4. Int corridors. **Pets:** Other species. $25 one-time fee/room. Designated rooms, service with restrictions, crate.

[SAVE] [S☷] [✕] [&M] [☷] [▥] [▤] [▥] [¶] [⊇] [✕]

▼▼▼▼ **Ramada Continental Hotel** SH
(303) 433-6677. **$69-$129.** 2601 Zuni St. I-25, exit 212B, just w on Speer Blvd, then just e. **Pets:** $35 one-time fee/pet. Service with restrictions, supervision.

[ASK] [S☷] [☷] [▥] [▤] [▥] [¶] [⊇]

▼▼▼▼ **Ramada Inn Denver Downtown** LH ❖
(303) 831-7700. **$69-$174.** 1150 E Colfax Ave. I-25, exit 210 (E Colfax Ave), 1 mi e on US 40; 0.5 mi e of State Capitol. Int corridors. **Pets:** Other species. $100 deposit/room. Service with restrictions.

[ASK] [S☷] [✕] [&M] [☷] [▥] [▤] [⊇]

AAA ▼▼▼▼ **Ramada Limited & Suites** SH
(303) 373-1600. **$79-$99.** 7020 Tower Rd. I-70, exit 186 (Tower Rd), 4.5 mi n. Int corridors. **Pets:** Accepted.

[SAVE] [S☷] [✕] [&M] [☷] [▥] [▤] [▥] [⊇] [✕]

▼▼▼▼ **Red Lion Denver Central** SH ❖
(303) 321-6666. **$74.** 4040 Quebec St. I-70, exit 278, just s. Ext/int corridors. **Pets:** Other species. $25 one-time fee/room. No service.

[ASK] [✕] [☷] [▥] [▤] [▥] [¶] [⊇]

AAA ▼▼▼▼ **Red Lion Hotel Denver Downtown at Invesco Field** SH
(303) 433-8331. **$119-$139.** 1975 Bryant St. I-25, exit 210B, just w. Int corridors. **Pets:** Accepted.

[SAVE] [S☷] [✕] [▥] [¶] [⊇]

AAA ▼▼▼▼ **Red Roof Inn & Suites** SH ❖
(303) 371-5300. **$58-$83.** 6890 Tower Rd. I-70, exit 286, 4.2 mi n; 0.8 mi s of Pena Blvd. Int corridors. **Pets:** Service with restrictions, supervision.

[SAVE] [S☷] [✕] [&M] [☷] [▥] [▤] [▥] [⊇]

▼▼▼▼ **Residence Inn by Marriott Denver Downtown** 🆂🅷
(303) 458-5318. **$119-$199.** 2777 Zuni St. I-25, exit 212B, just w. Ext corridors. **Pets:** Accepted.
🅰🆂🅺 🆂🔄 ⊠ 🖊 🍴 💻 🏊 ⊠

▼▼▼ **TownePlace Suites by Marriott-Denver Southeast** 🆂🅷 🐾
(303) 759-9393. **$49-$99.** 3699 S Monaco Pkwy. I-25, exit 201, just e to Monaco Pkwy, then s. Int corridors. **Pets:** Other species. $25 daily fee/room. Service with restrictions, supervision.
⊠ 🔧 🍴 💻 🏊

▼▼▼ **TownePlace Suites by Marriott Downtown Denver** 🆂🅷 🐾
(303) 722-2322. **$129-$159.** 685 Speer Blvd. I-25, exit Speer Blvd S, 1.5 mi s, stay in right lane, just past second Bannock St, exit towards Broadway, then right on Acoma St. Int corridors. **Pets:** $25 daily fee/room, $200 one-time fee/room. Service with restrictions, crate.
🅰🆂🅺 🆂🔄 ⊠ 🔧 🍴 💻

🅰🅰🅰 ▼▼▼▼ **The Warwick Hotel-Denver** 🆂🅷 🐾
(303) 861-2000. **$210.** 1776 Grant St at 18th Ave. I-25, exit 210 (E Colfax Ave) to Logan St, n to 18th St, then just w. Int corridors. **Pets:** Dogs only. Designated rooms, service with restrictions, supervision.
🆂🅰🆅🅴 🆂🔄 ⊠ 🖊 🔧 💻 🍽 🏊

🅰🅰🅰 ▼▼▼▼ **The Westin Tabor Center Denver** 🅻🅷
(303) 572-9100. **$99-$179.** 1672 Lawrence St. I-25, exit 212A, 1 mi s to Lawrence St, then e. Int corridors. **Pets:** Accepted.
🆂🅰🆅🅴 🆂🔄 ⊠ 🔧 🖊 🔧 💻 🍽 🏊 ⊠

ENGLEWOOD

🅰🅰🅰 ▼▼▼▼ **AmeriSuites (Denver/Tech Center)** 🆂🅷
(303) 804-0700. **$69-$109.** 8300 E Crescent Pkwy. I-25, exit 199 (Bellview Ave), 0.4 mi e to Crescent Pkwy, then s. Int corridors. **Pets:** Small. $10 daily fee/pet. Designated rooms, service with restrictions, supervision.
🆂🅰🆅🅴 🆂🔄 ⊠ 🖊 🔧 🔧 💻 🏊

▼▼▼▼ **Drury Inn & Suites-Denver Near the Tech Center** 🆂🅷
(303) 694-3400. **$55-$90.** 9445 E Dry Creek Rd. I-25, exit 196 (Dry Creek Rd), just w, on northwest corner. Int corridors. **Pets:** Large, other species. Service with restrictions, supervision.
🅰🆂🅺 ⊠ 🔧 🔧 💻 🏊 ⊠

▼▼▼ **Homestead Studio Suites Hotel-Denver/Tech South/Inverness** 🅼
(303) 708-8888. **$52-$76.** 9650 E Geddes Ave. I-25, exit 196 (Dry Creek Rd), just e, then n on S Clinton St. Ext corridors. **Pets:** Accepted.
🅰🆂🅺 🆂🔄 ⊠ 🖊 🔧 🔧 💻

▼▼▼ **Quality Suites by Choice Hotels** 🆂🅷
(303) 858-0700. **$80-$85.** 7374 S Clinton St. I-25, exit 196 (Dry Creek Rd), just e, then n. Int corridors. **Pets:** Accepted.
🅰🆂🅺 🆂🔄 ⊠ 🔧 🖊 🔧 🔧 💻 🏊

▼▼▼▼ **Residence Inn by Marriott-Denver Tech Center** 🆂🅷
(303) 740-7177. **$89-$179.** 6565 S Yosemite St. I-25, exit 197, just w on Arapahoe Rd, then n. Ext corridors. **Pets:** Accepted.
🅰🆂🅺 🆂🔄 ⊠ 🔧 🔧 💻 ⊠

▼▼▼▼ **Residence Inn Park Meadows** 🆂🅷
(720) 895-0200. **$89-$119.** 8322 S Valley Hwy. I-25, exit 195 (County Line Rd), just e to S Valley Hwy, then just s. Int corridors. **Pets:** Other species. $75 one-time fee/room. Service with restrictions, supervision.
🅰🆂🅺 🆂🔄 ⊠ 🔧 🖊 🔧 🔧 💻 🏊 ⊠

▼▼▼ **TownePlace Suites Denver Tech Center** 🆂🅷 🐾
(720) 875-1113. **$49-$85.** 7877 S Chester St. I-25, exit 196 (Dry Creek Rd), just w to Chester St, then 0.3 mi s. Int corridors. **Pets:** Other species. $25 daily fee/room. Service with restrictions.
🅰🆂🅺 🆂🔄 ⊠ 🔧 🔧 🔧 💻 🏊

GLENDALE

🅰🅰🅰 ▼▼▼▼ **Four Points Cherry Creek Denver** 🆂🅷 🐾
(303) 757-3341. **$109-$159.** 600 S Colorado Blvd. I-25, exit 204, 1.4 mi n. Int corridors. **Pets:** Medium. $25 one-time fee/room. Service with restrictions, supervision.
🆂🅰🆅🅴 🆂🔄 ⊠ 💻 🍴 🏊

▼▼▼ **Homestead Studio Suites Hotel-Denver/Cherry Creek** 🆂🅷
(303) 388-3880. **$64-$74.** 4444 Leetsdale Dr. I-25, exit 204, 1.5 mi n to E Virginia Ave, just e to S Birch St, then just n. Ext corridors. **Pets:** Small. $25 daily fee/room, $75 one-time fee/room. Designated rooms, no service, supervision.
🅰🆂🅺 🆂🔄 ⊠ 🔧 🖊 🔧 💻

🅰🅰🅰 ▼▼▼▼ **Loews Denver Hotel** 🅻🅷 🐾
(303) 782-9300. **$89-$199.** 4150 E Mississippi Ave. I-25, exit 204, 1 mi n on Colorado Blvd, then just e. Int corridors. **Pets:** Other species. Designated rooms, service with restrictions.
🆂🅰🆅🅴 🆂🔄 ⊠ 🔧 🖊 🔧 🔧 💻 🍴

▼▼▼ **Staybridge Suites** 🆂🅷
(303) 321-5757. **$119-$189.** 4220 E Virginia Ave. I-25, exit 204, 1.5 mi n on Colorado Blvd to Virginia Ave, then just e. Int corridors. **Pets:** $75 one-time fee/room. Service with restrictions.
🅰🆂🅺 🆂🔄 ⊠ 🔧 🖊 🔧 🔧 💻 ⊠

GOLDEN

▼▼▼ **Clarion Collection The Golden Hotel** 🆂🅷 🐾
(303) 279-0100. **$99-$259.** 800 11th St. At 11th St and Washington Ave; downtown. Int corridors. **Pets:** Medium. $10 daily fee/pet. Service with restrictions, supervision.
🅰🆂🅺 🆂🔄 ⊠ 🖊 🔧 💻 🍴

▼▼▼ **Days Inn Denver West** 🆂🅷
(303) 277-0200. **$59-$109.** 15059 W Colfax Ave. I-70, exit 262 (Colfax Ave), just e. Int corridors. **Pets:** Small. $8 daily fee/room. Service with restrictions, supervision.
🅰🆂🅺 🆂🔄 ⊠ 🖊 🔧 🔧 💻 🍴 🏊 ⊠

▼▼▼ **Denver Marriott West** 🅻🅷
(303) 279-9100. **$180.** 1717 Denver W Blvd. I-70, exit 263, just n, then w. Int corridors. **Pets:** $10 daily fee/pet. Designated rooms, service with restrictions, supervision.
🅰🆂🅺 🆂🔄 ⊠ 🔧 🖊 🔧 🔧 💻 🍴 🏊 ⊠

▼▼▼ **Holiday Inn Denver West** 🅻🅷
(303) 279-7611. **$74-$94, 3 day notice.** 14707 W Colfax Ave. I-70, exit 262 (Colfax Ave), just e. Ext/int corridors. **Pets:** Accepted.
🅰🆂🅺 🆂🔄 ⊠ 🔧 🖊 🔧 🔧 💻 🍴 🏊 ⊠

🅰🅰🅰 ▼▼▼▼ **La Quinta Inn Denver (Golden)** 🆂🅷
(303) 279-5565. **$74-$99.** 3301 Youngfield Service Rd. I-70, exit 264 (32nd Ave), just w, then n. Ext corridors. **Pets:** Other species. Service with restrictions, supervision.
🆂🅰🆅🅴 ⊠ 💻 🏊

▼▼▼ **Residence Inn by Marriott Denver West/Golden** 🆂🅷
(303) 271-0909. **$89-$129.** 14600 W 6th Ave Frontage Rd. US 6, exit Indiana Ave to frontage road, just e. Int corridors. **Pets:** Accepted.
⊠ 🔧 🔧 🔧 💻 🏊

🅰🅰🅰 ▼▼▼▼ **Table Mountain Inn** 🆂🅷 🐾
(303) 277-9898. **$100-$172.** 1310 Washington Ave. US 6, exit 19th St, 0.5 mi n to Washington Ave, 0.5 mi w; downtown, just s of arch. Int corridors. **Pets:** $10 daily fee/room. Designated rooms, service with restrictions, supervision.
🆂🅰🆅🅴 🆂🔄 ⊠ 🔧 🔧 🔧 💻 🍴

GREENWOOD VILLAGE

▽▽▽ Hampton Inn Denver Southeast SH
(303) 792-9999. **$79-$89.** 9231 E Arapahoe Rd. I-25, exit 197, just e.
Int corridors. **Pets:** Other species. $10 daily fee/pet. Designated rooms,
service with restrictions.

▽▽ Homestead Studio Suites Hotel-Denver/Tech South/
Greenwood Village SH
(303) 858-1669. **$59-$74.** 9253 E Costilla St. I-25, exit 197, just e on
Arapahoe Rd, se on Clinton St to Costilla St, then w. Int corridors.
Pets: Other species. $25 daily fee/room. Service with restrictions.

▲▲ ▽▽▽ La Quinta Inn & Suites Denver (Tech
Center) SH
(303) 649-9969. **$69-$99.** 7077 S Clinton St. I-25, exit 197, e to Clinton
St, then s. Int corridors. **Pets:** Small, other species. Service with restrictions, supervision.

▽▽▽ Sheraton Denver Tech Center Hotel SH ❋
(303) 799-6200. **$199, 3 day notice.** 7007 S Clinton St. I-25, exit 197,
e on Arapahoe Rd, then s. Int corridors. **Pets:** Medium, dogs only.
Designated rooms, service with restrictions, supervision.

▽▽ Sleep Inn Denver Tech Center SH
(303) 662-9950. **$54-$63.** 9257 Costilla Ave. I-25, exit 197, just e to
Clinton St, s to Costilla Ave, then w. Int corridors. **Pets:** Medium. $25
one-time fee/room. Designated rooms, service with restrictions, supervision.

▲▲▲ ▽▽▽▽ Summerfield Suites by Wyndham-Denver Tech
Center SH
(303) 706-1945. **$69-$99.** I-25, exit 197, e to Clinton St, then just s. Int
corridors. **Pets:** Medium, other species. $150 one-time fee/room. Service
with restrictions, crate.

▲▲▲ ▽▽▽▽ Woodfield Suites Denver-Tech
Center SH 🐾
(303) 799-4555. **$69-$150.** 9009 E Arapahoe Rd. I-25, exit 197, just e.
Int corridors. **Pets:** Other species. $25 deposit/pet. Service with restric-
tions, supervision.

HIGHLANDS RANCH

▽▽▽▽ Residence Inn Denver South Highlands Ranch SH
(303) 683-5500. **$125.** 93 Centennial Blvd. C-470, exit Broadway, just s,
then w. Int corridors. **Pets:** Accepted.

LAKEWOOD

▲▲▲ ▽▽▽▽ Comfort Suites SH
(303) 231-9929. **$89.** 11909 W 6th. US 6, exit Simms/Union, west-
bound travelers must turn right at stop light, but do not use right turn
lane, follow signs to frontage road. Int corridors. **Pets:** Small. $10 daily
fee/room. Designated rooms, service with restrictions, supervision.

▽▽▽ Hampton Inn-Denver Southwest SH
(303) 989-6900. **$79, 7 day notice.** 3605 S Wadsworth Blvd. Just sw of
jct US 285 (Hampden Ave) and S Wadsworth Blvd; entry on frontage
road. Int corridors. **Pets:** Accepted.

▲▲▲ ▽▽▽ Holiday Inn Lakewood SH
(303) 980-9200. **$59-$79.** 7390 W Hampden Ave. Just se of jct US 285
(W Hampden Ave) and Wadsworth Blvd, e on Jefferson Ave, then n
on frontage road. Int corridors. **Pets:** Accepted.

▲▲▲ ▽▽▽ Lakewood Inn-Denver Southwest SH
(303) 989-5500. **$50-$100.** 3440 S Vance St. Just ne of jct US 285
(Hampden Ave) and S Wadsworth Blvd, e on Girton Dr, then just s. Int
corridors. **Pets:** Other species. $25 one-time fee/room. Service with restric-
tions, supervision.

▲▲▲ ▽▽▽▽ La Quinta Inn & Suites Denver
(Southwest/Lakewood) M
(303) 969-9700. **$89-$99.** 7190 W Hampden Ave. Just se of jct US 285
(W Hampden Ave) and Wadsworth Blvd, e on Jefferson Ave, just n,
then e on frontage road. Int corridors. **Pets:** Accepted.

▽▽ ▽ Mile High Inn & Suites SH
(303) 238-7751. **$45-$125.** 11595 W 6th Ave. I-70, exit 261, 3 mi e on
US 6. Ext/int corridors. **Pets:** Accepted.

▽▽▽ Quality Suites Lakewood SH
(303) 988-8600. **$49-$149.** 7260 W Jefferson Ave. Just se of US 285
(W Hampden Ave) and Wadsworth Blvd, then e. Int corridors.
Pets: Other species. $10 daily fee/pet. Designated rooms, service with
restrictions, crate.

▽▽▽ Residence Inn by Marriott Denver
SW/Lakewood SH
(303) 985-7676. **$119.** 7050 W Hampden Ave. Just se of jct US 285 (W
Hampden Ave) and Wadsworth Blvd, e on Jefferson Ave, then n on
frontage road. Int corridors. **Pets:** Large, other species. $75 one-time
fee/room. Service with restrictions, crate.

▲▲▲ ▽▽▽▽ Sheraton-Denver West Hotel LH ❋
(303) 987-2000. **$69-$99.** 360 Union Blvd. US 6, exit Simms/Union, s
on Union Blvd; 3 mi e of jct I-70, exit 261. Int corridors. **Pets:** Large,
dogs only. Service with restrictions, supervision.

▽▽ ▽ TownePlace Suites by Marriott-Lakewood SH 🐾
(303) 232-7790. **$84-$129.** 800 Tabor St. US 6, exit Simms/Union, just
n to 8th, then w. Int corridors. **Pets:** Large, other species. $200 one-time
fee/room. Service with restrictions, supervision.

LITTLETON

▽▽▽▽ Denver Marriott South at Park Meadows SH
(303) 925-0004. **$69-$179.** 10345 Park Meadows Dr. I-25, exit 193
(Lincoln Ave), just w to Park Meadows Dr, then n and e. Int corridors.
Pets: Accepted.

LONE TREE

▲▲▲ ▽▽▽▽ AmeriSuites (Denver/Park Meadows) SH
(303) 662-8500. **$76-$107.** 9030 E Westview Rd. I-25, exit 195 (County
Line Rd), 0.5 mi w to Yosemite, then s, e to Parkland; C-470 eastbound, exit Yosemite. Int corridors. **Pets:** Other species. $10 daily fee/
room. Service with restrictions, crate.

▽▽▽▽ Staybridge Suites Denver South-Lone Tree SH
(303) 649-1010. **$99-$159.** 7820 Park Meadows Dr. I-25, exit 195, w on
County Line Rd to Acres Green, s to E Park Meadows Dr, then just w;
C-470, exit Quebec St, just se. Int corridors. **Pets:** Accepted.

NORTHGLENN

Holiday Inn Denver-Northglenn SH
(303) 452-4100. **$104-$119.** 10 E 120th Ave. I-25, exit 223, just e. Int corridors. **Pets:** Other species. $15 one-time fee/room. Designated rooms, service with restrictions, supervision.

THORNTON

Sleep Inn North Denver SH ❀
(303) 280-9818. **$54-$109.** 12101 Grant St. I-25, exit 223, e to Grant St, then n. Int corridors. **Pets:** Other species. $5 one-time fee/pet.

WESTMINSTER

DoubleTree Hotel Denver North SH
(303) 427-4000. **$79-$149.** 8773 Yates Dr. US 36 (Boulder Tpke), exit Sheridan Ave, n to 92nd Ave, e to Yates Dr, then 0.5 mi s. Int corridors. **Pets:** Service with restrictions, crate.

La Quinta Inn & Suites Westminster (Promenade) SH
(303) 438-5800. **$69-$109.** 10179 Church Ranch Way. US 36 (Boulder Tpke), exit Church Ranch Blvd, just s to 103rd Pl, then e. Int corridors. **Pets:** Other species. Service with restrictions, supervision.

La Quinta Inn Denver (Northglenn) SH
(303) 252-9800. **$59-$99.** 345 W 120th Ave. I-25, exit 223, just w. Ext/int corridors. **Pets:** Other species. Service with restrictions, crate.

La Quinta Inn Denver (Westminster Mall) SH
(303) 425-9099. **$74-$99.** 8701 Turnpike Dr. US 36 (Boulder Tpke), exit Sheridan Ave, just s, then left on Turnpike Dr at 87th Ave. Ext/int corridors. **Pets:** Accepted.

Residence Inn by Marriott SH
(303) 427-9500. **$90-$130.** 5010 W 88th Pl. US 36 (Boulder Tpke), exit Sheridan Ave, n to 92nd Ave, e to Yates Dr, then s. Int corridors. **Pets:** Accepted.

The Westin Westminster LH ❀
(303) 410-5000. **$109-$249.** 10600 Westminster Blvd. US 36 (Boulder Tpke), exit 104th Ave, just n. Int corridors. **Pets:** Other species. Service with restrictions, crate.

Westminster-Super 8 SH ❀
(303) 451-7200. **$60-$80.** 12055 Melody Dr. I-25, exit 223, just w. Int corridors. **Pets:** $5.38 daily fee/pet. Service with restrictions, supervision.

END METROPOLITAN AREA

DILLON

Best Western Ptarmigan Lodge SH
(970) 468-2341. **$60-$149, 7 day notice.** 652 Lake Dillon Dr. I-70, exit 205, 1.3 mi se on US 6, then 0.3 mi s. Ext/int corridors. **Pets:** Other species. $15 one-time fee/pet. Designated rooms, service with restrictions, supervision.

Dillon Super 8 Motel SH
(970) 468-8888. **$60-$126.** 808 Little Beaver Tr. I-70, exit 205, just s, then e. Int corridors. **Pets:** Other species. $15 one-time fee/pet. Service with restrictions, supervision.

DURANGO

Adobe Inn M ❀
(970) 247-2743. **$39-$86.** 2178 Main Ave. On US 550, 1.4 mi n of jct US 160. Ext corridors. **Pets:** $20 deposit/pet, $5 daily fee/pet. Service with restrictions, supervision.

Alpine Inn M
(970) 247-4042. **$44-$84.** 3515 N Main Ave. 2.7 mi n of jct US 160 W and 550, on US 550. Ext corridors. **Pets:** Other species. Service with restrictions, supervision.

Caboose Motel M
(970) 247-1191. **$48-$98.** 3363 Main Ave. 2.5 mi n of jct US 550 and 160. Ext corridors. **Pets:** Small, dogs only. $10 daily fee/pet. Service with restrictions, supervision.

Comfort Inn SH
(970) 259-5373. **$49-$129, 14 day notice.** 2930 N Main Ave. 2.1 mi n of jct US 160 and 550, on US 550. Ext corridors. **Pets:** Small. $10 one-time fee/pet. Designated rooms, service with restrictions, crate.

Days Inn Durango M
(970) 259-1430. **$69-$117.** 1700 CR 203. 4.5 mi n on US 550; entry just s of establishment, then w. Int corridors. **Pets:** Other species. Service with restrictions, supervision.

DoubleTree Hotel Durango SH
(970) 259-6580. **$69-$234.** 501 Camino Del Rio. Jct US 160 and 550. Int corridors. **Pets:** Accepted.

Holiday Inn SH ❀
(970) 247-5393. **$68-$139.** 800 Camino Del Rio. On US 550, just n of jct US 160. Ext corridors. **Pets:** Large. $10 daily fee/pet. Designated rooms, no service, crate.

Quality Inn & Suites SH
(970) 259-7900. **$89-$159.** 455 S Camino Del Rio. On US 160 (Frontage Rd), 1.5 mi e of jct US 550. Int corridors. **Pets:** $10 daily fee/room. Designated rooms, service with restrictions, supervision.

Residence Inn by Marriott SH
(970) 259-6200. **$109-$234, 3 day notice.** 21691 Hwy 160 W. On US 160, just w. Int corridors. **Pets:** Medium. $75 one-time fee/room. Service with restrictions, supervision.

The Rochester Hotel BB ❀
(970) 385-1920. **$109-$229, 14 day notice.** 726 E 2nd Ave. Just e of Main Ave via 7th St, then just n. Int corridors. **Pets:** Other species. $20 daily fee/pet. Designated rooms, service with restrictions, supervision.

Rodeway Inn M ❀
(970) 259-2540. **$39-$109.** 2701 Main Ave. On US 550, 2 mi n of jct US 160. Ext corridors. **Pets:** Dogs only. $10 one-time fee/pet. Service with restrictions, supervision.

(AAA) ▼▼ Siesta Motel M
(970) 247-0741. **$32-$75.** 3475 N Main Ave. 2.6 mi n of jct US 160 W and 550, on US 550. Ext corridors. **Pets:** Dogs only. $10 daily fee/pet. Designated rooms, service with restrictions, supervision.

⟨SAVE⟩ ⟨S⟩ ⟨X⟩ ⟨❚⟩ ⟨▦⟩

(AAA) ▼▼▼ Travelodge M
(970) 247-1741. **$58-$129.** 2970 Main Ave. 2.2 mi n of jct US 160 and 550, on US 550. Ext corridors. **Pets:** Other species. $8 one-time fee/pet. Designated rooms, service with restrictions, supervision.

⟨SAVE⟩ ⟨X⟩ ⟨❚⟩ ⟨▦⟩

EAGLE

▼▼ AmericInn Lodge & Suites SH
(970) 328-5155. **$89-$109.** 0085 Pond Rd. I-70, exit 147, just n, then w. Int corridors. **Pets:** Accepted.

⟨ASK⟩ ⟨S⟩ ⟨X⟩ ⟨M⟩ ⟨⟩ ⟨⟩ ⟨❚⟩ ⟨▦⟩ ⟨≈⟩ ⟨X⟩

(AAA) ▼▼▼ Best Western Eagle Lodge & Suites SH
(970) 328-6316. **$75-$90.** 200 Loren Ln. I-70, exit 147, just s. Int corridors. **Pets:** Accepted.

⟨SAVE⟩ ⟨S⟩ ⟨X⟩ ⟨⟩ ⟨❚⟩ ⟨▦⟩ ⟨≈⟩ ⟨X⟩

▼▼ Holiday Inn Express SH
(970) 328-8088. **$60-$129.** 0075 Pond Rd. I-70, exit 147, just n, then w. Int corridors. **Pets:** Other species. $20 one-time fee/room. Service with restrictions, supervision.

⟨ASK⟩ ⟨S⟩ ⟨X⟩ ⟨⟩ ⟨⟩ ⟨❚⟩ ⟨▦⟩ ⟨≈⟩

EDWARDS

(AAA) ▼▼▼ Inn and Suites at Riverwalk SH
(970) 926-0606. **$155-$800, 14 day notice.** 27 Main St. I-70, exit 163, 0.3 mi s. Int corridors. **Pets:** Large. $25 one-time fee/pet. Designated rooms, no service.

⟨SAVE⟩ ⟨S⟩ ⟨X⟩ ⟨⟩ ⟨❚⟩ ⟨▦⟩ ⟨🍴⟩ ⟨≈⟩ ⟨X⟩

ESTES PARK

(AAA) ▼▼ Budget Host Four Winds Motor Lodge M ✿
(970) 586-3313. **$43-$108, 5 day notice.** 1120 Big Thompson Ave. 1 mi e on US 34. Ext corridors. **Pets:** Small, other species. $15 daily fee/pet. Service with restrictions, supervision.

⟨SAVE⟩ ⟨S⟩ ⟨X⟩ ⟨❚⟩ ⟨▦⟩ ⟨≈⟩ ⟨X⟩

(AAA) ▼▼▼ Castle Mountain Lodge CA
(970) 586-3664. **$70-$225, 30 day notice.** 1520 Fall River Rd. 1 mi w on US 34. Ext corridors. **Pets:** Dogs only. $15 daily fee/pet. Designated rooms, supervision.

⟨SAVE⟩ ⟨S⟩ ⟨❚⟩ ⟨X⟩ ⟨AC⟩ ⟨☎⟩

(AAA) ▼▼▼ Holiday Inn SH ✿
(970) 586-2332. **$72-$144, 3 day notice.** 101 S St Vrain Ave. 0.5 mi se; on SR 7 at jct US 36. Int corridors. **Pets:** Large. $10 daily fee/room. Service with restrictions, supervision.

⟨SAVE⟩ ⟨S⟩ ⟨X⟩ ⟨⟩ ⟨⟩ ⟨⟩ ⟨❚⟩ ⟨▦⟩ ⟨🍴⟩ ⟨≈⟩ ⟨X⟩

(AAA) ▼▼▼ Lake Estes Inn & Suites M
(970) 586-3386. **$59-$260, 7 day notice.** 1650 Big Thompson Ave. 1.7 mi e on US 34. Ext corridors. **Pets:** $25 daily fee/pet. Designated rooms, no service.

⟨SAVE⟩ ⟨S⟩ ⟨X⟩ ⟨❚⟩ ⟨▦⟩ ⟨≈⟩ ⟨X⟩ ⟨AC⟩

(AAA) ▼▼▼ Silver Moon Inn M
(970) 586-6006. **$74-$140, 7 day notice.** 175 Spruce Dr. Just w on US 34 business route, then just ne. Ext corridors. **Pets:** Dogs only. Designated rooms, service with restrictions, supervision.

⟨SAVE⟩ ⟨X⟩ ⟨❚⟩ ⟨▦⟩ ⟨≈⟩

▼▼ Timber Creek Chalets CA
(970) 586-8803. **$60-$265, 30 day notice.** 2115 Fall River Rd. Jct US 34 and 36, 2.9 mi w. Ext corridors. **Pets:** Accepted.

⟨X⟩ ⟨❚⟩ ⟨▦⟩ ⟨≈⟩ ⟨AC⟩

EVANS

(AAA) ▼▼▼ Sleep Inn Greeley/Evans SH ✿
(970) 356-2180. **$54-$94.** 3025 8th Ave. Just sw of jct US 34 and 85 Bypass. Int corridors. **Pets:** Large. $15 one-time fee/pet. Service with restrictions, supervision.

⟨SAVE⟩ ⟨S⟩ ⟨X⟩ ⟨M⟩ ⟨⟩ ⟨⟩ ⟨❚⟩ ⟨▦⟩ ⟨≈⟩

EVERGREEN

▼▼▼ Quality Suites Evergreen SH ✿
(303) 526-2000. **$69-$109.** I-70, exit 252 (Evergreen Pkwy), on west side of El Rancho Restaurant; exit 251 eastbound. Int corridors. **Pets:** Other species. $50 deposit/room. Designated rooms, service with restrictions, crate.

⟨ASK⟩ ⟨S⟩ ⟨X⟩ ⟨M⟩ ⟨⟩ ⟨⟩ ⟨❚⟩ ⟨▦⟩ ⟨≈⟩ ⟨X⟩

FAIRPLAY

(AAA) ▼▼▼ The Western Inn M
(719) 836-2026. **$53-$75.** 490 Hwy 285. US 285, 0.3 mi n of jct SR 9. Ext corridors. **Pets:** $5 one-time fee/room. Service with restrictions, supervision.

⟨SAVE⟩ ⟨S⟩ ⟨X⟩ ⟨❚⟩ ⟨▦⟩ ⟨AC⟩

FLORENCE

▼▼ Super 8 M
(719) 784-4800. **$66-$76.** 4540 S State Hwy 67. 0.8 mi s on SR 67 from jct SR 115. Int corridors. **Pets:** Very small. $10 one-time fee/pet. Designated rooms, service with restrictions, supervision.

⟨ASK⟩ ⟨S⟩ ⟨X⟩ ⟨❚⟩ ⟨▦⟩

FORT COLLINS

(AAA) ▼▼▼ Best Western University Inn M
(970) 484-1984. **$59-$99.** 914 S College Ave. I-25, exit 268, 4 mi w to College Ave, just n on US 287. Ext/int corridors. **Pets:** Other species. $10 daily fee/pet. Designated rooms, service with restrictions, supervision.

⟨SAVE⟩ ⟨S⟩ ⟨X⟩ ⟨❚⟩ ⟨▦⟩

▼▼▼▼ Comfort Suites by Choice Hotels SH
(970) 206-4597. **$85-$105.** 1415 Oakridge Dr. I-25, exit 265, 3.3 mi w to McMurray Ave, just s, then w. Int corridors. **Pets:** Medium. $15 daily fee/room. Service with restrictions, supervision.

⟨ASK⟩ ⟨S⟩ ⟨X⟩ ⟨⟩ ⟨⟩ ⟨❚⟩ ⟨▦⟩ ⟨≈⟩

▼▼▼▼ Courtyard by Marriott SH
(970) 282-1700. **$80-$150.** 1200 Oakridge Dr. I-25, exit 265, 3.3 mi w; entry via Lemay Ave. Int corridors. **Pets:** Large. $25 daily fee/pet. Designated rooms, service with restrictions, supervision.

⟨ASK⟩ ⟨S⟩ ⟨X⟩ ⟨M⟩ ⟨⟩ ⟨⟩ ⟨❚⟩ ⟨▦⟩ ⟨🍴⟩ ⟨≈⟩ ⟨X⟩

▼▼▼▼ Fort Collins Marriott LH
(970) 226-5200. **$75-$127.** 350 E Horsetooth Rd. I-25, exit 265, 4 mi w to John F Kennedy, then n; just beyond Horsetooth Rd. Int corridors. **Pets:** Medium. $10 daily fee/pet. Designated rooms, service with restrictions, crate.

⟨X⟩ ⟨M⟩ ⟨⟩ ⟨⟩ ⟨❚⟩ ⟨▦⟩ ⟨🍴⟩ ⟨≈⟩

▼▼▼ Hampton Inn SH
(970) 229-5927. **$89-$149.** 1620 Oakridge Dr. I-25, exit 265, 3.3 mi w, s on McMurray Ave to Oakridge Dr, then just e. Int corridors. **Pets:** Medium, dogs only. $25 one-time fee/pet. Service with restrictions, crate.

⟨ASK⟩ ⟨S⟩ ⟨X⟩ ⟨M⟩ ⟨⟩ ⟨❚⟩ ⟨▦⟩ ⟨≈⟩

(AAA) ▼▼▼ Hilton Fort Collins SH
(970) 482-2626. **$107-$139.** 425 W Prospect Rd. I-25, exit 268, 4.3 mi w. Int corridors. **Pets:** Accepted.

⟨SAVE⟩ ⟨S⟩ ⟨X⟩ ⟨⟩ ⟨⟩ ⟨❚⟩ ⟨▦⟩ ⟨🍴⟩ ⟨≈⟩ ⟨X⟩

[AAA] ♦♦♦ **Quality Inn & Suites** [SH]
(970) 282-9047. **$89-$139.** 4001 S Mason St. I-25, exit 265, 4.6 mi w to Mason St, then 0.5 mi n. Int corridors. **Pets:** Other species. $25 deposit/room. Designated rooms, service with restrictions, supervision.
[SAVE] [SD] ⊠ [♿M] 👂 ♿ ☎ 📺 🏊

♦♦♦ **Residence Inn Fort Collins** [SH] 🐾
(970) 223-5700. **$114-$169.** 1127 Oakridge Dr. I-25, exit 265, 3.3 mi w on Harmony Rd to Lemay Ave, then s to Oakridge Dr. Int corridors. **Pets:** Other species. $75 one-time fee/pet.
[A$K] [SD] ⊠ ♿ ☎ 📺 🏊 ⚒

♦♦ **Sleep Inn** [SH]
(970) 484-5515. **$69-$119.** 3808 E Mulberry St. I-25, exit 269B, just nw. Int corridors. **Pets:** Large, other species. $25 one-time fee/room. Service with restrictions, supervision.
[A$K] [SD] ⊠ ♿ ☎ 📺

♦♦ **Super 8 Motel** [SH]
(970) 493-7701. **$45-$105.** 409 Centro Way. I-25, exit 269B, just w. Int corridors. **Pets:** Accepted.
[A$K] [SD] ⊠ ☎ ⚒

FORT MORGAN

♦♦ **Affordable Inns** [M]
(970) 867-9481. **$57-$87.** 1409 Barlow Rd. I-76, exit 82, just n. Ext/int corridors. **Pets:** Large. $15 daily fee/room. Service with restrictions, supervision.
[A$K] [SD] ⊠ ☎ 🍴 🏊

♦♦ **Best Western Park Terrace Inn** [SH] 🐾
(970) 867-8256. **$64-$80.** 725 Main St. I-76, exit 80, 0.5 mi s. Ext corridors. **Pets:** Other species. $10 daily fee/room. Designated rooms, service with restrictions, supervision.
[A$K] [SD] ⊠ ☎ 📺 🍴 🏊

[AAA] ♦♦ **Central Motel** [M]
(970) 867-2401. **$44-$61.** 201 W Platte Ave. I-76, exit 80, 0.6 mi s, then w on US 34. Ext corridors. **Pets:** Other species. $5 one-time fee/room. Service with restrictions, supervision.
[SAVE] [SD] ⊠ ☎ 📺

FRISCO

[AAA] ♦♦♦ **Best Western Lake Dillon Lodge** [SH]
(970) 668-5094. **$69-$199, 7 day notice.** 1202 Summit Blvd. I-70, exit 203, just s. Int corridors. **Pets:** Accepted.
[SAVE] [SD] ⊠ ☎ 📺 🍴 🏊 ⚒

[AAA] ♦♦♦ **Holiday Inn-Frisco** [SH]
(970) 668-5000. **$99-$159, 14 day notice.** 1129 N Summit Blvd. I-70, exit 203, just s. Ext/int corridors. **Pets:** Accepted.
[SAVE] [SD] ⊠ [♿M] 👂 ♿ ☎ 📺 🍴 🏊 ⚒

♦♦ **Hotel Frisco** [SH] 🐾
(970) 668-5009. **$59-$169, 14 day notice.** 308 Main St.. I-70, exit 201, 0.7 mi s; center. Ext/int corridors. **Pets:** Dogs only. $10 daily fee/pet. Designated rooms, service with restrictions, supervision.
[A$K] [SD] ⊠ ☎ 📺 [AC]

[AAA] ♦♦ **New Summit Inn** [SH]
(970) 668-3220. **$54-$130.** 1205 N Summit Blvd. I-70, exit 203, just s, then just e. Int corridors. **Pets:** Accepted.
[SAVE] [SD] ⊠ ☎ 📺

[AAA] ♦♦ **Ramada Limited Frisco** [SH] 🐾
(970) 668-8783. **$55-$139.** 990 Lakepoint Dr. I-70, exit 203, just s. Int corridors. **Pets:** Other species. $10 daily fee/room. Designated rooms, service with restrictions, supervision.
[SAVE] [SD] ⊠ [♿M] ♿ ☎ 📺

[AAA] ♦♦ **Snowshoe Motel** [M]
(970) 668-3444. **$45-$125, 14 day notice.** 521 Main St. I-70, exit 203 westbound, 1 mi s to Main St, then just w; exit 201 eastbound. Ext corridors. **Pets:** $10 deposit/pet, $10 one-time fee/pet. Designated rooms, service with restrictions, supervision.
[SAVE] ⊠ ☎ 📺 [AC]

FRUITA

[AAA] ♦ **Balanced Rock Motel** [M]
(970) 858-7333. **$40-$55.** 126 S Coulson. I-70, exit 19, just n to Aspen Ave, then just w. Ext corridors. **Pets:** $5 daily fee/pet. Designated rooms, service with restrictions, supervision.
[SAVE] ⊠ ☎

[AAA] ♦♦♦ **Comfort Inn** [SH]
(970) 858-1333. **$59-$135.** 400 Jurassic Ave. I-70, exit 19 (use caution), 0.3 mi s; just e of Dinosaur Discovery Museum. Int corridors. **Pets:** Other species. Service with restrictions, supervision.
[SAVE] [SD] ⊠ [♿M] 👂 ♿ ☎ 📺 🏊

[AAA] ♦ **H-Motel** [M]
(970) 858-7198. **$35-$55, 3 day notice.** 333 Hwy 6 & 50. I-70, exit 19, 0.5 mi e. Ext corridors. **Pets:** Accepted.
[SAVE] ⊠ ☎

[AAA] ♦♦ **Super 8** [SH]
(970) 858-0808. **$48-$85.** 399 Jurassic Ave. I-70, exit 19, 0.3 mi s; just e of Dinosaur Discovery Museum. Int corridors. **Pets:** Other species. $5 daily fee/pet. Service with restrictions, crate.
[SAVE] [SD] ⊠ [♿M] 👂 ♿ ☎ 🏊

GEORGETOWN

[AAA] ♦♦ **Georgetown Mountain Inn** [M]
(303) 569-3201. **$59-$79.** 1100 Rose St. I-70, exit 228, just s, then 0.3 mi w. Ext corridors. **Pets:** Other species. $10 one-time fee/room. Designated rooms, service with restrictions, crate.
[SAVE] [SD] ⊠ ☎ 🏊 ⚒ [AC]

GLENWOOD SPRINGS

[AAA] ♦♦ **Caravan Inn** [M]
(970) 945-7451. **$59-$109.** 1826 Grand Ave. I-70, exit 116, 1.3 mi s on SR 82. Ext corridors. **Pets:** Other species. $50 deposit/room, $8 daily fee/pet. Designated rooms, service with restrictions, crate.
[SAVE] [SD] ⊠ ☎ 🏊

[AAA] ♦♦♦ **Hotel Colorado** [SH] 🐾
(970) 945-6511. **$145-$165.** 526 Pine St. I-70, exit 116, just ne. Int corridors. **Pets:** $10 daily fee/room. Service with restrictions.
[SAVE] [SD] ⊠ ♿ ☎ 📺 🍴 ⚒ [AC]

♦♦♦ **Quality Inn & Suites** [SH]
(970) 945-5995. **$79-$169.** 2650 Gilstrap. I-70, exit 114, just s, then w. Int corridors. **Pets:** Accepted.
[A$K] [SD] ⊠ [♿M] 👂 ♿ ☎ 📺 🏊 ⚒

♦♦♦ **Ramada Inn & Suites** [SH] 🐾
(970) 945-2500. **$70-$130.** 124 W 6th St. I-70, exit 116, just w. Ext/int corridors. **Pets:** Medium, other species. $10 one-time fee/room. Service with restrictions, supervision.
[A$K] [SD] ⊠ ☎ 📺 🍴 🏊

[AAA] ♦♦ **Silver Spruce Motel** [M] 🐾
(970) 945-5458. **$45-$110.** 162 W 6th St. I-70, exit 116, just w on frontage road. Ext corridors. **Pets:** Other species. $5 daily fee/pet. Designated rooms, service with restrictions, crate.
[SAVE] [SD] ⊠ ☎

GRANBY

⧉ ▼▼▼▼ The Inn at Silver Creek [LH]
(970) 887-2131. **$59-$338, 15 day notice.** 62927 Hwy 40. 2 mi se on US 40. Int corridors. **Pets:** $25 one-time fee/room. Designated rooms, service with restrictions, supervision.

[icons]

GRAND JUNCTION

⧉ ▼▼▼▼ Best Western Horizon Inn [SH]
(970) 245-1410. **$55-$85.** 754 Horizon Dr. I-70, exit 31, 0.3 mi n. Ext corridors. **Pets:** Other species. Service with restrictions, supervision.

[icons]

⧉ ▼▼▼▼ Best Western Sandman Motel [SH] 🐾
(970) 243-4150. **$45-$105.** 708 Horizon Dr. I-70, exit 31, 0.3 mi s. Ext/int corridors. **Pets:** Designated rooms, supervision.

[icons]

⧉ ▼▼ Budget Host Inn [M] 🐾
(970) 243-6050. **$50-$85.** 721 Horizon Dr. I-70, exit 31, 0.3 mi s. Ext corridors. **Pets:** Other species. $50 deposit/room. Service with restrictions, supervision.

[icons]

⧉ ▼▼▼ Grand Junction Super 8 [SH]
(970) 248-8080. **$45-$70.** 728 Horizon Dr. I-70, exit 31, just s. Int corridors. **Pets:** Accepted.

[icons]

⧉ ▼▼▼ Grand Vista Hotel [SH]
(970) 241-8411. **$75-$79.** 2790 Crossroads Blvd. I-70, exit 31, 0.3 mi n. Int corridors. **Pets:** Small. $10 one-time fee/room. Designated rooms, service with restrictions, supervision.

[icons]

▼▼▼ Hampton Inn [SH]
(970) 243-3222. **$90-$117.** 205 Main St. At 2nd and Main sts; downtown. Int corridors. **Pets:** Medium, other species. $25 daily fee/room. Service with restrictions, crate.

[icons]

▼▼▼ Hawthorn Suites [SH]
(970) 242-2525. **$89-$269.** 225 Main St. At 2nd and Main sts; downtown. Int corridors. **Pets:** $25 daily fee/room. Service with restrictions, crate.

[icons]

⧉ ▼▼▼▼ Holiday Inn [SH] 🐾
(970) 243-6790. **$79-$99.** 755 Horizon Dr. I-70, exit 31, northwest corner. Ext/int corridors. **Pets:** Other species. Service with restrictions, supervision.

[icons]

⧉ ▼▼▼▼ La Quinta Inn & Suites Grand Junction [SH]
(970) 241-2929. **$84-$119.** 2761 Crossroads Blvd. I-70, exit 31, n to Crossroads Blvd, then just w. Int corridors. **Pets:** Service with restrictions, crate.

[icons]

⧉ ▼▼ Mesa Inn [M]
(970) 245-3080. **$40-$70.** 704 Horizon Dr. I-70, exit 31, 0.5 mi s. Ext corridors. **Pets:** $50 deposit/room. Designated rooms, service with restrictions, supervision.

[icons]

⧉ ▼▼▼ Quality Inn of Grand Junction [SH]
(970) 245-7200. **$50-$90.** 733 Horizon Dr. I-70, exit 31, just s. Int corridors. **Pets:** $50 deposit/room. Designated rooms, service with restrictions, supervision.

[icons]

⧉ ▼▼▼ Ramada Inn [SH] 🐾
(970) 243-5150. **$49-$79.** 752 Horizon Dr. I-70, exit 31, just n. Int corridors. **Pets:** Other species. $10 one-time fee/room. Crate.

[icons]

⧉ ▼▼▼ West Gate Inn [M]
(970) 241-3020. **$54-$74.** 2210 Hwy 6 & 50. I-70, exit 26, 0.3 mi se. Ext corridors. **Pets:** Other species. $50 deposit/room. Designated rooms, service with restrictions, crate.

[icons]

GRAND LAKE

⧉ ▼▼▼ Spirit Lake Lodge [M]
(970) 627-3344. **$65-$160, 7 day notice.** 829 Grand Ave. Just e of US 34; downtown. Ext corridors. **Pets:** Other species. $10 daily fee/pet. No service, supervision.

[icons]

GREAT SAND DUNES NATIONAL PARK AND PRESERVE

▼▼▼ Great Sand Dunes Lodge [M]
(719) 378-2900. **$85-$99.** 7900 Hwy 150 N. From Alamosa, 16 mi e on US 160, 16 mi n on SR 150; at entrance to Great Sand Dunes National Monument. Ext corridors. **Pets:** Medium. $10 one-time fee/room. Service with restrictions, supervision.

[icons]

GREELEY

⧉ ▼▼▼ Best Western Regency Hotel [SH]
(970) 353-8444. **$69-$95.** 701 8th St. On US 85 business route; downtown. Int corridors. **Pets:** Accepted.

[icons]

⧉ ▼▼▼ Country Inn & Suites By Carlson [SH]
(970) 330-3404. **$77-$104.** 2501 W 29th St. US 34 Bypass, exit 23rd Ave, just s, then w. Int corridors. **Pets:** Small. $10 daily fee/pet. Designated rooms, service with restrictions, supervision.

[icons]

▼▼▼ Holiday Inn Express [SH]
(970) 330-7495. **$70-$90.** 2563 W 29th St. US 34 Bypass, exit 23rd Ave, just s, then w. Int corridors. **Pets:** Accepted.

[icons]

⧉ ▼▼▼ Super 8 Motel [SH]
(970) 330-8880. **$55-$115.** 2423 W 29th St. US 34 Bypass, exit 23rd Ave, just s, then just w. Int corridors. **Pets:** $20 one-time fee/pet. Service with restrictions, supervision.

[icons]

GUNNISON

⧉ ▼▼▼ ABC Motel [M]
(970) 641-2400. **$42-$79.** 212 E Tomichi Ave. On US 50; near Western State College. Ext corridors. **Pets:** $5 daily fee/pet. Designated rooms, service with restrictions, supervision.

[icons]

⧉ ▼▼ Hylander Inn [M]
(970) 641-0700. **$40-$75.** 412 E Tomichi Ave. On US 50; near Western State College. Ext corridors. **Pets:** Other species. $5 daily fee/pet. Service with restrictions, supervision.

[icons]

▼▼ Ramada Limited [M]
(970) 641-2804. **$59-$125, 15 day notice.** 1011 W Rio Grande. On US 50, 0.5 mi w. Int corridors. **Pets:** Accepted.

[icons]

△△△ ▽▽▽▽ **Water Wheel Inn** SH
(970) 641-1650. **$49-$99.** 37478 W Hwy 50. On US 50, 2.5 mi w. Ext/int corridors. **Pets:** Large. Designated rooms, service with restrictions, supervision.
SAVE S❑ ✕ ❏ ▣

HERMOSA

▽▽▽▽ **The Inn at Durango Mountain & Silverpick Condos & Townhomes** M
(970) 247-9669. **$69-$179.** 49617 US 550 N. 16.4 mi n, then just w. Int corridors. **Pets:** Accepted.
ASK S❑ ✕ ❏ ▣ ⅋ ⌖ ✕ ⌖

HOT SULPHUR SPRINGS

△△△ ▽ **Canyon Motel** M ❖
(970) 725-3395. **$54-$99.** 221 Byers Ave. On US 40. Ext corridors. **Pets:** $10 daily fee/room. Supervision.
SAVE S❑ ✕ ❏ ▣ ⌖

JULESBURG

△△△ ▽ **Budget Host Platte Valley Inn** SH
(970) 474-3336. **$44-$60.** 15225 Hwy 385 & I-76. I-76, exit 180, just n. Ext corridors. **Pets:** Dogs only. $7 daily fee/pet. Designated rooms, service with restrictions, supervision.
SAVE S❑ ✕ ▣ ⅋ ⌖

KEYSTONE

△△△ ▽▽▽▽ **The Inn at Keystone** SH
(970) 496-4825. **$75-$169, 21 day notice.** 23044 Hwy 6. I-70, exit 205, 6.5 mi e on US 6; at Keystone Ski Area. Int corridors. **Pets:** Other species. $20 daily fee/pet. Designated rooms, service with restrictions.
SAVE ✕ ⌖ ❏ ▣ ⅋ ✕ ⌖

LA JUNTA

▽ **Holiday Inn Express** M ❖
(719) 384-2900. **$79-$99.** 27994 US Hwy 50 Frontage Rd. On US 50, 0.8 mi w. Int corridors. **Pets:** Other species. $10 daily fee/room. Service with restrictions, supervision.
ASK S❑ ✕ ⌖ ⌖ ❏ ▣ ⌖

▽ **Travel Inn** M
(719) 384-2504. **$38-$42.** 110 E 1st St. On US 50. Ext corridors. **Pets:** Accepted.
ASK S❑ ✕ ❏

LAKE CITY

△△△ ▽ **Matterhorn Mountain Motel** M
(970) 944-2210. **$80-$85, 14 day notice.** 409 Bluff St. SR 149, just w via 4th St. Ext corridors. **Pets:** Other species. $10 one-time fee/pet. No service, supervision.
SAVE ✕ ⌖ ❏ ▣ ⌖ ⌖

LAMAR

△△△ ▽▽▽▽ **Best Western Cow Palace Inn** M
(719) 336-7753. **$89-$114.** 1301 N Main St. 0.8 mi n on US 50 and 287. Ext/int corridors. **Pets:** Accepted.
SAVE S❑ ✕ ⌖ ⌖ ❏ ▣ ⅋ ⌖

△△△ ▽▽ **Blue Spruce Motel** M
(719) 336-7454. **$45-$70.** 1801 S Main St. 1.3 mi s on US 287 and 385. Ext corridors. **Pets:** Other species. $5 daily fee/pet. Designated rooms, service with restrictions, supervision.
SAVE S❑ ✕ ❏ ▣ ⌖

△△△ ▽▽ **El Mar Budget Host Motel** M
(719) 336-4331. **$44-$48.** 1210 S Main St. 1 mi s on US 287 and 385. Ext corridors. **Pets:** Dogs only. $20 deposit/pet, $5 daily fee/pet. Designated rooms, service with restrictions, supervision.
SAVE S❑ ✕ ⌖ ❏ ▣ ⌖

▽ **Passport Inn** M
(719) 336-7746. **$40-$45.** 113 N Main St. Jct US 50 and 385, just e. Ext corridors. **Pets:** $5 daily fee/pet. Service with restrictions, crate.
ASK S❑ ✕ ❏

LAS ANIMAS

△△△ ▽▽▽▽ **Best Western Bent's Fort Inn** M
(719) 456-0011. **$53-$69.** 10950 E US 50. On US 50, 1.5 mi e. Int corridors. **Pets:** Other species.
SAVE S❑ ✕ ❏ ▣ ⅋ ⌖

LEADVILLE

△△△ ▽▽▽ **Alps Motel** M
(719) 486-1223. **$59-$109, 3 day notice.** S Hwy 24. Just s on US 24. Int corridors. **Pets:** $10 daily fee/pet. Designated rooms, service with restrictions, supervision.
SAVE ✕ ❏ ⌖

LIMON

△△△ ▽▽▽ **Best Western Limon Inn** SH
(719) 775-0277. **$60-$105.** 925 T Ave. I-70, exit 359. Int corridors. **Pets:** Large, other species. $10 one-time fee/room. Designated rooms, service with restrictions.
SAVE S❑ ✕ ❏ ▣ ⌖

△△△ ▽▽▽ **Midwest Country Inn** M
(719) 775-2373. **$55-$65.** 795 Main St. I-70, exit 361, 1 mi w. Ext/int corridors. **Pets:** Other species. $15 daily fee/pet. Service with restrictions.
SAVE S❑ ✕

△△△ ▽▽▽ **Safari Motel** M
(719) 775-2363. **$42-$76.** 637 Main St. I-70, exit 361, 0.8 mi w. Ext corridors. **Pets:** Other species. $5 daily fee/pet. Service with restrictions, supervision.
SAVE S❑ ✕ ⌖

△△△ ▽▽▽ **Super 8 Motel** SH
(719) 775-2889. **$57-$79.** 937 Hwy 24. I-70, exit 359, just s. Int corridors. **Pets:** Other species. $10 one-time fee/room. Service with restrictions, supervision.
SAVE S❑ ✕

△△△ ▽▽▽▽ **Tyme Square Inn** SH ❖
(719) 775-0700. **$61-$105, 7 day notice.** 2505 6th St. I-70, exit 359, then s. Int corridors. **Pets:** Other species. $15 daily fee/pet. No service, supervision.
SAVE S❑ ✕ ⌖ ⌖ ⌖ ❏ ▣ ⌖ ✕

LONGMONT

▽▽▽▽ **Hawthorn Suites** SH ❖
(303) 774-7100. **$109-$162.** 2000 Sunset Way. 1 mi s on US 287, 1.3 mi sw on SR 119, just n on Sunset St, then just w on Korte Pkwy. Int corridors. **Pets:** Other species. $50 deposit/room. Service with restrictions, crate.
ASK ✕ ⌖ ⌖ ❏ ▣ ⌖ ✕

▽▽▽▽ **Radisson Hotel & Conference Center Longmont-Boulder** SH ❖
(303) 776-2000. **$89-$135.** 1900 Ken Pratt Blvd. 1 mi s on US 287, 1.3 mi sw on SR 119. Int corridors. **Pets:** Large. $50 deposit/pet. Designated rooms, service with restrictions, crate.
ASK S❑ ✕ ⌖ ⌖ ❏ ▣ ⅋ ⌖ ✕

▽▽▽▽ **Residence Inn by Marriott Boulder/Longmont** SH
(303) 702-9933. **$149-$199.** 1450 Dry Creek Dr. I-25, exit 235, jct Hover Rd and SR 119. Int corridors. **Pets:** $50 one-time fee/room. Service with restrictions, supervision.
ASK S❑ ✕ ⌖ ⌖ ⌖ ❏ ▣ ⌖ ✕

▼◇▼ Super 8 Motel **SH** ❀
(303) 772-0888. **$50-$86.** 10805 Turner Blvd. I-25, exit 240, jct SR 119; 7 mi e of town. Int corridors. **Pets:** Other species. Service with restrictions, supervision.

A$K S6 X

LOUISVILLE

▼◇▼ ▼◇▼ Comfort Inn of Boulder County **SH**
(303) 604-0181. **$119-$124.** 1196 Dillon Rd. US 36 (Boulder Tpke), exit Superior (SR 170), just n on McCaslin Blvd, then just w. Int corridors. **Pets:** Accepted.

SAVE S6 X 6M

▼◇▼ ▼◇▼ La Quinta Inn Denver (Louisville/Boulder) **SH**
(303) 664-0100. **$79-$124.** 902 Dillon Rd. US 36 (Boulder Tpke), exit Superior (SR 170), just n on McCaslin Blvd, then e. Int corridors. **Pets:** Accepted.

SAVE X 6M

▼◇▼ ▼◇▼ Residence Inn by Marriott-Boulder/Louisville **SH**
(303) 665-2661. **$139.** 845 Coal Creek Cir. US 36 (Boulder Tpke), exit Superior (SR 170), n on McCaslin Blvd to Dillon Rd, then 0.6 mi e. Int corridors. **Pets:** $75 one-time fee/room. Service with restrictions.

A$K S6 X 6M

LOVELAND

▼◇▼ ▼◇▼ Best Western Coach House **SH**
(970) 667-7810. **$59-$135.** 5542 E US Hwy 34. I-25, exit 257B, just w. Ext/int corridors. **Pets:** Accepted.

SAVE S6 X

▼◇▼ Budget Host Exit 254 Inn **M** ❀
(970) 667-5202. **$49-$76.** 2716 SE Frontage Rd. I-25, exit 254, just e. Ext corridors. **Pets:** Dogs only. $5 daily fee/pet. Service with restrictions, supervision.

SAVE S6 X

MARBLE

▼◇▼ ▼◇▼ Ute Meadows Inn Bed & Breakfast **BB**
(970) 963-7088. **$119-$159, 14 day notice.** 2880 CR 3. SR 133, 3 mi to town. Int corridors. **Pets:** Accepted.

A$K X

MESA VERDE NATIONAL PARK

▼◇▼ ▼◇▼ Far View Lodge in Mesa Verde **M**
(970) 529-4421. **$119-$139.** 1 Navajo Hill. 10 mi e of Cortez; 8 mi w of Mancos on US 160; 15 mi within the park; near park visitors center. Ext corridors. **Pets:** Small, other species. $75 deposit/pet. Designated rooms, service with restrictions, crate.

SAVE S6 X

MONTE VISTA

▼◇▼ ▼◇▼ Best Western Movie Manor Motel **SH**
(719) 852-5921. **$55-$115.** 2830 W Hwy 160. On US 160, 2 mi w. Ext corridors. **Pets:** Accepted.

SAVE X

▼◇▼ ▼◇▼ Comfort Inn **M** ❀
(719) 852-0612. **$80-$105.** 1519 Grande Ave. 0.3 mi e on US 160. Int corridors. **Pets:** Other species. Service with restrictions, supervision.

SAVE S6 X

MONTROSE

▼◇▼ ▼◇▼ Affordable Inns **M**
(970) 249-6644. **$46-$86.** 1480 S Townsend Ave. 1 mi s on US 550. Ext corridors. **Pets:** Dogs only. $6 daily fee/room. Designated rooms, service with restrictions, supervision.

SAVE X

▼◇▼ ▼◇▼ Best Western Red Arrow **SH** ❀
(970) 249-9641. **$69-$109.** 1702 E Main St. 1 mi e on US 50. Ext/int corridors. **Pets:** $8 daily fee/room. Service with restrictions.

SAVE S6 X

▼◇▼ ▼◇▼ Black Canyon Motel **M**
(970) 249-3495. **$45-$95.** 1605 E Main St. 1 mi e on US 50. Ext corridors. **Pets:** Accepted.

SAVE S6 X

▼◇▼ ▼◇▼ Canyon Trails Inn **M**
(970) 249-3426. **$37-$60.** 1225 E Main St. 0.8 mi e on US 50. Ext corridors. **Pets:** Accepted.

SAVE S6 X

▼◇▼ ▼◇▼ Days Inn **SH**
(970) 249-3411. **$39-$69.** 1655 E Main St. 1 mi e on US 50. Int corridors. **Pets:** Accepted.

A$K S6 X

▼◇▼ ▼◇▼ Holiday Inn Express Hotel & Suites **SH**
(970) 240-1800. **$89-$149.** 1391 S Townsend Ave. 1 mi s on US 550, e on Niagara Ave. Int corridors. **Pets:** Accepted.

SAVE S6 X 6M

▼◇▼ ▼◇▼ Quality Inn & Suites-Montrose **SH** ❀
(970) 249-1011. **$69-$109.** 2751 Commercial Way. 2 mi s on US 550, w on O'Delle. Int corridors. **Pets:** Dogs only. $10 one-time fee/room. Designated rooms, service with restrictions, supervision.

A$K S6 X

▼◇▼ ▼◇▼ Uncompahgre Bed & Breakfast **BB**
(970) 240-4000. **$60-$105.** 21049 Uncompahgre Rd. 8 mi s on US 550. Int corridors. **Pets:** Large, dogs only. Service with restrictions, supervision.

A$K X

▼◇▼ ▼◇▼ Western Motel **M**
(970) 249-3481. **$42-$95.** 1200 E Main St. 0.8 mi e on US 50. Ext corridors. **Pets:** Small, dogs only. $25 deposit/room, $5 daily fee/pet. Designated rooms, service with restrictions, supervision.

SAVE S6 X

NEDERLAND

▼◇▼ ▼◇▼ Best Western Lodge at Nederland **SH**
(303) 258-9463. **$89-$109, 3 day notice.** 55 Lakeview Dr. SR 119; across street from Visitor's Center. Int corridors. **Pets:** Accepted.

SAVE S6 X

NEW CASTLE

▼◇▼ ▼◇▼ New Castle Rodeway Inn **SH**
(970) 984-2363. **$59-$109.** 781 Burning Mountain Rd. I-70, exit 105, just n, then w. Int corridors. **Pets:** Accepted.

A$K S6 X

OURAY

▼◇▼ ▼◇▼ Comfort Inn **M**
(970) 325-7203. **$53-$110.** 191 5th Ave. Just w of US 550. Ext corridors. **Pets:** Dogs only. $10 daily fee/pet. Designated rooms, supervision.

SAVE S6 X 6M

▼◇▼ ▼◇▼ Ouray Victorian Inn & Resort Accommodations **M**
(970) 325-7222. **$65-$100.** 50 3rd Ave. Just w of US 550. Ext corridors. **Pets:** Designated rooms, service with restrictions, supervision.

SAVE S6 X

▼◇▼ ▼◇▼ Rivers Edge Motel **M**
(970) 325-4621. **$50-$100.** 110 7th Ave. Just w of US 550 via 7th Ave. Ext corridors. **Pets:** Dogs only. $10 daily fee/pet. Service with restrictions, supervision.

SAVE S6 X

(AAA) ▼▼ ▼▼ Riverside Inn M
(970) 325-4061. **$33-$160.** 1805 N Main St. Just n on US 550. Ext corridors. **Pets:** $50 deposit/room. Designated rooms, supervision.
[SAVE] [✕] [🛏] [💻] [☕]

PAGOSA SPRINGS

(AAA) ▼▼▼▼ Best Value High Country Lodge M
(970) 264-4181. **$70-$96.** 3821 E Hwy 160. On US 160, 3 mi e. Ext corridors. **Pets:** Other species. $15 one-time fee/pet. Service with restrictions, supervision.
[SAVE] [Sₒ] [✕] [🛏] [💻] [🍴] [✕]

(AAA) ▼▼ ▼▼ Best Western Oak Ridge Lodge M
(970) 264-4173. **$49-$150, 3 day notice.** 158 Hot Springs Blvd. Just s of US 160. Int corridors. **Pets:** Other species. $100 deposit/pet, $15 one-time fee/pet. Service with restrictions, supervision.
[SAVE] [Sₒ] [✕] [🛏] [💻] [🍴] [🏊] [✕]

▼▼ ▼▼ Econo Lodge M
(970) 731-2701. **$59-$109.** 315 Navajo Trail Dr. 4 mi w on US 160. Int corridors. **Pets:** Accepted.
[ASK] [Sₒ] [✕] [♿] [🛏] [☕]

▼▼ ▼▼ Fireside Inn Cabins CA 🐾
(970) 264-9204. **$85-$144, 15 day notice.** 1600 E Hwy 160. 1.3 mi e on US 160. Ext corridors. **Pets:** Other species. $5 daily fee/pet. No service, crate.
[ASK] [Sₒ] [✕] [🛏] [💻] [✕] [✕]

▼▼▼▼ The Pagosa Springs Inn & Suites SH
(970) 731-3400. **$60-$129.** 519 Village Dr. 3.8 mi w on US 160. Int corridors. **Pets:** Medium, dogs only. $10 daily fee/pet. Designated rooms, service with restrictions, supervision.
[ASK] [Sₒ] [✕] [🛏] [💻] [✕] [✕]

(AAA) ▼▼ Super 8 Motel M
(970) 731-4005. **$40-$100.** 8 Solomon Dr. 2.5 mi w on US 160. Ext/int corridors. **Pets:** Other species. Supervision.
[SAVE] [Sₒ] [✕] [🛏]

PUEBLO

(AAA) ▼▼ ▼▼ Best Western Town House Motel M
(719) 543-6530. **$50-$81.** 730 N Santa Fe Ave. I-25, exit 99B, just w, then just s. Ext corridors. **Pets:** Large, other species. $10 one-time fee/room. Service with restrictions.
[SAVE] [Sₒ] [✕] [♿] [🛏] [💻] [🍴] [☕]

▼▼▼▼ Hampton Inn SH
(719) 544-4700. **$69-$99.** 4703 N Freeway. I-25, exit 102, just w. Ext corridors. **Pets:** Accepted.
[ASK] [Sₒ] [✕] [🛏] [💻] [☕]

▼▼▼▼ Holiday Inn Pueblo SH
(719) 543-8050. **Call for rates.** 4001 N Elizabeth St. I-25, exit 101 (US 50 W), 0.3 mi n on service road. Ext/int corridors. **Pets:** Accepted.
[✕] [🛏] [💻] [🍴] [☕] [✕]

▼▼▼▼ La Quinta Inn & Suites Pueblo SH
(719) 542-3500. **$79-$109.** 4801 N Elizabeth St. I-25, exit 102, just nw. Int corridors. **Pets:** Small, other species. Service with restrictions, supervision.
[ASK] [✕] [⏰] [♿] [🛏] [💻] [☕]

(AAA) ▼▼ ▼▼ Microtel Inn & Suites SH
(719) 242-2020. **$54-$95.** 3343 Gateway Dr. I-25, exit 94. Int corridors. **Pets:** Other species. $50 deposit/room. Service with restrictions, supervision.
[SAVE] [Sₒ] [✕] [♿M] [🛏] [💻]

▼▼ Motel 6–1186 M
(719) 543-8900. **$40-$53.** 960 Hwy 50 W. I-25, exit 101, 0.3 mi w. Ext corridors. **Pets:** Other species. Service with restrictions, supervision.
[Sₒ] [✕] [♿] [🛏]

▼▼ ▼▼ Sleep Inn SH
(719) 583-4000. **$65-$109.** 3626 N Freeway. I-25, exit 101, just ne on frontage road. Int corridors. **Pets:** Small, dogs only. $15 daily fee/pet. Service with restrictions, supervision.
[ASK] [Sₒ] [✕] [♿M] [♿] [🛏] [💻] [☕]

PUEBLO WEST

▼▼ ▼▼ Inn at Pueblo West M
(719) 547-2111. **$79-$99.** 201 S McCulloch Blvd. I-25, exit 101, 8 mi w on US 50, then 0.5 mi s. Ext/int corridors. **Pets:** Accepted.
[ASK] [Sₒ] [✕] [♿M] [♿] [🛏] [💻] [🍴] [☕]

RIDGWAY

(AAA) ▼▼▼▼ Chipeta Sun Lodge and Spa BB
(970) 626-3737. **$125-$250, 30 day notice.** 304 S Lena St. Jct US 550, just w on SR 62, then just s. Ext/int corridors. **Pets:** Medium. $35 one-time fee/room. Designated rooms, service with restrictions, crate.
[SAVE] [Sₒ] [✕] [🛏] [💻] [☕] [✕] [🐾]

(AAA) ▼▼ ▼▼ Ridgway-Ouray Lodge & Suites M
(970) 626-5444. **$60-$88.** 373 Palomino Tr. From US 550, just ne on SR 62, then just e. Int corridors. **Pets:** $10 daily fee/pet. Designated rooms, service with restrictions, supervision.
[SAVE] [Sₒ] [✕] [🛏] [💻] [✕]

RIFLE

(AAA) ▼▼ ▼▼ Rusty Cannon Motel M
(970) 625-4004. **$70-$78.** 701 Taughenbaugh Blvd. I-70, exit 90, just s. Ext corridors. **Pets:** Dogs only. $25 one-time fee/pet. Designated rooms, service with restrictions, supervision.
[SAVE] [Sₒ] [✕] [🛏] [💻] [🏊]

SALIDA

(AAA) ▼▼ ▼▼ Aspen Leaf Lodge M 🐾
(719) 539-6733. **$49-$79.** 7350 W Hwy 50. Just w of Hot Springs Pool. Ext corridors. **Pets:** Medium, other species. $5 daily fee/room. Service with restrictions, supervision.
[SAVE] [✕] [🛏]

(AAA) ▼▼▼▼ Best Western Colorado Lodge M
(719) 539-2514. **$49-$88.** 352 W Rainbow Blvd. On US 50. Ext corridors. **Pets:** $10 one-time fee/pet. Supervision.
[SAVE] [Sₒ] [✕] [🛏] [💻] [🏊] [✕]

(AAA) ▼▼ Circle R Motel M
(719) 539-6296. **$39-$74.** 304 E US Hwy 50. Ext corridors. **Pets:** Medium. $5 one-time fee/pet. Service with restrictions, crate.
[SAVE] [Sₒ] [✕] [🛏]

(AAA) ▼▼ ▼▼ Days Inn SH
(719) 539-6651. **$50-$100.** 407 E Hwy 50. US 50. Int corridors. **Pets:** Other species. $10 one-time fee/pet. Designated rooms, service with restrictions, supervision.
[SAVE] [Sₒ] [✕] [🛏] [💻]

(AAA) ▼▼▼▼ Econo Lodge SH
(719) 539-2895. **$49-$129.** 1310 E Hwy 50. Just e on US 50; between Blake and Palmer sts. Ext corridors. **Pets:** Medium, dogs only. $10 daily fee/pet. Designated rooms, supervision.
[SAVE] [Sₒ] [✕] [🛏] [💻]

(AAA) ▼▼ ▼▼ Silver Ridge Lodge M
(719) 539-2553. **$40-$100, 3 day notice.** 545 W Rainbow Blvd. US 50, just w of Chamber of Commerce. Ext corridors. **Pets:** Small, dogs only. $10 daily fee/pet. Designated rooms, service with restrictions, supervision.
[SAVE] [Sₒ] [✕] [🛏] [💻] [☕]

▼▼ ▼▼ Super 8 Motel M
(719) 539-6689. **$59-$119.** 525 W Rainbow Blvd. On US 50. Ext corridors. **Pets:** Medium. Service with restrictions, supervision.
[ASK] [Sₒ] [✕] [🛏] [💻] [☕] [✕]

♦♦♦ ▼▼▼▼ Travelodge M
(719) 539-2528. **$59-$109.** 7310 Hwy 50. On US 50 W. Ext corridors.
Pets: Other species. $5 daily fee/pet. Service with restrictions.
[SAVE] [S🐾] [✕] [🛏] [💻] [🏊]

▼▼▼▼ The Tudor Rose Bed & Breakfast BB
(719) 539-2002. **$75-$165, 7 day notice.** 6720 CR 104. Just e on US
50, s on CR 104, 0.5 mi up the hill, follow signs. Int corridors.
Pets: Accepted.
[✕] [🛏] [🐾] [🎾]

♦♦♦ ▼▼▼ Woodland Motel M ❄
(719) 539-4980. **$42-$107.** 903 W 1st St. From center of historic downtown, 1 mi w on 1st St (SR 291). Ext corridors. **Pets:** Large, other
species.
[SAVE] [✕] [🛏] [💻] [🐾]

SILVERTHORNE

♦♦♦ ▼▼▼ Days Inn Summit County SH
(970) 468-8661. **$59-$229.** 580 Silverthorne Ln. I-70, exit 205, just n on
SR 9, just e on Rainbow Dr, then just e on Tanglewood Ln. Int
corridors. **Pets:** Accepted.
[SAVE] [S🐾] [✕] [&M] [🎾] [♿] [🛏] [🏊]

▼▼▼▼ Four Points by Sheraton Silverthorne SH
(970) 468-6200. **Call for rates.** 560 Silverthorne Ln. I-70, exit 205, just
n on SR 9, just e on Rainbow Rd, then just e on Tanglewood Ln. Int
corridors. **Pets:** Accepted.
[S🐾] [✕] [&M] [🎾] [♿] [🛏] [💻] [🍴] [🏊] [🐾]

▼▼▼▼ Quality Inn & Suites SH
(970) 513-1222. **$69-$239.** 530 Silverthorne Ln. I-70, exit 205, just n on
SR 9, just e on Rainbow Rd, then just e on Tanglewood Ln. Int
corridors. **Pets:** Accepted.
[ASK] [S🐾] [✕] [&M] [🎾] [♿] [🛏] [💻] [🏊]

SILVERTON

**♦♦♦ ▼▼▼ Silverton's Inn of the Rockies at the Historic
Alma House BB**
(970) 387-5336. **$69-$99, 7 day notice.** 220 E 10th St. SR 110, off US
550 to 10th St, then just se. Int corridors. **Pets:** Medium, dogs only. $15
daily fee/pet. Designated rooms, service with restrictions, supervision.
[SAVE] [S🐾] [✕] [🐾] [🎾] [🎾]

▼▼▼ ◆ Villa Dallavalle B & B BB
(970) 387-5555. **$75-$165.** 1257 Blair St. SR 110, off US 550, se on
12th to Blair St, then just n. Int corridors. **Pets:** Medium, dogs only. $15
one-time fee/room. Service with restrictions, supervision.
[ASK] [S🐾] [✕] [💻] [🎾]

♦♦♦ ▼▼▼▼ The Wyman Hotel & Inn BB ❄
(970) 387-5372. **$135-$235, 14 day notice.** 1371 Greene (Main) St.
Northeast corner of Greene (Main) and 14th sts. Int corridors.
Pets: Other species. $25 one-time fee/room. Designated rooms, service
with restrictions, supervision.
[SAVE] [✕] [🛏] [🍴] [🎾]

SNOWMASS VILLAGE

▼▼▼▼ Silvertree Hotel LH ❄
(970) 923-3520. **$79-$659.** 100 Elbert Ln. 4 mi sw of SR 82 via Brush
Creek and Snowmelt rds, Lot 8. Int corridors. **Pets:** Other species. $10
daily fee/room.
[ASK] [S🐾] [✕] [🎾] [🛏] [💻] [🍴] [🏊] [🐾] [🎾]

♦♦♦ ▼▼▼◆ Snowmass Mountain Chalet SH ❄
(970) 923-3900. **$79-$325, 45 day notice.** 115 Daly Ln. 4 mi sw of SR
82 via Brush Creek and Lower Village rds, Lot 5. Ext/int corridors.
Pets: Large, other species. $10 daily fee/pet. Designated rooms.
[SAVE] [S🐾] [✕] [🛏] [🏊] [🐾] [🎾]

SOUTH FORK

▼▼▼ Comfort Inn M
(719) 873-5600. **$100-$110.** 0182 E Frontage Rd. On US 160. Int
corridors. **Pets:** Accepted.
[ASK] [S🐾] [✕] [🛏] [💻] [🏊]

▼▼ Ute Bluff Lodge M ❄
(719) 873-5595. **$59-$64, 14 day notice.** 27680 W Hwy 160. 2.5 mi e
of jct US 160 and SR 149. Ext corridors. **Pets:** Medium. $7 daily fee/pet.
Service with restrictions, supervision.
[ASK] [S🐾] [✕] [🛏] [💻] [🎾]

♦♦♦ ▼▼▼ ◆ Wolf Creek Ski Lodge M ❄
(719) 873-5547. **$59-$109, 15 day notice.** 31042 Hwy 160 W. On US
160. Ext corridors. **Pets:** Medium, dogs only. $10 daily fee/pet. Designated
rooms, service with restrictions, supervision.
[SAVE] [✕] [🛏] [💻] [🍴] [🐾]

STEAMBOAT SPRINGS

♦♦♦ ▼▼▼ The Alpiner Lodge M
(970) 879-1430. **$52-$99, 3 day notice.** 424 Lincoln Ave. US 40, just w
of Hot Springs Pool. Ext/int corridors. **Pets:** Dogs only. $15 one-time
fee/pet. Designated rooms, service with restrictions, supervision.
[SAVE] [S🐾] [✕] [🛏] [💻]

▼▼ Comfort Inn SH
(970) 879-6669. **$65-$180.** 1055 Walton Creek Rd. 2.8 mi e on US 40.
Int corridors. **Pets:** Dogs only. $10 daily fee/pet. Designated rooms, super-
vision.
[ASK] [S🐾] [✕] [&M] [♿] [🛏] [💻] [🏊] [🐾]

♦♦♦ ▼▼▼▼ Fairfield Inn & Suites by Marriott SH ❄
(970) 870-9000. **$79-$159.** 3200 S Lincoln Ave. 3 mi e on US 40. Int
corridors. **Pets:** Other species. $50 deposit/pet, $10 daily fee/pet. Designated rooms, service with restrictions, supervision.
[SAVE] [S🐾] [✕] [🎾] [♿] [🛏] [🏊] [🐾]

▼▼▼◆ Hampton Inn & Suites SH 🐾
(970) 871-8900. **$109-$339.** 725 S Lincoln Ave. 1.1 mi e on US 40. Int
corridors. **Pets:** $10 daily fee/room. Designated rooms, service with restric-
tions.
[ASK] [S🐾] [✕] [&M] [🎾] [♿] [🛏] [💻] [🏊] [🐾]

♦♦♦ ▼▼▼◆ Holiday Inn Steamboat SH
(970) 879-2250. **$79-$179, 3 day notice.** 3190 S Lincoln Ave. 3 mi e
on US 40. Int corridors. **Pets:** Accepted.
[SAVE] [S🐾] [✕] [🎾] [♿] [🛏] [💻] [🍴] [🏊] [🐾]

♦♦♦ ▼▼▼ Iron Horse Inn-Steamboat Springs SH
(970) 879-6505. **$70-$150, 3 day notice.** 333 S Lincoln Ave. 1 mi e on
US 40. Ext/int corridors. **Pets:** Accepted.
[SAVE] [S🐾] [✕] [🛏] [💻] [🐾]

♦♦♦ ▼▼▼ Rabbit Ears Motel M ❄
(970) 879-1150. **$69-$125, 3 day notice.** 201 Lincoln Ave. Just e on
US 40. Ext corridors. **Pets:** $12 one-time fee/room. Service with restric-
tions, supervision.
[SAVE] [S🐾] [✕] [🛏] [💻]

▼▼▼◆ Sheraton Steamboat Resort LH
(970) 879-2220. **$119-$329, 30 day notice.** 2200 Village Inn Ct. 2.3 mi
e on US 40, 1 mi n on Mt Werner Rd; at ski area. Int corridors.
Pets: Large, dogs only. $25 one-time fee/room. Designated rooms, service
with restrictions, supervision.
[ASK] [S🐾] [✕] [🎾] [♿] [🛏] [💻] [🍴] [🏊] [🐾]

▼▼▼ Super 8 Motel SH
(970) 879-5230. **$65-$108.** 3195 S Lincoln Ave. 3 mi e on US 40. Int
corridors. **Pets:** Dogs only. $20 deposit/room. Designated rooms, service
with restrictions, supervision.
[ASK] [S🐾] [✕] [🏊]

STERLING

AAA ▼▼▼ **Best Western Sundowner M**
(970) 522-6265. **$79-$119.** 125 Overland Trail St. I-76, exit 125, just w. Ext/int corridors. **Pets:** Accepted.
SAVE S⃝ ✕ 🔒 🖥 ⊃

AAA ▼ **Colonial Motel M**
(970) 522-3382. **$43-$62.** 915 S Division. I-76, exit 125, 1.8 mi w on US 6 to 2nd traffic light (4th St), then s. Ext corridors. **Pets:** Accepted.
SAVE S⃝ ✕ 🔒

AAA ▼▼▼ **Ramada Inn SH**
(970) 522-2625. **$69-$99.** 22140 E Hwy 6. I-76, exit 125, 0.5 mi e on US 6. Ext/int corridors. **Pets:** Other species. $25 deposit/room. Service with restrictions, supervision.
SAVE S⃝ ✕ 🤿 🔒 🖥 🍴 ⊃ ✕

STRATTON

AAA ▼▼▼ **Best Western Golden Prairie Inn SH**
(719) 348-5311. **$65-$89.** 700 Colorado Ave. I-70, exit 419, just n. Ext corridors. **Pets:** Accepted.
SAVE S⃝ ✕ 🔒 🖥 🍴 ⊃

TELLURIDE

AAA ▼▼▼ **Hotel Columbia SH** 🐾
(970) 728-0660. **$145-$450, 30 day notice.** 300 W San Juan Ave. Just s of SR 145 Spur, at Aspen St and San Juan Ave; opposite gondola. Int corridors. **Pets:** Dogs only. $20 daily fee/room. Designated rooms, service with restrictions.
SAVE S⃝ ✕ 🔒 🖥 🍴 ✕

▼▼▼ **The Hotel Telluride SH**
(970) 369-1188. **$129-$579.** 199 N Cornet St. Just n of jct SR 145 (Colorado Ave). Int corridors. **Pets:** Accepted.
ASK S⃝ ✕ &M 🤿 📷 🔒 🖥 🍴 ✕

AAA ▼▼▼ ▼▼▼ **Wyndham Peaks Resort & Golden Door (R) Spa LH**
(970) 728-6800. **$199-$299.** 136 Country Club Dr. 1.8 mi s of jct SR 145 (Colorado Ave) and 145 Spur, 2 mi e on Mountain Village Blvd, follow ski area signs; in Telluride Mountain Village. Ext/int corridors. **Pets:** Accepted.
SAVE ✕ &M 🔒 🖥 🍴 ⊃ ✕ 🦮

TRINIDAD

AAA ▼▼▼ **Best Western Trinidad Inn M**
(719) 846-2215. **$59-$119.** 900 W Adams St. I-25, exit 13A, just ne. Ext corridors. **Pets:** Accepted.
SAVE S⃝ ✕ 🔒 🖥 🍴 ⊃

AAA ▼ **Budget Host Derrick Motel M**
(719) 846-3307. **$54-$59.** 10301 Santa Fe Trail Dr. I-25, exit 11, 0.5 mi ne. Ext corridors. **Pets:** Small. $10 one-time fee/room. Service with restrictions, supervision.
SAVE S⃝ ✕ 🔒 🖥

▼▼ **Budget Summit Inn M**
(719) 846-2251. **$45-$65.** 9800 Santa Fe Trail Dr. I-25, exit 11, just se. Ext/int corridors. **Pets:** Small, dogs only. $10 one-time fee/room. Service with restrictions, supervision.
ASK S⃝ ✕ 🤿 📷 🔒

AAA ▼▼▼ **Quality Inn Trinidad SH**
(719) 846-4491. **$89-$139.** 3125 Toupal Dr. I-25, exit 11, just w. Int corridors. **Pets:** Medium, dogs only. $50 deposit/pet, $15 one-time fee/pet. Designated rooms, service with restrictions, supervision.
SAVE S⃝ ✕ 🔒 🖥 🍴 ⊃ ✕

▼▼ **Super 8 Motel M**
(719) 846-8280. **$55-$80, 20 day notice.** 1924 Freedom Rd. I-25, exit 15, just ne. Int corridors. **Pets:** Medium. $10 one-time fee/room. Designated rooms, service with restrictions, supervision.
ASK S⃝ ✕ 🔒 🖥

VAIL

AAA ▼▼▼ **Antlers at Vail CO** 🐾
(970) 476-2471. **$125-$475, 30 day notice.** 680 W Lionshead Pl. I-70, exit 176, 0.5 mi w, then just s on Lionshead Cir. Ext corridors. **Pets:** Other species. $15 daily fee/pet. Designated rooms, service with restrictions, crate.
SAVE S⃝ ✕ 🤿 🔒 🖥 ⊃ ✕ 🦮

AAA ▼▼▼ ▼▼▼ **Sonnenalp Resort of Vail LH**
(970) 476-5656. **$240-$2055.** 20 Vail Rd. I-70, exit 176, just s. Int corridors. **Pets:** Accepted.
SAVE S⃝ ✕ 🤿 🍴 ⊃ ✕

WALSENBURG

AAA ▼ **Anchor Motel M**
(719) 738-2800. **$45-$65.** 1001 Main St. I-25, exit 49, 0.5 mi nw. Ext corridors. **Pets:** Small, other species. $5 one-time fee/room. Designated rooms, service with restrictions, supervision.
SAVE ✕ 🔒 🖥

AAA ▼▼ **Best Western Rambler SH**
(719) 738-1121. **$63-$98.** 457 US Hwy 85-87. I-25, exit 52, just w. Ext corridors. **Pets:** Accepted.
SAVE S⃝ ✕ 🖥 🍴 ⊃

AAA ▼ **Country Budget Host Motel M**
(719) 738-3800. **$42-$64.** 553 US Hwy 85 & 87. I-25, exit 52, 0.3 mi w. Ext corridors. **Pets:** Dogs only. $10 daily fee/pet. Designated rooms, no service, supervision.
SAVE S⃝ ✕

WINDSOR

AAA ▼▼▼ **AmericInn Lodge & Suites SH** 🐾
(970) 226-1232. **$79-$159.** 7645 Westgate Dr. I-25, exit 262, just se off SR 392. Int corridors. **Pets:** Medium. $10 daily fee/room. Designated rooms, service with restrictions, supervision.
SAVE ✕ &M 🤿 📷 🔒 🖥 ⊃ ✕

AAA ▼▼▼ **Super 8 Motel SH**
(970) 686-5996. **$57-$63.** 1265 Main St. I-25, exit 262, 3.8 mi e; in shopping/restaurant complex. Int corridors. **Pets:** Accepted.
SAVE S⃝ ✕ &M 🔒 🖥

WINTER PARK

AAA ▼▼▼ **Winter Park Mountain Lodge SH** 🐾
(970) 726-4211. **$60-$529.** 81699 US Hwy 40. 2.3 mi se on US 40; near ski area. Int corridors. **Pets:** Large, other species. Designated rooms, service with restrictions, supervision.
SAVE ✕ &M 🔒 🖥 🍴 ⊃ ✕

YAMPA

AAA ▼▼▼ **Oak Tree Inn SH**
(970) 638-1000. **$75.** 98 Moffat Ave. Just off SR 131. Int corridors. **Pets:** $10 one-time fee/room. Service with restrictions, supervision.
SAVE S⃝ ✕ 🔒 🖥 🍴

CONNECTICUT

BETHEL

◆◆◆ ▼▼▼ Microtel Inn & Suites SH
(203) 748-8318. **$70-$122.** 80 Benedict Rd. I-84, exit 8, 1 mi e on US 6. Int corridors. **Pets:** $100 deposit/room, $10 daily fee/pet. Service with restrictions, supervision.

SAVE S/D ✕ ⊘ ☁ ⬛ 🖵

BRANFORD

◆◆◆ ▼▼▼ Days Inn & Conference Center M
(203) 488-8314. **$59-$299.** 375 E Main St. I-95, exit 55, just n on US 1. Ext/int corridors. **Pets:** Medium, dogs only. $20 one-time fee/room. Designated rooms, service with restrictions, crate.

SAVE S/D ✕ ⬛ 🖵 ⇋

▼▼ Motel 6–1279 SH
(203) 483-5828. **$45-$63.** 320 E Main St. I-95, exit 55, 0.3 mi n on US 1. Int corridors. **Pets:** Medium, other species. Designated rooms, service with restrictions, supervision.

S/D ✕ ☁

BRIDGEPORT

▼▼▼ Bridgeport Holiday Inn & Convention Center SH
(203) 334-1234. **$109-$159, 7 day notice.** 1070 Main St. SR 8, exit 2 northbound, 0.7 mi se; SR 8, exit southbound, just s, then just e. Int corridors. **Pets:** Accepted.

ASK ✕ ⬛ 🖵 ⊘ ⇋

BROOKFIELD

▼▼▼ Twin Tree Inn M
(203) 775-0220. **$85-$95.** 1030 Federal Rd (Rt 7 & 202). Jct SR 25 and US 202, 1 mi n. Ext/int corridors. **Pets:** Other species. $10 one-time fee/room. Designated rooms, service with restrictions, crate.

ASK S/D ✕ ☁ ⬛

DANBURY

◆◆◆ ▼▼▼ Ethan Allen Hotel SH
(203) 744-1776. **$129.** 21 Lake Ave Extension. I-84, exit 4, 0.3 mi w on US 6 and 202. Int corridors. **Pets:** Accepted.

SAVE S/D ✕ ⊘ ⬛ 🖵 ⊘ ⇋

◆◆◆ ▼▼▼ Holiday Inn SH
(203) 792-4000. **$129.** 80 Newtown Rd. I-84, exit 8 (Newtown Rd), 0.5 mi s on US 6 W. Int corridors. **Pets:** Large. $25 one-time fee/room. Designated rooms, service with restrictions, supervision.

SAVE S/D ✕ ⊘ ⬛ 🖵 ⊘ ⇋

◆◆◆ ▼▼▼ Maron Hotel & Suites SH
(203) 791-2200. **$99-$179.** 42 Lake Ave Extension. I-84, exit 4 westbound, 0.5 mi w on US 6 and 202. Int corridors. **Pets:** Medium, other species. $10 one-time fee/pet. Service with restrictions.

SAVE S/D ✕ ⊘M ⊘ ⊘ ⬛ 🖵 ⊘

◆◆◆ ▼▼▼ Residence Inn by Marriott SH ✿
(203) 797-1256. **$109-$139.** 22 Segar St. I-84, exit 4 eastbound, just n; exit westbound, just e on Lake Ave Extension, then just s. Int corridors. **Pets:** Other species. $75 one-time fee/pet. Designated rooms, service with restrictions.

SAVE S/D ✕ ⊘ ⊘ ⬛ 🖵 ⇋

▼▼▼ Sheraton Danbury LH ✿
(203) 794-0600. **$89-$189.** 18 Old Ridgebury Rd. I-84, exit 2 eastbound; exit 2A westbound. Int corridors. **Pets:** Medium, dogs only. Designated rooms, service with restrictions, supervision.

ASK ✕ ⊘ ⊘ ⬛ 🖵 🍴 ⇋ ✕

◆◆◆ ▼▼▼ Super 8 Motel SH
(203) 743-0064. **$74.** 3 Lake Ave Extension. I-84, exit 4, just w on US 6 and 202. Int corridors. **Pets:** $10 daily fee/pet. Designated rooms, service with restrictions, supervision.

SAVE ✕ ⬛

◆◆◆ ▼▼▼ Wellesley Inn (Danbury) SH
(203) 792-3800. **$89-$129, 30 day notice.** 116 Newtown Rd. I-84, exit 8 (Newtown Rd), northeast corner. Int corridors. **Pets:** Accepted.

SAVE ✕ ⊘ ⬛ 🖵 🍴 ⇋

DAYVILLE

▼▼▼ Holiday Inn Express SH
(860) 779-3200. **$108-$128.** 16 Tracy Rd. I-395, exit 94, just w. Int corridors. **Pets:** Small. $10 one-time fee/pet. Designated rooms, service with restrictions, crate.

ASK S/D ✕ ⊘M ⊘ ⬛ 🖵 ⇋

GRISWOLD

◆◆◆ ▼▼▼ AmericInn Lodge & Suites SH
(860) 376-3200. **$69-$179.** 375 Voluntown Rd. I-395, exit 85, w on SR 138. Int corridors. **Pets:** Small. $100 deposit/pet. Designated rooms, service with restrictions, supervision.

SAVE S/D ✕ ⊘M ⊘ ⬛ 🖵 ⇋

GROTON

◆◆◆ ▼▼▼ Clarion Inn SH
(860) 446-0660. **$69-$169.** 156 Kings Hwy. I-95, exit 86, 0.3 mi ne on SR 184. Int corridors. **Pets:** Dogs only. $15 daily fee/pet. Designated rooms, service with restrictions, supervision.

SAVE S/D ✕ ⬛ 🖵 ⇋ ✕

HARTFORD METROPOLITAN AREA

BERLIN

WWWW Hawthorne Inn SH ❖
(860) 828-4181. **$89-$175.** 2387 Berlin Tpke. I-91, exit 17 northbound, 4.7 mi n on SR 15 (Berlin Tpke); exit 22N southbound, 2.5 mi n on SR 9 to exit 22, follow signs onto US 5 and SR 15 S (Berlin Tpke) for 3 mi. Int corridors. **Pets:** Other species. Service with restrictions, supervision.
[SAVE] [S₀] [✕] [☞] [❸] [↑↓] [⇌] [⊗]

CROMWELL

WW Comfort Inn SH
(860) 635-4100. **$59-$129.** 111 Berlin Rd. I-91, exit 21, just e on SR 372. Int corridors. **Pets:** Accepted.
[ASK] [S₀] [✕] [❸] [⬛]

WWWW Radisson Hotel and Conference Center Cromwell/ Hartford South LH
(860) 635-2000. **$99-$149.** 100 Berlin Rd. I-91, exit 21, just e on SR 372. Int corridors. **Pets:** Accepted.
[ASK] [S₀] [✕] [☞M] [❸] [⬛] [↑↓] [⇌] [⊗]

EAST HARTFORD

WWWW Holiday Inn SH
(860) 528-9611. **$71-$107.** 363 Roberts St. I-84, exit 58, just w. Int corridors. **Pets:** Medium, dogs only. $25 deposit/room, $25 one-time fee/ room. Service with restrictions, supervision.
[SAVE] [S₀] [✕] [⊘] [☞] [❸] [⬛] [↑↓] [⇌]

WWWW Sheraton Hartford Hotel SH ❖
(860) 528-9703. **$79-$119.** 100 E River Dr. I-84, exit 53 eastbound, just s; exit 54 westbound to exit 3 (Darlin St), just n. Int corridors. **Pets:** Medium, dogs only. Designated rooms, service with restrictions, supervision.
[SAVE] [S₀] [✕] [☞M] [⊘] [☞] [❸] [⬛] [↑↓] [⇌]

EAST WINDSOR

WWWW Holiday Inn Express Hartford Airport Area M
(860) 627-6585. **$89-$109.** 260 Main St (US 5). I-91, exit 44, just s. Int corridors. **Pets:** Small, other species. $35 one-time fee/pet. Service with restrictions, supervision.
[ASK] [S₀] [✕] [☞M] [⊘] [☞] [❸] [⬛]

ENFIELD

WW Motel 6 Hartford-Enfield #1042 M
(860) 741-3685. **$45-$65.** 11 Hazard Ave. I-91, exit 47E, just e. Ext corridors. **Pets:** Large, other species. Service with restrictions, supervision.
[S₀] [✕] [☞]

WWWW Radisson Hotel Springfield-Enfield SH ❖
(860) 741-2211. **$85-$100.** 1 Bright Meadow Blvd. I-91, exit 49, just e on service road. Int corridors. **Pets:** $50 one-time fee/room. Designated rooms, service with restrictions, crate.
[ASK] [S₀] [✕] [☞M] [⊘] [☞] [❸] [⬛] [↑↓] [⇌] [⊗]

WW Red Roof Inn M
(860) 741-2571. **$50-$75.** 5 Hazard Ave. I-91, exit 47E. Ext corridors. **Pets:** Accepted.
[✕] [☞M] [⊘] [☞] [❸]

WWW Super 8 Motel-Enfield M
(860) 741-3636. **$64-$99.** 1543 King St. I-91, exit 46, 0.3 mi n on US 5. Ext corridors. **Pets:** $10 daily fee/room. Service with restrictions, supervision.
[SAVE] [S₀] [✕] [❸] [⬛]

FARMINGTON

WWWW Centennial Inn Suites CO ❖
(860) 677-4647. **$109-$169.** 5 Spring Ln. US 6, 0.3 mi e of jct SR 177. Ext/int corridors. **Pets:** Other species. $15 daily fee/pet. Service with restrictions, crate.
[ASK] [S₀] [✕] [☞M] [☞] [❸] [⬛] [⇌] [⊗]

WWWW Homewood Suites by Hilton SH
(860) 321-0000. **$149.** 2 Farm Glen Blvd. I-84, exit 39, 0.6 mi e on SR 4. Int corridors. **Pets:** Large, other species. $150 one-time fee/pet. Service with restrictions, supervision.
[ASK] [S₀] [✕] [☞M] [☞] [❸] [⬛] [⇌]

HARTFORD

WWWW Crowne Plaza Hartford Downtown LH
(860) 549-2400. **$130-$180.** 50 Morgan St. I-91, exit 32B; I-84, exit 50 eastbound; exit 52 westbound. Int corridors. **Pets:** Very small. $50 one-time fee/room. Designated rooms, service with restrictions, crate.
[ASK] [S₀] [✕] [☞M] [⊘] [☞] [❸] [⬛] [↑↓] [⇌]

WWWW Goodwin Hotel SH
(860) 246-7500. **$109-$1050.** 1 Haynes St. Downtown; entrance on Asylum St. Int corridors. **Pets:** Accepted.
[ASK] [S₀] [✕] [☞M] [☞] [❸] [↑↓]

WWWW Residence Inn by Marriott Downtown Hartford SH ❖
(860) 524-5550. **$179-$199.** 942 Main St. I-91, exit 29A northbound; exit 31 southbound. Int corridors. **Pets:** Large. $75 one-time fee/pet. Service with restrictions, supervision.
[SAVE] [✕] [☞] [❸] [⬛]

MANCHESTER

WWWW Residence Inn Manchester SH
(860) 432-4242. **$144-$194.** 201 Hale Rd. I-84, exit 63, 0.5 mi nw, then 0.6 mi sw. Int corridors. **Pets:** Accepted.
[ASK] [S₀] [✕] [☞M] [⊘] [☞] [❸] [⬛] [⇌] [⊗]

MIDDLETOWN

WWWW Inn at Middletown SH ❖
(860) 854-6300. **$99-$159.** 70 Main St. SR 9, exit 15, just sw on Dr. Martin Luther King Jr Way, then 0.4 mi se. Int corridors. **Pets:** Medium. $75 one-time fee/pet. Designated rooms, service with restrictions, crate.
[SAVE] [S₀] [✕] [☞M] [⊘] [☞] [❸] [⬛] [↑↓] [⇌]

MILLDALE

WW Days Inn M
(860) 621-9181. **$63.** 1845 Meriden Waterbury Tpke. I-84, exit 28, just e on SR 322. Int corridors. **Pets:** Large. $10 daily fee/room. Designated rooms, service with restrictions, supervision.
[ASK] [S₀] [✕] [❸] [⬛]

PLAINVILLE

WWW Ramada Inn SH
(860) 747-6876. **$80-$110.** 400 New Britain Ave. I-84, exit 34, just ne on Crooked St. Int corridors. **Pets:** $50 deposit/room. Designated rooms, service with restrictions, supervision.
[SAVE] [S₀] [✕] [❸] [⬛] [↑↓] [⇌]

SIMSBURY

WWW The Ironhorse Inn M
(860) 658-2216. **$86-$96.** 969 Hopmeadow St. On US 202/SR 10, 0.4 mi n. Int corridors. **Pets:** Accepted.
[SAVE] [S₀] [✕] [❸] [⇌]

SOUTHINGTON

Motel 6–1018 M
(860) 621-7351. **$45-$57.** 625 Queen St. I-84, exit 32, just ne. Ext corridors. **Pets:** Accepted.

Residence Inn by Marriott SH
(860) 621-4440. **$114-$225.** 778 West St. I-84, exit 31, just s. Int corridors. **Pets:** Accepted.

WETHERSFIELD

Best Western Camelot Inn SH
(860) 563-2311. **$79-$109.** 1330 Silas Deane Hwy. I-91, exit 24, 0.4 mi n. Int corridors. **Pets:** Medium. $10 daily fee/pet. Designated rooms, service with restrictions, crate.

Motel 6–1028 M
(860) 563-5900. **$45-$62.** 1341 Silas Deane Hwy. I-91, exit 24, just n on SR 99. Ext corridors. **Pets:** Accepted.

WINDSOR

The Residence Inn by Marriott Hartford-Windsor SH
(860) 688-7474. **$159.** 100 Dunfey Ln. I-91, exit 37, just w on SR 305 to Dunfey Ln, then 0.3 mi n. Ext corridors. **Pets:** Other species. $75 one-time fee/room. Service with restrictions.

WINDSOR LOCKS

Baymont Inn & Suites Hartford-Airport SH
(860) 623-3336. **$79-$89.** 64 Ella T Grasso Tpke. I-91, exit 40, 2.5 mi w on SR 20, then just n on SR 75. Int corridors. **Pets:** Accepted.

Homewood Suites by Hilton SH
(860) 627-8463. **$79-$149.** 65 Ella T Grasso Tpke. I-91, exit 40, 2.5 mi w on SR 20, then just n on SR 75. Ext/int corridors. **Pets:** Accepted.

Motel 6–763 M
(860) 292-6200. **$47-$61.** 3 National Dr. Jct SR 20, 0.7 mi n on SR 75, then just e. Ext corridors. **Pets:** Other species. Service with restrictions, supervision.

Ramada Inn Bradley International Airport SH
(860) 623-9494. **$99-$135.** 5 Ella T Grasso Tpke. I-91, exit 40, 2.5 mi w on SR 20, then just n on SR 75. Int corridors. **Pets:** Small, other species. Service with restrictions, supervision.

Sheraton Hotel At Bradley International Airport LH
(860) 627-5311. **$215-$235.** 1 Bradley International Airport. At Bradley International Airport terminal. Int corridors. **Pets:** Medium. Service with restrictions, supervision.

END METROPOLITAN AREA

LAKEVILLE

Inn at Iron Masters M
(860) 435-9844. **$95-$195.** 229 Main St (Rt 44 & 41). 0.5 mi ne. Ext corridors. **Pets:** Dogs only. Designated rooms, service with restrictions, supervision.

Interlaken Inn Resort and Conference Center SH
(860) 435-9878. **$139-$349, 7 day notice.** 74 Interlaken Rd. On SR 112, 0.5 mi w of jct SR 41. Ext/int corridors. **Pets:** Other species. $10 daily fee/room. Designated rooms, service with restrictions, supervision.

LEDYARD

The Mare's Inn B & B BB
(860) 572-7556. **$100-$200, 14 day notice.** 333 Colonel Ledyard Hwy. I-95, exit 89, 1 mi ne to Gold Star Hwy, 0.6 mi w, then 0.7 mi n. Int corridors. **Pets:** Other species. Designated rooms, service with restrictions.

LITCHFIELD

Litchfield Inn CI
(860) 567-4503. **$150-$250, 3 day notice.** 432 Bantam Rd. 1.5 mi w on US 202. Int corridors. **Pets:** Medium, dogs only. $25 daily fee/pet. Designated rooms, service with restrictions, supervision.

MERIDEN

Four Points by Sheraton Meriden SH
(203) 238-2380. **$89-$229.** 275 Research Pkwy. I-91, exit 17 southbound; exit 16 northbound, 0.5 mi e, then 0.5 mi s. Int corridors. **Pets:** Accepted.

Residence Inn by Marriott SH
(203) 634-7770. **$129-$139.** 390 Bee St. I-91, exit 17 northbound, just e on E Main St, then 0.7 mi n. Ext/int corridors. **Pets:** Accepted.

MILFORD

Comfort Inn SH
(203) 877-9411. **$71-$80.** 278 Old Gate Ln. I-95, exit 40, just s. Int corridors. **Pets:** Accepted.

MYSTIC

AmeriSuites (Mystic/I-95 & Seaport) SH
(860) 536-9997. **$129-$234.** 224 Greenmanville Ave. I-95, exit 90, just se. Int corridors. **Pets:** Accepted.

The Inn at Mystic M
(860) 536-9604. **$85-$295.** 3 Williams Ave. On US 1 at SR 27. Ext/int corridors. **Pets:** $15 daily fee/pet. Designated rooms, service with restrictions, supervision.

Residence Inn by Marriott SH
(860) 536-5150. **$149-$399.** 40 Whitehall Ave. I-95, exit 90, just n on SR 27. Int corridors. **Pets:** Accepted.

NEW HAVEN

Omni New Haven Hotel at Yale LH
(203) 772-6664. **$189-$239.** 155 Temple St. Center of downtown. Int corridors. **Pets:** Small. $50 one-time fee/pet. Service with restrictions, supervision.

▼▼▼▼ **Residence Inn by Marriott** 🆂🅷 🐾
(203) 777-5337. **$134-$161.** 3 Long Wharf Dr. I-95, exit 46, 0.6 mi nw. Ext corridors. **Pets:** Other species. $75 one-time fee/room. No service, supervision.
🅰🆂🅺 ⊠ 🕖 🖥 💻 🛏 ⊠

NEW LONDON

▼▼ **Red Roof Inn #7145** 🅼
(860) 444-0001. **$58-$96.** 707 Colman St. I-95, exit 82A northbound, 0.8 mi n, just w, then 0.6 mi on Bayonet St; exit 83 southbound, 0.6 mi s. Ext corridors. **Pets:** Medium, other species. Service with restrictions, supervision.
⊠ 🕖

NEW MILFORD

🅰🅰🅰 ▼▼▼▼ **The Homestead Inn** 🅱🅱
(860) 354-4080. **$105-$165.** 5 Elm St. Just e of village green off Main St; center. Ext/int corridors. **Pets:** Other species. $10 daily fee/room. Designated rooms, service with restrictions, crate.
🆂🅰🆅🅴 🆂🔟 ⊠ 🖥

NIANTIC

▼ **Motel 6–1063** 🅼
(860) 739-6991. **$45-$85.** 269 Flanders Rd. I-95, exit 74 northbound, just e; exit southbound, just s, then e. Ext corridors. **Pets:** Other species. Service with restrictions, supervision.
🆂🔟 ⊠ 🐾 🖥 🛏

NORTH STONINGTON

▼▼▼▼ **Antiques and Accommodations** 🅱🅱 🐾
(860) 535-1736. **$99-$229, 14 day notice.** 32 Main St. I-95, exit 92, 2.5 mi nw on SR 2, then 0.3 mi n. Ext/int corridors. **Pets:** $50 deposit/room. Designated rooms, service with restrictions, supervision.
🅰🆂🅺 🆂🔟 ⊠ 🖥 💻 🕖

🅰🅰🅰 ▼▼▼▼ **Cedar Park Inn & Whirlpool Suites** 🅼
(860) 535-7829. **$79-$249, 3 day notice.** 85 Norwich Westerly Rd. I-95, exit 92, 1 mi w on SR 2. Ext corridors. **Pets:** Medium. $50 deposit/room. Designated rooms, no service, supervision.
🆂🅰🆅🅴 🆂🔟 ⊠ 🅶🅼 🐾 🖥 🛏

▼▼▼▼ **The Inn at Lower Farm** 🅱🅱
(860) 535-9075. **$85-$150, 7 day notice.** 119 Mystic Rd. I-95, exit 90, 1.5 mi n on SR 27, 1.4 mi e on SR 184, then 3.4 mi n on SR 201. Int corridors. **Pets:** Small. $25 one-time fee/pet. Designated rooms, service with restrictions, supervision.
🅰🆂🅺 🆂🔟 ⊠ 🅆 🕖

NORWALK

▼▼ **Homestead Studio Suites Hotel-Norwalk** 🆂🅷
(203) 847-6888. **$119-$139.** 400 Main Ave. I-95, exit 15, 3.5 mi n via US 7, just e, then 1 mi s. Int corridors. **Pets:** Accepted.
🅰🆂🅺 🆂🔟 ⊠ 🕖 🐾 🖥 💻

NORWICH

🅰🅰🅰 ▼▼ ▼ **Ramada Hotel Norwich/Mystic** 🆂🅷
(860) 889-5201. **$79-$159.** 10 Laura Blvd. I-395, exit 80 southbound; exit 80W northbound, just w on SR 82. Int corridors. **Pets:** Small, dogs only. $25 one-time fee/pet. Service with restrictions, crate.
🆂🅰🆅🅴 🆂🔟 ⊠ 🕖 🖥 💻 🛏

OLD LYME

🅰🅰🅰 ▼▼▼▼ **Old Lyme Inn** 🅲🅸 🐾
(860) 434-2600. **$135-$185, 10 day notice.** 85 Lyme St. I-95, exit 70 northbound, just n on SR 156, then 0.5 mi e on US 1; exit southbound, just n. Int corridors. **Pets:** $50 deposit/room. Designated rooms, service with restrictions, crate.
🆂🅰🆅🅴 ⊠ 🖥 🍴

OLD SAYBROOK

🅰🅰🅰 ▼▼▼▼ **Saybrook Point Inn & Spa** 🆂🅷 🐾
(860) 395-2000. **$179-$649, 3 day notice.** 2 Bridge St. On SR 154, 2.2 mi s of jct US 1; at Saybrook Point. Int corridors. **Pets:** Medium, dogs only. $50 one-time fee/room. Designated rooms, service with restrictions, supervision.
🆂🅰🆅🅴 ⊠ 🅶🅼 🖥 💻 🍴 🛏 ⊠

PUTNAM

🅰🅰🅰 ▼▼ ▼ **King's Inn** 🆂🅷
(860) 928-7961. **$68-$98.** 5 Heritage Rd. I-395, exit 96, just w. Int corridors. **Pets:** Accepted.
🆂🅰🆅🅴 🆂🔟 ⊠ 🖥 💻 🍴 🛏

RIVERTON

▼▼▼▼ **Old Riverton Inn** 🅲🅸
(860) 379-8678. **$95-$225, 10 day notice.** 436 E River Rd (SR 20). Center. Int corridors. **Pets:** Accepted.
🅰🆂🅺 ⊠ 🖥 🍴

SHELTON

▼▼▼▼ **Homestead Studio Suites Hotel-Shelton** 🆂🅷
(203) 926-6868. **$106-$126.** 945 Bridgeport Ave. SR 8, exit 11, 0.5 mi w. Int corridors. **Pets:** Accepted.
🅰🆂🅺 🆂🔟 ⊠ 🅶🅼 🐾 🖥 💻

▼▼▼▼ **Residence Inn by Marriott** 🆂🅷
(203) 926-9000. **$149-$189.** 1001 Bridgeport Ave. SR 8, exit 11, 0.3 mi w. Ext corridors. **Pets:** Accepted.
🅰🆂🅺 🆂🔟 ⊠ 🖥 💻 🛏 ⊠

SOUTHBURY

▼▼▼ **Hilton Southbury** 🆂🅷
(203) 598-7600. **$89-$169.** 1284 Strongtown Rd. I-84, exit 16, just n on SR 188. Int corridors. **Pets:** Medium, other species. $50 deposit/room. Designated rooms, service with restrictions, supervision.
🅰🆂🅺 🆂🔟 ⊠ 🅶🅼 🖥 💻 🍴 🛏 ⊠

STAMFORD

▼▼▼ **Marriott Stamford Hotel** 🅻🅷
(203) 357-9555. **$265-$285.** Two Stamford Forum. I-95, exit 8, just n under viaduct, then n on Tresser Blvd. Int corridors. **Pets:** Accepted.
🅰🆂🅺 🆂🔟 ⊠ 🅶🅼 🕖 🐾 🖥 💻 🍴 🛏 ⊠

🅰🅰🅰 ▼ **Rodeway Inn-Greenwich/Stamford** 🆂🅷
(203) 327-4300. **$80-$100.** 19 Clark's Hill Ave. I-95, exit 8 northbound, just n on Atlantic St, 0.6 mi ne on Tresser Blvd, then just s; southbound, just nw on Elm St, ne on E Main St, then just s. Int corridors. **Pets:** $20 daily fee/pet. Service with restrictions, crate.
🆂🅰🆅🅴 ⊠ 🖥 💻

▼▼▼▼ **Sheraton Stamford Hotel** 🅻🅷
(203) 359-1300. **$99-$219.** 2701 Summer St. I-95, exit 8 northbound, 1.7 mi w on Atlantic and Bedford sts; exit 7 (North St) southbound, n on Atlantic and Bedford sts. Int corridors. **Pets:** Accepted.
🅰🆂🅺 🆂🔟 ⊠ 🐾 🖥 💻 🍴 🛏 ⊠

🅰🅰🅰 ▼▼ ▼ **Super 8 Motel** 🆂🅷
(203) 324-8887. **$99-$109.** 32 Grenhart Rd. I-95, exit 6, just n. Int corridors. **Pets:** Large. $20 daily fee/room. Designated rooms, service with restrictions, supervision.
🆂🅰🆅🅴 🆂🔟 ⊠ 🖥

▼▼▼▼ **The Westin Stamford** 🅻🅷
(203) 967-2222. **$89-$199.** 1 First Stamford Pl. I-95, exit 7 northbound, just s on Greenwich Ave, then just w; exit 6 southbound, just s on West Ave, 0.3 mi w on Baxter Ave, just n on Fairfield Ave, then just e. Int corridors. **Pets:** Accepted.
⊠ 🕖 🐾 🖥 💻 🍴 🛏 ⊠

STRATFORD

▼▼▼ Staybridge Suites SH
(203) 377-3322. **$139, 7 day notice.** 6905 Main St. SR 15, exit 53, just
n. Int corridors. **Pets:** Accepted.

ASK S✗ ✗ &M (✓) 🔒 💻 ⚓ ✗

TORRINGTON

◆◆◆ ▼▼◆ Days Inn M
(860) 496-8808. **$90-$253, 3 day notice.** 395 Winsted Rd. SR 8 N, exit
45, just w, then 0.6 mi s. Ext/int corridors. **Pets:** Accepted.

SAVE S✗ ✗ (✓) 🔒 💻 ⚓

WATERBURY

▼▼▼ House on the Hill Bed & Breakfast BB
(203) 757-9901. **$150-$200, 7 day notice.** 92 Woodlawn Terrace. I-84,
exit 21, 0.6 mi n on Meadow St, then 0.4 mi ne on Pine St. Int
corridors. **Pets:** Service with restrictions, supervision.

ASK S✗ ✗ 🔒 💻

WATERFORD

◆◆◆ ▼▼▼ Oakdell Motel M
(860) 442-9446. **$60-$150.** 983 Hartford Tpke. I-95, exit 82, 2 mi n on
SR 85. Ext/int corridors. **Pets:** Large.

SAVE 🔒 ⚓

WESTBROOK

▼▼ Beach Plum Inn M
(860) 399-9345. **$60-$175, 14 day notice.** 1935 Boston Post Rd. I-95,
exit 65, 1.5 mi e of jct SR 153 on US 1. Ext corridors. **Pets:** Other
species. Designated rooms, service with restrictions, crate.

ASK S✗ ✗ 🔒 💻 ⚓ ✗

WESTPORT

▼▼▼ The Westport Inn M ❀
(203) 259-5236. **$139-$189.** 1595 Post Rd E. I-95, exit 18 northbound,
n to US 1, then 1.5 mi e; exit 19 southbound, 1 mi w. Ext/int corridors.
Pets: Small, other species. Service with restrictions.

ASK S✗ ✗ (✓) 🔒 💻 ⚓

WILLINGTON

◆◆◆ ▼▼◆ Econo Lodge SH
(860) 684-1400. **$85-$95.** 327 Ruby Rd. I-84, exit 71, just s. Int corridors. **Pets:** Accepted.

SAVE S✗ ✗ &M (✓) (✓) ⚓

DELAWARE

CITY INDEX

CLAYMONT

 ▼▼▼▼ **Holiday Inn Select Wilmington** 🔲
(302) 792-2700. **$99-$159.** 630 Naamans Rd. I-95, exit 11, just w on SR 92; I-495, exit 6 (Naamans Rd). Int corridors. **Pets:** Accepted.
[SAVE] [S☉] [✕] [&M] [⌂] [&] [🛏] [📶] [¶] [⚓]

DEWEY BEACH

▼▼▼ **Atlantic Oceanside Motel** Ⓜ ❖
(302) 227-8811. **$35-$199, 7 day notice.** 1700 Hwy 1. Jct SR 1 and McKinley St. Ext corridors. **Pets:** Dogs only. $5 daily fee/pet. Service with restrictions, crate.
[SAVE] [✕] [🛏] [⚓]

▼▼ **Bellbuoy Motel** Ⓜ ❖
(302) 227-6000. **$50-$175, 7 day notice.** 21 Van Dyke St. SR 1, on oceanside block of Van Dyke St. Ext corridors. **Pets:** Large, dogs only. $10 daily fee/pet. Service with restrictions.
[✕] [🛏] [📶] [🔒]

▼▼▼ **Best Western Gold Leaf** 🔲
(302) 226-1100. **$69-$289, 3 day notice.** 1400 Hwy 1. On SR 1; center. Int corridors. **Pets:** Accepted.
[SAVE] [S☉] [✕] [⌂] [🛏] [📶] [⚓]

▼▼▼ **Sea-Esta Motel I** Ⓜ
(302) 227-7666. **$45-$159, 3 day notice.** 2306 Hwy 1. SR 1 at Houston St. Ext corridors. **Pets:** Accepted.
[SAVE] [S☉] [🛏]

▼▼▼ **Sea-Esta Motel III** Ⓜ
(302) 227-4343. **$44-$189, 3 day notice.** 1409 Hwy 1. Jct SR 1 and Rodney St. Ext corridors. **Pets:** Accepted.
[SAVE] [✕] [🛏]

DOVER

▼▼▼▼ **Little Creek Inn** 🅱🅱
(302) 730-1300. **$150-$195.** 2623 N Little Creek Rd. SR 1, exit 98, 1 mi e on SR 8; 2.2 mi e of jct US 13. Int corridors. **Pets:** Dogs only. Designated rooms.
[ASK] [✕] [⚓]

▼▼▼ **Red Roof Inn Dover** 🔲
(302) 730-8009. **Call for rates.** 652 N DuPont Hwy. SR 1, exit 104, 2.7 mi s on US 13. Int corridors. **Pets:** Accepted.
[✕] [&] [🛏]

FENWICK ISLAND

▼▼ **Atlantic Coast Inn** Ⓜ
(302) 539-7673. **$59-$179, 5 day notice.** Lighthouse Rd & Coastal Hwy. Jct SR 1 and 54. Ext corridors. **Pets:** Accepted.
[✕] [🛏] [⚓]

GEORGETOWN

▼▼▼▼ **Comfort Inn & Suites-Georgetown** 🔲
(302) 854-9400. **$79-$249, 3 day notice.** 507 N DuPont Hwy. On US 113, 0.5 mi n of jct SR 404. Int corridors. **Pets:** Other species. $15 daily fee/pet. Designated rooms, service with restrictions, supervision.
[SAVE] [S☉] [✕] [⌂] [🛏] [📶] [⚓]

HARRINGTON

▼▼▼ **AmericInn Lodge & Suites of Harrington** 🔲 ❖
(302) 398-3900. **$90-$110.** 1259 Corn Crib Rd. On US 13, 0.6 mi s of jct SR 14. Int corridors. **Pets:** Medium, dogs only. $20 daily fee/pet. Service with restrictions, supervision.
[ASK] [S☉] [✕] [&M] [⌂] [&] [🛏] [📶] [⚓] [🔒]

LEWES

▼▼▼▼ **The Inn at Canal Square** 🔲 ❖
(302) 644-3377. **$105-$265, 7 day notice.** 122 Market St. On the canal. Int corridors. **Pets:** Large. $25 one-time fee/room. Designated rooms, service with restrictions.
[SAVE] [S☉] [✕] [🛏] [📶]

▼▼▼ **Sleep Inn & Suites** 🔲 ❖
(302) 645-6464. **$49-$209.** 1595 Hwy 1. On SR 1, 1.5 mi s. Int corridors. **Pets:** Large, other species. $15 daily fee/pet. Designated rooms, service with restrictions, supervision.
[SAVE] [S☉] [✕] [⌂] [&] [🛏] [📶] [⚓]

LONG NECK

▼▼▼ **Sea Esta II** Ⓜ
(302) 945-5900. **$42-$139.** A19 Long Neck Rd. On SR 23, 1.1 mi s of jct SR 24, 5 and 23. Ext corridors. **Pets:** Accepted.
[SAVE] [✕] [🛏] [⚓]

MILLSBORO

▼▼▼ **Atlantic Inn-Millsboro** Ⓜ
(302) 934-6711. **$69-$219.** US 113, just s of SR 24. Ext corridors. **Pets:** Small. $15 daily fee/pet. Designated rooms, service with restrictions, supervision.
[✕] [🛏] [⚓]

NEWARK

▼▼▼ **Best Western Delaware Inn and Conference Center-Wilmington/Newark** 🔲
(302) 738-3400. **$89-$169.** 260 Chapman Rd. I-95, exit 3 southbound; exit 3A northbound, 0.3 mi e on SR 273 E, then just n. Int corridors. **Pets:** Accepted.
[SAVE] [S☉] [✕] [⌂] [🛏] [📶] [¶] [⚓]

▼▼▼ **Days Inn Wilmington/Newark** Ⓜ
(302) 368-2400. **$55-$125.** 900 Churchmans Rd. I-95, exit 4B, 0.3 mi n on SR 7, exit 166, then 0.3 mi w on SR 58 (Churchmans Rd). Ext corridors. **Pets:** Other species. $10 daily fee/pet. Service with restrictions, supervision.
[SAVE] [S☉] [✕] [🛏] [📶] [⚓]

▼▼▼▼ **Hilton Wilmington/Christiana** 🔲 ❖
(302) 454-1500. **$99-$219.** 100 Continental Dr. I-95, exit 4B, 0.3 mi n on SR 7, exit 166, then 0.4 mi w on SR 58 (Churchmans Rd). Int corridors. **Pets:** Small. $25 one-time fee/room. Designated rooms, service with restrictions, supervision.
[SAVE] [S☉] [✕] [⌂] [🛏] [📶] [¶] [⚓] [🔒]

Homestead Studio Suites
Hotel-Newark/Christiana 🆂🅷
(302) 283-0800. **$84-$104.** 333 Continental Dr. I-95, exit 4B, 0.3 mi n on SR 7, exit 166, then 0.4 mi w on SR 58 (Churchmans Rd). Int corridors. **Pets:** $81 one-time fee/pet. Designated rooms, service with restrictions, crate.

🅰🆂🅺 📶 ☒ 🔽M 🎵 🌀 🎁 🖥️

🔺🔺🔺 **Howard Johnson Inn &**
Suites–Wilmington/Newark 🆂🅷 🐾
(302) 368-8521. **$55-$99.** 1119 S College Ave. I-95, exit 1B southbound; exit 1 northbound, 0.3 mi n on SR 896. Int corridors. **Pets:** $10 daily fee/pet. Designated rooms, service with restrictions, crate.

🆂🅰🆅🅴 📶 ☒ 🎵 🎁 🖥️ ⦿ ⊳⊷

🔺🔺🔺 **Quality Inn by Choice Hotels-University** Ⓜ
(302) 368-8715. **$59-$99.** 1120 S College Ave. I-95, exit 1B southbound; exit 1 northbound, 0.3 mi n on SR 896. Ext corridors. **Pets:** Other species. $10 one-time fee/room. Designated rooms, service with restrictions, supervision.

🆂🅰🆅🅴 📶 ☒ 🎁 🖥️ ⊳⊷

🔺 **Red Roof Inn-Wilmington** Ⓜ
(302) 292-2870. **$56-$81.** 415 Stanton Christiana Rd. I-95, exit 4B, 0.5 mi n on SR 7. Ext corridors. **Pets:** Accepted.

☒

🔺🔺🔺 **Residence Inn by Marriott** 🆂🅷
(302) 453-9200. **$99-$169.** 240 Chapman Rd. I-95, exit 3 southbound; exit 3A northbound, 0.3 mi e on SR 273 E, then 0.5 mi s. Ext corridors. **Pets:** Accepted.

☒ 🎵 🎮 🎁 🖥️ ⊳⊷ ☒

NEW CASTLE

🔺 **Dutch Inn** Ⓜ
(302) 328-6246. **$55-$60.** 111 S DuPont Hwy. I-295, exit Dover/Shore Points, 2.5 mi s on US 13, 40 and 301. Ext corridors. **Pets:** Large, other species. $10 daily fee/pet. Service with restrictions, supervision.

🅰🆂🅺 📶 ☒ 🎁 🖥️

🔺🔺🔺 **Quality Inn Skyways** Ⓜ 🐾
(302) 328-6666. **$94-$104.** 147 N DuPont Hwy. I-95, exit 5A, 0.8 mi s on SR 141, exit 1B, 0.5 mi s on US 13, 40 and 301; I-295, exit New Castle Airport/US 13 S, 1.8 mi s on US 13, 40 and 301. Ext/int corridors. **Pets:** Medium, other species. $10 daily fee/room. Designated rooms, service with restrictions, supervision.

🆂🅰🆅🅴 📶 ☒ 🔽M 🎵 🎮 🎁 🖥️ ⊳⊷

REHOBOTH BEACH

🔺🔺 **AmericInn Lodge & Suites of Rehoboth**
Beach 🆂🅷 🐾
(302) 226-0700. **$79-$199.** 329Z Airport Rd. Just w of SR 1; 1.3 mi n of jct SR 1A. Int corridors. **Pets:** Dogs only. $20 daily fee/pet. Designated rooms, service with restrictions, supervision.

🅰🆂🅺 📶 ☒ 🔽M 🎵 🎮 🎁 🖥️ ⊳⊷

🔺🔺 **The Atlantis Inn** Ⓜ
(302) 227-9446. **$59-$209, 7 day notice.** 154 Rehoboth Ave. At Rehoboth Ave and 2nd St; downtown. Ext corridors. **Pets:** Dogs only. $15 daily fee/pet. Designated rooms, service with restrictions, supervision.

🅰🆂🅺 📶 ☒ 🎁 🖥️ ⊳⊷

🔺🔺🔺 **Sea-Esta IV, III & I** Ⓜ
(302) 227-5882. **$39-$169, 3 day notice.** 3101 Hwy 1. 1 mi s. Ext corridors. **Pets:** Accepted.

🆂🅰🆅🅴 📶 ☒ 🎁 ⊳⊷

WILMINGTON

🔺🔺🔺 **Best Western Brandywine Valley Inn** Ⓜ
(302) 656-9436. **$99-$159.** 1807 Concord Pike. I-95, exit 8, 1 mi n on US 202. Ext corridors. **Pets:** Accepted.

🆂🅰🆅🅴 📶 ☒ 🎵 🎁 🖥️ ⊳⊷

🔺🔺🔺 **Days Inn Wilmington** Ⓜ
(302) 478-0300. **$75-$129.** 5209 Concord Pike. I-95, exit 8, 4 mi n on US 202; jct SR 92 (Naamans Rd). Ext corridors. **Pets:** Medium. $15 daily fee/pet. Designated rooms, service with restrictions, supervision.

🆂🅰🆅🅴 📶 ☒ 🔽M 🎁 🖥️

🔺🔺🔺 **Sheraton Suites Wilmington** 🅻🅷
(302) 654-8300. **$99-$225.** 422 Delaware Ave. I-95, exit 7, 0.3 mi e; downtown. Int corridors. **Pets:** Accepted.

🆂🅰🆅🅴 📶 ☒ 🔽M 🎵 🎁 🖥️ 🍴 ⊳⊷

🔺🔺🔺🔺 **Wyndham Wilmington** 🅻🅷
(302) 655-0400. **$99-$149.** 700 N King St. King and 7th sts; downtown. Int corridors. **Pets:** Accepted.

🆂🅰🆅🅴 ☒ 🔽M 🎵 🎮 🎁 🖥️ 🍴 ⊳⊷

DISTRICT OF COLUMBIA

WASHINGTON

Best Western-New Hampshire Suites Hotel SH
(202) 457-0565. **$179-$260.** 1121 New Hampshire Ave NW. Just ne of 22nd; between L and M sts NW. Int corridors. **Pets:** Accepted.

Doubletree Guest Suites, Washington DC SH
(202) 785-2000. **$109-$279.** 801 New Hampshire Ave NW. Just sw at Washington Circle. Int corridors. **Pets:** Medium. $20 daily fee/pet. Designated rooms, service with restrictions.

The Fairmont Washington, D.C. LH 🐾
(202) 429-2400. **$149-$529, 7 day notice.** 2401 M St NW. 24th and M sts NW. Int corridors. **Pets:** Other species. Service with restrictions, supervision.

Four Seasons Hotel Washington D.C. LH 🐾
(202) 342-0444. **$500-$1550.** 2800 Pennsylvania Ave NW. Located in Georgetown. Int corridors. **Pets:** Very small. Service with restrictions, supervision.

Grand Hyatt Washington at Washington Center LH
(202) 582-1234. **$149-$340, 3 day notice.** 1000 H St NW. Jct 11th and H St NW. Int corridors. **Pets:** Accepted.

Hamilton Crowne Plaza Hotel Washington LH
(202) 682-0111. **$94-$324.** 1001 14th St NW. 14th and K sts NW. Int corridors. **Pets:** Accepted.

The Hay-Adams SH
(202) 638-6600. **$550-$5500.** 16th & H Sts NW. 16th and H sts NW, just n of the White House. Int corridors. **Pets:** Accepted.

Holiday Inn-Central LH
(202) 483-2000. **$189-$209.** 1501 Rhode Island Ave NW. Just e of Scott Circle. Int corridors. **Pets:** Accepted.

Holiday Inn Downtown LH
(202) 737-1200. **$159-$229.** 1155 14th St NW. Massachusetts Ave, at Thomas Circle NW. Int corridors. **Pets:** Small. $35 one-time fee/pet. Designated rooms, service with restrictions, supervision.

The Hotel George SH 🐾
(202) 347-4200. **$174-$434.** 15 E St NW. On Capitol Hill, just n of Capitol grounds. Int corridors. **Pets:** Large. $50 deposit/pet. Service with restrictions, supervision.

Hotel Helix SH 🐾
(202) 462-9001. **$119-$309.** 1430 Rhode Island Ave NW. Just e of Scott Circle. Int corridors. **Pets:** Other species. Designated rooms, service with restrictions, crate.

Hotel Madera SH
(202) 296-7600. **$149-$349.** 1310 New Hampshire Ave NW. Between 20th and N sts NW. Int corridors. **Pets:** Accepted.

Hotel Monaco Washington DC LH
(202) 628-7177. **$149-$479.** 700 F St NW. Between 7th and 8th sts NW. Int corridors. **Pets:** Accepted.

Hotel Rouge SH 🐾
(202) 232-8000. **$129-$309.** 1315 16th St NW. Just n of Scott Circle. Int corridors. **Pets:** Other species. Designated rooms, service with restrictions, supervision.

Hotel Washington LH
(202) 638-5900. **$200-$325.** 515 15th St NW. 1 blk e of the White House at Pennsylvania Ave and 15th St NW; 2 blks from Metro Center. Int corridors. **Pets:** Accepted.

The Jefferson, A Loews Hotel SH
(202) 347-2200. **$195-$405, 3 day notice.** 1200 16th St NW. 16th and M sts NW. Int corridors. **Pets:** Accepted.

Lincoln Suites Downtown SH
(202) 223-4320. **$125-$195.** 1823 L St NW. Between 18th and 19th sts NW. Int corridors. **Pets:** Accepted.

Loews L'Enfant Plaza Hotel LH 🐾
(202) 484-1000. **$144-$274.** 480 L'Enfant Plaza SW. I-395, exit L'Enfant Plaza/12th St. Int corridors. **Pets:** Other species.

The Madison LH 🐾
(202) 862-1600. **$179-$299.** 1177 15th St NW. 15th and M sts NW. Int corridors. **Pets:** Other species. Service with restrictions.

Mandarin Oriental, Washington D.C. LH
(202) 554-8588. **$350-$8000.** 1330 Maryland Ave SW. Jct Independence Ave SW, just s on 12th St SW. Int corridors. **Pets:** Accepted.

Marriott Wardman Park Hotel LH
(202) 328-2000. **$124-$344, 7 day notice.** 2660 Woodley Rd NW. Just w of Connecticut Ave; at Woodley Park/Zoo Metro Station. Int corridors. **Pets:** Accepted.

The Melrose Hotel, Washington DC LH
(202) 955-6400. **$169-$209.** 2430 Pennsylvania Ave NW. Between 24th and 25th sts NW. Int corridors. **Pets:** Medium. $100 one-time fee/pet. Service with restrictions, crate.

Omni Shoreham Hotel LH
(202) 234-0700. **$349-$389.** 2500 Calvert St NW. Just w of Connecticut Ave. Int corridors. **Pets:** Small. $50 one-time fee/room.

Park Hyatt Washington, D.C. LH
(202) 789-1234. **$306-$410, 3 day notice.** 1201 24th St NW. 24th and M sts NW. Int corridors. **Pets:** Accepted.

Red Roof Inn Downtown Washington, D.C. SH
(202) 289-5959. **$100-$150.** 500 H St NW. At 5th and H sts NW; in Chinatown. Int corridors. **Pets:** Large. Service with restrictions, supervision.

(AAA) ▼▼ ▼▼▼ **Renaissance Mayflower Hotel** 🄻🄷 ❀
(202) 347-3000. **$149-$409.** 1127 Connecticut Ave NW. Just n of K St NW; in business district. Int corridors. **Pets:** Small. $100 one-time fee/pet. Service with restrictions, supervision.
[SAVE] [S🄳] [✕] [🄵🄼] [🅿] [🍴]

(AAA) ▼▼▼▼ **Residence Inn by Marriott-Dupont Circle** 🅂🄷
(202) 466-6800. **$149-$299.** 2120 P St NW. Between 21st and 22nd sts NW; just w of Dupont Circle. Int corridors. **Pets:** Accepted.
[SAVE] [✕] [🄵🄼] [🅿] [🔒] [💻]

(AAA) ▼▼▼ **Residence Inn by Marriott-Washington DC-Vermont Ave** 🄻🄷
(202) 898-1100. **$259.** 1199 Vermont Ave NW. Jct 14th St and Vermont Ave NW, at Thomas Circle. Int corridors. **Pets:** Large. $8 daily fee/pet, $150 one-time fee/room. Service with restrictions, crate.
[SAVE] [S🄳] [✕] [🄵🄼] [🅿] [🔒] [💻]

▼▼◆▼▼ **The Ritz-Carlton, Georgetown** 🅂🄷 ❀
(202) 912-4100. **$260-$550.** 3100 South St NW. Just s of jct M St and Wisconsin Ave, off Wisconsin, just e. Int corridors. **Pets:** Small. $50 one-time fee/pet. Service with restrictions, supervision.
[✕] [🅿] [🔒] [💻] [🍴] [✕]

▼▼◆▼▼ **The Ritz-Carlton, Washington, DC** 🄻🄷
(202) 835-0500. **$259-$645.** 1150 22nd St NW. At 22nd and M sts NW. Int corridors. **Pets:** Accepted.
[✕] [🅿] [🔒] [💻] [🍴] [🏊] [✕]

(AAA) ▼▼▼ **The River Inn** 🅂🄷
(202) 337-7600. **$99-$405.** 924 25th St NW. Between K and I sts NW. Int corridors. **Pets:** Accepted.
[SAVE] [S🄳] [✕] [🅿] [🔒] [💻] [🍴]

▼▼▼▼ **Sofitel Lafayette Square Washington DC** 🅂🄷
(202) 730-8800. **$300-$480.** 806 15th St NW. Jct 15th and H sts NW. Int corridors. **Pets:** Accepted.
[✕] [🄵🄼] [🅿] [🔒] [🍴]

(AAA) ▼▼▼▼ **The St. Regis Washington** 🄻🄷 ❀
(202) 638-2626. **$230-$385.** 923 16th St NW. Just n of the White House, 16th and K sts. Int corridors. **Pets:** Accepted.
[SAVE] [S🄳] [✕] [🅿] [🍴]

(AAA) ▼▼▼ **Topaz Hotel** 🅂🄷
(202) 393-3000. **$139-$339.** 1733 N St NW. Just e of Connecticut Ave. Int corridors. **Pets:** Accepted.
[SAVE] [S🄳] [✕] [🅿] [🔒] [🍴]

(AAA) ▼▼▼ **Travelodge Gateway** 🅂🄷
(202) 832-8600. **$95-$110.** 1917 Bladensburg Rd NE. US 50 and Alternate Rt 1; just w of entrance to Baltimore-Washington Pkwy, New York Ave. Ext/int corridors. **Pets:** Accepted.
[SAVE] [S🄳] [✕] [🅿] [🔒] [🔒] [💻] [🍴] [🏊]

▼▼▼▼ **The Washington Court Hotel** 🄻🄷
(202) 628-2100. **$139-$359, 7 day notice.** 525 New Jersey Ave NW. 3 blks from Capitol grounds. Int corridors. **Pets:** Dogs only. Supervision.
[A$K] [S🄳] [✕] [🅿] [🔒] [💻] [🍴]

(AAA) ▼▼▼▼ **Washington Suites Georgetown** 🅂🄷
(202) 333-8060. **$148-$248.** 2500 Pennsylvania Ave NW. Jct 25th St NW and Pennsylvania Ave; 2 blks from Foggy Bottom Metro Station. Int corridors. **Pets:** Small. $20 daily fee/pet. Designated rooms, service with restrictions, crate.
[SAVE] [S🄳] [✕] [🄵🄼] [🅿] [🔒] [🔒] [💻]

▼▼◆▼▼ **The Westin Embassy Row** 🄻🄷 ❀
(202) 293-2100. **$209-$289.** 2100 Massachusetts Ave NW. Just w of Dupont Circle; at 21st St. Int corridors. **Pets:** Small. $100 deposit/pet. Service with restrictions.
[A$K] [S🄳] [✕] [🅿] [💻] [🍴] [✕]

▼▼▼ **The Westin Grand** 🄻🄷
(202) 429-0100. **$209-$289.** 2350 M St NW. 24th and M sts NW. Int corridors. **Pets:** Accepted.
[A$K] [S🄳] [✕] [🅿] [🔒] [💻] [🍴] [🏊]

▼▼▼ ▼▼▼ **The Willard InterContinental** 🄻🄷 ❀
(202) 628-9100. **$209-$610.** 1401 Pennsylvania Ave NW. Just e of the White House. Int corridors. **Pets:** Medium, other species. Service with restrictions, supervision.
[A$K] [S🄳] [✕] [🄵🄼] [🅿] [🔒] [💻] [🍴]

FLORIDA

ALACHUA

Comfort Inn/FL-339 SH ✿
(386) 462-2414. **$75, 7 day notice.** 15920 NW US Hwy 441. I-75, exit 399, just e. Ext corridors. **Pets:** Small, dogs only. $10 daily fee/pet. Designated rooms, service with restrictions, supervision.

Quality Inn Alachua SH
(386) 462-2244. **$70-$80.** 15960 NW Hwy 441. I-75, exit 399, just e. Ext corridors. **Pets:** Accepted.

APALACHICOLA

Gibson Inn 🅲 ✿
(850) 653-2191. **$90-$160, 14 day notice.** Market St & Ave C. On US 98 at west end of bridge. Int corridors. **Pets:** Other species. $25 daily fee/pet. Designated rooms, supervision.

ARCADIA

Best Western Arcadia Inn Ⓜ
(863) 494-4884. **$45-$125.** 504 S Brevard Ave. 0.6 mi s of SR 70 on US 17. Ext corridors. **Pets:** Accepted.

BOCA RATON

Doubletree Guest Suites-Boca Raton SH
(561) 997-9500. **$99-$239.** 701 NW 53rd St. I-95, exit 48B (Yamato Rd), just w; in Arvida Corporate Park. Ext corridors. **Pets:** Accepted.

Homestead Studio Suites Hotel-Boca Raton/Commerce Ⓜ
(561) 994-2599. **$59-$119.** 501 NW 77th St. I-95, exit 50, just s on Congress Ave to NW 6th Ave. Ext corridors. **Pets:** Accepted.

Radisson Suite Hotel Boca Raton SH
(561) 483-3600. **$179-$299.** 7920 Glades Rd. Florida Tpke, exit 75 (SR 808/Glades Rd); in Arvida Parkway Center. Int corridors. **Pets:** Accepted.

Residence Inn-By Marriott-Boca Raton SH
(561) 994-3222. **$189-$209.** 525 NW 77th St. I-95, exit 50, just w of Congress Ave. Ext corridors. **Pets:** Accepted.

TownePlace Suites by Marriott SH
(561) 994-7232. **$54-$199.** 5110 NW 8th Ave. I-95, exit 48B (Yamato Rd), just w; in Arvida Corporate Park. Int corridors. **Pets:** Other species. $75 one-time fee/room. Service with restrictions, supervision.

BONITA SPRINGS

AmericInn Hotel & Suites SH ✿
(239) 495-9255. **$69-$170.** 28600 Trails Edge Blvd. I-75, exit 116, 0.7 mi s of Bonita Beach Rd on US 41. Int corridors. **Pets:** Small. $10 daily fee/pet, service with restrictions, supervision.

Comfort Inn Hotel SH
(239) 992-5001. **$59-$149.** 9800 Bonita Beach Rd. I-75, exit 116, 2.5 mi w on CR 865. Int corridors. **Pets:** Small. $25 one-time fee/room. Service with restrictions.

Staybridge Suites by Holiday Inn SH
(239) 949-5913. **$99-$239.** 8900 Brighton Ln. I-75, exit 116, 3.5 mi w on CR 865, 1.4 mi n on US 41 (Tamiami Tr), then e on Highland Woods Blvd. Int corridors. **Pets:** Medium, other species. $100 one-time fee/pet. Service with restrictions, supervision, crate.

BRADENTON

△△△ ▽▽ **◈** Comfort Inn & Suites **SH**
(941) 795-4633. **$70-$100.** 4450 47th St W. Just s of jct SR 684 (Cortez Rd). Int corridors. **Pets:** Accepted.
[SAVE] [S🐾] [✕] [🐾] [🐾] [🛏] [💻] [🏊]

▽▽ **◈** Days Inn Bradenton **M**
(941) 746-1141. **$69-$109.** 3506 1st St W. On US 41, just e of jct US 301. Ext corridors. **Pets:** Accepted.
[ASK] [S🐾] [✕] [🛏] [🍴] [🏊]

△△△ ▽▽ **◈** Econo Lodge Airport **M**
(941) 758-7199. **$59-$99.** 6727 14th St W. US 41, 2 mi s of jct SR 70. Ext corridors. **Pets:** Small, dogs only. $25 one-time fee/pet. Designated rooms, service with restrictions, supervision.
[SAVE] [S🐾] [✕] [🛏] [💻] [🏊]

△△△ ▽▽ **◈** Howard Johnson Express Inn **M**
(941) 756-8399. **$64-$104.** 6511 14th St W. On US 41, 1.5 mi s of jct SR 70. Ext corridors. **Pets:** Accepted.
[SAVE] [S🐾] [✕] [🛏] [💻] [🏊]

▽ Motel 6 #678 **M**
(941) 747-6005. **$45-$67.** 660 67th St Cir E. I-75, exit 220 southbound; exit 220B northbound, just w on SR 64. Ext corridors. **Pets:** Accepted.
[S🐾] [✕] [🏊]

BRADENTON BEACH

△△△ ▽▽▽ **◈** Tortuga Inn Beach Resort **M**
(941) 778-6611. **$114-$379, 14 day notice.** 1325 Gulf Dr N. On SR 789, 0.3 mi n of jct SR 684. Ext corridors. **Pets:** Accepted.
[SAVE] [S🐾] [✕] [🛏] [💻] [🏊] [✕]

△△△ ▽▽▽ **◈** Tradewinds Resort **M**
(941) 779-0010. **$159-$319, 14 day notice.** 1603 Gulf Dr N. On SR 789, 0.5 mi n of jct SR 684. Ext corridors. **Pets:** Accepted.
[SAVE] [S🐾] [✕] [🛏] [💻] [🏊]

BROOKSVILLE

△△△ ▽▽▽ **◈** Best Western Brooksville I-75 **M** 🐾
(352) 796-9481. **$64-$99.** 30307 Cortez Blvd. I-75, exit 301, just w on US 98/SR 50. Ext corridors. **Pets:** Other species. $25 one-time fee/room. Designated rooms, service with restrictions, supervision.
[SAVE] [S🐾] [✕] [🐾M] [🐾] [🛏] [💻] [🍴] [🏊]

△△△ ▽▽ **◈** Days Inn Heritage Inn **M**
(352) 796-9486. **$59-$74.** 6320 Windmere Rd. I-75, exit 301, just e on US 98/SR 50. Ext corridors. **Pets:** Accepted.
[SAVE] [S🐾] [✕] [🐾M] [🐾] [🐾] [🛏] [💻] [🍴] [🏊]

BUSHNELL

△△△ ▽▽▽ **◈** Best Western Guest House Inn **M**
(352) 793-5010. **$54-$79.** 2224 W Hwy 48. I-75, exit 314, just e. Ext corridors. **Pets:** Accepted.
[SAVE] [S🐾] [✕] [🛏] [💻] [🏊]

CAPE CORAL

▽▽▽ **◈** Quality Inn-Nautilus **SH**
(239) 542-2121. **$66-$122.** 1538 Cape Coral Pkwy. Jct Del Prado Blvd. Int corridors. **Pets:** Accepted.
[ASK] [S🐾] [✕] [🐾] [🛏] [💻] [🏊]

CARRABELLE

▽▽ **◈** The Moorings At Carrabelle **SH**
(850) 697-2800. **$125-$275.** 1000 US 98. On US 98, just e of bridge. Ext corridors. **Pets:** Large, other species. $50 deposit/room, $10 daily fee/pet. Service with restrictions, supervision.
[ASK] [S🐾] [🛏] [💻] [🏊] [✕]

CEDAR KEY

△△△ ▽▽ **◈** Park Place Motel & Condominiums **M**
(352) 543-5737. **$65-$100.** 211 2nd St. At A St. Ext corridors. **Pets:** Small, other species. $7 daily fee/pet. Designated rooms, service with restrictions, supervision.
[SAVE] [✕] [🛏] [💻]

▽▽▽ **◈** Seahorse Landing Condominiums **CO**
(352) 543-5860. **$125-$150, 3 day notice.** 4050 G St. Just w on 6th St. Ext corridors. **Pets:** Large, other species. $15 daily fee/room. Designated rooms, no service, crate.
[✕] [🛏] [💻] [🏊] [✕]

CHARLOTTE HARBOR

△△△ ▽ **◈** Banana Bay Waterfront Motel **M**
(941) 743-4441. **$39-$99.** 23285 Bayshore Rd. Jct US 41. Ext corridors. **Pets:** Small. $4 daily fee/pet. Service with restrictions, crate.
[SAVE] [✕] [🛏] [💻] [✕]

CHIEFLAND

▽▽▽ **◈** Holiday Inn Express **SH**
(352) 493-9400. **$65-$91.** 809 NW 21st Ave. US 19/98, 1.5 mi n of jct US 129. Ext corridors. **Pets:** Medium, other species. $15 daily fee/pet. Designated rooms, service with restrictions, crate.
[ASK] [S🐾] [✕] [🐾M] [🐾] [🐾] [🛏] [🏊]

CHIPLEY

▽▽ **◈** Super 8 Motel **M**
(850) 638-8530. **$45-$75.** 1150 Motel Dr. I-10, exit 120, just n. Ext corridors. **Pets:** Accepted.
[ASK] [S🐾] [✕] [🛏]

COCOA

△△△ ▽▽▽ **◈** Best Western Cocoa Inn **SH**
(321) 632-1065. **$69-$129.** 4225 W King St. I-95, exit 201 (SR 520), 0.3 mi e. Ext corridors. **Pets:** Small, other species. $10 daily fee/pet. Service with restrictions, supervision.
[SAVE] [S🐾] [✕] [🐾] [🐾] [🛏] [💻] [🏊]

△△△ ▽▽▽ **◈** Econo Lodge-Space Center **SH**
(321) 632-4561. **$55-$150.** 3220 N Cocoa Blvd. US 1, just n of jct SR 528. Ext corridors. **Pets:** Medium, other species. $10 one-time fee/room. Designated rooms, service with restrictions, supervision.
[SAVE] [S🐾] [✕] [🐾] [🛏] [💻] [🍴] [🏊]

△△△ ▽▽▽ **◈** Holiday Inn Express Hotel & Suites **SH**
(321) 635-9975. **$79-$109.** 301 Tucker Ln. I-95, exit 201 (SR 520), just w. Int corridors. **Pets:** Accepted.
[SAVE] [S🐾] [✕] [🛏] [💻] [🏊]

△△△ ▽▽▽ **◈** Ramada Inn Cocoa Beach Area/KSC **SH**
(321) 631-1210. **$69-$119.** 900 Friday Rd. I-95, exit 202 (SR 524), just w. Ext corridors. **Pets:** Accepted.
[SAVE] [S🐾] [✕] [🐾] [🛏] [💻] [🍴] [🏊] [✕]

△△△ ▽▽▽ **◈** Super 8 Motel Cocoa Beach Area/KSC **M** 🐾
(321) 631-1212. **$59-$109.** 900A Friday Rd. I-95, exit 202 (SR 524), 0.5 mi sw. Ext corridors. **Pets:** Very small. $5 daily fee/pet. Service with restrictions, supervision.
[SAVE] [S🐾] [✕] [🛏] [💻] [🏊] [✕]

COCOA BEACH

△△△ ▽▽▽ **◈** Holiday Inn Cocoa Beach Oceanfront Resort **SH**
(321) 783-2271. **$119-$299.** 1300 N Atlantic Ave. SR A1A, 1.8 mi s of jct SR 520. Ext corridors. **Pets:** Medium, other species. $10 daily fee/pet. Service with restrictions, supervision.
[SAVE] [S🐾] [✕] [🐾M] [🐾] [🐾] [🛏] [💻] [🍴] [🏊] [✕]

🔺 ▽▽ **South Beach Inn** Ⓜ
(321) 784-3333. **$70-$150, 10 day notice.** 1701 S Atlantic Ave. SR A1A northbound, 5 mi s of jct SR 520 at Indian Village Tr; 1.5 mi n of Patrick AFB. Ext corridors. **Pets:** Medium. $15 daily fee/pet. No service, supervision.
[SAVE] 🈁 🖵 ⊠

▽▽ 🔻 **Surf Studio Beach Resort** Ⓜ
(321) 783-7100. **$75-$185, 7 day notice.** 1801 S Atlantic Ave. SR A1A northbound, 5 mi s of jct SR 520 at Francis St; 1.3 mi n of Partrick AFB. Ext corridors. **Pets:** Medium. $20 daily fee/pet. Service with restrictions, supervision.
🈯 🈁 🖵 ⇋

CRESCENT BEACH

🔺 ▽▽ **Beacher's Lodge** 🆂🅷
(904) 471-8849. **$79-$245.** 6970 A1A S. Just s of jct SR 206. Ext corridors. **Pets:** Small, dogs only. $50 one-time fee/pet. Designated rooms, service with restrictions, supervision.
[SAVE] 🆂 ⊠ 🈁 🖵 ⇋

CRESCENT CITY

▽▽ **Lake View Motel** Ⓜ
(386) 698-1090. **$55-$75.** 1004 N Summit St. 1 mi n on US 17. Ext corridors. **Pets:** Small. $5 daily fee/pet. Designated rooms, service with restrictions, supervision.
⊠ 🈁 🖵 ⇋

CRESTVIEW

▽▽ **Holiday Inn** 🆂🅷
(850) 682-6111. **$68.** 4050 S Ferdon Blvd. I-10, exit 56, 0.5 mi s. Ext corridors. **Pets:** Accepted.
⊠ 🈳 🈁 🖵 🍽 ⇋

▽▽▽▽ **Jameson Inn** 🆂🅷
(850) 683-1778. **$49-$104.** 151 Cracker Barrel Dr. I-10, exit 56, just s. Int corridors. **Pets:** Very small, other species. $10 daily fee/room. Service with restrictions, supervision.
[ASK] ⊠ 🈁 🖵 ⇋

🔺 ▽▽ **Super 8 Motel** Ⓜ
(850) 682-9649. **$43-$62.** 3925 S Ferdon Blvd. I-10, exit 56, 0.3 mi s. Ext corridors. **Pets:** Other species. $5 one-time fee/room. Designated rooms, service with restrictions, supervision.
[SAVE] 🆂 ⊠ 🈁

CRYSTAL RIVER

🔺 ▽▽ **Best Western Crystal River Resort** 🆂🅷
(352) 795-3171. **$87-$127.** 614 NW Hwy 19. On US 19/98, 0.8 mi n of jct SR 44. Ext corridors. **Pets:** Small, other species. $3 daily fee/pet. Service with restrictions, supervision.
[SAVE] 🆂 ⊠ 🈯 🈳 🈁 🖵 ⇋ ⊠

🔺 ▽▽ **Days Inn** 🆂🅷 🐾
(352) 795-2111. **$60-$120.** 2380 NW US 19. US 19, 2.2 mi n of jct SR 44. Ext corridors. **Pets:** Other species. $10 daily fee/pet. Service with restrictions, supervision.
[SAVE] 🆂 ⊠ 🈳 🈁 🍽

DAYTONA BEACH

🔺 ▽▽ **Days Inn Speedway** Ⓜ
(386) 255-0541. **$49-$249.** 2900 W International Speedway Blvd. I-95, exit 261B southbound; exit 261 northbound, just w on US 92. Ext corridors. **Pets:** Accepted.
[SAVE] 🆂 ⊠ 🈁 🍽 ⇋

🔺 ▽▽ **La Quinta Inn Daytona Beach** Ⓜ
(386) 255-7412. **$75-$105.** 2725 International Speedway Blvd. I-95, exit 261 northbound; exit 261B southbound, just e. Int corridors. **Pets:** Accepted.
[SAVE] ⊠ 🈳 🈯 🈳 🈁 🖵 ⇋

🔺 ▽▽▽▽ **Plaza Ocean Club** 🆂🅷
(386) 239-9800. **$89-$309, 7 day notice.** 640 N Atlantic Ave. On SR A1A, 1 mi n of jct SR 90. Int corridors. **Pets:** Small, dogs only. $25 daily fee/pet. Designated rooms, service with restrictions, crate.
[SAVE] 🆂 ⊠ 🈳 🈯 🈳 🈁 🖵 🍽 ⇋

🔺 ▽▽▽ **Ramada Inn Speedway** 🆂🅷
(386) 255-2422. **$89-$325, 7 day notice.** 1798 W International Speedway Blvd. I-95, exit 261, 2 mi e on US 92; across from Daytona International Speedway. Ext corridors. **Pets:** Medium, other species. $25 one-time fee/room. Designated rooms, service with restrictions.
[ASK] 🆂 ⊠ 🈯 🈁 🖵 🍽 ⇋

🔺 ▽ **Scottish Inns** Ⓜ
(386) 258-5742. **$45-$195.** 1515 S Ridgewood Ave. I-95, exit 260A, 2.5 mi e on SR 400, then just n on US 1. Ext corridors. **Pets:** Very small, dogs only. $10 daily fee/pet. Designated rooms, service with restrictions, supervision.
[SAVE] 🆂 ⊠ 🈁 ⇋

DAYTONA BEACH SHORES

🔺 ▽▽ **Atlantic Ocean Palm Inn** Ⓜ
(386) 761-8450. **$39-$109, 30 day notice.** 3247 S Atlantic Ave. On SR A1A, 5 mi s of jct US 92. Ext corridors. **Pets:** Small. $15 daily fee/pet. Designated rooms, service with restrictions, supervision.
[SAVE] 🆂 ⊠ 🈁 🖵 ⇋

🔺 ▽▽▽▽ **Quality Inn Ocean Palms** 🆂🅷
(386) 255-0476. **$65-$200.** 2323 S Atlantic Ave. On SR A1A, 2.5 mi s of jct US 92. Ext corridors. **Pets:** Accepted.
[SAVE] 🆂 ⊠ 🈳 🈯 🈳 🈁 🖵 ⇋

DE FUNIAK SPRINGS

▽▽ **Best Western Crossroads Inn** 🆂🅷
(850) 892-5111. **$69-$99, 14 day notice.** 2343 Freeport Rd. I-10, exit 85, just s. Ext/int corridors. **Pets:** Accepted.
[ASK] 🆂 ⊠ 🈁 🖵 🍽 ⇋

🔺 ▽▽ **Days Inn** 🆂🅷
(850) 892-6115. **$55-$90, 3 day notice.** 472 Hugh Adams Rd. I-10, exit 85, just n. Ext corridors. **Pets:** Accepted.
[SAVE] 🆂 ⊠ 🈁 ⇋

DELAND

🔺 ▽▽▽▽ **Holiday Inn** 🆂🅷
(386) 738-5200. **$49-$209, 3 day notice.** 350 E International Speedway Blvd. 0.3 mi ne on US 92 from jct US 17. Int corridors. **Pets:** Small. $25 one-time fee/room. Service with restrictions.
[SAVE] 🆂 ⊠ 🈯 🈳 🈁 🖵 🍽 ⇋

🔺 ▽▽ **University Inn** Ⓜ
(386) 734-5711. **$59-$175.** 644 N Woodland Blvd. US 17, 0.9 mi n of jct SR 44. Ext corridors. **Pets:** Small, dogs only. $10 daily fee/pet. Service with restrictions, supervision.
[SAVE] 🆂 ⊠ 🈳 🈁 🖵 ⇋

DELRAY BEACH

🔺 ▽▽▽▽ **The Colony Hotel & Cabana Club** 🆂🅷 🐾
(561) 276-4123. **$99-$275, 3 day notice.** 525 E Atlantic Ave. On SR 806 (Atlantic Ave) at US 1 northbound; center. Int corridors. **Pets:** Other species. $25 daily fee/pet. Service with restrictions.
[SAVE] ⊠ 🈯 🈳 🈁 🖵 ⇋

▽▽▽▽ **Residence Inn Delray Beach** 🆂🅷
(561) 276-7441. **$299-$599.** 1111 E Atlantic Ave. I-95, exit 52, 1.7 mi e. Int corridors. **Pets:** Accepted.
[ASK] 🆂 ⊠ 🈳 🈯 🈳 🈁 🖵 ⇋ ⊠

DELTONA

△△△ ▽▽▽▽ Best Western Deltona Inn M
(386) 860-3000. **$59-$235, 3 day notice.** 481 Deltona Blvd. I-4, exit 108, just ne. Ext corridors. **Pets:** Small. $10 daily fee/pet. Designated rooms, service with restrictions, supervision.
[SAVE] [S] [X] [⟨] [⬚] [💻] [🍴] [≈]

ELKTON

△△△ ▽▽▽ Comfort Inn St. Augustine SH
(904) 829-3435. **$69-$109.** 2625 SR 207. I-95, exit 311, just w. Ext corridors. **Pets:** Other species. $15 one-time fee/room. Service with restrictions, crate.
[SAVE] [S] [X] [⬚] [💻] [≈]

ELLENTON

▽▽▽ GuestHouse International Inn M
(941) 729-0600. **$60-$110.** 4915 17th St E. I-75, exit 224, 0.3 mi s on US 301, just w on 51st Ave E, then just n. Ext corridors. **Pets:** Other species. $10 one-time fee/room. Service with restrictions, supervision.
[ASK] [S] [X] [⟨M] [⟨] [⟨⟩] [⬚] [💻] [≈]

FLAGLER BEACH

△△△ ▽▽▽ Sleep Inn & Suites M
(941) 721-4933. **$74-$135.** 5605 18th St E. I-75, exit 224, just n on US 301, just e on 19th St E, then 0.3 mi sw. Int corridors. **Pets:** Accepted.
[ASK] [S] [X] [⟨M] [⟨] [⬚] [💻] [≈]

△△△ ▽▽▽ Beach Front Motel M
(386) 439-0089. **$49-$57, 3 day notice.** 1544 S A1A. On SR A1A, 1 mi s of SR 100. Ext corridors. **Pets:** Medium, dogs only. $15 one-time fee/room. Service with restrictions, crate.
[SAVE] [S] [X] [⬚] [💻] [≈]

△△△ ▽▽▽ Topaz Motel SH
(386) 439-3301. **$55-$175, 14 day notice.** 1224 S Oceanshore Blvd. On SR A1A, 0.5 mi s of SR 100. Ext/int corridors. **Pets:** Accepted.
[SAVE] [X] [⬚] [💻] [🍴] [≈]

FLORAL CITY

▽▽▽ Moonrise Resort CA
(352) 726-2553. **$60-$85 (no credit cards), 14 day notice.** 8801 E Moonrise Ln, Lot 18. Just e on CR 48, then 1.5 mi n on Old Floral City Rd. Ext corridors. **Pets:** $20 daily fee/pet. No service.
[⬚] [💻] [X] [⟨]

THE FLORIDA KEYS AREA

ISLAMORADA

△△△ ▽▽▽ Sands of Islamorada M
(305) 664-2791. **$99-$275, 3 day notice.** 80051 Overseas Hwy. US 1 at MM 80. Ext corridors. **Pets:** Other species. $15 daily fee/pet.
[SAVE] [⟨] [⬚] [💻] [≈] [X]

KEY LARGO

▽▽▽ Howard Johnson Resort Key Largo SH
(305) 451-1400. **Call for rates.** 102400 Overseas Hwy. US 1 at MM 102 (Bayside). Int corridors. **Pets:** Accepted.
[X] [⟨M] [⟨] [⟨] [⬚] [💻] [≈] [X]

△△△ ▽▽▽ Marina Del Mar Resort & Marina SH
(305) 451-4107. **$99-$199, 3 day notice.** 527 Caribbean Dr. US 1 at MM 100. Ext corridors. **Pets:** Accepted.
[SAVE] [S] [X] [⟨] [⬚] [💻] [🍴] [≈] [X]

KEY WEST

▽▽▽▽ Ambrosia Too At Fleming St BB
(305) 296-9838. **$120-$425, 30 day notice.** 622 Fleming St. Just n of Simonton St; in Old Town. Ext corridors. **Pets:** Accepted.
[X] [⬚] [💻] [≈]

▽▽▽▽ Center Court Historic Inn & Cottages BB
(305) 296-9292. **$98-$598, 30 day notice.** 915 Center St. 0.5 mi n of jct US 1; between Duval and Simonton sts; in Old Town. Ext/int corridors. **Pets:** Accepted.
[X] [⬚] [≈] [X]

△△△ ▽▽▽ Chelsea House BB
(305) 296-2211. **$89-$275, 10 day notice.** 707 Truman Ave. Corner of Elizabeth St and Truman Ave. Ext/int corridors. **Pets:** Accepted.
[SAVE] [X] [⬚] [💻] [≈]

△△△ ▽▽▽ Courtney's Place Historic Cottages & Inn CA
(305) 294-3480. **$79-$249, 21 day notice.** 720 Whitmarsh Ln. Just e of jct Petronia and Simonton sts; in Old Town. Ext corridors. **Pets:** Accepted.
[SAVE] [⟨] [⬚] [💻] [≈]

▽▽▽▽ The Cuban Club Suites M
(305) 294-5269. **$179-$399.** 1108 Duval St. Corner of Duval and Amelia sts; in Old Town. Int corridors. **Pets:** Accepted.
[ASK] [X] [⬚] [💻]

△△△ ▽▽▽ Curry Mansion Inn BB
(305) 294-5349. **$175-$325, 14 day notice.** 511 Caroline St. Just n of jct Duval St; in Old Town. Ext/int corridors. **Pets:** Accepted.
[SAVE] [X] [⬚] [≈] [X]

△△△ ▽▽▽▽ Frances Street Bottle Inn BB
(305) 294-8530. **$89-$189, 14 day notice.** 535 Frances St. US 1/Roosevelt Blvd, w on White St, then just s on Southard St; corner of Frances and Southard sts; in Old Town. Int corridors. **Pets:** Accepted.
[SAVE] [X] [⬚] [≈]

▽▽▽ The Grand BB
(305) 294-0590. **$88-$188, 14 day notice.** 1116 Grinnell St. From Truman Ave, just e; between Virginia and Catherine sts. Ext corridors. **Pets:** Accepted.
[X] [⬚] [💻]

△△△ ▽▽▽ The Palms Hotel BB
(305) 294-3146. **$110-$250, 7 day notice.** 820 White St. Just w of Truman Ave. Ext corridors. **Pets:** Accepted.
[SAVE] [≈] [X]

△△△ ▽▽▽▽ Pier House Resort & Caribbean Spa LH
(305) 296-4600. **$200-$460, 7 day notice.** One Duval St. At the foot of Duval St; in Old Town. Ext/int corridors. **Pets:** Accepted.
[SAVE] [X] [⟨] [⟨] [⬚] [💻] [🍴] [≈] [X]

▽▽▽ Travelers Palm Inn & Guesthouses BB
(305) 294-9560. **$98-$308, 30 day notice.** 915 Center St. US 1, just n; in Old Town. Ext corridors. **Pets:** Accepted.
[X] [⬚] [💻] [≈]

MARATHON

△△△ ▽▽▽ Ramada Marathon Oceanview Florida Keys SH
(305) 743-8550. **$69-$399.** 13351 Overseas Hwy. US 1 at MM 54. Int corridors. **Pets:** Accepted.
[SAVE] [S] [X] [⬚] [💻] [≈]

END AREA

FORT LAUDERDALE METROPOLITAN AREA

CORAL SPRINGS

⒜ ▼▼▼ Coral Springs Marriott Hotel Golf Club & Convention Center 🄻🄷 ❀
(954) 753-5598. **$89-$169.** 11775 Heron Bay Blvd. Sawgrass Expwy/SR 869, exit 10 (Coral Ridge Dr), 0.3 mi n, then 0.3 mi w. Int corridors. **Pets:** Medium. $50 deposit/room. Service with restrictions, crate.
[SAVE] 🖺 ⊠ 🕮 🖾 🖥 💻 🍽 ≋ ⊠

⒜ ▼▼▼ La Quinta Inn Ft. Lauderdale (Coral Springs) 🅂🄷
(954) 753-9000. **$75-$135.** 3701 University Dr. SR 817, just n of jct SR 834 (Sample Rd). Int corridors. **Pets:** Small, other species. Service with restrictions, supervision.
[SAVE] 🖺 ⊠ 🖾🄼 🕮 🖾 🖥 💻 ≋

▼▼ Studio 6 #6027 🄼
(954) 796-0011. **$60-$80.** 5645 University Dr. SR 869 (Sawgrass Expwy), exit 12 (University Dr), just s. Ext corridors. **Pets:** Accepted.
🖺 ⊠ 🕮 🖾 🖥 💻

⒜ ▼▼ Wellesley Inn (Coral Springs) 🅂🄷
(954) 344-2200. **$99-$119.** 3100 N University Dr. SR 817, just s of jct Sample Rd (SR 834). Int corridors. **Pets:** Accepted.
[SAVE] ⊠ 🕮 🖾 🖥 💻 ≋

DANIA BEACH

▼ Motel 6–Dania Beach #376 🄼
(954) 921-5505. **$45-$75.** 825 E Dania Beach Blvd. I-95, exit 22, 1.1 mi e on Stirling Rd, just n on US 1 (Federal Hwy), then 0.8 mi e. Ext corridors. **Pets:** Accepted.
🖺 ⊠ 🖾 ≋

⒜ ▼▼▼ Sheraton Fort Lauderdale Airport Hotel 🄻🄷
(954) 920-3500. **$95-$149.** 1825 Griffin Rd. I-95, exit 23. Int corridors. **Pets:** Accepted.
[SAVE] 🖺 ⊠ 🖾🄼 🕮 🖾 🖥 💻 🍽 ≋ ⊠

DAVIE

▼▼ Homestead Studio Suites Hotel-Plantation/Davie 🄼
(954) 476-1211. **$74-$109.** 7550 SR 84 E. I-595, exit University Dr/SR 817, 0.1 mi. Ext corridors. **Pets:** Accepted.
[ASK] 🖺 ⊠ 🖾🄼 🕮 🖾 🖥 💻

DEERFIELD BEACH

⒜ ▼▼▼ Comfort Suites 🅂🄷
(954) 570-8887. **$79-$159.** 1040 E Newport Center Dr. I-95, exit 41, jct SW 10th St to SW 12th Ave, then s; in Newport Center Complex. Ext corridors. **Pets:** Medium. $10 daily fee/pet, $25 one-time fee/pet. Designated rooms, service with restrictions, supervision.
[SAVE] 🖺 ⊠ 🕮 🖾 🖥 💻

⒜ ▼▼▼ Embassy Suites-Deerfield Beach Resort 🄻🄷 ❀
(954) 426-0478. **$129-$399.** 950 Ocean Dr (SR A1A). SR A1A, 0.5 mi s of jct SR 810 (Hillsboro Blvd). Int corridors. **Pets:** Small, dogs only. $25 daily fee/pet. Service with restrictions, supervision.
[SAVE] ⊠ 🕮 🖾 🖥 💻 🍽 ≋ ⊠

⒜ ▼▼▼ La Quinta Inn Ft. Lauderdale (Deerfield Beach) 🄼
(954) 421-1004. **$65-$131.** 351 W Hillsboro Blvd. I-95, exit 42A, 0.3 mi e on SR 810. Ext corridors. **Pets:** Medium, other species. Service with restrictions, crate.
[SAVE] ⊠ 🖾🄼 🕮 🖥 💻 ≋

⒜ ▼▼▼ Ramada Inn Deerfield Beach/Boca Raton 🅂🄷
(954) 427-2200. **$30-$259.** 1250 W Hillsboro Blvd. I-95, exit 42B, just w on SR 810 (Hillsboro Blvd), then just s on 12th Ave SW. Ext corridors. **Pets:** Accepted.
[SAVE] 🖺 ⊠ 🕮 🖾 🖥 💻 🍽 ≋

⒜ ▼▼ Travelers Inn 🄼
(954) 421-5000. **$65-$149.** 1401 S Federal Hwy. On US 1, 1.3 mi s of jct SR 810 (Hillsboro Blvd). Ext/int corridors. **Pets:** Medium. $10 daily fee/pet. Designated rooms, service with restrictions, supervision.
[SAVE] 🖺 ⊠ 🖥 💻 🍽 ≋

⒜ ▼▼ Wellesley Inn (Deerfield Beach) 🅂🄷
(954) 428-0661. **$49-$119.** 100 12th Ave SW. I-95, exit 42B, just w on SR 810 (Hillsboro Blvd), then just s. Int corridors. **Pets:** Small. $10 daily fee/pet. Designated rooms, service with restrictions, supervision.
[SAVE] ⊠ 🖾🄼 🕮 🖾 🖥 💻 ≋

FORT LAUDERDALE

⒜ ▼▼▼ AmeriSuites (Fort Lauderdale/17th Street) 🅂🄷 ❀
(954) 763-7670. **$119-$169.** 1851 SE Tenth Ave. SR A1A/17th St Cswy, just s. Int corridors. **Pets:** Small, other species. $10 daily fee/pet. Designated rooms, service with restrictions, crate.
[SAVE] ⊠ 🖾🄼 🕮 🖾 🖥 💻 ≋

▼▼ Birch Patio Motel 🄼
(954) 563-9540. **$35-$105, 28 day notice.** 617 N Birch Rd. 0.4 mi s on SR A1A from jct SR 838 (Sunrise Blvd), w on Aurumar St. Ext corridors. **Pets:** $100 deposit/pet, $10 daily fee/pet. Designated rooms, service with restrictions.
[ASK] 🖺 ⊠ 🖥 💻 ≋

▼▼▼ The Doubletree Guest Suites/Fort Lauderdale Galleria 🅂🄷
(954) 565-3800. **$69-$269, 3 day notice.** 2670 E Sunrise Blvd. Intracoastal Bridge on SR 838 (Sunrise Blvd), 3 blks w of jct SR A1A. Int corridors. **Pets:** Accepted.
⊠ 🕮 🖥 💻 🍽 ≋ ⊠

⒜ ▼▼ Flying Cloud Motel 🄼
(954) 563-7062. **$49-$135, 14 day notice.** 533 Orton Ave. Just w of SR A1A; between Terramar and Rio Mar sts, 0.5 mi s of SR 838 (Sunrise Blvd). Ext corridors. **Pets:** Small. $50 one-time fee/pet. Service with restrictions, supervision.
[SAVE] 🖥 ≋

▼▼▼ Hampton Inn Fort Lauderdale Airport North 🅂🄷
(954) 524-9900. **$94-$149, 3 day notice.** 2301 SW 12th Ave. I-95, exit 25 (SR 84), 0.7 mi e to SW 12th Ave, then just n. Int corridors. **Pets:** Accepted.
[ASK] 🖺 ⊠ 🖾🄼 🕮 🖾 🖥 💻 ≋

⒜ ▼▼▼ La Quinta Inn Ft. Lauderdale (Cypress Creek/I-95) 🅂🄷
(954) 491-7666. **$66-$126.** 999 W Cypress Creek Rd. I-95, exit 33 southbound, 0.8 mi; exit 33B northbound, at Powerline Rd. Int corridors. **Pets:** Accepted.
[SAVE] ⊠ 🕮 🖥 💻 ≋

▼ Motel 6–Ft. Lauderdale #55 🅂🄷
(954) 760-7999. **$47-$77.** 1801 SR 84. I-95, exit 25 (SR 84 E), just e, then U-turn at light. Int corridors. **Pets:** Accepted.
🖺 ⊠ 🕮 ≋

▼▼ Red Roof Inn 🆂🅷
(954) 776-6333. **$47-$87.** 4800 Powerline Rd. I-95, exit 32, just w of jct Commercial Blvd, then n. Int corridors. **Pets:** Medium, other species. Service with restrictions, supervision.

🅧 🕖 🖋 ➦

⬥⬥⬥ ▼▼ Royal Saxon Apartments 🅼 ☀
(954) 566-7424. **$55-$125, 14 day notice.** 551 Breakers Ave. Just w of SR A1A, 0.5 mi s of SR 838 (Sunrise Blvd); corner of Breakers Ave and Terramar St. Ext corridors. **Pets:** Other species. $20 deposit/pet. Service with restrictions.

🆂🅰🆅🅴 🆂🔂 ➦

⬥⬥⬥ ▼ Sea Chateau Resort Motel 🅼
(954) 566-8331. **$50-$100 (no credit cards), 7 day notice.** 555 N Birch Rd & Terramar St. 2 blks w of SR A1A, 0.5 mi s of SR 838 (Sunrise Blvd). Ext corridors. **Pets:** Designated rooms, supervision.

🆂🅰🆅🅴 🖋 ➦

⬥⬥⬥ ▼▼▼ Sheraton Suites Cypress Creek 🅻🅷
(954) 772-5400. **$89-$329.** 555 NW 62nd St. I-95, exit 33B northbound, then w; exit 33 southbound, then w (Cypress Creek Rd). Int corridors. **Pets:** Accepted.

🆂🅰🆅🅴 🆂🔂 🅧 🕖 🖋 💻 🍽 ➦

▼▼▼ TownePlace Suites by Marriott 🆂🅷 ☀
(954) 484-2214. **$54-$189.** 3100 Prospect Rd. I-95, exit 33, 2.7 mi w, then 0.5 mi s on NW 31st St. Int corridors. **Pets:** $75 one-time fee/room. Designated rooms, service with restrictions.

🅰🆂🅺 🆂🔂 🅧 🕖 🖋 💻 ➦

▼▼▼ The Westin, Fort Lauderdale 🅻🅷 ☀
(954) 772-1331. **$89-$269.** 400 Corporate Dr. I-95, exit 33 southbound, then e; exit 33A northbound; in Radice Corporate Park. Int corridors. **Pets:** Medium. $50 one-time fee/room. Designated rooms, service with restrictions, supervision.

🅰🆂🅺 🅧 🕖 🖋 💻 🍽 ➦ 🅧

HOLLYWOOD

▼▼▼ Comfort Inn-Airport/Cruise Port South 🅼
(954) 922-1600. **$69-$139.** 2520 Stirling Rd. I-95, exit 22, just e, 2 mi s of airport. Ext corridors. **Pets:** Accepted.

🅰🆂🅺 🆂🔂 🅧 🖋 🕖 🖋 💻 🍽 ➦

▼▼▼ Days Inn Fort Lauderdale/Hollywood Airport South 🆂🅷
(954) 923-7300. **$59-$229.** 2601 N 29th Ave. I-95, exit 21, just nw on SR 822 (Sheridan St). Int corridors. **Pets:** Accepted.

🅰🆂🅺 🆂🔂 🅧 🖋 🖋 💻 ➦

⬥⬥⬥ ▼▼▼ Econo Lodge Inn & Suites Hollywood Blvd 🅼 ☀
(954) 981-1800. **$49-$189.** 4900 Hollywood Blvd. I-95, exit 20, 1.6 mi w; Florida Tpke, exit 49, 1.3 mi e. Ext corridors. **Pets:** Medium, other species. $50 deposit/pet, $15 daily fee/pet. Service with restrictions.

🆂🅰🆅🅴 🆂🔂 🅧 🕖 🖋 🖋 💻 ➦

⬥⬥⬥ ▼▼▼ La Quinta Inn & Suites Ft. Lauderdale (Airport) 🆂🅷
(954) 922-2295. **$95-$145.** 2620 N 26th Ave. I-95, exit 21, just e to Oakwood, then just left. Int corridors. **Pets:** Accepted.

🆂🅰🆅🅴 🅧 🖋 🕖 🖋 🖋 💻 ➦ 🅧

⬥⬥⬥ ▼ Sandy Shores Motel & Family Lodging 🅼
(954) 923-3750. **$55-$95, 7 day notice.** 342 Van Buren St. From Hollywood Blvd (SR 820), just s on S Ocean Dr (SR A1A), then e. Ext corridors. **Pets:** Accepted.

🆂🅰🆅🅴 🆂🔂 🅧 🖋 🅩

LAUDERDALE-BY-THE-SEA

▼▼ The Pier Point Resort 🆂🅷
(954) 776-5121. **$59-$249.** 4320 El Mar Dr. SR 870 (Commerical Blvd) just s. Ext corridors. **Pets:** Accepted.

🅰🆂🅺 🆂🔂 🅧 🖋 💻 ➦

PLANTATION

⬥⬥⬥ ▼▼▼ Holiday Inn Plantation/Sawgrass 🆂🅷 🐾
(954) 472-5600. **$89-$129.** 1711 N University Dr. SR 817, just s of jct SR 838 (Sunrise Blvd). Ext/int corridors. **Pets:** $25 one-time fee/room. Service with restrictions.

🆂🅰🆅🅴 🆂🔂 🅧 🖋 🖋 💻 🍽 ➦

⬥⬥⬥ ▼▼▼ La Quinta Inn & Suites Ft. Lauderdale (Plantation) 🆂🅷
(954) 476-6047. **$94-$134.** 8101 Peters Rd. I-595, exit 5 (University Dr/SR 817 N), just n, then just w; in Crossroad Office Park. Int corridors. **Pets:** Accepted.

🆂🅰🆅🅴 🅧 🖋🅼 🕖 🖋 🖋 💻 ➦

▼▼▼ Residence Inn by Marriott-Ft. Lauderdale/Plantation 🆂🅷
(954) 723-0300. **$109-$189.** 130 N University Dr. I-595, exit 5, 0.7 mi n on University Dr (SR 817), then just n of jct Broward Blvd (SR 842). Int corridors. **Pets:** Accepted.

🅰🆂🅺 🆂🔂 🅧 🖋🅼 🕖 🖋 🖋 💻 ➦ 🅧

⬥⬥⬥ ▼▼▼ Sheraton Suites-Plantation 🅻🅷
(954) 424-3300. **$199-$550.** 311 N University Dr. I-595, exit 5, 0.7 mi n on University Dr (SR 817), 0.3 mi n of jct Broward Blvd (SR 842); at Fashion Mall. Int corridors. **Pets:** Accepted.

🆂🅰🆅🅴 🆂🔂 🅧 🕖 🖋 💻 🍽 ➦ 🅧

⬥⬥⬥ ▼▼▼ Staybridge Suites Ft Lauderdale-Plantation 🆂🅷
(954) 577-9696. **$103-$195.** 410 N Pine Island Rd. I-595, exit 4, 1.7 mi n. Int corridors. **Pets:** Medium, other species. $30 one-time fee/room. Service with restrictions, crate.

🆂🅰🆅🅴 🆂🔂 🅧 🖋🅼 🕖 🖋 🖋 💻 ➦ 🅧

⬥⬥⬥ ▼▼▼ Wellesley Inn (Plantation) 🆂🅷
(954) 473-8257. **$79-$139.** 7901 SW 6th St. 0.3 mi w of University Dr (SR 817); 0.5 mi sw of jct Broward Blvd (SR 842). Int corridors. **Pets:** Accepted.

🆂🅰🆅🅴 🆂🔂 🅧 🕖 🖋 🖋 💻 ➦

POMPANO BEACH

▼ Motel 6–Pompano Beach #371 🅼
(954) 977-8011. **$45-$67.** 1201 NW 31st Ave. Florida Tpke, exit 67 Coconut Creek Pkwy/Martin Luther King Blvd, just s. **Pets:** Accepted.

🆂🔂 🅧 🖋 ➦

⬥⬥⬥ ▼▼▼ Sea Castle Resort Inn 🅼
(954) 941-2570. **$48-$149, 7 day notice.** 730 N Ocean Blvd. SR A1A, 1 mi n of jct SR 814 (Atlantic Blvd). Ext corridors. **Pets:** Accepted.

🆂🅰🆅🅴 🆂🔂 🅧 🖋 💻 ➦

⬥⬥⬥ ▼▼▼ Wellesley Inn & Suites (Ft. Lauderdale/Cypress Creek) 🆂🅷
(954) 783-1050. **$67-$118.** 1401 SW 15th St. I-95, exit 33B (Cypress Creek Rd) to Andrews Ave, just s, then left on McNab St. Int corridors. **Pets:** Small. $25 daily fee/room. Service with restrictions, supervision.

🆂🅰🆅🅴 🅧 🕖 🖋 🖋 💻 ➦

SUNRISE

Baymont Inn & Suites Sunrise at Sawgrass 𝗦𝗛
(954) 846-1200. **$69-$99.** 13651 NW 2nd St. SW 136th Ave, 0.3 mi n of jct I-595, exit 1A and SR 84; 0.5 mi e of jct I-75 and Sawgrass Expwy. Int corridors. **Pets:** Medium. $25 deposit/pet. Designated rooms, service with restrictions, supervision.

Wellesley Inn & Suites (Sunrise) 𝗦𝗛
(954) 845-9929. **$89-$129.** 13600 NW 2nd St. SW 136th Ave, 0.3 mi n of jct I-595, exit 1A and SR 84; 0.5 mi e of jct I-75 and Sawgrass Expwy. Int corridors. **Pets:** Accepted.

TAMARAC

Baymont Inn & Suites Ft. Lauderdale 𝗦𝗛
(954) 485-7900. **$54-$92.** 3800 W Commercial Blvd. On SR 870 (Commercial Blvd), 0.8 mi e of Florida Tpke, exit 62, then just e of jct SR 7 and US 441. Int corridors. **Pets:** Accepted.

Homestead Studio Suites Hotel-Ft Lauderdale/Tamarac 𝗠
(954) 733-6644. **$64-$104.** 3873 W Commercial Blvd. SR 870 (Commercial Blvd), 0.7 mi e of Florida Tpke, exit 62, then just e of jct US 441 and SR 7. Ext corridors. **Pets:** Accepted.

WESTON

AmeriSuites (Ft. Lauderdale/Weston) 𝗦𝗛
(954) 659-1555. **$89-$119.** 2201 N Commerce Pkwy. I-75, exit 15, 0.5 mi w on Arvida Pkwy to Weston Rd, n to N Commerce Pkwy, then just e. Int corridors. **Pets:** Accepted.

Residence Inn by Marriott Weston 𝗦𝗛
(954) 659-8585. **$119-$229.** 2605 Weston Rd. I-75, exit 15 to Weston Rd, just s. Int corridors. **Pets:** Other species. $75 one-time fee/room. Service with restrictions.

TownePlace Suites by Marriott Weston 𝗦𝗛
(954) 659-2234. **$69-$159.** 1545 Three Village Rd. I-75, exit 15, 1 mi e on Arvida Pkwy to Bonaventure Blvd, n to Three Village Rd, then w. Int corridors. **Pets:** Large, other species. $75 one-time fee/room. Service with restrictions.

END METROPOLITAN AREA

FORT MYERS

Best Western Airport Inn 𝗦𝗛
(239) 561-7000. **$69-$169.** 8955 Daniels Pkwy. I-75, exit 131, 0.6 mi w. Int corridors. **Pets:** Small. $10 daily fee/pet. Designated rooms, service with restrictions, supervision.

Best Western Coral Bridge Inn & Suites 𝗦𝗛
(239) 454-6363. **$49-$139.** 9200 College Pkwy. 1.3 mi w of US 41 at McGregor Blvd; in Southpointe Commons. Int corridors. **Pets:** Accepted.

Best Western Fort Myers Island Gateway 𝗦𝗛
(239) 466-1200. **$99-$199.** 20091 Summerlin Rd SW. Jct John Morris Rd. Ext corridors. **Pets:** Other species. $25 one-time fee/pet. Service with restrictions, crate.

Best Western Springs Resort 𝗠
(239) 267-7900. **$69-$139.** 18051 S Tamiami Tr. On US 41 at Constitution Blvd. Ext corridors. **Pets:** Accepted.

Comfort Inn-Ft. Myers 𝗦𝗛
(239) 694-9200. **$79-$129.** 4171 Boatways Rd. I-75, exit 141, just e on SR 80, then just s on Orange River Blvd. Int corridors. **Pets:** Other species. $20 one-time fee/pet. No service, supervision.

Comfort Suites Airport/University 𝗠
(239) 768-0005. **$80-$140.** 13651 Indian Paint Ln. I-75, exit 131, just w. Int corridors. **Pets:** Small, other species. $10 daily fee/pet. Designated rooms, service with restrictions, supervision.

Country Inn & Suites By Carlson Sanibel-Gateway 𝗦𝗛
(239) 454-9292. **$99-$179.** 13901 Shell Point Plaza. Jct McGregor Blvd; in Shell Point. Int corridors. **Pets:** Medium, other species. $10 daily fee/room. Service with restrictions, crate.

Homewood Suites by Hilton-Ft. Myers 𝗦𝗛
(239) 275-6000. **$109-$239, 3 day notice.** 5255 Big Pine Way. Just e of jct US 41; in Bell Tower Shops. Int corridors. **Pets:** Medium. $75 one-time fee/room. Service with restrictions, crate.

La Quinta Inn Fort Myers 𝗠
(239) 275-3300. **$65-$151.** 4850 S Cleveland Ave. On US 41, just s of jct N Airport Rd. Ext corridors. **Pets:** Accepted.

Quality Hotel Historic District 𝗦𝗛
(239) 332-3232. **$57-$155.** 2431 Cleveland Ave. On US 41, just n. Int corridors. **Pets:** Small, dogs only. $15 daily fee/pet. Designated rooms, service with restrictions, supervision.

Residence Inn by Marriott 𝗦𝗛 🐾
(239) 936-0110. **$104-$209.** 2960 Colonial Blvd. I-75, exit 136, 3.5 mi w on SR 884 (Colonial Blvd). Int corridors. **Pets:** Other species. $75 one-time fee/room.

Suburban Extended Stay Hotel 𝗦𝗛
(239) 938-0100. **$55-$130.** 10150 Metro Pkwy. I-75, exit 136, 3.5 mi w on SR 884 (Colonial Blvd). Int corridors. **Pets:** Medium. $25 one-time fee/pet. Designated rooms, service with restrictions, supervision.

Ta Ki-Ki Riverfront Inn 𝗠
(239) 334-2135. **$46-$105, 7 day notice.** 2631 First St. I-75, exit 141, 4.5 mi w on SR 80. Ext corridors. **Pets:** Accepted.

▼▼▼▼ **Wynstar Inn & Suites** SH
(239) 791-5000. **$69-$179, 3 day notice.** 10150 Daniels Pkwy. I-75, exit 131, just e. Int corridors. **Pets:** Small. $100 deposit/pet, $25 daily fee/pet. Designated rooms, service with restrictions, supervision.
A$K ⬛ ✕ ⬛ 🔧 ❓ 🔓 🅿 🏊

FORT MYERS BEACH

▲▲▲ ▼▼ **Best Western Beach Resort** SH
(239) 463-6000. **$129-$399, 7 day notice.** 684 Estero Blvd. 0.4 mi n of Matanzas Pass Bridge. Ext corridors. **Pets:** Accepted.
SAVE ⬛ ✕ ❓ 🔧 🔓 🅿 🏊 ✕

▲▲▲ ▼▼▼▼ **Casa Playa Resort** M ❀
(239) 765-0510. **$83-$250, 30 day notice.** 510 Estero Blvd. 0.5 mi n of Matanzas Pass Bridge via 5th St. Ext corridors. **Pets:** $15 daily fee/pet. Designated rooms, service with restrictions.
SAVE ⬛ ✕ 🔧 🔓 🅿 🏊

▲▲▲ ▼▼ **Lighthouse Resort Inn & Suites** SH
(239) 463-9392. **$52-$275, 3 day notice.** 1051 5th St. Jct SR 865 and 5th St; at south end of Matanzas Pass Bridge. Ext corridors. **Pets:** Small, other species. $25 one-time fee/room. Service with restrictions, supervision.
SAVE ⬛ ✕ 🔧 🔓 🅿 🏊 ✕

▼▼ **Silver Sands Villas** SH
(239) 463-6554. **$79-$187, 21 day notice.** 1207 Estero Blvd. Just s of Matanzas Pass Bridge. Ext corridors. **Pets:** Medium, other species. $50 one-time fee/room. No service, crate.
✕ 🔧 🔓 🅿 🏊

▲▲▲ ▼▼ **Sun Deck Resort** M
(239) 463-1842. **$49-$235, 30 day notice.** 1051 Third St. Just s of Matanzas Pass Bridge. Ext corridors. **Pets:** Accepted.
SAVE ⬛ ✕ 🔧 🔓 🅿 🖨

FORT PIERCE

▲▲▲ ▼▼▼ **Days Inn Hutchinson Island** M
(772) 461-8737. **$69-$105.** 1920 Seaway Dr. SR A1A southbound, Hutchinson Island, 2.5 mi e of jct US 1. Ext/int corridors. **Pets:** Accepted.
SAVE ⬛ ✕ ❓ 🔧 🔓 🅿 🏊 ✕

▼▼▼▼ **Holiday Inn Express** SH
(772) 464-5000. **$79-$159.** 7151 Okeechobee Rd. I-95, exit 129, 0.7 mi w on SR 70; Florida Tpke, exit 152. Ext corridors. **Pets:** Small, other species. $25 one-time fee/room. Service with restrictions, supervision.
A$K ⬛ ✕ 🔧 ❓ 🔓 🅿 🏊

▼▼▼▼ **Motel 6-Fort Pierce #1207** M
(772) 461-9937. **$43-$65.** 2500 Peters Rd. I-95, exit 129, just w, then n. Ext corridors. **Pets:** Small. Service with restrictions, supervision.
⬛ ✕ 🏊

FORT WALTON BEACH

▲▲▲ ▼▼ **Marina Motel & Marina** M
(850) 244-1129. **$50-$100.** 1345 Miracle Strip Pkwy SE. 1 mi e on US 98. Ext/int corridors. **Pets:** Accepted.
SAVE ⬛ ✕ 🔧 🔓 🅿 🏊 ✕

GAINESVILLE

▲▲▲ ▼▼▼▼ **Baymont Inn & Suites-Gainesville** SH
(352) 376-0004. **$82-$119.** 3905 SW 43rd St. I-75, exit 384, just w; behind Cracker Barrel Restaurant. Int corridors. **Pets:** Medium, other species. $10 daily fee/room. Designated rooms, service with restrictions, supervision.
SAVE ⬛ ✕ 🔧 ❓ 🔓 🅿 🏊

▲▲▲ ▼▼▼▼ **Best Western Gateway Grand** SH
(352) 331-3336. **$79-$99.** 4200 NW 97th Blvd. I-75, exit 390, just n of SR 222, then just w. Int corridors. **Pets:** Accepted.
SAVE ⬛ ✕ 🔧 ❓ 🔓 🅿 🍴 🏊 ✕

▼▼▼▼ **Comfort Inn West** SH
(352) 264-1771. **$69-$119.** 3440 SW 40th Blvd. I-75, exit 384, just e, then just n. Int corridors. **Pets:** $10 daily fee/pet. Designated rooms, service with restrictions, supervision.
A$K ⬛ ✕ 🔧 ❓ 🔓 🅿 🏊

▲▲▲ ▼▼ **Econo Lodge University** M
(352) 373-7816. **$43-$110.** 2649 SW 13th St. I-75, exit 382, 2 mi e on SR 331, then 0.5 mi n on US 441. Ext corridors. **Pets:** Small, other species. $10 daily fee/pet. Designated rooms, no service, supervision.
SAVE ⬛ ✕ 🔧 🔓 🅿 🏊

▲▲▲ ▼▼▼▼ **Holiday Inn-West** SH
(352) 332-7500. **$78-$109, 14 day notice.** 7417 Newberry Rd. I-75, exit 387, just w. Ext corridors. **Pets:** Accepted.
SAVE ⬛ ✕ 🔧 🔓 🅿 🍴 🏊

▼▼▼▼ **La Quinta Inn Gainesville** SH
(352) 332-6466. **$75-$105.** 920 NW 69th Terrace. I-75, exit 387, just e, then just n. Ext corridors. **Pets:** Accepted.
A$K ✕ ❓ 🔧 🔓 🅿 🏊

▼▼ **Motel 6 #414** SH
(352) 373-1604. **$40-$75.** 4000 SW 40th Blvd. I-75, exit 384, just e. Ext corridors. **Pets:** Accepted.
⬛ ✕ 🔧 🏊

▼▼ **Quality Inn** SH
(352) 378-2405. **$60-$129.** 3455 SW Williston Rd. I-75, exit 382, just w. Ext/int corridors. **Pets:** Other species. $10 daily fee/room. Service with restrictions, supervision.
A$K ⬛ ✕ 🔧 🔓 🅿 🏊

▲▲▲ ▼▼▼ **Ramada Limited** SH
(352) 332-8001. **$55-$79, 14 day notice.** 7413 W Newberry Rd. I-75, exit 387, just w. Ext corridors. **Pets:** Accepted.
SAVE ⬛ ✕ 🔧 🔓 🅿 🍴 🏊

▼▼ **Red Roof Inn-Gainesville** SH
(352) 336-3311. **$46-$57.** 3500 SW 42nd St. I-75, exit 384, just e. Int corridors. **Pets:** Medium. Service with restrictions, supervision.
✕ 🔧 ❓ ❓ 🔧 🏊

HAINES CITY

▲▲▲ ▼▼▼▼ **Best Western Lake Hamilton** M
(863) 421-6929. **$62-$99.** 605 B Moore Rd. On US 27, just s of jct SR 544, 2 mi s of jct US 17-92. Ext corridors. **Pets:** Accepted.
SAVE ⬛ ✕ 🔧 ❓ 🔓 🅿 🏊 ✕

▲▲▲ ▼▼▼ **Howard Johnson Inn** M
(863) 422-8621. **$49-$69.** 33224 Hwy 27 S. On US 27, 1.8 mi s of jct US 17-92. Ext corridors. **Pets:** Accepted.
SAVE ⬛ ✕ ❓ 🔧 🔓 🅿 🍴 🏊

HERNANDO

▼▼▼▼ **Best Western Citrus Hills Lodge** SH
(352) 527-0015. **$78-$103.** 350 E Norvell Bryant Hwy. CR 486 at Citrus Hills Blvd, 3.3 mi w of US 41. Ext corridors. **Pets:** Small. $10 one-time fee/pet. Designated rooms, service with restrictions, supervision.
A$K ⬛ ✕ 🔧 ❓ 🔧 🔓 🅿 🍴 🏊

HOMOSASSA SPRINGS

▼▼ **Park Inn** SH
(352) 628-4311. **$69-$89.** 4076 S Suncoast Blvd. Just s of jct CR 490 and US 19. Ext corridors. **Pets:** Accepted.
A$K ⬛ ✕ 🔧 🔓 🅿 🏊 ✕

INDIALANTIC

▼▼▼▼ Hilton Melbourne Beach Oceanfront SH ❀
(321) 777-5000. **$119-$249.** 3003 N SR A1A. N SR A1A, 3 mi n of jct US 192. Int corridors. **Pets:** Medium. $50 one-time fee/room. Designated rooms, service with restrictions, supervision.

ASK ⊠ 🕭 🛢 💷 🍽 ➹ 🚫

▼▼▼▼ Melbourne Quality Suites Oceanfront Hotel SH
(321) 723-4222. **$119-$219.** 1665 N SR A1A. SR A1A, 1.5 mi n of jct US 192. Ext corridors. **Pets:** Medium. $75 one-time fee/pet. Designated rooms, service with restrictions, crate.

ASK 🕭 ⊠ 🕭 🛢 💷 🍽 ➹ 🚫

▼▼▼ Oceanfront Cottages CA
(321) 725-8474. **$790-$1390 (weekly), 60 day notice.** 612 Wavecrest Ave. Just s of east end of US 192. Ext corridors. **Pets:** Small, other species. $30 one-time fee/pet. No service, crate.

⊠ 🛢 💷 ➹

INDIAN HARBOUR BEACH

AAA ▼▼▼ Wellesley Inn-Melbourne/Indian Harbour Beach M
(321) 773-0325. **$79-$119.** 1894 S Patrick Dr. I-95, exit 183, 8 mi e, then 1 mi n on SR 513. Int corridors. **Pets:** Accepted.

SAVE 🕭 ⊠ 🕭 🛢 🛢 💷 ➹ 🚫

INVERNESS

▼▼▼ Van der Valk Inverness VH
(352) 637-1140. **$1130-$1300 (weekly), 28 day notice.** 4555 E Windmill Dr. 2.7 mi n on US 41. **Pets:** Accepted.

ASK 🕭 ⊠ 🛢 💷 ➹

JACKSONVILLE METROPOLITAN AREA

BALDWIN

AAA ▼▼▼ Best Western Baldwin Inn M
(904) 266-9759. **$54-$159.** 1088 US 301 & I-10. I-10, exit 343, just s. Ext corridors. **Pets:** Medium, other species. $8 daily fee/pet. Service with restrictions, supervision.

SAVE 🕭 ⊠ 💷 ➹

FERNANDINA BEACH

AAA ▼▼▼ Florida House Inn CI
(904) 261-3300. **$99-$219, 7 day notice.** 22 S 3rd St. In Fernandina Beach; just s of Centre St; in historic district. Ext/int corridors. **Pets:** Accepted.

SAVE 🕭 ⊠ 💷 🍽

JACKSONVILLE

AAA ▼▼▼▼ AmeriSuites (Jacksonville/Baymeadows) SH
(904) 737-4477. **$75-$80.** 8277 Western Way Cir. I-95, exit 341, just e. Int corridors. **Pets:** Accepted.

SAVE 🕭 ⊠ 🕭 🛢 🛢 💷 ➹

AAA ▼▼▼ Baymont Inn & Suites Jacksonville SH
(904) 268-9999. **$54-$75.** 3199 Hartley Rd. I-295, exit 5A northbound; exit 5 southbound at SR 13. Int corridors. **Pets:** Accepted.

SAVE 🕭 ⊠ 🕭 🛢 💷 ➹

AAA ▼▼▼ Best Western Hotel JTB/Southpoint LH
(904) 281-0900. **$65-$199.** 4660 Salisbury Rd. I-95, exit 344, just e. Int corridors. **Pets:** Accepted.

SAVE 🕭 ⊠ 🕭 🛢 💷 🍽 ➹ 🚫

▼▼▼ Candlewood Suites SH
(904) 296-7785. **$99-$399.** 4990 Belfort Rd. I-95, exit 344, e to Belfort Rd, then just s. Int corridors. **Pets:** Accepted.

ASK 🕭 ⊠ 🕭M 🕭 🛢 🛢 💷

AAA ▼▼▼ Hampton Inn Jacksonville Airport M
(904) 741-4980. **$69-$99.** 1170 Airport Entrance Rd. I-95, exit 363, jct Airport Rd. Ext corridors. **Pets:** Accepted.

SAVE 🕭 ⊠ 🕭M 🕭 🛢 🛢 💷 ➹

▼▼▼ Holiday Inn Airport SH
(904) 741-4404. **$119-$139.** 14670 Duval Rd. I-95, exit 363, just w. Ext/int corridors. **Pets:** Medium. Designated rooms, service with restrictions.

ASK ⊠ 🕭 🛢 🛢 💷 🍽 ➹ 🚫

▼▼▼ Holiday Inn Baymeadows SH
(904) 737-1700. **$64-$99.** 9150 Baymeadows Rd. I-95, exit 341, 0.3 mi e. Ext/int corridors. **Pets:** Accepted.

ASK 🕭 ⊠ 🕭 🛢 💷 🍽 ➹

▼▼▼ Homestead Studio Suites Hotel-Jacksonville/Baymeadows SH
(904) 739-1881. **$74-$89.** 8300 Western Way. I-95, exit 341, just e to Western Way, then just s. Int corridors. **Pets:** Accepted.

ASK 🕭 ⊠ 🕭 🛢 💷 ➹

▼▼▼ Homestead Studio Suites Hotel-Jacksonville/Southeast SH
(904) 296-0661. **$79-$104.** 4693 Salisbury Rd S. I-95, exit 344, e on J Turner Butler Blvd, then just s. Int corridors. **Pets:** Accepted.

ASK 🕭 ⊠ 🕭M 🕭 🛢 🛢 💷 ➹

▼▼▼ Homestead Studio Suites Hotel-Jacksonville/Southside M
(904) 642-9911. **$64-$84.** 10020 Skinner Lake Dr. I-95, exit 344, 3.5 mi on J Turner Butler Blvd to Gate Pkwy, just n, then just w. Ext corridors. **Pets:** Accepted.

ASK 🕭 ⊠ 🕭M 🕭 🛢 💷

▼▼▼ Homewood Suites by Hilton SH
(904) 733-9299. **$135-$200.** 8737 Baymeadows Rd. I-95, exit 341, 0.3 mi w. Ext/int corridors. **Pets:** Other species. $75 one-time fee/room. Service with restrictions, crate.

ASK 🕭 ⊠ 🛢 💷 ➹ 🚫

▼▼▼ Inn 2000 SH
(904) 741-1133. **Call for rates.** 14585 Duval Rd. I-95, exit 363B, just sw. Int corridors. **Pets:** Accepted.

⊠ 🛢

▼▼▼ Jameson Inn SH
(904) 296-0968. **$49-$104.** 7030 Bonneval Rd. I-95, exit 344, just w. Int corridors. **Pets:** Small, other species. $10 one-time fee/room. Designated rooms, service with restrictions, supervision.

ASK ⊠ 🛢 💷 ➹

▼▼▼ La Quinta Inn & Suites Jacksonville (Butler Blvd) SH
(904) 296-0703. **$89-$109.** 4686 Lenoir Ave S. I-95, exit 344, just w, then just n. Int corridors. **Pets:** Small. Service with restrictions, supervision.

ASK ⊠ 🕭M 🕭 🛢 🛢 💷 ➹

▼▼▼ La Quinta Inn Jacksonville (Airport/North) SH
(904) 751-6960. **$85-$105.** 812 Dunn Ave. I-95, exit 360, southwest corner. Ext corridors. **Pets:** Accepted.

ASK ⊠ 🕭 🛢 💷 ➹

▼▼▼▼ La Quinta Inn Jacksonville (Baymeadows) Ⓜ
(904) 731-9940. $89-$99. 8255 Dix Ellis Tr. I-95, exit 341, southwest corner. Ext corridors. Pets: Accepted.
ⒶⓈⓀ ⊠ 🛢 💻 ⇉

AAA ▼▼▼▼ La Quinta Inn Jacksonville (Orange Park) SH
(904) 778-9539. $81-$93. 8555 Blanding Blvd. I-295, exit 12, just s on SR 21. Ext corridors. Pets: Accepted.
SAVE ⊠ ⌨ 🛢 💻 ⇉

AAA ▼▼ Masters Inn JT Butler/Southpoint Ⓜ
(904) 281-2244. $49-$59. 4940 Mustang Rd. I-95, exit 344, just w, then just n. Int corridors. Pets: Small. $15 daily fee/pet. Designated rooms, service with restrictions, supervision.
SAVE SD ⊠ ♿M ⌨ 🛢

▼▼ Motel 6 Jacksonville SW (Orange Park) #415 Ⓜ
(904) 777-6100. $43-$59. 6107 Youngerman Cir. I-295, exit 12, just s. Ext corridors. Pets: Accepted.
SD ⊠ ⇉

AAA ▼▼▼▼ Ramada Inn Conference Center SH ✿
(904) 268-8080. $82. 3130 Hartley Rd. I-295, exit 5A northbound; exit 5 southbound, just n on SR 13. Ext corridors. Pets: Other species. $50 one-time fee/room. Service with restrictions, supervision.
SAVE SD ⊠ ⌨ 🛢 💻 🍴 ⇉

▼▼ Red Roof Inn-Airport Ⓜ
(904) 741-4488. $50-$55. 14701 Airport Entrance Rd. I-95, exit 363. Ext corridors. Pets: Accepted.
⊠ ⇉

▼▼ Red Roof Inn-South Ⓜ
(904) 777-1000. $51-$61. 6099 Youngerman Cir. I-295, exit 12. Ext corridors. Pets: Accepted.
⊠ ⇉

▼▼▼▼ Residence Inn by Marriott SH
(904) 996-8900. $74-$169. 10551 Deerwood Park Blvd. I-95, exit 344, 3.5 mi e on J Turner Butler Blvd to Gate Blvd, just s, then just w. Int corridors. Pets: Accepted.
ⒶⓈⓀ SD ⊠ ♿M ⌨ ⌨ 🛢 💻 ⇉ ⊠

▼▼ Residence Inn by Marriott SH
(904) 733-8088. $69-$189. 8365 Dix Ellis Tr. I-95, exit 341, sw off Baymeadows Rd. Ext corridors. Pets: Other species. $75 one-time fee/room. Service with restrictions.
ⒶⓈⓀ SD ⊠ ⌨ ♿ 🛢 💻 ⇉ ⊠

JACKSONVILLE BEACH

AAA ▼▼▼▼ Quality Suites Oceanfront SH ✿
(904) 435-3535. $159-$269. 11 1st St N. Just n of Beach Blvd (US 90). Int corridors. Pets: Medium. $35 daily fee/pet. Designated rooms, service with restrictions, supervision.
SAVE SD ⊠ 🛢 💻 ⇉

AAA ▼▼▼ Surfside Inn Ⓜ
(904) 246-1583. $69-$179. 1236 N 1st St. 1.2 mi n of Beach Blvd (US 90). Ext corridors. Pets: Accepted.
SAVE SD ⊠ 🛢 💻 ⇉

ORANGE PARK

AAA ▼▼▼ Comfort Inn SH ✿
(904) 644-4444. $71-$91. 341 Park Ave. I-295, exit 10, just s on US 17. Ext corridors. Pets: Medium, other species. $30 one-time fee/pet. Service with restrictions, supervision.
SAVE SD ⊠ 🛢 💻 ⇉

AAA ▼▼▼ Days Inn SH
(904) 269-8887. $69-$389. 4280 Eldridge Loop. I-295, exit 10, just s on US 17. Int corridors. Pets: Accepted.
SAVE SD ⊠ 🛢 💻

PONTE VEDRA BEACH

AAA ▼▼▼▼ The Sawgrass Marriott Resort & Beach Club LH
(904) 285-7777. $135-$259. 1000 PGA Tour Blvd. 2.5 mi s of J Turner Butler Blvd. Int corridors. Pets: $25 daily fee/room. Designated rooms, service with restrictions.
SAVE SD ⊠ 🛢 💻 🍴 ⇉ ⊠

END METROPOLITAN AREA

JENSEN BEACH

▼▼▼▼ River Palm Cottages CA
(772) 334-0401. $119-$199, 14 day notice. 2325 NE Indian River Dr. On SR 707 (NE Indian River Dr), 1.4 mi s of jct SR 732. Ext corridors. Pets: Accepted.
ⒶⓈⓀ ⊠ 🛢 💻 ⇉ ⊠

JUNO BEACH

▼▼▼▼ Holiday Inn Express-North Palm Beach SH
(561) 622-4366. $69-$400. 13950 US Hwy 1. Jct Donald Ross Rd. Ext/int corridors. Pets: Accepted.
ⒶⓈⓀ SD ⊠ ⌨ ♿ 🛢 💻 ⇉

JUPITER

AAA ▼▼▼▼ Jupiter Beach Resort LH
(561) 746-2511. $129-$559, 7 day notice. 5 N A1A. SR A1A, 1 mi se of jct US 1; jct SR 706 (Indiantown Rd). Int corridors. Pets: Accepted.
SAVE SD ⊠ ♿ 🛢 💻 🍴 ⇉ ⊠

AAA ▼▼▼▼ Wellesley Inn (Jupiter) SH
(561) 575-7201. $69-$149. 34 Fishermans Wharf. SR 706 (Indiantown Rd); 0.3 mi w of jct US 1; in Fisherman's Wharf Plaza. Int corridors. Pets: Accepted.
SAVE SD ⊠ ⌨ ♿ 🛢 💻 ⇉

LAKE CITY

AAA ▼▼▼▼ Best Western Inn SH
(386) 752-3801. $55-$100. 3598 W US Hwy 90. I-75, exit 427, just w. Ext corridors. Pets: Medium. $10 daily fee/pet. Designated rooms, service with restrictions, supervision.
SAVE SD ⊠ 🛢 💻 ⇉ ⊠

AAA ▼▼▼ Days Inn I-10 SH
(386) 758-4224. $50-$75. US 441. I-10, exit 303, just s. Ext corridors. Pets: Medium, other species. $10 daily fee/pet. Designated rooms, service with restrictions, crate.
SAVE SD ⊠ 🛢 💻 ⇉

AAA ▼▼▼ Driftwood Inn Ⓜ
(386) 755-3545. $35-$49. 2764 W US Hwy 90. I-75, exit 427, 0.7 mi e. Ext corridors. Pets: Very small, dogs only. $10 daily fee/pet. Designated rooms, service with restrictions, supervision.
SAVE ⊠ 🛢

AAA ▼▼▼ Econo Lodge South Ⓜ
(386) 755-9311. $46-$49, 7 day notice. 14113 S US Hwy 441. I-75, exit 414, at US 441. Ext corridors. Pets: Small. $10 daily fee/pet. No service, supervision.
SAVE SD ⊠ 💻 ⇉

▽▽▽ **Jameson Inn** SH
(386) 758-8440. **$49-$104.** 285 SW Commerce Blvd. I-75, exit 427, just e, then just s. Int corridors. **Pets:** Very small, other species. $10 daily fee/room. Service with restrictions, supervision.
ASK ✕ &M 🕉 🛒 🖪 🖵 ⌷⌷⌷

⟨AAA⟩ ▽▽ **Rodeway Inn** M ✿
(386) 755-5203. **$45.** 205 SW Commerce Dr. I-75, exit 427, just e. Ext corridors. **Pets:** Other species. $5 daily fee/pet. Designated rooms, service with restrictions, crate.
SAVE S⌷ ✕ 🖪 🖵

⟨AAA⟩ ▽▽ **Scottish Inns** M
(386) 755-0230. **$39-$59.** 2916 W US Hwy 90. I-75, exit 427, 0.6 mi e. Ext corridors. **Pets:** Small, dogs only. $5 daily fee/pet. Designated rooms, service with restrictions, supervision.
SAVE S⌷ ✕ 🖪

LAKELAND

⟨AAA⟩ ▽▽▽ **AmeriSuites (Lakeland Center)** SH
(863) 413-1122. **$79-$159.** 525 W Orange St. I-4, exit 32, 3.2 mi s on US 98, then just w. Int corridors. **Pets:** Accepted.
SAVE S⌷ ✕ &M 🕉 🛒 🖪 🖵 ⌷⌷⌷

⟨AAA⟩ ▽▽▽ **Baymont Inn & Suites Lakeland** SH
(863) 815-0606. **$49-$129.** 4315 Lakeland Park Dr. I-4, exit 33; jct SR 33, just nw. Int corridors. **Pets:** Accepted.
SAVE S⌷ ✕ &M 🕉 🛒 🖪 🖵 ⌷⌷⌷

⟨AAA⟩ ▽▽▽ **Comfort Inn & Suites** SH
(863) 859-0100. **$89-$109.** 3520 Hwy US 98 N. I-4, exit 32, just nw; at Lakeland Square Mall. Int corridors. **Pets:** Accepted.
SAVE S⌷ ✕ &M 🕉 🛒 🖪 🖵 ⌷⌷⌷

▽▽▽ **Jameson Inn** SH
(863) 858-9070. **$49-$104.** 4375 Lakeland Park Dr. I-4, exit 33, just nw. Int corridors. **Pets:** Very small, other species. $10 daily fee/room. Service with restrictions, supervision.
ASK ✕ &M 🕉 🛒 🖪 🖵 ⌷⌷⌷

▽▽▽ **Lakeland Residence Inn by Marriott** SH
(863) 680-2323. **$130-$350.** 3701 Harden Blvd. I-4, exit 27 (Polk Pkwy), se on SR 570 (toll) to exit 5, then just n. Int corridors. **Pets:** Accepted.
ASK S⌷ ✕ 🕉 🛒 🖪 🖵 ⌷⌷⌷ ✕

⟨AAA⟩ ▽◆▽ **La Quinta Inn & Suites Lakeland** SH
(863) 859-2866. **$84-$124.** 1024 Crevasse St. I-4, exit 32, just n on US 98. Int corridors. **Pets:** Accepted.
SAVE ✕ &M 🕉 🛒 🖪 🖵 ⌷⌷⌷

⟨AAA⟩ ▽▽▽ **Super 8 Motel** SH
(863) 683-5961. **$54-$70, 3 day notice.** 601 E Memorial Blvd. Just e of jct SR 33. Ext/int corridors. **Pets:** Medium. $10 daily fee/pet. Designated rooms, service with restrictions, crate.
SAVE S⌷ ✕ 🖪 ⌷⌷⌷

LAKE WORTH

⟨AAA⟩ ▽▽ **Lago Motor Inn** M
(561) 585-5246. **$60-$75, 7 day notice.** 714 S Dixie Hwy. I-95, exit 63, 0.7 mi e, then just s on US 1; US 1, just s of jct 6th Ave S. Ext corridors. **Pets:** Other species. $10 deposit/pet, $10 daily fee/pet. Designated rooms, service with restrictions, supervision.
SAVE ✕ 🖪 ⌷⌷⌷

▽▽▽ **Parador Inn of the Palm Beaches** BB
(561) 540-1443. **$75-$150, 14 day notice.** 1000 S Federal Hwy. I-95, exit 63, 1 mi e on 6th Ave S, then 0.5 mi s on SR 5 (Federal Hwy). Ext/int corridors. **Pets:** Medium, other species. Designated rooms, service with restrictions.
ASK S⌷ ✕ 🖪 🖵 ✇

LANTANA

▽ **Motel 6 Lantana #688** M
(561) 585-5833. **$45-$73.** 1310 W Lantana Rd. I-95, exit 61 (SR 812), just e, then s. Ext corridors. **Pets:** Accepted.
S⌷ ✕ ⌷⌷⌷

LIVE OAK

⟨AAA⟩ ▽▽▽ **Econo Lodge** SH ✿
(386) 362-7459. **$49-$89, 14 day notice.** 6811 N US 129 & I-10. I-10, exit 283, just s. Ext corridors. **Pets:** Large, other species. $10 one-time fee/room. Service with restrictions.
SAVE S⌷ ✕ 🖪 🖵 ⌷⌷⌷

⟨AAA⟩ ▽▽▽ **Suwannee River Best Western Inn** SH
(386) 362-6000. **$45-$140.** 6819 US 129 N. I-10, exit 283, 0.3 mi s. Ext corridors. **Pets:** Accepted.
SAVE S⌷ ✕ 🖪 🖵 ⌷⌷⌷

LONGBOAT KEY

⟨AAA⟩ ▽▽▽▽ **Hilton Longboat Key Beachfront Resort** SH
(941) 383-2451. **$155-$600, 3 day notice.** 4711 Gulf of Mexico Dr. On SR 789, 6.2 mi n of New Pass Bridge. Ext/int corridors. **Pets:** Very small. $100 one-time fee/pet. Supervision.
SAVE S⌷ ✕ 🕉 &⌷ 🖪 🖵 🍴 ⌷⌷⌷ ✕

▽▽ **Riviera Beach Resort** M
(941) 383-2552. **$700-$1300 (weekly), 30 day notice.** 5451 Gulf of Mexico Dr. On SR 789, 5 mi s of jct SR 684 (Cortez Rd). Ext corridors. **Pets:** Small, other species. $15 daily fee/pet. No service, supervision.
ASK S⌷ ✕ 🖪 🖵 ⌷⌷⌷ ✕

MACCLENNY

⟨AAA⟩ ▽▽ **Econo Lodge** M
(904) 259-3000. **$47-$85.** 151 Woodlawn Rd. I-10, exit 335, just s of jct SR 121. Ext corridors. **Pets:** Large, other species. $10 one-time fee/room. Service with restrictions, supervision.
SAVE S⌷ ✕ 🖪 🖵 ⌷⌷⌷

MANALAPAN

⟨AAA⟩ ▽▽▽▽ **The Ritz-Carlton, Palm Beach** LH
(561) 533-6000. **$225-$3500, 14 day notice.** 100 S Ocean Blvd. On SR A1A; 9 mi s of Palm Beach. Int corridors. **Pets:** Accepted.
SAVE ✕ 🕉 🖪 🖵 🍴 ⌷⌷⌷ ✕

MARIANNA

⟨AAA⟩ ▽▽ **Best Western Marianna Inn** SH
(850) 526-5666. **$55-$65, 15 day notice.** 2086 Hwy 71 S. I-10, exit 142, 0.3 mi s. Ext corridors. **Pets:** Medium. $12 daily fee/pet. Service with restrictions, supervision.
SAVE S⌷ ✕ 🖪 🖵 ⌷⌷⌷

⟨AAA⟩ ▽▽ **Comfort Inn** SH
(850) 526-5600. **$65-$95.** 2175 Hwy 71 S. I-10, exit 142, just n. Ext corridors. **Pets:** Small. $12 daily fee/pet. Service with restrictions, supervision.
SAVE S⌷ ✕ 🖪 🖵 ⌷⌷⌷

MELBOURNE

⟨AAA⟩ ▽▽▽ **Baymont Inn & Suites Melbourne** SH
(321) 242-9400. **$70-$110.** 7200 George T Edwards Dr. I-95, exit 191 (CR 509), just w. Int corridors. **Pets:** Accepted.
SAVE S⌷ ✕ 🕉 &⌷ 🖪 🖵 ⌷⌷⌷

▼▼▼ Crane Creek Inn Waterfront Bed &
    Breakfast 🅑🅑 ❖
(321) 768-6416. **$100-$175, 14 day notice.** 907 E Melbourne Ave. Jct
US 192, just s on Babcock, then 0.9 mi e. Ext/int corridors. **Pets:** Dogs
only. $25 daily fee/pet. Designated rooms, supervision.
☒ 🖥 🖵 🌊 ☒

▼▼▼ Hilton Melbourne Rialto Place 🆂🅷
(321) 768-0200. **$109-$249.** 200 Rialto Pl. 1 mi w of US 1, 0.8 mi n of
US 192. Int corridors. **Pets:** Large, other species. $50 deposit/room.
Service with restrictions.
🆂🅾 ☒ ♿ 🖥 🖵 🍴 🌊 ☒

▼▼▼ Holiday Inn Melbourne 🆂🅷
(321) 724-4422. **$63-$80, 30 day notice.** 964 S Harbor City Blvd. 1 mi
n of US 192 on US 1, jct Nasa Blvd. Int corridors. **Pets:** Accepted.
🅰🆂🅺 🆂🅾 ☒ 🗝 🖥 🖵 🍴 🌊

▼▼▼ Ramada Inn 🆂🅷
(321) 723-5320. **$50-$95.** 420 S Harbor City Blvd. US 1, 1.7 mi n of US
192. Ext corridors. **Pets:** Accepted.
🅰🆂🅺 🆂🅾 ☒ 🗝 🖥 🖵 🍴 🌊

🅐🅐🅐 ▼▼▼ Super 8 🅜
(321) 723-4430. **$49-$79.** 1515 S Harbor City Blvd. I-95, exit 180, 7 mi
e to US 1 on SR 192, then 0.5 mi n. Int corridors. **Pets:** Medium, other
species. $20 deposit/room, $10 one-time fee/pet. Service with restrictions,
supervision.
🆂🅰🆅🅴 🆂🅾 ☒ ♿ 🖥

MIAMI-MIAMI BEACH METROPOLITAN AREA

AVENTURA

▼▼▼▼ The Fairmont Turnberry Isle Resort &
    Club 🅛🅗 ❖
(305) 932-6200. **$169-$4200, 3 day notice.** 19999 W Country Club Dr.
0.5 mi w of SR A1A via SR 856; from US 1 at NE 199th St and
Biscayne Blvd. Ext/int corridors. **Pets:** Small. Service with restrictions.
🅰🆂🅺 🆂🅾 ☒ 🗝 🖥 🖵 🍴 🌊 ☒

🅐🅐🅐 ▼▼▼ Residence Inn by Marriott-Aventura
    Mall 🆂🅷 ❖
(786) 528-1001. **$99-$409.** 19900 W Country Club Dr. 0.5 mi w of SR
A1A via SR 856; from US 1 at NE 199th St and Biscayne Blvd. Int
corridors. **Pets:** Medium. $75 one-time fee/room.
🆂🅰🆅🅴 🆂🅾 ☒ ♿ 🗝 ♿ 🖥 🖵 🌊 ☒

BAL HARBOUR

🅐🅐🅐 ▼▼▼▼ Bay Harbor Inn & Suites 🆂🅷
(305) 868-4141. **$79-$209.** 9660 E Bay Harbor Dr. Just s of SR A1A.
Ext/int corridors. **Pets:** Large, other species. $50 deposit/room, $10 one-
time fee/pet. Designated rooms, service with restrictions.
🆂🅰🆅🅴 🆂🅾 ☒ 🖥 🖵 🍴 🌊

🅐🅐🅐 ▼▼▼▼ Sheraton Bal Harbour Beach Resort 🅛🅗
(305) 865-7511. **$459, 3 day notice.** 9701 Collins Ave. On SR A1A,
just n on SR 922. Int corridors. **Pets:** Accepted.
🆂🅰🆅🅴 🆂🅾 ☒ 🗝 ♿ 🖥 🖵 🍴 🌊 ☒

COCONUT GROVE

🅐🅐🅐 ▼▼▼ ▼▼▼ Mayfair House Hotel 🆂🅷
(305) 441-0000. **$149-$800.** 3000 Florida Ave. At Florida Ave and Virginia St; center. Ext/int corridors. **Pets:** Accepted.
🆂🅰🆅🅴 🆂🅾 ☒ 🗝 ♿ 🍴 ☒

▼▼▼▼ Residence Inn by Marriott 🆂🅷 ❖
(305) 285-9303. **$99-$149.** 2835 Tigertail Ave. S Bayshore Dr, w on
SW 27th Ave/Cornelia Dr, then s; in CocoWalk and May Fair Shops.
Ext corridors. **Pets:** Other species. $75 one-time fee/room.
🅰🆂🅺 🆂🅾 ☒ 🖥 🌊

CUTLER RIDGE

🅐🅐🅐 ▼▼▼▼ Baymont Inn & Suites Miami-Cutler Ridge 🆂🅷
(305) 278-0100. **$60-$90.** 10821 Caribbean Blvd. Florida Tpke, exit 12
(US 1), northwest corner. Int corridors. **Pets:** Accepted.
🆂🅰🆅🅴 🆂🅾 ☒ ♿ 🗝 🖥 🖵 🌊

🅐🅐🅐 ▼▼▼▼ Best Western Floridian Hotel 🆂🅷
(305) 253-9960. **$69-$169.** 10775 Caribbean Blvd. Florida Tpke, exit 12
(US 1), then w. Ext corridors. **Pets:** Small, dogs only. $45 deposit/room,
$15 daily fee/pet. Designated rooms, service with restrictions, supervision.
🆂🅰🆅🅴 🆂🅾 ☒ 🖥 🖵 🍴 🌊

FLORIDA CITY

🅐🅐🅐 ▼▼▼ Coral Roc Motel 🅜
(305) 246-2888. **$32-$129, 3 day notice.** 1100 N Krome Ave. On SR
997; just w of US 1; 0.5 mi s of Homestead. Ext corridors.
Pets: Medium. $50 deposit/pet. Service with restrictions, supervision.
🆂🅰🆅🅴 🆂🅾 ☒ 🖥 🌊

▼▼▼▼ Hampton Inn 🅜
(305) 247-8833. **$84-$124.** 124 E Palm Dr. On US 1, 0.3 mi s of Florida
Tpke terminus. Ext corridors. **Pets:** Accepted.
🅰🆂🅺 🆂🅾 ☒ 🗝 🖥 🖵 🌊

HIALEAH

🅐🅐🅐 ▼▼▼ Days Inn Miami Lakes/Westland Mall 🆂🅷
(305) 823-2121. **$59-$89, 3 day notice.** 1950 W 49th St. SR 826
(Palmetto Expwy), exit NW 103rd St, just e. Int corridors.
Pets: Accepted.
🆂🅰🆅🅴 🆂🅾 ☒ 🖥 🖵

🅐🅐🅐 ▼▼▼ Ramada Inn-Miami Airport North 🆂🅷
(305) 823-2000. **$69-$99.** 1950 W 49th St. SR 826 (Palmetto Expwy),
exit NW 103rd St, just e. Int corridors. **Pets:** Accepted.
🆂🅰🆅🅴 🆂🅾 ☒ 🗝 🖥 🖵 🌊

HIALEAH GARDENS

🅐🅐🅐 ▼▼▼ Howard Johnson Plaza Hotel & Conference
    Center-Miami Airport 🅛🅗 ❖
(305) 825-1000. **$89-$119.** 7707 NW 103rd St. SR 826 (Palmetto
Expwy), exit NW 103rd St, just w. Int corridors. **Pets:** Medium, other
species. $100 one-time fee/room. Designated rooms, service with restric-
tions, crate.
🆂🅰🆅🅴 🆂🅾 ☒ 🖥 🖵 🍴 🌊 ☒

HOMESTEAD

▼▼▼ Days Inn Homestead 🅜
(305) 245-1260. **$75-$149, 3 day notice.** 51 S Homestead Blvd. US 1,
1.2 mi n of Florida Tpke, jct 320 St SW and US 1. Ext corridors.
Pets: Small. $10 daily fee/pet. Designated rooms, service with restrictions,
supervision.
🅰🆂🅺 🆂🅾 ☒ ♿ 🖥 🍴 🌊

🅐🅐🅐 ▼▼ Everglades Motel 🅜
(305) 247-4117. **$32-$109, 3 day notice.** 605 S Krome Ave. Just w of
US 1; between Lucy and 6th sts; on SR 997, 0.5 mi s of center of
town. Ext corridors. **Pets:** Accepted.
🆂🅰🆅🅴 🆂🅾 ☒ 🖥 🌊

KENDALL

AAA ▼▼▼▼ AmeriSuites (Miami/Kendall) SH
(305) 279-8688. **$119-$179.** 11520 SW 88th St. Florida Tpke, exit 20 (SW 88th/Kendall Dr), just e on SR 94, then 0.3 mi s. Int corridors. **Pets:** Accepted.
SAVE S❍ ✕ 🖑M ⟠ 🔊 🛏 🖵 ⊇

AAA ▼▼▼ Wellesley Inn (Miami/Kendall) SH
(305) 270-0359. **$85-$105.** 11750 Mills Dr. Florida Tpke, exit 20, SW 88th (Kendall Dr), 0.3 mi e on SR 94, then 0.3 mi n on SW 117 Ave. Int corridors. **Pets:** Accepted.
SAVE S❍ ✕ 🖑M ⟠ 🔊 🛏 🖵 ⊇

KEY BISCAYNE

▼▼▼▼ The Ritz-Carlton, Key Biscayne LH
(305) 365-4500. **$199-$779, 7 day notice.** 455 Grand Bay Dr. Crandon Blvd, just e. Int corridors. **Pets:** Accepted.
✕ 🛏 🍴 ⊇ ⊠

MIAMI

AAA ▼▼▼ AmeriSuites (Miami/Airport West) SH
(305) 718-8292. **$84-$159.** 3655 NW 82nd Ave. 0.4 mi w on NW 36th St from jct SR 826 (Palmetto Expwy). Int corridors. **Pets:** Small. $10 daily fee/pet. Service with restrictions, supervision.
SAVE S❍ ✕ 🖑M ⟠ 🔊 🛏 🖵 ⊇

AAA ▼▼▼ AmeriSuites (Miami/Blue Lagoon) SH
(305) 265-0144. **$109-$129.** 6700 NW 7th St. SR 836, exit NW 72nd Ave S. Int corridors. **Pets:** Accepted.
SAVE ✕ ⟠ 🔊 🛏 🖵 ⊇

▼▼▼ Best Inn-Miami Airport M
(305) 592-5440. **$49-$75.** 7330 NW 36th St. Just e of jct SR 826 (Palmetto Expwy). Int corridors. **Pets:** Accepted.
ASK S❍ ✕ 🖵 ⊇

▼▼▼ Candlewood Suites Miami Airport West SH
(305) 591-9099. **Call for rates.** 8855 NW 27th St. SR 826 (Palmetto Expwy), 0.8 mi w on nw 36th St, then 0.4 mi s. Int corridors. **Pets:** Accepted.
✕ 🖑M ⟠ 🔊 🛏 🖵 ⊇ ⊠

▼▼▼ Four Seasons Hotel Miami LH
(305) 358-3535. **$275-$525.** 1435 Brickell Ave. On US 1 (Brickell Ave) and 14th. Int corridors. **Pets:** Accepted.
✕ 🖑M ⟠ 🔊 🛏 🖵 🍴 ⊇ ⊠

▼▼▼ Hampton Inn-Miami Airport West SH
(305) 513-0777. **$82-$119.** 3620 NW 79th Ave. SR 826 (Palmetto Expwy), exit NW 36th St, just s of jct NW 58th St, then exit s; in Boykin Center. Int corridors. **Pets:** Small. $50 one-time fee/pet. Designated rooms, service with restrictions, supervision.
✕ 🖑M ⟠ 🔊 🛏 🖵 ⊇

▼▼ Homestead Studio Suites Hotel-Miami/Airport/Blue Lagoon M
(305) 260-0085. **$64-$94.** 6605 NW 7th St. SR 836 (Dolphin Expwy), exit Milam Dairy Rd S, 0.3 mi e; in Blue Lagoon Office Park. Ext corridors. **Pets:** Small. $75 one-time fee/pet. Service with restrictions, supervision.
ASK S❍ ✕ 🖑M ⟠ 🔊 🛏 🖵

▼▼▼ Homestead Studio Suites Hotel-Miami/Airport/Doral M
(305) 436-1811. **$74-$114.** 8720 NW 33rd St. SR 826 (Palmetto Expwy), 0.8 mi w on NW 36th St, just s; in Westpoint Office Park. Ext corridors. **Pets:** Small, other species. $75 one-time fee/pet. Service with restrictions, supervision.
ASK S❍ ✕ ⟠ 🔊 🛏 🖵 ⊇

▼▼▼▼ Homewood Suites by Hilton-Miami Airport/Blue Lagoon SH
(305) 261-3335. **$125-$188.** 5500 Blue Lagoon Dr. Se of jct SR 836 (Dolphin Expwy), exit Red Rd. Int corridors. **Pets:** Accepted.
ASK S❍ ✕ 🖑M ⟠ 🔊 🛏 🖵 ⊇ ⊠

▼▼▼▼ La Quinta Inn & Suites Miami (Airport West) SH
(305) 436-0830. **$88-$125.** 8730 NW 27th St. SR 836 (Dolphin Expwy), just n on 87th NW Ave. Int corridors. **Pets:** Small, other species. Service with restrictions, supervision.
ASK ✕ 🖑M ⟠ 🔊 🛏 🖵 ⊇

▼▼▼▼ La Quinta Inn Miami (Airport North) M
(305) 599-9902. **$74-$114.** 7401 NW 36th St. Just e of jct SR 826 (Palmetto Expwy). Ext corridors. **Pets:** Small. Service with restrictions, supervision.
ASK ✕ ⟠ 🛏 🖵 ⊇

AAA ▼▼▼▼ Mandarin Oriental, Miami LH 🐾
(305) 913-8288. **$445-$825.** 500 Brickell Key Dr. US 1 (Brickell Ave), just e on SE 8th St (Brickell Key Dr). Int corridors. **Pets:** Small, dogs only. $100 deposit/room, $100 one-time fee/room. Supervision.
SAVE ✕ 🖑M ⟠ 🔊 🛏 🖵 ⊇ ⊠

▼▼ Miami River Inn BB 🐾
(305) 325-0045. **$69-$199, 5 day notice.** 118 SW South River Dr. I-95, exit 1B (SW 7th St), just w to SW 5th Ave, just n to SW 2nd St, then e. Ext/int corridors. **Pets:** Other species. $25 one-time fee/room. Service with restrictions.
ASK S❍ ✕ ⊇

AAA ▼▼▼▼ Quality Inn-South M
(305) 251-2000. **$77-$117.** 14501 S Dixie Hwy (US 1). US 1 at SW 145th St. Ext corridors. **Pets:** Accepted.
SAVE S❍ ✕ ⟠ 🛏 🖵 🍴 ⊇

▼▼▼▼ Residence Inn by Marriott SH
(305) 591-2211. **$99-$184.** 1212 NW 82nd Ave. SR 836 (Dolphin Expwy), exit 87th Ave NW, just n to NW 82nd Ave, then e. Ext corridors. **Pets:** Other species. $75 one-time fee/room. Service with restrictions, crate.
ASK S❍ ✕ ⟠ 🔊 🛏 🖵 ⊇ ⊠

AAA ▼▼▼▼ Sheraton Miami-Biscayne Bay Hotel LH
(305) 373-6000. **$114-$329.** 495 Brickell Ave. 0.5 mi s on US 1. Int corridors. **Pets:** Accepted.
SAVE S❍ ✕ ⟠ 🔊 🛏 🖵 🍴 ⊇

▼▼▼▼ Sofitel Miami LH
(305) 264-4888. **$199-$219.** 5800 Blue Lagoon Dr. Just sw of jct SR 836 (Dolphin Expwy), exit Red Rd. Int corridors. **Pets:** Accepted.
ASK S❍ ✕ 🛏 🍴 ⊇ ⊠

▼▼▼▼ Staybridge Suites Miami-Airport West SH
(305) 500-9100. **$99-$125.** 3265 NW 87th Ave. 0.4 mi s of jct NW 36th St. Int corridors. **Pets:** Other species. $125 one-time fee/pet. Service with restrictions, crate.
ASK S❍ ✕ ⟠ 🛏 🖵 ⊇ ⊠

AAA ▼▼▼▼ Summerfield Suites by Wyndham-Miami Airport SH
(305) 269-1922. **$89-$149.** 5710 Blue Lagoon Dr. Se of jct SR 836 (Dolphin Expwy), exit Red Rd, just w. Int corridors. **Pets:** Medium. $150 one-time fee/room. Designated rooms, service with restrictions, supervision.
SAVE ✕ ⟠ 🛏 🖵 ⊇ ⊠

▼▼▼▼ TownePlace Suites by Marriott SH 🐾
(305) 718-4144. **$59-$159.** 10505 NW 36th St. Florida Tpke, exit 29, 1.2 mi e to 107th Ave, then just s. Int corridors. **Pets:** Other species. $75 one-time fee/room. Service with restrictions, supervision.
ASK S❍ ✕ ⟠ 🛏 🖵 ⊇

(AAA) ▼▼▼ Wellesley Inn (Miami Airport) SH
(305) 592-4799. $58-$72. 8436 NW 36th St. 0.8 mi w of jct SR 826 (Palmetto Expwy). Int corridors. Pets: Accepted.
[SAVE] [S] [X] [P] [H] [P] [🏊]

MIAMI BEACH

▼▼▼ Abbey Hotel SH
(305) 531-0031. $79-$185. 300 21st St. Collins Ave, just w. Int corridors. Pets: Accepted.
[X] [�]

▼▼▼ Century Hotel SH
(305) 674-8855. $85-$155, 7 day notice. 140 Ocean Dr. Just e of SR A1A (Collins Ave), just s of 2nd St. Int corridors. Pets: Accepted.
[ASK] [S] [�]

▼▼▼ Crowne Plaza Royal Palm on South Beach LH
(305) 604-5700. $264-$454, 3 day notice. 1545 Collins Ave. On SR A1A at Collins Ave, just s of 16th Ave. Ext/int corridors. Pets: Accepted.
[ASK] [S] [X] [P] [�] [🏊] [X]

▼▼▼ Eden Roc Miami Beach A Renaissance Resort & Spa LH
(305) 531-0000. $224-$261, 3 day notice. 4525 Collins Ave. SR A1A (Collins Ave), just n of 41st St. Int corridors. Pets: Accepted.
[ASK] [S] [X] [P] [&] [H] [P] [♦] [🏊] [X]

▼▼▼ Fontainebleau Hilton Resort LH
(305) 538-2000. Call for rates. 4441 Collins Ave. On SR A1A. Int corridors. Pets: Accepted.
[X] [P] [&] [H] [P] [♦] [🏊] [X]

▼▼▼ Hotel Ocean SH 🐾
(305) 672-2579. $179-$600, 3 day notice. 1230 Ocean Dr. E of jct SR A1A (Collins Ave) and 12th St. Int corridors. Pets: Large, other species. $15 daily fee/room. Service with restrictions.
[ASK] [S] [X] [H] [♦]

▼▼▼ The Kent SH
(305) 604-5068. $130-$165, 3 day notice. 1131 Collins Ave. On SR A1A, at Collins Ave and 11th St. Int corridors. Pets: Small. $100 one-time fee/room. Service with restrictions, crate.
[ASK] [S] [X] [P] [&] [H]

(AAA) ▼▼▼ ▼▼ Loews Miami Beach Hotel LH 🐾
(305) 604-1601. $279-$489, 3 day notice. 1601 Collins Ave. On SR A1A, at Collins and 16th aves. Int corridors. Pets: Other species. Service with restrictions.
[SAVE] [S] [X] [&M] [P] [&] [H] [P] [♦] [🏊] [X]

▼▼▼ The Marlin SH
(305) 604-5063. Call for rates. 1200 Collins Ave. On SR A1A, at Collins Ave and 12th St. Int corridors. Pets: Accepted.
[P] [H] [P] [♦] [X]

▼▼▼ The Tides Hotel SH 🐾
(305) 604-5070. $420-$3000, 3 day notice. 1220 Ocean Dr. E of jct SR A1A (Collins Ave) and 12th St. Int corridors. Pets: Small. $100 one-time fee/room. Service with restrictions, crate.
[X] [&M] [P] [&] [H] [♦] [🏊]

▼▼▼ Villa Capri All Suites Hotel SH
(305) 531-7742. Call for rates. 3010 Collins Ave. On SR A1A; at 30th St. Int corridors. Pets: Medium. $30 one-time fee/room. Service with restrictions.
[X] [H] [P] [♦] [🏊]

▼▼▼ The Waldorf Towers Hotel SH
(305) 531-7684. $109-$219. 860 Ocean Dr. Corner of 8th St and Ocean Dr. Int corridors. Pets: Accepted.
[ASK] [S] [X] [H] [♦]

MIAMI LAKES

▼▼ TownePlace Suites by Marriott SH
(305) 512-9191. Call for rates. 8079 NW 154th St. SR 826 (Palmetto Expwy), exit 154th St, 0.4 mi w. Int corridors. Pets: Accepted.
[X] [H] [P] [🏊]

(AAA) ▼▼▼ Wellesley Inn (Miami Lakes) SH
(305) 821-8274. $79-$189. 7925 NW 154th St. Jct SR 826 (Palmetto Expwy), just w. Int corridors. Pets: Accepted.
[SAVE] [S] [X] [P] [&] [H] [P] [🏊]

MIAMI SPRINGS

(AAA) ▼▼▼ Baymont Inn & Suites Miami-Airport SH
(305) 871-1777. $80-$110. 3501 NW Le Jeune Rd. SR 953 (Le Jeune Rd) at jct SR 112. Int corridors. Pets: Accepted.
[SAVE] [S] [X] [P] [H] [P] [🏊]

(AAA) ▼▼▼ Comfort Inn & Suites-Miami International Airport SH
(305) 871-6000. $89-$199. 5301 NW 36th St. Between Le Jeune Rd and SR 826 (Palmetto Expwy). Int corridors. Pets: Accepted.
[SAVE] [S] [X] [P] [H] [P] [♦] [🏊] [X]

(AAA) ▼▼▼ Holiday Inn Express Miami International Airport SH
(305) 887-2153. $109-$169. 5125 NW 36th St. Between Le Jeune Rd and SR 826 (Palmetto Expwy). Int corridors. Pets: Accepted.
[SAVE] [S] [X] [P] [&] [H]

▼▼ Homestead Studio Suites Hotel-Miami/Airport/Miami Springs SH
(305) 870-0448. $84-$109. 101 Fairway Dr. I-95 to SR 112 W, exit NW 36th St, then w, right on Palmetto Dr, then w; between Le Jeune Rd and SR 826 (Palmetto Expwy); behind Clarion Hotel. Int corridors. Pets: Medium. $25 daily fee/pet. Service with restrictions.
[ASK] [S] [X] [P] [H] [P] [🏊] [X]

▼▼ Red Roof Inn Miami Airport SH
(305) 871-4221. $55-$85. 3401 NW Le Jeune Rd. On SR 953 at SR 112; 0.5 mi n of airport entrance. Int corridors. Pets: Medium, other species. Designated rooms, service with restrictions, supervision.
[X] [P] [🏊]

(AAA) ▼▼ Sleep Inn-Miami Airport SH
(305) 871-7553. $75-$159. 105 Fairway Dr. I-95 to SR 112 W, exit NW 36th St, then w, right on Palmetto Dr, then w; between Le Jeune Rd and SR 826 (Palmetto Expwy). Int corridors. Pets: Small. $10 daily fee/room, $25 one-time fee/room. Service with restrictions, supervision.
[SAVE] [S] [X] [P] [H] [P] [X]

SUNNY ISLES BEACH

(AAA) ▼▼▼ Newport Beachside Hotel & Resort LH
(305) 949-1300. $99-$289. 16701 Collins Ave. SR A1A, jct SR 826 and Sunny Isles Blvd. Int corridors. Pets: Small. Service with restrictions, supervision.
[SAVE] [S] [P] [H] [P] [♦] [🏊] [X]

(AAA) ▼▼▼ Trump International Sonesta Beach Resort LH
(305) 692-5600. $169-$425, 3 day notice. 18001 Collins Ave. On SR A1A, just s of The William Lehman Cswy. Int corridors. Pets: Small, dogs only. $100 one-time fee/room. Service with restrictions, crate.
[SAVE] [S] [X] [P] [H] [P] [♦] [🏊] [X]

END METROPOLITAN AREA

MILTON

AAA **♥♥** Comfort Inn **SH**
(850) 623-1511. **$59-$119.** 8936 Hwy 87 S. I-10, exit 31, just s. Int corridors. **Pets:** Accepted.
[SAVE] [S🐾] [✕] [📞] [💻] [🌊]

♥♥ Red Roof Inn & Suites **SH**
(850) 995-6100. **$44-$110.** 2672 Avalon Blvd. I-10, exit 22, just s. Int corridors. **Pets:** Large, other species. Service with restrictions, supervision.
[ASK] [S🐾] [✕] [🖊M] [♿] [📞] [💻] [🌊]

MOSSY HEAD

♥♥ Ramada Limited **SH**
(850) 951-9780. **$44-$49.** 326 Green Acres Dr. I-10, exit 70, just s. Ext corridors. **Pets:** Accepted.
[ASK] [✕] [💻] [🍴]

NAPLES

AAA **♥♥♥** Baymont Inn & Suites Naples **SH**
(239) 352-8400. **$59-$99.** 185 Bedzel Cir. I-75, exit 101, just w. Int corridors. **Pets:** Accepted.
[SAVE] [S🐾] [✕] [🖊M] [🔷] [♿] [📞] [💻] [🌊]

♥♥♥ Clarion Inn & Suites **SH**
(239) 649-5500. **$65-$275.** 4055 Tamiami Tr N. I-75, exit 107, 3.5 mi n on US 41, then just n of Park Shore Dr. Int corridors. **Pets:** Small. $5 daily fee/pet, $25 one-time fee/pet. Service with restrictions, supervision.
[ASK] [S🐾] [✕] [♿] [📞] [💻] [🌊]

AAA **♥♥♥** The Fairways Resort **M**
(239) 597-8181. **$60-$280, 3 day notice.** 103 Palm River Blvd. I-75, exit 111, 2.2 mi w on CR 846. Ext corridors. **Pets:** Small. $50 one-time fee/pet. Service with restrictions, supervision.
[SAVE] [S🐾] [✕] [📞] [💻] [🌊] [🚫]

AAA **♥♥♥♥** The Hawthorn Suites of Naples **SH**
(239) 593-1300. **$139-$239.** 3557 Pine Ridge Rd. I-75, exit 107, 0.7 mi w. Int corridors. **Pets:** Medium. $125 one-time fee/room. Designated rooms, service with restrictions, crate.
[SAVE] [S🐾] [✕] [🖊M] [🔷] [♿] [📞] [💻] [🌊] [🚫]

AAA **♥♥♥♥** Holiday Inn **M**
(239) 263-3434. **$89-$169.** 1100 Tamiami Tr N. I-75, exit 107, 3.8 mi w on CR 896, then 3.8 mi s on US 41 (Tamiami Tr). Ext corridors. **Pets:** Medium, other species. $20 daily fee/room. Designated rooms, service with restrictions, supervision.
[SAVE] [S🐾] [✕] [📞] [💻] [🍴] [🌊]

♥♥♥♥ Hotel Escalante & Spa **SH**
(239) 659-3466. **$255-$725, 5 day notice.** 290 5th Ave S. 0.5 mi w of US 41 (Tamiami Tr); in Old Naples area. Ext corridors. **Pets:** Accepted.
[ASK] [S🐾] [✕] [📞] [💻] [🌊] [🚫]

♥♥♥♥ LaPlaya Beach & Golf Resort **LH** ✿
(239) 597-3123. **$219-$699, 14 day notice.** 9891 Gulf Shore Dr. North end of town; US 41 (Tamiami Tr), 1.3 mi w on Vanderbilt Beach Rd (SR 862), then 0.5 mi n. Ext/int corridors. **Pets:** Small. $200 deposit/room, $50 one-time fee/pet. Designated rooms, service with restrictions, crate.
[ASK] [S🐾] [✕] [♿] [📞] [🍴] [🌊] [🚫]

♥♥ Red Roof Inn **M**
(239) 774-3117. **$45-$93.** 1925 Davis Blvd. I-75, exit 101, 6.5 mi w on SR 84; just e of jct US 41 (Tamiami Tr). Ext corridors. **Pets:** Accepted.
[✕] [♿] [📞] [💻] [🌊]

♥♥♥♥ Residence Inn by Marriott, Naples **SH**
(239) 659-1300. **$89-$199.** 4075 Tamiami Tr N. I-75, exit 107, 3.8 mi w on CR 896 (Pine Ridge Rd), then 1 mi s on US 41 (Tamiami Tr). Int corridors. **Pets:** Other species. $75 one-time fee/room. Service with restrictions.
[ASK] [S🐾] [✕] [🖊M] [🔷] [♿] [📞] [💻] [🌊] [🚫]

AAA **♥♥** Spinnaker Inn of Naples **M**
(239) 434-0444. **$41-$86.** 6600 Dudley Dr. I-75, exit 107, just w. Ext corridors. **Pets:** Other species. $10 daily fee/pet. Designated rooms, service with restrictions, supervision.
[SAVE] [S🐾] [✕] [📞] [🌊]

♥♥♥♥ Staybridge Suites by Holiday Inn **SH**
(239) 643-8002. **$87-$270, 3 day notice.** 4805 Tamiami Tr N. I-75, exit 107, 3.8 mi w on Pine Ridge Rd to US 41 (Tamiami Tr), then just s. Int corridors. **Pets:** Other species. $75 one-time fee/room. Service with restrictions.
[ASK] [S🐾] [✕] [🖊M] [🔷] [♿] [📞] [💻] [🌊] [🚫]

AAA **♥♥♥** Wellesley Inn (Naples) **SH**
(239) 793-4646. **$65-$120.** 1555 5th Ave S. I-75, exit 101, 6.5 mi w on SR 84. Int corridors. **Pets:** Accepted.
[SAVE] [✕] [🔷] [♿] [📞] [💻] [🌊]

NEW SMYRNA BEACH

♥♥ Buena Vista Inn and Apartments **M** ✿
(386) 428-5565. **$65-$85, 14 day notice.** 500 North Cswy. 2 mi e on SR Business Rt 44, at west end of North Causeway Bridge. Ext corridors. **Pets:** Other species. $5 daily fee/pet. Service with restrictions.
[ASK] [S🐾] [✕] [📞] [💻] [🚫]

♥♥♥♥ Night Swan Intracoastal Bed & Breakfast **BB**
(386) 423-4940. **$100-$200, 3 day notice.** 512 S Riverside Dr. Just s of SR 44 Intracoastal Waterway bridge; west side of Intracoastal Waterway. Ext/int corridors. **Pets:** Small, other species. Designated rooms, service with restrictions, supervision.
[ASK] [S🐾] [✕] [♿] [📞] [💻]

NICEVILLE

♥♥♥ Holiday Inn Express **SH**
(850) 678-9131. **$80-$99.** 106 Bayshore Dr. SR 85, just se on jct SR 20. Int corridors. **Pets:** Accepted.
[ASK] [S🐾] [✕] [♿] [📞] [💻] [🌊]

NORTH FORT MYERS

AAA **♥♥** Econo Lodge **M**
(239) 995-0571. **$49-$145.** 13301 N Cleveland Ave. On US 41, 1.1 mi n of Caloosahatchee Bridge. Ext corridors. **Pets:** Large. $10 one-time fee/room. Service with restrictions, supervision.
[SAVE] [S🐾] [✕] [📞] [💻] [🌊]

AAA **♥♥** Howard Johnson Express Inn **M**
(239) 656-4000. **$69-$139.** 13000 N Cleveland Ave. On US 41, 1 mi n of Caloosahatchee Bridge. Ext corridors. **Pets:** Accepted.
[SAVE] [S🐾] [✕] [🔷] [📞] [💻] [🌊]

OCALA

AAA **♥♥♥** Budget Host Inn **M**
(352) 732-6940. **$45-$72.** 4013 NW Bonnie Heath Blvd. I-75, exit 354, 0.3 mi w on US 27. Ext corridors. **Pets:** Medium, other species. $10 daily fee/pet. Service with restrictions, supervision.
[SAVE] [S🐾] [✕] [📞]

AAA **♥♥** Comfort Inn **M**
(352) 629-8850. **$65-$150.** 4040 W Silver Springs Blvd. I-75, exit 352, just w on SR 40. Ext corridors. **Pets:** Large, other species. $5 daily fee/pet. Service with restrictions, crate.
[SAVE] [S🐾] [✕] [📞] [💻] [🍴] [🌊]

AAA **♥♥** Days Inn **SH**
(352) 629-7041. **$60-$150.** 3811 NW Bonnie Heath Blvd. I-75, exit 354, just n on US 27. Ext/int corridors. **Pets:** Large. $5 daily fee/pet. Service with restrictions, supervision.
[SAVE] [S🐾] [✕] [📞] [💻] [🌊]

▼◆◆ Days Inn SH
(352) 629-0091. **$54-$100.** 3620 W Silver Springs Blvd. I-75, exit 352, just e. Ext/int corridors. **Pets:** Medium. $10 daily fee/pet. Service with restrictions.
(ASK) (SD) (X) (▣) (≈)

▼◆◆◆ Hilton Ocala LH ❀
(352) 854-1400. **$79-$129, 3 day notice.** 3600 SW 36th Ave. I-75, exit 350, 0.3 mi e on SR 200. Int corridors. **Pets:** Large. Designated rooms, service with restrictions, supervision.
(ASK) (SD) (X) (Ⓐ) (🛏) (▣) (🍴) (≈) (X)

◆◆◆ Howard Johnson Inn M
(352) 629-7021. **$50-$200.** 3951 NW Bonnie Heath Blvd. I-75, exit 354, just w. Ext corridors. **Pets:** Other species. $10 daily fee/pet. Service with restrictions, supervision.
(SAVE) (SD) (X) (🛏) (▣) (🍴) (≈) (X)

◆◆◆ ▼◆◆◆ La Quinta Inn & Suites Ocala SH
(352) 861-1137. **$94-$134.** 3530 SW 36th Ave. I-75, exit 350, just e on SR 200. Int corridors. **Pets:** Accepted.
(SAVE) (X) (🛦) (Ⓐ) (Ⓐ) (🛏) (▣) (≈)

▼◆◆ Quality Inn Ocala Hotel and Conference
Center SH ❀
(352) 629-0381. **$39-$129.** 3621 W Silver Springs Blvd. I-75, exit 352, just e on SR 40. Ext corridors. **Pets:** Other species. $20 one-time fee/room. Service with restrictions.
(ASK) (SD) (X) (🛏) (▣) (🍴) (≈)

▼◆◆◆ Red Roof Inn & Suites SH
(352) 732-4590. **$60-$90.** 120 NW 40th Ave. I-75, exit 352, just w. Int corridors. **Pets:** Accepted.
(X) (🛏) (▣) (≈)

◆◆◆ ▼◆◆◆ Steinbrenner's Ramada Inn & Conference
Center SH
(352) 732-3131. **$69-$139.** 3810 NW Bonnie Heath Blvd. I-75, exit 354, just w. Ext corridors. **Pets:** Medium. $25 one-time fee/room. Service with restrictions, supervision.
(SAVE) (SD) (X) (Ⓐ) (🛏) (▣) (🍴) (≈) (X)

OKEECHOBEE

◆◆◆ ▼◆◆ Budget Inn M
(863) 763-3185. **$89-$185.** 201 S Parrott Ave (US 441). US 98 and 441, just s of jct SR 70. Ext corridors. **Pets:** Very small. $10 one-time fee/pet. Designated rooms, service with restrictions, supervision.
(SAVE) (SD) (X) (🛏) (≈)

◆◆◆ ▼ Economy Inn M
(863) 763-1148. **$55-$129, 3 day notice.** 507 N Parrott Ave. US 441, 0.3 mi n of jct SR 70. Ext corridors. **Pets:** Small. $10 daily fee/pet. Service with restrictions, supervision.
(SAVE) (SD) (X) (🛏)

OLD TOWN

◆◆◆ ▼◆◆ Suwanee Gables Motel M
(352) 542-7752. **$76-$86.** HC 3, Box 208. US 19, 98 and 27A; 2 mi s of jct SR 349. Ext corridors. **Pets:** Medium, other species. $10 daily fee/pet. Designated rooms, service with restrictions, supervision.
(SAVE) (SD) (X) (🛏) (≈)

ORANGE CITY

◆◆◆ ▼◆◆◆ Comfort Inn M
(386) 775-7444. **$64-$215.** 445 S Volusia Ave. I-4, exit 114, 2.8 mi w on SR 472, then 2 mi s on US 17-92. Ext corridors. **Pets:** Large. $25 deposit/room, $10 daily fee/room. Designated rooms, service with restrictions, crate.
(SAVE) (SD) (X) (🛏) (▣) (≈)

ORLANDO METROPOLITAN AREA

ALTAMONTE SPRINGS

▼◆◆◆ Candlewood Suites SH
(407) 767-5757. **$79-$109.** 644 Raymond Ave. I-4, exit 92, just w to Douglas Ave, 0.8 mi n to Central Pkwy, then just e. Int corridors. **Pets:** Accepted.
(ASK) (SD) (X) (🛦) (Ⓐ) (Ⓐ) (🛏) (▣) (≈)

◆◆◆ ▼◆◆◆ Days Inn SH
(407) 788-1411. **$50-$150, 3 day notice.** 150 S Westmonte Dr. I-4, exit 92, 0.3 mi w, then just s of SR 436. Ext corridors. **Pets:** Other species. $10 daily fee/pet. Designated rooms, crate.
(SAVE) (SD) (X) (Ⓐ) (Ⓐ) (🛏) (▣) (≈)

◆◆◆ ▼◆◆◆ Embassy Suites Orlando North SH
(407) 834-2400. **$120-$229.** 225 E Altamonte Dr. I-4, exit 92, 0.3 mi e on SR 436, then just n on North Lake Blvd. Int corridors. **Pets:** Other species. $20 daily fee/pet. No service.
(SAVE) (X) (🛦) (Ⓐ) (Ⓐ) (🛏) (▣) (🍴) (≈) (X)

▼◆◆◆ Hampton Inn SH
(407) 869-9000. **$69-$95.** 151 N Douglas Ave. I-4, exit 92, just nw. Ext corridors. **Pets:** Medium, other species. $60 one-time fee/room. Service with restrictions.
(ASK) (SD) (X) (🛦) (Ⓐ) (Ⓐ) (🛏) (▣) (≈)

◆◆◆ ▼◆◆◆ Holiday Inn Orlando North/Altamonte
Springs SH
(407) 862-4455. **$85-$288.** 230 W SR 436. I-4, exit 92, just sw. Ext/int corridors. **Pets:** Accepted.
(SAVE) (SD) (X) (🛦) (Ⓐ) (Ⓐ) (🛏) (▣) (🍴) (≈)

▼◆◆◆ Homestead Studio Suites Hotel-Orlando/Altamonte
Springs SH
(407) 332-9300. **$59-$74.** 302 S North Lake Blvd. I-4, exit 92, just e, then 0.3 mi s. Int corridors. **Pets:** Accepted.
(ASK) (SD) (X) (🛦) (Ⓐ) (Ⓐ) (🛏) (▣)

▼◆◆◆ Residence Inn by Marriott SH ❀
(407) 788-7991. **$79-$229.** 270 Douglas Ave. I-4, exit 92, just w on SR 436, then just n. Ext corridors. **Pets:** Small. $75 one-time fee/room. Service with restrictions, crate.
(ASK) (SD) (X) (🛦) (Ⓐ) (Ⓐ) (🛏) (▣) (≈) (X)

CLERMONT

▼◆◆◆ Highlands Reserve-Superior Resorts VH
(863) 424-8411. **Call for rates.** 9230 US Hwy 192. On US 192, 1 mi e of US 27. Ext corridors. **Pets:** Accepted.
(🛏) (▣) (≈) (X)

DAVENPORT

◆◆◆ ▼◆◆◆ Best Western Central Florida SH
(863) 424-2596. **$79-$95.** 2425 Frontage Rd. I-4, exit 55, just s on US 27. Ext corridors. **Pets:** Small. $10 daily fee/room. Service with restrictions, crate.
(SAVE) (SD) (X) (🛦) (Ⓐ) (🛏) (▣) (≈)

▼◆◆◆ Calabay Parc-The Florida Store VH
(407) 846-1722. **$110-$215, 30 day notice.** 3479 W Vine St. I-4, exit 68, 3.5 mi s on SR 535, then 3.8 mi e on US 192. Ext corridors. **Pets:** Accepted.
(ASK) (SD) (X) (🛏) (▣) (≈)

▼▼▼▼ **Hampton Inn Orlando-S of Walt Disney Resort** 🆂🅷
(863) 420-9898. **$79-$120.** 44117 Hwy 27. I-4, exit 55, just nw. Int corridors. **Pets:** Medium, other species. $20 daily fee/room. Designated rooms, service with restrictions, crate.
(A$K) 🆂🔊 ✕ 🕭M 🖉 🕸 🖥 💻 ⌇

▼▼ ▼▼ **Royal Palms Inn and Suites** 🆂🅷
(863) 424-2811. **$39-$69.** 44089 US 27. I-4, exit 55, just w. Ext corridors. **Pets:** Accepted.
(A$K) 🆂🔊 ✕ 🖉 🖥 💻 ⌇

▼▼▼▼ **Southern Dunes-The Florida Store** 🆅🅷
(407) 846-1722. **$115-$215, 30 day notice.** 3479 W Vine St. I-4, exit 68, 3.5 mi s on SR 535, then 3.8 mi e on US 192. Ext corridors. **Pets:** Accepted.
(A$K) 🆂🔊 ✕ 🖥 💻 🍴 ⌇ 🗙

▼▼ ▼▼ **Super 8 Motel Maingate South** 🆂🅷
(863) 420-8888. **$39-$120.** 44199 Hwy 27. I-4, exit 55, 0.5 mi n. Ext corridors. **Pets:** Medium, other species. $10 daily fee/room. Designated rooms, service with restrictions.
(A$K) 🆂🔊 ✕ 🖉 🕸 🖥 💻 ⌇

KISSIMMEE

🅐🅐🅐 ▼▼▼▼ **AmeriSuites (Orlando/Lake Buena Vista South)** 🆂🅷
(407) 997-1300. **$79-$169.** 4991 Calypso Cay Way. I-4, exit 68, 3 mi s on SR 535. Int corridors. **Pets:** Accepted.
(SAVE) 🆂🔊 ✕ 🕭M 🖉 🕸 🖥 💻 ⌇ 🗙

🅐🅐🅐 ▼▼▼ **Best Western Maingate East Hotel & Suites** 🆂🅷
(407) 870-2000. **$52-$149.** 4018 W Vine St. I-4, exit 64A, 7 mi e on US 192. Ext corridors. **Pets:** Accepted.
(SAVE) 🆂🔊 ✕ 🖉 🖥 💻 🍴 ⌇ 🗙

▼▼▼▼ **Clear Creek-The Florida Store** 🆅🅷
(407) 846-1722. **$110-$215, 30 day notice.** 3479 W Vine St. I-4, exit 68, 3.5 mi s on SR 535, then 3.8 mi e on US 192. Ext corridors. **Pets:** Accepted.
(A$K) 🆂🔊 ✕ 🖥 💻 ⌇

🅐🅐🅐 ▼▼▼▼ **Country Inn & Suites** 🆂🅷
(407) 997-1400. **$69-$149.** 5001 Calypso Cay Way. I-4, exit 68, 3 mi s on SR 535, just s of Osceola Pkwy, then just n of US 192. Int corridors. **Pets:** Accepted.
(SAVE) 🆂🔊 ✕ 🕭M 🖉 🕸 🖥 💻 ⌇ 🗙

▼▼▼▼ **Days Inn-Kissimmee** 🆂🅷
(407) 846-7136. **$40-$100, 3 day notice.** 2095 E Irlo Bronson Memorial Hwy. Florida Tpke, exit 244, 0.8 mi w on US 192. Ext corridors. **Pets:** Accepted.
(A$K) 🆂🔊 ✕ 🖥 🍴 ⌇

🅐🅐🅐 ▼▼ ▼▼ **Days Inn Maingate East** 🆂🅷
(407) 396-7969. **$39-$109, 3 day notice.** 5840 W Irlo Bronson Memorial Hwy. I-4, exit 64A, 1 mi e on US 192. **Pets:** Medium, other species. $10 daily fee/pet. Designated rooms, service with restrictions.
(SAVE) 🆂🔊 ✕ 🖉 🕸 🍴 ⌇

▼▼ ▼▼ **Eastgate Inn** 🆂🅷
(407) 396-0707. **$42-$138.** 5565 W Irlo Bronson Memorial Hwy. I-4, exit 64A, 2 mi e on US 192. Ext corridors. **Pets:** Accepted.
(A$K) 🆂🔊 ✕ 🖉 🖥 💻 🍴 ⌇ 🗙

🅐🅐🅐 ▼▼ ▼▼ **Econo Lodge Maingate Resort** 🆂🅷
(407) 396-2000. **$30-$54.** 7514 W Hwy 192. I-4, exit 64B, 2.4 mi w, 1 mi w of Disney World main gate. Ext corridors. **Pets:** Accepted.
(SAVE) 🆂🔊 ✕ 🖉 🕸 🖥 💻 🍴 ⌇ 🗙

🅐🅐🅐 ▼▼▼▼ **Fantasy World Club Villas** 🅒🅞
(407) 396-1808. **$99-$195.** 5005 Kyngs Heath Rd. I-4, exit 64A, 3.5 mi e on US 192 and just n; at MM 11. Ext corridors. **Pets:** Small, dogs only. $30 daily fee/pet. Designated rooms, service with restrictions, crate.
(SAVE) 🆂🔊 ✕ 🖥 💻 ⌇ 🗙

🅐🅐🅐 ▼▼▼ **Flamingo Inn** 🅼
(407) 846-1935. **$27-$37, 3 day notice.** 801 E Vine St. 0.3 mi e of jct US 441 and 192 on US 192. Ext corridors. **Pets:** Small, dogs only. $8 daily fee/pet. No service.
(SAVE) 🆂🔊 ✕ 🖉 🕸 🖥 ⌇

▼▼▼▼ **Florida Pines-The Florida Store** 🆅🅷
(407) 846-1722. **$115-$215, 30 day notice.** 3479 W Vine St. I-4, exit 68, 3.5 mi s on SR 535, then 3.8 mi e on US 192. Ext corridors. **Pets:** Accepted.
(A$K) 🆂🔊 ✕ 🖥 💻 ⌇

🅐🅐🅐 ▼▼▼▼ **Hampton Lakes-The Florida Store** 🆅🅷
(407) 846-1722. **$105-$215, 30 day notice.** 3479 W Vine St. I-4, exit 68, 3.5 mi s on SR 535, then 3.8 mi e on US 192. Ext corridors. **Pets:** Accepted.
(SAVE) 🆂🔊 ✕ 🖥 💻 ⌇

🅐🅐🅐 ▼▼▼▼ **Holiday Inn Maingate West** 🆂🅷
(407) 396-1100. **$45-$119.** 7601 Black Lake Rd. I-4, exit 64B, 2.9 mi w on US 192, then just n; 1 mi w of Disney World main gate access road. Ext corridors. **Pets:** Accepted.
(SAVE) 🆂🔊 ✕ 🖉 🕸 🖥 💻 🍴 ⌇ 🗙

🅐🅐🅐 ▼▼▼▼ **Homewood Suites by Hilton** 🆂🅷
(407) 396-2229. **$69-$129.** 3100 Parkway Blvd. I-4, exit 64A, 0.3 mi e on US 192, then 0.5 mi n. Ext/int corridors. **Pets:** Accepted.
(SAVE) 🆂🔊 ✕ 🖉 🖥 💻 ⌇ 🗙

🅐🅐🅐 ▼▼ ▼▼ **Howard Johnson Express Inn Parkside** 🆂🅷
(407) 396-7100. **$40-$70, 7 day notice.** 4311 W Vine St/W Hwy 192. I-4, exit 64A, 3.5 mi w of jct US 17-92 and 441. Ext corridors. **Pets:** Other species. $10 daily fee/pet. Designated rooms, service with restrictions, supervision.
(SAVE) 🆂🔊 ✕ 🖥 💻 ⌇

▼▼ ▼▼ **Howard Johnson Hotel** 🆂🅷
(407) 846-4900. **$40-$50.** 2323 E Irlo Bronson Memorial Hwy. US 192 and 441; Florida Tpke, exit 244, just e. Int corridors. **Pets:** Accepted.
(A$K) 🆂🔊 ✕ 🖉 🕸 🖥 💻 🍴 ⌇

🅐🅐🅐 ▼▼ ▼▼ **Howard Johnson Maingate Resort West** 🆂🅷
(407) 396-4500. **$39-$99.** 8660 W Irlo Bronson Memorial Hwy. I-4, exit 64B, 5.6 mi w on SR 192. Ext corridors. **Pets:** Accepted.
(SAVE) 🆂🔊 ✕ 🖉 🕸 🖥 💻 🍴 ⌇ 🗙

▼▼▼▼ **Indian Creek-Absolute Premier Vacation Homes** 🆅🅷
(407) 396-2401. **$111-$249, 31 day notice.** 3160 Vineland Rd, Suite 1. I-4, exit 68, 2.5 mi e on SR 535 (Apopka-Vineland Rd). Ext corridors. **Pets:** Accepted.
(A$K) ✕ 🖉 🖥 💻 ⌇

▼▼▼▼ **Indian Creek-The Florida Store** 🆅🅷
(407) 846-1722. **$110-$215, 30 day notice.** 3479 W Vine St. I-4, exit 68, 3.5 mi s on SR 535, then 3.8 mi e on US 192; behind the SunTrust Bank. Ext corridors. **Pets:** Accepted.
(A$K) 🆂🔊 ✕ 🖥 💻 ⌇

▼▼▼▼ **Indian Point-Absolute Premier Vacation Homes** 🆅🅷
(407) 396-2401. **$111-$249, 31 day notice.** 3160 Vineland Rd, Suite 1. I-4, exit 68, 2.5 mi e on SR 535 (Apopka-Vineland Rd). Ext corridors. **Pets:** Accepted.
(A$K) ✕ 🖥 💻 ⌇

▼▼▼ Indian Ridge Oaks-Absolute Premier Vacation Homes VH
(407) 396-2401. **$111-$249, 31 day notice.** 3160 Vineland Rd, Suite 1. I-4, exit 68, 2.5 mi e on SR 535 (Apopka-Vineland Rd). Ext corridors. **Pets:** Accepted.
ASK ✕ 🖥 🖵 🏊

△△△ ▼▼▼ La Quinta Inn & Suites Kissimmee (Orlando Maingate) SH
(407) 997-1700. **$59-$139.** 3484 Polynesian Isle Blvd. I-4, exit 68, s on SR 535, then just e. Int corridors. **Pets:** Accepted.
SAVE S🐾 ✕ 🕐 🖥 🖵 🏊 ✕

△△△ ▼▼▼ La Quinta Inn Lakeside LH
(407) 396-2222. **$59-$129.** 7769 W Irlo Bronson Memorial Hwy. I-4, exit 64B westbound on US 192; exit 64A eastbound, 3 mi w; 1.8 mi w of Disney World main gate. Ext corridors. **Pets:** Accepted.
SAVE S🐾 ✕ 🕐M 🕐 🕹 🖥 🖵 🍴 🏊 ✕

△△△ ▼▼▼ MainStay Suites Maingate SH 🐾
(407) 396-2056. **$79-$189.** 4786 W Irlo Bronson Memorial Hwy. I-4, exit 64A, 4 mi e on US 192; 4.8 mi w of jct US 17-92 and 441. Ext corridors. **Pets:** Medium, other species. $10 daily fee/room. Service with restrictions.
SAVE S🐾 ✕ 🕐 🖥 🖵 🏊 ✕

△△△ ▼▼▼ Masters Inn-Kissimmee M
(407) 396-4020. **$37-$69, 3 day notice.** 5367 W Irlo Bronson Memorial Hwy. I-4, exit 25, 2.5 mi e on US 192. Ext corridors. **Pets:** Accepted.
SAVE S🐾 ✕ 🕐 🖥 🏊

△△△ ▼▼▼ Masters Inn-Main Gate SH
(407) 396-7743. **$39-$99, 3 day notice.** 2945 Entry Point Blvd. I-4, exit 25, 2.5 mi w on US 192; 1 mi w of Disney World main gate. Ext corridors. **Pets:** Accepted.
SAVE S🐾 ✕ 🕐 🖥 🏊

▼▼ Motel 6–#0436 SH
(407) 396-6422. **$35-$65.** 7455 W Irlo Bronson Memorial Hwy. I-4, exit 64B, 1.3 mi w on US 192. Ext corridors. **Pets:** Accepted.
S🐾 ✕ 🕐 🕹 🏊

▼ Motel 6–#0464 M
(407) 396-6333. **$35-$65.** 5731 W Hwy 192. I-4, exit 64A, 2 mi e. Ext corridors. **Pets:** Small. Service with restrictions, supervision.
S🐾 ✕ 🕐M 🕐 🕹 🖥 🏊

△△△ ▼▼▼ Park Inn & Suites Orlando Maingate East SH
(407) 396-6100. **$39-$89, 3 day notice.** 6075 W Irlo Bronson Memorial Hwy. I-4, exit 64A, 1 mi e on US 192; between MM 8 and 9. Ext corridors. **Pets:** Accepted.
SAVE S🐾 ✕ 🕐 🕹 🖥 🖵 🍴 🏊 ✕

△△△ ▼▼▼ Ramada Inn Resort Eastgate SH 🐾
(407) 396-1111. **$49-$129.** 5150 W Irlo Bronson Memorial Hwy. I-4, exit 64A, 2.8 mi e on US 192. Int corridors. **Pets:** Medium. $10 daily fee/pet. Service with restrictions, supervision.
SAVE S🐾 ✕ 🕐 🕹 🖥 🖵 🍴 🏊 ✕

△△△ ▼▼▼ Ramada Plaza Hotel and Inn Gateway LH
(407) 396-4400. **$59-$129, 3 day notice.** 7470 W Irlo Bronson Memorial Hwy. I-4, exit 64B, 2.3 mi w on US 192; 1 mi w of Disney World main gate. Ext/int corridors. **Pets:** Accepted.
SAVE S🐾 ✕ 🕐 🕹 🖥 🖵 🍴 🏊 ✕

△△△ ▼▼▼ Red Roof Inn M
(407) 396-0065. **$40-$63.** 4970 Kyngs Heath Rd. I-4, exit 64A, 3.6 mi e on US 192; jct SR 535. Ext corridors. **Pets:** Accepted.
SAVE ✕ 🖥 🏊

△△△ ▼▼▼ Rodeway Inn Maingate SH
(407) 396-4300. **$35-$90.** 5995 W Irlo Bronson Memorial Hwy. I-4, exit 64A, 1 mi e. Ext corridors. **Pets:** Accepted.
SAVE S🐾 ✕ 🕐 🖥 🖵 🏊

▼▼▼ Summerfield Condo Resort CO
(407) 847-7222. **$99-$159, 14 day notice.** 2422 Summerfield Way. SR 423 (John Young Pkwy), 0.8 mi n of US 192; Florida Tpke, exit 249, 2.5 mi w, then 1.7 mi s. Ext corridors. **Pets:** Accepted.
✕ 🕐 🖥 🖵 🏊 ✕

▼▼▼ Sunset Lakes-Absolute Premier Vacation Homes VH
(407) 396-2401. **$111-$249, 31 day notice.** 3160 Vineland Rd, Suite 1. I-4, exit 68, 2.5 mi e on SR 535 (Apopka-Vineland Rd). Ext corridors. **Pets:** Accepted.
ASK ✕ 🖥 🖵 🏊

△△△ ▼▼ Super 8 Motel Maingate SH
(407) 396-8883. **$40-$70.** 5875 W Irlo Bronson Hwy. I-4, exit 64A, 1.5 mi e on US 192. Ext corridors. **Pets:** Accepted.
SAVE S🐾 ✕ 🕐 🖥 🏊

▼▼▼ The Tradition Hotel & Suites Main Gate East SH
(407) 396-4488. **$59-$129.** 5678 W Irlo Bronson Memorial Hwy. I-4, exit 64A; between MM 9 and 10. Ext corridors. **Pets:** Accepted.
ASK S🐾 ✕ 🕐M 🕐 🕹 🖥 🖵 🍴 🏊 ✕

△△△ ▼▼ Travelodge SH
(407) 846-2221. **$44-$79.** 2261 E Irlo Bronson Memorial Hwy. US 192 and 441 at Florida Tpke, exit 244. Ext corridors. **Pets:** Accepted.
SAVE S🐾 ✕ 🕐 🖥 🖵 🍴 🏊 ✕

△△△ ▼▼ Travelodge Hotel Maingate East SH 🐾
(407) 396-4222. **$49-$129.** 5711 W Irlo Bronson Memorial Hwy. I-4, exit 64A, 2 mi e on US 192. Int corridors. **Pets:** Medium. $25 one-time fee/pet. Service with restrictions, supervision.
SAVE S🐾 ✕ 🕐 🖥 🖵 🍴 🏊 ✕

LADY LAKE

▼▼▼ Holiday Inn Express Hotel & Suites SH
(352) 750-3888. **$92-$97.** 1205 Avenida Central N. Just n on US 441. Int corridors. **Pets:** Small. $35 one-time fee/pet. Designated rooms, service with restrictions, supervision.
ASK S🐾 ✕ 🖥 🖵 🏊

▼▼▼ Microtel Inn & Suites SH 🐾
(352) 259-0184. **$49-$94.** 850 US 27/441. 1 mi s. Int corridors. **Pets:** Small. $25 one-time fee/pet. Designated rooms, service with restrictions, supervision.
ASK ✕ 🖥 🖵 🏊

LAKE BUENA VISTA

▼▼▼ Comfort Inn Lake Buena Vista SH
(407) 996-7300. **$49-$89.** 8442 Palm Pkwy. I-4, exit 68, 0.6 mi n on SR 535, then 0.5 mi e. Ext corridors. **Pets:** Medium, other species. $50 deposit/room, $10 daily fee/room. Service with restrictions.
ASK S🐾 ✕ 🕐M 🕐 🕹 🖥 🖵 🍴 🏊

△△△ ▼▼▼ Days Inn Lake Buena Vista Hotel SH
(407) 239-4441. **$65-$129.** 12799 Apopka-Vineland Rd. I-4, exit 68, just n. Int corridors. **Pets:** Small. $10 daily fee/pet. Designated rooms, no service, supervision.
SAVE S🐾 ✕ 🕐 🕹 🖥 🖵 🏊

▼▼▼ Embassy Suites Hotel-Lake Buena Vista Resort SH 🐾
(407) 239-1144. **$109-$229, 3 day notice.** 8100 Lake Ave. I-4, exit 68, 0.6 mi n on SR 535, 1 mi e on Palm Pkwy, then just se. Ext/int corridors. **Pets:** Small, dogs only. $25 daily fee/room. Designated rooms, service with restrictions.
ASK S🐾 ✕ 🕐M 🕐 🕹 🖥 🖵 🍴 🏊 ✕

Holiday Inn-SunSpree Resort-Lake Buena Vista LH
(407) 239-4500. **$89-$139.** 13351 SR 535. I-4, exit 68, 0.3 mi se. Ext corridors. **Pets:** Small. $25 one-time fee/pet. Service with restrictions, supervision.

Marriott Residence Inn Lake Buena Vista North SH
(407) 465-0075. **Call for rates.** 11450 Marbella Palms Ct. I-4, exit 68, 0.6 mi n on SR 535, then 0.5 mi e on Palm Pkwy. Int corridors. **Pets:** Accepted.

Sheraton Safari Hotel SH
(407) 239-0444. **$109-$209, 3 day notice.** 12205 Apopka-Vineland Rd. I-4, exit 68, 0.5 mi n on SR 535. Ext/int corridors. **Pets:** Accepted.

LAKE MARY

Candlewood Suites Lake Mary-Heathrow SH
(407) 585-3000. **$89.** 1130 Greenwood Blvd. I-4, exit 98, just e to Lake Emma Rd, 0.5 mi s to Greenwood Blvd, then 0.6 mi w. Int corridors. **Pets:** Large, other species. $75 one-time fee/room. Service with restrictions.

Homestead Studio Suites Hotel-Orlando/Lake Mary SH
(407) 829-2332. **$69-$79.** 1040 Greenwood Blvd. I-4, exit 98, 0.5 mi s on Lake Emma Rd; in Commerce Park. Int corridors. **Pets:** Accepted.

La Quinta Inn & Suites Orlando (Lake Mary) SH
(407) 805-9901. **$75-$115.** 1060 Greenwood Blvd. I-4, exit 98, just se via Lake Mary Blvd. Int corridors. **Pets:** Accepted.

LEESBURG

Super 8 Motel M
(352) 787-6363. **$45-$99.** 1392 North Blvd W. Jct US 27 and 441. Int corridors. **Pets:** Large, other species. $10 daily fee/pet. Service with restrictions, supervision.

LONGWOOD

Comfort Inn & Conference Center SH
(407) 862-4000. **$79-$89, 3 day notice.** 2025 W SR 434. I-4, exit 94, just nw. Ext corridors. **Pets:** Accepted.

MAITLAND

Homewood Suites Orlando North SH ❀
(407) 875-8777. **$129-$143.** 290 Southhall Ln. I-4, exit 90, just w, then just s on Lake Destiny. Int corridors. **Pets:** Other species. $75 one-time fee/room. Service with restrictions, crate.

Hotel Orlando North SH
(407) 660-9000. **$59-$285.** 600 N Lake Destiny Dr. I-4, exit 90, just w on SR 414 (Maitland Blvd). Int corridors. **Pets:** Medium. $50 one-time fee/pet. Designated rooms, service with restrictions, supervision.

MOUNT DORA

The Lakeside Inn SH
(352) 383-4101. **$169.** 100 N Alexander St. Just s from downtown. Int corridors. **Pets:** Accepted.

OCOEE

Best Western Turnpike West-Orlando SH
(407) 656-5050. **$79-$89.** 10945 W Colonial Dr. I-4, exit 84, 10 mi w on SR 50; 0.5 mi e of Florida Tpke, exit 267B. Ext corridors. **Pets:** Accepted.

Red Roof Inn Orlando West SH
(407) 347-0140. **$65-$97.** 11241 W Colonial Dr. I-4, exit 84, 10 mi w on SR 50; 0.6 mi e of Florida Tpke, exit 267. Int corridors. **Pets:** Accepted.

ORLANDO

AmeriSuites (Orlando Airport/Northeast) SH
(407) 240-3939. **$79-$129.** 7500 Augusta National Dr. SR 528 (Bee Line Expwy), exit 11, 0.5 mi n on SR 436, just e on TG Lee Blvd, then just s. Int corridors. **Pets:** Accepted.

AmeriSuites (Orlando Airport/Northwest) SH
(407) 816-7800. **$79-$149.** 5435 Forbes Pl. SR 528 (Bee Line Expwy), exit 11, 0.5 mi n on SR 436, then just w. Int corridors. **Pets:** Medium. $10 daily fee/pet. Designated rooms, service with restrictions, supervision.

AmeriSuites (Orlando/Convention Center) SH
(407) 370-4720. **$99-$149.** 8741 International Dr. I-4, exit 74A, just e, then 0.7 mi s of SR 482 (Sand Lake Rd). Int corridors. **Pets:** Accepted.

AmeriSuites (Orlando/Universal) SH
(407) 351-0627. **$89-$139.** 5895 Caravan Ct. I-4, exit 75B, 0.6 mi ne. Int corridors. **Pets:** Small. $10 daily fee/room. Service with restrictions, supervision.

Baymont Inn & Suites Orlando South SH
(407) 240-0500. **$65-$85.** 2051 Consulate Dr. US 17-92 and 441, just s of SR 528 (Bee Line Expwy); off Florida Tpke, exit 254. Int corridors. **Pets:** Accepted.

Best Western Orlando West SH
(407) 841-8600. **$59-$125.** 2014 W Colonial Dr. I-4, exit 84, 1.5 mi w on SR 50; 0.4 mi e of SR 423. Int corridors. **Pets:** Accepted.

Comfort Inn-North SH
(407) 629-4000. **$63-$68.** 830 Lee Rd. I-4, exit 88, 0.4 mi w on SR 423. Int corridors. **Pets:** Very small. $10 daily fee/pet, $25 one-time fee/pet. Designated rooms, service with restrictions, crate.

Comfort Suites Orlando SH ❀
(407) 351-5050. **$59-$99.** 9350 Turkey Lake Rd. I-4, exit 74A, just w on SR 482 (Sand Lake Rd), then 1.5 mi s. Ext corridors. **Pets:** Other species. $10 daily fee/room. Service with restrictions, crate.

Crestwood Suites-UCF SH
(407) 249-0044. **Call for rates.** 11424 University Blvd. 2 mi e of SR 417. Int corridors. **Pets:** Accepted.

Days Inn Maingate To Universal SH
(407) 351-3800. **$39-$99, 3 day notice.** 5827 Caravan Ct. I-4, exit 75B, 0.5 mi n on SR 435 (Kirkman Rd), then just e. Ext corridors. **Pets:** Accepted.

Days Inn North of Universal SH
(407) 841-3731. **$49-$69.** 2500 W 33rd St. I-4, exit 79, just e. Ext corridors. **Pets:** Accepted.

Hard Rock Hotel at Universal Orlando LH ❀
(407) 503-2000. **$229-$409, 5 day notice.** 5800 Universal Blvd. I-4, exit 75A. Int corridors. **Pets:** Other species. $50 deposit/room. Designated rooms.

Hawthorn Suites Orlando Airport SH ❀
(407) 438-2121. **$79-$119.** 7450 Augusta National Dr. SR 528 (Bee Line Expwy), exit 11, 0.5 mi n on SR 436, just e, then just s. Int corridors. **Pets:** Medium, dogs only. $20 daily fee/room. Designated rooms, service with restrictions, crate.

Holiday Inn & Suites At Universal Orlando SH
(407) 351-3333. **$99-$169, 3 day notice.** 5905 S Kirkman Rd. I-4, exit 75B, 0.5 mi n on SR 435 (Kirkman Rd). Int corridors. **Pets:** Other species. $50 one-time fee/pet. Service with restrictions, crate.

Holiday Inn Express International Drive M
(407) 351-4430. **$69-$109.** 6323 International Dr. I-4, exit 74A, just e on SR 482 (Sand Lake Rd), then 0.7 mi n. Int corridors. **Pets:** Accepted.

Holiday Inn-International Drive Resort SH
(407) 351-3500. **$119-$139.** 6515 International Dr. I-4, exit 74A, just e on SR 482 (Sand Lake Rd), then 0.5 mi n. Ext/int corridors. **Pets:** Other species. $100 deposit/pet, $25 one-time fee/pet. Service with restrictions, crate.

Homestead Studio Suites Hotel-Orlando/South SH
(407) 352-5577. **$64-$74.** 4101 Equity Row. Just sw of jct SR 423 (John Young Pkwy) and 482 (Sand Lake Rd). Int corridors. **Pets:** Large, other species. $75 deposit/room. Service with restrictions, supervision.

Howard Johnson Inn-International Drive SH ❀
(407) 351-2900. **$80-$125.** 6603 International Dr. I-4, exit 74A, just e on SR 482 (Sand Lake Rd), then 0.4 mi n. Ext corridors. **Pets:** Small, dogs only. $25 daily fee/pet. Designated rooms, no service, supervision.

Howard Johnson Plaza Resort Universal Gateway SH
(407) 351-2000. **$39-$149.** 7050 S Kirkman Rd. I-4, exit 75A, 0.8 mi s on SR 435 (Kirkman Rd). Int corridors. **Pets:** Small, other species. $10 daily fee/pet. Service with restrictions.

La Quinta Inn & Suites Orlando (Airport North) SH
(407) 240-5000. **$71-$101.** 7160 N Frontage Rd. SR 528 (Bee Line Expwy), exit 11, 0.5 mi n on SR 436, just w. Int corridors. **Pets:** Small. Service with restrictions, supervision.

La Quinta Inn & Suites Orlando (Convention Center) SH
(407) 345-1365. **$65-$115.** 8504 Universal Blvd. I-4, exit 74A, 0.5 mi e on SR 482 (Sand Lake Rd), then 0.5 mi s. Int corridors. **Pets:** Other species. Service with restrictions, supervision.

La Quinta Inn & Suites Orlando (U.C.F.) SH
(407) 737-6075. **$69-$104.** 11805 Research Pkwy. Just se of jct University Blvd and SR 434 (Alafaya Tr). Int corridors. **Pets:** Accepted.

La Quinta Inn Orlando (Airport West) SH
(407) 857-9215. **$65-$85.** 7931 Daetwyler Dr. SR 528 (Bee Line Expwy), exit 9 (Tradeport), via McCoy Rd. Ext corridors. **Pets:** Accepted.

La Quinta Inn Orlando (International Drive) SH
(407) 351-1660. **$75-$105.** 8300 Jamaican Ct. I-4, exit 74A, just e on SR 482 (Sand Lake Rd), then just s on International Dr. Ext corridors. **Pets:** Accepted.

La Quinta Inn Orlando-Winter Park SH
(407) 645-5600. **$70-$90.** 626 Lee Rd. I-4, exit 88 (Lee Rd), just w on SR 438. Int corridors. **Pets:** Medium. Designated rooms, service with restrictions, supervision.

Masters Inn International Drive SH
(407) 345-1172. **$39-$89, 3 day notice.** 8222 Jamaican Ct. I-4, exit 74A, e on SR 482 (Sand Lake Rd), then just s on International Dr. Ext corridors. **Pets:** Accepted.

Motel 6 Orlando-International Drive #1079 SH
(407) 351-6500. **$43-$57.** 5909 American Way. I-4, exit 75A, just w of SR 435, then just n. Int corridors. **Pets:** Accepted.

Motel 6 Orlando-Winter Park #791 M
(407) 647-1444. **$43-$55.** 5300 Adanson Rd. I-4, exit 88, 0.5 mi w on SR 423 (Lee Rd). Ext corridors. **Pets:** Accepted.

Quality Inn International SH
(407) 996-1600. **$49-$89.** 7600 International Dr. I-4, exit 74A, just e on SR 482 (Sand Lake Rd), then just n. Ext corridors. **Pets:** Medium, other species. $10 daily fee/pet. Service with restrictions, supervision.

Quality Inn Plaza SH ❀
(407) 996-8585. **$49-$89.** 9000 International Dr. I-4, exit 74A, just e on SR 482 (Sand Lake Rd), then 1 mi s. Ext corridors. **Pets:** Medium, other species. $50 deposit/pet, $10 daily fee/pet. Service with restrictions, crate.

Ramada Inn at International Drive SH
(407) 351-4410. **$69-$89.** 5858 International Dr. I-4, exit 75A, just s on (SR 435) (Kirkman Rd), then just w. Ext corridors. **Pets:** Accepted.

Red Horse Inn SH
(407) 351-4100. **$69-$99, 3 day notice.** 5825 International Dr. I-4, exit 75A, just w. Ext corridors. **Pets:** Small. $10 daily fee/pet. Service with restrictions, crate.

Red Roof Inn Convention Center SH
(407) 352-1507. **$40-$100.** 9922 Hawaiian Ct. I-4, exit 72, 0.9 mi e on SR 528 (Bee Line Expwy) to exit 1, then just n. Ext corridors. **Pets:** Accepted.

Red Roof Inn Universal Studios SH
(407) 313-3100. **$59-$79.** 5621 Major Blvd. I-4, exit 75B, just n, then just e. Int corridors. **Pets:** Accepted.

▼▼▼ **Residence Inn by Marriott Orlando Convention Center** 🅂🄷
(407) 226-0288. **$89-$189.** 8800 Universal Blvd. I-4, exit 74A, 0.5 mi e on SR 482 (Sand Lake Rd), then 0.8 mi s. Int corridors. **Pets:** Accepted.
(ASK) 🔊 ✕ 🔌 📺 🛎 💻 ➳ ✕

▼▼▼ **Residence Inn by Marriott/Orlando East** 🅂🄷 ❀
(407) 513-9000. **$139-$169.** 11651 University Blvd. 2.2 mi e of SR 417 on University Blvd, just w of SR 434 (Alafaya Tr). Int corridors. **Pets:** Large, other species. $125 one-time fee/room. Service with restrictions.
(ASK) 🔊 ✕ 🔌 📺 🛎 💻 ➳ ✕

🄰🄰🄰 ▼▼▼ **Residence Inn by Marriott-Orlando International Dr** 🅂🄷
(407) 345-0117. **$79-$159.** 7975 Canada Ave. I-4, exit 74A, just e on SR 482 (Sand Lake Rd). Ext corridors. **Pets:** Accepted.
(SAVE) ✕ 🔌 📺 🛎 💻 ➳ ✕

▼▼▼ **Residence Inn by Marriott SeaWorld International Center** 🅂🄷
(407) 313-3600. **$82-$164.** 11000 Westwood Blvd. I-4, exit 72. Int corridors. **Pets:** Medium, other species. $150 one-time fee/room. Service with restrictions, supervision.
(ASK) 🔊 ✕ 🔌 📺 🛎 💻 🍴 ➳ ✕

▼▼ **Rodeway Inn International** 🅂🄷
(407) 996-4444. **$46-$69.** 6327 International Dr. I-4, exit 74A, just e on SR 482 (Sand Lake Rd), then 0.7 mi n. Ext/int corridors. **Pets:** Medium. $10 daily fee/pet. Designated rooms, service with restrictions, crate.
(ASK) 🔊 ✕ 🔌 📺 🛎 💻 🍴 ➳

🄰🄰🄰 ▼▼▼ **Sheraton Suites Orlando Airport** 🅂🄷 ❀
(407) 240-5555. **$99-$159.** 7550 Augusta National Dr. 2 mi n of airport terminal via SR 436 and TG Lee Blvd. Int corridors. **Pets:** Medium, dogs only. $150 deposit/room, $25 one-time fee/pet. Designated rooms, service with restrictions, supervision.
(SAVE) 🔊 ✕ 🔌 📺 🛎 💻 🍴 ➳

▼▼▼ **Sheraton World Resort** 🄻🄷
(407) 352-1100. **$289-$309, 3 day notice.** 10100 International Dr. I-4, exit 72, just s on International Dr; SR 528 (Bee Line Expwy), exit 1, just e. Ext/int corridors. **Pets:** Accepted.
(ASK) 🔊 ✕ 🔌 📺 🛎 💻 🍴 ➳ ✕

▼▼▼ **TownePlace Suites by Marriott Orlando East/UCF** 🅂🄷
(407) 243-6100. **$109-$139.** 11801 High Tech Ave. 2.2 mi e of SR 417 on University Blvd. Int corridors. **Pets:** Other species. $75 one-time fee/room. Service with restrictions.
(ASK) 🔊 ✕ 🔌 📺 🛎 💻 ➳

🄰🄰🄰 ▼▼▼ **Universal's Portofino Bay Hotel a Loews Hotel** 🄻🄷 ❀
(407) 503-1000. **$259-$429, 5 day notice.** 5601 Universal Blvd. I-4, exit 74B westbound; exit 75A eastbound, 1 mi n, follow signs. Int corridors. **Pets:** Other species. $50 deposit/room.
(SAVE) ✕ 🔌 📺 🛎 💻 ➳ ✕

🄰🄰🄰 ▼▼▼ **Universal's Royal Pacific Resort** 🄻🄷 ❀
(407) 503-3000. **$199-$369, 5 day notice.** 6300 Hollywood Way. I-4, exit 74B, just n. Int corridors. **Pets:** Other species. $50 deposit/room. Designated rooms.
(SAVE) ✕ 🔌 📺 🛎 💻 🍴 ➳ ✕

▼▼▼ **Ventura Resort Rentals-Kissimmee** 🅅🄷
(407) 273-8770. **$72-$165, 15 day notice.** 5946 Curry Ford Rd. 0.6 mi e of SR 436. Ext corridors. **Pets:** Accepted.
(ASK) 🔊 🔌 🛎 💻 ➳ ✕

▼▼▼ **Ventura Resort Rentals Orlando** 🄲🄾
(407) 273-8770. **$56-$215, 15 day notice.** 5946 Curry Ford Rd. 0.6 mi e of SR 436. Ext corridors. **Pets:** Accepted.
(ASK) 🔊 🔌 🛎 💻 ➳ ✕

🄰🄰🄰 ▼▼▼ **Wellesley Inn & Suites (Orlando/Maitland)** 🅂🄷
(407) 659-0066. **$75-$105.** 1951 Summit Tower Blvd. I-4, exit 90, 1 mi w. Int corridors. **Pets:** Accepted.
(SAVE) 🔊 ✕ 🔌 📺 🛎 💻 ➳

🄰🄰🄰 ▼▼▼ **Wellesley Inn & Suites (Orlando/Southpark)** 🅂🄷
(407) 248-8010. **$85-$119.** 8687 Commodity Cir. Just sw of jct SR 423 (John Young Pkwy) and 482 (Sand Lake Rd). Int corridors. **Pets:** Accepted.
(SAVE) 🔊 ✕ 🔌 📺 🛎 💻 ➳

🄰🄰🄰 ▼▼▼▼ **Westin Grand Bohemian** 🄻🄷
(407) 313-9000. **$169-$389.** 325 S Orange Ave. Downtown. Int corridors. **Pets:** Accepted.
(SAVE) ✕ 🔌 📺 🛎 💻 🍴 ➳ ✕

🄰🄰🄰 ▼▼▼▼ **Wyndham Orlando Resort** 🄻🄷
(407) 351-2420. **$93-$143, 3 day notice.** 8001 International Dr. I-4, exit 74A, just e at SR 482 (Sand Lake Rd). Ext/int corridors. **Pets:** Accepted.
(SAVE) ✕ 🔌 📺 🛎 💻 🍴 ➳ ✕

ST. CLOUD

🄰🄰🄰 ▼▼▼ **Budget Inn of St Cloud** 🄼
(407) 892-2858. **$45, 3 day notice.** 602 13th St. On US 192, 0.5 mi e of The Water Tower, 2 mi w of jct CR 15. Ext corridors. **Pets:** Very small, dogs only. $10 daily fee/pet. Service with restrictions, supervision.
(SAVE) 🔊 ✕ 🔌 🛎 💻

SANFORD

▼▼▼ **Rose Cottage Inn** 🄱🄱
(407) 323-9448. **Call for rates.** 1301 Park Ave. From 1st St, 0.8 mi s on Park Ave; downtown. Int corridors. **Pets:** Accepted.
✕ 🛎 🍴 📶 🎧

TAVARES

▼ **Budget Inn** 🄼
(352) 343-4666. **$45-$99, 7 day notice.** 101 W Burleigh Blvd. On US 441, 0.3 mi e of jct SR 19 S. Ext corridors. **Pets:** Accepted.
(ASK) 🔊 ✕ 🛎 💻

🄰🄰🄰 ▼▼▼ **Inn On The Green** 🄼
(352) 343-6373. **$65-$79.** 700 E Burleigh Blvd. On US 441, 1 mi e of jct SR 19. Ext corridors. **Pets:** Accepted.
(SAVE) 🔊 ✕ 🛎 💻 ➳ ✕

END METROPOLITAN AREA

ORMOND BEACH

AAA ▼▼▼ **Comfort Inn On The Beach M**
(386) 677-8550. **$75-$200, 10 day notice.** 507 S Atlantic Ave. On SR A1A, 1 mi s of jct SR 40. Ext corridors. **Pets:** Very small. $10 daily fee/pet. Service with restrictions, supervision.
SAVE S👁 ✕ 🛏 💻 ➰

▼▼▼ **Jameson Inn SH**
(386) 672-3675. **$49-$104.** 175 Interchange Blvd. I-95, exit 268, just w, then just s. Int corridors. **Pets:** Very small, other species. $10 daily fee/room. Service with restrictions, supervision.
ASK ✕ 👁M 📶 📶 🛏 💻 ➰

OSPREY

AAA ▼▼▼ **Ramada Inn-Sarasota South M**
(941) 966-2121. **$59-$129.** 1660 S Tamiami Tr. On US 41, 1.8 mi n of jct SR 681. Ext/int corridors. **Pets:** Small. $25 one-time fee/pet. Designated rooms, service with restrictions, supervision.
SAVE S👁 ✕ 🛏 💻 🍴 ➰

PALM BAY

▼▼▼ **Jameson Inn SH**
(321) 725-2952. **$49-$104.** 890 Palm Bay Rd. I-95, exit 176. Int corridors. **Pets:** Very small, other species. $10 daily fee/room. Service with restrictions, supervision.
ASK ✕ 👁M 📶 📶 🛏 💻 ➰

PALM BEACH

AAA ▼▼▼▼ **The Chesterfield Hotel SH**
(561) 659-5800. **$109-$1600, 3 day notice.** 363 Cocoanut Row. Just w of SR A1A; at Australian Ave and Cocoanut Row. Int corridors. **Pets:** Accepted.
SAVE S👁 ✕ 📶 🛏 🍴 ➰ ✕

AAA ▼▼▼▼ **The Four Seasons Resort, Palm Beach LH**
(561) 582-2800. **$285-$760, 7 day notice.** 2800 S Ocean Blvd. SR A1A, 0.3 mi n of jct SR 802. Int corridors. **Pets:** Accepted.
SAVE ✕ 👁M 📶 📶 💻 🍴 ➰ ✕

▼▼▼▼ **Heart of Palm Beach Hotel SH**
(561) 655-5600. **$169-$299, 3 day notice.** 160 Royal Palm Way. Just e of SR A1A; center. Int corridors. **Pets:** Medium. $100 one-time fee/pet. Designated rooms, no service.
ASK S👁 ✕ 🛏 🍴 ➰ ✕

▼▼▼▼ **Palm Beach Hilton Oceanfront Resort SH**
(561) 586-6542. **$104-$494, 10 day notice.** 2842 S Ocean Blvd. On SR A1A; just n of jct SR 802. Int corridors. **Pets:** Medium, other species. $100 one-time fee/pet. Service with restrictions, supervision.
ASK ✕ 📶 💻 🍴 ➰ ✕

▼▼▼▼ **Plaza Inn SH** 🐾
(561) 832-8666. **$145-$285, 3 day notice.** 215 Brazilian Ave. At Brazilian Ave and SR A1A (S County Rd); center. Int corridors. **Pets:** Medium. Designated rooms, service with restrictions, supervision.
ASK S👁 ✕ 📶 🛏 ➰

PALM BEACH SHORES

AAA ▼▼▼ **Best Western Seaspray Inn SH**
(561) 844-0233. **$70-$200.** 123 S Ocean Ave. On Singer Island; 0.5 mi s of SR A1A. Int corridors. **Pets:** Small. $15 daily fee/pet. Service with restrictions, supervision.
SAVE ✕ 🛏 💻 🍴 ➰

PALM COAST

▼▼▼ **Microtel Inn & Suites SH**
(386) 445-8976. **$59-$199.** 16 Kingswood Dr. I-95, exit 289, just e, then just s. Int corridors. **Pets:** Small, dogs only. $25 one-time fee/pet. Designated rooms, service with restrictions, supervision.
ASK S👁 ✕ 👁M 📶 🛏 💻 ➰

AAA ▼▼▼ **Palm Coast Villas M** 🐾
(386) 445-3525. **$54-$74.** 5454 N Oceanshore Blvd. I-95, exit 289, 2.8 mi e to SR A1A, then 1.8 mi n. Int corridors. **Pets:** Other species. $5 daily fee/pet. Designated rooms, service with restrictions.
SAVE S👁 ✕ 🛏 💻 ➰

PANAMA CITY

AAA ▼▼▼ **Days Inn Bayside SH**
(850) 763-4622. **$58-$136.** 711 W Beach Dr. Business US 98, 0.5 mi w of jct US 231. Ext corridors. **Pets:** Accepted.
SAVE S👁 ✕ 🛏 💻 🍴 ➰

▼▼▼ **Howard Johnson Inn SH**
(850) 785-0222. **$79-$125, 3 day notice.** 4601 W Hwy 98. US 98, 0.8 mi e of Hathaway Bridge. Ext/int corridors. **Pets:** Accepted.
ASK ✕ 🛏 💻 ➰

AAA ▼▼▼▼ **La Quinta Inn & Suites Panama City SH**
(850) 914-0022. **$100-$122.** 1030 E 23rd St. Jct US 231 and CR 390A. Int corridors. **Pets:** Other species. Service with restrictions, crate.
SAVE ✕ 👁M 📶 🛏 💻 ➰

▼▼ **Super 8 Motel M**
(850) 784-1988. **$55-$105.** 207 Hwy 231 N. Just n of jct US 98. Ext/int corridors. **Pets:** Small, dogs only. $15 daily fee/pet. Designated rooms, service with restrictions.
ASK S👁 ✕ 🛏 ➰

PENSACOLA

▼▼▼ **Ashton Inn & Suites SH**
(850) 454-0280. **$55-$85.** 4 New Warrington Rd. Just n of jct US 98 and SR 292. Int corridors. **Pets:** Accepted.
ASK S👁 ✕ 🛏 💻 ➰

▼▼ **Best Value Inn and Suites SH**
(850) 479-1099. **$49-$79.** 8240 N Davis Hwy. I-10, exit 13, 0.8 mi n. Ext/int corridors. **Pets:** $10 one-time fee/pet. Service with restrictions.
ASK S👁 ✕ 📶 🛏 💻 ➰

AAA ▼▼▼ **Comfort Inn SH**
(850) 484-8070. **$49-$159.** 8080 N Davis Hwy. I-10, exit 13, just n on SR 291. Int corridors. **Pets:** Small. $20 daily fee/pet. Designated rooms, service with restrictions, supervision.
SAVE S👁 ✕ 🛏 💻 ➰

AAA ▼▼▼ **Comfort Inn-NAS Corry SH**
(850) 455-3233. **$57-$79.** 3 New Warrington Rd. Just n of jct US 98 and SR 292. Ext corridors. **Pets:** Large, other species. $30 one-time fee/room. Designated rooms, service with restrictions, crate.
SAVE S👁 ✕ 🛏 💻 ➰

AAA ▼▼▼ **Days Inn North SH**
(850) 476-9090. **$45-$99.** 7051 Pensacola Blvd. I-10, exit 10A, 0.3 mi s on US 29. Int corridors. **Pets:** Other species. $10 daily fee/pet. Service with restrictions, supervision.
SAVE S👁 ✕ 🛏 ➰

AAA ▼▼▼ **Holiday Inn-University Mall SH**
(850) 474-0100. **$65, 3 day notice.** 7200 Plantation Rd. I-10, exit 13, just s of University Mall entrance. Ext corridors. **Pets:** Medium. $25 deposit/room. Designated rooms, service with restrictions, supervision.
SAVE S👁 ✕ 📶 📶 🛏 💻 🍴 ➰

◊◊ **Hospitality Inn** 🅂🅷
(850) 477-2333. **$55-$120.** 6900 Pensacola Blvd. I-10, exit 10A, 0.5 mi s on US 29. Ext/int corridors. **Pets:** Accepted.
🅰🆂🅺 🆂📶 ✕ 🈁 💻 ⊇

🆔 ◊◊◊ **La Quinta Inn Pensacola** 🅂🅷
(850) 474-0411. **$66-$99.** 7750 N Davis Hwy. I-10, exit 13, just n. Ext corridors. **Pets:** Large, other species. Service with restrictions.
🆂🅰🆅🅴 ✕ 🔧 🈁 💻 ⊇

◊ **Motel 6 #1105** 🅼
(850) 474-1060. **$39-$51.** 7226 Plantation Rd. I-10, exit 13, sw on Mall Rd. Ext corridors. **Pets:** Accepted.
🆂📶 ✕ ⊇

◊ **Motel 6 #1183** 🅼
(850) 476-5386. **$37-$53.** 7827 N Davis Hwy. I-10, exit 13, 0.3 mi n. Ext corridors. **Pets:** Accepted.
🆂📶 ✕ 🔧 ⊇

🆔 ◊◊ **Quality Inn** 🅂🅷
(850) 477-0711. **$54-$74.** 6550 N Pensacola Blvd. I-10, exit 10A, 1.2 mi s on US 29. Ext/int corridors. **Pets:** Other species. $25 one-time fee/room. Service with restrictions, supervision.
🆂🅰🆅🅴 🆂📶 ✕ 🈂 🈁 💻 🍴 ⊇

🆔 ◊◊ **Ramada Inn Bayview** 🅂🅷
(850) 477-7155. **$69-$150.** 7601 Scenic Hwy. I-10, exit 17, just s on US 90. Int corridors. **Pets:** Small. $25 one-time fee/pet. Designated rooms, service with restrictions, supervision.
🆂🅰🆅🅴 🆂📶 ✕ 🈁 💻 🍴 ⊇

🆔 ◊◊ **Ramada Limited** 🅂🅷
(850) 944-0333. **$50-$100.** 8060 Lavalle Way. I-10, exit 7, just s. Ext corridors. **Pets:** Accepted.
🆂🅰🆅🅴 🆂📶 ✕ 🈁 💻 ⊇

◊◊ **Red Roof Inn** 🅼
(850) 476-7960. **$43-$58.** 7340 Plantation Rd. I-10, exit 13, just s. Ext corridors. **Pets:** Accepted.
✕ 🈁

◊◊◊ **Residence Inn By Marriott** 🅂🅷
(850) 479-1000. **$109.** 7230 Plantation Rd. I-10, exit 13, just s. Ext corridors. **Pets:** Small. $75 one-time fee/room. Service with restrictions, crate.
🅰🆂🅺 🆂📶 ✕ 🈂 🈁 💻 ⊇ ✕

◊◊◊ **Travelodge Inn & Suites** 🅂🅷
(850) 473-0222. **$85-$150.** 6950 Pensacola Blvd. I-10, exit 10A, 0.5 mi s. Int corridors. **Pets:** Medium. $10 daily fee/room. Designated rooms, service with restrictions, crate.
🅰🆂🅺 🆂📶 ✕ 🈁 💻 ⊇

PENSACOLA BEACH

🆔 ◊◊◊◊ **Beachside Resort & Conference Center** 🅂🅷
(850) 932-5331. **$69-$229, 3 day notice.** 14 Via De Luna. SR 399, just e of traffic light. Int corridors. **Pets:** Accepted.
🆂🅰🆅🅴 🆂📶 ✕ 🔧 🈁 💻 🍴 ⊇

◊◊ **Comfort Inn Pensacola Beach** 🅂🅷
(850) 934-5400. **$69-$185.** 40 Fort Pickens Rd. Just off SR 399. Ext corridors. **Pets:** Accepted.
🅰🆂🅺 🆂📶 ✕ 🈂 🔧 🈁 💻 ⊇

PERRY

🆔 ◊ **Best Budget Inn** 🅼
(850) 584-6231. **$43-$46.** 2220 US 19 S. US 19 and 98, 0.4 mi s jct US 221. Ext corridors. **Pets:** Small, other species. $5 daily fee/pet. Designated rooms, service with restrictions, supervision.
🆂🅰🆅🅴 🆂📶 ✕ 🈁 ⊇

PORT CHARLOTTE

◊◊ **Days Inn of Port Charlotte** 🅂🅷
(941) 627-8900. **$54-$144.** 1941 Tamiami Tr. On US 41, just s of jct Toledo Blade Blvd. Ext corridors. **Pets:** Accepted.
✕ 🈂 🈁 💻 ⊇

PORT ST. LUCIE

🆔 ◊◊◊ **Holiday Inn-Port St Lucie** 🅂🅷 🐾
(772) 337-2200. **$99-$179.** 10120 S Federal Hwy, Rt 1. US 1, 0.5 mi n of jct SR 716, Port St Lucie Blvd. Int corridors. **Pets:** Medium. $50 one-time fee/room. Designated rooms, service with restrictions, supervision.
🆂🅰🆅🅴 🆂📶 ✕ 🈂 🈁 💻 🍴 ⊇

PUNTA GORDA

🆔 ◊◊◊ **Best Western Waterfront** 🅂🅷
(941) 639-1165. **$76-$395, 3 day notice.** 300 Retta Esplanade. On US 41; just s of Peace River Bridge. Int corridors. **Pets:** Accepted.
🆂🅰🆅🅴 🆂📶 ✕ 🈂 🈁 💻 🍴 ⊇ ✕

🆔 ◊◊◊ **Holiday Inn Harborside** 🅼
(941) 639-2167. **$69-$250.** 33 Tamiami Tr. On US 41; at Peace River Bridge. Int corridors. **Pets:** Accepted.
🆂🅰🆅🅴 🆂📶 ✕ 🆖 🔧 🈁 💻 🍴 ⊇ ✕

◊ **Motel 6 #1231** 🅼
(941) 639-9585. **$38-$68.** 9300 Knights Dr. I-75, exit 161, just w on CR 768. Ext corridors. **Pets:** Accepted.
🆂📶 ✕ 🆖 🔧 🈁 ⊇

QUINCY

◊◊◊ **Allison House Inn** 🅱🅱 🐾
(850) 875-2511. **$95-$120, 14 day notice.** 215 N Madison St. Just e of town center; in historic district. Int corridors. **Pets:** Small, dogs only. Service with restrictions, crate.
🅰🆂🅺 🆂📶 ✕

ST. AUGUSTINE

🆔 ◊◊ **Best Western St. Augustine I-95** 🅂🅷
(904) 829-1999. **$59-$110.** 2445 SR 16. I-95, exit 318, just w. Ext corridors. **Pets:** Accepted.
🆂🅰🆅🅴 🆂📶 ✕ 💻 ⊇

◊◊ **Conch House Marina Resort** 🅂🅷
(904) 829-8646. **Call for rates.** 57 Comares Ave. 1 mi s of Bridge of Lions on SR A1A, 0.3 mi n. Ext corridors. **Pets:** Accepted.
🈁 💻 🍴 ⊇ ✕ 🈑

🆔 ◊◊ **The Cozy Inn** 🅼
(904) 824-2449. **$49-$99.** 202 San Marco Ave. 0.3 mi s of jct SR 16. Ext corridors. **Pets:** Large, other species. $25 one-time fee/room.
🆂🅰🆅🅴 🆂📶 ✕ 🈁 💻

🆔 ◊◊ **Days Inn Historic** 🅂🅷
(904) 829-6581. **$59-$109.** 2800 N Ponce de Leon Blvd. US 1 at SR 16; in historic district. Ext corridors. **Pets:** Medium, dogs only. $10 daily fee/pet. Designated rooms, service with restrictions, supervision.
🆂🅰🆅🅴 🆂📶 ✕ 🈂 🈁 🍴 ⊇

🆔 ◊◊ **Days Inn-West** 🅂🅷 🐾
(904) 824-4341. **$69-$350.** 2560 SR 16. I-95, exit 318, just w. Ext corridors. **Pets:** $10 daily fee/pet. Designated rooms, service with restrictions.
🆂🅰🆅🅴 🆂📶 ✕ 🈁 💻 🍴 ⊇

🆔 ◊◊ **La Quinta Inn St. Augustine** 🅂🅷
(904) 824-3383. **$49-$150.** 1300 Ponce de Leon Blvd. US 1, 1 mi n. Ext corridors. **Pets:** Accepted.
🆂🅰🆅🅴 ✕ 🔧 🈁 💻 🍴 ⊇

♦♦♦ ▼▼▼ Ramada Limited SH
(904) 829-5643. **$69-$109.** 2535 SR 16. I-95, exit 318, just w. Ext corridors. **Pets:** Accepted.
[SAVE] [S] [X] [■] [💻] [≈]

♦♦♦ ▼▼▼▼ St. Francis Inn BB
(904) 824-6068. **$119-$229, 7 day notice.** 279 St George St. Just s; in the historic district. Ext/int corridors. **Pets:** Small, other species. $10 daily fee/pet. Designated rooms, service with restrictions, crate.
[SAVE] [S] [X] [■] [💻] [≈] [X]

♦♦♦ ▼▼▼ Scottish Inns M
(904) 824-2871. **$50-$100.** 110 San Marco Ave. Old Mission and San Marco aves; center. Ext corridors. **Pets:** Accepted.
[SAVE] [S] [X] [≈]

ST. AUGUSTINE BEACH

♦♦♦ ▼▼▼ Holiday Inn-St Augustine Beach SH 🐾
(904) 471-2555. **$114-$169.** 860 A1A Beach Blvd. On Business Rt SR A1A, 1.8 mi s of jct SR 312 and A1A. Ext/int corridors. **Pets:** Medium, other species. $20 daily fee/pet. Designated rooms, service with restrictions, supervision.
[SAVE] [S] [X] [♿] [■] [💻] [🍴] [≈]

♦♦♦ ▼▼▼ Super 8 By The Beach SH
(904) 471-2330. **$69-$109.** 311 A1A Beach Blvd. On Business Rt SR A1A, 1 mi s of jct SR 312 and A1A. Ext corridors. **Pets:** Other species. $15 one-time fee/room. Supervision.
[SAVE] [S] [X] [📶] [■] [💻] [≈]

SARASOTA

▼▼▼▼ AmericInn Hotel & Suites SH
(941) 342-8778. **$89-$229.** 5931 Fruitville Rd. I-75, exit 210, 0.4 mi w, just n on N Cattlemen Rd, then just e on Commercial Way. Int corridors. **Pets:** Small, other species. $15 daily fee/pet. Service with restrictions, supervision.
[ASK] [S] [X] [♿M] [📶] [♿] [■] [💻] [≈]

♦♦♦ ▼▼▼ Coquina on the Beach Resort M 🐾
(941) 388-2141. **$89-$359, 14 day notice.** 1008 Benjamin Franklin Dr. On St. Armands Key of Lido Beach, 0.9 mi s of St. Armands Circle. Ext corridors. **Pets:** Other species. $35 one-time fee/room. Service with restrictions.
[SAVE] [S] [■] [💻] [≈]

♦♦♦ ▼▼▼ Hibiscus Suites Inn M 🐾
(941) 921-5797. **$100-$750, 10 day notice.** 1735 Stickney Point Rd. On SR 72, 0.3 mi sw of jct US 41. Ext corridors. **Pets:** Large, dogs only. $25 daily fee/pet. Service with restrictions, supervision.
[SAVE] [S] [X] [■] [💻] [≈]

♦♦♦ ▼▼▼ Ramada Limited SH
(941) 921-7812. **$75-$139, 3 day notice.** 5774 Clark Rd. I-75, exit 205, just w on SR 72. Int corridors. **Pets:** Small. $10 daily fee/pet. Designated rooms, service with restrictions, supervision.
[SAVE] [S] [X] [📶] [■] [💻] [≈]

▼▼▼▼ The Ritz-Carlton, Sarasota LH
(941) 309-2000. **$175-$395, 5 day notice.** 1111 Ritz-Carlton Dr. On US 41, jct John Ringling Blvd. Int corridors. **Pets:** Accepted.
[S] [X] [♿M] [📶] [♿] [💻] [🍴] [≈] [X]

▼▼ The Sunset Lodge Motel M
(941) 925-1151. **$65-$105, 21 day notice.** 1765 Dawn St. 0.3 mi sw of jct US 41 on SR 72, just s on Ave C, then just w. Ext corridors. **Pets:** Small, dogs only. $50 one-time fee/pet. Designated rooms, service with restrictions, crate.
[X] [■] [💻] [≈] [X]

▼ The Tides Inn M
(941) 924-7541. **$60-$120, 21 day notice.** 1800 Stickney Point Rd. On SR 72, 0.3 mi sw of jct US 41. Ext corridors. **Pets:** Other species. $10 daily fee/pet, $15 one-time fee/pet. Designated rooms, no service, supervision.
[ASK] [S] [X] [■] [💻] [≈] [X]

SATELLITE BEACH

♦♦♦ ▼▼▼ Days Inn M
(321) 777-3552. **$59-$175.** 180 SR A1A. 0.3 mi s of jct SR 404. Ext corridors. **Pets:** Accepted.
[SAVE] [S] [X] [📶] [♿] [■] [💻] [≈] [X]

SEBRING

▼▼▼▼ The Chateau Elan Hotel & Spa SH
(863) 655-6252. **$129-$159, 3 day notice.** 150 Midway Dr. From US 27, 2.2 mi e on SR 98; at entrance to Sebring International Raceway. Int corridors. **Pets:** Accepted.
[ASK] [S] [X] [📶] [♿] [■] [💻] [🍴] [≈] [X]

♦♦♦ ▼▼▼▼ Inn On The Lakes SH
(863) 471-9400. **$69-$109.** 3100 Golfview Rd. On US 27, 1.5 mi n of jct SR 17. Ext/int corridors. **Pets:** Accepted.
[SAVE] [S] [X] [■] [💻] [🍴] [≈] [X]

♦♦♦ ▼▼ Kenilworth Lodge SH 🐾
(863) 385-0111. **$64-$110, 3 day notice.** 836 SE Lakeview Dr. US 27, 1 mi e on SR 17. Ext/int corridors. **Pets:** Large, other species. $15 daily fee/room. Designated rooms, service with restrictions.
[SAVE] [S] [X] [■] [💻] [≈] [X]

▼▼▼▼ Quality Inn & Suites Conference Center SH
(863) 385-4500. **$69-$99.** 6525 US 27 N. On US 27, 7 mi n of jct SR 17. Ext corridors. **Pets:** Other species. $10 daily fee/pet. Service with restrictions, crate.
[ASK] [S] [X] [♿M] [📶] [■] [💻] [🍴] [≈]

SIESTA KEY

♦♦♦ ▼▼▼ Tropical Breeze Resort of Siesta Key M
(941) 349-1125. **$85-$499, 14 day notice.** 5150 Ocean Blvd. Jct Avenida Messina; in Siesta Village. Ext corridors. **Pets:** Other species. $50 one-time fee/pet. No service.
[SAVE] [S] [X] [■] [💻] [🍴] [≈] [X]

▼▼▼ Turtle Beach Resort M
(941) 349-4554. **$250-$430.** 9049 Midnight Pass Rd. 2.8 mi s of jct SR 72. Ext corridors. **Pets:** Other species. No service.
[X] [■] [💻] [≈] [X]

SILVER SPRINGS

♦♦♦ ▼▼ Days Inn M
(352) 236-2891. **$55-$90.** 5001 E Silver Springs Blvd. SR 40, 0.5 mi w of jct CR 35. Ext corridors. **Pets:** Other species. $10 daily fee/pet. Service with restrictions.
[SAVE] [S] [X] [■] [≈]

♦♦♦ ▼▼ Sun Plaza Motel M
(352) 236-2343. **$45-$75.** 5461 E Silver Springs Blvd. SR 40, jct CR 35. Ext corridors. **Pets:** Medium, dogs only. $10 daily fee/pet. Designated rooms, service with restrictions, supervision.
[SAVE] [X] [■] [💻] [≈]

STARKE

♦♦♦ ▼▼▼ Best Western Motor Inn SH
(904) 964-6744. **$65-$135.** 1290 N Temple Ave. 1 mi n on US 301 from jct SR 100. Ext corridors. **Pets:** Medium. $10 daily fee/pet. Service with restrictions, supervision.
[SAVE] [S] [X] [■] [💻] [≈]

Days Inn SH
(904) 964-7600. **$65-$179, 30 day notice.** 1101 N Temple Ave. 10 mi s of jct SR 16. Ext corridors. **Pets:** Other species. $10 daily fee/pet. Designated rooms, service with restrictions, crate.

STEINHATCHEE

Steinhatchee Landing Resort CO
(352) 498-3513. **$132-$425, 14 day notice.** SR 51 N. SR 51, 8 mi w of jct US 19/98. Ext corridors. **Pets:** Accepted.

Steinhatchee River Inn M
(352) 498-4049. **$60-$89, 14 day notice.** 1111 Riverside Dr. Center. Ext corridors. **Pets:** Small, dogs only. $10 daily fee/pet. Designated rooms, service with restrictions, supervision.

STUART

Hutchinson Island Marriott Beach Resort & Marina LH
(772) 225-3700. **$109-$239, 3 day notice.** 555 NE Ocean Blvd. 4 mi ne on SR A1A, on south end of Hutchinson Island at east end of causeway. Ext/int corridors. **Pets:** $75 one-time fee/room. Designated rooms, supervision.

Pirates Cove Resort & Marina SH
(772) 287-2500. **$150-$175.** 4307 SE Bayview St. 0.3 mi e of SR A1A. Ext corridors. **Pets:** Medium, other species. $20 one-time fee/room. Designated rooms, service with restrictions, supervision.

TALLAHASSEE

Best Western Seminole Inn M
(850) 656-2938. **$60-$139, 3 day notice.** 6737 Mahan Dr. I-10, exit 209A, just w on US 90. Ext corridors. **Pets:** Accepted.

Homewood Suites by Hilton SH
(850) 402-9400. **$89-$259.** 2987 Apalachee Pkwy. US 27, 3.5 mi s. Int corridors. **Pets:** Accepted.

Howard Johnson Express Inn M
(850) 386-5000. **$49-$69.** 2726 N Monroe St. I-10, exit 199, 0.5 mi s. Ext corridors. **Pets:** Accepted.

La Quinta Inn Tallahassee (North) SH
(850) 385-7172. **$75-$115.** 2905 N Monroe St. I-10, exit 199, just s on US 27. Ext corridors. **Pets:** Accepted.

La Quinta Inn Tallahassee (South) SH
(850) 878-5099. **$75-$115.** 2850 Apalachee Pkwy. 3 mi se on US 27. Ext corridors. **Pets:** Accepted.

Motel 6 SH
(850) 877-6171. **Call for rates.** 1027 Apalachee Pkwy. 1 mi se on US 27. Ext corridors. **Pets:** Accepted.

Motel 6 #1191 SH
(850) 386-7878. **$39-$55.** 2738 N Monroe St. I-10, exit 199, just s on US 27. Ext corridors. **Pets:** Accepted.

Motel 6–420 M
(850) 668-2600. **$45-$55.** 1481 Timberlane Rd. I-10, exit 203, just n, then w. Ext corridors. **Pets:** Accepted.

Super 8 Motel SH
(850) 386-8818. **$40-$65.** 2702 N Monroe St. I-10, exit 199, 0.4 mi s on US 27. Int corridors. **Pets:** Accepted.

TAMPA BAY METROPOLITAN AREA

APOLLO BEACH

Ramada Inn on Tampa Bay M
(813) 641-2700. **$65-$150.** 6414 Surfside Blvd. I-75, exit 246, 1.8 mi w on CR 672; 1.8 mi s on US 41, 2.4 mi w on Apollo Beach Blvd. Ext corridors. **Pets:** Small, other species. $15 daily fee/pet. Designated rooms, service with restrictions, supervision.

BRANDON

Behind the Fence Bed & Breakfast BB
(813) 685-8201. **$79-$99 (no credit cards), 10 day notice.** 1400 Viola Dr. I-75, exit 254, just s on US 301 northbound; 1.5 mi s on US 301 southbound, 2.5 mi e on Bloomingdale Ave, then just n on Country Side St. Ext/int corridors. **Pets:** Accepted.

Homestead Studio Suites Hotel-Tampa/Brandon M
(813) 643-5900. **$74-$104.** 330 Grand Regency Blvd. I-75, exit 257, just e on SR 60, then 0.4 mi n; in Regency Office Park. Ext corridors. **Pets:** Other species. $25 daily fee/room. Service with restrictions.

La Quinta Inn & Suites Tampa Bay (Brandon) SH
(813) 643-0574. **$95-$141.** 310 Grand Regency Blvd. I-75, exit 257, just e on SR 60, then 0.5 mi n; in Regency Office Park. Int corridors. **Pets:** Other species. Service with restrictions.

CLEARWATER

Belleview Biltmore Resort & Spa SH
(727) 373-3000. **$169-$209.** 25 Belleview Blvd. Jct Alternate US 19 and SR 60, 2 mi s to Belleview Blvd, 0.5 mi w. Int corridors. **Pets:** Small. $25 deposit/pet, $25 daily fee/pet. Designated rooms, service with restrictions, supervision.

Days Inn-St. Pete/Clearwater Airport SH
(727) 573-3334. **$69-$99.** 3910 Ulmerton Rd. I-275, exit 31B southbound; exit 30 northbound, 2 mi w on SR 688. Int corridors. **Pets:** Accepted.

Homestead Studio Suites Hotel-Tampa/Clearwater SH
(727) 572-4800. **$64-$104.** 2311 Ulmerton Rd. I-275, exit 31B southbound; exit 30 northbound, 1.3 mi w on SR 688. Ext corridors. **Pets:** Accepted.

Homewood Suites by Hilton SH
(727) 573-1500. **$99-$169.** 2233 Ulmerton Rd. I-275, exit 31B southbound; exit 30 northbound, 1.3 mi w on SR 688. Int corridors. **Pets:** Medium. $150 one-time fee/room. Designated rooms, service with restrictions.

🔺 ◈◈◈ La Quinta Inn Tampa Bay (Clearwater-Airport) 🆂🅷
(727) 572-7222. **$89-$124.** 3301 Ulmerton Rd. I-275, exit 31B southbound; exit 30 northbound, 1.7 mi w on SR 688; in The Centres Office Park. Int corridors. **Pets:** Accepted.
[SAVE] [✕] [🖉] [✎] [🛏] [🖥] [≋] [✕]

◈◈◈ Radisson Hotel Clearwater Central 🆂🅷
(727) 799-1181. **$69-$79.** 20967 US 19 N. On US 19, just n of jct SR 60. Ext/int corridors. **Pets:** Accepted.
[ASK] [🅢] [✕] [🅗M] [🖉] [✎] [🛏] [🖥] [🍴] [≋] [✕]

◈◈◈ Residence Inn by Marriott 🆂🅷
(727) 573-4444. **$115-$225.** 5050 Ulmerton Rd. On SR 688, 1 mi e of jct US 19. Ext corridors. **Pets:** Medium. $75 one-time fee/pet. Service with restrictions, supervision.
[ASK] [🅢] [✕] [🖉] [✎] [🛏] [🖥] [≋] [✕]

🔺 ◈◈◈ Super 8 Clearwater/St. Petersburg Airport 🆂🅷
(727) 572-8881. **$49-$119.** 13260 34th St N. I-275, exit 31B southbound; exit 30 northbound, 1.8 mi w on SR 688, then just s. Int corridors. **Pets:** Large. $10 daily fee/pet. Designated rooms, service with restrictions, supervision.
[SAVE] [🅢] [✕] [🛏] [≋]

◈◈◈ TownePlace Suites by Marriott St. Petersburg/Clearwater 🆂🅷
(727) 299-9229. **$62-$116.** 13200 49th St N. I-275, exit 31B southbound; exit 30 northbound, 3 mi w on SR 688, then just s; in Turtle Creek. Int corridors. **Pets:** Accepted.
[ASK] [✕] [🅗M] [🖉] [✎] [🛏] [🖥] [≋]

CLEARWATER BEACH

🔺 ◈ Bel Crest Beach Resort 🅼
(727) 442-4923. **$68-$208, 60 day notice.** 706 Bayway Blvd. 1 mi s of jct roundabout via Gulfview Blvd. Ext corridors. **Pets:** $5 daily fee/pet. Designated rooms, service with restrictions, supervision.
[SAVE] [🅢] [🛏] [≋] [✕]

HOLIDAY

◈◈ Tahitian Resort 🅼 🐾
(727) 937-4121. **$49-$99.** 2337 US 19. On US 19, 3 mi n of jct SR 582, 1.5 mi s of jct SR 54. Ext corridors. **Pets:** Other species. $5 daily fee/pet. Designated rooms, service with restrictions, supervision.
[✕] [🖉] [🛏] [🖥] [≋]

INDIAN ROCKS BEACH

◈◈ Sea Star Motel & Apartments 🅼 ❀
(727) 596-2525. **$60-$90, 30 day notice.** 1805 Gulf Blvd. On SR 699, 1.2 mi n of jct SR 688 (Walsingham Rd). Ext corridors. **Pets:** Other species. $10 daily fee/pet. No service, crate.
[ASK] [✕] [🛏] [🖥] [✕] [🐾]

MADEIRA BEACH

🔺 ◈◈◈ Snug Harbor Inn Waterfront Bed & Breakfast 🅼 ❀
(727) 395-9256. **$50-$110, 21 day notice.** 13655 Gulf Blvd. On SR 699, 0.9 mi s of jct Tom Stuart Cswy. Ext corridors. **Pets:** Other species. Designated rooms, service with restrictions.
[SAVE] [✕] [🛏] [🖥] [≋] [✕]

NEW PORT RICHEY

🔺 ◈◈ Econo Lodge 🅼
(727) 845-4990. **$50-$150.** 7631 US 19. On US 19, 0.8 mi n of jct Main St. Ext corridors. **Pets:** Small. $6 daily fee/room. Designated rooms, no service, supervision.
[SAVE] [🅢] [✕] [🛏] [🖥] [≋]

PALM HARBOR

🔺 ◈◈◈ Best Western Palm Harbor Hotel 🆂🅷
(727) 942-0358. **$69-$175, 3 day notice.** 37611 US 19 N. On US 19, 3 mi s of jct SR 582. Ext corridors. **Pets:** Medium. $10 daily fee/pet. Designated rooms, service with restrictions, supervision.
[SAVE] [🅢] [✕] [✎] [🛏] [🖥] [🍴] [≋] [✕]

◈◈ Knights Inn-Clearwater/Palm Harbor 🅼
(727) 789-2002. **$35-$99.** 34106 US 19 N. On US 19, 1.8 mi n of CR 752 (Tampa Rd). Ext corridors. **Pets:** Other species. $10 daily fee/room. Service with restrictions, crate.
[ASK] [🅢] [✕] [🛏] [🖥] [≋]

🔺 ◈◈◈ Red Roof Inn 🅼
(727) 786-2529. **$51-$96.** 32000 US 19 N. On US 19, 0.4 mi s of jct CR 752 (Tampa Rd). Ext corridors. **Pets:** Medium. Service with restrictions, supervision.
[SAVE] [🅢] [✕] [🖉] [✎] [🛏] [🖥] [≋]

PINELLAS PARK

🔺 ◈◈◈ La Quinta Inn Tampa (Pinellas Park/Clearwater) 🆂🅷
(727) 545-5611. **$74-$100.** 7500 US Hwy 19 N. I-275, exit 28, 1.4 mi s on Gandy Blvd (SR 694), then just n. Ext/int corridors. **Pets:** Accepted.
[SAVE] [✕] [🅗M] [🖉] [🛏] [🖥] [≋]

PORT RICHEY

◈◈ Comfort Inn 🅼
(727) 863-3336. **$52-$85.** 11810 US 19. On US 19, just s of jct SR 52. Ext corridors. **Pets:** Accepted.
[ASK] [🅢] [✕] [🖉] [🛏] [🖥] [≋]

REDINGTON BEACH

◈◈ The Royal Orleans Condotel 🅲🅾
(727) 391-4456. **Call for rates.** 16333 Gulf Blvd. On SR 699, 1.3 mi n of Tom Stuart Cswy. Ext corridors. **Pets:** Accepted.
[✕] [🛏] [≋] [✕]

RUSKIN

🔺 ◈◈◈ Mariner's Club Bahia Beach Resort 🅲🅾
(813) 645-3291. **$99-$129, 7 day notice.** 611 Destiny Dr. 3.5 mi w of US 41 via Shell Point Rd, follow signs. Ext/int corridors. **Pets:** Accepted.
[SAVE] [✕] [🅗M] [🖉] [✎] [🛏] [🖥] [🍴] [≋] [✕]

SAFETY HARBOR

🔺 ◈◈◈ Safety Harbor Resort and Spa on Tampa Bay 🆂🅷
(727) 726-1161. **$102-$195, 3 day notice.** 105 N Bayshore Dr. Jct SR 590 (Main St); downtown. Int corridors. **Pets:** Small. $35 daily fee/room. Designated rooms, service with restrictions.
[SAVE] [🅢] [✕] [🅗M] [🖉] [✎] [🛏] [🖥] [🍴] [≋] [✕]

ST. PETE BEACH

◈◈ Bay Palm Resort 🅼
(727) 360-7642. **$55-$99, 14 day notice.** 4237 Gulf Blvd. On SR 699, 0.5 mi n of Pinellas Bayway. Ext corridors. **Pets:** Other species. $7 daily fee/pet. Service with restrictions.
[✕] [🛏] [≋] [✕]

🔺 ◈◈◈◈ The Don CeSar Beach Resort A Loews Hotel 🅻🅷
(727) 360-1881. **$219-$499, 5 day notice.** 3400 Gulf Blvd. On SR 699, jct Pinellas Bayway. Int corridors. **Pets:** Accepted.
[SAVE] [🅢] [✕] [🅗M] [🖉] [✎] [🛏] [🖥] [🍴] [≋] [✕]

Lamara Motel Apartments **M**
(727) 360-7521. **$50-$100, 7 day notice.** 520 73rd Ave. Just w of Gulf Blvd (SR 699). Ext corridors. **Pets:** Accepted.

ST. PETERSBURG

La Quinta Inn Tampa Bay Area (St. Petersburg) **M**
(727) 527-8421. **$74-$100.** 4999 34th St N. I-275, exit 26 southbound; exit 26B northbound, just w on 54th Ave N, then just s on US 19. Ext corridors. **Pets:** Accepted.

Mansion House B & B and The Courtyard on Fifth **BB**
(727) 821-9391. **$99-$220, 30 day notice.** 105 5th Ave NE. 0.5 mi n at 1st St N; downtown. Ext/int corridors. **Pets:** Accepted.

Ramada Inn Mirage **M**
(727) 525-1181. **$49-$85.** 5005 34th St N. I-275, exit 26 southbound; exit 26B northbound, just w on 54th Ave N, then just s on US 19. Ext corridors. **Pets:** Small. $25 one-time fee/pet. Service with restrictions, crate.

St. Petersburg Bayfront Hilton **LH** ❀
(727) 894-5000. **$120-$220.** 333 1st St S. I-275, exit 22, 1.5 mi s on 5th Ave, then just e. Int corridors. **Pets:** Medium, other species. $50 daily fee/pet. Service with restrictions, crate.

TAMPA

AmeriSuites (Tampa Airport/Westshore) **SH**
(813) 282-1037. **$99-$159.** 4811 W Main St. I-275, exit 40A, 0.5 mi w on Westshore Blvd; exit 39A northbound, 1 mi n on Kennedy Blvd, then 1 mi w on Westshore Blvd. Int corridors. **Pets:** Small. $10 daily fee/pet. Designated rooms, service with restrictions, supervision.

AmeriSuites (Tampa near Busch Gardens) **SH**
(813) 979-1922. **$109-$125.** 11408 N 30th St. I-275, exit 51, 1.8 mi e on SR 582, then just s. Int corridors. **Pets:** $10 daily fee/room. Service with restrictions, supervision.

AmeriSuites (Tampa/Sabal Corporate Park) **M**
(813) 622-8557. **$109-$149.** 10007 Princess Palm Ave. I-75, exit 260 southbound; exit 260B northbound, 0.5 mi w on SR 574 (Dr. Martin Luther King Blvd), just s on Falkenburg Rd, then just w; in the Sabal Corporate Park. Int corridors. **Pets:** Small, other species. Service with restrictions, supervision.

Baymont Inn & Suites Tampa-Brandon **SH**
(813) 684-4007. **$69-$104, 18 day notice.** 602 S Falkenburg Rd. I-75, exit 257, just w on SR 60, then just n. Int corridors. **Pets:** Accepted.

Baymont Inn & Suites Tampa/near Busch Gardens **SH**
(813) 930-6900. **$60-$100.** 9202 N 30th St. I-275, exit 50, 2 mi e on SR 580, then just n. Int corridors. **Pets:** Large, other species. Designated rooms, service with restrictions, supervision.

Baymont Inn Tampa-Fairgrounds **M**
(813) 626-0885. **$50-$90.** 4811 US 301 N. I-4, exit 6 westbound; exit 6A eastbound, just se. Int corridors. **Pets:** Accepted.

Best Western All Suites Hotel Near USF Behind Busch Gardens **SH**
(813) 971-8930. **$99-$119.** 3001 University Center Dr. I-275, exit 51, 1.8 mi e on SR 582, then 0.5 mi s on N 30th St; behind Busch Gardens. Ext corridors. **Pets:** Accepted.

Best Western-The Westshore Hotel **LH**
(813) 282-3636. **$89-$119.** 1200 N Westshore Blvd. I-275, exit 40A southbound, 0.4 mi n; exit 39A northbound, 0.5 mi e on Kennedy Blvd, then 1.2 mi n. Ext corridors. **Pets:** Accepted.

Chase Suite Hotel by Woodfin **M** ❀
(813) 281-5677. **$129-$229.** 3075 N Rocky Point Dr. I-275, exit 39 southbound; exit 39B northbound, 3 mi w on SR 60, then just n; in Rocky Point Harbor. Ext corridors. **Pets:** Small, other species. $5 daily fee/pet, $50 one-time fee/room. Service with restrictions, supervision.

Clarion Hotel Tampa Airport Westshore **LH** ❀
(813) 289-1950. **$79-$159.** 5303 W Kennedy Blvd. I-275, exit 40A, 0.4 mi e on Westshore Blvd, then 0.5 mi s; exit 39A northbound, just e. Ext/int corridors. **Pets:** Small, dogs only. $25 one-time fee/pet. Designated rooms, service with restrictions, crate.

Days Inn-Tampa North **SH**
(813) 977-1550. **$40-$79.** 701 E Fletcher Ave. I-275, exit 52, just e. Ext corridors. **Pets:** Small, other species. $15 daily fee/pet. Service with restrictions, supervision.

Hampton Inn Veterans Expressway **SH**
(813) 901-5900. **$109-$139.** 5628 W Waters Ave. SR 589 (Veteran's Expwy), exit 6A, just e on CR 584. Int corridors. **Pets:** Small. $8 daily fee/room. Service with restrictions, supervision.

Hard Rock Seminole Casino & Hotel **LH**
(813) 627-7625. **$140-$280, 3 day notice.** 5223 N Orient Rd. I-4, exit 6, just w. Int corridors. **Pets:** Accepted.

Holiday Inn Express & Suites **SH**
(813) 910-7171. **$90-$113.** 8310 Galbraith Rd. I-75, exit 270, 0.7 mi n on Bruce B Downs Blvd, just w on Highwoods Preserve Pkwy, then just n. Int corridors. **Pets:** Small, other species. $100 deposit/pet, $50 one-time fee/pet. Designated rooms, service with restrictions, supervision.

Holiday Inn Express Hotel & Suites **SH**
(813) 885-3700. **$119-$149.** 9402 Corporate Lake Dr. SR 589 (Veteran's Expwy), exit 6B, just e; in Westlake Corporate Center. Int corridors. **Pets:** Small. $35 one-time fee/room. Service with restrictions, supervision.

Holiday Inn Express Hotel & Suites Tampa Stadium/Airport **M**
(813) 877-6061. **$65-$143, 3 day notice.** 4732 N Dale Mabry Hwy. I-275, exit 41B, 2 mi n. Ext corridors. **Pets:** Other species. $35 one-time fee/room. Service with restrictions.

Holiday Inn Tampa Near Busch Gardens **SH**
(813) 971-4710. **$109-$169.** 2701 E Fowler Ave. I-275, exit 51, 1.5 mi e on SR 582. Ext/int corridors. **Pets:** Accepted.

▼▼ **Homestead Studio Suites Hotel-Tampa/North Airport M**
(813) 243-1913. **$64-$105.** 5401 Beaumont Ctr Blvd. SR 589 (Veterans Expwy), exit 4, just w on SR 580. Ext/int corridors. **Pets:** Accepted.
🅰$🄺 🅂🄳 ✖ 🄻🄼 🛗 🛎 📺 💻

◆◆◆ ▼▼▼▼ **La Quinta Inn & Suites Tampa Bay (U.S.F./Near Busch Gardens) SH**
(813) 910-7500. **$85-$125.** 3701 E Fowler. I-275, exit 51, 2.2 mi e on SR 582. Int corridors. **Pets:** Accepted.
(SAVE) ✖ 🄻🄼 🛗 🛎 🛎 📺 💻 🏊

◆◆◆ ▼▼▼▼ **La Quinta Inn Tampa Bay (Airport) M**
(813) 287-0440. **$74-$120.** 4730 Spruce St. I-275, exit 40A southbound; exit 39A (Westshore Blvd) northbound, 0.8 mi w. Ext corridors. **Pets:** Accepted.
(SAVE) ✖ 🛗 🛎 💻 🏊

▼▼▼▼ **La Quinta Inn Tampa South SH**
(813) 835-6262. **$100-$130.** 4620 W Gandy Blvd. Just e of jct S West Shore Blvd. Int corridors. **Pets:** Small. Designated rooms, service with restrictions, supervision.
🅰$🄺 🅂🄳 ✖ 🛗 🛎 🛎 🛎 💻 🏊

▼ **Motel 6 #1192 M**
(813) 628-0888. **$43-$61.** 6510 US 301 N. I-4, exit 6 westbound; exit 6B eastbound, 0.7 mi n. Ext corridors. **Pets:** Accepted.
🅂🄳 ✖ 🏊

▼ **Motel 6–483 M**
(813) 932-4948. **$42-$55.** 333 E Fowler Ave. I-275, exit 51, just w on SR 582. Ext corridors. **Pets:** Accepted.
🅂🄳 ✖ 🏊

▼▼ **Red Roof Inn M**
(813) 932-0073. **$44-$70.** 2307 E Busch Blvd. I-275, exit 50, 1.4 mi e on SR 580. Ext corridors. **Pets:** Medium. Service with restrictions, crate.
✖ 🏊

▼▼ **Red Roof Inn-Brandon M**
(813) 681-8484. **$48-$88.** 10121 Horace Ave. I-75, exit 257, just w on SR 60, then just n on Falkenburg Rd. Ext corridors. **Pets:** Accepted.
✖ 🛎 🛎 🏊

▼▼ **Red Roof Inn-Fairgrounds M**
(813) 623-5245. **$42-$84.** 5001 N US 301. I-4, exit 7 westbound; exit 7A eastbound, just se. Ext corridors. **Pets:** Accepted.
✖ 🛎 🛎

▼▼▼▼ **Residence Inn by Marriott Sabal Park SH**
(813) 627-8855. **$109-$179.** 9719 Princess Palm Ave. I-75, exit 260 southbound; exit 260B northbound, just w on SR 574, just s on Falkenburg Rd, then 0.4 mi w; in Sabal Corporate Center. Int corridors. **Pets:** Accepted.
✖ 🄻🄼 🛎 🛎 🛎 💻 🏊 🛎

▼▼▼▼ **Residence Inn by Marriott Tampa Downtown SH**
(813) 221-4224. **Call for rates.** 101 E Tyler St. I-275, exit 44, 0.5 mi se via Tampa St; downtown. Int corridors. **Pets:** Accepted.
✖ 🄻🄼 🛎 🛎 🛎 💻 🏊 🛎

◆◆◆ ▼▼▼▼ **Sheraton Suites Hotel LH**
(813) 873-8675. **$300.** 4400 W Cypress St. I-275, exit 40B, n to Cypress St, then 0.3 mi w. Int corridors. **Pets:** Accepted.
(SAVE) 🅂🄳 ✖ 🛎 🛎 🛎 🛎 💻 🍴 🏊 🛎

◆◆◆ ▼▼▼▼ **Tahitian Inn M**
(813) 877-6721. **$104-$209.** 601 S Dale Mabry Hwy. I-275, exit 41A, 1.1 mi s. Ext/int corridors. **Pets:** Accepted.
(SAVE) 🅂🄳 ✖ 🛎 🛎 💻 🍴 🏊 🛎

◆◆◆ ▼▼▼▼ **Wellesley Inn & Suites (Tampa/Westshore) SH**
(813) 637-8990. **$69-$159, 30 day notice.** 1805 N Westshore Blvd. I-275, exit 40A southbound, 0.5 mi n; exit 39A northbound, 0.5 mi e on Kennedy Blvd, then 1.3 mi n. Int corridors. **Pets:** Small. $25 daily fee/room. Service with restrictions, crate.
(SAVE) ✖ 🄻🄼 🛎 🛎 🛎 💻 🏊

◆◆◆ ▼▼▼▼ **Wyndham Westshore-Tampa LH**
(813) 286-4400. **$99-$215.** 4860 W Kennedy Blvd. I-275, exit 40A, 0.5 mi s; jct SR 60 and Westshore Blvd. Int corridors. **Pets:** Medium. $50 one-time fee/pet. Service with restrictions, supervision.
(SAVE) ✖ 🛎 🛎 🛎 🛎 💻 🍴 🏊

TEMPLE TERRACE

▼▼▼ **Residence Inn by Marriott Tampa North SH**
(813) 972-4400. **Call for rates.** 13420 N Telecom Pkwy. I-75, exit 266, 1.1 mi w on Fletcher Ave (CR 582A); in Telecom Tampa Park. Int corridors. **Pets:** Accepted.
🅂🄳 ✖ 🄻🄼 🛎 🛎 🛎 🛎 💻 🏊 🛎

TREASURE ISLAND

◆◆◆ ▼▼▼ **Best Western Sea Castle Suites M**
(727) 367-2704. **$75-$180, 3 day notice.** 10750 Gulf Blvd. On SR 699, jct Treasure Island Cswy. Ext corridors. **Pets:** Very small, other species. $50 deposit/pet. Service with restrictions, crate.
(SAVE) 🅂🄳 ✖ 🛎 🛎 💻 🏊 🛎

▼▼ **Bilmar Beach Resort LH**
(727) 360-5531. **$105-$310, 3 day notice.** 10650 Gulf Blvd. On SR 699, jct Treasure Island Cswy. Ext corridors. **Pets:** Accepted.
🅰$🄺 🅂🄳 ✖ 🛎 🛎 🛎 🛎 💻 🏊 🛎

WESLEY CHAPEL

◆◆◆ ▼▼▼ **Masters Inn Tampa North M**
(813) 973-0155. **$43-$63.** 27807 SR 54 W. I-75, exit 279, just w. Ext corridors. **Pets:** Medium, other species. $10 one-time fee/room. Designated rooms, service with restrictions, supervision.
(SAVE) 🅂🄳 ✖ 🛎 🛎 🍴 🏊

END METROPOLITAN AREA

TITUSVILLE

◆◆◆ ▼▼▼▼ **Best Western Space Shuttle Inn Kennedy Space Center SH** 🐾
(321) 269-9100. **$69-$149.** 3455 Cheney Hwy. I-95, exit 215, just e on SR 50. Ext corridors. **Pets:** Other species. $5 daily fee/room. Designated rooms, service with restrictions.
(SAVE) 🅂🄳 ✖ 🛎 🛎 🛎 💻 🍴 🏊 🛎

◆◆◆ ▼▼▼ **Comfort Inn Titusville SH**
(321) 269-7110. **$69-$255.** 3655 Cheney Hwy. I-95, exit 215, just w. Ext corridors. **Pets:** Small. $10 daily fee/pet. Service with restrictions, supervision.
(SAVE) 🅂🄳 🛎 💻 🏊

(AAA) ◆◆◆◆ Days Inn-Kennedy Space Center SH
(321) 269-4480. **$54-$139.** 3755 Cheney Hwy. I-95, exit 215 (SR 50). Ext corridors. **Pets:** Large, other species. $10 daily fee/room. Service with restrictions, crate.
SAVE S⚡ ✕ ⊘ 🛏 💻 ⊇

(AAA) ◆◆◆ Holiday Inn Riverfront-Kennedy Space Center SH
(321) 269-2121. **$99-$179.** 4951 S Washington Ave. US 1, 0.5 mi s of jct SR 50; 1.7 mi n of jct SR 405. Ext corridors. **Pets:** Accepted.
SAVE S⚡ ✕ ⚡M ⊘ ⚡ 🛏 💻 ❙❙ ⊇ ✕

(AAA) ◆◆◆ Ramada Inn & Suites-Kennedy Space Center SH
(321) 269-5510. **$99-$149.** 3500 Cheney Hwy. I-95, exit 215, just e on SR 50. Int corridors. **Pets:** Medium. $25 one-time fee/pet. Service with restrictions, supervision.
SAVE S⚡ ✕ ⊘ 🛏 💻 ❙❙ ⊇ ✕

VENICE

(AAA) ◆◆◆◆ Holiday Inn Venice M ❀
(941) 485-5411. **$65-$149.** 455 US 41 Bypass N. 0.5 mi s of jct US 41. Ext/int corridors. **Pets:** Small, other species. $30 one-time fee/room. Supervision.
SAVE S⚡ ✕ ⚡M ⊘ ⚡ 🛏 💻 ❙❙ ⊇ ✕

◆◆◆ Horse and Chaise Inn A Bed & Breakfast BB
(941) 488-2702. **$89-$149.** 317 Ponce de Leon. Just s of jct Venice Ave on Nassau St, just sw; downtown. Ext/int corridors. **Pets:** Accepted.
ASK ✕ 🛏 ⊇

◆ Motel 6-364 M
(941) 485-8255. **$43-$71.** 281 US 41 Bypass N. On US 41, just n of jct Venice Ave. Ext corridors. **Pets:** Accepted.
S⚡ ✕ ⊘ ⚡ ⊇

WEEKI WACHEE

(AAA) ◆◆◆ Best Western Weeki Wachee Resort M
(352) 596-2007. **$65-$90.** 6172 Commercial Way. On US 19, jct SR 50 (Cortez Blvd). Ext corridors. **Pets:** Other species. No service, supervision.
SAVE S⚡ ✕ ⊘ 💻 ⊇

WEST MELBOURNE

◆◆◆ Howard Johnson SH
(321) 768-8877. **$69-$99.** 4431 W New Haven Ave. I-95, exit 180, just e on US 192. Ext corridors. **Pets:** Accepted.
ASK S⚡ ✕ ⊘ 🛏 💻 ⊇

◆◆ Ramada Limited West Melbourne SH
(321) 724-2051. **Call for rates.** 4500 W New Haven Ave. I-95, exit 180, just e. Ext corridors. **Pets:** Accepted.
✕ ⊘ ⚡ 🛏 💻

WEST PALM BEACH

(AAA) ◆◆◆◆ Comfort Inn-Palm Beach Lakes M
(561) 689-6100. **$89-$139.** 1901 Palm Beach Lakes Blvd. I-95, exit 71, just w. Int corridors. **Pets:** Medium. $10 daily fee/room, $25 one-time fee/room. Designated rooms, service with restrictions, supervision.
SAVE S⚡ ✕ ⊘ 🛏 💻 ⊇

◆◆◆ Hibiscus House Bed & Breakfast BB
(561) 863-5633. **$85-$190, 14 day notice.** 501 30th St. 1.2 mi n on Flagler Dr from jct Palm Beach Lakes Blvd, 0.3 mi w. Int corridors. **Pets:** Other species.
ASK S⚡ ✕ 🛏 ⊇

◆◆ Red Roof Inn-West Palm Beach M
(561) 697-7710. **$52-$95.** 2421 Metrocenter Blvd E. I-95, exit 74 (45th St), just w on CR 702; in Metrocenter Corporate Park. Ext/int corridors. **Pets:** Small. Service with restrictions, supervision.
✕ ⚡M ⊘ ⚡ 🛏 ⊇

◆◆◆ Residence Inn by Marriott West Palm Beach SH
(561) 687-4747. **$114-$154.** 2461 Metrocenter Blvd. I-95, exit 74, just w on 45th St; in Metrocenter Corporate Park. Int corridors. **Pets:** Other species. $75 one-time fee/room. Service with restrictions.
✕ ⚡M ⊘ ⚡ 🛏 💻 ⊇ ✕

◆◆ Studio 6 Extended Stay #6026 M
(561) 640-3335. **$65-$75.** 1535 Centrepark Dr N. I-95, exit 69 (Belvedere Rd), w to Australian Ave, n to Centrepark Dr, then e straight ahead. Ext corridors. **Pets:** Accepted.
S⚡ ✕ ⚡M ⚡ 🛏 💻

(AAA) ◆◆ Wellesley Inn (West Palm Beach) SH
(561) 689-8540. **$59-$109.** 1910 Palm Beach Lakes Blvd. I-95, exit 71, just w. Int corridors. **Pets:** Small. Designated rooms, service with restrictions, supervision.
SAVE S⚡ ✕ ⊘ ⚡ 🛏 💻 ⊇

WILLISTON

◆ Williston Motor Inn M
(352) 528-4801. **$38-$209.** 606 W Noble Ave. 0.5 mi n on US 27 Alternate. Ext corridors. **Pets:** Accepted.
✕ 🛏 💻 ❙❙ ⊇

WINTER HAVEN

(AAA) ◆◆◆◆ Best Western Admiral's Inn SH
(863) 324-5950. **$79-$115, 14 day notice.** 5665 Cypress Gardens Blvd. SR 540, 3 mi e of jct US 17; 3.9 mi w of jct US 27. Ext/int corridors. **Pets:** Accepted.
SAVE S⚡ ✕ ⊘ 🛏 💻 ❙❙ ⊇ ✕

◆◆ Cypress Motel M
(863) 324-5867. **$49-$80.** 5651 Cypress Gardens Rd. 1.7 mi w of US 27 on SR 540; or 2 mi e of Cypress Gardens Theme Park, then 500 yds n. Ext corridors. **Pets:** Medium. $10 one-time fee/pet. No service, supervision.
ASK S⚡ ✕ ⊘ 🛏 💻 ⊇ ✕

GEORGIA

ADAIRSVILLE

Comfort Inn SH
(770) 773-2886. **$50-$80.** 107 Princeton Blvd. I-75, exit 306, just w. Ext corridors. **Pets:** Small. $5 daily fee/pet. Service with restrictions, supervision.

Ramada Ltd SH
(770) 769-9726. **$49-$109.** 500 Georgia North Cir. I-75, exit 306, 0.3 mi w. Ext corridors. **Pets:** Accepted.

ADEL

Hampton Inn SH
(229) 896-3099. **$70-$72.** 1500 W 4th St. I-75, exit 39, just w. Int corridors. **Pets:** Other species. $10 daily fee/pet. Designated rooms, service with restrictions, supervision.

Super 8 Motel I-75 SH
(229) 896-2244. **$42-$52.** 1103 W 4th St. I-75, exit 39, just e. Ext corridors. **Pets:** Accepted.

ALBANY

Jameson Inn SH
(229) 435-3737. **$49-$104.** 2720 Dawson Rd. 0.5 mi s of jct US 82 and SR 520. Ext corridors. **Pets:** Very small, other species. $10 daily fee/room. Service with restrictions, supervision.

Motel 6 #172 SH
(229) 439-0078. **$37-$47.** 201 S Thorton Dr. Just e of US 19/82. Ext corridors. **Pets:** Accepted.

Wingate Inn SH
(229) 883-9800. **$100.** 2735 Dawson Rd. Jct US 82 and SR 520, 0.4 mi s. Int corridors. **Pets:** Other species. $50 one-time fee/room. Service with restrictions, crate.

AMERICUS

1906 Pathway Inn Bed & Breakfast BB
(229) 928-2078. **$89-$145.** 501 S Lee St. 0.5 mi s of US 280 on SR 377. Int corridors. **Pets:** Small. $50 deposit/pet, $20 daily fee/pet. Designated rooms, service with restrictions, supervision.

Holiday Inn Express SH
(229) 928-5400. **$70-$80.** 1611 E Lomar St. On US 280, just w of jct US 27. Ext corridors. **Pets:** Small. $15 one-time fee/pet. Service with restrictions, supervision.

ASHBURN

Best Western Ashburn Inn SH
(229) 567-0080. **$44-$55.** 820 Shoney's Dr. I-75, exit 82, just w. Ext corridors. **Pets:** Small. $6 daily fee/pet. Designated rooms, service with restrictions, supervision.

Days Inn SH
(229) 567-3346. **$42-$52.** 823 E Washington Ave. I-75, exit 82, just w on SR 112. Ext corridors. **Pets:** Small. $6 daily fee/pet. Designated rooms, service with restrictions, supervision.

Ramada Limited SH
(229) 567-3295. **$46-$52.** 156 Whittle Cir. I-75, exit 82, just w. Ext corridors. **Pets:** Other species. $5 daily fee/pet. Service with restrictions, supervision.

Super 8 Motel SH
(229) 567-4688. **$50-$76, 3 day notice.** 749 E Washington Ave. I-75, exit 82, just w. Ext corridors. **Pets:** $5 one-time fee/pet. Supervision.

ATHENS

Best Western-Colonial Inn SH
(706) 546-7311. **$59-$119, 7 day notice.** 170 N Milledge Ave. Jct US 78 business route (Broad St), 0.5 mi w on SR 15. Ext corridors. **Pets:** Accepted.

▼▼▼▼ Holiday Inn 🆑
(706) 549-4433. **$79-$119.** 197 E Broad St. On US 78 business route (Broad St); center. Ext/int corridors. **Pets:** Small, other species. Designated rooms, service with restrictions, supervision.
A$K 🆂 ✖ 🕗 🖥 🍴 ➾

▼▼▼ Holiday Inn Express 🆂🅷
(706) 546-8122. **$76-$85.** 513 W Broad St. On US 78 business route (Broad St); center. Int corridors. **Pets:** Accepted.
A$K 🆂 ✖ 🕗 🖥 ➾

ATLANTA METROPOLITAN AREA

ACWORTH

🆎 ▼▼▼ Best Western Acworth Inn 🆂🅷
(770) 974-0116. **$50-$65.** 5155 Cowan Rd. I-75, exit 277, just w. Ext corridors. **Pets:** Medium. $10 daily fee/pet. Service with restrictions, supervision.
SAVE 🆂 ✖ 🖥 ➾

🆎 ▼▼▼ Days Inn 🅼
(770) 974-1700. **$50-$80.** 5035 Cowan Rd. I-75, exit 277, just w. Ext corridors. **Pets:** Accepted.
SAVE 🆂 ✖ ➾

🆎 ▼▼▼ Econo Lodge 🆂🅷
(770) 974-1922. **$50-$80.** 4980 Cowan Rd. I-75, exit 277, just w. Ext corridors. **Pets:** Accepted.
SAVE 🆂 ✖ 🖥 ➾

🆎 ▼▼▼ Red Roof Inn 🅼
(770) 974-5400. **$45-$50, 7 day notice.** 5320 Glade Rd. I-75, exit 278, just w. Ext corridors. **Pets:** Medium, other species. Service with restrictions, supervision.
SAVE 🆂 ✖ 🕗 🖥 ➾

🆎 ▼▼▼ Super 8 Motel 🆂🅷
(770) 966-9700. **$45-$79.** 4970 Cowan Rd. I-75, exit 277, just w. Ext corridors. **Pets:** Medium. $7 daily fee/pet. Service with restrictions, supervision.
SAVE 🆂 ✖ 🕗 🖥 ➾

ALPHARETTA

🆎 ▼▼▼ AmeriSuites (Atlanta Alpharetta/North Point Mall) 🆂🅷
(770) 594-8788. **$99, 30 day notice.** 7500 North Point Pkwy. SR 400, exit 8, just e to North Point Pkwy, then just n. Int corridors. **Pets:** Small, dogs only. $10 one-time fee/pet. Service with restrictions, supervision.
SAVE 🆂 ✖ 🅼 🕗 🖥 ➾

🆎 ▼▼▼ AmeriSuites (Atlanta Alpharetta/Windward Parkway) 🆂🅷
(770) 343-9566. **$109-$119.** 5595 Windward Pkwy. SR 400, exit 11, just w. Int corridors. **Pets:** Small. $10 daily fee/pet. Service with restrictions, supervision.
SAVE 🆂 ✖ 🅼 🕗 🖥 ➾

🆎 ▼▼▼ Homewood Suites 🆂🅷
(770) 998-1622. **$89-$139.** 10775 Davis Dr. SR 400, exit 8, northwest corner. Int corridors. **Pets:** Other species. $100 one-time fee/room.
SAVE 🆂 ✖ 🅼 🕗 🖥 ➾

🆎 ▼▼▼ La Quinta Inn & Suites Atlanta (Alpharetta) 🆂🅷
(770) 754-7800. **$74-$104.** 1350 North Point Dr. SR 400, exit 9, 0.5 mi e. Int corridors. **Pets:** Medium, other species. Service with restrictions, crate.
SAVE ✖ 🅼 🕗 🖥 ➾

▼▼▼ Residence Inn by Marriott 🆂🅷
(770) 664-0664. **Call for rates.** 5465 Windward Pkwy W. SR 400, exit 11, 0.4 mi w. Ext/int corridors. **Pets:** Accepted.
✖ 🅼 🕗 🖥 ➾ ✖

▼▼▼ Sleep Inn 🆂🅷
(678) 347-0022. **$49-$69.** 2925 Jordan Ct. SR 400, exit 11, 0.7 mi w. Int corridors. **Pets:** Accepted.
A$K 🆂 ✖ 🅼 🕗 🖥 ➾

▼▼▼ Staybridge Suites 🆂🅷
(770) 569-7200. **$129-$169.** 3980 North Point Pkwy. SR 400, exit 10, 0.5 mi e. Int corridors. **Pets:** Medium. $150 one-time fee/room. Service with restrictions.
A$K 🆂 ✖ 🅼 🕗 🖥 ➾

▼▼▼ TownePlace Suites by Marriott 🆂🅷
(770) 664-1300. **$81-$104.** 7925 S Westside Pkwy. SR 400, exit 9, 0.3 mi w. Int corridors. **Pets:** $75 one-time fee/room. Service with restrictions.
A$K 🆂 ✖ 🅼 🕗 🖥 ➾

🆎 ▼▼▼ Wellesley Inn & Suites (Atlanta/Alpharetta) 🆂🅷
(770) 569-1730. **$65-$99.** 3329 Old Milton Pkwy. SR 400, exit 10, just e. Int corridors. **Pets:** Accepted.
SAVE 🆂 ✖ 🅼 🕗 🖥 ➾

▼▼▼ Wingate Inn 🆂🅷
(770) 649-0955. **$69-$107.** 1005 Kingswood Pl. SR 400, exit 8, 0.7 mi w. Int corridors. **Pets:** Small. Service with restrictions, crate.
A$K 🆂 ✖ 🅼 🕗 🖥

ATLANTA

🆎 ▼▼▼▼ AmeriSuites (Atlanta/Buckhead) 🆂🅷
(404) 869-6161. **$69-$299.** 3242 Peachtree Rd NE. Jct Peachtree and Piedmont rds NE, just s. Int corridors. **Pets:** Small, other species. $10 daily fee/pet. Service with restrictions, supervision.
SAVE 🆂 ✖ 🅼 🕗 🖥 ➾

🆎 ▼▼▼▼ AmeriSuites (Atlanta/Perimeter Center) 🆂🅷
(770) 730-9300. **$79-$179.** 1005 Crestline Pkwy. SR 400, exit 5A (Dunwoody), 0.3 mi e. Int corridors. **Pets:** Other species. $10 daily fee/room. Service with restrictions, supervision.
SAVE 🆂 ✖ 🅼 🕗 🖥 ➾

🆎 ▼▼▼ Baymont Inn & Suites Atlanta-Lenox/Buckhead 🆂🅷
(404) 321-0999. **$75-$80.** 2535 Chantilly Dr NE. I-85, exit 88 southbound; exit 86 northbound, 2 mi on Buford Hwy to Lenox Rd, then just e under highway. Int corridors. **Pets:** Accepted.
SAVE 🆂 ✖ 🕗 🖥

🆎 ▼▼▼▼ Best Western Granada Suite Hotel 🆂🅷
(404) 876-6100. **$95-$229, 14 day notice.** 1302 W Peachtree St. I-75/85, exit 250 (14th St), just e, then just n on W Peachtree St to 16th St. Int corridors. **Pets:** Accepted.
SAVE 🆂 ✖ 🕗 🖥

🆎 ▼▼▼▼ Best Western Inn at the Peachtrees 🆂🅷
(404) 577-6970. **$91-$229, 14 day notice.** 330 W Peachtree St. I-75/85, exit 248C northbound, 0.4 mi w to Peachtree St, then 0.3 mi n; exit 249C southbound, just s to Peachtree Pl, then just e. Ext/int corridors. **Pets:** Accepted.
SAVE 🆂 🕗 🖥

▼▼ Beverly Hills Inn BB
(404) 233-8520. **$110-$165, 3 day notice.** 65 Sheridan Dr NE. Jct Piedmont and Peachtree rds, 1.1 mi s on Peachtree Rd to Sheridan Dr, then just e. Int corridors. **Pets:** $50 one-time fee/room. Service with restrictions, supervision.

(ASK) (🔊) (🈵) (📼)

▼▼▼ Crowne Plaza Atlanta Perimeter NW LH
(770) 955-1700. **$69-$149.** 6345 Powers Ferry Rd NW. I-285, exit 22, southeast corner. Int corridors. **Pets:** Small. $75 one-time fee/room. Service with restrictions, supervision.

(ASK) (🔊) (✖) (👤) (📼) (🈵) (📺) (🍴) (🏊)

△△△ ▼▼▼▼ Four Seasons Hotel Atlanta SH
(404) 881-9898. **$295-$375.** 75 14th St. I-75/85, exit 250 (14th St), 0.3 mi e; in art and business district. Int corridors. **Pets:** Accepted.

(✖) (👤) (📼) (📺) (🍴) (🏊) (📺)

△△△ ▼▼▼ Grand Hyatt Atlanta LH
(404) 365-8100. **$119-$275, 3 day notice.** 3300 Peachtree Rd. Corner of Peachtree and Piedmont rds. Int corridors. **Pets:** Small, other species. $100 one-time fee/room. Service with restrictions.

(SAVE) (✖) (👤) (📼) (📺) (📼) (🍴) (🏊) (📺)

△△△ ▼▼▼ Hawthorn Suites-Atlanta NW SH
(770) 952-9595. **$109-$189, 3 day notice.** 1500 Parkwood Cir. I-75, exit 260 (Windy Hill Rd), 0.5 mi e, then 0.3 mi s on Powers Ferry Rd. Ext corridors. **Pets:** Accepted.

(SAVE) (🔊) (✖) (📼) (📺) (📺) (🏊) (📺)

▼▼▼▼ Holiday Inn Select Atlanta Perimeter SH
(770) 457-6363. **$119-$139.** 4386 Chamblee-Dunwoody Rd. I-285, exit 30 eastbound, southwest corner; westbound, follow access road 1.3 mi to Chamblee-Dunwoody Rd, then just s. Int corridors. **Pets:** Accepted.

(ASK) (🔊) (✖) (👤) (📼) (📺) (📺) (🍴) (🏊)

▼▼ Homestead Studio Suites Hotel-Atlanta/North Druid Hills SH
(404) 325-1223. **$62-$82.** 1339 Executive Park Dr NE. I-85, exit 89, just e to Executive Park Dr, then just s. Ext corridors. **Pets:** Accepted.

(ASK) (🔊) (✖) (👤) (📼) (📺) (📼) (📺)

▼▼▼ Homestead Studio Suites Hotel-Atlanta/Perimeter SH
(770) 522-0025. **$66-$86.** 1050 Hammond Dr. I-285, exit 26 eastbound, 0.5 mi n to Hammond Dr, then 0.5 mi e; exit 28 westbound, just n to Hammond Dr, then just w. Ext corridors. **Pets:** Small, other species. $25 one-time fee/room. Service with restrictions, supervision.

(ASK) (🔊) (✖) (👤) (📼) (📺) (📼) (📺)

▼▼▼ Homewood Suites-Cumberland SH
(770) 988-9449. **$99-$189.** 3200 Cobb Pkwy SW. I-285, exit 19 eastbound; exit 20 westbound, 0.7 mi se on US 41 (Cobb Pkwy). Ext/int corridors. **Pets:** Medium. $150 one-time fee/room. Service with restrictions, supervision.

(ASK) (🔊) (✖) (👤) (📼) (📼) (📺) (🏊) (📺)

▼▼▼ La Quinta Inn & Suites Atlanta (Paces Ferry/Vinings) SH
(770) 801-9002. **$94-$109.** 2415 Paces Ferry Rd SE. I-285, exit 18, just w. Int corridors. **Pets:** Accepted.

(ASK) (✖) (👤) (📼) (📺) (📼) (📺) (🏊)

△△△ ▼▼▼ La Quinta Inn & Suites Atlanta (Perimeter/ Medical Center) SH ✿
(770) 350-6177. **$79-$99.** 6260 Peachtree-Dunwoody. I-285, exit 28 westbound, 0.7 mi n; exit 26 eastbound, 0.5 mi n to Hammond Dr, 0.7 mi e, then 0.5 mi n. Int corridors. **Pets:** Other species. Service with restrictions, supervision.

(SAVE) (✖) (👤) (📼) (📺) (📼) (📼) (📺)

△△△ ▼▼▼▼ Omni Hotel at CNN Center LH
(404) 659-0000. **$149-$279.** 100 CNN Center. I-75/85, exit 248C northbound, 0.8 mi w; exit 249C southbound to International Blvd, 0.5 mi w. Int corridors. **Pets:** Small. $50 one-time fee/room. Designated rooms, service with restrictions, supervision.

(SAVE) (🔊) (✖) (📼) (📺) (📼) (📼) (🍴) (🏊) (📺)

▼▼ Red Roof Inn-Druid Hills M
(404) 321-1653. **$53-$66.** 1960 N Druid Hills Rd. I-85, exit 89, just w. Ext corridors. **Pets:** Accepted.

(✖) (📼)

▼▼▼ Residence Inn Atlanta Midtown at 17th Street SH
(404) 745-1000. **$99-$299.** 1365 Peachtree St. I-75/85, exit 250 (14th St), 0.5 mi e to Peachtree St, then 0.3 mi n. Int corridors. **Pets:** Medium. $75 one-time fee/room. Service with restrictions, crate.

(ASK) (🔊) (✖) (👤) (📼) (📼) (📼) (📺)

▼▼▼ Residence Inn-Buckhead/Lenox SH
(404) 467-1660. **$79-$169.** 2220 Lake Blvd. I-85, exit 89, 1.6 mi w on N Druid Hills which becomes E Roxboro, then just n on Lenox Park Blvd. Int corridors. **Pets:** Medium. $75 one-time fee/room. Service with restrictions.

(ASK) (🔊) (✖) (👤) (📼) (📼) (📼) (📺) (🏊) (📺)

▼▼▼ Residence Inn by Marriott-Atlanta/Buckhead SH
(404) 239-0677. **$159.** 2960 Piedmont Rd NE. Jct Piedmont and Pharr rds, just s. Ext corridors. **Pets:** Accepted.

(ASK) (🔊) (✖) (👤) (📼) (📼) (📼) (📺) (🏊) (📺)

▼▼▼ Residence Inn by Marriott-Atlanta Downtown SH ✿
(404) 522-0950. **$139-$169.** 134 Peachtree St NW. I-75/85, exit 248C northbound, 0.4 mi w, then just s; exit 249A southbound to International Blvd, just w, then just s. Int corridors. **Pets:** Large, other species. $75 one-time fee/pet. Service with restrictions, supervision.

(ASK) (🔊) (✖) (👤) (📼) (📼) (📼)

▼▼▼ Residence Inn by Marriott Atlanta Dunwoody SH ✿
(770) 455-4446. **Call for rates.** 1901 Savoy Dr. I-285, exit 30, just e. Ext corridors. **Pets:** Other species. $75 one-time fee/room. Service with restrictions.

(✖) (📼) (📼) (📼) (📺) (🏊) (📺)

▼▼▼ Residence Inn by Marriott Midtown SH
(404) 872-8885. **$74-$234.** 1041 W Peachtree St. I-75/85, exit 250 (10th St), just e to W Peachtree St, then just n; corner of 11th St. Int corridors. **Pets:** Accepted.

(ASK) (🔊) (✖) (👤) (📼) (📼) (📼) (📺)

▼▼▼ Residence Inn by Marriott-Perimeter West SH
(404) 252-5066. **$79-$159.** 6096 Barfield Rd. I-285, exit 26 eastbound, 0.5 mi n on Glenridge to Hammond Dr, then 0.3 mi e to Barfield Rd; exit 28 westbound (Peachtree-Dunwoody Rd), 0.5 mi n to Hammond Dr, then just w. Ext corridors. **Pets:** Accepted.

(ASK) (🔊) (✖) (📼) (📼) (📺) (🏊) (📺)

△△△ ▼▼▼▼ The Ritz-Carlton, Buckhead LH
(404) 237-2700. **$379-$449.** 3434 Peachtree Rd NE. I-85, exit 86, 1.8 mi n on Cheshire Bridge-Lenox Rd. Int corridors. **Pets:** Accepted.

(✖) (📼) (📼) (📼) (📺) (🍴) (🏊) (📺)

▼▼▼ Sheraton Atlanta Hotel LH ✿
(404) 659-6500. **$99-$139.** 165 Courtland St. I-75/85, exit 249A southbound; exit 248C northbound, just w. Int corridors. **Pets:** Medium, dogs only. Designated rooms, service with restrictions, supervision.

(ASK) (🔊) (✖) (📼) (📼) (📺) (🍴) (🏊) (📺)

▼▼▼ Sheraton Buckhead Hotel Atlanta LH ✿
(404) 261-9250. **$89-$139.** 3405 Lenox Rd NE. I-85, exit 88 southbound; exit 86 northbound, 1.8 mi n. Int corridors. **Pets:** Service with restrictions.

(ASK) (🔊) (✖) (📼) (📼) (📼) (📺) (🍴) (🏊)

AAA ◇◇◇ Sheraton Midtown Atlanta Hotel at Colony Square **SH** ❖
(404) 892-6000. **$259-$309.** 188 14th St NE. I-75/85, exit 250 (14th St), 0.5 mi e. Int corridors. Pets: Medium, dogs only. $25 daily fee/pet. Designated rooms, service with restrictions, supervision.
SAVE S✗M ✗ ✎ ✦ 🔒 💻 ⊞ ⊞

AAA ◇◇◇ Sheraton Suites Galleria **LH**
(770) 955-3900. **$89-$249.** 2844 Cobb Pkwy SE. I-285, exit 20 westbound; exit 19 eastbound, just s on US 41 (Cobb Pkwy). Int corridors. **Pets:** Accepted.
SAVE S✗M ✗ ✎ ✦ 🔒 💻 ⊞ ⊞ ⊠

◇◇◇ Staybridge Suites **SH**
(404) 842-0800. **$146-$199.** 540 Pharr Rd. Jct Pharr and Piedmont rds, just w. Int corridors. **Pets:** Medium. $150 one-time fee/room. Service with restrictions.
ASK S✗M ✗ ✎ ✦ 🔒 💻 ⊞ ⊠

◇◇◇ Staybridge Suites-Atlanta-Mt. Vernon **SH**
(404) 250-0110. **$160.** 760 Mt Vernon Hwy NE. I-285, exit 25, 0.8 mi n on Roswell Rd, then 1 mi e. Ext/int corridors. **Pets:** Accepted.
ASK S✗M ✗ ✎ 🔒 💻 ⊞ ⊠

◇◇◇ Staybridge Suites Atlanta Perimeter **SH**
(678) 320-0111. **$127.** 4601 Ridgeview Rd. I-285, exit 29, 0.5 mi n, 0.5 mi w on Perimeter Center W to Crowne Pointe Dr, then just n. Int corridors. **Pets:** Other species. $75 one-time fee/room. Service with restrictions, supervision.
ASK S✗M ✗ ✎M ✎ ✦ 🔒 💻 ⊞

◇◇◇ Summerfield Suites by Wyndham-Atlanta/Buckhead **SH**
(404) 262-7880. **$80-$120.** 505 Pharr Rd. Jct Pharr Rd and Maple Dr, just w of Piedmont Rd. Ext/int corridors. **Pets:** Medium. $150 one-time fee/room. Service with restrictions, supervision.
ASK ✗ ✎ 🔒 💻 ⊞ ⊠

AAA ◇◇ Super 8 Motel **M**
(404) 873-5731. **$69-$99.** 1641 Peachtree St NE. I-75/85, exit 250 (10th St), 0.3 mi e to W Peachtree St, then 1 mi n. Ext/int corridors. **Pets:** Other species. $10 daily fee/pet. Service with restrictions, crate.
SAVE S✗M ✗ ✦ 🔒

AAA ◇◇ University Inn at Emory **SH** 🐾
(404) 634-7327. **$65-$149.** 1767 N Decatur Rd. I-85, exit 91, 3.8 mi s on Clairmont Rd to N Decatur Rd, then 0.8 mi w. Ext corridors. **Pets:** Large, other species. $15 daily fee/pet.
SAVE S✗M ✗ ✎ 🔒 💻

◇◇◇ W Atlanta **LH** ❖
(770) 396-6800. **$179-$369.** 111 Perimeter Center W. I-285, exit 29, 0.3 mi n. Int corridors. **Pets:** Large, other species. $25 daily fee/pet, $100 one-time fee/pet. Service with restrictions, supervision.
ASK ✗ ✎M 🔒 💻 ⊞ ⊞ ⊠

AAA ◇◇◇ Wellesley Inn & Suites (Atlanta/Windy Hill) **SH**
(770) 226-0242. **$75-$89.** 2225 Interstate North Pkwy. I-75, exit 260 (Windy Hill Rd), just e to Interstate North Pkwy, then just s. Int corridors. **Pets:** Accepted.
SAVE S✗M ✗ ✎M ✎ ✦ 🔒 💻 ⊞

◇◇◇ The Westin Atlanta North **LH**
(770) 395-3900. **$109-$189.** 7 Concourse Pkwy. I-285, exit 28 westbound; exit 26 eastbound, 0.5 mi n to Hammond Dr, then 0.4 mi e. Int corridors. **Pets:** Accepted.
ASK S✗M ✗ ✎ ✦ 🔒 💻 ⊞ ⊞ ⊠

AAA ◇◇◇ The Westin Buckhead Atlanta **LH**
(404) 365-0065. **$239, 3 day notice.** 3391 Peachtree Rd NE. Adjacent to Lenox Mall. Int corridors. **Pets:** Accepted.
SAVE S✗M ✗ ✎ 🔒 💻 ⊞ ⊞ ⊠

◇◇◇ The Westin Peachtree Plaza **LH** ❖
(404) 659-1400. **Call for rates.** 210 Peachtree St. I-75/85, exit 248C northbound, 0.4 mi w; exit 249C southbound, 0.5 mi s. Int corridors. **Pets:** Medium, dogs only. Service with restrictions, supervision.
✗ ✎ ✦ 🔒 💻 ⊞ ⊞

AUSTELL

◇◇◇ La Quinta Inn Atlanta (West/Near Six Flags) **SH**
(770) 944-2110. **$75-$95.** 7377 Six Flags Dr. I-20, exit 46 eastbound; exit 46B westbound, just n. Ext/int corridors. **Pets:** Accepted.
ASK ✗ ✎ 🔒 💻 ⊞

COLLEGE PARK

AAA ◇◇◇ AmeriSuites (Atlanta/Airport) **SH**
(770) 994-2997. **$89-$95.** 1899 Sullivan Rd. I-85, exit 71, just e to Sullivan Rd, then just s; I-285, exit 60 (Riverdale Rd N), 1 mi to Sullivan Rd, then just s. Int corridors. **Pets:** Small. $20 daily fee/room. Service with restrictions, crate.
SAVE S✗M ✗ ✎M 🔒 💻 ⊞

◇◇ Howard Johnson Express Inn **SH**
(404) 766-0000. **$49-$69, 7 day notice.** 2480 Old National Pkwy. I-285, exit 62, just s. Int corridors. **Pets:** Small, other species. $15 daily fee/pet. Designated rooms, no service.
ASK S✗M ✗ 🔒 💻

◇◇ Motel 6-1487 Atlanta Airport **M**
(404) 761-9701. **$45-$57.** 2471 Old National Pkwy. I-85, exit 69; I-285, exit 62, just s. Ext corridors. **Pets:** Accepted.
S✗M ✗ ✎

AAA ◇◇◇ Ramada Hotel Atlanta Airport South **SH**
(770) 996-4321. **$69-$99.** 1551 Phoenix Blvd. I-285, exit 60 (Riverdale Rd N), just sw. Ext/int corridors. **Pets:** Medium, other species. $10 daily fee/room. Designated rooms, service with restrictions.
SAVE S✗M ✗ ✎ 🔒 💻 ⊞

DECATUR

◇◇ Best Inn & Suites **SH**
(404) 286-2500. **$59-$65.** 4095 Covington Hwy. I-285, exit 43, just w. Ext corridors. **Pets:** Accepted.
ASK S✗M ✗ ✎M ✎ ✦ 🔒 ⊞

◇◇ Days Inn I-20 East **SH**
(770) 981-5670. **Call for rates.** 4300 Snapfinger Woods Dr. I-20, exit 68, just e. Ext corridors. **Pets:** Accepted.
✗ ✎M ✎ 🔒 💻 ⊞

DORAVILLE

AAA ◇◇ Masters Inn **M**
(770) 454-8373. **$43-$63.** 3092 Presidential Pkwy. I-85, exit 94, just e, then n. Ext corridors. **Pets:** Accepted.
SAVE S✗M ✗ ✎ 🔒 ⊞

DULUTH

AAA ◇◇◇ AmeriSuites (Atlanta/Duluth-John's Creek) **SH**
(770) 622-5858. **$69-$109, 14 day notice.** 11505 Medlock Bridge Rd. Jct SR 141 and 120, 0.7 mi n. Int corridors. **Pets:** Accepted.
SAVE S✗M ✗ ✎M ✎ ✦ 🔒 💻 ⊞

AAA ◇◇◇ AmeriSuites (Atlanta/Gwinnett Mall) **SH**
(770) 623-9699. **$89-$109, 14 day notice.** 3530 Venture Pkwy. I-85, exit 104, just w to Venture Pkwy, then just n. Int corridors. **Pets:** Accepted.
SAVE S✗M ✗ ✎M ✎ 🔒 💻 ⊞

ᗺᗺ Candlewood Suites-Atlanta 🆂🅷
(678) 380-0414. **$72-$93.** 3665 Shackleford Rd. I-85, exit 104, just e, then just s. Int corridors. **Pets:** Medium. $25 one-time fee/room. Designated rooms, service with restrictions, supervision.
[ASK] [S🅳] [✕] [&M] [🖉] [🐾] [🗄] [💻] [🏊]

🅐🅐🅐 ᗺᗺᗺ Days Inn Gwinnett Place 🆂🅷
(770) 476-8700. **$70-$100.** 1920 Pleasant Hill Rd. I-85, exit 104; northwest corner. Int corridors. **Pets:** Medium. $25 deposit/room, $10 daily fee/pet. Service with restrictions, crate.
[SAVE] [S🅳] [✕]

🅐🅐🅐 ᗺᗺᗺᗺ Hampton Inn & Suites-Gwinnett 🆂🅷
(770) 931-9800. **$59-$79.** 1725 Pineland Rd. I-85, exit 104, 0.3 mi e to Crestwood, then just s. Int corridors. **Pets:** Accepted.
[SAVE] [S🅳] [✕] [&M] [🖉] [🐾] [🗄] [💻] [🏊]

ᗺᗺᗺᗺ Holiday Inn-Gwinnett Center 🆂🅷
(770) 476-2022. **Call for rates.** 6310 Sugarloaf Pkwy. I-85, exit 108, just se. Int corridors. **Pets:** Accepted.
[✕] [🗄] [💻] [🍴] [🏊]

🅐🅐🅐 ᗺᗺᗺᗺ La Quinta Inn Duluth 🆂🅷 ✿
(678) 957-0500. **$79-$89.** 2370 Stephen Center Dr. I-85, exit 107, just w. Int corridors. **Pets:** Service with restrictions, supervision.
[SAVE] [S🅳] [✕] [&M] [🖉] [🐾] [🗄] [💻] [🏊]

ᗺᗺᗺ Residence Inn-Atlanta Gwinnett 🆂🅷 🐾
(770) 921-2202. **$134-$179.** 1760 Pineland Rd. I-85, exit 104, just e to Shackleford Rd, just s to Pineland Rd, then just e. Int corridors. **Pets:** Medium, other species. $75 one-time fee/room. Service with restrictions.
[ASK] [✕] [&M] [🖉] [🐾] [🗄] [💻] [🏊] [✕]

ᗺᗺᗺ Studio 6 #6023 🆂🅷
(770) 931-3113. **$43-$61.** 3525 Breckinridge Blvd. I-85, exit 104, just e to Breckinridge Blvd, then just n. Ext corridors. **Pets:** Accepted.
[ASK] [S🅳] [✕] [&M] [🗄] [💻]

🅐🅐🅐 ᗺᗺᗺᗺ Wellesley Inn & Suites (Atlanta/Gwinnett Mall) 🆂🅷
(770) 623-6800. **$69-$109.** 3390 Venture Pkwy NW. I-85, exit 104, just w to Venture Pkwy, then just n. Int corridors. **Pets:** Small. $10 daily fee/room. Designated rooms, service with restrictions, supervision.
[SAVE] [S🅳] [✕] [&M] [🖉] [🗄] [💻] [🏊]

EAST POINT

🅐🅐🅐 ᗺᗺᗺᗺ AmeriSuites (Atlanta Airport/North) 🆂🅷
(404) 768-8484. **$85-$105.** 3415 Norman Berry Dr. I-85, exit 73 southbound, just e to Bobby Brown Pkwy, then just n; exit 73B northbound. Int corridors. **Pets:** Accepted.
[SAVE] [S🅳] [✕] [&M] [🖉] [🐾] [🗄] [💻] [🏊]

ᗺᗺᗺᗺ Comfort Inn & Suites Atlanta Airport North 🆂🅷
(404) 762-5566. **$79-$119.** 3601 N Desert Dr. I-285, exit 2, just e. Int corridors. **Pets:** Accepted.
[ASK] [S🅳] [✕] [&M] [🖉] [🗄] [💻]

🅐🅐🅐 ᗺᗺᗺ Crowne Plaza Hotel and Resort Atlanta Airport 🅛🅗
(404) 768-6660. **$139.** 1325 Virginia Ave. I-85, exit 73 southbound; exit 73B northbound, just w. Int corridors. **Pets:** $25 one-time fee/pet. Service with restrictions, supervision.
[SAVE] [S🅳] [✕] [&M] [🖉] [🐾] [🗄] [💻] [🍴] [🏊]

ᗺᗺᗺᗺ Drury Inn & Suites Atlanta Airport 🆂🅷
(404) 761-4900. **$73-$123.** 1270 Virginia Ave. I-85, exit 73 southbound; exit 73A northbound, just e. Int corridors. **Pets:** Large, other species. Service with restrictions, supervision.
[ASK] [✕] [&M] [🖉] [🐾] [🗄] [💻] [🏊]

🅐🅐🅐 ᗺᗺᗺ Holiday Inn Atlanta Airport North 🅛🅗
(404) 762-8411. **$109.** 1380 Virginia Ave. I-85, exit 73 southbound; exit 73B northbound, just w. Ext/int corridors. **Pets:** Medium, other species. $50 one-time fee/room. Designated rooms, service with restrictions, crate.
[SAVE] [S🅳] [✕] [&M] [🖉] [🐾] [🗄] [💻] [🍴] [🏊]

🅐🅐🅐 ᗺᗺᗺ Red Roof Inn-Atlanta Airport North 🆂🅷
(404) 209-1800. **$71-$76.** 1200 Virginia Ave. I-85, exit 73 southbound; exit 73A northbound, just e. Int corridors. **Pets:** Accepted.
[SAVE] [S🅳] [✕] [&M] [🖉] [🐾] [🏊]

🅐🅐🅐 ᗺᗺᗺ Wellesley Inn (Atlanta/Hartsfield Int'l Airport) 🆂🅷
(404) 762-5111. **$65-$95.** 1377 Virginia Ave. I-85, exit 73 southbound; exit 73B northbound, just w. Int corridors. **Pets:** Accepted.
[SAVE] [S🅳] [✕] [🖉] [🐾] [🗄] [💻] [🍴] [🏊]

FOREST PARK

ᗺᗺ Days Inn-Airport East 🆂🅷
(404) 768-6400. **$50-$90.** 5116 Hwy 85. I-75, exit 237A southbound; exit 237 northbound, 0.5 mi w. **Pets:** Medium, other species. $20 daily fee/room. No service, supervision.
[ASK] [S🅳] [✕] [🗄] [💻] [🏊]

🅐🅐🅐 ᗺᗺ Econo Lodge 🅜
(404) 363-6429. **$46-$65.** 5060 Frontage Rd. I-75, exit 237, southeast corner. Int corridors. **Pets:** Large. $5 daily fee/pet. Service with restrictions, supervision.
[SAVE] [S🅳] [✕]

🅐🅐🅐 ᗺᗺᗺ Super 8 Motel 🆂🅷
(404) 363-8811. **$45-$55.** 410 Old Dixie Way. I-75, exit 235, just e. Ext corridors. **Pets:** Accepted.
[SAVE] [S🅳] [✕] [🐾] [🗄] [🏊]

HAPEVILLE

🅐🅐🅐 ᗺᗺᗺᗺ Hilton Atlanta Airport 🅛🅗
(404) 767-9000. **$89-$219.** 1031 Virginia Ave. I-85, exit 73 southbound; exit 73A northbound, just e. Int corridors. **Pets:** Large. $100 deposit/room. Service with restrictions, supervision.
[SAVE] [S🅳] [✕] [&M] [🖉] [🗄] [💻] [🍴] [🏊] [✕]

ᗺᗺᗺ Residence Inn Atlanta Airport 🆂🅷
(404) 761-0511. **$156.** 3401 International Blvd. I-85, exit 73 southbound; exit 73A northbound, 0.5 mi e to International Blvd, then just n. Ext/int corridors. **Pets:** Accepted.
[ASK] [✕] [🖉] [🐾] [🗄] [💻] [🏊] [✕]

JONESBORO

🅐🅐🅐 ᗺᗺᗺ Holiday Inn Atlanta South Jonesboro 🆂🅷
(770) 968-4300. **$80-$100.** 6288 Old Dixie Hwy. I-75, exit 235, just w. Int corridors. **Pets:** Medium. $15 one-time fee/room. Service with restrictions.
[SAVE] [S🅳] [✕] [&M] [🖉] [🐾] [🗄] [💻] [🍴] [🏊]

ᗺᗺ Shoneys Inn-Atlanta South 🆂🅷
(770) 968-5018. **$54-$59.** 6358 Old Dixie Rd. I-75, exit 235, just w. Ext corridors. **Pets:** Accepted.
[ASK] [S🅳] [✕] [🗄] [💻] [🏊]

KENNESAW

🅐🅐🅐 ᗺᗺᗺ Best Western Kennesaw Inn 🆂🅷
(770) 424-7666. **$69-$74.** 3375 Busbee Dr. I-75, exit 271, just e. Ext corridors. **Pets:** Medium. $10 daily fee/pet. Designated rooms, service with restrictions, supervision.
[SAVE] [S🅳] [✕] [🗄] [💻] [🏊]

▼▼ ▼▼ Red Roof Inn-Town Center Mall **M**
(770) 429-0323. **$45-$52.** 520 Roberts Ct NW. I-75, exit 269, southeast corner. Ext corridors. **Pets:** Medium. Service with restrictions, supervision.
⊠ ⓛ ⌂ ⌂ ⏢

▼▼▼▼ Residence Inn by Marriott Town Center **SH**
(770) 218-1018. **$71-$159.** 3443 Busbee Dr. I-75, exit 271, just e. Int corridors. **Pets:** Medium. $75 one-time fee/room. Service with restrictions, supervision.
A$K Ⓢ ⊠ ⓛ ⌂ ⌂ ⏢ ⏥ ⇶ ⊠

▲▲▲ ▼▼ Rodeway Inn **M**
(770) 590-0519. **$45-$60.** 1460 George Busbee Pkwy. I-75, exit 273, just e. Ext corridors. **Pets:** Accepted.
SAVE ⊠ ⏢ ⏥ ⇶

▼▼▼▼ TownePlace Suites by Marriott **SH** 🐾
(770) 794-8282. **$125.** 1074 Cobb Place Blvd NW. I-75, exit 269, 1.1 mi w to Second Cobb Place Blvd entrance. Int corridors. **Pets:** Other species. $150 one-time fee/room. Service with restrictions, supervision.
A$K Ⓢ ⊠ ⓛ ⌂ ⌂ ⏢ ⏥ ⇶

LAWRENCEVILLE

▼▼ ▼▼ Days Inn **M**
(770) 995-7782. **$57-$65.** 731 Duluth Hwy. Jct SR 316, just e on SR 120. Ext corridors. **Pets:** Accepted.
A$K Ⓢ ⊠ ⏢

▼▼▼▼ Hampton Inn **SH** 🐾
(770) 338-9600. **$59-$89.** 1135 Lakes Pkwy. I-85, exit 106 northbound, 4 mi e to Riverside Pkwy, then just n; exit 115 southbound, 4.4 mi s on SR 20 to SR 316, then 1.1 mi w. Int corridors. **Pets:** Small. $25 one-time fee/room. Service with restrictions, supervision.
A$K Ⓢ ⊠ ⓛ ⌂ ⌂ ⏢ ⏥ ⇶

LITHIA SPRINGS

▼▼ ▼▼ SuiteOne Hotel of Douglas County **SH**
(770) 948-8331. **$69-$99.** 637 W Market Cir. I-20, exit 44, 1 mi n. Ext corridors. **Pets:** Accepted.
A$K Ⓢ ⊠ ⌂ ⏢ ⏥ ⇶

LITHONIA

▲▲▲ ▼▼▼▼ AmeriSuites (Lithonia/Stonecrest Mall) **SH**
(770) 484-4384. **$79-$149.** 7900 Mall Ring Rd. I-20, exit 75, just s on Turner Hill Rd, 0.7 mi w; the rear of Stonecrest Mall. Int corridors. **Pets:** Accepted.
SAVE ⊠ ⌂ ⏢ ⏥

MARIETTA

▼▼▼▼ Comfort Inn-Marietta **SH**
(770) 952-3000. **$79-$109.** 2100 Northwest Pkwy. I-75, exit 261, 0.3 mi w to Franklin Rd, then just s. Ext corridors. **Pets:** Accepted.
A$K Ⓢ ⊠ ⌂ ⏢ ⏥ ⇶

▼▼▼▼ Drury Inn & Suites-Atlanta Northwest **SH**
(770) 612-0900. **$63-$97.** 1170 Powers Ferry Pl. I-75, exit 261, just e. Int corridors. **Pets:** Large, other species. Service with restrictions, supervision.
A$K ⊠ ⓛ ⌂ ⌂ ⏢ ⏥ ⇶

▼▼▼▼ Homestead Studio Suites Hotel-Atlanta/Powers Ferry/Galleria Area **SH**
(770) 303-0043. **$62-$82.** 2239 Powers Ferry Rd. I-285, exit 22, just n. Int corridors. **Pets:** Accepted.
A$K Ⓢ ⊠ ⓛ ⌂ ⌂ ⏢

▲▲▲ ▼▼▼▼ Hyatt Regency Suites Perimeter Northwest **LH**
(770) 956-1234. **$75-$195, 3 day notice.** 2999 Windy Hill Rd. I-75, exit 260, 0.5 mi e at Powers Ferry Rd. Int corridors. **Pets:** Small. $50 one-time fee/pet. Designated rooms, service with restrictions.
SAVE ⊠ ⓛ ⌂ ⌂ ⏢ ⏥ ⑪ ⇶ ⊠

▲▲▲ ▼▼▼▼ La Quinta Inn Atlanta (Marietta) **SH**
(770) 951-0026. **$71-$81.** 2170 Delk Rd. I-75, exit 261, 0.3 mi w. Ext/int corridors. **Pets:** Accepted.
SAVE ⊠ ⌂ ⏢ ⏥ ⇶

▲▲▲ ▼▼ Masters Inn Marietta **M**
(770) 951-2005. **$43-$63.** 2682 Windy Hill Rd. I-75, exit 260, just w to Circle 75 Pkwy, then just s. Ext corridors. **Pets:** Accepted.
SAVE Ⓢ ⊠ ⏢

▲▲▲ ▼▼▼▼ Quality Inn Atlanta/Marietta **SH**
(770) 955-0004. **$59-$89.** 1255 Franklin Rd. I-75, exit 261, 0.3 mi w to Franklin Rd, then just s. Int corridors. **Pets:** Medium, other species. $10 daily fee/pet. Service with restrictions, supervision.
SAVE Ⓢ ⊠ ⌂ ⏢ ⏥ ⇶

▲▲▲ ▼▼▼▼ Ramada Limited Suites **SH** 🐾
(770) 919-7878. **$48-$54.** 630 Franklin Rd. I-75, exit 263, 0.3 mi w to Franklin Rd, then 0.3 mi s. Ext corridors. **Pets:** Other species. $7 daily fee/pet. Service with restrictions, supervision.
SAVE Ⓢ ⊠ ⌂ ⌂ ⏢ ⏥ ⇶

▲▲▲ ▼▼▼▼ Super 8 Motel **SH** 🐾
(770) 919-2340. **$45-$54.** 610 Franklin Rd. I-75, exit 263, 0.3 mi w to Franklin Rd, then 0.3 mi s. Ext corridors. **Pets:** Other species. $7 daily fee/pet. Service with restrictions, supervision.
SAVE Ⓢ ⊠ ⌂ ⏢ ⏥ ⇶

▲▲▲ ▼▼▼▼ Wyndham Garden Hotel-Atlanta Northwest **SH**
(770) 428-4400. **$69-$109.** 1775 Parkway Pl NW. I-75, exit 263, southwest corner. Int corridors. **Pets:** Accepted.
SAVE ⊠ ⓛ ⌂ ⌂ ⏢ ⏥ ⑪ ⇶

MORROW

▲▲▲ ▼▼ ▼▼ Best Western Southlake Inn **SH**
(770) 961-6300. **$59-$109.** 6437 Jonesboro Rd. I-75, exit 233, just e. Ext corridors. **Pets:** Small. $10 daily fee/pet. Service with restrictions, supervision.
SAVE Ⓢ ⊠ ⌂ ⏢ ⏥ ⇶

▲▲▲ ▼▼ ▼▼ Days Inn **SH**
(770) 961-6044. **$49-$99.** 1599 Adamson Pkwy. I-75, exit 233, just e. Ext/int corridors. **Pets:** Small. $25 deposit/room, $10 daily fee/room. Designated rooms, service with restrictions, supervision.
SAVE Ⓢ ⊠ ⓛ ⌂ ⌂ ⏢ ⇶

▼▼ ▼▼ ▼▼ Drury Inn & Suites-Atlanta South **SH**
(770) 960-0500. **$62-$102.** 6520 S Lee St. I-75, exit 233, just e. Int corridors. **Pets:** Large, other species. Service with restrictions, supervision.
A$K ⊠ ⓛ ⌂ ⌂ ⏢ ⏥ ⇶

▲▲▲ ▼▼ ▼▼ Quality Inn & Suites **SH**
(770) 960-1957. **$49-$79.** 6597 Hwy 54. I-75, exit 233, just w. Ext corridors. **Pets:** $10 daily fee/pet. Designated rooms, service with restrictions, crate.
SAVE Ⓢ ⊠ ⌂ ⏢ ⏥ ⇶

▼▼ ▼▼ Red Roof Inn-South **M**
(770) 968-1483. **$45-$65.** 1348 Southlake Plaza Dr. I-75, exit 233, just e to Southlake Plaza Dr, then just n. Ext corridors. **Pets:** Accepted.
⊠ ⌂ ⏢

[AAA] ◆◆ **Sleep Inn** [SH]
(770) 472-9800. **$54-$154.** 2185 Mt Zion Pkwy. I-75, exit 231, just w to Mt Zion Pkwy, then just s. Int corridors. **Pets:** Accepted.
[SAVE] [SD] ⊠ ♿M ☎ ☕ 🏊

NORCROSS

[AAA] ◆◆◆ **Amberley Suite Hotel** [SH]
(770) 263-0515. **$69-$79.** 5885 Oakbrook Pkwy. I-85, exit 99, 0.5 mi e to Live Oak Pkwy, 0.8 mi n, then w. Int corridors. **Pets:** Other species. $25 one-time fee/room. Service with restrictions, supervision.
[SAVE] [SD] ⊠ ♿M 👂 ☎ ☕ 🍴 🏊 🏋

[AAA] ◆◆◆ **AmeriSuites (Atlanta/Peachtree Corners)** [SH]
(770) 416-7655. **$99-$109.** 5600 Peachtree Pkwy. I-285, exit 31B, 4 mi n on SR 141, then 1 mi n. Int corridors. **Pets:** Medium. $10 daily fee/pet. Designated rooms, service with restrictions, supervision.
[SAVE] [SD] ⊠ ♿M 👂 ♿ ☎ ☕ 🏊

◆◆◆ **ClubHouse Inn & Suites** [SH]
(770) 368-9400. **$59-$89.** 5945 Oakbrook Pkwy. I-85, exit 99, 0.5 mi e to Live Oak Pkwy, then 0.8 mi w. Int corridors. **Pets:** Small. $10 daily fee/pet. Service with restrictions, supervision.
[A$K] [SD] ⊠ ♿ ☎ ☕ 🏊

[AAA] ◆◆ **Days Inn Atlanta NE** [SH]
(770) 368-0218. **$49.** 5990 Western Hills Dr. I-85, exit 99, 0.8 mi w to Norcross Tucker Rd to Western Hills Dr, then just n. Ext corridors. **Pets:** Very small. $10 daily fee/pet. Service with restrictions, supervision.
[SAVE] [SD] ⊠ ☎ 🏊

◆◆◆ **Drury Inn & Suites-Atlanta Northeast** [SH]
(770) 729-0060. **$55-$108.** 5655 Jimmy Carter Blvd. I-85, exit 99, just w. Int corridors. **Pets:** Large, other species. Service with restrictions, supervision.
[A$K] ⊠ ♿M 👂 ♿ ☎ ☕ 🏊

[AAA] ◆◆ **GuestHouse Inn** [SH]
(770) 564-0492. **$49-$69, 7 day notice.** 2050 Willowtrail Pkwy. I-85, exit 101, just e. Ext corridors. **Pets:** Small. $20 one-time fee/pet. Designated rooms, service with restrictions, supervision.
[SAVE] [SD] ⊠ ☎ ☕ 🏊

◆◆◆ **Hilton Atlanta Northeast** [LH]
(770) 447-4747. **$72-$160.** 5993 Peachtree Industrial Blvd. I-285, exit 31B, 4.5 mi ne. Int corridors. **Pets:** Medium. $25 deposit/room, $25 one-time fee/room. Service with restrictions, crate.
[A$K] [SD] ⊠ ♿M 👂 ☎ ☕ 🍴 🏊 🏋

◆◆ **Homestead Studio Suites Hotel-Atlanta/Norcross** [SH]
(770) 449-9966. **$43-$63.** 7049 Jimmy Carter Blvd. I-85, exit 99, 4 mi n; I-285, exit 31B, 4 mi n. Ext corridors. **Pets:** Accepted.
[A$K] [SD] ⊠ ♿M ♿ ☎ ☕

[AAA] ◆◆◆ **Homewood Suites by Hilton** [SH]
(770) 448-4663. **$134-$174.** 450 Technology Pkwy. I-85, exit 99, 4 mi w to Peachtree Industrial Blvd, 0.4 mi n, w on Holcomb Bridge Rd, then 2 blks n on Peachtree Pkwy; I-285, exit 31B, 5 mi n on SR 141. Ext/int corridors. **Pets:** Accepted.
[SAVE] [SD] ⊠ ♿M 👂 ☎ ☕ 🏊 🏋

[AAA] ◆◆◆ **La Quinta Inn** [SH]
(770) 448-8686. **$79.** 6187 Dawson Blvd. I-85, exit 99, just e to McDonough Dr, then just s. Ext corridors. **Pets:** Accepted.
[SAVE] [SD] ⊠ ☕ 🏊

◆◆◆ **La Quinta Inn Atlanta (Peachtree Industrial)** [SH]
(770) 449-5144. **$65-$75.** 5375 Peachtree Industrial Blvd. I-285, exit 31B, 5.5 mi n; I-85, exit 99, 4 mi w to Peachtree Industrial Blvd, then 1.5 mi n. Ext/int corridors. **Pets:** Accepted.
[A$K] ⊠ 👂 ☎ ☕ 🏊

◆◆ **Ramada Limited** [SH]
(770) 449-7322. **$69-$99.** 6045 Oakbrook Pkwy. I-85, exit 99, just e to Live Oak Pkwy, 1 mi n, then w. Ext/int corridors. **Pets:** Accepted.
[A$K] [SD] ⊠ ☎ ☕ 🏊

◆◆ **Red Roof Inn & Suites** [SH]
(770) 446-2882. **$48-$63.** 5395 Peachtree Industrial Blvd. I-285, exit 31B, 5.5 mi n; I-85, exit 99, 4 mi w to Peachtree Industrial Blvd, then 1.5 mi n. Int corridors. **Pets:** Small, other species. Designated rooms, service with restrictions, supervision.
[A$K] [SD] ⊠ 👂 ☎ ☕ 🏊

◆◆ **Red Roof Inn-Indian Trail** [M]
(770) 448-8944. **$41-$54.** 5171 Brook Hollow Pkwy. I-85, exit 101, just w to Brook Hollow Pkwy, then just s. Ext corridors. **Pets:** Accepted.
⊠ 👂 ♿

ROSWELL

[AAA] ◆◆◆ **Baymont Inn & Suites Atlanta-Roswell** [SH]
(770) 552-0200. **$59-$69.** 575 Old Holcomb Bridge Rd. SR 400, exit 7B, just w. Int corridors. **Pets:** Accepted.
[SAVE] [SD] ⊠ ♿M 👂 ☎ ☕ 🏊

◆◆◆ **Brookwood Inn** [SH]
(770) 587-5161. **$45-$59.** 9995 Old Dogwood Rd. SR 400, exit 7B, just w to Old Dogwood Rd, just n. Ext corridors. **Pets:** $25 one-time fee/room. Designated rooms, no service, crate.
[A$K] [SD] ⊠ 👂 ☎ ☕ 🏊

◆◆ **Studio 6 #6025** [M]
(770) 992-9449. **$45-$61.** 9955 Old Dogwood Rd. SR 400, exit 7B, just w. Ext corridors. **Pets:** Small. $50 one-time fee/pet. Service with restrictions.
[SD] ♿M 👂 ♿ ☎ ☕

SMYRNA

[AAA] ◆◆ **AmeriHost Inn-Smyrna** [SH]
(404) 794-1600. **$69-$89.** 5130 S Cobb Dr. I-285, exit 15, 0.3 mi w. Int corridors. **Pets:** Accepted.
[SAVE] [SD] ⊠ ♿M 👂 ♿ ☎ ☕ 🏊 🏋

[AAA] ◆◆◆ **AmeriSuites (Atlanta/Galleria)** [SH]
(770) 384-0060. **$98-$109, 3 day notice.** 2876 Springhill Pkwy. I-285, exit 20 westbound; exit 19 eastbound, just n to Spring Rd, then just w. Int corridors. **Pets:** Medium. $10 daily fee/room. Service with restrictions, crate.
[SAVE] [SD] ⊠ ♿M 👂 ☎ ☕ 🏊

◆◆◆ **Best Western, Atlanta Galleria Inn and Suites** [SH]
(770) 541-1499. **Call for rates.** 2221 Corporate Plaza. I-75, exit 260, just w. Int corridors. **Pets:** Accepted.
⊠ ♿M 👂 ♿ ☎ ☕ 🏊 🏋

◆◆◆ **Comfort Inn & Suites** [SH]
(678) 309-1200. **$40-$159.** 2800 Highlands Pkwy. I-285, exit 15, just w to Highlands Pkwy, then just s. Int corridors. **Pets:** Other species.
[A$K] ⊠ ♿M 👂 ♿ ☎ ☕ 🏊

◆◆ **Holiday Inn Express, Vinings/Smyrna** [SH]
(770) 333-9910. **$75-$85.** 1200 Winchester Pkwy. I-285, exit 16, just w. Int corridors. **Pets:** Accepted.
[A$K] ⊠ ☎ ☕ 🏊

◆◆ **Homestead Studio Suites Hotel-Atlanta/Cumberland** [SH]
(770) 432-4000. **$52-$72.** 3103 Sports Ave. I-285, exit 20 westbound; exit 19 eastbound, just n to Spring Rd, 0.3 mi w. Ext corridors. **Pets:** Small. $25 daily fee/pet. Service with restrictions.
[A$K] [SD] ⊠ ♿M 👂 ♿ ☎ ☕

▼▼ ▼▼ **Red Roof Inn-North** Ⓜ
(770) 952-6966. **$44-$51.** 2200 Corporate Plaza. I-75, exit 260, just w to Corporate Plaza, then just s. Ext corridors. **Pets:** Medium, other species. Service with restrictions, supervision.
✕ 🅜 🖊 🖫

▼▼◆▼▼ **Residence Inn-Atlanta Cumberland** 🆂🅷
(770) 433-8877. **$74-$149.** 2771 Cumberland Blvd. I-285, exit 20 westbound; exit 19 eastbound, just n to Spring Rd, 0.3 mi w to Cumberland Blvd, then just n. Ext corridors. **Pets:** Accepted.
✕ 🅜 🖊 🖫 🖨 🖳 ➳ ✕

SUWANEE

▼▼ ◆▼▼ **Admiral Benbow Inn** 🆂🅷
(770) 945-4921. **Call for rates.** 2955 Hwy 317. I-85, exit 111, just e. Ext corridors. **Pets:** Accepted.
✕ 🅜 🖨 🖳 🍴 ➳

◆◆◆ ▼▼◆▼▼ **Comfort Inn** 🆂🅷
(770) 945-1608. **$65-$115.** 2945 Hwy 317. I-85, exit 111, just e. Ext corridors. **Pets:** Medium. $25 one-time fee/room. Service with restrictions.
SAVE 🅢 ✕ 🖨 🖳 ➳

▼▼ **Days Inn** 🆂🅷
(770) 945-8372. **Call for rates.** 3103 Hwy 317. I-85, exit 111, just w. Ext corridors. **Pets:** Accepted.
✕ 🖨 ➳

TUCKER

▼▼◆▼▼ **Atlanta Northlake TownePlace Suites** 🆂🅷
(770) 938-0408. **Call for rates.** 3300 Northlake Pkwy. I-285, exit 36 southbound, just w; exit 37 northbound, just w to Parklake Dr, 0.5 mi n, then just w. Int corridors. **Pets:** Accepted.
✕ 🅜 🖊 🖫 🖨 🖳 ➳

◆◆◆ ▼▼ **Masters Inn Tucker** Ⓜ 🐾
(770) 938-3552. **$43-$63.** 1435 Montreal Rd. I-285, exit 38, just w. Ext corridors. **Pets:** Small. $5 daily fee/pet. Designated rooms, service with restrictions, supervision.
SAVE 🅢 ✕ 🖨 ➳

▼▼◆▼▼ **Red Roof Inn-Atlanta Tucker NE** Ⓜ
(770) 496-1311. **$43-$53.** 2810 Lawrenceville Hwy. I-285, exit 38, just w. Ext corridors. **Pets:** Accepted.
✕ 🖊

UNION CITY

▼▼◆▼▼ **Holiday Inn Express Hotel & Suites** 🆂🅷
(770) 969-4567. **$59-$129.** 6743 Shannon Pkwy. I-85, exit 64, 0.3 mi w, then just n. Int corridors. **Pets:** Accepted.
ASK 🅢 ✕ 🅜 🖊 🖫 🖨 🖳 ➳

◆◆◆ ▼▼◆▼▼ **Microtel Inn & Suites** 🆂🅷 🐾
(770) 306-3800. **$40-$46.** 6690 Shannon Pkwy. I-85, exit 64, 0.3 mi w to Shannon Pkwy, then just n. Int corridors. **Pets:** Small, other species. $10 daily fee/pet. Designated rooms, service with restrictions, supervision.
SAVE 🅢 ✕ 🅜 🖊 🖫 🖨 🖳

▼▼◆▼▼ **Ramada Limited** 🆂🅷
(770) 964-5100. **$80-$84.** 7420 Oakley Rd. I-85, exit 64, just e. Ext corridors. **Pets:** Accepted.
ASK 🅢 ✕ 🖨 🖳

▼▼◆▼▼ **Red Roof Inn** 🆂🅷
(770) 306-7750. **Call for rates.** 6710 Shannon Pkwy. I-85, exit 64, 0.3 mi w, then just n. Int corridors. **Pets:** Accepted.
✕ 🖫 🖨 ➳

END METROPOLITAN AREA

AUGUSTA

◆◆◆ ▼▼◆▼▼ **AmeriSuites (Augusta/River Watch Pkwy)** 🆂🅷 🐾
(706) 733-4656. **$79-$89.** 1062 Claussen Rd. I-20, exit 200 westbound, 0.4 mi sw on service road; exit 199 eastbound, 0.3 mi w, then 0.6 mi nw on service road. Int corridors. **Pets:** Medium. $10 daily fee/pet. Service with restrictions, supervision.
SAVE ✕ 🅜 🖊 🖫 🖨 🖳 ➳ ✕

▼▼◆▼▼ **Augusta Inn and Conference Center** 🆂🅷
(706) 738-8811. **$79.** 1075 Stevens Creek Rd. I-20, exit 199 (Washington Rd), just w, then n. Ext corridors. **Pets:** Accepted.
ASK 🅢 ✕ 🖫 🖨 🖳 🍴 ➳ ✕

◆◆◆ ▼▼◆▼▼ **Augusta Suites Inn** 🆂🅷
(706) 868-1800. **$99, 3 day notice.** 3038 Washington Rd. I-20, exit 199 (Washington Rd), just w. Ext corridors. **Pets:** Small. $50 one-time fee/pet. Service with restrictions, crate.
SAVE 🅢 ✕ 🖨 🖳 🍴 ➳

◆◆◆ ▼▼◆▼▼ **Comfort Inn** 🆂🅷
(706) 855-6060. **$63-$350.** 629 Frontage Rd NW. I-20, exit 196B, 0.3 mi n to Scott Nixon Memorial, just w, then 0.3 mi s. Int corridors. **Pets:** Other species. $50 one-time fee/room. Designated rooms, service with restrictions, crate.
SAVE 🅢 ✕ 🖨 🖳 ➳

◆◆◆ ▼▼◆▼▼ **Comfort Inn Medical Center** 🆂🅷
(706) 722-2224. **$66.** 1455 Walton Way. I-20, exit 199 (Washington Rd), 4.5 mi e on SR 28, then just sw on 15th St. Ext corridors. **Pets:** Medium, other species. $50 deposit/pet. Service with restrictions, supervision.
SAVE 🅢 ✕ 🖫 🖨 🖳 ➳

◆◆◆ ▼▼◆▼▼ **Country Suites Augusta Riverwalk** 🆂🅷
(706) 774-1400. **$119.** 3 9th St. I-20, exit 200 (River Watch Pkwy), 5.4 mi se, then just n. Int corridors. **Pets:** Small. Service with restrictions, crate.
SAVE 🅢 ✕ 🅜 🖊 🖫 🖨 🖳 ➳ ✕

▼▼◆▼▼ **Holiday Inn Gordon Highway at Bobby Jones** 🆂🅷
(706) 737-2300. **$59-$89.** 2155 Gordon Hwy. I-520, exit 3A (US 78), just w. Ext corridors. **Pets:** Accepted.
ASK 🅢 ✕ 🖨 🖳 🍴 ➳

▼▼ ▼▼ **Howard Johnson Inn** Ⓜ
(706) 863-2882. **$49-$54.** 601 Frontage Rd NW. I-20, exit 196B (Bobby Jones Expwy), just nw. Ext corridors. **Pets:** Small. $10 daily fee/pet. Designated rooms, service with restrictions, crate.
ASK 🅢 ✕ 🖨 🖳 ➳

◆◆◆ ▼▼◆▼▼ **La Quinta Inn Augusta** 🆂🅷 🐾
(706) 733-2660. **$65-$75.** 3020 Washington Rd. I-20, exit 199 (Washington Rd), just w. Ext/int corridors. **Pets:** Small. No service, crate.
SAVE ✕ 🅜 🖊 🖨 🖳 ➳

◆◆◆ ▼▼◆▼▼ **The Partridge Inn** 🆂🅷
(706) 737-8888. **$119-$129.** 2110 Walton Way. 1.3 mi w off 15th St. Int corridors. **Pets:** Accepted.
SAVE 🅢 ✕ 🖨 🖳 🍴 ➳

◆◆◆◆ Radisson Riverfront Hotel LH
(706) 722-8900. **$129.** 2 10th St. I-20, exit 200 (River Watch Pkwy), 5.4 mi se, then just n; downtown. Int corridors. **Pets:** Small. Service with restrictions, crate.
[SAVE] [S&] [✕] [&M] [🗲] [🛏] [💻] [🍴] [⇆] [⊠]

◆◆◆◆ Sheraton Augusta Hotel SH
(706) 855-8100. **$89-$159.** 2651 Perimeter Pkwy. I-520, exit 1C (Wheeler Rd), just w to Perimeter Pkwy, then just n. Int corridors. **Pets:** Accepted.
[ASK] [S&] [✕] [&M] [🛏] [💻] [🍴] [⇆] [⊠]

BAINBRIDGE

◆◆ Jameson Inn SH
(229) 243-7000. **$49-$104.** 1403 Tallahassee Hwy. Just s of US 84 Bypass on US 27. Ext corridors. **Pets:** Very small, other species. $10 daily fee/room. Service with restrictions, supervision.
[ASK] [✕] [&] [🛏] [💻] [⇆]

BAXLEY

◆ Scottish Inn M
(912) 367-3652. **Call for rates.** 1179 Hatch Pkwy S. Jct US 1 and SR 15, just s. Ext corridors. **Pets:** Accepted.
[✕] [🛏]

BLUE RIDGE

◆◆ Douglas Inn & Suites M
(706) 258-3600. **Call for rates.** 1192 Windy Ridge Rd. Just off SR 515 and US 76. Ext corridors. **Pets:** Medium, other species. $10 daily fee/pet. Service with restrictions, supervision.
[✕] [🛏] [💻] [⇆]

BRASELTON

◆◆◆ Chateau Elan Lodge by Holiday Inn Express SH
(770) 867-8100. **$89-$129.** 2069 Hwy 211 NW. I-85, exit 126, just w. Int corridors. **Pets:** Other species. $20 one-time fee/room. Service with restrictions, crate.
[SAVE] [S&] [💻] [⇆]

BREMEN

◆◆◆ Days Inn SH
(770) 537-4646. **$45-$60.** 35 Price Creek Rd. I-75, exit 11, just n. Ext corridors. **Pets:** $5 daily fee/pet. Service with restrictions.
[SAVE] [S&] [✕] [🛏] [💻] [⇆]

BRUNSWICK

◆◆◆ Baymont Inn & Suites Brunswick SH
(912) 265-7725. **$54-$74.** 165 Warren Mason Blvd. I-95, exit 36A (New Jesup Hwy/US 25), just se, then sw on Tourist Dr. Int corridors. **Pets:** Accepted.
[SAVE] [S&] [✕] [🗲] [🛏] [💻] [⇆]

◆◆◆ Best Western Brunswick Inn SH
(912) 264-0144. **$70-$74.** 5323 New Jesup Hwy. I-95, exit 36B (New Jesup Hwy/US 25), just nw. Ext corridors. **Pets:** Small, other species. Service with restrictions.
[SAVE] [S&] [✕] [🛏] [💻] [🍴] [⇆]

◆◆◆ Embassy Suites Hotel SH 🐾
(912) 264-6100. **$119-$279.** 500 Mall Blvd. I-95, exit 38 (Golden Isles Pkwy), 2 mi se, then just e. Int corridors. **Pets:** $15 daily fee/room. Service with restrictions, supervision.
[✕] [🗲] [🛏] [💻] [⇆]

◆◆◆ Holiday Inn I-95 SH
(912) 264-4033. **$89-$129.** 5252 New Jesup Hwy. I-95, exit 36B (New Jesup Hwy/US 25), just nw. Ext corridors. **Pets:** Other species. $25 daily fee/room. Service with restrictions, supervision.
[SAVE] [S&] [✕] [&] [🛏] [💻] [🍴] [⇆]

◆◆ Jameson Inn Brunswick SH
(912) 267-0800. **$49-$104.** 661 Scranton Rd. I-95, exit 38 (Golden Isles Pkwy), 1.6 mi se, then just sw. Ext corridors. **Pets:** Very small, other species. $10 daily fee/room. Service with restrictions, supervision.
[ASK] [✕] [🛏] [💻] [⇆]

◆ Motel 6 #790 M
(912) 264-8582. **$40-$55.** 403 Butler Dr. I-95, exit 36B (New Jesup Hwy/US 25), just nw, then sw on I-95 south entrance service road. Ext corridors. **Pets:** Small, other species. Service with restrictions, supervision.
[S&] [✕] [&] [⇆]

◆◆◆ Ramada Inn I-95 SH
(912) 264-3621. **$89.** 3040 Scarlett St. I-95, exit 36A (New Jesup Hwy/US 25), just e. Ext corridors. **Pets:** Accepted.
[SAVE] [S&] [✕] [🗲] [&] [🛏] [💻] [🍴] [⇆]

◆◆◆ Red Roof Inn & Suites I-95 SH
(912) 264-4720. **$59-$212.** 25 Tourist Dr. I-95, exit 36A (New Jesup Hwy/US 25), just se. Int corridors. **Pets:** Large, other species. Service with restrictions, supervision.
[SAVE] [S&] [✕] [🗲] [🛏] [💻] [⇆]

◆◆ Super 8 Motel M
(912) 264-8800. **$56-$76.** 5280 New Jesup Hwy. I-95, exit 36B (New Jesup Hwy/US 25), just nw. Int corridors. **Pets:** $10 daily fee/pet. Service with restrictions, supervision.
[S&] [✕] [🛏]

BYRON

◆◆◆ Best Western Inn and Suites SH
(478) 956-3056. **$59.** 101 Dunbar Rd. I-75, exit 149 (SR 49), just ne. Ext corridors. **Pets:** Accepted.
[SAVE] [S&] [✕] [&] [🛏] [💻] [⇆]

◆◆◆ Comfort Inn SH
(478) 956-1600. **$59-$89.** 115 Chapman Rd. I-75, exit 149 (SR 49), just sw, then n. Ext corridors. **Pets:** Very small. $10 daily fee/pet. No service, supervision.
[SAVE] [S&] [✕] [&] [🛏] [💻] [⇆]

CALHOUN

◆◆ Best Inns M
(706) 625-1511. **$35-$60.** 1438 US Hwy 41 N. I-75, exit 318, just w. Ext corridors. **Pets:** Medium. $8 daily fee/pet. Service with restrictions, supervision.
[SAVE] [✕] [🛏] [💻] [⇆]

◆◆◆ Budget Host Shepherd Motel M 🐾
(706) 629-8644. **$39-$49.** 1007 Fairmount Hwy 53. I-75, exit 312, just e. Ext corridors. **Pets:** Other species. Service with restrictions.
[SAVE] [S&] [✕] [&] [🛏] [⇆]

◆◆ Comfort Inn SH 🐾
(706) 629-8271. **$55-$60.** 742 Hwy 53 SE. I-75, exit 312, just w. Ext corridors. **Pets:** Other species. $4 daily fee/pet. Service with restrictions.
[ASK] [S&] [✕] [🛏] [💻] [🍴] [⇆]

◆◆ Jameson Inn SH
(706) 629-8133. **$49-$104.** 189 Jameson St. I-75, exit 312, just w. Ext corridors. **Pets:** Small, other species. $10 daily fee/room. Service with restrictions, supervision.
[ASK] [✕] [🗲] [&] [🛏] [💻] [⇆]

◆◆ Knights Inn of Calhoun M
(706) 629-4521. **$40-$60.** 2261 US 41 NE. I-75, exit 318, just e. Ext corridors. **Pets:** Other species. $5 daily fee/pet. Designated rooms, no service, supervision.
[ASK] [S&] [✕] [🛏]

AAA ▼▼ Quality Inn SH
(706) 629-9501. **$65-$75.** 915 Hwy 53 E SE. I-75, exit 312, just e. Ext corridors. **Pets:** Small. $6 daily fee/pet. Service with restrictions, supervision.
SAVE 🅂 ⌧ 🛡 ▯ ⓣ 🌊

AAA ▼▼ Ramada Limited SH
(706) 629-9207. **$45-$99, 14 day notice.** 1204 Red Bud Rd NE. I-75, exit 315, just w. Ext corridors. **Pets:** Accepted.
SAVE 🅂 ⌧ 🔯 🛡 ▯ 🌊

CARROLLTON

▼▼ Jameson Inn SH
(770) 834-2600. **$49-$104.** 700 S Park St. On US 27, just s of downtown. Ext corridors. **Pets:** Very small, other species. $10 daily fee/room. Service with restrictions, supervision.
ASK 🅶 🅼 🛡 ▯ 🌊

▼▼ Quality Inn SH
(770) 832-2611. **Call for rates.** 1202 S Park St. Jct US 27 and SR 166. Ext corridors. **Pets:** Accepted.
⌧ 🛡 ▯ ⓣ 🌊

CARTERSVILLE

▼ Budget Host Inn M
(770) 386-0350. **$36-$41.** 851 Cass-White Rd. I-75, exit 296, just w. Ext corridors. **Pets:** Other species. $3 daily fee/pet. No service.
ASK 🅂 ⌧ 🌊

AAA ▼▼ Comfort Inn SH
(770) 387-1800. **$48-$70.** 28 SR 20 Spur. I-75, exit 290, 0.3 mi se. Ext corridors. **Pets:** $5 daily fee/pet. Service with restrictions, supervision.
SAVE 🅂 ⌧ 🛡 ▯ 🌊

▼▼▼ Country Inn & Suites by Carlson SH
(770) 386-5888. **$85.** 43 SR 20 Spur. I-75, exit 290, 0.3 mi se. Int corridors. **Pets:** Accepted.
ASK 🅂 ⌧ 🅶 🛡 ▯ 🌊

AAA ▼▼▼ Days Inn SH
(770) 382-1824. **$44-$88, 7 day notice.** 5618 Hwy 20 SE. I-75, exit 290, just w. Ext corridors. **Pets:** Medium. $5 daily fee/pet. Service with restrictions, supervision.
SAVE 🅂 ⌧ 🛡 🌊

AAA ▼▼▼ Holiday Inn SH
(770) 386-0830. **$75.** 2336 Hwy 411 NE. I-75, exit 293, southwest corner. Int corridors. **Pets:** Accepted.
SAVE 🅂 ⌧ 🅶 🔯 🛡 ▯ ⓣ 🌊

AAA ▼▼ Howard Johnson Express M
(770) 386-0700. **$40-$55.** 25 Carson Loop NW. I-75, exit 296, northwest corner. Ext corridors. **Pets:** Accepted.
SAVE 🅂 ⌧ 🛡 ▯ ⓣ 🌊

AAA ▼▼ Knights Inn M
(770) 386-7263. **$50-$70, 14 day notice.** 420 E Church St. I-75, exit 288, 1.5 mi w. Ext corridors. **Pets:** Medium. $10 one-time fee/pet. Service with restrictions, crate.
SAVE 🅂 ⌧ 🛡 🌊

▼▼ Motel 6—4046 M
(770) 386-1449. **$42-$46, 3 day notice.** 5657 Hwy 20 NE. I-75, exit 290, 0.3 mi e. Ext corridors. **Pets:** Small, other species. Service with restrictions, supervision.
🅂 ⌧ 🔯 🛡 🌊

AAA ▼▼▼ Quality Inn SH
(770) 386-0510. **$57-$61.** 235 Dixie Ave. I-75, exit 288, 2.5 mi w. Ext corridors. **Pets:** Small. $5 daily fee/pet. Service with restrictions, supervision.
SAVE 🅂 ⌧ 🛡 ▯ ⓣ 🌊

AAA ▼▼ Super 8 Motel M
(770) 382-8881. **$40-$60.** 41 SR 20 Spur SE. I-75, exit 290, 0.3 mi e. Int corridors. **Pets:** Accepted.
SAVE 🅂 ⌧ 🔯 🛡

CEDARTOWN

▼▼ Country Hearth Inn SH
(770) 749-9951. **$45-$85.** 925 N Main St. 1.5 mi n on US 27. Int corridors. **Pets:** $10 one-time fee/pet. Supervision.
ASK 🅂 ⌧ 🅶 🔯 🅶 🛡 ▯

CHATSWORTH

▼▼ Key West Inn M
(706) 517-1155. **$49-$60.** 501 GI Maddox Pkwy. Jct SR 76 and US 411. Ext corridors. **Pets:** Medium. $5 daily fee/pet. Service with restrictions, supervision.
ASK 🅂 ⌧ 🛡

CLAYTON

▼▼ Quality Inn & Suites SH
(706) 782-2214. **$59-$99, 15 day notice.** 834 Hwy 441 S. 0.8 mi s. Ext corridors. **Pets:** Accepted.
ASK 🅂 ⌧ 🛡 ▯ 🌊

AAA ▼ Regal Inn M
(706) 782-4269. **$37-$95, 3 day notice.** 707 Hwy 441 S. 0.8 mi s. Ext corridors. **Pets:** Small, dogs only. $5 daily fee/pet. Designated rooms, service with restrictions, supervision.
SAVE 🅂 ⌧ 🛡

AAA ▼▼▼ Stonebrook Inn SH
(706) 782-4702. **$37-$99.** 698 Hwy 441 S. 0.8 mi s. Int corridors. **Pets:** Small. $50 deposit/pet, $6 daily fee/pet. No service, supervision.
SAVE 🅂 ⌧ 🛡 ▯

COLUMBUS

AAA ▼▼▼ Baymont Inn & Suites Columbus SH
(706) 323-4344. **$65-$89.** 2919 Warm Springs Rd. I-185, exit 7 southbound; exit 7A northbound, just e. Int corridors. **Pets:** Accepted.
SAVE 🅂 ⌧ 🔯 🛡 ▯ 🌊

▼▼ Howard Johnson Inn & Suites SH
(706) 322-6641. **$70-$80.** 1011 Veterans Pkwy. I-185, exit 7 southbound; exit 7A northbound, 1.2 mi w to Veterans Pkwy, then 3.2 mi s. Ext corridors. **Pets:** Other species. $25 one-time fee/room. Service with restrictions, supervision.
ASK 🅂 ⌧ 🛡 ▯ ⓣ 🌊

▼▼ La Quinta Inn Columbus SH
(706) 568-1740. **$85-$99.** 3201 Macon Rd. I-185, exit 6, just w. Ext corridors. **Pets:** Accepted.
ASK ⌧ 🔯 🛡 ▯ 🌊

▼▼ Motel 6 M
(706) 687-7214. **$39-$49.** 3050 Victory Dr. I-185, exit 1B, 3 mi w. Ext corridors. **Pets:** Small, other species. Service with restrictions, supervision.
🅂 ⌧ 🅶 🌊

▼▼ Super 8 Motel of Columbus M ✿
(706) 322-6580. **Call for rates.** 2935 Warm Springs Rd. I-185, exit 7 southbound; exit 7A northbound, just e. Int corridors. **Pets:** Small, dogs only. $25 deposit/room. Service with restrictions, supervision.
⌧ 🅶 🛡

COMMERCE

▼▼ Comfort Inn SH
(706) 335-9001. **$90-$130.** 165 Eisenhower Dr. I-85, exit 149, just nw. Ext corridors. **Pets:** Accepted.
⌧ 🔯 🛡 🌊

▼▼ Howard Johnson Inn & Suites SH
(706) 335-5581. **$45-$80.** 148 Eisenhower Dr. I-85, exit 149, just w. Ext corridors. **Pets:** $10 one-time fee/room. Service with restrictions, supervision.
[A$K] [S6] [X] [icons] [◼] [icon]

AAA ▼ Scottish Inn M ❖
(706) 335-5147. **$40-$50.** 30934 US 441 S. I-85, exit 149, 0.3 mi e. Ext corridors. **Pets:** $10 daily fee/pet. Designated rooms, service with restrictions, supervision.
[SAVE] [S6] [X] [icons]

▼▼ Super 8 Motel SH
(706) 336-8008. **$39-$79.** 152 Eisenhower Dr. I-85, exit 149, just w. Ext corridors. **Pets:** $10 one-time fee/room. Service with restrictions, supervision.
[A$K] [S6] [X]

CONYERS

▼▼▼ Hampton Inn SH
(770) 483-8838. **$75-$95.** 1340 Dogwood Dr. I-20, exit 82, just n, then just e. Int corridors. **Pets:** Accepted.
[A$K] [S6] [X] [icons]

▼▼ Holiday Inn SH
(770) 483-3220. **$85.** 1351 Dogwood Dr. I-20, exit 80, just n to Dogwood Dr, then 0.4 mi w. Ext corridors. **Pets:** Small. $25 one-time fee/pet. Service with restrictions, supervision.
[A$K] [S6] [X] [icons]

▼▼ Jameson Inn M
(770) 760-1230. **$49-$104.** 1164 Dogwood Dr. I-20, exit 82, just n to Dogwood Dr, then just w. Ext corridors. **Pets:** Very small, other species. $10 daily fee/room. Service with restrictions, supervision.
[A$K] [X] [icons]

▼◆▼ La Quinta Inn & Suites Atlanta (Conyers) SH
(770) 918-0092. **$95-$125.** 1184 Dogwood Dr. I-20, exit 82, just n to Dogwood Dr, then just w. Int corridors. **Pets:** Small, other species. Service with restrictions, crate.
[A$K] [X] [icons]

▼◆▼ Ramada Limited M
(770) 760-0777. **Call for rates.** 1070 Dogwood Dr. I-20, exit 82, just n to Dogwood Dr, then 0.5 mi w. Ext corridors. **Pets:** Accepted.
[X] [icons]

CORDELE

AAA ▼▼▼ Best Western Colonial Inn SH
(229) 273-5420. **$63-$65.** 1706 E 16th Ave (US 280). I-75, exit 101 (US 280), just w. Ext/int corridors. **Pets:** Medium. $10 daily fee/pet. Service with restrictions, supervision.
[SAVE] [S6] [X] [icons]

AAA ▼▼▼ Ramada Inn SH ❖
(229) 273-5000. **$70.** 2016 E 16th Ave (US 280). I-75, exit 101 (US 280), just e. Ext corridors. **Pets:** Small. $15 daily fee/room. Service with restrictions, supervision.
[SAVE] [S6] [X] [icons]

AAA ▼ Super 8 M ❖
(229) 273-2456. **$45-$55.** 1618 16th Ave E (US 280). I-75, exit 101 (US 280), just w. Ext corridors. **Pets:** Other species. Supervision.
[SAVE] [S6] [X] [◼]

COVINGTON

AAA ▼▼▼ Best Western Colonial Inn SH
(770) 786-5800. **$65-$125.** 10130 Alcovy Rd. I-20, exit 92, just n. Ext corridors. **Pets:** Very small. $10 daily fee/room, $30 one-time fee/pet. Service with restrictions, supervision.
[SAVE] [S6] [X] [icons]

▼▼▼ Holiday Inn Express SH
(770) 787-4900. **Call for rates.** 10111 Alcovy Rd. I-20, exit 92, just n. Ext corridors. **Pets:** Accepted.
[X] [icons]

CUMMING

▼▼▼ Hampton Inn SH
(770) 889-0877. **$79-$94.** 915 Baptist Medical Center Dr. SR 400, exit 14, just e. Int corridors. **Pets:** Large. $20 daily fee/pet. Service with restrictions, crate.
[A$K] [S6] [X] [icons]

DALTON

AAA ▼▼▼ Best Western Inn of Dalton SH
(706) 226-5022. **$59-$89.** 2106 Chattanooga Rd. I-75, exit 336, just w. Ext corridors. **Pets:** Small. $5 daily fee/pet. Service with restrictions, supervision.
[SAVE] [S6] [X] [icons]

AAA ▼▼▼ Comfort Inn & Suites SH
(706) 259-2583. **$65-$95.** 905 Westbridge Rd. I-75, exit 333, just w to Westbridge Rd, then just s. Int corridors. **Pets:** Small. $10 daily fee/pet. Designated rooms, service with restrictions, supervision.
[SAVE] [S6] [X] [icons]

▼▼ Econo Lodge M
(706) 278-4300. **$65.** 2007 Tampico Way. I-75, exit 336, just e. Int corridors. **Pets:** Accepted.
[A$K] [S6] [X] [icons]

▼▼ Jameson Inn SH
(706) 281-1880. **$49-$104.** 422 Holiday Dr. I-75, exit 333, just w, then 0.3 mi n. Ext corridors. **Pets:** Very small, other species. $10 daily fee/room. Service with restrictions, supervision.
[A$K] [X] [icons]

▼ Motel 6-#761 M
(706) 278-5522. **$37-$47.** 2200 Chattanooga Rd. I-75, exit 336, 0.3 mi w. Ext corridors. **Pets:** Accepted.
[S6] [X] [icons]

▼▼▼ Quality Inn & Suites SH
(706) 278-0500. **$59-$79, 7 day notice.** 515 Holiday Dr. I-75, exit 333, northwest corner. Ext corridors. **Pets:** Accepted.
[A$K] [S6] [X] [icons]

DARIEN

AAA ▼▼▼ Comfort Inn SH
(912) 437-4200. **$89-$139.** 703 Frontage Rd. I-95, exit 49 (SR 251), just nw. Int corridors. **Pets:** Accepted.
[SAVE] [S6] [X] [icons]

DAWSONVILLE

AAA ▼▼▼ Best Western (Dawson Village Inn) SH
(706) 216-4410. **$59-$119.** 76 N Georgia Ave. Jct SR 400 and 53, 0.5 mi s. Int corridors. **Pets:** Small, dogs only. $5 daily fee/pet. No service, supervision.
[SAVE] [S6] [X] [icons]

▼▼▼ Comfort Inn SH
(706) 216-1900. **$64-$94.** 127 Beartooth Pkwy. Jct SR 400/53, 0.5 mi s. Int corridors. **Pets:** Accepted.
[A$K] [S6] [X] [icons]

DILLARD

AAA ▼▼▼ Dillard House SH
(706) 746-5348. **$49-$149.** 768 Franklin St. US 441, just e via Old Dillard Rd. Ext corridors. **Pets:** Medium. $5 one-time fee/pet. Service with restrictions.
[SAVE] [X] [icons]

(AAA) ▽▽ Ramada Limited **M**
(706) 746-5321. **$59-$149.** 3 Best Inn Way. Center. Ext corridors.
Pets: Accepted.
[SAVE] [S♦] [✕] [🛏] [💻] [🏊]

DOUGLAS

(AAA) ▽▽ Holiday Inn Douglas **M**
(912) 384-9100. **$79-$92.** 1750 S Peterson Ave (US 221/441). 2 mi s of
center on US 221/441. Ext corridors. **Pets:** Medium. $20 one-time fee/
pet. Service with restrictions, supervision.
[SAVE] [S♦] [✕] [🛏] [💻] [🍴] [🏊]

DUBLIN

(AAA) ▽▽▽ Best Western Executive Inn & Suites **SH**
(478) 275-2650. **$64, 3 day notice.** 2121 Hwy 441 S. I-16, exit 51 (US
441), 0.5 mi n. Ext corridors. **Pets:** Medium. Designated rooms, service
with restrictions, supervision.
[SAVE] [S♦] [✕] [✎] [🛏] [💻] [🏊]

▽▽ Comfort Inn **SH**
(478) 274-8000. **$55-$70.** 2110 Hwy 441 S. I-16, exit 51 (US 441), 0.6
mi n. Ext corridors. **Pets:** Accepted.
[ASK] [S♦] [✕] [&M] [✎] [🛏] [💻] [🏊]

▽ Econo Lodge **M**
(478) 296-1223. **$49-$59.** 2184 Hwy 441 S. I-16, exit 51 (US 441), just
n. Ext corridors. **Pets:** Accepted.
[ASK] [S♦] [✕] [🛏]

▽▽ Jameson Inn **M**
(478) 275-3008. **$49-$104.** 100 PM Watson Dr. I-16, exit 51 (US 441),
just n. Ext corridors. **Pets:** Very small, other species. $10 daily fee/room.
Service with restrictions, supervision.
[ASK] [✕] [🛏] [💻] [🏊]

FITZGERALD

▽▽ Country Hearth Inn **SH**
(229) 409-9911. **$50-$95.** 125 Stuart Way. Just n of US 319/107, just e.
Int corridors. **Pets:** Accepted.
[ASK] [S♦] [✕] [🛏] [💻]

▽▽ Jameson Inn **SH**
(229) 424-9500. **$49-$104.** 111 Bull Run Rd. Just n of US 319/107, on
US 129. Ext corridors. **Pets:** Very small, other species. $10 daily fee/
room. Service with restrictions, supervision.
[ASK] [✕] [🛏] [💻] [🏊]

FORSYTH

(AAA) ▽▽▽ Econo Lodge **SH** ❀
(478) 994-5603. **$48-$64.** 320 Cabiness Rd. I-75, exit 187 (SR 83), just
ne. Int corridors. **Pets:** Medium. $4 daily fee/pet. No service, supervision.
[SAVE] [S♦] [💻] [🏊]

▽▽▽ Hampton Inn **SH**
(478) 994-9697. **$66-$80.** 520 Holiday Cir. I-75, exit 186 (Juliette Rd),
just w, then just s on Aaron St. Int corridors. **Pets:** Small. Service with
restrictions, supervision.
[ASK] [S♦] [✕] [&M] [🛏] [💻]

▽▽▽ Holiday Inn Forsyth **SH** ❀
(478) 994-5691. **$87.** 480 Holiday Cir. I-75, exit 186 (Juliette Rd), just w,
then just s on Aaron St. Ext corridors. **Pets:** Other species. $25 one-time
fee/room. Service with restrictions, supervision.
[ASK] [S♦] [✕] [✎] [🐾] [🛏] [💻] [🍴] [🏊]

GAINESVILLE

(AAA) ▽▽ GuestHouse Inn & Suites **SH** ❀
(770) 535-8100. **$55-$70.** 520 Queen City Pkwy SW. I-985, exit 20, 1.8
mi nw on SR 60. Ext corridors. **Pets:** Other species. $10 daily fee/pet.
Service with restrictions.
[SAVE] [S♦] [✕] [🛏] [💻] [🏊]

GARDEN CITY

(AAA) ▽▽▽ Masters Inn Garden City **SH**
(912) 964-4344. **$43-$73.** 4200 Hwy 21 N (Augusta Rd). I-95, exit 109
(SR 21), 6.7 mi s. Ext/int corridors. **Pets:** Accepted.
[SAVE] [S♦] [✕] [✎] [🛏] [🏊]

GLENNVILLE

(AAA) ▽ Cheeri-O Inn **M**
(912) 654-2176. **$40-$42.** 820 Musgrove St. 0.8 mi s on US 25 and
301. Ext corridors. **Pets:** Medium. $5 daily fee/pet. Designated rooms,
service with restrictions, supervision.
[SAVE] [S♦] [✕] [🛏] [💻]

GOLDEN ISLES AREA

JEKYLL ISLAND

(AAA) ▽▽ Quality Inn & Suites **SH**
(912) 635-2202. **$199-$250, 7 day notice.** 700 N Beachview Dr. Jct
Ben Fortson Pkwy (SR 50)/Beachview Dr, 1.5 mi n. Ext corridors.
Pets: Small, other species. $10 daily fee/pet. Service with restrictions,
supervision.
[SAVE] [S♦] [✕] [🐾] [🛏] [💻] [🏊] [✕]

(AAA) ▽▽▽ Villas by the Sea [CO] ❀
(912) 635-2521. **$84-$139, 7 day notice.** 1175 N Beachview Dr. Jct
Ben Fortson Pkwy (SR 50)/Beachview Dr, 4 mi n. Ext corridors.
Pets: Medium. $100 one-time fee/room. Designated rooms, service with
restrictions, crate.
[SAVE] [S♦] [✕] [&M] [✎] [🐾] [🛏] [💻] [🍴] [🏊] [✕]

END AREA

GRAY

▽▽ Days Inn **M**
(478) 986-4200. **$58.** 288 W Clinton St. Jct SR 44/US 129, 0.9 mi w on
US 129. Ext/int corridors. **Pets:** Accepted.
[ASK] [S♦] [✕] [🐾] [🛏] [🏊]

GREENSBORO

▽ Microtel Inn **SH**
(706) 453-7300. **$55-$90.** 2470 Old Eatonton Hwy. I-20, exit 130, just n.
Int corridors. **Pets:** Accepted.
[ASK] [S♦] [✕] [&M] [✎] [🐾] [🛏]

GRIFFIN

▼▼ Howard Johnson Inn & Suites 🆂🅷
(770) 227-1516. **$55-$189.** 1690 N Expressway. 1.5 mi n on US 41 and 19. Ext corridors. **Pets:** Medium, other species. $25 one-time fee/pet. Designated rooms, service with restrictions, crate.

A$K S🐾 ☒ ♿ 🛢 💻 🏊

GROVETOWN

▼▼ Motel 6 of Augusta 🆂🅷
(706) 651-8300. **$48-$50, 14 day notice.** 459 Parkwest Dr. I-20, exit 194 (SR 383), just s, then w. Int corridors. **Pets:** Small, other species. Service with restrictions, supervision.

A$K S🐾 ☒ ♿ 🛢 🏊

HAHIRA

▼▼ Super 8 Motel I-75 🆂🅷
(229) 794-8000. **$39-$49.** 1300 Georgia Hwy 122 W. I-75, exit 29, just w. Ext corridors. **Pets:** Accepted.

A$K S🐾 ☒

HAMPTON

▼▼ Country Hearth Inn 🆂🅷
(770) 707-1477. **$59-$79, 7 day notice.** 1078 Bear Creek Blvd. 1 mi w of center of town; at US 41 and 19. Int corridors. **Pets:** Medium. $7 daily fee/room. Service with restrictions, crate.

A$K S🐾 ☒ 🅼 🌀 ♿ 🛢 💻

HELEN

♦♦♦ ▼▼▼ Blue Ridge Cabin Rentals 🅲🅰
(706) 878-1773. **$99-$399, 8 day notice.** 2990 Hwy 356. 1 mi n on SR 75, then 2.9 mi e. Ext corridors. **Pets:** Other species. $30 one-time fee/pet. No service, crate.

SAVE 🛢 💻

▼▼ The Helendorf River Inn & Conference Center 🆂🅷
(706) 878-2271. **$34-$109, 10 day notice.** 33 Munichstrasse. SR 17 and 75; center. Ext corridors. **Pets:** Other species. $10 daily fee/pet. Designated rooms, service with restrictions, supervision.

☒ 🛢 💻 🏊

▼▼ Kountry Peddler Tanglewood Resort Cabins 🅲🅰
(706) 878-3286. **$100-$585, 14 day notice.** 3387 Hwy 356. 1 mi n on SR 75, then 3 mi ne. Ext corridors. **Pets:** Small, other species. $25 one-time fee/pet. Designated rooms, no service, crate.

A$K S🐾 ☒ 🛢 💻 ☒

♦♦♦ ▼▼▼ Premier Vacation Rentals Inc 🆅🅷
(706) 348-8323. **$85-$595, 14 day notice.** 5156 Helen Hwy. 3.5 mi s on SR 75. Ext corridors. **Pets:** Small, dogs only. $15 daily fee/pet. Designated rooms, no service, supervision.

SAVE S🐾 🛢 💻

HIAWASSEE

▼▼▼ Enota B & B, Cabins & Conference Lodge 🅲🅰
(706) 896-9966. **$100-$165, 30 day notice.** 1000 Hwy 180. E on US 76 to SR 75/15, 6 mi s to SR 180, 3 mi w. Ext corridors. **Pets:** Other species. $15 daily fee/pet. Service with restrictions, supervision.

☒ 🛢 💻 ☒ 🌀

HINESVILLE

▼▼▼▼ Quality Inn at Fort Stewart 🆂🅷
(912) 876-4466. **$65.** 706 E Oglethrope Hwy. Just sw of jct US 84 and SR 38C. Ext corridors. **Pets:** Large. $10 daily fee/room. Service with restrictions, crate.

A$K S🐾 ☒ 🌀 ♿ 🛢 💻 🏊

HIRAM

▼▼▼ Country Inn & Suites By Carlson 🆂🅷
(770) 222-0456. **$69-$110, 3 day notice.** 70 Enterprise Path. Jct SR 92/6 and US 278, 0.3 mi w. Int corridors. **Pets:** Very small, other species. $10 daily fee/room. Service with restrictions, supervision.

A$K S🐾 ☒ ♿ 🛢 💻 🏊

HOGANSVILLE

▼▼ Days Inn 🆂🅷
(706) 637-5400. **$50-$55.** 1630 Bass Cross Rd. I-85, exit 28, just w. Ext corridors. **Pets:** Accepted.

A$K S🐾 ☒ 🛢 💻 🏊

♦♦♦ ▼▼ Econo Lodge 🆂🅷
(706) 637-9395. **$49-$59, 7 day notice.** 1888 E Main St. I-85, exit 28, just w. Ext corridors. **Pets:** Accepted.

SAVE S🐾 ☒ 🛢 💻 🏊

JASPER

▼▼ Super 8 Motel 🆂🅷
(706) 253-3297. **$66-$90.** 100 Whitfield Dr. Jct SR 515/53; in Lawsons Crossing. Ext corridors. **Pets:** Medium. $5 daily fee/pet. Service with restrictions, supervision.

A$K S🐾 ☒ 🅼 ♿ 🛢 💻 🏊

JESUP

▼▼ Jameson Inn of Jesup 🅼
(912) 427-6800. **$49-$104.** 205 N Hwy 301. Jct US 341, just n. Ext corridors. **Pets:** Very small, other species. $10 daily fee/room. Service with restrictions, supervision.

A$K ☒ 🌀 🛢 💻 🏊

KINGSLAND

♦♦♦ ▼▼▼ Best Western/Kings Bay Inn 🆂🅷
(912) 729-7666. **$75.** 1353 Hwy 40 E. I-95, exit 3 (SR 40), just se. Ext corridors. **Pets:** Accepted.

SAVE S🐾 ☒ 🌀 🛢 💻 🏊

▼▼ Econo Lodge 🅼
(912) 673-7336. **$45-$65.** 1135 E King Ave. I-95, exit 3 (SR 40), just nw. Ext corridors. **Pets:** Small. $5 one-time fee/pet. Service with restrictions, supervision.

A$K S🐾 ☒ 🅼 🌀 ♿ 🛢 💻 🏊

▼▼ Jameson Inn 🅼
(912) 729-9600. **$49-$104.** 105 May Creek Blvd. I-95, exit 3 (SR 40), just nw, then s at Boone Ave. Ext corridors. **Pets:** Very small, other species. $10 daily fee/pet. Service with restrictions, supervision.

A$K ☒ 🅼 🛢 💻 🏊

♦♦♦ ▼▼▼ Ramada Inn & Suites 🆂🅷
(912) 729-3000. **$49-$79.** 930 Hwy 40 E. I-95, exit 3 (SR 40), just nw. Ext corridors. **Pets:** Accepted.

SAVE S🐾 ☒ ♿ 🛢 💻 🍴 🏊

♦♦♦ ♦ Super 8 Motel 🆂🅷
(912) 729-6888. **$35-$85.** 120 Edenfield Dr. I-95, exit 3 (SR 40), just se. Int corridors. **Pets:** Accepted.

SAVE ☒ 🛢

LA FAYETTE

♦♦♦ ▼▼▼ Days Inn 🆂🅷
(706) 639-9362. **$50-$100.** 2209 N Main St. 2.5 mi n on US 27. Ext corridors. **Pets:** $10 daily fee/pet. Service with restrictions, supervision.

SAVE S🐾 ☒ 🛢 🏊

LAGRANGE

(AAA) ▼▼▼▼ Best Western Lafayette Garden Inn SH
(706) 884-6175. **$55-$84, 7 day notice.** 1513 Lafayette Pkwy. I-85, exit 18 (Lafayette Pkwy), just w. Ext corridors. **Pets:** Accepted.
SAVE Sᴅ ✕ 🖥 🖵 🍴 ⊷

(AAA) ▼▼▼ Days Inn-LaGrange/Callaway Gardens SH
(706) 882-8881. **$55, 14 day notice.** 2606 Whitesville Rd. I-85, exit 13, just e. Ext corridors. **Pets:** $10 daily fee/pet. Service with restrictions, supervision.
SAVE Sᴅ ✕ 🔊 🖥 🖵 ⊷

▼▼▼ Econo Lodge SH
(706) 882-9540. **$53-$65, 3 day notice.** 1601 Lafayette Pkwy. I-85, exit 18 (Lafayette Pkwy), just e. Ext corridors. **Pets:** Accepted.
ASK Sᴅ ✕ 🖥 🖵 ⊷

▼▼▼ Jameson Inn SH
(706) 882-8700. **$49-$104.** 110 Jameson Dr. I-85, exit 18 (Lafayette Pkwy), 0.3 mi w. Ext corridors. **Pets:** Very small, other species. $10 daily fee/room. Service with restrictions, supervision.
ASK ✕ ᴋᴍ 🔊 🖥 🖵 ⊷

LAKE PARK

▼▼▼ Days Inn SH
(229) 559-0229. **$55-$60.** 4913 Timber Dr. I-75, exit 5, just w, then n. Ext corridors. **Pets:** Small. $7 daily fee/room. Service with restrictions, supervision.
ASK Sᴅ ✕ 🖵 ⊷

▼▼▼ Holiday Inn Express SH
(229) 559-5181. **$75.** 1198 Lakes Blvd. I-75, exit 5, just e. Ext corridors. **Pets:** Accepted.
✕ 🖥 🖵 ⊷

▼▼▼ Lake Park Inn SH
(229) 559-4939. **Call for rates.** 6972 Bellville Rd. I-75, exit 2, just w. Ext corridors. **Pets:** Accepted.
✕ 🖵 ⊷

(AAA) ▼▼▼ Super 8 Motel SH
(229) 559-8111. **$50-$65.** 4907 Timber Dr. I-75, exit 5, just w, then n. Ext corridors. **Pets:** Accepted.
SAVE Sᴅ ✕ 🖥

▼▼▼ Travelodge SH
(229) 559-0110. **Call for rates.** 4912 Timber Dr. I-75, exit 5, just w, then just n. Int corridors. **Pets:** Accepted.
✕ ᴋᴍ 🖥 🖵 ⊷

LAVONIA

(AAA) ▼▼▼ GuestHouse International Inn SH
(706) 356-8848. **$45-$75.** 14227 Jones St. I-85, exit 173, just w. Ext corridors. **Pets:** $10 daily fee/pet. Service with restrictions, supervision.
SAVE Sᴅ ✕ ᴋᴍ 🔊 🔊 🖥 🖵 ⊷

LOCUST GROVE

(AAA) ▼▼▼ Econo Lodge M
(770) 957-2601. **$45-$100, 3 day notice.** 4829 Bill Gardner Pkwy. I-75, exit 212, just e. Ext corridors. **Pets:** Small. $7 daily fee/pet. Service with restrictions, supervision.
SAVE Sᴅ ✕ 🖥 🖵

(AAA) ▼▼▼▼ Red Roof Inn & Suites SH 🐾
(678) 583-0004. **$54-$89.** 4832 Bill Gardner Pkwy. I-75, exit 212, just e. Int corridors. **Pets:** Large, other species. Service with restrictions, supervision.
SAVE Sᴅ ✕ ᴋᴍ 🔊 🔊 🖥 🖵 ⊷

LOUISVILLE

(AAA) ▼▼▼ Louisville Motor Lodge M
(478) 625-7168. **$43-$48.** 308 Hwy 1 Bypass. Jct SR 24/US 1 Bypass, 0.6 mi n. Ext corridors. **Pets:** Very small. $5 one-time fee/pet. Service with restrictions, supervision.
SAVE ✕ 🖥

MACON

▼▼▼ Best Inns & Suites M
(478) 405-0106. **$45-$55.** 130 Holiday North Dr. I-75, exit 169 (Arkwright Rd), just sw to US 23 (Riverside Dr), just se to Holiday North Dr, then just sw. Ext corridors. **Pets:** Accepted.
ASK Sᴅ ✕ 🖥 🖵 ⊷

(AAA) ▼▼▼▼ Best Western Inn & Suites of Macon M 🐾
(478) 781-5300. **$59.** 4681 Chambers Rd. I-475, exit 3 (Eisenhower Pkwy/US 80), just ne, then just se. Ext corridors. **Pets:** Medium. $10 one-time fee/room. Designated rooms, service with restrictions, supervision.
SAVE Sᴅ ✕ 🔊 🖥 🖵 ⊷

(AAA) ▼▼▼ Best Western Riverside Inn SH 🐾
(478) 743-6311. **$59-$69.** 2400 Riverside Dr. I-75, exit 167 (Riverside Dr), just w, then 0.4 mi se. Int corridors. **Pets:** Medium. $10 daily fee/pet. Designated rooms, service with restrictions, supervision.
SAVE Sᴅ ✕ 🖥 🖵 ⊷

(AAA) ▼▼▼▼ Crowne Plaza Hotel LH
(478) 746-1461. **$64-$129.** 108 First St. Between Walnut St and Riverside Dr; downtown. Int corridors. **Pets:** Accepted.
SAVE ✕ 🖥 🖵 ⊷ ✕

▼▼▼ Days Inn-Macon West M
(478) 784-1000. **$60-$80, 7 day notice.** 6000 Harrison Rd. I-475, exit 3 (Eisenhower Pkwy/US 80), just w. Ext corridors. **Pets:** Accepted.
ASK Sᴅ ✕ 🔊 🖥 ⊷

(AAA) ▼▼▼ Econo Lodge M
(478) 474-1661. **$36-$50.** 4951 Romeiser Dr. I-475, exit 3 (Eisenhower Pkwy/US 80), just sw, then s. Ext corridors. **Pets:** Small. $5 daily fee/pet. Designated rooms, service with restrictions, supervision.
SAVE Sᴅ ✕ 🖥 🖵 ⊷

▼▼▼ Hawthorn Inn & Suites SH
(478) 471-2121. **$59-$73.** 107 Holiday North Dr. I-75, exit 169 (Arkwright Rd), just sw to Riverside Dr, then just se. Ext corridors. **Pets:** Medium. $25 one-time fee/pet. Service with restrictions, crate.
ASK Sᴅ ✕ 🔊 🖥 🖵 ⊷

▼▼▼ Holiday Inn Macon Conference Center SH
(478) 474-2610. **$72.** 3590 Riverside Dr. I-75, exit 169 (Arkwright Rd), just sw, then just se. Ext corridors. **Pets:** Accepted.
ASK Sᴅ ✕ 🖥 🖵 🍴 ⊷

▼▼▼ Jameson Inn M
(478) 474-8004. **$49-$104.** 150 Plantation Inn Dr. I-475, exit 9 (Zebulon Rd), just e to Peake Rd, then just s. Ext corridors. **Pets:** Very small, other species. $10 daily fee/room. Service with restrictions, supervision.
ASK ✕ 🖥 ⊷

(AAA) ▼▼▼▼ La Quinta Inn & Suites Macon SH 🐾
(478) 475-0206. **$85-$115.** 3944 River Place Dr. I-75, exit 169 (Arkwright Rd), just n, then e. Int corridors. **Pets:** Other species. Service with restrictions.
SAVE ✕ ᴋᴍ 🔊 🖥 🖵 ⊷

▼▼▼ Motel 6 M
(478) 474-2870. **Call for rates.** 4991 Harrison Rd. I-475, exit 3 (Eisenhower Pkwy/US 80), just ne, then n. Ext corridors. **Pets:** Accepted.
✕ 🖥 ⊷

▼▼ **Quality Inn & Conference Center** M ☘
(478) 781-7000. **Call for rates.** 4630 Chambers Rd. I-475, exit 3 (Eisenhower Pkwy/US 80), just ne, then just se. Ext corridors. **Pets:** Medium. $10 daily fee/pet. Service with restrictions, supervision.

⊠ 🛢 🍴 💻 ⌒

▼▼ **Red Roof Inn** SH
(478) 477-7477. **$41-$54.** 3950 River Place Dr. I-75, exit 169 (Arkwright Rd), just n, then e. Int corridors. **Pets:** Accepted.

⊠ 🐾 🍴 ⌒

🔺 ▼▼ **Rodeway Inn** M ☘
(478) 781-4343. **$49.** 4999 Eisenhower Pkwy. I-475, exit 3 (Eisenhower Pkwy/US 80), just ne. Ext corridors. **Pets:** Medium. $5 one-time fee/room. Service with restrictions, supervision.

SAVE 🛢 ⊠ 🍴 💻 ⌒

▼▼ **Sleep Inn I-475** SH
(478) 476-8111. **$65-$69.** 140 Plantation Inn Dr. I-475, exit 9 (Zebulon Rd), just e to Peake Rd, then just s. Int corridors. **Pets:** Medium. $10 daily fee/pet. Designated rooms, service with restrictions, supervision.

ASK 🛢 ⊠ 🐾 🍴 🐾 🍴 💻 ⌒

MADISON

🔺 ▼▼ **Days Inn** SH
(706) 342-1839. **$44-$90, 14 day notice.** 2001 Eatonton Hwy. I-20, exit 114, just n. Ext corridors. **Pets:** Accepted.

SAVE 🛢 ⊠ 🍴 💻 ⌒

▼▼ **Super 8 Motel** SH
(706) 342-7800. **Call for rates.** 2091 Eatonton Hwy. I-20, exit 114, 0.3 mi s. Int corridors. **Pets:** Accepted.

⊠ 🍴

MCDONOUGH

🔺 ▼▼▼ **Comfort Inn** SH
(770) 954-9110. **$75-$80.** 80 Hwy 81 W. I-75, exit 218, just nw. Ext corridors. **Pets:** Medium. $6 daily fee/pet. Service with restrictions, supervision.

SAVE 🛢 ⊠ 🐾 🍴 💻 ⌒

🔺 ▼▼ **Days Inn** SH
(770) 957-5261. **$48-$68.** 744 SR 155 S & I-75. I-75, exit 216, just e. Ext corridors. **Pets:** Medium, other species. $7 daily fee/pet. Service with restrictions, supervision.

SAVE 🛢 ⊠ 🐾 🍴 💻 ⌒

▼ **Econo Lodge** M
(770) 957-2651. **$45.** 1279 Hampton Rd. I-75, exit 218, just w. Ext corridors. **Pets:** Small. $5 one-time fee/pet. Service with restrictions, supervision.

ASK 🛢 ⊠ 🍴 💻 ⌒

🔺 ▼▼ **Masters Inn** M
(770) 957-5818. **$43-$140.** 1311 Hampton Rd. I-75, exit 218, just w. Ext corridors. **Pets:** Small. $5 one-time fee/pet. Service with restrictions, supervision.

SAVE 🛢 ⊠ 🍴 ⌒

🔺 ▼▼▼ **Quality Inn & Suites Conference Center** SH
(770) 957-5291. **$64-$89.** 930 Hwy 155 S. I-75, exit 216, just w. Ext corridors. **Pets:** Other species. $5 daily fee/room. Service with restrictions.

SAVE 🛢 ⊠ 🐾 🍴 🐾 🍴 🍽 ⌒

🔺 ▼▼▼ **Super 8 Motel** M
(770) 957-2458. **$50.** 1170 Hampton Rd. I-75, exit 218, just e. Ext/int corridors. **Pets:** Accepted.

SAVE 🛢 ⊠ 🍴

MILLEDGEVILLE

▼▼▼▼ **Holiday Inn Express** SH
(478) 454-9000. **$69-$78.** 1839 N Columbia St. US 441, 2 mi n of downtown. Int corridors. **Pets:** Small. $15 one-time fee/room. Supervision.

ASK 🛢 ⊠ 🐾 🍴 🐾 🍴 💻 ⌒

MONROE

▼▼ **Country Hearth Inn** SH
(770) 207-1977. **$65-$70.** 1222 W Spring St. 1 mi w of downtown on Business Rt SR 10. Int corridors. **Pets:** Very small. $10 daily fee/pet. No service, supervision.

⊠ 🐾 🍴 🍴 💻

NEWNAN

🔺 ▼▼▼ **Best Western-Shenandoah Inn** SH
(770) 304-9700. **$60-$69.** 620 Hwy 34 E. I-85, exit 47, just w. Ext corridors. **Pets:** Medium. $10 daily fee/pet. Designated rooms, service with restrictions, supervision.

SAVE 🛢 ⊠ 🐾 🍴 🍴 💻 ⌒

▼▼▼ **Jameson Inn** SH
(770) 252-1236. **$49-$104.** 40 Lakeside Way. I-85, exit 47, 0.6 mi e. Int corridors. **Pets:** Very small, other species. $10 daily fee/room. Service with restrictions, supervision.

ASK ⊠ 🍴 🐾 🍴 🍴 💻 ⌒

▼▼ **Ramada Limited** SH
(770) 683-1499. **$52.** 1310 Hwy 29 S. I-85, exit 41, just w. Ext corridors. **Pets:** Accepted.

⊠ 🐾 🍴 💻 ⌒

OAKWOOD

▼▼▼ **Country Inn & Suites By Carlson** SH
(770) 535-8080. **$66-$145.** 4535 Oakwood Rd. I-985, exit 16, just sw. Int corridors. **Pets:** Accepted.

ASK 🛢 ⊠ 🐾 🍴 🍴 💻 ⌒

▼▼ **Jameson Inn of Oakwood/Gainesville** SH
(770) 533-9400. **$49-$104.** 3780 Merchants Way. I-985, exit 16, 0.4 mi nw. Ext corridors. **Pets:** Very small, other species. $10 daily fee/room. Service with restrictions, supervision.

ASK ⊠ 🍴 🍴 💻 ⌒

PEACHTREE CITY

▼▼ **Sleep Inn** SH
(770) 486-0044. **Call for rates.** 109 City Cir. Jct SR 74 and 54; downtown. Int corridors. **Pets:** Small. $10 daily fee/pet. Designated rooms, service with restrictions, supervision.

⊠ 🍴 🐾 🍴 💻

PERRY

▼▼ **Best Inns** SH
(478) 987-4454. **$36-$45.** 110 Perimeter Rd. I-75, exit 136 (Sam Nunn Blvd), just se. Ext corridors. **Pets:** Other species. $9 daily fee/room. Service with restrictions.

ASK 🛢 ⊠ 🍴

▼▼▼ **Best Western Bradbury Inn & Suites** SH ☘
(478) 218-5200. **$55-$121.** 205 Lect Dr. I-75, exit 135 (US 41), just e, then just n. Int corridors. **Pets:** Medium. $10 daily fee/pet. Service with restrictions, supervision.

ASK 🛢 ⊠ 🐾 🍴 💻 ⌒

🔺 ▼▼▼ **Comfort Inn Perry** SH
(478) 987-7710. **$50-$90.** 1602 Sam Nunn Blvd. I-75, exit 136 (Sam Nunn Blvd), just nw. Ext corridors. **Pets:** Accepted.

SAVE 🛢 ⊠ 🐾 🍴 💻 ⌒

Henderson Village CI
(478) 988-8696. **$175-$350, 3 day notice.** 125 S Langston Cir. I-75, exit 127 (SR 26), 1.3 mi w. Ext/int corridors. **Pets:** Designated rooms, service with restrictions, crate.

Jameson Inn-Perry M
(478) 987-5060. **$49-$104.** 200 Market Place Dr. I-75, exit 136 (Sam Nunn Blvd), just se, then sw. Ext corridors. **Pets:** Very small, other species. $10 daily fee/room. Service with restrictions, supervision.

New Perry Hotel SH
(478) 987-1000. **$59-$94.** 800 Main St. I-75, exit 136 (Sam Nunn Blvd) southbound, 1.2 mi se on US 341, then just w; exit 135 (US 41) northbound, 1.5 mi ne, then just s. Ext/int corridors. **Pets:** Medium. $10 daily fee/pet. Designated rooms, service with restrictions, supervision.

Quality Inn M
(478) 987-1345. **$52-$57.** 1504 Sam Nunn Blvd. I-75, exit 136 (Sam Nunn Blvd), just nw. Ext corridors. **Pets:** Medium. $10 daily fee/room. Service with restrictions, crate.

Super 8 Motel SH
(478) 987-0999. **$45-$50.** 102 Plaza Dr. I-75, exit 136 (Sam Nunn Blvd), just se. Ext corridors. **Pets:** Medium, other species. $10 daily fee/pet. Service with restrictions, crate.

PINE MOUNTAIN

Days Inn SH
(706) 663-2121. **$60-$84.** 368 S Main Ave. Just s on US 27 and SR 18. Ext corridors. **Pets:** Accepted.

White Columns Motel M
(706) 663-8008. **$59-$65.** 524 S Main St. 1 mi s on US 27. Ext corridors. **Pets:** Other species. $10 one-time fee/room. Designated rooms, service with restrictions, supervision.

POOLER

Best Western Bradbury Suites SH
(912) 330-0330. **$79-$159.** 155 Bourne Ave. I-95, exit 102 (US 80), just e. Int corridors. **Pets:** Other species. Service with restrictions.

Comfort Inn and Suites Conference Center SH
(912) 748-6464. **$59, 3 day notice.** 301 Governor Treutlen Dr. I-95, exit 102 (US 80), just nw, then just se. Int corridors. **Pets:** Accepted.

Econo Lodge–Savannah Pooler M
(912) 748-4124. **$54-$99.** 500 E Hwy 80. I-95, exit 102 (US 80), just nw. Ext corridors. **Pets:** Other species. $10 daily fee/pet. Designated rooms, service with restrictions.

Jameson Inn SH
(912) 748-0017. **$49-$104.** 125 Bourne Ave. I-95, exit 102 (US 80), just e. Int corridors. **Pets:** Very small, other species. $10 daily fee/room. Service with restrictions, supervision.

Red Roof Inn & Suites SH
(912) 748-4050. **$67-$107.** 20 Mill Creek Cir. I-95, exit 104 (Pooler Pkwy), just w. Int corridors. **Pets:** Other species. Service with restrictions, supervision.

Travelodge Suites SH
(912) 748-6363. **$65-$99.** 130 Continental Blvd. I-95, exit 102 (US 80), just e. Int corridors. **Pets:** Small. $10 daily fee/pet. Designated rooms, service with restrictions, supervision.

RINCON

Days Inn SH
(912) 826-6966. **$45-$99.** 582 Columbia Ave. I-95, exit 109 (SR 21), 6.1 mi nw. Ext corridors. **Pets:** Accepted.

RINGGOLD

Comfort Inn SH
(706) 935-4000. **$59-$95.** 177 Industrial Blvd. I-75, exit 348, just w. Int corridors. **Pets:** Small. $10 daily fee/pet. Designated rooms, service with restrictions, supervision.

Super 8 Motel M
(706) 965-7080. **$47-$100.** 5400 Alabama Hwy. I-75, exit 348, just e. Ext corridors. **Pets:** Accepted.

ROCKMART

Days Inn SH
(770) 684-9955. **$55-$60.** 105 GTM Pkwy. Jct US 278 and SR 101, just n. Ext corridors. **Pets:** Medium. Service with restrictions, supervision.

ROME

Holiday Inn-Sky Top Center SH
(706) 295-1100. **$80.** 20 US 411 E. 2 mi e. Ext corridors. **Pets:** Accepted.

Howard Johnson Express Inn of Rome SH
(706) 291-1994. **$52-$60.** 1610 Martha Berry Blvd. 2 mi n on US 27. Ext corridors. **Pets:** Medium. $5 daily fee/pet. Designated rooms, service with restrictions.

Jameson Inn SH
(706) 291-7797. **$49-$104.** 40 Grace Dr. On US 411, 2.2 mi e. Int corridors. **Pets:** Very small, other species. $10 daily fee/room. Service with restrictions, supervision.

SANDERSVILLE

Villa South Motor Inn M
(478) 552-1234. **$47-$55.** 725 S Harris St (SR 15). Jct SR 15/242, just s on SR 15. Ext corridors. **Pets:** Accepted.

SAVANNAH

Ballastone Inn BB
(912) 236-1484. **$215-$395, 15 day notice.** 14 E Oglethorpe Ave. Between Bull and Drayton sts. Int corridors. **Pets:** Accepted.

Baymont Inn & Suites Savannah SH
(912) 927-7660. **$64-$84.** 8484 Abercorn St. 2.4 mi s of jct SR 21/204 (Abercorn St). Int corridors. **Pets:** $50 deposit/room. Service with restrictions, supervision.

△△△ ▼▼▼ Best Value Inn M
(912) 927-2999. **$45-$65, 5 day notice.** 390 Canebrake Rd. I-95, exit 94 (SR 204), just e, then just s. Ext corridors. **Pets:** Small, other species. $5 daily fee/pet. Designated rooms, service with restrictions, supervision.
SAVE 🐾 ✕ 🖉 🖥 🖨 🏊

△△△ ▼▼▼ Best Western Central SH
(912) 355-1000. **$70-$90.** 45 Eisenhower Dr. 1.3 mi s of jct SR 21/204 (Abercorn St), then just w. Ext corridors. **Pets:** Accepted.
SAVE 🐾 ✕ 🖉 🖥 🖨 🏊

▼▼▼▼ Catherine Ward House Inn BB
(912) 234-8564. **$149-$400, 14 day notice.** 118 E Walburg St. Between Drayton and Abercorn sts. Ext/int corridors. **Pets:** Small. $10 daily fee/pet. Designated rooms, service with restrictions.
ASK ✕ 🖥

△△△ ▼▼▼▼ ClubHouse Inn & Suites SH
(912) 356-1234. **$76-$109.** 6800 Abercorn St. 1 mi s of jct SR 21 and 204 (Abercorn St). Int corridors. **Pets:** Accepted.
SAVE 🐾 ✕ 🖥 🖨 🏊

▼▼▼▼ Days Inn-I-95/204 M
(912) 925-3680. **$75-$82.** 4 Gateway Blvd E. I-95, exit 94 (SR 204), just e. Int corridors. **Pets:** Accepted.
ASK 🐾 ✕ 🖉 🏊

△△△ ▼▼▼▼ East Bay Inn CI
(912) 238-1225. **$99-$189, 7 day notice.** 225 E Bay St. I-16, exit 167 (Montgomery St), 0.8 mi ne, then 0.4 mi se; in historic district. Int corridors. **Pets:** Accepted.
SAVE 🐾 ✕ 🖥 🍴

▼▼▼▼ Econo Lodge Gateway M
(912) 925-2280. **$49-$129.** 7 Gateway Blvd W. I-95, exit 94 (SR 204), just nw, then just ne. Ext corridors. **Pets:** Accepted.
ASK 🐾 ✕ 🖥 🏊

▼▼▼▼ The Forsyth Park Inn BB 🐾
(912) 233-6800. **$130-$230, 7 day notice.** 102 W Hall St. Between Whitaker and Howard sts; on Forsyth Park. Int corridors. **Pets:** Small. $40 one-time fee/room. Designated rooms, service with restrictions.
ASK 🐾 ✕ 🖥

△△△ ▼▼▼▼ Hawthorn Suites SH
(912) 966-0020. **$119.** 4 Stephen S Green Ave. I-95, exit 104, 0.4 mi e. Int corridors. **Pets:** Accepted.
SAVE 🐾 ✕ 🖥 🖨 🏊

▼▼▼▼ Homewood Suites by Hilton SH
(912) 353-8500. **$151-$217.** 5820 White Bluff Rd. Jct SR 21/204, 0.5 mi s. Ext/int corridors. **Pets:** Large, other species. $45 one-time fee/room. Service with restrictions.
ASK 🐾 ✕ 🖥 🖨 🏊 ✕

▼▼▼ Joan's on Jones B & B BB 🐾
(912) 234-3863. **$145-$160 (no credit cards), 7 day notice.** 17 W Jones St. Between Whitaker and Bull sts. Ext corridors. **Pets:** Dogs only. $50 one-time fee/room. Crate.
✕ 🖥 🖨

△△△ ▼▼▼ La Quinta Inn Savannah (I-95) M
(912) 925-9505. **$74-$94.** 6 Gateway Blvd S. I-95, exit 94 (SR 204), just e, then s. Ext corridors. **Pets:** Service with restrictions, supervision.
SAVE ✕ 🖨 🖉 🖥 🏊

▼▼▼▼ La Quinta Inn Savannah (Midtown) SH 🐾
(912) 355-3004. **$76-$95.** 6805 Abercorn St. 1 mi s of jct SR 21/204 (Abercorn St). Ext/int corridors. **Pets:** Small, other species. Service with restrictions, supervision.
ASK ✕ 🖉 🖥 🖨 🏊

△△△ ▼▼▼▼ The Olde Georgian Inn BB
(912) 236-2911. **$105-$195, 7 day notice.** 212 W Hall St. Between Jefferson and Barnard sts; just w of Forsyth Park. Ext/int corridors. **Pets:** Small, dogs only. $100 deposit/pet, $15 daily fee/pet. Designated rooms, no service, crate.
SAVE ✕ 🖥 🖨 🖉

△△△ ▼▼▼▼ Olde Harbour Inn BB 🐾
(912) 234-4100. **$169-$350, 7 day notice.** 508 E Factors Walk. Lincoln St ramp off E Bay St; in historic riverfront district. Ext corridors. **Pets:** Small, other species. $35 one-time fee/pet. Service with restrictions, supervision.
SAVE 🐾 ✕ 🖥

△△△ ▼▼▼ Quality Inn Savannah South M
(912) 925-2770. **$59-$129.** 3 Gateway Blvd S. I-95, exit 94 (SR 204), just e, then just s. Ext corridors. **Pets:** Accepted.
SAVE 🐾 ✕ 🖉 🖥 🍴 🏊

△△△ ▼▼▼ Red Roof Inn SH
(912) 920-3535. **$53-$87.** 405 Al Henderson Blvd. I-95, exit 94 (SR 204), just e. Int corridors. **Pets:** Small, other species. Designated rooms, no service, supervision.
SAVE 🐾 ✕ 🖥 🖨 🏊

▼▼▼ Savannah Residence Inn by Marriott SH
(912) 356-3266. **$99-$179.** 5710 White Bluff Rd. Jct SR 21, 0.5 mi s. Int corridors. **Pets:** Accepted.
🐾 ✕ 🖥 🖨 🏊 ✕

△△△ ▼▼▼ Travelodge M
(912) 925-2640. **$45-$199.** 1 Fort Argyle Rd. I-95, exit 94 (SR 204), just w. Ext corridors. **Pets:** $15 daily fee/pet. Designated rooms, supervision.
SAVE 🐾 ✕ 🖥 🖨 🏊

△△△ ▼▼▼▼ Westin Savannah Harbor Resort and Spa LH
(912) 201-2000. **$149-$279, 3 day notice.** 1 Resort Dr. On Hutchinson Island; 1 mi se of first exit after Eugene Talmadge Memorial Bridge and US 17. Int corridors. **Pets:** Accepted.
SAVE 🐾 ✕ 🖉 🖥 🍴 🏊 ✕

STATESBORO

▼▼▼ Best Western University Inn M
(912) 681-7900. **$53-$64.** 1 Jameson Ave. Jct US 25/301 and SR 67, 0.9 mi s on US 25/301. Ext corridors. **Pets:** Accepted.
ASK 🐾 ✕ 🖥 🖨 🏊

▼▼▼ Hometown Inn M 🐾
(912) 681-4663. **Call for rates.** 126 Rushing Ln. Jct US 301 Bypass and SR 67, just n, then w. Ext corridors. **Pets:** Other species. $5 daily fee/room. Designated rooms, service with restrictions, crate.
✕ 🖥

▼▼▼ Statesboro Inn & Restaurant CI
(912) 489-8628. **$85-$150.** 106 S Main St (US 301/25). US 301/25, just s of town center; downtown. Int corridors. **Pets:** Accepted.
ASK 🐾 ✕ 🖥 🖨 🍴

STOCKBRIDGE

▼▼▼ Best Western Atlanta South SH
(770) 474-8771. **$60-$100.** 619 Hwy 138. I-75, exit 228, just e; I-675, exit 1, 0.5 mi w. Ext corridors. **Pets:** Accepted.
ASK 🐾 ✕ 🖥 🖨 🍴 🏊

▼▼▼ Motel 6–1117 M
(770) 389-1142. **$45-$57.** 7233 Davidson Pkwy N. I-675, exit 1, northeast corner; I-75, exit 228, 1 mi e. Ext corridors. **Pets:** Accepted.
🐾 ✕ 🖉 🖨 🖥

▽▽◇ Shoney's Inn SH
(770) 389-5179. **Call for rates.** 110 Hwy 138. I-675, exit 1, just e; I-75, exit 228, 1.1 mi e. Ext corridors. **Pets:** Accepted.

☒ ⚗ 🛏 💻 ≈

❀❀ ▽▽▽ Super 8 Motel Atlanta South SH
(770) 474-5758. **$59.** 1451 Hudson Bridge Rd. I-75, exit 224, just w. Ext corridors. **Pets:** Accepted.

SAVE S✆ ☒ 🛏 💻 ≈

SWAINSBORO

❀❀ ▽▽▽ Bradford Inn M
(478) 237-2400. **$50-$59, 10 day notice.** 688 S Main St. I-16, exit 90 (US 1), 12.4 mi n. Ext corridors. **Pets:** Small. $10 daily fee/pet. Service with restrictions, supervision.

SAVE S✆ ☒ 🛏 💻

TALLAPOOSA

▽▽▽▽ Comfort Inn SH
(770) 574-5575. **$55-$225.** 788 Hwy 100. I-20, exit 5, just s. Int corridors. **Pets:** Very small, other species. $10 daily fee/pet. Designated rooms, service with restrictions, supervision.

ASK S✆ ☒ ⓂM ⓦ 🛏 💻 ≈

THOMASTON

❀❀ ▽▽▽ Best Western Thomaston Inn SH
(706) 648-2900. **$55-$65.** 1207 Hwy 19 N. 2.8 mi n; center of town. Ext corridors. **Pets:** Small, dogs only. $8 daily fee/pet. Service with restrictions, supervision.

SAVE S✆ ☒ 🛏 💻 ≈

▽▽ Jameson Inn SH
(706) 648-2232. **$49-$104.** 1010 Hwy 19 N. Jct SR 74, 2.3 mi n. Ext corridors. **Pets:** Accepted.

ASK ☒ 🛏 💻 ≈

THOMASVILLE

▽▽▽▽ Hampton Inn Thomasville SH
(229) 227-0040. **$86-$136.** 1950 GA Hwy 122 (Pavo Rd). Jct of SR 300/I-19 and I-84 and SR 122, southeast corner. Int corridors. **Pets:** Accepted.

ASK S✆ ☒ ⓂM ⓦ 🛏 💻 ≈ ☒

▽▽ Jameson Inn SH
(229) 227-9500. **$49-$104.** 1670 Remington Ave. US 19, just w on CR 122. Ext corridors. **Pets:** Very small, other species. $10 daily fee/room. Service with restrictions, supervision.

ASK ☒ ⓂM ⚗ ⓦ 🛏 💻 ≈

▽▽▽▽ Quality Inn & Suites Conference Center SH
(229) 225-2134. **$73.** 15138 Hwy 19 S. 0.3 mi s of US 319. Ext corridors. **Pets:** Accepted.

ASK S✆ ☒ ⓂM ⚗ 🛏 💻 ⅊ ≈

THOMSON

❀❀ ▽▽◇ Best Western White Columns Inn SH ❀
(706) 595-8000. **$65-$85.** 1890 Washington Rd. I-20, exit 172 (US 78), just s. Ext corridors. **Pets:** Medium. $10 daily fee/room. Designated rooms, service with restrictions, crate.

SAVE S✆ ☒ 🛏 💻 ⅊ ≈ ☒

❀❀ ▽▽ Days Inn M
(706) 595-2262. **$55-$60, 30 day notice.** 2658 Cobbham Rd. I-20, exit 175 (SR 150), just n. Ext corridors. **Pets:** $15 daily fee/pet. No service, supervision.

SAVE S✆ ☒ 🛏

TIFTON

▽▽ ▽▽ Days Inn & Suites SH
(229) 382-8505. **$55-$75.** 1199 Hwy 82 W. I-75, exit 62, just w. Int corridors. **Pets:** Accepted.

ASK S✆ ☒ 🛏 💻 ≈

▽▽◇▽ Hampton Inn SH
(229) 382-8800. **$89-$97.** 720 Hwy 319 S. I-75, exit 62, just e. Ext corridors. **Pets:** Medium, other species. No service, supervision.

ASK S✆ ☒ 🛏 💻 ≈

❀❀ ▽▽▽ Holiday Inn SH
(229) 382-6687. **$62-$68.** 1208 Hwy 82 W. I-75, exit 62, at jct US 82 and 319. Ext corridors. **Pets:** Service with restrictions, supervision.

SAVE S✆ ☒ 🛏 💻 ⅊ ≈

▽▽ ▽▽ Microtel Inns & Suites SH
(229) 387-0112. **$39-$90.** 196 S Virginia Ave. I-75, exit 62, just n. Int corridors. **Pets:** Medium, other species. $10 one-time fee/room. Service with restrictions, supervision.

ASK S✆ ☒ ⓂM ⓦ 🛏 💻 ≈

❀❀ ▽▽ Motel 6 #4074 SH
(229) 388-8777. **$38, 7 day notice.** 579 Old Omega Rd. I-75, exit 61, just w. Int corridors. **Pets:** Small, other species. Service with restrictions, supervision.

SAVE S✆ ☒ ≈

❀❀ ▽▽▽ Ramada Limited and Conference Center SH
(229) 382-8500. **$52-$63.** 1211 Hwy 82 W. I-75, exit 62, just w. Ext corridors. **Pets:** Accepted.

SAVE S✆ ☒ 🛏 💻 ≈

TOWNSEND

◇ Days Inn M
(912) 832-4411. **$60-$65.** I-95, exit 58 (SR 57), just nw. Ext corridors. **Pets:** Accepted.

ASK S✆ ☒ 🛏 ≈

UNADILLA

▽ Scottish Inn M
(478) 627-3228. **$36-$39, 4 day notice.** 1062 Pine St (US 41). I-75, exit 121 (US 41), just ne. Ext corridors. **Pets:** Small. $5 daily fee/pet. Service with restrictions, supervision.

ASK S✆ ☒ 🛏 ≈

VALDOSTA

❀❀ ▽▽▽ Best Western King of the Road SH
(229) 244-7600. **$59-$69.** 1403 N St Augustine Rd. I-75, exit 18, just w off of SR 94. Ext corridors. **Pets:** Small. $7 daily fee/room. Service with restrictions, supervision.

SAVE S✆ ☒ ⚗ 🛏 💻 ⅊ ≈

▽▽ ▽▽ Comfort Inn Conference Center SH
(229) 242-1212. **$78-$174.** 2101 W Hill Ave. I-75, exit 16, just w. Ext/int corridors. **Pets:** Small, other species. Designated rooms, service with restrictions, supervision.

ASK S✆ ☒ 🛏 💻 ⅊ ≈

▽▽ ▽▽ Days Inn Conference Center SH
(229) 249-8800. **$46-$62.** 1827 W Hill Ave. I-75, exit 16, just e. Ext corridors. **Pets:** Accepted.

ASK S✆ ☒ ⓂM ⓦ 🛏 💻 ≈

▽▽ ▽▽ Days Inn I-75 North SH
(229) 244-4460. **$46-$59.** 4598 N Valdosta Rd. I-75, exit 22, just w. Ext corridors. **Pets:** Accepted.

ASK S✆ ☒ 🛏 ≈

ⒶⒶⒶ ▼▼▼ Holiday Inn 🆂🅷
(229) 242-3881. **$69-$89.** 1309 St Augustine Rd. I-75, exit 18, just e on SR 94. Ext corridors. **Pets:** Accepted.
🆂🅰🆅🅴 🆂🅾 ⊠ 🗐 🖵 🍽 ⇌

▼▼▼ Howard Johnson Express Inn & Suites 🆂🅷
(229) 249-8900. **$48-$58.** 1330 St Augustine Rd. I-75, exit 18, just e. Ext corridors. **Pets:** Accepted.
🅰🆂🅺 🆂🅾 ⊠ 🗐 🖵 ⇌

▼▼ Jameson Inn 🆂🅷
(229) 253-0009. **$49-$104.** 1725 Gornto Rd. I-75, exit 18, 0.3 mi e on north side of SR 94. Ext corridors. **Pets:** Very small, other species. $10 daily fee/room. Service with restrictions, supervision.
🅰🆂🅺 ⊠ 🖫 🗐 🖵 ⇌

▼▼▼▼ La Quinta Inn & Suites Valdosta 🆂🅷
(229) 247-7755. **$69-$94.** 1800 Clubhouse Dr. I-75, exit 18, 0.3 mi e, then just s off of SR 94. Int corridors. **Pets:** Accepted.
🅰🆂🅺 🆂🅾 ⊠ 🖉 🗐 🖵 ⇌

ⒶⒶⒶ ▼▼ Quality Inn North 🆂🅷 🐾
(229) 244-8510. **$55-$75.** 1209 St Augustine Rd. I-75, exit 18, 0.3 mi e on SR 94. Ext corridors. **Pets:** Small. $5 daily fee/pet. Designated rooms, service with restrictions, supervision.
🆂🅰🆅🅴 🆂🅾 ⊠ 🖫 🗐 🖵 ⇌ ⊠

▼▼ Quality Inn South 🆂🅷
(229) 244-4520. **$45-$75.** 1902 W Hill Ave. I-75, exit 16, just e on US 84. Ext corridors. **Pets:** Other species. Service with restrictions, crate.
🅰🆂🅺 🆂🅾 ⊠ 🗐 🖵 ⇌

ⒶⒶⒶ ▼▼▼ Ramada Limited 🆂🅷
(229) 242-1225. **$75, 7 day notice.** 2008 W Hill Ave. I-75, exit 16, just e on US 84. Ext corridors. **Pets:** Accepted.
🆂🅰🆅🅴 🆂🅾 ⊠ 🖫 🗐 🖵 ⇌

▼▼ Super 8 Motel I-75 🆂🅷
(229) 249-8000. **$46-$62.** 1825 W Hill Ave. I-75, exit 16, just e. Int corridors. **Pets:** Accepted.
🅰🆂🅺 🆂🅾 ⊠ 🖫 🗐 🖵 ⇌

VIDALIA

ⒶⒶⒶ ▼▼ Days Inn 🆂🅷
(912) 537-9251. **$50-$60, 7 day notice.** 1503 Lyons E. 1 mi e on US 280. Ext corridors. **Pets:** Small. $5 daily fee/pet. Designated rooms, service with restrictions, supervision.
🆂🅰🆅🅴 🆂🅾 ⊠ 🖉 🗐 🖵 ⇌

▼▼▼ Holiday Inn Express 🆂🅷
(912) 537-9000. **$69-$75, 7 day notice.** 2619 E First St. 2.5 mi e on US 280. Ext corridors. **Pets:** Accepted.
🅰🆂🅺 🆂🅾 ⊠ 🖫 🗐 ⇌ ⊠

WARM SPRINGS

ⒶⒶⒶ ▼▼▼ Best Western White House Inn 🆂🅷
(706) 655-2750. **$79-$145.** 2526 White House Pkwy. Jct US 41/27, 1.4 mi s. Ext/int corridors. **Pets:** Medium. $15 one-time fee/pet. Designated rooms, service with restrictions, supervision.
🆂🅰🆅🅴 🆂🅾 ⊠ �figM 🖫 🗐 🖵 ⇌

WARNER ROBINS

ⒶⒶⒶ ▼▼ Best Western Peach Inn 🆂🅷
(478) 953-3800. **$56-$65.** 2739 Watson Blvd. I-75, exit 146 (SR 247C), 4.1 mi e. Ext corridors. **Pets:** Small. $8 daily fee/pet. Designated rooms, service with restrictions, supervision.
🆂🅰🆅🅴 🆂🅾 ⊠ 🖫 🗐 🖵 ⇌

ⒶⒶⒶ ▼▼▼ Comfort Inn & Suites 🆂🅷
(478) 922-7555. **$66-$140.** 95 S Hwy 247. Jct SR 247C and US 129/SR 247, 1.6 mi s on US 129/SR 247. Ext/int corridors. **Pets:** Small, other species. $25 one-time fee/room. Service with restrictions, supervision.
🆂🅰🆅🅴 🆂🅾 ⊠ 🖉 🖫 🗐 🖵 ⇌

▼▼▼ Jameson Inn-Warner Robins 🆂🅷
(478) 953-5522. **$49-$104.** 2731 Watson Blvd. I-75, exit 146 (SR 247C), 4.1 mi e. Ext corridors. **Pets:** Very small, other species. $10 daily fee/room. Service with restrictions, supervision.
🅰🆂🅺 ⊠ 🖫 🗐 🖵 ⇌

▼▼▼ SuiteOne of Warner Robins 🆂🅷
(478) 329-9222. **$54-$84.** 2103 Moody Rd. Jct US 129/SR 247 and Russell Pkwy; 1.8 mi e on Russell Pkwy, then just n. Ext corridors. **Pets:** Accepted.
⊠ 🖫 🗐 🖵

WAYCROSS

▼▼ Comfort Inn Waycross 🆂🅷
(912) 283-3300. **$59-$95.** 1903 Memorial Dr. Between US 1 and 82, at S City Blvd. Ext corridors. **Pets:** Small. $10 daily fee/pet. Designated rooms, service with restrictions, supervision.
🅰🆂🅺 🆂🅾 ⊠ 🖫 🗐 🖵 ⇌

▼▼▼ Holiday Inn Waycross 🆂🅷
(912) 283-4490. **$90-$100.** 1725 Memorial Dr. Jct US 1 and 82. Ext corridors. **Pets:** Accepted.
🅰🆂🅺 🆂🅾 ⊠ 🖉 🖫 🗐 🖵 🍽 ⇌ ⊠

▼▼ Jameson Inn Ⓜ
(912) 283-3800. **$49-$104.** 950 City Blvd. Between US 1 and 82, east of city. Ext corridors. **Pets:** Very small, other species. $10 daily fee/room. Service with restrictions, supervision.
🅰🆂🅺 ⊠ �figM 🖉 🗐 🖵 ⇌

WAYNESBORO

▼▼ Jameson Inn Ⓜ
(706) 437-0500. **$49-$104.** 1436 N Liberty St. 0.9 mi n of downtown center on US 25. Ext corridors. **Pets:** Very small, other species. $10 daily fee/room. Service with restrictions, supervision.
🅰🆂🅺 ⊠ 🖉 🗐 🖵 ⇌

WEST POINT

▼▼ Travelodge Ⓜ
(706) 643-9922. **$51.** 1870 SR 18. I-85, exit 2, just e. Int corridors. **Pets:** Accepted.
🅰🆂🅺 🆂🅾 ⊠ 🗐 🖵 ⇌

WINDER

▼▼ Jameson Inn Ⓜ
(770) 867-1880. **$49-$104.** 9 Stafford St. Jct SR 81, 11, 53 and 8; center. Ext corridors. **Pets:** Very small, other species. $10 daily fee/room. Service with restrictions, supervision.
🅰🆂🅺 ⊠ 🖉 🗐 🖵 ⇌

WOODSTOCK

▼▼ SuiteOne of Woodstock 🆂🅷
(770) 592-7848. **$54-$79.** 470 Parkway 575. I-575, exit 7, just n. Ext corridors. **Pets:** Accepted.
🅰🆂🅺 🆂🅾 ⊠ �figM 🖉 🗐 🖵

HAWAII

KAANAPALI

◆◆◆ ◆◆◆ The Westin Maui ⛟
(808) 667-2525. **$360-$540, 3 day notice.** 2365 Kaanapali Pkwy. Off SR 30; via Kaanapali Pkwy; in Kaanapali Beach resort area. Int corridors. **Pets:** Accepted.

ASK ✕ 🛏 🖥 🍴 ➙ ✕

KAUPULEHU

AAA ◆◆◆◆ Four Seasons Resort Hualalai at Historic Ka'upulehu ⛟ 🐾
(808) 325-8000. **$540-$810, 21 day notice.** 100 Ka'upulehu Dr. Off SR 19; 6 mi n of Kona International Airport. Ext corridors. **Pets:** Very small. Supervision.

SAVE ✕ ⚷M 🗀 🔥 🖥 🍴 ➙ ✕

KOHALA COAST

◆◆◆ ◆◆◆ The Fairmont Orchid, Hawaii ⛟ 🐾
(808) 885-2000. **$299-$859, 14 day notice.** 1 N Kaniku Dr. On SR 19, 20 mi n of Kona International Airport, then 2 mi w; in Kohala Coast/Mauna Lani resort area. Int corridors. **Pets:** Medium, other species. $25 one-time fee/room. Designated rooms, service with restrictions, supervision.

ASK ✕ ⚷M 🗀 🔥 🛏 🖥 🍴 ➙ ✕

WAILEA

AAA ◆◆◆◆ Four Seasons Resort, Maui at Wailea ⛟ 🐾
(808) 874-8000. **$345, 21 day notice.** 3900 Wailea Alanui Dr. From end of SR 31, 0.5 mi s. Int corridors. **Pets:** Small. Service with restrictions, supervision.

SAVE ✕ ⚷M 🗀 🔥 🛏 🖥 🍴 ➙ ✕

IDAHO

AMERICAN FALLS

⚠️ Hillview Motel M

(208) 226-5151. **$38-$58.** 2799 Lakeview Rd. I-86, exit 40, just s, then just w. Ext corridors. **Pets:** Medium. Service with restrictions, supervision.

BLACKFOOT

⚠️ Best Western Blackfoot Inn SH

(208) 785-4144. **$59-$99.** 750 Jensen Grove Dr. I-15, exit 93, just e on Bergener, then 0.4 mi n on Parkway. Int corridors. **Pets:** Other species. Service with restrictions, supervision.

Super 8 SH

(208) 785-9333. **$62-$79.** 1279 Parkway Dr. I-15, exit 93, just e; shared driveway with McDonald's Restaurant. Int corridors. **Pets:** Other species. $10 one-time fee/room. Service with restrictions, supervision.

BLISS

⚠️ Amber Inn Motel SH

(208) 352-4441. **$42.** 17286 US Hwy 30. I-84, exit 141, just s. Int corridors. **Pets:** Medium. $8 daily fee/pet. Service with restrictions, supervision.

BOISE

⚠️ AmeriSuites (Boise/Towne Square Mall) SH

(208) 375-1200. **$99-$119.** 925 N Milwaukee St. I-84, exit 49 (Franklin St), just w, then 0.5 mi n. Int corridors. **Pets:** Small, other species. Service with restrictions, supervision.

⚠️ Best Value University Inn M 🐾

(208) 345-7170. **$61-$78.** 2360 University Dr. I-84, exit 53 (Vista Ave), 2.5 mi n. Ext corridors. **Pets:** Small. $10 one-time fee/pet. Designated rooms, service with restrictions, crate.

⚠️ Best Western Safari Motor Inn SH 🐾

(208) 344-6556. **$72-$89.** 1070 Grove St. At 11th and Grove sts; center. Int corridors. **Pets:** $10 one-time fee/room. Designated rooms, service with restrictions, supervision.

Boise Super 8 Motel SH 🐾

(208) 344-8871. **$48-$70.** 2773 Elder St. I-84, exit 53 (Vista Ave), just n. Int corridors. **Pets:** Large, other species. $25 deposit/room. Designated rooms, service with restrictions, supervision.

⚠️ Budget Host Inn M

(208) 322-4404. **$65-$75, 5 day notice.** 8002 Overland Rd. I-84, exit 50A westbound, just s, just w, then just n; exit 50B eastbound, just w, then just n. Ext corridors. **Pets:** $10 one-time fee/room. Service with restrictions.

Doubletree Club Hotel SH

(208) 345-2002. **$79-$179.** 475 W Parkcenter Blvd. I-84, exit 54 (Broadway Ave), 2 mi n, then 0.3 mi e on Beacon and Parkcenter Blvd. Int corridors. **Pets:** Accepted.

Doubletree Hotel Riverside SH

(208) 343-1871. **$76-$300.** 2900 Chinden Blvd. I-184, exit Fairview Ave, just n, then just w on Garden. Int corridors. **Pets:** Medium, other species. $25 one-time fee/room. Designated rooms, service with restrictions, crate.

⚠️ Econo Lodge Boise SH

(208) 344-4030. **$65-$75.** 4060 Fairview Ave. I-184, exit Fairview Ave, just n. Int corridors. **Pets:** Dogs only. $10 one-time fee/pet. Designated rooms, service with restrictions, supervision.

Extended Stay America SH

(208) 363-9040. **$60-$70.** 2500 S Vista Ave. I-84, exit 53 (Vista Ave), 0.7 mi n. Int corridors. **Pets:** Accepted.

Fairfield Inn by Marriott SH

(208) 331-5656. **$66-$94.** 3300 S Shoshone St. I-84, exit 53 (Vista Ave), just n to Elder St, then just w. Int corridors. **Pets:** Medium. $10 one-time fee/room. Designated rooms, service with restrictions, supervision.

Hampton Inn SH

(208) 331-5600. **$99-$129.** 3270 S Shoshone St. I-84, exit 53 (Vista Ave), just n to Elder St, then just w. Int corridors. **Pets:** Medium. $10 daily fee/pet. Service with restrictions, supervision.

Holiday Inn Boise Airport SH 🐾

(208) 343-4900. **$89-$109.** 3300 Vista Ave. I-84, exit 53 (Vista Ave), just n. Int corridors. **Pets:** Other species. $25 one-time fee/room. Designated rooms, service with restrictions, supervision.

Owyhee Plaza Hotel SH

(208) 343-4611. **$85-$145.** 1109 Main St. At 11th and Main sts; center. Ext/int corridors. **Pets:** Medium, dogs only. $25 one-time fee/room. Designated rooms, service with restrictions, supervision.

Red Lion Hotel Boise Downtowner LH

(208) 344-7691. **$79-$139.** 1800 Fairview Ave. I-184, exit Fairview Ave, 1 mi n. Int corridors. **Pets:** Accepted.

Red Lion ParkCenter Suites–Boise SH

(208) 342-1044. **$59-$119.** 424 E Parkcenter Blvd. I-84, exit 54 (Broadway Ave), 2.3 mi n, then just e on Beacon and Parkcenter Blvd. Int corridors. **Pets:** Accepted.

▼▼▼ Residence Inn by Marriott 🆂🅷 ❀
(208) 344-1200. **$89-$137.** 1401 Lusk Ave. I-84, exit 53 (Vista Ave), 2.4 mi n. Ext corridors. **Pets:** Other species. $75 one-time fee/room. Service with restrictions.
(Ⓐ🆂🅺) 🆂 ⊠ 🖥 📠 ≈ ⊠

🔷 ▼▼▼ Rodeway Inn of Boise 🆂🅷
(208) 376-2700. **$65-$99.** 1115 N Curtis Rd. I-184, exit 2, just se. Ext/int corridors. **Pets:** Medium. $25 deposit/room, $10 one-time fee/pet. Service with restrictions, supervision.
(SAVE) 🆂 ⊠ 🖥 📠 ⑪ ≈ ⊠

▼▼ Shilo Inn-Boise Riverside 🆂🅷
(208) 344-3521. **$49-$92.** 3031 Main St. I-184, exit Fairview Ave, 0.5 mi n, then just w on S 30th St. Int corridors. **Pets:** Accepted.
(Ⓐ🆂🅺) 🆂 ⊠ 📷 🖥 📠 ≈ ⊠

▼▼🔷 Shilo Inn Suites-Boise Airport 🆂🅷 ❀
(208) 343-7662. **$52-$109.** 4111 Broadway Ave. I-84, exit 54 (Broadway Ave), just sw. Int corridors. **Pets:** Other species. $10 daily fee/pet. Service with restrictions, supervision.
(Ⓐ🆂🅺) 🆂 ⊠ 📷 (⑆) 🖥 📠 ≈ ⊠

BONNERS FERRY

🔷🔷 ▼▼🔷 Best Western Kootenai River Inn & Casino 🆂🅷
(208) 267-8511. **$79-$125.** 7169 Plaza St. On US 95; city center. Int corridors. **Pets:** Medium. $15 one-time fee/pet. Service with restrictions, supervision.
(SAVE) 🆂 ⊠ 📷 ⑆ 🖥 📠 ⑪ ≈ ⊠

BURLEY

🔷🔷 ▼▼🔷 Best Western Burley Inn & Convention Center 🆂🅷
(208) 678-3501. **$60-$73.** 800 N Overland Ave. I-84, exit 208, just s. Ext/int corridors. **Pets:** Small. Service with restrictions, supervision.
(SAVE) 🆂 ⊠ 📷 ⑆ 🖥 📠 ⑪ ≈ ⊠

🔷🔷 ▼🔷 Budget Motel 🅼
(208) 678-2200. **$50-$68.** 900 N Overland Ave. I-84, exit 208, just s. Ext corridors. **Pets:** Small. Service with restrictions, supervision.
(SAVE) 🆂 ⊠ (♿) 📷 ⑆ ≈

CALDWELL

🔷🔷 ▼▼🔷 Best Western Caldwell Inn & Suites 🅼 ❀
(208) 454-7225. **$64-$154.** 908 Specht Ave. I-84, exit 29, just s. Int corridors. **Pets:** Large, other species. $50 deposit/room. Service with restrictions, supervision.
(SAVE) 🆂 ⊠ 📷 ⑆ 🖥 📠 ≈

🔷🔷 ▼▼ La Quinta Inn Caldwell 🆂🅷
(208) 454-2222. **$65-$90.** 901 Specht Ave. I-84, exit 29, just s. Int corridors. **Pets:** Accepted.
(SAVE) 🆂 ⊠ 🖥 📠 ≈

COEUR D'ALENE

🔷🔷 ▼▼🔷🔷 Best Western Coeur d'Alene Inn & Conference Center 🆂🅷
(208) 765-3200. **$89-$169.** W 414 Appleway Ave. I-90, exit 12, just nw. Int corridors. **Pets:** Dogs only. $25 daily fee/room. Service with restrictions, supervision.
(SAVE) 🆂 ⊠ (♿) 📷 ⑆ 🖥 📠 ⑪ ≈ ⊠

🔷🔷 ▼▼🔷▼🔷 The Coeur d'Alene Resort 🅻🅷
(208) 765-4000. **$89-$399, 7 day notice.** 115 S 2nd St. I-90, exit 11, 2 mi s. Ext/int corridors. **Pets:** $50 one-time fee/pet. Service with restrictions, crate.
(SAVE) ⊠ 📠 ⑪ ≈ ⊠

▼▼ ▼▼ Days Inn-Coeur d'Alene 🆂🅷
(208) 667-8668. **$43-$114.** 2200 Northwest Blvd. I-90, exit 11, just se. Int corridors. **Pets:** Accepted.
(Ⓐ🆂🅺) 🆂 ⊠ (♿) 📷 ⑆ 🖥 📠 ⊠

🔷🔷 ▼▼🔷 La Quinta Inn & Suites Coeur D'Alene (East) 🆂🅷 ❀
(208) 667-6777. **$39-$179.** 2209 E Sherman Ave. I-90, exit 15 (Sherman Ave), just s. Int corridors. **Pets:** Other species. Service with restrictions, crate.
(SAVE) 🆂 ⊠ (♿) 📷 🖥 📠 ≈ ⊠

🔷🔷 ▼▼🔷 La Quinta Inn Coeur D'Alene (Appleway) 🆂🅷 ❀
(208) 765-5500. **$46-$113.** 280 W Appleway Ave. I-90, exit 12, just ne. Int corridors. **Pets:** Service with restrictions, supervision.
(SAVE) ⊠ (♿) 📷 🖥 📠 ≈

🔷🔷 ▼🔷 Rodeway Inn Pines Resort 🅼
(208) 664-8244. **$52-$105.** 1422 Northwest Blvd. I-90, exit 11, 0.8 mi s. Ext corridors. **Pets:** $50 deposit/room. Service with restrictions, supervision.
(SAVE) 🆂 ⊠ (♿) 📷 ⑆ 🖥 📠 ≈

🔷🔷 ▼▼▼ The Roosevelt, A Bed & Breakfast Inn 🅱🅱 ❀
(208) 765-5200. **$79-$289, 14 day notice.** 105 Wallace Ave. I-90, exit 13, 2 mi s, then just w; downtown. Int corridors. **Pets:** $25 one-time fee/room. Designated rooms, service with restrictions, supervision.
(SAVE) 🆂 ⊠ ⑆ 📷 🖥 📠 🅦 ≈

▼▼🔷 Shilo Inn Suites Coeur d'Alene 🆂🅷 ❀
(208) 664-2300. **$79-$163.** 702 W Appleway Ave. I-90, exit 12, just n, then just w. Int corridors. **Pets:** Large. $10 one-time fee/room. Designated rooms, service with restrictions, supervision.
(Ⓐ🆂🅺) 🆂 ⊠ (♿) 📷 ≈

DRIGGS

🔷🔷 ▼▼ Best Western Teton West Motel 🆂🅷
(208) 354-2363. **$70-$120.** 476 N Main St. 0.7 mi n on SR 33. Int corridors. **Pets:** Accepted.
(SAVE) 🆂 ⊠ 🖥 📠 ≈

HAGERMAN

🔷🔷 ▼▼ Hagerman Valley Inn 🅼
(208) 837-6196. **$49-$69.** 661 Frog's Landing. South end of town on US 30. Ext/int corridors. **Pets:** $5 daily fee/pet. Service with restrictions, supervision.
(SAVE) 🆂 ⊠ 🖥

HAILEY

▼▼ Airport Inn 🅼
(208) 788-2477. **$73-$87.** 820 4th Ave S. Just n of SR 75 at 4th Ave; near airport. Ext corridors. **Pets:** $10 daily fee/pet. Service with restrictions, supervision.
⊠ 🖥 📠

▼▼🔷 Wood River Inn 🆂🅷
(208) 578-0600. **$82-$159.** 603 N Main. Just n of downtown on SR 75. Int corridors. **Pets:** Accepted.
(Ⓐ🆂🅺) 🆂 ⊠ (♿) ⑆ 🖥 📠 ≈

HEYBURN

▼▼ Super 8–Burley 🆂🅷
(208) 678-7000. **$52-$69.** 336 S 600 W. I-84, exit 208, just n. Int corridors. **Pets:** Other species. $5 one-time fee/pet. Service with restrictions, supervision.
🆂 ⊠ (♿) 📷 ⑆ 🖥 📠

IDAHO FALLS

Best Western Driftwood Inn SH
(208) 523-2242. **$59-$115.** 575 River Pkwy. I-15, exit 118 (Broadway), 0.5 mi e, then 0.3 mi n. Ext corridors. **Pets:** Other species. $10 daily fee/room. Service with restrictions, supervision.

Comfort Inn SH
(208) 528-2804. **$59-$149, 14 day notice.** 195 S Colorado Ave. I-15, exit 118 (Broadway), just w to Colorado Ave, then just s. Int corridors. **Pets:** Other species. $10 daily fee/pet. Service with restrictions, supervision.

GuestHouse Inn & Suites SH
(208) 523-6260. **$54-$89.** 850 Lindsay Blvd. I-15, exit 119, just e. Ext/int corridors. **Pets:** Large, other species. $20 deposit/room. Supervision.

Le Ritz Hotel & Suites SH
(208) 528-0880. **$89-$209.** 720 Lindsay Blvd. I-15, exit 118 (Broadway), 0.5 mi e, then just n. Int corridors. **Pets:** $15 one-time fee/room. Service with restrictions, supervision.

Red Lion Hotel on the Falls SH
(208) 523-8000. **$115.** 475 River Pkwy. I-15, exit 118 (Broadway), 0.5 mi e, then just n. Ext/int corridors. **Pets:** Medium, other species. $50 deposit/room. Designated rooms, service with restrictions, supervision.

Shilo Inn Suites Conference Hotel SH
(208) 523-0088. **$90-$200.** 780 Lindsay Blvd. I-15, exit 119, just se. Int corridors. **Pets:** Accepted.

JEROME

Best Western Sawtooth Inn and Suites SH
(208) 324-9200. **$79-$99.** 2653 S Lincoln. I-84, exit 168, just n on SR 79. Int corridors. **Pets:** Other species. $50 deposit/room. Service with restrictions, supervision.

KELLOGG

Silverhorn Motor Inn SH
(208) 783-1151. **$63-$73.** 699 W Cameron Ave. I-90, exit 49, just ne. Int corridors. **Pets:** Other species. Supervision.

Super 8 Motel-Kellogg SH
(208) 783-1234. **$52-$92.** 601 Bunker Ave. I-90, exit 49, 0.5 mi s. Int corridors. **Pets:** $25 deposit/room. Service with restrictions, supervision.

KETCHUM

Best Western Tyrolean Lodge SH
(208) 726-5336. **$85-$144, 3 day notice.** 260 Cottonwood. South end of town, just w of SR 75 (Main St) on Rivers St, just s on 3rd Ave. Int corridors. **Pets:** Accepted.

KOOSKIA

Reflections Inn (formerly Looking Glass Inn) BB
(208) 926-0855. **$69-$94, 3 day notice.** HCR 75, Box 32, US Hwy 12. 11 mi e on US 12, between MM 84 and 85. Ext corridors. **Pets:** Accepted.

LEWISTON

Comfort Inn SH
(208) 798-8090. **$69-$149.** 2128 8th Ave. 1.2 mi s on US 12 from jct US 95, just s on 21st St. Int corridors. **Pets:** Other species. $10 daily fee/room. Supervision.

Holiday Inn Express SH
(208) 750-1600. **$79.** 2425 Nez Perce Dr. 1.2 mi s on US 12 from jct US 95, 1.2 mi s on 21st St, then just e. Int corridors. **Pets:** Other species. $25 one-time fee/room. Service with restrictions, supervision.

Red Lion Hotel Lewiston SH
(208) 799-1000. **$74-$203.** 621 21st St. 1.2 mi s on US 12 from jct US 95, just s. Int corridors. **Pets:** Small. $15 one-time fee/room. Designated rooms, service with restrictions, crate.

Sacajawea Motor Inn M
(208) 746-1393. **$63-$89.** 1824 Main St. 1.5 mi s on US 12 from jct US 95. Ext/int corridors. **Pets:** Other species. $2 daily fee/pet. Designated rooms, service with restrictions, supervision.

Super 8 Motel M
(208) 743-8808. **$45-$54.** 3120 North & South Hwy. Just e on US 12 from jct US 95. Int corridors. **Pets:** Accepted.

LUCILE

Steelhead Inn M
(208) 628-3044. **Call for rates.** 5 mi n on US 95 at MM 210. Ext corridors. **Pets:** Other species. $5 one-time fee/room. Service with restrictions.

MACKAY

Wagon Wheel Motel M
(208) 588-3331. **$50-$80.** 809 W Custer. 0.3 mi n on US 93. Ext corridors. **Pets:** Accepted.

MCCALL

Best Western McCall SH
(208) 634-6300. **$60-$120.** 415 3rd St. SR 55, just s of jct with Lake St. Ext/int corridors. **Pets:** Service with restrictions, supervision.

McCall Super 8 Lodge M
(208) 634-4637. **$57-$129.** 303 S 3rd St. South end of town on SR 55. Int corridors. **Pets:** Other species. $5 daily fee/pet. Designated rooms, supervision.

MONTPELIER

Best Western Clover Creek Inn SH
(208) 847-1782. **$67-$99.** 243 N 4th St. Just n on US 30 from jct US 89 S. Ext corridors. **Pets:** Medium, dogs only. $10 one-time fee/pet. Service with restrictions, supervision.

The Fisher Inn M
(208) 847-1772. **$38-$62.** 601 N 4th St. 0.8 mi n on US 30 from jct US 89 S. Ext corridors. **Pets:** Accepted.

MOSCOW

Best Western University Inn SH
(208) 882-0550. **$94-$135, 3 day notice.** 1516 Pullman Rd. Jct US 95, 1 mi w on SR 8. Int corridors. **Pets:** Small, other species. $25 daily fee/room. Designated rooms, service with restrictions, crate.

MOUNTAIN HOME

Best Western Foothills Motor Inn SH
(208) 587-8477. **$67-$89.** 1080 Hwy 20. I-84, exit 95, just n. Ext corridors. **Pets:** $5 daily fee/pet. Service with restrictions, supervision.

Sleep Inn SH
(208) 587-9743. **$65-$70.** 1180 Hwy 20. I-84, exit 95, just n. Int corridors. **Pets:** $5 daily fee/pet. Service with restrictions, supervision.

NAMPA

Shilo Inn-Nampa Boulevard SH
(208) 466-8993. **$50-$85.** 617 Nampa Blvd. I-84, exit 35, just sw. Int corridors. **Pets:** Other species. $10 daily fee/room. Service with restrictions, crate.

Shilo Inn Nampa Suites SH 🐾
(208) 465-3250. **$73-$113.** 1401 Shilo Dr. I-84, exit 36, just nw. Int corridors. **Pets:** $10 daily fee/room. Service with restrictions, crate.

NEW MEADOWS

Hartland Inn & Motel M
(208) 347-2114. **$59-$150, 3 day notice.** 211 Norris St. US 95, just n of jct SR 55. Ext/int corridors. **Pets:** Accepted.

OROFINO

Konkolville Motel M
(208) 476-5584. **$50-$55.** 2000 Konkolville Rd. 2.7 mi e on Michigan Ave. Ext corridors. **Pets:** Medium, other species. $10 daily fee/pet. Designated rooms, service with restrictions, supervision.

POCATELLO

Best Western CottonTree Inn SH
(208) 237-7650. **$77-$92.** 1415 Bench Rd. I-15, exit 71, just e. Int corridors. **Pets:** Accepted.

Comfort Inn SH
(208) 237-8155. **$56-$89.** 1333 Bench Rd. I-15, exit 71, just e. Int corridors. **Pets:** Accepted.

Econo Lodge-University SH
(208) 233-0451. **Call for rates.** 835 S 5th Ave. I-15, exit 67, 1.8 mi n. Int corridors. **Pets:** Accepted.

Holiday Inn-Pocatello SH
(208) 237-1400. **$63-$89.** 1399 Bench Rd. I-15, exit 71, just e. Ext/int corridors. **Pets:** Medium, other species. $10 daily fee/room. Designated rooms, service with restrictions.

Pocatello Super 8 Motel SH
(208) 234-0888. **$53-$73.** 1330 Bench Rd. I-15, exit 71, just e. Int corridors. **Pets:** Accepted.

Ramada Inn & Convention Center SH
(208) 237-0020. **$70-$100.** 133 W Burnside. I-86, exit 61, just n. Int corridors. **Pets:** Designated rooms, supervision.

Red Lion Hotel Pocatello SH
(208) 233-2200. **$63-$73.** 1555 Pocatello Creek Rd. I-15, exit 71, just e. Int corridors. **Pets:** Medium. Designated rooms, service with restrictions.

Thunderbird Motel M
(208) 232-6330. **$46-$55.** 1415 S 5th Ave. I-15, exit 67, 1.3 mi n; just s of Idaho State University. Ext corridors. **Pets:** Accepted.

PONDERAY

Monarch Mountain Lodge SH
(208) 263-1222. **$52-$95.** 363 Bonner Mall Way. 0.5 mi n on US 95 N from jct SR 200. Int corridors. **Pets:** Accepted.

Sandpoint Motel 6–4163 SH
(208) 263-5383. **$46-$56.** 477255 Hwy 95 N. 1.2 mi n on US 95 from jct SR 200. Int corridors. **Pets:** Large, other species. Designated rooms, service with restrictions, supervision.

Super 8 Motel SH 🐾
(208) 263-2210. **$33-$66.** 476841 Hwy 95 N. 0.7 mi n on US 95 from jct SR 200. Int corridors. **Pets:** Other species. $5 one-time fee/room. Service with restrictions, supervision.

POST FALLS

Holiday Inn Express SH 🐾
(208) 773-8900. **$72-$139.** 3175 E Seltice Way. I-90, exit 7, just sw. Int corridors. **Pets:** $20 one-time fee/room. Service with restrictions, crate.

Howard Johnson Express SH 🐾
(208) 773-4541. **$49-$139.** 3647 W 5th Ave. I-90, exit 2, just ne. Int corridors. **Pets:** Other species. $10 daily fee/pet. Service with restrictions, supervision.

Red Lion Templin's Hotel on the River–Post Falls SH
(208) 773-1611. **$79-$149, 3 day notice.** 414 E First Ave. I-90, exit 5 eastbound, just s to First Ave; exit 6 westbound, 0.7 mi w on Seltice Way to Spokane St, 0.5 mi s, then just e. Int corridors. **Pets:** Other species. $5 daily fee/pet. Designated rooms, service with restrictions, crate.

Sleep Inn SH
(208) 777-9394. **$59-$149.** 157 S Pleasant View Rd. I-90, exit 2, just s. Int corridors. **Pets:** Accepted.

PRIEST RIVER

Eagle's Nest Motel M
(208) 448-2000. **$50-$110.** 1007 Albeni Hwy (US 2). US 2, 0.5 mi w. Ext corridors. **Pets:** $100 deposit/room. Designated rooms, service with restrictions, supervision.

REXBURG

Best Western CottonTree Inn SH
(208) 356-4646. **$74-$101.** 450 W 4th St S. US 20, exit 332 (S Rexburg), 1 mi e. Int corridors. **Pets:** Small, dogs only. $20 deposit/room. Designated rooms, service with restrictions, supervision.

AAA ▼▼▼ Comfort Inn SH
(208) 359-1311. **$55-$109.** 885 W Main St. US 20, exit 333 (Salmon), just e. Int corridors. **Pets:** Other species. Service with restrictions, supervision.
[SAVE] [S◐] [✕] [🛏] [◫] [≋]

AAA ▼▼▼ Days Inn M
(208) 356-9222. **$56-$71.** 271 S 2nd W. US 20, exit 332 (S Rexburg), 1.8 mi e, then just n. Ext corridors. **Pets:** Accepted.
[SAVE] [S◐] [✕] [🛏] [≋]

RIGGINS

AAA ▼▼▼ Best Western Salmon Rapids Lodge SH
(208) 628-2743. **$79-$119.** 1010 S Main St. Just e of US 95; downtown. Int corridors. **Pets:** Accepted.
[SAVE] [S◐] [✕] [⚙] [🛏] [◫] [≋]

▼▼ Pinehurst Resort Cottages CA
(208) 628-3323. **$45-$70, 7 day notice.** MM 182 on US 95. On US 95, 13 mi s. Ext corridors. **Pets:** Accepted.
[✕] [🛏] [◫] [⚙] [冊] [⌘] [🛁]

SAGLE

▼▼ Bottle Bay Resort & Marina CA
(208) 263-5916. **$80-$100, 60 day notice.** 115 Resort Rd. 8.3 mi e on Bottle Bay Rd from US 95. Ext corridors. **Pets:** Accepted.
[🛏] [◫] [冊] [⚙] [冊] [🛁]

ST. ANTHONY

▼▼ Best Western Henry's Fork Inn SH
(208) 624-3711. **$49-$89.** 115 S Bridge St. US 20, exit St. Anthony, just w. Ext corridors. **Pets:** Other species. $10 deposit/room. No service, crate.
[ASK] [S◐] [✕] [◫] [冊]

SALMON

▼▼ Motel DeLuxe M
(208) 756-2231. **$39-$74, 7 day notice.** 112 S Church St. Just s of Main St; downtown. Ext corridors. **Pets:** Other species. $5 one-time fee/pet. Service with restrictions, supervision.
[ASK] [S◐] [✕] [🛏]

SANDPOINT

▼▼▼ Best Western Edgewater Resort SH
(208) 263-3194. **$89-$159.** 56 Bridge St. Just e of US 95 N; downtown. Int corridors. **Pets:** $100 deposit/pet, $5 daily fee/pet. Service with restrictions, supervision.
[ASK] [S◐] [✕] [◫] [冊] [≋] [🛁]

▼▼▼ Coit House Bed & Breakfast BB
(208) 265-4035. **$75-$110, 3 day notice.** 502 N Fourth Ave. Just ne of US 95 at Fourth Ave and Alder St. Int corridors. **Pets:** Medium, dogs only. $20 one-time fee/room. Service with restrictions, supervision.
[ASK] [S◐] [✕]

▼▼ The K2 Inn M
(208) 263-3441. **$30-$109.** 501 N Fourth Ave. US 95, just e. Ext corridors. **Pets:** Dogs only. $10 one-time fee/room. Service with restrictions.
[ASK] [S◐] [✕] [🛏] [◫]

AAA ▼▼▼ La Quinta Inn Sandpoint SH
(208) 263-9581. **$99-$139.** 415 Cedar St. Jct US 95 and 2; downtown. Ext/int corridors. **Pets:** Dogs only. Service with restrictions, supervision.
[SAVE] [S◐] [✕] [⚙M] [🛈] [⚙] [🛏] [◫] [冊] [≋]

▼▼ Quality Inn Sandpoint SH
(208) 263-2111. **$59-$129.** 807 N 5th. US 2 and 95, just s of jct SR 200. Int corridors. **Pets:** $100 deposit/pet, $5 daily fee/pet. Service with restrictions, supervision.
[ASK] [S◐] [✕] [⚙] [🛏] [◫] [冊] [≋]

SODA SPRINGS

▼▼ J-R Inn M
(208) 547-3366. **$53.** 179 W 2nd S. US 30. Ext corridors. **Pets:** Accepted.
[S◐] [✕] [🛏] [◫] [⚙]

STANLEY

▼▼ Mountain Village Lodge SH
(208) 774-3661. **$54-$74.** Corner US 75 & SR 21. Jct US 75 and SR 21. Ext corridors. **Pets:** Other species. $8 one-time fee/pet. Service with restrictions, supervision.
[ASK] [✕] [🛏] [◫] [冊] [⚙]

AAA ▼ Salmon River Cabins & Motel CA
(208) 774-3566. **$75-$95.** 1 mi n on US 75 from jct SR 21. Ext corridors. **Pets:** $10 daily fee/pet. Service with restrictions, supervision.
[SAVE] [✕] [🛏] [◫] [⚙]

TETONIA

AAA ▼▼▼ Teton Mountain View Lodge M
(208) 456-2741. **$39-$89.** 510 Egbert Ave (Hwy 33). On SR 33. Ext corridors. **Pets:** $10 daily fee/pet. Designated rooms, supervision.
[SAVE] [S◐] [✕] [🛏] [✕]

TWIN FALLS

AAA ▼▼▼ Best Western Apollo Motor Inn M
(208) 733-2010. **$56-$82.** 296 Addison Ave W. I-84, exit 173, 5.7 mi s on US 93, then 1.2 mi w. Ext corridors. **Pets:** Small, other species. $8 daily fee/room. Designated rooms, service with restrictions, supervision.
[SAVE] [S◐] [✕] [🛏] [◫] [≋]

▼▼ Comfort Inn M
(208) 734-7494. **$65-$115.** 1893 Canyon Springs Rd. I-84, exit 173, 3.5 mi s on US 93. Int corridors. **Pets:** Other species. $10 daily fee/pet. Service with restrictions, supervision.
[ASK] [✕] [🛏] [◫] [≋]

AAA ▼▼▼ Days Inn M
(208) 324-6400. **$65-$95.** 1200 Centennial Spur. I-84, exit 173, just n on US 93. Int corridors. **Pets:** Medium. $10 daily fee/pet. Designated rooms, service with restrictions, supervision.
[SAVE] [S◐] [✕] [⚙] [🛏] [◫] [✕]

AAA ▼▼▼▼ Red Lion Hotel Canyon Springs SH
(208) 734-5000. **$70-$112.** 1357 Blue Lakes Blvd N. I-84, exit 173, 4 mi s on US 93. Int corridors. **Pets:** Accepted.
[SAVE] [S◐] [✕] [⚙M] [🛈] [⚙] [🛏] [◫] [冊] [≋] [✕]

▼▼▼ Shilo Inn, Twin Falls, LLC SH
(208) 733-7545. **$79-$144.** 1586 Blue Lakes Blvd N. I-84, exit 173, 3.7 mi s on US 93. Int corridors. **Pets:** Accepted.
[ASK] [S◐] [✕] [⚙] [🛏] [◫] [≋] [✕]

▼▼▼ Twin Falls Super 8 Motel M
(208) 734-5801. **$64-$118.** 1260 Blue Lakes Blvd N. I-84, exit 173, 4.1 mi s on US 93. Int corridors. **Pets:** Medium, dogs only. $10 one-time fee/pet. Designated rooms, service with restrictions, supervision.
[ASK] [S◐] [✕] [🛏] [◫]

WALLACE

▼▼▼ Best Western Wallace Inn SH
(208) 752-1252. **$80-$90.** 100 Front St. I-90, exit 61 (Business Rt 90), just se. Int corridors. **Pets:** Other species. $15 daily fee/pet. Service with restrictions, supervision.
[ASK] [S◐] [✕] [⚙M] [⚙] [🛏] [◫] [冊] [≋] [✕]

WORLEY

AAA ▼▼▼▼ Coeur d'Alene Casino Resort Hotel SH
(208) 686-0248. **$60-$100.** 27068 S Hwy 95. On US 95, 3 mi n. Int corridors. **Pets:** Accepted.
[SAVE] [S◐] [✕] [⚙] [🛏] [◫] [冊] [≋] [✕]

ILLINOIS

CITY INDEX

ALTON

▽▽▽▽ Comfort Inn SH
(618) 465-9999. $85-$100. 11 Crossroads Ct. Off SR 3, jct SR 140. Int corridors. **Pets:** Other species. Service with restrictions, crate.
ASK SD X ⓑM 🐾 ⓕ 🔵 🔵 ≈

▽▽ ▽▽ Super 8 Motel SH
(618) 465-8885. $63-$83. 1800 Homer Adams Pkwy. On SR 111, 1.8 mi e of jct US 67. Int corridors. **Pets:** Medium. $50 deposit/room. Service with restrictions, supervision.
ASK SD X ⓑM ⓕ 🔵

ARCOLA

▽▽ ▽▽ Comfort Inn SH
(217) 268-4000. $39-$99. 610 E Springfield Rd. I-57, exit 203, just w. Int corridors. **Pets:** Small, other species. $7 daily fee/pet. Service with restrictions, crate.
X 🐾 ⓕ 🔵 ≈

BEARDSTOWN

▽▽ Super 8 Motel SH
(217) 323-5858. **Call for rates.** 9918 Grand Ave. US 67, just w from SR 125. Int corridors. **Pets:** Accepted.
X ⓕ ≈

BELLEVILLE

⏺⏺ ▽▽ ▽▽ The Shrine Hotel SH
(618) 397-1162. $67. 451 S Demazenod Dr. I-255, exit 17A, 1 mi e on SR 15. Int corridors. **Pets:** Small, other species. Service with restrictions, crate.
SAVE SD X ⓕ 🔵 ⓘⓘ ⊠

BLOOMINGTON

▽▽▽▽ The Chateau LH
(309) 662-2020. $109-$179. 1601 Jumer Dr. I-55, exit 167, follow I-55 business route (Veterans Pkwy); 1.3 mi n of jct SR 9; 1 mi s of jct I-55. Int corridors. **Pets:** Other species. $25 one-time fee/room. Designated rooms, service with restrictions, supervision.
ASK SD X 🐾 ⓕ 🔵 ⓘⓘ ≈ ⊠

▽▽▽▽ Country Inn & Suites By Carlson Bloomington/Normal-Airport SH 🐾
(309) 662-3100. $69-$89. 2403 E Empire St. Jct I-55 business route (Veterans Pkwy) and SR 9 (Empire St), 0.8 mi e. Int corridors. **Pets:** Medium. $10 one-time fee/room. Designated rooms, service with restrictions, crate.
ASK SD X 🐾 ⓛⓕ ⓕ 🔵 ≈

▽▽▽▽ Country Inn & Suites By Carlson Bloomington/Normal-West SH 🐾
(309) 828-7177. $86-$103. 923 Maple Hill Rd. I-55/74, exit 160B (SR 9), 0.3 mi n to Wylie Dr, just n, then just e. Int corridors. **Pets:** Medium, other species. $10 one-time fee/pet. Service with restrictions.
ASK SD X ⓑM ⓛⓕ ⓕ 🔵 ≈

▽▽ ▽▽ Days Inn-Bloomington SH
(309) 829-6292. $65-$75. 1707 W Market St. I-55/74, exit 160A (SR 9), 0.5 mi e. Int corridors. **Pets:** Large, other species. $10 daily fee/pet. Designated rooms, service with restrictions, supervision.
ASK SD X ⓑM ⓕ ≈

▽▽ ▽▽ Eastland Suites Hotel & Conference Center SH
(309) 662-0000. $89. 1801 Eastland Dr. Jct Business Rt 55 (Veteran's Pkwy) and SR 9, just s to Eastland Dr, then just e. Ext/int corridors. **Pets:** Accepted.
ASK X ⓕ 🔵 ≈ ⊠

▽▽ ▽▽ Econo Lodge M
(309) 829-3100. $49-$110. 403 Brock Dr. I-55/74, exit 106A (SR 9), just e. Ext corridors. **Pets:** Large. $10 daily fee/pet. Service with restrictions, crate.
ASK SD X ⓕ 🔵

⏺⏺ ▽▽▽▽ Radisson Hotel & Conference Center-Bloomington LH
(309) 664-6446. $95. 10 Brickyard Dr. I-55 business route (Veterans Pkwy), just n of US 150. Int corridors. **Pets:** Other species. $25 deposit/room. Service with restrictions, crate.
SAVE SD X 🐾 ⓛⓕ ⓕ 🔵 ⓘⓘ ≈ ⊠

▽▽ ▽▽ Ramada Limited & Suites Bloomington/Normal-West SH 🐾
(309) 828-0900. $77-$119. 919 Maple Hill Rd. I-55/74, exit 160B (SR 9), 0.3 mi w to Wylie Rd, just n, then just e. Int corridors. **Pets:** Medium, other species. $10 one-time fee/pet. Service with restrictions.
ASK SD X ⓕ 🔵 ≈

▼▼▼ **Wingate Inn** 🆂🅷
(309) 820-9990. **$79.** 1031 Wylie Dr. I-55/74, exit 160B (SR 9), just w, then just n. Int corridors. **Pets:** $10 deposit/pet. Designated rooms, service with restrictions, supervision.

(A$K) 🆂 ⊗ 🕖 ⌨ 🛢 🖵 🏊

BOURBONNAIS

▼▼▼ **Hampton Inn Bradley/Kankakee** 🆂🅷
(815) 932-8369. **$88-$127.** 60 Ken Hayes Dr. I-57, exit 315 (SR 50). Int corridors. **Pets:** Small, dogs only. $50 deposit/room. Service with restrictions, supervision.

(A$K) 🆂 ⊗ ⌨ 🛢 🖵 🏊

CARBONDALE

▼▼▼ **Hampton Inn** 🆂🅷
(618) 549-6900. **$86-$119.** 2175 Reed Station Pkwy. I-57, exit 54B, 12 mi w on SR 13. Int corridors. **Pets:** Accepted.

(A$K) 🆂 ⊗ 🅼 🕖 ⌨ 🛢 🖵 🏊

▼ **Motel 6** 🅼
(618) 457-5566. **Call for rates.** 700 E Main St. 1 mi e on SR 13. Ext corridors. **Pets:** Small. Service with restrictions, supervision.

⊗ 🛢

▼ **Super 8 Motel** 🆂🅷
(618) 457-8822. **$54-$80.** 1180 E Main St. 1 mi e on SR 13. Int corridors. **Pets:** Service with restrictions, supervision.

(A$K) 🆂 ⊗ 🕖 🛢 🖵

CARLINVILLE

(AAA) ▼▼▼ **Carlin Villa-Best Value Inn** 🅼
(217) 854-3201. **$39-$115, 7 day notice.** 18891 Rt 4. Jct SR 4 and 108, 0.5 mi s. Ext/int corridors. **Pets:** Accepted.

(SAVE) 🆂 ⊗ 🛢 🖵 🏊

CASEY

(AAA) ▼▼▼ **Comfort Inn** 🆂🅷
(217) 932-2212. **$65-$70.** 933 SR 49. I-70, exit 129, 0.3 mi se. Int corridors. **Pets:** Other species. $5 one-time fee/pet. Service with restrictions, supervision.

(SAVE) 🆂 ⊗ 🛢 🖵 🏊

CASEYVILLE

(AAA) ▼▼▼ **Best Inns** 🆂🅷
(618) 397-3300. **$48-$70.** 2423 Old Country Inn Dr. I-64, exit 9 (SR 157), just s. Int corridors. **Pets:** Accepted.

(SAVE) 🆂 ⊗ 🕖 ⌨ 🛢 🏊

CHAMPAIGN

(AAA) ▼▼▼ **Baymont Inn & Suites** 🆂🅷
(217) 356-8900. **$70-$125.** 302 W Anthony Dr. I-74, exit 182 (Neil St), just nw. Int corridors. **Pets:** Other species. Service with restrictions, supervision.

(SAVE) 🆂 ⊗ 🕖 ⌨ 🛢 🖵

▼▼▼ **Country Inn & Suites By Carlson** 🆂🅷
(217) 355-6666. **$85.** 602 W Marketview Dr. I-74, exit 181 (Prospect Rd), just n, then just e. Int corridors. **Pets:** Small. Designated rooms, no service, supervision.

(A$K) 🆂 ⊗ 🅼 🕖 ⌨ 🛢 🖵 🏊

▼▼▼ **Drury Inn & Suites-Champaign** 🆂🅷
(217) 398-0030. **$75-$115.** 905 W Anthony Dr. I-74, exit 181 (Prospect Blvd), just n. Int corridors. **Pets:** Large, other species. Service with restrictions, supervision.

(A$K) ⊗ 🅼 🕖 ⌨ 🛢 🖵 🏊

(AAA) ▼▼▼ **La Quinta Inn Champaign** 🆂🅷 🐾
(217) 356-4000. **$69-$116.** 1900 Center Dr. I-74, exit 182B (Neil St), just n. Int corridors. **Pets:** Small. Service with restrictions, crate.

(SAVE) ⊗ 🅼 🕖 🛢 🖵 🏊

(AAA) ▼▼▼ **Microtel Inn** 🆂🅷
(217) 398-4136. **$55-$91, 14 day notice.** 1615 Rion Dr. I-57, exit 238, just w. Int corridors. **Pets:** Small. $10 one-time fee/room. Designated rooms, supervision.

(SAVE) 🆂 ⊗ 🛢

▼▼ **Red Roof Inn #170** 🆂🅷
(217) 352-0101. **$42-$64.** 212 W Anthony Dr. I-74, exit 182B (Neil St), just n to Anthony Dr, then just w. Ext corridors. **Pets:** Medium. Service with restrictions, crate.

⊗ 🕖 🛢

CHESTER

(AAA) ▼▼▼ **Best Western Reids' Inn** 🆂🅷
(618) 826-3034. **$64.** 2150 State St. SR 150, 1 mi e of SR 3. Int corridors. **Pets:** Accepted.

(SAVE) 🆂 ⊗ 🅼 🛢 🖵 🏊

CHICAGO METROPOLITAN AREA

ALSIP

▼▼ **Baymont Inn-Midway South** 🆂🅷
(708) 597-3900. **$59-$70.** 12801 S Cicero Ave. I-294, exit Cicero Ave S. Int corridors. **Pets:** Medium, dogs only. $50 deposit/room. Designated rooms, service with restrictions, crate.

(A$K) 🆂 ⊗ 🕖 ⌨ 🛢 🖵

▼▼ **Days Inn** 🅼
(708) 371-5600. **Call for rates.** 5150 W 127th St. I-294, exit Cicero Ave S, 0.3 mi w. Ext corridors. **Pets:** Accepted.

⊗

(AAA) ▼▼▼ **Doubletree Hotel Chicago/Alsip** 🅻🅷
(708) 371-7300. **$79-$159.** 5000 W 127th St. I-294, exit Cicero Ave S, just w. Int corridors. **Pets:** Medium, other species. $50 deposit/room. Designated rooms, service with restrictions.

(SAVE) 🆂 ⊗ 🅼 🕖 🛢 🖵 🍴 🏊

ANTIOCH

(AAA) ▼▼▼ **Best Western Regency Inn** 🆂🅷
(847) 395-3606. **$79-$145.** 350 Rt 173. SR 173, 0.5 mi w of jct SR 83. Int corridors. **Pets:** Small. $25 deposit/room. Service with restrictions, crate.

(SAVE) 🆂 ⊗ 🛢 🖵 🏊

ARLINGTON HEIGHTS

(AAA) ▼▼▼▼ **AmeriSuites (Chicago/Arlington Heights)** 🆂🅷
(847) 956-1400. **$85-$94.** 2111 S Arlington Heights Rd. I-90, exit Arlington Heights Rd, 0.6 mi n. Int corridors. **Pets:** Accepted.

(SAVE) 🆂 ⊗ 🕖 ⌨ 🛢 🖵 ⊗

▼ **Best Value Inn** 🅼
(847) 255-2900. **$60-$75.** 948 E Northwest Hwy. US 14 (Northwest Hwy), 0.3 mi e of Arlington Heights Rd; downtown. Ext corridors. **Pets:** Accepted.

(A$K) 🆂 ⊗ 🛢 🍴

▼▼▼▼ La Quinta Inn Chicago (Arlington Heights) 🆂🅷
(847) 253-8777. **$86-$116.** 1415 W Dundee Rd. SR 53, exit Dundee Rd, just e. Int corridors. **Pets:** Accepted.
🅰🆂🅺 ✖ 🕭 🛢 📺 🕿

▼ Motel 6–1048 🆂🅷
(847) 806-1230. **$48-$60.** 441 W Algonquin Rd. I-90, exit Arlington Heights Rd, 0.5 mi n, then 0.5 mi w. Int corridors. **Pets:** Accepted.
🆂🅳 ✖ 🕭

▼▼▼▼ Park Plaza Chicago-Arlington Heights 🅻🅷
(847) 364-7600. **Call for rates.** 75 W Algonquin Rd. I-90, exit Arlington Heights Rd, just n to Algonquin Rd, then just w. Int corridors. **Pets:** Accepted.
✖ 🕭 🛢 📺 🍴 🕿 🗙

▼ Red Roof Inn #7102 🅼
(847) 228-6650. **$49-$73.** 22 W Algonquin Rd. I-90, exit Arlington Heights Rd, 0.5 mi n, then just w. Ext corridors. **Pets:** Accepted.
✖ 🕭

▼▼▼▼ Sheraton Chicago Northwest 🅻🅷 ❖
(847) 394-2000. **$79-$159.** 3400 W Euclid Ave. SR 53, exit Euclid Ave, just e. Int corridors. **Pets:** Medium, dogs only. $50 one-time fee/room. Service with restrictions, crate.
🅰🆂🅺 🆂🅳 ✖ 🕭 🛢 📺 🍴 🕿 🗙

BANNOCKBURN

🅰🅰🅰 ▼▼▼▼ Woodfield Suites
Chicago-Bannockburn/Deerfield 🆂🅷
(847) 317-7300. **$71-$120.** 2000 Lakeside Dr. I-94, exit Half Day Rd (SR 22), just e to Lakeside Dr, then just s. Int corridors. **Pets:** Accepted.
🆂🅰🆅🅴 🆂🅳 ✖ 🕭 🛢 🅫 📺 🕿 🗙

BLOOMINGDALE

▼▼▼▼ Residence Inn by Marriott 🆂🅷 ❖
(630) 893-9200. **$99-$149, 14 day notice.** 295 Knollwood Dr. I-355, exit Army Trail Rd, 4 mi w, then just n. Int corridors. **Pets:** Medium, other species. $100 one-time fee/room. Service with restrictions, supervision.
✖ 🕭 🛢 📺 🕿 🗙

BOLINGBROOK

▼▼▼▼ Holiday Inn Hotel & Suites 🅻🅷
(630) 679-1600. **$129.** 205 Remington Blvd. I-55, exit 267, just n, then 0.4 mi w. Int corridors. **Pets:** Accepted.
🅰🆂🅺 🆂🅳 ✖ 🕭 🛢 📺 🍴 🕿 🗙

🅰🅰🅰 ▼▼▼▼ La Quinta Inn Bolingbrook 🆂🅷 ❖
(630) 226-0000. **$67-$116.** 225 W South Frontage Rd. I-55, exit 267, 0.5 mi sw. Int corridors. **Pets:** Small. Designated rooms, service with restrictions, supervision.
🆂🅰🆅🅴 🆂🅳 ✖ 🕭 🛢 📺 🕿

BRIDGEVIEW

🅰🅰🅰 ▼ Exel Inn of Bridgeview 🆂🅷
(708) 430-1818. **$65-$85.** 9625 S 76th Ave. I-294, exit 95th St, just s. Int corridors. **Pets:** Small, other species. Designated rooms, service with restrictions, supervision.
🆂🅰🆅🅴 🆂🅳 ✖ 🕭 📺

BURR RIDGE

▼▼ Ramada Inn 🆂🅷
(630) 325-2900. **Call for rates.** 300 S Frontage Rd. I-55, exit 276A (County Line Rd), just sw. Int corridors. **Pets:** Accepted.
✖ 🕭 📺 🍴 🕿 🗙

CALUMET CITY

▼▼ Baymont Inn & Suites Chicago-Calumet City 🆂🅷
(708) 891-2900. **$89-$99.** 510 E End Ave. I-94, exit 71B (Sibley Blvd), just e. Int corridors. **Pets:** Other species. $25 one-time fee/pet. Service with restrictions, supervision.
🅰🆂🅺 🆂🅳 ✖ 🕭 🛢 📺 🕿

CALUMET PARK

🅰🅰🅰 ▼▼▼▼ Best Western Chicago Southwest 🆂🅷
(708) 389-2600. **$79-$109.** 12800 S Ashland Ave. I-57, exit 353, just e. Int corridors. **Pets:** Accepted.
🆂🅰🆅🅴 🆂🅳 ✖ 🕭 📺 🕿

▼▼ Super 8 Motel Chicago Southwest 🆂🅷
(708) 385-9100. **$68-$88.** 12808 S Ashland Ave. I-57, exit 353, just e. Int corridors. **Pets:** Accepted.
🅰🆂🅺 🆂🅳 ✖ 🕭 🛢 🕭

CHICAGO

🅰🅰🅰 ▼▼▼▼ Allegro Chicago, A Kimpton Hotel 🆂🅷 ❖
(312) 236-0123. **$119-$139.** 171 W Randolph St. Jct La Salle St; in theater district. Int corridors. **Pets:** Service with restrictions, crate.
🆂🅰🆅🅴 🆂🅳 ✖ 🕭 📺 🍴

▼▼▼▼ Allerton Crowne Plaza 🅻🅷
(312) 440-1500. **$109-$229.** 701 N Michigan Ave. Jct Huron St. Int corridors. **Pets:** Accepted.
🅰🆂🅺 🆂🅳 ✖ 🕭 🛢 📺 🍴 🗙

🅰🅰🅰 ▼▼▼▼ Amalfi Hotel Chicago 🆂🅷 ❖
(312) 395-9000. **$139-$309.** 20 W Kinzie St. Between State and Dearborn sts. Int corridors. **Pets:** Small. Service with restrictions.
🆂🅰🆅🅴 ✖ 🕭 🛢 📺 🗙

🅰🅰🅰 ▼▼ Best Western Hawthorne Terrace 🆂🅷
(773) 244-3434. **$149-$199.** 3434 N Broadway St. Between Belmont Ave and Addison St. Int corridors. **Pets:** Accepted.
🆂🅰🆅🅴 🆂🅳 ✖ 🕭 📺 🗙

🅰🅰🅰 ▼▼ Carlton Inn Midway 🅼 ❖
(773) 582-0900. **$85-$129.** 4944 S Archer Ave. I-55, exit 287 (Pulaski), 1.8 mi s to Archer Ave, then just e. Ext corridors. **Pets:** Medium. $50 deposit/pet. Service with restrictions, supervision.
🆂🅰🆅🅴 ✖ 🕭 🛢 📺

▼▼▼▼ Clarion Barcelo Hotel O'Hare International 🆂🅷
(773) 693-5800. **$119-$149.** 5615 N Cumberland Ave. I-90, exit N Cumberland Ave S, just s. Int corridors. **Pets:** Accepted.
🅰🆂🅺 🆂🅳 ✖ 🕭 🛢 📺 🍴 🕿

▼▼▼▼ The Drake Hotel, Chicago 🅻🅷
(312) 787-2200. **$249-$409.** 140 E Walton Pl. N Michigan Ave at Lake Shore Dr and Walton Pl. Int corridors. **Pets:** Accepted.
🅰🆂🅺 🆂🅳 ✖ 🕭 📺 🍴

▼▼▼▼ The Fairmont Chicago 🅻🅷
(312) 565-8000. **$139-$469.** 200 N Columbus Dr. Jct Michigan Ave and Wacker Dr, just e. Int corridors. **Pets:** Accepted.
🅰🆂🅺 🆂🅳 ✖ 🕭 🍴

🅰🅰🅰 ▼▼▼▼ Four Seasons Hotel Chicago 🅻🅷
(312) 280-8800. **$445-$3500, 3 day notice.** 120 E Delaware Pl. Jct Michigan Ave, just nw of the John Hancock building. Int corridors. **Pets:** Accepted.
🆂🅰🆅🅴 ✖ 🕭 🛢 📺 🍴 🕿 🗙

🅰🅰🅰 ▼▼▼▼ Hard Rock Hotel Chicago 🅻🅷 ❖
(312) 345-1000. **$149-$219.** 230 N Michigan Ave. Between Lake St and Wacker Dr. Int corridors. **Pets:** Other species. $50 one-time fee/room. Service with restrictions, crate.
🆂🅰🆅🅴 🆂🅳 ✖ 🕭 🛢 📺 🗙

Hilton Chicago LH
(312) 922-4400. **$134-$324.** 720 S Michigan Ave. I-290 (Congress Pkwy), just s. Int corridors. **Pets:** Accepted.

Hilton Chicago O'Hare Airport LH
(773) 686-8000. **$134-$324.** Opposite and connected to terminal buildings at O'Hare International Airport, accessed via I-190. Int corridors. **Pets:** Designated rooms, service with restrictions, crate.

Holiday Inn Chicago Mart Plaza LH
(312) 836-5000. **$189-$309.** 350 N Orleans. Atop the Apparel Center; 14th thru 23rd floors. Int corridors. **Pets:** Accepted.

Hotel Burnham Chicago SH 🐾
(312) 782-1111. **$139-$299.** One W Washington St. Jct State St. Int corridors. **Pets:** Other species. Designated rooms, service with restrictions, crate.

Hotel Monaco Chicago LH 🐾
(312) 960-8500. **$299-$349.** 225 N Wabash Ave. Jct Wacker Dr. Int corridors. **Pets:** Other species. Service with restrictions, crate.

House of Blues Hotel, A Loews Hotel LH 🐾
(312) 245-0333. **$119-$299.** 333 N Dearborn St. Between Dearborn and State sts. Int corridors. **Pets:** Other species.

Hyatt on Printers Row SH
(312) 986-1234. **$99-$219, 14 day notice.** 500 S Dearborn St. Jct Congress Pkwy. Int corridors. **Pets:** Accepted.

Le Meridien Chicago LH
(312) 645-1500. **$319-$2500.** 521 N Rush St at Michigan Ave. Jct Grand Ave. Int corridors. **Pets:** Accepted.

Omni Ambassador East LH 🐾
(312) 787-7200. **$219-$289.** 1301 N State Pkwy. Jct Goethe St and N State Pkwy. Int corridors. **Pets:** Small. $50 one-time fee/room. Designated rooms, service with restrictions, crate.

Omni Chicago Hotel LH
(312) 944-6664. **$329-$1000.** 676 N Michigan Ave. Jct Huron St. Int corridors. **Pets:** Small, dogs only. $50 one-time fee/room. Service with restrictions, crate.

The Palmer House Hilton LH
(312) 726-7500. **$99-$374.** 17 E Monroe St. Between State St and Wabash Ave. Int corridors. **Pets:** Large, other species. Service with restrictions, supervision.

Park Hyatt Chicago LH
(312) 335-1234. **$225-$425, 14 day notice.** 800 N Michigan Ave. Jct Chicago and Michigan aves at Water Tower Square. Int corridors. **Pets:** Accepted.

The Peninsula Chicago LH 🐾
(312) 337-2888. **$445-$890.** 108 E Superior St. Jct Michigan Ave. Int corridors. **Pets:** Small, other species. Service with restrictions.

Radisson Hotel & Suites Chicago LH
(312) 787-2900. **$189-$309.** 160 E Huron St. Just e of N Michigan Ave. Int corridors. **Pets:** Small. $75 deposit/room. Service with restrictions, supervision.

Red Roof Inn Chicago Downtown #7281 SH
(312) 787-3580. **$87-$150.** 162 E Ontario St. Just e of Michigan Ave. Int corridors. **Pets:** Large, other species. Service with restrictions, supervision.

Residence Inn by Marriott Chicago Downtown SH
(312) 943-9800. **Call for rates.** 201 E Walton St. Just e of Michigan Ave at Mies van der Rohe. Int corridors. **Pets:** Accepted.

The Ritz-Carlton, Chicago (A Four Seasons Hotel) LH
(312) 266-1000. **$455-$530.** 160 E Pearson St. Jct N Michigan Ave. Int corridors. **Pets:** Accepted.

Sheraton Chicago Hotel & Towers LH
(312) 464-1000. **$129-$319, 3 day notice.** 301 E North Water St. Columbus Dr at the Chicago River, just e of Michigan Ave. Int corridors. **Pets:** Accepted.

Sofitel Chicago Water Tower LH 🐾
(312) 324-4000. **$329-$399.** 20 E Chestnut St. Jct Wabash Ave and Chestnut St, 0.5 blk w of Rush St. Int corridors. **Pets:** Small, dogs only. Service with restrictions, supervision.

The Sutton Place Hotel LH 🐾
(312) 266-2100. **$169-$289.** 21 E Bellevue Pl. Jct Rush St. Int corridors. **Pets:** Small, dogs only. $200 deposit/pet, $50 one-time fee/pet. Service with restrictions, crate.

W Chicago-City Center LH 🐾
(312) 332-1200. **Call for rates.** 172 W Adams St. Between La Salle and Wells sts. Int corridors. **Pets:** Medium. $100 one-time fee/room. Service with restrictions, supervision.

W Chicago Lakeshore LH
(312) 943-9200. **$209-$369.** 644 N Lake Shore Dr. Jct Ontario St. Int corridors. **Pets:** Accepted.

Westin Chicago River North LH
(312) 744-1900. **$159-$339, 3 day notice.** 320 N Dearborn St. Just n of the Chicago River; between Dearborn and Clark sts; in the River North area. Int corridors. **Pets:** Accepted.

The Westin Michigan Avenue Chicago LH 🐾
(312) 943-7200. **$149-$269.** 909 N Michigan Ave. Across from John Hancock Center. Int corridors. **Pets:** Accepted.

CRYSTAL LAKE

Comfort Inn SH
(815) 444-0040. **$74-$94.** 595 E Tracy Tr. Jct US 14 and SR 31, 0.4 mi w, then just s on Pingree St. Int corridors. **Pets:** Large. $40 daily fee/pet. Service with restrictions, supervision.

(AAA) (W) Crystal Lake Super 8 SH
(815) 788-8888. **$48-$92, 7 day notice.** 577 Crystal Point Dr. On US 14, 1 mi w of jct SR 31. Int corridors. **Pets:** $10 daily fee/pet. Service with restrictions, supervision.
SAVE 🆂 ✕ 🅗 🖵

DEERFIELD

(W)(W) Residence Inn by Marriott SH
(847) 940-4644. **Call for rates.** 530 Lake Cook Rd. I-94, exit Lake Cook Rd, 1.8 mi e, then 3 blks n on Corporate 500 Dr access road. Ext corridors. **Pets:** Accepted.
✕ 🖉 🅗 🖵 🏊 ✕

DOWNERS GROVE

(W) Red Roof Inn #7087 M
(630) 434-4205. 1113 Butterfield Rd. I-355, exit Butterfield Rd (SR 56), on frontage road; I-88, exit Highland Ave N, just w. Ext corridors. **Pets:** Accepted.
✕ 🖉

ELGIN

(W)(W) Best Western Plaza Hotel and Convention
Center SH
(847) 695-5000. **Call for rates.** 345 W River Rd. I-90, exit SR 31 S, just s to W River Rd, then 0.5 mi e. Int corridors. **Pets:** Accepted.
✕ 🖉 🅗 🖵 🍴 🏊 ✕

(AAA) (W)(W) Quality Inn-Elgin SH 🐾
(847) 608-7300. **$60-$85.** 500 Tollgate Rd. I-90, exit SR 31 N, just n. Int corridors. **Pets:** Other species. $10 daily fee/room. Designated rooms, service with restrictions, crate.
SAVE 🆂 ✕ 🅜 🖉 🅙 🅗 🖵

ELK GROVE VILLAGE

(AAA) (W) Exel Inn of Elk Grove Village SH
(847) 895-2085. **$56-$76.** 1000 W Devon Ave. I-290, exit Thorndale Ave, 0.5 mi w to Rohlwing Rd, 0.3 mi n to Devon Ave, then 0.3 mi e. Int corridors. **Pets:** Small, other species. Designated rooms, service with restrictions, supervision.
SAVE 🆂 ✕ 🖉 🅗 🖵

(AAA) (W) Exel Inn of O'Hare SH
(847) 803-9400. **$65-$85.** 2881 Touhy Ave. Jct SR 72 (Higgins Rd) and 83 (Busse Rd), 1.5 mi e on SR 72 (Higgins Rd). Int corridors. **Pets:** Small, other species. Designated rooms, service with restrictions, supervision.
SAVE 🆂 ✕ 🖉 🅗 🖵

(W)(W) Holiday Inn of Elk Grove LH
(847) 437-6010. **$109-$139.** 1000 Busse Rd. 0.3 mi s of jct SR 72 (Higgins Rd). Int corridors. **Pets:** Accepted.
ASK 🆂 ✕ 🖉 🅗 🖵 🍴 🏊 ✕

(W)(W)(W) La Quinta Inn Chicago (O'Hare Airport) SH
(847) 439-6767. **$79-$115.** 1900 E Oakton St. Jct SR 72 (Higgins Rd) and 83 (Busse Rd). Int corridors. **Pets:** Small, other species. Designated rooms, service with restrictions, crate.
ASK ✕ 🖉 🅗 🖵 🏊

(W)(W)(W) Sheraton Suites Elk Grove Village LH
(847) 290-1600. **$89-$219.** 121 Northwest Point Blvd. I-90, exit Arlington Heights Blvd, just s; in Northwest Point Corporate Park. Int corridors. **Pets:** Accepted.
ASK 🆂 ✕ 🅜 🖉 🖵 🍴 🏊 ✕

(AAA) (W)(W) Super 8 Motel O'Hare SH
(847) 827-3133. **$59-$69.** 2951 Touhy Ave. Jct SR 72 (Higgins Rd) and 83 (Busse Rd), 1.5 mi e on SR 72 (Higgins Rd). Int corridors. **Pets:** Small. $10 daily fee/pet. Service with restrictions, supervision.
SAVE 🆂 ✕ 🅜 🖉 🅗 🖵 🏊

ELMHURST

(AAA) (W)(W)(W) Holiday Inn Chicago-Elmhurst SH
(630) 279-1100. **$85-$95.** 624 N York St. I-290, exit 12 (York Rd), just n. Int corridors. **Pets:** Small. $20 daily fee/pet. Designated rooms, service with restrictions, supervision.
SAVE 🆂 ✕ 🖉 🅗 🖵 🍴 🏊 ✕

FRANKLIN PARK

(W)(W) Comfort Inn SH
(847) 233-9292. **$89.** 3001 N Mannheim Rd. Jct US 12/45 (Mannheim Rd) and Grand Ave, just n. Int corridors. **Pets:** Medium. $50 deposit/pet. No service, supervision.
ASK 🆂 ✕ 🅙 🅗 🖵 🏊

(AAA) (W)(W)(W) Super 8 O'Hare South SH
(847) 288-0600. **$49-$149.** 3010 N Mannheim Rd. Jct US 12/45 (Mannheim Rd) and Grand Ave, just n. Int corridors. **Pets:** Accepted.
SAVE 🆂 ✕ 🅗

GLEN ELLYN

(W)(W) Holiday Inn-Glen Ellyn SH
(630) 629-6000. **$74-$94.** 1250 Roosevelt Rd. I-355, exit Roosevelt Rd, 0.8 mi e on SR 38. Int corridors. **Pets:** Small, other species. $25 one-time fee/room. Designated rooms, service with restrictions, supervision.
ASK 🆂 ✕ 🅜 🖉 🅙 🅗 🖵 🍴 🏊

GLENVIEW

(AAA) (W)(W)(W) Baymont Inn & Suites Chicago-Glenview SH
(847) 635-8300. **$44-$90.** 1625 Milwaukee Ave. I-294, exit Willow Rd, 0.4 mi e to Landwehr Rd, 1.3 mi s to Lake Ave, then 0.5 mi w. Int corridors. **Pets:** $50 deposit/room. Designated rooms, service with restrictions, crate.
SAVE 🆂 ✕ 🖉 🅗 🖵

GURNEE

(AAA) (W)(W)(W) Baymont Inn & Suites Chicago-Gurnee SH
(847) 662-7600. **$64-$125.** 5688 N Ridge Rd. I-94, exit Grand Ave (SR 132 E), just e via service road. Int corridors. **Pets:** Accepted.
SAVE 🆂 ✕ 🅜 🖉 🅙 🅗 🖵 🏊

(W)(W)(W) Comfort Suites SH
(847) 782-0890. **Call for rates.** 5430 Grand Ave. I-94, exit Grand Ave (SR 132 E), 0.5 mi e. Int corridors. **Pets:** Small, dogs only. $30 deposit/room. Service with restrictions, crate.
🆂 ✕ 🅜 🖉 🅙 🅗 🖵 🏊 ✕

(W)(W)(W) Country Inn & Suites By Carlson SH
(847) 625-9700. **Call for rates.** 5420 Grand Ave. I-94, exit Grand Ave (SR 132 E), 0.5 mi e. Int corridors. **Pets:** Accepted.
✕ 🅜 🖉 🅙 🅗 🖵 🏊

HAMPSHIRE

(W)(W) Super 8 Motel-Hampshire SH
(847) 683-0888. **Call for rates.** 115 Arrowhead Dr. I-90, exit Marango-Hampshire, just ne. Int corridors. **Pets:** Accepted.
✕ 🅙 🅗 🖵

HOFFMAN ESTATES

(AAA) (W)(W)(W) Baymont Inn & Suites Chicago-Hoffman
Estates SH
(847) 882-8848. **$79-$100.** 2075 Barrington Rd. I-90, exit Barrington Rd westbound, 0.3 mi s; exit SR 59 eastbound, 0.5 mi n to SR 72 (Higgins Rd), 2 mi e to Barrington Rd, then just n. Int corridors. **Pets:** $50 deposit/room. Designated rooms, service with restrictions, supervision.
SAVE 🆂 ✕ 🖉 🅗 🖵

AAA ♦♦♦♦ Chicago Marriott Northwest at Hoffman Estates LH

(847) 645-9500. **$99-$159.** 4800 Columbine Blvd. I-90, exit SR 59. Int corridors. **Pets:** Medium. $50 deposit/room. Service with restrictions, supervision.

SAVE 🅢 ✕ Ⓜ 🐾 🄲 🛏 🖥 🍴 ⚊ ✕

AAA ♦♦♦♦ La Quinta Inn Chicago (Hoffman Estates) SH

(847) 882-3312. **$81-$105.** 2280 Barrington Rd. I-90, exit Barrington Rd westbound, 0.3 mi s; exit SR 59 eastbound, 0.5 mi n to SR 72 (Higgins Rd), 2 mi e to Barrington Rd, then just n. Int corridors. **Pets:** Other species. Service with restrictions, crate.

SAVE ✕ 🐾 🄲 🛏 🖥 ⚊

♦ Red Roof Inn #7199 M 🐾

(847) 885-7877. **$52-$86.** 2500 Hassell Rd. I-90, exit Barrington Rd westbound, 0.3 mi s; exit SR 59 eastbound, 0.5 mi n to SR 72 (Higgins Rd), 2 mi e to Barrington Rd, then just n. Ext corridors. **Pets:** Other species. Service with restrictions, supervision.

✕ 🐾 🛏

ITASCA

AAA ♦♦♦♦ AmeriSuites (Chicago/Itasca) SH

(630) 875-1400. **$104-$119.** 1150 Arlington Heights Rd. I-290, exit Thorndale Ave, 0.6 mi e on Thorndale Heights Rd, then 0.5 mi n. Int corridors. **Pets:** Accepted.

SAVE 🅢 ✕ Ⓜ 🐾 🄲 🛏 🖥 ⚊

JOLIET

♦♦ Comfort Inn by Choice Hotels North SH

(815) 436-5141. **$75-$95.** 3235 Norman Ave. I-55, exit 257, just e. Int corridors. **Pets:** Accepted.

ASK 🅢 ✕ 🐾 🛏 🖥 ⚊

♦♦ Comfort Inn by Choice Hotels-South SH

(815) 744-1770. **$80-$100.** 135 S Larkin Ave. I-80, exit 130B, 0.5 mi n. Int corridors. **Pets:** Accepted.

ASK 🅢 ✕ 🐾 🛏 🖥 ⚊

♦♦ Holiday Inn Express-Joliet SH

(815) 729-2000. **$59-$139.** 411 S Larkin Ave. I-80, exit 130B. Int corridors. **Pets:** Small, dogs only. Designated rooms, service with restrictions, supervision.

ASK 🅢 ✕ Ⓜ 🄲 🛏 🖥 ⚊

♦ Motel 6 Joliet I-55—1296 SH

(815) 439-1332. **$40-$53.** 3551 Mall Loop Dr. I-55, exit 257, 0.4 mi e on US 30, then 0.4 mi s. Int corridors. **Pets:** Accepted.

🅢 ✕ Ⓜ 🐾 🄲

♦ Red Roof Inn #7071 M

(815) 741-2304. **$42-$70.** 1750 McDonough St. I-80, exit 130B, just off Larkin Ave. Ext corridors. **Pets:** Accepted.

✕ 🐾 🛏

AAA ♦♦♦ Super 8 Motel I-55 North SH

(815) 439-3838. **$53-$63.** 3401 Mall Loop Dr. I-55, exit 257, 0.4 mi e on US 30, then just s. Int corridors. **Pets:** Accepted.

SAVE 🅢 ✕ 🐾 🄲 🛏 ⚊

LANSING

♦ Red Roof Inn #7078 M

(708) 895-9570. **$49-$85.** 2450 E 173rd St. I-80/94, exit 161 (Torrence Ave), just n. Ext corridors. **Pets:** Small, other species. No service, supervision.

✕ 🐾 🛏

LIBERTYVILLE

AAA ♦♦♦ Best Western Hitch-Inn Post SH

(847) 362-8700. **$69-$109.** 1765 N Milwaukee Ave. Jct SR 21 (Milwaukee Ave) and 137 (Buckley Rd). Int corridors. **Pets:** Accepted.

SAVE 🅢 ✕ 🐾 🛏 🖥 ⚊ ✕

♦♦ Candlewood Suites Chicago-Libertyville SH

(847) 247-9900. **$97-$127.** 1100 N US 45. I-94, exit SR 137 (Buckley Rd), 5.6 mi w to US 45, then 1.4 mi s. Int corridors. **Pets:** Large. $75 one-time fee/room. Service with restrictions.

ASK 🅢 ✕ Ⓜ 🐾 🄲 🛏 🖥

♦ Days Inn SH

(847) 816-8006. **$65-$85.** 1809 N Milwaukee Ave. Jct SR 21 (Milwaukee Ave) and 137 (Buckley Rd). Int corridors. **Pets:** Medium, other species. $5 daily fee/pet. Service with restrictions, supervision.

ASK 🅢 ✕ 🐾 🛏 🖥 ⚊

♦♦♦ Holiday Inn Express Hotel & Suites SH

(847) 549-7878. **$101-$106.** 77 W Buckley Rd. I-94, exit SR 137 (Buckley Rd), 2.3 mi w. Int corridors. **Pets:** Small, dogs only. $50 one-time fee/pet. Designated rooms, service with restrictions, supervision.

ASK 🅢 ✕ 🄲 🛏 🖥 ⚊

LINCOLNSHIRE

AAA ♦♦♦♦ Lincolnshire Marriott Resort LH

(847) 634-0100. **$89-$219.** 10 Marriott Dr. I-94, exit Half Day Rd, 2 mi w to jct US 45, SR 21 and 22, then just s. Int corridors. **Pets:** Accepted.

SAVE ✕ Ⓜ 🐾 🄲 🛏 🖥 🍴 ⚊ ✕

♦♦♦ Staybridge Suites SH

(847) 821-0002. **$129-$299.** 100 Barclay Blvd. I-94, exit Half Day Rd, 2.2 mi w to Barclay Blvd, then just s; just w of jct US 45 and SR 21; in Lincolnshire Corporate Center. Int corridors. **Pets:** Accepted.

ASK 🅢 ✕ Ⓜ 🐾 🄲 🛏 🖥 ⚊ ✕

LOMBARD

AAA ♦♦♦ AmeriSuites (Chicago/Lombard/Oakbrook) SH

(630) 932-6501. **$89-$99.** 2340 S Fountain Square Dr. I-88, exit Highland Ave, just n to Butterfield Rd (SR 56), 0.9 mi e, then just n. Int corridors. **Pets:** Very small, dogs only. $10 daily fee/pet. Designated rooms, service with restrictions, supervision.

SAVE 🅢 ✕ Ⓜ 🐾 🄲 🛏 🖥 ⚊

♦♦ Homestead Studio Suites Hotel-Chicago/Lombard/Oak Brook SH

(630) 928-0202. **$74-$89.** 2701 Technology Dr. I-88, exit Highland Ave, just n, 0.6 mi e on Butterfield Rd (SR 56), then just s. Int corridors. **Pets:** Other species. $75 one-time fee/room. Service with restrictions, crate.

ASK 🅢 ✕ Ⓜ 🐾 🄲 🛏 🖥

MATTESON

AAA ♦♦♦ Baymont Inn & Suites Chicago-Matteson SH 🐾

(708) 503-0999. **$70-$100.** 5210 W Southwick Dr. I-57, exit 340A, 0.3 mi e on US 30, then 0.3 mi s on Cicero Ave. Int corridors. **Pets:** Medium, other species. $50 deposit/room. Service with restrictions, crate.

SAVE 🅢 ✕ 🐾 🛏 🖥

MUNDELEIN

♦♦♦ Crowne Plaza Chicago North Shore SH

(847) 949-5100. **$125.** 510 SR 83 E. Jct US 45 and SR 83. Int corridors. **Pets:** Designated rooms, service with restrictions, crate.

ASK 🅢 ✕ 🐾 🛏 🖥 🍴 ⚊

◆ **Super 8 Motel** SH
(847) 949-8842. **Call for rates.** 1950 S Lake St. Jct US 45, SR 60 and 83. Int corridors. **Pets:** Accepted.
⊠ ▤

NAPERVILLE

AAA ◆ **Exel Inn of Naperville** SH
(630) 357-0022. **$56-$76.** 1585 N Naperville/Wheaton Rd. I-88, exit Naperville Rd, 0.5 mi s. Int corridors. **Pets:** Small, other species. $100 deposit/pet. Designated rooms, service with restrictions, supervision.
SAVE S🐾 ⊠ ▤ 🖃

◆◆◆ **Fairfield Inn & Suites by Marriott** SH
(630) 548-0966. **$99-$130.** 1847 W Diehl Rd. I-88, exit SR 59, just s. Int corridors. **Pets:** Accepted.
⊠ 🅼 📶 📺 ▤ 🖃 ➰

◆◆◆ **Hawthorn Suites** SH
(630) 548-0881. **$110, 5 day notice.** 1843 W Diehl Rd. I-88, exit SR 59, just s to Diehl Rd, then just w. Int corridors. **Pets:** Accepted.
ASK ⊠ 📶 📺 ▤ 🖃 ➰ ⊠

AAA ◆◆◆ **Holiday Inn Select Chicago/Naperville** LH
(630) 505-4900. **$69-$149.** 1801 N Naper Blvd. I-88, exit Naperville Rd, just s. Int corridors. **Pets:** Accepted.
SAVE S🐾 ⊠ 📶 ▤ 🖃 🍽 ➰ ⊠

◆ **Homestead Studio Suites**
   Hotel-Chicago/Naperville SH
(630) 577-0200. **$70-$85.** 1827 Centre Point Cir. I-88, exit Naperville Rd, just s to Diehl Rd, 0.8 mi w, then just n. Int corridors. **Pets:** Other species. $75 one-time fee/pet. Service with restrictions, supervision.
ASK S🐾 ⊠ 📶 🅼 📺 ▤ 🖃

◆ **Red Roof Inn #7195** M
(630) 369-2500. **$56-$78.** 1698 W Diehl Rd. I-88, exit SR 59, just s. Ext corridors. **Pets:** Accepted.
⊠ ▤

NORTH AURORA

AAA ◆◆◆ **Baymont Inn & Suites North Aurora** SH
(630) 897-7695. **$74-$109.** 308 S Lincoln Way. I-88, exit SR 31. Int corridors. **Pets:** Service with restrictions, supervision.
SAVE S🐾 ⊠ 📺 ▤ 🖃 ➰

NORTHBROOK

◆ **Red Roof Inn #7188** M
(847) 205-1755. **$54-$79.** 340 Waukegan Rd. I-94, exit SR 43 (Waukegan Rd). Ext corridors. **Pets:** Accepted.
⊠

OAK BROOK

◆◆◆ **Residence Inn by Marriott Chicago/Oak Brook** SH
(630) 571-1200. **$149.** 790 Jorie Blvd. I-88, exit Midwest Rd eastbound, just n to 22nd St (Cermak Rd), 1.7 mi e to Jorie Blvd, then just sw; exit 22nd St (Cermak Rd) westbound, 0.4 mi e to Jorie Blvd. Int corridors. **Pets:** Large, other species. $75 one-time fee/room. Designated rooms, service with restrictions, crate.
ASK S🐾 ⊠ 🅼 📶 📺 ▤ 🖃 ➰ ⊠

OAKBROOK TERRACE

AAA ◆◆◆ **La Quinta Inn Chicago (Oakbrook)** SH
(630) 495-4600. **$82-$119.** 1 S 666 Midwest Rd. I-88, exit Midwest Rd eastbound, 0.4 mi n, then just n of 22nd St (Cermak Rd); exit 22nd St (Cermak Rd) westbound, 1.1 mi w to Midwest Rd, then just n. Int corridors. **Pets:** Accepted.
SAVE ⊠ 📶 ▤ 🖃 ➰

◆◆◆ **Staybridge Suites Chicago-Oakbrook Terrace** SH
(630) 953-9393. **$139-$159.** 200 Royce Blvd. I-88, exit Midwest Rd eastbound to 22nd St, 0.4 mi w to SR 56, just n, then just n on Renaissance Blvd; exit Cermak Rd/22nd St westbound, 2.5 mi w on 22nd St to SR 56, just n, then just. Int corridors. **Pets:** Medium, other species. $75 one-time fee/room. Service with restrictions.
ASK S🐾 ⊠ 🅼 📶 📺 ▤ 🖃 ⊠

OAK LAWN

◆◆◆ **Holiday Inn-Oak Lawn/Chicago Southwest** SH
(708) 425-7900. **$139-$239.** 4140 W 95th St. US 12 and 20, 1 mi e of jct Cicero Ave. Int corridors. **Pets:** Accepted.
ASK S🐾 ⊠ 📶 📺 ▤ 🖃 🍽 ➰

PALATINE

◆◆◆ **Holiday Inn Express Palatine/Arlington Heights** SH
(847) 934-4900. **$64-$84.** 1550 E Dundee Rd. SR 53, exit Dundee Rd (SR 68), just w. Int corridors. **Pets:** Medium, other species. Designated rooms, service with restrictions, supervision.
ASK S🐾 ⊠ 📶 📺 ▤ 🖃 ➰ ⊠

PROSPECT HEIGHTS

AAA ◆ **Exel Inn of Prospect Heights** SH
(847) 459-0545. **$51-$71.** 540 Milwaukee Ave. Jct SR 21 and US 45. Int corridors. **Pets:** Small, other species. Designated rooms, service with restrictions, supervision.
SAVE S🐾 ⊠ 📶 ▤ 🖃

ROSEMONT

AAA ◆◆◆◆ **Crowne Plaza Chicago O'Hare** LH
(847) 671-6350. **$80-$179.** 5440 N River Rd. I-190, exit 1B, just s. Int corridors. **Pets:** Accepted.
SAVE S🐾 ⊠ 🅼 📶 📺 ▤ 🖃 🍽 ➰ ⊠

◆◆◆ **Doubletree Hotel Chicago O'Hare**
   Airport-Rosemont LH
(847) 292-9100. **$85-$199.** 5460 N River Rd. I-190, exit 1B, just s. Int corridors. **Pets:** Accepted.
ASK S🐾 ⊠ 🅼 📶 📺 🖃 🍽 ➰ ⊠

AAA ◆◆◆◆ **Embassy Suites Hotel O'Hare Rosemont** LH
(847) 678-4000. **$109-$325.** 5500 N River Rd. I-190, exit 1B, just s. Int corridors. **Pets:** Medium. Service with restrictions, supervision.
SAVE S🐾 ⊠ 📶 📺 ▤ 🖃 🍽 ➰ ⊠

◆◆◆ **Residence Inn by Marriott Chicago-O'Hare** SH
(847) 375-9000. **$139-$189.** 7101 Chestnut St. Jct US 12/45 (Mannheim Rd) and Touhy Ave. Int corridors. **Pets:** Accepted.
ASK ⊠ 📶 📺 ▤ 🖃 ➰ ⊠

AAA ◆◆◆ **Sheraton Gateway Suites O'Hare** LH
(847) 699-6300. **$89-$259.** 6501 N Mannheim Rd. On US 12 and 45, at SR 72 (Higgins Rd). Int corridors. **Pets:** Accepted.
SAVE S🐾 ⊠ 📶 📺 ▤ 🖃 🍽 ➰ ⊠

◆◆◆ **Sofitel Chicago O'Hare** LH
(847) 678-4488. **$259.** 5550 N River Rd. I-190, exit 1B, just s. Int corridors. **Pets:** Accepted.
ASK S🐾 ⊠ 📶 ▤ 🖃 🍽 ➰ ⊠

AAA ◆◆◆◆ **The Westin O'Hare** LH 🐾
(847) 698-6000. **$99-$289.** 6100 N River Rd. I-190, exit 1B, just n. Int corridors. **Pets:** Small. Service with restrictions, supervision.
SAVE S🐾 ⊠ 📶 📺 ▤ 🖃 🍽 ➰ ⊠

AAA ◆◆◆◆ **Wyndham O'Hare** LH
(847) 297-1234. **$79-$149.** 6810 N Mannheim Rd. On US 12 and 45, 0.3 mi n of SR 72 (Higgins Rd). Int corridors. **Pets:** Accepted.
SAVE S🐾 ⊠ 📶 📺 ▤ 🖃 🍽 ➰ ⊠

ST. CHARLES

[AAA] ◆◆ **Best Western Inn of St. Charles** [SH]
(630) 584-4550. **$79-$89.** 1635 E Main St. On SR 64, 0.5 mi e of SR 25. Ext/int corridors. **Pets:** Medium, dogs only. $7 daily fee/pet. Service with restrictions, supervision.
[SAVE] [SD] ⊠ ▣ 📺 🏊

[AAA] ◆ **Super 8 Motel-St. Charles** [SH]
(630) 377-8388. **$76-$109, 4 day notice.** 1520 E Main St. On SR 64, 1 mi e. Int corridors. **Pets:** Medium. $50 deposit/room, $6 daily fee/pet. Service with restrictions, supervision.
[SAVE] [SD] ⊠ ▣

SCHAUMBURG

[AAA] ◆◆◆ **AmeriSuites (Chicago/Schaumburg)** [SH] 🐾
(847) 330-1060. **$79-$130.** 1851 McConnor Pkwy. I-290, exit 1A (Woodfield/Golf rds) northbound, just n to Golf Rd, just w to McConnor Pkwy, then just n; exit 1B (Woodfield/Golf rds) southbound. Int corridors. **Pets:** Small, other species. $50 one-time fee/room. Designated rooms.
[SAVE] [SD] ⊠ ♿M 🦻 ♿ ▣ 📺 🏊

◆◆◆ **Drury Inn-Schaumburg** [SH]
(847) 517-7737. **$67-$105.** 600 N Martingale Rd. I-290, exit Higgins Rd (SR 72) westbound, just w, then just n. Int corridors. **Pets:** Large, other species. Service with restrictions, supervision.
[ASK] ⊠ 🦻 ▣ 📺 🏊

◆◆◆ **Hawthorn Suites Schaumburg** [SH]
(847) 706-9007. **$69-$149.** 1251 E American Ln. I-290, exit 1A (Woodfield/Golf rds), 0.5 mi w to Meacham Rd, just n to American Ln, then just w. Int corridors. **Pets:** Accepted.
[ASK] [SD] ⊠ ♿M ♿ ▣ 📺 🏊 ⚒

◆◆◆ **Holiday Inn Schaumburg** [SH]
(847) 310-0500. **$89-$115.** 1550 N Roselle Rd. I-90, exit Roselle Rd, 0.8 mi s. Int corridors. **Pets:** Medium, other species. Service with restrictions, crate.
[ASK] [SD] ⊠ 🦻 ▣ 📺 🏊

◆◆ **Homestead Studio Suites Hotel-Chicago/Schaumburg** [SH]
(847) 882-6900. **$74-$89.** 51 E State Pkwy. I-90, exit Roselle Rd, 0.8 mi s, then just e. Int corridors. **Pets:** Accepted.
[ASK] [SD] ⊠ ♿M 🦻 ♿ ▣ 📺

◆◆◆ **Homewood Suites by Hilton-Schaumburg** [SH]
(847) 605-0400. **$79-$139.** 815 E American Ln. I-290, exit Higgins Rd (SR 72), 0.5 mi w, 0.8 mi n on Meacham Rd, then 0.8 mi w. Ext/int corridors. **Pets:** Accepted.
[ASK] [SD] ⊠ ♿M 🦻 ▣ 📺 🏊 ⚒

[AAA] ◆◆◆ **La Quinta Inn Chicago (Schaumburg)** [SH]
(847) 517-8484. **$81-$129.** 1730 E Higgins Rd. I-290, exit Higgins Rd (SR 72) westbound, just w. Int corridors. **Pets:** Accepted.
[SAVE] ⊠ 🦻 ▣ 📺 🏊

◆◆◆ **Residence Inn by Marriott-Chicago/Schaumburg** [SH]
(847) 517-9200. **$169-$229.** 1610 McConnor Pkwy. I-290, exit 1A (Woodfield/Golf rds) northbound, follow signs just n to Golf Rd, just w to McConnor Pkwy, then just n; exit 1B (Woodfield/Golf rds) southbound. Int corridors. **Pets:** Accepted.
[ASK] ⊠ ♿M 🦻 ♿ ▣ 📺 🏊 ⚒

◆◆◆ **Staybridge Suites Chicago/Schaumburg** [SH]
(847) 619-6677. **$129-$189.** 901 E Woodfield Office Ct. I-290, exit SR 72 (Higgins Rd), 1.5 mi w, then 0.3 mi n on Plum Grove Rd. Ext/int corridors. **Pets:** Medium, other species. $200 one-time fee/room. Service with restrictions, crate.
[ASK] [SD] ⊠ 🦻 ▣ 📺 🏊 ⚒

SKOKIE

[AAA] ◆◆◆ **Comfort Inn Northshore-Skokie** [SH]
(847) 679-4200. **$119-$149.** 9333 Skokie Blvd. I-94, exit Old Orchard Rd, 0.4 mi e to Skokie Blvd (US 41), then 0.3 mi s. Int corridors. **Pets:** Other species. Service with restrictions, supervision.
[SAVE] [SD] ⊠ ♿ ▣ 📺 🍴 🏊 ⚒

[AAA] ◆◆◆ **Holiday Inn Chicago-Skokie** [SH]
(847) 679-8900. **$89-$179.** 5300 W Touhy Ave. I-94, exit 39A, 0.5 mi w. Ext/int corridors. **Pets:** Medium. $25 one-time fee/room. Designated rooms, service with restrictions, supervision.
[SAVE] [SD] ⊠ 🦻 ♿ ▣ 📺 🍴 🏊 ⚒

SOUTH HOLLAND

◆ **Motel 6-1483** [M]
(708) 331-1621. **$38-$52.** 17301 S Halsted St. I-80/294, exit Halsted St northbound, just ne. Ext corridors. **Pets:** Accepted.
[SD] ⊠

TINLEY PARK

[AAA] ◆◆ **Baymont Inn & Suites Chicago-Tinley Park** [SH]
(708) 633-1200. **$70-$100.** 7255 W 183rd St. I-80, exit 148B, 0.5 mi n to 183rd St, then just w to North Creek Business Center. Int corridors. **Pets:** Medium. $50 one-time fee/room. Designated rooms, service with restrictions, supervision.
[SAVE] [SD] ⊠ ♿M ♿ ▣ 📺 🏊

VERNON HILLS

◆◆ **Homestead Studio Suites Hotel-Chicago/Vernon Hills/Lincolnshire** [SH] 🐾
(847) 955-1111. **$74-$89.** 675 Woodlands Pkwy. I-94, exit SR 60 (Town Line Rd), 2.1 mi w to SR 21 (Milwaukee Ave), 1.9 mi s to Woodlands Pkwy, then just w. Int corridors. **Pets:** Other species. $75 one-time fee/room. Designated rooms, service with restrictions, supervision.
⊠ 🦻 ♿ ▣ 📺

WARRENVILLE

◆◆◆ **Residence Inn Marriott Chicago Naperville/Warrenville** [SH]
(630) 393-3444. **$129-$149, 14 day notice.** 28500 Bella Vista Pkwy. I-88, exit Winfield Rd, just n to Ferry Rd, then just e. Int corridors. **Pets:** $75 one-time fee/pet. Service with restrictions.
[ASK] [SD] ⊠ ♿M 🦻 ♿ ▣ 📺 🏊 ⚒

WAUKEGAN

[AAA] ◆◆ **Best Western of Waukegan** [SH]
(847) 244-6100. **$59-$149.** 411 S Green Bay Rd. I-94, exit Belvidere Rd (SR 120) eastbound, 2.3 mi e to Green Bay Rd, then just n. Ext/int corridors. **Pets:** Accepted.
[SAVE] [SD] ⊠ ▣ 📺 🏊

◆◆ **Candlewood Suites Chicago/Waukegan** [SH]
(847) 578-5250. **$79-$119.** 1151 S Waukegan Rd. I-94, exit Buckley Rd (SR 137), 0.5 mi e to SR 43 (Waukegan Rd), then 1.9 mi n. Int corridors. **Pets:** Medium. $25 one-time fee/pet. Service with restrictions.
[ASK] [SD] ⊠ 🦻 ♿ ▣ 📺

◆◆◆ **Residence Inn by Marriott-Waukegan** [SH]
(847) 689-9240. **$119-$159.** 1440 S White Oak Dr. I-94, exit SR 137 (Buckley Rd), 0.5 mi e to SR 43 (Waukegan Rd), 1.5 mi n to Lakeside Dr, then just e. Int corridors. **Pets:** Other species. $75 one-time fee/room.
[ASK] ⊠ ♿M 🦻 ♿ ▣ 📺 🏊 ⚒

WEST DUNDEE

◆◆ **TownePlace Suites by Marriott** [SH] 🐾
(847) 608-6320. **$59-$109.** 2185 Marriott Dr. I-90, exit SR 31, 0.4 mi n to Marriott Dr, then just e. Int corridors. **Pets:** Medium, other species. $75 one-time fee/room. Service with restrictions.
[ASK] ⊠ 🦻 ♿ ▣ 📺 🏊

WESTMONT

♦♦ ♦♦ Homestead Studio Suites Hotel-Chicago/Westmont/Oak Brook 🆂🅷
(630) 323-9292. **$65-$80.** 855 Pasquinelli Dr. SR 83, exit US 34 (Ogden Ave), just w to Pasquinelli Dr, then 0.5 mi n. Int corridors. **Pets:** Medium, other species. $75 one-time fee/room. Service with restrictions, crate.
🆂🅢 🆂🅓 ⊠ 🔧 ⟋ 🅵 🔒 💻

WILLOWBROOK

♦♦♦ ♦♦ ♦♦ Baymont Inn & Suites Chicago-Willowbrook 🆂🅷
(630) 654-0077. **$79-$94.** 855 79th St. I-55, exit 274, just n. Int corridors. **Pets:** Accepted.
🆂🅐🆅🅔 🆂🅓 ⊠ ⟋ 🔒 💻

♦♦ Red Roof Inn #7167 🅼
(630) 323-8811. **$57-$90.** 7535 Kingery Hwy. I-55, exit 274, 0.5 mi n on SR 83. Ext corridors. **Pets:** Accepted.
⊠ ⟋ 🔒

WOODSTOCK

♦♦♦ ♦♦ Super 8 Motel 🆂🅷
(815) 337-8808. **$55-$106, 3 day notice.** 1220 Davis Rd. On SR 47, s of jct US 14. Int corridors. **Pets:** Medium, dogs only. $5 daily fee/pet. Service with restrictions, supervision.
🆂🅐🆅🅔 🆂🅓 ⊠ 🔒

END METROPOLITAN AREA

CHILLICOTHE

♦♦ ♦♦ Super 8 Motel 🆂🅷
(309) 274-2568. **$52-$57, 3 day notice.** 615 S Fourth St. 1.1 mi s on SR 29. Int corridors. **Pets:** Medium, other species. $50 deposit/room. Service with restrictions, supervision.
🆂🅐🆂🅚 ⊠ 🔒

COLLINSVILLE

♦♦♦ ♦♦ ♦♦ Best Western/Pear Tree Inn-Collinsville 🆂🅷
(618) 345-9500. **$42-$93.** 552 Ramada Blvd. I-55/70, exit 11 (SR 157), just s. Ext corridors. **Pets:** Accepted.
🆂🅐🆅🅔 ⊠ 🔧 ⟋ 🅵 🔒 💻 ⨝

♦♦♦♦ Drury Inn St. Louis/Collinsville 🆂🅷
(618) 345-7700. **$62-$111.** 602 N Bluff Rd. I-55/70, exit 11 (SR 157), just n. Int corridors. **Pets:** Large, other species. Service with restrictions, supervision.
🆂🅐🆂🅚 ⊠ 🔧 ⟋ 🔒 💻 ⨝

♦♦♦ ♦♦♦♦ Holiday Inn Collinsville/St. Louis 🆂🅷
(618) 345-2800. **$110.** 1000 Eastport Plaza Dr. I-55/70, exit 11 (SR 157), just nw. Int corridors. **Pets:** Accepted.
🆂🅐🆅🅔 ⊠ 🔒 💻 🍴 ⨝ 🅧

DANVILLE

♦♦♦ ♦♦ Best Western Regency Inn 🆂🅷
(217) 446-2111. **$70-$90.** 360 Eastgate Dr. I-74, exit 220 (Lynch Dr), just n. Ext/int corridors. **Pets:** Small. $10 daily fee/pet. Designated rooms, service with restrictions, supervision.
🆂🅐🆅🅔 🆂🅓 ⊠ 🔒 💻 ⨝

♦♦♦ ♦♦ Best Western Riverside Inn 🆂🅷
(217) 431-0020. **$70-$90.** 57 S Gilbert St. I-74, exit 215B, 0.8 mi n, on US 150 and SR 1. Ext/int corridors. **Pets:** Small. $10 daily fee/pet. Designated rooms, service with restrictions, supervision.
🆂🅐🆅🅔 🆂🅓 ⊠ 🔒 💻 ⨝

♦♦ ♦♦ Comfort Inn by Choice Hotels 🆂🅷
(217) 443-8004. **$55-$96.** 383 Lynch Dr. I-74, exit 220 (Lynch Dr), just n. Int corridors. **Pets:** Other species. Service with restrictions, supervision.
🆂🅐🆂🅚 ⊠ 🔒 ⟋ 💻 ⨝

♦♦ ♦♦ Sleep Inn & Suites 🆂🅷
(217) 442-6600. **$65-$99.** 361 Lynch Dr. I-74, exit 220 (Lynch Dr), just n. Int corridors. **Pets:** Small, dogs only. $10 daily fee/room. Designated rooms, service with restrictions, supervision.
🆂🅐🆂🅚 🆂🅓 ⊠ 🔒 💻 ⨝

♦♦ ♦♦ Super 8 🆂🅷
(217) 443-4499. **$51-$64.** 377 Lynch Dr. I-74, exit 220 (Lynch Dr), just n. Int corridors. **Pets:** Accepted.
🆂🅐🆂🅚 🆂🅓 ⊠ 🔒 💻

DECATUR

♦♦♦ ♦♦ Baymont Inn Decatur 🆂🅷
(217) 875-5800. **$59-$79.** 5100 Hickory Point Frontage Rd. I-72, exit 141B (US 51 N), s on frontage road. Int corridors. **Pets:** Accepted.
🆂🅐🆅🅔 🆂🅓 ⊠ ⟋ 🔒 💻

♦♦♦♦ Country Inn & Suites By Carlson 🆂🅷
(217) 872-2402. **$79.** 5150 Hickory Point Frontage Rd. I-72, exit 141B (US 51 N), s on frontage road. Int corridors. **Pets:** Accepted.
🆂🅐🆂🅚 🆂🅓 ⊠ 🔧 ⟋ 🅵 🔒 💻 ⨝ 🅧

♦♦♦♦ Holiday Inn Select Conference Hotel 🅻🅷
(217) 422-8800. **$99-$119, 3 day notice.** 4191 W Hwy 36. I-72, exit 133A (US 36), 1 mi e. Int corridors. **Pets:** Accepted.
🆂🅐🆂🅚 🆂🅓 ⊠ ⟋ 🅵 🔒 💻 🍴 ⨝ 🅧

♦♦ ♦♦ Ramada Limited Decatur 🆂🅷
(217) 876-8011. **$73-$79.** 355 E Hickory Point Rd. I-72, exit 141B (US 51 N), just n, then s via frontage road. Int corridors. **Pets:** Accepted.
🆂🅐🆂🅚 🆂🅓 ⊠ ⟋ 🅵 🔒 💻 ⨝ 🅧

♦♦♦ ♦♦ Sleep Inn of Decatur 🆂🅷
(217) 872-7700. **$64-$79, 14 day notice.** 3920 E Hospitality Ln. I-72, exit 144 (SR 48), just s to Brush College Rd, then just e. Int corridors. **Pets:** Accepted.
🆂🅐🆅🅔 🆂🅓 ⊠ ⟋ 🅵 🔒 💻 ⨝

♦♦ Super 8 Motel-Decatur 🆂🅷
(217) 877-8888. **Call for rates.** 3141 N Water St. I-72, exit 141A (US 51 S), 1.8 mi s; downtown. Int corridors. **Pets:** Accepted.
⊠ 🔒

♦♦♦ Wingate Inn 🆂🅷
(217) 875-5500. **$79.** 5170 Wingate Dr. I-72, exit 141, 0.5 mi n on US 51, then just e. Int corridors. **Pets:** Accepted.
🆂🅐🆂🅚 🆂🅓 ⊠ 🔧 ⟋ 🅵 🔒 💻 ⨝

DEKALB

♦♦ ♦♦ Baymont Inn & Suites Dekalb/Sycamore 🆂🅷
(815) 748-4800. **Call for rates.** 1314 W Lincoln Hwy. I-88, exit Annie Glidden Rd, 2 mi n to W Lincoln Hwy (SR 38), then 0.4 mi w. Int corridors. **Pets:** Other species. $20 one-time fee/room. Service with restrictions, supervision.
⊠ 🔧 ⟋ 🅵 🔒 💻 ⨝

AAA ▽▽▽ **Best Western DeKalb Inn & Suites** SH
(815) 758-8661. **$79.** 1212 W Lincoln Hwy. I-88, exit Annie Glidden Rd,
2 mi n to W Lincoln Hwy (SR 38), then just w. Ext/int corridors.
Pets: Accepted.
SAVE 🔊 ✕ 📶 🖥 🖶 🏊

DIXON

AAA ▽▽▽ **Comfort Inn** SH 🐾
(815) 284-0500. **$69-$94.** 136 Plaza Dr. I-88, exit SR 26, just n, then
just e. Int corridors. **Pets:** Medium, other species. $100 deposit/room, $15
daily fee/room. Designated rooms, service with restrictions, supervision.
SAVE 🔊 ✕ 🖥 🖶 🏊

AAA ▽▽▽ **Quality Inn & Suites** SH 🐾
(815) 288-2001. **$79-$160.** 154 Plaza Dr. I-88, exit SR 26, just n, then
just e. Int corridors. **Pets:** Medium, other species. $100 deposit/room, $15
daily fee/room. Designated rooms, service with restrictions, supervision.
SAVE 🔊 ✕ 🖥 🖶 🏊 ✕

EAST MOLINE

▽ **Super 8 Motel-East Moline** SH
(309) 796-1999. **$60-$90.** 2201 John Deere Rd. I-80, exit 4A (John
Deere Rd), 5.5 mi w on SR 5. Int corridors. **Pets:** Accepted.
ASK 🔊 ✕ 🖥

EAST PEORIA

▽▽ **Super 8 Motel** SH 🐾
(309) 698-8889. **$56-$85.** 725 Taylor St. I-74, exit 96, just e. Int corridors. **Pets:** Other species. $50 deposit/room. Designated rooms, service
with restrictions, supervision.
ASK 🔊 ✕ 🖥 🖶

EFFINGHAM

AAA ▽▽▽ **Best Western Raintree Inn** SH
(217) 342-4121. **$45-$65.** 1811 W Fayette Ave. I-57/70, exit 159, just n.
Ext/int corridors. **Pets:** Medium. Designated rooms, service with restrictions, supervision.
SAVE 🔊 ✕ 🖥 🖶 🏊

▽▽ **Comfort Inn** SH
(217) 347-5050. **$59-$89.** 1304 W Evergreen Dr. I-57/70, exit 160 (SR
32/33), just e, then just n. Int corridors. **Pets:** Accepted.
ASK 🔊 ✕ 🗚 📶 📦 🖥 🖶 🏊 ✕

▽▽▽ **Comfort Suites** SH
(217) 342-3151. **$59-$75.** 1310 W Fayette Ave. I-57/70, exit 159, 0.4 mi
e. Int corridors. **Pets:** Other species. Service with restrictions, supervision.
ASK 🔊 ✕ 🗚 📦 🖥 🖶

AAA ▽▽ **Days Inn** M
(217) 342-9271. **$61-$68, 10 day notice.** 1412 W Fayette Ave. I-57/70,
exit 159, just e. Ext corridors. **Pets:** Other species. $5 daily fee/pet.
Service with restrictions, supervision.
SAVE 🔊 ✕ 🖥 🖶 🏊

▽▽▽ **Holiday Inn Express** SH
(217) 540-1111. **Call for rates.** 1103 Ave of Mid-America. I-57/70, exit
160 (SR 32/33), just n. Int corridors. **Pets:** Other species. $10 one-time
fee/room. Designated rooms, service with restrictions, supervision.
✕ 🗚 🖥 🖶 🏊

AAA ▽ **Paradise Inn** M
(217) 342-2165. **$39-$45.** 1000 W Fayette Ave. I-57/70, exit 159, 1 mi
e. Ext corridors. **Pets:** Small. $6 daily fee/pet. Designated rooms, service
with restrictions, supervision.
SAVE ✕ 🖥

▽▽▽ **Super 8 Motel-Effingham** M
(217) 342-6888. **$60-$96.** 1400 Thelma Keller Ave. I-57/70, exit 160
(SR 32/33), 0.5 mi n. Int corridors. **Pets:** Very small, other species.
Service with restrictions, supervision.
ASK 🔊 ✕ 📶 🖥 🖶 🖥

FAIRVIEW HEIGHTS

▽▽▽ **Drury Inn & Suites Fairview Heights** SH
(618) 398-8530. **$70-$116.** 12 Ludwig Dr. I-64, exit 12 (SR 159). Int
corridors. **Pets:** Large, other species. Service with restrictions, supervision.
ASK ✕ 🖥 🖶 🏊

AAA ▽▽▽ **Ramada Inn Fairview Heights** LH
(618) 632-4747. **$82-$109.** 6900 N Illinois Ave. I-64, exit 12 (SR 159),
just n. Int corridors. **Pets:** Other species. $15 one-time fee/room. Desig-
nated rooms, service with restrictions, crate.
SAVE 🔊 ✕ 🖥 🖶 🍽 🏊

▽▽ **Super 8 Motel** SH 🐾
(618) 398-8338. **$68-$90.** 45 Ludwig Dr. I-64, exit 12 (SR 159). Int
corridors. **Pets:** Service with restrictions, supervision.
ASK 🔊 ✕ 📶 🖥

FLORA

▽▽▽ **Best Western** SH
(618) 662-3054. **$66-$86.** 201 Gary Hagen Dr. Jct US 45 and 50. Int
corridors. **Pets:** Other species. $25 deposit/room. Service with restrictions,
supervision.
ASK 🔊 ✕ 🗚 🖥 🖶

FORSYTH

▽▽ **Comfort Inn by Choice Hotels** SH
(217) 875-1166. **$59.** 134 Barnett Ave. I-72, exit 141B (US 51), 0.5 mi
n. Int corridors. **Pets:** Accepted.
ASK 🔊 ✕ 📶 🖥 🖶 🏊

FREEPORT

AAA ▽▽▽ **AmeriHost Inn & Suites-Freeport** SH
(815) 599-8510. **$75-$80, 14 day notice.** 1060 Riverside Dr. Jct US 20
Bypass and SR 26, just s. Int corridors. **Pets:** Small. $25 one-time
fee/room. Service with restrictions, supervision.
SAVE 🔊 ✕ 🖥 🖶 🏊

GALENA

AAA ▽▽▽ **Best Western Quiet House & Suites** SH
(815) 777-2577. **$65-$215.** 9915 US 20 W. 1 mi e. Ext/int corridors.
Pets: Large, other species. $15 daily fee/pet. Designated rooms, supervi-
sion.
SAVE 🔊 ✕ 🖥 🖶 🏊

AAA ▽▽▽ **Eagle Ridge Resort & Spa** LH
(815) 777-2444. **$149-$309.** 444 Eagle Ridge Dr. 6 mi e on US 20,
then 4.5 mi n. Ext/int corridors. **Pets:** Medium. $75 one-time fee/pet.
Service with restrictions, crate.
SAVE ✕ 📶 🖥 🖶 🍽 🏊 ✕

GALESBURG

AAA ▽▽▽ **Best Western Prairie Inn** SH
(309) 343-7151. **$68-$86.** 300 S Soangetaha Rd. I-74, exit 48 (Main
St), just e, then just s. Int corridors. **Pets:** Medium, other species. Designated rooms, service with restrictions, supervision.
SAVE 🔊 ✕ 📶 📦 🖥 🖶 🍽 🏊 ✕

▽▽▽ **Comfort Inn by Choice Hotels** SH
(309) 344-5445. **$60-$90.** 907 W Carl Sandburg Dr. US 34, exit US 150
E. Int corridors. **Pets:** Accepted.
ASK 🔊 ✕ 🗚 📶 🖥 🖶

▼▼ ▼▼ **Holiday Inn Express** SH
(309) 343-7100. **Call for rates.** 2285 Washington St. I-74, exit 48A (US 150), just w to Michigan Ave, just s to Washington St, then just e. Int corridors. **Pets:** Accepted.
☒ ⚙ ♿ 🛏 ▣ ≋

GILMAN

▲▲▲ ▼▼ ▼▼ **Super 8 Motel** SH 🐾
(815) 265-7000. **$63-$73.** 1301 S Crescent St. I-57, exit 283, 0.3 mi e. Int corridors. **Pets:** Small. $25 deposit/pet, $5 daily fee/pet. Service with restrictions, supervision.
SAVE 🔟 ☒ 🗍 🛏

▼▼ ▼▼ **Travel Inn** M
(815) 265-7283. **$55-$65.** 834 US 24 W. I-57, exit 283, just e. Ext/int corridors. **Pets:** $5 daily fee/room. Designated rooms, service with restrictions, supervision.
ASK ☒ ≋

GRAYVILLE

▲▲▲ ▼▼ ▼▼ **Best Western Windsor Oaks Inn** SH
(618) 375-7930. **$65-$105.** 2200 S Court St. I-64, exit 130 (SR 1), just n. Int corridors. **Pets:** Accepted.
SAVE 🔟 ☒ 🗍 🛏 ▣ ❚❚ ≋

▼▼ ▼▼ **Super 8 Motel** SH
(618) 375-7288. **$79, 14 day notice.** 2060 Co Rd. I-64, exit 130, just n. Int corridors. **Pets:** Medium. $25 one-time fee/room. Service with restrictions, supervision.
ASK 🔟 ☒ ⚙ 🗍 🛏 ▣

GREENVILLE

▲▲▲ ▼▼ ▼▼ **Best Western Country View Inn** SH
(618) 664-3030. **$45-$85.** Rt 127 & I-70. I-70, exit 45, just n. Ext/int corridors. **Pets:** Small, other species. $10 daily fee/pet. Designated rooms, service with restrictions, supervision.
SAVE 🔟 ☒ 🗍 🛏 ▣ ≋

HIGHLAND

▼▼ ▼▼ **Holiday Inn Express** SH
(618) 651-1100. **$81-$142, 3 day notice.** 20 Central Blvd. I-70, exit 24 (SR 143), 4 mi s. Int corridors. **Pets:** Accepted.
ASK 🔟 ☒ 🛏 ▣ ≋

JACKSONVILLE

▼▼ **Super 8 Motel** SH 🐾
(217) 479-0303. **$40-$70.** 1003 W Morton Ave. I-72, exit 64, 2.3 mi n on SR 267 (Main St) to SR 104 (Morton Ave), then 0.8 mi w. Int corridors. **Pets:** Medium. $10 daily fee/pet. Service with restrictions.
ASK 🔟 ☒

LINCOLN

▼▼ ▼▼ **Holiday Inn Express** SH
(217) 735-5800. **$79-$125.** 130 Olson Dr. I-55, exit 126 (US 121), just e to Heitman Dr, just w to Olson Dr, then just n. Int corridors. **Pets:** Other species. Service with restrictions, crate.
🔟 ☒ ⚙ ♿ 🛏 ▣ ≋

LITCHFIELD

▲▲▲ ▼▼ ▼▼ ▼▼ **Baymont Inn-Litchfield** SH
(217) 324-4556. **$72-$87.** 1405 W Hudson Dr. I-55, exit 52 (SR 16), just e to Ohren Ln, just s to W Hudson Dr, then just w. Int corridors. **Pets:** Small, dogs only. Designated rooms, service with restrictions, supervision.
SAVE 🔟 ☒ 🛏 ▣ ≋

▼▼▼▼ **Litchfield Comfort Inn** SH 🐾
(217) 324-9260. **$74.** 1010 E Columbian Blvd N. I-55, exit 52 (SR 16), 0.7 mi e to Old SR 66, then 0.3 mi n. Int corridors. **Pets:** Other species. $15 one-time fee/room.
ASK 🔟 ☒ 🛏 ▣ ≋

LOVES PARK

▼▼ ▼▼ **Days Inn & Suites Rockford/Loves Park** SH
(815) 282-9300. **$64-$104.** 4313 Bell School Rd. I-90, exit Riverside Blvd, just nw. Int corridors. **Pets:** Accepted.
ASK 🔟 ☒ ⚙ ♿ 🛏 ▣ ≋

MACOMB

▼▼ **Super 8 Motel** SH
(309) 836-8888. **$50-$130.** 313 University Dr. 1.1 mi n on US 67 to University Dr, 0.5 mi w. Int corridors. **Pets:** Medium. $10 daily fee/pet. Service with restrictions, supervision.
ASK 🔟 ☒ 🗍 🛏

MANTENO

▲▲▲ ▼▼▼▼ **Country Inn & Suites by Carlson** SH
(815) 468-2600. **$79-$199.** 380 S Cypress St. I-57, exit 322, just se via frontage road. Int corridors. **Pets:** Medium. $100 deposit/room, $15 daily fee/room. Designated rooms, service with restrictions, supervision.
SAVE 🔟 ☒ ⚙ ♿ 🗍 🛏 ▣ ≋

MARION

▼▼ ▼▼ ▼▼ **Drury Inn-Marion** SH
(618) 997-9600. **$63-$105.** 2706 W DeYoung St. I-57, exit 54B (SR 13), 0.5 mi w. Int corridors. **Pets:** Large, other species. Service with restrictions, supervision.
ASK ☒ ♿ 🗍 ♿ 🛏 ▣ ≋

▼▼ ▼▼ **Super 8 Motel** SH
(618) 993-5577. **$56-$88.** 2601 W DeYoung St. I-57, exit 54B (SR 13), just w. Int corridors. **Pets:** Other species. Service with restrictions, supervision.
ASK 🔟 ☒ 🗍 🛏 ▣

MATTOON

▼▼ ▼▼ **Super 8 Motel** SH
(217) 235-8888. **$49-$105.** 205 McFall Rd. I-57, exit 190B, just w. Int corridors. **Pets:** Small, dogs only. $10 one-time fee/pet. Designated rooms, service with restrictions, supervision.
ASK 🔟 ☒ 🛏

METROPOLIS

▼▼ ▼▼ ▼▼ **Holiday Inn Express** SH
(618) 524-8899. **$79-$125.** 2179 E 5th St. I-24, exit 37, just w. Int corridors. **Pets:** Accepted.
ASK 🔟 ☒ ⚙ ♿ 🛏 ▣ ≋

▼▼ ▼▼ ▼▼ **Isle of View Bed & Breakfast** BB
(618) 524-5838. **Call for rates.** 205 Metropolis St. I-24, exit 37, 3 mi w, then 0.3 mi s of US 45. Int corridors. **Pets:** Accepted.

▲▲▲ ▼▼ ▼▼ **Super 8** SH
(618) 524-8200. **$56-$77.** 2055 E 5th St. I-24, exit 37, just w. Int corridors. **Pets:** Accepted.
SAVE 🔟 ☒ 🗍 ♿ 🛏 ▣ ≋

MONTICELLO

▲▲▲ ▼▼ ▼▼ ▼▼ **Best Western Monticello Gateway Inn** SH
(217) 762-9436. **$54-$110, 3 day notice.** 805 Iron Horse Pl. I-72, exit 166, just s. Ext/int corridors. **Pets:** $10 one-time fee/pet. Designated rooms, supervision.
SAVE 🔟 ☒ 🛏 ▣ ≋

MORRIS

▼▼ Days Inn & Suites 🅂🄷
(815) 942-9000. **$60-$70.** 80 Hampton Rd. I-80, exit 112, just n. Int corridors. **Pets:** Other species. Service with restrictions.
🄰🅂🄺 🆂🄳 ✕ 🄺 🄴 🄻 ⛲

▼▼ Holiday Inn 🅂🄷
(815) 942-6600. **$90-$100.** 200 Gore Rd. I-80, exit 112, 0.3 mi nw. Int corridors. **Pets:** Accepted.
🄰🅂🄺 🆂🄳 ✕ 🄺 🄴 🄻 🍴 ⛲

MORTON

ⒶⒶⒶ ▼▼▼ Best Western Ashland House Inn & Conference Center 🅂🄷
(309) 263-5116. **$64-$84.** 201 E Ashland St. I-74, exit 102, 0.3 mi ne. Int corridors. **Pets:** Accepted.
🆂🄰🆅🄴 🆂🄳 ✕ 🄴 🄻 🍴 ⛲ 🄭

▼▼▼ Holiday Inn Express 🅂🄷
(309) 266-8310. **$59-$69.** 115 E Ashland St. I-74, exit 102B, just w. Ext/int corridors. **Pets:** Accepted.
🄰🅂🄺 🆂🄳 ✕ 🄴 🄻

MOUNT VERNON

▼▼▼ Drury Inn-Mount Vernon 🅂🄷
(618) 244-4550. **$60-$100.** 145 N 44th St. I-57/64, exit 95 (SR 15), just e, then just n; entry through restaurant parking lot. Int corridors. **Pets:** Large, other species. Service with restrictions, supervision.
🄰🅂🄺 ✕ 🄽 🄴 🄻 ⛲

ⒶⒶⒶ ▼▼▼ Holiday Inn 🄻🄷
(618) 244-7100. **$70-$95.** 222 Potomac Blvd. I-57/64, exit 95 (SR 15), just w to Potomac Blvd, then just n. Int corridors. **Pets:** Medium, other species. $10 one-time fee/pet. Designated rooms, service with restrictions, crate.
🆂🄰🆅🄴 🆂🄳 ✕ 🄶🄼 🄽 🄺 🄴 🄻 🍴 ⛲ 🄭

▼▼ Motel 6-1180 🅂🄷
(618) 244-2383. **$35-$50.** 333 S 44th St. I-57/64, exit 95 (SR 15), just e to Mateer Dr, then 0.4 mi s. Ext corridors. **Pets:** Small, other species. Service with restrictions, supervision.
🆂🄳 ✕ ⛲

▼▼ Super 8 Motel 🅂🄷 🐾
(618) 242-8800. **$59-$85.** 401 S 44th St. I-57/64, exit 95 (SR 15), just e, then just s. Int corridors. **Pets:** Other species. Service with restrictions, supervision.
🄰🅂🄺 🆂🄳 ✕ 🄴 🄻

▼▼ Thrifty Inn-Mt. Vernon 🅂🄷
(618) 244-7750. **$45-$75.** 100 N 44th St. I-57/64, exit 95 (SR 15), just e. Ext corridors. **Pets:** Large, other species. Service with restrictions, supervision.
🄰🅂🄺 ✕ 🄽

NASHVILLE

ⒶⒶⒶ ▼▼▼ Best Western U S Inn 🅂🄷
(618) 478-5341. **$69-$79.** 11640 SR 127. I-64, exit 50 (SR 127), 0.3 mi s. Int corridors. **Pets:** Small. $10 daily fee/pet. Designated rooms, service with restrictions, supervision.
🆂🄰🆅🄴 🆂🄳 ✕ 🄶🄼 🄴 🄻 ⛲

NORMAL

ⒶⒶⒶ ▼▼▼ Best Western University Inn 🅂🄷 🐾
(309) 454-4070. **$70-$85.** 6 Traders Cir. I-55, exit 165A (US 51), just s, then return on frontage road. Int corridors. **Pets:** $20 one-time fee/room. Service with restrictions, crate.
🆂🄰🆅🄴 🆂🄳 ✕ 🄽 🄴 🄻 ⛲

▼▼▼ Comfort Suites by Choice Hotels of Bloomington 🅂🄷
(309) 452-8588. **$74-$110.** 310 B Greenbriar Dr. I-55, exit 167, follow I-55 business route (Veterans Pkwy), 1.3 mi s; jct Fort Jesse Rd. Int corridors. **Pets:** Small. $20 daily fee/room. Service with restrictions, supervision.
🄰🅂🄺 🆂🄳 ✕ 🄶🄼 🄺 🄴 🄻 ⛲

ⒶⒶⒶ ▼▼▼ Holiday Inn Bloomington-Normal 🅂🄷 🐾
(309) 452-8300. **$89-$99.** 8 Traders Cir. I-55, exit 165A, 0.5 mi e, return on service road. Int corridors. **Pets:** Supervision.
🆂🄰🆅🄴 🆂🄳 ✕ 🄽 🄴 🄻 🍴 ⛲ 🄭

▼▼▼ Holiday Inn Express Hotel & Suites 🅂🄷 🐾
(309) 862-1600. **$69-$109.** 1715 Parkway Plaza Dr. I-55, exit 167, follow I-55 business route (Veterans Pkwy), 1.7 mi s to Parkway Plaza Dr, then just e. Int corridors. **Pets:** $15 deposit/room.
🄰🅂🄺 🆂🄳 ✕ 🄽 🄺 🄴 🄻 ⛲ 🄭

▼▼ Signature Inn-Normal 🅂🄷
(309) 454-4044. **$49-$104.** 101 S Veterans Pkwy. I-55, exit 167; I-55 business route (Veterans Pkwy), 1.5 mi s. Int corridors. **Pets:** Very small, other species. $10 daily fee/pet. Service with restrictions, supervision.
🄰🅂🄺 ✕ 🄽 🄴 🄻 ⛲

O'FALLON

ⒶⒶⒶ ▼▼ Comfort Inn 🅂🄷
(618) 624-6060. **$65-$129.** 1100 Eastgate Dr. I-64, exit 19B (SR 158), 0.5 mi n, then just sw. Int corridors. **Pets:** $50 deposit/pet. Service with restrictions, crate.
🆂🄰🆅🄴 🆂🄳 ✕ 🄴 🄻 ⛲

ⒶⒶⒶ ▼▼ Econo Lodge 🅂🄷
(618) 628-8895. **$64-$99.** 1409 W Hwy 50. I-64, exit 14 (US 50), 0.4 mi w. Int corridors. **Pets:** Other species. $40 deposit/room, $5 daily fee/room, $10 one-time fee/room. Designated rooms, service with restrictions, supervision.
🆂🄰🆅🄴 🆂🄳 ✕ 🄺 🄴 🄻 ⛲

ⒶⒶⒶ ▼▼▼ Howard Johnson Express Inn & Suites 🅂🄷
(618) 628-1200. **$73-$83, 3 day notice.** 116 Regency Park. I-64, exit 14 (US 50), just n. Int corridors. **Pets:** Small. $20 daily fee/pet. Designated rooms, service with restrictions, supervision.
🆂🄰🆅🄴 🆂🄳 ✕ 🄶🄼 🄴 🄻 ⛲

OGLESBY

▼▼ Holiday Inn Express 🅂🄷
(815) 883-3535. **$72-$150.** 900 Holiday St. I-39, exit 54, just e. Int corridors. **Pets:** Other species. Designated rooms, service with restrictions.
🄰🅂🄺 🆂🄳 ✕ 🄴 🄻 ⛲

OTTAWA

▼▼▼ Hampton Inn 🅂🄷
(815) 434-6040. **$84.** 4115 Holiday Ln. I-80, exit 90 (SR 23), just n. Int corridors. **Pets:** Accepted.
🄰🅂🄺 🆂🄳 ✕ 🄶🄼 🄽 🄺 🄴 🄻 ⛲ 🄭

▼▼ Holiday Inn Express 🅂🄷
(815) 433-0029. **$85-$115.** 120 W Stevenson Rd. I-80, exit 90 (SR 23), just n. Int corridors. **Pets:** Accepted.
🄰🅂🄺 🆂🄳 ✕ 🄴 🄻 ⛲

PEKIN

▼▼ Comfort Inn 🅂🄷
(309) 353-4047. **Call for rates.** 3240 Vandever Ave. Just n of SR 9; 3 mi e of jct SR 29. Int corridors. **Pets:** Accepted.
✕ 🄽 🄴 🄻 ⛲

PEORIA

▽▽ AmericInn Lodge & Suites SH
(309) 692-9200. **$90-$160.** 9106 N Lindbergh Dr. SR 6, exit 6, 0.5 mi s. Int corridors. **Pets:** Accepted.

ASK SD ☒ ⬚ ⬚ ⬚ ⬚ ⬚ ☒

▽▽ Best Western Signature Inn SH
(309) 685-2556. **$49-$104.** 4112 N Brandywine Dr. I-74, exit 89 (US 150/War Memorial Dr), just e, then just n. Int corridors. **Pets:** Very small, other species. $10 daily fee/room. Service with restrictions, supervision.

ASK ☒ ⬚ ⬚ ⬚ ⬚

▽▽ Comfort Suites by Choice Hotels SH
(309) 688-3800. **$79-$105.** 1812 W War Memorial Dr. I-74, exit 89 (US 150/War Memorial Dr), just e, then just s. Int corridors. **Pets:** Accepted.

ASK SD ☒ ⬚ ⬚ ⬚ ⬚

AAA ▽▽▽ Holiday Inn City Centre LH
(309) 674-2500. **$135-$350.** 500 Hamilton Blvd. I-74, exit 92 (Glendale Ave) eastbound, just se; exit Jefferson St westbound, just nw; downtown. Int corridors. **Pets:** Accepted.

SAVE SD ☒ ⬚ ⬚ ⬚ ⬚ ⬚ ☒

▽▽ Mark Twain Hotel SH
(309) 676-3600. **Call for rates.** 225 NE Adams St. I-74, exit 98B (Adams St) westbound, just w; exit 93 eastbound; downtown. Int corridors. **Pets:** Accepted.

☒ ⬚ ⬚ ⬚ ☒

▽▽ Red Roof Inn #7057 M
(309) 685-3911. **$45-$64.** 1822 W War Memorial Dr. I-74, exit 89 (US 150/Memorial Dr), just e. Ext corridors. **Pets:** Accepted.

☒ ⬚ ⬚ ⬚

▽▽▽ Residence Inn by Marriott SH
(309) 681-9000. **$119-$150.** 2000 N War Memorial Dr. I-74, exit 89 (US 150/War Memorial Dr), just w; entrance through Northwoods Mall. Int corridors. **Pets:** Large, other species. $75 one-time fee/room. Service with restrictions, supervision.

ASK SD ☒ ⬚ ⬚ ⬚ ⬚ ☒

▽▽▽ Staybridge Suites Peoria-Downtown SH
(309) 673-7829. **$129-$199.** 300 W Romeo B Garrett Ave. I-74, exit 92 (Glendale Ave), 0.5 mi w (Glendale Ave becomes William Kumpf St), then just w on Fourth Ave. Int corridors. **Pets:** Small, dogs only. $75 one-time fee/pet. Designated rooms, service with restrictions, crate.

ASK SD ☒ ⬚ ⬚ ⬚ ⬚ ☒

▽▽ Super 8 Motel SH
(309) 688-8074. **$62-$82.** 1816 W War Memorial Dr. I-74, exit 89 (US 150/War Memorial Dr), just e. Int corridors. **Pets:** $50 deposit/pet. Service with restrictions, supervision.

ASK SD ☒ ⬚ ⬚ ⬚

PERU

▽▽▽ La Quinta Inn Peru SH
(815) 224-9000. **$68-$125.** 4389 Venture Dr. I-80, exit 75 (SR 251), 0.4 mi s to 38th St, just w to Venture Dr, then 0.4 mi nw. Int corridors. **Pets:** Accepted.

ASK SD ☒ ⬚ ⬚ ⬚ ⬚ ☒

PONTIAC

▽▽ Comfort Inn SH
(815) 842-2777. **$74-$99, 14 day notice.** 1821 W Reynolds St. I-55, exit 197, just e. Int corridors. **Pets:** Accepted.

ASK SD ☒ ⬚ ⬚ ⬚

PONTOON BEACH

AAA ▽▽▽ Best Western Camelot Inn SH
(618) 931-2262. **$49-$75.** 1240 E Old Chain of Rocks Rd. I-270, exit 6B (SR 111), just n. Int corridors. **Pets:** Small. $10 daily fee/pet. Designated rooms, service with restrictions, supervision.

SAVE SD ☒ ⬚ ⬚ ⬚

QUAD CITIES AREA

MOLINE

▽▽ Comfort Inn by Choice Hotels SH
(309) 762-7000. **$60-$90.** 2600 52nd Ave. I-280/74, exit 18A eastbound; exit 5B westbound, just s to traffic light, then 0.5 mi w on 27th St. Int corridors. **Pets:** Accepted.

ASK SD ☒ ⬚ ⬚ ⬚

AAA ▽ Exel Inn of Moline SH
(309) 797-5580. **$43-$63.** 2501 52nd Ave. I-280/74, exit 18A eastbound; exit 5B westbound, just s on US 6 and 150, then 1 mi nw on 27th St. Int corridors. **Pets:** Small, other species. Designated rooms, service with restrictions, supervision.

SAVE SD ☒ ⬚ ⬚

AAA ▽▽▽ Holiday Inn Express-Moline Airport SH
(309) 762-8300. **$69-$109.** 6910 27th St. I-280/74, exit 18A eastbound; exit 5B westbound, just s on US 6 and 150, then just nw. Int corridors. **Pets:** Other species. $5 one-time fee/room. Service with restrictions, supervision.

SAVE SD ☒ ⬚ ⬚ ⬚

AAA ▽▽▽ Holiday Inn-Moline Convention Center Airport SH
(309) 762-8811. **$52-$129.** 6902 27th St. I-280/74, exit 18A eastbound; exit 5B westbound, just s on US 6 and 150, then just nw. Int corridors. **Pets:** Accepted.

SAVE SD ☒ ⬚ ⬚ ⬚ ⬚ ⬚ ⬚ ☒

AAA ▽▽▽ La Quinta Inn Moline SH 🐾
(309) 762-9008. **$72-$102.** 5450 27th St. I-280/74, exit 18A eastbound; exit 5B westbound, just s on US 6 and 150 to traffic light, then just nw. Int corridors. **Pets:** Other species. Service with restrictions.

SAVE ☒ ⬚ ⬚ ⬚ ⬚

END AREA

QUINCY

▽▽ Comfort Inn by Choice Hotels SH
(217) 228-2700. **$54-$94.** 4122 Broadway. I-172, exit 14 (SR 104), 1.3 mi w. Int corridors. **Pets:** Accepted.

ASK SD ☒ ⬚ ⬚ ⬚

▽▽ Super 8 Motel SH
(217) 228-8808. **$58-$85.** 224 N 36th St. I-172, exit 14 (SR 104), 1.8 mi w, then just s. Int corridors. **Pets:** Accepted.

ASK SD ☒ ⬚ ⬚

RANTOUL

Best Western Heritage Inn 🆂🅷
(217) 892-9292. **$54.** 420 S Murray Rd. I-57, exit 250 (US 136), 0.5 mi e, then just s. Ext corridors. **Pets:** Accepted.
⬛ ⬛ ⬛ ⬛ ⬛ ⬛

Super 8 Motel 🆂🅷
(217) 893-8888. **$55-$100.** 207 S Murray Rd. I-57, exit 250 (US 136), just e. Int corridors. **Pets:** Small, dogs only. $10 one-time fee/pet. Designated rooms, service with restrictions, supervision.
⬛ ⬛

ROBINSON

Best Western Robinson Inn 🆂🅷
(618) 544-8448. **$71-$110.** 1500 W Main St. 1 mi w on SR 33. Int corridors. **Pets:** Other species. $5 daily fee/room. Service with restrictions, crate.
⬛ ⬛ ⬛ ⬛ ⬛ ⬛

ROCHELLE

Comfort Inn & Suites 🆂🅷
(815) 562-5551. **$74-$84.** 1131 N 7th St. I-39, exit 99 (SR 38), 2.5 mi w; jct SR 38 and 251; downtown. Int corridors. **Pets:** Accepted.
⬛ ⬛ ⬛ ⬛ ⬛ ⬛ ⬛ ⬛

ROCK FALLS

Holiday Inn Rock Falls/Sterling 🆂🅷
(815) 626-5500. **$78-$102, 7 day notice.** 2105 First Ave. I-88, exit 41 (SR 40), 0.4 mi n. Int corridors. **Pets:** Medium, other species. $25 one-time fee/room. Designated rooms, service with restrictions, supervision.
⬛ ⬛ ⬛ ⬛ ⬛ ⬛ ⬛ ⬛

Rock Falls Super 8 🆂🅷
(815) 626-8800. **$45-$65.** 2100 First Ave. I-88, exit 41 (SR 40), 0.3 mi n, just w on W 21st St. Int corridors. **Pets:** Accepted.
⬛ ⬛ ⬛

ROCKFORD

Baymont Inn & Suites Rockford 🆂🅷 🐾
(815) 229-8200. **$49-$200.** 662 N Lyford Rd. I-90, exit US 20 business route, just e, then just n. Int corridors. **Pets:** Medium, other species. Service with restrictions, supervision.
⬛ ⬛ ⬛ ⬛ ⬛ ⬛ ⬛

Exel Inn of Rockford 🆂🅷
(815) 332-4915. **$46-$80.** 220 S Lyford Rd. I-90, exit US 20 business route, just e, then just s. Int corridors. **Pets:** Small, other species. Designated rooms, service with restrictions, supervision.
⬛ ⬛ ⬛

Quality Suites 🆂🅷 🐾
(815) 227-1300. **$85-$159.** 7401 Walton St. I-90, exit US 20 business route, just w to Bell School Rd, then just s. Int corridors. **Pets:** Medium, other species. Service with restrictions, supervision.
⬛ ⬛ ⬛ ⬛ ⬛ ⬛ ⬛ ⬛

Red Roof Inn #7035 Ⓜ
(815) 398-6100. **$49-$79.** 7434 E State St. I-90, exit US 20 business route, just w. Ext corridors. **Pets:** Accepted.
⬛ ⬛ ⬛

Residence Inn by Marriott 🆂🅷
(815) 227-0013. **$79-$159.** 7542 Colosseum Dr. I-90, exit US 20 business route, just w. Int corridors. **Pets:** Medium, other species. $75 one-time fee/room. Service with restrictions, crate.
⬛ ⬛ ⬛ ⬛ ⬛ ⬛ ⬛ ⬛ ⬛

Sleep Inn-Rockford 🆂🅷
(815) 398-8900. **$79-$279.** 725 Clark Dr. I-90, exit US 20 business route, just w to Bell School Rd, just n to Clark Dr, then 0.4 mi ne. Int corridors. **Pets:** Medium. $15 daily fee/pet. Designated rooms, service with restrictions, supervision.
⬛ ⬛ ⬛ ⬛ ⬛ ⬛

Sweden House Lodge 🆂🅷
(815) 398-4130. **$50-$75.** 4605 E State St. I-90, exit US 20 business route, 4 mi w. Ext/int corridors. **Pets:** Accepted.
⬛ ⬛ ⬛ ⬛ ⬛ ⬛

SALEM

Super 8 Motel of Salem 🆂🅷
(618) 548-5882. **$66-$87.** 118 Woods Ln. I-57, exit 116 (US 50), just w. Ext/int corridors. **Pets:** Large, other species. Service with restrictions, supervision.
⬛ ⬛ ⬛ ⬛ ⬛ ⬛ ⬛

SAVOY

Best Western Paradise Inn 🆂🅷
(217) 356-1824. **$72-$82.** 709 N Dunlap. I-57, exit 229, 1 mi e to US 45, then 2.5 mi n. Ext corridors. **Pets:** Small. $5 daily fee/pet. Service with restrictions, crate.
⬛ ⬛ ⬛ ⬛ ⬛ ⬛

SOUTH JACKSONVILLE

Comfort Inn-South Jacksonville 🆂🅷
(217) 245-8372. **$79-$100.** 200 Comfort Dr. I-72, exit 64, just n. Int corridors. **Pets:** Other species. $25 daily fee/room. Service with restrictions, supervision.
⬛ ⬛ ⬛ ⬛ ⬛

SPRINGFIELD

Baymont Inn Springfield 🆂🅷
(217) 529-6655. **$67-$69.** 5871 S 6th St. I-55, exit 90 (Toronto Rd), just e to 6th St, then just n. Int corridors. **Pets:** Small, dogs only. $25 daily fee/room. Designated rooms, service with restrictions, supervision.
⬛ ⬛ ⬛ ⬛ ⬛ ⬛ ⬛ ⬛

Comfort Inn by Choice Hotels 🆂🅷
(217) 787-2250. **$69-$90.** 3442 Freedom Dr. I-72, exit 93 (Veterans Pkwy), 0.7 mi n to Lindbergh Blvd, just w to Freedom Dr, then just s. Int corridors. **Pets:** Accepted.
⬛ ⬛ ⬛ ⬛ ⬛ ⬛ ⬛

Days Inn Ⓜ
(217) 529-0171. **$68-$70.** 3000 Stevenson Dr. I-55, exit 94 (Stevenson Dr), just w. Ext corridors. **Pets:** Accepted.
⬛ ⬛ ⬛ ⬛ ⬛

Drury Inn & Suites-Springfield 🆂🅷
(217) 529-3900. **$75-$105.** 3180 S Dirksen Pkwy. I-55, exit 94 (Stevenson Dr), just w to Dirksen Pkwy, then just n. Int corridors. **Pets:** Large, other species. Service with restrictions, supervision.
⬛ ⬛ ⬛ ⬛ ⬛ ⬛ ⬛ ⬛ ⬛

Howard Johnson Inn & Suites Ⓜ
(217) 541-8762. **$65-$95.** 1701 J David Jones Pkwy. 1.5 mi s of Capital Airport on SR 29; opposite west entrance to Lincoln's tomb. Ext corridors. **Pets:** Other species. $10 daily fee/room. Service with restrictions, crate.
⬛ ⬛ ⬛ ⬛ ⬛ ⬛ ⬛

Microtel Inn & Suites 🆂🅷
(217) 753-2636. **$64-$84, 3 day notice.** 2636 Sunrise Dr. I-55, exit 94 (Stevenson Dr), just w to Dirksen Pkwy, then 0.4 mi n. Int corridors. **Pets:** Accepted.
⬛ ⬛ ⬛ ⬛ ⬛ ⬛ ⬛ ⬛ ⬛

▼▼ Pear Tree Inn by Drury-Springfield SH
(217) 529-9100. **$60-$75.** 3190 S Dirksen Pkwy. I-55, exit 94 (Stevenson Dr), just w. Int corridors. **Pets:** Large, other species. Service with restrictions, supervision.
ASK ✕ 🐾 ▣

AAA ▼▼▼ Quality Inn & Suites-State House SH
(217) 528-5100. **$79-$129.** 101 E Adams St. Jct 1st and Adams sts; just n of the State House. Int corridors. **Pets:** Accepted.
SAVE 🐾 ✕ &M ⊘ 🐾 🖪 ▣

▼▼ Ramada Limited (South) SH
(217) 529-1410. **$65-$89.** 5970 S 6th St. I-55, exit 90 (Toronto Rd), 0.3 mi e. Int corridors. **Pets:** Medium. $10 daily fee/pet. Designated rooms, service with restrictions, supervision.
ASK 🐾 ✕ 🖪 ▣ 🏊

▼ Red Roof Inn #7040 M
(217) 753-4302. **$47-$70.** 3200 Singer Ave. I-55, exit 96B, just w. Ext corridors. **Pets:** Small. Service with restrictions, supervision.
✕ ⊘ 🐾

▼▼▼ Signature Inn & Conference Center SH
(217) 529-6611. **$49-$104.** 3090 Stevenson Dr. I-55, exit 94 (Stevenson Dr), just w. Int corridors. **Pets:** Small. $10 daily fee/room. No service, supervision.
ASK ✕ &M ⊘ 🐾 🖪 ▣ 🏊 ✕

▼▼ Sleep Inn by Choice Hotels SH
(217) 787-6200. **$60-$110.** 3470 Freedom Dr. I-72, exit 93 (Veterans Pkwy), 0.7 mi n to Lindbergh Blvd, just w to Freedom Dr, then just s. Int corridors. **Pets:** Other species. $25 one-time fee/room. Service with restrictions, crate.
ASK 🐾 ✕ ⊘ 🐾 🖪 ▣

▼▼▼ Staybridge Suites Springfield South SH
(217) 793-6700. **Call for rates.** 4231 Schooner Dr. I-72, exit 93, 0.4 mi se. Int corridors. **Pets:** Medium. $75 deposit/room, $75 one-time fee/room. Designated rooms, service with restrictions, supervision.
✕ &M ⊘ 🐾 🖪 ▣ 🏊 ✕

▼ Super 8 Springfield South SH
(217) 529-8898. **Call for rates.** 3675 S 6th St. I-55, exit 92A (Business Rt US 55), just n to Hazel Bell, just w to Access Rd, then just n. Int corridors. **Pets:** Accepted.
✕ 🖪 ▣

STAUNTON

▼▼◇ Staunton Super 8 SH
(618) 635-5353. **$52-$54.** 1527 Herman Rd. I-55, exit 41, 0.3 mi w. Int corridors. **Pets:** Medium. Service with restrictions, supervision.
ASK 🐾 ✕ ⊘ 🖪 ▣

STOCKTON

▼▼▼ Country Inn & Suites by Carlson SH
(815) 947-6060. **$79-$179.** 200 Dillon Ave. On US 20, just e of SR 78. Int corridors. **Pets:** Medium, other species. $10 daily fee/room. Designated rooms, service with restrictions, supervision.
ASK 🐾 ✕ &M 🐾 🖪 ▣ 🏊

SYCAMORE

▼▼ Microtel Inn & Suites SH
(815) 899-6500. **$59-$72.** 1860 Dekalb Ave. On SR 23, 0.9 mi s of Peace Rd. Int corridors. **Pets:** Accepted.
ASK 🐾 ✕ &M 🐾 🖪 ▣

TROY

▼▼ Red Roof Inn SH
(618) 667-2222. **Call for rates.** 2030 Formosa Rd. I-55/70, exit 18, just w. Int corridors. **Pets:** Accepted.
✕ &M ⊘ 🐾 🖪 🏊

TUSCOLA

▼▼▼ Holiday Inn Express SH
(217) 253-6363. **$67-$90.** 1201 Tuscola Blvd. I-57, exit 212 (US 36), 0.3 mi w to Progress Blvd, just s to Tuscola Blvd, then 0.4 mi se. Int corridors. **Pets:** Medium. Designated rooms, no service, supervision.
ASK 🐾 ✕ &M 🐾 🖪 ▣ 🏊

▼▼ Super 8 Motel-Tuscola SH
(217) 253-5488. **$54-$84, 10 day notice.** 1007 E Southline Rd. I-57, exit 212 (US 36), 0.4 mi w. Int corridors. **Pets:** Other species. $10 one-time fee/pet. Designated rooms, service with restrictions, supervision.
ASK 🐾 ✕ 🖪 ▣

URBANA

AAA ▼▼▼ Ramada Limited-Urbana/Champaign SH 🐾
(217) 328-4400. **$79-$92.** 902 W Killarney St. I-74, exit 183 (Lincoln Ave), just s to Killarney St, then just w. Int corridors. **Pets:** $50 deposit/room. Service with restrictions, supervision.
SAVE 🐾 ✕ 🖪 ▣ 🏊

▼▼ Sleep Inn SH 🐾
(217) 367-6000. **$72-$115.** 1908 N Lincoln Ave. I-74, exit 183 (Lincoln Ave), 0.5 mi s. Int corridors. **Pets:** Other species. $75 deposit/pet, $7 one-time fee/room. Designated rooms, service with restrictions, supervision.
ASK 🐾 ✕ 🐾 🖪 ▣ 🏊

VANDALIA

AAA ▼▼ Days Inn M
(618) 283-4400. **$68-$135.** 1920 Kennedy Blvd. I-70, exit 63 (US 51), 0.6 mi n. Ext corridors. **Pets:** Other species. $10 deposit/room. Designated rooms, service with restrictions, crate.
SAVE 🐾 ✕ 🖪 ▣ 🏊

AAA ▼▼ Jay's Inn M
(618) 283-1200. **$48-$60.** 720 Gochenour St. I-70, exit 63 (US 51), just s. Ext corridors. **Pets:** Other species. Service with restrictions.
SAVE 🐾 ✕ 🖪 ▣

AAA ▼▼▼ Ramada Limited Vandalia SH 🐾
(618) 283-1400. **$58-$62.** 2707 Veterans Ave. I-70, exit 61, just s. Int corridors. **Pets:** Other species. $10 one-time fee/pet. Designated rooms, crate.
SAVE 🐾 ✕ 🖪 ▣ 🏊

WASHINGTON

▼ Super 8 Motel SH
(309) 444-8811. **$55-$95.** 1884 Washington Rd. On Business Rt SR 24, 1.5 mi w. Int corridors. **Pets:** $8 daily fee/pet. Designated rooms, no service, supervision.
ASK 🐾 ✕ 🖪

WATSEKA

AAA ▼▼ Super 8 Motel SH 🐾
(815) 432-6000. **$63-$73.** 710 W Walnut. On US 24; center of downtown. Int corridors. **Pets:** Small. $25 deposit/pet, $5 daily fee/pet. Service with restrictions, supervision.
SAVE 🐾 ✕ 🖪

WEST CITY

▼▼ Days Inn of Benton/West City SH
(618) 439-3183. **$55-$89.** 711 W Main St. I-57, exit 71 (SR 14), just e. Int corridors. **Pets:** Small. $10 daily fee/pet. Service with restrictions, supervision.
ASK 🐾 ✕ &M 🐾 🖪 🍴

INDIANA

ANGOLA

Ramada Inn 🆂🅷
(260) 665-9471. **$85-$200, 7 day notice.** 3855 N SR 127. I-69, exit 154, just e, then 0.4 mi s. Int corridors. **Pets:** Other species. $25 one-time fee/pet. Service with restrictions, supervision.

AUBURN

Holiday Inn Express 🆂🅷
(260) 925-1900. **$90-$117.** 404 Touring Dr. I-69, exit 129, just e off SR 8. Int corridors. **Pets:** Other species. Designated rooms, service with restrictions, supervision.

La Quinta Inn Auburn 🆂🅷
(260) 920-1900. **$79-$105.** 306 Touring Dr. I-69, exit 129, 0.5 mi e on SR 8. Int corridors. **Pets:** Other species. Service with restrictions, supervision.

Super 8 Motel-Auburn 🆂🅷
(260) 927-8800. **$65-$78, 30 day notice.** 503 Ley Dr. I-69, exit 129, just e. Int corridors. **Pets:** Accepted.

BEDFORD

Bedford Super 8 🆂🅷
(812) 275-8881. **$65-$99.** 501 Bell Back Rd. Jct SR 37 and 58, just e on SR 58. Int corridors. **Pets:** Medium. $10 daily fee/pet.

BLOOMINGTON

Hampton Inn 🆂🅷
(812) 334-2100. **$94-$249, 30 day notice.** 2100 N Walnut St. 1 mi e of jct SR 37 on SR 45/46 Bypass, then just s on College Ave/Walnut St. Int corridors. **Pets:** Accepted.

TownePlace Suites By Marriott 🆂🅷
(812) 334-1234. **$69-$119.** 105 S Franklin Rd. Just e from SR 37 at 3rd St, then 0.3 mi n. Int corridors. **Pets:** Accepted.

BLUFFTON

Budget Inn Ⓜ
(260) 824-0820. **$38-$40.** 1090 N Main St. Jct SR 1 and 116; north side of town. Ext corridors. **Pets:** Accepted.

CHESTERTON

Gray Goose Inn 🅱🅱 🐾
(219) 926-5781. **$90-$185, 10 day notice.** 350 Indian Boundary Rd. I-94, exit 26A, 0.6 mi s to Indian Boundary Rd, then 0.3 mi w. Int corridors. **Pets:** Medium. Service with restrictions, supervision.

NEARBY OHIO
CINCINNATI METROPOLITAN AREA

LAWRENCEBURG

Quality Inn & Suites 🆂🅷
(812) 539-4770. **$89-$129.** 1000 E Eads Pkwy. I-275, exit 16, 0.5 mi w on US 50. Int corridors. **Pets:** Medium. $20 one-time fee/pet. Service with restrictions, crate.

END METROPOLITAN AREA

CLARKSVILLE

Best Western Green Tree Inn Ⓜ
(812) 288-9281. **$70-$90.** 1425 Broadway St. I-65, exit 4, just w. Ext corridors. **Pets:** Accepted.

CLOVERDALE

Holiday Inn Express 🆂🅷
(765) 795-5050. **$76-$85.** 1017 N Main St. I-70, exit 41, just s. Int corridors. **Pets:** $10 one-time fee/room. Crate.

Super 8 Motel Cloverdale/Greencastle SH
(765) 795-7373. **$50-$70.** 1020 N Main St. I-70, exit 41, just s. Int corridors. **Pets:** Small, dogs only. $10 daily fee/room. Service with restrictions, supervision.

COLUMBIA CITY

AmeriHost Inn & Suites SH
(260) 248-4551. **$79-$99.** 701 W Connexion Way. 1 mi w, just off US 30. Int corridors. **Pets:** $50 deposit/room. Service with restrictions, supervision.

COLUMBUS

Columbus Holiday Inn and Conference Center SH
(812) 372-1541. **$85-$129.** 2480 Jonathan Moore Pike. I-65, exit 68, just e on SR 46. Ext/int corridors. **Pets:** Accepted.

Days Inn Columbus SH
(812) 376-9951. **$64-$74.** 3445 Jonathan Moore Pike. I-65, exit 68, just w. Int corridors. **Pets:** Accepted.

Ramada Inn SH
(812) 376-3051. **$89-$109.** 2485 Jonathan Moore Pike. I-65, exit 68, just e on SR 46. Int corridors. **Pets:** Dogs only. $100 deposit/pet. Designated rooms, service with restrictions, crate.

CRAWFORDSVILLE

Comfort Inn SH
(765) 361-0665. **$79-$199.** 2991 N Gandhi Dr. I-74, exit 34, just s on US 231. Int corridors. **Pets:** $10 daily fee/room. Designated rooms, service with restrictions, supervision.

Holiday Inn-Crawfordsville SH
(765) 362-8700. **$66-$139.** 2500 N Lafayette Rd. I-74, exit 34, 0.3 mi s on US 231. Ext corridors. **Pets:** Small. $10 daily fee/pet. Designated rooms, service with restrictions, supervision.

DALE

Baymont Inn & Suites Dale SH
(812) 937-7000. **$70-$230.** 1339 N Washington St. I-64, exit 57 (US 231), just s. Int corridors. **Pets:** Medium, other species. $50 deposit/room. Designated rooms, service with restrictions, supervision.

Motel 6 #4068 SH
(812) 937-2294. **$43-$96.** 1334 N Washington St. I-64, exit 57 (US 231), just s. Int corridors. **Pets:** Medium. Service with restrictions, supervision.

DECATUR

AmeriHost Inn Decatur SH
(260) 728-4600. **$84-$89.** 1201 S 13th St. On US 27 and 33, 1 mi s of jct US 224. Int corridors. **Pets:** Accepted.

Comfort Inn of Decatur SH
(260) 724-8888. **$69-$89.** 1302 S 13th St. 1 mi s on US 27 and 33. Int corridors. **Pets:** Small, dogs only. $5 daily fee/pet. Service with restrictions, crate.

Days Inn SH
(260) 728-2196. **$49-$79.** 1033 N 13th St. On US 27 and 33, 0.5 mi n of jct US 224. Ext/int corridors. **Pets:** Small, dogs only. $5 daily fee/pet. Service with restrictions, crate.

ELKHART

Econo Lodge M
(574) 262-0540. **$35-$59, 7 day notice.** 3440 Cassopolis St. I-80/90, exit 92, 0.3 mi n. Ext corridors. **Pets:** Medium. $5 daily fee/pet. Service with restrictions, supervision.

Ramada Inn SH
(574) 262-1581. **$79-$129, 30 day notice.** 3011 Belvedere Rd. I-80/90, exit 92, 0.3 mi s on SR 19. Int corridors. **Pets:** Small. $10 one-time fee/pet. Designated rooms, service with restrictions, crate.

Red Roof Inn-Elkhart #7018 M 🐾
(574) 262-3691. **$47-$75.** 2902 Cassopolis St. I-80/90, exit 92, 0.5 mi s. Ext corridors. **Pets:** Medium, other species. Service with restrictions, supervision.

Signature Inn Elkhart SH
(574) 264-7222. **$49-$104.** 3010 Brittany Ct. I-80/90, exit 92, 0.3 mi s on SR 19. Int corridors. **Pets:** Very small, other species. $10 daily fee/room. Service with restrictions, supervision.

Super 8 Motel-Elkhart SH
(574) 264-4457. **Call for rates.** 345 Windsor Ave. I-80/90, exit 92, 0.3 mi s on SR 19. Int corridors. **Pets:** Accepted.

EVANSVILLE

Baymont Inn & Suites Evansville East SH
(812) 477-2677. **$65-$125.** 8005 E Division St. I-164, exit 7B (SR 66/Lloyd Expwy), 0.5 mi w to Cross Pointe Blvd, just n to Division St, then 0.5 mi e. Int corridors. **Pets:** Other species. $25 deposit/room. Designated rooms, service with restrictions, crate.

Baymont Inn & Suites Evansville West SH
(812) 421-9773. **$79-$99.** 5737 Pearl Dr. Jct US 41 and SR 62, 5.7 mi w on SR 62, then just s on Boehne Camp Rd. Int corridors. **Pets:** Small. $15 one-time fee/pet. Service with restrictions, supervision.

Casino Aztar Hotel LH
(812) 433-4000. **$74-$114.** 421 NW Riverside Dr. SR 62 (Lloyd Expwy), just s on Fulton. Int corridors. **Pets:** Small, dogs only. $100 deposit/pet. Service with restrictions.

Comfort Inn East SH
(812) 476-3600. **$69-$190.** 8331 E Walnut St. I-164, exit 7B (SR 66/Lloyd Expwy), 0.5 mi w to Eagle Crest Blvd, 0.3 mi se to Fuquay St, just s to Walnut St, then 0.4 mi e. Int corridors. **Pets:** Medium. $10 daily fee/room. Service with restrictions, crate.

Drury Inn & Suites Evansville East SH
(812) 471-3400. **$65-$100.** 100 Cross Pointe Blvd. I-164, exit 7B (SR 66/Lloyd Expwy), 0.5 mi w. Int corridors. **Pets:** Large, other species. Service with restrictions, supervision.

Drury Inn-Evansville North SH
(812) 423-5818. **$65-$95.** 3901 US 41 N. On US 41, 2.5 mi n of jct SR 62 and 66 (Lloyd Expwy), 3.3 mi sw of Regional Airport entrance. Int corridors. **Pets:** Large, other species. Service with restrictions, supervision.

▼▼ ◆◆ **Econo Lodge** SH
(812) 477-2211. **$55-$79.** 5006 Morgan Ave. I-164, exit 9, 1.5 mi w on SR 62. Int corridors. **Pets:** Other species. $5 one-time fee/pet. Service with restrictions, supervision.

SAVE ⊠ ⟨⟩ 🛏 ▦ 🌊

▼▼ **Evansville Microtel Inn & Suites** SH
(812) 471-9340. **$49-$109.** 1930 Cross Pointe Blvd. I-164, exit 9, just w. Int corridors. **Pets:** Accepted.

ASK 🐾 ⊠ 🛏

▼▼ **HomeLife Studios & Suites** M
(812) 475-1700. **$35-$99.** 100 S Green River Rd. I-164, exit 7B (SR 66/Lloyd Expwy), 2 mi w to Green River Rd, then just s. Ext corridors. **Pets:** Medium. $99 deposit/room. Service with restrictions, crate.

ASK 🐾 ⊠ ⟨⟩ ⟨⟩ 🛏 ▦ 🌊

▲▲ ▼▼▼ **Quality Inn & Suites East** SH
(812) 471-3414. **$70-$100.** 8015 E Division St. I-164, exit 7B (SR 66/Lloyd Expwy), 0.5 mi w to Cross Pointe Blvd, just n, then 0.5 mi e. Int corridors. **Pets:** Small. $10 one-time fee/room. No service, supervision.

SAVE 🐾 ⊠ 🔊 ⟨⟩ 🛏 ▦ 🌊

▼▼▼▼ **Residence Inn Hotel** SH
(812) 471-7191. **$105-$165.** 8283 E Walnut St. I-164, exit 7B (SR 66/Lloyd Expwy), 0.5 mi w to Eagle Crest Blvd, 0.3 mi se to Fuquay St, then 0.3 mi e. Int corridors. **Pets:** Accepted.

ASK 🐾 ⊠ 🔊 ⟨⟩ ⟨⟩ 🛏 ▦ 🌊 ⊠

▼▼ **Signature Inn Evansville** SH
(812) 476-9626. **$49-$104.** 1101 N Green River Rd. I-164, exit 9 (SR 62 E/Morgan Ave), 1.5 mi w on SR 62, then just s. Int corridors. **Pets:** Very small, other species. $10 daily fee/room. Service with restrictions, supervision.

ASK ⊠ ⟨⟩ 🛏 ▦ 🌊

▼▼ **Super 8** SH
(812) 476-4008. **$39-$47.** 4600 Morgan Ave. I-164, exit 9 (SR 62 E/Morgan Ave), 1.7 mi w on SR 62. Int corridors. **Pets:** Accepted.

ASK 🐾 ⊠ 🛏

FORT WAYNE

▲▲ ▼▼◆ **AmeriSuites (Ft Wayne)** SH
(260) 471-8522. **$69-$94.** 111 W Washington Center Rd. I-69, exit 112A, just w of Coldwater Rd. Int corridors. **Pets:** Accepted.

SAVE 🐾 ⊠ 🛏 🌊

▼▼ **Baymont Inn Fort Wayne** SH
(260) 489-2220. **$61-$71.** 1005 W Washington Center Rd. I-69, exit 111A, just w on SR 3, then just n. Int corridors. **Pets:** Accepted.

ASK 🐾 ⊠ ⟨M ⟨⟩ 🛏 ▦

▲▲ ▼▼▼ **Best Western Luxbury Inn Fort Wayne** SH
(260) 436-0242. **$76-$149.** 5501 Coventry Ln. I-69, exit 102. Int corridors. **Pets:** $10 one-time fee/room. Service with restrictions, supervision.

SAVE 🐾 ⊠ 🛏

▲▲ ▼▼▼ **Don Hall's Guesthouse** SH
(260) 489-2524. **$89.** 1313 W Washington Center Rd. I-69, exit 111B, just n on SR 3, then 0.3 mi e. Ext/int corridors. **Pets:** Medium, dogs only. Service with restrictions, supervision.

SAVE 🐾 ⊠ 🛏 ▦ 🍴 🌊 ⊠

▼▼▼ **Fort Wayne Marriott** LH
(260) 484-0411. **$179.** 305 E Washington Center Rd. I-69, exit 112A. Int corridors. **Pets:** Medium. $50 one-time fee/pet. Service with restrictions, crate.

ASK ⊠ 🔊 🛏 ▦ 🍴 🌊 ⊠

▲▲ ▼▼◆ **Quality Hotel and Fundome** SH
(260) 484-7711. **$104.** 3330 W Coliseum Blvd. I-69, exit 109A, just s to Coliseum Blvd, then 0.4 mi w. Int corridors. **Pets:** $20 one-time fee/room. Service with restrictions, crate.

SAVE 🐾 ⊠ 🔊 🛏 ▦ 🍴 🌊 ⊠

▼▼▼ **Red Roof Inn-Fort Wayne** M 🐾
(260) 484-8641. **$48-$68.** 2920 Goshen Rd. I-69, exit 109A, just e. Ext corridors. **Pets:** Medium. Service with restrictions, supervision.

⊠ ⟨⟩

▼▼▼▼ **Residence Inn by Marriott Fort Wayne** SH 🐾
(260) 484-4700. **$89-$149.** 4919 Lima Rd. I-69, exit 111A, just s on US 27. Ext corridors. **Pets:** $75 one-time fee/room.

ASK 🐾 ⊠ 🛏 ▦ 🌊 ⊠

▼▼▼ **Residence Inn Southwest** SH
(260) 432-8000. **$99-$119.** 7811 W Jefferson Blvd. I-69, exit 102, just e. Int corridors. **Pets:** Accepted.

ASK 🐾 ⊠ ⟨⟩ 🛏 ▦ 🌊 ⊠

FRANKFORT

▼▼▼ **Holiday Inn Express** SH
(765) 659-4400. **$64.** 592 S CR 200 W. I-65, exit 158, 6.1 mi e; jct US 421/SR 38/39, 1.8 mi w. Int corridors. **Pets:** Accepted.

ASK 🐾 ⊠ 🔊 ⟨⟩ 🛏 ▦ 🌊

▼▼ **Super 8 Motel** SH
(765) 654-0088. **Call for rates.** 1875 W SR 28. I-65, exit 158, 6.4 mi e; jct US 421/SR 38/39, 1.6 mi w. Int corridors. **Pets:** Accepted.

⊠ 🛏 🌊

GEORGETOWN

▼ **Motel 6–4097** SH
(812) 923-0441. **Call for rates.** 1079 N Luther Rd. I-64, exit 118, just w on SR 64. Int corridors. **Pets:** Accepted.

⊠ ⟨⟩ 🛏 🌊

GOSHEN

▲▲ ▼▼▼ **Best Western Inn** M
(574) 533-0408. **$69-$74.** 900 Lincolnway E. 1 mi se on US 33. Ext corridors. **Pets:** Service with restrictions, supervision.

SAVE 🐾 ⊠ 🛏 ▦

GREENCASTLE

▲▲ ▼ **College Inn** M
(765) 653-4167. **$45-$60.** 315 Bloomington St. I-70, exit 41, 8 mi n on US 231. Ext corridors. **Pets:** Accepted.

SAVE 🐾 ⊠ 🛏

GREENSBURG

▼▼▼▼ **Holiday Inn Express** SH
(812) 663-5500. **$79.** 915 Ann Blvd. I-74, exit 134A, 1.4 mi s on SR 3. Int corridors. **Pets:** Medium. Designated rooms, service with restrictions, crate.

ASK 🐾 ⊠ ⟨M ⟨⟩ ⟨⟩ 🛏 ▦ 🌊

HAMMOND

▼▼ **Best Western Northwest Indiana Inn** SH
(219) 844-2140. **$99-$129.** 3830 179th St. I-80/94, exit 5 (Cline Ave), 0.6 mi s to frontage road, then 0.6 mi n. Int corridors. **Pets:** Accepted.

ASK 🐾 ⊠ 🔊 🛏 ▦ 🍴 🌊

▼▼▼▼ **Residence Inn by Marriott Chicago Southeast** SH
(219) 844-8440. **$159-$219.** 7740 Corinne Dr. I-80/94, exit 3 (Kennedy Ave S), just s. Int corridors. **Pets:** Small. $75 one-time fee/room. Service with restrictions, crate.

ASK ⊠ ⟨M ⟨⟩ 🛏 ▦ 🌊 ⊠

HAUBSTADT

▼▼▼ **Holiday Inn Express** SH
(812) 867-1100. **$72-$104.** 19600 Elpers Rd. I-64, exit 25A (US 41), 0.5 mi s. Int corridors. **Pets:** Accepted.

ASK 🐾 ⊠ ⟨M ⟨⟩ 🛏 ▦ 🌊

AAA ▼▼▼▼ **Quality Inn Evansville North** SH
(812) 768-5878. **$69-$99.** RR 1, Box 252 (Hwy 41 & I-64). I-64, exit 25B, 0.4 mi n on US 41 to Warrenton Rd, just w to frontage road, then 0.3 mi s. Int corridors. **Pets:** $15 one-time fee/pet. Service with restrictions, crate.

[SAVE] [S6] [X] [&] [▤] [▦] [⇒]

HOWE

AAA ▼▼▼ **Super 8 Motel** SH
(260) 562-2828. **$64-$99.** 7333 N SR 9. I-80/90, exit 121 (US 266), 0.5 mi s. Int corridors. **Pets:** Other species. Service with restrictions, supervision.

[SAVE] [S6] [X] [&M] [⊘] [&] [▤]

HUNTINGBURG

AAA ▼▼▼ **Quality Inn** SH
(812) 683-2334. **$59-$119.** 406 E 22nd St. I-64, exit 57, 9 mi n on US 231, then just w. Ext corridors. **Pets:** Small. $40 deposit/room, $10 daily fee/pet. Service with restrictions, supervision.

[SAVE] [S6] [X] [▤] [▦] [⊞] [⇒]

HUNTINGTON

AAA ▼▼▼ **AmeriHost Inn & Suites Huntington** SH
(260) 359-9000. **$59-$145.** 2820 Hotel Ave. 0.6 mi nw of jct US 24/224 and SR 5. Int corridors. **Pets:** Accepted.

[SAVE] [S6] [X] [⊘] [&] [▤] [▦] [⇒]

INDIANAPOLIS METROPOLITAN AREA

ANDERSON

▼▼▼▼ **Hampton Inn** SH
(765) 622-0700. **$89-$94.** 2312 Hampton Dr. I-69, exit 26, just e. Int corridors. **Pets:** Accepted.

[ASK] [S6] [X] [&M] [&] [▤] [▦] [⇒]

▼▼▼ **Super 8 Motel** SH
(765) 642-2222. **$58-$68.** 2215 E 59th St. I-69, exit 26, just w. Int corridors. **Pets:** Accepted.

[ASK] [S6] [X] [▤] [▦] [⇒]

CARMEL

▼▼▼▼ **Residence Inn by Marriott Indianapolis/Carmel** SH
(317) 846-2000. **$109-$199.** 11895 N Meridian St. I-465, exit 31, 2 mi n on US 31, just e on 116th St, then just n on Pennsylvania Rd. Int corridors. **Pets:** Accepted.

[ASK] [S6] [X] [&] [▤] [▦] [⇒] [X]

▼▼▼ **Signature Inn Carmel** SH
(317) 816-1616. **$49-$104.** 10201 N Meridian St. I-465, exit 31, 0.3 mi n on US 31. Int corridors. **Pets:** Very small, other species. $10 daily fee/room. Service with restrictions, supervision.

[ASK] [X] [⊘] [▤] [▦] [⇒] [X]

CHESTERFIELD

▼▼▼ **Super 8 Motel** SH
(765) 378-0888. **$47-$57.** 15701 W Commerce Rd. I-69, exit 34, just w. Ext/int corridors. **Pets:** $25 deposit/room, $5 one-time fee/room. Service with restrictions, supervision.

[ASK] [S6] [X] [▤]

EDINBURGH

AAA ▼▼▼ **Best Western Horizon Inn** SH
(812) 526-9883. **$55-$149.** 11780 N US 31. I-65, exit 76B, just n. Int corridors. **Pets:** Medium, dogs only. $20 one-time fee/room. Service with restrictions, supervision.

[SAVE] [S6] [X] [▤] [▦] [⇒]

FISHERS

AAA ▼▼▼▼ **Comfort Suites** SH 🐾
(317) 578-1200. **$74-$119, 30 day notice.** 9760 Crosspoint Blvd. I-69, exit 3, just w on 96th St, then just n. Int corridors. **Pets:** Other species. $10 daily fee/room. Service with restrictions.

[SAVE] [S6] [X] [&] [▤] [▦] [⇒]

▼▼▼▼ **Frederick-Talbott Inn** BB
(317) 578-3600. **$99-$179, 7 day notice.** 13805 Allisonville Rd. I-465, exit 35 (Allisonville Rd), 6.2 mi n; I-69, exit 5, 1.8 mi w on 116th St to Allisonville Rd, then 2.2 mi n. Int corridors. **Pets:** Accepted.

[ASK] [S6] [X]

▼▼ **Ramada Inn Indianapolis Northeast** SH
(317) 558-4100. **$84-$200.** 9791 North by Northeast Blvd. I-69, exit 3, just ne. Int corridors. **Pets:** Accepted.

[ASK] [S6] [X] [&] [▤] [▦] [⇒]

▼▼▼▼ **Residence Inn by Marriott Indianapolis/Fishers** SH 🐾
(317) 842-1111. **$89-$189.** 9765 Crosspoint Blvd. I-69, exit 3, just nw. Int corridors. **Pets:** Medium, other species. $75 one-time fee/room. Service with restrictions.

[ASK] [S6] [X] [&M] [⊘] [&] [▤] [▦] [⇒] [X]

▼▼▼▼ **Staybridge Suites Indianapolis-Fishers** SH
(317) 577-9500. **$109-$169.** 9780 Crosspoint Blvd. I-69, exit 3, just nw. Int corridors. **Pets:** Accepted.

[ASK] [S6] [X] [&M] [⊘] [&] [▤] [▦] [⇒] [X]

GREENWOOD

▼▼▼▼ **Lees Inn & Suites** SH
(317) 865-0100. **Call for rates.** 1281 S Park Dr. I-65, exit 99. Int corridors. **Pets:** Accepted.

[X] [&M] [⊘] [&] [▤] [▦] [⇒]

▼▼▼ **Red Roof Inn** M
(317) 887-1515. **$54-$135.** 110 Sheek Rd. I-65, exit 99. Ext corridors. **Pets:** Medium. Service with restrictions, crate.

[ASK] [S6] [X] [▤] [▦] [⇒]

INDIANAPOLIS

AAA ▼▼▼▼ **AmeriSuites (Indianapolis/Airport-Speedway)** SH
(317) 227-0950. **$79-$119.** 5500 Bradbury Ave. I-465, exit 11A, 0.3 mi e on Airport Expwy to Executive Dr exit. Int corridors. **Pets:** Medium. $10 one-time fee/pet. Designated rooms, service with restrictions, supervision.

[SAVE] [S6] [X] [&M] [▤] [▦] [⇒]

AAA ▼▼▼▼ **AmeriSuites (Indianapolis/Keystone)** SH
(317) 843-0064. **$109.** 9104 Keystone Crossing. I-465, exit 33, 0.5 mi s on SR 431, just e on 86th St, then 0.5 mi n. Int corridors. **Pets:** Accepted.

[SAVE] [S6] [X] [⊘] [&] [▤] [▦] [⇒]

AAA ▼▼▼ **Baymont Inn & Suites Indianapolis-Airport** SH
(317) 244-8100. **$79-$99.** 2650 Executive Dr. I-465, exit 11, 0.3 mi e, exit Executive Dr. Int corridors. **Pets:** Accepted.

[SAVE] [S6] [X] [⊘] [&] [▤] [▦] [⇒]

AAA ▼▼▼ **Baymont Inn & Suites Indianapolis East** SH
(317) 897-2300. **$79-$99.** 2349 Post Dr. I-70, exit 91 (Post Rd), just n. Int corridors. **Pets:** Accepted.

[SAVE] [S6] [X] [&M] [⊘] [&] [▤] [▦]

▼▼▼ **Comfort Inn & Suites City Centre** SH
(317) 631-9000. **$129-$250.** 530 S Capitol Ave. Just s of South St. Int corridors. **Pets:** Accepted.
[ASK] [S$] [X] [&M] [🖉] [&] [🛏] [💻] [➔] [⊠]

▼▼▼ **Drury Inn-Indianapolis** SH
(317) 876-9777. **$69-$99.** 9320 N Michigan Rd. I-465, exit 27, just s. Int corridors. **Pets:** Large, other species. Service with restrictions, supervision.
[ASK] [X] [🖉] [🛏] [💻] [➔]

◆◆◆ ▼▼▼ **Four Points by Sheraton Indianapolis East** SH
(317) 897-4000. **$69-$119.** 7701 E 42nd St. I-465, exit 42 (Pendleton Pike), just e. Int corridors. **Pets:** Small, other species. $20 one-time fee/room. Designated rooms, service with restrictions, supervision.
[SAVE] [S$] [X] [&] [🛏] [💻] [¶¶] [➔]

▼▼▼ **Hawthorn Suites East** SH
(317) 322-0011. **$89-$109.** 7035 Western Select Dr. I-70, exit 89, 0.5 mi w of jct I-465. Int corridors. **Pets:** Accepted.
[ASK] [S$] [X] [&] [🛏] [💻] [➔]

◆◆◆ ▼▼▼ **Hilton Indianapolis North Hotel** LH
(317) 849-6668. **$99-$259.** 8181 N Shadeland Ave. I-69, exit 1, just e. Int corridors. **Pets:** Medium, dogs only. $25 one-time fee/room. Service with restrictions.
[SAVE] [X] [🖉] [&] [🛏] [💻] [¶¶] [➔]

▼▼▼ **Holiday Inn East** SH
(317) 359-5341. **$99-$129.** 6990 E 21st St. I-70, exit 89, 0.5 mi w of jct I-465. Int corridors. **Pets:** Accepted.
[ASK] [S$] [X] [🖉] [💻] [¶¶] [➔] [⊠]

▼▼ **Holiday Inn-Southeast** SH
(317) 783-7751. **$76-$96.** 5120 Victory Dr. I-465, exit 52 (Emerson Ave), just s. Int corridors. **Pets:** Accepted.
[ASK] [S$] [X] [&] [🛏] [💻] [¶¶] [➔]

▼▼ **Homestead Studio Suites Hotel-Indianapolis/Northwest** SH
(317) 334-7829. **$81-$96.** 8520 Northwest Blvd. I-465, exit 23, just e. Int corridors. **Pets:** Accepted.
[ASK] [S$] [X] [&M] [🖉] [&] [🛏] [💻] [➔]

▼▼▼ **Indianapolis Marriott East** LH
(317) 352-1231. **$89-$139.** 7202 E 21st St. I-70, exit 89, 0.3 mi se; 0.5 mi w of jct I-465. Int corridors. **Pets:** Accepted.
[ASK] [S$] [X] [🖉] [🛏] [💻] [¶¶] [➔] [⊠]

◆◆◆ ▼▼ **La Quinta Inn Indianapolis (Airport)** SH
(317) 247-4281. **$89-$129.** 5316 W Southern Ave. I-465, exit 11A, 0.5 mi e on Airport Expwy to Lynhurst Dr. Int corridors. **Pets:** Small. Service with restrictions, crate.
[SAVE] [X] [🖉] [🛏] [💻] [➔]

▼▼ **La Quinta Inn Indianapolis (East)** SH
(317) 359-1021. **$59-$99.** 7304 E 21st St. I-70, exit 89, just s, then just e; 0.5 mi w of jct I-465. Int corridors. **Pets:** Accepted.
[ASK] [S$] [X] [🖉] [➔]

▼▼ **Microtel Inn & Suites** SH
(317) 870-7765. **$45-$170.** 9140 N Michigan Rd. I-465, exit 27, just s. Int corridors. **Pets:** Accepted.
[ASK] [S$] [X] [🛏] [💻]

◆◆◆ ▼▼ ▼▼ **Omni Severin Hotel** LH
(317) 634-6664. **$139-$219.** 40 W Jackson Pl. Opposite Union Station. Int corridors. **Pets:** Small. $50 one-time fee/room. Service with restrictions, crate.
[SAVE] [S$] [X] [🖉] [&] [🛏] [💻] [¶¶] [➔]

▼▼ ▼▼ **Quality Inn & Suites Airport** SH
(317) 381-1000. **$79-$199.** 2631 S Lynhurst Dr. I-465, exit 11A, 0.5 mi e on Airport Expwy to Lynhurst Dr. Int corridors. **Pets:** Medium, other species. $10 daily fee/pet. Designated rooms, service with restrictions, supervision.
[ASK] [S$] [X] [&] [🛏] [💻] [➔]

▼▼ **Quality Inn South** SH
(317) 788-0811. **$59-$119, 14 day notice.** 450 Bixler Rd. I-465, exit 2B, just s. Int corridors. **Pets:** Accepted.
[ASK] [S$] [X] [🛏] [💻] [➔]

▼ **Red Roof Inn-South #7013** M
(317) 788-9551. **$47-$63.** 5221 Victory Dr. I-465/74, exit 52 (Emerson Ave), just s. Ext corridors. **Pets:** Accepted.
[X] [🖉] [🛏]

▼ **Red Roof Inn-Speedway #7074** M
(317) 293-6881. **$46-$62.** 6415 Debonair Ln. I-465, exit 16A, just se. Ext corridors. **Pets:** Accepted.
[X] [🖉] [&]

▼▼▼ **Residence Inn by Marriott Indianapolis Airport** SH 🐾
(317) 244-1500. **$149-$199.** 5224 W Southern Ave. I-465, exit 11A, 0.5 mi e on Airport Expwy to Lynhurst Dr. Int corridors. **Pets:** Other species. $75 one-time fee/room. Service with restrictions, supervision.
[ASK] [S$] [X] [🖉] [&] [🛏] [💻] [➔] [⊠]

▼▼▼ **Residence Inn by Marriott Indianapolis Downtown on the Canal** SH
(317) 822-0840. **$149-$399.** 350 W New York St. At New York St and Senate Ave. Int corridors. **Pets:** Accepted.
[S$] [X] [&M] [🖉] [&] [🛏] [💻] [➔] [⊠]

▼▼▼ **Sheraton Indianapolis Hotel & Suites** LH
(317) 846-2700. **$249-$289.** 8787 Keystone Crossing. I-465, exit 33, jct SR 431. Int corridors. **Pets:** Accepted.
[ASK] [S$] [X] [&M] [🖉] [&] [🛏] [💻] [¶¶] [➔] [⊠]

▼▼ **Signature Inn-Indianapolis East** SH
(317) 353-6966. **$49-$104.** 7610 Old Trails Rd. I-465, exit 46, just sw. Int corridors. **Pets:** Very small, other species. $10 daily fee/room. Service with restrictions, supervision.
[ASK] [X] [🖉] [🛏] [💻] [➔]

▼▼ **Signature Inn-South** SH
(317) 784-7006. **$49-$104.** 4402 E Creekview Dr. I-65, exit 103, just w. Int corridors. **Pets:** Very small, other species. $10 daily fee/room. Service with restrictions, supervision.
[ASK] [X] [🖉] [🛏] [💻] [➔]

▼▼ **Super 8 Indianapolis-Northeast** SH
(317) 841-8585. **$55-$59.** 7202 E 82nd St. I-69, exit 1, 0.3 mi e to Clear Vista, just n, then just w on Clear Vista Ln. Ext corridors. **Pets:** Small, dogs only. $10 daily fee/room, $25 one-time fee/room. Service with restrictions, supervision.
[ASK] [S$] [X] [&] [🛏] [💻] [➔]

◆◆◆ ▼▼ **Wellesley Inn & Suites (Indianapolis/Airport)** SH
(317) 241-0700. **$79-$99.** 5350 W Southern Ave. I-465, exit 11A, just e to Lynhurst Dr, just s, then just w. Int corridors. **Pets:** Small. $25 one-time fee/room. Service with restrictions, supervision.
[SAVE] [X] [🖉] [&] [🛏] [💻] [➔]

◆◆◆ ▼▼ ▼▼ **The Westin Indianapolis** LH 🐾
(317) 262-8100. **$159-$339.** 50 S Capitol Ave. At Washington and Maryland sts and Capitol Ave. Int corridors. **Pets:** Small, dogs only. Supervision.
[SAVE] [S$] [X] [🖉] [&] [💻] [¶¶] [➔]

LEBANON

△△△ ▼▼▼▼ Comfort Inn SH
(765) 482-4800. **$79-$100, 7 day notice.** 210 N Sam Ralston Rd. I-65,
exit 140. Int corridors. **Pets:** Other species. $10 daily fee/pet. Service with
restrictions, supervision.
[SAVE] 🔊 ⊗ 📶 🖵 ⇌

▼▼ Super 8 Motel SH
(765) 482-9999. **$56-$149.** 405 N Mount Zion Rd. I-65, exit 140, just w.
Int corridors. **Pets:** Accepted.
[ASK] 🔊 ⊗ 📶 ⇌

NOBLESVILLE

▼▼▼ Quality Inn & Suites SH
(317) 770-6772. **$59-$159.** 16025 Prosperity Dr. 1.7 mi s of jct SR 32,
37 and 38. Int corridors. **Pets:** Accepted.
⊗ 📶 ⇌

PLAINFIELD

▼▼▼▼ Lees Inn & Suites SH
(317) 837-9000. **Call for rates.** 6010 Gateway Dr. I-70, exit 66, just n.
Int corridors. **Pets:** Accepted.
⊗ 🗝 📶 🖵 ⇌

END METROPOLITAN AREA

JASPER

▼▼ Days Inn Jasper SH
(812) 482-6000. **$45-$84.** 272 Brucke Strasse. On SR 162 and 164,
0.5 mi e of jct US 231. Ext/int corridors. **Pets:** Other species. $10 daily
fee/pet. Service with restrictions, crate.
[ASK] 🔊 ⊗ 🗝 📶 🖵 🍽 ⇌ 🗙

JEFFERSONVILLE

▼▼▼▼ TownePlace Suites by Marriott SH
(812) 280-8200. **$75-$89.** 703 N Shore Dr. I-65, exit 0, just w. Int
corridors. **Pets:** Accepted.
[ASK] 🔊 ⊗ 🗝 📶 🖵 ⇌

KENDALLVILLE

△△△ ▼▼▼ Best Western Kendallville Inn SH
(260) 347-5263. **$69-$129.** 621 Professional Way. 1 mi e on US 6. Int
corridors. **Pets:** Accepted.
[SAVE] 🔊 ⊗ 📶 🖵 ⇌ 🗙

KOKOMO

▼▼▼ Comfort Inn by Choice Hotels SH 🐾
(765) 452-5050. **$65-$85.** 522 Essex Dr. US 31, just n of jct US 35. Int
corridors. **Pets:** Small, other species. Designated rooms, service with
restrictions, crate.
[ASK] 🔊 ⊗ 🗝 📶 🖵 ⇌

▼▼ Days Inn & Suites M
(765) 453-7100. **$57-$87.** 264 S 00 EW. US 31, 2.8 mi s of jct US 35.
Ext corridors. **Pets:** Medium. $7 daily fee/room. Service with restrictions,
supervision.
[ASK] 🔊 ⊗ 📶 🖵 🍽 ⇌

▼▼▼▼ Hampton Inn & Suites SH
(765) 455-2900. **$79-$99.** 2920 S Reed Rd (US Hwy 31). US 31, 2 mi
s of jct US 35. Int corridors. **Pets:** Other species. Designated rooms,
service with restrictions, crate.
[ASK] 🔊 ⊗ 🗝 🗝 🗝 📶 🖵 ⇌ 🗙

▼▼ Super 8 Motel SH
(765) 455-3288. **$54-$81.** 5110 Clinton Dr. US 31, 2.8 mi s of jct US 35.
Int corridors. **Pets:** Accepted.
[ASK] 🔊 ⊗ 🗝 📶 ⇌

LAFAYETTE

**△△△ ▼▼▼ Best Western Lafayette Executive Plaza &
       Conference Center** SH
(765) 447-0575. **$84-$199.** 4343 SR 26 E. I-65, exit 172, just n. Int
corridors. **Pets:** Very small. $15 daily fee/room. Designated rooms, service
with restrictions, supervision.
[SAVE] 🔊 ⊗ 🗝 🗝 📶 🖵 🍽 ⇌ 🗙

△△△ ▼▼▼▼ Comfort Suites-Lafayette SH
(765) 447-0016. **$79-$200, 3 day notice.** 31 Frontage Rd. I-65, exit
172, just e. Int corridors. **Pets:** Other species. $10 one-time fee/pet.
Service with restrictions, supervision.
[SAVE] 🔊 ⊗ 🗝 🗝 🗝 📶 🖵 ⇌ 🗙

▼▼ Days Inn & Suites SH
(765) 446-8558. **$69-$99.** 151 Frontage Rd. I-65, exit 172, just e. Int
corridors. **Pets:** Accepted.
[ASK] 🔊 ⊗ 📶 🖵

△△△ ▼▼▼▼ Holiday Inn Express SH
(765) 449-4808. **$89-$200.** 201 Frontage Rd. I-65, exit 172, just e on
SR 26, then just n. Int corridors. **Pets:** Small. Service with restrictions,
supervision.
[SAVE] 🔊 ⊗ 🗝 📶 🖵

▼▼▼▼ Homewood Suites by Hilton SH
(765) 448-9700. **$124-$189.** 3939 SR 26 E. I-65, exit 172, 0.8 mi w.
Ext/int corridors. **Pets:** Medium, other species. $10 daily fee/pet, $50
one-time fee/pet. Service with restrictions, crate.
⊗ 🗝 📶 🖵 ⇌ 🗙

△△△ ▼▼ Lafayette Inn M
(765) 447-7566. **$45-$115.** 139 Frontage Rd. I-65, exit 172. Ext corridors. **Pets:** Large, other species. Service with restrictions, supervision.
[SAVE] 🔊 🗙

▼▼▼▼ Lees Inn & Suites SH
(765) 447-3434. **Call for rates.** 4701 Meijer Ct. I-65, exit 172, just e on
SR 26. Int corridors. **Pets:** Other species. Designated rooms, service with
restrictions, supervision.
⊗ 🗝 🗝 📶 🖵 ⇌

▼▼▼▼ Loeb House Inn BB
(765) 420-7737. **$95-$175, 14 day notice.** 708 Cincinnati St. SR 38,
0.4 mi n on 9th St, then just w. Int corridors. **Pets:** Accepted.
[ASK] 🔊 🗙

▼▼ Red Roof Inn-Lafayette #7062 M
(765) 448-4671. **$46-$62.** 4201 SR 26 E. I-65, exit 172, 0.3 mi w. Ext
corridors. **Pets:** Accepted.
⊗ 🗝

▼▼ Signature Inn Lafayette SH
(765) 447-4142. **$49-$104.** 4320 SR 26 E. I-65, exit 172. Int corridors.
Pets: Very small, other species. $10 daily fee/room. Service with restric-
tions, supervision.
[ASK] ⊗ 🗝 📶 🖵 ⇌

▼▼▼▼ TownePlace Suites by Marriott SH
(765) 446-8668. **$79-$259.** 163 Frontage Rd. I-65, exit 172, just e. Int
corridors. **Pets:** Accepted.
[ASK] 🔊 ⊗ 📶 🖵 ⇌

LOGANSPORT

▼▼ ▼▼ Holiday Inn SH
(574) 753-6351. **$90-$94.** 3550 E Market St. 1.5 mi e on Business Rt US 24. Int corridors. **Pets:** Medium. Designated rooms, service with restrictions, supervision.
ASK 🛇 ✕ 🔥M 🐾 🛢 🖵 🍽 ⇀

MADISON

▲▲ ▼▼▼▼ Super 8 Motel SH
(812) 273-4443. **$80.** 3767 Clifty Dr. Jct SR 56/62/256. Int corridors. **Pets:** Medium. $10 daily fee/pet. Designated rooms, service with restrictions, supervision.
SAVE 🛇 ✕ 🐾 🛢 🖵 ⇀

MARION

▲▲ ▼▼▼▼ Comfort Suites-Marion SH
(765) 651-1006. **$79-$125.** 1345 N Baldwin Ave. 1.5 mi n of jct SR 9 and 18. Int corridors. **Pets:** Other species. $10 one-time fee/room. Designated rooms, service with restrictions, crate.
SAVE 🛇 ✕ 🔁 🐾 🛢 🖵 ⇀ 🚫

▲▲ ▼▼▼▼ Country Inn & Suites SH
(765) 664-5840. **$89.** 6138 E Corridor Dr. I-69, exit 64, just w. Int corridors. **Pets:** Medium. $15 one-time fee/pet. Designated rooms, service with restrictions.
SAVE 🛇 ✕ 🔥M 🛢 🖵 ⇀

MARKLE

▼▼ ▼▼ Super 8 Motel Fort Wayne South/Markle SH 🐾
(260) 758-8888. **$56.** 610 Annette Dr. I-69, exit 86, just e. Int corridors. **Pets:** Medium. $7 daily fee/pet. No service, supervision.
ASK 🛇 ✕ 🛢 🖵

MERRILLVILLE

▲▲ ▼▼▼▼ La Quinta Inn Merrillville SH
(219) 738-2870. **$71-$95.** 8210 Louisiana St. I-65, exit 253A (US 30), 0.3 mi se. Int corridors. **Pets:** Medium, other species. Designated rooms, service with restrictions, crate.
SAVE ✕ 🔁 🛢 🖵 ⇌

▼▼▼▼ Residence Inn by Marriott Merrillville SH 🐾
(219) 791-9000. **$149-$159.** 8018 Delaware Pl. I-65, exit 253B (US 30), 0.3 mi nw. Int corridors. **Pets:** $75 one-time fee/room. Service with restrictions, crate.
ASK 🛇 ✕ 🔥M 🔁 🐾 🛢 🖵 ⇀ 🚫

▲▲ ▼▼▼▼ Super 8 Motel SH
(219) 736-8383. **$44-$65, 7 day notice.** 8300 Louisiana St. I-65, exit 253A (US 30), 0.5 mi se. Int corridors. **Pets:** Medium. Service with restrictions, supervision.
SAVE 🛇 ✕ 🔥M 🔁 🛢

MICHIGAN CITY

▼▼ ▼▼ Red Roof Inn-Michigan City #7007 M
(219) 874-5251. **$49-$86.** 110 W Kieffer Rd. I-94, exit 34B, 0.3 mi n on US 421. Ext corridors. **Pets:** Accepted.
✕ 🐾 🛢

MONTGOMERY

▲▲ ▼▼▼▼ Gasthof Village Inn SH
(812) 486-2600. **$59-$99, 3 day notice.** CR 650 E. US 50, 1 mi n on First St. Int corridors. **Pets:** Accepted.
SAVE ✕ 🔁 🐾 🛢 🖵 🍽 ⇀ 🚫

MONTICELLO

▲▲ ▼▼▼▼ Best Western Brandywine Inn & Suites SH
(574) 583-6333. **$75-$210.** 728 S 6th St. SR 24, just s. Int corridors. **Pets:** Other species. $10 daily fee/room. Service with restrictions, crate.
SAVE 🛇 ✕ 🔥M 🛢 🖵 ⇀ 🚫

MOUNT VERNON

▼▼ ▼▼ Four Seasons Motel M
(812) 838-4821. **$85.** 70 Hwy 62 W. 1.8 mi w of jct SR 69 N. Ext corridors. **Pets:** Accepted.
ASK ✕ 🛢 🖵 ⇀

▼▼ ▼▼ Super 8 Motel SH
(812) 838-8888. **$49-$60, 5 day notice.** 6225 Hwy 69 S. On SR 69 Bypass, just n of SR 62. Int corridors. **Pets:** Other species. $6 daily fee/pet. Service with restrictions, supervision.
ASK 🛇 ✕ 🛢 🖵 ⇀

MUNCIE

▼▼ ▼▼ Muncie Days Inn SH
(765) 288-2311. **$48-$78.** 3509 N Everbrook Ln. I-69, exit 41, 6.3 mi e on SR 332, then just n. Int corridors. **Pets:** Dogs only. $10 one-time fee/room. Service with restrictions, supervision.
ASK 🛇 ✕ 🛢 🖵

▼▼▼▼ The Roberts Hotel LH
(765) 741-7777. **$89-$325.** 420 S High St. Opposite Horizon Convention Center. Int corridors. **Pets:** Accepted.
ASK 🛇 ✕ 🛢 🍽 ⇀

▼▼▼▼ Signature Inn-Muncie SH
(765) 284-4200. **$49-$104.** 3400 N Chadam Ln. I-69, exit 41, 6.3 mi e on SR 332. Int corridors. **Pets:** Very small, other species. $10 daily fee/room. Service with restrictions, supervision.
ASK ✕ 🔁 🛢 🖵 ⇀

▼▼ ▼▼ Super 8 Motel SH
(765) 286-4333. **$49-$55.** 3601 W Fox Ridge Ln. I-69, exit 41, 6.3 mi e on SR 332. Int corridors. **Pets:** Accepted.
ASK 🛇 ✕ 🛢

NEW ALBANY

▲▲ ▼▼▼▼ Holiday Inn Express SH
(812) 945-2771. **$75-$129.** 411 W Spring St. I-64, exit 123. Int corridors. **Pets:** Medium. $10 daily fee/pet. Designated rooms, service with restrictions, supervision.
SAVE 🛇 ✕ 🐾 🛢 🖵 ⇀

NEW CASTLE

▲▲ ▼▼ ▼▼ Best Western Raintree Inn SH
(765) 521-0100. **$78, 10 day notice.** 2836 S SR 3. I-70, exit 123, 2.5 mi n. Ext/int corridors. **Pets:** Other species. $20 one-time fee/pet. Service with restrictions, crate.
SAVE 🛇 ✕ 🐾 🛢 🖵 🍽 ⇀ 🚫

NORTH VERNON

▼▼ ▼▼ Comfort Inn SH
(812) 352-9999. **$79-$109.** 150 FDR Dr. Jct US 50, 0.6 mi n on SR 7. Int corridors. **Pets:** Small. $20 deposit/pet. Service with restrictions, crate.
ASK 🛇 ✕ 🐾 🛢 🖵 ⇀

PERU

▼▼▼▼ Best Western Circus City Inn SH
(765) 473-8800. **$79-$160.** 2642 Business 31 S. Just e of jct US 31. Int corridors. **Pets:** Accepted.
ASK 🛇 ✕ 🔁 🐾 🛢 🖵 ⇀

PLYMOUTH

WW Super 8 Motel SH
(574) 936-8856. **$55-$130.** 2160 N Oak Rd. US 30, just s. Int corridors. **Pets:** Accepted.
A$K S6 X 8 ⌨ ⇌

PORTLAND

WW Hoosier Inn M
(260) 726-7113. **$45-$60.** 1620 Meridian St. 1.4 mi n on US 27. Ext corridors. **Pets:** Dogs only. $5 daily fee/pet. Service with restrictions, supervision.
A$K S6 X 8 ⌨

REMINGTON

WW Super 8 Motel-Remington SH
(219) 261-2883. **$75-$85.** 4278 W US 24. I-65, exit 201, 0.5 mi w. Int corridors. **Pets:** Small, dogs only. $10 daily fee/pet. Designated rooms, service with restrictions, supervision.
A$K S6 X ☾ 8 ⇌

RENSSELAER

AAA WWWW Holiday Inn Express SH
(219) 866-7111. **$82-$102, 7 day notice.** 4788 Nesbitt Dr. I-65, exit 215, just e. Int corridors. **Pets:** Accepted.
SAVE S6 X ☾M ☾ 8

RICHMOND

AAA WW Best Western Imperial Motor Lodge SH
(765) 966-1505. **$49-$87.** 3020 E Main St. I-70, exit 156A, 2 mi w. Ext corridors. **Pets:** $5 daily fee/pet. Service with restrictions, supervision.
SAVE S6 X 8 ⌨ ⇌

WW Days Inn M
(765) 966-4900. **$55-$75.** 5775 National Rd E. I-70, exit 156A, just s. Ext corridors. **Pets:** Other species. $10 daily fee/room. Service with restrictions, crate.
A$K S6 X

WWWW Holiday Inn-Richmond SH
(765) 966-7511. **$99-$325, 3 day notice.** 5501 National Rd E. I-70, exit 156A, 0.3 mi w. Int corridors. **Pets:** Accepted.
A$K S6 X ☾M ⌂ ☾ 8 ⌨ ⎕ ⌿ ⇌ ⌧

WWWW Lees Inn & Suites SH
(765) 966-6559. **Call for rates.** 6030 National Rd E. I-70, exit 156A, jct US 40. Int corridors. **Pets:** Accepted.
X 8 ⌨ ⇌

WW Motel 6 Richmond #4170 M
(765) 966-6682. **Call for rates.** 419 Commerce Dr. I-70, exit 156A, just s on US 40. Ext corridors. **Pets:** Small. Service with restrictions, supervision.
X 8 ⇌

ROCKVILLE

AAA WW Billie Creek Village & Inn SH
(765) 569-3430. **$49-$215, 3 day notice.** 1659 E US Hwy 36. On US 36, 1.4 mi e. Int corridors. **Pets:** Other species. $10 one-time fee/pet. Designated rooms, service with restrictions, crate.
SAVE X ☾M ⌨ ⇌

ROSELAND

AAA WWWW Comfort Suites South Bend SH
(574) 272-1500. **$89-$295, 30 day notice.** 52939 SR 933 N. I-80/90, exit 77, just e to Business Rt US 31/33, then 1 mi n. Int corridors. **Pets:** Medium. $20 one-time fee/room. Designated rooms, service with restrictions, supervision.
SAVE S6 X ☾ 8 ⌨ ⇌ ⌧

WW Quality Inn-University Area SH
(574) 272-6600. **$70-$100.** 515 Dixie Way N. I-80/90, exit 77, on US 31 and SR 933, 0.8 mi n. Ext/int corridors. **Pets:** Medium. $25 deposit/room. Service with restrictions, supervision.
A$K S6 X ☾ 8 ⌨ ⌿ ⇌ ⌧

WW Ramada Inn South Bend SH
(574) 272-5220. **$69-$99.** 52890 SR 933 N. I-80/90, exit 77, 1 mi n. Ext/int corridors. **Pets:** Other species. $10 daily fee/pet. Designated rooms, service with restrictions, supervision.
A$K S6 X 8 ⌨ ⌿ ⇌

SCOTTSBURG

AAA WW Mariann Travel Inn M
(812) 752-3396. **$54-$58.** SR 56. I-65, exit 29A, just e. Ext corridors. **Pets:** Accepted.
SAVE S6 X 8 ⌿ ⇌ ⌧

SELLERSBURG

WW Home Lodge SH
(812) 246-6332. **$299 (weekly).** 363 Triangle Dr. I-65, exit 9, just e. Int corridors. **Pets:** Accepted.
X ☾ 8 ⌨

AAA WWWW Ramada Limited & Suites SH
(812) 246-3131. **$109-$129.** 360 Triangle Dr. I-65, exit 9, just e. Int corridors. **Pets:** Accepted.
SAVE S6 X 8 ⌨ ⇌

SEYMOUR

WW Holiday Inn SH
(812) 522-6767. **$86-$116.** 2025 E Tipton St. I-65, exit 50B, just w on US 50. Ext corridors. **Pets:** Large. Service with restrictions, crate.
A$K S6 X 8 ⌨ ⌿ ⇌

W Motel 6 Seymour #4153 SH
(812) 524-7443. **$41-$50.** 365 Tanger Blvd. I-65, exit 50A. Int corridors. **Pets:** Service with restrictions, supervision.
A$K S6 X ☾M ☾ 8 ⇌

SHIPSHEWANA

AAA WW Super 8 Motel SH
(260) 768-4004. **$55-$110.** 740 S Van Buren St. US 20, 0.8 mi n on SR 5. Int corridors. **Pets:** Medium, other species. $10 daily fee/pet. Service with restrictions, supervision.
SAVE S6 X ⌿ ☾ 8 ⌨

SOUTH BEND

WWWW Oliver Inn Bed & Breakfast BB ✿
(574) 232-4545. **$130-$190, 14 day notice.** 630 W Washington St. 0.3 mi w of jct US 933 and 31 S. Int corridors. **Pets:** $10 one-time fee/pet. Designated rooms, service with restrictions, supervision.
A$K S6 X

WW Quality Inn & Suites SH
(574) 288-3800. **$79-$149.** 4124 Lincolnway W. I-80/90, exit 72 (US 31) south, follow US 31, 1.5 mi s to South Bend Airport exit, follow signs to airport, then 2 mi e. Int corridors. **Pets:** Accepted.
A$K S6 X ☾M ☾ 8 ⌨ ⇌

WW Super 8 Motel SH
(574) 243-0200. **$59-$74.** 4124 Ameritech Dr. I-80/90, exit 72, just n on Cleveland Rd, then just e. Int corridors. **Pets:** Accepted.
A$K S6 X ☾ 8 ⌨ ⇌

STACER

[AAA] ◆◆◆ **Best Western Gateway Inn & Suites** [SH] 🐾
(812) 868-8000. **$50-$100.** 324 Rusher Creek Rd. I-64, exit 25A (US 41), 0.5 mi s, then just w. Int corridors. **Pets:** Other species. $15 one-time fee/pet. Service with restrictions, supervision.
[SAVE] [SD] 🚭 [♿M] ♿ ☎ ☕ 🏊

TAYLORSVILLE

◆◆ **Red Roof Inn** [M]
(812) 526-9747. **$54-$120.** 10330 US 31. I-65, exit 76A, just s. Ext corridors. **Pets:** Accepted.
[A$K] [SD] 🚭 ☎ ☕ 🏊

TELL CITY

◆◆ **Ramada Limited** [SH]
(812) 547-3234. **$59.** 235 Orchard Hill Dr. Just off SR 66, 1.7 mi se of jct SR 37. Int corridors. **Pets:** Other species. $50 deposit/room. Service with restrictions, crate.
[A$K] [SD] 🚭 [♿M] ♿ ☎ ☕ 🏊

TERRE HAUTE

◆◆◆ **Drury Inn-Terre Haute** [SH]
(812) 238-1206. **$79-$120.** 3040 Hwy 41 S. I-70, exit 7 (US 41/150), just n. Int corridors. **Pets:** Large, other species. Service with restrictions, supervision.
[A$K] 🚭 [♿M] ♿ ☎ ☕ 🏊 🏋

◆ **Econo Lodge** [M]
(812) 234-9931. **$44-$125.** 401 E Margaret Ave. I-70, exit 7 (US 41/150), just n, then e. Ext corridors. **Pets:** Large. $10 daily fee/room. Designated rooms, service with restrictions.
[A$K] [SD] 🚭 ☎ ☕ 🏊

◆◆◆ **Holiday Inn** [SH]
(812) 232-6081. **$119-$180, 3 day notice.** 3300 US 41 S. I-70, exit 7 (US 41/150), just s. Int corridors. **Pets:** Accepted.
[A$K] [SD] 🚭 🦻 ☎ ☕ 🍴 🏊 🏋

◆◆ **Pear Tree Inn by Drury-Terre Haute** [SH]
(812) 234-4268. **$60-$89.** 3050 US 41 S. I-70, exit 7 (US 41/150), just n. Int corridors. **Pets:** Large, other species. Service with restrictions, supervision.
[A$K] 🚭 ♿ ☕

◆ **Super 8 Motel-Terre Haute** [SH]
(812) 232-4890. **$47-$60.** 3089 S 1st St. I-70, exit 7 (US 41/150), just nw. Int corridors. **Pets:** Accepted.
[A$K] [SD] 🚭 ☎

VALPARAISO

◆◆ **Best Western Expressway Inn** [SH]
(219) 464-8555. **$74-$99.** 760 Morthland Dr. 0.8 mi e on US 30. Ext/int corridors. **Pets:** Accepted.
[A$K] [SD] 🚭 ♿ ☎ ☕

◆◆◆ **Courtyard by Marriott Valparaiso** [SH]
(219) 465-1700. **$89-$139.** 2301 E Morthland Dr. US 30, w of jct SR 49 Bypass. Int corridors. **Pets:** Accepted.
[A$K] [SD] 🚭 🦻 ☎ ☕ 🍴 🏊

WARREN

◆◆◆ **La Quinta Inn Warren** [SH]
(260) 375-4800. **$61.** 7275 S 75 E. I-69, exit 78, just n on SR 5. Int corridors. **Pets:** Accepted.
[A$K] [SD] 🚭 [♿M] ♿ ☎ ☕ 🏊

◆◆ **Super 8 Motel** [SH]
(260) 375-4688. **$45.** 7281 S 75 E. I-69, exit 78. Int corridors. **Pets:** Accepted.
[A$K] [SD] 🚭

WARSAW

[AAA] ◆◆◆ **Hampton Inn & Suites-Warsaw** [SH]
(574) 269-6655. **$72-$132.** 3328 E Center St. 3.2 mi e of SR 15 on US 30. Int corridors. **Pets:** $25 one-time fee/pet. Service with restrictions, supervision.
[SAVE] [SD] 🚭 🦻 ♿ ☎ ☕ 🏊 🏋

◆◆◆ **Ramada Plaza Hotel of Warsaw** [SH]
(574) 269-2323. **$86-$94.** 2519 E Center St. 2.8 mi e of SR 15 on US 30, just s. Int corridors. **Pets:** Other species. Service with restrictions.
[A$K] [SD] 🚭 ☎ ☕ 🍴 🏊 🏋

WASHINGTON

◆◆◆ **Baymont Inn & Suites Washington** [SH]
(812) 254-7000. **$69-$86.** 7 Cumberland Dr. Just ne of jct US 50 and SR 57. Int corridors. **Pets:** Small. $50 deposit/pet. Service with restrictions, supervision.
[A$K] [SD] 🚭 🦻 ☎ ☕ 🏊 🏋

WEST LAFAYETTE

◆◆ **Super 8 Motel-West Lafayette** [SH]
(765) 567-7100. **$60-$70.** 2030 Northgate Dr. I-65, exit 178, just n on SR 43. Int corridors. **Pets:** Other species. $15 one-time fee/room. Service with restrictions, supervision.
[A$K] [SD] 🚭 [♿M] ♿ ☎ ☕

IOWA

ADAIR

Adair Budget Inn M
(641) 742-5553. **$39-$45.** 100 S 5th St. I-80, exit 76. Ext corridors. **Pets:** $20 deposit/room. Designated rooms, service with restrictions, supervision.
SAVE S XX

Adair Super 8 SH
(641) 742-5251. **$54-$79.** 111 S 5th St. I-80, exit 76, just n. Int corridors. **Pets:** Very small. $20 deposit/room. Designated rooms, service with restrictions, supervision.
ASK S XX

ALBIA

Indian Hills Inn SH
(641) 932-7181. **$61-$97.** 100 Hwy 34 E. Just e of jct US 34 and SR 5. Ext/int corridors. **Pets:** $6 one-time fee/pet. Designated rooms, service with restrictions, supervision.
SAVE XX

ALGONA

AmericInn Motel SH
(515) 295-3333. **$73-$135.** 600 Hwy 18 W. Just w of jct US 169/18. Int corridors. **Pets:** Accepted.
ASK XX

ALTOONA

Heartland Inn-Altoona SH
(515) 967-2400. **$76-$95.** 300 34th Ave NW. I-80, exit 142, 0.5 mi s. Int corridors. **Pets:** Small. $5 daily fee/room. Designated rooms, service with restrictions, supervision.
ASK S XX

Motel 6 Des Moines East #1420 SH
(515) 967-5252. **$43-$65.** 3225 Adventureland Dr. I-80, exit 142A. Int corridors. **Pets:** Accepted.
S XX

Settle Inn & Suites-Altoona SH
(515) 967-7888. **$69-$89.** 2101 Adventureland Dr. I-80, exit 142A, just se. Int corridors. **Pets:** Accepted.
ASK S XX

AMANA COLONIES AREA

AMANA

Amana Holiday Inn SH
(319) 668-1175. **$189.** 2211 U Ave. I-80, exit 225 (US 151). Int corridors. **Pets:** Accepted.
ASK S XX

HOMESTEAD

Die Heimat Country Inn & Bed & Breakfast BB
(319) 622-3937. **$65-$89, 14 day notice.** 4430 V St. Just s of US 6, e on Main St, then just e of jct US 151. Int corridors. **Pets:** Medium, dogs only. $10 daily fee/pet. Designated rooms, service with restrictions, supervision.
XX

END AREA

AMES

AmericInn & Suites SH
(515) 233-1005. **$69-$109.** 2507 SE 16th St. I-35, exit 111B, just w on US 30, then exit 150. Int corridors. **Pets:** Other species. $50 deposit/room. Designated rooms, supervision.
ASK S XX

Baymont Inn & Suites SH
(515) 296-2500. **$79-$159.** 2500 Elwood Dr. I-35, exit 111B, 3.7 mi w on US 30, exit 146 (Elwood Dr). Int corridors. **Pets:** Service with restrictions, supervision.
SAVE S XX

▼▼▼ Comfort Inn-Ames 🔲
(515) 232-0689. **$60-$90.** 1605 S Dayton Ave. I-35, exit 111B, just w on US 30 then exit 150. Int corridors. **Pets:** Accepted.
[ASK] [S🔲] [X] [🔲] [🔲] [🏊]

▲▲▲ ▼▼▼ Comfort Suites 🔲
(515) 268-8808. **$99-$149.** 2609 Elwood Dr. I-35, exit 111B, 3.5 mi w on US 30, exit 146 (Elwood Dr), then just s. Int corridors. **Pets:** Medium. $10 one-time fee/pet. Designated rooms, service with restrictions, supervision.
[SAVE] [S🔲] [X] [🖴M] [🔌] [🐾] [🔲] [🔲] [🏊] [X]

▼▼▼ Heartland Inn-Ames 🔲
(515) 233-6060. **$140-$150.** 2600 SE 16th St. I-35, exit 111B, just w on US 30, then exit 150. Int corridors. **Pets:** Small. $5 daily fee/room. Designated rooms, service with restrictions, supervision.
[ASK] [S🔲] [X] [🔲] [🔲] [🏊]

▼▼▼ The Hotel at Gateway Center 🔲
(515) 292-8600. **$139-$179.** US 30 & Elwood Dr. I-35, exit 111B, 3.5 mi w on US 30, exit 146 (Elwood Dr). Int corridors. **Pets:** Medium. Designated rooms, service with restrictions, supervision.
[ASK] [S🔲] [X] [🖴M] [🔌] [🐾] [🔲] [🔲] [🍴] [🏊] [X]

▲▲▲ ▼▼▼ Quality Inn & Suites Starlite Village Conference Center 🔲
(515) 232-9260. **$70-$100.** 2601 E 13th St. I-35, exit 113 (US 30), 0.5 mi w. Int corridors. **Pets:** Medium. $10 daily fee/room. Service with restrictions, crate.
[SAVE] [S🔲] [X] [🔌] [🐾] [🔲] [🔲] [🍴] [🏊] [X]

ANAMOSA

▼▼▼ Super 8 Motel-Anamosa 🔲
(319) 462-3888. **$50-$70.** 100 Grant Wood Dr. Just e on US 64 from US 151. Int corridors. **Pets:** Accepted.
[ASK] [S🔲] [X] [🔌]

ANKENY

▲▲▲ ▼▼▼ Best Western Metro North 🔲
(515) 964-1717. **$68-$84, 30 day notice.** 133 SE Delaware Ave. I-35, exit 92, just w. Int corridors. **Pets:** $10 one-time fee/room. Designated rooms, service with restrictions, supervision.
[SAVE] [S🔲] [X] [🔲] [🔲] [🍴] [🏊] [X]

▼▼▼ Heartland Inn 🔲
(515) 964-8202. **$76-$86.** 201 SE Delaware Ave. I-35, exit 92, just w. Int corridors. **Pets:** Small. $5 daily fee/room. Designated rooms, service with restrictions, supervision.
[ASK] [S🔲] [X] [🔌] [🔲] [🔲] [🏊]

ARNOLDS PARK

▼▼▼ Fillenwarth Beach 🔲
(712) 332-5646. **$290-$4000 (weekly) (no credit cards), 21 day notice.** 87 Lake Shore Dr. Just w of US 71; on West Lake Okoboji. Ext corridors. **Pets:** Other species. Service with restrictions.
[X] [🔲] [🔲] [🏊] [X]

ATLANTIC

▲▲▲ ▼▼▼ Days Inn 🔲
(712) 243-4067. **$49-$79.** 64968 Boston Rd. I-80, exit 60 (US 71), 0.5 mi s. Int corridors. **Pets:** Small, other species. $25 deposit/room. Designated rooms, service with restrictions, supervision.
[SAVE] [S🔲] [X] [🔲] [🏊]

▼▼▼ Super 8 Motel 🔲
(712) 243-4723. **$54-$79.** 1902 E 7th St. I-80, exit 60 (US 71), 6 mi s, then 2 mi w; east side of town. Int corridors. **Pets:** Small, other species. Designated rooms, service with restrictions, supervision.
[ASK] [S🔲] [X] [🔌] [🔲] [🔲] [🏊]

BURLINGTON

▲▲▲ ▼▼▼ Best Western Pzazz Motor Inn 🔲
(319) 753-2223. **$89-$139.** 3001 Winegard Dr. Jct US 61 and 34, just n. Int corridors. **Pets:** Other species. Service with restrictions.
[SAVE] [S🔲] [X] [🖴M] [🔌] [🐾] [🔲] [🔲] [🍴] [🏊] [X]

▼▼▼ Comfort Inn-Burlington 🔲
(319) 753-0000. **$69-$99.** 3051 Kirkwood Ave. Jct US 61 and 34, just n. Int corridors. **Pets:** Accepted.
[ASK] [S🔲] [X] [🔲] [🔲] [🏊]

▼▼▼ Super 8 Motel-Burlington 🔲
(319) 752-9806. **$55-$72.** 3001 Kirkwood Ave. Jct US 61 and 34, just n. Int corridors. **Pets:** Medium. $10 daily fee/pet. Service with restrictions, supervision.
[ASK] [S🔲] [X] [🔲]

CARROLL

▼▼▼ Super 8 Motel 🔲
(712) 792-4753. **Call for rates.** 1757 US 71 N. Just n of jct US 30 and 71. Int corridors. **Pets:** Accepted.
[X]

CARTER LAKE

▲▲▲ ▼▼▼ Super 8 Motel 🔲 🐾
(712) 347-5588. **$70-$80, 10 day notice.** 3000 Airport Dr. I-480 E, exit 3A; to 14th St; follow Eppley Airfield signs; 1.5 mi s of airport. Int corridors. **Pets:** Other species. $10 one-time fee/room. Service with restrictions, supervision.
[SAVE] [S🔲] [X] [🖴M] [🔌] [🔲] [🏊]

CEDAR FALLS

▲▲▲ ▼◆▼ University Inn 🔲 🐾
(319) 277-1412. **$44-$120.** 4711 University Ave. 2 mi w of US 63. Ext/int corridors. **Pets:** $30 deposit/pet, $5 one-time fee/room. Designated rooms, service with restrictions, supervision.
[SAVE] [S🔲] [X] [🔲] [🔲] [X]

CEDAR RAPIDS

▼▼▼ Best Western Cooper's Mill Hotel & Restaurant 🔲
(319) 366-5323. **$59-$79.** 100 F Ave NW. I-380, exit 19C northbound, take a right at end of the exit, make an immediate U-turn and go under I-380; exit 20A southbound, cross river, right on 1st St NW. Int corridors. **Pets:** Accepted.
[ASK] [S🔲] [X] [🔲] [🔲] [🍴] [🏊] [X]

▲▲▲ ▼▼▼▼ Best Western Longbranch Hotel & Convention Center 🔲
(319) 377-6386. **$79-$99.** 90 Twixt Town Rd NE. I-380, exit 24A (SR 100/Collins Rd), 2.5 mi e, then just n. Int corridors. **Pets:** $5 daily fee/room. Service with restrictions, crate.
[SAVE] [S🔲] [X] [🔲] [🔲] [🍴] [🏊] [X]

▲▲▲ ▼◆◆▼ Clarion Hotel & Convention Center 🔲 🐾
(319) 366-8671. **$55-$89.** 525 33rd Ave SW. I-380, exit 17 (33rd Ave SW), just w. Int corridors. **Pets:** $25 deposit/room. Service with restrictions.
[SAVE] [S🔲] [X] [🔌] [🔲] [🔲] [🍴] [🏊] [X]

▼▼▼ Comfort Inn by Choice Hotels North 🔲
(319) 393-8247. **$64-$89.** 5055 Rockwell Dr. I-380, exit 24A (SR 100/Collins Rd), 1.3 mi e. Int corridors. **Pets:** Other species. Designated rooms, service with restrictions, supervision.
[ASK] [S🔲] [X] [🔌] [🔲] [🔲]

▼▼▼ Comfort Inn by Choice Hotels-South 🔲
(319) 363-7934. **$64-$89.** 390 33rd Ave SW. I-380, exit 17 (33rd Ave SW), just w. Int corridors. **Pets:** Accepted.
[ASK] [S🔲] [X] [🔲] [🔲]

Crowne Plaza Five Seasons LH
(319) 363-8161. **$90-$130.** 350 1st Ave NE. I-380, exit 20B, just e; downtown. Int corridors. **Pets:** Small. $25 deposit/pet. Designated rooms, no service, supervision.
SAVE Sb ⊠ ♿ 🛏 🖵 ❚❙ ⚓ ⊠

Days Inn of Cedar Rapids SH
(319) 365-4339. **$56-$80.** 3245 Southgate Pl SW. I-380, exit 17 (33rd Ave SW), just w. Int corridors. **Pets:** Accepted.
ASK Sb ⊠ ⌇ 🛏 🖵

Exel Inn of Cedar Rapids SH
(319) 366-2475. **$41-$61.** 616 33rd Ave SW. I-380, exit 17 (33rd Ave SW), 0.3 mi w. Int corridors. **Pets:** Small, other species. Designated rooms, service with restrictions, supervision.
SAVE Sb ⊠ 🛏 🖵

GuestHouse International Inns & Suites SH
(319) 378-3948. **$57-$62.** 2215 Blairs Ferry Rd NE. I-380, exit 24B, just e. Int corridors. **Pets:** Small, other species. $25 one-time fee/room. Designated rooms, service with restrictions.
ASK Sb ⊠ ♿ 🛏 🖵 ⚓

Hawthorn Suites Ltd SH 🐾
(319) 294-8700. **$92-$98.** 4444 Czech Ln NE. I-380, exit 24A (SR 100/Collins Rd), just s. Int corridors. **Pets:** Other species. Service with restrictions, crate.
ASK Sb ⊠ ♿ ⌇ 🏷 🛏 🖵 ⚓

Heartland Inn SH
(319) 362-9012. **$76-$86.** 3315 Southgate Ct SW. I-380, exit 17 (33rd Ave SW), just sw. Int corridors. **Pets:** Small. $5 daily fee/room. Designated rooms, service with restrictions, supervision.
ASK Sb ⊠ ⌇ 🛏 🖵 ⚓ ⊠

Howard Johnson Airport Express Inn & Suites SH
(319) 363-3789. **$80-$110.** 9100 Atlantic Dr SW. I-380, exit 13, just w. Int corridors. **Pets:** Other species. $10 daily fee/pet. Service with restrictions, crate.
ASK Sb ⊠ ♿ 🏷 🛏 🖵 ⚓ ⊠

Mainstay Suites SH
(319) 363-7829. **$69-$149.** 5145 Rockwell Dr NE. I-380, exit 24A (SR 100/Collins Rd), 1 mi e, then just n. Int corridors. **Pets:** $50 deposit/ room, $10 daily fee/pet. Service with restrictions, crate.
ASK Sb ⊠ ♿ 🛏 🖵 ⚓ ⊠

Marriott Cedar Rapids LH
(319) 393-6600. **$125-$145.** 1200 Collins Rd NE. I-380, exit 24A (SR 100/Collins Rd), 1 mi e. Int corridors. **Pets:** Accepted.
SAVE Sb ⊠ ⌇ 🏷 🛏 🖵 ❚❙ ⚓ ⊠

Motel 6 #1485 M
(319) 366-7523. **$35-$45.** 3325 Southgate Ct SW. I-380, exit 17 (33rd Ave SW), just sw. Ext corridors. **Pets:** Accepted.
Sb ⊠ ♿ ⌇ 🏷

Ramada Limited SH
(319) 396-5000. **$65-$75.** 4011 16th Ave SW. I-380, exit 16 (US 30), 2.4 mi w, 1.4 mi n (exit 250) on Edgewood Rd to 16th Ave, then just w. Int corridors. **Pets:** Small. Service with restrictions, crate.
ASK Sb ⊠ ♿ 🛏 🖵 ⚓

Ramada Limited Suites SH
(319) 378-8888. **$65-$85.** 2025 Werner Ave NE. I-380, exit 24A (SR 100/Collins Rd), just se. Int corridors. **Pets:** Small. Service with restrictions, crate.
ASK Sb ⊠ 🏷 🛏 🖵 ⚓

Residence Inn by Marriott SH
(319) 395-0111. **$79-$149.** 1900 Dodge Rd NE. I-380, exit 24A (SR 100/Collins Rd), just e. Int corridors. **Pets:** Other species. $5 daily fee/ room, $50 one-time fee/room. Service with restrictions.
ASK Sb ⊠ ♿ ⌇ 🏷 🛏 🖵 ⚓ ⊠

Super 8 Motel SH
(319) 362-6002. **$55-$60.** 720 33rd Ave SW. I-380, exit 17 (33rd Ave SW), 0.4 mi w. Int corridors. **Pets:** Accepted.
ASK Sb ⊠ ♿ ⌇ 🛏

Super 8 Motel SH
(319) 363-1755. **$50-$60.** 400 33rd Ave SW. I-380, exit 17 (33rd Ave SW), just w. Int corridors. **Pets:** Medium. $10 one-time fee/pet. Service with restrictions, crate.
ASK Sb ⊠ ⌇ 🛏

CHARLES CITY

Hartwood Inn M
(641) 228-4352. **$45-$55.** 1312 Gilbert St. Jct US 18 and 218 (exit 229), 3 mi e. Ext corridors. **Pets:** Accepted.
SAVE Sb ⊠ ♿ 🛏 🖵 ⚓

CHEROKEE

Best Western La Grande Hacienda SH
(712) 225-5701. **$59-$69, 3 day notice.** 1401 N 2nd St. Jct US 59 and SR 2, 0.4 mi s. Int corridors. **Pets:** Medium, other species. $50 deposit/ room. Service with restrictions, supervision.
SAVE Sb ⊠ ♿ ⌇ 🖵 ❚❙ ⚓

CLARINDA

Clarinda Super 8 Motel SH
(712) 542-6333. **$55-$70.** 1203 S 12th St. Jct US 71 and SR 2, just e. Int corridors. **Pets:** Other species. Service with restrictions, supervision.
ASK Sb ⊠ ♿ 🛏 🖵 ⚓

CLEAR LAKE

Budget Inn SH
(641) 357-8700. **$45-$60.** 1306 N 25th St. I-35, exit 194 (US 18), just nw. Int corridors. **Pets:** Accepted.
SAVE Sb ⊠ 🛏 🖵 ⚓

Heartland Inn SH
(641) 357-5123. **$76-$115.** 1603 S Shore Dr. I-35, exit 193, 1.3 mi w to S Shore Dr, then 1 mi s. Int corridors. **Pets:** Small. $5 daily fee/room. Designated rooms, service with restrictions, supervision.
ASK Sb ⊠ 🛏 🖵 ⚓ ⊠

Lake Country Inn M 🐾
(641) 357-2184. **$55-$70.** 518 Hwy 18 W. I-35, exit 194 (US 18), 2 mi w. Ext corridors. **Pets:** Dogs only. $5 daily fee/room. Designated rooms, service with restrictions, supervision.
ASK Sb ⊠ 🛏

Microtel Inn SH
(641) 357-0966. **$58-$72.** 1305 N 25th St. I-35, exit 194 (SR 122), just nw. Int corridors. **Pets:** Accepted.
ASK ⊠ ♿ ⌇ 🛏 🖵

Super 8 Motel SH
(641) 357-7521. **$49-$60, 30 day notice.** 2809 4th Ave S. I-35, exit 193, just e. Int corridors. **Pets:** Other species. $10 deposit/room. Designated rooms, service with restrictions, supervision.
ASK Sb ⊠

CLINTON

Best Western-Frontier Motor Inn SH
(563) 242-7112. **$69-$99.** 2300 Lincoln Way. On US 30, just e of jct US 30 and 67. Ext/int corridors. **Pets:** Accepted.
SAVE Sb ⊠ ⌇ 🏷 🛏 🖵 ❚❙ ⚓ ⊠

Country Inn & Suites By Carlson SH
(563) 244-9922. **$69-$99.** 2224 Lincoln Way. On US 30, just e of jct US 30 and 67. Int corridors. **Pets:** Accepted.
SAVE Sb ⊠ ♿ ⌇ 🏷 🛏 🖵 ⚓

▼▼ **Super 8 Motel-Clinton** SH ❀
(563) 242-8870. **$49-$72.** 1711 Lincoln Way. On US 30 and 67, 2.4 mi w. Int corridors. **Pets:** Other species. $10 one-time fee/room. Service with restrictions, supervision.
ASK SO ✕ &M 🐾 🛢

CLIVE

AAA ▼▼▼ **Baymont Inn & Suites West Des Moines-Clive** SH
(515) 221-9200. **$59-$109.** 1390 NW 118th St. I-80/35, exit 124 (University Ave). Int corridors. **Pets:** Medium, other species. $25 deposit/room. Designated rooms, service with restrictions, supervision.
SAVE SO ✕ &M 🐾 & 🛢 🖳 ≈

AAA ▼▼▼ **Chase Suite Hotel by Woodfin** M
(515) 223-7700. **$89-$209.** 11428 Forest Ave. I-80/35, exit 124 (University Ave), just ne. Ext corridors. **Pets:** Accepted.
SAVE SO ✕ 🐾 & 🛢 🖳 ≈ ✕

▼▼ **Heartland Inn-West Des Moines** SH
(515) 226-0414. **$76-$86.** 11414 Forest Ave. I-80/35, exit 124 (University Ave), just e. Int corridors. **Pets:** Small. $5 daily fee/room. Designated rooms, service with restrictions, supervision.
ASK SO ✕ 🛢 🖳 ✕

COLUMBUS JUNCTION

▼▼ **Columbus Motel** M
(319) 728-8080. **$48-$55.** 265 Colonels Dr. Just e of jct US 92 and SR 70 on US 92. Int corridors. **Pets:** Accepted.
ASK ✕ 🛢 🖳

CORALVILLE

▼▼ **Days Inn** M ❀
(319) 354-4400. **$59-$79.** 205 2nd St. I-80, exit 242, 1 mi s to 2nd St, then just w. Ext corridors. **Pets:** Medium. $10 daily fee/pet. Service with restrictions, supervision.
ASK SO ✕

▼▼ **Heartland Inn** SH
(319) 351-8132. **$80-$90.** 87 2nd St. I-80, exit 242, 1 mi s on US 6, then just e. Int corridors. **Pets:** Small. $5 daily fee/room. Designated rooms, service with restrictions, supervision.
ASK SO ✕ 🐾 🛢 🖳 ≈

▼▼ **Super 8 Motel-Iowa City** SH
(319) 337-8388. **$56-$88.** 611 1st Ave. I-80, exit 242, 0.4 mi s. Int corridors. **Pets:** Other species. $10 daily fee/pet. Service with restrictions, supervision.
ASK SO ✕ &M 🐾

COUNCIL BLUFFS

AAA ▼▼▼ **Best Western Crossroads of the Bluffs** SH
(712) 322-3150. **$59-$129.** 2216 27th Ave. I-80, exit 1B (24th St). Int corridors. **Pets:** Accepted.
SAVE SO ✕ 🐾 & 🛢 🖳 ≈ ✕

AAA ▼▼▼▼ **Comfort Suites** SH
(712) 323-9760. **$69-$129.** 1801 S 35th St. I-29, exit 52, just e. Int corridors. **Pets:** $10 daily fee/room. Designated rooms, service with restrictions, supervision.
SAVE SO ✕ &M 🐾 & 🛢 🖳 ≈

▼▼ **Days Inn** SH
(712) 323-2200. **$54-$94, 15 day notice.** 3619 9th Ave. I-29, exit 53A (9th Ave). Int corridors. **Pets:** Medium. $10 daily fee/pet. Designated rooms, service with restrictions, supervision.
ASK ✕ 🐾 🛢 🖳

▼▼ **Days Inn** SH ❀
(712) 366-9699. **$45-$90, 7 day notice.** 3208 S 7th St. I-80, exit 3, just s. Int corridors. **Pets:** Medium. $10 daily fee/pet. Service with restrictions, supervision.
ASK SO ✕ 🐾 & 🛢 🖳

▼▼ **Heartland Inn** SH
(712) 322-8400. **$76-$86.** 1000 Woodbury Ave. I-80, exit 5 (Madison Ave). Int corridors. **Pets:** Small. $5 daily fee/room. Designated rooms, service with restrictions, supervision.
ASK SO ✕ 🐾 🛢 🖳 ≈

▼▼ **Motel 6 Council Bluffs, IA #1153** SH
(712) 366-2405. **$45-$65.** 3032 S Expressway St. I-29/80, exit 3 (US 92). Int corridors. **Pets:** Accepted.
SO ✕ 🐾 & 🛢 ≈

AAA ▼▼▼ **Quality Inn & Suites** SH
(712) 328-3171. **$59-$95.** 3537 W Broadway. I-29, exit 53A (9th Ave), just e, 0.5 mi n on S 35th St, then just w. Ext/int corridors. **Pets:** Accepted.
SAVE SO ✕ 🐾 & 🛢 🖳 ≈

▼ **Super 8 Motel** SH
(712) 322-2888. **$56-$62.** 2712 S 24th St. I-80, exit 1B (24th St). Int corridors. **Pets:** Service with restrictions, supervision.
ASK SO ✕ 🐾

AAA ▼▼▼ **Western Inn** SH
(712) 322-4499. **$73-$93.** 1842 Madison Ave. I-80, exit 5 (Madison Ave). Int corridors. **Pets:** Small, other species. $10 one-time fee/room. Designated rooms, service with restrictions, crate.
SAVE SO ✕ & ≈

CRESCO

AAA ▼▼ **Cresco Motel** M
(563) 547-2240. **$46-$73.** 620 2nd Ave SE. On SR 9; on east side of town. Ext corridors. **Pets:** Other species. Service with restrictions, supervision.
SAVE SO ✕ &M & 🛢

DECORAH

▼▼ **Heartland Inn** SH
(563) 382-2269. **$74-$84.** 705 Commerce Dr. Jct US 52, 1.8 mi e on SR 9. Int corridors. **Pets:** Small. $5 daily fee/room. Designated rooms, service with restrictions, supervision.
ASK SO ✕ 🛢 🖳 ≈

DENISON

▼▼ **Denison Super 8** SH
(712) 263-5081. **Call for rates.** 502 Boyer Valley Rd. Jct US 30/59 and SR 141, 0.3 mi sw. Int corridors. **Pets:** Accepted.
✕ 🛢

DES MOINES

AAA ▼▼▼ **American Inn & Suites** M
(515) 265-7511. **$45-$95.** 5020 NE 14th St. I-80/35, exit 136 (US 69), just n. Ext/int corridors. **Pets:** Other species. Service with restrictions, crate.
SAVE SO ✕ & 🖳

▼▼ **Bavarian Inn** SH
(515) 265-5611. **$59-$69.** 5220 NE 14th St. I-80/35, exit 136 (US 69), 0.3 mi n. Int corridors. **Pets:** Accepted.
ASK SO ✕ 🛢 🖳 🍴 ≈

▼▼ **Comfort Inn by Choice Hotels** SH
(515) 287-3434. **$64-$109.** 5231 Fleur Dr. Opposite the airport. Int corridors. **Pets:** $10 one-time fee/room. Designated rooms, service with restrictions, supervision.
ASK SO ✕ &M 🐾 🛢 🖳 ≈

Des Moines Marriott Downtown 🔲
(515) 245-5500. **$99-$189.** 700 Grand Ave. Downtown. Int corridors.
Pets: Accepted.

Four Points Sheraton Des Moines Airport 🔲
(515) 287-6464. **$109-$159.** 1810 Army Post Rd. Just s of Des Moines
Airport entrance. Int corridors. **Pets:** Accepted.

Heartland Inn-Airport 🔲
(515) 256-0603. **$80-$90.** 1901 Hackley Ave. Opposite the airport. Int
corridors. **Pets:** Small. $5 daily fee/room. Designated rooms, service with
restrictions, supervision.

Hickman Motor Lodge 🅜
(515) 276-8591. **$49-$56.** 6500 Hickman Rd. I-80/35, exit 125, 2.5 mi e.
Ext corridors. **Pets:** Medium. $10 daily fee/pet. Supervision.

Motel 6-30 🅜
(515) 287-6364. **$40-$50.** 4817 Fleur Dr. Opposite the airport. Ext
corridors. **Pets:** Other species. Supervision.

Quality Inn & Suites 🔲
(515) 278-2381. **$59-$140.** 4995 Merle Hay Rd. I-80/35, exit 131 (Merle
Hay Rd), just s. Int corridors. **Pets:** $25 deposit/room. Designated rooms,
service with restrictions, supervision.

Quality Inn & Suites Iowa Event Center 🔲
(515) 282-5251. **$72-$100.** 929 3rd St. I-235, exit 3rd St; downtown. Int
corridors. **Pets:** Large. $10 one-time fee/room. Service with restrictions,
supervision.

Red Roof Inn & Suites 🔲
(515) 266-6800. **$68-$92.** 4950 NE 14th St. I-80, exit 136. Int corridors.
Pets: Medium. Service with restrictions, supervision.

Super 8 Lodge 🔲
(515) 278-8858. **$54-$89.** 4755 Merle Hay Rd. I-80/35, exit 131 (Merle
Hay Rd), just s. Int corridors. **Pets:** Medium. $10 daily fee/pet. Service
with restrictions, supervision.

DE SOTO

Edgetowner Motel 🅜
(515) 834-2641. **$40-$60.** 804 Guthrie. I-80, exit 110, just s. Ext corridors. **Pets:** Accepted.

DUBUQUE

Best Western Dubuque Inn 🔲
(563) 556-7760. **$79-$109.** 3434 Dodge St. US 20, 3 mi w of jct US
52/61/151 and Mississippi Bridge. Int corridors. **Pets:** Medium. $10 daily
fee/pet. Designated rooms, service with restrictions, crate.

Best Western Midway Hotel 🔲
(563) 557-8000. **$95-$125.** 3100 Dodge St. US 20, 2.3 mi w of jct US
52/61/151 and Mississippi Bridge. Int corridors. **Pets:** Medium. Service
with restrictions, supervision.

Comfort Inn by Choice Hotels 🔲
(563) 556-3006. **$59-$99.** 4055 McDonald Dr. US 20, 3.8 mi w of jct
US 52/61/151 and Mississippi Bridge. Int corridors. **Pets:** Large. $10
one-time fee/room. Designated rooms, no service, supervision.

Days Inn-Dubuque 🔲
(563) 583-3297. **$69-$99.** 1111 Dodge St. US 20, 0.8 mi w of jct US
52/61/151 and Mississippi Bridge, exit Hill/Bryant. Ext corridors.
Pets: Other species. $5 daily fee/pet. Service with restrictions, crate.

Heartland Inn-South 🔲
(563) 556-6555. **$76-$86.** 2090 Southpark Ct. US 151 and 61 at jct US
52; 2.5 mi s of jct US 20 and Mississippi Bridge. Int corridors.
Pets: Small. $5 daily fee/room. Designated rooms, service with restrictions,
supervision.

Heartland Inn-West 🔲
(563) 582-3752. **$76-$86.** 4025 McDonald Dr. US 20, 3.8 mi w of jct
US 52/61/151 and Mississippi Bridge. Int corridors. **Pets:** Small. $5
daily fee/room. Designated rooms, service with restrictions, supervision.

Holiday Inn Dubuque/Galena 🔲
(563) 556-2000. **$89-$109.** 450 Main St. At Main and 4th sts; downtown. Int corridors. **Pets:** Accepted.

MainStay Suites 🔲
(563) 557-7829. **$69-$119.** 1275 Associates Dr. Just n of jct US 20 and
NW Arterial Rd; west side of town. Int corridors. **Pets:** Accepted.

DYERSVILLE

Comfort Inn-Dyersville 🔲
(563) 875-7700. **$75-$160.** 527 16th Ave SE. US 20, exit 294, just nw.
Int corridors. **Pets:** Medium. $6 daily fee/room. Designated rooms, service
with restrictions, supervision.

ELDRIDGE

Quality Inn & Suites 🔲
(563) 285-4600. **$64-$129.** 1000 E Iowa St. Just w of jct US 61 and CR
F45 (exit 127). Int corridors. **Pets:** Other species. $12.50 daily fee/room.
Service with restrictions.

ELK HORN

AmericInn Motel & Suites 🔲
(712) 764-4000. **$76-$119.** 4037 Main St. I-80, exit 54 (SR 173), 6 mi n.
Int corridors. **Pets:** $50 deposit/room. Designated rooms, service with
restrictions, crate.

ESTHERVILLE

Sleep Inn & Suites 🔲
(712) 362-5522. **$79-$89.** 2008 Central Ave. Jct SR 4 and 9, 1 mi e. Int
corridors. **Pets:** Other species. $15 one-time fee/pet. Service with restric-
tions, supervision.

EVANSDALE

Ramada Limited 🔲
(319) 235-1111. **$74-$79.** 450 Evansdale Dr. I-380, exit 68, just n. Int
corridors. **Pets:** Accepted.

FAIRFIELD

Best Western Fairfield Inn 🔲
(641) 472-2200. **$62-$71.** 2200 W Burlington Ave. On US 34, 1 mi w of
jct SR 1. Int corridors. **Pets:** Other species. $10 one-time fee/pet. Desig-
nated rooms, service with restrictions, supervision.

FORT DODGE

AAA ▼▼▼ Comfort Inn SH
(515) 573-5000. **$70-$80.** 2938 5th Ave S. US 20, exit 124 (Coalville), 6 mi n on CR P59, then 2 mi w on 5th Ave and Business Rt US 20. Int corridors. **Pets:** $10 daily fee/pet. Designated rooms, service with restrictions, supervision.
[SAVE] [S₀] [✕] [&M] [⌖] [🛏] [📺] [≈]

▼▼ Days Inn SH
(515) 576-8000. **$49-$64.** 3040 5th Ave S. US 20, exit 124 (Coalville), 3.7 mi n on CR P59, then 1.2 mi w on Business Rt US 20. Int corridors. **Pets:** $25 daily fee/pet. Designated rooms, service with restrictions, supervision.
[ASK] [S₀] [✕] [🖉] [🛏] [📺]

▼▼▼ Holiday Inn SH
(515) 955-3621. **$63.** 2001 US 169 S. US 20, 2 mi n. Ext/int corridors. **Pets:** Small. $10 one-time fee/pet. Service with restrictions, supervision.
[ASK] [S₀] [✕] [&M] [🛏] [🍴] [≈] [✕]

▼▼ Super 8 Motel-Fort Dodge Iowa SH
(515) 576-8788. **$65-$80.** 3638 Maple Dr. US 20, exit 124 (Coalville), 6 mi n, then just w. Int corridors. **Pets:** $10 daily fee/pet. Designated rooms, supervision.
[ASK] [S₀] [✕] [🖉] [🛏]

FORT MADISON

AAA ▼▼▼ The Madison Inn Motel M
(319) 372-7740. **$48-$85.** 3440 Ave L. US 2 and 61, 2 mi w. Ext corridors. **Pets:** Medium. $5 daily fee/pet. Designated rooms, service with restrictions, supervision.
[SAVE] [S₀] [✕] [🛏] [📺]

▼▼ Super 8 Motel-Ft Madison SH
(319) 372-8500. **$49-$59.** US 61 W, 5107 Ave O. US 61, 1 mi e of jct US 61 and SR 2. Ext/int corridors. **Pets:** $10 daily fee/pet. Service with restrictions, crate.
[ASK] [S₀] [✕] [⌖] [🛏]

GLENWOOD

▼ Lincoln Bluff View Motel SH
(712) 622-8191. **$48-$53.** 57902 190 St. I-29, exit 35 (US 34). Int corridors. **Pets:** Accepted.
[✕] [🛏] [🍴]

GRIMES

▼▼▼ AmericInn Motel & Suites SH ☙
(515) 986-9900. **$69-$179.** 251 Gateway. Just sw of jct US 44 and SR 141. Int corridors. **Pets:** Dogs only. $50 deposit/room, $10 daily fee/pet. Designated rooms, service with restrictions, supervision.
[ASK] [✕] [&M] [🖉] [🛏] [📺] [≈] [✕]

HAMPTON

▼▼▼ AmericInn Lodge & Suites SH
(641) 456-5559. **$76-$130.** 702 Central Ave W. On SR 3 (Central Ave W), 0.7 mi w of jct US 65 and SR 3. Int corridors. **Pets:** Medium. $100 deposit/pet. Supervision.
[ASK] [✕] [⌖] [🖉] [🛏] [📺] [≈] [✕]

IDA GROVE

▼ Delux Motel M
(712) 364-3317. **$45-$60.** 5981 US Hwy 175. Jct US 59 S and 175. Ext corridors. **Pets:** Large. $10 daily fee/pet. Designated rooms, service with restrictions, supervision.
[✕] [🛏]

INDEPENDENCE

▼▼ Super 8 Motel SH
(319) 334-7041. **$59-$99, 30 day notice.** 2000 1st St W. US 20, exit 252, 1.4 mi n. Int corridors. **Pets:** Very small. $10 daily fee/pet. Designated rooms, service with restrictions, crate.
[ASK] [S₀] [✕] [&M] [🛏]

IOWA CITY

AAA ▼▼▼ Quality Inn & Suites LH
(319) 354-2000. **$79-$109.** 2525 N Dodge. I-80, exit 246, just ne. Int corridors. **Pets:** Medium. $10 daily fee/room. Designated rooms, service with restrictions, supervision.
[SAVE] [S₀] [✕] [🖉] [🛏] [📺] [🍴] [≈] [✕]

AAA ▼▼▼▼ Sheraton Iowa City Hotel LH ☙
(319) 337-4058. **$99-$239.** 210 S Dubuque St. Dubuque and Burlington sts (SR 1); downtown. Int corridors. **Pets:** Medium, dogs only. Designated rooms, service with restrictions, supervision.
[SAVE] [S₀] [✕] [&M] [⌖] [🖉] [🛏] [📺] [🍴] [≈] [✕]

AAA ▼▼▼ Travelodge SH ☙
(319) 351-1010. **$69-$139.** 2216 N Dodge St. I-80, exit 246, just sw on SR 1. Ext/int corridors. **Pets:** Medium. $6 one-time fee/pet. Service with restrictions.
[SAVE] [S₀] [✕] [&M] [⌖] [🖉] [🛏] [📺] [≈]

JEFFERSON

AAA ▼▼ The Redwood Motel M
(515) 386-3116. **$40-$45, 3 day notice.** 209 E Gallup Rd. Just e of jct US 30 and SR 4. Ext corridors. **Pets:** Accepted.
[SAVE] [S₀] [✕]

JOHNSTON

AAA ▼▼▼ Best Inns of America SH
(515) 270-1111. **$59-$85.** 5050 Merle Hay Rd. I-80/35, exit 131 (Merle Hay Rd), just n. Int corridors. **Pets:** Other species. $10 one-time fee/room. Service with restrictions, supervision.
[SAVE] [S₀] [✕] [&M] [⌖] [🛏] [📺] [≈]

▼▼▼ Best Western-Des Moines North SH
(515) 276-5411. **$74-$87, 30 day notice.** 5055 Merle Hay Rd. I-80/35, exit 131 (Merle Hay Rd), just n. Int corridors. **Pets:** $10 one-time fee/room. Designated rooms, service with restrictions, supervision.
[ASK] [S₀] [✕] [⌖] [🛏] [📺] [🍴] [≈]

KEOKUK

▼▼ Super 8 Motel-Keokuk SH
(319) 524-3888. **$49-$59.** 3511 Main St. US 218, 2 mi nw. Int corridors. **Pets:** Medium. $10 daily fee/pet. Service with restrictions, crate.
[ASK] [S₀] [✕] [&M] [🛏] [📺]

LE CLAIRE

AAA ▼▼▼ Comfort Inn Riverview SH
(563) 289-4747. **$69-$149.** 902 Mississippi View Ct. I-80, exit 306 (US 67), 0.5 mi n to Eagle Ridge Rd, then just sw. Int corridors. **Pets:** Medium. $25 deposit/room. Service with restrictions, crate.
[SAVE] [S₀] [✕] [&M] [🖉] [🛏] [📺] [≈]

AAA ▼▼▼ Super 8 of LeClaire SH
(563) 289-5888. **$62-$75.** 1552 Welcome Center Dr. I-80, exit 306 (US 67), 0.5 mi n to Eagle Ridge Rd, then just sw to Mississippi View Ct. Int corridors. **Pets:** Medium. $25 deposit/room. Service with restrictions, crate.
[SAVE] [S₀] [✕] [&M] [🖉] [🛏] [📺]

LE MARS

◆◆ **Super 8 Motel** 🆂🅷
(712) 546-8800. **$56-$80.** 1201 Hawkeye Ave SW. 1.2 mi s of jct US 75/SR 3, on US 75; south end of town. Int corridors. **Pets:** Dogs only. $10 daily fee/room. Designated rooms, service with restrictions, supervision.

🆂🅾 ✖ 🔊ᴹ 📟 💻 🏊

MANCHESTER

◆◆ **Super 8 of Manchester** 🆂🅷
(563) 927-2533. **$58-$96.** 1020 W Main. Jct US 20 and SR 13, exit 275, 1.3 mi n, then 0.3 mi e. Int corridors. **Pets:** Medium. $6 daily fee/pet. Designated rooms, service with restrictions, supervision.

A$K 🆂🅾 ✖ 🔊ᴹ 📟 💻

MARION

◆◆ **Microtel Inn & Suites** 🆂🅷
(319) 373-7400. **$59-$64.** 5500 Dyer Ave. Jct US 151 and SR 13. Int corridors. **Pets:** Accepted.

A$K 🆂🅾 ✖ 🔊ᴹ 🐾 📟 💻

MARQUETTE

◆ **The Frontier Motel** 🅼
(563) 873-3497. **$55-$95.** 101 S 1st St. Just s of jct US 18 and SR 76; between Mississippi River Bridge and casino. Ext corridors. **Pets:** Accepted.

✖ 📟 💻 🏊

MARSHALLTOWN

◆◆◆ **Best Western Regency Inn** 🆂🅷
(641) 752-6321. **$77-$97, 7 day notice.** 3303 S Center St. Jct US 30 and SR 14. Int corridors. **Pets:** Other species. $10 one-time fee/room. Service with restrictions, supervision.

A$K 🆂🅾 ✖ 🅿 🐾 📟 💻 🍽 🏊 ✖

◆◆ **Comfort Inn** 🆂🅷
(641) 752-6000. **$70-$90, 7 day notice.** 2613 S Center St. 0.5 mi n of jct US 30 and SR 14. Int corridors. **Pets:** Other species. $10 one-time fee/room. Service with restrictions, supervision.

A$K 🆂🅾 ✖ 🔊ᴹ 🅿 🐾 📟 💻 🏊

◆◆ **Econo Lodge** 🆂🅷
(641) 753-3333. **$50-$70, 7 day notice.** 3315 S Center St. Just n of jct US 30 and SR 14. Int corridors. **Pets:** Other species. $10 one-time fee/room. Service with restrictions, supervision.

A$K 🆂🅾 ✖ 🅿 📟 💻

◆◆ **Super 8 Motel-Marshalltown** 🆂🅷
(641) 753-8181. **Call for rates.** 18 E Berle Rd. Just n of jct US 30 and SR 14. Int corridors. **Pets:** Accepted.

✖

MASON CITY

🅐🅐🅐 ◆◆ **Best Value Inn** 🅼
(641) 424-2910. **$50-$69.** 24 5th St SW. Just w of jct US 65 and SR 122. Ext/int corridors. **Pets:** Medium, other species. Service with restrictions, crate.

SAVE ✖ 📟 🏊

◆◆ **Days Inn Mason City** 🆂🅷
(641) 424-0210. **$54-$66.** 2301 4th St SW. I-35, exit 194 (SR 122), 6 mi e. Int corridors. **Pets:** Accepted.

A$K 🆂🅾 ✖ 🐾 📟 💻

🅐🅐🅐 ◆◆ **Holiday Inn** 🆂🅷
(641) 423-1640. **$72-$129.** 2101 4th St SW (Hwy 122). 1.5 mi w of jct US 18 and 65, on SR 122; 8 mi e of jct I-35 and US 18. Ext/int corridors. **Pets:** $10 one-time fee/room. Designated rooms, service with restrictions, supervision.

SAVE ✖ 🔊ᴹ 🐾 📟 💻 🍽 🏊 ✖

◆◆ **Mason City Super 8 Motel & Suites** 🆂🅷
(641) 423-8855. **Call for rates.** 3010 4th St SW. I-35, exit 194 (SR 122), 6 mi e. Int corridors. **Pets:** Accepted.

✖ 🔊ᴹ 🐾 📟 💻 🏊

MONTICELLO

◆◆ **The Blue Inn** 🆂🅷
(319) 465-6116. **$62-$100.** 250 N Main St. North end of town on US 151. Int corridors. **Pets:** Accepted.

A$K 🆂🅾 ✖ 💻 🍽 🏊

MOUNT PLEASANT

◆◆ **Heartland Inn** 🆂🅷
(319) 385-2102. **$73-$83.** 810 N Grand Ave. US 218/27, exit 45, 0.6 mi s. Int corridors. **Pets:** Small. $5 daily fee/room. Designated rooms, service with restrictions, supervision.

A$K 🆂🅾 ✖ 📟 💻 🏊 ✖

◆◆ **Ramada Limited** 🆂🅷
(319) 385-0571. **Call for rates.** 1200 E Baker. US 218/27, exit 45, 0.6 mi s on Grand Ave. Int corridors. **Pets:** Large, other species. $8 daily fee/pet. Designated rooms, service with restrictions, supervision.

✖ 🎞 🐾 📟 💻 🏊 ✖

◆◆ **Super 8 Motel-Mt Pleasant** 🆂🅷
(319) 385-8888. **$46-$85.** 1000 N Grand Ave. US 218/27, exit 45, 0.6 mi s. Int corridors. **Pets:** Other species. $10 daily fee/room. Service with restrictions, supervision.

A$K 🆂🅾 ✖ 📟 💻

MOUNT VERNON

🅐🅐🅐 ◆◆◆◆ **Sleep Inn & Suites** 🆂🅷
(319) 895-0055. **$69-$149.** 310 Virgil Ave. Jct US 30 and SR 1, just se. Int corridors. **Pets:** Medium. $15 one-time fee/room. Service with restrictions, supervision.

SAVE 🆂🅾 ✖ 📟 💻 🏊

MUSCATINE

◆◆◆ **Holiday Inn Muscatine** 🆂🅷
(563) 264-5550. **$90.** 2915 N Hwy 61. Jct US 61 and SR 38, just n. Int corridors. **Pets:** Medium, other species. $50 deposit/room, $10 one-time fee/room. Service with restrictions, crate.

A$K 🆂🅾 ✖ 📟 💻 🍽 🏊 ✖

◆◆ **Super 8 Motel-Muscatine** 🆂🅷
(563) 263-9100. **$46-$69.** 2900 N Hwy 61. Jct US 61 and SR 38. Int corridors. **Pets:** $5 daily fee/room. Service with restrictions, supervision.

A$K 🆂🅾 ✖ 🎞 📟

NEWTON

◆◆◆ **Days Inn of Newton** 🆂🅷
(641) 792-2330. **$65-$120.** 1605 W 19th St S. I-80, exit 164 (SR 14), just n. Int corridors. **Pets:** Other species. $10 daily fee/pet. Service with restrictions, supervision.

A$K 🆂🅾 ✖ 🐾 📟 💻

◆◆◆ **Holiday Inn Express** 🆂🅷
(641) 792-7722. **$64-$80.** 1700 W 19th St S. I-80, exit 164 (SR 14), just nw. Int corridors. **Pets:** Medium. $20 one-time fee/pet. Service with restrictions, supervision.

A$K 🆂🅾 ✖ 🐾 📟 💻 🏊

🅐🅐🅐 ◆◆ **Ramada Limited** 🆂🅷
(641) 792-8100. **$70-$85.** 1405 W 19th St S. I-80, exit 164 (SR 14), just n. Int corridors. **Pets:** Small. $10 daily fee/pet. Designated rooms, service with restrictions, supervision.

SAVE 🆂🅾 ✖ 📟 💻

OKOBOJI

▼▼ AmericInn Lodge & Suites SH
(712) 332-9000. **$75-$195, 7 day notice.** 1005 Brooks Park Dr. Jct US 71 and SR 9, 2.5 mi s on US 71. Int corridors. **Pets:** Large, dogs only. $10 one-time fee/room. Service with restrictions, supervision.

⊠ ⅗ᴹ ⟨᠂⟩ 🛏 🖵 ⚊ ⊠

▼▼▼ Arrowwood Resort & Conference Center SH
(712) 332-2161. **$79-$189, 7 day notice.** 1405 US 71. Jct US 71 and SR 9, 3 mi s. Ext/int corridors. **Pets:** Service with restrictions, crate.

A$K ⅗ ⊠ ⅗ᴹ ⟨⟩ ⟨᠂⟩ 🛏 🖵 ⁙ ⚊ ⊠

OSCEOLA

▼▼▼ AmericInn Lodge & Suites SH
(641) 342-9400. **$79-$144.** 111 Ariel Cir. I-35, exit 33. Int corridors. **Pets:** Medium. $50 deposit/room, $10 one-time fee/room. Designated rooms, service with restrictions, supervision.

A$K ⅗ ⊠ ⅗ᴹ ⟨᠂⟩ 🛏 🖵 ⚊

OSKALOOSA

▼▼▼ Comfort Inn SH
(641) 672-0375. **$85-$119.** 2401 A Ave W. Just e of jct SR 163, exit 57 (SR 92). Int corridors. **Pets:** Medium. $20 one-time fee/room. Designated rooms, service with restrictions, supervision.

A$K ⅗ ⊠ ⟨᠂⟩ 🛏 🖵 ⚊ ⊠

△△△ ▼▼ Rodeway Inn M
(641) 673-8351. **$55-$75.** 1315 A Ave E. On SR 92, just w of jct SR 23. Ext/int corridors. **Pets:** Accepted.

SAVE ⅗ ⊠ 🛏 🖵

OTTUMWA

▼▼ Colonial Motor Inn M
(641) 683-1661. **$40-$46.** 1534 Albia Rd. W on US 34, s at Quincy St, 0.5 mi to Albia Rd, then just w. Ext/int corridors. **Pets:** Accepted.

A$K ⅗ ⊠ 🛏

▼▼ Heartland Inn SH
(641) 682-8526. **$110-$120.** 125 W Joseph Ave. 2 mi n on US 63. Int corridors. **Pets:** Small. $5 daily fee/room. Designated rooms, service with restrictions, supervision.

A$K ⅗ ⊠ ⟨⟩ 🛏 🖵 ⚊

PELLA

△△△ ▼▼▼ AmeriHost Inn & Suites-Pella SH
(641) 628-0085. **$69-$129.** 2104 Washington St. SR 163 Bypass at CR G28, exit 40. Int corridors. **Pets:** Other species. $75 deposit/pet. Designated rooms, service with restrictions, supervision.

SAVE ⅗ ⊠ ⅗ᴹ ⟨᠂⟩ 🛏 🖵 ⚊ ⊠

▼▼ Super 8 Motel-Pella SH
(641) 628-8181. **$49-$59.** 105 E Oskaloosa St. SR 163, exit 42, 1 mi n, then 0.5 mi e. Int corridors. **Pets:** $5 daily fee/pet. Designated rooms, service with restrictions, supervision.

A$K ⅗ ⊠ ⅗ᴹ ⟨⟩ 🛏 🖵

PERCIVAL

▼▼ Nebraska City Super 8 Motel SH
(712) 382-2828. **$56-$76.** 2103 249th St. I-29, exit 10, just w. Int corridors. **Pets:** Dogs only. $5 daily fee/pet. Designated rooms, service with restrictions, supervision.

A$K ⅗ ⊠ ⅗ᴹ ⟨᠂⟩ 🛏 🖵

QUAD CITIES AREA

BETTENDORF

▼▼ Heartland Inn-Bettendorf SH
(563) 355-6336. **$76-$86.** 815 Golden Valley Dr. I-74, exit 2, just e, just n on Utica Ridge Rd, then just w. Int corridors. **Pets:** Small. $5 daily fee/room. Designated rooms, service with restrictions, supervision.

A$K ⅗ ⊠ 🛏 🖵 ⚊ ⊠

▼▼▼▼ The Lodge-Hotel & Conference Center LH
(563) 359-7141. **$95-$105.** 900 Spruce Hills Dr. I-74, exit 2, just e. Int corridors. **Pets:** Accepted.

A$K ⅗ ⊠ ⟨⟩ 🛏 🖵 ⁙ ⚊ ⊠

▼▼▼ Signature Inn Bettendorf SH
(563) 355-7575. **$49-$104.** 3020 Utica Ridge Rd. I-74, exit 2, just e. Int corridors. **Pets:** Very small, other species. $10 daily fee/room. Service with restrictions, supervision.

A$K ⊠ ⅗ᴹ 🛏 🖵 ⚊

DAVENPORT

△△△ ▼▼▼ Baymont Inn & Suites Davenport SH
(563) 386-1600. **$59-$89.** 400 Jason Way Ct. I-80, exit 295A (US 61), just s to 65th St, then 0.5 mi ne on frontage road. Int corridors. **Pets:** Designated rooms, service with restrictions, supervision.

SAVE ⊠ ⟨⟩ ⟨᠂⟩ 🛏 🖵 ⚊

△△△ ▼▼▼▼ Best Western SteepleGate Inn SH 🐾
(563) 386-6900. **$89-$119.** 100 W 76th St. I-80, exit 295A (US 61), 0.5 mi s to 65th St and frontage road entrance, then just nw. Int corridors. **Pets:** Medium. $10 daily fee/pet. Designated rooms, service with restrictions, crate.

SAVE ⅗ ⊠ ⟨⟩ 🛏 🖵 ⁙ ⚊ ⊠

▼▼ Comfort Inn Davenport SH 🐾
(563) 391-8222. **$54-$140, 30 day notice.** 7222 Northwest Blvd. I-80, exit 292 (Northwest Blvd), 0.3 mi s. Ext corridors. **Pets:** $5 daily fee/room. Service with restrictions.

A$K ⅗ ⊠ ⟨᠂⟩ 🛏 🖵

▼▼▼ Country Inn & Suites by Carlson SH 🐾
(563) 388-6444. **$69-$99.** 140 E 55th St. I-80, exit 295A (US 61), 1.4 mi s. Int corridors. **Pets:** $25 one-time fee/room. Designated rooms, service with restrictions, crate.

A$K ⅗ ⊠ ⅗ᴹ ⟨᠂⟩ 🛏 🖵 ⚊

△△△ ▼▼▼▼ Davenport Holiday Inn SH
(563) 391-1230. **$69-$109.** 5202 Brady St. I-80, exit 295A (US 61), 1.6 mi s. Int corridors. **Pets:** Accepted.

SAVE ⅗ ⊠ ⅗ᴹ ⟨᠂⟩ 🛏 🖵 ⁙ ⚊ ⊠

△△△ ▼▼▼ Davenport Super 8 Motel SH
(563) 388-9810. **$45-$100.** 410 E 65th St. I-80, exit 295A (US 61), 0.5 mi s, then just e. Int corridors. **Pets:** Small, other species. $5 daily fee/pet. Service with restrictions, supervision.

SAVE ⊠ ⅗ᴹ 🛏

△△△ ▼▼▼ Exel Inn of Davenport SH
(563) 386-6350. **$43-$63.** 6310 N Brady St. I-80, exit 295A (US 61), 0.5 mi s. Int corridors. **Pets:** Small, other species. Designated rooms, service with restrictions, supervision.

SAVE ⅗ ⊠ ⟨⟩ 🛏 🖵

▼▼ Heartland Inn SH
(563) 386-8336. **$76-$86.** 6605 Brady St. I-80, exit 295A (US 61), just se. Int corridors. **Pets:** Small. $5 daily fee/room. Service with restrictions, supervision.

A$K ⅗ ⊠ 🛏 🖵 ⚊ ⊠

▼▼▼▼ **Residence Inn by Marriott** SH
(563) 391-8877. **$99-$149, 14 day notice.** 120 E 55th St. I-80, exit 295 (US 61), 1.4 mi s. Int corridors. **Pets:** Medium, other species. $75 one-time fee/room. Service with restrictions, supervision.
ASK Sb ✕ 🕎 🕭 🛏 💻 🌊 📵

▼▼ **Rhythm City Casino Blackhawk Hotel** LH
(563) 328-6000. **$54-$79.** 200 E 3rd St. Between Brady St (US 61 N) and Pershing Ave; downtown. Int corridors. **Pets:** Medium, other species. $25 deposit/room. Designated rooms, service with restrictions, supervision.
ASK Sb ✕ 🛏 💻

END AREA

SIBLEY

▼▼ **Super 8 Motel** SH
(712) 754-3603. **$48-$90.** 1108 2nd Ave. On SR 60. Int corridors. **Pets:** $8 daily fee/room. Designated rooms, service with restrictions, crate.
ASK Sb ✕ 🕎 🛏

SIOUX CITY

▼▼▼ **AmericInn Lodge & Suites** SH 🐾
(712) 255-1800. **$75-$80.** 4230 S Lewis Blvd. I-29, exit 143, just e. Int corridors. **Pets:** Other species. $50 deposit/room, $10 daily fee/room. Designated rooms, service with restrictions, supervision.
ASK Sb ✕ 🕎 🕭 🛏 💻 🌊 📵

▼▼ **Comfort Inn by Choice Hotels** SH
(712) 274-1300. **$69-$99.** 4202 S Lakeport St. I-29, exit 144A, 1 mi e on US 20, then just s; do not use Business Rt US 20. Int corridors. **Pets:** Accepted.
ASK Sb ✕ 🖉 🛏 💻 🌊

▼ **Motel 6-45** SH
(712) 277-3131. **$35-$51.** 6166 Harbor Dr. I-29, exit 141, just w. Int corridors. **Pets:** Accepted.
Sb ✕ 🕭 🌊

🅰🅰🅰 ▼▼▼▼ **Plaza Hotel & Conference Center** LH
(712) 277-4101. **$59-$80.** 707 4th St. Downtown. Int corridors. **Pets:** Accepted.
SAVE Sb ✕ 🕭 🛏 💻 🍴 🌊 📵

🅰🅰🅰 ▼▼▼ **Qualtiy Inn Hotel & Conference Center** M
(712) 277-3211. **$49-$69.** 1401 Zenith Dr. I-29, exit 149 (Hamilton Blvd). Int corridors. **Pets:** Service with restrictions, supervision.
SAVE Sb ✕ 🖉 🛏 💻 🍴 🌊 📵

▼▼ **Super 8 Motel** M
(712) 274-1520. **$55-$70.** 4307 Stone Ave. I-29, exit 144A, 4.2 mi e on US 20/75 to Business Rt 20 (exit 4B), 1.2 mi w. Int corridors. **Pets:** Small, dogs only. $10 daily fee/pet. Designated rooms, service with restrictions, supervision.
ASK Sb ✕ 🕎 🛏 💻

SLOAN

▼▼ **Winna Vegas Inn** SH
(712) 428-4280. **$53-$58.** 1862 Hwy 141. I-29, exit 127, just e. Int corridors. **Pets:** Accepted.
ASK Sb ✕ 🕎 🕭 🛏 💻

SPIRIT LAKE

▼▼ **Oaks Motel** M
(712) 336-2940. **$56-$100, 10 day notice.** 1701 Chicago. Jct US 71 and SR 9, just e. Ext corridors. **Pets:** Other species. $20 deposit/room. Designated rooms, service with restrictions, supervision.
✕ 🛏

▼ **Shamrock Inn** SH
(712) 336-2668. **$49-$109, 3 day notice.** 1905 18th St. 0.6 mi e on SR 9 from jct US 71. Ext/int corridors. **Pets:** $10 daily fee/room. Designated rooms, supervision.
ASK Sb ✕ 🛏 💻 🌊

▼▼ **Spirit Lake Super 8** SH
(712) 336-4901. **$55-$120, 3 day notice.** 2203 Circle Dr W. Jct US 71 and SR 9. Int corridors. **Pets:** $10 one-time fee/room. Service with restrictions, supervision.
ASK ✕ 🕎 🛏 💻

STORY CITY

🅰🅰🅰 ▼▼▼▼ **Comfort Inn** SH 🐾
(515) 733-6363. **$70-$86.** 425 Timberland Dr. I-35, exit 124, just sw. Int corridors. **Pets:** Other species. $15 one-time fee/room. Service with restrictions, supervision.
SAVE Sb ✕ 🕭 🛏 💻 🌊 📵

▼▼ **Viking Motor Inn** M
(515) 733-4306. **$58.** 1520 Broad St. I-35, exit 124, just w. Int corridors. **Pets:** Medium. Service with restrictions, supervision.
ASK Sb ✕ 🛏 💻

STUART

▼▼▼ **AmericInn Motel & Suites** SH
(515) 523-9000. **$49-$149.** 420 SW 8th St. I-80, exit 93, just w. Int corridors. **Pets:** Medium. $50 deposit/room, $10 daily fee/pet. Service with restrictions, supervision.
ASK Sb ✕ 🕎 🖉 🕭 🛏 💻 🌊 📵

▼▼ **Super 8 Motel** SH
(515) 523-2888. **Call for rates.** 203 SE 7th St. I-80, exit 93. Int corridors. **Pets:** Accepted.
✕ 🕎 🛏 💻 🌊

TOLEDO

▼▼ **Super 8 Motel-Toledo** SH
(641) 484-5888. **$49-$79.** 207 Hwy 30 W. On US 30, just w of jct US 63 and 30. Ext/int corridors. **Pets:** Accepted.
ASK Sb ✕ 🕎 🛏 💻

URBANA

▼▼ **Super 8 Urbana Iowa** SH
(319) 443-8888. **$67-$148.** 5369 Hutton Dr. I-380, exit 43, just s on east access road. Int corridors. **Pets:** Medium. $15 one-time fee/room. Designated rooms, service with restrictions, supervision.
ASK Sb ✕ 🛏 💻 🌊 📵

URBANDALE

🅰🅰🅰 ▼▼▼ **Comfort Inn-Merle Hay** SH
(515) 270-1037. **$64-$99.** 5900 Sutton Dr. I-80, exit 131, just s, then w. Int corridors. **Pets:** Other species. $5 daily fee/pet. Service with restrictions, supervision.
SAVE Sb ✕ 🖉 🛏 💻 🌊 📵

▼▼▼ **Holiday Inn Northwest** SH
(515) 278-0271. **$76-$84.** 5000 Merle Hay Rd. I-80/35, exit 131 (Merle Hay Rd), just s. Ext/int corridors. **Pets:** Large. $10 one-time fee/room. Service with restrictions, supervision.
ASK Sb ✕ 🕎 🛏 💻 🍴 🌊 📵

◆◆ **Microtel Inn and Suites** [SH] 🐾
(515) 727-5424. **$65.** 8711 Plum Dr. I-35/80, exit 129. Int corridors. **Pets:** Other species. $25 deposit/room. Service with restrictions, supervision.
[A$K] [SD] ⊠ ♿M ♿ ▣ 📺

◆◆◆ **Sleep Inn** [SH]
(515) 270-2424. **$75-$105.** 11211 Hickman Rd. I-35/80, exit 125 (Hickman Rd), just ne. Int corridors. **Pets:** Accepted.
[A$K] [SD] ⊠ ♿M 👂 ♿ ▣ 📺 🏊 🏋

WALNUT

◆◆ **Super 8 Motel** [SH]
(712) 784-2221. **$55-$85.** 2109 Antique City Dr. I-80, exit 46, just n. Int corridors. **Pets:** $10 one-time fee/pet. Designated rooms, service with restrictions, supervision.
[A$K] [SD] ⊠ ♿M ♿ ▣ 🏊

WASHINGTON

◆◆ **Super 8 Motel-Washington** [M]
(319) 653-6621. **$56-$62.** 119 Westview Dr. 1.5 mi w on SR 1 and 92. Int corridors. **Pets:** $25 deposit/pet. Designated rooms, service with restrictions, supervision.
[A$K] [SD] ⊠ ▣ 📺

WATERLOO

◆◆ **Comfort Inn by Choice Hotels** [SH]
(319) 234-7411. **$64-$99.** 1945 La Porte Rd. I-380, exit 72 (E San Marnan). Int corridors. **Pets:** Small. Designated rooms, service with restrictions, supervision.
[A$K] [SD] ⊠ 👂 ▣ 📺 🏊

◆◆ **Heartland Inn-Crossroads** [SH]
(319) 235-4461. **$122-$132.** 1809 La Porte Rd. I-380, exit 72 (E San Marnan), just nw. Int corridors. **Pets:** Small. $5 daily fee/room. Designated rooms, service with restrictions, supervision.
[A$K] [SD] ⊠ ♿ ▣ 📺 🏊

◆◆ **Heartland Inn-Greyhound Park** [SH]
(319) 232-7467. **$110-$120.** 3052 Marnie Ave. 1 mi n of jct US 20 and 63, exit 227. Int corridors. **Pets:** Small. $5 daily fee/room. Designated rooms, service with restrictions, supervision.
[A$K] [SD] ⊠ ▣ 📺 🏊 🏋

[AAA] ◆◆◆ **Holiday Inn Express** [SH]
(319) 233-9191. **$82-$105.** 2141 La Porte Rd. I-380, exit 72 (E San Marnan). Int corridors. **Pets:** Small. $10 one-time fee/room. Designated rooms, service with restrictions, supervision.
[SAVE] [SD] ⊠ ♿ ▣ 📺 🏊 🏋

◆◆ **Motel 6-4081** [SH]
(319) 236-3238. **Call for rates.** 2343 Logan Ave. On US 63, 2.5 mi n of jct US 218 and 63. Int corridors. **Pets:** Accepted.
⊠ ♿M ▣ 📺 🏊

[AAA] ◆◆◆ **Quality Inn & Suites** [SH]
(319) 235-0301. **$54-$99.** 226 W 5th St. Downtown. Int corridors. **Pets:** Accepted.
[SAVE] [SD] ⊠ ♿M ♿ ▣ 📺

◆◆ **Ramada Inn & 5 Sullivan Brothers Convention Center** [LH]
(319) 233-7560. **$89-$109.** 205 W 4th St. 4th and Commercial sts; downtown. Int corridors. **Pets:** Other species. Designated rooms, service with restrictions, supervision.
[A$K] [SD] ⊠ ♿M 👂 ▣ 📺 🍴 🏊 🏋

WAVERLY

◆◆ **AmeriHost Inn-Waverly** [SH]
(319) 352-0399. **$79-$149, 7 day notice.** 404 29th Ave SW. US Business Rt 218, exit 198, 0.5 mi n. Int corridors. **Pets:** Other species. $10 daily fee/pet. Designated rooms, service with restrictions, supervision.
[A$K] [SD] ⊠ ♿M ♿ ▣ 📺 🏊 🏋

[AAA] ◆◆ **Red Fox Inn** [SH]
(319) 352-5330. **$56-$195.** 1900 Heritage Way. On SR 3, 2 mi e of jct US 218 and SR 3 (exit 203). Ext/int corridors. **Pets:** Accepted.
[SAVE] ⊠ 👂 ▣ 📺 🍴 🏊 🏋

◆◆ **Super 8 Waverly** [SH]
(319) 352-0888. **$59-$90.** 301 13th Ave SW. Business Rt US 218 S, exit 198, 1.2 mi n. Int corridors. **Pets:** Accepted.
[A$K] [SD] ⊠ ♿M ▣

WEBSTER CITY

◆◆ **The Executive Inn** [SH]
(515) 832-3631. **$45-$75.** 1700 Superior St. Jct US 20 and SR 17, exit 140, 0.5 mi n. Int corridors. **Pets:** Accepted.
⊠ ▣ 📺 🏊

WEST BURLINGTON

◆◆ **AmericInn** [SH]
(319) 758-9000. **$65-$125.** 628 S Gear Ave. US 34, exit 260 (Gear Ave), just ne. Int corridors. **Pets:** Other species. Designated rooms, service with restrictions, supervision.
[A$K] [SD] ⊠ ♿M 👂 ♿ ▣ 📺 🏊 🏋

WEST DES MOINES

◆◆◆ **Candlewood Suites-West Des Moines** [SH]
(515) 221-0001. **$75-$119.** 7625 Office Plaza Dr N. I-80, exit 121 (74th St), just sw. Int corridors. **Pets:** Medium. $25 one-time fee/pet. Service with restrictions, crate.
[A$K] [SD] ⊠ ♿M ♿ ▣ 📺

◆◆◆ **Hawthorn Suites Ltd** [SH]
(515) 223-0000. **$102-$112.** 6905 Lake Dr. I-80, exit 121 (74th St), just ne. Int corridors. **Pets:** Large, dogs only. Service with restrictions, supervision.
[A$K] [SD] ⊠ ♿ ▣ 📺 🏊 🏋

◆◆ **Motel 6-1408** [SH]
(515) 267-8885. **$41-$55.** 7655 Office Plaza Dr N. I-80, exit 121 (74th St), just sw. Int corridors. **Pets:** Service with restrictions, supervision.
[SD] ⊠ ♿M ♿ 🏊

[AAA] ◆◆◆ **Sheraton West Des Moines** [LH] 🐾
(515) 223-1800. **$125-$129.** 1800 50th St. I-80/35, exit 124 (University Ave), just e. Int corridors. **Pets:** Medium. $25 one-time fee/room. Designated rooms, service with restrictions, supervision.
[SAVE] [SD] ⊠ ♿M 👂 ♿ ▣ 📺 🍴 🏊 🏋

◆◆◆ **Valley West Inn** [SH]
(515) 225-2524. **$69-$119.** 3535 Westown Pkwy. I-235, exit 1 (35th St), just n. Int corridors. **Pets:** $10 daily fee/pet. Designated rooms, service with restrictions, crate.
[A$K] [SD] ⊠ 👂 ▣ 📺 🍴 🏊 🏋

◆◆◆ **West Des Moines Marriott** [LH]
(515) 267-1500. **$89-$119.** 1250 Jordan Creek Pkwy. I-80, exit 121 (74th St). Int corridors. **Pets:** Medium. $50 one-time fee/room. No service, supervision.
[A$K] [SD] ⊠ ♿M ♿ ▣ 📺 🍴 🏊 🏋

WEST LIBERTY

◆ **Econo Lodge** [M]
(319) 627-2171. **$49-$70.** 1943 Garfield Ave. I-80, exit 259, just sw. Ext corridors. **Pets:** Medium. $5 daily fee/pet. Service with restrictions, supervision.
[A$K] [SD] ⊠ 📺

WILLIAMS

▽▽ ◆◆ Best Western Norseman Inn 🅼
(515) 854-2281. **$60-$70.** 3086 220th St. I-35, exit 144, just e. Int corridors. **Pets:** Medium, dogs only. Designated rooms, service with restrictions, supervision.

Ⓐ🅂🅅 🅂🄳 ⊠ 🄱 💻

WILLIAMSBURG

◉◉◉ ▽▽◆◆ Best Western Quiet House Suites 🆂🅷
(319) 668-9777. **$85-$140.** 1708 N Highland St. I-80, exit 220, 0.8 mi n. Int corridors. **Pets:** Accepted.

🆂🅰🆅🅴 🅂🄳 ⊠ 🎜 🅺 🄱 💻 🛋

▽▽◆◆ Comfort Inn Amana Colonies 🆂🅷
(319) 668-2700. **$68-$140.** 2185 U Ave. I-80, exit 225 (US 151), just n. Int corridors. **Pets:** Accepted.

Ⓐ🅂🅺 🅂🄳 ⊠ 🅺🅼 🅺 🄱 💻 🛋

◉◉◉ ▽▽◆◆ Crest Country Inn 🅼
(319) 668-1522. **$57-$65.** 340 W Evans St. I-80, exit 220, just nw. Ext corridors. **Pets:** Medium. $5 daily fee/pet. Designated rooms, supervision.

🆂🅰🆅🅴 🅂🄳 ⊠ 🅺

◉◉◉ ▽▽◆◆ Super 8 Motel 🆂🅷
(319) 668-9718. **$70-$100.** 1708 N Highland St. I-80, exit 220, 0.8 mi n. Ext/int corridors. **Pets:** Accepted.

🆂🅰🆅🅴 🅂🄳 ⊠ 🎜

KANSAS

ABILENE

Best Western President's Inn SH
(785) 263-2050. **$44-$80.** 2210 N Buckeye. I-70, exit 275. Ext corridors.
Pets: Service with restrictions, supervision.

Days Inn-Abilene Pride SH
(785) 263-2800. **$39-$68.** 1709 N Buckeye Ave. I-70, exit 275, 0.5 mi s.
Ext/int corridors. **Pets:** Accepted.

Diamond Motel M
(785) 263-2360. **$34-$46.** 1407 NW 3rd St. I-70, exit 275, 1.3 mi s, then
1 mi w. Ext corridors. **Pets:** Small. $5 deposit/pet. Designated rooms,
service with restrictions, supervision.

Holiday Inn Express Hotel & Suites SH
(785) 263-4049. **$76-$99.** 110 E Lafayette Ave. I-70, exit 275, just n. Int
corridors. **Pets:** Accepted.

Super 8 Motel SH
(785) 263-4545. **$54-$67.** 2207 N Buckeye. I-70, exit 275, just s. Int
corridors. **Pets:** $50 deposit/room, $10 one-time fee/pet. Service with
restrictions, supervision.

ATCHISON

Comfort Inn SH
(913) 367-7666. **$54-$90.** 509 S 9th. Just s of jct US 59, on US 73. Int
corridors. **Pets:** Accepted.

BAXTER SPRINGS

Baxter Inn-4-Less SH
(620) 856-2106. **$40-$50.** 2451 Military Ave. On US 69 alternate route,
1 mi s of jct US 166. Int corridors. **Pets:** Supervision.

BELLEVILLE

Super 8 Motel SH
(785) 527-2112. **$45-$95.** 1410 28th St. On US 36, 0.5 mi e of jct US
81. Int corridors. **Pets:** Accepted.

BELOIT

Super 8 Motel-Beloit SH
(785) 738-4300. **$54-$75.** 205 W Hwy 24. Just e of jct SR 14. Ext/int
corridors. **Pets:** Medium. Designated rooms, service with restrictions, crate.

BURLINGTON

Country Haven Inn SH
(620) 364-8260. **$60.** 207 Cross St. Just e of US 75; 1 mi n of center.
Int corridors. **Pets:** Small, dogs only. $25 deposit/pet. Service with restric-
tions, supervision.

CHANUTE

Guest House Motor Inn M
(620) 431-0600. **$33-$38.** 1814 S Santa Fe. US 169, exit 35th St, 2.5
mi ne. Ext corridors. **Pets:** Small. $5 daily fee/pet. Service with restric-
tions.

CLAY CENTER

Cedar Court Motel SH
(785) 632-2148. **$45-$65.** 905 Crawford. On US 24, just e of jct SR 15.
Ext corridors. **Pets:** Small, dogs only. $5 deposit/pet. Designated rooms,
service with restrictions, supervision.

COFFEYVILLE

Appletree Inn M
(620) 251-0002. **$67-$96.** 820 E 11th St. 0.8 mi e of center. Int corridors. **Pets:** Very small. $3 daily fee/pet. Designated rooms, service with
restrictions, supervision.

Super 8 Motel M
(620) 251-2250. **$64-$74, 7 day notice.** 104 W 11th St. On US 169
and 166; center. Ext corridors. **Pets:** Medium, dogs only. $10 one-time
fee/room. Service with restrictions, supervision.

COLBY

Best Western Crown Motel M ❖
(785) 462-3943. **$65-$90.** 2320 S Range. I-70, exit 53 (SR 25), just s.
Ext corridors. **Pets:** Other species.

Comfort Inn SH
(785) 462-3833. **$79-$119.** 2225 S Range. I-70, exit 53 (SR 25), just s.
Int corridors. **Pets:** Other species. $5 daily fee/pet. Designated rooms,
service with restrictions, supervision.

Days Inn SH
(785) 462-8691. **$55-$85.** 1925 S Range. I-70, exit 53 (SR 25), 0.3 mi
n. Int corridors. **Pets:** Other species. $5 daily fee/pet. Service with restric-
tions, supervision.

Holiday Inn Express Hotel & Suites SH
(785) 462-8787. **$85-$110.** 645 W Willow. I-70, exit 53 (SR 25), just ne. Int corridors. **Pets:** Other species. $10 daily fee/room. Service with restrictions, supervision.

Motel 6 SH
(785) 462-8201. **$45-$56.** 1985 S Range. I-70, exit 53 (SR 25), just n. Ext/int corridors. **Pets:** Accepted.

Quality Inn SH
(785) 462-3933. **$55-$85, 7 day notice.** 1950 S Range. I-70, exit 53 (SR 25), just n. Ext/int corridors. **Pets:** Other species. $20 deposit/room.

Super 8 Motel SH
(785) 462-8248. **$47-$74.** 1040 Zelfer Ave. I-70, exit 53 (SR 25), 0.3 mi n, then just w. Int corridors. **Pets:** Accepted.

CONCORDIA

Super 8 Motel-Concordia SH
(785) 243-4200. **$59-$69.** 1320 Lincoln. On US 81, 1 mi s of center. Ext/int corridors. **Pets:** Accepted.

COTTONWOOD FALLS

Grand Central Hotel CI
(620) 273-6763. **$180.** 215 Broadway. Just w of US 177; center of downtown. Int corridors. **Pets:** Dogs only. Service with restrictions, supervision.

COUNCIL GROVE

The Cottage House Hotel & Motel SH
(620) 767-6828. **$58-$175, 7 day notice.** 25 N Neosho. Just n of Main St; downtown. Ext/int corridors. **Pets:** Other species. $10 daily fee/pet. Service with restrictions, supervision.

DODGE CITY

Econo Lodge of Dodge City SH
(620) 225-0231. **$47-$60.** 1610 W Wyatt Earp Blvd. 1 mi w on US 50 business route. Int corridors. **Pets:** Medium. $5 daily fee/pet. Service with restrictions, supervision.

Holiday Inn Express SH
(620) 227-5000. **$90-$100.** 2320 W Wyatt Earp Blvd. 1.4 mi w on US 50 business route. Int corridors. **Pets:** Medium, other species. Service with restrictions, supervision.

Super 8 Motel SH
(620) 225-3924. **$61-$71.** 1708 W Wyatt Earp Blvd. 1.2 mi w on US 50 business route. Int corridors. **Pets:** Other species. No service, supervision.

EL DORADO

Best Western Red Coach Inn SH
(316) 321-6900. **$63-$110, 3 day notice.** 2525 W Central Ave. I-35, exit 71, 0.5 mi e. Ext corridors. **Pets:** Small, dogs only. $10 one-time fee/pet. Designated rooms, service with restrictions, supervision.

ELLSWORTH

Best Western Garden Prairie Inn SH
(785) 472-3116. **$74-$81.** Jct SR 140 & 156. Jct SR 140 and 156. Ext/int corridors. **Pets:** No service, supervision.

EMPORIA

Best Value Inn M
(620) 342-7567. **$45-$70.** 2913 W Hwy 50. I-35, exit 127, 0.8 mi e. Int corridors. **Pets:** Dogs only. $10 one-time fee/room. Supervision.

Days Inn SH
(620) 342-1787. **$58-$95.** 3032 W Hwy 50. I-35, exit 127, 0.5 mi e. Ext/int corridors. **Pets:** Other species. Service with restrictions, supervision.

Motel 6 #4148 SH
(620) 343-1240. **$42-$48.** 2630 W 18th Ave. I-35, exit 128 (Industrial St), just s, then e. Int corridors. **Pets:** Accepted.

FORT SCOTT

1st Interstate Inn M
(620) 223-5330. **$44-$59, 15 day notice.** 2222 1/2 S Main. On US 69 Bypass, 2.5 mi s of US 54. Int corridors. **Pets:** Accepted.

Best Western Fort Scott Inn SH
(620) 223-0100. **$63.** 101 State St. On US 69 Bypass, exit US 54 southbound; exit 3rd St northbound. Ext/int corridors. **Pets:** Accepted.

GARDEN CITY

AmericInn Lodge & Suites SH
(620) 272-9860. **$85-$160.** 3020 E Kansas Ave. Jct US 50, 83 and SR 156. Int corridors. **Pets:** $50 deposit/room, $10 daily fee/pet. Service with restrictions, supervision.

Best Value Inn SH
(620) 275-5095. **$50-$57.** 1818 Commanche Dr. W of US 50 and 83 Bypass, on SR 156. Ext corridors. **Pets:** Accepted.

Best Western Red Baron Hotel SH
(620) 275-4164. **$59-$67.** Jct US 50 & 83. 2.3 mi e on US 50 business route, at US 83 Bypass. Ext corridors. **Pets:** Other species. Service with restrictions, supervision.

Best Western Wheat Lands Hotel & Conference Center SH
(620) 276-2387. **$64-$94.** 1311 E Fulton. 1 mi e on US 50 business route. Ext corridors. **Pets:** Other species. Service with restrictions, crate.

Comfort Inn SH
(620) 275-5800. **$60-$115.** 2608 E Kansas Ave. Jct US 50, 83 and SR 156. Int corridors. **Pets:** Medium, other species. $10 daily fee/pet. Service with restrictions, crate.

Holiday Inn Express Hotel & Suites SH
(620) 275-5900. **$89-$100.** 2502 E Kansas Ave. Jct US 50, 83 and SR 156. Int corridors. **Pets:** Large, other species. Service with restrictions, crate.

▼▼▼ National 9 Inn **M**
(620) 275-0677. **Call for rates.** 123 Honey Bee Ct. 2.3 mi e on US 50 business route, at US 83 Bypass. Ext corridors. **Pets:** Other species. Service with restrictions, supervision.

⊠ 🖃 ➣

▼▼▼ Plaza Hotel **SH**
(620) 275-7471. **$82-$88.** 1911 E Kansas Ave. 0.5 mi w of US 50 and 83 Bypass, on SR 156. Int corridors. **Pets:** Other species. Service with restrictions, supervision.

SAVE 🖬 ⊠ 🖃 🖃 ⑪ ➣ ⊠

▼▼▼ Super 8 Motel-Garden City **M**
(620) 275-9625. **Call for rates.** 2808 N Taylor. 0.7 mi s of jct US 50 and 83, on US 83 business route. Int corridors. **Pets:** Accepted.

⊠ 🖉 🖃 ➣

GODDARD

🔺 ▼▼▼ Express Inn **M**
(316) 794-3366. **$46-$48.** 19941 W Kellogg Dr. Just se of jct US 54/400 and 199th St. Ext corridors. **Pets:** Medium, other species. $5 one-time fee/room. Service with restrictions, supervision.

SAVE ⊠ 🖃

GOODLAND

🔺 ▼▼▼ Best Western Buffalo Inn **SH**
(785) 899-3621. **$59-$80.** 830 W Hwy 24. I-70, exit 17 or 19, n to jct US 24 and SR 27. Ext corridors. **Pets:** $25 deposit/room. Service with restrictions, supervision.

SAVE 🖬 ⊠ 🖃 🖃 ⑪ ➣

🔺 ▼▼▼ Comfort Inn **SH**
(785) 899-7181. **$84-$120, 30 day notice.** 2519 Enterprise Rd. I-70, exit 17, just n. Int corridors. **Pets:** Medium. $15 daily fee/pet. Service with restrictions, supervision.

SAVE 🖬 ⊠ 🖾ᴹ 🖃 🖃 🖃 ➣

GREAT BEND

🔺 ▼▼▼ Best Western Angus Inn **SH**
(620) 792-3541. **$75.** 2920 10th St. 0.8 mi w on US 56 and SR 96/156. Ext/int corridors. **Pets:** Small, dogs only. Service with restrictions, supervision.

SAVE 🖬 ⊠ 🖉 🖃 🖃 ⑪ ➣ ⊠

🔺 ▼▼▼ Highland Hotel & Convention Center **SH**
(620) 792-2431. **$72-$100.** 3017 10th St. 1 mi w on US 56 and SR 96/156. Ext/int corridors. **Pets:** Large. $10 daily fee/pet. Service with restrictions, supervision.

SAVE 🖬 ⊠ 🖃 🖃 🖃 ⑪ ➣ ⊠

GREENSBURG

▼▼ Best Western J-Hawk Motel **SH**
(620) 723-2121. **$49-$72.** 515 W Kansas Ave. Just w on US 54. Ext corridors. **Pets:** Small. Service with restrictions, supervision.

ASK 🖬 ⊠ 🖃 ➣

HAYS

▼▼ Best Western Vagabond Motel **M**
(785) 625-2511. **$55-$72.** 2524 Vine St. I-70, exit 159 (US 183), 1 mi s. Ext corridors. **Pets:** Service with restrictions, supervision.

ASK 🖬 ⊠ 🖃 🖃 🖃 ⑪ ➣

🔺 ▼▼▼ Hampton Inn-Hays **SH** ❀
(785) 625-8103. **$61-$73.** 3801 Vine St. I-70, exit 159 (US 183), just sw. Ext/int corridors. **Pets:** Service with restrictions, supervision.

SAVE 🖬 ⊠ 🖉 🖃 🖃

▼▼▼ Holiday Inn-Hays **SH**
(785) 625-7371. **$59-$99.** 3603 Vine St. I-70, exit 159 (US 183), just s. Ext/int corridors. **Pets:** Other species. $10 one-time fee/room. Service with restrictions, supervision.

ASK ⊠ 🖾ᴹ 🖉 🖃 🖃 🖃 ⑪ ➣ ⊠

▼▼▼ Motel 6-167 **M**
(785) 625-4282. **$45-$60.** 3404 Vine St. I-70, exit 159 (US 183), 0.3 mi s. Ext corridors. **Pets:** Accepted.

🖬 ⊠ ➣

HAYSVILLE

🔺 ▼▼▼ Haysville Inn **M**
(316) 522-1000. **$42-$48.** 301 E 71st St. I-35, exit 39, just w. Ext corridors. **Pets:** Medium. Service with restrictions, supervision.

SAVE 🖬 ⊠ 🖃 🖃

HESSTON

▼▼▼ AmericInn Lodge & Suites-Hesston **SH**
(620) 327-2053. **$68-$99.** 2 Leonard Ct. I-135, exit 40, just e. Int corridors. **Pets:** Other species. Service with restrictions, supervision.

🖬 ⊠ 🖃 🖃 ➣

HILLSBORO

▼▼▼ Country Haven Inn **SH**
(620) 947-2929. **$55-$59, 3 day notice.** 804 Western Heights. On US 56; center. Int corridors. **Pets:** Accepted.

ASK 🖬 ⊠ 🖃

HUTCHINSON

🔺 ▼▼ Astro Motel **M**
(620) 663-1151. **$50-$70.** 15 E 4th Ave. Just e of Main St. Ext corridors. **Pets:** Accepted.

SAVE 🖬 ⊠ 🖃 ➣

▼▼▼ Comfort Inn **SH**
(620) 663-7822. **$59-$119.** 1621 Super Plaza. Just w of jct SR 61 and N 17th Ave. Int corridors. **Pets:** Accepted.

ASK 🖬 ⊠ 🖉 🖃 🖃 🖃 ➣

▼▼▼ Holiday Inn Express Hotel & Suites **SH**
(620) 669-5200. **$90-$100.** 1601 Super Plaza. Just w of jct SR 61 and N 17th Ave. Int corridors. **Pets:** $50 deposit/room. Service with restrictions, supervision.

ASK 🖬 ⊠ 🖾ᴹ 🖉 🖃 🖃 🖃 ➣

▼▼▼ Microtel Inn & Suites **SH** ❀
(620) 665-3700. **$64-$70.** 1420 N Lorraine. Just nw of jct SR 61 and N 11th Ave. Int corridors. **Pets:** Medium. Service with restrictions, crate.

ASK 🖬 ⊠ 🖃 🖃 🖃

▼▼▼ Super 8 Motel-Hutchinson **M**
(620) 662-6394. **$45-$70.** 1315 E 11th Ave. Just se of jct SR 61. Int corridors. **Pets:** Dogs only. $10 one-time fee/room. Service with restrictions, supervision.

ASK 🖬 ⊠ 🖉 🖃

INDEPENDENCE

▼▼▼ Appletree Inn **SH**
(620) 331-5500. **$73-$76.** 201 N 8th St. At 8th and Laurel sts. Ext/int corridors. **Pets:** Accepted.

⊠ 🖃 ➣

🔺 ▼▼▼▼ Glencliff Farm Bed, Breakfast & Spa **BB**
(620) 331-1277. **$79-$189, 15 day notice.** 448 Glencliff Rd. 1.5 mi n on US 75. Int corridors. **Pets:** Accepted.

SAVE ⊠ 🖃 🖃 ➣ ⊠

⚫ ♦♦♦ Knights Inn 🆂🅷

(620) 331-7300. **$44-$69.** 3222 W Main St. 1.4 mi e of jct US 75 and 160. Ext corridors. **Pets:** Medium. $10 daily fee/pet. Service with restrictions, supervision.

🆂🅰🆅🅴 🆂🅾 ✖ ❘❘ 🖵 ⊇

♦♦♦ Microtel Inn & Suites 🆂🅷

(620) 331-0088. **$60-$76.** 2917 W Main St. 1.2 mi e of jct US 75 and 160. Int corridors. **Pets:** Other species. $6 one-time fee/room. Service with restrictions, crate.

🅰🆂🅺 🆂🅾 ✖ 🕭ᴹ 🖉 🛆 ❘❘ 🖵

IOLA

⚫ ♦♦♦ Best Western Inn 🅼

(620) 365-5161. **$54-$58.** 1315 N State St. Jct US 54 and 169, 1.5 mi w on US 54, then 0.8 mi n. Ext corridors. **Pets:** Small. Service with restrictions, supervision.

🆂🅰🆅🅴 🆂🅾 ✖ 🕭ᴹ 🖉 🛆 ❘❘ 🖵 🍴 ⊇

JUNCTION CITY

♦♦♦ Days Inn 🆂🅷

(785) 762-2727. **$55-$75, 7 day notice.** 1024 S Washington St. I-70, exit 296, just n. Ext/int corridors. **Pets:** Other species. Designated rooms, service with restrictions, supervision.

🅰🆂🅺 🆂🅾 ✖ 🖉 ❘❘ 🖵 ⊇ ✖

KANSAS CITY METROPOLITAN AREA

DE SOTO

♦♦♦ Super 8 Motel 🆂🅷

(913) 583-3880. **Call for rates.** 34085 Commerce Dr. Just ne of jct SR 10 and DeSoto exit. Int corridors. **Pets:** Accepted.

✖ ❘❘

GARDNER

♦♦♦ Super 8 🆂🅷

(913) 856-8887. **$45-$120.** 2001 E Santa Fe. I-35, exit 210. Int corridors. **Pets:** Medium, other species. $10 daily fee/pet. Designated rooms, service with restrictions, supervision.

🅰🆂🅺 🆂🅾 ✖ 🕭ᴹ ❘❘

KANSAS CITY

⚫ ♦♦♦ Best Western Inn and Conference Center 🆂🅷

(913) 677-3060. **$89.** 501 Southwest Blvd. I-35, exit 234 (7th St), just s. Int corridors. **Pets:** Service with restrictions, supervision.

🆂🅰🆅🅴 🆂🅾 ✖ ❘❘ 🖵 ⊇

♦♦ Microtel Inn & Suites at the Speedway 🆂🅷

(913) 334-3028. **$59-$69.** 7721 Elizabeth St. I-70, exit 414 (78th St N), just ne. Int corridors. **Pets:** Other species. Service with restrictions, supervision.

🅰🆂🅺 🆂🅾 ✖ 🕭ᴹ 🛆 ❘❘ 🖵 ⊇

LENEXA

♦♦ Days Inn Lenexa 🅼

(913) 492-7200. **$57-$62.** 9630 Rosehill Rd. I-35, exit 224 (95th St), just e. Ext corridors. **Pets:** Small. Service with restrictions, supervision.

🅰🆂🅺 🆂🅾 ✖ 🕭ᴹ 🛆 ❘❘ ⊇

♦♦♦♦ La Quinta Inn Kansas City (Lenexa) 🆂🅷

(913) 492-5500. **$79-$99.** 9461 Lenexa Dr. I-35, exit 224 (95th St), just ne; entrance left on Monrovia Rd, off 95th St. Int corridors. **Pets:** Other species. No service, supervision.

🅰🆂🅺 ✖ 🛆 ❘❘ 🖵 ⊇

⚫ ♦♦♦ Econo Lodge 🅼

(785) 238-8181. **$40-$80.** 211 Flint Hills Blvd. I-70, exit 299 (Grandview Plaza). Int corridors. **Pets:** Accepted.

🆂🅰🆅🅴 🆂🅾 ✖ ❘❘ 🖵

⚫ ♦♦♦ Golden Wheat Budget Host 🅼

(785) 238-5106. **$30-$75, 3 day notice.** 820 S Washington St. I-70, exit 296, 0.5 mi n. Ext corridors. **Pets:** Dogs only. $5 daily fee/pet. Designated rooms, service with restrictions, supervision.

🆂🅰🆅🅴 🆂🅾 ✖ ❘❘

♦♦♦ Holiday Inn Express 🆂🅷

(785) 762-4200. **$55-$110, 15 day notice.** 120 N East St. I-70, exit 298, just nw. Int corridors. **Pets:** Small. $25 deposit/pet, $5 daily fee/pet. Service with restrictions, supervision.

🅰🆂🅺 🆂🅾 ✖ 🕭ᴹ 🖉 ❘❘ 🖵 ⊇ ✖

♦♦ Ramada Limited 🆂🅷

(785) 238-1141. **$62-$72.** 1133 S Washington St. I-70, exit 296. Ext corridors. **Pets:** Accepted.

🅰🆂🅺 🆂🅾 ✖ ❘❘ 🖵

⚫ ♦♦♦♦ Wellesley Inn & Suites (Kansas City/Lenexa) 🆂🅷

(913) 894-5550. **$69-$139.** 8015 Lenexa Dr. I-35, exit 227 (75th St), 1 mi s on east frontage road. Ext corridors. **Pets:** Accepted.

🆂🅰🆅🅴 🆂🅾 ✖ 🕭ᴹ 🖉 🛆 ❘❘ 🖵 ⊇

MERRIAM

⚫ ♦♦♦ Comfort Inn-Merriam 🆂🅷

(913) 262-2622. **$45-$75.** 6401 E Frontage Rd. I-35, exit 228B (Shawnee Mission Pkwy), just se. Int corridors. **Pets:** Medium. $5 deposit/pet. Designated rooms, service with restrictions, supervision.

🆂🅰🆅🅴 🆂🅾 ✖ 🖉 ❘❘ 🖵 ⊇

♦♦♦♦ Drury Inn Merriam/Shawnee Mission Parkway 🆂🅷

(913) 236-9200. **$60-$103.** 9009 W Shawnee Mission Pkwy. I-35, exit 228B (Shawnee Mission Pkwy). Int corridors. **Pets:** Large, other species. Service with restrictions, supervision.

🅰🆂🅺 ✖ 🕭ᴹ 🖉 ❘❘ 🖵 ⊇

♦♦♦♦ Hampton Inn & Suites 🆂🅷

(913) 722-0800. **$98-$105.** 7400 W Frontage Rd. I-35, exit 227, just nw. Int corridors. **Pets:** Other species. Service with restrictions, supervision.

🅰🆂🅺 🆂🅾 ✖ 🕭ᴹ ❘❘ 🖵 ⊇

♦♦♦♦ Homestead Studio Suites Hotel-Kansas City/Shawnee Mission 🅼

(913) 236-6006. **$52-$71.** 6451 E Frontage Rd. I-35, exit 228B (Shawnee Mission Pkwy), just se. Ext corridors. **Pets:** Accepted.

🅰🆂🅺 🆂🅾 ✖ 🕭ᴹ 🖉 🛆 ❘❘ 🖵

OLATHE

♦♦♦ Sleep Inn 🆂🅷

(913) 390-9500. **$54-$94.** 20662 W 151st St. I-35, exit 215 (151st St), 0.4 mi sw. Int corridors. **Pets:** Medium, other species. $10 one-time fee/pet. Service with restrictions, supervision.

🅰🆂🅺 🆂🅾 ✖ 🕭ᴹ 🖉 🛆 ❘❘ 🖵 ⊇

OVERLAND PARK

AmeriSuites (Overland Park/Metcalf) SH
(913) 451-2553. **$115-$125.** 6801 W 112th St. I-435, exit 79 (Metcalf Ave/US 169), 0.6 mi s. Int corridors. **Pets:** Small. $25 one-time fee/room. Service with restrictions, supervision.

Candlewood Suites SH
(913) 469-5557. **$92-$149.** 11001 Oakmont. I-435, exit 82 (Quivira Rd), 0.5 mi s, 0.3 mi w on College Ave, then just n. Int corridors. **Pets:** Small. $75 one-time fee/pet. Service with restrictions.

Chase Suites by Woodfin SH
(913) 491-3333. **$69-$139.** 6300 W 110th. I-435, exit 79 (Metcalf Ave/US 169), 0.3 mi s on US 169, 0.5 mi e on College Blvd to Lamar Ave, then just n. Ext corridors. **Pets:** Other species. $150 deposit/pet, $10 daily fee/pet. Designated rooms, service with restrictions, crate.

ClubHouse Inn & Suites SH
(913) 648-5555. **$67-$76.** 10610 Marty Ave. I-435, exit 79 (Metcalf Ave/US 169). Int corridors. **Pets:** Accepted.

Drury Inn & Suites-Overland Park SH
(913) 345-1500. **$65-$115.** 10963 Metcalf Ave. I-435, exit 79 (Metcalf Ave/US 169), just se. Int corridors. **Pets:** Large, other species. Service with restrictions, supervision.

Holiday Inn of Mission-Overland Park LH
(913) 262-3010. **$69-$99.** 7240 Shawnee Mission Pkwy. I-35, exit 228B (Shawnee Mission Pkwy), 1 mi e. Ext/int corridors. **Pets:** Accepted.

Holtze Executive Village SH
(913) 344-8100. **$98-$107.** 11400 College Blvd. I-435, exit 82 (Quivira Rd), 0.5 mi s, then just e. Ext/int corridors. **Pets:** Medium, other species. $200 deposit/room, $5 daily fee/pet. Service with restrictions, supervision.

Homestead Studio Suites Hotel-Kansas City/Overland Park SH
(913) 661-7111. **$71-$90.** 5401 W 110th St. I-435, exit 77B (Nall Ave), just s. Int corridors. **Pets:** Accepted.

Microtel Inn and Suites of Overland Park/Lenexa SH
(913) 541-2664. **Call for rates.** 8750 Ballentine St. I-35, exit 225A, just se. Int corridors. **Pets:** Accepted.

Pear Tree Inn-Overland Park SH
(913) 451-0200. **$50-$95.** 10951 Metcalf Ave. I-435, exit 79 (Metcalf Ave/US 169), just se. Int corridors. **Pets:** Large, other species. Service with restrictions, supervision.

Red Roof Inn-Overland Park M
(913) 341-0100. **$49-$72.** 6800 W 108th St. I-435, exit 79 (Metcalf Ave/US 169), just ne. Ext corridors. **Pets:** Large, other species. Service with restrictions, supervision.

Super 8 Motel SH
(913) 341-4440. **$44-$89.** 10750 Barkley St. I-435, exit 79 (Metcalf Ave/US 169), just n to 107th St, then just e. Int corridors. **Pets:** Medium. $25 one-time fee/room. Service with restrictions, supervision.

Wellesley Inn & Suites (Kansas City/Overland Park) SH
(913) 642-2299. **$71-$90.** 7201 W 106th St. I-435, exit 79 (Metcalf Ave/US 169), just nw. Int corridors. **Pets:** Medium, other species. $75 one-time fee/room. Service with restrictions, supervision.

White Haven Motor Lodge M
(913) 649-8200. **$54-$60.** 8039 Metcalf Ave. I-435, exit 79 (Metcalf Ave/US 169), 3.5 mi n. Ext corridors. **Pets:** Medium, dogs only. Service with restrictions, supervision.

END METROPOLITAN AREA

LANSING

Econo Lodge SH
(913) 727-2777. **$55-$59.** 504 N Main. I-70, exit Leavenworth, 10 mi n on US 73 and SR 7. Int corridors. **Pets:** Accepted.

Holiday Inn Express Hotel & Suites SH
(913) 250-1000. **$71-$80.** 120 Express Dr. On SR 7, just s of jct SR 5; downtown. Int corridors. **Pets:** Medium. $20 one-time fee/room. Service with restrictions, crate.

LARNED

Best Western Townsman Inn SH
(620) 285-3114. **$50-$74.** 123 E 14th. Jct US 56 and SR 156. Ext corridors. **Pets:** Small, dogs only. Service with restrictions, supervision.

LAWRENCE

Best Value Hallmark Inn M
(785) 841-6500. **$59-$99, 5 day notice.** 730 Iowa St. I-70, exit 202, 1 mi s. Ext corridors. **Pets:** Accepted.

Best Western Lawrence SH
(785) 843-9100. **$69-$99.** 2309 Iowa St. On US 59; jct SR 10. Ext/int corridors. **Pets:** Large, other species. Designated rooms, service with restrictions, supervision.

Quality Inn SH
(785) 842-5100. **$65-$70.** 801 N Iowa St. I-70, exit 202. Ext/int corridors. **Pets:** Accepted.

Super 8 Motel SH
(785) 842-5721. **$45-$70.** 515 McDonald Dr. I-70, exit 202; US 59, 1 mi s. Int corridors. **Pets:** Small, dogs only. $10 one-time fee/room. Service with restrictions, supervision.

LEAVENWORTH

▼▼ Days Inn **M**
(913) 651-6000. **$50-$129.** 3211 S 4th St. On US 73 and SR 7. Ext corridors. **Pets:** Accepted.
🅰🆂🅺 ✕ 📶 💻 ⊇

LIBERAL

▼▼ Best Western LaFonda Motel **SH**
(620) 624-5601. **$46-$94.** 229 W Pancake Blvd. Just w of jct US 54 and 83B (Kansas Ave). Ext corridors. **Pets:** Accepted.
🅰🆂🅺 🆂 ✕ 🅿 📶 💻 🍴 ⊇

⚠ ▼ Cimarron Inn **M**
(620) 624-6203. **$45.** 564 E Pancake Blvd. 0.8 w of jct US 54 and 83. Ext corridors. **Pets:** $5 one-time fee/pet. Service with restrictions, supervision.
🆂🅰🆅🅴 🆂 ✕ 📶 💻 ⊇

⚠ ▼▼ Liberal Inn **SH**
(620) 624-7254. **$60-$75.** 603 E Pancake Blvd. 0.5 mi w of jct US 54 and 83. Int corridors. **Pets:** Medium. Designated rooms, service with restrictions, crate.
🆂🅰🆅🅴 🆂 ✕ 📶 💻 🍴 ⊇

LINDSBORG

▼▼ Viking Motel **M**
(785) 227-3336. **$48-$62.** 446 Harrison. I-135, exit 78, 4 mi sw. Ext corridors. **Pets:** Small. $5 daily fee/pet. Designated rooms, service with restrictions, supervision.
✕ ⊇

MANHATTAN

▼▼▼ Hampton Inn **SH**
(785) 539-5000. **$81-$85.** 501 E Poyntz Ave. SR 177, 0.3 mi e on US 24 (Frontage Rd). Int corridors. **Pets:** Medium, other species. Supervision.
🅰🆂🅺 🆂 ✕ 🅼 🅿 📶 💻 ⊇

⚠ ▼▼▼ Holiday Inn/Holidome **LH**
(785) 539-5311. **$79-$149.** 530 Richards Dr. 2.5 mi sw on SR 18 (Ft Riley Blvd), 0.3 mi e of jct SR 113. Ext/int corridors. **Pets:** Medium. $20 one-time fee/room. Service with restrictions, supervision.
🆂🅰🆅🅴 🆂 ✕ 🅿 📶 💻 🍴 ⊇ 🐾

▼ Motel 6–152 **M**
(785) 537-1022. **$43-$55.** 510 Tuttle Creek Blvd. 0.3 mi ne on US 24 (Frontage Rd) and SR 177. Ext corridors. **Pets:** Small, other species. Service with restrictions, supervision.
🆂 ✕ 🅼 🅿 🅿 ⊇

▼▼▼ Ramada Plaza Hotel **SH**
(785) 539-7531. **$89-$149.** 1641 Anderson. 1 mi n of SR 18 (Ft Riley Blvd). Int corridors. **Pets:** Accepted.
🅰🆂🅺 🆂 ✕ 📶 💻 🍴 ⊇

MARYSVILLE

▼▼ Best Western Surf Motel **SH**
(785) 562-2354. **$49-$69.** 2105 Center St. 1 mi e on US 36 (Pony Express Hwy). Ext/int corridors. **Pets:** Accepted.
🅰🆂🅺 🆂 ✕ 🅿 📶 💻 🐾

⚠ ▼▼▼ Oak Tree Inn-Marysville **SH**
(785) 562-1234. **$64-$72.** 1127 Pony Express Hwy. 1.6 mi e on US 36 (Pony Express Hwy). Int corridors. **Pets:** Accepted.
🆂🅰🆅🅴 🆂 ✕ 🅼 🅿 📶 💻 🍴

▼▼ Super 8 Motel **SH**
(785) 562-5588. **$64-$84, 7 day notice.** 1155 Pony Express Hwy. 2 mi e on US 36 (Pony Express Hwy). Int corridors. **Pets:** Other species. $10 one-time fee/room. Designated rooms, service with restrictions, supervision.
🅰🆂🅺 🆂 ✕ 📶

MCPHERSON

▼▼ ▼▼ Best Western Holiday Manor Motel **SH**
(620) 241-5343. **$62-$74.** 2211 E Kansas Ave. I-135, exit 60, just w. Ext/int corridors. **Pets:** Accepted.
🅰🆂🅺 🆂 ✕ 🅿 📶 💻 🍴 ⊇

▼▼ ▼▼ McPherson Super 8 Motel **M**
(620) 241-8881. **$45-$70.** 2110 E Kansas Ave. I-135, exit 60, just w. Int corridors. **Pets:** Accepted.
🅰🆂🅺 🆂 ✕ 🅼 🅿 💻

⚠ ▼ Red Coach Inn **SH**
(620) 241-6960. **$59-$111.** 2111 E Kansas Ave. I-135, exit 60, just w. Ext/int corridors. **Pets:** Accepted.
🆂🅰🆅🅴 🆂 ✕ 🍴 ⊇ 🐾

NEWTON

▼ Best Value Inn **M**
(316) 283-7611. **$45-$70.** 1620 E 2nd St. I-135, exit 31, just e. Int corridors. **Pets:** Accepted.
🅰🆂🅺 🆂 ✕ 🅿 💻

⚠ ▼▼ Best Western Red Coach Inn **SH**
(316) 283-9120. **$61-$89.** 1301 E 1st St. I-135, exit 31. Ext/int corridors. **Pets:** Other species. Service with restrictions, supervision.
🆂🅰🆅🅴 🆂 ✕ 🅿 📶 💻 🍴 ⊇ 🐾

▼▼ Days Inn Newton **SH**
(316) 283-3330. **$63-$65.** 105 Manchester St. I-135, exit 31, just e. Int corridors. **Pets:** $10 one-time fee/room. Service with restrictions, supervision.
🅰🆂🅺 🆂 ✕ 📶 💻 ⊇

OAKLEY

▼▼ Best Western Golden Plains Motel **M**
(785) 672-3254. **$49-$58.** 3506 US 40. I-70, exit 76, 1.7 mi w. Ext corridors. **Pets:** Small. Service with restrictions, supervision.
✕ 💻 ⊇

OBERLIN

⚠ ▼ Frontier Motel **M**
(785) 475-2203. **$45-$49.** 207 E Frontier Pkwy. On US 36, 0.5 mi e of jct US 83. Ext corridors. **Pets:** Medium. Service with restrictions, crate.
🆂🅰🆅🅴 ✕ 📶 🍴 ⊇

OTTAWA

▼▼ Days Inn **M**
(785) 242-4842. **$50-$85, 7 day notice.** 1641 S Main. I-35, exit 183 (US 59), 1 mi n. Ext corridors. **Pets:** Small. $10 one-time fee/pet. Designated rooms, service with restrictions, supervision.
🅰🆂🅺 🆂 ✕ 🅼 📶 💻

▼▼ Econo Lodge **SH**
(785) 242-3400. **$49-$59.** 2331 S Cedar Rd. I-35, exit 183 (US 59). Int corridors. **Pets:** Small, other species. $10 daily fee/pet. Designated rooms, service with restrictions, supervision.
🅰🆂🅺 🆂 ✕ 💻 ⊇

▼▼ Holiday Inn Express **SH**
(785) 242-2224. **Call for rates.** 606 E 23rd St. I-35, exit 183 (US 59). Ext/int corridors. **Pets:** Very small. Designated rooms, service with restrictions, supervision.
✕ 🅼 📶 💻 ⊇

▼▼ Travelodge **M**
(785) 242-7000. **Call for rates.** 2209 S Princeton Rd. I-35, exit 183 (US 59). Ext corridors. **Pets:** Accepted.
✕ 📶 💻 ⊇

PARK CITY

◆ **Super 8 Motel-Wichita North/Park City** [SH]
(316) 744-2071. **$53-$73.** 6075 Air Cap Dr. I-135, exit 14, just sw. Int corridors. **Pets:** $10 daily fee/pet. Designated rooms, service with restrictions, supervision.
[ASK] [S/D] ⊠ 👂 ▣

PHILLIPSBURG

[AAA] ◆◆ **Cottonwood Inn** [M]
(785) 543-2125. **$70-$100, 7 day notice.** 1200 State St. 2 mi e on US 36. Ext corridors. **Pets:** Accepted.
[SAVE] [S/D] ⊠ ♿ 🏊

PRATT

[AAA] ◆◆ **Best Western Hillcrest Motel** [SH]
(620) 672-6407. **$50-$65.** 1336 E 1st St. 1 mi e on US 54. Ext corridors. **Pets:** Accepted.
[SAVE] [S/D] ⊠ ▣ ☕ 🏊

◆◆ **Days Inn** [SH] 🐾
(620) 672-9465. **$47-$85.** 1901 E 1st St. 1.7 mi e on US 54. Ext corridors. **Pets:** Other species. $3 daily fee/pet. Service with restrictions, supervision.
[ASK] [S/D] ⊠ ▣ ☕ 🏊

[AAA] ◆ **Economy Inn** [M]
(620) 672-5588. **$36-$46, 4 day notice.** 1401 E 1st St. 1 mi e on US 54. Ext corridors. **Pets:** Medium. Designated rooms, no service, supervision.
[SAVE] [S/D] ⊠ ▣ 🏊

◆ **Evergreen Inn** [M]
(620) 672-6431. **$46.** 20001 W US Hwy 54. On US 54, 3 mi w. Ext corridors. **Pets:** Small, dogs only. $5 one-time fee/pet. Service with restrictions, supervision.
[ASK] ⊠ ▣ 🏊

◆◆◆ **Pratt Leisure Hotel** [SH]
(620) 672-9433. **$82-$93.** 1401 W Hwy 54. On US 54, 2 mi w. Int corridors. **Pets:** Other species. Service with restrictions, supervision.
[ASK] [S/D] ⊠ 👂 ♿ ▣ ☕ 🏊

◆◆ **Super 8 Motel of Pratt** [SH]
(620) 672-5945. **$47-$53.** 1906 E 1st St. 1.7 mi e on US 54. Int corridors. **Pets:** Accepted.
[ASK] [S/D] ⊠

RUSSELL

◆◆◆ **AmericInn Lodge & Suites** [SH] 🐾
(785) 483-4200. **$66-$130.** 1430 S Fossil St. I-70, exit 184 (US 281), just n. Int corridors. **Pets:** Medium. $50 deposit/pet, $10 daily fee/pet. Designated rooms, service with restrictions, supervision.
[ASK] ⊠ [♿M] 👂 ♿ ▣ ☕ 🏊 ⊗

◆ **Days Inn** [M]
(785) 483-6660. **$60-$70, 30 day notice.** 1225 S Fossil St. I-70, exit 184 (US 281), just n. Ext corridors. **Pets:** Other species. $5 daily fee/pet. Service with restrictions, supervision.
[ASK] [S/D] ⊠ ▣ 🏊

SABETHA

◆◆ **Sabetha Country Inn** [SH]
(785) 284-2300. **$51-$56.** 1423 S 75 Hwy. US 75, 1 mi s of jct SR 246 and US 75. Int corridors. **Pets:** $10 daily fee/pet. Designated rooms, crate.
⊠ ♿ ▣

SALINA

◆ **1st Inn Gold** [SH]
(785) 827-5511. **$49-$64.** 2403 S 9th St. I-135, exit 90 (Magnolia), just e. Ext corridors. **Pets:** Large, other species. Supervision.
[ASK] [S/D] ⊠ ▣ ☕ 🏊

◆◆ **Baymont Inn & Suites** [SH]
(785) 493-9800. **$70-$90.** 745 W Schilling Rd. I-135, exit 89 (Schilling Rd), just w. Int corridors. **Pets:** $10 one-time fee/pet. Service with restrictions, supervision.
[ASK] [S/D] ⊠ [♿M] ♿ ▣ ☕ 🏊 ⊗

◆◆ **Best Inn** [SH]
(785) 825-2500. **$49-$59.** 429 W Diamond Dr. I-70, exit 252, just n. Int corridors. **Pets:** Medium, dogs only. $5 one-time fee/pet. Designated rooms, service with restrictions, supervision.
[ASK] [S/D] ⊠ [♿M] ▣

[AAA] ◆◆ **Best Western Mid-America Inn** [SH]
(785) 827-0356. **$64-$77.** 1846 N 9th St. I-70, exit 252, just s. Ext corridors. **Pets:** $50 deposit/pet. Designated rooms, service with restrictions, crate.
[SAVE] [S/D] ⊠ [♿M] ♿ ☕ 🍴 🏊

◆◆◆ **Candlewood Suites** [SH]
(785) 823-6939. **$49-$119.** 2650 Planet Ave. I-135, exit 89 (Schilling Rd), just e to S 9th St, 0.5 mi n to Belmont, then just w. Int corridors. **Pets:** Small. $20 one-time fee/pet. Service with restrictions, crate.
[ASK] ⊠ [♿M] 👂 ♿ ▣ ☕

◆◆ **Comfort Inn** [SH]
(785) 826-1711. **$90.** 1820 W Crawford St. I-135, exit 92, just e. Int corridors. **Pets:** Small, dogs only. $20 one-time fee/room. Service with restrictions, supervision.
[ASK] [S/D] ⊠ 👂 ▣ ☕ 🏊

◆◆◆ **Holiday Inn Express Hotel & Suites-Salina** [SH]
(785) 827-9000. **$69-$99.** 201 E Diamond Dr. I-70, exit 252, just ne. Int corridors. **Pets:** Other species. $10 one-time fee/pet. Service with restrictions, crate.
[ASK] ⊠ [♿M] 👂 ♿ ▣ ☕ 🏊

◆◆◆ **Holiday Inn of Salina** [SH]
(785) 823-1739. **Call for rates.** 1616 W Crawford St. I-135, exit 92, 0.5 mi e. Int corridors. **Pets:** Accepted.
⊠ 👂 ♿ ▣ ☕ 🍴 🏊 ⊗

[AAA] ◆◆ **Red Coach Inn** [SH]
(785) 825-2111. **$60-$125.** 2110 W Crawford St. I-135, exit 92, just w. Int corridors. **Pets:** Accepted.
[SAVE] ⊠ [♿M] 👂 ♿ ▣ ☕ 🍴 🏊 ⊗

[AAA] ◆◆ **Super 8 I-70** [SH]
(785) 823-8808. **$56-$79.** 120 E Diamond Dr. I-70, exit 252, just ne. Int corridors. **Pets:** Medium, other species. $5 daily fee/pet. Service with restrictions, supervision.
[SAVE] [S/D] ⊠ [♿M] ♿ ▣ 🏊

◆◆ **TraveLodge** [SH]
(785) 825-8211. **$54-$65.** 1949 N 9th St. I-70, exit 252, just s. Ext corridors. **Pets:** Accepted.
[ASK] [S/D] ⊠ ▣ ☕ 🍴 🏊

SHARON SPRINGS

◆◆ **Oak Tree Inn** [SH]
(785) 852-4664. **$75.** 801 N Hwy 27. Jct US 40 and SR 27. Ext/int corridors. **Pets:** Other species. $10 deposit/pet. Service with restrictions, supervision.
[ASK] [S/D] ⊠ 👂 ♿ ▣ ☕ 🍴 ⊗

TOPEKA

AAA ▼▼▼▼ **AmeriSuites (Topeka/Northwest)** SH
(785) 273-0066. **$109.** 6021 SW Sixth Ave. I-70, exit 356 (Wanamaker Rd), just n. Int corridors. **Pets:** Small. Service with restrictions, supervision.
SAVE ✕ ৬M ⚹ 🛢 💻 ➹

▼▼ **Best Western Candlelight Inn** M
(785) 272-9550. **$55-$139.** 2831 SW Fairlawn Rd. I-470, exit 3. Ext corridors. **Pets:** Small. $8 daily fee/pet. Designated rooms, service with restrictions, crate.
ASK S⁄o ✕ ⚹ 🛢 💻 ➹ ✕

AAA ▼▼◆ **Best Western Meadow Acres Motel** M
(785) 267-1681. **$50-$100.** 2950 S Topeka Blvd. I-470, exit 6, 1.5 mi n. Ext corridors. **Pets:** Accepted.
SAVE S⁄o ✕ 🛢 💻 ➹

AAA ▼▼◆▼ **Capitol Plaza Hotel** LH
(785) 431-7200. **$89-$129.** 1717 SW Topeka Blvd. I-70, exit SE 8th Ave, 1.6 mi s; I-470, exit Topeka Blvd, 2.9 mi n. Int corridors. **Pets:** Accepted.
SAVE S⁄o ✕ ৬M ⁄⁄ ⚹ 🛢 💻 ▯▯ ➹ ✕

▼▼◆▼ **ClubHouse Inn & Suites** SH
(785) 273-8888. **$74-$94.** 924 SW Henderson. I-70, exit 356 (Wanamaker Rd). Int corridors. **Pets:** Accepted.
ASK S⁄o ✕ ⁄⁄ ⚹ 🛢 💻 ➹

▼▼◆ **Comfort Inn by Choice Hotels** SH
(785) 273-5365. **$59-$129.** 1518 SW Wanamaker Rd. I-470, exit 1 (Wanamaker Rd). Int corridors. **Pets:** Accepted.
ASK S⁄o ✕ 🛢 💻 ➹

▼▼◆ **Country Inn & Suites By Carlson-Topeka-West** SH
(785) 478-9800. **$79-$99.** 6020 SW 10th St. I-70, exit 356 (Wanamaker Rd). Int corridors. **Pets:** Accepted.
ASK S⁄o ✕ ৬M ⚹ 🛢 💻 ➹

AAA ▼▼◆ **Quality Inn** SH
(785) 273-6969. **$59-$129.** 1240 SW Wanamaker Rd. I-470, exit 1 (Wanamaker Rd), just ne; I-70, exit 356A (Wanamaker Rd), 1 mi s. Int corridors. **Pets:** Accepted.
SAVE S⁄o ✕ ⁄⁄ 🛢 💻 ➹

▼▼◆▼ **Ramada Inn Downtown** LH
(785) 234-5400. **$65-$109.** 420 SE Sixth Ave. I-70, exit 362B, just e. Int corridors. **Pets:** Medium. No service, supervision.
ASK S⁄o ✕ ৬M ⚹ 🛢 💻 ▯▯ ➹ ✕

▼▼◆▼ **Residence Inn by Marriott** SH
(785) 271-8903. **$119-$179, 14 day notice.** 1620 SW Westport Dr. I-470, exit 1 (Wanamaker Rd). Int corridors. **Pets:** Accepted.
ASK S⁄o ✕ ৬M ⁄⁄ ⚹ 🛢 💻 ➹ ✕

ULYSSES

▼▼◆ **Single Tree Inn** SH
(620) 356-1500. **$67-$77.** 2033 W Oklahoma St. 1.5 mi w on US 160. Int corridors. **Pets:** Other species. $25 deposit/room. Designated rooms, service with restrictions, supervision.
ASK S⁄o ✕ ⁄⁄ 🛢 💻

WAMEGO

AAA ▼◆ **Simmer Motel** M
(785) 456-2304. **$48-$60.** 1215 Hwy 24 W. Jct SR 99, 0.5 mi w. Ext corridors. **Pets:** Other species. $5 daily fee/room. Designated rooms, supervision.
SAVE ✕ 🛢 💻 ➹

WICHITA

AAA ▼▼◆ **Best Western Airport Inn & Convention Center** SH
(316) 942-5600. **$89-$109, 4 day notice.** 6815 W Kellogg. I-235, exit 7, 0.6 mi w on US 54 (S Frontage Rd). Int corridors. **Pets:** Supervision.
SAVE S⁄o ✕ ⚹ 🛢 💻 ▯▯ ➹ ✕

AAA ▼▼◆ **Best Western Governors Inn & Suites** SH
(316) 522-0775. **$69-$79.** 4742 S Emporia. I-135, exit 1B, just sw. Int corridors. **Pets:** Small, dogs only. $10 daily fee/pet. Service with restrictions, supervision.
SAVE ✕ 🛢 💻 ➹

AAA ▼▼◆ **Best Western Wichita North/Park City** SH
(316) 832-9387. **$71-$81.** 915 E 53rd St N. I-135, exit 13, just w. Ext/int corridors. **Pets:** Medium. $25 one-time fee/room. Service with restrictions, supervision.
SAVE S⁄o ✕ ⁄⁄ 🛢 💻 ▯▯ ➹ ✕

▼▼◆ **Candlewood Suites-Wichita Northeast** SH
(316) 634-6070. **Call for rates.** 3141 N Webb Rd. SR 96, exit Webb Rd, just nw. Int corridors. **Pets:** Accepted.
✕ ৬M ⁄⁄ ⚹ 🛢 💻

▼▼◆ **ClubHouse Inn & Suites** SH
(316) 684-1111. **$69-$79.** 515 S Webb Rd. I-35, exit 50, just e. Int corridors. **Pets:** Accepted.
ASK S⁄o ✕ ⁄⁄ 🛢 💻 ➹

AAA ▼▼◆ **Comfort Inn** SH
(316) 522-1800. **$60.** 4849 S Laura. I-135, exit 1A/B (47th St S), just e. Int corridors. **Pets:** Medium. $10 daily fee/room. Service with restrictions, crate.
SAVE S⁄o ✕ ⚹ 🛢 💻 ➹

▼▼◆ **Comfort Inn by Choice Hotels** SH
(316) 686-2844. **$64-$99.** 9525 E Corporate Hills. I-35, exit 50, just ne. Int corridors. **Pets:** Accepted.
ASK S⁄o ✕ ⁄⁄ 🛢 💻 ➹

AAA ▼▼◆ **Comfort Suites Airport** SH 🐾
(316) 945-2600. **$88-$116.** 658 Westdale. Jct I-235 and US 54. Int corridors. **Pets:** Medium, other species. $10 daily fee/pet. Designated rooms, service with restrictions, supervision.
SAVE S⁄o ✕ ⁄⁄ 🛢 💻 ➹

◆ **Days Inn Wichita North** M
(316) 832-1131. **$52-$63, 3 day notice.** 901 E 53rd St N. I-135, exit 13, just w. Int corridors. **Pets:** Medium. $10 daily fee/room. Designated rooms, service with restrictions, crate.
ASK S⁄o ✕ ⁄⁄

AAA ▼▼◆▼ **Four Points By Sheraton** SH
(316) 942-7911. **$109.** 5805 W Kellogg. I-235, exit 7A, just w. Int corridors. **Pets:** Small, other species. $25 one-time fee/room. Service with restrictions, crate.
SAVE S⁄o ✕ ⁄⁄ 🛢 💻 ▯▯ ➹

▼▼◆▼ **Hampton Inn by Hilton** SH
(316) 686-3576. **$74-$104.** 9449 E Corporate Hills. I-35, exit 50, just ne. Int corridors. **Pets:** Accepted.
ASK S⁄o ✕ ৬M ⁄⁄ ⚹ 🛢 💻 ➹

▼▼◆▼ **Hawthorn Suites at Reflection Ridge** SH
(316) 729-5700. **$81-$101.** 2405 N Ridge Rd. I-235, exit 10, 1.7 mi w on Zoo Blvd/21st St N, then just n. Int corridors. **Pets:** Other species. $20 one-time fee/room. Service with restrictions, crate.
ASK S⁄o ✕ ⁄⁄ 🛢 💻 ✕

▼▼◆▼ **Holiday Inn Express-North** SH
(316) 634-3900. **$74-$104.** 7824 E 32nd St N. SR 96 E, exit Rock Rd, just sw. Int corridors. **Pets:** Accepted.
ASK S⁄o ✕ ⁄⁄ ⚹ 🛢 ➹

Holiday Inn Select LH
(316) 686-7131. **$79-$129.** 549 S Rock Rd. I-35, exit 50, 0.5 mi w. Ext/int corridors. **Pets:** Small, other species. $25 one-time fee/pet. Designated rooms, service with restrictions, crate.

Holiday Inn Wichita/Airport SH
(316) 943-2181. **$109.** 5500 W Kellogg. I-235, exit 7, just w. Int corridors. **Pets:** Small, dogs only. $25 one-time fee/room. Service with restrictions, supervision.

The Inn at Willowbend BB
(316) 636-4032. **$99-$109.** 3939 Comotara. SR 96, exit Rock Rd, 0.5 mi n to 37th St, 0.3 mi e, then just n. Int corridors. **Pets:** Accepted.

The Kansas Inn SH ❀
(316) 269-9999. **$55-$57.** 1011 N Topeka Ave. I-135, exit 8 (13th St), 0.7 mi w, then 0.3 mi s. Int corridors. **Pets:** Other species. $25 deposit/room, $10 daily fee/pet. Designated rooms, service with restrictions, supervision.

La Quinta Inn & Suites Wichita Downtown SH
(316) 269-2090. **$60-$149.** 221 E Kellogg. Just sw of jct US 54/400 and Broadway. Ext corridors. **Pets:** Small, other species. Service with restrictions, crate.

La Quinta Inn Wichita (Towne East Mall) SH
(316) 681-2881. **$79-$99.** 7700 E Kellogg. I-35, exit 50, 0.5 mi w. Int corridors. **Pets:** Other species. Service with restrictions, crate.

Quality Inn-Airport SH
(316) 722-8730. **$55-$65.** 600 S Holland. I-235, exit 7, 1.1 mi w on US 54. Int corridors. **Pets:** Medium, other species. $10 one-time fee/room. Designated rooms, service with restrictions, crate.

Residence Inn by Marriott SH
(316) 686-7331. **$69-$134.** 411 S Webb Rd. I-35, exit 50, just ne. Ext corridors. **Pets:** Other species. $75 one-time fee/room. Service with restrictions.

Super 8 Motel-Wichita/East M
(316) 686-3888. **$53-$73.** 527 S Webb Rd. I-35, exit 50, just e. Int corridors. **Pets:** Medium, dogs only. $25 daily fee/room. Designated rooms, no service, supervision.

TownePlace Suites by Marriott SH
(316) 631-3773. **$89-$119, 3 day notice.** 9444 E 29th St N. SR 96, exit Webb Rd, just sw. Int corridors. **Pets:** Other species. $75 one-time fee/room. Service with restrictions.

Wesley Inn SH
(316) 858-3343. **$68-$78.** 3343 E Central Ave. I-135, exit 7 (Central Ave), 1 mi e. Int corridors. **Pets:** Small. $25 one-time fee/room. Designated rooms, service with restrictions, crate.

WINFIELD

Comfort Inn SH
(620) 221-7529. **$75-$85.** Hwy 77 at Quail Ridge Dr. On US 77, 1 mi s. Ext/int corridors. **Pets:** Accepted.

YATES CENTER

Star Motel M
(620) 625-2175. **$33-$39.** 206 S Fry. On US 54, at US 75. Ext corridors. **Pets:** Accepted.

CITY INDEX

ASHLAND

🔷 ▽▽▽ Knights Inn Ⓜ
(606) 928-9501. **$46-$60.** 7216 US Rt 60. I-64, exit 185, 5 mi sw on US 60, then 4.3 mi n. Ext corridors. **Pets:** Small, other species. $5 daily fee/room. Service with restrictions, supervision.

SAVE 🔖 ✕ 🖥 💻 🏊

BARDSTOWN

🔷 ▽▽▽ Bardstown-Parkview Motel Ⓜ
(502) 348-5983. **$60-$85.** 418 E Stephen Foster Ave. 0.5 mi e on US 150; e of jct US 62. Ext corridors. **Pets:** Accepted.

SAVE 🔖 ✕ 🖥 🍴 🏊

▽▽ Best Western General Nelson Motel ⓈⒽ
(502) 348-3977. **$59-$69.** 411 W Stephen Foster Ave. 0.5 mi w on US 62. Ext corridors. **Pets:** Medium. $10 one-time fee/room. Service with restrictions, crate.

ASK 🔖 ✕ 🖥 💻 🏊

🔷 ▽▽▽ Days Inn-Bardstown ⓈⒽ
(502) 348-9253. **$59-$89.** 1875 New Haven Rd. Bluegrass Pkwy, exit 21. Ext corridors. **Pets:** Medium, other species. $10 one-time fee/room. Service with restrictions, supervision.

SAVE 🔖 ✕ 🖥 💻 🍴 🏊 ✕

▽▽▽ Hampton Inn ⓈⒽ
(502) 349-0100. **$75-$95.** 985 Chambers Blvd. Just s of US 245. Int corridors. **Pets:** Accepted.

ASK 🔖 ✕ 🏊 🖥 💻 🏊

🔷 ▽ Old Kentucky Home Motel Ⓜ
(502) 348-5979. **$35-$75.** 414 W Stephen Foster Ave. 0.5 mi w on US 62. Ext corridors. **Pets:** Medium, other species. $20 deposit/room. Service with restrictions, crate.

SAVE 🔖 ✕ 🖥 💻 🏊

🔷 ▽▽ Ramada Inn ⓈⒽ
(502) 349-0363. **$39-$130.** 523 N 3rd St. 0.5 mi n on US 150. Ext corridors. **Pets:** Other species. $10 daily fee/pet. Service with restrictions, supervision.

SAVE 🔖 ✕ 🖥 💻 🏊

BEAVER DAM

▽▽▽ Days Inn Beaver Dam ⓈⒽ
(270) 274-0851. **$64-$69.** 1750 US Hwy 231. Kentucky Pkwy, exit 75, just n. Int corridors. **Pets:** Accepted.

ASK 🔖 ✕ 🖥 💻 🏊

BENTON

▽▽▽ Holiday Inn Express Hotel & Suites ⓈⒽ
(270) 527-5300. **$80-$140.** 173 Carroll Rd. Purchase Pkwy, exit 47. Int corridors. **Pets:** Accepted.

✕ 🏊 🖥 💻 🏊

BEREA

🔷 ▽▽▽▽ Boone Tavern Hotel-Berea College ⓈⒽ
(859) 985-3700. **$138.** 100 Main St. I-75, exit 76, 1.5 mi ne on SR 21. Int corridors. **Pets:** Accepted.

SAVE 🔖 ✕ 🖥 💻 🍴

▽▽▽ Comfort Inn & Suites ⓈⒽ
(859) 985-5500. **$59-$89.** 1003 Paint Lick Rd. I-75, exit 76, just w. Int corridors. **Pets:** Small. $5 daily fee/pet. Service with restrictions, supervision.

ASK 🔖 ✕ 🏊 🖥 💻 💻 🏊

🔷 ▽▽ Knights Inn Berea Ⓜ
(859) 986-2384. **$40-$60.** 715 Chestnut St. I-75, exit 76, 0.3 mi e. Ext corridors. **Pets:** Other species. $5 daily fee/pet. Service with restrictions.

SAVE 🔖 ✕ 🖥

🔷 ▽▽ Super 8 Motel ⓈⒽ
(859) 986-8426. **$45-$64.** 196 Prince Royal Dr. I-75, exit 76, 0.3 mi e. Ext corridors. **Pets:** Accepted.

SAVE 🔖 ✕ 🖥 🏊

BOWLING GREEN

🔷 ▽▽ Baymont Inn & Suites-Bowling Green ⓈⒽ
(270) 843-3200. **$59-$99.** 165 Three Springs Rd. I-65, exit 22 (Scottsville Rd), 0.3 mi w. Int corridors. **Pets:** Dogs only. $25 deposit/pet. Designated rooms, service with restrictions, supervision.

SAVE 🔖 ✕ 🏊 🖥 💻

🔷 ▽ Best Value Inn ⓈⒽ
(270) 781-9594. **$45-$70.** 250 Cumberland Trace Rd. I-65, exit 22 (Scottsville Rd), just ne. Int corridors. **Pets:** $20 deposit/pet. Designated rooms, service with restrictions, supervision.

SAVE 🔖 ✕ 🏊 🖥 🏊

🔷 ▽▽ Continental Inn ⓈⒽ
(270) 781-5200. **$49-$65.** 700 Interstate Dr. I-65, exit 28, 0.3 mi w. Ext corridors. **Pets:** Very small. $10 daily fee/room. Designated rooms, service with restrictions, supervision.

SAVE 🔖 ✕ 🖥 🏊

▽▽ Country Hearth Inn ⓈⒽ
(270) 783-4443. **$54-$64.** 395 Corvette Dr. I-65, exit 28, just w. Int corridors. **Pets:** Accepted.

ASK ✕ 🏊 🖥 💻

🔷 ▽▽▽ Days Inn ⓈⒽ
(270) 781-6470. **$60-$130.** 4617 Scottsville Rd. I-65, exit 22 (Scottsville Rd), 0.3 mi e. Int corridors. **Pets:** Medium. $10 daily fee/pet. Designated rooms, service with restrictions, supervision.

SAVE 🔖 ✕ 🏊 🖥 💻 🏊

▼▼▼▼ Drury Inn-Bowling Green SH
(270) 842-7100. **$67-$105.** 3250 Scottsville Rd. I-65, exit 22 (Scottsville Rd), just w. Int corridors. **Pets:** Large, other species. Service with restrictions, supervision.
(ASK) ✕ 🔊 🖥 🍴 🛏 🖥 🏊

▼▼▼▼ Holiday Inn University Plaza LH
(270) 745-0088. **$99-$139.** 1021 Wilkinson Trace. I-65, exit 22 (Scottsville Rd), 2.5 mi w, then just n. Int corridors. **Pets:** Other species. $25 one-time fee/room. Designated rooms, service with restrictions, supervision.
(SAVE) 🔊 ✕ 🖥 🛏 🖥 🍴 🏊 ✕

▼▼▼ News Inn of Bowling Green M
(270) 781-3460. **$49-$69.** 3160 Scottsville Rd. I-65, exit 22 (Scottsville Rd). Ext corridors. **Pets:** Large. $5 daily fee/pet. Service with restrictions, supervision.
(SAVE) 🔊 ✕ 🛏 🏊

▼▼ Travelodge Hotel SH
(270) 781-6610. **$65-$95.** 1000 Executive Way. I-65, exit 22 (Scottsville Rd), just ne. Int corridors. **Pets:** Large, other species. $10 daily fee/pet. Service with restrictions.
(ASK) 🔊 ✕ 🛏 🖥 🍴 🏊

CADIZ

▼▼▼▼ Holiday Inn Express SH
(270) 522-3700. **$54-$75.** 153 Broad Bent Blvd. I-24, exit 65, just s. Int corridors. **Pets:** Accepted.
(ASK) 🔊 ✕ 🛏 🖥 🏊

▼▼ Super 8 Motel SH
(270) 522-7007. **$59-$79.** 154 Hospitality Ln. I-24, exit 65. Ext corridors. **Pets:** Other species. $5 daily fee/pet. Designated rooms, service with restrictions, supervision.
(ASK) 🔊 ✕ 🏊

CAMPBELLSVILLE

▼▼▼ Best Western Campbellsville Lodge SH
(270) 465-7001. **$66-$72.** 1400 E Broadway. 2 mi e on US 68 and SR 55. Int corridors. **Pets:** Very small. $10 daily fee/pet. Service with restrictions, crate.
(SAVE) 🔊 ✕ 🛏 🖥 🏊

▼▼▼ Holiday Inn Express SH
(270) 465-2727. **$69-$129.** 102 Plantation Dr. Jct US 68 and SR 55, 0.5 mi n. Int corridors. **Pets:** Other species. $10 daily fee/pet. Service with restrictions, supervision.
(ASK) 🔊 ✕ 🖥 🛏 🖥 🏊

CARROLLTON

▼▼▼ Best Western Executive Inn SH
(502) 732-8444. **$59-$99, 15 day notice.** 10 Slumber Ln. I-71, exit 44, just nw. Int corridors. **Pets:** Accepted.
(SAVE) 🔊 ✕ 🖥 🛏 🖥 🏊

▼▼▼ Days Inn Carrollton SH
(502) 732-9301. **$59-$99.** 61 Inn Rd. I-71, exit 44, just nw. Int corridors. **Pets:** Accepted.
(SAVE) 🔊 ✕ 🛏 🖥 🏊

▼▼ Super 8 Carrollton SH
(502) 732-0252. **$55-$99.** 130 Slumber Ln. I-71, exit 44, just nw. Int corridors. **Pets:** Accepted.
(ASK) 🔊 ✕

CAVE CITY

▼▼▼ Best Western Kentucky Inn SH
(270) 773-3161. **$34-$75.** 1009 Doyle Ave. I-65, exit 53, just e. Ext corridors. **Pets:** Large. $10 daily fee/pet. Designated rooms, service with restrictions, crate.
(SAVE) 🔊 ✕ 🛏 🖥 🏊

▼▼▼ Comfort Inn SH
(270) 773-2030. **$45-$130.** 801 Mammoth Cave St. I-65, exit 53, just ne. Ext corridors. **Pets:** Very small. $5 daily fee/pet. Designated rooms, no service, supervision.
(SAVE) 🔊 ✕ 🛏 🖥 🏊

▼▼▼ Ramada Limited SH
(270) 773-3121. **$42-$70.** 807 Mammoth Cave Rd. I-65, exit 53, just e. Ext corridors. **Pets:** $10 daily fee/pet. Designated rooms, service with restrictions, supervision.
(SAVE) 🔊 ✕ 🖥 🏊

▼▼▼ Super 8 Motel SH
(270) 773-2500. **$45-$129.** 799 Mammoth Cave Rd. I-65, exit 53, just ne. Ext corridors. **Pets:** Accepted.
(SAVE) 🔊 ✕ 🖥 🛏 🖥 🏊

CORBIN

▼▼▼ Baymont Inn & Suites-Corbin SH
(606) 523-9040. **$59-$79.** 174 Adams Rd. I-75, exit 29. Int corridors. **Pets:** Medium, other species. $8 daily fee/pet. Designated rooms, service with restrictions, supervision.
(ASK) 🔊 ✕ 🖥 🗂 🖥 🛏 🖥 🏊

▼▼▼ Best Western-Corbin Inn SH
(606) 528-2100. **$49-$89.** 2630 Cumberland Falls Hwy. I-75, exit 25. Ext corridors. **Pets:** Small. $10 daily fee/pet. Service with restrictions, supervision.
(SAVE) 🔊 ✕ 🛏 🖥 🏊

COVINGTON

▼▼▼ Embassy Suites Cincinnati RiverCenter LH
(859) 261-8400. **$129-$249.** 10 E RiverCenter Blvd. I-71/75, exit 192, 0.8 mi e on 5th St, then 0.3 mi n on Madison Ave. Int corridors. **Pets:** Small. $25 one-time fee/room. Designated rooms, service with restrictions, crate.
✕ 🖥 🗂 🛏 🖥 🖥 🍴 🏊 ✕

DANVILLE

▼▼▼ Holiday Inn Express-Danville SH
(859) 236-8600. **$59-$79.** 96 Daniel Dr. Just e of US 127 on US 150 Bypass. Int corridors. **Pets:** Accepted.
(ASK) 🔊 ✕ 🖥 🖥 🖥 🏊

▼▼ Super 8 Motel SH
(859) 236-8881. **$50-$70.** 3663 Hwy 150/127 Bypass. Just e of US 127 on US 150 Bypass. Int corridors. **Pets:** Accepted.
(ASK) 🔊 ✕ 🗂 🛏

DRY RIDGE

▼▼▼ Holiday Inn Express SH
(859) 824-7121. **$64-$79.** 1050 Fashion Ridge Rd. I-75, exit 159, just nw. Int corridors. **Pets:** Medium. $7 one-time fee/pet. Service with restrictions, supervision.
(ASK) 🔊 ✕ 🖥 🛏 🖥

▼▼ Microtel Inn and Suites SH
(859) 824-2000. **$45-$55.** 79 Blackburn Ln. I-75, exit 159, just ne. Int corridors. **Pets:** Medium. $5 one-time fee/pet. Service with restrictions, supervision.
(ASK) 🔊 ✕ 🖥 🛏 🖥

EDDYVILLE

▼▼ Eddy Creek Resort & Marina CA
(270) 388-2271. **$74, 45 day notice.** 7612 SR 93 S. I-24, exit 45, 4 mi s. Ext corridors. **Pets:** $100 deposit/room. Service with restrictions, supervision.
✕ 🛏 🖥 🍴 🏊 ✕ 🖥

ELIZABETHTOWN

Best Western Cardinal Inn SH
(270) 765-6139. **$75-$109, 7 day notice.** 642 E Dixie Ave. I-65, exit 91 (US 31 W), 0.3 mi nw. Ext/int corridors. **Pets:** Other species. $15 one-time fee/pet. Service with restrictions, supervision.
ASK SD X 🖵 ➰

Comfort Inn Atrium Gardens SH
(270) 769-3030. **$55-$109.** 1043 Executive Dr. I-65, exit 94, just nw. Int corridors. **Pets:** Accepted.
ASK SD X 🛏 🖵 ➰

Days Inn SH
(270) 769-5522. **$64-$79.** 2010 N Mulberry St. I-65, exit 94, just ne. Ext corridors. **Pets:** Small. $10 one-time fee/room. Service with restrictions, crate.
SAVE SD X 🛏 🖵 ➰

Holiday Inn SH
(270) 769-2344. **$89.** 1058 N Mulberry St. I-65, exit 94, just nw. Ext corridors. **Pets:** Medium. Service with restrictions, supervision.
ASK SD X 🐾 🛏 🖵 🍴 ➰

Quality Inn & Suites SH
(270) 765-4166. **$69-$99.** 2009 N Mulberry St. I-65, exit 94, just sw. Int corridors. **Pets:** Medium. $10 daily fee/room. Designated rooms, no service, supervision.
SAVE SD X ᏔM 🐾 🛏 🖵 ➰

Super 8 Motel SH
(270) 737-1088. **$50-$85.** 2028 N Mulberry St. I-65, exit 94, just ne. Int corridors. **Pets:** Accepted.
SD X ᏔM 🐾 🛏 ➰

ERLANGER

Baymont Inn & Suites Cincinnati-Airport (Erlanger, KY) SH
(859) 746-0300. **$79-$110.** 1805 Airport Exchange Blvd. I-275, exit 2. Int corridors. **Pets:** Accepted.
ASK SD X ᏔM 🐾 🐾 🛏 🖵 ➰

Residence Inn by Marriott, Cincinnati Airport SH
(859) 282-7400. **$109-$169.** 2811 Circleport Dr. I-275, exit 2. Int corridors. **Pets:** Accepted.
ASK SD X ᏔM 🐾 🛏 🖵 ➰ ⊠

FLORENCE

AmeriSuites (Cincinnati/Airport) SH
(859) 647-1170. **$79-$89, 30 day notice.** 300 Meijer Dr. I-71/75, exit 182, 0.4 mi sw. Int corridors. **Pets:** Accepted.
SAVE SD X ᏔM 🐾 🐾 🛏 🖵 ➰

Ashley Quarters SH
(859) 525-9997. **$82-$110.** 4880 Houston Rd. I-71/75, exit 182, 0.6 mi w on Turfway and Houston rds. Int corridors. **Pets:** Medium. $50 one-time fee/room. Designated rooms, service with restrictions.
SAVE SD X 🐾 🛏 🖵 ➰

Best Western Inn Florence SH
(859) 525-0090. **$50-$125.** 7821 Commerce Dr. I-71/75, exit 181, just ne. Int corridors. **Pets:** Medium, dogs only. $10 daily fee/pet. Supervision.
SAVE SD X ᏔM 🐾 🛏 🖵 ➰

Cross Country Inn Florence M
(859) 283-2030. **$43-$59.** 7810 Commerce Dr. I-71/75, exit 181, just ne. Ext corridors. **Pets:** Accepted.
ASK SD X 🐾 ➰

Florence Super 8 SH 🐾
(859) 283-1221. **$44-$79.** 7928 Dream St. I-71/75, exit 180, just e on US 42, then just n. Int corridors. **Pets:** Medium. $5 one-time fee/pet. Service with restrictions, supervision.
SAVE SD X 🛏

Knights Inn Florence M
(859) 371-9711. **$45-$59.** 8049 Dream St. I-71/75, exit 180, just e on US 42, then just n. Ext corridors. **Pets:** Medium. $10 daily fee/pet. Designated rooms, service with restrictions, crate.
ASK SD X 🛏 🖵 ➰

Motel 6-Florence SH
(859) 283-0909. **$35-$47, 5 day notice.** 7937 Dream St. I-75/71, exit 180, just e on US 42, then just n. Ext corridors. **Pets:** Small, other species. Service with restrictions, supervision.
SD X ᏔM 🐾 ➰

Quality Inn & Suites SH
(859) 371-4700. **$74-$85.** 7915 US Hwy 42. I-71/75, exit 180, just e. Int corridors. **Pets:** Accepted.
ASK SD X 🛏 🖵 🍴 ➰

Red Roof Inn M 🐾
(859) 647-2700. **$45-$70.** 7454 Turfway Rd. I-71/75, exit 182, 0.8 mi sw. Int corridors. **Pets:** Medium. Service with restrictions, supervision.
ASK SD X 🛏 🖵

Suburban Extended Stay Hotel-Cincinnati Int'l Airport SH
(859) 746-2400. **$45-$50.** 8035 Action Blvd. I-71/75, exit 181, just w. Ext corridors. **Pets:** Accepted.
ASK SD X ᏔM 🐾 🛏 🖵

Travelodge of Florence SH
(859) 371-0227. **$49-$135.** 8075 Steilen Dr. I-71/75, exit 180, just w. Int corridors. **Pets:** Accepted.
ASK SD X 🛏 🖵

FORT MITCHELL

Holiday Inn Fort Mitchell SH
(859) 331-1500. **$69-$129.** 2100 Dixie Hwy. I-71/75, exit 188, just w. Ext/int corridors. **Pets:** Accepted.
ASK SD X ᏔM 🐾 🖵 🍴 ➰ ⊠

FRANKFORT

Bluegrass Inn M
(502) 695-1800. **$48-$64.** 635 Versailles Rd. I-64, exit 58, 1 mi n on US 60. Ext corridors. **Pets:** Medium. $10 daily fee/pet. Designated rooms, service with restrictions, supervision.
SAVE SD X 🛏 ➰

Holiday Inn Capital Plaza LH
(502) 227-5100. **$86-$94.** 405 Wilkinson Blvd. Adjacent to Frankfort Civic Center. Int corridors. **Pets:** Small. $25 one-time fee/pet. Service with restrictions, crate.
SAVE SD X ᏔM 🐾 🐾 🛏 🖵 🍴 ➰

Super 8 Motel SH
(502) 875-3220. **$47-$67.** 1225 US Hwy 127 S. I-64, exit 53B, 1.2 mi n. Int corridors. **Pets:** Accepted.
ASK SD X 🖵

FRANKLIN

Best Value Inn & Suites-Franklin SH
(270) 586-5090. **$37-$43.** 3811 Nashville Rd. I-65, exit 2, just w. Ext corridors. **Pets:** Accepted.
ASK SD X ᏔM 🛏 🖵 ➰

AAA ▼▼▼ Best Western Franklin Inn SH
(270) 598-0070. **$37-$75.** 162 Anand Dr. I-65, exit 2, just w. Ext corridors. **Pets:** Accepted.
[SAVE] [S&] [✕] [&M] [✉] [▣] [≈]

AAA ▼▼ Comfort Inn SH
(270) 586-6100. **$55-$65.** 3794 Nashville Rd. I-65, exit 2. Ext corridors. **Pets:** $5 daily fee/pet. Service with restrictions, supervision.
[SAVE] [S&] [✕] [&M] [✆] [▣] [≈]

AAA ▼▼ Days Inn SH
(270) 598-0163. **$50-$70.** 103 Trotter Ln. I-65, exit 6, just w. Ext corridors. **Pets:** $5 daily fee/pet. Service with restrictions.
[SAVE] [S&] [✕] [&M] [✉] [✆] [▣] [≈]

GEORGETOWN

AAA ▼▼▼ Days Inn of Georgetown M
(502) 863-5000. **$35-$65.** 385 Cherry Blossom Way. I-75, exit 129, just se. Ext corridors. **Pets:** $5 daily fee/pet. Service with restrictions, supervision.
[SAVE] [S&] [✕] [&] [✆] [▣] [≈]

▼▼▼ Super 8 Motel SH
(502) 863-4888. **$50-$100.** 250 Shoney Dr. I-75, exit 126. Ext/int corridors. **Pets:** Accepted.
[ASK] [S&] [✕] [&M] [✆] [≈]

GLASGOW

▼▼ Comfort Inn SH
(270) 651-9099. **$59-$80.** 210 Calvary Dr. Cumberland Pkwy, exit 11, just n. Ext corridors. **Pets:** Medium, other species. $10 daily fee/room. Service with restrictions, supervision.
[ASK] [S&] [✕] [&] [✆] [▣] [≈]

GRAND RIVERS

AAA ▼▼▼ Best Western Kentucky-Barkley Lakes Inn SH
(270) 928-2700. **$56-$72.** 720 Complex Dr. I-24, exit 31 (SR 453), just s. Ext/int corridors. **Pets:** Medium. $10 daily fee/pet. Supervision.
[SAVE] [S&] [✕] [✆] [▣] [≈]

▼▼ Microtel Inn & Suites SH
(270) 928-2740. **$50-$93.** 1017 Dover Rd. I-24, exit 31 (SR 453), just n. Int corridors. **Pets:** Accepted.
[✕] [&M] [▱] [&] [✆] [≈]

GRAYSON

AAA ▼▼▼ Super 8 Motel SH
(606) 474-8811. **$39-$89.** 125 Super 8 Ln. I-64, exit 172, just s. Int corridors. **Pets:** Small. $25 deposit/room. Designated rooms, service with restrictions, supervision.
[SAVE] [S&] [✕] [&M] [▱] [&] [✆] [▣]

HARLAN

▼▼▼ Holiday Inn Express Harlan SH
(606) 573-3385. **$69-$79.** 2608 S Hwy 421. On US 421, 2.8 mi s. Int corridors. **Pets:** Very small, dogs only. $50 one-time fee/room. Designated rooms, service with restrictions, supervision.
[ASK] [S&] [▱] [&] [✆] [▣] [≈]

HARRODSBURG

▼▼▼ Country Hearth Inn SH
(859) 734-2400. **$54-$70.** 105 Commercial Dr. 0.6 mi n on College St. Int corridors. **Pets:** Small. $20 one-time fee/pet. Service with restrictions, supervision.
[ASK] [S&] [✕] [✆] [▣]

HEBRON

▼▼▼ Radisson Hotel Cincinnati Airport LH
(859) 371-6166. **$89-$139.** Cincinnati N KY Airport. I-71/75 via I-275, 4 mi w, exit 4B from I-275 (SR 212), then 1.3 mi w on SR 212. Int corridors. **Pets:** Small. Service with restrictions, supervision.
[ASK] [S&] [✕] [▱] [✆] [▣] [¶] [≈] [✕]

HENDERSON

AAA ▼▼▼ Ramada Inn SH
(270) 826-6600. **$69.** 2044 US 41 N. 1 mi n on US 41. Int corridors. **Pets:** Accepted.
[SAVE] [✕] [▱] [✆] [▣] [¶] [≈]

HOPKINSVILLE

▼▼▼ Holiday Inn SH
(270) 886-4413. **$80.** 2910 Ft Campbell Blvd. Pennyrile Pkwy, exit 7A, 0.6 mi n on US 41A. Int corridors. **Pets:** Very small. Service with restrictions, supervision.
[ASK] [S&] [✕] [✆] [▣] [¶] [≈] [✕]

AAA ▼▼▼ Hopkinsville Best Western SH
(270) 886-9000. **$65-$75.** 4101 Ft Campbell Blvd. Pennyrile Pkwy, exit 7A, just s on US 41A. Int corridors. **Pets:** Accepted.
[SAVE] [S&] [✕] [✆] [▣] [≈]

HORSE CAVE

AAA ▼▼▼ Budget Host Inn SH
(270) 786-2165. **$33-$77.** I-65 & Hwy 218. I-65, exit 58, just ne. Ext corridors. **Pets:** Very small. $5 daily fee/pet. Designated rooms, service with restrictions, supervision.
[SAVE] [✕] [✆] [¶] [≈]

▼▼▼ Hampton Inn SH
(270) 786-5000. **$59-$79.** 750 Flint Ridge Rd. I-65, exit 58, just nw. Int corridors. **Pets:** Accepted.
[ASK] [S&] [✕] [✆] [▣] [≈]

IRVINE

▼▼ Oak Tree Inn SH
(606) 723-2600. **$40-$70.** 1075 Richmond Rd. 1 mi w on SR 52. Ext corridors. **Pets:** Accepted.
[ASK] [S&] [✕] [▣]

KUTTAWA

▼▼ Days Inn SH 🐾
(270) 388-4060. **$60-$78.** 139 Days Inn Dr. I-24, exit 40 (US 62), just s. Ext corridors. **Pets:** Other species. $10 one-time fee/room.
[ASK] [S&] [✕] [&M] [&] [✆] [▣] [≈]

LEBANON

▼▼ Country Hearth Inn SH
(270) 692-4445. **$60-$75.** 720 W Main St. 1.4 mi s on SR 55 and US 68. Int corridors. **Pets:** $25 one-time fee/room. Service with restrictions, crate.
[ASK] [S&] [✕] [&M] [✆] [▣]

LEITCHFIELD

▼▼ Hatfield Inn SH
(270) 259-0464. **$58-$99.** 769 White St. Western Kentucky Pkwy, exit 107, just nw. Int corridors. **Pets:** Medium. $10 daily fee/pet. Service with restrictions, supervision.
[ASK] [S&] [✕] [✆]

LEWISPORT

▼▼▼ Best Western Hancock Inn M
(270) 295-3234. **$62.** 9040 US Hwy 60 W. On US 60. Int corridors. **Pets:** Accepted.
[✕] [✆] [▣] [≈]

LEXINGTON

AAA ▼▼▼ **Days Inn-South** SH
(859) 263-3100. **$47-$57.** 5575 Athens-Boonesboro Rd. I-75, exit 104, just e. Ext corridors. **Pets:** Medium. $5 daily fee/pet. Designated rooms, service with restrictions, supervision.
SAVE SD ✕ ♿M 🖥 🖵

AAA ▼▼▼▼ **Hampton Inn I-75** SH
(859) 299-2613. **$69-$149.** 2251 Elkhorn Rd. I-75, exit 110, 0.4 mi nw. Int corridors. **Pets:** Service with restrictions, crate.
SAVE SD ✕ ♿M 🖥 🖵

AAA ▼▼▼▼ **Holiday Inn-Lexington North** SH
(859) 233-0512. **$99-$139.** 1950 Newtown Pike. I-75/64, exit 115, just s. Ext/int corridors. **Pets:** $25 one-time fee/room. Designated rooms, service with restrictions, crate.
SAVE SD ✕ ♿M 🌀 🖥 🖵 ¶ 🏊 ✕

▼▼▼ **Holiday Inn Lexington South** SH
(859) 263-5241. **$79-$89.** 5532 Athens-Boonesboro Rd. I-75, exit 104, just e. Int corridors. **Pets:** Small, other species. $25 deposit/pet. Service with restrictions, supervision.
ASK SD ✕ 🌀 🖵 ¶ 🏊 ✕

▼▼▼▼ **La Quinta Inn Lexington** SH
(859) 231-7551. **$71-$105.** 1919 Stanton Way. I-75/64, exit 115, just se off SR 922. Int corridors. **Pets:** Medium. Supervision.
✕ 🖥 🏊

AAA ▼▼▼ ▼▼▼ **Marriott's Griffin Gate Resort** LH
(859) 231-5100. **$89-$159, 4 day notice.** 1800 Newtown Pike. I-75/64, exit 115, 0.5 mi sw. Int corridors. **Pets:** Other species. $50 one-time fee/room. Designated rooms, service with restrictions, supervision.
SAVE SD ✕ ♿M 🌀 🖴 🖥 🖵 ¶ 🏊 ✕

▼▼ ▼▼ **Microtel Inn** SH
(859) 299-9600. **$41-$71.** 2240 Buena Vista Rd. I-75, exit 110, just w. Int corridors. **Pets:** Medium, other species. $25 one-time fee/room. Service with restrictions, supervision.
ASK SD ✕

▼▼ ▼▼ **Quality Inn Northwest** SH
(859) 233-0561. **$50-$85.** 750 Newtown Pike. I-75/64, exit 115, 1.5 mi w on SR 922. Ext corridors. **Pets:** Accepted.
ASK SD ✕ 🖥 🏊

AAA ▼▼▼▼ **Radisson Plaza Hotel Lexington** LH
(859) 231-9000. **$99-$139.** 369 W Vine St. Corner of Vine St and Broadway. Int corridors. **Pets:** Small, dogs only. $100 deposit/pet, $40 one-time fee/pet. Service with restrictions, supervision.
SAVE SD ✕ ♿M 🌀 🖴 🖥 🖵 ¶ 🏊 ✕

▼▼ ▼▼ **Ramada Inn & Conference Center** SH
(859) 299-1261. **$99-$129.** 2143 N Broadway. I-75, exit 113, just e. Int corridors. **Pets:** Accepted.
ASK SD ✕ ♿M 🌀 🖴 🖥 🖵 ¶ 🏊 ✕

▼▼ ▼▼ **Red Roof Inn-North** SH
(859) 293-2626. **$45-$66.** 1980 Haggard Ct. I-75/64, exit 113, 0.3 mi nw. Ext corridors. **Pets:** Large, other species. Service with restrictions, supervision.
✕

▼▼ ▼▼ **Red Roof Inn South** SH
(859) 277-9400. **$55-$73.** 2651 Wilhite Dr. Jct US 27 and SR 4. Ext corridors. **Pets:** Accepted.
✕ ♿M 🖥

▼▼ ▼▼ **Red Roof Inn Southeast** SH
(859) 543-1877. **$45-$65.** 100 Canebrake Dr. I-75, exit 104, just e. Int corridors. **Pets:** Accepted.
ASK SD ✕ 🖥 🖵 🏊

▼▼▼ **Residence Inn** SH ❀
(859) 263-9979. **$99-$149.** 2688 Pink Pigeon Pkwy. I-75, exit 108, just se. Int corridors. **Pets:** Other species. $75 one-time fee/room.
ASK SD ✕ ♿M 🌀 🖴 🖥 🖵 ¶ 🏊 ✕

▼▼▼ **Residence Inn by Marriott** SH ❀
(859) 231-6191. **$109-$126.** 1080 Newtown Pike. I-75/64, exit 115, 1 mi s on SR 922. Ext corridors. **Pets:** Other species. $75 one-time fee/room.
ASK SD ✕ 🖴 🖥 🖵 🏊 ✕

▼▼ ▼▼ **Sleep Inn Lexington** SH ❀
(859) 543-8400. **$69-$119.** 1920 Plaudit Pl. I-75, exit 108, just sw. Int corridors. **Pets:** Other species. $15 one-time fee/room. Service with restrictions, supervision.
ASK SD ✕ 🖴 🖥 🖵 🏊

LIBERTY

AAA ▼▼ **Royal Inn Express** SH
(606) 787-6224. **$42-$44.** 579 N Wallace Wilkinson Blvd. 1 mi n on US 127; 0.5 mi n of jct SR 70. Ext corridors. **Pets:** Large. $5 daily fee/pet. Service with restrictions, supervision.
SAVE ✕ 🖥

LONDON

▼▼ **Budget Host Westgate Inn** SH ❀
(606) 878-7330. **$45-$54, 3 day notice.** 254 W Daniel Boone Pkwy. I-75, exit 41, just w on SR 80. Ext/int corridors. **Pets:** Small. Designated rooms, service with restrictions, supervision.
SD ✕ ♿M 🖴 🖥 🏊

▼▼▼ **Holiday Inn Express** SH
(608) 862-0077. **$80-$150.** 506 Minton Dr. I-75, exit 38, just e. Int corridors. **Pets:** Accepted.
ASK SD ✕ ♿M 🌀 🖴 🖥 🏊

▼▼ ▼▼ **Park Inn** SH
(606) 878-7678. **Call for rates.** 400 GOP St. I-75, exit 41. Ext corridors. **Pets:** Accepted.
✕ 🖥 🖵 🏊

AAA ▼▼ ▼▼ **Red Roof Inn** SH
(606) 862-8844. **$45-$70.** 110 Melcon Ln. I-75, exit 41, southwest corner. Int corridors. **Pets:** Medium. $6 one-time fee/pet. Designated rooms, service with restrictions, supervision.
SAVE SD ✕ ♿M 🖥 🖵 🏊

LOUISVILLE METROPOLITAN AREA

BROOKS

▼▼▼▼ Comfort Inn SH
(502) 957-6900. **$69.** 149 Willabrook Dr. I-65, exit 121, just nw. Int corridors. **Pets:** Large, other species. $10 daily fee/room. Service with restrictions, supervision.

ASK S6 X 8 9 a X

HURSTBOURNE

▼▼▼▼ Drury Inn & Suites-Louisville SH
(502) 326-4170. **$70-$100.** 9501 Blairwood Rd. I-64, exit 15. Int corridors. **Pets:** Large, other species. Service with restrictions, supervision.

ASK X 6M 9 6 8 9 a

▼ Red Roof Inn Louisville–East #034 SH
(502) 426-7621. **$43-$67.** 9330 Blairwood Rd. I-64, exit 15, 0.3 mi nw of Hurstbourne Pkwy. Ext corridors. **Pets:** Accepted.

X 6M

JEFFERSONTOWN

▲▲▲ ▼▼▼▼ AmeriSuites (Louisville/East) SH
(502) 426-0119. **$98-$108, 7 day notice.** 701 S Hurstbourne Pkwy. I-64, exit 15, 1 mi n. Int corridors. **Pets:** Small, dogs only. $10 daily fee/pet. Service with restrictions, crate.

SAVE S6 X 6 8 9 a

▼▼▼ Best Western Signature Inn East SH
(502) 267-8100. **$49-$104.** 1301 Kentucky Mills Dr. I-64, exit 17. Ext/int corridors. **Pets:** Accepted.

ASK X 6M 6 8 9 a X

▲▲▲ ▼▼▼▼ Clarion Hotel and Conference Center LH
(502) 491-4830. **$69-$99.** 9700 Bluegrass Pkwy. I-64, exit 15, 0.5 mi se of Hurstbourne Pkwy. Int corridors. **Pets:** Small. $25 one-time fee/room. Service with restrictions, crate.

SAVE S6 X 6 8 9 TI a X

▼▼▼▼ Comfort Suites SH
(502) 266-6509. **$64-$81.** 1850 Resource Way. I-64, exit 17, 0.5 mi s of Blankenbaker Rd. Int corridors. **Pets:** Medium. $10 daily fee/room. Service with restrictions.

ASK S6 X 6M 8 9 a

▲▲▲ ▼▼▼▼ Holiday Inn-Hurstbourne LH
(502) 426-2600. **$89-$119.** 1325 S Hurstbourne Pkwy. I-64, exit 15. Ext/int corridors. **Pets:** Accepted.

SAVE S6 X 6 8 9 TI a X

**▼▼▼ Homestead Studio Suites
Hotel-Louisville/East** SH ❀
(502) 267-4454. **$54-$79.** 1650 Alliant Ave. I-64, exit 17, just s. Int corridors. **Pets:** Medium, other species. $25 daily fee/pet, $75 one-time fee/pet. Designated rooms, service with restrictions.

ASK S6 X 6M 6 8 9 a

▲▲▲ ▼▼▼ Microtel Inn SH
(502) 266-6590. **$50-$65.** 1221 Kentucky Mills Dr. I-64, exit 17. Int corridors. **Pets:** Small. $20 one-time fee/pet. Service with restrictions, supervision.

SAVE S6 X 6M 6 6

▼▼ Sleep Inn SH
(502) 266-6776. **$55-$200.** 1850 Priority Way. I-64, exit 17, 0.5 mi s of Blankenbaker Rd. Int corridors. **Pets:** Accepted.

ASK S6 X 8 9

▼▼▼ Super 8 Motel & Suites SH
(502) 267-8889. **$60-$170.** 1501 Alliant Ave. I-64, exit 17, just e. Int corridors. **Pets:** Medium, other species. $15 daily fee/pet. Designated rooms, no service, supervision.

ASK S6 X 6M 6 8 a

LA GRANGE

▼▼▼▼ Comfort Suites SH
(502) 225-4125. **$72-$180.** 1500 Crystal Dr. I-71, exit 22, just e. Int corridors. **Pets:** Large. $10 one-time fee/room. Service with restrictions, supervision.

ASK S6 X 6M 6 8 9 a X

LOUISVILLE

▼▼▼▼ Aleksander House Bed and Breakfast BB ❀
(502) 637-4985. **$95-$169, 3 day notice.** 1213 S 1st St. I-65, exit 135 (St Catherine St), just s. Int corridors. **Pets:** $20 one-time fee/room. Service with restrictions, crate.

ASK X 8 9

▼▼▼ Breckinridge Inn LH
(502) 456-5050. **$69-$79.** 2800 Breckinridge Ln. I-264, exit 18A, just s. Int corridors. **Pets:** $25 one-time fee/pet. Service with restrictions, crate.

ASK S6 X 8 9 a X

▲▲▲ ▼▼▼ Executive West LH
(502) 367-2251. **$99-$139.** 830 Phillips Ln. I-264, exit 11 (Fairgrounds/Expo Center Main Gate). Int corridors. **Pets:** Other species. $100 one-time fee/room. Designated rooms, service with restrictions.

SAVE S6 X 6 8 9 TI a X

▲▲▲ ▼▼▼▼ Holiday Inn Airport East SH
(502) 452-6361. **$85-$136.** 4004 Gardiner Point Dr. I-264, exit 15B westbound; exit 15 eastbound. Int corridors. **Pets:** Medium, dogs only. $25 one-time fee/pet. Designated rooms, service with restrictions, supervision.

SAVE X 6 8 9 TI a

▲▲▲ ▼▼▼▼ Holiday Inn Louisville (Downtown) SH
(502) 582-2241. **$136.** 120 W Broadway. Just w on US 60 business route and 150. Int corridors. **Pets:** Medium. Designated rooms, service with restrictions, crate.

SAVE S6 X 6 6 9 TI a

▼▼▼ Holiday Inn South-Airport LH
(502) 964-3311. **$105-$145.** 3317 Fern Valley Rd. I-65, exit 128 (Fern Valley Rd), northeast corner. Int corridors. **Pets:** Large. $35 one-time fee/room. Service with restrictions, supervision.

ASK S6 X 6M 6 6 8 9 TI a X

▼▼▼ La Quinta Inn & Suites Airport & Expo-Louisville SH
(502) 368-0007. **$79-$99.** 4125 Preston Hwy. I-65, exit 130, 1 mi w. Int corridors. **Pets:** Designated rooms, service with restrictions, supervision.

ASK S6 X 6M 6 6 8 9

▼▼▼ Red Roof Inn-Airport-Fairgrounds SH
(502) 968-0151. **$45-$74.** 4704 Preston Hwy. I-65, exit 130, northeast corner. Ext corridors. **Pets:** Accepted.

X

▼▼▼ Red Roof Inn-Southeast-Fairgrounds SH ❀
(502) 456-2993. **$47-$64.** 3322 Red Roof Inn Pl. I-264, 15B westbound, 0.3 mi s; exit 15 eastbound. Ext corridors. **Pets:** Medium, other species. Service with restrictions, crate.

X

▼▼▼ Residence Inn by Marriott SH ❀
(502) 363-8800. **$99-$229.** 700 Phillips Ln. I-264, exit 11 (Fairgrounds/Expo Center Main Gate), 0.4 mi w. Int corridors. **Pets:** $75 one-time fee/room. Service with restrictions, supervision.

ASK S6 X 6M 6 6 8 9 a X

▼▼▼ **Residence Inn by Marriott-Louisville NE** 🆂🅷 ❀
(502) 412-1311. **$139-$149.** 3500 Springhurst Commons Dr. I-265, exit 32, 0.5 mi w on Westport Rd, then just n. Int corridors. **Pets:** Accepted.
(A$K) 🆂 ✖ 🅼 🖪 🖬 🖳 ➣ ✖

▼▼▼ **Residence Inn Louisville East** 🆂🅷
(502) 425-1821. **$89-$134.** 120 N Hurstbourne Pkwy. I-64, exit 15, 1.8 mi n. Ext corridors. **Pets:** Other species. $75 one-time fee/room. Service with restrictions.
(A$K) ✖ 🖪 🖬 ➣ ✖

🆀 ▼▼▼ ▼▼▼ **The Seelbach Hilton Louisville** 🅻🅷
(502) 585-3200. **$119-$199.** 500 4th St. I-65, exit 136C (Muhammad Ali), 0.3 mi w, then just s. Int corridors. **Pets:** Large, other species. $50 deposit/pet.
(SAVE) ✖ 🅼 🖇 🖬 🖪 🖬 🍴 ✖

▼▼▼ **Signature Inn South** 🆂🅷
(502) 968-4100. **$49-$104.** 6515 Signature Dr. I-65, exit 128 (Fern Valley Rd), southeast corner. Int corridors. **Pets:** Very small, other species. $10 daily fee/room. Service with restrictions, supervision.
(A$K) ✖ 🖪 🖬 ➣

▼▼ **Sleep Inn Fairgrounds** 🆂🅷 ❀
(502) 368-9597. **$49-$275.** 3330 Preston Hwy. I-264, exit 11 (Fairgrounds/Expo Center Main Gate), 0.5 mi e on Phillips Ln, then just n. Int corridors. **Pets:** Other species. $10 daily fee/room. Service with restrictions.
(A$K) 🆂 ✖ 🖇 🖪 🖬

▼▼▼ **Staybridge Suites by Holiday Inn** 🆂🅷
(502) 244-9511. **$82-$90.** 11711 Gateworth Way. I-64, exit 17, just n. Int corridors. **Pets:** Accepted.
(A$K) 🆂 ✖ 🅼 🖇 🖇 🖪 🖬 ➣

SHEPHERDSVILLE

🆀 ▼▼▼ **Best Western South** 🆂🅷
(502) 543-7097. **$69-$79, 30 day notice.** 211 S Lakeview Dr. I-65, exit 117 (SR 44 W), just se. Int corridors. **Pets:** Accepted.
(SAVE) 🆂 ✖ 🖪 🖬 ➣

SHIVELY

▼▼▼ **Holiday Inn-Southwest** 🅻🅷
(502) 448-2020. **$84-$134, 3 day notice.** 4110 Dixie Hwy. I-264, exit 8B, just n on US 31 W and 60. Int corridors. **Pets:** Accepted.
(A$K) 🆂 ✖ 🖇 🖪 🖬 🍴 ➣

END METROPOLITAN AREA

MADISONVILLE

▼▼ **Days Inn Madisonville** 🆂🅷
(270) 821-8620. **$59-$64.** 1900 Lantaff Blvd. Pennyrile Pkwy, exit 44. Int corridors. **Pets:** Small, other species. $10 daily fee/room. Service with restrictions, supervision.
(A$K) 🆂 ✖ 🖇 🖪 🖬 🍴 ➣

MAYSVILLE

▼▼ **Super 8 Motel, Maysville KY** 🆂🅷
(606) 759-8888. **$61-$66, 5 day notice.** 550 Tucker Dr. Just e of US 68. Int corridors. **Pets:** Accepted.
(A$K) 🆂 ✖ 🖪

MOREHEAD

🆀 ▼▼▼ **Comfort Inn & Suites** 🆂🅷
(606) 780-7378. **$52-$92.** 2650 Kentucky 801 N. I-64, exit 133, just s. Int corridors. **Pets:** Accepted.
(SAVE) 🆂 ✖ 🅼 🖇 🖪 🖬 ➣

▼▼▼ **Holiday Inn Express of Morehead** 🆂🅷
(606) 784-5796. **$58-$89.** 110 Toms Dr. I-64, exit 137 (SR 32), just sw. Int corridors. **Pets:** Medium, other species. $10 daily fee/pet. Service with restrictions, supervision.
(A$K) 🆂 ✖ 🅼 🖇 🖪 🖬 ➣

MORGANTOWN

▼▼ **Motel 6 #4120** 🆂🅷
(270) 526-9481. **Call for rates.** 1460 S Main St. William H Natcher Pkwy, exit 26, just w. Int corridors. **Pets:** Accepted.
✖ 🅼 🖇 🖇 🖪 ➣

MORTONS GAP

🆀 ▼▼ **Best Western Pennyrile Inn** 🆂🅷
(270) 258-5201. **$49-$68.** White City Rd. Pennyrile Pkwy, exit 37 (US 41). Ext corridors. **Pets:** Accepted.
(SAVE) 🆂 ✖ 🖪 🖬 ➣

MOUNT STERLING

▼▼▼ **Ramada Limited** 🆂🅷
(859) 497-9400. **$70.** 115 Stone Trace Dr. I-64, exit 110. Int corridors. **Pets:** Other species. $10 daily fee/room. Service with restrictions.
(A$K) 🆂 ✖ 🅼 🖇 🖪 🖬 ➣

MOUNT VERNON

🆀 ▼ **Kastle Inn Motel** 🅼
(606) 256-5156. **$52-$70, 3 day notice.** Hwy 25 S. I-75, exit 59. Ext corridors. **Pets:** Medium, other species. Service with restrictions, supervision.
(SAVE) 🆂 ✖ 🍴 ➣

MURRAY

▼▼ **Days Inn-Murray, KY** 🆂🅷
(270) 753-6706. **$49-$64, 7 day notice.** 517 S 12th St. 1 mi s on US 641. Ext corridors. **Pets:** Accepted.
(A$K) 🆂 ✖ 🖪 🖬 ➣

🆀 ▼ **Murray Plaza Court** 🆂🅷
(270) 753-2682. **$39.** 504 12th St. 1 mi s on US 641. Ext corridors. **Pets:** Accepted.
(SAVE) ✖ 🖪

OAK GROVE

🆀 ▼▼ **Comfort Inn-Oak Grove** 🆂🅷
(270) 439-3311. **$64-$89.** 201 Auburn St. I-24, exit 86, just s. Ext corridors. **Pets:** Small. $10 daily fee/pet. Designated rooms, no service, supervision.
(SAVE) 🆂 ✖ 🅼 🖇 🖇 🖪 🖬 ➣

▼▼▼ **Days Inn Ft. Campbell** 🆂🅷
(270) 640-3888. **$64-$69.** 212 Auburn St. I-24, exit 86, just s. Ext corridors. **Pets:** Accepted.
(A$K) 🆂 ✖ 🅼 🖇 🖪 ➣

▼▼▼ **Holiday Inn Express** 🆂🅷
(270) 439-0022. **$89.** 12759 Ft Campbell Blvd. I-24, exit 86. Int corridors. **Pets:** $10 daily fee/pet. Designated rooms, service with restrictions, crate.
(A$K) 🆂 ✖ 🅼 🖇 🖪 🖬 ➣

OWENSBORO

▼ **Motel 6 #205** 🆂🅷
(270) 686-8606. **$40-$60.** 4585 Frederica St. US 60 Bypass, exit 4 at jct US 431, just n. Ext corridors. **Pets:** Small, other species. Service with restrictions, supervision.
🆂 ✖ 🅼 🖇 🖇 🖪 ➣

▼▼ ▼▼ **Super 8 Motel-Owensboro** SH
(270) 685-3388. **$75.** 1027 Goetz Dr. US 60 Bypass, exit 4 at jct US 431. Int corridors. **Pets:** Small, other species. $5 daily fee/pet. Designated rooms, service with restrictions, supervision.
A$K S⌀ ✕ &M 🛅 🖥 🖵

PADUCAH

▼▼ ▼▼ **Baymont Inn-Paducah** SH
(270) 443-4343. **$59-$69.** 5300 Old Cairo Rd. I-24, exit 3 (SR 305), just w. Int corridors. **Pets:** Accepted.
A$K S⌀ ✕ 🐾 🐕 🛅 🖥 🖵

▼▼ ▼▼ **Days Inn** SH
(270) 442-7501. **$55-$95.** 3901 Hinkleville Rd. I-24, exit 4 (US 60), just e. Ext corridors. **Pets:** Accepted.
A$K S⌀ ✕ 🛅 🖥 🖵 ⤴

▼▼▼▼ **Drury Inn-Paducah** SH
(270) 443-3313. **$67-$98.** 3975 Hinkleville Rd. I-24, exit 4 (US 60), just e. Int corridors. **Pets:** Large, other species. Service with restrictions, supervision.
A$K ✕ 🐕 🛅 🖥 🖵 ⤴

▼▼▼▼ **Drury Suites-Paducah** SH
(270) 441-0024. **$77-$105.** 2930 James-Sanders Blvd. I-24, exit 4 (US 60), just w. Int corridors. **Pets:** Large, other species. Service with restrictions, supervision.
A$K ✕ &M 🐕 🛅 🖥 ⤴ ✕

▼▼▼▼ **Hampton Inn-Paducah** SH
(270) 442-4500. **$74-$114.** 5006 Hinkleville Rd. I-24, exit 4 (US 60), just w. Int corridors. **Pets:** Accepted.
A$K ✕ &M 🐾 🖥 ⤴

▼▼ ▼▼ **Holiday Inn Express** SH
(270) 442-8874. **$105-$115.** 3994 Hinkleville Rd. I-24, exit 4 (US 60), just e. Int corridors. **Pets:** Accepted.
A$K S⌀ ✕ 🛅 🖥 🖵 ⤴

▼▼ ▼▼ **Pear Tree Inn-Paducah** SH
(270) 444-7200. **$56-$80.** 5002 Hinkleville Rd. I-24, exit 4 (US 60), just w. Ext corridors. **Pets:** Large, other species. Service with restrictions, supervision.
A$K ✕ 🛅 🖥 🖵 ⤴

PRESTONSBURG

▼▼ ▼▼ **Super 8 Prestonsburg** M
(606) 886-3355. **$44-$58.** 550 US 23 S. Jct US 114 and US 23. Int corridors. **Pets:** Large, other species. $20 one-time fee/pet. Service with restrictions, supervision.
A$K S⌀ ✕ 🖵

RICHMOND

▼▼▼▼ **Holiday Inn Express Hotel & Suites** SH
(859) 624-4005. **$76-$149.** 1990 Colby Taylor Dr. I-75, exit 87, just w. Int corridors. **Pets:** Accepted.
A$K S⌀ ✕ &M 🐾 🐕 🛅 🖥 🖵 ⤴

▼▼▼▼ **Jameson Inn** SH
(859) 623-0063. **$49-$104.** 1007 Colby Taylor Dr. I-75, exit 87, just w. Int corridors. **Pets:** Very small, other species. $10 daily fee/room. Service with restrictions, supervision.
A$K ✕ &M 🐾 🐕 🛅 🖥 🖵 ⤴

▲▲▲ ▼▼ ▼▼ **La Quinta Inn Richmond** SH
(859) 623-9121. **$54-$69.** 1751 Lexington Rd. I-75, exit 90 northbound; exit 90A southbound. Int corridors. **Pets:** Accepted.
SAVE S⌀ ✕ 🐾 🛅 🖥 🖵 ⤴

▼▼ ▼▼ **Red Roof Inn** M
(859) 625-0084. **$50-$70, 14 day notice.** 111 Bahama Ct. I-75, exit 90 northbound; exit 90A southbound. Int corridors. **Pets:** Accepted.
A$K ✕ 🐕 🛅 🖥 🖵 ⤴

▲▲▲ ▼▼ ▼▼ **Super 8 Motel** SH
(859) 624-1550. **$55-$60.** 107 N Keeneland Dr. I-75, exit 90. Int corridors. **Pets:** Accepted.
SAVE S⌀ ✕ &M 🛅 🖥 🖵

SCOTTSVILLE

▲▲▲ ▼▼ ▼▼ **Executive Inn** SH
(270) 622-7770. **$55.** 57 Burnley Rd. US 31 E, jct SR 231. Ext corridors. **Pets:** Accepted.
SAVE S⌀ ✕ 🛅 ⤴

SHELBYVILLE

▲▲▲ ▼▼ ▼▼ **Best Western Shelbyville Lodge** SH
(502) 633-4400. **$69-$145.** 115 Isaac Shelby Dr. I-64, exit 32, 0.5 mi n on SR 55. Int corridors. **Pets:** Accepted.
SAVE S⌀ ✕ 🛅 🖥 ⤴

▼▼ ▼▼ **Days Inn Shelbyville** SH
(502) 633-4005. **$55-$65.** 101 Howard Dr. I-64, exit 32, 0.8 mi n on SR 55. Ext corridors. **Pets:** Accepted.
A$K S⌀ ✕ 🛅 🖥

▼▼▼▼ **Holiday Inn Express** SH
(502) 647-0109. **$78-$83.** 110 Club House Dr. I-64, exit 35, just s. Int corridors. **Pets:** Accepted.
A$K S⌀ ✕ &M 🐾 🐕 🛅 🖥 ⤴

SMITHS GROVE

▲▲▲ ▼▼ ▼▼ **Bryce Inn** SH
(270) 563-5141. **$49-$59.** 592 S Main St. I-65, exit 38, 0.3 mi w. Ext corridors. **Pets:** Accepted.
SAVE S⌀ ✕ 🛅 🖥 ⤴

SOMERSET

▼▼▼▼ **Comfort Inn** SH
(606) 677-1500. **$69-$119, 3 day notice.** 82 Jolin Dr. Cumberland Pkwy, 4.3 mi s on US 27. Int corridors. **Pets:** Accepted.
A$K S⌀ ✕ &M 🐕 🛅 🖥 ⤴

VERSAILLES

▼▼▼▼ **1823 Historic Rose Hill Inn** BB
(859) 873-5957. **$109-$169, 7 day notice.** 233 Rose Hill. Just s on SR 33 (S Main St), then just w. Ext/int corridors. **Pets:** Accepted.
✕ 🛅 🖥

WILLIAMSTOWN

▲▲▲ ▼▼ ▼▼ **Best Value Inn & Suites** SH
(859) 824-7177. **$40-$52.** 10 Skyway Dr. I-75, exit 154, just w. Ext corridors. **Pets:** Accepted.
SAVE S⌀ ✕ 🛅 ⤴

▲▲▲ ▼▼ ▼▼ **Days Inn** SH
(859) 824-5025. **$49-$66, 3 day notice.** 211 SR 36 W. I-75, exit 154, just n. Ext corridors. **Pets:** Accepted.
SAVE S⌀ ✕ 🛅 🖥 ⤴

WINCHESTER

▲▲▲ ▼▼ ▼▼ **Best Western-Country Squire** SH
(859) 744-7210. **$54-$69.** 1307 W Lexington Rd. I-64, exit 94 (US 60), 0.9 mi se. Ext corridors. **Pets:** Accepted.
SAVE S⌀ ✕ 🛅 🖥 ⤴

LOUISIANA

ALEXANDRIA

AAA ◆◆◆◆ **Best Western of Alexandria Inn & Suites & Conference Center** SH
(318) 445-5530. **$72-$88.** 2720 W MacArthur Dr. 0.9 mi n of jct SR 28 and US 71/165 (MacArthur Dr). Ext/int corridors. **Pets:** Very small. $10 daily fee/room. Designated rooms, service with restrictions, crate.
SAVE S X 🖐 🛢 💻 ❚❙ ⇒

AAA ◆◆◆ **Clarion Hotel Alexandria** SH
(318) 487-4261. **$96.** 2716 N MacArthur Dr. 0.9 mi n of jct SR 28 and US 71/165 (MacArthur Dr). Ext/int corridors. **Pets:** Medium. $15 daily fee/pet. Service with restrictions, supervision.
SAVE S X 🛢 💻 ⇒

AAA ◆◆◆ **Days Inn** M
(318) 443-1841. **$55-$59.** 1146 MacArthur Dr. 0.7 mi s of jct SR 28 and US 71/165 (MacArthur Dr). Ext corridors. **Pets:** Accepted.
SAVE X 🛢 💻 ⇒

◆◆◆ **La Quinta Inn & Suites Alexandria** SH
(318) 442-3700. **$86-$115.** 6116 W Calhoun Dr. I-49, exit 90 (Air Base Rd), just w. Int corridors. **Pets:** Accepted.
ASK X 🖐 🛢 💻 ⇒

◆ **Motel 6 Alexandria #458** M
(318) 445-2336. **$42-$55.** 546 MacArthur Dr. Jct SR 28. Ext corridors. **Pets:** Accepted.
S X 🖐 ⇒

AAA ◆◆◆ **Ramada Limited** SH
(318) 448-1611. **$60-$70.** 742 MacArthur Dr. 0.4 mi s of jct SR 28 and US 71/165 (MacArthur Dr). Ext corridors. **Pets:** Accepted.
SAVE S X 🛢 💻 ⇒

AAA ◆◆ **Super 8 Motel** M
(318) 445-6541. **$45-$65.** 700 MacArthur Dr. 0.4 mi s of jct SR 28 and US 71/65 (MacArthur Dr). Ext/int corridors. **Pets:** Accepted.
SAVE S X 💻 ⇒

BATON ROUGE

AAA ◆◆◆◆ **AmeriSuites (Baton Rouge/East)** SH
(225) 769-4400. **$78-$115.** 6080 Bluebonnet Blvd. I-10, exit 162. Int corridors. **Pets:** Medium, other species. $10 one-time fee/room. Service with restrictions, supervision.
SAVE S X 🖐 🛢 💻 ⇒

AAA ◆◆◆ **Baymont Inn & Suites Baton Rouge** SH
(225) 291-6600. **$55-$75.** 10555 Rieger Rd. I-10, exit 163 (Siegen Ln), just n, then just e. Int corridors. **Pets:** Medium. $50 deposit/room. Designated rooms, service with restrictions, supervision.
SAVE S X 🖐 🛢 💻 ⇒

◆◆◆◆ **Chase Suites by Woodfin** SH
(225) 927-5630. **$144-$179.** 5522 Corporate Blvd. I-10, exit 158, just n on College Dr, then just e. Ext corridors. **Pets:** Other species. $150 deposit/room. Service with restrictions, crate.
ASK S X 🖐 🛢 💻 ⇒ X

◆◆◆◆ **Comfort Inn** SH
(225) 236-4000. **$60.** 2445 S Acadian Thruway. I-10, exit 157B, just n. Int corridors. **Pets:** Medium, other species. $25 daily fee/pet. Service with restrictions, supervision.
SAVE S X 🖐 🛢 💻 ⇒

AAA ◆◆◆ **La Quinta Inn Baton Rouge** SH
(225) 924-9600. **$78-$103.** 2333 S Acadian Thruway. I-10, exit 157B. Ext corridors. **Pets:** Accepted.
SAVE X 🖐 🛢 💻 ⇒

◆◆ **Microtel Inn & Suites** SH
(225) 927-9997. **$40-$50.** 10311 Plaza Americana Dr. I-12, exit 2B, just n, then e. Int corridors. **Pets:** Accepted.
ASK S X 🖐 🛢 💻 ⇒

◆ **Motel 6 Baton Rouge Southeast #1124** M
(225) 291-4912. **$43-$53.** 10445 Rieger Rd. I-10, exit 163, just n. Ext corridors. **Pets:** Small, other species. Service with restrictions, supervision.
S X 🖐 ⇒

◆◆◆ **Residence Inn by Marriott-Baton Rouge** SH
(225) 293-8700. **$89-$119.** 10333 N Mall Dr. I-10, exit 163 westbound, just s on Siegen Ln, then just e; exit eastbound, 0.5 mi to S Mall Dr, just e to Andrea (at Lowe's), then just n. Int corridors. **Pets:** $75 one-time fee/room. Designated rooms, service with restrictions, supervision.
ASK X 🖐 🛢 💻 ⇒ X

◆◆◆ **Sheraton Baton Rouge Convention Center Hotel** LH
(225) 242-2600. **$209.** 102 France St. I-110, exit 1A (Government St), 0.8 mi w to St. James, then just s. Int corridors. **Pets:** Accepted.
ASK S X 🖐 🛢 💻 ❚❙ ⇒

◆◆◆ **TownePlace Suites by Marriott** SH
(225) 819-2112. **$75-$99.** 8735 Summa Ave. I-10, exit 162 (Bluebonnet Blvd), just s to Picardy, just w to Summa Ave, then 0.5 mi nw. Int corridors. **Pets:** Accepted.
ASK S X 🖐 🛢 💻 ⇒

BOSSIER CITY

AAA ◆◆◆ **Best Western-Airline Motor Inn** SH 🐾
(318) 742-6000. **$75-$95, 10 day notice.** 1984 Airline Dr. I-20, exit 22 (Airline Dr), just n. Ext corridors. **Pets:** Medium, other species. $10 daily fee/room.
SAVE S X 💻 ❚❙ ⇒

◆◆◆ **Econo Lodge Inn & Suites** SH
(318) 746-5050. **$49-$59.** 4300 Industrial Dr. I-20, exit 23 (Industrial Dr). Ext corridors. **Pets:** $20 one-time fee/pet. Designated rooms, service with restrictions, supervision.
ASK S X 🛢 💻 ⇒

◆◆◆ **Hampton Inn** SH
(318) 752-1112. **$79-$104.** 1005 Gould Dr. I-20, exit 21, 0.5 mi ne on service road. Int corridors. **Pets:** Accepted.
ASK X 🖐 🛢 💻 ⇒

▽▽▽▽ **La Quinta Inn Bossier City** SH
(318) 747-4400. **$65-$100.** 309 Preston Blvd. I-20, exit 21, just n. Ext corridors. **Pets:** Accepted.
SAVE ✕ 🐾 ▥ ⌦

▽▽▽ **Microtel Inn & Suites** SH
(318) 742-7882. **$45.** 2713 Village Ln. I-20, exit 22 (Airline Dr), just s, then just w. Int corridors. **Pets:** Accepted.
ASK 🐾 ✕ 🐾M 🐾 🐾 🗋 ▥

▽▽ **Motel 6 #391** M
(318) 742-3472. **$35-$55.** 210 John Wesley Blvd. I-20, exit 121, just sw. Ext corridors. **Pets:** Accepted.
🐾 ✕ 🐾 ⌦

▽▽▽▽ **Quality Inn & Suites** SH 🐾
(318) 742-7890. **$82.** 2717 Village Ln. I-20, exit 22 (Airline Dr), just s, then just w. Int corridors. **Pets:** Other species. $25 one-time fee/room. Service with restrictions.
ASK 🐾 ✕ 🐾M 🐾 🐾 🗋 ▥ ⌦

▽▽▽▽ **Residence Inn by Marriott-Shreveport/Bossier**
        City SH
(318) 747-6220. **$139-$199.** 1001 Gould Dr. I-20, exit 21, just ne. Ext corridors. **Pets:** Other species. $75 one-time fee/room. Service with restrictions.
ASK 🐾 ✕ 🐾 🗋 ▥ ⌦ ✕

▽▽ **Shoney's Inn-Bossier City** SH
(318) 747-7700. **$69.** 1836 Old Minden Rd. I-20, exit 21, just n. Ext corridors. **Pets:** Accepted.
ASK 🐾 ✕ 🐾 🗋 ▥ ⌦

BREAUX BRIDGE

▲▲▲ ▽▽▽ **Best Western of Breaux Bridge** M
(337) 332-1114. **$54-$66.** 2088-B Rees St. I-10, exit 109 (Breaux Bridge). Ext corridors. **Pets:** $10 daily fee/pet. Service with restrictions.
SAVE 🐾 ✕ 🗋 ▥ ⌦

▽▽▽ **Holiday Inn Express of Breaux Bridge** SH
(337) 667-8913. **Call for rates.** 2942 H Grand Point Hwy. I-10, exit 115, just n. Int corridors. **Pets:** Accepted.
✕ 🐾M 🐾 🗋 ▥ ⌦

CONVENT

▲▲▲ ▽▽▽▽ **Poche Plantation Bed & Breakfast** BB
(225) 562-7728. **$119, 7 day notice.** 6554 Louisiana Hwy 44. Jct SR 44 and 641; 10.1 mi s of Sunshine Bridge (SR 70), then 10.2 mi n. Ext corridors. **Pets:** Accepted.
SAVE 🐾 ✕ 🗋 ▥ ⌦

DELHI

▽▽ **Days Inn** SH
(318) 878-9000. **$65-$75.** 113 Snider Rd. I-20, exit 153, just s. Ext corridors. **Pets:** $10 daily fee/pet. Service with restrictions, supervision.
ASK 🐾 ✕ 🗋 ▥ ⌦

DERIDDER

▲▲▲ ▽▽▽ **Stagecoach Inn** SH
(337) 462-0022. **$69-$74.** 505 E 1st St. 2 mi on east side; between US 171 NS. Ext corridors. **Pets:** Very small. $25 daily fee/pet. Service with restrictions, crate.
SAVE 🐾 ✕ 🐾M 🗋 ▥ ⌦

HAMMOND

▲▲▲ ▽▽▽ **Best Western Hammond Inn & Suites** SH
(985) 419-2001. **$60-$80.** 107 Duo Dr. I-12, exit 40 (US 51), just ne. Ext corridors. **Pets:** Other species. $10 daily fee/room. Supervision.
SAVE 🐾 ✕ 🐾 ▥ ⌦

▲▲▲ ▽▽▽ **Michabelle-A Little Inn** CI
(985) 419-0550. **$75-$125, 5 day notice.** 1106 S Holly St. I-12, exit 40 (US 51), 0.8 mi n, just e on Old Covington Hwy, then n, follow signs. Ext/int corridors. **Pets:** Small. Service with restrictions, supervision.
SAVE 🐾 ✕ ▥ 🍴 ☎

▽▽▽▽ **Rockwood Inn & Suites** SH
(985) 345-1980. **Call for rates.** 42309 S Morrison Blvd. I-55, exit 28 (US 51), just e. Int corridors. **Pets:** Accepted.
✕ 🗋 ▥ ⌦

IOWA

▽▽ **Howard Johnson Express Inn** SH
(337) 582-2440. **$55-$64.** 107 E Frontage Rd. I-10, exit 43, just n, then just e. Int corridors. **Pets:** Other species. $10 one-time fee/room. Service with restrictions.
ASK 🐾 ✕ 🗋 ▥

KINDER

▲▲▲ ▽▽▽▽ **Best Western Inn At Coushatta** SH
(337) 738-4800. **$89-$119.** 12102 US Hwy 165 N. 5 mi n of jct US 190/165. Int corridors. **Pets:** Small, other species. $25 deposit/room. No service, supervision.
SAVE 🐾 ✕ 🗋 ▥ ⌦

▽▽▽▽ **Holiday Inn Express Hotel & Suites** SH
(337) 738-3381. **$79-$150.** 11750 US Hwy 165. 5.2 mi n of jct US 190/165, 5.1 mi on US 165. Ext/int corridors. **Pets:** Accepted.
ASK 🐾 ✕ 🐾M 🐾 🗋 ▥ ⌦

LAFAYETTE

▽▽▽ **Best Suites of Lafayette** SH
(337) 235-1367. **$79-$159.** 125 E Kaliste Saloom Rd. I-10, exit 103A, 1 mi w of jct E Kaliste Saloom Rd and US 90 (SW Evangeline Thruway). Int corridors. **Pets:** Accepted.
ASK 🐾 ✕ 🐾 🗋 ▥ ⌦

▲▲▲ ▽▽▽ **Best Western Hotel Acadiana** SH
(337) 233-8120. **$79, 3 day notice.** 1801 W Pinhook Rd. SR 182, 1.5 mi s of US 90 (Evangeline Thruway). Int corridors. **Pets:** Medium. $25 one-time fee/room. Service with restrictions, supervision.
SAVE 🐾 ✕ 🐾 🗋 ▥ 🍴 ⌦

▽▽▽ **Comfort Inn Lafayette** SH
(337) 232-9000. **$81.** 1421 SE Evangeline Thruway. 3 mi s of I-10 at jct US 90 (Evangeline Thruway). Int corridors. **Pets:** Other species. Service with restrictions, supervision.
ASK 🐾 ✕ 🐾 🗋 ▥ 🍴 ⌦

▽▽▽ **Days Inn-Lafayette** M
(337) 237-8880. **$55-$65.** 1620 N University. I-10, exit 101. Ext corridors. **Pets:** Other species. $10 one-time fee/pet. Service with restrictions, crate.
ASK 🐾 ✕ 🗋 ▥ ⌦

▽▽▽ **Hilton Lafayette & Towers** LH
(337) 235-6111. **$79-$189.** 1521 W Pinhook Rd. SR 182, 1.3 mi sw of US 90 (Evangeline Thruway). Int corridors. **Pets:** Small, other species. $25 one-time fee/room. Designated rooms, service with restrictions, supervision.
✕ 🐾 🗋 ▥ 🍴 ⌦

▽▽▽ **La Quinta Inn & Suites Lafayette Oil Center** SH
(337) 291-1088. **$72-$90.** 1015 W Pinhook Rd. I-10, exit 101 (University Ave), 3.5 mi to SR 182 (Pinhook Rd), then 0.5 mi w. Int corridors. **Pets:** Other species. Service with restrictions, crate.
ASK 🐾 ✕ 🗋 ▥ ⌦

▲▲▲ ▽▽▽ **La Quinta Inn Lafayette (North)** SH
(337) 233-5610. **$65-$100.** 2100 NE Evangeline Thruway. I-10, exit 103A, 0.3 mi s on US 167. Ext corridors. **Pets:** Other species. Service with restrictions.
SAVE ✕ 🐾 🗋 ▥ ⌦

▼ Motel 6 #461
(337) 233-2055. **$37-$50.** 2724 NE Evangeline Thruway. I-49, exit 1B (Pont des Mouton Rd), just e, then just s on frontage road. Ext corridors. **Pets:** Accepted.

🏊 ✕

▼▼ Ramada Inn **SH**
(337) 235-0858. **$64-$79.** 120 E Kaliste Saloom Rd. I-10, exit 103A, 4.4 mi e on US 90 (Evangeline Thruway), then 1 mi s. Ext corridors. **Pets:** Medium. $10 one-time fee/pet. Supervision.

ASK 🏊 ✕ ♿ 📺 🖥 🏊

▼▼ Red Roof Inn **M**
(337) 233-3339. **$40-$53.** 1718 N University Ave. I-10, exit 101, just n. Ext corridors. **Pets:** Accepted.

✕ 🛗

LAKE CHARLES

▼▼▼ Best Suites of America **SH**
(337) 439-2444. **$94-$150.** 401 Lakeshore Dr. I-10, exit 29 (business district/tourist bureau) eastbound; exit 30B (Ryan St business district) westbound, just s to Pine, then just w. Int corridors. **Pets:** Accepted.

ASK 🏊 ✕ 🖥 🛗 📺 🖥 🏊

AAA ▼▼▼ La Quinta Inn Lake Charles **SH**
(337) 436-5998. **$60-$100.** 1320 MLK Hwy 171 N. I-10, exit 33, 0.8 mi n. Int corridors. **Pets:** Medium, other species. $50 deposit/room. Service with restrictions, supervision.

SAVE 🏊 ✕ ♿ 📺 🖥 🏊

LIVONIA

▼▼ Oak Tree Inn **SH**
(225) 637-2590. **$53.** 7875 Airline Hwy. Jct SR 77 and US 190, 0.3 mi w. Ext corridors. **Pets:** Accepted.

ASK 🏊 ✕ ♿ 📺 🖥

MINDEN

AAA ▼▼▼ Best Western Minden Inn **SH**
(318) 377-1001. **$60.** 1411 Sibley Rd. I-20, exit 47, just n. Ext corridors. **Pets:** $10 daily fee/room. Service with restrictions, supervision.

SAVE 🏊 ✕ 🖥 ♿ 📺 🖥 🏊

MONROE

AAA ▼▼▼ Days Inn **SH**
(318) 345-2220. **$52-$66, 5 day notice.** 5650 Frontage Rd. I-20, exit 120, just s, 0.5 mi e on south service road. Ext corridors. **Pets:** Accepted.

SAVE 🏊 ✕ 🖥 📺 🖥 🏊

▼▼▼ La Quinta Inn Monroe **SH**
(318) 322-3900. **$64-$89.** 1035 Hwy 165 Bypass. I-20, exit 118B, just ne on US 165 service road. Ext corridors. **Pets:** Accepted.

ASK ✕ 🖥 🖥 🏊

▼▼ Motel 6 Monroe #481 **M**
(318) 322-5430. **$40-$50.** 1501 Martin Luther King Dr. I-20, exit 118A, just s. Ext corridors. **Pets:** Accepted.

🏊 ✕ 🛗 🏊

▼▼▼ Residence Inn by Marriott **SH**
(318) 387-0210. **Call for rates.** 4960 Millhaven Rd. I-20, exit 120, just n of Pecanland Mall. Int corridors. **Pets:** Accepted.

✕ 🛗 🖥 📺 🖥 🏊 ✕

MORGAN CITY

▼▼▼ Holiday Inn-Morgan City **SH**
(985) 385-2200. **$85-$200.** 520 Roderick St. 1.5 mi s of jct US 90 and SR 70. Ext corridors. **Pets:** Small, other species. $50 one-time fee/room. Supervision.

ASK 🏊 ✕ ♿ 🖥 📺 🖥 🍴 🏊

NEW IBERIA

AAA ▼▼▼ Best Western Inn & Suites **SH**
(337) 364-3030. **$62-$72.** 2714 Hwy 14. 0.3 mi e of jct US 90. Ext/int corridors. **Pets:** $50 deposit/room. Service with restrictions, supervision.

SAVE 🏊 ✕ 📺 🖥 🏊

▼▼▼ Holiday Inn New Iberia-Avery Island **SH**
(337) 367-1201. **$75-$77.** 2915 Hwy 14. SR 14, just e of jct US 90. Ext corridors. **Pets:** Accepted.

ASK 🏊 ✕ 📺 🖥 🍴 🏊

NEW ORLEANS METROPOLITAN AREA

CHALMETTE

AAA ▼▼▼ Econo Lodge Marina **M**
(504) 277-5353. **$64-$130.** 5353 Paris Rd. I-10, exit 246A, 5 mi s to SR 47. Ext corridors. **Pets:** Accepted.

SAVE 🏊 ✕ 📺 🖥 🍴 🏊 ✕

GRETNA

▼▼▼ La Quinta Inn New Orleans (West Bank) **SH**
(504) 368-5600. **$75-$106.** 50 Terry Pkwy. S US 90 business route, exit 9A (Terry Pkwy); N US 90 (Westbank Expwy), exit 9 (Terry Pkwy/General DeGaulle). Ext corridors. **Pets:** Accepted.

ASK ✕ 🖥 📺 🖥 🏊

KENNER

AAA ▼▼▼ Hilton New Orleans Airport **LH**
(504) 469-5000. **$99-$249.** 901 Airline Dr. I-10, exit 223A (Williams Blvd), 2 mi s, then 0.8 mi w. Int corridors. **Pets:** Medium. $50 one-time fee/room. Service with restrictions, crate.

SAVE ✕ 🖥 🖥 📺 🖥 🍴 🏊 ✕

▼▼▼ La Quinta Inn New Orleans (Airport) **SH**
(504) 466-1401. **$86-$111.** 2610 Williams Blvd. I-10, exit 223A (Williams Blvd), 0.3 mi s. Int corridors. **Pets:** Accepted.

ASK ✕ 📺 🖥 🏊

LA PLACE

AAA ▼▼▼ Best Western La Place Inn **SH**
(985) 651-4000. **$79-$179.** 4289 Main St. I-10, exit 209, just s. Ext corridors. **Pets:** Accepted.

SAVE 🏊 ✕ 🖥 📺 🖥 🏊

METAIRIE

▼▼▼ Four Points by Sheraton New Orleans Airport **SH**
(504) 885-5700. **$79-$99.** 6401 Veterans Memorial Blvd. I-10, exit 225, just s. Int corridors. **Pets:** Accepted.

ASK 🏊 ✕ 🖥 ♿ 📺 🖥 🍴 🏊

▼▼▼ La Quinta Inn New Orleans (Causeway) **SH**
(504) 835-8511. **$76-$101.** 3100 I-10 Service Rd. I-10, exit 228 (Causeway Blvd), just s. Ext corridors. **Pets:** Accepted.

ASK ✕ 🖥 ♿ 📺 🖥 🏊

▼▼▼ La Quinta Inn New Orleans (Veterans) **SH**
(504) 456-0003. **$76-$101.** 5900 Veterans Memorial Blvd. I-10, exit 225, just n. Ext corridors. **Pets:** Accepted.

ASK ✕ 🖥 ♿ 📺 🖥 🏊

▼▼▼ **Residence Inn by Marriott-Metairie** 🏨
(504) 832-0888. **$109-$129, 3 day notice.** 3 Galleria Blvd. I-10, exit 228 (Causeway Blvd), just se to 36th St, then just e. Int corridors. **Pets:** Accepted.

A$K 🛏 ✕ 🖥 🖨 💻 🏊 ✕

NEW ORLEANS

◢◣ ▼▼▼ **Ambassador Hotel** 🏨
(504) 527-5271. **$69-$229.** 535 Tchoupitoulas St. Between Poydras and Lafayette; downtown. Int corridors. **Pets:** Accepted.

SAVE 🛏 ✕ 🖥 🖨 💻 🍽

◢◣ ▼▼ **Best Western Patio Downtown Motel** Ⓜ
(504) 822-0200. **$69-$259.** 2820 Tulane Ave. I-10, exit 232, jct Carrollton and Tulane (US 61) aves, 1.3 mi e. Int corridors. **Pets:** Other species. Service with restrictions.

SAVE 🛏 ✕ 🖨 💻 🏊

◢◣ ▼▼▼ **Chateau Sonesta Hotel** 🏨
(504) 586-0800. **$99-$199, 3 day notice.** 800 Iberville St. Between Dauphine and Bourbon sts. Int corridors. **Pets:** Accepted.

SAVE ✕ 🖥 🖨 💻 🍽 🏊

▼▼▼ **Drury Inn & Suites-New Orleans** 🏨
(504) 529-7800. **$80-$155.** 820 Poydras St. Between Baronne and Carondelet sts. Int corridors. **Pets:** Large, other species. Service with restrictions, supervision.

A$K ✕ 🖥 🖥 🖨 💻 🏊

◢◣ ▼▼▼▼ **Elysian Fields Inn** 🅱🅱
(504) 948-9420. **$99-$250, 14 day notice.** 930 Elysian Fields Ave. I-610, exit 3 (Elysian Fields), 1.2 mi s. Int corridors. **Pets:** Accepted.

SAVE ✕

◢◣ ▼▼▼▼ **The Fairmont New Orleans** 🏨 🐾
(504) 529-7111. **$99-$289, 3 day notice.** 123 Baronne St. Between Canal and University sts; entrance on University St; downtown. Int corridors. **Pets:** Small. $25 daily fee/pet. Designated rooms, service with restrictions, supervision.

SAVE 🛏 ✕ 🖥 🖨 💻 🍽 🏊 ✕

◢◣ ▼▼▼ **French Quarter Courtyard Hotel** 🏨
(504) 522-7333. **$69-$229.** 1101 N Rampart St. Between Ursulines and Governor Nicholls sts. Ext/int corridors. **Pets:** Other species. $25 one-time fee/pet. Service with restrictions, supervision.

SAVE 🛏 ✕ 🖥 💻 🏊

◢◣ ▼▼▼ **Garden District Hotel Clarion Collection** 🏨
(504) 566-1200. **$69-$209, 3 day notice.** 2203 St. Charles Ave. 1 mi w of US 90; at corner of Jackson Ave. Int corridors. **Pets:** Medium, other species. $50 one-time fee/pet. Crate.

SAVE ✕ 🖥 🖨 💻 🍽

◢◣ ▼▼▼▼ **Hotel Monaco New Orleans** 🏨 🐾
(504) 561-0010. **$189-$339.** 333 St. Charles Ave. Jct Perdido St. Int corridors. **Pets:** Other species.

SAVE 🛏 ✕ 🖨 💻 🍽

◢◣ ▼▼▼▼ **The Iberville Suites** 🏨
(504) 523-2400. **$84-$263.** 910 Iberville St. Between Burgundy and Dauphine sts. Int corridors. **Pets:** Accepted.

SAVE 🛏 ✕ 🖨 🖨 💻

▼▼▼ **La Quinta Inn & Suites New Orleans (Downtown)** 🏨
(504) 598-9977. **$109-$209.** 301 Camp St. Corner of Gravier and Camp sts; downtown. Int corridors. **Pets:** Small, dogs only. No service, supervision.

A$K ✕ 🖥 🖥 🖨 🖨 💻 🏊

▼▼ **La Quinta Inn New Orleans (Bullard)** 🏨
(504) 246-3003. **$60-$95.** 12001 I-10 Service Rd. I-10, exit 245 (Bullard Rd). Ext corridors. **Pets:** Accepted.

A$K ✕ 🖥 🖨 💻 🏊

▼▼ **La Quinta Inn New Orleans (Crowder)** Ⓜ
(504) 246-5800. **$64-$99.** 8400 I-10 Service Rd. I-10, exit 242 (Crowder Blvd). Ext corridors. **Pets:** Service with restrictions, supervision.

A$K ✕ 🖥 🖨 💻 🏊

◢◣ ▼▼▼ **Loews New Orleans Hotel** 🏨 🐾
(504) 595-3300. **$149-$319, 3 day notice.** 300 Poydras St. Corner of S Peters St; downtown. Int corridors. **Pets:** Other species.

SAVE 🛏 ✕ 🖥 🖨 💻 🍽 🏊 ✕

◢◣ ▼▼▼▼ **The Maison Orleans-Ritz Carlton** 🏨 🐾
(504) 670-2900. **$419-$509.** 904 Iberville St. Between Burgundy and Dauphine sts. Int corridors. **Pets:** Small. $250 one-time fee/room. Service with restrictions, supervision.

SAVE ✕ 🖥 🖥 🍽 🏊 ✕

▼▼ **Motel 6- Six Flags Area** Ⓜ
(504) 240-2862. **$42-$60.** 12330 I-10 Service Rd. I-10, exit 245 (Bullard Rd), just s, then 0.4 mi e on eastbound access road. Int corridors. **Pets:** Small, other species. Service with restrictions, supervision.

✕ 🖥 🖥

▼▼▼ **Omni Royal Crescent Hotel** 🏨
(504) 527-0006. **$129-$209.** 535 Gravier St. 0.3 mi w of Canal St; downtown. Int corridors. **Pets:** Accepted.

A$K 🛏 ✕ 🖥 🖥 🖨 💻 🍽 ✕

◢◣ ▼▼▼▼ **Omni Royal Orleans Hotel** 🏨
(504) 529-5333. **$99-$399, 3 day notice.** 621 St. Louis St. At Royal and St. Louis sts. Int corridors. **Pets:** Small. $50 one-time fee/pet. Service with restrictions, supervision.

SAVE 🛏 ✕ 🖨 🖨 💻 🏊

▼▼▼ **Residence Inn by Marriott** 🏨
(504) 522-1300. **$119-$209, 3 day notice.** 345 St. Joseph's St. Jct Tchoupitoulas St. Int corridors. **Pets:** Large. $75 one-time fee/pet. Service with restrictions, crate.

A$K ✕ 🖥 🖨 🖨 💻 🏊 ✕

◢◣ ▼▼▼▼▼ **The Ritz-Carlton New Orleans** 🏨 🐾
(504) 524-1331. **$109-$276.** 921 Canal St. Between Dauphine and Burgundy sts. Int corridors. **Pets:** Small. $250 one-time fee/room. Service with restrictions, crate.

SAVE 🛏 ✕ 🖥 🖥 🖨 🍽 🏊

◢◣ ▼▼▼▼ **Royal Sonesta Hotel New Orleans** 🏨
(504) 586-0300. **$109-$329, 3 day notice.** 300 Bourbon St. Garage entrance on Conti or Bienville sts. Int corridors. **Pets:** Small. $50 one-time fee/room. Service with restrictions, supervision.

SAVE 🛏 ✕ 🖥 🖥 🖨 🖨 🍽 🏊

▼▼▼▼ **St. James Hotel** 🏨 🐾
(504) 304-4000. **$59-$149, 3 day notice.** 330 Magazine St. Jct Magazine and Natchez sts; downtown. Int corridors. **Pets:** Small. $75 one-time fee/room. Service with restrictions.

A$K 🛏 ✕ 🖥 💻 🍽 ✕

◢◣ ▼▼▼▼ **The Sheraton New Orleans Hotel** 🏨 🐾
(504) 525-2500. **$449-$549.** 500 Canal St. Between Camp and Magazine sts. Int corridors. **Pets:** Medium. Service with restrictions, supervision.

SAVE 🛏 ✕ 🖥 🖥 🖨 🖨 💻 🍽 🏊 ✕

▼▼ **Studio 6 New Orleans #6000** 🏨
(504) 240-9778. **$49-$73.** 12330 I-10 Service Rd. I-10, exit 245 (Bullard Rd), 0.4 mi e on eastbound access road. Int corridors. **Pets:** Accepted.

🛏 ✕ 💻 🏊

▼▼▼▼ W French Quarter **SH**
(504) 581-1200. **$479-$519, 3 day notice.** 316 rue Chartres St. Between Conti and Bienville sts. Int corridors. **Pets:** Accepted.
(ASK) (S✆) (X) (✆) (▦) (¶¶) (⊷)

△△△ ▼▼▼▼ Windsor Court Hotel **LH** ✿
(504) 523-6000. **$195-$450.** 300 Gravier St. Between Magazine and Tchoupitoulas sts. Int corridors. **Pets:** Medium. $150 one-time fee/room. Service with restrictions, crate.
(SAVE) (X) (⊘) (▦) (¶¶) (⊷) (X⃠)

△△△ ▼▼▼▼ W New Orleans **LH**
(504) 525-9444. **$469-$499, 3 day notice.** 333 Poydras St. Close to Riverfront area/convention center; jct Poydras and S Peters sts; downtown. Int corridors. **Pets:** Accepted.
(SAVE) (S✆) (X) (▵M) (⊘) (✆) (¶¶) (⊷)

END METROPOLITAN AREA

OPELOUSAS

△△△ ▼▼ Best Western of Opelousas **SH**
(337) 942-5540. **$54-$104.** 5791 I-49 S Service Rd. I-49, exit 18 (Creswell Ln), on west service road. Ext corridors. **Pets:** $10 daily fee/pet. Service with restrictions.
(SAVE) (S✆) (X) (▦) (▬) (⊷)

△△△ ▼▼ Days Inn & Suites **SH**
(337) 407-0004. **$75-$86, 3 day notice.** 5761 I-49 S Service Rd. I-49, exit 18 (Creswell Ln). Ext corridors. **Pets:** Accepted.
(SAVE) (S✆) (X) (✆) (▦) (▬) (⊷)

PORT ALLEN

△△△ ▼▼ Best Western Magnolia Manor **SH**
(225) 344-3638. **$55.** 234 Lobdell Hwy. I-10, exit 151, just n. Int corridors. **Pets:** Accepted.
(SAVE) (S✆) (X) (▦) (▬) (⊷)

▼ Motel 6 Baton Rouge-Port Allen #406 **M**
(225) 389-5803. **$40-$50.** 2800 I-10 Frontage Rd. I-10, exit 151, just s. Ext corridors. **Pets:** Accepted.
(S✆) (X) (▦) (▬) (⊷)

RAYVILLE

▼▼▼ Days Inn **SH**
(318) 728-4500. **$50-$70, 3 day notice.** 125 Maxwell St. I-20, exit 138, just n. Ext corridors. **Pets:** Accepted.
(ASK) (S✆) (X) (▦) (▬) (⊷)

△△△ ▼▼ Ramada Limited **SH**
(318) 728-5985. **$64-$69.** 116 Cottonland Dr. I-20, exit 138, just s. Ext corridors. **Pets:** Small. Supervision.
(SAVE) (S✆) (X) (▦) (▬) (⊷)

RUSTON

▼▼ Econo Lodge **SH**
(318) 255-0354. **$54-$64, 3 day notice.** 1301 Goodwin Rd. I-20, exit 85, just n on US 167, then just e on N Service Rd. Ext corridors. **Pets:** Accepted.
(ASK) (S✆) (X) (⊘) (▦) (▬) (¶¶) (⊷) (X⃠)

▼▼ Ramada Inn **SH**
(318) 255-5901. **$59-$99.** 401 N Service Rd. I-20, exit 85, just ne. Ext corridors. **Pets:** Accepted.
(ASK) (S✆) (X) (▦) (▬) (¶¶) (⊷)

ST. FRANCISVILLE

▼▼▼▼ Green Springs Inn & Cottages **BB**
(225) 635-4232. **$120-$180.** 7463 Tunica Trace. US 61, 2.7 mi n of jct US 61 and SR 10 to SR 66, then 0.9 mi w. Ext/int corridors. **Pets:** Medium, other species. Designated rooms, service with restrictions, supervision.
(X) (▦) (▬) (✿)

▼▼ Lake Rosemound Inn Bed & Breakfast **BB**
(225) 635-3176. **$75-$125, 3 day notice.** 10473 Lindsey Ln. 13 mi n on SR 61, then 3 mi w using Rosemound Loop, Sligo Rd, Lake Rosemound Rd and Lindsey Ln, follow signs. Ext/int corridors. **Pets:** Other species. Service with restrictions.
(X) (X⃠)

SCOTT

▼▼ Howard Johnson **SH**
(337) 593-0849. **$60-$70.** 103 Harold Gauthe. I-10, exit 97. Int corridors. **Pets:** Other species. $25 deposit/room. Service with restrictions, crate.
(ASK) (S✆) (X) (▦) (▬) (⊷)

SHREVEPORT

▼▼▼ Clarion Hotel Shreveport **LH**
(318) 797-9900. **$109-$139.** 1419 E 70th St. I-20, exit 19A (SR 1 S), 6 mi s to E 70th St, then 0.4 mi w. Int corridors. **Pets:** Small. $50 deposit/room. No service.
(ASK) (S✆) (X) (⊘) (▦) (▬) (¶¶) (⊷)

▼▼▼ Holiday Inn Downtown **LH**
(318) 222-7717. **$79-$139.** 102 Lake St. I-20, exit 19A (Spring St), just n. Int corridors. **Pets:** Accepted.
(ASK) (S✆) (X) (▵M) (⊘) (▦) (▬) (¶¶) (⊷)

△△△ ▼▼ Howard Johnson Express **SH**
(318) 636-0000. **$49-$89.** 2610 Claiborne Ave. I-20, exit 16A (Hearne Ave), just se. Ext corridors. **Pets:** Accepted.
(SAVE) (S✆) (X) (▦) (▬) (⊷)

▼▼▼ Jameson Inn **SH**
(318) 671-0731. **$49-$104.** 6715 Rasberry Ln. I-20, exit 10 (Pines Rd), 0.6 mi on frontage road. Int corridors. **Pets:** Very small, other species. $10 daily fee/room. Service with restrictions, supervision.
(ASK) (X) (⊘) (✆) (▦) (▬) (⊷)

▼▼▼ La Quinta Inn & Suites Shreveport **SH**
(318) 671-1100. **$89-$109.** 6700 Financial Cir. I-20, exit 10 (Pines Rd), 0.5 mi e on frontage road. Int corridors. **Pets:** Medium. Service with restrictions, supervision.
(ASK) (X) (▵M) (✆) (▦) (▬) (⊷)

SLIDELL

△△△ ▼▼▼▼ La Quinta Inn New Orleans/Slidell **SH**
(985) 643-9770. **$60-$85.** 794 E I-10 Service Rd. I-10, exit 266 (Gause Blvd), just se. Ext corridors. **Pets:** Accepted.
(SAVE) (X) (✆) (▦) (▬) (⊷)

▼▼ Sleep Inn **SH**
(985) 641-2143. **$49-$99.** 142 Oak Ct. I-10, exit 261, just n. Int corridors. **Pets:** Accepted.
(ASK) (S✆) (X) (▵M) (✆) (▦) (⊷)

◈◈ Red Roof Inn **M**
(318) 938-5342. **$41-$55.** 7296 Greenwood Rd. I-20, exit 8, just nw. Ext corridors. **Pets:** Accepted.

⊠ 🛏

SULPHUR

◈◈ La Quinta Inn Sulphur **SH**
(337) 527-8303. **$59-$94.** 2600 S Ruth St. I-10, exit 20 (SR 27). Ext corridors. **Pets:** Other species. Service with restrictions, crate.

(A$K) ⊠ 🛏M 🛏 💻 �'t

◈◈◈ Wingate Inn **SH**
(337) 527-5151. **$79-$89.** 300 Texaco Rd. I-10, exit 20 (SR 27), just s, then just w. Int corridors. **Pets:** Accepted.

(A$K) (S🛏) ⊠ 🛏 🛏 💻 ➟

WEST MONROE

◈◈◈ Quality Inn & Suites-West Monroe **SH**
(318) 387-2711. **$89.** 503 Constitution Dr. I-20, exit 114 (Thomas Rd), just s to Constitution Dr, then 0.6 mi w. Int corridors. **Pets:** Medium. $25 one-time fee/room. Service with restrictions, crate.

(A$K) (S🛏) ⊠ 🛏M ✈ 🛏 🛏 💻 ➟

◈◈ Red Roof Inn **M**
(318) 388-2420. **$40-$55.** 102 Constitution Dr. I-20, exit 114 (Thomas Rd), just s. Ext corridors. **Pets:** Medium, other species. Service with restrictions, supervision.

⊠ 🛏

◈◈ Shoney's Inn **M**
(318) 325-5780. **$44-$49.** 310 Thomas Rd. I-20, exit 114 (Thomas Rd), just n. Ext corridors. **Pets:** Large. $10 one-time fee/room. Service with restrictions.

(A$K) (S🛏) ⊠ 🛏 💻 ➟

MAINE

AUBURN

A Fireside Inn & Suites SH
(207) 777-1777. **$70-$120, 3 day notice.** 1777 Washington St. I-95 (Maine Tpke), exit 75, 5 mi s on US 202, SR 4 and 100. Ext/int corridors. **Pets:** Dogs only. Service with restrictions, crate.

AUGUSTA

Best Western Senator Inn & Spa SH
(207) 622-5804. **$109-$259.** 284 Western Ave. I-95, exit 109 (Augusta-Winthrop) northbound; exit 109A southbound, on US 202, SR 11 and 100. Ext/int corridors. **Pets:** Medium, other species. $9 daily fee/pet. Designated rooms, service with restrictions, supervision.

Comfort Inn SH
(207) 623-1000. **$89-$189, 3 day notice.** 281 Civic Center Dr. I-95, exit 112B northbound; exit 112 southbound. Int corridors. **Pets:** $100 deposit/room. Service with restrictions, supervision.

Econo Lodge Inn & Suites SH
(207) 622-6371. **$59-$209.** 390 Western Ave. I-95, exit 109 (Augusta-Winthrop); exit 109B southbound on US 202, SR 11 and 100. Ext corridors. **Pets:** Service with restrictions, supervision.

Holiday Inn SH
(207) 622-4751. **$95-$169, 3 day notice.** 110 Community Dr. I-95, exit 112A northbound; exit 112 southbound, just s on SR 8, 11 and 27. Int corridors. **Pets:** $100 deposit/room. Service with restrictions, supervision.

BANGOR

Best Inn SH
(207) 942-1234. **$80-$115, 7 day notice.** 570 Main St. I-395, exit 3B. Int corridors. **Pets:** Large. Service with restrictions, supervision.

Best Western White House SH 🐾
(207) 862-3737. **$68-$127.** 155 Littlefield Ave. I-95, exit 180 (Coldbrook Rd), 5.5 mi s of downtown. Ext/int corridors. **Pets:** Other species. $100 deposit/room. Service with restrictions, supervision.

Comfort Inn SH
(207) 942-7899. **$69-$119.** 750 Hogan Rd. I-95, exit 187 (Hogan Rd), 0.5 mi w. Int corridors. **Pets:** Other species. $6 daily fee/room. Service with restrictions, supervision.

Days Inn SH
(207) 942-8272. **$59-$99.** 250 Odlin Rd. I-95, exit 182B, 0.3 mi e on US 2 and SR 100. Int corridors. **Pets:** Other species. $6 one-time fee/room. Service with restrictions, supervision.

Econo Lodge M
(207) 945-0111. **$40-$120.** 327 Odlin Rd. I-95, exit 182B, just e on US 2 and SR 100. Int corridors. **Pets:** Other species. $6 one-time fee/pet. Service with restrictions, supervision.

Four Points by Sheraton Bangor SH
(207) 947-6721. **$129-$159.** 308 Godfrey Blvd. At Bangor International Airport. Int corridors. **Pets:** Accepted.

Holiday Inn-Bangor SH
(207) 947-0101. **$99-$107.** 404 Odlin Rd. I-95, exit 182B; jct Odlin Rd and I-395. Int corridors. **Pets:** Designated rooms, service with restrictions, supervision.

Holiday Inn Bangor-Civic Center SH
(207) 947-8651. **$95-$150.** 500 Main St. I-395, exit 3B, just n. Int corridors. **Pets:** Designated rooms, service with restrictions, supervision.

Main Street Inn M
(207) 942-5282. **$52-$62.** 480 Main St. I-395, exit 3B, just n. Ext/int corridors. **Pets:** Small. Designated rooms, service with restrictions, crate.

Ramada Inn SH
(207) 947-6961. **$69-$119.** 357 Odlin Rd. I-95, exit 182B; jct Odlin Rd and I-395. Int corridors. **Pets:** Accepted.

Riverside Inn SH
(207) 973-4100. **$69-$129, 7 day notice.** 495 State St. Adjacent to Eastern Maine Medical Center. Int corridors. **Pets:** Accepted.

Travelodge M
(207) 942-6301. **$60-$90.** 482 Odlin Rd. I-95, exit 182B, just left. Ext corridors. **Pets:** Medium. $10 daily fee/pet. Service with restrictions, supervision.

BAR HARBOR

Anchorage Motel M
(207) 288-3959. **$54-$129, 3 day notice.** 51 Mt Desert St. In town on SR 3. Ext corridors. **Pets:** $15 daily fee/pet. Service with restrictions, supervision.

A Wonder View Inn & Suites SH
(207) 288-3358. **$50-$230, 3 day notice.** 50 Eden St. 0.5 mi w on SR 3. Ext corridors. **Pets:** Medium. $15 daily fee/pet. Supervision.

AAA ▼▼▼▼ **Balance Rock Inn 1903** BB
(207) 288-2610. **$115-$625, 14 day notice.** 21 Albert Meadow. S on Main St, just e; center. Ext/int corridors. **Pets:** Other species. $30 daily fee/pet. Service with restrictions, supervision.
SAVE ⊠ 🗎 🏊

AAA ▼▼▼▼ **Best Western Inn** SH
(207) 288-5823. **$74-$145.** 452 State Hwy 3. 4.8 mi w. Ext corridors. **Pets:** Accepted.
SAVE S🔒 ⊠ 🗎 💻 🏊

▼▼ ◇ **Days Inn** M
(207) 288-3321. **$89-$229.** 120 Eden St. 1 mi w on SR 3. Ext corridors. **Pets:** Accepted.
ASK S🔒 ⊠ 🗎

▼▼ **Dreamwood Pines Motel** M
(207) 288-9717. **$150, 7 day notice.** 389 State Hwy 3. 4.5 mi w. Ext corridors. **Pets:** Accepted.
🗎 💻 🏊

▼ **Hutchins Mountain View Cottages** CA
(207) 288-4833. **$46-$98, 14 day notice.** 286 State Rt 3. 4 mi w. Ext corridors. **Pets:** Other species. Service with restrictions, supervision.
🗎 💻 🏊 🐾 🐾

AAA ▼▼▼ ◇ **The Ledgelawn Inn** BB
(207) 288-4596. **$65-$325, 14 day notice.** 66 Mt Desert St. Center. Ext/int corridors. **Pets:** Other species. $30 daily fee/pet. Service with restrictions, supervision.
SAVE ⊠ 🏊

▼▼▼ **Primrose Inn Bed and Breakfast** BB
(207) 288-4031. **$85-$215, 14 day notice.** 73 Mt Desert St. Center. Int corridors. **Pets:** Accepted.
⊠ 🗎

BATH

AAA ▼▼▼▼ **Holiday Inn Bath/Brunswick** SH
(207) 443-9741. **$90-$210.** 139 Richardson St. 0.3 mi s on US 1. Int corridors. **Pets:** Accepted.
SAVE S🔒 ⊠ 🔒M 🐾 🐾 🗎 💻 🍴 🏊 🐾

BELFAST

AAA ▼▼▼▼ **Belfast Bay Meadows Inn** CI
(207) 338-5715. **$75-$165, 14 day notice.** 192 Northport Ave (US 1). US 1, 2 mi s from jct SR 3. Ext/int corridors. **Pets:** Large. $15 one-time fee/room. Designated rooms, service with restrictions, crate.
SAVE S🔒 ⊠ 🗎 🍴

AAA ▼▼ ◇ **Belfast Harbor Inn** SH 🐾
(207) 338-2740. **$54-$129.** 91 Searsport Ave (Rt 1). On US 1, 1.2 mi n from jct SR 3. Ext/int corridors. **Pets:** Dogs only. $10 daily fee/pet. Service with restrictions, supervision.
SAVE S🔒 ⊠ 🏊

▼▼▼ **Comfort Inn Ocean's Edge** SH 🐾
(207) 338-2090. **$79-$189.** 159 Searsport Ave. On US 1, 2 mi n from jct SR 3. Int corridors. **Pets:** $10 daily fee/room. Designated rooms, service with restrictions, supervision.
ASK S🔒 ⊠ 🔒M 🐾 🐾 🗎 💻 🍴 🏊 🐾

▼▼ **Gull Motel** M
(207) 338-4030. **$39-$89, 3 day notice.** US Rt 1. On US 1, 3 mi n from jct SR 3. Ext corridors. **Pets:** $10 daily fee/pet. Service with restrictions, supervision.
ASK ⊠ 🗎

AAA ▼▼ ◇ **Seascape Motel & Cottages** M
(207) 338-2130. **$49-$123, 3 day notice.** 202 Searsport Ave. On US 1, 3 mi n from jct SR 3. Ext corridors. **Pets:** Small. $10 one-time fee/pet. Designated rooms, service with restrictions, supervision.
SAVE S🔒 ⊠ 🗎 🏊

BETHEL

▼▼▼ **Briar Lea Inn & Restaurant** CI 🐾
(207) 824-4717. **$69-$129, 14 day notice.** 150 Mayville Rd (US 2). 1 mi n of jct US 2, SR 5 and 26. Int corridors. **Pets:** Other species. $10 daily fee/room. Service with restrictions, crate.
ASK S🔒 ⊠ 🍴

▼▼ ◇ **The Inn At the Rostay** M
(207) 824-3111. **$50-$130, 14 day notice.** 186 Mayville Rd (US 2). On US 2, 2 mi e. Ext corridors. **Pets:** Other species. $10 one-time fee/pet. Designated rooms, service with restrictions, supervision.
ASK S🔒 ⊠ 🗎 🍴 🏊

AAA ▼▼▼▼ **L'Auberge Country Inn & Bistro** CI
(207) 824-2774. **$99-$247, 14 day notice.** 22 Mill Hill Rd/L'Auberge Ln. Center. Int corridors. **Pets:** Accepted.
SAVE ⊠ 🍴 🐾 🐾 🐾

BOOTHBAY

▼▼ **Hillside Acres Cabins & Motel** M
(207) 633-3411. **$45-$80, 3 day notice.** 301 Adams Pond Rd. US 1, 9 mi s on SR 27, then just w. Ext/int corridors. **Pets:** Designated rooms, service with restrictions, supervision.
⊠ 🗎 💻 🏊 🐾 🐾

▼▼▼ **Kenniston Hill Inn** BB
(207) 633-2159. **$80-$140, 14 day notice.** 988 Wiscasset Rd. US 1 to SR 27, 10 mi s. Ext/int corridors. **Pets:** Medium. $5 one-time fee/pet. Designated rooms, supervision.
ASK S🔒 ⊠ 🐾 🐾

AAA ▼▼▼ **White Anchor Inn** M
(207) 633-3788. **$45-$75.** 609 Wiscasset Rd. US 1 to SR 27, 7.5 mi s. Ext/int corridors. **Pets:** Large, other species. $10 one-time fee/pet. Designated rooms, service with restrictions, supervision.
SAVE ⊠ 🗎

BOOTHBAY HARBOR

▼▼ **The Pines Motel** M
(207) 633-4555. **Call for rates.** 30 Sunset Rd. 1 mi e of SR 27 via Atlantic Ave, on the east side of Boothbay Harbor. Ext corridors. **Pets:** Accepted.
⊠ 🗎 🏊

AAA ▼▼▼▼ **Welch House Inn** BB
(207) 633-3431. **$85-$195, 14 day notice.** 56 McKown St. Center. Ext/int corridors. **Pets:** $25 one-time fee/room. Designated rooms, service with restrictions, supervision.
SAVE ⊠

BREWER

AAA ▼ **Brewer Motor Inn** SH
(207) 989-4476. **$49-$62.** 359 Wilson St. I-395, exit 4, n on SR 15 to US 1A, then 0.7 mi e. Ext/int corridors. **Pets:** Small. Designated rooms, service with restrictions, crate.
SAVE ⊠ 🍴

BRIDGTON

AAA ▼▼▼ **Pleasant Mountain Inn** M 🐾
(207) 647-4505. **$60-$125, 7 day notice.** N High St. On US 302, 3 mi w of center. Ext corridors. **Pets:** Dogs only. $10 daily fee/pet. Service with restrictions, supervision.
SAVE ⊠ 🗎 💻 🍴

BRUNSWICK

AAA ▼▼▼ **Viking Motor Inn** M
(207) 729-6661. **$59-$139.** 287 Bath Rd. US 1, exit Cooks Corner, left on Bath Rd, then 1 mi w. Ext/int corridors. **Pets:** Medium. $10 daily fee/pet. Service with restrictions, supervision.
SAVE ⊠ 🗎

BRYANT POND

◈◈◈ **Mollyockett Motel & Swim Spa** **M**
(207) 674-2345. **$70-$95.** 1132 S Main St. 1.3 mi n on SR 26, from jct SR 219. Ext/int corridors. **Pets:** Service with restrictions, supervision.
🆔 [S🐾] ✖ 📶 💻 ⮐ ✖

CALAIS

◈◈◈ **Calais Motor Inn** **SH**
(207) 454-7111. **$44-$84.** 633 Main St. 0.5 mi s on US 1. Ext/int corridors. **Pets:** Accepted.
[SAVE] [S🐾] ✖ 📶 💻 🍴 ⟲

◈◈ **International Motel** **M**
(207) 454-7515. **$50-$80.** 626 Main St. 0.5 mi s on US 1. Ext corridors. **Pets:** Accepted.
[SAVE] [S🐾] ✖ 📶 💻

CAMDEN

◈◈◈◈ **Blue Harbor House, A Village Inn** **CI** 🐾
(207) 236-3196. **$125-$155, 14 day notice.** 67 Elm St. On US 1; center. Ext/int corridors. **Pets:** Small. $25 one-time fee/room. Designated rooms, service with restrictions, supervision.
🆔 ✖ 🍴

◈◈◈◈ **Camden Harbour Inn** **BB**
(207) 236-4200. **$155-$275, 7 day notice.** 83 Bayview St. Off US 1, 0.3 mi e; center. Int corridors. **Pets:** Accepted.
✖ [🐾]

◈◈◈◈ **The Camden Riverhouse Hotel & Inns** **SH** 🐾
(207) 236-0500. **$99-$250, 14 day notice.** 11 Tannery Ln. Center. Int corridors. **Pets:** Dogs only. $25 daily fee/pet. Designated rooms, service with restrictions, supervision.
🆔 [S🐾] ✖ 📶 💻 ⟲

◈◈◈ **Lord Camden Inn** **BB** 🐾
(207) 236-4325. **$98-$268.** 24 Main St. Center. Int corridors. **Pets:** Other species. $20 daily fee/room. Service with restrictions, supervision.
[SAVE] [S🐾] ✖ 📶 💻

CAPE ELIZABETH

◈◈◈ ◈◈◈◈ **Inn By The Sea** **SH** 🐾
(207) 799-3134. **$249-$689, 14 day notice.** 40 Bowery Beach Rd (SR 77). On SR 77, 7 mi s. Ext/int corridors. **Pets:** Other species. Designated rooms, service with restrictions, supervision.
[SAVE] [S🐾] ✖ [♿M] 📶 💻 🍴 ⟲ ✖ [🐾]

CARIBOU

◈◈◈ ◈◈◈◈ **Caribou Inn & Convention Center** **SH** 🐾
(207) 498-3733. **$72-$120.** 19 Main St. 3 mi s on US 1. Int corridors. **Pets:** Other species. Service with restrictions.
[SAVE] [S🐾] ✖ 📶 💻 🍴 ⟲ ✖

CASTINE

◈◈◈◈ **Pentagoet Inn** **CI**
(207) 326-8616. **$95-$205, 14 day notice.** 26 Main St. Center. Int corridors. **Pets:** Accepted.
✖ 🍴 [🐾] [W] [🐾]

CORNISH

◈◈ **Midway Motel** **M**
(207) 625-8835. **$49-$99, 7 day notice.** 712 S Hiram Rd. 0.7 mi w on SR 25, just past jct SR 25. Ext/int corridors. **Pets:** Small, dogs only. $5 daily fee/pet. Service with restrictions, supervision.
✖ 📶 💻 ⟲

EAGLE LAKE

◈◈◈ **Overlook Motel & Lakeside Cabins** **M**
(207) 444-4535. **$49-$150.** 3232 Aroostook Rd. On SR 11; center. Ext/int corridors. **Pets:** Other species. $3 daily fee/pet. Service with restrictions, supervision.
📶 💻 ✖

EAST BOOTHBAY

◈◈◈ ◈◈◈ **Smuggler's Cove Motor Inn** **SH**
(207) 633-2800. **$69-$249.** 727 Ocean Point Rd. Jct SR 27, 4.5 mi e on SR 96. Ext corridors. **Pets:** Accepted.
[SAVE] ✖ 📶 💻 🍴 ⟲ ✖

EDGECOMB

◈◈◈ **Sheepscot River Inn** **SH**
(207) 882-6343. **$79-$149.** 306 Eddy Rd. 1 mi w on US 1; on east side of Davies Bridge, 1 mi e of Wiscasset. Ext/int corridors. **Pets:** Accepted.
🆔 [S🐾] ✖ 📶 💻 ✖

ELLSWORTH

◈◈◈ **The Colonial Inn** **SH** 🐾
(207) 667-5548. **$68-$160.** 321 High St. 1.3 mi e on SR 3. Ext/int corridors. **Pets:** Small, dogs only. Supervision.
🆔 [S🐾] ✖ [♿] 📶 💻 🍴 ⟲

◈◈ **Comfort Inn** **SH**
(207) 667-1345. **$70-$150.** 130 High St. Center. Int corridors. **Pets:** Accepted.
[S🐾] ✖ [♿M] [♿] 📶 💻

◈◈◈ **Holiday Inn** **SH**
(207) 667-9341. **$62-$155.** 215 High St. Jct US 1, 1A and SR 3. Int corridors. **Pets:** Large. $10 daily fee/pet. Designated rooms, service with restrictions, supervision.
🆔 [S🐾] ✖ [♿M] 📶 💻 🍴 ⟲ ✖

◈◈◈ ◈◈◈ **Jasper's Motel** **SH**
(207) 667-5318. **$49-$99, 3 day notice.** 200 High St. 1 mi e on US 1 and SR 3. Ext corridors. **Pets:** Accepted.
[SAVE] [S🐾] ✖ 📶 🍴

◈◈◈ ◈◈◈ **Twilite Motel** **M** 🐾
(207) 667-8165. **$56-$94, 3 day notice.** 147 Bucksport Rd. Jct US 1A, 1.5 mi w on US 1/SR 3. Ext corridors. **Pets:** Small, dogs only. $10 daily fee/pet. Designated rooms, service with restrictions, supervision.
[SAVE] ✖ 📶 💻

◈◈ **The White Birches** **SH**
(707) 667-3621. **$50-$200.** Thorsen Rd. US 1, 1.5 mi n of jct SR 3. Ext corridors. **Pets:** Other species. Service with restrictions, supervision.
🆔 [S🐾] ✖ 📶 🍴

FARMINGTON

◈◈◈ ◈◈ **Mount Blue Motel** **M**
(207) 778-6004. **$48-$60.** 454 Wilton Rd. 2 mi w on US 2 and SR 4. Ext corridors. **Pets:** Accepted.
[SAVE] [S🐾] ✖ 📶

FREEPORT

◈◈◈ ◈◈◈◈ **Best Western Freeport Inn** **SH**
(207) 865-3106. **$80-$165.** 31 US 1 S. I-295, exit 17, 1 mi n. Ext/int corridors. **Pets:** Other species. Designated rooms, service with restrictions.
[SAVE] [S🐾] ✖ 📶 💻 🍴 ⟲

◈◈ ◈◈ **Econo Lodge** **M**
(207) 865-3777. **$59-$159.** 537 US Rt 1. I-295, exit 20, 0.3 mi s. Ext corridors. **Pets:** Accepted.
🆔 [S🐾] ✖ 📶 💻

◇◇ ▽▽ ▽▽ Harraseeket Inn **CI** ☙
(207) 865-9377. **$110-$289, 3 day notice.** 162 Main St. I-295, exit 22, 0.5 mi e. Int corridors. **Pets:** Dogs only. $25 daily fee/pet. Designated rooms, service with restrictions.
SAVE ⊠ &M ◎ ◎ 🛢 🖵 ❨◯❩ ≈

GRAND LAKE STREAM

▽▽ Weatherby's-The Fisherman's Resort **CA**
(207) 796-5558. **$240, 60 day notice.** 1 Church St. 10 mi w off US 1. Ext corridors. **Pets:** $10 daily fee/pet. Service with restrictions, crate.
❨◯❩ ⊠ ◎ ◎ ◎

GREENVILLE

▽▽ Chalet Moosehead Lakefront Motel **M**
(207) 695-2950. **$67-$130.** 12 N Birch St. 1.5 mi w on SR 15. Ext corridors. **Pets:** Large, dogs only. $10 daily fee/pet. Designated rooms, service with restrictions, supervision.
⊠ 🛢 🖵 ⊠

◇◇ ▽▽ Kineo View Motor Lodge **M**
(207) 695-4470. **$55-$99.** Overlook Dr. 2.5 mi s on SR 15. Ext corridors. **Pets:** $10 daily fee/pet. Designated rooms, service with restrictions, supervision.
SAVE S◎ ⊠ 🛢 🖵

HOULTON

◇◇ ▽▽ Scottish Inns **M**
(207) 532-2236. **$50-$70.** 239 Bangor St. I-95, exit 302, 1 mi s on US 1, then 1 mi sw on US 2A. Ext/int corridors. **Pets:** Accepted.
SAVE S◎ ⊠ 🛢

KENNEBUNKPORT

◇◇ ▽▽▽ The Captain Jefferds Inn **BB** ☙
(207) 967-2311. **$130-$350, 14 day notice.** 5 Pearl St. From Dock Square, 0.3 mi e on Maine St, just s; corner of Pearl and Pleasant sts. Ext/int corridors. **Pets:** Dogs only. $30 daily fee/room. Supervision.
SAVE ⊠ 🛢

◇◇ ▽▽▽ The Colony Hotel **SH** ☙
(207) 967-3331. **$170-$500, 3 day notice.** 140 Ocean Ave. From Dock Square, 1 mi s. Int corridors. **Pets:** Other species. $25 daily fee/pet.
SAVE ⊠ ◎ 🛢 ❨◯❩ ≈ ⊠

◇◇ ▽▽▽ Lodge At Turbat's Creek **M**
(207) 967-8700. **$79-$169, 14 day notice.** 7 Turbat's Creek Rd. From Dock Square, 0.5 mi e on Maine St, 0.6 mi ne on Wildes, then just se. Ext corridors. **Pets:** Other species. Designated rooms, service with restrictions, supervision.
SAVE S◎ ⊠ &M 🛢 ≈

◇◇ ▽▽▽ ▽▽▽ The Yachtsman Lodge & Marina **M** ☙
(207) 967-2511. **$199-$314, 30 day notice.** 57 Ocean Ave. From Dock Square, 0.3 mi e. Ext corridors. **Pets:** Medium, dogs only. $19 daily fee/pet. Designated rooms, supervision.
SAVE ⊠ 🛢 🖵 ⊠

KITTERY

▽▽ Enchanted Nights Bed & Breakfast **BB** ☙
(207) 439-1489. **$56-$280, 15 day notice.** 29 Wentworth St. I-95, exit 2 (Kittery), 1 mi s on SR 236, then just w on SR 103. Ext/int corridors. **Pets:** Other species. $15 one-time fee/room. Supervision.
⊠ 🛢 🖵

LEWISTON

▽▽ Chalet Motel **SH** ☙
(207) 784-0600. **$60-$70.** 1243 Lisbon St. I-95 (Maine Tpke), exit 80. Ext/int corridors. **Pets:** $20 deposit/room. Designated rooms, service with restrictions.
❨◯❩ S◎ ⊠ 🛢 ❨◯❩ ≈ ⊠

▽▽ Motel 6–1223 **SH**
(207) 782-6558. **$45-$71.** 516 Pleasant St. I-95 (Maine Tpke), exit 80, follow signs for Lisbon, just w. Ext/int corridors. **Pets:** Other species. Service with restrictions, supervision.
S◎ ⊠ ◎ ◎

LINCOLNVILLE

▽▽ Abbingtons Seaview Motel & Cottages **M** ☙
(207) 236-3471. **$60-$130, 3 day notice.** 6 Seaview Dr. On US 1, 1.2 mi s of jct SR 173. Ext corridors. **Pets:** Other species. $10 daily fee/pet. Designated rooms, supervision.
❨◯❩ S◎ ⊠ 🛢 🖵 ≈

▽▽ Pine Grove Cottages **CA**
(207) 236-2929. **$50-$150, 7 day notice.** 2076 Atlantic Hwy. On US 1, 2 mi s of jct SR 173. Ext corridors. **Pets:** Large, other species. $7 daily fee/pet. Service with restrictions, supervision.
⊠ 🛢 🖵

LUBEC

◇◇ ▽▽ The Eastland Motel **M**
(207) 733-5501. **$51-$71.** 395 County Rd. Jct US 1 and SR 189, 8.4 mi e on SR 189. Ext/int corridors. **Pets:** Medium, dogs only. $10 daily fee/pet. Designated rooms, supervision.
SAVE ⊠ 🛢

MACHIAS

◇◇ ▽▽ The Bluebird Motel **M**
(207) 255-3332. **$60-$70.** Dublin St. On US 1, 1 mi s. Ext corridors. **Pets:** Medium, other species. Designated rooms, service with restrictions, supervision.
SAVE S◎ ⊠ &M 🛢

◇◇ ▽▽ Machias Motor Inn **M**
(207) 255-4861. **$69-$95, 5 day notice.** 26 E Main St. 0.5 mi e on US 1. Ext corridors. **Pets:** Medium, dogs only. $5 daily fee/pet. Service with restrictions, supervision.
SAVE S◎ ⊠ 🛢 🖵

MEDWAY

▽▽ Katahdin Shadows Motel **M**
(207) 746-5162. **$49-$59, 5 day notice.** I-95, exit 244, 1.5 mi w on SR 157. Ext corridors. **Pets:** Service with restrictions, supervision.
⊠ 🛢 ≈ ⊠

MILFORD

▽▽ Milford Motel On The River **M**
(207) 827-3200. **$57-$95.** 154 Main Rd. 0.5 mi n on US 2. Ext/int corridors. **Pets:** Medium, dogs only. $35 deposit/room. Designated rooms, service with restrictions, supervision.
⊠ 🛢

MILLINOCKET

▽▽ Best Value Inn **SH**
(207) 723-9777. **$79-$89.** 935 Central St. 0.8 mi e on SR 11 and 157. Int corridors. **Pets:** Service with restrictions, supervision.
❨◯❩ ⊠ 🖵 ❨◯❩

◇◇ ▽▽ The Katahdin Inn **SH** ☙
(207) 723-4555. **$69-$125, 3 day notice.** 740 Central St. On SR 157; center. Int corridors. **Pets:** Medium, other species. $10 one-time fee/pet. Designated rooms, service with restrictions, supervision.
SAVE ⊠ 🛢 ≈ ⊠

OGUNQUIT

▽▽ Studio East Motor Inn **M**
(207) 646-7297. **$49-$149, 7 day notice.** 267 Main St. On US 1; center. Ext corridors. **Pets:** Small. $10 daily fee/room. Designated rooms.
⊠ 🛢

OLD ORCHARD BEACH

▼▼ ▼▼ **Alouette Beach Resort** Ⓜ ❖
(207) 934-4151. **$49-$265, 14 day notice.** 91 E Grand Ave. 0.9 mi e on SR 9 (E Grand Ave). Ext/int corridors. **Pets:** Medium, dogs only. $50 deposit/room, $8 daily fee/pet. Designated rooms, service with restrictions, crate.
⊠ 🔓 🖳 🍴 ⚤

▼▼ ▼▼ **Beau Rivage Motel** Ⓜ
(207) 934-4668. **$55-$249, 14 day notice.** 54 E Grand Ave. 0.3 mi e of Old Orchard St. Ext corridors. **Pets:** Small, dogs only. $25 deposit/pet, $10 daily fee/pet. Designated rooms, service with restrictions, supervision.
⊠ 🖋 🔓 ⚤

ⒶⒶⒶ ▼▼ ▼▼ **Old Colonial Motel** Ⓜ ❖
(207) 934-9862. **$70-$220, 14 day notice.** 61 W Grand Ave. On SR 9 (W Grand Ave), 0.5 mi w. Ext corridors. **Pets:** Medium. $5 daily fee/pet. Service with restrictions, crate.
SAVE S🔓 ⊠ 🔓 ⚤ ⊠

ⒶⒶⒶ ▼▼ ▼▼ **Sea View Motel** SH
(207) 934-4180. **$50-$245, 3 day notice.** 65 W Grand Ave. 0.5 mi w on SR 9 (W Grand Ave). Ext corridors. **Pets:** Medium. $100 deposit/pet, $10 daily fee/pet. Supervision.
SAVE S🔓 ⊠ 🔓 ⚤

ORONO

▼▼▼▼ **Best Western Black Bear Inn & Conference Center** SH
(207) 866-7120. **$89-$129.** 4 Godfrey Dr. I-95, exit 193 (Stillwater Ave). Int corridors. **Pets:** $3 daily fee/pet. Designated rooms, service with restrictions, supervision.
A$K S🔓 ⊠ ♿M 🔓 🖳

▼▼ ▼▼ **University Inn Academic Suites** SH
(207) 866-4921. **$69-$82.** 5 College Ave. I-95, exit 191, 0.4 mi n on US 2; 8 mi n of Bangor. Int corridors. **Pets:** Other species. Designated rooms, service with restrictions, supervision.
⊠ 🔓 🖳 ⚤

PORTLAND

▼▼▼▼ **Doubletree Hotel** LH
(207) 774-5611. **$89-$239.** 1230 Congress St. I-295, exit 5 southbound, w on SR 22; exit 5B northbound. Int corridors. **Pets:** Accepted.
A$K ⊠ ♿M 🖋 🔓 🖳 🍴 ⚤

ⒶⒶⒶ ▼▼▼▼ **Eastland Park Hotel** LH ❖
(207) 775-5411. **$99-$159.** 157 High St. At Congress Square; center. Int corridors. **Pets:** Other species. $25 one-time fee/room. Service with restrictions.
SAVE S🔓 ⊠ 🔓 🖳 🍴 ⊠

ⒶⒶⒶ ▼▼▼▼ **Embassy Suites Hotel** LH ❖
(207) 775-2200. **$129-$229.** 1050 Westbrook St. At Portland International Jetport. Int corridors. **Pets:** Other species. Service with restrictions.
SAVE S🔓 ⊠ ♿M 🖉 🔓 🖳 ⚤ ⊠

ⒶⒶⒶ ▼▼▼▼ **Holiday Inn-West** SH
(207) 774-5601. **$100-$195.** 81 Riverside St. I-95 (Maine Tpke), exit 48. Int corridors. **Pets:** Large. Designated rooms, service with restrictions, supervision.
SAVE S🔓 ⊠ ♿M 🖉 🖋 🔓 🖳 🍴 ⚤ ⊠

ⒶⒶⒶ ▼▼▼▼ **Howard Johnson Plaza Hotel** SH
(207) 774-5861. **$85-$195.** 155 Riverside St. I-95 (Maine Tpke), exit 48, jct SR 25. Int corridors. **Pets:** $50 deposit/room. Service with restrictions, supervision.
SAVE S🔓 ⊠ 🔓 🖳 🍴 ⚤

ⒶⒶⒶ ▼▼ ▼▼ ▼▼ **Portland Harbor Hotel** SH
(207) 775-9090. **$169-$245.** 468 Fore St. In the Old Port. Int corridors. **Pets:** Accepted.
SAVE S🔓 ⊠ ♿M 🔓 🍴

PRESQUE ISLE

ⒶⒶⒶ ▼▼ **Northern Lights Motel** Ⓜ ❖
(207) 764-4441. **$50-$70.** 72 Houlton Rd. 2 mi s on US 1. Ext corridors. **Pets:** Designated rooms, supervision.
SAVE ⊠ 🔓

ⒶⒶⒶ ▼▼ ▼▼ **Presque Isle Inn & Convention Center** SH ❖
(207) 764-3321. **$108-$132.** 116 Main St. 1 mi s on US 1. Int corridors. **Pets:** Other species. Service with restrictions.
SAVE S🔓 ⊠ 🔓 🖳 🍴 ⚤

RANGELEY

▼▼ ▼▼ **Country Club Inn** CI
(207) 864-3831. **$116, 7 day notice.** 56 Country Club Rd. 2.5 mi w on SR 4 and 16, 0.8 mi s, follow signs. Ext/int corridors. **Pets:** $10 daily fee/pet. Designated rooms, service with restrictions, crate.
A$K ⊠ 🍴 ⚤ 🖋 📺 📼

ROCKLAND

ⒶⒶⒶ ▼▼ ▼▼ **Navigator Motor Inn** SH
(207) 594-2131. **$59-$139.** 520 Main St. On US 1. Ext/int corridors. **Pets:** Designated rooms, service with restrictions.
SAVE ⊠ 🔓 🍴

ⒶⒶⒶ ▼▼ ▼▼ **Trade Winds Motor Inn** SH ❖
(207) 596-6661. **$55-$149.** 2 Park Dr. On US 1; center. Ext/int corridors. **Pets:** Other species. Designated rooms, supervision.
SAVE S🔓 ⊠ 🔓 🍴 ⚤ ⊠

RUMFORD

ⒶⒶⒶ ▼▼ ▼▼ **Linnell Motel & RestInn Conference Center** SH ❖
(207) 364-4511. **$60-$75.** 986 Prospect Ave. 2 mi w, just off US 2. Ext/int corridors. **Pets:** Other species. $5 daily fee/room. Supervision.
SAVE S🔓 ⊠ 🔓

SACO

ⒶⒶⒶ ▼▼▼▼ **Hampton Inn** SH ❖
(207) 282-7222. **$69-$159.** 48 Industrial Park Rd. I-95 (Maine Tpke), exit 36; I-195, exit 1. Int corridors. **Pets:** Service with restrictions, supervision.
SAVE S🔓 ⊠ ♿M 🖋 🔓 🖳 ⚤

ⒶⒶⒶ ▼▼ **Saco Motel** Ⓜ
(207) 284-6952. **$45-$80.** 473 Main St. I-95 (Maine Tpke), exit 36, 0.5 mi s on US 1. Ext corridors. **Pets:** Small, dogs only. $5 daily fee/pet. Service with restrictions, supervision.
SAVE S🔓 ⊠ 🔓 ⚤

▼▼ ▼▼ **Wagon Wheel Motel** Ⓜ ❖
(207) 284-6387. **$48-$95, 3 day notice.** 726 Portland Rd. 1.8 mi n on US 1; 0.8 mi n of jct I-95, exit 36. Ext corridors. **Pets:** Small, dogs only. $3 daily fee/pet. Designated rooms, service with restrictions, supervision.
A$K S🔓 ⊠ 🔓 🖳 ⚤

SANFORD

▼▼ ▼▼ **Super 8 Motel** SH
(207) 324-8823. **$55-$99.** 1892 Main St (Rt 109). I-95 (Maine Tpke), exit 19, 7 mi w. Int corridors. **Pets:** $15 daily fee/pet. Service with restrictions, supervision.
A$K S🔓 ⊠ 🖉

SCARBOROUGH

◆ **Pride Motel & Cottages** CA
(207) 883-4816. **$40-$100.** 677 US 1. I-95 (Maine Tpke), exit 36, 0.5 mi e to US 1, then 4.5 mi n. Ext corridors. **Pets:** Other species. $5 daily fee/room. Service with restrictions, supervision.

◆◆◆◆ **Residence Inn by Marriott** SH
(207) 883-0400. **$129-$229.** 800 Roundwood Dr. I-95 (Maine Tpke), exit 42, 1.5 mi n on Payne Rd. Int corridors. **Pets:** Other species. $75 one-time fee/room. Supervision.

◆◆◆◆ **TownePlace Suites by Marriott** SH
(207) 883-6800. **$79-$169.** 700 Roundwood Dr. I-95 (Maine Tpke), exit 42, 1.5 mi n on Payne Rd. Int corridors. **Pets:** Other species. $75 one-time fee/room. Service with restrictions.

SEARSPORT

◆◆ ◆◆◆ **The Yardarm Motel** M
(207) 548-2404. **$59-$115, 3 day notice.** 172 E Main St. 0.5 mi n on US 1. Ext corridors. **Pets:** Medium. $5 daily fee/pet. Designated rooms, service with restrictions, supervision.

SKOWHEGAN

◆◆ ◆ **Breezy Acres Motel** M
(207) 474-2703. **$58-$68.** 315 Waterville Rd. 1.5 mi s on US 201. Ext corridors. **Pets:** Accepted.

SOUTHPORT

◆◆ ◆◆◆ **The Lawnmere Inn** CI ❀
(207) 633-2544. **$90-$185, 14 day notice.** 65 Hendricks Hill Rd. 2 mi s of Boothbay Harbor on SR 27, just s of bridge to Southport Island. Ext/int corridors. **Pets:** Large. $20 daily fee/pet. Designated rooms, service with restrictions, supervision.

SOUTH PORTLAND

◆◆◆◆ **Best Western Merry Manor Inn** SH
(207) 774-6151. **$99-$159.** 700 Main St. I-95 (Maine Tpke), exit 45, 1.3 mi e to US 1. Ext/int corridors. **Pets:** Dogs only. Service with restrictions, supervision.

◆◆ **Econo Lodge** M
(207) 772-3838. **$60-$120.** 80 John Roberts Rd. I-95 (Maine Tpke), exit 45 to Maine Mall Rd, right turn, continue to Philbrook Ave; corner of Philbrook Ave and John Roberts Rd. Ext corridors. **Pets:** Accepted.

◆◆ ◆◆◆ **Howard Johnson Hotel** SH
(207) 775-5343. **$79-$179.** 675 Main St. I-95 (Maine Tpke), exit 45, 1.3 mi e to US 1. Int corridors. **Pets:** Designated rooms, service with restrictions, supervision.

◆◆◆◆ **Portland Marriott Hotel & Golf Resort** LH
(207) 871-8000. **$109-$229.** 200 Sable Oaks Dr. I-95 (Maine Tpke), exit 45, just n on Maine Mall Rd, then just w on Running Hill Rd. Int corridors. **Pets:** Accepted.

◆◆ ◆◆◆ **Sable Oaks Suites** SH
(207) 775-3900. **$99-$179.** 303 Sable Oaks Dr. I-95 (Maine Tpke), exit 45, just n on Maine Mall Rd, then just w on Running Hill Rd. Int corridors. **Pets:** Accepted.

◆◆◆◆ **Sheraton South Portland** LH
(207) 775-6161. **$318.** 363 Maine Mall Rd. I-95 (Maine Tpke), exit 45. Int corridors. **Pets:** Accepted.

SPRUCE HEAD

◆◆ ◆◆◆ **Craignair Inn** CI ❀
(207) 594-7644. **$65-$155, 14 day notice.** 5 Third St. 2.5 mi w on SR 73, 1.5 mi s on Clark Island Rd; 10 mi s of Rockland. Ext/int corridors. **Pets:** Medium. $10 daily fee/pet. Designated rooms, service with restrictions, supervision.

WATERVILLE

◆◆ ◆◆◆ **Best Western Waterville** SH
(207) 873-3335. **$89-$160, 30 day notice.** 356 Main St. I-95, exit 130 (Main St). Int corridors. **Pets:** Other species. $25 deposit/room. Designated rooms, service with restrictions, supervision.

◆◆ ◆◆◆ **Budget Host Airport Inn** SH
(207) 873-3366. **$40-$110.** 400 Kennedy Memorial Dr. I-95, exit 127, 0.3 mi e on SR 11 (Kennedy Memorial Dr). Ext/int corridors. **Pets:** $10 daily fee/pet. Designated rooms, service with restrictions, supervision.

◆◆ ◆◆◆ **Econo Lodge** SH
(207) 872-5577. **$35-$109.** 455 Kennedy Memorial Dr. I-95, exit 127 on SR 11 (Kennedy Memorial Dr) at Waterville-Oakland. Ext/int corridors. **Pets:** Dogs only. $5 daily fee/pet. Service with restrictions.

◆◆◆◆ **Holiday Inn** SH
(207) 873-0111. **$109-$135.** 375 Main St. I-95, exit 130 (Main St) on SR 104. Int corridors. **Pets:** Other species. Service with restrictions.

WELLS

◆◆ **Ne'r Beach Motel** M
(207) 646-2636. **$49-$119, 14 day notice.** 395 Post Rd (Rt 1). US 1, 0.8 mi s of jct SR 9B. Ext corridors. **Pets:** Accepted.

WEST FORKS

◆◆ **Inn by the River** CI
(207) 663-2181. **$65-$200, 30 day notice.** US Rt 201. Center. Int corridors. **Pets:** Designated rooms, service with restrictions.

WESTPORT

◆◆◆◆ **The Squire Tarbox Inn** CI
(207) 882-7693. **$80-$190, 14 day notice.** 1181 Main Rd. Jct US 1 and SR 144; in Wiscasset; 8.5 mi s on SR 144, follow signs. Ext/int corridors. **Pets:** Accepted.

WILTON

◆◆ ◆ **Whispering Pines Motel** M ❀
(207) 645-3721. **$65-$90, 3 day notice.** 183 Lake Rd. SR 2, 1 mi w of jct SR 4. Ext corridors. **Pets:** $3 daily fee/pet. Service with restrictions, supervision.

YARMOUTH

◆◆ ◆◆◆ **Down-East Village Motel** M
(207) 846-5161. **$59-$115.** 705 US Rt 1. I-295, exit 15 northbound; exit 17 southbound. Ext corridors. **Pets:** $8 daily fee/pet. Service with restrictions, supervision.

MARYLAND

BALTIMORE METROPOLITAN AREA

ABERDEEN

▽▽▽▽ **Four Points by Sheraton Aberdeen** SH
(410) 273-6300. **$89-$114.** 980 Hospitality Way. I-95, exit 85, just e on SR 22. Int corridors. **Pets:** Medium, other species. Service with restrictions, crate.

Ⓐ ▽▽▽▽ **Holiday Inn Chesapeake House** SH
(410) 272-8100. **$104-$130.** 1007 Beards Hill Rd. I-95, exit 85, just e on SR 22. Int corridors. **Pets:** Medium. Service with restrictions, supervision.

▽▽ **Red Roof Inn** SH
(410) 273-7800. **$54-$71.** 988 Hospitality Way. I-95, exit 85, just e on SR 22. Ext corridors. **Pets:** Accepted.

ANNAPOLIS

▽▽ **Homestead Studio Suites Hotel-Annapolis** SH
(410) 571-6600. **$86-$106.** 120 Admiral Cochrane Dr. 2.3 mi sw on US 50 and 301, exit 22, just s, then just e. Int corridors. **Pets:** Accepted.

ⒶⒶ ▽▽▽▽ **Loews Annapolis Hotel** LH 🐾
(410) 263-7777. **$99-$259.** 126 West St. US 50 and 301, exit 24 eastbound; exit 24A westbound, 1.4 mi s on SR 70, just sw on Calvert St, then just w. Int corridors. **Pets:** Other species.

ⒶⒶⒶ ▽▽▽▽ **Radisson Hotel Annapolis** SH
(410) 224-3150. **$89-$125.** 210 Holiday Ct. 2.3 mi sw on US 50 and 301, exit 22 to Riva Rd, then 0.3 mi n on Riva Rd. Int corridors. **Pets:** Accepted.

▽▽▽▽ **Residence Inn by Marriott-Annapolis** SH
(410) 573-0300. **$99-$289.** 170 Admiral Cochrane Dr. 2.3 mi sw on US 50 and 301, exit 22 to Riva Rd, just s on Riva Rd, then just e. Ext corridors. **Pets:** Medium. $150 one-time fee/room. Designated rooms, service with restrictions.

▽▽▽▽ **Sheraton Barcelo Hotel Annapolis** LH
(410) 266-3131. **$99-$259.** 173 Jennifer Rd. North side of US 50 and 301, exit 23B westbound; exit 23 eastbound. Int corridors. **Pets:** Accepted.

ANNAPOLIS JUNCTION

▽▽▽▽ **TownePlace Suites by Marriott-Baltimore/Ft. Meade** SH
(301) 498-7477. **$59-$139.** 120 National Business Pkwy. I-95, exit 38A, 2 mi e on SR 32 to exit 11 (Dorsey Run Rd), then just nw. Int corridors. **Pets:** Other species. $75 one-time fee/room.

BALTIMORE

▽▽▽▽ **Admiral Fell Inn** SH
(410) 522-7377. **$199-$239.** 888 S Broadway St. Corner of Broadway and Thames sts; facing the waterfront. Int corridors. **Pets:** Accepted.

▽▽▽ **Brookshire Suites** SH 🐾
(410) 625-1300. **$179-$209.** 120 E Lombard St. Corner of Calvert and Lombard sts. Int corridors. **Pets:** Medium, other species. $25 deposit/room. Service with restrictions, crate.

▽▽ **Days Inn** SH
(410) 747-8900. **$79-$129.** 5701 Baltimore National Pike. I-695, exit 15A, just e. Int corridors. **Pets:** Accepted.

ⒶⒶⒶ ▽▽▽▽ **Peabody Court-A Clarion Hotel** SH
(410) 727-7101. **$149-$350.** 612 Cathedral St. Cathedral St and Mount Vernon Square. Int corridors. **Pets:** Accepted.

COLUMBIA

▽▽▽▽ **Homewood Suites by Hilton** SH 🐾
(410) 872-9200. **$99-$199.** 8320 Benson Dr. I-95, exit 41B (Little Patuxent Pkwy), w on SR 175, then right on SR 108, left on Lark Brown, continue on Benson Dr. Int corridors. **Pets:** Other species. $75 one-time fee/room. Service with restrictions, crate.

ⒶⒶⒶ ▽▽▽▽ **Sheraton Columbia Hotel** LH
(410) 730-3900. **$109-$235.** 10207 Wincopin Cir. 1.2 mi w on SR 175 (Little Patuxent Pkwy) from jct US 29, then just s; center. Int corridors. **Pets:** Accepted.

▽▽▽▽ **Staybridge Suites by Holiday Inn Baltimore-Columbia** SH 🐾
(410) 964-9494. **$89-$209.** 8844 Columbia 100 Pkwy. I-95, exit 43B, 4 mi w on SR 100, exit 1B. Int corridors. **Pets:** Medium. $75 one-time fee/room. Service with restrictions, crate.

...WOOD

 **Best Western Invitation Inn** SH
(410) 679-9700. **$69-$99.** 1709 Edgewood Rd. I-95, exit 77A, just e on SR 24. Ext corridors. **Pets:** Other species. $15 daily fee/room. Designated rooms, service with restrictions, crate.

ELLICOTT CITY

Residence Inn by Marriott Columbia SH
(410) 997-7200. **$79-$159.** 4950 Beaver Run Way. I-95, exit 43B, 4 mi w on SR 100, exit 1B (Executive Park Dr). Int corridors. **Pets:** Large, other species. $75 one-time fee/room. Service with restrictions, supervision.

GLEN BURNIE

Days Inn-Glen Burnie SH
(410) 761-8300. **$109-$124.** 6600 Ritchie Hwy. I-695, exit 3B eastbound; exit 2 westbound, 0.5 mi s on SR 2. Ext corridors. **Pets:** Accepted.

HANOVER

Red Roof Inn-BWI Parkway M
(410) 712-4070. **$60-$93.** 7306 Parkway Dr S. 0.7 mi w of SR 295, exit 100, to exit 8, 0.5 mi se. Ext corridors. **Pets:** Accepted.

Residence Inn by Marriott-Arundel Mills/BWI SH
(410) 799-7332. **$95-$219.** 7035 Arundel Mills Cir. I-95, exit 43A, 5 mi e on SR 100 to exit 10A, then just n. Int corridors. **Pets:** Accepted.

JESSUP

Red Roof Inn-Columbia/Jessup M
(410) 796-0380. **$74-$96.** 8000 Washington Blvd. I-95, exit 41A; 0.3 mi s of jct US 1 and SR 175. Ext corridors. **Pets:** Accepted.

LINTHICUM HEIGHTS

AmeriSuites (Baltimore/BWI Airport) SH
(410) 859-3366. **$170-$209.** 940 International Dr. I-695, exit 7A, 1 mi s on SR 295, just e on W Nursery Rd. Int corridors. **Pets:** Small. $10 one-time fee/pet. Designated rooms, service with restrictions, crate.

Comfort Inn Airport SH
(410) 789-9100. **$119-$139.** 6921 Baltimore Annapolis Blvd. I-695, exit 6A eastbound; exit 5 westbound, at jct SR 170 and 648. Int corridors. **Pets:** Other species. Service with restrictions.

Comfort Suites-BWI Airport SH
(410) 691-1000. **$79-$249.** 815 Elkridge Landing Rd. I-695, exit 7A, 1 mi s on SR 295, then 1.3 mi e on W Nursery Rd. Int corridors. **Pets:** Small, other species. $25 one-time fee/pet. Service with restrictions, crate.

Four Points by Sheraton BWI Airport SH
(410) 859-3300. **$89-$239.** 7032 Elm Rd. I-195, exit 1A, 0.5 mi n on SR 170, just e. Int corridors. **Pets:** Large. $25 daily fee/pet. Service with restrictions, supervision.

Hampton Inn BWI Airport SH
(410) 850-0600. **$89-$179.** 829 Elkridge Landing Rd. I-695, exit 7A, 1 mi s on SR 295, 1.3 mi e on W Nursery Rd, then just w. Int corridors. **Pets:** Accepted.

Holiday Inn-BWI Airport LH
(410) 859-8400. **$98-$199.** 890 Elkridge Landing Rd. I-695, exit 7A, 1 mi s on SR 295, 1.3 mi e on W Nursery Rd, then 0.5 mi w. Int corridors. **Pets:** Accepted.

Homestead Studio Suites Hotel-Baltimore Washington Int'l Airport M
(410) 691-2500. **$96-$106.** 939 International Dr. I-695, exit 7A, 1 mi s on SR 295, then just e on W Nursery Rd. Ext corridors. **Pets:** Accepted.

Homewood Suites by Hilton-BWI Airport SH
(410) 684-6100. **$109-$189.** 1181 Winterson Rd. I-695, exit 7A, 1 mi s on SR 295, 0.7 mi e on W Nursery Rd, then just n. Int corridors. **Pets:** Accepted.

Red Roof Inn-BWI Airport SH
(410) 850-7600. **$71-$99.** 827 Elkridge Landing Rd. I-695, exit 7A, 1 mi s on SR 295, 1.3 mi e on W Nursery Rd, then just w. Ext corridors. **Pets:** Accepted.

Residence Inn by Marriott-BWI Airport SH
(410) 691-0255. **$119-$199.** 1160 Winterson Rd. I-695, exit 7A, 1 mi s on SR 295, 0.7 mi e on W Nursery Rd, then just n. Int corridors. **Pets:** Accepted.

Sleep Inn & Suites Airport SH
(410) 789-7223. **$119-$129.** 6055 Belle Grove Rd. I-695, exit 6A eastbound; exit 5 westbound, 0.3 mi n to jct SR 170/648. Int corridors. **Pets:** Other species. Service with restrictions.

OWINGS MILLS

AmeriSuites (Baltimore/Owings Mills) SH
(410) 998-3630. **$134-$199.** 4730 Painters Mill Rd. I-795, exit 4 (Owings Mills Blvd), 0.5 mi s, 0.7 mi w on Red Run Blvd. Int corridors. **Pets:** Small. $10 daily fee/pet. Service with restrictions, supervision.

TIMONIUM

Red Roof Inn-Timonium M
(410) 666-0380. **$61-$96.** 111 W Timonium Rd. I-83, exit 16A northbound; exit 16 southbound, just e. Ext corridors. **Pets:** Other species. Service with restrictions.

TOWSON

Comfort Inn Towson SH
(410) 882-0900. **$99-$179.** 8801 Loch Raven Blvd. I-695, exit 29B, just e. Int corridors. **Pets:** Small. $15 one-time fee/pet. Service with restrictions, supervision.

Holiday Inn-Cromwell Bridge SH
(410) 823-4410. **$80-$134.** 1100 Cromwell Bridge Rd. I-695, exit 29A, just s. Int corridors. **Pets:** Accepted.

WESTMINSTER

The Boston Inn M
(410) 848-9095. **$46-$62.** 533 Baltimore Blvd. 0.9 mi se on SR 97/140 from jct SR 27. Ext corridors. **Pets:** Dogs only. $100 deposit/room. Service with restrictions, supervision.

WHITE MARSH

♦♦♦ **Residence Inn by Marriott Baltimore/White Marsh** 🅢🅗
(410) 933-9554. **$119-$199.** 4980 Mercantile Rd. I-95, exit 67B, just w. Int corridors. **Pets:** Other species. $75 one-time fee/room. Service with restrictions, supervision.

END METROPOLITAN AREA

CAMBRIDGE

♦♦ **Commodore's Cottage Bed and Breakfast** 🅒🅐
(410) 228-6938. **$85-$100, 7 day notice.** 215 Glenburn Ave. US 50, 0.7 mi s on Maryland Ave, just w on Academy and Spring sts, just s on High St, 0.5 mi w on Locust St, then just n. Ext corridors. **Pets:** Accepted.

🅐🅐🅐 ♦♦ ♦♦ **Hyatt Regency Chesapeake Bay Golf Resort, Spa and Marina** 🅛🅗 🐾
(410) 901-1234. **$130-$215, 3 day notice.** 100 Heron Blvd. US 50 E, 1.2 mi e of Frederick C Malkus Jr Bridge. Int corridors. **Pets:** Medium, dogs only. $25 one-time fee/room. Designated rooms, service with restrictions, supervision.

CUMBERLAND

♦♦♦ **Holiday Inn** 🅢🅗
(301) 724-8800. **$79-$109, 3 day notice.** 100 S George St. I-68, exit 43C, just n; downtown. Int corridors. **Pets:** Large. $10 one-time fee/room. Service with restrictions, supervision.

🅐🅐🅐 ♦♦♦ ♦♦♦ **Rocky Gap Lodge & Golf Resort** 🅛🅗 🐾
(301) 784-8400. **$89-$195, 3 day notice.** 16701 Lakeview Rd NE. I-68, exit 50, just n. Int corridors. **Pets:** Large, other species. $50 one-time fee/room. Designated rooms, service with restrictions.

DISTRICT OF COLUMBIA AREA

BELTSVILLE

♦♦♦ **Sheraton-College Park** 🅢🅗 🐾
(301) 937-4422. **$89-$139.** 4095 Powder Mill Rd. I-95, exit 29B, just w on SR 212; 2 mi n of I-495 (Capital Beltway). Int corridors. **Pets:** Medium, dogs only. Service with restrictions, supervision.

BETHESDA

♦♦♦ **Residence Inn by Marriott-Bethesda-Downtown** 🅢🅗
(301) 718-0200. **$239-$279.** 7335 Wisconsin Ave. I-495, exit 34, 2.5 mi s on SR 355; entrance on Waverly St. Int corridors. **Pets:** Medium, other species. $10 daily fee/room, $200 one-time fee/room. Service with restrictions, supervision.

BOWIE

♦♦♦ **Hampton Inn-Bowie** 🅢🅗 🐾
(301) 809-1800. **$89-$139.** 15202 Major Lansdale Blvd. US 50, exit 11, 0.4 mi s on SR 197. Int corridors. **Pets:** Small. $20 daily fee/pet. Service with restrictions, supervision.

CAMP SPRINGS

🅐🅐🅐 ♦♦♦ **Days Inn-Camp Springs/Andrews AFB** 🅢🅗
(301) 423-2323. **$59-$99.** 5001 Mercedes Blvd. I-95/495, exit 7B, 0.3 mi n on Auth Rd. Int corridors. **Pets:** Other species. $10 daily fee/pet. Service with restrictions, crate.

GAITHERSBURG

🅐🅐🅐 ♦♦♦ **Comfort Inn Shady Grove** 🅢🅗 🐾
(301) 330-0023. **$59-$129.** 16216 Frederick Rd. I-270, exit 8, 1 mi e on Shady Grove Rd at jct SR 355. Int corridors. **Pets:** Other species. $10 daily fee/pet. Service with restrictions, crate.

🅐🅐🅐 ♦♦♦ **Holiday Inn-Gaithersburg** 🅛🅗
(301) 948-8900. **$79-$129.** 2 Montgomery Village Ave. I-270, exit 11, 0.3 mi e. Int corridors. **Pets:** Accepted.

♦♦♦ **Homestead Studio Suites Hotel-Gaithersburg/Rockville** 🅢🅗
(301) 987-9100. **$90-$110.** 2621 Research Blvd. I-270, exit 8, just w, then just n. Int corridors. **Pets:** Accepted.

♦♦♦ **Residence Inn by Marriott-Gaithersburg** 🅢🅗
(301) 590-3003. **$99-$179.** 9721 Washingtonian Blvd. I-270, exit 9B (I-370/Sam Eig Hwy), just w to Fields Rd, 0.8 mi se, then just ne. Int corridors. **Pets:** Accepted.

♦♦♦ **Summerfield Suites by Wyndham-Gaithersburg** 🅢🅗 🐾
(301) 527-6000. **$135-$175.** 200 Skidmore Blvd. I-370, exit SR 355, just n to Westland Rd. Ext corridors. **Pets:** Large. $200 one-time fee/room. Designated rooms, service with restrictions.

♦♦♦ **TownePlace Suites by Marriott-Gaithersburg** 🅢🅗
(301) 590-2300. **$59-$149.** 212 Perry Pkwy. I-270, exit 11, just e on SR 124 to SR 355, 0.3 mi s, then 0.5 mi sw. Int corridors. **Pets:** Accepted.

GERMANTOWN

♦♦ **Homestead Studio Suites Hotel-Germantown** 🅜
(301) 515-4500. **$77-$97.** 20141 Century Blvd. I-270, exit 15B, just w to Aircraft Dr, then just n. Ext corridors. **Pets:** Accepted.

NBELT

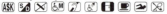 Residence Inn by Marriott-Greenbelt SH
(301) 982-1600. **$129-$249.** 6320 Golden Triangle Dr. I-95/495, exit 23, 0.5 mi sw of jct SR 201; off SR 193, just n on Walker Dr. Int corridors. **Pets:** Large. Designated rooms, service with restrictions, supervision.

LANHAM

Red Roof Inn-Lanham M
(301) 731-8830. **$62-$89.** 9050 Lanham Severn Rd. I-95/495, exit 20A, 0.3 mi e on SR 450. Ext corridors. **Pets:** Accepted.

LARGO

Doubletree Club Hotel Washington DC-Largo LH
(301) 773-0700. **$69-$149.** 9100 Basil Ct. I-95/495, exit 17A (SR 202); off Capital Beltway. Int corridors. **Pets:** Accepted.

LAUREL

Quality Inn & Suites Laurel SH
(301) 725-8800. **$95-$249.** One Second St. On US 1, 0.5 mi n of jct SR 198. Ext/int corridors. **Pets:** Small. $15 daily fee/room. Designated rooms, service with restrictions, crate.

Red Roof Inn-Laurel M
(301) 498-8811. **$61-$84.** 12525 Laurel Bowie Rd. On SR 197, 0.3 mi w of Baltimore-Washington Pkwy. Ext corridors. **Pets:** Accepted.

ROCKVILLE

Best Western Washington Gateway Hotel LH
(301) 424-4940. **$79-$179, 3 day notice.** 1251 W Montgomery Ave. I-270, exit 6B, just w on SR 28. Int corridors. **Pets:** Small, other species. $10 daily fee/pet. Designated rooms, service with restrictions, supervision.

Quality Suites and Conference Center SH 🐾
(301) 840-0200. **$109-$169.** 3 Research Ct. I-270, exit 8 (Shady Grove Rd), just sw. Int corridors. **Pets:** Medium. $10 one-time fee/pet. Designated rooms, service with restrictions.

Red Roof Inn-Rockville SH
(301) 987-0965. **$63-$96.** 16001 Shady Grove Rd. I-270, exit 8 (Shady Grove Rd), 0.5 mi e. Ext corridors. **Pets:** Accepted.

Woodfin Suites Hotel SH
(301) 590-9880. **$124.** 1380 Piccard Dr. I-270, exit 8 (Shady Grove Rd), 0.3 mi s; 1 mi w of SR 355 via Redland Rd. Ext corridors. **Pets:** Medium. $10 one-time fee/pet. Service with restrictions, supervision.

END AREA

EMMITSBURG

Sleep Inn & Suites in Emmitsburg SH 🐾
(301) 447-0044. **$69-$129.** 501 Silo Hill Pkwy. US 15. Int corridors. **Pets:** Large. $25 daily fee/room. Designated rooms, no service, supervision.

FREDERICK

Frederick Residence Inn by Marriott SH
(301) 360-0010. **$99-$134.** 5230 Westview Dr. I-270, exit 31B, 0.5 mi sw on SR 85, 0.3 mi n on Crestwood Blvd. Int corridors. **Pets:** Other species. $75 one-time fee/room. Service with restrictions, crate.

Hampton Inn SH
(301) 698-2500. **$99-$110, 21 day notice.** 5311 Buckeystown Pike (SR 85). I-270, exit 31B, 0.6 mi w. Int corridors. **Pets:** Accepted.

Holiday Inn Express-FSK Mall SH
(301) 695-2881. **$74-$94.** 5579 Spectrum Dr. I-270, exit 31A, just e on SR 85. Int corridors. **Pets:** Large, other species. $25 deposit/room. Service with restrictions, supervision.

Holiday Inn-Francis Scott Key Mall SH 🐾
(301) 694-7500. **$99-$114.** 5400 Holiday Dr. I-270, exit 31A, just se of SR 85. Int corridors. **Pets:** Medium. Service with restrictions, supervision.

Holiday Inn-Frederick/Ft Detrick SH
(301) 662-5141. **$67-$98.** 999 W Patrick St. Just w on US 40 from jct US 15. Ext corridors. **Pets:** Accepted.

MainStay Suites SH
(301) 668-4600. **$129-$149.** 7310 Executive Way. I-270, exit 31B. Int corridors. **Pets:** Other species. $10 daily fee/pet. Service with restrictions, crate.

Quality Inn Historic Frederick SH
(301) 695-6200. **$69-$99.** 420 Prospect Blvd. US 15, exit Jefferson St, just se. Int corridors. **Pets:** Large, other species. Service with restrictions, crate.

GRANTSVILLE

Grantsville Inn SH
(301) 895-5993. **$64-$109.** 2541 Chestnut Ridge Rd. I-68, exit 22, just s on US 219. Int corridors. **Pets:** Medium. $25 deposit/pet. Designated rooms, service with restrictions, crate.

GRASONVILLE

Comfort Inn Kent Narrows M 🐾
(410) 827-6767. **$79-$179.** 3101 Main St. US 50 and 301, exit 42; at Kent Narrows Bridge. Ext corridors. **Pets:** Medium. $10 daily fee/room. Service with restrictions, supervision.

HAGERSTOWN

AAA ▼▼◆ Clarion Hotel & Conference Center Antietam Creek **SH** ☞
(301) 733-5100. **$69-$99.** 901 Dual Hwy. I-70, exit 32B, 2.3 mi w on US 40. Int corridors. **Pets:** Small, other species. $10 daily fee/pet. Designated rooms, service with restrictions, crate.
〔SAVE〕 〔S♦〕 ✕ 🎞 🔒 💻 🍽 ⊶

AAA ▼◆▼◆ Four Points by Sheraton Hagerstown **SH**
(301) 790-3010. **$79-$109.** 1910 Dual Hwy. I-70, exit 32B, 0.5 mi n. Int corridors. **Pets:** Accepted.
〔SAVE〕 〔S♦〕 ✕ 🔒 💻 🍽 ⊶

▼◆▼◆ Halfway Hagerstown Super 8 **M**
(301) 582-1992. **$53-$69.** 16805 Blake Rd. I-81, exit 5B, just w. Int corridors. **Pets:** Medium. $15 deposit/pet, $10 one-time fee/pet. Service with restrictions, supervision.
〔ASK〕 〔S♦〕 ✕ 〔♿〕 🔒 💻

▼◆▼◆ Motel 6–1259 **M**
(301) 582-4445. **$47-$57.** 11321 Massey Blvd. I-81, exit 5, 0.5 mi e, 0.5 mi n of jct I-81 and 70. Ext corridors. **Pets:** Medium. Service with restrictions, supervision.
〔S♦〕 ✕ 〔♿〕 ⊶

AAA ▼◆▼◆ Sleep Inn & Suites **SH**
(301) 766-9449. **$70-$130.** 18216 Col Henry K Douglas Dr. I-70, exit 29, just s. Int corridors. **Pets:** Other species. $10 one-time fee/pet. Service with restrictions, supervision.
〔SAVE〕 〔S♦〕 ✕ 〔♿〕 🔒 💻 ⊶

INDIAN HEAD

AAA ▼◆ Super 8 Motel **SH**
(301) 753-8100. **$58-$78.** 4694 Indian Head Hwy. SR 210, 0.6 mi s of jct SR 225. Int corridors. **Pets:** Small, dogs only. $6 daily fee/pet. Service with restrictions, supervision.
〔SAVE〕 〔S♦〕 ✕ 〔♿M〕 🔒

LA PLATA

AAA ▼◆▼◆ Best Western La Plata Inn **SH**
(301) 934-4900. **$69-$119, 3 day notice.** 6900 Crain Hwy. Jct SR 6, 0.4 mi s on US 301. Int corridors. **Pets:** Small. $25 one-time fee/room. Designated rooms, service with restrictions, supervision.
〔SAVE〕 〔S♦〕 ✕ 〔♿M〕 🎞 🔒 💻 ⊶

LA VALE

AAA ▼◆▼◆ Oak Tree Inn **SH**
(301) 729-6700. **$69-$79.** 12310 Winchester Rd SW. I-68, exit 40, 0.6 mi s. Ext/int corridors. **Pets:** Other species. $5 daily fee/pet. Service with restrictions, supervision.
〔SAVE〕 〔S♦〕 ✕ 🎞 〔♿〕 🔒 💻

AAA ▼◆▼◆ Super 8 Motel **M**
(301) 729-6265. **$54.** 1301 National Hwy. I-68, exit 40, 0.4 mi n. Int corridors. **Pets:** $10 deposit/pet. Service with restrictions, supervision.
〔SAVE〕 ✕ 🔒

LEXINGTON PARK

AAA ▼◆▼◆ Best Western Lexington Park **SH**
(301) 862-4100. **$74-$92.** Rt 235. 3.2 mi n. Int corridors. **Pets:** Accepted.
〔SAVE〕 〔S♦〕 ✕ 🔒 💻 ⊶ 〔✕〕

AAA ▼◆▼◆ Days Inn Lexington Park **M** ☞
(301) 863-6666. **$84-$89.** 21847 Three Notch Rd. On SR 235. Ext corridors. **Pets:** Other species. $8 daily fee/pet. Designated rooms, service with restrictions.
〔SAVE〕 〔S♦〕 ✕ 〔♿M〕 🎞 🔒 💻 🍽 ⊶

MCHENRY

▼◆▼◆ Comfort Inn at Deep Creek **SH**
(301) 387-4200. **$69-$129.** 2704 Deep Creek Dr. 1 mi s on US 219 from jct SR 42. Int corridors. **Pets:** Other species. $15 daily fee/room. Designated rooms, no service, supervision.
〔ASK〕 〔S♦〕 ✕ 🔒 💻 ⊶

▼◆▼◆ Wisp Mountain Resort/Hotel & Conference Center **SH**
(301) 387-5581. **$89-$199, 7 day notice.** 290 Marsh Hill Rd. 1 mi s on US 219 from jct SR 42, just w on Sang Run Rd, 0.3 mi s. Int corridors. **Pets:** Accepted.
〔ASK〕 〔S♦〕 ✕ 🎞 〔♿〕 🔒 💻 🍽 ⊶ 〔✕〕

OCEAN CITY

AAA ▼◆▼◆ Best Western Sea Bay Inn **SH**
(410) 524-6100. **$34-$429, 3 day notice.** 6007 Coastal Hwy. Jct 60th St and Coastal Hwy. Int corridors. **Pets:** Accepted.
〔SAVE〕 〔S♦〕 ✕ 🔒 💻 🍽 ⊶

AAA ▼◆▼◆ Clarion Resort Fontainebleau Hotel **LH**
(410) 524-3535. **$129-$369, 3 day notice.** 10100 Coastal Hwy. 101st St and the ocean. Int corridors. **Pets:** Dogs only. $30 daily fee/pet. Designated rooms, service with restrictions, supervision.
〔SAVE〕 〔S♦〕 ✕ 🎞 🔒 💻 🍽 ⊶ 〔✕〕

AAA ▼◆▼◆ Fenwick Inn **SH**
(410) 250-1100. **$49-$229, 3 day notice.** 13801 Coastal Hwy. 138th St and Coastal Hwy. Int corridors. **Pets:** Accepted.
〔SAVE〕 〔S♦〕 ✕ 🔒 🍽 ⊶ 〔✕〕

PERRYVILLE

▼◆▼◆ Ramada Inn Perryville **SH**
(410) 642-2866. **$69-$99.** 61 Heather Ln. I-95, exit 93, just e. Ext corridors. **Pets:** Accepted.
〔ASK〕 〔S♦〕 ✕ 🎞 🔒 💻

PRINCESS ANNE

▼◆▼◆▼◆ Waterloo Country Inn **CI** ☞
(410) 651-0883. **$125-$255, 7 day notice.** 28822 Mt. Vernon Rd. 3.3 mi w on SR 362 from jct US 13. Int corridors. **Pets:** Other species. Designated rooms.
✕ 🔒 💻 🍽 ⊶ 〔✕〕

ROCK HALL

▼◆▼◆ Inn at Huntingfield Creek **BB**
(410) 639-7779. **$130-$225, 5 day notice.** 4928 Eastern Neck Rd. 1.8 mi s on SR 445 from jct SR 20. Ext/int corridors. **Pets:** Accepted.
〔ASK〕 ✕ 🔒 💻 ⊶ 〔✕〕 〔✓〕

▼◆ Mariners Motel **M** ☞
(410) 639-2291. **$70-$85.** 5681 S Hawthorne Ave. 0.3 mi e of SR 20. Ext corridors. **Pets:** Other species. Supervision.
✕ 🔒 💻 ⊶ 〔✕〕

ST. MICHAELS

AAA ▼◆▼◆ The Parsonage Inn **BB**
(410) 745-5519. **$125-$195, 10 day notice.** 210 N Talbot St. 0.3 mi w on SR 33. Ext/int corridors. **Pets:** Small, dogs only. $25 one-time fee/pet. Designated rooms, service with restrictions, supervision.
〔SAVE〕 〔S♦〕 ✕ 〔✕〕 〔✓〕

SALISBURY

AAA ▼◆▼◆ Best Value Inn Salisbury **SH**
(410) 742-7194. **$49-$149, 3 day notice.** 2625 N Salisbury Blvd. US 13, 1 mi n of jct US 50 Bypass. Ext corridors. **Pets:** $10 daily fee/pet. Service with restrictions.
〔SAVE〕 〔S♦〕 ✕ 🔒 💻 🍽 ⊶

Best Western Salisbury Plaza M
(410) 546-1300. **$59-$145.** 1735 N Salisbury Blvd. US 13 business route, 0.5 mi s of US 50 Bypass. Ext corridors. **Pets:** Other species. $10 daily fee/pet. Service with restrictions, supervision.

Comfort Inn Salisbury SH
(410) 543-4666. **$79-$149.** 2701 N Salisbury Blvd. US 13, 0.5 mi n of jct US 13 business route and Bypass. Int corridors. **Pets:** Other species. Service with restrictions, supervision.

Ramada Inn and Conference Center LH
(410) 546-4400. **$65-$139.** 300 S Salisbury Blvd. US 13 business route, 0.4 mi s of jct Business US 50. Int corridors. **Pets:** Other species. $25 one-time fee/pet. Service with restrictions, supervision.

SNOW HILL

River House Inn BB 🐾
(410) 632-2722. **$125-$250, 7 day notice.** 201 E Market St. 1 mi w on SR 394 from jct SR 113. Ext/int corridors. **Pets:** Dogs only. $20 daily fee/pet.

WALDORF

Hampton Inn Waldorf SH
(301) 632-9600. **$96-$129.** 3750 Crain Hwy. On US 301; opposite St Charles Towne Plaza. Int corridors. **Pets:** Accepted.

WHITEHAVEN

Whitehaven Bed & Breakfast BB
(410) 873-3294. **$90-$100, 7 day notice.** 23844 River St. SR 352 to Whitehaven Rd, then w. Int corridors. **Pets:** Accepted.

WILLIAMSPORT

Red Roof Inn SH
(301) 582-3500. **$49-$69.** 310 E Potomac St. I-81, exit 2, 0.3 mi sw on US 11. Ext corridors. **Pets:** Accepted.

MASSACHUSETTS

AMHERST

The Lord Jeffery Inn SH
(413) 253-2576. **$79-$249.** 30 Boltwood Ave. I-91, exit 19, 6 mi e on SR 9 to Commons. Int corridors. **Pets:** Other species. $15 daily fee/room. Designated rooms, supervision.

University Lodge M
(413) 256-8111. **$59-$159.** 345 N Pleasant St. 0.6 mi n. Ext corridors. **Pets:** Large, other species. $20 daily fee/room. Designated rooms, supervision.

AUBURN

Baymont Inn & Suites Worcester-Auburn SH
(508) 832-7000. **$84-$104.** 446 Southbridge St. I-90, exit 10, 1.2 mi n on SR 12. Int corridors. **Pets:** Service with restrictions, supervision.

Best Western Yankee Drummer Inn SH
(508) 832-3221. **$99-$115.** 624 Southbridge St. I-90, exit 10; I-290, exit 8 to SR 12 S. Int corridors. **Pets:** Accepted.

BARRE

Jenkins Inn CI
(978) 355-6444. **$165-$195, 7 day notice.** 7 West St. On SR 122 and 32. Int corridors. **Pets:** Dogs only. $5 daily fee/pet. Supervision.

BOSTON METROPOLITAN AREA

ANDOVER

Comfort Suites SH
(978) 475-6000. **$90-$145.** 4 Riverside Dr. I-93, exit 45, 0.5 mi e. Int corridors. **Pets:** Accepted.

Residence Inn by Marriott Boston-Andover SH
(978) 683-0382. **$99-$179.** 500 Minuteman Rd. I-93, exit 45, 0.3 mi w, then 0.5 mi n. Int corridors. **Pets:** Other species. $75 one-time fee/room. Service with restrictions.

Staybridge Suites Boston/Andover SH
(978) 686-2000. **$89-$129.** 4 Tech Dr. I-93, exit 45, just sw via Shattuck Rd. Int corridors. **Pets:** Other species. $75 one-time fee/room. Service with restrictions, crate.

Wyndham Andover LH
(978) 975-3600. **$89-$165.** 123 Old River Rd. I-93, exit 45, just e on River Rd. Int corridors. **Pets:** Small. $50 one-time fee/pet. Service with restrictions, supervision.

ARLINGTON

Hawthorn Suites Ltd SH
(781) 643-7258. **$119-$229.** 1 Massachusetts Ave. On SR 2A, just n of SR 16. Int corridors. **Pets:** Accepted.

BILLERICA

Homewood Suites by Hilton SH
(978) 670-7111. **$139-$179.** 35 Middlesex Tpke. I-95, exit 32B, 2.5 mi n. Int corridors. **Pets:** Accepted.

BOSTON

Boston Harbor Hotel LH
(617) 439-7000. **$285-$575.** 70 Rowes Wharf. At Rowes Wharf. Int corridors. **Pets:** Accepted.

Boston Omni Parker House Hotel LH
(617) 227-8600. **$159-$309.** 60 School St. Corner of Tremont and School sts; northeast corner of Boston Common. Int corridors. **Pets:** Small. $50 one-time fee/pet. Service with restrictions.

The Boston Park Plaza Hotel & Towers LH
(617) 426-2000. **$119-$309.** 64 Arlington St. Just s of Boston Common and the Public Gardens. Int corridors. **Pets:** Accepted.

Comfort Inn Boston SH
(617) 287-9200. **$99-$189.** 900 William T Morrissey Blvd. I-93, exit 13 northbound, 0.5 mi sw; exit 12 southbound, follow signs. Int corridors. **Pets:** Large, other species. Service with restrictions, crate.

▼▼▼ **Courtyard by Marriott Boston, Copley Square** 🆂🅷
(617) 437-9300. **$139-$299.** 88 Exeter St. I-90, exit 22, just n; between Huntington Ave and Boylston St. Int corridors. **Pets:** Accepted.
[ASK] [S🐾] [✕] [&M] [🌙] [🔌] [🛁] [🍽]

▼▼▼ **DoubleTree Guest Suites-Boston/Cambridge** 🆂🅷
(617) 783-0090. **$89-$309.** 400 Soldiers Field Rd. I-90, exit 20 westbound; exit 18 eastbound. Int corridors. **Pets:** Small. $250 deposit/room. Service with restrictions, crate.
[✕] [🌙] [🛁] [🔌] [💻] [🍽] [🏊] [✕]

▲▲▲ ▼▼▼ ▼▼▼ **The Eliot Hotel** 🆂🅷 🐾
(617) 267-1607. **$275-$415.** 370 Commonwealth Ave. Corner of Commonwealth and Massachusetts aves. Int corridors. **Pets:** Other species. Service with restrictions, crate.
[SAVE] [✕] [🌙] [&🅼] [🍽]

▲▲▲ ▼▼▼ **Embassy Suites Boston at Logan Airport** 🆂🅷
(617) 567-5000. **$109-$229.** 207 Porter St. I-90, exit 20, at Logan Airport; rental car returns. Int corridors. **Pets:** Accepted.
[SAVE] [S🐾] [✕] [&M] [🔌] [🛁] [🔌] [💻] [🍽] [🏊]

▲▲▲ ▼▼▼ ▼▼▼ **The Fairmont Copley Plaza Boston** 🅻🅷
(617) 267-5300. **$145-$449.** 138 St. James Ave. At Copley Square. Int corridors. **Pets:** Accepted.
[SAVE] [S🐾] [✕] [&M] [🌙] [🔌] [🛁] [💻] [🍽]

▲▲▲ ▼▼▼▼ **Fifteen Beacon** 🆂🅷
(617) 670-1500. **$395-$1400.** 15 Beacon St. Just e of the State House; just ne of Boston Common; center. Int corridors. **Pets:** Accepted.
[SAVE] [✕] [🌙] [🔌] [🍽] [✕]

▲▲▲ ▼▼▼▼ ▼▼▼ **Four Seasons Hotel Boston** 🅻🅷
(617) 338-4400. **$425-$795.** 200 Boylston St. Between Arlington and Charles sts. Int corridors. **Pets:** Accepted.
[SAVE] [✕] [&M] [🌙] [🔌] [🍽] [🏊] [✕]

▲▲▲ ▼▼▼▼ ▼▼▼ **Hilton Boston Logan Airport** 🅻🅷
(617) 568-6700. **$99-$279.** 85 Terminal Rd. At General Edward Lawrence Logan International Airport. Int corridors. **Pets:** Other species. Designated rooms.
[SAVE] [✕] [🌙] [🔌] [🛁] [💻] [🍽] [🏊] [✕]

▲▲▲ ▼▼▼▼ ▼▼▼ **Hotel Commonwealth** 🅻🅷 🐾
(617) 933-5000. **$239-$329.** 500 Commonwealth Ave. On SR 2 at Beacon St and Brookline Ave. Int corridors. **Pets:** Small. $25 one-time fee/room. Supervision.
[SAVE] [✕] [&M] [🛁] [🍽]

▼▼▼ **Howard Johnson Hotel Fenway** 🆂🅷
(617) 267-8300. **$109-$279.** 1271 Boylston St. I-90, exit Brookline Ave S, backing onto Fenway Park. Int corridors. **Pets:** Service with restrictions, supervision.
[ASK] [S🐾] [✕] [🛁] [💻] [🍽] [🏊]

▲▲▲ ▼▼▼ ▼▼▼ **Langham Hotel Boston** 🅻🅷
(617) 451-1900. **$325-$420.** 250 Franklin St. Center; on Post Office Square. Int corridors. **Pets:** Accepted.
[SAVE] [🌙] [🔌] [💻] [🏊] [✕]

▼▼▼▼ **Marriott Residence Inn Boston Harbor** 🆂🅷
(617) 242-9000. **$189-$299.** 44 Charles River Ave. Just se of SR 99 at Charlestown Bridge. Int corridors. **Pets:** $75 one-time fee/room.
[ASK] [✕] [&M] [🌙] [🔌] [🛁] [💻] [🍽] [🏊]

▲▲▲ ▼▼▼ **The Midtown Hotel** 🆂🅷
(617) 262-1000. **$99-$239, 7 day notice.** 220 Huntington Ave. 3 blks sw of Copley Pl; just n of Symphony Hall and Massachusetts Ave; downtown. Int corridors. **Pets:** Medium. Service with restrictions, crate.
[SAVE] [S🐾] [✕] [🛁] [💻] [🍽] [🏊]

▲▲▲ ▼▼▼ ▼▼▼ **Onyx Hotel** 🆂🅷 🐾
(617) 557-9955. **$209-$309.** 155 Portland St. Just n of corner of Merrimac and Traverse sts; 3 blks s of Fleet Center. Int corridors. **Pets:** Other species. Designated rooms, service with restrictions, supervision.
[SAVE] [S🐾] [✕] [🌙] [🔌] [💻] [🍽]

▲▲▲ ▼▼▼ **Ramada Inn Boston** 🆂🅷
(617) 287-9100. **$99-$189.** 800 William T Morrisey Blvd. I-93, exit 13 northbound, 0.5 mi sw; exit 12 southbound, follow signs. Int corridors. **Pets:** Large, other species. Service with restrictions, supervision.
[SAVE] [S🐾] [✕] [🛁] [💻] [🏊]

▼▼▼ ▼▼▼ **The Ritz-Carlton, Boston** 🅻🅷
(617) 536-5700. **$305-$525.** 15 Arlington St. At Arlington and Newbury sts; overlooks the Public Gardens. Int corridors. **Pets:** Accepted.
[✕] [🌙] [🔌] [🍽] [✕]

▼▼▼ ▼▼▼ **The Ritz-Carlton Boston Common** 🆂🅷 🐾
(617) 574-7100. **$305-$505.** 10 Avery St. At Washington and Avery sts; 1 blk e of Boston Common. Int corridors. **Pets:** Medium. $125 one-time fee/room. Service with restrictions.
[✕] [&M] [🌙] [🔌] [🍽] [🏊]

▲▲▲ ▼▼▼ ▼▼▼ **Seaport Hotel** 🅻🅷
(617) 385-4000. **$169-$299.** 1 Seaport Ln. At World Trade Center/Commonwealth Pier. Int corridors. **Pets:** Medium, other species. Service with restrictions, supervision.
[SAVE] [S🐾] [✕] [&M] [🌙] [🔌] [💻] [🍽] [🏊] [✕]

▲▲▲ ▼▼▼ ▼▼▼ **Sheraton Boston** 🅻🅷
(617) 236-2000. **$309-$1800.** 39 Dalton St. I-90, exit 22. Int corridors. **Pets:** Accepted.
[SAVE] [✕] [&M] [🌙] [🔌] [🛁] [💻] [🍽] [🏊] [✕]

▲▲▲ ▼▼▼ ▼▼▼ **The Westin Copley Place Boston** 🅻🅷 🐾
(617) 262-9600. **$249-$459.** 10 Huntington Ave. I-90, exit 22, at Copley Square. Int corridors. **Pets:** Medium, dogs only. $25 one-time fee/pet. Designated rooms, service with restrictions, supervision.
[SAVE] [✕] [🌙] [🔌] [💻] [🍽] [🏊] [✕]

BOXBOROUGH

▼▼▼ **Holiday Inn Boxborough Woods** 🆂🅷
(978) 263-8701. **$129-$219.** 242 Adams Pl. I-495, exit 28, just e on SR 111. Int corridors. **Pets:** Accepted.
[ASK] [✕] [🌙] [🛁] [🔌] [💻] [🏊]

BRAINTREE

▲▲▲ ▼▼▼ **Holiday Inn Express-Braintree** 🆂🅷 🐾
(781) 848-1260. **$89-$189.** 190 Wood Rd. I-93, exit 6, just n on SR 37, then 0.4 mi w. Int corridors. **Pets:** Medium. $100 deposit/room. Service with restrictions, supervision.
[SAVE] [S🐾] [✕] [🔌] [🛁] [💻]

▲▲▲ ▼▼▼ **Sheraton Braintree Hotel** 🅻🅷
(781) 848-0600. **$140-$179.** 37 Forbes Rd. I-93, exit 6, just s on SR 37, then just w. Int corridors. **Pets:** Accepted.
[SAVE] [✕] [🌙] [🔌] [🛁] [💻] [🍽] [🏊] [✕]

BROOKLINE

▼▼▼ **Holiday Inn Brookline** 🆂🅷
(617) 277-1200. **$169-$199.** 1200 Beacon St. 1 mi sw of Kenmore Square; at Beacon and St. Paul sts. Int corridors. **Pets:** Accepted.
[ASK] [✕] [&M] [🌙] [🔌] [🛁] [💻] [🍽] [🏊]

BURLINGTON

▼▼ ▼▼ **Homestead Studio Suites Hotel-Boston/Burlington** 🆂🅷
(781) 359-9099. **$97-$117.** 40 South Ave. I-95/SR 128, exit 32B, just n. Int corridors. **Pets:** Accepted.
🅰🆂🅺 🆂🔟 ✖ 🎯 🅔 🔋 🖥

▼▼▼▼ **Staybridge Suites Boston-Burlington** 🆂🅷
(781) 221-2233. **$126-$171.** 11 Old Concord Rd. I-95/SR 128, exit 32B, just s on Middlesex Tpke. Int corridors. **Pets:** Accepted.
🅰🆂🅺 🆂🔟 ✖ 🅶🅼 🎯 🅔 🔋 🖥 🏊

▼▼▼ **Summerfield Suites by Wyndham-Boston/Burlington** 🆂🅷
(781) 270-0800. **$109-$189.** 2 Van de Graaff Dr. I-95/SR 128, exit 33A, just s on US 3, then 0.5 mi w on Wayside Rd. Int corridors. **Pets:** Medium. $150 one-time fee/room. Service with restrictions, supervision.
🅰🆂🅺 ✖ 🅶🅼 🎯 🅔 🔋 🖥 🏊 ✖

CAMBRIDGE

🆎🆎 ▼▼▼ **Best Western Hotel Tria** 🆂🅷
(617) 491-8000. **$139-$249, 3 day notice.** 220 Alewife Brook Pkwy. Jct SR 2, 16 and US 3; in N Cambridge; I-90 (Massachusetts Tpke), exit Cambridge/Allston to SR 2 W (Fresh Pond Pkwy). Int corridors. **Pets:** $25 daily fee/pet. Service with restrictions.
🆂🅰🆅🅴 🆂🔟 ✖ 🔋 🖥 🔟 🏊

🆎🆎 ▼▼▼▼ **The Charles Hotel, Harvard Square** 🅻🅷
(617) 864-1200. **$350-$575.** One Bennett St. Corner of Eliot and Bennett sts; just s of Harvard Square. Int corridors. **Pets:** Accepted.
🆂🅰🆅🅴 🆂🔟 ✖ 🅶🅼 🎯 🅔 🔋 🔟 🏊 ✖

🆎🆎 ▼▼▼▼ **Hotel @ MIT** 🆂🅷
(617) 577-0200. **$109-$399.** 20 Sidney St. On SR 2A, 1 mi n of the river. Int corridors. **Pets:** Accepted.
🆂🅰🆅🅴 ✖ 🅶🅼 🎯 🅔 🔋 🖥 🔟

🆎🆎 ▼▼▼▼ **Hotel Marlowe** 🆂🅷 🐾
(617) 868-8000. **$299-$329.** 25 Edwin H Land Blvd. Just sw of jct SR 28. Int corridors. **Pets:** Other species. Service with restrictions, supervision.
🆂🅰🆅🅴 🆂🔟 ✖ 🅶🅼 🎯 🅔 🖥 🔟 ✖

🆎🆎 ▼▼▼▼ **Hyatt Regency Cambridge** 🅻🅷
(617) 492-1234. **$129-$265, 14 day notice.** 575 Memorial Dr. On US 3 and SR 2. Int corridors. **Pets:** Accepted.
🆂🅰🆅🅴 ✖ 🅶🅼 🎯 🅔 🔋 🖥 🔟 🏊 ✖

▼▼▼ **Residence Inn by Marriott Cambridge** 🅻🅷 🐾
(617) 349-0700. **$179-$399.** 6 Cambridge Center. Corner of Ames St and Broadway. Int corridors. **Pets:** Large, other species. $150 one-time fee/pet. Designated rooms, service with restrictions.
🅰🆂🅺 🆂🔟 ✖ 🅶🅼 🎯 🅔 🔋 🖥 🏊

▼▼▼ **Sheraton Commander Hotel** 🆂🅷 🐾
(617) 547-4800. **$129-$405.** 16 Garden St. Just n of Harvard Square. Int corridors. **Pets:** Medium, dogs only. Designated rooms, service with restrictions, supervision.
🅰🆂🅺 🆂🔟 ✖ 🎯 🅔 🔋 🖥 🔟

CONCORD

▼▼ ▼▼ **Best Western at Historic Concord** 🆂🅷
(978) 369-6100. **$99-$149.** 740 Elm St. 1.8 mi w, just off SR 2 and 2A. Int corridors. **Pets:** Other species. $10 daily fee/room. Designated rooms, service with restrictions, supervision.
🅰🆂🅺 🆂🔟 ✖ 🔋 🖥 🏊

DANVERS

▼▼▼ **Residence Inn by Marriott** 🆂🅷
(978) 777-7171. **$139-$189.** 51 Newbury St (Rt 1). US 1 N, just s of jct SR 114. Ext corridors. **Pets:** $75 one-time fee/room. Service with restrictions, crate.
🅰🆂🅺 ✖ 🅔 🔋 🖥 🏊 ✖

🆎🆎 ▼▼▼ **Sheraton Ferncroft Resort** 🅻🅷
(978) 777-2500. **$79-$149.** 50 Ferncroft Rd. I-95, exit 50, follow signs for US 1 S to Ferncroft Village. Int corridors. **Pets:** Accepted.
🆂🅰🆅🅴 🆂🔟 ✖ 🅶🅼 🎯 🅔 🔋 🖥 🔟 🏊 ✖

▼▼▼ **TownePlace Suites by Marriott** 🆂🅷
(978) 777-6222. **$99-$129.** 238 Andover St. Southwest corner of jct US 1 and SR 114; SR 114 eastbound, enter just w of US 1 (no westbound entrance); US 1 southbound, enter through shopping center. Int corridors. **Pets:** Accepted.
🅰🆂🅺 🆂🔟 ✖ 🅶🅼 🎯 🅔 🔋 🖥 🏊

DEDHAM

🆎🆎 ▼▼▼ **Residence Inn by Marriott** 🆂🅷
(781) 407-0999. **$139-$169.** 259 Elm St. I-95, exit 15A, just n, then 0.4 mi e. Int corridors. **Pets:** Other species. $75 one-time fee/pet.
🆂🅰🆅🅴 🆂🔟 ✖ 🎯 🅔 🔋 🖥 🏊 ✖

FOXBORO

▼▼▼ **Foxborough Residence Inn by Marriott** 🆂🅷
(508) 698-2800. **$99-$169.** 250 Foxborough Blvd. I-95, exit 7A, 0.6 mi s on SR 140, 0.7 mi e, then just n. Int corridors. **Pets:** Accepted.
🅰🆂🅺 🆂🔟 ✖ 🅶🅼 🎯 🅔 🔋 🖥 🏊 ✖

FRAMINGHAM

▼▼ ▼▼ **Best Western Framingham** 🆂🅷
(508) 872-8811. **$80-$110.** 130 Worcester Rd. I-90 (Massachusetts Tpke), exit 13, 0.5 mi s to SR 9, 1 mi w of Speen St; just w of Shopper's World Mall. Int corridors. **Pets:** Accepted.
🅰🆂🅺 🆂🔟 ✖ 🔋 🖥 🔟 🏊

▼▼ ▼▼ **Red Roof Inn #7068** 🅼
(508) 872-4499. **$66-$96.** 650 Cochituate Rd. I-90 (Massachusetts Tpke), exit 13, e on SR 9 in Natick, 0.8 mi n on Speen St, then just w on SR 30, follow signs for Massachusetts Tpke. Ext corridors. **Pets:** Accepted.
✖ 🔋 🖥

🆎🆎 ▼▼▼ **Residence Inn by Marriott** 🆂🅷
(508) 370-0001. **$169-$199.** 400 Staples Dr. SR 9 W to Crossing Blvd, then s. Int corridors. **Pets:** $75 one-time fee/room. Service with restrictions, crate.
🆂🅰🆅🅴 🆂🔟 ✖ 🅶🅼 🎯 🅔 🔋 🖥 🏊

▼▼▼ **Sheraton-Framingham** 🅻🅷 🐾
(508) 879-7200. **$99-$259.** 1657 Worcester Rd. I-90 (Massachusetts Tpke), exit 12, follow signs to SR 9 W. Int corridors. **Pets:** Medium, dogs only. Service with restrictions, supervision.
🅰🆂🅺 🆂🔟 ✖ 🎯 🅔 🔋 🖥 🔟 🏊 ✖

FRANKLIN

▼▼▼ **Franklin Residence Inn by Marriott** 🆂🅷 🐾
(508) 541-8188. **$99-$189.** 4 Forge Pkwy. I-495, exit 17, 0.7 mi nw off SR 140 N. Int corridors. **Pets:** Other species. $75 one-time fee/pet. Service with restrictions, crate.
🅰🆂🅺 ✖ 🅶🅼 🎯 🅔 🔋 🖥 🏊

▼▼▼ **Hawthorn Suites Ltd** 🆂🅷
(508) 553-3500. **$99-$220.** 835 Upper Union St. I-495, exit 16, just s, then 0.3 mi e. Int corridors. **Pets:** Accepted.
🅰🆂🅺 🆂🔟 ✖ 🅶🅼 🎯 🅔 🔋 🖥 🏊

GLOUCESTER

▼▼▼ Cape Ann Motor Inn 🅼
(978) 281-2900. **$75-$160, 7 day notice.** 33 Rockport Rd. 2 mi n of terminus of SR 128 via SR 127A. Ext corridors. **Pets:** Other species. Service with restrictions, crate.
[✕] [🛏] [Ⓐ🅲]

LAWRENCE

▼▼▼ Hampton Inn Boston/North Andover 🆂🅷
(978) 975-4050. **$79-$129.** 224 Winthrop Ave. I-495, exit 42A, just s on SR 114. Int corridors. **Pets:** $15 daily fee/pet. Service with restrictions, supervision.
[A$K] [🛏] [✕] [🦽M] [🕗] [🛏] [▣]

LEXINGTON

🅐🅐🅐 ▼▼▼ Sheraton Lexington Hotel 🆂🅷 🐾
(781) 862-8700. **$89-$159.** 727 Marrett Rd. Jct I-95 and SR 128, exit 30B (SR 2A). Int corridors. **Pets:** Medium. $20 one-time fee/pet. Designated rooms, crate.
[SAVE] [🛏] [✕] [🦽] [🛏] [▣] [🍽]

MARLBOROUGH

▼▼▼ Embassy Suites Hotel-Boston Marlborough 🅛🅗
(508) 485-5900. **$119-$189.** 123 Boston Post Rd W. I-495, exit 24B, 0.5 mi w; just off US 20. Int corridors. **Pets:** Accepted.
[A$K] [🛏] [✕] [🦽M] [🕗] [🦽] [🛏] [▣] [🍽] [🏊] [✕]

▼▼ Homestead Studio Suites
Hotel-Boston/Marlborough 🆂🅷
(508) 490-9911. **$97-$117.** 19 Northborough Rd E. I-495, exit 24B, just w on US 20. Int corridors. **Pets:** Medium. $25 daily fee/pet. Service with restrictions.
[A$K] [🛏] [✕] [🕗] [🦽] [🛏] [▣]

MEDFORD

🅐🅐🅐 ▼▼▼ AmeriSuites (Boston/Medford) 🆂🅷
(781) 395-8500. **$129.** 116 Riverside Ave NE. I-93, exit 32, just sw via SR 60 and River St. Int corridors. **Pets:** Accepted.
[SAVE] [🛏] [✕] [🦽M] [🕗] [🦽] [🛏] [▣] [🏊]

NATICK

🅐🅐🅐 ▼▼▼ Boston/Natick Travelodge 🅼 🐾
(508) 655-2222. **$64-$99.** 1350 Worcester St. I-90 (Massachusetts Tpke), exit 13, SR 9W; eastbound side. Ext corridors. **Pets:** Large, other species. $20 one-time fee/room. Service with restrictions, crate.
[SAVE] [🛏] [✕] [🛏] [▣]

NEEDHAM

▼▼▼ Sheraton Needham Hotel 🅛🅗 🐾
(781) 444-1110. **$129-$189.** 100 Cabot St. I-95, exit 19A, just e. Int corridors. **Pets:** Medium, dogs only. Designated rooms, service with restrictions, supervision.
[A$K] [🛏] [✕] [🦽] [🛏] [▣] [🍽] [🏊] [✕]

NEWTON

🅐🅐🅐 ▼▼▼ Holiday Inn Newton 🆂🅷
(617) 969-5300. **$149-$219.** 399 Grove St. I-95, exit 22, just e; 0.3 mi s of I-90. Int corridors. **Pets:** Medium. $25 one-time fee/room. Service with restrictions, supervision.
[SAVE] [✕] [🕗] [🦽] [🛏] [▣] [🍽] [🏊]

▼▼▼ Sheraton Newton Hotel 🅛🅗
(617) 969-3010. **$329-$354.** 320 Washington St. I-90 (Massachusetts Tpke), exit 17 (SR 16). Int corridors. **Pets:** Accepted.
[A$K] [🛏] [✕] [🕗] [🕗] [🛏] [▣] [🍽] [🏊]

NORTH CHELMSFORD

▼▼▼▼ Hawthorn Suites, LTD 🆂🅷
(978) 256-5151. **$89.** 25 Research Pl. US 3, exit 32, 0.3 mi ne on SR 4. Int corridors. **Pets:** Accepted.
[A$K] [🛏] [✕] [🦽M] [🕗] [🦽] [🛏] [▣] [🏊]

PEABODY

▼▼▼ Homestead Studio Suites
Hotel-Boston/Peabody 🆂🅷
(978) 531-6632. **$90-$120.** 200 Jubilee Dr. SR 128, exit 28, just s to Centennial Dr, w to the end, n to Jubilee Dr, then 1.1 mi e. Int corridors. **Pets:** Accepted.
[A$K] [🛏] [✕] [🕗] [🦽] [🛏] [▣] [🏊]

▼▼▼ Homewood Suites by Hilton 🆂🅷
(978) 536-5050. **$99-$159.** 57 Newbury St. On US 1, northbound; I-95 and SR 128, exit 44B, just n, then left on Dearborn Rd. Int corridors. **Pets:** Accepted.
[A$K] [✕] [🦽M] [🕗] [🦽] [🛏] [▣] [🏊]

REVERE

🅐🅐🅐 ▼▼▼▼ Comfort Inn & Suites Boston Airport 🆂🅷
(781) 485-3600. **$99-$199.** 85 American Legion Hwy. Jct SR 1A and 60, 3 mi n of General Edward Lawrence Logan International Airport. Int corridors. **Pets:** Medium, other species. $10 daily fee/room. Service with restrictions.
[SAVE] [🛏] [✕] [🦽] [🛏] [▣] [🍽] [🏊]

▼▼▼ Hampton Inn Boston Logan Airport 🆂🅷
(781) 286-5665. **$89-$179.** 230 Lee Burbank Hwy. On SR 1A, 1.9 mi n of General Edward Lawrence Logan International Airport; 0.6 mi s of terminus of SR 60. Int corridors. **Pets:** Medium. $25 daily fee/pet. Service with restrictions, crate.
[✕] [🦽M] [🕗] [🦽] [🛏] [▣] [🏊]

SALEM

▼▼▼ Hawthorne Hotel 🆂🅷 🐾
(978) 744-4080. **$125-$309, 3 day notice.** 18 Washington Square W. On SR 1A. Int corridors. **Pets:** Other species. $10 daily fee/room. Service with restrictions, supervision.
[A$K] [🛏] [✕] [🛏] [🍽]

▼▼▼ The Salem Inn 🅱🅱
(978) 741-0680. **$129-$240, 7 day notice.** 7 Summer St. On SR 114 at Essex St; SR 128, exit 25A, 3 mi e. Int corridors. **Pets:** Other species. $15 daily fee/pet. Designated rooms, service with restrictions, supervision.
[✕] [🛏] [▣]

SAUGUS

▼▼ Red Roof Inn #7305 🆂🅷
(781) 941-1400. **$89-$104.** 920 Broadway (US 1). I-95, exit 44 northbound, 3.2 mi s on US 1; exit Main St/Saugus southbound to U-turn. Int corridors. **Pets:** Supervision.
[✕] [🦽M] [🕗]

SUDBURY

▼▼▼ Clarion Carriage House Inn 🆂🅷
(978) 443-2223. **$119-$250.** 738 Boston Post Rd. I-495, exit 24A, 7.5 mi e on US 20; 4.7 mi w of jct SR 27 on US 20. Int corridors. **Pets:** Other species. $10 daily fee/pet. Service with restrictions, supervision.
[A$K] [🛏] [✕] [🛏] [▣]

TEWKSBURY

🅐🅐🅐 ▼▼▼ Holiday Inn Tewksbury/Andover 🆂🅷
(978) 640-9000. **$95-$129.** 4 Highwood Dr. I-495, exit 39, just w on SR 133. Int corridors. **Pets:** Accepted.
[SAVE] [🛏] [✕] [🕗] [🛏] [▣] [🍽] [🏊] [✕]

▼▼▼ Motel 6 Boston-Tewksbury #1403 M
(978) 851-8677. **$61-$75.** 95 Main St. I-495, exit 38, just s on SR 38. Ext corridors. **Pets:** Small. Service with restrictions, supervision.
⬛⬛⬛⬛

▼▼▼▼ Residence Inn by Marriott-Boston/Tewksbury SH
(978) 640-1003. **$79-$159.** 1775 Andover St. I-495, exit 39, 0.3 mi w on SR 133. Ext corridors. **Pets:** Other species. $75 one-time fee/room. Service with restrictions, crate.
⬛⬛⬛⬛⬛⬛⬛⬛⬛

▼▼▼ TownePlace Suites by Marriott SH
(978) 863-9800. **$84-$129.** 20 International Pl. I-495, exit 39, 0.3 mi nw. Int corridors. **Pets:** Accepted.
⬛⬛⬛⬛⬛⬛⬛

WAKEFIELD

▼▼▼ Sheraton Colonial Hotel & Golf Club Boston North LH
(781) 245-9300. **$109-$229.** 1 Audubon Rd. I-95, exit 42, just n. Int corridors. **Pets:** Accepted.
⬛⬛⬛⬛⬛⬛⬛⬛⬛⬛

WALTHAM

▼▼▼ Homestead Studio Suites Hotel-Boston/Waltham SH
(781) 890-1333. **$87-$117.** 52 Fourth Ave. I-95, exit 27A, just se; behind The Westin, Waltham-Boston. Int corridors. **Pets:** Accepted.
⬛⬛⬛⬛⬛⬛⬛

AAA ▼▼▼ Summerfield Suites by Wyndham-Waltham/Boston SH
(781) 290-0026. **$89-$135.** 54 Fourth Ave. I-95, exit 27A, just e; behind The Westin, Waltham-Boston. Int corridors. **Pets:** Medium. $150 one-time fee/room. Designated rooms, service with restrictions, crate.
⬛⬛⬛⬛⬛⬛⬛⬛⬛

▼▼▼ ▼▼▼ The Westin, Waltham-Boston LH
(781) 290-5600. **$175-$255.** 70 Third Ave. I-95, exit 27A, just se. Int corridors. **Pets:** Accepted.
⬛⬛⬛⬛⬛⬛⬛⬛⬛

WESTFORD

▼▼▼ Residence Inn by Marriott SH
(978) 392-1407. **$149-$199.** 7 Lan Dr. I-495, exit 32, just s, then 0.5 w on SR 110. Int corridors. **Pets:** Accepted.
⬛⬛⬛⬛⬛⬛⬛⬛⬛

WOBURN

▼▼▼ Crowne Plaza Hotel and Resort Boston/Woburn LH
(781) 932-0999. **$169-$219.** 2 Forbes Rd. I-95, exit 36, 0.5 mi s via Washington St, then just e at Getty Station; jct Cedar St. Int corridors. **Pets:** Medium, other species. $50 deposit/room. Designated rooms, service with restrictions, crate.
⬛⬛⬛⬛⬛⬛⬛⬛⬛

▼▼▼ Radisson Hotel Woburn SH
(781) 935-8760. **$109-$145.** 15 Middlesex Canal Park Rd. I-95, exit 35, s via SR 38. Int corridors. **Pets:** Accepted.
⬛⬛⬛⬛⬛⬛⬛⬛⬛

▼▼▼ Red Roof Inn Woburn #7238 SH
(781) 935-7110. **$75-$110.** 19 Commerce Way. I-95, exit 36, just n, then just w on Mishawum Rd. Int corridors. **Pets:** Accepted.
⬛⬛⬛⬛⬛

▼▼▼ Residence Inn by Marriott-Boston/Woburn SH
(781) 376-4000. **$79-$169.** 300 Presidential Way. I-93, exit 37C, just nw. Int corridors. **Pets:** Accepted.
⬛⬛⬛⬛⬛⬛⬛⬛

END METROPOLITAN AREA

BROCKTON

▼▼▼ Residence Inn by Marriott SH
(508) 583-3600. **$89-$209.** 124 Liberty St. SR 24, exit 17B, just w, just s on Pearl St, then 0.3 mi se via Mill St connector. Int corridors. **Pets:** Accepted.
⬛⬛⬛⬛⬛⬛⬛⬛⬛

CAPE COD AREA

BUZZARDS BAY

AAA ▼▼▼ Bay Motor Inn CA
(508) 759-3989. **$51-$119, 10 day notice.** 223 Main St. SR 25, 0.5 mi w of Bourne rotary, exit 2. Ext corridors. **Pets:** $10 daily fee/pet. Service with restrictions, supervision.
⬛⬛⬛⬛⬛⬛

CENTERVILLE

AAA ▼▼▼ The Inn at Centerville Corners M
(508) 775-7223. **$50-$160, 14 day notice.** 369 S Main St. 1 mi s of SR 28, jct Craigville Beach Rd. Ext corridors. **Pets:** Medium, dogs only. $5 daily fee/pet. Service with restrictions, supervision.
⬛⬛⬛⬛

FALMOUTH

▼▼▼ Capeside Cottage Bed & Breakfast BB 🐾
(508) 548-6218. **$100-$160, 14 day notice.** 320 Woods Hole Rd. 2.2 mi s on SR 28. Int corridors. **Pets:** Large. Designated rooms, supervision.
⬛⬛⬛⬛⬛

AAA ▼▼▼ Mariner Motel M
(508) 548-1331. **$59-$169, 14 day notice.** 555 Main St. 0.5 mi e on SR 28. Ext corridors. **Pets:** Accepted.
⬛⬛⬛⬛

HYANNIS

▼▼▼ Comfort Inn SH
(508) 771-4804. **$89-$209.** 1470 Iyanough Rd. On SR 132; US 6, exit 6, 1.3 mi se. Ext/int corridors. **Pets:** Other species. $50 deposit/room. Designated rooms, service with restrictions, supervision.
⬛⬛⬛⬛⬛⬛⬛⬛

ORLEANS

AAA ▼▼▼ Skaket Beach Motel M
(508) 255-1020. **$59-$169, 10 day notice.** 203 Cranberry Hwy (Rt 6A). US 6, exit 12, just e. Ext corridors. **Pets:** $9 deposit/pet. Designated rooms, service with restrictions, supervision.
⬛⬛⬛⬛⬛

PROVINCETOWN

▼▼▼ **Bayshore & Chandler** CO
(508) 487-9133. **$95-$295, 30 day notice.** 493 Commercial St. 0.8 mi
e of Town Hall. Ext corridors. **Pets:** Accepted.
⊠ 🖪 🖭

△△△ ▼▼▼ **Cape Inn** SH
(508) 487-1711. **$99-$179, 3 day notice.** 698 Commercial St. 1.5 mi se
on SR 6A. Ext corridors. **Pets:** Other species. Service with restrictions,
supervision.
SAVE S☆ ⊠ 🖉 🖪 🖭 🍴 ⇝

△△△ ▼▼▼ **Surfside Hotel & Suites** SH ☙
(508) 487-1726. **$129-$329, 21 day notice.** 542-543 Commercial St. 1
mi e of Town Hall. Ext corridors. **Pets:** Large, dogs only. $20 daily
fee/pet. Designated rooms, service with restrictions.
SAVE S☆ ⊠ 🖪 🖭 ⇝

▼▼▼▼ **White Wind Inn** BB
(508) 487-1526. **$80-$235, 14 day notice.** 174 Commercial St. Just w
of Town Hall. Int corridors. **Pets:** Dogs only. $100 deposit/pet, $15 daily
fee/pet. Designated rooms, service with restrictions, crate.
⊠ 🖪

SANDWICH

▼▼▼ **The Earl of Sandwich Motel** M
(508) 888-1415. **$55-$109, 7 day notice.** 378 SR 6A. At MM 5.1. Ext
corridors. **Pets:** Accepted.
⊠ 🖪 ⇝

△△△ ▼▼▼ **Sandwich Lodge & Resort** M
(508) 888-2275. **$59-$129, 7 day notice.** 54 SR 6A. On SR 6A, 1 mi
w. Ext/int corridors. **Pets:** Other species. $10 daily fee/pet. Designated
rooms, service with restrictions, supervision.
SAVE S☆ ⊠ 🖪 ⇝ ⊠

END AREA

CHICOPEE

▼ **Motel 6–1059** M
(413) 592-5141. **$45-$65.** 36 Johnny Cake Hollow Rd. I-90 (Massachusetts Tpke), exit 6, just n. Ext corridors. **Pets:** Accepted.
S☆ ⊠ ⇝

△△△ ▼▼▼ **Super 8 Motel-Chicopee** SH ☙
(413) 592-6171. **$55-$109.** 463 Memorial Dr. I-90 (Massachusetts
Tpke), exit 5, just ne; upon exiting, use jug handle overpass to SR 33
N. Int corridors. **Pets:** Other species. $15 one-time fee/room. Crate.
SAVE S☆ ⊠ 🖪 🖭 ⇝

DARTMOUTH

▼▼▼▼ **Residence Inn by Marriott** SH
(508) 984-5858. **$109-$219.** 181 Faunce Corner Rd. I-195, exit 12A,
just s. Int corridors. **Pets:** Medium, other species. $75 one-time fee/room.
Service with restrictions.
ASK S☆ ⊠ ☾M 🖉 🖪 🖭 ⇝ ⊠

DEERFIELD

▼▼▼▼ **Deerfield Inn** CI ☙
(413) 774-5587. **$105-$250, 7 day notice.** 81 Old Main St. Center. Int
corridors. **Pets:** Medium, dogs only. $15 daily fee/room. Designated rooms,
service with restrictions, crate.
ASK S☆ ⊠ 🍴

EAST WAREHAM

△△△ ▼▼▼ **Atlantic Motel** M
(508) 295-0210. **$69-$189, 10 day notice.** 7 Depot St. Between eastbound and westbound lanes of US 6/SR 28; jct SR 25, exit 1. Ext
corridors. **Pets:** Small, dogs only. $20 daily fee/pet. Designated rooms,
service with restrictions, supervision.
SAVE S☆ ⊠ 🖪 ⇝

FITCHBURG

△△△ ▼▼▼▼ **Best Western Royal Plaza Hotel & Trade**
          Center LH ☙
(978) 342-7100. **$79-$169.** 150 Royal Plaza Dr. Just s on SR 31; SR 2,
exit 28. Int corridors. **Pets:** Large, other species. $50 deposit/room. Des-
ignated rooms, service with restrictions, crate.
SAVE S☆ ⊠ 🖉 🖪 🖭 🍴 ⇝ ⊠

GARDNER

▼▼ **Super 8 Motel** M
(978) 630-2888. **$79-$105.** 22 Pearson Blvd. SR 2, exit 23, just n. Int
corridors. **Pets:** Large. $10 daily fee/pet. Service with restrictions, supervi-
sion.
ASK S☆ ⊠ 🖪

GREAT BARRINGTON

△△△ ▼▼▼ **Barrington Court Motel** M
(413) 528-2340. **$55-$179, 14 day notice.** 400 Stockbridge Rd. On US
7, 1.2 mi s of jct SR 183. Ext corridors. **Pets:** $10 daily fee/room.
Designated rooms, service with restrictions, supervision.
SAVE S☆ ⊠ 🖪 ⇝

△△△ ▼ **Monument Mountain Motel** M ☙
(413) 528-3272. **$60-$200, 14 day notice.** 249 Stockbridge Rd. On US
7, 1.2 mi s of jct SR 183. Ext corridors. **Pets:** Dogs only. $10 daily
fee/pet. Designated rooms, service with restrictions, supervision.
SAVE S☆ ⊠ 🖪 ⇝

GREENFIELD

△△△ ▼▼▼▼ **The Brandt House B&B** BB ☙
(413) 774-3329. **$105-$300.** 29 Highland Ave. I-91, exit 26, 1.8 mi e on
SR 2A, then se via Cresent St. Int corridors. **Pets:** Dogs only. $25
one-time fee/pet. Supervision.
SAVE S☆ ⊠ 🖪

HADLEY

△△△ ▼▼▼▼ **Howard Johnson** SH
(413) 586-0114. **$69-$197.** 401 Russell St. I-91, exit 19 northbound, 4.3
mi e on SR 9; exit 24 southbound, 10 mi s on SR 116, then just w on
SR 9. Int corridors. **Pets:** Large, other species. $20 daily fee/room. Des-
ignated rooms, supervision.
SAVE S☆ ⊠ ☾M 🖉 🖪 🖭 ⇝

△△△ ▼▼▼ **Quality Inn** SH
(413) 584-9816. **$65-$185.** 237 Russell St. I-91, exit 19 northbound;
exit 20 southbound, 3 mi e on SR 9. Int corridors. **Pets:** Medium, dogs
only. $25 one-time fee/pet. No service, supervision.
SAVE S☆ ⊠ ♿ 🖪 🖭 ⇝

LANESBORO

AAA ▼▼ **Mt View Motel** **M**
(413) 442-1009. **$48-$145, 7 day notice.** 499 S Main St. 1 mi s on US 7. Ext corridors. **Pets:** Medium. $10 daily fee/pet. Designated rooms, service with restrictions, supervision.
SAVE Sö X ⊞

AAA ▼▼ **The Weathervane Motel** **M**
(413) 443-3230. **$35-$125, 15 day notice.** 475 S Main St. 1.3 mi s on US 7. Ext corridors. **Pets:** Small. $10 one-time fee/pet. Designated rooms, no service, supervision.
SAVE Sö X ⊞ ⊑

LENOX

▼▼ **Seven Hills Country Inn & Restaurant** **SH** ❀
(413) 637-0060. **$85-$340, 15 day notice.** 40 Plunkett St. Jct US 7/20, 0.6 mi se on US 20, 0.8 mi w. Ext/int corridors. **Pets:** Other species. $20 daily fee/pet. Designated rooms.
ASK X ⌨ ⊞ ⊑ ⊓ ⇌ ⊠

MANSFIELD

▼▼▼ **Holiday Inn Mansfield** **SH**
(508) 339-2200. **$89-$175.** 31 Hampshire St. I-95, exit 7A, 0.5 mi s on SR 140, then 1 mi w on Forbes Rd; I-495, exit 12, 2 mi n on SR 140, then w on Forbes Rd. Int corridors. **Pets:** Large. $10 daily fee/room. Service with restrictions, crate.
ASK Sö X ⊞ ⊑ ⊓ ⇌ ⊠

MIDDLEBORO

AAA ▼▼▼ **Days Inn-Plymouth/Middleboro** **SH** ❀
(508) 946-4400. **$74-$119.** 30 E Clark St. I-495, exit 4, at SR 105. Int corridors. **Pets:** Other species. $3 daily fee/pet. Service with restrictions, supervision.
SAVE Sö X ⌨ ⊞ ⊑ ⇌

MILFORD

AAA ▼▼ **Days Inn** **SH**
(508) 634-2499. **$65-$105.** 3 Fortune Blvd. I-495, exit 20, 0.3 mi s on SR 85, then just e. Int corridors. **Pets:** Small. $25 one-time fee/pet. Service with restrictions, supervision.
SAVE Sö X ⌨ ⊞ ⊑

▼▼▼ **Holiday Inn Express** **SH**
(508) 634-1054. **$89-$139.** 50 Fortune Blvd. I-495, exit 20, just sw on SR 85, then just se. Int corridors. **Pets:** Accepted.
ASK X ⌨M ⌀ ⌨ ⊞ ⊑ ⇌

NORTHAMPTON

▼▼▼▼ **Clarion Hotel & Conference Center** **SH**
(413) 586-1211. **$79-$235.** One Atwood Dr. I-91, exit 18, just s on US 5. Int corridors. **Pets:** $20 daily fee/pet. Designated rooms, service with restrictions, supervision.
ASK Sö X ⌨M ⌀ ⌨ ⊞ ⊑ ⊓ ⇌ ⊠

ORANGE

AAA ▼▼ **Executive Inn** **M**
(978) 544-8864. **$55-$85, 7 day notice.** 110 Daniel Shay Hwy. US 202, exit 16, just n of jct SR 2. Ext/int corridors. **Pets:** $7 daily fee/pet. Service with restrictions, supervision.
SAVE Sö X ⊞

PITTSFIELD

▼▼▼▼ **Crowne Plaza Hotel and Resort Pittsfield Berkshires** **LH**
(413) 499-2000. **$129-$289.** 1 West St, Berkshire Common. Center. Int corridors. **Pets:** Accepted.
ASK Sö X ⌨M ⌀ ⌨ ⊞ ⊑ ⊓ ⇌ ⊠

RAYNHAM

▼▼▼ **Days Inn Taunton** **M**
(508) 824-8647. **$69-$99, 15 day notice.** 164 New State Hwy. SR 24, exit 13B, 0.8 mi w on US 44. Ext/int corridors. **Pets:** Small. Service with restrictions, supervision.
X ⌨ ⇌

REHOBOTH

▼▼▼ **Five Bridge Inn Bed & Breakfast** **BB** ❀
(508) 252-3190. **$98-$145, 7 day notice.** 154 Pine St. 1.6 mi n of US 44, 3.3 mi w of jct SR 118; US 44, n on Blanding, e on Broad, n on Salisbury, then w. Int corridors. **Pets:** Other species. $10 one-time fee/room. Service with restrictions, supervision.
X ⊞ ⊑ ⇌ ⊠

ROCKLAND

▼▼▼ **Holiday Inn Express-Boston/Rockland** **SH** ❀
(781) 871-5660. **$119-$150.** 909 Hingham St. SR 3, exit 14, 0.3 mi sw on SR 228. Int corridors. **Pets:** Other species. $20 daily fee/room. Service with restrictions, supervision.
ASK Sö X ⊞ ⊑

SEEKONK

▼▼ **Motel 6-1289** **SH**
(508) 336-7800. **$55-$85.** 821 Fall River Ave. I-195, exit 1, just n on SR 114A. Int corridors. **Pets:** Medium, other species. Service with restrictions, supervision.
Sö X ⌀ ⌨

▼▼▼ **Ramada Inn-Providence** **SH**
(508) 336-7300. **$89-$135.** 940 Fall River Ave. I-195, exit 1, just s. Int corridors. **Pets:** Accepted.
ASK Sö X ⊞ ⊑ ⊓ ⇌ ⊠

SOMERSET

AAA ▼▼▼ **Quality Inn-Fall River/Somerset** **SH**
(508) 678-4545. **$74-$179.** 1878 Wilbur Ave. Jct SR 103 and I-195, exit 4 eastbound; exit 4A westbound. Int corridors. **Pets:** Accepted.
SAVE Sö X ⊞ ⊑ ⇌ ⊠

SOUTHBOROUGH

▼▼ **Red Roof Inn #7075** **M**
(508) 481-3904. **$64-$94.** 367 Turnpike Rd. I-495, exit 23A, just e on SR 9. Ext corridors. **Pets:** Accepted.
X ⊞

SPRINGFIELD

AAA ▼▼▼ **Holiday Inn** **LH**
(413) 781-0900. **$114-$149.** 711 Dwight St. I-291, exit 2A, just e. Int corridors. **Pets:** Other species. $35 daily fee/room. Service with restrictions, supervision.
SAVE Sö X ⌨M ⌀ ⊞ ⊑ ⊓ ⇌ ⊠

▼▼▼ **Sheraton Springfield Monarch Place** **LH**
(413) 781-1010. **$209.** 1 Monarch Pl. I-91, exit 6 northbound; exit 7 southbound, just n; downtown. Int corridors. **Pets:** Large, other species. $300 one-time fee/room. Service with restrictions, supervision.
ASK Sö X ⌨M ⌀ ⊞ ⊑ ⊓ ⇌ ⊠

STURBRIDGE

AAA ▼▼▼ **Best Western-American Motor Lodge** **M**
(508) 347-9121. **$69-$109.** 350 Main St. Jct US 20 and SR 131. Int corridors. **Pets:** Accepted.
SAVE Sö X ⊓ ⇌

AAA ▽▽▽▽ Comfort Inn & Suites Colonial **SH**
(508) 347-3306. **$89-$215.** 215 Charlton Rd. I-90 (Massachusetts Tpke), exit 9, 0.5 mi e; I-84, exit 3A. Ext/int corridors. **Pets:** Other species. $15 daily fee/pet. Designated rooms.
[SAVE] [S☼] [✕] [&M] [♪] [♿] [🛏] [◻] [≈]

AAA ▽▽ Days Inn **M**
(508) 347-3391. **$59-$150, 7 day notice.** 66-68 Haynes St (SR 15). I-84, exit 2, 0.5 mi n, follow signs to SR 131, on I-84 service road. Ext/int corridors. **Pets:** $7 daily fee/pet. Service with restrictions, supervision.
[SAVE] [S☼] [✕] [◻] [≈]

AAA ▽ Green Acres Motel **M**
(508) 347-3496. **$55-$139.** 2 Shepard Rd (SR 131). 1.5 mi s of jct US 20. Ext corridors. **Pets:** Small. $10 one-time fee/pet. Designated rooms, no service, supervision.
[SAVE] [S☼] [✕] [🛏] [≈]

AAA ▽▽▽ Publick House Historic Inn & Country Lodge **SH**
(508) 347-3313. **$71-$112.** 295 Main St. I-90, I-90 (Massachusetts Tpke), exit 9; I-84, exit 3B, 0.5 mi s of jct US 20. Ext/int corridors. **Pets:** Other species. $10 daily fee/pet. Designated rooms, service with restrictions, crate.
[SAVE] [S☼] [✕] [🛏] [◻] [♨] [≈]

▽▽▽ Quality Inn & Conference Center **SH** 🐾
(508) 347-1978. **$59-$149.** 400 Haynes Rd (SR 15). I-84, exit 1, 0.5 mi w. Int corridors. **Pets:** $10 daily fee/pet. Designated rooms, service with restrictions.
[ASK] [S☼] [✕] [♪] [♿] [🛏] [◻] [♨] [≈]

AAA ▽ Rodeway Inn **M**
(508) 347-9673. **$55-$130.** 172 Main St. On SR 131, 1.4 mi s of jct US 20. Ext corridors. **Pets:** Medium. $10 daily fee/pet. Service with restrictions, supervision.
[SAVE] [S☼] [✕] [🛏] [◻]

AAA ▽▽ Sturbridge Coach Motor Lodge **M**
(508) 347-7327. **$49-$140.** 408 Main St. I-90 (Massachusetts Tpke), exit 9, 0.8 mi w on US 20; I-84, exit 3B. Ext corridors. **Pets:** Accepted.
[SAVE] [S☼] [✕] [◻] [≈]

AAA ▽▽▽▽ Sturbridge Host Hotel and Conference Center on Cedar Lake **LH**
(508) 347-7393. **$109-$169.** 366 Main St. I-90 (Massachusetts Tpke), exit 9, just w on US 20; I-84, exit 3B. Int corridors. **Pets:** Large. $25 deposit/room. Service with restrictions, supervision.
[SAVE] [S☼] [✕] [♪] [🛏] [◻] [♨] [≈] [✕]

WESTBOROUGH

AAA ▽▽▽▽ Residence Inn by Marriott Boston/Westborough **SH** 🐾
(508) 366-7700. **$89-$209.** 25 Connector Rd. I-495, exit 23B, just w on SR 9, exit Computer/Research Dr, 0.3 mi s. Ext/int corridors. **Pets:** Large, other species. $75 one-time fee/room. Designated rooms.
[SAVE] [S☼] [✕] [&M] [♪] [♿] [🛏] [◻] [≈] [✕]

AAA ▽▽▽▽ Wyndham Westborough **LH**
(508) 366-5511. **$99-$185.** 5400 Computer Dr. I-495, exit 23B, just w on SR 9, exit Computer/Research Dr. Int corridors. **Pets:** Accepted.
[SAVE] [✕] [&M] [♪] [♿] [🛏] [◻] [♨] [≈] [✕]

WEST SPRINGFIELD

AAA ▽▽▽▽ Hampton Inn **SH** 🐾
(413) 732-1300. **$89-$99.** 1011 Riverdale St (US 5). I-91, exit 13B, 0.3 mi s. Int corridors. **Pets:** Other species. $75 one-time fee/room. Supervision.
[SAVE] [S☼] [✕] [&M] [♪] [♿] [🛏] [◻] [≈]

AAA ▽▽▽ Quality Inn **SH**
(413) 739-7261. **$59-$159.** 1150 Riverdale St. I-91, exit 13B, at jct US 5. Int corridors. **Pets:** Small, other species. $25 one-time fee/pet. Designated rooms, service with restrictions, supervision.
[SAVE] [S☼] [✕] [🛏] [◻] [♨] [≈]

▽ Red Roof Inn #7193 **M**
(413) 731-1010. **$59-$87.** 1254 Riverdale St. I-91, exit 13A. Ext corridors. **Pets:** Accepted.
[✕] [&M] [♪] [🛏]

▽▽▽ Residence Inn by Marriott **SH** 🐾
(413) 732-9543. **$149-$180.** 64 Border Way. I-91, exit 13A, on US 5. Int corridors. **Pets:** Other species. $75 one-time fee/room. Service with restrictions, crate.
[ASK] [S☼] [✕] [&M] [♪] [♿] [🛏] [◻] [≈] [✕]

WEST STOCKBRIDGE

AAA ▽ Pleasant Valley Motel **M**
(413) 232-8511. **$45-$195.** 42 Stockbridge Rd. I-90 (Massachusetts Tpke), exit B3 eastbound, 0.5 mi s on SR 22, then 3.5 mi e on SR 102; exit 1 westbound, 0.4 mi e. Ext corridors. **Pets:** Medium. $15 daily fee/pet. Designated rooms, no service.
[SAVE] [✕] [🛏] [≈]

WILLIAMSTOWN

▽▽ Cozy Corner Motel **M**
(413) 458-8006. **$50-$125, 10 day notice.** 284 Sand Springs Rd (US 7). On US 7, 1.5 mi n of jct SR 2. Ext corridors. **Pets:** Other species. $10 one-time fee/pet. Service with restrictions, crate.
[✕] [🛏]

AAA ▽▽ The Villager Motel **M**
(413) 458-4046. **$55-$125, 14 day notice.** 953 Simonds Rd. On US 7, 1.7 mi n of jct SR 2. Ext corridors. **Pets:** Medium. $10 daily fee/pet. Designated rooms, service with restrictions, supervision.
[SAVE] [S☼] [✕] [🛏]

WORCESTER

AAA ▽▽▽▽ Crowne Plaza Hotel **LH** 🐾
(508) 791-1600. **$89-$200.** 10 Lincoln Square. I-290, exit 17 eastbound; exit 18 westbound, 0.3 mi n. Int corridors. **Pets:** Medium. $20 daily fee/pet. Designated rooms, service with restrictions, crate.
[SAVE] [S☼] [✕] [&M] [♪] [♿] [🛏] [◻] [♨] [≈] [✕]

AAA ▽▽▽ Holiday Inn **SH**
(508) 852-4000. **$100-$159.** 500 Lincoln St. I-290, exit 20, 0.5 mi n on SR 70. Int corridors. **Pets:** $25 daily fee/room. Service with restrictions, supervision.
[SAVE] [✕] [&M] [♪] [♿] [🛏] [◻] [♨] [≈]

ALANSON

◆◆◆◆ **Crooked River Lodge** SH
(231) 548-5000. **$75-$290.** 6845 US 31 N. On US 31, just n. Int corridors. **Pets:** Accepted.
ASK S✆ ✕ 🛈 🛏 💻 ➾ ✕

ALGONAC

◆◆ **Linda's Lighthouse Inn** BB
(810) 794-2992. **$95-$135, 7 day notice.** 5965 Pointe Tremble Rd (SR 29). I-94, exit 243, 14 mi e. Int corridors. **Pets:** $15 daily fee/pet. Service with restrictions, crate.
✕ ✕ 🅆 ☎

ALLENDALE

◆◆ **Sleep Inn & Suites** SH
(616) 892-8000. **$59-$149.** 4869 Becker Dr. I-96, exit 16, 6 mi s, then 2.5 mi e on SR 45. Int corridors. **Pets:** Accepted.
ASK S✆ ✕ 🛈 🛏 💻 ➾

ALPENA

◆◆◆◆ **Holiday Inn** SH
(989) 356-2151. **$81-$109.** 1000 Hwy 23 N. On US 23, 1 mi n. Int corridors. **Pets:** Accepted.
ASK S✆ ✕ 🛈 🛏 💻 🍴 ➾ ✕

ANN ARBOR

◆◆ **Candlewood Suites** SH
(734) 663-2818. **$74-$169.** 701 Waymarket Way. I-94, exit 175 (Ann Arbor/Saline Rd), just e on Eisenhower Rd. Int corridors. **Pets:** Large, other species. $75 one-time fee/room. Service with restrictions.
ASK ✕ 🛁 🛈 🛏 💻

◆◆ **Extended Stay America** SH
(734) 332-1980. **$66-$71.** 1501 Briarwood Circle Dr. I-94, exit 177 (State St), just nw. Int corridors. **Pets:** Medium, other species. $75 one-time fee/pet. Service with restrictions, crate.

✕ 🛁 🍳 🛈 🛏 💻

◆◆◆◆ **Hampton Inn-North** SH
(734) 996-4444. **$84-$164.** 2300 Green Rd. US 23, exit 41 (Plymouth Rd), just nw. Int corridors. **Pets:** Accepted.
ASK S✆ ✕ 🛁 🍳 🛈 🛏 💻 🍴 ➾

◆◆◆◆ **Hawthorn Suites** SH
(734) 327-0011. **$110-$145.** 3535 Green Rd. US 23, exit 41 (Plymouth Rd), just sw. Int corridors. **Pets:** $100 one-time fee/room. Service with restrictions, crate.
ASK S✆ ✕ 🛁 🍳 🛈 🛏 💻 ➾ ✕

◆◆◆ **Red Roof Inn #7045** M
(734) 996-5800. **$58-$79.** 3621 Plymouth Rd. US 23, exit 41 (Plymouth Rd), just nw. Ext corridors. **Pets:** Small. $25 one-time fee/pet. No service, supervision.
✕ 🍳 🛈 🛏

◆◆◆◆ **Residence Inn by Marriott** SH ❖
(734) 996-5666. **$99-$199.** 800 Victor's Way. I-94, exit 177 (State St), just ne. Ext/int corridors. **Pets:** Large, other species. $20 daily fee/room. Service with restrictions.
ASK ✕ 🍳 🛈 🛏 💻 ➾ ✕

◆◆◆◆ **Super 8 Motel** SH
(734) 741-8888. **Call for rates.** 2910 Jackson Ave. I-94, exit 172 (Jackson Ave), just e. Ext/int corridors. **Pets:** Accepted.
✕ 🛈 🛏 💻

AU GRES

◆◆◆ **Best Western Pinewood Lodge** SH
(989) 876-4060. **$74-$84.** 510 W US 23. Just w on US 23. Int corridors. **Pets:** Other species. $10 one-time fee/pet. Supervision.
ASK S✆ ✕ 🛈 🛏 💻 ➾

BAD AXE

◆◆◆ **Econo Lodge Inns & Suites** SH
(989) 269-3200. **$69-$99.** 898 N Van Dyke Rd. Just s of jct SR 142 and 53 (Van Dyke Rd). Int corridors. **Pets:** Accepted.
ASK S✆ ✕ ➾

BARAGA

◆◆◆ **Super 8 Motel** SH
(906) 353-6680. **$54-$59.** 790 Michigan Ave. 1 mi w on SR 38. Int corridors. **Pets:** Medium. $5 one-time fee/room. Supervision.
ASK S✆ ✕ 🛈 🛏

BATTLE CREEK

AAA WWW **Baymont Inn & Suites-Battle Creek** **SH**
(269) 979-5400. **$69-$119.** 4725 Beckley Rd. I-94, exit 97 (Capital Ave), just sw. Int corridors. **Pets:** Other species. Designated rooms.
[SAVE] [S6] [X] [≈] [⌖] [♿] [📼] [🛏]

WWW **Days Inn** **M** ❀
(269) 979-3561. **$40-$79, 3 day notice.** 4786 Beckley Rd. I-94, exit 97 (Capital Ave), just s. Ext corridors. **Pets:** Other species. Crate.
[ASK] [S6] [X] [♿]

WWW **Motel 6–4250** **M**
(269) 979-1141. **$42-$54.** 4775 Beckley Rd. I-94, exit 97 (Capital Ave), just sw. Ext corridors. **Pets:** Accepted.
[ASK] [S6] [X] [&M] [⌖] [🛏]

WWW **Ramada Inn & Suites** **M**
(269) 979-1100. **$55-$120.** 5050 Beckley Rd. I-94, exit 97 (Capital Ave), just s. Ext corridors. **Pets:** Accepted.
[ASK] [S6] [X] [♿] [📼] [🍴] [🛏]

BAY CITY

WWW **AmericInn of Bay City** **SH** ❀
(989) 671-0071. **Call for rates.** 3915 3 Mile Rd. I-75, exit 164. Int corridors. **Pets:** Other species. $25 deposit/room. Designated rooms, service with restrictions, supervision.
[X] [⌖] [♿] [📼] [🛏]

WWW **Holiday Inn** **SH**
(989) 892-3501. **$79-$93.** 501 Saginaw St. Center line on I-75 business loop, SR 15 and 25; downtown. Int corridors. **Pets:** Other species. Service with restrictions, supervision.
[ASK] [S6] [X] [⌖] [📼] [🍴] [🛏]

BAY VIEW

AAA WWW **Comfort Inn** **SH** ❀
(231) 347-3220. **$60-$200.** 1314 US 31 N. Jct US 31 and SR 119. Int corridors. **Pets:** Other species. Supervision.
[SAVE] [S6] [X] [♿] [📼]

BEAR LAKE

AAA WWW **Bella Vista Inn** **M**
(231) 864-3000. **$55-$99.** 12273 US 31. Center; on US 31. Ext corridors. **Pets:** Medium, dogs only. $10 daily fee/pet. Service with restrictions, crate.
[SAVE] [X] [♿] [📼] [🛏]

BENTON HARBOR

AAA WWW **Best Western T.C. Inn & Suites** **SH**
(269) 925-1880. **$49-$99.** 1598 Mall Dr. I-94, exit 29 (Pipestone Rd), just n to Mall Dr, then just w. Int corridors. **Pets:** Accepted.
[SAVE] [X] [♿] [🛏]

WWW **Ramada Inn** **SH**
(269) 927-1172. **$69-$99.** 798 Ferguson Dr. I-94, exit 28, just sw. Int corridors. **Pets:** Accepted.
[ASK] [S6] [X] [♿] [📼] [🍴] [🛏] [X]

WWW **Red Roof Inn #7043** **M**
(269) 927-2484. **$43-$72.** 1630 Mall Dr. I-94, exit 29 (Pipestone Rd), just n, then just w. Ext corridors. **Pets:** Other species. Service with restrictions, supervision.
[X] [&M] [≈] [♿]

BIG RAPIDS

WWWW **Holiday Inn Hotel & Conference Center** **SH**
(231) 796-4400. **$86-$95.** 1005 Perry St. US 131, exit 139, 1.3 mi e on SR 20. Int corridors. **Pets:** Large. $10 daily fee/room. Supervision.
[ASK] [S6] [X] [&M] [⌖] [♿] [📼] [🍴] [🛏] [X]

BIRCH RUN

AAA WWW **Super 8 Motel** **SH**
(989) 624-4440. **$47-$72.** 9235 E Birch Run Rd. I-75, exit 136 (Birch Run Rd), just e. Int corridors. **Pets:** Small. Service with restrictions, supervision.
[SAVE] [S6] [X] [♿] [X]

BREVORT

WWW **Chapel Hill Motel** **M**
(906) 292-5521. **$35-$54, 3 day notice.** 4422 W US 2. Center. Ext/int corridors. **Pets:** Accepted.
[X] [♿] [📼] [X]

BRIDGEPORT

AAA WWW **Baymont Inn & Suites-Frankenmuth/Bridgeport** **SH**
(989) 777-3000. **$59-$119.** 6460 Dixie Hwy. I-75, exit 144A. Int corridors. **Pets:** Accepted.
[SAVE] [S6] [X] [⌖] [♿] [📼] [🛏]

BROOKLYN

WWW **Super 8 Motel** **SH**
(517) 592-0888. **$58-$130.** 155 Wamplers Rd. Jct SR 50 and 124; downtown. Int corridors. **Pets:** Other species. $5 daily fee/pet. Service with restrictions, supervision.
[ASK] [S6] [X] [&M] [⌖] [♿]

BYRON CENTER

AAA WWW **AmeriHost Inn-Grand Rapids South** **SH**
(616) 827-9900. **$89-$99.** 7625 Caterpillar Ct SW. US 131, exit 76. Int corridors. **Pets:** Accepted.
[SAVE] [S6] [X] [⌖] [♿] [📼] [🛏]

CADILLAC

AAA WWW **Econo Lodge** **SH**
(231) 775-6700. **$50-$90.** 2501 Sunnyside Dr. Jct SR 55 and 115. Ext/int corridors. **Pets:** Medium. $10 one-time fee/room. Service with restrictions, supervision.
[SAVE] [S6] [X] [♿] [📼]

AAA WWW **McGuires Resort** **SH** ❀
(231) 775-9947. **$79-$199, 7 day notice.** 7880 Mackinaw Tr. US 131, exit 177, 0.7 mi n, then 0.5 mi w. Int corridors. **Pets:** $15 daily fee/room. Designated rooms, service with restrictions, crate.
[SAVE] [X] [⌖] [♿] [📼] [🍴] [🛏] [X]

CALUMET

WWW **AmericInn of Calumet** **SH**
(906) 337-6463. **$81-$131.** 56925 S 6th St. US 41; just w of Visitors Center. Int corridors. **Pets:** Accepted.
[ASK] [S6] [X] [⌖] [♿] [📼] [🛏] [X]

CASCADE

AAA WWW **AmeriSuites Grand Rapids/Airport** **SH**
(616) 940-8100. **$79-$99.** 5401 28th St Ct SE. I-96, exit 43B, just e on SR 11. Int corridors. **Pets:** Accepted.
[SAVE] [S6] [X] [♿] [📼] [🛏] [X]

WWW **Baymont Inn-Grand Rapids Airport** **SH**
(616) 956-3300. **$69-$99.** 2873 Kraft Ave SE. I-96, exit 43B, just e. Int corridors. **Pets:** Accepted.
[ASK] [S6] [X] [♿] [📼]

WWW **Country Inn & Suites by Carlson of Grand Rapids** **SH**
(616) 977-0909. **$69-$79.** 5399 28th St. I-96, exit 43B, just e on SR 11. Int corridors. **Pets:** Accepted.
[ASK] [S6] [X] [&M] [≈] [⌖] [♿] [📼] [🛏]

▽▽▽▽ Crowne Plaza Hotel-Grand Rapids M ☙
(616) 957-1770. **$89-$109.** 5700 28th St SE. I-96, exit 43B, 0.3 mi e on SR 11. Int corridors. **Pets:** Small. $50 deposit/room, $10 daily fee/pet. Designated rooms, service with restrictions, supervision.
A$K S🐾 ✕ 🌁 🐾 🖥 🖥 🍽 🏊 ✕

▽▽ Days Inn Airport SH
(616) 949-8400. **$65-$75.** 5500 28th St SE. I-96, exit 43B, just e on SR 11. Int corridors. **Pets:** Accepted.
A$K ✕ 🖥 🖥 🏊 ✕

Ⓐ ▽ Exel Inn of Grand Rapids SH
(616) 957-3000. **$46-$66.** 4855 28th St SE. I-96, exit 43A, 0.5 mi w on SR 11. Int corridors. **Pets:** Small, other species. Designated rooms, service with restrictions, supervision.
SAVE S🐾 ✕ 🖥 🖥

Ⓐ ▽▽▽ Hampton Inn SH ☙
(616) 956-9304. **$83-$99.** 4981 28th St SE. I-96, exit 43A, 0.5 mi w on SR 11. Int corridors. **Pets:** Other species. Service with restrictions, supervision.
SAVE S🐾 ✕ 🌁 🖥 🖥 🏊

▽▽ Howard Johnson Express Inn & Suites SH
(616) 940-1777. **$69-$109.** 2985 Kraft Ave SE. I-96, exit 43B, 0.5 mi se. Int corridors. **Pets:** Accepted.
A$K S🐾 🖥 🖥

CEDARVILLE

Ⓐ ▽▽▽ Cedarville Inn M
(906) 484-2266. **$79-$139.** 106 W M-134. On SR 134; just w of SR 129. Int corridors. **Pets:** Designated rooms, supervision.
SAVE ✕ 🖥 🖥 🏊 ✕

CHARLEVOIX

▽▽ AmericInn Lodge & Suites SH
(231) 237-0988. **$79-$179.** 11800 US 31 N. On US 31, 2.4 mi n. Int corridors. **Pets:** Accepted.
A$K S🐾 ✕ 🖥M 🖥 🖥 🖥 🏊 🏊

CHARLOTTE

Ⓐ ▽▽ Super 8 Motel SH
(517) 543-8288. **$60-$82.** 828 E Shepherd St. I-69, exit 60 (SR 50), just w. Int corridors. **Pets:** Other species. Service with restrictions, supervision.
SAVE ✕ 🖥

CHEBOYGAN

Ⓐ ▽ Birch Haus Motel M
(231) 627-5862. **$40-$65.** 1301 Mackinaw Ave. On US 23, 0.8 mi nw. Ext corridors. **Pets:** Medium. $5 daily fee/pet. Designated rooms, service with restrictions, supervision.
SAVE ✕ 🖥

▽ Continental Inn M
(231) 627-7164. **$39-$120.** 613 N Main St. Jct US 23 and SR 27. Ext corridors. **Pets:** $6 daily fee/room. Service with restrictions, crate.
A$K S🐾 ✕ 🖥 🖥 🏊

Ⓐ ▽ Pine River Motel M
(231) 627-5119. **$30-$80, 3 day notice.** 102 Lafayette. 0.5 mi e on US 23. Ext corridors. **Pets:** $10 one-time fee/pet. Supervision.
SAVE ✕ 🖥

CHELSEA

▽▽▽ Chelsea Comfort Inn & Conference Center SH
(734) 433-8000. **$94-$194.** 1645 Commerce Park Dr. I-94, exit 159 (SR 52/Main St), just n. Int corridors. **Pets:** Other species. Service with restrictions, supervision.
A$K S🐾 ✕ 🖥M 🖥 🖥 🖥 🏊

CHRISTMAS

Ⓐ ▽▽▽ Pair-A-Dice Inn SH
(906) 387-3500. **$69-$99.** E7889 W M-28. On SR 28; center. Int corridors. **Pets:** Dogs only. $10 deposit/room. Service with restrictions, supervision.
SAVE ✕ 🖥 🖥

COLDWATER

Ⓐ ▽▽▽ Ramada Inn SH
(517) 278-2017. **$59-$189.** 1000 Orleans Blvd. I-69, exit 13 (US 12), 0.3 mi w, just n on N Michigan Ave, then just e. Int corridors. **Pets:** Medium, other species. $10 one-time fee/pet. Designated rooms, service with restrictions, supervision.
SAVE S🐾 ✕ 🖥 🖥 🍽 🏊 ✕

▽▽ Red Roof Inn SH
(517) 279-1199. **$49-$89.** 348 S Willowbrook Rd. I-69, exit 13 (US 12), just e. Int corridors. **Pets:** Medium. $25 deposit/pet. Service with restrictions, supervision.
A$K S🐾 ✕ 🖥M 🖥 🖥

Ⓐ ▽▽▽ Super 8 Motel SH
(517) 278-8833. **$61-$75.** 600 Orleans Blvd. I-69, exit 13 (US 12), 0.3 mi w on E Chicago St, just n on N Michigan Ave, then just e. Int corridors. **Pets:** Accepted.
SAVE S🐾 ✕ 🖥M 🖥 🖥

COMSTOCK PARK

▽▽ Swan Inn SH
(616) 784-1224. **$48-$80.** 5182 Alpine Ave. Jct I-96 and Alpine Ave, 3 mi n on SR 37. Ext corridors. **Pets:** Other species.
S🐾 ✕ 🖥 🖥 🍽 🏊

COPPER HARBOR

▽ Lake Fanny Hooe Resort M
(906) 289-4451. **$69-$99, 7 day notice.** 505 2nd St. Just s on Manganese Rd. Ext corridors. **Pets:** Other species. $7 daily fee/pet. Service with restrictions, supervision.
✕ 🖥 🖥 🖥 ✕ 🖥 🖥

DETROIT METROPOLITAN AREA

ALLEN PARK

Best Western Greenfield Inn SH ☙
(313) 271-1600. **$99-$139.** 3000 Enterprise Dr. I-94, exit 206 (Oakwood Blvd), just s, then just w. Int corridors. **Pets:** Medium, dogs only. $100 deposit/room. Designated rooms, service with restrictions, supervision.

Holiday Inn Express & Suites SH ☙
(313) 323-3500. **$120-$190.** 3600 Enterprise Dr. I-94, exit 206 (Oakwood Blvd), just s, then just w. Int corridors. **Pets:** Medium, dogs only. $50 deposit/room. Service with restrictions, supervision.

AUBURN HILLS

AmeriSuites (Detroit/Auburn Hills) SH ☙
(248) 475-9393. **$75-$129.** 1545 Opdyke Rd. I-75, exit 79 (University Dr), just w to Opdyke Rd, then just n. Int corridors. **Pets:** Small, other species. Service with restrictions, supervision.

Homestead Studio Suites Hotel-Detroit/Auburn Hills SH
(248) 340-8888. **$80-$95.** 3315 University Dr. I-75, exit 79 (University Dr), 0.9 mi e. Int corridors. **Pets:** Accepted.

Staybridge Suites SH
(248) 322-4600. **$169-$189.** 2050 Featherstone Rd. I-75, exit 79 (University Dr), just w, 0.5 mi s on Opdyke Rd, then just e. Int corridors. **Pets:** Accepted.

Wellesley Inn & Suites (Detroit/Auburn Hills) SH
(248) 335-5200. **$85-$95.** 2100 Featherstone Rd. I-75, exit 79 (University Dr), just w to Opdyke Rd, then 0.5 mi s. Int corridors. **Pets:** Medium. $25 one-time fee/room. Service with restrictions, supervision.

BELLEVILLE

Comfort Inn SH
(734) 697-8556. **$59-$179.** 45945 S I-94 Service Dr. I-94, exit 190 (Belleville Rd), just s to Service Dr, then 0.6 mi w. Int corridors. **Pets:** Accepted.

Red Roof Inn Metro Airport #7183 M
(734) 697-2244. **$59-$73.** 45501 N I-94 Service Dr. I-94, exit 190 (Belleville Rd), just n. Ext corridors. **Pets:** Accepted.

Super 8 Motel SH
(734) 699-1888. **$55-$95.** 45707 S I-94 Service Dr. I-94, exit 190 (Belleville Rd), just s. Int corridors. **Pets:** Accepted.

BIRMINGHAM

Barclay Inn Birmingham SH
(248) 646-7300. **$79-$189.** 34952 Woodward Ave. On SR 1, jct Woodward Ave and Maple Rd; center. Ext/int corridors. **Pets:** Accepted.

Hamilton Hotel SH
(248) 642-6200. **$151-$161.** 35270 Woodward Ave. Jct Woodward Ave and Maple Rd; center. Int corridors. **Pets:** Medium, dogs only. $25 daily fee/room. Service with restrictions, supervision.

CANTON

Baymont Inn & Suites Detroit-Canton SH
(734) 981-1808. **$64-$104.** 41211 Ford Rd. I-275, exit 25 (Ford Rd), just w to jct Haggerty Rd. Int corridors. **Pets:** Medium. Service with restrictions, crate.

Motel 6-1070 M
(734) 981-5000. **$45-$55.** 41216 Ford Rd. I-275, exit 25 (Ford Rd), just w to jct Haggerty Rd. Ext corridors. **Pets:** Accepted.

Super 8 Motel-Canton SH ☙
(734) 722-8880. **$64-$89.** 3933 Lotz Rd. I-275, exit 22 (Michigan Ave), just e on US 12, then just s. Int corridors. **Pets:** Medium, dogs only. $10 daily fee/pet. Service with restrictions.

DEARBORN

Red Roof Inn-Dearborn #7182 M
(313) 278-9732. **$68-$94.** 24130 Michigan Ave. Jct US 12 (Michigan Ave) and SR 24 (Telegraph Rd). Ext corridors. **Pets:** Accepted.

The Ritz-Carlton, Dearborn LH ☙
(313) 441-2000. **$219-$295.** 300 Town Center Dr. SR 39 (Southfield Frwy), between Ford Rd and Michigan Ave exits, on Service Dr. Int corridors. **Pets:** Medium. $150 one-time fee/room. Service with restrictions, crate.

TownePlace Suites SH
(313) 271-0200. **$99-$109.** 6141 Mercury Dr. SR 39 (Southfield Frwy), exit 7 (Ford Rd), just e, then 0.8 mi n. Int corridors. **Pets:** Medium, other species. $5 daily fee/room, $125 one-time fee/pet. Service with restrictions.

DETROIT

Comfort Inn-Downtown Detroit SH
(313) 567-8888. **$79-$189.** 1999 E Jefferson Ave. I-375, exit E Jefferson Ave, 0.5 mi e. Int corridors. **Pets:** Accepted.

Holiday Inn Express LH
(313) 887-7000. **$80-$170.** 1020 Washington Blvd. Corner of Washington Blvd and Michigan Ave. Int corridors. **Pets:** Accepted.

Residence Inn By Marriott-Dearborn SH ☙
(313) 441-1700. **$59-$199.** 5777 Southfield Service Dr. SR 39 (Southfield Frwy), exit Ford Rd, just w. Ext corridors. **Pets:** Other species. $75 one-time fee/room. Service with restrictions.

FARMINGTON HILLS

Candlewood Suites SH
(248) 324-0540. **$89-$109.** 37555 Hills Tech Dr. I-696, exit I-96 E/I-275 S/SR 5, just s to SR 5 N, 2 mi n to 12 Mile Rd, 1.3 mi e on 12 Mile Rd, then 0.3 mi s on Halsted Rd. Int corridors. **Pets:** Medium. $75 one-time fee/pet. Service with restrictions, supervision.

Red Roof Inn-Farmington Hills #7038 M
(248) 478-8640. **$52-$71.** 24300 Sinacola Ct. I-96/275 and SR 5, exit 165 (Grand River Ave), just w. Ext corridors. **Pets:** Accepted.

LAKE ORION

AAA ▼▼▼▼ Best Western Palace Inn 🆂🅷
(248) 391-2755. **$80-$90.** 2755 N Lapeer Rd. I-75, exit 81 (Lapeer Rd), 3.3 mi n. Ext/int corridors. **Pets:** Small. $25 one-time fee/pet. Designated rooms, service with restrictions, supervision.
🆂🅰🆅 Ⓢ⑥ ☒ ⓒ🅼 ⓒ 📠 💻 🏊 ☒

LIVONIA

AAA ▼▼▼▼ AmeriSuites (Detroit/Livonia) 🆂🅷
(734) 953-9224. **$79-$109.** 19300 Haggerty Rd. I-275, exit 169A (7 Mile Rd), just w. Int corridors. **Pets:** Medium. $10 daily fee/room. Service with restrictions, crate.
🆂🅰🆅 Ⓢ⑥ ☒ ⓒ 📠 💻 🏊

▼▼▼▼ Residence Inn Detroit-Livonia 🆂🅷
(734) 462-4201. **$89-$139.** 17250 Fox Dr. I-275, exit 170 (6 Mile Rd), just w. Int corridors. **Pets:** Accepted.
🅰🆂🅺 Ⓢ⑥ ☒ ⓒ🅼 🅐 ⓒ 📠 💻 🏊 ☒

MADISON HEIGHTS

▼ Motel 6 Madison Heights #1109 🅼
(248) 583-0500. **$45-$58.** 32700 Barrington Rd. I-75, exit 65A (14 Mile Rd), just e. Ext corridors. **Pets:** Service with restrictions, supervision.
Ⓢ⑥ ☒ ⓒ

▼▼ Red Roof Inn #7084 🅼 🐾
(248) 583-4700. **$54-$76.** 32511 Concord Dr. I-75, exit 65A (14 Mile Rd), just e, then just s. Ext corridors. **Pets:** Large. Service with restrictions, crate.
☒ 🅐 📠

▼▼▼▼ Residence Inn by Marriott-Madison Heights 🆂🅷
(248) 583-4322. **$159.** 32650 Stephenson Hwy. I-75, exit 65B (W 14 Mile Rd), just w, then just s. Ext corridors. **Pets:** Medium, other species. $75 one-time fee/room. Service with restrictions, crate.
☒ 🅐 📠 💻 🏊 ☒

NOVI

▼▼▼ Residence Inn by Marriott-Detroit/Novi 🆂🅷 🐾
(248) 735-7400. **$99-$599.** 27477 Caberet Dr. I-96, exit 162 (Novi Rd), just n to 12 Mile Rd, then just w. Int corridors. **Pets:** Large, other species. $75 one-time fee/room. Service with restrictions, supervision.
🅰🆂🅺 Ⓢ⑥ ☒ ⓒ🅼 🅐 ⓒ 📠 💻 🏊

▼▼ TownePlace Suites 🆂🅷
(248) 305-5533. **$114-$124.** 42600 11 Mile Rd. I-96, exit 162 (Novi Rd), just s, 0.5 mi e on Crescent Dr, then just s on Town Center Dr. Int corridors. **Pets:** Medium. $200 one-time fee/room. Service with restrictions, crate.
☒ ⓒ 📠 💻 🏊

PLYMOUTH

▼▼ Red Roof Inn-Plymouth #7016 🅼
(734) 459-3300. **$54-$76.** 39700 Ann Arbor Rd. I-275, exit 28 (Ann Arbor Rd), just e. Ext corridors. **Pets:** Large. Service with restrictions, supervision.
☒ 🅐 ⓒ 📠

PONTIAC

▼▼▼▼ Residence Inn by Marriott Detroit Pontiac/Auburn Hills 🆂🅷 🐾
(248) 858-8664. **$139-$179.** 3333 Centerpoint Pkwy. I-75, exit 75 (Square Lake Rd), w via Opdyke Rd. Int corridors. **Pets:** Large, other species. $75 one-time fee/room. Service with restrictions.
🅰🆂🅺 Ⓢ⑥ ☒ 🅐 ⓒ 📠 💻 🏊 ☒

ROCHESTER HILLS

▼▼ Red Roof Inn #719 🅼
(248) 853-6400. **$58-$85.** 2580 Crooks Rd. Jct Hall (SR 59) and Crooks rds. Ext corridors. **Pets:** Medium, other species. Service with restrictions, supervision.
☒ 🅐 ⓒ 📠

ROMULUS

AAA ▼▼▼ Baymont Inn & Suites Detroit-Airport 🆂🅷
(734) 722-6000. **$59-$84.** 9000 Wickham Rd. I-94, exit 198 (Merriman Rd), just n, then just w. Int corridors. **Pets:** Accepted.
🆂🅰🆅 Ⓢ⑥ ☒ 🅐 📠 💻

▼▼▼ Detroit Metro Airport Marriott 🆂🅷
(734) 729-7555. **$79-$169.** 30559 Flynn Dr. I-94, exit 198 (Merriman Rd), just n, then 0.3 mi e. Int corridors. **Pets:** Accepted.
🅰🆂🅺 Ⓢ⑥ ☒ ⓒ🅼 🅐 📠 💻 🍴 🏊

AAA ▼▼▼ Four Points by Sheraton Detroit Metro Airport 🆂🅷
(734) 729-9000. **$79-$99.** 8800 Wickham Rd. I-94, exit 198 (Merriman Rd), just n, then just e. Int corridors. **Pets:** Accepted.
🆂🅰🆅 Ⓢ⑥ ☒ 🅐 📠 💻 🍴 🏊

▼▼ Super 8 Motel-Romulus 🆂🅷
(734) 946-8808. **$54-$79.** 9863 Middlebelt Rd. I-94, exit 199 (Middlebelt Rd), 0.8 mi s. Int corridors. **Pets:** Accepted.
🅰🆂🅺 Ⓢ⑥ ☒ ⓒ🅼 📠

AAA ▼▼▼▼ The Westin Detroit Metropolitan Airport 🅻🅷
(734) 942-6500. **$79-$259.** 2501 Worldgateway Pl. I-94, exit 198 (Merriman Rd); at McNamara Terminal. Int corridors. **Pets:** Medium, dogs only. $25 deposit/room. Service with restrictions, supervision.
🆂🅰🆅 Ⓢ⑥ ☒ ⓒ🅼 ⓒ 📠 💻 🍴 🏊

ROSEVILLE

AAA ▼▼ Baymont Inn & Suites Detroit-Roseville 🆂🅷
(586) 296-6910. **$59-$84.** 20675 13 Mile Rd. I-94, exit 232 (Little Mack Ave), just s. Int corridors. **Pets:** Accepted.
🆂🅰🆅 Ⓢ⑥ ☒ 🅐 📠 💻

AAA ▼▼▼ Best Western Georgian Inn 🅼
(586) 294-0400. **$69-$179.** 31327 Gratiot Ave. I-94, exit 232 (Little Mack Ave), just s, 0.5 mi n on 13 Mile Rd, then just n. Ext corridors. **Pets:** Medium, dogs only. $8 daily fee/pet. Service with restrictions, crate.
🆂🅰🆅 Ⓢ⑥ ☒ 📠 💻 🍴 🏊

▼▼ Red Roof Inn #7012 🅼
(586) 296-0310. **$48-$75.** 31800 Little Mack Ave. I-94, exit 232 (Little Mack Ave), just n. Ext corridors. **Pets:** Medium, other species. Service with restrictions, crate.
☒ ⓒ 📠

SOUTHFIELD

▼▼ Candlewood Suites 🆂🅷
(248) 945-0010. **$69-$159.** 1 Corporate Dr. SR 10 (Northwestern Hwy), exit Lasher Rd, just e. Int corridors. **Pets:** $25 one-time fee/pet. Service with restrictions.
☒ ⓒ🅼 ⓒ 📠 💻

▼▼▼ Hawthorn Suites Ltd 🆂🅷
(248) 350-2400. **$89-$149.** 25100 Northwestern Hwy. SR 10 (Northwestern Hwy), exit 10 Mile Rd. Int corridors. **Pets:** Medium. $150 one-time fee/room. Crate.
🅰🆂🅺 ☒ ⓒ🅼 ⓒ 📠 💻 🏊

▼▼ Holiday Inn-Southfield LH
(248) 353-7700. **$85-$149.** 26555 Telegraph Rd. I-696, exit 9 (Telegraph Rd), just s on US 24 (Telegraph Rd). Int corridors. **Pets:** $10 one-time fee/room. Designated rooms, service with restrictions, supervision.

ASK ✕ 🔥M 🐾 🛏 🍴 ➛ ✕

▼▼ Homestead Studio Suites
Hotel-Detroit/Southfield SH
(248) 213-4500. **$74-$89.** 28500 Northwestern Hwy. I-696, exit 9, just nw of jct US 24 (Telegraph Rd). Int corridors. **Pets:** Accepted.

ASK S✕ 🔥M 🐾 🛏

▼▼ Red Roof Inn-Southfield #7133 M
(248) 353-7200. **$66-$80.** 27660 Northwestern Hwy. I-696, exit 9, just nw of Telegraph Rd. Ext corridors. **Pets:** Medium. Service with restrictions, supervision.

✕ 🔥M 🐾 🛏

AAA ▼▼▼▼ Westin Hotel Southfield-Detroit LH
(248) 827-4000. **$89-$270.** 1500 Town Center. SR 10 (Northwestern Hwy), exit 10 (Mile/Evergreen rds), 0.3 mi n. Int corridors. **Pets:** Accepted.

SAVE S✕ 🔥M 🐾 🛏 🍴 ➛ ✕

SOUTHGATE

AAA ▼▼▼ Baymont Inn & Suites Detroit-Southgate SH
(734) 374-3000. **$64-$89.** 12888 Reeck Rd. I-75, exit 37 (Northline Rd), just w. Int corridors. **Pets:** Medium, other species. $25 deposit/room. Designated rooms, service with restrictions, supervision.

SAVE S✕ 🐾 🛏

AAA ▼▼▼ Best Value Inn & Suites M
(734) 287-8340. **$54-$70.** 18777 Northline Rd. I-75, exit 37 (Northline Rd), just w. Ext corridors. **Pets:** Accepted.

SAVE S✕ 🐾 🛏 ➛

STERLING HEIGHTS

▼▼ TownePlace Suites SH 🐾
(586) 566-0900. **$89-$119.** 14800 Lakeside Cir. 1 mi e of jct SR 53 (Van Dyke Ave) and SR 59 (Hall Rd). Int corridors. **Pets:** Other species. $75 one-time fee/room. Service with restrictions, crate.

ASK S✕ 🔥M 🐾 🛏 ➛

TAYLOR

▼▼ Red Roof Inn-Taylor #7189 M
(734) 374-1150. **$55-$80.** 21230 Eureka Rd. I-75, exit 36 (Eureka Rd), just w. Ext corridors. **Pets:** Accepted.

✕

TROY

▼▼▼ Drury Inn & Suites-Troy SH
(248) 524-3330. **$75-$135.** 575 W Big Beaver Rd. I-75, exit 69 (Big Beaver Rd), just e. Int corridors. **Pets:** Large, other species. Service with restrictions, supervision.

ASK ✕ 🐾 🛏 🍴 ➛

▼▼ Holiday Inn-Troy SH
(248) 689-7500. **$79-$139.** 2537 Rochester Ct. I-75, exit 67 (Rochester Rd), 0.3 mi sw, then just w. Int corridors. **Pets:** $25 one-time fee/room. Service with restrictions.

ASK S✕ 🛏 🍴 ➛

▼▼ Red Roof Inn-Troy #7021 M
(248) 689-4391. **$58-$83.** 2350 Rochester Ct. I-75, exit 67 (Rochester Rd), 0.3 mi sw. Ext corridors. **Pets:** Accepted.

✕ 🐾

▼▼▼ Residence Inn by Marriott SH
(248) 689-6856. **$134.** 2600 Livernois Rd. I-75, exit 69 (Big Beaver Rd), 0.5 mi e to Livernois Rd, then 0.5 mi s. Ext corridors. **Pets:** Accepted.

ASK S✕ 🐾 🛏 ➛ ✕

UTICA

AAA ▼▼▼ AmeriSuites (Detroit/Utica) SH
(586) 803-0100. **$79-$149.** 45400 Park Ave. Jct Van Dyke Ave (SR 53) and Hall Rd (SR 59). Int corridors. **Pets:** Other species. $10 daily fee/room. Service with restrictions, crate.

SAVE S✕ 🔥M 🐾 🛏 ➛

AAA ▼▼▼ Baymont Inn & Suites Detroit-Utica SH
(586) 731-4700. **$79-$99.** 45311 Park Ave. Jct Van Dyke Ave (SR 53) and Hall Rd (SR 59), just n. Int corridors. **Pets:** Accepted.

SAVE S✕ 🐾 🛏 ➛

AAA ▼▼▼ Staybridge Suites-Utica SH
(586) 323-0101. **$129-$189.** 46155 Utica Park Blvd. Jct Van Dyke Ave (SR 53) and Hall Rd (SR 59), just n. Int corridors. **Pets:** Accepted.

SAVE S✕ 🛏 ➛

WARREN

AAA ▼▼▼ Baymont Inn & Suites Detroit-Warren Tech
Center SH
(586) 574-0550. **$60-$90.** 30900 Van Dyke Ave. I-696, exit 23 (Van Dyke Ave), 2 mi n on SR 53. Int corridors. **Pets:** Service with restrictions, supervision.

SAVE S✕ 🐾 🛏

AAA ▼▼▼ Hawthorn Suites Ltd SH
(586) 264-8800. **$89.** 7601 Chicago Rd. I-696, exit 23 (Van Dyke Ave), 1.8 mi n. Int corridors. **Pets:** Accepted.

SAVE S✕ 🛏 ➛

▼▼▼ Homewood Suites by Hilton SH
(586) 558-7870. **$79-$159, 3 day notice.** 30180 N Civic Center Blvd. I-696, exit 23 (Van Dyke Ave), 2 mi n. Ext/int corridors. **Pets:** Accepted.

ASK S✕ 🔥M 🐾 🛏 ➛

▼▼ Red Roof Inn-Warren #7070 M
(586) 573-4300. **$57-$75.** 26300 Dequindre Rd. I-696, exit 20 (Dequindre Rd), just ne. Ext corridors. **Pets:** Accepted.

✕ 🐾 🛏

END METROPOLITAN AREA

DOUGLAS

▼▼ AmericInn of Saugatuck/Douglas SH 🐾
(269) 857-8581. **$63-$254, 7 day notice.** 2905 Blue Star Hwy. I-196, exit 36, 0.3 mi n. Int corridors. **Pets:** Medium, dogs only. $30 daily fee/room. Designated rooms, service with restrictions, supervision.

ASK ✕ 🔥M 🐾 🛏 ➛

EAGLE HARBOR

AAA ▼▼ Shoreline Resort M
(906) 289-4441. **$70-$77.** 201 Front St, F #2015. On SR 26. Ext corridors. **Pets:** Other species. Supervision.

SAVE S✕ 🍴 ✕ 🐾

EAST LANSING

▼▼▼ Residence Inn by Marriott SH
(517) 332-7711. **$124-$159.** 1600 E Grand River Ave. US 127, exit Grand River Ave, 2.6 mi se on SR 43. Ext corridors. **Pets:** Accepted.

ASK SD ✕ 🐾 🏢 💻 🏊 ✕

▼▼ TownePlace Suites SH
(517) 203-1000. **$89-$109.** 2855 Hannah Blvd. I-96, exit 110 (Okemos Rd), just n, 0.5 mi w on Jolly Rd, then 0.4 mi n on Hagedorn Rd. Int corridors. **Pets:** Accepted.

ASK SD ✕ 🐾 🏢 💻 🏊

EAST TAWAS

▼▼▼ Holiday Inn-Tawas Bay Resort SH
(989) 362-8601. **$65-$156, 3 day notice.** 300 E Bay St. On US 23 N. Int corridors. **Pets:** $30 one-time fee/room. Crate.

ASK SD ✕ 🏢 💻 🍴 🏊 ✕

ESCANABA

◬◬ ▼ Hiawatha Motel M
(906) 786-1341. **$50-$60.** 2400 Ludington St. 0.5 mi w on US 2/41. Ext corridors. **Pets:** Other species. $5 daily fee/room. Service with restrictions, supervision.

SAVE SD ✕ 🏢

FENTON

▼▼▼ Holiday Inn Express Hotel & Suites SH
(810) 714-7171. **$70-$160.** 17800 Silver Pkwy. US 23, exit 78 (Owen Rd), just w, then 1 mi n. Int corridors. **Pets:** Small. Service with restrictions, supervision.

ASK SD ✕ 🐾 🐾 🏢 💻 🏊

FLINT

▼▼ AmericInn Flint SH 🐾
(810) 233-9000. **Call for rates.** 6075 Hill 23 Dr. US 23, exit 90 (Hill Rd). Int corridors. **Pets:** Other species. Designated rooms, service with restrictions, supervision.

✕ 🏢 💻 🏊 ✕

◬◬ ▼▼◈ Baymont Inn & Suites-Flint SH
(810) 732-2300. **$69-$109, 30 day notice.** 4160 Pier North Blvd. I-75, exit 122 (Pierson Rd), just w. Int corridors. **Pets:** Medium, other species. $25 deposit/room. Service with restrictions, supervision.

SAVE SD ✕ 🐾 🏢 💻 🏊

◬◬ ▼▼▼ Holiday Inn Express SH
(810) 238-7744. **$72-$199.** 1150 Robert T Longway Blvd. I-475, 8A (Robert T Longway Blvd), just w. Int corridors. **Pets:** Medium, other species. $25 one-time fee/room. Service with restrictions, crate.

SAVE SD ✕ 🐾 🏢 💻

▼ Howard Johnson Lodge M
(810) 733-5910. **$59-$69.** G-3277 Miller Rd. I-75, exit 117B (Miller Rd). Ext corridors. **Pets:** Accepted.

ASK ✕ 🏢 💻 🏊

▼▼ Red Roof Inn-Flint #7004 M
(810) 733-1660. **$49-$70.** G-3219 Miller Rd. I-75, exit 117B (Miller Rd), just w. Ext corridors. **Pets:** Small, other species. Service with restrictions, supervision.

🐾 🐾 🏢

▼▼▼ Residence Inn by Marriott SH
(810) 424-7000. **$110-$160.** 2202 W Hill Rd. US 23, exit 90 (Hill Rd), just e. Int corridors. **Pets:** Accepted.

ASK SD ✕ 🐾 🐾 🏢 💻 🏊

FRANKENMUTH

▼▼▼ Drury Inn & Suites SH
(989) 652-2800. **$85-$140.** 260 S Main St. On SR 83; downtown. Int corridors. **Pets:** Large, other species. Service with restrictions, supervision.

ASK ✕ 🐾 🐾 🏢 💻 🏊

GAYLORD

◬◬ ▼▼◈ Best Value Royal Crest Inn SH 🐾
(989) 732-6451. **$49-$99.** 803 S Otsego Ave. I-75, exit 279, 2.3 mi ne on I-75 business loop. Int corridors. **Pets:** Medium, dogs only. $10 daily fee/room. Service with restrictions, supervision.

SAVE SD ✕ 🏢 💻 🏊 ✕

◬◬ ▼▼▼ Best Western Alpine Lodge SH 🐾
(989) 732-2431. **$69-$109, 7 day notice.** 833 W Main St. I-75, exit 282, 0.3 mi e on SR 32. Ext/int corridors. **Pets:** Small. Designated rooms, service with restrictions, supervision.

SAVE SD ✕ 🏢 💻 🍴 🏊 ✕

◬◬ ▼ Downtown Motel M
(989) 732-5010. **$46-$66.** 208 S Otsego Ave. I-75, exit 282, 0.5 mi e and 0.3 mi s on I-75 business loop. Ext/int corridors. **Pets:** $5 daily fee/pet. Designated rooms, service with restrictions, supervision.

SAVE SD ✕ 🏢

▼▼ Red Roof Inn SH
(989) 731-6331. **$49-$99.** 510 S Wisconsin. I-75, exit 282, just e on SR 32, then 0.4 mi s. Int corridors. **Pets:** Medium. Service with restrictions, supervision.

✕ 🐾 🐾 🏢 💻 🏊

◬◬ ▼ Timberly Motel M
(989) 732-5166. **$48-$84.** 881 S Otsego Ave. I-75, exit 279, 2.5 mi n on I-75 business loop (Old US 27). Ext corridors. **Pets:** Other species. $6 daily fee/pet. Designated rooms, service with restrictions, supervision.

SAVE SD ✕

GRAND MARAIS

◬◬ ▼ ArborGate Inn M
(906) 494-2681. **$40-$65.** Randolph Rd. Just e of SR 77. Ext corridors. **Pets:** Accepted.

SAVE SD ✕ 🏢 ✕ 🅰 🐾

▼ Voyageur's Motel M
(906) 494-2389. **$78.** E Wilson St. 0.5 mi e of SR 77. Ext corridors. **Pets:** Accepted.

ASK ✕ 🏢 💻 ✕ 🅰

GRAND RAPIDS

▼▼ Days Inn-Downtown SH
(616) 235-7611. **$66-$96.** 310 Pearl St NW. US 131, exit Pearl St. Int corridors. **Pets:** Medium. $10 one-time fee/room. Service with restrictions, supervision.

ASK SD ✕ 🏢 💻 🍴 🏊

▼▼▼ Homewood Suites by Hilton SH 🐾
(616) 285-7100. **$99-$129.** 3920 Stahl Dr SE. I-96, exit 43A (28th St SW), 1.5 mi w to E Paris Ave, then just n. Int corridors. **Pets:** $80 one-time fee/pet. Service with restrictions, crate.

ASK SD ✕ 🐾 🐾 🏢 💻 🏊

◬◬ ▼▼▼ Radisson Hotel Grand Rapids Riverfront LH
(616) 363-9001. **$79-$129.** 270 Ann St NW. US 131, exit 88, 1.8 mi n. Int corridors. **Pets:** $20 one-time fee/room. Service with restrictions, supervision.

SAVE SD ✕ 🏢 💻 🍴 🏊 ✕

GRANDVILLE

ⒶⒶⒶ ▽▽▽▽ Comfort Suites 🆂🅷
(616) 667-0733. **$79-$147.** 4520 Kenowa Ave SW. I-196, exit 67, just sw. Int corridors. **Pets:** Accepted.
🆂🅰🆅🅴 🆂🅾 ✖ 🖥 🍽 🏊 ✖

▽▽▽▽ Residence Inn by Marriott Grand Rapids West 🆂🅷
(616) 538-1100. **$79-$169.** 3451 Rivertown Point Ct SW. I-196, exit 67, 1.7 mi e. Int corridors. **Pets:** Small. $75 one-time fee/room. Service with restrictions, crate.
🅰🆂🅺 ✖ 🖥 🍽 🏊 ✖

GRAYLING

ⒶⒶⒶ ▽▽▽ Holiday Inn 🆂🅷 ✿
(989) 348-7611. **$79-$147.** 2650 S Business Loop. I-75 business loop, 0.8 mi s. Ext/int corridors. **Pets:** Service with restrictions, supervision.
🆂🅰🆅🅴 🆂🅾 ✖ 🖥 🍽 🏊 ✖

ⒶⒶⒶ ▽ North Country Lodge Ⓜ
(989) 348-8471. **$58-$160.** 617 N I-75 Business Loop. 1 mi n. Ext corridors. **Pets:** Accepted.
🆂🅰🆅🅴 🆂🅾 ✖ 🖥

▽▽ Super 8 Motel 🆂🅷
(989) 348-8888. **$57-$74.** 5828 Nelson A Miles Pkwy. I-75, exit 251, just w. Int corridors. **Pets:** Accepted.
🅰🆂🅺 ✖ 🖥 🏊 ✖

HANCOCK

▽▽ Best Western Copper Crown Motel 🆂🅷
(906) 482-6111. **$55-$61.** 235 Hancock Ave. On US 41 S; downtown. Ext/int corridors. **Pets:** Accepted.
🅰🆂🅺 🆂🅾 ✖ 🖥 🏊 ✖

HART

▽ Budget Host Hart Motel 🆂🅷
(231) 873-1855. **$49-$119, 14 day notice.** 4143 Polk Rd. US 31, exit Mears/Hart, just e on US 31 business route. Int corridors. **Pets:** Very small, dogs only. $25 deposit/pet. Designated rooms, no service, supervision.
✖ 🖥

ⒶⒶⒶ ▽▽▽ Comfort Inn 🆂🅷
(231) 873-3456. **$65-$179.** 2248 N Comfort Dr. US 31, exit Mears/Hart, just e on US 31 business route. Int corridors. **Pets:** Other species. $10 daily fee/pet. Service with restrictions, supervision.
🆂🅰🆅🅴 🆂🅾 ✖ 🖥 🍽 🏊 ✖

HOLLAND

ⒶⒶⒶ ▽▽▽▽ Best Western Kelly Inn & Suites 🆂🅷
(616) 994-0400. **$99-$159.** 2888 W Shore Dr. US 31, exit Felch St E, just n. Ext/int corridors. **Pets:** Other species. Service with restrictions, supervision.
🆂🅰🆅🅴 🆂🅾 ✖ 🖥 🍽 🏊 ✖

▽▽▽▽ Residence Inn by Marriott 🆂🅷
(616) 393-6900. **$129-$179.** 631 Southpoint Ridge Rd. I-196, exit 49, 0.7 mi n on SR 40. Int corridors. **Pets:** Other species. $75 one-time fee/room. Service with restrictions, crate.
🅰🆂🅺 ✖ 🖥 🍽 🏊 ✖

HOUGHTON

▽▽ Best Value King's Inn 🆂🅷
(906) 482-5000. **$69-$110.** 215 Shelden Ave. On US 41; downtown. Int corridors. **Pets:** Other species. $6 daily fee/room. Service with restrictions.
🅰🆂🅺 🆂🅾 ✖ 🖥 🍽 🏊 ✖

ⒶⒶⒶ ▽▽▽ Best Western-Franklin Square Inn 🆂🅷
(906) 487-1700. **$91-$107.** 820 Shelden Ave. On US 41; downtown. Int corridors. **Pets:** Other species. $9 daily fee/room. Designated rooms, service with restrictions, supervision.
🆂🅰🆅🅴 🆂🅾 ✖ 🖥 🍽 🍴 🏊 ✖

HOUGHTON LAKE

ⒶⒶⒶ ▽▽▽▽ Comfort Suites Lakeside 🆂🅷
(989) 422-4000. **$119-$509, 3 day notice.** 100 Clearview Dr. On Old US 27, 0.5 mi n of SR 55. Int corridors. **Pets:** Small. $20 daily fee/pet. Designated rooms, service with restrictions, crate.
🆂🅰🆅🅴 ✖ 🖥 🍽 🍴 🏊 ✖

▽ Hillside Motel Ⓜ 🐾
(989) 366-5711. **$64-$74, 3 day notice.** 3419 W Houghton Lake Dr. On SR 55, 6 mi e of US 27; 10 mi w of I-75. Ext corridors. **Pets:** Other species. Service with restrictions, supervision.
🅰🆂🅺 🆂🅾 ✖ 🖥

▽▽▽ Holiday Inn Express 🆂🅷
(989) 422-7829. **$59-$189.** 200 Cloverleaf Ln. Jct US 127 and SR 55, just e. Int corridors. **Pets:** Other species. $25 one-time fee/room. Service with restrictions, supervision.
🅰🆂🅺 🆂🅾 ✖ 🖥 🏊

ⒶⒶⒶ ▽▽▽ Super 8 Motel 🆂🅷
(989) 422-3119. **$76-$109.** 9580 W Lake City Rd. Jct US 27 and SR 55. Int corridors. **Pets:** Accepted.
🆂🅰🆅🅴 🆂🅾 ✖ 🖥 🏊 ✖

HOWELL

ⒶⒶⒶ ▽▽▽ Best Western Howell Ⓜ
(517) 548-2900. **$85-$145.** 1500 Pinckney Rd. I-96, exit 137 (Pickney Rd), just s on CR D19. Ext corridors. **Pets:** Small, dogs only. $15 daily fee/pet. Designated rooms, service with restrictions, supervision.
🆂🅰🆅🅴 🆂🅾 ✖ 🖥 🍽 🏊

ⒶⒶⒶ ▽▽ Kensington Inn Ⓜ
(517) 548-3510. **$44-$59.** 124 Holiday Ln. I-96, exit 137 (Pickney Rd), just n. Ext corridors. **Pets:** Other species. $10 daily fee/pet. Service with restrictions, supervision.
🆂🅰🆅🅴 🆂🅾 ✖ 🖥 🏊

▽▽ Quality Inn Banquet & Conference Center Ⓜ 🐾
(517) 546-6800. **$59-$89.** 125 Holiday Ln. I-96, exit 137 (Pickney Rd), just n. Int corridors. **Pets:** Other species. $15 daily fee/pet. Service with restrictions, supervision.
🅰🆂🅺 🆂🅾 ✖ 🖥 🍽 🍴 🏊

IMLAY CITY

ⒶⒶⒶ ▽▽▽ Days Inn 🆂🅷
(810) 724-8005. **$80-$85.** 6692 Newark Rd. I-69, exit 168 (SR 53/Van Dyke Rd), 0.3 mi n, then w. Int corridors. **Pets:** Other species. $50 deposit/room, $8 one-time fee/room. Supervision.
🆂🅰🆅🅴 🆂🅾 ✖ 🖥 🍽 🏊

▽▽ Super 8 Motel-Imlay City 🆂🅷
(810) 724-8700. **$49-$89, 30 day notice.** 6951 Newark Rd. I-69, exit 168 (SR 53/Van Dyke Rd), just n to Newark Rd, then just e. Int corridors. **Pets:** Large. $10 one-time fee/pet. Designated rooms, service with restrictions, supervision.
🅰🆂🅺 🆂🅾 ✖ 🖥

INDIAN RIVER

ⒶⒶⒶ ▽ Nor Gate Motel Ⓜ
(231) 238-7788. **$44-$50, 3 day notice.** 4846 S Straits Hwy. I-75, exit 310, 0.3 mi w, then 2 mi s on Old US 27. Ext corridors. **Pets:** Small, dogs only. $10 one-time fee/room. Designated rooms, service with restrictions, supervision.
🆂🅰🆅🅴 ✖ 🖥 🍽 ✖

▼ **Star Gate Motel** Ⓜ
(231) 238-7371. **$44-$52, 3 day notice.** 4646 S Straits Hwy. I-75, exit 310, 0.3 mi w, then 1.8 mi s on Old US 27. Ext corridors. **Pets:** Accepted.
🅰🆂🅺 ⊠ 🛏 ⊠

IONIA

🔺 ▼ ◆ **Super 8 Motel** 🆂🅷
(616) 527-2828. **$48-$110.** 7245 S State Rd. I-96, exit 67 (SR 66). Int corridors. **Pets:** Accepted.
🆂🅰🆅🅴 🆂🅳 ⊠ 🅼 🅰 🛏 💻

IRON MOUNTAIN

▼ **Best Inn** 🆂🅷
(906) 776-8000. **$60-$250.** 1609 S Stephenson Ave. 1 mi e on US 2. Ext/int corridors. **Pets:** Accepted.
🅰🆂🅺 🆂🅳 ⊠ 💻

🔺 ▼ **Budget Host Inn** Ⓜ 🐾
(906) 774-6797. **$50-$55.** 1663 N Stephenson Ave. 1.5 mi nw on US 2 and 141. Ext corridors. **Pets:** Medium. $5 daily fee/room. Service with restrictions, supervision.
🆂🅰🆅🅴 🆂🅳 ⊠ 🛏

▼ ▼ **Days Inn** 🆂🅷
(906) 774-2181. **$50-$120.** W8176 S US 2. 1.8 mi e on US 2. Ext/int corridors. **Pets:** Dogs only. $10 one-time fee/room. Designated rooms, service with restrictions, supervision.
🅰🆂🅺 🆂🅳 ⊠ 🛏 ⊅

▼ ▼ **Super 8 Motel** 🆂🅷
(906) 774-3400. **Call for rates.** 2702 N Stephenson Ave. 2 mi nw on US 2 and 141. Int corridors. **Pets:** Accepted.
⊠ 🛏 💻 ⊅ ⊠

IRONWOOD

🔺 ▼ ◆ **AmericInn of Ironwood** 🆂🅷
(906) 932-7200. **$69-$149.** 1117 E Cloverland Dr. 0.8 mi e on US 2. Int corridors. **Pets:** Medium. $25 one-time fee/room. Designated rooms, service with restrictions, supervision.
🆂🅰🆅🅴 🆂🅳 ⊠ 🅴 🛏 💻 ⊅ ⊠

🔺 ▼ **Crestview Motel** Ⓜ
(906) 932-4845. **$45-$75, 5 day notice.** US 2. 0.4 mi w on US 2. Ext corridors. **Pets:** Supervision.
🆂🅰🆅🅴 ⊠ 🛏 💻

🔺 ▼ **Royal Motel** Ⓜ
(906) 932-4230. **$41-$46, 7 day notice.** 715 W Cloverland Dr. 0.7 mi w on US 2. Ext corridors. **Pets:** Accepted.
🆂🅰🆅🅴 ⊠

▼ **Super 8 Motel** 🆂🅷
(906) 932-3395. **$68-$98, 30 day notice.** 160 E Cloverland Dr. Jct US 2 and US 2 business route. Int corridors. **Pets:** Other species. $10 one-time fee/room. Designated rooms, service with restrictions, supervision.
🅰🆂🅺 🆂🅳 ⊠ 🛏 💻 ⊠

ISHPEMING

🔺 ▼ ▼ **Best Western Country Inn** 🆂🅷
(906) 485-6345. **$75-$99.** 850 US 41 W. On US 41, just n of town. Int corridors. **Pets:** Designated rooms, service with restrictions, supervision.
🆂🅰🆅🅴 🆂🅳 ⊠ 🍴 ⊅ ⊠

JACKSON

▼ ▼ ◆ **Holiday Inn** 🆂🅷
(517) 783-2681. **$75-$143.** 2000 Holiday Inn Dr. I-94, exit 138 (US 127), just n to Springport Rd, then just w. Ext/int corridors. **Pets:** Accepted.
🅰🆂🅺 🆂🅳 ⊠ 🅰 🅴 🛏 💻 🍴 ⊅ ⊠

▼ **Motel 6–1088** Ⓜ
(517) 789-7186. **$41-$55.** 830 Royal Dr. I-94, exit 138 (US 127), just se. Ext corridors. **Pets:** Accepted.
🆂🅳 ⊠ 🅰 🅴 ⊅

JONESVILLE

🔺 ▼ **Pinecrest Motel** Ⓜ
(517) 849-2137. **$43-$55.** 516 W Chicago St. 1 mi w of jct SR 99 and US 12. Ext corridors. **Pets:** $5 one-time fee/pet. No service, supervision.
🆂🅰🆅🅴 🆂🅳 ⊠ 🛏

KALAMAZOO

🔺 ▼ ▼ **Clarion Hotel** 🆂🅷
(269) 385-3922. **$69-$179.** 3600 E Cork St. I-94, exit 80 (Sprinkle Rd), just n, then just w. Int corridors. **Pets:** Accepted.
🆂🅰🆅🅴 🆂🅳 ⊠ 🛏 💻 🍴 ⊅ ⊠

▼ ▼ **Days Inn Airport** 🆂🅷
(269) 381-7070. **$55-$95.** 3522 Sprinkle Rd. I-94, exit 80 (Sprinkle Rd), just s. Int corridors. **Pets:** Small. $10 daily fee/pet. Service with restrictions, supervision.
🅰🆂🅺 🆂🅳 ⊠ 💻 ⊅

🔺 ▼ **Knights Inn** Ⓜ
(269) 381-5000. **$50-$90.** 1211 S Westnedge Ave. I-94, exit 76B, 3 mi n, w on Park Place, then just s. Ext/int corridors. **Pets:** Other species. $25 one-time fee/room. No service, supervision.
🆂🅰🆅🅴 🆂🅳 ⊠ 🛏

▼ ▼ **Red Roof Inn-East #7003** Ⓜ
(269) 382-6350. **$50-$77.** 3701 E Cork St. I-94, exit 80 (Sprinkle Rd), just n, then just w. Ext corridors. **Pets:** Accepted.
⊠ 🅼 🅴

▼ ▼ **Red Roof Inn-West #7025** 🆂🅷
(269) 375-7400. **$47-$69.** 5425 W Michigan Ave. US 131, exit 36B, just nw. Ext corridors. **Pets:** Accepted.
⊠ 🅴 🛏

KENTWOOD

🔺 ▼ ▼ **Best Western Midway Hotel** 🆂🅷
(616) 942-2550. **$79-$119.** 4101 28th St SE. I-96, exit 43A, 1.5 mi w on SR 11. Int corridors. **Pets:** Medium. Designated rooms, service with restrictions.
🆂🅰🆅🅴 🆂🅳 ⊠ 🛏 💻 🍴 ⊅ ⊠

▼ ▼ **Comfort Inn** 🆂🅷
(616) 957-2080. **$59-$119.** 4155 28th St SE. I-96, exit 43A, 1.5 mi w on SR 11. Int corridors. **Pets:** Other species. Service with restrictions, crate.
🅰🆂🅺 🆂🅳 ⊠ 🅴 🛏 💻

▼ ▼ ▼ **Residence Inn by Marriott East** 🆂🅷
(616) 957-8111. **$69-$169.** 2701 E Beltline Ave. Jct SR 11 and E Beltline Ave (SR 37). Ext corridors. **Pets:** Accepted.
🅰🆂🅺 ⊠ 🅰 🛏 💻 ⊅ ⊠

▼ ▼ ◆ **Staybridge Suites by Holiday Inn** 🆂🅷
(616) 464-3200. **$99-$149.** 3000 Lake Eastbrook Blvd SE. I-96, exit 43A, 2 mi w on SR 11, then just s. Int corridors. **Pets:** Accepted.
🅰🆂🅺 🆂🅳 ⊠ 🅼 🅴 🛏 💻 ⊅

LAKE CITY

🔺 ▼ **Northcrest Motel** Ⓜ
(231) 839-2075. **$59-$79.** 1341 S Lakeshore. 1 mi s on SR 55 and 66. Ext corridors. **Pets:** Accepted.
🆂🅰🆅🅴 🆂🅳 💻 ⊅

LAKESIDE

▼▼▼▼ White Rabbit Inn BB
(269) 469-4620. **$95-$155, 7 day notice.** 14634 Red Arrow Hwy. I-94, exit 6 (Union Pier Rd), 1 mi w, then 2 mi n. Ext corridors. **Pets:** Accepted.
⊠ 🖪 🖵 ☎

LANSING

▲▲▲ ▼▼▼ Best Western Midway Hotel SH
(517) 627-8471. **$79-$109.** 7711 W Saginaw Hwy. I-96, exit 93B (SR 43/Saginaw Hwy), just e. Int corridors. **Pets:** Accepted.
SAVE S🖪 ⊠ 🖪 🖵 🍴 🏊 🖾

▲▲▲ ▼▼▼▼ Hampton Inn of Lansing SH
(517) 627-8381. **$69-$89.** 525 N Canal Rd. I-96, exit 93B (SR 43/Saginaw Hwy), just e. Int corridors. **Pets:** Medium, dogs only. $100 deposit/room. Designated rooms, service with restrictions, supervision.
SAVE S🖪 ⊠ ⌦ 🖪 🖵

▲▲▲ ▼▼▼▼ Lansing's Quality Suites Hotel SH
(517) 886-0600. **$65-$99.** 901 Delta Commerce Dr. I-96, exit 93B (SR 43/Saginaw Hwy), 0.3 mi e to Bennigans Restaurant, then just n. Int corridors. **Pets:** Other species. $25 one-time fee/room. Designated rooms.
SAVE S🖪 ⊠ 🖪 🖵 🖾

▼▼▼ Red Roof Inn-East #7029 M
(517) 332-2575. **$56-$73.** 3615 Dunckel Rd. Just e of I-496 and US 127, exit 11 (Jolly Rd). Ext corridors. **Pets:** Other species. Service with restrictions, supervision.
⊠ ⌦ 🖪

▼▼▼ Red Roof Inn-West #7020 SH
(517) 321-7246. **$52-$67.** 7412 W Saginaw Hwy. I-96, exit 93B (SR 43/Saginaw Hwy), just e. Ext corridors. **Pets:** Medium. Service with restrictions, supervision.
⊠

▼▼▼▼ Residence Inn by Marriott West SH
(517) 886-5030. **$89-$120.** 922 Delta Commerce Dr. I-96, exit 96B (SR 43/Saginaw Hwy), 0.4 mi e; behind Bennigans. Int corridors. **Pets:** Other species. $75 one-time fee/room. Service with restrictions, crate.
ASK S🖪 ⊠ 🖪ᴹ 🖪 🖵 🏊 🖾

▼▼▼▼ Sheraton Lansing Hotel SH 🐾
(517) 323-7100. **$169-$184.** 925 S Creyts Rd. I-496, exit 1 (Creyts Rd), just n. Int corridors. **Pets:** Medium, dogs only. $30 one-time fee/room. Service with restrictions, supervision.
ASK S🖪 ⊠ ⌦ 🖪 🖵 🍴 🏊 🖾

LUDINGTON

▼▼▼ Holiday Inn Express SH 🐾
(231) 845-7004. **$67-$225.** 5323 W US 10. Jct US 31, 1.3 mi w on US 10. Int corridors. **Pets:** Other species. $10 one-time fee/pet. Designated rooms, service with restrictions, supervision.
ASK S🖪 ⊠ 🖪 🖵 🏊 🖾

▲▲▲ ▼▼▼ Super 8 Motel SH
(231) 843-2140. **$54-$279.** 5005 W US 10. Jct US 31, 1 mi w on US 10. Int corridors. **Pets:** $10 daily fee/room. Designated rooms, service with restrictions, supervision.
SAVE S🖪 ⊠ 🖪 🖵 🏊 🖾

MACKINAW CITY

▲▲▲ ▼▼▼ Baymont Inn & Suites-Mackinaw City SH 🐾
(231) 436-7737. **$59-$149.** 109 S Nicolet St. I-75, exit 338. Int corridors. **Pets:** Medium. $50 deposit/room. Designated rooms, service with restrictions, supervision.
SAVE S🖪 ⊠ 🖪 🖵 🏊

▲▲▲ ▼▼▼ Beachcomber Motel on the Water M 🐾
(231) 436-8451. **$42-$125, 3 day notice.** 1011 S Huron Ave. 1 mi s on US 23. Ext corridors. **Pets:** Small, dogs only. $5 one-time fee/pet. Designated rooms, service with restrictions, supervision.
SAVE S🖪 ⊠ 🖪

▲▲▲ ▼▼▼ The Beach House CA
(231) 436-5353. **$44-$160, 14 day notice.** 11490 W US 23. 1.3 mi s. Ext corridors. **Pets:** Large, dogs only. $15 one-time fee/pet. Service with restrictions, supervision.
SAVE 🖪 🏊 🖾 ☎

▲▲▲ ▼▼▼ Budget Inns-Starlite M 🐾
(231) 436-5959. **$26-$129.** 116 Old US 31. I-75, exit 338 southbound, 0.3 mi e; exit 337 northbound, just ne. Ext corridors. **Pets:** Medium, dogs only. $15 daily fee/pet. Designated rooms, no service, supervision.
SAVE S🖪 ⊠ 🖪 🖵 🖾

▲▲▲ ▼▼▼ Capri Motel M
(231) 436-5498. **$39-$89.** 801 S Nicolet St. I-75, exit 338, just s. Ext corridors. **Pets:** Large. $5 daily fee/pet. Service with restrictions, supervision.
SAVE S🖪 ⊠ 🖪 🖵 🏊 🖾

▼▼▼ Chief Motel M
(231) 436-7981. **$39-$99, 4 day notice.** 10470 US 23. 1 mi s. Ext corridors. **Pets:** Accepted.
ASK S🖪 ⊠ 🏊

▲▲▲ ▼▼▼ Days Inn & Suites "Bridgeview Lodge" M
(231) 436-8961. **$39-$249.** 206 N Nicolet St. I-75, exit 339; at bridge. Ext/int corridors. **Pets:** Small, dogs only. $50 deposit/pet. Designated rooms, service with restrictions, supervision.
SAVE S🖪 ⊠ 🖵 🏊

▲▲▲ ▼▼▼ Days Inn Lakeview M
(231) 436-5557. **$39-$169.** 825 S Huron Ave. I-75, exit 337 northbound, 0.5 mi n to US 23, 0.3 mi e; exit 338 southbound, 0.8 mi se on US 23. Ext corridors. **Pets:** Accepted.
SAVE S🖪 ⊠ 🖪 🖵 🍴 🏊

▲▲▲ ▼▼▼▼ Holiday Inn Express at the Bridge SH
(231) 436-7100. **$39-$269.** 364 Louvigny. I-75, exit 339. Int corridors. **Pets:** Accepted.
SAVE S🖪 ⊠ 🖪ᴹ 🖪 🖵 🏊 🖾

▲▲▲ ▼▼ Kings Inn M
(231) 436-5322. **$39-$99, 3 day notice.** 1020 S Nicolet St. I-75, exit 337 northbound, 0.5 mi n; exit 338 southbound, 0.5 mi s. Ext corridors. **Pets:** Accepted.
SAVE S🖪 ⊠ 🖪 🏊

▼▼▼ Ramada Inn Conference Resort SH
(231) 436-5535. **$79-$209.** 450 S Nicolet. I-75, exit 338. Int corridors. **Pets:** Accepted.
ASK S🖪 ⊠ 🖪 🖵 🍴 🏊 🖾

▲▲▲ ▼▼▼ Super 8 Motel Bridgeview SH
(231) 436-5252. **$38-$179, 3 day notice.** 601 N Huron Ave. I-75, exit 339 northbound (Nicolet St), just n, then just e. Ext/int corridors. **Pets:** Accepted.
SAVE S🖪 ⊠ 🖪 🖪 🖵 🏊 🖾

MANISTIQUE

▲▲▲ ▼▼ Beachcomber Motel M
(906) 341-2567. **$50-$88.** 795 E Lakeshore Dr. 1 mi e on US 2. Ext corridors. **Pets:** Designated rooms.
SAVE S🖪 ⊠ 🖪

▼▼ ▼▼ **Comfort Inn** 🆂🅷
(906) 341-6981. **$70-$159.** 617 E Lakeshore Dr. 0.5 mi e on US 2. Int corridors. **Pets:** Other species. $10 daily fee/pet. Service with restrictions, supervision.
Ⓐ🆂🅺 🆂🔧 ⊗ 🔒 💻 ⊠

Ⓐ Ⓐ ▼▼ **Kewadin Casino Inn** 🆂🅷
(906) 341-6911. **$47-$70.** 6596 W US Hwy 2. 2.5 mi e on US 2. Int corridors. **Pets:** Accepted.
🆂🅰🆅🅴 🆂🔧 ⊗ 🔒 💻 ≈

MARQUETTE

Ⓐ Ⓐ ▼▼ **Birchmont Motel** Ⓜ ✿
(906) 228-7538. **$45-$72.** 2090 US 41 S. On US 41 and SR 28, 4.3 mi s. Ext corridors. **Pets:** Other species. $6 daily fee/pet. Designated rooms, service with restrictions, supervision.
🆂🅰🆅🅴 ⊗ 🔒 ≈

▼▼ ▼▼ **Holiday Inn** 🆂🅷
(906) 225-1351. **$85-$99.** 1951 US 41 W. On US 41 and SR 28, 1.8 mi w. Int corridors. **Pets:** Medium, dogs only. $25 daily fee/pet. Designated rooms, service with restrictions, supervision.
Ⓐ🆂🅺 🆂🔧 ⊗ 🅼♿ ♿ 🔒 💻 🍴 ≈ ⊠

Ⓐ Ⓐ Ⓐ ▼▼ ▼▼ **Nordic Bay Lodge** Ⓜ
(906) 226-7516. **$60-$85.** 1880 US 41 S. On US 41 and SR 28, 1.8 mi se. Ext corridors. **Pets:** Dogs only. Designated rooms, service with restrictions, supervision.
🆂🅰🆅🅴 🆂🔧 ⊗ 🔒 💻 🍴 ⊠

▼▼ ▼▼ **Ramada Inn** 🆂🅷
(906) 228-6000. **$114-$119, 3 day notice.** 412 W Washington St. 0.5 w on US 41 business route. Int corridors. **Pets:** Other species. $10 daily fee/pet. Designated rooms, service with restrictions, supervision.
Ⓐ🆂🅺 🆂🔧 ⊗ 🔒 💻 🍴 ≈ ⊠

Ⓐ Ⓐ Ⓐ ▼▼ **Travelodge** 🆂🅷
(906) 249-1712. **$59-$74.** 1010 M-28 E. Jct US 41 S and SR 28 E. Int corridors. **Pets:** Other species. $6 one-time fee/pet. Service with restrictions, supervision.
🆂🅰🆅🅴 🆂🔧 ⊗ 🔒 💻 ≈

MARSHALL

Ⓐ Ⓐ Ⓐ ▼▼ **Arbor Inn of Historic Marshall** Ⓜ
(269) 781-7772. **$50-$69.** 15435 W Michigan Ave. I-69, exit 36 (Michigan Ave), just w. Ext corridors. **Pets:** Other species. $5 daily fee/pet. Designated rooms, service with restrictions, crate.
🆂🅰🆅🅴 🆂🔧 ⊗ 🔒 ≈

MENOMINEE

Ⓐ Ⓐ Ⓐ ▼▼ ▼▼ **Econo Lodge On The Bay** 🆂🅷
(906) 863-4431. **$67-$139.** 2516 10th St. 1 mi n on US 41. Int corridors. **Pets:** Accepted.
🆂🅰🆅🅴 🆂🔧 ⊗ 🔒 💻

MIDLAND

Ⓐ Ⓐ Ⓐ ▼▼ **Best Western Valley Plaza Resort** 🆂🅷
(989) 496-2700. **$85-$129.** 5221 Bay City Rd. US 10, exit Midland/Bay City Rd. Int corridors. **Pets:** Accepted.
🆂🅰🆅🅴 🆂🔧 ⊗ 🔒 💻 🍴 ≈ ⊠

▼▼ ▼▼ **Fairview Inn & Suites** 🆂🅷
(989) 631-0070. **$69-$99.** 2200 W Wackerly St. Jct US 10 and Eastman Rd. Int corridors. **Pets:** Accepted.
⊗ 🔒 💻 ≈

Ⓐ Ⓐ Ⓐ ▼▼ ▼▼ ▼▼ **Holiday Inn** 🆂🅷
(989) 631-4220. **$90.** 1500 W Wackerly St. Jct US 10 and Eastman Rd. Ext/int corridors. **Pets:** Accepted.
🆂🅰🆅🅴 🆂🔧 ⊗ 🔒 💻 🍴 ≈ ⊠

Ⓐ Ⓐ Ⓐ ▼▼ ▼▼ **Plaza Suites Hotel** 🆂🅷
(989) 496-0100. **$107-$139.** 5221 Bay City Rd. US 10, exit Midland/Bay City Rd. Int corridors. **Pets:** Accepted.
🆂🅰🆅🅴 🆂🔧 ⊗ 🔒 💻 ⊠

▼▼ ▼▼ **Sleep Inn of Midland** 🆂🅷
(989) 837-1010. **Call for rates.** 2100 W Wackerly. Jct US 10 and Eastman Rd. Int corridors. **Pets:** Other species. Service with restrictions, supervision.
⊗ 🅼♿ ♿ 🔒 💻 ≈

MONROE

Ⓐ Ⓐ Ⓐ ▼▼ ▼▼ ▼▼ **Comfort Inn** 🆂🅷
(734) 384-1500. **$55-$200.** 6500 Albain Rd. I-75, exit 11 (Laplaisance Rd), just w. Int corridors. **Pets:** $10 daily fee/pet. Service with restrictions, supervision.
🆂🅰🆅🅴 🆂🔧 ⊗ ♿ 🔒 💻 ≈ ⊠

Ⓐ Ⓐ Ⓐ ▼▼ ▼▼ ▼▼ **Hometown Inn** Ⓜ ❀
(734) 289-1080. **$50-$55.** 1885 Welcome Way. I-75, exit 15 (SR 50), just e. Ext corridors. **Pets:** Other species. $5 daily fee/room. Service with restrictions, supervision.
🆂🅰🆅🅴 🆂🔧 ⊗ 🔒

MOUNT PLEASANT

▼▼ ▼▼ ▼▼ **Holiday Inn** 🆂🅷
(989) 772-2905. **$89-$159, 3 day notice.** 5665 E Pickard Ave. Jct US 27 and SR 20 E. Ext/int corridors. **Pets:** Medium. Designated rooms, service with restrictions, supervision.
Ⓐ🆂🅺 🆂🔧 ⊗ 🅼♿ ♿ 🔒 💻 🍴 ≈ ⊠

MUNISING

Ⓐ Ⓐ Ⓐ ▼▼ **Alger Falls Motel** Ⓜ
(906) 387-3536. **$40-$65.** E9427 SR 28. 2 mi e on SR 28 and 94. Ext corridors. **Pets:** Small, dogs only. Designated rooms, service with restrictions, supervision.
🆂🅰🆅🅴 ⊗ 🔒 ⊠

Ⓐ Ⓐ Ⓐ ▼▼ ▼▼ ▼▼ **Best Western** Ⓜ
(906) 387-4864. **$59-$119.** M-28. On SR 28, 3 mi e. Ext/int corridors. **Pets:** Designated rooms, service with restrictions, crate.
🆂🅰🆅🅴 🆂🔧 ⊗ 🔒 💻 🍴 ≈ ⊠

▼▼ ▼▼ **Comfort Inn** 🆂🅷
(906) 387-5292. **$75-$110.** M-28 E. 1.5 mi e on SR 28. Int corridors. **Pets:** Dogs only. Designated rooms, service with restrictions, supervision.
Ⓐ🆂🅺 🆂🔧 ⊗ 💻 ≈ ⊠

▼▼ **Days Inn** 🆂🅷
(906) 387-2493. **$75-$110.** On M-28. 0.5 mi e on SR 28. Int corridors. **Pets:** Dogs only. Designated rooms, service with restrictions, supervision.
Ⓐ🆂🅺 🆂🔧 ⊗ 🔒 💻 ≈ ⊠

Ⓐ Ⓐ Ⓐ ▼▼ **Sunset Motel on the Bay** Ⓜ
(906) 387-4574. **$45-$78.** 1315 Bay St. 1 mi e on E Munising Ave (CR 58). Ext corridors. **Pets:** Dogs only. $10 one-time fee/pet. Designated rooms, service with restrictions, supervision.
🆂🅰🆅🅴 ⊗ 🔒 💻 ⊠ 🅩

Ⓐ Ⓐ Ⓐ ▼▼ **Terrace Motel** Ⓜ
(906) 387-2735. **$40-$55, 3 day notice.** 420 Prospect. 0.5 mi e, just off SR 28. Ext corridors. **Pets:** Medium, other species. $3 daily fee/room. Designated rooms, service with restrictions, crate.
🆂🅰🆅🅴 ⊗ ⊠ 🅰 🅩

NORWAY

▼▼ ▼▼ **AmericInn of Norway** 🆂🅷
(906) 563-7500. **$78-$80.** W 6002 US Hwy 2. 0.7 mi w. Int corridors. **Pets:** Accepted.
Ⓐ🆂🅺 ⊗ 🔒 💻 ≈ ⊠

PAW PAW

▽▽ Comfort Inn & Suites 🆂🅷
(269) 655-0303. **$55-$109.** 153 Ampey Rd. I-94, exit 60 (SR 40), just nw. Int corridors. **Pets:** Large, other species. Service with restrictions, crate.

(ASK) (S🅳) (✕) (🔬M) (🖉) (♿) (🛏) (💻) (🏊)

PELLSTON

🅰 ▽▽▽ Holiday Inn Express Pellston 🆂🅷
(231) 539-7000. **$99-$239.** 1600 US 31 N. 1.2 mi n. Int corridors. **Pets:** Accepted.

(SAVE) (S🅳) (✕) (♿) (🛏) (🏊) (✕)

PETOSKEY

🅰 ▽▽▽ Days Inn Petoskey 🅼
(231) 348-3900. **$58-$148.** 1420 US 131 S. 1.3 mi s. Ext corridors. **Pets:** Other species. $10 daily fee/pet. Service with restrictions, supervision.

(SAVE) (S🅳) (✕) (🛏) (💻) (🍴)

PLAINWELL

🅰 ▽▽▽▽ Comfort Inn 🆂🅷
(269) 685-9891. **$75-$200.** 622 Allegan St. US 131, exit 49A, just e. Int corridors. **Pets:** $10 daily fee/room. Service with restrictions, supervision.

(SAVE) (S🅳) (✕) (🛏) (💻) (🏊)

PORTLAND

🅰 ▽▽▽▽ Best Western American Heritage Inn 🆂🅷
(517) 647-2200. **$74-$84.** 1681 Grand River Ave. I-96, exit 77, just n. Int corridors. **Pets:** Medium, dogs only. $10 one-time fee/pet. Service with restrictions, supervision.

(SAVE) (S🅳) (✕) (🔬M) (♿) (🛏) (💻) (🏊) (✕)

PRUDENVILLE

🅰 ▽▽ East Bay Lodge 🆂🅷
(989) 366-5910. **$48-$108, 10 day notice.** 125 12th St. I-75, exit 227, 8 mi w on SR 55. Ext/int corridors. **Pets:** Accepted.

(SAVE) (🛏) (💻) (✕) (🐾) (☎)

ROGERS CITY

▽▽ Driftwood Motel 🅼
(989) 734-4777. **$70-$95.** 540 W Third St. 1 mi nw on US 23 business route. Ext corridors. **Pets:** Small. $10 daily fee/pet. Designated rooms, service with restrictions, supervision.

(ASK) (S🅳) (✕) (💻) (🏊)

SAGINAW

▽▽ ▽▽ Best Western–Saginaw 🆂🅷
(989) 755-0461. **$59-$99.** 1408 S Outer Dr. I-75, exit 149B (SR 46). Int corridors. **Pets:** Other species. $25 one-time fee/room. Service with restrictions, supervision.

(ASK) (S🅳) (✕) (🛏) (💻) (🏊) (✕)

▽▽▽▽ Four Points by Sheraton Saginaw 🆂🅷
(989) 790-5050. **$79.** 4960 Towne Centre Rd. I-675, exit 6, just w on Tittabawassee Rd. Int corridors. **Pets:** Accepted.

(ASK) (S🅳) (✕) (🛏) (💻) (🍴) (🏊) (✕)

▽▽ Howard Johnson Plaza Hotel 🆂🅷
(989) 753-6608. **$79-$189.** 400 Johnson St. I-675, exit 2, just s. Int corridors. **Pets:** Accepted.

(ASK) (S🅳) (✕) (♿) (🛏) (💻) (🍴) (🏊)

▽▽ Motel 6 Saginaw #1496 🅼
(989) 754-8414. **$41-$55.** 966 S Outer Dr. I-75, exit 149B (SR 46). Ext corridors. **Pets:** Large, other species. Service with restrictions, supervision.

(S🅳) (✕) (🛏)

🅰 ▽▽▽ Ramada Inn & Suites 🆂🅷 🐾
(989) 793-7900. **$69-$139.** 3325 Davenport Ave. I-675, exit 3, 2 mi w on SR 58. Int corridors. **Pets:** Medium. Designated rooms, service with restrictions.

(SAVE) (S🅳) (✕) (♿) (🛏) (💻) (🍴)

🅰 ▽▽ Super 8 Motel 🆂🅷
(989) 791-3003. **$65-$125.** 4848 Towne Centre Rd. I-675, exit 6, 0.3 mi w, then just s. Int corridors. **Pets:** $10 one-time fee/room. Service with restrictions, supervision.

(SAVE) (S🅳) (✕) (🛏)

ST. IGNACE

▽▽ Bay View Motel 🅼 🐾
(906) 643-9444. **$32-$76.** 1133 N State St. 3 mi n of bridge tollgate on I-75 business route. Ext corridors. **Pets:** $5 one-time fee/pet. Designated rooms, service with restrictions, supervision.

(✕) (☎)

🅰 ▽▽▽ Budget Host Inn 🆂🅷
(906) 643-9666. **$58-$167.** 700 N State St. 1.8 mi n of bridge tollgate on I-75 business route. Ext/int corridors. **Pets:** Other species. $40 deposit/room. Designated rooms, service with restrictions, supervision.

(SAVE) (S🅳) (✕) (🛏) (💻) (🏊) (✕)

🅰 ▽▽▽ Econo Lodge Inn & Suites 🅼
(906) 643-9688. **$49-$130.** 680 W US 2. Just e on I-75 business route and US 2. Ext/int corridors. **Pets:** $10 daily fee/room. Service with restrictions, supervision.

(SAVE) (S🅳) (✕) (🛏) (💻) (🏊) (✕)

▽▽▽ Quality Inn St. Ignace 🆂🅷 🐾
(906) 643-9700. **$59-$159.** 913 Boulevard Dr. Jct I-75 and US 2 W. Int corridors. **Pets:** $10 daily fee/pet. Service with restrictions, supervision.

(ASK) (S🅳) (✕) (💻) (🏊) (✕)

🅰 ▽▽ Wayside Motel 🅼
(906) 643-8944. **$40-$65, 7 day notice.** 751 N State St. 2 mi n of bridge tollgate on I-75 business route. Ext corridors. **Pets:** Medium, dogs only. $5 daily fee/pet. Designated rooms, service with restrictions, supervision.

(SAVE) (S🅳) (✕) (💻)

ST. JOSEPH

🅰 ▽▽ Econo Lodge St. Joseph 🅼
(269) 982-3333. **$49-$89.** 2723 Niles Ave. I-94, exit 27 (Niles Ave), 2 mi w. Ext corridors. **Pets:** Accepted.

(SAVE) (✕) (🛏) (🏊)

SAULT STE. MARIE

🅰 ▽▽▽ Best Western Sault Ste Marie 🆂🅷 🐾
(906) 632-2170. **$59-$109.** 4281 I-75 business loop. I-75, exit 392, 0.3 mi ne. Ext/int corridors. **Pets:** Other species. $15 one-time fee/room. Designated rooms, service with restrictions, crate.

(SAVE) (S🅳) (✕) (♿) (🛏) (💻) (🏊) (✕)

🅰 ▽▽ Budget Host Crestview Inn 🅼
(906) 635-5213. **$59-$79.** 1200 Ashmun St. I-75, exit 392, 2.8 mi ne on I-75 business loop. Ext corridors. **Pets:** Other species. Designated rooms, service with restrictions, supervision.

(SAVE) (S🅳) (✕) (🛏)

🅰 ▽▽▽ Days Inn 🆂🅷
(906) 635-5200. **$55-$90.** 3651 I-75 Business Spur. I-75, exit 392, 0.8 mi ne on I-75 business loop. Int corridors. **Pets:** Other species. $10 one-time fee/room. Designated rooms, service with restrictions, crate.

(SAVE) (S🅳) (✕) (🛏) (💻) (🏊) (✕)

▼▼ **Econo Lodge** 🆂🅷
(906) 632-6000. **$44-$89.** 3525 I-75 Business Spur. I-75, exit 392, 0.7 mi ne. Int corridors. **Pets:** Large. $10 one-time fee/room. Designated rooms, service with restrictions, supervision.
🅰🆂🅺 🆂🔟 🗙 🅜 ☕ 🛢 🖵

▲▲▲ ▼ **La France Terrace Motel** 🅼
(906) 632-7823. **$42-$75.** 1608 Ashmun St. I-75, exit 392, 2.3 mi ne on I-75 business loop. Ext corridors. **Pets:** Dogs only. Designated rooms, service with restrictions, supervision.
🆂🅰🆅🅴 🆂🔟 🗙 🛢 🏊

▲▲▲ ▼ **Mid-City Motel** 🅼
(906) 632-6832. **$46-$58.** 304 E Portage Ave. Just e of town, on I-75 business loop. Ext corridors. **Pets:** Dogs only. Service with restrictions, supervision.
🆂🅰🆅🅴 🆂🔟 🗙

▼ **Royal Motel** 🅼
(906) 632-6323. **$44-$52.** 1707 Ashmun St. I-75, exit 392, 2 mi ne on I-75 business loop. Ext corridors. **Pets:** Small, dogs only. Service with restrictions, supervision.
🅰🆂🅺 🆂🔟 🗙 🖵

▲▲▲ ▼ **Sunset Motel** 🅼
(906) 632-3906. **$42-$48.** 8929 S Mackinaw Tr. I-75, exit 386, 0.3 mi e to jct SR 28 and CR H-63. Ext corridors. **Pets:** Accepted.
🆂🅰🆅🅴 🗙 🛢 🖵

▼▼ **Super 8 Motel** 🆂🅷
(906) 632-8882. **$55-$78.** 3826 I-75 Business Loop. I-75, exit 392, 0.5 mi ne. Int corridors. **Pets:** Other species. $50 deposit/room. Service with restrictions, supervision.
🅰🆂🅺 🆂🔟 🗙 🅜

SILVER CITY

▼▼ **AmericInn Lodge & Suites** 🆂🅷
(906) 885-5311. **$79-$140.** 120 Lincoln Ave. On SR 107, 0.3 mi w of SR 64. Int corridors. **Pets:** Large, dogs only. $10 daily fee/room. Service with restrictions, supervision.
🅰🆂🅺 🗙 🅜 🛢 🖵 🍽 🏊 🗙

▼ **Mountain View Lodges** 🅲🅰
(906) 885-5256. **$134-$149, 30 day notice.** 237 SR 107. Jct SR 107 and 64, 0.8 mi w. Ext corridors. **Pets:** Dogs only. $40 one-time fee/pet. Crate.
🗙 🛢 🖵 🐾

▲▲▲ ▼ **Tomlinson's Rainbow Lodging** 🅼
(906) 885-5348. **$49-$85, 30 day notice.** 32739 W State Hwy M 64. SR 64, just e of jct SR 107. Ext corridors. **Pets:** Accepted.
🆂🅰🆅🅴 🆂🔟 🗙 🛢 🖵 🗙

SPRING LAKE

▼▼▼ **Grand Haven Waterfront Holiday Inn** 🆂🅷
(616) 846-1000. **$89-$185.** 940 W Savidge St. On SR 104, just e of US 131. Int corridors. **Pets:** Medium, dogs only. $25 daily fee/pet. Designated rooms, service with restrictions, supervision.
🅰🆂🅺 🆂🔟 🗙 🅜 🛢 🖵 🍽 🏊 🗙

STEVENSVILLE

▲▲▲ ▼ **Baymont Inn & Suites-St. Joseph
(Stevensville)** 🆂🅷
(269) 428-9111. **$49-$99.** 2601 W Marquette Woods Rd. I-94, exit 23 (Red Arrow Hwy), just w. Int corridors. **Pets:** Medium, other species. Service with restrictions, crate.
🆂🅰🆅🅴 🆂🔟 🗙 🅜 ☕ 🛢 🖵

▲▲▲ ▼▼ **Candlewood Suites** 🆂🅷
(269) 428-4400. **$69-$149.** 2567 W Marquette Woods Rd. I-94, exit 23 (Red Arrow Rd), just w. Int corridors. **Pets:** Other species. $25 one-time fee/room.
🆂🅰🆅🅴 🆂🔟 🗙 🅜 ☕ 🛢 🖵

▼▼▼ **Hampton Inn** 🆂🅷
(269) 429-2700. **$74-$129, 7 day notice.** 5050 Red Arrow Hwy. I-94, exit 23 (Red Arrow Hwy), just se. Int corridors. **Pets:** Other species. $40 deposit/room. Service with restrictions, supervision.
🅰🆂🅺 🆂🔟 🗙 🅜 ☕ 🛢 🖵 🏊

▲▲▲ ▼▼ **Park Inn International** 🆂🅷
(269) 429-3218. **$69-$149.** 4290 Red Arrow Hwy. I-94, exit 23 (Red Arrow Hwy), 0.5 mi n. Ext/int corridors. **Pets:** Other species. Service with restrictions, supervision.
🆂🅰🆅🅴 🆂🔟 🗙 ☕ 🛢 🖵 🍽 🏊 🗙

STURGIS

▲▲▲ ▼ **Best Value Green Briar Inn** 🅼 🐾
(269) 651-2361. **$35-$59.** 71381 S Centerville Rd. I-80/90, exit 121 (SR 66), 0.4 mi n. Ext corridors. **Pets:** Small, dogs only. $5 daily fee/pet. Service with restrictions, supervision.
🆂🅰🆅🅴 🆂🔟 🗙 🏊

SUTTONS BAY

▼ **Red Lion Motor Lodge** 🅼
(231) 271-6694. **$59-$135.** 4290 S West Bay Shore Rd. 5 mi s on SR 22. Ext corridors. **Pets:** $10 daily fee/pet. Service with restrictions, supervision.
🗙 🛢 🖵 🐾

TAWAS CITY

▲▲▲ ▼ **Tawas Motel-Resort** 🅼
(989) 362-3822. **$40-$95, 3 day notice.** 1124 US 23 S. On US 23, 1.8 mi s. Ext corridors. **Pets:** Other species. $5 one-time fee/room. Service with restrictions.
🆂🅰🆅🅴 🆂🔟 🗙 🛢 🖵 🏊 🗙

TECUMSEH

▼ **Tecumseh Inn Motel** 🅼
(517) 423-7401. **$49-$150.** 1445 W Chicago Blvd. On SR 50, 1.5 mi w of city center. Int corridors. **Pets:** Other species. $25 deposit/room.
🅰🆂🅺 🆂🔟 🗙 🛢 🖵 🍽

THREE RIVERS

▼▼ **Super 8 Motel** 🆂🅷
(269) 279-8888. **$59-$89.** 711 US 131. Jct US 131 and SR 60 (Broadway St). Int corridors. **Pets:** Accepted.
🗙 🅜 ☕ 🛢 🏊

TRAVERSE CITY

▲▲▲ ▼▼ **Best Western Four Seasons** 🅼 🐾
(231) 946-8424. **$44-$179.** 305 Munson Ave. 2 mi e on US 31. Ext/int corridors. **Pets:** Other species. $10 daily fee/pet. Designated rooms, service with restrictions, supervision.
🆂🅰🆅🅴 🆂🔟 🗙 🛢 🖵 🏊

▲▲▲ ▼▼ **Days Inn & Suites** 🆂🅷 🐾
(231) 941-0208. **$45-$199.** 420 Munson Ave. 2 mi e on US 31. Int corridors. **Pets:** Large, other species. $100 deposit/pet, $10 daily fee/pet. Designated rooms, service with restrictions, supervision.
🆂🅰🆅🅴 🆂🔟 🗙 🛢 🖵 🏊 🗙

▼▼▼ **Holiday Inn** 🆂🅷 🐾
(231) 947-3700. **$89-$199.** 615 E Front St. 0.5 mi e on US 31. Int corridors. **Pets:** Other species. $10 daily fee/room. Designated rooms, service with restrictions, supervision.
🅰🆂🅺 🗙 🅜 ☕ 🛢 🖵 🍽 🏊 🗙

◆◆ **Motel 6–4065** 🆂🅷
(231) 938-3002. **Call for rates.** 1582 US 31 N. On US 31, 4.3 mi e. Int corridors. **Pets:** Accepted.
⊠ ⓛⓜ ⇒

◆◆ **Park Place Hotel** 🆂🅷
(231) 946-5000. **$119-$209.** 300 E State St. Corner of E State and Park sts; downtown. Int corridors. **Pets:** Medium. Designated rooms, service with restrictions, supervision.
(ASK) 🆂 ⊠ 🖊 🔲 🔲 🍴 ⇒ ⊠

◆◆ **Quality Inn** 🆂🅷 🐾
(231) 929-4423. **$39-$169.** 1492 US 31 N. On US 31, 3.3 mi e. Ext/int corridors. **Pets:** Other species. $10 daily fee/room. Designated rooms, service with restrictions, supervision.
(SAVE) 🆂 ⊠ 🖊 🔲 🔲 ⇒

◆◆ **Traverse Victorian Inn** 🆂🅷
(231) 947-5525. **$59-$149.** 461 Munson Ave. 2.4 mi e on US 31. Int corridors. **Pets:** Accepted.
(ASK) 🆂 ⊠ 🔲 🔲 ⇒

WALKER

◆◆ **Baymont Inn & Suites-Grand Rapids North** 🆂🅷
(616) 735-9595. **$69-$99.** 2151 Holton Ct NW. I-96, exit 28 (Walker Ave), just s. Int corridors. **Pets:** Accepted.
(ASK) 🆂 ⊠ 🖊 🔲 🔲 ⇒

WATERSMEET

◆◆ **Dancing Eagles Resort Lac Vieux Desert Casino** 🆂🅷
(906) 358-4949. **$59-$149.** N5384 US Hwy 45. 1.8 mi n of US 2. Int corridors. **Pets:** Medium. $100 deposit/room, $10 daily fee/room. Designated rooms, service with restrictions, supervision.
(ASK) 🆂 ⊠ 🖊 🔲 🔲 ⇒ ⊠

WEST BRANCH

(AAA) ◆◆ **Super 8 Motel** 🆂🅷
(989) 345-8488. **$81-$179.** 2596 Austin's Way. I-75, exit 212 (Cook Rd). Int corridors. **Pets:** Large. Service with restrictions, supervision.
(SAVE) 🆂 ⊠ 🖊 🔲 🔲 ⇒

WHITEHALL

(AAA) ◆ **Lake Land Motel** 🅼 🐾
(231) 894-5644. **$40-$75.** 1002 E Colby St. On US 31 business route, 0.8 mi w of US 31. Ext corridors. **Pets:** Other species. $5 one-time fee/pet. Service with restrictions.
(SAVE) ⊠ 🔲

WHITMORE LAKE

(AAA) ◆◆ **Best Western Whitmore Lake** 🅼
(734) 449-2058. **$69-$99, 3 day notice.** 9897 Main St. US 23, exit 53, just e. Ext corridors. **Pets:** Medium. $25 daily fee/pet. Designated rooms, service with restrictions, crate.
(SAVE) 🆂 ⊠ 🔲 🔲 ⇒

WYOMING

◆ **Super 8 Motel** 🅼
(616) 530-8588. **$54-$80, 3 day notice.** 727 44th St SW. US 131, exit 79. Int corridors. **Pets:** Other species. $10 one-time fee/pet. Designated rooms, service with restrictions, supervision.
(ASK) 🆂 ⊠ 🔲

MINNESOTA

AITKIN

▼▼ 40 Club Inn SH
(218) 927-2903. **$59-$89.** 950 2nd St NW. SR 210, 1 mi w of jct US 169. Int corridors. **Pets:** $5 daily fee/pet. Designated rooms, service with restrictions, supervision.
(ASK) ✕ 🛏 🍴 📺 🏊

▼ Ripple River Motel & RV Park M
(218) 927-3734. **$55-$85.** 701 Minnesota Ave S. US 169, 0.8 mi s of jct SR 210. Ext corridors. **Pets:** $5 daily fee/pet. Designated rooms, service with restrictions, supervision.
(ASK) ✕ 🛏

ALBERT LEA

◆◆◆ ▼◆▼ Albert Lea Countryside Inn Motel M ❖
(507) 373-2446. **$40-$79, 3 day notice.** 2102 E Main St. I-35, exit 11, 1.3 mi w on CR 46. Ext/int corridors. **Pets:** Medium. $5 daily fee/pet. Designated rooms, service with restrictions, supervision.
(SAVE) (S₀) ✕ 🛏

◆◆◆ ▼◆▼◆▼ Comfort Inn SH ❖
(507) 377-1100. **$59-$89.** 810 Happy Trails Ln. I-35, exit 11, just se. Int corridors. **Pets:** Other species. $10 one-time fee/pet. Designated rooms, service with restrictions, supervision.
(SAVE) (S₀) ✕ 🛁 🐾 🛏 📺 🏊 🏊

◆◆◆ ▼◆▼◆▼ Country Inn & Suites By Carlson SH
(507) 373-5513. **$71-$116.** 2214 E Main St. I-35, exit 12 southbound; exit 11 northbound, 1 mi w. Int corridors. **Pets:** Small. $20 one-time fee/room. Designated rooms, service with restrictions, supervision.
(SAVE) (S₀) ✕ 🛁 🐾 🛏 📺 🏊

◆◆◆ ▼◆▼ Days Inn SH
(507) 373-8291. **$75-$90, 3 day notice.** 2301 E Main St. I-35, exit 11, 1 mi w on CR 46. Int corridors. **Pets:** Medium, other species. $8 daily fee/pet. Designated rooms, service with restrictions, supervision.
(SAVE) (S₀) ✕ 🐾 🛏 🍴 🏊 🏊

ALEXANDRIA

◆◆◆ ▼◆▼◆▼ Country Inn & Suites By Carlson SH
(320) 763-9900. **$76-$109.** 5304 Hwy 29 S. I-94, exit 103, just sw. Int corridors. **Pets:** Small. $10 one-time fee/room. Designated rooms, service with restrictions, supervision.
(SAVE) (S₀) ✕ 🐾 🛁 🛏 📺 🏊

▼▼▼ Holiday Inn Alexandria SH
(320) 763-6577. **$77-$150.** 5637 State Hwy 29 S. I-94, exit 103, just s. Int corridors. **Pets:** Other species. Designated rooms, service with restrictions, supervision.
(ASK) ✕ 🛏 📺 🍴 🏊 🏊

◆◆◆ ▼◆▼ Super 8 Motel SH
(320) 763-6552. **$56-$81, 14 day notice.** 4620 SR 29 S. I-94, exit 103, 0.3 mi n. Int corridors. **Pets:** Small. $50 deposit/room, $6 one-time fee/pet. Designated rooms, service with restrictions, crate.
(SAVE) (S₀) ✕ 🛏

AUSTIN

◆◆◆ ▼◆▼ Country Side Inn SH
(507) 437-7774. **$45-$60.** 3303 Oakland Ave W. I-90, exit 175 (Oakland Ave), just nw. Int corridors. **Pets:** Other species. $5 one-time fee/room. Service with restrictions.
(SAVE) (S₀) ✕ 🛏 📺

▼▼ Days Inn SH
(507) 433-8600. **$65-$75.** 700 16th Ave NW. I-90, exit 178A (4th St NW), just nw. Int corridors. **Pets:** Other species. $10 one-time fee/room. Designated rooms, service with restrictions, supervision.
(ASK) (S₀) ✕ 🛁 🛏 📺

▼▼▼ Holiday Inn & Austin Conference Center SH ❖
(507) 433-1000. **$70-$200.** 1701 4th St NW. I-90, exit 178A (4th St NW), just nw. Int corridors. **Pets:** Small, other species. $25 one-time fee/pet. Designated rooms, service with restrictions, crate.
(ASK) (S₀) ✕ 🐾 🛁 🛏 📺 🍴 🏊 🏊

BABBITT

▼▼▼ Timber Bay Lodge & Houseboats CA
(218) 827-3682. **$140-$300, 60 day notice.** 8347 Timber Bay Rd. 2.8 mi e of jct CR 21 via CR 70 and 623. Ext corridors. **Pets:** $15 daily fee/pet. No service.
🛏 📺 ✕ 🎿 ☎

BAUDETTE

▼▼▼ AmericInn Lodge & Suites Lake of the Woods SH
(218) 634-3200. **$74-$140.** 1179 Main St W. 0.5 mi w on SR 11. Int corridors. **Pets:** Medium. $20 one-time fee/room. Designated rooms, service with restrictions, supervision.
(ASK) (S₀) ✕ 🛁 🛏 📺 🏊 🏊

BAXTER

▼▼▼▼ Country Inn & Suites by Carlson SH
(218) 828-2161. **$79-$99.** 15058 Dellwood Dr N. Jct SR 371 and 210,
1 mi n on SR 371. Int corridors. **Pets:** Dogs only. Designated rooms,
service with restrictions, supervision.

[ASK] [S🐾] [✕] [🕎M] [🔌] [🐾] [🛏] [💻] [➳]

▼▼▼▼ Hawthorn Inn & Suites SH
(218) 822-1133. **$89-$349.** 2300 Fairview Rd N. Just nw of jct SR 371
on SR 210. Int corridors. **Pets:** Medium. $50 deposit/pet. Designated
rooms, service with restrictions, supervision.

[ASK] [S🐾] [✕] [🕎M] [🔌] [🐾] [🛏] [💻] [➳] [✕]

BEMIDJI

▲▲▲ ▼▼▼▼ Best Western Bemidji SH ❖
(218) 751-0390. **$45-$99.** 2420 Paul Bunyan Dr. Jct US 71 N and SR
197. Int corridors. **Pets:** Medium, other species. $10 one-time fee/room.
Designated rooms, service with restrictions, supervision.

[SAVE] [S🐾] [✕] [🐾] [🛏] [💻] [➳] [✕]

▲▲▲ ▼▼▼▼ Ruttger's Birchmont Lodge CA
(218) 444-3463. **$46-$249, 30 day notice.** 7598 Bemidji Rd NE. Jct SR
197, 3.6 mi n on CR 21 (Bemidji Ave N). Ext/int corridors. **Pets:** Other
species. $10 daily fee/pet. Designated rooms, service with restrictions.

[SAVE] [S🐾] [✕] [🛏] [💻] [🍴] [➳] [✕]

BIWABIK

▲▲▲ ▼▼▼▼ The Lodge at Giants Ridge SH
(218) 865-7170. **$69-$189, 14 day notice.** 6373 Wynne Creek Dr. 2.7
mi e on CR 135, then 4 mi e. Int corridors. **Pets:** Accepted.

[SAVE] [S🐾] [✕] [🐾] [🛏] [💻] [🍴] [➳] [✕]

BLUE EARTH

▼▼ AmericInn of Blue Earth SH
(507) 526-4215. **$49-$150.** 1495 Domes Dr. I-90, exit 119 (US 169),
just se. Int corridors. **Pets:** Accepted.

[ASK] [S🐾] [✕] [🕎M] [🐾] [🛏] [🛏] [💻] [➳]

▼▼ Super 8 Motel SH
(507) 526-7376. **$60-$70.** 1420 Giant Dr. I-90, exit 119 (US 169), just s.
Int corridors. **Pets:** Other species. $5 one-time fee/room. Designated
rooms, service with restrictions, supervision.

[ASK] [S🐾] [✕] [🛏] [💻]

BRAINERD

▲▲▲ ▼▼▼▼ Ramada Inn Brainerd SH
(218) 829-1441. **$69-$95, 7 day notice.** 2115 S 6th St. On SR 371
business route, 1.8 mi s of jct SR 210. Ext/int corridors. **Pets:** Medium.
$10 daily fee/room. Service with restrictions, supervision.

[SAVE] [S🐾] [✕] [🐾] [🛏] [💻] [🍴] [➳] [✕]

BRECKENRIDGE

▲▲▲ ▼▼▼ Select Inn of Breckenridge/Wahpeton SH
(218) 643-9201. **$49-$59.** 821 Hwy 75 N. Just sw of jct US 75 N and
210. Int corridors. **Pets:** Other species. $50 deposit/room, $10 one-time
fee/room. Designated rooms.

[SAVE] [S🐾] [✕] [🐾] [🛏] [➳]

CALEDONIA

▲▲▲ ▼▼▼▼ AmericInn Lodge & Suites SH
(507) 725-8000. **$68-$111.** 508 N Kruckow Ave. Just n of Main St on
SR 44, just w on Esch Dr. Int corridors. **Pets:** Small. $50 deposit/pet.
Service with restrictions, supervision.

[SAVE] [✕] [🐾] [🛏] [💻] [➳]

CANNON FALLS

▲▲▲ ▼▼▼ Best Western Saratoga Inn SH
(507) 263-7272. **$69-$135.** 31591 64th Ave. 1 mi s on US 52. Int
corridors. **Pets:** Medium, other species. $15 daily fee/room. Designated
rooms, service with restrictions, crate.

[SAVE] [S🐾] [✕] [🛏] [💻] [➳]

CLOQUET

▼▼ Super 8 Motel SH
(218) 879-1250. **$66-$136.** 121 Big Lake Rd. I-35, exit 237 (SR 33), 2
mi nw. Int corridors. **Pets:** Dogs only. $50 deposit/room. Designated
rooms, service with restrictions, supervision.

[ASK] [S🐾] [✕] [🕎M] [🐾] [🛏]

CROOKSTON

▼▼ Northland Inn of Crookston SH
(218) 281-5210. **$69-$89.** 2200 University Ave. On US 2 W and 75 N,
1.5 mi n. Int corridors. **Pets:** Large, other species. $10 one-time fee/room.
Designated rooms, supervision.

[ASK] [S🐾] [✕] [🐾] [🍴] [➳]

DETROIT LAKES

▲▲▲ ▼▼▼▼ AmericInn Lodge & Suites SH
(218) 847-8795. **$64-$126.** 777 Hwy 10 E. 1.4 mi se. Int corridors.
Pets: Other species. $10 daily fee/pet. Service with restrictions, supervision.

[SAVE] [S🐾] [✕] [🕎M] [🔌] [🐾] [🛏] [💻] [➳] [✕]

▲▲▲ ▼▼▼▼ Best Western Holland House & Suites SH
(218) 847-4483. **$79-$209, 3 day notice.** 615 Hwy 10 E. 1.3 mi se.
Ext/int corridors. **Pets:** Accepted.

[SAVE] [✕] [🔌] [🛏] [💻] [➳] [✕]

▲▲▲ ▼▼▼ Budget Host Inn M ❖
(218) 847-4454. **$48-$62.** 895 Hwy 10 E. 1.5 mi se. Ext corridors.
Pets: Other species. $10 daily fee/room. Service with restrictions, supervision.

[SAVE] [S🐾] [✕] [🛏] [💻]

DULUTH

**▲▲▲ ▼▼▼▼ AmericInn Hotel & Suites of
Duluth/Proctor** SH
(218) 624-1026. **$80-$190.** 185 US 2. Jct I-35 and US 2, 0.8 mi n. Int
corridors. **Pets:** Dogs only. $10 daily fee/pet. Service with restrictions,
supervision.

[SAVE] [S🐾] [✕] [🔌] [🐾] [🛏] [💻] [🍴] [➳]

▲▲▲ ▼▼▼▼ Best Western Downtown Motel M
(218) 727-6851. **$39-$119.** 131 W 2nd St. 2nd St at 2nd Ave W; center.
Ext/int corridors. **Pets:** Accepted.

[SAVE] [S🐾] [✕] [🛏] [💻]

▲▲▲ ▼▼▼▼ Best Western Edgewater Motel M
(218) 728-3601. **$69-$219.** 2400 London Rd. I-35, exit 258 (21st Ave
E), just nw. Ext/int corridors. **Pets:** Accepted.

[SAVE] [S🐾] [✕] [🐾] [🛏] [💻] [➳] [✕]

▼▼▼ Days Inn-Duluth SH
(218) 727-3110. **$59-$159.** 909 Cottonwood Ave. SR 194, just n of jct
US 53. Int corridors. **Pets:** Other species. Service with restrictions, supervision.

[ASK] [S🐾] [✕] [🐾] [🛏]

▲▲▲ ▼▼▼ Hawthorn Suites at Waterfront Plaza SH ❖
(218) 727-4663. **$95-$275.** 325 Lake Ave S. In Canal Park area. Int
corridors. **Pets:** Large, other species. $50 deposit/room. Designated
rooms, service with restrictions, supervision.

[SAVE] [S🐾] [✕] [🕎M] [🔌] [🐾] [🛏] [💻] [🍴] [➳] [✕]

▼▼▼▼ Radisson Hotel Duluth-Harborview 🄻🄷
(218) 727-8981. **$99-$149.** 505 W Superior St. At 5th Ave W; center. Int corridors. **Pets:** Medium. $10 daily fee/room. Designated rooms, service with restrictions, supervision.
(A$K) (S🛏) (✕) (🛎) (💻) (🍴) (🏊) (✕)

▼▼▼ Voyageur Lakewalk Inn 🄼
(218) 722-3911. **$35-$68.** 333 E Superior St. I-35, exit 256 (Superior St), just n at jct 4th Ave E and Superior St. Ext corridors. **Pets:** Large. $10 one-time fee/room. Crate.
(A$K) (S🛏) (✕) (🛎) (💻)

ELY

🄰🄰🄰 ▼▼▼▼ Grand Ely Lodge Resort and Conference
          Center 🆂🅷 🐾
(218) 365-6565. **$90-$175, 14 day notice.** 400 N Pioneer Rd. SR 169 to Central Ave, just n to Pioneer Rd, then 1 mi n. Ext/int corridors. **Pets:** Other species. $15 daily fee/pet. Designated rooms, service with restrictions, supervision.
(SAVE) (S🛏) (✕) (🌀) (🛎) (💻) (🍴) (🏊) (✕)

▼▼ Motel Ely-Budget Host 🄼
(218) 365-3237. **$69-$89.** 1047 E Sheridan St. SR 1 and 169. Ext corridors. **Pets:** $10 daily fee/room. Designated rooms, service with restrictions, supervision.
(A$K) (S🛏) (✕) (💻)

EVELETH

▼▼ Super 8 Motel 🆂🅷
(218) 744-1661. **$56-$127.** 1080 Industrial Park Dr. On US 53, 0.5 mi n of jct SR 37. Int corridors. **Pets:** Accepted.
(A$K) (S🛏) (✕) (🅜) (🛎) (💻) (🏊) (✕)

FAIRMONT

▼▼▼ Comfort Inn 🆂🅷
(507) 238-5444. **$75-$95.** 2225 N State St. I-90, exit 102 (SR 15), just sw. Int corridors. **Pets:** Accepted.
(A$K) (S🛏) (✕) (🅜) (🛎) (💻) (🏊)

▼▼▼ Holiday Inn 🆂🅷
(507) 238-4771. **$89-$109.** 1201 Torgerson Dr. I-90, exit 102 (SR 15), just se. Int corridors. **Pets:** Accepted.
(A$K) (S🛏) (✕) (🛎) (💻) (🍴) (🏊) (✕)

▼▼ Super 8 Motel 🆂🅷
(507) 238-9444. **$47-$65.** 1200 Torgerson Dr. I-90, exit 102 (SR 15), just se. Int corridors. **Pets:** Designated rooms, service with restrictions, supervision.
(A$K) (S🛏) (✕)

FARIBAULT

🄰🄰🄰 ▼▼▼ AmericInn Motel 🆂🅷
(507) 334-9464. **$74-$150.** 1801 Lavender Dr. I-35, exit 59 (SR 21), 0.3 mi e. Int corridors. **Pets:** $15 one-time fee/pet. Designated rooms, service with restrictions, supervision.
(SAVE) (S🛏) (✕) (🌀) (🛎) (💻) (🏊) (✕)

▼▼ Days Inn & Suites 🆂🅷
(507) 334-6835. **$50-$80.** 1920 Cardinal Ln. I-35, exit 59 (SR 21), just ne. Int corridors. **Pets:** Medium. $10 daily fee/pet. Service with restrictions, supervision.
(A$K) (✕) (🅜) (🌀) (🛎) (💻) (🏊)

🄰🄰🄰 ▼▼▼ Select Inn 🄼
(507) 334-2051. **$45-$60.** 4040 SR 60 W. I-35, exit 56, just w. Int corridors. **Pets:** Accepted.
(SAVE) (✕) (🛎) (💻) (🏊)

FERGUS FALLS

🄰🄰🄰 ▼▼▼ AmericInn Lodge & Suites 🆂🅷 🐾
(218) 739-3900. **$72-$95.** 526 Western Ave N. I-94, exit 54 (SR 210), just se. Int corridors. **Pets:** Other species. $50 deposit/room, $10 one-time fee/room. Designated rooms, service with restrictions, crate.
(SAVE) (✕) (🅜) (🌀) (🛎) (💻) (🏊) (✕)

FINLAYSON

▼▼▼ Banning Junction-North Country Inn 🆂🅷
(320) 245-5284. **$50-$90.** 60671 State Hwy 23. I-35, exit 195 (SR 23), just ne. Int corridors. **Pets:** Accepted.
(A$K) (S🛏) (✕) (🛎)

FOSSTON

▼▼ Super 8 Motel 🆂🅷
(218) 435-1088. **$53-$82.** 108 S Amber. US 2, 0.5 mi e. Int corridors. **Pets:** Dogs only. $5 one-time fee/room. Supervision.
(A$K) (S🛏) (✕) (🛎)

GARRISON

▼▼▼▼ Garrison Inn & Suites by Ruttger's 🆂🅷
(320) 692-4050. **$69-$115.** 9243 Hwy 169. SR 169, just s of jct SR 18. Int corridors. **Pets:** Dogs only. $50 deposit/room, $10 daily fee/pet. Designated rooms, service with restrictions, supervision.
(A$K) (S🛏) (✕) (🛎) (💻) (🏊)

GAYLORD

▼▼▼ Gold Leaf Inn & Suites 🄼
(507) 237-5860. **$54-$130.** 330 Main Ave E. 1.5 mi e. Int corridors. **Pets:** Medium. Designated rooms, service with restrictions, supervision.
(✕) (🌀) (🛎)

GRAND MARAIS

🄰🄰🄰 ▼▼▼▼ Best Western Superior Inn & Suites 🆂🅷 🐾
(218) 387-2240. **$69-$259, 3 day notice.** 104 1st Ave E. SR 61, just ne of center. Int corridors. **Pets:** Other species. $10 daily fee/pet. Designated rooms, service with restrictions, supervision.
(SAVE) (✕) (🌀) (🌀) (🛎) (💻)

▼▼▼▼ Gunflint Lodge 🆅🅷 🐾
(218) 388-2294. **$105-$459, 42 day notice.** 143 S Gunflint Lake. 43 mi n of town; 0.8 mi e of jct CR 12 (Gunflint Tr) and 50. Ext corridors. **Pets:** Other species. $15 daily fee/pet.
(🅜) (🛎) (💻) (🍴) (✕) (🗙) (🌀)

🄰🄰🄰 ▼▼▼ Nor'Wester Lodge and Outfitter 🄲🄰
(218) 388-2252. **$920-$1400 (weekly), 60 day notice.** 7778 Gunflint Tr. 30 mi nw on CR 12 (Gunflint Tr) from jct SR 61. Ext corridors. **Pets:** Dogs only. $15 daily fee/pet. Designated rooms, supervision.
(SAVE) (🛎) (💻) (✕) (🗙) (🌐) (🌀)

▼▼ Outpost Motel 🄼
(218) 387-1833. **$45-$95.** 2935 SR 61 E. 9 mi ne. Ext corridors. **Pets:** Other species. $10 daily fee/pet. Service with restrictions, supervision.
(✕) (🛎) (💻) (✕) (🗙)

🄰🄰🄰 ▼▼ Wedgewood Motel 🄼
(218) 387-2944. **$44-$59, 3 day notice.** 1663 E Hwy 61. On SR 61, 2.5 mi ne. Ext corridors. **Pets:** Dogs only. $5 daily fee/pet. Designated rooms, service with restrictions, supervision.
(SAVE) (S🛏) (✕) (🛎) (🗙) (🌀)

GRAND RAPIDS

🄰🄰🄰 ▼▼▼ Budget Host Inn 🄼
(218) 326-3457. **$50-$78.** 311 E Hwy 2. Jct US 2 E and 169 N. Ext/int corridors. **Pets:** $50 deposit/pet. Designated rooms, service with restrictions, crate.
(SAVE) (S🛏) (✕)

Country Inn By Carlson SH ❀
(218) 327-4960. **$88-$94, 30 day notice.** 2601 Hwy 169 S. US 2, 2 mi s. Int corridors. **Pets:** Medium, other species. Supervision.
[SAVE] ☒ 🅰M 🗐 🖍 🔒 💻 ⊿

Sawmill Inn M ❀
(218) 326-8501. **$76-$99.** 2301 S Pokegama Ave. US 2, 2 mi s on US 169. Ext/int corridors. **Pets:** Service with restrictions, supervision.
[SAVE] 🗐 ☒ 🗐 🔒 💻 ⊪ ⊿ ☒

GRANITE FALLS

Super 8 Motel SH
(320) 564-4075. **Call for rates.** 845 W SR 212. Jct SR 23 and 212, 0.5 mi w. Int corridors. **Pets:** Accepted.
☒ 🅰M 🖍 🔒 ⊿

HARMONY

Country Lodge Motel SH
(507) 886-2515. **$55-$90.** 525 Main Ave N. 0.4 mi n on US 52. Int corridors. **Pets:** Accepted.
☒ 🖍 🔒 💻

HINCKLEY

Days Inn SH
(320) 384-7751. **$59-$129.** 104 Grindstone Ct. I-35, exit 183 (SR 48), just e. Int corridors. **Pets:** Other species. $16 daily fee/room. Service with restrictions, supervision.
[SAVE] 🗐 ☒ 🖍 🔒 💻 ⊿

Hinckley Gold Pine Inn M
(320) 384-6112. **$45-$109.** 325 Fire Monument. I-35, exit 183 (SR 48), just w. Ext/int corridors. **Pets:** Other species. $6 daily fee/pet. Service with restrictions, supervision.
[SAVE] 🗐 ☒ 🗐 🔒 💻

HUTCHINSON

AmericInn Motel SH ❀
(320) 587-5515. **$65-$139.** 1115 Hwy 7 E. On SR 7, just e. Int corridors. **Pets:** Other species. $10 daily fee/room. Designated rooms, service with restrictions, supervision.
[SAVE] 🗐 ☒ 🅰M 🗐 🖍 🔒 💻 ⊿ ☒

INTERNATIONAL FALLS

Hilltop Motel M
(218) 283-2505. **$46-$79.** 2002 2nd Ave W. US 53, 1 mi s of jct US 53 and SR 11. Ext corridors. **Pets:** Small, dogs only. $10 daily fee/pet. Service with restrictions, supervision.
[ASK] 🗐 ☒

Holiday Inn SH
(218) 283-8000. **$89-$175.** 1500 US 71 W. 1.5 mi w on US 71 and SR 11 W. Int corridors. **Pets:** Accepted.
[ASK] 🗐 ☒ 🖍 🔒 💻 ⊪ ⊿ ☒

JACKSON

Budget Host Inn Praire Winds M
(507) 847-2020. **$40-$56.** 950 US 71. I-90, exit 73 (US 71), 0.4 mi s. Ext corridors. **Pets:** Accepted.
[SAVE] ☒ 🅰M 🔒

Super 8 Motel SH
(507) 847-3498. **$65-$70.** 2025 Hwy 71 N. I-90, exit 73 (US 71), just n. Int corridors. **Pets:** Accepted.
[ASK] 🗐 ☒ 🅰M 🖍 🔒

LAMBERTON

Lamberton Motel M
(507) 752-7242. **$35-$55.** 601 1st Ave W. Just s of jct US 14 and Ilex St. Ext corridors. **Pets:** Accepted.
[ASK] 🗐 ☒ 🔒 💻

LITCHFIELD

ScotWood Motel M
(320) 693-2496. **$55-$69.** 1017 E Frontage Rd. On US 12. Int corridors. **Pets:** Accepted.
[ASK] 🗐 ☒ 🔒 ⊿

LITTLE FALLS

Country Inn & Suites By Carlson SH
(320) 632-1000. **$94-$139.** 209 16th St NE. Just ne of jct SR 10 and 27. Int corridors. **Pets:** Accepted.
[SAVE] 🗐 ☒ 🅰M 🖍 🔒 💻 ⊿

LONG PRAIRIE

Budget Host Inn M
(320) 732-6118. **$43-$70, 3 day notice.** 417 Lake St. On US 71 and SR 27, just s of jct SR 287. Ext corridors. **Pets:** Large. $5 daily fee/pet. Designated rooms, service with restrictions, supervision.
[SAVE] 🗐 ☒ 🔒 💻

LUTSEN

Cascade Lodge CI
(218) 387-1112. **$45-$99, 14 day notice.** 3719 W Hwy 61. On SR 61, 7 mi ne of jct CR 4. Ext/int corridors. **Pets:** Accepted.
[SAVE] ☒ 🔒 💻 ⊪ ☒

Lutsen Lodging Company "The Mountain Inn" SH
(218) 663-7244. **$59-$134, 45 day notice.** 360 Ski Hill Rd. On CR 5 (Ski Hill Rd), 1.3 mi n of jct SR 61. Int corridors. **Pets:** Accepted.
☒ 🔒 ☒

Solbakken Resort M
(218) 663-7566. **$49-$145, 14 day notice.** 4874 W SR 61. On SR 61, 1.3 mi n of jct CR 4 (Caribou Tr). Ext corridors. **Pets:** Medium. $10 daily fee/pet. Designated rooms, supervision.
[SAVE] 🗐 ☒ 🖍 🔒 💻 ☒ 🗝

MANKATO

Best Western Hotel, Restaurant & Conference Center SH
(507) 625-9333. **$70-$110.** 1111 Range St. 1.3 mi n on US 169. Int corridors. **Pets:** Designated rooms, service with restrictions, crate.
[SAVE] 🗐 ☒ 🔒 💻 ⊪ ⊿ ☒

Comfort Inn by Choice Hotels SH
(507) 388-5107. **$60-$109.** 131 Apache Pl. Just s of jct US 14 and SR 22 S. Int corridors. **Pets:** Accepted.
[ASK] 🗐 ☒ 🖍 🔒 💻 ⊿

Days Inn SH ❀
(507) 387-3332. **$50-$90.** 1285 Range St. US 169, 0.3 mi s of jct US 14. Int corridors. **Pets:** Other species. $5 daily fee/pet. Designated rooms, service with restrictions, supervision.
[SAVE] 🗐 ☒ 🔒 💻 ⊿

Grandstay Residential Suites SH
(507) 388-8688. **$99-$119.** 1000 Raintree Rd. 1.3 mi s of jct US 14 and SR 22 on CR 3. Int corridors. **Pets:** Accepted.
[ASK] 🗐 ☒ 🗐 🖍 🔒 💻 ⊿

Holiday Inn SH
(507) 345-1234. **$70-$100.** 101 E Main St. Main St at Riverfront Dr; downtown. Int corridors. **Pets:** Accepted.
[ASK] 🗐 ☒ 🅰M 🗐 🖍 🔒 💻 ⊪ ⊿ ☒

▼▼/▼▼ **Super 8 Motel** SH
(507) 387-4041. **$60-$105, 3 day notice.** 51578 US Hwy 169. Jct US 169 N and 14, just n. Int corridors. **Pets:** Accepted.

[ASK] [S̅o̅] [✕] [🛏] [💻] [⊠]

MARSHALL

AAA ▼▼/▼▼ **Best Western Marshall Inn** SH
(507) 532-3221. **$66-$96.** 1500 E College Dr. SR 19, just w of jct SR 23. Int corridors. **Pets:** Other species. $10 one-time fee/room. Service with restrictions, supervision.

[SAVE] [S̅o̅] [✕] [🛏] [💻] [¶¶] [⇘] [⊠]

▼▼/▼▼ **Comfort Inn** SH
(507) 532-3070. **$68-$108.** 1511 E College Dr. SR 19, w of jct SR 23. Int corridors. **Pets:** $5 daily fee/pet. Service with restrictions, crate.

[ASK] [S̅o̅] [✕] [&M] [⊘] [🖉] [🛏] [💻] [⇘]

▼▼/▼▼ **Super 8 Motel** SH ❀
(507) 537-1461. **$60-$75.** 1106 E Main St. 0.3 mi se on US 59 from jct SR 23. Int corridors. **Pets:** Other species. $50 deposit/room, $10 one-time fee/room. Service with restrictions, supervision.

[ASK] [S̅o̅] [✕] [⊘] [🛏]

MCGREGOR

▼▼/▼▼ **Country Meadows Inn** SH
(218) 768-7378. **$60-$109.** Jct SR 65 and 210. Int corridors. **Pets:** Accepted.

[✕] [🖉] [🛏] [💻] [⇘]

MINNEAPOLIS-ST. PAUL METROPOLITAN AREA

ANNANDALE

▼▼/▼▼ **AmericInn Lodge & Suites** SH
(320) 274-3006. **$69-$129.** 620 Elm St E. On SR 55. Int corridors. **Pets:** Small, other species. $50 deposit/room. Designated rooms, service with restrictions, crate.

[ASK] [S̅o̅] [✕] [&M] [⊘] [🖉] [🛏] [💻] [⇘]

ARDEN HILLS

▼▼/▼▼ **Super 8 Arden Hills/Minneapolis/St. Paul** SH
(651) 484-6557. **$59-$89.** 1125 Red Fox Rd. I-694, exit 43A (Lexington Ave), just sw. Int corridors. **Pets:** Medium. $50 deposit/room, $8 daily fee/pet. Service with restrictions, supervision.

[ASK] [S̅o̅] [✕] [🛏] [💻]

BECKER

AAA ▼▼/▼▼ **Sleep Inn & Suites** SH
(763) 262-7700. **$69-$139.** 14435 Bank St. On US 10. Int corridors. **Pets:** $100 deposit/room, $10 daily fee/pet. Service with restrictions, supervision.

[SAVE] [S̅o̅] [✕] [🛏] [💻] [⇘] [⊠]

BLOOMINGTON

AAA ▼▼/▼▼ **AmeriSuites (Minneapolis/Mall of America)** SH
(952) 854-0700. **$79-$159.** 7800 International Dr. I-494, exit 1B (34th Ave), just sw. Int corridors. **Pets:** Medium, other species. $10 one-time fee/room. Service with restrictions, supervision.

[SAVE] [S̅o̅] [✕] [&M] [🖉] [🛏] [💻] [⇘]

AAA ▼▼/▼▼ **Baymont Inn Minneapolis-Airport (Bloomington)** SH
(952) 881-7311. **$70-$95.** 7815 Nicollet Ave S. I-494, exit 4A (Nicollet Ave), just s. Int corridors. **Pets:** Accepted.

[SAVE] [S̅o̅] [✕] [⊘] [🛏] [💻]

AAA ▼▼/▼▼ **Hilton Minneapolis/St. Paul Airport Mall of America** LH
(952) 854-2100. **$89-$189.** 3800 E 80th St. I-494, exit 1B (34th Ave), just se. Int corridors. **Pets:** Accepted.

[SAVE] [S̅o̅] [✕] [♿] [⊘] [🖉] [🛏] [💻] [¶¶] [⇘] [⊠]

AAA ▼▼/▼▼ **Homewood Suites by Hilton** SH
(952) 854-0900. **$109-$209.** 2261 Killebrew Dr. I-494, exit 2A (24th Ave), 1 mi s, then just w. Int corridors. **Pets:** Accepted.

[SAVE] [S̅o̅] [✕] [🖉] [🛏] [💻] [⇘]

▼▼/▼▼ **Hospitality Inn & Suites** SH
(952) 854-1687. **$64-$154.** 1601 79th St E. I-494, exit 3, 0.5 mi s. Int corridors. **Pets:** Small. $20 daily fee/pet. Designated rooms, service with restrictions, crate.

[ASK] [S̅o̅] [✕] [🛏] [💻] [¶¶] [⇘]

AAA ▼▼/▼▼ **Park Inn Suites Bloomington** SH
(952) 893-9999. **$105-$120.** 7770 Johnson Ave. I-494, exit 6B (France Ave), 0.5 mi nw on frontage road (78th St). Int corridors. **Pets:** Accepted.

[SAVE] [✕] [&M] [⊘] [🛏] [💻] [⇘] [⊠]

▼▼/▼▼ **Ramada Inn Mall of America** SH
(952) 854-3411. **$79-$139.** 2201 E 78th St. I-494, exit 2A (24th Ave), just s. Int corridors. **Pets:** Accepted.

[ASK] [S̅o̅] [✕] [&M] [⊘] [🛏] [💻] [¶¶] [⇘] [⊠]

▼▼/▼▼ **Residence Inn by Marriott** SH ❀
(952) 876-0900. **$159-$220.** 7850 Bloomington Ave S. I-494, exit 3, on south frontage road. Int corridors. **Pets:** Other species. $50 one-time fee/room. No service.

[ASK] [✕] [⊘] [🖉] [🛏] [💻] [⇘]

▼▼/▼▼ **Sheraton Bloomington Hotel Minneapolis South** LH
(952) 835-7800. **$89-$229.** 7800 Normandale Blvd. I-494, exit 7 (SR 100). Int corridors. **Pets:** Accepted.

[ASK] [S̅o̅] [✕] [🖉] [🛏] [💻] [¶¶] [⇘] [⊠]

AAA ▼▼/▼▼ **Sofitel Minneapolis** LH ❀
(952) 835-1900. **$204-$234.** 5601 W 78th St. Just nw of jct I-494 and SR 100, access via SR 100 and Industrial Blvd. Int corridors. **Pets:** Service with restrictions, supervision.

[SAVE] [S̅o̅] [✕] [&M] [⊘] [🖉] [🛏] [¶¶] [⊠]

▼▼/▼▼ **Staybridge Suites** SH
(952) 831-7900. **$109-$139.** 5150 American Blvd. I-494, exit 6B (France Ave), just se of SR 100, then 1 mi w on frontage road. Int corridors. **Pets:** Accepted.

[ASK] [S̅o̅] [✕] [&M] [⊘] [🖉] [🛏] [💻] [⇘] [⊠]

BROOKLYN CENTER

AAA ▼▼/▼▼ **Baymont Inn & Suites Minneapolis-Brooklyn Center** SH
(763) 561-8400. **$59-$90.** 6415 James Cir N. I-94/694, exit 34 (Shingle Creek Pkwy), just ne. Int corridors. **Pets:** Service with restrictions, supervision.

[SAVE] [S̅o̅] [✕] [⊘] [🛏] [💻]

▼▼ Comfort Inn by Choice Hotels 🆂🅷
(763) 560-7464. **$64-$99.** 1600 James Cir N. I-694, exit 34 (Shingle Creek Pkwy), just ne. Int corridors. **Pets:** Accepted.
🅰🆂🅚 🆂💰 ☒ 🅛🅜 🖉 🛋 🛎 🖥

🅐🅐🅐 ▼▼▼ Holiday Inn Select Minneapolis North 🆂🅷
(763) 566-8000. **$82-$100.** 2200 Freeway Blvd. I-94/694, exit 34 (Shingle Creek Pkwy). Int corridors. **Pets:** Medium. $100 deposit/pet, $25 daily fee/pet. Crate.
🆂🅐🆅🅴 🆂💰 ☒ 🖉 🛋 🛎 🖥 🍽 🏊 ⊠

BROOKLYN PARK

🅐🅐🅐 ▼▼ Sleep Inn 🆂🅷
(763) 971-8000. **$74-$99.** 7011 Northland Cir. I-94/694, exit 30 (Boone Ave), just ne. Int corridors. **Pets:** Accepted.
🆂🅐🆅🅴 🆂💰 ☒ 🅛🅜 🖉 🛋 🛎 🖥 🏊

BURNSVILLE

▼▼ Red Roof Inn 🅼
(952) 890-1420. **$41-$74.** 12920 Aldrich Ave S. I-35W, exit 2 (Burnsville Pkwy), just sw. Ext corridors. **Pets:** Accepted.
☒ 🖉

▼▼ Super 8 Motel 🅼
(952) 894-3400. **$52-$72.** 1101 Burnsville Pkwy. I-35W, exit 2 (Burnsville Pkwy), just sw. Int corridors. **Pets:** Accepted.
🅰🆂🅚 🆂💰 ☒ 🖥

CHANHASSEN

🅐🅐🅐 ▼▼▼ AmericInn Hotel & Suites 🆂🅷
(952) 934-3888. **$101-$185.** 570 Pond Promenade. Just se of jct SR 5 and 101 N. Int corridors. **Pets:** Small. $100 deposit/room, $30 one-time fee/pet. Designated rooms, service with restrictions, crate.
🆂🅐🆅🅴 🆂💰 ☒ 🅛🅜 🖉 🛋 🛎 🖥 ⊠

COON RAPIDS

🅐🅐🅐 ▼▼▼ Comfort Inn-Northtown 🆂🅷
(763) 785-4746. **$60-$100.** 9052 University Ave NE. Just ne of jct US 10, exit University Ave. Int corridors. **Pets:** Accepted.
🆂🅐🆅🅴 🆂💰 ☒ 🛋 🛎 🖥 🏊

🅐🅐🅐 ▼▼▼ Country Suites By Carlson 🆂🅷
(763) 780-3797. **$109-$124.** 155 Coon Rapids Blvd. 0.5 mi e of SR 610. Int corridors. **Pets:** Small. $10 daily fee/pet. Designated rooms, service with restrictions, crate.
🆂🅐🆅🅴 🆂💰 ☒ 🖉 🛋 🛎 🖥 🏊

EAGAN

▼▼ Homestead Studio Suites Hotel-Airport/Eagan 🆂🅷
(651) 905-1778. **$69-$84.** 3015 Denmark Ave. I-35E, exit 98 (Lone Oak Rd), just se. Int corridors. **Pets:** Other species. $75 one-time fee/pet. Designated rooms, service with restrictions, crate.
🅰🆂🅚 🆂💰 ☒ 🖉 🛋 🖥

▼▼ Microtel Inn 🆂🅷
(651) 405-0988. **$60.** 3000 Denmark Ave. I-35E, exit 98 (Lone Oak Rd), just se. Int corridors. **Pets:** $10 one-time fee/room. Designated rooms, service with restrictions, supervision.
🅰🆂🅚 ☒ 🛋 🛎 🖥

▼▼ Residence Inn by Marriott-Mpls/St. Paul Airport 🆂🅷
(651) 688-0363. **$75-$139.** 3040 Eagandale Pl. I-35E, exit 98 (Lone Oak Rd), just sw. Ext corridors. **Pets:** Large, other species. $75 one-time fee/room. Supervision.
☒ 🖉 🖥 🏊 ⊠

▼▼▼ Staybridge Suites 🆂🅷
(651) 994-7810. **$119-$139.** 4675 Rahncliff Rd. I-35E, exit 93 (Cliff Rd), just w, then just s. Int corridors. **Pets:** Other species. $75 one-time fee/room. Service with restrictions.
🅰🆂🅚 🆂💰 ☒ 🖉 🛋 🛎 🖥 🏊

▼▼▼ TownePlace Suites 🆂🅷
(651) 994-4600. **$79-$159.** 3615 Crestridge Dr. I-35E, exit 71 (Pilot Knob Rd), just se. Int corridors. **Pets:** Accepted.
🅰🆂🅚 🆂💰 ☒ 🛋 🛎 🖥 🏊

EDEN PRAIRIE

🅐🅐🅐 ▼▼▼ AmeriSuites (Minneapolis/Eden Prairie) 🆂🅷
(952) 944-9700. **$99-$129.** 11369 Viking Dr. I-494, exit 11A, just w. Int corridors. **Pets:** Accepted.
🆂🅐🆅🅴 🆂💰 ☒ 🅛🅜 🖉 🛋 🛎 🖥 🏊

▼▼ Homestead Studio Suites Hotel-Minneapolis/Eden Prairie 🆂🅷
(952) 942-6818. **$69-$84.** 11905 Technology Dr. Just sw of jct I-494 and US 212 (Flying Cloud Dr). Int corridors. **Pets:** $75 one-time fee/pet. Service with restrictions.
🅰🆂🅚 🆂💰 ☒ 🅛🅜 🖉 🛋 🛎 🖥

▼▼▼ The Residence Inn by Marriott-Minneapolis SW 🆂🅷
(952) 829-0033. **$89-$159.** 7780 Flying Cloud Dr. I-494, exit 11A, on US 169 S and 212 (Flying Cloud Dr). Int corridors. **Pets:** Accepted.
🅰🆂🅚 ☒ 🛋 🛎 🖥 🏊

▼▼▼ TownePlace Suites By Marriott 🆂🅷
(952) 942-6001. **$51-$129.** 11588 Leona Rd. I-494, se of jct US 212 (Flying Cloud Dr). Int corridors. **Pets:** Accepted.
☒ 🛋 🛎 🖥 🏊

EDINA

▼▼▼ Residence Inn Minneapolis-Edina 🆂🅷
(952) 893-9300. **$161-$199.** 3400 Edinborough Way. I-494, exit 6B (France Ave), 0.3 mi n to Minnesota Dr, then just e. Int corridors. **Pets:** Small, dogs only. $150 deposit/pet, $50 one-time fee/pet. Designated rooms, service with restrictions, supervision.
🅰🆂🅚 🆂💰 ☒ 🖉 🛋 🛎 🖥

ELK RIVER

▼▼ AmericInn Lodge & Suites of Elk River 🅼 🐾
(763) 441-8554. **$75-$149.** 17432 Hwy 10. 1.5 mi se on US 10/169. Int corridors. **Pets:** $10 daily fee/pet. Service with restrictions, crate.
🅰🆂🅚 🆂💰 ☒ 🖥

FOREST LAKE

▼▼ AmericInn Motel 🆂🅷
(651) 464-1930. **$64-$95.** 1291 W Broadway. I-35, exit 131 (CR 2), just ne. Int corridors. **Pets:** Accepted.
🅰🆂🅚 🆂💰 ☒ 🖉 🛋 🛎 🖥 🏊

HASTINGS

🅐🅐🅐 ▼▼▼ Country Inn & Suites By Carlson 🆂🅷
(651) 437-8870. **$79-$149.** 300 33rd St. Just e of US 61. Int corridors. **Pets:** Accepted.
🆂🅐🆅🅴 🆂💰 ☒ 🖉 🛋 🛎 🖥 🏊

LAKE ELMO

🅐🅐🅐 ▼▼▼ A Wildwood Lodge 🆂🅷
(651) 714-8068. **$159.** 8511 Hudson Blvd. I-94, exit 250 (Inwood/Radio), just ne. Int corridors. **Pets:** Medium, other species. $50 deposit/room, $10 daily fee/pet. Designated rooms, service with restrictions, crate.
🆂🅐🆅🅴 🆂💰 ☒ 🅛🅜 🖉 🛋 🛎 🖥 🍽 🏊 ⊠

LAKEVILLE

AAA ▼▼▼ Super 8 Conference Center SH
(952) 469-1134. **$79-$111.** 20800 Kenrick Ave. I-35, exit 81 (CR 70), just se. Int corridors. **Pets:** Accepted.
[SAVE] [S▼] [✕] [✦] [🚪] [≋]

MAPLE GROVE

▼▼▼ Staybridge Suites Minneapolis-Maple Grove SH
(763) 494-8856. **$119-$339.** 7821 Elm Creek Blvd. Just ne of jct I-94/ 494/694. Int corridors. **Pets:** Medium. $150 one-time fee/pet. Service with restrictions, supervision.
[ASK] [S▼] [✕] [&M] [🔇] [✦] [🚪] [🖳] [≋] [✕]

MINNEAPOLIS

AAA ▼▼▼▼ DoubleTree Guest Suites LH
(612) 332-6800. **$79-$229.** 1101 LaSalle Ave. Corner of S 11th St and LaSalle Ave. Int corridors. **Pets:** Accepted.
[SAVE] [S▼] [✕] [🔇] [🚪] [🖳] [🍴]

▼▼▼▼ Hilton Minneapolis LH
(612) 376-1000. **$115-$339.** 1001 Marquette Ave. Between S 10th and S 11th sts. Int corridors. **Pets:** Accepted.
[ASK] [S▼] [✕] [🔇] [✦] [🚪] [🖳] [🍴] [≋] [✕]

▼▼▼▼ Holiday Inn Minneapolis Metrodome LH
(612) 333-4646. **$129-$169.** 1500 Washington Ave S. Jct Washington and S 15th aves. Int corridors. **Pets:** Accepted.
[✕] [🔇] [✦] [🚪] [🖳] [🍴] [≋] [✕]

AAA ▼▼▼▼ The Marquette Hotel LH
(612) 333-4545. **$119-$329.** 7th St & Marquette Ave. Jct Marquette Ave and S 7th St. Int corridors. **Pets:** Accepted.
[SAVE] [S▼] [✕] [🔇] [🚪] [🖳] [🍴] [✕]

AAA ▼▼▼▼ Millenium Hotel Minneapolis LH 🐾
(612) 332-6000. **$89-$141.** 1313 Nicollet Mall. Jct Nicollet Ave and Grant St. Int corridors. **Pets:** Other species. $10 daily fee/room. Service with restrictions.
[SAVE] [S▼] [✕] [&M] [🔇] [🚪] [🖳] [🍴] [≋] [✕]

▼▼▼▼ Minneapolis Marriott City Center LH 🐾
(612) 349-4000. **$199-$239.** 30 S 7th St. Between Hennepin and Nicollet aves; in City Center Shopping Complex. Int corridors. **Pets:** Other species. Service with restrictions, crate.
[✕] [&M] [🔇] [🚪] [🖳] [🍴] [✕]

AAA ▼▼▼▼ Radisson Plaza Hotel Minneapolis LH
(612) 339-4900. **$199-$279.** 35 S 7th St. Between Nicollet and Hennepin aves. Int corridors. **Pets:** Accepted.
[SAVE] [S▼] [✕] [&M] [🔇] [✦] [🚪] [🖳] [🍴] [✕]

▼▼▼▼ Residence Inn Milwaukee Road Depot SH
(612) 340-1300. **$99-$229.** 425 S 2nd St. Jct S 2nd St and 5th Ave S. Int corridors. **Pets:** Accepted.
[ASK] [✕] [🔇] [✦] [🚪] [🖳]

MINNETONKA

▼▼▼▼ Minneapolis Marriott-Southwest LH 🐾
(952) 935-5500. **$149-$169.** 5801 Opus Pkwy. Just nw of jct US 169 and Cross Town SR 62, exit Bren Rd off US 169. Int corridors. **Pets:** Small. $100 deposit/pet. Service with restrictions, crate.
[✕] [🔇] [🚪] [🖳] [🍴] [≋] [✕]

AAA ▼▼▼▼ Sheraton Minneapolis West Hotel SH 🐾
(952) 593-0000. **$89-$159.** 12201 Ridgedale Dr. I-394, exit 1C (Plymouth Rd), 0.3 mi s. Int corridors. **Pets:** Medium, dogs only. Service with restrictions, supervision.
[SAVE] [S▼] [✕] [🚪] [🖳] [🍴] [≋] [✕]

MONTICELLO

AAA ▼▼▼ Best Western Silver Fox Inn SH
(763) 295-4000. **$72-$140.** 1114 Cedar St. I-94, exit 193, 0.3 mi se. Int corridors. **Pets:** Small. $10 daily fee/pet. Designated rooms, service with restrictions, supervision.
[SAVE] [S▼] [✕] [🚪] [🖳] [🍴] [≋]

AAA ▼▼▼ Days Inn SH
(763) 295-1111. **$59-$79.** 200 E Oakwood Dr. I-94, exit 193, 0.3 mi se. Int corridors. **Pets:** Other species. $12 daily fee/pet. Designated rooms, service with restrictions, crate.
[SAVE] [S▼] [✕] [🚪] [🖳]

OAKDALE

▼▼▼▼ Wingate Inn SH
(651) 578-8466. **$105-$155.** 970 Helena Ave N. I-694, exit 57, just e, then just s. Int corridors. **Pets:** Accepted.
[ASK] [S▼] [✕] [&M] [🔇] [✦] [🚪] [🖳]

PLYMOUTH

AAA ▼▼▼▼ Best Western Kelly Inn SH
(763) 553-1600. **$99-$119.** 2705 N Annapolis Ln. I-494, exit 22 (SR 55), just e. Int corridors. **Pets:** Medium. Designated rooms, service with restrictions, crate.
[SAVE] [S▼] [✕] [✦] [🚪] [🖳] [🍴] [≋] [✕]

AAA ▼▼▼▼ Radisson Hotel & Conference Center Minneapolis LH 🐾
(763) 559-6600. **$89-$135.** 3131 Campus Dr. I-494, exit 22 (SR 55), just e to CR 61 (Northwest Blvd), then 0.8 mi nw. Int corridors. **Pets:** $50 deposit/room. Service with restrictions, crate.
[SAVE] [S▼] [✕] [🔇] [✦] [🖳] [🍴] [≋] [✕]

▼▼ Red Roof Inn M
(763) 553-1751. **$53-$91.** 2600 Annapolis Ln N. I-494, exit 22 (SR 55), just se. Ext corridors. **Pets:** Large, other species. Service with restrictions, supervision.
[✕]

RICHFIELD

AAA ▼▼▼▼ Candlewood Suites SH
(612) 869-7704. **$95-$115.** 351 W 77th St. I-494, exit 4B (Lyndale Ave), just ne. Int corridors. **Pets:** Medium. $75 one-time fee/pet. Service with restrictions, crate.
[SAVE] [S▼] [✕] [&M] [🔇] [✦] [🚪] [🖳]

ROGERS

▼▼ AmericInn Lodge & Suites SH
(763) 428-4346. **$69-$159.** 21800 Industrial Blvd. I-94, exit 207 (SR 101), just sw. Int corridors. **Pets:** $6 one-time fee/pet. Designated rooms, service with restrictions, supervision.
[ASK] [S▼] [✕] [✦] [🚪] [🖳] [≋]

ROSEVILLE

▼▼▼ Residence Inn SH
(651) 636-0680. **$159-$179.** 2985 Centre Pointe Dr. I-35W, exit 25A (CR C), just se. Int corridors. **Pets:** Accepted.
[ASK] [✕] [&M] [✦] [🚪] [🖳] [≋] [✕]

ST. LOUIS PARK

AAA ▼ Lakeland Inn SH
(952) 926-6575. **$60-$75.** 4025 Hwy 7. SR 7, 0.5 mi e of SR 100. Int corridors. **Pets:** Medium. $5 daily fee/pet. Designated rooms, service with restrictions, supervision.
[SAVE] [S▼] [✕] [🚪]

▼▼▼▼ TownePlace Suites-Minneapolis West 🆂🅷 ❀
(952) 847-6900. **$79-$149.** 1400 Zarthan Ave S. I-394, exit 5 (Park Place Blvd), 0.3 mi w on 16th, then just n. Int corridors. **Pets:** Medium. $75 one-time fee/room. Service with restrictions, crate.

🅰🆂🅺 🆂🅾 ✕ 🄻 🄳 🄳 🅿 ➳

ST. PAUL

🅰🅰🅰 ▼▼▼▼ Best Western Kelly Inn 🆂🅷
(651) 227-8711. **$89-$119.** 161 St. Anthony Ave. Jct I-35E and 94. Int corridors. **Pets:** Accepted.

🆂🅰🆅🅴 🆂🅾 ✕ 🄻 🄳 🅿 ¶¶ ➳

🅰🅰🅰 ▼▼▼ Exel Inn of St. Paul 🆂🅷
(651) 771-5566. **$46-$76.** 1739 Old Hudson Rd. I-94, exit 245 (White Bear Ave), just nw. Int corridors. **Pets:** Small, other species. Designated rooms, service with restrictions, supervision.

🆂🅰🆅🅴 🆂🅾 ✕ 🄲 🄳 🅿

🅰🅰🅰 ▼▼▼▼ Holiday Inn Express Bandana
Square 🆂🅷 🐾
(651) 647-1637. **$69-$109.** 1010 Bandana Blvd W. I-94, exit 239B (Lexington Pkwy), 1.3 mi n, then 0.3 mi w on Energy Park Dr. Int corridors. **Pets:** Other species. $10 one-time fee/room. Service with restrictions, supervision.

🆂🅰🆅🅴 🆂🅾 ✕ 🄶🄼 🄲 🄻 🄳 🅿 ➳ ✕

SHAKOPEE

▼▼▼ Park Inn & Suites International 🆂🅷
(952) 445-3644. **$69-$119.** 1244 Canterbury Rd. Just nw of US 169. Int corridors. **Pets:** Dogs only. $10 daily fee/pet. Service with restrictions, supervision.

🅰🆂🅺 🆂🅾 ✕ 🄲 🄳 🅿 ¶¶ ➳ ✕

🅰🅰🅰 ▼▼▼ Sandalwood Studios & Suites 🆂🅷
(952) 277-0100. **$49-$109.** 3910 12th Ave E. Just nw of US 169. Int corridors. **Pets:** Very small. $10 daily fee/room. Designated rooms, service with restrictions, supervision.

🆂🅰🆅🅴 ✕ 🄳

STILLWATER

🅰🅰🅰 ▼▼▼▼ Best Western Stillwater Inn 🆂🅷
(651) 430-1300. **$59-$99.** 1750 W Frontage Rd. SR 36 at Washington Ave, 3 mi sw. Int corridors. **Pets:** Medium. $10 daily fee/room. Designated rooms, service with restrictions, supervision.

🆂🅰🆅🅴 🆂🅾 ✕ 🄶🄼 🄲 🄳 🅿 ➳

▼▼ Super 8 Motel 🅼
(651) 430-3990. **$61-$81.** 2190 W Frontage Rd. SR 36 at Washington Ave, 3.3 mi sw. Int corridors. **Pets:** Other species. Supervision.

✕ 🄲 🄳

TAYLORS FALLS

🅰🅰🅰 ▼▼▼▼ The Springs Country Inn 🅼
(651) 465-6565. **$45-$95.** 361 Government St. US 8 and SR 95, just w. Ext corridors. **Pets:** Other species. $7 daily fee/room. Designated rooms, crate.

🆂🅰🆅🅴 ✕ 🄳

WACONIA

▼▼▼ Super 8 Motel 🅼
(952) 442-5147. **Call for rates.** 301 E Frontage Rd. On SR 5 at jct CR 10. Int corridors. **Pets:** Accepted.

✕ 🄲 🄻 🄳 🅿

WHITE BEAR LAKE

🅰🅰🅰 ▼▼▼▼ Best Western White Bear Country Inn 🆂🅷
(651) 429-5393. **$89-$169.** 4940 N Hwy 61. Jct SR 96, 1 mi n. Int corridors. **Pets:** $10 daily fee/room. Service with restrictions, supervision.

🆂🅰🆅🅴 🆂🅾 ✕ 🄳 🅿 ¶¶ ➳ ✕

WOODBURY

▼▼▼▼ Hampton Inn by Hilton 🆂🅷
(651) 578-2822. **$80-$110.** 1450 Weir Dr. I-494, exit 59 (Valley Creek Rd), just nw. Int corridors. **Pets:** Accepted.

🅰🆂🅺 🆂🅾 ✕ 🄶🄼 🄲 🄻 🄳 🅿 ➳

🅰🅰🅰 ▼▼▼▼ Holiday Inn Express Hotels & Suites 🆂🅷
(651) 702-0200. **$109.** 9840 Norma Ln. I-94, exit 251, just sw. Int corridors. **Pets:** Designated rooms, service with restrictions, supervision.

🆂🅰🆅🅴 🆂🅾 ✕ 🄻 🄳 🅿 ➳ ✕

▼▼ Red Roof Inn #7063 🅼
(651) 738-7160. **$45-$80.** 1806 Wooddale Dr. I-494, exit 59 (Valley Creek Rd), just se. Ext corridors. **Pets:** Accepted.

✕ 🄲

END METROPOLITAN AREA

MONTEVIDEO

▼▼▼▼ Country Inn & Suites By Carlson 🆂🅷
(320) 269-8000. **$75-$145.** 1805 E Hwy 7. On SR 7. Int corridors. **Pets:** $200 deposit/room. Designated rooms, service with restrictions, supervision.

🅰🆂🅺 🆂🅾 ✕ 🄳 🅿 ➳

MOORHEAD

🅰🅰🅰 ▼▼▼ Days Inn 🆂🅷
(218) 287-7100. **$72-$156.** 600 30th Ave SW. I-94, exit 1A (US 75), just sw. Int corridors. **Pets:** Other species. $10 daily fee/room. Designated rooms, service with restrictions, supervision.

🆂🅰🆅🅴 🆂🅾 ✕ 🄳 🅿 ¶¶ ➳ ✕

🅰🅰🅰 ▼▼ Motel 75 🆂🅷
(218) 233-7501. **$46-$54.** 810 Belsly Blvd. I-94, exit 1A (US 75), 0.5 mi s. Int corridors. **Pets:** Other species. Designated rooms, service with restrictions, supervision.

🆂🅰🆅🅴 🆂🅾 ✕

🅰🅰🅰 ▼▼▼ Travelodge & Suites 🆂🅷
(218) 233-5333. **$54-$90.** 3027 S Frontage Rd. Just s of US 10 E. Int corridors. **Pets:** Designated rooms, service with restrictions, supervision.

🆂🅰🆅🅴 🆂🅾 ✕ 🄶🄼 🄲 🄳 🅿 ➳

MORRIS

🅰🅰🅰 ▼▼▼ Best Western Prairie Inn 🆂🅷
(320) 589-3030. **$53-$90.** 200 SR 28 E. Jct US 59 and SR 28, just sw. Int corridors. **Pets:** Accepted.

🆂🅰🆅🅴 🆂🅾 ✕ 🄳 🅿 ¶¶ ➳ ✕

NEW ULM

▼▼▼ Holiday Inn 🆂🅷
(507) 359-2941. **$65-$150.** 2101 S Broadway. SR 15/68, 1.8 mi se. Int corridors. **Pets:** Accepted.

🅰🆂🅺 ✕ 🄳 🅿 ¶¶ ➳ ✕

Microtel Inn & Suites SH

(507) 354-9800. **$69-$84.** 424 20th St S. Just e of jct SR 15/68 and CR 37. Int corridors. **Pets:** Other species. $10 daily fee/room. Service with restrictions, supervision.

NISSWA

Nisswa Motel M

(218) 963-7611. **$49-$81.** 5370 Merrill Ave. Just sw of Main St; center. Ext corridors. **Pets:** Accepted.

OLIVIA

The Sheep Shedde Inn SH

(320) 523-5000. **$55.** 2425 W Lincoln Ave. Just e of jct US 71 and 212. Int corridors. **Pets:** Supervision.

ONAMIA

Econo Lodge SH

(320) 532-3838. **$40-$80.** 40847 US 169. On US 169; 6 mi n. Int corridors. **Pets:** Accepted.

ORR

AmericInn Lodge & Suites SH

(218) 757-3613. **$80-$230.** 4675 Hwy 53. Just n on US 53. Int corridors. **Pets:** $20 one-time fee/room. Designated rooms, service with restrictions, supervision.

North Country Inn SH

(218) 757-3778. **$60-$90.** 4483 Hwy 53. 0.3 mi s. Int corridors. **Pets:** Other species. $10 one-time fee/pet. Service with restrictions, supervision.

OWATONNA

Microtel Inn & Suites SH

(507) 446-0228. **$45-$54.** 150 St. John Dr NW. I-35, exit 41 (Bridge St), just nw. Int corridors. **Pets:** Medium. $10 one-time fee/room. Service with restrictions, supervision.

Owatonna Grand Hotel SH ❀

(507) 455-0606. **$55.** 1212 N I-35. I-35, exit 42B, 0.3 mi nw. Int corridors. **Pets:** Small. $75 one-time fee/room. Designated rooms, service with restrictions, crate.

PEQUOT LAKES

AmericInn Lodge & Suites SH

(218) 568-8400. **$69-$149.** 32912 Paul Bunyan Trail Dr (SR 371/CR 16). SR 371, n of downtown. Int corridors. **Pets:** Small, dogs only. $10 daily fee/pet. Designated rooms, service with restrictions, supervision.

PERHAM

Super 8 Motel SH

(218) 346-7888. **Call for rates.** 106 Jake St SE. SR 78, just nw of jct US 10. Int corridors. **Pets:** $5 daily fee/pet. Service with restrictions, supervision.

PINE RIVER

Econo Lodge M

(218) 587-4499. **$69-$99.** 2684 SR 371 SW. 1 mi s. Ext corridors. **Pets:** Dogs only. $5 daily fee/pet. Service with restrictions, supervision.

RED WING

Best Western Quiet House & Suites SH

(651) 388-1577. **$100-$180.** 752 Withers Harbor Dr. 1.5 mi n on US 61, at Withers Harbor Dr; opposite side of US 61 from Pottery Mall. Ext/int corridors. **Pets:** Medium. $15 daily fee/pet. Designated rooms, service with restrictions, supervision.

Days Inn M

(651) 388-3568. **$53-$96.** 955 E 7th St. US 61/63, 1.7 mi se. Ext corridors. **Pets:** Accepted.

ROCHESTER

Best Value Inn M

(507) 288-1855. **$49-$59.** 519 3rd Ave SW. 3rd Ave SW at 5th St SW; just s of Mayo Clinic. Ext corridors. **Pets:** Accepted.

Days Inn-South M

(507) 286-1001. **$49-$79.** 111 28th St SE. Jct US 52 and 63 (Broadway), 0.5 mi n. Int corridors. **Pets:** Accepted.

Econo Lodge-South SH

(507) 282-9905. **$50-$60.** 1850 S Broadway. Jct US 52 and 63 (Broadway), 1 mi s. Int corridors. **Pets:** Accepted.

Executive Suites and Economy Inn by Kahler SH

(507) 289-8646. **$80-$110.** 9 NW 3rd Ave. Just n of Mayo Clinic. Int corridors. **Pets:** Other species. $20 daily fee/room. Service with restrictions, crate.

Holiday Inn South SH

(507) 288-1844. **$69-$109.** 1630 S Broadway. On US 63 (Broadway), 0.5 mi s of jct US 14. Ext/int corridors. **Pets:** Service with restrictions, supervision.

The Kahler Grand Hotel LH

(507) 282-2581. **$75-$135.** 20 2nd Ave SW. Opposite Mayo Clinic and Methodist Hospital. Int corridors. **Pets:** Accepted.

Marriott Hotel LH

(507) 280-6000. **$199.** 101 1st Ave SW. Just e of Mayo Clinic. Int corridors. **Pets:** Accepted.

Microtel Inn & Suites SH

(507) 286-8780. **$53-$67.** 4210 Hwy 52 N. US 52, exit 41st St NW, just w. Int corridors. **Pets:** Other species. $5 daily fee/room. Service with restrictions.

Quality Inn & Suites SH

(507) 282-8091. **$73-$109.** 1620 1st Ave SE. On US 63 (Broadway) from jct US 14, 0.5 mi s, just e on 16th St, then just s. Ext/int corridors. **Pets:** Other species.

Radisson Plaza Hotel LH

(507) 281-8000. **$119-$179.** 150 S Broadway. On US 63 (Broadway); downtown. Int corridors. **Pets:** Large. $3 daily fee/pet. Designated rooms, service with restrictions, crate.

AAA ◈◈◈ Sleep Inn & Suites SH
(507) 536-7000. **$65-$99.** 7320 Airport View Dr SW. On US 63 (Broadway), airport exit. Int corridors. **Pets:** $10 one-time fee/room. Service with restrictions, crate.

SAVE ⬚ ✕ ⬚ ⬚ ⬚ ⬚ ✕

◈◈◈ Staybridge Suites SH
(507) 289-6600. **$129-$209.** 1211 2nd St SW. US 52, exit 2nd St SW, just e. Int corridors. **Pets:** Other species. $75 one-time fee/room. Service with restrictions.

✕ ⬚ ⬚ ⬚ ⬚ ⬚ ⬚ ✕

◈◈ Super 8 Motel-South #1 SH
(507) 288-8288. **Call for rates.** 1230 S Broadway. Jct US 63 (Broadway) and 14. Int corridors. **Pets:** Accepted.

✕ ⬚ ⬚ ⬚ ⬚

ROSEAU

◈◈ AmericInn Lodge & Suites SH
(218) 463-1045. **Call for rates.** 1090 3rd St NW. 1 mi w on SR 11. Int corridors. **Pets:** Other species. $25 one-time fee/room. Designated rooms, service with restrictions, supervision.

✕ ⬚ ⬚ ⬚ ⬚ ⬚ ✕

ST. CLOUD

AAA ◈◈◈ AmericInn Motel & Suites SH
(320) 253-6337. **$60-$126.** 4385 Clearwater Rd. I-94, exit 171 (CR 75), just ne. Int corridors. **Pets:** Medium, other species. $10 daily fee/pet. Designated rooms, service with restrictions, crate.

SAVE ⬚ ✕ ⬚ ⬚ ⬚ ⬚ ⬚

AAA ◈◈◈◈ Best Western Americanna Inn & Conference Center SH
(320) 252-8700. **$62-$128, 7 day notice.** 520 S US Hwy 10. Jct SR 23, 0.3 mi s. Ext/int corridors. **Pets:** Accepted.

SAVE ⬚ ✕ ⬚ ⬚ ⬚ ⬚ ⬚ ⬚ ✕

AAA ◈◈◈◈ Best Western Kelly Inn SH
(320) 253-0606. **$84-$145.** 100 4th Ave S. SR 23 at 4th Ave S; center. Int corridors. **Pets:** Other species. Service with restrictions, supervision.

SAVE ⬚ ✕ ⬚ ⬚ ⬚ ⬚ ⬚ ⬚ ✕

AAA ◈◈◈◈ Country Inn & Suites By Carlson SH
(320) 259-8999. **$78-$99.** 235 S Park Ave. Jct SR 15 and 23 W, just w. Int corridors. **Pets:** Small. $10 daily fee/pet. Designated rooms, service with restrictions, supervision.

SAVE ⬚ ✕ ⬚ ⬚ ⬚ ⬚

◈◈◈◈ Holiday Inn Express SH
(320) 240-8000. **$59-$169.** 4322 Clearwater Rd. I-94, exit 171 (CR 75), just ne. Int corridors. **Pets:** Designated rooms, service with restrictions, supervision.

ASK ⬚ ✕ ⬚ ⬚ ⬚ ⬚ ⬚ ⬚ ✕

◈◈◈◈ Holiday Inn Hotel & Suites SH
(320) 253-9000. **$68-$110.** 75 S 37th Ave. Jct SR 15 and 23. Int corridors. **Pets:** Service with restrictions, crate.

ASK ⬚ ✕ ⬚ ⬚ ⬚ ⬚ ⬚ ✕

AAA ◈◈◈ Quality Inn Hotel and Waterslide SH
(320) 253-4444. **$55-$120.** 70 37th Ave S. Jct SR 15 and 23, just e. Int corridors. **Pets:** Medium, dogs only. $10 daily fee/room. Service with restrictions, supervision.

SAVE ⬚ ✕ ⬚ ⬚ ⬚ ⬚ ⬚

AAA ◈◈◈◈ Ramada Limited & Suites SH
(320) 253-3200. **$70-$95.** 121 Park Ave S. Jct SR 15 and 23, just w. Int corridors. **Pets:** Accepted.

SAVE ✕ ⬚ ⬚ ⬚ ⬚ ✕

◈ Thrifty Motel M
(320) 253-6320. **$36-$78.** 130 14th Ave NE. Jct US 10 and SR 23, 0.3 mi e. Int corridors. **Pets:** Medium, other species. $5 daily fee/pet. Service with restrictions, supervision.

✕ ⬚ ⬚

SAUK CENTRE

AAA ◈◈ AmericInn Lodge & Suites SH 🐾
(320) 352-2800. **$71-$129.** 1230 Timberlane Dr. I-94, exit 127, just ne. Int corridors. **Pets:** Medium. $10 one-time fee/pet. Designated rooms, service with restrictions, supervision.

SAVE ✕ ⬚ ⬚ ⬚ ⬚ ✕

SILVER BAY

AAA ◈◈◈ AmericInn Lodge & Suites SH 🐾
(218) 226-4300. **$80-$150, 3 day notice.** 150 Mensing Dr. On SR 61, 0.5 mi ne of jct SR 61 and Outer Dr. Int corridors. **Pets:** Large, dogs only. $50 deposit/room, $10 daily fee/pet. Designated rooms, service with restrictions, supervision.

SAVE ✕ ⬚ ⬚ ⬚ ⬚ ⬚ ⬚ ✕

AAA ◈◈ Mariner Motel M 🐾
(218) 226-4488. **$50-$70, 3 day notice.** 46 Outer Dr. Just w off SR 61; at traffic signal. Ext corridors. **Pets:** Dogs only. $5 daily fee/pet. Service with restrictions, supervision.

SAVE ✕ ⬚ ⬚ ✕

SLEEPY EYE

AAA ◈◈◈ Inn of Seven Gables SH
(507) 794-5390. **$65-$89.** 1100 E Main St. US 14, 0.8 mi e of jct CR 4 and US 14. Int corridors. **Pets:** Accepted.

SAVE ⬚ ✕ ⬚ ⬚ ⬚

SPICER

◈◈ Northern Inn Hotel & Suites SH
(320) 796-2091. **$99-$119.** 154 Lake Ave S. On SR 23; center. Int corridors. **Pets:** Medium, other species. $10 daily fee/pet. Designated rooms, service with restrictions, supervision.

ASK ✕ ⬚ ⬚ ⬚

THIEF RIVER FALLS

◈ Hartwood Motel M
(218) 681-2640. **Call for rates.** 1010 N Main Ave. Jct US 59 and SR 32, 0.5 mi n on SR 32. Ext/int corridors. **Pets:** Accepted.

✕ ⬚

TOFTE

AAA ◈◈ AmericInn Lodge & Suites SH
(218) 663-7899. **$59-$229.** 7261 W SR 61. On SR 61. Int corridors. **Pets:** $10 daily fee/room. Designated rooms, service with restrictions, supervision.

SAVE ⬚ ✕ ⬚ ⬚ ⬚ ⬚ ✕

◈◈◈ Bluefin Bay on Lake Superior CO
(218) 663-7296. **$59-$595, 7 day notice.** 7198 W SR 61. On SR 61. Ext corridors. **Pets:** Large. $25 one-time fee/room. Designated rooms, service with restrictions, supervision.

✕ ⬚ ⬚ ⬚ ✕ ✕

TWO HARBORS

AAA ◈◈ AmericInn Lodge and Suites SH 🐾
(218) 834-3000. **$65-$220.** 1088 SR 61. On SR 61, 0.7 mi s. Int corridors. **Pets:** Medium, dogs only. $20 daily fee/room. Service with restrictions, supervision.

SAVE ⬚ ✕ ⬚ ⬚ ⬚ ⬚ ⬚ ✕

(AAA) ▼▼▼▼ **Superior Shores Resort** CO
(218) 834-5671. **$49-$189, 14 day notice.** 1521 Superior Shores Dr. On SR 61, 1.5 mi n of center. Ext/int corridors. **Pets:** Accepted.
SAVE Sd ✕ 🛏 💻 🍴 ≈ ✕

VIRGINIA

▼▼ **AmericInn Lodge & Suites** SH ❁
(218) 741-7839. **$69-$162.** 5480 Mountain Iron Dr. US 53, just s of jct US 169. Int corridors. **Pets:** Dogs only. Designated rooms, service with restrictions, supervision.
✕ ♿M ♿ 🛏 💻 ≈ ✕

▼ **Lakeshor Motor Inn Downtown** M
(218) 741-3360. **$52-$56.** 404 6th Ave N. Just n of Chestnut St; center. Ext corridors. **Pets:** Accepted.
ASK Sd ✕ 🛏 💻

▼▼▼ **Park Inn** SH
(218) 749-1000. **$69-$95.** 502 Chestnut St. Jct 5th Ave W; downtown. Int corridors. **Pets:** Accepted.
ASK Sd ✕ 🛏 💻 🍴 ≈ ✕

▼ **Ski-View Motel** M
(218) 741-8918. **$44-$70.** 903 N 17th St. Jct US 53 and 169, 0.5 mi n on US 53, 0.7 mi e on 9th St N, then 0.5 mi n on 9th Ave W. Ext/int corridors. **Pets:** Other species. $5 daily fee/room. Service with restrictions, supervision.
✕ 💻

WABASHA

▼▼▼ **AmericInn Lodge & Suites** SH
(651) 565-5366. **$64-$169.** 150 Commerce Dr. Just ne of jct US 61 and SR 60. Int corridors. **Pets:** Accepted.
ASK ✕ ♿M ♿ 🛏 💻 ≈

WALKER

▼▼▼ **Country Inn & Suites By Carlson** SH
(218) 547-1400. **$81-$106.** 442 Walker Bay Blvd. 1 mi s on SR 371. Int corridors. **Pets:** Other species. $50 deposit/pet. Designated rooms, service with restrictions, crate.
ASK Sd ✕ ♿M 🛏 💻 ≈

WARROAD

▼▼ **Can-Am Motel** SH
(218) 386-3807. **$51-$63.** 406 Main Ave NE. 1 mi w on SR 11. Int corridors. **Pets:** Medium. Designated rooms, service with restrictions, supervision.
ASK Sd ✕ ♿M ♿

▼▼ **The Patch Motel** SH
(218) 386-2723. **$56-$66.** SR 11 W. 1 mi w. Int corridors. **Pets:** Medium. $10 one-time fee/room.
ASK Sd ✕ ♿M ♿ 🛏

WILLMAR

▼▼▼ **Comfort Inn** SH
(320) 231-2601. **$69-$149.** 2200 E US 12. 1.8 mi e. Int corridors. **Pets:** Medium. Designated rooms, service with restrictions, supervision.
ASK Sd ✕ ♿ 🛏 💻 ≈ ✕

▼▼ **Days Inn-Willmar** SH
(320) 231-1275. **$59-$129.** 225 28th St SE. 2.3 mi e on US 12. Int corridors. **Pets:** Medium. Designated rooms, service with restrictions, supervision.
ASK Sd ✕ ♿ 🛏 💻

▼▼▼ **Holiday Inn & Willmar Conference Center** SH
(320) 235-6060. **$89-$119.** 2100 US 12 E. 1.8 mi e. Int corridors. **Pets:** Medium. Designated rooms, service with restrictions, supervision.
ASK Sd ✕ ♿ 🛏 💻 🍴 ≈ ✕

WINDOM

(AAA) ▼▼ **Guardian Inn Motel** M
(507) 831-1809. **$60-$82.** 225 1st Ave. Just ne on SR 60 from jct US 71. Int corridors. **Pets:** $6 one-time fee/pet. Designated rooms, service with restrictions, supervision.
SAVE Sd ✕ 🛏 💻

▼▼ **Super 8 of Windom** M
(507) 831-1120. **$48-$59.** 222 3rd Ave S. Jct US 71 and SR 60, just n. Int corridors. **Pets:** Accepted.
ASK Sd ✕ 🛏 💻

WINONA

(AAA) ▼▼▼▼ **Best Western Riverport Inn & Suites** SH ❁
(507) 452-0606. **$80-$110.** 900 Bruski Dr. Jct US 14/61 and SR 43. Int corridors. **Pets:** Other species. $15 one-time fee/room. Designated rooms, service with restrictions, supervision.
SAVE Sd ✕ 🛏 💻 🍴 ≈

▼▼▼ **Holiday Inn Hotel and Suites** SH
(507) 453-0303. **$99-$179.** 1025 Hwy 61 E. Jct SR 43, just sw. Int corridors. **Pets:** Accepted.
ASK Sd ✕ ♿M ♿ 🛏 💻 🍴 ≈ ✕

▼▼ **Quality Inn** SH
(507) 454-4390. **$70-$150.** 956 Mankato Ave. Jct US 14/61 and SR 43. Ext/int corridors. **Pets:** Accepted.
ASK Sd ✕ 🛏 💻 🍴 ≈ ✕

WORTHINGTON

(AAA) ▼▼▼ **AmericInn Motel** SH ❁
(507) 376-4500. **$69-$109, 7 day notice.** 1475 Darling Dr. I-90, exit 43 (US 59), just se. Int corridors. **Pets:** Other species. $10 one-time fee/room. Service with restrictions, supervision.
SAVE ✕ ♿M ♿ ♿ 🛏 💻 ≈ ✕

▼▼ **Days Inn** SH
(507) 376-6155. **$62-$89.** 207 Oxford St. I-90, exit 42, 1 mi se on SR 266. Ext/int corridors. **Pets:** Medium, other species. $6 one-time fee/pet. Service with restrictions, supervision.
ASK Sd ✕ ♿ 🛏 💻 ≈

(AAA) ▼▼ **Super 8 Motel** SH
(507) 372-7755. **$58-$109.** 850 Lucy Dr. I-90, exit 42, just sw. Int corridors. **Pets:** $10 daily fee/room. Service with restrictions, supervision.
SAVE Sd ✕ 🛏 💻

MISSISSIPPI

ABERDEEN

Best Western Aberdeen Inn SH
(662) 369-4343. **$59-$65.** 801 E Commerce St. On US 45, just n of jct SR 25 and Tenn-Tom Bridge. Ext corridors. **Pets:** Medium, other species. Service with restrictions, supervision.

BATESVILLE

Comfort Inn SH
(662) 563-1188. **$54-$85.** 290 Power Dr. I-55, exit 243B, just ne on frontage road. Ext corridors. **Pets:** Accepted.

BAY ST. LOUIS

Casino Magic Inn LH
(228) 467-9257. **$39-$109.** 711 Casino Magic Dr. US 90, 0.6 mi n on Meadow Rd, then e, follow signs. Int corridors. **Pets:** Accepted.

Key West Inn SH
(228) 466-0444. **$50-$135, 3 day notice.** 1000 Hwy 90. 2.5 mi e of jct SR 603. Ext corridors. **Pets:** Accepted.

BILOXI

Father Ryan House Bed & Breakfast Inn BB
(228) 435-1189. **Call for rates.** 1196 Beach Blvd. I-110, exit 1B, 0.8 mi w on US 90. Ext/int corridors. **Pets:** Accepted.

Gulf Beach Resort Hotel SH
(228) 385-5555. **$40-$95.** 2428 Beach Blvd. I-110, exit 1B, 5.5 mi w on US 90. Int corridors. **Pets:** Accepted.

Holiday Inn Express SH
(228) 388-1000. **Call for rates.** 2416 Beach Blvd. I-110, exit 1B, 5.5 mi w on US 90. Ext corridors. **Pets:** Accepted.

BOONEVILLE

Super 8 Motel SH
(662) 720-1688. **$55-$65.** 110 Hospitality Ave. Jct US 45 and SR 4/30, 1.7 mi e to SR 145, then 0.5 mi s. Int corridors. **Pets:** Accepted.

CANTON

Best Western-Canton Inn SH
(601) 859-8600. **$55, 4 day notice.** 137 Soldier Colony Rd. I-55, exit 119, just se. Int corridors. **Pets:** Other species. $10 one-time fee/pet. Service with restrictions, crate.

CLARKSDALE

Best Western Executive Inn SH
(662) 627-9292. **$65-$74.** 710 S State St. US 61, 1 mi s of jct US 49. Ext/int corridors. **Pets:** Accepted.

Econo Lodge M
(662) 621-1110. **$49-$54, 3 day notice.** 350 S State St. On US 61. Ext corridors. **Pets:** Very small, dogs only. $10 one-time fee/pet. Service with restrictions, supervision.

CLEVELAND

Comfort Inn of Cleveland SH
(662) 843-4060. **$59-$79.** 721 N Davis Ave. On US 61, 1 mi n of jct US 61 and SR 8. Ext corridors. **Pets:** Accepted.

COLUMBIA

Comfort Inn SH
(601) 731-9955. **$65-$100.** 820 Hwy 98 Bypass. Just e of jct US 98 Bypass and SR 13. Int corridors. **Pets:** Accepted.

COLUMBUS

Master Hosts Inns & Suites SH
(662) 328-5202. **$54-$64.** 506 Hwy 45 N. US 82, exit US 45 N, just s. Ext corridors. **Pets:** $5 daily fee/pet. Service with restrictions, crate.

CORINTH

Comfort Inn SH
(662) 287-4421. **$49-$59.** 2101 Hwy 72 W. Jct US 72 and 45, just e. Ext corridors. **Pets:** Other species. $25 deposit/room.

DIAMONDHEAD

Ramada Inn Diamondhead SH
(228) 255-1300. **$55-$129.** 103 Live Oak Dr. I-10, exit 16, just nw. Ext/int corridors. **Pets:** Other species. $5 daily fee/pet. Designated rooms, service with restrictions.

D'IBERVILLE

Wingate Inn D'Iberville/Biloxi SH
(228) 396-0036. **$49-$99.** 3641 Sangani Dr. I-10, exit 46B, just ne. Int corridors. **Pets:** Small, other species. $10 daily fee/pet. Service with restrictions, supervision.

FOREST

△△△ ▽▽▽▽ Apple Tree Inn SH
(601) 469-2640. **$54-$59.** 1846 Hwy 35 S. I-20, exit 88, just n. Ext corridors. **Pets:** Other species. Service with restrictions.
[SAVE] [S⬦] [✕] [🔒] [💻] [➜]

△△△ ▽▽▽▽ Comfort Inn SH
(601) 469-2100. **$55.** 1250 Hwy 35 S. I-20, exit 88, just n. Ext corridors. **Pets:** Accepted.
[SAVE] [S⬦] [✕] [🔒] [💻] [➜]

GREENVILLE

▽▽ ▽▽ Comfort Inn of Greenville SH
(662) 378-4976. **$59-$89.** 3080 US 82 E. 3 mi e of center. Ext corridors. **Pets:** Accepted.
[A$K] [S⬦] [✕] [♿] [🔒] [💻] [➜]

GREENWOOD

▽▽ ▽▽ Comfort Inn SH
(662) 453-5974. **$64-$79.** 401 Hwy 82 W. On US 82; center. Ext corridors. **Pets:** Accepted.
[A$K] [S⬦] [✕] [🔒] [💻] [➜]

GRENADA

△△△ ▽▽▽▽ Best Western Grenada SH 🐾
(662) 226-7816. **$54-$69.** 1750 Sunset Dr. I-55, exit 206, just ne on frontage road. Ext corridors. **Pets:** Small. $5 daily fee/pet. Designated rooms, service with restrictions, supervision.
[SAVE] [S⬦] [✕] [🔒] [💻] [🍴] [➜]

▽▽▽▽ Country Inn & Suites by Carlson SH
(662) 227-8444. **$59-$78.** 255 SW Frontage Rd. I-55, exit 206, southwest corner. Int corridors. **Pets:** $25 one-time fee/pet. Service with restrictions, supervision.
[A$K] [S⬦] [✕] [🔒] [💻] [➜]

▽▽ ▽▽ Days Inn-Grenada SH
(662) 226-8888. **$39-$69.** 1632 Sunset Dr. I-55, exit 206, just ne on frontage road. Ext corridors. **Pets:** Other species. $8 daily fee/pet. Designated rooms, service with restrictions, supervision.
[A$K] [S⬦] [✕] [🔒] [➜]

▽▽ Holiday Inn SH
(662) 226-2851. **$67-$71.** 1796 Sunset Dr. I-55, exit 206, just ne on frontage road. Ext/int corridors. **Pets:** Accepted.
[A$K] [S⬦] [✕] [🔒] [💻] [🍴] [➜] [✕]

GULFPORT

△△△ ▽▽▽▽ Best Western Seaway Inn SH
(228) 864-0050. **$50-$225.** 9475 Hwy 49. I-10, exit 34A, just sw. Ext corridors. **Pets:** Small, other species. $11 daily fee/pet. Designated rooms, service with restrictions, supervision.
[SAVE] [✕] [♿] [💻] [➜]

▽▽▽▽ Crystal Inn SH
(228) 822-9600. **$69-$109.** 9379 Canal Rd. I-10, exit 31, just s. Int corridors. **Pets:** Small. $10 daily fee/pet. Designated rooms, service with restrictions, supervision.
[A$K] [S⬦] [✕] [♿] [🔒] [💻] [➜] [✕]

▽▽▽▽ Holiday Inn Airport SH
(228) 868-8200. **$49-$89.** 9415 Hwy 49. I-10, exit 34A, 0.6 mi s. Ext corridors. **Pets:** Accepted.
[A$K] [S⬦] [✕] [♿] [🔒] [💻] [🍴] [➜]

▽▽▽▽ Holiday Inn Beachfront SH
(228) 864-4310. **$75-$105.** 1600 E Beach Blvd. US 90, 0.8 mi e of jct US 49. Ext/int corridors. **Pets:** Accepted.
[A$K] [S⬦] [✕] [♿] [🔒] [💻] [🍴] [➜]

△△△ ▽▽▽▽ Holiday Inn Express SH
(228) 864-7222. **$69-$129, 3 day notice.** 9435 Hwy 49. I-10, exit 34A, 0.6 mi s. Ext corridors. **Pets:** Small, other species. $35 one-time fee/room. Service with restrictions, supervision.
[SAVE] [S⬦] [✕] [♿] [♿] [🔒] [💻]

▽▽ Motel 6 #416 M
(228) 863-1890. **$39-$55.** 9355 US Hwy 49. I-10, exit 34A, just s. Ext corridors. **Pets:** Accepted.
[S⬦] [✕] [♿] [➜]

▽▽ ▽▽ Ramada Limited SH
(228) 868-8500. **$69-$135.** 9375 Hwy 49. I-10, exit 34A, just sw. Ext corridors. **Pets:** Accepted.
[A$K] [S⬦] [✕] [🔒] [💻] [➜]

HATTIESBURG

▽▽▽▽ Comfort Inn University-The Lodge SH
(601) 264-1881. **$69-$79.** 6541 US Hwy 49. I-59, exit 67A, just s. Ext/int corridors. **Pets:** Accepted.
[A$K] [S⬦] [✕] [🔒] [💻] [➜]

▽▽▽▽ Dunhopen Inn CI
(601) 543-0707. **Call for rates.** 3875 Veterans Memorial Dr. I-59, exit 60, 0.6 mi ne on US 11. Int corridors. **Pets:** Accepted.
[✕] [💻] [🍴] [➜]

△△△ ▽▽▽▽ Hampton Inn of Hattiesburg SH
(601) 264-8080. **$76-$84.** 4301 Hardy St. I-59, exit 65, just nw. Ext/int corridors. **Pets:** Medium. Service with restrictions, supervision.
[SAVE] [S⬦] [✕] [♿] [🔒] [💻] [➜]

△△△ ▽▽▽▽ Holiday Inn-Hattiesburg SH
(601) 268-2850. **$79.** 6563 Hwy 49 N. I-59, exit 67A, just se. Int corridors. **Pets:** Accepted.
[SAVE] [S⬦] [✕] [💻] [🍴] [➜]

△△△ ▽▽▽▽ Inn on the Hill SH 🐾
(601) 599-2001. **$59-$72.** 6595 Hwy 49 N. I-59, exit 67A, just se. Ext corridors. **Pets:** $25 one-time fee/room. Service with restrictions, crate.
[SAVE] [S⬦] [✕] [🔒] [💻] [🍴] [➜]

▽▽ Motel 6 #0235 M
(601) 544-6096. **$40-$50.** 6508 US Hwy 49 N. I-59, exit 67A, 0.5 mi e. Ext corridors. **Pets:** Small. Service with restrictions, supervision.
[S⬦] [✕] [♿] [➜]

HOLLY SPRINGS

▽▽▽▽ Days Inn SH
(662) 252-1120. **Call for rates.** 120 Heritage Dr. US 78, exit 30. Ext corridors. **Pets:** Accepted.
[✕] [🔒] [🍴] [➜]

▽▽▽▽ Hampton Inn SH
(662) 252-5444. **$89-$99.** 100 Brooks Rd. US 78, exit Oxford/Holly Springs (SR 7/4), just s. Int corridors. **Pets:** Medium, other species. $25 deposit/pet, $10 daily fee/pet. Designated rooms, service with restrictions, supervision.
[A$K] [S⬦] [✕] [♿] [♿] [🔒] [💻] [➜]

HORN LAKE

△△△ ▽▽▽▽ Days Inn SH
(662) 349-3493. **$59-$79.** 801 Desoto Cove. I-55, exit 289, just nw. Ext corridors. **Pets:** Small, dogs only. $10 one-time fee/pet. Designated rooms, service with restrictions, supervision.
[SAVE] [S⬦] [✕] [♿M] [♿] [🔒] [💻] [➜]

▽▽▽▽ Drury Inn & Suites-Memphis South SH
(662) 349-6622. **$67-$104.** 735 Goodman Rd W. I-55, exit 289, just sw. Int corridors. **Pets:** Large, other species. Service with restrictions, supervision.
[A$K] [✕] [♿M] [♿] [♿] [🔒] [💻] [➜]

▼ Motel 6 **M**
(662) 349-4439. **$55-$65.** 701 Southwest Dr. I-55, exit 289, just se. Int corridors. **Pets:** Accepted.
❌ 🛗 🏊

▼▼ Sleep Inn **SH**
(662) 349-2773. **$65-$79.** 708 Desoto Cove. I-55, exit 289, just nw. Int corridors. **Pets:** Accepted.
ASK 🛅 ❌ 🛗 🍴 🏊

JACKSON

ⓐⓐⓐ ▼▼▼▼ Best Suites of America-Jackson **SH**
(601) 899-9000. **$66-$74.** 5411 I-55 N. I-55, exit 102A northbound; exit 102 southbound, s on west service road. Int corridors. **Pets:** Accepted.
SAVE 🛅 ❌ 🕐 🛗 🍴 🏊

ⓐⓐ ▼▼▼▼ Clarion Hotel & Convention Center **SH**
(601) 969-2141. **$89-$99.** 400 Greymont Ave. I-55, exit 96B, just w, then just s. Ext/int corridors. **Pets:** Other species. $25 one-time fee/room. Service with restrictions, supervision.
SAVE 🛅 ❌ 🛗 🕐 🍴 🏊

▼▼▼▼ The Edison Walthall Hotel **LH**
(601) 948-6161. **$89-$99.** 225 E Capitol St. I-55, exit 96A (Pearl St), 0.8 mi w; between West and Lamar sts; downtown. Ext/int corridors. **Pets:** Accepted.
ASK ❌ 🕐 🍴 🏊

ⓐⓐ ▼▼▼▼ Holiday Inn Hotel & Suites **LH**
(601) 366-9411. **$105-$112.** 5075 I-55 N. I-55, exit 102A, s on west frontage road. Ext/int corridors. **Pets:** Accepted.
SAVE 🛅 ❌ 🛗 🕐 🍴 🏊

▼▼▼▼ Jameson Inn **SH**
(601) 206-8923. **$49-$104.** 585 Beasley Rd. I-55, exit 102, just w. Int corridors. **Pets:** Very small, other species. $10 daily fee/room. Service with restrictions, supervision.
ASK ❌ 🛐 🕐 🛗 🍴 🏊

ⓐⓐ ▼▼▼▼ La Quinta Inn Jackson (North) **SH**
(601) 957-1741. **$56-$85.** 616 Briarwood Dr. I-55, exit 102A northbound, just ne on Frontage Rd. Ext corridors. **Pets:** Accepted.
SAVE ❌ 🕐 🍴 🏊

▼▼ Microtel Inn & Suites **SH**
(601) 352-8282. **$50-$68.** 614 Monroe St. I-55, exit 96B (High St), just nw. Int corridors. **Pets:** Accepted.
ASK 🛅 ❌ 🛗 🕐 🍴

▼ Motel 6–1167 **M**
(601) 956-8848. **$41-$51.** 6145 I-55 N/Frontage Rd. I-55, exit 103, 0.5 mi sw on Frontage Rd. Ext corridors. **Pets:** Accepted.
🛅 ❌ 🏊

ⓐⓐ ▼▼▼▼ Quality Inn & Suites **SH**
(601) 969-2230. **$79-$89.** 400 Greymont Ave. I-55, exit 96B (High St), just w, then just s. Ext corridors. **Pets:** Small. $25 daily fee/pet. Service with restrictions, supervision.
SAVE 🛅 ❌ 🛗 🕐 🍴 🏊

▼▼ Red Roof Inn Fairgrounds **M**
(601) 969-5006. **$43-$60.** 700 Larson St. I-55, exit 96B (High St), e to Greymont, then just ne. Ext corridors. **Pets:** Accepted.
❌ 🛗

▼▼▼▼ Residence Inn by Marriott **SH**
(601) 355-3599. **Call for rates.** 881 E River Pl. I-55, exit 96C, just e. Ext corridors. **Pets:** Accepted.
❌ 🛗 🕐 🍴 🏊 ❌

KOSCIUSKO

ⓐⓐⓐ ▼▼▼ Best Western Parkway Inn **SH**
(662) 289-6252. **$52-$66.** 1052 Veterans Memorial Dr/Hwy 35 Bypass. Just sw of jct SR 35 and Natchez Trace Pkwy. Ext corridors. **Pets:** Accepted.
SAVE 🛅 ❌ 🕐 🍴 🏊

LAUREL

▼▼▼▼ Ramada Inn & Convention Center **SH**
(601) 649-9100. **$75-$135.** 1105 Sawmill Rd. I-59, exit 95B, 0.5 mi n to Sawmill Rd, 0.4 mi e. Ext corridors. **Pets:** Accepted.
ASK 🛅 ❌ 🕐 🍴 🍴 🏊

MCCOMB

ⓐⓐⓐ ▼▼▼ Days Inn McComb **SH**
(601) 684-5566. **$65-$71, 14 day notice.** 2298 Delaware Ave. I-55, exit 17, just nw. Ext corridors. **Pets:** Accepted.
SAVE 🛅 ❌ 🍴 🍴 🏊

ⓐⓐⓐ ▼▼▼ Hawthorn Inn & Suites **SH**
(601) 684-8655. **$80-$110.** 2001 Veteran's Blvd. I-55, exit 18, just off interstate. Int corridors. **Pets:** Medium. $125 one-time fee/room. Service with restrictions, crate.
SAVE 🛅 ❌ 🛐 🕐 🍴 🍴 🏊

MERIDIAN

ⓐⓐ ▼▼▼▼ Baymont Inn & Suites Meridian **SH**
(601) 693-2300. **$52-$69.** 1400 Roebuck Dr. I-20/59, exit 153, just s. Int corridors. **Pets:** Accepted.
SAVE 🛅 ❌ 🕐 🍴 🏊

▼ Days Inn **M**
(601) 483-3812. **Call for rates.** 145 Hwy 11 & 80 E. I-20/59, exit 154 westbound; exit 154B eastbound, just n to Frontage Rd, then just e. Ext corridors. **Pets:** Other species. $6 daily fee/pet. Service with restrictions, supervision.
❌ 🍴 🏊

▼▼ Econo Lodge **M**
(601) 693-9393. **$40-$50.** 2405 S Frontage Rd. I-20/59, exit 153, 0.5 mi sw. Ext corridors. **Pets:** Accepted.
ASK 🛅 ❌ 🍴

▼▼ Econo Lodge of Meridian **SH**
(601) 485-3254. **$48-$70.** 109 US Hwy 11 & 80. I-20/59, exit 154 westbound; exit 154B eastbound, just n to Frontage Rd, then just e. Ext corridors. **Pets:** Accepted.
ASK 🛅 ❌ 🛗 🕐 🍴

ⓐⓐ ▼▼▼ Holiday Inn Northeast **SH**
(601) 485-5101. **$93-$103.** 111 US 11 & 80. I-20/59, exit 154 westbound, just n to frontage road, then just e; exit 154B eastbound. Ext corridors. **Pets:** Accepted.
SAVE 🛅 ❌ 🛐 🕐 🛗 🍴 🍴 🏊

▼▼ Jameson Inn **SH**
(601) 483-3315. **$49-$104.** 524 Bonita Lakes Dr. I-20/59, exit 154 southbound; exit 154A northbound, just s. Ext corridors. **Pets:** Very small, other species. $10 daily fee/room. Service with restrictions, supervision.
ASK ❌ 🛐 🕐 🛗 🍴 🏊

▼▼ Quality Inn **SH**
(601) 693-4521. **$60-$70.** 1401 Roebuck Dr. I-20/59, exit 153, just s. Ext corridors. **Pets:** Medium. Service with restrictions, supervision.
ASK 🛅 ❌ 🕐 🍴 🏊

MOSS POINT

Best Western Flagship Inn SH
(228) 475-5000. **$45-$70.** 4830 Amoco Dr. I-10, exit 69, just s. Ext corridors. **Pets:** Accepted.

Holiday Inn Express SH
(228) 474-2100. **$59-$89.** 4800 Amoco Dr. I-10, exit 69, just s. Int corridors. **Pets:** Accepted.

NATCHEZ

Natchez Eola Hotel LH
(601) 445-6000. **$98-$145.** 110 N Pearl St. Corner of Main St; downtown. Int corridors. **Pets:** Accepted.

NEWTON

Days Inn M
(601) 683-3361. **$50-$75.** 261 Eastside Dr. I-20, exit 109, just s on SR 15. Ext corridors. **Pets:** Accepted.

OCEAN SPRINGS

Days Inn SH
(228) 872-8255. **$64-$159, 20 day notice.** 7305 Washington Ave. I-10, exit 50, just s. Ext corridors. **Pets:** Medium, other species. $10 daily fee/pet. Designated rooms, service with restrictions.

Holiday Inn Express SH
(228) 875-7555. **$149.** 7304 Washington Ave. I-10, exit 50, 0.4 mi s on SR 609. Ext corridors. **Pets:** Accepted.

Ramada Limited SH
(228) 872-2323. **$64-$159, 10 day notice.** 8011 Tucker Rd. I-10, exit 50, just n. Ext corridors. **Pets:** Medium, other species. $10 daily fee/pet. Designated rooms, service with restrictions, supervision.

OLIVE BRANCH

Comfort Inn SH
(662) 895-0456. **$67.** 7049 Enterprise. US 78, exit SR 302, just w. Int corridors. **Pets:** Small. $10 one-time fee/pet. Service with restrictions, supervision.

Whispering Woods Hotel and Conference Center LH 🐾
(662) 895-2941. **$139.** 11200 E Goodman Rd. US 78, exit SR 302, 2.5 mi e. Int corridors. **Pets:** Other species. $100 deposit/room, $25 one-time fee/room.

OXFORD

Days Inn SH
(662) 234-9500. **$55-$159, 30 day notice.** 1101 Frontage Rd. SR 6, exit Lamar Blvd, just sw. Ext corridors. **Pets:** Small. $15 one-time fee/room. Service with restrictions, supervision.

PASCAGOULA

LaFont Inn SH
(228) 762-7111. **$49-$89.** 2703 Denny Ave. I-10, exit 69, 3.5 mi s on SR 63, then 2 mi w on US 90. Ext corridors. **Pets:** Accepted.

Super 8 Motel M
(228) 762-9414. **$109-$180, 14 day notice.** 4919 Denny Ave. I-10, exit 69, 3.5 mi s on SR 63, then just w on US 90. Int corridors. **Pets:** Accepted.

PASS CHRISTIAN

Harbour Oaks Inn BB
(228) 452-9399. **$83-$128, 14 day notice.** 126 W Scenic Dr. Just off US 90. Int corridors. **Pets:** Dogs only. $20 one-time fee/pet. Designated rooms, service with restrictions, supervision.

PEARL

Jameson Inn SH
(601) 932-6030. **$49-$104.** 434 Riverwind Dr. I-20, exit 48, just nw. Int corridors. **Pets:** Very small, other species. $10 daily fee/room. Service with restrictions, supervision.

La Quinta Inn & Suites Jackson Airport (Pearl) SH
(601) 664-0065. **$70-$85, 7 day notice.** 501 S Pearson Rd. I-20, exit 48, just s. Int corridors. **Pets:** Accepted.

PHILADELPHIA

Deluxe Inn & Suites SH
(601) 656-0052. **$39-$89.** 1004 Central Dr. Jct SR 15 and 16. Ext corridors. **Pets:** Small. $10 daily fee/pet. No service, crate.

PICAYUNE

Days Inn SH
(601) 799-1339. **$59-$99.** 450 S Lofton Ave. I-59, exit 4, just nw. Ext corridors. **Pets:** Medium. $10 daily fee/pet. Designated rooms, service with restrictions, supervision.

PONTOTOC

Days Inn M
(662) 489-5200. **$52-$90.** 217 Hwy 15 N. On SR 15, just n of jct SR 6. Ext corridors. **Pets:** Small. $7 daily fee/pet. Designated rooms, service with restrictions, supervision.

RICHLAND

Days Inn SH
(601) 932-5553. **$55.** 1035 US Hwy 49 S. I-20, exit 47A, 4 mi s on US 49. Ext corridors. **Pets:** Small. $5 daily fee/pet. Service with restrictions, crate.

Executive Inn & Suites SH
(601) 664-3456. **$49-$59.** 390 Hwy 49 S. I-20, exit 47, just s. Ext corridors. **Pets:** Large. $20 deposit/room, $5 one-time fee/room. Service with restrictions, supervision.

RIDGELAND

Drury Inn & Suites-Jackson, MS SH
(601) 956-6100. **$65-$115.** 610 E County Line Rd. I-55, exit 103 (County Line Rd), just w. Int corridors. **Pets:** Large, other species. Service with restrictions, supervision.

▼▼ **Econo Lodge** Ⓜ
(601) 956-7740. **$54-$79, 7 day notice.** 839 Ridgewood Rd. I-55, exit 103 (County Line Rd), just e, then just n. Ext corridors. **Pets:** Small. $10 daily fee/room. Designated rooms, no service, supervision.

ⒶⓈⓀ Ⓢ⬧ ☒ 🖥 💻

▼▼▼▼ **Homewood Suites by Hilton** ⓈⒽ
(601) 899-8611. **$129.** 853 Centre St. I-55, exit 103 (County Line Rd), just e to Ridgewood Rd, 0.4 mi ne, then just e. Int corridors. **Pets:** Accepted.

ⒶⓈⓀ Ⓢ⬧ ☒ ⚿ᴹ ☒ 🖥 💻 🏊

Ⓐ Ⓐ Ⓐ ▼▼▼ **Quality Inn North** ⓈⒽ
(601) 956-6203. **$54-$79, 7 day notice.** 839 Ridgewood Rd. I-55, exit 103 (County Line Rd), just ne. Ext corridors. **Pets:** Small. $10 daily fee/room. Designated rooms, no service, supervision.

ⓈⒶⓋⒺ Ⓢ⬧ ☒ 🖥 💻 🏊

▼▼ **Red Roof Inn Ridgeland** Ⓜ
(601) 956-7707. **$45-$57.** 810 Adcock St. I-55, exit 103 (County Line Rd), just ne on Frontage Rd. Ext corridors. **Pets:** Accepted.

☒ 🚿 🖥

SARDIS

▼▼ **Knights Inn** ⓈⒽ
(662) 487-2424. **$45-$55.** 598 E Lee St. I-55, exit 252. Ext corridors. **Pets:** Large, other species. $3 one-time fee/room. Service with restrictions.

ⒶⓈⓀ Ⓢ⬧ ☒ 🖥 💻 🍽 🏊

SOUTHAVEN

▼▼ **Super 8-Southaven** Ⓜ
(662) 280-8826. **Call for rates.** 5115 Pepper Chase Dr. I-55, exit 287, just w. Int corridors. **Pets:** Accepted.

☒ ⚿ᴹ 🚿 🖥 🏊

STARKVILLE

Ⓐ Ⓐ Ⓐ ▼▼▼▼ **Best Western Starkville Inn** ⓈⒽ
(662) 324-5555. **$75-$95.** 119 Hwy 12 W. SR 12, 1.5 mi w of jct US 82. Ext corridors. **Pets:** Accepted.

ⓈⒶⓋⒺ ☒ 🖥 💻 🏊

▼▼▼▼ **Comfort Suites Starkville** ⓈⒽ
(662) 324-9595. **Call for rates.** 801 Russell St. 0.5 mi w of jct US 82 and SR 12. Int corridors. **Pets:** Accepted.

☒ 🚿 🖥 💻 🏊

TUNICA

▼ **Delta Plantation Inn** Ⓜ
(662) 363-1532. **Call for rates.** 3515 Hwy 61 N. On US 61; at Tunica Expo Center and Museum. Ext corridors. **Pets:** Accepted.

☒ 🖥 💻 🏊

▼ **Key West Inn Tunica** Ⓜ
(662) 363-0021. **$50-$99.** 11635 Hwy 61 N. US 61, 0.3 mi n of SR 304. Ext corridors. **Pets:** Small. $10 daily fee/pet. Designated rooms, service with restrictions, supervision.

☒ 🖥 💻

TUPELO

Ⓐ Ⓐ Ⓐ ▼▼▼ **Days Inn** ⓈⒽ
(662) 842-0088. **$60-$68, 7 day notice.** 1015 N Gloster St. SR 145, w on McCullough Blvd to N Gloster St, just n. Ext corridors. **Pets:** Small. $20 one-time fee/room. Designated rooms, service with restrictions, crate.

ⓈⒶⓋⒺ Ⓢ⬧ ☒ 🖥 💻 🏊

Ⓐ Ⓐ Ⓐ ▼▼▼ **Howard Johnson Express Inn** ⓈⒽ
(662) 842-8811. **$49-$99.** 923 N Gloster St. On SR 145, just s of McCullough Blvd. Ext corridors. **Pets:** Other species. $25 deposit/room.

ⓈⒶⓋⒺ Ⓢ⬧ ☒ 🚿 🚿 🖥 💻 🏊

▼▼ **Jameson Inn** ⓈⒽ
(662) 840-2380. **$49-$104.** 879 Mississippi Dr. SR 145, exit Barnes Crossing, 1 mi sw. Ext corridors. **Pets:** Very small, other species. $10 daily fee/room. Service with restrictions, supervision.

ⒶⓈⓀ ☒ 🚿 🖥 💻 🏊

▼▼ **Red Roof Inn Tupelo** Ⓜ
(662) 844-1904. **$46-$56.** 1500 McCullough Blvd. On McCullough Blvd, just w of jct SR 145. Ext corridors. **Pets:** Accepted.

☒ 🚿 🏊

Ⓐ Ⓐ Ⓐ ▼▼▼ **Super 8 Motel** Ⓜ
(662) 842-0448. **$47-$58.** 3898 McCullough Blvd. On McCullough Blvd, exit 81, just ne. Ext corridors. **Pets:** Accepted.

ⓈⒶⓋⒺ Ⓢ⬧ ☒ 🖥 🏊

VICKSBURG

Ⓐ Ⓐ Ⓐ ▼▼▼ **Battlefield Inn** ⓈⒽ
(601) 638-5811. **$50-$75.** 4137 I-20 N Frontage Rd. I-20, exit 4B, 1 mi ne. Ext/int corridors. **Pets:** Other species. $5 daily fee/pet. Service with restrictions.

ⓈⒶⓋⒺ Ⓢ⬧ ☒ 🖥 🍽 🏊 ☒

▼▼▼▼ **The Corners Bed & Breakfast Inn** ⒷⒷ
(601) 636-7421. **$90-$130, 3 day notice.** 601 Klein St. I-20, exit 1A, 2.3 mi n on Washington St, just w. Ext/int corridors. **Pets:** Service with restrictions, supervision.

ⒶⓈⓀ ☒ 🖥 💻

▼ **Econo Lodge of Vicksburg** Ⓜ
(601) 634-8766. **$44-$74.** 3330-A Clay St. I-20, exit 4B (Clay St), just n. Ext corridors. **Pets:** Other species. $10 one-time fee/room. Service with restrictions, supervision.

ⒶⓈⓀ Ⓢ⬧ ☒ 🖥 💻

▼▼▼▼ **Hampton Inn of Vicksburg** ⓈⒽ
(601) 636-6100. **$74-$89.** 3332 Clay St. I-20, exit 4B (Clay St), just n. Ext corridors. **Pets:** Other species. Designated rooms, service with restrictions, supervision.

 ⒶⓈⓀ Ⓢ⬧ ☒ 🖥 💻 🏊

▼▼ **Jameson Inn** ⓈⒽ
(601) 619-7799. **$49-$104.** 3975 S Frontage Rd. I-20, exit 4A, on southeast frontage road. Ext corridors. **Pets:** Very small, other species. $10 daily fee/room. Service with restrictions, supervision.

ⒶⓈⓀ ☒ ⚿ᴹ 🚿 🚿 🖥 💻 🏊

▼▼ **Motel 6 #4189** ⓈⒽ
(601) 638-5077. **$46-$76.** 4127 N Frontage Rd. I-20, exit 4B (Clay St), just ne on Frontage Rd. Int corridors. **Pets:** Accepted.

Ⓢ⬧ ☒ 🏊

WAVELAND

▼▼▼▼ **Coast Inn & Suites** ⓈⒽ 🐾
(228) 467-9261. **$59-$69.** 404 Hwy 90. Just w of jct SR 603/43. Ext corridors. **Pets:** Small, other species. $35 one-time fee/room. Designated rooms, service with restrictions, crate.

ⒶⓈⓀ Ⓢ⬧ ☒ 🚿 🖥 💻 🍽 🏊

WIGGINS

▼▼▼ **Best Western Woodstone** ⓈⒽ
(601) 928-1616. **$59.** 535 Frontage Dr E. Jct US 49 and SR 26. Int corridors. **Pets:** Accepted.

ⒶⓈⓀ Ⓢ⬧ ☒ 💻 🏊

YAZOO CITY

Ⓐ Ⓐ Ⓐ ▼▼▼ **Comfort Inn** ⓈⒽ
(662) 746-6444. **$67.** 1600 Jerry Clower Blvd. US 49 E, 1.8 mi n of jct US 49 W. Int corridors. **Pets:** Accepted.

ⓈⒶⓋⒺ Ⓢ⬧ ☒ 🖥 💻 🏊

MISSOURI

ARNOLD

▼▼▼▼◆ Drury Inn-St. Louis/Arnold 🆂🇭
(636) 296-9600. **$57-$102.** 1201 Drury Ln. I-55, exit 191 (SR 141), 0.3 mi e. Int corridors. **Pets:** Large, other species. Service with restrictions, supervision.
🄰🅂🄺 ⊠ 🛡 💻 🏊

AVA

▼▼ ◆ Ava Super 8 🆂🇭
(417) 683-1343. **$55-$65.** 1711 S Jefferson St. Jct SR 5 S and 76. Int corridors. **Pets:** Accepted.
🄰🅂🄺 🆂🄳 ⊠ 🄲🄼 🛡 💻

BETHANY

▼▼ ▼▼ Best Western Bethany Inn 🆂🇭
(660) 425-8006. **$62-$80.** 496 S 39th St. I-35, exit 92, just nw. Int corridors. **Pets:** Medium. $10 daily fee/pet. Service with restrictions, supervision.
🄰🅂🄺 🆂🄳 ⊠ 🄲🄼 🛡 💻 🏊

▼▼ ▼▼ Family Budget Inn 🄼
(660) 425-7915. **$47-$49.** 4014 Miller St. I-35, exit 92. Int corridors. **Pets:** $5 daily fee/room. Designated rooms, service with restrictions, supervision.
🄰🅂🄺 🆂🄳 ⊠ 🄲🄼 🛡 🏊

BOLIVAR

🄰🄰🄰 ▼▼ Welcome Inn 🄼
(417) 326-5268. **$47-$50.** 4688 Bus 83 E. On Frontage Rd, 0.3 mi s of jct SR 83. Ext corridors. **Pets:** Accepted.
🆂🄰🅅🄴 🆂🄳 ⊠ 🏊

BOONVILLE

🄰🄰🄰 ▼▼ Boonville Comfort Inn 🆂🇭 🐾
(660) 882-5317. **$49-$99.** 2427 Mid American Industrial Dr. I-70, exit 102, just sw. Int corridors. **Pets:** Small, dogs only. $10 daily fee/pet. Designated rooms, service with restrictions, supervision.
🆂🄰🅅🄴 🆂🄳 ⊠ 🛡 💻 🏊

BRANSON

▼▼ ▼▼ 1st Inn Gold 🆂🇭
(417) 334-7000. **$54-$69.** 2719 W Hwy 76. 2.5 mi w of jct US 65. Ext/int corridors. **Pets:** Accepted.
🄰🅂🄺 🆂🄳 ⊠ 🛡 🏊

🄰🄰🄰 ▼▼▼ Best Western Branson Landing 🆂🇭
(417) 334-6464. **$54-$94.** 403 W Main (Hwy 76). 0.3 mi e from SR 76 and US 65. Ext corridors. **Pets:** Accepted.
🆂🄰🅅🄴 🆂🄳 ⊠ 🎧 🛡 💻 🏊 🏊⊠

🄰🄰🄰 ▼▼▼ ▼▼▼ Chateau on the Lake Resort Spa &
Convention Center 🇱🇭 🐾
(417) 334-1161. **$89-$299, 3 day notice.** 415 N State Hwy 265. Just n of jct SR 165 and 265. Int corridors. **Pets:** Small. $25 one-time fee/room. Designated rooms, service with restrictions, crate.
🆂🄰🅅🄴 🆂🄳 ⊠ 🄲🄼 🎧 🄲🄸 🛡 💻 🍴 🏊 🏊⊠

🄰🄰🄰 ▼▼▼ Days Inn of Branson 🆂🇭
(417) 334-5544. **$59-$74.** 3524 Keeter St. Jct SR 376, 0.5 mi e on SR 76 (Country Music Blvd), then 0.3 mi w. Ext corridors. **Pets:** $10 daily fee/pet. Service with restrictions, crate.
🆂🄰🅅🄴 🆂🄳 ⊠ 🎧 🄲🄸 💻 🍴 🏊

▼▼▼▼ Holiday Inn Express Hotel & Suites 🆂🇭 🐾
(417) 336-1100. **$72-$102.** 1970 W Hwy 76. 1.8 mi w of jct SR 76 (Country Music Blvd) and US 65. Int corridors. **Pets:** Other species. $25 one-time fee/room. Designated rooms, service with restrictions.
🄰🅂🄺 🆂🄳 ⊠ 🄲🄼 🎧 🄲🄸 🛡 💻 🏊

🄰🄰🄰 ▼▼ Ozark Valley Inn 🄼
(417) 336-4666. **$35-$70.** 2693 Shephard of the Hills Expwy. Jct SR 76 (Country Music Blvd), 0.9 mi e. Ext corridors. **Pets:** Medium. $10 one-time fee/room. Designated rooms, service with restrictions, crate.
🆂🄰🅅🄴 ⊠ 🏊

▼▼ ▼▼ Quality Inn-Branson 🆂🇭 🐾
(417) 335-6776. **$45-$90.** 3269 Shepherd of the Hills Expwy. 0.3 mi e of jct SR 76 (Country Music Blvd). Ext/int corridors. **Pets:** Small, dogs only. $10 daily fee/pet. Designated rooms, service with restrictions, crate.
🄰🅂🄺 🆂🄳 ⊠ 🎧 🛡 💻 🍴 🏊 🏊⊠

▼▼▼▼ Ramada Inn & Conference Center 🆂🇭 🐾
(417) 334-1000. **$39-$79.** 1700 Hwy 76 W. Jct SR 76 (Country Music Blvd) and US 65, 1.5 mi w. Ext corridors. **Pets:** Medium. $20 one-time fee/pet. Designated rooms, service with restrictions, supervision.
🄰🅂🄺 🆂🄳 ⊠ 🄲🄸 💻 🍴 🏊 🏊⊠

▼▼▼▼ Ramada Limited 🆂🇭
(417) 337-5207. **$49-$99.** 2316 Shepherd of the Hills Expwy. Jct SR 76 (Country Music Blvd), 1.3 mi e. Ext corridors. **Pets:** Other species. $10 daily fee/room. Service with restrictions.
🄰🅂🄺 🆂🄳 ⊠ 🄲🄸 💻 🏊

▼▼▼▼ **Residence Inn by Marriott** 🅂🅷
(417) 336-4077. **$79-$119.** 280 Wildwood Dr S. 2 mi w on SR 76 (Country Music Blvd), just s. Int corridors. **Pets:** Other species. $75 one-time fee/room. Service with restrictions, crate.
🅰🅢🅚 ⊠ 𝄜 🖥 🛏 ⌦

▼▼ **Rock View Resort** 🅼
(417) 334-4678. **$53-$87, 21 day notice.** 1049 Park View Dr. Jct US 65, 4.4 mi w on SR 165, 0.3 mi s via Dale Dr, then 0.7 mi w. Ext corridors. **Pets:** Accepted.
🛏 🖥 ⌦ ⊠ 🅩

▲▲▲ ▼▼▼ **Scenic Hills Inn** 🅂🅷
(417) 336-8855. **$39-$59.** 2422 Shepherd of the Hills Expwy. Jct SR 76 (Country Music Blvd), 1.1 mi e. Int corridors. **Pets:** Other species. $5 daily fee/pet. Designated rooms, service with restrictions, crate.
🆂🅰🆅🅴 🆂🅾 ⊠ 🛏 🖥 ⌦

▲▲▲ ▼▼▼ **Settle Inn Resort & Conference Center** 🅂🅷
(417) 335-4700. **$58-$119.** 3050 Green Mountain Dr. Jct SR 76 (Country Music Blvd) and US 65, 3 mi w on SR 76, 0.8 mi s. Int corridors. **Pets:** Other species. $10 daily fee/pet. Designated rooms, service with restrictions, supervision.
🆂🅰🆅🅴 🆂🅾 ⊠ 𝄜 🆒 🛏 🖥 🍴 ⌦ ⊠

▼▼ **White Wing Resort** 🅼 🐾
(417) 338-2318. **$50-$140, 21 day notice.** 1028 Jakes Creek Tr. Jct SR 76 and 265, 0.6 mi w, 1 mi s on Indian Point Rd, then 1 mi e. Ext corridors. **Pets:** Dogs only. $25 one-time fee/pet. No service.
⊠ 🛏 🖥 ⌦ ⊠ 🅩

BRANSON WEST

▼▼▼ **Shady Acre Motel** 🅼
(417) 338-2316. **$36-$42.** 8722 Hwy 76. Jct SR 265, 1.1 mi w. Ext corridors. **Pets:** Very small, dogs only. $10 one-time fee/pet. Service with restrictions, crate.
⊠ 🛏 🖥 ⌦

BUFFALO

▲▲▲ ▼ **Goodnite Inn** 🅼
(417) 345-2345. **$40-$55.** 642 S Ash. US 65, just s of jct SR 32. **Pets:** Accepted.
🆂🅰🆅🅴 🆂🅾 ⊠ 🛏 ⌦

BUTLER

▼▼▼ **Days Inn** 🅂🅷
(660) 679-4544. **$45-$90.** 100 S Fran Ave. Just e of jct US 71 and SR 52. Int corridors. **Pets:** Medium. $5 daily fee/pet. No service, supervision.
🅰🅢🅚 🆂🅾 ⊠ 🛏 ⌦

▼ **Super 8 Motel–Butler** 🅼
(660) 679-6183. **$45-$80.** 1114 W Fort Scott St. Just e of jct US 71 and SR 52. Ext corridors. **Pets:** Other species. $5 daily fee/pet. Service with restrictions, supervision.
🅰🅢🅚 🆂🅾 ⊠ 🛏

CAMERON

▲▲▲ ▼▼▼ **Best Western Acorn Inn** 🅼
(816) 632-2187. **$69-$89.** 2210 E US 36. I-35, exit 54, 0.3 mi e. Ext corridors. **Pets:** Other species. Supervision.
🆂🅰🆅🅴 🆂🅾 ⊠ 𝄜 🆒 🛏 🖥 ⌦

▼▼▼ **Comfort Inn** 🅂🅷 🐾
(816) 632-5655. **Call for rates.** 1803 Comfort Ln. I-35, exit 54, just e. Int corridors. **Pets:** Medium. Designated rooms, service with restrictions, supervision.
⊠ 🅼 🛏 🖥 ⌦

▲▲▲ ▼▼▼ **Econo Lodge** 🅼
(816) 632-6571. **$45-$59.** 220 E Grand. I-35, exit 54, 0.5 mi w on US 36, then just s on US 69. Ext corridors. **Pets:** Other species. $5 one-time fee/pet. Service with restrictions, supervision.
🆂🅰🆅🅴 🆂🅾 ⊠ 🛏 ⌦

▼▼ **Super 8 Motel** 🅂🅷
(816) 632-8888. **$60.** 1710 N Walnut St. I-35, exit 54, 0.5 mi w on US 36. Int corridors. **Pets:** Small. $10 one-time fee/pet. Designated rooms, service with restrictions, supervision.
🅰🅢🅚 🆂🅾 ⊠ 🆒 🛏 ⌦

CANTON

▲▲▲ ▼▼▼ **Comfort Inn Canton** 🅂🅷
(573) 288-8800. **$60-$105.** 1701 Oak St. US 61, exit CR-P, just e. Int corridors. **Pets:** $20 deposit/pet, $10 daily fee/pet. Designated rooms, service with restrictions, crate.
🆂🅰🆅🅴 🆂🅾 ⊠ 🛏 🖥 ⌦ ⊠

CAPE GIRARDEAU

▼▼▼ **Drury Lodge-Cape Girardeau** 🅂🅷
(573) 334-7151. **$78-$98.** 104 S Vantage Dr. I-55, exit 96 (William St), just e. Ext/int corridors. **Pets:** Large, other species. Service with restrictions, supervision.
🅰🅢🅚 ⊠ 𝄜 🛏 🖥 🍴 ⌦

▼▼▼ **Drury Suites-Cape Girardeau** 🅂🅷
(573) 339-9500. **$88-$108.** 3303 Campster Dr. I-55, exit 96 (William St), just w. Int corridors. **Pets:** Large, other species. Service with restrictions, supervision.
🅰🅢🅚 ⊠ 🅼 𝄜 🆒 🛏 🖥 ⌦ ⊠

▼▼▼ **Hampton Inn-Cape Girardeau** 🅂🅷
(573) 651-3000. **$89-$126.** 103 Cape W Pkwy. I-55, exit 96 (William St), 0.3 mi sw. Int corridors. **Pets:** Accepted.
🅰🅢🅚 ⊠ 🅼 𝄜 🛏 🖥

▼▼▼ **Pear Tree Inn by Drury-Cape Girardeau** 🅂🅷
(573) 334-3000. **$65-$90.** 3248 William St. I-55, exit 96 (William St), just e. Int corridors. **Pets:** Large, other species. Service with restrictions, supervision.
🅰🅢🅚 ⊠ 🖥 ⌦

▼▼▼ **Victorian Inn & Suites** 🅂🅷 🐾
(573) 651-4486. **$69-$99.** 3265 William St. I-55, exit 96 (William St), just e. Ext/int corridors. **Pets:** Medium, other species. $50 deposit/room. Service with restrictions, supervision.
🅰🅢🅚 🆂🅾 ⊠ 🅼 𝄜 🆒 🛏 🖥 ⌦ ⊠

CARTHAGE

▲▲▲ ▼▼▼ **Carthage Inn** 🅼
(417) 358-2499. **$51-$56.** 2244 Grand Ave. Just n of jct SR HH. Ext corridors. **Pets:** Small. $10 one-time fee/pet. Designated rooms, service with restrictions, supervision.
🆂🅰🆅🅴 🆂🅾 ⊠ 🛏 ⌦

▲▲▲ ▼▼▼ **Econo Lodge** 🅂🅷
(417) 358-3900. **$55-$65.** 1441 W Central. On SR 96; jct US 71. Ext/int corridors. **Pets:** Accepted.
🆂🅰🆅🅴 🆂🅾 ⊠ 🆒 🛏 ⌦

▼▼ **Super 8 Motel** 🅂🅷 🐾
(417) 359-9000. **Call for rates.** 416 W Fir Rd. Just e of jct US 71 and SR HH. Int corridors. **Pets:** Medium. $5 one-time fee/pet. Service with restrictions.
⊠ 🛏

CASSVILLE

◇ Budget Inn M ☙
(417) 847-4196. **$34-$58.** Hwy 112/248. On SR 76, 86 and 112, just e of jct SR 248; downtown. Ext corridors. **Pets:** Very small, dogs only. $10 deposit/pet. Service with restrictions, supervision.
ASK S6 X 🗐 🖭 ⚊

◇◇ Super 8 Motel SH
(417) 847-4888. **$58-$65.** 101 S Hwy 37. Just s of jct SR 76, 86 and 37 business route. Int corridors. **Pets:** Small, dogs only. $20 deposit/pet. Designated rooms, service with restrictions, supervision.
ASK S6 X 🗐 ⚊

CHILLICOTHE

◇◇ Best Western Inn SH
(660) 646-0572. **$55-$101.** 1020 S Washington St. Jct US 36 and 65 (Washington St). Ext/int corridors. **Pets:** Accepted.
ASK S6 X 🗐 🖭 ⚊

◇◇ Chillicothe Super 8 Motel SH
(660) 646-7888. **$58-$63.** 580 Old Hwy 36 E. Jct US 36 and 65 (Washington St), 0.8 mi e. Int corridors. **Pets:** Small. $10 one-time fee/pet. Service with restrictions, supervision.
ASK S6 X 🗐

CLINTON

◬◬◬ ◇ Motel USA Inn M
(660) 885-2267. **$35-$55.** 1508 N 2nd St. Jct SR 7 and 13. Ext corridors. **Pets:** Very small, dogs only. $10 daily fee/pet. Designated rooms, service with restrictions, supervision.
SAVE S6 X 🗐

COLUMBIA

◇◇ Candlewood Suites SH
(573) 817-0525. **$79-$179.** 3100 Wingate Ct. I-70, exit 128A, just s to I-70 Dr SE, 0.3 mi e to Keene St, 0.3 mi s to Wingate Ct, then just ne. Int corridors. **Pets:** Accepted.
ASK S6 X 📁 🗐 🖭

◇◇◇◇ Drury Inn-Columbia SH
(573) 445-1800. **$72-$117.** 1000 Knipp St. I-70, exit 124 (Stadium Blvd), just s. Int corridors. **Pets:** Large, other species. Service with restrictions, supervision.
ASK X 📁 🗐 🖭 ⚊

◇◇◇◇ Holiday Inn Select Executive Center LH
(573) 445-8531. **$109-$129.** 2200 I-70 Dr SW. I-70, exit 124 (Stadium Blvd), just w. Int corridors. **Pets:** Medium. $100 deposit/room. Service with restrictions, crate.
ASK X 6M 📁 🔆 🗐 🖭 🍴 ⚊ ⊠

◬◬◬ ◇◇ La Quinta Inn Columbia SH
(573) 443-4141. **$90-$110.** 901 Conley Rd. I-70, exit 128A (US 63). Int corridors. **Pets:** Accepted.
SAVE X 6M 🗐 🖭 ⚊

◬◬◬ ◇◇◇ Quality Inn Columbia SH
(573) 449-2491. **$69-$99.** 1612 N Providence Rd. I-70, exit 126 (Providence Rd). Ext/int corridors. **Pets:** Accepted.
SAVE S6 X 6M 🗐 🖭 ⚊ ⊠

◇ Red Roof Inn-Columbia M
(573) 442-0145. **$48-$71.** 201 E Texas Ave. I-70, exit 126 (Providence Rd), just n. Ext corridors. **Pets:** Accepted.
X 🔆

◇◇ Travelodge M ☙
(573) 449-1065. **$59-$99.** 900 Vandiver Dr. I-70, exit 127 (US 63), just n. Ext corridors. **Pets:** Medium. $5 daily fee/pet. Service with restrictions, crate.
ASK S6 X 🗐 🖭 ⚊

◇◇◇ Wingate Inn SH
(573) 817-0500. **$81.** 3101 Wingate Ct. I-70, exit 128A, just s to I-70 Dr SE, 0.3 mi e to Keene St, 0.3 mi s, then just w. Int corridors. **Pets:** Accepted.
ASK S6 X 6M 🔆 🗐 🖭 ⚊

CUBA

◬◬◬ ◇◇ Best Western Cuba Inn M
(573) 885-7707. **$55-$70.** 246 Hwy P. I-44, exit 208, just ne. Ext corridors. **Pets:** Small. $10 one-time fee/room. Designated rooms, service with restrictions, supervision.
SAVE S6 X 🗐 🖭 ⚊

FESTUS

◇◇◇ Drury Inn St. Louis/Festus SH
(636) 933-2400. **$55-$96.** 1001 Veterans Blvd. I-55, exit 175, just e. Int corridors. **Pets:** Large, other species. Service with restrictions, supervision.
ASK X 🗐 🖭 ⚊

FULTON

◇◇◇ Loganberry Inn Bed & Breakfast Inc BB
(573) 642-9229. **$99-$189, 14 day notice.** 310 W 7th St. 1 mi e of jct US 54 and CR F, n on Westminster, then just e. Int corridors. **Pets:** Other species. $10 one-time fee/room. Designated rooms, service with restrictions, crate.
ASK S6 X 🗐 🖭 ⊠

HANNIBAL

◬◬◬ ◇◇ Hannibal Travelodge M
(573) 221-4100. **$46-$82.** 500 Mark Twain Ave. I-72, exit 157, 0.6 mi se on US Business Rt 36/SR 29. Ext corridors. **Pets:** Medium, other species. $10 daily fee/pet. Designated rooms, service with restrictions, supervision.
SAVE S6 X 🗐 🖭 ⚊

◬◬◬ ◇◇◇ Quality Inn & Suites SH
(573) 221-4001. **$79-$109.** 120 Lindsey Dr. 2 mi w on US 36, south service road. Int corridors. **Pets:** Small. $10 daily fee/pet. Designated rooms, service with restrictions, supervision.
SAVE S6 X 🗐 🖭 ⚊ ⊠

HARRISONVILLE

◬◬◬ ◇◇ Best Western Harrisonville M
(816) 884-3200. **$60-$92.** 2201 Rockhaven Rd. Just n of jct US 71 and SR 291. Ext corridors. **Pets:** Small. $10 daily fee/pet. Designated rooms, service with restrictions, supervision.
SAVE S6 X 🗐 🖭 ⚊

◇ Budget Host Caravan Motel M
(816) 884-4100. **$39-$60.** 1705 Hwy 291 N. Just n of jct US 71. Ext corridors. **Pets:** Small. Service with restrictions, supervision.
ASK S6 X 🗐

◬◬◬ ◇ Slumber Inn Motel M ☙
(816) 884-3100. **$37-$48, 7 day notice.** 21400 E 275th St. Jct US 71 and SR 7 S (Clinton exit), just w. Ext corridors. **Pets:** Medium. $6 daily fee/pet. Service with restrictions, supervision.
SAVE X 🗐 ⚊

HAYTI

◇◇◇ Drury Inn & Suites-Hayti SH
(573) 359-2702. **$60-$120.** 1317 Hwy 84. I-55, exit 19 (US 412/SR 84), just w. Int corridors. **Pets:** Large, other species. Service with restrictions, supervision.
ASK X 📁 🗐 🖭 ⚊

HIGGINSVILLE

▼▼▼ Super 8 Motel-Higginsville 🆂🅷
(660) 584-7781. **$59-$75.** 6471 Oakview Ln. I-70, exit 49 (SR 13), just se. Int corridors. **Pets:** Accepted.
🅰🆂🅺 🆂🔊 ✕

HOUSTON

▼▼ Southern Inn Motel 🆂🅷
(417) 967-4591. **$45-$50.** 1493 S Hwy 63. 1.3 mi s on US 63. Ext corridors. **Pets:** Accepted.
🅰🆂🅺 🆂🔊 ✕ 🖥

JACKSON

▼▼▼ Drury Inn & Suites-Jackson 🆂🅷
(573) 243-9200. **$70-$105.** 225 Drury Ln. I-55, exit 105 (SR 61), 0.3 mi w. Int corridors. **Pets:** Large, other species. Service with restrictions, supervision.
🅰🆂🅺 ✕ &M 🖥 🖥 ⌨ ⊇

JEFFERSON CITY

⬥⬥⬥ ▼▼▼ Capitol Plaza Hotel 🅻🅷
(573) 635-1234. **$109-$139.** 415 W McCarty St. On US 50 and 63 S, just e of jct US 54. Int corridors. **Pets:** Medium, dogs only. Service with restrictions, supervision.
🆂🅰🆅🅴 🆂🔊 ✕ &M 🖥 🖥 🍴 ⊇ ⊗

⬥⬥⬥ ▼▼▼ Ramada Inn-Jefferson City 🆂🅷
(573) 635-7171. **$70.** 1510 Jefferson St. US 54, exit Ellis Blvd, 0.5 mi nw. Ext/int corridors. **Pets:** $10 daily fee/room. Designated rooms, service with restrictions, crate.
🆂🅰🆅🅴 🆂🔊 ✕ &M 🖥 🖥 🍴 ⊇

▼▼ Super 8 Motel-Jefferson City 🅼
(573) 636-5456. **$52-$89.** 1710 Jefferson St. US 54, exit Ellis Blvd, 0.3 mi nw on frontage road. Int corridors. **Pets:** Small, other species. $5 daily fee/room. Service with restrictions, supervision.
🅰🆂🅺 🆂🔊 ✕ 🖥 🖥

JOPLIN

⬥⬥⬥ ▼▼▼ Baymont Inn & Suites 🆂🅷
(417) 623-0000. **$66-$86.** 3510 S Range Line Rd. I-44, exit 8B, just n. Ext/int corridors. **Pets:** Accepted.
🆂🅰🆅🅴 🆂🔊 ✕ &M 🖥 🖥 ⊇

⬥⬥⬥ ▼▼▼ Best Western Oasis Inn & Suites 🆂🅷
(417) 781-6776. **$66-$86.** 3508 S Range Line Rd. I-44, exit 8B, just nw. Ext corridors. **Pets:** Medium. $10 daily fee/pet. Service with restrictions, supervision.
🆂🅰🆅🅴 🆂🔊 ✕ 🖥 🖥 ⊇

▼▼▼ Drury Inn & Suites-Joplin 🆂🅷
(417) 781-8000. **$63-$117.** 3601 Range Line Rd. I-44, exit 8B, just ne. Int corridors. **Pets:** Large, other species. Service with restrictions, supervision.
🅰🆂🅺 ✕ ⊘ 🖥 🖥 ⊇ ⊗

⬥⬥⬥ ▼▼▼▼ Holiday Inn 🆂🅷 🐾
(417) 782-1000. **$59-$119.** 3615 Range Line Rd. I-44, exit 8B, just ne. Int corridors. **Pets:** Small. $25 deposit/room. Designated rooms, service with restrictions, supervision.
🆂🅰🆅🅴 🆂🔊 ✕ ⊘ 🖥 🖥 🍴 ⊇ ⊗

▼▼ Microtel Inn & Suites Joplin 🆂🅷
(417) 626-8282. **$53-$61.** 4101 Richard Joseph Blvd. I-44, exit 8A, just s. Int corridors. **Pets:** Accepted.
🅰🆂🅺 🆂🔊 ✕ ⊘ &M 🖥 🖥 ⊇

⬥⬥⬥ ▼▼ Sleep Inn 🆂🅷
(417) 782-1212. **$69.** I-44 & State Hwy 43 S. I-44, exit 4, just s. Int corridors. **Pets:** Accepted.
🆂🅰🆅🅴 🆂🔊 ✕ &M 🖥

⬥⬥⬥ ▼▼ Super 8 Motel-Joplin 🅼
(417) 782-8765. **$50-$95.** 2830 E 36th St. I-44, exit 8B, just n. Int corridors. **Pets:** Accepted.
🆂🅰🆅🅴 🆂🔊 ✕ 🖥

KANSAS CITY METROPOLITAN AREA

BLUE SPRINGS

▼▼ Days Inn & Suites 🆂🅷
(816) 224-1122. **$55-$94.** 3120 NW Jefferson Rd. I-70, exit 18, just n to NW Jefferson St, then 0.5 mi e. Int corridors. **Pets:** Other species. $5 daily fee/pet. Designated rooms, service with restrictions, supervision.
🅰🆂🅺 🆂🔊 ✕ &M 🖥 🖥 🖥

▼▼ Motel 6 Kansas City-Blue Springs #384 🅼
(816) 228-9133. **$36-$46.** 901 NW Jefferson St. I-70, exit 20, 0.5 mi w. Ext corridors. **Pets:** Accepted.
🆂🔊 ✕ &M 🖥 ⊇

⬥⬥⬥ ▼▼ Sleep Inn 🆂🅷
(816) 224-1199. **$60.** 451 NW Jefferson St. I-70, exit 20, just n on SR 7 to NW Jefferson St, then just e. Int corridors. **Pets:** Other species.
🆂🅰🆅🅴 🆂🔊 ✕ &M 🖥 🖥 🖥 ⊇

GRAIN VALLEY

▼▼ Comfort Inn 🆂🅷
(816) 847-2700. **Call for rates.** 210 Jefferson St. I-70, exit 24, just nw. Int corridors. **Pets:** Accepted.
✕ 🖥 🖥 🖥 ⊇

INDEPENDENCE

⬥⬥⬥ ▼▼▼ Best Western Truman Inn 🅼
(816) 254-0100. **$59-$89.** 4048 S Lynn Court Dr. I-70, exit 12, just n on Noland Rd, then just w. Ext corridors. **Pets:** Medium. $30 deposit/room, $8 daily fee/room. Designated rooms, service with restrictions, crate.
🆂🅰🆅🅴 🆂🔊 ✕ 🖥 ⊇

▼▼ Red Roof Inn 🅼
(816) 373-2800. **$49-$75.** 13712 E 42nd Terrace. I-70, exit 12, just sw. Ext corridors. **Pets:** Accepted.
✕ &M 🖥

⬥⬥⬥ ▼▼ Super 8 Motel 🆂🅷
(816) 833-1888. **$44-$89.** 4032 S Lynn Court Dr. I-70, exit 12, just nw. Int corridors. **Pets:** Medium. $30 deposit/room, $8 daily fee/room. Designated rooms, service with restrictions, crate.
🆂🅰🆅🅴 🆂🔊 ✕ ⊇

KANSAS CITY

⬥⬥⬥ ▼▼▼ AmeriSuites KCI Airport 🆂🅷
(816) 891-0871. **$89-$98.** 7600 NW 97th Terr. I-29, exit 10, just sw. Int corridors. **Pets:** Accepted.
🆂🅰🆅🅴 🆂🔊 ✕ ⊘ 🖥 🖥 ⊇

⬥⬥⬥ ▼▼▼ Baymont Inn & Suites Kansas City South 🆂🅷
(816) 822-7000. **$49-$69.** 8601 Hillcrest Rd. I-435, exit 69 (87th St). Int corridors. **Pets:** Medium. $25 deposit/pet. Designated rooms, service with restrictions, supervision.
🆂🅰🆅🅴 🆂🔊 ✕ &M ⊘ &M 🖥 🖥

Chase Suites by Woodfin SH
(816) 891-9009. **$89-$159.** 9900 NW Prairie View Rd. I-29, exit 10. Ext corridors. **Pets:** Other species. $150 deposit/pet, $10 daily fee/pet. Service with restrictions.

Clarion Hotel KCI SH
(816) 464-2345. **$59-$119.** 11832 Plaza Cir. I-29, exit 13, just e. Int corridors. **Pets:** Accepted.

Days Inn M
(816) 746-1666. **$70-$190.** 11120 NW Ambassador Dr. I-29, exit 12, just e, then s. Int corridors. **Pets:** Medium, other species. $15 daily fee/pet. Service with restrictions, crate.

Doubletree Hotel Kansas City SH
(816) 474-6664. **$89-$219.** 1301 Wyandotte St. Just s of I-70, US 24 and 40. Int corridors. **Pets:** Accepted.

Drury Inn & Suites-Kansas City Airport SH
(816) 880-9700. **$60-$113.** 7900 NW Tiffany Springs Pkwy. I-29, exit 10, just w. Int corridors. **Pets:** Large, other species. Service with restrictions, supervision.

Drury Inn & Suites-Kansas City Stadium SH
(816) 923-3000. **$60-$113.** 3830 Blue Ridge Cutoff. I-70, exit 9 (Blue Ridge Cutoff), just nw. Int corridors. **Pets:** Large, other species. Service with restrictions, supervision.

Embassy Suites Hotel KCI Airport SH
(816) 891-7788. **$99-$209.** 7640 NW Tiffany Springs Pkwy. I-29, exit 10, just e. Int corridors. **Pets:** Small, other species. $50 one-time fee/room. Service with restrictions, supervision.

The Fairmont Kansas City at the Plaza LH
(816) 756-1500. **$159-$529.** 401 Ward Pkwy. Corner of Wornall and Ward Pkwy. Int corridors. **Pets:** Small. $25 daily fee/pet. Service with restrictions, crate.

Four Points by Sheraton Kansas City Country Club Plaza A Barcelo Hotel SH
(816) 753-7400. **$199.** One E 45th St. In Country Club Plaza. Int corridors. **Pets:** Accepted.

Hampton Inn SH
(816) 483-7900. **$72-$109.** 1051 N Cambridge Ave. I-435, exit 57, just w to Cambridge Ave, then just s. Int corridors. **Pets:** Medium. $10 one-time fee/room. Service with restrictions, supervision.

Holiday Inn Express Westport Plaza SH
(816) 931-1000. **$79-$129.** 801 Westport Rd. In Westport Plaza area. Int corridors. **Pets:** Accepted.

Holiday Inn-Sports Complex SH
(816) 353-5300. **$79, 14 day notice.** 4011 Blue Ridge Cutoff. I-70, exit 9 (Blue Ridge Cutoff), just se. Int corridors. **Pets:** Accepted.

Homestead Studio Suites Hotel-Kansas City/Country Club Plaza SH
(816) 531-2212. **$80-$99.** 4535 Main St. Just ne of Country Club Plaza. Int corridors. **Pets:** Accepted.

Homestead Studio Suites Hotel-Kansas City/KCI Airport SH
(816) 891-8500. **$57-$76.** 9701 N Shannon Ave. I-29, exit 10. Int corridors. **Pets:** Medium, other species. $25 daily fee/pet. Service with restrictions, supervision.

Homewood Suites by Hilton SH
(816) 880-9880. **$89-$179.** 7312 NW Polo Dr. I-29, exit 10, just e. Int corridors. **Pets:** Small, other species. $50 one-time fee/room. Designated rooms, service with restrictions.

Kansas City Marriott Downtown LH
(816) 421-6800. **$139-$240.** 200 W 12th St. Just s of I-70, US 24 and 40. Int corridors. **Pets:** Accepted.

Quality Inn & Suites Airport SH
(816) 587-6262. **$65-$145.** 6901 NW 83rd St. I-29, exit 8. Int corridors. **Pets:** Other species.

Radisson Hotel Kansas City Airport SH
(816) 464-2423. **$88-$98.** 11828 NW Plaza Cir. I-29, exit 13, just se. Int corridors. **Pets:** Small. $10 daily fee/room. Designated rooms, service with restrictions, crate.

Red Roof Inn-North M
(816) 452-8585. **$48-$76.** 3636 NE Randolph Rd. I-435, exit 55B northbound; exit 55 southbound, just e on SR 210, then just n. Ext corridors. **Pets:** Accepted.

Residence Inn by Marriott Union Hill SH
(816) 561-3000. **$139-$189.** 2975 Main St. Just e of 31st St. Ext corridors. **Pets:** Medium. $75 one-time fee/room. Service with restrictions, crate.

Sheraton Suites Country Club Plaza LH
(816) 931-4400. **$145-$165.** 770 W 47th St. Corner of Summit and 47th St; in Country Club Plaza. Int corridors. **Pets:** Other species. $15 daily fee/room. Service with restrictions, supervision.

Westin Crown Center LH
(816) 474-4400. **$104-$169.** 1 Pershing Rd. 0.5 mi s. Int corridors. **Pets:** Accepted.

KEARNEY

Kearney Super 8 Motel SH
(816) 628-6800. **$61-$100.** 210 Platte Clay Way. I-35, exit 26, just e on SR 92, then just n. Int corridors. **Pets:** Medium, dogs only. $10 one-time fee/pet. Service with restrictions, crate.

LEE'S SUMMIT

Comfort Inn by Choice Hotels SH
(816) 524-8181. **$64-$94.** 607 SE Oldham Pkwy. Jct of US 50 and SR 291 N. Int corridors. **Pets:** Accepted.

Lee's Summit Holiday Inn Express SH
(816) 795-6400. **$84-$109.** 4825 NE Lakewood Way. I-470, exit 14, just e on Bowlin Rd, then 0.4 mi s. Int corridors. **Pets:** Accepted.

▼▼▼ Summit Inn and Suites 🅂🄷
(816) 525-1400. **$62-$72.** 625 NW Murray Rd. I-470, exit 7A, just s of jct US 50, exit Chipman Rd. Int corridors. **Pets:** Medium, other species. Designated rooms, service with restrictions, supervision.
🄰🅂🄺 🅂🄳 ⊠ ⟨⟩ ⟨⟩ ⬛ ⬛ ⟿

LIBERTY

🄰🄰🄰 ▼▼▼ Days Inn 🄼
(816) 781-8770. **$50-$65, 7 day notice.** 209 N Hwy 291. I-35, exit 16 (SR 152), 0.7 mi e on SR 152, then just n on SR 291. Ext corridors. **Pets:** Small. $15 daily fee/pet. Service with restrictions, supervision.
🅂🄰🅅🄴 🅂🄳 ⊠ ⬛ ⬛ ⟿

NORTH KANSAS CITY

🄰🄰🄰 ▼▼▼ Baymont Inn & Suites Kansas City North 🅂🄷
(816) 221-1200. **$59-$99.** 2214 Taney Rd. I-29/35, exit 6A, just e on SR 210, then just n. Int corridors. **Pets:** Medium, dogs only. $25 deposit/pet. Designated rooms, supervision.
🅂🄰🅅🄴 🅂🄳 ⊠ ⟨⟩ ⬛ ⬛

END METROPOLITAN AREA

KIMBERLING CITY

🄰🄰🄰 ▼▼ Kimberling Heights Resort 🄼
(417) 779-4158. **$48-$59.** 9687 State Hwy 13. On US 13, 1.5 mi s. Ext corridors. **Pets:** Accepted.
🅂🄰🅅🄴 🅂🄳 ⬛ ⬛ ⟿ ⟿

KINGDOM CITY

▼▼ Super 8 Motel-Kingdom City 🄼
(573) 642-2888. **$45-$74.** 3370 Gold Ave. I-70, exit 148 (US 54), 0.3 mi s. Int corridors. **Pets:** Other species. $5 daily fee/pet. Service with restrictions, supervision.
🄰🅂🄺 🅂🄳 ⊠ 🄶🄼 ⟨⟩ ⬛

KIRKSVILLE

▼▼ Comfort Inn by Choice Hotels 🄼
(660) 665-2205. **$59-$89.** 2209 N Baltimore. US 63 N. Int corridors. **Pets:** Accepted.
🄰🅂🄺 🅂🄳 ⊠ 🄶🄼 ⟨⟩ ⬛ ⬛

🄰🄰🄰 ▼▼▼ Days Inn 🅂🄷 🐾
(660) 665-8244. **$64.** 3805 S Baltimore. 3 mi s on US 63; 0.5 mi s of jct SR 6. Int corridors. **Pets:** $10 one-time fee/room. Service with restrictions, supervision.
🅂🄰🅅🄴 🅂🄳 ⊠ 🄶🄼 ⟨⟩ ⟨⟩ ⬛ ⬛ ⟦⟧ ⟿ ⟨⟩

▼▼ Shamrock Inn 🄼
(660) 665-8352. **$50.** 2521 S Business Rt 63. 0.3 mi w of jct US 63. Ext corridors. **Pets:** Medium, dogs only. $10 daily fee/pet. Designated rooms, service with restrictions, supervision.
🄰🅂🄺 🅂🄳 ⊠ ⬛ ⬛ ⟿

▼▼ Super 8 Motel-Kirksville 🄼
(660) 665-8826. **$45-$75.** 1101 Country Club Dr. On US 63 and SR 6. Int corridors. **Pets:** Other species. $10 daily fee/pet. Designated rooms, service with restrictions, supervision.
🄰🅂🄺 🅂🄳 ⊠ ⬛

LAKE OZARK

🄰🄰🄰 ▼▼▼ Holiday Inn SunSpree Resort & Conference Center 🄻🄷 🐾
(573) 365-2334. **$99-$170, 3 day notice.** 120 Holiday Ln. 2.6 mi s of Bagnell Dam, on US 54 business route. **Pets:** Dogs only. $50 deposit/pet, $6 daily fee/pet. Service with restrictions, supervision.
🅂🄰🅅🄴 🅂🄳 ⊠ 🄶🄼 ⟨⟩ ⟨⟩ ⬛ ⬛ ⟦⟧ ⟿ ⟨⟩

▼▼ Days Inn-North 🅂🄷
(816) 421-6000. **$45-$75.** 2232 Taney St. I-29/35, exit 6A, just e on SR 210, then just n. Int corridors. **Pets:** Accepted.
🄰🅂🄺 🅂🄳 ⊠ 🄶🄼 ⟨⟩ ⟨⟩ ⬛

OAK GROVE (JACKSON COUNTY)

🄰🄰🄰 ▼▼▼ Econo Lodge 🄼
(816) 690-3681. **$59-$69.** 410 SE 1st St. I-70, exit 28, just s on Broadway St, just e on SE 4th St, then just n. Ext corridors. **Pets:** Small. $5 daily fee/pet. Service with restrictions, crate.
🅂🄰🅅🄴 🅂🄳 ⊠ ⬛

LAMAR

▼▼ Blue Top Inn 🄼
(417) 682-3333. **$39-$46.** 65 SE 1st Ln. Just se of jct US 71 and 160. Ext corridors. **Pets:** Other species. $25 deposit/room. No service, supervision.
🄰🅂🄺 🅂🄳 ⊠ ⬛ ⬛ ⟿

LEBANON

🄰🄰🄰 ▼▼▼ Best Western Wyota Inn 🅂🄷
(417) 532-6171. **$67-$70.** 1225 Mill Creek Rd. I-44, exit 130, just nw. Ext corridors. **Pets:** Medium, other species. $10 daily fee/pet. Designated rooms, service with restrictions, supervision.
🅂🄰🅅🄴 🅂🄳 ⊠ ⬛ ⬛ ⟦⟧ ⟿

LICKING

▼▼ Best Value Inn 🅂🄷
(573) 674-4809. **$46.** 209 S Hwy 63. On US 63. Ext corridors. **Pets:** Small. $10 daily fee/room. Service with restrictions, supervision.
🄰🅂🄺 🅂🄳 ⊠ ⟨⟩

LOUISIANA

🄰🄰🄰 ▼▼ River's Edge Motel 🄼
(573) 754-4522. **$50-$60.** 201 Mansion St. On US 54; at Champ Clark Bridge. Ext corridors. **Pets:** Dogs only. $25 deposit/room. Service with restrictions, supervision.
🅂🄰🅅🄴 🅂🄳 ⊠ ⬛ ⬛

MACON

▼▼ Best Western Inn 🄼
(660) 385-2125. **$51-$63.** 28933 Sunset Dr. On Outer Rd S; at US 36 and Long Branch Lake exit. Ext corridors. **Pets:** $20 deposit/pet. Service with restrictions, supervision.
🄰🅂🄺 🅂🄳 ⊠ ⬛ ⬛ ⟿

▼▼ Super 8 Motel 🅂🄷
(660) 385-5788. **$56-$66.** 203 E Briggs Dr. Jct US 36 and 63. Int corridors. **Pets:** Other species. $10 daily fee/pet.
🄰🅂🄺 🅂🄳 ⊠ ⬛

MARSHFIELD

▼▼▼ Holiday Inn Express 🅂🄷
(417) 859-6000. **$69-$89.** 1301 Banning St. I-44, exit 100 (SR 38), on southeast corner. Int corridors. **Pets:** Medium. $25 deposit/room. Service with restrictions, supervision.
🄰🅂🄺 🅂🄳 ⊠ 🄶🄼 ⬛ ⬛ ⟿

MARSTON

WWW **Super 8 Motel** M
(573) 643-9888. **$54.** 501 SE Outer Rd. I-55, exit 40, just se. Int corridors. **Pets:** Medium. $25 deposit/room. Service with restrictions, supervision.
(ASK) (S6) (X) (B) (IMG)

MARYVILLE

WWW **Super 8 Motel-Maryville** SH
(660) 582-8088. **$40-$47.** 222 Summit Dr. On Business Rt US 71; just n of US 71 Bypass. Int corridors. **Pets:** Other species. $20 deposit/room. Service with restrictions, supervision.
(ASK) (S6) (X) (B) (IMG)

MINER

AAA WWW **Best Western Coach House Inn** SH
(573) 471-9700. **$65-$130.** 220 S Interstate Dr. I-55, exit 67, just e, then 0.5 mi s on Interstate Dr (frontage road). Int corridors. **Pets:** Small. $25 one-time fee/room. Designated rooms, service with restrictions, supervision.
(SAVE) (S6) (X) (IMG) (B) (IMG) (IMG)

WWW **Drury Inn-Sikeston** SH
(573) 471-4100. **$70-$106.** 2602 E Malone. I-55, exit 67, just sw. Int corridors. **Pets:** Large, other species. Service with restrictions, supervision.
(ASK) (X) (S6M) (IMG) (IMG) (B) (IMG) (IMG)

WWW **Pear Tree Inn by Drury-Sikeston** SH
(573) 471-8660. **$52-$76.** 2602 E Malone Rear. I-55, exit 67, just sw. Ext corridors. **Pets:** Large, other species. Service with restrictions, supervision.
(ASK) (X) (S6M) (IMG) (IMG) (IMG)

MOBERLY

WWW **Best Western Moberly Inn** SH
(660) 263-6540. **$63-$127, 10 day notice.** 1200 Hwy 24 E. Jct US 24 and 63 business route. Ext/int corridors. **Pets:** Medium, dogs only. $30 one-time fee/pet. Service with restrictions, supervision.
(X) (S6M) (B) (IMG) (IMG) (IMG)

WWW **Super 8 Motel-Moberly** SH
(660) 263-8862. **$45-$75.** 300 Hwy 24 E. Jct US 24 and 63 business route. Int corridors. **Pets:** Accepted.
(ASK) (S6) (X) (B)

MOUNTAIN GROVE

AAA WWW **Best Western Ranch House Inn** M
(417) 926-3152. **$57-$70.** 111 E 17th St. Jct US 60 and 95, just s. Ext corridors. **Pets:** Accepted.
(SAVE) (S6) (X) (IMG) (IMG)

WWW **Days Inn of Mountain Grove** SH
(417) 926-5555. **$48-$64.** 300 E 19th St. Jct US 60 and 95, just se. Ext corridors. **Pets:** Accepted.
(ASK) (S6) (X) (IMG)

MOUNT VERNON

AAA WW **Motel USA Inn** M
(417) 466-2125. **$35-$55.** 1015 E Mt Vernon Blvd. I-44, exit 46, just n. Ext corridors. **Pets:** Other species. $10 daily fee/pet. Service with restrictions, supervision.
(SAVE) (S6) (X) (IMG)

WWW **Super 8** SH
(417) 461-0230. **$62-$95, 7 day notice.** 1200 E Industrial Blvd. I-44, exit 46, just n, then just se. Int corridors. **Pets:** Small. $10 one-time fee/pet. Service with restrictions, supervision.
(ASK) (S6) (X) (IMG) (B) (IMG)

NEOSHO

WWW **Super 8 Motel-Neosho** SH
(417) 455-1888. **$52-$69.** 3085 Gardner/Edgewood Dr. Just s of jct US 60B and 71B. Int corridors. **Pets:** Accepted.
(ASK) (S6) (X) (IMG) (B)

NEVADA

AAA WWW **Days Inn of Nevada** SH ✿
(417) 667-6777. **$64-$74.** 2345 Marvel Rd. US 71, exit Camp Clark, just w. Ext/int corridors. **Pets:** Small. $5 daily fee/pet. Designated rooms, service with restrictions, supervision.
(SAVE) (S6) (X) (B) (IMG) (IMG)

WWW **Super 8 Motel** SH
(417) 667-8888. **$54-$56.** 2301 E Austin Blvd. US 71, exit Camp Clark, just w. Int corridors. **Pets:** Accepted.
(ASK) (S6) (X) (B) (IMG)

NEW FLORENCE

WW **Days Inn Booneslick Lodge** SH
(573) 835-7777. **Call for rates.** 403 Booneslick Rd. I-70, exit 175, just w. Int corridors. **Pets:** Accepted.
(X) (B) (IMG)

OSAGE BEACH

AAA WWW **Best Western Dogwood Hills Resort Inn** SH
(573) 348-1735. **$39-$129.** 1252 State Hwy KK. 0.5 mi n, off US 54. Ext corridors. **Pets:** Accepted.
(SAVE) (S6) (X) (B) (IMG) (IMG) (IMG)

AAA WWW **Lake Chateau Resort** M
(573) 348-2791. **$49-$145.** 5066 Hwy 54. Just s of Grand Glaize Bridge. Ext corridors. **Pets:** Medium. $10 one-time fee/pet. Designated rooms, service with restrictions, supervision.
(SAVE) (S6) (X) (B) (IMG) (IMG) (X)

AAA WW **Scottish Inns** M
(573) 348-3123. **$40-$90, 3 day notice.** 5404 Hwy 54. 1 mi w of Grand Glaize Bridge. Ext/int corridors. **Pets:** Small. $5 daily fee/pet. Designated rooms, service with restrictions, crate.
(SAVE) (S6) (X) (IMG)

POPLAR BLUFF

WW **Comfort Inn** SH
(573) 686-5200. **$75-$110.** 2582 N Westwood Blvd. 1.3 mi s from jct US 60 E. Int corridors. **Pets:** Accepted.
(ASK) (S6) (X) (S6M) (X) (B) (IMG) (IMG)

WWWW **Drury Inn-Poplar Bluff** SH
(573) 686-2451. **$70-$106.** 2220 N Westwood Blvd. On US 67, 1.4 mi s from jct US 60 E. Int corridors. **Pets:** Large, other species. Service with restrictions, supervision.
(ASK) (X) (IMG) (B) (IMG) (IMG)

WWW **Pear Tree Inn by Drury-Poplar Bluff** M
(573) 785-7100. **$55-$80.** 2218 N Westwood Blvd. On US 67, 1.4 mi s from jct US 60 E. Ext corridors. **Pets:** Large, other species. Service with restrictions, supervision.
(ASK) (X) (IMG) (IMG) (IMG)

WWW **Super 8** SH
(573) 785-0176. **$50-$55, 15 day notice.** 2831 N Westwood Blvd. On US 67, 0.8 mi s from jct US 60 E. Int corridors. **Pets:** Medium. $25 one-time fee/room. Service with restrictions, supervision.
(ASK) (S6) (X) (IMG) (B)

RICH HILL

Apache Motel M
(417) 395-2161. **$36-$40.** Hwy 71 and B. Just e of jct US 71 and CR B.
Ext corridors. **Pets:** Accepted.
SAVE SD X

ROLLA

Best Western Coachlight M
(573) 341-2511. **$48-$85.** 1403 Martin Springs Dr. Jct I-44 and Business Rt 44 S, exit 184. Ext corridors. **Pets:** Accepted.
SAVE SD X B P

Days Inn M
(573) 341-3700. **$60-$80.** 1207 Kingshighway. I-44, exit 184, just s. Ext
corridors. **Pets:** Other species. No service, supervision.
X

Drury Inn SH
(573) 364-4000. **$50-$94.** 2006 N Bishop. I-44, exit 186 (US 63), just
ne. Ext/int corridors. **Pets:** Large, other species. Service with restrictions,
supervision.
ASK X B P

Econo Lodge M
(573) 341-3130. **$50-$65.** 1417 Martin Springs Dr. I-44, exit 184, just n.
Ext corridors. **Pets:** Medium, other species. Designated rooms, service
with restrictions, crate.
SAVE SD X B P

Holiday Inn Express SH
(573) 364-8200. **Call for rates.** 1507 Martin Springs Dr. I-44, exit 184.
Int corridors. **Pets:** Small. $10 daily fee/pet. Designated rooms, service
with restrictions, supervision.
X B P

Super 8 Motel-Rolla M
(573) 364-4156. **$45-$60.** 1201 Kingshighway. I-44, exit 184, just ne.
Ext/int corridors. **Pets:** $5 daily fee/pet. No service, supervision.
SAVE SD X B

ST. CLAIR

Budget Lodging M
(636) 629-1000. **$59-$79.** 866 S Outer Rd W. I-44, exit 240, just w.
Ext/int corridors. **Pets:** Other species. $5 daily fee/pet. Designated rooms,
service with restrictions, supervision.
SAVE SD X B P

ST. JOSEPH

Drury Inn-St. Joseph SH
(816) 364-4700. **$50-$93.** 4213 Frederick Blvd. I-29, exit 47. Int corridors. **Pets:** Large, other species. Service with restrictions, supervision.
ASK X GM B P X

Holiday Inn Historic Riverfront District LH
(816) 279-8000. **$74-$139.** 102 S Third St. I-229, exit Edmond St
northbound; exit Felix St southbound; downtown. Int corridors.
Pets: Other species. $10 daily fee/room. Service with restrictions, supervi-
sion.
ASK SD X GM B P X

Ramada Inn LH
(816) 233-6192. **$70-$90.** 4016 Frederick Blvd. I-29, exit 47. Int corridors. **Pets:** Accepted.
SAVE SD X B P X

ST. LOUIS METROPOLITAN AREA

BRIDGETON

Red Roof Inn-Bridgeton M
(314) 291-3350. **$45-$73.** 3470 Hollenberg Dr. I-270, exit 20B (St.
Charles Rock Rd), 0.4 mi w. Ext corridors. **Pets:** Medium. Designated
rooms, service with restrictions, crate.
X

CHESTERFIELD

Homewood Suites by Hilton SH
(636) 530-0305. **$129-$139.** 840 Chesterfield Pkwy W. I-64, exit 20, 1
mi n. Int corridors. **Pets:** Accepted.
ASK SD X B P

CLAYTON

The Ritz-Carlton, St. Louis LH
(314) 863-6300. **$179-$215.** 100 Carondelet Plaza. I-64/US 40, exit 31
(Brentwood Blvd), 1.3 mi n, then 1 mi e. Int corridors. **Pets:** Medium,
dogs only. $125 one-time fee/pet. Service with restrictions, supervision.
SAVE X B P X

Sheraton Clayton Plaza Hotel SH
(314) 863-0400. **$99-$129.** 7730 Bonhomme Ave. I-64/US 40, exit 31
(Brentwood Blvd), 1.3 mi n, then 0.7 mi e. Int corridors. **Pets:** Medium.
Designated rooms, service with restrictions.
SAVE SD X B P

CREVE COEUR

Drury Inn & Suites-St. Louis/Creve Coeur SH
(314) 989-1100. **$73-$133.** 11980 Olive Blvd. I-270, exit 14 (Olive Blvd).
Int corridors. **Pets:** Large, other species. Service with restrictions, supervision.
ASK X GM B P

EARTH CITY

Residence Inn St. Louis Airport/Earth City SH
(314) 209-0995. **$134-$169.** 3290 River Tr S. I-70, exit 231B (Earth City
Expwy N), just e. Int corridors. **Pets:** Large, other species. $100 one-time
fee/pet. Service with restrictions.
ASK X GM B P X

EDMUNDSON

Drury Inn-St. Louis Airport SH
(314) 423-7700. **$60-$121.** 10490 Natural Bridge Rd. I-70, exit 236
(Lambert Airport), just se. Int corridors. **Pets:** Large, other species. Service with restrictions, supervision.
ASK X GM B P

EUREKA

Holiday Inn at Six Flags SH
(636) 938-6661. **$89-$229.** 4901 Six Flags Rd. I-44, exit 261 (Allenton
Rd). Ext/int corridors. **Pets:** $10 daily fee/room. Service with restrictions,
crate.
SAVE SD X B P X

FENTON

Drury Inn & Suites St. Louis Fenton SH
(636) 343-7822. **$65-$105.** 1088 S Highway Dr. I-44, exit 274 (Bowles
Ave), just se. Int corridors. **Pets:** Large, other species. Service with
restrictions, supervision.
ASK X B P

▼▼ ◆▼ **Pear Tree Inn by Drury-Fenton** 🆂🅷
(636) 343-8820. **$55-$93.** 1100 S Highway Dr. I-44, exit 274 (Bowles Ave), just s. Int corridors. **Pets:** Large, other species. Service with restrictions, supervision.
🅰🆂🅺 ⊠ 🕭 🛢 🖵 🏊

▼▼ ▼▼ **Towne Place Suites by Marriott** 🆂🅷
(636) 305-7000. **$83-$135.** 1662 Fenton Business Park Ct. I-44, exit 275 westbound; exit 274 eastbound, to S Highway Dr, then just s. Int corridors. **Pets:** Accepted.
🅰🆂🅺 🆂🄳 ⊠ 🕭🄼 🕭 🖵 🏊

FORISTELL

🆎🆎🆎 ▼▼ ◆▼ **Best Western West 70 Inn** 🆂🅷
(636) 673-2900. **$70-$90.** 12 Hwy W. I-70, exit 203 (CR W), just n. Int corridors. **Pets:** Medium. $10 one-time fee/pet. Service with restrictions, supervision.
🆂🄰🆅🄴 🆂🄳 ⊠ 🕭 🖵 🏊

FRONTENAC

▼▼▼▼ **Hilton St. Louis Frontenac** 🆂🅷
(314) 993-1100. **$99-$229.** 1335 S Lindbergh Blvd. I-64/US 40, exit 28A (S Lindbergh Blvd), just s. Int corridors. **Pets:** Accepted.
🅰🆂🅺 ⊠ 🕭 🖵 🍴 🏊 🕱

HAZELWOOD

🆎🆎🆎 ▼▼ ◆▼ **Baymont Inn & Suites St. Louis-Hazelwood** 🆂🅷
(314) 731-4200. **$69-$89.** 318 Taylor Rd. I-270, exit 25B (N Lindbergh Blvd), just s. Int corridors. **Pets:** Medium. $50 deposit/room. Designated rooms, service with restrictions, supervision.
🆂🄰🆅🄴 🆂🄳 ⊠ 🕭 🖵

▼▼ ▼▼ **La Quinta Inn St. Louis (Airport)** 🆂🅷
(314) 731-3881. **$75-$105.** 5781 Campus Ct. I-270, exit 23 (McDonnell Blvd), just s. Int corridors. **Pets:** Accepted.
⊠ 🕭 🛢 🖵 🏊

KIRKWOOD

🆎🆎🆎 ▼▼◆▼ **Best Western Kirkwood Inn** 🆂🅷 ✿
(314) 821-3950. **$69-$119, 7 day notice.** 1200 S Kirkwood Rd. I-44, exit 277B (Lindbergh Blvd), just n. Int corridors. **Pets:** Large, other species. $10 daily fee/pet. Designated rooms, service with restrictions, crate.
🆂🄰🆅🄴 🆂🄳 ⊠ 🕭 🛢 🖵 🍴 🏊

MARYLAND HEIGHTS

▼▼▼▼ **ClubHouse Inn & Suites** 🆂🅷
(314) 205-8000. **$69-$149.** 1970 Craig Rd. I-270, exit 16A (Page Ave), 0.8 mi e to Lackland Rd exit, 0.3 mi w to Craig Rd, then just s. Int corridors. **Pets:** Medium, other species. $10 daily fee/room. Service with restrictions, supervision.
🅰🆂🅺 🆂🄳 ⊠ 🕭🄼 🛢 🖵 🏊 🕱

🆎🆎🆎 ▼▼ ▼▼ **Comfort Inn Westport** 🆂🅷
(314) 878-1400. **$60-$96.** 12031 Lackland Rd. I-270, exit 16A (Page Ave), just e to Lackland Rd, then just w. Int corridors. **Pets:** Accepted.
🆂🄰🆅🄴 🆂🄳 ⊠ 🕭 🛢 🖵 🍴 🏊

▼▼ ▼▼ **Drury Inn & Suites-St. Louis Westport** 🆂🅷
(314) 576-9966. **$63-$110.** 12220 Dorsett Rd. I-270, exit 17 (Dorsett Rd), just se. Int corridors. **Pets:** Large, other species. Service with restrictions, supervision.
🅰🆂🅺 ⊠ 🕭 🛢 🖵 🏊

▼▼ ▼▼ **Red Roof Inn-Westport** 🄼
(314) 991-4900. **$48-$75.** 11837 Lackland Rd. I-270, exit 16A (Page Ave), 1.5 mi se. Ext corridors. **Pets:** Medium. Service with restrictions, crate.
⊠ 🕭🄼 🖵

▼▼ ◆▼ **Staybridge Suites** 🆂🅷
(314) 878-1555. **$81-$171.** 1855 Craigshire Rd. I-270, exit 16A (Page Ave), 0.8 mi e, exit Lackland Rd, 1 mi w, then s via Lackland and Craigshire rds. Ext corridors. **Pets:** Accepted.
🅰🆂🅺 🆂🄳 ⊠ 🕭 🛢 🖵 🏊 🕱

MEHLVILLE

▼▼◆▼ **Holiday Inn St. Louis-South I-55** 🆂🅷
(314) 894-0700. **$89-$129.** 4234 Butler Hill Rd. I-55, exit 195 (Butler Hill Rd), just se. Ext/int corridors. **Pets:** Accepted.
🅰🆂🅺 🆂🄳 ⊠ 🕭 🛢 🖵 🍴 🏊 🕱

O'FALLON

🆎🆎🆎 ▼▼▼▼ **Comfort Inn & Suites** 🆂🅷
(636) 696-8000. **$81-$159.** 100 Comfort Inn Ct. I-70, exit 219, just sw. Int corridors. **Pets:** $10 daily fee/pet. Service with restrictions, crate.
🆂🄰🆅🄴 🆂🄳 ⊠ 🕭 🛢 🖵 🏊 🕱

RICHMOND HEIGHTS

▼▼▼▼ **Residence Inn By Marriott-St. Louis Galleria** 🆂🅷
(314) 862-1900. **Call for rates.** 1100 McMorrow Ave. I-170, exit 1C (Brentwood Ave) northbound; exit Brentwood Ave southbound, 0.5 mi e of Galleria via Galleria Pkwy. Ext corridors. **Pets:** Accepted.
⊠ 🕭🄼 🛢 🖵 🏊 🕱

ST. ANN

▼▼◆▼ **Hampton Inn-St. Louis Airport** 🆂🅷
(314) 429-2000. **$89-$99.** 10820 Pear Tree Ln. I-70, exit 236 (Airport Dr), just sw. Int corridors. **Pets:** Small. Service with restrictions, supervision.
🅰🆂🅺 ⊠ 🕭 🖵 🏊

▼▼ ▼▼ **Pear Tree Inn-St. Louis Airport** 🆂🅷
(314) 427-3400. **$50-$101.** 10810 Pear Tree Ln. I-70, exit 236 (Airport Dr), just sw. Int corridors. **Pets:** Accepted.
🅰🆂🅺 ⊠ 🕭 🖵 🏊

ST. CHARLES

🆎🆎🆎 ▼▼◆▼▼ **Comfort Suites-St. Charles** 🆂🅷
(636) 949-0694. **$90-$120.** 1400 S 5th St. I-70, exit 229 (5th St), just ne. Int corridors. **Pets:** Other species. Service with restrictions, crate.
🆂🄰🆅🄴 🆂🄳 ⊠ 🕭 🛢 🖵 🏊

ST. LOUIS

▼▼◆▼ **Drury Inn & Suites St. Louis Convention Center** 🅻🅷
(314) 231-8100. **$73-$118.** 711 N Broadway. I-70, exit 250B, at convention center. Int corridors. **Pets:** Large, other species. Service with restrictions, supervision.
🅰🆂🅺 ⊠ 🕭 🛢 🖵 🍴 🏊 🕱

▼▼◆▼ **Drury Inn St. Louis/Union Station** 🆂🅷
(314) 231-3900. **$72-$150.** 201 S 20th St. Just e of Jefferson Ave; between Market St and Clark Ave. Int corridors. **Pets:** Large, other species. Service with restrictions, supervision.
🅰🆂🅺 ⊠ 🕭 🛢🄼 🛢 🖵 🍴 🏊

▼▼◆▼ **Drury Plaza Hotel-St. Louis At the Arch** 🆂🅷
(314) 231-3003. **$82-$152.** 2 S Fourth St. I-70, 250B (Stadium/Memorial Dr), just w on Pine St to Broadway, just s to Walnut St, just e to Fourth St, then just n. Int corridors. **Pets:** Large, other species. Service with restrictions, supervision.
🅰🆂🅺 ⊠ 🕭🄼 🛢 🖵 🍴 🏊

▼▼◆▼ **Hampton Inn St. Louis/Union Station** 🆂🅷
(314) 241-3200. **$82-$142.** 2211 Market St. I-64/US 40, exit 39, just n on Jefferson Ave, then just e. Int corridors. **Pets:** Accepted.
🅰🆂🅺 ⊠ 🕭 🖵 🍴 🏊 🕱

▼▼▼▼ **Holiday Inn-Forest Park** SH
(314) 645-0700. **$99-$145.** 5915 Wilson Ave. I-44, exit 286 (Hampton Ave), just se. Int corridors. **Pets:** Other species. $75 deposit/room, $25 one-time fee/room. Service with restrictions, supervision.

(ASK) (S&) (×) (&M) (🐾) (&) (🛏) (💻) (🍴) (≈)

AAA ▼▼▼▼ **Holiday Inn Select St. Louis Downtown Convention Center** SH
(314) 421-4000. **$69-$109.** 811 N 9th St. I-70, exit 249C, just w of convention center. Int corridors. **Pets:** Service with restrictions, supervision.

(SAVE) (S&) (×) (🐾) (&) (🛏) (💻) (🍴) (≈) (⊠)

▼▼▼▼ **Omni Majestic Hotel** SH
(314) 436-2355. **$174-$204, 12 day notice.** 1019 Pine St. Between 10th and 11th sts. Int corridors. **Pets:** Accepted.

(ASK) (S&) (×) (🐾) (🛏) (💻) (🍴)

▼▼ **Red Roof Inn-Hampton** M
(314) 645-0101. **$70-$108.** 5823 Wilson Ave. I-44, exit 286 (Hampton Ave), 0.3 mi se. Ext corridors. **Pets:** Accepted.

(×) (🐾)

▼▼▼ ▼▼▼ **Renaissance Grand Hotel St. Louis** LH
(314) 621-9600. **$169-$219.** 800 Washington Ave. Across from America's Center (Convention Center). Int corridors. **Pets:** Accepted.

(ASK) (×) (&M) (🐾) (&) (🛏) (💻) (🍴) (≈)

AAA ▼▼▼ ▼▼▼ **Sheraton St. Louis City Center Hotel & Suites** LH 🐾
(314) 231-5007. **$299-$439.** 400 S 14th St. I-40, exit 39B (14th St), just ne. Int corridors. **Pets:** Medium, dogs only. Service with restrictions, supervision.

(SAVE) (S&) (×) (🐾) (&) (🛏) (💻) (🍴) (≈) (⊠)

AAA ▼▼▼ ▼▼▼ **The Westin St. Louis** LH 🐾
(314) 621-2000. **$334.** 811 Spruce St. Just w of Busch Stadium. Int corridors. **Pets:** Other species.

(SAVE) (×) (&M) (🐾) (&) (🛏) (🍴)

ST. PETERS

▼▼▼▼ **Drury Inn-St. Charles/St. Peters** SH
(636) 397-9700. **$72-$127.** 170 Westfield Dr. I-70, exit 222 (Mid Rivers Mall Dr), just se. Int corridors. **Pets:** Large, other species. Service with restrictions, supervision.

(ASK) (×) (&M) (🐾) (&) (🛏) (💻) (≈)

SUNSET HILLS

AAA ▼▼▼ ▼▼▼ **Holiday Inn-Southwest & Viking Conference Center** SH
(314) 821-6600. **$84-$104.** 10709 Watson Rd. I-44, exit 277B, just s. Int corridors. **Pets:** Small. $25 one-time fee/pet. Service with restrictions, supervision.

(SAVE) (S&) (×) (🐾) (&) (🛏) (💻) (≈) (⊠)

TOWN AND COUNTRY

AAA ▼▼▼ ▼▼▼ **St. Louis Marriott West** LH
(314) 878-2747. **$109-$209.** 660 Maryville Centre Dr. I-64/US40, exit 23 (Maryville Centre Dr), just n. Int corridors. **Pets:** Accepted.

(SAVE) (×) (🐾) (🛏) (≈) (⊠)

VALLEY PARK

▼▼▼ ▼▼▼ **Drury Inn & Suites-St. Louis Southwest** SH
(636) 861-8300. **$75-$130.** 5 Lambert Drury Pl. I-44, exit 272 (SR 141), just sw. Int corridors. **Pets:** Large. Service with restrictions, supervision.

(ASK) (×) (&) (🛏) (💻) (≈)

▼▼▼ ▼▼▼ **Hampton Inn-St. Louis Southwest** SH
(636) 529-9020. **$92-$112.** 9 Lambert Drury Pl. I-44, exit 272 (SR 141), just sw. Int corridors. **Pets:** Service with restrictions, supervision.

(×) (🛏) (💻) (≈)

WENTZVILLE

AAA ▼▼▼ ▼▼▼ **Holiday Inn-Wentzville/O'Fallon** SH
(636) 327-7001. **$96-$129.** 900 Corporate Pkwy. I-70, exit 212A, 0.3 mi w on service road. Int corridors. **Pets:** Accepted.

(SAVE) (S&) (×) (🐾) (🛏) (💻) (🍴) (≈)

END METROPOLITAN AREA

ST. ROBERT

AAA ▼▼▼ **Best Western Montis Inn** M
(573) 336-4299. **$69-$79.** 14086 Hwy Z. I-44, exit 163, just se. Ext corridors. **Pets:** Medium. Service with restrictions, crate.

(SAVE) (S&) (×) (🛏) (💻) (≈)

SEDALIA

AAA ▼▼▼ ▼▼ **Hotel Bothwell, A Clarion Collection** SH
(660) 826-5588. **$60-$185.** 103 E 4th St. Corner of 4th and S Ohio sts; downtown. Int corridors. **Pets:** Small. $25 one-time fee/pet. Designated rooms, service with restrictions, crate.

(SAVE) (S&) (×) (🛏) (💻) (🍴)

SPRINGFIELD

AAA ▼▼▼ **Baymont Inn & Suites** SH
(417) 889-8188. **$78-$125.** 3776 S Glenstone Ave. On US 60. Int corridors. **Pets:** Accepted.

(SAVE) (S&) (×) (&M) (🐾) (🛏) (💻) (≈)

AAA ▼▼▼ **Best Western Coach House Inn** M 🐾
(417) 862-0701. **$59-$79.** 2535 N Glenstone Ave. I-44, exit 80A, just s. Ext corridors. **Pets:** Large, other species. Service with restrictions, supervision.

(SAVE) (S&) (×) (🛏) (💻) (≈) (⊠)

AAA ▼▼ ▼▼ **Best Western Route 66 Rail Haven** M
(417) 866-1963. **$54-$74.** 203 S Glenstone Ave. I-44, exit 80A, 3 mi s. Ext corridors. **Pets:** Accepted.

(SAVE) (S&) (×) (&M) (🛏) (💻) (≈)

AAA ▼▼▼ ▼▼ **Clarion Hotel** SH
(417) 883-6550. **$70-$80.** 3333 S Glenstone Ave. On US 60 (James River Expwy), 0.5 mi n. Int corridors. **Pets:** $10 one-time fee/pet. Service with restrictions, supervision.

(SAVE) (S&) (×) (&M) (🐾) (&) (🛏) (💻) (🍴) (≈)

AAA ▼▼▼ **Comfort Suites** SH
(417) 886-5090. **$89-$129.** 1260 E Independence St. US 60 (James River Expwy), exit National Ave. Ext corridors. **Pets:** Accepted.

(SAVE) (S&) (×) (🐾) (🛏) (💻) (≈)

▼▼▼ ▼▼▼ **Drury Inn & Suites-Springfield** SH
(417) 863-8400. **$70-$102.** 2715 N Glenstone Ave. I-44, exit 80A (Glenstone Ave), just s. Int corridors. **Pets:** Large, other species. Service with restrictions, supervision.

(ASK) (×) (&M) (🐾) (&) (🛏) (💻) (≈)

AAA ▼▼▼ ▼▼ **Holiday Inn North** SH
(417) 865-8600. **$89-$119.** 2720 N Glenstone Ave. I-44, exit 80A, just se. Int corridors. **Pets:** Other species. $15 one-time fee/room. Designated rooms, service with restrictions, supervision.

(SAVE) (S&) (×) (🐾) (&) (🛏) (💻) (🍴) (≈) (⊠)

△△△ ▽▽▽ ◇ Krystal Aire-A Non-Smoking Hotel SH
(417) 869-0001. **$74-$96.** 2745 N Glenstone Ave. I-44, exit 80A, just sw. Ext/int corridors. **Pets:** Other species. Service with restrictions, crate.

SAVE Sð ✕ 🖬 🖵 ➔

△△△ ▽▽▽ Lamplighter Inn Convention Center North SH
(417) 869-3900. **$61-$81.** 2820 N Glenstone Ave. I-44, exit 80A, just se. Ext/int corridors. **Pets:** Accepted.

SAVE Sð ✕ ᏜM ⬡ 🖬 🖵 ➔

▽▽▽ La Quinta Inn Springfield SH
(417) 520-8800. **$59-$85, 30 day notice.** 1610 E Evergreen. I-44, exit 80A. Int corridors. **Pets:** Accepted.

ASK ✕ ᏜM ⬡ 🖬 🖵 ➔

△△△ ▽▽▽ Merigold Inn M
(417) 881-2833. **$44-$68.** 2006 S Glenstone Ave. On Business Rt US 65, just s of CR D. Ext corridors. **Pets:** Accepted.

SAVE Sð ✕ ➔

▽▽▽ Red Roof Inn M
(417) 831-2100. **$39-$55.** 2655 N Glenstone Ave. I-44, exit 80A, just s. Ext corridors. **Pets:** Large, other species. Service with restrictions, crate.

✕ ⬡ ⬡

△△△ ▽▽◇▽ Residence Inn-Springfield SH
(417) 890-0020. **$69-$179.** 1303 E Kingsley St. James River Expwy, exit National St, just s, then just e. Int corridors. **Pets:** Other species. $50 one-time fee/room.

SAVE Sð ✕ ᏜM ⬡ ⬡ 🖬 🖵 ➔ ✕

▽▽▽ Sheraton Hawthorn Park Hotel SH ☙
(417) 831-3131. **$79-$99.** 2431 N Glenstone Ave. I-44, exit 80A, just s. Int corridors. **Pets:** Medium, other species. $25 one-time fee/room. Service with restrictions.

ASK Sð ✕ ⬡ 🖬 🖵 🍴 ➔ ✕

▽▽▽ Sleep Inn of Springfield SH
(417) 886-2464. **$63-$72.** 233 E Camino Alto. US 60 (James River Expwy), exit Campbell Ave, just se. Int corridors. **Pets:** Medium, other species. $10 daily fee/pet. Designated rooms, service with restrictions, supervision.

ASK Sð ✕ ⬡ ⬡ 🖬 🖵 ➔

△△△ ▽▽◇▽ University Plaza Hotel and Convention Center LH
(417) 864-7333. **$89-$149.** 333 John Q Hammons Pkwy. 0.5 mi e on St. Louis St. Int corridors. **Pets:** Other species. $10 daily fee/room. Designated rooms, service with restrictions, supervision.

SAVE ✕ ᏜM ⬡ ⬡ 🖬 🖵 🍴 ➔ ✕

STE. GENEVIEVE

△△△ ▽ Family Budget Inn SH
(573) 543-2272. **$49-$54, 3 day notice.** 17030 New Bremen Rd. I-55, exit 143, just w on CR M. Ext/int corridors. **Pets:** Medium. $5 daily fee/pet. Designated rooms, service with restrictions, supervision.

SAVE Sð ✕ 🖬 ➔

SWEET SPRINGS

△△△ ▽ People's Choice Motel M
(660) 335-6315. **$34-$37.** 1001 N Locust St. I-70, exit 66, just se. Ext corridors. **Pets:** $20 deposit/room. Service with restrictions, supervision.

SAVE Sð ✕

▽▽ ▽▽ Super 8 Motel SH
(660) 335-4888. **$60-$70.** 208 W 40 Hwy. I-70, exit 66, just se. Int corridors. **Pets:** Medium, other species. $20 deposit/room. Service with restrictions, supervision.

ASK Sð ✕ 🖬

TIPTON

▽▽ Twin Pine Motel M
(660) 433-5525. **$40-$55.** 442 Hwy 50 W. On US 50 and SR 5, just w. Ext corridors. **Pets:** Designated rooms, service with restrictions, supervision.

✕ 🖬

TRENTON

▽▽ Super 8 Motel SH
(660) 359-2988. **$49-$75.** 1845A E 28th St. US 65, 1 mi n of jct SR 6 and US 65. Int corridors. **Pets:** Accepted.

ASK Sð ✕

WAPPAPELLO

▽▽ ◇ Millers Motor Lodge M
(573) 222-8579. **Call for rates.** 8920 Hwy T. On CR T, 2 mi s of Wappapello Dam. Ext corridors. **Pets:** Accepted.

🖬 🖵 ➔ ✕

WARRENSBURG

▽▽ ▽▽ University Inn SH ☙
(660) 747-5125. **$59-$79.** 403 E Russell Ave. Jct US 50 and SR 13, just se. Ext corridors. **Pets:** Small, other species. $20 deposit/pet, $5 daily fee/pet. Designated rooms, service with restrictions, supervision.

ASK Sð ✕ 🖬 🖵 🍴 ➔

WARSAW

▽▽ ▽▽ Super 8 Motel-Warsaw SH
(660) 438-2882. **$56-$94.** 1603 Commercial St. US 65 and SR 7, exit Clinton. Ext corridors. **Pets:** Medium, dogs only. $40 deposit/pet. Service with restrictions, supervision.

ASK Sð ✕ 🖬 🖵 ➔

WASHINGTON

▽▽ ▽▽ Super 8 Washington SH ☙
(636) 390-0088. **$70-$100.** 2081 Eckelkamp Ct. Jct SR 100 and 47, just s. Int corridors. **Pets:** Medium, dogs only. $25 deposit/room, $10 daily fee/pet. Service with restrictions, supervision.

ASK Sð ✕ 🖵

WEST PLAINS

△△△ ▽▽▽ Ramada Inn SH
(417) 256-8191. **$69-$76.** 1301 Preacher Roe Blvd. 2 mi sw, jct US 160 and 63 Bypass. Ext/int corridors. **Pets:** Large, other species. $10 daily fee/room. Service with restrictions, supervision.

SAVE Sð ✕ 🖵 🍴 ➔

▽▽ ▽▽ Super 8 Motel-West Plains SH
(417) 256-8088. **$45-$75.** 1210 Porter Wagoner Blvd. On US 63B. Int corridors. **Pets:** Large, other species. Service with restrictions, supervision.

ASK Sð ✕

MONTANA

BELGRADE

Gallatin River Lodge CI
(406) 388-0148. **$170-$270, 7 day notice.** 9105 Thorpe Rd. I-90, exit 298, 2.7 mi s on SR 85, 1 mi w on Valley Center Rd (gravel), then 0.5 mi s, follow sign. Int corridors. **Pets:** Other species. $20 one-time fee/room. Crate.

Holiday Inn Express SH
(406) 388-0800. **$85-$105.** 6261 Jackrabbit Ln. I-90, exit 298, just s on SR 85. Int corridors. **Pets:** Accepted.

La Quinta Inn & Suites Belgrade
(Bozeman/Belgrade) SH
(406) 388-2222. **$59-$149.** 6445 Jackrabbit Ln. I-90, exit 298, just s on SR 85. Int corridors. **Pets:** Service with restrictions, supervision.

Super 8 Motel-Belgrade/Bozeman Airport SH
(406) 388-1493. **$57-$104.** 6450 Jackrabbit Ln. I-90, exit 298, just s. Int corridors. **Pets:** Accepted.

BIGFORK

Mountain Lake Lodge SH
(406) 837-3800. **$85-$265, 7 day notice.** 1950 Sylvan Dr. On US 35, 5 mi s. Ext corridors. **Pets:** Medium. $15 daily fee/pet. Designated rooms.

Timbers Motel M
(406) 837-6200. **$52-$128, 7 day notice.** 8540 Hwy 35. Just n on US 35 from jct of SR 209. Ext corridors. **Pets:** $5 daily fee/pet. No service, supervision.

BIG SKY

320 Guest Ranch RA
(406) 995-4283. **$100-$338, 30 day notice.** 205 Buffalo Horn Creek Rd. 11.8 mi s on US 191; in Gallatin National Forest. Ext corridors. **Pets:** Other species. $10 daily fee/pet. Service with restrictions, crate.

Best Western Buck's T-4 Lodge SH
(406) 995-4111. **$79-$159, 7 day notice.** 46625 Gallatin Rd. US 191, 1 mi s of Big Sky entrance. Ext/int corridors. **Pets:** Large, other species. $10 daily fee/pet. Service with restrictions, supervision.

BIG TIMBER

Big Timber Budget Host M
(406) 932-4943. **$58-$78.** 600 W 2nd St. I-90, exit 367, just n, then 0.6 mi e. Int corridors. **Pets:** Small, other species. $10 one-time fee/room. Service with restrictions, supervision.

Big Timber Super 8 Motel SH
(406) 932-8888. **$54-$94.** 20A Big Timber Loop Rd. I-90, exit 367. Int corridors. **Pets:** Medium, dogs only. $10 daily fee/pet. Designated rooms, service with restrictions, supervision.

BILLINGS

Best Western Billings SH
(406) 248-9800. **$75-$115.** 5610 S Frontage Rd. I-90, exit 446, just s. Ext/int corridors. **Pets:** Large. Designated rooms, service with restrictions, supervision.

Best Western Ponderosa Inn SH
(406) 259-5511. **$69-$84, 3 day notice.** 2511 1st Ave N. On I-90 business loop; downtown. Ext/int corridors. **Pets:** Small, dogs only. $25 deposit/pet. Designated rooms, service with restrictions, supervision.

Billings Hotel and Convention Center SH
(406) 248-7151. **$99-$109.** 1223 Mullowney Ln. I-90, exit 446, just s. Int corridors. **Pets:** Medium. $10 one-time fee/room. Service with restrictions, supervision.

Billings Super 8 Motel SH
(406) 248-8842. **$56-$96.** 5400 Southgate Dr. I-90, exit 447, just n on S Billings Blvd, 0.8 mi w on King Ave, then just s on Parkway Ln. Int corridors. **Pets:** Medium. $20 deposit/pet. Designated rooms, service with restrictions, supervision.

Cherry Tree Inn M
(406) 252-5603. **$55-$65.** 823 N Broadway. I-90, exit 450, 2 mi n on 27th St, then just w on 9th Ave. Int corridors. **Pets:** Other species. Service with restrictions, supervision.

Comfort Inn by Choice Hotels SH
(406) 652-5200. **$80-$100.** 2030 Overland Ave. I-90, exit 446, 0.5 mi n, then just s. Int corridors. **Pets:** Accepted.

Days Inn SH
(406) 252-4007. **$54-$96.** 843 Parkway Ln. I-90, exit 447, just n on S Billings Blvd, 0.8 mi w on King Ave, then just s. Int corridors. **Pets:** Other species. $5 one-time fee/pet. Service with restrictions, supervision.

Dude Rancher Lodge M
(406) 259-5561. **$50-$75.** 415 N 29th St. Just w of the 400 block of N 27th st; downtown. Ext/int corridors. **Pets:** Medium. $5 daily fee/room. Designated rooms, service with restrictions, supervision.

AAA ▼▼ Hilltop Inn SH
(406) 245-5000. **$62-$72.** 1116 N 28th St. I-90, exit 450, 2 mi n, just w on 11th Ave, then just n. Int corridors. **Pets:** $5 daily fee/pet. Designated rooms, service with restrictions, supervision.
SAVE S6 ✕ &M 📶 🖵

AAA ▼▼▼ Holiday Inn Grand Montana Billings LH
(406) 248-7701. **$85-$95.** 5500 Midland Rd. I-90, exit 446. Int corridors. **Pets:** Other species. $25 one-time fee/room. Designated rooms, service with restrictions, crate.
SAVE ✕ &M 🌀 & 📶 🖵 ▊ ➳ ✕

▼▼ Howard Johnson Express Inn SH ❀
(406) 248-4656. **$69-$99.** 1001 S 27th St. I-90, exit 450, just n on SR 3 (S 27th St). Int corridors. **Pets:** Other species. Designated rooms, service with restrictions, crate.
ASK S6 ✕ &M 🌀 & 📶 🖵

AAA ▼▼ Kelly Inn SH ❀
(406) 252-2700. **$62-$99.** 5425 Midland Rd. I-90, exit 446, just se. Ext/int corridors. **Pets:** Small, other species. Service with restrictions, supervision.
SAVE S6 ✕ & 📶 🖵 ➳

▼ Motel 6 #178 M
(406) 252-0093. **$37-$63.** 5400 Midland Rd. I-90, exit 446, just se. Ext corridors. **Pets:** Accepted.
S6 ✕ &M 🌀 &

▼▼▼ Quality Inn Homestead SH
(406) 652-1320. **$64-$94.** 2036 Overland Ave. I-90, exit 446, n on King Ave W, then just s, first stoplight. Int corridors. **Pets:** Large, other species. $25 deposit/room. Service with restrictions, crate.
ASK S6 ✕ & 📶 🖵 ➳ ✕

▼▼ Red Roof Inn #269 SH
(406) 248-7551. **$40-$68.** 5353 Midland Rd. I-90, exit 446, just se. Int corridors. **Pets:** Medium, other species. Service with restrictions, supervision.
✕ &M 🌀 & 📶 ➳

AAA ▼▼ Rimview Inn M
(406) 248-2622. **$62-$72.** 1025 N 27th St. I-90, exit 450, 2 mi n. Ext/int corridors. **Pets:** Dogs only. $10 one-time fee/pet. Service with restrictions, supervision.
SAVE ✕ 📶

AAA ▼▼ Riverstone Billings Inn SH
(406) 252-6800. **$62-$72.** 880 N 29th St. I-90, exit 27th St, 2 mi n, then just w on 9th Ave. Int corridors. **Pets:** $5 daily fee/pet. Designated rooms, service with restrictions, supervision.
SAVE S6 ✕ 📶 🖵

▼▼▼▼ Sheraton Downtown Billings Hotel LH ❀
(406) 252-7400. **$115-$135.** 27 N 27th St. I-90 business loop and SR 3. Int corridors. **Pets:** Small, dogs only. $50 deposit/pet. Designated rooms, service with restrictions, supervision.
ASK S6 ✕ & 📶 🖵 ▊ ➳ ✕

AAA ▼▼ Western Executive Inn SH
(406) 294-8888. **$75-$100.** 3121 King Ave W. I-90, exit 446, 2.5 mi w. Int corridors. **Pets:** $10 one-time fee/pet. Supervision.
SAVE S6 ✕ &M & 📶 🖵

BOZEMAN

▼▼▼ AmericInn Lodge & Suites SH
(406) 522-8686. **$89-$169.** 1121 Reeves Rd W. I-90, exit 305, just n. Int corridors. **Pets:** Accepted.
ASK ✕ &M & 📶 🖵 ➳ ✕

▼▼ Best Value Inn SH
(406) 585-7888. **$44-$84.** 817 Wheat Dr. I-90, exit 306, just n. Int corridors. **Pets:** Accepted.
ASK ✕ &M & 📶 ➳

AAA ▼▼▼ Best Western GranTree Inn SH
(406) 587-5261. **$89-$139.** 1325 N 7th Ave. I-90, exit 306, just s. Int corridors. **Pets:** Accepted.
SAVE S6 ✕ & 📶 🖵 ▊ ➳

▼▼ Bozeman Days Inn SH
(406) 587-5251. **$55-$105.** 1321 N 7th Ave. I-90, exit 306, just s. Int corridors. **Pets:** Accepted.
ASK S6 ✕ & 📶 🖵 ✕

AAA ▼▼ Bozeman Inn M
(406) 587-3176. **$39-$80.** 1235 N 7th Ave. I-90, exit 306, just s. Ext corridors. **Pets:** Other species. $5 one-time fee/room. Service with restrictions.
SAVE S6 ✕ 📶 🖵 ➳

▼▼ Bozeman Super 8 SH
(406) 586-1521. **Call for rates.** 800 Wheat Dr. I-90, exit 306, just n, then just w. Int corridors. **Pets:** $5 one-time fee/room. Designated rooms, supervision.
✕

AAA ▼▼ Bozeman's Western Heritage Inn SH
(406) 586-8534. **$49-$98.** 1200 E Main St. I-90 business loop, exit 309, 0.5 mi w. Int corridors. **Pets:** Accepted.
SAVE S6 ✕ 📶 🖵 ✕

AAA ▼▼▼ Holiday Inn Bozeman SH
(406) 587-4561. **$89-$129, 5 day notice.** 5 Baxter Ln. I-90, exit 306, just s. Int corridors. **Pets:** Accepted.
SAVE S6 ✕ & 📶 🖵 ▊ ➳ ✕

▼▼ Microtel Inn & Suites SH
(406) 586-3797. **$49-$89.** 612 Nikles Dr. I-90, exit 306, just ne. Int corridors. **Pets:** Accepted.
ASK S6 ✕ & 📶 🖵 ➳

AAA ▼▼ Rainbow Motel M
(406) 587-4201. **$45-$75.** 510 N 7th Ave. I-90, exit 306, 0.8 mi s. Ext corridors. **Pets:** Accepted.
SAVE ✕ 📶 🖵 ➳

▼▼ Ramada Limited M
(406) 585-2626. **$52-$99.** 2020 Wheat Dr. I-90, exit 306, just n, then just w. Int corridors. **Pets:** Small, dogs only. $10 daily fee/pet. Service with restrictions, supervision.
ASK S6 ✕ 📶 🖵 ➳

AAA ▼▼ Royal "7" Budget Inn M
(406) 587-3103. **$45-$66.** 310 N 7th Ave. I-90, exit 306, 0.8 mi s. Ext corridors. **Pets:** Medium. $2 daily fee/pet. Supervision.
SAVE S6 ✕ 📶 ➳

BROWNING

AAA ▼ Western Motel LLC M
(406) 338-7572. **$45-$98.** 121 Central Ave E. On US 2; center. Ext corridors. **Pets:** Other species. $20 daily fee/pet. Service with restrictions, supervision.
SAVE ✕ 📶

BUTTE

AAA ▼▼▼ Best Western Butte Plaza Inn SH
(406) 494-3500. **$77-$99.** 2900 Harrison Ave. I-90/15, exit 127 (Harrison Ave). Int corridors. **Pets:** Other species. $50 deposit/pet. Designated rooms, service with restrictions, supervision.
SAVE S6 ✕ 📶 🖵 ▊ ➳ ✕

▼▼ Comfort Inn of Butte SH
(406) 494-8850. **$99.** 2777 Harrison Ave. I-90/15, exit 127 (Harrison Ave), just s. Int corridors. **Pets:** Medium, other species. $5 daily fee/pet. Service with restrictions, supervision.
ASK S6 ✕ 🌀 & 📶 🖵 ➳ ✕

△△△ ▽▽▽ Copper King Lodge & Convention Center SH
(406) 494-6666. **$59-$109.** 4655 Harrison Ave S. I-90/15, exit 127A, 2 mi s on SR 2 (Harrison Ave). Int corridors. **Pets:** Large, other species. $10 deposit/room. Service with restrictions, supervision.
[SAVE] [S♦] [✕] [♿M] [⚟] [🚪] [💲] [📶] [♨] [⊗]

▽▽▽ Days Inn SH
(406) 494-7000. **$79-$99, 3 day notice.** 2700 Harrison Ave. I-90/15, exit 127 (Harrison Ave), just n. Int corridors. **Pets:** Medium. Designated rooms, service with restrictions, supervision.
[A$K] [S♦] [✕] [♿M] [⚟] [♿] [🚪] [💲] [♨]

△△△ ▽▽▽ Red Lion Hotel SH ❖
(406) 494-7800. **$69-$109.** 2100 Cornell Ave. I-90/15, exit 127B (Harrison Ave), just n, then just e. Int corridors. **Pets:** Other species. Service with restrictions.
[SAVE] [S♦] [✕] [⚟] [♿] [🚪] [💲] [📶] [♨] [⊗]

△△△ ▽▽▽ Rocker Inn M
(406) 723-5464. **$45-$57.** 122001 W Brown's Gulch Rd. I-90/15, exit 122 (Rocker). Int corridors. **Pets:** Medium. $5 daily fee/room. Designated rooms, service with restrictions.
[SAVE] [✕] [🚪]

△△△ ▽▽▽ Super 8 Motel of Butte SH
(406) 494-6000. **$59-$92, 4 day notice.** 2929 Harrison Ave. I-90/15, exit 127 (Harrison Ave), just s. Int corridors. **Pets:** Medium. $50 deposit/room, $5 daily fee/room. Designated rooms, service with restrictions, supervision.
[A$K] [S♦] [✕]

CHINOOK

△△△ ▽▽▽ Chinook Motor Inn SH
(406) 357-2248. **$60-$75.** 100 Indiana St. On US 2. Int corridors.
Pets: Accepted.
[SAVE] [S♦] [✕] [💲] [🍴]

COLSTRIP

▽▽▽ Super 8 Motel of Colstrip LLC M
(406) 748-3400. **$56-$70.** 6227 Main St. SR 39. Int corridors.
Pets: Other species. $5 daily fee/pet. Designated rooms, service with restrictions, supervision.
[A$K] [S♦] [✕] [🚪] [💲]

COLUMBIA FALLS

△△△ ▽▽▽▽ Meadow Lake Resort CO
(406) 892-8700. **$95-$565, 30 day notice.** 100 St Andrews Dr. Jct US 2 and SR 40, 1.4 mi e on US 2, 1.1 mi n on Meadow Lake Blvd. Ext/int corridors. **Pets:** Accepted.
[SAVE] [S♦] [✕] [🚪] [💲] [🍴] [♨] [⊗]

COLUMBUS

▽▽▽ Super 8 of Columbus SH ❖
(406) 322-4101. **$55-$75.** 602 8th Ave N. I-90, exit 408, just s on SR 78. Int corridors. **Pets:** Large, other species. $5 daily fee/room. Service with restrictions, supervision.
[A$K] [S♦] [✕] [♿M] [⚟] [♿] [🚪] [💲]

CONRAD

▽▽▽ Super 8 Motel SH
(406) 278-7676. **$55-$75.** 215 N Main. I-15, exit 339, just w. Int corridors. **Pets:** Accepted.
[A$K] [S♦] [✕] [⚟] [🚪] [💲]

CUT BANK

△△△ ▽▽▽ Glacier Gateway Inn SH
(406) 873-5544. **$56-$74.** 1121 E Railroad St. US 2, just e from town center. Int corridors. **Pets:** Other species. $6 daily fee/pet. Designated rooms, service with restrictions.
[SAVE] [S♦] [✕] [🚪]

DEER LODGE

△△△ ▽▽▽ Super 8 Motel M
(406) 846-2370. **$88-$90.** 1150 N Main St. I-90, exit 184, 0.3 mi s. Int corridors. **Pets:** Accepted.
[SAVE] [S♦] [✕] [🚪] [💲]

▽▽▽ Western Big Sky Inn M
(406) 846-2590. **$40-$56.** 210 N Main St. I-90, exit 184, 1 mi w. Ext corridors. **Pets:** Designated rooms, service with restrictions, supervision.
[A$K] [✕] [🚪] [💲]

DILLON

△△△ ▽▽▽ Best Western Paradise Inn M
(406) 683-4214. **$55-$79.** 650 N Montana St. I-15, exit 63, 0.3 mi s on SR 41. Ext corridors. **Pets:** Accepted.
[SAVE] [S♦] [✕] [💲] [🍴] [♨]

▽▽▽ Comfort Inn of Dillon M
(406) 683-6831. **$65-$99.** 450 N Interchange. I-15, exit 63. Int corridors. **Pets:** Medium, other species. $5 daily fee/pet. Service with restrictions, supervision.
[A$K] [S♦] [✕] [⚟] [🚪] [💲] [♨]

△△△ ▽ Dillon Beaverhead Inn M 🐾
(406) 683-6600. **$58-$79.** 20 Swenson Way. I-15, exit 63, just e, then just s. Ext corridors. **Pets:** Medium, dogs only. $100 deposit/room, $5 daily fee/room. Designated rooms, service with restrictions, supervision.
[SAVE] [S♦] [✕] [♿M] [♿]

▽▽▽▽ GuestHouse International Inns & Suites SH
(406) 683-3636. **$59-$89.** 580 Sinclair St. I-15, exit 63. Int corridors.
Pets: Other species. $10 one-time fee/room. Designated rooms, service with restrictions, supervision.
[A$K] [S♦] [✕] [♿M] [♿] [🚪] [💲] [♨]

△△△ ▽▽ Sundowner Motel M
(406) 683-2375. **$38-$43.** 500 N Montana St. I-15, exit 63, just s. Ext corridors. **Pets:** Other species. Designated rooms, service with restrictions, supervision.
[SAVE] [✕] [🚪]

▽▽▽ Super 8 Motel M
(406) 683-4288. **$50-$57, 5 day notice.** 550 N Montana St. I-15, exit 63, just n on US 91. Int corridors. **Pets:** Dogs only. $50 deposit/room, $5 daily fee/pet. Service with restrictions, supervision.
[A$K] [S♦] [✕] [🚪]

EAST GLACIER PARK

△△△ ▽▽ Dancing Bears Inn LLC M
(406) 226-4402. **$55-$146.** 40 Montana Ave. Just off US 2, follow signs; center. Ext/int corridors. **Pets:** Other species. $20 daily fee/pet. Service with restrictions, supervision.
[SAVE] [S♦] [✕] [🚪] [💲]

ENNIS

△△△ ▽▽▽ Fan Mountain Inn M
(406) 682-5200. **$50-$75, 14 day notice.** 204 N Main. US 287, just nw of city center. Ext corridors. **Pets:** Accepted.
[SAVE] [✕] [♿M] [⚟] [🚪]

▽ Sportsman's CA
(406) 682-4242. **$60-$100, 10 day notice.** 310 US Hwy 287 N. US 287, just nw of city center. Ext corridors. **Pets:** Accepted.
[✕] [🚪] [💲] [🍴]

FORSYTH

△△△ ▽▽▽ Best Western Sundowner Inn M
(406) 346-2115. **$74-$85.** 1018 Front St. I-94, exit 95, 0.5 mi nw on north frontage road. Ext corridors. **Pets:** $10 daily fee/pet. Service with restrictions, supervision.
[SAVE] [S♦] [✕] [🚪] [💲]

Rails Inn Motel SH
(406) 346-2242. **$62-$67, 3 day notice.** 3rd & Front sts. I-94, exit 93, just n, then 0.5 mi e on frontage road. Int corridors. **Pets:** $5 daily fee/pet. Service with restrictions, supervision.
SAVE [S6] [X] [B] [TI]

Restwel Motel M
(406) 346-2771. **$47-$60.** 810 Front St. I-94, exit 95, 0.8 mi nw on north frontage road. Ext corridors. **Pets:** Medium. $5 daily fee/pet. Designated rooms, no service, supervision.
SAVE [S6] [X] [L] [B]

Westwind Motor Inn M
(406) 346-2038. **$60-$65, 3 day notice.** 225 Westwind Ln. I-94, exit 93, 0.3 mi n. Int corridors. **Pets:** $5 daily fee/pet. Service with restrictions, supervision.
SAVE [S6] [X] [B]

GARDINER

Best Western by Mammoth Hot Springs SH
(406) 848-7311. **$49-$115.** S Hwy 89. 0.5 mi n. Ext/int corridors. **Pets:** Other species. $5 daily fee/pet. Designated rooms, service with restrictions, supervision.
SAVE [S6] [X] [L] [B] [P] [TI] [⇌] [X]

Yellowstone River Motel M
(406) 848-7303. **$45-$85.** 14 E Park St. Just e of US 89. Ext corridors. **Pets:** Accepted.
SAVE [S6] [X] [LM] [B] [P] [X]

Yellowstone Super 8-Gardiner SH
(406) 848-7401. **$39-$99.** Hwy 89 S. On US 89. Int corridors. **Pets:** Other species. $5 daily fee/pet. Designated rooms, supervision.
ASK [S6] [X] [B] [P] [⇌]

GLASGOW

Cottonwood Inn SH
(406) 228-8213. **$65-$75.** 45 1st Ave NE. 0.5 mi e on US 2. Int corridors. **Pets:** Other species. Designated rooms, service with restrictions, supervision.
ASK [S6] [X] [B] [TI] [⇌]

GLENDIVE

Best Western Jordan Inn SH
(406) 377-5555. **$68-$80, 10 day notice.** 223 N Merrill Ave. I-94, exit 215, on I-94 business loop; downtown. Ext/int corridors. **Pets:** Accepted.
SAVE [S6] [X] [B] [P] [TI] [⇌]

Super 8 Glendive M
(406) 365-5671. **$48-$66.** 1904 Merrill Ave. I-94, exit 215, just n. Int corridors. **Pets:** Other species. $5 one-time fee/room. Service with restrictions, supervision.
ASK [S6] [X]

GREAT FALLS

Best Western Heritage Inn SH
(406) 761-1900. **$80-$110.** 1700 Fox Farm Rd. I-15, exit 278, 0.8 mi e on 10th Ave S and US 87/89 and SR 3/200. Int corridors. **Pets:** Medium. Designated rooms, service with restrictions, supervision.
SAVE [S6] [X] [Ø] [B] [P] [TI] [⇌] [X]

Comfort Inn by Choice Hotels SH
(406) 454-2727. **$80-$100.** 1120 9th St S. I-15, exit 278, 3 mi e on 10th Ave S and US 87/89 and SR 3/200, then just s. Int corridors. **Pets:** Accepted.
ASK [S6] [X] [LM] [Ø] [B] [P] [⇌]

Crystal Inn SH
(406) 727-7788. **$59-$89.** 3701 31st St SW. I-15, exit 277, just e. Int corridors. **Pets:** Large, other species. $10 daily fee/room. Service with restrictions, crate.
ASK [S6] [X] [Ø] [L] [B] [P] [⇌]

Days Inn of Great Falls M
(406) 727-6565. **$63-$87.** 101 14th Ave NW. I-15, exit 280 (Central Ave), 1.3 mi e on Central Ave/Business Rt I-15, 0.8 mi n on 3rd St NW, then just w. Int corridors. **Pets:** Dogs only. $5 daily fee/room. Designated rooms, service with restrictions, supervision.
ASK [S6] [X] [Ø] [B] [P]

The Great Falls Inn SH 🐾
(406) 453-6000. **$66-$69.** 1400 28th St S. I-15, exit 278, 5.3 mi e on 10th Ave s, 0.3 mi s on 26th St S, then just e on 15th Ave S. Int corridors. **Pets:** Large, other species. $5 daily fee/pet. Designated rooms, supervision.
SAVE [S6] [X] [LM] [Ø] [L] [B] [P]

Great Falls Super 8 Motel SH
(406) 727-7600. **$44-$55, 7 day notice.** 1214 13th St S. I-15, exit 278, 2.7 mi e on 10th Ave S and US 87/89 and SR 3/200, then just s. Int corridors. **Pets:** $3 daily fee/room. Service with restrictions, supervision.
SAVE [S6] [Ø] [B] [P]

Hampton Inn SH
(406) 453-2675. **$79-$149.** 2301 14th St SW. I-15, exit 278, just sw. Int corridors. **Pets:** Small, dogs only. $20 one-time fee/pet. Service with restrictions, supervision.
ASK [S6] [X] [LM] [Ø] [L] [B] [P] [⇌]

Howard Johnson Ponderosa Inn SH
(406) 761-3410. **$55-$90, 7 day notice.** 220 Central Ave. Downtown. Ext/int corridors. **Pets:** Accepted.
SAVE [S6] [X] [B] [P] [TI] [⇌]

La Quinta Inn & Suites Great Falls SH
(406) 761-2600. **$79-$99.** 600 River Dr S. I-15, exit 278, 1.7 mi e on 10th Ave S, then 0.8 mi n. Int corridors. **Pets:** Service with restrictions, supervision.
SAVE [S6] [X] [LM] [Ø] [L] [B] [P] [⇌] [X]

Motel 6 #4238 M
(406) 453-1602. **$52-$65.** 2 Treasure State Dr. I-15, exit 278, 0.8 mi e on 10th Ave S and US 87/89 and SR 3/200; next to Best Western. Int corridors. **Pets:** Large. Service with restrictions, supervision.
SAVE [S6] [X] [Ø] [P]

Plaza Inn M
(406) 452-9594. **$45-$55, 3 day notice.** 1224 10th Ave S. I-15, exit 278, 2.4 mi e on 10th Ave S and US 87/89 and SR 3/200. Ext corridors. **Pets:** Medium. $10 one-time fee/room. Designated rooms, service with restrictions, supervision.
SAVE [S6] [X] [B]

Ski's Western Motel M 🐾
(406) 453-3281. **$45-$55, 3 day notice.** 2420 10th Ave S. I-15, exit 278, 5.2 mi e on 10th Ave S and US 87/89 and SR 3/200. Ext corridors. **Pets:** Small. $10 daily fee/room. Service with restrictions, supervision.
SAVE [S6] [X] [B]

HAMILTON

Comfort Inn of Hamilton SH
(406) 363-6600. **$65-$99.** 1113 N 1st St. N of city center on US 93. Int corridors. **Pets:** Other species. $4 deposit/pet. Service with restrictions, supervision.
ASK [S6] [X] [LM] [Ø] [B] [P]

HARDIN

△△△ ▼▼ American Inn of Hardin SH
(406) 665-1870. **$50-$89.** 1324 N Crawford Ave. I-90, exit 495, just s on SR 47. Ext corridors. **Pets:** Medium. $5 one-time fee/room. Designated rooms, service with restrictions, supervision.

SAVE S✗ ✗ 🐾 🔲 🍽 ➤ ✗

▼▼ Western Motel M
(406) 665-2296. **$33-$75.** 830 W 3rd St. I-90, exit 495 eastbound, 1.3 mi s on SR 47 and CR 313, just e; exit 497 westbound, 0.3 mi w on I-90 business loop, continue straight on 3rd St for 0.7 mi. Ext corridors. **Pets:** Service with restrictions, supervision.

✗ 🔲

HARLOWTON

▼ Corral Motel M
(406) 632-4331. **$50-$55.** 0.5 mi e at jct US 12 and 191. Ext corridors. **Pets:** Medium, dogs only. $5 one-time fee/pet. Service with restrictions, supervision.

✗ 🔲

▼ Countryside Inn M
(406) 632-4119. **$55-$65.** 309 3rd St NE. US 12 E. Ext corridors. **Pets:** Small, dogs only. $5 daily fee/pet. Designated rooms, service with restrictions, supervision.

S✗ ✗ 🔲 ✗

HELENA

▼▼▼ Barrister Bed & Breakfast BB 🐾
(406) 443-7330. **$95-$110, 3 day notice.** 416 N Ewing. I-15, exit 192 (Prospect Ave), 1.5 mi sw via Prospect and Montana aves to 9th Ave, 0.8 mi w, then just s. Int corridors. **Pets:** Dogs only.

ASK ✗ ☎

▼▼▼▼ Best Western Helena Great Northern Hotel SH
(406) 457-5500. **$90-$130.** 835 Great Northern Blvd. I-15, exit 193 (Cedar St), just e of jct Lyndale and Benton aves; downtown. Int corridors. **Pets:** Accepted.

ASK S✗ ✗ 🆖 🐾 ✗ 🔲 🖥 ➤ ✗

▼▼ Comfort Inn by Choice Hotels SH
(406) 443-1000. **$75-$95.** 750 N Fee St. I-15, exit 192 (Prospect Ave), just w. Int corridors. **Pets:** Accepted.

ASK S✗ ✗ 🆖 🔲 🖥 ➤

▼▼ Days Inn Helena SH
(406) 442-3280. **$59-$99.** 2001 Prospect Ave. I-15, exit 192 (Prospect Ave), just w. Int corridors. **Pets:** Other species. $10 daily fee/pet. Service with restrictions, supervision.

ASK S✗ ✗ 🆖 🐾 ✗ 🔲 🖥 ✗

△△△ ▼▼▼ Elkhorn Mountain Inn SH 🐾
(406) 442-6625. **$65-$71.** 1 Jackson Creek Rd. I-15, exit 187 (Montana City). Int corridors. **Pets:** $5 daily fee/pet. Supervision.

SAVE S✗ ✗ 🆖 ✗ 🔲 🖥

▼▼▼ Hampton Inn-Helena SH
(406) 443-5800. **$79-$109.** 3000 Hwy 12 E. I-15, exit 192 eastbound; exit 192A westbound, just e on SR 12/287, then just n. Int corridors. **Pets:** Accepted.

ASK ✗ 🆖 🐾 ✗ 🔲 🖥 ➤

△△△ ▼ Mountain Valley Inn & Suites M
(406) 443-2300. **$55-$109.** 2101 E 11th Ave. I-15, exit 192B (capitol area), just sw. Ext/int corridors. **Pets:** Other species. $10 daily fee/pet. Service with restrictions, supervision.

SAVE S✗ ✗ 🔲 🖥 ➤

△△△ ▼▼▼ Red Lion Colonial Hotel SH
(406) 443-2100. **$89-$129.** 2301 Colonial Dr. I-15, exit 192 southbound; exit 192B northbound. Int corridors. **Pets:** $10 one-time fee/room. Service with restrictions, supervision.

SAVE S✗ ✗ 🔲 🖥 🍽 ➤

▼▼▼▼ Super 8 Motel SH
(406) 443-2450. **Call for rates.** 2200 11th Ave. I-15, exit 192B (capitol area) southbound; exit west business district northbound on US 12. Int corridors. **Pets:** Accepted.

✗ 🐾 🆖 🔲 🖥

▼▼▼▼ Wingate Inn SH
(406) 449-3000. **$94-$110.** 2007 Oakes. I-15, exit 193, just sw. Int corridors. **Pets:** $10 one-time fee/room. Designated rooms, service with restrictions, supervision.

ASK S✗ ✗ 🆖 🐾 ✗ 🔲 🖥 🏊

HUNGRY HORSE

△△△ ▼▼▼ Mini Golden Inns Motel M
(406) 387-4313. **$58-$96, 30 day notice.** 8955 US 2 E. East end of town. Ext corridors. **Pets:** Accepted.

SAVE ✗ 🆖 ✗ 🔲 🖥

KALISPELL

△△△ ▼▼ Aero Inn M
(406) 755-3798. **$42-$83.** 1830 US 93 S. 1.3 mi s on US 93 from jct US 2. Int corridors. **Pets:** Other species. $10 deposit/room. Designated rooms, service with restrictions, supervision.

SAVE S✗ ✗ 🐾 ✗ 🔲 ➤

▼▼ Days Inn Kalispell SH
(406) 756-3222. **$57-$103.** 1550 Hwy 93 N. 1.3 mi n on US 93 from jct US 2. Int corridors. **Pets:** Accepted.

ASK S✗ ✗ 🔲

△△△ ▼▼▼ Four Seasons Motor Inn SH
(406) 755-6123. **$53-$98, 21 day notice.** 350 N Main St. US 93, just n of jct US 2. Ext/int corridors. **Pets:** Medium. $10 daily fee/room. Designated rooms, service with restrictions, supervision.

SAVE S✗ ✗ 🔲 🖥 🍽

△△△ ▼▼ Glacier Gateway Motel M
(406) 755-3330. **$59-$94, 3 day notice.** 264 N Main St. Northwest corner of jct US 2 and 93. Ext corridors. **Pets:** Accepted.

SAVE ✗ 🔲 🖥

▼▼ Kalispell/Glacier Int'l Airport area Super 8 Motel SH
(406) 755-1888. **$67-$123.** 1341 1st Ave E. 1.2 mi s on US 93 from jct US 2. Int corridors. **Pets:** Other species. $10 one-time fee/room. Designated rooms, service with restrictions, supervision.

ASK S✗ ✗ 🆖 🐾 🔲 🖥

▼▼ Kalispell Grand Hotel SH
(406) 755-8100. **$72-$115.** 100 Main St. On US 93; downtown. Int corridors. **Pets:** Other species. Service with restrictions, crate.

ASK S✗ ✗ 🍽

△△△ ▼▼▼ La Quinta Inn & Suites Kalispell SH
(406) 257-5255. **$59-$159.** 255 Montclair Dr. Jct US 93 and 2, 1 mi e. Int corridors. **Pets:** Other species. Service with restrictions, supervision.

SAVE S✗ ✗ 🆖 🐾 ✗ 🔲 🖥 🏊 ✗

△△△ ▼▼▼ Red Lion Inn Kalispell SH
(406) 755-6700. **$69-$141.** 1330 Hwy 2 W. 1 mi w on US 2 from jct US 93. Int corridors. **Pets:** $15 one-time fee/pet. Service with restrictions, supervision.

SAVE S✗ ✗ 🔲 🖥 🍽 🏊

△△△ ▼▼▼▼ WestCoast Kalispell Center Hotel SH
(406) 751-5050. **$69-$111.** 20 N Main St. Just s on US 93 from jct of US 2; connected to Kalispell Center Mall. Int corridors. **Pets:** Other species. $20 one-time fee/room. Service with restrictions, supervision.

SAVE S✗ ✗ 🆖 🔲 🖥 🍽 ➤ ✗

◆◆◆ ▼▼▼ **WestCoast Outlaw Hotel-Kalispell** 🆂🅷
(406) 755-6100. **$69-$111.** 1701 Hwy 93 S. 1.4 mi s on US 93 from jct US 2. Int corridors. **Pets:** Other species. $20 one-time fee/room. Service with restrictions, supervision.

🆂🅰🆅🅴 🆂🅾 ⊠ 🈁 💻 🍽 ⇌ ⊠

LAKESIDE

▼▼ **Bayshore Resort Motel Inc** Ⓜ
(406) 844-3131. **$50-$165.** 616 Lakeside Blvd. On US 93; center. Ext corridors. **Pets:** Other species. $7 daily fee/room. Designated rooms, service with restrictions, crate.

🅰🆂🅺 ⊠ 🈁 💻 ⊠ 🄰🄲

▼▼ **Sunrise Vista Inn** Ⓜ
(406) 844-0231. **$80-$125, 14 day notice.** 7005 US 93. North edge of town. Ext corridors. **Pets:** Accepted.

⊠ 🈁 💻

LAUREL

▼▼▼ **Laurel Super 8** 🆂🅷
(406) 628-6888. **$74-$89, 14 day notice.** 205 SE 4th St. I-90, exit 434, just n, then just e. Int corridors. **Pets:** Large, other species. $10 daily fee/pet. Service with restrictions, supervision.

🅰🆂🅺 🆂🅾 ⊠ 🄼 ⟳ 🄺 🈁 💻 ⇌

LEWISTOWN

◆◆◆ ▼ **B & B Motel** Ⓜ
(406) 538-5496. **$40-$65.** 520 E Main St. Downtown. Ext corridors. **Pets:** Accepted.

🆂🅰🆅🅴 ⊠ 🈁

LIBBY

▼▼ **Sandman Motel** Ⓜ
(406) 293-8831. **$39-$62.** 688 US Hwy 2 W. Just w on US 2 from jct SR 37. Ext corridors. **Pets:** Dogs only. $20 deposit/room. Designated rooms, service with restrictions, supervision.

🅰🆂🅺 🆂🅾 ⊠ 🈁

◆◆◆ ▼▼ **Super 8 Motel** 🆂🅷
(406) 293-2771. **$60-$90.** 448 US 2 W. Just w on US 2 from jct SR 37. Int corridors. **Pets:** Other species. $5 daily fee/pet. Service with restrictions, supervision.

🆂🅰🆅🅴 🆂🅾 ⊠ ⟳ 🈁 ⇌

LINCOLN

◆◆◆ ▼ **Leeper's Ponderosa Motel** Ⓜ
(406) 362-4333. **$54-$65.** Hwy 200 & 1st Ave. On SR 200, just w. Ext corridors. **Pets:** Dogs only. $5 daily fee/pet. Service with restrictions, supervision.

🆂🅰🆅🅴 🆂🅾 ⊠ 🈁 💻 🄰🄲

LIVINGSTON

◆◆◆ ▼▼ **Best Western Yellowstone Inn & Conference Center** 🆂🅷 🐾
(406) 222-6110. **$75-$135.** 1515 W Park St. I-90, exit 333, just n. Int corridors. **Pets:** $10 daily fee/pet. Service with restrictions, supervision.

🆂🅰🆅🅴 ⊠ 🈁 💻 🍽 ⇌

◆◆◆ ▼ **Del Mar Motel Inc** Ⓜ 🐾
(406) 222-3120. **$44-$76, 3 day notice.** 1201 Hwy 10 W. I-90, exit 330, 1.9 mi e on I-90 business loop. Ext corridors. **Pets:** Other species. $5 daily fee/pet. Designated rooms, service with restrictions, supervision.

🆂🅰🆅🅴 🆂🅾 ⊠ 🈁 💻 ⇌ ⊠

◆◆◆ ▼▼ **Econo Lodge** 🆂🅷
(406) 222-0555. **$45-$100.** 111 Rogers Ln. I-90, exit 333, just n on US 89, then just w. Int corridors. **Pets:** Other species. $25 deposit/room, $5 daily fee/pet. Service with restrictions, supervision.

🆂🅰🆅🅴 🆂🅾 ⊠ 🄼 ⟳ 🄺 🈁 💻 ⇌

◆◆◆ ▼▼ **Travelodge Livingston** Ⓜ
(406) 222-6320. **$59-$110.** 102 Rogers Ln. I-90, exit 333, just n. Ext/int corridors. **Pets:** Other species. $5 daily fee/pet. Service with restrictions, supervision.

🆂🅰🆅🅴 ⊠ 🈁 💻 🍽 ⇌

LOLO

▼▼ **Days Inn** 🆂🅷 🐾
(406) 273-2121. **$59-$99.** 11225 US 93 S. North edge of town. Ext/int corridors. **Pets:** Medium, dogs only. $10 daily fee/pet. Service with restrictions, supervision.

🅰🆂🅺 🆂🅾 ⊠ 🄼 🈁 💻

MILES CITY

◆◆◆ ▼▼ **Best Western War Bonnet Inn** Ⓜ 🐾
(406) 234-4560. **$88.** 1015 S Haynes Ave. I-94, exit 138 (Broadus), 0.3 mi n. Ext corridors. **Pets:** Other species. $5 daily fee/pet. Service with restrictions, supervision.

🆂🅰🆅🅴 🆂🅾 ⊠ 🈁 💻 ⇌ ⊠

▼▼▼ **GuestHouse International Inn & Suites** 🆂🅷
(406) 232-3661. **$75-$150.** 3111 Steel St. I-94, exit 138 (Broadus), just s. Int corridors. **Pets:** Large, other species. $10 daily fee/room. Designated rooms, service with restrictions, supervision.

🅰🆂🅺 🆂🅾 ⊠ 🄼 🄺 🈁 💻 ⇌

MISSOULA

◆◆◆ ▼▼▼ **Best Inn & Conference Center-South** 🆂🅷
(406) 251-2665. **$65-$89.** 3803 Brooks St. I-90, exit 101 (Reserve St), 5 mi s to Brooks (US 93), then just w. Int corridors. **Pets:** Large, other species. $7 daily fee/room. Designated rooms.

🆂🅰🆅🅴 🆂🅾 ⊠ 🄼 ⟳ 🄺 🈁 💻

▼▼ **Best Inn North** 🆂🅷
(406) 542-7550. **$65-$89.** 4953 N Reserve St. I-90 W, exit 101 (Reserve St), just s. Int corridors. **Pets:** Large, other species. $7 daily fee/room. Designated rooms.

🅰🆂🅺 🆂🅾 ⊠ ⟳ 🄺 🈁 💻

◆◆◆ ▼▼▼ **Best Western Grant Creek Inn** 🆂🅷
(406) 543-0700. **$85-$149.** 5280 Grant Creek Rd. I-90, exit 101 (Reserve St), just n. Int corridors. **Pets:** Small. $10 daily fee/room. Service with restrictions, supervision.

🆂🅰🆅🅴 🆂🅾 ⊠ 🄼 ⟳ 🄺 🈁 💻 ⇌ ⊠

▼▼ **Campus Inn** Ⓜ 🐾
(406) 549-5134. **$80-$120.** 744 E Broadway. I-90, exit 105 (Van Buren St), just s to Broadway, then just w. Ext/int corridors. **Pets:** Medium, other species. $6 daily fee/pet. Service with restrictions, supervision.

🅰🆂🅺 🆂🅾 ⊠ ⟳ 🄺 🈁 ⇌

▼▼▼ **Comfort Inn** 🆂🅷
(406) 542-0888. **$70-$160.** 4545 N Reserve St. I-90, exit 101 (Reserve St), 0.5 mi s. Int corridors. **Pets:** Medium. $10 daily fee/room. Service with restrictions, supervision.

🅰🆂🅺 🆂🅾 ⊠ 🄼 ⟳ 🄺 🈁 💻 ⇌

◆◆◆ ▼▼▼ **Days Inn/Missoula Airport** 🆂🅷 🐾
(406) 721-9776. **$61-$94.** 8600 Truck Stop Rd. I-90, exit 96, just n. Int corridors. **Pets:** Other species. $5 daily fee/pet. Designated rooms, service with restrictions, supervision.

🆂🅰🆅🅴 🆂🅾 ⊠ 🈁

◆◆◆ ▼▼▼ **Days Inn University** 🆂🅷
(406) 543-7221. **$64-$84.** 201 E Main St. I-90, exit 104 (Orange St), 0.5 mi s to Broadway, 0.5 mi e to Washington, just s to Main St, then just w. Ext corridors. **Pets:** $50 deposit/room. Service with restrictions, supervision.

🆂🅰🆅🅴 🆂🅾 ⊠ 🈁 💻 ⇌

Doubletree Hotel Missoula/Edgewater 🆂🅷
(406) 728-3100. **$109-$285.** 100 Madison. I-90, exit 105 (Van Buren St), just s, then w on Front St. Int corridors. **Pets:** Accepted.

Downtown Motel Ⓜ ❀
(406) 549-5191. **$40-$49.** 502 E Broadway. I-90, exit 105 (Van Buren St), just w. Ext corridors. **Pets:** Medium. $6 one-time fee/pet. Service with restrictions.

Family Inn Ⓜ
(406) 543-7371. **$70-$78.** 1031 E Broadway. I-90, exit 105 (Van Buren St), just s, then just e. Ext corridors. **Pets:** Accepted.

Hampton Inn 🆂🅷 ❀
(406) 549-1800. **$70-$119, 7 day notice.** 4805 N Reserve St. I-90, exit 101 (Reserve St), just s. Int corridors. **Pets:** Other species. $15 one-time fee/room. Service with restrictions, supervision.

Holiday Inn Missoula-Parkside 🆂🅷
(406) 721-8550. **$79-$169.** 200 S Pattee St. I-90, exit 104 (Orange St), 0.5 mi s to Broadway, just e to Pattee St, then just s. Int corridors. **Pets:** $25 one-time fee/room. Designated rooms, service with restrictions, supervision.

Microtel Inn & Suites 🆂🅷
(406) 543-0959. **$65-$110.** 5059 N Reserve St. I-90, exit 101 (Reserve St), just s. Int corridors. **Pets:** Very small. $10 one-time fee/pet. Designated rooms, supervision.

Ponderosa Lodge Ⓜ
(406) 543-3102. **$49-$69.** 800 E Broadway. I-90, exit 105 (Van Buren St), just s to Broadway, then w. Ext/int corridors. **Pets:** Dogs only. $10 daily fee/pet. Designated rooms, service with restrictions, supervision.

Ramada Limited 🆂🅷
(406) 721-3610. **$85.** 801 N Orange St. I-90, exit 104 (Orange St), just s. Int corridors. **Pets:** $10 one-time fee/pet. Designated rooms, service with restrictions, supervision.

Red Lion Inn 🆂🅷
(406) 728-3300. **$60-$200.** 700 W Broadway. I-90, exit 104 (Orange St), just s, then just w. Ext corridors. **Pets:** Large. $5 daily fee/pet. Service with restrictions.

Redwood Lodge Ⓜ
(406) 721-2110. **$65-$70.** 8060 Hwy 93 N. I-90, exit 96, just s. Ext corridors. **Pets:** Accepted.

Royal Motel Ⓜ
(406) 542-2184. **$40-$54.** 338 Washington St. I-90, exit 105 (Van Buren St), just s, then 0.5 mi w on Broadway. Ext corridors. **Pets:** $5 daily fee/pet. Designated rooms, no service, supervision.

Ruby's Inn & Convention Center 🆂🅷
(406) 721-0990. **$70-$120.** 4825 N Reserve St. I-90, exit 101 (Reserve St), just s. Ext/int corridors. **Pets:** Other species. $10 one-time fee/room. Designated rooms, service with restrictions.

Sleep Inn by Choice Hotels 🆂🅷
(406) 543-5883. **$65-$85.** 3425 Dore Ln. I-90, exit 101 (Reserve St), 5 mi s, then just e on Brooks St. Int corridors. **Pets:** Accepted.

Southgate Inn 🆂🅷
(406) 251-2250. **$49-$85.** 3530 Brooks St. I-90, exit 101 (Reserve St), 5 mi s to Brooks St, then just e. Ext corridors. **Pets:** $5 daily fee/pet. Designated rooms, service with restrictions, supervision.

Super 8-Brooks St 🆂🅷
(406) 251-2255. **$48-$81, 7 day notice.** 3901 Brooks St. I-90, exit 101 (Reserve St), 5 mi s, then just w. Int corridors. **Pets:** Medium, dogs only. $5 daily fee/pet. Designated rooms, service with restrictions, supervision.

Travelers Inn Motel Ⓜ
(406) 728-8330. **$49-$69.** 4850 N Reserve St. I-90, exit 101 (Reserve St), just s. Ext corridors. **Pets:** Small, dogs only. $5 daily fee/pet. Designated rooms, service with restrictions, supervision.

OVANDO

Lake Upsata Guest Ranch 🆁🅰
(406) 793-5890. **$75-$220, 30 day notice.** 201 Lower Lakeside Ln. 7.5 mi w on SR 200 to MM 38, 3.4 mi n on Woodworth Rd, then 1 mi e. Ext corridors. **Pets:** Other species. Crate.

POLSON

Bayview Inn Ⓜ
(406) 883-3120. **Call for rates.** 914 Hwy 93. Just s; downtown. Ext corridors. **Pets:** Accepted.

RED LODGE

Best Western Lu Pine Inn 🆂🅷
(406) 446-1321. **$69-$99.** 702 S Hauser. 0.4 mi s, just w of US 212. Int corridors. **Pets:** Other species. Service with restrictions, supervision.

Comfort Inn of Red Lodge 🆂🅷
(406) 446-4469. **$60-$120.** 612 N Broadway. Jct US 212 and SR 78, north entrance. Int corridors. **Pets:** $25 deposit/room. Service with restrictions, supervision.

Super 8 of Red Lodge Ⓜ
(406) 446-2288. **$49-$139.** 1223 S Broadway Ave. Just s on US 212. Ext/int corridors. **Pets:** Other species. $5 daily fee/room. Supervision.

Yodeler Motel Ⓜ
(406) 446-1435. **$49-$99.** 601 S Broadway. Just s on US 212. Ext corridors. **Pets:** Dogs only. $10 one-time fee/room. Designated rooms, service with restrictions, supervision.

RONAN

Starlite Motel Ⓜ
(406) 676-7000. **$58-$79.** 18 Main St SW. Just w of jct US 93 and Main St. Ext corridors. **Pets:** Accepted.

ST. IGNATIUS

Sunset Motel Ⓜ
(406) 745-3900. **$49-$120.** 333 Mountain View. Just s of downtown, exit on US 93. Ext corridors. **Pets:** Medium, dogs only. $5 daily fee/pet. Service with restrictions, supervision.

ST. REGIS

AAA **WW** Little River Motel **M**
(406) 649-2713. **$40-$65.** 50 Old US Hwy 10 W. I-90, exit 33, just n to flashing light, just w, then just sw. Ext corridors. **Pets:** Small. $5 daily fee/pet. Service with restrictions, supervision.

SAVE S6 X 🛏 🖥 ⚿ ☎

SEELEY LAKE

AAA **WWW** Wilderness Gateway Inn **M**
(406) 677-2095. **$50-$63.** 2996 Hwy 83 N. South end of town on SR 83. Ext corridors. **Pets:** Medium, other species. $5 daily fee/pet. Supervision.

SAVE X

SHELBY

WW **WW** Comfort Inn of Shelby **SH**
(406) 434-2212. **$65-$95.** 455 McKinley Ave. I-15, exit 363, just e, then just s. Int corridors. **Pets:** Other species. $5 daily fee/pet. Designated rooms, service with restrictions, supervision.

ASK S6 X 🐾 🖥 💻 ⌧

AAA **WW** Crossroads Inn **M**
(406) 434-5134. **$52-$60, 7 day notice.** 1200 Roosevelt Hwy. Just w of town center on US 2. Int corridors. **Pets:** Other species. $10 daily fee/pet. Designated rooms, service with restrictions, supervision.

SAVE X 🐾 🖥 🏊

AAA **WW** O'Haire Manor Motel **M**
(406) 434-5555. **$50-$70.** 204 2nd St S. Just s of Main St via Maple St. Ext/int corridors. **Pets:** Medium. $5 daily fee/pet. Designated rooms, service with restrictions, supervision.

SAVE S6 X 🖥

SIDNEY

AAA **WW** Richland Motor Inn **M**
(406) 433-6400. **$78.** 1200 S Central Ave. 1.5 mi n of jct SR 200 and 16. Int corridors. **Pets:** Other species. $50 deposit/room. Service with restrictions.

SAVE S6 X 🖥 💻 ⌧

SUPERIOR

AAA **WW** Budget Host Big Sky Motel **M**
(406) 822-4831. **$56-$60.** 103 4th Ave E. I-90, exit 47, just n. Ext corridors. **Pets:** Accepted.

SAVE S6 X 🖥

THOMPSON FALLS

AAA **WW** The Riverfront **M**
(406) 827-3460. **$62-$92.** 4907 Hwy 200 W. 1 mi w of city center. Ext corridors. **Pets:** $7 daily fee/pet.

SAVE X 🖥 💻 ⌧

THREE FORKS

AAA **WW** Broken Spur Motel **M**
(406) 285-3237. **$50-$68.** 124 W Elm (Hwy 2). I-90, exit 278 westbound, 1.3 mi sw on SR 2; exit 274 eastbound, 1 mi s on SR 287 to jct SR 2, then 3 mi se on SR 2. Ext corridors. **Pets:** Other species. $5 one-time fee/pet. Service with restrictions, supervision.

SAVE S6 X 🖥

WW **WW** Fort Three Forks Motel & RV Park **M**
(406) 285-3233. **Call for rates.** 10776 Hwy 287. I-90, exit 274. Ext corridors. **Pets:** Accepted.

X 🖥 💻

VICTOR

AAA **WWW** Wildlife Adventures Guest Ranch **RA** 🐾
(406) 642-3262. **$105-$170, 45 day notice.** 1765 Pleasant View Dr. Jct US 93 and Fifth St, 0.9 mi w, 3.2 mi s. Int corridors. **Pets:** Other species. $25 deposit/room, $10 daily fee/pet. Designated rooms, service with restrictions, supervision.

SAVE S6 X ⌧ ⚿ 🗝 ☎

WEST YELLOWSTONE

AAA **WW** Best Western Cross Winds Motor Inn **SH**
(406) 646-9557. **$49-$129, 3 day notice.** 201 Firehole Ave. Just w of US 191 and 287, on US 20 at Dunraven St and Firehole Ave. Ext corridors. **Pets:** Dogs only. Designated rooms, service with restrictions, supervision.

SAVE S6 X 💻 🏊

AAA **WWWW** Best Western Desert Inn **M**
(406) 646-7376. **$59-$169, 3 day notice.** 133 Canyon Ave. US 191 at US 20; corner of Canyon and Firehole aves. Int corridors. **Pets:** Dogs only. Designated rooms, service with restrictions, supervision.

SAVE S6 X 🅼 🐾 🗝 🖥 💻 🏊

AAA **WWW** Days Inn West Yellowstone **SH**
(406) 646-7656. **$79-$125, 14 day notice.** 301 Madison Ave. W off US 191; just nw of park entrance. Ext/int corridors. **Pets:** Medium, dogs only. $10 daily fee/pet. Designated rooms, service with restrictions, supervision.

SAVE S6 X 🅼 🗝 🖥 💻 🍴 🏊 ⌧

AAA **WWWW** Fairfield Inn by Marriott **SH**
(406) 646-4892. **$59-$149.** 105 S Electric St. Just sw of jct US 191, 187 and 20, just w of park entrance. Int corridors. **Pets:** Other species. Service with restrictions, supervision.

SAVE S6 🅼 🐾 🖥 💻 🏊

AAA **WWW** Gray Wolf Inn & Suites **M**
(406) 646-0000. **$59-$139.** 250 S Canyon Ave. Just w of park entrance. Int corridors. **Pets:** Other species. $50 deposit/room. Designated rooms, service with restrictions, supervision.

SAVE S6 X 🅼 🐾 🗝 🖥 💻 🏊

AAA **WW** Hebgen Lake Mountain Inn **SH**
(406) 646-5100. **$85-$145, 10 day notice.** 15475 Hebgen Lake Rd. 8 mi n on US 191, w at jct US 191/287, then 7 mi w on US 287. Ext corridors. **Pets:** Accepted.

SAVE S6 X 💻 🍴 ⌧

AAA **WW** Kelly Inn **SH**
(406) 646-4544. **$59-$149.** 104 S Canyon Ave. S of jct US 191, 287 and 20, just w of park entrance. Ext/int corridors. **Pets:** Accepted.

SAVE S6 X 🗝 🖥 💻 🏊

AAA **WWW** Roundup Motel & Dude Motor Inn **M**
(406) 646-7301. **$65-$129.** 3 Madison Ave. Just n of park entrance. Ext corridors. **Pets:** Accepted.

SAVE S6 X 🖥 💻

AAA **WWWW** Stage Coach Inn **SH**
(406) 646-7381. **$49-$139.** 209 Madison Ave. Corner of Dunraven St and Madison Ave, just w of park entrance. Ext/int corridors. **Pets:** $50 deposit/room. Designated rooms, supervision.

SAVE S6 X 🐾 🗝 🖥 💻 🍴 ⌧

AAA **WWWW** The Three Bear Lodge **M**
(406) 646-7353. **$50-$90.** 217 Yellowstone Ave. Just w of park entrance. Ext/int corridors. **Pets:** Other species. $5 daily fee/pet. Service with restrictions, supervision.

SAVE X 🖥 💻 🍴 🏊 ⌧

 Yellowstone Lodge **SH**
(406) 646-0020. **$59-$139.** 251 S Electric St. Just w of park entrance. Int corridors. **Pets:** Other species. $10 one-time fee/pet. Designated rooms, service with restrictions, supervision.

SAVE S⬠X ⬠ ⬠ ⬠ ⬠

WHITEFISH

 Bay Point on the Lake **CO**
(406) 862-2331. **$89-$185, 30 day notice.** 300 Bay Point Dr. Jct US 93 and SR 487, 0.6 mi n on SR 487 to Skyles Pl, 0.3 mi w to Dakota Ave, 0.3 mi n, then just w. Ext corridors. **Pets:** Other species. Designated rooms, service with restrictions, supervision.

SAVE S⬠X ⬠ ⬠ ⬠ X

⬠⬠ Cheap Sleep Motel **SH**
(406) 862-5515. **$45-$70.** 6400 Hwy 93 S. US 93, 1 mi s. Int corridors. **Pets:** Medium, dogs only. $5 daily fee/pet. Service with restrictions, supervision.

X ⬠

⬠⬠ Kristianna Mountain Homes **CO**
(406) 862-2860. **$150-$525.** 3842 Winter Ln. Jct US 93 and SR 487, 2.4 mi n on SR 487, at flashing light go 5.2 mi on Big Mountain Rd, just n on Gelande, then just w on Kristanna Close. Ext/int corridors. **Pets:** Accepted.

SAVE X ⬠ ⬠ X ⬠

⬠⬠⬠ North Forty Resort **CA**
(406) 862-7740. **$69-$215, 14 day notice.** 3765 Hwy 40 W. 2.5 mi e on SR 40 from jct of US 93. Ext corridors. **Pets:** $10 daily fee/pet. Designated rooms, service with restrictions, supervision.

X ⬠ ⬠ X ⬠

⬠⬠⬠ Pine Lodge **SH**
(406) 862-7600. **$80-$139.** 920 Spokane Ave. 1 mi s on US 93. Int corridors. **Pets:** Large. Service with restrictions, supervision.

SAVE S⬠X ⬠M ⬠ ⬠ ⬠ ⬠ ⬠

⬠⬠ Super 8 Motel **SH**
(406) 862-8255. **$48-$90.** 800 Spokane Ave. 1 mi s on US 93 from jct SR 487. Int corridors. **Pets:** Medium, dogs only. $5 daily fee/pet. Designated rooms, service with restrictions, supervision.

SAVE S⬠X

WHITE SULPHUR SPRINGS

⬠⬠ All Seasons Super 8 Motel **M**
(406) 547-8888. **$60-$87.** 808 3rd Ave SW. On US 89, south end of town. Int corridors. **Pets:** $20 deposit/room, $6 one-time fee/pet. Service with restrictions, supervision.

SAVE S⬠X ⬠M ⬠ ⬠

NEBRASKA

AINSWORTH

Comfort Inn SH
(402) 387-1050. **$74-$84.** 1124 E 4th St. 0.5 mi e on US 20. Int corridors. **Pets:** Medium, other species. $10 daily fee/pet. Designated rooms, service with restrictions, crate.

Super 8 Motel SH
(402) 387-0700. **$49-$51.** 1025 E 4th St. 0.5 mi e on US 20. Int corridors. **Pets:** Accepted.

ALLIANCE

Alliance Days Inn SH
(308) 762-8000. **$64-$100.** 117 Cody Ave. Jct US 385 and SR 2, 0.4 mi e, just s. Int corridors. **Pets:** Large. $5 daily fee/pet. Service with restrictions, supervision.

Sunset Motel & RV Park M
(308) 762-8660. **$49-$69.** 1210 E Hwy 2. Jct US 87, 1 mi e. Ext/int corridors. **Pets:** Medium. $5 daily fee/pet. Designated rooms, service with restrictions, supervision.

AURORA

Budget Host, Ken's Motel M
(402) 694-3141. **$40.** 1515 11th St. I-80, exit 332, 3 mi n on SR 14, then 0.3 mi w on US 34. Ext corridors. **Pets:** Accepted.

BEATRICE

Beatrice Super 8 Motel SH
(402) 228-8808. **$59-$75.** 3721 N 6th St. 1 mi n on US 77. Int corridors. **Pets:** Accepted.

Holiday Inn Express Hotel & Suites SH
(402) 228-7000. **$70.** 4005 N 6th St. 1 mi n on US 77. Int corridors. **Pets:** Accepted.

BELLEVUE

Days Inn SH
(402) 292-3800. **$61-$185.** 1811 Hillcrest Dr. Jct US 75 and SR 370, 0.8 mi on SR 370. Int corridors. **Pets:** $35 one-time fee/pet. Designated rooms, service with restrictions, supervision.

Settle Inn and Suites SH
(402) 292-1155. **$59-$200.** 2105 Pratt Ave. US 75, exit Cornhusker, just w. Int corridors. **Pets:** Small, dogs only. $15 daily fee/room. Designated rooms, service with restrictions, supervision.

CENTRAL CITY

Super 8 Motel SH
(308) 946-5055. **$60-$70.** 1701 31st St. SR 14, 1 mi s of jct US 30. Ext/int corridors. **Pets:** Other species. $5 daily fee/room. Service with restrictions, supervision.

CHADRON

Best Western West Hills Inn SH
(308) 432-3305. **$56-$152, 30 day notice.** 1100 W 10th St. Jct US 385 and 20. Ext/int corridors. **Pets:** Medium. $10 daily fee/room. Service with restrictions, crate.

Chadron Super 8 Motel SH
(308) 432-4471. **$45-$103.** 840 W Hwy 20. 0.8 mi w on US 20, just e of jct US 385. Int corridors. **Pets:** Medium. Service with restrictions, supervision.

Grand Westerner Motel M
(308) 432-5595. **$40-$55.** 1050 W Hwy 20. 0.8 mi w on US 20, just e of jct US 385. Ext corridors. **Pets:** Dogs only. Service with restrictions, supervision.

Westerner Motel M
(308) 432-5577. **$40-$55.** 300 Oak St. On US 20, 0.5 mi e of jct US 385 and SR 87. Ext corridors. **Pets:** Dogs only. Designated rooms, service with restrictions, supervision.

COLUMBUS

Days Inn SH
(402) 564-2527. **$48-$59.** 371 33rd Ave. Jct US 30 and 81, 1 mi s. Int corridors. **Pets:** $10 one-time fee/room. Service with restrictions, supervision.

Sleep Inn & Suites Hotel SH
(402) 562-5200. **$67-$125.** 303 23rd St. On US 30, 2 mi e of jct US 30 and 81; east side of town. Int corridors. **Pets:** Medium. $10 daily fee/pet. Designated rooms, service with restrictions, crate.

Super 8 Motel-Columbus SH
(402) 563-3456. **$49-$59.** 3324 20th St. On US 30 and 81, just s. Int corridors. **Pets:** Small. $10 one-time fee/pet. Service with restrictions, supervision.

COZAD

Motel 6-Cozad–4091 SH
(308) 784-4900. **$41-$53.** 809 S Meridian. I-80, exit 222, just n. Int corridors. **Pets:** Large, other species. Service with restrictions, supervision.

CRETE

▽▽ Super 8 Motel ⚡
(402) 826-3600. **$61-$88.** 1880 W 12th St. 1.3 mi sw at jct SR 33/103; west end of town. Int corridors. **Pets:** Medium, dogs only. $5 daily fee/pet. Service with restrictions, supervision.

(ASK) [S🐾] [✕] [🛏] [🖨]

FREMONT

▽▽ Comfort Inn by Choice Hotels ⚡
(402) 721-1109. **$59-$99.** 1649 E 23rd Ave. 2 mi e on US 30, just e of Business Rt US 275. Int corridors. **Pets:** Accepted.

(ASK) [S🐾] [✕] [📷] [🛏] [🖨] [🌊]

◆◆◆ ▽▽◆ Holiday Lodge & Conference Center ⚡
(402) 727-1110. **$60-$80.** 1220 E 23rd St. US 30, jct Business Rt US 275 and 30. Ext/int corridors. **Pets:** Accepted.

[SAVE] [S🐾] [✕] [🛏] [🖨] [🍴] [🌊] [🐾]

FULLERTON

▽▽ The Fullerton Inn Ⓜ
(308) 536-2699. **$58-$63.** S Hwy 14. Just s of center. Int corridors. **Pets:** Other species. Service with restrictions, crate.

[S🐾] [✕] [&M]

GERING

▽▽ Microtel Inn & Suites ⚡
(308) 436-1950. **$60-$65.** 1130 M St. On SR 92, 1 mi e of SR 71. Int corridors. **Pets:** Other species. $10 one-time fee/room. Service with restrictions, supervision.

(ASK) [S🐾] [✕] [&M] [🖨] [🛏] [🖨]

GOTHENBURG

◆◆◆ ▽▽ Gothenburg Super 8 ⚡
(308) 537-2684. **$56-$69.** 401 Platte River Dr. I-80, exit 211 (SR 47), just n. Int corridors. **Pets:** Large. Designated rooms, service with restrictions, supervision.

[SAVE] [S🐾] [✕] [🖨] [🛏] [🖨] [🌊]

GRAND ISLAND

▽▽▽ Holiday Inn-Interstate 80 ⚡ ⚡
(308) 384-7770. **$64-$109.** 7838 S US Hwy 281. I-80, exit 312 (US 281), just s. Int corridors. **Pets:** Other species. $15 daily fee/room. Service with restrictions, supervision.

[✕] [&M] [📷] [🖨] [🛏] [🖨] [🍴] [🌊] [🐾]

▽▽ Super 8 Motel ⚡
(308) 384-4380. **$59-$82.** 2603 S Locust St. I-80, exit 314, 4.7 mi n. Int corridors. **Pets:** Medium. $5 daily fee/room. Service with restrictions, supervision.

(ASK) [S🐾] [✕] [🛏] [🖨] [🌊]

◆ ▽▽ Travelodge ⚡
(308) 382-5003. **$51-$57.** 1311 S Locust St. I-80, exit 314, 5.2 mi n. Int corridors. **Pets:** Accepted.

[✕] [🖨] [🛏] [🖨]

◆◆◆ ▽▽ USA Inns of America Ⓜ
(308) 381-0111. **$50-$60.** 7000 S Nine Bridge Rd. I-80, exit 312 (US 281), just n. Ext/int corridors. **Pets:** Medium. $5 daily fee/pet. Designated rooms, service with restrictions, supervision.

[SAVE] [S🐾] [✕] [🛏] [🖨]

HASTINGS

◆◆◆ ▽▽▽ Holiday Inn-Hastings ⚡ ⚡
(402) 463-6721. **$89-$129.** 2205 Osborne Dr E. Jct US 34 and 281, 2 mi n. Ext/int corridors. **Pets:** Small. $10 one-time fee/pet. Designated rooms, service with restrictions, crate.

[SAVE] [✕] [♿] [&M] [📷] [🖨] [🛏] [🖨] [🍴] [🌊] [🐾]

HOLDREGE

▽▽ Super 8 ⚡
(402) 463-2428. **$40-$54, 7 day notice.** 910 W J St. Jct US 6, 34 and 281. Ext corridors. **Pets:** Large, other species. Designated rooms, service with restrictions, supervision.

[SAVE] [S🐾] [✕] [🛏] [🌊]

▽▽ Super 8 ⚡
(402) 463-8888. **$54-$74.** 2200 N Kansas Ave. Jct US 34 and 281, 2 mi n. Int corridors. **Pets:** $10 daily fee/pet. Service with restrictions, supervision.

(ASK) [S🐾] [✕] [📷] [♿] [🛏] [🖨]

HOLDREGE

▽▽ Super 8 ⚡
(308) 995-2793. **$62-$87.** 420 Broadway. US 183, 0.5 mi w on US 6/34. Int corridors. **Pets:** Small. $10 daily fee/room. Service with restrictions, supervision.

(ASK) [S🐾] [✕] [🛏] [🌊] [🐾]

KEARNEY

◆◆◆ ▽▽▽ Best Western Inn of Kearney ⚡ ⚡
(308) 237-5185. **$60-$95.** 1010 3rd Ave. I-80, exit 272 (SR 44), 1 mi n, then just w. Ext/int corridors. **Pets:** Other species. $10 one-time fee/room.

[SAVE] [S🐾] [✕] [📷] [🛏] [🖨] [🍴] [🌊] [🐾]

◆◆◆ ▽▽▽ Ramada Inn-Kearney ⚡
(308) 237-3141. **$69-$99.** 301 2nd Ave. I-80, exit 272 (SR 44), 0.7 mi n. Int corridors. **Pets:** Accepted.

[SAVE] [S🐾] [✕] [🛏] [🖨] [🍴] [🌊] [🐾]

KIMBALL

▽▽ Days Inn-Kimball Ⓜ
(308) 235-4671. **$60-$107.** 611 E 3rd St. I-80, exit 20, 1.5 ne on SR 71, then 0.5 mi e on US 30. Ext corridors. **Pets:** Other species. $10 daily fee/pet. Service with restrictions, supervision.

(ASK) [S🐾] [✕] [🛏] [🖨]

LEXINGTON

◆ Budget Host Minute Man Motel Ⓜ ⚡
(308) 324-5544. **$39-$50, 3 day notice.** 801 Plum Creek Pkwy. I-80, exit 237 (US 283), 2 mi n. Ext corridors. **Pets:** Medium. $5 daily fee/pet. Designated rooms, service with restrictions, supervision.

(ASK) [✕]

◆◆◆ ▽▽ Days Inn ⚡
(308) 324-6440. **$50-$85.** 2506 Plum Creek Pkwy. I-80, exit 237 (US 283), 0.6 mi n. Int corridors. **Pets:** Dogs only. $6 daily fee/pet. Designated rooms, service with restrictions, supervision.

[SAVE] [S🐾] [✕] [🛏]

◆◆◆ ▽▽▽ Holiday Inn Express Hotel & Suites ⚡
(308) 324-9900. **$65-$109.** 2605 Plum Creek Pkwy. I-80, exit 237 (US 283), 0.5 mi n. Int corridors. **Pets:** $10 one-time fee/room. Designated rooms, service with restrictions, supervision.

[SAVE] [S🐾] [✕] [&M] [📷] [♿] [🛏] [🖨] [🌊]

▽▽ Lexington Comfort Inn ⚡
(308) 324-3747. **$64-$85.** 2810 Plum Creek Pkwy. I-80, exit 237 (US 283), 0.3 mi n. Ext/int corridors. **Pets:** Accepted.

[✕] [🛏] [🖨] [🌊]

LINCOLN

◆◆◆ ▽▽▽ Baymont Inn & Suites ⚡
(402) 477-1100. **$69-$130.** 3939 N 26th St. I-80, exit 403 (27th St), 2 mi s. Int corridors. **Pets:** Small. Service with restrictions, supervision.

[SAVE] [S🐾] [✕] [&M] [📷] [♿] [🛏] [🖨] [🌊] [🐾]

▽▽ Best Western Crown Inn ⚡
(402) 438-4700. **Call for rates.** 6501 N 28th St. I-80, exit 403 (27th St), 0.3 mi s via Wildcat Dr. Int corridors. **Pets:** Accepted.

[✕] [📷] [♿] [🛏] [🖨] [🌊]

AAA ▼▼▼ Best Western Villager Courtyard & Gardens Hotel SH ✿
(402) 464-9111. **$60-$75.** 5200 O St. 3 mi e on US 6 city route and 34. Ext corridors. **Pets:** Large, other species. Service with restrictions.
[SAVE] [S6] [✕] [&M] [✍] [&] [■] [▣] [▥] [¶] [≈] [✕]

▼▼▼▼ Chase Suites Hotel SH
(402) 483-4900. **$88-$159.** 200 S 68th St Pl. On US 34, 4.3 mi e, just s of jct 68th St. Ext corridors. **Pets:** Medium. $150 deposit/pet, $5 daily fee/pet. Service with restrictions.
[ASK] [S6] [✕] [&M] [✍] [&] [■] [▣] [≈] [✕]

▼▼ Comfort Inn by Choice Hotels SH
(402) 475-2200. **$59-$89.** 2940 NW 12th St. I-80, exit 399, enter at Perkins Restaurant. Int corridors. **Pets:** Accepted.
[ASK] [S6] [✕] [&] [■] [▣]

▼▼▼▼ Country Inns & Suites By Carlson SH ✿
(402) 476-5353. **$89-$99.** 5353 N 27th St. I-80, exit 403 (27th St), 1.5 mi s. Int corridors. **Pets:** Medium. $75 deposit/room, $10 daily fee/pet. Service with restrictions, supervision.
[ASK] [S6] [✕] [&M] [&] [■] [▣] [¶] [≈]

AAA ▼▼▼ Days Inn South SH
(402) 423-7111. **$53-$68.** 1140 Calvert St. 2.5 mi s on SR 2. Ext/int corridors. **Pets:** Medium, dogs only. $5 daily fee/pet. Service with restrictions, supervision.
[SAVE] [S6] [✕] [■] [▣]

▼▼▼▼ Holiday Inn Express SH ✿
(402) 435-0200. **$76-$89.** 1133 Belmont Ave. I-80, exit 401A; 2 mi s on I-180, exit 2 (Cornhusker Hwy), then just e. Int corridors. **Pets:** Service with restrictions, supervision.
[ASK] [S6] [✕] [&M] [✍] [&] [■] [▣] [≈] [✕]

▼▼▼▼ Quality Inn & Suites SH
(402) 464-4400. **$74-$99.** 216 N 48th St. 2.5 mi e on US 6 and 34; just ne of jct O St; entrance off or 48th St. Int corridors. **Pets:** Accepted.
[ASK] [S6] [✕] [&M] [✍] [&] [■] [▣] [≈]

▼▼ Settle Inn & Suites SH
(402) 435-8100. **$69-$109.** 2800 Husker Cir. I-80, exit 403, just s to Wildcat Dr, just e, then just n. Int corridors. **Pets:** Accepted.
[ASK] [S6] [✕] [&M] [&] [■] [▣] [≈]

▼▼▼ Staybridge Suites Lincoln-I-80 SH
(402) 438-7829. **$89-$199.** 2701 Fletcher Ave. I-80, exit 403, 0.4 mi s on N 27th St. Int corridors. **Pets:** Other species. $25 one-time fee/room. Service with restrictions.
[ASK] [✕] [&M] [&] [■] [▣] [≈] [✕]

▼▼▼ Super 8 Motel-Lincoln/Cornhusker SH
(402) 467-4488. **$53-$65.** 2545 Cornhusker Hwy. I-80, exit 403, 2.5 mi s. Int corridors. **Pets:** $10 daily fee/room. Service with restrictions, supervision.
[ASK] [S6] [✕] [&M] [✍] [&] [■] [▣]

▼▼ Super 8 Motel-Lincoln/West "O" Street SH
(402) 476-8887. **$53-$65.** 2635 W O St. I-80, exit 395, 2 mi e. Int corridors. **Pets:** Other species. $10.70 one-time fee/room. Designated rooms, service with restrictions, supervision.
[ASK] [S6] [✕] [&M] [✍] [■] [▣]

AAA ▼▼▼ Town House Motel SH
(402) 475-3000. **$55-$75.** 1744 M St. Jct 18th and M St; downtown. Int corridors. **Pets:** Other species. Service with restrictions, supervision.
[SAVE] [S6] [✕] [✍] [■] [▣]

MCCOOK

▼▼▼ Days Inn & Suites McCook SH
(308) 345-7115. **$45-$75.** 901 N Hwy 83. Jct US 6 and 34, 0.3 mi n. Int corridors. **Pets:** Large, other species. $10 daily fee/pet. Designated rooms, service with restrictions, supervision.
[ASK] [S6] [✕] [■] [▣] [≈]

▼▼ Holiday Inn Express SH
(308) 345-4505. **$60.** 1 Holiday Bison Dr. On US 83, just n of jct US 6 and 34. Int corridors. **Pets:** Accepted.
[ASK] [S6] [✕] [&M] [✍] [■]

AAA ▼▼ Super 8 Motel M
(308) 345-1141. **$44, 7 day notice.** 1103 E B St. Jct US 6 and 34, 0.5 mi e; east side of town. Ext corridors. **Pets:** Medium. Service with restrictions, supervision.
[SAVE] [S6] [✕]

MORRILL

▼▼▼ Oak Tree Inn SH
(308) 247-2111. **$52-$62.** 707 E Webster. 0.5 mi e. Ext/int corridors. **Pets:** $5 one-time fee/room. Designated rooms, service with restrictions, supervision.
[ASK] [S6] [✕] [&M] [&] [■] [¶] [✕]

NEBRASKA CITY

AAA ▼▼▼ Apple Inn SH
(402) 873-5959. **$56-$64.** 502 S 11th St. Jct 11th St and 4th Corso; center. Ext/int corridors. **Pets:** Small, dogs only. $5 daily fee/pet. Designated rooms, service with restrictions, supervision.
[SAVE] [S6] [✕] [✍] [■] [▣] [≈]

NORFOLK

AAA ▼▼▼ Norfolk Country Inn SH ✿
(402) 371-4430. **$62.** 1201 S 13th St. Jct US 275 Bypass and US 81. Ext corridors. **Pets:** Service with restrictions, supervision.
[SAVE] [S6] [✕] [&] [■] [▣] [¶] [≈]

▼▼ Super 8 Motel-Norfolk SH
(402) 379-2220. **$49-$59.** 1223 Omaha Ave. Jct US 81 and 275, just e. Int corridors. **Pets:** Medium. $10 daily fee/room. No service, supervision.
[ASK] [S6] [✕] [✍] [■] [▣]

▼▼ White House Inn SH
(402) 371-3133. **$55-$60.** 2206 Market Ln. On US 275 Bypass, 1 mi w of jct US 81. Int corridors. **Pets:** $25 deposit/room, $5 daily fee/room. Designated rooms, supervision.
[ASK] [S6] [✕] [✍] [&] [■] [▣] [✕]

NORTH PLATTE

AAA ▼▼ Best Value Travelers Inn M
(308) 534-4020. **$36-$55.** 602 E 4th St. I-80, exit 177 (US 83), 1.5 mi n, then just e. Ext corridors. **Pets:** Medium, other species. Service with restrictions, supervision.
[SAVE] [S6] [✕] [■] [≈]

AAA ▼▼▼ Best Western Chalet Lodge M
(308) 532-2313. **$49-$79.** 920 N Jeffers St. I-80, exit 177 (US 83), 2 mi n on US 30 and 83. Ext corridors. **Pets:** Other species. $5 daily fee/pet. Service with restrictions, supervision.
[SAVE] [S6] [✕] [■] [▣] [≈]

AAA ▼▼▼▼ Holiday Inn Express Hotel & Suites SH
(308) 532-9500. **$79-$159.** 300 Holiday Frontage Rd. I-80, exit 177 (US 83), just s. Int corridors. **Pets:** Accepted.
[SAVE] [S6] [✕] [&M] [✍] [&] [■] [▣] [≈] [✕]

▼▼▼ Howard Johnson Inn SH
(308) 532-0130. **$50-$90.** 1209 S Dewey. I-80, exit 177 (US 83), 0.5 mi n. Ext corridors. **Pets:** Accepted.
[ASK] [S6] [✕] [■] [▣] [¶] [≈]

▼▼▼▼ La Quinta Inn & Suites SH
(308) 534-0700. **$89-$179.** 2600 Eagles Wings Pl. I-80, exit 179, just n, then just w. Int corridors. **Pets:** Other species. No service, supervision.
[ASK] [S6] [✕] [&M] [✍] [&] [■] [▣] [≈]

ⒶⒶⒶ 🔷🔷🔷🔷 **Quality Inn & Suites** 🆂🅷 🐾
(308) 532-9090. **$79-$129.** 2102 S Jeffers St. I-80, exit 177 (US 83), just n. Ext/int corridors. **Pets:** Other species. $10 daily fee/pet. Designated rooms.
[SAVE] [S🐾] [✕] [&M] [🔌] [🅵] [🅷] [🖥] [🍽] [🏊] [✕]

ⒶⒶⒶ 🔷🔷🔷 **Ramada Limited** 🆂🅷 🐾
(308) 534-3120. **$49-$79.** 3201 S Jeffers St. I-80, exit 177 (US 83), 0.3 mi s. Int corridors. **Pets:** Other species. $10 one-time fee/room. Service with restrictions, supervision.
[SAVE] [✕] [🅷] [🖥] [🍽] [🏊]

OGALLALA

ⒶⒶⒶ 🔷🔷🔷 **Best Western Stagecoach Inn** 🆂🅷 🐾
(308) 284-3656. **$59-$99.** 201 Stagecoach Tr. I-80, exit 126 (US 26/SR 61), just ne on frontage road. Ext corridors. **Pets:** Other species. Supervision.
[SAVE] [S🐾] [✕] [🅷] [🖥] [🍽] [🏊] [✕]

ⒶⒶⒶ 🔷🔷🔷 **Days Inn** 🅼 🐾
(308) 284-6365. **$69-$89.** 601 Stagecoach Tr. I-80, exit 126 (US 26/SR 61), just ne on frontage road. Int corridors. **Pets:** Other species. $6 one-time fee/room. Designated rooms, service with restrictions, crate.
[SAVE] [S🐾] [✕] [🅷]

🔷🔷 **Holiday Inn Express** 🆂🅷
(308) 284-2266. **$64-$94.** 501 Stagecoach Dr. I-80, exit 126 (US 26/SR 61), just n, then just e on service road. Ext/int corridors. **Pets:** Large. $7 daily fee/pet. Service with restrictions, supervision.
[ASK] [S🐾] [✕] [🔌] [&'] [🅷] [🖥]

OMAHA

ⒶⒶⒶ 🔷🔷🔷 **Baymont Inn Omaha** 🆂🅷
(402) 592-5200. **$54-$64.** 10760 M St. I-80, exit 445 (L St E), 0.3 mi; entry off 108th St. Int corridors. **Pets:** Other species. No service, supervision.
[SAVE] [S🐾] [✕] [🔌] [🅷] [🖥]

🔷🔷 **Best Western Redick Plaza Hotel** 🅻🅷
(402) 342-1500. **$99-$169.** 1504 Harney St. Downtown. Int corridors. **Pets:** Accepted.
[ASK] [S🐾] [✕] [🔌] [🅷] [🖥] [🍽] [✕]

🔷🔷 **Best Western Settle Inn** 🆂🅷 🐾
(402) 431-1246. **$69-$109.** 650 N 109th Ct. I-680, exit 3 (Dodge St W), 0.8 mi to 108th St to 108th Ave and N Old Mill Rd exit, just n on 108th Ave, then just w on Mill Valley Rd. Int corridors. **Pets:** Small, dogs only. $15 daily fee/room. Designated rooms, service with restrictions, supervision.
[ASK] [S🐾] [✕] [🔌] [&'] [🅷] [🖥] [🏊]

🔷🔷🔷 **Candlewood Suites** 🆂🅷
(402) 758-2848. **$69-$109.** 360 S 108th Ave. I-680, exit 3 (Dodge St W), 0.7 mi to 108th St, then 0.8 mi s. Int corridors. **Pets:** Other species. $75 one-time fee/room. Service with restrictions.
[ASK] [S🐾] [✕] [&M] [🔌] [&'] [🅷] [🖥]

🔷🔷 **Clarion Hotel-West** 🆂🅷
(402) 895-1000. **$59-$249.** 4888 S 118th St. I-80, exit 445 (L St W), 0.3 mi w on US 275/SR 92, then just s on 120th St. Int corridors. **Pets:** Medium. $10 daily fee/room. No service, supervision.
[ASK] [S🐾] [✕] [&M] [🔌] [&'] [🅷] [🖥] [🍽] [🏊] [✕]

ⒶⒶⒶ 🔷🔷🔷 **Comfort Inn** 🆂🅷
(402) 896-6300. **$55-$190.** 9595 S 145th St. I-80, exit 440, just n, then w. Int corridors. **Pets:** Other species. $10 daily fee/pet. Designated rooms, service with restrictions, supervision.
[SAVE] [S🐾] [✕] [&'] [🅷] [🖥] [🏊]

ⒶⒶⒶ 🔷🔷🔷🔷 **Comfort Inn Omaha-Southwest** 🆂🅷 🐾
(402) 593-2380. **$70-$149.** 10728 L St. I-80, exit 445 (L St E), just n on 108th St, then e. Int corridors. **Pets:** Medium. $10 daily fee/pet. Service with restrictions.
[SAVE] [S🐾] [✕] [🅷] [🖥] [🏊]

ⒶⒶⒶ 🔷🔷🔷 **Countryside Suites** 🅼
(402) 884-2644. **$60-$80.** 9477 S 142nd St. I-80, exit 440, just ne. Ext corridors. **Pets:** Very small, dogs only. $20 deposit/pet, $5 one-time fee/pet. Designated rooms, service with restrictions, supervision.
[SAVE] [✕] [&M] [🅷] [🖥]

🔷🔷🔷🔷 **Crowne Plaza Hotel and Resort Omaha-Old Mill** 🅻🅷
(402) 496-0850. **$79-$189.** 655 N 108th Ave. I-680, exit 3 (Dodge St W), 0.7 mi to 108th St to 108th Ave and N Old Mill Rd exits, then just n. Int corridors. **Pets:** Large, other species. $100 deposit/pet, $25 one-time fee/pet. Service with restrictions, crate.
[ASK] [S🐾] [✕] [🔌] [&'] [🅷] [🖥] [🍽] [🏊] [✕]

ⒶⒶⒶ 🔷🔷🔷🔷 **Doubletree Guest Suites Omaha** 🅻🅷
(402) 397-5141. **$69-$189.** 7270 Cedar St. I-80, exit 449 (72nd St), 1.3 mi n. Int corridors. **Pets:** Medium. $50 one-time fee/room. Designated rooms, service with restrictions, supervision.
[SAVE] [✕] [🔌] [&'] [🅷] [🖥] [🍽] [🏊] [✕]

ⒶⒶⒶ 🔷🔷🔷🔷 **DoubleTree Hotel & Executive Meeting Center-Omaha Downtown** 🅻🅷
(402) 346-7600. **$79-$189.** 1616 Dodge St. Downtown. Int corridors. **Pets:** Other species. $50 deposit/room.
[SAVE] [✕] [&M] [🔌] [&'] [🅷] [🖥] [🍽] [🏊] [✕]

🔷 **Econo Lodge West Dodge** 🅼
(402) 391-7100. **$46-$74.** 7833 Dodge St. I-680, exit 3 (Dodge St E), 2.2 mi e. Ext corridors. **Pets:** Accepted.
[✕] [🅷] [🖥] [🏊]

ⒶⒶⒶ 🔷🔷🔷 **Hawthorn Suites** 🆂🅷
(402) 331-0101. **$89-$99.** 11025 M St. I-80, exit 445 (L St E), 0.3 mi e, just s on 108th St, then just w. Ext corridors. **Pets:** Medium. $6 one-time fee/pet. Service with restrictions, crate.
[SAVE] [S🐾] [✕] [🔌] [🅷] [🖥] [🏊] [✕]

🔷🔷🔷 **Homewood Suites** 🆂🅷
(402) 397-7500. **$89-$129.** 7010 Hascall St. I-80, exit 449 (72nd St), just n, then just e. Ext/int corridors. **Pets:** Accepted.
[ASK] [S🐾] [✕] [🔌] [&'] [🅷] [🖥] [🏊]

ⒶⒶⒶ 🔷🔷🔷🔷 **La Quinta Inn Omaha** 🆂🅷
(402) 493-1900. **$75-$105.** 3330 N 104th Ave. I-680, exit 4 (Maple St), just w to 108th St, just n to Bedford, then just e. Int corridors. **Pets:** Service with restrictions, supervision.
[SAVE] [✕] [🔌] [🅷] [🖥] [🏊]

🔷🔷 **Ramada Limited** 🆂🅷
(402) 896-9500. **$68-$99, 5 day notice.** 9505 S 142nd St. I-80, exit 440, just ne. Int corridors. **Pets:** Medium, dogs only. $10 daily fee/pet. No service, crate.
[ASK] [S🐾] [✕] [&'] [🅷] [🖥] [🏊]

ⒶⒶⒶ 🔷🔷 **Relax Inn Motel & Suites** 🅼
(402) 731-7300. **$48-$60.** 4578 S 60th St. I-80, exit 450 (60th St), 0.8 mi s. Ext corridors. **Pets:** Very small, dogs only. $20 deposit/pet, $5 daily fee/pet. Designated rooms, service with restrictions, supervision.
[SAVE] [✕] [🅷] [🖥]

ⒶⒶⒶ 🔷🔷🔷🔷 **Residence Inn by Marriott** 🆂🅷
(402) 553-8898. **$126-$132.** 6990 Dodge St. I-680, exit 3 (Dodge St E), 3 mi e. Ext corridors. **Pets:** Accepted.
[SAVE] [✕] [🅷] [🖥] [🏊] [✕]

ⒶⒶⒶ 🔷🔷 **Satellite Motel** 🅼
(402) 733-7373. **$44-$46.** 6006 L St. I-80, exit 450 (60th St), 0.8 mi s; just n of US 275 and SR 92. Ext/int corridors. **Pets:** Very small, dogs only. $20 deposit/pet, $5 daily fee/pet. Designated rooms, service with restrictions, supervision.
[SAVE] [✕] [🅷] [🖥]

▼▼▼▼ Sheraton Omaha Hotel 🏨
(402) 342-2222. **$75-$199.** 1615 Howard St. Downtown. Int corridors.
Pets: Accepted.
(A$K) (S🐾) ⊗ 🐕 🐾 🐶 📶 💻 ▥ ⊠

▼▼ Super 8 Motel-Omaha/West Dodge 🆂🅷
(402) 492-8845. **$55-$65.** 11610 W Dodge Rd. I-680, exit 3 (Dodge St
W), 1.3 mi to 120 St, just n, then just e on Webster. Int corridors.
Pets: Other species. $10 daily fee/room. Designated rooms, service with
restrictions, crate.
(A$K) (S🐾) ⊗ (🐾M) 🐶 🐾

▼▼ Super 8 Motel-Omaha/West L 🆂🅷
(402) 339-2250. **$55-$65.** 10829 M St. I-80, exit 445 (L St E), just e;
entry off 108th St. Int corridors. **Pets:** Medium. $10 daily fee/pet. Service
with restrictions, supervision.
(A$K) (S🐾) ⊗ 🐶 🐾

O'NEILL

🅐🅐🅐 ▼ Elms Motel 🅜
(402) 336-3800. **$45-$55.** 414 E Hwy 20. 1 mi se on US 20/275. Ext
corridors. **Pets:** Medium, dogs only. Service with restrictions, supervision.
(SAVE) (S🐾) ⊗ 💻

🅐🅐🅐 ▼▼▼ Golden Hotel 🆂🅷 🐾
(402) 336-4436. **$36-$54.** 406 E Douglas St. Jct US 20/275/281; center. Ext/int corridors. **Pets:** Large. $7 one-time fee/pet. Service with restric-
tions, supervision.
(SAVE) (S🐾) ⊗ 🐶

▼▼▼▼ Holiday Inn Express Hotel & Suites 🆂🅷
(402) 336-4500. **$68-$85.** 1020 E Douglas St. 0.4 mi e on US 20/275.
Int corridors. **Pets:** Dogs only. $10 daily fee/pet. Service with restrictions.
(A$K) ⊗ (🐾M) 🐶 💻 🐾

▼▼ Super 8 Motel-O'Neill 🆂🅷
(402) 336-3100. **$49-$65.** 106 E Hwy 20. 0.5 mi e on US 20/275. Int
corridors. **Pets:** $10 daily fee/pet. Service with restrictions, supervision.
(A$K) (S🐾) ⊗ (🐾M) 🐶 🐾 🐶

PAXTON

🅐🅐🅐 ▼▼▼ Paxton Days Inn 🅜
(308) 239-4510. **$55-$75.** 851 Paxton Rd. I-80, exit 145, just n. Ext
corridors. **Pets:** Other species. $10 daily fee/room. Designated rooms,
service with restrictions, supervision.
(SAVE) (S🐾) ⊗ 🐾 🐶 💻 ▥ ⊠

ST. PAUL

▼▼ Super 8 Motel 🆂🅷
(308) 754-4554. **$58-$61.** 116 Howard Ave. Just e of downtown, jct US
281. Ext/int corridors. **Pets:** Accepted.
(A$K) (S🐾) ⊗ 🐶 🐶

SCOTTSBLUFF

🅐🅐🅐 ▼ Capri Motel 🅜
(308) 635-2057. **$38-$45.** 2424 Ave I. 1.5 mi nw, just s of 27th St. Ext
corridors. **Pets:** Other species. $5 daily fee/room. Service with restrictions,
crate.
(SAVE) (S🐾) ⊗ 🐶 💻

▼▼▼ Comfort Inn 🆂🅷
(308) 632-7510. **$66-$80.** 1902 21st Ave. 1.8 mi e on US 26, just n.
Ext/int corridors. **Pets:** Other species. Service with restrictions, supervision.
(A$K) (S🐾) ⊗ 🐾 🐶 🐶 💻 🐾

▼▼▼ Lamplighter American Inn 🆂🅷
(308) 632-7108. **$38-$48.** 606 E 27th St. US 26 business route, 0.5 mi
e of jct SR 71, just s. Int corridors. **Pets:** Dogs only. $6 daily fee/pet.
Service with restrictions, supervision.
(A$K) (S🐾) ⊗ 🐶 ▥ 🐾

SEWARD

▼▼ Seward Super 8 🅜
(402) 643-3388. **$51-$61.** 1329 Progressive Rd. I-80, exit 379, 3 mi n
on SR 15. Ext/int corridors. **Pets:** Accepted.
(A$K) (S🐾) ⊗ 🐶 🐶

SIDNEY

🅐🅐🅐 ▼▼▼ AmericInn Motel & Suites of Sidney 🆂🅷 🐾
(308) 254-0100. **$84-$159.** 645 Cabela Dr. I-80, exit 59, just nw. Int
corridors. **Pets:** Other species. Service with restrictions, crate.
(SAVE) (S🐾) ⊗ (🐾M) 🐾 🐶 🐶 💻 🐾

🅐🅐🅐 ▼▼▼ Days Inn 🆂🅷
(308) 254-2121. **$54-$110, 5 day notice.** 3042 Silverberg Dr. I-80, exit
59, just n. Int corridors. **Pets:** Medium. $10 one-time fee/pet. Designated
rooms, service with restrictions, supervision.
(SAVE) (S🐾) ⊗ 🐶 💻 🐾

▼▼▼▼ Holiday Inn & Conference Center 🆂🅷
(308) 254-2000. **Call for rates.** 664 Chase Blvd. I-80, exit 59, just s. Int
corridors. **Pets:** $10 daily fee/pet.
⊗ (🐾M) 🐾 🐶 🐶 💻 ▥ 🐾 ⊠

SOUTH SIOUX CITY

▼▼▼▼ Marina Inn Conference Center 🆂🅷
(402) 494-4000. **$94-$109.** 4th & B sts. I-29, exit 148, on banks of
Missouri River (e at stop light by Nebraska side of bridge). Int corridors. **Pets:** Accepted.
(A$K) (S🐾) ⊗ (🐾M) 🐾 🐶 🐶 💻 ▥ 🐾

SYRACUSE

🅐🅐🅐 ▼▼▼ Sleep Inn & Suites 🆂🅷
(402) 269-2700. **$66-$125.** 130 N 30th Rd. Jct SR 2, 1 mi n on SR 50.
Int corridors. **Pets:** Other species. $10 daily fee/pet.
(SAVE) (S🐾) ⊗ (🐾M) 🐾 🐶 🐶 💻 🐾

THEDFORD

🅐🅐🅐 ▼▼▼ Rodeway Inn 🆂🅷
(308) 645-2284. **$56-$72.** HC 58 Box 1D. 1 mi e on SR 2, just w of US
83. Int corridors. **Pets:** Other species. $25 deposit/room, $7 daily fee/
room. Designated rooms, service with restrictions, supervision.
(SAVE) (S🐾) ⊗ (🐾M) 🐾 🐶 💻

VALENTINE

▼▼▼ Dunes Motel 🅜
(402) 376-3131. **$44-$74.** 304 E Hwy 20 & 83. Jct US 20/83, 0.3 mi e.
Ext corridors. **Pets:** $10 daily fee/pet. Designated rooms, service with
restrictions, supervision.
(A$K) (S🐾) ⊗ 🐶

🅐🅐🅐 ▼ Motel Raine 🅜
(402) 376-2030. **$40-$60.** 618 W Hwy 20 W. Jct US 20/83, 0.5 mi sw.
Ext corridors. **Pets:** Accepted.
(SAVE) ⊗ 💻

🅐🅐🅐 ▼▼▼ Trade Winds Motel 🅜
(402) 376-1600. **$40-$69.** E Hwy 20 & 83. Jct US 20/83, 1 mi se. Ext
corridors. **Pets:** Other species. $3 daily fee/pet. Service with restrictions,
supervision.
(SAVE) (S🐾) ⊗ 🐶 💻 🐾

WAHOO

▼▼ Wahoo Heritage Inn 🆂🅷
(402) 443-1288. **$55-$79.** 950 N Chestnut. On US 77 and SR 92, just
nw of downtown. Ext/int corridors. **Pets:** $25 deposit/pet, $10 daily fee/
pet. Service with restrictions, supervision.
(A$K) (S🐾) ⊗ (🐾M) 🐶 💻

YORK

Best Western Palmer Inn [M]
(402) 362-5585. **$45-$62.** 2426 S Lincoln Ave. I-80, exit 353 (US 81), 1 mi n. Ext corridors. **Pets:** $10 daily fee/room. Designated rooms, supervision.
[SAVE] [S/D] [X] [🖥] [📺] [➰]

Yorkshire Inn Motel [M]
(402) 362-6633. **$42-$59.** 3402 S Lincoln Ave. I-80, exit 353 (US 81), 0.5 mi n. Ext/int corridors. **Pets:** Accepted.
[ASK] [S/D] [X] [🖥]

NEVADA

AMARGOSA VALLEY

▼▼▼▼ Longstreet Inn, Casino & RV Park SH
(775) 372-1777. **$69-$99.** 373 Stateline. 7 mi n of jct SR 127 and 190 (Death Valley Jct) on SR 373; 15 mi s of jct SR 95 and 373 on SR 373. Int corridors. **Pets:** Dogs only. $150 deposit/pet. Service with restrictions.
(ASK) (S🐾) (✕) (🍴) (➦)

BATTLE MOUNTAIN

AAA ▼▼▼ Big Chief Motel M
(775) 635-2416. **$39-$42.** 434 W Front St. I-80, exit 229 or 233, just n. Ext corridors. **Pets:** Other species. $5 one-time fee/pet. Designated rooms, supervision.
(SAVE) (✕) (🖉) (🎞) (➦)

AAA ▼▼▼ Comfort Inn M
(775) 635-5880. **$50-$89.** 521 E Front St. I-80, exit 229 or 233, just n. Int corridors. **Pets:** Other species. $10 one-time fee/room. Designated rooms, service with restrictions, crate.
(SAVE) (S🐾) (✕) (🖉) (🎞) (📺) (➦)

BEATTY

▼ Amargosa River Inn M
(775) 553-2250. **$27-$44.** 350 First St. Just off SR 95. Ext corridors. **Pets:** Other species. $5 one-time fee/pet. Designated rooms, supervision.
(ASK) (S🐾) (✕) (🎞)

▼ Burro Inn M
(775) 553-2225. **$44.** Third St & Hwy 95. 4 blks s on SR 95. Ext corridors. **Pets:** Accepted.
(ASK) (S🐾) (✕) (🖉) (🍴)

AAA ▼▼▼ Stagecoach Hotel Casino M
(775) 553-2419. **$40-$75.** Hwy 95 N. North end of town, west side of US 95. Ext/int corridors. **Pets:** Other species. $10 deposit/room, $5 one-time fee/room. Designated rooms, service with restrictions, supervision.
(SAVE) (✕) (♿M) (📶) (🎞) (📺) (🍴) (➦)

CARLIN

AAA ▼▼▼ Comfort Inn M
(775) 754-6110. **$59-$89.** 1018 Fir St. I-80, exit 280, just s. Int corridors. **Pets:** Large, other species. $100 deposit/room, $10 daily fee/room. Service with restrictions, supervision.
(SAVE) (S🐾) (✕) (♿M) (🖉) (📶) (🎞) (📺)

CARSON CITY

AAA ▼▼▼ Best Value Inn M
(775) 882-2007. **$42-$250.** 2731 S Carson St. 1.3 mi s on US 50 and 395. Ext corridors. **Pets:** Other species. $50 deposit/pet. Service with restrictions, supervision.
(SAVE) (S🐾) (✕) (🎞) (➦)

AAA ▼▼▼ Best Western Trailside Inn M
(775) 883-7300. **$55-$199.** 1300 N Carson St. 0.5 mi n on US 395. Ext corridors. **Pets:** Other species. $10 daily fee/pet. Service with restrictions, supervision.
(SAVE) (S🐾) (✕) (🎞) (📺) (➦)

AAA ▼▼ Carson City Super 8 M
(775) 883-7800. **$34-$199.** 2829 S Carson. South end of town. Int corridors. **Pets:** Medium, other species. $8 daily fee/pet. Designated rooms, service with restrictions, supervision.
(SAVE) (S🐾) (✕) (🎞)

AAA ▼▼ Days Inn M
(775) 883-3343. **$46-$160.** 3103 N Carson St. US 395 N, north end of city. Ext corridors. **Pets:** Large. $50 deposit/room, $10 daily fee/pet. Service with restrictions, supervision.
(SAVE) (S🐾) (✕) (🎞) (📺)

▼▼▼ Holiday Inn Express & Suites M
(775) 283-4055. **$99-$269, 7 day notice.** 4055 N Carson St. US 395; north end of town. Int corridors. **Pets:** $20 one-time fee/room. Designated rooms, service with restrictions, supervision.
(ASK) (S🐾) (✕) (♿M) (🎞) (🎞) (📺) (➦)

ELKO

AAA ▼▼▼▼ Best Western Gold Country Motor Inn M
(775) 738-8421. **$79-$109.** 2050 Idaho St. I-80, exit 303, just s. Ext corridors. **Pets:** Other species. $15 one-time fee/room. Designated rooms.
(SAVE) (S🐾) (✕) (♿M) (🖉) (📶) (🎞) (📺) (🍴) (➦)

AAA ▼▼▼▼ Comfort Inn M
(775) 777-8762. **$59-$89.** 2970 Idaho St. I-80, exit 303, just s, then just e. Int corridors. **Pets:** Small, dogs only. $10 one-time fee/pet. Designated rooms, service with restrictions, supervision.
(SAVE) (S🐾) (✕) (♿M) (📶) (🎞) (📺) (➦) (✕)

AAA ▼▼▼▼ High Desert Inn SH
(775) 738-8425. **$69.** 3015 Idaho St. I-80, exit 303, just s. Ext/int corridors. **Pets:** Accepted.
(SAVE) (S🐾) (✕) (🖉) (🎞) (📺) (🍴) (➦)

AAA ▼▼▼ Oak Tree Inn M
(775) 777-2222. **$49-$79.** 95 Spruce Rd. I-80, exit 301, just n. Int corridors. **Pets:** Other species. $10 daily fee/pet. Service with restrictions, crate.
(SAVE) (S🐾) (✕) (♿M) (📶) (🎞) (📺)

AAA ▼▼▼▼ Red Lion Inn Hotel & Casino Elko SH
(775) 738-2111. **$89-$109.** 2065 Idaho St. I-80, exit 303, just s. Int corridors. **Pets:** Large, other species. $15 one-time fee/room. No service, supervision.
(SAVE) (S🐾) (✕) (♿M) (🖉) (📺) (🍴) (➦)

▼▼▼ Shilo Inn M 🐾
(775) 738-5522. **$80-$129.** 2401 Mountain City Hwy. I-80, exit 301, just n. Int corridors. **Pets:** $10 daily fee/pet. Service with restrictions, supervision.
(ASK) (S🐾) (✕) (🎞) (📺) (➦) (✕)

AAA ▼▼▼ Thunderbird Motel M
(775) 738-7115. **$59-$69.** 345 Idaho St. I-80, exit 301 or 303, 1 mi s. Ext corridors. **Pets:** Accepted.
(SAVE) (✕) (🖉) (🎞) (➦)

ELY

4 Sevens Motel M
(775) 289-4747. **$30-$45.** 500 High St. Just n of 5th St; downtown. Ext corridors. **Pets:** Service with restrictions, crate.

Fireside Inn M
(775) 289-3765. **$46.** McGill Hwy. 2 mi n on US 95. Ext corridors. **Pets:** Medium. $5 daily fee/pet. Service with restrictions, supervision.

Historic Hotel Nevada & Gambling Hall SH
(775) 289-6665. **$30-$85.** 501 Aultman St. Downtown. Int corridors. **Pets:** Designated rooms, service with restrictions, crate.

Ramada Inn-Copper Queen Casino M
(775) 289-4884. **$67-$115.** 805 Great Basin Blvd. 0.3 mi s of jct US 6, 50 and 93. Ext/int corridors. **Pets:** Large, other species. Service with restrictions, supervision.

FALLON

Comfort Inn M
(775) 423-5554. **$60-$150.** 1830 W Williams Ave. US 50, 1 mi w of US 95. Int corridors. **Pets:** Other species. $50 deposit/pet, $6 daily fee/pet. Service with restrictions, supervision.

Motel 6 #4140 M
(775) 423-2277. **$46-$70.** 1705 S Taylor St. 0.5 mi s of US 50. Ext corridors. **Pets:** Medium. Service with restrictions, supervision.

Super 8 Motel M
(775) 423-6031. **$50.** 855 W Williams Ave. US 50, 0.5 mi w of US 95. Ext/int corridors. **Pets:** Other species. $5 daily fee/pet. Designated rooms, no service.

FERNLEY

Best Western Fernley Inn M
(775) 575-6776. **$67-$90, 5 day notice.** 1405 E Newlands Dr. I-80, exit 48, just s. Ext corridors. **Pets:** $7 daily fee/pet. Designated rooms, service with restrictions, supervision.

GARDNERVILLE

Best Western Topaz Lake Inn M
(775) 266-4661. **$50-$139.** 3410 Sandy Bowers Ave. US 395 at Topaz Lake, 22 mi s. Ext/int corridors. **Pets:** Medium. $10 daily fee/pet. Designated rooms, service with restrictions, supervision.

Topaz Lodge M
(775) 266-3338. **$29-$79.** 1979 US 395 S. US 395 S at Topaz Lake, 22 mi s. Ext corridors. **Pets:** Small, dogs only. $10 daily fee/pet. Designated rooms, service with restrictions.

Westerner Motel M
(775) 782-3602. **$40-$70.** 1353 US 395 N. US 395 S; end of town. Ext corridors. **Pets:** Other species. Designated rooms, service with restrictions, supervision.

HAWTHORNE

El Capitan Resort Casino M
(775) 945-3321. **$50-$55.** 540 F St. Just n of US 95. Ext corridors. **Pets:** Accepted.

JACKPOT

Horseshu Hotel & Casino SH
(775) 755-7777. **$29-$85.** 1385 Hwy 93. On SR 93. Int corridors. **Pets:** Large, other species. Designated rooms, service with restrictions, crate.

West Star Resort M
(775) 755-2600. **$32-$125.** Hwy 93 & Poker St. Just w of SR 93. Int corridors. **Pets:** Accepted.

NEARBY CALIFORNIA
LAKE TAHOE AREA

STATELINE

Harrah's Hotel & Casino LH
(775) 588-6611. **$69-$299, 3 day notice.** Hwy 50. In casino area. Int corridors. **Pets:** Accepted.

Harveys Casino & Resort LH
(775) 588-2411. **$39-$289, 3 day notice.** US 50, in casino center. Int corridors. **Pets:** Accepted.

Lake Village Resort CO
(775) 589-6065. **$155-$450, 30 day notice.** 301 Hwy 50. Near casino center. Ext corridors. **Pets:** Dogs only. $100 deposit/room, $20 daily fee/pet. Designated rooms, service with restrictions.

END AREA

LAS VEGAS METROPOLITAN AREA

BOULDER CITY

El Rancho Boulder Motel M
(702) 293-1085. **$65-$105, 7 day notice.** 725 Nevada Way. On US 93. Ext corridors. **Pets:** Accepted.

SAVE ⊠ 🔒 📺 ⇝

Super 8 Motel M
(702) 294-8888. **$59-$128.** 704 Nevada Way. On US 93. Ext corridors. **Pets:** Medium, dogs only. $10 daily fee/pet. Designated rooms, service with restrictions, supervision.

A$K S⊙ ⊠ ⟨ 🔒 ⇝

ECHO BAY

Echo Bay Resort M
(702) 394-4000. **$60-$115, 3 day notice.** 4 mi e of SR 167; on Lake Mead. Int corridors. **Pets:** Accepted.

SAVE ⊠ ♿ ⟨ 📺 ⊞ ⌐

HENDERSON

Green Valley Ranch LH
(702) 617-7777. **$250-$500.** 2300 S Paseo Verde Dr. I-215, exit Green Valley Pkwy, just s. **Pets:** Accepted.

SAVE S⊙ ⊠ ♿ ⟨ 📺 ⊞ ⇝ ⌐

Hawthorn Inn & Suites M ❧
(702) 568-7800. **$99-$199, 3 day notice.** 910 S Boulder Hwy. S of Lake Mead Blvd. Int corridors. **Pets:** Other species. $20 daily fee/room. Service with restrictions.

SAVE S⊙ ⊠ ⟨ 🔒 ⇝

Holiday Inn Express & Suites M
(702) 990-2323. **$89-$199.** 441 Astaire Dr. I-215, exit Stephanie St N, 1.8 mi; exit Warm Springs Rd, just e, then just s. Ext/int corridors. **Pets:** Accepted.

A$K S⊙ ⊠ 🔒 📺 ⇝

Residence Inn-Green Valley M
(702) 434-2700. **$139.** 2190 Olympic Ave. I-215, exit Green Valley Pkwy N, at Sunset Rd. Int corridors. **Pets:** Accepted.

⊠ ♿ ⟨ 🔒 📺 ⇝ ⌐

The Ritz-Carlton, Lake Las Vegas LH ❧
(702) 567-4700. **$199-$589.** 1610 Lake Las Vegas Pkwy. I-215, e to end, n on Lake Las Vegas Pkwy, then 0.5 mi on right. Int corridors. **Pets:** Small. $125 one-time fee/room. Designated rooms, service with restrictions, supervision.

SAVE ⊠ ♿ ⟨ 📺 ⊞ ⇝ ⌐

INDIAN SPRINGS

Indian Springs Motor Hotel M
(702) 879-3700. **$41-$51.** 300 Tonopah Hwy. On US 95, 45 mi n of Las Vegas. Int corridors. **Pets:** Medium, other species. $50 deposit/room, $5 daily fee/pet. Service with restrictions, crate.

SAVE S⊙ ⊠ 🔒 ⊞

LAS VEGAS

AmeriSuites (Las Vegas/Paradise Road) SH
(702) 369-3366. **$69-$159.** 4520 Paradise Rd. Cross streets Harmon Ave and Paradise Rd, e of the Strip. Int corridors. **Pets:** Small. $10 daily fee/pet. Designated rooms, service with restrictions, supervision.

SAVE S⊙ ⊠ ♿ ⟨ ⟨ 🔒 📺 ⇝

Best Western Main Street Inn M
(702) 382-3455. **$49-$159.** 1000 N Main St. I-15, exit 43E northbound; exit 44E southbound. Ext corridors. **Pets:** Other species. $15 daily fee/pet. Service with restrictions, supervision.

SAVE S⊙ ⊠ 🔒 📺 ⊞ ⇝

Best Western Nellis Motor Inn M
(702) 643-6111. **$55-$200.** 5330 E Craig Rd. I-15, exit 48 eastbound, 7 mi ne; 0.3 mi from Nellis AFB. Ext corridors. **Pets:** Large, other species. $10 daily fee/pet. Designated rooms, service with restrictions, supervision.

SAVE S⊙ ⊠ 🔒 📺 ⇝

Best Western Parkview Inn M
(702) 385-1213. **$49-$169, 14 day notice.** 921 Las Vegas Blvd N. I-15, exit US 93-95, 0.3 mi n at Washington. Ext corridors. **Pets:** Small, other species. $8 daily fee/pet. Service with restrictions, supervision.

SAVE S⊙ ⊠ 📺 ⇝

Candlewood Suites SH
(702) 836-3660. **$89-$209.** 4034 S Paradise Rd. I-15, exit E Flamingo Rd to Paradise Rd, just ne. Int corridors. **Pets:** Accepted.

A$K S⊙ ⊠ ♿ ⟨ 🔒 📺 ⇝

Comfort Inn M
(702) 399-1500. **$79-$299.** 910 E Cheyenne Ave. I-15, exit 46 (Cheyenne Ave W). Int corridors. **Pets:** $10 daily fee/pet. Designated rooms, service with restrictions, supervision.

A$K S⊙ ⊠ ♿ ⟨ 🔒 📺 ⇝

Hawthorn Suites-Las Vegas M
(702) 739-7000. **$79-$169, 3 day notice.** 5051 Duke Ellington Way. I-15, exit E Tropicana Ave, 0.8 mi e to Duke Ellington Way, then just s. Ext corridors. **Pets:** Accepted.

A$K S⊙ ⊠ ♿ ⟨ ⟨ 🔒 📺 ⇝ ⌐

Holiday Inn Express M ❧
(702) 256-3766. **$79-$169.** 8669 W Sahara Ave. I-15, exit Sahara Ave, 6.5 mi w at Durango. Int corridors. **Pets:** Medium. $25 daily fee/pet. Service with restrictions, crate.

SAVE S⊙ ⊠ ⟨ 🔒 📺 ⇝

Holiday Inn Express SH
(702) 736-0098. **$89-$229.** 5760 Polaris Ave. I-15, exit Russell Rd, just w. Int corridors. **Pets:** Accepted.

A$K S⊙ ⊠ ♿ ⟨ 🔒 📺 ⇝

Holiday Inn Express Hotel & Suites N Las Vegas M
(702) 649-3000. **$99-$149.** 4540 Donovan Way. I-15, exit W Craig Rd. Int corridors. **Pets:** Small, other species. $25 one-time fee/pet. Designated rooms, supervision.

A$K ⊠ ♿ ⟨ 🔒 📺 ⇝

Homestead Studio Suites Hotel-Las Vegas/Midtown M ❧
(702) 369-1414. **$69-$84.** 3045 S Maryland Pkwy. I-15, exit Sahara Ave E, just s. Int corridors. **Pets:** Other species. $75 daily fee/room. Service with restrictions, supervision.

A$K S⊙ ⊠ ♿ ⟨ 🔒 📺

Howard Johnson Airport Inn M
(702) 798-2777. **$32-$129.** 5100 Paradise Rd. I-15, exit E Tropicana Ave, 1.8 mi to Paradise Rd, then 0.3 mi s. Ext corridors. **Pets:** Other species. $50 one-time fee/room. Designated rooms, service with restrictions, supervision.

A$K S⊙ ⊠ ⟨ ⟨ 🔒 📺 ⊞ ⇝

Howard Johnson Las Vegas Strip M
(702) 388-0301. **$49-$169.** 1401 Las Vegas Blvd S. I-15, exit Las Vegas Blvd, just n. Ext/int corridors. **Pets:** Small. $10 daily fee/pet. Designated rooms, service with restrictions, supervision.

SAVE S⊙ ⊠ 🔒 📺 ⊞ ⇝

▼▼▼ **La Quinta Inn & Suites Las Vegas (Summerlin Tech Center)** Ⓜ
(702) 360-1200. **$105-$125.** 7101 Cascade Valley Ct. US 95, exit W Cheyenne Ave. Int corridors. **Pets:** Accepted.
🅰🆂🅺 ☒ 🏃M 🛎 🍴 💻 ≈

Ⓐ ▼▼▼ **La Quinta Inn & Suites Las Vegas (West/Lakes)** Ⓜ
(702) 243-0356. **$89-$309.** 9570 W Sahara Ave. Just w of Fort Apache. Int corridors. **Pets:** Accepted.
🆂🅰🆅🅴 ☒ 🏃M 🛎 🍴 💻 ≈

▼▼▼ **La Quinta Inn Las Vegas (Convention Center)** Ⓜ
(702) 796-9000. **$109-$159.** 3970 Paradise Rd. I-15, exit E Flamingo Rd, 0.8 mi s of convention center; 0.5 mi e of the Strip. Int corridors. **Pets:** Accepted.
🅰🆂🅺 ☒ 🛎 🍴 💻 🍴 ≈

▼▼▼ **La Quinta Inn Las Vegas (Nellis)** Ⓜ 🐾
(702) 632-0229. **$89-$199, 3 day notice.** 4288 N Nellis Blvd. I-15, exit Craig Rd, e to N Las Vegas Blvd. Int corridors. **Pets:** Other species. Service with restrictions.
🅰🆂🅺 ☒ 🏃M 🖊 🛎 🍴 💻 ≈

Ⓐ ▼▼▼ **La Quinta Inn Las Vegas (Tropicana)** Ⓜ
(702) 798-7736. **$59-$160, 14 day notice.** 4975 S Valley View Blvd. I-15, exit Tropicana Ave W. Int corridors. **Pets:** Accepted.
🆂🅰🆅🅴 ☒ 🏃M 🛎 🍴 💻 ≈

▼ **Motel 6 Boulder Highway** Ⓜ
(702) 457-8051. **$42-$100.** 4125 Boulder Hwy. Just s of Sahara Ave. Ext corridors. **Pets:** Accepted.
☒ 🛎 ≈

▼▼ **Ramada Inn-Speedway Casino** Ⓜ
(702) 399-3297. **Call for rates.** 3227 Civic Ctr Dr. I-15, exit 46E (Cheyenne Ave). Int corridors. **Pets:** Small. $10 daily fee/pet. Designated rooms, service with restrictions, crate.
🆂🅰 ☒ 🏃M 🛎 🍴 ≈

▼▼▼ **Residence Inn by Marriott Las Vegas South** Ⓜ
(702) 795-7378. **Call for rates.** 5875 Industrial Rd. I-15, exit Russell Rd, just sw. Int corridors. **Pets:** Small, other species. $75 one-time fee/room. Service with restrictions.
☒ 🏃M 🛎 🍴 💻 ≈ ☒

▼▼▼ **Residence Inn-Hughes Center** Ⓜ
(702) 650-0040. **$139-$299.** 370 Hughes Center Dr. I-15, exit Paradise Rd. Int corridors. **Pets:** Accepted.
🅰🆂🅺 🆂🅰 ☒ 🏃M 🖊 🛎 🍴 💻 ≈

▼▼▼ **Residence Inn Las Vegas Convention Center** Ⓜ
(702) 796-9300. **$139-$349.** 3225 Paradise Rd. Opposite the convention center. Ext corridors. **Pets:** Accepted.
🆂🅰 ☒ 🏃M 🖊 🛎 🍴 💻 ≈

▼▼▼ **St. Tropez All Suite Hotel** 🆂🅷
(702) 369-5400. **$69-$189.** 455 E Harmon Ave. 2 mi s of convention center at Paradise Rd. Ext/int corridors. **Pets:** Accepted.
🅰🆂🅺 🆂🅰 ☒ 🏃M 🖊 🖊 🛎 🍴 💻 ≈

▼▼▼ **Super 8 Motel Las Vegas Strip** Ⓜ
(702) 794-0888. **$61-$150.** 4250 S Koval Ln. I-15, exit S Koval Ln. Int corridors. **Pets:** Large, other species. $15 daily fee/pet. Designated rooms, service with restrictions, supervision.
🅰🆂🅺 🆂🅰 ☒ 🖊 ≈

Ⓐ ▼▼▼ **Wellesley Inn & Suites (Las Vegas/East Flamingo)** Ⓜ
(702) 731-3111. **$99-$149.** 1550 E Flamingo Rd. I-15, exit E Flamingo Rd, 2 mi. Int corridors. **Pets:** Accepted.
🆂🅰🆅🅴 🆂🅰 ☒ 🏃M 🖊 🖊 🛎 🍴 💻 ≈

Ⓐ ▼▼▼ **The Westin Casuarina Las Vegas Hotel & Spa** 🅻🅷
(702) 836-9775. **$139-$299, 3 day notice.** 160 E Flamingo Rd. I-15, exit Flamingo Rd E. Int corridors. **Pets:** Accepted.
🆂🅰🆅🅴 🆂🅰 ☒ 🏃M 🖊 💻 🍴 ≈ ☒

LAUGHLIN

▼▼▼ **Don Laughlin's Riverside Resort Hotel & Casino** 🅻🅷
(702) 298-2535. **$39-$199, 7 day notice.** 1650 S Casino Dr. 2 mi s of Davis Dam. Int corridors. **Pets:** Accepted.
🅰🆂🅺 ☒ 🏃M 🖊 🖊 🛎 🍴 💻 🍴 ≈ ☒

Ⓐ ▼▼▼ **Edgewater Hotel/Casino** 🅻🅷
(702) 298-2453. **$39-$350.** 2020 S Casino Dr. 2.3 mi s of Davis Dam. Int corridors. **Pets:** Small. $100 deposit/room. Designated rooms.
🆂🅰🆅🅴 ☒ 🏃M 🖊 🖊 💻 🍴 ≈

MESQUITE

Ⓐ ▼▼ **Best Western Mesquite Inn** Ⓜ
(702) 346-7444. **$65-$85.** 390 N Sandhill. I-15, exit 122. Ext corridors. **Pets:** Medium. $10 daily fee/pet. Designated rooms, service with restrictions, supervision.
🆂🅰🆅🅴 🆂🅰 ☒ 🖊 🛎 🍴 💻 ≈

▼▼ **Virgin River Hotel Casino Bingo** Ⓜ
(702) 346-7777. **$22-$99.** 100 Pioneer Blvd. I-15, exit 122, just w. Ext corridors. **Pets:** Other species. $25 deposit/room. Designated rooms, service with restrictions, supervision.
☒ 🏃M 🖊 🍴 ≈ ☒

OVERTON

▼▼▼ **Best Western North Shore Inn at Lake Mead** Ⓜ
(702) 397-6000. **$55-$79.** 520 N Moapa Valley Blvd. I-15, exit 93, 10 mi ne on SR 169. Int corridors. **Pets:** Medium. $10 daily fee/room. Designated rooms, service with restrictions, supervision.
🅰🆂🅺 🆂🅰 ☒ 🛎 💻 ≈

PAHRUMP

Ⓐ ▼▼ **Best Western Pahrump Station** Ⓜ
(775) 727-5100. **$61-$95, 7 day notice.** 1101 S Hwy 160. Downtown. Ext corridors. **Pets:** Small, dogs only. $7 daily fee/pet. Designated rooms, service with restrictions.
🆂🅰🆅🅴 🆂🅰 ☒ 🏃M 🖊 🛎 🍴 💻 🍴 ≈

Ⓐ ▼▼ **Saddle West Hotel & Casino** Ⓜ
(775) 727-1111. **$46-$86.** 1220 S Hwy 160. Downtown. Ext corridors. **Pets:** Medium. $100 deposit/room. Designated rooms, service with restrictions, supervision.
🆂🅰🆅🅴 🆂🅰 ☒ 🏃M 🖊 🛎 💻 🍴 ≈

END METROPOLITAN AREA

LOVELOCK

WWWW Ramada Inn-Sturgeon's Casino M
(775) 273-2971. **$63-$70.** 1420 Cornell Ave. I-80, exit 105 or 107, just n. Ext corridors. **Pets:** Other species. $5 one-time fee/room. Designated rooms, service with restrictions, supervision.

MINDEN

AAA WWWW Best Western Minden Inn M
(775) 782-7766. **$65-$109.** 1795 Ironwood Dr. US 395, exit Ironwood Dr W, 0.5 mi n of jct US 395 and SR 88. Ext corridors. **Pets:** Dogs only. $15 daily fee/pet. Service with restrictions, supervision.

WWWW Holiday Lodge M
(775) 782-2288. **$39-$50.** 1591 US 395 N. Center. Ext corridors. **Pets:** Small, dogs only. $20 deposit/pet, $5 daily fee/pet. Designated rooms, service with restrictions, supervision.

RENO

AAA WWWW A&A's Rodeway Inn & Spa M ❀
(775) 786-2500. **$45-$200.** 2050 Market St. I-395, exit W Mill St. Int corridors. **Pets:** Medium, other species. $10 one-time fee/pet. Service with restrictions, supervision.

AAA WWWW Airport Travelodge M ❀
(775) 786-2506. **$46-$200.** 2050-B Market St. I-395, exit W Mill St, just w. Int corridors. **Pets:** Medium, other species. $10 one-time fee/pet. Service with restrictions, supervision.

AAA WWWW Atlantis Casino Resort–Reno LH
(775) 825-4700. **$49-$169.** 3800 S Virginia St. 3 mi s on US 395. Ext/int corridors. **Pets:** Accepted.

AAA WWW Best Western Airport Plaza Hotel SH ❀
(775) 348-6370. **$59-$249.** 1981 Terminal Way. US 395, exit E Plumb Villanova. Int corridors. **Pets:** Small. $50 deposit/room, $10 daily fee/pet. Designated rooms, service with restrictions, supervision.

AAA WWW Days Inn M
(775) 786-4070. **$35-$185.** 701 E 7th St. I-80, exit Wells Ave, just s. Ext corridors. **Pets:** Accepted.

AAA WWW Easy 8 Motel M
(775) 322-4587. **$29-$200, 5 day notice.** 255 W 5th St. I-80, exit Keystone, 4 blks e. Ext corridors. **Pets:** Small. $25 deposit/pet. Designated rooms, service with restrictions.

WWWW Golden Phoenix Hotel & Casino LH
(775) 785-7100. **Call for rates.** 255 N Sierra St. I-80, exit S Virginia St. Int corridors. **Pets:** Accepted.

AAA WWWW Holiday Inn-Downtown SH ❀
(775) 786-5151. **$59-$269.** 1000 E 6th St. I-80, exit Wells Ave, 2 blks e. Int corridors. **Pets:** $15 daily fee/pet. Designated rooms, service with restrictions, supervision.

WWWW La Quinta Inn Reno (Airport) M
(775) 348-6100. **$75-$95.** 4001 Market St. US 395, exit airport northbound; exit Villanova Dr southbound. Ext corridors. **Pets:** Large, other species. Service with restrictions, supervision.

AAA WWWW Reno Downtown Travelodge M
(775) 329-3451. **$29-$199.** 655 W 4th St. I-80, exit Keystone, just e. Ext corridors. **Pets:** $8 daily fee/room. Designated rooms, service with restrictions, supervision.

AAA WWWW Residence Inn by Marriott M ❀
(775) 853-8800. **$79-$209.** 9845 Gateway Dr. US 395, exit S Meadows Pkwy, then e. Int corridors. **Pets:** $75 one-time fee/room.

WWWW Speakeasy Hotel SH
(775) 329-7400. **Call for rates.** 200 E 6th St. I-80, exit Wells Ave S, 3 blks w. Int corridors. **Pets:** Other species. $50 deposit/room, $15 daily fee/pet. Service with restrictions, supervision.

AAA WWWW Super 8 Motel-University M
(775) 329-3464. **$39-$140.** 1651 N Virginia St. Opposite University of Nevada. Ext corridors. **Pets:** Accepted.

AAA WWWW Super 8 Motel at Meadow Wood Courtyard M ❀
(775) 829-4600. **$49-$139.** 5851 S Virginia St. US 395 at S McCarran Blvd. Ext corridors. **Pets:** Other species. $10 daily fee/pet. Designated rooms, service with restrictions, supervision.

WWW Truckee River Lodge M
(775) 786-8888. **$53-$73.** 501 W 1st St. I-80, exit Virginia St, just w. Int corridors. **Pets:** Accepted.

AAA WWW Vagabond Inn M
(775) 825-7134. **$45-$79.** 3131 S Virginia St. 2.5 mi s on US 395. Ext corridors. **Pets:** $10 daily fee/pet. Designated rooms, service with restrictions, supervision.

SPARKS

AAA WWWW Quality Inn M
(775) 358-6900. **$69-$99, 3 day notice.** 55 E Nugget Ave. I-80, exit E McCarran Blvd, just s. Int corridors. **Pets:** Accepted.

TONOPAH

AAA WWWW Best Western Hi-Desert Inn M
(775) 482-3511. **$69-$89.** 320 Main St. On US 6 and 95. Int corridors. **Pets:** Dogs only. Designated rooms, service with restrictions, supervision.

AAA WWW Jim Butler Motel M
(775) 482-3577. **$52-$56.** 100 S Main St. On US 6 and 95; downtown. Ext corridors. **Pets:** Accepted.

WWW Ramada Inn-Tonopah Station M
(775) 482-9777. **$65-$70.** 1100 Main St. On US 6 and 95. Int corridors. **Pets:** Accepted.

UNIONVILLE

AAA WWW Old Pioneer Garden BB ❀
(775) 538-7585. **$85-$95 (no credit cards).** 2805 Unionville Rd. I-80, exit 149, 16 mi s, then 2.5 mi w. Int corridors. **Pets:** Large, other species.

VIRGINIA CITY

◆◆ Gold Hill Hotel BB
(775) 847-0111. **$45-$250.** 1540 Main St. 1 mi s on SR 342. Ext/int corridors. **Pets:** Small. $15 one-time fee/room. Designated rooms, service with restrictions, supervision.

ASK 🛏 🖵 🍽

WELLS

◆◆◆ ◆◆ Best Western Sage Inn M
(775) 752-3353. **$54-$74.** 576 6th St. I-80, exit 351 eastbound, 1 mi n, then 0.5 mi e; exit 352A westbound, 0.3 mi n, then 0.7 mi w. Ext corridors. **Pets:** Accepted.

SAVE 🛏 ✕ 🛏 🖵 🏊

◆◆◆ ◆◆ Super 8 Motel M
(775) 752-3384. **$38-$69.** 930 6th St. I-80, exit 351 eastbound, 1 mi n, then 0.8 mi e; 352A westbound, 0.3 mi n, then 0.5 mi w. Ext corridors. **Pets:** Accepted.

SAVE 🛏 ✕ 🛏 🏊

WEST WENDOVER

◆◆ Wendover Super 8 M
(775) 664-2888. **$39-$99, 3 day notice.** 1325 Wendover Blvd. I-80, exit 410, 0.5 mi w. Int corridors. **Pets:** Other species. $7 one-time fee/room. Service with restrictions, supervision.

ASK 🛏 ✕ 🐾 🛏

WINNEMUCCA

◆◆◆ ◆◆◆ Best Western Gold Country Inn M 🐾
(775) 623-6999. **$89-$119.** 921 W Winnemucca Blvd. I-80, exit 176 or 178, just s. Int corridors. **Pets:** Other species. $10 one-time fee/pet. Designated rooms, service with restrictions, supervision.

SAVE 🛏 ✕ 🛏 🖵 🏊

◆◆◆ ◆◆◆ Best Western Holiday Motel M
(775) 623-3684. **$49-$89.** 670 W Winnemucca Blvd. I-80, exit 176 or 178, just s. Ext corridors. **Pets:** Other species. $20 deposit/room. Designated rooms, service with restrictions, supervision.

SAVE 🛏 ✕ 🛏 🖵 🏊

◆◆◆ ◆◆◆ Days Inn M
(775) 623-3661. **$59-$89.** 511 W Winnemucca Blvd. I-80, exit 176 or 178, just s. Ext corridors. **Pets:** Other species. $10 one-time fee/room. Service with restrictions, crate.

SAVE 🛏 ✕ 🛏 🖵 🏊

◆◆◆ Holiday Inn Express M
(775) 623-3100. **$79-$109, 30 day notice.** 1987 W Winnemucca Blvd. I-80, exit 176, just s. Int corridors. **Pets:** Medium. $50 deposit/pet, $10 daily fee/pet, $10 one-time fee/pet. Designated rooms, service with restrictions, supervision.

ASK 🛏 ✕ 🛏 🐾 🛏 🛏 🖵 🏊

◆◆◆ ◆◆◆ Red Lion Hotel & Casino SH
(775) 623-2565. **$89-$119.** 741 W Winnemucca Blvd. I-80, exit 176 or 178, just s. Int corridors. **Pets:** Medium, other species. Service with restrictions, supervision.

SAVE 🛏 ✕ 🐾 🛏 🖵 🍽 🏊

◆◆◆ ◆◆ Scott Shady Court Motel M
(775) 623-3646. **$38-$55.** 400 First St. I-80, exit 176 or 178, 0.3 mi n on Pavilion. Ext corridors. **Pets:** Service with restrictions, supervision.

SAVE 🖵 🏊

◆◆ Super 8 Motel M
(775) 625-1818. **$54-$99.** 1157 W Winnemucca Blvd. I-80, exit 176, 0.5 mi e. Int corridors. **Pets:** Other species. $50 deposit/room, $10 one-time fee/room. Service with restrictions, supervision.

ASK 🛏 ✕ 🛏

◆◆◆ ◆◆◆ Town House Motel M
(775) 623-3620. **$40-$62.** 375 Monroe St. I-80, exit 176 or 178, just s. Ext corridors. **Pets:** Medium, dogs only. Service with restrictions, supervision.

SAVE 🛏 ✕ 🛏 🖵 🏊

NEW HAMPSHIRE

BARTLETT

AAA ▼▼ The Villager Motel **M**
(603) 374-2742. **$39-$149, 10 day notice.** US 302. 1 mi e on US 302; 1.3 mi w of Attitash Mountain. Ext corridors. **Pets:** Medium, other species. $8 daily fee/pet. Service with restrictions, supervision.

BETHLEHEM

▼▼▼ The Mulburn Inn at Bethlehem **BB** ❀
(603) 869-3389. **$90-$175, 14 day notice.** 2370 Main St. I-93, exit 40, 3.5 mi e on US 302. Int corridors. **Pets:** Other species. $25 one-time fee/pet. Designated rooms, supervision.

CHESTERFIELD

▼▼▼ Chesterfield Inn **CI**
(603) 256-3211. **$150-$250, 5 day notice.** 399 Cross Rd. I-91, exit 3, 2 mi e on SR 9. Ext/int corridors. **Pets:** Medium, other species. Service with restrictions, crate.

CHOCORUA

▼▼▼ The Lazy Dog Inn **BB** ❀
(603) 323-8350. **$85-$205, 14 day notice.** 201 White Mountain Hwy. On SR 16, 2.8 mi n of jct SR 25. Int corridors. **Pets:** Dogs only. Supervision.

CLAREMONT

AAA ▼▼ Best Budget Inn **M**
(603) 542-9567. **$53-$72, 3 day notice.** 24 Sullivan St. Just n of jct SR 11/12/103/120; center. Ext corridors. **Pets:** Medium, dogs only. $12 daily fee/pet. Designated rooms, service with restrictions, supervision.

COLEBROOK

AAA ▼▼▼ Northern Comfort Motel **M**
(603) 237-4440. **$64-$78, 3 day notice.** 1 Trooper Scott Phillips Hwy. 1.5 mi s on US 3. Ext corridors. **Pets:** Medium. $5 daily fee/pet. Service with restrictions, supervision.

CONCORD

AAA ▼▼▼ Best Western Concord Inn & Suites **SH**
(603) 228-4300. **$59-$199.** 97 Hall St. I-93, exit 13, just n on Main St, then 0.5 mi w. Int corridors. **Pets:** $15 daily fee/pet. Service with restrictions, supervision.

CONWAY

▼▼ White Deer Motel **M**
(603) 447-5366. **$59-$149, 7 day notice.** 379 White Mountain Hwy. 2.1 mi s of jct US 302; 0.5 mi n of village center on SR 16. Ext/int corridors. **Pets:** Large, other species. $35 deposit/room, $10 daily fee/pet. Designated rooms, service with restrictions, supervision.

DOVER

▼▼ Days Inn **M**
(603) 742-0400. **$79-$159.** 481 Central Ave. Spaulding Tpke, exit 7, 2 mi n on SR 108; downtown. Ext/int corridors. **Pets:** Other species. $50 deposit/room. Supervision.

DURHAM

▼▼ Hickory Pond Inn & Golf Course **CI**
(603) 659-2227. **$89-$149, 3 day notice.** 1 Stagecoach Rd. 2.8 mi s on SR 108. Int corridors. **Pets:** Accepted.

EATON CENTER

▼▼▼ Inn at Crystal Lake & Restaurant **CI**
(603) 447-2120. **$89-$239, 14 day notice.** 2356 Eaton Rd. On SR 153; center. Ext/int corridors. **Pets:** Accepted.

FRANCONIA

AAA ▼▼ Franconia Hotel **SH**
(603) 823-7422. **$69-$139, 3 day notice.** 87 Wallace Hill Rd. I-93, exit 38, just e. Int corridors. **Pets:** Accepted.

AAA ▼▼▼ Gale River Motel **M** ❀
(603) 823-5655. **$50-$105, 7 day notice.** 1 Main St. I-93, exit 38, 0.8 mi n on SR 18. Ext corridors. **Pets:** $10 daily fee/pet. Service with restrictions, supervision.

▼▼▼ Lovetts Inn by Lafayette Brook **CI**
(603) 823-7761. **$125-$335, 7 day notice.** 1474 Profile Rd. I-93, exit 38, just w on Wallace Hill Rd, then 2.1 mi s on SR 18. Ext/int corridors. **Pets:** Accepted.

GORHAM

▼▼ Colonial Comfort Inn **M**
(603) 466-2732. **$45-$125, 3 day notice.** 370 Main St. Jct US 2 and SR 16. Ext corridors. **Pets:** Other species. Service with restrictions, supervision.

▼▼ Moose Brook Motel **M**
(603) 466-5400. **$39-$79, 5 day notice.** 65 Lancaster Rd. Jct SR 16, 0.5 mi w on US 2. Ext corridors. **Pets:** Other species. $5 one-time fee/pet. Designated rooms, service with restrictions, supervision.

Mt Madison Motel M
(603) 466-3622. **$47-$124, 3 day notice.** 365 Main St. On US 2, at jct SR 16 N. Ext corridors. **Pets:** Accepted.

Royalty Inn SH
(603) 466-3312. **$61-$104.** 130 Main St. On US 2 and SR 16; center. Ext/int corridors. **Pets:** Other species. $5 daily fee/pet. Designated rooms, service with restrictions.

Top Notch Inn M
(603) 466-5496. **$44-$142.** 265 Main St. On US 2 and SR 16; center. Ext/int corridors. **Pets:** Medium, dogs only. Designated rooms, service with restrictions, supervision.

Town & Country Motor Inn SH
(603) 466-3315. **$60-$110.** US Rt 2. 0.5 mi e of jct SR 16. Ext/int corridors. **Pets:** $6 daily fee/pet. Designated rooms, service with restrictions, supervision.

HAMPTON

The Inn of Hampton and Conference Center SH
(603) 926-6771. **$99-$189.** 815 Lafayette Rd. 0.5 mi n on US 1. Int corridors. **Pets:** Medium. Designated rooms, service with restrictions, supervision.

Lamie's Inn & Tavern CI
(603) 926-0330. **$115-$135, 3 day notice.** 490 Lafayette Rd. Jct SR 27 on US 1. Int corridors. **Pets:** Accepted.

HAMPTON FALLS

Hampton Falls Inn M
(603) 926-9545. **$69-$169.** 11 Lafayette Rd. I-95, exit 1, 0.5 mi e on SR 107, then 1 mi n on US 1. Int corridors. **Pets:** Medium, dogs only. $50 deposit/pet. Supervision.

HANCOCK

The Hancock Inn CI
(603) 525-3318. **$120-$275, 15 day notice.** 33 Main St. Jct of SR 123 and 137; center. Int corridors. **Pets:** Accepted.

HARTS LOCATION

Notchland Inn CI
(603) 374-6131. **$195-$245, 14 day notice.** US 302. On US 302, 6.4 mi w of Bartlett. Ext/int corridors. **Pets:** $10 daily fee/pet. Designated rooms, supervision.

JACKSON

The Inn at Jackson BB
(603) 383-4321. **$99-$209, 14 day notice.** Thorn Hill Rd. Jct SR 16, 0.4 mi e on SR 16A (through covered bridge). Ext/int corridors. **Pets:** $25 one-time fee/room. Designated rooms, service with restrictions.

KEENE

Best Western Sovereign Hotel SH
(603) 357-3038. **$79-$195.** 401 Winchester St. SR 10, just s of jct SR 12 and 101. Int corridors. **Pets:** Medium, other species. $10 daily fee/pet. Designated rooms, service with restrictions, supervision.

Holiday Inn Express SH
(603) 352-7616. **$119-$269.** 175 Key Rd. SR 101, just n, via Winchester St, then 0.3 mi w. Int corridors. **Pets:** $25 daily fee/pet. Service with restrictions, supervision.

Super 8 Keene SH
(603) 352-9780. **$69-$200.** 3 Ashbrook Rd. Jct SR 9 and 12, just w. Int corridors. **Pets:** $20 one-time fee/room. Service with restrictions, supervision.

LEBANON

Days Inn M
(603) 448-5070. **$89-$189.** 135 SR 120. I-89, exit 18, 0.8 mi n. Ext/int corridors. **Pets:** Accepted.

Residence Inn by Marriott-Lebanon SH
(603) 643-4511. **$119-$219.** 32 Centerra Pkwy. I-89, exit 18, 2.5 mi n on SR 120. Int corridors. **Pets:** Accepted.

LINCOLN

Parker's Motel M
(603) 745-8341. **$39-$99, 3 day notice.** 750 US Rt 3. I-93, exit 33 (US 3), 2 mi ne. Ext corridors. **Pets:** $5 daily fee/pet. Designated rooms, service with restrictions, supervision.

LITTLETON

Beal House Inn CI
(603) 444-2661. **$115-$245, 30 day notice.** 2 W Main St. I-93, exit 42, 0.8 mi e on US 302 and SR 10. Int corridors. **Pets:** Dogs only. $35 daily fee/pet. Designated rooms, service with restrictions, supervision.

Eastgate Motor Inn M
(603) 444-3971. **$59-$109.** 335 Cottage St. I-93, exit 41, just e. Ext/int corridors. **Pets:** Accepted.

Thayers Inn SH
(603) 444-6469. **$59-$99, 3 day notice.** 111 Main St. I-93, exit 42, 1.3 mi e on US 302 and SR 10; center. Int corridors. **Pets:** Medium, dogs only. Designated rooms, supervision.

LOUDON

Lovejoy Farm Bed & Breakfast BB
(603) 783-4007. **$112-$139, 14 day notice.** 268 Lovejoy Rd. Jct SR 106 and 129, just w on SR 129, just nw on Village Rd, then 1.2 mi n. Int corridors. **Pets:** Accepted.

MANCHESTER

Comfort Inn SH
(603) 668-2600. **$65-$269.** 298 Queen City Ave. I-293, exit 4, just w. Int corridors. **Pets:** Accepted.

Holiday Inn Express Hotel & Suites–Manchester Airport SH
(603) 669-6800. **$119-$179.** 1298 S Porter St. I-293, exit 1. Int corridors. **Pets:** Medium, other species. $50 deposit/room. Service with restrictions, crate.

WWW Homewood Suites by Hilton SH
(603) 668-2200. **$99-$199.** 1000 N Perimeter Rd. I-293, exit 2, follow signs to Manchester Airport. Int corridors. **Pets:** Large, other species. $100 one-time fee/room. Service with restrictions, crate.

ASK SD ✕ ⓒ 🛏 🖵 ⓦ

WWW Radisson Hotel Manchester LH
(603) 625-1000. **$109-$189.** 700 Elm St. Jct Granite St; downtown. Int corridors. **Pets:** Accepted.

ASK SD ✕ 🔊M ⬆ ⓒ 🛏 🖵 ⓦ 🔵 ✕

WWW ◆ TownePlace Suites by Marriott SH 🐾
(603) 641-2288. **$99-$169.** 686 Huse Rd. I-293, exit 1, 0.5 mi se on SR 28. Int corridors. **Pets:** Other species. $75 one-time fee/pet. Supervision.

ASK ✕ 🔊M 🛏 🖵 🔵

MERRIMACK

AAA WWW Days Inn Merrimack M
(603) 429-4600. **$55-$65.** 242 Daniel Webster Hwy. Everett Tpke, exit 11, just e, then 0.7 mi s on US 3. Int corridors. **Pets:** Accepted.

SAVE SD ✕ 🔊M ⬆ 🛏 🖵

WWW Residence Inn by Marriott SH 🐾
(603) 424-8100. **$109-$199.** 246 Daniel Webster Hwy. Everett Tpke, exit 11, just e, then 0.6 mi s on US 3. Ext/int corridors. **Pets:** Large, other species. $5 daily fee/room, $75 one-time fee/room. Designated rooms.

ASK ✕ 🔊M ⬆ ⓒ 🛏 🖵 🔵 ✕

NASHUA

WWW Holiday Inn Nashua SH
(603) 888-1551. **$89-$139.** 9 Northeastern Blvd. US 3 (Everett Tpke), exit 4, just w, then 0.3 mi n. Int corridors. **Pets:** $25 one-time fee/room. Service with restrictions, supervision.

ASK SD ✕ 🔊M ⬆ 🛏 🖵 ⓦ ✕

WWW Nashua Marriott LH
(603) 579-6005. **$89-$165.** 2200 Southwood Dr. US 3 (Everett Tpke), exit 8, just w. Int corridors. **Pets:** Accepted.

ASK ✕ 🔊M ⬆ 🛏 🖵 ⓦ ✕

WW Red Roof Inn #7122 M
(603) 888-1893. **$57-$80.** 77 Spitbrook Rd. US 3 (Everett Tpke), exit 1, just e. Ext corridors. **Pets:** Large, other species. Service with restrictions, crate.

✕ 🔊M ⬆ ⓒ 🛏

AAA WWW Sheraton Nashua Hotel LH 🐾
(603) 888-9970. **$79-$239.** 11 Tara Blvd. US 3 (Everett Tpke), exit 1, just w. Int corridors. **Pets:** Medium, dogs only. Service with restrictions, supervision.

SAVE SD ✕ 🔊M ⬆ ⓒ 🛏 🖵 ⓦ 🔵 ✕

NEWBURY

AAA WWW Best Western Sunapee Lake Lodge SH
(603) 763-2010. **$99-$299, 14 day notice.** 1403 SR 103. Jct SR 103B, just e. Int corridors. **Pets:** Other species. $8 daily fee/pet. Designated rooms, service with restrictions, supervision.

SAVE ✕ 🔊M ⬆ ⓒ 🛏 🖵 🔵 ✕

NEW CASTLE

AAA WWWW Wentworth By The Sea Marriott Hotel & Spa LH
(603) 422-7322. **$119-$729, 3 day notice.** 588 Wentworth Rd. On SR 1B, 2 mi e of SR 1A. Ext/int corridors. **Pets:** Accepted.

SAVE SD ✕ ⓒ 🛏 🖵 ⓦ 🔵 ✕

NORTH CONWAY

WW WW Cranmore Mountain Lodge BB
(603) 356-2044. **$59-$295, 14 day notice.** 859 Kearsarge Rd. Jct US 302/SR 16 eastbound, 1.2 mi n on Hurricane Mt Rd, then 0.5 mi e; westbound 1.4 mi n. Ext/int corridors. **Pets:** Dogs only. $10 one-time fee/room, no service.

✕ 🛏 🖵 🔵 ✕

AAA WWW North Conway Mountain Inn M
(603) 356-2803. **$59-$169, 3 day notice.** 2114 White Mountain Hwy. 1 mi s on US 302/SR 16. Ext corridors. **Pets:** Supervision.

SAVE ✕

WWW Spruce Moose Lodge and Cottages BB 🐾
(603) 356-6239. **$49-$159, 21 day notice.** 207 Seavey St. US 302/SR 16, 0.5 mi e; village center. Ext/int corridors. **Pets:** Dogs only. $10 daily fee/pet, service with restrictions, crate.

✕ 🛏 🖵

PITTSBURG

WW WW The Glen CA
(603) 538-6500. **$188-$204 (no credit cards), 7 day notice.** 118 Glen Rd. 9 mi n on US 3, from jct SR 145 to Varney Rd, then 0.3 mi s to Glen Rd, follow signs. Ext/int corridors. **Pets:** Other species. Designated rooms, service with restrictions, supervision.

✕ 🛏 🖵 ⓦ ✕ 🔊 ⓦ 🔵

PLYMOUTH

WWWW The Common Man Inn & Spa SH 🐾
(603) 536-2200. **$99-$199.** 231 Main St. I-93, exit 26, on US 3. Int corridors. **Pets:** $50 deposit/pet. Designated rooms, service with restrictions.

ASK SD ✕ 🔊M 🛏 ⓦ 🔵 ✕

PORTSMOUTH

WW WW Meadowbrook Inn M
(603) 436-2700. **$69-$129.** 549 US Hwy 1 Bypass. I-95, exit 5; jct US 1 Bypass and Portsmouth Traffic Circle. Ext/int corridors. **Pets:** Accepted.

ASK SD ✕ 🛏

WW Motel 6 Portsmouth M
(603) 334-6606. **$55-$91.** 3 Gosling Rd. I-95, exit 4 to Spaulding Tpke (US 4 and SR 16), exit 1, just e. Int corridors. **Pets:** Accepted.

SD ✕ 🛏 🔵

WWW Residence Inn by Marriott SH
(603) 436-8880. **$89-$219.** 1 International Dr. SR 4/16, exit 1, just s. Int corridors. **Pets:** $75 one-time fee/room. Service with restrictions, supervision.

ASK SD ✕ 🔊M ⬆ ⓒ 🛏 🖵 🔵 ✕

ROCHESTER

AAA WWW Anchorage Inn M 🐾
(603) 332-3350. **$59-$119.** 13 Wadleigh Rd. Jct Spaulding Tpke and SR 125, exit 12. Ext corridors. **Pets:** $50 deposit/room, $15 daily fee/pet. Designated rooms, service with restrictions, supervision.

SAVE SD ✕ 🛏 🔵

SALEM

WW Red Roof Inn #7151 M
(603) 898-6422. **$52-$90.** 15 Red Roof Ln. I-93, exit 2, just se. Ext corridors. **Pets:** Accepted.

✕ 🔊M ⬆

SUGAR HILL

WWW The Hilltop Inn BB 🐾
(603) 823-5695. **$90-$195, 8 day notice.** 1348 Main St. I-93, exit 38, 0.5 mi n on SR 18, then 2.8 mi w on SR 117. Int corridors. **Pets:** Dogs only. $10 daily fee/room. Supervision.

✕ 🛏 ✕ 🔊 ⓦ

SUNAPEE

▼▼▼ Dexter's Inn BB ❖
(603) 763-5571. **$125-$185, 14 day notice.** 258 Stagecoach Rd. Jct SR 103B and 11, 0.4 mi w on SR 11, 1.75 mi s (Winn Hill Rd). Ext/int corridors. **Pets:** Other species. $10 daily fee/pet. Designated rooms, service with restrictions.

ASK 🇸🇩 ✕ 🖥 ⬛ 🐾 ✕

TAMWORTH

▼▼▼ Tamworth Inn CI
(603) 323-7721. **$115-$290.** 15 Cleveland Hill Rd. Jct SR 16 and 113, 3 mi w on SR 113; center. Int corridors. **Pets:** Accepted.

ASK ✕ 🍴 🐾 ✕ 🐾 🖋

THORNTON

▼ Shamrock Motel M
(603) 726-3534. **$40-$60, 7 day notice.** 2913 US 3. I-93, exit 29, 2.3 mi n. Ext corridors. **Pets:** Accepted.

ASK 🇸🇩 ✕ 🖥 🐾 🐾 🖋

WEST LEBANON

◬◬◬ ▼▼▼ Airport Economy Inn M
(603) 298-8888. **$60-$115.** 45 Airport Rd. I-89, exit 20 (SR 12A), just s, then just e. Int corridors. **Pets:** Other species. $10 daily fee/room. Designated rooms, supervision.

SAVE 🇸🇩 ✕ ♿ 🖥 🐾

▼▼▼ Fireside Inn and Suites SH
(603) 298-5900. **$99-$159.** 25 Airport Rd. I-89, exit 20 (SR 12A), just s. Int corridors. **Pets:** Dogs only. $10 one-time fee/pet. Designated rooms, service with restrictions, supervision.

ASK 🇸🇩 ✕ 🖥 🖥 🍴 🐾

WOLFEBORO

▼▼ The Lake Motel M
(603) 569-1100. **$75-$134, 14 day notice.** 280 S Main St. 0.5 mi se on SR 28. Ext/int corridors. **Pets:** Accepted.

✕ 🖥 🖥 ✕

WOODSVILLE

◬◬◬ ▼ All Seasons Motel M
(603) 747-2157. **$55-$95.** 36 Smith St. I-91, exit 17, 4.1 mi e on US 302, then just s. Ext corridors. **Pets:** Accepted.

SAVE 🇸🇩 ✕ 🖥 🐾 ✕

◬◬◬ ▼▼ Nootka Lodge M
(603) 747-2418. **$65-$139.** Jct 10 & 302. I-91, exit 17, 4.5 mi e on US 302. Ext corridors. **Pets:** Accepted.

SAVE 🇸🇩 ✕ 🖥 🐾 ✕

NEW JERSEY

ATLANTIC CITY METROPOLITAN AREA

ATLANTIC CITY

AAA ▼▼▼▼ **Sheraton Atlantic City Convention Center Hotel** 🄛🄷 🐾
(609) 344-3535. **$79-$399.** 2 Miss America Way. Garden State Expwy, exit 38 to Atlantic City Expwy to Artic, just e to Michigan, then just n. Int corridors. **Pets:** Large, dogs only. Designated rooms, service with restrictions, supervision.
[SAVE] [S6] [X] [🌀] [🏃] [📶] [💻] [🍴] [🏊]

SOMERS POINT

▼▼▼ **Residence Inn by Marriott** 🄢🄷 🐾
(609) 927-6400. **$139-$309.** 900 Mays Landing Rd. Garden State Pkwy, exit 30 southbound; exit 29 northbound, 1 mi e. Ext corridors. **Pets:** Medium, other species. $75 one-time fee/room. Service with restrictions.
[ASK] [S6] [X] [🌀] [🏃] [📶] [💻] [🏊]

END METROPOLITAN AREA

BASKING RIDGE

AAA ▼▼▼▼ **The Inn at Somerset Hills** 🄢🄷
(908) 580-1300. **$129-$225.** 80 Allen Rd. I-78, exit 33, 0.3 mi n on CR 525, then 0.3 mi w. Int corridors. **Pets:** Accepted.
[SAVE] [S6] [X] [🌀] [🏃] [📶] [💻] [🍴]

BEACH HAVEN

AAA ▼▼ **Engleside Inn** 🄢🄷
(609) 492-1251. **$90-$417, 30 day notice.** 30 Engleside Ave. 6.9 mi s of SR 72 Cswy to Engleside Ave, then just e. Ext corridors. **Pets:** Other species. $10 daily fee/pet. Designated rooms, service with restrictions, supervision.
[SAVE] [X] [🏃] [📶] [💻] [🍴] [🏊]

BRIDGEWATER

▼▼▼▼ **Hilton Garden Inn-Bridgewater** 🄢🄷
(732) 271-9030. **$89-$179.** 500 Promenade Blvd. I-287, exit 13B northbound, just w; exit 13 southbound. Int corridors. **Pets:** $50 one-time fee/room. Designated rooms, service with restrictions.
[S6] [X] [🌀] [🏃] [📶] [💻] [🏊]

▼▼▼▼ **Marriott Bridgewater Hotel** 🄛🄷
(908) 927-9300. **$229-$269.** 700 Commons Way. I-287, exit 17 to US 202/206 S, 0.5 mi to Commons Way, then 0.4 mi e. Int corridors. **Pets:** Accepted.
[ASK] [S6] [X] [🗲M] [🌀] [🏃] [📶] [💻] [🍴] [🏊]

▼▼▼▼ **Summerfield Suites by Wyndham-Bridgewater** 🄢🄷
(908) 725-0800. **$119-$205.** 530 Rt 22 E. I-287, exit 14B northbound; exit 17 southbound to US 22 W, then 0.8 mi. Ext corridors. **Pets:** Accepted.
[ASK] [X] [🗲M] [🌀] [🏃] [📶] [💻] [🏊] [🐾]

CRANBURY

▼▼▼▼ **Residence Inn by Marriott/Cranbury** 🄢🄷
(609) 395-9447. **$84-$189.** 2662 Rt 130. New Jersey Tpke, exit 8A to SR 32 W toward town, 2 mi w on S River Rd. Int corridors. **Pets:** Accepted.
[ASK] [S6] [X] [🗲M] [🌀] [🏃] [📶] [💻] [🐾] [🗲]

▼▼▼▼ **Staybridge Suites/Cranbury** 🄢🄷
(609) 409-7181. **$149-$169.** 1272 S River Rd. New Jersey Tpke, exit 8A to SR 32 toward Cranbury, 2 mi w. Int corridors. **Pets:** Other species. $75 one-time fee/room. Service with restrictions, crate.
[ASK] [X] [📶] [💻] [🏊]

DENVILLE

AAA ▼▼▼▼ **Hampton Inn-The Inn At Denville** 🄢🄷
(973) 664-1050. **$89-$159, 7 day notice.** 350 Morris Ave. I-80, exit 37 westbound, just s on Green Pond Rd, then just e; eastbound, just n on Hibernia Ave, then just e. Int corridors. **Pets:** Medium, other species. $20 daily fee/pet. Service with restrictions.
[SAVE] [S6] [X] [🗲M] [🌀] [🏃] [📶] [💻] [🏊] [🗲]

EAST BRUNSWICK

▼▼ **Motel 6, East Brunswick #1083** 🄢🄷
(732) 390-4545. **$61-$73.** 244 Rt 18 N. New Jersey Tpke, exit 9 (SR 18) to SR 18 S, 1 mi, exit at Edgeboro Rd, w at U-turn, then just e. Ext/int corridors. **Pets:** Accepted.
[S6] [X] [🗲M] [🌀] [🏃]

▼▼ **Studio 6 East Brunswick #6020** 🄢🄷
(732) 238-3330. **$71-$81.** 246 Rt 18 @ Edgeboro Rd. New Jersey Tpke, exit 9 (SR 18) to SR 18 S, 1 mi, exit at Edgeboro Rd, w at U-turn, then just e. Int corridors. **Pets:** Accepted.
[S6] [X] [🗲M] [🌀] [🏃] [📶] [💻]

EAST HANOVER

AAA ▼▼▼▼ **Ramada Inn & Conference Center** 🄢🄷
(973) 386-5622. **$109-$149.** 130 Rt 10 W. I-287, exit 39, 3 mi e. Int corridors. **Pets:** Accepted.
[SAVE] [S6] [X] [🗲M] [🌀] [🏃] [📶] [💻] [🍴]

EAST RUTHERFORD

▼▼ **Homestead Studio Suites Hotel-Meadowlands/East Rutherford** 🄢🄷
(201) 939-8866. **$96-$116.** 300 SR 3 E. New Jersey Tpke, exit 16W (from western spur), sports complex right after toll. Int corridors. **Pets:** Medium. $25 one-time fee/pet. Service with restrictions, supervision.
[ASK] [S6] [X] [🗲M] [🌀] [🏃] [📶] [💻]

▼▼ Sheraton (East Rutherford/Meadowlands) 🄻🄷
...300. **$169-$194.** 2 Meadowlands Plaza. New Jersey Tpke, ...w (from western spur), sports complex right after toll to ...ton Plaza Dr. Int corridors. **Pets:** Medium. Service with restrictions.

EDISON

▼▼▼▼ Courtyard by Marriott Edison/Woodbridge 🅂🄷
(732) 738-1991. **$134, 7 day notice.** 3105 Woodbridge Ave. New Jersey Tpke, exit 10, 0.5 mi se on CR 514, then just e. Int corridors. **Pets:** Accepted.

▼▼ Red Roof Inn #7194 Ⓜ
(732) 248-9300. **$77-$96.** 860 New Durham Rd. I-287, exit 2A northbound, 0.3 mi w via Bridge St, then left; exit 3 southbound, just w. Ext corridors. **Pets:** Accepted.

▼▼▼▼ Sheraton Edison 🄻🄷 🐾
(732) 225-8300. **$249-$279.** 125 Raritan Center Pkwy. New Jersey Tpke, exit 10, 0.5 mi se on CR 514, keep right after tolls. Int corridors. **Pets:** Medium. $50 deposit/room. Service with restrictions.

ⒶⒶⒶ ▼▼▼ Wellesley Inn (Edison) 🅂🄷
(732) 287-0171. **$65-$110.** 831 US 1 S. 1.3 mi s of I-287. Int corridors. **Pets:** Accepted.

ELIZABETH

▼▼▼▼ Hilton Newark Airport 🄻🄷
(908) 351-3900. **$189-$229.** 1170 Spring St. New Jersey Tpke, exit 13A, on US 1 and 9 N, U-turn on McClellan St. Int corridors. **Pets:** Accepted.

▼▼▼▼ Residence Inn by Marriott 🅂🄷
(908) 352-4300. **$149-$179.** 83 Glimcher Realty Way. New Jersey Tpke, exit 13A, after toll follow signs to Jersey Garden Blvd, 1 mi, left on Kapkowski Rd, then just e. Int corridors. **Pets:** $75 one-time fee/room. Designated rooms, service with restrictions.

FAIR LAWN

ⒶⒶⒶ ▼▼▼▼ AmeriSuites (Fair Lawn/Paramus) 🅂🄷
(201) 475-3888. **$149-$165.** 41-01 Broadway (Rt 4 W). Garden State Pkwy, exit 161 northbound, 0.7 mi w; exit 163 southbound. Int corridors. **Pets:** Small, other species. $10 daily fee/pet. Designated rooms, service with restrictions, crate.

FLEMINGTON

ⒶⒶⒶ ▼▼▼ The Ramada Inn Ⓜ
(908) 782-7472. **$79-$102.** 250 Hwy 202 & SR 31. 0.5 mi s of the circle. Ext corridors. **Pets:** Accepted.

HAZLET

ⒶⒶⒶ ▼▼▼ Wellesley Inn (Hazlet) 🅂🄷
(732) 888-2800. **$89-$159.** 3215 SR 35 N. Garden State Pkwy, exit 117, 1.5 mi s on SR 35, U-turn on Hazlet Ave. Int corridors. **Pets:** Medium, other species. $10 one-time fee/pet. Service with restrictions, supervision.

ISELIN

▼▼▼▼ Sheraton at Woodbridge Place 🄻🄷
(732) 634-3600. **$95-$169.** 515 Rt 1 S. Garden State Pkwy, exit 131A northbound, 0.7 mi e, s on Middlesex Essex Tpke, 0.4 mi to Gill Ln, then 1.5 mi w; exit 130 southbound, 0.7 mi on US 1 N to Gill Ln, then U-turn; diago. Int corridors. **Pets:** Accepted.

LAWRENCEVILLE

ⒶⒶⒶ ▼▼▼ Howard Johnson Inn Ⓜ
(609) 896-1100. **$75-$135.** 2995 Rt 1 S. On US 1 southbound, 0.5 mi s of I-295. Ext/int corridors. **Pets:** Accepted.

▼▼ Red Roof Inn-Princeton #7111 Ⓜ
(609) 896-3388. **$60-$85.** 3203 Brunswick Pike (US 1). I-295, exit 67A, just n. Ext corridors. **Pets:** Accepted.

LEDGEWOOD

ⒶⒶⒶ ▼▼▼ Days Inn 🅂🄷
(973) 347-5100. **$92-$125.** 1691 US 46 W. I-80, exit 27, 2 mi e (thru US 206 N and 183 N). Int corridors. **Pets:** Accepted.

LYNDHURST

▼▼ Quality Inn Meadowlands 🅂🄷
(201) 933-9800. **$79-$149.** 10 Polito Ave. New Jersey Tpke, exit 16W (SR 3 W), s on SR 17 S. Int corridors. **Pets:** Accepted.

MAHWAH

▼▼▼▼ Homewood Suites by Hilton 🅂🄷
(201) 760-9994. **$159-$199, 60 day notice.** 375 Corporate Dr. I-278, exit 66, 1.7 mi on SR 17 S to MacArthur Blvd, then 0.4 mi w. Int corridors. **Pets:** Accepted.

ⒶⒶⒶ ▼▼▼▼ Sheraton Crossroads Hotel 🄻🄷 🐾
(201) 529-1660. **$215-$239.** 1 International Blvd (Rt 17). I-287, exit 66, at SR 17 N. Int corridors. **Pets:** Dogs only. Designated rooms, service with restrictions, supervision.

MIDDLETOWN

ⒶⒶⒶ ▼▼▼ Comfort Inn Ⓜ 🐾
(732) 671-3400. **$107-$172.** 750 Hwy 35 S. Garden State Pkwy, exit 114, 2 mi on Red Hill Rd, 1 mi s on King's Hwy to SR 35, then 0.3 mi s. Int corridors. **Pets:** Other species. $19 daily fee/room. Service with restrictions, supervision.

MILLVILLE

▼▼▼ Country Inn By Carlson 🅂🄷
(856) 825-3100. **$75-$79, 4 day notice.** 1125 Village Dr. SR 55, exit 26, just w to Wade Blvd, then 0.7 mi s on Wade Blvd. Int corridors. **Pets:** Service with restrictions, crate.

MONMOUTH JUNCTION

▼▼ Red Roof Inn/North Princeton #7198 Ⓜ
(732) 821-8800. **$51-$75.** 208 New Rd. On US 1 S. Ext corridors. **Pets:** Accepted.

⚑⚑⚑ ◈◈◈ Residence Inn by Marriott 🅂🅷 ❀
(732) 329-9600. **$169-$179.** 4225 Rt 1 S. 0.5 mi s of Raymond Rd. Int corridors. **Pets:** Other species. $75 one-time fee/room. Service with restrictions, crate.

[SAVE] [S⍴] [✕] [&M] [🐾] [&] [🛏] [💻] [🌊] [⊠]

MORRISTOWN

⚑⚑⚑ ◈◈◈ Summerfield Suites by Wyndham-Morristown 🅂🅷 ❀
(973) 971-0008. **$109-$199.** 194 Park Ave. SR 24, exit 2A (Morristown), stay in far left lane. Int corridors. **Pets:** Other species. $150 one-time fee/room. Service with restrictions, supervision.

[SAVE] [✕] [&M] [🐾] [&] [🛏] [💻] [🌊] [⊠]

◈◈◈ The Westin Governor Morris-Morristown 🅻🅷 ❀
(973) 539-7300. **$229-$239.** 2 Whippany Rd. I-287, exit 36 southbound, left lane to light, left to stop, then left 1 mi; exit 36A northbound thru Morris Ave, 0.8 mi, follow signs. Int corridors. **Pets:** Medium, dogs only. $50 one-time fee/pet. Supervision.

[ASK] [S⍴] [✕] [🐾] [&] [🛏] [💻] [🍴] [🌊] [⊠]

NEWARK

◈◈◈ Hilton Gateway 🅻🅷
(973) 622-5000. **$119-$349.** 3312 Raymond Blvd. New Jersey Tpke, exit 15E, 3 mi w via Raymond Blvd. Int corridors. **Pets:** Accepted.

[S⍴] [✕] [🐾] [&] [🛏] [💻] [🍴] [🌊]

◈◈◈ Sheraton Newark Airport Hotel 🅻🅷
(973) 690-5500. **$99-$269.** 128 Frontage Rd. New Jersey Tpke, exit 14 via Frontage Rd, 2nd right after toll booth. Int corridors. **Pets:** Accepted.

[ASK] [S⍴] [✕] [&M] [🐾] [&] [🛏] [💻] [🍴] [🌊] [⊠]

NORTH BERGEN

◈◈ Days Inn 🅂🅷
(201) 348-3600. **$109-$139.** 2750 Tonnelle Ave (US 1 & 9). Jct SR 3, 0.4 mi s. Int corridors. **Pets:** Other species. $100 deposit/room. Designated rooms, service with restrictions, supervision.

[ASK] [S⍴] [✕] [🐾] [🛏] [💻] [🍴]

PARK RIDGE

◈◈◈ Park Ridge Marriott Hotel 🅻🅷 ❀
(201) 307-0800. **$109-$250.** 300 Brae Blvd. Garden State Pkwy S, U-turn thru Food Fuel Service Plaza; exit 172 northbound, right 300 yds on Grand Ave, then 0.5 mi s on Mercedes. Int corridors. **Pets:** $75 one-time fee/room. Service with restrictions, supervision.

[ASK] [S⍴] [✕] [🐾] [&] [🛏] [💻] [🍴] [🌊] [⊠]

PARSIPPANY

◈◈◈ Embassy Suites 🅻🅷 ❀
(973) 334-1440. **$109-$299.** 909 Parsippany Blvd. I-80, exit 42 to US 202 N, just ne of jct US 202 and 46 W. Int corridors. **Pets:** Medium. $20 daily fee/room. Designated rooms, service with restrictions, crate.

[✕] [🐾] [🛏] [💻] [🍴] [🌊] [⊠]

◈◈ Red Roof Inn #7072 Ⓜ
(973) 334-3737. **$73-$86.** 855 US 46 E. I-80, exit 47 westbound; exit 45 eastbound, 0.5 mi e. Ext corridors. **Pets:** Accepted.

[✕] [🐾] [🛏]

◈◈◈ Sheraton Parsippany Hotel 🅻🅷 ❀
(973) 515-2000. **$180-$204.** 199 Smith Rd. I-287, exit 41A northbound; exit 42 to US 46 E, 0.4 mi s. Int corridors. **Pets:** Medium, dogs only. Service with restrictions, supervision.

[ASK] [S⍴] [✕] [🐾] [&] [🛏] [💻] [🍴] [🌊] [⊠]

NEARBY PENNSYLVANIA
PHILADELPHIA METROPOLITAN AREA

BORDENTOWN

⚑⚑⚑ ◈ Imperial Inn Ⓜ
(609) 298-3355. **$55-$75.** 3312 Rt 206 S. New Jersey Tpke, exit 7, 0.8 mi s. Ext corridors. **Pets:** Dogs only. $20 deposit/pet, $5 daily fee/pet. Service with restrictions, supervision.

[SAVE] [✕] [🛏]

CARNEYS POINT

⚑⚑⚑ ◈◈◈ Holiday Inn Express Hotel & Suites 🅂🅷
(856) 351-9222. **$90-$100.** 506 Pennsville-Auburn Rd. I-295, exit 2B, just e. Int corridors. **Pets:** Accepted.

[SAVE] [S⍴] [✕] [&] [🛏] [💻]

CHERRY HILL

⚑⚑⚑ ◈◈◈ Holiday Inn Philadelphia-Cherry Hill 🅂🅷
(856) 663-5300. **$85-$149.** Rt 70 & Sayer Ave. I-295, exit 34B, 2.5 mi w. Int corridors. **Pets:** Medium. $75 deposit/room. Service with restrictions, supervision.

[SAVE] [S⍴] [✕] [🐾] [&] [🛏] [💻] [🍴] [🌊]

◈◈◈ Residence Inn by Marriott 🅂🅷
(856) 429-6111. **$169-$219.** 1821 Old Cuthbert Rd. I-295, exit 34A, just e to Marlkress Rd jughandle, back to Old Cuthbert Rd, then just n. Ext corridors. **Pets:** Accepted.

[ASK] [✕] [🐾] [🛏] [💻] [🌊] [⊠]

DEPTFORD

◈◈◈ Residence Inn by Marriott 🅂🅷 ❀
(856) 686-9188. **$80-$120.** 1154 Hurffville Rd. SR 42, exit Deptford, Woodbury, Runnemede to CR 544, just e to CR 415. Int corridors. **Pets:** Other species. $75 one-time fee/room. Designated rooms, service with restrictions, supervision.

[ASK] [S⍴] [✕] [🐾] [&] [🛏] [💻] [🌊] [⊠]

HADDONFIELD

◈◈◈ Haddonfield Inn 🅱🅱
(856) 428-2195. **$129-$309, 14 day notice.** 44 W End Ave. I-295, exit 28, 0.7 mi n on SR 168, 2.6 mi e on Kings Hwy, then just n. Int corridors. **Pets:** Accepted.

[ASK] [✕] [&] [🛏]

MOUNT HOLLY

⚑⚑⚑ ◈◈ Best Western Burlington Inn 🅂🅷
(609) 261-3800. **$84-$129, 3 day notice.** 2020 Rt 541, Rd 1. New Jersey Tpke, exit 5, just n. Int corridors. **Pets:** Accepted.

[SAVE] [S⍴] [✕] [🐾] [🛏] [💻] [🌊]

MOUNT LAUREL

⚑⚑⚑ ◈◈◈ AmeriSuites (Mt. Laurel/Philadelphia) 🅂🅷
(856) 840-0770. **$69-$149.** 8000 Crawford Pl. New Jersey Tpke, exit 4, 1 mi se on SR 73; I-295, exit 36A, 1.7 mi se on SR 73. Int corridors. **Pets:** Accepted.

[SAVE] [S⍴] [✕] [&M] [🐾] [&] [🛏] [💻] [🌊]

▼▼ Candlewood Suites SH
(856) 642-7567. **$109.** 4000 Crawford Pl. New Jersey Tpke, exit 4, 1 mi s on SR 73 S. Int corridors. **Pets:** Accepted.
[ASK] [S6] [✗] [⬥] [⬛] [▣]

🔺 ▼▼▼ Radisson Hotel Mount Laurel LH ❀
(856) 234-7300. **$113.** 915 Rt 73 N. New Jersey Tpke, exit 4, northeast corner; I-295, exit 36A, just se. Int corridors. **Pets:** Large. $50 one-time fee/pet. Designated rooms, service with restrictions, supervision.
[SAVE] [S6] [✗] [🌀] [⬥] [⬛] [▣] [🍽] [≈] [✗]

▼▼ Red Roof Inn #7066 M
(856) 234-5589. **$52-$75.** 603 Fellowship Rd. New Jersey Tpke, exit 4, just nw on SR 73 to Fellowship Rd, then just s; I-295, exit 36A, just se on SR 73 to Fellowship Rd, then just s. Ext corridors. **Pets:** Accepted.
[✗] [🌀] [⬛]

▼▼▼▼ Summerfield Suites by Wyndham-Mount Laurel SH
(856) 222-1313. **$95-$139.** 3000 Crawford Pl. New Jersey Tpke, exit 4, 1 mi s on SR 73; I-295, exit 36A, 1.5 mi s on SR 73. Ext corridors. **Pets:** Accepted.
[ASK] [✗] [⬥M] [🌀] [⬥] [⬛] [▣] [≈] [✗]

END METROPOLITAN AREA

PHILLIPSBURG

▼▼▼ Clarion Hotel & Conference Center SH
(908) 454-9771. **$99-$109.** 1314 US Rt 22. I-78, exit 3, just n. Ext/int corridors. **Pets:** Accepted.
[ASK] [S6] [✗] [⬥M] [🌀] [⬥] [⬛] [▣] [🍽] [≈]

PISCATAWAY

▼ Motel 6 Piscataway SH
(732) 981-9200. **$62-$96.** 1012 Stelton Rd. I-287, exit 5, just e. Ext/int corridors. **Pets:** Accepted.
[⬥]

PRINCETON

🔺 ▼▼▼ AmeriSuites (Princeton/Carnegie Center West) SH
(609) 720-0200. **$149-$179.** 3565 US 1 S. 1.5 mi s of jct CR 526 and 571. Int corridors. **Pets:** Medium. $10 one-time fee/room. Service with restrictions, supervision.
[SAVE] [S6] [✗] [⬥M] [⬥] [⬛] [▣] [≈]

🔺 ▼▼▼ Holiday Inn Princeton SH
(609) 520-1200. **$159.** 100 Independence Way. I-295, exit 67A (SR 1) northbound; exit 67 (SR 1) southbound, 7 mi n. Int corridors. **Pets:** Accepted.
[SAVE] [S6] [✗] [🌀] [⬛] [▣] [🍽] [≈]

🔺 ▼▼▼ Nassau Inn SH ❀
(609) 921-7500. **$198-$288.** 10 Palmer Square. Center. Int corridors. **Pets:** Small. $75 one-time fee/room. Designated rooms, service with restrictions, crate.
[SAVE] [S6] [✗] [🌀] [⬥] [⬛] [🍽]

▼▼▼ Staybridge Suites SH
(609) 951-0009. **Call for rates.** 4375 US 1 S. Just past Ridge Rd. Ext corridors. **Pets:** Accepted.
[✗] [🌀] [⬛] [▣] [≈] [✗]

🔺 ▼▼▼ Westin Princeton at Forrestal Village LH ❀
(609) 452-7900. **$279-$319.** 201 Village Blvd. On US 1 southbound, 1.5 mi n of CR 571. Int corridors. **Pets:** Medium, dogs only. Service with restrictions, supervision.
[SAVE] [S6] [✗] [⬥M] [⬥] [⬛] [▣] [🍽] [≈] [✗]

RAMSEY

🔺 ▼▼ Best Western SH
(201) 327-6700. **$109-$165.** 1315 Rt 17 S. Jct I-287 and SR 17 S, 3 mi s. Int corridors. **Pets:** Small. $10 one-time fee/pet. Service with restrictions, supervision.
[SAVE] [S6] [✗] [⬛] [▣]

🔺 ▼▼▼ Wellesley Inn (Ramsey) SH
(201) 934-9250. **$79-$109.** 946 Rt 17 N. At Airmont Rd. Int corridors. **Pets:** Accepted.
[SAVE] [✗] [⬥M] [🌀] [⬥] [⬛] [▣]

ROCKAWAY

▼▼ Best Western-The Inn at Rockaway SH
(973) 625-1200. **$129.** 14 Green Pond Rd. I-80, exit 37, just n. Int corridors. **Pets:** Accepted.
[S6] [✗] [🌀] [▣] [≈]

SECAUCUS

🔺 ▼▼▼ AmeriSuites (Secaucus/Meadowlands) SH
(201) 422-9480. **$169-$179.** 575 Park Plaza Dr. New Jersey Tpke, exits 16E, 17 or 16W via SR 3 to Harmon Meadow Blvd, then just w. Int corridors. **Pets:** Accepted.
[SAVE] [✗] [⬥M] [🌀] [⬥] [⬛] [▣]

▼▼▼ Homestead Studio Suites Hotel-Secaucus/Meadowlands SH 🐾
(201) 553-9700. **$109-$129.** 1 Park Plaza Dr. New Jersey Tpke, exit 16E northbound; exit 17E southbound, 0.3 mi e. Int corridors. **Pets:** $25 daily fee/room. Service with restrictions, crate.
[ASK] [S6] [✗] [⬥M] [🌀] [⬥] [⬛] [▣] [≈]

🔺 ▼▼▼ PRIME Suites Secaucus/Meadowlands LH
(201) 863-8700. **$89-$189.** 350 Rt 3 W, at Mill Creek Dr. Between eastern and western spurs of New Jersey Tpke, exits 16E, 17 or 16W via SR 3 W and Harmon Meadow Blvd; in Mill Creek Mall. Int corridors. **Pets:** Accepted.
[SAVE] [✗] [🌀] [⬛] [▣] [🍽] [≈]

▼▼ Red Roof Inn-Meadowlands #7150 M
(201) 319-1000. **$83-$110.** 15 Meadowlands Pkwy. Between eastern and western spurs of New Jersey Tpke, exits 16E, 17 or 16W to SR 3, exit Meadowlands Pkwy. Ext corridors. **Pets:** Medium, other species. Service with restrictions, crate.
[✗] [⬥]

SHORT HILLS

🔺 ▼▼▼ ▼▼ Hilton Short Hills and Spa LH
(973) 379-0100. **$179-$399.** 41 John F Kennedy Pkwy. I-78, exit 48 (SR 24), 2.5 mi to Kennedy Pkwy. Int corridors. **Pets:** Accepted.
[SAVE] [✗] [⬥M] [🌀] [⬥] [⬛] [▣] [🍽] [≈] [✗]

SOMERSET

🔺 ▼▼▼ Holiday Inn-Somerset SH
(732) 356-1700. **$69-$159.** 195 Davidson Ave. I-287, exit 10 (CR 527), just n (direction Bound Brook), then 0.5 mi sw. Int corridors. **Pets:** Other species. Service with restrictions, crate.
[SAVE] [S6] [✗] [⬥M] [🌀] [⬥] [⬛] [▣] [🍽] [≈]

▼▼▼▼ Residence Inn by Marriott-Somerset SH
(732) 627-0881. **$90-$153.** 37 World Fair Dr. I-287, exit 10 (CR 527), left on ramp (CR 527 S/Easton Ave) 0.3 mi, then 0.5 mi w. Int corridors. **Pets:** Accepted.
[ASK] [S6] [✗] [⬥M] [🌀] [⬥] [⬛] [▣] [≈] [✗]

▽▽▽▽ **Staybridge Suites** 𝖲𝖧
(732) 356-8000. **$149-$189.** 260 Davidson Ave. I-287, exit 10 (CR 527), just n (direction Bound Brook) to Davidson Ave, then 0.8 mi sw. Ext corridors. **Pets:** Accepted.
⊠ 🕭 🛏 🖵 ⤵ ⊠

SOUTH PLAINFIELD

ⒶⒶⒶ ▽▽▽ **Best Western** 𝖲𝖧
(908) 561-4488. **$59-$105.** 101 New World Way. I-287, exit 5, just s. Int corridors. **Pets:** Accepted.
[SAVE] 🕭 ⊠ 🛏 🖵

ⒶⒶⒶ ▽▽▽▽ **Holiday Inn** 𝖲𝖧
(908) 753-5500. **$126-$135.** 4701 Stelton Rd. I-287, exit 5, just s. Int corridors. **Pets:** Other species. Service with restrictions, supervision.
[SAVE] ⊠ 🕭 🛏 🖵 ⍾ ⤵ ⊠

SPRINGFIELD

▽▽▽▽ **Holiday Inn Springfield** 𝖲𝖧
(973) 376-9400. **$140-$145.** 304 Rt 22 W. Garden State Pkwy, exit 140 northbound, 4 mi w; exit 140A southbound. Int corridors. **Pets:** Service with restrictions, crate.
[ASK] 🕭 ⊠ 🕭 🛏 🖵 ⍾ ⤵

TINTON FALLS

ⒶⒶⒶ ▽▽▽▽ **Holiday Inn at Tinton Falls** 𝖲𝖧 ❖
(732) 544-9300. **$160-$170.** 700 Hope Rd. Garden State Pkwy, exit 105. Int corridors. **Pets:** Small. $30 one-time fee/room. Designated rooms, service with restrictions, crate.
[SAVE] 🕭 ⊠ 🕭 🕭 🛏 🖵 ⍾ ⤵

▽▽▽ **Red Roof Inn #7211** Ⓜ
(732) 389-4646. **$66-$105.** 11 Centre Plaza. Garden State Pkwy, exit 105, just right at 1st light after toll. Ext corridors. **Pets:** Medium. Designated rooms, service with restrictions, supervision.
⊠ 🕭 🕭 🛏

▽▽▽ **Residence Inn by Marriott** 𝖲𝖧
(732) 389-8100. **$139-$229.** 90 Park Rd. Garden State Pkwy, exit 105, 1st jughandle after toll, immediate left before Courtyard by Marriott, just n, then e. Ext corridors. **Pets:** Accepted.
[ASK] 🕭 ⊠ 🕭 🕭 🛏 🖵 ⤵ ⊠

▽▽▽▽ **Sunrise Suites Hotel** 𝖲𝖧
(732) 389-4800. **$89-$159.** 3 Centre Plaza. Garden State Pkwy, exit 105, 1st right at Hope Rd after toll. Ext/int corridors. **Pets:** Accepted.
[ASK] ⊠ 🕭 🕭 ⊠

VINELAND

▽▽▽ **Ramada Inn Vineland** 𝖲𝖧
(856) 696-3800. **$75-$85.** 2216 W Landis Ave. SR 55, exit 32A, just e. Int corridors. **Pets:** Medium. $10 daily fee/pet. Designated rooms, service with restrictions, supervision.
[ASK] 🕭 ⊠ 🛏 🖵 ⍾ ⤵

WANTAGE

▽▽ **High Point Country Inn** Ⓜ ❖
(973) 702-1860. **$80-$90.** 1328 SR 23 N. 1 mi n of Colesville Village Center. Ext corridors. **Pets:** Other species. $10 one-time fee/pet.
⊠ 🛏 ⤵

WARREN

▽▽▽▽ **Somerset Hills Hotel** 𝖲𝖧
(908) 647-6700. **$129-$215.** 200 Liberty Corner Rd. I-78, exit 33, just n on CR 525. Int corridors. **Pets:** Large. $25 daily fee/room. Designated rooms, service with restrictions, crate.
[ASK] 🕭 ⊠ 🕭 🛏 🖵 ⍾ ⤵ ⊠

WAYNE

▽▽ ▽▽ **Holiday Inn Wayne-Fairfield** 𝖲𝖧
(973) 256-7000. **$81-$108.** 334 Rt 46 E/Service Rd. I-80, exit 53 westbound (Butler-Verona) thru SR 23 S, service road off US 46 eastbound Caldwells; exit 47B eastbound, 7 mi e on US 46 to service road. Ext corridors. **Pets:** Medium, dogs only. $50 deposit/room, $15 daily fee/pet. Designated rooms, service with restrictions, crate.
[ASK] 🕭 ⊠ 🛏 🖵 ⍾ ⤵

ⒶⒶⒶ ▽▽▽▽ **Wellesley Inn (Wayne)** 𝖲𝖧
(973) 696-8050. **$109-$119.** 1850 Rt 23 & Ratzer Rd. I-80, exit 53 (Butler-Verona) westbound to SR 23 N, 3 mi to Ratzer Rd (service road); exit 54 eastbound to Minisink Rd to U-turn for I-80 W to exit 53. Int corridors. **Pets:** Small. $10 daily fee/room. Service with restrictions, crate.
[SAVE] 🕭 ⊠ 🕭 🕭 🕭 🛏 🖵 ⤵

WEEHAWKEN

ⒶⒶⒶ ▽▽▽▽ **Sheraton Suites On The Hudson** 🅻🅷
(201) 617-5600. **$179-$329.** 500 Harbor Blvd. I-495 E toward Lincoln Tunnel, exit Weekawken/Hoboken, bear right at bottom of hill, then 0.4 mi e to Lincoln Harbor Complex. Int corridors. **Pets:** Accepted.
[SAVE] 🕭 ⊠ 🕭 🕭 🛏 🖵 ⍾ ⤵

WEST ORANGE

▽▽▽▽ **Residence Inn by Marriott-West Orange** 𝖲𝖧 🐾
(973) 669-4700. **$199-$299.** 107 Prospect Ave. I-280, exit 8B, 1 mi n on CR 527 (Prospect Ave). Int corridors. **Pets:** Other species. $15 daily fee/pet, $75 one-time fee/room. Service with restrictions.
[ASK] ⊠ 🕭 🛏 🖵 ⤵ ⊠

WHIPPANY

▽▽▽ **Homestead Studio Suites Hotel-Hanover/Parsippany** 𝖲𝖧
(973) 463-1999. **$90-$110.** 125 Rt 10 E. I-287, exit 39, 3.6 mi e. Int corridors. **Pets:** Other species. $75 one-time fee/room. Service with restrictions.
[ASK] 🕭 ⊠ 🕭 🕭 🕭 🛏 🖵

ⒶⒶⒶ ▽▽▽▽ **Summerfield Suites by Wyndham-Parsippany/Whippany** 𝖲𝖧
(973) 605-1001. **$109-$189.** 1 Ridgedale Ave. I-287, exit 39, just nw. Int corridors. **Pets:** Medium. $150 one-time fee/room. Service with restrictions, supervision.
[SAVE] ⊠ 🕭 🕭 🕭 🛏 🖵 ⤵

ⒶⒶⒶ ▽▽ ▽▽ **Wellesley Inn (Whippany)** 𝖲𝖧
(973) 539-8350. **$79.** 1255 Rt 10 E. I-287, exit 39B southbound; exit 39 northbound, just w. Int corridors. **Pets:** Other species. Service with restrictions, crate.
[SAVE] 🕭 ⊠ 🕭 🕭 🛏 🖵 ⤵

WOODBRIDGE

▽▽ ▽▽ **Homestead Studio Suites Hotel-Woodbridge** 𝖲𝖧
(732) 442-8333. **$90-$110.** 1 Hoover Way. New Jersey Tpke, exit 11, 1.4 mi to US 9 N, then just w on King George Post Rd. Int corridors. **Pets:** Accepted.
[ASK] 🕭 ⊠ 🕭 🕭 🛏 🖵

NEW MEXICO

ABIQUIU

▼▼▼ Casa del Rio BB
(505) 753-2035. **$109-$135, 21 day notice.** Hwy 84, MM 199.46. 2.3 mi n from jct US 285, then just e on gated drive. Ext/int corridors. **Pets:** Accepted.
[ASK] [X] [⚙] [📶] [▦] [🐾] [W] [✉]

ALAMOGORDO

ⒶⒶⒶ ▼▼▼ Best Western Desert Aire Inn SH
(505) 437-2110. **$47-$109.** 1021 S White Sands Blvd. 1.5 mi s of jct US 54/70 and 82. Ext corridors. **Pets:** Small. $50 deposit/room, $10 one-time fee/room. Designated rooms, no service, supervision.
[SAVE] [Sᴅ] [X] [📶] [▦] [▥] [🐾] [X]

▼▼▼ Holiday Inn Express-Alamogordo SH
(505) 437-7100. **$69-$85.** 1401 S White Sands Blvd. 1.6 mi s of jct US 54/70 and 82. Int corridors. **Pets:** Accepted.
[ASK] [Sᴅ] [X] [Ġᴍ] [▦] [▥] [🐾]

▼▼ Super 8 Motel-Alamogordo SH
(505) 434-4205. **$55-$61.** 3204 N White Sands Blvd. Just s of jct US 54/70 and 82. Int corridors. **Pets:** Medium, other species. Designated rooms, service with restrictions, supervision.
[ASK] [Sᴅ] [X] [▦]

ALBUQUERQUE

ⒶⒶⒶ ▼▼▼ Airport University Inn SH
(505) 247-0512. **$69-$89, 7 day notice.** 1901 University Blvd SE. I-25, exit 228A southbound; exit 222 northbound, just e. Int corridors. **Pets:** Accepted.
[SAVE] [Sᴅ] [X] [📶] [▥] [🍴] [🐾]

ⒶⒶⒶ ▼▼▼ AmeriSuites (Albuquerque/Airport) SH
(505) 242-9300. **$104-$135.** 1400 Sunport Place Blvd SE. I-25, exit 221, 0.3 mi e to University Blvd exit, then just n to Woodward Rd. Int corridors. **Pets:** Accepted.
[SAVE] [Sᴅ] [X] [Ġᴍ] [📶] [▦] [▥] [🐾]

ⒶⒶⒶ ▼▼▼ AmeriSuites (Albuquerque/Midtown) SH
(505) 881-0544. **$90.** 2500 Menaul Blvd NE. I-40, exit 160, just n to Menaul Blvd, then 0.6 mi w. Int corridors. **Pets:** Accepted.
[SAVE] [Sᴅ] [X] [Ġᴍ] [📶] [▦] [▥] [🐾]

ⒶⒶⒶ ▼▼▼ AmeriSuites (Albuquerque/Uptown) SH
(505) 872-9000. **$69-$139.** 6901 Arvada Ave NE. I-40, exit 162 westbound; exit 162B eastbound, 0.7 mi n. Int corridors. **Pets:** $10 daily fee/pet. Service with restrictions, supervision.
[SAVE] [Sᴅ] [X] [📶] [▦] [▥] [🐾]

ⒶⒶⒶ ▼▼▼ Baymont Inn & Suites Albuquerque North SH
(505) 345-7500. **$59-$129.** 7439 Pan American Frwy NE. I-25, exit 231, just w. Int corridors. **Pets:** Accepted.
[SAVE] [Sᴅ] [X] [📶] [▦] [▥] [🐾]

ⒶⒶⒶ ▼▼▼ Best Western American Motor Inn SH
(505) 298-7426. **$69-$89.** 12999 Central Ave NE. I-40, exit 167 westbound, 0.3 mi w on Central Ave; exit 166 eastbound, right on Juan Tabo, left on Central Ave, then 0.5 mi e. Ext corridors. **Pets:** Accepted.
[SAVE] [Sᴅ] [X] [▦] [▥] [🍴] [🐾]

ⒶⒶⒶ ▼▼▼ Best Western InnSuites Hotel & Suites-Airport Albuquerque SH 🐾
(505) 242-7022. **$59-$99.** 2400 Yale Blvd SE. I-25, exit 222 northbound; exit 222A southbound, 1 mi e, then just s. Int corridors. **Pets:** Medium, other species. $25 one-time fee/pet. Designated rooms, service with restrictions, crate.
[SAVE] [Sᴅ] [X] [📶] [▦] [▥] [🐾]

ⒶⒶⒶ ▼▼▼ Best Western Winrock Inn SH
(505) 883-5252. **$89-$99.** 18 Winrock Center NE. I-40, exit 162 westbound; exit 162B eastbound, just n via Americas Pkwy. Ext/int corridors. **Pets:** Accepted.
[SAVE] [Sᴅ] [X] [📶] [▦] [▥] [🐾]

ⒶⒶⒶ ▼▼▼ Brittania & W E Mauger Estate Bed & Breakfast BB 🐾
(505) 242-8755. **$79-$259, 10 day notice.** 701 Roma Ave NW. I-25, exit 225, 1 mi w, then just s on 7th Ave. Int corridors. **Pets:** Dogs only. $30 one-time fee/room. Designated rooms, service with restrictions, crate.
[SAVE] [Sᴅ] [X] [▦] [▥]

▼▼▼ Candlewood Suites SH
(505) 888-3424. **$85-$160.** 3025 Menaul Blvd NE. I-40, exit 160, just n to Menaul Blvd, then 0.5 mi w. Int corridors. **Pets:** Accepted.
[ASK] [Sᴅ] [X] [Ġᴍ] [⚙] [▥]

ⒶⒶⒶ ▼▼▼ ClubHouse Inn & Suites SH
(505) 345-0010. **$69-$109.** 1315 Menaul Blvd NE. I-25, exit 227A, just e to University Blvd, 0.5 mi s to Menaul Blvd, then 0.5 mi w. Int corridors. **Pets:** Accepted.
[SAVE] [Sᴅ] [X] [Ġᴍ] [📶] [▦] [▥] [🐾]

ⒶⒶⒶ ▼▼▼ Comfort Inn-Airport SH
(505) 243-2244. **$55-$105, 3 day notice.** 2300 Yale Blvd SE. I-25, exit 222A southbound; exit 222 northbound, 1 mi n, then just s. Ext/int corridors. **Pets:** Accepted.
[SAVE] [Sᴅ] [X] [Ġᴍ] [📶] [⚙] [▦] [🐾]

▼▼▼ Comfort Inn & Suites by Choice Hotels SH
(505) 822-1090. **$70-$90.** 5811 Signal Ave NE. I-25, exit 233, just e via Alameda. Int corridors. **Pets:** Other species. $10 daily fee/pet. Service with restrictions, supervision.
[ASK] [Sᴅ] [X] [Ġᴍ] [📶] [⚙] [▦] [▥] [🐾]

ⒶⒶⒶ ▼▼▼ Comfort Inn East SH 🐾
(505) 294-1800. **$61-$71.** 13031 Central Ave NE. I-40, exit 167, just w. Ext corridors. **Pets:** Very small, other species. $3 daily fee/room. Service with restrictions, crate.
[SAVE] [Sᴅ] [X] [📶] [⚙] [▦] [▥] [🍴] [🐾]

♥♥ Comfort Inn-Midtown SH

(505) 881-3210. **$49-$110.** 2015 Menaul Blvd NE. I-25, exit 225 northbound, 1.6 mi n of Frontage Rd to Menaul Blvd, then just e; exit 227 (Commanche Rd) southbound, s on Frontage Rd, 0.8 mi n to Menaul Blvd, then just e. Ext corridors. **Pets:** Medium. $10 daily fee/pet. Designated rooms, service with restrictions, supervision.

ASK SD X H ⬛ ⇌

♠♠♠ ♥♥♥ Days Inn-Hotel Circle SH

(505) 275-3297. **$48-$60.** 10321 Hotel Cir NE. I-40, exit 165 (Eubank Blvd), just n. Ext corridors. **Pets:** Medium, other species. $10 one-time fee/pet. Service with restrictions, supervision.

SAVE SD X ⇌

♥♥♥ Days Inn West M

(505) 836-3297. **$55-$90.** 6031 Iliff Rd NW. I-40, exit 155, just s on Coors Rd, then just w. Ext corridors. **Pets:** Medium. $7 daily fee/pet. Designated rooms, service with restrictions, supervision.

ASK SD X 5M ⌀ ⌂ ⇌

♥♥♥♥ Drury Inn & Suites-Albuquerque SH

(505) 341-3600. **$73-$103.** 4310 The 25 Way NE. I-25, exit Jefferson St NE, northwest quadrant of exchange. Int corridors. **Pets:** Large, other species. Service with restrictions, supervision.

ASK X 5M ⌂ H ⬛ ⇌

♠♠♠ ♥♥♥ Econo Lodge Downtown/University SH ❀

(505) 243-1321. **$39-$89.** 817 Central Ave NE. I-25, 224A northbound; exit 224B southbound, just e. Ext corridors. **Pets:** Medium. $50 deposit/room. Service with restrictions, supervision.

SAVE SD X H ⬛ ⇌

♠♠♠ ♥♥♥ Econo Lodge Old Town SH

(505) 243-8475. **$40-$105.** 2321 Central Ave NW. I-40, exit 157A, 0.6 mi s on Rio Grande Blvd, then 0.4 mi w. Ext corridors. **Pets:** Medium, dogs only. $10 daily fee/pet. Designated rooms, service with restrictions, crate.

SAVE SD X H ⬛ ⇌

♥♥ Equus Hotel Suites M

(505) 883-8888. **$49.** 2401 Wellsley Dr NE. I-40, exit 160, just n to Menaul Blvd, just w, then just s. Ext corridors. **Pets:** Medium. $75 one-time fee/room. Service with restrictions, supervision.

ASK SD X H ⬛ ⇌

♠♠♠ ♥♥♥ Fairfield Inn Airport SH

(505) 247-1621. **$69-$89.** 2300 Centre Ave SE. I-25, exit 222 northbound; exit 222A southbound, 1 mi e to Yale Blvd, ne jct of Gibson and Yale blvds. Int corridors. **Pets:** $75 one-time fee/room. Service with restrictions, crate.

SAVE SD X 5M ⌀ ⌂ H ⬛ ⇌

♠♠♠ ♥♥♥ GuestHouse Inn & Suites SH

(505) 271-8500. **$40-$70, 7 day notice.** 10331 Hotel Ave NE. I-40, exit 165, 2 blks n. Int corridors. **Pets:** Medium. $10 one-time fee/pet. Designated rooms, service with restrictions, supervision.

SAVE SD X H

♠♠♠ ♥♥♥ Hacienda Antigua Inn BB

(505) 345-5399. **$134-$189, 10 day notice.** 6708 Tierra Dr NW. I-25, exit 230 (Osuna Dr), 2 mi w, then just n. Ext/int corridors. **Pets:** Accepted.

SAVE SD X H ⬛ ⇌

♠♠♠ ♥♥♥ Hampton Inn-North SH

(505) 344-1555. **$72-$125.** 5101 Ellison NE. I-25, exit 231, just w. Ext corridors. **Pets:** Other species. Service with restrictions, supervision.

SAVE SD X ⌀ H ⬛ ⇌

♥♥♥♥ Hawthorn Inn & Suites SH ❀

(505) 242-1555. **$79-$149.** 1511 Gibson Blvd SE. I-25, exit 222 northbound; exit 222A southbound, just e. Int corridors. **Pets:** Large. $5 daily fee/pet. Designated rooms, service with restrictions, supervision.

ASK SD X 5M ⌀ ⌂ H ⬛ ¶ ⇌

♠♠♠ ♥♥♥ Holiday Inn Express SH

(505) 275-8900. **$69.** 10330 Hotel Ave NE. I-40, exit 165 (Eubank Blvd), 2 blks n. Ext corridors. **Pets:** Medium, other species. $5 daily fee/pet. Service with restrictions, supervision.

SAVE SD X ⌀ ⌂ H ⬛ ⇌ ⊠

♠♠♠ ♥♥♥♥ Holiday Inn Express-West SH

(505) 836-8600. **$90-$110.** 6100 Iliff Rd NW. I-40, exit 155, just sw. Ext/int corridors. **Pets:** Other species. $10 one-time fee/room. Service with restrictions, supervision.

SAVE SD X 5M ⌀ ⌂ H ⬛ ⇌ ⊠

♠♠♠ ♥♥♥♥ The Hotel Blue SH

(505) 924-2400. **$79-$109.** 717 Central Ave NW. 8th and Central Ave; downtown. Ext corridors. **Pets:** Accepted.

SAVE SD X ⌀ ⌂ H ⬛ ⇌

♠♠♠ ♥♥♥♥ Howard Johnson Express Inn SH

(505) 828-1600. **$60-$130.** 7630 Pan American Frwy NE. I-25, exit 231, 0.8 mi n on frontage road. Int corridors. **Pets:** Large, other species. $10 daily fee/pet. Designated rooms, service with restrictions, supervision.

SAVE SD X ⌀ ⌂ H ⬛ ⇌

♥♥♥♥ La Quinta Inn Albuquerque (Airport) SH

(505) 243-5500. **$89-$109.** 2116 Yale Blvd SE. I-25, exit 222 northbound; exit 222A southbound, 1 mi e. Ext/int corridors. **Pets:** Accepted.

ASK X 5M ⌀ ⌂ H ⬛ ⇌

♥♥♥♥ La Quinta Inn Albuquerque (I-40 East) SH

(505) 884-3591. **$84-$104.** 2424 San Mateo Blvd NE. I-40, exit 161 westbound; exit 161B eastbound, just n. Ext corridors. **Pets:** Accepted.

ASK X ⌀ ⌂ H ⬛ ⇌

♠♠♠ ♥♥♥♥ La Quinta Inn Albuquerque (North) SH

(505) 821-9000. **$89-$109.** 5241 San Antonio Dr NE. I-25, exit 231, just e. Ext corridors. **Pets:** Accepted.

SAVE X 5M ⌀ ⌂ H ⬛ ⇌

♥♥♥♥ La Quinta Inn & Suites Albuquerque (West) SH

(505) 839-1744. **$99-$119.** 6101 Iliff Rd NW. I-40, exit 155, just sw. Int corridors. **Pets:** Accepted.

ASK X ⌀ ⌂ H ⬛ ⇌

♥♥♥ Le Baron Courtyard & Suites SH

(505) 884-0250. **$59-$79.** 2120 Menaul Blvd NE. I-40, exit 160, just n to Menaul Blvd, then 0.8 mi w. Ext corridors. **Pets:** Other species. $25 one-time fee/room. Service with restrictions.

ASK SD X 5M ⌀ H ⬛ ⇌

♥♥♥♥ MCM Elegante Hotel SH

(505) 884-2511. **$76-$154.** 2020 Menaul Blvd NE. I-40, exit 160, 0.3 mi n to Menaul Blvd, then 1 mi w. Int corridors. **Pets:** Accepted.

ASK SD X 5M ⌀ ⌂ ⬛ ¶ ⇌ ⊠

♥♥♥ Microtel Inn & Suites SH

(505) 836-1686. **$65.** 9910 Avalon NW. I-40, exit 153, just s; on western edge of city. Int corridors. **Pets:** Accepted.

ASK SD X ⬛

♥ Motel 6 #1349 M

(505) 243-8017. **$41-$53.** 1000 Avenida Cesar Chavez. I-25, exit 223, just w. Ext corridors. **Pets:** Accepted.

SD X 5M ⌂ H ⇌

♥ Motel 6 Albuquerque East #49 M

(505) 294-4600. **Call for rates.** 13141 Central Ave NE. I-40, exit 167 (Tramway Blvd), just s, then just w. Ext corridors. **Pets:** Accepted.

X ⇌

♥ Motel 6 Albuquerque North #1290 SH

(505) 821-1472. **$41-$53.** 8510 Pan American Frwy NE. I-25, exit 232 (Paseo del Norte), just n on Frontage Rd. Int corridors. **Pets:** Accepted.

SD X 5M ⌂ ⇌

(AAA) ▼▼▼ Motel 76 SH
(505) 836-3881. **$34-$39.** 1521 Coors Blvd NW. I-40, exit 155 (Coors Blvd), just s. Ext corridors. **Pets:** Medium. $25 deposit/room. Service with restrictions, supervision.
SAVE S✆ ✕

(AAA) ▼▼▼ Plaza Inn Albuquerque SH
(505) 243-5693. **$89-$109.** 900 Medical Arts NE. I-25, exit 225, just e. Int corridors. **Pets:** $25 one-time fee/room. Service with restrictions, crate.
SAVE S✆ ✕ 🛏 💻 ⊇

▼▼ Quality Inn & Suites Albuquerque Downtown SH
(505) 242-5228. **$59-$69.** 411 McKnight Ave NW. I-40, exit 159A, just s via 4th St N. Int corridors. **Pets:** Medium, other species. $50 deposit/room, $15 one-time fee/pet. Service with restrictions, crate.
ASK S✆ ✕ 💻 ⊇

▼▼▼▼ Radisson Hotel & Conference Center LH
(505) 888-3311. **$89-$179.** 2500 Carlisle Blvd NE. I-40, exit 160, just n. Ext/int corridors. **Pets:** Accepted.
ASK S✆ ✕ ᏭM 🐾 Ꮜ 🛏 💻 🍴 ⊇ ✕

▼▼▼▼ Ramada Limited SH
(505) 858-3297. **$59-$159, 7 day notice.** 5601 Alameda Blvd NE. I-25, exit 233, just w. Int corridors. **Pets:** Accepted.
ASK S✆ ✕ ᏭM 🐾 Ꮜ 🛏 💻 ⊇

▼▼▼▼ Ramada Limited (Airport) SH 🐾
(505) 242-0036. **$64-$79.** 1801 Yale Blvd SE. I-25, exit 222 northbound; exit 222A southbound, 1 mi e, then just n. Int corridors. **Pets:** Other species. $10 daily fee/room. Designated rooms, service with restrictions, crate.
ASK S✆ ✕ ᏭM Ꮜ 🛏 ⊇ ✕

▼▼ Red Roof Inn SH
(505) 831-3400. **$38-$56.** 6015 Iliff Rd NW. I-40, exit 155 (Coors Blvd), just s, then just w. Ext corridors. **Pets:** Accepted.
✕ ᏭM 🐾 Ꮜ ⊇

▼▼▼ Residence Inn by Marriott SH
(505) 881-2661. **$79-$139.** 3300 Prospect Dr NE. I-40, exit 160, just n to Menaul Blvd, then just w. Ext corridors. **Pets:** Accepted.
ASK ✕ 🐾 🛏 💻 ⊇ ✕

▼▼▼ Residence Inn North by Marriott SH
(505) 761-0200. **$109-$149.** 4331 The Lane at 25 NE. I-25, exit 229 (Jefferson St), just w, just n to The Lane at 25 NE, then just e. Int corridors. **Pets:** Accepted.
ASK ✕ ᏭM Ꮜ 🛏 💻 ⊇ ✕

(AAA) ▼▼▼ Sheraton Albuquerque Uptown LH
(505) 881-0000. **$79-$189.** 2600 Louisiana Blvd NE. I-40, exit 162, 0.8 mi n. Int corridors. **Pets:** Accepted.
SAVE S✆ ✕ ᏭM 🐾 Ꮜ 🛏 💻 🍴 ⊇ ✕

▼▼▼▼ Sheraton Old Town LH
(505) 843-6300. **$89-$159.** 800 Rio Grande Blvd NW. I-40, exit 157A, 0.4 mi s. Int corridors. **Pets:** Accepted.
ASK S✆ ✕ 🐾 💻 🍴 ⊇ ✕

▼▼ Sleep Inn Airport SH
(505) 244-3325. **Call for rates.** 2300 International Ave SE. I-25, exit 222, northbound; exit 222A southbound, 1 mi e to Yale Blvd, then just n. Int corridors. **Pets:** Accepted.
✕ ᏭM 🐾 Ꮜ ⊇

(AAA) ▼▼ Stardust Inn M
(505) 243-2891. **$30-$79.** 801 Central Ave NE. I-25, 224A northbound; exit 224B southbound, just e. Ext corridors. **Pets:** Medium. $25 deposit/pet, $5 daily fee/pet. Service with restrictions, supervision.
SAVE S✆ ✕ 🛏 ⊇

▼▼▼ Sun Village Corporate Suites CO
(505) 842-6640. **$60-$90, 7 day notice.** 801 Locust NE. From University Blvd, just w on Indian School Rd, then just n. Ext corridors. **Pets:** Accepted.
✕ 🛏 💻 ⊇ ✕

▼▼ Super 8 Motel East SH
(505) 271-4807. **$58-$108, 14 day notice.** 450 Paisano NE. I-40, exit 166 (Juan Tabo Blvd), just n to Copper, then just s. Int corridors. **Pets:** Accepted.
ASK S✆ ✕ Ꮜ

▼▼ Super 8 Motel of Albuquerque SH
(505) 888-4884. **$58-$108, 14 day notice.** 2500 University Blvd NE. I-25, exit 225 northbound, 1.9 mi n on frontage road to Menaul Blvd, then just e; exit 227 (Comanche Rd) southbound, 0.9 mi s to Menaul Blvd, then just e. Int corridors. **Pets:** Accepted.
ASK S✆ ✕ 🐾 Ꮜ 🛏

▼▼ Super 8 Motel West (Albuquerque) SH
(505) 836-5560. **$59-$89, 14 day notice.** 6030 Iliff Rd NW. I-40, exit 155, 0.5 mi s. Int corridors. **Pets:** Accepted.
ASK S✆ ✕ 🛏

(AAA) ▼▼▼ TownePlace Suites SH 🐾
(505) 232-5800. **$69-$109.** 2400 Centre Ave SE. I-25, exit 222 northbound; exit 222A southbound, 1 mi e to Yale Blvd, at northeast jct of Gibson and Yale blvds, then just e. Int corridors. **Pets:** Other species. $75 one-time fee/pet. Service with restrictions, supervision.
SAVE S✆ ✕ ᏭM Ꮜ 🛏 💻 ⊇ ✕

ALGODONES

(AAA) ▼▼▼▼ Hacienda Vargas Bed and Breakfast Inn BB
(505) 867-9115. **$89-$149, 10 day notice.** 1431 SR 313 (El Camino Real). I-25, exit 248, 0.5 mi w. Int corridors. **Pets:** Accepted.
SAVE S✆ ✕ ⨎ ⊘

ALTO

▼▼ High Country Lodge CA
(505) 336-4321. **$89-$124, 7 day notice.** Hwy 48. Center. Ext corridors. **Pets:** Small, other species. $11 one-time fee/pet. Supervision.
🛏 💻 ⊇ ✕ 🎿

▼▼ Rancho Ruidoso Condominiums CO
(505) 336-8103. **$140-$165, 14 day notice.** 6 Little Creek Rd. Jct SR 48, 4.2 mi e on Little Creek Rd (SR 220), just s at sign. Ext corridors. **Pets:** Accepted.
🛏 💻 ⊇ ✕ 🎿 ⊘

ARROYO SECO

▼▼▼ Adobe and Stars B & B BB
(505) 776-2776. **$95-$185, 30 day notice.** 584 SR 150. 1.1 mi ne on SR 150 at Valdez Rd. Ext/int corridors. **Pets:** Accepted.
ASK ✕ 🛏 🎿 ⨎

ARTESIA

(AAA) ▼▼ Artesia Inn M
(505) 746-9801. **$45-$55.** 1820 S 1st St. 1.5 mi s on US 285. Ext corridors. **Pets:** Accepted.
SAVE S✆ ✕ 🛏 💻 ⊇

▼▼▼▼ Holiday Inn Express-Artesia SH
(505) 748-3904. **$80-$95.** 2210 W Main. 1.6 mi w of jct US 82 and 285. Int corridors. **Pets:** Small, dogs only. $20 one-time fee/pet. Designated rooms, no service, supervision.
ASK S✆ ✕ ᏭM 🐾 Ꮜ 🛏 💻 ⊇

BELEN

AAA ▼▼▼ Best Western-Belen **SH**
(505) 861-3181. **$79.** 2111 Camino del Llano Blvd. I-25, exit 191, just w. Ext/int corridors. **Pets:** Accepted.
[SAVE] [S⚡] [✕] [🔒] [🛏] [📺] [🏊]

▼▼▼ Holiday Inn Express **SH**
(505) 861-5000. **$89.** 2110 Camino del Llano. I-25, exit 191, just w. Int corridors. **Pets:** Accepted.
[ASK] [S⚡] [✕] [🔒M] [♿] [🛏] [📺] [🏊]

BERNALILLO

▼▼ Days Inn **SH**
(505) 771-7000. **$45-$100.** 107 N Camino del Pueblo. I-25, exit 242, just w. Int corridors. **Pets:** Small, dogs only. $30 deposit/pet. Service with restrictions, supervision.
[ASK] [S⚡] [✕] [🏊]

▼▼▼ La Hacienda Grande **BB**
(505) 867-1887. **$109, 10 day notice.** 21 Barros Rd. I-25, exit 242, 0.3 mi w to Camino del Pueblo, then 0.5 mi n. Ext/int corridors. **Pets:** Other species. $10 one-time fee/room. Supervision.
[ASK] [S⚡] [✕] [☎]

▼▼▼ Quality Inn & Suites **SH**
(505) 771-9500. **$66-$126, 10 day notice.** 210 N Hill Rd. I-25, exit 242, just w. Int corridors. **Pets:** Small. $20 one-time fee/room. Service with restrictions, supervision.
[ASK] [S⚡] [✕] [🔒M] [🛏] [📺]

BLOOMFIELD

▼▼ Super 8 Motel **M**
(505) 632-8886. **$50.** 525 W Broadway Blvd. Jct of US 64 and SR 44. Int corridors. **Pets:** $10 one-time fee/room. Service with restrictions, supervision.
[ASK] [S⚡] [✕] [🎵] [🛏]

CARLSBAD

AAA ▼▼▼ Best Western Stevens Inn **SH**
(505) 887-2851. **$79-$99.** 1829 S Canal St. 1 mi s on US 62, 180 and 285. Ext corridors. **Pets:** Small. $10 deposit/pet. No service.
[SAVE] [S⚡] [✕] [🔒] [🛏] [📺] [🍴] [🏊]

AAA ▼▼▼ Carlsbad Inn **M** 🐾
(505) 887-1171. **$36-$49.** 2019 S Canal St. 1.5 mi s on US 62, 180 and 285. Ext corridors. **Pets:** Small. $5 daily fee/pet. Designated rooms, service with restrictions, supervision.
[SAVE] [✕] [🛏] [🏊]

▼▼▼ Comfort Inn **SH**
(505) 887-1994. **$71-$81.** 2429 W Pierce St. N on US 285. Int corridors. **Pets:** Accepted.
[ASK] [S⚡] [✕] [🔒M] [♿] [🛏] [📺] [🏊]

AAA ▼▼▼ Continental Inn **M**
(505) 887-0341. **$36-$49.** 3820 National Parks Hwy. 3.5 mi sw on US 62 and 180. Ext corridors. **Pets:** Accepted.
[SAVE] [✕] [🛏] [🏊]

AAA ▼▼▼ Days Inn of Carlsbad **SH**
(505) 887-7800. **$59, 14 day notice.** 3910 National Parks Hwy. 3.5 mi sw on US 62 and 180. Ext corridors. **Pets:** Accepted.
[SAVE] [S⚡] [✕] [🔒M] [🎵] [🛏] [🏊]

AAA ▼▼▼ Quality Inn **SH** 🐾
(505) 887-2861. **$54-$79.** 3706 National Parks Hwy. 3 mi sw on US 62 and 180. Ext corridors. **Pets:** Large, other species. Designated rooms, service with restrictions, supervision.
[SAVE] [S⚡] [✕] [🎵] [🛏] [📺] [🏊]

CHAMA

AAA ▼▼▼ Branding Iron Motel **M**
(505) 756-2162. **$69-$109.** 1511 W Main. 0.5 mi s. Ext corridors. **Pets:** Small. $10 daily fee/pet. Service with restrictions, supervision.
[SAVE] [S⚡] [✕] [📺] [🍴]

AAA ▼▼▼▼ Vista del Rio Lodge **M**
(505) 756-2138. **$60-$90.** 2595 US Hwy 84/64. 0.5 mi s of SR 17. Ext corridors. **Pets:** Small, dogs only. Service with restrictions, crate.
[SAVE] [S⚡] [✕] [🛏] [📺] [✕] [🐾]

CHIMAYO

▼▼ Casa Escondida Bed & Breakfast **BB** 🐾
(505) 351-4805. **$85-$145, 14 day notice.** 64 CR 0100. SR 68, 7.1 mi e on SR 76, 0.5 mi nw on CR 100, follow signs. Ext/int corridors. **Pets:** Other species. $15 daily fee/pet. Designated rooms, service with restrictions, supervision.
[✕] [🛏] [W] [☎]

CIMARRON

AAA ▼ Cimarron Inn & RV Park **M**
(505) 376-2268. **$55-$65.** 212 10th St. On US 64. Ext corridors. **Pets:** Accepted.
[SAVE] [✕] [🛏] [📺] [🐾]

CLAYTON

AAA ▼▼▼▼ Best Western Kokopelli Lodge **SH** 🐾
(505) 374-2589. **$69-$125.** 702 S 1st St. US 87, 0.5 mi se of jct US 56 and 64. Ext corridors. **Pets:** Medium. $5 daily fee/pet. Designated rooms, service with restrictions, crate.
[SAVE] [S⚡] [✕] [🔒] [🛏] [📺] [🍴] [🏊] [✕]

AAA ▼▼▼ Days Inn & Suites **SH**
(505) 374-0133. **$64-$139.** 1120 S 1st St. US 87, 1 mi s of jct US 56 and 64. Int corridors. **Pets:** $5 daily fee/pet. Service with restrictions, supervision.
[SAVE] [S⚡] [✕] [🔒] [🛏] [📺] [🏊]

▼▼ Super 8 Motel **M**
(505) 374-8127. **$65-$70.** 1425 S 1st St. US 87, 1 mi se of jct US 56 and 64. Int corridors. **Pets:** Accepted.
[ASK] [S⚡] [✕] [🎵]

CLOUDCROFT

AAA ▼▼▼ The Lodge **SH** 🐾
(505) 682-2566. **$109-$159, 14 day notice.** 1 Corona Pl. US 82, 0.3 mi s. Int corridors. **Pets:** $25 one-time fee/room. Designated rooms, supervision.
[SAVE] [S⚡] [✕] [🔒M] [🔒] [🛏] [📺] [🍴] [🏊] [✕]

CLOVIS

AAA ▼▼▼ Comfort Inn **SH**
(505) 762-4591. **$59-$79.** 1616 Mabry Dr. 1 mi e on US 60, 70 and 84. Ext corridors. **Pets:** Large, other species. $10 one-time fee/room. Service with restrictions, supervision.
[SAVE] [S⚡] [✕] [🛏] [📺] [🏊]

AAA ▼▼▼ Econo Lodge **M**
(505) 763-3439. **$59-$99.** 1400 E Mabry Dr. 0.5 mi e on US 60, 70 and 84. Ext corridors. **Pets:** Accepted.
[SAVE] [S⚡] [✕] [🔒] [🛏] [🏊]

▼▼ Stagecoach Inn **M**
(505) 887-1148. **$44-$52.** 1819 S Canal St. 1 mi s on US 62, 180 and 285. Ext corridors. **Pets:** Medium. $5 daily fee/pet. Service with restrictions, supervision.
[SAVE] [S⚡] [✕] [🛏] [🍴] [🏊]

▼▼▼ **Holiday Inn Clovis** SH
(505) 762-4491. **$80.** 2700 E Mabry Dr. 1.5 mi e on US 60, 70 and 84. Ext corridors. **Pets:** Very small, other species. Service with restrictions, supervision.
(ASK) (S&) ☒ (&M) ◐ (&) ▤ 💻 (¶¶) ⇌ (✕)

▼▼ **Howard Johnson Expressway Inn** SH
(505) 769-1953. **$52-$66.** 2920 Mabry Dr. US 60, 70 and 84, just e. Int corridors. **Pets:** Accepted.
(ASK) (S&) ☒ ▤ 💻 ⇌

(AAA) ▼▼▼▼ **La Quinta Inn & Suites Clovis** SH
(505) 763-8777. **$80-$105.** 4521 N Prince St. Jct US 60/84 and Prince St, 3 mi n. Int corridors. **Pets:** Other species. Service with restrictions, crate.
(SAVE) (S&) ☒ (⌀) (&) ▤ 💻 ⇌

▼ **Motel 6 Clovis #217** M
(505) 762-2995. **Call for rates.** 2620 Mabry Dr. Jct US 60/70/84. Ext corridors. **Pets:** Accepted.
☒ (&) ⇌

DEMING

▼▼ **Best Western Mimbres Valley Inn** SH ❀
(505) 546-4544. **$49-$75.** 1500 W Pine. I-10, exit 81, just e. Ext corridors. **Pets:** Very small, other species. $5 daily fee/pet. Designated rooms, service with restrictions, supervision.
(ASK) (S&) ☒ ▤ 💻 ⇌

(AAA) ▼▼ **Days Inn** M ❀
(505) 546-8813. **$47-$57.** 1601 E Pine St. I-10, exit 85 westbound, 2 mi w on business loop; exit 81 eastbound, 1 mi e on business loop. Ext corridors. **Pets:** Small. $5 daily fee/pet. Service with restrictions, supervision.
(SAVE) (S&) ☒ ▤ 💻 (¶¶) ⇌

(AAA) ▼▼▼ **Grand Motor Inn** SH
(505) 546-2632. **$48.** 1721 E Pine St. I-10, exit 85 westbound, 2 mi w on business loop; exit 82 eastbound, 1 mi e on business loop. Ext corridors. **Pets:** Medium, other species. $6 daily fee/room. Designated rooms, service with restrictions, supervision.
(SAVE) (S&) ☒ ▤ (¶¶) ⇌

(AAA) ▼▼▼ **Holiday Inn** SH
(505) 546-2661. **$49-$99.** 4600 E Pine St. I-10, exit 85, just w. Ext corridors. **Pets:** Service with restrictions, supervision.
(SAVE) (S&) ☒ (&M) (⌀) (&) ▤ 💻 (¶¶) ⇌

EDGEWOOD

▼▼▼ **Alta Mae's Heritage Inn** BB
(505) 281-5000. **$95, 14 day notice.** 1950-C Old Route 66. I-40, exit 187, just s to stop sign, then just e. Ext corridors. **Pets:** Accepted.
(ASK) ☒ (✕) (☎)

ELEPHANT BUTTE

(AAA) ▼▼▼▼ **Elephant Butte Inn** SH
(505) 744-5431. **$69-$89.** 401 Hwy 195. I-25, exit 83, 4 mi e. Ext corridors. **Pets:** Accepted.
(SAVE) (S&) ☒ (&M) (&) ▤ 💻 (¶¶) ⇌

(AAA) ▼ **Marina Suites Motel** M
(505) 744-5269. **$75-$95.** 200 Country Club Dr. I-25, exit 83, 4.7 mi e. Ext corridors. **Pets:** Dogs only. $10 deposit/room. Service with restrictions, supervision.
(SAVE) (S&) ▤ 💻 (☎)

ESPANOLA

(AAA) ▼▼▼ **Comfort Inn** SH
(505) 753-2419. **$55-$125.** 604-B S Riverside Dr. US 84 and 285, just s of jct SR 68. Int corridors. **Pets:** Accepted.
(SAVE) (S&) ☒ ▤ 💻 ⇌

▼▼ **Espanola Days Inn** SH
(505) 747-1242. **$50-$76.** 807 S Riverside Dr. US 84 and 285, 0.7 mi s of jct SR 68. Ext corridors. **Pets:** $6 daily fee/pet. Service with restrictions, supervision.
(ASK) (S&) ☒

(AAA) ▼▼▼ **Super 8 Motel** SH
(505) 753-5374. **$41-$106.** 811 S Riverside Dr. US 84 and 285, 0.5 mi s of jct SR 68. Int corridors. **Pets:** Other species. Service with restrictions, supervision.
(SAVE) (S&) ☒ ▤ 💻

FARMINGTON

(AAA) ▼▼▼ **Best Western Inn & Suites** SH
(505) 327-5221. **$89-$99.** 700 Scott Ave. 0.8 mi e on US 64 at Bloomfield Blvd and Scott Ave. Int corridors. **Pets:** Other species. $10 one-time fee/room. Designated rooms, service with restrictions, supervision.
(SAVE) (S&) ☒ (⌀) ▤ 💻 (¶¶) ⇌ (✕)

(AAA) ▼▼▼ **Comfort Inn** M
(505) 325-2626. **$69-$109.** 555 Scott Ave. 0.8 mi e on US 64 (Bloomfield Blvd), just n. Int corridors. **Pets:** Accepted.
(SAVE) (S&) ☒ ▤ 💻 ⇌

▼▼ **Days Inn** M
(505) 325-3700. **$60-$80.** 1901 E Broadway. 1.7 mi e on US 64 (Bloomfield Blvd). Int corridors. **Pets:** Accepted.
(ASK) (S&) ☒ (&M) (⌀) (&) ▤ 💻

(AAA) ▼▼▼▼ **Holiday Inn Express** M 🐾
(505) 325-2545. **$63-$94, 14 day notice.** 2110 Bloomfield Blvd. 1.6 mi e on US 64 (Bloomfield Blvd). Int corridors. **Pets:** Small. $10 one-time fee/room. Service with restrictions, supervision.
(SAVE) (S&) ☒ (&M) (⌀) (&) ▤ 💻 ⇌

(AAA) ▼▼▼ **Holiday Inn of Farmington** SH
(505) 327-9811. **$65-$75.** 600 E Broadway. 0.8 mi e on US 64 at Bloomfield Blvd and Scott Ave. Int corridors. **Pets:** $20 one-time fee/room. No service, supervision.
(SAVE) (S&) ☒ (⌀) ▤ 💻 (¶¶) ⇌ (✕)

(AAA) ▼▼▼ **La Quinta Inn Farmington** M
(505) 327-4706. **$75-$95.** 675 Scott Ave. 0.8 mi e on US 64 at Bloomfield Blvd and Scott Ave. Ext/int corridors. **Pets:** Other species. Service with restrictions, supervision.
(SAVE) ☒ (&M) (⌀) ▤ 💻 ⇌

(AAA) ▼▼▼ **Super 8 Motel** M
(505) 325-1813. **$55-$105.** 1601 E Broadway. Just n of jct SR 44. Int corridors. **Pets:** $5 daily fee/pet.
(SAVE) (S&) ☒ (&) ▤

GALLUP

(AAA) ▼▼▼ **Best Western Inn & Suites** SH
(505) 722-2221. **$59-$89.** 3009 US 66 W. I-40, exit 16, 1 mi e. Int corridors. **Pets:** Accepted.
(SAVE) (S&) ☒ ▤ 💻 (¶¶) ⇌ (✕)

(AAA) ▼▼▼ **Best Western Royal Holiday Motel** SH
(505) 722-4900. **$59-$149.** 1903 W Hwy 66. I-40, exit 20, 0.5 mi s to US 66, then 0.8 mi w. Int corridors. **Pets:** Accepted.
(SAVE) (S&) ☒ ▤ 💻 ⇌

(AAA) ▼▼▼ **Comfort Inn** M
(505) 722-0982. **$49-$99.** 3208 US 66 W. I-40, exit 16, 0.3 mi e. Int corridors. **Pets:** Small. $5 daily fee/pet. Service with restrictions, supervision.
(SAVE) (S&) ☒ ▤ 💻 ⇌

AAA ▼▼▼ Days Inn-West SH
(505) 863-6889. **$60-$90, 7 day notice.** 3201 W Hwy 66. I-40, exit 16, 0.3 mi e. Ext corridors. **Pets:** Accepted.
〔SAVE〕〔S◈〕〔✕〕〔▤〕〔▣〕〔⇌〕

AAA ▼▼▼ Econo Lodge SH
(505) 722-3800. **$35-$60.** 3101 US 66 W. I-40, exit 16, 0.8 mi e. Int corridors. **Pets:** Other species. $5 daily fee/pet. Service with restrictions, supervision.
〔SAVE〕〔S◈〕〔✕〕

AAA ▼▼▼ Gallup Travelodge SH
(505) 722-2100. **$38.** 3275 US 66 W. I-40, exit 16, just e. Int corridors. **Pets:** $8 daily fee/pet. Designated rooms, service with restrictions, supervision.
〔SAVE〕〔S◈〕〔✕〕〔占M〕〔占〕〔▣〕〔⇌〕

AAA ▼▼▼ Ramada Limited SH
(505) 726-2700. **$64-$99.** 1440 W Maloney Ave. I-40, exit 20, 1 mi w. Int corridors. **Pets:** Medium, dogs only. $5 daily fee/pet. Designated rooms, service with restrictions, supervision.
〔SAVE〕〔S◈〕〔✕〕〔占M〕〔▤〕〔▣〕〔⇌〕

AAA ▼▼▼ Red Roof Inn M
(505) 722-7765. **$36-$60.** 3304 W Hwy 66. I-40, exit 16, just se. Ext corridors. **Pets:** Large. $3 daily fee/pet. Service with restrictions, supervision.
〔SAVE〕〔S◈〕〔✕〕〔▤〕〔▣〕〔⇌〕

▼ Road Runner Motel M
(505) 863-3804. **$36.** 3012 US 66 E. I-40, exit 26, 1 mi w. Ext corridors. **Pets:** Other species. Service with restrictions.
〔SAVE〕〔S◈〕〔✕〕〔¶〕〔⇌〕

▼▼ Sleep Inn SH
(505) 863-3535. **$55-$70.** 3820 E US 66. I-40, exit 26, just e. Int corridors. **Pets:** $8 daily fee/pet. Service with restrictions, crate.
〔ASK〕〔S◈〕〔✕〕〔占M〕〔占〕〔▣〕〔⇌〕

AAA ▼▼▼ Super 8 Motel M
(505) 722-5300. **$45-$88.** 1715 W US 66. I-40, exit 20, s to US 66, then 0.5 mi w. Int corridors. **Pets:** $7 daily fee/pet. Designated rooms, service with restrictions, supervision.
〔SAVE〕〔S◈〕〔✕〕〔▤〕〔▣〕〔⇌〕

GRANTS

AAA ▼▼▼ Best Western Inn & Suites SH
(505) 287-7901. **$69-$89.** 1501 E Santa Fe Ave. I-40, exit 85, just w. Int corridors. **Pets:** $10 one-time fee/room. Designated rooms, service with restrictions, supervision.
〔SAVE〕〔S◈〕〔✕〕〔∅〕〔▤〕〔▣〕〔¶〕〔⇌〕〔✕〕

▼▼▼ Comfort Inn SH
(505) 287-8700. **$54-$79.** 1551 E Santa Fe Ave. I-40, exit 85, 0.3 mi n. Int corridors. **Pets:** Medium, dogs only. $5 daily fee/pet. Designated rooms, service with restrictions, supervision.
〔ASK〕〔S◈〕〔✕〕〔占M〕〔▤〕〔▣〕〔⇌〕

AAA ▼▼▼ Days Inn SH
(505) 287-8883. **$50-$90, 14 day notice.** 1504 E Santa Fe Ave. I-40, exit 85, 0.3 mi n. Ext corridors. **Pets:** Other species. $5 one-time fee/pet. Service with restrictions.
〔SAVE〕〔S◈〕〔✕〕

AAA ▼▼▼ Grants Travelodge SH
(505) 287-7800. **$49-$64.** 1608 E Santa Fe Ave. I-40, exit 85, 0.3 mi n. Ext corridors. **Pets:** Medium, dogs only. $5 daily fee/pet. Designated rooms, service with restrictions, supervision.
〔SAVE〕〔S◈〕〔✕〕〔占M〕〔占〕〔▣〕〔⇌〕

▼▼▼ Holiday Inn Express SH
(505) 285-4676. **$80-$120, 3 day notice.** 1496 E Sante Fe Ave. I-40, exit 85, 0.3 mi n. Int corridors. **Pets:** Small. $10 daily fee/pet. Designated rooms, service with restrictions, supervision.
〔ASK〕〔S◈〕〔✕〕〔▤〕〔▣〕〔⇌〕

AAA ▼▼▼ Sands Motel M
(505) 287-2996. **$40-$43.** 112 McArthur St. I-40, exit 85, 1.5 mi w on Business Loop 40. Ext corridors. **Pets:** Medium. $5 one-time fee/pet. Service with restrictions, supervision.
〔SAVE〕〔S◈〕〔✕〕〔▤〕

▼▼ Super 8 Grants SH
(505) 287-8811. **$45-$65.** 1604 E Santa Fe Ave. I-40, exit 85, just n. Int corridors. **Pets:** Accepted.
〔ASK〕〔S◈〕〔✕〕〔▤〕〔⇌〕

HOBBS

AAA ▼▼▼ Best Western Executive Inn SH
(505) 397-7171. **$60-$70.** 309 N Marland Blvd. US 62/180 and Snyder St. Ext corridors. **Pets:** Accepted.
〔SAVE〕〔S◈〕〔✕〕〔▤〕〔▣〕〔⇌〕

AAA ▼▼▼ Days Inn M
(505) 397-6541. **$55-$65, 3 day notice.** 211 N Marland Blvd. 2 mi e on US 62 and 180. Ext corridors. **Pets:** Accepted.
〔SAVE〕〔S◈〕〔✕〕〔∅〕〔占〕〔▤〕〔▣〕〔⇌〕

AAA ▼▼▼ Econo Lodge SH
(505) 397-3591. **$44-$54.** 619 N Marland Blvd. 2.5 mi e on US 62 and 180. Ext corridors. **Pets:** Accepted.
〔SAVE〕〔S◈〕〔✕〕〔▤〕〔▣〕〔⇌〕

AAA ▼▼▼ Howard Johnson-Hobbs SH
(505) 397-3251. **$65-$72, 5 day notice.** 501 N Marland Blvd. 2.5 mi e on US 62 and 180. Ext/int corridors. **Pets:** $7 one-time fee/pet. Service with restrictions, supervision.
〔SAVE〕〔S◈〕〔✕〕〔占〕〔▤〕〔▣〕〔¶〕〔⇌〕

AAA ▼▼▼ Rodeway Inn M
(505) 393-4101. **$46-$55, 3 day notice.** 200 N Marland Blvd. On US 62/180, 2 mi e. Ext corridors. **Pets:** Accepted.
〔ASK〕〔S◈〕〔✕〕〔▤〕〔▣〕

LAS CRUCES

AAA ▼▼▼ Baymont Inn & Suites Las Cruces SH
(505) 523-0100. **$49-$64.** 1500 Hickory Dr. I-10, exit 140, just se of jct I-25 and Avenida de Mesilla. Int corridors. **Pets:** Small. $25 deposit/room. Service with restrictions, supervision.
〔SAVE〕〔S◈〕〔✕〕〔占M〕〔占〕〔▤〕〔▣〕〔⇌〕

AAA ▼▼▼ Best Western Mesilla Valley Inn SH
(505) 524-8603. **$62-$89.** 901 Avenida de Mesilla. I-10, exit 140, just n. Ext/int corridors. **Pets:** Medium, other species. Service with restrictions.
〔SAVE〕〔S◈〕〔✕〕〔∅〕〔▤〕〔▣〕〔¶〕〔⇌〕

AAA ▼▼▼ Best Western Mission Inn SH
(505) 524-8591. **$65-$75.** 1765 S Main St. I-10, exit 142, 1 mi n. Ext corridors. **Pets:** Accepted.
〔SAVE〕〔S◈〕〔✕〕〔▤〕〔▣〕〔¶〕〔⇌〕

▼▼▼ Comfort Suites by Choice Hotels SH
(505) 522-1300. **$65-$85.** 2101 S Triviz. I-25, exit 1. Int corridors. **Pets:** Medium, dogs only. $15 one-time fee/room. Designated rooms, service with restrictions, supervision.
〔ASK〕〔S◈〕〔✕〕〔占M〕〔∅〕〔占〕〔▤〕〔▣〕〔⇌〕

AAA ▼▼▼ Hampton Inn SH
(505) 526-8311. **$72-$74.** 755 Avenida de Mesilla. I-10, exit 140. Ext corridors. **Pets:** Small. Service with restrictions, supervision.
〔SAVE〕〔S◈〕〔✕〕〔▤〕〔▣〕〔⇌〕

▼▼▼▼ Hilton Las Cruces LH
(505) 522-4300. **$65-$129.** 705 S Telshore Blvd. I-25, exit 3 (Lohman Dr), just e. Int corridors. **Pets:** Small, dogs only. $25 one-time fee/room. Designated rooms, service with restrictions, supervision.
ASK ✕ ⓜ 🕭 🛢 🖳 🍴 🏊

▼▼▼▼ Holiday Inn de Las Cruces SH
(505) 526-4411. **$71-$78.** 201 E University Ave. I-10, exit 142, just n. Int corridors. **Pets:** Accepted.
ASK Sⓓ ✕ ⓜ 🕭 🖖 🛢 🖳 🍴 🏊

▼▼▼▼ Holiday Inn Express SH
(505) 527-9947. **$59-$149.** 2200 S Valley Dr. I-10, exit 142, 2 blks w. Ext corridors. **Pets:** Very small. Service with restrictions, supervision.
ASK Sⓓ ✕ ⓜ 🕭 🛢 🖳 🏊

▼▼▼▼ La Quinta Inn Las Cruces SH
(505) 524-0331. **$85-$105.** 790 Avenida de Mesilla. I-10, exit 140. Int corridors. **Pets:** Accepted.
ASK ✕ ⓜ 🕭 🛢 🖳 🏊

▼▼▼▼ Lundeen's Inn of the Arts BB 🐾
(505) 526-3326. **$72.** 618 S Alameda Blvd. Center. Int corridors. **Pets:** Medium. $15 one-time fee/pet. Service with restrictions, crate.
ASK ✕

▼▼ Motel 6–363 M
(505) 525-1010. **$38-$52.** 235 La Posada Ln. I-10, exit 142, just n. Ext corridors. **Pets:** Accepted.
ASK ✕ ⓜ 🕭 🖖 🛢 🏊

▼▼▼ Royal Host Motel M
(505) 524-8536. **$38-$46.** 2146 W Picacho St. I-10, exit 139, 1 mi n, then 0.5 mi e on I-10 business route (Picacho St). Ext corridors. **Pets:** Medium. $10 daily fee/pet. No service, supervision.
✕ 🛢 🏊

▼▼▼▼ Sleep Inn by Choice Hotels SH
(505) 522-1700. **$65-$85.** 2121 S Triviz. I-25, exit 1. Int corridors. **Pets:** Medium, dogs only. $15 one-time fee/room. Designated rooms, service with restrictions, supervision.
ASK Sⓓ ✕ ⓜ 🕭 🖖 🛢 🖳 🏊

▼▼ Super 8 Motel M
(505) 523-8695. **Call for rates.** 245 La Posada Ln. I-10, exit 142, 2.8 mi s on US 80, 85 and 180. Int corridors. **Pets:** Accepted.
✕ 🛢

▼▼▼ TRH Smith Mansion Bed and Breakfast BB
(505) 525-2525. **Call for rates.** 909 N Alameda Blvd. Center. Int corridors. **Pets:** Accepted.
✕

LAS VEGAS

▲▲▲ ▼▼▼ Comfort Inn SH
(505) 425-1100. **$75-$100.** 2500 N Grand Ave. I-25, exit 347, just sw, US 85 and I-25 business route. Int corridors. **Pets:** Other species. Designated rooms, service with restrictions, supervision.
SAVE Sⓓ ✕ 🖖 🛢 🖳 🏊

▲▲▲ ▼▼▼ El Camino Motel M
(505) 425-5994. **$50-$65.** 1152 N Grand Ave. I-25, exit 345, 0.3 mi w, US 85 and I-25 business route. Ext corridors. **Pets:** Small, other species. $6 daily fee/pet. Service with restrictions, supervision.
SAVE Sⓓ ✕ 🍴

▲▲▲ Inn on the Santa Fe Trail M 🐾
(505) 425-6791. **$59-$84.** 1133 N Grand Ave. I-25, exit 345, 0.5 mi n; I-25 business route and US 84, 0.3 mi w. Ext corridors. **Pets:** $5 daily fee/room. Designated rooms, service with restrictions, supervision.
SAVE Sⓓ ✕ 🛢 🖳 🍴 🏊

▲▲▲ ▼▼ Plaza Hotel CI
(505) 425-3591. **$96-$124.** 230 Plaza. I-25, exit 343W, just w, follow signs to Old Town Plaza. Int corridors. **Pets:** $10 daily fee/room.
SAVE Sⓓ ✕ 🛢 🖳 🍴

LORDSBURG

▲▲▲ ▼▼▼ Best Western-Western Skies Inn SH 🐾
(505) 542-8807. **$59-$89.** 1303 S Main St. I-10, exit 22, just s. Ext corridors. **Pets:** $5 daily fee/pet. Designated rooms, service with restrictions, supervision.
SAVE Sⓓ ✕ 🛢 🖳 🍴 🏊

▼▼▼ Holiday Inn Express SH
(505) 542-3666. **$73-$90.** 1408 S Main St. I-10, exit 22, just s. Ext corridors. **Pets:** Accepted.
ASK Sⓓ ✕ ⓜ 🛢 🖳 🏊

▲▲▲ ▼▼▼ Super 8 Motel SH
(505) 542-8882. **$49-$69.** 110 E Maple. I-10, exit 22, just s. Int corridors. **Pets:** $10 daily fee/pet. Designated rooms, no service, supervision.
SAVE Sⓓ ✕

LOS ALAMOS

▲▲▲ ▼▼▼ Los Alamos Inn SH
(505) 662-7211. **$69-$99, 3 day notice.** 2201 Trinity Dr. Center. Int corridors. **Pets:** Accepted.
SAVE ✕ 🛢 🖳 🏊

LOS LUNAS

▼▼▼ Days Inn SH
(505) 865-5995. **$53-$89.** 1919 Main St SW. I-25, exit 203, just s to entrance at southeast corner. Int corridors. **Pets:** Other species. $15 one-time fee/room. Service with restrictions.
ASK Sⓓ ✕ 🛢 🖳 🏊

▼▼▼ Western Skies Inn & Suites SH
(505) 865-0001. **$58-$69.** 2258 Sun Ranch Village Loop. I-25, exit 203, just n. Int corridors. **Pets:** Medium. $10 daily fee/pet. Designated rooms, service with restrictions, supervision.
ASK Sⓓ ✕ ⓜ 🖖 🏊

LOVINGTON

▲▲▲ ▼▼▼ Lovington Inn SH
(505) 396-5346. **$75-$90.** 1600 W Ave D. Jct US 82 and SR 18, 1 mi w. Ext corridors. **Pets:** Medium. $10 deposit/pet. No service.
SAVE Sⓓ ✕ 🖖 🛢 🖳 🍴

MESILLA

▼▼▼ Meson de Mesilla CI
(505) 525-9212. **$57-$185.** 1803 Avenida de Mesilla. I-10, exit 140, 0.4 mi s. Ext/int corridors. **Pets:** Accepted.
✕ 🛢 🍴 🏊

MORIARTY

▲▲▲ ▼▼▼ Days Inn SH
(505) 832-4451. **$45-$55.** 1809 Route 66 W. I-40, exit 194. Int corridors. **Pets:** $10 daily fee/pet. Service with restrictions, crate.
SAVE Sⓓ ✕ 🛢

▲▲▲ ▼▼▼ Econo Lodge SH
(505) 832-4457. **$45-$65.** 1316 Route 66 W. I-40, exit 194, 0.5 mi se on US 66 and I-40 business loop. Int corridors. **Pets:** Other species. $5 daily fee/pet. Service with restrictions, supervision.
SAVE Sⓓ ✕ 🛢 🖳

▲▲▲ ▼▼▼▼ Holiday Inn Express SH
(505) 832-5000. **$74-$95.** 1507 Route 66. I-40, exit 194, 0.4 mi e. Int corridors. **Pets:** Medium, other species. $10 one-time fee/room. Designated rooms, service with restrictions, supervision.
SAVE Sⓓ ✕ ⓜ 🛢 🖳 🏊

▼▼ ▼▼ Motel 6 #4069 **SH**
(505) 832-6666. **Call for rates.** 119 Route 66 E. I-40, exit 197, 1 mi e, then 0.5 mi e. Int corridors. **Pets:** Medium, other species. Service with restrictions, supervision.

[X] [⅙M] [🐾] [🐾] [≋]

AAA ▼▼ Sunset Motel **M**
(505) 832-4234. **$41-$50.** 501 E Route 66. I-40, exit 197, 1 mi w, then 0.5 mi e. Ext corridors. **Pets:** Accepted.

[SAVE] [⅚6] [X] [📞] [📺]

AAA ▼▼▼ Super 8 Motel **SH**
(505) 832-6730. **$52-$75.** 1611 W Old Route 66. I-40, exit 194, 0.5 mi e on Central Ave. Int corridors. **Pets:** $20 deposit/room. Designated rooms, service with restrictions, supervision.

[SAVE] [⅚6] [X] [🐾] [📞]

PINOS ALTOS

▼▼ ▼▼ Bear Creek Motel & Cabins **CA** 🐾
(505) 388-4501. **$89-$159, 10 day notice.** 88 Main St. 1 mi n on SR 15. Ext corridors. **Pets:** Medium. $10 daily fee/pet. No service, supervision.

[ASK] [⅚6] [📞] [📺] [🐾]

POJOAQUE PUEBLO

AAA ▼▼▼ Cities of Gold Hotel **SH**
(505) 455-0515. **$92-$119.** 10A Cities of Gold Rd. On US 84/265, just n. Int corridors. **Pets:** Large, other species. $20 deposit/room.

[SAVE] [⅚6] [X] [⅙M] [♿] [📞] [📺] [🍽]

RANCHOS DE TAOS

AAA ▼▼ Budget Host Inn **M**
(505) 758-2524. **$48-$70, 14 day notice.** 1798 Paseo Del Pueblo Sur. On SR 68; center. Ext corridors. **Pets:** Other species. $5 one-time fee/pet. Service with restrictions, crate.

[SAVE] [X] [📞] [📺]

RATON

AAA ▼▼▼ Budget Host Raton **M**
(505) 445-3655. **$44-$55.** 136 Canyon Dr. I-25, exit 454, 0.8 mi s on I-25 business loop. Ext corridors. **Pets:** Medium. $2 daily fee/pet. Service with restrictions, supervision.

[SAVE] [⅚6] [X] [⅙M] [📞]

▼▼ Motel 6 Raton #279 **M**
(505) 445-2777. **$41-$65.** 1600 Cedar St. I-25, exit 451, just w. Ext corridors. **Pets:** Accepted.

[⅚6] [X] [≋]

▼▼ The Pass Inn **M**
(505) 445-3641. **$36-$46.** 308 Canyon Dr. I-25, exit 454, 0.8 mi s. Ext corridors. **Pets:** $2 one-time fee/room. Designated rooms, service with restrictions, supervision.

[ASK] [⅚6] [X] [📞]

RIO RANCHO

AAA ▼▼▼ Best Western Rio Rancho Inn & Conference Center **SH**
(505) 892-1700. **$69-$144, 60 day notice.** 1465 Rio Rancho Blvd. I-25, exit 233 (Alameda Blvd), 6.5 mi w; I-40, exit 155, 10 mi n on Coors Rd/Coors Bypass to SR 528, 1 mi n. Ext corridors. **Pets:** Accepted.

[SAVE] [⅚6] [X] [🐾] [📞] [📺] [🍽] [≋]

AAA ▼▼▼ Days Inn **SH**
(505) 892-8800. **$50-$95.** 4200 Crestview Dr. I-25, exit 233 (Alameda Blvd), 8 mi w on SR 528; I-40, exit 155, 8 mi n on Coors Rd (SR 448). Ext corridors. **Pets:** Very small. $10 one-time fee/pet. Service with restrictions, supervision.

[SAVE] [⅚6] [X] [📞] [≋]

AAA ▼▼▼ Ramada Limited Hotel **SH**
(505) 892-5998. **$55-$108.** 4081 High Resort Blvd. I-25, exit 233 (Alameda Blvd), 8 mi w; I-40, exit 155, 8 mi n on Coors Rd (SR 448). Int corridors. **Pets:** Other species. $10 daily fee/pet. Service with restrictions.

[SAVE] [⅚6] [X] [📞] [📺] [≋]

AAA ▼▼▼ Rio Rancho Super 8 Motel **SH**
(505) 896-8888. **$45-$85.** 4100 Barbara Loop. I-25, exit 233 (Alameda Blvd), 0.5 mi w, 3.8 mi nw on SR 528, then just e. Int corridors. **Pets:** Other species. $6 daily fee/pet. Service with restrictions, supervision.

[ASK] [⅚6] [X]

AAA ▼▼▼ Wellesley Inn & Suites
(Albuquerque/North) **SH**
(505) 892-7900. **$79-$159.** 2221 Rio Rancho Blvd. I-25, exit 233 (Alameda Blvd), 6 mi w (becomes SR 528/Rio Rancho Blvd). Int corridors. **Pets:** Small. $25 daily fee/pet. Service with restrictions, crate.

[SAVE] [⅚6] [X] [🐾] [🐾] [📞] [📺] [≋] [🐾]

ROSWELL

AAA ▼▼ ▼▼ Best Western El Rancho Palacio **SH**
(505) 622-2721. **$60-$80, 7 day notice.** 2205 N Main St. 1.8 mi n on US 70 and 285. Ext corridors. **Pets:** Service with restrictions, supervision.

[SAVE] [⅚6] [X] [📞] [📺] [≋]

AAA ▼▼▼▼ Best Western Sally Port Inn & Suites **SH**
(505) 622-6430. **$89-$100, 7 day notice.** 2000 N Main St. 1.5 mi n on US 70 and 285. Int corridors. **Pets:** Other species. $10 daily fee/pet. Designated rooms, service with restrictions, supervision.

[SAVE] [⅚6] [X] [📞] [📺] [🍽] [≋] [🐾]

AAA ▼▼▼ Budget Inn-North **M**
(505) 623-6050. **$35-$50, 10 day notice.** 2101 N Main St. 1.8 mi n on US 70 and 285. Ext corridors. **Pets:** Medium. $5 daily fee/pet. Designated rooms, service with restrictions, supervision.

[SAVE] [X] [📞] [📺]

AAA ▼▼▼ Budget Inn West **SH**
(505) 623-3811. **$35-$50.** 2200 W 2nd St. 2 mi w on US 70 and 380. Ext corridors. **Pets:** Small, dogs only. $2 daily fee/pet. Designated rooms, service with restrictions, supervision.

[SAVE] [⅚6] [X] [📞] [≋]

AAA ▼▼▼▼ Comfort Inn **SH**
(505) 623-4567. **$69-$109.** 3595 N Main St. On US 70 and 285, 3 mi n. Int corridors. **Pets:** Small. Designated rooms, service with restrictions, supervision.

[SAVE] [X] [⅙M] [🐾] [📞] [📺] [≋]

AAA ▼▼▼ Days Inn **SH**
(505) 623-4021. **$60-$90, 7 day notice.** 1310 N Main St. 0.8 mi n on US 70 and 285. Ext corridors. **Pets:** Service with restrictions, supervision.

[SAVE] [⅚6] [X] [🐾] [📞] [📺] [🍽] [≋]

AAA ▼▼▼ Frontier Motel **M**
(505) 622-1400. **$36-$44.** 3010 N Main St. 2.5 mi n on US 70 and 285. Ext corridors. **Pets:** Other species. Service with restrictions, supervision.

[SAVE] [⅚6] [X] [📞] [≋]

AAA ▼▼▼ Leisure Inn **SH**
(505) 622-2575. **$32-$42.** 2700 W 2nd St. 2.5 mi w on US 70 and 380. Ext corridors. **Pets:** Small, dogs only. $5 one-time fee/pet. Designated rooms, no service, supervision.

[SAVE] [⅚6] [X] [📞] [📺] [≋] [🐾]

AAA ▼▼ National 9 Inn **M**
(505) 622-0110. **$38-$50.** 2001 N Main St. 1.5 mi n on US 70 and 285. Ext corridors. **Pets:** Other species. $5 daily fee/pet. Service with restrictions, supervision.

[SAVE] [⅚6] [X] [📞] [≋]

◊◊ Ramada Limited SH
(505) 623-9440. **$68.** 2803 W 2nd St. 2.5 mi w on US 70 and 380. Ext/int corridors. **Pets:** Accepted.

(ASK) (S6) (X) (📁) (💻)

◊◊ Western Inn M
(505) 623-9425. **$62-$67.** 2331 N Main St. Jct US 70/285/380, 2.2 mi n. Ext corridors. **Pets:** Accepted.

(ASK) (S6) (X) (📁) (💻) (≈)

RUIDOSO

◊◊◊ ◊◊ Dan Dee Cabins CA
(505) 257-2165. **$84-$240, 14 day notice.** 310 Main Rd. 0.8 mi w on Upper Canyon Rd. Ext corridors. **Pets:** Other species. $10 one-time fee/pet. No service, supervision.

(SAVE) (S6) (📁) (💻) (X) (☎)

◊◊◊ Hawthorn Suites Convention & Golf Resort SH
(505) 258-5500. **$184-$205.** 107 Sierra Blanca Dr. 2.5 mi n on SR 48. Int corridors. **Pets:** Service with restrictions, supervision.

(X) (🐾) (&) (📁) (💻) (≈) (X)

◊◊ Travelodge SH
(505) 378-4471. **$45-$180.** 159 W Hwy 70. Jct of US 70 and SR 48 (the "Y"). Ext corridors. **Pets:** Small. $10 daily fee/room. Designated rooms, supervision.

(ASK) (S6) (X) (📁) (💻) (≈)

◊◊◊ Village Lodge Suites CO ✿
(505) 258-5442. **$69-$250, 7 day notice.** 1000 Mechem Dr. 2 mi n on SR 48. Ext corridors. **Pets:** Medium, other species. $10 one-time fee/room. Service with restrictions, supervision.

(ASK) (S6) (X) (📁) (💻)

RUIDOSO DOWNS

◊◊ Best Western Pine Springs Inn SH ✿
(505) 378-8100. **$59-$139.** 1420 W Hwy 70. Just n; center. Ext corridors. **Pets:** Other species. Service with restrictions.

(ASK) (S6) (X) (📁) (💻) (≈) (X)

SANTA FE

◊◊◊ ◊◊ Alexander's Inn BB ✿
(505) 986-1431. **$85-$200, 14 day notice.** 529 E Palace Ave. Just e of jct Paseo De Peralta and 6 blks e of the historic plaza. Ext/int corridors. **Pets:** $20 one-time fee/pet. Service with restrictions.

(SAVE) (X) (📁) (💻) (X)

◊◊◊ ◊◊ Best Western Inn of Santa Fe SH
(505) 438-3822. **$45-$145.** 3650 Cerrillos Rd. I-25, exit 278, 2.8 mi n. Int corridors. **Pets:** Service with restrictions, supervision.

(SAVE) (S6) (X) (🐾) (📁) (💻) (≈)

◊◊◊ ◊◊ Bishop's Lodge Resort & Spa LH
(505) 983-6377. **$159-$499, 3 day notice.** 1297 N Bishop's Lodge Rd. 3.5 mi n of jct Paseo De Peralta. Ext/int corridors. **Pets:** Accepted.

(SAVE) (S6) (X) (🐾) (📁) (💻) (🍴) (≈) (X)

◊◊◊ ◊◊ Cactus Lodge Motel M
(505) 471-7699. **$40-$78, 3 day notice.** 2864 Cerrillos Rd. 3.8 mi sw on US 85. Ext corridors. **Pets:** Dogs only. Service with restrictions, supervision.

(SAVE) (S6) (X) (📁)

◊◊◊ ◊◊ Camel Rock Suites M
(505) 989-3600. **$89-$99, 3 day notice.** 3007 S St Frances Dr. 0.8 mi n on S St. Francis Dr, just e on Zia via access drive. Ext corridors. **Pets:** $100 deposit/room, $25 one-time fee/room. Designated rooms, service with restrictions, supervision.

(SAVE) (S6) (X) (&M) (🐾) (&) (📁) (💻)

◊◊◊ Casapueblo Inn SH
(505) 988-4455. **$109-$239, 3 day notice.** 138 Park Ave. Jct Guadalupe St. Ext corridors. **Pets:** Large, other species. $50 one-time fee/room. Designated rooms, service with restrictions, supervision.

(ASK) (S6) (X) (&) (💻)

◊◊◊ ◊◊ Comfort Inn SH
(505) 474-7330. **$59-$169.** 4312 Cerrillos Rd. I-25, exit 278, 1.6 mi n. Int corridors. **Pets:** Medium. Service with restrictions, supervision.

(SAVE) (S6) (X) (🐾) (&) (📁) (💻) (≈)

◊◊ Dancing Ground of the Sun Bed and Breakfast BB
(505) 986-9797. **Call for rates.** 711 Paseo de Peralta. 5 blks e of The Plaza. Ext corridors. **Pets:** Medium, other species. $30 one-time fee/pet. Service with restrictions.

(X) (📁) (💻)

◊◊◊ ◊◊◊ ◊◊ Eldorado Hotel LH ✿
(505) 988-4455. **$209-$1500, 3 day notice.** 309 W San Francisco. Just w of The Plaza at Sandoval St. Int corridors. **Pets:** Other species. $50 one-time fee/pet. Service with restrictions, supervision.

(SAVE) (S6) (X) (&M) (🐾) (📁) (💻) (🍴) (≈) (X)

◊◊◊ ◊◊◊ El Paradero Bed & Breakfast BB
(505) 988-1177. **$80-$165, 14 day notice.** 220 W Manhattan Ave. 0.3 mi s on Cerrillos Rd, 1/2 blk e. Ext/int corridors. **Pets:** Dogs only. $15 daily fee/room. Designated rooms, crate.

(SAVE) (X) (💻)

◊◊◊ ◊◊◊ ◊◊ The Hacienda at Hotel Santa Fe SH ✿
(505) 982-1200. **$189-$499, 3 day notice.** 1501 Paseo de Peralta. At Cerrillos Rd, 0.6 mi s of The Plaza. Int corridors. **Pets:** Medium, dogs only. $20 daily fee/pet. Designated rooms, service with restrictions, crate.

(SAVE) (S6) (X) (📁) (💻) (🍴) (X)

◊◊◊ ◊◊◊ El Paradero... Hacienda Nicholas BB ✿
(505) 986-1431. **$100-$190, 14 day notice.** 320 E Marcy St. Just e of jct Paseo De Paralta and 4 blks e of the historic plaza. Ext/int corridors. **Pets:** $20 one-time fee/pet. Service with restrictions, crate.

(SAVE) (X)

◊◊◊ ◊◊◊ Hampton Inn Santa Fe SH
(505) 474-3900. **$69-$169.** 3625 Cerrillos Rd. I-25, exit 278B, 2.5 mi n. Int corridors. **Pets:** Other species. Service with restrictions.

(SAVE) (S6) (X) (&M) (🐾) (&) (📁) (💻) (≈) (X)

◊◊◊ ◊◊ Hotel Plaza Real SH ✿
(505) 988-4900. **$89-$199, 3 day notice.** 125 Washington Ave. Just ne of The Plaza; center. Ext/int corridors. **Pets:** Dogs only. $50 one-time fee/room. Service with restrictions, supervision.

(ASK) (S6) (X) (🐾) (📁) (💻) (🍴)

◊◊◊ ◊◊◊ Hotel Santa Fe SH
(505) 982-1200. **$99-$499, 3 day notice.** 1501 Paseo de Peralta. At Cerrillos Rd, 0.6 mi s of The Plaza. Int corridors. **Pets:** Accepted.

(SAVE) (S6) (X) (🐾) (📁) (🍴) (≈) (X)

◊◊◊ ◊◊◊ Inn On The Alameda SH ✿
(505) 984-2121. **$129-$295, 3 day notice.** 303 E Alameda Ave. 4 blks e of The Plaza; at Paseo de Peralta. Ext/int corridors. **Pets:** Small, other species. $20 daily fee/pet. Designated rooms.

(SAVE) (S6) (X) (🐾) (&) (📁) (💻) (X)

◊◊◊ ◊◊◊ La Quinta Inn Santa Fe SH
(505) 471-1142. **$85-$135.** 4298 Cerrillos Rd. I-25, exit 278, 1.8 mi n. Ext/int corridors. **Pets:** Medium, dogs only. Service with restrictions, crate.

(SAVE) (X) (&) (📁) (💻) (X)

◊◊◊ ◊◊◊ Las Palomas M
(505) 982-5560. **$139-$259, 7 day notice.** 460 W San Francisco St. Just w of jct Guadalupe St. Ext corridors. **Pets:** Accepted.

(SAVE) (X) (&) (📁) (💻) (X)

▼▼ ▼▼ Motel 6–150 **M**
(505) 473-1380. **$45-$71.** 3007 Cerrillos Rd. I-25, exit 278B, 3.8 mi n.
Ext corridors. **Pets:** Accepted.
⬛ ⬛ ⬛ ⬛ ⬛

AAA ▼▼▼▼ Park Inn **SH**
(505) 471-3000. **$49-$104.** 2907 Cerrillos Rd. I-25, exit 278, 7 mi n. Ext
corridors. **Pets:** Accepted.
⬛ ⬛ ⬛ ⬛ ⬛ ⬛

AAA ▼▼▼▼ Quality Inn **SH**
(505) 471-1211. **$75-$120.** 3011 Cerrillos Rd. I-25, exit 278B, 3.8 mi n.
Int corridors. **Pets:** Accepted.
⬛ ⬛ ⬛ ⬛ ⬛ ⬛ ⬛

▼▼▼▼ Residence Inn by Marriott **SH**
(505) 988-7300. **$159-$259.** 1698 Galisteo St. I-25, exit 282, 1.7 mi n
on St Francis Dr to St Michaels Dr, then just e. Ext corridors.
Pets: Accepted.
⬛ ⬛ ⬛ ⬛ ⬛ ⬛ ⬛ ⬛

AAA ▼▼ ▼▼ Santa Fe Motel & Inn **M** ❖
(505) 982-1039. **$89-$139, 3 day notice.** 510 Cerrillos Rd. 4 blks sw of
The Plaza. Ext corridors. **Pets:** Medium. $15 daily fee/pet. Designated
rooms.
⬛ ⬛ ⬛ ⬛ ⬛

AAA ▼▼ ▼▼ Santa Fe Plaza Travelodge **SH**
(505) 982-3551. **$89-$199.** 646 Cerrillos Rd. 0.8 mi sw of The Plaza.
Ext/int corridors. **Pets:** $10 daily fee/pet. Service with restrictions, crate.
⬛ ⬛ ⬛ ⬛ ⬛ ⬛ ⬛

▼▼ ▼▼ Sleep Inn **SH** ❖
(505) 474-9500. **$69-$189.** 8376 Cerrillos Rd. I-25, exit 278, 0.3 mi n.
Int corridors. **Pets:** Other species. $10 one-time fee/room. Designated
rooms, service with restrictions, supervision.
⬛ ⬛ ⬛ ⬛ ⬛ ⬛ ⬛ ⬛ ⬛

SANTA ROSA

AAA ▼▼ ▼▼ Best Western Adobe Inn **SH**
(505) 472-3446. **$52-$75.** 1501 Historic Route 66. I-40, exit 275. Ext
corridors. **Pets:** Small. Service with restrictions, supervision.
⬛ ⬛ ⬛ ⬛ ⬛

AAA ▼▼ ▼▼ Best Western Santa Rosa Inn **M**
(505) 472-5877. **$56-$76.** 3022 Historic Route 66. I-40, exit 277, 0.5 mi
w. Ext corridors. **Pets:** Small. $10 daily fee/pet. Designated rooms, service
with restrictions, supervision.
⬛ ⬛ ⬛ ⬛ ⬛ ⬛

▼▼ ▼▼ Comfort Inn **SH**
(505) 472-5570. **$64-$85.** 3343 E Historic Route 66. I-40, exit 277, 0.3
mi w. Ext corridors. **Pets:** $25 daily fee/pet. Designated rooms, service
with restrictions, supervision.
⬛ ⬛ ⬛ ⬛ ⬛ ⬛

AAA ▼▼ ▼▼ Days Inn of Santa Rosa **SH**
(505) 472-5985. **$55-$95.** 1830 Historic Route 66. I-40, exit 275. Ext
corridors. **Pets:** Small. $5 daily fee/pet. Designated rooms, service with
restrictions, supervision.
⬛ ⬛ ⬛ ⬛ ⬛

AAA ▼▼▼▼ La Quinta Inn-Santa Rosa **SH**
(505) 472-4800. **$81-$91.** 1701 Historic Route 66. I-40, exit 275, just e.
Int corridors. **Pets:** Service with restrictions, supervision.
⬛ ⬛ ⬛ ⬛ ⬛ ⬛

▼▼ Motel 6–273 **M**
(505) 472-3045. **$43-$53.** 3400 Historic Route 66. I-40, exit 277, 0.3 mi
w. Ext corridors. **Pets:** Accepted.
⬛ ⬛ ⬛ ⬛ ⬛ ⬛

AAA ▼▼ ▼▼ Ramada Inn **SH**
(505) 472-5411. **$69-$79.** 3300 Historic Route 66. I-40, exit 277, 0.3 mi
w. Int corridors. **Pets:** Accepted.
⬛ ⬛ ⬛ ⬛ ⬛

▼▼ ▼▼ Super 8 Motel-Santa Rosa **M**
(505) 472-5388. **$55-$65.** 1201 Historic Route 66. I-40, exit 275, just w.
Int corridors. **Pets:** Other species. $10 daily fee/pet. Designated rooms,
service with restrictions, supervision.
⬛ ⬛ ⬛ ⬛ ⬛ ⬛

SILVER CITY

▼▼▼▼ Comfort Inn **SH**
(505) 534-1883. **$55-$150.** 1060 E Hwy 180. 1.5 mi e on US 180 and
SR 90. Int corridors. **Pets:** Accepted.
⬛ ⬛ ⬛ ⬛ ⬛ ⬛

AAA ▼▼ ▼▼ Econo Lodge Silver City **SH**
(505) 534-1111. **$45-$89.** 1120 Hwy 180 E. 1.5 mi ne on US 180 and
SR 90. Int corridors. **Pets:** $25 deposit/room, $7 daily fee/room. Designated rooms, service with restrictions, crate.
⬛ ⬛ ⬛ ⬛ ⬛ ⬛ ⬛ ⬛

▼▼▼▼ Holiday Inn Express **SH**
(505) 538-2525. **$90.** 1103 Superior St. 3 mi ne on US 180 and SR 90.
Int corridors. **Pets:** Accepted.
⬛ ⬛ ⬛ ⬛

▼▼ ▼▼ Holiday Motor Hotel **SH**
(505) 538-3711. **$42-$46.** 3420 Hwy 180 E. 3 mi ne on jct US 180 and
SR 90. Ext corridors. **Pets:** Accepted.
⬛ ⬛ ⬛ ⬛

▼▼ ▼▼ Super 8 Motel **SH**
(505) 388-1983. **$34-$65.** 1040 E Hwy 180. 1.5 mi ne on US 180 and
SR 90. Int corridors. **Pets:** Accepted.
⬛ ⬛ ⬛ ⬛

SOCORRO

AAA ▼▼ ▼▼ Econo Lodge **SH** ❖
(505) 835-1500. **$39-$75.** 713 California Ave. I-25, exit 150, 1 mi s. Ext
corridors. **Pets:** Small, dogs only. $5 daily fee/pet, $5 one-time fee/pet.
Designated rooms, service with restrictions, supervision.
⬛ ⬛ ⬛ ⬛ ⬛ ⬛ ⬛

▼▼▼▼ Holiday Inn Express **SH**
(505) 838-0556. **$90.** 1100 California Ave NE. Center. Ext/int corridors.
Pets: Medium. $10 daily fee/pet. Designated rooms, service with restric-
tions, supervision.
⬛ ⬛ ⬛ ⬛ ⬛ ⬛ ⬛ ⬛ ⬛

▼▼ ▼▼ Motel 6 #392 **SH**
(505) 835-4300. **$39-$51.** 807 S US 85. I-25, exit 147. Ext corridors.
Pets: Accepted.
⬛ ⬛ ⬛ ⬛ ⬛ ⬛ ⬛

TAOS

AAA ▼▼ ▼▼ Adobe Sun God Lodge **M** ❖
(505) 758-3162. **$54-$119, 14 day notice.** 919 Paseo del Pueblo Sur.
SR 68, 1.8 mi sw of jct US 64 and Taos Plaza. Ext corridors.
Pets: Other species. $10 one-time fee/pet. Service with restrictions.
⬛ ⬛ ⬛ ⬛ ⬛

AAA ▼▼▼▼ American Artists Gallery House Bed &
　　　　 Breakfast **BB**
(505) 758-4446. **$95-$195, 14 day notice.** 132 Frontier Ln. 1 mi s of jct
US 64 and Taos Plaza, 0.3 mi e. Ext/int corridors. **Pets:** Dogs only. $25
daily fee/pet. Designated rooms, service with restrictions, supervision.
⬛ ⬛ ⬛ ⬛ ⬛ ⬛ ⬛

(AAA) ▼▼▼ Brooks Street Inn Bed and Breakfast BB ❖
(505) 758-1489. **$89-$169, 14 day notice.** 119 Brooks St. 0.3 mi n on US 64 from jct SR 68 and Taos Plaza, just e. Ext/int corridors. **Pets:** Small, dogs only. $10 daily fee/pet. Designated rooms, service with restrictions, supervision.
⟦SAVE⟧ ⟦S⟧ ⟦✕⟧ ⟦🖥⟧ ⟦💻⟧ ⟦K⟧ ⟦Z⟧

(AAA) ▼▼ Burch Street Casitas M ❖
(505) 737-9038. **$99-$135, 21 day notice.** 310 Burch St. US 64, just e of jct SR 68, just s. Ext corridors. **Pets:** Medium, dogs only. $50 deposit/pet. No service, supervision.
⟦SAVE⟧ ⟦S⟧ ⟦✕⟧ ⟦🖥⟧ ⟦💻⟧ ⟦K⟧

(AAA) ▼▼▼ Casa Encantada BB ❖
(505) 758-7477. **$110-$200, 10 day notice.** 416 Liebert St. Jct SR 68 and Taos Plaza, 0.6 mi e on US 64, then just s. Ext corridors. **Pets:** Other species. $15 daily fee/room. Service with restrictions, supervision.
⟦SAVE⟧ ⟦S⟧ ⟦✕⟧ ⟦🖥⟧ ⟦💻⟧ ⟦K⟧ ⟦Z⟧

(AAA) ▼▼▼ Casa Europa Inn & Gallery BB
(505) 758-9798. **$105-$195, 14 day notice.** 840 Upper Ranchitos Rd. 1.7 mi s from jct US 64. Ext/int corridors. **Pets:** Medium, dogs only. $25 one-time fee/pet. Designated rooms, service with restrictions, supervision.
⟦SAVE⟧ ⟦✕⟧ ⟦🖥⟧ ⟦💻⟧ ⟦✕⟧ ⟦K⟧

(AAA) ▼▼ El Pueblo Lodge M
(505) 758-8700. **$89.** 412 Paseo del Pueblo Norte. US 64, 0.5 mi n of jct SR 68 and Taos Plaza. Ext corridors. **Pets:** $10 daily fee/pet. Designated rooms, service with restrictions, supervision.
⟦SAVE⟧ ⟦S⟧ ⟦✕⟧ ⟦🖊⟧ ⟦🖥⟧ ⟦💻⟧ ⟦➰⟧

(AAA) ▼▼▼ Fechin Inn SH ❖
(505) 751-1000. **$114-$512, 3 day notice.** 227 Paseo del Pueblo Norte. Just n on US 64 of jct SR 68 and Taos Plaza. Int corridors. **Pets:** Small, dogs only. $50 one-time fee/pet. Designated rooms, service with restrictions, supervision.
⟦SAVE⟧ ⟦S⟧ ⟦✕⟧ ⟦M⟧ ⟦🖊⟧ ⟦🖥⟧ ⟦💻⟧ ⟦✕⟧

(AAA) ▼▼▼ Inn On The Rio M
(505) 758-7199. **$99-$129, 15 day notice.** 910 Kit Carson Rd. US 64, 1.5 mi e of jct SR 68 and Taos Plaza. Ext corridors. **Pets:** Dogs only. $20 daily fee/pet. Designated rooms, service with restrictions, supervision.
⟦SAVE⟧ ⟦S⟧ ⟦✕⟧ ⟦💻⟧ ⟦➰⟧ ⟦K⟧

(AAA) ▼▼▼ Orinda Bed & Breakfast BB
(505) 758-8581. **$89-$145, 14 day notice.** 461 Valverde St. 0.5 mi ne of Taos Plaza; center. Ext/int corridors. **Pets:** Medium, dogs only. $10 daily fee/pet. Service with restrictions, supervision.
⟦SAVE⟧ ⟦S⟧ ⟦✕⟧ ⟦🖥⟧ ⟦💻⟧

(AAA) ▼▼▼ Quality Inn SH
(505) 758-2200. **$59-$109.** 1043 Paseo del Pueblo Sur. SR 68, 2 mi sw of jct US 64 and Taos Plaza. Ext/int corridors. **Pets:** Other species. $7 daily fee/pet. Designated rooms, service with restrictions, supervision.
⟦SAVE⟧ ⟦S⟧ ⟦✕⟧ ⟦🖊⟧ ⟦🖥⟧ ⟦💻⟧ ⟦🍴⟧ ⟦➰⟧

▼▼▼ Ramada Inn de Taos SH
(505) 758-2900. **$58-$100.** 615 Paseo del Pueblo Sur. SR 68, 1 mi sw of jct US 64 and Taos Plaza. Ext corridors. **Pets:** Medium, other species. $7 one-time fee/room.
⟦ASK⟧ ⟦S⟧ ⟦✕⟧ ⟦🖥⟧ ⟦💻⟧ ⟦🍴⟧ ⟦➰⟧

(AAA) ▼▼▼ Sagebrush Inn SH
(505) 758-2254. **$85-$165.** 1508 Paseo del Pueblo Sur. SR 68, 3 mi sw of jct US 64 and Taos Plaza. Ext corridors. **Pets:** Other species. $7 daily fee/room. Designated rooms, service with restrictions, supervision.
⟦SAVE⟧ ⟦S⟧ ⟦✕⟧ ⟦🖊⟧ ⟦🖥⟧ ⟦💻⟧ ⟦🍴⟧ ⟦➰⟧

(AAA) ▼▼▼ San Geronimo Lodge BB
(505) 751-3776. **$95-$150, 10 day notice.** 1101 Witt Rd. 1.3 mi e of jct SR 68 & Taos Plaza on US 64 (Kit Carson Rd), 0.6 mi s. Ext/int corridors. **Pets:** Accepted.
⟦SAVE⟧ ⟦S⟧ ⟦✕⟧ ⟦🖊⟧ ⟦➰⟧ ⟦✕⟧ ⟦K⟧

THOREAU

▼▼ Zuni Mountain Lodge BB ❖
(505) 862-7769. **$95-$500 (no credit cards), 3 day notice.** 40 W Perch Dr. I-40, exit 53, 13 mi s on SR 612, then w. Ext/int corridors. **Pets:** Other species. Supervision.
⟦✕⟧ ⟦K⟧ ⟦W⟧ ⟦Z⟧

TRUTH OR CONSEQUENCES

(AAA) ▼▼ Best Western Hot Springs Motor Inn M ❖
(505) 894-6665. **$62-$75.** 2270 N Date St. I-25, exit 79. Ext corridors. **Pets:** Other species. Service with restrictions.
⟦SAVE⟧ ⟦S⟧ ⟦✕⟧ ⟦🖥⟧ ⟦💻⟧ ⟦🍴⟧ ⟦➰⟧

▼▼▼ Holiday Inn SH
(505) 894-1660. **Call for rates.** 2250 N Date St. I-25, exit 79, just e. Int corridors. **Pets:** Medium, other species. Service with restrictions, supervision.
⟦M⟧ ⟦✎⟧ ⟦🖊⟧ ⟦🖥⟧ ⟦💻⟧ ⟦➰⟧

(AAA) ▼▼▼ Super 8 Motel M
(505) 894-7888. **$40-$50.** 2151 N Date St. I-25, exit 79, just s. Int corridors. **Pets:** Other species. Service with restrictions, supervision.
⟦SAVE⟧ ⟦S⟧ ⟦✕⟧

TUCUMCARI

(AAA) ▼▼ Americana Motel M
(505) 461-0431. **$28-$38.** 406 E Tucumcari Blvd. I-40, exit 332, 1.5 mi n on SR 18, then 0.5 mi e on US 66. Ext corridors. **Pets:** Designated rooms, no service, supervision.
⟦SAVE⟧ ⟦✕⟧

(AAA) ▼▼▼ Best Western Discovery Inn SH
(505) 461-4884. **$58-$84.** 200 E Estrella. I-40, exit 332. Ext corridors. **Pets:** Accepted.
⟦SAVE⟧ ⟦S⟧ ⟦✕⟧ ⟦🖥⟧ ⟦💻⟧ ⟦🍴⟧ ⟦➰⟧

(AAA) ▼▼ Budget Inn M
(505) 461-4139. **$30-$45.** 824 W Tucumcari Blvd. I-40, exit 332, 1 mi n to Tucumari Blvd, then 1 mi w. Ext corridors. **Pets:** Medium. $5 one-time fee/room. No service, supervision.
⟦SAVE⟧ ⟦S⟧ ⟦✕⟧ ⟦🖥⟧

▼▼▼ Comfort Inn SH
(505) 461-4094. **$55-$85.** 2800 E Tucumcari Blvd. I-40, exit 335, 0.5 mi w. Ext corridors. **Pets:** Medium. $6 one-time fee/pet. No service, supervision.
⟦ASK⟧ ⟦S⟧ ⟦✕⟧ ⟦💻⟧ ⟦➰⟧

(AAA) ▼▼▼ Days Inn SH
(505) 461-3158. **$53-$67, 14 day notice.** 2623 S First St. I-40, exit 332, just n. Ext/int corridors. **Pets:** Other species. $6 daily fee/pet. Service with restrictions, supervision.
⟦SAVE⟧ ⟦S⟧ ⟦✕⟧

(AAA) ▼▼▼ Holiday Inn SH ❖
(505) 461-3780. **$79-$99.** 3716 E Tucumcari Blvd. I-40, exit 335, 0.3 mi w on US 66. Ext corridors. **Pets:** Medium, other species. $10 one-time fee/room. Service with restrictions, supervision.
⟦SAVE⟧ ⟦S⟧ ⟦✕⟧ ⟦M⟧ ⟦✎⟧ ⟦🖥⟧ ⟦💻⟧ ⟦🍴⟧ ⟦➰⟧ ⟦✕⟧

▼▼ Howard Johnson Express Inn SH
(505) 461-2747. **$55-$65.** 3604 E Route 66. I-40, exit 335, 0.5 mi w. Int corridors. **Pets:** $6 daily fee/room. Service with restrictions, supervision.
⟦ASK⟧ ⟦S⟧ ⟦✕⟧ ⟦🖥⟧ ⟦💻⟧

Microtel Inn-Tucumcari SH
(505) 461-0600. **$60-$80.** 2420 S 1st St. I-40, exit 332, just n. Int corridors. **Pets:** Small, other species. $6 daily fee/pet. Designated rooms, service with restrictions, supervision.

Motel 6 Tucumcari #380 M
(505) 461-4791. **$41-$55.** 2900 E Tucumcari Blvd. I-40, exit 335. Ext corridors. **Pets:** Accepted.

Pow Wow Inn M
(505) 461-0500. **$54-$59.** 801 W Tucumcari Blvd. I-40, exit 332, 1.5 mi n on SR 18, then 0.5 mi w on US 66. Ext corridors. **Pets:** Large, other species. $10 one-time fee/pet. Service with restrictions, supervision.

Rodeway Inn East M
(505) 461-0360. **$55-$65.** 1023 E Tucumcari Blvd. I-40, exit 333, n to Tucumcari Blvd, then 0.6 mi w. Ext corridors. **Pets:** Other species. $5 daily fee/pet. Service with restrictions, supervision.

Super 8 Motel M
(505) 461-4444. **$50-$75.** 4001 E Tucumcari Blvd. I-40, exit 335, just w. Int corridors. **Pets:** Medium. $5 one-time fee/room. No service, supervision.

VAUGHN

Bel-Air Motel M
(505) 584-2241. **$38-$44.** 1004 US 54/60/285. 1 mi e on US 54, 60 and 285. Ext corridors. **Pets:** Medium. Service with restrictions, supervision.

Oak Tree Inn SH
(505) 584-8733. **$70-$90, 3 day notice.** Jct State Hwy 54/60 & 285. 1.5 mi e on US 54, 60 and 285. Int corridors. **Pets:** Medium, other species. $5 one-time fee/pet. Service with restrictions.

WHITES CITY

Best Western Cavern Inn SH
(505) 785-2291. **$70-$110.** 17 Carlsbad Caverns Hwy. US 62 and 180 at SR 7. Ext corridors. **Pets:** Small. $10 one-time fee/room. Service with restrictions, supervision.

NEW YORK

CITY INDEX

ALBANY

[AAA] ♦♦♦ **Albany Mansion Hill Inn & Restaurant** [BB] 🐾
(518) 465-2038. **$195-$215, 5 day notice.** 115 Philip St at Park Ave. I-787, exit 3B (Madison Ave/US 20 W) to Philip St, 0.4 mi s. Ext/int corridors. **Pets:** Other species. Crate.
[SAVE] [SD] ⊠ ▣ ☕ 🍴

♦♦♦ **CrestHill Suites** [SH]
(518) 454-0007. **$129-$229.** 1415 Washington Ave. I-90, exit 2 westbound, just s on Fuller Rd, then just e; exit eastbound, just e. Int corridors. **Pets:** Accepted.
[ASK] [SD] ⊠ ♿M 🦻 ▣ ☕ 🏊

[AAA] ♦♦♦ **Ramada Inn Albany (Exit 23)** [SH]
(518) 462-6555. **$69-$129.** 416 Southern Blvd. On US 9W; I-87, exit 23. Ext/int corridors. **Pets:** Accepted.
[SAVE] [SD] ⊠ ▣ ☕ 🏊 ✂

♦♦♦ **TownePlace Suites by Marriott** [SH]
(518) 435-1900. **$100-$180.** 1379 Washington Ave. I-90, exit 2 westbound, just s on Fuller Rd, then 0.6 mi e; exit eastbound, just e. Int corridors. **Pets:** Accepted.
[ASK] [SD] ⊠ ♿M ♿ ▣ ☕ 🏊

ALLEGANY

[AAA] ♦♦ **Microtel Inn & Suites-Olean/Allegany** [SH]
(716) 373-5333. **$39-$89.** 3234 W State Rd. I-86, exit 24. Int corridors. **Pets:** Accepted.
[SAVE] [SD] ⊠ ♿M ▣ ☕

ANGELICA

♦♦ **Angelica Inn B&B** [BB]
(585) 466-3063. **$75-$150, 14 day notice.** 64 W Main St. SR 17, exit 31, 0.5 mi w. Ext/int corridors. **Pets:** Designated rooms, service with restrictions.
[ASK] [SD] ⊠ ▣ ☕ ☎

APALACHIN

♦♦ **The Dolphin Inn** [SH]
(607) 625-4441. **$55-$75.** 7666 SR 434. SR 17, exit 66, just e. Int corridors. **Pets:** Other species. $10 one-time fee/pet. Service with restrictions, crate.
[ASK] [SD] ⊠ ♿ ▣ ☕

AUBURN

♦♦ **Finger Lakes Inn & Suites** [SH]
(315) 253-5000. **$79-$149.** 12 Seminary Ave. Jct SR 34/38, just e on US 20/SR 5; center. Int corridors. **Pets:** Medium. $15 one-time fee/pet. Designated rooms, service with restrictions, supervision.
[ASK] [SD] ⊠ ♿M 🦻 ♿ ▣ ☕

[AAA] ♦♦♦ **Holiday Inn-Auburn/Finger Lakes** [SH]
(315) 253-4531. **$67-$102.** 75 North St. SR 34, just n of US 20/SR 5. Int corridors. **Pets:** $10 daily fee/room. Designated rooms, service with restrictions, supervision.
[SAVE] [SD] ⊠ ♿M ▣ ☕ 🍴 🏊

AVERILL PARK

♦♦♦ **La Perla at the Gregory House Country Inn & Restaurant** [CI]
(518) 674-3774. **$100-$140, 14 day notice.** 3016 SR 43. Center. Int corridors. **Pets:** Accepted.
[ASK] ⊠ 🍴 🏊

BALDWINSVILLE

[AAA] ♦♦ **Microtel Inn & Suites** [SH]
(315) 635-9556. **$60-$100.** 131 Downer St. SR 690, exit SR 31 W, 0.6 mi e. Int corridors. **Pets:** Other species. $5 daily fee/pet. Service with restrictions, crate.
[SAVE] [SD] ⊠ ♿M ♿ ▣ ☕

BATAVIA

[AAA] ♦ **Budget Inn** [M]
(585) 343-7921. **$45-$99.** 301 Oak St. I-90, exit 48, just n. Int corridors. **Pets:** Medium. $5 daily fee/pet. Designated rooms, service with restrictions, supervision.
[SAVE] [SD] ⊠ ▣

△△△ ▽◈▽ Comfort Inn 🆂🅷
(585) 344-9999. **$69-$189.** 4371 Federal Dr. I-90, exit 48, just n on SR 98. Int corridors. **Pets:** $10 one-time fee/pet. Supervision.
🆂🅰🆅🅴 🆂🅳 ⊠ 🔧 ✍ 🖥 ≋

△△△ ▽◈▽ Days Inn 🆂🅷 🐾
(585) 343-6000. **$49-$109.** 200 Oak St. I-90, exit 48, just s. Ext/int corridors. **Pets:** Large, other species. $10 one-time fee/pet. Service with restrictions, supervision.
🆂🅰🆅🅴 🆂🅳 ⊠ 🔧 🖥 🍴 ≋

△△△ ▽◈▽ Holiday Inn-Darien Lake 🆂🅷
(585) 344-2100. **$59-$129.** 8250 Park Rd. I-90, exit 48, just w. Int corridors. **Pets:** Small, other species. $15 one-time fee/pet. Service with restrictions, supervision.
🆂🅰🆅🅴 ⊠ 🔧 🖥 🍴 ≋ ⊠

△△△ ▽◈▽ Ramada Limited 🆂🅷
(585) 343-1000. **$49-$119.** 8204 Park Rd. I-90, exit 48, just w. Int corridors. **Pets:** Accepted.
🆂🅰🆅🅴 🆂🅳 ⊠ 🖥 ≋

BATH

▽◈▽ Bath Super 8 🆂🅷
(607) 776-2187. **$66-$96.** 333 W Morris St. I-86, exit 38, just n. Int corridors. **Pets:** Other species. Service with restrictions, supervision.
⊠ 🔧

▽◈▽ Days Inn 🆂🅷
(607) 776-7644. **$80-$115.** 330 W Morris St. I-86, exit 38, just n. Int corridors. **Pets:** Accepted.
🅰🆂🅺 🆂🅳 ⊠ 🔧 🖥 ≋

BELLPORT

▽◈▽◈▽ The Great South Bay Inn 🅱🅱
(631) 286-8588. **$115-$150, 7 day notice.** 160 S Country Rd. SR 27, exit 56, 2.2 mi s on Station Rd, then just e. Int corridors. **Pets:** Accepted.
⊠ 🛗

BINGHAMTON

▽◈▽ Days Inn 🆂🅷
(607) 724-3297. **$90-$175.** 1000 Front St. I-81, exit 5, 1 mi n on US 11 (Front St). Int corridors. **Pets:** Other species. $5 daily fee/room. Designated rooms, service with restrictions, supervision.
🅰🆂🅺 🆂🅳 ⊠ 🔧 🖥 ≋ ⊠

▽◈▽ Holiday Inn Arena 🅻🅷 🐾
(607) 722-1212. **$89-$145.** 2-8 Hawley St. Downtown. Int corridors. **Pets:** Medium. $25 one-time fee/room. Service with restrictions, crate.
🅰🆂🅺 ⊠ 🔧 🖥 🍴 ≋

▽◈▽ Motel 6–1222 🆂🅷
(607) 771-0400. **$41-$55.** 1012 Front St. I-81, exit 6 southbound, 2 mi s on US 11 (Front St); exit 5 northbound, 1 mi n on US 11 (Front St). Int corridors. **Pets:** Accepted.
🆂🅳 ⊠ 🔧 ✍

△△△ ▽◈▽ Quality Inn & Suites 🆂🅷
(607) 722-5353. **$79-$189.** 1156 Front St. I-81, exit 6; just n of Broome Community College. Int corridors. **Pets:** Other species. $15 one-time fee/room. Designated rooms, service with restrictions, crate.
🆂🅰🆅🅴 🆂🅳 ⊠ 🔧 🖥

△△△ ▽◈▽ Sai Bless Inn 🆂🅷
(607) 724-2412. **$55-$99.** 65 Front St. I-81, exit 5, 2 mi s; SR 17 E, exit 72, 1 mi s. Int corridors. **Pets:** Medium. $20 deposit/pet. Service with restrictions, crate.
🆂🅰🆅🅴 🆂🅳 ⊠ 🔧 🖥 ≋

BOONVILLE

△△△ ▽◈▽ Headwaters Motor Lodge 🅼
(315) 942-4493. **$59-$85, 3 day notice.** 13524 Rt 12. Jct SR 12 and 120, 0.7 mi n. Int corridors. **Pets:** Small. Service with restrictions, supervision.
🆂🅰🆅🅴 🆂🅳 ⊠ 🔧

BRIGHTON

△△△ ▽◈▽ Wellesley Inn (Rochester/South) 🆂🅷
(585) 427-0130. **$55-$105.** 797 E Henrietta Rd. I-390, exit 16 northbound; exit 16B (Henrietta Rd) southbound, just s. Int corridors. **Pets:** Accepted.
🆂🅰🆅🅴 🆂🅳 ⊠ 🐾 ✍ 🔧 🖥

BROCKPORT

▽◈▽◈▽ Holiday Inn Express 🆂🅷
(585) 395-1000. **$83-$143.** 4908 Lake Rd S. Just s of jct SR 31 and 19. Int corridors. **Pets:** Medium, other species. $15 one-time fee/room. No service, supervision.
🅰🆂🅺 🆂🅳 ⊠ ✍ 🔧 🖥

BUFFALO METROPOLITAN AREA

AMHERST

△△△ ▽◈▽ Buffalo Marriott-Niagara 🅻🅷
(716) 689-6900. **$99-$179.** 1340 Millersport Hwy. I-290, exit 5B, 0.5 mi n on SR 263 (Millersport Hwy). Int corridors. **Pets:** Other species. $50 one-time fee/room. Designated rooms, service with restrictions, crate.
🆂🅰🆅🅴 🆂🅳 ⊠ ✍ 🐾 ✍ 🔧 🖥 🍴 ≋ ⊠

△△△ ▽◈▽ Comfort Inn 🆂🅷 🐾
(716) 688-0811. **$94-$144.** 1 Flint Rd. I-290, exit 5B, 0.5 mi n on SR 263 (Millersport Hwy), then just w. Int corridors. **Pets:** Medium, other species. $15 daily fee/pet. Service with restrictions, supervision.
🆂🅰🆅🅴 🆂🅳 ⊠ 🔧 🖥

△△△ ▽◈▽ Lord Amherst Motor Hotel 🅼
(716) 839-2200. **$65-$109.** 5000 Main St. I-290, exit 7A, just w on SR 5. Ext/int corridors. **Pets:** Service with restrictions, supervision.
🆂🅰🆅🅴 🆂🅳 ⊠ ✍ 🔧 🖥 🍴 ≋

▽◈▽ Motel 6 Buffalo-Amherst #1298 🅼 🐾
(716) 834-2231. **$55-$91.** 4400 Maple Rd. I-290, exit 5B, just n to Maple Rd, then 0.7 mi w. Int corridors. **Pets:** Other species. Designated rooms, service with restrictions, supervision.
🆂🅳 ⊠

▽◈▽ Red Roof Inn #7104 🅼
(716) 689-7474. **$47-$88.** 42 Flint Rd. I-290, exit 5B, 0.5 mi n on SR 263 (Millersport Hwy). Ext corridors. **Pets:** Accepted.
⊠ ✍ 🔧

BLASDELL

△△△ ▽◈▽ Clarion Hotel 🆂🅷
(716) 648-5700. **$59-$129.** 3950 McKinley Pkwy. I-90, exit 56, 0.4 mi e on SR 179, then 0.8 mi s. Int corridors. **Pets:** Accepted.
🆂🅰🆅🅴 🆂🅳 ⊠ ✍ 🔧 🖥

Econo Lodge South 🅼
(716) 825-7530. **$54-$99.** 4344 Milestrip Rd. I-90, exit 56, just e on SR 179. Ext corridors. **Pets:** Designated rooms, service with restrictions, supervision.

BOWMANSVILLE

Red Roof Inn-Buffalo Airport #7137 🅼
(716) 633-1100. **$44-$82.** 146 Maple Dr. Just e of SR 78; just n of entrance to I-90 (New York Thruway), exit 49. Ext corridors. **Pets:** Accepted.

BUFFALO

Best Western Inn-On The Avenue 🆂🅷
(716) 886-8333. **$99-$155.** 510 Delaware Ave. Between Virginia and Allen sts; downtown. Int corridors. **Pets:** Medium, dogs only. $150 deposit/pet. Designated rooms, service with restrictions, crate.

Holiday Inn-Downtown 🆂🅷
(716) 886-2121. **$69-$149.** 620 Delaware Ave. Between Allen and North sts; downtown. Int corridors. **Pets:** Accepted.

CHEEKTOWAGA

Holiday Inn Express Hotel & Suites-Buffalo Airport 🆂🅷
(716) 631-8700. **$100-$130.** 131 Buell Ave. I-90, exit 33E. Int corridors. **Pets:** Accepted.

Homewood Suites by Hilton 🆂🅷
(716) 685-0700. **$124-$199, 3 day notice.** 760 Dick Rd. SR 33, exit Dick Rd, 0.3 mi sw. Int corridors. **Pets:** Large, other species. $100 one-time fee/room. Service with restrictions, crate.

Oak Tree Inn 🆂🅷
(716) 681-2600. **$46-$105.** 3475 Union Rd. Just s of Walden Ave. Int corridors. **Pets:** Medium, other species. $5 daily fee/room. Service with restrictions.

Residence Inn by Marriott 🆂🅷
(716) 892-5410. **$69-$169.** 107 Anderson Rd. I-90, exit 52 westbound, stay to the left off exit ramp. Int corridors. **Pets:** Other species. $75 one-time fee/room. Service with restrictions.

CLARENCE

Asa Ransom House 🅲🅸
(716) 759-2315. **$105-$185, 7 day notice.** 10529 Main St. Jct SR 78 (Transit Rd), 5.3 mi e on SR 5 (Main St). Int corridors. **Pets:** Dogs only. $50 deposit/pet. Designated rooms, service with restrictions, crate.

GRAND ISLAND

Chateau Motor Lodge 🅼
(716) 773-2868. **$39-$99, 3 day notice.** 1810 Grand Island Blvd. I-190, exit 18A northbound, 0.5 mi n on SR 324 W. Ext corridors. **Pets:** Accepted.

HAMBURG

Comfort Inn & Suites 🆂🅷
(716) 648-2922. **$69-$179.** 3615 Commerce Pl. I-90, exit 57, just w. Int corridors. **Pets:** Accepted.

Holiday Inn Hamburg 🆂🅷
(716) 649-0500. **$64-$129.** 5440 Camp Rd. I-90, exit 57, 0.3 mi se on SR 75. Int corridors. **Pets:** Accepted.

Red Roof Inn #7055 🅼
(716) 648-7222. **$43-$82.** 5370 Camp Rd. I-90, exit 57, just se on SR 75. Ext corridors. **Pets:** Accepted.

Tallyho-tel 🅼 🐾
(716) 648-2000. **$30-$125.** 5245 Camp Rd. I-90, exit 57, just nw on SR 75. Ext corridors. **Pets:** Other species. $15 one-time fee/pet. Service with restrictions, supervision.

KENMORE

Super 8-Buffalo/Niagara Falls 🆂🅷
(716) 876-4020. **$48-$76.** 1288 Sheridan Dr. I-190, exit 15, 1.5 mi e on SR 324 (Sheridan Dr). Int corridors. **Pets:** Accepted.

SPRINGVILLE

Microtel Inn & Suites 🆂🅷
(716) 592-3141. **$49-$59.** 270 S Cascade Dr. On SR 219 S. Int corridors. **Pets:** $10 daily fee/room. Service with restrictions, crate.

TONAWANDA

Days Inn 🅼
(716) 835-5916. **$49-$125.** 1120 Niagara Falls Blvd. I-290, exit 3 (Niagara Falls Blvd), 1.3 mi s on US 62. Ext corridors. **Pets:** Other species. Service with restrictions, crate.

Microtel-Tonawanda 🆂🅷
(716) 693-8100. **$46-$70.** 1 Hospitality Centre Way. I-290, exit 1B westbound; exit 1 eastbound, 0.5 mi e on Crestmount Ave, then just n on SR 384 (Delaware St). Int corridors. **Pets:** Medium. $10 daily fee/pet. Service with restrictions, supervision.

WILLIAMSVILLE

Microtel-Lancaster 🆂🅷
(716) 633-6200. **$42-$70.** 50 Freeman Rd. I-90, exit 49 (SR 78), just n, then just e. Int corridors. **Pets:** Accepted.

Residence Inn by Marriott Buffalo/Amherst 🆂🅷 🐾
(716) 632-6622. **$89-$139.** 100 Maple Rd. I-290, exit 5B, just e on Maple Rd from jct SR 263 (Millersport Hwy). Ext corridors. **Pets:** Other species. $75 one-time fee/room. Service with restrictions, crate.

END METROPOLITAN AREA

CALCIUM

▼▼ ▼▼ Microtel Inn Watertown 🆂🅷
(315) 629-5000. **$60.** 8000 Virginia Smith Dr. 4 mi e on SR 342; jct US 11. Int corridors. **Pets:** Other species. $3 daily fee/room. Service with restrictions, supervision.
🅰🆂🅺 🆂🔟 ✖️ 🎱

CANANDAIGUA

🆎🆎 ▼▼▼▼ Canandaigua Inn on the Lake 🆂🅷
(585) 394-7800. **$94-$304.** 770 S Main St. I-90, exit 44 (Canandaigua), jct SR 332, just s across US 20 and SR 5. Int corridors. **Pets:** Accepted.
🆂🅰🆅🅴 🆂🔟 ✖️ 🛗 ⤵️ 🅢 🎱 🖥️ 🍴 ⤳ ✖️

🆎🆎 ▼▼▼ Econo Lodge Canandaigua 🆂🅷
(585) 394-9000. **$54-$122.** 170 Eastern Blvd. Jct SR 332, 5 and US 20, 0.5 mi e. Int corridors. **Pets:** Supervision.
🆂🅰🆅🅴 🆂🔟 ✖️ 🎱 🖥️

CANASTOTA

▼▼ ▼▼ Days Inn 🆂🅷 🐾
(315) 697-3309. **$59-$139.** 377 N Peterboro St. I-90, exit 34, on SR 13. Int corridors. **Pets:** Other species. Service with restrictions, supervision.
🅰🆂🅺 🆂🔟 ✖️ 🎱

CATSKILL

🆎🆎 ▼▼ ▼▼ Catskill Quality Inn & Conference Center 🆂🅷
(518) 943-5800. **$59-$269.** 704 Rt 23B. I-87 (New York State Thruway), exit 21, just w. Ext/int corridors. **Pets:** Accepted.
🆂🅰🆅🅴 🆂🔟 ✖️ 🎱 🖥️ 🍴 ⤳

CICERO

🆎🆎 ▼▼ Budget Inn 🅼
(315) 458-3510. **$65-$110.** 901 S Bay Rd. I-481, exit 10, just s. Ext corridors. **Pets:** Small. $10 daily fee/pet. Service with restrictions, supervision.
🆂🅰🆅🅴 🆂🔟 ✖️ 🎱

CLINTON

▼▼▼▼▼ The Hedges 🅱🅱 🐾
(315) 853-3031. **$110-$150, 7 day notice.** 180 Sanford Ave. College St, 0.3 mi n on Elm St. Int corridors. **Pets:** Large, dogs only. $25 one-time fee/room. Service with restrictions, supervision.
✖️ 🎱 🖥️ ⤳

COBLESKILL

🆎🆎 ▼▼▼▼ Best Western Inn of Cobleskill 🆂🅷
(518) 234-4321. **$80-$160.** 121 Burgin Dr. I-88, exit 21 eastbound on SR 7, 0.8 mi e of jct SR 10; exit 22 westbound, 2.9 mi w on SR 27. Int corridors. **Pets:** Other species. $15 daily fee/room. Service with restrictions.
🆂🅰🆅🅴 🆂🔟 ✖️ 🅢 ⤵️ 🎱 🖥️ 🍴 ⤳

▼▼ ▼▼ Super 8 🆂🅷
(518) 234-4888. **$70-$145.** 955 E Main St. I-88, exit 22 westbound, 2.4 mi w on SR 7; exit 21 eastbound, 3.1 mi e on SR 7. Int corridors. **Pets:** Other species. $10 one-time fee/room. Service with restrictions, supervision.
🅰🆂🅺 🆂🔟 ✖️ 🅢 ⤵️ 🅢

COLONIE

▼▼ ▼▼ Albany Super 8 Motel 🅼
(518) 869-8471. **$59-$85.** 1579 Central Ave. I-87, exit 2, just nw on SR 5. Ext corridors. **Pets:** Other species. $5 daily fee/room. Designated rooms, service with restrictions, supervision.
🅰🆂🅺 🆂🔟 ✖️ 🎱

▼▼ Ambassador Motor Inn 🅼
(518) 456-8982. **$59-$109, 3 day notice.** 1600 Central Ave. I-87, exit 2, 0.8 mi w; 5.4 mi w on SR 5. Ext corridors. **Pets:** Accepted.
🅰🆂🅺 🆂🔟 ✖️

🆎🆎 ▼▼▼ Ramada Limited 🅼
(518) 456-0222. **$75-$200, 3 day notice.** 1630 Central Ave. I-87, exit 2, 0.8 mi w on 5.5 mi w on SR 5. Ext corridors. **Pets:** Accepted.
🆂🅰🆅🅴 🆂🔟 ✖️ 🎱

▼▼ ▼▼ Red Roof Inn #7112 🅼
(518) 459-1971. **$61-$94.** 188 Wolf Rd. I-87, exit 4, just se to Wolf Rd, then just sw. Ext corridors. **Pets:** Accepted.
✖️ 🅢 🎱

CORNING

▼▼▼▼ Radisson Hotel Corning 🆂🅷
(607) 962-5000. **$116-$129.** 125 Denison Pkwy E. On I-86/SR 17; center. Int corridors. **Pets:** Accepted.
🅰🆂🅺 🆂🔟 ✖️ 🎱 🖥️ 🍴 ⤳

▼▼▼▼ Staybridge Suites by Holiday Inn 🆂🅷
(607) 936-7800. **$94-$200.** 201 Townley Ave. I-86/SR 17, exit 46, just s. Int corridors. **Pets:** Accepted.
🅰🆂🅺 🆂🔟 ✖️ 🅢 ⤵️ 🅢 🎱 🖥️ ⤳ ✖️

CORTLAND

▼▼ ▼▼ Comfort Inn 🆂🅷
(607) 753-7721. **$79-$179.** 2 1/2 Locust Ave. I-81, exit 11, just e. Int corridors. **Pets:** Accepted.
🅰🆂🅺 🆂🔟 ✖️ 🎱 🖥️ 🍴

🆎🆎 ▼▼ Econo Lodge 🅼
(607) 756-2856. **$52-$159, 3 day notice.** 10 Church St. I-81, exit 11, 0.8 mi s on SR 13/41 and US 11. Ext corridors. **Pets:** Small. $20 fee/pet. Designated rooms, service with restrictions, supervision.
🆂🅰🆅🅴 🆂🔟 ✖️ 🎱

▼▼▼▼ Holiday Inn Cortland 🆂🅷
(607) 756-4431. **$80-$110.** 2 River St. I-81, exit 11, just s on SR 13. Int corridors. **Pets:** Small. $25 one-time fee/room. Service with restrictions, supervision.
🅰🆂🅺 🆂🔟 ✖️ 🎱 🖥️ 🍴 ⤳ ✖️

🆎🆎 ▼▼▼ Quality Inn Cortland 🆂🅷
(607) 756-5622. **$79-$159.** 188 Clinton St. I-81, exit 11, just n. Int corridors. **Pets:** Medium. $20 one-time fee/room. Service with restrictions.
🆂🅰🆅🅴 🆂🔟 ✖️ 🎱

CUBA

🆎🆎 ▼▼ ▼▼ Cuba Coachlight Motel 🅼
(585) 968-1992. **$49-$69.** 1 N Branch Rd. I-86, exit 28, n to N Branch Rd, then e. Int corridors. **Pets:** Large, other species. $5 daily fee/room. Service with restrictions, crate.
🆂🅰🆅🅴 🆂🔟 ✖️ 🎱

DELHI

🆎🆎 ▼▼▼ Buena Vista Motel 🅼
(607) 746-2135. **$79-$89.** 18718 State Hwy 28. Jct SR 10, 0.8 mi e. Ext corridors. **Pets:** Medium, dogs only. $12 daily fee/pet. Designated rooms, service with restrictions, supervision.
🆂🅰🆅🅴 🆂🔟 ✖️ 🎱

DE WITT

🆎🆎 ▼▼▼ Econo Lodge 🅼
(315) 446-3300. **$65-$120, 3 day notice.** 3400 Erie Blvd E. I-481, exit 3, 1.2 mi w on SR 5. Ext corridors. **Pets:** Small. $10 daily fee/pet. Service with restrictions, supervision.
🆂🅰🆅🅴 🆂🔟 ✖️ 🎱 🖥️

DOVER PLAINS

▽▽▽▽ Old Drovers Inn **CI**
(845) 832-9311. **$190-$550, 14 day notice.** 196 E Duncan Hill Rd. 3 mi s of SR 22 on Old Rt 22 (CR 6). Int corridors. **Pets:** Accepted.

⊠ ⑪ 🕊 ☎

DUNKIRK

🐾 ▽▽▽▽ Best Western Dunkirk/Fredonia **SH**
(716) 366-7100. **$69-$139.** 3912 Vineyard Dr. I-90, exit 59, just w. Int corridors. **Pets:** Large. $10 daily fee/pet. Service with restrictions, supervision.

SAVE S🔊 ⊠ ✍ 🗄 🖥 ≈

🐾 ▽▽▽▽ Comfort Inn **SH**
(716) 672-4450. **$59-$139.** 3925 Vineyard Dr. I-90, exit 59, just w of jct SR 60. Int corridors. **Pets:** Large. $10 daily fee/pet. Service with restrictions, supervision.

SAVE S🔊 ⊠ ✍ 🗄 🖥

🐾 ▽▽▽▽ Ramada Inn & Conference Center **SH** 🐾
(716) 366-8350. **$80-$160.** 30 Lake Shore Dr E. Jct SR 60, 0.3 mi w on SR 5. Int corridors. **Pets:** Other species. $10 daily fee/room. Service with restrictions, supervision.

SAVE S🔊 ⊠ ✍ 🗄 🖥 ⑪ ≈ ⊠

EAST HAMPTON

▽ Dutch Motel & Cottages **M**
(631) 324-4550. **$89-$349.** 488 Montauk Hwy. 1.3 mi e on SR 27 (Montauk Hwy). Ext corridors. **Pets:** Accepted.

A$K 🗄

EAST SYRACUSE

🐾 ▽▽▽▽ Comfort Inn-Carrier Circle **SH**
(315) 437-0222. **$72-$90.** 6491 Thompson Rd S. I-90, exit 35 (Carrier Cir). Ext/int corridors. **Pets:** $50 one-time fee/room. Service with restrictions, supervision.

SAVE S🔊 ⊠ 🗄 🖥

▽▽▽▽ CrestHill Suites **SH**
(315) 432-5595. **$114-$199.** 6410 New Venture Gear Dr. I-90, exit 35 (Carrier Cir) to SR 298 E, just s. Int corridors. **Pets:** Other species. $50 one-time fee/room. Service with restrictions.

A$K S🔊 ⊠ ✍ 🗄 🖥 ≈

▽▽▽ East Syracuse Super 8 **SH**
(315) 432-5612. **$44-$84.** 6620 Old Collamer Rd. I-90, exit 35 (Carrier Cir), just e on SR 298, then just n. Int corridors. **Pets:** Dogs only. $10 one-time fee/pet. Service with restrictions, supervision.

A$K S🔊 ⊠ 🖥M ✍ ✍ 🗄

▽▽▽ Holiday Inn East-Carrier Circle **SH**
(315) 437-2761. **$99-$179.** 6555 Old Collamer Rd. I-90, exit 35 (Carrier Cir) to SR 298 E to Old Collamer Rd, just n. Ext/int corridors. **Pets:** Accepted.

A$K S🔊 ⊠ ✍ 🗄 🖥 ⑪ ≈ ⊠

▽▽ Microtel Inn Syracuse **SH**
(315) 437-3500. **$46-$72.** 6608 Old Collamer Rd. I-90, exit 35 (Carrier Cir) to SR 298 E. Int corridors. **Pets:** Small, other species. $10 one-time fee/pet. Service with restrictions, supervision.

A$K S🔊 ⊠ 🖥M ✍

▽▽ Red Roof Inn #7157 **M**
(315) 437-3309. **$49-$76.** 6614 N Thompson Rd. I-90, exit 35 (Carrier Cir), just n. Ext corridors. **Pets:** Medium, other species. Service with restrictions, supervision.

⊠ ✍ ✍ 🗄

▽▽▽▽ Residence Inn by Marriott **SH**
(315) 432-4488. **$154-$174.** 6420 Yorktown Cir. I-90, exit 35 (Carrier Cir) to SR 298, just e to Old Collamer Rd, then 0.5 mi n. Ext corridors. **Pets:** Accepted.

A$K ⊠ 🖥M ✍ ✍ 🗄 🖥 ≈ ⊠

ELLICOTTVILLE

🐾 ▽▽▽▽ The Jefferson Inn of Ellicottville **BB**
(716) 699-5869. **$79-$209, 30 day notice.** 3 Jefferson St. Western jct US 219 and SR 242, just n; eastern jct US 219 and 242, 0.8 mi w. Ext/int corridors. **Pets:** $15 daily fee/room. Designated rooms, no service.

SAVE ⊠ 🗄 🖥

🐾 ▽▽▽▽ Sugar Pine Lodge **BB** 🐾
(716) 699-4855. **$89-$260, 30 day notice.** 6158 Jefferson St. Jct US 219 and SR 242, 0.5 mi s on US 219. Ext/int corridors. **Pets:** $20 one-time fee/room. Designated rooms.

SAVE ⊠ 🗄 🖥 ≈

ELMIRA

🐾 ▽▽▽ Coachman Motor Lodge **M**
(607) 733-5526. **$70.** 908 Pennsylvania Ave. SR 17, exit 56 (Water St), 0.5 mi w on SR 352 (Church St), 0.5 mi s on Madison Ave, then 1.4 mi s. Ext corridors. **Pets:** Medium. Service with restrictions, supervision.

SAVE S🔊 🗄 🖥

ENDWELL

🐾 ▽▽▽ Kings Inn **M**
(607) 754-8020. **$39-$100.** 2603 E Main St. SR 17 W, exit 69, 2.4 mi w on SR 17C; SR 17 E, exit 67N, 1.3 mi e. Ext corridors. **Pets:** Small. $10 one-time fee/pet. Service with restrictions, supervision.

SAVE S🔊 ⊠ 🗄 🖥 ≈

ERWIN

🐾 ▽ Erwin Motel **M**
(607) 962-7411. **$42-$79, 4 day notice.** Rt 417. US 15, exit Erwin Addison, 0.5 mi e. Ext corridors. **Pets:** $7 daily fee/pet. Designated rooms, service with restrictions, supervision.

SAVE ⊠ 🗄 ≈

FALCONER

▽▽▽ Red Roof Inn Jamestown/Falconer #7273 **SH**
(716) 665-3670. **$53-$73.** 1980 E Main St. I-86, exit 13, just w. Int corridors. **Pets:** Accepted.

⊠

FARMINGTON

🐾 ▽▽▽ Budget Inn **M**
(585) 924-5020. **$54-$79, 3 day notice.** 6001 Rt 96. I-90, exit 44, 1 mi s on SR 332, then just e. Ext corridors. **Pets:** Very small, dogs only. $10 daily fee/pet. Service with restrictions, supervision.

SAVE S🔊 ⊠ 🗄 🖥

FISHKILL

▽▽▽ Homestead Studio Suites Hotel-Fishkill **SH**
(845) 897-2800. **$119-$139.** 25 Merritt Blvd. I-84, exit 13, just n. Int corridors. **Pets:** Accepted.

A$K S🔊 ⊠ ✍ ✍ 🗄 🖥

🐾 ▽▽▽▽ Residence Inn by Marriott **SH**
(845) 896-5210. **$179-$209.** 14 Schuyler Blvd. I-84, exit 13, just n. Ext corridors. **Pets:** Accepted.

SAVE S🔊 ⊠ 🖥M ✍ 🗄 🖥 ≈ ⊠

🐾 ▽▽▽ Wellesley Inn (Fishkill) **SH**
(845) 896-4995. **$99-$119.** 20 Schuyler Blvd & Rt 9. I-84, exit 13, just n. Int corridors. **Pets:** Small. $10 daily fee/pet. Designated rooms, service with restrictions, supervision.

SAVE S🔊 ⊠ 🖥M ✍ ✍ 🗄 🖥

FREDONIA

🐾 ▽▽▽ Days Inn Dunkirk-Fredonia **SH**
(716) 673-1351. **$62-$121.** 10455 Bennett Rd. I-90, exit 59, just s on SR 60. Ext/int corridors. **Pets:** Large, other species. Designated rooms, service with restrictions.

SAVE S🔊 ⊠ 🗄 🖥 ⑪ ≈

FULTON

▼▼ ▼▼ **Riverside Inn** 🆂🅷
(315) 593-2444. **$49-$109, 7 day notice.** 930 S 1st St. On SR 481. Int corridors. **Pets:** Accepted.
Ⓐ🆂🅚 🆂🅙 ☒ 🔒 🖥 🍴 ⚊

GATES

▼▼ ◆ **Comfort Inn Central** 🆂🅷
(585) 436-4400. **$49-$85, 3 day notice.** 395 Buell Rd. I-390, exit 18B (SR 204), 0.3 mi w; opposite entrance to Rochester-Monroe County Airport. Int corridors. **Pets:** Large, other species. Designated rooms, service with restrictions, supervision.
Ⓐ🆂🅚 🆂🅙 ☒ 🕖 🔒 🖥

▼▼▼▼ **Holiday Inn-Rochester Airport** 🆂🅷
(585) 328-6000. **$79-$109.** 911 Brooks Ave. I-390, exit 18A (SR 204), just e. Int corridors. **Pets:** Accepted.
Ⓐ🆂🅚 🆂🅙 ☒ 🕖 🔒 🖥 🍴 ⚊ ☒

GENEVA

🆎🅐 ▼▼▼▼ **Ramada Inn Geneva Lakefront** 🆂🅷 🐾
(315) 789-0400. **$92-$150.** 41 Lakefront Dr. I-90, exit 42, 8 mi s on SR 14. Int corridors. **Pets:** $10 daily fee/pet. Service with restrictions, supervision.
🆂🅐🆅🅴 🆂🅙 ☒ 🕖 🔒 🖥 🍴 ⚊

GREAT NECK

🆎🅐 ▼▼▼▼ **The Andrew Hotel** 🆂🅷
(516) 482-2900. **$175-$395, 7 day notice.** 75 N Station Plaza. Jct SR 25A, 0.8 mi n on Middle Neck Rd, just e. Int corridors. **Pets:** Small. $150 one-time fee/room. Service with restrictions, supervision.
🆂🅐🆅🅴 ☒

▼▼▼▼ ◆ **Inn at Great Neck** 🆂🅷
(516) 773-2000. **$199-$239.** 30 Cutter Mill Rd. Jct SR 25A, 0.8 mi n on Middle Neck Rd, just w. Int corridors. **Pets:** $250 deposit/pet, $25 daily fee/pet. Service with restrictions, supervision.
Ⓐ🆂🅚 🆂🅙 ☒ 🕖 🔒 🔒 🍴

GREECE

🆎🅐 ▼▼▼▼ **Hampton Inn-Rochester North** 🆂🅷
(585) 663-6070. **$99-$119.** 500 Center Place Dr. I-390, exit 24A, just e on SR 104 (Ridge Rd), then just n on Buckman Rd. Int corridors. **Pets:** Accepted.
Ⓐ🆂🅚 🆂🅙 ☒ 🕖🅼 🔒 🔒 🖥

▼▼▼▼ **Residence Inn by Marriott-West** 🆂🅷
(585) 865-2090. **$109-$249.** 500 Paddy Creek Cir. I-390, exit 24A, just e on SR 104 (Ridge Rd), just s on Hoover Dr, then just w. Int corridors. **Pets:** Accepted.
Ⓐ🆂🅚 🆂🅙 ☒ 🕖 🔒 🖥 ⚊ ☒

🆎🅐 ▼▼▼▼ **Wellesley Inn (Rochester/North)** 🆂🅷
(585) 621-2060. **$55-$105.** 1635 W Ridge Rd. I-390, exit 24A, just e on SR 104 (Ridge Rd). Int corridors. **Pets:** Medium. $5 daily fee/room. Service with restrictions, crate.
🆂🅐🆅🅴 🆂🅙 ☒ 🕖🅼 🕖 🕖 🔒 🖥

GUILDERLAND

🆎🅐 ▼▼▼▼ **Best Western Sovereign Hotel Albany** 🆂🅷
(518) 489-2981. **$99-$149.** 1228 Western Ave. I-90, exit 2, 0.7 mi s, follow signs to US 20 (Western Ave). Int corridors. **Pets:** Small. $10 one-time fee/pet. Service with restrictions, supervision.
🆂🅐🆅🅴 🆂🅙 ☒ 🕖 🕖 🔒 🖥 🍴 ⚊ ☒

HANCOCK

▼▼ ▼▼ **Smith's Colonial Motel** Ⓜ
(607) 637-2989. **$55-$110.** 23085 State Hwy 97. SR 17, exit 87, 2.5 mi. Ext corridors. **Pets:** Accepted.

HAUPPAUGE

🆎🅐 ▼▼▼▼▼ **Hyatt Regency WindWatch** 🅻🅷
(631) 232-9800. **$109-$229, 3 day notice.** 1717 Long Island Motor Pkwy. I-495, exit 57, just n to Long Island Motor Pkwy, then 1.3 mi ne. Int corridors. **Pets:** Accepted.
🆂🅐🆅🅴 ☒ 🆂🅼 🕖 🔒 🖥 🍴 ⚊ ☒

▼▼▼▼ **Residence Inn by Marriott** 🆂🅷
(631) 724-4188. **$129-$299.** 850 Veterans Memorial Hwy. I-495, exit 57, 1.2 mi nw. Int corridors. **Pets:** Accepted.
Ⓐ🆂🅚 ☒ 🆂🅼 🕖 🕖 🔒 🖥 ⚊ ☒

🆎🅐 ▼▼▼▼ **Sheraton Long Island Hotel Smithtown** 🅻🅷 🐾
(631) 231-1100. **$104-$166.** 110 Vanderbilt Motor Pkwy. I-495, exit 53 (Wicks Rd), just n, then 0.3 mi e. Int corridors. **Pets:** Medium, dogs only. Designated rooms, service with restrictions, supervision.
🆂🅐🆅🅴 🆂🅙 ☒ 🆂🅼 🕖 🕖 🔒 🖥 🍴 ⚊ ☒

HENRIETTA

▼▼▼▼ **Comfort Suites by Choice Hotels of Rochester** 🆂🅷
(585) 334-6620. **$100-$160.** 2085 Hylan Dr. I-390, exit 13, just e. Int corridors. **Pets:** Other species. $75 one-time fee/pet. Service with restrictions, crate.
Ⓐ🆂🅚 🆂🅙 ☒ 🆂🅼 🕖 🔒 🖥 ⚊

▼▼ ▼▼ **Econo Lodge-Rochester South** 🆂🅷
(585) 427-2700. **$49-$85, 3 day notice.** 940 Jefferson Rd. I-390, exit 14A southbound; exit 14 northbound, just w on SR 252 (Jefferson Rd). Int corridors. **Pets:** Large, other species. Designated rooms, service with restrictions, supervision.
Ⓐ🆂🅚 🆂🅙 ☒ 🕖 🔒 🖥

▼▼ ▼▼ **Homewood Suites by Hilton-Rochester** 🆂🅷
(585) 334-9150. **$109-$149.** 2095 Hylan Dr. I-390, exit 13, just e. Int corridors. **Pets:** Accepted.
Ⓐ🆂🅚 🆂🅙 ☒ 🆂🅼 🕖 🕖 🔒 🖥 ⚊

▼▼ ◆ **Microtel-Rochester** 🆂🅷
(585) 334-3400. **$39-$69.** 905 Lehigh Station Rd. I-390, exit 12 northbound; exit 12A southbound, just w on SR 253. Int corridors. **Pets:** Other species. $75 deposit/room, $5 daily fee/room. Designated rooms, service with restrictions, supervision.
Ⓐ🆂🅚 🆂🅙 ☒ 🔒

▼▼ ▼▼ **Ramada Inn Rochester** 🆂🅷
(585) 475-9190. **$69-$119.** 800 Jefferson Rd. I-390, exit 14A southbound; exit 14 northbound, 0.5 mi w on SR 252 (Jefferson Rd). Int corridors. **Pets:** Large. Service with restrictions.
Ⓐ🆂🅚 🆂🅙 ☒ 🔒 🖥 🍴 ⚊

▼▼ ▼▼ **Red Roof Inn-Henrietta #7042** Ⓜ
(585) 359-1100. **$39-$75.** 4820 W Henrietta Rd. I-390, exit 12 northbound; exit 12A southbound, 0.5 mi w on SR 253, then just s on SR 15 (W Henrietta Rd). Ext corridors. **Pets:** Accepted.
☒ 🔒

▼▼▼▼ **Residence Inn by Marriott** 🆂🅷
(585) 272-8850. **$149-$205.** 1300 Jefferson Rd. I-390, exit 14A southbound, 0.5 mi e on SR 252 (Jefferson Rd); exit 14 northbound, just n on SR 15A, then 0.5 mi e on SR 252 (Jefferson Rd). Ext corridors. **Pets:** Other species. $75 one-time fee/room. Service with restrictions, crate.
Ⓐ🆂🅚 🆂🅙 ☒ 🕖 🔒 🖥 ⚊ ☒

▼▼▼▼ **R I T Inn & Conference Center** 🆂🅷
(585) 359-1800. **$89-$125.** 5257 W Henrietta Rd. I-390, exit 12 northbound; exit 12A southbound, 0.5 mi w on SR 253, then 0.7 mi s. Int corridors. **Pets:** $50 one-time fee/room. Service with restrictions.
Ⓐ🆂🅚 🆂🅙 ☒ 🕖 🔒 🖥 🍴 ⚊ ☒

HERKIMER

Herkimer Motel M
(315) 866-0490. **$68-$88.** 100 Marginal Rd. I-90, exit 30, just n on SR 28. Ext/int corridors. **Pets:** Service with restrictions, supervision.

HORNELL

Econo Lodge M
(607) 324-0800. **$49-$69.** 7462 Seneca Rd. Jct I-86 and SR 36, exit 34, just s to SR 21, just e to Seneca Rd, then just s. Ext/int corridors. **Pets:** Other species. $7 daily fee/room. Service with restrictions, crate.

HORSEHEADS

Hilton Garden Inn Elmira/Corning SH
(607) 795-1111. **$94-$179.** 35 Arnot Rd. SR 17 (I-86), exit 51 eastbound; exit 51A westbound. Int corridors. **Pets:** Small. $35 one-time fee/pet. Designated rooms, service with restrictions, supervision.

HUNTER

Hunter Inn SH
(518) 263-3777. **$79-$285, 14 day notice.** Rt 23A. Jct SR 296, 1.9 mi e. Int corridors. **Pets:** Accepted.

ITHACA

Comfort Inn SH 🐾
(607) 272-0100. **$79-$279.** 356 Elmira Rd. Jct SR 96, 89 and 79, 1.5 mi sw on SR 13. Ext/int corridors. **Pets:** Other species. $25 one-time fee/room. Service with restrictions, supervision.

Hampton Inn SH
(607) 277-5500. **$99-$299.** 337 Elmira Rd. On SR 13. Int corridors. **Pets:** Accepted.

Holiday Inn Ithaca Downtown SH
(607) 272-1000. **$107-$152.** 222 S Cayuga St. Just n of SR 96B. Int corridors. **Pets:** Accepted.

La Tourelle Country Inn CI
(607) 273-2734. **$99-$299.** 1150 Danby Rd. 2.7 mi s on SR 96B. Int corridors. **Pets:** Large, other species. $50 deposit/pet. Designated rooms, service with restrictions, supervision.

Meadow Court Inn M
(607) 273-3885. **$60-$195.** 529 S Meadow St. 1.5 mi s on SR 13 and 96. Ext/int corridors. **Pets:** $10 daily fee/pet. Designated rooms.

JAMESTOWN

Comfort Inn SH
(716) 664-5920. **$69-$169.** 2800 N Main St Extension. I-86, exit 12, just s. Int corridors. **Pets:** Small, other species. $10 one-time fee/pet. Service with restrictions, supervision.

Holiday Inn LH
(716) 664-3400. **$79-$149.** 150 W 4th St. I-86, exit 12, 2 mi s on SR 60 (Washington St); center. Int corridors. **Pets:** Accepted.

JOHNSON CITY

Best Western of Johnson City SH
(607) 729-9194. **$65-$115.** 569 Harry L Dr. SR 17, exit 70, 0.3 mi n. Int corridors. **Pets:** Medium. $10 daily fee/room. Designated rooms, service with restrictions, crate.

Red Roof Inn-Binghamton #7203 M
(607) 729-8940. **$49-$72.** 590 Fairview St. SR 17, exit 70, 0.3 mi n, then just n on Reynolds Rd. Ext corridors. **Pets:** Accepted.

JOHNSTOWN

Holiday Inn SH
(518) 762-4686. **$96-$156.** 308 N Comrie Ave. Jct SR 30A and 29 E, 1.3 mi n. Ext/int corridors. **Pets:** Accepted.

KINGSTON

Holiday Inn SH
(845) 338-0400. **$139-$179, 3 day notice.** 503 Washington Ave. I-87, exit 19, just e of traffic circle. Int corridors. **Pets:** Medium. $10 daily fee/room. Service with restrictions, supervision.

LAKE GEORGE

Balmoral Motel M
(518) 668-2673. **$49-$119, 10 day notice.** 444 Canada St. I-87, exit 22, 0.3 mi s on US 9. Ext corridors. **Pets:** Other species. $12 daily fee/pet. Designated rooms, crate.

Fort William Henry Resort Hotel & Conference Center LH
(518) 668-3081. **$89-$359, 3 day notice.** 48 Canada St. I-87, exit 21, 1 mi n on US 9. Ext/int corridors. **Pets:** Accepted.

Green Haven M
(518) 668-2489. **$54-$109, 10 day notice.** 3136 Lake Shore Dr. I-87, exit 22, 0.8 mi n on SR 9N. Ext corridors. **Pets:** Large, dogs only. $10 one-time fee/pet. Service with restrictions, supervision.

Lake Haven Motel M
(518) 668-2260. **$49-$139, 10 day notice.** 442 Canada St. I-87, exit 22, 0.4 mi s on US 9. Ext corridors. **Pets:** Medium, dogs only. $15 daily fee/room. Designated rooms, service with restrictions, crate.

Travelodge of Lake George M 🐾
(518) 668-5421. **$69-$169.** 2011 SR 9. I-87, exit 21. Ext corridors. **Pets:** Small. $20 daily fee/room. Designated rooms, service with restrictions, supervision.

LAKE LUZERNE

Luzerne Court M 🐾
(518) 696-2734. **$66-$176, 14 day notice.** 508 Lake Ave. I-87, exit 21, 8.7 mi s on SR 9N. Ext corridors. **Pets:** Dogs only. Designated rooms, service with restrictions, supervision.

LAKE PLACID

Art Devlin's Olympic Motor Inn M
(518) 523-3700. **$58-$148, 10 day notice.** 350 Main St. 0.5 mi e on SR 86. Ext corridors. **Pets:** Dogs only. Supervision.

(AAA) ▽▽▽ **Best Western Golden Arrow Hotel** SH ❁
(518) 523-3353. **$79-$219, 30 day notice.** 150 Main St. On SR 86; center. Int corridors. **Pets:** $100 deposit/pet, $50 one-time fee/pet. Designated rooms, service with restrictions, supervision.
[SAVE] [S🐾] [✕] [🖋] [🛗] [📺] [¶¶] [🏊] [⊠]

▽▽▽ **Comfort Inn on Lake Placid** SH
(518) 523-9555. **$85-$200.** 2125 Saranac Ave. 0.5 mi w on SR 86. Ext/int corridors. **Pets:** Large, other species. Service with restrictions, supervision.
[ASK] [S🐾] [✕] [🖋] [🛗] [📺] [¶¶] [🏊] [⊠]

(AAA) ▽▽▽ **Edge of the Lake Motel** M
(518) 523-9430. **$49-$139.** 56 Saranac Ave. 0.5 mi w on SR 86. Ext/int corridors. **Pets:** Medium. $10 daily fee/pet. No service, supervision.
[SAVE] [🛗] [📺] [🏊] [⊠]

▽▽▽▽ **Hilton Lake Placid Resort** SH
(518) 523-4411. **$79-$269, 7 day notice.** 1 Mirror Lake Dr. 0.3 mi w on SR 86. Int corridors. **Pets:** Accepted.
[✕] [♿] [🖋] [🛗] [📺] [¶¶] [🏊] [⊠]

(AAA) ▽▽▽ **Lake Placid Ramada Inn** SH
(518) 523-2587. **$69-$179, 3 day notice.** 8-12 Saranac Ave. 0.3 mi w on SR 86. Int corridors. **Pets:** Medium, dogs only. $25 daily fee/room. Designated rooms, service with restrictions, supervision.
[SAVE] [S🐾] [✕] [🖋] [🛗] [📺] [¶¶] [🏊]

▽▽▽ **Lake Placid Resort Hotel & Golf Club/Holiday Inn** SH
(518) 523-2556. **$69-$219, 30 day notice.** 1 Olympic Dr. Downtown. Ext/int corridors. **Pets:** Other species. $25 one-time fee/room. Designated rooms, service with restrictions, supervision.
[✕] [🖋] [🛗] [🛗] [📺] [🏊] [⊠]

(AAA) ▽▽▽ **Swiss Acres Inn** SH
(518) 523-3040. **$48-$278, 7 day notice.** 189 Saranac Ave. 1 mi w on SR 86. Ext/int corridors. **Pets:** Medium. $15 daily fee/room. Service with restrictions, supervision.
[SAVE] [✕] [🛗] [📺] [¶¶] [🏊] [⊠]

LANSING

▽▽ **The Clarion University Hotel & Conference Center** SH
(607) 257-2000. **$89-$199, 3 day notice.** SR 13, exit Triphammer Rd, just s; n of Ithaca. Int corridors. **Pets:** Medium, other species. $20 one-time fee/room. Designated rooms, service with restrictions, supervision.
[ASK] [S🐾] [✕] [🛗] [📺] [🏊] [⊠]

(AAA) ▽▽▽ **Econo Lodge** SH
(607) 257-1400. **$66-$160.** 2303 N Triphammer Rd. Jct SR 13 and Triphammer Rd. Int corridors. **Pets:** $15 daily fee/pet. Service with restrictions, supervision.
[SAVE] [S🐾] [✕] [🛗] [📺]

▽▽▽ **Ramada Inn-Airport** SH
(607) 257-3100. **$99-$199, 3 day notice.** 2310 N Triphammer Rd. Jct SR 13 and 34, 3.5 mi n on SR 13, exit Triphammer Rd, just w. Int corridors. **Pets:** Medium, other species. $20 one-time fee/room. Designated rooms, service with restrictions, supervision.
[ASK] [S🐾] [✕] [♿] [🛗] [📺] [¶¶] [🏊] [⊠]

LATHAM

(AAA) ▽▽▽ **Century House Restaurant & Hotel** SH ❁
(518) 785-0931. **$115-$225.** 997 New Loudon Rd. I-87, exit 7 (SR 7), just e, then 0.5 mi n on US 9 (New Loudon Rd). Int corridors. **Pets:** $15 daily fee/pet. Designated rooms, service with restrictions, supervision.
[SAVE] [S🐾] [✕] [🛗] [📺] [¶¶] [🏊] [⊠]

▽▽▽ **Comfort Inn At Albany Airport** SH
(518) 783-1900. **$99-$149.** 20 Airport Park Blvd. I-87, exit 4, 2.2 mi nw on Albany Shaker Rd. Int corridors. **Pets:** Accepted.
[ASK] [S🐾] [✕] [🛗] [📺] [¶¶]

▽▽▽▽ **Holiday Inn Express-Airport** SH
(518) 783-6161. **$85-$125.** 946 New Loudon Rd. I-87, exit 7 (SR 7), just e, then just n on US 9 (New Loudon Rd). Ext corridors. **Pets:** Accepted.
[ASK] [S🐾] [✕] [🖋] [🛗] [📺] [🏊]

(AAA) ▽▽▽ **Microtel Inn** SH
(518) 782-9161. **$45-$129.** 7 Rensselaer Ave. I-87, exit 6, just w. Int corridors. **Pets:** Medium, dogs only. $10 daily fee/pet. Service with restrictions, supervision.
[SAVE] [S🐾] [✕] [♿] [🖋] [🖋] [🛗] [📺]

▽▽▽ **Residence Inn by Marriott Albany Airport** SH ❁
(518) 783-0600. **$199-$249.** 1 Residence Inn Dr. I-87, exit 6, 2 mi w on SR 7. Ext corridors. **Pets:** $75 one-time fee/room. Service with restrictions.
[ASK] [S🐾] [✕] [🖋] [🛗] [📺] [🏊] [⊠]

LITTLE FALLS

(AAA) ▽▽▽ **Best Western Little Falls Motor Inn** SH
(315) 823-4954. **$65-$105.** 20 Albany St. On SR 5 and 167. Int corridors. **Pets:** Other species. $10 deposit/pet. Designated rooms, service with restrictions, crate.
[SAVE] [S🐾] [✕] [📺] [¶¶]

LIVERPOOL

(AAA) ▽▽▽ **Best Western Inn & Suites** SH
(315) 701-4400. **$79-$129, 3 day notice.** 136 Transistor Pkwy. I-90, exit 37 (Electronics Pkwy), just n; I-81, exit 25 (7th North St), 1.3 mi w, just n on Electronics Pkwy, then just w. Int corridors. **Pets:** Small, dogs only. $10 daily fee/pet. Designated rooms, service with restrictions, supervision.
[SAVE] [✕] [🛗] [📺] [🏊]

▽▽▽▽ **Holiday Inn Syracuse Airport** LH
(315) 457-1122. **$149-$199.** 441 Electronics Pkwy. I-90, exit 37 (Electronics Pkwy); I-81, exit 25 (7th North St), 1.3 mi nw. Int corridors. **Pets:** Other species. $50 deposit/room. Designated rooms, service with restrictions, crate.
[ASK] [S🐾] [✕] [♿] [🖋] [🖋] [🛗] [📺] [🏊] [⊠]

▽▽▽ **Homewood Suites** SH
(315) 451-3800. **$139-$219.** 275 Elwood Davis Rd. I-81, exit 25 (7th North St), 1 mi w; I-90, exit 36. Int corridors. **Pets:** Small. $100 one-time fee/room. Service with restrictions, crate.
[ASK] [✕] [🛗] [📺] [🏊] [⊠]

(AAA) ▽▽▽ **Knights Inn** M 🐾
(315) 453-6330. **$42-$124.** 430 Electronics Pkwy. I-90, exit 37 (Electronics Pkwy), just s; I-81, exit 25 (7th North St), 1.3 mi nw, then just s. Ext corridors. **Pets:** Large. $10 daily fee/pet. Service with restrictions, supervision.
[SAVE] [S🐾] [✕] [🛗]

▽▽ **Super 8 Motel Syracuse/Liverpool** SH
(315) 451-8888. **$69-$99.** 421 7th North St. I-81, exit 25 (7th North St), just nw; I-90, exit 36. Int corridors. **Pets:** $25 deposit/room. Designated rooms, service with restrictions, supervision.
[ASK] [S🐾] [✕] [🛗]

LONG LAKE

▽▽ **Long View Lodge** CI
(518) 624-2862. **$65-$110, 7 day notice.** Deerland Rd (Rt 30). On SR 30/28N, 2.2 mi s. Ext/int corridors. **Pets:** Other species. Designated rooms, service with restrictions, supervision.
[✕] [🛗] [¶¶] [⊠] [🐾]

LOWMAN

ⒶⒶⒶ ▽▽▽ Red Jacket Motel M ❀
(607) 734-1616. **$40-$95, 3 day notice.** 1744 Rt 17 W. SR 17, just e of CR 8; between MM 195 and 196. Ext corridors. **Pets:** Dogs only. $10 daily fee/pet. No service, supervision.
SAVE S6 ✕ & 🗂 ⌕

MALONE

ⒶⒶⒶ ▽▽▽ Four Seasons Motel M
(518) 483-3490. **$45-$79.** 206 W Main St. 1 mi w on US 11. Ext corridors. **Pets:** Large, other species. Service with restrictions, supervision.
SAVE S6 ✕ 🗂 💻 ⌕

▽▽ Sunset Inn M
(518) 483-3367. **$50-$65.** 3899 US 11. 1.5 mi e. Ext corridors. **Pets:** Accepted.
ASK S6 ✕ 🗂 💻 ⌕

ⒶⒶⒶ ▽▽▽ Super 8 Motel at Jons SH
(518) 483-8123. **$70-$95.** 42 Finney Blvd. On SR 30, just s of jct US 11. Int corridors. **Pets:** Small. Designated rooms, service with restrictions, supervision.
SAVE S6 ✕ &M 🗂

MALTA

▽▽▽ Fairfield Inn & Suites by Marriott SH
(518) 899-6900. **$119-$309.** 101 Saratoga Village Blvd. I-87, exit 12, just e. Int corridors. **Pets:** Accepted.
ASK S6 ✕ &M & 🗂 💻 ⌕

MASSENA

ⒶⒶⒶ ▽▽▽ Econo Lodge-Meadow View Motel SH ❀
(315) 764-0246. **$75-$99.** 15054 SR 37. On SR 37, 2.7 mi sw. Ext/int corridors. **Pets:** Small. $5 daily fee/pet. Designated rooms, service with restrictions.
SAVE S6 ✕ 🗂 💻 ⑪

MCGRAW

ⒶⒶⒶ ▽▽▽ Cortland Days Inn SH
(607) 753-7594. **$64-$129.** 3775 US Rt 11. I-81, exit 10 (McGraw/Cortland), just n. Int corridors. **Pets:** Accepted.
SAVE S6 ✕ 🗂

MIDDLETOWN

▽▽ Super 8 Motel SH
(845) 692-5828. **$88-$110, 3 day notice.** 563 Rt 211 E. I-84, exit 4, 0.5 mi w on SR 17 to exit 120, then 0.3 mi e. Int corridors. **Pets:** Other species. $25 deposit/room. No service, supervision.
ASK S6 ✕ 🗂

MONTOUR FALLS

ⒶⒶⒶ ▽ Relax Inn M
(607) 535-7183. **$39-$89, 4 day notice.** 100 Clawson Blvd. Jct SR 14 and 224. Ext corridors. **Pets:** Small. $10 daily fee/pet. Designated rooms, service with restrictions, supervision.
SAVE S6 ✕ 🗂

NEW HAMPTON

ⒶⒶⒶ ▽▽▽ Days Inn M
(845) 374-2411. **$64-$139.** 4939 Rt 17M. I-84, 0.8 mi e on US 6 and SR 17M. Ext/int corridors. **Pets:** Large. Designated rooms, service with restrictions, supervision.
SAVE S6 ✕ 🗂 💻 ⌕

NEW HARTFORD

▽▽▽ Holiday Inn Utica SH
(315) 797-2131. **$89-$159.** 1777 Burrstone Rd. I-90 (New York State Thruway), exit 31, 4.5 mi w on SR 5 W and 12 S, exit Burrstone Rd, then 1 mi nw. Ext/int corridors. **Pets:** Other species. $25 deposit/room. Service with restrictions, crate.
ASK S6 ✕ 🐾 🗂 💻 ⑪ ⌕ ✕

NEW YORK METROPOLITAN AREA

ELMSFORD

ⒶⒶⒶ ▽▽▽ Wellesley Inn (Elmsford) SH
(914) 592-3300. **$119-$159.** 540 Saw Mill River Rd. SR 9A, 1.5 mi n of SR 119; 1 mi n of I-287, exit 2 westbound; exit 1 eastbound, jct SR 100C. Int corridors. **Pets:** Small, other species. $20 deposit/room. Service with restrictions, supervision.
SAVE S6 ✕ &M 🐾 & 🗂 💻 ⑪ ⌕

JAMAICA

ⒶⒶⒶ ▽▽▽ Ramada Plaza Hotel at JFK LH
(718) 995-9000. **$109-$149, 3 day notice.** Bldg 144/JFK International Airport. In Jamaica; Van Wyck Expwy at Belt Pkwy; southwest corner. Int corridors. **Pets:** Accepted.
SAVE S6 ✕ 🐾 🗂 💻 ⑪ ✕

LONG ISLAND CITY

ⒶⒶⒶ ▽▽▽ Holiday Inn Express SH
(718) 706-6700. **$125-$169.** 3805 Hunters Point Ave. In Long Island City; I-278, exit I-495 (Midtown tunnel) westbound, exit 15 (Van Dam St), just n to Hunters Point Blvd, w on Greenpoint Ave, n at 39th St; I-278 westbound, exit 35 (. Int corridors. **Pets:** Accepted.
SAVE S6 ✕ 🐾 & 🗂 💻

MOUNT KISCO

ⒶⒶⒶ ▽▽▽▽ Holiday Inn SH
(914) 241-2600. **$179-$199.** 1 Holiday Inn Dr. Saw Mill River Pkwy, exit 37, just e. Int corridors. **Pets:** Other species. $10 daily fee/pet. Service with restrictions, crate.
SAVE ✕ &M 🐾 & 🗂 💻 ⑪ ⌕

NANUET

ⒶⒶⒶ ▽▽▽ Days Inn Nanuet SH
(845) 623-4567. **$69-$99.** 367 W Rt 59. I-287/87, exit 14 (SR 59), just w. Ext/int corridors. **Pets:** $8 daily fee/pet. Service with restrictions, crate.
SAVE S6 ✕ 🗂 💻 ⌕

NEW YORK

ⒶⒶⒶ ▽▽▽ Affinia 50 SH ❀
(212) 751-5710. **$189-$399.** 155 E 50th St. Between 3rd and Lexington aves. Int corridors. **Pets:** Other species. Service with restrictions.
SAVE ✕ 🐾 🗂 💻

ⒶⒶⒶ ▽▽▽ Affinia Dumont SH ❀
(212) 481-7600. **$189-$399.** 150 E 34th St. Between Lexington and 3rd aves. Int corridors. **Pets:** Other species. Service with restrictions.
SAVE ✕ 🐾 & 🗂 💻 ⑪ ✕

ⒶⒶⒶ ▽▽▽ Beekman Tower Hotel SH
(212) 355-7300. **$139-$339.** 3 Mitchell Pl. 49th St and 1st Ave. Int corridors. **Pets:** Accepted.
SAVE ✕ 🐾 & 🗂 💻 ⑪

The Benjamin Hotel SH
(212) 715-2500. **$219-$459.** 125 E 50th St. Between Lexington and 3rd aves. Int corridors. **Pets:** Other species. Service with restrictions.

The Carlyle SH
(212) 744-1600. **$550-$5000.** 35 E 76th St. At Madison Ave. Int corridors. **Pets:** Accepted.

Crowne Plaza at the United Nations LH
(212) 986-8800. **$239-$599.** 304 E 42nd St. Between 1st and 2nd aves. Int corridors. **Pets:** Small. $500 deposit/room, $50 one-time fee/room. Service with restrictions.

DoubleTree Metropolitan Hotel New York City SH
(212) 752-7000. **$290-$419.** 569 Lexington Ave. At E 51st St. Int corridors. **Pets:** Small. Service with restrictions, supervision.

Eastgate Tower Hotel SH
(212) 687-8000. **$139-$319.** 222 E 39th St. Between 2nd and 3rd aves. Int corridors. **Pets:** Other species. Service with restrictions.

Embassy Suites Hotel New York LH
(212) 945-0100. **$189-$439.** 102 N End Ave. Between Murray and Vesey sts. Int corridors. **Pets:** $75 one-time fee/room. Supervision.

The Essex House-A Westin Hotel LH
(212) 247-0300. **$469-$649.** 160 Central Park S. Between 6th (Ave of the Americas) and 7th aves. Int corridors. **Pets:** Accepted.

Four Points by Sheraton Manhattan Chelsea SH
(212) 627-1888. **$169-$479.** 160 W 25th St. Between 6th (Ave of the Americas) and 7th aves. Int corridors. **Pets:** Accepted.

Four Seasons Hotel, New York LH
(212) 758-5700. **$450-$995.** 57 E 57th St. Between Park and Madison aves. Int corridors. **Pets:** Accepted.

Hampton Inn-Manhattan/Chelsea SH
(212) 414-1000. **$129-$229.** 108 W 24th St. Between 6th (Ave of the Americas) and 7th aves. Int corridors. **Pets:** Small. $20 one-time fee/room. Service with restrictions, supervision.

Hilton New York LH
(212) 586-7000. **$199-$729.** 1335 Ave of the Americas. Between 53rd and 54th sts. Int corridors. **Pets:** Medium. No service, crate.

Hilton Times Square LH
(212) 840-8222. **$179-$1000.** 234 W 42nd St. Between 7th and 8th aves. Int corridors. **Pets:** Accepted.

The Holiday Inn Martinique on Broadway SH
(212) 736-3800. **$179-$329.** 49 W 32nd St. Corner of Broadway. Int corridors. **Pets:** Accepted.

Hotel Gansevoort SH
(212) 206-6700. **$325-$505.** 18 9th Ave. At 13th St. Int corridors. **Pets:** Medium. $65 one-time fee/room. Service with restrictions, crate.

Hotel Plaza Athenee SH
(212) 734-9100. **$545-$695.** 37 E 64th St. Between Madison and Park aves. Int corridors. **Pets:** Accepted.

Hotel Wales SH
(212) 876-6000. **$375.** 1295 Madison Ave. Between 92 and 93 sts E. Int corridors. **Pets:** Accepted.

Jolly Hotel Madison Towers LH
(212) 802-0600. **$220-$275.** 22 E 38th St. Between Park and Madison aves. Int corridors. **Pets:** Accepted.

Le Parker Meridien New York LH
(212) 245-5000. **$460-$555.** 118 W 57th St. Between 6th (Ave of the Americas) and 7th aves; vehicle entrance on 56th St. Int corridors. **Pets:** Other species. Service with restrictions.

The Lowell Hotel SH
(212) 838-1400. **$495-$625.** 28 E 63rd St. Between Park and Madison aves. Int corridors. **Pets:** Other species.

Lyden Gardens Hotel SH
(212) 355-1230. **$179-$339.** 215 E 64th St. Between 2nd and 3rd aves. Int corridors. **Pets:** Other species. Service with restrictions, supervision.

Mandarin Oriental, New York LH
(212) 805-8800. **$625-$9999.** 80 Columbus Circle. At 60th St. Int corridors. **Pets:** Accepted.

The Mansfield SH
(212) 944-6050. **Call for rates.** 12 W 44th St. Between 5th and 6th (Ave of the Americas) aves. Int corridors. **Pets:** Accepted.

The Mark, New York SH
(212) 744-4300. **$600-$730.** 25 E 77th St. Madison Ave at E 77th St. Int corridors. **Pets:** Accepted.

Millenium Hilton LH
(212) 693-2001. **$199-$599.** 55 Church St. Between Dey and Fulton sts. Int corridors. **Pets:** Medium, dogs only. Service with restrictions, supervision.

Millennium Broadway LH
(212) 768-4400. **$319-$499.** 145 W 44th St. Between 6th (Ave of the Americas) and 7th aves. Int corridors. **Pets:** Accepted.

The Muse Hotel SH
(212) 485-2400. **$289-$349.** 130 W 46th St. Between 6th (Ave of the Americas) and 7th aves. Int corridors. **Pets:** Service with restrictions, crate.

New York Marriott Marquis LH
(212) 398-1900. **$259-$619.** 1535 Broadway. Between 45th and 46th sts; motor entrance on 46th St. Int corridors. **Pets:** Accepted.

The New York Palace LH
(212) 888-7000. **$450-$690.** 455 Madison Ave. Between 50th and 51st sts. Int corridors. **Pets:** Very small. Service with restrictions, supervision.

Novotel New York LH ❀
(212) 315-0100. **$179-$349.** 226 W 52nd St. At Broadway. Int corridors. **Pets:** Medium. Service with restrictions, crate.
[SAVE] [S🐾] [✕] [🐾] [¶]

Omni Berkshire Place LH
(212) 753-5800. **$369-$950.** 21 E 52nd St. Between Madison and 5th aves. Int corridors. **Pets:** Accepted.
[ASK] [S🐾] [✕] [&M] [🐾] [🐾] [🛏] [🖥] [¶] [✕]

On The Ave Hotel SH
(212) 362-1100. **$209-$279.** 2178 Broadway. At 77th St. Int corridors. **Pets:** Accepted.
[ASK] [✕] [🛏] [🖥]

The Peninsula New York LH ❀
(212) 956-2888. **$475-$660.** 700 5th Ave. At 55th St. Int corridors. **Pets:** Small, dogs only. $25 one-time fee/pet. No service, supervision.
[SAVE] [✕] [🐾] [&] [🛏] [¶] [🏊] [✕]

The Pierre New York-A Four Seasons Hotel LH
(212) 838-8000. **Call for rates.** 2 E 61st St. At 5th Ave. Int corridors. **Pets:** Accepted.
[✕] [&M] [🐾] [&] [🛏] [¶] [✕]

The Regency Hotel LH
(212) 759-4100. **$249-$509.** 540 Park Ave. At 61st St. Int corridors. **Pets:** Accepted.
[SAVE] [S🐾] [✕] [&M] [🐾] [&] [🛏] [¶]

Renaissance New York Hotel Times Square LH ❀
(212) 765-7676. **$239-$569.** 2 Times Square, 7th Ave at W 48th St. Broadway and 7th Ave; auto access from 7th Ave, s of W 48th St. Int corridors. **Pets:** Medium, dogs only. $65 one-time fee/pet. Service with restrictions, crate.
[SAVE] [✕] [🐾] [🖥] [¶]

The Ritz-Carlton New York, Battery Park SH ❀
(212) 344-0800. **$550-$780.** Two West St. Jct Battery Pl. Int corridors. **Pets:** Small. $125 one-time fee/pet. Designated rooms, service with restrictions.
[SAVE] [✕] [&M] [🐾] [&] [🛏] [¶]

The Ritz-Carlton New York, Central Park LH ❀
(212) 308-9100. **$750-$995.** 50 Central Park S. Between 5th and 6th (Ave of the Americas) aves. Int corridors. **Pets:** Large. Service with restrictions, supervision.
[SAVE] [✕] [&M] [🐾] [&] [🛏] [¶]

The Roger Smith Hotel SH
(212) 755-1400. **$260-$320.** 501 Lexington Ave. Between 47th and 48th sts. Int corridors. **Pets:** Accepted.
[ASK] [S🐾] [✕] [🐾] [🛏] [🖥] [¶]

Royalton LH
(212) 869-4400. **$375-$450.** 44 W 44th St. Between 5th and 6th (Ave of the Americas) aves. Int corridors. **Pets:** Accepted.
[✕] [🐾] [¶] [✕]

The St. Regis New York LH
(212) 753-4500. **$695-$895.** 2 E 55th St. Between Madison and 5th aves. Int corridors. **Pets:** Accepted.
[SAVE] [✕] [&M] [🐾] [🛏] [🖥] [¶] [✕]

Shelburne Murray Hill Hotel SH ❀
(212) 689-5200. **$159-$339.** 303 Lexington Ave. Between 37th and 38th sts. Int corridors. **Pets:** Other species. Service with restrictions.
[SAVE] [✕] [🐾] [&] [🛏] [🖥] [¶]

Sheraton Manhattan Hotel LH
(212) 581-3300. **$179-$299.** 790 7th Ave. Between 51st and 52nd sts. Int corridors. **Pets:** Accepted.
[ASK] [S🐾] [✕] [&M] [🐾] [&] [🛏] [🖥] [¶] [🏊] [✕]

Sheraton New York Hotel & Towers LH
(212) 581-1000. **$179-$299.** 811 7th Ave. At 52nd St. Int corridors. **Pets:** Accepted.
[ASK] [S🐾] [✕] [&M] [🐾] [&] [🛏] [🖥] [¶] [✕]

Sheraton Russell Hotel SH ❀
(212) 685-7676. **$179-$299.** 45 Park Ave. At 37th St. Int corridors. **Pets:** Dogs only. Service with restrictions.
[ASK] [S🐾] [✕] [&M] [🐾] [🛏] [🖥]

The Shoreham Hotel SH
(212) 247-6700. **Call for rates.** 33 W 55th St. Between 5th and 6th (Ave of the Americas) aves. Int corridors. **Pets:** Accepted.
[✕] [&M] [&] [🛏] [¶] [✕]

Sofitel New York LH
(212) 354-8844. **$379-$599.** 45 W 44th St. Between 5th and 6th (Ave of the Americas) aves. Int corridors. **Pets:** Medium, other species. Service with restrictions, crate.
[SAVE] [S🐾] [✕] [🐾] [&] [🛏] [¶]

The SoHo Grand Hotel SH
(212) 965-3000. **$309-$3500.** 310 W Broadway. In SoHo; jct Grand St. Int corridors. **Pets:** Accepted.
[✕] [&] [🖥]

Southgate Tower Suite Hotel LH ❀
(212) 563-1800. **$159-$319.** 371 7th Ave. At 31st St. Int corridors. **Pets:** Other species. Service with restrictions.
[SAVE] [✕] [🐾] [&] [🛏] [🖥] [¶]

The Stanhope Park Hyatt New York SH
(212) 774-1234. **$299-$385, 14 day notice.** 995 5th Ave. At 81st St. Int corridors. **Pets:** Medium, other species. $100 one-time fee/room. Service with restrictions, supervision.
[ASK] [✕] [🐾] [🛏] [¶] [✕]

Surrey Hotel SH ❀
(212) 288-3700. **$259-$435.** 20 E 76th St. E 76th St and Madison Ave. Int corridors. **Pets:** Other species. Service with restrictions.
[SAVE] [✕] [🐾] [🛏] [🖥] [¶]

Swissotel The Drake, New York SH
(212) 421-0900. **$270-$430.** 440 Park Ave. At 56th St; between Park and Madison aves. Int corridors. **Pets:** Accepted.
[SAVE] [✕] [🐾] [&] [🛏] [¶] [✕]

Tribeca Grand Hotel SH
(212) 519-6600. **$309-$2300.** 2 Ave of the Americas. At 6th Ave (Ave of the Americas) and White St. Int corridors. **Pets:** Accepted.
[✕] [&] [¶]

Trump International Hotel & Tower SH
(212) 299-1000. **$595-$695.** 1 Central Park W. Jct Central Park S; at Columbus Circle. Int corridors. **Pets:** Accepted.
[SAVE] [✕] [🐾] [🛏] [🖥] [¶] [🏊] [✕]

The Wall Street District Hotel LH
(212) 232-7700. **$169-$349.** 15 Gold St. Corner of Gold and Platt sts. Int corridors. **Pets:** Small. $10 daily fee/pet. Service with restrictions.
[ASK] [S🐾] [✕] [&M] [🐾] [&] [🛏] [🖥] [¶]

The Westin New York at Times Square LH
(212) 201-2700. **$449-$599.** 270 W 43rd St. Corner of 8th Ave. Int corridors. **Pets:** Accepted.
[ASK] [S🐾] [✕] [🐾] [&] [🛏] [🖥] [¶] [✕]

WWWW **W New York** LH ❀
(212) 755-1200. **$429-$519.** 541 Lexington Ave. At 49th St. Int corridors. **Pets:** Medium. $25 daily fee/room, $100 one-time fee/room. Service with restrictions.
ASK S🐾 ⊠ ♿M 🗗 🏃 🖪 🖵 🍴

WWWW **W New York Times Square** LH ❀
(212) 930-7400. **$429-$519.** 1567 Broadway at 47th St. Corner of 47th St. Int corridors. **Pets:** Large. $25 daily fee/room, $100 one-time fee/room. Service with restrictions.
ASK S🐾 ⊠ ♿M 🗗 🏃 🖪 🖵 🍴

AAA WWW WWW **W New York-Union Square** SH
(212) 253-9119. **$549-$649.** 201 Park Ave S. At 17th St. Int corridors. **Pets:** Accepted.
SAVE ⊠ ♿M 🗗 🏃 🖪 🖵 🍴

PEEKSKILL

AAA WWW **Peekskill Inn** M
(914) 739-1500. **$125-$140.** 634 Main St. Jct US 6 and 9, e to top of Main St. Ext corridors. **Pets:** Accepted.
SAVE S🐾 ⊠ 🖪 🍴 ➰

RYE BROOK

AAA WWWW **Hilton Rye Town** LH
(914) 939-6300. **$159-$409.** 699 Westchester Ave. I-287 (Cross Westchester Expwy), exit 10 eastbound, 0.6 mi ne on SR 120A; exit westbound, 0.3 mi n on Webb Ave, then 0.4 mi ne on SR 120A. Int corridors. **Pets:** Accepted.
SAVE ⊠ ♿M 🗗 🏃 🖪 🖵 🍴 ➰ 🐾

STATEN ISLAND

AAA WWWW **Hilton Garden Inn Staten Island** SH ❀
(718) 477-2400. **$159-$189.** 1100 South Ave. I-278, exit 6 (South Ave) westbound, just s; exit 5 eastbound to SR 440 S, exit South Ave, just s to South Ave, 1 mi n to Lois Ln, then just w. Int corridors. **Pets:** Very small. $35 daily fee/pet. Service with restrictions, crate.
SAVE S🐾 ⊠ 🏃 🖪 🖵 🍴 ➰ 🐾

AAA WWWW **The Staten Island Hotel** LH
(718) 698-5000. **$154-$159.** 1415 Richmond Ave. I-278, exit Richmond Ave, 0.5 mi se. Int corridors. **Pets:** Other species. Designated rooms, service with restrictions, crate.
SAVE S🐾 ⊠ 🖪 🖵 🍴

SUFFERN

AAA WWW **Wellesley Inn (Suffern)** SH
(845) 368-1900. **$99.** 17 N Airmont Rd. I-87/287, exit 14B, just s. Int corridors. **Pets:** Accepted.
SAVE S🐾 ⊠ ♿M 🗗 🏃 🖪 🖵

TARRYTOWN

WWWW **Hilton of Tarrytown** LH
(914) 631-5700. **Call for rates.** 455 S Broadway. I-87 (New York State Thruway), exit 9, just s on US 9. Int corridors. **Pets:** Accepted.
⊠ 🗗 🖪 🖵 🍴 ➰ 🐾

WHITE PLAINS

WWWW **Renaissance Westchester Hotel** LH
(914) 694-5400. **$130-$239.** 80 W Red Oak Ln. I-287 (Cross Westchester Expwy), exit 9N-S eastbound, 0.5 mi e on Westchester Ave, just n on Kenilworth Rd, then 0.7 mi w on Westchester Ave; exit westbound, 0.8 mi w on Westcheste. Int corridors. **Pets:** $90 one-time fee/room. Service with restrictions.
ASK ⊠ ♿M 🗗 🖪 🖵 🍴 ➰ 🐾

WWWW **Summerfield Suites By Wyndham-Westchester** SH
(914) 251-9700. **$139-$189.** 101 Corporate Park Dr. I-287 (Cross Westchester Expwy), exit 9A eastbound, 0.6 mi e on Westchester Ave, then 0.3 mi n; exit 9N-S westbound, 0.9 mi w on Westchester Ave. Int corridors. **Pets:** Medium. $150 one-time fee/room. Service with restrictions, crate.
ASK ⊠ 🗗 🏃 🖪 🖵 ➰ 🐾

NIAGARA FALLS METROPOLITAN AREA

LOCKPORT

WWWW **Holiday Inn Lockport** SH
(716) 434-6151. **$99-$129.** 515 S Transit Rd. 1 mi s on SR 78. Int corridors. **Pets:** Accepted.
ASK S🐾 ⊠ 🗗 🏃 🖪 🖵 🍴 ➰

NEWFANE

WWW **Lake Ontario Motel** M
(716) 778-5004. **$50-$68.** 3330 Lockport-Olcott Rd. 2.5 mi n of jct SR 104 on SR 78. Int corridors. **Pets:** $5 daily fee/room. Service with restrictions, supervision.
ASK ⊠ 🖪

NIAGARA FALLS

AAA WWW WWW **Best Western Summit Inn** SH
(716) 297-5050. **$59-$159.** 9500 Niagara Falls Blvd. I-190, exit 22, 2.1 mi e on US 62 S. Int corridors. **Pets:** Accepted.
SAVE S🐾 ⊠ 🖪 🖵 ➰

AAA WWW **Budget Host Inn** M
(716) 283-3839. **$59-$239.** 6621 Niagara Falls Blvd. I-190, exit 22, just e on US 62 S. Ext corridors. **Pets:** Medium. $10 one-time fee/room. Service with restrictions, supervision.
SAVE S🐾 ⊠ 🖪 ➰

AAA WWW WWW **Howard Johnson Hotel (Closest to the Falls)** SH
(716) 285-5261. **$79-$215.** 454 Main St. I-190, exit 21 (Robert Moses Pkwy), 2 mi e, just n to Rainbow Blvd, then just s. Int corridors. **Pets:** Accepted.
SAVE S🐾 ⊠ ♿M 🖪 🖵 ➰

WWW WWW **Quality Hotel and Suites "At the Falls"** SH
(716) 282-1212. **$79-$299.** 240 Rainbow Blvd. Downtown. Int corridors. **Pets:** Other species. $20 daily fee/pet. Service with restrictions, supervision.
ASK S🐾 ⊠ 🗗 🖪 🖵 🍴 ➰

AAA WW Thriftlodge M
(716) 297-2660. **$55-$99.** 9401 Niagara Falls Blvd. I-190, exit 22, 1.8 mi e. Ext corridors. **Pets:** Medium. $10 daily fee/pet. Designated rooms, service with restrictions, supervision.
SAVE ✕ 🛏 ➹

WHEATFIELD

AAA WW Driftwood Suites M
(716) 692-6650. **$35-$75.** 2754 Niagara Falls Blvd. I-190, exit 22, 5 mi e on US 62 S. Ext corridors. **Pets:** Accepted.
SAVE S6 ✕ 🛏 ➹

END METROPOLITAN AREA

NORTH SYRACUSE

WWWW Candlewood Suites Syracuse Airport SH
(315) 454-8999. **$99-$149.** 5414 South Bay Rd. I-90, exit 36; I-81, exit 26 (Mattydale Rd), follow South Bay Rd signs. Int corridors. **Pets:** Medium. $75 deposit/pet. Service with restrictions, supervision.
ASK S6 ✕ 🗡 🖊 🛏 🖵

WWWW Doubletree Club Hotel/Syracuse Airport SH
(315) 457-4000. **$79-$119.** 6701 Buckley Rd. I-81, exit 25 (7th North St), 0.8 mi w; I-90, exit 36. Int corridors. **Pets:** Accepted.
ASK ✕ 🗡 🛏 🖵 🍴 ➹ ✕

AAA WWW Quality Inn North M
(315) 451-1212. **$69-$169.** 1308 Buckley Rd. I-81, exit 25 (7th North St), 0.3 mi w, then just n. Ext/int corridors. **Pets:** Accepted.
SAVE S6 ✕ 🛏 🖵 🍴 ➹

NORWICH

WWW Howard Johnson Hotel SH
(607) 334-2200. **$75-$199, 3 day notice.** 75 N Broad St. On SR 12; downtown. Int corridors. **Pets:** Medium, dogs only. $10 one-time fee/pet. Service with restrictions, supervision.
ASK S6 ✕ 🛏 🖵 🍴 ➹

WWW Super 8 Motel of Norwich SH
(607) 336-8880. **$65-$115, 7 day notice.** 6067 State Hwy 12. On SR 12, 0.9 mi n. Int corridors. **Pets:** $3.50 deposit/pet. Service with restrictions, supervision.
ASK S6 ✕ 🛏 🖵

OGDENSBURG

AAA WWW Quality Inn Gran-View M
(315) 393-4550. **$82-$145.** 6765 State Hwy 37. On SR 37, 3 mi sw. Ext/int corridors. **Pets:** Accepted.
SAVE S6 ✕ 🛏 🖵 🍴 ➹ ✕

AAA WWWW The Stonefence Resort & Motel M
(315) 393-1545. **$77-$153.** 7191 SR 37. Jct SR 68, 0.5 mi w. Ext/int corridors. **Pets:** Medium. $25 daily fee/room. Designated rooms, service with restrictions, supervision.
SAVE S6 ✕ 🛏 🖵 🍴 ➹ ✕

OLD FORGE

AAA WWW Best Western Sunset Inn M
(315) 369-6836. **$59-$229, 8 day notice.** 2752 SR 28. 0.3 mi s. Ext/int corridors. **Pets:** Accepted.
ASK S6 ✕ 🛏 🖵 ➹ ✕

ONEONTA

AAA WWWW Holiday Inn Oneonta/Cooperstown Area SH
(607) 433-2250. **$79-$199.** 5206 State Hwy 23. I-88, exit 15 (SR 23 and 28), 1.5 mi e. Int corridors. **Pets:** Accepted.
SAVE S6 ✕ 🗡 🖊 🛏 🖵 🍴 ➹ ✕

WWW Super 8 Motel SH
(607) 432-9505. **$62-$150, 3 day notice.** 4973 SR 23. I-88, exit 15 (SR 23 and 28), 0.3 mi e. Int corridors. **Pets:** Accepted.
ASK S6 ✕ 🖱 🛏

OWEGO

AAA WW Sunrise Motel M
(607) 687-5667. **$51-$55.** 3778 Waverly Rd. SR 17, exit 64 (SR 96 N) across river w to SR 17C, 2 mi w. Ext corridors. **Pets:** Very small. $5 daily fee/pet. Service with restrictions, supervision.
SAVE S6 ✕

PAINTED POST

AAA WWW Best Western Lodge on the Green M
(607) 962-2456. **$50-$100.** 3171 Canada Rd. Jct US 15 and SR 17, exit 44, s to Gang Mills exit, then n. Ext corridors. **Pets:** Other species. Service with restrictions.
SAVE ✕ 🛏 🖵 🍴 ➹

WW Econo Lodge SH
(607) 962-4444. **$49-$99.** 200 Robert Dann Dr. Jct US 15 and SR 17, exit 44, s to Gang Mills exit. Int corridors. **Pets:** Other species. $10 daily fee/room. Service with restrictions, supervision.
ASK S6 ✕ 🖱M 🗡 🛏 🖵

PEMBROKE

WW Darien Lakes Econo Lodge SH 🐾
(585) 599-4681. **$44-$119.** 8493 SR 77. I-90, exit 48A, just s. Int corridors. **Pets:** Other species. Designated rooms, service with restrictions, supervision.
ASK S6 ✕ 🛏 🖵

PINE VALLEY

AAA WWWW Best Western Marshall Manor M
(607) 739-3891. **$52-$87, 7 day notice.** 3527 Watkins Rd. SR 17, exit 52, 5 mi n on SR 14. Ext corridors. **Pets:** Large, other species. $4 daily fee/pet. Designated rooms, service with restrictions, crate.
SAVE S6 ✕ 🛏 🖵 ➹

PLAINVIEW

WWWW Residence Inn by Marriott SH
(516) 433-6200. **$189-$209.** 9 Gerhard Rd. I-495, exit 44, 1.6 mi s on SR 135, exit 10, then just e on Old Country Rd. Int corridors. **Pets:** Accepted.
✕ 🖱M 🗡 🛏 🖵 🍴 ➹ ✕

PLATTSBURGH

AAA WWWW Baymont Inn & Suites Plattsburgh SH
(518) 562-4000. **$67-$99.** 16 Plaza Blvd. I-87, exit 37, just w. Int corridors. **Pets:** Accepted.
SAVE ✕ 🖱M 🗡 🖊 🛏 🖵 ➹

AAA WWW Best Western The Inn at Smithfield SH 🐾
(518) 561-7750. **$69-$129.** 446 Rt 3. I-87, exit 37, just w. Int corridors. **Pets:** Other species. Service with restrictions, supervision.
SAVE S6 ✕ 🛏 🖵 🍴 ➹ ✕

PORT JERVIS

AAA WWW Comfort Inn SH
(845) 856-6611. **$69-$199.** 2247 Greenville Tpke. I-84, exit 1, just se. Int corridors. **Pets:** Small. $20 one-time fee/room. Designated rooms, service with restrictions, crate.
SAVE S6 ✕ 🛏 🖵 ➹

POUGHKEEPSIE

(AAA) ▼▼▼▼ Best Western Inn & Conference Center SH
(845) 462-4600. **$90-$140.** 2170 South Rd (US 9). Jct US 44 and SR 55, 4.7 mi s. Int corridors. **Pets:** Other species. $50 deposit/room. Supervision.
SAVE S☉ ✕ 🛏 💻 🍴 ⇌

PULASKI

(AAA) ▼ Redwood Motel M
(315) 298-4717. **$53-$60.** 3723 SR 13. I-81, exit 36, just e. Ext/int corridors. **Pets:** Dogs only. $20 deposit/room. Service with restrictions, supervision.
SAVE ✕ 🛏 🍴 ⇌

RHINEBECK

▼▼▼ Beekman Arms & Delamater Inn and Conference Center CI
(845) 876-7077. **$100-$300, 7 day notice.** 6387 Mill St (Rt 9). Jct US 9 and SR 308; center of village. Ext/int corridors. **Pets:** Accepted.
✕ 🖾 🛏 💻 🍴

RICHMONDVILLE

▼▼ Econo Lodge Cobleskill/Richmondville M
(518) 294-7739. **$49-$200.** 555 Ploss Rd. I-88, exit 20, just e on SR 7, then just s. Ext corridors. **Pets:** Accepted.
ASK S☉ ✕ 🛏 💻

RIVERHEAD

▼▼▼ Best Western East End SH
(631) 369-2200. **$139-$209, 3 day notice.** 1830 SR 25. I-495, exit 72 (SR 25 E). Int corridors. **Pets:** Medium, dogs only. $50 one-time fee/room. Designated rooms, service with restrictions, supervision.
ASK S☉ ✕ 🖾 🛏 💻 🍴 ⇌

ROCK HILL

(AAA) ▼▼▼ The Lodge at Rock Hill SH
(845) 796-3100. **$99-$189.** 283 Rock Hill Dr. SR 17, exit 109, just e. Int corridors. **Pets:** Other species. $25 one-time fee/pet. Service with restrictions, crate.
SAVE S☉ ✕ 🖨 🖾 🛏 💻 ⇌ ⊠

ROCKVILLE CENTRE

▼▼▼ Best Western SH
(516) 678-1300. **$159.** 173 Sunrise Hwy. On SR 27; between N Village and N Centre aves. Ext corridors. **Pets:** Other species. $15 daily fee/room. Designated rooms, service with restrictions.
ASK S☉ ✕ 🖳 🖨 🖾 🛏 💻 🍴 ⇌

ROME

▼▼ Adirondack Thirteen Pines Motel M ☘
(315) 337-4930. **$45-$70, 3 day notice.** 7353 River Rd. Jct SR 49, 0.5 mi e on SR 365. Ext corridors. **Pets:** Other species. No service.
ASK S☉ 🛏 ⇌ ⊠

(AAA) ▼▼▼ Inn at the Beeches M
(315) 336-1776. **$79-$118, 3 day notice.** 7900 Turin Rd. Jct SR 46, 2 mi n on SR 26 (Turin Rd). Ext corridors. **Pets:** Accepted.
SAVE S☉ ✕ 🛏 🍴 ⇌

(AAA) ▼▼▼ Quality Inn of Rome SH
(315) 336-4300. **$80-$100.** 200 S James St. On SR 49; downtown. Ext/int corridors. **Pets:** Other species. $25 daily fee/pet. Designated rooms, service with restrictions, supervision.
SAVE S☉ ✕ 🛏 💻 🍴 ⇌

RONKONKOMA

▼▼▼ Courtyard by Marriott Long Island MacArthur Airport SH
(631) 612-5000. **$149-$159.** 5000 Express Dr S. I-495, exit 60 (Express Dr S), 0.5 mi e. Int corridors. **Pets:** Accepted.
ASK S☉ ✕ 🖾 🛏 💻 🍴 ⇌

ROSCOE

(AAA) ▼ Roscoe Motel M
(607) 498-5220. **$55-$70, 7 day notice.** 2054 Old Rt 17. SR 17, exit 94, 0.5 mi n on SR 206, then just w. Ext corridors. **Pets:** Accepted.
SAVE 🛏 💻

ROTTERDAM

▼▼ Super 8 Schenectady SH
(518) 355-2190. **$55-$85.** 3083 Carman Rd. I-890, exit 9 (Curry Rd), 0.4 mi w; I-90, exit 25. Int corridors. **Pets:** Medium, dogs only. $10 daily fee/pet. Service with restrictions, supervision.
ASK S☉ ✕

SACKETS HARBOR

▼▼ Ontario Place Hotel SH
(315) 646-8000. **$69-$175.** 103 General Smith Dr. Center. Int corridors. **Pets:** Accepted.
✕ 🛏 💻

SALAMANCA

▼▼▼ Holiday Inn Express Hotel & Suites SH ☘
(716) 945-7600. **$100-$160, 14 day notice.** 779 Broad St. I-86, exit 20, just n. Int corridors. **Pets:** Other species. $50 deposit/pet, $25 one-time fee/pet. Service with restrictions, supervision.
ASK S☉ ✕ 🖳 🖨 🖾 🛏 💻 ⇌ ⊠

SARANAC LAKE

(AAA) ▼ Adirondack Motel M
(518) 891-2116. **$60-$160, 3 day notice.** 248 Lake Flower Ave. 0.7 mi e on SR 86. Ext corridors. **Pets:** Dogs only. $10 daily fee/room. Service with restrictions, supervision.
SAVE ✕ 🛏 💻 ⊠

(AAA) ▼▼▼ Best Western Mountain Lake Inn SH
(518) 891-1970. **$74-$160.** 487 Lake Flower Ave. 0.8 mi e on SR 86. Int corridors. **Pets:** Other species. $20 one-time fee/pet. Designated rooms, supervision.
SAVE S☉ ✕ 🖳 💻 🍴 ⇌

(AAA) ▼▼▼ The Hotel Saranac of Paul Smith's College SH
(518) 891-2200. **$60-$145, 3 day notice.** 100 Main St. Center. Int corridors. **Pets:** Other species. $15 daily fee/pet. Designated rooms, service with restrictions, supervision.
SAVE S☉ ✕ 🖨 🛏 💻 🍴

▼ Lake Flower Inn M
(518) 891-2310. **$48-$128, 14 day notice.** 234 Lake Flower Ave. 0.6 mi e on SR 86. Ext corridors. **Pets:** Dogs only. Designated rooms, supervision.
✕ 🛏 ⇌ ⊠

SARATOGA SPRINGS

▼▼ Adirondack Inn M
(518) 584-3510. **Call for rates.** 230 West Ave. 0.7 mi e of jct SR 29; 0.5 mi e of SR 50. Ext/int corridors. **Pets:** Accepted.
✕ 🖳 🛏 ⇌

(AAA) ▼▼▼ Holiday Inn SH
(518) 584-4550. **$139-$549.** 232 Broadway. On US 9, jct SR 50. Int corridors. **Pets:** Other species. Service with restrictions, supervision.
SAVE S☉ ✕ 🖨 🛏 💻 🍴 ⇌

AAA ▼▼▼ Union Gables Bed & Breakfast BB ✿
(518) 584-1558. **$140-$410, 14 day notice.** 55 Union Ave. I-87, exit 14, 1.5 mi w. Int corridors. **Pets:** $35 one-time fee/room. Designated rooms, service with restrictions.
SAVE Sᴅ ✕ 🖥

SAUGERTIES

AAA ▼▼ Comfort Inn SH ✿
(845) 246-1565. **$89-$159, 14 day notice.** 2790 SR 32. I-87, exit 20, just n. Int corridors. **Pets:** Other species. $25 one-time fee/room. Designated rooms, service with restrictions, supervision.
SAVE Sᴅ ✕ 🖥 🖥

SCHENECTADY

▼▼ Days Inn SH
(518) 370-3297. **$79-$139.** 167 Nott Terrace. Jct State St (SR 5) and Nott Terrace, 2 blks e; downtown. Int corridors. **Pets:** Very small. $15 daily fee/pet. No service, supervision.
ASK Sᴅ ✕ 🔊 🖥 🖥

▼▼▼ Holiday Inn-Downtown Schenectady SH
(518) 393-4141. **$129-$189.** 100 Nott Terrace. Jct State St (SR 5) and Nott Terrace, 2 blks e; center. Int corridors. **Pets:** Small. $100 one-time fee/room. Designated rooms, service with restrictions, supervision.
ASK Sᴅ ✕ 🖥 🖥 🍴 🏊 ✕

SCHROON LAKE

AAA ▼ Blue Ridge Motel M ✿
(518) 532-7521. **$85-$95, 14 day notice.** 2455 US Rt 9. I-87, exit 28, 4 mi n. Ext/int corridors. **Pets:** Medium. $10 daily fee/pet. Service with restrictions, supervision.
SAVE Sᴅ ✕ 🖥 🖥 🏊 ✕ ✈

SCHUYLERVILLE

AAA ▼▼ Burgoyne Motor Inn M
(518) 695-3282. **$49-$145, 3 day notice.** 220 Broad St. US 4 and SR 32, just n of jct SR 29. Ext/int corridors. **Pets:** Very small, dogs only. Designated rooms, service with restrictions, supervision.
SAVE ᴸᴹ 🖥 🖥

SKANEATELES

AAA ▼▼▼ Skaneateles Suites M
(315) 685-7568. **$125-$195, 11 day notice.** 4114 W Genesee St. On US 20, 2 mi w. Ext corridors. **Pets:** $35 one-time fee/pet. Designated rooms.
SAVE Sᴅ ✕ 🖥 🖥

SOLVAY

AAA ▼▼▼▼ Best Western Fairgrounds SH
(315) 484-0044. **$85-$179, 7 day notice.** 670 State Fair Blvd. I-690, exit 7, 1.3 mi nw, just past fairgrounds. Int corridors. **Pets:** Small. $200 deposit/room, $50 one-time fee/room. Service with restrictions, supervision.
SAVE Sᴅ ✕ ᴸᴹ ✂ 🖥 🖥 🍴

▼▼▼ Comfort Inn Fairgrounds SH
(315) 453-0045. **$79-$159.** 7010 Interstate Island Rd. I-90, exit 39 to I-690 E, exit 2 (Jones Rd), just sw. Int corridors. **Pets:** $15 one-time fee/room. Service with restrictions, supervision.
ASK Sᴅ ✕ 🖥 🖥

▼▼▼ Holiday Inn/Farrell Road SH
(315) 457-8700. **$79-$189.** 100 Farrell Rd. I-90, exit 39 to I-690 E, exit John Glenn Blvd. Int corridors. **Pets:** Accepted.
ASK Sᴅ ✕ 🔊 ✂ 🖥 🖥 🍴 🏊

SOUTHAMPTON

AAA ▼▼▼ Southampton Inn SH ✿
(631) 283-6500. **$119-$489, 30 day notice.** 91 Hill St. 0.3 mi n from corner of Main St and Jobs Ln. Ext corridors. **Pets:** Medium, other species. $39 daily fee/pet. Designated rooms, service with restrictions, supervision.
SAVE Sᴅ ✕ ✂ 🖥 🍴 🏊 ✕

SYLVAN BEACH

▼ Cinderella's Comfort Sleep Suites M
(315) 762-4280. **$59-$179, 16 day notice.** 1208 N Main St. On SR 13; center. Ext corridors. **Pets:** Accepted.
ASK Sᴅ ✕ 🖥 🖥 🍴

SYRACUSE

AAA ▼▼ Econo Lodge University/Downtown M
(315) 425-0015. **$60-$100, 15 day notice.** 454 James St. Downtown. Ext corridors. **Pets:** Accepted.
SAVE Sᴅ ✕ 🖥

▼▼▼ Radisson Syracuse Hotel & Conference Center LH
(315) 479-7000. **$99-$139.** 701 E Genesee St. Jct Almond St; downtown. Int corridors. **Pets:** Medium, dogs only. $25 daily fee/room. Designated rooms, service with restrictions.
ASK Sᴅ ✕ ᴸᴹ 🔊 ✂ 🖥 🖥 🍴

AAA ▼▼▼ Sheraton Syracuse University Hotel & Conference Center LH ✿
(315) 475-3000. **$139-$599.** 801 University Ave. I-81, exit 18. Int corridors. **Pets:** Large, dogs only. Service with restrictions, supervision.
SAVE ✕ 🖥 🖥 🍴 🏊 ✕

TICONDEROGA

AAA ▼ Circle Court Motel M
(518) 585-7660. **$58-$77.** 6 Montcalm St. SR 9N; at Liberty Monument traffic circle. Ext corridors. **Pets:** Service with restrictions, supervision.
SAVE Sᴅ ✕ 🖥 🖥

TROY

AAA ▼▼ Best Western-Rensselaer Inn SH
(518) 274-3210. **$89-$104.** 1800 6th Ave. I-787, exit 9, 0.5 mi e, exit downtown, then 0.5 mi s. Int corridors. **Pets:** Designated rooms, service with restrictions, supervision.
SAVE Sᴅ ✕ 🖥 🖥 🍴 🏊

TUPPER LAKE

AAA ▼▼ Red Top Inn M
(518) 359-9209. **$55-$80, 3 day notice.** 1562 SR 30. 3 mi s. Ext/int corridors. **Pets:** Other species. Designated rooms, service with restrictions, supervision.
SAVE ✕ 🖥 🖥 ✕

UTICA

AAA ▼ A-1 Motel M
(315) 735-6698. **$50-$65, 3 day notice.** 238 N Genesee St. I-90 (New York State Thruway), exit 31, just s. Int corridors. **Pets:** Small, dogs only. $10 one-time fee/pet. Service with restrictions, supervision.
SAVE Sᴅ ✕ 🖥

▼▼ Best Western Gateway Adirondack Inn SH
(315) 732-4121. **$89-$190.** 175 N Genesee St. I-90 (New York State Thruway), exit 31, 0.5 mi s. Int corridors. **Pets:** $25 deposit/room. Service with restrictions, supervision.
ASK Sᴅ ✕ 🔊 🖥 🖥

▼▼ Red Roof Inn #7180 M
(315) 724-7128. **$51-$94.** 20 Weaver St. I-90 (New York State Thruway), exit 31. Ext corridors. **Pets:** Accepted.
✕ 🖥

VALATIE

AAA ▼▼ Blue Spruce Inn & Suites **M**
(518) 758-9711. **$75-$95.** 3093 Rt 9. I-90 (New York State Thruway), exit 12, 4 mi s on US 9 via New York Thruway Extension, exit B1. Ext corridors. **Pets:** Service with restrictions, supervision.

SAVE Sᴅ ⊠ 🛏 🖵 🍴 ⇨

VESTAL

▼▼▼ Holiday Inn at the University **SH**
(607) 729-6371. **$79-$189.** 4105 Vestal Pkwy E. SR 17, exit 70, 2.5 mi s on US 201 to SR 434 W, then right on Bunn Hill Rd. Int corridors. **Pets:** Medium, other species. $25 one-time fee/room. Designated rooms, service with restrictions, crate.

ASK Sᴅ ⊠ � &M 🛏 🖵 🍴 ≈

VICTOR

AAA ▼▼▼ Hampton Inn and Suites-Rochester/Victor **SH**
(585) 924-4400. **$119-$149.** 7637 NY SR 96. I-90 (New York State Thruway), exit 45, just n. Int corridors. **Pets:** Small. Designated rooms, service with restrictions, supervision.

SAVE Sᴅ ⊠ ⌨ 🛏 🖵 ⇨

WARRENSBURG

▼▼ Super 8 Warrensburg **M**
(518) 623-2811. **$65-$150, 7 day notice.** 3619 SR 9. I-87, exit 23, just w. Int corridors. **Pets:** Other species. $20 one-time fee/room. Designated rooms, service with restrictions.

⊠

WATERLOO

AAA ▼▼▼▼ Holiday Inn Waterloo-Seneca Falls **SH**
(315) 539-5011. **$80-$153.** 2468 SR 414. I-90 (New York State Thruway), exit 41, 4 mi s; just n of jct SR 414/5 and US 20. Int corridors. **Pets:** Accepted.

SAVE ⊠ 🛏 🖵 🍴 ≈ ⊠

AAA ▼▼▼ Microtel Inn & Suites **SH**
(315) 539-8438. **$51-$90.** 1966 Rt 5 & 20. I-90 (New York State Thruway), exit 41, 4 mi s on SR 414, then just e. Int corridors. **Pets:** $5 daily fee/room. Supervision.

SAVE Sᴅ ⊠ &M ⌨ 🛏 🖵

WATERTOWN

AAA ▼▼ Ramada Inn **SH** 🐾
(315) 788-0700. **$80-$135.** 6300 Arsenal St. I-81, exit 45, just w. Int corridors. **Pets:** Other species. $100 deposit/room. Designated rooms, service with restrictions, supervision.

SAVE Sᴅ ⊠ 🛏 🖵 🍴 ≈ ⊠

WATKINS GLEN

AAA ▼▼ Anchor Inn and Marina **M** 🐾
(607) 535-4159. **$69-$150, 10 day notice.** 3425 Salt Point Rd. 1.2 mi n on SR 14. Ext corridors. **Pets:** Medium. $25 deposit/pet. Service with restrictions, supervision.

SAVE Sᴅ ⊠ ⌨ 🛏 ⊠

AAA ▼ Budget Inn **M**
(607) 535-4800. **$48-$135, 10 day notice.** 435 S Franklin St. On SR 14. Ext corridors. **Pets:** Very small, dogs only. $10 daily fee/pet. Designated rooms, service with restrictions, crate.

SAVE ⊠ 🛏

AAA ▼▼ Chieftain Motel **M** 🐾
(607) 535-4759. **$59-$135, 10 day notice.** 3815 State Rt 14. Jct SR 14A, 3 mi n. Ext corridors. **Pets:** Medium, other species. $25 deposit/pet. Service with restrictions, supervision.

SAVE Sᴅ ⊠ ⌨ 🛏 ⇨

WELLSVILLE

AAA ▼ Long Vue Inn & Suites **M** 🐾
(585) 593-2450. **$49-$89.** 5081 Rt 417 W. Jct SR 19, 3 mi w. Ext corridors. **Pets:** Other species. $7 daily fee/room. Designated rooms, supervision.

SAVE Sᴅ ⊠ 🛏 🖵

WEST COXSACKIE

AAA ▼▼ Best Western New Baltimore Inn **SH**
(518) 731-8100. **$89-$139.** 12600 Rt 9W. I-87 (New York State Thruway), exit 21B, 0.5 mi s. Int corridors. **Pets:** Accepted.

SAVE Sᴅ ⊠ ⌨ 🛏 🖵 ⇨ ⊠

WESTMORELAND

AAA ▼ Carriage Motor Inn **M**
(315) 853-3561. **$42-$65, 5 day notice.** 5370 SR 233. I-90 (New York State Thruway), exit 32, just n. Ext corridors. **Pets:** Medium. $20 deposit/room, $5 daily fee/pet. Service with restrictions, supervision.

SAVE Sᴅ ⊠ 🛏

WILMINGTON

AAA ▼ Grand View Motel **M**
(518) 946-2209. **$59-$99.** 5941 NYS Rt 86. On SR 86, 1 mi e. Ext corridors. **Pets:** Accepted.

SAVE Sᴅ ⊠ ⇨ ⊠

AAA ▼▼ Hungry Trout Resort **M** 🐾
(518) 946-2217. **$79-$129, 7 day notice.** 5239 Rt 86. On SR 86, 2 mi w. Ext corridors. **Pets:** Medium, dogs only. $5 daily fee/pet. Service with restrictions, crate.

SAVE ⊠ 🛏 🖵 🍴 ⇨ ⊠

AAA ▼▼▼ Ledge Rock at Whiteface Mountain **M**
(518) 946-2379. **$69-$109, 10 day notice.** 5078 NYS Rt SR 86. On SR 86, 3 mi w. Ext corridors. **Pets:** Medium. $10 one-time fee/pet. Service with restrictions, crate.

SAVE Sᴅ ⊠ 🛏 🖵 ⇨ ⊠

▼▼ Mountain Brook Lodge **M**
(518) 946-2262. **$60-$99, 14 day notice.** 5712 Rt 86. Center. Ext corridors. **Pets:** Medium, dogs only. $3 daily fee/room. Designated rooms, no service, supervision.

⊠ 🛏 🖵 ⇨

AAA ▼▼ North Pole Motor Inn **M**
(518) 946-7733. **$49-$99, 7 day notice.** 5636 NYS Rt 86. On SR 86, just w of jct CR 431. Ext corridors. **Pets:** Dogs only. $5 daily fee/pet. Service with restrictions, supervision.

SAVE Sᴅ ⊠ 🛏 🖵 ⇨ ⊠

CITY INDEX

ABERDEEN

Best Western Pinehurst Motor Inn M
(910) 944-2367. **$55-$80.** 1500 Sandhills Blvd. Jct of US 15 and 501, 0.3 mi s on US 1. Ext corridors. **Pets:** Small, dogs only. $10 daily fee/room. Service with restrictions.

Innkeeper Southern Pines M
(910) 944-2324. **$58-$71, 3 day notice.** 1405 N Sandhills Blvd. Jct US 15 and 501, just s on US 1. Ext/int corridors. **Pets:** Accepted.

Motel 6-1234 M
(910) 944-5633. **$43-$53.** 1408 Sandhills Blvd. Jct US 15 and 501, 0.3 mi s on US 1. Ext corridors. **Pets:** Accepted.

ALBEMARLE

Comfort Inn SH
(704) 983-6990. **$59-$65.** 735 SR 24/27 Bypass. 1.5 mi e of US 52 S. Ext corridors. **Pets:** Accepted.

Sleep Inn & Suites SH
(704) 983-2770. **Call for rates.** 621 Hwy 24/27 Bypass. 1.5 mi e of US 52 S. Int corridors. **Pets:** Accepted.

ANDREWS

Hawkesdene House Mountain Retreat BB
(828) 321-6027. **$85-$125, 3 day notice.** 381 Phillips Creek Rd. US 19 business route, 3.2 mi s on Cherry St, then 0.5 mi s. Ext/int corridors. **Pets:** Accepted.

ARCHDALE

Best Western-High Point SH
(336) 861-3000. **$55-$199.** 1202 Liberty Rd. I-85, exit 113, just s on SR 62. Int corridors. **Pets:** Small, dogs only. $10 daily fee/pet. Designated rooms, no service, supervision.

Comfort Inn Archdale SH
(336) 434-4797. **$72-$199.** 10123 N Main St. I-85, exit 111, just n on US 311, then just sw on Balfour Dr. Int corridors. **Pets:** Small. $25 daily fee/pet. Designated rooms, service with restrictions, supervision.

ARDEN

Quality Inn & Suites Asheville South SH
(828) 684-6688. **$79-$189.** 1 Skyland Inn Dr. I-26, exit 6. Int corridors. **Pets:** Accepted.

ASHEBORO

Comfort Inn SH
(336) 626-3680. **$69-$130, 10 day notice.** 242 Lake Crest Rd. US 64, just w on SR 42. Ext corridors. **Pets:** Accepted.

Ramada Limited M 🐾
(336) 626-4414. **$50-$95.** 825 W Dixie Dr. From US 220, exit US 64 E/SR 49 N Raleigh, just e. Int corridors. **Pets:** Medium. $20 one-time fee/room. Service with restrictions, supervision.

ASHEVILLE

Best Western of Asheville Biltmore East M
(828) 298-5562. **$49-$109.** 501 Tunnel Rd. I-240, exit 7, 0.5 mi e on SR 70. Ext corridors. **Pets:** Small. $10 daily fee/pet. Service with restrictions, supervision.

Black Walnut B&B Inn BB 🐾
(828) 254-3878. **$195-$250, 15 day notice.** 288 Montford Ave. I-240, exit 4C (Montford Ave/Haywood St), 0.5 mi n; in historic district. Ext/int corridors. **Pets:** Other species. $50 deposit/room. Designated rooms, service with restrictions.

Comfort Suites-Biltmore Square Mall SH 🐾
(828) 665-4000. **$80-$140.** 890 Brevard Rd. I-26, exit 33, 0.3 mi w. Int corridors. **Pets:** Other species. $20 daily fee/room. Designated rooms, service with restrictions, crate.

Days Inn-Asheville Mall M
(828) 252-4000. **$30-$179.** 201 Tunnel Rd. I-240, exit 6, 0.5 mi e, on south side of road. Ext corridors. **Pets:** Other species. $5 daily fee/pet. No service.

Days Inn-Biltmore East SH
(828) 298-4000. **$35-$149.** 1435 Tunnel Rd. I-40, exit 55, just n. Int corridors. **Pets:** Medium, dogs only. $15 daily fee/pet. Service with restrictions, crate.

(AAA) ▼▼▼ Great Smokies Holiday Inn SunSpree Golf & Tennis Resort 🆂🅷

(828) 254-3211. **$71-$134, 7 day notice.** 1 Holiday Inn Dr. I-240, exit 3B (Holiday Inn Dr), just w. Int corridors. **Pets:** Other species. $20 daily fee/room. Designated rooms, service with restrictions, supervision.

🆂🅰🆅🅴 🆂🄳 ⊠ 🕖 🈁 🖥 🍽 ⊅ ⊠

▼▼▼ Holiday Inn-Biltmore East at the Blue Ridge Parkway 🆂🅷 🐾

(828) 298-5611. **$59-$149.** 1450 Tunnel Rd. I-40, exit 55, just n. Int corridors. **Pets:** Other species. $10 daily fee/room. Service with restrictions.

🄰🆂🄺 🆂🄳 ⊠ 🈁 🖥 🍽 ⊅

(AAA) ▼ The Log Cabin Motor Court 🄲🄰

(828) 645-6546. **$50-$250, 14 day notice.** 330 Weaverville Hwy. 4 mi n on US 19 and 23, exit New Bridge northbound, then 1 mi n on Weaverville Hwy; exit New Stock Rd southbound, 1 mi s. Ext corridors. **Pets:** Other species. $15 daily fee/pet. Service with restrictions.

🆂🅰🆅🅴 🈁 🖥 ⓩ

▼ Motel 6-1134 🄼

(828) 299-3040. **$39-$51.** 1415 Tunnel Rd. I-40, exit 55. Ext corridors. **Pets:** Accepted.

🆂🄳 ⊠ ♿ ⊅

(AAA) ▼▼▼ The Pines Cottages 🄲🄰

(828) 645-9661. **$55-$185, 14 day notice.** 346 Weaverville Hwy. 4 mi n on US 19 and 23, exit New Bridge northbound, 1.1 mi n on Weaverville Hwy; exit New Stock Rd southbound, 1 mi s. Ext corridors. **Pets:** Other species. $50 deposit/room. Service with restrictions, crate.

🆂🅰🆅🅴 🈁 🖥 ⓩ

(AAA) ▼▼▼ Quality Inn & Suites 🆂🅷

(828) 298-5519. **$50-$150.** 1430 Tunnel Rd. I-40, exit 55, just n. Ext corridors. **Pets:** Medium, other species. $20 deposit/pet. Designated rooms, service with restrictions, supervision.

🆂🅰🆅🅴 🆂🄳 ⊠ ♿ 🈁 🖥 ⊅

▼▼ Red Roof Inn-West 🄼

(828) 667-9803. **$40-$80.** 16 Crowell Rd. I-40, exit 44, just n on US 19 and 23, just w on Old Haywood Rd, then just s. Ext corridors. **Pets:** Medium, other species. Service with restrictions.

⊠ ♿ 🈁

▼▼ Sleep Inn Biltmore 🆂🅷

(828) 277-1800. **$79-$189.** 117 Hendersonville Rd. I-40, exit 50, 0.3 mi n on US 25. Int corridors. **Pets:** Accepted.

⊠ ♿ᴹ ♿ 🖥

▼▼ Sleep Inn Biltmore West 🆂🅷

(828) 670-7600. **$76-$143.** 1918 Old Haywood Rd. I-40, exit 44, just n on US 19 and 23, then just w. Int corridors. **Pets:** Other species. $8 daily fee/room. Service with restrictions, crate.

🄰🆂🄺 🆂🄳 ⊠ ♿ 🈁 🖥

(AAA) ▼▼▼ Super 8 Biltmore East 🆂🅷

(828) 298-7952. **$49-$199.** 1329 Tunnel Rd. I-40, exit 55, 0.3 mi w. Ext corridors. **Pets:** Other species. $15 one-time fee/pet. Service with restrictions, supervision.

🆂🅰🆅🅴 🆂🄳 ⊠ 🈁 🖥 ⊅ ⊠

▼▼ Super 8 Motel at Biltmore Square 🆂🅷

(828) 670-8800. **$39-$129.** 9 Wedgefield Dr. I-26, exit 33, just nw. Int corridors. **Pets:** Medium, other species. $15 one-time fee/room. Service with restrictions, supervision.

🄰🆂🄺 🆂🄳 ⊠ ♿ᴹ ♿ 🈁 🖥

▼ Super 8 Motel Central 🄼 🐾

(828) 667-8706. **$39-$129.** 8 Crowell Rd. I-40, exit 44, just n on US 19 and 23. Int corridors. **Pets:** Medium, other species. $15 one-time fee/pet. Service with restrictions, supervision.

🄰🆂🄺 🆂🄳 ⊠ ♿ᴹ 🖥

BANNER ELK

▼▼▼ Banner Elk Inn B&B and Cottages 🅱🅱

(828) 898-6223. **$100-$175, 30 day notice.** 407 Main St E. Jct SR 184 and 194, 0.3 mi n on SR 194. Int corridors. **Pets:** Large. Designated rooms, service with restrictions, supervision.

⊠ 🈁 🖥

▼▼▼ Best Western Mountain Lodge at Banner Elk 🆂🅷 🐾

(828) 898-4571. **$80-$170, 3 day notice.** 1615 Tynecastle Hwy. 1 mi se on SR 184. Ext corridors. **Pets:** Other species. $25 deposit/room. Designated rooms, service with restrictions, crate.

🄰🆂🄺 🆂🄳 ⊠ ♿ᴹ 🕖 🈁 🖥 🍽 ⊅

BURLINGTON

▼▼▼ Holiday Inn 🆂🅷

(336) 229-5203. **$89-$250.** 2444 Maple Ave. I-40/85, exit 145, just n. Int corridors. **Pets:** Accepted.

🄰🆂🄺 🆂🄳 ⊠ ♿ᴹ 🕖 🈁 🖥 🍽 ⊅

▼ Motel 6-1257 🆂🅷

(336) 226-1325. **$41-$51.** 2155 Hanford Rd. I-40/85, exit 145, just s on SR 49, then just w. Ext corridors. **Pets:** Accepted.

🆂🄳 ⊠ 🕖 ♿ ⊅

(AAA) ▼▼▼ Red Roof Inn 🆂🅷

(336) 227-1270. **$45-$105, 3 day notice.** 2133 W Hanford Rd. I-40/85, exit 145, just s on SR 49, then just w. Int corridors. **Pets:** Medium. Service with restrictions, supervision.

🆂🅰🆅🅴 🆂🄳 ⊠ 🈁 ⊅

CARY

(AAA) ▼▼▼▼ Best Western Cary Inn & Suites 🆂🅷

(919) 481-1200. **$59-$79.** 1722 Walnut St. I-40, exit 293, 0.3 mi sw on US 1 and 64 W, exit Walnut St, then just w. Ext/int corridors. **Pets:** Other species. $75 one-time fee/room. Supervision.

🆂🅰🆅🅴 🆂🄳 ⊠ 🕖 🈁 🖥 ⊅ ⊠

▼▼▼ Candlewood Suites 🆂🅷

(919) 468-4222. **$119-$139.** 1020 Buck Jones Rd. I-40, exit 293, just sw on US 1 and 64, exit Walnut St, just w, then 0.5 mi n; in Buck Jones Village. Int corridors. **Pets:** Large, other species. $12 daily fee/room. Service with restrictions, supervision.

🄰🆂🄺 🆂🄳 ⊠ 🕖 ♿ 🈁 🖥

▼▼▼ Comfort Suites Hotel 🆂🅷

(919) 852-4318. **$69-$79.** 350 Ashville Ave. US 1 and 64, exit 98A, 0.8 mi e on Tryon Rd, then just n. Int corridors. **Pets:** Large, other species. $50 one-time fee/pet. Designated rooms, service with restrictions, crate.

🄰🆂🄺 🆂🄳 ⊠ ♿ᴹ ♿ 🈁 🖥 ⊅ ⊠

▼▼▼ La Quinta Inn & Suites Raleigh (Cary) 🆂🅷

(919) 851-2850. **$70-$99.** 191 Crescent Commons Dr. US 1 and 64, exit 98A, 0.5 mi e on Tryon Rd, then just n. Int corridors. **Pets:** Accepted.

🄰🆂🄺 ⊠ ♿ᴹ 🕖 ♿ 🈁 🖥 ⊅

▼▼ Red Roof Inn 🆂🅷

(919) 469-3400. **$45-$57.** 1800 Walnut St. I-40, exit 293, 0.3 mi sw on US 1 and 64 W; exit Walnut St, just e. Int corridors. **Pets:** Large, other species. Service with restrictions, supervision.

⊠ ♿ᴹ 🕖 ♿ 🈁

▼▼▼ Residence Inn 🆂🅷 🐾

(919) 467-4080. **$99-$159.** 2900 Regency Pkwy. US 1 and 64, exit 98A, 0.5 mi e on Tryon Rd, then just s. Int corridors. **Pets:** Large, other species. $75 one-time fee/room. Designated rooms, service with restrictions.

🄰🆂🄺 ⊠ ♿ᴹ ♿ 🈁 🖥 ⊅ ⊠

CASHIERS

◆◆◆◆ High Hampton Inn & Country Club SH
(828) 743-2411. **$157-$244, 10 day notice.** 1525 Hwy 107 S. Jct US 64, 1.5 mi s. Ext/int corridors. **Pets:** Accepted.
⊬ ⊠ ⊮ 〽 ⊠

CHAPEL HILL

◆◆◆ ◆◆◆◆ Carolina Inn SH
(919) 933-2001. **$129-$239.** 211 Pittsboro St. Jct Columbia and Franklin sts, 0.3 mi s on SR 86. Int corridors. **Pets:** Accepted.
SAVE ⊠ ⌂M ⊘ ⊠ 目 ⊒ ⊬

◆◆◆ ◆◆◆◆ ◆◆◆◆ The Siena Hotel SH ❀
(919) 929-4000. **$119-$245.** 1505 E Franklin St. I-40, exit 270, 2 mi s on US 15/501, then 0.5 mi w. Int corridors. **Pets:** Medium, dogs only. $75 one-time fee/pet. Designated rooms, service with restrictions, supervision.
SAVE ⊠ ⌂M ⊘ ⊠ 目 ⊬

CHARLOTTE METROPOLITAN AREA

CHARLOTTE

◆◆◆ ◆◆◆◆ AmeriSuites (Charlotte/Airport) SH
(704) 423-9931. **$94-$159.** 2950 Oak Lake Blvd. I-85, exit 33 (Billy Graham Pkwy), 2 mi s, exit Tyvola/Coliseum, 0.3 mi sw. Int corridors. **Pets:** Accepted.
SAVE Ⓢ ⊠ 目 ⊒ ⊱

◆◆◆ ◆◆◆◆ AmeriSuites (Charlotte/Arrowood) SH ❀
(704) 522-8400. **$94-$159.** 7900 Forest Point Blvd. I-77, exit 3 southbound; exit 2 northbound, just e. Int corridors. **Pets:** Small. $10 one-time fee/pet. Service with restrictions, supervision.
SAVE Ⓢ ⊠ ⌂M ⊘ ⊠ 目 ⊒ ⊱

◆◆◆ ◆◆◆◆ AmeriSuites (Charlotte/Coliseum) SH
(704) 357-8555. **$89-$159.** 4119 S Stream Blvd. I-77, exit 6B, 2 mi e on Billy Graham Pkwy, then 1.3 mi sw on Tyvola Rd. Int corridors. **Pets:** Accepted.
SAVE Ⓢ ⊠ 目 ⊒ ⊱

◆◆◆ ◆◆◆◆ ◆◆◆◆ Ballantyne Resort LH
(704) 248-4000. **$159-$229.** 10000 Ballantyne Commons Pkwy. I-485, exit 61, just s. Int corridors. **Pets:** Accepted.
SAVE Ⓢ ⊠ ⌂M ⊠ 目 ⊒ ⊬ ⊱ ⊠

◆◆◆ ◆◆◆◆ Best Value Inn & Suites M
(704) 398-3144. **$43-$89, 3 day notice.** 3200 S I-85 Service Rd. I-85, exit 33 (Billy Graham Pkwy), just n. Ext corridors. **Pets:** Accepted.
SAVE Ⓢ ⊠ 目 ⊱

◆◆◆ ◆◆◆◆ Clarion Hotel SH ❀
(704) 523-1400. **$69-$130.** 321 W Woodlawn Rd. I-77, exit 6B, just w. Int corridors. **Pets:** Other species. $25 one-time fee/pet. Designated rooms, service with restrictions.
SAVE Ⓢ ⊠ ⌂M ⊘ ⊠ 目 ⊒ ⊬ ⊱ ⊠

◆◆◆◆ Comfort Inn Carowinds SH
(704) 339-0574. **$49-$159.** 3725 Avenue of the Carolinas. I-77, exit 90, just w. Int corridors. **Pets:** Other species. $25 one-time fee/room. Service with restrictions.
ASK Ⓢ ⊠ ⊘ 目 ⊒ ⊱

◆◆◆ ◆◆◆◆ Comfort Inn-Executive Park SH
(704) 525-2626. **$69-$129.** 5822 Westpark Dr. I-77, exit 5 (Tyvola Rd), just e, then 0.4 mi s. Int corridors. **Pets:** Medium, other species. $25 one-time fee/room. Service with restrictions, supervision.
SAVE Ⓢ ⊠ ⊘ ⊠ 目 ⊒ ⊱

◆◆◆◆ Comfort Suites-University SH
(704) 547-0049. **$79-$129.** 7735 University City Blvd. I-85, exit 45A, 1 mi e on WT Harris Blvd, then 0.5 mi s on SR 49. Int corridors. **Pets:** $25 one-time fee/pet. Service with restrictions, supervision.
ASK Ⓢ ⊠ ⌂M ⊘ ⊠ 目 ⊒ ⊱

◆◆◆◆ Drury Inn & Suites-Charlotte North SH
(704) 593-0700. **$58-$102.** 415 West WT Harris Blvd. I-85, exit 45A, just e. Int corridors. **Pets:** Large, other species. Service with restrictions, supervision.
ASK ⊠ ⌂M ⊘ ⊠ 目 ⊒ ⊱

◆◆◆◆ Holiday Inn Airport SH
(704) 394-4301. **$92.** 2707 Little Rock Rd. I-85, exit 32, just e. Int corridors. **Pets:** Small, other species. $25 one-time fee/pet. Designated rooms, service with restrictions, supervision.
ASK Ⓢ ⊠ ⊘ ⊠ 目 ⊒ ⊬ ⊱

◆◆◆◆ Holiday Inn at University Executive Park SH
(704) 547-0999. **$99-$139.** 8520 University Executive Park Dr. I-85, exit 45A, 0.3 mi e, then s. Int corridors. **Pets:** $25 one-time fee/room. Designated rooms, service with restrictions, crate.
ASK Ⓢ ⊠ ⌂M ⊘ ⊠ 目 ⊒ ⊬ ⊱

◆◆◆ Homestead Studio Suites
Hotel-Charlotte/Coliseum SH
(704) 676-0083. **$54-$64.** 710 Yorkmont Rd. I-77, exit 6B, 0.3 mi w. Ext corridors. **Pets:** Accepted.
ASK Ⓢ ⊠ ⊘ 目 目

◆◆◆◆ La Quinta Inn & Suites Charlotte (Coliseum) SH
(704) 523-5599. **$74-$95.** 4900 S Tryon St. I-77, exit 6B, just w. Int corridors. **Pets:** Accepted.
ASK ⊠ ⌂M ⊘ ⊠ 目 ⊒ ⊱

◆◆◆◆ La Quinta Inn Charlotte (Airport) SH
(704) 393-5306. **$61-$76.** 3100 S I-85 Service Rd. I-85, exit 33 (Billy Graham Pkwy), just w, then just n. Ext/int corridors. **Pets:** Accepted.
ASK ⊠ ⊘ 目 ⊒ ⊱

◆◆ MainStay Suites SH
(704) 521-3232. **$79-$129.** 7926 Forest Pine Dr. I-77, exit 3, just e. Int corridors. **Pets:** Accepted.
ASK Ⓢ ⊠ ⌂M ⊘ ⊠ 目 ⊒ ⊱

◆◆◆ ◆◆◆◆ ◆◆◆◆ Omni Charlotte Hotel LH
(704) 377-0400. **$139-$199, 7 day notice.** 132 E Trade St. I-77, exit 10B (Trade St E); I-277, exit College St; jct Trade and Tryon sts. Int corridors. **Pets:** Accepted.
SAVE Ⓢ ⊠ ⊘ 目 ⊒ ⊬ ⊱ ⊠

◆◆◆ ◆◆◆◆ Quality Inn & Suites-Crown Point SH
(704) 845-2810. **$69-$79.** 2501 Sardis Rd N. I-485, exit 51A (US 74 W), 3.3 mi w. Int corridors. **Pets:** Accepted.
SAVE Ⓢ ⊠ ⊘ 目 ⊒

◆◆ Red Roof Inn-Airport M ❀
(704) 392-2316. **$47-$69.** 3300 S I-85 Service Rd. I-85, exit 33 (Billy Graham Pkwy), just w, then just s. Ext corridors. **Pets:** Large, other species. Service with restrictions, crate.
⊠ ⌂M ⊘ 目

▼▼▼▼ **Residence Inn by Marriott** SH
(704) 547-1122. **$84-$104.** 8503 N Tryon St. I-85, exit 45A, 0.3 mi e, then just s. Ext corridors. **Pets:** $100 one-time fee/room. Service with restrictions, crate.
ASK SÓ ✕ ᳖M 🝔 🏊 🖵 🖨 🌊 ⌧

▼▼▼▼ **Residence Inn by Marriott-Charlotte Uptown** SH
(704) 340-4000. **$149-$199.** 404 S Mint St. I-77, exit 10 (Trade St), 0.5 mi e, then just s. Int corridors. **Pets:** Other species. $5 daily fee/room, $100 one-time fee/room. Service with restrictions, crate.
ASK SÓ ✕ ᳖M 🝔 🖵 🖨

▼▼▼▼ **Residence Inn by Marriott-Piper Glen** SH
(704) 319-3900. **$89-$134.** 5115 Piper Station Dr. I-485, exit 59 (Tyvola Rd), just s, then e. Int corridors. **Pets:** Large, other species. $75 one-time fee/room. Service with restrictions.
ASK SÓ ✕ ᳖M 🝔 🏊 🖵 🖨 🌊 ⌧

▼▼▼▼ **Residence Inn by Marriott-Tyvola Executive Park** CO
(704) 527-8110. **$79-$109.** 5816 Westpark Dr. I-77, exit 5 (Tyvola Rd), just e, then 0.4 mi s. Ext/int corridors. **Pets:** Accepted.
ASK SÓ ✕ ᳖M 🝔 🏊 🖵 🖨 🌊 ⌧

▼▼▼▼ **Sheraton Charlotte Airport Plaza Hotel** LH
(704) 392-1200. **$209-$229.** 3315 I-85 S Service Rd. I-85, exit 33 (Billy Graham Pkwy), just e. Int corridors. **Pets:** Accepted.
ASK SÓ ✕ 🝔 🏊 🖵 🖨 🍴 🌊

ΛΛΛ ▼▼▼ **Sleep Inn** SH
(704) 549-4544. **$59-$169.** 8525 N Tryon St. I-85, exit 45A, 0.3 mi e on WT Harris Blvd, just s on US 29. Int corridors. **Pets:** Medium, other species. $25 one-time fee/room. Service with restrictions, supervision.
SAVE SÓ ✕ ᳖M 🝔 🏊 🖵 🖨

▼▼▼▼ **Staybridge Suites Charlotte-Ballantyne** SH 🐾
(704) 248-5000. **$119-$159.** 15735 John J Delaney Dr. I-485, exit 61, just s. Int corridors. **Pets:** $100 one-time fee/room. Service with restrictions, crate.
ASK SÓ ✕ ᳖M 🝔 🏊 🖵 🖨 🌊 ⌧

▼▼▼ **Studio 6 Airport-#6006** SH 🐾
(704) 394-4993. **$48-$59.** 3420 S I-85 Service Rd. I-85, exit 33, just w, then just s. Int corridors. **Pets:** Medium, other species. $10 daily fee/pet. Service with restrictions, crate.
SÓ ✕ ᳖M 🏊 🖵 🖨

▼▼▼▼ **TownePlace Suites by Marriott** SH
(704) 548-0388. **$56-$94.** 8710 Research Dr. I-85, exit 45B, just w, then n. Int corridors. **Pets:** Accepted.
ASK ✕ ᳖M 🝔 🏊 🖵 🖨 🌊

▼▼▼▼ **TownePlace Suites by Marriott** SH 🐾
(704) 227-2000. **$49-$59, 14 day notice.** 7805 Forest Point Blvd. I-77, exit 3 southbound; exit 2 northbound, just e. Int corridors. **Pets:** Medium. $75 one-time fee/room. Service with restrictions, crate.
ASK SÓ ✕ ᳖M 🝔 🏊 🖵 🖨 🌊 ⌧

▼▼▼ ▼▼▼ **The Westin Charlotte** LH 🐾
(704) 375-2600. **$249.** 601 S College St. I-277, exit 9; corner of College and E Stonewall sts. Int corridors. **Pets:** Supervision.
ASK SÓ ✕ ᳖M 🝔 🏊 🖵 🖨 🍴 🌊 ⌧

CORNELIUS

ΛΛΛ ▼▼▼ **Best Western Lake Norman** SH
(704) 896-0660. **$77-$89, 14 day notice.** 19608 Liverpool Pkwy. I-77, exit 28, just w, then s. Int corridors. **Pets:** Small, other species. $20 one-time fee/pet. Designated rooms, service with restrictions, supervision.
SAVE SÓ ✕ 🖵 🖨 🌊

▼▼▼ ◆ **Holiday Inn Lake Norman** SH
(704) 892-9120. **$65.** 19901 Holiday Ln. I-77, exit 28, just e, then just n. Ext corridors. **Pets:** Other species. $25 one-time fee/room. Service with restrictions, supervision.
ASK SÓ ✕ ᳖M 🝔 🖵 🖨 🍴 🌊

HUNTERSVILLE

▼▼▼▼ **Candlewood Suites** SH
(704) 895-3434. **Call for rates.** 16530 Northcross Dr. I-77, exit 25 (Sam Kurr Rd), just w, then s. Int corridors. **Pets:** Medium, other species. $75 one-time fee/pet. Designated rooms, service with restrictions, crate.
✕ 🝔 🖵 🖨

▼▼▼▼ **Ramada Limited** SH
(704) 892-6597. **$49-$119.** 16825 Caldwell Creek Dr. I-77, exit 25 (Sam Kurr Rd), just e, then n. Ext/int corridors. **Pets:** Medium, other species. $25 one-time fee/room. Service with restrictions.
ASK SÓ ✕ 🝔 🖵 🖨

▼▼▼▼ **Residence Inn by Marriott-Lake Norman** SH 🐾
(704) 584-0000. **Call for rates.** 16830 Kenton Dr. I-77, exit 25 (Sam Kurr Rd), 1 mi w, then just n. Int corridors. **Pets:** Medium. $75 one-time fee/room. Service with restrictions, supervision.
✕ ᳖M 🝔 🏊 🖵 🖨 ⌧

MATTHEWS

ΛΛΛ ▼▼▼▼ **Country Inn & Suites-Matthews** SH
(704) 846-8000. **$74-$79.** 2001 Mount Harmony Church Rd. I-485, exit 51B (Independence Blvd). Int corridors. **Pets:** $5 daily fee/pet. Service with restrictions, crate.
SAVE SÓ ✕ ᳖M 🝔 🏊 🖵 🖨 🌊

PINEVILLE

▼▼▼◆ **Quality Suites** SH
(704) 889-7095. **$79-$125.** 9840 Pineville Matthews Rd. I-485, exit 64B, 0.3 mi s on SR 51. Int corridors. **Pets:** Accepted.
ASK SÓ ✕ ᳖M 🝔 🏊 🖵 🖨 🌊

END METROPOLITAN AREA

CHEROKEE

ΛΛΛ ▼▼▼ **Baymont Inn-Cherokee/Smoky Mountains** SH
(828) 497-2102. **$59-$149.** 1455 Acquoni Rd. 2.5 mi n, just w off US 441 N. Int corridors. **Pets:** Accepted.
SAVE SÓ ✕ ᳖M 🝔 🏊 🖵 🖨 🌊

ΛΛΛ ▼▼▼ **Best Western Great Smokies Inn** M
(828) 497-2020. **$49-$159.** 1636 Acquoni Rd. US 441 N, 2.5 mi n; downtown. Ext corridors. **Pets:** $10 daily fee/room. Designated rooms, service with restrictions.
SAVE SÓ ✕ 🝔 🏊 🖵 🖨 🍴 🌊

▼▼ **Microtel Inn & Suites** SH
(828) 497-7800. **$39-$119.** 674 Casino Tr. Jct US 441 and Business Rt US 441 S. Int corridors. **Pets:** Small. $25 daily fee/pet. Designated rooms, service with restrictions, supervision.
ASK SÓ ✕ ᳖M 🝔 🏊 🖵 🖨 🌊

ΛΛΛ ▼▼ **Pioneer Motel** M
(828) 497-2435. **$38-$78, 3 day notice.** 0.8 mi w on US 19 S. Ext corridors. **Pets:** Small, dogs only. $10 one-time fee/pet. Designated rooms, service with restrictions, supervision.
SAVE SÓ ✕ 🏊 🖵 🖨 🌊 ⌧

CLAYTON

▼▼▼▼ **Quality Inn & Suites** 🆂🅷
(919) 773-1110. **Call for rates.** 126 Cleveland Crossing Dr. I-40, exit 312, just e on SR 42, then 0.4 mi s. Int corridors. **Pets:** Accepted.
[icons]

▼▼▼ **Sleep Inn** 🆂🅷
(919) 772-7771. **$50-$70.** 105 Commerce Pkwy. I-40, exit 312, just w on SR 42, then just s. Int corridors. **Pets:** Accepted.
[icons]

▼▼ **Super 8 Motel** 🆂🅷
(919) 661-1991. **Call for rates.** 101 Leone Ct. I-40, exit 312, just e on SR 42, then just s. Ext corridors. **Pets:** Accepted.
[icons]

CLEMMONS

▼▼ **The Village Inn Golf & Conference Center** 🆂🅷
(336) 766-9121. **$66.** 6205 Ramada Dr. I-40, exit 184, just s, then just e. Int corridors. **Pets:** Accepted.
[icons]

DORTCHES

▼▼ **Econo Lodge** 🅼
(252) 937-6300. **Call for rates.** 5350 Dortches Blvd. I-95, exit 141, just w, then just n on service road. Ext corridors. **Pets:** Accepted.
[icons]

DUNN

▼▼ **Jameson Inn** 🅼
(910) 891-5758. **$49-$104.** 901 Jackson Rd. I-95, exit 73, just w, then just s. Ext corridors. **Pets:** Very small. $10 daily fee/room. Service with restrictions, supervision.
[icons]

DURHAM

🅰🅰🅰 ▼▼▼ **Best Value Carolina Duke Inn** 🅼
(919) 286-0771. **$43-$60.** 2517 Guess Rd. I-85, exit 175, just e. Ext corridors. **Pets:** $5 daily fee/pet. Designated rooms, service with restrictions, crate.
[icons]

🅰🅰🅰 ▼▼▼ **Best Western Skyland Inn** 🅼
(919) 383-2508. **$62-$72, 7 day notice.** 5400 US 70 W. I-85, exit 170, 0.3 mi e on US 70, then just n. Ext corridors. **Pets:** Accepted.
[icons]

▼▼▼ **Candlewood Suites** 🆂🅷
(919) 484-9922. **$81-$99.** 1818 E NC Hwy 54. I-40, exit 278, just s, then just w. Int corridors. **Pets:** $75 one-time fee/room.
[icons]

▼▼ **Homestead Studio Suites Hotel-Durham/University** 🅼
(919) 402-1700. **$64-$74.** 1920 Ivy Creek Blvd. I-40, exit 270, 2 mi n on US 15/501, then just e on Martin Luther King Jr Pkwy; in University Place. Ext corridors. **Pets:** Accepted.
[icons]

▼▼ **Homestead Studio Suites Hotel-Raleigh/Durham/Research Triangle Park** 🆂🅷
(919) 544-9991. **$64-$74.** 4515 NC Hwy 55. I-40, exit 278, just s. Ext corridors. **Pets:** Accepted.
[icons]

▼▼▼ **La Quinta Inn & Suites Raleigh (Durham-Chapel Hill)** 🆂🅷
(919) 401-9660. **$83-$100.** 4414 Chapel Hill Blvd. I-40, exit 270, 1.7 mi n on US 15/501. Int corridors. **Pets:** Other species. Service with restrictions.
[icons]

▼▼▼▼ **La Quinta Inn & Suites Raleigh (Research Triangle Park)** 🆂🅷
(919) 484-1422. **$65-$101.** 1910 W Park Dr. I-40, exit 278, just n, then just e. Int corridors. **Pets:** Medium. Service with restrictions, supervision.
[icons]

▼▼▼ **Residence Inn** 🆂🅷
(919) 361-1266. **$119-$144.** 201 Residence Inn Blvd. I-40, exit 278, just s, then just w. Ext/int corridors. **Pets:** Accepted.
[icons]

▼▼▼ **Sheraton Imperial Hotel & Convention Center** 🅻🅷
(919) 941-5050. **$145-$165.** 4700 Emperor Blvd. I-40, exit 282, just s, then just e. Int corridors. **Pets:** Accepted.
[icons]

▼▼ **Sleep Inn-RTP** 🆂🅷
(919) 993-3393. **$84, 7 day notice.** 5208 New Page Rd. I-40, exit 282, just s. Int corridors. **Pets:** Medium. Designated rooms, service with restrictions, supervision.
[icons]

🅰🅰 ▼▼▼▼ **Wellesley Inn & Suites (Durham Research Triangle Park)** 🆂🅷
(919) 998-0400. **$94-$129.** 4919 S Miami Blvd. I-40, exit 281, just s. Int corridors. **Pets:** Accepted.
[icons]

▼▼▼▼ **Wyndham Garden Hotel-Durham** 🆂🅷 🐾
(919) 941-6066. **$99-$149.** 4620 S Miami Blvd. I-40, exit 281, just n. Int corridors. **Pets:** $50 one-time fee/pet. Service with restrictions, supervision.
[icons]

EDEN

▼▼ **Jameson Inn** 🆂🅷
(336) 627-0472. **$49-$104.** 716 Linden Dr. Jct SR 700/770, 1.4 mi s on SR 87/14, then just e. Ext corridors. **Pets:** Very small, other species. $10 daily fee/room. Service with restrictions, supervision.
[icons]

ELIZABETH CITY

▼ **Days Inn** 🆂🅷
(252) 335-4316. **Call for rates.** 308 S Hughes Blvd (US 17). Jct US 158/17, 0.6 mi se on US 17. Ext corridors. **Pets:** Accepted.
[icons]

🅰🅰🅰 ▼▼ **Quality Inn** 🆂🅷
(252) 338-3951. **$80-$160, 3 day notice.** 522 S Hughes Blvd. Jct Halstead Blvd and US 17 Bypass. Ext corridors. **Pets:** Accepted.
[icons]

FAYETTEVILLE

🅰🅰🅰 ▼▼▼ **Comfort Inn-Fayetteville** 🅼
(910) 323-8333. **$66-$91.** 1957 Cedar Creek Rd. I-95, exit 49, just w. Ext corridors. **Pets:** Accepted.
[icons]

🅰🅰🅰 ▼▼▼ **Econo Lodge I-95** 🅼
(910) 433-2100. **$60-$90.** 1952 Cedar Creek Rd. I-95, exit 49, just w. Ext corridors. **Pets:** Accepted.
[icons]

🅰🅰🅰 ▼▼▼ **Fayetteville Inn & Suites** 🆂🅷
(910) 486-8300. **$69-$89.** 3136 Bordeaux Park Dr. Jct I-95 business route/US 301, 1.7 mi w on Owen Dr, then just s. Int corridors. **Pets:** Very small, other species. Designated rooms, service with restrictions, supervision.
[icons]

AAA ▼▼▼▼ Holiday Inn Bordeaux SH
(910) 323-0111. **$75-$95.** 1707 Owen Dr. Jct I-95 business route/US 301 S, 2.3 mi w. Ext/int corridors. **Pets:** Accepted.
SAVE Sₒ ✕ 🐾 🖺 🖵 ¶ ⇌

AAA ▼▼▼▼ Holiday Inn I-95 SH
(910) 323-1600. **$84-$116.** 1944 Cedar Creek Rd. I-95, exit 49, just w. Ext/int corridors. **Pets:** Accepted.
SAVE Sₒ ✕ 🐾 🖼 🖺 🖵 ¶ ⇌

▼ Motel 6 #1075 M
(910) 485-8122. **$41-$53.** 2076 Cedar Creek Rd. I-95, exit 49, just e. Ext corridors. **Pets:** Accepted.
Sₒ ✕ 🖼 ⇌

AAA ▼▼▼▼ Ramada Limited SH
(910) 485-6866. **$55-$75, 14 day notice.** 1725 Jim Johnson Rd. I-95, exit 49, just w, then just s. Int corridors. **Pets:** Accepted.
SAVE Sₒ ✕ 🖐M 🐾 🖼 🖺 ⇌

AAA ▼▼▼▼ Red Roof Inn SH
(910) 321-1460. **$60-$75.** 1569 Jim Johnson Rd. I-95, exit 49, just w on SR 53, then just n. Int corridors. **Pets:** Small. $10 daily fee/room. Designated rooms, service with restrictions, supervision.
SAVE Sₒ ✕ 🖐M 🖼 🖺 ⇌

FLETCHER

▼▼▼▼ Holiday Inn Asheville-Airport SH
(828) 684-1213. **$72-$99.** 550 Airport Rd. I-26, exit 9, just e. Int corridors. **Pets:** Medium. $50 one-time fee/room. Service with restrictions, supervision.
ASK ✕ 🐾 🖼 🖺 🖵 ¶ ⇌

FOREST CITY

▼▼ Jameson Inn SH
(828) 287-8788. **$49-$104.** 164 Jameson Inn Dr. US 74 Bypass, exit 181, 1.8 mi nw on US 74A. Ext corridors. **Pets:** Very small, other species. $10 daily fee/room. Service with restrictions, supervision.
ASK ✕ 🖐M 🐾 🖼 🖺 🖵 ⇌

FRANKLIN

▼ Colonial Inn M
(828) 524-6600. **$40-$85.** 3157 Georgia Rd. US 441 Bypass, 2.4 mi s on US 441 and 23. Ext corridors. **Pets:** $10 one-time fee/room. Designated rooms, service with restrictions, supervision.
ASK Sₒ ✕ 🖼 🖺 🖵 ⇌

AAA ▼ Country Inn Town Motel M
(828) 524-4451. **$35-$99, 3 day notice.** 668 E Main St. 0n US 441 S business route. Ext corridors. **Pets:** Medium. $7 daily fee/pet. Designated rooms, service with restrictions, supervision.
SAVE Sₒ ✕ 🖺 ⇌

▼▼ Days Inn-Franklin M
(828) 524-6491. **$44-$119.** 1320 E Main St. Jct US 23 and 441 Bypass, just nw on US 441 business route. Ext corridors. **Pets:** $15 one-time fee/pet. Service with restrictions, supervision.
ASK Sₒ ✕ 🖺 ⇌

AAA ▼ Franklin Motel Inn & Suites M
(828) 524-4431. **$40-$70.** 17 W Palmer St. Jct US 441 Bypass, 1 mi n on US 441 business route; downtown. Ext corridors. **Pets:** Other species. $10 one-time fee/room.
SAVE Sₒ ✕ 🖼 🖺 ⇌

▼▼▼ Microtel Inn & Suites SH 🐾
(828) 349-9000. **$39-$99.** 81 Allman Dr. Jct US 441 Bypass, 0.4 mi s on US 441 and 23. Int corridors. **Pets:** Other species. $20 one-time fee/room.
ASK Sₒ ✕ 🖼 🖺 🖵

▼▼▼ Mountainside Vacation Lodging M
(828) 524-6209. **$60-$80, 7 day notice.** 8356 Sylva Rd. 4.8 mi n on US 441 and 23. Ext corridors. **Pets:** Medium. $5 daily fee/pet. No service, crate.
ASK Sₒ ✕ 🖼 🖺 🖵 ✆

GARNER

▼▼▼ Holiday Inn Express SH
(919) 662-4890. **$85-$100.** 1595 Mechanical Blvd. I-40, exit 298A, 2.3 mi e on US 70, then just n. Int corridors. **Pets:** Small. $20 daily fee/pet. Designated rooms, service with restrictions, supervision.
ASK Sₒ ✕ 🖼 🖺

GOLDSBORO

▼▼ Best Western Goldsboro Inn M 🌼
(919) 735-7911. **$63-$66.** 801 US 70 E Bypass. US 70 E Bypass, exit Williams St, just n, then 0.4 mi e on service road. Ext corridors. **Pets:** Dogs only. $10 daily fee/pet. Service with restrictions, crate.
ASK Sₒ ✕ 🖼 🖺 🖵 ¶ ⇌

▼▼▼ Jameson Inn SH
(919) 778-9759. **$49-$104.** 1408 S Harding Dr. US 70 E Bypass, exit Spence Ave, just n, then just e on North Park Dr. Int corridors. **Pets:** Very small, other species. $10 daily fee/room. Service with restrictions, supervision.
ASK ✕ 🖐M 🐾 🖼 🖺 🖵 ⇌

GREENSBORO

AAA ▼▼▼▼ AmeriSuites (Greensboro/Wendover) SH
(336) 852-1443. **$229.** 1619 Stanley Rd. I-40, exit 214 westbound; exit 214B eastbound, just s, then just e. Int corridors. **Pets:** Accepted.
SAVE Sₒ ✕ 🐾 🖼 🖺 🖵

▼▼▼ Biltmore Greensboro Hotel SH
(336) 272-3474. **$79-$199, 3 day notice.** 111 W Washington St. Just s on Elm St, then just w; downtown. Int corridors. **Pets:** Accepted.
ASK Sₒ ✕ 🖺 🖵

AAA ▼▼▼ Comfort Inn SH
(336) 294-6220. **$83-$179.** 2001 Veasley St. I-40, exit 217, just s, then just w. Int corridors. **Pets:** Small. $10 daily fee/pet. Designated rooms, service with restrictions, supervision.
SAVE Sₒ ✕ 🐾 🖼 🖵 ⇌

▼▼ Crestwood Suites SH
(336) 886-1250. **Call for rates.** 501 Americhase Dr. I-40, exit 210, 0.5 mi s on SR 68. Int corridors. **Pets:** Accepted.
✕ 🖺 🖵

▼▼▼▼ Drury Inn & Suites SH
(336) 856-9696. **$70-$105.** 3220 High Point Rd. I-40, exit 217, just s. Int corridors. **Pets:** Large, other species. Service with restrictions, supervision.
ASK ✕ 🐾 🖼 🖺 🖵 ⇌

▼▼▼▼ La Quinta Inn & Suites Greensboro SH
(336) 316-0100. **$85-$116.** 1201 Lanada Rd. I-40, exit 214 or 214A, just w on Wendover Ave, just s on Stanley Rd, then just e. Int corridors. **Pets:** Large.
ASK ✕ 🖐M 🐾 🖼 🖺 🖵 ⇌

▼▼▼ Red Roof Inn Greensboro-Airport M
(336) 271-2636. **$44-$60.** 615 Regional Rd S. I-40, exit 210 (SR 68), just s via service road. Ext corridors. **Pets:** Accepted.
✕ 🖐M 🐾 🖼 🖺

▼▼▼ Residence Inn by Marriott SH
(336) 294-8600. **$89-$144.** 2000 Veasley St. I-40, exit 217, just s, then 0.4 mi w. Ext corridors. **Pets:** Accepted.
✕ 🐾 🖺 🖵 ⇌ ✕

GREENVILLE

▽▽ Jameson Inn M
(252) 752-7382. **$49-$104.** 920 Crosswinds St. Jct US 264 business route, just s on US 13/SR 11, then just w. Ext corridors. **Pets:** Very small, other species. $10 daily fee/room. Service with restrictions, supervision.

ASK ✕ ᏧM 🎵 🛏 💻 ⇌

HAYESVILLE

▽ Chatuge Mountain Inn M
(828) 389-9340. **$39-$59.** 4238 Hwy 64 E. Jct SR 69, 4.2 mi e. Ext corridors. **Pets:** Accepted.

ASK ᏚᎶ ✕ 🛏 💻

▽▽ Deerfield Inn M ❀
(828) 389-8272. **$55-$80.** 40 Chatuge Ln. 3 mi e on US 64. Ext corridors. **Pets:** Other species. $10 daily fee/pet. Service with restrictions, supervision.

ASK ᏚᎶ ✕ 🛏 💻

HENDERSON

▽▽ Jameson Inn SH
(252) 430-0247. **$49-$104.** 400 N Cooper Dr. I-85, exit 212, just w on Ruin Creek Rd, then just n. Int corridors. **Pets:** Very small, other species. $10 daily fee/room. Service with restrictions, supervision.

ASK ✕ ᏧM 🎵 🚶 🛏 ☕ ⇌

▽▽ Lamplight Inn BB ❀
(252) 438-6311. **$80-$120, 5 day notice.** 1680 Flemingtown Rd. I-85, exit 220, 1.5 mi nw. Int corridors. **Pets:** Small. Service with restrictions, crate.

ASK ᏚᎶ ✕ ✕ 🎵

HENDERSONVILLE

ⒶⒶⒶ ▽▽ Best Western Hendersonville Inn M ❀
(828) 692-0521. **$49-$119.** 105 Sugarloaf Rd. I-26, exit 18A, just e. Ext corridors. **Pets:** Other species. $10 one-time fee/room. Service with restrictions, supervision.

SAVE ᏚᎶ ✕ 🛏 💻 🍴 ⇌

ⒶⒶⒶ ▽▽ Comfort Inn SH
(828) 693-8800. **$69-$149.** 206 Mitchell Dr. I-26, exit 18B, just w. Ext corridors. **Pets:** Other species. $10 daily fee/pet. Service with restrictions, supervision.

SAVE ᏚᎶ ✕ 🎵 🛏 💻 ⇌

ⒶⒶⒶ ▽▽ Quality Inn & Suites SH
(828) 692-7231. **$50-$190.** 201 Sugarloaf Rd. I-26, exit 49A, just e. Ext/int corridors. **Pets:** Accepted.

SAVE ᏚᎶ ✕ 🎵 🛏 💻 🍴 ⇌ ✕

HICKORY

▽▽ Jameson Inn M
(828) 304-0410. **$49-$104.** 1120 13th Ave Dr SE. I-40, exit 125, just s, then 0.4 mi w. Ext corridors. **Pets:** Very small, other species. $10 daily fee/room. Service with restrictions, supervision.

ASK ✕ ᏧM 🚶 🛏 💻 ⇌

▽▽ Park Inn Gateway Conference Center SH
(828) 328-5101. **$69-$89.** 909 US 70 SW. I-40, exit 123, just n on US 321, then just e at jct US 70 E. Ext/int corridors. **Pets:** Very small, dogs only. $200 deposit/room, $50 one-time fee/room. Designated rooms, service with restrictions, crate.

ASK ᏚᎶ ✕ 🎵 🚶 🛏 💻 ⇌

▽ Red Roof Inn Hickory M
(828) 323-1500. **$47-$61.** 1184 Lenoir Rhyne Blvd. I-40, exit 125, just n. Ext corridors. **Pets:** Accepted.

✕ 🎵 🚶 🛏

HIGHLANDS

ⒶⒶⒶ ▽▽▽ Kelsey & Hutchinson Lodge SH
(828) 526-4746. **$91-$294, 7 day notice.** 450 Spring St. Jct US 64, just s on SR 28 (Fourth St), then just e. Ext corridors. **Pets:** Accepted.

SAVE ✕ 🛏 💻 ✕

ⒶⒶⒶ ▽▽▽ Mountain High Lodge M
(828) 526-2790. **$49-$209, 7 day notice.** 200 Main St. Just w on US 64; downtown. Ext corridors. **Pets:** Other species. $10 daily fee/pet. Designated rooms, service with restrictions, supervision.

SAVE ᏚᎶ ✕ 🛏 💻

HIGH POINT

▽▽ Crestwood Suites SH
(336) 886-5665. **Call for rates.** 2860 N Main St. Jct SR 68, 1.1 mi n on US 311 business route. Int corridors. **Pets:** Medium, other species. $25 daily fee/room. Designated rooms, service with restrictions, supervision.

✕ 🚶 🛏 💻

HILLSBOROUGH

ⒶⒶⒶ ▽▽▽ Microtel Inn & Suites SH
(919) 245-3102. **$50-$70.** 120 Old Dogwood St. I-85, exit 164, just w, then s. Int corridors. **Pets:** Other species. $25 one-time fee/room. Service with restrictions.

SAVE ᏚᎶ ✕ 🛏 💻

JACKSONVILLE

▽▽ Super 8 Motel SH
(910) 455-6888. **$55-$75.** 2149 N Marine Blvd. 2.8 mi n on US 17. Int corridors. **Pets:** Accepted.

ASK ᏚᎶ ✕ 🛏 💻 ⇌

JONESVILLE

ⒶⒶⒶ ▽▽ Comfort Inn SH ❀
(336) 835-9400. **$62-$96.** 1633 Winston Rd. I-77, exit 82, just w. Ext corridors. **Pets:** Medium, other species. $10 daily fee/pet. Designated rooms, service with restrictions, supervision.

SAVE ᏚᎶ ✕ ᏧM 🎵 🛏 💻 ⇌ ✕

▽▽▽ Holiday Inn Express SH
(336) 835-6000. **$59-$79.** 1713 NC 67 Hwy. I-77, exit 82, just n. Int corridors. **Pets:** Medium. $10 daily fee/pet. Designated rooms, no service, supervision.

ASK ᏚᎶ ✕ ᏧM 🎵 🚶 🛏 💻 ⇌

KENLY

ⒶⒶⒶ ▽▽▽ Days Inn M
(919) 284-3400. **$60-$70.** 1139 Johnston Pkwy. I-95, exit 106, just w, then just n. Ext corridors. **Pets:** Accepted.

SAVE ᏚᎶ ✕ ᏧM ⇌

KINGS MOUNTAIN

ⒶⒶⒶ ▽▽▽ Comfort Inn SH ❀
(704) 739-7070. **$69-$119.** 720-A York Rd. I-85, exit 8, just nw on SR 161. Ext corridors. **Pets:** Medium, other species. $15 daily fee/room. Service with restrictions.

SAVE ᏚᎶ ✕ 🛏 💻 ⇌

LAURINBURG

▽▽▽ Hampton Inn SH
(910) 277-1516. **$63-$67.** 115 Hampton Cir. Just s on US 15/401 Bypass from jct US 74/501, then just e. Int corridors. **Pets:** Accepted.

ASK ✕ 🎵 🚶 🛏 💻 ⇌

▽▽ Jameson Inn M
(910) 277-0080. **$49-$104.** 14 Jameson Inn Ct. Just n on US 15/401 Bypass from US 74/501 Bypass. Ext corridors. **Pets:** Very small, other species. $10 daily fee/room. Service with restrictions, supervision.

ASK ✕ 🛏 💻 ⇌

LENOIR

◆◆ **Jameson Inn** [M]
(828) 758-1200. **$49-$104.** 350 Wilkesboro Blvd. Jct US 321, 0.4 mi ne on SR 18. Ext corridors. **Pets:** Very small, other species. $10 daily fee/room. Service with restrictions, supervision.
[A$K] ⊠ ♿M ▣ 🖥 🏊

LEXINGTON

◆◆ **Comfort Suites of Lexington** [SH] 🐾
(336) 357-2333. **$90.** 1620 Cotton Grove Rd. I-85, exit 91, just s on SR 8. Ext/int corridors. **Pets:** Small. $10 daily fee/room, $25 one-time fee/room. Designated rooms, no service.
[A$K] [S/D] ⊠ ♿M ▣ 🖥 🏊

[AAA] ◆◆ **Quality Inn** [SH]
(336) 249-0111. **$60-$114.** 418 Piedmont Dr. I-85, exit 96, 3.5 mi w on US 64. Ext corridors. **Pets:** Medium, other species. $25 one-time fee/pet. Designated rooms, service with restrictions, supervision.
[SAVE] [S/D] ⊠ ▣ 🖥 🏊

LINCOLNTON

◆◆ **Days Inn** [M]
(704) 735-8271. **$54-$60.** 614 Clark Dr. US 321, exit 24, 1 mi w on SR 150. Ext corridors. **Pets:** Other species. $10 daily fee/room. No service, supervision.
[A$K] [S/D] ⊠ ▣ 🖥 🏊

LITTLE SWITZERLAND

[AAA] ◆◆◆ **Switzerland Inn** [CI]
(828) 765-2153. **$105-$190, 7 day notice.** Jct SR 226A and Blue Ridge Pkwy, MM 334. Ext/int corridors. **Pets:** Other species. Designated rooms, service with restrictions.
[SAVE] [S/D] ⊠ ▣ 🖥 🍴 🏊 ⊗

LUMBERTON

[AAA] ◆◆ **Best Western Inn** [M]
(910) 618-9799. **$69-$129.** 201 Jackson Ct. I-95, exit 22, just e, then just s. Ext corridors. **Pets:** Small. $10 daily fee/pet. Service with restrictions, supervision.
[SAVE] [S/D] ⊠ ♿ ▣ 🖥 🏊

[AAA] ◆◆ **Quality Inn and Suites** [SH]
(910) 738-8261. **$60-$90.** 3608 Kahn Dr. I-95, exit 20, just e, enter at K-Mart entrance, then just w. Ext/int corridors. **Pets:** $10 daily fee/room. Service with restrictions.
[SAVE] [S/D] ⊠ ▣ 🖥 🍴 🏊

MAGGIE VALLEY

◆ **Applecover Inn Motel** [M]
(828) 926-9100. **$35-$135, 3 day notice.** 4077 Soco Rd. US 19, 4.5 mi w of US 276. Ext corridors. **Pets:** Accepted.
⊠ ▣

MARION

◆◆◆ **Comfort Inn** [SH]
(828) 652-4888. **$60-$110.** 178 Hwy 70 W. I-40, exit 85, 5 mi n to jct US 221 N Bypass and US 70. Int corridors. **Pets:** Small. $35 one-time fee/room. Service with restrictions, supervision.
[A$K] [S/D] ⊠ ♿ ▣ 🖥 🏊

MOCKSVILLE

◆◆ **Comfort Inn** [SH] 🐾
(336) 751-7310. **$66-$125.** 1500 Yadkinville Rd. I-40, exit 170, 0.3 mi s on US 601. Ext corridors. **Pets:** $25 one-time fee/pet. Designated rooms, supervision.
[A$K] [S/D] ⊠ 🦻 ▣ 🖥 🏊

MOREHEAD CITY

◆◆◆ **Holiday Inn Express Hotel & Suites** [SH]
(252) 247-5001. **$85-$169.** 5063 Executive Dr. Jct US 70 and SR 24. Int corridors. **Pets:** Medium. $25 one-time fee/room. Designated rooms, service with restrictions, supervision.
[A$K] ⊠ ♿ ▣ 🖥 🏊 ⊗

MORGANTON

◆◆◆ **Comfort Inn & Suites** [SH]
(828) 430-4000. **$50-$90, 3 day notice.** 1273 Burkemont Ave. I-40, exit 103, just s. Int corridors. **Pets:** Accepted.
[A$K] [S/D] ⊠ ♿M 🦻 ♿ ▣ 🖥 🏊

◆◆◆ **Holiday Inn** [SH]
(828) 437-0171. **$76.** 2400 S Sterling St. I-40, exit 105 (SR 18), just s. Ext corridors. **Pets:** Other species. $25 one-time fee/room. Crate.
[A$K] [S/D] ⊠ ♿M 🦻 ♿ ▣ 🖥 🍴 🏊

◆◆ **Sleep Inn** [SH]
(828) 433-9000. **$56.** 2400A S Sterling St. I-40, exit 105 (SR 18), just s. Int corridors. **Pets:** Accepted.
[A$K] [S/D] ⊠ 🦻 ▣ 🖥

MORRISVILLE

[AAA] ◆◆◆ **AmeriSuites (Raleigh/RDU Airport-RTP)** [SH]
(919) 405-2400. **$54-$109.** 200 Airgate Dr. I-40, exit 284 and 284B, just n, just w on Pleasant Grove Church Rd, then just s. Int corridors. **Pets:** Small. $10 daily fee/pet. Designated rooms, service with restrictions, supervision.
[SAVE] [S/D] ⊠ ♿M ♿ ▣ 🖥 🏊

[AAA] ◆◆◆ **Baymont Inn & Suites Raleigh-Airport** [SH]
(919) 481-3600. **$70-$90.** 1001 Aerial Center Pkwy. I-40, exit 284 and 284A, 0.3 mi s; in Aerial Center Park. Int corridors. **Pets:** Accepted.
[SAVE] [S/D] ⊠ ♿M 🦻 ▣ 🖥 🏊

◆◆◆ **La Quinta Inn & Suites Raleigh (Raleigh-Durham Int'l Airport)** [SH]
(919) 461-1771. **$77-$132.** 1001 Hospitality Ct. I-40, exit 284 and 284A, just s, just e on Aerial Center Pkwy, then just ne; in Aerial Center Park. Int corridors. **Pets:** Small. Service with restrictions, crate.
[A$K] ⊠ ♿M 🦻 ♿ ▣ 🖥 🏊

◆◆◆ **Staybridge Suites Raleigh Durham Airport** [SH]
(919) 468-0180. **$81-$151, 3 day notice.** 1012 Airport Blvd. I-40, exit 284 and 284A, just s; enter between Hampton Inn and Holiday Inn Express. Int corridors. **Pets:** $150 one-time fee/room. Service with restrictions, supervision.
[A$K] [S/D] ⊠ ♿M 🦻 ♿ ▣ 🖥 ⊗

MOUNT AIRY

◆◆ **Comfort Inn** [M] 🐾
(336) 789-2000. **$62-$125.** 2136 Rockford St. Jct US 52, 0.6 mi s on US 601. Ext corridors. **Pets:** $25 one-time fee/pet. Designated rooms, supervision.
[A$K] [S/D] ⊠ 🦻 ▣ 🖥 🏊

MURPHY

[AAA] ◆◆ **Best Western of Murphy** [M]
(828) 837-3060. **$59-$119.** 1522 Andrews Rd. US 74, 19 and SR 129, exit Andrews Rd. Ext corridors. **Pets:** Small. $10 daily fee/pet. Designated rooms, service with restrictions, supervision.
[SAVE] [S/D] ⊠ ▣ 🖥 🏊

[AAA] ◆◆ **Comfort Inn** [M]
(828) 837-8030. **$59-$119.** 754 Hwy 64 W. US 64 W/19 S/74 W and 129 S. Ext corridors. **Pets:** Accepted.
[SAVE] [S/D] ⊠ ▣ 🖥 🏊

OUTER BANKS AREA

BUXTON

WWWW Outer Banks Motel M
(252) 995-5601. **Call for rates.** 46577 Hwy 12. On SR 12, 1.3 mi ne. Ext corridors. **Pets:** Large. $5 daily fee/pet. Designated rooms, service with restrictions, supervision.

KILL DEVIL HILLS

WWW Ramada Plaza Outer Banks Resort & Conference Center SH 🐾
(252) 441-2151. **$69-$280.** 1701 S Virginia Dare Tr. SR 12, at MM 9.5. Int corridors. **Pets:** $10 daily fee/pet. Designated rooms, supervision.

WWW Travelodge-Nags Head Beach SH 🐾
(252) 441-0411. **$29-$289, 3 day notice.** 804 N Virginia Dare Tr. SR 12, at MM 8.1. Ext/int corridors. **Pets:** Other species. $10 daily fee/pet. Designated rooms, service with restrictions.

NAGS HEAD

WWW Dolphin Oceanfront Motel M
(252) 441-7488. **$49-$329, 30 day notice.** 8017 Old Oregon Inlet Rd (SR 1243). Jct SR 12/1243, just s, at MM 16.5. Ext corridors. **Pets:** Other species. $10 daily fee/pet. Service with restrictions.

OCRACOKE

WWW The Anchorage Inn SH
(252) 928-1101. **$89-$165, 3 day notice.** 205 Irving Garrish Hwy (SR 12). From Cedar Island Ferry, just n. Ext corridors. **Pets:** Other species. $20 daily fee/room. Designated rooms, service with restrictions, supervision.

END AREA

PINEHURST

WWWW Homewood Suites by Hilton SH 🐾
(910) 255-0300. **$104-$250.** 250 Central Park Ave. Jct SR 5 and 211; in Olmsted Village. Int corridors. **Pets:** Other species. $50 one-time fee/pet. Designated rooms, service with restrictions.

RALEIGH

WWW AmeriSuites (Raleigh/Wake Forest Rd) SH
(919) 877-9997. **$93-$179.** 1105 Navaho Dr. I-440, exit 10 (Wake Forest Rd), just n, then just w. Int corridors. **Pets:** Small. $10 daily fee/pet. Designated rooms, service with restrictions, crate.

WWWW Best Western Raleigh North SH
(919) 872-5000. **$63.** 2715 Capital Blvd. I-440, exit 11 or 11B, just n on US 1. Int corridors. **Pets:** Accepted.

WWW Candlewood Suites-Crabtree SH
(919) 789-4840. **$79.** 4433 Lead Mine Rd. I-440, exit 7 or 7B, just w, then just n. Int corridors. **Pets:** Medium, dogs only. $75 one-time fee/room. Designated rooms, service with restrictions.

WWW Econo Lodge M
(919) 856-9800. **$59-$89.** 2641 Appliance Ct. I-440, exit 11 or 11B, just n, then 0.3 mi e. Ext/int corridors. **Pets:** Other species. $20 deposit/pet, $20 daily fee/pet. Service with restrictions, supervision.

WWW Fairfield Inn & Suites–Crabtree SH
(919) 881-9800. **Call for rates.** 2201 Summit Park Ln. I-440, exit 7 or 7B, just w on US 70, just s on Blue Ridge Rd, then just e. Int corridors. **Pets:** Accepted.

WWWW Holiday Inn at Crabtree Valley Mall LH
(919) 782-8600. **$129-$139.** 4100 Glenwood Ave. I-440, exit 7, just w on US 70. Int corridors. **Pets:** Medium. $25 one-time fee/room. Designated rooms, service with restrictions, supervision.

WWWW Holiday Inn-Brownstone SH
(919) 828-0811. **$94-$134.** 1707 Hillsborough St. I-440, exit 3, 3 mi e. Int corridors. **Pets:** Accepted.

WWWW Holiday Inn Raleigh-North LH
(919) 872-3500. **$69-$104.** 2805 Highwoods Blvd. I-440, exit 11 or 11B, just n on US 1. Int corridors. **Pets:** Other species. $75 one-time fee/room. Service with restrictions, supervision.

WWW Homestead Studio Suites Hotel-Raleigh/Crabtree Valley SH
(919) 510-8551. **$54-$64.** 4810 Bluestone Dr. I-440, exit 7 or 7B, 1 mi w on US 70, then just s. Ext corridors. **Pets:** Service with restrictions, supervision.

WWW Homestead Studio Suites Hotel-Raleigh/North SH
(919) 981-7353. **$64-$74.** 3531 Wake Forest Rd. I-440, exit 10 (Wake Forest Rd), 0.5 mi n. Ext corridors. **Pets:** Accepted.

WWW Homestead Studio Suites Hotel-Raleigh/Northeast SH
(919) 807-9970. **$54-$69.** 2601 Appliance Ct. I-440, exit 11, just n on US 1, then just e. Int corridors. **Pets:** Medium. $25 daily fee/room. Service with restrictions, supervision.

WWWW La Quinta Inn & Suites Raleigh (Crabtree) SH
(919) 785-0071. **$70-$89.** 2211 Summit Park Ln. I-440, exit 7 or 7B, just w on US 70, just s on Blue Ridge Rd, then just e. Int corridors. **Pets:** Small. Designated rooms, service with restrictions, supervision.

WWWW Quality Suites Hotel SH
(919) 876-2211. **$69-$109.** 4400 Capital Blvd. I-440, exit 11 and 11B, 2.5 mi n on US 1. Int corridors. **Pets:** Accepted.

AAA ▼▼▼ **Red Roof Inn-North** **M**
(919) 878-9310. **$49-$64.** 3201 Wake Forest Rd. I-440, exit 10 (Wake Forest Rd), just n, then just w. Ext corridors. **Pets:** Small, other species. Service with restrictions, supervision.
[SAVE] [S☼] [✕] [⊘] [⊟] [⇆]

▼▼ **Red Roof Inn-South** **SH**
(919) 833-6005. **$53-$66.** 1813 S Saunders St. I-40, exit 298B, just n. Int corridors. **Pets:** Medium, other species. Service with restrictions, supervision.
[✕] [&M] [⊘] [&] [⊟]

▼▼▼ **Residence Inn by Marriott** **SH**
(919) 878-6100. **$69-$139.** 1000 Navaho Dr. I-440, exit 10 (Wake Forest Rd), just n, then w. Ext corridors. **Pets:** Accepted.
[ASK] [✕] [&M] [⊘] [&] [⇆] [✕]

▼▼▼ **Residence Inn by Marriott Crabtree** **SH**
(919) 279-3000. **$89-$125, 3 day notice.** 2200 Summit Park Ln. I-440, exit 7 or 7B, just w on US 70, just s on Blue Ridge Rd, then just e. Int corridors. **Pets:** Accepted.
[✕] [&M] [&] [⊟] [⊡] [⇆] [✕]

AAA ▼▼▼▼ **Sheraton Capital Center** **LH**
(919) 834-9900. **$189.** 421 S Salisbury St. Downtown; just s. Int corridors. **Pets:** Accepted.
[SAVE] [✕] [&] [⊟] [⊡] [¶] [⇆]

REIDSVILLE

▼▼ **Best Value Inn & Suites** **M**
(336) 342-0341. **$60-$70.** 2100 Barnes St. US 29, exit 150 (Barnes St), just e. Ext corridors. **Pets:** Accepted.
[ASK] [S☼] [✕] [⊟] [⊡] [¶] [⇆]

AAA ▼▼▼ **Comfort Inn** **M**
(336) 634-1275. **$55-$205.** 2203 Barnes St. US 29, exit 150 (Barnes St), just e. Ext corridors. **Pets:** Accepted.
[SAVE] [S☼] [✕] [&M] [⊟] [⊡] [⇆]

ROANOKE RAPIDS

▼▼ **Jameson Inn** **M**
(252) 533-0022. **$49-$104.** 101 Old Farm Rd. I-95, exit 173, 0.5 mi w on US 158, then just s. Ext corridors. **Pets:** Very small, other species. $10 daily fee/room. Service with restrictions, supervision.
[ASK] [✕] [⊘] [⊟] [⊡] [⇆]

ROBBINSVILLE

▼▼ **Microtel Inn & Suites** **SH**
(828) 479-6772. **$50.** 111 Rodney Orr Bypass (US 129). Center of downtown. Int corridors. **Pets:** Other species. $25 one-time fee/room. Service with restrictions, supervision.
[ASK] [S☼] [✕] [&M] [⊘] [&] [⊟] [⊡]

ROCKY MOUNT

AAA ▼▼▼ **Best Western Inn I-95 Gold Rock** **M**
(252) 985-1450. **$64-$97, 10 day notice.** 7095 NC 4. I-95, exit 145, just e. Ext corridors. **Pets:** Medium, other species. $5 daily fee/pet. Service with restrictions.
[SAVE] [S☼] [✕] [⊟] [⊡] [⇆]

AAA ▼▼▼ **Comfort Inn** **SH**
(252) 937-7765. **$70-$85.** 200 Gateway Blvd. I-95, exit 138, 1 mi e on US 64, exit Winstead Ave, then just s. Int corridors. **Pets:** Other species. $25 one-time fee/room. Designated rooms, service with restrictions, crate.
[SAVE] [S☼] [✕] [⊘] [⊟] [⊡] [⇆]

AAA ▼▼▼ **GuestHouse International Inn Battleboro/Rocky Mt.** **M**
(252) 407-8100. **$54-$64.** 7797 NC Hwy 48. I-95, exit 145, just e, then just n. Ext corridors. **Pets:** Accepted.
[SAVE] [S☼] [✕] [&M] [&] [⊟] [⊡] [⇆]

▼▼▼ **Red Roof Inn** **SH**
(252) 984-0907. **$43-$58.** 1370 N Weslyan Blvd. Jct US 64 Bypass, 1.5 mi n on US 301. Int corridors. **Pets:** Accepted.
[✕] [⊘] [&] [⊟]

AAA ▼▼▼▼ **Residence Inn by Marriott** **SH** 🐾
(252) 451-5600. **$125-$185.** 230 Gateway Blvd. I-95, exit 138, 1 mi e on US 64, exit Winstead Ave, then just s. Int corridors. **Pets:** Other species. $100 one-time fee/room. Service with restrictions.
[SAVE] [S☼] [✕] [&M] [⊘] [&] [⊟] [⊡] [⇆] [✕]

ROWLAND

▼▼ **Holiday Inn Express** **M**
(910) 422-3377. **$51-$100.** 14733 US Hwy 301. I-95, exit 1B, just w. Ext corridors. **Pets:** Medium. $15 one-time fee/room. Service with restrictions, supervision.
[ASK] [S☼] [✕] [⊘] [&] [⊟] [⇆]

SALISBURY

▼▼ **Hampton Inn** **SH**
(704) 637-8000. **$85-$160.** 1001 Klumac Rd. I-85, exit 75, just w. Int corridors. **Pets:** Other species. Service with restrictions, supervision.
[ASK] [S☼] [✕] [⊘] [⊟] [⊡] [⇆]

SALUDA

▼▼ **The Oaks Bed & Breakfast** **BB**
(828) 749-9613. **$85-$175, 3 day notice.** 339 Greenville St. I-26, exit 28, 1.1 mi sw, 0.3 mi s, then cross railway tracks. Ext/int corridors. **Pets:** Designated rooms.
[ASK] [S☼] [✕] [⊟] [⊠]

SANFORD

▼▼ **Jameson Inn** **SH**
(919) 708-7400. **$49-$104.** 2614 S Horner Blvd. 2.5 mi s on SR 87. Ext corridors. **Pets:** Very small, dogs only. $10 daily fee/room. Designated rooms, service with restrictions, supervision.
[ASK] [✕] [&M] [⊟] [⊡] [⇆]

SMITHFIELD

▼▼ **Jameson Inn** **M**
(919) 989-5901. **$49-$104.** 125 S Equity Dr. I-95, exit 95, just w, then just n on Industrial Park Blvd. Ext corridors. **Pets:** Very small, other species. $10 daily fee/room. Service with restrictions, supervision.
[ASK] [✕] [&M] [⊘] [⊟] [⊡] [⇆]

AAA ▼▼ **Log Cabin Motel** **M**
(919) 934-1534. **$45-$47.** 2491 US 70 E (Business Route). I-95, exit 95, 0.5 mi e. Ext corridors. **Pets:** Accepted.
[SAVE] [✕] [⊟] [¶] [⇆]

AAA ▼▼▼ **Super 8 Motel** **SH**
(919) 989-8988. **$53-$99.** 735 Industrial Park Dr. I-95, exit 95, just w on US 70, then just n. Int corridors. **Pets:** $4 daily fee/room. Designated rooms, service with restrictions, supervision.
[SAVE] [S☼] [✕] [&M] [⊘] [&] [⊟] [⇆]

SOUTHERN PINES

▼▼▼ **Hampton Inn** **SH**
(910) 692-9266. **$79-$99.** 1675 US 1 S. On US 1, 1 mi s. Ext corridors. **Pets:** Small, dogs only. $10 daily fee/room. Service with restrictions, supervision.
[ASK] [S☼] [✕] [⊟] [⊡] [⇆]

SPRING LAKE

Super 8 Motel M
(910) 436-8588. **Call for rates.** 256 S Main St. Jct SR 24, just s. Int corridors. **Pets:** Accepted.

SPRUCE PINE

Richmond Inn BB
(828) 765-6993. **$75-$80, 5 day notice.** 51 Pine Ave. Exit off US 19 E and 226 to Oak Ave, just n on Walnut Ave, follow signs; center. Int corridors. **Pets:** Accepted.

STATESVILLE

Best Western Statesville Inn SH
(704) 881-0111. **$70-$99.** 1121 Morland Dr. I-77, exit 49A, just e on US 70 E. Ext/int corridors. **Pets:** Medium, other species. $15 daily fee/pet. No service, supervision.

Hampton Inn Statesville SH
(704) 878-2721. **$65-$74.** 715 Sullivan Rd. I-40, exit 151, just s. Ext corridors. **Pets:** Large. Service with restrictions, supervision.

Holiday Inn Express Hotel & Suites M
(704) 872-4101. **$69-$129.** 740 Sullivan Rd. I-40, exit 151, just s. Ext corridors. **Pets:** Accepted.

Super 8 Motel M
(704) 878-9888. **$42-$120.** 1125 Greenland Rd. I-77, exit 49A, just e. Ext/int corridors. **Pets:** Small, dogs only. $5 daily fee/pet. Designated rooms, service with restrictions, supervision.

SUNSET BEACH

Sea Trail Golf Resort & Conference Center CO
(910) 287-1100. **$62-$343, 30 day notice.** 211 Clubhouse Rd. US 17, 4 mi e to jct SR 904 and 179, then 1.5 mi s on SR 179. Ext corridors. **Pets:** $70 one-time fee/pet. Designated rooms, service with restrictions, supervision.

TRYON

Pine Crest Inn & Restaurant CI
(828) 859-9135. **$90-$199, 7 day notice.** 85 Pine Crest Ln. I-26, exit 36, 4 mi s, follow signs. Ext/int corridors. **Pets:** Accepted.

WAYNESVILLE

The Lodge of Waynesville M
(828) 452-0353. **$39-$125.** 909 Russ Ave. US 23/74, exit 102, just se. Ext corridors. **Pets:** Accepted.

WELDON

Days Inn M
(252) 536-4867. **$61-$67.** 1611 Julian Allsbrook Hwy. I-95, exit 173, just e on US 158. Ext corridors. **Pets:** Accepted.

WILLIAMSTON

Holiday Inn SH
(252) 792-3184. **$62-$79.** 101 East Blvd. US 64, exit 514, 1.5 mi n on US 17. Ext/int corridors. **Pets:** Medium. Service with restrictions, supervision.

WILMINGTON

Comfort Inn Wilmington SH 🐾
(910) 791-4841. **$60-$130.** 151 S College Rd. US 17, just s on SR 132. Int corridors. **Pets:** Large, other species. $25 daily fee/pet. Designated rooms, service with restrictions, crate.

Days Inn M 🐾
(910) 799-6300. **$45-$99.** 5040 Market St. Jct SR 132, 0.6 mi s on US 17. Ext corridors. **Pets:** Large. $15 daily fee/room. Designated rooms, service with restrictions, crate.

Hilton Wilmington Riverside LH
(910) 763-5900. **$109-$250.** 301 N Water St. On Cape Fear River waterfront. Int corridors. **Pets:** Accepted.

Jameson Inn SH
(910) 452-5660. **$49-$104.** 5102 Dunlea Ct. Jct SR 132, 0.5 mi s on US 17, then just w on New Centre Dr. Int corridors. **Pets:** Small, other species. $10 daily fee/room. Service with restrictions, supervision.

MainStay Suites SH
(910) 392-1741. **$79-$200.** 5229 Market St. 4 mi n on US 17 and 74. Int corridors. **Pets:** Small. $100 one-time fee/room. Designated rooms, service with restrictions.

Residence Inn-Landfall Business Center SH
(910) 256-0098. **$99-$189.** 1200 Culbreth Dr. 2.8 mi e on US 74 from jct SR 132, 0.4 mi n on Military Cutoff Rd, then just e. Int corridors. **Pets:** Large. $75 one-time fee/room. Service with restrictions, crate.

WILSON

Holiday Inn Express & Suites SH
(252) 246-1588. **Call for rates.** 2308 Montgomery Dr. US 264, exit 40, 3.2 mi e on SR 42, then just n. Int corridors. **Pets:** Accepted.

WINSTON-SALEM

Augustus T Zevely Inn BB
(336) 748-9299. **$80-$125.** 803 S Main St. In Old Salem Historical District. Ext/int corridors. **Pets:** Accepted.

Best Western Salem Inn & Suites SH
(336) 725-8561. **$65-$110.** 127 S Cherry St. I-40 business route, exit 5C (Cherry St) eastbound; exit 5D westbound, just s. Ext corridors. **Pets:** Medium. $25 one-time fee/room. Service with restrictions, supervision.

Comfort Inn Coliseum SH
(336) 767-8240. **$73-$156.** 531 Akron Dr. US 52, exit 112, just e. Int corridors. **Pets:** Small. $15 daily fee/pet. Service with restrictions, crate.

The Hawthorne Inn & Conference Center SH
(336) 777-3000. **$59-$99.** 420 High St. I-40 business route, exit 5C (Cherry St) eastbound, just e; exit westbound, just w on 1st St, then just s on Marshall St. Int corridors. **Pets:** Medium. $15 daily fee/room. Designated rooms, service with restrictions, crate.

Holiday Inn Hanes Mall SH
(336) 765-6670. **$59.** 2008 S Hawthorne Rd. I-40 business route, exit Silas Creek Pkwy S, just e. Ext corridors. **Pets:** Large. $25 one-time fee/room. Service with restrictions, crate.

▼▼▼ **La Quinta Inns & Suites Winston-Salem** SH
(336) 765-8777. **$85-$105.** 2020 Griffith Rd. I-40, exit 189 (Stratford Rd), just s, then just e on Hanes Mall Blvd. Int corridors. **Pets:** Small, other species. Service with restrictions.
(A$K) ⊠ 🖎M 🖉 🖎 🖬 🖵 🖘

▼▼▼ **Residence Inn by Marriott** CO ✿
(336) 759-0777. **$94-$114.** 7835 N Point Blvd. US 52 N, exit 115B, 2 mi s on University Pkwy, then just e. Ext corridors. **Pets:** Other species. $75 one-time fee/room. Designated rooms, service with restrictions.
(A$K) S🖎 ⊠ 🖉 🖬 🖵 🖘 🖎

YANCEYVILLE

▼▼ **Days Inn** SH
(336) 694-9494. **$65-$125.** 1858 NC Hwy 86 N. Jct US 158 W, just s. Ext corridors. **Pets:** $10 daily fee/pet. Service with restrictions, supervision.
S🖎 ⊠ 🖎 🖬 🖘

NORTH DAKOTA

BEULAH

▼▼▼ **AmericInn Motel & Suites** 🆂🅷
(701) 873-2220. **$76-$126.** 2100 2nd Ave NW. Jct SR 49/200, 1.2 mi s. Int corridors. **Pets:** $100 deposit/room. Service with restrictions, supervision.

BISMARCK

🆊🆊🆊 ▼▼ **Best Western Doublewood Inn** 🆂🅷
(701) 258-7000. **$83-$109.** 1400 E Interchange Ave. I-94, exit 159 (US 83), just s. Int corridors. **Pets:** Medium. $10 daily fee/room. Designated rooms, service with restrictions, supervision.

🆊🆊🆊 ▼▼◆ **Best Western Ramkota Hotel** 🆂🅷
(701) 258-7700. **$99-$125.** 800 S 3rd St. Just s of jct I-94 business loop and S 3rd St. Int corridors. **Pets:** $10 one-time fee/room. Designated rooms, service with restrictions, supervision.

▼▼ **Comfort Inn** 🆂🅷
(701) 223-1911. **$60-$85.** 1030 Interstate Ave. I-94, exit 159 (US 83), 0.3 mi nw. Int corridors. **Pets:** Small. Service with restrictions, supervision.

🆊🆊🆊 ▼▼ **Days Inn-Bismarck** 🆂🅷
(701) 223-9151. **$69-$79, 7 day notice.** 1300 E Capitol Ave. I-94, exit 159 (US 83), just s. Int corridors. **Pets:** $10 one-time fee/pet. Designated rooms, service with restrictions.

▼▼ **Expressway Inn** 🆂🅷
(701) 222-2900. **$60-$80.** 200 Bismarck Expwy. Jct I-94 business loop (Bismarck Expwy) and S 3rd St. Int corridors. **Pets:** Large, other species. $5 one-time fee/room. Designated rooms, service with restrictions, supervision.

🆊🆊🆊 ▼▼ **Kelly Inn** 🆂🅷
(701) 223-8001. **$69-$89.** 1800 N 12 St. I-94, exit 159 (US 83), 0.3 mi s. Int corridors. **Pets:** Designated rooms, supervision.

🆊🆊🆊 ▼▼▼ **Radisson Hotel Bismarck** 🅻🅷
(701) 255-6000. **$84.** 605 E Broadway Ave. Jct 6th St; center. Int corridors. **Pets:** Accepted.

🆊🆊🆊 ▼ **Select Inn** 🆂🅷
(701) 223-8060. **$40-$72.** 1505 Interchange Ave. I-94, exit 159 (US 83), just se. Int corridors. **Pets:** $25 deposit/room, $5 daily fee/pet. Designated rooms, service with restrictions, supervision.

BOWMAN

🆊🆊🆊 ▼▼▼ **North Winds Lodge** 🅼
(701) 523-5641. **$40-$56.** 503 Hwy 85 S. On US 85, just s of US 12. Ext corridors. **Pets:** Accepted.

CARRINGTON

▼▼▼ **Chieftain Conference Center** 🆂🅷
(701) 652-3131. **$55-$75.** 60 4th Ave S. Jct US 52 and 281, 0.5 mi e on US 52; just s of jct SR 200. Ext/int corridors. **Pets:** Small. $5 daily fee/pet. Designated rooms, service with restrictions, crate.

▼▼ **Super 8 Motel** 🆂🅷
(701) 652-3982. **$50-$60.** 101 4th Ave S. Jct US 52 and 281, 0.5 mi e on US 52; just s of jct SR 200. Int corridors. **Pets:** Medium. $5 daily fee/pet. Designated rooms, service with restrictions, supervision.

DEVILS LAKE

▼▼ **Comfort Inn** 🆂🅷
(701) 662-6760. **$60-$80.** 215 Hwy 2 E. Jct US 2 and SR 20. Int corridors. **Pets:** Service with restrictions, supervision.

▼▼ **Days Inn Devils Lake** 🆂🅷
(701) 662-5381. **$58-$85.** 1109 Hwy 20 S. On SR 20, just s of jct US 2. Ext corridors. **Pets:** Accepted.

🆊🆊🆊 ▼ **Trails West Motel** 🅼
(701) 662-5011. **$44-$47.** 309 1st St W. 0.8 mi sw on US 2. Int corridors. **Pets:** $5 daily fee/pet. Service with restrictions, supervision.

DICKINSON

▼▼ **AmericInn Motel & Suites of Dickinson** 🆂🅷
(701) 225-1400. **$71-$130.** 229 15th St W. I-94, exit 61 (SR 22), just n, then e. Int corridors. **Pets:** Other species. Designated rooms, service with restrictions, supervision.

▼▼ **Comfort Inn** 🆂🅷
(701) 264-7300. **$65-$95.** 493 Elks Dr. I-94, exit 61 (SR 22), just n, then w. Int corridors. **Pets:** Other species. Service with restrictions, supervision.

🆊🆊🆊 ▼▼▼ **Hartfiel Inn** 🅱🅱
(701) 225-6710. **$79.** 509 3rd Ave W. I-94, exit 61 (SR 22), 0.8 mi s. Int corridors. **Pets:** Medium, dogs only. Designated rooms, supervision.

▼▼▼ **Holiday Inn Express Hotel & Suites** 🆂🅷
(701) 456-8000. **$69-$85.** 103 14th St W. I-94, exit 61 (SR 22), just n, then just e. Int corridors. **Pets:** Other species. $10 daily fee/room. Designated rooms.

FARGO

▼▼ **Airport/Dome Days Inn & Suites** 🆂🅷
(701) 232-0000. **$77-$97.** 1507 19th Ave N. I-29, exit 67, 1.2 mi e. Int corridors. **Pets:** Medium. $15 one-time fee/room. Designated rooms, service with restrictions, supervision.

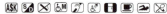

AAA WWW AmericInn Lodge & Suites SH ❀
(701) 234-9946. **$69-$134.** 1423 35th St SW. I-29, exit 64 (13th Ave S), just se. Int corridors. **Pets:** Other species. $10 one-time fee/room. Designated rooms, service with restrictions, supervision.

SAVE ⊗ ⌂ ⌨ ⊟ 💻 ⇋ ⊗

AAA WWW Best Western Fargo Doublewood Inn SH ❀
(701) 235-3333. **$76-$94.** 3333 13th Ave S. I-29, exit 64 (13th Ave S), 0.3 mi e. Int corridors. **Pets:** Medium, dogs only. $25 deposit/room. Service with restrictions, supervision.

SAVE ⓢ ⊗ ⌂ᴹ ⌂ ⌂ ⊟ 💻 ¶¶ ⇋ ⊗

AAA WWW Best Western Kelly Inn SH ❀
(701) 282-2143. **$89-$105.** 3800 Main Ave. I-29, exit 65 (Main Ave), just w. Ext/int corridors. **Pets:** Medium. Service with restrictions, supervision.

SAVE ⓢ ⊗ ⌂ ⌂ ⊟ 💻 ¶¶ ⇋ ⊗

WWW Comfort Inn by Choice Hotels East SH
(701) 280-9666. **$60-$99.** 1407 35th St S. I-29, exit 64 (13th Ave S), just se. Int corridors. **Pets:** Accepted.

ASK ⓢ ⊗ ⌂ ⊟ 💻 ⇋

WWW Comfort Inn by Choice Hotels West SH
(701) 282-9596. **$60-$99.** 3825 9th Ave SW. I-29, exit 64 (13th Ave S), just nw. Int corridors. **Pets:** Other species. Designated rooms, service with restrictions, supervision.

ASK ⓢ ⊗ ⊟ 💻 ⇋

WWWW Comfort Suites by Choice Hotels SH
(701) 237-5911. **$69-$109.** 1415 35th St SW. I-29, exit 64 (13th Ave S), just se. Int corridors. **Pets:** Accepted.

ASK ⓢ ⊗ ⌂ᴹ ⌂ ⌂ ⊟ 💻 ⇋ ⊗

WWW Econo Lodge by Choice Hotels SH
(701) 232-3412. **$50-$80.** 1401 35th St S. I-29, exit 64 (13th Ave S), just se. Int corridors. **Pets:** Accepted.

ASK ⓢ ⊗ ⌂ ⌂ ⊟ 💻

WWW Expressway Inn SH
(701) 235-3141. **$72.** 1340 21st Ave S. I-94, exit 351, just sw. Ext/int corridors. **Pets:** Medium. $5 daily fee/room. Designated rooms, service with restrictions, crate.

ASK ⓢ ⊗ ⌂ᴹ ⌂ ⌂ ⊟ 💻 ¶¶ ⇋ ⊗

AAA WWWW Holiday Inn LH
(701) 282-2700. **$129-$149.** 3803 13th Ave S. I-29, exit 64 (13 Ave S), just nw. Int corridors. **Pets:** Other species. Service with restrictions, supervision.

SAVE ⓢ ⊗ ⌂ᴹ ⌂ ⌂ ⊟ 💻 ¶¶ ⇋ ⊗

WWWW Holiday Inn Express Fargo SH
(701) 282-2000. **$85-$95.** 1040 40th St S. I-29, exit 64 (13th Ave S), just nw. Int corridors. **Pets:** Accepted.

ⓢ ⊗ ⌂ᴹ ⌂ ⌂ ⊟ 💻 ⇋ ⊗

AAA WWW Kelly Inn 13th Avenue SH
(701) 277-8821. **$71-$114.** 4207 13th Ave SW. I-29, exit 64 (13th Ave S), 0.5 mi w. Ext/int corridors. **Pets:** Medium. Service with restrictions, supervision.

SAVE ⓢ ⊗ ⌂ᴹ ⌂ ⌂ ⊟ 💻

WWWW MainStay Suites SH
(701) 277-4627. **$79-$139.** 1901 44th St SW. I-94, exit 348 (45th St), just n, then just e. Int corridors. **Pets:** Accepted.

ASK ⓢ ⊗ ⌂ᴹ ⌂ ⌂ ⊟ 💻 ⇋ ⊗

WWW Motel 6 #1158 M
(701) 232-9251. **$41-$53.** 1202 36th S. I-29, exit 64 (13th Ave S), just n on east frontage road. Int corridors. **Pets:** Other species. Service with restrictions, supervision.

ⓢ ⊗ ⌂ ⊟ ⇋

AAA WW Motel 75 SH
(701) 232-1321. **$46-$54.** 3402 14th Ave S. I-29, exit 64 (13th Ave S), just se. Int corridors. **Pets:** Other species. Designated rooms, service with restrictions, supervision.

SAVE ⓢ ⊗ ⌂

AAA WW Select Inn SH ❀
(701) 282-6300. **$45-$75.** 1025 38th St SW. I-29, exit 64 (13th Ave S), just w, then n. Int corridors. **Pets:** Large, other species. $25 deposit/room, $5 daily fee/room. Designated rooms, service with restrictions, supervision.

SAVE ⓢ ⊗ ⌂ ⌂ ⊟ 💻

WWW Sleep Inn SH
(701) 281-8240. **$64-$79.** 1921 44 St SW. I-94, exit 348 (45th St), just n, then just e. Int corridors. **Pets:** Accepted.

ASK ⓢ ⊗ ⌂ᴹ ⌂ ⌂ ⊟ 💻 ⇋ ⊗

WW WWW Super 8 Motel SH
(701) 232-9202. **$54-$125.** 3518 Interstate Blvd. I-29, exit 64 (13th Ave S), just n on east frontage road. Int corridors. **Pets:** $4 daily fee/pet. Designated rooms, service with restrictions, supervision.

ASK ⓢ ⊗ ⌂ ⊟ 💻 ⇋

GRAND FORKS

AAA WW Best Value Inn of Grand Forks M
(701) 775-0555. **$50-$60.** 1000 N 42nd St. I-29, exit 141 (Gateway Dr), jct US 2, then just se. Int corridors. **Pets:** Other species. $6 daily fee/pet. Designated rooms, service with restrictions, supervision.

SAVE ⓢ ⊗ ⊟ 💻

WW WW Best Western Town House SH
(701) 746-5411. **Call for rates.** 710 1st Ave N. I-29, exit 140 (DeMers Ave), 3 mi e; downtown. Int corridors. **Pets:** Small, dogs only. $15 daily fee/room. Designated rooms, service with restrictions, supervision.

⊗ ⌂ ⊟ ⌂ 💻 ¶¶ ⇋ ⊗

AAA WWW Days Inn SH
(701) 775-0060. **$59-$89.** 3101 34th St S. I-29, exit 138 (32nd Ave), 0.5 mi e. Int corridors. **Pets:** $5 daily fee/pet. Designated rooms, service with restrictions, supervision.

SAVE ⓢ ⊗ ⊟ ⇋

AAA WWWW Holiday Inn Grand Forks SH
(701) 772-7131. **$89-$129.** 1210 N 43rd St. I-29, exit 141 (Gateway Dr), just e on US 2. Ext/int corridors. **Pets:** Small. $50 deposit/pet. Designated rooms, service with restrictions, supervision.

SAVE ⓢ ⊗ ⌂ ⌂ ⊟ 💻 ¶¶ ⇋ ⊗

WW WW Travelodge SH
(701) 772-8151. **$69-$99.** 2100 S Washington St. I-29, exit 140 (DeMers Ave), 2.5 mi e, then 1.5 mi s. Int corridors. **Pets:** Small, dogs only. $3 daily fee/room. Designated rooms, service with restrictions, supervision.

ASK ⓢ ⊗ ⌂ ⊟ 💻 ⇋ ⊗

JAMESTOWN

WW WW Comfort Inn by Choice Hotels SH
(701) 252-7125. **$74-$104.** 811 20 St SW. I-94, exit 258 (US 281), just n, then just w. Int corridors. **Pets:** Accepted.

ASK ⓢ ⊗ ⊟ 💻 ⇋

AAA WW Ranch House Motel M
(701) 252-0222. **$35.** 408 Business Loop W. I-94, exit 258 (US 281), 0.8 mi n. Ext/int corridors. **Pets:** $35 deposit/room. Service with restrictions, supervision.

SAVE ⓢ ⊗ ⌂ ⇋

KENMARE

WW WW Quilt Inn SH
(801) 385-4100. **$50.** 1232 Central Ave N. Just n on US 52. Int corridors. **Pets:** Accepted.

ASK ⊗ ⌂ ⇋

MANDAN

Best Western Seven Seas Inn & Conference Center SH

(701) 663-7401. **$81.** 2611 Old Red Tr. I-94, exit 152, just nw. Int corridors. **Pets:** $25 deposit/room. Service with restrictions.

MEDORA

AmericInn Motel & Suites SH

(701) 623-4800. **$69-$227.** 75 E River Rd S. I-94, exit 24, just se of downtown. Int corridors. **Pets:** Other species. $12 one-time fee/room. Designated rooms, no service, supervision.

MINOT

Best Western Kelly Inn SH

(701) 852-4300. **$66-$149.** 1510 26th Ave SW. US 2 and 52 Bypass, at 16th St SW. Ext/int corridors. **Pets:** Other species. Designated rooms, service with restrictions, crate.

Comfort Inn SH

(701) 852-2201. **$64-$150.** 1515 22nd Ave SW. US 2 and 52 Bypass, at 16th St SW. Int corridors. **Pets:** Other species. Service with restrictions, supervision.

Dakota Inn SH

(701) 838-2700. **$54.** 2401 US 2 & 52 Bypass. Jct US 83, 1 mi w. Int corridors. **Pets:** Small, dogs only. Designated rooms, service with restrictions, supervision.

Days Inn SH

(701) 852-3646. **$52-$68.** 2100 4th St SW. Jct US 2 and 52 Bypass, just n. Int corridors. **Pets:** Medium, dogs only. Designated rooms, service with restrictions, supervision.

Holiday Inn Riverside Minot LH

(701) 852-2504. **$64-$104.** 2200 Burdick Expwy E. 1.3 mi e on US 2 business route (Burdick Expwy E). Int corridors. **Pets:** Small, dogs only. $50 one-time fee/pet. Designated rooms, service with restrictions, supervision.

International Inn LH

(701) 852-3161. **$65-$95.** 1505 N Broadway. 1.5 mi n on US 83. Int corridors. **Pets:** Designated rooms, supervision.

VALLEY CITY

AmericInn Lodge & Suites SH

(701) 845-5551. **$66-$155.** 280 Winter Show Rd SE. I-94, exit 292, just ne. Int corridors. **Pets:** $10 daily fee/room. Service with restrictions, supervision.

Super 8 Motel-Valley City M

(701) 845-1140. **$51-$66.** 860 11th St SW. I-94, exit 292, just nw. Int corridors. **Pets:** Accepted.

Wagon Wheel Inn & Suites SH

(701) 845-5333. **$52-$62.** 455 Winter Show Rd. I-94, exit 292, just ne. Ext/int corridors. **Pets:** Medium, dogs only. Designated rooms, service with restrictions, supervision.

WAHPETON

AmericInn Lodge & Suites SH

(701) 642-8365. **$75-$105, 3 day notice.** 2029 Two-Ten Dr. 1 mi n on SR 210 Bypass. Int corridors. **Pets:** Medium. $25 deposit/room. Designated rooms, service with restrictions, supervision.

Comfort Inn by Choice Hotels SH

(701) 642-1115. **$54-$74.** 209 13th St S. SR 13, 0.3 mi e of jct SR 210 Bypass. Int corridors. **Pets:** Other species. Designated rooms, service with restrictions, supervision.

Hospitality Inn & Suites SH

(701) 642-5000. **$59-$99.** 1800 Two-Ten Dr. 1 mi n on SR 210 Bypass. Int corridors. **Pets:** Medium. $25 deposit/room. Designated rooms, service with restrictions, supervision.

Wahpeton Super 8 SH

(701) 642-8731. **$55-$69.** 995 21st Ave N. 1.5 mi n on SR 210 Bypass. Int corridors. **Pets:** $5 one-time fee/room. Designated rooms, service with restrictions, supervision.

WATFORD CITY

McKenzie Inn M

(701) 444-3980. **$47-$52.** 132 SW 3rd St. US 85, just w. Ext corridors. **Pets:** Small, dogs only. Designated rooms, service with restrictions, supervision.

Roosevelt Inn & Suites SH

(701) 842-3686. **$48-$52.** 600 2nd Ave SW. US 85, 0.3 mi w. Int corridors. **Pets:** Designated rooms, service with restrictions, supervision.

WEST FARGO

West Fargo Days Inn SH

(701) 281-0000. **$65.** 525 E Main Ave. I-29, exit 65 (Main Ave), 2.3 mi w. Int corridors. **Pets:** Accepted.

WILLISTON

El Rancho Motor Hotel SH

(701) 572-6321. **$49-$54.** 1623 2nd Ave W. 1 mi n on US 2 and 85 N Bypass. Ext/int corridors. **Pets:** Accepted.

Marquis Plaza & Suites SH

(701) 774-3250. **$53-$110.** 1525 9th Ave NW. US 2 and 85, 4 mi e of jct US 85. Int corridors. **Pets:** Small, dogs only. $25 deposit/room. Designated rooms, service with restrictions, crate.

OHIO

AKRON

🚩 Days Inn Akron South/Airport **M**
(330) 644-1204. **Call for rates.** 3237 S Arlington Rd. I-77, exit 120, just s. Ext corridors. **Pets:** Accepted.
⊠ 🛢 🏊

🔷 🚩🚩🚩 Quality Inn Conference Center **SH**
(330) 644-7126. **$79-$129.** 2940 Chenoweth Rd. I-77, exit 120, just n. Int corridors. **Pets:** Accepted.
SAVE S₀ ⊠ 🐾 🛢 🖳 🏊

🚩🚩 Red Roof Inn-Akron South #0207 **M**
(330) 644-7748. **$47-$72.** 2939 S Arlington Rd. I-77, exit 120, just n. **Pets:** Accepted.
⊠

ALLIANCE

🚩🚩🚩🚩 Holiday Inn Express Hotel & Suites **SH**
(330) 821-6700. **$90-$99.** 2341 W State St. 2 mi w on US 62. Int corridors. **Pets:** Medium. $10 one-time fee/pet. Designated rooms, service with restrictions, crate.
ASK S₀ ⊠ 🐾 🛢 🖳 🏊

🔷 🚩🚩🚩 Super 8 Motel **M**
(330) 821-5688. **$49-$77.** 2330 W State St. 2 mi w on US 62. Ext corridors. **Pets:** $5 daily fee/pet. Service with restrictions, crate.
SAVE S₀ ⊠ 🐾 🛢 🏊

AMHERST

🚩🚩 Days Inn **M**
(440) 985-1428. **$45-$95.** 934 N Leavitt Rd. SR 58, 0.3 mi n of SR 2. Ext/int corridors. **Pets:** Accepted.
ASK S₀ ⊠ 🛢 🖳 🏊

ASHLAND

🔷 🚩🚩 Days Inn **M**
(419) 289-0101. **$40-$70.** 1423 CR 1575. I-71, exit 186, just w. Ext corridors. **Pets:** Service with restrictions, crate.
SAVE S₀ ⊠ 🛢 🖳 🏊

🚩🚩 The Surrey Inn **SH**
(419) 289-7700. **$59-$120, 3 day notice.** 1065 Claremont Ave. 1 mi s. Int corridors. **Pets:** Small, dogs only. $15 one-time fee/room. Designated rooms, service with restrictions, supervision.
ASK ⊠ 🛢 🖳

ASHTABULA

🔷 🚩 Cedars Motel **M**
(440) 992-5406. **$55-$75.** 2015 W Prospect Rd. Jct SR 11, 3 mi w on US 20. Ext corridors. **Pets:** Other species. $10 daily fee/pet. Service with restrictions, supervision.
SAVE ⊠ 🛢

🔷 🚩 Ho Hum Motel **M**
(440) 969-1136. **$55-$80.** 3801 N Ridge Rd W. I-90, exit 223, 3 mi n on SR 45, then 1 mi e on SR 20. Ext corridors. **Pets:** $5 daily fee/pet. Service with restrictions, crate.
SAVE ⊠ 🛢

ATHENS

🔷 🚩 Budget Host-Coach Inn **M**
(740) 594-2294. **$41-$85.** 100 Albany Rd (Hwy 50 W). US 50 W, just past Richland Ave exit; US 50 E, e on Township Rd 60. Ext corridors. **Pets:** Very small, dogs only. $10 daily fee/pet. Designated rooms, service with restrictions, supervision.
SAVE ⊠ 🛢

🔷 🚩🚩 Super 8 Motel **SH**
(740) 594-4900. **$50-$130, 21 day notice.** 2091 E State St. US 33, exit State St, 2.7 mi e. Int corridors. **Pets:** $5 daily fee/pet. Designated rooms, service with restrictions, crate.
SAVE S₀ ⊠ 🛢

AUSTINBURG

🚩🚩🚩 Comfort Inn-Ashtabula **SH** 🐾
(440) 275-2711. **$69-$99.** 1860 Austinburg Rd. I-90, exit 223, just n. Int corridors. **Pets:** Medium. $10 one-time fee/pet. Designated rooms, service with restrictions, supervision.
ASK S₀ ⊠ 🐾 🛢 🖳 🍴 🏊

AUSTINTOWN

Austintown Super 8 Motel M
(330) 793-7788. **$50-$89.** 5280 76 Dr. I-80, exit 223, just s on SR 46. Int corridors. **Pets:** Medium. $8 daily fee/pet. Service with restrictions, supervision.

Best Western Meander Inn SH
(330) 544-2378. **$69-$150.** 870 N Canfield-Niles Rd. I-80, exit 223, 0.3 mi s on SR 46. Int corridors. **Pets:** Accepted.

Econo Lodge M
(330) 270-2865. **$60-$85.** 5431 1/2 76th Dr. I-80, exit 223, just s on SR 46. Ext corridors. **Pets:** Accepted.

Motel 6–4066 M
(330) 793-9305. **$46-$61.** 5431 76 Dr. I-80, exit 223, just s on SR 46. Ext corridors. **Pets:** Accepted.

BEAVERCREEK

Residence Inn by Marriott SH
(937) 427-3914. **$109-$149.** 2779 Fairfield Commons. I-675, exit 17, just e, just s on New Germany-Trebein, then just e. Int corridors. **Pets:** Accepted.

BLUFFTON

Comfort Inn SH
(419) 358-6000. **$75-$99.** 117 Commerce Ln. I-75, exit 142, just w on SR 103. Int corridors. **Pets:** Medium, other species. $15 one-time fee/pet. Service with restrictions, supervision.

BOARDMAN

Days Inn M
(330) 758-2371. **$36-$88, 3 day notice.** 8392 Market St. I-76, exit 232, 1.8 mi n on SR 7. Ext corridors. **Pets:** Other species. $6 daily fee/pet. Service with restrictions, supervision.

Microtel Inn Youngstown SH
(330) 758-1816. **$45-$105.** 7393 South Ave. Jct I-680 and US 224, 0.3 mi w. Int corridors. **Pets:** Medium, other species. $25 one-time fee/pet. Service with restrictions, supervision.

Ramada Limited SH
(330) 549-0157. **$59-$79.** 9988 Market St. 0.5 mi n on SR 7. Int corridors. **Pets:** $10 daily fee/pet. Designated rooms, service with restrictions, supervision.

BOWLING GREEN

Days Inn M
(419) 352-5211. **$59-$99.** 1550 E Wooster St. I-75, exit 181, just w. Ext corridors. **Pets:** Large, other species. $10 one-time fee/pet. Service with restrictions, supervision.

Quality Inn & Suites SH
(419) 352-2521. **$59-$129.** 1630 E Wooster St. I-75, exit 181, just w. Int corridors. **Pets:** Medium, other species. $10 daily fee/room. No service.

BROOKVILLE

Brookville Days Inn M
(937) 833-4003. **$55.** 100 Parkview Dr. I-70, exit 21, just s. Ext corridors. **Pets:** Other species. $10 one-time fee/room. Designated rooms.

BRUNSWICK

Sleep Inn SH
(330) 273-1112. **$48-$72.** 1435 S Carpenter Rd. I-71, exit 226, just w. Ext corridors. **Pets:** Accepted.

CAMBRIDGE

Best Western Cambridge SH
(740) 439-3581. **$40-$80.** 1945 Southgate Pkwy. I-70, exit 178, 0.3 mi n on SR 209. Ext corridors. **Pets:** Accepted.

Budget Inn M
(740) 432-2304. **$30-$40.** 6405 Glenn Hwy. I-70, exit 176, e on US 40. Ext/int corridors. **Pets:** Small. $10 daily fee/pet. Designated rooms, service with restrictions, supervision.

Comfort Inn SH
(740) 435-3200. **$64-$135.** 2327 Southgate Pkwy. I-70, exit 178, just n on SR 209. Int corridors. **Pets:** Other species. $10 one-time fee/pet. Designated rooms, service with restrictions, supervision.

Days Inn-Cambridge SH
(740) 432-5691. **$49-$89, 3 day notice.** 2328 Southgate Pkwy. I-70, exit 178, just n on SR 209. Int corridors. **Pets:** Accepted.

Deer Creek Express M
(740) 432-6391. **$35-$69.** 2321 Southgate Pkwy. I-70, exit 178, just n on SR 209. Ext corridors. **Pets:** Small. $5 one-time fee/room. Designated rooms, service with restrictions, crate.

Holiday Inn Cambridge/Salt Fork Area SH
(740) 432-7313. **$89-$109.** 2248 Southgate Pkwy. I-70, exit 178, just n on SR 209. Int corridors. **Pets:** Medium. Service with restrictions, crate.

Super 8 Motel-Cambridge SH
(740) 435-8080. **$44-$89.** 8779 Georgetown Rd. I-70, exit 178, just n. Ext corridors. **Pets:** Other species. $5 daily fee/pet. Designated rooms, service with restrictions, supervision.

CANTON

Red Roof Inn #7019 M
(330) 499-1970. **$46-$74.** 5353 Inn Circle Ct NW. I-77, exit 109, just w on Everhard Rd. Ext corridors. **Pets:** Accepted.

Residence Inn by Marriott SH
(330) 493-0004. **$99-$129.** 5280 Broadmoor Cir NW. I-77, exit 109, 0.5 mi e on Everhard Rd. Int corridors. **Pets:** Other species. $200 one-time fee/room. Service with restrictions, crate.

CARROLLTON

Carrollton Days Inn SH
(330) 627-9314. **$81-$130, 7 day notice.** 1111 Canton Rd. On SR 43, 0.5 mi n of SR 39. Int corridors. **Pets:** $20 one-time fee/pet. Service with restrictions, crate.

CEDARVILLE

▼▼▼▼ Hearthstone Inn & Suites 🆂🅷
(937) 766-3000. **$94-$119.** 10 S Main St. I-70, exit 54, 11 mi s. Int corridors. **Pets:** Small, dogs only. $15 daily fee/pet. Supervision.
🅰🆂🅺 ✕ 🖥 🔲 💻

CELINA

🆔 ▼▼▼ Comfort Inn Grand Lake 🆂🅷
(419) 586-4656. **$69-$199, 30 day notice.** 1421 SR 703 E. Jct SR 29. Ext corridors. **Pets:** Small. $20 daily fee/pet. Designated rooms, service with restrictions, supervision.
🆂🅰🆅🅴 🆂🅳 ✕ 🖥 🔲 💻

CHILLICOTHE

▼▼▼ Adena Inn Chillicothe 🆂🅷
(740) 775-7000. **$59-$79.** 1250 N Bridge St. US 35, exit Bridge St, 0.8 mi n. Int corridors. **Pets:** $12 daily fee/room. Service with restrictions, supervision.
🅰🆂🅺 🆂🅳 ✕ 🖥 🔲 💻 ⊃

▼▼▼ Christopher Inn & Suites 🆂🅷
(740) 774-6835. **$65-$89.** 30 N Plaza Blvd. US 35, exit Bridge St. Int corridors. **Pets:** Small. Service with restrictions, crate.
🅰🆂🅺 🆂🅳 ✕ ♿ 🖥 🔲 💻 ⊃ ✕

▼▼▼ Comfort Inn 🆂🅷
(740) 775-3500. **Call for rates.** 20 N Plaza Blvd. Jct US 35 and 23 business route. Int corridors. **Pets:** Accepted.
✕ 🗐 🖥 🔲 💻 ⊃

CINCINNATI METROPOLITAN AREA

BATAVIA

▼▼▼▼ Fairfield Inn & Suites by Marriott Cincinnati 🆂🅷
(513) 947-9402. **$75-$95.** 4521 Eastgate Blvd. I-275, exit 63B (SR 32), 0.5 mi e to Eastgate Blvd exit, then 0.5 mi n. Int corridors. **Pets:** Accepted.
🅰🆂🅺 🆂🅳 ✕ 🗐 ♿ 🖥 🔲 💻 ⊃

🆔 ▼▼▼▼ Hampton Inn-Cincinnati Eastgate 🆂🅷
(513) 752-8584. **$71-$109.** 858 Eastgate North Dr. I-275, exit 63B (SR 32), just e, just n on Gleneste Withamsville Rd, then just w; behind Longhorn Steak House. Int corridors. **Pets:** Medium, other species. Service with restrictions, crate.
🆂🅰🆅🅴 🆂🅳 ✕ �figuresM 🗐 🖥 🔲 💻 ⊃

🆔 ▼▼▼▼ Holiday Inn-Cincinnati Eastgate 🆂🅷
(513) 752-4400. **$100-$129.** 4501 Eastgate Blvd. I-275, exit 63B (SR 32), 0.5 mi e to Eastgate Mall exit, then 0.5 mi n. Int corridors. **Pets:** Other species. Service with restrictions, crate.
🆂🅰🆅🅴 🆂🅳 ✕ 🗐 🖥 🔲 💻 🍴 ⊃ ✕

BLUE ASH

🆔 ▼▼▼▼ AmeriSuites (Cincinnati/Blue Ash) 🆂🅷
(513) 489-3666. **$79-$109.** 11435 Reed-Hartman Hwy. I-275, exit 47, 0.8 mi s. Int corridors. **Pets:** Accepted.
🆂🅰🆅🅴 🆂🅳 ✕ �figuresM 🗐 🖥 🔲 💻 ⊃

▼▼▼ Homestead Studio Suites Hotel-Cincinnati/Blue Ash 🆂🅷
(513) 985-9992. **$70-$85.** 4630 Creek Rd. I-275, exit 47, 2.3 mi s on Reed-Hartman Hwy, then just e. Int corridors. **Pets:** Accepted.
🅰🆂🅺 🆂🅳 ✕ 🗐 ♿ 🖥 🔲 💻 ⊃ ✕

▼ Red Roof Inn Northeast (Blue Ash) 🅼 🐾
(513) 793-8811. **$49-$76.** 5900 Pfeiffer Rd. I-71, exit 15, just w. Ext corridors. **Pets:** Medium. Service with restrictions, crate.
✕ �figuresM ♿ 🖥

▼▼▼ Residence Inn by Marriott-Blue Ash 🆂🅷 🐾
(513) 530-5060. **$129-$139.** 11401 Reed-Hartman Hwy. I-275, exit 47, 0.8 mi s. Ext corridors. **Pets:** Large, other species. $75 one-time fee/room. Service with restrictions.
🅰🆂🅺 🆂🅳 ✕ �figuresM 🗐 ♿ 🖥 🔲 💻 ⊃ ✕

▼▼▼ TownePlace Suites by Marriott Blue Ash 🆂🅷 🐾
(513) 469-8222. **$89-$94.** 4650 Cornell Rd. I-275, exit 47, 0.9 mi s on Reed-Hartman Hwy, then just w. Int corridors. **Pets:** Large, other species. $75 one-time fee/room. Service with restrictions.
🅰🆂🅺 🆂🅳 ✕ ♿ 🖥 🔲 💻 ⊃

CHERRY GROVE

▼▼▼ Best Western Clermont 🅼
(513) 528-7702. **Call for rates.** 4004 Williams Dr. I-275, exit 65, just w, then just s. Ext corridors. **Pets:** Accepted.
✕ 🗐 ♿ 🔲 💻 ⊃

▼▼▼ Red Roof Inn Cincinnati East 🅼
(513) 528-2741. **$45-$70.** 4035 Mt. Carmel-Tobasco Rd. I-275, exit 65, just w on SR 125, then just n. Ext corridors. **Pets:** Accepted.
✕ ♿ 🖥

CINCINNATI

🆔 ▼▼▼▼ Four Points by Sheraton Cincinnati Downtown 🅻🅷 🐾
(513) 357-5800. **$59-$169.** 150 W 5th St. Between Elm and Race sts. Int corridors. **Pets:** Other species. $65 deposit/pet, $35 one-time fee/pet. Designated rooms, service with restrictions, supervision.
🆂🅰🆅🅴 🆂🅳 ✕ 🗐 ♿ 🖥 🔲 💻 🍴 ⊃

🆔 ▼▼▼▼ Millennium Hotel Cincinnati 🅻🅷 🐾
(513) 352-2100. **$59-$169.** 141 W 6th St. Between Elm and Race sts. Int corridors. **Pets:** Large, other species. $65 deposit/pet, $35 one-time fee/pet. Designated rooms, service with restrictions, supervision.
🆂🅰🆅🅴 🆂🅳 ✕ ♿ 🖥 🔲 🍴 ⊃

🆔 ▼▼▼▼ The Vernon Manor Hotel 🅻🅷
(513) 281-3300. **$115-$225.** 400 Oak St. I-71, exit 2 (Reading Rd) northbound, 1 mi n; exit 3 (Taft Rd) southbound, just w, just on Reading Rd, then just w. Int corridors. **Pets:** Medium. $75 deposit/room, $10 daily fee/room. Service with restrictions, crate.
🆂🅰🆅🅴 🆂🅳 ✕ 🗐 ♿ 🖥 🔲 🍴

🆔 ▼▼▼▼ The Westin Cincinnati 🅻🅷 🐾
(513) 621-7700. **$153-$295.** 21 E 5th St. Between Vine and Walnut sts. Int corridors. **Pets:** Medium, dogs only. Service with restrictions, supervision.
🆂🅰🆅🅴 ✕ �figuresM 🗐 ♿ 🔲 🍴 ⊃

FAIRFIELD

▼▼▼ Holiday Inn Express 🆂🅷
(513) 860-2900. **$87-$105.** 6755 Fairfield Business Park Dr. I-275, exit 41 (SR 4), 1.5 mi n. Int corridors. **Pets:** Small. Designated rooms, service with restrictions, supervision.
🅰🆂🅺 🆂🅳 ✕ �figuresM 🗐 ♿ 🖥 🔲 💻

FOREST PARK

🆔 ▼▼▼▼ AmeriSuites (Cincinnati/North) 🆂🅷
(513) 825-9035. **$89-$119.** 12001 Chase Plaza Dr. I-275, exit 39, just s, then just w. Int corridors. **Pets:** Accepted.
🆂🅰🆅🅴 ✕ 🗐 🖥 🔲 💻 ⊃

▼▼▼▼ Lees Inn & Suites Cincinnati SH
(513) 825-9600. **Call for rates.** 11967 Chase Plaza Dr. I-275, exit 39, just s on Winton Rd. Int corridors. **Pets:** Accepted.
⊠ ⊾M ⟨⟩ 🖬 💻 ⤳ ⊠

HAMILTON

◈◈◈ ▼▼▼▼ The Hamiltonian Hotel SH
(513) 896-6200. **$72-$82.** 1 Riverfront Plaza. Just off High St, on Front St. Int corridors. **Pets:** Accepted.
SAVE S⚡ ⊠ ⟨⟩ 🖬 💻 ⑪ ⤳

HARRISON

◈◈◈ ▼▼▼ Comfort Inn SH
(513) 367-9666. **$59-$94.** 391 Comfort Dr. I-74, exit 1, just n on New Haven Rd, then just e. Int corridors. **Pets:** Small. $20 one-time fee/pet. Designated rooms, service with restrictions, supervision.
SAVE S⚡ ⊠ ⊾M ⟨⟩ 🖬 💻 ⤳

MASON

◈◈◈ ▼▼▼▼ AmeriSuites (Cincinnati/Deerfield Crossing) SH
(513) 754-0003. **$99-$149.** 5070 Natorp Blvd. I-71, exit 19, 0.5 mi w. Int corridors. **Pets:** Medium. $10 daily fee/pet. Designated rooms, service with restrictions, supervision.
SAVE ⊠ ⊾M ⟨⟩ 🖬 💻 ⤳

◈◈◈ ▼▼▼ Baymont Inn & Suites Cincinnati-Mason/near Kings Island SH
(513) 459-1111. **$54-$109.** 9918 Escort Dr. I-71, exit 19, just w, then just s. Int corridors. **Pets:** Accepted.
SAVE S⚡ ⊠ ⟨⟩ 🖬 💻 ⤳

◈◈◈ ▼▼▼ The Inn at Kings Island SH
(513) 398-8075. **$89-$229.** 5589 Kings Mills Rd. I-71, exit 25, just w, then just s. Ext corridors. **Pets:** Accepted.
SAVE S⚡ ⊠ ⊾M ⟨⟩ 🖬 💻 ⤳ ⊠

◈◈◈ ▼▼▼ Microtel Inn & Suites SH
(513) 754-1500. **$49-$159.** 5324 Beach Blvd. I-71, exit 25, just nw. Int corridors. **Pets:** Small. $20 one-time fee/pet. Designated rooms, service with restrictions, supervision.
SAVE S⚡ ⊠ ⊾M ⟨⟩ 🖬 💻

◈◈◈ ▼▼▼ Ramada Limited Kings Island Area SH
(513) 336-7911. **$55-$80.** 9665 Mason-Montgomery Rd. I-71, exit 19, just w. Int corridors. **Pets:** Small, dogs only. Designated rooms, no service, supervision.
SAVE S⚡ ⊠ ⊾M ⟨⟩ 🖬 💻 ⤳

▼▼▼ Red Roof Inn-Kings Island M
(513) 398-3633. **$30-$120.** 9847 Bards Rd. I-71, exit 19, just w. Ext corridors. **Pets:** Medium. Supervision.
SAVE S⚡ ⊠ ⊾M ⟨⟩ ⟨⟩ 🖬 💻 ⤳

▼▼▼ TownePlace Suites by Marriott SH ❀
(513) 774-0610. **$79-$139.** 9369 Waterstone Blvd. I-71, exit 19, 0.5 mi e on Fields-Ertel Rd, then 0.9 mi n. Int corridors. **Pets:** Other species. $75 one-time fee/room. Service with restrictions, crate.
ASK S⚡ ⊠ ⊾M ⟨⟩ 🖬 💻 ⤳

MIDDLETOWN

◈◈◈ ▼▼▼▼ Best Western SH
(513) 424-3551. **$65-$145, 3 day notice.** 6475 Culbertson Rd. I-75, exit 32. Int corridors. **Pets:** Dogs only. $5 daily fee/room, $25 one-time fee/room. Designated rooms, service with restrictions, supervision.
SAVE S⚡ ⟨⟩ 🖬 💻 ⤳

▼▼▼▼ Fairfield Inn by Marriott SH
(513) 424-5444. **$75-$95.** 6750 Roosevelt Pkwy. I-75, exit 32, 0.5 mi w on SR 122. Int corridors. **Pets:** Accepted.
ASK S⚡ ⊠ ⊾M ⟨⟩ 🖬 ⤳

◈◈◈ ▼▼▼▼ The Manchester Inn & Conference Center SH
(513) 422-5481. **$74-$145.** 1027 Manchester Ave. Just w of SR 4 and 73. Int corridors. **Pets:** Small. $20 deposit/room. Service with restrictions, crate.
SAVE S⚡ ⊠ 🖬 💻 ⑪

▼▼▼ Ramada Inn Middletown SH ❀
(513) 424-1201. **$79-$85.** 6147 W SR 122. I-75, exit 32, just e. Int corridors. **Pets:** Medium. $10 daily fee/pet. Service with restrictions.
ASK S⚡ ⊠ ⟨⟩ 🖬 💻 ⑪ ⤳

▼▼▼ Super 8 Motel Middletown SH
(513) 422-4888. **$49-$69.** 3553 Commerce Dr. I-75, exit 32, just e, then just n. Int corridors. **Pets:** $10 one-time fee/room. Service with restrictions, supervision.
ASK S⚡ ⊠ 🖬

MOUNT ORAB

◈◈◈ ▼▼▼▼ Best Western Mt. Orab Inn SH
(937) 444-6666. **$59-$99.** 100 Leininger St. Jct US 68 and SR 32, just n on US 68. Int corridors. **Pets:** Accepted.
SAVE S⚡ ⊠ ⟨⟩ 🖬 💻 ⤳

NORWOOD

◈◈◈ ▼▼▼ Howard Johnson East SH
(513) 631-8500. **$60-$74.** 5410 Ridge Rd. I-71, exit 8 southbound; exit 8B northbound, 0.4 mi nw. Int corridors. **Pets:** Other species. $25 deposit/room. Crate.
SAVE S⚡ ⊠ 🖬 💻 ⑪ ⤳

SHARONVILLE

◈◈◈ ▼▼▼▼ Arcadia Residential Suites SH ❀
(513) 354-1000. **$99-$169.** 11180 Dowlin Dr. I-75, exit 15, just e on Sharon Rd, then just n. Int corridors. **Pets:** Small, other species. $50 one-time fee/room. Crate.
SAVE S⚡ ⊠ ⟨⟩ 🖬 💻 ⤳

▼▼▼▼ Homewood Suites by Hilton-Cincinnati North SH ❀
(513) 772-8888. **$89-$139.** 2670 E Kemper Rd. I-275, exit 44, jct Mosteller Rd. Int corridors. **Pets:** Other species. $15 daily fee/room. Service with restrictions.
ASK S⚡ ⊠ 🖬 💻 ⤳ ⊠

▼▼▼ Red Roof Inn-Sharon Road #7171 M
(513) 771-5552. **$48-$69.** 2301 E Sharon Rd. I-75, exit 15, just e. Ext corridors. **Pets:** Large, other species. Service with restrictions, supervision.
⊠ ⟨⟩ 🖬

▼▼▼▼ Residence Inn by Marriott SH ❀
(513) 771-2525. **$89-$209.** 11689 Chester Rd. I-75, exit 15, 0.3 mi w on Sharon Rd, then 1 mi n. Ext corridors. **Pets:** $75 one-time fee/room. Service with restrictions, crate.
ASK ⊠ ⊾M ⟨⟩ 🖬 💻 ⤳ ⊠

◈◈◈ ▼▼▼▼ Woodfield Suites Cincinnati-Sharonville SH
(513) 771-0300. **$99-$119.** 11029 Dowlin Dr. I-75, exit 15, just e. Int corridors. **Pets:** $50 deposit/room. Designated rooms, service with restrictions, supervision.
SAVE S⚡ ⊠ ⊾M ⟨⟩ ⟨⟩ 🖬 💻 ⤳ ⊠

WEST CHESTER

▼▼◆▼▼ **Staybridge Suites Cincinnati North** 🆂🅷 ❖
(513) 874-1900. **$98-$159.** 8955 Lakota Dr W. I-75, exit 19, just w on Union Center Blvd, then just n. Int corridors. **Pets:** Service with restrictions, crate.

A$K 🆂🅳 ☒ ᯤ 🕭 ❤ 🍴 🖵 ≈ ☒

WILMINGTON

▼▼◆▼▼ **Holiday Inn Express** 🆂🅷
(937) 382-5858. **$75-$109.** 155 Holiday Dr. 1.6 mi e on US 22. Int corridors. **Pets:** Medium. $20 one-time fee/room. Service with restrictions, supervision.

A$K 🆂🅳 ☒ ᯤ 🕭 ❤ 🍴 🖵 ≈ ☒

🆑 ▼▼◆▼▼ **Ramada Plaza-Wilmington** 🅻🅷
(937) 283-3200. **$109.** 123 Gano Rd. I-71, exit 50, just w. Int corridors. **Pets:** Other species. $250 deposit/room. Service with restrictions, supervision.

SAVE 🆂🅳 ☒ ᯤ 🕭 ❤ 🖵 🍴 ≈

CLEVELAND METROPOLITAN AREA

BEACHWOOD

▼▼◆▼▼ **Holiday Inn-Beachwood** 🆂🅷 ❖
(216) 831-3300. **$69-$109.** 3750 Orange Pl. I-271, exit Chagrin Blvd, just e. Int corridors. **Pets:** Small. $50 deposit/room. Designated rooms, service with restrictions, crate.

A$K 🆂🅳 ☒ 🕭 ❤ 🖵 🍴 ≈ ☒

▼▼ ▼▼ **Homestead Studio Suites**
Hotel-Cleveland/Beachwood 🆂🅷
(216) 896-5555. **$70-$85.** 3625 Orange Pl. I-271, exit Chagrin Blvd, just e. Int corridors. **Pets:** Accepted.

A$K 🆂🅳 ☒ ᯤ 🕭 🖵

▼▼◆▼▼ **Residence Inn by Marriot**
Cleveland-Beachwood 🆂🅷
(216) 831-3030. **$99-$169.** 3628 Park East Dr. Jct US 422 and I-271, exit Chagrin Blvd, just w. Int corridors. **Pets:** Other species. $75 one-time fee/room. Service with restrictions, crate.

A$K 🆂🅳 ☒ ᯤ 🕭 ❤ 🖵 ≈ ☒

BROADVIEW HEIGHTS

🆎 ▼▼ **Tallyho-tel** 🅼
(440) 526-0640. **$34-$59.** 4501 E Royalton Rd. I-77 and SR 82, exit 149B southbound; exit 149 northbound. Ext corridors. **Pets:** Accepted.

SAVE 🆂🅳 ☒ 🕭 ≈

CLEVELAND

🆎 ▼▼◆▼▼ **Baymont Inn & Suites Cleveland-Airport** 🆂🅷
(216) 251-8500. **$69-$104.** 4222 W 150th St. I-71, exit 240, just n. Int corridors. **Pets:** Other species. Supervision.

SAVE 🆂🅳 ☒ 🕭 🖵

🆎 ▼▼◆▼▼ **Cleveland Airport Marriott** 🅻🅷
(216) 252-5333. **$109-$189.** 4277 W 150th St. I-71, exit 240, just s. Int corridors. **Pets:** Accepted.

SAVE ☒ ᯤ ❤ 🕭 🖵 🍴 ≈

🆎 ▼▼◆▼▼ **InterContinental Hotel & Conference**
Center 🅻🅷
(216) 707-4100. **$209-$349.** 9801 Carnegie Ave. Northeast corner of Carnegie Ave and E 96th St. Int corridors. **Pets:** Small. $250 deposit/room, $50 one-time fee/pet. Service with restrictions, supervision.

SAVE 🆂🅳 ☒ ᯤ 🕭 ❤ 🖵 🍴 ☒

▼▼◆▼▼ **Residence Inn by Marriott** 🆂🅷
(216) 443-9043. **$99-$169.** 527 Prospect Ave. Int corridors. **Pets:** Accepted.

A$K 🆂🅳 ☒ 🕭 🖵 ☒

🆎 ▼▼◆▼▼ **The Ritz-Carlton, Cleveland** 🅻🅷 ❖
(216) 623-1300. **$259-$279.** 1515 W 3rd St. In Tower City Center (3rd St side). Int corridors. **Pets:** Small, other species. $50 daily fee/pet. Designated rooms.

SAVE ☒ ᯤ ❤ 🕭 🍴 ≈ ☒

▼▼◆▼▼ **Sheraton Cleveland Airport Hotel** 🆂🅷
(216) 267-1500. **$69-$200.** 5300 Riverside Dr. I-71, exit 237, follow signs; just s of I-480 on SR 237. Int corridors. **Pets:** Accepted.

A$K 🆂🅳 ☒ ᯤ 🕭 ❤ 🕭 🖵 🍴 ≈ ☒

INDEPENDENCE

🆎 ▼▼◆▼▼ **AmeriSuites (Cleveland/Independence)** 🆂🅷
(216) 328-1060. **$89-$93.** 6025 Jefferson Dr. I-77, exit Rockside Rd, just w to W Creek Rd, then just n. Int corridors. **Pets:** Medium, other species. $10 daily fee/room. Designated rooms, service with restrictions, crate.

SAVE ☒ ᯤ 🕭 ❤ 🕭 🖵 ≈

🆎 ▼▼ ▼▼ **Baymont Inn & Suites**
Cleveland-Independence 🆂🅷
(216) 447-1133. **$59-$79.** 6161 Quarry Ln. I-77, exit Rockside Rd, just e. Int corridors. **Pets:** Large, other species. Designated rooms, service with restrictions, supervision.

SAVE 🆂🅳 ☒ ᯤ 🕭 🖵

▼▼◆▼▼ **Clarion Hotel & Conference Center Cleveland**
South 🆂🅷
(216) 524-0700. **$59-$189.** 5300 Rockside Rd. I-77, exit Rockside Rd, just w. Int corridors. **Pets:** Other species. $25 deposit/room, $10 daily fee/pet. Service with restrictions.

A$K 🆂🅳 ☒ ᯤ 🕭 🖵 🍴 ≈ ☒

▼▼ ▼▼ **Red Roof Inn #7028** 🅼 ❖
(216) 447-0030. **$56-$72.** 6020 Quarry Ln. I-77, exit Rockside Rd, just e. Ext corridors. **Pets:** Large, other species. Service with restrictions, supervision.

☒ ᯤ 🕭 🕭

▼▼◆▼▼ **Residence Inn by Marriott** 🆂🅷
(216) 520-1450. **$99-$139.** 5101 W Creek Rd. I-77, exit Rockside Rd, just w to W Creek Rd, then just n. Ext corridors. **Pets:** Large, other species. $75 one-time fee/room. Service with restrictions, crate.

A$K 🆂🅳 ☒ ᯤ 🕭 🕭 🖵 ≈ ☒

LAKEWOOD

▼▼ **Days Inn** 🆂🅷
(216) 226-4800. **$59-$79.** 12019 Lake Ave. I-90, exit 166, 1 mi n on W 117th St, then just w. **Pets:** Accepted.

A$K 🆂🅳

▼ Travelodge 🆂🅷
(216) 221-9000. **$59-$79.** 11837 Edgewater Dr. I-90, exit 166, 1 mi n on W 117th St, then just w. Int corridors. **Pets:** Accepted.
⊠ 🅱 💻

MACEDONIA

🔷 ▼▼▼ Baymont Inn & Suites
　　　　 Cleveland-Macedonia 🆂🅷
(330) 468-5400. **$70-$125.** 268 E Highland Rd. I-271, exit 18, just s; I-80/90 (Ohio Tpke), exit 180, just n. Int corridors. **Pets:** Medium, other species. $50 deposit/room. Designated rooms, service with restrictions, supervision.
🆂🅰🆅🅴 🆂💲 ⊠ 🆕 🅰 🅴 🅱 💻 🌊

🔷 ▼▼ Cleveland/Akron Travelodge 🅼
(330) 467-1516. **$45-$85.** 275 Highland Rd. I-271, exit 18, just s; I-80/90 (Ohio Tpke), exit 180, 3 mi n. Ext corridors. **Pets:** Accepted.
🆂🅰🆅🅴 🆂💲 ⊠ 🅰 🅱 💻 🌊

▼ Knights Inn-Cleveland/Macedonia 🅼
(330) 467-1981. **$45-$75.** 240 E Highland Rd. I-271, exit 18, just s; I-80/90 (Ohio Tpke), exit 180, 3 mi n. Ext corridors. **Pets:** Medium. $5 daily fee/room. Service with restrictions, supervision.
🅰💲🅺 🆂💲 ⊠ 🅱 💻 🌊

MAYFIELD HEIGHTS

🔷 ▼▼ Baymont Inn & Suites-Cleveland (Mayfield
　　　　 Heights) 🆂🅷 🐾
(440) 442-8400. **$74-$89.** 1421 Golden Gate Blvd. I-271, exit 34, 0.3 mi w off US 322. Int corridors. **Pets:** Large, other species. $10 daily fee/pet. Service with restrictions, supervision.
🆂🅰🆅🅴 🆂💲 ⊠ 🅰 🅱 💻

MEDINA

🔷 ▼ Best Value Inn Cleveland-Medina 🅼
(330) 722-4335. **$56-$89, 14 day notice.** 5200 Montville Dr. I-71, exit 218, just e. Ext corridors. **Pets:** Accepted.
🆂🅰🆅🅴 🆂💲 ⊠ 🅱 🌊

🔷 ▼▼ Best Western Medina Inn 🆂🅷
(330) 725-4571. **$36-$41.** 2875 Medina Rd. I-71, exit 218, just e. Int corridors. **Pets:** Accepted.
🆂🅰🆅🅴 🆂💲 ⊠ 🅱 💻 🌊

MIDDLEBURG HEIGHTS

🔷 ▼▼▼ Comfort Inn-Cleveland Airport 🆂🅷
(440) 234-3131. **$69-$109.** 17550 Rosbough Dr. I-71, exit 235, 0.3 mi w to Engle Rd, then 0.3 mi n. Int corridors. **Pets:** $10 daily fee/room, $35 one-time fee/room. Service with restrictions, supervision.
🆂🅰🆅🅴 🆂💲 ⊠ 🆕 🅱 💻 🌊

▼▼ Red Roof Inn-Middleburg Heights #7060 🆂🅷
(440) 243-2441. **$50-$72.** 17555 Bagley Rd. I-71, exit 235, just w. Ext/int corridors. **Pets:** Small. Service with restrictions, supervision.
⊠ 🅴 🅱

▼▼▼ Residence Inn by Marriott 🆂🅷
(440) 234-6688. **$99-$139.** 17525 Rosbough Dr. I-71, exit 235, just w on Bagley Rd, then just n on Engle Rd. Ext/int corridors. **Pets:** Other species. $75 one-time fee/room. Service with restrictions.
🅰💲🅺 🆂💲 ⊠ 🅴 🅱 💻 🆇

▼▼▼ TownePlace Suites 🆂🅷
(440) 816-9300. **$109-$139.** 7325 S Engle Rd. I-71, exit 235, just w on Bagley Rd. Int corridors. **Pets:** Accepted.
🅰💲🅺 🆂💲 ⊠ 🅴 🅱 💻 🌊

NORTH OLMSTED

▼▼ Homestead Studio Suites Hotel-Cleveland/Airport/North
　　　 Olmsted 🆂🅷
(440) 777-8585. **$50-$65.** 24851 Country Club Blvd. I-480, exit 6B, just n on SR 252. Ext corridors. **Pets:** Other species. $75 one-time fee/pet. Service with restrictions, supervision.
🅰💲🅺 🆂💲 ⊠ 🆕🅼 🆕 🅴 🅱 💻

🔷 ▼▼▼ Radisson Hotel Cleveland Airport 🆂🅷
(440) 734-5060. **$89-$139.** 25070 Country Club Blvd. I-480, exit 6B, just n on SR 252. Int corridors. **Pets:** Other species. $50 deposit/room. Service with restrictions.
🆂🅰🆅🅴 🆂💲 ⊠ 🆕🅼 🆕 🅱 💻 🍽 🌊 🆇

NORTH RIDGEVILLE

🔷 ▼ Travelers Inn, Cleveland/North Ridgeville 🅼
(440) 327-6311. **$40-$56.** 32751 Lorain Rd. I-80, exit 152, 0.6 mi ne on SR 10. Ext corridors. **Pets:** Medium, other species. $10 daily fee/pet. Service with restrictions, supervision.
🆂🅰🆅🅴 🆂💲 ⊠ 💻

SOLON

▼▼▼ Hampton Inn 🆂🅷
(440) 542-0400. **$89-$109, 7 day notice.** 6035 Enterprise Pkwy. US 422, exit Harper Rd, 0.6 mi s, then 0.4 mi e. Int corridors. **Pets:** Service with restrictions, crate.
🆂💲 ⊠ 🆕🅼 🆕 🅴 🅱 💻 🌊

STRONGSVILLE

▼▼ Motel 6-Strongsville #1497 🅼
(440) 238-0170. **$41-$55.** 15385 Royalton Rd. I-71, exit 231A, just e; I-76 (Ohio Tpke), exit 161, 1 mi s. Ext corridors. **Pets:** Accepted.
🆂💲 ⊠ 🆕

TWINSBURG

🔷 ▼▼ Twinsburg Super 8 Motel 🆂🅷
(330) 425-2889. **$45-$80.** 8848 Twins Hills Dr. I-480, exit 36, just w on SR 82. Int corridors. **Pets:** Other species. $5 daily fee/pet. Service with restrictions, supervision.
🆂🅰🆅🅴 🆂💲 ⊠ 💻

WESTLAKE

▼▼ Red Roof Inn-Westlake #7094 🅼
(440) 892-7920. **$52-$80.** 29595 Clemens Rd. I-90, exit 156, just n. Ext corridors. **Pets:** Medium, other species. Service with restrictions, supervision.
⊠ 🆕 🅱

▼▼ Residence Inn by Marriott 🆂🅷
(440) 892-2254. **$89-$139.** 30100 Clemens Rd. I-90, exit 156, just n. Ext corridors. **Pets:** Accepted.
🅰💲🅺 🆂💲 ⊠ 🆕 🅱 💻 🌊 🆇

WICKLIFFE

▼▼▼ Clarion Hotel Cleveland East 🆂🅷
(440) 585-2750. **Call for rates.** 28500 Euclid Ave. I-90, exit 186, just n. Int corridors. **Pets:** Other species. $10 daily fee/room. Service with restrictions, crate.
⊠ 🆕 🅱 💻 🍽 🌊 🆇

WILLOUGHBY

▼▼▼ Red Roof Inn-East #7053 🅼 🐾
(440) 946-9872. **$49-$87.** 4166 SR 306. I-90, exit 193, just s. Ext corridors. **Pets:** Other species. Service with restrictions, crate.
⊠ 🆕 🅴 🅱

END METROPOLITAN AREA

CLYDE

◆◆◆ **Red Roof Inn** [SH]
(419) 547-6660. **$54-$109.** 1363 W McPherson Hwy. 1 mi w on SR 20. Int corridors. **Pets:** Medium, dogs only. $50 deposit/pet. Designated rooms, service with restrictions, supervision.
[A$K] [S/D] ⊠ [♿M] ♿ ▣ 🏊

COLUMBUS METROPOLITAN AREA

COLUMBUS

[AAA] ◆◆◆ **AmeriSuites (Columbus/Worthington)** [SH]
(614) 846-4355. **$109.** 7490 Vantage Dr. I-270, exit 23, just ne. Int corridors. **Pets:** Small, other species. Service with restrictions, supervision.
[SAVE] ⊠ [♿M] 🦻 ▣ ☕ 🏊

[AAA] ◆◆◆ **Baymont Inn & Suites-Polaris** [SH] 🐾
(614) 791-9700. **$79-$159.** 8400 Lyra Dr. I-71, exit 121, just w. Int corridors. **Pets:** Large. $25 one-time fee/room. Service with restrictions, supervision.
[SAVE] [S/D] ⊠ ▣ ☕ 🏊

[AAA] ◆◆◆ **Best Western Columbus North** [SH]
(614) 888-8230. **$63.** 888 E Dublin-Granville Rd. I-71, exit 117, 0.5 mi w on SR 161. Int corridors. **Pets:** Small, other species. $25 deposit/room. Service with restrictions, crate.
[SAVE] [S/D] ⊠ ♿ ▣ ☕ 🍴 🏊 ✂

[AAA] ◆◆◆ **Columbus Marriott North** [SH]
(614) 885-1885. **$99-$169.** 6500 Doubletree Ave. I-71, exit 117, 0.3 mi w on SR 161, then 0.8 mi on Busch Blvd to Kingsmill Pkwy. Int corridors. **Pets:** Dogs only. $50 one-time fee/room. Designated rooms, service with restrictions, supervision.
[SAVE] ⊠ [♿M] 🦻 ♿ ▣ ☕ 🍴 🏊 ✂

◆◆ **Cross Country Inn Airport** [M]
(614) 237-3403. **$69-$89.** 4240 International Gateway. At Port Columbus International Airport. Ext corridors. **Pets:** Other species. Service with restrictions, supervision.
[A$K] [S/D] ⊠ ♿ 🏊

[AAA] ◆◆ **Days Inn Fairgrounds** [M]
(614) 299-4300. **$50-$80.** 1700 Clara St. I-71, exit 111, just w. Ext corridors. **Pets:** Dogs only. $10 daily fee/room. Service with restrictions.
[SAVE] [S/D] ⊠ ▣ ☕ 🏊

◆◆◆ **Doubletree Guest Suites** [LH]
(614) 228-4600. **$99-$169.** 50 S Front St. Corner of Front and State sts, just n. Int corridors. **Pets:** Accepted.
⊠ 🦻 ▣ ☕ 🍴

◆◆◆ **Drury Inn & Suites-Columbus Convention Center** [SH]
(614) 221-7008. **$94-$145.** 88 E Nationwide Blvd. 0.3 mi n on US 23. Int corridors. **Pets:** Large, other species. Service with restrictions, supervision.
[A$K] ⊠ [♿M] 🦻 ♿ ▣ ☕ 🏊

[AAA] ◆◆◆ **Holiday Inn Columbus East** [SH]
(614) 868-1380. **$99-$209.** 4560 Hilton Corporate Dr. I-70, exit 107. Int corridors. **Pets:** Other species. $25 one-time fee/room. Designated rooms, service with restrictions.
[SAVE] [S/D] ⊠ [♿M] ♿ ▣ ☕ 🍴 🏊 ✂

[AAA] ◆◆◆ **Holiday Inn-Columbus/Worthington Area** [LH]
(614) 885-3334. **$99-$139.** 175 Hutchinson Ave. I-270, exit 23, just n of jct US 23 N. Int corridors. **Pets:** Accepted.
[SAVE] [S/D] ⊠ [♿M] 🦻 ♿ ▣ ☕ 🍴 🏊 ✂

[AAA] ◆◆◆ **Holiday Inn on the Lane** [SH] 🐾
(614) 294-4848. **$92-$99.** 328 W Lane Ave. 0.5 mi e of SR 315, exit Lane Ave. Int corridors. **Pets:** Service with restrictions, crate.
[SAVE] [S/D] ⊠ [♿M] 🦻 ▣ ☕ 🍴 🏊 ✂

[AAA] ◆◆ **Knights Inn-Columbus East** [M]
(614) 864-0600. **$50-$90.** 4320 Groves Rd. I-70, exit 107, just sw. Ext corridors. **Pets:** Medium. $35 deposit/pet. Service with restrictions, crate.
[SAVE] [S/D] ⊠ ▣

◆◆ **Microtel Inn-Columbus/Worthington** [SH]
(614) 436-0556. **$43-$73.** 7500 Vantage Dr. I-270, exit 23, just n of US 23 N. Int corridors. **Pets:** Other species. $15 one-time fee/pet. Service with restrictions, supervision.
[A$K] [S/D] ⊠ [♿M] ▣

◆◆ **Motel 6 OSU #1491** [M]
(614) 846-8520. **$41-$51.** 750 Morse Rd. I-71, exit 116. Ext corridors. **Pets:** Accepted.
[S/D] ⊠ [♿M] ♿

◆◆ **Red Roof Inn-Downtown #7262** [SH]
(614) 224-6539. **$87-$115.** 111 E Nationwide Blvd. Nationwide Blvd at Third St. Int corridors. **Pets:** Medium. Service with restrictions, crate.
⊠ [♿M] 🦻 ♿ ▣

◆◆ **Red Roof Inn-OSU #7121** [SH]
(614) 267-9941. **$60-$74.** 441 Ackerman Rd. SR 315, exit Ackerman Rd, 0.3 mi e. Ext corridors. **Pets:** Large, other species. Service with restrictions.
⊠ ♿

◆◆ **Red Roof Inn-West #7009** [M]
(614) 878-9245. **$50-$78.** 5001 Renner Rd. I-70, exit 91 eastbound; exit 91B westbound, just nw. Ext corridors. **Pets:** Medium. Service with restrictions, supervision.
⊠ [♿M] ♿ ▣

◆◆ **Red Roof Inn-Worthington #7310** [SH]
(614) 846-3001. **$54-$70.** 7480 N High St. I-270, exit 23, jct US 23 N, just n. Ext/int corridors. **Pets:** Large, other species. Service with restrictions, supervision.
⊠ ♿ ▣

◆◆◆ **Residence Inn by Marriott** [SH]
(614) 885-0799. **$69-$159.** 7300 Huntington Park Dr. I-270, exit 23, just e of Vantage Dr. Int corridors. **Pets:** Accepted.
[A$K] [S/D] ⊠ ♿ ▣ ☕ 🏊 ✂

◆◆◆ **The Residence Inn by Marriott-Columbus North** [SH]
(614) 431-1819. **$89-$139.** 6191 W Zumstein Dr. I-71, exit 117, just nw. Ext corridors. **Pets:** Accepted.
[A$K] [S/D] ⊠ ♿ ▣ ☕ 🏊 ✂

◆◆◆ **Residence Inn by Marriott-Columbus Southeast** [SH]
(614) 864-8844. **$129-$189.** 2084 S Hamilton Rd. I-70, exit 107, just e. Ext corridors. **Pets:** Accepted.
[A$K] [S/D] ⊠ [♿M] ♿ ▣ ☕ 🏊 ✂

◆◆◆ **Residence Inn by Marriott Easton** [SH]
(614) 414-1000. **Call for rates.** 3999 Easton Loop W. I-270, exit 33, 1 mi w, then just n. Int corridors. **Pets:** Accepted.
⊠ ♿ ▣ ☕ 🏊 ✂

▼▼▼ **Sheraton Suites Columbus** 〔LH〕 🐾
(614) 436-0004. **$99-$200.** 201 Hutchinson Ave. I-270, exit 23, just ne. Int corridors. **Pets:** Large, other species. Service with restrictions, supervision.
〔ASK〕 〔S◐〕 〔✕〕 〔&M〕 〔🐾〕 〔&〕 〔🗎〕 〔🖃〕 〔❚❚〕 〔🏊〕

▼▼▼ **Signature Inn Columbus North** 〔SH〕
(614) 890-8111. **$49-$104.** 6767 Schrock Hill Ct. I-270, exit 27, n off Cleveland Ave; enter off Schrock Rd. Int corridors. **Pets:** Very small, other species. $10 daily fee/room. Service with restrictions, supervision.
〔ASK〕 〔✕〕 〔🐾〕 〔🗎〕 〔🖃〕 〔🏊〕

▼▼▼ **TownePlace Suites by Marriott** 〔SH〕
(614) 885-1557. **$89-$109.** 7272 Huntington Park Dr. I-270, exit 23, just e of Vantage Dr. Int corridors. **Pets:** Accepted.
〔ASK〕 〔S◐〕 〔✕〕 〔&〕 〔🗎〕 〔🖃〕 〔🏊〕

◈◈◈ ▼▼▼ **The University Plaza Hotel & Conference Center** 〔SH〕
(614) 267-7461. **$89-$119.** 3110 Olentangy River Rd. 0.5 mi s of N Broadway, exit off SR 315. Int corridors. **Pets:** Accepted.
〔SAVE〕 〔S◐〕 〔✕〕 〔🗎〕 〔🖃〕 〔❚❚〕 〔🏊〕

◈◈◈ ▼▼▼ **Wellesley Inn & Suites (Columbus/Polaris)** 〔SH〕
(614) 431-5522. **$89-$109.** 8555 Lyra Dr. I-71, exit 121, just w on Polaris Pkwy. Int corridors. **Pets:** Accepted.
〔SAVE〕 〔S◐〕 〔✕〕 〔&M〕 〔&〕 〔🗎〕 〔🖃〕 〔🏊〕

◈◈◈ ▼▼▼ ▼▼▼ **The Westin Great Southern Columbus** 〔LH〕
(614) 228-3800. **$119-$155.** 310 S High St. Corner of Main and High sts. Int corridors. **Pets:** Accepted.
〔SAVE〕 〔S◐〕 〔✕〕 〔🐾〕 〔&〕 〔🗎〕 〔🖃〕 〔❚❚〕

DELAWARE

▼▼ **Delaware Hotel** 〔SH〕
(740) 363-1262. **$49-$129, 3 day notice.** 351 S Sandusky St. 0.5 mi s. Int corridors. **Pets:** Accepted.
〔ASK〕 〔S◐〕 〔✕〕 〔🗎〕 〔🖃〕 〔🏊〕 〔✕〕

◈◈◈ ▼ **Travelodge** 〔M〕
(740) 369-4421. **$58-$140.** 1001 US Rt 23 N. 0.5 mi n of downtown. Ext/int corridors. **Pets:** Other species. $10 daily fee/room. Service with restrictions, supervision.
〔SAVE〕 〔S◐〕 〔✕〕 〔🗎〕 〔🖃〕

DUBLIN

◈◈◈ ▼▼▼ **AmeriSuites (Columbus/Dublin)** 〔SH〕
(614) 799-1913. **$79-$129.** 6161 Park Center Cir. I-270, exit 15 (Tuttle Crossing Blvd), just e. Int corridors. **Pets:** Small. Service with restrictions, supervision.
〔SAVE〕 〔S◐〕 〔✕〕 〔&M〕 〔🐾〕 〔&〕 〔🗎〕 〔🖃〕 〔🏊〕

◈◈◈ ▼▼▼ **Baymont Inn & Suites Columbus-Dublin** 〔SH〕
(614) 792-8300. **$65-$85.** 6145 Park Center Cir. I-270, exit 15 (Tuttle Crossing Blvd), just e. Int corridors. **Pets:** Large, other species. Service with restrictions, supervision.
〔SAVE〕 〔S◐〕 〔✕〕 〔&M〕 〔&〕 〔🗎〕 〔🖃〕

◈◈◈ ▼▼▼ **Columbus Marriott Northwest** 〔LH〕
(614) 791-1000. **$159-$189.** 5605 Paul Blazer Memorial Pkwy. I-270, exit 15 (Tuttle Crossing Blvd), 0.3 mi e. Int corridors. **Pets:** Accepted.
〔SAVE〕 〔S◐〕 〔✕〕 〔&M〕 〔🐾〕 〔&〕 〔🗎〕 〔🖃〕 〔❚❚〕 〔🏊〕

▼▼▼ **Drury Inn & Suites-Columbus Northwest** 〔SH〕
(614) 798-8802. **$75-$120.** 6170 Parkcenter Cir. I-270, exit 15 (Tuttle Crossing), just e. Int corridors. **Pets:** Large, other species. Service with restrictions, supervision.
〔ASK〕 〔✕〕 〔&〕 〔🗎〕 〔🖃〕 〔🏊〕

▼▼▼ **Homewood Suites by Hilton** 〔SH〕
(614) 791-8675. **$89-$139.** 5300 Parkcenter Ave. I-270, exit 15 (Tuttle Crossing Blvd), just e, just n on Blazer Pkwy, then just e. Int corridors. **Pets:** Accepted.
〔ASK〕 〔S◐〕 〔✕〕 〔&M〕 〔🐾〕 〔&〕 〔🗎〕 〔🖃〕 〔🏊〕 〔✕〕

▼▼ **Red Roof Inn-Dublin** 〔M〕
(614) 764-3993. **$57-$73.** 5125 Post Rd. I-270, exit 17A, just ne. Ext corridors. **Pets:** Accepted.
〔✕〕 〔&M〕 〔&〕 〔🗎〕

▼▼▼ **Residence Inn by Marriott** 〔SH〕
(614) 791-0403. **$79-$129.** 435 Metro Pl S. I-270, exit 17A, 0.5 mi e to Frantz Rd, then 0.5 mi s. Ext/int corridors. **Pets:** Other species. $100 one-time fee/room.
〔ASK〕 〔S◐〕 〔✕〕 〔&M〕 〔🐾〕 〔&〕 〔🗎〕 〔🖃〕 〔🏊〕 〔✕〕

▼▼▼ **Staybridge Suites by Holiday Inn** 〔SH〕
(614) 734-9882. **$109-$199.** 6095 Emerald Pkwy. I-270, exit 15 (Tuttle Crossing Blvd), just w. Int corridors. **Pets:** Accepted.
〔ASK〕 〔S◐〕 〔✕〕 〔🗎〕 〔🖃〕 〔🏊〕 〔✕〕

◈◈◈ ▼▼▼ **Wellesley Inn & Suites (Columbus/Dublin)** 〔SH〕
(614) 760-0245. **$64-$125.** 5530 Tuttle Crossing Blvd. I-270, exit 15 (Tuttle Crossing Blvd), 0.3 mi w. Int corridors. **Pets:** Accepted.
〔SAVE〕 〔S◐〕 〔✕〕 〔&M〕 〔&〕 〔🗎〕 〔🖃〕

▼▼▼ **Woodfin Suites Hotel** 〔SH〕
(614) 766-7762. **$99-$150.** 4130 Tuller Rd. I-270, exit 20, 0.3 mi s on Sawmill Rd via Dublin Center Dr. Ext corridors. **Pets:** Other species. $50 one-time fee/room. Designated rooms, service with restrictions, crate.
〔ASK〕 〔✕〕 〔🐾〕 〔🗎〕 〔🖃〕 〔🏊〕

GAHANNA

▼▼ **Candlewood Suites Columbus Airport** 〔SH〕
(614) 863-4033. **$89-$109.** 590 Taylor Rd. I-270, exit 37, just e, 0.6 mi s on Morrison Rd, then just e. Int corridors. **Pets:** Accepted.
〔ASK〕 〔S◐〕 〔✕〕 〔🗎〕 〔🖃〕

▼▼ **TownePlace Suites by Marriott** 〔SH〕
(614) 861-1400. **$69-$109.** 695 Taylor Rd. I-270, exit 37, just e, 0.6 mi s on Morrison Rd, then just e. Int corridors. **Pets:** Other species.
〔ASK〕 〔S◐〕 〔✕〕 〔🐾〕 〔&〕 〔🗎〕 〔🖃〕 〔🏊〕

GROVE CITY

◈◈◈ ▼▼ **Best Western Executive Inn** 〔M〕
(614) 875-7770. **$59-$69.** 4026 Jackpot Rd. I-71, exit 100, just e. Ext corridors. **Pets:** Medium, dogs only. $10 daily fee/pet. Designated rooms, service with restrictions, crate.
〔SAVE〕 〔S◐〕 〔✕〕 〔🗎〕 〔🖃〕 〔🏊〕

▼▼ **Motel 6-South Columbus #1492** 〔M〕
(614) 875-8543. **$42-$55.** 1900 Stringtown Rd. I-71, exit 100, just w. Ext corridors. **Pets:** Accepted.
〔S◐〕 〔✕〕 〔&〕

HEATH

◈◈◈ ▼▼▼ **Quality Inn** 〔SH〕
(740) 522-1165. **$55-$110.** 733 Hebron Rd. I-70, exit 129B, 7 mi n on SR 79. Ext corridors. **Pets:** Medium. $5 daily fee/pet. Service with restrictions, crate.
〔SAVE〕 〔S◐〕 〔✕〕 〔🗎〕 〔🖃〕 〔❚❚〕 〔🏊〕

HEBRON

▼▼ **Red Roof Inn** 〔SH〕
(740) 467-7663. **$58-$63.** 10668 Lancaster Rd SW. I-70, exit 126, just s. Int corridors. **Pets:** Other species. Service with restrictions, supervision.
〔ASK〕 〔S◐〕 〔✕〕 〔&M〕 〔&〕

HILLIARD

▼▼▼▼ Comfort Suites by Choice Hotels-Columbus 🆂🅷
(614) 529-8118. **$70-$90.** 3831 Park Mill Run Dr. I-270, exit 13A northbound; exit 13 southbound. Int corridors. **Pets:** Accepted.
(ASK) (S�０) (✕) (&M) (🔊) (🖘) (🔒) (🖳) (🛥)

▼▼▼▼ Homewood Suites by Hilton-Columbus 🆂🅷
(614) 529-4100. **$89-$149.** 3841 Park Mill Run Dr. I-270, exit 13 southbound; exit 13A northbound. Int corridors. **Pets:** Accepted.
(ASK) (S�０) (✕) (&M) (🔊) (🖘) (🔒) (🖳) (🛥) (🗶)

LANCASTER

▲▲▲ ▼▼▼ Best Western Lancaster Inn 🆂🅷 ✿
(740) 653-3040. **$67-$75, 3 day notice.** 1858 N Memorial Dr. 2 mi nw on US 33. Ext/int corridors. **Pets:** Small. Service with restrictions, crate.
(SAVE) (S�０) (✕) (🔒) (🖳) (🍽) (🛥)

LONDON

▲▲▲ ▼▼▼▼ Alexandra's Bed & Breakfast 🅱🅱
(740) 852-5993. **$70-$135.** 117 N Main St. I-70, exit 79, 4 mi s on SR 42, then just w. Int corridors. **Pets:** Small. Service with restrictions, supervision.
(SAVE) (S�０) (✕) (🔒) (🖳) (🖉)

MARYSVILLE

▼▼ ▼ Days Inn Marysville 🆂🅷
(937) 644-8821. **$69, 7 day notice.** 16510 Square Dr. Just e of US 36, exit off US 33. Ext corridors. **Pets:** Other species. $10 one-time fee/pet. Service with restrictions, crate.
(ASK) (S�０) (✕) (🔒) (🖳)

REYNOLDSBURG

▲▲▲ ▼▼▼ Days Inn & Suites 🆂🅷
(614) 864-1280. **$54-$64.** 2100 Brice Rd. I-70, exit 110 westbound; exit 110B eastbound, just n. Int corridors. **Pets:** Other species. Service with restrictions, supervision.
(SAVE) (S�０) (✕) (🖘) (🔒) (🖳) (🍽) (🛥)

▲▲▲ ▼▼▼▼ La Quinta Inn Columbus (Airport) 🆂🅷
(614) 866-6456. **$75-$105.** 2447 Brice Rd. I-70, exit 110 westbound; exit 110B eastbound, 0.3 mi n. Int corridors. **Pets:** Accepted.
(SAVE) (✕) (🔒) (🖳) (🛥)

▼▼ ▼ Red Roof Inn-East #7033 Ⓜ
(614) 864-3683. **$52-$72.** 2449 Brice Rd. I-70, exit 110 westbound; exit 110B eastbound. Ext corridors. **Pets:** Accepted.
(✕) (🖘)

SUNBURY

▲▲▲ ▼▼▼ Days Inn of Sunbury 🆂🅷
(740) 362-6159. **$65-$80.** 7323 SR 37 E. I-71, exit 131, just w. Int corridors. **Pets:** Other species. $10 daily fee/pet. Service with restrictions, supervision.
(SAVE) (S�０) (✕) (♿) (🔒) (🛥)

▼▼▼▼ Hampton Inn-Columbus/Delaware 🆂🅷
(740) 363-4700. **$79-$139.** 7329 SR 36 & 37. I-71, exit 131, just nw. Int corridors. **Pets:** Small. $25 daily fee/pet. Designated rooms, service with restrictions, supervision.
(ASK) (S�０) (✕) (&M) (🔊) (🖘) (🔒) (🖳) (🛥)

END METROPOLITAN AREA

CONNEAUT

▲▲▲ ▼▼▼ Days Inn of Conneaut 🆂🅷
(440) 593-6000. **$65-$179.** 600 Days Blvd. I-90, exit 241, 0.3 mi n. Int corridors. **Pets:** Large, other species. $10 daily fee/room. Service with restrictions, crate.
(SAVE) (S�０) (✕) (🖳) (🛥)

CUYAHOGA FALLS

▲▲▲ ▼▼▼▼ Akron Sheraton Suites Cuyahoga Falls 🆂🅷 ✿
(330) 929-3000. **$114-$214.** 1989 Front St. SR 8, exit Broad Blvd, just w. Int corridors. **Pets:** Other species. Service with restrictions.
(SAVE) (S�０) (✕) (&M) (🔊) (🔒) (🖳) (🍽) (🛥) (🗶)

▲▲▲ ▼▼▼ Economy Inn Ⓜ
(330) 929-8200. **$63-$109.** 1070 Graham Rd. SR 8, exit Graham Rd, just w. Ext corridors. **Pets:** Small, dogs only. $10 one-time fee/pet. Designated rooms, service with restrictions, crate.
(SAVE) (✕) (🔒)

DAYTON

▼▼▼▼ Dayton Marriott Hotel 🅻🅷 ✿
(937) 223-1000. **Call for rates.** 1414 S Patterson Blvd. I-75, exit 51 (Edwin C Moses Blvd), 1 mi e. Int corridors. **Pets:** $100 one-time fee/pet. Designated rooms, service with restrictions, supervision.
(✕) (🔊) (🖘) (🔒) (🖳) (🍽) (🛥) (🗶)

▲▲▲ ▼▼▼ Howard Johnson Express Inn 🆂🅷
(937) 454-0550. **$60-$65.** 7575 Poe Ave. I-75, exit 60 (Little York Rd) northbound, just n; southbound, n on Miller Ln, then n on Little York Rd. Int corridors. **Pets:** Large. $50 deposit/room.
(SAVE) (S�０) (✕) (🔊) (🔒) (🖳) (🛥)

▼ Motel 6-603 🆂🅷
(937) 898-3606. **$41-$51.** 7130 Miller Ln. I-75, exit 60 (Little York Rd), just sw. Ext corridors. **Pets:** Accepted.
(S�０) (✕) (🖘) (🛥)

▲▲▲ ▼▼▼▼ Ramada Inn Dayton Mall 🆂🅷
(937) 847-8422. **$65-$99, 14 day notice.** 3555 Miamisburg-Centerville Rd. I-75, exit 44, just w on SR 725; I-675, exit 2, just w on SR 725. Int corridors. **Pets:** Accepted.
(SAVE) (S�０) (✕) (🖘) (🔒) (🖳) (🍽) (🛥) (🗶)

▼▼ ▼ Ramada Inn-North 🆂🅷
(937) 890-9500. **$65-$90.** 4079 Little York Rd. I-75, exit 60 (Little York Rd), 0.5 mi s of jct I-70. Ext/int corridors. **Pets:** Other species. $10 one-time fee/pet. Service with restrictions.
(ASK) (S�０) (✕) (🔊) (🔒) (🖳) (🍽) (🛥)

▼▼ ▼ Red Roof Inn-North #7023 🆂🅷
(937) 898-1054. **$45-$70.** 7370 Miller Ln. I-75, exit 60 (Little York Rd); 0.5 mi s of jct I-70, just nw. Ext corridors. **Pets:** Accepted.
(✕) (🔊) (🖘)

▼▼▼▼ Residence Inn by Marriott-Dayton North 🆂🅷
(937) 898-7764. **$119-$199.** 7070 Poe Ave. I-75, exit 60 (Little York Rd). Ext corridors. **Pets:** Accepted.
(ASK) (S�０) (✕) (🔊) (🖘) (🔒) (🖳) (🛥) (🗶)

DOVER

▼ Hospitality Inn Ⓜ ✿
(330) 364-7724. **$40-$75.** 889 Commercial Pkwy. I-77, exit 83, just e. Ext corridors. **Pets:** Other species. $10 one-time fee/pet. Service with restrictions, supervision.
(ASK) (S�０) (✕) (🔊) (🔒) (🛥)

ELYRIA

▼▼ Comfort Inn 🆂🅷
(440) 324-7676. **$59-$119.** 739 Leona St. I-80, exit 145, just n on SR 57, exit Midway Blvd. Int corridors. **Pets:** Other species. $8 daily fee/pet. Service with restrictions, supervision.

🄰🅂🄺 🆂🄳 ☒ 🄴 💻

▼▼ Super 8 Motel 🆂🅷
(440) 323-7488. **$49-$104.** 910 Lorain Blvd. I-80, exit 145, 0.5 mi s on SR 57. Int corridors. **Pets:** Accepted.

🄰🅂🄺 🆂🄳 ☒ 🄺 💻 ⚓

ENGLEWOOD

▼▼▼ Holiday Inn-Dayton Northwest Airport 🆂🅷
(937) 832-1234. **$90-$115.** 10 Rockridge Rd. I-70, exit 29, just n. Int corridors. **Pets:** Accepted.

🄰🅂🄺 🆂🄳 ☒ 🄺 🄴 💻 🍴 ⚓

▼▼ Red Roof Inn-Dayton NW 🄼 🐾
(937) 836-8339. **Call for rates.** 9325 N Main St. I-70, exit 29, just s. Ext corridors. **Pets:** Large, other species. Designated rooms, service with restrictions, supervision.

☒ 🄺 🄴 ⚓

▼▼ Super 8 Motel-Englewood 🄼
(937) 832-3350. **$39-$69.** 15 Rockridge Rd. I-70, exit 29, just n. Ext corridors. **Pets:** Accepted.

🄰🅂🄺 🆂🄳 ☒

FAIRBORN

🄰🄰🄰 ▼▼▼ Comfort Inn-Wright Patterson 🆂🅷
(937) 879-7666. **$60-$100.** 616 N Broad St. I-675, exit 24, 1.8 mi sw on SR 444. Int corridors. **Pets:** $75 deposit/room, $5 daily fee/pet. Service with restrictions, supervision.

🆂🄰🅅🄴 🆂🄳 ☒ 🄰 🄴 💻 ⚓

🄰🄰🄰 ▼▼▼▼ Hawthorn Inn & Suites 🆂🅷
(937) 754-9109. **$89-$109.** 730 E Xenia Dr. I-675, exit 23, just w. Int corridors. **Pets:** Accepted.

🆂🄰🅅🄴 🆂🄳 ☒ 🄰 🄺 🄴 💻

🄰🄰🄰 ▼▼▼▼ Homewood Suites by Hilton-Fairborn/Dayton 🆂🅷
(937) 429-0600. **$129-$169.** 2750 Presidential Dr. I-675, exit 17 (N Fairfield Rd). Ext/int corridors. **Pets:** Accepted.

🆂🄰🅅🄴 ☒ 🄰 🄴 💻 ⚓

▼▼▼ Ramada Limited & Suites-Wright Patterson 🆂🅷
(937) 490-2000. **$68-$110, 30 day notice.** 2540 University Blvd. I-675, exit 15 (Colonel Glen Hwy), 1.5 mi e, then just s. Int corridors. **Pets:** Accepted.

🄰🅂🄺 🆂🄳 ☒ 🄺 🄴 💻 ⚓

▼▼ Red Roof Inn-Fairborn #7205 🆂🅷
(937) 426-6116. **$51-$69.** 2580 Colonel Glenn Hwy. I-675, exit 17 (N Fairfield Rd). Ext corridors. **Pets:** Accepted.

☒ 🄰 🄴 💻

FAIRLAWN

🄰🄰🄰 ▼▼ Akron Super 8 Motel 🆂🅷
(330) 666-8887. **$39-$75.** 79 Rothrock Rd. I-77, exit 137A, just e. Int corridors. **Pets:** $5 daily fee/pet. No service.

🆂🄰🅅🄴 🆂🄳 ☒ 🄰 🄴 💻

▼▼ Motel 6 Akron North #2000 🄼
(330) 666-0566. **$42-$53.** 99 Rothrock Rd. I-77, exit 137A, just e. Ext corridors. **Pets:** Accepted.

🆂🄳 ☒ 🄰

▼▼▼▼ The Residence Inn by Marriott 🆂🅷
(330) 666-4811. **$139-$199.** 120 W Montrose Ave. I-77, exit 137B, just w. Ext corridors. **Pets:** Large, other species. $150 one-time fee/room. Service with restrictions.

🄰🅂🄺 🆂🄳 ☒ 🄴 💻 ⚓ ☒

FINDLAY

▼ Days Inn Findlay 🄼
(419) 423-7171. **$65-$76.** 1305 W Main Cross St. I-75, exit 157, just e. Int corridors. **Pets:** Accepted.

🄰🅂🄺 🆂🄳 ☒ 🄴 💻 🍴 ⚓

🄰🄰🄰 ▼▼▼ Econo Lodge 🄼
(419) 422-0154. **$42-$70.** 316 Emma St. I-75, exit 157, just w. Ext corridors. **Pets:** $10 daily fee/pet. Service with restrictions, crate.

🆂🄰🅅🄴 🆂🄳 ☒ 🄴 💻

▼▼▼ Hawthorn Suites Ltd 🆂🅷
(419) 425-9696. **$79, 10 day notice.** 2355 Tiffin Ave. 3 mi e on US 224. Int corridors. **Pets:** Small, dogs only. $50 deposit/room, $10 daily fee/room. Service with restrictions, supervision.

🄰🅂🄺 🆂🄳 ☒ 🄰 🄺 🄴 💻 ⚓ ☒

🄰🄰🄰 ▼▼▼ Red Roof Inn 🄼
(419) 424-0466. **$70-$80.** 1951 Broad Ave. I-75, exit 159, 0.5 mi e. Ext corridors. **Pets:** Medium. $10 daily fee/room. No service, supervision.

🆂🄰🅅🄴 🆂🄳 ☒ 🄰 ⚓

🄰🄰🄰 ▼▼ Rodeway Inn 🄼 🐾
(419) 424-1133. **$35-$49.** 1901 Broad Ave. I-75, exit 159, 0.5 mi e. Ext corridors. **Pets:** $10 one-time fee/room. Service with restrictions, crate.

🆂🄰🅅🄴 🆂🄳 ☒ 🄴 💻 ⚓

▼▼ Super 8 Motel-Findlay 🆂🅷
(419) 422-8863. **$47-$55.** 1600 Fox St. I-75, exit 159, just e. Int corridors. **Pets:** Accepted.

🄰🅂🄺 🆂🄳 ☒ 🄰 🄴

FOSTORIA

🄰🄰🄰 ▼▼ Country Club Inn and Suites 🄼
(419) 435-6511. **$50-$75.** 737 Independence Rd. SR 12, 1 mi w of SR 23. Ext corridors. **Pets:** Accepted.

🆂🄰🅅🄴 🆂🄳 ☒ 🄰 🄴

FREDERICKTOWN

▼▼▼ Heartland Country Resort 🄲🄰 🐾
(419) 768-9300. **$120-$175, 7 day notice.** 3020 Township Rd 190. I-71, exit 151, 2 mi e on SR 95, 2 mi s on SR 314, then 1 mi e on SR 179. Ext corridors. **Pets:** Other species. $15 daily fee/room. Crate.

🄰🅂🄺 ☒ 🄰 🄴 💻 ☒

FREMONT

🄰🄰🄰 ▼▼▼▼ Comfort Inn & Suites 🆂🅷 🐾
(419) 355-9300. **$84-$200.** 840 Sean Dr. I-80/90, exit 91, 2 mi s on SR 53. Int corridors. **Pets:** Other species. $15 one-time fee/pet. Service with restrictions, supervision.

🆂🄰🅅🄴 🆂🄳 ☒ 🄺 🄰 🄴 💻 ⚓

🄰🄰🄰 ▼▼▼▼ Holiday Inn-Fremont 🆂🅷
(419) 334-2682. **$159.** 3422 Port Clinton Rd. I-80/90, exit 91, just s. Int corridors. **Pets:** Service with restrictions, supervision.

🆂🄰🅅🄴 🆂🄳 ☒ 🄼 🄰 🄴 💻 🍴 ⚓ ☒

GALION

▼▼ Hometown Inn 🄼
(419) 468-9909. **$40-$150.** 172 N Portland Way. 1 mi w on SR 598, n of jct SR 309/61/19. Ext/int corridors. **Pets:** Other species. $10 daily fee/room. Service with restrictions, supervision.

🄰🅂🄺 🆂🄳 ☒ 🄰 💻

GREEN

AAA ◈◈◈ Super 8 Motel SH
(330) 899-9888. **$65-$130.** 1605 Corporate Woods Pkwy. I-77, exit 118, just w. **Pets:** Small. $6 daily fee/pet. Service with restrictions, supervision.
SAVE S6 ✕ 🖥 🖵 ⌇

GREENVILLE

AAA ◈◈◈ Greenville Inn SH
(937) 548-3613. **$60-$80, 7 day notice.** 851 E Martin. Jct US 36 and 127, 0.3 mi w on SR 571. Int corridors. **Pets:** $75 deposit/room, $10 one-time fee/room. Service with restrictions, supervision.
SAVE ✕ 🖉 🖥 🖵 ⍾

HOLLAND

AAA ◈◈◈ Best Value Inn & Suites M
(419) 866-6565. **$46-$64.** 1201 E Mall Dr. I-475, exit 8, just w on SR 2. Ext corridors. **Pets:** Small. Designated rooms, no service.
SAVE S6 ✕ ♿ 🖥 🖵 ⌇

◈◈ Red Roof Inn Toledo/Holland #7058 M
(419) 866-5512. **$36-$62.** 1214 Corporate Dr. I-475, exit 8, just e on Holland-Sylvania Rd, then just n to Trust Dr. Ext corridors. **Pets:** Accepted.
✕ 🖉 🖥

◈◈◈ Residence Inn by Marriott SH
(419) 867-9555. **$66-$109.** 6101 Trust Dr. I-475, exit 8, just e to Holland-Sylvania Rd, then just n. Ext corridors. **Pets:** Accepted.
ASK ✕ 🖥 🖵 ⌇

HUBER HEIGHTS

◈◈◈ Holiday Inn Express Hotel & Suites SH
(937) 235-2000. **$84-$109.** 5612 Merily Way. I-70, exit 36, just s on SR 202. Int corridors. **Pets:** Other species. Service with restrictions, supervision.
ASK S6 ✕ 🖉 🖥 🖵 ⌇

◈ Travelodge Dayton/Huber Heights M
(937) 236-9361. **$50-$85.** 7911 Brandt Pike. I-70, exit 38, just s at SR 201. Ext/int corridors. **Pets:** Accepted.
ASK S6 ✕ 🖥 🖵 ⌇

HURON

AAA ◈ Plantation Motel M ❀
(419) 433-4790. **$38-$95, 3 day notice.** 2815 E Cleveland Rd. 3 mi e of town, on US 6. Ext corridors. **Pets:** Medium, other species. $9 daily fee/pet. Designated rooms, service with restrictions, supervision.
SAVE ✕ 🖥 🖵 ⌇

JACKSON

◈◈ Knights Inn M
(740) 286-2135. **$47-$61.** 404 Chillicothe St. 0.7 mi n on US 35 business route. Ext corridors. **Pets:** Other species. $20 deposit/room. Service with restrictions.
ASK S6 ✕ 🖥

◈◈ Red Roof Inn M
(740) 288-1200. **$60-$70.** 1000 Acy Ave. US 35, exit McCarty Ln, just nw. Int corridors. **Pets:** Medium. $25 deposit/pet. Service with restrictions, supervision.
ASK S6 ✕ ♿ 🖥

JEFFERSONVILLE

AAA ◈◈◈ AmeriHost Inn-Jeffersonville North SH
(740) 426-6400. **$51-$99.** 10160 Carr Rd NW. I-71, exit 69 (SR 41), just w. Int corridors. **Pets:** Accepted.
SAVE S6 ✕ ♿ 🖉 🖥 🖵 ⌇

KENT

◈ Alden Inn M
(330) 678-9927. **Call for rates.** I-76, exit 33. Ext/int corridors. **Pets:** Accepted.
✕ 🖥

◈◈ Days Inn-Akron Kent M
(330) 677-9400. **$69-$85, 14 day notice.** 4422 Edsen Rd. I-76, exit 33. Ext corridors. **Pets:** Accepted.
ASK S6 ✕ 🖉 ♿ 🖥 🖵 ⌇

AAA ◈◈◈ Ramada Inn-Akron/Kent SH
(330) 678-0101. **$59-$129.** 4363 SR 43. I-76, exit 33. Ext corridors. **Pets:** Dogs only. $10 daily fee/pet. Designated rooms, service with restrictions, supervision.
SAVE S6 ✕ 🖉 🖥 🖵 ⍾ ⌇ ✕

◈◈ Super 8 Motel SH
(330) 678-8817. **$50-$85, 7 day notice.** 4380 Edson Rd. I-76, exit 33. Int corridors. **Pets:** Accepted.
ASK S6 ✕ 🖉 🖥

LIMA

◈◈◈◈ Holiday Inn Lima SH
(419) 222-0004. **$99-$111.** 1920 Roschman Ave. I-75, exit 125A, just se. Int corridors. **Pets:** Accepted.
ASK ✕ 🖉 ♿ 🖥 🖵 ⍾ ⌇ ✕

◈ Motel 6–586 M
(419) 228-0456. **$42-$55.** 1800 Harding Hwy. I-75, exit 125A, just se. Ext corridors. **Pets:** Accepted.
S6 ✕ ♿

LOGAN

AAA ◈◈◈ AmeriHost Inn-Logan SH
(740) 385-1700. **$55-$199.** 12819 SR 664. Jct US 33, just n. Int corridors. **Pets:** Small, dogs only. $10 daily fee/room. Designated rooms, service with restrictions, supervision.
SAVE S6 ✕ ♿M 🖉 ♿ 🖥 🖵 ⌇

◈◈◈◈ Holiday Inn Express Hocking Hills SH
(740) 385-7700. **$89-$159.** 12916 Grey St. SR 664, just w to Lake Logan Rd, then just n. Int corridors. **Pets:** Service with restrictions, supervision.
ASK S6 ✕ ♿M 🖉 ♿ 🖥 🖵

LOUDONVILLE

◈◈ Little Brown Inn M
(419) 994-5525. **$47-$74.** 940 S Market St. 1 mi s on SR 3. Int corridors. **Pets:** Very small. $10 one-time fee/pet. Designated rooms, no service, supervision.
ASK S6 ✕ 🖥

MANSFIELD

AAA ◈◈◈ AmeriHost Inn Mansfield SH
(419) 756-6670. **$54-$199.** 180 E Hanley Rd. I-71, exit 169, jct SR 13. Int corridors. **Pets:** Medium. $25 daily fee/pet. Service with restrictions, supervision.
SAVE S6 ✕ 🖉 ♿ 🖥 🖵 ⌇ ✕

AAA ◈◈◈ Baymont Inn & Suites Mansfield SH
(419) 774-0005. **$70-$100.** 120 Stander Ave. I-71, exit 169. Int corridors. **Pets:** Large, other species. Designated rooms, service with restrictions, supervision.
SAVE S6 ✕ ♿M 🖉 ♿ 🖥 🖵 ⌇

◈◈ Comfort Inn North SH
(419) 529-1000. **$65-$135.** 500 N Trimble Rd. Jct US 30. Int corridors. **Pets:** Accepted.
ASK S6 ✕ 🖉 🖥 🖵 ⌇ ✕

Econo Lodge SH
(419) 589-3333. **$48-$60.** 1017 Koogle Rd. I-71, exit 176, just e. Int corridors. **Pets:** $5 daily fee/pet. Service with restrictions, supervision.

Fairfield Inn by Marriott SH
(419) 747-2200. **$65-$85.** 1065 N Lexington-Springmill Rd. Jct US 30, on south side. Int corridors. **Pets:** Accepted.

Knights Inn M
(419) 529-2100. **$50-$90.** 555 N Trimble Rd. Jct US 30. Ext corridors. **Pets:** Accepted.

Super 8 Motel SH
(419) 756-8875. **$61-$67, 7 day notice.** 2425 Interstate Cir. I-71, exit 169. Int corridors. **Pets:** Other species. $50 deposit/room. Service with restrictions, supervision.

Travelodge M
(419) 756-7600. **$49-$90, 3 day notice.** 90 W Hanley Rd. I-71, exit 169. Ext corridors. **Pets:** Accepted.

MARIETTA

Best Value Inn M
(740) 373-7373. **$47-$70.** 506 Pike St. I-77, exit 1. Ext corridors. **Pets:** $5 one-time fee/pet. Service with restrictions, crate.

Econo Lodge M
(740) 374-8481. **$40-$85.** 702 Pike St. I-77, exit 1. Ext corridors. **Pets:** Medium. $7 daily fee/pet. No service, crate.

The Lafayette Hotel LH
(740) 373-5522. **$65-$125, 3 day notice.** 101 Front St. Center. Int corridors. **Pets:** Accepted.

Super 8 Motel-Marietta SH
(740) 374-8888. **$52-$57.** 46 Acme St. I-77, exit 1, just w. Int corridors. **Pets:** Accepted.

MARION

Comfort Inn by Choice Hotels SH
(740) 389-5552. **$65-$85.** 256 James Way. Jct US 23 and SR 95. Int corridors. **Pets:** Large, other species. $10 daily fee/pet. Service with restrictions, crate.

MASSILLON

Hampton Inn-Canton/Massillon SH
(330) 834-1144. **$79-$109.** 44 First St SW. Downtown. Int corridors. **Pets:** Small. Service with restrictions, crate.

MAUMEE

Arrowhead Super 8 Motel-Maumee/Toledo SH
(419) 897-3800. **$44-$59.** 1390 Arrowhead Rd. I-475, exit 6, just e. Int corridors. **Pets:** Small. $10 daily fee/pet. Service with restrictions, supervision.

Comfort Inn Toledo West/Maumee SH
(419) 893-2800. **$69-$85.** 1426 S Reynolds Rd. I-80/90, exit 59, just s. Int corridors. **Pets:** Small. $10 daily fee/pet. Service with restrictions, supervision.

Country Inn & Suites by Carlson of Toledo SH
(419) 893-8576. **$80-$100.** 541 W Dussel Dr. I-475, exit 6, just e. Int corridors. **Pets:** Accepted.

Days Inn-Toledo/Maumee M
(419) 897-6900. **$34-$69.** 1704 Tollgate Dr. I-80/90, exit 59, just s. Ext corridors. **Pets:** Medium. $10 daily fee/room. Designated rooms, service with restrictions, supervision.

Econ Lodge-Toledo/Maumee M
(419) 893-9960. **$40-$95.** 150 Dussel Dr. I-80/90, exit 59, just s. Ext corridors. **Pets:** Other species. $10 deposit/pet. Designated rooms, service with restrictions, crate.

Homewood Suites by Hilton-Toledo SH
(419) 897-0980. **$89-$129.** 1410 Arrowhead Rd. I-475, exit 6, just e. Int corridors. **Pets:** Accepted.

Red Roof Inn-Maumee #7046 M ❀
(419) 893-0292. **$49-$76.** 1570 S Reynolds Rd. I-80/90, exit 59, just s. Ext/int corridors. **Pets:** Service with restrictions, supervision.

MENTOR

Best Western Lawnfield Inn & Suites SH ❀
(440) 205-7378. **$79-$149, 14 day notice.** 8434 Mentor Ave. I-90, exit 193, 2 mi n on SR 306, then 2 mi e. Int corridors. **Pets:** Medium. Designated rooms, service with restrictions, crate.

Residence Inn by Marriott SH
(440) 392-0800. **$99-$139.** 5660 Emerald Ct. Jct SR 2 and Heisley Rd, just s. Int corridors. **Pets:** Other species. $75 one-time fee/room. Service with restrictions.

Studio 6 #6019 M
(440) 946-0749. **$49-$61.** 7677 Reynolds Rd. Just s of SR 2 on SR 306. Ext corridors. **Pets:** Accepted.

Super 8 Motel SH
(440) 951-8558. **$40-$70.** 7325 Palisades Pkwy. On SR 306, just s of SR 2. Int corridors. **Pets:** Accepted.

MIAMISBURG

Holiday Inn-Dayton Mall SH
(937) 434-8030. **$89-$199.** 31 Prestige Plaza Dr. I-75, exit 44, just e on SR 725, then just s. Int corridors. **Pets:** Accepted.

Homewood Suites by Hilton-Dayton South SH
(937) 432-0000. **Call for rates.** 3100 Contemporary Ln. I-75, exit 44, just e on SR 725, then just s. Int corridors. **Pets:** Accepted.

Red Roof Inn-South #7006 SH
(937) 866-0705. **$45-$65.** 222 Byers Rd. I-75, exit 44, just w on SR 725. Ext corridors. **Pets:** Medium. Service with restrictions, supervision.

▼▼▼▼ **Residence Inn by Marriott-Dayton South** SH
(937) 434-7881. **$150-$175.** 155 Prestige Pl. I-75, exit 44, just e on SR 725, then just s. Ext corridors. **Pets:** Other species. $75 one-time fee/pet. Service with restrictions.
(ASK) (S⌀) (✕) (⚿) (🛏) (🖥) (⇄) (✕)

▼▼▼ **Signature Inn Dayton South** SH
(937) 865-0077. **$49-$104.** 250 Byers Rd. I-75, exit 44, just w on SR 725. Int corridors. **Pets:** Very small, other species. $10 daily fee/room. Service with restrictions, supervision.
(ASK) (✕) (🐾) (🛏) (🖥) (⇄)

(AAA) ▼▼▼ **Wellesley Inn South Dayton** SH
(937) 866-5500. **$64-$69.** 155 Monarch Ln. I-75, exit 44, 0.5 mi w on SR 725. Int corridors. **Pets:** Accepted.
(SAVE) (S⌀) (✕) (🐾) (🛏) (🖥)

MILAN

▼▼ **Motel 6-4016** SH
(419) 499-8001. **$36-$149, 3 day notice.** 11406 US 250 N. I-80/90, exit 118, 1.5 mi n. Int corridors. **Pets:** Other species. Service with restrictions, supervision.
(ASK) (✕) (⚿) (⇄)

▼▼ **Super 8 Motel** SH
(419) 499-4671. **$38-$138.** 11313 Milan Rd. I-80/90, exit 118, 0.5 mi n on SR 250. Int corridors. **Pets:** Medium, dogs only. $50 deposit/pet. Designated rooms, service with restrictions, supervision.
(ASK) (S⌀) (✕) (🛏) (🍴) (⇄)

MONTPELIER

▼▼ **Ramada Inn & Suites** SH
(419) 485-5555. **$99-$129.** 13508 SR 15. I-80/90, exit 13, just s. Int corridors. **Pets:** Other species. Service with restrictions, supervision.
(ASK) (✕) (🐾) (🛏) (🖥) (🍴) (⇄) (✕)

MORAINE

▼▼▼ **Holiday Inn Hotel & Suites** SH
(937) 294-1471. **$86-$116.** 2455 Dryden Rd. I-75, exit 50A, just w. Int corridors. **Pets:** Accepted.
(ASK) (S⌀) (✕) (🐾) (⚿) (🛏) (🖥) (🍴) (⇄) (✕)

▼▼ **Super 8 Motel-Moraine** M
(937) 298-0380. **$39-$99.** 2450 Dryden Rd. I-75, exit 50A, just w. Ext corridors. **Pets:** Accepted.
(ASK) (S⌀) (✕) (🛏) (⇄)

MOUNT GILEAD

(AAA) ▼ **Knights Inn** M
(419) 946-6010. **$43-$58.** 5898 SR 95. I-71, exit 151, 0.3 mi w. Ext corridors. **Pets:** Dogs only. $15 deposit/room. Designated rooms, service with restrictions, supervision.
(SAVE) (S⌀) (✕) (🛏)

MOUNT VERNON

▼▼▼ **AmeriHost Inn-Mount Vernon** SH
(740) 392-6886. **$69-$125.** 150 Howard St. Jct SR 13; south of downtown. Int corridors. **Pets:** Accepted.
(ASK) (S⌀) (✕) (🛏) (🖥) (⇄) (✕)

▼▼▼ **Holiday Inn Express** SH
(740) 392-1900. **$79-$190.** 11555 Upper Gilchrist Rd. 3 mi e on US 36. Int corridors. **Pets:** Small, other species. Designated rooms, service with restrictions, supervision.
(ASK) (S⌀) (✕) (♿) (⚿) (🛏) (🖥) (⇄)

NEWCOMERSTOWN

▼▼▼ **Hampton Inn** SH 🐾
(740) 498-9800. **$70-$92.** 200 Morris Crossing. I-77, exit 65, 0.8 mi w. Int corridors. **Pets:** Dogs only. Designated rooms, service with restrictions, supervision.
(ASK) (S⌀) (✕) (🛏) (🖥) (⇄)

NEW PHILADELPHIA

▼▼▼ **Hampton Inn** SH
(330) 339-7000. **$72-$95.** 1299 W High St. I-77, exit 81, just e. **Pets:** Small, dogs only. $50 deposit/room. Service with restrictions, crate.
(ASK) (S⌀) (✕) (L.M) (🛏) (🖥) (⇄) (✕)

▼ **Motel 6-254** M
(330) 339-6446. **$35-$45.** 181 Bluebell Dr SW. I-77, exit 81, 0.4 mi e. Ext corridors. **Pets:** Accepted.
(S⌀) (✕) (⚿) (⇄)

▼▼▼ **Schoenbrunn Inn by Christopher** SH
(330) 339-4334. **$62-$89.** 1186 W High Ave. I-77, exit 81, 0.6 mi e. Int corridors. **Pets:** Accepted.
(ASK) (S⌀) (✕) (⚿) (🛏) (🖥) (⇄) (✕)

▼▼ **Super 8 Motel** SH
(330) 339-6500. **$42-$79.** 131 1/2 Bluebell Dr SE. I-77, exit 81, 0.4 mi e. Int corridors. **Pets:** Accepted.
(ASK) (S⌀) (✕) (🖥)

NEWTON FALLS

(AAA) ▼▼▼ **Econo Lodge** M 🐾
(330) 872-0988. **$37-$85.** 4248 SR 5. I-80, exit 209, just w. Ext corridors. **Pets:** Other species. $7 daily fee/pet. Service with restrictions, crate.
(SAVE) (S⌀) (✕) (🛏)

NORTH CANTON

▼▼ **Super 8 Motel Canton North** M
(330) 492-5030. **$40-$130.** 3950 Convenience Cir NW. I-77, exit 109 southbound, 0.3 mi e on Everhard, then 0.3 mi s on Whipple; exit 109A northbound, 0.3 mi s on Whipple. Ext corridors. **Pets:** Accepted.
(ASK) (S⌀) (✕) (🛏) (🖥) (⇄)

NORTH LIMA

▼ **Liberty Inn** M
(330) 549-3988. **$50.** 10650 Market St. I-76, exit 232, 0.3 mi s on SR 7. Ext corridors. **Pets:** Accepted.
(ASK) (S⌀) (✕)

NORTHWOOD

▼▼ **Comfort Inn South** SH
(419) 666-2600. **$59-$120.** 2426 Oregon Rd. I-75, exit 198, just e; jct Wales and Oregon rds. Int corridors. **Pets:** Accepted.
(ASK) (S⌀) (✕) (🛏) (🖥) (🍴) (⇄)

NORWALK

▼▼ **Econo Lodge** M
(419) 668-5656. **$36-$139.** 342 Milan Ave. 3 mi n on SR 250; 6 mi s of I-80/90 (Ohio Tpke). Ext corridors. **Pets:** Medium, dogs only. $50 deposit/pet. Designated rooms, service with restrictions, supervision.
(ASK) (S⌀) (✕) (🛏) (🖥) (⇄)

OBERLIN

▼▼▼ **Oberlin Inn** CI
(440) 775-1111. **$109-$189.** 7 N Main St. On SR 58; jct College and Main sts; center. Int corridors. **Pets:** Accepted.
(ASK) (S⌀) (✕) (🛏) (🖥) (🍴)

OREGON

▼▼▼ Comfort Inn East SH
(419) 691-8911. **$74-$84.** 2930 Navarre Ave. I-280, exit 7, just n on access road, then 0.5 mi e on SR 2 (Navarre Ave). Int corridors. **Pets:** $12 one-time fee/room. Designated rooms, service with restrictions, supervision.
(ASK) (S♦) (✕) (🐾) (🔒) (🔋) (💻) (🏊)

▼▼ Sleep Inn & Suites SH
(419) 697-7800. **$79-$94.** 1761 Meijer Cir. I-280, exit 6, just w. Int corridors. **Pets:** Other species. $12 one-time fee/room. Designated rooms, service with restrictions, supervision.
(ASK) (S♦) (✕) (🔒) (🔋) (💻) (🏊)

PERRYSBURG

⚑ ▼▼▼ Baymont Inn & Suites
Toledo-Perrysburg SH ✿
(419) 872-0000. **$69-$79.** 1154 Professional Dr. I-75, exit 193, just w. Int corridors. **Pets:** Other species. Designated rooms, service with restrictions, supervision.
(SAVE) (S♦) (✕) (🐾) (🔒) (🔋) (💻)

⚑ ▼▼▼ Howard Johnson Inn Toledo South M
(419) 837-5245. **$44-$74.** 3555 Hanley Rd. I-80/90 (Ohio Tpke), exit 71 to I-280, exit 1B. Ext/int corridors. **Pets:** Accepted.
(SAVE) (S♦) (✕) (🐾) (🔋) (💻) (🏊)

PIQUA

▼▼▼ Comfort Inn-Piqua SH
(937) 778-8100. **$68-$72.** 987 E Ash St. I-75, exit 82, just w. Int corridors. **Pets:** $25 deposit/pet. Designated rooms, service with restrictions, crate.
(ASK) (S♦) (✕) (🐾) (🔒) (🔋) (💻) (🏊)

▼▼▼ La Quinta Inn Piqua SH
(937) 615-0140. **$70-$89.** 950 E Ash St. I-75, exit 82, just w. Int corridors. **Pets:** Other species. Designated rooms, service with restrictions, crate.
(ASK) (S♦) (✕) (🔒) (🔋) (💻) (🏊)

POLAND

▼▼▼ Red Roof Inn #7253 SH
(330) 758-1999. **$46-$77.** 1051 Tiffany S. I-680, exit 11, just w. Int corridors. **Pets:** Medium. Service with restrictions, supervision.
(✕) (🐾) (🔒) (🔋) (💻)

▼▼▼ Residence Inn by Marriott-Youngstown SH
(330) 726-1747. **$89-$169.** 7396 Tiffany S. I-680, exit 11, just w. Int corridors. **Pets:** Medium. $75 one-time fee/room. Designated rooms, service with restrictions, crate.
(ASK) (S♦) (✕) (🐾) (🔒) (🔋) (💻) (🏊) (✕)

PORT CLINTON

▼▼ Best Western Port Clinton SH
(419) 734-2274. **$42-$149.** 1734 E Perry St. 1.7 mi e on SR 163, w of jct SR 2. Int corridors. **Pets:** Medium, dogs only. $50 deposit/pet. Designated rooms, service with restrictions, supervision.
(ASK) (S♦) (✕) (🏊)

▼▼ Country Hearth Inn M
(419) 732-2111. **$45-$95.** 1815 E Perry St. 1.2 mi e on SR 163, w of jct SR 2. Ext/int corridors. **Pets:** Accepted.
(ASK) (S♦) (✕) (🔋) (💻) (🏊)

▼▼ Super 8 SH
(419) 734-4446. **$39-$149.** 1704 E Perry St. 1.7 mi e on SR 163, w of jct SR 2. Int corridors. **Pets:** Accepted.
(ASK) (S♦) (✕) (💻)

RIO GRANDE

▼ College Hill Motel M
(740) 245-5326. **$49-$79.** 10987 State Rt 588. US 35, exit Rio Grande. Ext corridors. **Pets:** Medium. $10 daily fee/pet. Service with restrictions, crate.
(✕) (🔋)

ST. CLAIRSVILLE

⚑ ▼▼▼ Best Value Inn St. Clairsville/Wheeling M
(740) 695-5038. **$49-$73.** 51260 National Rd. I-70, exit 218, 0.5 mi ne on US 40. Ext corridors. **Pets:** Medium, other species. $10 one-time fee/room. Service with restrictions, supervision.
(SAVE) (S♦) (✕) (🐾) (🔋) (💻) (🏊)

▼▼ Red Roof Inn M
(740) 695-4057. **$45-$79.** 68301 Red Roof Ln. I-70, exit 218, just n. Ext corridors. **Pets:** Accepted.
(✕) (🔋)

ST. MARYS

⚑ ▼▼▼ AmeriHost Inn-St. Marys SH
(419) 394-2710. **$99-$109, 3 day notice.** 1410 Commerce Dr. Jct US 33 and SR 29, just s. Int corridors. **Pets:** Accepted.
(SAVE) (S♦) (✕) (🐾) (🔒) (🔋) (💻) (🏊)

⚑ ▼▼▼ Best Value Inn & Suites SH
(419) 394-2341. **$55-$99.** 1321 Celina Rd. SR 29, 0.8 mi w on SR 703. Ext corridors. **Pets:** Medium. $10 daily fee/room. Designated rooms, supervision.
(SAVE) (S♦) (✕) (🔋) (💻) (🏊) (✕)

SANDUSKY

⚑ ▼▼ Best Budget Inn M
(419) 626-3610. **$39-$128.** 2027 Cleveland Rd. US 6, just e of Cedar Point Cswy. Ext/int corridors. **Pets:** Medium, dogs only. $50 deposit/pet. Designated rooms, service with restrictions, supervision.
(SAVE) (S♦) (✕) (🏊)

▼▼ Clarion Inn Sandusky SH
(419) 625-6280. **$55-$189.** 1119 Sandusky Mall Blvd. On US 250, 1.5 mi n of SR 2. Int corridors. **Pets:** Accepted.
(ASK) (S♦) (✕) (🐾) (🔋) (💻) (🍴) (🏊) (✕)

▼▼ Knights Inn Sandusky M
(419) 621-9000. **$40-$150, 3 day notice.** 2405 Cleveland Rd. US 6, 2 mi e of Cedar Point Cswy. Ext/int corridors. **Pets:** Small. $25 deposit/pet. Designated rooms, service with restrictions, supervision.
(ASK) (S♦) (✕) (🔋) (💻) (🏊)

SEVILLE

⚑ ▼▼▼ Super 8 Motel-Seville SH
(330) 769-8880. **$60-$100.** 6116 Speedway Dr. Jct SR 224 and Lake Rd. Int corridors. **Pets:** Small. $50 deposit/room, $20 one-time fee/room. Service with restrictions, supervision.
(SAVE) (S♦) (✕) (S♦M) (🔒) (🔋)

SIDNEY

⚑ ▼▼▼ Comfort Inn SH
(937) 492-3001. **$69-$95.** 1959 W Michigan Ave. I-75, exit 92, just sw of SR 47. Int corridors. **Pets:** Accepted.
(SAVE) (S♦) (✕) (🔋) (💻) (🏊)

▼▼ Days Inn Sidney M
(937) 492-1104. **$50-$80, 3 day notice.** 420 Folkerth Ave. I-75, exit 92, just nw. Ext corridors. **Pets:** Medium. $5 daily fee/pet. Service with restrictions, supervision.
(ASK) (S♦) (✕) (🔋) (🏊)

▼▼▼ Holiday Inn 🆂🅷
(937) 492-1131. **$66-$99.** 400 Folkerth Ave. I-75, exit 92, just w. Int corridors. **Pets:** Accepted.
🄰🅂🄺 🆂🄳 ⊠ 🕭 🖭 🗂 🖥 🍴 ⇌

SPRINGFIELD

▼▼▼ Holiday Inn South Springfield Ohio 🆂🅷
(937) 323-8631. **$99.** 383 E Leffel Ln. I-70, exit 54, just n, then e. Int corridors. **Pets:** Other species. Service with restrictions, supervision.
🄰🅂🄺 🆂🄳 ⊠ 🗂 🖥 🖭 🍴 ⇌ ⊠

▲▲ ▼ Knights Inn 🅼
(937) 325-8721. **$45-$60.** 2207 W Main St. I-70, exit 52, 1.7 mi n on US 68, then just e on US 40. Ext corridors. **Pets:** $10 daily fee/pet. Service with restrictions, supervision.
🆂🄰🆅🄴 🆂🄳 ⊠ 🖥 ⇌

▲▲ ▼▼ Ramada Limited 🆂🅷
(937) 328-0123. **$49-$99.** 319 E Leffel Ln. I-70, exit 54, just n, then e. Int corridors. **Pets:** $10 daily fee/pet. Designated rooms, service with restrictions, supervision.
🆂🄰🆅🄴 🆂🄳 ⊠ 🕭 🖥 🖭 ⇌

▲▲ ▼▼ Red Roof Inn 🆂🅷
(937) 325-5356. **$59-$99.** 155 W Leffel Ln. I-70, exit 54, just n, then w. Int corridors. **Pets:** Accepted.
🆂🄰🆅🄴 🆂🄳 ⊠ 🗂 🖥 🖭 ⇌

STRASBURG

▲▲ ▼▼▼ Ramada Limited Dover/Strasburg 🆂🅷
(330) 878-1400. **$65-$110.** 509 S Wooster Ave. I-77, exit 87, 0.4 mi n on US 250 and SR 21. Int corridors. **Pets:** $10 daily fee/room. Service with restrictions, supervision.
🆂🄰🆅🄴 🆂🄳 ⊠ 🄲🄼 🕭 🗂 🖥 🖭 ⇌

STREETSBORO

▼▼ Comfort Inn 🆂🅷
(330) 626-5511. **$50-$110.** 9789 SR 14. I-80, exit 187, 0.5 mi s. Int corridors. **Pets:** Accepted.
🄰🅂🄺 🆂🄳 ⊠ 🗂 🖭

▼▼ Microtel Inn & Suites of Streetsboro 🆂🅷
(330) 422-1234. **$66-$106.** 9371 SR 14. I-80, exit 187, 1.2 mi s. Int corridors. **Pets:** Accepted.
🄰🅂🄺 🆂🄳 ⊠ 🖥 🖭 ⇌

▼▼▼ TownePlace Suites by Marriott 🆂🅷
(330) 422-1855. **$69-$149.** 795 Mondial Pkwy. I-80, exit 187, 0.8 mi s. Int corridors. **Pets:** Accepted.
🄰🅂🄺 🆂🄳 ⊠ 🗂 🖭 ⇌

SWANTON

▼▼ Super 8 Toledo Airport 🆂🅷
(419) 865-2002. **$69.** 10753 Airport Hwy. I-80/90, exit 3A, just s, then e. Int corridors. **Pets:** Other species. Supervision.
🄰🅂🄺 🆂🄳 ⊠ 🗂 🖭

TIFFIN

▼▼▼ Holiday Inn Express 🆂🅷
(419) 443-5100. **$75.** 78 Shaffer Park Dr. Just w of mall. Int corridors. **Pets:** Other species. $20 one-time fee/pet. Service with restrictions, supervision.
🄰🅂🄺 🆂🄳 ⊠ 🖥 🖭 ⇌

▼▼ Quality Inn 🆂🅷
(419) 447-6313. **$68-$75.** 1927 S SR 53. Jct US 224 and SR 53, 2 mi sw. Ext/int corridors. **Pets:** $15 daily fee/pet. Designated rooms, service with restrictions, crate.
🄰🅂🄺 🆂🄳 ⊠ 🕭 🗂 🖥 🖭 🍴 ⇌

TOLEDO

▲▲ ▼▼▼ Comfort Inn-North 🆂🅷
(419) 476-0170. **$70-$160.** 445 E Alexis Rd. I-75, exit 210, 2 mi w on SR 184; just e of jct US 24 and SR 184. Int corridors. **Pets:** Accepted.
🆂🄰🆅🄴 🆂🄳 ⊠ 🕭 🖥 🖭

▲▲ ▼▼ ▼ Hotel Seagate 🆂🅷
(419) 242-8885. **$79-$229.** 141 N Summit St. Between Jefferson and Monroe sts; downtown. Int corridors. **Pets:** $25 one-time fee/room. Service with restrictions, crate.
🆂🄰🆅🄴 🆂🄳 ⊠ 🕭 🖥 🖭 🍴 ⇌

▲▲ ▼▼▼ Radisson Hotel Toledo 🆂🅷
(419) 241-3000. **$89.** 101 N Summit St. Between Jefferson and Monroe sts; downtown. Int corridors. **Pets:** Medium. Service with restrictions, supervision.
🆂🄰🆅🄴 🆂🄳 ⊠ 🖭 🍴

▼▼ ▼▼ Red Roof Inn Toledo University #7196 🅼
(419) 536-0118. **$49-$62.** 3530 Executive Pkwy. I-475, exit 17, 0.5 mi s on Secor Rd, then just e. Ext corridors. **Pets:** Accepted.
⊠ 🕭 🗂 🖥

TROY

▼▼▼ Holiday Inn Express Hotel & Suites 🆂🅷
(937) 332-1700. **$75-$99.** 60 Troy Town Dr. I-75, exit 74, just w. Int corridors. **Pets:** Small, other species. $20 one-time fee/room. Designated rooms, service with restrictions, crate.
🄰🅂🄺 🆂🄳 ⊠ 🕭 🗂 🖥 🖭 ⇌

▼▼▼ Residence Inn By Marriott 🆂🅷
(937) 440-9303. **$89-$129.** 87 Troy Town Dr. I-75, exit 74, just w. Int corridors. **Pets:** Accepted.
🄰🅂🄺 🆂🄳 ⊠ 🕭 🗂 🖥 🖭 ⇌ ⊠

UHRICHSVILLE

▲▲ ▼▼ ▼ Best Western Country Inn 🅼
(740) 922-0774. **$50-$70.** 111 McCauley Dr. US 250, exit McCauley Dr. Ext corridors. **Pets:** Other species. $5 one-time fee/room. Service with restrictions, supervision.
🆂🄰🆅🄴 🆂🄳 ⊠ 🕭 🖥 🖭

URBANA

▲▲ ▼▼ ▼ Econo Lodge Urbana 🅼
(937) 652-2188. **$56-$70.** 2551 S US Hwy 68. 1.3 mi s. Ext corridors. **Pets:** $15 daily fee/pet. Service with restrictions, supervision.
🆂🄰🆅🄴 🆂🄳 ⊠ ⇌

VANDALIA

▲▲ ▼▼ ▼ Super 8 Motel-Vandalia 🅼
(937) 898-7636. **$49-$89.** 550 E National Rd. I-75, exit 63, just w. Ext corridors. **Pets:** Service with restrictions, supervision.
🆂🄰🆅🄴 🆂🄳 ⊠ 🕭 🖥 ⇌

▲▲ ▼▼ ▼ Travelodge Dayton Airport 🅼
(937) 898-8321. **$39-$99, 10 day notice.** 75 Corporate Center Dr. Off National Rd. Ext corridors. **Pets:** Small. $10 daily fee/room. Designated rooms, service with restrictions, supervision.
🆂🄰🆅🄴 🆂🄳 ⊠ 🕭 🖥 🖭 ⇌

VERMILION

▼▼▼ Holiday Inn Express 🆂🅷
(440) 967-8770. **$79-$149.** 2417 SR 60. Jct SR 2 and 60. Int corridors. **Pets:** Medium, other species. $15 one-time fee/pet. Designated rooms, service with restrictions, supervision.
🄰🅂🄺 🆂🄳 ⊠ 🕭 🗂 🖥 🖭 ⇌

AAA ◆ Motel Plaza M
(440) 967-3191. **$65-$89, 3 day notice.** 4645 Liberty Ave. On US 6, 2 mi e of SR 60. Ext corridors. **Pets:** Accepted.
[SAVE] [S0] [X] [B] [D]

WADSWORTH

AAA ◆ Legacy Inn M
(330) 336-6671. **$42-$51, 3 day notice.** 810 High St. I-76, exit 9, just s. Ext corridors. **Pets:** Service with restrictions, supervision.
[SAVE] [S0] [X] [B] [2~]

WAPAKONETA

AAA ◆◆◆ Best Western Wapakoneta SH
(419) 738-8181. **$66-$129.** 1510 Saturn Dr. I-75, exit 111, just w. Int corridors. **Pets:** Accepted.
[SAVE] [S0] [X] [2] [B] [D] [2~]

◆◆ Super 8 Motel-Wapakoneta SH
(419) 738-8810. **$55.** 1011 Lunar Dr. I-75, exit 111, just w. Ext/int corridors. **Pets:** Accepted.
[ASK] [X] [B] [D]

◆◆ Travelodge SH
(419) 739-9600. **$44-$60.** 413 Apollo Dr. I-75, exit 111, just w. Ext corridors. **Pets:** Dogs only. $5 one-time fee/room. Service with restrictions, supervision.
[ASK] [S0] [X] [B] [D]

WARREN

AAA ◆◆ Best Western M
(330) 392-2515. **$54-$68.** 777 Mahoning Ave. 0.3 mi n of Courthouse Square. Ext corridors. **Pets:** Other species. Service with restrictions, supervision.
[SAVE] [S0] [X] [2] [B] [D] [2~]

AAA ◆◆◆ Comfort Inn SH
(330) 393-1200. **$70-$80.** 136 N Park Ave. Downtown; east side of Courthouse Square. Int corridors. **Pets:** Small. $10 daily fee/pet. Service with restrictions, supervision.
[SAVE] [S0] [X] [B] [D] [11]

WAUSEON

AAA ◆◆ Best Western Del Mar M
(419) 335-1565. **$65-$159.** 8319 SR 108. I-80/90, exit 34, just s. Ext corridors. **Pets:** Other species. $17 one-time fee/pet. Service with restrictions, supervision.
[SAVE] [S0] [X] [2] [6] [B] [D] [2~]

WINCHESTER

AAA ◆◆ Budget Host Inn M
(937) 695-0381. **$55-$65.** 18760 SR 136. Jct US 32. Ext corridors. **Pets:** Accepted.
[SAVE] [S0] [X] [B]

WOOSTER

AAA ◆◆◆ Econo Lodge M
(330) 264-8883. **$59-$69.** 2137 E Lincoln Way. US 30, 3 mi e. Ext corridors. **Pets:** Accepted.
[SAVE] [X] [2] [B] [D] [2~]

◆◆◆ The Wooster Inn CI
(330) 263-2660. **$80-$225.** 801 E Wayne Ave. 0.5 mi e on Liberty St, 1 mi n on Beall Ave. Int corridors. **Pets:** Accepted.
[X] [B] [11] [X]

XENIA

AAA ◆◆ Regency Inn SH
(937) 372-9954. **$45-$70.** 600 Little Main St. 1 mi w. Ext corridors. **Pets:** Other species. $10 daily fee/pet, $10 one-time fee/pet. Service with restrictions, supervision.
[SAVE] [S0] [X] [B] [D]

ZANESVILLE

AAA ◆◆ Best Value Inn SH
(740) 452-4511. **$50-$95.** 135 N 7th St. I-70, exit 155, on SR 60 via signs; downtown. Ext corridors. **Pets:** Accepted.
[SAVE] [S0] [X] [2] [B] [D] [11]

AAA ◆◆◆ Comfort Inn SH
(740) 454-4144. **$69-$164.** 500 Monroe St. I-70, exit 155 westbound; exit 7th St eastbound, e on Elberon to light, just n on Underwood. Int corridors. **Pets:** Medium, other species. $10 one-time fee/room. Designated rooms, service with restrictions, supervision.
[SAVE] [S0] [X] [2] [6] [B] [D] [2~]

◆◆◆ Holiday Inn Conference Center SH ❀
(740) 453-0771. **$69-$109.** 4645 E Pike. I-70, exit 160, on US 22 and 40. Int corridors. **Pets:** $20 one-time fee/room. Designated rooms, service with restrictions, supervision.
[ASK] [S0] [X] [2] [6] [B] [D] [11] [2~] [X]

◆◆ Red Roof Inn SH
(740) 453-6300. **$55-$82.** 4929 E Pike. I-70, exit 160, just s. Int corridors. **Pets:** Other species. Service with restrictions, supervision.
[ASK] [S0] [X] [6M] [6] [B] [2~]

AAA ◆◆ Super 8 Motel-Zanesville SH ❀
(740) 455-3124. **$39-$79.** 2440 National Rd. I-70, exit 152, just n. Int corridors. **Pets:** Medium, other species. $10 daily fee/pet. Service with restrictions, supervision.
[SAVE] [S0] [X] [2] [B]

AAA ◆ Travelodge SH
(740) 453-0611. **$50-$70.** 58 N 6th St. I-70, exit 155, on US 22 and SR 60 at Market St. Ext/int corridors. **Pets:** $10 one-time fee/room. Service with restrictions, supervision.
[SAVE] [S0] [X] [B] [D]

OKLAHOMA

ALTUS

 Best Western Altus SH
(580) 482-9300. **$69-$79.** 2804 N Main St. 2 mi n on US 283. Ext corridors. **Pets:** Service with restrictions, supervision.
[SAVE] [S/D] [✕] [🛏] [📺] [🏊] [✕]

Days Inn M
(580) 477-2300. **$55-$65.** 3202 N Main St. 2.3 mi n on US 283. Ext corridors. **Pets:** Small, dogs only. $10 daily fee/pet. Designated rooms, service with restrictions, supervision.
[ASK] [S/D] [✕] [🛏] [📺]

ARDMORE

 Best Western Inn SH
(580) 223-7525. **$75-$85.** 6 Holiday Dr. I-35, exit 31A, just ne. Int corridors. **Pets:** Small. $8 daily fee/pet. Designated rooms, service with restrictions, supervision.
[SAVE] [S/D] [✕] [🛏] [📺] [🏊]

Holiday Inn SH
(580) 223-7130. **$63-$89.** 2705 W Broadway. I-35, exit 31A, just e. Ext corridors. **Pets:** Medium. $10 one-time fee/room. Service with restrictions.
[ASK] [✕] [🔊] [🛏] [📺] [🍴] [🏊] [✕]

La Quinta Inn Ardmore SH
(580) 223-7976. **Call for rates.** 2432 Veterans Blvd. I-35, exit 33, just e. Ext corridors. **Pets:** Other species. No service, supervision.
[✕] [🔊] [🛏] [📺] [🏊]

Microtel Inn & Suites SH
(580) 224-2600. **$43-$52.** 1904 Cooper Dr. I-35, exit 32, just w. Int corridors. **Pets:** Accepted.
[ASK] [S/D] [✕] [🔊] [🛏] [📺]

Super 8 Motel SH
(580) 223-2201. **$40-$50.** 2120 Veterans Blvd. I-35, exit 33, just e. Int corridors. **Pets:** Accepted.
[ASK] [S/D] [✕] [🛏] [📺]

BARTLESVILLE

Econo Lodge M
(918) 333-0710. **$60.** 3910 SE Nowata Rd. Just e of jct US 60 and 75. Ext corridors. **Pets:** Accepted.
[ASK] [S/D] [✕] [🛏] [📺]

Holiday Inn SH
(918) 333-8320. **$56-$72.** 1410 SE Washington Blvd. Just s of jct US 60 W and 75. Int corridors. **Pets:** Accepted.
[ASK] [✕] [🛏] [📺] [🍴] [🏊]

Super 8 Motel M
(918) 335-1122. **$54, 3 day notice.** 211 SE Washington Blvd. 0.7 mi n of jct US 60 and 75. Ext/int corridors. **Pets:** Small. Service with restrictions, supervision.
[ASK] [S/D] [✕] [🛏] [📺]

BIG CABIN

Big Cabin Super 8 Motel M
(918) 783-5888. **$48-$54.** 30954 S Hwy 69. I-44, exit 283, just ne. Ext/int corridors. **Pets:** Other species. $20 deposit/room. Designated rooms, service with restrictions.
[ASK] [S/D] [✕] [🛏] [🏊]

BLACKWELL

Comfort Inn SH
(580) 363-7000. **$65-$70.** 1201 N 44th St. I-35, exit 222, just ne. Int corridors. **Pets:** Small. $10 daily fee/pet. Service with restrictions, supervision.
[SAVE] [S/D] [✕] [🖍] [🛏] [📺] [🏊]

BROKEN BOW

Microtel Inn SH
(580) 584-7708. **$59.** 1701 S Park Dr. 1 mi s. Int corridors. **Pets:** Accepted.
[ASK] [S/D] [✕] [🛏] [🏊]

CHECOTAH

Days Inn of Eufaula M
(918) 689-3999. **$50-$100.** Hwy 69 & 150. Just w of jct US 69 and SR 150. Ext corridors. **Pets:** Accepted.
[ASK] [S/D] [✕] [🛏]

Lake Eufaula Inn M 🐾
(918) 473-2376. **$19-$79.** SR 150 & I-40. I-40, exit 259, just s. Ext corridors. **Pets:** Large, other species. No service, supervision.
[ASK] [S/D] [✕] [🛏] [🏊]

CHICKASHA

Best Western Inn SH 🐾
(405) 224-4890. **$55-$65.** 2101 S 4th St. I-44, exit 80, just nw. Ext/int corridors. **Pets:** Small. $10 one-time fee/pet. Designated rooms, service with restrictions, crate.
[SAVE] [S/D] [✕] [🛏] [📺] [🍴] [🏊] [✕]

DUNCAN

Chisholm Suite Hotel SH
(580) 255-0551. **$59-$77.** 1204 N Hwy 81. Center. Int corridors. **Pets:** Accepted.
[ASK] [S/D] [✕] [🛏] [📺] [🏊]

DURANT

Comfort Inn & Suites of Durant SH
(580) 924-8881. **$77.** 2112 W Main St. Just e of jct US 75/69 and 70. Int corridors. **Pets:** Accepted.
[ASK] [S/D] [✕] [🔊] [🖍] [🛏] [📺] [🏊]

ELK CITY

▼ Bedford Inn Ⓜ
(580) 225-6775. **$55-$75.** 2004 S Main. I-40, exit 38, just ne. Ext corridors. **Pets:** Accepted.
ASK 🛇 ✕ 🛏 🖵 ⚓

ⒶⒶⒶ ▼▼▼ Holiday Inn 🆂🅷 🐾
(580) 225-6637. **$109-$159.** 101 Meadow Ridge Dr. I-40, exit 38, just sw. Ext/int corridors. **Pets:** Other species. Designated rooms, service with restrictions, supervision.
SAVE ✕ 🖉 🛏 🖵 🍴 ⚓ ⊠

▼▼ Ramada Inn 🆂🅷
(580) 225-8140. **$58.** 102 B J Hughes Access Rd. I-40, exit 38, just s. Ext corridors. **Pets:** Accepted.
ASK 🛇 ✕ 🛏 🖵 🍴 ⚓

▼ Travelodge Ⓜ
(580) 225-6661. **$41-$49.** 2500 E Hwy 66. I-40, exit 41, 0.5 mi nw. Ext corridors. **Pets:** Accepted.
ASK 🛇 ✕ 🛁 🛏 🖵 ⚓

ENID

▼▼ Comfort Inn 🆂🅷
(580) 234-1200. **$70-$100.** 210 N Van Buren St. 0.7 mi n on US 81. Ext/int corridors. **Pets:** Dogs only. $7 one-time fee/pet. Designated rooms, service with restrictions, supervision.
ASK 🛇 ✕ 🛏 🖵 🏊

ERICK

▼▼ Comfort Inn 🆂🅷
(580) 526-8124. **$81-$109, 5 day notice.** 1001 N Sheb Wooley. I-40, exit 7, just nw. Ext corridors. **Pets:** Medium. $6 daily fee/pet. Designated rooms, service with restrictions, supervision.
ASK 🛇 ✕ 🖉 🛏 🖵 ⚓

FREDERICK

ⒶⒶⒶ ▼ Scottish Inns Ⓜ
(580) 335-2129. **$39-$59.** 1015 S Main St. 1 mi s. Ext corridors. **Pets:** Dogs only. Designated rooms, service with restrictions, supervision.
SAVE 🛇 ✕ 🛏 🖵 ⚓

GUYMON

▼▼ Ambassador Inn 🆂🅷
(580) 338-5555. **$50-$80.** Hwy 64 N at 21st. 1.5 mi n on US 64 and SR 136. Ext corridors. **Pets:** Other species. Service with restrictions, supervision.
ASK 🛇 ✕ 🖵 🍴 ⚓

▼▼ Best Western Townsman Inn 🆂🅷
(580) 338-6556. **$59-$99.** 212 NE Hwy 54. 0.7 mi s of jct US 64. Ext corridors. **Pets:** Small. Service with restrictions, crate.
ASK 🛇 ✕ 🛁 🛏 🖵 ⚓

ⒶⒶⒶ ▼▼ Econo Lodge Ⓜ
(580) 338-5431. **$52.** 923 Hwy 54 E. Just s of jct US 64. Ext corridors. **Pets:** Small. $8 one-time fee/pet. Service with restrictions, supervision.
SAVE 🛇 ✕ 🛏

ⒶⒶⒶ ▼▼▼ Guymon Super 8 🆂🅷
(580) 338-0507. **$50-$90.** 1201 Hwy 54 NE. Jct US 54 and 64. Int corridors. **Pets:** Large. $5 daily fee/room. Service with restrictions, supervision.
SAVE 🛇 ✕ 🛏 🖵

HENRYETTA

ⒶⒶⒶ ▼ Green Country Inn Ⓜ
(918) 652-9988. **$38-$42, 3 day notice.** 2004 Old Hwy 75 W. I-40, exit 237, just ne. Ext corridors. **Pets:** Accepted.
SAVE 🛇 ✕ 🛏 🏊

IDABEL

▼▼▼ Comfort Suites 🆂🅷
(580) 286-9393. **$75-$85.** 400 SE Lincoln Blvd. Just s of jct US 70 and 259. Int corridors. **Pets:** $15 one-time fee/pet. Service with restrictions, supervision.
ASK 🛇 ✕ 🛁 🛏 🖵 ⚓

LAWTON

▼▼ Baymont Inn & Suites 🆂🅷
(580) 353-5581. **$69-$89.** 1203 NW 40th St. I-44, exit 39A, 3.7 mi w. Int corridors. **Pets:** Accepted.
ASK 🛇 ✕ 🛁 🛏 🖵 ⚓

ⒶⒶⒶ ▼▼▼ Best Western Hotel & Convention Center 🆂🅷
(580) 353-0200. **$88, 14 day notice.** 1125 E Gore Blvd. I-44, exit 37, just e. Ext/int corridors. **Pets:** Medium. $40 one-time fee/pet. Designated rooms, service with restrictions, supervision.
SAVE 🛇 ✕ 🛏 🖵 🍴 ⚓ ⊠

▼ Motel 6 Lawton #1412 Ⓜ
(580) 355-9765. **$45-$55.** 202 SE Lee Blvd. I-44, exit 36 A/B, just w. Ext corridors. **Pets:** Accepted.
🛇 ✕ ⚓

▼▼ Ramada Inn 🆂🅷
(580) 355-7155. **$58-$64.** 601 NW 2nd St. I-44, exit 37 northbound; exit 39B southbound. Ext/int corridors. **Pets:** Small. $15 daily fee/pet. Designated rooms, service with restrictions, supervision.
ASK 🛇 ✕ 🛏 🖵 🍴 ⚓

ⒶⒶⒶ ▼▼▼ Red Lion Hotel-Lawton 🆂🅷
(580) 353-1682. **$68-$77.** 3134 NW Cache Rd. I-44, exit 39A, 2.5 mi w. Ext corridors. **Pets:** $25 one-time fee/room. Service with restrictions, supervision.
SAVE 🛇 ✕ 🛏 🍴 ⚓ ⊠

MCALESTER

▼▼ Best Western Inn of McAlester 🆂🅷
(918) 426-0115. **$70-$80, 3 day notice.** 1215 George Nigh Expwy. 3 mi s on US 69. Ext corridors. **Pets:** Accepted.
ASK 🛇 ✕ 🖉 🛏 🖵 ⚓

▼▼▼ Holiday Inn Express Hotel & Suites 🆂🅷
(918) 302-0001. **$91-$129.** 650 George Nigh Expwy. 1.2 mi s on US 69. Int corridors. **Pets:** Other species. $25 one-time fee/pet. Service with restrictions, crate.
ASK 🛇 ✕ 🛁 🛏 🖵 ⚓

▼ Microtel Inn 🆂🅷
(918) 429-0910. **$55-$65.** 1400 S George Nigh Expwy. 3.3 mi s on US 69. Int corridors. **Pets:** Small. $10 one-time fee/room. Service with restrictions, supervision.
ASK 🛇 ✕ 🛁 🛏 🖵 ⚓

▼ Super 8 Motel Ⓜ
(918) 426-5400. **$49-$64.** 2400 S Main St. Just n of jct US 69. Ext corridors. **Pets:** Accepted.
✕ 🛏 ⚓

MIAMI

ⒶⒶⒶ ▼▼▼ Best Western Inn of Miami 🆂🅷
(918) 542-6681. **$62-$79.** 2225 E Steve Owens Blvd. I-44, exit 313, just w. Ext corridors. **Pets:** Other species. Service with restrictions, crate.
SAVE 🛇 ✕ 🛏 🖵 🍴 ⚓

MUSKOGEE

ⒶⒶⒶ ▼▼▼ Days Inn of Muskogee Ⓜ
(918) 683-3911. **$59-$69.** 900 S 32nd St. 3 mi s on US 64 and 69. Ext corridors. **Pets:** Small. $5 daily fee/pet. Service with restrictions, supervision.
SAVE 🛇 ✕ 🛏 🖵 ⚓

OKLAHOMA CITY METROPOLITAN AREA

DEL CITY

AAA ▼▼▼▼ **La Quinta Inn Oklahoma City East (Del City)** SH
(405) 672-0067. **$79-$99.** 5501 Tinker Diagonal Rd. I-40, exit 156A (Sooner Rd), just nw. Ext/int corridors. **Pets:** Other species. Service with restrictions, supervision.
[SAVE] ⊗ 🐾 🖨 💻 ➿

EDMOND

AAA ▼▼▼▼ **Best Western Edmond Inn & Suites** SH
(405) 216-0300. **$79-$84, 3 day notice.** 2700 E 2nd St. I-35, exit 141, 1.1 mi w. Int corridors. **Pets:** Accepted.
[SAVE] [S🐾] ⊗ 🖨 💻 ➿

AAA ▼▼▼ **Ramada Plaza Hotel** SH
(405) 341-3577. **$69-$79, 14 day notice.** 930 E 2nd St. I-35, exit 141, 2.3 mi w. Int corridors. **Pets:** Accepted.
[SAVE] [S🐾] ⊗ 🐾 🖨 💻 [¶] ➿

EL RENO

AAA ▼▼▼ **Best Western Hensley's** SH
(405) 262-6490. **$50-$70.** 2701 S Country Club Rd. I-40, exit 123, just s. Ext corridors. **Pets:** Medium, other species. $25 deposit/room, $5 one-time fee/room. Service with restrictions, supervision.
[SAVE] [S🐾] ⊗ 🐾 🖨 💻 ➿

GUTHRIE

AAA ▼▼▼ **Best Western Territorial Inn** SH
(405) 282-8831. **$66-$79.** 2323 Territorial Tr. I-35, exit 157, just sw. Int corridors. **Pets:** Accepted.
[SAVE] [S🐾] ⊗ 🐾 🖨 💻 ➿

MIDWEST CITY

AAA ▼▼▼▼ **AmeriSuites (Midwest City/Tinker Air Force Base)** SH
(405) 737-7777. **$89-$99.** 5701 Tinker Diagonal Rd. I-40, exit 156A (Sooner Rd), just n. Int corridors. **Pets:** Small, dogs only. $10 daily fee/pet. Designated rooms, service with restrictions, supervision.
[SAVE] [S🐾] ⊗ 🐾 🐾 🖨 💻 ➿

▼ **Studio 6 #6003** M
(405) 737-8851. **$49-$62.** 5801 Tinker Diagonal Rd. I-40, exit 156A (Sooner Rd), just ne. Ext corridors. **Pets:** Accepted.
[S🐾] ⊗ 🖨 💻 ➿

MOORE

AAA ▼▼▼ **Best Western Green Tree Inn & Suites** SH
(405) 912-8882. **$85-$95.** 1811 N Moore Ave. I-35, exit 118, just n on westbound frontage road. Int corridors. **Pets:** Small. $5 daily fee/pet. Service with restrictions, supervision.
[SAVE] [S🐾] ⊗ 🐾 🖨 💻 ➿

AAA ▼▼▼ **Microtel Inn & Suites** SH
(405) 799-8181. **$54-$69.** 2400 S Service Rd. I-35, exit 116, just s on east service road. Int corridors. **Pets:** Medium. $7 daily fee/pet. Service with restrictions, supervision.
[SAVE] [S🐾] ⊗ 🐾 🖨 💻 ➿

NORMAN

▼▼▼▼ **Holiday Inn** SH
(405) 364-2882. **$164.** 1000 N Interstate Dr. I-35, exit 110 (Robinson St), w to south service road. Int corridors. **Pets:** Accepted.
[ASK] ⊗ 🐾 🖨 💻 [¶] ➿

▼▼▼ **La Quinta Inn & Suites Oklahoma City (Norman)** SH
(405) 579-4000. **$89-$109.** 930 Ed Noble Dr. I-35, exit 108B (Lindsey), just nw. Int corridors. **Pets:** Accepted.
⊗ 🐾 🖨 💻 ➿

AAA ▼▼▼ **Quality Inn** M
(405) 364-5554. **$75-$85.** 100 SW 26th Dr. I-35, exit 109 (Main St), just se. Ext corridors. **Pets:** Very small. $5 daily fee/pet. Service with restrictions, supervision.
[SAVE] [S🐾] ⊗ 💻

AAA ▼▼▼▼ **The Residence Inn by Marriott** SH
(405) 366-0900. **$89-$119.** 2681 Jefferson St. I-35, exit 108A, just se. Ext corridors. **Pets:** Accepted.
[SAVE] [S🐾] ⊗ 🐾 🐾 🖨 💻 ➿ ⊗

OKLAHOMA CITY

AAA ▼▼▼ **AmeriSuites (Oklahoma City/Airport)** SH
(405) 682-3900. **$99-$104.** 1818 S Meridian Ave. I-40, exit 145 (Meridian Ave), 1 mi s. Int corridors. **Pets:** Accepted.
[SAVE] [S🐾] ⊗ 🐾 🐾 🖨 💻 ➿

AAA ▼▼▼ **AmeriSuites (Oklahoma City/Quail Springs)** SH
(405) 749-1595. **$99-$104.** 3201 W Memorial Rd. John Kilpatrick Tpke, exit May Ave, 0.4 mi w on north service road. Int corridors. **Pets:** Small. $10 daily fee/pet. Designated rooms, service with restrictions, supervision.
[SAVE] [S🐾] ⊗ 🐾 🖨 💻 ➿

AAA ▼▼▼ **Best Western Saddleback Inn** LH
(405) 947-7000. **$94.** 4300 SW 3rd St. I-40, exit 145, just ne. Ext/int corridors. **Pets:** Accepted.
[SAVE] [S🐾] ⊗ 🐾 🖨 💻 [¶] ➿ ⊗

▼▼▼ **Candlewood Suites Hotel** SH
(405) 680-8770. **$79-$98.** 4400 River Park Dr. I-40, exit 145 (Meridian Ave), 1.1 mi s. Int corridors. **Pets:** Medium, other species. $75 one-time fee/pet. Service with restrictions, supervision.
[ASK] [S🐾] ⊗ [🐾M] 🐾 🖨 💻

▼▼▼ **Clarion Meridian Hotel and Convention Center** SH
(405) 942-8511. **$76-$80.** 737 S Meridian Ave. I-40, exit 145 (Meridian Ave), just s. Ext/int corridors. **Pets:** Accepted.
[ASK] [S🐾] ⊗ [🐾M] 🐾 🐾 🖨 💻 ➿

AAA ▼▼▼ **Comfort Inn** SH
(405) 943-4400. **$70.** 4240 W I-40 Service Rd. I-40, exit 145 (Meridian Ave), just e on south frontage road. Ext/int corridors. **Pets:** Small. $20 one-time fee/room. Service with restrictions, supervision.
[SAVE] [S🐾] ⊗ 🐾 🖨 💻 ➿

AAA ▼▼▼ **Comfort Inn at Founders Tower** SH
(405) 810-1100. **$62-$149.** 5704 Mosteller Dr. 0.5 mi e of jct SR 74 and 3. Int corridors. **Pets:** Accepted.
[SAVE] [S🐾] ⊗ 🖨 💻 ➿

AAA ▼▼▼ **Comfort Inn North** SH
(405) 478-7282. **$65-$125.** 4625 NE 120th. I-35, exit 137 (122nd St), just sw. Int corridors. **Pets:** Large, other species. $10 daily fee/pet. Service with restrictions, crate.
[SAVE] [S🐾] ⊗ 🐾 🖨 💻 ➿

AAA ▼▼▼ **Courtyard by Marriott-Downtown/Bricktown** SH
(405) 232-2290. **$94-$134, 30 day notice.** 2 W Reno Ave. Gaylord and Reno aves; downtown. Int corridors. **Pets:** Small. $50 deposit/room. Service with restrictions, supervision.
[SAVE] [S🐾] ⊗ [🐾M] 🐾 🐾 🖨 💻 [¶] ➿

▼▼▼ Courtyard by Marriott-NW SH
(405) 848-0808. **$79-$160.** 1515 Northwest Expwy. I-44, exit 125C westbound; exit 125B eastbound, just e. Int corridors. **Pets:** Medium. $40 one-time fee/pet. Designated rooms, service with restrictions, crate.

ASK ✕ &M ✦ 🛏 💻 ﹖ ♒ ✕

▼▼ Days Inn & Suites North SH
(405) 478-2554. **$52-$89.** 12013 N I-35 Service Rd. I-35, exit 137, just sw. Ext/int corridors. **Pets:** Accepted.

ASK S6 ✕ 🛏 💻 ♒

⊕ ▼▼ Days Inn West SH
(405) 942-8294. **$49.** 504 S Meridian Ave. I-40, exit 145 (Meridian Ave), just ne. Ext corridors. **Pets:** Other species. $10 one-time fee/room. Service with restrictions, supervision.

SAVE S6 ✕ 🛏 💻 ♒

⊕ ▼▼ Econo Lodge SH
(405) 942-5955. **$43-$54.** 4601 SW 3rd. I-40, exit 145 (Meridian Ave), just nw. Ext corridors. **Pets:** Accepted.

SAVE S6 ✕ 💻 ♒

▼▼▼ Embassy Suites LH ✿
(405) 682-6000. **$99-$179.** 1815 S Meridian Ave. I-40, exit 145 (Meridian Ave), 1 mi s. Int corridors. **Pets:** $35 one-time fee/pet. Service with restrictions, supervision.

ASK S6 ✕ ⊘ 🛏 💻 ﹖ ♒ ✕

▼▼▼ Four Points by Sheraton Oklahoma City SH
(405) 681-3500. **$90.** 6300 Terminal Dr. I-40, exit 145 (Meridian Ave), 4 mi s. Int corridors. **Pets:** Very small. $30 one-time fee/room. Service with restrictions, supervision.

ASK S6 ✕ &' 🛏 💻 ♒ ✕

▼▼▼ Hilton Oklahoma City Northwest LH
(405) 848-4811. **Call for rates.** 2945 Northwest Expwy. 0.5 mi e of jct SR 74 and 3. Ext/int corridors. **Pets:** Medium. $20 daily fee/room. Designated rooms, service with restrictions, crate.

✕ ⊘ &' 🛏 💻 ﹖ ♒ ✕

▼▼▼ Holiday Inn Express-Quail Springs SH
(405) 755-8686. **$65-$85.** 13520 Plaza Terrace. John Kilpatrick Tpke, exit May Ave, just e on south frontage road. Int corridors. **Pets:** Accepted.

ASK S6 ✕ &' 🛏 💻 ♒

▼▼▼ Holiday Inn Hotel & Suites SH ✿
(405) 843-5558. **$77.** 6200 N Robinson Ave. I-44, exit 127, just nw. Ext/int corridors. **Pets:** Small, dogs only. $25 one-time fee/pet. Designated rooms, service with restrictions, crate.

ASK S6 ✕ &' 🛏 💻 ﹖

⊕ ▼▼ Howard Johnson Express Inn-Airport M
(405) 943-9841. **$51, 7 day notice.** 400 S Meridian Ave. I-40, exit 145 (Meridian Ave), just n. Int corridors. **Pets:** Other species. $6 daily fee/pet. Service with restrictions, crate.

SAVE S6 ✕ ⊘ 🛏 💻 ♒

▼▼▼ La Quinta Inn & Suites Oklahoma City (Northwest Expressway) SH
(405) 773-5575. **$99-$109.** 4829 Northwest Expwy. 1.9 mi w of jct SR 74 and 3. Int corridors. **Pets:** Small. Service with restrictions, supervision.

ASK ✕ ⊘ &' 🛏 💻 ♒

⊕ ▼▼▼ La Quinta Inn Oklahoma City (Airport) SH
(405) 942-0040. **$89-$99.** 800 S Meridian Ave. I-40, exit 145 (Meridian Ave), just se. Ext/int corridors. **Pets:** Other species. Service with restrictions.

SAVE ✕ &' 🛏 💻 ﹖ ♒

▼▼▼ La Quinta Inn Oklahoma City (South) SH
(405) 631-8661. **$79-$89.** 8315 I-35 S. I-35, exit 121A (82nd St), just sw. Ext corridors. **Pets:** Other species. Service with restrictions, crate.

ASK ✕ 🛏 💻 ♒

▼▼ Motel 6-1182 M
(405) 478-4030. **$35-$52.** 12121 Northeast Expwy. I-35, exit 137, just sw. Ext corridors. **Pets:** Small. Service with restrictions, supervision.

S6 ✕ ⊘ &' ♒

▼▼ Motel 6 Airport-116 M
(405) 946-6662. **$41-$51.** 820 S Meridian Ave. I-40, exit 145 (Meridian Ave), just se. Ext corridors. **Pets:** Medium, other species. Service with restrictions, supervision.

S6 ✕ ⊘ &' ♒

▼▼ Motel 6 West-1128 SH
(405) 947-6550. **$43-$55.** 4200 I-40 Service Rd. I-40, exit 145 (Meridian Ave), just e on south frontage road. Ext/int corridors. **Pets:** Accepted.

S6 ✕ 🛏 ♒

▼▼▼ Oklahoma City Marriott LH
(405) 842-6633. **$132-$169.** 3233 Northwest Expwy. Just e of jct SR 74 and 3. Int corridors. **Pets:** Accepted.

ASK ✕ ⊘ &' 🛏 💻 ﹖ ♒ ✕

⊕ ▼▼▼ Quality Inn SH ✿
(405) 632-6666. **$70-$80.** 7800 CA Henderson Blvd. I-240, exit 2A, just s. Ext corridors. **Pets:** Small, dogs only. $10 one-time fee/pet. Designated rooms, service with restrictions.

SAVE S6 ✕ ⊘ &' 🛏 💻 ♒

⊕ ▼▼ Quality Inn at Frontier City SH
(405) 478-0400. **$60-$70.** 12001 N I-35 Service Rd. I-35, exit 137, just sw. Ext corridors. **Pets:** Medium, other species. $10 daily fee/pet. Service with restrictions, crate.

SAVE S6 ✕ &' 💻 ♒

⊕ ▼▼ Ramada Limited SH
(405) 948-8000. **$69-$129.** 2727 W I-44 Service Rd. I-44, exit 124, just n. Int corridors. **Pets:** Medium. $10 one-time fee/pet. Designated rooms, service with restrictions, supervision.

SAVE S6 ✕ &' 🛏 💻 ♒

⊕ ▼▼▼▼ Renaissance Oklahoma City Hotel LH
(405) 228-8000. **$209.** 10 N Broadway Ave. Sheridan and Broadway aves; downtown. Int corridors. **Pets:** Medium. Service with restrictions, supervision.

SAVE ✕ &M ⊘ &' 🛏 💻 ﹖ ♒ ✕

▼▼▼ Residence Inn by Marriott South-Crossroads Mall SH
(405) 634-9696. **$109-$145, 14 day notice.** 1111 E I-240 Service Rd. I-240, exit 4C eastbound, 0.4 mi nw; exit 5 westbound, 0.8 mi nw. Int corridors. **Pets:** Accepted.

ASK S6 ✕ &' 🛏 💻 ♒

▼▼▼ Residence Inn by Marriott-West SH ✿
(405) 942-4500. **$105-$135.** 4361 W Reno Ave. I-40, exit 145 (Meridian Ave), 0.3 mi n, then just e. Ext corridors. **Pets:** Other species. $75 one-time fee/room.

ASK ✕ ⊘ 🛏 💻 ♒ ✕

⊕ ▼▼▼▼ Sheraton Oklahoma City LH
(405) 235-2780. **$199-$239.** One N Broadway Ave. Sheridan and Broadway aves; downtown. Int corridors. **Pets:** Medium, dogs only. Service with restrictions, crate.

SAVE S6 ✕ ⊘ &' 🛏 💻 ﹖ ♒

PURCELL

⊕ ▼▼ Econo Lodge M
(405) 527-5603. **$65-$70.** 2122 Hwy 74 S. I-35, exit 91, just e. Ext corridors. **Pets:** Small. $5 daily fee/pet. Service with restrictions, supervision.

SAVE S6 ✕ ⊘ 🛏

SHAWNEE

▼ **Motel 6–1236** **M**
(405) 275-5310. **$43-$55.** 4981 N Harrison. I-40, exit 186, just ne. Int corridors. **Pets:** Accepted.
[icons]

YUKON

(AAA) ▼▼▼▼ **Best Western Inn & Suites Yukon** **SH**
(405) 265-2995. **$71-$86.** 11440 W I-40 Service Rd. I-40, exit 138, just sw. Ext/int corridors. **Pets:** Other species. $25 deposit/room, $5 daily fee/room. Service with restrictions, supervision.
[icons]

END METROPOLITAN AREA

OKMULGEE

(AAA) ▼▼▼ **Best Western Okmulgee** **SH**
(918) 756-9200. **$69-$99.** 3499 N Wood Dr. Just n of jct US 75 and SR 56. Int corridors. **Pets:** Small. $50 deposit/pet. Service with restrictions, supervision.
[icons]

PAULS VALLEY

(AAA) ▼▼▼ **Days Inn** **SH**
(405) 238-7548. **$70-$75.** 2606 W Grant Ave. I-35, exit 72, just e. Int corridors. **Pets:** Accepted.
[icons]

PONCA CITY

▼▼ **Holiday Inn Ponca City** **SH**
(580) 762-8311. **$79-$82.** 2215 N 14th St. 2.8 mi n on US 77. Ext corridors. **Pets:** Small. Service with restrictions, supervision.
[icons]

PRYOR

▼▼▼ **Comfort Inn & Suites** **SH**
(918) 476-6660. **$69-$119.** 307 Mid America Dr. 5 mi s on US 69. Int corridors. **Pets:** Accepted.
[icons]

▼ **Microtel Inn & Suites** **SH**
(918) 476-4661. **Call for rates.** 315 Mid America Dr. 5.1 mi s on US 69. Int corridors. **Pets:** Accepted.
[icons]

ROLAND

▼▼ **Days Inn of Roland** **SH**
(918) 427-1000. **$55, 15 day notice.** 207 Cherokee Blvd. I-40, exit 325, just ne. Int corridors. **Pets:** Accepted.
[icons]

SALLISAW

(AAA) ▼▼ **Best Western Blue Ribbon Inn** **SH**
(918) 775-6294. **$60-$100.** 706 S Kerr Blvd (US 59). I-40, exit 308 (US 59), just n. Ext/int corridors. **Pets:** Small. $20 one-time fee/pet. Designated rooms, service with restrictions, supervision.
[icons]

▼▼ **Microtel Inn & Suites** **SH**
(918) 774-0400. **$48-$64.** 710 S Kerr Blvd. I-40, exit 308 (US 59), just n. Int corridors. **Pets:** Medium, dogs only. $10 one-time fee/pet. Service with restrictions, supervision.
[icons]

SAVANNA

(AAA) ▼▼ **Travelodge** **M**
(918) 548-3506. **$50-$75.** Hwy 69 & Panola. 2 mi sw of jct Indian Nation Tpke. Ext corridors. **Pets:** Accepted.
[icons]

SAYRE

▼▼ **AmericInn Lodge & Suites of Sayre** **SH**
(580) 928-2700. **$75-$137, 30 day notice.** 2405 S El Camino Rd. I-40, exit 20, just n. Int corridors. **Pets:** Small. $15 one-time fee/pet. Designated rooms, service with restrictions, supervision.
[icons]

STILLWATER

(AAA) ▼▼ **Best Western Stillwater** **SH**
(405) 377-7010. **$70-$95.** 600 E McElroy. 1 mi n on US 177 (Perkins Rd). Int corridors. **Pets:** Accepted.
[icons]

▼▼ **Holiday Inn** **SH**
(405) 372-0800. **$77-$142.** 2515 W 6th Ave. 1.8 mi w on SR 51. Ext/int corridors. **Pets:** Accepted.
[icons]

TULSA METROPOLITAN AREA

BROKEN ARROW

(AAA) ▼▼▼ **Holiday Inn Tulsa South** **SH**
(918) 258-7085. **$109.** 2600 N Aspen Ave. Just s of jct SR 51. Int corridors. **Pets:** Accepted.
[icons]

CATOOSA

(AAA) ▼ **Super 8 Motel** **M**
(918) 266-7000. **$40-$55, 7 day notice.** 19250 Timbercrest Cir. I-44, exit 240A, just nw. Ext corridors. **Pets:** Accepted.
[icons]

CLAREMORE

(AAA) ▼ **Claremore Motor Inn** **M** ❀
(918) 342-4545. **$45-$55.** 1709 N Lynn Riggs. 1.2 mi n on SR 66. Ext/int corridors. **Pets:** Small. $50 deposit/room, $5 daily fee/pet. Service with restrictions, supervision.
[icons]

▼▼ **Days Inn Claremore** **SH**
(918) 343-3297. **$64-$90.** 1720 S Lynn Riggs. 1.6 mi s on SR 66. Int corridors. **Pets:** Large, other species. $10 daily fee/pet. Supervision.
[icons]

▼▼ **Microtel Inn & Suites** **SH**
(918) 343-2868. **$58.** 10600 E Mallard Lake Rd. 2.6 mi s on SR 66. Int corridors. **Pets:** Medium. $25 one-time fee/pet. Designated rooms, service with restrictions, supervision.
[icons]

🔺🔺 ▽▽ Super 8 Motel SH
(918) 341-2323. **$59-$69.** 1100 E Will Rogers Blvd. I-44, exit 255, just w. Ext/int corridors. **Pets:** Small. $25 deposit/room, $5 daily fee/pet. Designated rooms, service with restrictions, supervision.
🅂🄰🅅🄴 🛇 ✕ 🅿

🔺🔺 ▽ Travel Inn M
(918) 341-3254. **$40-$50, 7 day notice.** 812 E Will Rogers Blvd. I-44, exit 255, 0.5 mi w. Ext corridors. **Pets:** Accepted.
🅂🄰🅅🄴 🛇 ✕ 🅿

GLENPOOL

🔺🔺 ▽▽ Best Western Glenpool/Tulsa SH
(918) 322-5201. **$63-$69.** 14831 S Casper St. I-44, exit 224, 9.5 mi s on US 75. Ext corridors. **Pets:** Small. $50 deposit/room. Service with restrictions, supervision.
🅂🄰🅅🄴 🛇 ✕ 🅿 🖭 🏊

SAND SPRINGS

🔺🔺 ▽▽ Best Western Sand Springs Inn & Suites SH
(918) 245-4999. **$63-$120.** 211 S Lake Dr. US 64 and 412, exit 81st W Ave, just sw. Ext/int corridors. **Pets:** Accepted.
🅂🄰🅅🄴 🛇 ✕ 🅿 🖭 🏊

SAPULPA

▽▽ Sapulpa Super 8 Motel SH
(918) 227-3300. **$49-$54.** 1505 New Sapulpa Rd. 0.5 mi e on SR 66. Int corridors. **Pets:** Other species. Designated rooms, service with restrictions, supervision.
🄰🅂🄺 🛇 ✕ 🅐 🅿 🏊

TULSA

🔺🔺 ▽▽▽ AmeriSuites (Tulsa/Hyde Park) SH
(918) 491-4010. **$109-$115.** 7037 S Zurich Ave. I-44, exit 229 (Yale Ave/SR 66), 3 mi s to 71st St, then just e. Int corridors. **Pets:** Other species. Service with restrictions, supervision.
🅂🄰🅅🄴 🛇 ✕ 🅐 🅔 🅿 🖭 🏊

▽▽ Baymont Inn & Suites Tulsa SH
(918) 488-8777. **$59-$79.** 4530 E Skelly Dr. I-44, exit 229 (Yale Ave/SR 66), just s, then w. Int corridors. **Pets:** Accepted.
🄰🅂🄺 🛇 ✕ 🅐 🅿 🖭 🏊

🔺🔺 ▽▽ Best Western Trade Winds Central Inn SH
(918) 749-5561. **$59-$79.** 3141 E Skelly Dr. I-44, exit 228 (Harvard Ave), on northwest frontage road. Ext/int corridors. **Pets:** Very small. $10 one-time fee/room. Service with restrictions, crate.
🅂🄰🅅🄴 🛇 ✕ 🅐 🅿 🖭 🍴 🏊

🔺🔺 ▽ Days Inn-Tulsa West SH
(918) 446-1561. **$45-$47.** 5525 W Skelly Dr. I-44, exit 222B eastbound, just w on south service road; exit 222A westbound, just e on south service road. **Pets:** Medium. $8 daily fee/pet. Service with restrictions, supervision.
🅂🄰🅅🄴 🛇 ✕ 🅿 🏊

▽▽▽ Doubletree Hotel At Warren Place LH ❀
(918) 495-1000. **$79-$189.** 6110 S Yale Ave. I-44, exit 229 (Yale Ave/SR 66), 1.3 mi s. Int corridors. **Pets:** Medium. $25 one-time fee/pet. Service with restrictions, supervision.
✕ 🅐 🅿 🖭 🍴 🏊 🏓

▽▽▽ Doubletree Hotel Downtown Tulsa LH
(918) 587-8000. **$89-$179.** 616 W 7th St. 7th St and Houston. Int corridors. **Pets:** $50 one-time fee/room. Supervision.
✕ 🅐 🅿 🖭 🍴 🏊

▽▽ Holiday Inn Express SH
(918) 459-5321. **$70-$90.** 9010 E 71st St. US 169, exit 71st St, 1 mi w. Int corridors. **Pets:** Medium, other species. $50 one-time fee/pet. Designated rooms, no service, supervision.
🄰🅂🄺 🛇 ✕ 🅐 🅔 🅿 🖭 🏊

▽▽▽ Holiday Inn-International Airport SH
(918) 437-7660. **$84.** 1010 N Garnett Rd. I-244, exit 14 (Garnett Rd), just n. Int corridors. **Pets:** Small, dogs only. $25 one-time fee/room. Service with restrictions, supervision.
🄰🅂🄺 🛇 ✕ 🅐 🅔 🅿 🖭 🍴 🏊 🏓

▽▽▽ Holiday Inn Select SH
(918) 622-7000. **$129.** 5000 E Skelly Dr. I-44, exit 229 (Yale Ave/SR 66); on south frontage road. Ext/int corridors. **Pets:** Accepted.
🄰🅂🄺 🛇 ✕ 🅐 🅿 🖭 🍴 🏊

▽▽▽ Hotel Ambassador SH
(918) 587-8200. **$149-$240.** 1324 S Main St. 14th and Main sts. Int corridors. **Pets:** Small, other species. $200 deposit/room. Service with restrictions, supervision.
🄰🅂🄺 🛇 ✕ 🅔 🅿 🖭 🍴

🔺🔺 ▽▽◆ La Quinta Inn Tulsa (Airport) SH
(918) 836-3931. **$70-$80.** 35 N Sheridan Rd. I-244, exit 11 (Sheridan Rd). Ext corridors. **Pets:** Other species. Service with restrictions, supervision.
🅂🄰🅅🄴 ✕ 🅐 🅿 🖭 🏊

🔺🔺 ▽▽▽ La Quinta Inn Tulsa Central SH
(918) 665-2630. **$65-$89.** 6030 E Skelly Dr. I-44, exit 230, just s. Int corridors. **Pets:** Medium, other species. Service with restrictions, supervision.
🅂🄰🅅🄴 🛇 ✕ 🅿 🖭 🏊

🔺🔺 ▽▽◆ La Quinta Inn Tulsa (East) SH
(918) 665-0220. **$69-$79.** 10829 E 41st St. US 169, exit E 41st St. Ext corridors. **Pets:** Medium. Service with restrictions, supervision.
🅂🄰🅅🄴 🛇 ✕ 🅐 🅿 🖭 🏊

▽▽ La Quinta Inn Tulsa (South) SH
(918) 254-1626. **$79-$89.** 12525 E 52nd St S. Broken Arrow Expwy (SR 51), exit 129th and 51st sts, just s. Ext corridors. **Pets:** Other species. Supervision.
🄰🅂🄺 ✕ 🅐 🅿 🖭 🏊

▽▽ Microtel Inn & Suites SH
(918) 234-9100. **$49-$89, 3 day notice.** 16518 E Admiral Pl. I-44, exit 238 (161st Ave), just s. Int corridors. **Pets:** Accepted.
🄰🅂🄺 🛇 ✕ 🅐 🅔 🅿 🖭

▽▽ Microtel Inn & Suites SH
(918) 858-3775. **$39-$65.** 4531 E 21st St. Just w of 21st St and Yale Ave. Int corridors. **Pets:** Other species. $25 one-time fee/room. Service with restrictions, supervision.
🄰🅂🄺 🛇 ✕ 🅔 🅿 🖭

🔺🔺 ▽▽ Ramada Inn SH
(918) 743-9811. **$65-$85.** 3131 E 51st St. I-44, exit 228 (Harvard Ave), just sw. Ext/int corridors. **Pets:** Accepted.
🅂🄰🅅🄴 🛇 ✕ 🅿 🖭 🏊

▽▽ Red Roof Inn M
(918) 622-6776. **$52-$90.** 4717 S Yale Ave. I-44, exit 229 (Yale Ave), just s. Ext corridors. **Pets:** Medium. Service with restrictions, supervision.
🄰🅂🄺 🛇 ✕ 🅿 🏊

🔺🔺 ▽▽▽ ▽▽▽ Renaissance Tulsa Hotel & Convention Center LH
(918) 307-2600. **$98-$189.** 6808 S 107th E Ave. Just ne of jct US 169 and 71st St. Int corridors. **Pets:** Large, other species. Service with restrictions, crate.
🅂🄰🅅🄴 🛇 ✕ 🅜 🅐 🅿 🖭 🍴 🏊 🏓

▽▽▽ Residence Inn by Marriott [SH]
(918) 250-4850. **$89-$119, 14 day notice.** 11025 E 73rd St. US 169, exit 71st St, just e. Int corridors. **Pets:** Accepted.
[ASK] [S🐾] [✕] [🔋] [💻] [🏊] [✕]

▽▽▽ Rodeway Inn & Suites [SH]
(918) 664-7241. **$60-$95.** 8181 E 41st St. 1.7 mi w of jct US 169. Ext corridors. **Pets:** Accepted.
[ASK] [S🐾] [✕] [🗝] [🔋] [💻] [🏊] [✕]

▽▽▽ Sheraton Tulsa Hotel [LH] 🐾
(918) 627-5000. **$99-$165.** 10918 E 41st St. Just e of US 169. Int corridors. **Pets:** Dogs only. Service with restrictions, crate.
[ASK] [S🐾] [✕] [🗝] [🔋] [🔋] [💻] [🍴] [🏊] [✕]

AAA ▽▽▽ Sleep Inn & Suites Tulsa [SH]
(918) 663-2777. **$59-$85, 3 day notice.** 8021 E 33rd St S. I-44, exit 231 eastbound; exit 232 (Memorial Dr) westbound, just sw. Int corridors. **Pets:** Small. $10 daily fee/pet. Service with restrictions, supervision.
[SAVE] [S🐾] [✕] [🗝] [🔋] [🔋] [💻] [🏊] [✕]

▽▽▽ Staybridge Suites [SH]
(918) 461-2100. **$105-$110.** 11111 E 73rd St. Just se of jct US 169 and 71st St. Int corridors. **Pets:** Small, other species. $75 one-time fee/pet. Designated rooms, service with restrictions, crate.
[ASK] [✕] [🗝M] [🔋] [🔋] [💻] [🏊] [✕]

AAA ▽▽▽ Super 8 Motel [SH] 🐾
(918) 446-6000. **$40-$60.** 5811 S 49th West Ave. I-44, exit 222A, just e on south service road. Ext corridors. **Pets:** No service.
[SAVE] [S🐾] [✕] [🔋] [🏊]

▽▽▽ Tulsa Hilton Southern Hills [LH]
(918) 492-5000. **$69-$169.** 7902 S Lewis. I-44, exit 227, 3 mi s. Int corridors. **Pets:** Accepted.
[S🐾] [✕] [🗝] [🔋] [🔋] [💻] [🍴] [🏊]

END METROPOLITAN AREA

WEATHERFORD

AAA ▽▽▽ Best Western Mark Motor Hotel [SH]
(580) 772-3325. **$59-$79.** 525 E Main St. I-40, exit 82, 0.5 mi n. Ext corridors. **Pets:** Accepted.
[SAVE] [S🐾] [✕] [🗝] [🔋] [🔋] [💻] [🏊]

WOODWARD

AAA ▽▽▽ Northwest Inn [SH]
(580) 256-7600. **$75-$85.** Hwy 270 S & 1st St. 1.4 mi s on US 183, 270, SR 3 and 34. Ext/int corridors. **Pets:** Other species. $15 one-time fee/room. Service with restrictions, supervision.
[SAVE] [S🐾] [✕] [🔋] [💻] [🍴] [🏊] [✕]

OREGON

ALBANY

Best Western Albany Inn SH
(541) 928-6322. **$69-$110.** 315 Airport Rd SE. I-5, exit 234B southbound; exit 234 northbound, just w, then just s. Ext corridors. **Pets:** Accepted.

Days Inn & Suites SH
(541) 928-5050. **$69-$89.** 1100 Price Rd SE. I-5, exit 233, just e, then just n. Int corridors. **Pets:** Large. $20 one-time fee/pet. Designated rooms, service with restrictions, supervision.

La Quinta Inn & Suites Albany SH
(541) 928-0921. **$69-$89.** 251 Airport Rd SE. I-5, exit 234B southbound; exit 234 northbound, just w. Int corridors. **Pets:** Other species. Service with restrictions, supervision.

Motel 6 #4124 SH
(541) 926-4233. **$62-$74, 15 day notice.** 2735 E Pacific Blvd. I-5, exit 234B southbound; exit 234 northbound, 0.5 mi w. Ext corridors. **Pets:** Medium, other species. Service with restrictions, supervision.

Phoenix Inn Suites-Albany SH
(541) 926-5696. **$69-$99.** 3410 Spicer Rd SE. I-5, exit 233, just e. Int corridors. **Pets:** Medium. $20 daily fee/room. Service with restrictions, supervision.

ASHLAND

Ashland Springs Hotel SH
(541) 488-1700. **$89-$209.** 212 E Main St. Corner of 1st St; center. Int corridors. **Pets:** Accepted.

Best Western Bard's Inn SH
(541) 482-0049. **$80-$156.** 132 N Main St. Just n on SR 99 (N Main St) from Downtown Plaza. Ext/int corridors. **Pets:** Other species. $15 daily fee/pet. Designated rooms, service with restrictions, supervision.

Best Western Windsor Inn SH
(541) 488-2330. **$69-$169.** 2520 Ashland St. I-5, exit 14, just e on SR 66. Ext corridors. **Pets:** Other species. $15 daily fee/pet. Service with restrictions, supervision.

Cedarwood Inn M
(541) 488-2000. **$59-$105, 3 day notice.** 1801 Siskiyou Blvd. I-5, exit 11 northbound, 2.8 mi w; exit 14 southbound, just w on SR 66, 0.6 mi s on Tolman Creek Rd, then 0.6 mi w. Ext corridors. **Pets:** Accepted.

Flagship Inn of Ashland M
(541) 482-2641. **$59-$109, 3 day notice.** 1193 Siskiyou Blvd. I-5, exit 14, 1.3 mi w on SR 66, just n on SR 99 (Siskiyou Blvd). Ext corridors. **Pets:** Medium, other species. $10 daily fee/pet. Designated rooms, service with restrictions, crate.

Knights Inn Motel M
(541) 482-5111. **$58-$88, 3 day notice.** 2359 Hwy 66. I-5, exit 14, just w. Ext corridors. **Pets:** Other species. $10 daily fee/pet. Designated rooms, service with restrictions, supervision.

La Quinta Inn & Suites Ashland SH
(541) 482-6932. **$79-$149.** 434 Valley View Rd. I-5, exit 19, just w. Int corridors. **Pets:** Accepted.

Plaza Inn & Suites At Ashland Creek SH
(541) 488-8900. **$69-$249.** 98 Central Ave. I-5, exit 19, 0.5 mi w, 1.9 mi s on SR 99 (N Main St), just e on Water St, then just n. Int corridors. **Pets:** Accepted.

Super 8 Motel-Ashland SH
(541) 482-8887. **$65-$110.** 2350 Ashland St. I-5, exit 14, just w. Int corridors. **Pets:** Small, dogs only. $10 daily fee/pet. Service with restrictions, supervision.

Timbers Motel M 🐾
(541) 482-4242. **$46-$97, 3 day notice.** 1450 Ashland St. I-5, exit 14, 0.8 mi w. Ext corridors. **Pets:** Other species. Designated rooms, service with restrictions, crate.

Windmill Inn & Suites of Ashland SH 🐾
(541) 482-8310. **$64-$160.** 2525 Ashland St. I-5, exit 14, just e. Int corridors. **Pets:** Large, other species. Designated rooms, service with restrictions, crate.

ASTORIA

▽▽▽▽ Astoria Holiday Inn Express Hotel & Suites SH ❖
(503) 325-6222. **$79-$229.** 204 W Marine Dr. On US 30; west side of town. Int corridors. **Pets:** $15 daily fee/pet. Designated rooms, service with restrictions, supervision.
(ASK) (S/D) (✕) (&M) (🗐) (🖘) (🛢) (🖵) (🏊) (✕)

◬◬ ▽▽▽ Best Western Lincoln Inn SH ❖
(503) 325-2205. **$79-$259.** 555 Hamburg Ave. On US 101/30, at east end of Young's Bay Bridge. Int corridors. **Pets:** Other species. $10 daily fee/room. Service with restrictions, supervision.
(SAVE) (S/D) (✕) (&M) (🛢) (🖵) (🏊) (✕)

▽▽ ▽▽ Clementine's Bed & Breakfast BB ❖
(503) 325-2005. **$75-$160, 7 day notice.** 847 Exchange St. At 8th and Exchange sts; in historic downtown. Int corridors. **Pets:** $20 one-time fee/room. Designated rooms, service with restrictions, supervision.
(✕) (🛢) (🖵) (🎦) (🗲)

◬◬◬ ▽▽▽ Crest Motel M
(503) 325-3141. **$63-$138.** 5366 Leif Erickson Dr. 4 mi e of Astoria Bridge on US 30. Ext corridors. **Pets:** Other species. Service with restrictions, supervision.
(SAVE) (✕) (🛢) (🖵) (🎦)

◬◬◬ ▽▽▽ Red Lion Inn Astoria M ❖
(503) 325-7373. **$69-$199.** 400 Industry St. Just w of Astoria Bridge on US 30, just n on Basin St (Caution: do not turn onto Astoria-Megler Bridge). Ext corridors. **Pets:** Other species. $10 daily fee/pet. Designated rooms, service with restrictions.
(SAVE) (S/D) (✕) (🗐) (🛢) (🖵) (🎦)

BAKER CITY

◬◬◬ ▽▽▽▽ Best Western Sunridge Inn SH
(541) 523-6444. **$70-$88.** 1 Sunridge Ln. I-84, exit 304, just w. Int corridors. **Pets:** Accepted.
(SAVE) (S/D) (✕) (&M) (🗐) (🛢) (🖵) (🍴) (🏊)

▽▽▽▽ Geiser Grand Hotel SH
(541) 523-1889. **$89-$209.** 1996 Main St. I-84, exit 304, 0.9 mi w on Campbell St, then 0.3 mi s; downtown. Int corridors. **Pets:** Other species. $15 daily fee/pet, $75 one-time fee/room. Service with restrictions, crate.
(ASK) (S/D) (✕) (🖘) (🍴)

BANDON

◬◬◬ ▽▽▽ Best Western Inn at Face Rock SH ❖
(541) 347-9441. **$106-$264.** 3225 Beach Loop Dr. 1 mi s on US 101, 0.8 mi w on Seabird Rd, then just s. Ext corridors. **Pets:** Other species. $25 one-time fee/room. Designated rooms, service with restrictions, supervision.
(SAVE) (S/D) (✕) (🗐) (🖘) (🛢) (🖵) (🍴) (🏊) (✕) (🎦)

◬◬◬ ▽▽▽ Driftwood Motel M
(541) 347-9022. **$65-$100.** 460 Hwy 101. On US 101; center. Ext corridors. **Pets:** Dogs only. $10 daily fee/pet. Designated rooms, service with restrictions, supervision.
(SAVE) (✕) (🛢) (🖵) (🎦)

◬◬◬ ▽▽▽ Harbor View Motel M ❖
(541) 347-4417. **$69-$129.** 355 Hwy 101. Center. Ext corridors. **Pets:** Medium. $15 daily fee/pet. Designated rooms, supervision.
(SAVE) (✕) (🗐) (🛢) (🖵) (🎦)

BEND

▽▽ ▽▽ Bend Super 8 Motel SH
(541) 388-6888. **$59-$97.** 1275 S Business Hwy 97. US 97, exit 139 (Reed Market Rd), just s; jct US 20 E, 3.5 mi s. Int corridors. **Pets:** Accepted.
(ASK) (S/D) (✕) (🛢) (🏊)

◬◬◬ ▽▽▽ Best Western Inn & Suites of Bend SH
(541) 382-1515. **$69-$149.** 721 NE 3rd St. On Business Rt US 97, just s of jct US 20. Ext corridors. **Pets:** Other species. $10 daily fee/pet. Designated rooms, service with restrictions, supervision.
(SAVE) (S/D) (✕) (🗐) (🛢) (🖵) (🏊)

▽▽▽▽ Cricketwood Country Bed & Breakfast BB ❖
(541) 330-0747. **$95-$130, 7 day notice.** 63520 Cricketwood Rd. 3.8 mi se on Deschutes Market Rd, 0.5 mi e on Hamehook Rd, 0.5 mi on Repine Rd, then just n. Ext/int corridors. **Pets:** Dogs only. $10 daily fee/room. Designated rooms, no service.
(✕) (🛢) (🖵)

◬◬◬ ▽▽▽ Econo Lodge SH
(541) 382-2211. **$40-$89.** 3705 N US Hwy 97 business loop. On US 97 business loop, 2 mi n. Ext corridors. **Pets:** Dogs only. $5 one-time fee/pet. Designated rooms, supervision.
(SAVE) (S/D) (✕) (🛢) (🏊)

▽▽▽ Entrada Lodge SH
(541) 382-4080. **$69-$119.** 19221 SW Century Dr. 5.7 mi w on Mt. Bachelor Rt via Division St/Colorado Ave from jct US 20 W/97 N. Ext corridors. **Pets:** Accepted.
(SAVE) (S/D) (✕) (🛢) (🖵) (🏊)

▽▽▽▽ Fairfield Inn & Suites by Marriott SH ❖
(541) 318-1747. **$79-$149.** 1626 NW Hill St. US 97, exit 137 (Revere Ave), just s; downtown. Int corridors. **Pets:** Other species. $75 one-time fee/room. Service with restrictions, supervision.
(ASK) (S/D) (✕) (&M) (🗐) (🖘) (🛢) (🖵) (🏊) (✕)

◬◬◬ ▽▽▽▽ Hampton Inn SH
(541) 388-4114. **$79-$129.** 15 NE Butler Market Rd. US 97, exit 136, just n. Ext corridors. **Pets:** Medium. $10 one-time fee/pet. Designated rooms, service with restrictions, supervision.
(SAVE) (S/D) (✕) (🛢) (🖵) (🏊)

◬◬◬ ▽▽▽▽ Holiday Inn Express Hotel & Suites SH ❖
(541) 317-8500. **$60-$200.** 20615 Grandview Dr. On US 97; north end of town. Int corridors. **Pets:** Other species. $10 daily fee/pet. Service with restrictions, supervision.
(SAVE) (S/D) (✕) (&M) (🗐) (🖘) (🛢) (🖵) (🏊) (✕)

◬◬◬ ▽▽▽▽ La Quinta Inn Bend SH
(541) 388-2227. **$69-$119.** 61200 S Business Hwy 97. Jct US 20 E, 3 mi s. Int corridors. **Pets:** Accepted.
(SAVE) (✕) (&M) (🗐) (🛢) (🖵) (🏊)

◬◬◬ ▽▽▽ Plaza Motel M
(541) 382-1621. **$44-$79.** 1430 NW Hill St. US 97, exit 137 (Revere Ave), just s; downtown. Ext corridors. **Pets:** Very small, dogs only. $10 one-time fee/pet. Designated rooms, service with restrictions, supervision.
(SAVE) (S/D) (✕) (🛢) (🖵)

◬◬◬ ▽▽▽ Quality Inn SH
(541) 318-0848. **$59-$99.** 20600 Grandview Dr. On US 97; north end of town. Int corridors. **Pets:** Medium. $10 daily fee/pet. Service with restrictions, supervision.
(SAVE) (S/D) (✕) (&M) (🗐) (🖘) (🛢) (🖵) (🏊)

▽▽▽ Red Lion Inn/North SH ❖
(541) 382-7011. **$62-$94.** 1415 NE 3rd St. US 97, just n of jct US 20. Ext corridors. **Pets:** Large, other species. Service with restrictions, supervision.
(ASK) (S/D) (✕) (&M) (🗐) (🖘) (🛢) (🖵) (🍴) (🏊) (✕)

▽▽▽ Red Lion Inn/South SH ❖
(541) 382-8384. **$62-$94.** 849 NE 3rd St. US 97, just s of jct US 20. Ext corridors. **Pets:** Large, other species. Service with restrictions, supervision.
(ASK) (S/D) (✕) (&M) (🗐) (🖘) (🛢) (🖵) (🏊) (✕)

The Riverhouse Resort Hotel SH

(541) 389-3111. **$79-$125.** 3075 N Business 97. US 97, exit 136 (Butler Market Rd) northbound, just n; exit 135B southbound. Ext/int corridors. **Pets:** Other species. Supervision.

Sleep Inn of Bend SH

(541) 330-0050. **$69-$89.** 600 NE Bellevue. On US 20 E, 2 mi e of jct US 97. Int corridors. **Pets:** Medium. $8 one-time fee/room. Service with restrictions, supervision.

BOARDMAN

Econo Lodge M

(541) 481-2375. **$55-$79.** 105 SW Front St. I-84, exit 164, just s. Ext corridors. **Pets:** Other species. Designated rooms, service with restrictions, supervision.

BROOKINGS

Best Western Beachfront Inn SH

(541) 469-7779. **$109-$285.** 16008 Boat Basin Rd. Jct US 101, 0.6 mi w on Benham Ln. Ext corridors. **Pets:** Large, other species. $5 daily fee/pet. Designated rooms, service with restrictions, supervision.

Westward Motel M

(541) 469-7471. **$52-$85, 3 day notice.** 1026 Chetco Ave. On US 101; north end of town. Ext corridors. **Pets:** Small, dogs only. $10 daily fee/pet. Designated rooms, service with restrictions, supervision.

BURNS

Best Inn M

(541) 573-1700. **$47-$67, 3 day notice.** 999 Oregon Ave. 1 mi w on US 395/20 from jct SR 78. Ext/int corridors. **Pets:** Medium. $20 deposit/room, $5 one-time fee/pet. Designated rooms, service with restrictions, supervision.

Days Inn Burns M

(541) 573-2047. **$41-$60.** 577 W Monroe St. Just w on US 395/20 from jct SR 78. Ext corridors. **Pets:** Other species. $5 one-time fee/pet. Designated rooms, service with restrictions, supervision.

Silver Spur Motel M

(541) 573-2077. **$55.** 789 N Broadway. US 395/20, at edge of town. Ext corridors. **Pets:** Large, other species. $5 daily fee/pet. Designated rooms, service with restrictions, supervision.

CANNON BEACH

Cannon Beach Ecola Creek Lodge M

(503) 436-2776. **$52-$157, 3 day notice.** 208 5th St. 0.3 mi w of US 101 via north exit to Ecola State Park. Ext corridors. **Pets:** Accepted.

Hallmark Resort at Cannon Beach SH

(503) 436-1566. **$79-$349, 3 day notice.** 1400 S Hemlock St. US 101, exit Sunset Blvd, just s. Ext corridors. **Pets:** $12 daily fee/pet. Designated rooms, service with restrictions, supervision.

Haystack Resort Motel M

(503) 436-1577. **$99-$239, 3 day notice.** 3339 S Hemlock St. US 101, exit Tolovana Park, just w. Ext corridors. **Pets:** Accepted.

Inn at Cannon Beach M

(503) 436-9085. **$99-$229, 3 day notice.** 3215 S Hemlock St. US 101, exit Tolovana Park, just w, then just n. Ext corridors. **Pets:** Other species. $10 daily fee/pet. Designated rooms, service with restrictions, supervision.

Ocean Lodge SH

(503) 436-2241. **$199-$309, 3 day notice.** 2864 S Pacific. US 101, exit Tolovana Park, 1 mi s, then just w on Chisana. Ext/int corridors. **Pets:** Other species. $15 daily fee/pet. Designated rooms, service with restrictions, supervision.

Surfsand Resort & Meeting Facility M

(503) 436-2274. **$89-$349, 3 day notice.** Ocean Front & Gower. US 101, exit Cannon Beach (2nd exit); downtown. Ext corridors. **Pets:** Dogs only. $12 daily fee/pet. Supervision.

Tolovana Inn CO

(503) 436-2211. **$65-$329, 3 day notice.** 3400 S Hemlock St. 2 mi s off US 101 Beach Loop. Ext corridors. **Pets:** $12 daily fee/pet. Designated rooms, service with restrictions, supervision.

CANYONVILLE

Best Western Canyonville Inn & Suites SH

(541) 839-4200. **$65-$139.** 200 Creekside Rd. I-5, exit 99, just w. Int corridors. **Pets:** Small. $15 daily fee/pet. Designated rooms, service with restrictions, supervision.

CASCADE LOCKS

Best Western Columbia River Inn SH

(541) 374-8777. **$59-$139.** 735 WaNaPa St. I-84, exit 44. Int corridors. **Pets:** Other species. $10 daily fee/pet. Service with restrictions, supervision.

COOS BAY

Best Western Holiday Motel SH

(541) 269-5111. **$79-$101.** 411 N Bayshore Dr. Just n of downtown on US 101. Ext/int corridors. **Pets:** Small, dogs only. $10 daily fee/pet. Service with restrictions, supervision.

Edgewater Inn M

(541) 267-0423. **$85-$94.** 275 E Johnson Ave. Just s of downtown on US 101, then e. Ext/int corridors. **Pets:** Accepted.

Motel 6—1244 SH

(541) 267-7171. **$41-$69.** 1445 Bayshore Dr. 0.6 mi n of downtown on US 101. Ext corridors. **Pets:** Other species. Service with restrictions, supervision.

Red Lion Hotel Coos Bay SH

(541) 267-4141. **$134-$167.** 1313 N Bayshore Dr. 0.5 mi n of downtown on US 101. Ext corridors. **Pets:** Other species. Service with restrictions.

COQUILLE

Myrtle Lane Motel M

(541) 396-2102. **$45.** 787 N Central Blvd. SR 42, 0.4 mi n. Ext corridors. **Pets:** Medium. $4 daily fee/pet. Designated rooms, service with restrictions, supervision.

CORVALLIS

Best Western Grand Manor Inn SH
(541) 758-8571. **$80-$110.** 925 NW Garfield. 1.5 mi n on 9th St; downtown. Int corridors. **Pets:** Large, other species. $100 deposit/room, $10 daily fee/room. Designated rooms, service with restrictions, supervision.

Days Inn SH
(541) 754-7474. **$58-$77.** 1113 NW 9th St. 1.3 mi n. Int corridors. **Pets:** Medium, other species. $5 daily fee/pet. Designated rooms, service with restrictions, supervision.

Holiday Inn Express On The River SH ✿
(541) 752-0800. **$69-$89.** 781 NE 2nd St. I-5, exit 228, 9.8 mi w on SR 34, then 0.4 mi nw. Int corridors. **Pets:** Other species. $15 daily fee/room. Designated rooms, service with restrictions, supervision.

Motel 6 #4243 SH
(541) 758-9125. **$56-$65.** 935 NW Garfield Ave. 1.5 mi n on 9th St; downtown. Int corridors. **Pets:** Medium, dogs only. Designated rooms, service with restrictions, supervision.

Super 8 Motel SH ✿
(541) 758-8088. **$76-$86.** 407 NW 2nd St. US 20, just n of jct SR 34; downtown. Int corridors. **Pets:** Medium, other species. $25 deposit/room. Service with restrictions, supervision.

COTTAGE GROVE

Comfort Inn SH
(541) 942-9747. **$69-$109, 7 day notice.** 845 Gateway Blvd. I-5, exit 174, just w. Ext/int corridors. **Pets:** Accepted.

Holiday Inn Express SH
(541) 942-1000. **$69-$89.** 1601 Gateway Blvd. I-5, exit 174, just w. Int corridors. **Pets:** Medium, dogs only. $10 one-time fee/pet. Service with restrictions, supervision.

Village Green Resort M
(541) 942-2491. **$79-$99, 3 day notice.** 725 Row River Rd. I-5, exit 174, just e. Ext corridors. **Pets:** Accepted.

CRESCENT

The Woodsman Country Lodge M ✿
(541) 433-2710. **$45-$89.** 136740 Hwy 97 N. Center. Ext corridors. **Pets:** Large. $10 daily fee/pet. Designated rooms, service with restrictions, supervision.

CRESWELL

Best Western Creswell Inn M
(541) 895-3341. **$69-$139.** 345 E Oregon Ave. I-5, exit 182, just w. Ext corridors. **Pets:** Other species. $25 one-time fee/room. Designated rooms, no service, supervision.

DALLAS

Best Western Dallas Inn & Suites SH
(503) 623-6000. **$79-$89.** 250 Orchard Dr. SR 223, just n. Int corridors. **Pets:** Accepted.

THE DALLES

Best Western River City Inn SH
(541) 296-9107. **$69-$98.** 112 W 2nd St. I-84, exit 84 eastbound, just se; exit 85 westbound, 0.8 mi nw; at Liberty and W 2nd St; downtown. Ext/int corridors. **Pets:** Medium, other species. $10 daily fee/pet. Designated rooms.

Comfort Inn Columbia Gorge SH
(541) 298-2800. **$60-$129.** 351 Lone Pine Dr. I-84, exit 87, just n. Int corridors. **Pets:** Small. $10 daily fee/pet. Service with restrictions, supervision.

Cousins Country Inn SH ✿
(541) 298-5161. **$60-$95.** 2114 W 6th. I-84, exit 83 eastbound, just n; exit 84 westbound, just nw on W 2nd St, just sw on Webber St, then just n. Ext corridors. **Pets:** $10 daily fee/pet. Service with restrictions, supervision.

Super 8 Motel SH
(541) 296-6888. **$60-$84.** 609 Cherry Heights Rd. I-84, exit 84, just se. Int corridors. **Pets:** Accepted.

DEPOE BAY

Crown Pacific Inn M
(541) 765-7773. **$70-$95.** 50 NE Bechill St. Center. Ext/int corridors. **Pets:** Medium. $10 daily fee/pet. Designated rooms, service with restrictions, supervision.

Gracie's Sea Hag Inn BB ✿
(541) 765-2322. **$99-$135, 7 day notice.** 235 SE Bay View Ave. US 101, just e on SE Bay St. Int corridors. **Pets:** Other species. $9 daily fee/pet. Designated rooms, service with restrictions, supervision.

ENTERPRISE

Ponderosa Motel M
(541) 426-3186. **$65-$76.** 102 E Greenwood St. Center. Ext corridors. **Pets:** Dogs only. $10 daily fee/pet. Supervision.

The Wilderness Inn M
(541) 426-4535. **$49-$71.** 301 W North St. Corner of NW 2nd. Ext corridors. **Pets:** Small, dogs only. $10 daily fee/pet. Designated rooms, service with restrictions, supervision.

EUGENE

Best Value Inn M
(541) 343-0730. **$44-$74.** 1140 W 6th Ave. I-5, exit 194B, 3 mi w on I-105, then just w on SR 99 N (6th Ave). Ext corridors. **Pets:** Other species. $5 daily fee/pet. Designated rooms, service with restrictions, crate.

Best Western Greentree Inn SH ✿
(541) 485-2727. **$82-$96.** 1759 Franklin Blvd. I-5, exit 194B southbound to I-105, then University of Oregon Rt; exit 192 northbound, 1.2 mi w. Ext/int corridors. **Pets:** $5 deposit/pet. Service with restrictions, supervision.

Best Western New Oregon Motel SH ✿
(541) 683-3669. **$82-$96.** 1655 Franklin Blvd. I-5, exit 192 northbound, 1.3 mi w; exit 194B southbound to I-105, follow University of Oregon signs. Ext/int corridors. **Pets:** $50 deposit/pet. Service with restrictions, supervision.

AAA **W** Courtesy Inn **M**
(541) 345-3391. **$50-$80.** 345 W 6th Ave. I-5, exit 194B, 2 mi w on I-105 (to end of freeway) to 7th Ave, just e to Lincoln, then just n; downtown. Ext corridors. **Pets:** Dogs only. $7 daily fee/pet. Service with restrictions, supervision.
[SAVE] [S] [X] [1] [P]

AAA **WW** Days Inn **SH**
(541) 342-6383. **$59-$112.** 1859 Franklin Blvd. I-5, exit 192 northbound, 1 mi w; exit 194B southbound to I-105, follow signs to University of Oregon. Ext/int corridors. **Pets:** Accepted.
[SAVE] [S] [X] [1] [P]

WWWW Eugene/Springfield Residence Inn by Marriott **SH** ✿
(541) 342-7171. **$79-$189.** 25 Club Rd. I-5, exit 194B, 1.3 mi w on I-105, exit 2 (Coburg Rd), just s, just w on Martin Luther King Jr Blvd (Centennial Blvd), then just se. Int corridors. **Pets:** Other species. $75 one-time fee/room. Service with restrictions, supervision.
[ASK] [X] [GM] [2] [1] [P] [2] [X]

AAA **WW** Express Inn & Suites **M**
(541) 868-1520. **$55-$65, 3 day notice.** 990 W 6th Ave. I-5, exit 194B, 3 mi w on I-105, then just w on SR 99 N (6th Ave). Ext corridors. **Pets:** $10 daily fee/pet. Supervision.
[SAVE] [S] [X] [1]

AAA **WW** Franklin Inn **M**
(541) 342-4804. **$44-$79.** 1857 Franklin Blvd. I-5, exit 191 southbound; exit 192 northbound, just e, follow University of Oregon signs. Ext corridors. **Pets:** Small, dogs only. $10 daily fee/pet. Designated rooms, service with restrictions, supervision.
[SAVE] [S] [X] [1] [P] [2]

WWWW Hilton Eugene **LH**
(541) 342-2000. **$129-$184.** 66 E 6th Ave. At 6th Ave and Oak St; center. Int corridors. **Pets:** Medium. $15 daily fee/room. Service with restrictions, supervision.
[X] [2] [1] [P] [11] [2]

AAA **WWW** La Quinta Inn & Suites Eugene **SH** ✿
(541) 344-8335. **$89-$170.** 155 Day Island Rd. I-5, exit 194B, 1.3 mi w on I-105, exit 2 (Coburg Rd), just s, just w on Martin Luther King Jr Blvd (Centennial Blvd), then 0.5 mi se on Country Club Rd. Int corridors. **Pets:** Other species. $50 deposit/pet. Service with restrictions, supervision.
[SAVE] [X] [2] [1] [P] [2]

WW Motel 6-36 **M**
(541) 687-2395. **$45-$61.** 3690 Glenwood Dr. I-5, exit 191, just sw. Ext corridors. **Pets:** Accepted.
[S] [X] [GM] [2] [1] [2]

WW Ramada Inn-Eugene **SH**
(541) 342-5181. **$59-$108.** 225 Coburg Rd. I-5, exit 194B southbound, 1.3 mi w on I-105, exit 2 (Coburg Rd), then just n. Ext/int corridors. **Pets:** Other species. $15 one-time fee/room. Service with restrictions, supervision.
[ASK] [S] [X] [2] [2] [1] [P] [11] [2]

WW Red Lion Hotel Eugene **SH**
(541) 342-5201. **$74-$109.** 205 Coburg Rd. I-5, exit 194B southbound, 1.3 mi w on I-105, exit 2 (Coburg Rd), then just n. Ext corridors. **Pets:** Service with restrictions.
[X] [2] [2] [1] [P] [11] [2]

AAA **WWWW** Valley River Inn, a WestCoast Hotel **SH** ✿
(541) 743-1000. **$109-$180.** 1000 Valley River Way. I-5, exit 194B southbound, 2.5 mi w on I-105, exit 1, follow Valley River Center signs, just s of mall. Int corridors. **Pets:** Designated rooms, service with restrictions, supervision.
[SAVE] [S] [X] [2] [2] [1] [P] [11] [2] [X]

FLORENCE

AAA **W** Le Chateau Motel **SH**
(541) 997-3481. **$49-$84.** 1084 Hwy 101 N. SR 126, just n. Ext corridors. **Pets:** Accepted.
[SAVE] [S] [X] [1] [P] [2] [K]

AAA **WW** Oceanbreeze Motel **M**
(541) 997-2642. **$45-$115.** 85165 Hwy 101 S. SR 126, 2 mi s. Ext corridors. **Pets:** Dogs only. Supervision.
[SAVE] [S] [X] [1] [P] [K]

AAA **W** Old Town Inn **M**
(541) 997-7131. **$53-$86.** 170 Hwy 101. SR 126, 0.5 mi s. Ext corridors. **Pets:** $10 one-time fee/pet. Designated rooms, service with restrictions, supervision.
[SAVE] [S] [X] [P] [K]

AAA **W** Park Motel **M** ✿
(541) 997-2634. **$49-$129.** 85034 Hwy 101 S. SR 126, 2.2 mi s. Ext corridors. **Pets:** Large, other species. $8 daily fee/pet. Service with restrictions, supervision.
[SAVE] [S] [X] [1] [P] [K]

FOREST GROVE

WW Best Value Inn & Suites **SH**
(503) 357-9000. **$49-$69.** 3306 Pacific Ave. West end of town on SR 8. Int corridors. **Pets:** Small, dogs only. $10 daily fee/pet. Service with restrictions, supervision.
[ASK] [S] [X] [GM] [1] [P] [2]

AAA **WWW** Best Western University Inn & Suites **SH** ✿
(503) 992-8888. **$79-$149.** 3933 Pacific Ave. East end of town on SR 8. Int corridors. **Pets:** Small, dogs only. $10 daily fee/pet. Designated rooms, service with restrictions, supervision.
[SAVE] [S] [X] [GM] [2] [2] [1] [P] [2] [X]

GARIBALDI

WW Inn at Garibaldi **SH**
(503) 322-3338. **$59-$119.** 502 Garibaldi Ave. On US 101 at jct 5th St; center. Int corridors. **Pets:** Dogs only. $10 one-time fee/room. Designated rooms, service with restrictions, supervision.
[ASK] [S] [X] [2] [1] [P] [2] [X]

GEARHART

AAA **WWW** Gearhart By The Sea **CO**
(503) 738-8331. **$63-$260, 3 day notice.** 1157 N Marion. 1 mi w off US 101 via City Center exit (Pacific Way). Ext corridors. **Pets:** $11 daily fee/pet. Designated rooms, service with restrictions, supervision.
[SAVE] [S] [X] [1] [P] [2] [K]

GLENEDEN BEACH

AAA **WWWW** Salishan Lodge & Golf Resort **LH**
(541) 764-2371. **$195-$365, 3 day notice.** 7760 Hwy 101 N. Just e of US 101; center. Ext corridors. **Pets:** Accepted.
[SAVE] [S] [X] [2] [2] [1] [P] [11] [2] [X] [K]

GLIDE

AAA **WWW** Steelhead Run B & B and Fine Art Gallery **BB** ✿
(541) 496-0563. **$62-$180, 7 day notice.** 23049 N Umpqua (Hwy 138). I-5, exit 124, 0.8 mi e, just n to SR 138, then 20.7 mi e; just e of MM 20. Ext/int corridors. **Pets:** Other species. $20 daily fee/room. Designated rooms, crate.
[SAVE] [S] [X] [1] [P] [X]

GOLD BEACH

BREAKERS Gold Beach M 🐾
(541) 247-6606. **$45-$139.** 29171 Ellensburg Ave. On US 101; south end of town. Ext corridors. **Pets:** $10 daily fee/pet. Designated rooms, supervision.
[SAVE] [S🐾] [✕] [🔌] [📺] [K]

Clear Sky Lodging CA
(541) 247-6456. **$80-$150, 7 day notice.** 29350 Clear Sky Ln. Jct US 101, just e on 10th St. Ext corridors. **Pets:** Medium, other species. $50 one-time fee/pet. Service with restrictions, supervision.
[SAVE] [S🐾] [✕] [🔌] [📺] [✕] [K] [Z]

Gold Beach Inn M 🐾
(541) 247-7091. **$48-$119.** 29346 Ellensburg Ave. On US 101; center. Ext corridors. **Pets:** Other species. Designated rooms, service with restrictions.
[SAVE] [✕] [🔌] [📺] [K]

Inn of the Beachcomber M
(541) 247-6691. **$65-$180.** 29266 Ellensburg Ave. On US 101; south end of town. Ext/int corridors. **Pets:** Accepted.
[SAVE] [S🐾] [✕] [🔌] [📺] [🏊]

Ireland's Rustic Lodges CA
(541) 247-7718. **$60-$95.** 29330 Ellensburg Ave. On US 101; center. Ext corridors. **Pets:** Other species. $10 daily fee/pet. Designated rooms, service with restrictions, crate.
[SAVE] [✕] [🔌] [📺] [K] [Z]

Jot's Resort M
(541) 247-6676. **$60-$195, 3 day notice.** 94360 Wedderburn Loop. Just w of US 101, north end of bridge. Ext corridors. **Pets:** Other species. $15 daily fee/pet. Designated rooms, service with restrictions, supervision.
[SAVE] [S🐾] [✕] [🔌] [🔌] [📺] [🍴] [🏊] [✕] [K]

Motel 6–4047 M
(541) 247-4533. **Call for rates.** 94433 Jerry's Flat Rd. Just e of jct US 101. Ext corridors. **Pets:** Medium, other species. Service with restrictions, supervision.
[✕] [🔌] [📺] [K]

Sand 'n Sea Motel M
(541) 247-6658. **$49-$119.** 29362 Ellensburg Ave. On US 101; center. Ext/int corridors. **Pets:** Other species. $5 daily fee/pet. Designated rooms, service with restrictions, supervision.
[SAVE] [S🐾] [✕] [♿] [🔌] [📺] [K]

GOVERNMENT CAMP

Mt. Hood Inn SH
(503) 272-3205. **$149-$169.** 87450 E Government Camp. 0.5 mi w of center. Int corridors. **Pets:** $10 daily fee/pet. Service with restrictions, supervision.
[ASK] [S🐾] [✕] [🔌] [🔌] [📺] [K]

GRANTS PASS

Best Western Grants Pass Inn SH
(541) 476-1117. **$70-$116.** 111 NE Agness Ave. I-5, exit 55, just w. Ext corridors. **Pets:** Other species. $10 one-time fee/room. Designated rooms, service with restrictions, supervision.
[SAVE] [S🐾] [✕] [♿] [🔌] [📺] [🏊]

Best Western Inn at the Rogue SH
(541) 582-2200. **$65-$125, 3 day notice.** 8959 Rogue River Hwy. I-5, exit 48, just w. Int corridors. **Pets:** Large, other species. $20 daily fee/pet. Designated rooms, service with restrictions, supervision.
[SAVE] [S🐾] [✕] [🔌] [📺] [🏊]

Comfort Inn SH
(541) 479-8301. **$70-$114.** 1889 NE 6th St. I-5, exit 58, just s on SR 99. Int corridors. **Pets:** Large, other species. $100 deposit/room, $10 daily fee/room. Designated rooms, service with restrictions, supervision.
[SAVE] [S🐾] [✕] [🔌] [📺] [🏊]

Holiday Inn Express SH
(541) 471-6144. **$79-$129.** 105 NE Agness Ave. I-5, exit 55, just w. Int corridors. **Pets:** Other species. $5 daily fee/pet. Designated rooms, service with restrictions, supervision.
[SAVE] [S🐾] [✕] [♿] [🔌] [📺]

Knights Inn Motel M 🐾
(541) 479-5595. **$60-$95.** 104 SE 7th St. I-5, exit 58, 1.5 mi s on SR 99 to G St, then 1 blk e. Ext corridors. **Pets:** Small, dogs only. $50 deposit/pet, $10 one-time fee/pet. Designated rooms, service with restrictions, supervision.
[SAVE] [S🐾] [✕] [🔌]

La Quinta Inn & Suites Grants Pass SH 🐾
(541) 472-1808. **$69-$130.** 243 NE Morgan Ln. I-5, exit 58, 0.4 mi s on SR 99, just e on Hillcrest Dr to SR 99 northbound, then just n. Int corridors. **Pets:** Designated rooms, service with restrictions, supervision.
[SAVE] [✕] [♿M] [♿] [🔌] [📺] [🏊]

Motel 6–253 M
(541) 474-1331. **$45-$61.** 1800 NE 7th St. I-5, exit 58, 0.3 mi s on SR 99. Ext corridors. **Pets:** Accepted.
[S🐾] [✕] [♿M] [♿] [🔌] [🏊]

Redwood Motel M
(541) 476-0878. **$50-$240.** 815 NE 6th St. I-5, exit 58, 1.2 mi s on SR 99. Ext corridors. **Pets:** Accepted.
[SAVE] [S🐾] [✕] [♿M] [♿] [🔌] [📺] [🏊]

Riverside Inn Resort SH
(541) 476-6873. **$79-$125.** 971 SE 6th St. I-5, exit 58, 2.5 mi s on SR 99. Ext corridors. **Pets:** Large, other species. $10 daily fee/pet. Designated rooms, service with restrictions, supervision.
[SAVE] [S🐾] [✕] [🔌] [📺] [🍴] [🏊] [✕]

Sunset Inn M
(541) 479-3305. **$50-$135.** 1400 NW 6th St. I-5, exit 58, 0.6 mi s on SR 99. Ext corridors. **Pets:** Small, dogs only. $25 deposit/pet, $5 daily fee/pet. Designated rooms, service with restrictions, supervision.
[SAVE] [S🐾] [✕] [🔌] [📺] [🏊]

Super 8 Motel-Grants Pass M
(541) 474-0888. **$61-$76.** 1949 NE 7th St. I-5, exit 58, 0.4 mi s on SR 99, just e on Hillcrest Dr to SR 99 northbound, then just n. Int corridors. **Pets:** Accepted.
[ASK] [S🐾] [✕] [♿M] [🔌] [🏊]

Sweet Breeze Inn M
(541) 471-4434. **$58-$110.** 1627 NE 6th St. I-5, exit 58, 0.5 mi s on SR 99. Ext/int corridors. **Pets:** Very small. Designated rooms, service with restrictions, supervision.
[SAVE] [S🐾] [✕] [♿] [🔌]

Travelodge M
(541) 479-6611. **$49-$69.** 1950 NW Vine St. I-5, exit 58, just s on SR 99. Ext corridors. **Pets:** Small, other species. $5 daily fee/pet. Designated rooms, service with restrictions, supervision.
[SAVE] [S🐾] [✕] [🔌] [📺] [🏊]

HALSEY

Best Western Pioneer Lodge M
(541) 369-2804. **$69-$82.** 33180 SR 228. I-5, exit 216, just e. Ext corridors. **Pets:** $5 daily fee/pet. Service with restrictions.
[ASK] [S🐾] [✕] [📺] [🍴] [🏊]

HERMISTON

AAA ◇◇ Oak Tree Inn SH
(541) 567-2330. **$59-$69.** 1110 SE 4th St. 0.4 mi s on US 395, just w. Int corridors. **Pets:** Medium. $10 daily fee/pet. Service with restrictions, crate.
SAVE Sₒ ✕ 🛢 ▣

◇◇◇ Oxford Suites SH ❀
(541) 564-8000. **$85-$125.** 1050 N 1st St. 0.3 mi n on US 395. Int corridors. **Pets:** Small, dogs only. $20 one-time fee/pet. Designated rooms, service with restrictions, supervision.
ASK Sₒ ✕ ᴹ 🍴 🛢 ▣ ⇌ ✕

HINES

◇◇ Comfort Inn SH
(541) 573-3370. **$72-$75.** 504 N Hwy 20. On US 20 (Hines/Burns). Int corridors. **Pets:** Accepted.
ASK Sₒ ✕ 🍴 🛢 ▣ ⇌

HOOD RIVER

AAA ◇◇ Best Western Hood River Inn SH
(541) 386-2200. **$79-$149.** 1108 E Marina Way. I-84, exit 64, just n, then just e. Int corridors. **Pets:** Accepted.
SAVE Sₒ ✕ ᴹ 🍴 🛢 ▣ 🍴 ⇌ ✕

AAA ◇◇◇ Columbia Gorge Hotel CI ❀
(541) 386-5566. **$189-$409, 14 day notice.** 4000 Westcliff Dr. I-84, exit 62, just w of overpass. Int corridors. **Pets:** Other species. $25 one-time fee/pet. Designated rooms, supervision.
SAVE ✕ 🛢 🍴

AAA ◇◇ Vagabond Lodge M
(541) 386-2992. **$49-$83.** 4070 Westcliff Dr. I-84, exit 62, just n, then just w. Ext corridors. **Pets:** Accepted.
SAVE ✕ 🛢 ▣

JACKSONVILLE

AAA ◇◇◇◇ Jacksonville Inn CI
(541) 899-1900. **$149-$189, 3 day notice.** 175 E California St. On SR 238; in historic district. Ext/int corridors. **Pets:** Service with restrictions.
SAVE Sₒ ✕ 🛢 ▣ 🍴

◇◇ The Stage Lodge M
(541) 899-3953. **$98-$185, 3 day notice.** 830 N 5th St. On N 5th St (SR 238). 0.3 mi ne. Ext corridors. **Pets:** Accepted.
ASK Sₒ ✕ 🍴 🛢 ▣

JOHN DAY

AAA ◇◇◇ Best Western John Day Inn M
(541) 575-1700. **$70-$135.** 315 W Main St. Just w on US 26 and 395. Ext corridors. **Pets:** Medium, other species. $10 daily fee/pet. Designated rooms, service with restrictions, supervision.
SAVE Sₒ ✕ 🍴 🛢 ▣ ⇌

AAA ◇◇◇ Dreamers Lodge M
(541) 575-0526. **$49-$70.** 144 N Canyon Blvd. Just n of jct US 26 and 395. Ext corridors. **Pets:** Medium, dogs only. $5 one-time fee/pet. Supervision.
SAVE Sₒ ✕ 🛢 ▣

KLAMATH FALLS

AAA ◇◇◇ Best Western Klamath Inn SH
(541) 882-1200. **$65-$80.** 4061 S 6th St. Just w on 6th St (SR 140) from jct SR 140 E/39 S and SR 39 N/US 97 business route. Ext corridors. **Pets:** Accepted.
SAVE Sₒ ✕ 🍴 🍴 🛢 ▣ ⇌

AAA ◇◇ Golden West Motel M ❀
(541) 882-1758. **$42-$56, 3 day notice.** 6402 S 6th St. S 6th St (SR 140) at eastern edge of town. Ext corridors. **Pets:** Large, other species. Designated rooms, supervision.
SAVE Sₒ ✕ 🛢

AAA ◇◇ Majestic Inn & Suites M
(541) 883-7771. **$35-$65.** 5543 S 6th St. 1 mi e on 6th St (SR 140) from jct SR 140 E/39 S and SR 39 N/US 97 business route. Ext corridors. **Pets:** Dogs only. Designated rooms, service with restrictions, supervision.
SAVE ✕ 🛢

AAA ◇◇ Maverick Motel M
(541) 882-6688. **$39-$69.** 1220 Main St. US 97 N to City Center exit, 0.3 mi e. Ext corridors. **Pets:** Dogs only. Designated rooms, service with restrictions, supervision.
SAVE Sₒ ✕ 🛢 ⇌

◇◇ Motel 6-226 SH ❀
(541) 884-2110. **$43-$63.** 5136 S 6th St. 0.5 mi e on 6th St E (SR 140) from jct SR 39/US 97 business route. Ext corridors. **Pets:** Other species. Service with restrictions, supervision.
Sₒ ✕ ᴹ 🍴 🍴 🛢 ▣ ⇌

AAA ◇◇ Oregon Motel 8 M
(541) 883-3431. **$43-$63.** 5225 Hwy 97 N. On US 97, between MM 270 and 271, east side of highway. Ext corridors. **Pets:** Medium. $5 one-time fee/room. Service with restrictions, supervision.
SAVE Sₒ ✕ 🛢 ▣ ⇌

AAA ◇◇◇ Quality Inn SH
(541) 882-4666. **$59-$99.** 100 Main St. Just e of US 97, exit City Center. Ext corridors. **Pets:** Medium, other species. $10 daily fee/room. Service with restrictions, supervision.
SAVE Sₒ ✕ ᴹ 🍴 🍴 🛢 ▣ 🍴 ⇌

◇◇ Red Lion Inn Klamath Falls SH
(541) 882-8864. **$69-$99.** 3612 S 6th St. 0.3 mi w on 6th St (SR 140) from jct SR 140 E/39 S and SR 39 N/US 97 business route. Ext corridors. **Pets:** Accepted.
ASK Sₒ ✕ 🍴 🍴 🛢 ▣ 🍴 ⇌ ✕

◇◇◇ The Running Y Ranch Resort SH
(541) 850-5500. **$119-$269, 3 day notice.** 5500 Running Y Rd. On SR 140, 7.2 mi n from jct US 66 and SR 140. Int corridors. **Pets:** Medium. $10 daily fee/room. Designated rooms, service with restrictions, supervision.
ASK Sₒ ✕ ᴹ 🍴 🍴 🛢 ▣ 🍴 ⇌ ✕

◇◇ Super 8 Motel SH ❀
(541) 884-8880. **$58-$73.** 3805 Hwy 97. On US 97, 2 mi n. Int corridors. **Pets:** Other species. $25 deposit/pet. Service with restrictions, crate.
ASK Sₒ ✕ ᴹ

LA GRANDE

AAA ◇◇ Royal Motor Inn M
(541) 963-4154. **$40-$50.** 1510 Adams Ave. I-84, exit La Grande on US 30, just n of jct SR 82; downtown. Ext corridors. **Pets:** Accepted.
SAVE Sₒ ✕ 🍴 🛢

LAKEVIEW

AAA ◇◇◇ Best Western Skyline Motor Lodge SH
(541) 947-2194. **$89-$109.** 414 N G St. Jct US 395 and SR 140. Ext corridors. **Pets:** Very small, dogs only. $10 daily fee/pet. Designated rooms, service with restrictions, supervision.
SAVE Sₒ ✕ 🍴 🛢 ▣ ⇌

LA PINE

▼▼▼▼ Best Western Newberry Station 🆂🅷
(541) 536-5130. **$79-$99.** 16515 Reed Rd. North end of town, just off SR 97. Int corridors. **Pets:** Small, dogs only. $15 deposit/room, $10 one-time fee/room. Service with restrictions, supervision.
🅰🆂🅺 🆂🐾 ⊠ 🔤 🖋 🎒 🖥 ⤴

LINCOLN CITY

🆎 ▼▼ Coho Inn Ⓜ
(541) 994-3684. **$62-$160.** 1635 NW Harbor. US 101, exit N 17th St, just w. Ext corridors. **Pets:** Small, other species. $8 deposit/pet. Designated rooms, supervision.
🆂🅰🆅🅴 ⊠ 🎒 🖥 ⤴ ⊠ 🎾

🆎 ▼ Crown Pacific Inn Express 🆂🅷 🐾
(541) 994-7559. **$50-$85.** 1070 SE 1st St. On US 101 near D River. Int corridors. **Pets:** Other species. $10 daily fee/pet. Designated rooms, service with restrictions, supervision.
🆂🅰🆅🅴 🆂🐾 ⊠ 🎒 🖥 🎾

🆎 ▼▼ Lincoln City Inn Ⓜ 🐾
(541) 996-4400. **$60-$89.** 1091 SE 1st St. On US 101 at D River. Int corridors. **Pets:** Medium, dogs only. $10 one-time fee/pet. Service with restrictions, supervision.
🆂🅰🆅🅴 🆂🐾 ⊠ 🔤 🖋 🎒 🖥

MADRAS

🆎 ▼▼ Best Western Rama Inn Ⓜ 🐾
(541) 475-6141. **$69-$99.** 12 SW 4th St. On US 97/26 southbound; downtown. Ext corridors. **Pets:** $10 one-time fee/pet. Service with restrictions, supervision.
🆂🅰🆅🅴 🆂🐾 ⊠ 🔤 🖋 🎒 🖥 ⤴

🆎 ▼ Budget Inn Ⓜ
(541) 475-3831. **$50-$70.** 133 NE 5th St. On US 97/26 northbound; downtown. Ext corridors. **Pets:** Accepted.
🆂🅰🆅🅴 🆂🐾 ⊠ 🎒

MCMINNVILLE

▼▼▼▼ Red Lion Inn & Suites 🆂🅷
(503) 472-1500. **$97-$134.** 2535 NE Cumulus Ave. Jct SR 99W, 3.7 mi e on SR 18. Int corridors. **Pets:** Accepted.
🅰🆂🅺 🆂🐾 ⊠ 🔤 🖋 🎒 🖥 ⤴

MEDFORD

🆎 ▼▼▼▼ Best Western Horizon Inn 🆂🅷
(541) 779-5085. **$71-$110.** 1154 E Barnett Rd. I-5, exit 27, just e. Ext corridors. **Pets:** Other species. $10 daily fee/room. Service with restrictions, supervision.
🆂🅰🆅🅴 🆂🐾 ⊠ 🖋 🖋 🎒 🖥 ⤴ ⊠

🆎 ▼ Cedar Lodge Motor Inn Ⓜ
(541) 773-7361. **$52-$72.** 518 N Riverside Ave. I-5, exit 27, 0.5 mi w on Barnett Rd, then 1.2 mi n on SR 99. Ext corridors. **Pets:** Accepted.
🆂🅰🆅🅴 🆂🐾 ⊠ 🎒 ⤴

🆎 ▼ Knights Inn Ⓜ
(541) 773-3676. **$55-$70.** 500 N Riverside Ave. I-5, exit 27, 0.4 mi w on Barnett Rd, then 1.2 mi n on SR 99. Ext corridors. **Pets:** Accepted.
🆂🅰🆅🅴 🆂🐾 ⊠ 🖋 🎒 ⤴

🆎 ▼▼ Medford Inn and Suites 🆂🅷
(541) 773-8266. **$61-$98.** 1015 S Riverside Ave. I-5, exit 27, 0.4 mi w, then just n. Ext corridors. **Pets:** Small, other species. $100 deposit/pet. Designated rooms, service with restrictions, supervision.
🆂🅰🆅🅴 🆂🐾 ⊠ 🖋 🖋 🎒 🖥 ⤴

▼▼ Motel 6-Medford North–739 Ⓜ
(541) 779-0550. **$51-$68.** 2400 Biddle Rd. I-5, exit 30 northbound, just s; exit southbound, follow signs. Ext corridors. **Pets:** Accepted.
🆂🐾 ⊠ 🖋 🖋 🎒 ⤴

▼▼ Motel 6-Medford South–89 Ⓜ
(541) 773-4290. **$47-$63.** 950 Alba Dr. I-5, exit 27, just e on Barnett Rd, then just n. Ext corridors. **Pets:** Medium, other species. Service with restrictions, supervision.
🆂🐾 ⊠ 🔤 🖋 🖋 🎒 ⤴

🆎🆎🆎 ▼▼▼▼ Red Lion Hotel Medford 🆂🅷
(541) 779-5811. **$69-$84.** 200 N Riverside Ave. I-5, exit 27, 0.4 mi w on Barnett Rd, then 1 mi n. Ext corridors. **Pets:** Other species. Service with restrictions.
🆂🅰🆅🅴 ⊠ 🔤 🖋 🎒 🖥 🍴 ⤴

▼▼▼▼ Shilo Inn Medford 🆂🅷 🐾
(541) 770-5151. **$60-$100.** 2111 Biddle Rd. I-5, exit 30 northbound, just s; exit southbound, follow signs for Biddle Rd, then just s. Int corridors. **Pets:** Large. $10 daily fee/pet. Service with restrictions, supervision.
🅰🆂🅺 🆂🐾 ⊠ 🎒

🆎🆎🆎 ▼▼ Windmill Inn of Medford 🆂🅷 🐾
(541) 779-0050. **$81-$101.** 1950 Biddle Rd. I-5, exit 30 northbound, just s; exit southbound, follow signs for Biddle Rd, then just s. Int corridors. **Pets:** Other species. Service with restrictions, supervision.
🆂🅰🆅🅴 🆂🐾 ⊠ 🖋 🖋 🎒 ⤴ ⊠

MYRTLE POINT

🆎🆎🆎 ▼ Myrtle Trees Motel Ⓜ
(541) 572-5811. **$52-$58, 3 day notice.** 1010 8th St (Hwy 42). On SR 42, 0.5 mi e. Ext corridors. **Pets:** Accepted.
🆂🅰🆅🅴 🆂🐾 ⊠ 🎒 🎾

NEWBERG

▼▼ Travelodge Suites 🆂🅷
(503) 537-5000. **$64.** 2816 Portland Rd. North end on SR 99W. Int corridors. **Pets:** Medium. $7 daily fee/pet. Designated rooms, service with restrictions, supervision.
🅰🆂🅺 🆂🐾 ⊠ 🎒 🖥 ⤴ ⊠

NEWPORT

🆎🆎🆎 ▼▼▼▼ The Best Western Agate Beach Inn 🆂🅷 🐾
(541) 265-9411. **$81-$152.** 3019 N Coast Hwy. US 20, 1.5 mi n on US 101. Int corridors. **Pets:** Other species. $15 one-time fee/pet. Designated rooms, service with restrictions, supervision.
🆂🅰🆅🅴 🆂🐾 ⊠ 🖋 🎒 🖥 🍴 ⤴ ⊠ 🎾

🆎🆎🆎 ▼▼ Econo Lodge Ⓜ 🐾
(541) 265-7723. **$42-$95.** 606 SW Coast Hwy 101. 0.5 mi s of US 20. Ext/int corridors. **Pets:** Large, other species. Service with restrictions, supervision.
🆂🅰🆅🅴 🆂🐾 ⊠ 🖋 🎒 🎾

🆎🆎🆎 ▼▼▼▼ Hallmark Resort 🆂🅷 🐾
(541) 265-2600. **$69-$224.** 744 SW Elizabeth St. US 20, 0.7 mi s on US 101, just w on SW Bay St. Ext corridors. **Pets:** $5 daily fee/pet. Designated rooms, service with restrictions, supervision.
🆂🅰🆅🅴 🆂🐾 ⊠ 🔤 🖋 🖋 🎒 🖥 🍴 ⤴ ⊠ 🎾

🆎🆎🆎 ▼▼▼▼ La Quinta Inn & Suites Newport 🆂🅷 🐾
(541) 867-7727. **$64-$124.** 45 SE 32nd St. US 101, just s of Yaquina Bay Bridge. Int corridors. **Pets:** Other species. Designated rooms, service with restrictions, supervision.
🆂🅰🆅🅴 🆂🐾 ⊠ 🔤 🖋 🖋 🎒 🖥 ⤴ ⊠

▼▼ ▼▼ Val-U Inn Ⓜ
(541) 265-6203. **$50-$100.** 531 SW Fall St. US 20, 0.5 mi s on US 101, just w. Int corridors. **Pets:** Accepted.
🅰🆂🅺 🆂🐾 ⊠ 🎒 🖥 🎾

◬ ▽▽▽ Waves of Newport Motel and Vacation Rentals Ⓜ

(541) 265-4661. **$58-$103.** 820 NW Coast St. US 101, 0.6 mi n from jct US 20, just w on NW 11th St, then just s. Ext corridors. **Pets:** Medium. $5 daily fee/pet. Service with restrictions, supervision.

[SAVE] [S🐾] [✕] [🛏] [💻] [🐾]

◬ ▽▽▽ Whaler Motel Ⓜ 🐾

(541) 265-9261. **$82-$162.** 155 SW Elizabeth St. Just s on US 101 from jct US 20, just w on SW 2nd St. Ext corridors. **Pets:** Dogs only. $5 daily fee/pet. Designated rooms, service with restrictions, supervision.

[SAVE] [S🐾] [✕] [⅄M] [🐾] [🛏] [💻] [🏊] [🐾]

NORTH BEND

◬ ▽▽▽ Comfort Inn Ⓜ

(541) 756-3191. **$165-$275, 3 day notice.** 1503 Virginia Ave. 0.5 mi w of US 101. Ext/int corridors. **Pets:** Accepted.

[SAVE] [✕] [⅄M] [🐾] [🛏] [💻] [🍴]

OAKLAND

◬ ▽▽▽ Best Western Rice Hill Ⓜ

(541) 849-3335. **$50-$100.** 621 John Long Rd. I-5, exit 148, just e. Ext corridors. **Pets:** Small. $10 daily fee/pet. Designated rooms, service with restrictions, supervision.

[SAVE] [S🐾] [✕] [🐾] [🛏] [💻] [🏊] [🐾]

OAKRIDGE

◬ ▽▽▽ Best Western Oakridge Inn Ⓜ

(541) 782-2212. **$59-$79.** 47433 SR 58. West end of SR 58. Ext corridors. **Pets:** Medium, dogs only. $10 one-time fee/pet. Service with restrictions, supervision.

[SAVE] [S🐾] [✕] [⅄M] [🐾] [🛏] [💻] [🏊]

ONTARIO

◬ ▽▽▽ Holiday Inn-Ontario, OR SH 🐾

(541) 889-8621. **$70-$80.** 1249 Tapadera Ave. I-84, exit 376B, just ne. Int corridors. **Pets:** Other species. $10 one-time fee/room. Designated rooms, service with restrictions, supervision.

[SAVE] [S🐾] [✕] [🐾] [🛏] [💻] [🍴] [🏊]

◬ ▽ Holiday Motel SH

(541) 889-9188. **$46-$50.** 615 E Idaho. I-84, exit 376A, just nw. Ext corridors. **Pets:** Other species. Designated rooms, service with restrictions.

[SAVE] [S🐾] [✕] [🍴] [🏊]

◬ ▽▽▽ Sleep Inn SH

(541) 881-0007. **$89-$99.** 1221 SE First Ave. I-84, exit 376B, just se. Int corridors. **Pets:** Accepted.

[SAVE] [S🐾] [✕] [⅄M] [🐾] [🛏] [💻] [🏊]

PACIFIC CITY

◬ ▽▽▽▽ Inn at Cape Kiwanda SH 🐾

(503) 965-7001. **$109-$239.** 33105 Cape Kiwanda Dr. Just w on Pacific Ave, 1 mi n. Ext corridors. **Pets:** $20 daily fee/pet. Designated rooms, service with restrictions, crate.

[SAVE] [S🐾] [✕] [⅄M] [💻] [🏊] [🐾]

◬ ▽ Pacific City Inn Ⓜ

(503) 965-6464. **$59-$99.** 35280 Brooten Rd. Center. Ext corridors. **Pets:** Large, dogs only. $15 daily fee/pet. Designated rooms, service with restrictions, supervision.

[SAVE] [✕] [🛏] [💻] [🍴] [🐾]

PENDLETON

◬ ▽▽▽ Best Western Pendleton Inn SH

(541) 276-2135. **$71.** 400 SE Nye Ave. I-84, exit 210, just se. Int corridors. **Pets:** Accepted.

[SAVE] [S🐾] [✕] [⅄M] [🐾] [🛏] [💻] [🏊]

◬ ▽▽▽ Econo Lodge Ⓜ

(541) 276-8654. **$59-$65.** 620 SW Tutuilla Rd. I-84, exit 209, just s on US 395. Ext corridors. **Pets:** Dogs only. $7 one-time fee/pet. Designated rooms, service with restrictions, supervision.

[SAVE] [S🐾] [✕] [🛏] [💻]

◬ ▽▽▽ Holiday Inn Express SH

(541) 966-6520. **$72-$84.** 600 SE Nye Ave. I-84, exit 210, just se. Int corridors. **Pets:** Large. $20 deposit/room, $10 one-time fee/pet. Service with restrictions, supervision.

[SAVE] [S🐾] [✕] [🛏] [💻] [🏊]

▽ Motel 6–349 Ⓜ

(541) 276-3160. **$41-$55.** 325 SE Nye Ave. I-84, exit 210, just se. Ext corridors. **Pets:** Accepted.

[S🐾] [✕] [🛏] [🏊]

▽▽▽ Oxford Suites SH

(541) 276-6000. **$89-$159.** 2400 SW Court Pl. I-84, exit 209, just n on US 395; at northwest corner. Int corridors. **Pets:** Small. $15 one-time fee/room. Service with restrictions, supervision.

[ASK] [S🐾] [✕] [⅄M] [🐾] [🐾] [🛏] [💻] [🏊] [🐾]

◬ ▽▽▽ Red Lion Hotel Pendleton SH 🐾

(541) 276-6111. **$66-$86.** 304 SE Nye Ave. I-84, exit 210, just s. Ext/int corridors. **Pets:** $25 deposit/room. Service with restrictions.

[SAVE] [✕] [🐾] [🐾] [🛏] [💻] [🍴] [🏊] [🐾]

▽▽▽ Super 8 Motel SH

(541) 276-8881. **$62-$77.** 601 SE Nye Ave. I-84, exit 210, just se. Int corridors. **Pets:** Accepted.

[ASK] [S🐾] [✕] [🐾] [🛏] [🏊]

◬ ▽▽▽ Travelodge Ⓜ

(541) 276-7531. **$65-$95.** 411 SW Dorion Ave. I-84, exit 209, just w of town center on corner of SW 4th St; downtown. Ext corridors. **Pets:** Dogs only. $10 one-time fee/pet. Designated rooms, service with restrictions, supervision.

[SAVE] [S🐾] [✕] [🛏] [💻]

PHOENIX

◬ ▽▽▽ Super 8 Motel & RV Park Ⓜ

(541) 535-4445. **$55-$95.** 300 Pear Tree Ln. I-5, exit 24, just e, then just s. Ext corridors. **Pets:** Accepted.

[SAVE] [S🐾] [✕] [🐾] [🐾] [🛏] [💻] [🏊]

PORTLAND METROPOLITAN AREA

BEAVERTON

▽▽▽ Best Western Greenwood Inn & Suites **M**
(503) 643-7444. **Call for rates.** 10700 SW Allen Blvd. SR 217, exit Allen Blvd, just e. Ext/int corridors. **Pets:** Accepted.

▽▽ Comfort Inn & Suites **SH**
(503) 643-9100. **$49-$159.** 13455 SW Canyon Rd. SR 217, exit Canyon Rd (SR 8), 1 mi w. Int corridors. **Pets:** Medium, other species. $15 one-time fee/room. Service with restrictions, supervision.

▽▽ Homestead Studio Suites Hotel-Beaverton **M**
(503) 690-3600. **$65-$85.** 875 SW 158th Ave. US 26, exit 65 westbound, just s on Cornell Rd, 1.1 mi se on 158th Ave; exit eastbound, just straight on feeder road, then same directions as westbound. Ext corridors. **Pets:** $25 daily fee/room. Designated rooms, service with restrictions, crate.

▽▽▽ Homewood Suites By Hilton **SH** ❖
(503) 614-0900. **$109-$119.** 15525 NW Gateway Ct. US 26, exit 65, s on 158th Ave, then just e on Waterhouse Ave. Int corridors. **Pets:** Small. $15 daily fee/pet. Designated rooms.

CLACKAMAS

▲▲▲ ▽▽ Clackamas Inn **SH**
(503) 650-5340. **$69-$109.** 16010 SE 82nd Dr. I-205, exit 12A southbound; exit 12 (SR 212) northbound. Int corridors. **Pets:** $10 daily fee/pet. Service with restrictions.

GLADSTONE

▽▽▽ Oxford Suites **SH** ❖
(503) 722-7777. **$89-$109.** 75 82nd Dr. I-205, exit 11, just w. Int corridors. **Pets:** Medium, other species. Service with restrictions, supervision.

GRESHAM

▲▲▲ ▽▽▽ Best Western Pony Soldier Inn **SH**
(503) 665-1591. **$93.** 1060 NE Cleveland Ave. I-84, exit 16, 2.7 mi s on NE 238th Dr, just w on Division St, then just n; I-205, exit 19, 5.5 mi e on Division St, then just n. Int corridors. **Pets:** Small. Designated rooms, service with restrictions, supervision.

▲▲▲ ▽▽▽ Hawthorn Inn & Suites **SH**
(503) 492-4000. **$69-$109.** 2323 NE 181st Ave. I-84, exit 13, just e. Int corridors. **Pets:** Small, other species. $25 deposit/room, $10 one-time fee/pet. Designated rooms, service with restrictions, supervision.

▲▲▲ ▽▽ Sleep Inn-Portland Gresham **SH**
(503) 618-8400. **$58-$119.** 2261 NE 181st Ave. I-84, exit 13, just s. Int corridors. **Pets:** Accepted.

▲▲▲ ▽▽ Super 8 Motel **M**
(503) 661-5100. **$54-$69.** 121 NE 181st Ave. I-84, exit 13, 1.4 mi s. Int corridors. **Pets:** Medium, dogs only. $10 daily fee/pet. Designated rooms, supervision.

HILLSBORO

▲▲▲ ▽▽ The Dunes Motel **M**
(503) 648-8991. **$40-$55.** 452 SE 10th Ave (SR 8). US 26, exit 62, 1 mi s on NW Cornelius Pass Rd, then 4.4 mi w on NE Cornell Rd. Int corridors. **Pets:** Small, dogs only. $25 deposit/pet, $5 one-time fee/pet. Designated rooms, service with restrictions, supervision.

▲▲▲ ▽▽▽ Red Lion Hotel Hillsboro **SH**
(503) 648-3500. **$62-$105.** 3500 NE Cornell Rd. US 26, exit 62, 1.1 mi s on Cornelius Pass Rd, then 2.5 mi w. Int corridors. **Pets:** Accepted.

▽▽▽▽ Residence Inn by Marriott Portland West **SH** ❖
(503) 531-3200. **$85-$149.** 18855 NW Tanasbourne Dr. US 26, exit 64, just s. Ext/int corridors. **Pets:** Other species. $75 one-time fee/room.

▽▽▽ TownePlace Suites by Marriott-Portland Hillsboro **SH**
(503) 268-6000. **$69-$139.** 6550 NE Brighton St. US 26, exit 62, just s; 1 mi on Cornelius Pass Rd, 0.7 mi w on Cornell Rd, just n on 229th Ave, then just w. Ext/int corridors. **Pets:** Large, other species. $75 one-time fee/room. Designated rooms, service with restrictions, crate.

▲▲▲ ▽▽▽ Wellesley Inn & Suites (Portland/Hillsboro) **SH**
(503) 439-0706. **$85-$105.** 19311 NW Cornell Rd. US 26, exit 64, 0.5 mi s on 185th Ave, then 0.4 mi w. Int corridors. **Pets:** Medium. $25 one-time fee/pet. Service with restrictions, supervision.

KING CITY

▲▲▲ ▽▽▽ Best Western Northwind Inn & Suites **SH**
(503) 431-2100. **$84-$89, 7 day notice.** 16105 SW Pacific Hwy. I-5, exit 292, just nw on SR 217, exit SR 99W, then 2.5 mi s. Int corridors. **Pets:** Medium. $10 daily fee/pet. Service with restrictions, supervision.

LAKE OSWEGO

▲▲▲ ▽▽▽ Crowne Plaza Hotel **SH** ❖
(503) 624-8400. **$69-$179.** 14811 Kruse Oaks Dr. I-5, exit 292B northbound; exit 292 southbound, just e. Int corridors. **Pets:** $25 one-time fee/room. Designated rooms, service with restrictions, crate.

▲▲▲ ▽▽▽ Phoenix Inn Suites-Lake Oswego **SH** ❖
(503) 624-7400. **$79-$109.** 14905 SW Bangy Rd. I-5, exit 292 southbound, just e, then just s; exit 292B northbound, just s. Int corridors. **Pets:** Medium. $15 daily fee/pet. Service with restrictions, supervision.

▽▽▽ Residence Inn by Marriott-Portland South **SH** ❖
(503) 684-2603. **$119-$199.** 15200 SW Bangy Rd. I-5, exit 292B northbound; exit 292 southbound, just e, then 0.3 mi s. Ext corridors. **Pets:** Other species. $75 one-time fee/room.

MILWAUKIE

▲▲▲ ▽▽▽ Econo Lodge Suites Inn **M**
(503) 654-2222. **$59-$69.** 17330 SE McLoughlin Blvd. I-205, exit 9 (Oregon City/Gladstone), 2.3 mi n on SR 99E (McLoughlin Blvd). Ext corridors. **Pets:** Small, dogs only. $10 daily fee/pet. Service with restrictions, supervision.

OREGON CITY

◇◇◇ Rivershore Hotel 🔲 ❈
(503) 655-7141. **$78-$125.** 1900 Clackamette Dr. I-205, exit 9, just n. Int corridors. **Pets:** Large, other species. $5 daily fee/pet. Service with restrictions, supervision.

PORTLAND

◇◇◇◇ 5th Avenue Suites Hotel 🔲 ❈
(503) 222-0001. **$109-$199.** 506 SW Washington St. At SW 5th Ave and SW Washington St. Int corridors. **Pets:** Other species. Service with restrictions, supervision.

◇◇◇◇ The Benson Hotel, a Coast Hotel 🔲 ❈
(503) 228-2000. **$119-$199.** 309 SW Broadway. At SW Broadway and Oak. Int corridors. **Pets:** $75 one-time fee/room. Designated rooms.

◇◇◇ Best Western Inn at the Meadows 🔲 ❈
(503) 286-9600. **$79-$99.** 1215 N Hayden Meadows Dr. I-5, exit 306B, just e. Int corridors. **Pets:** $22 one-time fee/room. Service with restrictions, supervision.

◇◇◇ Country Inn & Suites at Portland Airport 🔲
(503) 255-2700. **$89.** 7205 NE Alderwood Rd. I-205, exit 24A (Airport Way) northbound; exit 24 southbound, 1 mi w on Airport Way, just sw on NE 82nd Ave, then just w. Int corridors. **Pets:** Accepted.

◇◇ Days Inn-Portland North 🔲
(503) 289-1800. **$70-$95.** 9930 N Whitaker Rd. I-5, exit 306B, just e. Int corridors. **Pets:** Accepted.

◇◇◇ Doubletree Hotel-Columbia River 🔲
(503) 283-2111. **$79-$139.** 1401 N Hayden Island Dr. I-5, exit 308, just w. Int corridors. **Pets:** $35 one-time fee/room. Service with restrictions, crate.

◇◇◇ Doubletree Hotel-Jantzen Beach 🔲
(503) 283-4466. **$79-$149.** 909 N Hayden Island Dr. I-5, exit 308, just e. Int corridors. **Pets:** $35 one-time fee/room. Service with restrictions, crate.

◇◇◇ Four Points by Sheraton Portland Downtown 🔲
(503) 221-0711. **$79-$199.** 50 SW Morrison St. At Morrison St and Naito Pkwy (formerly Front Ave). Int corridors. **Pets:** Other species. No service, supervision.

◇◇◇ The Heathman Hotel 🔲
(503) 241-4100. **$150-$775.** 1001 SW Broadway. At SW Broadway and Salmon St. Int corridors. **Pets:** Small, other species. $25 daily fee/pet. Service with restrictions, crate.

◇◇◇ Hilton Portland & Executive Tower 🔲
(503) 226-1611. **$99-$179.** 921 SW 6th Ave. I-405, 1B (6th Ave); at 6th Ave and Taylor St. Int corridors. **Pets:** Medium. $25 one-time fee/room. Service with restrictions, supervision.

◇◇ Hospitality Inn 🔲
(503) 244-6684. **$78-$89.** 10155 SW Capitol Hwy. I-5, exit 295 southbound; exit 294 northbound, just s. Int corridors. **Pets:** Accepted.

◇◇◇ Hotel Lucia 🔲 ❈
(503) 225-1717. **$130-$575.** 400 SW Broadway. At SW Broadway and Stark St. Int corridors. **Pets:** Designated rooms, service with restrictions, supervision.

◇◇◇◇ Hotel Vintage Plaza 🔲 ❈
(503) 228-1212. **$109-$189.** 422 SW Broadway. At Broadway and Washington St. Int corridors. **Pets:** Other species. Designated rooms, service with restrictions, supervision.

◇◇◇ La Quinta Inn & Suites Portland Airport 🔲
(503) 382-3820. **$64-$89.** 11207 NE Holman St. I-205, exit 24B northbound; exit 24 southbound, just e on Airport Way. Int corridors. **Pets:** Large. Service with restrictions, crate.

◇◇◇ La Quinta Inn & Suites Portland (NW) 🔲
(503) 497-9044. **$72-$96.** 4319 NW Yeon. I-5, exit 302 B southbound, 2.5 mi w on US 30; I-5 to I-405, exit 3 (US 30) northbound, 2.5 mi w. Int corridors. **Pets:** Accepted.

◇◇ La Quinta Inn Portland (Lloyd Center) 🔲
(503) 233-7933. **$94-$104.** 431 NE Multnomah St. I-5, exit 302A, just e, then just s on Martin Luther King Blvd. Int corridors. **Pets:** Other species. Service with restrictions, crate.

◇◇◇ Mallory Hotel 🔲 ❈
(503) 223-6311. **$110-$165.** 729 SW 15th Ave. I-5 to I-405, exit Salmon St northbound, just n on 14th Ave, w on Morrison St, then s; exit Couch-Burnside southbound; at SW 15th Ave and Yamhill. Int corridors. **Pets:** Large, other species. $25 one-time fee/pet. Service with restrictions, supervision.

◇◇◇ The Mark Spencer Hotel 🔲
(503) 224-3293. **$59-$109.** 409 SW 11th Ave. At SW Stark St and SW 11th Ave. Int corridors. **Pets:** Accepted.

◇◇◇ Marriott City Center 🔲
(503) 226-6300. **$89-$179.** 520 SW Broadway. At Washington St and SW Broadway. Int corridors. **Pets:** Accepted.

◇◇◇ Motel 6 North Portland #4198 🔲
(503) 247-3700. **$51-$61.** 1125 N Schmeer Rd. I-5, exit 306B, 0.4 mi s on N Whitaker Rd, then just e. Int corridors. **Pets:** Accepted.

◇◇◇ Oxford Suites 🔲
(503) 283-3030. **$79-$199.** 12226 N Jantzen Dr. I-5, exit 308, just e on Hayden Island Dr. Int corridors. **Pets:** Medium. $25 daily fee/room. Service with restrictions, supervision.

◇◇◇ The Paramount Hotel, a Coast Hotel 🔲
(503) 223-9900. **$109-$195.** 808 SW Taylor St. At SW 8th Ave and SW Taylor St. Int corridors. **Pets:** Medium, other species. $200 deposit/room, $50 one-time fee/pet. Designated rooms, service with restrictions, supervision.

◇◇◇ Park Lane Suites 🔲
(503) 226-6288. **$89-$179.** 809 SW King Ave. I-405, exit Burnside St southbound, 0.5 mi w, then just s; exit Everett St northbound, 0.4 mi w on Glisan St, just s on NW 21st Ave, just w on Burnside St, then just s. Ext corridors. **Pets:** Accepted.

AAA ▼▼ The Portlander Inn SH ☸
(503) 345-0300. **$69.** 10350 N Vancouver Way. I-5, exit 307, follow signs for Marine Dr E, just ne, then 0.7 mi se. Int corridors. **Pets:** Other species. $10 daily fee/room. Service with restrictions, supervision.
SAVE ✕ 🗗 💻 ⫾⫿ ✕

AAA ▼▼ Quality Inn Portland Airport SH
(503) 256-4111. **$69-$109.** 8247 NE Sandy Blvd. I-84, exit 5, 1.5 mi n on 82nd Ave; I-205, exit 23A southbound/23B northbound (US 30 business route/Sandy Blvd W), 1 mi w. Ext/int corridors. **Pets:** Other species. $15 daily fee/room. Designated rooms, service with restrictions.
SAVE 🗐 ✕ 🖥 💻 ⇆

▼▼▼ Red Lion Hotel Portland-Convention Center SH ☸
(503) 235-2100. **$99-$159.** 1021 NE Grand Ave. I-5, exit 302A, just e on Weidler, then just s on Martin Luther King Blvd. Int corridors. **Pets:** $100 deposit/room, $10 daily fee/room. Designated rooms, service with restrictions, crate.
ASK 🗐 ✕ 🗗 🖥 💻 ⫾⫿

▼▼▼ Red Lion Inn & Suites-Portland Airport SH
(503) 252-6397. **$79-$109.** 5019 NE 102nd Ave. I-205, exit 23A, just e on NE Sandy Blvd. Int corridors. **Pets:** Other species. $15 one-time fee/pet. Service with restrictions, supervision.
ASK 🗐 ✕ 🗗 🖥 💻 ⇆

AAA ▼▼ Residence Inn by Marriott-Lloyd Center SH
(503) 288-1400. **$129-$199.** 1710 NE Multnomah St. I-5, exit 302A, 0.8 mi e on Weidler St, then just s on 15th Ave; I-84, exit 1 (Lloyd Center) westbound, just n on 13th St, then just e. Ext corridors. **Pets:** Accepted.
SAVE ✕ 🗗M 🗗 🖥 💻 ⇆ ✕

▼▼ Residence Inn Portland Downtown at RiverPlace SH ☸
(503) 552-9500. **$109-$209.** 2115 SW River Pkwy. At SW Moody and SW River Pkwy; on the Willamette River Waterfront. Int corridors. **Pets:** Other species. $10 daily fee/room.
ASK 🗐 ✕ 🗗 🖥 🗗 🖥 💻 ⇆

AAA ▼▼ ▼▼ RiverPlace Hotel SH ☸
(503) 228-3233. **$149-$259.** 1510 SW Harbor Way. At Naito Pkwy (formerly Front Ave) and SW Harbor Way. Int corridors. **Pets:** Other species. $45 one-time fee/room.
SAVE 🗐 ✕ 🗗M 🗗 🖥 🗗 🖥 💻 ⫾⫿ ✕

AAA ▼▼ ▼▼ Sheraton Portland Airport Hotel LH
(503) 281-2500. **$178-$204.** 8235 NE Airport Way. I-205, exit 24A northbound; exit 24 southbound, 1.5 mi w. Int corridors. **Pets:** Small, dogs only. $25 one-time fee/room. Service with restrictions, supervision.
SAVE 🗐 ✕ 🗗 🖥 💻 ⫾⫿ ⇆ ✕

▼▼ Staybridge Suites Portland-Airport SH
(503) 262-8888. **Call for rates.** 11936 NE Glenn Widing Dr. I-205, exit 24B northbound; exit 24 southbound, just e. Int corridors. **Pets:** Accepted.
✕ 🗗M 🗗 🖥 🗗 🖥 💻 ⇆ ✕

AAA ▼▼ ▼▼ Travelodge Suites Portland M
(503) 788-9394. **$69-$81.** 7740 SE Powell Blvd. I-205, exit 19, 1 mi w. Ext/int corridors. **Pets:** Accepted.
SAVE 🗐 ✕ 🖥 💻 ⇆

AAA ▼▼ ▼▼ The Westin Portland LH
(503) 294-9000. **$109-$169.** 750 SW Alder St. At Park Ave and SW Alder St. Int corridors. **Pets:** Accepted.
SAVE 🗐 ✕ 🗗M 🗗 🖥 🗗 🖥 💻 ⫾⫿ ✕

TIGARD

AAA ▼▼ Days Inn M
(503) 246-8451. **$60-$75.** 11455 SW Pacific Hwy. I-5, exit 294, just w. Ext corridors. **Pets:** Small, dogs only. $10 one-time fee/pet. Designated rooms, service with restrictions, supervision.
SAVE 🗐 ✕ 🖥 ⇆

▼▼▼ Embassy Suites Hotel-Portland Washington Square LH ☸
(503) 644-4000. **$119-$179.** 9000 SW Washington Square Rd. SR 217, exit Progress/Scholls Ferry Rd, just e, then just s on Hall Blvd. Int corridors. **Pets:** Other species. $25 one-time fee/room. Designated rooms, service with restrictions.
✕ 🗗M 🗗 🗗 🖥 💻 ⫾⫿ ⇆ ✕

▼▼ Homestead Studio Suites Hotel-Tigard/Lake Oswego SH
(503) 670-0555. **$61-$104.** 13009 SW 68th Pkwy. I-5, exit 293 (Haines), 0.5 mi s on SW 68th Ave; SR 217 S, exit 72nd Ave, just ne, just e on Hampton St, then just s. Ext corridors. **Pets:** Accepted.
ASK 🗐 ✕ 🗗 🖥 💻

▼▼ Shilo Inn-Portland I-5 South SH
(503) 639-2226. **$59-$79.** 7300 SW Hazel Fern Rd. I-5, exit 290, just w, then just s. Ext corridors. **Pets:** $10 daily fee/room. Service with restrictions, supervision.
ASK 🗐 ✕ 🗗 🖥 💻 ⇆ ✕

TROUTDALE

AAA ▼▼ ▼▼ Comfort Inn & Suites, Columbia Gorge West SH ☸
(503) 669-6500. **$59-$129.** 477 NW Phoenix Dr. I-84, exit 17. Int corridors. **Pets:** Small, other species. $10 daily fee/room. Designated rooms, service with restrictions, crate.
SAVE 🗐 ✕ 🗗 🖥 💻 ⇆

▼▼▼ Holiday Inn Express-Portland East SH
(503) 492-2900. **$69-$89.** 1000 NW Graham Rd. I-84, exit 17, on north frontage road. Int corridors. **Pets:** Accepted.
ASK 🗐 ✕ 🗗 🗗 🖥 💻 ✕

▼▼ Motel 6-Portland Troutdale-407 M
(503) 665-2254. **$41-$53.** 1610 NW Frontage Rd. I-84, exit 17, just s. Ext corridors. **Pets:** Accepted.
🗐 ✕ 🗗M 🗗 🗗 ⇆

TUALATIN

AAA ▼▼ ▼▼ Comfort Inn & Suites SH
(503) 612-9952. **$79-$149.** 7640 SW Warm Springs St. I-5, exit 289, w on Nyberg Rd; behind the Fred Meyer. Int corridors. **Pets:** Accepted.
SAVE 🗐 ✕ 🗗M 🗗 🗗 🖥 💻 ⇆

AAA ▼▼ ▼▼ The Sweetbrier Inn & Suites SH
(503) 692-5800. **$69-$79.** 7125 SW Nyberg Rd. I-5, exit 289, just e. Ext/int corridors. **Pets:** Accepted.
SAVE 🗐 ✕ 🗗M 🗗 🗗 🖥 💻 ⫾⫿ ⇆ ✕

WILSONVILLE

AAA ▼▼ ▼▼ Best Western Willamette Inn SH
(503) 682-2288. **$83-$93.** 30800 SW Parkway Ave. I-5, exit 283, just e, then just s. Int corridors. **Pets:** Small. Designated rooms, service with restrictions, supervision.
SAVE 🗐 ✕ 🗗M 🖥 💻 ⇆ ✕

AAA ▼▼ Comfort Inn SH ☸
(503) 682-9000. **$59-$119.** 8855 SW Citizens Dr. I-5, exit 283, just e, then just n on Town Center Loop W. Int corridors. **Pets:** Other species. $10 daily fee/room. Service with restrictions, supervision.
SAVE 🗐 ✕ 🗗M 🗗 🗗 🖥 💻 ⇆

(AAA) ▼▼ Days Inn & Suites SH
(503) 682-3184. $79-$129. 8815 SW Sun Pl. I-5, exit 286, just e, then just n. Int corridors. Pets: $20 daily fee/pet. Service with restrictions, supervision.
[SAVE] [S☉] [✕] [✍] [🛏] [📺] [🌊]

▼▼▼ Holiday Inn-Wilsonville SH
(503) 682-2211. $79-$89. 25425 SW 95th Ave. I-5, exit 286, just w. Int corridors. Pets: $15 daily fee/room. Service with restrictions, supervision.
[ASK] [S☉] [✕] [�525M] [✍] [�] [🛏] [📺] [🍽] [🌊]

WOOD VILLAGE

(AAA) ▼▼ Portland/Troutdale Travelodge SH ❄
(503) 666-6623. $38-$89. 23705 NE Sandy Blvd. I-84, exit 16, just n. Int corridors. Pets: $5 daily fee/pet. Service with restrictions, supervision.
[SAVE] [S☉] [✕] [�] [🛏] [📺] [🍽]

END METROPOLITAN AREA

PORT ORFORD

(AAA) ▼ Castaway by the Sea M
(541) 332-4502. $55-$145, 3 day notice. 545 W 5th St. Jct US 101, just w on Oregon St. Ext corridors. Pets: Accepted.
[SAVE] [✕] [🛏] [📺] [🎿]

(AAA) ▼ Sea Crest Motel M
(541) 332-3040. $49-$76. 44 Hwy 101. On US 101, 1 mi s. Ext corridors. Pets: Accepted.
[SAVE] [✕] [🛏] [📺] [🎿]

PRINEVILLE

▼▼▼ Best Western Prineville Inn SH ❄
(541) 447-8080. $68-$78. 1475 NE 3rd St. 1.4 mi e on US 26 from SR 126. Int corridors. Pets: Medium, other species. $10 daily fee/room. Service with restrictions.
[ASK] [S☉] [✕] [�525M] [🛏] [📺] [🌊]

▼▼▼ Stafford Inn SH
(541) 447-7100. $69-$109. 1773 NE 3rd St. On US 26. Int corridors. Pets: $20 one-time fee/room. Service with restrictions, supervision.
[✕] [�] [🛏] [📺] [🌊]

PROSPECT

▼▼ Prospect Historical Hotel-Motel & Dinner
House M ❄
(541) 560-3664. $50-$150. 391 Mill Creek Dr. Jct SR 62, 0.3 mi s on 1st St (0.7 mi e of MM 43), just w. Ext/int corridors. Pets: Large. Designated rooms, service with restrictions, supervision.
[✕] [🛏] [📺] [🍽] [🎿]

REDMOND

▼▼▼ Comfort Suites-Airport SH
(541) 504-8900. $74-$164. 2243 SW Yew Ave. US 97, just w. Int corridors. Pets: Accepted.
[ASK] [S☉] [✕] [�] [🛏] [📺] [🌊]

▼▼▼ Eagle Crest Resort SH ❄
(541) 923-2453. $82-$152. 1522 Cline Falls Rd. 5 mi w on SR 126, 1 mi s. Int corridors. Pets: Dogs only. $125 one-time fee/pet. Designated rooms, service with restrictions, supervision.
[ASK] [S☉] [✕] [�525M] [✍] [�] [🛏] [📺] [🍽] [🌊] [🎿]

(AAA) ▼▼ Motel 6 Redmond-4076 SH
(541) 923-2100. $49-$69. 2247 S Hwy 97. 1 mi s on US 97 from jct SR 126 W. Int corridors. Pets: Small, other species. Designated rooms, service with restrictions, supervision.
[SAVE] [S☉] [✕] [�525M] [✍] [�] [🛏]

(AAA) ▼▼ Redmond Inn M
(541) 548-1091. $55-$70. 1545 Hwy 97 S. 0.5 mi s on US 97 from jct SR 126 W. Ext corridors. Pets: Other species. $5 daily fee/pet. Service with restrictions, supervision.
[SAVE] [S☉] [✕] [🛏] [📺] [🌊]

▼▼ Redmond Super 8 Motel SH ❄
(541) 548-8881. $63-$68. 3629 21st Pl SW. US 97, exit Yew Ave. Int corridors. Pets: Other species. $10 one-time fee/room. Service with restrictions, supervision.
[ASK] [S☉] [✕] [�525M] [✍] [�] [🌊]

REEDSPORT

(AAA) ▼ Anchor Bay Inn M
(541) 271-2149. $45-$77. 1821 Winchester Ave (Hwy 101). On US 101, 0.8 mi s of jct SR 38. Ext corridors. Pets: Other species. $7 daily fee/pet. Designated rooms, service with restrictions, supervision.
[SAVE] [S☉] [✕] [🛏] [📺] [🌊] [🎿]

(AAA) ▼▼▼ Best Western Salbasgeon Inn M
(541) 271-4831. $76-$90. 1400 Hwy Ave 101 S. Just s on US 101 from jct SR 38. Ext corridors. Pets: Medium, dogs only. $10 daily fee/pet. Designated rooms, supervision.
[SAVE] [S☉] [✕] [🛏] [📺] [🌊]

(AAA) ▼ Economy Inn M
(541) 271-3671. $39-$90. 1593 Hwy 101. On US 101; center. Ext corridors. Pets: Other species. $5 one-time fee/pet. Service with restrictions, supervision.
[SAVE] [S☉] [✕] [🛏] [📺] [🌊] [🎿]

(AAA) ▼ Salbasgeon Inn of the Umpqua SH ❄
(541) 271-2025. $68-$180. 45209 Hwy 38. Jct US 101, 7.3 mi e. Ext corridors. Pets: Large, dogs only. $15 daily fee/pet. Designated rooms, service with restrictions, supervision.
[SAVE] [✕] [🛏] [📺] [🎿]

ROCKAWAY BEACH

(AAA) ▼▼ Sea Treasures Inn M
(503) 355-8220. $49-$99. 301 N Miller St. Jct 3rd Ave N; center. Ext corridors. Pets: Dogs only. $10 one-time fee/pet. Designated rooms, service with restrictions, supervision.
[SAVE] [✕] [🛏] [📺] [🎿]

(AAA) ▼▼ Silver Sands Motel M
(503) 355-2206. $75-$154. 215 S Pacific St. US 101, exit S 2nd Ave, just w. Ext corridors. Pets: Accepted.
[SAVE] [S☉] [✕] [�] [🛏] [📺] [🌊] [🎿] [🎿]

(AAA) ▼▼ Tradewinds Motel M ❄
(503) 355-2112. $47-$135, 7 day notice. 523 N Pacific St. Just w of US 101, off N 6th Ave. Ext corridors. Pets: Medium, dogs only. $10 daily fee/pet. Designated rooms, service with restrictions, supervision.
[SAVE] [✕] [🛏] [📺] [🎿]

ROSEBURG

(AAA) ▼▼▼ Best Western Garden Villa Inn M
(541) 672-1601. $69-$99. 760 NW Garden Valley Blvd. I-5, exit 125, just w. Ext corridors. Pets: Accepted.
[SAVE] [S☉] [✕] [✍] [�] [🛏] [📺] [🌊]

AAA ▽▽▽ Holiday Inn Express SH ❀
(541) 673-7517. **$71-$99.** 375 W Harvard Blvd. I-5, exit 124, just e. Ext/int corridors. **Pets:** Other species. $5 daily fee/room. Designated rooms, service with restrictions, supervision.
SAVE S🐾 ✕ ⛊M 🕅 ⛊ 🖥 💻 ⇝ ✕

AAA ▽▽▽ Howard Johnson Express Inn M
(541) 673-5082. **$55-$76.** 978 NE Stephen St. I-5, exit 125, 0.6 mi e on Garden Valley Blvd, then 0.4 mi s. Ext corridors. **Pets:** Small. $10 daily fee/pet. Designated rooms, service with restrictions, supervision.
SAVE S🐾 ✕ 🖥 💻

AAA ▽▽▽ Quality Inn SH
(541) 673-5561. **$69-$109.** 427 NW Garden Valley Blvd. I-5, exit 125, just e. Ext corridors. **Pets:** Large, other species. $100 deposit/room, $7 daily fee/room. Designated rooms, service with restrictions, supervision.
SAVE S🐾 ✕ 🕅 ⛊ 🖥 💻

AAA ▽▽▽ Roseburg Travelodge M
(541) 672-4836. **$67-$91.** 315 W Harvard Blvd. I-5, exit 124, just e. Ext corridors. **Pets:** Accepted.
SAVE S🐾 ✕ 🖥 💻 ⇝

AAA ▽ Shady Oaks Motel M
(541) 672-2608. **$41-$49.** 2954 Old Hwy 99 S. I-5, exit 120, 0.5 mi n. Ext corridors. **Pets:** Accepted.
SAVE ✕ 🖥

▽▽ Sleep Inn and Suites SH
(541) 464-8338. **$54-$94.** 2855 NW Edenbower Blvd. I-5, exit 127, just n. Int corridors. **Pets:** Large. $7 one-time fee/pet. Service with restrictions, crate.
A$K S🐾 ✕ 🕅 ⛊ 🖥 💻

▽▽ Super 8 Motel SH
(541) 672-8880. **$51-$65.** 3200 NW Aviation Dr. I-5, exit 127, just ne. Int corridors. **Pets:** Medium, other species. $25 deposit/pet. Service with restrictions, supervision.
A$K S🐾 ✕ ⛊M 🕅 ⛊ 🖥 ⇝

AAA ▽▽▽ Windmill Inn of Roseburg SH ❀
(541) 673-0901. **$65-$95.** 1450 NW Mulholland Dr. I-5, exit 125, just ne. Int corridors. **Pets:** Other species. Designated rooms, service with restrictions, supervision.
SAVE S🐾 ✕ 🕅 ⛊ 🖥 💻 ⇝ ✕

ST. HELENS

AAA ▽▽▽ Best Western Oak Meadows Inn SH
(503) 397-3000. **$79-$139.** 585 S Columbia River Hwy. South end of town on US 30. Int corridors. **Pets:** Accepted.
SAVE S🐾 ✕ 🖥 💻 ⇝

SALEM

AAA ▽▽▽ Best Western New Kings Inn SH
(503) 581-1559. **$67-$90.** 1600 Motor Ct NE. I-5, exit 256, just e. Ext corridors. **Pets:** Accepted.
SAVE S🐾 ✕ ⛊M 🕅 ⛊ 🖥 💻 🍴 ⇝ ✕

AAA ▽▽▽ Best Western Pacific Hwy Inn SH
(503) 390-3200. **$73-$87.** 4646 Portland Rd NE. I-5, exit 258, just e. Ext corridors. **Pets:** Accepted.
SAVE S🐾 ✕ ⛊M 🕅 ⛊ 🖥 💻 ⇝

AAA ▽▽▽ Holiday Inn Express SH
(503) 391-7000. **$69-$89.** 890 Hawthorne Ave SE. I-5, exit 253, just w, then just n. Int corridors. **Pets:** Accepted.
SAVE ✕ ⛊M 🕅 ⛊ 🖥 💻

AAA ▽▽ Holiday Lodge M
(503) 585-2323. **$50-$90.** 1400 Hawthorne Ave NE. I-5, exit 256, just w, then just s. Ext corridors. **Pets:** $10 daily fee/pet. Designated rooms, service with restrictions, supervision.
SAVE S🐾 ✕ ⛊ 🖥 ⇝

◇ Motel 6–1343 M
(503) 371-8024. **$45-$59.** 1401 Hawthorne Ave NE. I-5, exit 256, just w, then just s. Ext corridors. **Pets:** Accepted.
S🐾 ✕ 🕅 ⛊ ⇝

AAA ▽▽▽ Phoenix Inn Suites-North Salem SH ❀
(503) 581-7004. **$79-$99.** 1590 Weston Ct NE. I-5, exit 256, just w, then just s. Int corridors. **Pets:** $10 daily fee/room. Service with restrictions, supervision.
SAVE S🐾 ✕ ⛊M 🕅 ⛊ 🖥 💻 ⇝ ✕

AAA ▽▽▽ Phoenix Inn Suites-South Salem SH ❀
(503) 588-9220. **$79-$99.** 4370 Commercial SE. I-5, exit 252, 1.5 mi w on Kuebler Rd, then 0.7 mi n. Int corridors. **Pets:** Large. $10 one-time fee/room. Designated rooms, service with restrictions, supervision.
SAVE S🐾 ✕ ⛊M 🕅 ⛊ 🖥 💻 ⇝ ✕

▽▽▽▽ Red Lion Hotel Salem SH
(503) 370-7888. **$59-$99.** 3301 Market St NE. I-5, exit 256, just w. Int corridors. **Pets:** Medium. $10 daily fee/pet. Service with restrictions, crate.
A$K ✕ 🕅 ⛊ 🖥 💻 🍴 ⇝

▽▽▽▽ Residence Inn by Marriott SH ❀
(503) 585-6500. **$100-$120.** 640 Hawthorne Ave SE. I-5, exit 253, just w, then n. Int corridors. **Pets:** Small, other species. $75 one-time fee/room. Service with restrictions, supervision.
A$K S🐾 ✕ ⛊M 🕅 ⛊ 🖥 💻 ⇝ ✕

▽▽▽ Salem Inn SH
(503) 588-0515. **$69-$89.** 1775 Freeway Ct NE. I-5, exit 256, just w. Int corridors. **Pets:** Other species. $50 deposit/room, $10 daily fee/pet. Service with restrictions, supervision.
A$K S🐾 ✕ ⛊M 🕅 ⛊ 🖥 💻 ⇝

▽▽ Salem Super 8 SH
(503) 370-8888. **$54-$79.** 1288 Hawthorne Ave NE. I-5, exit 256, just w, then just s. Int corridors. **Pets:** Accepted.
A$K S🐾 ✕ ⛊M 🕅 ⛊ 🖥

▽▽▽ Shilo Inn Suites-Salem SH
(503) 581-4001. **$59-$149.** 3304 Market St NE. I-5, exit 256, just w. Int corridors. **Pets:** Small, dogs only. $10 daily fee/pet. Service with restrictions, supervision.
A$K S🐾 ✕ 🖥 💻 ⇝ ✕

AAA ▽▽ Travelodge Salem Capital M
(503) 581-2466. **$51-$59.** 1555 State St. I-5, exit 253, just w on SR 22/99 (Mission St), 0.7 mi n on Hawthorne Ave SE, then 1.6 mi w. Ext corridors. **Pets:** Small. $10 daily fee/room. Designated rooms, service with restrictions, supervision.
SAVE S🐾 ✕ ⛊ 🖥 💻 ⇝

SANDY

▽▽▽ Best Western Sandy Inn SH
(503) 668-7100. **$90-$125.** 37465 Hwy 26. West side of town. Int corridors. **Pets:** Dogs only. $10 daily fee/pet. Service with restrictions, supervision.
A$K S🐾 ✕ ⛊M 🕅 🖥 💻 ⇝

SEASIDE

AAA ▽▽▽ Best Western Ocean View Resort SH ❀
(503) 738-3334. **$59-$399, 3 day notice.** 414 N Prom. US 101, exit 1st Ave, just w, just n on Necanicum Dr, then just w on 4th Ave. Ext/int corridors. **Pets:** $20 one-time fee/room. Designated rooms, service with restrictions, supervision.
SAVE S🐾 ✕ ⛊ 🖥 💻 🍴 ⇝

Colonial Motor Inn M
(503) 738-6295. **$57-$210, 7 day notice.** 1120 N Holladay Dr. US 101, exit 12th Ave, just w, then just s. Ext corridors. **Pets:** Accepted.

Comfort Inn Boardwalk SH
(503) 738-3011. **$79-$259.** 545 Broadway. US 101, exit Ave A, just w; downtown. Ext/int corridors. **Pets:** $10 daily fee/room. Designated rooms, service with restrictions, supervision.

Seaside Convention Center Inn M
(503) 738-9581. **$69-$139, 3 day notice.** 441 2nd Ave. US 101, exit 1st Ave, 0.4 mi w. Ext/int corridors. **Pets:** $10 daily fee/pet. Service with restrictions, crate.

Sea Side Oceanfront Inn Bed & Breakfast Hotel BB
(503) 738-6403. **$95-$315, 5 day notice.** 581 S Prom. US 101, exit Ave G, 0.6 mi w, then just n. Int corridors. **Pets:** Medium. $25 one-time fee/pet. Designated rooms, service with restrictions, supervision.

SHADY COVE

The Edgewater Inn on the Rogue River M
(541) 878-3171. **$67-$158.** 7800 Rogue River Dr. Off SR 62. Ext corridors. **Pets:** Medium. $7 daily fee/pet. Service with restrictions, supervision.

SISTERS

Best Western Ponderosa Lodge SH
(541) 549-1234. **$89-$199.** 500 Hwy 20 W. West end of town, just w on US 20 from jct SR 242. Ext corridors. **Pets:** Large. $15 one-time fee/room. Designated rooms.

Comfort Inn at Sisters SH
(541) 549-7829. **$90-$100.** 540 Hwy 20 W. West end of town, just w on US 20 from jct SR 242. Ext corridors. **Pets:** Large, other species. Designated rooms, supervision.

Sun Ranch Inn BB
(541) 549-0123. **$70-$150 (no credit cards).** 69013 Camp Polk Rd. East end of town, just w on US 20 from jct SR 126, 0.5 mi n on Locust Rd. Int corridors. **Pets:** Medium, dogs only. $10 one-time fee/room. Designated rooms, service with restrictions, supervision.

SPRINGFIELD

Best Western Grand Manor Inn SH
(541) 726-4769. **$79-$110.** 971 Kruse Way. I-5, exit 195A, just e. Int corridors. **Pets:** Dogs only. $100 deposit/pet, $6 daily fee/pet. Designated rooms, service with restrictions, supervision.

Comfort Suites Eugene/Springfield SH
(541) 746-5359. **$89-$154.** 969 Kruse Way. I-5, exit 195A, just e. Int corridors. **Pets:** Medium, dogs only. $10 daily fee/pet. Designated rooms, service with restrictions, supervision.

Holiday Inn Express SH
(541) 746-8471. **$89-$119.** 3480 Hutton St. I-5, exit 195A, just e. Int corridors. **Pets:** Medium, dogs only. $10 daily fee/pet. Designated rooms, service with restrictions, supervision.

Motel 6 #418 M
(541) 741-1105. **$43-$55.** 3752 International Ct. I-5, exit 195A, just e, then just n on Gateway St. Ext corridors. **Pets:** Accepted.

Super 8 Motel SH
(541) 746-1314. **$50-$67.** 3315 Gateway St. I-5, exit 195A, just e, then just s. Int corridors. **Pets:** Medium. Service with restrictions, supervision.

Village Inn SH
(541) 747-4546. **$62.** 1875 Mohawk Blvd. I-5, exit 194A, 2.5 mi e, then just n. Ext corridors. **Pets:** Small. Service with restrictions, supervision.

SUMMER LAKE

Summer Lake Inn CI
(541) 943-3983. **$105-$145, 14 day notice.** 47531 Hwy 31. 10 mi s; between MM 81 and 82. Ext corridors. **Pets:** Dogs only. $10 one-time fee/pet. Service with restrictions, supervision.

SUNRIVER

Sunriver Resort LH
(541) 593-1000. **$119-$199, 21 day notice.** 1 Center Dr. 2 mi w of US 97. Ext corridors. **Pets:** $75 one-time fee/room. Designated rooms.

SUTHERLIN

Sutherlin Inn SH
(541) 459-6800. **$45-$90.** 1400 Hospitality Pl. I-5, exit 136, just se. Int corridors. **Pets:** Other species. $10 daily fee/room. Service with restrictions, supervision.

Umpqua Regency Inn M
(541) 459-1424. **$61-$79.** 150 Myrtle St. I-5, exit 136, just e. Ext corridors. **Pets:** Accepted.

SWEET HOME

Sweet Home Inn M
(541) 367-5137. **$64-$79.** 805 Long St. Just e of jct US 20 and SR 228; just s on 10th Ave, just w. Ext corridors. **Pets:** Medium, dogs only. $10 daily fee/pet. Service with restrictions, supervision.

TILLAMOOK

Mar-Clair Inn M
(503) 842-7571. **$65-$86.** 11 Main Ave. US 101, just n of jct SR 6. Ext/int corridors. **Pets:** Very small, dogs only. $10 daily fee/pet. Designated rooms, service with restrictions, supervision.

UMATILLA

Desert River Inn SH
(541) 922-1000. **$81.** 705 Willamette Ave. I-82, exit 1 (US 730), 1.3 mi e, then just n. Int corridors. **Pets:** $10 daily fee/pet. Service with restrictions, supervision.

WALDPORT

Alsea Manor Motel M
(541) 563-3249. **$43-$83.** 190 SW Hwy 101. SR 34, just s on US 101; downtown. Ext corridors. **Pets:** Small, dogs only. $5 daily fee/pet. Designated rooms, service with restrictions, supervision.

WELCHES

(AAA) ▼▼▼▼ The Resort at the Mountain 🏨 🐾
(503) 622-3101. **$99-$450, 3 day notice.** 68010 E Fairway Ave. 0.8 mi s of US 26 on E Welches Rd. Ext corridors. **Pets:** Large, other species. $25 one-time fee/room. Designated rooms, service with restrictions.
[SAVE] [S🐾] [✕] [🐾] [✆] [🛏] [💻] [🍽] [🏊] [✕]

WHEELER

(AAA) ▼ Wheeler on the Bay Lodge and Marina Ⓜ
(503) 368-5858. **$50-$145, 3 day notice.** 580 Marine Dr. On US 101; center. Ext corridors. **Pets:** Accepted.
[SAVE] [✕] [🛏] [💻] [✕] [🐾]

WINSTON

(AAA) ▼▼ Sweet Breeze Inn II Ⓜ
(541) 679-2420. **$60-$70.** 251 NE Main St. I-5, exit 119, 3 mi w. Ext corridors. **Pets:** Accepted.
[SAVE] [S🐾] [✕] [✆] [🛏]

WOODBURN

(AAA) ▼▼▼ Best Western Woodburn 🆂🅷
(503) 982-6515. **$75-$115.** 2887 Newberg Hwy. I-5, exit 271, just e. Int corridors. **Pets:** Medium. $10 daily fee/pet. Designated rooms, service with restrictions, supervision.
[SAVE] [S🐾] [✕] [♿M] [🐾] [✆] [🛏] [💻] [🏊]

(AAA) ▼▼▼▼ La Quinta Inn & Suites Woodburn 🆂🅷 🐾
(503) 982-1727. **$59-$117.** 120 Arney Rd NE. I-5, exit 271, just w. Int corridors. **Pets:** Other species. Service with restrictions, supervision.
[SAVE] [✕] [🐾] [🛏] [💻] [🏊]

YACHATS

(AAA) ▼▼▼ The Adobe Resort 🆂🅷 🐾
(541) 547-3141. **$75-$405.** 1555 Hwy 101. 0.5 mi n. Int corridors. **Pets:** Other species. $10 daily fee/pet. Designated rooms, service with restrictions.
[SAVE] [S🐾] [✕] [🐾] [✆] [🛏] [💻] [🍽] [🏊] [✕] [🐾]

▼ The Dublin House Ⓜ
(541) 547-3200. **$49-$160.** 251 W 7th St. US 101 at 7th St; downtown. Ext corridors. **Pets:** Small, dogs only. $10 one-time fee/pet. Supervision.
[A$K] [S🐾] [✕] [🛏] [💻] [🏊] [🐾]

(AAA) ▼▼▼ Fireside Motel Ⓜ
(541) 547-3636. **$55-$120.** 1881 Hwy 101 N. 0.6 mi n; just w of US 101. Ext corridors. **Pets:** Accepted.
[SAVE] [S🐾] [✕] [🛏] [💻] [🏊] [🐾]

▼▼ Shamrock Lodgettes 🅲🅰
(541) 547-3312. **$59-$200, 3 day notice.** 105 Hwy 101 S. On US 101, just s. Ext corridors. **Pets:** Accepted.
[A$K] [S🐾] [✕] [🛏] [💻] [🏊] [🐾]

PENNSYLVANIA

ABBOTTSTOWN

🛆🛆🛆 ▽▽▽ The Altland House CI
(717) 259-9535. **$99-$150.** Center Square Rt 30. Jct SR 194. Int corridors. **Pets:** Small, other species. $15 one-time fee/pet. Service with restrictions, supervision.
[SAVE] [X] [■] [YI]

ALLENTOWN

🛆🛆🛆 ▽▽▽ Allentown Howard Johnson Inn & Suites SH 🐾
(610) 439-4000. **$49-$199.** 3220 Hamilton Blvd. I-78, exit 54 (Hamilton Blvd), 0.8 mi n. Int corridors. **Pets:** Other species. $20 one-time fee/room. Service with restrictions.
[SAVE] [S🐾] [X] [🕭M] [🖉] [🐾] [■] [◧] [🏊]

🛆🛆🛆 ▽▽▽ Allenwood Motel M 🐾
(610) 395-3707. **$55-$125.** 1058 Hausman Rd. I-476, exit 56, 0.5 mi e on US 22, then 0.8 mi s on SR 309; I-78, exit 53 westbound; exit 51 eastbound, 1 mi n on SR 309, w on Tilghman St to light, then 0.8 mi n to dead end. Ext corridors. **Pets:** Medium. $10 daily fee/pet. Designated rooms, service with restrictions, supervision.
[SAVE] [S🐾] [X] [■]

▽▽▽ Days Inn Conference Center SH 🐾
(610) 395-3731. **$78-$150.** 1151 Bulldog Dr. I-476, exit 56, 0.5 mi e on US 22, then 0.6 mi n on SR 309 via Bulldog Dr access road. Ext/int corridors. **Pets:** Other species. $15 daily fee/room. Designated rooms, service with restrictions, crate.
[ASK] [S🐾] [X] [🕭M] [🖉] [🐾] [■] [◧] [YI] [🏊] [X]

▽▽▽ Four Points by Sheraton Hotel & Suites Lehigh Valley Airport SH
(610) 266-1000. **$89-$159.** 3400 Airport Rd. On SR 987 N (Airport Rd), 0.5 mi n of jct US 22. Int corridors. **Pets:** Accepted.
[ASK] [S🐾] [X] [🕭M] [🖉] [🐾] [■] [◧] [YI] [🏊]

🛆🛆🛆 ▽▽▽ Microtel Inn SH
(610) 266-9070. **$35-$139.** 1880 Steelstone Rd. US 22, exit Airport Rd S. Int corridors. **Pets:** Large, other species. Service with restrictions, supervision.
[SAVE] [S🐾] [X] [🕭M] [🖉] [🐾] [■] [◧]

🛆🛆🛆 ▽▽▽▽ Quality Inn M
(610) 434-9550. **$45-$199.** 1033 Airport Rd. US 22, exit Airport Rd S, 1.1 mi s. Int corridors. **Pets:** Small. $20 daily fee/pet. No service, supervision.
[SAVE] [S🐾] [X] [🕭M] [🖉] [■] [◧]

▽▽▽ Red Roof Inn #7110 M
(610) 264-5404. **$55-$86.** 1846 Catasauqua Rd. US 22, exit Airport Rd S, just s. Ext corridors. **Pets:** Accepted.
[X] [🕭M] [🖉] [🐾] [■]

▽▽▽ Staybridge Suites Allentown-Airport SH
(610) 443-5000. **$89-$169.** 1787-A Airport Rd. US 22, exit Airport Rd S, 0.3 mi s. Int corridors. **Pets:** Other species. $100 one-time fee/room. Service with restrictions, supervision.
[ASK] [X] [🕭M] [🖉] [🐾] [■] [◧] [🏊] [X]

🛆🛆🛆 ▽▽▽▽ Super 8 Motel-Allentown SH
(610) 435-7880. **$65-$95.** 1715 Plaza Ln. US 22, exit 15th St, just n. Int corridors. **Pets:** $10 daily fee/pet. Service with restrictions, supervision.
[SAVE] [S🐾] [X] [🖉] [■]

ALTOONA

🛆🛆🛆 ▽▽▽ Econo Lodge M
(814) 944-3555. **$66, 7 day notice.** 2906 Pleasant Valley Blvd. I-99/US 220, exit 32 (Frankstown Rd), 0.4 mi w, then 0.5 mi n. Ext corridors. **Pets:** Other species. Service with restrictions, crate.
[SAVE] [S🐾] [X] [■] [◧] [YI]

▽▽ Motel 6 #1415 M
(814) 946-7601. **$45-$61.** 1500 Sterling St. I-99/US 220, exit 31 (Plank Rd), just w. Ext corridors. **Pets:** Accepted.
[S🐾] [X] [🕭M] [🖉] [🏊]

▽▽ Super 8 Motel Altoona M
(814) 942-5350. **$50-$55.** 3535 Fairway Dr. I-99/US 220, exit 32 (Frankstown Rd), just w. Int corridors. **Pets:** Small. $6 daily fee/pet. Designated rooms, service with restrictions, supervision.
[ASK] [S🐾] [X] [🕭M] [■]

BARKEYVILLE

Comfort Inn-Barkeyville M
(814) 786-7901. **$65-$120, 3 day notice.** 137 Gibb Rd. I-80, exit 29, just n on SR 8. Ext corridors. **Pets:** Medium. $10 one-time fee/room. No service, supervision.

Super 8 Motel-Barkeyville M
(814) 786-8375. **$48-$69, 3 day notice.** 1010 Dholu Rd. I-80, exit 29, just n. Int corridors. **Pets:** $5 daily fee/pet. Designated rooms, service with restrictions, supervision.

BEDFORD

Best Western Bedford Inn SH
(814) 623-9006. **$67-$87.** 4517 Business Rt 220. I-70/76 (Pennsylvania Tpke), exit 146, 0.3 mi n. Ext/int corridors. **Pets:** Medium, other species. $50 deposit/room, $10 daily fee/room. Service with restrictions, supervision.

Budget Host Inn M
(814) 623-8107. **$40-$85.** 4378 Business Rt 220. I-70/76 (Pennsylvania Tpke), exit 146, just n. Ext corridors. **Pets:** Small. $5 one-time fee/pet. Service with restrictions, supervision.

Janey Lynn Motel M
(814) 623-9515. **Call for rates.** 3567 Business Rt 220. I-70/76 (Pennsylvania Tpke), exit 146, 1.6 mi s. Ext corridors. **Pets:** Accepted.

Motel Town House M
(814) 623-5138. **$40-$65.** 200 S Richard St. I-70/76 (Pennsylvania Tpke), exit 146, 2.5 mi s on US 220 business route. Ext corridors. **Pets:** Accepted.

Quality Inn Bedford SH
(814) 623-5188. **$70-$150.** 4407 Business Rt 220 N. I-70/76 (Pennsylvania Tpke), exit 146, just n. Ext/int corridors. **Pets:** Medium, other species. $10 daily fee/pet. Designated rooms, service with restrictions, supervision.

Super 8 Motel M
(814) 623-5880. **$55-$60.** 4498 Business Rt 220. I-70/76 (Pennslyvania Tpke), exit 146, 0.3 mi n. Int corridors. **Pets:** $5 daily fee/pet. Service with restrictions, supervision.

Travelodge M
(814) 623-7800. **$44-$109.** 4271 Business Rt 220. I-70/76 (Pennsylvania Tpke), exit 146, just s. Ext/int corridors. **Pets:** Other species. $7 daily fee/pet. Designated rooms, no service, supervision.

BETHEL

Comfort Inn-Bethel/Midway SH
(717) 933-8888. **$69-$139.** 41 Diner Dr. I-78, exit 16, just w. Int corridors. **Pets:** Other species. $10 daily fee/pet. Service with restrictions, crate.

BETHLEHEM

Comfort Inn SH
(610) 865-6300. **$89-$135.** 3191 Highfield Dr. US 22, exit SR 191, just s. Ext/int corridors. **Pets:** Other species. $10 daily fee/pet. Service with restrictions, supervision.

Comfort Suites SH
(610) 882-9700. **$79-$149.** 120 W 3rd St. SR 378, exit 3rd St, W 3rd and Brodhead sts; center. Int corridors. **Pets:** Designated rooms, supervision.

Holiday Inn Bethlehem at the Gateway Conference Center SH
(610) 866-5800. **$99-$129.** 300 Gateway Dr. US 22, exit Center St and SR 512. Ext/int corridors. **Pets:** Medium, dogs only. $10 daily fee/room. Designated rooms, service with restrictions.

Residence Inn by Marriott SH
(610) 317-2662. **$169-$209.** 2180 Motel Dr. US 22, exit Airport Rd S, 0.8 mi se on Catasauqua Rd. Int corridors. **Pets:** Accepted.

BLOOMSBURG

Econo Lodge at Bloomsburg SH
(570) 387-0490. **$62-$99.** 189 Columbia Mall Dr. I-80, exit 232, just n on SR 42. Int corridors. **Pets:** Large. $25 one-time fee/room. Designated rooms, service with restrictions, supervision.

The Inn at Turkey Hill CI
(570) 387-1500. **$109-$119.** 991 Central Rd. I-80, exit 236 eastbound; exit 236A westbound, just s. Ext/int corridors. **Pets:** Other species. $15 daily fee/room. Service with restrictions, supervision.

BLUE MOUNTAIN

Kenmar Motel M
(717) 423-5915. **$60-$75.** 17788 Cumberland Hwy. I-76, exit 201, just e on SR 997 N. Ext corridors. **Pets:** Dogs only. $5 daily fee/pet. Designated rooms, service with restrictions, supervision.

BOYERTOWN

Mel-Dor Motel M
(610) 367-2626. **$54.** 1 Spring Garden Dr. SR 100, exit New Berlinville; 1 mi n of town. Ext corridors. **Pets:** Small, dogs only. $5 daily fee/pet. Service with restrictions, supervision.

BRADFORD

Best Western Bradford Inn SH
(814) 362-4501. **$80-$90.** 100 Davis St S. US 219, exit Forman St southbound, just w to Davis St, then 0.3 mi s; norhtbound, exit Elm St, just w. Ext/int corridors. **Pets:** $10 daily fee/room. Designated rooms, service with restrictions, crate.

Glendorn CI
(814) 362-6511. **$495-$795, 30 day notice.** 1000 Glendorn Dr. Main and Corydon, 4.3 mi w to W Corydon, follow signs. Ext/int corridors. **Pets:** Large, dogs only. $75 daily fee/pet. Designated rooms, service with restrictions, supervision.

BREEZEWOOD

Breezewood Ramada Inn SH
(814) 735-4005. **$49-$79.** 16620 Lincoln Hwy. I-76, exit 161, just e on US 30; I-70, exit 147, just e on US 30. Int corridors. **Pets:** $10 daily fee/room. Supervision.

Heritage Inn M
(814) 735-2200. **$59-$79.** 16550 Lincoln Hwy. I-76, exit 161, just e on US 30; I-70, exit 147, just e on US 30. Int corridors. **Pets:** Accepted.

AAA ▼ Wiltshire Motel M
(814) 735-4361. **$40-$50.** 140 S Breezewood Rd. I-76, exit 161, just w on US 30; I-70, exit 147. Ext corridors. **Pets:** Small. Service with restrictions, supervision.
[SAVE] [S6] [X] [▭]

BROOKVILLE

AAA ▼ Budget Host Gold Eagle Inn M
(814) 849-7344. **$50-$75.** 250 W Main St. I-80, exit 78, 0.5 mi s on SR 36. Ext corridors. **Pets:** Other species. Supervision.
[SAVE] [X] [🛏] [▭] [¶]

AAA ▼▼ Holiday Inn Express M
(814) 849-8381. **$79-$99, 5 day notice.** 235 Allegheny Blvd. I-80, exit 78, just s on SR 36. Int corridors. **Pets:** $15 one-time fee/pet. Service with restrictions, supervision.
[SAVE] [S6] [X] [🛏] [▭]

▼ Super 8 Motel M
(814) 849-8840. **$55-$65, 30 day notice.** 251 Allegheny Blvd. I-80, exit 78, just s on SR 36. Int corridors. **Pets:** Other species. $10 daily fee/pet. Supervision.
[ASK] [X] [🛏]

CAMBRIDGE SPRINGS

AAA ▼ Riverside Inn CI ❖
(814) 398-4645. **$65-$170, 10 day notice.** 1 Fountain Ave. I-79, exit 154 northbound, 2.9 mi e on SR 198, then 8.4 mi n on US 19; exit 166 southbound, 2.4 mi e on US 6 N, then 7 mi s on SR 99. Int corridors. **Pets:** Other species. Service with restrictions.
[SAVE] [X] [🛏] [¶] [🏊] [X] [Z]

CARLISLE

▼▼▼ Comfort Suites Hotel SH
(717) 960-1000. **$104-$179, 3 day notice.** 10 S Hanover St. Just s of the square; downtown. Int corridors. **Pets:** Medium, other species. $10 daily fee/pet. Service with restrictions, crate.
[ASK] [S6] [X] [&M] [&] [🛏] [▭] [¶]

AAA ▼▼ Days Inn & Suites-Carlisle SH
(717) 258-4147. **$72-$130.** 101 Alexander Spring Rd. I-81, exit 45, just sw. Int corridors. **Pets:** Accepted.
[SAVE] [S6] [X] [&M] [&] [🛏] [▭]

AAA ▼▼ Econo Lodge M
(717) 249-7775. **$70-$118.** 1460 Harrisburg Pike. I-81, exit 52 southbound; exit 52A northbound; I-76 (Pennsylvania Tpke), exit 226, 0.8 mi n. Ext corridors. **Pets:** Small, other species. $10 daily fee/pet. Designated rooms, service with restrictions, supervision.
[SAVE] [S6] [X] [🛏] [▭] [X]

AAA ▼▼▼ Hampton Inn Carlisle SH
(717) 240-0200. **$69-$159.** 1164 Harrisburg Pike. I-76 (Pennsylvania Tpke), exit 226, just n; I-81, exit 52 southbound; exit 52B northbound, 0.8 mi s. Int corridors. **Pets:** Medium. Service with restrictions, supervision.
[SAVE] [S6] [X] [&M] [&] [🛏] [▭] [🏊]

AAA ▼▼▼ Holiday Inn Carlisle SH
(717) 245-2400. **$88-$158.** 1450 Harrisburg Pike. I-81, exit 52 southbound; exit 52A northbound, just se; I-76 (Pennsylvania Tpke), exit 226, 0.8 mi n. Int corridors. **Pets:** Medium. $10 daily fee/pet. Designated rooms, service with restrictions, supervision.
[SAVE] [S6] [X] [🛏] [▭] [¶] [🏊]

AAA ▼▼▼ Hotel Carlisle SH ❖
(717) 243-1717. **$99-$174.** 1700 Harrisburg Pike. I-81, exit 52 southbound; exit 52A northbound, 0.4 mi n; I-76 (Pennsylvania Tpke), exit 226, 1.2 mi n. Int corridors. **Pets:** Medium, other species. $10 daily fee/pet. Designated rooms, service with restrictions, crate.
[SAVE] [S6] [X] [🛏] [▭] [¶] [🏊] [X]

AAA ▼▼▼ Howard Johnson Inn SH
(717) 243-5411. **$49-$139.** 1245 Harrisburg Pike. I-81, exit 52 (US 11) southbound; exit 52B northbound, 0.5 mi s; I-72 (Pennsylvania Tpke), exit 226, 0.8 mi n on US 11. Ext/int corridors. **Pets:** Accepted.
[SAVE] [S6] [X] [&M] [🛏] [▭] [¶] [🏊]

AAA ▼▼▼ Pheasant Field Bed & Breakfast BB ❖
(717) 258-0717. **$95-$175, 3 day notice.** 150 Hickorytown Rd. I-76 (Pennsylvania Tpke), exit 226, 0.4 mi n on US 11, 2.3 mi se on S Middlesex Rd, 0.4 mi e on Ridge Dr, then just s (left turn). Ext/int corridors. **Pets:** Other species. $10 daily fee/room. Designated rooms, service with restrictions, supervision.
[SAVE] [X] [🛏] [X]

AAA ▼▼▼ Quality Inn Carlisle SH
(717) 243-6000. **$70-$150.** 1255 Harrisburg Pike. I-81, exit 52 southbound; exit 52B northbound; I-76 (Pennsylvania Tpke), exit 226, 0.8 mi n. Int corridors. **Pets:** Large. Designated rooms, service with restrictions, crate.
[SAVE] [S6] [X] [&] [🛏] [▭] [🏊]

AAA ▼▼ Ramada Ltd SH
(717) 243-8585. **$65-$79.** 1252 Harrisburg Pike. I-81, exit 52 southbound; exit 52B northbound; I-76 (Pennsylvania Tpke), exit 226, 1 mi n on US 11. Ext/int corridors. **Pets:** Large, other species. $10 daily fee/pet. Designated rooms, service with restrictions, crate.
[SAVE] [S6] [X] [&] [▭]

AAA ▼ Rodeway Inn M
(717) 249-2800. **$59-$124, 3 day notice.** 1239 Harrisburg Pike. I-81, exit 52 southbound; exit 52B northbound, 0.3 mi s; I-76 (Pennsylvania Tpke), exit 226, 0.8 mi s. Ext corridors. **Pets:** Small. $8 daily fee/pet. Designated rooms, service with restrictions.
[SAVE] [S6] [X] [🛏] [▭]

AAA ▼ Sleep Inn Carlisle SH
(717) 249-8863. **$59-$155.** 5 E Garland Dr. I-81, exit 47 northbound, just ne; exit 47A southbound. Int corridors. **Pets:** Other species. $10 daily fee/pet. No service, supervision.
[SAVE] [S6] [X] [🛏] [▭] [🏊]

AAA ▼ Super 8 Motel/North Carlisle M
(717) 249-7000. **$32-$129, 3 day notice.** 1800 Harrisburg Pike. I-81, exit 52A northbound; exit 52 (US 11) southbound, 0.5 mi n; I-76 (Pennsylvania Tpke), exit 226, 1.3 mi n. Ext/int corridors. **Pets:** Small. $5 daily fee/pet. Designated rooms, service with restrictions, supervision.
[SAVE] [S6] [X] [&M] [🛏] [🏊]

▼▼ Super 8 Motel-South M
(717) 245-9898. **$48-$68.** 100 Alexander Spring Rd. I-81, exit 45, just se. Int corridors. **Pets:** Accepted.
[ASK] [S6] [X] [&M] [🛏]

CHAMBERSBURG

AAA ▼▼▼ Best Western Chambersburg SH
(717) 262-4994. **$50-$169.** 211 Walker Rd. I-81, exit 16, just w on US 30, then just n. Int corridors. **Pets:** Small. $9 daily fee/pet. Designated rooms, service with restrictions, supervision.
[SAVE] [S6] [X] [&] [🛏] [▭] [🏊]

AAA ▼▼▼ Chambersburg Travelodge M
(717) 264-4187. **$40-$89.** 565 Lincoln Way E. I-81, exit 16, 0.8 mi w on US 30. Ext corridors. **Pets:** Other species. $5 daily fee/pet. Service with restrictions, supervision.
[SAVE] [S6] [X] [🛏] [▭] [¶]

▼▼ Comfort Inn-Chambersburg SH
(717) 263-6655. **$59-$89.** 3301 Black Gap Rd. I-81, exit 20, just e, then just s on SR 997. Int corridors. **Pets:** $10 daily fee/pet. Designated rooms, service with restrictions, supervision.
[ASK] [S6] [X] [🛏] [▭]

Days Inn SH
(717) 263-1288. **$69-$119.** 30 Falling Spring Rd. I-81, exit 16, just e on US 30. Int corridors. **Pets:** Medium, other species. $10 daily fee/pet. Designated rooms, service with restrictions, supervision.

Econo Lodge M
(717) 264-8005. **$57-$65.** 1110 Sheller Ave. I-81, exit 14, just w on SR 316. Int corridors. **Pets:** Other species. $10 one-time fee/pet. Service with restrictions, supervision.

CLARION

Holiday Inn SH
(814) 226-8850. **$79-$95.** 45 Holiday Inn Rd. I-80, exit 62, 0.5 mi n on SR 68. Int corridors. **Pets:** $10 one-time fee/room. Service with restrictions, supervision.

Microtel Inn & Suites-Clarion SH
(814) 227-2700. **$54-$74.** 151 Hotel Dr. I-80, exit 62, just n on SR 68, then just e. Int corridors. **Pets:** Medium. $10 daily fee/room. Service with restrictions, supervision.

Super 8 Motel-Clarion M
(814) 226-4550. **$42-$80, 14 day notice.** 135 Hotel Rd. I-80, exit 62, just n. Ext corridors. **Pets:** Other species. Designated rooms, service with restrictions, supervision.

CLARKS SUMMIT

Comfort Inn-Clarks Summit/Scranton SH
(570) 586-9100. **$69-$150.** 811 Northern Blvd. I-81, exit 194 on US 6 and 11; I-476 (Pennsylvania Tpke), exit 131. Int corridors. **Pets:** Accepted.

The Inn at Nichols Village SH
(570) 587-1135. **$89-$220.** 1101 Northern Blvd. I-81, exit 194; I-476 (Pennsylvania Tpke), exit 131, 0.5 mi w on US 6 and 11. **Pets:** Dogs only. $10 one-time fee/room. Designated rooms, service with restrictions, crate.

Ramada Plaza Hotel SH
(570) 586-2730. **$79-$169.** 820 Northern Blvd. I-81, exit 194; I-476 (Pennsylvania Tpke), exit 131, 0.3 mi w on US 6 and 11. **Pets:** $15 daily fee/pet.

CLEARFIELD

Budget Inn M
(814) 765-2639. **$38-$62.** 6321 Woodland Hwy (Rt 322 E). I-80, exit 120, 1.5 mi sw on SR 879, then 1.2 mi e. Ext/int corridors. **Pets:** $5 daily fee/pet. Designated rooms, service with restrictions, supervision.

Comfort Inn Clearfield SH
(814) 768-6400. **$59-$150.** 1821 Industrial Rd. I-80, exit 120, just s. Int corridors. **Pets:** Other species. Service with restrictions, crate.

Super 8 Motel-Clearfield M
(814) 768-7580. **$48-$81, 7 day notice.** 14597 Clearfield/Shawville Hwy (Rt 879). I-80, exit 120, just s. Int corridors. **Pets:** Other species. $5 one-time fee/room. Designated rooms, service with restrictions, supervision.

COOKSBURG

Clarion River Lodge Resort & Spa SH
(814) 744-8171. **$122-$551.** River Rd. SR 36 southbound, 5.2 mi e on River Rd along the Clarion River; northbound, 1.5 mi ne on SR 899 to River Rd, 3 mi sw, follow signs. Int corridors. **Pets:** Dogs only. $25 one-time fee/pet. Designated rooms.

COOPERSBURG

Econo Lodge M
(610) 282-1212. **$49-$99.** 321 Rt 309 S. On SR 309; center. Ext corridors. **Pets:** $10 daily fee/pet. Service with restrictions.

COUDERSPORT

Big Moore's Run Lodge CI
(814) 647-5300. **$80, 7 day notice.** 2218 Big Moore's Run Rd. From jct US 6, 2 mi s on SR 872 to top of hill, 1 mi e on paved road, 5.5 mi e on dirt road, across two bridges, then 1 mi s. Ext corridors. **Pets:** Small. $25 deposit/pet. Service with restrictions, supervision.

DANVILLE

Hampton Inn SH
(570) 271-2500. **$129-$199.** 97 Valley School Rd. I-80, exit 224, just s on SR 54. Int corridors. **Pets:** Other species. $30 one-time fee/room. Service with restrictions.

Quality Inn & Suites Danville M
(570) 275-5100. **$89-$139.** 15 Valley West Rd. I-80, exit 224, just n on SR 54. Int corridors. **Pets:** Medium. $25 one-time fee/room. Designated rooms, service with restrictions, supervision.

DICKSON CITY

Days Inn Scranton SH
(570) 383-9979. **$68-$120.** 1946 Scranton-Carbondale Hwy. I-81, exit 191A, 2 mi on US 6; I-476 (Pennsylvania Tpke Northeast Extension), exit 131 (Clarks Summit), 4.5 mi e on US 6. Int corridors. **Pets:** Other species. $20 one-time fee/pet. Service with restrictions, crate.

Residence Inn by Marriott-Scranton SH
(570) 343-5121. **$79-$169.** 947 Viewmont Dr. I-81, exit 190, just e, follow signs to Viewmont Dr. Int corridors. **Pets:** Other species. $75 one-time fee/pet. Service with restrictions, supervision.

DOUGLASSVILLE

Econo Lodge M
(610) 385-3016. **$60-$89.** 387 Ben Franklin Hwy (Rt 422) W. From Pottstown, 6 mi w on US 422; from Reading, 8 mi e on US 422. Ext corridors. **Pets:** Other species. $12 daily fee/pet. Service with restrictions, supervision.

DU BOIS

Holiday Inn DuBois SH
(814) 371-5100. **$75-$83.** US 219 & I-80. I-80, exit 97, just s. Int corridors. **Pets:** Designated rooms, service with restrictions, supervision.

DUNMORE

Days Inn SH
(570) 348-6101. **$50-$150.** 1226 O'Neill Hwy. I-81, exit 188, just e at SR 347. Int corridors. **Pets:** $5 daily fee/pet. Service with restrictions, supervision.

▼▼▼ Holiday Inn-Scranton East SH
(570) 343-4771. **$69-$179.** 200 Tigue St. I-84/380, exit 1 (Tigue St), 0.3 mi e of jct I-81. Ext/int corridors. **Pets:** Medium, other species. $10 daily fee/pet. Designated rooms, service with restrictions, crate.
[ASK] [S/D] [×] [🐾] [&] [🖥] [💻] [🍴] [≈] [X]

EASTON

AAA ▼▼▼ Best Western Easton Inn SH
(610) 253-9131. **$69-$109.** 185 S 3rd St. I-78, exit 75, 1 mi n, follow signs; US 22, exit 4th St (SR 611), just e to 3rd St, then 0.5 mi s; downtown. Int corridors. **Pets:** Small, other species. $50 deposit/pet. Service with restrictions, crate.
[SAVE] [S/D] [×] [🖥] [💻] [🍴] [≈]

EBENSBURG

▼▼▼ Comfort Inn SH
(814) 472-6100. **$72-$79.** 111 Cook Rd. Jct US 219, just e on US 22. Int corridors. **Pets:** Other species. $25 deposit/room, $8 daily fee/pet. Designated rooms, service with restrictions, supervision.
[ASK] [S/D] [×] [&M] [&] [🖥] [💻] [≈]

ERIE

AAA ▼▼▼ Best Western Erie Inn & Suites SH
(814) 864-1812. **$49-$129, 7 day notice.** 7820 Perry Hwy. I-90, exit 27, just n on SR 97. Int corridors. **Pets:** $10 daily fee/pet. Service with restrictions.
[SAVE] [S/D] [×] [&] [🖥] [💻] [≈]

AAA ▼▼▼ Best Western Presque Isle Country Inn SH
(814) 838-7647. **$54-$99.** 6467 Sterrettania Rd. I-90, exit 18, just s on SR 832. Int corridors. **Pets:** Accepted.
[SAVE] [S/D] [×] [&] [🖥] [💻] [🍴] [≈]

AAA ▼▼▼ Country Inn & Suites SH
(814) 864-5810. **$49-$129.** 8040 Oliver Rd. I-90, exit 24, just s, then 0.5 mi w. Int corridors. **Pets:** Small. $25 one-time fee/pet. Service with restrictions, supervision.
[SAVE] [S/D] [×] [&] [🖥] [💻] [≈]

▼▼▼ Days Inn SH
(814) 868-8521. **$59-$159, 4 day notice.** 7415 Schultz Rd. I-90, exit 27, just n on SR 97. Int corridors. **Pets:** Other species. $5 daily fee/pet. Service with restrictions, supervision.
[ASK] [S/D] [×] [🖥] [💻] [≈]

▼▼▼ Hampton Inn Erie South SH
(814) 866-6800. **$89-$139.** 8050 Old Oliver Rd. I-90, exit 24, just s, then 0.5 mi w. Int corridors. **Pets:** Medium. $25 one-time fee/room. Service with restrictions, supervision.
[ASK] [S/D] [×] [&M] [&] [🖥] [💻] [≈]

▼▼▼ Homewood Suites by Hilton SH 🐾
(814) 866-8292. **$89-$149.** 2084 Interchange Rd. I-79, exit 180, just e. Int corridors. **Pets:** $75 one-time fee/pet. Service with restrictions, crate.
[ASK] [S/D] [×] [🖥] [💻] [≈] [X]

◆ Microtel Inn-Erie M
(814) 864-1010. **$50-$77.** 8100 Peach St. I-90, exit 24, just s. Int corridors. **Pets:** $15 one-time fee/room. Designated rooms, service with restrictions, supervision.
[ASK] [S/D] [×] [🐾] [&] [🖥]

▼▼ Motel 6 #4020 M
(814) 864-4811. **$49-$109.** 7875 Peach St. I-90, exit 24, just n. Int corridors. **Pets:** Accepted.
[ASK] [S/D] [×] [🖥] [≈]

▼▼ Quality Inn & Suites SH
(814) 864-4911. **$49-$109.** 8040 Perry Hwy. I-90, exit 27, just s. Ext corridors. **Pets:** Medium. $10 daily fee/pet. Service with restrictions, crate.
[ASK] [S/D] [×] [🖥] [💻] [🍴] [≈]

▼▼▼ Red Roof Inn #7054 M 🐾
(814) 868-5246. **$45-$78.** 7865 Perry Hwy. I-90, exit 27, just n on SR 97. Ext/int corridors. **Pets:** Medium. Service with restrictions, supervision.
[×] [&] [🖥]

▼▼▼ Residence Inn by Marriott SH
(814) 864-2500. **$129-$299.** 8061 Peach St. I-90, exit 24, just s. Int corridors. **Pets:** Other species. $75 one-time fee/pet. Service with restrictions, crate.
[ASK] [S/D] [×] [🐾] [&] [🖥] [💻] [≈] [X]

▼▼▼ Super 8 Motel SH
(814) 864-9200. **$42-$98.** 8040 Perry Hwy. I-90, exit 27, just s. Int corridors. **Pets:** Medium. $10 daily fee/pet. Service with restrictions, crate.
[ASK] [S/D] [×] [🖥] [🍴]

FAYETTEVILLE

AAA ▼ Rite Spot Scottish Inn M 🐾
(717) 352-2144. **$35-$70.** 5651 Lincoln Way E. On US 30, 1 mi w of jct SR 997. Ext corridors. **Pets:** Medium, other species. $10 daily fee/pet. Designated rooms, no service, crate.
[SAVE] [S/D] [×] [🖥]

FOGELSVILLE

▼▼▼ Comfort Inn Lehigh Valley-West SH
(610) 391-0344. **$80-$120.** I-78, exit 49B (SR 100), just n. Int corridors. **Pets:** Other species. $25 one-time fee/pet. Service with restrictions, supervision.
[ASK] [S/D] [×] [🐾] [🖥] [💻]

▼▼▼ Glasbern CI
(610) 285-4723. **$140-$460, 7 day notice.** 2141 Packhouse Rd. I-78, exit 49B (SR 100), 0.3 mi n to 1st light, 0.3 mi w on Main St, 0.6 mi w on Church St, then 0.8 mi nw. Ext/int corridors. **Pets:** $25 daily fee/room. Designated rooms, service with restrictions.
[×] [🖥] [💻] [🍴] [≈] [X]

▼▼▼ Holiday Inn Conference Center SH
(610) 391-1000. **$89-$159.** 7736 Adrienne Dr. I-78, exit 49A, 0.3 mi s on SR 100. Int corridors. **Pets:** Dogs only. $10 daily fee/room. Designated rooms, service with restrictions, crate.
[ASK] [S/D] [×] [&M] [🐾] [🖥] [💻] [🍴] [≈] [X]

AAA ▼▼▼ Sleep Inn SH
(610) 395-6603. **$59-$99.** 327 Star Rd. I-78, exit 49A, 0.3 mi s on SR 100, left at 1st traffic light, then immediate left on service road. Int corridors. **Pets:** Medium. $15 daily fee/pet. Designated rooms, no service, supervision.
[SAVE] [S/D] [×] [&M] [🐾] [&] [🖥] [💻]

FRACKVILLE

AAA ▼▼▼ Econo Lodge M
(570) 874-3838. **$55-$85.** 501 S Middle St. I-81, exit 124B, 0.4 mi n on SR 61. Ext corridors. **Pets:** Accepted.
[SAVE] [S/D] [×] [🐾] [🖥] [💻]

AAA ▼▼▼ Granny's Motel & Restaurant SH
(570) 874-0408. **$39-$48.** 115 W Coal St. I-81, exit 124B, 0.3 mi nw on SR 61, then 0.3 mi n on Altamont Blvd. Ext/int corridors. **Pets:** Medium. $5 one-time fee/room. Designated rooms, service with restrictions, supervision.
[SAVE] [×] [🖥] [💻] [🍴]

▼▼ Motel 6–4043 M 🐾
(570) 874-1223. **Call for rates.** 701 Altamont Blvd. I-81, exit 124B, 0.3 mi nw on SR 61, then 0.3 mi n. Ext/int corridors. **Pets:** $5 daily fee/room. Service with restrictions, crate.
[×] [🖥]

FRANKLIN

◆◆ Franklin Super 8 Motel SH
(814) 432-2101. **$65.** 847 Allegheny Ave. 2 mi on SR 8. Int corridors.
Pets: Other species. $10 daily fee/room. Service with restrictions, supervision.
[ASK] [S6] [✕] [🔲]

GALETON

◆ Pine Log Motel M
(814) 435-6400. **$60-$65, 7 day notice.** 5156 US Rt 6 W. On US 6, 9
mi w. Ext corridors. **Pets:** Dogs only. $8 daily fee/pet. Designated rooms,
service with restrictions, supervision.
[✕] [🔲] [✕] [🐾]

GETTYSBURG

◆◆◆ ◆◆ America's Best Inn M
(717) 334-1188. **$45-$136.** 301 Steinwehr Ave. 1 mi s on US 15 business route, just s of jct SR 134. Ext/int corridors. **Pets:** Accepted.
[SAVE] [S6] [✕] [🔲]

◆◆ ◆◆ Gettysburg Travelodge M
(717) 334-9281. **$59-$165.** 613 Baltimore St. On SR 97 at US 15
business route. Ext/int corridors. **Pets:** Other species. Service with
restrictions, supervision.
[ASK] [S6] [✕] [🔲] [🔲] [🔲]

◆◆◆◆ Holiday Inn-Battlefield SH
(717) 334-6211. **$79-$196.** 516 Baltimore St. Jct US 15 business route
and SR 97. Ext/int corridors. **Pets:** Other species. Designated rooms,
service with restrictions, supervision.
[ASK] [S6] [✕] [🔲] [🔲] [🔲] [🍴] [🔲]

◆◆ ◆◆ Holiday Inn Express of Gettysburg M 🐾
(717) 337-1400. **$59-$117.** 869 York Rd. 1 mi e on US 30. Int corridors.
Pets: Medium, other species. Designated rooms, service with restrictions,
crate.
[ASK] [S6] [✕] [🔲] [🔲]

◆◆◆ ◆◆ Red Carpet Inn-Perfect Rest Motel M
(717) 334-1345. **$50-$130, 30 day notice.** 2450 Emmitsburg Rd. 4.5
mi s on US 15 business route. Ext corridors. **Pets:** Dogs only. $5 daily
fee/pet. Service with restrictions, supervision.
[SAVE] [S6] [✕] [🔲] [🔲]

GIRARD

◆◆ ◆◆ The Green Roof Inn M 🐾
(814) 774-7072. **$55-$80.** 8790 Rt 18. I-90, exit 9, 1.9 mi s on SR 18.
Ext corridors. **Pets:** Other species. $10 daily fee/pet. Service with restrictions, crate.
[ASK] [S6] [✕] [🔲] [🔲]

GRANTVILLE

◆◆◆ ◆◆ Econo Lodge M
(717) 469-0631. **$45-$90.** 252 Bow Creek Rd. I-81, exit 80. Ext corridors. **Pets:** Medium. $6 daily fee/pet. Designated rooms, service with
restrictions, supervision.
[SAVE] [S6] [✕] [🔲] [🔲] [🔲]

◆◆◆ ◆◆◆◆ Holiday Inn Harrisburg-Hershey Area, I-81 SH
(717) 469-0661. **$99-$199.** 604 Station Rd. I-81, exit 80. Int corridors.
Pets: Other species. $75 deposit/room. Service with restrictions, supervision.
[SAVE] [S6] [✕] [🔲] [🔲] [🔲] [🔲] [🔲] [🍴] [🔲] [🔲]

GREENCASTLE

◆◆◆ ◆◆ Comfort Inn SH
(717) 597-8164. **$50-$80.** 50 Pine Dr. I-81, exit 3, just s on US 11. Int
corridors. **Pets:** Other species. $6.54 one-time fee/pet. Service with restrictions, supervision.
[SAVE] [S6] [✕] [🔲] [🔲] [🔲]

GROVE CITY

◆◆ ◆◆ Old Arbor Rose Bed & Breakfast BB
(724) 458-6425. **$65-$75, 3 day notice.** 114 W Main St. Jus
corridors. **Pets:** $10 daily fee/pet. Service with restrictions, supervision
[ASK] [S6] [✕] [🔲]

HAMBURG

◆◆ ◆◆ Microtel Inn & Suites SH
(610) 562-4234. **$50-$140, 30 day notice.** 50 Industrial Dr. I-78, exit
29B, 0.3 mi n on SR 61, then just e. Int corridors. **Pets:** Other species.
$10 daily fee/pet. Service with restrictions, supervision.
[ASK] [✕] [🔲] [🔲] [🔲] [🔲]

HANOVER

◆◆◆ ◆◆ ◆◆ Howard Johnson Inn M
(717) 646-1000. **$39-$119.** 1080 Carlisle St. 1.5 mi n on SR 94, just e.
Ext corridors. **Pets:** Accepted.
[SAVE] [S6] [✕] [🔲] [🔲] [🔲] [🔲]

HARRISBURG

◆◆◆ ◆◆ ◆◆ Baymont Inn & Suites Harrisburg-Airport SH
(717) 939-8000. **$59-$99.** 990 Eisenhower Blvd. I-283, exit 2, just se;
I-76 (Pennsylvania Tpke), exit 247, 1 mi n. Int corridors.
Pets: Accepted.
[SAVE] [S6] [✕] [🔲] [🔲] [🔲]

◆◆◆ ◆◆ ◆◆ Best Western Capital Plaza SH
(717) 545-9089. **$79-$86.** 150 Nationwide Dr. I-81, exit 69, just n.
Ext/int corridors. **Pets:** Accepted.
[SAVE] [S6] [✕] [🔲] [🔲] [🔲] [🔲]

**◆◆◆ ◆◆◆◆ Best Western Harrisburg/Hershey Hotel &
Suites** SH
(717) 652-7180. **$69-$130.** 300 N Mountain Rd. I-81, exit 72 southbound; exit 72B northbound. Int corridors. **Pets:** Accepted.
[SAVE] [S6] [✕] [🔲] [🔲] [🔲] [🔲] [🔲] [🔲]

◆◆ ◆◆ Comfort Inn Harrisburg East SH
(717) 561-8100. **$89-$129, 3 day notice.** 4021 Union Deposit Rd. I-83,
exit 48, just w. Int corridors. **Pets:** Medium, other species. $10 daily
fee/pet. Service with restrictions, crate.
[ASK] [S6] [✕] [🔲] [🔲] [🔲] [🔲] [🔲]

◆◆◆ ◆◆◆ Comfort Inn Harrisburg/Hershey SH
(717) 540-8400. **$69-$189.** 7744 Linglestown Rd. I-81, exit 77, 0.5 mi
w. Int corridors. **Pets:** Accepted.
[SAVE] [S6] [✕] [🔲] [🔲] [🔲] [🔲] [🔲] [🔲]

◆◆◆ ◆◆◆ Comfort Inn-Riverfront SH
(717) 233-1611. **$65-$149.** 525 S Front St. I-83, exit 43, 0.5 mi n.
Ext/int corridors. **Pets:** Accepted.
[SAVE] [S6] [✕] [🔲] [🔲] [🔲] [🍴] [🔲]

◆◆◆ Days Inn-Harrisburg Airport SH 🐾
(717) 939-4147. **$94-$99.** 800 S Eisenhower Blvd S. I-76 (Pennsylvania
Tpke), exit 247, just n; I-283, exit 1B (Highspire). Ext corridors.
Pets: Dogs only. $50 deposit/room, $10 daily fee/pet. Service with restrictions.
[ASK] [S6] [✕] [🔲] [🔲] [🔲] [🔲]

◆◆◆ ◆◆ Greenlawn Motel M
(717) 652-1530. **$69-$79, 3 day notice.** 7490 Allentown Blvd. W of jct
SR 39 and US 22. Ext corridors. **Pets:** Medium. $15 one-time fee/pet.
Designated rooms, no service, crate.
[SAVE] [✕] [🔲]

◆◆◆ ◆◆◆ Holiday Inn Express Hotel & Suites SH
(717) 657-2200. **$69-$189.** 5680 Allentown Blvd. I-81, exit 72, just s on
S Mountain Rd, then just w on SR 22. Int corridors. **Pets:** Accepted.
[SAVE] [S6] [✕] [🔲] [🔲] [🔲] [🔲] [🔲]

...urg East-Airport SH

...e Rd. I-283, exit 2, just e. Int

...nn SH

...lestown Rd. I-81, exit 77. Int cor-
...Service with restrictions, supervision.

(AAA) ▼▼▼ Quality Inn SH
(717) 540-9339. **$69-$135.** 200 N Mountain Rd. I-81, exit 72A northbound; exit 72 southbound. Int corridors. **Pets:** Other species. Service
with restrictions, supervision.
SAVE S6 ☒ ◷ 🖥 💻

▼▼ Ramada Limited SH
(717) 545-6944. **$69-$119.** 7965 Jonestown Rd. I-81, exit 77, just s. Int
corridors. **Pets:** Accepted.
S6 ☒ 🖥 ⌇

▼▼ Red Roof Inn-North #7037 M
(717) 657-1445. **$46-$79.** 400 Corporate Cir. I-81, exit 69, just n on
Progress Ave. Ext/int corridors. **Pets:** Accepted.
☒ ◷ ♿ 🖥

▼▼ Red Roof Inn-South #7027 M
(717) 939-1331. **$46-$79.** 950 Eisenhower Blvd. I-283, exit 2, just e.
Ext/int corridors. **Pets:** Accepted.
☒ ◷ ♿

▼▼▼ Residence Inn by Marriott Harrisburg-Hershey SH
(717) 561-1900. **$169-$269.** 4480 Lewis Rd. US 322, exit Penhar Dr,
just e. Ext corridors. **Pets:** $75 one-time fee/room. Service with restric-
tions, supervision.
ASK S6 ☒ ◷ 🖥 💻 ⌇ ☒

(AAA) ▼ Super 8 Motel-North M
(717) 233-5891. **$65-$139.** 4125 N Front St. I-81, exit 66, 0.8 mi n. Ext
corridors. **Pets:** Accepted.
SAVE S6 ☒ 🖥 ¶¶ ⌇

(AAA) ▼▼▼ Wyndham Harrisburg-Hershey LH
(717) 564-5511. **$149-$159.** 4650 Lindle Rd. I-283, exit 2, just e. Int
corridors. **Pets:** Other species. $50 one-time fee/room. Service with restric-
tions.
SAVE ☒ 6M ◷ ♿ 🖥 💻 ¶¶ ⌇ ☒

HAZLETON

(AAA) ▼▼ Best Western Genetti Lodge SH
(570) 454-2494. **$79-$99, 3 day notice.** 32nd & N Church St. I-80, exit
262, 6 mi s on SR 309. Ext/int corridors. **Pets:** Medium. $10 one-time
fee/pet. Service with restrictions, supervision.
SAVE S6 ☒ ◷ 🖥 💻 ⌇

(AAA) ▼ Hazleton Motor Inn M
(570) 459-1451. **$35-$50.** 615 E Broad St. I-81, exit 143, 2 mi n on SR
924, then 1 mi s on SR 93. Int corridors. **Pets:** Large, other species. $5
daily fee/pet. Service with restrictions, supervision.
SAVE S6 ☒ 🖥

HERSHEY

(AAA) ▼▼▼ Best Western Inn-Hershey SH
(717) 533-5665. **$89-$229.** US 422 & Sipe Ave. Jct US 322, just e.
Ext/int corridors. **Pets:** Small. $25 deposit/room. Designated rooms, serv-
ice with restrictions, supervision.
SAVE S6 ☒ ◷ 🖥 💻 ⌇

▼▼ Days Inn Hershey SH
(717) 534-2162. **$89-$199.** 350 W Chocolate Ave. On US 422; center.
Int corridors. **Pets:** Accepted.
ASK S6 ☒ 6M ◷ 🖥 💻 ⌇ ☒

(AAA) ▼▼▼ Hampton Inn & Suites SH
(717) 533-8400. **$89-$239.** 749 E Chocolate Ave. 0.9 mi e on US 422.
Int corridors. **Pets:** Small. $10 daily fee/pet. Designated rooms, service
with restrictions, supervision.
SAVE S6 ☒ 6M ◷ ♿ 🖥 💻 ⌇ ☒

(AAA) ▼ Hershey Travel Inn M
(717) 533-7950. **$45-$95, 3 day notice.** 905 E Chocolate Ave. 1.3 mi e
on US 422. Ext corridors. **Pets:** Very small, other species. $15 one-time
fee/pet. No service, supervision.
SAVE S6 ☒ 🖥

(AAA) ▼▼▼ Holiday Inn Express SH
(717) 583-0500. **$89-$219.** Just nw of jct US 322, 422 and SR 39
(Hershey Park Dr); just off Hershey Park Dr. Int corridors. **Pets:** Small,
other species. $10 daily fee/pet. Designated rooms, service with restrictions,
crate.
SAVE S6 ☒ 6M ◷ ♿ 🖥 💻 ⌇ ☒

HUNTINGDON

▼▼ Huntingdon Motor Inn M 🐾
(814) 643-1133. **$51-$65, 3 day notice.** Motor Inn Rd. On US 22 at SR
26. Ext corridors. **Pets:** Other species. $25 one-time fee/pet. Service with
restrictions, supervision.
☒ ◷ 🖥 💻

INDIANA

(AAA) ▼▼▼ Best Western University Inn SH
(724) 349-9620. **$64-$84.** 1545 Wayne Ave. US 422, exit Wayne Ave,
0.6 mi n. Int corridors. **Pets:** Accepted.
SAVE S6 ☒ 🖥 💻 ⌇

▼▼▼ Holiday Inn Holidome SH
(724) 463-3561. **$66-$99.** 1395 Wayne Ave. US 422, exit Wayne Ave, 1
mi n. Ext/int corridors. **Pets:** Service with restrictions, crate.
ASK S6 ☒ ♿ 🖥 💻 ¶¶ ⌇ ☒

JONESTOWN

(AAA) ▼▼▼ Days Inn Lebanon/Lickdale SH
(717) 865-4064. **$75-$120, 7 day notice.** 3 Everest Ln. I-81, exit 90. Int
corridors. **Pets:** Accepted.
SAVE S6 ☒ ♿ 🖥 💻

▼▼ Red Carpet Inn & Suites-Jonestown SH
(717) 865-6600. **$48-$100.** 16 Marsenna Ln. I-81, exit 90, just w. Int
corridors. **Pets:** Accepted.
ASK S6 ☒ 🖥 ⌇

▼▼▼ Strawberry Patch Bed & Breakfast BB 🐾
(717) 865-7219. **$125-$189.** 115 Moore Rd. I-81, exit 90, 2.8 mi s on
SR 72, 1 mi e on Jonestown Rd, 0.8 mi s on S Lancaster St, then just
e. Ext/int corridors. **Pets:** Large. $25 daily fee/pet. Designated rooms,
service with restrictions, crate.
☒ ☒

KITTANNING

▼▼▼ Comfort Inn SH
(724) 543-5200. **$77.** 13 Hilltop Plaza. SR 28, exit 19A. Int corridors.
Pets: Accepted.
ASK S6 ☒ ♿ 🖥 💻 ⌇

(AAA) ▼▼▼ Quality Inn Royle SH
(724) 543-1159. **$59-$95.** 405 Butler Rd. SR 28, exit I-422 W (Belmont). Ext/int corridors. **Pets:** Large. Designated rooms, service with
restrictions, supervision.
SAVE S6 ☒ ◷ 🖥 💻

▼ Rodeway Inn Kittanning M
(724) 543-1100. **$55-$60.** US 422 E. E of jct Business Rt US 422, SR
66 and 28. Ext corridors. **Pets:** Accepted.
ASK S6 ☒ 🖥 💻

KUTZTOWN

ΑΑΑ ▼▼▼ Campus Inn M
(610) 683-8721. **$55-$75, 3 day notice.** 15080 Kutztown Rd. US 222, exit Kutztown Rd/Virginsville, 1 mi e. Ext corridors. **Pets:** Designated rooms, no service, supervision.
SAVE S♂ ✕ 🖥 ➢

ΑΑΑ ▼▼▼ Lincoln Motel M
(610) 683-3456. **$50-$70, 3 day notice.** 12 Lincoln Dr. US 222, exit Kutztown Rd/Virginsville. Ext corridors. **Pets:** Accepted.
SAVE S♂ ✕ 🖥

LAMAR

ΑΑΑ ▼▼▼ Comfort Inn of Lamar SH
(570) 726-4901. **$70-$140.** 31 Comfort Inn Ln. I-80, exit 173, just n on SR 64. Int corridors. **Pets:** $10 daily fee/room. Designated rooms, service with restrictions, supervision.
SAVE S♂ ✕ 🖥 🖥 ➢

LAUREL HIGHLANDS AREA

CHALK HILL

▼▼▼▼ Historic Summit Inn LH
(724) 438-8594. **$89-$211, 3 day notice.** On US 40; center. Int corridors. **Pets:** Small, dogs only. $15 daily fee/pet. Service with restrictions, supervision.
ASK S♂ ✕ 🖥 🖥 🍴 ➢ ✕

ΑΑΑ ▼▼▼ The Lodge at Chalk Hill M
(724) 438-8880. **$54-$84.** Just w. Ext corridors. **Pets:** Other species. $10 daily fee/pet. Service with restrictions, supervision.
SAVE S♂ ✕ 🖥 🖥 ✕

GREENSBURG

▼▼▼▼ Comfort Inn Greensburg SH 🐾
(724) 832-2600. **$84-$165.** 1129 E Pittsburgh St. I-76, exit 75, 5.6 mi on US 119 N, 4 mi e on US 30. Int corridors. **Pets:** Small. $10 daily fee/room. Designated rooms, service with restrictions, crate.
ASK S♂ ✕ 🖥 🖥 ➢

▼▼▼▼ Four Points by Sheraton SH
(724) 836-6060. **$129-$149.** 100 Sheraton Dr. I-76 (Pennsylvania Tpke), exit 75, 5.6 mi on US 119 N, 3 mi e on US 30, then just n. Int corridors. **Pets:** Medium, other species. $10 daily fee/pet. Service with restrictions, crate.
ASK S♂ ✕ 🖥 🖥 🖥 🍴 ➢ ✕

▼▼ ▼▼ Knights Inn-Greensburg SH
(724) 836-7100. **$85.** 1215 S Main St. I-76 (Pennsylvania Tpke), exit 75, 4 mi s on US 119; just s of US 30. Ext corridors. **Pets:** Accepted.
ASK S♂ ✕ 🖥 🖥 ➢

JOHNSTOWN

▼▼▼▼ Comfort Inn & Suites SH
(814) 266-3678. **$79-$140.** 455 Theatre Dr. US 219, exit Elton (SR 756), just e. Int corridors. **Pets:** $25 deposit/room, $15 daily fee/room. Designated rooms, service with restrictions, supervision.
ASK S♂ ✕ 🖥M 📷 🖥 🖥 ➢

▼▼ ▼▼ Econo Lodge M
(814) 536-1114. **$55-$65.** 430 Napoleon Pl. Jct SR 271 and 403; downtown. Int corridors. **Pets:** Other species. Service with restrictions, supervision.
ASK S♂ ✕ 🖥M 📷 🖥 🖥 🖥

▼▼▼▼ Holiday Inn Downtown SH
(814) 535-7777. **$90-$109.** 250 Market St. Corner of Market and Vine sts; downtown. Int corridors. **Pets:** Service with restrictions, supervision.
ASK S♂ ✕ 🖥 🖥 🖥 🍴 ➢ ✕

▼▼ ▼▼ Holiday Inn Express Johnstown M
(814) 266-8789. **$85-$109.** 1440 Scalp Ave. US 219, exit Windber (SR 56 E), just e. Int corridors. **Pets:** Accepted.
ASK S♂ ✕ 🖥M 📷 🖥 🖥

▼▼ ▼▼ Sleep Inn SH
(814) 262-9292. **$65-$89.** 453 Theatre Dr. US 219, exit Elton (SR 756), just e. Int corridors. **Pets:** $25 deposit/room, $15 daily fee/room. Designated rooms, service with restrictions, supervision.
ASK S♂ ✕ 🖥M 📷 🖥 🖥 🖥

▼▼ ▼▼ Super 8 Motel Johnstown SH
(814) 535-5600. **$43-$48.** 627 Solomon Run Rd. US 219, exit Galleria Dr, just w. Int corridors. **Pets:** Accepted.
ASK S♂ ✕ 🖥 🖥

LIGONIER

ΑΑΑ ▼▼▼▼ Lady of the Lake Bed & Breakfast BB
(724) 238-6955. **$95-$135, 14 day notice.** 157 Rt 30 E. US 30 E, just w of jct SR 711; beside Idlewild Park. Ext/int corridors. **Pets:** Other species. $10 daily fee/pet. Designated rooms, service with restrictions, supervision.
SAVE ✕ 🖥 🖥 ➢ ✕ 🖥

NEW STANTON

ΑΑΑ ▼▼ ▼▼ Howard Johnson Inn M
(724) 925-3511. **$49-$99, 14 day notice.** 112 W Byers Ave. I-76, exit 75, 0.5 mi sw; I-70, exit 57B westbound; exit 57 eastbound. Ext/int corridors. **Pets:** Other species. $7 daily fee/pet. Designated rooms, service with restrictions, supervision.
SAVE S♂ ✕ 🖥 🖥 ➢

▼▼ ▼▼ Quality Inn New Stanton SH
(724) 925-6755. **$60-$90, 10 day notice.** 110 N Main St/Byers Ave. I-76, exit 75, 0.5 mi se; I-70, exit 57B westbound; exit 57 eastbound. Int corridors. **Pets:** Accepted.
ASK S♂ ✕ 🖥 🖥 🍴 ➢

▼▼ ▼▼ Super 8 Motel-New Stanton M 🐾
(724) 925-8915. **$56-$77.** 103 Bair Blvd. I-76, exit 75, 0.5 mi se; I-70, 57B westbound; exit 57 eastbound. Int corridors. **Pets:** Medium. $10 daily fee/pet. Designated rooms, service with restrictions, supervision.
ASK S♂ ✕ 🖥

SOMERSET

ΑΑΑ ▼▼▼▼ Best Western Executive Inn SH
(814) 445-3996. **$55-$125.** 165 Water Works Rd. I-70/76 (Pennsylvania Tpke), exit 110, just e. Int corridors. **Pets:** Medium, other species. $7 daily fee/pet. Designated rooms, service with restrictions, supervision.
SAVE S♂ ✕ 🖥 🖥 🖥 ✕

ΑΑΑ ▼▼ Budget Host Inn M
(814) 445-7988. **$40-$85, 7 day notice.** 799 N Center Ave. I-70/76 (Pennsylvania Tpke), exit 110, 0.3 mi s. Ext corridors. **Pets:** Small. $7 daily fee/pet. Designated rooms, no service, crate.
SAVE S♂ ✕ 🖥

▼ The Budget Inn M
(814) 443-6441. **$32-$75.** 736 N Center Ave. I-70/76 (Pennsylvania Tpke), exit 110, 0.4 mi s. Ext corridors. **Pets:** Large, other species. Designated rooms, service with restrictions, supervision.

(ASK) [S🐾] [✕] [🍴]

▼ Days Inn-Somerset M
(814) 445-9200. **$50-$100.** 220 Water Works Rd. I-70/76 (Pennsylvania Tpke), exit 110, just e. Ext corridors. **Pets:** $6 daily fee/pet. Service with restrictions, supervision.

(ASK) [S🐾] [✕] [🍴] [💻]

⏣ ▼ Dollar Inn M
(814) 445-2977. **$35-$75.** 1146 N Center Ave. I-70/76 (Pennsylvania Tpke), exit 110, just e via Water Works Rd, then just n on SR 601, at top of hill. Ext corridors. **Pets:** Medium. $5 daily fee/pet. Designated rooms, supervision.

(SAVE) [S🐾] [✕] [🍴]

▼ ▼ Glades Pike Inn BB
(814) 443-4978. **$70-$125, 7 day notice.** 2684 Glades Pike. I-70/76 (Pennsylvania Tpke), exit 110, 7.9 mi w on SR 31. Int corridors. **Pets:** Other species. $5 one-time fee/pet. Supervision.

(ASK) [S🐾] [✕] [✕]

⏣ ▼▼▼ Holiday Inn SH
(814) 445-9611. **$89-$119.** 202 Harmon St. I-70/76 (Pennsylvania Tpke), exit 110, just s. Int corridors. **Pets:** Accepted.

(SAVE) [S🐾] [✕] [🏊] [💻] [🍴] [🏊]

▼▼▼ The Inn at Georgian Place BB
(814) 443-1043. **$95-$185, 10 day notice.** 800 Georgian Place Dr. I-70/76 (Pennsylvania Tpke), exit 110, just e via Water Works Rd, then 0.5 mi n on SR 601. Int corridors. **Pets:** Medium. Service with restrictions, supervision.

(ASK) [S🐾] [✕] [🍴]

▼▼ Knights Inn M
(814) 445-8933. **$60-$65.** 585 Ramada Rd. I-70/76 (Pennsylvania Tpke), exit 110, just s. Ext corridors. **Pets:** Accepted.

(ASK) [S🐾] [✕] [🍴] [💻] [🏊]

⏣ ▼▼▼ Ramada Inn SH
(814) 443-4646. **$69-$109.** 215 Ramada Rd. I-70/76 (Pennsylvania Tpke), exit 110, just s. Int corridors. **Pets:** Other species. Service with restrictions, supervision.

(SAVE) [S🐾] [✕] [🍴] [💻] [🍴] [🏊] [✕]

▼ Super 8 Motel M
(814) 445-8788. **$44-$88.** 125 Lewis Dr. I-70/76 (Pennsylvania Tpke), exit 110, just s. Int corridors. **Pets:** Accepted.

(ASK) [S🐾] [✕] [🍴] [💻]

UNIONTOWN

▼▼▼▼ Uniontown Holiday Inn SH
(724) 437-2816. **$79-$129.** 700 W Main St. 1.8 mi w on US 40. Int corridors. **Pets:** Designated rooms, service with restrictions, supervision.

(ASK) [S🐾] [✕] [🏊] [🍴] [🍴] [💻] [🍴] [🏊] [✕]

END AREA

LEBANON

⏣ ▼▼▼▼ Quality Inn-Lebanon/Hershey SH
(717) 273-6771. **$89-$149.** 625 Quentin Rd. 0.5 mi s on SR 72. Ext/int corridors. **Pets:** Medium, other species. $5 daily fee/pet. Designated rooms, service with restrictions, supervision.

(SAVE) [S🐾] [✕] [🍴M] [🏊] [🍴] [🍴] [💻] [🍴] [🏊] [✕]

LEWISBURG

⏣ ▼▼ Days Inn-Lewisburg SH
(570) 523-1171. **$83-$110, 3 day notice.** US Rt 15. 0.5 mi n of jct SR 45. Ext corridors. **Pets:** Other species. Service with restrictions, crate.

(SAVE) [S🐾] [✕] [🍴] [💻] [🏊]

LINCOLN FALLS

▼▼ Morgan Century Farm BB
(570) 924-4909. **$85-$125, 7 day notice.** Rt 154. In village. Ext/int corridors. **Pets:** Medium. $10 one-time fee/room. Designated rooms, service with restrictions, supervision.

[S🐾] [✕] [🍴] [💻] [🏊]

LOCK HAVEN

▼▼ Best Western-Lock Haven SH
(570) 748-3297. **$75-$135, 3 day notice.** 101 E Walnut St. Just w of jct US 220. Int corridors. **Pets:** $7 daily fee/pet. Service with restrictions.

(ASK) [S🐾] [✕] [🍴] [🍴] [💻]

MANSFIELD

⏣ ▼▼▼ Comfort Inn SH
(570) 662-3000. **$69-$119.** 300 Gateway Dr. Jct US 6 and 15. Int corridors. **Pets:** Other species. $10 one-time fee/room. Service with restrictions, supervision.

(SAVE) [S🐾] [✕] [🍴] [💻] [✕]

⏣ ▼▼▼ Mansfield Inn M
(570) 662-2136. **$55-$70, 3 day notice.** 26 S Main St. Jct US 6, just s on Business Rt 15; downtown. Ext corridors. **Pets:** $5 daily fee/pet. Service with restrictions, supervision.

(SAVE) [S🐾] [✕] [🍴] [💻]

⏣ ▼ West's Deluxe Motel M
(570) 659-5141. **$50-$65.** Rt 15, 2848 S Main St. 3.5 mi s. Ext corridors. **Pets:** Accepted.

(SAVE) [S🐾] [✕] [🍴] [💻] [🏊]

MEADVILLE

▼ Days Inn Conference Center SH
(814) 337-4264. **$55-$129.** 18360 Conneaut Lake Rd. I-79, exit 147A, just e on US 322. Int corridors. **Pets:** Medium. $50 deposit/room. Designated rooms, service with restrictions.

(ASK) [S🐾] [✕] [🍴] [💻] [🍴] [🏊]

▼ Motel 6 M
(814) 724-6366. **$60-$100.** 11237 Shaw Ave. I-79, exit 147A, just e on US 322. Int corridors. **Pets:** Other species. Service with restrictions, supervision.

[S🐾] [✕] [🍴]

▼ Super 8 Motel M
(814) 333-8883. **Call for rates.** 17259 Conneaut Lake Rd. I-79, exit 147B, just w on US 322. Ext/int corridors. **Pets:** Small, other species. $50 deposit/room. Service with restrictions, supervision.

[✕] [🍴]

MECHANICSBURG

⏣ ▼▼▼ Comfort Inn Capital City SH
(717) 766-3700. **$89-$139.** 1012 Wesley Dr. I-76 (Pennsylvania Tpke), exit 236 (US 15), 1 mi n to Wesley Dr exit, then just w. Int corridors. **Pets:** Accepted.

(SAVE) [S🐾] [✕] [🍴M] [🍴] [🍴] [💻] [🏊]

▼▼▼ Hampton Inn-Harrisburg West **SH**
(717) 691-1300. **$111-$136.** 4950 Ritter Rd. I-76 (Pennsylvania Tpke), exit 236 (US 15), 1 mi n to Rossmoyne Rd exit. Int corridors. **Pets:** Other species. Designated rooms, service with restrictions, supervision.

[ASK] [S6] [X] [♿M] [♨] [▣] [🏊] [X]

▼▼▼ Holiday Inn Harrisburg-West **SH**
(717) 697-0321. **$94-$134.** 5401 Carlisle Pike. Jct Carlisle Pike and US 11, just w. Ext corridors. **Pets:** Medium, other species. $10 one-time fee/room. Service with restrictions, crate.

[SAVE] [S6] [X] [♨] [▣] [🍴] [🏊] [X]

▼▼▼ Homewood Suites-Harrisburg West **SH**
(717) 697-4900. **$109-$128.** 5001 Ritter Rd. I-76 (Pennsylvania Tpke), exit 236 (US 15), 1 mi n to Rossmoyne Rd exit. **Pets:** Accepted.

[ASK] [S6] [X] [♿] [🖋] [♿] [♨] [▣] [🏊] [X]

MERCER

▼ Colonial Inn Motel **M**
(724) 662-5600. **$35-$40.** 383 N Perry Hwy. I-80, exit 15, 3 mi n; I-79, exit 121, 4 mi w on SR 62 S, then 0.5 mi n on US 19. Ext corridors. **Pets:** Other species. $4 daily fee/pet. Service with restrictions, supervision.

[ASK] [S6] [X] [♨] [▣]

▼▼▼ Howard Johnson Inn **SH**
(724) 748-3030. **$88-$90.** 835 Perry Hwy. I-80, exit 15, just n on US 19. Int corridors. **Pets:** Accepted.

[ASK] [S6] [X] [🖋] [♨] [▣] [🍴] [🏊] [X]

MIFFLINVILLE

▼▼ Super 8 Motel **M**
(570) 759-6778. **$35-$89.** 450 3rd St. I-80, exit 242, just n on SR 339. Ext corridors. **Pets:** Accepted.

[ASK] [S6] [X]

MILESBURG

▼▼▼ Holiday Inn **SH**
(814) 355-7521. **$90-$260, 7 day notice.** 971 N Eagle Valley Rd. I-80, exit 158, 0.4 mi n. Int corridors. **Pets:** Accepted.

[ASK] [S6] [X] [♿M] [🖋] [♿] [♨] [▣] [🍴] [🏊] [X]

MOOSIC

▲▲▲ ▼▼ Rodeway Inn-Scranton **M**
(570) 457-6713. **$39-$110, 15 day notice.** 4130 Birney Ave. I-81, exit 182B southbound, 0.7 mi w, then 2.3 mi s on US 11; exit 180 northbound, just n on US 11. Ext corridors. **Pets:** Medium. $10 daily fee/pet. Designated rooms, service with restrictions, supervision.

[SAVE] [S6] [X] [♿] [♨] [▣]

MORGANTOWN

▲▲▲ ▼▼▼ Holiday Inn **SH**
(610) 286-3000. **$109-$119.** 6170 Morgantown Rd. I-76, exit 298, just s on SR 10. Int corridors. **Pets:** Medium. $10 daily fee/pet. Designated rooms, service with restrictions, crate.

[SAVE] [S6] [X] [🖋] [♨] [▣] [🍴] [🏊] [X]

NEW CASTLE

▼▼ Comfort Inn-New Castle **M**
(724) 658-7700. **$64-$94.** 1740 New Butler Rd. Jct SR 65, 1 mi e on US 422, then 1 mi w on US 422 business route. Int corridors. **Pets:** Small, dogs only. $6 daily fee/pet. Service with restrictions, supervision.

[ASK] [S6] [X] [♨] [▣]

NEW COLUMBIA

▼▼▼ New Columbia Comfort Inn **SH**
(570) 568-8000. **$63-$110.** 330 Commerce Park Dr. I-80, exit 210A (US 15/New Columbia), just s. Int corridors. **Pets:** Other species.

[ASK] [S6] [X] [♿M] [♨] [▣] [🍴] [🏊]

NEW CUMBERLAND

▲▲▲ ▼▼ Days Inn Harrisburg South **SH**
(717) 774-4156. **$59-$115.** 353 Lewisberry Rd. I-83, exit 39A, just ne. Int corridors. **Pets:** Accepted.

[SAVE] [S6] [X] [♨] [▣] [🏊]

▲▲▲ ▼▼▼ Holiday Inn Hotel & Conference
    Center-Harrisburg **SH**
(717) 774-2721. **$94-$189.** 148 Sheraton Dr. I-83, exit 40A, just se. Int corridors. **Pets:** Medium. $10 daily fee/pet. Service with restrictions, supervision.

[SAVE] [S6] [X] [♿] [♨] [▣] [🍴] [🏊] [X]

NORTH EAST

▲▲▲ ▼ Super 8 Motel **M**
(814) 725-4567. **$58-$78.** 11021 Side Hill Rd. I-90, exit 41, just n on SR 89. Ext corridors. **Pets:** $5 one-time fee/room. No service, supervision.

[SAVE] [S6] [X]

PENNSYLVANIA DUTCH COUNTRY AREA

ADAMSTOWN

▼▼▼ The Barnyard Inn B & B and Suites **BB** ✿
(717) 484-1111. **$85-$100, 10 day notice.** 2145 Old Lancaster Pike. 1 mi ne via Main St/Old Lancaster Pike; SR 272, just w on Willow St to Main St, 1 mi n bearing left at fork, then just n. Int corridors. **Pets:** Other species. $20 one-time fee/room. Designated rooms.

[X] [♨] [▣] [🖉]

▲▲▲ ▼ Black Forest Inn **M**
(717) 484-4801. **$59-$109.** 2828 N Reading Rd. I-76 (Pennsylvania Tpke), exit 286, 2.8 mi n on SR 272. Ext corridors. **Pets:** Very small. $10 daily fee/pet. No service, supervision.

[SAVE] [S6] [X] [♨]

DENVER

▲▲▲ ▼▼▼ Black Horse Lodge and Suites **SH**
(717) 336-7563. **$69-$159.** 2180 N Reading Rd. I-76 (Pennsylvania Tpke), exit 286, 1 mi w to SR 272, then 0.3 mi n. Ext/int corridors. **Pets:** Other species. Service with restrictions, supervision.

[SAVE] [S6] [X] [♨] [▣] [🍴] [🏊]

▲▲▲ ▼▼▼ Comfort Inn **SH**
(717) 336-4649. **$69-$159, 3 day notice.** 2017 N Reading Rd. I-76 (Pennsylvania Tpke), exit 286, 1 mi w to SR 272, then just s. Int corridors. **Pets:** Medium, dogs only. $20 daily fee/room. Designated rooms, service with restrictions, supervision.

[SAVE] [S6] [X] [🖋] [♨] [▣]

Holiday Inn-Lancaster County SH
(717) 336-7541. **$79-$159.** 1 Denver Rd. I-76 (Pennsylvania Tpke), exit 286, 1 mi w to SR 272, then just s. Int corridors. **Pets:** Small, other species. $10 daily fee/room. Designated rooms, service with restrictions, supervision.

EPHRATA

Historic Smithton Inn BB
(717) 733-6094. **$95-$150, 14 day notice.** 900 W Main St. On US 322, just w of jct SR 272. Int corridors. **Pets:** Dogs only. Designated rooms, service with restrictions, supervision.

GORDONVILLE

Motel 6-Lancaster #4174 M
(717) 687-3880. **$51-$81.** 2959 Lincoln Hwy E. On US 30; center. Int corridors. **Pets:** Medium, dogs only. $25 deposit/pet. Service with restrictions, supervision.

LANCASTER

Best Western Eden Resort Inn & Suites LH
(717) 569-6444. **$89-$189.** 222 Eden Rd. Jct US 30 (Lincoln Hwy) and SR 272 (Oregon Pike). Ext/int corridors. **Pets:** Medium, other species. $20 one-time fee/pet. Designated rooms, service with restrictions, crate.

Hawthorn Inn & Suites SH
(717) 290-7100. **$69-$139.** 2045 Lincoln Hwy E. Jct US 30 E and Lincoln Hwy. Int corridors. **Pets:** Large, other species. $25 one-time fee/room. Service with restrictions, crate.

Holiday Inn Visitors Center SH
(717) 299-2551. **$80-$89.** 521 Greenfield Rd. 3.3 mi e on US 30 (Lincoln Hwy), exit Greenfield Rd, just n. Ext/int corridors. **Pets:** Medium. $25 one-time fee/room. Designated rooms, service with restrictions, supervision.

Lancaster Host Resort & Conference Center LH
(717) 299-5500. **$49-$179.** 2300 Lincoln Hwy E. On US 30 (Lincoln Hwy), 5 mi e. Int corridors. **Pets:** Accepted.

Lancaster Travelodge & Conference Center SH
(717) 393-0771. **$49-$99.** 1492 Lititz Pike. US 30 (Lincoln Hwy), exit Lititz Pike (SR 501), just s. Ext corridors. **Pets:** Accepted.

Ramada Inn Brunswick LH
(717) 397-4801. **$75-$105.** 151 N Queen St. Center. Int corridors. **Pets:** Small. $25 one-time fee/room. Service with restrictions, supervision.

LITITZ

General Sutter Inn CI ❀
(717) 626-2115. **$87-$120.** 14 E Main St. Jct SR 501 and 772; downtown. Int corridors. **Pets:** Other species. $10 one-time fee/room. Service with restrictions, supervision.

MANHEIM

Rodeway Inn-Penns Woods M
(717) 665-2755. **$42-$70.** 2931 Lebanon Rd. I-76 (Pennsylvania Tpke), exit 266, just s on SR 72. Ext corridors. **Pets:** Medium, other species. $5 daily fee/pet. No service, supervision.

MOUNTVILLE

MainStay Suites SH
(717) 285-2500. **$85-$200.** 314 Primrose Ln. US 30 (Lincoln Hwy), exit Mountville. Int corridors. **Pets:** Accepted.

STRASBURG

Carriage House Motor Inn M
(717) 687-7651. **$49-$99.** 144 E Main St. 0.3 mi e on SR 896 and 741. Ext corridors. **Pets:** Small, dogs only. $50 deposit/pet. Service with restrictions, crate.

Netherlands Inn & Spa SH ❀
(717) 687-7691. **$69-$169, 3 day notice.** One Historic Dr. 0.5 mi n on SR 896; 2.5 mi s of US 30 (Lincoln Hwy). Ext/int corridors. **Pets:** Medium, other species. $20 daily fee/room. Designated rooms, service with restrictions, supervision.

PHILADELPHIA METROPOLITAN AREA

BENSALEM

Holiday Inn-Philadelphia Northeast SH
(215) 638-1500. **$119-$139.** 3499 Street Rd. I-276 (Pennsylvania Tpke), exit 351, just s on US 1, then 0.3 mi e on SR 132. Ext/int corridors. **Pets:** Medium, other species. $50 deposit/room. Service with restrictions, supervision.

Sleep Inn & Suites-Bensalem SH
(215) 244-2300. **$69-$159.** 3427 Street Rd. I-276 (Pennsylvania Tpke), exit 351, just s on US 1, then 0.3 mi e on SR 132. Int corridors. **Pets:** Medium. $100 deposit/pet, $10 daily fee/pet. Service with restrictions, supervision.

BERWYN

Residence Inn by Marriott SH
(610) 640-9494. **$169.** 600 W Swedesford Rd. US 202, exit Valley Forge Rd, 1 mi s. Ext corridors. **Pets:** Accepted.

CHADDS FORD

Brandywine River Hotel SH
(610) 388-1200. **$125-$169.** Rt 1 & Creek Rd. Jct US 1 and SR 100, 2 mi w of US 202. Int corridors. **Pets:** Medium, dogs only. Designated rooms, service with restrictions, crate.

CONSHOHOCKEN

Residence Inn by Marriott Philadelphia/Conshohocken SH
(610) 828-8800. **$99-$229.** 191 Washington St. I-76 (Schuylkill Expwy), exit 332; I-476, exit 16 (SR 23), 0.3 mi over Fayette Bridge to Elm St, then just se along the river. Int corridors. **Pets:** Accepted.

EAST NORRITON

▼▼▼ Summerfield Suites Hotel by Wyndham-Plymouth
Meeting East Norriton SH
(610) 313-9990. **$119-$149.** 501 E Germantown Pike. I-476, exit 20;
I-276 (Pennsylvania Tpke), exit 333, 2.5 mi w. Int corridors.
Pets: Accepted.
ASK ✕ 🐾 ♿ 🛏 💻 🏊

ERWINNA

▼▼▼ Golden Pheasant Inn CI ❀
(610) 294-9595. **$95-$225, 21 day notice.** 763 River Rd. SR 32, 0.5 mi
n of jct Dark Hollow Rd. Ext/int corridors. **Pets:** Medium, other species.
$20 daily fee/room. Designated rooms, service with restrictions, crate.
ASK ✕ 🛏 💻 🍴 ✕

ESSINGTON

AAA ▼▼▼ Comfort Inn Airport SH
(610) 521-9800. **$150.** 53 Industrial Hwy. I-95, exit 9A, 0.3 mi sw on SR
291. Int corridors. **Pets:** Small. $50 deposit/room, $10 daily fee/pet. Designated rooms, service with restrictions, supervision.
SAVE 🐾 ✕ ♿ 🐾 🛏 💻

AAA ▼▼▼ Holiday Inn-Airport LH ❀
(610) 521-2400. **$145-$175.** 45 Industrial Hwy. I-95, exit 9A, 0.3 mi sw
on SR 291. Int corridors. **Pets:** Large. $30 one-time fee/room. Designated
rooms, service with restrictions, supervision.
SAVE 🐾 ✕ ♿ 🐾 🛏 💻 🍴 🏊

▼▼ Red Roof Inn-Airport #7119 M
(610) 521-5090. **$82-$92.** 49 Industrial Hwy. I-95, exit 9A, 0.3 mi sw on
SR 291. Ext corridors. **Pets:** Medium, other species. Service with restrictions, crate.
✕ ♿ 🐾 🐾 🛏

EXTON

AAA ▼▼▼ Holiday Inn Express SH
(610) 524-9000. **$77-$109.** 120 N Pottstown Pike. I-76 (Pennsylvania
Tpke), exit 312, 3 mi s at jct Business Rt US 30 and SR 100. Int
corridors. **Pets:** Accepted.
SAVE 🐾 ✕ ♿ 🐾 🛏 💻 🏊

HORSHAM

AAA ▼▼▼ Days Inn-Horsham/Willow Grove SH
(215) 674-2500. **$89-$119.** 245 Easton Rd. I-276 (Pennsylvania Tpke),
exit 343, 1 mi n. Int corridors. **Pets:** Other species. $10 daily fee/pet.
Service with restrictions, supervision.
SAVE 🐾 ✕ ♿ 🐾 🛏 💻

▼▼▼ Homestead Studio Suites Hotel-Horsham/Willow
Grove SH
(215) 956-9966. **$100-$110.** 537 Dresher Rd. I-276 (Pennsylvania
Tpke), exit 343, 1.5 mi n on SR 611 (Easton Rd), just w on Horsham
Rd, then 0.5 mi s. Int corridors. **Pets:** $75 one-time fee/room. Service
with restrictions.
ASK 🐾 ✕ ♿ 🐾 🐾 🛏 💻

▼▼▼ Residence Inn by Marriott-Willow Grove SH
(215) 443-7330. **$164-$184.** 3 Walnut Grove Dr. I-276 (Pennsylvania
Tpke), exit 343, 1 mi n on SR 611 (Easton Rd), then 1.3 mi w on
Dresher Rd. Ext corridors. **Pets:** Accepted.
✕ ♿ 🐾 🐾 🛏 💻 🏊 ✕

KING OF PRUSSIA

▼▼▼ Homestead Studio Suites Hotel-King of
Prussia SH
(610) 962-9000. **$81-$101.** 400 American Ave. I-76 (Pennsylvania
Tpke), exit 326 (Valley Forge); Schuylkill Expwy, exit 328A (Mall Blvd),
1.3 mi n on N Gulph Rd, then 1 mi ne on 1st Ave. Int corridors.
Pets: Accepted.
ASK 🐾 ✕ ♿ 🐾 🐾 🛏 💻

AAA ▼▼▼ MainStay Suites SH
(484) 690-3000. **$129-$139.** 440 American Ave. I-76 (Pennsylvania
Tpke), exit 326 (Valley Forge); Schuylkill Expwy, exit 328A (Mall Blvd),
1.3 mi n on N Gulph Rd, 1 mi ne on 1st Ave, then just e. Int corridors.
Pets: Medium. $150 deposit/room, $10 daily fee/room. Service with restrictions.
SAVE 🐾 ✕ ♿ 🐾 🛏 💻 🏊

▼▼ Motel 6 Philadelphia-King of Prussia #1280 SH
(610) 265-7200. **$61-$75.** 815 W DeKalb Pike. I-76 (Pennsylvania
Tpke), exit 326 (Valley Forge), 1.3 mi e to jct US 202 N and S Gulph
Rd; Schuylkill Expwy, exit 328A (US 202 N), just e. Int corridors.
Pets: Service with restrictions, supervision.
🐾 ✕ 🐾 🏊

▼▼▼ The Sheraton Park Ridge Hotel and Conference
Center LH
(610) 337-1800. **$120-$195.** 480 N Gulph Rd. I-76 (Pennsylvania
Tpke), exit 327 (Valley Forge), 0.3 mi w. Int corridors. **Pets:** Accepted.
ASK 🐾 ✕ ♿ 🐾 🐾 🛏 💻 🍴 🏊 ✕

KULPSVILLE

▼▼▼ Best Western-The Inn at Towamencin SH
(215) 368-3800. **$104-$109.** 1750 Sumneytown Pike. I-476, exit 31, just
e. Int corridors. **Pets:** Accepted.
ASK 🐾 ✕ 🐾 🛏 💻 🍴 🏊 ✕

LANGHORNE

▼▼ Red Roof Inn-Oxford Valley #7165 M
(215) 750-6200. **$65-$120.** 3100 Cabot Blvd W. I-95, exit 46A (Oxford
Valley Rd), just e off US 1 N; 0.5 mi n of Sesame Place. Ext corridors.
Pets: Accepted.
✕ 🐾 🐾 🛏

▼▼▼ Sheraton Bucks County Hotel LH
(215) 547-4100. **$209-$279, 3 day notice.** 400 Oxford Valley Rd. I-95,
exit 46A (Oxford Valley Rd), 0.8 mi e, exit off US 1 N. Int corridors.
Pets: Accepted.
ASK 🐾 ✕ 🐾 🐾 🐾 🛏 💻 🍴 🏊 ✕

LIONVILLE

AAA ▼▼▼ Hampton Inn SH
(610) 363-5555. **$79-$119.** 4 N Pottstown Pike. I-76 (Pennsylvania
Tpke), exit 312, 0.5 mi s; jct SR 113 and 100. Int corridors. **Pets:** Other
species. Service with restrictions, crate.
SAVE 🐾 ✕ ♿ 🐾 🛏 💻 🏊

▼▼▼ Residence Inn by Marriott-Exton SH
(610) 594-9705. **$100-$200.** 10 N Pottstown Pike. I-76 (Pennsylvania
Tpke), exit 312, 1 mi s on SR 100. Int corridors. **Pets:** Accepted.
ASK 🐾 ✕ 🐾 🛏 💻 🏊 ✕

MALVERN

▼▼▼ Homestead Studio Suites Hotel-Malvern SH
(610) 695-9200. **$87-$107.** 8 E Swedesford Rd. Just w of US 202 and
SR 29 N. Int corridors. **Pets:** Accepted.
ASK 🐾 ✕ 🐾 🐾 🛏 💻

▼▼▼ Homewood Suites by Hilton SH
(610) 296-3500. **$89-$109.** 12 E Swedesford Rd. US 202, exit SR 29,
follow signs. Int corridors. **Pets:** Accepted.
ASK 🐾 ✕ 🐾 🐾 🛏 💻 🏊

AAA ▼▼▼ Sheraton Great Valley Hotel LH
(610) 524-5500. **$139-$159.** 707 Lancaster Pike. Jct US 30 and 202.
Int corridors. **Pets:** Accepted.
SAVE 🐾 ✕ 🐾 🐾 🐾 🛏 💻 🍴 🏊

▼▼▼ **Staybridge Suites By Holiday Inn** 🆂🅷
(610) 296-4343. **$99-$199.** 20 Morehall Rd. Jct US 30 and SR 29, just nw. Ext/int corridors. **Pets:** Large. $10 daily fee/room. Service with restrictions, supervision.

Ⓐ🆂🅺 ⊠ 🗐 🖴 💻 🏊 ⊠

NEW HOPE

▼▼▼▼ **1870 Wedgwood Inn of New Hope** 🅱🅱 ❁
(215) 862-2570. **$99-$265, 10 day notice.** 111 W Bridge St (SR 179). 0.5 mi w of SR 32; downtown. Ext/int corridors. **Pets:** Medium, dogs only. $20 daily fee/pet. Service with restrictions, supervision.

⊠ 🖴 💻

▼◆▼ **Aaron Burr House Inn & Conference Center** 🅱🅱 ❁
(215) 862-2520. **$99-$275, 10 day notice.** 80 W Bridge St (SR 179). 0.5 mi w of SR 32; at W Bridge and Chestnut sts. Int corridors. **Pets:** Medium, dogs only. $25 daily fee/pet. Service with restrictions, supervision.

⊠ 🖴 🕅

▲▲▲ ▼◆▼ **Best Western New Hope Inn** 🆂🅷
(215) 862-5221. **$89-$169.** 6426 Lower York Rd. 2 mi s on US 202, 1 mi w of jct SR 179. Ext corridors. **Pets:** Accepted.

🆂🅰🆅🅴 🆂🗷 ⊠ 🗐 🖴 💻 🍴 🏊 ⊠

▲▲▲ ▼◆▼ **The New Hope Motel in the Woods** Ⓜ ❁
(215) 862-2800. **$69-$149, 14 day notice.** 400 W Bridge St. 1 mi s on SR 179, e of jct US 202. Ext corridors. **Pets:** Medium, dogs only. $25 one-time fee/pet. Designated rooms, service with restrictions, supervision.

🆂🅰🆅🅴 🆂🗷 ⊠ 🖴 🏊

PHILADELPHIA

▲▲▲ ▼◆▼ **Best Western Center City Hotel** 🆂🅷
(215) 568-8300. **$119-$149.** 501 N 22nd St. Just n of Benjamin Franklin Pkwy. Int corridors. **Pets:** Medium, other species. $10 daily fee/room. Service with restrictions.

🆂🅰🆅🅴 🆂🗷 ⊠ 🗐 🖴 💻 🍴 🏊

▲▲▲ ▼◆▼ **Best Western Independence Park Inn** 🆂🅷
(215) 922-4443. **$159-$214, 7 day notice.** 235 Chestnut St. Between 2nd and 3rd sts. Int corridors. **Pets:** Small, other species. $50 one-time fee/room. Service with restrictions.

🆂🅰🆅🅴 🆂🗷 ⊠ 🗐 🖴 💻

▲▲▲ ▼◆▼ **The Doubletree Hotel Philadelphia** 🅻🅷
(215) 893-1600. **$139-$219.** 237 S Broad St. Jct Broad and Locust sts. Int corridors. **Pets:** Accepted.

🆂🅰🆅🅴 🆂🗷 ⊠ 🗐 🖴 🖴 💻 🍴 🏊 ⊠

▼◆▼ **Four Points by Sheraton Philadelphia Airport** 🆂🅷 ❁
(215) 492-0400. **$189.** 4101 Island Ave. Jct I-95 and SR 291, exit 13 northbound; exit 15 southbound. Int corridors. **Pets:** Medium, dogs only. Service with restrictions.

Ⓐ🆂🅺 🆂🗷 ⊠ 🗐 🖴 💻 🍴 🏊

▲▲▲ ▼◆▼◆ **Four Seasons Hotel Philadelphia** 🅻🅷 ❁
(215) 963-1500. **$360-$2600.** 1 Logan Square. Corner of 18th St and Benjamin Franklin Pkwy. Int corridors. **Pets:** Very small. Service with restrictions, supervision.

🆂🅰🆅🅴 ⊠ 🗄🅼 🗐 🗷 🖴 💻 🍴 🏊 ⊠

▲▲▲ ▼◆▼◆ **Hampton Inn-Center City** 🅻🅷
(215) 665-9100. **$88-$169.** 1301 Race St. At 13th and Race sts. Int corridors. **Pets:** Small, dogs only. $100 deposit/room. Designated rooms, service with restrictions, supervision.

🆂🅰🆅🅴 🆂🗷 ⊠ 🗐 🗷 🖴 💻 🏊

▲▲▲ ▼◆▼◆ **Loews Philadelphia Hotel** 🅻🅷
(215) 627-1200. **$154-$304.** 1200 Market St. Corner of 12th and Market sts. Int corridors. **Pets:** Accepted.

🆂🅰🆅🅴 🆂🗷 ⊠ 🗄🅼 🗐 🗷 🖴 💻 🍴 🏊 ⊠

▼◆▼◆ **Marriott Residence Inn Center City Philadelphia** 🅻🅷
(215) 557-0005. **$189-$349.** 1 E Penn Square. Market and Juniper sts. Int corridors. **Pets:** Accepted.

Ⓐ🆂🅺 🆂🗷 ⊠ 🗐 🗷 🖴 💻 🏊

▲▲▲ ▼◆▼◆ **Philadelphia Airport Residence Inn** 🆂🅷
(215) 492-1611. **$159-$184.** 4630 Island Ave. I-95, exit 13 northbound; exit 15 southbound, 0.3 mi e on SR 291. Ext/int corridors. **Pets:** $100 one-time fee/room. Service with restrictions, crate.

🆂🅰🆅🅴 ⊠ 🗄🅼 🗐 🗷 🖴 💻 🏊 ⊠

▼◆▼ **Philadelphia Downtown Marriott Hotel** 🅻🅷
(215) 625-2900. **$239-$269.** 1201 Market St. Between 12th and 13th sts. Int corridors. **Pets:** Accepted.

Ⓐ🆂🅺 🆂🗷 ⊠ 🗐 🗷 🖴 💻 🍴 🏊 ⊠

▲▲▲ ▼◆▼◆ **The Radisson Plaza-Warwick Hotel Philadelphia** 🅻🅷
(215) 735-6000. **$119-$169.** 1701 Locust St. Jct 17th and Locust sts. Int corridors. **Pets:** Small. $50 one-time fee/room. Designated rooms, service with restrictions, crate.

🆂🅰🆅🅴 ⊠ 🗐 🖴 🍴

▲▲▲ ▼◆▼◆ **The Rittenhouse Hotel and Condominium Residences** 🅻🅷 ❁
(215) 546-9000. **$380-$420.** 210 W Rittenhouse Square. On Rittenhouse Square. Int corridors. **Pets:** Service with restrictions, supervision.

🆂🅰🆅🅴 ⊠ 🗄🅼 🗐 🗷 🍴 🏊 ⊠

▼◆▼◆ **The Ritz-Carlton Philadelphia** 🅻🅷 🐾
(215) 523-8000. **$249-$519.** Ten Avenue of the Arts. Chestnut and Broad sts. Int corridors. **Pets:** Medium, dogs only. $25 daily fee/room. Service with restrictions, supervision.

⊠ 🗐 🗷 🍴 ⊠

▼◆▼ **Sheraton Society Hill** 🅻🅷
(215) 238-6000. **$289.** One Dock St. I-95, exit 20 (Historic District Center City), then 0.5 mi n on Delaware Ave to Dock St; at 2nd and Walnut sts. Int corridors. **Pets:** Accepted.

Ⓐ🆂🅺 ⊠ 🗐 🖴 💻 🍴 🏊 ⊠

▼◆▼ **Sheraton Suites Philadelphia Airport** 🅻🅷 ❁
(215) 365-6600. **$225.** 4101 Island Ave. Jct I-95 and SR 291, exit 13 northbound; exit 15 southbound. Int corridors. **Pets:** Medium, dogs only. Service with restrictions.

Ⓐ🆂🅺 🆂🗷 ⊠ 🗐 🖴 💻 🍴 ⊠

▲▲▲ ▼◆▼◆ **Sheraton University City** 🅻🅷
(215) 387-8000. **$279-$299.** 36th & Chestnut sts. I-76 (Pennsylvania Tpke), exit 345, 0.5 mi w. Int corridors. **Pets:** Accepted.

🆂🅰🆅🅴 ⊠ 🗄🅼 🗐 🗷 🖴 💻 🍴 🏊

▼◆▼ **Sofitel Philadelphia** 🅻🅷 ❁
(215) 569-8300. **$199.** 120 S 17th St. Jct Sansom and 17th sts. Int corridors. **Pets:** Other species. Service with restrictions, supervision.

Ⓐ🆂🅺 🆂🗷 ⊠ 🗄🅼 🗐 🗷 🍴

▲▲▲ ▼◆▼ ▼◆▼ **The Westin Philadelphia** 🅻🅷 ❁
(215) 563-1600. **$139-$259.** 99 S 17th St at Liberty Pl. On 17th St; between Market and Chestnut sts. Int corridors. **Pets:** Medium, dogs only. Designated rooms, service with restrictions, crate.

🆂🅰🆅🅴 ⊠ 🗷 💻 🍴 ⊠

▲▲▲ ▼◆▼◆ **Wyndham Philadelphia at Franklin Plaza** 🅻🅷
(215) 448-2000. **$99-$199.** 2 Franklin Plaza. Jct 17th and Race sts. Int corridors. **Pets:** Accepted.

🆂🅰🆅🅴 ⊠ 🗐 🗷 🖴 💻 🍴 🏊 ⊠

PLYMOUTH MEETING

▼▼▼▼ Doubletree Guest Suites Plymouth Meeting 🏨
(610) 834-8300. **$89-$249.** 640 W Germantown Pike. I-476, exit 20; I-276 (Pennsylvania Tpke), exit 333, just w on Plymouth Rd (Norristown), just e on Germantown Pike, then just e on Hickory Rd. Int corridors. **Pets:** $100 one-time fee/pet. Service with restrictions, crate.
⊠ 🔊 🛏 🖥 🍴 🏊 ⊠

POTTSTOWN

▼▼▼▼ Comfort Inn 🆘
(610) 326-5000. **$69-$118.** 99 Robinson St. SR 100, 1 mi n of jct US 422. Int corridors. **Pets:** Other species. $50 deposit/room. Service with restrictions, supervision.
A$K 🔊 ⊠ 🕹M 🔊 ⌖ 🛏 🖥 🏊

▲▲▲ ▼▼▼ Days Inn 🅼
(610) 970-1101. **$42-$79.** 29 High St. Just off SR 663, 0.5 mi e of jct SR 100. Ext corridors. **Pets:** Medium. $10 daily fee/pet. Service with restrictions, supervision.
SAVE 🔊 ⊠ 🛏

▼▼▼ Motel 6 🅼
(610) 819-1288. **$55-$70.** 78 Robinson St. Jct US 422, 1 mi n on SR 100, just w in Tri-County Business Campus. Int corridors. **Pets:** Accepted.
🔊 ⊠ 🕹M 🛏

▲▲▲ ▼▼▼ Quality Inn 🆘
(610) 326-6700. **$69-$99.** 61 W King St. Just e of SR 100. Ext corridors. **Pets:** Accepted.
SAVE 🔊 ⊠ 🛏 🖥 🍴 🏊

QUAKERTOWN

▲▲▲ ▼▼▼ Rodeway Inn Quakertown 🅼
(215) 536-7600. **$69-$79.** 1920 John Fries Hwy (SR 663). I-476 (Pennsylvania Tpke), exit 44, just e. Ext corridors. **Pets:** Accepted.
SAVE 🔊 ⊠ 🛏 🖥

TREVOSE

▲▲▲ ▼▼▼ Knights Inn-Philadelphia/Bucks County 🅼
(215) 639-4900. **$49-$149.** 2707 Super Hwy, US Rt 1 N. I-276 (Pennsylvania Tpke), exit 351, just s on US 1. Ext corridors. **Pets:** Very small, dogs only. $20 daily fee/pet. Designated rooms, service with restrictions, supervision.
SAVE 🔊 ⊠ 🛏

▼▼▼▼ Radisson Hotel of Philadelphia Northeast 🏨 🐾
(215) 638-8300. **$119-$126.** 2400 Old Lincoln Hwy. I-276 (Pennsylvania Tpke), exit 351, 1 mi s on US 1; jct Roosevelt Blvd and Old Lincoln Hwy. Int corridors. **Pets:** Other species. Designated rooms, service with restrictions, supervision.
A$K 🔊 ⊠ ♿ 🔊 ⌖ 🛏 🖥 🍴 🏊

▼▼ ▼▼ Red Roof Inn #7185 🅼
(215) 244-9422. **$60-$71.** 3100 Lincoln Hwy. I-276 (Pennsylvania Tpke), exit 351, 0.5 mi s on US 1 at US 132. Ext corridors. **Pets:** Accepted.
⊠ 🕹M 🔊 ⌖ 🛏

WEST CHESTER

▲▲▲ ▼▼▼ Microtel Inn & Suites 🆘
(610) 738-9111. **$69-$84.** 500 Willowbrook Ln. Just se of US 202, exit Matlack St. Int corridors. **Pets:** $10 daily fee/pet. Service with restrictions, supervision.
SAVE 🔊 ⊠ 🕹M 🔊 🛏 🖥

END METROPOLITAN AREA

PHILIPSBURG

▲▲▲ ▼▼ Main Liner Motel 🅼
(814) 342-2004. **$36-$59.** 1896 Philipsburg Bigler Hwy. 1 mi w of jct SR 53 N. Ext corridors. **Pets:** Small. $10 daily fee/pet. Designated rooms, service with restrictions, supervision.
SAVE 🔊 ⊠ 🛏

PIGEON

▼▼ The Forest Lodge & Campground 🅼 🐾
(814) 927-8790. **$45-$60.** SR 66, 6 mi n of Marienville. Ext corridors. **Pets:** Other species. $6 daily fee/pet. Designated rooms, service with restrictions, supervision.
A$K 🔊 ⊠ 🛏 🖥

PINE GROVE

▲▲▲ ▼▼▼ Comfort Inn 🆘
(570) 345-8031. **$70-$110.** SR 443. I-81, exit 100. Int corridors. **Pets:** Medium, other species. $10 daily fee/pet. Designated rooms, service with restrictions, crate.
SAVE 🔊 ⊠ 🕹M 🔊 🛏 🖥 🏊

▲▲▲ ▼▼▼ Econo Lodge 🆘
(570) 345-4099. **$40-$70.** 419 Suedberg Rd. I-81, exit 100, just e on SR 443. Ext/int corridors. **Pets:** Medium, other species. $10 daily fee/pet. Designated rooms, service with restrictions, supervision.
SAVE 🔊 ⊠ 🔊 🛏 🖥

PITTSBURGH METROPOLITAN AREA

BEAVER FALLS

▼▼▼▼ Holiday Inn 🆘 🐾
(724) 846-3700. **$99-$129.** 7195 Eastwood Rd. I-76 (Pennsylvania Tpke), exit 13, just n. Int corridors. **Pets:** $25 one-time fee/room. Service with restrictions, crate.
A$K 🔊 ⊠ 🔊 🛏 🖥 🍴 🏊 ⊠

BRIDGEVILLE

▲▲▲ ▼▼ Knights Inn-Pittsburgh/Bridgeville 🅼
(412) 221-8110. **$50-$55.** 111 Hickory Grade Rd. I-79, exit 54 (SR 50). Ext corridors. **Pets:** Accepted.
SAVE 🔊 ⊠ 🔊 ♿ 🛏 🖥

BUTLER

▼▼▼▼ Comfort Inn 🆘
(724) 287-7177. **$69-$149.** 1 Comfort Ln. 4 mi s on SR 8. Int corridors. **Pets:** Accepted.
A$K 🔊 ⊠ ♿ 🛏 🖥 🏊

▼▼ ▼▼ Super 8 Motel 🅼
(724) 287-8888. **$55.** 138 Pittsburgh/SR 8. 2 mi s. Int corridors. **Pets:** $20 deposit/pet, $5 daily fee/pet. Service with restrictions, supervision.
A$K 🔊 ⊠ 🛏

CANONSBURG

Super 8 Motel M
(724) 873-8808. **$58-$69.** 8 Curry Ave. I-79, exit 45, follow signs. Int corridors. **Pets:** Accepted.
SAVE 🔌 ⊠ 🈁 🛗

CORAOPOLIS

Embassy Suites-Pittsburgh International Airport LH
(412) 269-9070. **$89-$199.** 550 Cherrington Pkwy. Business Rt SR 60, exit Thorn Run Rd. Int corridors. **Pets:** $25 one-time fee/room. Designated rooms, service with restrictions, supervision.
ASK ⊠ ⌚M 🈁 🛗 ⊟ ▦ ⊯ ➿ ⊠

Hampton Inn Airport-Pittsburgh SH
(412) 264-0020. **$89-$99.** 8514 University Blvd. Business Rt SR 60, 0.5 mi n. Int corridors. **Pets:** Small. $25 one-time fee/room. Service with restrictions, supervision.
ASK 🔌 ⊠ 🈁 🛗 ▦

Holiday Inn-Pittsburgh Airport LH
(412) 262-3600. **$79-$169.** 8256 University Blvd. Busines Rt SR 60, 1 mi n. Int corridors. **Pets:** Small, other species. $25 one-time fee/room. Designated rooms, service with restrictions, supervision.
SAVE 🔌 ⊠ ⌚M 🈁 🛗 ⊟ ▦ ⊯ ➿

La Quinta Inn Pittsburgh (Airport) SH
(412) 269-0400. **$81-$106.** 8507 University Blvd. 1 mi n of Business Rt SR 60. Int corridors. **Pets:** Medium. Designated rooms, service with restrictions, supervision.
SAVE ⊠ ⌚M 🈁 🛗 ▦

CRANBERRY TOWNSHIP

AmeriSuites (Pittsburgh/Cranberry) SH
(724) 779-7900. **$89-$114.** 136 Emeryville Dr. I-76 (Pennsylvania Tpke), exit 28; I-79, exit 76 northbound; exit 78 southbound, 0.3 mi s on US 19. Int corridors. **Pets:** Accepted.
SAVE 🔌 ⊠ ⌚M 🈁 🛗 ⊟ ▦ ➿

Hampton Inn Cranberry SH
(724) 776-1000. **$104, 3 day notice.** 210 Executive Dr. I-76 (Pennsylvania Tpke), exit 28, 0.5 mi n on US 19, then 0.3 mi w on Freedom Rd; I-79, exit 78 southbound, 0.5 mi w on Freedom Rd. Int corridors. **Pets:** Accepted.
ASK ⊠ 🈁 🛗 ▦ ➿ ⊠

Holiday Inn Express SH
(724) 772-1000. **$89.** 20003 Rt 19. I-76 (Pennsylvania Tpke), exit 28, jct US 19 and I-76 (Pennsylvania Tpke); I-79, exit 76 northbound; exit 78 southbound, just s. Int corridors. **Pets:** Accepted.
ASK 🔌 ⊠ 🛗 ▦

Red Roof Inn-Cranberry Township-Pittsburgh North #7079 M
(724) 776-5670. **$54-$74.** 20009 Rt 19. I-76 (Pennsylvania Tpke), exit 28; I-79, exit 76 northbound; exit 78 southbound. Ext corridors. **Pets:** Service with restrictions, supervision.
⊠ 🈁

DELMONT

Super 8 Motel M
(724) 468-4888. **$53.** 180 Sheffield Dr. SR 66, just s of US 22. Int corridors. **Pets:** Other species. $5 daily fee/pet. Service with restrictions, supervision.
ASK 🔌 ⊠ ⌚M 🛗

GIBSONIA

Comfort Inn Gibsonia M
(724) 444-8700. **$59-$99.** 5137 Rt 8. I-76 (Pennsylvania Tpke), exit 39, just n. Ext corridors. **Pets:** Other species. $6 daily fee/pet. Service with restrictions, supervision.
ASK 🔌 ⊠ ⌚ 🛗 ▦

GREEN TREE

Hampton Inn Hotel Green Tree SH
(412) 922-0100. **$74-$94.** 555 Trumbull Dr. I-279, exit 4A to jct US 22 and 30, 1 mi nw via Mansfield Ave. Int corridors. **Pets:** Accepted.
ASK 🔌 ⊠ 🈁 🛗 ▦

Hawthorn Suites SH
(412) 279-6300. **$119-$149.** 700 Mansfield Ave. I-279, exit 4A to jct US 22 and 30, 1.5 mi nw. Ext corridors. **Pets:** Accepted.
ASK 🔌 ⊠ ⌚ 🈁 ⌚ 🛗 ➿ ⊠

Holiday Inn-Pittsburgh Central Greentree SH
(412) 922-8100. **$79-$109.** 401 Holiday Dr. I-279, exit 4A to jct US 22 and 30, 1 mi nw via Mansfield Ave. Int corridors. **Pets:** Medium. Service with restrictions, supervision.
SAVE 🔌 ⊠ ⌚ 🛗 ▦ ⊯ ➿

HARMARVILLE

Days Inn Harmarville M
(412) 828-5400. **$57-$75.** 6 Landings Dr. I-76 (Pennsylvania Tpke), exit 48, just s on Freeport Rd. Ext corridors. **Pets:** Medium, other species. $10 one-time fee/pet. Service with restrictions, crate.
ASK 🔌 ⊠ 🛗 ▦

MARS

Comfort Inn SH
(724) 772-2700. **$64-$99.** 924 Sheraton Dr. I-76 (Pennsylvania Tpke), exit 28; I-79, exit 76 northbound; exit 78 southbound, 0.5 mi s on US 19. Int corridors. **Pets:** Accepted.
ASK 🔌 ⊠ 🈁 🛗 ▦

Motel 6 Pittsburgh North Cranberry #42 M
(724) 776-4333. **$41-$55.** 19025 Perry Hwy. I-76 (Pennsylvania Tpke), exit 28, jct US 19; I-79, exit 76 northbound; exit 78 southbound on US 19. Ext corridors. **Pets:** Accepted.
🔌 ⊠ ⌚ 🛗

MONROEVILLE

Comfort Inn Pittsburgh East SH
(412) 244-1600. **$79-$119.** 699 Rodi Rd. I-376, exit 11, just n. Int corridors. **Pets:** Accepted.
ASK 🔌 ⊠ ⌚ 🛗 ▦ ⊯ ➿ ⊠

Days Inn-Monroeville M
(412) 856-1610. **$40-$85.** 2727 Mosside Blvd. I-76 (Pennsylvania Tpke), exit 57; I-376, exit 14A, 1 mi s on SR 48. Ext corridors. **Pets:** Dogs only. $25 daily fee/pet. Service with restrictions, supervision.
SAVE 🔌 ⊠ 🛗

Hampton Inn Monroeville/Pittsburgh SH
(412) 380-4000. **$114-$144.** 3000 Mosside Blvd. I-76 (Pennsylvania Tpke), exit 57; I-376, exit 14A, 0.3 mi s on SR 48. Int corridors. **Pets:** Accepted.
ASK 🔌 ⊠ 🈁 ⌚ 🛗 ▦ ➿

Holiday Inn Pittsburgh-Monroeville SH
(412) 372-1022. **$99-$145.** 2750 Mosside Blvd. I-76 (Pennsylvania Tpke), exit 57, 0.4 mi s on SR 48; I-376, exit 14A, 0.4 mi s on SR 48. Int corridors. **Pets:** Accepted.
SAVE 🔌 ⊠ 🈁 ⌚ 🛗 ⊟ ▦ ⊯ ➿

▼▼ Red Roof Inn-Monroeville #7174
(412) 856-4738. **$54-$74.** 2729 Mosside Blvd. I-76 (Pennsylvania Tpke), exit 57; I-376, exit 14A, 0.8 mi s on SR 48. Ext corridors. **Pets:** Other species. No service, supervision.
⊠

▼▼ Super 8 Motel Pittsburgh/Monroeville M
(724) 733-8008. **$53-$57.** 1807 Rt 286. I-76 (Pennsylvania Tpke), exit 57; I-376, exit 14A, 2 mi e on US 22 E, then 2 mi e. Int corridors. **Pets:** Other species. $5 daily fee/room. Service with restrictions, supervision.
ASK S⊘ ⊠ ⊟

MOON RUN

◈◈ ▼▼◈ AmeriSuites (Pittsburgh/Airport) SH
(412) 494-0202. **$99-$109.** 6011 Campbells Run Rd. Jct US 22 and 30, exit Moon Run Rd, just w. Int corridors. **Pets:** Accepted.
SAVE S⊘ ⊠ ⊛M ⊘ ⊛ ⊟ ⊡ ≈

◈◈ ▼▼ Comfort Inn-Pittsburgh Airport SH
(412) 787-2600. **$60-$95.** 7011 Old Steubenville Pike. US 22 and 30, jct SR 60; 4 mi w of jct I-279 and 79. Ext/int corridors. **Pets:** Other species. $10 daily fee/pet. Designated rooms, service with restrictions.
SAVE S⊘ ⊠ ⊘ ⊟ ⊡ ⊺⊺

▼▼◈ Comfort Suites SH
(412) 494-5750. **$69-$89.** 750 Aten Rd. SR 60, exit 2 (Montour Run Rd). Int corridors. **Pets:** Accepted.
ASK S⊘ ⊠ ⊛ ⊟ ⊡ ≈

▼▼ MainStay Suites Pittsburgh Airport SH
(412) 490-7343. **$82.** 1000 Park Lane Dr. SR 60, exit 2 (Montour Run Rd), just w on Cliff Mine Rd, then just s. Int corridors. **Pets:** Medium, other species. $100 deposit/room, $10 daily fee/room. Service with restrictions, supervision.
ASK S⊘ ⊠ ⊛ ⊟ ⊡

▼ Motel 6 Pittsburgh #657 M
(412) 922-9400. **$35-$45.** 211 Beecham Dr. I-79, exit 60A, just s on Steubenville Pike (SR 60), then e. Ext corridors. **Pets:** Accepted.
S⊘ ⊠ ⊛M ⊛

▼ Red Roof Inn South Airport #7030 M
(412) 787-7870. **$42-$64.** 6404 Steubenville Pike. I-79, exit 60A, 3.2 mi w on SR 60. Ext/int corridors. **Pets:** Accepted.
⊠ ⊘ ⊛

▼▼◈ Residence Inn-Pittsburgh Airport SH ❀
(412) 787-3300. **$139-$189.** 1500 Park Lane Dr. SR 60, exit 2 (Montour Run Rd), just w on Cliff Mine Dr to Summit Park Dr, just s to Park Lane Dr, then just e. Int corridors. **Pets:** Large, other species. $75 one-time fee/room. Service with restrictions, crate.
ASK S⊘ ⊠ ⊛M ⊘ ⊛ ⊟ ⊡ ≈ ⊠

◈◈ ▼▼◈ Sleep Inn Pittsburgh Airport SH
(412) 859-4000. **$59-$129.** 2500 Marketplace Blvd. SR 60, exit 2 (Montour Run Rd), 0.5 mi e, then 0.5 mi n. Int corridors. **Pets:** Other species. $25 deposit/room. Service with restrictions.
SAVE S⊘ ⊠ ⊘ ⊛ ⊟ ≈

◈◈ ▼▼◈ Wyndham Pittsburgh Airport LH
(412) 788-8800. **$99-$159.** 777 Aten Rd. SR 60, exit 2 (Montour Run Rd). Int corridors. **Pets:** Other species. $50 daily fee/pet. Service with restrictions, supervision.
SAVE ⊠ ⊟ ⊡ ⊺⊺ ≈ ⊠

NEW KENSINGTON

▼▼◈ Clarion Hotel SH
(724) 335-9171. **$74-$94, 3 day notice.** 300 Tarentum Bridge Rd. SR 366, 1.5 mi s of SR 28, exit 14; at south end of Tarentum Bridge. Int corridors. **Pets:** Other species. Supervision.
ASK S⊘ ⊠ ⊛ ⊟ ⊡ ⊺⊺ ≈

PITTSBURGH

◈◈◈ ▼▼◈ Days Inn Pittsburgh M
(412) 531-8900. **$60-$90.** 1150 Banksville Rd. 3.5 mi s on US 19. Ext/int corridors. **Pets:** Medium, dogs only. $15 one-time fee/pet. Service with restrictions, supervision.
SAVE S⊘ ⊠ ⊛ ⊟ ⊺⊺ ≈

◈◈◈ ▼▼▼ Hilton Pittsburgh LH ❀
(412) 391-4600. **$94-$234.** 600 Commonwealth Pl. On Commonwealth Pl; in Gateway Center. Int corridors. **Pets:** Small. $25 one-time fee/room. Service with restrictions, supervision.
SAVE ⊠ ⊛M ⊘ ⊟ ⊡ ⊺⊺

◈◈◈ ▼▼▼ Holiday Inn Pittsburgh North Hills SH
(412) 366-5200. **$139-$149.** 4859 McKnight Rd. I-279, exit 11, 7 mi n. Int corridors. **Pets:** Other species. $25 one-time fee/room. Designated rooms, service with restrictions.
SAVE S⊘ ⊠ ⊘ ⊟ ⊡ ⊺⊺ ≈

▼▼▼ Omni William Penn Hotel LH
(412) 281-7100. **$189-$209.** 530 William Penn Pl. Jct 6th St and William Penn Pl. Int corridors. **Pets:** Small. $50 one-time fee/room. Service with restrictions, crate.
ASK ⊠ ⊛ ⊟ ⊡ ⊺⊺

▼▼▼ Pittsburgh Comfort Inn SH
(412) 922-7555. **$59-$79.** 4770 Steubenville Pike. I-79, exit 60A, just s on Steubenville Pike (SR 60). Int corridors. **Pets:** Accepted.
ASK S⊘ ⊠ ⊛M ⊟ ⊡

▼▼▼ Residence Inn by Marriott SH
(412) 621-2200. **$169-$179.** 3896 Bigelow Blvd. On SR 380. Int corridors. **Pets:** Accepted.
ASK ⊠ ⊛ ⊟ ⊡ ≈ ⊠

▼▼▼ Sheraton Station Square Hotel LH ❀
(412) 261-2000. **$129-$239.** 300 W Station Square St. I-376, exit Grant St, south end of Smithfield St Bridge. Int corridors. **Pets:** Medium, dogs only. Service with restrictions, supervision.
ASK S⊘ ⊠ ⊛ ⊟ ⊡ ⊺⊺ ≈ ⊠

▼▼▼ The Westin Convention Center Pittsburgh LH
(412) 281-3700. **$119-$249.** 1000 Penn Ave. At Liberty Center; adjacent to convention center. Int corridors. **Pets:** Accepted.
ASK S⊘ ⊠ ⊘ ⊟ ⊡ ⊺⊺ ≈ ⊠

▼▼▼ Wyndham Garden Pittsburgh University Place LH
(412) 683-2040. **$109-$189.** 3454 Forbes Ave. Just w of Bundary St. Int corridors. **Pets:** Accepted.
ASK ⊠ ⊛ ⊟ ⊡ ⊺⊺

WASHINGTON

◈◈◈ ▼▼◈ Holiday Inn-Meadowlands SH
(724) 222-6200. **$79-$139.** 340 Race Track Rd. I-79, exit 41, 0.5 mi e. Int corridors. **Pets:** Accepted.
SAVE S⊘ ⊠ ⊛M ⊘ ⊛ ⊟ ⊡ ⊺⊺ ≈ ⊠

◈◈◈ ▼▼◈ Ramada Inn SH
(724) 225-9750. **$65-$97.** 1170 W Chestnut St. I-70, exit 15, 0.5 mi e on US 40. Ext/int corridors. **Pets:** Small. $30 one-time fee/room. Designated rooms, service with restrictions, crate.
SAVE S⊘ ⊠ ⊟ ⊡ ≈

▼▼◈ Red Roof Inn #7048 M
(724) 228-5750. **$45-$55.** 1399 W Chestnut St. I-70, exit 15, just e on US 40. Ext/int corridors. **Pets:** Accepted.
⊠ ⊛ ⊟

PITTSTON

AAA ▼▼▼ Knights Inn-Scranton/Pittston M
(570) 654-6020. **$42-$75.** 310 SR 315. I-81, exit 175 northbound, just s on SR 315; exit 175A southbound; I-476 (Northeast Extension Pennslyvania Tpke), exit 115. Ext corridors. **Pets:** Very small. Designated rooms, service with restrictions, supervision.
SAVE S⬛ ✕ ⬛

AAA ▼▼ Super 8 Motel SH
(570) 654-3301. **$45-$150.** 307 Rt 315 Hwy. I-81, exit 48 northbound, just s on SR 315; exit 48A southbound and 37 (Northeast Pennsylvania Tpke). Int corridors. **Pets:** Medium, other species. $10 daily fee/pet. Designated rooms, service with restrictions, supervision.
SAVE S⬛ ✕ ⬛ ⬛

▼▼ Victoria Inns and Suites SH
(570) 655-1234. **$99-$179.** 400 SR 315. I-81, exit 175 northbound; exit 175B southbound; I-476 (Northeast Extension Pennsylvania Tpke), exit 115. Int corridors. **Pets:** Accepted.
ASK S⬛ ✕ ⬛ ⬛ ⬛

POCONO MOUNTAINS AREA

BLAKESLEE

AAA ▼▼▼▼ Best Western Inn-Blakeslee/Pocono SH
(570) 646-6000. **$80-$190.** New Ventures Business Park. I-80, exit 284, just n. Int corridors. **Pets:** Small. $50 deposit/room. Service with restrictions, supervision.
SAVE S⬛ ✕ ⬛M ⬛ ⬛ ⬛ ⬛

AAA ▼▼▼▼ Blue Berry Mountain Inn BB
(570) 646-7144. **$90-$135, 30 day notice.** Thomas Rd. I-80, exit 284, 3 mi n on SR 115, just n on Thomas Rd, then to the end of Edmund Dr. Int corridors. **Pets:** Medium, other species. $10 daily fee/pet. Designated rooms, service with restrictions, supervision.
SAVE S⬛ ✕ ⬛ ⬛ ⬛ ⬛

EAST STROUDSBURG

AAA ▼▼▼▼ Budget Motel SH ❀
(570) 424-5451. **$59-$94, 3 day notice.** I-80, exit 308. I-80, exit 308, just se on Greentree Rd. Ext/int corridors. **Pets:** Medium. $25 deposit/pet. Designated rooms, service with restrictions, crate.
SAVE S⬛ ✕ ⬛ ⬛

▼▼ Super 8 Motel M
(570) 424-7411. **$58-$80.** 340 Greentree Rd. I-80, exit 308, just se. Int corridors. **Pets:** Small, dogs only. $10 daily fee/pet. Designated rooms, service with restrictions, supervision.
ASK S⬛ ✕ ⬛M ⬛

HAMLIN

AAA ▼▼▼ Comfort Inn SH
(570) 689-4148. **$70-$150.** SR 191. I-84, exit 17, just n. Int corridors. **Pets:** Accepted.
SAVE S⬛ ✕ ⬛ ⬛ ⬛

HAWLEY

▼▼ The Falls Port Inn & Restaurant CI
(570) 226-2600. **$70-$120, 3 day notice.** 330 Main Ave. At Main Ave (US 6) and Church St; downtown. Int corridors. **Pets:** Medium, dogs only. $20 one-time fee/room. No service.
ASK ✕ ⬛ ⬛

LAKE HARMONY

AAA ▼▼▼▼ Ramada Inn-Pocono SH
(570) 443-8471. **$80-$175.** I-80, exit 277 (Lake Harmony); I-476 (Northeast Extension Pennsylvania Tpke), exit 95 (Pocono), 0.5 mi e. Int corridors. **Pets:** Small. $50 deposit/room. Service with restrictions, supervision.
SAVE S⬛ ✕ ⬛ ⬛ ⬛ ⬛ ⬛ ⬛ ⬛

MATAMORAS

AAA ▼▼▼▼ Best Western Inn at Hunt's Landing SH
(570) 491-2400. **$79-$179.** 120 Rt 6 & 209. I-84, exit 53. Int corridors. **Pets:** Medium, dogs only. $10 daily fee/pet. Designated rooms, service with restrictions, supervision.
SAVE S⬛ ✕ ⬛ ⬛ ⬛ ⬛ ⬛ ⬛

MILFORD

AAA ▼▼ Milford Motel M ❀
(570) 296-6411. **$50-$95, 3 day notice.** 591 Rt 6 & 209. On US 6 and 209 N, 0.7 mi e. Ext corridors. **Pets:** Dogs only. Designated rooms, service with restrictions, supervision.
SAVE S⬛ ✕ ⬛

AAA ▼▼ Red Carpet Inn-Milford M ❀
(570) 296-9444. **$65-$115, 7 day notice.** 240 Rt 6. I-84, exit 46, just s. Ext corridors. **Pets:** Small. $7 daily fee/pet. Designated rooms, no service, supervision.
SAVE S⬛ ✕ ⬛

AAA ▼▼ Scottish Inns M
(570) 491-4414. **$50-$95.** 274 Rt 6 & 209. I-84, exit 53, 1 mi s. Ext corridors. **Pets:** Accepted.
SAVE S⬛ ✕ ⬛ ⬛

END AREA

PUNXSUTAWNEY

▼▼ Pantall Hotel SH
(814) 938-6600. **$59-$105.** 135 E Mahoning St. On US 119/SR 36; downtown. Int corridors. **Pets:** Medium. Service with restrictions, supervision.
ASK S⬛ ✕ ⬛ ⬛

READING

AAA ▼▼▼▼ Best Western Dutch Colony Inn & Suites SH
(610) 779-2345. **$84-$98.** 4635 Perkiomen Ave. US 422, 0.3 mi e of jct US 422 business route. Ext/int corridors. **Pets:** Accepted.
SAVE S⬛ ✕ ⬛ ⬛ ⬛ ⬛ ⬛ ⬛ ⬛

AAA ▼▼▼ **Econo Lodge M**
(610) 378-1145. **$49-$79.** 2310 Fraver Dr. US 222 business route (5th St); just s of Warren St Bypass (SR 12 E). Ext corridors. **Pets:** Medium, dogs only. $10 daily fee/pet. Service with restrictions, supervision.
[SAVE] [S] [X] [H] [P]

AAA ▼▼▼ **Quality Inn Airport SH**
(610) 736-0400. **$60-$70.** 2017 Bernville Rd. US 222, exit SR 183, 2 mi s. Int corridors. **Pets:** Small. $20 daily fee/pet. Designated rooms, service with restrictions, supervision.
[SAVE] [S] [X] [H] [P]

ST. MARYS

▼▼▼ **Comfort Inn SH**
(814) 834-2030. **$65-$84.** 195 Comfort Ln. SR 255, south end of town. Int corridors. **Pets:** Other species. Service with restrictions, supervision.
[ASK] [S] [X] [&] [H] [P] [≈]

AAA ▼▼▼ **Towne House Inn SH**
(814) 781-1556. **$53-$85.** 138 Center St. Just n of "Diamond" and jct SR 255 and 120; downtown. Int corridors. **Pets:** Accepted.
[SAVE] [S] [X] [H] [P] [TI] [≈]

SELINSGROVE

AAA ▼▼▼ **Comfort Inn SH**
(570) 374-8880. **$65-$150.** 710 S US Hwy 11 & 15. Just n of jct US 522. Int corridors. **Pets:** Other species. $10 daily fee/pet, $25 one-time fee/pet. Service with restrictions, crate.
[SAVE] [S] [X] [H] [P] [≈]

SHAMOKIN DAM

AAA ▼▼▼ **Hampton Inn SH**
(570) 743-2223. **$129-$179, 30 day notice.** 3 Stettler Ave. US 11 and 15, 1 mi s of jct SR 61. Int corridors. **Pets:** Accepted.
[SAVE] [S] [X] [&M] [∅] [&] [H] [P] [≈]

AAA ▼▼▼ **Quality Inn & Suites M**
(570) 743-1111. **$59-$199, 3 day notice.** 2 Susquehanna Tr. US 11 and 15; just n of jct SR 61. Ext corridors. **Pets:** Medium. $25 one-time fee/pet. Service with restrictions.
[SAVE] [S] [X] [H] [P] [TI] [≈]

SHARTLESVILLE

AAA ▼▼ **Budget Inn Shartlesville M**
(610) 488-1578. **$49-$125.** Roadside Dr. I-78, exit 23, just s to Old Rt 22, just w to Roadside Dr, then just nw. Ext corridors. **Pets:** Accepted.
[SAVE] [S] [X] [H]

AAA ▼▼ **Dutch Motel M**
(610) 488-1479. **$45-$65.** 1 Motel Dr. I-78, exit 23, just nw. Ext corridors. **Pets:** $5 daily fee/pet. No service.
[SAVE] [S] [X] [H] [P]

SHICKSHINNY

▼▼ **The Blue Heron Bed & Breakfast BB**
(570) 864-3740. **$60-$90 (no credit cards), 3 day notice.** 1270 Bethel Hill Rd. Jct US 11, 6.2 mi n on SR 239, then 2 mi n on CR 4016 (Harveyville/Bethel Hill Rd). Int corridors. **Pets:** Accepted.
[X] [K] [W]

SLIPPERY ROCK

▼▼ **Evening Star Motel M**
(724) 794-3211. **$49-$55.** 915 New Castle Rd. I-79, exit 105, 0.5 mi e on SR 108. Ext corridors. **Pets:** Accepted.
[ASK] [S] [X] [H] [P]

SOUTH WILLIAMSPORT

AAA ▼▼▼ **Quality Inn Williamsport SH**
(570) 323-9801. **$59-$139.** 234 Montgomery Pike. 0.8 mi s on US 15. Int corridors. **Pets:** Large. $25 one-time fee/room. Designated rooms, service with restrictions, crate.
[SAVE] [S] [X] [∅] [H] [P] [≈]

AAA ▼▼▼ **Ridgemont Motel M**
(570) 321-5300. **$43-$53.** 637 Rt 15 Hwy. 1.2 mi s on US 15. Ext corridors. **Pets:** Small, dogs only. $5 one-time fee/pet. Designated rooms, service with restrictions, supervision.
[SAVE] [S] [X] [H]

STATE COLLEGE

▼▼ **The Autoport Motel & Restaurant Inc SH**
(814) 237-7666. **$59-$95.** 1405 S Atherton St. US 322 business route, 1.4 mi e of jct SR 26. Ext/int corridors. **Pets:** Other species. $10 daily fee/pet. Designated rooms, service with restrictions, crate.
[ASK] [S] [X] [H] [P] [TI] [≈]

AAA ▼▼▼ **Days Inn Penn State LH**
(814) 238-8454. **$93-$240, 30 day notice.** 240 S Pugh St. Just e of SR 26 northbound, 0.4 mi n of jct US 322 business route; downtown. Int corridors. **Pets:** Accepted.
[SAVE] [X] [∅] [&] [H] [P] [TI] [≈] [X]

AAA ▼▼ **Happy Valley Motor Inn M**
(814) 234-1111. **$48-$85, 30 day notice.** 1245 S Atherton St. 1.3 mi e on US 322 business route. Ext/int corridors. **Pets:** Other species. $20 one-time fee/room. Service with restrictions, supervision.
[SAVE] [S] [X] [H]

▼▼ **Motel 6 State College M**
(814) 234-1600. **$51-$66.** 1274 N Atherton St. US 322 business route, 1 mi w of jct SR 26. Int corridors. **Pets:** Accepted.
[S] [X] [&M] [∅] [&] [H]

▼ **Nittany Budget Motel M**
(814) 238-0015. **$44-$50.** 2070 Cato Ave. SR 26, 2.6 mi s of jct US 322 business route. Ext corridors. **Pets:** Other species. $5 daily fee/pet. Service with restrictions, crate.
[ASK] [S] [X] [&] [H]

AAA ▼▼▼ **Super 8 State College SH**
(814) 237-8005. **$49-$89.** 1663 S Atherton St. US 322 business route, 1.6 mi e of jct SR 26. Int corridors. **Pets:** Medium, other species. $25 one-time fee/room. Designated rooms, service with restrictions, supervision.
[SAVE] [S] [X] [H] [P] [X]

TOWANDA

AAA ▼▼▼ **Towanda Motel & Restaurant M**
(570) 265-2178. **$55-$79, 3 day notice.** 383 York Ave. 0.8 mi w on US 6. Ext corridors. **Pets:** Accepted.
[SAVE] [S] [X] [H] [TI]

TOWN HILL

▼ **Days Inn Breezewood SH**
(814) 735-3860. **Call for rates.** 9650 Old 126. I-70, exit 156, just n. Int corridors. **Pets:** $10 daily fee/pet. Designated rooms, crate.
[X] [H] [P] [TI]

WARREN

AAA ▼▼▼ **Holiday Inn of Warren SH**
(814) 726-3000. **$80-$100.** 210 Ludlow St. Jct US 6, just n on Ludlow St (US 62 N). Int corridors. **Pets:** Small. Service with restrictions, supervision.
[SAVE] [S] [X] [∅] [H] [P] [TI] [≈]

Warren Super 8 Motel SH
(814) 723-8881. **$71-$72.** 204 Struthers St. 1.5 mi w on US 6, exit Ludlow St, w on Allegheny, then s. Ext/int corridors. **Pets:** Accepted.
ASK X

WAYNESBORO

Best Western of Waynesboro M
(717) 762-9113. **$70-$85, 3 day notice.** 239 W Main St. 0.5 mi w on SR 16. Ext corridors. **Pets:** Other species. $10 daily fee/pet. Designated rooms, service with restrictions, supervision.
SAVE X TI

WAYNESBURG

Comfort Inn SH
(724) 627-3700. **$59-$89.** 100 Comfort Ln. I-79, exit 14, just e. Int corridors. **Pets:** Large, other species. Service with restrictions, supervision.
ASK X

Econo Lodge M
(724) 627-5544. **$48-$68.** 126 Miller Ln. I-79, exit 14, just w. Ext corridors. **Pets:** Medium, other species. Service with restrictions, crate.
SAVE X

Super 8 Motel-Waynesburg M
(724) 627-8880. **$45-$95.** 100 Stanley Dr. I-79, exit 14, just w. Int corridors. **Pets:** Accepted.
ASK X

WELLSBORO

Penn Wells Lodge M
(570) 724-3463. **$50-$100.** 4 Main St. Just n on US 6 and SR 287. Ext/int corridors. **Pets:** Medium. $20 daily fee/room. Designated rooms.
SAVE X TI

WEST HAZLETON

Comfort Inn Hazleton West Hazleton SH
(570) 455-9300. **$99-$180.** 58 SR 93. I-81, exit 145, 0.3 mi se; I-80, exit 256, 3.8 mi se. Int corridors. **Pets:** Other species. Service with restrictions.
SAVE X TI

Forest Hill Inn M
(570) 459-2730. **$60.** 18202 SR 93. I-81, exit 145, 0.3 mi se; I-80, exit 256, 3.8 mi se. Ext corridors. **Pets:** Other species. Service with restrictions, supervision.
SAVE X

WEST MIDDLESEX

Super 8 Motel-West Middlesex/Sharon SH
(724) 528-3888. **$55-$80.** 3369 New Castle Rd. I-80, exit 4B (SR 18), just s. Int corridors. **Pets:** Small. $10 daily fee/pet. Designated rooms, service with restrictions, supervision.
ASK X

WILKES-BARRE

Best Western Genetti Hotel & Conference Center LH
(570) 823-6152. **$109-$119.** 77 E Market St. Market and Washington sts; downtown. Int corridors. **Pets:** Accepted.
SAVE X TI

Holiday Inn SH
(570) 824-8901. **$93-$99.** 880 Kidder St. I-81, exit 170B, exit 1 (SR 309 S business route). Ext corridors. **Pets:** Medium, other species. $15 one-time fee/pet. Service with restrictions, supervision.
ASK X TI

Host Inn Residential Suites SH
(570) 270-4678. **$109-$199.** 860 Kidder St. I-81, exit 170B, exit 1 off the expressway, then 0.5 mi w. Int corridors. **Pets:** Medium, other species. $15 one-time fee/pet. Service with restrictions, supervision.
ASK X

Red Roof Inn #7139 M
(570) 829-6422. **$49-$62.** 1035 Hwy 315. I-81, exit 170B, jct SR 115, 0.7 mi w, exit 1 (SR 309 S business route) to SR 315, then just n. Ext corridors. **Pets:** Other species. Service with restrictions, supervision.
X

WILLIAMSPORT

Genetti Hotel & Suites SH
(570) 326-6600. **$71-$106, 7 day notice.** 200 W Fourth St. Jct William St; downtown. Int corridors. **Pets:** Large, other species. Service with restrictions, supervision.
SAVE X TI

Holiday Inn-Williamsport SH
(570) 326-1981. **$63-$113, 30 day notice.** 1840 E 3rd St. I-180, exit 25 (Faxon St), just e; 1 mi w of W 3rd St. Ext corridors. **Pets:** Other species. $15 one-time fee/room. Service with restrictions, crate.
X TI

Radisson Hotel Williamsport SH
(570) 327-8231. **$114-$119.** 100 Pine St. Jct US 220 and SR 15 S; downtown. Int corridors. **Pets:** Small. Designated rooms, service with restrictions, supervision.
ASK X TI

WIND GAP

Travel Inn of Wind Gap M
(610) 863-4146. **$50-$90, 3 day notice.** 499 E Moorestown Rd. SR 512, e of jct SR 33, exit Bath/Wind Gap. Ext corridors. **Pets:** $5 daily fee/pet. Service with restrictions, crate.
SAVE X

WYOMISSING

Econo Lodge SH
(610) 378-5105. **$57-$84.** 635 Spring St. Just off US 422, exit Papermill Rd. Int corridors. **Pets:** Small. $10 daily fee/pet. Service with restrictions, crate.
ASK X

Homewood Suites-Reading/Wyomissing SH
(610) 736-3100. **$164-$179.** 2801 Papermill Rd. US 422, exit Papermill Rd, 1.8 mi nw; US 222, exit Spring Ridge Rd. Int corridors. **Pets:** Accepted.
ASK X

The Inn at Reading SH
(610) 372-7811. **$69-$149.** 1040 Park Rd. US 222, exit N Wyomissing Blvd, just n, then 0.3 mi e. Int corridors. **Pets:** Accepted.
SAVE X TI

Sheraton Reading Hotel SH
(610) 376-3811. **$119-$169.** 1741 W Papermill Rd. US 422, exit Papermill Rd. Int corridors. **Pets:** Accepted.
SAVE X TI

Wellesley Inn (Reading) SH
(610) 374-1500. **$89-$129.** 910 Woodland Rd. US 422 W, exit Papermill Rd, just e. Int corridors. **Pets:** Accepted.
SAVE X

WYSOX

Comfort Inn SH
(570) 265-5691. **$99-$125.** US 6. Center. Int corridors. **Pets:** Other species. $15 one-time fee/room. Service with restrictions, supervision.
ASK X

YORK

◆◆◆ ▽▽▽ Best Western-Westgate 🆂🅷
(717) 767-6931. **$82-$88.** 1415 Kenneth Rd. I-83, exit 21B northbound, 2 mi w on US 30, then just n; exit 22 southbound, 0.5 mi s on SR 181, 1.7 mi w on US 30, then just n. Int corridors. **Pets:** Other species. $100 deposit/pet, $5 daily fee/pet. Designated rooms, service with restrictions, supervision.

[SAVE] [S🐾] [✕] [🚹] [💻]

▽▽▽ Four Points by Sheraton Hotel and Suites 🆂🅷
(717) 846-4940. **$149-$159, 3 day notice.** 1650 Toronita St. I-83, exit 21A northbound; exit 21 southbound, just ne. Int corridors. **Pets:** Accepted.

[ASK] [S🐾] [✕] [🐕] [🚹] [💻] [🍽] [🏊]

▽▽▽ Holiday Inn Holidome & Conference
Center 🆂🅷 🐾
(717) 846-9500. **$124.** 2000 Loucks Rd. I-83, exit 21B northbound, 2.5 mi w on US 30, then just n; exit 22 southbound, 0.5 mi s on SR 181, 2.2 mi w on US 30, then just n. Int corridors. **Pets:** Other species. Service with restrictions, supervision.

[ASK] [S🐾] [✕] [🔈] [🐕] [🚹] [💻] [🍽] [🏊] [✕]

◆◆◆ ▽▽▽ Holiday Inn York I-83 & Rt 30 🆂🅷
(717) 845-5671. **$92-$110.** 334 Arsenal Rd. I-83, exit 21A northbound; exit 21 southbound, just e on US 30. Ext corridors. **Pets:** Accepted.

[SAVE] [S🐾] [✕] [🔈] [🐕] [🚹] [💻] [🍽] [🏊]

▽▽▽ Red Roof Inn #7172 🅼
(717) 843-8181. **$46-$79.** 323 Arsenal Rd. I-83, exit 21A northbound; exit 21 southbound; just e on US 30. Ext corridors. **Pets:** Accepted.

[✕] [🐕]

▽▽ Super 8 Motel 🅼
(717) 852-8686. **$55-$90, 7 day notice.** 40 Arsenal Rd. I-83, exit 21B northbound, 0.3 mi w on US 30; exit 21 southbound, 0.5 mi s on SR 181 to US 30. Int corridors. **Pets:** Accepted.

[ASK] [S🐾] [✕] [🚹]

RHODE ISLAND

CRANSTON

AAA ♦♦♦ Days Inn **M**
(401) 942-4200. **$79-$109, 14 day notice.** 101 New London Ave. I-95, exit 14B to SR 37, exit 2B westbound, then 0.5 mi ne. Ext corridors. **Pets:** Dogs only. $10 daily fee/pet. Service with restrictions, supervision.
[SAVE] [S] [X]

MIDDLETOWN

♦♦♦ The Bay Willows Inn **M** ❧
(401) 847-8400. **$39-$179, 3 day notice.** 1225 Aquidneck Ave. Jct SR 138 and 138A. Ext corridors. **Pets:** Other species. $10 daily fee/room. Designated rooms, service with restrictions.
[X] [■]

AAA ♦♦♦ Howard Johnson Inn-Newport **SH**
(401) 849-2000. **$49-$244.** 351 W Main Rd. On SR 114, 0.3 mi s of jct SR 138. Int corridors. **Pets:** Accepted.
[SAVE] [S] [X] [&M] [♪] [&] [■] [▣] [¶] [≈] [X]

♦♦♦ SeaView Inn **M** ❧
(401) 846-5000. **$59-$229, 7 day notice.** 240 Aquidneck Ave (SR 138A). Jct SR 214. Ext corridors. **Pets:** Other species. $10 daily fee/room. Designated rooms, service with restrictions.
[ASK] [S] [X] [■] [▣]

NEWPORT

AAA ♦♦♦♦ Beech Tree Inn **BB**
(401) 847-9794. **$115-$350, 15 day notice.** 34 Rhode Island Ave. Just e of SR 114, 0.8 mi s of jct SR 138. Int corridors. **Pets:** Other species. $25 daily fee/pet. Designated rooms, no service.
[SAVE] [X] [■]

AAA ♦♦♦♦ The Hotel Viking **LH**
(401) 847-3300. **$139-$349, 7 day notice.** One Bellevue Ave. Corner of Kay St, Church and Bellevue Ave. Int corridors. **Pets:** Medium. $35 one-time fee/pet. Designated rooms, service with restrictions, supervision.
[SAVE] [S] [X] [■] [▣] [¶] [≈] [X]

NORTH KINGSTOWN

♦♦♦ Hamilton Village Inn **M**
(401) 295-0700. **$79-$119, 7 day notice.** 642 Boston Neck Rd. SR 1A, 1.3 mi s of jct SR 102. Ext corridors. **Pets:** Other species. Designated rooms, service with restrictions, supervision.
[■] [▣] [¶]

PORTSMOUTH

AAA ♦♦♦ Founder's Brook Motel & Suites **M**
(401) 683-1244. **$59-$159, 3 day notice.** 314 Boyd's Ln. Jct SR 24, exit Mt. Hope Blvd, on SR 138. Ext corridors. **Pets:** Small, dogs only. $10 daily fee/pet. Designated rooms, service with restrictions, supervision.
[SAVE] [S] [X] [■]

PROVIDENCE

♦♦♦♦ Providence Biltmore Hotel **LH**
(401) 421-0700. **$149-$249.** 11 Dorrance St. I-95, exit 22A; downtown. Int corridors. **Pets:** Accepted.
[ASK] [S] [X] [&M] [♪] [&] [■] [▣] [¶]

AAA ♦♦♦♦ The Westin Providence **LH** ❧
(401) 598-8000. **$419-$444.** One W Exchange St. I-95, exit 22A; downtown. Int corridors. **Pets:** Small, dogs only. Service with restrictions, supervision.
[SAVE] [S] [X] [&M] [♪] [&] [▣] [¶] [≈] [X]

WAKEFIELD

♦♦♦ The Kings' Rose Bed & Breakfast Inn **BB**
(401) 783-5222. **$120-$170, 7 day notice.** 1747 Mooresfield Rd (SR 138). I-95, exit 3A, 11 mi e on SR 138; 3.3 mi w of US 1. Int corridors. **Pets:** Service with restrictions, supervision.
[X]

WARWICK

♦♦♦ Crowne Plaza Hotel at the Crossings **LH**
(401) 732-6000. **$119-$209.** 801 Greenwich Ave. I-95, exit 12A southbound; exit 12 northbound, 0.3 mi e on SR 5. Int corridors. **Pets:** Accepted.
[ASK] [S] [X] [&M] [♪] [■] [▣] [¶] [≈] [X]

AAA ♦♦♦ Hampton Inn & Suites Providence-Warwick Airport **SH** ❧
(401) 739-8888. **$95-$150.** 2100 Post Rd. I-95, exit 13, e to US 1, then just n. Int corridors. **Pets:** Medium. Service with restrictions, supervision.
[SAVE] [S] [X] [♪] [&] [■] [▣]

AAA ♦♦♦ Holiday Inn Express Hotel & Suites **SH**
(401) 736-5000. **$89-$159.** 901 Jefferson Blvd. I-95, exit 13, 0.4 mi on Airport Connector Rd, exit Jefferson Blvd. Int corridors. **Pets:** $50 deposit/pet. Service with restrictions, supervision.
[SAVE] [S] [X] [&M] [♪] [&] [■] [▣] [≈]

♦♦ Homestead Studio Suites Hotel-Providence/Airport/Warwick **SH**
(401) 732-6667. **$97-$117.** 268 Metro Center Blvd. I-95, exit 12A, 0.4 mi e on SR 113, 0.4 mi n on SR 5, then 0.4 mi e. Int corridors. **Pets:** Medium, other species. $75 one-time fee/room. Service with restrictions, crate.
[ASK] [S] [X] [&M] [♪] [&] [■] [▣] [X]

♦♦♦ Residence Inn by Marriott **SH**
(401) 737-7100. **$79-$209.** 500 Kilvert St. I-95, exit 13 to Jefferson Blvd, 0.4 mi n, then 0.6 mi w. Ext corridors. **Pets:** Accepted.
[ASK] [S] [X] [♪] [■] [▣] [≈] [X]

♦♦♦ Sheraton Providence Airport Hotel **LH** ❧
(401) 738-4000. **$129-$179.** 1850 Post Rd. I-95, exit 13, 0.6 mi s on US 1. Int corridors. **Pets:** Dogs only. Service with restrictions, supervision.
[ASK] [S] [X] [&M] [♪] [&] [■] [▣] [¶] [≈] [X]

WESTERLY

AAA ♦♦ The Pine Lodge **CA**
(401) 322-0333. **$68-$104, 14 day notice.** 92 Old Post Rd. On US 1, 1.8 mi ne of jct SR 78. Ext corridors. **Pets:** Small, dogs only. $150 deposit/pet, $25 one-time fee/room. Designated rooms, no service, supervision.
[SAVE] [S] [X] [■] [X]

WOONSOCKET

♦♦♦ Holiday Inn Express Hotel & Suites **SH**
(401) 769-5000. **$107-$145.** 194 Fortin Dr. I-295, exit 9 on SR 122, 3.5 mi n via SR 146/99/122. Int corridors. **Pets:** $10 daily fee/room. Service with restrictions, crate.
[ASK] [S] [X] [&M] [♪] [&] [■] [▣] [≈]

SOUTH CAROLINA

AIKEN

▼▼ Days Inn-Downtown Ⓜ
(803) 649-5524. **$48-$65.** 1204 Richland Ave W. Jct US 1/78 and SR 19, 0.9 mi w on US 1/78. Ext corridors. **Pets:** Accepted.
ⒶⓈⓀ Ⓢ Ⓧ Ⓐ Ⓗ Ⓟ ⓐ

▼▼ Econo Lodge Ⓜ ❀
(803) 649-3968. **$48-$55, 7 day notice.** 3560 Richland Ave W. Jct US 1/78 and SR 19, 2.6 mi w on US 1/78. Ext corridors. **Pets:** Medium, other species. $10 daily fee/pet. Service with restrictions, crate.
ⒶⓈⓀ Ⓢ Ⓧ Ⓗ Ⓟ ⓐ

▼▼▼ Holiday Inn Express Ⓢ🅷
(803) 648-0999. **$100.** 155 Colony Pkwy/Whiskey Rd. Jct US 1/78 and SR 19, 1.8 mi s on SR 19. Ext corridors. **Pets:** Medium, other species. $30 one-time fee/room. Service with restrictions, supervision.
ⒶⓈⓀ Ⓢ Ⓧ Ⓐ Ⓚ Ⓗ Ⓟ ⓐ

🆔 ▼▼ Quality Inn & Suites Ⓢ🅷
(803) 641-1100. **$60-$80.** 3608 Richland Ave W. Jct US 1/78 and SR 19, 2.9 mi w on US 1/78. Ext corridors. **Pets:** Large, other species. $10 daily fee/pet. Service with restrictions, crate.
ⓈⒶⓋⒺ Ⓢ Ⓧ Ⓐ Ⓚ Ⓗ Ⓟ ⓐ

🆔 ▼▼ Ramada Ltd Ⓢ🅷
(803) 648-6821. **$49-$54.** 1850 Richland Ave W. Jct US 1/78 and SR 19, 1.6 mi w on US 1/78. Ext corridors. **Pets:** Accepted.
ⓈⒶⓋⒺ Ⓢ Ⓧ Ⓚ Ⓗ Ⓟ ⓐ

▼▼ Sleep Inn Ⓢ🅷 ❀
(803) 644-9900. **$49-$219.** 1002 Monterey Dr. Jct US 78 and SR 302/19 (Whiskey Rd), 0.5 mi s on SR 19, then just e. Int corridors. **Pets:** Medium. $20 daily fee/pet. Designated rooms, service with restrictions, supervision.
ⒶⓈⓀ Ⓢ Ⓧ Ⓚ Ⓜ Ⓚ Ⓗ Ⓟ ⓐ

▼▼ Town & Country Inn 🅱🅱 ❀
(803) 642-0270. **$70-$95.** 2340 Sizemore Cir. Jct US 78 and SR 302/19 (Whiskey Rd), 2.3 mi s on SR 19, then just w. Int corridors. **Pets:** Large, other species. Supervision.
ⒶⓈⓀ Ⓢ Ⓧ ⓐ Ⓩ

ANDERSON

▼▼ Days Inn Ⓜ
(864) 375-0375. **$69-$119.** 1007 Smith Mill Rd. I-85, exit 19A, jct US 76, just se. Ext corridors. **Pets:** Small. $10 daily fee/room. Service with restrictions, crate.
ⒶⓈⓀ Ⓢ Ⓧ Ⓜ Ⓐ Ⓗ Ⓟ ⓐ

🆔 ▼▼▼ Holiday Inn Express Ⓢ🅷
(864) 231-0231. **$69-$159.** 103 Anderson Business Park. I-85, exit 27, just s on SR 81. Int corridors. **Pets:** Very small, dogs only. $25 one-time fee/room. Designated rooms, service with restrictions, supervision.
ⓈⒶⓋⒺ Ⓢ Ⓧ Ⓜ Ⓐ Ⓚ Ⓗ Ⓟ ⓐ

▼▼▼▼ La Quinta Inn Anderson Ⓢ🅷
(864) 225-3721. **$65-$80.** 3430 Clemson Blvd. I-85, exit 19A, 2.5 mi se on US 76. Ext corridors. **Pets:** Accepted.
ⒶⓈⓀ Ⓧ Ⓐ Ⓚ Ⓗ Ⓟ ⓐ

BEAUFORT

▼▼ Ramada Limited of Beaufort Ⓢ🅷
(843) 524-2144. **$59-$199.** 2001 Boundary St. I-95, exit 33 (Point South/US 17); jct SR 281/US 21, just w on US 21. Ext corridors. **Pets:** Accepted.
ⒶⓈⓀ Ⓢ Ⓧ Ⓐ Ⓗ Ⓟ ⓐ

BENNETTSVILLE

🆔 ▼▼ Holiday Inn Express Ⓜ ❀
(843) 479-1700. **$65-$85.** 213 US Hwy 15 & 401 Bypass E. US 15 and 401 Bypass. Ext corridors. **Pets:** $10 daily fee/room. Designated rooms, service with restrictions.
ⓈⒶⓋⒺ Ⓢ Ⓧ Ⓐ Ⓚ Ⓗ Ⓟ ⓐ

BLUFFTON

▼▼▼ Holiday Inn Express Hotel & Suites Ⓢ🅷
(843) 757-2002. **$79-$139.** 35 Bluffton Rd. Jct William Hilton Pkwy (US 278/Bluffton Rd US 46), just se. Int corridors. **Pets:** Large. $40 one-time fee/pet. Service with restrictions.
ⒶⓈⓀ Ⓢ Ⓧ Ⓜ Ⓚ Ⓗ Ⓟ ⓐ

CAMDEN

🆔 ▼▼ Colony Inn Ⓜ
(803) 432-5508. **$55-$59.** 2020 W DeKalb St. Jct US 521/1/601, 1.6 mi w on US 1/601. Ext/int corridors. **Pets:** Medium. $5 one-time fee/room. Designated rooms, service with restrictions, supervision.
ⓈⒶⓋⒺ Ⓢ Ⓧ Ⓣ ⓐ

CAYCE

🆔 ▼▼▼ Ramada Limited Airport Ⓢ🅷
(803) 794-7500. **$50-$59.** 3020 Charleston Hwy. I-26, exit 115 (US 21), just s. Ext corridors. **Pets:** Accepted.
ⓈⒶⓋⒺ Ⓢ Ⓧ Ⓚ Ⓗ Ⓟ ⓐ

🆔 ▼▼ Riverside Inn Ⓜ
(803) 939-4688. **$60-$65.** 111 Knox Abbott Dr. US 21, just w of Congaree River Bridge. Ext corridors. **Pets:** $20 one-time fee/room. Service with restrictions, supervision.
ⓈⒶⓋⒺ Ⓧ Ⓚ Ⓗ Ⓟ ⓐ Ⓧ

CHARLESTON METROPOLITAN AREA

CHARLESTON

▼▼▼▼▼ Best Western Sweetgrass Inn SH ❀
(843) 571-6100. **$49-$139, 3 day notice.** 1540 Savannah Hwy. US 17 S, 3.6 mi w of Ashley River Bridge; jct I-526 W (end) and US 17 N, 1.7 mi e. Ext corridors. **Pets:** Medium. $25 one-time fee/room. Service with restrictions, supervision.

ASK S🐾 ✕ 🛁 💻 ➔

▼▼▼ Howard Johnson Riverfront SH
(843) 722-4000. **$64-$149.** 250 Spring St. I-26, exit 221A (US 17 S), 1.2 mi sw; just e of Ashley River. Int corridors. **Pets:** $10 daily fee/room. Designated rooms, service with restrictions.

ASK S🐾 ✕ 🛁 💻 🍴 ➔

▼▼▼▼ Residence Inn by Marriott SH ❀
(843) 571-7979. **$89-$229.** 90 Ripley Point Dr. US 17 S, just over Ashley River Bridge to Albermarle Rd, then just s. Int corridors. **Pets:** $75 one-time fee/room.

ASK S🐾 ✕ 🅜 🏇 🐾 🛁 💻 ➔ ✕

▼▼▼▼▼ Town & Country Inn & Conference Center SH
(843) 571-1000. **Call for rates.** 2008 Savannah Hwy. US 17 S, 3.5 mi nw of Ashley River Bridge; jct I-526 W (end) and US 17 N, just se. Ext corridors. **Pets:** Accepted.

✕ 🛁 💻 🍴 ➔ ✕

MOUNT PLEASANT

▼▼ Comfort Inn East SH
(843) 884-5853. **$59-$129.** 310 Hwy 17 (Johnnie Dodds Blvd). US 17, 0.7 mi n of Cooper River Bridge. Ext corridors. **Pets:** Medium, dogs only. $10 one-time fee/pet. Service with restrictions, supervision.

ASK S🐾 ✕ 🛁 💻 ➔

▲▲▲ ▼▼▼▼ Homewood Suites by Hilton SH
(843) 881-6950. **$99-$189, 14 day notice.** 1998 Riviera Dr. I-526, exit 32 (Georgetown/US 17 N), 1.4 mi ne on US 17, 1 mi se on Isle of Palms connector (SR 517), then just sw. Int corridors. **Pets:** Small. $75 one-time fee/room. Service with restrictions, supervision.

SAVE S🐾 ✕ 🅜 🏇 🐾 🛁 💻 ➔ ✕

▼▼▼▼ MainStay Suites Mount Pleasant SH ❀
(843) 881-1722. **$59-$169.** 400 McGrath-Darby Blvd. Base of Cooper River Bridge, just ne on US 17, then just n. Int corridors. **Pets:** Dogs only. $10 daily fee/pet. Service with restrictions.

ASK S🐾 ✕ 🅜 🐾 🛁 💻 ➔

▼▼ Red Roof Inn M
(843) 884-1411. **$50-$83.** 301 Johnnie Dodds Blvd. Just e of base of Cooper River Bridge, on US 17, then just s on McGrath-Darby Blvd. Ext corridors. **Pets:** Medium. Service with restrictions, supervision.

✕ 🏇 🐾 🛁 ➔

▼▼▼▼ Residence Inn by Marriott SH ❀
(843) 881-1599. **$89-$199.** 1116 Isle of Palms Connector. I-526, exit 32 (Georgetown/US 17 N), 1.4 mi ne on US 17 to Isle of Palms connector (SR 517), then just se. Int corridors. **Pets:** Other species. $75 one-time fee/room. Designated rooms, service with restrictions.

ASK S🐾 ✕ 🅜 🛁 💻 ➔ ✕

▼▼ Sleep Inn Mt Pleasant SH
(843) 856-5000. **$49-$139.** 299 Wingo Way. Just e of base of Cooper River Bridge, then just n at McGrath-Darby Blvd. Int corridors. **Pets:** Accepted.

ASK S🐾 ✕ 🅜 🏇 🐾 🛁 💻 ➔

NORTH CHARLESTON

▲▲▲ ▼▼▼▼ Best Western Charleston Airport Hotel SH
(843) 744-1621. **$59-$99.** 6099 Fain St. I-26, exit 211A (Aviation Ave), just w. Ext corridors. **Pets:** Medium, other species. $25 one-time fee/pet. Designated rooms, service with restrictions.

SAVE S🐾 ✕ 🏇 🛁 💻 🍴 ➔

▲▲▲ ▼▼▼▼ Charleston Super 8 Motel M
(843) 572-2228. **$54-$119.** 2311 Ashley Phosphate Rd. I-26, exit 209 (Ashley Phosphate Rd), just e. Ext corridors. **Pets:** Accepted.

SAVE S🐾 ✕ 🛁 ➔

▼▼▼ Comfort Inn Coliseum SH
(843) 554-6485. **$70-$80.** 5055 N Arco Ln. I-26, exit 213 westbound; exit 213A eastbound, just s, then n. Ext corridors. **Pets:** Accepted.

ASK S🐾 ✕ 🏇 🛁 💻 ➔

▼▼▼ Homestead Studio Suites
Hotel-Charleston/Airport SH
(843) 740-3440. **$94-$104.** 5045 N Arco Ln. I-26, exit 213 westbound; exit 213A eastbound, just s, then n. Int corridors. **Pets:** Accepted.

ASK S🐾 ✕ 🅜 🏇 🐾 🛁 💻 ➔

▼▼▼▼ La Quinta Inn Charleston SH
(843) 797-8181. **$66-$90.** 2499 La Quinta Ln. I-26, exit 209 (Ashley Phosphate Rd), just w. Ext corridors. **Pets:** Accepted.

ASK ✕ 🏇 🛁 💻 ➔

▼▼ Motel 6 #642 M
(843) 572-6590. **$43-$53.** 2551 Ashley Phosphate Rd. I-26, exit 209 (Ashley Phosphate Rd), just w. Ext corridors. **Pets:** Accepted.

S🐾 ✕ 🐾 ➔

▼▼ Red Roof Inn M 🐾
(843) 572-9100. **$48-$69.** 7480 Northwoods Blvd. I-26, exit 209 (Ashley Phosphate Rd), just e, then just n. Ext corridors. **Pets:** Medium, other species. Service with restrictions, crate.

✕ 🏇 🐾 🛁

▼▼▼▼ Residence Inn by Marriott SH
(843) 572-5757. **$126-$166.** 7645 Northwoods Blvd. I-26, exit 209 (Ashley Phosphate Rd), just e, then n. Ext corridors. **Pets:** Accepted.

ASK S🐾 ✕ 🏇 🛁 💻 ➔ ✕

▲▲▲ ▼▼▼▼ Sheraton Hotel North Charleston Convention
Center LH 🐾
(843) 747-1900. **$89-$109.** 4770 Goer Dr. I-26, exit 213 westbound; exit 213B eastbound, just n. Int corridors. **Pets:** Medium, dogs only. $25 one-time fee/pet. Service with restrictions, supervision.

SAVE S🐾 ✕ 🏇 🛁 💻 🍴 ➔

▼▼ Sleep Inn Charleston North SH
(843) 572-8400. **$49-$119.** 7435 Northside Dr. I-26, exit 209 (Ashley Phosphate Rd), just w. Int corridors. **Pets:** Accepted.

ASK S🐾 ✕ 🛁 💻

ST. STEPHEN

▼▼ Econo Lodge SH
(843) 567-7397. **$66-$76.** 3986 Byrnes Dr. Center. Int corridors. **Pets:** Accepted.

ASK S🐾 ✕ 🛁 💻 ➔

SUMMERVILLE

AAA ▼▼▼ **Holiday Inn**

Express-Charleston/Summerville SH ☘
(843) 875-3300. **$62-$82.** 120 Holiday Inn Dr. I-26, exit 199A (US 17 alternate route), just w. Int corridors. **Pets:** Service with restrictions.

SAVE 🖎 ✕ ᘒM ⌔ ᶜ 💻 🛁

AAA ▼▼▼▼ **Woodlands Resort & Inn** CI ☘
(843) 875-2600. **$295-$450, 7 day notice.** 125 Parsons Rd. I-26, exit 199A, 2 mi s on US 17 alternate route, 1.5 mi w on W Richardson Ave (SR 165), then just s. Int corridors. **Pets:** Accepted.

SAVE 🖎 ✕ ⌔ ▯ 🍽 🛁 🕲

END METROPOLITAN AREA

CHERAW

AAA ▼▼ **Days Inn** M
(843) 537-5554. **$50-$110.** 820 Market St. US 52 and 1, jct SR 9. Ext corridors. **Pets:** Accepted.

SAVE 🖎 ✕ ▯ 💻 🛁

▼▼ **Jameson Inn** M
(843) 537-5625. **$49-$104.** 885 Chesterfield Hwy. Jct US 1 and 52, 1.5 mi n on SR 9. Ext corridors. **Pets:** Very small, other species. $10 daily fee/room. Service with restrictions, supervision.

ASK ✕ ᶜ ▯ 💻 🛁

CLEMSON

AAA ▼▼▼ **Comfort Inn-Clemson** SH
(864) 653-3600. **$79-$151, 7 day notice.** 1305 Tiger Blvd. Jct US 76 and 123. Int corridors. **Pets:** Small. $10 daily fee/room. Service with restrictions.

SAVE 🖎 ✕ ⌔ ▯ 💻 🛁

AAA ▼▼▼ **Ramada Inn of Clemson** SH
(864) 654-7501. **$64-$89.** 1310 Tiger Blvd. Jct US 76 and 123. Int corridors. **Pets:** Accepted.

SAVE 🖎 ✕ ᶜ ▯ 💻 🍽 🛁 🕲

CLINTON

AAA ▼▼▼ **Comfort Inn** SH
(864) 833-5558. **$69-$89.** 105 Trade St. I-26, exit 52, just e, then n. Ext corridors. **Pets:** Small. $10 daily fee/pet. Designated rooms, service with restrictions, supervision.

SAVE 🖎 ✕ ⌔ ▯ 💻 🛁

AAA ▼▼▼ **Days Inn** SH ☘
(864) 833-6600. **$55-$69.** 12374 Hwy 56 N. I-26, exit 52, just w. Ext corridors. **Pets:** Medium. $10 daily fee/pet. Designated rooms, service with restrictions.

SAVE 🖎 ✕ ▯ 💻 🛁

COLUMBIA

AAA ▼▼▼▼ **AmeriSuites (Columbia/Northeast)** SH
(803) 736-6666. **$99-$119.** 7525 Two Notch Rd. I-20, exit 74 (Two Notch Rd), just n; I-77, exit 17 (Two Notch Rd), 0.5 mi s. Int corridors. **Pets:** Small, dogs only. $10 daily fee/pet. Service with restrictions, supervision.

SAVE 🖎 ✕ ⌔ ᶜ ▯ 💻 🛁

AAA ▼▼▼ **Baymont Inn & Suites Columbia NE/Ft. Jackson Area** SH
(803) 736-6400. **$49-$75.** 1538 Horseshoe Dr. I-20, exit 74 (Two Notch Rd), just n; I-77, exit 17 (Two Notch Rd), 0.5 mi s. Int corridors. **Pets:** Accepted.

SAVE 🖎 ✕ ⌔ ▯ 💻 🛁

▼▼ **Best Inn** SH
(803) 798-9590. **Call for rates.** 1335 Garner Ln. I-20, exit 65 (US 176), just ne. Ext corridors. **Pets:** Accepted.

✕ ⌔ ▯ 💻 🛁

▼▼▼ **Chestnut Cottage Bed & Breakfast** BB
(803) 256-1718. **$110-$225, 14 day notice.** 1718 Hampton St. SR 12 (Taylor St), just s; between Henderson and Barnwell sts. Int corridors. **Pets:** Accepted.

ASK 🖎 ✕ ▯ 💻

▼▼▼ **Columbiana Hotel and Conference Center** LH
(803) 731-0300. **$84-$209.** 2100 Bush River Rd. I-20, exit 63 (Bush River Rd), just e; I-26, exit 108, 0.7 mi w. Int corridors. **Pets:** Accepted.

✕ ⌔ ᶜ ▯ 💻 🍽 🛁 🕲

▼▼▼ **Days Inn** SH
(803) 798-5101. **Call for rates.** 911 Bush River Rd. I-26, exit 108 (Bush River Rd), just e. Int corridors. **Pets:** Accepted.

✕ ⌔ ▯ 💻 🛁

▼▼ **Days Inn** M
(803) 754-4408. **$55-$65.** 133 Plumbers Rd. I-20, exit 71 (Wilson Blvd), just n, then just e. Ext corridors. **Pets:** Small. $8 daily fee/pet. Designated rooms, service with restrictions, supervision.

ASK 🖎 ✕ 🛁

AAA ▼▼▼▼ **Holiday Inn Express Hotel & Suites** SH
(803) 419-3558. **$70.** 1011 Clemson Frontage Rd. I-20, exit 80 (Clemson Rd), just n. Int corridors. **Pets:** Accepted.

SAVE 🖎 ᶜ ▯ 💻 🛁

AAA ▼▼▼▼ **Holiday Inn-Northeast** SH
(803) 736-3000. **$89-$99, 3 day notice.** 7510 Two Notch Rd. I-20, exit 74 (Two Notch Rd), just n; I-77, exit 17 (Two Notch Rd), 0.5 mi s. Int corridors. **Pets:** Accepted.

SAVE ✕ ▯ 💻 🍽 🛁 🕲

AAA ▼▼▼ **Microtel Inn** SH
(803) 736-3237. **$50-$55.** 1520 Barbara Dr. I-20, exit 74 (Two Notch Rd), just n; I-77, exit 17 (Two Notch Rd), 0.5 mi s. Int corridors. **Pets:** $7 daily fee/pet. Designated rooms, no service, supervision.

SAVE 🖎 ✕ ⌔ ᶜ ▯

▼▼ **Microtel Inn & Suites Harbison Area** SH
(803) 772-1914. **$50-$60, 5 day notice.** 411 Piney Grove Rd. I-26, exit 104 (Piney Grove Rd), just sw. Int corridors. **Pets:** Accepted.

ASK 🖎 ✕ ᘒM ⌔ ▯ 💻

▼ **Motel 6 #1291** SH
(803) 736-3900. **$43-$53.** 7541 Nates Rd. I-20, exit 74 (Two Notch Rd), just n, then just e; I-77, exit 17 (Two Notch Rd), 0.5 mi s, then e. Int corridors. **Pets:** Accepted.

🖎 ✕ ᘒM ᶜ 🛁

▼▼▼ **Ramada Plaza Hotel** SH
(803) 736-5600. **$94.** 8105 Two Notch Rd. I-77, exit 17 (Two Notch Rd), just ne. Int corridors. **Pets:** Medium, other species. $75 deposit/room.

ASK ✕ ⌔ ▯ 💻 🍽 🛁 🕲

▼ **Red Roof Inn-West** M
(803) 798-9220. **$38-$45.** 10 Berryhill Rd. I-26, exit 106A westbound; exit 106 eastbound, just w. Ext corridors. **Pets:** Accepted.

✕ ⌔ ▯

▼▼▼▼ **Residence Inn by Marriott** 🆂🅷
(803) 779-7000. **$89-$179.** 150 Stoneridge Dr. I-126, exit Greystone Blvd, just n, then just e. Ext corridors. **Pets:** Medium, other species. $10 daily fee/room, $50 one-time fee/room. Service with restrictions, crate.
[A$K] [S🐾] [✕] [✍] [📋] [💻] [🏊] [✕]

▼▼ ▼▼ **Super 8** 🆂🅷
(803) 772-7275. **$55-$120.** 773 St Andrews Rd. I-26, exit 106A westbound; exit 106 eastbound, just w. Ext corridors. **Pets:** Small. $10 daily fee/pet. Service with restrictions, supervision.
[A$K] [S🐾] [✕] [📋] [💻] [🏊]

▼▼▼▼ **TownePlace Suites by Marriott** 🆂🅷 🐾
(803) 781-9391. **$44-$79.** 350 Columbiana Dr. I-26, exit 103 (Harbison Blvd), just sw to Columbiana Dr, then 0.7 mi nw. Int corridors. **Pets:** Other species. $75 one-time fee/room. Service with restrictions, crate.
[A$K] [S🐾] [✕] [♿M] [📋] [💻] [🏊]

DUNCAN

▼▼▼ **Days Inn** 🆂🅷
(864) 433-1122. **$49-$74.** 1386 E Main St. I-85, exit 63, just w on SR 290. Ext corridors. **Pets:** Small. $25 one-time fee/room. Service with restrictions, supervision.
[A$K] [✕] [✍] [📋] [💻] [🏊]

🆂🅷🆂 ▼▼▼ **Quality Inn** 🆂🅷
(864) 433-1333. **$50-$60.** 1391 E Main St. I-85, exit 63, just w. Ext corridors. **Pets:** Accepted.
[SAVE] [S🐾] [✕] [📋] [💻] [🏊]

EASLEY

▼▼ ▼▼ **Jameson Inn** 🆂🅷
(864) 306-9000. **$49-$104.** 211 Dayton School Rd. Jct US 123 and SR 93, 1.2 mi ne on US 123; jct US 123 and SR 153, 1.5 mi sw. Ext corridors. **Pets:** Very small, other species. $10 daily fee/room. Service with restrictions, supervision.
[A$K] [✕] [♿] [📋] [💻] [🏊]

FLORENCE

🆂🅷🆂 ▼▼ ▼▼ **Comfort Inn** 🅼
(843) 665-4558. **$50-$89.** 1916 W Lucas St. I-95, exit 164, just e on US 52. Ext/int corridors. **Pets:** Accepted.
[SAVE] [S🐾] [✕] [📋] [💻] [🏊]

🆂🅷🆂 ▼▼ **Country Hearth Inn** 🅼 🐾
(843) 662-9421. **$45-$58.** 831 S Irby St. 1.3 mi s on US 301 and 52. Ext corridors. **Pets:** Medium. Designated rooms, service with restrictions, supervision.
[SAVE] [✕] [📋] [💻] [🍽] [🏊]

▼▼ ▼▼ **Days Inn Florence** 🆂🅷
(843) 665-4444. **$150.** 2111 W Lucas St. I-95, exit 164, just nw. Ext corridors. **Pets:** Medium, other species. Service with restrictions, supervision.
[A$K] [S🐾] [✕] [📋] [🏊] [✕]

🆂🅷🆂 ▼▼ ▼▼ **Econo Lodge** 🅼
(843) 665-8558. **$39-$45.** 1811 W Lucas St. I-95, exit 164, just e. Ext corridors. **Pets:** Accepted.
[SAVE] [S🐾] [✕] [📋] [💻] [🏊]

▼▼ ▼▼ **Holiday Inn Express Civic Center** 🅼 🐾
(843) 664-2400. **Call for rates.** 150 Dunbarton Dr. I-95, exit 160A, just e, then just n. Ext corridors. **Pets:** Medium. Service with restrictions.
[✕] [✍] [♿] [📋] [💻] [🏊]

🆂🅷🆂 ▼▼▼▼ **Holiday Inn Hotel & Suites** 🆂🅷
(843) 665-4555. **$69.** 1819 W Lucas St. I-95, exit 164, just e on US 52. Ext corridors. **Pets:** Accepted.
[SAVE] [S🐾] [✕] [♿M] [✍] [♿] [📋] [💻] [🍽] [🏊]

🆂🅷🆂 ▼▼ ▼▼ **Howard Johnson Express Inn &**
Suites 🅼 🐾
(843) 664-9494. **$95, 30 day notice.** 3821 Bancroft Rd. I-95, exit 157, 0.4 mi e on US 76. Ext corridors. **Pets:** Medium, other species. $10 one-time fee/room. No service, supervision.
[SAVE] [S🐾] [✕] [♿] [📋] [💻] [🏊]

▼▼ **Motel 6 #1250** 🅼
(843) 667-6100. **$37-$51.** 1834 W Lucas St. I-95, exit 164, just e. Ext corridors. **Pets:** Accepted.
[S🐾] [✕] [♿] [🏊]

🆂🅷🆂 ▼▼ ▼▼ **Ramada Inn** 🆂🅷 🐾
(843) 669-4241. **$69-$75.** 2038 W Lucas St. I-95, exit 164, just w. Ext/int corridors. **Pets:** Other species. Designated rooms, service with restrictions, supervision.
[SAVE] [S🐾] [✕] [📋] [💻] [🍽] [🏊] [✕]

▼▼ ▼▼ **Red Roof Inn** 🅼
(843) 678-9000. **$41-$55.** 2690 David McLeod Blvd. I-95, exit 160A, just e on service road. Ext corridors. **Pets:** Medium. Service with restrictions, supervision.
[✕] [♿M] [✍] [♿]

🆂🅷🆂 ▼▼ ▼▼ **Thunderbird Inn** 🅼
(843) 669-1611. **$45-$53.** 2004 W Lucas St. I-95, exit 164, just w. Ext corridors. **Pets:** Accepted.
[SAVE] [✕] [📋] [🍽] [🏊]

GAFFNEY

▼▼ ▼▼ **Comfort Inn** 🅼
(864) 487-4200. **$60-$70.** 143 Corona Dr. I-85, exit 92, just w of SR 11. Ext corridors. **Pets:** $10 one-time fee/room. Service with restrictions, supervision.
[A$K] [S🐾] [✕] [✍] [📋] [💻] [🏊]

▼▼ ▼▼ **Jameson Inn** 🅼
(864) 489-0240. **$49-$104.** 101 Stuard St. I-85, exit 92, just e at jct SR 11. Ext corridors. **Pets:** Very small, other species. $10 daily fee/room. Service with restrictions, supervision.
[A$K] [✕] [♿] [📋] [💻] [🏊]

THE GRAND STRAND AREA

GEORGETOWN

△△△ ▽▽▽ Carolinian Inn M
(843) 546-5191. **$54-$79.** 706 Church St. US 17, 0.7 mi se of jct US 17/17 alternate route/701. Ext corridors. **Pets:** Medium. Service with restrictions.
[SAVE] [S♦] [✕] [🐾] [🛏] [💻] [≈]

▽▽▽ Jameson Inn Georgetown M
(843) 546-6090. **$49-$104.** 120 Church St. US 17, just w of the Intracoastal Waterway Bridge. Ext corridors. **Pets:** Very small, other species. $10 daily fee/room. Service with restrictions, supervision.
[ASK] [✕] [🐾] [🖊] [🛏] [💻] [≈]

▽▽▽ Winyah Bay Inn Bed & Breakfast BB
(843) 546-0464. **$95-$135 (no credit cards), 10 day notice.** 3030 South Island Rd. 0.5 mi s of Sylvan L Rosen Bridge on US 17, 2 mi e. Ext/int corridors. **Pets:** Accepted.
[ASK] [S♦] [✕] [🛏] [💻] [✏]

LITTLE RIVER

▽▽▽ Holiday Inn Hotel & Suites-North Myrtle Beach SH ☆
(843) 281-9400. **$39-$299.** 722 Hwy 17. At Coquina Harbor. Int corridors. **Pets:** $35 one-time fee/room. Service with restrictions, supervision.
[ASK] [S♦] [✕] [🛏] [💻] [🍴] [≈]

MYRTLE BEACH

△△△ ▽▽▽ A Summer Wind M
(843) 946-6960. **$31-$159, 3 day notice.** 1903 S Ocean Blvd. Jct 19th Ave S. Ext corridors. **Pets:** Small. $25 one-time fee/pet. Designated rooms, service with restrictions, crate.
[SAVE] [S♦] [✕] [🛏] [≈]

△△△ ▽▽▽ El Dorado Motel M
(843) 626-3559. **$35-$135, 10 day notice.** 2800 S Ocean Blvd. Jct 28th Ave S. Ext corridors. **Pets:** Small. $25 one-time fee/pet. Service with restrictions.
[SAVE] [S♦] [✕] [🛏] [💻] [≈] [✕]

△△△ ▽ Hurl Rock Motel M
(843) 626-3531. **$22-$98, 14 day notice.** 2010 S Ocean Blvd. Jct 21st Ave S. Ext corridors. **Pets:** Small, dogs only. $25 one-time fee/room. Designated rooms, no service, supervision.
[SAVE] [✕] [🛏] [≈]

▽▽▽ La Quinta Inn & Suites Myrtle Beach SH
(843) 916-8801. **$75-$185.** 1561 21st Ave N. US 17 Bypass, just e. Int corridors. **Pets:** Small. Service with restrictions, supervision.
[ASK] [✕] [⚙M] [🐾] [🖊] [🛏] [💻] [≈]

△△△ ▽▽▽ Mariner M ☆
(843) 449-5281. **$29-$149.** 7003 N Ocean Blvd. Jct 71st Ave N. Ext corridors. **Pets:** Dogs only. $9 daily fee/pet. Service with restrictions.
[SAVE] [S♦] [✕] [🛏] [💻] [≈] [✕]

▽▽▽ Red Roof Inn & Suites SH
(843) 626-4444. **$32-$99.** 2801 S Kings Hwy. 28th Ave S and US 17 business route. Int corridors. **Pets:** No service, supervision.
[✕] [🖊] [🛏] [💻] [≈]

△△△ ▽▽▽ St. John's Inn M
(843) 449-5251. **$36-$99, 7 day notice.** 6803 N Ocean Blvd. Jct 68th Ave N. Ext corridors. **Pets:** Medium, dogs only. $50 deposit/pet, $10 daily fee/pet. Designated rooms, service with restrictions, supervision.
[SAVE] [S♦] [✕] [🛏] [≈] [✕]

△△△ ▽▽▽ Sea Mist Oceanfront Resort LH ☆
(843) 448-1551. **$26-$192, 14 day notice.** 1200 S Ocean Blvd. Jct 12th Ave S. Ext/int corridors. **Pets:** $50 one-time fee/pet. Designated rooms, service with restrictions, crate.
[SAVE] [✕] [🐾] [🖊] [🛏] [🍴] [≈] [✕]

▽▽▽ Staybridge Suites-Fantasy Harbour SH ☆
(843) 903-4000. **$69-$169.** 3163 Outlet Blvd. Jct US 17 Bypass, 0.7 mi n on US 501, exit River Oaks Rd/George Bishop Pkwy, just w on River Oaks Rd, then 0.4 mi s. Int corridors. **Pets:** Medium. $12 daily fee/room. Designated rooms, service with restrictions, crate.
[ASK] [S♦] [✕] [🐾] [🖊] [🛏] [💻] [≈] [✕]

NORTH MYRTLE BEACH

▽▽ Red Roof Inn SH
(843) 280-4555. **Call for rates.** 1601-B US 17 N. Jct SR 9, just s. Int corridors. **Pets:** Accepted.
[✕] [🖊] [🛏] [≈]

PAWLEYS ISLAND

▽▽ Best Western Hammock Inn M ☆
(843) 237-4261. **$60-$135.** 7903 Ocean Hwy. 1 mi s on US 17. Ext corridors. **Pets:** Medium. Service with restrictions, supervision.
[ASK] [S♦] [✕] [🛏] [💻] [≈]

END AREA

GREENVILLE

△△△ ▽▽▽▽ AmeriSuites (Greenville/Haywood) SH
(864) 232-3000. **$71-$119.** 40 W Orchard Park Dr. I-385, exit 39 (Haywood Rd), just n, then w. Int corridors. **Pets:** Medium, other species. $25 one-time fee/pet. Service with restrictions, supervision.
[SAVE] [S♦] [✕] [⚙M] [🐾] [🖊] [🛏] [💻] [≈]

△△△ ▽▽▽ Comfort Inn Executive Center SH ☆
(864) 271-0060. **$45-$65.** 540 N Pleasantburg Dr. I-385, exit 40B, just w, then just s. Ext corridors. **Pets:** Other species. $15 one-time fee/room. Service with restrictions.
[SAVE] [S♦] [✕] [🐾] [🛏] [≈]

▽▽▽▽ Crowne Plaza Hotel and Resort Greenville SH
(864) 297-6300. **$98, 3 day notice.** 851 Congaree Rd. I-385, exit 37, just w, then n. Int corridors. **Pets:** Medium, other species. $50 one-time fee/room. Service with restrictions, supervision.
[ASK] [S♦] [✕] [⚙M] [🐾] [🖊] [🛏] [💻] [🍴] [≈] [✕]

▽▽ Days Inn SH
(864) 288-6900. **$60-$74, 7 day notice.** 2756 Laurens Rd. I-85, exit 48B, just nw; entry between auto dealership. Int corridors. **Pets:** Small. $10 daily fee/pet. Service with restrictions, supervision.
[ASK] [S♦] [✕] [🛏] [💻] [≈]

▽▽▽▽ Hilton Greenville 🆂🅷
(864) 232-4747. **$99-$169, 3 day notice.** 45 W Orchard Park Dr. I-385, exit 39 (Haywood Rd), just n, then w. Int corridors. **Pets:** Accepted.
🅰🆂🅺 🆂🖧 ⊠ 🔊M 🖉 📧 🖥 🖳 ⑪ 🏊 ⊠

▽▽▽▽ Holiday Inn Express Hotel & Suites 🆂🅷
(864) 213-9331. **$88.** 2681 Dry Pocket Rd. I-85, exit 54 (Pelham Rd), just nw, 0.3 mi ne on The Parkway to Parkway Rd, then 0.3 mi e. Int corridors. **Pets:** Medium, other species. $15 one-time fee/pet. Service with restrictions, crate.
🅰🆂🅺 🆂🖧 ⊠ 🖉 🔊 📧 🖥 🖳 🏊 ⊠

▽▽▽▽ Holiday Inn Express Hotel & Suites-I-85/385 🆂🅷
(864) 678-5555. **$97-$127.** 1036 Woodruff Rd. I-85, exit 51A, 0.5 mi n on SR 146. Int corridors. **Pets:** Accepted.
🅰🆂🅺 🆂🖧 ⊠ 🔊M 🖉 🔊 📧 🖥 🖳

▽▽▽▽ Holiday Inn I-85/Augusta Rd 🆂🅷
(864) 277-8921. **$78-$108.** 4295 Augusta Rd. I-85, exit 46A, just se. Int corridors. **Pets:** Large, other species. $30 one-time fee/pet. Service with restrictions, crate.
🅰🆂🅺 ⊠ 🔊M 🖉 🔊 📧 🖥 🖳 ⑪ 🏊

▽▽▽▽ La Quinta Inn Greenville (Woodruff Rd.) 🆂🅷
(864) 297-3500. **$65-$75.** 31 Old Country Rd. I-85, exit 51A, just n on SR 146. Ext corridors. **Pets:** Accepted.
🅰🆂🅺 ⊠ 🖉 📧 🖥 🖳 🏊

▽🔷▽ La Quinta Inns & Suites Greenville (Haywood) 🆂🅷
(864) 233-8018. **$69-$89.** 65 W Orchard Park Dr. I-385, exit 39 (Haywood Rd), just n, then w. Int corridors. **Pets:** Accepted.
🅰🆂🅺 ⊠ 🖉 🔊 📧 🖥 🖳 🏊 ⊠

▽🔷🔷 MainStay Suites-Greenville 🆂🅷
(864) 987-5566. **$74-$84.** 2671 Dry Pocket Rd. I-85, exit 54 (Pelham Rd), just nw on Pelham Rd, 0.3 mi ne on The Parkway to Parkway Rd, then 0.3 mi e. Int corridors. **Pets:** Other species. $10 daily fee/pet. Service with restrictions, crate.
🅰🆂🅺 ⊠ 🖉 🔊 📧 🖥 🖳 🏊 ⊠

▽🔷🔷 Marriott Hotel Greenville/Spartanburg Airport 🆂🅷
(864) 297-0300. **$66-$115.** 1 Parkway E. I-85, exit 54 (Pelham Rd), just n, then e. Int corridors. **Pets:** Accepted.
🅰🆂🅺 🆂🖧 ⊠ 🔊M 🖉 🔊 📧 🖥 🖳 ⑪ 🏊 ⊠

▽▽ Microtel Inn & Suites 🆂🅷
(864) 297-3811. **$42-$59.** 1024 Woodruff Rd. I-85, exit 51A, 0.5 mi n on SR 146. Int corridors. **Pets:** Other species. $25 one-time fee/room. Service with restrictions, supervision.
🅰🆂🅺 🆂🖧 ⊠ 🔊 📧 🖥 🖳

🔷🔷🔷 ▽▽▽ The Phoenix Greenville's Inn 🆂🅷
(864) 233-4651. **$75-$109, 3 day notice.** 246 N Pleasanturg Dr. I-385, exit 40B, 0.6 mi s on SR 291. Ext corridors. **Pets:** Other species. Designated rooms, service with restrictions, supervision.
🆂🅰🆅🅴 ⊠ 🔊 📧 🖥 🖳 ⑪ 🏊

▽▽ Red Roof Inn Ⓜ
(864) 297-4458. **$41-$61.** 2801 Laurens Rd. I-85, exit 48A, just s on frontage road to dead end. Ext corridors. **Pets:** Medium, other species. Service with restrictions, supervision.
⊠ 🖉

🔷🔷🔷 ▽▽▽ Sleep Inn Palmetto Expo Center 🆂🅷 🐾
(864) 240-2006. **$64-$109, 3 day notice.** 231 N Pleasanturg Dr. I-385, exit 40B, 0.6 mi s on SR 291. Int corridors. **Pets:** Medium. $20 one-time fee/room. Service with restrictions, supervision.
🆂🅰🆅🅴 🆂🖧 ⊠ 🔊M 📧 🖥 🖳

GREENWOOD

▽▽ Days Inn 🆂🅷
(864) 223-1818. **$50-$55.** 230 Birchtree Dr. Jct US 25/US 25 Bypass (SR 72 NE), just ne on US 25 Bypass (SR 72 NE), then just s. Int corridors. **Pets:** Accepted.
🅰🆂🅺 🆂🖧 ⊠ 📧 🖥 🖳

GREER

▽▽ Super 8 Motel 🆂🅷
(864) 848-1626. **$50-$55, 30 day notice.** 1515 Hwy 101 S. I-85, exit 60, just nw. Int corridors. **Pets:** Accepted.
🅰🆂🅺 🆂🖧 ⊠ 🔊M 🔊 📧 🖥 🏊

HARDEEVILLE

🔷🔷🔷 ▽▽▽ Comfort Inn 🆂🅷
(843) 784-2188. **$59-$89.** US 17 & I-95. I-95, exit 5 (US 17), just n. Ext/int corridors. **Pets:** Accepted.
🆂🅰🆅🅴 🆂🖧 ⊠ 🖳 🏊

▽▽▽▽ Quality Inn & Suites 🆂🅷
(843) 784-7060. **$55-$91.** I-95 & Hwy 17. I-95, exit 5 (US 17), just n. Ext corridors. **Pets:** Accepted.
🅰🆂🅺 🆂🖧 ⊠ 🔊M 🔊 📧 🖥 🖳

🔷🔷🔷 ▽▽▽ Sleep Inn Hardeeville 🆂🅷 🐾
(843) 784-7181. **$69-$109.** I-95 & US 17. I-95, exit 5 (US 17), just se. Int corridors. **Pets:** Medium. $7 daily fee/pet. Service with restrictions, supervision.
🆂🅰🆅🅴 🆂🖧 ⊠ 🔊M 🔊 🏊

HILTON HEAD ISLAND

🔷🔷🔷 ▽▽▽ Comfort Inn 🆂🅷
(843) 842-6662. **$49-$139.** 2 Tanglewood Dr. Sea Pines Circle, 1.1 mi se on Pope Ave, then just sw; at Coligny Plaza. Int corridors. **Pets:** Accepted.
🆂🅰🆅🅴 🆂🖧 ⊠ 🖉 📧 🖥 🖳 ⑪ 🏊 ⊠

🔷🔷🔷 ▽▽▽▽ Holiday Inn Express 🆂🅷
(843) 842-8888. **$60-$200.** 40 Waterside Dr. Sea Pines Circle, 0.7 mi se on Pope Rd, then just e. Ext corridors. **Pets:** Accepted.
🆂🅰🆅🅴 🆂🖧 ⊠ 🖉 🔊 📧 🖥 🖳 🏊

▽▽ Motel 6-#1129 Ⓜ 🐾
(843) 785-2700. **$45-$61.** 830 William Hilton Pkwy. J Wilton Graves Bridge, 9 mi e on US 278 business route. Ext corridors. **Pets:** Other species. No service, supervision.
🆂🖧 🖉 🔊 📧 🖥 🖳 🏊

▽▽▽▽ Quality Inn & Suites of Hilton Head Island 🆂🅷
(843) 681-3655. **$60-$150.** 200 Museum St. 3.3 mi e of J Wilton Graves Bridge on US 278 business route. Ext corridors. **Pets:** Small. $25 one-time fee/room. Designated rooms, service with restrictions, crate.
🅰🆂🅺 🆂🖧 ⊠ 🔊 📧 🖥 🖳

▽▽ Red Roof Inn-Hilton Head Ⓜ
(843) 686-6808. **$48-$88.** 5 Regency Pkwy. Over bridge, 9 mi e on US 278 business route; between Shipyard Plantation and Palmetto Dunes. Ext corridors. **Pets:** Accepted.
⊠ 🖉 📧 🏊

IRMO

🔷🔷🔷 ▽▽▽ AmeriSuites (Columbia/I-26) 🆂🅷
(803) 407-1560. **$99-$119.** 1130 Kinley Rd. I-26, exit 102B, just e, then n. Int corridors. **Pets:** Very small, dogs only. $10 daily fee/pet. Designated rooms, service with restrictions, supervision.
🆂🅰🆅🅴 🆂🖧 ⊠ 🔊M 🖉 🔊 📧 🖥 🖳 🏊

🔷🔷🔷 ▽▽▽ Wellesley Inn & Suites (Columbia/I-26) 🆂🅷
(803) 781-8590. **$89-$109.** 1170 Kinley Rd. I-26, exit 102B, just e, then n. Int corridors. **Pets:** Accepted.
🆂🅰🆅🅴 🆂🖧 ⊠ 🔊M 🖉 🔊 📧 🖥 🖳 🏊

LANCASTER

▽▽ Jameson Inn Ⓜ
(803) 283-1188. **$49-$104.** 114 Commerce Blvd. Jct SR 9 Bypass and US 521, 1 mi w on SR 9 Bypass. Ext corridors. **Pets:** Very small, other species. $10 daily fee/room. Service with restrictions, supervision.
🅰🆂🅺 ⊠ 🔊M 🖉 🔊 📧 🖥 🖳

LANDRUM

▼▼▼ The Red Horse Inn [CA] ♣
(864) 909-1575. **$110-$210, 7 day notice.** 310 N Campbell Rd. Jct SR 14, 1 mi w on SR 11 S, 1 mi s on Tugaloo Rd, then 1 mi e. Ext corridors. **Pets:** Medium. $20 one-time fee/pet. Designated rooms, service with restrictions, supervision.
[ASK] [S₆] [✕] [🛏] [💻] [⊠]

LUGOFF

▼▼ Best Western Camden West [SH]
(803) 438-9441. **$59-$109.** 850 Hwy 1 S. I-20, exit 92 (US 601), 2.9 mi n. Ext corridors. **Pets:** Other species. $25 one-time fee/room. Service with restrictions, supervision.
[ASK] [S₆] [✕] [🛁] [💻] [🍴] [≈]

▼▼ Ramada Limited [M]
(803) 438-1807. **$59.** 542 Hwy 601 S. I-20, exit 92 (US 601), just n. Ext corridors. **Pets:** Small. $10 one-time fee/pet. Designated rooms, service with restrictions, supervision.
[ASK] [S₆] [✕] [🛏] [💻] [≈]

MANNING

[AAA] ▼▼▼ Best Western Palmetto Inn [SH] ♣
(803) 473-4021. **$59-$99.** 2825 Paxville Hwy. I-95, exit 119 (SR 261), just se. Ext corridors. **Pets:** Medium. $5 one-time fee/room. Service with restrictions.
[SAVE] [S₆] [✕] [🛏] [💻] [≈]

[AAA] ▼▼▼ Comfort Inn [SH]
(803) 473-7550. **$59-$79.** 3031 Paxville Hwy. I-95, exit 119 (SR 261), just se. Ext corridors. **Pets:** Small, other species. $9 one-time fee/room. Designated rooms, service with restrictions.
[SAVE] [✕] [🛁] [🛏] [💻] [≈]

[AAA] ▼▼▼ Ramada Limited [SH]
(803) 473-5135. **$54-$130.** 2816 Paxville Hwy. I-95, exit 119 (SR 261), just se. Ext corridors. **Pets:** Accepted.
[SAVE] [S₆] [✕] [🛁] [🛏] [💻] [≈]

NEWBERRY

[AAA] ▼▼▼ Best Western Newberry Inn [SH]
(803) 276-5850. **$55-$65.** 11701 S Carolina Hwy 34. I-26, exit 74 (SR 34), just ne. Ext corridors. **Pets:** Small. $5 daily fee/pet. Service with restrictions, supervision.
[SAVE] [S₆] [✕] [🛏] [💻] [≈]

ORANGEBURG

[AAA] ▼▼▼ Comfort Inn & Suites [SH]
(803) 531-9200. **$73-$160.** 3671 St Matthews Rd. I-26, exit 145A (US 601), just sw. Ext corridors. **Pets:** Other species. $10 one-time fee/room. Designated rooms, service with restrictions.
[SAVE] [S₆] [✕] [🛁] [🛏] [💻] [≈]

[AAA] ▼▼▼ Days Inn [SH]
(803) 534-0500. **$58-$86.** 3402 Five Chop Rd. I-26, exit 154B (US 301), just e. Ext corridors. **Pets:** Accepted.
[SAVE] [S₆] [✕] [🛁] [🛏] [💻] [🍴] [≈]

▼▼ Jameson Inn Orangeburg [M]
(803) 534-1611. **$49-$104.** 2350 Chestnut St NE. I-26, exit 145A (US 601), 3.9 mi sw to jct US 601 and 21/178 Bypass, then 2 mi nw. Ext corridors. **Pets:** Very small, other species. $10 daily fee/room. Service with restrictions, supervision.
[ASK] [✕] [🛁] [🛏] [💻] [≈]

[AAA] ▼▼◆ Orangeburg Days Inn [SH]
(803) 531-2590. **$50-$150, 30 day notice.** 3691 St Matthews Rd. I-26, exit 145A (US 601), just sw. Ext corridors. **Pets:** Other species. $10 daily fee/pet. Service with restrictions, supervision.
[SAVE] [S₆] [✕] [🛏] [💻] [≈]

PICKENS

▼▼▼ The Schell Haus, A Resort Bed & Breakfast [BB]
(864) 878-0078. **$90-$165, 7 day notice.** 117 Hiawatha Tr. 9 mi n on SR 178, then 5 mi e on SR 11; just e of Table Rock State Park. Int corridors. **Pets:** Accepted.
[ASK] [✕] [💻] [≈] [☎]

POINT SOUTH

▼▼▼ Holiday Inn Express Point South/Yemassee [SH]
(843) 726-9400. **$73-$85.** 138 Frampton Dr. I-95, exit 33, just ne on US 17. Int corridors. **Pets:** $100 one-time fee/room. No service, supervision.
[ASK] [✕] [🔊M] [🛁] [🛏] [💻] [≈]

RIDGELAND

▼▼▼ Comfort Inn [SH]
(843) 726-2121. **$62-$92.** Hwy 336 & I-95. I-95, exit 21, just nw. Ext/int corridors. **Pets:** Large, dogs only. $10 daily fee/room. Service with restrictions, crate.
[ASK] [S₆] [✕] [🛁] [🛏] [💻] [≈]

▼▼ Days Inn Ridgeland [SH]
(843) 726-5553. **$47-$65.** 516 E Main St. I-95, exit 21, just nw. Ext corridors. **Pets:** Other species. $5 daily fee/pet. Service with restrictions, supervision.
[ASK] [S₆] [✕] [🛏] [💻]

ROCK HILL

[AAA] ▼▼▼ Best Western Inn [SH]
(803) 329-1330. **$65-$95.** 1106 N Anderson Rd. I-77, exit 82B, 0.6 mi w on US 21 to US 21 Bypass. Int corridors. **Pets:** Other species. $10 daily fee/room. Service with restrictions.
[SAVE] [S₆] [✕] [🛏] [💻] [🍴] [≈]

▼▼▼ The Book & the Spindle [BB] ♣
(803) 328-1913. **$95-$425, 14 day notice.** 626 Oakland Ave. I-77, exit 82B, 3.1 mi s on Business Rt US 21; before Aiken. Int corridors. **Pets:** Small, other species. Service with restrictions, crate.
[✕] [🛏] [💻] [☎]

▼▼▼ Holiday Inn [SH]
(803) 329-1122. **$71-$89.** 2640 N Cherry Rd. I-77, exit 82A, just e. Int corridors. **Pets:** Accepted.
[ASK] [S₆] [✕] [🛁] [🛏] [💻] [🍴] [≈]

ST. GEORGE

[AAA] ▼▼ Best Value Inn St George [M]
(843) 563-2360. **$31-$66.** 125 Motel Dr. I-95, exit 77 (US 78), just e. Ext corridors. **Pets:** Accepted.
[SAVE] [S₆] [✕] [🛏] [≈]

[AAA] ▼▼▼ Best Western-St. George [M]
(843) 563-2277. **$49-$79, 14 day notice.** 104 Interstate Dr. I-95, exit 77 (US 78), just w. Ext corridors. **Pets:** Accepted.
[SAVE] [S₆] [✕] [💻] [≈]

[AAA] ▼▼▼ Comfort Inn [M] ♣
(843) 563-4180. **$65.** 139 Motel Dr. I-95, exit 77 (US 78), just e. Ext corridors. **Pets:** Other species. $10 one-time fee/room.
[SAVE] [S₆] [✕] [💻] [≈]

[AAA] ▼▼ Econo Lodge [M]
(843) 563-4195. **$50-$80.** 5971 W Jim Bilton Blvd. I-95, exit 77 (US 78), just e. Ext corridors. **Pets:** Medium. $5 daily fee/pet. Designated rooms, service with restrictions, supervision.
[SAVE] [S₆] [✕] [🛏] [💻] [≈]

▼▼ Quality Inn-St. George [SH]
(843) 563-4581. **$54-$69.** 6014 W Jim Bilton Blvd. I-95, exit 77 (US 78), just e. Ext corridors. **Pets:** Accepted.
[ASK] [S₆] [✕] [🛁] [💻] [≈]

SANTEE

▽▽ Days Inn 🆂🅷
(803) 854-2175. **$45-$60, 7 day notice.** 9074 Old Hwy 6. I-95, exit 98 (SR 6), just se. Ext corridors. **Pets:** Accepted.
🅰🆂🅺 ✕ 🕭 🛏 🖵 🏊

🆔 ▽▽ Howard Johnson Express Inn Ⓜ
(803) 854-3870. **$48-$62.** 9112 Old Hwy 6. I-95, exit 98 (SR 6), 0.4 mi se. Ext corridors. **Pets:** Medium, dogs only. $10 daily fee/room. Service with restrictions, crate.
🆂🅰🆅🅴 🆂🄳 ✕ 🛏 🖵 🏊

🆔 ▽▽ Super 8 Motel Ⓜ
(803) 854-3456. **$50-$55.** 9125 Old Hwy 6. I-95, exit 98 (SR 6), 0.4 mi se. Ext corridors. **Pets:** Medium. $6 daily fee/pet. Designated rooms, service with restrictions, supervision.
🆂🅰🆅🅴 🆂🄳 ✕ 🛏 🖵 🏊

SENECA

▽▽ Jameson Inn Ⓜ
(864) 888-8300. **$49-$104.** 226 Hi-Tech Rd. Jct US 76, SR 28 and US 123, 1 mi s. Ext corridors. **Pets:** Very small, other species. $10 daily fee/room. Service with restrictions, supervision.
🅰🆂🅺 ✕ 🅶🅼 🛏 🅺 🛏 🖵 🏊

SIMPSONVILLE

▽▽ Days Inn 🆂🅷
(864) 963-7701. **$55-$79.** 45 Ray E Talley Ct. I-385, exit 27, 0.4 mi s, then just e. Ext corridors. **Pets:** Small. $10 daily fee/pet. No service, supervision.
🅰🆂🅺 🆂🄳 ✕ 🛏 🏊

SPARTANBURG

▽▽▽ Holiday Inn Express Hotel & Suites 🆂🅷
(864) 699-7777. **$89-$105.** 895 Spartan Blvd. I-26, exit 21B (US 29), just e, then 0.7 mi n on Blackstock Rd. Int corridors. **Pets:** Large, other species. $35 one-time fee/room. Service with restrictions, crate.
🅰🆂🅺 🆂🄳 ✕ 🅶🅼 🛏 🅺 🛏 🖵 🏊

SUMMERTON

🆔 ▽▽ Days Inn of Summerton Ⓜ
(803) 485-2865. **$40-$79.** 18 Bluff Blvd. I-95, exit 108, just n. Ext corridors. **Pets:** Accepted.
🆂🅰🆅🅴 🆂🄳 ✕ 🛏 🖵 🏊

SUMTER

▽◇▽ Magnolia House 🅱🅱 ❀
(803) 775-6694. **$95-$105.** 230 Church St. US 76 business route/521 (Broad St), just s; between Broad and Haynsworth sts. Int corridors. **Pets:** Other species. $10 one-time fee/pet. Supervision.
✕

🆔 ▽▽ Ramada Inn 🆂🅷 ❀
(803) 775-2323. **$75-$85.** 226 N Washington St. US 76 business route/521 (Broad St), just n. Ext corridors. **Pets:** Medium. $50 deposit/room, $5 daily fee/pet. Designated rooms, service with restrictions, crate.
🆂🅰🆅🅴 🆂🄳 ✕ 🕭 🛏 🖵 🍽 🏊

TURBEVILLE

🆔 ▽▽ Days Inn 🆂🅷
(843) 659-8060. **$45-$95.** Hwy 378. I-95, exit 135 (US 378), just e. Ext corridors. **Pets:** Accepted.
🆂🅰🆅🅴 🆂🄳 ✕ 🏊

🆔 ▽▽ Knights Inn-Turbeville Ⓜ
(843) 659-2175. **$40-$45.** 7840 Myrtle Beach Hwy. I-95, exit 135 (US 378), just e. Ext corridors. **Pets:** Other species. $5 one-time fee/pet. Service with restrictions.
🆂🅰🆅🅴 🆂🄳 ✕ 🛏 🍽

WALTERBORO

🆔 ▽▽▽ Best Western of Walterboro 🆂🅷
(843) 538-3600. **$59-$89.** 1428 Sniders Hwy. I-95, exit 53 (SR 63), just e. Ext corridors. **Pets:** Small. $10 daily fee/pet. Designated rooms, service with restrictions, supervision.
🆂🅰🆅🅴 🆂🄳 ✕ 🗭 🖵 🏊

🆔 ▽▽▽ Econo Lodge Ⓜ ❀
(843) 538-3830. **$45-$89.** 1145 Sniders Hwy. I-95, exit 53 (SR 63), just e. Ext corridors. **Pets:** Accepted.
🆂🅰🆅🅴 🆂🄳 ✕ 🛏 🖵

▽▽ Howard Johnson Express 🆂🅷
(843) 538-5473. **$55, 15 day notice.** 1286 Sniders Hwy. I-95, exit 53 (SR 63), just e. Ext corridors. **Pets:** Accepted.
🅰🆂🅺 🆂🄳 ✕ 🗭 🅺 🖵 🏊

▽▽ Ramada Inn of Walterboro 🆂🅷
(843) 538-5403. **$65-$70.** 1245 Sniders Hwy. I-95, exit 53 (SR 63), just e. Ext corridors. **Pets:** Small. $10 daily fee/pet. Designated rooms, service with restrictions, supervision.
🅰🆂🅺 🆂🄳 ✕ 🛏 🖵 🏊

🆔 ▽ Rice Planters Inn Ⓜ
(843) 538-8964. **$39.** I-95 & SR 63. I-95, exit 53 (SR 63), just e. Ext corridors. **Pets:** Other species. $5.55 daily fee/pet. Service with restrictions, supervision.
🆂🅰🆅🅴 ✕ 🏊

🆔 ▽▽ Super 8 Motel Ⓜ
(843) 538-5383. **$46-$65, 7 day notice.** 1972 Bells Hwy. I-95, exit 57 (SR 64), just nw. Ext corridors. **Pets:** Accepted.
🆂🅰🆅🅴 🆂🄳 ✕ 🛏 🏊

🆔 ▽ Thunderbird Inn Ⓜ
(843) 538-2503. **$34-$39.** I-95, exit 53 (SR 63), just e. Ext corridors. **Pets:** Other species. Supervision.
🆂🅰🆅🅴 🆂🄳 ✕

WINNSBORO

▽▽ Days Inn Ⓜ
(803) 635-1447. **$47-$60.** 1894 US Hwy 321 Bypass. I-77, exit 34 (SR 34), 6.5 mi w, jct US 321/SR 34/213. Ext corridors. **Pets:** Small. $7 daily fee/pet. Designated rooms, service with restrictions, supervision.
🅰🆂🅺 🆂🄳 ✕ 🗭 🛏 🏊

🆔 ▽▽ Fairfield Motel Ⓜ
(803) 635-3458. **$35-$55.** 56 US 321 Bypass S. Jct SR 213/US 321 Bypass S, 1.8 mi n. Ext corridors. **Pets:** Small. $5 daily fee/pet. Service with restrictions, supervision.
🆂🅰🆅🅴 🆂🄳 ✕ 🛏 🏊

SOUTH DAKOTA

ABERDEEN

▼▼▼ Aberdeen East Super 8 Motel 🆂🅷
(605) 229-5005. **$56-$131.** 2405 6th Ave SE. 1.8 mi e on US 12. Int corridors. **Pets:** $6 daily fee/pet. Service with restrictions, supervision.

▼▼ Aberdeen North Super 8 Motel 🆂🅷
(605) 226-2288. **$47-$92.** 770 NW Hwy 281. On US 281, 1.5 mi nw. Int corridors. **Pets:** $6 daily fee/pet. Service with restrictions, supervision.
🅰🆂🅺 🆂🔟 ✕

▼▼ Aberdeen West Super 8 Motel 🆂🅷
(605) 225-1711. **$49-$97.** 714 S Hwy 281. Jct US 12 and 281. Int corridors. **Pets:** Accepted.
🅰🆂🅺 🆂🔟 ✕ 🔌

▼▼▼ AmericInn Lodge & Suites of Aberdeen 🆂🅷
(605) 225-4565. **Call for rates.** 310 Centennial St. 2.2 mi e on US 12, just n. Int corridors. **Pets:** Accepted.
✕ 🅼 🔌 🔌 🛏 🏊 🐾

▼▼▼▼ Best Western Ramkota Hotel 🆂🅷
(605) 229-4040. **$89-$129.** 1400 8th Ave NW. 1.5 mi nw on US 281. Ext/int corridors. **Pets:** Large. Designated rooms, service with restrictions, crate.
🅰🆂🅺 🆂🔟 ✕ 🅼 🔌 🔌 🛏 🏊 🐾

📞 ▼▼▼ Comfort Inn 🆂🅷 🐾
(605) 226-0097. **$65-$85.** 2923 6th Ave SE. 2 mi e on US 12. Int corridors. **Pets:** Medium. $30 deposit/pet. Service with restrictions, supervision.
🆂🅰🆅🅴 🆂🔟 ✕ 🔌 🛏 🔌 🏊

▼▼▼▼ Holiday Inn Express Hotel & Suites 🆂🅷
(605) 725-4000. **$85-$250.** 3310 7th Ave SE. 2.1 mi e on US 12. Int corridors. **Pets:** Medium, dogs only. $15 daily fee/pet. Service with restrictions, crate.
🅰🆂🅺 ✕ 🅼 🔌 🔌 🛏 🔌 🏊 🐾

📞 ▼▼▼ Ramada Inn 🆂🅷
(605) 225-3600. **$69.** 2727 6th Ave SE. 2 mi e on US 12. Ext/int corridors. **Pets:** Dogs only. Designated rooms, service with restrictions, supervision.
🆂🅰🆅🅴 ✕ 🛏 🔌 🍴 🏊

BERESFORD

▼▼ Super 8 Motel 🆂🅷
(605) 763-2001. **$55-$58.** 1410 W Cedar. I-29, exit 47 (SR 46), just e. Int corridors. **Pets:** Large, other species. $10 one-time fee/room. Supervision.
🅰🆂🅺 🆂🔟 ✕ 🔌 🛏 🔌 🏊 🐾

BLACK HILLS AREA

BELLE FOURCHE

▼ Ace Motel 🅼
(605) 892-2612. **$28-$50.** 109 6th Ave. 0.5 mi n via US 85, just e; just s of US 212 Bypass. Ext corridors. **Pets:** $4 one-time fee/pet. Designated rooms, service with restrictions, supervision.
✕ 🔌

▼ Lariat Motel 🅼
(605) 892-4040. **$30-$45.** 1033 Elkhorn. 0.8 mi e of US 85 on Business 212 (State St). Ext corridors. **Pets:** Accepted.
✕ 🔌

BLACK HAWK

▼▼ Black Hawk Super 8 🆂🅷
(605) 787-4844. **Call for rates.** 7900 Stagestop Rd. I-90, exit 48, just s. Int corridors. **Pets:** Accepted.
✕ 🔌 🛏 🔌 🏊

CUSTER

📞 ▼▼▼ Bavarian Inn Motel 🆂🅷
(605) 673-2802. **$49-$116, 3 day notice.** 1000 N 5th St. 1 mi n on US 16 and 385. Ext/int corridors. **Pets:** Accepted.
🆂🅰🆅🅴 🆂🔟 ✕ 🔌 🔌 🍴 🏊 🐾

📞 ▼▼▼ Chief Motel 🅼
(605) 673-2318. **$49-$93.** 120 Mt. Rushmore Rd. Just w on US 16. Ext corridors. **Pets:** Accepted.
🆂🅰🆅🅴 ✕ 🔌 🔌 🏊 🐾

📞 ▼▼▼ Rock Crest Lodge and Cabins 🅲🅰 🐾
(605) 673-4323. **$55-$99, 3 day notice.** 15 W Mt. Rushmore Rd. US 16, 0.5 mi w. Ext/int corridors. **Pets:** Medium, dogs only. $25 deposit/pet, $5 daily fee/pet. Designated rooms, service with restrictions, crate.
🆂🅰🆅🅴 🆂🔟 ✕ 🔌 🔌 🏊 🐾

📞 ▼ Rocket Motel 🅼
(605) 673-4401. **$36-$64.** 211 Mt. Rushmore Rd. On US 16; center. Ext corridors. **Pets:** Medium. $4 daily fee/room. Service with restrictions, supervision.
🆂🅰🆅🅴 🆂🔟 ✕

▼ The Roost Resort 🅲🅰 🐾
(605) 673-2326. **$46-$86, 10 day notice.** US 16 A-E. 2 mi e on US Alternate Rt 16. Ext corridors. **Pets:** $50 deposit/room. No service, crate.
🆂🔟 ✕ 🔌 🔌 🐾

▼▼ Super 8 Custer 🆂🅷
(605) 673-2200. **$55-$109.** 415 W Mt. Rushmore Rd. US 16, 0.8 mi w. Int corridors. **Pets:** Other species. $5 daily fee/pet. Designated rooms, service with restrictions, supervision.
🅰🆂🅺 🆂🔟 ✕ 🔌 🏊

DEADWOOD

(AAA) ▼▼▼ First Gold Hotel & Gaming SH
(605) 578-9777. **$65-$195, 3 day notice.** 270 Main St. 0.7 mi n on US 85. Int corridors. **Pets:** Accepted.
[SAVE] [S6] [X] [C] [B] [T]

HILL CITY

(AAA) ▼▼▼ Best Western Golden Spike Inn & Suites SH ❀
(605) 574-2577. **$59-$139.** 106 Main St. Just n on US 16 and 385. Ext/int corridors. **Pets:** Medium. $20 one-time fee/pet. Designated rooms, service with restrictions, supervision.
[SAVE] [S6] [X] [C] [B] [L] [T] [☞] [X]

(AAA) ▼▼ Lantern Inn M
(605) 574-2582. **$44-$120.** 430 E Main St. On north side of town, on US 16 and 385. Ext corridors. **Pets:** Small. $4 daily fee/pet. Supervision.
[SAVE] [S6] [X] [B] [☞]

(AAA) ▼▼▼ The Lodge at Palmer Gulch SH ❀
(605) 574-2525. **$57-$150, 10 day notice.** 12620 SR 244. On SR 244, 5 mi w of Mt. Rushmore. Int corridors. **Pets:** Other species. Designated rooms, service with restrictions, supervision.
[SAVE] [S6] [X] [C] [B] [L] [T] [☞] [X]

HOT SPRINGS

(AAA) ▼▼▼ Best Value Inn By The River M
(605) 745-4292. **$39-$160.** 602 W River. On US 385; downtown. Ext corridors. **Pets:** Other species. $10 daily fee/room. Designated rooms, service with restrictions, supervision.
[SAVE] [S6] [X] [B] [☞]

(AAA) ▼▼▼ Best Western Sundowner Inn SH ❀
(605) 745-7378. **$59-$169.** 737 S 6th St. 0.5 mi se off US 18 and 385. Int corridors. **Pets:** Medium. Designated rooms, service with restrictions, supervision.
[SAVE] [S6] [X] [LM] [B] [L] [☞]

(AAA) ▼▼▼ Budget Host Hills Inn M
(605) 745-3130. **$54-$144, 3 day notice.** 640 S 6th St. 0.5 mi se off US 18 and 385. Ext corridors. **Pets:** Small. Designated rooms, service with restrictions, supervision.
[SAVE] [S6] [X] [B] [☞]

▼▼▼ Holiday Inn Express Hotel & Suites SH
(605) 745-4411. **$89-$295.** 1401 Hwy 18. Jct US 18 and 385, 0.7 mi w on US 18 Bypass. Int corridors. **Pets:** Medium. $20 daily fee/pet. Designated rooms, service with restrictions, supervision.
[X] [LM] [/] [C] [B] [L] [X]

(AAA) ▼▼ Hot Springs Super 8 Motel SH
(605) 745-3888. **$57-$121.** 800 Mammoth St. US 18 Bypass. Int corridors. **Pets:** Medium, other species. $10 one-time fee/room. Service with restrictions, supervision.
[SAVE] [S6] [X] [/] [B]

KEYSTONE

▼▼ The First Lady Inn M
(605) 666-4990. **$59-$169.** 702 Hwy 16A. On US 16A; west side of town. Ext/int corridors. **Pets:** Accepted.
[ASK] [S6] [X] [B] [L] [☞]

(AAA) ▼▼▼ Keystone/Mt Rushmore Super 8 SH
(605) 666-6666. **$59-$149.** 250 Winter St. On US 16A; downtown. Ext/int corridors. **Pets:** Accepted.
[SAVE] [S6] [X]

▼▼ Mt. Rushmore's White House Resort SH
(605) 666-4917. **$40-$100, 3 day notice.** 111 Swanzey St. Jct US 16A and SR 40. Ext/int corridors. **Pets:** Medium, dogs only. $10 daily fee/pet. Designated rooms, service with restrictions, supervision.
[ASK] [S6] [X] [LM] [C] [B] [T] [☞]

(AAA) ▼▼▼ Powder House Lodge CA
(605) 666-4646. **$65-$200, 3 day notice.** 24125 Hwy 16A. On US 16A, 1.5 mi n. Ext corridors. **Pets:** Other species. $15 daily fee/pet. Designated rooms, service with restrictions, crate.
[SAVE] [B] [L] [T] [☞]

LEAD

(AAA) ▼▼▼ Golden Hills Inn SH
(605) 584-1800. **$49-$150, 3 day notice.** 900 Miners Ave. US 85 and 14A; center. Int corridors. **Pets:** Accepted.
[SAVE] [S6] [X] [LM] [/] [B] [T]

RAPID CITY

(AAA) ▼▼▼ Alex Johnson Hotel SH
(605) 342-1210. **$59-$160.** 523 6th St. I-90, exit 57, s on I-190, then left at Omaha; downtown. Int corridors. **Pets:** Small. $25 one-time fee/room. Designated rooms, service with restrictions, supervision.
[SAVE] [S6] [X] [/] [B] [L] [T]

(AAA) ▼▼▼▼ Best Western Ramkota Hotel SH ❀
(605) 343-8550. **$89-$149.** 2111 N LaCrosse St. I-90, exit 59 (LaCrosse St), just n. Ext/int corridors. **Pets:** Service with restrictions.
[SAVE] [S6] [X] [LM] [/] [C] [B] [L] [T] [☞] [X]

▼▼ Econo Lodge of Rapid City SH
(605) 342-6400. **Call for rates.** 625 E Disk Dr. I-90, exit 59 (LaCrosse St), just ne. Ext/int corridors. **Pets:** Accepted.
[X] [B] [L] [☞] [X]

(AAA) ▼▼ Fair Value Inn M
(605) 342-8118. **$40-$75.** 1607 LaCrosse St. I-90, exit 59 (LaCrosse St), 0.3 mi s. Ext corridors. **Pets:** Very small, dogs only. Designated rooms, service with restrictions, supervision.
[SAVE] [S6] [X] [B]

(AAA) ▼▼▼ Foothills Inn SH ❀
(605) 348-5640. **$29-$329.** 1625 N LaCrosse St. I-90, exit 59 (LaCrosse St), just s. Int corridors. **Pets:** Small. $10 daily fee/room. Designated rooms, service with restrictions, supervision.
[SAVE] [S6] [X] [B] [☞]

(AAA) ▼▼▼ Gold Star Motel M
(605) 341-7051. **$36-$68.** 801 E North. I-90, exit 60, 1.5 mi sw on I-90 business loop, 1.2 mi s, then just e, from exit 59 (Lacrose St). Ext corridors. **Pets:** Medium, other species. $5 daily fee/pet. Service with restrictions, supervision.
[SAVE] [S6] [X] [L]

▼▼▼ Holiday Inn Express Hotel & Suites, I-90 SH
(605) 355-9090. **$74-$158.** 645 E Disk Dr. I-90, exit 59 (Lacrosse St), just ne. Int corridors. **Pets:** Accepted.
[ASK] [X] [LM] [/] [C] [B] [L] [☞] [X]

(AAA) ▼▼▼ Holiday Inn-Rushmore Plaza LH
(605) 348-4000. **$89-$140.** 505 N 5th St. I-90, exit 58, 1.3 mi s on Haines. Int corridors. **Pets:** Accepted.
[SAVE] [S6] [X] [LM] [/] [C] [B] [L] [T] [☞] [X]

(AAA) ▼▼▼ Microtel Inn & Suites SH
(605) 348-2523. **$57-$114.** 1740 Rapp St. I-90, exit 59 (LaCrosse St), just se. Int corridors. **Pets:** Small, dogs only. $10 daily fee/room. Designated rooms, service with restrictions, supervision.
[SAVE] [S6] [X] [LM] [/] [C] [B] [L] [☞]

WWW Motel 6–352 **M**
(605) 343-3687. **$37-$65.** 620 E Latrobe St. I-90, exit 59 (LaCrosse St), just se. Ext corridors. **Pets:** Accepted.
⬛⬛⬛⬛⬛

WWW Quality Inn **SH**
(605) 342-3322. **$59-$139.** 1902 LaCrosse St. I-90, exit 59 (LaCrosse St), just s. Ext/int corridors. **Pets:** Medium, other species. $10 daily fee/room. Service with restrictions, crate.
⬛⬛⬛⬛⬛⬛⬛⬛⬛⬛

WWW Ramada Inn Gold Key **SH** 🐾
(605) 342-1300. **$69-$349.** 1721 N LaCrosse St. I-90, exit 59 (LaCrosse St), just s. Int corridors. **Pets:** $10 daily fee/room. Designated rooms, service with restrictions, supervision.
⬛⬛⬛⬛⬛⬛⬛⬛⬛

WWW Red Roof Inn **SH**
(605) 343-5434. **$40-$120.** 620 Howard St. I-90, exit 58, just nw of Haines Ave. Int corridors. **Pets:** Medium, dogs only. Designated rooms, service with restrictions, supervision.
⬛⬛⬛⬛⬛

WWW Rodeway Inn **SH**
(605) 342-1303. **$50-$200.** 2208 Mt. Rushmore Rd. 1 mi s on US 16. Ext corridors. **Pets:** Designated rooms, service with restrictions, supervision.
⬛⬛⬛⬛⬛⬛⬛

WWW Super 8 Motel-I-90 **SH**
(605) 348-8070. **$45-$175.** 2124 Lacrosse St. I-90, exit 59 (Lacrosse St), just n. Int corridors. **Pets:** Accepted.
⬛⬛⬛⬛⬛⬛⬛

WWW Super 8 Motel-South **SH**
(605) 342-4911. **$40-$180.** 2520 Tower Rd. 1.4 mi s on US 16, then just e. Int corridors. **Pets:** Other species. $5 daily fee/pet. Service with restrictions, supervision.
⬛⬛⬛⬛

WWW Thrifty Motor Inn **M**
(605) 342-0551. **$40-$75.** 1303 LaCrosse St. I-90, exit 59 (LaCrosse St), 0.5 mi s. Ext corridors. **Pets:** Accepted.
⬛⬛⬛

ROCKERVILLE

WWW Rockerville Trading Post & Motel **M**
(605) 341-4880. **$60-$75, 3 day notice.** 13525 Main St. Center. Ext corridors. **Pets:** Other species. $2 daily fee/room. Service with restrictions.
⬛⬛⬛⬛

SPEARFISH

WWW Best Western Black Hills Lodge **SH**
(605) 642-7795. **$55-$99, 30 day notice.** 540 E Jackson. I-90, exit 12, just s. Ext/int corridors. **Pets:** Dogs only. $5 daily fee/pet. Designated rooms, service with restrictions, supervision.
⬛⬛⬛⬛⬛⬛⬛

WW Days Inn **SH** 🐾
(605) 642-7101. **$60-$130.** 240 Ryan Rd. I-90, exit 10, 1.2 mi s. Ext/int corridors. **Pets:** Other species. $10 daily fee/pet. Service with restrictions, supervision.
⬛⬛⬛⬛

WWW Holiday Inn Hotel & Convention Center **SH**
(605) 642-4683. **$70-$110.** 305 N 27th St. I-90, exit 14 (Spearfish Canyon), just n. Ext/int corridors. **Pets:** Large. $100 deposit/pet, $25 one-time fee/room. Designated rooms, service with restrictions, supervision.
⬛⬛⬛⬛⬛⬛⬛⬛⬛⬛

WWW Howard Johnson Express Inn **SH**
(605) 642-8105. **$50-$80.** 323 S 27th St. I-90, exit 14 (Spearfish Canyon), just s. Int corridors. **Pets:** Other species. $10 daily fee/room. Designated rooms, service with restrictions, supervision.
⬛⬛⬛⬛⬛⬛⬛

WWW Royal Rest Motel **M**
(605) 642-3842. **$30-$55.** 444 Main St. On US 14/85; downtown. Ext corridors. **Pets:** Accepted.
⬛⬛⬛

WWW Spearfish Canyon Lodge **SH** 🐾
(605) 584-3435. **$89-$159, 5 day notice.** 10619 Roughlock Falls Rd. I-90, exit 14 (Spearfish Canyon), 13 mi s. Int corridors. **Pets:** $15 one-time fee/room. Service with restrictions, supervision.
⬛⬛⬛⬛⬛

WW Travelodge of Spearfish **M**
(605) 642-4676. **$35-$120.** 346 W Kansas St. Downtown off of Main St; follow signs. Ext corridors. **Pets:** $10 daily fee/room. Service with restrictions, supervision.
⬛⬛⬛⬛⬛

STURGIS

WWW Best Western of Sturgis **SH**
(605) 347-3604. **$49-$109.** 2431 S Junction Ave. I-90, exit 32. Ext/int corridors. **Pets:** Other species. Designated rooms, service with restrictions, supervision.
⬛⬛⬛⬛⬛⬛⬛

WW Days Inn **SH**
(605) 347-3027. **$61-$91, 7 day notice.** I-90, exit 30, at jct US 14A. Ext/int corridors. **Pets:** Accepted.
⬛⬛⬛⬛

END AREA

BROOKINGS

WW Brookings Super 8 Motel **SH**
(605) 692-6920. **$48-$73.** 3034 Lefevre Dr. I-29, exit 132, just e. Int corridors. **Pets:** Medium. $5 daily fee/pet. Service with restrictions, supervision.
⬛⬛⬛⬛⬛

WWW Holiday Inn Express Hotel & Suites **SH**
(605) 692-9060. **$75-$125.** 3020 Lefevre Dr. I-29, exit 132, just se. Int corridors. **Pets:** Medium. $10 daily fee/pet. Service with restrictions, supervision.
⬛⬛⬛⬛⬛⬛⬛⬛⬛⬛

BUFFALO

Tipperary Lodge M
(605) 375-3721. **$48.** 604 1st St W. 0.5 mi n on US 85, turn at sign. Int corridors. **Pets:** Other species. Designated rooms, service with restrictions, supervision.
(ASK) (S$) (X) (🔒)

CANISTOTA

Best Western U-Bar Motel M
(605) 296-3466. **$42-$80.** 130 Ash St. I-90, exit 368, 6 mi s, follow signs. Ext corridors. **Pets:** Very small, dogs only. Service with restrictions, supervision.
(SAVE) (S$) (X) (🔒) (💻)

CHAMBERLAIN

AmericInn Lodge & Suites of Chamberlain SH
(605) 734-0985. **$85-$160.** 1981 E King St. I-90, exit 265, just e. Int corridors. **Pets:** Other species. $10 daily fee/pet. Service with restrictions, supervision.
(SAVE) (S$) (X) (♿) (🐾) (♿) (🔒) (💻) (🏊) (X)

Bel Aire Motel M
(605) 734-5595. **$40-$64, 4 day notice.** 312 E King St. On US 16 and I-90 business loop; downtown. Ext/int corridors. **Pets:** Accepted.
(SAVE) (S$) (X) (🔒)

Best Western Lee's Motor Inn SH
(605) 734-5575. **$50-$90, 5 day notice.** 220 W King St. On US 17 and I-90 business loop; downtown. Ext/int corridors. **Pets:** Very small. No service.
(SAVE) (S$) (X) (💻) (🏊) (X)

Cedar Shore Resort SH
(605) 734-6376. **$70-$150.** 1500 Shoreline Dr. I-90, exit 260, 2.5 mi e on Business Rt I-90, then 1 mi ne on Mickelson county road, follow signs. Int corridors. **Pets:** Large, other species. $10 daily fee/room. Service with restrictions, supervision.
(SAVE) (S$) (X) (♿) (🐾) (♿) (🔒) (💻) (🍴) (🏊) (X)

Holiday Inn Express SH
(605) 734-5593. **$70-$150.** 100 W Hwy 16. I-90, exit 260, just n. Int corridors. **Pets:** $10 daily fee/room. Designated rooms, no service, supervision.
(ASK) (S$) (X) (♿) (♿) (💻)

Lake Shore Motel M
(605) 234-5566. **$29-$64, 3 day notice.** 115 N River St. Just n of US 16 bridge (the northernmost bridge); just w of downtown. Ext corridors. **Pets:** $10 one-time fee/room.
(SAVE) (S$) (X)

Oasis Inn SH
(605) 734-6061. **$51-$119.** 1100 E Hwy 16. I-90, exit 260, 0.4 mi e on US 16 and I-90 business loop. Ext/int corridors. **Pets:** Other species. Service with restrictions, supervision.
(SAVE) (S$) (X) (♿) (🐾) (🔒) (💻) (🏊)

DELL RAPIDS

Super 8 Motel SH
(605) 428-4288. **$59-$72, 30 day notice.** 510 N Hwy 77. I-29, exit 98 (SR 115), 3 mi e, then just n. Int corridors. **Pets:** Accepted.
(ASK) (X) (♿) (🔒) (💻)

DE SMET

De Smet Super 8 SH
(605) 854-9388. **$89-$129.** 288 Hwy 14 E. US 14, just e. Int corridors. **Pets:** Accepted.
(ASK) (X) (♿) (🔒) (💻) (🏊)

FAITH

Prairie Vista Inn SH
(605) 967-2343. **$65-$85.** Hwy 212 & E 1st. On US 212; at east city edge. Int corridors. **Pets:** Medium. $10 daily fee/pet. Designated rooms, service with restrictions, crate.
(SAVE) (S$) (X) (♿) (💻)

FAULKTON

Super 8 Motel SH
(605) 598-4567. **$51-$61.** 700 Main St. On US 212; center. Int corridors. **Pets:** Accepted.
(ASK) (S$) (X)

FLANDREAU

Royal River Casino & Hotel SH
(605) 997-3746. **$55-$99.** 607 S Veterans St. I-29, exit 114, 7 mi e, follow signs. Int corridors. **Pets:** Other species. $50 deposit/pet. Designated rooms, service with restrictions, supervision.
(SAVE) (S$) (X) (♿) (🔒) (💻) (🍴) (🏊)

FORT PIERRE

Fort Pierre Motel M
(605) 223-3111. **$52-$60, 3 day notice.** 211 S 1st Ave. On US 83, 1.2 mi s of jct US 14. Ext corridors. **Pets:** Other species. Service with restrictions, crate.
(SAVE) (X) (🔒)

Holiday Inn Express Hotel & Suites SH
(605) 223-9045. **$65-$85.** 110 E Stanley Rd. On US 83, just s of jct US 14/SR 34. Int corridors. **Pets:** Small, dogs only. $5 daily fee/pet. Designated rooms, service with restrictions, supervision.
(ASK) (S$) (X) (♿) (🐾) (♿) (🔒) (💻) (🏊)

FREEMAN

Super 8 Motel SH
(605) 925-4888. **$47-$55.** 1019 S Hwy 81. On US 81, just s. Int corridors. **Pets:** Accepted.
(ASK) (X) (♿) (🔒)

HURON

Best Western of Huron SH
(605) 352-2000. **$57-$94.** 2000 Dakota Ave. 1.3 mi s on SR 37. Ext/int corridors. **Pets:** $10 daily fee/room. Service with restrictions, supervision.
(ASK) (S$) (X) (♿) (🐾) (♿) (🔒) (💻) (X)

The Crossroads Hotel & Huron Event Center SH
(605) 352-3204. **$80-$145, 3 day notice.** 100 4th St. Just w of Dakota Ave; downtown. Int corridors. **Pets:** Dogs only. $15 daily fee/room. Service with restrictions, supervision.
(SAVE) (S$) (X) (♿) (🔒) (💻) (🍴) (🏊) (X)

Holiday Inn Express SH
(605) 352-6655. **$69-$85.** 100 21st St SW. 1.3 mi s on SR 37. Ext/int corridors. **Pets:** Other species. $25 one-time fee/room. Service with restrictions, crate.
(ASK) (S$) (X) (♿) (🐾) (♿) (🔒) (💻) (X)

INTERIOR

Badlands Budget Host Motel M
(605) 433-5335. **$52-$58.** 900 SD Hwy 377. Jct SR 44 and 377, 2 mi s of Badlands National Park. Ext corridors. **Pets:** Accepted.
(SAVE) (S$) (💻) (🏊) (Z)

KADOKA

(AAA) ▽ Best Value Dakota Inn M
(605) 837-2151. **$45-$70.** 106 SD Hwy 73. I-90, exit 150, just n. Ext/int corridors. **Pets:** Medium, other species. $5 daily fee/pet. Designated rooms, service with restrictions, supervision.
[SAVE] [S0] [X] 🛆 🖵 [📶] ➤

(AAA) ▽▽▽ Best Western H & H El Centro Motel M ❀
(605) 837-2287. **$54-$115, 5 day notice.** 105 E Hwy 16. 1.5 mi w on I-90 business route from exit 152, 1.3 mi e from exit 150. Ext corridors. **Pets:** Medium, other species. Designated rooms, service with restrictions, crate.
[SAVE] [S0] [X] 🖵 [📶] ➤ ⊠

(AAA) ▽ West Motel M
(605) 837-2427. **$34-$70, 3 day notice.** 306 Hwy 16 W. I-90, exit 150, 1 mi e on I-90 business route. Ext corridors. **Pets:** Other species. $10 one-time fee/pet. Service with restrictions, supervision.
[SAVE] [S0] [X]

MITCHELL

▽▽ Americinn Motel & Suites SH
(605) 996-9700. **$68-$100.** 1421 S Burr St. I-90, exit 332, just n. Int corridors. **Pets:** Accepted.
[ASK] [S0] [X] [&M] [🅰] 🛆 🖵 ➤

(AAA) ▽▽▽ Hampton Inn SH
(605) 995-1575. **$74-$123.** 1920 Highland Way. I-90, exit 332, just se. Int corridors. **Pets:** Accepted.
[SAVE] [S0] [X] [&M] 🛆 [🅰] 🛆 🖵 ➤

(AAA) ▽▽▽ Holiday Inn SH ❀
(605) 996-6501. **$80-$159.** 1525 W Havens St. I-90, exit 330, 0.5 mi n. Ext/int corridors. **Pets:** $10 daily fee/room. Service with restrictions.
[SAVE] [S0] [X] [&M] 🛆 [🅰] 🖵 [📶] ➤ ⊠

(AAA) ▽▽▽ Kelly Inn & Suites SH
(605) 995-0500. **$69-$119.** 1010 Cabela Dr. I-90, exit 332, just sw. Ext/int corridors. **Pets:** Other species. Service with restrictions, supervision.
[SAVE] [S0] [X] [🅰] 🛆 🖵 ➤ ⊠

(AAA) ▽▽▽ Thunderbird Lodge M
(605) 996-6645. **$45-$89.** 1601 S Burr St. I-90, exit 332, just n. Ext/int corridors. **Pets:** Large, other species. $10 daily fee/room. Designated rooms, service with restrictions, supervision.
[SAVE] [S0] [X] [&M] 🛆 🖵

MOBRIDGE

(AAA) ▽▽▽ Best Value Wrangler Inn SH
(605) 845-3641. **$61-$79.** 820 W Grand Crossing. 0.5 mi w on US 12. Ext/int corridors. **Pets:** Dogs only. Designated rooms, service with restrictions, supervision.
[SAVE] [S0] [X] 🛆 🖵 [📶] ➤ ⊠

MURDO

(AAA) ▽▽▽ Best Western Graham's M
(605) 669-2441. **$55-$99.** 301 W 5th. On I-90 business loop, 0.5 mi w of jct US 83; I-90, exits 191 and 192. Ext corridors. **Pets:** Accepted.
[SAVE] [S0] [X] 🖵 ➤

NORTH SIOUX CITY

▽▽ Econo Lodge SH
(605) 232-9600. **$45-$65, 3 day notice.** 110 Sodrac Dr. I-29, exit 2, just w. Int corridors. **Pets:** Accepted.
[ASK] [S0] [X] [🅰] 🛆 🖵

▽▽▽ Hampton Inn SH
(605) 232-9739. **$75-$95.** 101 S Sodrac Dr. I-29, exit 2, just w. Int corridors. **Pets:** Medium, other species. $20 one-time fee/room. Designated rooms, service with restrictions, supervision.
[ASK] [S0] [X] [&M] 🛆 🖵 ➤

(AAA) ▽▽▽ Super 8 Motel SH
(605) 232-4716. **$50-$80.** 1300 River Dr. I-29, exit 2, just w. Int corridors. **Pets:** Accepted.
[SAVE] [S0] [X] 🛆 🖵

PICKSTOWN

▽▽ Fort Randall Inn M
(605) 487-7801. **$57.** 103 Hwy 18/281. On US 18/281; just e of the dam. Ext corridors. **Pets:** $10 daily fee/room. Service with restrictions.
[ASK] [S0] [X] 🛆

PIERRE

▽▽▽▽ Best Western Ramkota Hotel SH
(605) 224-6877. **$91-$98.** 920 W Sioux Ave. 1 mi w on US 14/83. Ext/int corridors. **Pets:** Other species. Service with restrictions, supervision.
[ASK] [S0] [X] [&M] 🛆 [🅰] 🛆 🖵 [📶] ➤ ⊠

(AAA) ▽▽▽ Comfort Inn SH ❀
(605) 224-0377. **$68-$109.** 410 W Sioux Ave. 0.3 mi w on US 14/83 and SR 34. Int corridors. **Pets:** Dogs only. $10 daily/room. Designated rooms, service with restrictions, supervision.
[SAVE] [S0] [X] [&M] [🅰] 🛆 🖵 ➤

(AAA) ▽▽▽ Days Inn SH ❀
(605) 224-0411. **$65-$90.** 520 W Sioux Ave. 0.5 mi w on US 14/83 and SR 34. Int corridors. **Pets:** $5 daily fee/pet. Designated rooms, service with restrictions, supervision.
[SAVE] [S0] [X] 🛆 [🅰] 🛆 🖵

(AAA) ▽▽▽ Governor's Inn SH
(605) 224-4200. **$69-$109.** 700 W Sioux Ave. 0.8 mi w on US 14/83 and SR 34. Ext/int corridors. **Pets:** Accepted.
[SAVE] [S0] [X] 🛆 [🅰] 🛆 🖵 ➤ ⊠

▽▽ Kelly Inn SH
(605) 224-4140. **$55-$60.** 713 W Sioux Ave. 0.8 mi w on US 14/83. Int corridors. **Pets:** Accepted.
[ASK] [S0] [X] 🛆 🖵

▽▽ Super 8 Motel SH
(605) 224-1617. **$40-$75.** 320 W Sioux Ave. 0.3 mi w on US 14/83 and SR 34. Int corridors. **Pets:** $5 daily fee/pet. Service with restrictions, crate.
[ASK] [S0] [X] [🅰] 🛆

PLANKINTON

▽▽ Super 8 Motel SH
(605) 942-7722. **$45-$80.** 801 S Main St. I-90, exit 308, just n. Int corridors. **Pets:** Other species. $8 daily fee/pet. Service with restrictions, supervision.
[ASK] [S0] [X]

SIOUX FALLS

▽▽ Baymont Inn SH
(605) 362-0835. **$69-$125.** 3200 Meadow Ave. I-29, exit 77 (41st St), just w, then just n. Int corridors. **Pets:** Small, other species. $25 one-time fee/room. Designated rooms, service with restrictions, supervision.
[ASK] [S0] [X] [&M] 🛆 [🅰] 🛆 🖵 ➤

▽▽▽▽ Best Western Ramkota Hotel & Conference Center SH
(605) 336-0650. **$89-$139.** 3200 W Maple. I-29, exit 81 (Airport/Russell St), just e. Ext/int corridors. **Pets:** Designated rooms, service with restrictions, supervision.
[ASK] [S0] [X] [&M] 🛆 [🅰] 🛆 🖵 [📶] ➤ ⊠

▼▼▼ Comfort Inn by Choice Hotels South 🆂🅷
(605) 361-2822. **$60-$104.** 3216 S Carolyn Ave. I-29, exit 77 (41st St), just e, then n. Int corridors. **Pets:** Accepted.
🅰🆂🅺 🆂🔂 ✖ 🎵 📶 🛏 💻 🌊

▲▲▲ ▼▼▼ Comfort Inn North 🆂🅷
(605) 331-4490. **$55-$110.** 5100 N Cliff Ave. I-90, exit 399 (Cliff Ave), 0.3 mi s. Int corridors. **Pets:** Other species. $10 daily fee/room. Designated rooms, service with restrictions, supervision.
🆂🅰🆅🅴 🆂🔂 ✖ 🔊 🎵 📶 🛏 💻 🌊

▼▼▼ Comfort Suites by Choice Hotels 🆂🅷
(605) 362-9711. **$70-$125.** 3208 S Carolyn Ave. I-29, exit 77 (41st St), just e, then n. Int corridors. **Pets:** Accepted.
🅰🆂🅺 🆂🔂 ✖ 🎵 🛏 💻 🌊

▼▼▼▼ Country Inn & Suites By Carlson 🆂🅷
(605) 373-0153. **$69-$179.** 200 E 8th St. Just e of Phillips Ave; downtown. Int corridors. **Pets:** Medium. $10 daily fee/room. Designated rooms, service with restrictions, supervision.
🅰🆂🅺 🆂🔂 ✖ 🔊 🎵 📶 🛏 💻 🍽 🌊

▲▲▲ ▼ Days Inn Airport 🆂🅷
(605) 331-5959. **$60-$139.** 5001 N Cliff Ave. I-90, exit 399 (Cliff Ave), just s. Int corridors. **Pets:** Other species. $10 daily fee/room. Service with restrictions, supervision.
🆂🅰🆅🅴 🆂🔂 ✖ 🔊 🎵 🛏 💻

▲▲▲ ▼▼▼▼ Homewood Suites By Hilton 🆂🅷 🐾
(605) 338-8585. **$99-$209.** 3620 W Avera Dr. I-229, exit 1C (Louise Ave), just s. Int corridors. **Pets:** Other species. $5 daily fee/room, $15 one-time fee/room. Service with restrictions, crate.
🆂🅰🆅🅴 ✖ 🔊 🎵 📶 🛏 💻 🌊 🍽

▲▲▲ ▼▼▼ Kelly Inn 🆂🅷 🐾
(605) 338-6242. **$60-$80.** 3101 W Russell St. I-29, exit 81 (Airport/Russell St), just e. Ext/int corridors. **Pets:** Other species. Designated rooms, service with restrictions, supervision.
🆂🅰🆅🅴 🆂🔂 ✖ 🎵 📶 🛏 💻 🍽

▲▲▲ ▼▼▼ Microtel Inn & Suites 🆂🅷
(605) 361-7484. **$49-$85.** 2901 S Carolyn Ave. I-29, exit 77 (41st St), just e, then n. Int corridors. **Pets:** Accepted.
🆂🅰🆅🅴 🆂🔂 ✖ 🔊 🎵 📶 🛏 💻

▼ Motel 6-0162 Ⓜ
(605) 336-7800. **$37-$55.** 3009 W Russell St. I-29, exit 81 (Airport/Russell St), just e. Ext corridors. **Pets:** Other species. Service with restrictions, supervision.
🆂🔂 ✖ 🔊 📶 🛏 🌊

▼▼ Ramada Limited 🆂🅷
(605) 330-0000. **$55-$80.** 407 S Lyons Ave. I-29, exit 79 (12th St), just e. Int corridors. **Pets:** Medium. $15 one-time fee/room. Service with restrictions, supervision.
🅰🆂🅺 🆂🔂 ✖ 🔊 📶 🛏 💻 🌊 🍽

▼▼ Red Roof Inn 🆂🅷
(605) 361-1864. **$48-$75.** 3500 S Gateway Blvd. I-29, exit 77 (41st St), just w. Int corridors. **Pets:** Accepted.
🅰🆂🅺 🆂🔂 ✖ 📶 🛏

▼▼▼▼ Residence Inn by Marriott 🆂🅷 🐾
(605) 361-2202. **$100-$200.** 4509 W Empire Pl. I-29, exit 77 (41st St), 0.5 mi se. Int corridors. **Pets:** Medium, other species. $75 one-time fee/room. No service, crate.
🅰🆂🅺 🆂🔂 ✖ 🔊 🎵 📶 🛏 💻 🌊 🍽

▲▲▲ ▼▼▼▼ Sheraton Sioux Falls Hotel 🅻🅷
(605) 331-0100. **$129-$149.** 1211 N West Ave. I-29, exit 81 (Airport/Russell St), 1.3 mi e. Int corridors. **Pets:** Accepted.
🆂🅰🆅🅴 🆂🔂 ✖ 🔊 🎵 📶 🛏 💻 🍽 🌊 🍽

▲▲▲ ▼▼▼ Sleep Inn 🆂🅷
(605) 339-3992. **$45-$80.** 1500 N Kiwanis Ave. I-29, exit 81 (Airport/Russell St), 0.7 mi e. Int corridors. **Pets:** Accepted.
🆂🅰🆅🅴 ✖ 🔊 📶 🛏 🌊

▼ Super 8/I-90/Airport East 🆂🅷
(605) 339-9212. **$65-$90.** 4808 N Cliff Ave. I-90, exit 399 (Cliff Ave), 0.3 mi s. Int corridors. **Pets:** Medium, dogs only. $10 one-time fee/room. Designated rooms, service with restrictions, crate.
🅰🆂🅺 🆂🔂 ✖ 🛏 💻 🌊

▼▼ Super 8 Motel-East 🆂🅷
(605) 338-8881. **$59-$110, 7 day notice.** 2616 E 10th St. I-229, exit 6, just e. Int corridors. **Pets:** Medium, dogs only. $10 daily fee/pet. No service, supervision.
✖ 🔊 📶 🛏 💻 🌊

▼▼▼▼ TownePlace Suites by Marriott 🆂🅷
(605) 361-2626. **$79-$139.** 4545 W Homefield Dr. I-29, exit 78 (26th St), just w. Int corridors. **Pets:** Small. $75 one-time fee/room. Designated rooms, service with restrictions, supervision.
🅰🆂🅺 ✖ 🔊 🎵 📶 🛏 💻 🌊

SISSETON

▼▼ Sisseton Super 8 🆂🅷
(605) 742-0808. **$55-$75.** 2104 SD Hwy 10. I-29, exit 232 (SR 10), 1.5 mi w; then just w of jct SR 127. Int corridors. **Pets:** Large, dogs only. Supervision.
🅰🆂🅺 🆂🔂 ✖ 📶 🛏 💻 🌊

VERMILLION

▲▲▲ ▼▼ Comfort Inn 🆂🅷
(605) 624-8333. **$65-$75.** 701 W Cherry St. I-29, exit 26, 7.5 mi w on Business Rt SR 50. Int corridors. **Pets:** Medium. $5 daily fee/pet. Service with restrictions, supervision.
🆂🅰🆅🅴 ✖ 📶 🛏 💻 🌊 🍽

▼▼▼▼ Holiday Inn Express Hotel & Suites-Vermillion 🆂🅷
(605) 624-7600. **$69-$149.** 1200 N Dakota St. I-29, exit 26, 7 mi w. Int corridors. **Pets:** Medium, other species. $5 daily fee/pet. Service with restrictions, supervision.
🅰🆂🅺 ✖ 🔊 🎵 📶 🛏 💻 🌊

WALL

▲▲▲ ▼▼▼ Best Western Plains Motel Ⓜ
(605) 279-2145. **$49-$159.** 712 Glenn St. I-90, exit 110, just n. Ext corridors. **Pets:** Other species. $10 one-time fee/pet. Service with restrictions, supervision.
🆂🅰🆅🅴 🆂🔂 ✖ 🛏 💻 🌊

▼▼ Days Inn 🆂🅷
(605) 279-2000. **$70-$169.** 212 10th Ave. I-90, exit 110, just n, then just w. Int corridors. **Pets:** Small. $15 one-time fee/pet. Designated rooms, service with restrictions, supervision.
🅰🆂🅺 🆂🔂 ✖ 🛏

▲▲▲ ▼▼▼ Econo Lodge Ⓜ 🐾
(605) 279-2121. **$59-$125.** 804 Glenn St. I-90, exit 110, just n. Ext corridors. **Pets:** Medium, other species. $10 daily fee/pet. Designated rooms, service with restrictions, supervision.
🆂🅰🆅🅴 🆂🔂 ✖ 🛏 💻 🌊

▲▲▲ ▼ Sunshine Inn Ⓜ
(605) 279-2178. **$47-$75.** 608 Main St. Downtown. Ext corridors. **Pets:** Other species. $5 one-time fee/room. Service with restrictions.
🆂🅰🆅🅴 🆂🔂 ✖

WATERTOWN

▼▼▼▼ Best Western Ramkota Hotel 🆂🅷
(605) 886-8011. **$89-$105.** 1901 9th Ave SW. I-29, exit 177 (US 212), 4 mi w. Int corridors. **Pets:** Accepted.
🅰🆂🅺 🆂🔂 ✖ 🔊 🎵 📶 🛏 💻 🍽 🌊 🍽

Comfort Inn SH
(605) 886-3010. **$80-$95.** 800 35th St Cir. I-29, exit 177 (US 212), just w. Ext/int corridors. **Pets:** Dogs only. $15 one-time fee/room. Designated rooms, service with restrictions, supervision.

Country Inn & Suites By Carlson SH
(605) 886-8900. **$79-$129.** 3400 8th Ave SE. I-29, exit 177 (US 212), just w. Int corridors. **Pets:** Small. $20 one-time fee/room. Designated rooms, service with restrictions, supervision.

Days Inn SH
(605) 886-3500. **$56-$85, 14 day notice.** 2900 9th Ave SE. I-29, exit 177 (US 212), 0.5 mi w. Ext/int corridors. **Pets:** $10 one-time fee/room. Service with restrictions, crate.

Holiday Inn Express Hotel & Suites SH
(605) 882-3636. **$79-$149, 3 day notice.** 3900 9th Ave SE. I-29, exit 177 (US 212), just e. Int corridors. **Pets:** $10 daily fee/room. Designated rooms, service with restrictions, supervision.

Travelers Inn Motel SH 🐾
(605) 882-2243. **$55-$60.** 920 14th St SE. I-29, exit 177 (US 212), 1.5 mi w, then just s. Int corridors. **Pets:** Other species. $6 daily fee/pet. Designated rooms.

Travel Host Motel M
(605) 886-6120. **$48-$54.** 1714 9th Ave SW. I-29, exit 177 (US 212), 4 mi w. Int corridors. **Pets:** Small. $5 one-time fee/room. Designated rooms, no service, supervision.

WINNER

Holiday Inn Express Hotel & Suites SH 🐾
(605) 842-2255. **$69-$129.** 1360 E Hwy 44. Just ne of jct US 18/183. Int corridors. **Pets:** Very small. $50 deposit/pet, $25 daily fee/pet. Service with restrictions, supervision.

YANKTON

Best Western Kelly Inn-Yankton SH
(605) 665-2906. **$79-$119.** 1607 Hwy 50 E. On US 50, 1.8 mi e. Ext/int corridors. **Pets:** Other species. Designated rooms, service with restrictions, supervision.

Days Inn SH
(605) 665-8717. **$60-$69.** 2410 Broadway. US 81, 1.7 mi n. Int corridors. **Pets:** Accepted.

Lewis & Clark Resort M
(605) 665-2680. **$50-$210, 30 day notice.** 43496 Shore Dr. 4 mi w on SR 52; in Lewis and Clark State Park, turn into park, just w of Marina. Ext corridors. **Pets:** Dogs only. $5 daily fee/pet. Service with restrictions, crate.

TENNESSEE

ALCOA

▼▼▼▼ Holiday Inn Express Hotel & Suites SH
(865) 981-9008. **$93.** 130 Associates Blvd. 1.5 mi s on US 129. Int corridors. **Pets:** Accepted.
ASK SD ✕ ৬ 🗔 💻 ➿

▼▼▼▼ Jameson Inn Alcoa SH
(865) 984-6800. **$49-$104.** 206 Corporate Pl. US 129, just s. Int corridors. **Pets:** Very small, other species. $10 daily fee/room. Service with restrictions, supervision.
ASK ✕ 🗔 💻 ➿

ATHENS

▼▼▼ Days Inn-Athens SH
(423) 745-5800. **$50-$60, 7 day notice.** 2541 Decatur Pike. I-75, exit 49. Ext corridors. **Pets:** Small, other species. $5 daily fee/pet. Service with restrictions, supervision.
ASK SD ✕ 🗔 ➿

▼▼▼ Motel 6 SH
(423) 745-4441. **Call for rates.** 2002 Whittaker Rd. I-75, exit 49, just e on SR 30. Int corridors. **Pets:** Accepted.
✕ ৬M ➿

▼▼▼ Ramada Inn SH
(423) 745-1212. **$75-$95.** 115 CR 247. I-75, exit 52, just w. Ext corridors. **Pets:** Accepted.
ASK SD ✕ 🗔 💻 ⁊ ➿

BOLIVAR

▼▼ The Bolivar Inn M
(731) 658-3372. **$40.** 626 W Market St. Jct US 64 and SR 18; downtown. Ext corridors. **Pets:** Other species. $10 one-time fee/room.
SD ✕ 🗔

▼▼ Rodeway Inn SH
(731) 658-7888. **$46-$75, 10 day notice.** 916 W Market St. Jct US 64 and SR 18. Ext corridors. **Pets:** Accepted.
ASK SD ✕ 🗔 ➿

BRENTWOOD

⏺⏺⏺ ▼▼▼ AmeriSuites (Nashville/Brentwood) SH 🐾
(615) 661-9477. **$79-$109.** 202 Summit View Dr. I-65, exit 74A. Int corridors. **Pets:** Large, other species. Service with restrictions, crate.
SAVE SD ✕ ৬M 🗔 💻 ➿

⏺⏺⏺ ▼▼▼ Baymont Inn & Suites SH
(615) 376-4666. **$63-$72.** 111 Penn Warren Dr. I-65, exit 74B, 1.5 mi w, then just s on West Park. Int corridors. **Pets:** Accepted.
SAVE SD ✕ ৬M ⁊ 🗔 💻 ➿

▼▼▼▼ Candlewood Suites SH
(615) 309-0600. **$63.** 5129 Virginia Way. I-65, exit 74B, 0.5 mi w, 0.5 mi s on Franklin Rd, 1.2 mi w on Marilyn Way, just s on Wade Cir, then just s. Int corridors. **Pets:** Accepted.
ASK SD ✕ 🗔 💻

▼▼▼▼ Hilton Suites Brentwood LH
(615) 370-0111. **$99-$159.** 9000 Overlook Blvd. I-65, exit 74B, 0.5 mi s on US 31, e on Church St. Int corridors. **Pets:** Accepted.
✕ ৬M ⁊ ৬ 🗔 💻 ⁊ ➿

▼▼▼▼ MainStay Suites-Brentwood SH
(615) 371-8477. **$65-$69.** 107 Brentwood Blvd. I-65, exit 74B, 1 mi w. Int corridors. **Pets:** Medium, other species. $50 one-time fee/room. Service with restrictions, supervision.
✕ ৬M ⁊ ৬ 🗔 💻 ➿

▼▼▼▼ Residence Inn Brentwood SH
(615) 371-0100. **$109.** 206 Ward Cir. I-65, exit 74B, 0.3 mi s on Franklin Pike Cir (US 31 S), 0.5 mi w on Maryland Way. Ext/int corridors. **Pets:** Accepted.
ASK SD ✕ ৬ 🗔 💻 ➿ ✕

▼▼▼ Sleep Inn SH
(615) 376-2122. **$64-$69.** 1611 Service Merchandise Blvd. I-65, exit 69 northbound, 0.4 mi, then just n; exit 69W southbound, just n. Int corridors. **Pets:** Other species. $10 daily fee/room. Service with restrictions.
ASK SD ✕ ৬M 🗔 💻 ➿

BROWNSVILLE

▼▼▼ Comfort Inn SH
(731) 772-4082. **$42-$82.** 2600 Anderson Ave. I-40, exit 56. Ext corridors. **Pets:** Accepted.
ASK SD ✕ 🗔 💻 ➿

▼▼▼ Days Inn SH
(731) 772-3297. **$42-$79.** 2530 Anderson Ave. I-40, exit 56. Ext corridors. **Pets:** Accepted.
ASK ✕ 🗔 💻

▼▼▼▼ Holiday Inn Express SH
(731) 772-4030. **$58.** 120 Sunny Hill Cove. I-40, exit 56. Int corridors. **Pets:** Accepted.
ASK SD ✕ 🗔 💻 ➿

BUCKSNORT

⏺⏺⏺ ▼ Travel Inn M
(931) 729-5450. **$36-$51.** 5032 Hwy 230 W. I-40, exit 152. Ext corridors. **Pets:** $10 deposit/pet. No service, supervision.
SAVE SD ✕ 💻

BULLS GAP

▼▼▼ **Comfort Inn** SH
(423) 235-9111. **$51-$180, 7 day notice.** 50 Speedway Ln. I-81, exit 23. Int corridors. **Pets:** Accepted.
ASK SA X & B ▣ ≈

▼ ▼ **Super 8 Motel** SH
(423) 235-4112. **$50-$70.** 90 Speedway Ln. I-81, exit 23. Ext corridors. **Pets:** Other species. $10 daily fee/room. Service with restrictions, supervision.
X & B ≈

BUTLER

▼▼▼▼ **Iron Mountain Inn B&B and Creekside Chalet** BB 🐾
(423) 768-2446. **$165-$250, 30 day notice.** 138 Moreland Dr. 1.6 mi w on Pine Orchard Rd from SR 67 at Stout Store, follow signs; 13 mi n on SR 67 from US 421 in Mountain City, follow sign at Stout Store area. Ext/int corridors. **Pets:** Other species. $100 deposit/room. Designated rooms, no service, supervision.
ASK SA X B ▣

CARYVILLE

▲▲▲ ▼ **Budget Host Inn** M
(423) 562-9595. **$25-$45.** 115 Woods Ave. I-75, exit 134, just w. Ext corridors. **Pets:** Accepted.
SAVE SA X

▼ ▼ **Super 8 Motel of Caryville** SH
(423) 562-8476. **$35-$65.** 200 John McGhee Blvd. I-75, exit 134, just e, then just s on CR 116. Ext corridors. **Pets:** $5 daily fee/pet. Designated rooms, service with restrictions, supervision.
ASK SA X ⑦ B ≈

CENTERVILLE

▼ ▼ **Days Inn** SH
(931) 729-5600. **$56.** 634 David St. On SR 100, 3 mi w of jct SR 48. Int corridors. **Pets:** Accepted.
ASK SA X ⑦ B ▣ ¶ ≈

CHATTANOOGA

▼▼▼ **Baymont Inn & Suites-Chattanooga** SH
(423) 821-1090. **$45-$110, 3 day notice.** 3540 Cummings Hwy. I-24, exit 174, 0.4 mi s. Int corridors. **Pets:** Small. Designated rooms, service with restrictions, supervision.
ASK SA X & B ▣ ≈

▼ ▼ **Best Inn-Hamilton Mall Area** SH
(423) 894-5454. **$40-$90.** 7717 Lee Hwy. I-75, exit 7B northbound; exit 7 southbound, 6.5 mi n of jct I-24. Ext corridors. **Pets:** Accepted.
X ⑦ B ▣ ≈

▲▲▲ ▼▼ **Best Western Heritage Inn** SH
(423) 899-3311. **$69-$89.** 7641 Lee Hwy. I-75, exit 7A northbound; exit 7 southbound, 6.5 mi n of jct I-24. Ext corridors. **Pets:** Very small, other species. $10 daily fee/pet. Service with restrictions, crate.
SAVE SA X B ▣ ¶ ≈

▲▲▲ ▼▼ **Best Western Royal Inn** SH
(423) 821-6840. **$60-$99.** 3644 Cummings Hwy. I-24, exit 174, 0.4 mi s. Ext corridors. **Pets:** Small. $10 daily fee/pet. Service with restrictions, supervision.
SAVE SA X B ▣ ≈

▼ ▼ **Comfort Inn** SH
(423) 821-1499. **$49-$125, 14 day notice.** 3109 Parker Ln. I-24, exit 175. Ext corridors. **Pets:** Other species. $5 daily fee/room. Service with restrictions, supervision.
ASK SA X B ▣ ≈

▼ ▼ **Days Inn Airport** SH
(423) 899-2288. **Call for rates.** 7725 Lee Hwy. I-75, exit 7A southbound; exit 7 northbound. Ext/int corridors. **Pets:** Accepted.
X B ≈

▲▲▲ ▼▼ **Days Inn-Lookout Mountain Tiftonia West** SH
(423) 821-6044. **$58-$78.** 3801 Cummings Hwy. I-24, exit 174, just n. Ext corridors. **Pets:** Medium. $10 daily fee/pet. Designated rooms, service with restrictions, supervision.
SAVE SA X ⑦ B ≈

▲▲▲ ▼▼ **La Quinta Inn Chattanooga** SH
(423) 855-0011. **$66-$76.** 7015 Shallowford Rd. I-75, exit 5 (Shallowford Rd), just w. Ext corridors. **Pets:** Other species. Service with restrictions, crate.
SAVE X ⑦ & B ▣ ≈

▼ ▼ **Microtel Inn-Chattanooga** SH
(423) 510-0761. **$30-$45, 21 day notice.** 7014 McCutcheon Rd. I-75, exit 5 (Shallowford Rd), just w, 0.3 mi n on Shallowford Village Dr, then just w. Int corridors. **Pets:** Small. $10 daily fee/pet. Service with restrictions, supervision.
ASK SA X & B

▼ ▼ **Motel 6 Downtown #4145** SH
(423) 265-7300. **$39-$99.** 2440 Williams St. I-24, exit 178 (Market St). Int corridors. **Pets:** Small. Designated rooms, service with restrictions, supervision.
ASK SA X & B

▼ ▼ **Red Roof Inn-Chattanooga** M
(423) 899-0143. **$38-$62.** 7014 Shallowford Rd. I-75, exit 5 (Shallowford Rd), just w. Ext corridors. **Pets:** Accepted.
X &

▼ ▼ **Residence Inn by Marriott** SH
(423) 266-0600. **$99-$199.** 215 Chestnut St. US 27, exit 1C (4th St), just n. Int corridors. **Pets:** Other species. $75 one-time fee/room. Service with restrictions.
ASK SA X ⓜ ⑦ & B ▣ ≈ ⊠

▼ ▼ **Super 8 Motel/Lookout Mountain** SH
(423) 821-8880. **$40-$110, 7 day notice.** 20 Birmingham Hwy. I-24, exit 174. Int corridors. **Pets:** Other species. $15 daily fee/pet. Service with restrictions, supervision.
ASK SA X B

CLARKSVILLE

▼ ▼ **Days Inn North** SH
(931) 552-1155. **$56-$66.** 130 Westfield Ct. I-24, exit 4, just s. Ext corridors. **Pets:** Accepted.
ASK SA X ⓜ B ≈

▼ ▼ **Days Inn of Clarksville** SH 🐾
(931) 358-3194. **$45-$85.** 1100 Hwy 76 Connector Rd. I-24, exit 11. Ext corridors. **Pets:** Medium, other species. $5 daily fee/pet. Service with restrictions, supervision.
ASK SA X B ≈

▲▲▲ ▼▼▼ **Holiday Inn-I-24** SH
(931) 648-4848. **$89-$119.** 3095 Wilma Rudolph Blvd. I-24, exit 4, just s. Ext corridors. **Pets:** Accepted.
SAVE SA X & B ▣ ¶ ≈ ⊠

▼ ▼ **Red Roof Inn** SH
(931) 905-1555. **$49-$79.** 197 Holiday Dr. I-24, exit 4, just se. Ext corridors. **Pets:** Accepted.
ASK SA X B ≈

CLEVELAND

Comfort Inn SH
(423) 478-5265. **$50-$90.** 153 James Asbury Dr. I-75, exit 27, just w on Paul Huff Pkwy. Ext/int corridors. **Pets:** Medium. $7 daily fee/pet. Service with restrictions, crate.

ASK ⬡ ✕ ⬡ ⬡ ⬳

Douglas Inn & Suites SH
(423) 559-5579. **$59-$89.** 2600 Westside Dr NW. I-75, exit 25, just s on SR 60, then just e. Ext/int corridors. **Pets:** Medium, other species. $10 daily fee/pet. Service with restrictions, supervision.

SAVE ⬡ ✕ ⬡ ⬡

Econo Lodge of Cleveland SH
(423) 472-3281. **$45-$70, 14 day notice.** 2655 Westside Dr NW. I-75, exit 25, just s. Ext corridors. **Pets:** Small. $10 daily fee/pet. Service with restrictions, supervision.

SAVE ⬡ ✕ ⬡ ⬡ ⬳

Holiday Inn Mountain View SH
(423) 472-1500. **$69-$79.** 2400 Executive Park Dr. I-75, exit 25. Ext/int corridors. **Pets:** Accepted.

SAVE ⬡ ✕ ⬡ ⬡ ⬡ 🍴 ⬳

Jameson Inn SH
(423) 614-5583. **$49-$104.** 360 Paul Huff Pkwy. I-75, exit 27, 1 mi e. Ext corridors. **Pets:** Very small, other species. $10 daily fee/room. Service with restrictions, supervision.

ASK ✕ ⬡ ⬡ ⬳

Quality Inn Chalet SH
(423) 476-8511. **$65-$85.** 2595 Georgetown Rd. I-75, exit 25. Ext corridors. **Pets:** Other species. $10 daily fee/pet. Designated rooms, supervision.

SAVE ⬡ ✕ ⬡ ⬡ ⬡ 🍴 ⬳

Ramada Limited SH
(423) 472-5566. **$65-$80.** 156 James Asbury Dr. I-75, exit 27. Ext corridors. **Pets:** Accepted.

ASK ⬡ ✕ ⬡ ⬡ ⬡ ⬳

Super 8 Motel SH
(423) 476-5555. **$50-$55.** 163 Bernham Dr. I-75, exit 27, just w on Paul Huff Pkwy, then s. Ext/int corridors. **Pets:** Accepted.

SAVE ⬡ ✕ ⬡ ⬡ ⬡ ⬳

CLINTON

Best Western Clinton Inn SH
(865) 457-2311. **$49-$120.** 720 Park Pl. I-75, exit 122, just w. Ext corridors. **Pets:** $10 daily fee/pet. Service with restrictions, supervision.

ASK ⬡ ✕ ⬡ ⬡ ⬡ ⬳

Clinton Super 8 Motel SH
(865) 457-0565. **$65-$125.** 2317 N Charles G Severs Blvd. I-75, exit 122, just w. Int corridors. **Pets:** Accepted.

ASK ⬡ ✕ ⬡ ⬡ ⬡ ⬡ ⬳

Holiday Inn Express Hotel & Suites SH
(865) 457-2233. **$79-$109, 7 day notice.** 141 Buffalo Rd. I-75, exit 122, just w. Ext corridors. **Pets:** Accepted.

ASK ⬡ ✕ ⬡ ⬡ ⬡ ⬡ ⬳

COLUMBIA

Best Value Inn SH
(931) 381-1410. **$39-$49.** 1548 Bear Creek Pike. I-65, exit 46, just w. Ext corridors. **Pets:** Other species. $5 one-time fee/pet. Service with restrictions, supervision.

SAVE ⬡ ✕ ⬡

Holiday Inn Express SH
(931) 380-1227. **$75-$83, 3 day notice.** 1554 Bear Creek Pike. I-65, exit 46, just w. Ext corridors. **Pets:** Other species. $10 daily fee/pet. Designated rooms, service with restrictions, supervision.

SAVE ⬡ ✕ ⬡ ⬡ ⬡ ⬡ ⬳

COOKEVILLE

Alpine Lodge & Suites SH
(931) 526-3333. **$38-$54.** 2021 E Spring St. I-40, exit 290, just s. Int corridors. **Pets:** Medium. $5 daily fee/pet. Designated rooms, service with restrictions, supervision.

SAVE ⬡ ✕ ⬡ ⬡ ⬡ ⬳

Baymont Inn & Suites Cookeville SH
(931) 525-6668. **$69-$99.** 1151 S Jefferson Ave. I-40, exit 387. Int corridors. **Pets:** Small, other species. Service with restrictions, supervision.

SAVE ⬡ ✕ ⬡ ⬡ ⬡ ⬡ ⬡ ⬳

Best Western Thunderbird Motel SH
(931) 526-7115. **$50-$90.** 900 S Jefferson Ave. I-40, exit 287. Ext corridors. **Pets:** Other species. $5 daily fee/pet. Service with restrictions.

SAVE ⬡ ✕ ⬡ ⬡ ⬡ ⬡ ⬡ ⬳

Days Inn SH
(931) 528-1511. **$34-$88.** 1296 S Walnut Ave. I-40, exit 287. Ext corridors. **Pets:** Other species. $10 one-time fee/room. Designated rooms, service with restrictions, supervision.

SAVE ⬡ ✕ ⬡ ⬡ ⬡ ⬳

Econo Lodge SH 🐾
(931) 528-1040. **$40-$80.** 1100 S Jefferson Ave. I-40, exit 287. Ext corridors. **Pets:** Large, other species. $10 one-time fee/pet. Designated rooms, service with restrictions, crate.

SAVE ⬡ ✕ ⬡ ⬡ ⬳

Hampton Inn SH
(931) 520-1117. **$75-$95.** 1025 Interstate Dr. I-40, exit 287, 0.5 mi n. Ext corridors. **Pets:** Other species. Service with restrictions.

SAVE ⬡ ✕ ⬡ ⬡ ⬡ ⬡ ⬡ ⬳

Holiday Inn SH
(931) 526-7125. **$59-$89.** 970 S Jefferson Ave. I-40, exit 287. Ext/int corridors. **Pets:** Designated rooms, service with restrictions, supervision.

ASK ⬡ ✕ ⬡ ⬡ ⬡ 🍴 ⬳

CORNERSVILLE

Econo Lodge M
(931) 293-2111. **$69-$79.** 3731 Pulaski Hwy. I-65, exit 22 at jct US 31A. Ext corridors. **Pets:** Accepted.

SAVE ⬡ ✕ ⬡ ⬳

CROSSVILLE

Ramada Limited SH
(931) 484-7581. **$79-$89, 30 day notice.** 4083 Hwy 127 N. I-40, exit 317, just n. Ext corridors. **Pets:** Medium. $10 daily fee/pet. Designated rooms, service with restrictions, supervision.

SAVE ⬡ ✕ ⬡ ⬡ ⬳

CUMBERLAND GAP

Ramada Inn of Cumberland Gap SH
(423) 869-3631. **$63-$87.** Hwy 58. On US 58, just e of jct US 25 E. Int corridors. **Pets:** Other species. $25 one-time fee/room. Service with restrictions.

SAVE ⬡ ✕ ⬡ ⬡ ⬡ 🍴 ⬳

DANDRIDGE

Tennessee Mountain Inn 5H
(865) 397-9437. **$29-$129.** 531 Patriot Dr. I-40, exit 417, just n. Ext corridors. **Pets:** $10 daily fee/pet. Designated rooms, service with restrictions, supervision.

DAYTON

Best Western Dayton 5H
(423) 775-6560. **$65-$105.** 7835 Rhea County Hwy. 1 mi n on US 27. Ext corridors. **Pets:** Other species. $5 daily fee/room. Service with restrictions.

Days Inn M
(423) 775-9718. **Call for rates.** 3914 Rhea County Hwy. 1 mi s on US 27. Ext corridors. **Pets:** Accepted.

DECHERD

Jameson Inn 5H
(931) 962-0130. **$49-$104.** 1838 Decherd Blvd. Jct Main St and SR 41A, just s. Ext corridors. **Pets:** Very small, other species. $10 daily fee/room. Service with restrictions, supervision.

DICKSON

Best Western Executive Inn 5H
(615) 446-0541. **$50-$60, 7 day notice.** 2338 Hwy 46. I-40, exit 172, just n. Ext corridors. **Pets:** Small, dogs only. $5 daily fee/pet. Designated rooms, service with restrictions, supervision.

Comfort Inn 5H
(615) 441-5252. **$60-$70.** 1025 E Christi Rd. I-40, exit 72. Int corridors. **Pets:** Accepted.

Days Inn 5H
(615) 740-7475. **$49-$59.** 2415 Hwy 46 S. I-40, exit 172, just s. Ext corridors. **Pets:** Medium. $20 deposit/room. Designated rooms, service with restrictions, supervision.

Holiday Inn 5H
(615) 446-9081. **$76-$83, 14 day notice.** 2420 Hwy 46 S. I-40, exit 172, just s. Ext corridors. **Pets:** Other species. Service with restrictions, supervision.

Motel 6 #4226 5H
(615) 446-2423. **$39-$49.** 2325 Hwy 46 S. I-40, exit 172, just n. Ext corridors. **Pets:** No service, supervision.

Super 8 Motel 5H
(615) 446-1923. **$49-$54.** 150 Suzanne Dr. I-40, exit 172, just n on SR 46, then just e. Int corridors. **Pets:** $10 daily fee/room. Service with restrictions, supervision.

DYERSBURG

Best Western Dyersburg 5H
(731) 285-8601. **$72-$75, 10 day notice.** 770 Hwy 51 Bypass W. I-155, exit 13, 0.5 mi s, jct of US 51 Bypass and SR 78. Ext corridors. **Pets:** Large, other species. $20 daily fee/pet. Service with restrictions, supervision.

Comfort Inn 5H
(731) 285-6951. **$65-$74.** 815 Reelfoot Dr. I-155, exit 13, just s. Ext corridors. **Pets:** Accepted.

Executive Inn & Suites 5H
(731) 287-0044. **$40-$70.** 2331 Lake Rd. I-155, exit 13, 0.5 mi s. Ext corridors. **Pets:** Accepted.

Hampton Inn 5H
(731) 285-4778. **$74-$89.** 2750 Mall Loop Rd. I-155, exit 13, just s. Int corridors. **Pets:** Accepted.

EAST RIDGE

Best Value Inn 5H
(423) 894-6110. **$39-$59.** 639 Camp Jordan Pkwy. I-75, exit 1 (Ringgold Rd), 0.3 mi e. Ext/int corridors. **Pets:** Accepted.

Howard Johnson Plaza Hotel 5H
(423) 892-8100. **$60-$80.** 6700 Ringgold Rd. I-75, exit 1 (Ringgold Rd). Int corridors. **Pets:** Other species. $15 daily fee/room. Service with restrictions, crate.

Ramada Limited 5H
(423) 894-1860. **$45-$100.** 6650 Ringgold Rd. I-75, exit 1 (Ringgold Rd). Int corridors. **Pets:** Small. $10 daily fee/pet. Designated rooms, service with restrictions, supervision.

ELIZABETHTON

Americourt 5H
(423) 542-4466. **$59-$79.** 1515 US 19 E Bypass. 1 mi e on US 19 E Bypass and 321. Int corridors. **Pets:** Medium, other species. Supervision.

ERWIN

Holiday Inn Express 5H
(423) 743-4100. **$70-$94, 3 day notice.** 2002 Temple Hill Rd. US 19 W and 23, exit 15, just e. Int corridors. **Pets:** $15 daily fee/pet. Service with restrictions, supervision.

FAIRVIEW

Deerfield Inn & Suites 5H
(615) 799-4700. **$39-$69.** 1407 Hwy 96 N. I-40, exit 182. Ext corridors. **Pets:** Small. $8 one-time fee/pet. Designated rooms, service with restrictions, supervision.

FARRAGUT

Baymont Inn & Suites-Knoxville West 5H
(865) 671-1010. **$60-$96.** 11341 Campbell Lakes Dr. I-40/75, exit 373 (Campbell Station Rd). Int corridors. **Pets:** Large, other species. Service with restrictions, supervision.

Super 8 5H
(865) 675-5566. **$49-$95.** 11748 Snyder Rd. I-40/75, exit 373 (Campbell Station Rd), just ne. Ext corridors. **Pets:** Medium. $6 daily fee/pet. Designated rooms, service with restrictions, supervision.

FAYETTEVILLE

Best Western-Fayetteville Inn SH
(931) 433-0100. **$66-$71.** 3021 Thornton Taylor Pkwy. 0.7 mi e of US 431, on US 64 and 231 Bypass. Ext corridors. **Pets:** Accepted.

FRANKLIN

AmeriSuites (Nashville/Cool Springs) SH
(615) 771-8900. **$89-$129.** 650 Bakers Bridge Ave. I-65, exit 69 (Galleria Blvd), 0.5 mi s, then just e. Int corridors. **Pets:** Accepted.

Baymont Inn & Suites Nashville-Franklin M
(615) 791-7700. **$59-$104.** 4207 Franklin Commons Ct. I-65, exit 65, just e. Int corridors. **Pets:** Accepted.

Best Western Franklin Inn SH
(615) 790-0570. **$69-$99.** 1308 Murfreesboro Rd. I-65, exit 65, just w. Ext corridors. **Pets:** $10 one-time fee/room. Service with restrictions, supervision.

Days Inn SH
(615) 790-1140. **$45-$65.** 4217 S Carothers Rd. I-65, exit 65, just e. Ext corridors. **Pets:** Very small, dogs only. $10 daily fee/pet. No service, supervision.

Holiday Inn Express Hotel & Suites SH
(615) 591-6660. **$99.** 4202 Franklin Commons Ct. I-65, exit 65, just e. Int corridors. **Pets:** Accepted.

Homestead Studio Suites Hotel-Nashville/Cool Springs/Brentwood SH
(615) 771-7600. **$54-$74.** 680 Bakers Bridge Ave. I-65, exit 69 (Galleria Blvd). Ext corridors. **Pets:** Accepted.

Namaste Acres Country Ranch Inn BB
(615) 791-0333. **$85-$95, 5 day notice.** 5436 Leipers Creek. SR 96, 5 mi w; SR 46, 6 mi sw, then 1.9 mi s. Ext/int corridors. **Pets:** Medium, other species. $15 one-time fee/room. No service, supervision.

Ramada Limited & Suites SH
(615) 791-4004. **$58.** 6210 Hospitality Dr. I-65, exit 65, 1 mi e. Int corridors. **Pets:** Large, other species. $5 daily fee/pet. Service with restrictions, crate.

GALLATIN

Jameson Inn SH
(615) 451-4494. **$49-$104.** 1001 Village Green Crossing. 2 mi s on US 31. Ext corridors. **Pets:** Very small, other species. $10 daily fee/room. Service with restrictions, supervision.

GATLINBURG

Cobbly Nob Rentals Inc CA
(865) 436-5298. **$75-$150, 30 day notice.** 3722 E Parkway (Hwy 321). 11 mi e on US 321 N (E Parkway). Ext corridors. **Pets:** Accepted.

Greenbrier Valley Resorts At Cobbly Nob CA
(865) 436-2015. **$100-$450, 30 day notice.** 3629 E Parkway. 10.8 mi e on US 321 N (E Parkway). Ext corridors. **Pets:** Other species. $100 deposit/room, $10 daily fee/pet. Designated rooms, crate.

Holiday Inn SunSpree Resort LH
(865) 436-9201. **$59-$119.** 520 Historic Nature Tr. US 441, 1 mi e at traffic light 8. Ext/int corridors. **Pets:** Medium, other species. $15 one-time fee/pet. Service with restrictions, supervision.

Microtel-Gatlinburg SH
(865) 436-0107. **$45-$199, 3 day notice.** 211 Historic Nature Tr. US 441, traffic light 8, just e. Int corridors. **Pets:** Medium. $10 daily fee/pet. Service with restrictions, supervision.

The Park Vista Hotel LH
(865) 436-9211. **$70-$169, 3 day notice.** 705 Cherokee Orchard Rd. US 441, 0.8 mi e, at traffic light 8 on Airport Rd. Int corridors. **Pets:** Accepted.

Terrace Motel M
(865) 436-4965. **$55-$85, 7 day notice.** 396 Parkway. US 441, between traffic lights 2 and 3. Ext corridors. **Pets:** Small, other species. Service with restrictions, crate.

GREENEVILLE

Comfort Inn of Greeneville SH
(423) 639-4185. **$63-$79.** 1790 E Andrew Johnson Hwy. US 11 E, 2.9 mi ne. Ext/int corridors. **Pets:** $10 daily fee/pet. Designated rooms, service with restrictions, supervision.

Days Inn M
(423) 639-2156. **$46-$180, 7 day notice.** 935 E Andrew Johnson Hwy. US 11 E, 2 mi ne. Ext corridors. **Pets:** Very small. $15 daily fee/pet. Designated rooms, no service, supervision.

HARRIMAN

Best Western Sundancer Motor Lodge M
(865) 882-6200. **$49-$60, 7 day notice.** 120 Childs Rd. I-40, exit 347, just n. Ext corridors. **Pets:** Small. $10 daily fee/pet. Designated rooms, no service, supervision.

Holiday Inn Express SH
(865) 882-5340. **$59-$109.** 1845 S Roane St. I-40, exit 347, just s. Ext corridors. **Pets:** Other species. $20 daily fee/room. Service with restrictions, supervision.

Super 8 Motel M
(865) 882-6600. **$49-$55.** 1867 S Roane St. I-40, exit 347, 0.3 mi s on US 27/SR 61. Ext corridors. **Pets:** Small, dogs only. $5 daily fee/pet. Designated rooms, service with restrictions, supervision.

HENDERSONVILLE

AmeriSuites (Nashville/Hendersonville) SH
(615) 826-4301. **$79-$99.** 330 E Main St. US 31, 1 mi n. Int corridors. **Pets:** Medium, other species. Service with restrictions, crate.

HIXSON

Home Away Extended Stay Studios SH
(423) 643-9663. **$69.** 1949 North Point Blvd. Center. Ext corridors. **Pets:** Medium, other species. $10 daily fee/pet, $50 one-time fee/pet. Service with restrictions, supervision.

HURRICANE MILLS

AAA ▽▽ Best Western of Hurricane Mills **M**
(931) 296-4251. **$70-$100.** 15542 Hwy 13 S. I-40, exit 143. Ext corridors. **Pets:** Medium. $12 daily fee/pet. Service with restrictions, supervision.
SAVE 🚭 ✕ 🐾 🔒 💻 🏊

AAA ▽▽▽ Holiday Inn Express **SH**
(931) 296-2999. **$67-$89.** 15368 Hwy 13 S. I-40, exit 143, just n. Int corridors. **Pets:** Other species. Service with restrictions, supervision.
SAVE 🚭 ✕ 🐾 🔒 💻 🏊

JACKSON

▽▽▽ Baymont Inn & Suites Jackson **SH** 🐾
(731) 664-1800. **$59-$89.** 2370 N Highland Ave. I-40, exit 82A. Int corridors. **Pets:** Other species. $25 deposit/room. No service, supervision.
ASK 🚭 ✕ 🔒 💻 🏊

▽▽▽ Best Western Inn & Suites **SH**
(731) 664-3030. **$60-$75.** 1936 Hwy 45 Bypass. I-40, exit 80A, just s. Ext corridors. **Pets:** Very small, dogs only. $5 daily fee/pet. Designated rooms, service with restrictions, supervision.
ASK 🚭 ✕ 🖥 🔒 💻 🏊

▽▽ Days Inn **SH**
(731) 668-3444. **$53-$70, 14 day notice.** 1919 US 45 Bypass. I-40, exit 80A, just s. Ext corridors. **Pets:** Medium, other species. $10 daily fee/pet. Designated rooms, service with restrictions, supervision.
ASK 🚭 ✕ 🔒 🏊

▽▽ Days Inn-West **SH**
(731) 668-4840. **$39-$50.** 2239 Hollywood Dr. I-40, exit 79. Ext corridors. **Pets:** Medium. $5 daily fee/room. Designated rooms, service with restrictions, supervision.
ASK 🚭 ✕ 🔒 🏊

▽▽▽ Doubletree Hotel Jackson **LH**
(731) 664-6900. **$89.** 1770 Hwy 45 Bypass. I-40, exit 80A, 0.5 mi s. Int corridors. **Pets:** Accepted.
ASK 🚭 ✕ 🐾 🔒 💻 🍴 🏊

▽▽▽ Jameson Inn **SH**
(731) 660-8651. **$49-$104.** 1292 Vann Dr. I-40, exit 80B, 0.6 mi w. Int corridors. **Pets:** Very small, other species. $10 daily fee/room. Service with restrictions, supervision.
ASK ✕ 🔒 💻 🏊

▽▽ Old Hickory Inn **SH**
(731) 668-4222. **$45-$49.** 1849 Hwy 45 Bypass. I-40, exit 80A, 0.3 mi s. Ext corridors. **Pets:** Accepted.
✕ 🔒 💻 🏊

JELLICO

▽▽ Best Western Holiday Plaza Motel **SH**
(423) 784-7241. **Call for rates.** 133 Holiday Dr. I-75, exit 160, just w. Ext corridors. **Pets:** Accepted.
✕ 💻 🏊

▽▽ Days Inn **SH**
(423) 784-7281. **$42-$66.** US 25 W. I-75, exit 160, just w. Ext corridors. **Pets:** Medium, other species. $8 daily fee/pet. Designated rooms, service with restrictions, supervision.
ASK 🚭 ✕ 💻 🍴 🏊

JOHNSON CITY

▽▽▽ Best Western Johnson City Hotel & Conference Center **SH**
(423) 282-2161. **$65-$75.** 2406 N Roan St. I-26, exit 35A northbound; exit 35 southbound, just e. Ext/int corridors. **Pets:** Small. $15 daily fee/room. Service with restrictions, crate.
ASK 🚭 ✕ 🖥 🔒 💻 🍴 🏊

▽▽ Comfort Inn of Johnson City **SH**
(423) 928-9600. **$54-$280.** 1900 S Roan St. I-181, exit 31, just w on US 321. Ext corridors. **Pets:** Accepted.
ASK 🚭 ✕ 🔒 💻 🏊

▽▽ Holiday Inn-Johnson City **SH**
(423) 282-4611. **$96-$110.** 101 W Springbrook Dr. I-181, exit 35A northbound; exit 35 southbound, just e on N Roan St, then just n. Int corridors. **Pets:** $50 deposit/room. Designated rooms, crate.
ASK ✕ 🐾 🔒 💻 🍴 🏊

▽▽ Jameson Inn **SH**
(423) 282-0488. **$49-$104.** 119 Pinnacle Dr. I-181, exit 38, just w on CR 354, then just s. Ext corridors. **Pets:** Very small, other species. $10 daily fee/room. Service with restrictions, supervision.
ASK ✕ 🖥 🔒 💻 🏊

▽▽ Red Roof Inn-Johnson City **SH**
(423) 282-3040. **$47-$71.** 210 Broyles Dr. I-181, exit 35B northbound; exit 35 southbound, just w on N Roan St, then s. Ext corridors. **Pets:** Accepted.
✕ 🐾 🔒

▽▽ Sleep Inn **SH**
(423) 915-0081. **$79.** 2020 Franklin Terrace Ct. I-181, exit 36, just w, then just n, follow signs; must enter on Oakland Ave at the light. Int corridors. **Pets:** Accepted.
ASK 🚭 ✕ 🖥 🐾 🖥 🔒 💻

KINGSPORT

▽▽▽ Jameson Inn **SH**
(423) 230-0534. **$49-$104.** 3004 Bay Meadow Pl. I-181, exit 51. Int corridors. **Pets:** Very small, other species. $10 daily fee/room. Service with restrictions, supervision.
ASK ✕ 🔒 💻 🏊

▽▽▽ La Quinta Inn Kingsport **SH**
(423) 323-0500. **$75-$85.** 10150 Airport Pkwy. I-81, exit 63, just e. Int corridors. **Pets:** Accepted.
ASK ✕ 🖥 🐾 🖥 🔒 💻 🏊

▽▽ Sleep Inn **SH**
(423) 279-1811. **$79.** 200 Hospitality Pl. I-81, exit 63, just s. Int corridors. **Pets:** Accepted.
ASK 🚭 ✕ 🖥 🔒 💻

KINGSTON

AAA ▽▽ Comfort Inn of Kingston **M**
(865) 376-4965. **$64-$90.** 905 N Kentucky St. I-40, exit 352, 0.3 mi s. Ext corridors. **Pets:** Accepted.
SAVE 🚭 ✕ 🔒 💻

AAA ▽▽ Days Inn **M**
(865) 376-2069. **$55-$90.** 495 Gallaher Rd. I-40, exit 356, just n. Ext corridors. **Pets:** Small. $10 daily fee/pet. Service with restrictions, supervision.
SAVE 🚭 ✕ 🐾 🔒 🏊

KINGSTON SPRINGS

AAA ▽▽▽ Best Western Harpeth Inn **SH**
(615) 952-3961. **$45-$80.** 116 Luy Ben Hills Rd. I-40, exit 188, just n. Ext corridors. **Pets:** Accepted.
SAVE 🚭 ✕ 🐾 🔒 💻 🏊

KNOXVILLE

▽▽▽ The Clarion Inn **SH**
(865) 687-8989. **$89-$99.** 5634 Merchant Center Blvd. I-75, exit 108 (Merchant Dr), 0.5 mi w, then 0.5 mi n. Int corridors. **Pets:** Accepted.
ASK 🚭 ✕ 🖥 🐾 🖥 🔒 💻 🏊

▼▼▼ **ClubHouse Inn & Suites Knoxville** SH
(865) 531-1900. **$69-$109.** 208 Market Place Ln. I-40/75, exit 378 (Cedar Bluff Rd). Int corridors. **Pets:** Accepted.
(A$K) (S🐾) (✕) (🔥M) (🎵) (🖥) (🖵) (🍴) (🏊)

▼▼ **Days Inn West** SH
(865) 966-5801. **$45-$90.** 326 Lovell Rd. I-40/75, exit 374 (Lovell Rd). Ext corridors. **Pets:** Accepted.
(A$K) (S🐾) (✕) (🎵) (🖥) (🖵) (🏊)

▲▲▲ ▼ **Econo Lodge West** M
(865) 693-6061. **$39-$99.** 9240 Park West Blvd. I-40/75, exit 378 (Cedar Bluff Rd), just n to Park West Blvd, then just w. Ext corridors. **Pets:** Medium. $5 daily fee/pet. Designated rooms, service with restrictions, supervision.
(SAVE) (S🐾) (✕) (🖥) (🖵) (🏊)

▼▼▼ **Hampton Inn-Knoxville West at Cedar Bluff** SH
(865) 693-1101. **$94-$109.** 9128 Executive Park Blvd. I-40/75, exit 378 (Cedar Bluff Rd). Ext/int corridors. **Pets:** Medium. Designated rooms, service with restrictions.
(A$K) (S🐾) (✕) (🔥M) (🎵) (🖇) (🖥) (🖵) (🏊)

▼▼▼ **Highway Host Inn & Suites** SH
(865) 688-8886. **Call for rates.** 5005 Central Ave Pike. I-75, exit 108 (Merchant Dr), just e. Ext/int corridors. **Pets:** Accepted.
(✕) (🎵) (🖥) (🖵)

▲▲▲ ▼▼▼ **Holiday Inn-Central/Papermill Road** LH 🐾
(865) 584-3911. **$110-$120.** 1315 Kirby Rd. I-40/75, exit 383 (Papermill Rd). Int corridors. **Pets:** Medium, other species. $10 daily fee/pet. Designated rooms, service with restrictions, crate.
(SAVE) (S🐾) (✕) (🔥M) (🎵) (🖇) (🖥) (🖵) (🍴) (🏊)

▲▲▲ ▼▼▼▼ **Holiday Inn Select-Cedar Bluff** LH
(865) 693-1011. **$129-$159.** 304 Cedar Bluff Rd. I-40/75, exit 378 (Cedar Bluff Rd). Int corridors. **Pets:** Medium. $10 daily fee/room. Designated rooms, service with restrictions, crate.
(SAVE) (S🐾) (✕) (🎵) (🖇) (🖥) (🖵) (🍴) (🏊) (✕)

▼▼ **Knights Inn-North** SH
(865) 687-3500. **$39-$44.** 114 Dante Rd. I-75, exit 110 (Callahan Dr), just e. Ext corridors. **Pets:** Accepted.
(A$K) (S🐾) (✕) (🖥)

▲▲▲ ▼▼▼▼ **La Quinta Inn Knoxville (West)** SH
(865) 690-9777. **$79-$91.** 258 Peters Rd N. I-40, exit 378 (Cedar Bluff Rd). Ext corridors. **Pets:** Medium, other species. Service with restrictions, crate.
(SAVE) (✕) (🔥M) (🎵) (🖥) (🖵) (🏊)

▼▼ **Microtel** SH
(865) 531-8041. **$44-$79.** 309 N Peters Rd. I-40/75, exit 378 (Cedar Bluff Rd), 0.5 mi s, then just w. Int corridors. **Pets:** $10 one-time fee/room. Designated rooms, service with restrictions.
(A$K) (S🐾) (✕) (🔥M) (🎵) (🖥)

▼▼ **Motel 6–1252** SH
(865) 675-7200. **$41-$53.** 402 Lovell Rd. I-40/75, exit 374 (Lovell Rd). Ext corridors. **Pets:** Accepted.
(S🐾) (✕) (🔥M) (🎵) (🖇) (🏊)

▼▼ **Motel 6 #1482** SH
(865) 689-7100. **$41-$55.** 5640 Merchant Center Blvd. I-75, exit 108 (Merchant Dr). Ext corridors. **Pets:** Accepted.
(S🐾) (✕) (🎵)

▲▲▲ ▼▼▼ **Quality Inn North** SH
(865) 689-6600. **$54-$70.** 6712 Central Ave Pike. I-75, exit 110 (Callahan Dr), just e. Ext/int corridors. **Pets:** Small. $10 daily fee/pet. Service with restrictions, crate.
(SAVE) (S🐾) (✕) (🖥) (🖵) (🏊)

▼▼▼ **Radisson Summit Hill** SH 🐾
(865) 522-2600. **$139.** 401 Summit Hill Dr. Corner of Walnut St; downtown. Int corridors. **Pets:** Large. $25 one-time fee/room. Service with restrictions.
(A$K) (S🐾) (✕) (🎵) (🖇) (🖥) (🖵) (🍴) (🏊)

▲▲▲ ▼▼▼ **Ramada Limited-East** M
(865) 546-7271. **$59-$89, 3 day notice.** 722 Brakebill Rd. I-40, exit 398 (Strawberry Plains), just n. Ext corridors. **Pets:** Very small. $10 daily fee/pet. Designated rooms, service with restrictions, supervision.
(SAVE) (S🐾) (✕) (🔥M) (🖥) (🖵) (🏊)

▼▼▼ **Ramada Suites Limited** SH
(865) 687-9922. **Call for rates.** 5317 Pratt Rd. I-75, exit 108 (Merchant Dr). Int corridors. **Pets:** Accepted.
(✕) (🔥M) (🎵) (🖥) (🖵) (🏊)

▼▼ **Red Roof Inn-West** SH
(865) 691-1664. **$45-$55.** 209 Advantage Pl. I-40/75, exit 378 (Cedar Bluff Rd), just sw. Ext corridors. **Pets:** Accepted.
(✕) (🔥M) (🎵) (🏊)

▼▼ **Super 8 Motel-Knoxville** SH
(865) 584-8511. **$48-$70.** 6200 Papermill Rd. I-40/75, exit 383 (Papermill Rd), 0.3 mi e. Ext corridors. **Pets:** Other species. Supervision.
(A$K) (S🐾) (✕) (🔥M) (🎵) (🖥) (🖵) (🏊)

LAWRENCEBURG

▼▼ **Best Western Villa Inn** SH
(931) 762-4448. **$66-$84.** 2126 N Locust Ave. On US 43, 2.2 mi n of jct US 64. Ext corridors. **Pets:** Medium. $15 daily fee/pet. Service with restrictions, supervision.
(✕) (🖥) (🖵) (🏊)

LEBANON

▲▲▲ ▼▼▼ **Best Value Inn & Suites** SH
(615) 449-5781. **$37-$129.** 822 S Cumberland St. I-40, exit 238. Ext corridors. **Pets:** Accepted.
(SAVE) (S🐾) (✕) (🖥) (🖵) (🏊)

▲▲▲ ▼▼▼ **Best Western Executive Inn** SH
(615) 444-0505. **$64-$94.** 631 S Cumberland St. I-40, exit 238, 0.5 mi n. Ext/int corridors. **Pets:** Medium, dogs only. $15 daily fee/pet. No service, crate.
(SAVE) (S🐾) (✕) (🔥M) (🖥) (🖵) (🏊)

▼▼ **Comfort Inn** SH
(615) 444-1001. **$49-$89.** 829 S Cumberland St. I-40, exit 238. Ext corridors. **Pets:** $5 daily fee/pet. Designated rooms, service with restrictions, crate.
(A$K) (S🐾) (✕) (🖥) (🖵) (🏊)

▼▼ **Days Inn** SH
(615) 444-5635. **$40-$80, 7 day notice.** 914 Murfreesboro Rd. I-40, exit 238. Ext corridors. **Pets:** Accepted.
(A$K) (S🐾) (✕) (🏊)

▲▲▲ ▼▼▼ **Hampton Inn** SH
(615) 444-7400. **$69-$129.** 704 S Cumberland St. I-40, exit 238. Ext corridors. **Pets:** Accepted.
(SAVE) (S🐾) (✕) (🔥M) (🎵) (🖥) (🖵) (🏊) (✕)

▼▼ **Super 8 Motel** SH
(615) 444-5637. **$35-$75, 7 day notice.** 914 Murfreesboro Rd. I-40, exit 238. Ext corridors. **Pets:** Accepted.
(A$K) (S🐾) (✕) (🖥) (🏊)

LENOIR CITY

▲▲▲ ▼▼▼ **Days Inn** SH
(865) 986-2011. **$55-$85.** 1110 Hwy 321 N. I-75, exit 81, just e. Ext corridors. **Pets:** Small. $10 daily fee/pet. Service with restrictions, supervision.
(SAVE) (S🐾) (✕) (🖥) (🏊)

⚫⚫ ▼▼▼ Econo Lodge 🆂🅷
(865) 986-0295. **$50-$80.** 1211 Hwy 321 N. I-75, exit 81, just w. Ext corridors. **Pets:** Small. $5 daily fee/pet. Service with restrictions, supervision.
🆂🅰🆅🅴 🆂🅳 ✖ 🈂 📠 ➾

LOUDON

⚫⚫ ▼▼▼ Knights Inn Ⓜ
(865) 458-5855. **$39-$69.** 15100 Hwy 72. I-75, exit 72, just w. Ext corridors. **Pets:** Medium. $5 daily fee/pet. Service with restrictions, supervision.
🆂🅰🆅🅴 🆂🅳 ✖ 📠 ➾

▼▼ Super 8 Motel 🆂🅷 🐾
(865) 458-5669. **$50-$60.** 12452 Hwy 72 N. I-75, exit 72, just e. Ext corridors. **Pets:** Other species. Service with restrictions, supervision.
🅰🆂🅺 🆂🅳 ✖ ♿ 🈂 📠 ➾

MANCHESTER

⚫⚫ ▼▼▼▼ Country Inn & Suites 🆂🅷
(931) 728-7551. **$85.** 126 Expressway Dr. I-24, exit 114, just w. Int corridors. **Pets:** Small. Service with restrictions, supervision.
🆂🅰🆅🅴 🆂🅳 ✖ ♿ 🏊 📠 📠 ➾

⚫⚫ ▼▼▼ Days Inn & Suites 🆂🅷
(931) 728-9530. **$60.** 2259 Hillsboro Blvd. I-24, exit 114, just w. Ext corridors. **Pets:** Medium, dogs only. $6 daily fee/pet. No service, supervision.
🆂🅰🆅🅴 🆂🅳 ✖ 📠 📠 ➾

▼▼ Econo Lodge Ⓜ
(931) 728-6023. **$50-$75, 5 day notice.** 890 Interstate Dr. I-24, exit 110, just n on SR 53. Ext corridors. **Pets:** Accepted.
🅰🆂🅺 🆂🅳 ✖ 📠 📠 ➾

⚫⚫ ▼▼ Ramada Inn 🆂🅷
(931) 728-0800. **$65-$89.** 2314 Hillsboro Blvd. I-24, exit 114, just n. Ext corridors. **Pets:** Small, other species. $8 daily fee/pet. Service with restrictions, crate.
🆂🅰🆅🅴 🆂🅳 ✖ 📠 📠 ➾

MCMINNVILLE

⚫⚫ ▼▼▼ McMinnville Inn 🆂🅷
(931) 473-7338. **$49-$69.** 2545 Sparta Hwy. I-24, exit 111, n on SR 55 to US 70 S Bypass. Ext corridors. **Pets:** Small. $8 daily fee/pet. Service with restrictions.
🆂🅰🆅🅴 🆂🅳 ✖ 📠 📠 ➾

MEMPHIS METROPOLITAN AREA

COLLIERVILLE

▼▼ Comfort Inn 🆂🅷
(901) 853-1235. **$65-$99, 7 day notice.** 1230 W Poplar Ave. 2.5 mi w on SR 57 and US 72. Ext corridors. **Pets:** $10 one-time fee/room. Service with restrictions, supervision.
🅰🆂🅺 🆂🅳 ✖ 🈂 📠 📠 ➾

CORDOVA

⚫⚫ ▼▼▼▼ Comfort Suites 🆂🅷
(901) 213-3600. **$79-$99.** 2427 N Germantown Pkwy. I-40, exit 16, just s. Int corridors. **Pets:** Other species. $25 daily fee/room. Designated rooms, service with restrictions, supervision.
🆂🅰🆅🅴 🆂🅳 ✖ 🏊 🈂 ♿ 📠 📠 ➾

⚫⚫ ▼▼▼ Quality Suites-Wolfchase 🆂🅷
(901) 386-4600. **$74-$150.** 8166 Varnavas Dr. I-40, exit 16, 0.3 mi s on Germantown Pkwy, then e. Int corridors. **Pets:** Accepted.
🆂🅰🆅🅴 🆂🅳 ✖ ♿ 📠 📠 ➾

COVINGTON

▼▼ Comfort Inn 🆂🅷
(901) 475-0380. **$70-$85.** 901 Hwy 51 N. 1 mi n of jct US 59. Ext corridors. **Pets:** Other species. $15 daily fee/pet. Service with restrictions, crate.
🅰🆂🅺 🆂🅳 ✖ 📠 📠 ➾

GERMANTOWN

▼▼ Comfort Inn & Suites-Germantown 🆂🅷
(901) 757-7800. **$59-$129, 7 day notice.** 7787 Wolf River Blvd. I-40, exit 16, 5 mi s on Germantown Pkwy. Int corridors. **Pets:** Accepted.
🅰🆂🅺 🆂🅳 ✖ 📠 📠 ➾

▼▼▼ Homewood Suites by Hilton-Germantown 🆂🅷
(901) 751-2500. **$119.** 7855 Wolf River Blvd. I-40, exit 16, 5.8 mi s on CR 177 at jct of Germantown Pkwy and Wolf River Blvd. Int corridors. **Pets:** Small, dogs only. $100 one-time fee/room. Service with restrictions, crate.
🅰🆂🅺 ✖ ♿ 📠 📠 ➾

▼▼▼ Residence Inn 🆂🅷
(901) 751-2500. **$113-$124.** 9314 Poplar Ave. I-240, exit 15 (Poplar Ave), 7 mi e. Int corridors. **Pets:** Other species. $75 one-time fee/room. Service with restrictions, crate.
🅰🆂🅺 ✖ 🏊 🈂 ♿ 📠 📠 ➾ ✖

LAKELAND

▼▼ Super 8 Motel 🆂🅷
(901) 372-4575. **$56-$75, 7 day notice.** 9779 Huff Puff Rd. I-40, exit 20. Ext corridors. **Pets:** Accepted.
🅰🆂🅺 🆂🅳 ✖ 📠 ➾

MEMPHIS

⚫⚫ ▼▼▼ AmeriSuites (Memphis/Cordova) 🆂🅷
(901) 371-0010. **$119.** 7905 Giacosa Pl. I-40, exit 16, just n on Germantown Rd, then just w. Int corridors. **Pets:** Accepted.
🆂🅰🆅🅴 🆂🅳 ✖ 🏊 🈂 ♿ 📠 📠 ➾

⚫⚫ ▼▼▼ AmeriSuites (Memphis/Primacy Pkwy) 🆂🅷
(901) 680-9700. **$89-$99, 14 day notice.** 1220 Primacy Pkwy. I-240, exit 15 (Poplar Ave), 0.3 mi e, s on Ridgeway, just w, then just s. Int corridors. **Pets:** Accepted.
🆂🅰🆅🅴 🆂🅳 ✖ 🏊 🈂 ♿ 📠 📠 ➾

▼▼ Baymont Inn & Suites Memphis-Airport 🆂🅷
(901) 396-5411. **$59-$89.** 3005 Millbranch Rd. I-240, exit 24, just s. Int corridors. **Pets:** Accepted.
🅰🆂🅺 🆂🅳 ✖ 🈂 📠 📠

▼▼▼ Baymont Inn & Suites Memphis East 🆂🅷
(901) 377-2233. **$59-$89.** 6020 Shelby Oaks Dr. I-40, exit 12, just n. Int corridors. **Pets:** Supervision.
🅰🆂🅺 🆂🅳 ✖ 🈂 📠 📠 ➾

⚫⚫ ▼▼ Comfort Inn Airport/Graceland 🆂🅷
(901) 345-3344. **$50-$100.** 1581 E Brooks Rd. I-55, exit 5A (Brooks Rd), 0.3 mi e. Ext corridors. **Pets:** $10 daily fee/pet. Service with restrictions.
🆂🅰🆅🅴 🆂🅳 ✖ 📠 ➾

Comfort Suites Thousand Oaks SH
(901) 365-2575. **$79-$179.** 2575 Thousand Oaks Dr. I-240, exit 18. Int corridors. **Pets:** Accepted.

Drury Inn & Suites-Memphis Northeast SH
(901) 373-8200. **$60-$95.** 1556 Sycamore View. I-40, exit 12, just n. Int corridors. **Pets:** Large, other species. Service with restrictions, supervision.

Hampton Inn & Suites SH
(901) 762-0056. **$109-$129.** 962 S Shady Grove Rd. I-240, exit 15 (Poplar Ave), 0.5 mi e. Int corridors. **Pets:** Small, dogs only. Service with restrictions, supervision.

Hawthorn Suites SH
(901) 682-1722. **$79-$149.** 1070 Ridge Lake Blvd. I-240, exit 15 (Poplar Ave), just e, then n under overpass. Int corridors. **Pets:** Accepted.

Holiday Inn-Sycamore View SH
(901) 388-7050. **$79-$85.** 6101 Shelby Oaks Dr. I-40, exit 12, just n. Int corridors. **Pets:** Accepted.

Holiday Inn-University of Memphis SH
(901) 678-8200. **$125, 3 day notice.** 3700 Central Ave. I-240 E, exit 20B, 1.7 mi w on Getwell Rd, 0.3 mi n on Park, 1 mi w on Goodlett, then just w; follow signs to university. Int corridors. **Pets:** Small. $50 one-time fee/room. Service with restrictions, supervision.

Homestead Studio Suites Hotel-Memphis/Airport SH
(901) 344-0010. **$69-$89.** 2541 Corporate Ave E. I-240, exit 23B (Airways Blvd S), just s to Democrat Rd, just w to Nonconnah Blvd, then 0.4 mi n to Corporate Ave, follow signs. Int corridors. **Pets:** Accepted.

Homestead Studio Suites Hotel-Memphis/Poplar SH
(901) 767-5522. **$64-$89.** 6500 Poplar Ave. I-240, exit 15 (Poplar Ave), 1 mi e. Int corridors. **Pets:** Accepted.

Homewood Suites SH
(901) 763-0500. **$139-$169.** 5811 Poplar Ave. I-240, exit 15 (Poplar Ave). Ext/int corridors. **Pets:** Small, dogs only. $100 one-time fee/room. Designated rooms, service with restrictions, crate.

La Quinta Inn & Suites Memphis (Primacy Parkway) SH
(901) 374-0330. **$77-$101.** 1236 Primacy Pkwy. I-240, exit 15 (Poplar Ave), 0.3 mi e, s on Ridgeway, just w, then just s. Int corridors. **Pets:** Medium. No service, supervision.

Marriott Memphis Downtown LH
(901) 527-7300. **$129-$249.** 250 N Main St. I-40, exit 1A westbound; exit 1 eastbound. Int corridors. **Pets:** Accepted.

Marriott Residence Inn SH
(901) 685-9595. **$79-$149.** 6141 Old Poplar Pike. I-240, exit 15 (Poplar Ave), 0.5 mi e. Ext/int corridors. **Pets:** Medium. $75 one-time fee/room. Designated rooms, no service.

Ramada Inn SH
(901) 382-2323. **$56-$89.** 6068 Macon Cove Rd. I-40, exit 12, just s. Ext corridors. **Pets:** $10 daily fee/room. Designated rooms, service with restrictions, supervision.

Red Roof Inn-East SH 🐾
(901) 388-6111. **$45-$58.** 6055 Shelby Oaks Dr. I-40, exit 12, just n. Ext corridors. **Pets:** Other species. Supervision.

The Ridgeway Inn SH
(901) 766-4000. **Call for rates.** 5679 Poplar Ave. I-240, exit 15 (Poplar Ave), just w. Int corridors. **Pets:** Accepted.

Wellesley Inn & Suites (Memphis/Horizon Center) SH
(901) 380-1525. **$84-$94.** 2520 Horizon Lake Dr. I-40, exit 16B, just n, then just w. Int corridors. **Pets:** Accepted.

END METROPOLITAN AREA

MONTEAGLE

Best Western Smoke House Lodge SH
(931) 924-2091. **$60-$90.** 850 W Main St. I-24, exit 134. Ext corridors. **Pets:** Accepted.

MORRISTOWN

Comfort Suites SH
(423) 585-4000. **Call for rates.** 3660 W Andrew Johnson Hwy. 3 mi w on US 11 E; downtown. Int corridors. **Pets:** Accepted.

Days Inn SH
(423) 587-2200. **$45-$65.** 2512 E Andrew Johnson Hwy. I-81, exit 8, 6 mi n on US 25 E to exit 2B (Greeneville-Morristown), then just w. Ext corridors. **Pets:** Accepted.

Holiday Inn SH
(423) 581-8700. **$63-$169.** 3304 W Andrew Johnson Hwy. 2.5 mi w on US 11 E; downtown. Ext corridors. **Pets:** Other species. $10 one-time fee/pet. Service with restrictions.

Holiday Inn Morristown Conference Center SH
(423) 587-2400. **$85-$170.** 5435 S Davy Crockett Pkwy. I-81, exit 8, just n. Int corridors. **Pets:** Accepted.

Super 8 Motel SH
(423) 318-8888. **$45-$50.** 5400 S Davy Crockett Pkwy. I-81, exit 8, just n. Int corridors. **Pets:** Medium. $9 daily fee/pet. Service with restrictions, supervision.

MOUNT JULIET

Microtel Inn & Suites SH
(615) 773-3600. **$60-$70.** 1000 Hershel Dr. I-40, exit 226. Int corridors. **Pets:** Small. $25 one-time fee/pet. Designated rooms, service with restrictions, supervision.

MURFREESBORO

Best Inn & Suites SH
(615) 890-1006. **$59.** 2135 S Church St. I-24, exit 81 westbound; exit 81B eastbound. Int corridors. **Pets:** Service with restrictions, supervision.

Best Western Chaffin Inn SH ❀
(615) 895-3818. **$56-$98.** 168 Chaffin Pl. I-24, exit 78B. Ext corridors. **Pets:** Small. $12 daily fee/pet. Designated rooms, service with restrictions, crate.

Hampton Inn SH ❀
(615) 896-1172. **$69-$139.** 2230 Armory Dr. I-24, exit 78B, just n. Ext corridors. **Pets:** Large. Designated rooms, service with restrictions, crate.

Howard Johnson Express Inn SH
(615) 896-5522. **$40-$90.** 2424 S Church St. I-24, exit 81A eastbound; exit 81 westbound. Int corridors. **Pets:** Small. $10 daily fee/pet. Service with restrictions, supervision.

Quality Inn SH
(615) 848-9030. **$45-$90.** 118 Westgate Blvd. I-24, exit 81A eastbound; exit 81 westbound. Int corridors. **Pets:** Small. $10 daily fee/pet. Service with restrictions, supervision.

Ramada Limited SH ❀
(615) 896-5080. **$60-$99.** 1855 S Church St. I-24, exit 81. Int corridors. **Pets:** Other species. $10 daily fee/pet. Service with restrictions, supervision.

Scarlet Hotels SH
(615) 896-2420. **$75-$99.** 2227 Old Fort Pkwy. I-24, exit 78B. Ext/int corridors. **Pets:** Accepted.

NASHVILLE METROPOLITAN AREA

GOODLETTSVILLE

Best Western Fairwinds Inn SH
(615) 851-1067. **$45-$95.** 100 Northcreek Blvd. I-65, exit 97 (Long Hollow Pike), 0.5 mi e. Ext corridors. **Pets:** Small. $10 daily fee/pet. Service with restrictions, supervision.

Red Roof Inn-Nashville North SH
(615) 859-2537. **$40-$54.** 110 Northgate Dr. I-65, exit 97 (Long Hollow Pike), 0.5 mi e. Ext corridors. **Pets:** Accepted.

Rodeway Inn M
(615) 859-1416. **$38-$50.** 650 Wade Cir. I-65, exit 96, just ne. Ext corridors. **Pets:** Accepted.

HERMITAGE

Best Inn SH
(615) 889-8940. **$45-$65.** 5770 Old Hickory Blvd. I-40, exit 221 westbound; exit 221B eastbound, just n. Ext corridors. **Pets:** Accepted.

Comfort Inn SH
(615) 889-5060. **$52-$70.** 5768 Old Hickory Blvd. I-40, exit 221 westbound; exit 221B eastbound, just n. Ext corridors. **Pets:** Accepted.

JOELTON

Days Inn SH
(615) 876-3261. **$55-$65.** 201 Gifford Pl. I-24, exit 35, just s. Ext corridors. **Pets:** Small. Service with restrictions, supervision.

NASHVILLE

AmeriSuites (Nashville/Airport) SH
(615) 493-5200. **$99.** 721 Royal Pkwy. I-40, exit 216C (Donelson Pike). Int corridors. **Pets:** Accepted.

AmeriSuites (Nashville/Opryland) SH
(615) 872-0422. **$99-$129.** 220 Rudy's Circle Dr. I-40, exit 215B (Briley Pkwy), 6 mi ne to exit 11 (McGavock Pike), then 0.3 mi left. Int corridors. **Pets:** Small. $10 daily fee/pet. Service with restrictions, crate.

Baymont Inn & Suites Nashville-Airport SH
(615) 885-3100. **$59-$89.** 531 Donelson Pike. I-40, exit 216C (Donelson Pike), 0.3 mi n. Int corridors. **Pets:** Other species. $25 deposit/room. Service with restrictions, supervision.

Best Value Inn M
(615) 226-9805. **$49-$89.** 2403 Brick Church Pike. I-65, exit 87 (Trinity Ln), just nw. Ext corridors. **Pets:** Medium. $10 daily fee/pet. Designated rooms, service with restrictions, supervision.

Best Western Airport Inn SH
(615) 889-9199. **$50-$80.** 701 Stewarts Ferry Pike. I-40, exit 219 (Stewarts Ferry Pike). Ext corridors. **Pets:** Small, other species. $10 daily fee/pet. Designated rooms, service with restrictions, crate.

Best Western Downtown Music Row SH
(615) 242-1631. **$59-$139.** 1407 Division St. I-40, exit 209, just w. Int corridors. **Pets:** Small, other species. $5 daily fee/pet. Service with restrictions.

Capstone Inn-Nashville South SH
(615) 834-7170. **$60-$80.** 341 Harding Pl. I-24, exit 56 (Harding Pl). Ext corridors. **Pets:** Large, other species. Service with restrictions, supervision.

ClubHouse Inn & Suites SH
(615) 883-0500. **$59-$109.** 2435 Atrium Way. Briley Pkwy to exit 7 (Elm Hill Pike), just e. Int corridors. **Pets:** Small. $10 daily fee/room. Service with restrictions, supervision.

Comfort Inn Opryland SH
(615) 889-0086. **$55-$99, 7 day notice.** 2516 Music Valley Dr. I-40, exit 215 (Briley Pkwy), 4 mi n; I-65, exit 90, exit McGavock Pike off Briley Pkwy. Int corridors. **Pets:** Small, other species. $5 daily fee/room. Service with restrictions, supervision.

Crestwood Suites SH
(615) 860-8500. **$49-$54.** 665 Myatt Dr. I-65, exit 96. Int corridors. **Pets:** Accepted.

Days Inn SH
(615) 399-0017. **$70.** 821 Murfreesboro Rd. I-24, exit 52 (Murfreesboro Rd), 0.5 mi e; I-40, exit 213. Ext corridors. **Pets:** Accepted.

Days Inn Bell Road SH
(615) 731-7800. **$49-$69.** 510 Collins Park Dr. I-24, exit 59 (Bell Rd). Ext corridors. **Pets:** Accepted.

Days Inn Vanderbilt SH
(615) 327-0922. **$67-$86.** 1800 West End Ave. I-40, exit 209A westbound; exit 209B eastbound. Ext/int corridors. **Pets:** Accepted.

Days Inn West SH
(615) 356-9100. **$45-$88, 7 day notice.** 269 White Bridge Pk. I-40, exit 204, just s. Ext corridors. **Pets:** Accepted.

Drury Inn & Suites-Nashville Airport SH
(615) 902-0400. **$65-$110.** 555 Donelson Pike. I-40, exit 216 (Donelson Pike). Int corridors. **Pets:** Large, other species. Service with restrictions, supervision.

Embassy Suites LH
(615) 871-0033. **$89-$169.** 10 Century Blvd. I-40, exit 215 (Briley Pkwy N), then exit 7 (Elm Hill Pike), 0.3 mi e to McGavock Pike, 0.3 mi s to Century Blvd, then 0.3 mi w. Int corridors. **Pets:** Small. $10 daily fee/room. Service with restrictions, supervision.

Fiddlers Inn SH
(615) 885-1440. **$50-$80.** 2410 Music Valley Dr. I-40, exit 215B (Briley Pkwy), 4 mi n to exit 11 (McGavock Pike), then just w. Ext corridors. **Pets:** Accepted.

GuestHouse International Inn & Suites SH ❁
(615) 885-4030. **$69-$109.** 2420 Music Valley Dr. Briley Pkwy, exit 12, 0.3 mi w, then 0.3 mi n. Int corridors. **Pets:** Medium. Service with restrictions, crate.

Hampton Inn & Suites at the University SH
(615) 320-6060. **$119-$169.** 2330 Elliston Pl. 3.5 mi w. Int corridors. **Pets:** Accepted.

The Hermitage Hotel LH
(615) 244-3121. **$199-$279.** 231 6th Ave N. Center. Int corridors. **Pets:** Accepted.

Holiday Inn Select-Vanderbilt SH
(615) 327-4707. **$94-$114.** 2613 West End Ave. I-40, exit 209B eastbound; exit 209A westbound, w on Broadway. Int corridors. **Pets:** Accepted.

Holiday Inn-The Crossings SH ❁
(615) 731-2361. **$69-$99.** 201 Crossings Pl. I-24, exit 60, 0.5 mi e. Int corridors. **Pets:** Large, other species. Service with restrictions, crate.

Homestead Studio Suites Hotel-Nashville/Airport SH
(615) 316-9020. **$44-$69.** 727 McGavock Pike. I-40, exit 215B (Briley Pkwy), 1 mi n to exit 7 (Elm Hill Pike), then just e. Ext corridors. **Pets:** Accepted.

Homewood Suites by Hilton SH
(615) 884-8111. **$89-$129.** 2640 Elm Hill Pike. I-40, exit 216C (Donelson Pike). Int corridors. **Pets:** Accepted.

Howard Johnson Inn SH
(615) 352-7080. **$55-$62.** 6834 Charlotte Pike. I-40, exit 201, 0.4 mi e on US 70. Int corridors. **Pets:** $5 one-time fee/pet. Designated rooms, service with restrictions, supervision.

La Quinta Inn Nashville (Airport) M
(615) 885-3000. **$71-$90.** 2345 Atrium Way. I-40, exit 215B (Briley Pkwy), 1 mi n to exit 7 (Elm Hill Pike), e to Atrium Way, then 0.3 mi n. Int corridors. **Pets:** Medium. Service with restrictions, supervision.

La Quinta Inn Nashville (South) SH
(615) 834-6900. **$65-$80.** 4311 Sidco Dr. I-65, exit 78A. Ext corridors. **Pets:** Accepted.

Loews Vanderbilt Hotel Nashville LH ❁
(615) 320-1700. **$139-$229.** 2100 West End Ave. I-40, exit 209 (Broadway), 1.3 mi w. Int corridors. **Pets:** Other species. Service with restrictions, supervision.

Marriott at Vanderbilt University SH
(615) 321-1300. **$199-$279.** 2555 West End Ave. I-40, exit 209B eastbound; exit 209A westbound, w on Broadway. Int corridors. **Pets:** Medium, dogs only. $50 one-time fee/room. Designated rooms, service with restrictions, supervision.

Microtel Inn & Suites SH
(615) 662-0004. **$55-$79.** 100 Coley Davis Ct. I-40, exit 196. Int corridors. **Pets:** $10 daily fee/pet. Service with restrictions, supervision.

Motel 6-156 SH
(615) 333-9933. **$35-$45.** 95 Wallace Rd. I-24, exit 56 (Harding Pl). Ext corridors. **Pets:** Accepted.

Pear Tree Inn-Nashville South SH
(615) 834-4242. **$50-$70.** 343 Harding Pl. I-24, exit 56 (Harding Pl). Ext corridors. **Pets:** Large, other species. Service with restrictions, supervision.

The Quarters Motor Inn M
(615) 731-5990. **$49-$125.** 1100 Bell Rd. I-24, exit 59 (Bell Rd), just w. Ext corridors. **Pets:** Medium, other species. Designated rooms, service with restrictions, supervision.

Red Roof Inn SH
(615) 889-0090. **$64-$79.** 2460 Music Valley Dr. I-40, exit 215B (Briley Pkwy), 4 mi n to exit 11 (McGavock Pike). Int corridors. **Pets:** Large, other species. Service with restrictions, crate.

Red Roof Inn Airport M
(615) 872-0735. **$45-$55.** 510 Claridge Dr. I-40, exit 216C (Donelson Pike). 0.3 mi n. Ext corridors. **Pets:** Accepted.

Red Roof Inn South SH
(615) 832-0093. **$46-$65.** 4271 Sidco Dr. I-65, exit 78. Ext corridors. **Pets:** Large, other species. Service with restrictions, crate.

Residence Inn SH ❁
(615) 889-8600. **$85-$114.** 2300 Elm Hill Pike. I-40, exit 215B (Briley Pkwy), 1.5 mi n. Ext corridors. **Pets:** Other species. $75 one-time fee/room. Service with restrictions.

Sheraton Music City Hotel LH ❁
(615) 885-2200. **$89-$155.** 777 McGavock Pike. I-40, exit 215B (Briley Pkwy), 1 mi n to exit 7 (Elm Hill Pike), 0.5 mi e, then s. Int corridors. **Pets:** Other species. Service with restrictions, crate.

▼▼▼▼ Super 8 SH
(615) 834-0620. **$55-$85.** 350 Harding Pl. I-24, exit 56. Int corridors.
Pets: Small, other species. $5 daily fee/pet. Service with restrictions.
(ASK) (S̄6) (×) (🛏) (💻) (⇌)

(AAA) ▼▼▼▼ Super 8 Motel-West SH
(615) 356-6005. **$55-$80.** 6924 Charlotte Pike. I-40, exit 201. Ext corridors. **Pets:** Medium, other species. $10 daily fee/pet. Service with restric-
tions, crate.
(SAVE) (S̄6) (×) (🛏)

END METROPOLITAN AREA

NEWPORT

(AAA) ▼▼▼▼ Best Western Newport Inn SH
(423) 623-8713. **$45-$130.** 1015 Cosby Hwy. I-40, exit 435, just w. Ext
corridors. **Pets:** Accepted.
(SAVE) (S̄6) (×) (ᴸᴹ) (🛍) (🛏) (💻) (⇌)

(AAA) ▼▼▼▼ Comfort Inn SH
(423) 623-5355. **$59-$179.** 1149 Smokey Mountain Ln. I-40, exit 432B.
Int corridors. **Pets:** Medium. $10 one-time fee/pet. Service with restrictions,
supervision.
(SAVE) (S̄6) (×) (ᴸᴹ) (🖊️) (🛏) (💻) (⇌)

▼▼▼▼ Holiday Inn SH
(423) 623-8622. **$54-$119.** 1010 Cosby Hwy. I-40, exit 435. Ext/int
corridors. **Pets:** Accepted.
(ASK) (S̄6) (×) (🛍) (🛏) (💻) (⍩) (⇌) (×)

▼▼▼ Motel 6-4090 M ♣
(423) 623-1850. **$40-$80.** 255 Heritage Blvd. I-40, exit 435. Int corridors. **Pets:** Large, other species. Designated rooms, service with restrictions, supervision.
(×) (ᴸᴹ) (ᴸ) (⇌)

OAK RIDGE

▼▼▼▼ Comfort Inn SH
(865) 481-8200. **$72-$97.** 433 S Rutgers Ave. 0.9 mi se of SR 95 on
SR 62. Int corridors. **Pets:** Small. $10 daily fee/pet. Designated rooms,
service with restrictions, supervision.
(ASK) (S̄6) (×) (ᴸᴹ) (🛏) (💻) (⇌)

ONEIDA

▼▼▼ The Galloway Inn M
(423) 569-8835. **$43.** 299 Galloway Dr. Jct SR 63, 3.3 mi n on US 27,
just e. Ext corridors. **Pets:** Accepted.
(ASK) (S̄6) (×) (🛏) (💻)

OOLTEWAH

▼▼▼ Super 8 Motel M
(423) 238-5951. **$45-$49, 7 day notice.** 5111 Hunter Rd. I-75, exit 11,
jct US 11 and 64. Ext corridors. **Pets:** Small. $6 daily fee/pet. Service
with restrictions.
(ASK) (S̄6) (×) (🛏) (⇌)

PARIS

▼▼▼▼ Hampton Inn SH
(731) 642-2838. **$65-$89.** 1510 E Wood St. 1.5 mi ne on US 79. Ext
corridors. **Pets:** Accepted.
(ASK) (S̄6) (×) (ᴸᴹ) (🛏) (💻) (⇌)

PIGEON FORGE

(AAA) ▼▼▼▼ Grand Resort Hotel SH
(865) 453-1000. **$39-$99.** 3171 Parkway. On US 441. Ext/int corridors.
Pets: Accepted.
(SAVE) (S̄6) (×) (🛏) (💻) (⍩) (⇌)

▼▼▼▼ Holiday Inn Resort SH
(865) 428-2700. **$50-$140.** 3230 Parkway. Just w of US 441. Int corridors. **Pets:** Accepted.
(ASK) (S̄6) (×) (🖊️) (🛏) (💻) (⍩) (⇌)

(AAA) ▼▼▼ Microtel SH
(865) 429-0150. **$30-$159, 3 day notice.** 202 Emert St. On US 441,
just w between traffic lights 7 and 8. Int corridors. **Pets:** Medium. $15
daily fee/pet. Designated rooms, service with restrictions.
(SAVE) (S̄6) (×) (ᴸᴹ) (🖊️) (ᴸ) (🛏) (⇌)

▼▼▼ Microtel Suites @ Music Road M
(865) 453-1116. **$35-$120.** 2045 Parkway. On US 441, between traffic
lights 1 and 1A. Int corridors. **Pets:** Large, other species. $25 one-time
fee/pet. Designated rooms, service with restrictions, crate.
(ASK) (S̄6) (×) (ᴸᴹ) (🛏) (💻) (⇌)

(AAA) ▼▼▼ Motel 6 #4021 SH ♣
(865) 908-1244. **$24-$99.** 336 Henderson Chapel Rd. On US 441, just
w of traffic light 1. Int corridors. **Pets:** Small, other species. Service with
restrictions, supervision.
(SAVE) (×) (ᴸᴹ) (ᴸ) (🛏) (⇌)

(AAA) ▼▼▼▼ National Parks Resort Lodge SH
(865) 453-4106. **$30-$120.** 2385 Parkway. On US 441 at traffic light 1.
Int corridors. **Pets:** Accepted.
(SAVE) (×) (🛏) (💻) (⇌)

(AAA) ▼▼▼ Smoky Shadows Motel & Conference
Center SH
(865) 453-7155. **$29-$99.** 4215 Parkway. On US 441, just s of traffic
light 9. Ext/int corridors. **Pets:** Small, other species. $10 daily fee/pet.
Service with restrictions, supervision.
(SAVE) (S̄6) (×) (🛏) (💻) (⇌)

POWELL

▼▼▼ Comfort Inn M
(865) 938-5500. **$59-$89.** 323 E Emory Rd. I-75, exit 112. Ext corridors.
Pets: Small. $10 daily fee/room. Service with restrictions, supervision.
(×) (🛏) (💻) (⇌)

PULASKI

(AAA) ▼▼▼ Super 8 Motel SH
(931) 363-4501. **$42-$72.** 2400 Hwy 64 E. I-65, exit 14, just e. Ext
corridors. **Pets:** Small, other species. $5 daily fee/pet. Service with restric-
tions, supervision.
(SAVE) (S̄6) (×) (🛏) (⇌)

ROGERSVILLE

▼▼▼▼ Holiday Inn Express SH
(423) 272-1842. **$73-$83.** 7139 Hwy 11 W. Jct SR 66 and US 11, just
sw. Int corridors. **Pets:** Accepted.
(ASK) (S̄6) (×) (ᴸ) (🛏) (💻) (⇌)

SELMER

Super 8 Motel-Selmer 🅂🄷
(731) 645-8880. **$50-$125, 7 day notice.** 644 Mulberry Ave. Jct SR 64 and 45, just s on SR 45. Ext corridors. **Pets:** Other species. Designated rooms, service with restrictions, supervision.

A$K 🆂 ☒ 🔟 ⤻

SEVIERVILLE

Best Western Dumplin Valley Inn 🅂🄷
(865) 933-3467. **$45-$125.** 3426 Winfield Dunn Pkwy. I-40, exit 407, 0.3 mi s. Ext corridors. **Pets:** Other species. $10 daily fee/pet. Service with restrictions, supervision.

SAVE 🆂 ☒ 🅿 🔟 💻 ⤻

Comfort Inn Mountain River Suites 🅂🄷
(865) 428-5519. **$39-$159.** 860 Winfield Dunn Pkwy. 2 mi n on SR 66. Ext corridors. **Pets:** Medium, other species. $10 daily fee/room. Designated rooms, service with restrictions, crate.

SAVE 🆂 ☒ 🅿 🔟 💻 ⤻

Holiday Inn Express Hotel & Suites 🅂🄷
(865) 933-9448. **$59-$149.** 2863 Winfield Dunn Pkwy. I-40, exit 407, 2 mi s. Int corridors. **Pets:** Small. $15 one-time fee/pet. Designated rooms, service with restrictions, crate.

A$K 🆂 ☒ 🅜 🅿 ♿ 🔟 💻 ⤻

SMYRNA

Days Inn 🅂🄷
(615) 355-6161. **$67-$90, 3 day notice.** 1300 Plaza Dr. I-24, exit 66, 2 mi ne. Ext corridors. **Pets:** Medium. $10 daily fee/pet. Designated rooms, service with restrictions, supervision.

A$K 🆂 ☒ 🔟 ⤻

SWEETWATER

Best Western Sweetwater Inn 🅂🄷
(423) 337-3541. **$69-$99.** 1421 Murray's Chapel Rd. I-75, exit 60, just w. Ext/int corridors. **Pets:** Very small. $15 one-time fee/room. Designated rooms, service with restrictions, supervision.

A$K 🆂 ☒ 🔟 💻 🍴 ⤻

Budget Host Inn 🅂🄷
(423) 337-9357. **$37-$59.** 207 Hwy 68. I-75, exit 60. Ext corridors. **Pets:** Accepted.

SAVE 🆂 ☒ 🔟

Comfort Inn 🅂🄷 🐾
(423) 337-6646. **$45-$65.** 731 S Main St. On US 11, jct SR 68. Ext/int corridors. **Pets:** Small. $5 daily fee/pet. Designated rooms, service with restrictions, crate.

SAVE 🆂 ☒ 🔟 💻 ⤻

Comfort Inn West 🅂🄷 🐾
(423) 337-3353. **$55-$99.** 249 Hwy 68. I-75, exit 60, just e. Ext/int corridors. **Pets:** Small. $5 daily fee/pet. Designated rooms, service with restrictions, supervision.

SAVE 🆂 ☒ 🔟 💻 ⤻

Days Inn 🅂🄷
(423) 337-4200. **$60-$69.** 229 Hwy 68. I-75, exit 60, just e. Ext corridors. **Pets:** Medium. $10 daily fee/pet. Service with restrictions, supervision.

SAVE 🆂 ☒ 🔟 💻 ⤻

Quality Inn 🅂🄷
(423) 337-4900. **$75-$200.** 1116 Hwy 68. I-75, exit 60. Int corridors. **Pets:** Other species. $10 one-time fee/pet. Service with restrictions, supervision.

SAVE 🆂 ☒ 🔟 💻 ⤻

TOWNSEND

Best Western Valley View Lodge 🅂🄷
(865) 448-2237. **$47-$102.** 7726 E Lamar Alexander Pkwy. On US 321; center. Ext corridors. **Pets:** Small, dogs only. $10 one-time fee/pet. Service with restrictions, supervision.

SAVE 🆂 ☒ 🅿 🔟 💻 ⤻

Comfort Inn 🅂🄷
(865) 448-9000. **$39-$179, 7 day notice.** 7824 E Lamar Alexander Pkwy. On US 321. Ext corridors. **Pets:** Small, dogs only. $20 daily fee/pet. Designated rooms, service with restrictions, supervision.

SAVE 🆂 ☒ 🔟 💻 ⤻

Maple Leaf Lodge 🄱🄱
(865) 448-6000. **Call for rates.** 137 Apple Valley Way. On US 321, 2 mi n. Ext/int corridors. **Pets:** Accepted.

☒ 🔟 💻 ☒

TULLAHOMA

Jameson Inn 🅂🄷
(931) 455-7891. **$49-$104.** 2113 N Jackson St. 3 mi n on SR 41A (N Jackson St). Ext corridors. **Pets:** Very small, other species. $10 daily fee/room. Service with restrictions, supervision.

A$K ☒ 🅦 🔟 💻 ⤻

VONORE

Grand Vista Hotel & Suites 🅂🄷
(423) 884-6200. **$90.** 117 Grand Vista Dr. I-75, exit 172, 14 mi e. Int corridors. **Pets:** Medium. $10 daily fee/pet. Supervision.

A$K 🆂 ☒ 🅜 🅿 ♿ 🔟 💻 ⤻

WHITE HOUSE

Days Inn Whitehouse 🅂🄷
(615) 672-3746. **$45-$48, 7 day notice.** 1009 Hwy 76. I-65, exit 108, just w. Ext corridors. **Pets:** Small. $5 daily fee/pet. Designated rooms, service with restrictions, supervision.

SAVE 🆂 ☒ 🔟 💻 ⤻

Holiday Inn Express 🅂🄷
(615) 672-7200. **$55-$69.** 354 Hester Ln. I-65, exit 108, just e. Ext corridors. **Pets:** Accepted.

A$K 🆂 ☒ 🅜 🅦 🔟 💻 ⤻

WHITE PINE

Days Inn 🅂🄷
(865) 674-2573. **$59-$159.** 3670 Roy Messer Hwy. I-81, exit 4, just w. Ext corridors. **Pets:** Accepted.

SAVE ☒ 🔟

WHITEVILLE

Super 8 🅂🄷
(731) 254-8884. **$50-$60.** 2040 Hwy 64. US 64 and SR 179. Ext corridors. **Pets:** Other species. $5 daily fee/pet. Service with restrictions, supervision.

☒ 🅜 🅦 🔟

WILDERSVILLE

Best Western Crossroads Inn 🅂🄷
(731) 968-2532. **$45-$55.** 21045 Hwy 22 N. I-40, exit 108, just s. Ext corridors. **Pets:** Other species. $10 daily fee/pet. Designated rooms, service with restrictions, supervision.

SAVE 🆂 ☒ 🔟 💻 ⤻

TEXAS

CITY INDEX

ABILENE

▼▼▼▼ Ambassador Suites Hotel SH
(325) 698-1234. **$104-$114.** 4250 Ridgemont Dr. 0.3 mi s of US 83/84, exit Ridgemont Dr. Ext/int corridors. **Pets:** $50 one-time fee/room. Service with restrictions, supervision.
[ASK] [S☐] [✕] [🔒] [💻] [🍴] [🏊] [✕]

▼▼ Antilley Inn M
(325) 695-3330. **$53.** 6550 US Hwy 83. US 83/84, exit Antilley Rd. Ext corridors. **Pets:** Medium. $10 one-time fee/room. Service with restrictions, supervision.
[ASK] [S☐] [✕] [🔒] [💻] [🏊]

▼▼▼▼ Best Western Abilene Inn & Suites SH
(325) 672-5501. **$89-$99, 7 day notice.** 350 I-20 W. I-20, exit 286C, just n. Int corridors. **Pets:** Accepted.
[ASK] [S☐] [✕] [🔖] [🔒] [💻] [🏊]

▲▲▲ ▼▼▼ Best Western Mall South SH
(325) 695-1262. **$75-$85.** 3950 Ridgemont Dr. US 83/84, exit Ridgemont Dr, just s. Ext corridors. **Pets:** Small. $10 daily fee/pet. Designated rooms, service with restrictions, supervision.
[SAVE] [S☐] [✕] [🔖] [🔒] [💻] [🏊]

▲▲▲ ▼▼▼ Budget Host Colonial Inn M
(325) 677-2683. **$35-$40.** 3210 Pine St. Jct I-20 and US 83 business route, exit 286A. Ext/int corridors. **Pets:** Medium. $10 daily fee/pet. Designated rooms, service with restrictions, supervision.
[SAVE] [S☐] [✕] [🌙] [🔒] [💻] [🏊]

▲▲▲ ▼▼▼ Civic Plaza Hotel SH
(325) 676-0222. **$49-$79.** 505 Pine St. Downtown. Ext corridors. **Pets:** Medium. $10 one-time fee/pet. Service with restrictions, supervision.
[SAVE] [S☐] [✕] [🔖] [🔒] [💻] [🍴] [🏊]

▲▲▲ ▼▼▼▼ Comfort Suites SH
(325) 795-8500. **$84-$159.** 3165 S Danville Dr. I-20, exit 279, s on US 83/84/277 to Southwest Dr, then just e. Int corridors. **Pets:** Other species. $30 one-time fee/room. Service with restrictions, supervision.
[SAVE] [S☐] [✕] [🔖] [🌙] [🔒] [🔒] [💻] [🏊]

▼▼▼ Days Inn M
(325) 672-6433. **$55-$60.** 1702 E Hwy 20. I-20, exit 288. Ext corridors. **Pets:** Small. $10 one-time fee/pet. Service with restrictions, crate.
[ASK] [S☐] [✕] [🌙] [🔒] [💻] [🏊]

▲▲▲ ▼▼▼ Econo Lodge M
(325) 673-5424. **$38-$45.** 1633 W Stamford. S Frontage Rd off I-20 and US 80, exit 285 eastbound; exit 286A westbound. Ext corridors. **Pets:** Very small. $10 daily fee/pet. Service with restrictions, supervision.
[SAVE] [S☐] [✕] [🔒] [💻]

▼▼▼ Executive Inn M
(325) 677-2200. **$60-$70.** 1650 I-20 E. I-20, exit 288. Ext corridors. **Pets:** Accepted.
[S☐] [✕] [🔒] [💻] [🏊]

▲▲▲ ▼▼▼▼ La Quinta Inn Abilene SH
(325) 676-1676. **$85-$95.** 3501 W Lake Rd. I-20, exit 286C. Ext corridors. **Pets:** Small. Service with restrictions, supervision.
[SAVE] [✕] [🌙] [🔒] [💻] [🏊]

▼▼▼ Motel 6 Abilene #79 M
(325) 672-8462. **$35-$45.** 4951 W Stamford St. I-20, exit 282, on eastbound frontage road. Ext corridors. **Pets:** Accepted.
[S☐] [✕] [🔖] [🏊]

▼▼ Regency Inn & Suites SH
(325) 695-7700. **$35-$62.** 3450 S Clack St. 5 mi sw on US 83/84, exit Southwest Dr. Int corridors. **Pets:** Medium. $15 one-time fee/pet. Designated rooms, service with restrictions, supervision.

[ASK] [S🐾] [✕] [🐾] [🛏] [💻] [🍴] [≈]

▼▼ Super 8 Motel M
(325) 673-5251. **$55-$75.** 1525 E I-20. I-20, exit 288. Ext corridors. **Pets:** Large, other species. $5 daily fee/pet. Service with restrictions, supervision.

[ASK] [S🐾] [✕] [🛏] [💻] [≈]

▼▼ Whitten Inn Expo SH
(325) 677-8100. **Call for rates.** 840 Hwy 80 E. I-20, exit 292A, 3 mi w on Business Rt 20. Ext corridors. **Pets:** Accepted.

[✕] [🛏] [🍴] [≈]

ALAMO

▼▼ Super 8 Motel SH
(956) 787-9444. **$50.** 714 N Alamo Rd. US 83, exit FM 907, just n. Ext corridors. **Pets:** Designated rooms.

[ASK] [S🐾] [✕] [🐾] [🛏] [≈]

ALPINE

◈◈ ▼▼▼ Oak Tree Inn SH
(432) 837-5711. **$70-$77.** 2407 E Holland (Hwy 90/67). US 90, 2 mi e. Int corridors. **Pets:** Accepted.

[SAVE] [S🐾] [✕] [&M] [🐾] [🐾] [🛏] [💻]

◈◈ ▼▼▼ Ramada Limited SH
(432) 837-1100. **$95-$105.** 2800 W Hwy 90. On US 90, 2 mi n. Int corridors. **Pets:** Large. $25 one-time fee/room. Service with restrictions.

[SAVE] [S🐾] [✕] [&M] [🐾] [🛏] [💻] [≈]

ALVIN

▼▼ ◈ Country Hearth Inn M
(281) 331-0335. **Call for rates.** 1588 S Hwy 35 Bypass. SR 35 Bypass, 0.5 mi sw of SR 6. Ext corridors. **Pets:** Accepted.

[✕] [🛏] [💻] [≈]

AMARILLO

◈◈◈ ▼▼▼▼ Ambassador Hotel LH
(806) 358-6161. **$139-$179.** 3100 I-40 W. I-40, exit 68, just w on north frontage road. Int corridors. **Pets:** $29 one-time fee/pet. Service with restrictions, crate.

[SAVE] [S🐾] [✕] [🐾] [🛏] [💻] [🍴] [≈] [✕]

◈◈◈ ▼▼▼ Best Western Amarillo Inn SH
(806) 358-7861. **$62-$72.** 1610 Coulter Dr. I-40, exit 65 (Coulter Dr), 0.6 mi n. Ext/int corridors. **Pets:** Small. $10 one-time fee/pet. Service with restrictions, supervision.

[SAVE] [S🐾] [✕] [🐾] [🛏] [💻] [🍴] [≈]

◈◈◈ ▼▼▼▼ Best Western Santa Fe SH
(806) 372-1885. **$70-$100.** 4600 I-40 E. I-40, exit 73 (Eastern St) eastbound; exit 73 (Bolton St) westbound, U-turn on south frontage road. Int corridors. **Pets:** Medium. $15 daily fee/pet. Designated rooms, no service, supervision.

[SAVE] [S🐾] [✕] [🛏] [💻] [≈]

◈◈◈ ▼▼ Big Texan Motel M
(806) 372-5000. **$40-$65, 7 day notice.** 7701 I-40 E. I-40, exit 75 (Lakeside Dr), 0.3 mi w on north frontage road. Ext corridors. **Pets:** Other species. $30 deposit/pet, $10 daily fee/pet. Service with restrictions, crate.

[SAVE] [S🐾] [✕] [🛏] [🍴] [≈]

◈◈◈ ▼▼▼ Days Inn SH
(806) 379-6255. **$59-$89.** 1701 I-40 E. I-40, exit 71 (Ross-Osage), just w on north frontage road. Int corridors. **Pets:** Other species. $10 daily fee/pet. Service with restrictions, supervision.

[SAVE] [S🐾] [✕] [🐾] [🛏] [💻] [≈]

◈◈◈ ▼▼▼ Days Inn SH
(806) 359-9393. **$69-$109.** 2102 S Coulter Dr. I-40, exit 65 (Coulter Dr), just n. Ext corridors. **Pets:** Small. $10 daily fee/pet. Service with restrictions, supervision.

[SAVE] [S🐾] [✕] [🐾] [🛏] [≈]

▼▼▼▼ Days Inn South SH
(806) 468-7100. **$55-$79.** 8601 Canyon Dr. I-27, exit 116, just n on east service road. Int corridors. **Pets:** Accepted.

[ASK] [S🐾] [✕] [🐾] [🛏] [≈]

◈◈◈ ▼▼▼▼ Hampton Inn SH
(806) 372-1425. **$64-$114.** 1700 I-40 E. I-40, exit 71 (Ross-Osage), just e on south frontage road. Int corridors. **Pets:** No service, supervision.

[SAVE] [S🐾] [✕] [🐾] [🛏] [💻] [≈]

▼▼▼▼ Holiday Inn Express SH
(806) 356-6800. **$89-$107.** 3411 I-40 W. I-40, exit 67, 0.3 mi e on south frontage road. Int corridors. **Pets:** Accepted.

[ASK] [S🐾] [✕] [🐾] [🛏] [💻] [≈]

▼▼▼▼ Holiday Inn-I-40 SH
(806) 372-8741. **$119-$134.** 1911 I-40 at Ross-Osage. I-40, exit 71 (Ross-Osage), on north frontage road. Int corridors. **Pets:** Other species. $25 one-time fee/room. Service with restrictions, supervision.

[ASK] [✕] [🐾] [🐾] [🛏] [💻] [🍴] [≈] [✕]

▼▼▼▼ La Quinta Inn Amarillo (East/Airport Area) SH
(806) 373-7486. **$71-$103.** 1708 I-40 E. I-40, exit 71 (Ross-Osage), just e on south frontage road. Ext corridors. **Pets:** Accepted.

[ASK] [✕] [🐾] [🛏] [💻] [≈]

◈◈◈ ▼▼▼▼ La Quinta Inn Amarillo (West/Medical Center) SH
(806) 352-6311. **$70-$102.** 2108 S Coulter Dr. I-40, exit 65 (Coulter Dr), just n. Ext corridors. **Pets:** Medium, other species. Service with restrictions, supervision.

[SAVE] [✕] [&M] [🐾] [🛏] [💻] [≈]

▼▼ Motel 6 Amarillo East #409 M
(806) 374-6444. **$39-$53.** 3930 I-40 E. I-40, exit 72B, on eastbound frontage road. Ext corridors. **Pets:** Other species. Service with restrictions, supervision.

[S🐾] [✕] [≈]

▼▼ Motel 6 Amarillo West #1146 M
(806) 359-7651. **$35-$52.** 6030 I-40 W. I-40, exit 66 (Bell St), just w, on north frontage road. Ext corridors. **Pets:** Accepted.

[S🐾] [✕] [🐾] [≈]

◈◈◈ ▼▼▼▼ Quality Inn SH
(806) 376-9993. **$49-$109.** 1515 I-40 E. I-40, exit 71 (Ross-Osage), just w on north frontage road. Ext corridors. **Pets:** Accepted.

[SAVE] [✕] [🐾] [🛏] [💻] [≈]

◈◈◈ ▼▼▼ Quality Inn & Suites SH
(806) 335-1561. **$65, 7 day notice.** 1803 Lakeside Dr. I-40, exit 75 (Lakeside Dr), just n. Ext/int corridors. **Pets:** Accepted.

[SAVE] [S🐾] [✕] [🐾] [🛏] [💻] [≈]

◈◈◈ ▼▼▼▼ Quality Inn & Suites West SH ❀
(806) 358-7943. **$79-$119.** 6800 I-40 W. I-40, exit 66, 0.5 mi w on north frontage road. Ext corridors. **Pets:** Small, other species. $10 one-time fee/pet. Designated rooms, service with restrictions, supervision.

[SAVE] [S🐾] [✕] [🛏] [💻] [≈]

Ramada Limited SH
(806) 374-2020. **$68-$75.** 1620 I-40 E. I-40, exit 71 (Ross-Osage), just e on south frontage road. Ext corridors. **Pets:** Other species. $10 one-time fee/pet. Service with restrictions, supervision.

Residence Inn by Marriott SH
(806) 354-2978. **$119, 14 day notice.** 6700 I-40 W. I-40, exit 66 (Bell St), 0.5 mi w on north frontage road. Int corridors. **Pets:** Accepted.

Ritz Plaza Hotel Airport SH
(806) 373-3303. **$40-$70, 3 day notice.** 7909 I-40 E. I-40, exit 75 (Lakeside Dr), just nw. Int corridors. **Pets:** Accepted.

Sleep Inn Amarillo SH
(806) 372-6200. **$75-$120, 7 day notice.** 2401 I-40 E. I-40, exit 72A (Nelson), 0.3 mi w on north frontage road. Int corridors. **Pets:** Small. $10 daily fee/pet. Service with restrictions, supervision.

Travelodge West M
(806) 353-3541. **$38-$59.** 2035 Paramount Blvd. I-40, exit 68A (Paramount Blvd), just s. Ext corridors. **Pets:** Small. $5 daily fee/room. No service.

ANGLETON

Best Western Angelton Inn SH
(979) 849-5822. **$70.** 1809 N Velasco (Business Rt 288). 1.5 mi n of jct SR 35 and Business Rt SR 288, e of SR 288. Ext corridors. **Pets:** Accepted.

ANTHONY

Holiday Inn Express SH
(915) 886-3333. **$79-$89.** 9401 S Desert Blvd. I-10, exit 0. Ext corridors. **Pets:** Very small. $25 daily fee/pet. Designated rooms, service with restrictions, supervision.

ARLINGTON

AmeriSuites (Dallas/Arlington) SH
(817) 649-7676. **$99-$129.** 2380 East Rd to Six Flags St. I-30, exit 30 (SR 360), 0.5 mi sw. Int corridors. **Pets:** Accepted.

Arlington TownePlace Suites by Marriott SH
(817) 861-8728. **$99-$109.** 1709 E Lamar Ave. 2 mi w of SR 360. Int corridors. **Pets:** Accepted.

Baymont Inn & Suites-Arlington SH
(817) 633-2434. **$59-$129.** 2401 Diplomacy Dr. I-30, exit 30 (SR 360), 0.5 mi s; off SR 360, exit Six Flags Dr northbound; exit Ave H/Lamar Blvd southbound, on southbound service road. Int corridors. **Pets:** $50 deposit/pet. Service with restrictions, supervision.

Country Inn & Suites By Carlson SH ✿
(817) 261-8900. **$69-$129.** 1075 Wet'N Wild Way. I-30, exit 28 (Collins St/FM 157), just e. Ext corridors. **Pets:** Very small, dogs only. $10 daily fee/pet. Designated rooms, service with restrictions, supervision.

Days Inn Ballpark at Arlington/Six Flags SH
(817) 261-8444. **$41-$97, 3 day notice.** 910 N Collins St. I-30, exit 28 (Collins St/FM 157), 1 mi s. Int corridors. **Pets:** Accepted.

Homestead Studio Suites Hotel-Arlington SH
(817) 633-7588. **$47-$62.** 1221 N Watson Rd. Jct SR 360, exit Ave K/Brown Blvd. Ext corridors. **Pets:** Accepted.

Homewood Suites by Hilton SH
(817) 633-1594. **$99-$189, 14 day notice.** 2401 East Rd to Six Flags St. I-30, exit 30 (SR 360), 0.5 mi sw. Int corridors. **Pets:** Accepted.

Howard Johnson Express Inn SH
(817) 461-1122. **$45-$105.** 2001 E Copeland Rd. I-30, exit 30 (SR 360) westbound, just s to Six Flags Dr, just w to Copeland Rd, then 0.9 mi w; exit 29 (Ball Pkwy) eastbound. Int corridors. **Pets:** Medium. $10 daily fee/pet. Service with restrictions, crate.

La Quinta Inn & Suites Dallas (Arlington South) SH
(817) 467-7756. **$109-$119.** 4001 Scott's Legacy. I-20, exit 450 (Matlock Rd) on westbound service road. Int corridors. **Pets:** Service with restrictions, supervision.

La Quinta Inn Dallas (Arlington Conference Center) SH
(817) 640-4142. **$79-$106.** 825 N Watson Rd. I-30, exit 30 (SR 360), exit Six Flags Dr northbound; exit Ave H/Lamar Blvd southbound. Ext corridors. **Pets:** Accepted.

Microtel Inn SH
(817) 557-8400. **$50-$70.** 1740 Oak Village Blvd. I-20, exit 449 (Cooper St) westbound; exit 449A (Cooper St) eastbound, just s. Int corridors. **Pets:** Small, dogs only. $10 daily fee/pet. Designated rooms, service with restrictions, supervision.

Motel 6–122 SH
(817) 649-0147. **$41-$65.** 2626 E Randol Mill Rd. Jct SR 360 and Randol Mill Rd. Ext corridors. **Pets:** Accepted.

Residence Inn by Marriott SH
(817) 649-7300. **Call for rates.** 1050 Brookhollow Plaza Dr. I-30, exit 30 (SR 360), just n to Lamar Blvd, then just w. Int corridors. **Pets:** Large. $5 daily fee/room, $100 one-time fee/room. Service with restrictions.

Sleep Inn Main Gate-Six Flags SH
(817) 649-1010. **$76-$110.** 750 Six Flags Dr. I-30, exit 30 (SR 360), 0.5 mi s. Int corridors. **Pets:** Small. $10 daily fee/pet. Designated rooms, service with restrictions, supervision.

Studio 6-South Arlington #6036 SH
(817) 465-8500. **$49-$61.** 1980 W Pleasant Ridge Rd. I-20, exit 449 (Cooper St), 0.3 mi n, then just w. Ext corridors. **Pets:** Small. $50 one-time fee/room. Service with restrictions, crate.

Whitten Inn SH
(817) 467-3535. **$59-$69.** 121 I-20 E. I-20, exit 450 (Matlock Rd), just nw. Ext corridors. **Pets:** Accepted.

AUSTIN

AmeriSuites (Austin/Airport) SH ✿
(512) 386-7600. **$60-$79.** 7601 Ben White Blvd. I-35, exit 230B (Ben White Blvd), 3.2 mi e. Int corridors. **Pets:** Other species. $50 one-time fee/room. Service with restrictions, crate.

AAA ▼▼▼ AmeriSuites (Austin/Arboretum) SH
(512) 231-8491. **$119-$169.** 3612 Tudor Blvd. Jct US 183 and SR 360, 1 blk e to Stonelake Blvd, 0.5 mi s to Tudor Blvd, then just e. Int corridors. **Pets:** Accepted.

AAA ▼▼▼ AmeriSuites (Austin/North Central) SH
(512) 323-2121. **$74-$105.** 7522 N I-35. I-35, exit 240A, on west frontage road. Int corridors. **Pets:** $10 one-time fee/room. Service with restrictions, crate.

▼▼▼ Austin Marriott at the Capitol LH
(512) 478-1111. **$125-$199.** 701 E 11th St. I-35, exit 234B, 0.3 mi e. Int corridors. **Pets:** Accepted.

▼▼▼ Best Western Atrium North SH
(512) 339-7311. **$80-$104.** 7928 Gessner Dr. I-35, exit 240A, 0.4 mi w on Anderson Ln. Int corridors. **Pets:** Small, other species. $25 deposit/room. Service with restrictions, crate.

▼▼ Best Western Seville Plaza Inn SH
(512) 447-5511. **$59-$89.** 4323 I-35 S. I-35, exit 230A (Stassney Rd) southbound; exit 230 (Ben White Blvd) northbound. Int corridors. **Pets:** Small. $50 deposit/room. Service with restrictions, supervision.

▼▼▼ Candlewood Suites Austin Northwest SH
(512) 338-1611. **$79-$119.** 9701 Stonelake Blvd. Jct US 183 and SR 360, on northwest corner. Int corridors. **Pets:** Accepted.

▼▼▼ Candlewood Suites-South SH
(512) 444-8882. **$79-$99.** 4320 I-35 S. I-35, exit 230 northbound; exit 230B southbound, on southbound frontage road. Int corridors. **Pets:** Accepted.

▼▼▼ Clarion Inn & Suites Conference Center SH
(512) 444-0561. **$79-$169.** 2200 S I-35. I-35, exit 232A (Oltorf Blvd), on west side access road. Ext/int corridors. **Pets:** Accepted.

▼▼▼ Crowne Plaza LH
(512) 480-8181. **$159-$199.** 500 N I-35. I-35, exit 234B southbound; exit 234C northbound, on southbound frontage road. Int corridors. **Pets:** Accepted.

AAA ▼▼▼ Days Inn University-Downtown M
(512) 478-1631. **$57-$99, 4 day notice.** 3105 N I-35. I-35, exit 236A at 32nd St from lower level. Ext corridors. **Pets:** Medium, other species. $7 one-time fee/room. Service with restrictions, supervision.

▼▼▼ Doubletree Club Hotel SH
(512) 479-4000. **$89-$149.** 1617 I-35 N. I-35, exit Martin Luther King Jr Blvd, just on northbound frontage road. Int corridors. **Pets:** Accepted.

▼▼▼ DoubleTree Guest Suites-Austin LH
(512) 478-7000. **$139-$199.** 303 W 15th St. Just nw of state capitol building. Int corridors. **Pets:** Accepted.

▼▼▼ Doubletree Hotel Austin LH
(512) 454-3737. **$89-$159.** 6505 I-35 N. I-35, exit 238A, on east frontage road. Int corridors. **Pets:** Other species. $75 deposit/room. Designated rooms, service with restrictions, supervision.

AAA ▼▼▼ ▼▼ The Driskill LH ❀
(512) 474-5911. **$195-$380.** 604 Brazos St. Jct US 6th St. Int corridors. **Pets:** Small, other species. $50 one-time fee/room. Service with restrictions, crate.

▼▼▼ Drury Inn & Suites-Austin North SH
(512) 467-9500. **$63-$99.** 6711 I-35 N. I-35, exit 238A, on east frontage road. Int corridors. **Pets:** Large, other species. Service with restrictions, supervision.

▼▼▼ Drury Inn Austin-Highland Mall SH
(512) 454-1144. **$58-$100.** 919 E Koenig Ln. I-35, exit 238A, on west frontage road. Int corridors. **Pets:** Large, other species. Service with restrictions, supervision.

AAA ▼▼▼ Embassy Suites Hotel-Downtown LH
(512) 469-9000. **$109-$199.** 300 S Congress Ave. Just s of Congress Ave Bridge. Int corridors. **Pets:** Small, other species. $25 one-time fee/pet. Designated rooms, service with restrictions, crate.

AAA ▼▼ Exel Inn Of Austin SH
(512) 462-9201. **$45-$75.** 2711 I-35 S. I-35, exit 231 (Woodward Ave) southbound; exit 232A (Oltorf St) northbound, on northbound frontage road; just n of jct I-35 and US 290/SR 71. Int corridors. **Pets:** Small, other species. Service with restrictions, supervision.

▼▼▼ Four Points by Sheraton SH
(512) 836-8520. **$122-$130.** 7800 I-35 N. I-35, exit 240A, on west frontage road. Int corridors. **Pets:** Other species. $50 deposit/room. Service with restrictions, crate.

AAA ▼▼▼ ▼▼ Four Seasons Hotel LH
(512) 478-4500. **$320-$405.** 98 San Jacinto Blvd. Bordering Town Lake. Int corridors. **Pets:** Accepted.

▼▼▼ Hampton Inn Northwest SH
(512) 349-9898. **$79-$99.** 3908 W Braker Ln. 1 mi n of US 183 on Loop 1 (Mo-Pac Expwy) to Braker Ln exit. Int corridors. **Pets:** Accepted.

AAA ▼▼▼ ▼▼ Hawthorn Suites Ltd-Austin-Bergstrom International Airport SH
(512) 247-6166. **$69-$149.** 7800 E Riverside Dr. I-35, exit 230B (Ben White Blvd/SR 71), 3.2 mi e. Int corridors. **Pets:** Accepted.

▼▼▼ Hilton Austin North LH
(512) 451-5757. **$89-$159.** 6000 Middle Fiskville Rd. I-35, exit 238A, just off west frontage road. Int corridors. **Pets:** Accepted.

AAA ▼▼ Holiday Inn Airport South SH
(512) 448-2444. **$59-$89.** 3401 I-35 S. I-35, exit 231 (Woodward St) southbound; exit 230 (Ben White Blvd/SR 71) northbound, on northbound frontage road. Ext/int corridors. **Pets:** Accepted.

▼▼▼ Holiday Inn Northwest/Arboretum SH ❀
(512) 343-0888. **$59-$109.** 8901 Business Park Dr. Jct US 183 and Loop 1 (Mo-Pac Expwy), on southwest corner. Int corridors. **Pets:** Medium. $25 one-time fee/room. Designated rooms, service with restrictions, supervision.

AAA ▼▼▼ **Holiday Inn-Town Lake** LH
(512) 472-8211. **$129.** 20 N I-35, exit 233. Int corridors.
Pets: Medium. $125 deposit/room, $25 one-time fee/room.
SAVE S✿ ✕ 🐾 📶 🖥 🛏 🍴 ➤ ✕

▼▼ **Homestead Studio Suites**
Hotel-Austin/Arboretum SH
(512) 837-6677. **$56-$71.** 9100 Waterford Centre Blvd. US 183, exit
Burnet Rd, on westbound frontage road. Ext corridors. **Pets:** Accepted.
ASK S✿ ✕ 🐾 📶 🛏 🖥 ➤

▼▼ **Homestead Studio Suites Hotel-Austin/Downtown/**
Town Lake SH
(512) 476-1818. **$84-$99.** 507 S First St. I-35, exit 234B southbound;
exit 234A northbound, 1.8 mi w on Caesar Chavez/E First St, then 0.5
mi s. Int corridors. **Pets:** Small. $75 one-time fee/room. Service with
restrictions, supervision.
ASK S✿ ✕ 🐾 📶 🛏 🖥

▼▼ **Homewood Suites by Hilton Arboretum NW** SH
(512) 349-9966. **$129.** 10925 Stonelake Blvd. US 183 N to Loop 1
(Mo-Pac Expwy), 1.5 mi n to Braker Ln; on northwest corner. Int
corridors. **Pets:** Large, other species. $75 one-time fee/room. Service with
restrictions, crate.
ASK ✕ 🐾M 🐾 📶 🛏 🖥 ➤ ✕

AAA ▼▼▼▼ **Hyatt Regency Austin** LH 🐾
(512) 477-1234. **$119-$209, 3 day notice.** 208 Barton Springs Rd. At
south end of Congress Bridge; on south bank of Town Lake. Int
corridors. **Pets:** Medium, other species. $25 one-time fee/pet. Service with
restrictions, supervision.
SAVE S✿ ✕ 🐾M 🐾 📶 🛏 🖥 🍴 ➤ ✕

AAA ▼▼▼▼ **La Quinta Inn & Suites Austin (Airport)** SH
(512) 386-6800. **$84-$104.** 7625 E Ben White Blvd. I-35, exit 230B
(Ben White Blvd/SR 71), 3.8 mi e. Int corridors. **Pets:** Other species.
Service with restrictions, crate.
SAVE ✕ 🐾M 🐾 📶 🛏 🖥 ➤

AAA ▼▼▼▼ **La Quinta Inn & Suites Austin (Mopac**
North) SH
(512) 832-2121. **$95-$119.** 11901 N Mo-Pac Expwy. US 183, 2 mi n on
Loop 1 (Mo-Pac Expwy) to Duval exit. Int corridors. **Pets:** Accepted.
SAVE ✕ 🐾M 🐾 📶 🛏 🖥 ➤

▼▼▼▼ **La Quinta Inn & Suites Austin (Southwest at**
Mopac) SH
(512) 899-3000. **$119-$139.** 4424 S Loop 1 (Mo-Pac Expwy). Jct Loop
1 (Mo-Pac Expwy), US 290 and SR 71 E, on southbound frontage
road. Int corridors. **Pets:** Accepted.
ASK ✕ 🐾M 🐾 📶 🛏 🖥 ➤

▼▼▼▼ **La Quinta Inn Austin (Capitol)** SH
(512) 476-1166. **$119-$129.** 300 E 11 St. Just e of state capitol building.
Ext/int corridors. **Pets:** Accepted.
ASK ✕ 🐾 📶 🛏 🖥 ➤

AAA ▼▼▼▼ **La Quinta Inn Austin (Highland Mall)** SH
(512) 459-4381. **$75-$95.** 5812 I-35 N. I-35, exit 238A, on west frontage road. Ext corridors. **Pets:** Accepted.
SAVE ✕ 🐾 🛏 🖥 ➤

AAA ▼▼▼▼ **La Quinta Inn Austin (I-35 South/Ben**
White) SH
(512) 443-1774. **$80-$100.** 4200 I-35 S. I-35, exit 230B (Ben White
Blvd/SR 71) southbound; exit 230 northbound, just s of jct I-35, US
290 and SR 71, on frontage road. Ext corridors. **Pets:** Medium, other
species. No service, crate.
SAVE ✕ 🐾M 🐾 📶 🛏 🖥 ➤

AAA ▼▼▼▼ **La Quinta Inn Austin (North)** SH
(512) 452-9401. **$75-$85.** 7100 I-35 N. I-35, exit 239, on west frontage
road. Ext corridors. **Pets:** Other species. Service with restrictions.
SAVE ✕ 🐾 🛏 🖥 ➤

▼▼▼▼ **La Quinta Inn Austin (Oltorf)** SH 🐾
(512) 447-6661. **$80-$105.** 1603 E Oltorf Blvd. I-35, exit 232A (Oltorf
Blvd), just s. Ext/int corridors. **Pets:** Service with restrictions, supervision.
ASK ✕ 🐾 🛏 🖥 ➤

AAA ▼▼▼▼ **The Mansion at Judge's Hill** SH
(512) 495-1800. **$129-$395, 3 day notice.** 1900 Rio Grande. Jct Rio
Grande and Martin Luther King Blvd. Int corridors. **Pets:** Accepted.
SAVE S✿ ✕ 🍴

▼▼ **Motel 6 Austin North–360** M
(512) 339-6161. **$35-$53.** 9420 N I-35. I-35, exit 241 (Rundberg St),
just w. Ext corridors. **Pets:** Small, other species. Service with restrictions,
supervision.
S✿ ✕ 🐾 ➤

▼▼▼▼ **North Austin Plaza Hotel** SH
(512) 459-4251. **$59-$89.** 6911 I-35 N. I-35, exit 238A, on east frontage
road. Ext corridors. **Pets:** Accepted.
ASK S✿ ✕ 🐾 📶 🛏 🖥 ➤

▼▼▼▼ **Omni Austin Hotel & Suites** LH 🐾
(512) 476-3700. **$129-$279.** 700 San Jacinto. 8th St and San Jacinto.
Int corridors. **Pets:** Small. $50 one-time fee/room. Service with restrictions,
crate.
ASK S✿ ✕ 🐾M 🐾 📶 🛏 🖥 🍴 ➤ ✕

▼▼▼▼ **Omni Austin Hotel Southpark** SH
(512) 448-2222. **$129-$179.** 4140 Governor's Row. I-35, exit 230B
southbound; exit 230 northbound, on east frontage road. Int corridors.
Pets: Accepted.
ASK S✿ ✕ 🐾 📶 🛏 🖥 🍴 ➤ ✕

▼▼▼▼ **Quality Suites Austin North** SH
(512) 251-9110. **$79-$109.** 14620 N I-35. I-35, exit 247, on west frontage road. Int corridors. **Pets:** Accepted.
ASK S✿ ✕ 🐾M 🐾 📶 🛏 🖥 ➤

AAA ▼▼▼ **Ramada Inn Airport South** SH
(512) 447-0151. **$69-$89.** 1212 W Ben White Blvd. I-35, exit 231, 1 mi
w to S First St exit, then 0.3 mi on north frontage road. Ext/int
corridors. **Pets:** Accepted.
SAVE S✿ ✕ 🛏 🖥 🍴 ➤

▼▼▼ **Ramada Limited Austin North** SH
(512) 836-0079. **$42-$95.** 9121 N I-35. I-35, exit 241 northbound; exit
240A southbound, on east frontage road. Int corridors. **Pets:** Accepted.
ASK S✿ ✕ 🛏 🖥 ➤

▼▼▼ **Red Lion Hotel Austin** SH
(512) 323-5466. **$69-$109.** 6121 I-35 N. I-35, exit 238A, on east frontage road. Int corridors. **Pets:** Medium. $25 one-time fee/room. Service
with restrictions.
ASK S✿ ✕ 🐾 🛏 🖥 🍴 ➤

▼▼ **Red Roof Inn Austin North** M
(512) 835-2200. **$39-$51.** 8210 I-35 N. I-35, exit 241, on west frontage
road. Ext corridors. **Pets:** Medium. Service with restrictions, crate.
✕ 🐾 🐾 🍴 ➤

▼▼ **Red Roof Inn-Austin South** SH
(512) 448-0091. **$45-$56.** 4701 I-35 S. I-35, exit 230B (Ben White
Blvd/SR 71) southbound; exit 229 (Stassney Rd) northbound, on
northbound frontage road. Int corridors. **Pets:** Accepted.
✕ 🐾M 🐾 🐾 🛏 ➤

AAA ▼▼▼▼ **Renaissance Austin Hotel** LH 🐾
(512) 343-2626. **$159-$199.** 9721 Arboretum Blvd. Jct US 183 and
Capital of Texas Hwy (SR 360); southwest corner. Int corridors.
Pets: Service with restrictions, supervision.
SAVE S✿ ✕ 🐾M 🐾 🛏 🖥 🍴 ➤ ✕

ﾠ▼▼▼▼ **Residence Inn by Marriott Austin Airport/South** 🆂🅷
(512) 912-1100. **$99-$139.** 4537 S I-35. I-35, exit 229 (Stassney Rd) southbound; exit 230 (Ben White Blvd/SR 71) northbound, on northbound frontage road. Int corridors. **Pets:** Other species. $75 one-time fee/room. Service with restrictions.
(A$K) 🆂🔟 ⊠ 🖉 🖾 🎫 💻 ⊷ ⊠

▼▼▼▼ **Residence Inn by Marriott-Austin North/Parmer Lane** 🆂🅷
(512) 977-0544. **$152-$169.** 12401 N Lamar Blvd. I-35, exit 245, just w. Int corridors. **Pets:** Accepted.
(A$K) 🆂🔟 ⊠ 🖐M 🖉 🖾 🎫 💻 ⊷ ⊠

▼▼▼▼ **Staybridge Suites Hotel** 🆂🅷
(512) 349-0888. **$102-$169.** 10201 Stonelake Blvd. Jct US 183 and Capital of Texas Hwy (SR 360); northwest corner. Int corridors. **Pets:** Accepted.
(A$K) 🆂🔟 ⊠ 🖐M 🖉 🖾 🎫 💻 ⊷ ⊠

▼▼▼ **Studio 6-Austin Midtown #6033** 🅼 🐾
(512) 458-5453. **$47-$59.** 937 Camino La Costa. I-35, exit 238A, on east frontage road. Ext corridors. **Pets:** Medium. $10 daily fee/pet, $50 one-time fee/pet. Service with restrictions.
🆂🔟 ⊠ 🖉 🖾 🎫 💻

▼▼▼ **Studio 6-Northwest #6032** 🅼
(512) 258-3556. **$47-$59.** 11901 Pavillon Blvd. US 183, exit Oak Knoll westbound; exit Duval/Balcones Woods eastbound, on eastbound frontage road. Ext corridors. **Pets:** Accepted.
🆂🔟 ⊠ 🖉 🖾 🎫 💻

▼▼▼ **Summerfield Suites by Wyndham-Northwest Austin** 🆂🅷
(512) 452-9391. **$69-$119.** 7685 Northcross Dr. Loop 1 (Mo-Pac Expwy), exit Anderson Rd, just e to Northcross Dr, then just s. Ext corridors. **Pets:** Accepted.
(A$K) ⊠ 🖉 🎫 💻 ⊷

▲▲▲ ▼▼▼ **Super 8 Austin North** 🆂🅷
(512) 339-1300. **$46-$61.** 8128 N I-35. I-35, exit 241, on west frontage road. Int corridors. **Pets:** Accepted.
(SAVE) 🆂🔟 ⊠ 🖉 🎫 💻 ⊷

▲▲▲ ▼▼▼ **Super 8 Central** 🅼
(512) 472-8331. **$59-$85, 3 day notice.** 1201 N I-35. I-35, exit 234, at 12th St. Ext corridors. **Pets:** Accepted.
(SAVE) 🆂🔟 ⊠ 🖾 🎫 💻 ⊷

▲▲▲ ▼▼▼▼ **Wellesley Inn & Suites (Austin/N Mopac)** 🆂🅷
(512) 833-0898. **$59-$109.** 2700 Gracy Farms Ln. 2 mi n of US 183 on Loop 1 (Mo-Pac Expwy), exit Burnet Rd (FM 1325). Int corridors. **Pets:** Accepted.
(SAVE) ⊠ 🖾 🎫 💻 ⊷

▲▲▲ ▼▼▼▼ **Wellesley Inn & Suites (Austin/North)** 🆂🅷
(512) 339-6005. **$55-$95.** 8221 N I-35. I-35, exit 241, on east frontage road. Int corridors. **Pets:** Accepted.
(SAVE) 🆂🔟 ⊠ 🖉 🖾 🎫 💻 ⊷

▲▲▲ ▼▼▼▼ **Wellesley Inn & Suites (Austin/NW)** 🆂🅷
(512) 219-6500. **$79-$99.** 12424 Research Blvd. US 183, exit Oak Knoll, on eastbound frontage road. Int corridors. **Pets:** Accepted.
(SAVE) 🆂🔟 ⊠ 🖐M 🖉 🖾 🎫 💻 ⊷

BASTROP

▼▼ **Days Inn Bastrop** 🆂🅷
(512) 321-1157. **$60-$75.** 4102 Hwy 71 E. On SR 71, 2 mi e of river at Loop 150 E. Ext corridors. **Pets:** Very small, dogs only. $25 one-time fee/pet. Designated rooms, supervision.
(A$K) 🆂🔟 ⊠ 🖾 🎫 💻 ⊷

▼▼▼▼ **Holiday Inn Express Hotel & Suites** 🆂🅷
(512) 321-1900. **$69-$129.** 491 Agnes St. Jct SR 71/95, 2 mi w. Int corridors. **Pets:** Accepted.
(A$K) 🆂🔟 ⊠ 🖐M 🖾 🎫 💻 ⊷

BEAUMONT

▲▲▲ ▼▼ **Best Western Beaumont Inn** 🆂🅷 🐾
(409) 898-8150. **$50-$70.** 2155 N 11th St. I-10, exit 853B (11th St), just n. Ext corridors. **Pets:** Other species. Service with restrictions.
(SAVE) 🆂🔟 ⊠ 🎫 💻 ⊷

▲▲▲ ▼▼ **Best Western Jefferson Inn** 🆂🅷 🐾
(409) 842-0037. **$50-$70.** 1610 I-10 S. I-10, exit 851 (College St), westbound service road, 0.5 mi s of jct US 90. Ext corridors. **Pets:** Other species. Service with restrictions.
(SAVE) 🆂🔟 ⊠ 🖉 🎫 💻 ⊷

▼▼▼▼ **Hilton Beaumont** 🆂🅷
(409) 842-3600. **$119, 3 day notice.** 2355 I-10 S. I-10, exit 850 (Washington Blvd), on eastbound service road. Int corridors. **Pets:** Medium. Designated rooms, service with restrictions, supervision.
(A$K) 🆂🔟 ⊠ 🖉 🖾 🎫 💻 🍴 ⊷

▲▲▲ ▼▼▼▼ **Holiday Inn Atrium Plaza** 🅻🅷
(409) 842-5995. **$99-$119.** 3950 I-10 S. I-10, exit 848 (Walden Rd), just n. Int corridors. **Pets:** Other species. $10 daily fee/pet. Service with restrictions.
(SAVE) 🆂🔟 ⊠ 🖉 🖾 🎫 💻 🍴 ⊷ ⊠

▲▲▲ ▼▼▼▼ **Holiday Inn Beaumont Midtown** 🆂🅷
(409) 892-2222. **$75-$85.** 2095 N 11th St. I-10, exit 853B (11th St), just n. Int corridors. **Pets:** Accepted.
(SAVE) ⊠ 🖐M 🖉 🖾 🎫 💻 🍴 ⊷

▼▼▼ **Howard Johnson Express Inn & Suites** 🆂🅷
(409) 832-0666. **$69-$109.** 2615 I-10 E. I-10, exit 853B (11th St). Ext corridors. **Pets:** Accepted.
(A$K) 🆂🔟 ⊠ 🖐M 🎫 💻 ⊷

▼▼▼▼ **La Quinta Inn & Suites** 🆂🅷
(409) 842-0002. **$83.** 5820 Walden Rd. I-10, exit 848, just n. Int corridors. **Pets:** Small. $50 deposit/pet. Designated rooms, service with restrictions, supervision.
(A$K) 🆂🔟 ⊠ 🖐M 🎫 💻 ⊷

▼▼▼ **La Quinta Inn Beaumont (Midtown)** 🆂🅷
(409) 838-9991. **$71-$81.** 220 I-10 N. I-10, exit 852B (Calder Ave) eastbound; exit 852A (Laurel Ave) westbound, on eastbound service road. Ext corridors. **Pets:** Accepted.
(A$K) ⊠ 🖉 🎫 💻 ⊷

▲▲▲ ▼▼▼ **Super 8 Beaumont** 🅼
(409) 899-3040. **$46-$58.** 2850 I-10 E. I-10, exit 853B (11th St), on westbound service road. Int corridors. **Pets:** Accepted.
(SAVE) 🆂🔟 ⊠ 🎫 ⊷

BEDFORD

▲▲▲ ▼▼▼▼ **Holiday Inn-DFW-Airport West** 🆂🅷
(817) 267-3181. **$49-$129.** 3005 W Airport Frwy. SR 183, just e of jct SR 121, exit Murphy Dr N. Int corridors. **Pets:** Large. $25 one-time fee/pet. Service with restrictions, supervision.
(SAVE) 🆂🔟 ⊠ 🖐M 🖉 🖾 🎫 💻 🍴 ⊷

▲▲▲ ▼▼▼▼ **La Quinta Inn Ft. Worth (Bedford/DFW Airport)** 🆂🅷 🐾
(817) 267-5200. **$66-$76.** 1450 Airport Frwy. SR 121/183, 0.3 mi e of jct Bedford Rd/Forest Ridge Dr exit. Ext corridors. **Pets:** Other species. Service with restrictions.
(SAVE) ⊠ 🖉 🎫 💻 ⊷

♦♦ **Super 8 Motel-Bedford** [SH]
(817) 545-8108. **$55-$59.** 1800 Airport Frwy. SR 183 at Bedford Rd, exit Forest Ridge Dr. Int corridors. **Pets:** Accepted.
[ASK] [S/D] ⊠ ♿[M] ♿ ▣

BEEVILLE

♦♦ **Beeville Inn** [SH]
(361) 358-4000. **Call for rates.** 400 A S US 181 Bypass. 0.3 mi s of jct US 59 and 181. Ext corridors. **Pets:** Accepted.
⊠ ▣ 🏊

♦♦ **Best Western Texan Inn** [SH]
(361) 358-9999. **$65-$95.** 2001 Hwy 59. US 181 at US 59, just e. Ext/int corridors. **Pets:** Accepted.
[ASK] [S/D] ⊠ ▣ ☕ 🏊

BELTON

[AAA] ♦♦ **Budget Host Inn** [SH]
(254) 939-0744. **$40-$60.** 1520 S I-35. I-35, exit 292 southbound; exit 293A northbound. Ext corridors. **Pets:** Accepted.
[SAVE] [S/D] ⊠ ▣ ☕ 🏊

♦♦ **Ramada Limited** [SH]
(254) 939-3745. **$62-$72.** 1102 E 2nd Ave. I-35, exit 294A southbound; exit 294B northbound. Ext corridors. **Pets:** Accepted.
[ASK] [S/D] ⊠ ▣ ☕ 🏊

♦♦ **River Forest Inn** [SH]
(254) 939-5711. **$60-$385, 3 day notice.** 1414 E 6th Ave. I-35, exit 294B. Ext corridors. **Pets:** Accepted.
[ASK] [S/D] ⊠ ▣ 🏊

BENBROOK

[AAA] ♦♦♦ **Best Western Winscott Inn & Suites** [SH]
(817) 249-0076. **$89-$189.** 590 Winscott Rd. I-20, exit 429B. Int corridors. **Pets:** Accepted.
[SAVE] [S/D] ⊠ ♿ ▣ ☕ 🏊

♦ **Motel 6-4051** [SH]
(817) 249-8885. **$51-$75.** 8601 Benbrook Blvd (Hwy 377 S). I-20, exit 429A, 0.7 mi s. Int corridors. **Pets:** Small. Service with restrictions, supervision.
[ASK] ⊠ ♿[M] ♿ ▣ 🏊

BIG SPRING

[AAA] ♦♦ **Super 8 Motel** [M]
(432) 267-1601. **$58-$65.** 700 W I-20. I-20, exit 177, just n. Ext corridors. **Pets:** Medium. Service with restrictions, supervision.
[SAVE] [S/D] ⊠ 🦻 ▣ ☕ 🏊

BOERNE

[AAA] ♦♦ **Best Western Texas Country Inn** [SH]
(830) 249-9791. **$72-$95.** 35150 I-10 W. I-10, exit 540 (SR 46), westbound access road. Ext corridors. **Pets:** Medium, other species. $20 one-time fee/pet. Service with restrictions, supervision.
[SAVE] [S/D] ⊠ ▣ ☕ 🏊

BONHAM

[AAA] ♦ **5 Star Inn** [M]
(903) 583-3121. **$43-$58.** 1515 Old Ector Rd. Jct SR 56 W and 121 S. Ext corridors. **Pets:** $10 one-time fee/room. Designated rooms, service with restrictions, supervision.
[SAVE] [S/D] ⊠ ▣ ☕ 🏊

BOWIE

[AAA] ♦♦ **Days Inn** [SH]
(940) 872-5426. **$55-$60, 7 day notice.** 2436 S US 287. Jct SR 59. Ext corridors. **Pets:** Medium. $5 daily fee/pet. Designated rooms, service with restrictions, supervision.
[SAVE] [S/D] ⊠ ▣ 🏊

[AAA] ♦ **Park's Inn** [M]
(940) 872-1111. **$46-$60.** 708 W Wise St. 0.5 mi n of jct SR 59; downtown. Ext corridors. **Pets:** Medium. $5 daily fee/pet. No service, supervision.
[SAVE] [S/D] ⊠ ▣ 🏊

BRADY

[AAA] ♦♦ **Best Western Brady Inn** [SH]
(325) 597-3997. **$55-$75.** 2200 S Bridge St. 1.1 mi s on US 87/377. Ext corridors. **Pets:** Accepted.
[SAVE] [S/D] ⊠ ▣ ☕ 🏊

[AAA] ♦♦ **Days Inn** [M]
(325) 597-0789. **$49-$79.** 2108 S Bridge St. 1 mi s on US 87/377 at US 190. Ext corridors. **Pets:** Service with restrictions, supervision.
[SAVE] [S/D] ⊠ ▣ ☕ 🏊

BRENHAM

♦♦♦ **Comfort Suites** [SH]
(979) 421-8100. **$59-$119.** 2350 S Day St. US 290, exit SR 36 S, just n on Business Rt SR 36. Int corridors. **Pets:** Accepted.
[ASK] [S/D] ⊠ ▣ ☕ 🏊

BROWNFIELD

♦♦ **Best Western Caprock Inn** [SH]
(806) 637-9471. **$69.** 321 Lubbock Rd. Jct US 385 and 82, 2 blks n. Ext corridors. **Pets:** Accepted.
[ASK] [S/D] ⊠ ♿ ▣ ☕ 🏊

BROWNSVILLE

♦♦♦ **Four Points by Sheraton** [SH]
(956) 547-1500. **Call for rates.** 3777 North Expwy. US 77 and 83, exit McAllen Rd, 0.5 mi s on west frontage road. Int corridors. **Pets:** Accepted.
⊠ 🦻 ▣ ☕ 🍴 🏊 ⊗

♦♦♦ **Hawthorn Suites** [SH]
(956) 574-6900. **$119-$149.** 3759 North Expwy. US 77, exit McAllen Rd; on southbound access lane. Int corridors. **Pets:** Small, other species. $125 one-time fee/room. Service with restrictions, supervision.
[ASK] [S/D] ⊠ ☕ 🏊 ⊗

[AAA] ♦♦ **Red Roof Inn** [M] 🐾
(956) 504-2300. **$48-$103.** 2377 North Expwy. US 83, exit FM 802, just s. Ext corridors. **Pets:** Medium. No service, supervision.
[SAVE] [S/D] ⊠ ♿ ▣ 🏊

♦♦♦ **Residence Inn by Marriott** [SH] 🐾
(956) 350-8100. **$84-$164.** 3975 North Expwy. US 83 and 77 Expwy, exit McAllen Rd. Int corridors. **Pets:** Medium. $75 one-time fee/room. Service with restrictions, supervision.
[ASK] [S/D] ⊠ ♿[M] ♿ ▣ ☕ 🏊 ⊗

BROWNWOOD

[AAA] ♦♦ **Best Western** [M]
(325) 646-3511. **$49-$89.** 410 E Commerce St. On US 67/84/377; just n of jct Main Ave. Ext corridors. **Pets:** Accepted.
[SAVE] [S/D] ⊠ ♿ ▣ ☕ 🏊

AAA ▼▼▼ Days Inn-Brownwood SH
(325) 646-2551. **$50-$74, 3 day notice.** 515 E Commerce St. On US 67/84/377, 0.4 mi n of jct Main Ave. Ext corridors. **Pets:** $15 one-time fee/room. Service with restrictions.
SAVE 🗑 ✕ 🖥 💻 🏊

BURLESON

AAA ▼▼▼ Comfort Suites SH
(817) 426-6666. **$79-$89.** 321 S Burleson Blvd. I-35, exit 36 (Renfro St) westbound, 0.6 mi s on frontage road east of interstate. Int corridors. **Pets:** Small. $10 daily fee/pet. Service with restrictions, supervision.
SAVE 🗑 ✕ 🖥 💻 🏊

AAA ▼▼▼ Days Inn SH
(817) 447-1111. **$59-$69.** 329 S Burleson Blvd. I-35, exit 36 (Renfro St), just w to east frontage road, then 0.5 mi s. Ext corridors. **Pets:** Accepted.
SAVE 🗑 ✕ 🖥 💻 🏊

CANTON

AAA ▼▼▼ Best Western Canton Inn SH
(903) 567-6591. **$59-$129.** 2251 N Trade Days Blvd. Jct I-20 and SR 19, exit 527. Ext corridors. **Pets:** Very small. $5 daily fee/pet. Service with restrictions, supervision.
SAVE 🗑 ✕ 🖥 💻 🏊

▼▼▼ Holiday Inn Express SH
(903) 567-0909. **Call for rates.** 2406 N Trade Days Blvd. I-20, exit 527. Ext corridors. **Pets:** Accepted.
✕ 🖥 💻 🏊

▼▼ Super 8 Motel SH
(903) 567-6567. **$52-$150, 3 day notice.** 17350 I-20. I-20, exit 527. Ext corridors. **Pets:** Other species. $10 daily fee/pet. Service with restrictions, supervision.
ASK 🗑 ✕ 🖥 💻 🏊

CANYON

AAA ▼▼▼ Holiday Inn Express Hotel & Suites SH
(806) 655-4445. **$67-$99.** 2901 4th Ave. I-27, exit 106, 2 mi w. Int corridors. **Pets:** Other species. $10 one-time fee/room. Service with restrictions, supervision.
SAVE 🗑 ✕ 🖥 💻 🏊

CEDAR PARK

▼▼ Comfort Inn SH
(512) 259-1810. **$70-$90.** 300 E Whitestone Blvd. I-35, exit 256, 8 mi w on FM 1431. Int corridors. **Pets:** $10 daily fee/pet. Service with restrictions, supervision.
ASK 🗑 ✕ 🖥 💻 🏊

CENTER

▼▼ Best Western Center Inn SH
(936) 598-3384. **$53-$69.** 1005 Hurst St. On US 96, jct SR 87. Int corridors. **Pets:** Small. $15 daily fee/pet. Designated rooms, service with restrictions, supervision.
ASK 🗑 ✕ 🖥 💻 🏊

CHILDRESS

AAA ▼▼▼ Best Western Childress M
(940) 937-6353. **$80-$90, 7 day notice.** 1801 Ave F NW (Hwy 287). On US 287, just s of jct US 62/83. Ext corridors. **Pets:** Medium. $20 daily fee/pet. Service with restrictions, supervision.
SAVE 🗑 ✕ 🖥 💻 🏊

▼▼▼ Comfort Inn SH
(940) 937-6363. **$74-$99.** 1804 Ave F NW (Hwy 287). US 287, just s of jct US 62/83. Ext corridors. **Pets:** Medium, other species. $5 daily fee/pet. Service with restrictions, supervision.
ASK ✕ 🖥 💻 🏊

AAA ▼▼▼ Days Inn SH
(940) 937-0622. **$64-$84.** 2220 Ave F (Hwy 287). 1.8 mi w on US 287, from jct US 62/83. Int corridors. **Pets:** Accepted.
SAVE 🗑 ✕ 🖥 💻 🏊

▼▼ Econo Lodge SH
(940) 937-3695. **$52-$75.** 1612 Ave F NW, Hwy 287. On US 287, just s of jct US 62/83. Ext corridors. **Pets:** $5 daily fee/pet. Service with restrictions, supervision.
ASK 🗑 ✕ 💻

AAA ▼▼▼ Super 8 Motel Childress M
(940) 937-8825. **$65-$85.** 411 Ave F NE (Hwy 287 S). Jct US 83/287, 1.5 mi e. Ext corridors. **Pets:** Other species. $15 daily fee/pet. Designated rooms, service with restrictions, supervision.
SAVE 🗑 ✕ 🖥 💻 🏊

CISCO

▼▼ Best Western Inn Cisco M 🐾
(254) 442-3735. **$59-$64.** 1898 Hwy 206 W. I-20, exit 330. Ext corridors. **Pets:** Small. $10 daily fee/pet. Service with restrictions, supervision.
ASK 🗑 ✕ 🖥 💻 🏊

CLARENDON

AAA ▼▼▼ Western Skies Motel M
(806) 874-3501. **$45-$55, 7 day notice.** 800 W 2nd St. 0.5 mi nw on US 287 and SR 70. Ext corridors. **Pets:** Medium, dogs only. $10 deposit/room. Designated rooms, service with restrictions, supervision.
SAVE 🗑 ✕ 🖥 🏊

CLAUDE

AAA ▼▼ L A Motel M
(806) 226-4981. **$40-$50, 7 day notice.** Hwy 287/200 E 1st St. 0.3 mi s. Ext corridors. **Pets:** Accepted.
SAVE 🗑 ✕ 🖥 💻 🍴

CLEBURNE

▼▼ Budget Host Inn M
(817) 556-3631. **$70.** 2107 N Main St. US 67, exit SR 174 (Main St), just e. Ext corridors. **Pets:** Accepted.
ASK 🗑 ✕ 🖥 💻 🏊

▼▼ Comfort Inn SH
(817) 641-4702. **$79-$125.** 2117 N Main St. On SR 174, just s of jct US 67. Int corridors. **Pets:** Small, other species. $10 daily fee/room. Service with restrictions, supervision.
ASK 🗑 ✕ 🖥 ⊘ 🖥 💻 🏊

CLUTE

AAA ▼▼▼ Best Western Clute Inn & Suites SH
(979) 388-0055. **$79-$129.** 900 Hwy 332. Just w of jct SR 288. Int corridors. **Pets:** Small, other species. $10 daily fee/pet. Service with restrictions, supervision.
SAVE 🗑 ✕ 🖥 💻 🏊

AAA ▼▼▼ La Quinta Inn Clute/Lake Jackson M
(979) 265-7461. **$69-$79.** 1126 Hwy 332 W. On SR 288/332, just w of jct Business Rt SR 288. Ext corridors. **Pets:** Accepted.
SAVE ✕ ⊘ 🖥 💻 🏊

AAA ▼▼▼ Mainstay Suites Clute/Lake Jackson SH
(979) 388-9300. **$99-$139.** 1003 W Hwy 332. Just w of jct SR 288. Int corridors. **Pets:** Small. $25 one-time fee/room. Service with restrictions, supervision.
SAVE 🗑 ✕ 🖥 💻 🏊 ⊠

COLLEGE STATION

AAA ▼▼▼ Hilton College Station and Conference Center LH 🐾
(979) 693-7500. **$99-$259, 21 day notice.** 801 University Dr E. SR 6, exit University Dr, 1.1 mi w. Int corridors. **Pets:** Other species. Service with restrictions, crate.
[SAVE] [X] [icons]

▼▼ Holiday Inn-College Station SH
(979) 693-1736. **$69-$115.** 1503 S Texas Ave. 1.3 mi s of jct CR 60. Int corridors. **Pets:** Medium. $15 one-time fee/pet. Service with restrictions, crate.
[ASK] [icons]

AAA ▼▼▼ La Quinta Inn College Station SH
(979) 696-7777. **$85-$105.** 607 Texas Ave. Just s on jct CR 60/SR 6 business route to Live Oak St, then just e. Ext corridors. **Pets:** Accepted.
[SAVE] [X] [icons]

▼▼▼ Manor House Inn SH
(979) 764-9540. **$70-$99.** 2504 Texas Ave S. 2.4 mi s of jct CR 60. Ext corridors. **Pets:** Accepted.
[ASK] [icons]

AAA ▼▼▼ Ramada Inn SH
(979) 693-9891. **$63.** 1502 Texas Ave S. 1.3 mi s of jct CR 60. Int corridors. **Pets:** Small. $15 one-time fee/room. Service with restrictions, supervision.
[SAVE] [icons]

▼▼ Super 8 Motel-College Station M
(979) 846-8800. **$70-$125, 14 day notice.** 301 Texas Ave. Just n of jct CR 60. Int corridors. **Pets:** Accepted.
[ASK] [icons]

▼▼▼ TownePlace Suites By Marriott SH
(979) 260-8500. **$89-$131.** 1300 E University Dr. SR 6, exit University Dr, 1 mi w. Ext corridors. **Pets:** Other species. $75 one-time fee/room. Service with restrictions.
[icons]

COLUMBUS

AAA ▼▼ Country Hearth Inn SH
(979) 732-6293. **$80-$200.** 2436 Hwy 71 S. I-10, exit 696 (SR 71). Ext corridors. **Pets:** Very small, dogs only. $10 daily fee/room. Designated rooms, service with restrictions, supervision.
[SAVE] [X] [icons]

▼▼▼ Holiday Inn Express Hotel & Suites SH
(979) 733-9300. **$89.** 4321 I-10. I-10, exit 696 (SR 71), just w on westbound service road. Int corridors. **Pets:** $40 deposit/room, $10 daily fee/room. Service with restrictions, supervision.
[ASK] [X] [icons]

CONWAY

AAA ▼▼▼ Budget Host S & S Motel M
(806) 537-5111. **$40, 3 day notice.** I-40 & SR 207. I-40, exit 96 (SR 207), 0.3 mi w on southbound access road. Ext corridors. **Pets:** Accepted.
[SAVE] [icons]

COPPERAS COVE

▼▼▼ Howard Johnson Express Inn SH
(254) 547-2345. **$60-$80.** 302 W US 190. On US 190, jct Georgetown Rd, 0.4 mi w of jct US 190 and SR 116. Ext corridors. **Pets:** Accepted.
[ASK] [icons]

CORPUS CHRISTI

AAA ▼▼▼ Best Western Garden Inn M
(361) 241-6675. **$69-$99.** 11217 I-37. I-37, exit 11B (Violet Rd), on southbound access road. Ext corridors. **Pets:** Small. $5 daily fee/pet. Designated rooms, service with restrictions, crate.
[SAVE] [icons]

AAA ▼▼▼ Best Western Marina Grand Hotel SH
(361) 883-5111. **$79-$195.** 300 N Shoreline Dr. Center of downtown. Int corridors. **Pets:** Medium. $25 one-time fee/room. Designated rooms, service with restrictions, supervision.
[SAVE] [icons]

▼▼◆ Christy Estate Suites CO
(361) 854-1091. **$109-$169.** 3942 Holly Rd. SR 358, exit Weber Rd, 0.5 mi s. Ext/int corridors. **Pets:** Accepted.
[ASK] [icons]

AAA ▼▼◆ Clarion Hotel SH
(361) 883-6161. **$74-$94.** 5224 I-37 (Navigation Blvd). I-37, exit 3A (Navigation Blvd), on northbound access lane. Ext corridors. **Pets:** Small. $25 one-time fee/room. Service with restrictions, supervision.
[SAVE] [icons]

▼▼ Days Inn-Airport SH
(361) 888-8599. **$40-$130.** 901 Navigation Blvd. I-37, exit 3A (Navigation Blvd), just w. Ext corridors. **Pets:** Small, other species. $15 daily fee/pet. Designated rooms, service with restrictions.
[ASK] [icons]

▼▼ Days Inn Corpus Christi South SH
(361) 854-0005. **$69-$189.** 2838 S Padre Island Dr. On SR 358 westbound access road, 0.4 mi w, exit Kostoryz Rd. Ext corridors. **Pets:** Small. $25 daily fee/pet. Service with restrictions, supervision.
[ASK] [icons]

▼▼▼ Drury Inn-Corpus Christi SH
(361) 289-8200. **$61-$95.** 2021 N Padre Island Dr. I-37, exit SR 358, just se at Leopard St. Int corridors. **Pets:** Large, other species. Service with restrictions, supervision.
[ASK] [icons]

AAA ▼▼▼ Holiday Inn-Airport and Conference Center LH
(361) 289-5100. **$89-$109.** 5549 Leopard St. Jct SR 358 and Leopard St, 5.5 mi w. Int corridors. **Pets:** Accepted.
[SAVE] [X] [icons]

AAA ▼▼▼ Holiday Inn-Emerald Beach LH
(361) 883-5731. **$120-$179.** 1102 S Shoreline Blvd. 1.5 mi s on bay from downtown marina. Ext/int corridors. **Pets:** Accepted.
[SAVE] [icons]

▼▼▼ La Quinta Inn Corpus Christi (North) SH
(361) 888-5721. **$76-$102.** 5155 I-37 N. I-37, exit 3A (Navigation Blvd), on southbound access road. Ext corridors. **Pets:** Small. Service with restrictions.
[ASK] [icons]

AAA ▼▼▼ La Quinta Inn Corpus Christi (South) SH
(361) 991-5730. **$80-$105.** 6225 S Padre Island Dr. SR 358 Expwy, exit Airline Rd. Ext corridors. **Pets:** Small. Service with restrictions, supervision.
[SAVE] [icons]

▼▼ Motel 6 #231 M
(361) 289-9397. **$35-$53.** 845 Lantana St. I-37, exit 4B (Lantana St), on southbound access road. Ext corridors. **Pets:** Small, other species. No service, supervision.
[icons]

◆◆ ▼▼ **Motel 6 SPI Drive–413** SH
(361) 991-8858. **$39-$71.** 8202 S Padre Island Dr. S Padre Island Dr at Paul Jones St. Ext corridors. **Pets:** Accepted.
⬛ ✕ 🏷 🏊

◆◆◆ ▼▼ **Quality Inn Sandy Shores** SH
(361) 883-7456. **$59-$179, 3 day notice.** 3202 Surfside Blvd. 1 mi n on US 181, at north end of Harbor Bridge, exit Bridge St. Ext/int corridors. **Pets:** Small. $20 daily fee/pet. Designated rooms, service with restrictions, supervision.
⬛ ⬛ ✕ 🖥 🏊

◆◆◆ ▼▼ **Red Roof Inn Corpus Christi Airport** M
(361) 289-6925. **$43-$115.** 6301 I-37. I-37, exit 5 (Corn Products Rd), southbound access road. Ext corridors. **Pets:** Small. $10 deposit/pet, $15 daily fee/pet. Service with restrictions, supervision.
⬛ ⬛ ✕ 🏷 🖥 🏊

DALHART

◆◆◆ ▼▼ **Best Western Nursanickel Motel** SH
(806) 244-5637. **$59-$79.** 102 Scott Ave (Hwy 87 S). Just s of jct US 54 and 87. Ext corridors. **Pets:** Small, dogs only. Service with restrictions, supervision.
⬛ ⬛ ✕ 🏷 🖥 🏊

◆◆◆ ▼ **Budget Inn** M
(806) 244-4557. **$38-$79.** 415 Liberal St (Hwy 54). US 54, just e of US 87 and 385. Ext corridors. **Pets:** Accepted.
⬛ ⬛ ✕ 🏷

◆◆◆ ▼▼▼ **Comfort Inn** M
(806) 249-8585. **$75-$95.** 1110 Hwy 54 E. 0.5 mi e of jct US 54 and 87. Ext corridors. **Pets:** Small. Designated rooms, service with restrictions, supervision.
⬛ ⬛ ✕ 🏷 🖥 🏊

◆◆◆ ▼▼▼ **Days Inn** SH
(806) 244-5246. **$79-$189, 3 day notice.** 701 Liberal St (Hwy 54). On US 54, 0.5 mi e. Int corridors. **Pets:** Accepted.
⬛ ⬛ ✕ 🏷 🖥 🏊

▼▼ **Holiday Inn Express** SH
(806) 249-1145. **$79-$199, 4 day notice.** 801 Liberal St (Hwy 54). 1 mi e of jct US 54 and 87. Int corridors. **Pets:** Medium. Designated rooms, service with restrictions, supervision.
⬛ ⬛ ✕ 🏷 🏷 🖥 🏊

◆◆◆ ▼ **Sands Motel** M
(806) 244-4568. **$40-$70.** 301 Liberal St (Hwy 54). US 54, just e of US 87 and 385. Ext corridors. **Pets:** Service with restrictions, supervision.
⬛ ⬛ ✕ 🏊

▼▼ **Super 8 Motel** M
(806) 249-8526. **$55-$65, 5 day notice.** 403 Tanglewood Rd. Jct US 87/54, 0.5 mi e. Int corridors. **Pets:** Medium. $25 deposit/pet. Designated rooms, service with restrictions, supervision.
⬛ ✕ 🏷

DALLAS METROPOLITAN AREA

ADDISON

◆◆◆ ▼▼▼ **Comfort Inn Hotel by the Galleria** SH
(972) 701-0881. **$44-$89.** 14975 Landmark Blvd. Jct Belt Line Rd and Landmark Blvd, just s. Int corridors. **Pets:** Medium. Service with restrictions, supervision.
⬛ ⬛ ✕ 🏷 🏷 🏷 🖥 🏊

▼▼▼ **Comfort Suites by Choice Hotels** SH
(972) 503-6500. **$62-$69.** 4555 Belt Line Rd. Just ne of jct Midway and Belt Line rds. Int corridors. **Pets:** Accepted.
⬛ ✕ 🏷 🏷 🏷 🖥 🏊

▼▼▼ **Crowne Plaza North Dallas/Near the Galleria** LH
(972) 980-8877. **Call for rates.** 14315 Midway Rd. 0.8 mi s of jct Belt Line and Midway rds. Int corridors. **Pets:** Accepted.
✕ 🏷 🏷 🏷 🖥 🍴 🏊 ✕

▼▼▼ **Homewood Suites by Hilton** SH
(972) 788-1342. **$119-$149.** 4451 Belt Line Rd. Just e of jct Belt Line and Midway rds. Ext/int corridors. **Pets:** Accepted.
⬛ ⬛ ✕ 🏷 🏷 🏷 🖥 🏊 ✕

▼▼▼ **La Quinta Inn & Suites Dallas (Addison-Galleria Area)** SH
(972) 404-0004. **$76-$96.** 14925 Landmark Blvd. Jct Belt Line Rd and Landmark Blvd, just s. Int corridors. **Pets:** Other species. Service with restrictions, crate.
⬛ ✕ 🏷 🏷 🏷 🖥 🏊

▼▼▼ **Summerfield Suites by Wyndham-Addison/North Dallas** SH
(972) 661-3113. **$69-$109.** 4900 Edwin Lewis Dr. Just n of jct Belt Line Rd and Quorum Dr to Edwin Lewis Dr, then just w. Ext/int corridors. **Pets:** Medium. $150 one-time fee/room. Service with restrictions, crate.
⬛ ✕ 🏷 🏷 🏷 🖥 🏊 ✕

CARROLLTON

▼▼ **Red Roof Inn-Carrollton** M
(972) 245-1700. **$37-$54.** 1720 S Broadway. I-35E, exit 442 (Valwood Pkwy), just ne. Ext corridors. **Pets:** Medium, other species. Service with restrictions, crate.
✕ 🏷

THE COLONY

◆◆◆ ▼▼▼ **Comfort Suites** SH
(972) 668-5555. **$84-$90.** 4796 Memorial Dr. Just n of jct SR 121. Int corridors. **Pets:** Medium, dogs only. $10 daily fee/pet. Service with restrictions, supervision.
⬛ ⬛ ✕ 🏷 🏷 🏷 🖥 🏊

COMMERCE

◆◆◆ ▼▼▼ **Holiday Inn Express Hotel & Suites** SH
(903) 886-4777. **$66-$82, 3 day notice.** 2207 Culver St. 0.9 mi e of jct SR 224, 24 and 50. Int corridors. **Pets:** Medium. $25 one-time fee/pet. Service with restrictions, crate.
⬛ ✕ 🏷 🏷 🖥 🏊

DALLAS

◆◆◆ ▼▼▼ **AmeriSuites (Dallas/Near the Galleria)** SH
(972) 716-2001. **$99-$109.** 5229 Spring Valley Rd. Jct Dallas Pkwy, just e. Int corridors. **Pets:** Very small. $10 daily fee/pet. Service with restrictions, supervision.
⬛ ⬛ ✕ 🏷 🏷 🖥 🏊

◆◆◆ ▼▼▼ **AmeriSuites (Dallas/Park Central)** SH
(972) 458-1224. **$99-$119.** 12411 N Central Expwy. US 75, exit 8B (Coit Rd) northbound; exit 8 (Coit Rd), on southbound access road. Int corridors. **Pets:** Accepted.
⬛ ⬛ ✕ 🏷 🏷 🖥 🏊

△△△ ▽▽▽▽ AmeriSuites (Dallas/West End) SH
(214) 999-0500. **$99-$134.** 1907 N Lamar St. Between Corbin Ave and Munger St. Int corridors. **Pets:** Accepted.
SAVE ✕ 🐾 🐕 🔋 💻 🏊

▽▽▽▽ Best Western Dallas Telecom Area Suites SH
(972) 669-0478. **$89-$149.** 13636 Goldmark Dr. US 75, exit 22 (Midpark Rd), just w. Ext/int corridors. **Pets:** Other species. $45 one-time fee/pet. Service with restrictions.
ASK S🐾 ✕ 🔋 💻 🏊

▽▽▽▽ Candlewood Dallas Market Center SH
(214) 631-3333. **$74-$144.** 7930 N Stemmons Frwy. I-35, exit 433B (Mockingbird Ln), just w. Int corridors. **Pets:** Accepted.
ASK S🐾 ✕ 🔋 💻 🏊

▽▽▽▽ Candlewood Suites-Dallas Hotel by the Galleria SH
(972) 233-6888. **$89.** 13939 Noel Rd. Jct Dallas Pkwy and Spring Valley, just e to Noel Rd, then just s. Int corridors. **Pets:** Accepted.
ASK S🐾 ✕ 🐾M 🔋 💻

▽▽▽▽ Candlewood Suites Dallas North/Richardson SH 🐾
(972) 669-9606. **$55-$75.** 12525 Greenville Ave. I-635, exit 18A (Greenville Ave), just n. Int corridors. **Pets:** Medium, other species. $75 one-time fee/room.
ASK S🐾 ✕ 🐾M 🐕 🔋 💻

▽▽▽▽ Comfort Inn & Suites Market Center SH
(214) 461-2677. **$69-$129.** 7138 N Stemmons Frwy. I-35E, exit 433B northbound; exit 432B southbound, turn under freeway, 0.7 mi on north access road. Int corridors. **Pets:** Small. $25 one-time fee/room. Designated rooms, no service, supervision.
ASK S🐾 ✕ 🐾 🐕 🔋 💻

▽▽▽▽ Country Inn & Suites Dallas Central SH
(972) 907-9500. **$63-$81.** 13185 N Central Expwy. US 75 N, exit 22 (Midpark Rd). Int corridors. **Pets:** Large. $5 daily fee/pet, $25 one-time fee/pet. Service with restrictions, supervision.
ASK S🐾 ✕ 🐾 🐕 🔋 💻 🏊

▽▽▽▽ Crowne Plaza Hotel and Resort Dallas Market Center LH
(214) 630-8500. **$119-$139.** 7050 Stemmons Frwy. I-35E, exit 433B northbound; exit 432B southbound. Int corridors. **Pets:** $25 one-time fee/room. Service with restrictions, supervision.
ASK S🐾 ✕ 🐕 🔋 💻 🍴 🏊 ✕

△△△ ▽▽▽▽ Crowne Plaza Suites Hotel Dallas Park Central LH
(972) 233-7600. **$159.** 7800 Alpha Rd. I-635, exit 19C (Coit Rd) eastbound; exit 19B (Coit Rd) westbound, 0.3 mi nw of jct US 75. Int corridors. **Pets:** Small. $125 deposit/room, $25 one-time fee/pet. Service with restrictions, crate.
SAVE S🐾 ✕ 🐾 🐕 🔋 💻 🍴 🏊

△△△ ▽▽▽▽ Dallas Marriott Suites Market Center SH
(214) 905-0050. **$89-$164.** 2493 N Stemmons Frwy. I-35, exit 431 (Motor St). Int corridors. **Pets:** Accepted.
SAVE ✕ 🐾M 🐾 🐕 🔋 💻 🍴 🏊

▽▽▽▽ Drury Inn & Suites-Dallas North SH
(972) 484-3330. **$50-$90.** 2421 Walnut Hill Ln. I-35E, exit 438 (Walnut Hill Ln). Int corridors. **Pets:** Large, other species. Service with restrictions, supervision.
ASK ✕ 🐾 🔋 💻 🏊

▽▽▽▽ Embassy Suites Dallas-Market Center LH
(214) 630-5332. **$199-$219.** 2727 Stemmons Frwy. I-35E, exit 432 (Inwood Rd). Int corridors. **Pets:** Accepted.
ASK ✕ 🐾 🐕 🔋 💻 🍴 🏊 ✕

▽▽▽▽ The Fairmont Dallas LH
(214) 720-2020. **$89-$209.** 1717 N Akard St. Corner of Ross Ave and N Akard St. Int corridors. **Pets:** Accepted.
ASK S🐾 ✕ 🐾M 🐾 🐕 🔋 💻 🍴 🏊

▽▽▽▽ Holiday Inn Express-Love Field SH
(214) 350-5577. **$80.** 2370 W Northwest Hwy. I-35E, exit 436 Northwest Hwy (Loop 12), 0.8 mi e. Int corridors. **Pets:** Accepted.
ASK S🐾 ✕ 🐾 🔋 💻 🏊

▽▽▽▽ Holiday Inn Select Dallas Central LH
(214) 373-6000. **$75-$95.** 10650 N Central Expwy. N US 75, exit 6 (Walnut Hill Ln/Meadow Rd). Int corridors. **Pets:** Accepted.
ASK S🐾 ✕ 🐾 🐕 🔋 💻 🍴 🏊

▽▽ Homestead Studio Suites Hotel-Dallas/North Addison/Tollway SH
(972) 447-1800. **$54-$69.** 17425 North Dallas Pkwy. On North Dallas Tollway, exit Trinity Mills, just s of jct Trinity Mills and Dallas Pkwy, on southbound access road. Ext corridors. **Pets:** Small, other species. $75 one-time fee/room. Service with restrictions.
ASK S🐾 ✕ 🐕 🔋 💻

▽▽ Homestead Studio Suites Hotel-Dallas/North/Park Central SH
(972) 663-1800. **$54-$69.** 12121 Coit Rd. I-635, exit 19C (Coit Rd), 0.7 mi s. Ext corridors. **Pets:** Accepted.
ASK S🐾 ✕ 🐾 🐕 🔋 💻

▽▽▽ Homestead Studio Suites Hotel-Dallas/Plano SH
(972) 248-2233. **$74-$89.** 18470 N Dallas Pkwy. North Dallas Tollway, exit Frankford, just ne. Int corridors. **Pets:** Accepted.
ASK S🐾 ✕ 🐾 🐕 🔋 💻 🏊

▽▽▽ Homewood Suites by Hilton SH
(214) 819-9700. **$125.** 2747 N Stemmons Frwy. I-35, exit 432 (Inwood Rd). Int corridors. **Pets:** Accepted.
ASK S🐾 ✕ 🐾M 🐕 🔋 💻 🏊

▽▽▽ Homewood Suites by Hilton–I-635 SH
(972) 437-6966. **$69-$109, 7 day notice.** 9169 Markville Dr. I-635, exit 18A (Greenville Ave S), just s, then just e. Int corridors. **Pets:** $100 one-time fee/room. Service with restrictions, supervision.
ASK S🐾 ✕ 🐕 🔋 💻 🏊 ✕

▽▽ Hotel Crescent Court LH 🐾
(214) 871-3200. **$365-$2500.** 400 Crescent Ct. Corner of Crescent Ct and McKinney Ave; uptown. Int corridors. **Pets:** Medium. $100 one-time fee/pet. Service with restrictions.
✕ 🐕 🍴 🏊 ✕

▽▽▽ Hotel Dallas Mockingbird SH
(214) 634-8850. **$69-$109.** 1893 W Mockingbird Ln. I-35E, exit 433C (Mockingbird Ln), 0.8 mi e. Int corridors. **Pets:** Accepted.
S🐾 ✕ 🐾 🐕 🔋 💻 🍴 🏊 ✕

▽▽▽ Hotel Lawrence SH 🐾
(214) 761-9090. **$99-$109.** 302 S Houston St. I-35E, exit 428A (Commerce St), 0.8 mi to Griffin, just s to Jackson St then just w. Int corridors. **Pets:** Medium. $25 one-time fee/room. Service with restrictions.
ASK S🐾 ✕ 🍴

△△△ ▽▽▽▽ Hotel St. Germain CI 🐾
(214) 871-2516. **$290-$650, 7 day notice.** 2516 Maple Ave. Woodall Rogers Pkwy, exit Pearl St, 0.3 mi n. Int corridors. **Pets:** Small, dogs only. $50 daily fee/pet. Designated rooms, service with restrictions, supervision.
SAVE 🍴

▽▽▽▽ Hotel ZaZa SH
(214) 468-8399. **$284-$350.** 2332 Leonard St. Jct Maple Ave/Routh St and McKinney Ave, northeast corner. Int corridors. **Pets:** Accepted.
ASK S🐾 ✕ 🐾M 🐕 🔋 🍴 🏊 ✕

▼▼▼▼ **La Quinta Inn & Suites Dallas (North Central)** SH
(214) 361-8200. **$96-$106.** 10001 N Central Expwy. US 75, exit 6
(Walnut Hill Ln/Meadow Rd) northbound, 0.5 mi n to Meadow Rd,
U-turn under highway; exit 7 (Royal/Meadow Rd) southbound, 1 mi s
on feeder. Int corridors. **Pets:** Small. Service with restrictions, crate.
ASK ✕ 🐾M 🖉 🕮 📺 🏊

▼▼▼▼ **La Quinta Inn & Suites Dallas Northwest** SH
(214) 904-9955. **$59-$69.** 2380 W Northwest Hwy. I-35, exit 436 Northwest Hwy (Loop 12), 0.8 mi e. Int corridors. **Pets:** Medium, other
species. Service with restrictions, supervision.
ASK 🐾 ✕ 🖉 🕮 📺 🏊

▼▼▼ **La Quinta Inn Dallas (City Place)** SH
(214) 821-4220. **$86-$102.** 4440 N Central Expwy. N off US 75, exit 2
(Henderson-Knox) northbound; exit 1B (Haskell/Blackburn) southbound. Ext corridors. **Pets:** Other species. Service with restrictions, supervision.
ASK ✕ 🖉 🕮 📺 🏊

▼▼▼ **La Quinta Inn Dallas (East)** SH
(214) 324-3731. **$72-$86.** 8303 E R L Thornton Frwy. I-30, exit 52A
(Jim Miller Rd). Ext corridors. **Pets:** Accepted.
ASK ✕ 🐾M 🖉 🕮 📺 🏊

▼▼▼ **La Quinta Inn Dallas (Love Field Airport)** SH 🐾
(214) 630-5701. **$66-$76.** 1625 Regal Row. I-35E, exit 434B (Regal
Row). Ext corridors. **Pets:** Other species. Service with restrictions.
ASK ✕ 🖉 🕮 📺 🏊

Ⓐ▼▼▼ **La Quinta Inn Dallas (Richardson)** SH
(972) 234-1016. **$62-$72.** 13685 N Central Expwy. US 75 N, exit 22
(Midpark Rd). Ext/int corridors. **Pets:** Accepted.
SAVE ✕ 🖉 🕮 📺 🏊

▼▼▼ **Magnolia Hotel Dallas** LH
(214) 915-6500. **$199-$220.** 1401 Commerce St. Corner of Commerce
and Akard sts. Int corridors. **Pets:** Accepted.
ASK 🐾 ✕ 🖉 🕮 🕮 📺 🏊

Ⓐ▼▼▼▼ **The Mansion On Turtle Creek** LH
(214) 559-2100. **$400-$2400.** 2821 Turtle Creek Blvd. 2 mi nw,
entrance on Gillespie St, just e of jct Gillespie and Lawn sts. Int
corridors. **Pets:** Accepted.
SAVE ✕ 🖉 🕮 📺 🍴 🏊

Ⓐ▼▼▼ **The Melrose Hotel** SH 🐾
(214) 521-5151. **$249-$279.** 3015 Oak Lawn Ave. I-35E, exit 430, 0.8
mi n, entrance off Cedar Springs, just n. Int corridors. **Pets:** Other
species. $50 deposit/room. Service with restrictions.
SAVE 🐾 ✕ 🕮 📺 🍴

▼▼ **Motel 6 #1479** M
(214) 388-8741. **$47-$57.** 8108 E R L Thornton Frwy. I-30, exit 52A
(Jim Miller Rd). Ext corridors. **Pets:** Other species. Service with restrictions, supervision.
🐾 ✕ 🖉

▼▼ **Motel 6 #1493** SH
(972) 506-8100. **$37-$47.** 10335 Gardner Rd. I-35E, exit 436, just sw of
jct Northwest Hwy (Loop 12) and Spur 348; 0.8 mi w of I-35E and US
77. Ext corridors. **Pets:** Large, other species. Service with restrictions,
supervision.
🐾 ✕ 🖉

▼▼ **Motel 6–560** SH
(972) 620-2828. **$37-$51.** 2753 Forest Ln. I-635, exit 26 (Josey Ln)
eastbound; exit 25 (Josey Ln) westbound, just s to Forest Ln, then just
w. Ext corridors. **Pets:** Accepted.
🐾 ✕ 🖉 🏊

▼▼ **Motel 6 Forest Lane-South #1119** M
(972) 484-9111. **$37-$47.** 2660 Forest Ln. I-635, exit 26 (Josey Ln)
eastbound, 0.5 mi s to Forest Ln, then just w; exit 25 (Josey Ln)
westbound, just s to Forest Ln, then just w. Ext corridors.
Pets: Accepted.
🐾 ✕ 🖉 🏊

Ⓐ ▼▼▼ **Quality Inn Dallas Market Center** SH 🐾
(214) 747-9551. **$79-$119.** 1955 Market Center Blvd. I-35E, exit 430B
(Market Center Blvd), 0.3 mi w. Ext corridors. **Pets:** Small, other species. $10 one-time fee/pet. Designated rooms, service with restrictions,
crate.
SAVE 🐾 ✕ 🖉 🕮 📺 🏊

Ⓐ ▼▼▼ **Radisson Hotel Central/Dallas** LH
(214) 750-6060. **$110-$115.** 6060 N Central Expwy. US 75, exit 3
(Mockingbird Ln). Int corridors. **Pets:** Small. $50 deposit/room. Service
with restrictions, supervision.
SAVE 🐾 ✕ 🖉 🕮 🕮 📺 🍴 🏊 🚫

▼▼ **Red Roof Inn-Market Center** M
(214) 638-5151. **$47-$56.** 1550 Empire Central Dr. I-35E, exit 434A
(Empire Central Dr), 0.3 mi e. Ext corridors. **Pets:** Accepted.
✕ 🖉

Ⓐ ▼▼▼ **Renaissance Dallas Hotel** LH
(214) 631-2222. **$79-$199.** 2222 Stemmons Frwy. I-35E, exit 430B
(Market Center Blvd), 0.3 mi nw on access road. Int corridors.
Pets: Accepted.
SAVE 🐾 ✕ 🖉 🕮 📺 🍴 🏊 🚫

▼▼▼ **Residence Inn by Marriott at Dallas Central** SH
(214) 750-8220. **$116.** 10333 N Central Expwy. US 75, exit 6 (Walnut
Hill Ln/Meadow Rd) northbound, 0.5 mi n to Meadow Rd, U-turn under
highway; exit 7 (Royal/Meadow Rd) southbound, 1 mi s on access
road. Ext corridors. **Pets:** Accepted.
ASK ✕ 🖉 🕮 📺 🏊 🚫

▼▼▼ **Residence Inn by Marriott-Dallas Market
Center** SH
(214) 631-2472. **$129-$159.** 6950 N Stemmons Frwy. I-35E, exit 432B
(Commonwealth), 0.6 mi n on northbound frontage road. Ext/int corri-
dors. **Pets:** Accepted.
ASK ✕ 🖉 🕮 📺 🏊 🚫

▼▼▼ **Residence Inn by Marriott-Dallas Park Central** SH
(972) 503-1333. **$119-$159, 30 day notice.** 7642 LBJ Frwy. I-635, exit
20 (Hillcrest), just e, on eastbound access road. Int corridors.
Pets: Accepted.
ASK 🐾 ✕ 🐾M 🖉 🕮 📺 🏊 🚫

▼▼ **Rodeway Inn** SH
(972) 572-1030. **Call for rates.** 8541 S Hampton Rd. I-20, exit 465, 0.3
mi e to S Hampton Rd, then just s. Ext corridors. **Pets:** Accepted.
✕ 🕮 📺 🏊

Ⓐ ▼▼▼ **Sheraton Dallas Brookhollow Hotel** LH
(214) 630-7000. **$79-$99.** 1241 W Mockingbird Ln. I-35E, exit 433B,
just nw of jct I-35E and W Mockingbird Ln. Int corridors.
Pets: Accepted.
SAVE ✕ 🖉 🕮 📺 🍴 🏊

▼▼▼ **Sheraton Suites Market Center-Dallas** LH
(214) 747-3000. **$125, 3 day notice.** 2101 Stemmons Frwy. Nw off
I-35E and US 77, exit 430B (Market Center Blvd). Int corridors.
Pets: Medium. Service with restrictions, crate.
✕ 🖉 🕮 📺 🍴 🏊

▼▼▼ **Staybridge Suites Dallas Park Central** SH
(972) 391-0000. **$129-$169.** 7880 Alpha Rd. I-635, exit 19B (Coit Rd),
0.3 mi n, then just w. Int corridors. **Pets:** Other species. $75 one-time
fee/pet. Supervision.
ASK 🐾 ✕ 🖉 🕮 📺 🏊

AAA ▼▼▼ **Sterling Hotel Dallas** 🆂🅷
(214) 634-8550. **$69-$129.** 1055 Regal Row. Southeast corner of jct SR 183 and Regal Row. Int corridors. **Pets:** Accepted.
[SAVE] [S🄳] [✕] [🕭] [🕭] [🛏] [💻] [🍽] [🏊] [✕]

AAA ▼▼▼ **Wellesley Inn & Suites (Dallas/Park Central)** 🆂🅷
(972) 671-7722. **$70.** 9019 Vantage Point Rd. I-635, exit 18A (Greenville Ave), just sw. Ext corridors. **Pets:** Accepted.
[SAVE] [✕] [🅼] [🕭] [🛏] [💻]

▼▼▼▼ **The Westin City Center, Dallas** 🅻🅷
(214) 979-9000. **$119-$169.** 650 N Pearl St. Between San Jacinto and Bryan St, 0.3 mi w of US 75 Central Expwy. Int corridors. **Pets:** Accepted.
[ASK] [✕] [🕭] [🕭] [🛏] [💻] [🍽] [✕]

▼▼▼▼ **The Westin Galleria, Dallas** 🅻🅷 🐾
(972) 934-9494. **$310, 3 day notice.** 13340 Dallas Pkwy. Just n of jct I-635 and N Dallas Pkwy. Int corridors. **Pets:** Small. Service with restrictions.
[ASK] [S🄳] [✕] [🅼] [🕭] [🕭] [💻] [🍽] [🏊]

DENTON

AAA ▼▼▼ **Exel Inn of Denton** 🆂🅷
(940) 383-1471. **$42-$62.** 4211 I-35E N. Jct US 380 and I-35, exit 469, just n. Int corridors. **Pets:** Small, other species. Designated rooms, service with restrictions, supervision.
[SAVE] [S🄳] [✕] [🕭] [🛏] [💻] [🏊]

▼▼▼▼ **La Quinta Inn Denton** 🆂🅷
(940) 387-5840. **$79-$92.** 700 Fort Worth Dr. I-35E, exit 465B (Fort Worth Dr), just n. Ext corridors. **Pets:** Accepted.
[ASK] [✕] [🅼] [🕭] [🕭] [🛏] [💻] [🏊]

▼ **Motel 6 Denton #97** 🅼
(940) 566-4798. **$41-$51.** 4125 I-35 N. I-35, exit 469. Ext corridors. **Pets:** Other species. Service with restrictions, supervision.
[S🄳] [✕] [🕭] [🏊]

▼▼▼▼ **Radisson Hotel Denton** 🆂🅷
(940) 565-8499. **$79-$99.** 2211 I-35E N. Off I-35E and US 77, exit 466B (N Texas Blvd), 2.5 mi sw. Int corridors. **Pets:** Medium. $100 deposit/room. Service with restrictions, crate.
[ASK] [S🄳] [✕] [🛏] [💻] [🍽] [🏊]

DESOTO

▼▼▼ **Red Roof Inn Dallas/DeSoto** 🆂🅷
(972) 224-7100. **$45-$54.** 1401 N Beckley Ave. I-35, exit 416, just s. Ext/int corridors. **Pets:** Medium, other species. Service with restrictions, supervision.
[✕] [🕭] [🕭] [🛏]

DUNCANVILLE

▼▼▼ **Motel 6-#1130** 🆂🅷
(972) 296-0345. **$42-$54.** 202 Jellison Blvd. I-20, exit 462A (Duncanville Rd) eastbound; exit 462B (Main St) westbound, just s to Camp Wisdom, just w to Duncanville Rd, just n to Jellison Blvd, then just w. Ext/int corridors. **Pets:** Other species. Service with restrictions, supervision.
[S🄳] [✕] [🕭] [🛏] [🏊]

▼▼▼ **Ramada Inn-Dallas Southwest** 🆂🅷
(972) 298-8911. **$59-$65, 7 day notice.** 711 E Camp Wisdom Rd. I-20, exit 463, 0.3 mi w of jct I-20 and Cockrell Hill Rd; 2 mi w of US 67. Ext/int corridors. **Pets:** Accepted.
[ASK] [S🄳] [✕] [🕭] [🛏] [💻] [🍽] [🏊]

FARMERS BRANCH

▼▼▼ **Comfort Inn of North Dallas** 🆂🅷
(972) 406-3030. **$51-$60.** 14040 Stemmons Frwy. I-35 E, exit 442 (Valwood Pkwy). Int corridors. **Pets:** Small. $10 daily fee/pet, $10 one-time fee/pet. Service with restrictions, supervision.
[ASK] [S🄳] [✕] [🕭] [🛏] [💻] [🏊]

AAA ▼▼▼ **Days Inn-North Dallas** 🆂🅷
(972) 488-0800. **$39-$55.** 13313 Stemmons Frwy. I-35E, exit 441 (Valley View Ln), on west side of frontage road. Int corridors. **Pets:** Accepted.
[SAVE] [S🄳] [✕] [🕭] [🛏] [💻] [🏊]

AAA ▼▼▼▼ **La Quinta Inn Dallas (NW-Farmers Branch)** 🆂🅷 🐾
(972) 620-7333. **$66-$76.** 13235 Stemmons Frwy N. I-35E, exit 441 (Valley View Ln), on southbound frontage road. Ext corridors. **Pets:** Other species. Service with restrictions.
[SAVE] [✕] [🕭] [🕭] [🛏] [🏊]

AAA ▼▼▼▼ **Omni Dallas Hotel Park West** 🅻🅷
(972) 869-4300. **$99-$209.** 1590 LBJ Frwy. Nw off I-635, 1.5 mi w of jct I-35E, exit 29 (Luna Rd). Int corridors. **Pets:** Accepted.
[SAVE] [S🄳] [✕] [🕭] [🕭] [🛏] [💻] [🍽] [🏊] [✕]

FRISCO

AAA ▼▼▼▼ **The Westin Stonebriar Resort, North Dallas** 🅻🅷
(972) 668-8000. **$119-$329.** 1549 Legacy Dr. 0.3 mi n of jct SR 121. Int corridors. **Pets:** Accepted.
[SAVE] [S🄳] [✕] [🅼] [🕭] [🛏] [💻] [🍽] [🏊] [✕]

GARLAND

AAA ▼▼▼▼ **Best Western Lakeview Inn** 🆂🅷
(972) 303-1601. **$59-$69.** 1635 E I-30 at Chaha Rd. I-30, exit 62 (Chaha Rd). Ext corridors. **Pets:** Medium, other species. $5 daily fee/pet. Service with restrictions, supervision.
[SAVE] [S🄳] [✕] [🕭] [🛏] [💻] [🏊]

▼▼▼▼ **Holiday Inn Select LBJ NE (Garland)** 🆂🅷
(214) 341-5400. **$89-$109.** 11350 LBJ Frwy. I-635, exit 13 (Jupiter/Kingsley rds), just sw. Int corridors. **Pets:** Accepted.
[ASK] [S🄳] [✕] [🛏] [💻] [🍽] [🏊]

AAA ▼▼▼▼ **La Quinta Inn Dallas (Garland)** 🆂🅷
(972) 271-7581. **$69-$76.** 12721 I-635. I-635, exit 11B, just nw. Ext/int corridors. **Pets:** Accepted.
[SAVE] [✕] [🕭] [🛏] [💻] [🏊]

AAA ▼▼▼ **Microtel Inn & Suites** 🆂🅷
(972) 270-7200. **$59-$75.** 1901 Pendleton Dr. I-635, exit 11B, just n to Pendleton Dr, then just e. Int corridors. **Pets:** Accepted.
[SAVE] [S🄳] [✕] [🅼] [🕭] [🛏] [💻]

▼ **Motel 6-0620** 🆂🅷
(972) 226-7140. **$39-$49.** 436 W I-30. I-30, exit 58 (Belt Line Rd). Ext corridors. **Pets:** Accepted.
[S🄳] [✕] [🕭] [🏊]

GRAND PRAIRIE

AAA ▼▼▼▼ **AmeriSuites (Dallas/Grand Prairie)** 🆂🅷
(972) 988-6800. **$69-$85.** 1542 N Hwy 360. SR 360, exit J/K aves. Int corridors. **Pets:** $25 one-time fee/pet. Service with restrictions, crate.
[SAVE] [S🄳] [✕] [🅼] [🕭] [🛏] [💻] [🏊]

AAA ▼▼▼▼ **La Quinta Inn Dallas (Grand Prairie)** 🆂🅷
(972) 641-3021. **$66-$76.** 1410 NW 19th St. I-30, exit 32, just e. Ext corridors. **Pets:** Accepted.
[SAVE] [✕] [🅼] [🕭] [🛏] [💻] [🏊]

▼▼ **Motel 6–446** 🆂🅷 🐾
(972) 642-9424. **$35-$45.** 406 E Palace Pkwy. I-30, exit 34 (Belt Line Rd), just n to Safari Pkwy, 0.6 mi w. Ext corridors. **Pets:** Very small. $25 one-time fee/room. Designated rooms, service with restrictions, supervision.
🆂📶 ✕ 🅒 🔌 🖥 ➤

GREENVILLE

▼▼ **Best Western Inn & Suites** 🆂🅷
(903) 454-1792. **$79.** 1216 I-30 W. I-30, exit 94B. Ext/int corridors. **Pets:** Accepted.
A$K 🆂📶 ✕ 🔌 🖥 ➤

▼▼▼ **Holiday Inn Express Hotel & Suites** 🆂🅷
(903) 454-8680. **$99-$150, 3 day notice.** 2901 Mustang Crossing. I-30, exit 93A. Int corridors. **Pets:** Small, other species. $100 deposit/room. Service with restrictions.
A$K 🆂📶 ✕ 🅜 🅒 🔌 🖥 ➤

IRVING

🅐🅐🅐 ▼▼▼ **AmeriSuites (Dallas Las Colinas/Hidden Ridge)** 🆂🅷
(972) 910-0302. **$65-$100.** 333 W John Carpenter Frwy. SR 114, exit Hidden Ridge. Int corridors. **Pets:** Small, other species. $10 daily fee/room. Designated rooms, service with restrictions, supervision.
SAVE 🆂📶 ✕ 🅜 🅒 🔌 🖥 ➤

🅐🅐🅐 ▼▼▼ **AmeriSuites (Dallas Las Colinas/Walnut Hill)** 🆂🅷
(972) 550-7400. **$90-$100.** 5455 Green Park Dr. SR 114, exit Walnut Hill Ln. Int corridors. **Pets:** Very small. Service with restrictions, supervision.
SAVE 🆂📶 ✕ 🅜 🅒 🔌 🖥 ➤

▼▼▼ **Candlewood Dallas/Las Colinas** 🆂🅷
(972) 714-9990. **$89.** 5300 Greenpark Dr. SR 114, exit Walnut Hill Ln, just s. Int corridors. **Pets:** Medium, other species. $25 one-time fee/pet. Service with restrictions, crate.
A$K 🆂📶 ✕ 🅜 🅒 🔌 🖥

▼▼▼ **Dallas Las Colinas TownePlace Suites** 🆂🅷
(972) 550-7796. **Call for rates.** 900 W Walnut Hill Ln. SR 114, exit Walnut Hill Ln, then w. Int corridors. **Pets:** Other species. $75 one-time fee/room. Service with restrictions, supervision.
✕ 🅜 🅒 🔌 🖥 ➤

▼▼▼ **Drury Inn & Suites-DFW Airport** 🆂🅷
(972) 986-1200. **$55-$90.** 4210 W Airport Frwy. SR 183, exit Esters Rd, on southbound access road. Int corridors. **Pets:** Large, other species. Service with restrictions, supervision.
A$K ✕ 🅒 🔌 🖥 ➤

🅐🅐🅐 ▼▼▼▼ **Four Seasons Resort and Club** 🅻🅷
(972) 717-0700. **$330-$500.** 4150 N MacArthur Blvd. Se off SR 114, 1.5 mi s of exit MacArthur Blvd. Int corridors. **Pets:** Accepted.
SAVE ✕ 🅜 🅒 🔌 🖥 🍴 ➤

▼▼▼ **Hampton Inn-DFW Airport South** 🆂🅷
(972) 986-3606. **$69-$119.** 4340 W Airport Frwy. SR 183, exit Valley View Ln, on southbound access road. Int corridors. **Pets:** Accepted.
A$K ✕ 🅒 🔌 🖥 ➤

▼▼▼ **Harvey Hotel-DFW Airport** 🅻🅷
(972) 929-4500. **$129-$189.** 4545 W John Carpenter Frwy. Nw off SR 114, exit Esters Blvd. Int corridors. **Pets:** Accepted.
A$K 🆂📶 ✕ 🅒 🔌 🖥 🍴 ➤

▼▼▼ **Harvey Suites-DFW Airport** 🆂🅷 🐾
(972) 929-4499. **$109-$149.** 4550 W John Carpenter Frwy. SR 114, exit Freeport Pkwy, on southbound service road. Int corridors. **Pets:** Medium, other species. $100 deposit/room, $25 one-time fee/room. Designated rooms, service with restrictions, supervision.
A$K 🆂📶 ✕ 🅜 🅒 🔌 🖥 ➤

▼▼▼ **Holiday Inn Select DFW Airport South** 🅻🅷
(972) 399-1010. **$129-$149.** 4440 W Airport Frwy. SR 183, exit Valley View Ln, on eastbound access road. Int corridors. **Pets:** Accepted.
A$K 🆂📶 ✕ 🅜 🅒 🔌 🖥 🍴 ➤

▼▼ **Homestead Studio Suites Hotel-Dallas/Las Colinas** 🆂🅷
(972) 756-0458. **$50-$65.** 5315 Carnaby St. SR 114, exit MacArthur Blvd, 0.5 mi s, then just e on Meadow Creek. Ext corridors. **Pets:** Medium, other species. $75 one-time fee/room. Service with restrictions.
A$K 🆂📶 ✕ 🅒 🖥

▼▼▼ **Homewood Suites by Hilton Las Colinas** 🆂🅷
(972) 556-0665. **$139-$199.** 4300 Wingren Dr. Ne off SR 114, exit O'Connor Rd/Wingren Dr eastbound, just n to Las Colinas Blvd, 0.4 mi e to Rochelle Rd, then just s; exit Rochelle Rd westbound. Ext/int corridors. **Pets:** Small. $50 one-time fee/room. Service with restrictions, crate.
A$K 🆂📶 ✕ 🅜 🅒 🖥 ➤

▼▼▼ **La Quinta Inn & Suites Dallas (DFW-Airport North)** 🆂🅷
(972) 915-4022. **$84-$115.** 4850 W John Carpenter Frwy. SR 114, exit Freeport Pkwy, on eastbound service road. Int corridors. **Pets:** Accepted.
A$K ✕ 🅜 🅒 🅒 🔌 🖥 ➤

▼▼▼ **La Quinta Inn & Suites Dallas DFW Airport South (Irving)** 🆂🅷
(972) 252-6546. **$109-$119.** 4105 W Airport Frwy. 3 mi nw off SR 183, exit Esters Rd; on northbound access road. Int corridors. **Pets:** Accepted.
A$K ✕ 🅒 🔌 🖥 ➤

▼▼ **MainStay Suites Hotel DFW Airport South** 🆂🅷
(972) 257-5400. **$59-$69.** 2323 Imperial Dr. SR 183, exit Story Rd, 0.6 mi w on westbound access road. Int corridors. **Pets:** Very small. $50 one-time fee/room. Service with restrictions, supervision.
✕ 🅜 🅒 🔌 🖥

▼ **Motel 6 #1274 DFW North** Ⓜ
(972) 915-3993. **$41-$51.** 7800 Heathrow Dr. SR 114, exit Freeport Pkwy, just se. Int corridors. **Pets:** Accepted.
🆂📶 ✕ 🅒 🔌 🖥 ➤

▼ **Motel 6–1335** 🆂🅷
(972) 438-4227. **$37-$50.** 510 S Loop 12. S Loop 12, exit SR 356 (Irving Blvd). Ext corridors. **Pets:** Accepted.
🆂📶 ✕ 🅒

▼ **Motel 6/DFW Airport South #1476** 🆂🅷
(972) 570-7500. **$35-$45.** 2611 W Airport Frwy. SR 183, exit Story Rd. Int corridors. **Pets:** Accepted.
🆂📶 ✕ 🅒 🔌 ➤

🅐🅐🅐 ▼▼▼ ▼▼▼ **Omni Mandalay Hotel at Las Colinas** 🅻🅷 🐾
(972) 556-0800. **$109-$249.** 221 E Las Colinas Blvd. Nw off SR 114, exit O'Connor Rd. Int corridors. **Pets:** Medium. $50 one-time fee/room. Designated rooms, service with restrictions, crate.
SAVE 🆂📶 ✕ 🅒 🅒 🔌 🖥 🍴 ➤

▼▼ **Quality Inn & Suites DFW Airport North** 🆂🅷
(972) 929-4008. **$59-$139.** 4100 W John Carpenter Frwy. Nw off SR 114, exit Esters Blvd, just s to Reese St, then just e. Ext corridors. **Pets:** Accepted.
A$K 🆂📶 ✕ 🅒 🅒 🔌 🖥 ➤

▼ **Red Roof Inn/DFW Airport North** Ⓜ
(972) 929-0020. **$50-$64.** 8150 Esters Blvd. SR 114, exit Esters Blvd, just n. Ext corridors. **Pets:** Medium. Service with restrictions, supervision.
✕ 🅒 🅒 🖥

▼▼▼ **Residence Inn by Marriott at Las Colinas** 🆂🅷
(972) 580-7773. **$79-$119.** 950 W Walnut Hill Ln. SR 114, exit Mac-Arthur Blvd, 0.5 mi s, then just e. Ext corridors. **Pets:** Accepted.
🅰🆂🅺 🆂🅳 ✖ � 🏊 ⊠

▼▼▼ **Residence Inn by Marriott-DFW/Irving** 🆂🅷
(972) 871-1331. **$159-$189.** 8600 Esters Blvd. SR 114, exit Esters Blvd, 0.9 mi n. Int corridors. **Pets:** Accepted.
🅰🆂🅺 ✖ ⊠

▼▼▼ **Sheraton Grand Hotel** 🅻🅷 ❀
(972) 929-8400. **$112.** 4440 W John Carpenter Frwy. SR 114, exit Esters Blvd, just s. Int corridors. **Pets:** Small. $200 deposit/pet. Service with restrictions.

▼▼▼ **Staybridge Suites Dallas-Las Colinas** 🆂🅷
(972) 465-9400. **Call for rates.** 1201 Executive Cir. SR 114, exit Mac-Arthur Blvd, just s to W Walnut Hill Ln, then just w. Int corridors. **Pets:** Accepted.

▼▼▼ **Summerfield Suites by Wyndham-Las Colinas** 🆂🅷
(972) 831-0909. **$69-$128.** 5901 N MacArthur Blvd. SR 114, exit Mac-Arthur Blvd, jct MacArthur Blvd and SR 114, northwest corner. Ext/int corridors. **Pets:** Accepted.

▼▼ **Super 8 Motel DFW Airport North/Irving** 🆂🅷
(214) 441-9000. **$49-$59.** 4770 W John Carpenter Frwy (SR 114). SR 114, exit Freeport Pkwy. Int corridors. **Pets:** Dogs only. $10 daily fee/pet. Service with restrictions, supervision.

▲▲▲ ▼▼▼ **Wellesley Inn & Suites (Dallas/Las Colinas)** 🆂🅷
(972) 751-0808. **$79-$129.** 5401 Green Park Dr. SR 114, exit Walnut Hill Ln, just s. Int corridors. **Pets:** Small, other species. Service with restrictions.

LEWISVILLE

▼▼▼ **Comfort Suites by Choice Hotels** 🆂🅷
(972) 315-6464. **$60-$80.** 755A Vista Ridge Mall Dr. I-35E, exit 448A, 0.5 mi s of jct I-35 and Round Grove Rd on southbound service road to Vista Ridge Mall Dr, then just w. Int corridors. **Pets:** Other species. $50 one-time fee/room. Service with restrictions, crate.

▼▼▼ **Country Inn & Suites by Carlson** 🆂🅷
(972) 315-6565. **$58-$78.** 755B Vista Ridge Mall Dr. I-35E, exit 448A, 0.5 mi s on service road to Vista Ridge Rd, then just w. Int corridors. **Pets:** Accepted.

▼▼▼ **La Quinta Inn Dallas (Lewisville)** 🆂🅷
(972) 221-7525. **$66-$76.** 1657 S Stemmons Frwy. I-35E, exit 449, just w. Ext corridors. **Pets:** Accepted.

▼ **Motel 6–1288** 🆂🅷
(972) 436-5008. **$40-$52.** 1705 Lakepointe Dr. I-35E, exit 449, just n on access road. Int corridors. **Pets:** Medium, other species. Service with restrictions, supervision.

▼▼▼ **Residence Inn by Marriott Dallas** 🆂🅷
(972) 315-3777. **$109-$149.** 755C Vista Ridge Mall Dr. I-35E, exit 448A, 0.5 mi s on service road; jct I-35 and Round Grove Rd to Vista Ridge Rd, just w. Int corridors. **Pets:** Accepted.

▼▼ **Super 8-Lewisville/Dallas North/Airport** 🅼
(972) 221-7511. **$40-$50.** 1305 S Stemmons Frwy. I-35E, exit 450, just sw. Ext corridors. **Pets:** Accepted.

MCKINNEY

▼▼ **Days Inn McKinney** 🆂🅷
(972) 548-8888. **Call for rates.** 2104 N Central Expwy. US 75, 0.5 mi n of jct US 380, exit 41. Ext corridors. **Pets:** Accepted.

▼▼ **Super 8 Motel-McKinney** 🆂🅷 ❀
(972) 548-8880. **$51-$100.** 910 N Central Expwy. US 75, exit 40A (Virginia/Louisiana sts), 0.5 mi n on northbound service road. Int corridors. **Pets:** $10 daily fee/pet. Service with restrictions, supervision.

MESQUITE

▼▼▼ **Country Inn & Suites By Carlson** 🆂🅷
(972) 216-7460. **$55-$125.** 118 Hwy 80 E. US 80 E, exit Belt Line Rd. Int corridors. **Pets:** Accepted.

▲▲▲ ▼▼▼ **Hampton Inn and Suites at Rodeo Center** 🆂🅷
(972) 329-3100. **$69-$149, 3 day notice.** 1700 Rodeo Dr. I-635, exit 4 (Military Pkwy), 0.5 mi s on Hickory Tree Rd. Int corridors. **Pets:** Accepted.

▲▲▲ ▼▼▼ **Super 8 Motel** 🆂🅷 ❀
(972) 289-5481. **$40-$55.** 121 Grand Junction. I-635, exit 4 (Military Pkwy). Ext corridors. **Pets:** Medium, other species. Service with restrictions, supervision.

MIDLOTHIAN

▲▲▲ ▼▼▼ **Best Western Midlothian Inn** 🆂🅷
(972) 775-1891. **$64-$69.** 220 N Hwy 67. On US 67, just n of jct US 287. Ext corridors. **Pets:** Medium, other species. $25 deposit/room. Service with restrictions, crate.

PLANO

▲▲▲ ▼▼▼ **AmeriSuites (Dallas/Plano)** 🆂🅷 ❀
(972) 378-3997. **$99-$129.** 3100 Dallas Pkwy. Dallas Pkwy, exit Park Blvd northbound; exit Parker Blvd southbound, on northbound service road. Int corridors. **Pets:** Medium, other species. $10 daily fee/room.

▼▼▼ **Best Western Park Suites Hotel** 🆂🅷
(972) 578-2243. **$59-$89.** 640 Park Blvd E. US 75, exit 29A northbound, just e; exit 29 southbound, 0.5 mi s on access road, just e on 15th St, then 0.5 mi n on access road. Int corridors. **Pets:** Other species. $25 one-time fee/pet. Service with restrictions, supervision.

▲▲▲ ▼▼▼ **Candlewood Suites-Plano** 🆂🅷
(972) 618-5446. **$73.** 4701 Legacy Dr. Jct SR 289 (Preston Rd) and Legacy Dr, just e. Int corridors. **Pets:** Accepted.

▼▼▼ **Hampton Inn Plano** 🆂🅷
(972) 519-1000. **Call for rates.** 4901 Old Shepherd Pl. 0.4 mi n of jct SR 289 (Preston Rd) and W Plano Pkwy, just e. Int corridors. **Pets:** Medium. $50 one-time fee/room. Service with restrictions, supervision.

[AAA] ◆◆◆ **Holiday Inn Express Hotel & Suites Plano Central** [SH]
(972) 881-1881. **$105-$205.** 700 Central Pkwy E. Just e of US 75; 0.3 mi ne of jct FM 544, exit 29A northbound; exit 29 southbound, 0.5 mi s on access road, just e on 15th St, then 0.5 mi n on access road. Int corridors. **Pets:** Accepted.
[SAVE] [SD] ⊠ 👂 ▣ 📺 🍴 🏊 🏋

◆◆◆ **Homestead Studio Suites Hotel-Dallas/Plano Parkway** [SH]
(972) 596-9966. **$69-$84.** 4709 W Plano Pkwy. Just n of jct Plano Pkwy and SR 289 (Preston Rd), then just e. Int corridors. **Pets:** Accepted.
[A$K] [SD] ⊠ 👂 ♿ ▣ 📺 🏊

◆◆◆ **Homewood Suites by Hilton** [SH]
(972) 758-8800. **$79-$129.** 4705 Old Shepherd Pl. Jct Plano Pkwy and SR 289 (Preston Rd), 0.4 mi n, then just e. Int corridors. **Pets:** Small. $75 one-time fee/pet. Service with restrictions, supervision.
[A$K] [SD] ⊠ [&M] 👂 ♿ ▣ 📺 🏊 🏋

◆◆◆ **La Quinta Inn & Suites Dallas (West Plano)** [SH]
(972) 599-0700. **$79-$99.** 4800 W Plano Pkwy. Just n of jct SR 289 (Preston Rd), then just e. Int corridors. **Pets:** Small, other species. Service with restrictions, crate.
[A$K] ⊠ [&M] 👂 ♿ ▣ 📺 🏊

[AAA] ◆◆◆ **La Quinta Inn Dallas (Plano)** [SH]
(972) 423-1300. **$66-$76.** 1820 N Central Expwy. US 75, exit 29A (Park Blvd), northbound, just ne; exit 29 southbound, 0.5 mi s on access road, just e on 15th St, then just n on northbound access road. Ext corridors. **Pets:** Accepted.
[SAVE] ⊠ [&M] 👂 ♿ ▣ 📺 🏊

◆ **Motel 6–1121** [SH]
(972) 578-1626. **$40-$52.** 2550 N Central Expwy. US 75, exit 29A (Park Blvd) northbound; exit 29 southbound, 1 mi n of jct Park Rd (SR 544), on east side of US 75. Ext/int corridors. **Pets:** Accepted.
[SD] ⊠ 👂 ♿ 🏊

◆◆ **Red Roof Inn Dallas-Plano** [SH]
(972) 881-8191. **$41-$58.** 301 Ruisseau Dr. SR 75, exit 30 (Parker Rd), 0.5 mi w to Premier, then just n. Ext/int corridors. **Pets:** Accepted.
⊠ [&M] 👂 ♿ ▣

◆◆◆ **Residence Inn by Marriott Dallas/Plano** [SH]
(972) 473-6761. **Call for rates.** 5001 White Stone Ln. North Dallas Tollway, exit Spring Creek Pkwy, 1.9 mi e, then n on Preston Rd; between Spring Creek Pkwy and Tennyson. Int corridors. **Pets:** Accepted.
⊠ ▣ 📺 🏊 🏋

◆◆ **Sleep Inn Plano** [SH]
(972) 867-1111. **$60-$72.** 4801 W Plano Pkwy. Just n of jct SR 289 (Preston Rd) and N Plano Pkwy, just e. Int corridors. **Pets:** Accepted.
[SD] ⊠ [&M] 👂 ♿ ▣ 📺 🏊

◆◆ **Super 8 Motel-Plano** [SH]
(972) 423-8300. **$49-$69.** 1704 N Central Expwy. US 75, exit 29A northbound, just e; exit 29 southbound, 0.5 mi s on access road, just e on 15th St, then just n on access road. Int corridors. **Pets:** Accepted.
[A$K] [SD] ⊠ [&M] 👂 📺

◆◆ **TownePlace Suites by Marriott** [SH]
(972) 943-8200. **$57-$107.** 5005 Whitestone Ln. North Dallas Tollway, exit Spring Creek Pkwy, 1.9 mi e, just n on SR 289 (Preston Rd), to Whitestone Ln, then just w. Int corridors. **Pets:** Accepted.
[A$K] [SD] ⊠ [&M] ♿ ▣ 📺 🏊

[AAA] ◆◆◆ **Wellesley Inn & Suites (Dallas/Plano)** [SH]
(972) 378-9978. **$89-$99.** 2900 Dallas Pkwy. Dallas Pkwy, exit Park Blvd northbound; exit Parker Blvd southbound, on northbound service road. Int corridors. **Pets:** Accepted.
[SAVE] [SD] ⊠ [&M] 👂 ♿ ▣ 📺 🏊

RICHARDSON

◆◆◆ **Homestead Studio Suites Hotel-Dallas/Richardson** [SH]
(972) 479-0500. **$74-$89.** 901 E Campbell Rd. US 75, exit 26 (Campbell Rd), just e. Int corridors. **Pets:** $75 one-time fee/pet. Service with restrictions.
[A$K] [SD] ⊠ [&M] 👂 ♿ ▣ 📺 🏊

[AAA] ◆◆◆◆ **Renaissance Dallas-Richardson Hotel** [LH]
(972) 367-2000. **$169-$299.** 900 E Lookout Dr. US 75, exit 27A (Gallatin Pkwy/Renner Rd) northbound; exit 26 (Gallatin Pkwy/Campbell Rd) southbound, just e. Int corridors. **Pets:** Accepted.
[SAVE] [SD] ⊠ 👂 ♿ ▣ 📺 🍴 🏊 🏋

◆◆◆ **Residence Inn by Marriott Richardson** [SH] 🐾
(972) 669-5888. **$69-$130.** 1040 Waterwood Dr. US 75, exit 26 (Campbell Rd), just e to Greenville Ave, 0.4 mi n to Glenville Rd, then just w. Int corridors. **Pets:** Medium, other species. $75 one-time fee/room. Service with restrictions.
⊠ 👂 ♿ ▣ 📺 🏊 🏋

◆◆ **Sleep Inn** [SH]
(972) 470-9440. **$44-$65.** 2458 N Central Expwy. US 75, exit 27 northbound; exit 26 southbound, 0.8 mi n on access road. Int corridors. **Pets:** Accepted.
[A$K] [SD] ⊠ ▣ 📺

ROANOKE

◆◆◆ **Comfort Suites Roanoke** [SH]
(817) 490-1455. **$60-$120.** 801 Byron Nelson Blvd/W Hwy 114 Bus. I-35, exit 70 (SR 114), 3.4 mi e, exit Rufe/Snow, then just se. Int corridors. **Pets:** Small. $20 one-time fee/room. Service with restrictions, crate.
[A$K] [SD] ⊠ [&M] ▣ 📺 🏊

[AAA] ◆◆◆ **Speedway Sleep Inn & Suites** [SH] 🐾
(817) 491-3120. **$70-$90.** 13471 Raceway Dr. I-35, exit 70 (SR 114), just e, then just s. Int corridors. **Pets:** Other species. $30 deposit/pet. Service with restrictions, supervision.
[SAVE] [SD] ⊠ [&M] ♿ ▣ 📺 🏊

TERRELL

[AAA] ◆◆ **Best Inn** [M]
(972) 563-2676. **$45-$65.** 309 I-20 E. Jct I-20 and SR 34, exit 501. Ext corridors. **Pets:** Small, other species. $5 one-time fee/pet. Service with restrictions, crate.
[SAVE] [SD] ⊠ ▣ 📺 🏊

[AAA] ◆◆ **Best Western Country Inn** [SH]
(972) 563-1521. **$50-$52.** 1604 Hwy 34 S. I-20, exit 501 (SR 34), just n. Ext corridors. **Pets:** Accepted.
[SAVE] ⊠ ▣ 📺 🏊

END METROPOLITAN AREA

DECATUR

(AAA) ▼▼▼ Best Western Decatur Inn M
(940) 627-5982. **$57-$67.** 1801 S Hwy 287. 0.6 mi s of jct Business Rt SR 380. Ext corridors. **Pets:** Small. $10 daily fee/pet. Service with restrictions, supervision.
[SAVE] [✕] [🛏] [💻] [🏊]

(AAA) ▼▼▼ Comfort Inn SH
(940) 627-6919. **$59-$120.** 1709 S US 287. 0.6 mi s of jct Business Rt SR 380. Ext corridors. **Pets:** Accepted.
[SAVE] [S🐾] [✕] [🛏] [💻] [🏊]

DEL RIO

(AAA) ▼▼▼▼ Best Western Inn of Del Rio SH
(830) 775-7511. **$69.** 810 Veterans Blvd. 0.8 mi nw on US 90, 277 and 377. Ext corridors. **Pets:** Small. $5 daily fee/pet. Service with restrictions, crate.
[SAVE] [S🐾] [✕] [🛏] [💻] [🏊]

▼▼▼ Comfort Inn & Suites SH
(830) 775-2933. **$55-$85.** 3616 Veterans Blvd. 3.2 mi nw on US 90. Ext/int corridors. **Pets:** Small. $10 one-time fee/pet. Service with restrictions, supervision.
[ASK] [S🐾] [✕] [🐾] [🛏] [💻] [🏊]

(AAA) ▼▼▼ Days Inn and Suites SH
(830) 775-0585. **$59-$79.** 3808 Veterans Blvd. 3.5 mi nw on US 90. Ext corridors. **Pets:** Medium, other species. $5 daily fee/room. Service with restrictions.
[SAVE] [S🐾] [✕] [🛏] [💻] [🏊]

▼▼▼▼ La Quinta Inns Del Rio SH
(830) 775-7591. **$70-$80.** 2005 Veterans Blvd. 1.8 mi nw on US 90, 277 and 377. Ext/int corridors. **Pets:** Medium. Designated rooms, service with restrictions, crate.
[ASK] [✕] [🐾] [🛏] [💻] [🏊]

▼ Motel 6 Del Rio #323 SH
(830) 774-2115. **$35-$45.** 2115 Veterans Blvd. Jct US 90/277 and Garner Dr. Ext corridors. **Pets:** Accepted.
[S🐾] [✕] [🏊]

(AAA) ▼▼▼▼ Ramada Inn SH 🐾
(830) 775-1511. **$89-$99.** 2101 Veterans Blvd. 1.8 mi nw on US 90, 277 and 377. Ext/int corridors. **Pets:** Small, other species. Designated rooms, service with restrictions, supervision.
[SAVE] [S🐾] [✕] [🛏] [💻] [🍴] [🏊] [✕]

DONNA

(AAA) ▼▼▼ Howard Johnson Express Inn & Suites SH
(956) 464-4656. **$64-$95.** 602 N Victoria Rd. US 83, exit Victoria Rd. Ext corridors. **Pets:** Accepted.
[SAVE] [S🐾] [✕] [🛏] [💻] [🍴] [🏊] [✕]

DUMAS

(AAA) ▼▼▼ Best Western Windsor Inn SH
(806) 935-9644. **$59-$89, 5 day notice.** 1701 S Dumas Ave. US 287, 2 mi s of US 87 and SR 152. Ext corridors. **Pets:** Small, dogs only. $10 daily fee/pet. Designated rooms, service with restrictions, supervision.
[SAVE] [S🐾] [✕] [🛏] [💻] [🏊] [✕]

▼▼ Dumas Inn Motel M
(806) 935-6441. **$55-$75, 3 day notice.** 1712 S Dumas Ave. US 287, 1.5 mi s from jct US 87 and SR 152. Ext/int corridors. **Pets:** Accepted.
[ASK] [S🐾] [✕] [🛏] [🏊]

(AAA) ▼▼▼ Econo Lodge SH
(806) 935-9098. **$45-$75.** 1719 S Dumas Ave. US 287, 2 mi s of US 87 and SR 152. Int corridors. **Pets:** Accepted.
[SAVE] [S🐾] [✕] [🛏]

▼▼▼ Holiday Inn Express SH
(806) 935-4000. **$69-$99.** 1525 S Dumas Ave. US 87, 1.1 mi s of US 87 and SR 152. Int corridors. **Pets:** Other species. $15 one-time fee/room. Service with restrictions, supervision.
[ASK] [S🐾] [✕] [🛏] [💻] [🏊]

(AAA) ▼▼▼ Super 8 Motel M 🐾
(806) 935-6222. **$79-$89.** 119 W 17th St. US 287, 2 mi s of jct US 87 and SR 152. Ext corridors. **Pets:** Very small. $10 daily fee/pet. Designated rooms, service with restrictions, supervision.
[SAVE] [S🐾] [✕] [🛏] [💻]

EAGLE PASS

(AAA) ▼▼▼▼ Best Western SH
(830) 758-1234. **$84.** 1923 Veterans Blvd. US 57, jct Loop 431 (US 277). Ext corridors. **Pets:** Accepted.
[SAVE] [S🐾] [✕] [🐾] [🛏] [💻] [🏊]

(AAA) ▼▼▼▼ Holiday Inn Express Hotel & Suites SH
(830) 757-3050. **$84-$89, 10 day notice.** 2007 Veterans Blvd. 1.5 mi n on Loop 431 (US 277). Int corridors. **Pets:** Other species. Designated rooms, service with restrictions, supervision.
[SAVE] [✕] [🄼] [🐾] [🛏] [💻] [🏊]

▼▼▼ La Quinta Inn Eagle Pass SH
(830) 773-7000. **$81-$91.** 2525 E Main St. US 57 and 277 at Loop 431. Ext corridors. **Pets:** Medium, other species. Service with restrictions, crate.
[ASK] [✕] [🐾] [🛏] [💻] [🏊]

▼▼▼ Super 8 Motel SH
(830) 773-9531. **$54-$59.** 2150 N US Hwy 277. On US 277, 4 mi n. Ext corridors. **Pets:** Accepted.
[ASK] [S🐾] [✕] [🐾] [🐾] [🛏] [🏊]

EASTLAND

▼▼▼ The Eastland BB
(254) 629-8397. **$70-$125.** 112 N Lamar St. I-20, exit 343, 1.7 mi n to Lamar St, then just e; downtown. Int corridors. **Pets:** Accepted.
[ASK] [✕] [💻] [🏊] [🄕]

▼▼ Super 8 Motel & RV Park M
(254) 629-3336. **$54-$59.** 3900 I-20 E. I-20, exit 343, on north service road. Ext corridors. **Pets:** Accepted.
[ASK] [S🐾] [✕] [🛏] [💻] [🏊]

EDINBURG

▼▼▼ La Copa Inn & Suites SH
(956) 381-8888. **$49-$79.** 1210 E Canton Rd. US 281, exit Canton Rd, just off southbound access road. Ext corridors. **Pets:** Medium, other species. $5 daily fee/pet. Service with restrictions, supervision.
[ASK] [S🐾] [✕] [🏊]

EL PASO

(AAA) ▼▼▼▼ AmeriSuites (El Paso/Airport) SH
(915) 771-0022. **$105.** 6030 Gateway Blvd E. I-10, exit 24B (Geronimo Dr) eastbound; exit 24 westbound, 0.6 mi to Trowbridge, U-turn under interstate. Int corridors. **Pets:** Small. $10 one-time fee/pet. Service with restrictions, crate.
[SAVE] [S🐾] [✕] [🄼] [🐾] [🐾] [🛏] [💻] [🏊]

(AAA) ▼▼▼▼ Baymont Inn & Suites El Paso East SH
(915) 591-3300. **$59-$70.** 7944 Gateway Blvd E. I-10, exit 28B. Int corridors. **Pets:** Accepted.
[SAVE] [S🐾] [✕] [🄼] [🐾] [🐾] [🛏] [💻] [🏊]

(AAA) ▼▼▼ Baymont Inn & Suites El Paso West SH
(915) 585-2999. **$49-$69.** 7620 N Mesa St. I-10, exit 11 (Mesa St). Int corridors. **Pets:** Accepted.
[SAVE] [S🐾] [✕] [🐾] [🛏] [💻] [🏊]

Best Western Airport Inn SH
(915) 779-7700. **$64.** 7144 Gateway Blvd E. I-10, exit 26 (Hawkins Blvd), on eastbound frontage road. Ext corridors. **Pets:** Accepted.

Best Western Sunland Park Inn M
(915) 587-4900. **$54-$89.** 1045 Sunland Park Dr. I-10, exit 13, just s. Ext corridors. **Pets:** Small. Designated rooms, service with restrictions, supervision.

Chase Suites by Woodfin SH ✿
(915) 772-8000. **$99.** 6791 Montana Ave. I-10, exit 25 (Airway Blvd), 1 mi n, then just e. Ext corridors. **Pets:** Small, other species. $150 deposit/ pet. No service, supervision.

Comfort Inn Airport East SH
(915) 594-9111. **$67-$76.** 900 Yarbrough Dr. I-10, exit 28B. Ext corridors. **Pets:** Accepted.

Days Inn M
(915) 845-3500. **$75-$80.** 5035 S Desert Blvd. I-10, exit 11 (Mesa St) eastbound; exit 9 (Redd) northbound, 1.5 mi e on eastbound service road. Ext corridors. **Pets:** Other species. $20 daily fee/pet. Designated rooms, no service, crate.

Hawthorn Inn & Suites SH
(915) 778-6789. **$69-$139.** 6789 Boeing. 7 mi e on US 62 and 180 to Airway Blvd, then just n. Int corridors. **Pets:** Accepted.

Hilton El Paso Airport LH
(915) 778-4241. **$132-$152.** 2027 Airway Blvd. I-10, exit 25 (Airway Blvd), 1.3 mi n. Int corridors. **Pets:** Medium. $200 deposit/room. Service with restrictions, supervision.

Holiday Inn El Paso Sunland Park SH
(915) 833-2900. **$98-$175.** 900 Sunland Park Dr. I-10, exit 13. Ext corridors. **Pets:** Medium, other species. $25 one-time fee/room. Service with restrictions, supervision.

Howard Johnson Inn SH
(915) 591-9471. **$62-$72.** 8887 Gateway Blvd W. I-10, exit 26 (Hawkins Blvd). Int corridors. **Pets:** Service with restrictions, supervision.

La Quinta Inn El Paso (Airport) M ✿
(915) 778-9321. **$70-$85.** 6140 Gateway Blvd E. I-10, exit 24B (Geronimo Dr) eastbound; exit 24 westbound. Ext corridors. **Pets:** Service with restrictions, crate.

La Quinta Inn El Paso (Cielo Vista) SH
(915) 593-8400. **$78-$94.** 9125 Gateway Blvd W. I-10, exit 28B westbound; exit 27 eastbound. Ext corridors. **Pets:** Accepted.

La Quinta Inn El Paso (Lomaland) SH
(915) 591-2244. **$65-$85.** 11033 Gateway Blvd W. I-10, exit 29 eastbound; exit 30 westbound, 1 mi w. Ext corridors. **Pets:** Accepted.

La Quinta Inn El Paso (West) M
(915) 833-2522. **$74-$85.** 7550 Remcon Cir. I-10, exit 11 (Mesa St). Ext corridors. **Pets:** Supervision.

Microtel Inn & Suites SH
(915) 772-3650. **$60-$85.** 2001 Airway Blvd. I-10, exit 25 (Airway Blvd), 1.3 mi n. Int corridors. **Pets:** Small, other species. $100 deposit/pet. Designated rooms, service with restrictions, supervision.

Microtel Inn & Suites El Paso East SH
(915) 858-1600. **$46-$66.** 12211 Gateway W at Don Haskins Rd. I-10, exit 34 (Joe Battle), on westbound frontage road. Int corridors. **Pets:** Large, other species. $100 deposit/room. Service with restrictions, crate.

Quality Inn & Suites SH
(915) 772-3300. **$70-$80.** 6099 Montana Ave. I-10, exit 24 (Geronimo Dr) westbound; exit 24B (Geronimo Dr) eastbound, 0.5 mi n. Ext corridors. **Pets:** Small. $10 daily fee/pet. Service with restrictions.

Red Roof Inn West SH
(915) 587-9977. **$42-$57.** 7530 Remcon Cir. I-10, exit 11 (Mesa St). Ext/int corridors. **Pets:** Accepted.

Residence Inn by Marriott El Paso SH
(915) 771-0504. **$122-$139, 14 day notice.** 6355 Gateway Blvd W. I-10, exit 24B (Geronimo Dr) eastbound, n to Edgemere, then just e; exit 25 (Airway Blvd) westbound on westbound frontage road. Int corridors. **Pets:** Accepted.

Sleep Inn by Choice Hotels SH
(915) 585-7577. **$55-$75.** 953 Sunland Park Dr. I-10, exit 13. Int corridors. **Pets:** $10 one-time fee/pet. Designated rooms, service with restrictions, supervision.

Studio 6 El Paso SH
(915) 594-8533. **$45-$52.** 11049 Gateway Blvd W. I-10, exit 29 (Lomaland) eastbound; exit 30 westbound. Ext corridors. **Pets:** Other species. $10 daily fee/room. Service with restrictions, crate.

Travelodge M
(915) 833-2613. **$49-$89.** 7815 N Mesa St. I-10, exit 11 (Mesa St). Ext corridors. **Pets:** Accepted.

Travelodge Hotel El Paso City Center SH
(915) 544-3333. **$59-$109.** 409 E Missouri St. I-10, exit 19B westbound (downtown); exit 19 eastbound, just e. Int corridors. **Pets:** Medium. $50 deposit/room. Service with restrictions.

Travelodge La Hacienda Airport M
(915) 772-4231. **$62-$95.** 6400 Montana Ave. I-10, exit 24 (Geronimo Dr) westbound; exit 24B (Geronimo Dr) eastbound, 0.5 mi n, then 0.5 mi e. Ext corridors. **Pets:** Medium. $10 daily fee/pet. Designated rooms, service with restrictions, supervision.

EULESS

La Quinta Inn Dallas (DFW Airport West-Euless) SH
(817) 540-0233. **$66-$76.** 1001 W Airport Frwy. SR 183, exit Industrial Blvd (FM 157). Ext corridors. **Pets:** Accepted.

Microtel Inn and Suites SH
(817) 545-1111. **$54-$74.** 901 W Airport Frwy. SR 183, exit Industrial Blvd (FM 157), just e. Int corridors. **Pets:** Small, dogs only. $25 deposit/ room. Service with restrictions, supervision.

Motel 6-Euless #1345 🅂🄷
(817) 545-0141. **$35-$45.** 110 Airport Frwy. SR 183, exit Euless/Main St, on westbound access road. Ext corridors. **Pets:** Accepted.

FORT DAVIS

Historical Prude Guest Ranch 🆁🄰 ❀
(432) 426-3202. **$58-$75.** 6 mi N Hwy 118. 4.5 mi n of jct SR 118 and 17. Ext corridors. **Pets:** Medium. $25 one-time fee/pet. Designated rooms, service with restrictions, crate.

FORT STOCKTON

Atrium West Inn 🅂🄷
(432) 336-6666. **$70-$130.** 1305 N Hwy 285. I-10, exit 257, just s. Ext corridors. **Pets:** Accepted.

Best Western Swiss Clock Inn 🅂🄷
(432) 336-8521. **$68-$88, 7 day notice.** 3201 W Dickinson Blvd. I-10, exit 256, 0.5 mi e. Ext corridors. **Pets:** Small. Designated rooms, service with restrictions, supervision.

Comfort Inn of Fort Stockton 🅂🄷
(432) 336-8531. **$66-$85.** 3200 W Dickinson Blvd. I-10, exit 256, just s. Int corridors. **Pets:** Other species. $5 daily fee/room. Designated rooms, no service, supervision.

Days Inn 🅂🄷
(432) 336-7500. **$56-$79, 7 day notice.** 1408 N US Hwy 285. I-10, exit 257, just s. Ext corridors. **Pets:** Very small. Service with restrictions, supervision.

Econo Lodge 🄼
(432) 336-9711. **$42-$46.** 800 E Dickinson Blvd. I-10, exit 261, 1.3 mi w on I-20 business route. Ext corridors. **Pets:** Other species. $7 daily fee/pet. Designated rooms, no service, supervision.

Holiday Inn Express 🅂🄷
(432) 336-5955. **$66-$100.** 1308 N US Hwy 285. I-10, exit 257, just s. Ext corridors. **Pets:** Medium. $10 daily fee/room. Designated rooms, service with restrictions, crate.

La Quinta Inn Fort Stockton 🅂🄷
(432) 336-9781. **$59-$74.** 1537 N Hwy 285. I-10, exit 257. Ext corridors. **Pets:** Medium, other species. Service with restrictions, crate.

Motel 6 Fort Stockton #333 🄼
(432) 336-9737. **$35-$49.** 3001 W Dickinson Blvd. I-10, exit 256, 0.5 mi e. Ext corridors. **Pets:** Accepted.

FORT WORTH

AmeriSuites (Ft Worth/Cityview) 🅂🄷
(817) 361-9797. **$89-$109.** 5900 Cityview Blvd. I-20, exit 431 (Bryant Irvin Rd). Int corridors. **Pets:** Small, other species. $10 daily fee/pet. Service with restrictions, supervision.

The Ashton Hotel 🅂🄷
(817) 332-0100. **$260-$780.** 610 Main St. Jct of 6th and Main sts; center. Int corridors. **Pets:** $150 deposit/room. Service with restrictions, supervision.

Best Western Inn 🅂🄷
(817) 847-8484. **$65-$125.** 6700 Fossil Bluff Dr. I-35W, exit 58 (Western Center Blvd), just n on service road, then just e. Int corridors. **Pets:** Accepted.

Candlewood Suites 🅂🄷
(817) 838-8229. **$69-$109.** 5201 Endicott Ave. I-820, exit 17B, just s. Int corridors. **Pets:** Accepted.

Comfort Inn 🅂🄷
(817) 535-2591. **$52-$69.** 2425 Scott Ave. I-30, exit 16C (Beach St). Int corridors. **Pets:** Other species. $25 one-time fee/room. Service with restrictions, crate.

Hampton Inn & Suites-FW Alliance Airport 🅂🄷
(817) 439-0400. **$79.** 13600 North Frwy. I-35W, exit 66 (Westport Pkwy). Int corridors. **Pets:** Accepted.

Holiday Inn Express Hotel & Suites-Fort Worth West 🅂🄷
(817) 560-4200. **$89-$125.** 2730 Cherry Ln. I-30, exit 7A. Int corridors. **Pets:** Other species. $50 deposit/room. Designated rooms, service with restrictions, crate.

Holiday Inn Ft. Worth South & Conference Center 🅂🄷
(817) 293-3088. **$89-$199.** 100 Altamesa E Blvd. I-35, exit 44. Int corridors. **Pets:** Small, other species. $25 one-time fee/room. Designated rooms, service with restrictions, supervision.

Holiday Inn North/Conference Center 🅂🄷
(817) 625-9911. **$89-$199.** 2540 Meacham Blvd. I-35W, exit 56A. Int corridors. **Pets:** Accepted.

Homestead Studio Suites Hotel-Fort Worth/Medical Center 🅂🄷
(817) 338-4808. **$66-$81.** 1601 River Run. I-30, exit 12 (University Dr), just s. Ext corridors. **Pets:** Accepted.

La Quinta Inn & Suites Fort Worth (North) 🅂🄷
(817) 222-2888. **$89-$99.** 4700 North Frwy. I-35W, exit 56A, just n. Int corridors. **Pets:** Large. Service with restrictions, supervision.

La Quinta Inn & Suites Fort Worth (Southwest) 🅂🄷 🐾
(817) 370-2700. **$99-$109.** 4900 Bryant Irving Rd. I-20, exit 431. Int corridors. **Pets:** Medium, other species. Service with restrictions, crate.

La Quinta Inn Fort Worth (West/Medical Center) 🅂🄷 🐾
(817) 246-5511. **$72-$86.** 7888 I-30 W. I-30, exit 7A. Ext/int corridors. **Pets:** Small, other species. Service with restrictions, supervision.

Microtel Inn & Suites 🅂🄷
(817) 222-3740. **$59-$89.** 3740 Tanacross Dr. I-820, exit 17B (Beach St), just s. Int corridors. **Pets:** Large, other species. $10 daily fee/pet. Service with restrictions, supervision.

Motel 6-#117 🅂🄷
(817) 244-9740. **$35-$45.** 8701 I-30 W. I-30, exit 6, just s on Las Vegas. Ext corridors. **Pets:** Accepted.

▼▼▼ Motel 6 East–1341 SH
(817) 834-7361. **$35-$45.** 1236 Oakland Blvd. I-30, exit 18. Ext corridors. **Pets:** Accepted.
SO ✕ ⚓

♦♦♦ ▼▼▼▼ The Renaissance Worthington Hotel LH
(817) 870-1000. **$154-$229.** 200 Main St. Northwest corner of 2nd and Main sts. Int corridors. **Pets:** Accepted.
SAVE ✕ 🐾 🏋 🛋 🔲 🍽 ⚓ ✕

▼▼▼▼ Residence Inn-Alliance Airport SH
(817) 750-7000. **$94-$139.** 13400 North Frwy. I-35W, exit 66. Int corridors. **Pets:** Accepted.
ASK SO ✕ 🏋 🛋 🔲 ⚓ ✕

▼▼▼ Residence Inn By Marriott Fort Worth-River
   Plaza SH 🐾
(817) 870-1011. **$139.** 1701 S University Dr. I-30, exit 12 (University Dr), 0.4 mi s. Ext corridors. **Pets:** Large, other species. $75 one-time fee/room. Service with restrictions.
ASK SO ✕ 🐾 🏋 🛋 🔲 ⚓ ✕

▼▼▼ Residence Inn by Marriott-Fossil Creek SH
(817) 439-1300. **Call for rates.** 5801 Sandshell. I-35W, exit 58 (Western Center Blvd) northbound to Sandshell, 0.7 mi s; exit southbound, take first road to the right through strip center, just s to Sandshell, then 0.7 mi s. Int corridors. **Pets:** Other species. $5 daily fee/pet, $75 one-time fee/room. Service with restrictions.
✕ 🐾 🛋 🔲 ⚓ ✕

▼▼▼ TownePlace Suites by Marriott-Fort Worth SH
(817) 732-2224. **$84.** 4200 International Plaza Dr. I-820, exit 433. Int corridors. **Pets:** Small. $75 one-time fee/room. Service with restrictions, crate.
ASK SO ✕ 🏋 🛋 🔲 ⚓

FREDERICKSBURG

♦♦♦ ▼▼▼▼ Best Western Fredericksburg SH
(830) 992-2929. **$85-$140.** 314 E Highway St. Jct US 87 and 290, 6 blks s. Int corridors. **Pets:** Small, dogs only. $10 one-time fee/pet. Designated rooms, no service, supervision.
SAVE SO ✕ 🏋 🛋 🔲 ⚓

♦♦♦ ▼▼ Budget Host Deluxe Inn M
(830) 997-3344. **$59-$79.** 901 E Main St. US 290, 0.5 mi e. Ext corridors. **Pets:** Small. $10 daily fee/pet. Designated rooms, service with restrictions, crate.
SAVE SO ✕ 🛋 🔲

▼▼▼ Comfort Inn & Suites SH
(830) 990-2552. **$99-$160.** 723 S Washington St. I-87, w on Main St, then left. Int corridors. **Pets:** Small. $20 one-time fee/room. Service with restrictions.
ASK SO ✕ 🛋 🔲 ⚓

♦♦♦ ▼▼ Dietzel Motel M
(830) 997-3330. **$47-$75.** 1141 W US 290. 1 mi w on US 290 at US 87. Ext corridors. **Pets:** Other species. $7 daily fee/pet. Service with restrictions.
SAVE ✕

♦♦♦ ▼▼ Econo Lodge SH
(830) 997-3437. **$59-$99.** 810 S Adams St. 0.7 mi sw of jct US 290 and SR 16. Ext corridors. **Pets:** Other species. $10 daily fee/room. Designated rooms, service with restrictions.
SAVE SO ✕ 🛋 🔲 ⚓

▼▼ Frontier Inn & RV Park M
(830) 997-4389. **$46-$64.** 1704 US Hwy 290 W. US 290, 1 mi w. Ext corridors. **Pets:** Accepted.
ASK SO ✕ 🛋 🔲

▼▼▼ Holiday Inn Express SH
(830) 990-4200. **$84-$119, 7 day notice.** 1220 N Hwy 87. 1 mi w on US 290 at US 87. Int corridors. **Pets:** Small. $25 one-time fee/pet. Service with restrictions, supervision.
ASK SO ✕ 🐾 🏋 🛋 🔲 ⚓

♦♦♦ ▼▼ Quality Inn SH
(830) 997-9811. **$69-$99.** 908 S Adams St. 0.8 mi sw on SR 16; 0.8 mi sw of jct US 87 and 290. Ext corridors. **Pets:** $10 daily fee/room. Service with restrictions, supervision.
SAVE SO ✕ 🐾 🛋 🔲 ⚓

▼▼ Sunday House Inn & Suites SH
(830) 997-4484. **$89-$139.** 501 E Main St. 0.4 mi e on US 290. Ext corridors. **Pets:** Accepted.
ASK ✕ 🛋 🔲 ⚓

♦♦♦ ▼ Sunset Inn M 🐾
(830) 997-9581. **$49-$69.** 900 S Adams St. 0.8 mi sw of jct US 290 and SR 16. Ext corridors. **Pets:** Dogs only. Service with restrictions, crate.
SAVE SO ✕ 🛋 🔲 🍽

♦♦♦ ▼▼▼ Super 8 Fredericksburg M
(830) 997-6568. **$79-$125.** 514 E Main St. US 290, just e of jct US 87. Ext corridors. **Pets:** Small. $10 one-time fee/room. No service, supervision.
SAVE SO ✕ 🛋 🔲 ⚓

FULTON

♦♦♦ ▼▼▼ Best Western Inn by the Bay M 🐾
(361) 729-8351. **$82-$97.** 3902 N Hwy 35. SR 35, 0.5 mi n of jct Business Rt SR 35 and FM 3063. Ext corridors. **Pets:** Other species. $10 daily fee/pet. Service with restrictions, crate.
SAVE SO ✕ 🐾 🛋 🔲 ⚓

GAINESVILLE

♦♦♦ ▼▼ Best Western Southwinds M 🐾
(940) 665-7737. **$70-$90.** 2103 N I-35. I-35, exit 499 northbound, 1.4 mi n on access road to S Frontage Rd; exit 498B southbound. Ext corridors. **Pets:** Dogs only. $10 daily fee/pet. Service with restrictions, crate.
SAVE SO ✕ 🛋 🔲 ⚓

♦♦♦ ▼▼ Budget Host Inn M
(940) 665-2856. **$40.** 1900 N I-35. I-35, exit 499 northbound; exit 498B southbound. Ext corridors. **Pets:** Small. $5 one-time fee/room. No service, supervision.
SAVE SO ✕

♦♦♦ ▼▼▼ Deluxe Inn/Super 8 SH
(940) 665-5599. **$61.** 1936 I-35 N. I-35, exit 499 northbound, exit 498A southbound. Int corridors. **Pets:** Small, dogs only. $10 daily fee/pet. No service, supervision.
SAVE SO ✕ 🛋 🔲 ⚓

GALVESTON

▼▼▼▼ La Quinta Inn Galveston Seawall South SH
(409) 763-1224. **$79-$156.** 1402 Seawall Blvd. Seawall Blvd at 14th St. Ext corridors. **Pets:** Small, other species. Service with restrictions, supervision.
ASK ✕ 🐾 🏋 🛋 🔲 ⚓

▼ Motel 6 Galveston #343 M
(409) 740-3794. **$39-$71.** 7404 Avenue J/Broadway St. I-45, exit 1B, on east frontage road. Ext corridors. **Pets:** Accepted.
SO ✕ 🏋 ⚓

GEORGETOWN

(AAA) ◆◆◆ La Quinta Inn Georgetown 🆂🅷
(512) 869-2541. **$76-$86.** 333 I-35 N. I-35, exit 264 northbound; exit 262 southbound; on west frontage road. Ext corridors. **Pets:** Medium, other species. Service with restrictions, crate.
[SAVE] 🗙 📁 🔋 💻 🌊

GEORGE WEST

(AAA) ◆◆◆ Best Western George West Executive Inn 🆂🅷
(361) 449-3300. **$70.** 208 N Nueces St. Just n of US 59 on SR 281. Ext corridors. **Pets:** Medium. Service with restrictions, supervision.
[SAVE] 🆑 🗙 📁 🔋 💻 🌊

GIDDINGS

(AAA) ◆◆ Ramada Limited Ⓜ
(979) 542-9666. **$80-$85, 3 day notice.** 4002 E Austin St. 2.5 mi e on US 290. Ext corridors. **Pets:** Small. $10 one-time fee/room. Designated rooms, service with restrictions.
[SAVE] 🆑 🗙 🔋 💻 🌊

(AAA) ◆◆ Super 8 Motel Ⓜ
(979) 542-5791. **$49-$59.** 3556 E Austin St. 2 mi e on US 290. Ext corridors. **Pets:** Accepted.
[SAVE] 🆑 🗙 🔋 💻 🌊

GLEN ROSE

(AAA) ◆◆◆ Best Western Dinosaur Valley Inn & Suites 🆂🅷
(254) 897-4818. **$105-$375.** 1311 NE Big Ben Tr. On US 67. Int corridors. **Pets:** Medium, dogs only. $40 one-time fee/room. Service with restrictions, supervision.
[SAVE] 🆑 🗙 📁 🔋 💻 🌊 🗙

GRANBURY

(AAA) ◆◆ Comfort Inn 🆂🅷
(817) 573-2611. **$85-$145.** 1201 Plaza Dr N. 2 mi e on US 377 Bypass. Ext corridors. **Pets:** Accepted.
[SAVE] 🆑 🗙 📁 🔋 💻 🌊

◆◆ Days Inn and Suites 🆂🅷
(817) 573-2691. **$49-$84.** 1339 N Plaza Dr. 2 mi e on US 377 Bypass. Ext corridors. **Pets:** Accepted.
[ASK] 🆑 🗙 🔋 💻 🌊

(AAA) ◆◆ Plantation Inn on the Lake 🆂🅷
(817) 573-8846. **$65-$85.** 1451 E Pearl St. 0.3 mi w of Business Rt US 377 at US 377 Bypass. Ext/int corridors. **Pets:** Large. $10 daily fee/pet. Service with restrictions, supervision.
[SAVE] 🆑 🗙 🔋 💻 🌊

GRAPEVINE

(AAA) ◆◆◆◆ AmeriSuites (Dallas/DFW Airport North) 🆂🅷
(972) 691-1199. **$149-$159.** 2220 Grapevine Mills Cir W. SR 121 N, exit Bass Pro Dr. Int corridors. **Pets:** Medium. $50 one-time fee/room. Service with restrictions, supervision.
[SAVE] 🆑 🗙 ♿ 🐾 🐕 🔋 💻 🌊

◆◆◆ Baymont Inn-Dallas-Ft Worth/Airport North 🆂🅷
(817) 329-9300. **$79-$89.** 301 Capital St. SR 114, exit Main St. Int corridors. **Pets:** Accepted.
[ASK] 🆑 🗙 🐾 🐕 🔋 💻 🌊

(AAA) ◆◆◆◆ Embassy Suites Outdoor World 🅻🅷
(972) 724-2600. **$119-$315.** 2401 Bass Pro Dr. US 121, exit Bass Pro Dr. Int corridors. **Pets:** Small. $250 deposit/room. Service with restrictions, supervision.
[SAVE] 🗙 ♿ 🐕 🔋 💻 🍴 🌊 🗙

◆◆◆◆ Homewood Suites by Hilton 🆂🅷
(972) 691-2427. **$149, 14 day notice.** 2214 Grapevine Mills Cir W. SR 121 N, exit Bass Pro Dr. Int corridors. **Pets:** Other species. $300 one-time fee/room. Service with restrictions, supervision.
[ASK] 🆑 🗙 ♿ 🐕 🔋 💻 🌊 🗙

◆◆◆ Super 8 Motel-Grapevine 🆂🅷
(817) 329-7222. **$59-$110.** 250 E Hwy 114. SR 114, exit Main St. Int corridors. **Pets:** $10 daily fee/pet. Service with restrictions, supervision.
[ASK] 🆑 🗙 ♿ 🐾 🐕 🔋 💻 🌊

HARLINGEN

◆◆◆ Country Inn & Suites By Carlson 🆂🅷
(956) 428-0043. **$64-$125, 3 day notice.** 3825 S Expwy 83. US 83 and 77 Expwy, exit Ed Carrey. Int corridors. **Pets:** Small. $25 one-time fee/pet. Service with restrictions, supervision.
[ASK] 🆑 🗙 🐕 🔋 💻 🌊 🗙

◆◆ Howard Johnson Inn 🆂🅷
(956) 425-7070. **$57.** 6779 W Expwy 83. Jct US 77, 2.3 mi w on US 83, exit Stuart Place Rd. Ext corridors. **Pets:** Accepted.
[ASK] 🆑 🔋 💻 🍴 🌊

◆◆◆ La Quinta Inn Harlingen 🆂🅷 🐾
(956) 428-6888. **$76-$91.** 1002 S Expwy 83. US 83 and 77 Expwy, exit M St. Ext corridors. **Pets:** Other species. Service with restrictions, supervision.
[ASK] 🗙 🐾 🐕 🔋 💻 🌊

(AAA) ◆◆ Super 8 Motel 🆂🅷
(956) 412-8873. **$56-$70.** 1115 S Expwy 83. US 83 and 77 Expwy, exit M St, just n. Int corridors. **Pets:** Accepted.
[SAVE] 🆑 🗙 🔋 💻 🌊

HEARNE

(AAA) ◆◆ Oak Tree Inn 🆂🅷
(979) 279-5599. **$67-$80.** 1051 N Market St. 0.6 mi n of jct US 79 and SR 6. Ext/int corridors. **Pets:** Accepted.
[SAVE] 🆑 🗙 📁 🔋 💻

HENDERSON

(AAA) ◆◆◆ Best Western Inn of Henderson 🆂🅷
(903) 657-9561. **$65-$85.** 1500 Hwy 259 S. 2 mi s on US 259, 0.7 mi s of jct US 79 and 259 S. Ext/int corridors. **Pets:** Accepted.
[SAVE] 🆑 🗙 🔋 💻 🌊

HEREFORD

◆◆ Best Western Red Carpet Inn 🆂🅷
(806) 364-0540. **$53-$75.** 830 W 1st St. Just w of jct US 385 and 60. Ext corridors. **Pets:** Medium. Service with restrictions, supervision.
[ASK] 🆑 🗙 🔋 💻 🌊

HILLSBORO

(AAA) ◆◆◆ Best Western Hillsboro Inn 🆂🅷
(254) 582-8465. **$65-$75.** 307 I-35. I-35, exit 368A northbound; exit 368B southbound, just w. Ext corridors. **Pets:** Medium. Service with restrictions, supervision.
[SAVE] 🆑 🗙 🔋 💻 🌊

◆ Motel 6–4136 🆂🅷
(254) 580-9000. **Call for rates.** 1506 Hillview Dr. I-35, exit 368 southbound; exit 368A northbound. Int corridors. **Pets:** Accepted.
🗙 ♿ 🔋 🌊

HONDO

▲▲▲ ▼▼▼ Hondo Executive Inn Ⓜ ❀
(830) 426-2535. **$45-$89.** 102 E 19th St. On US 90 W. Ext corridors.
Pets: $10 one-time fee/pet. Service with restrictions, supervision.
[SAVE] [S₀] [✕] [♿] [🅿] [◻] [🏊]

▲▲▲ ▼▼◆ Whitetail Lodge Ⓜ
(830) 426-3031. **$45-$75.** 401 Hwy 90 E. Jct SR 173. Ext corridors.
Pets: Small, dogs only. $10 one-time fee/pet. Designated rooms, service
with restrictions, supervision.
[SAVE] [S₀] [✕] [🅿] [🏊]

HOUSTON METROPOLITAN AREA

BAYTOWN

▲▲▲ ▼▼▼ Baymont Inn & Suites Houston-Baytown SH
(281) 421-7300. **$59-$89.** 5215 I-10 E. I-10, exit 792 (Garth Rd). Int
corridors. **Pets:** Accepted.
[SAVE] [S₀] [✕] [🐾] [♿] [🅿] [◻] [🏊]

▼▼ Holiday Inn Express SH
(281) 421-7200. **$71-$81.** 5222 I-10 E. I-10, exit 792 (Garth Rd). Int
corridors. **Pets:** $10 one-time fee/pet. Service with restrictions, supervision.
[ASK] [S₀] [✕] [♿M] [🐾] [🅿] [◻] [🏊]

▲▲▲ ▼▼ La Quinta Inn Houston (Baytown) Ⓜ
(281) 421-5566. **$69-$79.** 4911 I-10 E. I-10, exit 792 (Garth Rd). Ext
corridors. **Pets:** Medium. Service with restrictions, supervision.
[SAVE] [✕] [🐾] [🅿] [◻] [🏊]

▼ Motel 6-1136 Ⓜ
(281) 576-5777. **$40-$50.** 8911 Hwy 146. I-10, exit 797 (SR 146). Ext
corridors. **Pets:** Accepted.
[S₀] [✕] [♿] [🅿] [🏊]

CHANNELVIEW

▼▼ Travelodge Suites SH
(281) 862-0222. **Call for rates.** 15831 2nd St. I-10, exit 783 (Sheldon
Rd) eastbound, just n, then just e on 2nd St; exit westbound, 0.8 mi
on Frontage Rd. Ext corridors. **Pets:** Accepted.
[✕] [🅿] [◻] [🏊]

CONROE

▲▲▲ ▼▼▼ Baymont Inn-Conroe SH
(936) 539-5100. **$64-$69, 30 day notice.** 1506 I-45 S. I-45, exit 85
(Gladstell St) northbound; exit 84 (Frazier St) southbound. Int corridors. **Pets:** Medium. $50 deposit/room, $10 daily fee/room. Service with
restrictions, crate.
[SAVE] [S₀] [✕] [🐾] [♿] [🅿] [◻] [🏊]

▼▼▼ La Quinta Inn & Suites SH
(936) 228-0790. **$75-$95.** 4006 Sprayberry Ln. I-45, exit 91 (League
Line Rd), just e. Int corridors. **Pets:** Small. Service with restrictions,
supervision.
[ASK] [S₀] [✕] [♿M] [♿] [🅿] [◻] [🏊]

▼ Motel 6 Conroe #385 Ⓜ
(936) 760-4003. **$39-$49.** 820 I-45 S. I-45, exit 85 (Gladstell Rd). Ext
corridors. **Pets:** Accepted.
[S₀] [✕] [🏊]

HOUSTON

**▲▲▲ ▼▼▼ AmeriSuites (Houston Intercontinental
Airport/Greenspoint)** SH
(281) 820-6060. **$114-$124.** 300 Ronan Park Pl. Sam Houston Pkwy
(Beltway 8), exit Imperial Valley westbound, 0.8 mi w on frontage road;
exit Hardy Toll Rd eastbound, turn under parkway, 1.2 mi w on west
frontage road. Int corridors. **Pets:** Accepted.
[SAVE] [S₀] [✕] [♿M] [♿] [🅿] [◻] [🏊]

**▲▲▲ ▼▼▼ Baymont Inn & Suites
Houston-Greenspoint** SH
(281) 875-2000. **$65-$85.** 12701 North Frwy. I-45, exit 61 (Greens Rd),
on southbound frontage road; northbound, just w on Greens Rd, just n
on Northborough, then just e on Glenborough. Int corridors.
Pets: Accepted.
[SAVE] [S₀] [✕] [🐾] [♿] [🅿] [◻] [🏊]

**▲▲▲ ▼▼▼ Baymont Inn & Suites Houston
Northwest** SH
(713) 680-8282. **$49-$79.** 11130 Northwest Frwy. US 290 W, exit W
34th St, on southeast corner. Int corridors. **Pets:** Medium. Service with
restrictions, crate.
[SAVE] [S₀] [✕] [♿] [🅿] [◻] [🏊]

**▲▲▲ ◆▼▼ Baymont Inn & Suites Houston
Southwest** SH
(713) 784-3838. **$59-$79.** 6790 Southwest Frwy. US 59 (Southwest
Frwy), exit Hillcroft St/W Park eastbound; exit Hillcroft St westbound.
Int corridors. **Pets:** Other species. Service with restrictions.
[SAVE] [✕] [♿] [🅿] [◻] [🏊]

▼▼▼▼ Candlewood Suites Houston by the Galleria SH
(713) 839-9411. **$59-$104.** 4900 Loop Central Dr. I-610, exit 7 (Four-
nace Pl), on northbound frontage road. Int corridors. **Pets:** Accepted.
[ASK] [S₀] [✕] [🅿] [◻]

▼▼▼▼ Candlewood Suites-Houston-Clear Lake SH
(281) 461-3060. **$79-$136.** 2737 Bay Area Blvd. I-45, exit 26, 3.7 mi e.
Int corridors. **Pets:** Other species. $25 one-time fee/pet. Designated
rooms, service with restrictions, supervision.
[ASK] [S₀] [✕] [♿] [🅿] [◻] [✕]

▼▼▼▼ Candlewood Suites-Town & Country SH ❀
(713) 464-2677. **$87-$101.** 10503 Town & Country Way. I-10, exit 755
eastbound, 1.1 mi on frontage road to Town & Country Blvd, then 0.4
mi s; exit 756A westbound, U-turn under I-10, just e to Town &
Country Blvd, then 0.4 mi s. Int corridors. **Pets:** Small. $25 one-time
fee/room. Service with restrictions.
[ASK] [S₀] [✕] [♿M] [♿] [🅿] [◻] [✕]

▼▼▼ Candlewood Suites-Westchase SH
(713) 780-7881. **$65-$125.** 4033 W Sam Houston Pkwy S. Sam Houston Pkwy (Beltway 8), exit Westpark, southeast corner of Westpark
and Sam Houston Pkwy (Beltway 8) on northbound frontage road. Int
corridors. **Pets:** Medium, other species. $150 one-time fee/room. Service
with restrictions, supervision.
[ASK] [S₀] [✕] [♿M] [♿] [🅿] [◻]

▼▼▼ Champions Lodge Motel Ⓜ
(281) 587-9171. **$44-$57.** 4726 FM 1960 W. I-45, exit 66 (FM 1960),
4.7 mi sw. Ext corridors. **Pets:** Medium, other species. $10 daily fee/pet.
Service with restrictions.
[ASK] [S₀] [✕] [🅿] [🏊]

▼▼▼ Comfort Inn & Suites SH
(713) 623-4720. **$69-$99.** 4020 Southwest Frwy. US 59, exit Weslayan
St northbound; exit Edloe/Weslayan St southbound, on southbound
frontage road. Ext corridors. **Pets:** Accepted.
[ASK] [S₀] [✕] [♿] [🅿] [◻] [🏊]

Comfort Inn Galleria/Westchase SH
(713) 783-1400. **$77-$165.** 9041 Westheimer Rd. Just w of jct Fondren. Ext corridors. **Pets:** Other species. $25 one-time fee/pet. Designated rooms, service with restrictions, supervision.

Comfort Suites SH ❀
(281) 440-4448. **$84-$144.** 150 Overland Tr. I-45, exit 66 (FM 1960), on southbound frontage road. Int corridors. **Pets:** Small, other species. $50 deposit/room. No service, crate.

Comfort Suites Galleria SH
(713) 787-0004. **$98-$199.** 6221 Richmond Ave. US 59, exit Hillcroft, 1 mi n to Richmond Ave, then 0.6 mi e. Int corridors. **Pets:** Accepted.

Crowne Plaza Northwest Hotel LH
(713) 462-9977. **$62-$116.** 12801 Northwest Frwy. Nw on US 290, exit Hollister Rd, 0.7 mi e on south service road. Ext/int corridors. **Pets:** Accepted.

Doubletree Guest Suites LH
(713) 961-9000. **$99-$239.** 5353 Westheimer Rd. I-610, exit 8C (Westheimer Rd) northbound; exit 9A (San Felipe/Westheimer rds) southbound, 0.8 mi w. Int corridors. **Pets:** Accepted.

Doubletree Hotel at Allen Center LH
(713) 759-0202. **$89-$239.** 400 Dallas St. At Dallas and Bagby sts. Int corridors. **Pets:** Large. $75 deposit/pet, $25 one-time fee/pet. Service with restrictions, crate.

Drury Inn & Suites-Houston Hobby SH
(713) 941-4300. **$60-$108.** 7902 Mosley Rd. I-45, exit 36 (Airport Blvd/College Rd) off southbound service road. Int corridors. **Pets:** Large, other species. Service with restrictions, supervision.

Drury Inn & Suites-Houston Near Galleria SH
(713) 963-0700. **$70-$110.** 1615 W Loop S. I-610, exit 9 (San Felipe Rd) northbound; exit 9A (San Felipe/Westheimer rds) southbound, on east service road. Int corridors. **Pets:** Large, other species. Service with restrictions, supervision.

Drury Inn & Suites Houston West SH
(281) 558-7007. **$60-$106.** 1000 N Hwy 6. I-10, exit 751 (Addicks/SR 6), just n on SR 6. Int corridors. **Pets:** Large, other species. Service with restrictions, supervision.

Executive Inn & Suites Houston/Hobby Airport M
(713) 645-7666. **$47-$57.** 6711 Telephone Rd. I-610, exit 33, 2.1 mi s; 0.5 mi s of jct Telephone and Bellfort rds. Ext corridors. **Pets:** $8 one-time fee/pet. Designated rooms, service with restrictions, supervision.

Fairfield Inn by Marriott I-10 East SH
(713) 675-2711. **$75.** 10155 East Frwy. I-10, exit 776A (Mercury Dr), just nw. Ext corridors. **Pets:** Accepted.

Four Seasons Hotel Houston LH ❀
(713) 650-1300. **$390.** 1300 Lamar St. Lamar St and Austin. Int corridors. **Pets:** Small. Supervision.

Hampton Inn I-10 East SH
(713) 673-4200. **$65-$92.** 828 Mercury Dr. I-10, exit 776A (Mercury Dr), just n. Int corridors. **Pets:** Accepted.

Holiday Inn Express Hotel & Suites-Intercontinental SH
(281) 372-1000. **$89, 15 day notice.** 1330 N Sam Houston Pkwy. Off Sam Houston Pkwy (Beltway 8), exit Aldine Westfield eastbound, 0.8 mi e on service road; exit Hardy Toll Rd westbound, U-turn, then 1 mi e on service road. Int corridors. **Pets:** Very small, other species. $25 one-time fee/pet. Designated rooms, no service, supervision.

Holiday Inn Hotel and Suites Galleria SH
(713) 681-5000. **$79-$109.** 7787 Katy Frwy. I-10, exit 762 (Antoine Dr) westbound; exit 761B (Antoine Dr) eastbound, on eastbound service road. Ext/int corridors. **Pets:** Accepted.

Holiday Inn Houston Intercontinental Airport LH
(281) 449-2311. **$149.** 15222 John F Kennedy Blvd. Jct N Sam Houston Pkwy (Beltway 8) E and John F Kennedy Blvd. Int corridors. **Pets:** Other species. $25 one-time fee/room. Crate.

Holiday Inn Select I-10 SH
(281) 558-5580. **$139-$159.** 14703 Park Row. I-10, exit 751 (Addicks Rd/SR 6), just n. Int corridors. **Pets:** Accepted.

Homestead Studio Suites Hotel-Houston/Galleria Area SH
(713) 960-9660. **$64-$79.** 2300 W Loop S. Loop 610, exit 9A (San Felipe/Westheimer rds) southbound; exit 9 (San Felipe Rd) northbound, on southbound frontage road. Int corridors. **Pets:** Accepted.

Homestead Studio Suites Hotel-Houston/Medical Center/Reliant Park SH
(713) 797-0000. **$64-$79.** 7979 Fannin St. I-610, exit 1B, 0.8 mi n. Ext corridors. **Pets:** Accepted.

Homestead Studio Suites Hotel-Houston/Willowbrook SH
(281) 397-9922. **$49-$64.** 13223 Champions Center Dr. Jct SR 249 and FM 1960 W, 0.9 mi e to Champion Center Dr, just n to Champion Center Plaza, then just w. Ext corridors. **Pets:** Accepted.

Homewood Suites by Hilton SH
(281) 486-7677. **$89-$139.** 401 Bay Area Blvd. I-45, exit 26 (Bay Area Blvd), 1 mi e. Int corridors. **Pets:** Accepted.

Homewood Suites by Hilton-Westchase SH
(713) 334-2424. **$112-$124, 14 day notice.** 2424 Rogerdale Rd. Sam Houston Pkwy (Beltway 8), exit Westheimer Rd, just w to Rogerdale Rd, then just n. Int corridors. **Pets:** Accepted.

Homewood Suites by Hilton-Willowbrook SH
(281) 955-5200. **$119, 14 day notice.** 7655 W FM 1960. Just e of jct SR 249 and FM 1960. Int corridors. **Pets:** Other species. $100 one-time fee/room. Service with restrictions.

Homewood Suits by Hilton Intercontinental SH
(281) 219-9100. **$124.** 1340 N Sam Houston Pkwy E. Sam Houston Pkwy (Beltway 8), exit Aldine Westfield eastbound, 0.8 mi e on frontage road; exit Hardy Toll Rd westbound, U-turn, then 1 mi e on frontage road. Int corridors. **Pets:** Accepted.

Hotel Sofitel Houston LH
(281) 445-9000. **$219-$249.** 425 N Sam Houston Pkwy E. Sam Houston Pkwy (Beltway 8), exit Imperial Valley Dr westbound; exit Hardy Toll Rd eastbound, on westbound frontage road. Int corridors. **Pets:** Other species. Service with restrictions.

Houston Marriott Medical Center Hotel LH
(713) 796-0080. **$89-$199.** 6580 Fannin St. I-610, exit 2 (Main St), 2.5 mi ne to Holcombe St, 0.3 mi e, then just n. Int corridors. **Pets:** Accepted.

Howard Johnson Express Inn M ❀
(281) 447-6888. **$56-$60.** 6 N Sam Houston Pkwy E. I-45, exit 60A southbound; exit 60B northbound, just e. Ext corridors. **Pets:** Very small. $5 daily fee/pet, $10 one-time fee/pet. Service with restrictions, supervision.

InterContinental Houston LH
(713) 627-7600. **$259-$279.** 2222 W Loop S. I-610, exit 9 (San Felipe Rd) northbound; exit 9A (San Felipe/Westheimer rds) southbound. Int corridors. **Pets:** Accepted.

La Quinta Inn & Suites Houston (Bush Intercontinental Airport) SH
(281) 219-2000. **$109-$119.** 15510 John F Kennedy Blvd. Sam Houston Pkwy (Beltway 8), exit John F Kennedy Blvd/Vickery, just n. Int corridors. **Pets:** Accepted.

La Quinta Inn & Suites Houston (Galleria Area) SH ❀
(713) 355-3440. **$84-$129.** 1625 W Loop S. I-610, exit 9 (San Felipe Rd) northbound; exit 9A (San Felipe/Westheimer rds) southbound, on northbound service road. Int corridors. **Pets:** Small, other species. Service with restrictions, supervision.

La Quinta Inn & Suites Houston North Beltway SH
(832) 554-5000. **$65.** 10137 North Frwy. I-45, exit 59 (West Rd), on southbound frontage road. Int corridors. **Pets:** Small. $25 deposit/room. Designated rooms, service with restrictions, supervision.

La Quinta Inn & Suites Houston (Park 10) SH
(281) 646-9200. **$85-$105.** 15225 Katy Frwy. I-10, exit 748 (Barker Cypress Rd) eastbound, 2.6 mi on eastbound service road; exit 751 (SR 6) westbound, just s to Grisby Rd, then 0.5 mi w. Int corridors. **Pets:** Accepted.

La Quinta Inn Houston (Brookhollow) M
(713) 688-2581. **$66-$76.** 11002 Northwest Frwy. Nw on US 290, exit Magnum Rd-Watonga Blvd. Ext corridors. **Pets:** Service with restrictions, supervision.

La Quinta Inn Houston (Cyfair) SH
(281) 469-4018. **$79-$86.** 13290 FM 1960 W. Just w of jct US 290 and FM 1960. Ext corridors. **Pets:** Small, other species. Designated rooms, service with restrictions, supervision.

La Quinta Inn Houston (East) SH
(713) 453-5425. **$72-$82.** 11999 East Frwy. I-10, exit 778A (Federal Rd) eastbound; exit 776B (Holland Ave) westbound, just n. Ext corridors. **Pets:** Accepted.

La Quinta Inn Houston (Greenway Plaza) SH
(713) 623-4750. **$72-$82.** 4015 Southwest Frwy. Sw off US 59 (Southwest Frwy), exit Weslayan. Ext/int corridors. **Pets:** Accepted.

La Quinta Inn Houston (Hobby Airport) SH
(713) 941-0900. **$72-$82.** 9902 Gulf Frwy. I-45 S, exit 36 (Airport Blvd/College Rd), just s on southbound frontage road. Ext corridors. **Pets:** Accepted.

La Quinta Inn Houston (I-45 North) SH
(281) 444-7500. **$66-$76.** 17111 North Frwy. I-45, exit 66, southbound service road, 0.4 mi s of jct FM 1960 and I-45. Ext corridors. **Pets:** Accepted.

La Quinta Inn Houston (Medical Center/Astrodome) SH
(713) 668-8082. **$79-$96.** 9911 Buffalo Speedway. I-610, exit 2 (Buffalo Speedway/S Main St), just s. Ext corridors. **Pets:** Other species. Service with restrictions, supervision.

La Quinta Inn Houston (Wilcrest) SH
(713) 932-0808. **$69-$79.** 11113 Katy Frwy. I-10, exit 754 (Kirkwood Dr) westbound; exit 755 (Wilcrest Rd) eastbound, on eastbound service road. Ext corridors. **Pets:** Accepted.

Marriott Houston Hobby Airport LH
(713) 943-7979. **$99-$139.** 9100 Gulf Frwy. I-45, exit 36 (Airport Blvd/College Rd) southbound; exit 38 (Monroe) northbound, on southbound frontage road. Int corridors. **Pets:** Small, other species. $25 one-time fee/pet. Service with restrictions, supervision.

Motel 6–1140 M
(713) 937-7056. **$37-$51.** 16884 Northwest Frwy. US 290, exit Jones Rd westbound; exit Senate Ave eastbound, on westbound frontage road. Ext corridors. **Pets:** Accepted.

Motel 6–1401 M
(713) 334-9188. **$45-$55.** 2900 W Sam Houston Pkwy S. Sam Houston Pkwy (Beltway 8), exit Westheimer Rd. Int corridors. **Pets:** Accepted.

Omni Houston Hotel LH
(713) 871-8181. **$299-$319.** Four Riverway. I-610, exit 10 (Woodway Dr), 0.3 mi w. Int corridors. **Pets:** Accepted.

Omni Houston Westside LH ❀
(281) 558-8338. **$229.** 13210 Katy Frwy. I-10, exit 753A (Eldridge St), just n. Int corridors. **Pets:** Small, cats only. $50 one-time fee/room. Service with restrictions, supervision.

Palm Court Inn M
(713) 668-8000. **$55-$75.** 8200 S Main St. I-610, exit 2 (Main St), 1.4 mi ne. Ext corridors. **Pets:** Medium, dogs only. Service with restrictions, crate.

Park Plaza Reliant Center LH
(713) 748-3221. **$105-$155, 3 day notice.** 8686 Kirby Dr. I-610, exit 1C (Kirby Dr). Int corridors. **Pets:** Accepted.

▼▼▼ Quality Inn Hobby Airport SH
(713) 644-3800. **$65-$95, 30 day notice.** 7775 Airport Blvd. I-45, exit
36 (Airport Blvd/College Rd), 2 mi w. Int corridors. **Pets:** Small. $50
deposit/pet, $5 daily fee/pet. Designated rooms, service with restrictions,
supervision.

ASK Sⓓ ✕ ⓗ 🖵 ⇋

▼▼ Ramada Limited/S.H. 249 SH
(281) 970-5000. **$60-$85.** 18836 Tomball Pkwy. SR 249, exit Grant, on
northbound frontage road. Ext corridors. **Pets:** Accepted.

ASK Sⓓ ✕ ⓗ 🖵 ⇋

▼▼▼ Ramada Plaza Hotel Near the Galleria SH
(713) 688-2222. **$90-$109.** 7611 Katy Frwy. I-10, exit 762 (Silber Rd),
on eastbound frontage road. Int corridors. **Pets:** Accepted.

ASK Sⓓ ✕ ⓗ 🖵 ⑪ ⇋

▼▼ Red Roof Inn Hobby Airport SH
(713) 943-3300. **$46-$60.** 9005 Airport Blvd. I-45, exit 36 (Airport Blvd/
College Rd), just w. Int corridors. **Pets:** Accepted.

✕ 🐾 ⓖ ⓗ ⇋

▼▼ Red Roof Inn Houston West SH
(281) 579-7200. **$45-$53.** 15701 Park Ten Pl. I-10, exit 751 (Addicks
Rd/SR 6), 0.8 mi on west frontage road. Ext/int corridors. **Pets:** Small,
other species. Service with restrictions, supervision.

✕ 🐾 ⓖ ⓗ

▼▼ Red Roof Inns M
(713) 785-9909. **$47-$62.** 2960 W Sam Houston Pkwy S. SW Sam
Houston Pkwy (Beltway 8), exit Westheimer Rd. Ext/int corridors.
Pets: Accepted.

✕ ⓖ ⓗ ⇋

▼▼ Red Roof Inns SH
(713) 939-0800. **$45-$67.** 12929 Northwest Frwy. US 290, exit Hollister
and Tidwell rds, on eastbound service road. Ext/int corridors.
Pets: Accepted.

✕ 🐾 ⓖ ⓗ ⇋

**AAA ▼▼▼▼ Renaissance Houston Hotel Greenway
                    Plaza** LH
(713) 629-1200. **$89-$189.** 6 Greenway Plaza E. US 59 (Southwest
Frwy), exit Buffalo Speedway. Int corridors. **Pets:** Service with restrictions, supervision.

SAVE ✕ 🐾 ⓖ ⓗ 🖵 ⑪ ⇋ ⊠

**▼▼▼ Residence Inn by Marriott Houston by the
                    Galleria** SH 🐾
(713) 840-9757. **$129-$199.** 2500 McCue. I-610, exit 8C (Westheimer
Rd) northbound; exit 9A (San Felipe/Westheimer rds) southbound, just
w to McCue, then just n. Ext/int corridors. **Pets:** Medium, other species.
$75 one-time fee/pet.

ASK Sⓓ ✕ ⓖ ⓗ 🖵 ⇋

▼▼▼ Residence Inn by Marriott Houston Westchase SH
(713) 974-5454. **$94-$139.** 9965 Westheimer Rd. Sam Houston Pkwy
(Beltway 8), exit Westheimer Rd, 0.7 mi e to Elmside Dr, then just s.
Int corridors. **Pets:** Accepted.

ASK Sⓓ ✕ ⓖ ⓗ 🖵 ⇋ ⊠

▼▼▼ Residence Inn by Marriott-Medical Center SH
(713) 660-7993. **$89-$189.** 7710 Main St. I-610, exit 2 (S Main
St/Buffalo Speedway), 1.5 mi n. Ext corridors. **Pets:** Accepted.

ASK Sⓓ ✕ ⓗ 🖵 ⇋ ⊠

▼▼▼ Residence Inn by Marriott-West University SH
(713) 661-4660. **$79-$134.** 2939 Westpark Dr. US 59, exit Kirby, just s,
then just w. Int corridors. **Pets:** Medium, other species. $75 one-time
fee/room. Supervision.

ASK Sⓓ ✕ ⓖM ⓗ 🖵 ⇋ ⊠

▼▼▼ Residence Inn by Marriott Willowbrook SH
(832) 237-2002. **$119-$169, 14 day notice.** 7311 W Greens Rd. SR
249, exit Greens Rd, just e. Int corridors. **Pets:** Accepted.

ASK Sⓓ ✕ ⓖ ⓗ 🖵 ⇋ ⊠

▼▼▼ Residence Inn-Houston Clear Lake SH
(281) 486-2424. **$89-$162.** 525 Bay Area Blvd. I-45 S, exit 26 (Bay
Area Blvd), 1.2 mi e. Ext/int corridors. **Pets:** Accepted.

ASK Sⓓ ✕ 🐾 ⓖ ⓗ 🖵 ⇋ ⊠

▼▼ Robin's Nest Bed & Breakfast Inn BB
(713) 528-5821. **$126-$175, 3 day notice.** 4104 Greeley St. US 59
(Southwest Frwy), exit Richmond Ave, just e, then just n. Ext/int corridors. **Pets:** Accepted.

ASK Sⓓ ✕ ⓗ

▼▼ Rodeway Inn-Southwest Freeway M
(713) 526-1071. **$59-$69.** 3135 Southwest Frwy. US 59 (Southwest
Frwy), exit Buffalo Speedway, on eastbound service road. Ext corridors. **Pets:** Accepted.

ASK Sⓓ ✕ ⓗ 🖵 ⇋

AAA ▼▼▼▼ The St. Regis, Houston SH 🐾
(713) 840-7600. **$430-$2500.** 1919 Briar Oaks Ln. I-610, exit 9A (San
Felipe/Westheimer rds), 0.3 mi e. Int corridors. **Pets:** Medium. Service
with restrictions, supervision.

SAVE Sⓓ ✕ 🐾 ⓖ ⓗ 🖵 ⑪ ⇋ ⊠

AAA ▼▼▼ Sheraton North Houston Hotel LH
(281) 442-5100. **$199-$299.** 15700 John F Kennedy Blvd. Sam Houston Pkwy (Beltway 8), exit John F Kennedy Blvd, just n. Int corridors.
Pets: Medium. $25 one-time fee/room. Service with restrictions, supervi-
sion.

SAVE Sⓓ ✕ ⓖM 🐾 ⓖ ⓗ 🖵 ⑪ ⇋

**▼▼▼ Sheraton Suites Houston Near The
                    Galleria** SH 🐾
(713) 586-2444. **$279-$379.** 2400 W Loop S. I-610, exit 9 (San Felipe
Rd) northbound; exit 9A (San Felipe/Westheimer rds) southbound. Int
corridors. **Pets:** Medium, dogs only. Service with restrictions, supervision.

ASK Sⓓ ✕ ⓖ ⓗ 🖵 ⑪ ⇋

**▼▼▼ Staybridge Suites by Holiday Inn Houston-Near The
                    Galleria** SH
(713) 355-8888. **$80-$105.** 5190 Hidalgo St. I-610, exit 9A (San Felipe/
Westheimer rds) southbound; exit 8C (Westheimer Rd) northbound,
0.4 mi w to Sage Rd, then just s. Int corridors. **Pets:** Accepted.

ASK Sⓓ ✕ ⓖM ⓖ ⓗ 🖵 ⇋

▼▼ Studio 6 #6043 SH
(281) 579-6959. **$45-$60.** 1255 Hwy 6 N. I-10, exit 751 (Addicks Rd/SR
6), just n. Ext corridors. **Pets:** Accepted.

Sⓓ ✕ ⓖ ⓗ ⇋

▼▼ Studio 6-Cypress Station #6037 SH
(281) 580-2221. **$43-$53.** 220 Bammel-Westfield Rd. I-45, exit 66,
southbound frontage road, then just w. Ext corridors. **Pets:** Accepted.

Sⓓ ✕ 🐾 ⓖ ⓗ 🖵

▼▼ Studio 6-Houston Hobby South #6039 M
(281) 929-5400. **$45-$60.** 12700 Featherwood. I-45, exit 33 (Fugua St)
southbound, stay in right lane and cross over I-45, just e to Featherwood, then just s. Ext corridors. **Pets:** Accepted.

Sⓓ ✕ ⓖ ⓗ 🖵

▼▼ Super 8-Houston-Gessner M
(713) 772-3626. **Call for rates.** 8201 Southwest Frwy. Sw on US 59,
exit Gessner St. Ext corridors. **Pets:** Accepted.

✕ 🐾 ⓗ 🖵 ⇋

▼▼ Super 8 Motel SH
(281) 866-8686. **$65-$120.** 609 W FM 1960. I-45, exit 66 (FM 1960)
southbound; exit 66A northbound, just w. Int corridors. **Pets:** Medium,
other species. $25 deposit/pet. Service with restrictions, supervision.

ASK Sⓓ ✕ ⓖ ⓗ ⇋

▼▼ TownePlace Suites by Marriott-Central SH
(713) 690-4035. **$80.** 12820 Northwest Frwy (US 290). US 290, exit Bingle/43rd St eastbound; exit Bingle/Pinemont/43rd St westbound, on westbound feeder. Int corridors. **Pets:** Other species. $75 one-time fee/room. Service with restrictions.
ASK 🔊 ✕ 🕭 🛋 🛌 🖥 ⊠

▼▼ TownePlace Suites by Marriott-West SH ❀
(281) 646-0058. **$82-$119.** 15155 Katy Frwy. I-10, exit 751, just s on SR 6 to Grisby Rd, then w. Int corridors. **Pets:** Other species. $75 one-time fee/room. Designated rooms.
ASK 🔊 ✕ 🕭 🛌 🖥 ⇌

▼▼▼ The Warwick SH
(713) 526-1991. **$145-$175.** 5701 Main St. Jct Main and Ewing sts, just n of Herman Park. Int corridors. **Pets:** Accepted.
✕ 🕭 🕖 🛌 🛌 🖥 🍽 ⇌ ⊠

AAA ▼▼ Wellesley Inn & Suites (Houston/Reliant Park Medical Ctr) SH
(713) 794-0800. **$99-$129.** 1301 S Braeswood Blvd. I-610, exit 1B, 1.5 mi n, just e. Int corridors. **Pets:** Small. $75 one-time fee/pet. Service with restrictions, supervision.
SAVE 🔊 ✕ 🛌 🛌 🖥 ⇌ ⊠

AAA ▼▼ ▼▼ The Westin Galleria, Houston LH
(713) 960-8100. **$299-$309.** 5060 W Alabama St. I-610, exit 8C (Westheimer Rd) norhtbound; exit 9A (San Felipe/Westheimer rds) southbound, 0.5 mi w on Westheimer Rd to Sage, just s, then just e. Int corridors. **Pets:** Accepted.
SAVE 🔊 ✕ 🕭 🛌 🖥 🍽 ⇌

AAA ▼▼ ▼▼ The Westin Oaks, Houston LH
(713) 960-8100. **$299-$309.** 5011 Westheimer Rd. I-610, exit 8C (Westheimer Rd) northbound; exit 9A (San Felipe/Westheimer rds) southbound, just w. Int corridors. **Pets:** Accepted.
SAVE 🔊 ✕ 🛌 🖥 🍽 ⇌

HUMBLE

▼▼ Fairfield Inn by Marriott SH
(281) 540-3311. **$75-$95.** 20525 Hwy 59. US 59, exit Townsen Rd, on southbound access road. Int corridors. **Pets:** Accepted.
ASK 🔊 ✕ 🕭 🛌 🛌 🖥 ⇌

▼▼▼ Holiday Inn Express Hotel & Suites SH
(281) 446-9997. **$129-$139.** 7014 Will Clayton Pkwy. US 59, exit Will Clayton Pkwy, just w. Int corridors. **Pets:** Accepted.
ASK 🔊 ✕ 🕭 🛌 🛌 🖥 ⇌

KATY

AAA ▼▼ Best Western-Houston West M
(281) 392-9800. **$64-$74, 20 day notice.** 22455 I-10 (Katy Frwy). I-10, exit 743 (Grand Pkwy), just e on eastbound service road. Ext corridors. **Pets:** $10 daily fee/pet. Service with restrictions, supervision.
SAVE 🔊 ✕ 🛌 🖥 ⇌

KINGWOOD

AAA ▼▼▼ Homewood Suites by Hilton at Kingwood Parc SH
(281) 358-5566. **$79-$259, 3 day notice.** 23320 Hwy 59 N. US 59, exit Kingwood Dr, 1.4 mi n on northbound access road. Int corridors. **Pets:** Small. $500 deposit/room, $250 one-time fee/room. Designated rooms, service with restrictions, supervision.
SAVE ✕ 🕭 🛌 🛌 🖥 ⇌ ⊠

LA PORTE

▼▼▼ La Quinta Inn Houston (La Porte) SH
(281) 470-0760. **$72-$82.** 1105 Hwy 146 S. Jct SR 146, exit Fairmont Pkwy. Ext corridors. **Pets:** Other species.
ASK ✕ 🕖 🛌 🖥 ⇌

NASSAU BAY

AAA ▼▼ Holiday Inn Houston/NASA SH
(281) 333-2500. **$109.** 1300 NASA Pkwy. I-45, exit 25 (NASA Rd One), 2.5 mi n. Ext/int corridors. **Pets:** Medium, other species. $50 one-time fee/room. Service with restrictions.
SAVE 🔊 ✕ 🕖 🛌 🖥 🍽 ⇌

ROSENBERG

▼▼▼ Holiday Inn Express Hotel & Suites SH
(281) 342-7888. **$89.** 27927 Southwest Frwy. US 59, exit SR 36, just se of jct. Int corridors. **Pets:** Accepted.
ASK 🔊 ✕ 🕭 🛌 🛌 🖥 ⇌

STAFFORD

AAA ▼▼ La Quinta Inn Houston (Stafford/Sugarland) SH
(281) 240-2300. **$72-$86.** 12727 Southwest Frwy. US 59 eastbound service road, exit Corporate Dr southbound; exit Airport Blvd/Kirkwood Rd northbound. Int corridors. **Pets:** Accepted.
SAVE ✕ 🕖 🛌 🖥 ⇌

▼▼▼ Residence Inn by Marriott Houston/Sugar Land SH ❀
(281) 277-0770. **$129.** 12703 Southwest Frwy. US 59, exit Corporate Dr southbound; exit Airport Blvd/Kirkwood Rd northbound. Int corridors. **Pets:** Large, other species. $75 one-time fee/room. Service with restrictions, crate.
ASK 🔊 ✕ 🛌 🛌 🖥 ⇌ ⊠

▼▼ Studio 6 #6044 M
(281) 240-6900. **$45-$60.** 12827 Southwest Frwy. US 59, exit US 90 and SR 41 alternate route northbound, follow frontage road; exit US 90 southbound, first u-turn onto northbound frontage road. Ext corridors. **Pets:** Accepted.
🔊 ✕ 🛌 🛌 🖥

AAA ▼▼ Wellesley Inn & Suites (Houston/Stafford) SH
(281) 240-0025. **$62-$93.** 4726 Sugar Grove Blvd. US 59, exit W Airport Blvd/Kirkwood Dr, just w on Frontage Rd to Sugar Grove Blvd, then just n. Ext corridors. **Pets:** Accepted.
SAVE 🔊 ✕ 🛌 🛌 🖥 ⇌

SUGAR LAND

▼▼▼ Drury Inn & Suites-Houston/Sugar Land SH
(281) 277-9700. **$62-$105.** 13770 Southwest Frwy. Sw on US 59, exit Sugarland/Alternate Rt US 90, exit Sugar Creek Blvd northbound. Int corridors. **Pets:** Large, other species. Service with restrictions, supervision.
ASK ✕ 🕖 🛌 🛌 🖥 ⇌

WEBSTER

AAA ▼▼▼ Wellesley Inn & Suites (Houston/NASA Clear Lake) SH
(281) 338-7711. **$109-$129.** 720 W Bay Area Blvd. I-45, exit 26 (Bay Area Blvd), just e. Int corridors. **Pets:** Small, other species. $25 one-time fee/pet. Service with restrictions, supervision.
SAVE 🔊 ✕ 🕖 🛌 🛌 🖥 ⇌

WINNIE

AAA ▼▼ Best Western Gulf Coast Inn SH
(409) 296-9292. **$65-$75.** 46318 I-10 E. I-10, exit 829, on eastbound frontage road. Ext corridors. **Pets:** $5 daily fee/pet. Service with restrictions, crate.
SAVE 🔊 ✕ 🛌 🖥 ⇌

AAA ▼▼▼ Winnie Inn & Suites SH
(409) 296-2947. **$50-$65.** 205 Spur 5, Hwy 124. I-10, exit 829, just s. Ext corridors. **Pets:** Accepted.
SAVE 🔊 ✕ 🛌 🖥 ⇌

THE WOODLANDS

◇◇◇ Drury Inn & Suites-Houston The Woodlands SH
(281) 362-7222. **$60-$94.** 28099 I-45 N. I-45, exit 78 southbound; exit 77 northbound, on west service road. Int corridors. **Pets:** Large, other species. Service with restrictions, supervision.

ASK ✕ ☒ ☐ ☒ ☐ ☐ ☒

◇◇◇ Holiday Inn Express Hotel & Suites SH
(281) 681-8088. **$77.** 24888 I-45 N. I-45, exit 73 (Rayford/Sawdust Rd), on northbound access road. Int corridors. **Pets:** Accepted.

ASK ☒ ✕ ☒ ☐ ☐ ☒ ✕

◇◇◇◇ La Quinta Inn Houston, The Woodlands North SH
(281) 367-7722. **$69-$79.** 28673 I-45 N. I-45, exit 78 southbound; exit 79 (SR 242) northbound, on southbound frontage road. Ext/int corridors. **Pets:** Accepted.

SAVE ✕ ☒ ☐ ☐ ☒

◇◇◇ Residence Inn by Marriott SH
(281) 292-3252. **$109, 14 day notice.** 1040 Lake Front Cir. I-45, exit 78 southbound; exit 79 (SR 242) northbound, 0.8 mi s of jct I-45 and Research Forest Dr, just w. Int corridors. **Pets:** Accepted.

ASK ☒ ✕ ☒ ☐ ☐ ☒ ✕

END METROPOLITAN AREA

HUNTSVILLE

◇◇◇ Holiday Inn Express (Sam Houston) SH
(936) 293-8800. **$79-$99, 14 day notice.** 201 W Hill Park Cir. I-45, exit 116, just w on US 190. Ext corridors. **Pets:** Accepted.

ASK ☒ ✕ ☒ ☒ ☐ ☐ ☒

◇◇◇ La Quinta Inn Huntsville SH
(936) 295-6454. **$72-$80.** 124 I-45 N. I-45, exit 116. Ext corridors. **Pets:** Small. Service with restrictions, supervision.

SAVE ✕ ☒ ☐ ☐ ☒

HURST

◇◇◇ AmeriSuites (Ft Worth/Hurst) SH
(817) 577-3003. **$95-$105.** 1601 Hurst Town Center Dr. SR 183, exit Precinct Line Rd, just n to Thousand Oaks, then just w. Int corridors. **Pets:** Accepted.

SAVE ☒ ✕ ☒ ☒ ☒ ☐ ☐ ☒

JACKSONVILLE

◇◇◇ Holiday Inn Express SH
(903) 589-8500. **$80-$85.** 1848 S Jackson. 2 mi s of jct US 69 and 79, on US 69. Int corridors. **Pets:** Small. $15 daily fee/pet. Service with restrictions, supervision.

ASK ☒ ✕ ☒ ☐ ☐ ☒

JASPER

◇◇◇ Best Western Inn Of Jasper SH
(409) 384-7767. **$58.** 205 W Gibson. US 190 and SR 63, 0.5 mi w of jct US 96. Ext corridors. **Pets:** Accepted.

SAVE ☒ ✕ ☐ ☐ ☒

◇ Ramada Inn Jasper SH
(409) 384-9021. **$51.** 239 E Gibson (US 190). US 190 and SR 63, just w of jct US 96. Ext corridors. **Pets:** Accepted.

ASK ☒ ✕ ☐ ☐ ☐ ☒

JUNCTION

◇◇ Days Inn SH
(325) 446-3730. **$75, 5 day notice.** 111 S Martinez St. I-10, exit 457, 0.3 mi s. Ext corridors. **Pets:** Medium, other species. $4 daily fee/pet. Designated rooms, service with restrictions, supervision.

ASK ☒ ✕ ☐ ☐ ☒

◇ The Hills Motel M
(325) 446-2567. **$42.** 1520 Main St. I-10, exit 456, 1.3 mi s on US 377. Ext corridors. **Pets:** Other species. Designated rooms, service with restrictions, supervision.

ASK ✕ ☐ ☒

KERRVILLE

◇◇ ◇◇ Best Western Sunday House Inn SH
(830) 896-1313. **$69-$95.** 2124 Sidney Baker St. I-10, exit 508 (SR 16), just s. Ext corridors. **Pets:** Accepted.

SAVE ✕ ☐ ☐ ☐ ☒

◇◇ Budget Inn M
(830) 896-8200. **$45-$70.** 1804 Sidney Baker St. I-10, exit 508 (SR 16), 0.5 mi s on SR 16. Ext corridors. **Pets:** Small, dogs only. $5 daily fee/pet. Service with restrictions, supervision.

SAVE ☒ ✕ ☐ ☒

◇◇ Comfort Inn SH ❁
(830) 792-7700. **$67-$149.** 2001 Sidney Baker St. I-10, exit 508 (SR 16), 0.6 mi s. Int corridors. **Pets:** Small. $10 one-time fee/room. Service with restrictions, supervision.

SAVE ☒ ✕ ☐ ☐ ☐ ☒

◇◇◇ Days Inn of Kerrville M
(830) 896-1000. **$59-$139.** 2000 Sidney Baker St. I-10, exit 508 (SR 16), 0.5 mi s. Ext/int corridors. **Pets:** Small. $10 daily fee/pet. Service with restrictions, supervision.

ASK ☒ ✕ ☒ ☐ ☐ ☒

◇◇◇ Y. O. Ranch Resort Hotel & Conference Center LH
(830) 257-4440. **$89-$109.** 2033 Sidney Baker St. I-10, exit 508 (SR 16), 0.3 mi s. Ext/int corridors. **Pets:** Large, other species. $20 deposit/room. Service with restrictions, supervision.

SAVE ☒ ✕ ☒ ☐ ☐ ☐ ☒ ✕

KILGORE

◇◇◇ Best Western Inn of Kilgore SH
(903) 986-1195. **$67.** 1411 N Hwy 259. I-20, exit 589, 3.9 mi s. Ext corridors. **Pets:** Other species. Crate.

SAVE ✕ ☐ ☐ ☒

KILLEEN

◇◇◇ Holiday Inn Express SH
(254) 554-2727. **$99.** 1602 E Central Texas Expwy. US 190, exit Trimmier Rd. Ext corridors. **Pets:** Medium, other species. Service with restrictions, crate.

SAVE ☒ ✕ ☐ ☐

◇◇◇ La Quinta Inn Killeen SH
(254) 526-8331. **$91-$101.** 1112 S Fort Hood St. US 190, exit Fort Hood St, on westbound access road. Ext corridors. **Pets:** Accepted.

ASK ✕ ☒ ☐ ☐ ☒

KINGSVILLE

◇◇◇ Super 8 Motel M
(361) 592-6471. **$60-$75.** 105 S 77 Bypass. 0.8 mi e on US 77. Ext corridors. **Pets:** Accepted.

SAVE ☒ ✕ ☐ ☐ ☒

LAJITAS

▼▼▼▼ Lajitas The Ultimate Hideout SH
(432) 424-5000. **$235-$451.** 1 Main St. Center. Ext/int corridors.
Pets: Accepted.
✕ 🛢 💻 🍴 ☟ ✕

LAKE JACKSON

▼▼▼ Cherotel Brazosport Hotel & Conference
Center SH
(979) 297-1161. **$127-$158.** 925 Hwy 332. On SR 228/332, just w of jct
Business Rt SR 288. Int corridors. **Pets:** Other species. $100 deposit/
room. Service with restrictions, supervision.
ASK 🔊 ✕ 🛢 💻 🍴 ☟

▼▼▼ Super 8 Motel-Lake Jackson M
(979) 297-3031. **$55.** 915 Hwy 332. 3 mi e of jct SR 288 and 332. Ext
corridors. **Pets:** Very small. $10 daily fee/pet. Service with restrictions,
supervision.
ASK 🔊 ✕ 🛢 💻 ☟

LAKEWAY

▲▲▲ ▼▼▼▼ Lakeway Inn Conference Resort LH
(512) 261-6600. **$199-$239, 3 day notice.** 101 Lakeway Dr. Jct FM
620 and Lakeway Blvd W, 1.5 mi to Lakeway Dr, then 2.1 mi n. Ext/int
corridors. **Pets:** Medium. $50 deposit/room. Designated rooms, service
with restrictions, crate.
SAVE 🔊 ✕ ♿ 🏊 ♿ 🛢 💻 🍴 ☟ ✕

LAMESA

▼▼ Shiloh Inn M
(806) 872-6721. **$46-$53.** 1707 Lubbock Hwy. Jct US 87 and 180, 1 mi
n. Ext corridors. **Pets:** Accepted.
ASK 🔊 ✕ 🛢 💻 ☟

LAREDO

▲▲▲ ▼▼▼▼ La Quinta Inn Laredo (I-35) SH
(956) 722-0511. **$96-$122.** 3610 Santa Ursula Ave. I-35, exit 2 (US 59).
Ext corridors. **Pets:** Other species. Service with restrictions, crate.
SAVE ✕ 🛢 💻

▼▼ Motel 6 South-142 M
(956) 725-8187. **$50-$62.** 5310 San Bernardo Ave. I-35, exit 3B (Mann
Rd). Ext corridors. **Pets:** Medium, other species. Service with restrictions,
supervision.
🔊 ✕ ♿ ☟

▼▼ Red Roof Inn Laredo M
(956) 712-0733. **$59-$70.** 1006 W Calton Rd. I-35, exit 3A, 0.3 mi w.
Ext/int corridors. **Pets:** Accepted.
✕ ♿ 🛢 ☟

▼▼▼ Rio Grande Plaza Hotel SH
(956) 722-2411. **Call for rates.** One S Main Ave. I-35, exit 1, just w of
International Bridge. Int corridors. **Pets:** Accepted.
✕ 🏊 🛢 💻 🍴 ☟

LITTLEFIELD

▲▲▲ ▼ Crescent Park Motel M
(806) 385-4464. **$43-$70.** 2000 Hall Ave. Jct US 84, 0.3 mi n on SR
385. Ext corridors. **Pets:** Accepted.
SAVE 🔊 ✕ 🛢 💻

LLANO

▲▲▲ ▼▼▼ Best Western Llano SH
(325) 247-4101. **$59-$79.** 901 W Young St. 1 mi w on SR 71 and 29.
Ext corridors. **Pets:** Medium, dogs only. $5 daily fee/pet. Service with
restrictions, supervision.
SAVE 🔊 ✕ 🛢 💻 ☟

LOCKHART

▲▲▲ ▼▼▼ Best Western Plum Creek Inn M
(512) 398-4911. **$69-$99.** 2001 Hwy 183 S. US 183 S, 1 mi s. Ext
corridors. **Pets:** Small. $20 one-time fee/pet. Designated rooms, service
with restrictions, supervision.
SAVE 🔊 ✕ 🛢 💻 🍴 ☟

LONGVIEW

▼▼▼ Best Western Inn & Conference Center SH
(903) 758-0700. **$69-$150.** 3119 Estes Pkwy. I-20, exit 595A, just n.
Ext/int corridors. **Pets:** Small. Service with restrictions, crate.
ASK 🔊 ✕ 🛢 💻 🍴 ☟ ✕

▼▼▼ Hampton Inn SH
(903) 758-0959. **$63-$79.** 112 S Access Rd. I-20, exit 595A. Ext corridors. **Pets:** Accepted.
ASK 🔊 ✕ ♿ 🛢 💻 ☟

▲▲▲ ▼▼▼▼ La Quinta Inn Longview SH
(903) 757-3663. **$69-$79.** 502 S Access Rd. I-20, exit 595. Ext corridors. **Pets:** Other species. Service with restrictions, crate.
SAVE ✕ 🛢 💻 ☟

▼ Motel 6–158 M
(903) 758-5256. **$38-$48.** 110 S Access Rd. I-20, exit 595A. Ext corridors. **Pets:** Other species. Service with restrictions, crate.
🔊 ✕ ♿

LUBBOCK

▲▲▲ ▼▼▼ Best Western Lubbock Windsor Inn SH
(806) 762-8400. **$69-$119.** 5410 I-27. 3.5 mi s on I-27, exit 1B southbound; U-turn at exit 1A (50th St) northbound. Int corridors.
Pets: Large. $25 deposit/room, $8 daily fee/room. Service with restrictions,
crate.
SAVE 🔊 ✕ ♿ 🛢 💻 ☟

▼▼▼▼ Comfort Inn & Suites SH
(806) 763-6500. **$70-$100.** 5828 I-27 S. I-27, exit 1B, just s. Int corridors. **Pets:** Accepted.
ASK 🔊 ✕ ♿ 🛢 💻 ☟

▲▲▲ ▼▼▼ Days Inn Texas Tech SH
(806) 747-7111. **$55-$89.** 2401 4th St. I-27, exit 4 (4th St), 1.5 mi w. Ext
corridors. **Pets:** $25 deposit/room. Service with restrictions, crate.
SAVE 🔊 ✕ ♿ 🛢 💻 ☟

▲▲▲ ▼▼▼ Econo Lodge SH
(806) 747-3525. **$49-$99, 3 day notice.** 5401 Ave Q. I-27, exit 1A (US
84/Ave Q), 0.5 mi w. Ext/int corridors. **Pets:** Accepted.
SAVE 🔊 ✕ 🛢 🍴 ☟

▼▼▼ Four Points Sheraton Hotel SH
(806) 747-0171. **$81-$129.** 505 Ave Q. I-27, exit 4, 0.9 mi w to US 84
(Ave Q), then just s. Int corridors. **Pets:** Accepted.
ASK 🔊 ✕ 🏊 ♿ 🛢 💻 🍴 ☟

▼▼▼ La Quinta Inn Lubbock SH
(806) 763-9441. **$87-$107.** 601 Ave Q. 0.8 mi nw on US 84 (Ave Q).
Ext corridors. **Pets:** Accepted.
✕ 🏊 ♿ 🛢 💻

▼▼▼ La Quinta Inn Lubbock (West/Medical Center) SH
(806) 792-0065. **$89-$104.** 4115 Brownfield Hwy. 3.3 mi sw; 2.5 mi ne
of Loop 289 on US 62 and 82. Int corridors. **Pets:** Other species.
Service with restrictions, supervision.
ASK ✕ 🏊 ♿ 🛢 💻 ☟

▼▼ Lubbock Super 8 Motel M
(806) 762-8726. **$50-$90, 18 day notice.** 501 Ave Q. 1 mi nw on US
84. Ext corridors. **Pets:** $6 daily fee/pet. Service with restrictions, crate.
ASK 🔊 ✕ 🛢

Motel 6 Lubbock #298 **SH**
(806) 745-5541. **$38-$50.** 909 66th St. I-27, exit 1 northbound; exit 1B southbound, on westbound frontage road. Ext corridors. **Pets:** Accepted.

Ramada Inn and Conference Center **SH**
(806) 745-2208. **$65-$99.** 6624 I-27. 3.8 mi s on I-27 and US 87; just w of jct Loop 289, exit 1B southbound. Int corridors. **Pets:** Dogs only. $15 one-time fee/pet. Service with restrictions, crate.

Residence Inn by Marriott **SH**
(806) 745-1963. **$89-$105.** 2551 S Loop 289. Loop 289, exit University, 3 mi s, south frontage road. Ext corridors. **Pets:** Accepted.

TownePlace Suites by Marriott **SH**
(806) 799-6226. **$89.** 5310 W Loop 289. W Loop 289, exit US 62/82 (Brownfield Rd), 0.5 mi s on west frontage road. Int corridors. **Pets:** Other species. $75 one-time fee/pet. Service with restrictions, supervision.

LUFKIN

Days Inn **SH**
(936) 639-3301. **$77-$85.** 2130 S 1st St. 0.3 mi s of jct US 59 and Loop 287. Ext/int corridors. **Pets:** Medium. $25 one-time fee/room. Designated rooms, service with restrictions.

La Quinta Inn Lufkin **SH** 🐾
(936) 634-3351. **$86-$96.** 2119 S 1st St. US 59, exit Carriageway northbound, 0.3 mi s of jct S Loop 287 and US 59 business route. Ext corridors. **Pets:** Small, other species. Service with restrictions.

MADISONVILLE

Western Lodge **M**
(936) 348-7654. **$35-$50, 3 day notice.** 2007 E Main St. I-45, exit 142, 0.3 mi w. Ext corridors. **Pets:** Accepted.

MANSFIELD

Comfort Inn **SH**
(817) 453-8848. **$74-$79.** 175 N Hwy 287. US 287S, exit E Broad St. Int corridors. **Pets:** Accepted.

MARATHON

The Gage Hotel **CI**
(432) 386-4205. **$69-$189, 3 day notice.** Hwy 90. US 90; center. Ext/int corridors. **Pets:** Accepted.

MARBLE FALLS

Best Western Marble Falls Inn **SH**
(830) 693-5122. **$49-$119.** 1403 Hwy 281 N. 0.4 mi n of jct SR 281 and FM 1431. Ext/int corridors. **Pets:** Medium, other species. $10 one-time fee/pet. Designated rooms, service with restrictions, crate.

MARSHALL

Best Western Executive Inn **SH**
(903) 935-0707. **$69-$89.** 5201 E End Blvd S. I-20, exit 617, 0.4 mi n on US 59. Ext corridors. **Pets:** Small. $15 daily fee/pet. Designated rooms, service with restrictions, supervision.

La Quinta Inn & East Texas Conference Center **SH**
(903) 927-0009. **$79-$82.** 5301 E End Blvd S. I-20, exit 617, just n on US 59. Int corridors. **Pets:** Other species. Service with restrictions, supervision.

Motel 6 Marshall #422 **M**
(903) 935-4393. **$35-$45.** 300 I-20 E. I-20, exit 617, just e on access road. Ext corridors. **Pets:** Accepted.

MCALLEN

Drury Inn **SH**
(956) 687-5100. **$59-$101.** 612 W Expwy 83. US 83, exit 2nd St, northwest frontage road. Int corridors. **Pets:** Large, other species. Service with restrictions, supervision.

Drury Suites-McAllen **SH**
(956) 682-3222. **$86-$120.** 228 W Expwy 83. At US 83 and 6th St. Int corridors. **Pets:** Large, other species. Service with restrictions, supervision.

Hampton Inn-McAllen **SH**
(956) 682-4900. **$72-$109.** 300 W Expwy 83. US 83, exit 2nd St, northwest frontage road. Int corridors. **Pets:** Accepted.

La Quinta Inn McAllen **SH**
(956) 687-1101. **Call for rates.** 1100 S 10th St. 1.5 mi s on SR 336 (S 10th St); just n of jct US 83. Ext corridors. **Pets:** Service with restrictions.

Posada Ana Inn **SH**
(956) 631-6700. **$50-$76.** 620 W Expwy 83. US 83, exit 2nd St, on northwest frontage road. Int corridors. **Pets:** Large, other species. Service with restrictions, supervision.

Residence Inn by Marriott **SH**
(956) 994-8626. **$104.** 220 W Expwy 83. US 83, exit 2nd St, just w, then just n on 2nd St. Int corridors. **Pets:** Accepted.

Super 8 Motel **SH**
(956) 682-1190. **$50.** 1420 E Jackson Ave. US 83, exit Jackson Ave/ Sam Houston St, just s. Int corridors. **Pets:** Accepted.

MEMPHIS

Executive Inn **M**
(806) 259-3583. **$45-$343, 7 day notice.** 1600 Boykin Dr. On US 287, 1.3 mi n of jct SR 256. Ext corridors. **Pets:** Small. $5 daily fee/pet. No service, supervision.

MIDLAND

Best Western Atrium Inn **SH**
(432) 694-7774. **$53-$71.** 3904 W Wall St. I-20, exit 134, 1 mi n on Midkiff Rd, 0.3 mi w on I-20 business route. Ext/int corridors. **Pets:** $10 daily fee/pet. Service with restrictions, supervision.

Comfort Inn-Midland **SH**
(432) 683-1111. **$74-$104.** 902 I-20 W. I-20, exit 136. Int corridors. **Pets:** Accepted.

▼▼▼ Holiday Inn SH
(432) 697-3181. **$79-$150.** 4300 W Wall St. I-20, exit 134 (Midkiff Rd), 1 mi n to I-20 business loop, then 0.7 mi w. Ext/int corridors. **Pets:** Large. $25 one-time fee/room. Designated rooms, service with restrictions, crate.
[ASK] [S⊅] [✕] [📶] [🖥] [🍴] [⊒] [⊠]

▲▲▲ ▼▼▼▼ La Quinta Inn Midland SH
(432) 697-9900. **$63-$79.** 4130 W Wall St. I-20, exit 131, 0.9 mi n on SR 250 Loop to exit 1A; 1.2 mi e on I-20 business route. Ext corridors. **Pets:** Other species. Service with restrictions, supervision.
[SAVE] [S⊅] [✕] [🖥] [📶] [🖥] [⊒]

▼▼▼ Plaza Inn SH
(432) 686-8733. **$80-$110.** 4108 N Big Spring St. I-20, exit 144, 6.1 mi on SR 250 Loop to SR 349 (Big Spring St), just s on SR 349. Ext corridors. **Pets:** Accepted.
[ASK] [S⊅] [✕] [🖥] [📶] [🖥] [⊒]

▲▲▲ ▼▼▼ Ramada Limited SH
(432) 699-4144. **$59-$69.** 3100 W Wall St. 2 mi w on I-20 business loop. Int corridors. **Pets:** Medium. $7 daily fee/pet. Service with restrictions, supervision.
[SAVE] [S⊅] [✕] [📶] [🖥] [⊒]

▲▲▲ ▼▼▼ Sleep Inn SH
(432) 689-6822. **$64-$79.** 3828 W Wall St. I-20, exit 134 (Midkiff Rd), 1 mi n to Wall St, then just w. Int corridors. **Pets:** Accepted.
[SAVE] [S⊅] [✕] [🖥] [📶] [🖥] [⊒]

MINERAL WELLS

▲▲▲ ▼▼▼▼ Best Western Clubhouse Inn & Suites SH
(940) 325-2270. **$75-$95.** 4410 Hwy 180 E. Jct US 180 and SR 1195; in East Mineral Wells. Int corridors. **Pets:** Other species. $15 one-time fee/room. Service with restrictions.
[SAVE] [S⊅] [✕] [🖥M] [🖥] [📶] [🖥] [⊒]

MISSION

▼▼▼▼ Hawthorn Suites Ltd SH
(956) 519-9696. **$89-$99.** 3700 Plantation Grove Blvd. US 83, exit Sharyland Rd, 2.1 mi s to Plantation Grove Blvd. Ext corridors. **Pets:** Medium. $35 one-time fee/room. Service with restrictions, supervision.
[ASK] [S⊅] [✕] [🖥] [⊒]

MONAHANS

▲▲▲ ▼▼▼ Best Western Colonial Inn M
(432) 943-4345. **$45-$58.** 702 W I-20. I-20, exit 80, just s. Ext/int corridors. **Pets:** Accepted.
[SAVE] [S⊅] [✕] [🖥] [📶] [🖥] [⊒]

MOUNT PLEASANT

▲▲▲ ▼▼▼▼ Best Western Mt. Pleasant Inn SH
(903) 572-5051. **$74-$84.** 102 Burton St. I-30 and Business Rt US 271, exit 162. Ext corridors. **Pets:** Small. $10 daily fee/room. Designated rooms, service with restrictions, supervision.
[SAVE] [S⊅] [✕] [🖥] [📶] [🖥] [⊒]

▼▼▼▼ Holiday Inn Express Hotel & Suites SH
(903) 577-3800. **$89.** 2306 Greenhill Rd. I-30, exit 162, just n. Int corridors. **Pets:** Accepted.
[ASK] [S⊅] [✕] [🖥M] [🖥] [📶] [🖥] [⊒]

MOUNT VERNON

▲▲▲ ▼▼▼ Super 8 Motel of Mount Vernon SH ❀
(903) 588-2882. **$50-$60.** 401 W I-30. I-30, exit 146 (SR 37). Ext corridors. **Pets:** $5 daily fee/pet. Service with restrictions, supervision.
[SAVE] [S⊅] [✕] [🖥] [📶] [🖥]

MULESHOE

▲▲▲ ▼▼▼ Economy Inn M
(806) 272-4261. **$45-$50.** 2701 W American Blvd. US 70/84, just w. Ext corridors. **Pets:** Medium. $20 deposit/pet. Designated rooms, service with restrictions, supervision.
[SAVE] [S⊅] [✕] [🖥]

NACOGDOCHES

▲▲▲ ▼▼▼▼ La Quinta Inn Nacogdoches SH
(936) 560-5453. **$70-$80.** 3215 South St. US 59, jct Loop 224 and US 59 business route, south of town. Ext corridors. **Pets:** Accepted.
[SAVE] [✕] [🖥] [🖥] [📶] [⊒]

NEDERLAND

▼▼ Best Western-Airport Inn M
(409) 727-1631. **$54-$65, 7 day notice.** 200 Memorial Hwy 69. US 69, 96 and 287, exit Nederland Ave. Ext corridors. **Pets:** Accepted.
[ASK] [S⊅] [✕] [🖥] [📶] [⊒]

NEW BOSTON

▲▲▲ ▼▼▼ Best Western Inn of New Boston SH
(903) 628-6999. **$64-$99.** 1024 N Center. I-30, exit 201, on westbound access road. Ext corridors. **Pets:** Medium, other species. $25 daily fee/pet. Service with restrictions.
[SAVE] [S⊅] [✕] [🖥] [🖥] [📶] [⊒]

NORTH RICHLAND HILLS

▼▼▼ Benison Inn & Suites SH
(817) 268-6879. **$69-$129.** 5151 Thaxton Pkwy. I-820, exit 21 (Holiday Ln), 0.5 mi w on north access road to Thaxton Pkwy, just n. Int corridors. **Pets:** Small. $10 daily fee/pet. Service with restrictions, supervision.
[ASK] [S⊅] [✕] [🖥] [📶] [⊒]

▼▼ Studio 6 #6034 SH
(817) 788-6000. **$45-$58.** 7450 NE Loop 820. I-820, exit 21 (Holiday Ln), 0.4 mi e on south access road. Ext corridors. **Pets:** Accepted.
[S⊅] [✕] [🖥] [🖥] [🖥] [📶]

ODEM

▲▲▲ ▼▼▼ Days Inn-Odem M
(361) 368-2166. **$60-$120.** 1505 Voss Ave (US 77). US 77, 1 mi s of jct 631. Ext corridors. **Pets:** Accepted.
[SAVE] [S⊅] [✕] [🖥] [⊒]

ODESSA

▼▼ Best Western Garden Oasis SH
(432) 337-3006. **$74-$84.** 110 W I-20. Jct I-20 and US 385, exit 116. Ext/int corridors. **Pets:** Accepted.
[ASK] [S⊅] [✕] [🖥] [🖥] [📶] [🖥] [🍴] [⊒] [⊠]

▲▲▲ ▼▼▼ Days Inn SH
(432) 335-8000. **$60-$65, 14 day notice.** 3075 E Business Loop 20. I-20, exit 121, 0.7 mi n on Loop 338, then 0.5 mi w. Int corridors. **Pets:** $25 deposit/room. Service with restrictions, crate.
[SAVE] [S⊅] [✕] [🖥] [⊒]

▼▼▼▼ La Quinta Inn Odessa SH
(432) 333-2820. **$69-$79.** 5001 E Business Loop I-20. I-20, exit 121, 0.8 mi n on Loop 338, then just w. Ext corridors. **Pets:** Accepted.
[ASK] [✕] [🖥] [🖥] [📶] [⊒]

▲▲▲ ▼▼▼ MCM Grande Hotel SH
(432) 362-2311. **$63-$75, 3 day notice.** 6201 E Business I-20. I-20, exit 121, 0.8 mi n on Loop 338, then 1 mi e. Ext/int corridors. **Pets:** Other species. Service with restrictions, supervision.
[SAVE] [✕] [🖥] [🖥] [📶] [🖥] [🍴] [⊒] [⊠]

▼ Motel 6 Odessa #439 **M**
(432) 333-4025. **$35-$45.** 200 E I-20 Service Rd. I-20, exit 116, on eastbound frontage road. Ext corridors. **Pets:** Accepted.
🛆 ⊇

AAA ▼▼ Quality Inn **SH**
(432) 333-3931. **$69-$129.** 3001 E Business I-20. I-20, exit 121, 0.7 mi n on Loop 338, then 0.5 mi w. Ext/int corridors. **Pets:** Service with restrictions.
SAVE 🛆 ✕ 🖥 💻 ⊇ ✕

OZONA

AAA ▼▼ Best Value Inn **M**
(325) 392-2631. **$49-$59.** 820 11th St. I-10, exit 365 westbound to SR 163, 1 mi n; exit 363 eastbound to Loop 466, 2 mi e. Ext corridors. **Pets:** Small, other species. $5 one-time fee/pet. Designated rooms, service with restrictions, crate.
SAVE 🛆 ✕

AAA ▼▼ Travelodge **M**
(325) 392-2656. **$50-$55.** 8 11th St. I-10, exit 368 westbound, 2 mi w; exit 365 eastbound to Loop 466, 1 mi e. Ext corridors. **Pets:** Other species. $5 daily fee/pet. Service with restrictions, supervision.
SAVE 🛆 ✕ 🖥 💻 ⊇

PALESTINE

AAA ▼▼ Best Western Palestine Inn **SH**
(903) 723-4655. **$52-$70.** 1601 W Palestine Ave. Jct US 287/SR 19, 0.7 mi sw on US 79. Ext corridors. **Pets:** Small. Service with restrictions, supervision.
SAVE 🛆 ✕ 🖑 🖥 💻 ▮▮ ⊇

PARIS

AAA ▼▼ Best Western Inn of Paris **SH**
(903) 785-5566. **$54-$63.** 3755 NE Loop 286. Jct US 82 and E Loop 286, just n. Ext corridors. **Pets:** Medium. $10 daily fee/pet. Service with restrictions, crate.
SAVE 🛆 ✕ 🗆 🖑 🖥 💻 ⊇

PECOS

AAA ▼▼ Best Western Swiss Clock Inn **M**
(432) 447-2215. **$62-$64.** 133 S Frontage Rd. I-20 W. 1 mi w of jct US 285; 1 mi e of jct I-20 and SR 17, exit 40. Ext corridors. **Pets:** Small. $10 one-time fee/pet. Designated rooms, service with restrictions, supervision.
SAVE 🛆 ✕ 🗆 🖑 🖥 💻 ▮▮ ⊇

AAA ▼▼ LAURA LODGE **M**
(432) 445-4924. **$45-$55.** 1000 E Business 20. I-20, exit 42 (US 285), 1 mi nw to Business Rt I-20, then 0.5 mi e. Ext corridors. **Pets:** Small. $10 daily fee/pet. Designated rooms, service with restrictions, supervision.
SAVE 🛆 ✕ ⊇

AAA ▼▼ Oak Tree Inn **SH**
(432) 447-0180. **$64-$91.** 22 N Frontage Rd. I-20, exit 42, just w on north access road. Int corridors. **Pets:** Accepted.
SAVE 🛆 ✕ 🗆 🖑 🖥

▼▼ Quality Inn **SH**
(432) 445-5404. **Call for rates.** 4002 S Cedar St. Jct I-20 and US 285. Int corridors. **Pets:** Accepted.
✕ 🖥 💻 ▮▮ ⊇

PHARR

AAA ▼▼▼ Ramada Limited Suites **SH**
(956) 702-3330. **$65-$70.** 1130 E Expwy 83. Jct US 83 Expwy, exit I Rd. Ext corridors. **Pets:** Accepted.
SAVE 🛆 ✕ 🖑 🖥 💻 ⊇

PLAINVIEW

AAA ▼▼▼ Best Western Conestoga **SH**
(806) 293-9454. **$60-$100.** 600 N I-27. I-27, exit 49, just s of US 70, on eastbound access road. Ext corridors. **Pets:** Accepted.
SAVE 🛆 ✕ 🗆 🖥 💻 ⊇

▼▼▼ Holiday Inn Express Hotel & Suites **SH**
(806) 296-9900. **$90.** 4213 W 13th St. I-27, exit 49 northbound, just w to Mesa, then just n; exit 50 southbound, just s to 13th St, then just w. Int corridors. **Pets:** Very small. $20 one-time fee/room. No service, supervision.
ASK 🛆 ✕ 🖑M 🖑 🖥 💻 ⊇

▼▼ Plainview Hotel **SH**
(806) 293-4181. **Call for rates.** 4005 Olton Rd. I-27, exit 49. Ext/int corridors. **Pets:** Accepted.
✕ 🖥 💻 ⊇

PORT ARANSAS

▼▼ Captain's Quarters Inn **M** 🐾
(361) 749-6005. **$59-$129.** 235 W Cotter. Just w of N Alister St. Ext corridors. **Pets:** Medium, dogs only. $10 daily fee/room. Service with restrictions, supervision.
ASK 🛆 ✕ 🖑 🖥 ⊇

PORT ISABEL

▼▼ Southwind Inn **M**
(956) 943-3392. **$35-$130, 3 day notice.** 600 Davis St. Queen Isabella Cswy to Musina, 3 blks n. Ext corridors. **Pets:** Accepted.
ASK ✕ 🖥 💻 ⊇

PORTLAND

AAA ▼▼▼ Comfort Inn **SH**
(361) 643-2222. **$75-$100.** 1703 N Hwy 181. US 181 W access road, exit FM 3239 northbound; exit Lang St southbound. Ext corridors. **Pets:** Medium, other species. $5 daily fee/pet. Service with restrictions.
SAVE 🛆 ✕ 🖥 💻 ⊇ ✕

POST

▼▼ Best Western Post Inn **SH**
(806) 495-9933. **$71-$78.** 1011 N Broadway. 1 mi n on US 84. Int corridors. **Pets:** Small. $50 deposit/pet, $15 daily fee/pet. Designated rooms, service with restrictions, supervision.
ASK 🛆 ✕ 🖑 🖥 💻 ⊇

ROBSTOWN

AAA ▼▼▼ Days Inn **SH**
(361) 387-9416. **$55-$95.** 320 Hwy 77 S. On US 77, 1 mi s. Ext corridors. **Pets:** Accepted.
SAVE ✕ 🖥 ⊇

ROCKPORT

AAA ▼▼▼▼ Laguna Reef Hotel **CO**
(361) 729-1742. **$85-$295.** 1021 Water St. 0.5 mi s, just e of Business Rt SR 35; entrance on S Austin St. Ext corridors. **Pets:** Accepted.
SAVE 🛆 ✕ 🖥 💻 ⊇ ✕

AAA ▼▼▼ The Village Inn **M**
(361) 729-6370. **$55-$70.** 503 N Austin St. Just w of jct SR 35 and Business Rt SR 35. Ext corridors. **Pets:** $10 daily fee/pet. Designated rooms, service with restrictions, supervision.
SAVE 🛆 ✕ 🖥 💻 ⊇

ROUND ROCK

AAA ▽▽▽▽ Baymont Inn & Suites Austin-Round Rock 🆂🅷
(512) 246-2800. **$59-$69.** 150 Parker Dr. I-35, exit 250, on west frontage road. Int corridors. **Pets:** Accepted.
🆂🅰🆅🅴 🆂 ✕ 🅼 📶 🅫 🛏 🖵 🏊

AAA ▽▽▽ Best Western Executive Inn 🆂🅷
(512) 255-3222. **$49-$79.** 1851 N I-35. I-35, exit 253 northbound; exit 253A U-turn southbound. Ext corridors. **Pets:** $5 daily fee/room. Service with restrictions.
🆂🅰🆅🅴 🆂 ✕ 🅼 🅫 🛏 🖵 🏊

▽▽▽ Candlewood Suites 🆂🅷 🐾
(512) 828-0899. **$55-$119.** 521 S I-35. I-35, exit 252A, just n on northbound frontage road. Int corridors. **Pets:** Other species. $50 one-time fee/room. Service with restrictions.
🅰🆂🅺 🆂 ✕ 🅫 🛏 🖵

▽▽▽ Days Inn and Suites 🆂🅷
(512) 246-0055. **$59-$129.** 1802 S I-35. I-35, exit 251, just s. Ext/int corridors. **Pets:** Accepted.
🅰🆂🅺 🆂 ✕ 🅫 🛏 🖵 🏊

AAA ▽▽▽▽ La Quinta Inn Austin (Round Rock) 🆂🅷
(512) 255-6666. **$79-$89.** 2004 I-35 N. I-35, exit 254, on west frontage road. Int corridors. **Pets:** Other species. Service with restrictions, supervision.
🆂🅰🆅🅴 ✕ 📶 🛏 🖵 🏊

AAA ▽▽ Red Roof Inn 🆂🅷
(512) 310-1111. **$45-$65.** 1990 I-35 N. I-35, exit 254, on west frontage road. Int corridors. **Pets:** Accepted.
✕ 🅫 🛏 🏊

▽▽▽ Residence Inn by Marriott Austin Round Rock 🆂🅷
(512) 733-2400. **$107.** 2505 S I-35. I-35, exit 250 southbound; exit 251 northbound, on east frontage road. Int corridors. **Pets:** Other species. $75 one-time fee/room. Service with restrictions, crate.
🅰🆂🅺 ✕ 🅼 📶 🅫 🛏 🖵 🏊 ✕

▽▽▽ Staybridge Suites Austin-Round Rock 🆂🅷
(512) 733-0942. **$79-$159.** 520 I-35 S. I-35, exit 252B northbound; exit 252AB southbound, on west frontage road. Int corridors. **Pets:** Accepted.
🅰🆂🅺 🆂 ✕ 🅼 📶 🅫 🛏 🖵 🏊

SAN ANGELO

AAA ▽▽▽ Benchmark Comfort Inn 🆂🅷
(325) 944-2578. **$65-$70.** 2502 Loop 306. Loop 306, exit Knickebocker Rd. Ext corridors. **Pets:** Small. Service with restrictions, supervision.
🆂🅰🆅🅴 🆂 ✕ 🛏 🖵 🏊

AAA ▽▽▽ Best Value Inn 🅼
(325) 653-1323. **$50-$60.** 1601 S Bryant Blvd. US 87 and 277 at Ave L. Ext/int corridors. **Pets:** Small, dogs only. $25 deposit/pet, $2 daily fee/pet. Service with restrictions, supervision.
🆂🅰🆅🅴 ✕ 🛏 🖵 🏊

AAA ▽▽▽ Best Western San Angelo 🆂🅷
(325) 223-1273. **$70-$75.** 3017 W Loop 306. Loop 306, exit College Hills Blvd, just s. Ext corridors. **Pets:** Other species. Service with restrictions.
🆂🅰🆅🅴 🆂 ✕ 🅫 🛏 🖵 🏊

AAA ▽▽▽ Days Inn San Angelo 🆂🅷
(325) 658-6594. **$55-$70.** 4613 S Jackson St. Jct US US 87 and Jackson St. Ext corridors. **Pets:** Small. Service with restrictions, supervision.
🆂🅰🆅🅴 🆂 ✕ 🛏 🖵 🍴 🏊

AAA ▽▽▽▽ Holiday Inn Convention Center Hotel 🆂🅷
(325) 658-2828. **$119-$500.** 441 Rio Concho Dr. US 87 to Concho Ave, 0.5 mi e; downtown. Int corridors. **Pets:** Accepted.
🆂🅰🆅🅴 🆂 ✕ 📶 🛏 🖵 🍴 🏊

AAA ▽▽▽ Howard Johnson San Angelo 🆂🅷
(325) 653-2995. **$62-$74.** 415 W Beauregard. Just w on US 67 business route at US 87 southbound. Ext/int corridors. **Pets:** Accepted.
🆂🅰🆅🅴 🆂 ✕ 🛏 🖵 🍴 🏊

AAA ▽▽▽▽ La Quinta Inn San Angelo (Conference Center) 🆂🅷
(325) 949-0515. **$80-$90.** 2307 Loop 306. Loop 306, exit Knickerbocker Rd, just s. Ext corridors. **Pets:** Accepted.
🆂🅰🆅🅴 ✕ 📶 🛏 🖵 🏊

▽▽ Motel 6 San Angelo #229 🅼
(325) 658-8061. **$41-$53.** 311 N Bryant Blvd. Just n on US 87. Ext corridors. **Pets:** Accepted.
🆂 ✕ 🅫 🛏 🖵 🏊

SAN ANTONIO METROPOLITAN AREA

ELMENDORF

AAA ▽▽▽ Comfort Inn & Suites Braunig Lake 🆂🅷
(210) 633-1833. **$50-$89.** 13800 I-37. I-37, exit 130 (Donop, Southton Rd), on northbound access lane. Ext corridors. **Pets:** Other species. $5 daily fee/room. Service with restrictions, crate.
🆂🅰🆅🅴 🆂 ✕ 🛏 🖵 🏊

FLORESVILLE

AAA ▽▽▽▽ Best Western Floresville Inn 🆂🅷
(830) 393-0443. **$60-$89.** 1720 S 10th St. US 181, just s of downtown. Ext corridors. **Pets:** Small. $10 daily fee/room. Service with restrictions, crate.
🆂🅰🆅🅴 🆂 ✕ 🛏 🖵 🏊

LIVE OAK

▽▽▽▽ La Quinta Inn San Antonio (I-35 North at Toepperwein) 🆂🅷
(210) 657-5500. **$75-$115.** 12822 I-35 N. I-35, exit 170B (Toepperwein), on northbound access road. Ext/int corridors. **Pets:** Other species. Service with restrictions, crate.
🅰🆂🅺 ✕ 🅼 🛏 🖵 🏊

NEW BRAUNFELS

AAA ▽▽▽▽ Best Western Inn & Suites 🆂🅷
(830) 625-7337. **$49-$139.** 1493 I-35 N. I-35, exit 190, on southbound access lane. Ext/int corridors. **Pets:** Accepted.
🆂🅰🆅🅴 🆂 ✕ 🅫 🖵 🏊

▽▽▽▽ Executive Inn & Suites 🆂🅷
(830) 625-3932. **$39-$199.** 808 Hwy 46 S. I-35, exit 189, 0.4 mi e. Ext corridors. **Pets:** Accepted.
🅰🆂🅺 🆂 ✕ 🅼 🅫 🛏 🖵 🏊

▽▽▽ Holiday Inn 🆂🅷
(830) 625-8017. **$79-$199.** 1051 I-35 E. I-35, exit 189, on southbound access road. Ext corridors. **Pets:** Accepted.
🅰🆂🅺 🆂 ✕ 🅼 🛏 🖵 🍴 🏊

AAA ▽▽▽ Rodeway Inn 🆂🅷
(830) 629-6991. **$49-$89, 3 day notice.** 1209 I-35 E. I-35, exit 189, on southbound access road. Ext corridors. **Pets:** Medium, dogs only. $25 one-time fee/room. No service, supervision.
🆂🅰🆅🅴 🆂 ✕ 🛏 🖵 🏊

▼▼ Super 8 Motel-New Braunfels **M**
(830) 629-1155. **$44-$129.** 510 Hwy 46 S. I-35, exit 189 (SR 46), just e.
Ext corridors. **Pets:** $10 daily fee/pet. Service with restrictions.
(ASK) (S/D) (X) ⊟ ⊡ ⊇

SAN ANTONIO

(AAA) ▼▼▼ Alamo Travelodge **SH** ✿
(210) 222-1000. **$45-$100.** 405 Broadway. US 281, exit Broadway. Ext
corridors. **Pets:** Medium, dogs only. $5 daily fee/pet. Designated rooms,
service with restrictions.
(SAVE) (S/D) (X) ⊟ ⊡ ⊡ (YI) ⊇

(AAA) ▼▼▼ AmeriSuites (San Antonio/Airport) **SH**
(210) 930-2333. **$79-$109.** 7615 Jones Maltberger Rd. US 281, exit
Jones Maltsberger Rd, in Loop 410. Int corridors. **Pets:** Accepted.
(SAVE) (S/D) (X) (&') ⊟ ⊡ ⊇

(AAA) ▼▼▼ AmeriSuites (San Antonio/Northwest) **SH**
(210) 561-0099. **$90.** 4325 AmeriSuites Dr. I-10, exit Wurzbach Rd, 0.5
mi westbound frontage road. Int corridors. **Pets:** Accepted.
(SAVE) (X) (&M) (🌭) (&') ⊟ ⊡ ⊇

(AAA) ▼▼▼ AmeriSuites (San Antonio/Riverwalk) **SH**
(210) 227-6854. **$125-$152.** 601 S St. Mary's St. I-35, exit Durango St,
0.9 mi e. Int corridors. **Pets:** Small, other species. $10 daily fee/pet.
Service with restrictions, crate.
(SAVE) (S/D) (X) (&') ⊟ ⊡ ⊇

(AAA) ▼▼▼ Arbor House Suites Bed & Breakfast **BB**
(210) 472-2005. **$125-$225, 3 day notice.** 109 Arciniega St. Just n of
Durango St; near La Villita Historic District. Ext/int corridors.
Pets: Small.
(SAVE) (S/D) (X) ⊟ ⊡

(AAA) ▼▼▼ Best Western Fiesta Inn **SH**
(210) 696-2400. **$49-$139.** 13535 I-10 W. I-10, exit 557 westbound; exit
558 eastbound, on westbound access road. Ext corridors.
Pets: Accepted.
(SAVE) (S/D) (X) (&') ⊟ ⊡ ⊇

(AAA) ▼▼▼ Best Western Ingram Park Inn **SH**
(210) 520-8080. **$49-$139.** 6855 NW Loop 410. I-410, exit 10 westbound; exit 11 eastbound, on westbound access road. Ext corridors.
Pets: Accepted.
(SAVE) (S/D) (X) ⊟ ⊡ ⊇

(AAA) ▼▼▼ Best Western Lackland Inn & Suites **SH**
(210) 675-9690. **$56-$74.** 6815 Hwy 90 W. I-410, US 90 to Military Dr,
0.5 mi e on westbound access road. Ext corridors. **Pets:** Medium. $25
one-time fee/pet. Service with restrictions, crate.
(SAVE) (S/D) (X) ⊟ ⊡ ⊇

▼▼ Best Western-Northeast **SH**
(210) 599-0999. **$79-$159.** 11939 N I-35. I-35, exit 170, on southbound
access road, 0.5 mi s to Judson Rd exit. Ext corridors. **Pets:** Very
small. $10 daily fee/pet. No service, crate.
(ASK) (S/D) (X) (&') ⊟ ⊡ ⊇

▼▼▼ Best Western Posada Ana Inn-San Antonio
Airport **SH**
(210) 342-1400. **$73-$120.** 8600 Jones Maltsberger Rd. I-410, exit 21A
(Jones Maltsberger Rd), 0.5 mi s. Int corridors. **Pets:** Medium. Service
with restrictions, crate.
(ASK) (X) ⊟ ⊡ ⊇

(AAA) ▼▼▼ Best Western Posada Ana Inn San Antonio
Medical Center **SH**
(210) 561-9300. **$60-$119.** 9411 Wurzbach Rd. I-10 NW, exit 561
(Wurzbach Rd), on eastbound access road. Int corridors. **Pets:** Small.
Service with restrictions.
(SAVE) (X) ⊟ ⊡ ⊇

(AAA) ▼▼▼ Brackenridge House B & B **BB**
(210) 271-3442. **$110-$200, 14 day notice.** 230 Madison. In King
William Historic District. Ext/int corridors. **Pets:** Accepted.
(SAVE) (X) ⊟ ⊡

▼▼▼ Candlewood Suites Hotel **SH**
(210) 615-0550. **$89-$109.** 9350 I-10 W. I-10 W, exit 561 (Wurzbach
Rd), eastbound access road, between Wurzbach Rd and Callaghan.
Int corridors. **Pets:** Accepted.
(ASK) (S/D) (X) (&') ⊟ ⊡ ⊇

▼▼▼ The Clarion Hotel Riverwalk **LH**
(210) 223-9461. **Call for rates.** 110 Lexington Ave. 0.3 mi s of jct
Lexington Ave and I-35. Int corridors. **Pets:** Accepted.
(X) ⊟ ⊡ (YI) ⊇

(AAA) ▼▼▼ Comfort Inn Sea World **SH**
(210) 684-8606. **$69-$139.** 4 Piano Pl. I-410, Exit Evers Rd westbound,
U-turn; exit 14 Callahan/Babocks Rd eastbound. Ext corridors.
Pets: Small. $10 daily fee/pet. Service with restrictions, supervision.
(SAVE) (S/D) (X) ⊟ ⊡ ⊇

▼▼▼ Days Inn-Downtown Laredo St **SH**
(210) 271-3334. **$49-$99.** 1500 I-35 S. I-10/35, exit 154 (Laredo St).
Ext/int corridors. **Pets:** Small. $25 one-time fee/pet. Designated rooms,
service with restrictions, crate.
(ASK) (S/D) (X) ⊟ ⊡ ⊇

▼▼▼ Days Inn Northeast **SH**
(210) 225-4040. **$39-$99.** 3443 I-35 N. I-35, exit 160 (Splashtown), on
southbound access road. Ext corridors. **Pets:** Small. $25 one-time fee/
pet. Designated rooms, service with restrictions, crate.
(ASK) (S/D) (X) ⊟ ⊡ ⊇

(AAA) ▼ Delux Inn **M**
(210) 271-3100. **$45-$99.** 3370 I 35 N. I-35, exit 160 (Splashtown), on
northbound access lane. Ext corridors. **Pets:** Medium, other species. $30
deposit/pet. Designated rooms, service with restrictions, supervision.
(SAVE) (S/D) (X) ⊇

▼▼▼ Drury Inn & Suites San Antonio Airport **SH**
(210) 308-8100. **$84-$119.** 95 NE Loop 410. I-410, exit 21A (Jones
Maltsberger Rd), 1.8 mi w of airport. Int corridors. **Pets:** Large, other
species. Service with restrictions, supervision.
(ASK) (X) (&M) (&') ⊟ ⊡ ⊇

▼▼▼ Drury Inn & Suites-San Antonio Northwest **SH**
(210) 561-2510. **$71-$140.** 9806 I-10 W. I-10, exit Wurzbach Rd, on
southeast corner. Int corridors. **Pets:** Large, other species. Service with
restrictions, supervision.
(ASK) (X) ⊟ ⊡ ⊇

▼▼▼ Drury Inn & Suites San Antonio Riverwalk **SH**
(210) 212-5200. **$94-$193.** 201 N St. Mary's St. Just s of College St. Int
corridors. **Pets:** Large, other species. Service with restrictions, supervision.
(ASK) (X) (&') ⊟ ⊡ (YI) ⊇

▼▼▼ Drury Inn San Antonio Northeast **SH**
(210) 654-1144. **$66-$100.** 8300 I-35 N. I-35, exit 165 (Walzem Rd),
northbound access road. Ext/int corridors. **Pets:** Large, other species.
Service with restrictions, supervision.
(ASK) (X) (&M) ⊟ ⊡ ⊇

(AAA) ▼▼ Econo Lodge Airport **M**
(210) 247-4774. **$57-$74.** 2635 NE Loop 410. I-410, exit 25B (Perrin-
Beitel Rd), on westbound access lane. Ext/int corridors. **Pets:** $25
one-time fee/room. Service with restrictions, crate.
(ASK) (S/D) (X) ⊇

(AAA) ▼▼▼ The Fairmount Historic Hotel **SH**
(210) 224-8800. **$199-$555.** 401 S Alamo St. Opposite convention
center and Hemisfair Plaza. Ext/int corridors. **Pets:** Accepted.
(SAVE) (S/D) (X) (🌭) ⊡ (YI) (X)

▼▼▼▼ Hampton Inn-San Antonio Airport 🆂🅷
(210) 366-1800. **$85-$130.** 8818 Jones Maltsberger Rd. I-410, exit 21B (Jones Maltsberger Rd), on westbound access road. Int corridors. **Pets:** Medium. Service with restrictions.
(A$K) (✕) (🗾) (💻) (🏊)

Ⓐ ▼▼▼▼ Hampton Inn Six Flags Area 🆂🅷 🐾
(210) 561-9058. **$79-$99.** 11010 I-10 W. I-10, exit 560 westbound; exit 559 (Huebner Rd) eastbound. Int corridors. **Pets:** $10 daily fee/room. Service with restrictions, supervision.
(SAVE) (S🗾) (✕) (🖼) (📶) (💻) (🏊)

Ⓐ ▼▼ Hill Country Inn & Suites 🆂🅷
(210) 599-4204. **$54-$77.** 2383 NE Loop 410. I-410, exit 24B (Perrin Beitel Rd) eastbound; exit 25A (Starcrest) westbound. Ext corridors. **Pets:** Other species. $75 one-time fee/room. Service with restrictions, crate.
(SAVE) (S🗾) (✕) (🖼) (&M) (🖼) (📶) (💻) (🏊) (✕)

▼▼▼◆ Hilton Palacio del Rio 🅻🅷
(210) 222-1400. **$109-$289.** 200 S Alamo St. Adjacent to convention center. Int corridors. **Pets:** Small. $25 one-time fee/pet. Service with restrictions, crate.
(✕) (&M) (📶) (💻) (🍴) (🏊)

▼▼▼◆ Hilton San Antonio Airport 🅻🅷
(210) 340-6060. **$79-$245.** 611 NW Loop 410. I-410, exit San Pedro Ave, on westbound access road. Int corridors. **Pets:** Accepted.
(A$K) (✕) (🗾) (🖼) (📶) (💻) (🍴) (🏊) (✕)

Ⓐ ▼▼▼◆ Holiday Inn Crockett Hotel 🅻🅷
(210) 225-6500. **$135-$145, 3 day notice.** 320 Bonham St. Center. Ext/int corridors. **Pets:** Accepted.
(SAVE) (S🗾) (✕) (📶) (💻) (🍴) (🏊)

Ⓐ ▼▼▼◆ Holiday Inn-Downtown-Market Square 🆂🅷
(210) 225-3211. **$115-$159.** 318 W Durango St. I-35, exit Durango St, 2 blks e. Int corridors. **Pets:** Accepted.
(SAVE) (S🗾) (✕) (&M) (🖼) (📶) (💻) (🍴) (🏊) (✕)

▼▼▼▼ Holiday Inn Express-San Antonio Airport 🆂🅷
(210) 308-6700. **$75-$126.** 91 NE Loop 410. I-410, exit 21A (Jones Maltsberger Rd) eastbound; exit 20B westbound, on westbound access road; between San Pedro Ave and Jones Maltsberger Rd. Int corridors. **Pets:** Accepted.
(A$K) (✕) (&M) (🖼) (📶) (💻) (🏊)

Ⓐ ▼▼▼◆ Holiday Inn Riverwalk 🆂🅷
(210) 224-2500. **$127-$177.** 217 N St. Mary's St. Houston St, just s. Int corridors. **Pets:** Accepted.
(SAVE) (S🗾) (✕) (💻) (🍴) (🏊)

Ⓐ ▼▼▼◆ Holiday Inn Select 🆂🅷
(210) 349-9900. **$79-$109.** 77 NE Loop 410. I-410, exit 20B (McCullough St), on westbound access road. Int corridors. **Pets:** Small. $100 deposit/room, $25 daily fee/room. Service with restrictions, supervision.
(SAVE) (S🗾) (✕) (&M) (🗾) (🖼) (📶) (💻) (🍴) (🏊)

Ⓐ ▼▼◆ HomeGate Studios & Suites 🆂🅷
(210) 342-4800. **$54-$99.** 11221 San Pedro Ave. I-410, exit US 281 (San Pedro Ave), 2.3 mi n on US 281, exit Nakoma, on west frontage road. Ext corridors. **Pets:** Small. $50 one-time fee/pet. Service with restrictions, supervision.
(A$K) (S🗾) (✕) (💻) (🏊) (✕)

▼▼◆ Homestead Studio Suites Hotel-San Antonio/Airport 🅼 🐾
(210) 491-9009. **$64-$79.** 1015 Central Pkwy S. I-410, exit US 281 (San Pedro Ave), 4 mi n on US 281, exit Bitters Rd, on northbound access road. Ext corridors. **Pets:** $75 one-time fee/room. Service with restrictions, supervision.
(A$K) (S🗾) (✕) (📶) (💻)

▼▼▼ Howard Johnson Express Inn Fiesta 🆂🅷
(210) 558-7152. **Call for rates.** 13279 I-10 W. I-10 NW, exit 557 westbound; exit 558 eastbound, on westbound access road. Ext corridors. **Pets:** Accepted.
(✕) (🖼) (📶) (💻) (🏊)

Ⓐ ▼▼▼ Knights Inn Windsor Park 🅼
(210) 646-6336. **$80-$110.** 6370 I-35 N. I-410/35, exit Rittiman Rd, on northbound access road. Ext corridors. **Pets:** Small. $10 one-time fee/pet. Service with restrictions, crate.
(SAVE) (S🗾) (✕) (🗾) (📶) (🏊)

Ⓐ ▼▼▼◆ La Mansion del Rio 🅻🅷
(210) 518-1000. **$219-$369, 3 day notice.** 112 College St. Just s on the Riverwalk. Ext/int corridors. **Pets:** Accepted.
(SAVE) (S🗾) (✕) (🗾) (📶) (💻) (🍴) (🏊)

Ⓐ ▼▼▼◆ La Quinta Inn & Suites San Antonio Airport 🆂🅷
(210) 342-3738. **$115-$125.** 850 Halm. I-410, exit US 281 S, southwest corner. Int corridors. **Pets:** Accepted.
(SAVE) (✕) (📶) (💻) (🏊)

Ⓐ ▼▼▼◆ La Quinta Inn San Antonio (Convention Center) 🆂🅷
(210) 222-9181. **$115-$189.** 1001 E Commerce St. 0.5 mi ne. Ext/int corridors. **Pets:** Small. Service with restrictions, supervision.
(SAVE) (✕) (📶) (💻) (🏊)

Ⓐ ▼▼▼▼ La Quinta Inn San Antonio (I-35 North @ Windsor Park Mall) 🆂🅷
(210) 653-6619. **$72-$111.** 6410 I-35 N. I-35, exit 163B northbound, on I-35 northbound access road; between Rittiman and Eisenhauer rds; exit 164A (Rittiman Rd) southbound. Ext corridors. **Pets:** Other species. Service with restrictions, supervision.
(SAVE) (✕) (📶) (💻) (🏊)

▼▼▼▼ La Quinta Inn San Antonio (Lackland) 🆂🅷
(210) 674-3200. **$75-$105.** 6511 Military Dr W. Southwest of jct US 90 and Military Dr W. Ext corridors. **Pets:** Accepted.
(A$K) (✕) (📶) (💻) (🏊)

Ⓐ ▼▼▼▼ La Quinta Inn San Antonio (Market Square) 🆂🅷
(210) 271-0001. **$88-$119.** 900 Dolorosa. I-10/35, exit Durango St, just n on Santa Rosa St, then just w on Nueva St. Ext corridors. **Pets:** Accepted.
(SAVE) (✕) (&M) (📶) (💻) (🏊)

Ⓐ ▼▼▼▼ La Quinta Inn San Antonio (SeaWorld/Ingram Park) 🆂🅷
(210) 680-8883. **$79-$129.** 7134 NW Loop 410. I-410, exit 10 (Culebra Rd), on eastbound access road. Ext corridors. **Pets:** Other species. Service with restrictions.
(SAVE) (✕) (&M) (📶) (💻) (🏊)

▼▼▼▼ La Quinta Inn San Antonio (South Park) 🆂🅷
(210) 922-2111. **$80-$110.** 7202 S Pan American Expwy. I-35, exit 150A (Military Dr) northbound; exit 150B southbound, southeast of jct I-35 and Military Dr SW. Ext corridors. **Pets:** Small. Service with restrictions, supervision.
(✕) (&M) (💻) (🏊)

▼▼▼▼ La Quinta Inn San Antonio (Vance Jackson) 🆂🅷 🐾
(210) 734-7931. **$69-$99.** 5922 I-10 W. I-10, exit 565B eastbound; exit 565C (Vance Jackson Rd) westbound, on eastbound access road. Ext corridors. **Pets:** Other species. Service with restrictions, crate.
(A$K) (✕) (📶) (💻) (🏊)

La Quinta Inn San Antonio
(Wurzbach) SH ❖
(210) 593-0338. **$82-$112.** 9542 I-10 W. I-10, exit Wurzbach Rd, just e on eastbound access road. Ext corridors. **Pets:** Other species. Service with restrictions, supervision.

Marriott Plaza San Antonio LH ❖
(210) 229-1000. **$179-$239.** 555 S Alamo St. Opposite convention center and Hemisfair Plaza. Int corridors. **Pets:** Large, other species. $25 one-time fee/room. Designated rooms, service with restrictions.

Marriott Riverwalk LH
(210) 224-4555. **$334.** 711 E Riverwalk. Opposite convention center and Hemisfair Plaza. Int corridors. **Pets:** Accepted.

Motel 6–1122 M
(210) 225-1111. **$45-$75.** 211 N Pecos St. I-10/35, exit 155 B (Pecos St), on I-10 E/35 S access road. Ext corridors. **Pets:** Small, other species. No service, supervision.

Motel 6–134 M
(210) 650-4419. **$35-$55.** 9503 I-35 N. I-35, exit 167A (Randolf Blvd) southbound; exit 167 (Starlight Terrace) northbound. Ext corridors. **Pets:** Other species. Service with restrictions, supervision.

Motel 6–651 M
(210) 673-9020. **$35-$75.** 2185 SW Loop 410. I-410, exit 7 (Marbach Rd), on westbound access road. Ext corridors. **Pets:** Small. No service, crate.

Motel 6 East #183 SH
(210) 333-1850. **$35-$55.** 138 N W W White Rd. I-10, exit 580 (W W White Rd), just off westbound access road. Ext corridors. **Pets:** Accepted.

Motel 6 Fort Sam Houston #1350 M
(210) 661-8791. **$39-$55.** 5522 N PanAm Expwy. I-35/410, exit 164 (Rittiman Rd), just s on northbound access lane, just off Goldfield St. Ext corridors. **Pets:** Accepted.

Motel 6 San Antonio #1188 M
(210) 653-8088. **$35-$55.** 4621 E Rittiman Rd. I-35, exit 164 (Rittiman Rd), on north side of Rittiman Rd. Ext corridors. **Pets:** Small. Service with restrictions, supervision.

Pear Tree Inn San Antonio Airport SH
(210) 366-9300. **$61-$100.** 143 NE Loop 410. Loop 410 W, exit 21 (Jones Maltsberger Rd), on westbound access road; between San Pedro Ave and Jones Maltsberger Rd. Int corridors. **Pets:** Large, other species. Service with restrictions, supervision.

Quality Inn & Suites SH
(210) 359-7200. **$39-$129.** 222 S W W White Rd. I-10, exit 580 (W W White Rd), 0.4 mi s. Ext corridors. **Pets:** Accepted.

Quality Inn & Suites Coliseum SH
(210) 224-3030. **$39-$114.** 3817 I-35 N. I-35, exit 161 (Binz-Engleman Rd), follow signs to I-35 S access road northbound, exit Binz-Engleman Rd, continue southbound. Int corridors. **Pets:** Small, other species. $25 one-time fee/pet. Service with restrictions, crate.

Quality Inn & Suites North Airport SH ❖
(210) 545-5400. **$79-$119.** 1505 Bexar Crossing. US 281, exit 1604 (Anderson Loop), on southbound access lane. Int corridors. **Pets:** Medium. $25 one-time fee/room. Designated rooms, service with restrictions, crate.

Quality Inn Northwest SH
(210) 736-1900. **$49-$129.** 6023 NW I-10 W. I-10, exit 565B eastbound; exit 565C (Vance Jackson Rd) westbound, just n. Ext corridors. **Pets:** Small. $25 one-time fee/pet. Designated rooms, service with restrictions, crate.

Red Roof Inn Lackland SH
(210) 675-4120. **$47-$73.** 6861 Hwy 90 W. Northeast jct of US 90 and Military Dr W; access via Renwick St, off Military Dr, just n of jct US 90. Ext corridors. **Pets:** Accepted.

Red Roof Inn-San Antonio Airport SH
(210) 340-4055. **$43-$64.** 333 Wolfe Rd. On southbound access road, just s of US 281 at Isom Rd. Ext/int corridors. **Pets:** Small. Service with restrictions, supervision.

Red Roof Inn San Antonio (Downtown) M
(210) 229-9973. **$55-$95.** 1011 E Houston St. I-37, exit 141 northbound; exit 141B southbound. Int corridors. **Pets:** Accepted.

Red Roof Inn San Antonio (NW-SeaWorld) SH
(210) 509-3434. **$42-$79.** 6880 NW Loop 410. I-410, exit 11 (Alamo Downs Pkwy), on eastbound access road. Ext/int corridors. **Pets:** Accepted.

Residence Inn Alamo Plaza SH ❖
(210) 212-5555. **$189.** 425 Bonham St. I-37/281, exit Commerce St, just w to Bowie St, then 4 blks n. Int corridors. **Pets:** Other species. $75 one-time fee/pet. Service with restrictions, crate.

Residence Inn by Marriott San Antonio Downtown/
Market Square SH ❖
(210) 231-6000. **$152-$197.** 628 S Santa Rosa. I-10/35, exit Durango St, 0.5 mi e. Int corridors. **Pets:** $75 one-time fee/room. Service with restrictions, crate.

Residence Inn NW/Six Flags SH
(210) 561-9660. **$99-$159.** 4041 Bluemel Rd. I-10, exit Wurzbach Rd, 0.3 mi w on eastbound access road. Ext corridors. **Pets:** Accepted.

Residence Inn San Antonio-Airport SH
(210) 805-8118. **$89-$109.** 1014 NE Loop 410. On Loop 410, exit Broadway St, 0.4 mi e on access road. Ext corridors. **Pets:** Accepted.

Rodeway Inn Downtown SH
(210) 223-2951. **$59-$99.** 900 N Main Ave. I-35, exit San Pedro/Main aves, northeast corner. Ext corridors. **Pets:** Small. $20 one-time fee/room. Service with restrictions, crate.

Rodeway Inn-Six Flags Fiesta SH
(210) 698-3991. **$45-$135.** 19793 I-10 W. I-10, exit 554 (Camp Bullis), on eastbound access road. Ext corridors. **Pets:** Medium. $10 daily fee/room. Service with restrictions, supervision.

▼▼▼▼ San Antonio Marriott Rivercenter LH
(210) 223-1000. **$334.** 101 Bowie St. Corner of Bowie and Commerce sts. Int corridors. **Pets:** Accepted.
⊠ 🛇 💻 🍴 ⊃ ⊠

Ⓐ ▼▼▼▼ Sheraton Gunter SH ❀
(210) 227-3241. **$199.** 205 E Houston St. Center. Int corridors. **Pets:** Medium, dogs only. Service with restrictions, crate.
SAVE SD ⊠ ✑ 💻 🍴 ⊃

▼▼▼▼ Staybridge Suites San Antonio-Airport SH
(210) 341-3220. **$99-$168.** 66 NE Loop 410. I-410, exit 20B (McCullough St), on eastbound access lane. Int corridors. **Pets:** Accepted.
ASK ⊠ ᴹ 🛇 💻 ⊃

▼▼▼▼ Staybridge Suites San Antonio NW-Colonnade SH
(210) 558-9009. **$98-$208.** 4320 Spectrum One. I-10 W, exit 560 (Wurzbach Rd), follow westbound access road through light, then just n. Int corridors. **Pets:** Accepted.
ASK SD ⊠ 🔧 🛇 💻 ⊃ ⊠

▼▼ Studio 6 #6046 M
(210) 691-0121. **$46-$69.** 11802 I-10 W. I-10, exit 558 (De Zavala Rd), on eastbound access road. Ext corridors. **Pets:** Other species. $10 daily fee/pet. Service with restrictions.
SD ⊠ 🔧 💻

▼▼ Studio 6 #6047 M
(210) 349-3100. **$46-$69.** 7719 Louis Pasteur Ct. Loop 410, 1.5 mi nw on Fredericksburg Rd to Louis Pasteur Ct. Ext corridors. **Pets:** Accepted.
SD ⊠ 🔧 💻

▼▼ Super 8 Motel Downtown North M
(210) 227-8888. **$38-$78.** 3617 N PanAm Expwy. I-35, exit 160 (Splashtown), on southbound access road. Ext corridors. **Pets:** Small. $50 deposit/pet, $8 daily fee/pet. Designated rooms, no service, supervision.
ASK SD ⊠ ᴹ 🛇 ⊃

▼▼ Super 8 Motel of San Antonio Airport SH
(210) 637-1033. **Call for rates.** 11027 I-35 N. I-35, exit 168 (Weidner Rd), on southbound access road. Int corridors. **Pets:** Accepted.
⊠ ⊃

▼▼ Super 8 Motel-Six Flags Fiesta SH
(210) 696-6916. **Call for rates.** 5319 Casa Bella. I-10, exit 557 westbound; exit 558 eastbound, on westbound access road. Int corridors. **Pets:** Accepted.
⊠ 🔧 🛇 ⊃

Ⓐ ▼▼ Wellesley Inn (San Antonio/Airport) SH
(210) 653-9110. **$49-$69.** 2635 NE Loop 410. I-410, exit 25B (Perrin-Beitel Rd), on westbound access lane. Ext/int corridors. **Pets:** $25 one-time fee/room. Service with restrictions.
SAVE SD ⊠ 🛇 💻 ⊃

▼▼▼▼ Westin Riverwalk Hotel LH ❀
(210) 224-6500. **$329.** 420 W Market St. 2 blks w of Navarro St. Int corridors. **Pets:** Medium. Service with restrictions, supervision.
ASK SD ⊠ ᴹ 🛇 🔧 💻 🍴 ⊃ ⊠

Ⓐ ▼▼▼▼ Woodfield Suites San Antonio-Downtown SH
(210) 212-5400. **$99-$159.** 100 W Durango Blvd. I-35, exit 155B (Durango Blvd), 3 blks e of jct E Flores St. Int corridors. **Pets:** Accepted.
SAVE SD ⊠ ᴹ 🛇 🔧 🛇 💻 ⊃ ⊠

SEGUIN

▼▼▼▼ Holiday Inn Seguin SH
(830) 372-0860. **$76-$110.** 2950 N 123 Bypass. I-10, exit 610 (SR 123). Ext corridors. **Pets:** Small. $25 deposit/room. Designated rooms, service with restrictions, supervision.
ASK SD ⊠ 🛇 💻 🍴 ⊃

▼▼ Super 8 Motel of Seguin SH
(830) 379-6888. **$50-$110.** 1525 N Hwy 46. I-10, exit 607 (SR 46), on eastbound access road. Int corridors. **Pets:** Medium. $10 daily fee/pet. Service with restrictions, supervision.
ASK SD ⊠ 🔧 🛇 💻

UNIVERSAL CITY

Ⓐ ▼▼ Clarion Suites Hotel SH
(210) 655-9491. **$79-$149.** 13101 E Loop, 1604 N. Loop 1604 at Pat Booker Rd; 0.8 mi e of I-35. Ext corridors. **Pets:** Medium. $25 one-time fee/room. Designated rooms, service with restrictions, crate.
SAVE SD ⊠ 🔧 💻 ⊃

END METROPOLITAN AREA

SANDERSON

Ⓐ ▼ Desert Air Motel M
(432) 345-2572. **$34-$39.** 806 W Oak. 0.5 mi w on US 90, just e of jct US 285. Ext corridors. **Pets:** Accepted.
SAVE SD 🛇

SAN MARCOS

Ⓐ ▼▼ Best Western San Marcos SH
(512) 754-7557. **$49-$119.** 917 I-35 N. I-35, exit 204B, on westside access road. Int corridors. **Pets:** Accepted.
SAVE SD ⊠ 🛇 💻 ⊃

Ⓐ ▼▼ Days Inn SH
(512) 353-5050. **$40-$125.** 1005 I-35 N. I-35, exit 205 northbound; exit 204B southbound, on southbound frontage road, jct SR 80. Ext corridors. **Pets:** Dogs only. $10 daily fee/pet. Designated rooms, service with restrictions, supervision.
SAVE SD ⊠ 🛇 ⊃

Ⓐ ▼▼▼ La Quinta Inn San Marcos SH
(512) 392-8800. **$75-$111.** 1619 I-35 N. I-35, exit 206 southbound, 0.5 mi s on west frontage road; exit northbound, 1 mi n to turnaround to west frontage road, then 1.5 mi s. Ext/int corridors. **Pets:** Accepted.
SAVE ⊠ ᴹ 🛇 🔧 🛇 💻 ⊃

Ⓐ ▼▼▼ Ramada Limited SH
(512) 395-8000. **$33-$169.** 1701 I-35 N. I-35, exit 206 southbound, 0.4 mi s on west frontage road; exit northbound, 1 mi n to turnaround for west frontage road, then 1.4 mi s. Ext corridors. **Pets:** Very small. $10 daily fee/pet. Service with restrictions, crate.
SAVE SD ⊠ 🛇 💻 ⊃

Ⓐ ▼▼ Red Roof Inn SH
(512) 754-8899. **$39-$129.** 817 I-35 N. I-35, exit 204B southbound; exit 205 northbound, on westside access road. Int corridors. **Pets:** Service with restrictions, supervision.
SAVE SD ⊠ 🔧 🛇 ⊃

SEALY

Ⓐ ▼▼▼ Best Western Inn of Sealy SH
(979) 885-3707. **$65.** 2107 Hwy 36 S. I-10, exit 720. Ext corridors. **Pets:** Accepted.
SAVE SD ⊠ 🔧 💻 ⊃

SEMINOLE

AAA ▽▽▽ **Raymond Motor Inn** M
(432) 758-3653. **$40-$45.** 301 W Ave A. 0.3 mi w on US 62 and 180. Ext corridors. **Pets:** Other species. $5 daily fee/pet. Service with restrictions, supervision.
SAVE S6 X 8 ⌷

AAA ▽▽▽ **Seminole Inn** M
(432) 758-9881. **$47-$57, 3 day notice.** 2200 Hobbs Hwy. 1.5 mi w on US 62 and 180. Ext corridors. **Pets:** Small. $5 daily fee/pet. Service with restrictions, supervision.
SAVE S6 X 8 ⌷ 🏊

SHAMROCK

AAA ▽▽▽ **Econo Lodge** M
(806) 256-2111. **$48-$65.** 1006 E 12th St. I-40, exit 164 westbound; exit 161 or 163 eastbound, just e of US 83. Ext corridors. **Pets:** Medium. $5 daily fee/pet. Service with restrictions, supervision.
SAVE S6 X 8 ⌷ 🏊

AAA ▽▽▽ **Irish Inn** SH
(806) 256-2106. **$57-$72.** 301 I-40 E. I-40, exit 163, 0.3 mi e on north service road. Ext/int corridors. **Pets:** Other species. $9 one-time fee/room. Service with restrictions, crate.
SAVE S6 X 🐾 8 ⌷ 🍴 🏊

AAA ▽▽ **Western Motel** M
(806) 256-3244. **$49-$59.** 104 E 12th St. Business Rt I-40 and US 83. Ext corridors. **Pets:** Medium. $5 daily fee/pet. Service with restrictions, supervision.
SAVE S6 X 🍴

SHERMAN

▽▽▽▽ **Comfort Suites of Sherman** SH
(903) 893-0499. **$89.** 2900 US Hwy 75 N. US 75, exit 63, 0.3 mi s of jct US 82. Int corridors. **Pets:** Very small. $20 one-time fee/room. Service with restrictions, supervision.
ASK S6 X 🐾 8 ⌷ 🏊

▽▽▽▽ **La Quinta Inn & Suites Sherman/Denison** SH
(903) 870-1122. **$92-$109.** 2912 US 75 N. US 75, exit 63, just sw of jct US 82. Int corridors. **Pets:** Accepted.
ASK X 🐾 8 ⌷ 🏊

SMITHVILLE

▽▽ **Pine Point Inn** SH
(512) 237-2040. **$60-$70.** 1503 Dorothy Nichols Ln. Jct SR 71 and Dorothy Nichols Ln. Ext corridors. **Pets:** Accepted.
ASK S6 X 8 🏊

SNYDER

▽▽▽ **Best Western Snyder Inn** M
(325) 574-2200. **$70.** 810 E Coliseum Dr. 1.5 mi w of US 84/80. Ext corridors. **Pets:** Medium. $25 one-time fee/room. Service with restrictions.
ASK S6 X 8 ⌷ 🏊

AAA ▽▽▽ **Purple Sage Motel** M
(325) 573-5491. **$54-$72.** 1501 E Coliseum Dr. 1 mi w on US 180 from jct US 84. Ext corridors. **Pets:** Accepted.
SAVE S6 X 8 ⌷ 🏊

SONORA

AAA ▽▽ **Best Value Inn-Twin Oaks Motel** M
(325) 387-2551. **$45-$50.** 1009 N Crockett Ave. I-10, exit 400 westbound; exit 399 eastbound, 0.5 mi e, then 0.3 mi s on US 277. Ext corridors. **Pets:** Accepted.
SAVE X 8

AAA ▽▽▽ **Days Inn** M
(325) 387-3516. **$59-$69.** 1312 N Service Rd. I-10, exit 400, just n. Ext corridors. **Pets:** Medium, other species. $5 daily fee/pet. Service with restrictions, crate.
SAVE S6 X 8 ⌷ 🍴 🏊

AAA ▽▽ **Holiday Host Motel** M
(325) 387-2532. **$42-$50.** 127 Loop 467 (Hwy 290). Loop 467, exit 404 westbound, 3 mi w; exit 399 eastbound, 3 mi e. Ext corridors. **Pets:** $5 deposit/pet. No service, supervision.
SAVE X 8 🏊

SOUTH PADRE ISLAND

AAA ▽▽▽ **Best Western Fiesta Isles Hotel** SH
(956) 761-4913. **$49-$199, 3 day notice.** 5701 Padre Blvd. 3 mi n of Queen Isabella Cswy. Ext corridors. **Pets:** Large. $25 deposit/room. Service with restrictions, supervision.
SAVE X 8 ⌷ 🏊

▽▽▽ **Days Inn** SH
(956) 761-7831. **$39-$159, 3 day notice.** 3913 Padre Blvd. 2.6 mi n of Queen Isabella Cswy. Ext corridors. **Pets:** Accepted.
ASK S6 X 8 🏊

AAA ▽▽▽ **Econo Lodge** SH
(956) 761-8500. **$29-$299, 7 day notice.** 3813 Padre Blvd. 2.6 mi n of Queen Isabella Cswy. Int corridors. **Pets:** Small, other species. $10 daily fee/pet. Service with restrictions, supervision.
SAVE S6 X 8 🏊

▽▽▽ **Howard Johnson Inn-Resort** SH
(956) 761-5658. **$39-$249.** 1709 Padre Blvd. SR 100, 0.9 mi n at corner of W Palm St. Int corridors. **Pets:** Other species. $25 one-time fee/room. Service with restrictions, supervision.
ASK S6 X ⌷M 🐾 8 🏊

▽▽▽ **La Copa Beach Resort** SH
(956) 761-6000. **$49-$299.** 350 Padre Blvd. Just s of Queen Isabella Cswy. Int corridors. **Pets:** Small. $10 daily fee/pet. Service with restrictions, supervision.
ASK S6 X 8 ⌷ 🏊

▽▽▽ **La Quinta Inn and Suites South Padre Island** SH
(956) 772-7000. **$49-$349.** 7000 Padre Blvd. I-77, exit SR 100, over Queen Isabella Cswy, 3 mi n. Int corridors. **Pets:** Small. $10 daily fee/pet. Service with restrictions, supervision.
ASK X ⌷M 🐾 8 ⌷ 🏊 ✕

AAA ▽▽▽ **Ramada Limited** SH
(956) 761-4097. **$59-$209.** 4109 Padre Blvd. 2 mi n of Queen Isabella Cswy. Ext corridors. **Pets:** Small, dogs only. $25 deposit/room, $10 one-time fee/room. Designated rooms, service with restrictions, supervision.
SAVE S6 X 8 ⌷ 🏊

▽▽▽ **Super 8 Motel** SH
(956) 761-6300. **$65-$200.** 4205 Padre Blvd. 2.7 mi n of Queen Isabella Cswy. Ext corridors. **Pets:** Accepted.
ASK S6 X ⌷M 🐾 8

▽▽ **The Tiki Condominium Hotel** CO
(956) 761-2694. **$86-$325, 3 day notice.** 6608 Padre Blvd. 3.8 mi n of Queen Isabella Cswy. Ext corridors. **Pets:** Accepted.
ASK S6 X 8 🏊 ✕

▽▽▽ **Travelodge** SH
(956) 761-4744. **$35-$300, 3 day notice.** 6200 Padre Blvd. 3 mi n of Queen Isabella Cswy. Ext corridors. **Pets:** Small. $10 daily fee/pet. Service with restrictions, supervision.
ASK S6 X ⌷M 8 ⌷ 🏊

STEPHENVILLE

▼▼▼▼ Holiday Inn Stephenville 🆂🅷
(254) 968-5256. **$89-$99.** 2865 W Washington St. 1.5 mi s on US 377/167. Ext corridors. **Pets:** Medium. $100 deposit/room. Service with restrictions, supervision.
🅰🆂🅺 ⊠ 🕐 🖥 💻 🍴 ⊇

SULPHUR SPRINGS

▼▼▼▼ Best Western Trail Dust Inn 🆂🅷
(903) 885-7515. **$89-$99.** 1521 Shannon Rd. Jct I-30 and Loop 301, exit 127. Ext/int corridors. **Pets:** Small, other species. $50 deposit/room. Service with restrictions, supervision.
🅰🆂🅺 🆂🔟 ⊠ ⌨ 🖥 💻 ⊇

◆◆◆ ▼▼▼▼ Comfort Suites 🆂🅷
(903) 438-0918. **$79-$94.** 1521 E Industrial Dr. I-30, exit 127, just n. Int corridors. **Pets:** Medium. Service with restrictions, supervision.
🆂🅰🆅🅴 🆂🔟 ⊠ 🖥 ⌨ 🖥 💻 ⊇

◆◆◆ ▼▼▼▼ Holiday Inn 🆂🅷
(903) 885-0562. **$63-$81.** 1495 E Industrial Dr. I-30, exit 127. Ext/int corridors. **Pets:** Accepted.
🆂🅰🆅🅴 🆂🔟 ⊠ 🖥 💻 🍴 ⊇

SWEETWATER

◆◆◆ ▼▼ Comfort Inn 🆂🅷
(325) 235-5234. **$69-$125.** 216 SE Georgia Ave. I-20, exit 244. Ext corridors. **Pets:** Small. $25 deposit/pet. Service with restrictions, supervision.
🆂🅰🆅🅴 🆂🔟 ⊠ 🕐 ⌨ 🖥 💻 ⊇

◆◆◆ ▼▼ Holiday Inn 🆂🅷
(325) 236-6887. **$59-$125.** 500 NW Georgia St. I-20, exit 244, just w of jct SR 70 on north access road. Ext/int corridors. **Pets:** Other species. $25 one-time fee/room. Service with restrictions, crate.
🆂🅰🆅🅴 🆂🔟 ⊠ 🖥 💻 🍴 ⊇

◆◆◆ ▼▼ Ranch House Motel & Restaurant 🆂🅷
(325) 236-6341. **$49-$65.** 301 SW Georgia Ave. I-20, exit 244, just w of jct SR 70 on south access road. Ext/int corridors. **Pets:** Very small. $5 daily fee/room. Designated rooms, service with restrictions, crate.
🆂🅰🆅🅴 🆂🔟 ⊠ 🖥 💻 🍴 ⊇

TEMPLE

▼▼ Days Inn 🆂🅷
(254) 774-9223. **$79.** 1104 N General Bruce Dr. I-35, exit 302 (Nugent Ave). Ext corridors. **Pets:** Accepted.
🅰🆂🅺 🆂🔟 ⊠ ⌨ 🖥 💻 ⊇

◆◆◆ ▼▼▼ Howard Johnson Express Inn & Suites 🆂🅷
(254) 778-5521. **$64.** 1912 S 31st St. 0.4 mi ne of jct Loop 363, US 190 and SR 36. Ext corridors. **Pets:** Accepted.
🆂🅰🆅🅴 🆂🔟 ⊠ 🖥 ⊇

◆◆◆ ▼▼▼▼ La Quinta Inn Temple 🆂🅷 🌸
(254) 771-2980. **$82-$92.** 1604 W Barton Ave. SR 53, just e; jct I-35 and US 81, exit 301. Ext/int corridors. **Pets:** Service with restrictions.
🆂🅰🆅🅴 ⊠ 🖥 💻 ⊇

▼▼ Motel 6–257 🆂🅷
(254) 778-0272. **$35-$45.** 1100 N General Bruce Dr. I-35, exit 302 (Nugent Ave), just s on access road, follow signs. Ext corridors. **Pets:** Accepted.
🆂🔟 ⊠ ⊇

◆◆◆ ▼▼▼ Super 8 Motel 🆂🅷
(254) 778-0962. **$49-$65, 3 day notice.** 5505 S General Bruce Dr. I-35, exit 297 (Midway Dr). Ext corridors. **Pets:** Accepted.
🆂🅰🆅🅴 🆂🔟 ⊠ 🖥 💻 ⊇

TERLINGUA

◆◆◆ ▼▼▼▼ Big Bend Motor Inn Ⓜ
(432) 371-2218. **$85-$87, 7 day notice.** 300 N Jim Wright Frwy. SR 118, 2 mi from entrance of Big Bend National Park. Ext corridors. **Pets:** Medium, dogs only. $5 daily fee/pet. Designated rooms, service with restrictions, supervision.
🆂🅰🆅🅴 ⊠ 🖥 💻

TEXARKANA

◆◆◆ ▼▼▼ Best Western Northgate Motor Lodge 🆂🅷
(903) 793-6565. **$58-$68.** 400 W 53rd St. I-30, exit 223B, on northwest frontage road. Int corridors. **Pets:** Medium. $20 one-time fee/room. Service with restrictions, supervision.
🆂🅰🆅🅴 🆂🔟 ⊠ 🖥 💻 ⊇

◆◆◆ ▼▼▼ Comfort Inn 🆂🅷
(903) 792-6688. **$69-$79.** 5105 State Line Ave. I-30, exit 223A, just sw. Ext corridors. **Pets:** Small. $25 one-time fee/room. Designated rooms, supervision.
🆂🅰🆅🅴 ⊠ 🖥 💻 ⊇

◆◆◆ ▼▼▼▼ Four Points Hotel Sheraton Texarkana 🆂🅷
(903) 792-3222. **$75-$87.** 5301 N State Line Ave. I-30, exit 223B. Int corridors. **Pets:** Small. $50 one-time fee/pet. Designated rooms, service with restrictions, crate.
🆂🅰🆅🅴 🆂🔟 ⊠ 🖥 💻 🍴 ⊇

◆◆◆ ▼▼▼▼ Holiday Inn Express 🆂🅷
(903) 792-3366. **$71.** 5401 N State Line Ave. I-30, exit 223B, 0.3 mi n on US 71. Int corridors. **Pets:** Accepted.
🆂🅰🆅🅴 🆂🔟 ⊠ 🖥 💻 ⊇

◆◆◆ ▼▼▼▼ La Quinta Inn Texarkana 🆂🅷
(903) 794-1900. **$58-$80.** 5201 State Line Ave. I-30, exit 223A, sw of jct US 59 and 71. Ext corridors. **Pets:** Accepted.
🆂🅰🆅🅴 ⊠ 🖥 💻 ⊇

▼▼ Motel 6–201 🆂🅷
(903) 793-1413. **$38-$50.** 1924 Hampton Rd. I-30, exit 222 (Summerhill Rd). Ext corridors. **Pets:** Accepted.
🆂🔟 ⊠ ⌨ ⊇

TEXAS CITY

▼▼ La Quinta Inn Texas City 🆂🅷
(409) 948-3101. **$71-$91.** 1121 Hwy 146 N. Jct SR 146 S and FM 1764, 5 mi se of I-45, exit 16 southbound; exit 15 northbound. Ext corridors. **Pets:** Other species.
🅰🆂🅺 ⊠ 🕐 🖥 💻 ⊇

THREE RIVERS

▼▼ Bass Inn Ⓜ
(361) 786-3521. **Call for rates.** Hwy 72 W. SR 72, 7.5 mi w of jct US 281. Ext corridors. **Pets:** Accepted.
⊠ 🖥 💻 ⊇

TULIA

▼▼ Select Inn of Tulia Ⓜ
(806) 995-3248. **$56-$66.** Rt 1, Box 60. I-27, exit 74. Ext corridors. **Pets:** Very small, dogs only. $6 daily fee/pet. Designated rooms, service with restrictions, supervision.
🅰🆂🅺 ⊠ ⌨ 🖥 💻

TYLER

◆◆◆ ▼▼▼ Best Western Inn & Suites 🆂🅷
(903) 595-2681. **$58-$99.** 2828 W NW Loop 323. Jct US 69 N and Loop 323. Ext corridors. **Pets:** Accepted.
🆂🅰🆅🅴 🆂🔟 ⊠ 🖥 💻 ⊇

(AAA) ▼▼▽ Candlewood Suites SH
(903) 509-4131. **$70-$85.** 315 Rieck Rd. 1.1 mi s of jct Loop 323 and US 69 (S Broadway) to Rieck Rd, just e. Int corridors. **Pets:** Accepted.
[SAVE] [S🐾] [✕] [🛄M] [🐾] [🗄] [▣]

(AAA) ▼▼▽ Comfort Suites SH
(903) 534-0999. **$99-$129.** 303 E Rieck Rd. 1.1 mi s of jct Loop 323 and S Broadway (US 69) to E Rieck Rd, just e. Int corridors. **Pets:** Accepted.
[SAVE] [S🐾] [✕] [🛄M] [🐾] [🗄] [▣]

(AAA) ▼▼▽ La Quinta Inn Tyler SH
(903) 561-2223. **$80-$100.** 1601 W SW Loop 323. 1 mi w of S US 69. Ext corridors. **Pets:** Accepted.
[SAVE] [✕] [🐾] [▣] [🏊]

▼▼▽ Quality Hotel Tyler SH
(903) 597-1301. **$69-$89, 7 day notice.** 2843 W NW Loop 323. Just w of jct US 69. Int corridors. **Pets:** Medium, other species. $25 one-time fee/pet. Service with restrictions, crate.
[ASK] [S🐾] [✕] [🛄M] [🗄] [▣] [🍴] [🏊]

▼▼▽ Ramada Tyler Conference Center SH
(903) 593-3600. **$89.** 3310 Troup Hwy. 0.3 mi n of jct E Loop 323 and SR 110. Ext corridors. **Pets:** Accepted.
[ASK] [S🐾] [✕] [🐾] [🗄] [▣] [🍴] [🏊]

▼▼▽ Residence Inn by Marriott SH
(903) 595-5188. **$85-$135.** 3303 Troup Hwy. 0.3 mi n of jct E Loop 323 and SR 110. Ext corridors. **Pets:** Accepted.
[ASK] [✕] [🐾] [🗄] [▣] [🏊] [✕]

UVALDE

▼▼ Holiday Inn SH
(830) 278-4511. **$52-$57.** 920 E Main St. 0.5 mi e on US 90. Ext corridors. **Pets:** Accepted.
[ASK] [S🐾] [✕] [🗄] [▣] [🍴] [🏊]

VAN HORN

(AAA) ▼▼▽ Best Western American Inn M
(432) 283-2030. **$60-$95.** 1309 W Broadway. I-10, exit 138, 1 mi e. Ext corridors. **Pets:** Accepted.
[SAVE] [S🐾] [✕] [🗄] [▣] [🏊]

(AAA) ▼▼▽ Best Western Inn of Van Horn M 🐾
(432) 283-2410. **$90.** 1705 W Broadway St. I-10, exit 138, 0.3 mi e, then 1 mi w on US 80. Ext corridors. **Pets:** Other species. $8 one-time fee/room. Designated rooms, service with restrictions, supervision.
[SAVE] [S🐾] [✕] [🗄] [▣] [🏊]

(AAA) ▼▼ Budget Inn M
(432) 283-2019. **$30-$45.** 1303 W Broadway. I-10, exit 138, 0.7 mi e. Ext corridors. **Pets:** Accepted.
[SAVE] [S🐾] [✕] [🗄]

(AAA) ▼▼▽ Comfort Inn SH
(432) 283-2211. **$59-$129.** 1601 W Broadway St. I-10, exit 138, 0.5 mi e on Business Rt I-10. Ext corridors. **Pets:** Accepted.
[SAVE] [S🐾] [✕] [🗄] [▣] [🏊]

(AAA) ▼▼ Days Inn M
(432) 283-1007. **$85-$95, 15 day notice.** 600 E Broadway St. I-10, exit 140B, just w. Ext corridors. **Pets:** Medium. $8 daily fee/pet. Service with restrictions, supervision.
[SAVE] [S🐾] [✕] [🗄] [🏊]

(AAA) ▼▼ Economy Inn M
(432) 283-2754. **$32-$55.** 1500 W Broadway St. I-10, exit 138, 0.5 mi e on US 80. Ext corridors. **Pets:** $3 one-time fee/room. No service, supervision.
[SAVE] [S🐾] [✕] [🗄]

(AAA) ▼▼▽ Holiday Inn Express SH
(432) 283-7444. **$69-$109.** 1905 SW Frontage Rd. I-10, exit 138 (Golf Course Dr). Ext corridors. **Pets:** Accepted.
[SAVE] [S🐾] [✕] [🛄M] [🐾] [🗄] [▣] [🏊]

▼ Motel 6–4024 M
(432) 283-2992. **$46-$48, 7 day notice.** 1805 W Broadway St. I-10, exit 138. Ext corridors. **Pets:** Small, other species. Service with restrictions, supervision.
[ASK] [✕] [🏊]

(AAA) ▼▼ Ramada Limited SH
(432) 283-2780. **$68-$78.** 200 Golf Course Dr. I-10, exit 138 (Golf Course Dr). Ext/int corridors. **Pets:** Accepted.
[SAVE] [S🐾] [✕] [🗄] [▣] [🏊]

(AAA) ▼▼▽ Van Horn Super 8 M
(432) 283-2282. **$56-$95, 15 day notice.** 1807 E Service Rd. I-10, exit 138 (Golf Course Dr). Ext corridors. **Pets:** Medium. $8 daily fee/pet. Service with restrictions, supervision.
[SAVE] [S🐾] [✕] [🐾] [🗄]

VEGA

(AAA) ▼▼▽ Best Western Country Inn M 🐾
(806) 267-2131. **$69-$79.** 1800 W Vega Blvd. 0.5 mi w on US 40 business loop. Ext corridors. **Pets:** Large. Service with restrictions, supervision.
[SAVE] [S🐾] [✕] [🗄] [▣] [🏊]

VERNON

▼▼ Best Western Village Inn M
(940) 552-5417. **$59-$69.** 1615 Expwy. US 287, exit Main St, just w. Ext/int corridors. **Pets:** Very small. $5 daily fee/room. Designated rooms, service with restrictions, supervision.
[ASK] [S🐾] [✕] [🗄] [▣] [🍴] [🏊]

VICTORIA

(AAA) ▼▼▽ Comfort Inn SH
(361) 574-9393. **$80-$85, 30 day notice.** 1906 Houston Hwy. 3.5 mi ne on US 59. Ext corridors. **Pets:** Accepted.
[SAVE] [S🐾] [✕] [🗄] [▣] [🏊]

▼▼▼ Holiday Inn Holidome SH
(361) 575-0251. **$89.** 2705 E Houston Hwy (Business Rt 59). On Business Rt US 59, 2.5 mi ne. Ext/int corridors. **Pets:** Small. $125 deposit/room. Service with restrictions, supervision.
[ASK] [S🐾] [✕] [🗄] [🍴] [🏊] [✕]

(AAA) ▼▼▽ La Quinta Inn Victoria SH
(361) 572-3585. **$85-$100.** 7603 N Navarro St (US 77 N). 4 mi n; at Loop 463. Ext corridors. **Pets:** Accepted.
[SAVE] [✕] [🐾] [🗄] [▣] [🏊]

▼ Motel 6 Victoria #225 M
(361) 573-1273. **$40-$50.** 3716 Houston Hwy. On Business Rt US 59. Ext corridors. **Pets:** Accepted.
[S🐾] [✕] [🏊]

▼▽ Quality Inn-Victoria SH 🐾
(361) 578-2030. **$68-$110.** 3112 E Houston Hwy (Business Rt 59). On Business Rt US 59, 2 mi ne. Ext corridors. **Pets:** Medium. Service with restrictions, crate.
[ASK] [S🐾] [✕] [🗄] [▣] [🏊]

WACO

(AAA) ▼▼▽ Best Western Old Main Lodge SH 🐾
(254) 753-0316. **$90-$95.** I-35 & 4th St. I-35 and US 81, exit 335A (4th-5th sts). Ext corridors. **Pets:** Small. Service with restrictions, supervision.
[SAVE] [S🐾] [✕] [🗄] [▣] [🏊]

Days Inn SH
(254) 799-8585. **$69-$89.** 1504 I-35. I-35, exit 338B (Behrens Cir), just n. Ext corridors. **Pets:** Medium, dogs only. $10 daily fee/pet. Service with restrictions, supervision.

Holiday Inn-Waco I-35 SH
(254) 753-0261. **$100.** 1001 Martin Luther King Blvd. I-35, exit 335C (Lake Brazos Dr), just n. Int corridors. **Pets:** Accepted.

La Quinta Inn Waco (University) SH
(254) 752-9741. **$85-$105.** 1110 S 9th St. I-35, exit 334 (17th St) southbound; exit 334A (18th St) northbound. Ext corridors. **Pets:** Other species. Service with restrictions.

Residence Inn by Marriott SH
(254) 714-1386. **$119-$160.** 501 S University Parks Dr. I-35, exit 335B, 0.3 mi w. Int corridors. **Pets:** Accepted.

Super 8 Motel-Waco SH
(254) 754-1023. **$60-$100.** 1320 S Jack Kultgen Frwy. I-35, exit 334, just e. Int corridors. **Pets:** Accepted.

WAXAHACHIE

Best Western Gingerbread Inn SH
(972) 937-4202. **$56-$76.** 200 N I-35E. I-35E and US 287 business route, 1.8 mi s of jct US 287, exit 401B. Ext corridors. **Pets:** Accepted.

Super 8 Motel SH
(972) 938-9088. **$65-$75.** 400 I-35E. I-35E, exit 401B. Int corridors. **Pets:** Small. $5 daily fee/room. Service with restrictions, supervision.

WEATHERFORD

Best Western Santa Fe Inn SH 🐾
(817) 594-7401. **$69.** 1927 Santa Fe Dr. I-20, exit 409 (Clear Lake Rd/FM 2552), 0.3 mi nw. Ext corridors. **Pets:** Large. $10 daily fee/pet. Service with restrictions, supervision.

Hampton Inn SH
(817) 599-4800. **$75-$140.** 2524 S Main St. I-20, exit 408. Int corridors. **Pets:** Accepted.

Holiday Inn Express Hotel & Suites SH
(817) 599-3700. **$75-$200.** 2500 S Main St. I-20, exit 408. Ext/int corridors. **Pets:** Accepted.

Weatherford Comfort Suites SH
(817) 599-3300. **$75-$150.** 210 Alford Dr. I-20, exit 408, just s on SR 171, then just w. Int corridors. **Pets:** Medium, other species. $20 one-time fee/pet. Designated rooms, service with restrictions, supervision.

WEIMAR

Super 8 Motel M
(979) 725-9788. **$51-$73.** 102 Townsend Ln. I-10, exit 682, just w on north access road. Int corridors. **Pets:** Accepted.

WELLINGTON

Cherokee Inn & Restaurant M
(806) 447-2508. **$34-$56.** 1105 Houston St. US 83, just n of jct FM 338. Ext corridors. **Pets:** Accepted.

WESLACO

Best Western Palm Aire Hotel & Suites SH
(956) 969-2411. **$54-$111.** 415 S International Blvd. US 83, exit International Blvd. Ext corridors. **Pets:** Small. Service with restrictions, supervision.

Super 8 Motel SH
(956) 969-9920. **$50.** 1702 E Expwy 83. US 83, exit Airport Dr. Ext corridors. **Pets:** Accepted.

WESTLAKE

Dallas Marriott Solana SH
(817) 430-3848. **$74-$199.** 5 Village Cir. SR 114, exit Kirkwood Blvd, just s. Int corridors. **Pets:** Accepted.

WICHITA FALLS

Best Western Wichita Falls Inn SH
(940) 766-6881. **$59-$79.** 1032 Central Frwy. I-44, exit 2, just w. Ext corridors. **Pets:** Medium. $10 daily fee/room. Service with restrictions, supervision.

Comfort Inn & Suites SH 🐾
(940) 767-5653. **$65-$135.** 1740 Maurine St. US 287, exit Maurine St, just e. Ext/int corridors. **Pets:** $10 one-time fee/room. Service with restrictions.

Hampton Inn SH
(940) 766-3300. **$64-$104.** 1317 Kenley Ave. I-44, exit 2, just w. Int corridors. **Pets:** Small, other species. $30 one-time fee/room. Service with restrictions, crate.

Hawthorn Suites Limited SH 🐾
(940) 692-7900. **$84-$149.** 1917 Elmwood Ave N. US 281 S, exit Southwest Pkwy (CR 319), 2.3 mi w to Kemp, 2 blks n to Elmwood Ave, then just e. Int corridors. **Pets:** $5 daily fee/pet, $25 one-time fee/pet. Designated rooms, service with restrictions, crate.

La Quinta Inn Wichita Falls SH
(940) 322-6971. **$80-$90.** 1128 Central Frwy N. I-44, exit 2, just w. Ext corridors. **Pets:** Accepted.

Motel 6 #130 M
(940) 322-8817. **$43-$59.** 1812 Maurine St. I-44, exit 2, just e. Ext corridors. **Pets:** Accepted.

Quality Inn and Suites M
(940) 322-2477. **$59-$129.** 1750 Maurine St. I-44, exit 2, just e. Int corridors. **Pets:** $10 one-time fee/room. Service with restrictions.

Radisson Hotel LH
(940) 761-6000. **$89-$149, 14 day notice.** 100 Central Frwy. I-287, exit 1C, on west side access road. Int corridors. **Pets:** Accepted.

Ramada Limited M
(940) 855-0085. **$48-$55.** 3209 Northwest Frwy. US 287, exit Beverly (CR 11), just w. Ext corridors. **Pets:** Accepted.

Ⓐ ▽▽ Towne Crest Inn M
(940) 322-1182. **$37-$80.** 1601 8th St. US 287, exit Broad St/Business, w on 9th St, 1 blk n on Brook to 8th St, then just e. Ext corridors. **Pets:** Accepted.

SAVE Sᴏ ⊠ 🖬 💻

ZAPATA

Ⓐ ▽▽ Best Western Inn by the Lake SH
(956) 765-8403. **$80-$95.** Hwy 83 S. On US 83, 0.5 mi se. Ext corridors. **Pets:** Accepted.

SAVE Sᴏ ⊠ 🖬 💻 ⌦

UTAH

AMERICAN FORK

▼▼▼ Quality Inn & Suites M
(801) 763-8383. **$69-$129.** 712 S Utah Valley Dr. I-15, exit 276. Int corridors. **Pets:** Medium, other species. $25 deposit/room. Service with restrictions, crate.
[ASK] [S0] [X] [&] [=] [□] [≈]

BEAVER

▼▼▼ Beaver Super 8 Motel M
(435) 438-3888. **$39-$79.** 626 W 1400 N. I-15, exit 112, just w. Ext/int corridors. **Pets:** Accepted.
[ASK] [S0] [X] [∅] [=] [□]

◆◆◆ ▼▼▼ Best Western Butch Cassidy Inn M
(435) 438-2438. **$55-$105.** 161 S Main St. I-15, exit 109 or 112, just e. Ext corridors. **Pets:** Other species. $5 daily fee/pet. Service with restrictions, supervision.
[SAVE] [S0] [X] [&] [=] [□] [≈]

◆◆◆ ▼▼▼ Best Western Paradise Inn M
(435) 438-2455. **$55-$79.** 1451 N 300 W. I-15, exit 112, just e; north end of town. Ext corridors. **Pets:** Other species. Service with restrictions, supervision.
[SAVE] [S0] [X] [□] [††] [≈]

▼ Country Inn M ❀
(435) 438-2484. **$42-$55.** 1450 N 300 W. I-15, exit 112, 2 blks e. Ext corridors. **Pets:** Large. $3 daily fee/pet. Service with restrictions, supervision.
[ASK] [S0] [X] [=]

◆◆◆ ▼▼▼ DeLano Motel M
(435) 438-2418. **$34-$45, 3 day notice.** 480 N Main St. I-15, exit 112, just e; north end of town. Ext corridors. **Pets:** Accepted.
[SAVE] [S0] [X] [=]

▼▼▼ Motel 6 Beaver #4206 M
(435) 438-1666. **$43-$60.** 1345 N 450 W. I-15, exit 112, just se. Int corridors. **Pets:** Medium. Designated rooms, no service, supervision.
[X] [&] [=] [≈]

▼▼▼ Quality Inn M
(435) 438-5426. **$55-$75.** 781 W 1800 S. I-15, exit 109, just w. Int corridors. **Pets:** Small. Designated rooms, supervision.
[ASK] [S0] [X] [□] [≈]

▼▼▼ Sleepy Lagoon Motel M
(435) 438-5681. **$40-$50.** 882 S Main St. I-15, exit 109, 0.5 mi n. Ext corridors. **Pets:** Accepted.
[ASK] [S0] [X] [=] [≈]

BICKNELL

◆◆◆ ▼▼▼ Aquarius Motel and Restaurant M
(435) 425-3835. **$43-$50.** 240 W Main St. SR 24, 9 mi w of Capitol Reef National Park; downtown. Ext/int corridors. **Pets:** Large, other species. $25 deposit/room, $5 daily fee/pet. Service with restrictions, supervision.
[SAVE] [S0] [X] [=] [□] [††] [≈]

BLANDING

◆◆◆ ▼▼▼ Best Western Gateway Inn M
(435) 678-2278. **$43-$89.** 88 E Center St. East side on US 191. Ext corridors. **Pets:** Medium. $5 one-time fee/room. Designated rooms, supervision.
[SAVE] [S0] [X] [□] [≈]

◆◆◆ ▼▼ Four Corners Inn M
(435) 678-3257. **$48-$64.** 131 E Center St. On US 191. Ext corridors. **Pets:** Other species. $3 daily fee/room. Service with restrictions, supervision.
[SAVE] [S0] [X] [=]

BLUFF

◆◆◆ ▼ Kokopelli Inn M
(435) 672-2322. **$40-$50.** 161 E Main St. On US 191. Int corridors. **Pets:** Medium. $10 daily fee/pet. Service with restrictions, supervision.
[SAVE] [S0] [X]

◆◆◆ ▼▼ Recapture Lodge M ❀
(435) 672-2281. **$35-$60.** 220 E Main St. On US 191. Ext corridors. **Pets:** Other species. Designated rooms, service with restrictions, supervision.
[SAVE] [S0] [X] [∅] [=] [□] [≈] [X] [Z]

BOULDER

▼▼▼ Boulder Mountain Lodge M ❀
(435) 335-7460. **$69-$168, 14 day notice.** 20 N Hwy 12. Jct SR 12 and Burr Tr. Ext/int corridors. **Pets:** $10 daily fee/pet. Designated rooms, service with restrictions, supervision.
[X] [=] [□] [††] [X]

BRIGHAM CITY

▼▼▼ Crystal Inn M
(435) 723-0440. **$59-$99.** 480 Westland Dr. I-15 and 84, exit 362 (Logan and Brigham City), 1 mi e. Int corridors. **Pets:** Small, dogs only. $25 deposit/room. Designated rooms, service with restrictions, supervision.
[ASK] [S0] [X] [&] [=] [□] [≈]

▼▼ Howard Johnson Inn M
(435) 723-8511. **$51-$70.** 1167 S Main St. I-15 and 84, exit 362 (Logan and Brigham City), 2 mi e on US 89 and 91. Ext corridors. **Pets:** Service with restrictions, crate.
[ASK] [S0] [X] [=] [□] [≈]

BRYCE

ⒶⒶⒶ ▽▽ Best Western Ruby's Inn 🄢🄷 ❀
(435) 834-5341. **$52-$120.** UT Hwy 63. On SR 63, 1 mi s of SR 12, 1 mi n of Bryce Canyon National Park entrance. Ext/int corridors. **Pets:** Service with restrictions, supervision.
SAVE S⑩ ☒ ⬛M 🔕 🚳 ⬛ 💻 🍴 🏊 ☒

▽▽ Bryce Canyon Resort Ⓜ
(435) 834-5351. **$55-$105.** 13500 E Hwy 12. Jct of SR 12 and 63. Ext corridors. **Pets:** Other species. $10 daily fee/pet. Service with restrictions.
A$K S⑩ ☒ ⬛ 💻 🍴 🏊

ⒶⒶⒶ ▽▽▽ Bryce View Lodge Ⓜ ❀
(435) 834-5180. **$49-$78.** SR 63. On SR 63. Ext corridors. **Pets:** Service with restrictions, supervision.
SAVE S⑩ ☒ ⬛ 💻 🏊 ☒

CEDAR CITY

ⒶⒶⒶ ▽▽▽ Best Value Inn Ⓜ
(435) 586-6557. **$35-$95.** 323 S Main St. Cross streets 300 S and Main sts; downtown. Ext corridors. **Pets:** Small. $10 daily fee/pet. Service with restrictions, supervision.
SAVE S⑩ ☒ ⬛ 💻 🏊

ⒶⒶⒶ ▽▽▽ Cedar Rest Motel Ⓜ
(435) 586-9471. **$35-$60.** 479 S Main St. I-15, exit 59, just e. Ext corridors. **Pets:** Accepted.
SAVE S⑩ ☒ ⬛

▽▽▽▽ Comfort Inn Ⓜ
(435) 586-2082. **$47-$115.** 250 N 1100 W. I-15, exit 59, just e. Ext corridors. **Pets:** Other species. Designated rooms, service with restrictions, supervision.
A$K S⑩ ☒ 🔕 ⬛ 💻 🏊

▽▽▽▽ Crystal Inn 🄢🄷
(435) 586-8888. **$59-$99.** 1575 W 200 N. I-15, exit 59, just w. Ext/int corridors. **Pets:** Small, other species. $20 one-time fee/pet. Designated rooms, service with restrictions, supervision.
A$K S⑩ ☒ 🔕 ⬛ 💻 🍴 🏊 ☒

ⒶⒶⒶ ▽▽▽▽ Days Inn Ⓜ
(435) 867-8877. **$49-$89.** 1204 S Main St. I-15, exit 57, 0.4 mi e. Ext corridors. **Pets:** Small. $10 daily fee/pet. Designated rooms, service with restrictions, supervision.
SAVE S⑩ ☒ 🔕 ⬛ 🏊

▽▽▽ Holiday Inn Express Hotel & Suites Ⓜ
(435) 865-7799. **$89-$149, 5 day notice.** 1555 S Old Hwy 91. I-15, exit 57, just e, then s. Int corridors. **Pets:** Medium. $10 daily fee/room. Designated rooms.
A$K S⑩ ☒ 🔕 ⬛ 💻 🏊

▽▽▽ Motel 6 of Cedar City-4041 Ⓜ
(435) 586-9200. **Call for rates.** 1620 W 200 N. I-15, exit 59, just w. Int corridors. **Pets:** Other species. Service with restrictions, supervision.
S⑩ ☒ 🔕

▽▽▽▽ Ramada Limited Ⓜ
(435) 586-9916. **$45-$109.** 281 S Main St. I-15, exit 57, just e. Ext corridors. **Pets:** Small, dogs only. $7 daily fee/pet. Designated rooms, service with restrictions, supervision.
A$K S⑩ ☒ ⬛ 💻 🏊

ⒶⒶⒶ ▽▽ Super 7 Motel Ⓜ
(435) 586-6566. **$35-$80, 3 day notice.** 190 S Main St. I-15, exit 57, just e. Ext corridors. **Pets:** Small, dogs only. $8 daily fee/pet. Designated rooms, service with restrictions, supervision.
SAVE S⑩ ☒ ⬛

▽▽ Super 8 Motel Ⓜ ❀
(435) 586-8880. **$53-$63.** 145 N 1550 W. I-15, exit 59, just w. Int corridors. **Pets:** Medium. $25 deposit/pet, $7 daily fee/pet, $5 one-time fee/pet. Designated rooms, service with restrictions, supervision.
A$K S⑩ ☒ ⬛M 🔕 ⬛

ⒶⒶⒶ ▽▽ Valu-Inn Ⓜ
(435) 586-9114. **$30-$70.** 344 S Main St. I-15, exit 57, just e. Ext corridors. **Pets:** Accepted.
SAVE S⑩ ☒ ⬛

▽▽▽ Willow Glen Inn 🄱🄱
(435) 586-3275. **$59-$195, 5 day notice.** 3308 N Bulldog Rd. I-15, exit 62, 1.5 mi sw via 3000 N. Ext corridors. **Pets:** Medium. Designated rooms, service with restrictions, supervision.
A$K S⑩ ☒ ⬛ 💻 🍴 🕿

CLEARFIELD

▽▽▽ Clearfield Super 8 Ⓜ
(801) 825-8000. **$54-$84.** 572 N Main St. I-15, exit 335, just w. Int corridors. **Pets:** $50 deposit/room, $10 daily fee/pet. Service with restrictions, supervision.
A$K S⑩ ☒ 🔕 ⬛ ⬛

COALVILLE

▽▽▽ Best Western Holiday Hills Ⓜ
(435) 336-4444. **$69-$99.** 210 S 200 W. I-80, exit 162, just w. Int corridors. **Pets:** Medium, other species. $15 daily fee/pet. Designated rooms, service with restrictions, supervision.
A$K S⑩ ☒ 🔕 ⬛ 💻 🏊 ☒

DELTA

ⒶⒶⒶ ▽▽▽▽ Best Western Motor Inn Ⓜ
(435) 864-3882. **$63-$75.** 527 E Topaz Blvd. US 6, at jct US 50. Ext corridors. **Pets:** Other species. $25 one-time fee/room. Designated rooms, service with restrictions, supervision.
SAVE S⑩ ☒ 🔕 💻 🏊

DUCK CREEK VILLAGE

▽▽▽ Duck Creek Village Inn Ⓜ
(435) 682-2565. **$64-$74, 7 day notice.** Hwy 14. 30 mi e of Cedar City on SR 14; 10 mi w of US 89. Ext corridors. **Pets:** Accepted.
A$K S⑩ ☒ ⬛ 💻 🍴 🅧 🕿

ⒶⒶⒶ ▽▽▽ Pinewoods Resort Ⓜ
(435) 682-2512. **$50-$95, 30 day notice.** 121 Duck Greek Ridge Rd. Just s of SR 14 via Cedar Mountain Rd, 31 mi e of Cedar City; 10 mi w of jct US 89. Ext/int corridors. **Pets:** Accepted.
SAVE S⑩ ☒ ⬛ 💻 🍴 🅧 🅧 🕿

ESCALANTE

▽▽ Rainbow Country Bed & Breakfast 🄱🄱
(435) 826-4567. **$50-$75, 3 day notice.** 586 E 300 S. Just off SR 12; south end of town. Int corridors. **Pets:** Service with restrictions, supervision.
A$K S⑩ ☒ 🆆 🕿

FILLMORE

ⒶⒶⒶ ▽▽▽ Best Western Paradise Resort Ⓜ
(435) 743-6895. **$55-$79.** 905 N Main St. I-15, exit 167, just e. Ext corridors. **Pets:** Medium. Service with restrictions, supervision.
SAVE S⑩ ☒ ⬛ 💻 🍴 🏊

▽▽▽ Inn at Apple Creek Ⓜ
(435) 743-4334. **$59-$79.** 940 S Hwy 99. I-15, exit 163, just e. Int corridors. **Pets:** Other species. $6 one-time fee/pet. Designated rooms, service with restrictions, supervision.
A$K S⑩ ☒ 🔕 ⬛ 💻 🏊

GARDEN CITY

▼▼ Canyon Cove Inn M
(435) 946-3565. **$75-$125.** 315 W Logan (Hwy 89). On US Hwy 89, 3 blks w of downtown. Int corridors. **Pets:** Accepted.
[ASK] [S📶] [✕] [♿] [🛏] [🏊]

GLENDALE

▼▼ Historic Smith Hotel Bed & Breakfast BB ✿
(435) 648-2156. **$44-$70.** 295 N Main St. US 89, north end of town. Int corridors. **Pets:** Other species. $5 one-time fee/pet. Designated rooms, service with restrictions, supervision.
[ASK] [S📶] [✕] [📺] [🐾]

GREEN RIVER

▼▼▼ Holiday Inn Express M
(435) 564-4439. **$69-$89.** 965 E Main. I-70, exit 164, 1.8 mi w; exit 160 eastbound, 2.8 mi e on business loop. Int corridors. **Pets:** Large. $10 daily fee/room. Designated rooms, service with restrictions, supervision.
[ASK] [S📶] [✕] [♿] [🛏] [🖥] [🏊]

▼ Motel 6 #289 M
(435) 564-3436. **$41-$53.** 946 E Main St. I-70, exit 164, 1.8 mi w; exit 160 eastbound, 2.8 me e on business loop. Ext corridors. **Pets:** Medium, other species. Service with restrictions, supervision.
[S📶] [✕] [♿] [🛏] [🏊]

▼▼▼ Ramada Limited M ✿
(435) 564-8441. **$45-$74, 7 day notice.** 1117 E Main St. I-70, exit 164, 1 mi nw. Ext/int corridors. **Pets:** Other species. $5 daily fee/pet. Service with restrictions, supervision.
[ASK] [S📶] [✕] [♿] [🛏] [🖥] [🏊]

▼▼▼ Super 8 Motel M
(435) 564-8888. **$48-$85.** 1248 E Main St. I-70, exit 164. Int corridors. **Pets:** Accepted.
[S📶] [✕] [🐾] [♿] [🛏] [🏊]

HATCH

AAA ▼▼ Riverside Resort & RV Park M ✿
(435) 735-4223. **$40-$50, 3 day notice.** 594 US Hwy 89. On US 89, 1 mi n. Ext corridors. **Pets:** Other species. $50 deposit/room, $5 daily fee/pet. Service with restrictions, supervision.
[SAVE] [S📶] [✕] [🛏] [🖥] [🍴] [✕] [🐾]

HEBER CITY

AAA ▼▼ National 9 High Country Inn M
(435) 654-0201. **$60-$85.** 1000 S Main St. On US 40 E. Ext corridors. **Pets:** Small, other species. $10 daily fee/pet. Designated rooms, service with restrictions, supervision.
[SAVE] [S📶] [✕] [🛏] [🏊]

AAA ▼▼ Swiss Alps Inn M
(435) 654-0722. **$54-$72.** 167 S Main St. On US 40. Ext corridors. **Pets:** Other species. Service with restrictions, supervision.
[SAVE] [S📶] [✕] [🛏] [🏊] [✕]

HUNTSVILLE

▼▼ Jackson Fork Inn BB
(801) 745-0051. **$80-$130, 3 day notice.** 7345 E 900 S. On SR 39. Int corridors. **Pets:** Small. $20 one-time fee/room. Service with restrictions, supervision.
[ASK] [✕] [🍴] [🐾]

HURRICANE

AAA ▼▼▼ Motel 6–4050 M
(435) 635-4010. **$59-$139.** 650 W State. Just w on SR 9. Ext corridors. **Pets:** Small. $10 daily fee/pet. Service with restrictions, supervision.
[SAVE] [S📶] [✕] [🛏] [🏊]

▼▼ Super 8 M
(435) 635-0808. **$44-$120.** 65 S 700 W. Just s of SR 9. Ext corridors. **Pets:** Accepted.
[ASK] [S📶] [✕] [♿] [🛏] [🖥] [🏊]

▼▼ Travelodge M
(435) 635-4647. **$39-$109.** 280 W State. Just w on SR 9. Ext corridors. **Pets:** Small. $10 daily fee/pet. Service with restrictions, supervision.
[ASK] [S📶] [✕] [🛏] [🖥] [🏊]

KANAB

AAA ▼▼ Aikens Lodge M
(435) 644-2625. **$33-$66.** 79 W Center St. On US 89. Ext corridors. **Pets:** Small, dogs only. $10 daily fee/pet. Designated rooms, supervision.
[SAVE] [S📶] [✕] [♿] [🛏] [🏊]

AAA ▼▼ Bob-Bon Inn M
(435) 644-5094. **$26-$59, 3 day notice.** 236 Hwy 89 N. On US 89. Ext corridors. **Pets:** Accepted.
[SAVE] [✕] [🛏] [🏊]

▼▼▼ Clarion-Victorian Charm Inn M ✿
(435) 644-8660. **$74-$129.** 190 N Hwy 89. North end of town. Int corridors. **Pets:** Small, dogs only. $10 one-time fee/pet. Designated rooms, service with restrictions, supervision.
[ASK] [S📶] [✕] [♿] [🖥]

▼▼ Four Seasons Motel & Restaurant M
(435) 644-2635. **$49-$74.** 36 N 300 W. Ext corridors. **Pets:** Other species. $6 one-time fee/room. Designated rooms, service with restrictions.
[ASK] [S📶] [✕] [🛏] [🍴]

▼▼▼ Holiday Inn Express M
(435) 644-8888. **$53-$110.** 815 E Hwy 89. On US 89, just e. Int corridors. **Pets:** Large, other species. $10 daily fee/pet. Designated rooms, service with restrictions, supervision.
[ASK] [S📶] [✕] [🐾] [♿] [🛏] [🏊]

AAA ▼ Kanab Mission Motel M ✿
(435) 644-5373. **$35-$60.** 386 E 300 S. E on US 89. Int corridors. **Pets:** Other species. No service, supervision.
[SAVE] [S📶] [✕] [🛏]

AAA ▼▼ Parry Lodge M
(435) 644-2601. **$40-$78.** 89 E Center St. On US 89; corner of 100 E; center. Ext/int corridors. **Pets:** Accepted.
[SAVE] [S📶] [✕] [🛏] [🖥] [🍴] [🐾]

AAA ▼▼ Quail Park Lodge M
(435) 644-8700. **$43-$50.** 125 Hwy 89 N. On US 89. Ext corridors. **Pets:** Small, dogs only. $10 daily fee/pet. Designated rooms, service with restrictions, supervision.
[SAVE] [S📶] [✕] [🐾]

▼▼▼ Shilo Inn SH
(435) 644-2562. **$45-$95.** 296 W 100 N. N of downtown on US 89. Int corridors. **Pets:** Accepted.
[ASK] [S📶] [✕] [♿] [🛏] [🖥] [🏊]

AAA ▼ Sun N Sand Motel M
(435) 644-5050. **$32-$48.** 347 S 100 E. Jct US 89 and 89A. Ext corridors. **Pets:** Accepted.
[SAVE] [S📶] [✕] [🛏] [🐾]

▼▼ Super 8 M
(435) 644-5500. **$41-$78.** 70 S 200 W. Just s off US 89. Ext corridors. **Pets:** Other species. $6 daily fee/pet. Designated rooms, service with restrictions, supervision.
[ASK] [S📶] [✕] [🛏] [🐾]

LAKE POWELL

AAA ▽▽▽▽ Defiance House Lodge-Bullfrog Marina M
(435) 684-3000. **$65-$118, 3 day notice.** Bullfrog Marina. 70 mi s of Hanksville; 44 mi s off SR 95 on SR 276. Int corridors. **Pets:** Other species. Service with restrictions, supervision.

LAYTON

AAA ▽▽▽▽ Comfort Inn M
(801) 544-5577. **$50-$75.** 877 N 400 W. I-15, exit 331, then e. Int corridors. **Pets:** Small. Service with restrictions, supervision.

▽▽▽▽ Hampton Inn M
(801) 775-8800. **$99-$119.** 1700 Woodland Park Dr. I-15, exit 332, 0.3 mi se. Int corridors. **Pets:** Accepted.

▽▽▽▽ Holiday Inn Express M
(801) 773-3773. **$81-$135.** 1695 Woodland Park Dr. I-15, exit 332, 0.3 mi se. Int corridors. **Pets:** Accepted.

AAA ▽▽▽▽ La Quinta Inn Salt Lake City (Layton) M
(801) 776-6700. **$84-$99.** 1965 N 1200 W. I-15, exit 332, 1 blk e; corner of Antelope Dr and Angel Rd. Int corridors. **Pets:** Accepted.

▽▽▽▽ TownePlace Suites M
(801) 779-2422. **$79-$109.** 1743 Woodland Park Dr. I-15, exit 331, 0.3 mi se. Int corridors. **Pets:** Accepted.

LEHI

AAA ▽▽▽▽ Best Western Timpanogos Inn M
(801) 768-1400. **$59-$115.** 195 S 850 E. I-15, exit 279, southwest side. Int corridors. **Pets:** Accepted.

▽▽ Motel 6–1405 M
(801) 768-2668. **$41-$51.** 210 S 1200 E. I-15, exit 279, just e. Int corridors. **Pets:** Accepted.

▽▽▽ Super 8 M
(801) 766-8800. **$49-$89.** 125 S 850 E. I-15, exit 279, southwest side. Int corridors. **Pets:** Medium, other species. $50 deposit/room. Service with restrictions, supervision.

LOGAN

AAA ▽▽▽ Best Western Weston Inn M
(435) 752-5700. **$55-$89.** 250 N Main St. On US 89 and 91; downtown. Ext corridors. **Pets:** Small, dogs only. $5 daily fee/pet. Designated rooms, service with restrictions, supervision.

▽▽▽ Logan Days Inn M
(435) 753-5623. **$50-$80.** 364 S Main St. On US 89 and 91. Ext corridors. **Pets:** Accepted.

▽▽▽ Logan Super 8 M
(435) 753-8883. **$47-$80.** 865 S Hwy 89 and 91. South end of town. Int corridors. **Pets:** Other species. $5 daily fee/pet. Service with restrictions, supervision.

▽▽▽▽ Ramada Limited M
(435) 787-2060. **$60-$65.** 2002 S Hwy 89 and 91. South end of town. Int corridors. **Pets:** Other species. $50 deposit/pet. Service with restrictions, supervision.

MANTI

▽▽▽ Manti Country Village M
(435) 835-9300. **$57-$79.** 145 N Main St. On US 89. Ext corridors. **Pets:** Medium. $50 deposit/room. Designated rooms, service with restrictions, supervision.

MARYSVALE

▽▽▽ Big Rock Candy Mountain Resort M
(435) 326-2000. **$59-$99.** 4479 N Hwy 89. On US 89, 6 mi n. Ext corridors. **Pets:** Accepted.

MEXICAN HAT

AAA ▽▽▽ San Juan Inn & Trading Post M
(435) 683-2220. **$70-$72.** Hwy 163 & San Juan River. On US 163. Ext corridors. **Pets:** $4 daily fee/pet. Designated rooms, service with restrictions, supervision.

MOAB

AAA ▽▽▽ Adventure Inn Moab M
(435) 259-6122. **$45-$70.** 512 N Main St. US 191 N. Ext corridors. **Pets:** Medium. $10 one-time fee/room. Service with restrictions, supervision.

AAA ▽▽▽ Apache Motel M 🐾
(435) 259-5727. **$29-$89.** 166 S 400 E. Just e off US 191. Ext corridors. **Pets:** Medium. Service with restrictions, supervision.

▽▽▽ Best Inn of Moab M
(435) 259-8848. **$35-$110.** 988 N Main St. 1 mi n on US 191. Int corridors. **Pets:** $10 daily fee/room. Designated rooms, service with restrictions, supervision.

AAA ▽▽▽ Big Horn Lodge SH
(435) 259-6171. **$34-$89.** 550 S Main St. South end of town. Ext corridors. **Pets:** Other species. $5 daily fee/pet. Designated rooms, service with restrictions, supervision.

AAA ▽▽▽ Bowen Motel M
(435) 259-7132. **$40-$75.** 169 N Main St. Downtown. Ext corridors. **Pets:** Medium, dogs only. $20 deposit/room, $5 daily fee/pet. Service with restrictions, supervision.

AAA ▽▽▽▽ Cedar Breaks Condos CO
(435) 259-7830. **$60-$98, 7 day notice.** 400 East & Center St. Just s off US 191. Ext corridors. **Pets:** Medium, dogs only. $10 daily fee/pet. Designated rooms, service with restrictions, supervision.

▽▽▽▽ Comfort Suites M
(435) 259-5252. **$59-$119.** 800 S Main St. Int corridors. **Pets:** Accepted.

AAA ▽▽▽▽ The Gonzo Inn M
(435) 259-2515. **$129-$299.** 100 W 200 S. Downtown. Ext/int corridors. **Pets:** Other species. $25 daily fee/room. No service.

Kokopelli Lodge M
(435) 259-7615. **$45-$69.** 72 S 100 E. Downtown. Ext corridors. **Pets:** Dogs only. $5 daily fee/pet. No service, supervision.
ASK SO X 🖥 💻

La Quinta Inns Moab M
(435) 259-8700. **$50-$106.** 815 S Main St. South end of town. Int corridors. **Pets:** Service with restrictions, crate.
SAVE SO X 💺 🖥 💻 ➿

Moab Valley Inn M
(435) 259-4419. **$62-$105.** 711 S Main St. 1 mi s on US 191. Int corridors. **Pets:** $10 daily fee/room. Designated rooms, service with restrictions, supervision.
ASK SO X 💺 🖥 💻 ➿ ✕

Motel 6 Moab #4119 M
(435) 259-6686. **$29-$99.** 1089 N Main St. North end of town, west side of street. Int corridors. **Pets:** Small. $20 one-time fee/pet. Designated rooms, service with restrictions, supervision.
ASK SO X 🖉 💺 ➿

Ramada Inn of Downtown Moab M
(435) 259-7141. **$35-$135.** 182 S Main St. Downtown. Ext/int corridors. **Pets:** Small. $20 one-time fee/pet. Designated rooms, service with restrictions, supervision.
SAVE SO X 🖉 🖥 💻 🍴 ➿

Red Cliffs Adventure Lodge CI
(435) 259-2002. **$99-$169, 30 day notice.** Milepost 14 Hwy 128. 14 mi e on SR 128 from jct US 191. Ext corridors. **Pets:** Large. $20 daily fee/pet. Designated rooms, service with restrictions, supervision.
SAVE SO X 💺 🖥 🍴 ➿ ✕

Red Rock Lodge & Suites M
(435) 259-5431. **$55-$65.** 51 N 100 W. Just w of Main St. Ext/int corridors. **Pets:** $10 daily fee/pet. Supervision.
ASK SO X 🖥 💻 ➿

Red Stone Inn M
(435) 259-3500. **$34-$80.** 535 S Main St. Downtown. Int corridors. **Pets:** Other species. $5 daily fee/pet. Designated rooms, service with restrictions, supervision.
SAVE SO X 🖥 💻

River Canyon Lodge, An Extended Stay Inn & Suites M
(435) 259-8838. **$32-$135.** 71 W 200 N. Cross streets 100 W and 200 N; downtown. Int corridors. **Pets:** Small. $20 one-time fee/pet. Designated rooms, service with restrictions, supervision.
SAVE SO X 🖉 🖥 💻 ➿

Rustic Inn M
(435) 259-6177. **$30-$85.** 120 E 100 S. Ext corridors. **Pets:** Other species. $5 daily fee/room. Service with restrictions.
X 🖥 💻 ➿

Silver Sage Inn M
(435) 259-4420. **$25-$59.** 840 S Main St. South end of town on US 191. Int corridors. **Pets:** $10 deposit/pet. Service with restrictions.
SAVE X 🖥 💻

Sleep Inn M
(435) 259-4655. **$39-$99, 30 day notice.** 1051 S Main St. South end of town. Int corridors. **Pets:** Large, other species. Designated rooms, service with restrictions, supervision.
ASK SO X 💺M 🖉 💺 🖥 💻 ➿

The Virginian Motel M
(435) 259-5951. **$29-$79.** 70 E 200 S. Just e of US 191. Ext corridors. **Pets:** Other species. $10 daily fee/pet. Service with restrictions, supervision.
SAVE SO X 💺 🖥 💻

MONTICELLO

Best Western Wayside Inn M
(435) 587-2261. **$45-$75.** 173 E Central St. On US 491, just e of US 191. Ext corridors. **Pets:** Accepted.
SAVE SO X 🖉 🖥 💻 ➿

Go West Inn & Suites M
(435) 587-2489. **Call for rates.** 649 N Main St. On US 194 N; end of town. Int corridors. **Pets:** Accepted.
X 🖥 ➿

MOUNT CARMEL JUNCTION

Best Western Thunderbird Resort SH
(435) 648-2203. **$51-$103.** Jct US 89 & 9. Ext corridors. **Pets:** Accepted.
SAVE SO X 💻 🍴 ➿

Golden Hills Motel M
(435) 648-2268. **$45.** 4473 S State St. US 89, jct SR 9. Ext corridors. **Pets:** Accepted.
SAVE SO X 🖥 ➿

NEPHI

Best Western Paradise Inn M
(435) 623-0624. **$49-$85.** 1025 S Main St. I-15, exit 222, 0.5 mi n. Ext corridors. **Pets:** Small. $50 deposit/room, $5 daily fee/pet. Designated rooms, service with restrictions, supervision.
SAVE SO X 🖥 💻 ➿ ✕

Motel 6 M
(435) 623-0666. **Call for rates.** 2195 S Main St. I-15, exit 222, just s. Int corridors. **Pets:** Accepted.
SO X 🖥 ➿

Safari Motel M
(435) 623-1071. **$38-$47.** 413 S Main St. I-15, exit 222, 3 mi nw. Ext corridors. **Pets:** Other species. $3 one-time fee/pet. Service with restrictions, supervision.
SAVE SO X 🖥 ➿

OGDEN

Best Rest Inn M
(801) 393-8644. **$55-$65.** 1206 W 2100 S. I-15, exit 343, just e. Ext corridors. **Pets:** Other species. $20 deposit/room. Designated rooms, service with restrictions, crate.
ASK SO X 🖉 💺 🖥 💻 🍴 ➿

Best Western High Country Inn M
(801) 394-9474. **$59-$89.** 1335 W 12th St. I-15, exit 344 (12th St), then e. Ext corridors. **Pets:** Other species. $25 deposit/room. Service with restrictions, crate.
SAVE SO X 🖉 🖥 💻 🍴 ➿

Comfort Suites of Ogden M
(801) 621-2545. **$81-$165.** 2250 S 1200 W. I-15, exit 343E. Int corridors. **Pets:** Accepted.
ASK X 🖉 💺 🖥 💻 🍴 ➿ ✕

Days Inn of Ogden M
(801) 399-5671. **$49-$89.** 3306 Washington Blvd. I-15, exit 341A, 1.5 mi e via 31st St, then s. Ext/int corridors. **Pets:** Medium. $5 daily fee/pet. Service with restrictions, supervision.
ASK SO X 🖥 💻 ➿ ✕

Holiday Inn Express Hotel & Suites M
(801) 392-5000. **$81-$165.** 2245 S 1200 W. I-15, exit 343, just e. Int corridors. **Pets:** Accepted.
ASK X 🖉 💺 🖥 💻 ➿ ✕

Motel 6 Ogden #0111 M
(801) 627-4560. **$41-$51.** 1455 Washington Blvd. Downtown. Int corridors. **Pets:** Accepted.
SO X 🖥 ➿

▼▼ Red Roof Inn #7279 M ❋
(801) 627-2880. **$42-$60.** 1500 W Riverdale Rd. I-15, exit 340 southbound, 2 mi via Riverdale Rd; exit 342 northbound, 1 mi via Riverdale Rd. Ext/int corridors. **Pets:** Medium. Service with restrictions, supervision.
⊠ 🖐 📞 ➰

▼▼ Super 8 Motel M
(801) 731-7100. **$45-$56.** 1508 W 2100 S. I-15, exit 343, just w. Int corridors. **Pets:** Accepted.
ASK S❄ ⊠ 🖐 🖐 📞

ⒶⒶⒶ ▼▼ Western Colony Inn M
(801) 627-1332. **$35-$40.** 234 24th St. City Center. Ext corridors. **Pets:** Accepted.
SAVE S❄ ⊠ 📞 🍴

ⒶⒶⒶ ▼▼ Western Inn M
(801) 731-6500. **$64.** 1155 S 1700 W. I-15, exit 344, just w. Int corridors. **Pets:** Other species. $10 one-time fee/pet. Designated rooms, service with restrictions, supervision.
SAVE S❄ ⊠ 🖐 🖐 📞 ➡

OLD LA SAL

▼▼▼ Mt. Peale Inn & Spa BB ❋
(435) 686-2284. **$89-$199, 14 day notice.** 1415 E Hwy 46. 14 mi e from jct US 191 and SR 46. Ext/int corridors. **Pets:** Dogs only. $25 one-time fee/pet. Designated rooms, no service, supervision.
ASK S❄ ⊠ 📞 📞 🍴 ⊠ 🐾 ☎

OREM

ⒶⒶⒶ ▼▼▼▼ La Quinta Inn & Suites Orem (University Parkway) M
(801) 226-0440. **$89-$105.** 521 W University Pkwy. I-15, exit 269 to 12th St S, 1 mi e. Int corridors. **Pets:** Other species. Service with restrictions, supervision.
SAVE ⊠ 🐾 🖐 📞 📞 🏊

ⒶⒶⒶ ▼▼▼▼ La Quinta Inn Orem (North/Provo) M
(801) 235-9555. **$49-$89.** 1100 W 780 N. I-15, exit 272, east side. Int corridors. **Pets:** Accepted.
SAVE S❄ ⊠ 🐾 🖐 📞 📞 🏊

PANGUITCH

ⒶⒶⒶ ▼▼▼ Bryce Way Motel M
(435) 676-2400. **$35-$55.** 429 N Main St. On US 89. Ext corridors. **Pets:** Very small. $3 daily fee/pet. No service, supervision.
SAVE S❄ ⊠ 📞 📞

ⒶⒶⒶ ▼▼▼ Color Country Motel M
(435) 676-2386. **$35-$62.** 526 N Main St. On US 89. Ext corridors. **Pets:** Accepted.
SAVE S❄ ⊠ ➡

▼▼ Harold's Place Cabins CA
(435) 676-2350. **$45-$60.** 3066 Hwy 12. 1 mi e off US 89 at jct SR 12; 17 mi w of Bryce Canyon. Ext corridors. **Pets:** Medium. $20 deposit/room. Service with restrictions, supervision.
ASK S❄ ⊠ 📞 🍴 ☎

▼▼ Horizon Motel M
(435) 676-2651. **$39-$75.** 730 N Main St. US 89. Ext corridors. **Pets:** Very small, dogs only. $15 one-time fee/room. Designated rooms, service with restrictions, supervision.
ASK S❄ ⊠ 🖐 📞

ⒶⒶⒶ ▼▼▼ Marianna Inn Motel M
(435) 676-8844. **$30-$75.** 699 N Main St. On SR 89. Ext corridors. **Pets:** Accepted.
SAVE S❄ ⊠ 📞

▼▼ Silverado Wild West "Movie Town" M
(435) 676-8770. **$60-$89.** 3900 S Hwy 89. 0.3 mi n of jct SR 12 and 89, 5 mi s off Panguitch on US 89, then 17 mi w of Bryce Canyon. Ext corridors. **Pets:** Accepted.
ASK S❄ ⊠ 🖐 🍴 ⊠

PARK CITY

ⒶⒶⒶ ▼▼▼▼ Best Western Landmark Inn M ❋
(435) 649-7300. **$69-$169.** 6560 N Landmark Dr. I-80, exit 145, at Kimball Junction. Int corridors. **Pets:** Medium, other species. $100 deposit/pet, $10 daily fee/pet. Service with restrictions, supervision.
SAVE S❄ ⊠ 🖐M 🐾 🖐 📞 ➡ ⊠

▼▼▼▼ Holiday Inn Express Hotel & Suites M
(435) 658-1600. **$72-$189.** 1501 W Ute Blvd. I-80, exit 145, at Kimball Junction. Int corridors. **Pets:** Accepted.
ASK S❄ ⊠ 🐾 🖐 📞 📞 ➡ ⊠

ⒶⒶⒶ ▼▼▼▼ The Radisson Inn Park City SH
(435) 649-5000. **$79-$249, 46 day notice.** 2121 Park Ave. I-80, exit Kimball Junction; north end of town. Int corridors. **Pets:** Large, other species. $20 one-time fee/room. Service with restrictions, supervision.
SAVE ⊠ 🐾 📞 📞 🍴 ➡ ⊠

ⒶⒶⒶ ▼▼▼▼ WestGate Park City Resort & Spa LH
(435) 940-9444. **$89-$459.** 3000 The Canyons Resort Dr. I-80, exit 145, 3 mi sw on SR 224, follow signs. Int corridors. **Pets:** Accepted.
SAVE S❄ ⊠ 🖐 🖐 📞 🍴 ➡ ⊠

PAROWAN

ⒶⒶⒶ ▼▼▼ Days Inn M
(435) 477-3326. **$52-$99.** 625 W 200 S. I-15, exit 75, 1.5 mi e. Ext corridors. **Pets:** Medium. $10 daily fee/pet. Designated rooms, service with restrictions, supervision.
SAVE S❄ ⊠ 🖐 ➡ ⊠

PAYSON

▼▼▼ Comfort Inn M
(801) 465-4861. **$79-$99.** 830 N Main St. I-15, exit 250, just e. Int corridors. **Pets:** Large, other species. $20 deposit/room. Service with restrictions, supervision.
ASK S❄ ⊠ 🐾 🖐 📞 ➡ ⊠

PRICE

ⒶⒶⒶ ▼▼▼ Budget Host Inn M
(435) 637-2424. **$45-$57.** 145 N Carbonville Rd. US 6, exit 240, just e. Ext corridors. **Pets:** Medium. $10 daily fee/pet. Designated rooms, service with restrictions, crate.
SAVE S❄ ⊠ 🖐 📞 ➡

▼▼▼ National 9-Price River Inn M ❋
(435) 637-7000. **$42-$59.** 641 W Price River Dr. US 6, exit 240. Ext/int corridors. **Pets:** $5 daily fee/pet. Designated rooms, service with restrictions, supervision.
ASK S❄ ⊠ 🖐 📞

PROVO

ⒶⒶⒶ ▼▼ Colony Inn Suites-National 9 M
(801) 374-6800. **$45-$95.** 1380 S University Ave. I-15, exit 263. Ext corridors. **Pets:** Accepted.
SAVE ⊠ 🖐 ➡

▼▼▼▼ Days Inn M
(801) 375-8600. **$44-$89, 14 day notice.** 1675 N 200 W. I-15, exit 269, 3.5 mi e on University Pkwy. Ext corridors. **Pets:** Other species. $5 one-time fee/room. Service with restrictions, supervision.
ASK S❄ ⊠ 🐾 🖐 🖐 📞 ➡

▼▼ Econo Lodge Provo Airport M
(801) 373-0099. **$60-$80.** 1625 W Center St. I-15, exit 265A southbound; exit 265B northbound, 0.3 mi w. Ext corridors. **Pets:** Other species. $10 daily fee/pet. No service, supervision.
[A$K] [☉] [✕] [🛏] [💻]

▼▼▼ Hampton Inn M
(801) 377-6396. **$65-$99.** 1511 S 40 E. I-15, exit 263, just e. Int corridors. **Pets:** Accepted.
[A$K] [☉] [✕] [🏊] [♿] [🛏] [💻] [➰]

♦♦♦ ▼▼▼ Provo Travelers Inn M
(801) 373-8248. **$40-$60.** 469 W Center St. I-15, exit 265 southbound; exit 265A northbound. Ext corridors. **Pets:** Medium, other species. $50 deposit/room, $5 daily fee/pet. Designated rooms, service with restrictions, supervision.
[SAVE] [☉] [✕] [🛏] [➰]

▼▼▼ Residence Inn by Marriott M
(801) 374-1000. **$69-$149.** 252 W 2230 N. I-15, exit 269, 3.1 mi e via University Pkwy. Int corridors. **Pets:** Accepted.
[A$K] [☉] [✕] [🔟] [🏊] [♿] [🛏] [💻] [🏊] [✕]

▼▼ Sleep Inn M
(801) 377-6597. **$55-$85.** 1505 S 40 E. I-15, exit 263, just e. Int corridors. **Pets:** Other species. $10 one-time fee/pet. Crate.
[A$K] [☉] [✕] [🏊] [♿] [🛏] [💻]

▼▼▼ Super 8 Provo BYU/Orem UVSC M
(801) 374-6020. **$49-$79.** 1555 N Canyon Rd. I-15, exit 269, 3.5 mi e. Int corridors. **Pets:** Other species. Supervision.
[A$K] [☉] [✕] [♿] [🛏] [💻] [➰]

RICHFIELD

♦♦♦ ▼▼▼ AppleTree Inn M
(435) 896-5481. **$35-$75.** 145 S Main St. I-70, exit 37 or 40; center of downtown. Ext corridors. **Pets:** $6 one-time fee/room.
[SAVE] [☉] [✕] [🏊] [🛏] [💻] [➰]

♦♦♦ ▼▼▼ Budget Host Nights Inn M 🐾
(435) 896-8228. **$36-$48.** 69 S Main St. I-70, exit 37 or 40; center of downtown. Ext corridors. **Pets:** Large. $5 one-time fee/room. No service, supervision.
[SAVE] [☉] [✕] [🛏] [🍴] [➰]

♦♦♦ ▼▼▼ Days Inn SH
(435) 896-6476. **$52-$90.** 333 N Main St. I-70, exit 40, 1 mi s on US 89. Int corridors. **Pets:** Small, other species. $10 one-time fee/room. Designated rooms, service with restrictions, supervision.
[SAVE] [☉] [✕] [🛏] [💻] [🍴] [🏊] [✕]

▼▼ Luxury Inn M
(435) 893-0100. **$39-$79, 5 day notice.** 1335 N Main St. I-70, exit 40; north end of town. Int corridors. **Pets:** Accepted.
[A$K] [☉] [✕] [♿] [🛏] [➰]

♦♦♦ ▼ New West Motel M
(435) 896-4076. **$38-$44.** 447 S Main St. I-70, exit 37 or 40; downtown. Ext corridors. **Pets:** Accepted.
[SAVE] [☉] [✕] [🛏] [🔲]

▼▼▼ Richfield Travelodge M
(435) 896-9271. **$45-$85.** 647 S Main St. I-70, exit 37; south end of town. Int corridors. **Pets:** Accepted.
[A$K] [☉] [✕] [🛏] [💻] [🍴] [➰]

♦♦♦ ▼▼▼ Romanico Inn M
(435) 896-8471. **$33-$44.** 1170 S Main St. I-70, exit 37, just n. Ext corridors. **Pets:** Accepted.
[SAVE] [☉] [✕] [🛏]

ROOSEVELT

♦♦♦ ▼▼▼ Frontier Motel M
(435) 722-2201. **$47-$62.** 75 S 200 E. On US 40. Ext corridors. **Pets:** Accepted.
[SAVE] [☉] [✕] [🛏] [🍴] [➰]

♦♦♦ ▼▼▼ Western Hills Motel M
(435) 722-5115. **$35-$45, 3 day notice.** 737 E 200 N. On US 40. Ext corridors. **Pets:** Very small. $5 one-time fee/pet. No service, supervision.
[SAVE] [☉] [✕] [🛏]

ST. GEORGE

▼▼▼ An Olde Penny Farthing Inn Bed & Breakfast BB
(435) 673-7755. **$70-$145, 7 day notice.** 278 N 100 W. In historic district. Int corridors. **Pets:** Accepted.
[✕] [♿] [🛏] [🔲]

♦♦♦ ▼▼▼▼ Atkin's Singletree Inn M
(435) 673-6161. **$46-$129.** 260 E St George Blvd. I-15, exit 8, 1.5 mi w. Ext corridors. **Pets:** Medium. $16 one-time fee/pet. Designated rooms, service with restrictions, supervision.
[SAVE] [☉] [✕] [🛏] [➰]

▼▼ Best Value Inn M
(435) 673-4666. **$29-$99.** 60 W St. George Blvd. 1 blk w of Main; downtown. Ext corridors. **Pets:** Small. $7 daily fee/pet. Service with restrictions, supervision.
[A$K] [☉] [✕] [🛏] [💻] [➰]

▼▼ The Bluffs Inn & Suites M
(435) 628-6699. **$42-$99.** 1140 S Bluff St. I-15, exit 6 (Bluff St), just w. Ext corridors. **Pets:** Medium. $15 daily fee/pet. Service with restrictions, supervision.
[A$K] [☉] [✕] [♿] [🛏] [💻] [➰]

▼▼▼ Budget Inn & Suites M
(435) 673-6661. **$39-$166.** 1221 S Main St. I-15, exit 6 (Bluff St), just w. Ext corridors. **Pets:** Accepted.
[A$K] [☉] [✕] [♿] [🛏] [➰] [✕]

▼▼▼ Crystal Inn St. George SH
(435) 688-7477. **$79-$109.** 1450 S Hilton Dr. I-15, exit 6 (Bluff St), just w. Int corridors. **Pets:** Very small, other species. $25 one-time fee/pet. Designated rooms, service with restrictions, crate.
[A$K] [☉] [✕] [🛏] [💻] [🍴] [➰] [✕]

♦♦♦ ▼▼▼ Econo Lodge M
(435) 673-4861. **$40-$120.** 460 E St. George Blvd. Cross streets 500 E and St. George Blvd; downtown. Ext corridors. **Pets:** Small. $10 daily fee/pet. Designated rooms, service with restrictions, supervision.
[SAVE] [☉] [✕] [🏊] [♿] [🛏] [💻] [🍴] [➰]

♦♦♦ ▼▼▼ Fairfield Inn by Marriott M
(435) 673-6066. **$59-$89.** 1660 S Convention Center Dr. I-15, exit 6 (Bluff St), just e. Int corridors. **Pets:** Other species. $75 one-time fee/room. Service with restrictions, supervision.
[SAVE] [☉] [✕] [🏊] [♿] [🛏] [➰]

♦♦♦ ▼▼▼▼ Green Valley Spa & Coyote Inn SH 🐾
(435) 628-8060. **$395.** 1871 W Canyon View Dr. Bluff and S Main sts, 4 mi sw via Hilton Dr to Tonaquint Dr, to Dixie Dr, then to Canyon View Dr. Ext corridors. **Pets:** Small. $500 deposit/room, $25 daily fee/pet. Service with restrictions, crate.
[SAVE] [✕] [♿] [🛏] [💻] [➰] [✕]

♦♦♦ ▼▼▼ Holiday Inn SH
(435) 628-4235. **$72-$140.** 850 S Bluff St. I-15, exit 6 (Bluff St), just w. Ext/int corridors. **Pets:** Medium, other species. $25 one-time fee/pet. Designated rooms, service with restrictions, supervision.
[SAVE] [☉] [✕] [🏊] [♿] [🛏] [💻] [🍴] [➰] [✕]

(AAA) ▽▽▽▽ **Howard Johnson Express Inn &
Suites** M ❀
(435) 628-8000. **$49-$139.** 1040 S Main St. I-15, exit 6 (Bluff St), just w, then just e. Ext corridors. **Pets:** Dogs only. $10 daily fee/pet. Designated rooms, service with restrictions, supervision.
[SAVE] [S♦] [✕] [♿] [📶] [💻] [🏊]

(AAA) ▽▽▽▽ **Red Cliffs Inn & Suites** M
(435) 673-3537. **$59-$149.** 912 Red Cliffs Dr. I-15, exit 10, just e. Ext/int corridors. **Pets:** Accepted.
[SAVE] [S♦] [✕] [♿] [📶] [💻] [🍴] [🏊]

▽▽▽▽ **Seven Wives Inn** BB
(435) 628-3737. **$85-$250, 7 day notice.** 217 N 100 W. I-15, exit 8, 2.1 mi w, then right. Ext/int corridors. **Pets:** Accepted.
[ASK] [S♦] [✕] [♿] [📶] [🍴] [🏊]

▽▽▽ **Suntime Inn** M
(435) 673-6181. **$36-$99.** 420 E St. George Blvd. Cross streets 400 E and St. George Blvd; downtown. Ext corridors. **Pets:** Small. $5 daily fee/pet. Designated rooms, service with restrictions, supervision.
[✕] [📶] [🏊]

▽▽▽ **Super 8 Motel** M
(435) 688-8383. **$39-$99.** 915 S Bluff St. I-15, exit 6 (Bluff St), just w. Int corridors. **Pets:** Medium, other species. $10 daily fee/pet. Designated rooms, service with restrictions, supervision.
[ASK] [S♦] [✕] [🏊]

SALINA

▽▽▽ **Ranch Motel** M
(435) 529-7789. **$38-$52.** 80 N State St. On US 89; near town center. Ext/int corridors. **Pets:** Large, other species. $6 daily fee/pet. Service with restrictions, supervision.
[ASK] [S♦] [✕] [📶]

(AAA) ▽▽▽ **Scenic Hills Super 8** M
(435) 529-7483. **$50-$62.** 75 E 1500 S. I-70, exit 53, just n. Ext corridors. **Pets:** Other species. $10 daily fee/room. Service with restrictions, supervision.
[SAVE] [S♦] [✕] [📶] [🏊]

SALT LAKE CITY METROPOLITAN AREA

BOUNTIFUL

(AAA) ▽▽▽▽ **Country Inn & Suites** M
(801) 292-8100. **$75-$89.** 999 N 500 W. I-15, exit 317. Int corridors. **Pets:** Other species. $100 deposit/room. Service with restrictions, supervision.
[SAVE] [S♦] [✕] [🐾] [♿] [📶] [💻] [🏊]

COTTONWOOD HEIGHTS

▽▽▽▽ **Candlewood Suites Hotel** M
(801) 567-0111. **$77-$129.** 6990 S Park Centre Dr. I-15, exit 297, 2.5 mi via 7200 S and Fort Union Blvd. Int corridors. **Pets:** Accepted.
[ASK] [S♦] [✕] [🐾] [♿] [📶] [💻]

▽▽▽▽ **Residence Inn by Marriott at The
Cottonwoods** M ❀
(801) 453-0430. **$159-$269.** 6425 S 3000 E. I-215 S, exit 6200 S, 0.3 mi se. Int corridors. **Pets:** Large, other species. $75 one-time fee/room. Service with restrictions.
[ASK] [✕] [🐾] [♿] [📶] [💻] [🏊] [✕]

DRAPER

▽▽▽▽ **Holiday Inn Express** M
(801) 571-2511. **$59-$89.** 12033 S Factory Outlet Dr. I-15, exit 291, just n; on east side of interstate. Int corridors. **Pets:** Medium, other species. $30 deposit/pet. Service with restrictions, crate.
[ASK] [S♦] [✕] [♿] [📶] [💻]

▽▽▽▽ **Ramada Limited** M
(801) 571-1122. **$59-$79.** 12605 S Minuteman Dr. I-15, exit 291, 0.3 mi s on frontage road. Int corridors. **Pets:** Medium, other species. $30 deposit/room. Service with restrictions, crate.
[ASK] [S♦] [✕] [🐾] [♿] [📶] [💻]

MIDVALE

(AAA) ▽▽▽▽ **Best Western Executive Inn** M
(801) 566-4141. **$70.** 280 W 7200 S. I-15, exit 297, just e. Int corridors. **Pets:** Medium, other species. $15 daily fee/room. Service with restrictions, supervision.
[SAVE] [S♦] [✕] [🐾] [📶] [💻] [🏊]

(AAA) ▽▽▽▽ **La Quinta Inn Salt Lake City (Midvale)** M
(801) 566-3291. **$82-$95.** 7231 S Catalpa St. I-15, exit 297, just e. Int corridors. **Pets:** Other species. Service with restrictions, crate.
[SAVE] [✕] [🐾] [♿] [📶] [💻] [🏊]

▽▽▽ **Motel 6 #476** M
(801) 561-0058. **$42-$55.** 7263 S Catalpa Rd. I-15, exit 297, just e. Ext corridors. **Pets:** Small, other species. Service with restrictions, supervision.
[S♦] [✕] [📶] [🏊]

(AAA) ▽▽▽▽ **National 9 Discovery Inn** M
(801) 561-2256. **$52-$79.** 380 W 7200 S. I-15, exit 297, just e. Ext corridors. **Pets:** Medium. $25 deposit/pet, $5 daily fee/pet. Designated rooms, service with restrictions, supervision.
[SAVE] [S♦] [✕] [🐾] [📶] [💻] [🏊]

▽▽▽ **Super 8** M
(801) 255-5559. **$54-$79.** 7048 S 900 E. I-15, exit 297, 1.5 mi e on 7200 S to 900 E. Int corridors. **Pets:** Medium. $50 deposit/room. Service with restrictions, crate.
[ASK] [S♦] [✕] [🐾] [♿] [📶] [💻]

MURRAY

▽▽▽▽ **Holiday Inn Express** M
(801) 268-2533. **$63-$90.** 4465 S Century Dr. I-15, exit 301, just w. Int corridors. **Pets:** Accepted.
[ASK] [S♦] [✕] [🐾] [📶] [💻] [🏊]

▽▽▽▽ **Pavilion Inn** M
(801) 264-1054. **Call for rates.** 5335 College Dr. I-15, exit 300, 0.3 mi w. Int corridors. **Pets:** Accepted.
[S♦] [✕] [🐾] [📶] [🏊]

▽▽▽ **Studio 6 #6038** M
(801) 685-2102. **$49-$59.** 975 E 6600 S. I-215, exit 9 on 900 E, 0.5 mi e. Ext corridors. **Pets:** Accepted.
[S♦] [✕] [🐾] [♿] [📶] [💻]

NORTH SALT LAKE

(AAA) ▽▽▽▽ **Best Western Cottontree Inn** M
(801) 292-7666. **$89.** 1030 N 400 E. I-15, exit 315, just e. Int corridors. **Pets:** Large, other species. Service with restrictions, supervision.
[SAVE] [S♦] [✕] [🐾] [📶] [💻] [🏊]

SALT LAKE CITY

▽▽▽ **Airport Comfort Inn** SH ❀
(801) 746-5200. **$69-$99.** 200 N Admiral Byrd Rd. I-80, exit 113, 0.8 mi ne via 5600 W, Amelia Earhart Dr, then s. Int corridors. **Pets:** Other species. $15 one-time fee/room. Designated rooms, service with restrictions, supervision.
[ASK] [S♦] [✕] [🐾] [♿] [📶] [💻] [🍴] [🏊]

▼▼ Alpine Executive Suites ▣
(801) 533-8184. **$99-$109, 10 day notice.** 164 S 900 E. Cross streets 200 S and 900 E. Int corridors. **Pets:** $300 deposit/pet, $10 daily fee/room. Designated rooms, crate.

(ASK) ⬛ ✕ ⬛ ⬛

▼▼▼▼ Best Western Airport Inn Ⓜ
(801) 539-5005. **$69.** 315 N Admiral Byrd Rd. I-80, exit 113, 0.8 m ne via 5600 W and Amelia Earhart Dr, then s. Int corridors. **Pets:** $15 one-time fee/pet. Designated rooms, service with restrictions, supervision.

(ASK) ⬛ ✕ ⬛ ⬛ ⬛ ⬄

Ⓐ ▼▼▼▼ Best Western Garden Inn Ⓢ
(801) 521-2930. **$69-$109.** 154 W 600 S. Between cross streets 100-200 W. Ext/int corridors. **Pets:** Other species. $50 deposit/room. Designated rooms, supervision.

(SAVE) ⬛ ✕ ⬛ ⬛ ⬛ ⬛ ⬛ ⬄

Ⓐ ▼▼▼▼ Best Western Salt Lake Plaza Ⓛ
(801) 521-0130. **$69-$129, 3 day notice.** 122 W S Temple Dr. W of Temple Square. Int corridors. **Pets:** Accepted.

(SAVE) ⬛ ✕ ⬛ ⬛ ⬛ ⬛ ⬄

▼▼▼ Candlewood Suite Hotel Ⓜ
(801) 359-7500. **$47-$67.** 2170 W N Temple. 3 mi w of Temple Square. Int corridors. **Pets:** Medium. $25 one-time fee/room.

(ASK) ⬛ ✕ ⬛ ⬛ ⬛ ⬛

Ⓐ ▼▼▼▼ Chase Suite Hotel by Woodfin Ⓜ ❀
(801) 532-5511. **$99-$139.** 765 E 400 S. Cross streets 700 E and 400 S. Ext corridors. **Pets:** Other species. $50 deposit/pet, $5 daily fee/room. Service with restrictions, crate.

(SAVE) ⬛ ✕ ⬛ ⬛ ⬛ ⬛ ⬛ ⬄ ✕

Ⓐ ▼▼ City Creek Inn Ⓜ
(801) 533-9100. **$48-$74.** 230 W N Temple Dr. Cross street 200 W. Ext corridors. **Pets:** Accepted.

(SAVE) ⬛ ✕

▼▼▼ Days Inn-Salt Lake City Airport Ⓜ
(801) 539-8538. **$74.** 1900 W N Temple. W of Temple 59, 2.5 mi. Int corridors. **Pets:** Other species. $20 deposit/room. Designated rooms, service with restrictions, supervision.

(ASK) ⬛ ✕ ⬛ ⬛ ⬛ ⬛ ⬄

▼▼ Econo Lodge Downtown Ⓜ
(801) 363-0062. **$54-$64.** 715 W N Temple. W from Temple Square, 1 mi. Ext corridors. **Pets:** Other species. $15 deposit/room. Service with restrictions, supervision.

(ASK) ⬛ ✕ ⬛ ⬛ ⬄

▼▼▼ Hilton Salt Lake City Airport Ⓛ
(801) 539-1515. **$72-$162.** 5151 Wiley Post Way. I-80, exit 114 westbound, 0.4 mi nw via Wright Brothers Dr and Wiley Post; exit 113 eastbound, 1.3 mi ne via 5600 W, Amelia Earhart Dr then s on Charles Lindbergh Dr. Int corridors. **Pets:** Large, other species. $25 deposit/pet, $25 one-time fee/pet. Designated rooms, service with restrictions, crate.

(ASK) ⬛ ✕ ⬛ ⬛ ⬛ ⬛ ⬛ ⬄ ✕

Ⓐ ▼▼▼▼ Hilton Salt Lake City Center Ⓛ
(801) 328-2000. **$69-$179.** 255 S W Temple Dr. Int corridors. **Pets:** Accepted.

(SAVE) ⬛ ✕ ⬛ ⬛ ⬛ ⬛ ⬛ ⬛ ⬄ ✕

Ⓐ ▼▼▼▼ Holiday Inn-Downtown Ⓢ
(801) 359-8600. **$119-$129.** 999 S Main St. Cross streets 900 S & Main St. Int corridors. **Pets:** Small. $35 one-time fee/pet. Designated rooms, service with restrictions, supervision.

(SAVE) ✕ ⬛ ⬛ ⬛ ⬛ ⬛ ⬛ ⬄ ✕

▼▼ Homestead Studio Suites Hotel-Salt Lake City/Sugar House Ⓜ ❀
(801) 474-0771. **$71-$90.** 1220 E 2100 S. Cross streets 1300 E and 2100 S Sugarhouse. Ext corridors. **Pets:** Small, other species. $75 one-time fee/pet. Designated rooms, service with restrictions, supervision.

(ASK) ⬛ ✕ ⬛ ⬛ ⬛ ⬛ ⬛

Ⓐ ▼▼▼ ▼▼▼ Hotel Monaco Ⓛ
(801) 595-0000. **$219-$345.** 15 W 200 S. Cross streets 200 S and Main St. Int corridors. **Pets:** Accepted.

(SAVE) ⬛ ✕ ⬛ ⬛ ⬛ ⬛ ✕

Ⓐ ▼▼▼ Howard Johnson Express Inn Ⓜ
(801) 521-3450. **$49-$79.** 121 N 300 W. At N Temple and 300 W. Ext/int corridors. **Pets:** Accepted.

(SAVE) ⬛ ✕ ⬛ ⬛ ⬛ ⬄

Ⓐ ▼▼▼ La Quinta Inn & Suites Salt Lake City (Airport) Ⓜ
(801) 366-4444. **$99-$115.** 4905 W Wiley Post Way. I-80, exit 113 eastbound, 2 mi ne via 5600 W, Amelia Earhart Dr, s on Wright Brothers Dr, then 2 mi to Wiley Post Way; exit 114 westbound, 0.3 mi nw. Int corridors. **Pets:** Accepted.

(SAVE) ✕ ⬛ ⬛ ⬛ ⬛ ⬄

▼▼ Metropolitan Inn Ⓜ
(801) 531-7100. **$69-$119.** 524 SW Temple. Cross streets 500 S and Temple. Ext corridors. **Pets:** Medium. $25 one-time fee/pet. Designated rooms, service with restrictions, supervision.

(ASK) ⬛ ✕ ⬛ ⬛ ⬛ ⬄

▼▼ Microtel Inn & Suites Ⓜ
(801) 236-2800. **$49-$69.** 61 N Tommy Thompson Rd. I-80, exit 114 westbound, n on Wright Brothers Dr, e on Wiley Post Way; exit 113 eastbound, 2.4 mi ne via 5600 W, Amelia Earhart Dr, then s. Int corridors. **Pets:** Accepted.

✕ ⬛ ⬛ ⬛ ⬛

Ⓐ ▼▼▼ Red Lion Hotel Salt Lake Downtown Ⓛ
(801) 521-7373. **$169-$179.** 161 W 600 S. At W Temple and 600 S. Int corridors. **Pets:** Small, other species. $10 daily fee/pet. Service with restrictions.

(SAVE) ⬛ ✕ ⬛ ⬛ ⬛ ⬛ ⬛ ⬛ ⬄ ✕

▼▼▼ Renaissance Suites ▣
(801) 534-8500. **$124-$174, 3 day notice.** 267 W Broadway. Cross streets 200 W and 300 S. Int corridors. **Pets:** Small. $15 daily fee/pet. Service with restrictions, supervision.

(ASK) ⬛ ✕ ⬛ ⬛ ⬛

▼▼▼ Residence Inn by Marriott-City Center Ⓢ
(801) 355-3300. **$109-$219.** 285 W Broadway (300 S). Cross streets 300 W and Broadway (300 S). Int corridors. **Pets:** Medium. $75 one-time fee/room. Service with restrictions, crate.

(ASK) ✕ ⬛ ⬛ ⬛ ⬛ ⬄ ✕

▼▼▼ Residence Inn by Marriott Salt Lake City Airport Ⓢ
(801) 532-4101. **$107-$152.** 4883 W Douglas Corrigon Way. I-80, exit 114 westbound, via Wright Brothers Dr; exit 113 eastbound, via Amelia Earhart and Wright Brothers drs, then 2.6 mi se. Int corridors. **Pets:** Accepted.

(ASK) ⬛ ✕ ⬛M ⬛ ⬛ ⬛ ⬛ ⬛ ⬄ ✕

▼▼▼ Saltair Bed & Breakfast Ⓑ
(801) 533-8184. **$79-$109, 30 day notice.** 164 S 900 E. Cross streets 900 E and 200 S. Ext/int corridors. **Pets:** Accepted.

(ASK) ⬛ ✕ ⬛ ⬛

▼ Salt Lake Travelodge At Temple Square Ⓜ
(801) 533-8200. **$88.** 144 W N Temple. Just n of Genealogical Library. Ext/int corridors. **Pets:** Other species. Designated rooms, service with restrictions, crate.

(ASK) ⬛ ✕ ⬛ ⬛

▽▼▽▼ Sheraton City Centre 🔲 ❀
(801) 401-2000. **$70-$119.** 150 W 500 S. At 200 W and 500 S. Int corridors. **Pets:** Service with restrictions, supervision.
🅰🆂🅺 ⌷ ⊠ ⌀ ♿ 🛏 💻 🍴 ≈ ⊠

▽▼▽▼ Shilo Inn Hotel 🔲
(801) 521-9500. **$70-$140.** 206 S W Temple. Cross streets 200 S and W Temple. Int corridors. **Pets:** Accepted.
🅰🆂🅺 ⌷ ⊠ ⌀ ♿ 🛏 💻 🍴 ≈ ⊠

▵▵▵ The Skyline Inn **M**
(801) 582-5350. **$55-$67.** 2475 E 1700 S. E off Foothill Dr. Ext corridors. **Pets:** Accepted.
🆂🅰🆅🅴 ⌷ ⊠ ⌀ 🛏 ≈

▵▵▵ Super 8 Airport **M**
(801) 533-8878. **$59-$69.** 223 N Jimmy Doolittle Rd. I-80, exit 113, 0.7 mi ne via 5600 W, Amelia Earhart Dr and Admiral Byrd Rd, then e. Int corridors. **Pets:** Medium, other species. $50 deposit/room. Service with restrictions, supervision.
🆂🅰🆅🅴 ⌷ ⊠ ⌀ ♿ 🛏 💻 ≈

SANDY

▵▵▵ Best Western Cotton Tree Inn **M**
(801) 523-8484. **$75-$120.** 10695 S Auto Mall Dr. I-15, exit 293 eastbound, 0.3 mi e. Int corridors. **Pets:** Small. $10 one-time fee/room. Designated rooms, service with restrictions, supervision.
🆂🅰🆅🅴 ⌷ ⊠ ⌀ ♿ 🛏 💻 ≈

▽▼▽ Comfort Inn **M**
(801) 255-4919. **$59-$79, 7 day notice.** 8955 S 255 West. I-15, exit 295, just ne, follow signs. Int corridors. **Pets:** Other species. $10 daily fee/pet. Service with restrictions, supervision.
🅰🆂🅺 ⌷ ⊠ ⌀ ♿ 🛏 💻 ≈

▵▵▵ Country Inn & Suites **M** ❀
(801) 553-1151. **$83-$101.** 10499 S Jordan Gateway. I-15, exit 293 westbound, 1 mi w via 10600 S to Jordan Gate Way, then n. Int corridors. **Pets:** $25 deposit/room, $25 one-time fee/room. Service with restrictions, crate.
🆂🅰🆅🅴 ⌷ ⊠ ⌀ ♿ 🛏 💻 ≈ ⊠

▽▼▽▼ Residence Inn by Marriott **M** ❀
(801) 561-5005. **$109-$209.** 270 W 10000 S. From Stare St, 0.3 mi w on 10000 S. Int corridors. **Pets:** Other species. Designated rooms.
🅰🆂🅺 ⌷ ⊠ ⌀ ♿ 🛏 💻 ≈ ⊠

▽▼▽▼ Sandy Comfort Suites **M** ❀
(801) 495-1317. **$65-$85.** 10680 S Auto Mall Dr. I-15, exit 293 eastbound, 0.3 mi e. Int corridors. **Pets:** Other species. $10 daily fee/room. Service with restrictions, supervision.
🅰🆂🅺 ⌷ ⊠ ⌀ 🛏 💻 ≈ ⊠

▽▼ ▽▼ Sleep Inn **M**
(801) 572-2020. **$49-$79.** 10676 S 300 W. I-15, exit 293 westbound, just w. Int corridors. **Pets:** Medium, other species. $5 daily fee/pet. Service with restrictions, supervision.
🅰🆂🅺 ⌷ ⊠ 🛏 💻 ≈

▽▼▽ Super 8 Motel South Jordan/Sandy **M**
(801) 553-8888. **$45-$75.** 10722 S 300 W. I-15, exit 293 westbound, just w. Int corridors. **Pets:** Accepted.
🅰🆂🅺 ⌷ ⊠ ⌀ 🛏 💻 ≈ ⊠

SOUTH SALT LAKE

▽▼▽ Days Inn-Central **M**
(801) 486-8780. **$59-$99.** 315 W 3300 S. W from State St, 0.3 mi; I-15, just e. Ext corridors. **Pets:** Accepted.
🅰🆂🅺 ⌷ ⊠ ⌀ 🛏 💻 ≈ ⊠

▵▵▵ Ramada Limited Salt Lake City **M**
(801) 486-2400. **$81-$125.** 2455 S State St. Cross street Morris Ave. Int corridors. **Pets:** Small. Service with restrictions, supervision.
🆂🅰🆅🅴 ⌷ ⊠ ⌀ 🛏 💻 ≈

TAYLORSVILLE

▽▼▽ Homestead Studio Suites Hotel-Salt Lake City/Mid Valley **M**
(801) 269-9292. **$54-$74.** 5683 S Redwood Rd. I-215, exit 13, 0.5 mi n. Ext corridors. **Pets:** Medium, other species. $25 one-time fee/room. Service with restrictions.
🅰🆂🅺 ⌷ ⊠ ⌀ 🛏 💻

WEST VALLEY CITY

▽▼▽ Baymont Inn & Suites Salt Lake City-West Valley City **M**
(801) 886-1300. **$64-$84.** 2229 W City Center Ct. I-215, exit 18, just e. Int corridors. **Pets:** Other species. $50 deposit/room. Designated rooms, service with restrictions.
🅰🆂🅺 ⌷ ⊠ ⌀ 🛏 💻 ≈

▽▼▽▼ La Quinta Inn West Valley City (Salt Lake-West) **M**
(801) 954-9292. **Call for rates.** 3540 S 2200 W. I-215, exit 18; east side. Int corridors. **Pets:** Other species. Supervision.
⌷ ⊠ ⌀ ♿ 🛏 💻 ≈

▽▼ Sleep Inn **M**
(801) 975-1888. **$55-$99.** 3440 S 2200 W. I-215, exit 18, just e. Int corridors. **Pets:** Accepted.
🅰🆂🅺 ⌷ ⊠ ⌀ ♿ 🛏 💻

WOODS CROSS

▽▼▽▼ Hampton Inn **M**
(801) 296-1211. **$74-$89.** 2393 S 800 W. I-15, exit 315, just w of freeway. Int corridors. **Pets:** Medium. $50 deposit/room. Service with restrictions, supervision.
🅰🆂🅺 ⌷ ⊠ ⌀ ♿ 🛏 💻 ≈

▽▼ Motel 6 #1205 **M**
(801) 298-0289. **$43-$55.** 2433 S 800 W. I-15, exit 315 westbound, just w. Ext corridors. **Pets:** Accepted.
⌷ ⊠ ♿ 🛏 ≈

END METROPOLITAN AREA

SCIPIO

▽▼ ▽▼ Super 8 **M**
(435) 758-9188. **$55-$65.** 230 W 400 N. I-15, exit 188, just ne. Int corridors. **Pets:** Accepted.
🅰🆂🅺 ⌷ ⊠ ♿ 🛏 💻 ≈

SPANISH FORK

▵▵▵ Western Inn **M**
(801) 798-9400. **$54-$65.** 632 Kirby Ln. I-15, exit 258 southbound, 0.5 mi e; exit 257 northbound, 1 mi ne. Int corridors. **Pets:** Dogs only. $10 one-time fee/pet. Service with restrictions, supervision.
🆂🅰🆅🅴 ⌷ ⊠ 🛏

SPRINGDALE

Best Western Zion Park Inn M
(435) 772-3200. **$70-$113.** 1215 Zion Park Blvd. 2 mi s of park entrance. Int corridors. **Pets:** Small. $25 one-time fee/room. Designated rooms, service with restrictions, supervision.

Canyon Ranch Motel CA
(435) 772-3357. **$44-$92.** 668 Zion Park Blvd. SR 9, just s of south gate to Zion National Park. Ext corridors. **Pets:** Small, dogs only. $10 one-time fee/pet. Supervision.

Driftwood Lodge M
(435) 772-3262. **$72-$109.** 1515 Zion Park Blvd. SR 9, 2 mi s of south gate to Zion National Park. Ext corridors. **Pets:** Other species. $10 one-time fee/room. Designated rooms, service with restrictions, supervision.

SPRINGVILLE

Best Western CottonTree Inn M
(801) 489-3641. **$59-$94, 14 day notice.** 1455 N 1750 W. I-15, exit 261, just e; just s of Provo. Int corridors. **Pets:** Other species. $10 one-time fee/room. Service with restrictions, crate.

Days Inn M
(801) 491-0300. **$50-$60.** 520 S 2000 W. I-15, exit 259. Int corridors. **Pets:** Very small, dogs only. $25 deposit/pet. Service with restrictions, supervision.

TICABOO

Ticaboo Resort M
(435) 788-2110. **$59-$189.** 84533 Hwy 276. Jct SR 95 and 276, 28 mi s. Int corridors. **Pets:** Accepted.

TORREY

Cactus Hill Ranch Motel M
(435) 425-3578. **$45-$75, 3 day notice.** 830 S 1000 E. 5 mi s of SR 24 at Teasdale; 5 mi w of SR 12, exit Teasdale; 13 mi w of Capitol Reef National Park, 2 mi se of Town Center. Ext corridors. **Pets:** Small, dogs only. $5 one-time fee/pet. Service with restrictions.

Comfort Inn & Suites M
(435) 425-3866. **$39-$109.** 2424 E Hwy 24. On SR 24, 1.5 mi e of jct SR 12 and 24, 1.5 mi w of Capitol Rd. Ext corridors. **Pets:** Accepted.

Rim Rock Inn M
(435) 425-3398. **$42-$64.** 2523 E Hwy 24. 2.5 mi e of jct SR 12 and 24; east end of town. Ext corridors. **Pets:** Other species. $5 daily fee/pet. Service with restrictions, crate.

Torrey/Capitol Reef-Super 8 M
(435) 425-3688. **$37-$89.** 600 E Hwy 24. On SR 24, 0.3 mi w of SR 12; 3.3 mi w of Capitol Reef National Park. Int corridors. **Pets:** Medium, other species. $5 daily fee/pet. Designated rooms, service with restrictions, supervision.

Torrey Days Inn M
(435) 425-3111. **$55-$75.** 675 E Hwy 24. Jct SR 12 and 24. Int corridors. **Pets:** Small, other species. $10 one-time fee/room. Designated rooms, service with restrictions, supervision.

Wonderland Inn M
(435) 425-3775. **$40-$70.** Jct SR 12 & 24. Jct SR 12 and 24; 3 mi w of Capitol Reef National Park. Ext corridors. **Pets:** Other species. $10 daily fee/pet. Designated rooms, service with restrictions, crate.

TREMONTON

Sandman Motel M
(435) 257-5675. **$45-$54.** 585 W Main St. I-15/84, exit 376, 2.1 mi ne to 4-way stop, then 1.5 mi w; I-15, exit 383 southbound, 0.6 mi e to 4-way stop, s to Main St, then 0.5 mi w; I-84, exit 40, 1.5 mi e. Ext corridors. **Pets:** Accepted.

TROPIC

Bryce Pioneer Village M
(435) 679-8546. **$65-$75.** 80 S Main St. South end of town. Ext corridors. **Pets:** Accepted.

World Host Bryce Valley Inn M
(435) 679-8811. **$45-$125.** 199 N Main St. SR 12, 10 mi e of Bryce Canyon Park. Ext/int corridors. **Pets:** Medium. $10 daily fee/pet. Designated rooms, service with restrictions, supervision.

VERNAL

Econo Lodge M
(435) 789-2000. **$55-$65.** 311 E Main St. On US 40. Ext corridors. **Pets:** Other species. $5 daily fee/pet. Service with restrictions, supervision.

Motel 6 M
(435) 789-0666. **Call for rates.** 1092 W Hwy 40. North end of town on US 40. Int corridors. **Pets:** Dogs only. $5 daily fee/pet. No service, supervision.

Rodeway Inn M
(435) 789-8172. **$50-$60.** 590 W Main St. US 40. Ext corridors. **Pets:** Accepted.

Sage Motel & Restaurant M
(435) 789-1442. **$45-$80.** 54 W Main St. Center. Ext corridors. **Pets:** Other species. $5 daily fee/pet. Designated rooms, service with restrictions.

WELLINGTON

National 9 Inn M
(435) 637-7980. **$42-$59.** 50 S 700 E. On US 6. Ext/int corridors. **Pets:** Medium. $25 deposit/pet, $5 one-time fee/pet. Service with restrictions, supervision.

WENDOVER

Days Inn of Wendover M
(435) 665-2215. **$39-$79.** 685 E Wendover Blvd. I-80, exit 2. Int corridors. **Pets:** Other species. $5 daily fee/room. Service with restrictions, supervision.

Econo Lodge M
(435) 665-2226. **$35-$79.** 245 E Wendover Blvd. I-80, exit 2. Ext/int corridors. **Pets:** Other species. $5 daily fee/room. Service with restrictions, supervision.

Western Ridge Motel M
(435) 665-2211. **$28-$74.** 895 E Wendover Blvd. I-80, exit 2. Ext corridors. **Pets:** Small. $5 daily fee/pet. Service with restrictions, supervision.

VERMONT

ALBURG

▼▼ Ransom Bay Inn [BB]
(802) 796-3399. **$85-$95.** 4 Center Bay Rd. 0.5 mi s on US 2, from jct SR 78. Int corridors. **Pets:** Accepted.
⊠ 🕅 🖀

BARRE

⬥⬥⬥ ▼▼▼ The Hollow Inn & Motel [M] ❀
(802) 479-9313. **$80-$140.** 278 S Main St. Jct US 302, 1 mi s on SR 14; I-89, exit 6, 4.3 mi e on SR 63, then 0.7 mi n on SR 14. Ext/int corridors. **Pets:** Medium. $10 one-time fee/pet. Designated rooms, service with restrictions, supervision.
[SAVE] 🖀 🖵 ⊠ 🖾

BENNINGTON

⬥⬥⬥ ▼▼ Bennington Motor Inn [M] 🐾
(802) 442-5479. **$75-$110, 10 day notice.** 143 W Main St. Jct US 7, 0.4 mi w on SR 9. Ext corridors. **Pets:** $25 daily fee/room. Designated rooms, service with restrictions, supervision.
[SAVE] [S🖰] ⊠ 🖀 🖵

⬥⬥⬥ ▼ Darling Kelly's Motel [M]
(802) 442-2322. **$43-$105, 3 day notice.** 357 US 7 S. Jct SR 9 and US 7, 1.2 mi s. Ext corridors. **Pets:** Dogs only. $5 daily fee/pet. Designated rooms, supervision.
[SAVE] [S🖰] ⊠ 🖀 🖾

⬥⬥⬥ ▼ Fife 'N Drum Motel [M]
(802) 442-4074. **$47-$112, 3 day notice.** 693 US Rt 7 S. Jct SR 9 and US 7, 1.6 mi s. Ext corridors. **Pets:** Medium, dogs only. $6 daily fee/pet. Service with restrictions, supervision.
[SAVE] [S🖰] ⊠ 🖀 🖵 🖾 ⊠

⬥⬥⬥ ▼ Harwood Hill Motel [M]
(802) 442-6278. **$48-$80, 3 day notice.** 864 Harwood Hill Rd (Historic Rt 7A). Jct SR 9, 1.2 mi n on US 7, then 1.7 mi n on Historic SR 7A. Ext corridors. **Pets:** Medium, dogs only. $8 daily fee/room. Designated rooms, service with restrictions, crate.
[SAVE] ⊠ 🖀 🖵

▼ Knotty Pine Motel [M]
(802) 442-5487. **$51-$85.** 130 Northside Dr (SR 7A). Jct SR 9, 1.2 mi n on US 7, then just n on Historic SR 7A. Ext corridors. **Pets:** Service with restrictions, supervision.
⊠ 🖀 🖵 🖾

⬥⬥⬥ ▼ Vermonter Motor Lodge [M]
(802) 442-2529. **$60-$129, 3 day notice.** 2968 West Rd. 3.9 mi w on SR 9, from jct US 7. Ext corridors. **Pets:** Accepted.
[SAVE] [S🖰] ⊠ 🖀 🖾

BOLTON VALLEY

▼▼▼▼ Black Bear Inn [CI]
(802) 434-2126. **$99-$250, 21 day notice.** 4010 Bolton Access Rd. I-89, exit 10 northbound, 6.2 mi w on US 2, then 4 mi n; exit 11 southbound, 8.4 mi e on US 2, then 4 mi n. Ext/int corridors. **Pets:** Accepted.
⊠ 🖀 🖵 🍴 🖾

BRANDON

⬥⬥⬥ ▼▼▼ Brandon Motor Lodge [M]
(802) 247-9594. **$55-$95.** 2095 Franklin St. 2 mi s on US 7. Ext corridors. **Pets:** Dogs only. $5 one-time fee/pet. Designated rooms, service with restrictions, supervision.
[SAVE] [S🖰] ⊠ 🖀 🖾

▼▼▼▼ The Lilac Inn [CI]
(802) 247-5463. **$140-$325, 30 day notice.** 53 Park St. Just e on SR 73. Int corridors. **Pets:** Dogs only. $30 daily fee/pet. Service with restrictions, supervision.
[ASK] ⊠ 🍴 🖀

BRATTLEBORO

▼▼ Colonial Motel & Spa [SH]
(802) 257-7733. **$74-$140.** 889 Putney Rd. I-91, exit 3, just e on SR 9, then 0.5 mi s on US 5. Ext corridors. **Pets:** Accepted.
[ASK] ⊠ 🖀 🖵 🍴 🖾 🖾

⬥⬥⬥ ▼▼▼ Econo Lodge [M]
(802) 254-2360. **$40-$130.** 515 Canal St. I-91, exit 1, 0.3 mi n on US 5. Ext corridors. **Pets:** Small, dogs only. $10 daily fee/pet. Designated rooms, service with restrictions, crate.
[SAVE] [S🖰] ⊠ 🖀 🖵 🖾

⬥⬥⬥ ▼▼▼ Quality Inn & Suites [SH]
(802) 254-8701. **$79-$169.** 1380 Putney Rd. I-91, exit 3, 0.6 mi n on US 5. Int corridors. **Pets:** Medium, dogs only. $50 one-time fee/pet. Designated rooms, service with restrictions, supervision.
[SAVE] [S🖰] ⊠ 🏊 🖀 🖵 🍴 🖾 🖾

⬥⬥⬥ ▼▼▼ Super 8 Motel [M]
(802) 254-8889. **$50-$159.** 1043 Putney Rd. I-91, exit 3, just e on SR 9, then just s on US 5. Int corridors. **Pets:** Other species. $25 one-time fee/room. Service with restrictions, supervision.
[SAVE] ⊠ [⬆M] 🖀

BURLINGTON

⬥⬥⬥ ▼▼ Town & Country Motel [M] ❀
(802) 862-5786. **$59-$139, 3 day notice.** 490 Shelburne Rd. I-89, exit 13, just n on US 7 N. Ext corridors. **Pets:** Large, dogs only. $10 daily fee/pet. Designated rooms, service with restrictions.
[SAVE] ⊠ 🖀 🖵

CAVENDISH

⬥⬥⬥ ▼▼▼ Clarion Hotel at Cavendish Pointe [SH]
(802) 226-7688. **$89-$249, 14 day notice.** 2940 SR 103. On SR 103, just n of jct SR 131. Int corridors. **Pets:** $20 daily fee/room. Designated rooms, supervision.
[SAVE] [S🖰] ⊠ 🖀 🖵 🍴 🖾 🖾

CHITTENDEN

▼▼▼▼ The Mountain Top Inn & Resort 🅲 ❀
(802) 483-2311. **$130-$235, 21 day notice.** 195 Mountain Top Rd. Jct US 4, 1.8 mi n on Meadowlake Dr, 2.8 mi e on Chittenden Rd, then 2 mi n. Ext/int corridors. **Pets:** Other species. $200 deposit/pet, $25 daily fee/pet. Designated rooms, service with restrictions, supervision.
⊠ 🛢 🖵 🍴 ➔ ⊠

COLCHESTER

▼▼▼ Days Inn 🆂🄷
(802) 655-0900. **$55-$170.** 124 College Pkwy. I-89, exit 15 northbound, just e on SR 15; exit 16 southbound, 1.1 mi s on US 7, then 1 mi e on SR 15. Int corridors. **Pets:** Dogs only. $50 deposit/room, $10 daily fee/pet. Designated rooms, service with restrictions, crate.
🄰🅂🄺 🛢 ⊠ 🄼 🛢 ➔

▼▼▼▼ Hampton Inn & Conference Center 🆂🄷 ❀
(802) 655-6177. **$99-$169.** 42 Lower Mountain View Dr. I-89, exit 16, just n on US 7. Int corridors. **Pets:** $50 deposit/room. Designated rooms, supervision.
🄰🅂🄺 🛢 ⊠ 🄼 🄯 🄴 🛢 🖵 ➔

▼▼ Motel 6 #1407 🆂🄷
(802) 654-6860. **$45-$75.** 74 S Park Dr. I-89, exit 16, just s on US 7. Int corridors. **Pets:** Other species. Service with restrictions, supervision.
🛢 ⊠ 🛢 ➔

CRAFTSBURY COMMON

▼▼▼ Inn on the Common 🅲
(802) 586-9619. **$135-$299, 30 day notice.** 1162 N Craftsbury Rd. Center. Ext/int corridors. **Pets:** Accepted.
🄰🅂🄺 🛢 ⊠ 🛢 🖵 🍴 ➔ ⊠ 🄺 🅆 🄴

ESSEX JUNCTION

▲▲▲ ▼▼▼▼ The Inn at Essex 🆂🄷 ❀
(802) 878-1100. **$109-$269, 7 day notice.** 70 Essex Way. SR 289, exit 10, 0.3 mi s. Int corridors. **Pets:** Other species. $300 deposit/room, $25 daily fee/pet. Designated rooms, service with restrictions, crate.
🆂🄰🅅🄴 🛢 ⊠ 🄼 🄴 🛢 🖵 🍴 ➔ ⊠

▼▼▼▼ The Wilson Inn 🆂🄷
(802) 879-1515. **$78-$164.** 10 Kellogg Rd. I-89, exit 15 northbound, 2.1 mi e on SR 15, then 0.5 mi n on Susie Wilson Rd; exit 16 southbound, 1 mi s on US 7, 2.8 mi e on SR 15, then 0.5 mi n on Susie Wilson Rd. Int corridors. **Pets:** Accepted.
🄰🅂🄺 🛢 ⊠ 🛢 🖵 ➔ ⊠

FAIRLEE

▲▲▲ ▼▼▼ Silver Maple Lodge & Cottages 🄱🄱
(802) 333-4326. **$66-$89, 14 day notice.** 520 US 5 S. I-91, exit 15, 0.5 mi s. Ext/int corridors. **Pets:** Other species. Designated rooms.
🆂🄰🅅🄴 🛢 ⊠ 🛢 🖵 🄴

FLETCHER

▼▼▼ The Inn at Buck Hollow Farm 🄱🄱
(802) 849-2400. **$73-$98, 14 day notice.** 2150 Buck Hollow Rd. 6.4 mi n of jct SR 104 via Buck Hollow Rd. Int corridors. **Pets:** Accepted.
🄰🅂🄺 ⊠ ➔ ⊠ 🄴

JAMAICA

▲▲▲ ▼▼▼▼ Three Mountain Inn 🅲 ❀
(802) 874-4140. **$145-$345, 10 day notice.** 3732 Main St. On SR 30; center. Ext/int corridors. **Pets:** Dogs only. $25 daily fee/pet. Designated rooms, service with restrictions, crate.
🆂🄰🅅🄴 ⊠ 🍴 ➔ ⊠

JEFFERSONVILLE

▼▼ Deer Run Motor Inn 🄼
(802) 644-8866. **$100, 15 day notice.** 80 Deer Run Loop. 0.7 mi e on SR 15. Ext/int corridors. **Pets:** $10 daily fee/pet. Supervision.
🛢 ⊠ 🛢 🖵 ➔

KILLINGTON

▲▲▲ ▼▼▼ Butternut on the Mountain 🆂🄷
(802) 422-2000. **$75-$225, 30 day notice.** 63 Weathervane Rd. Jct SR 100/US 4, 1.1 mi s on Killington Rd, then just e. Ext/int corridors. **Pets:** Accepted.
🆂🄰🅅🄴 ⊠ 🛢 🖵 🍴 ➔

▲▲▲ ▼▼▼▼ The Cascades Lodge 🆂🄷
(802) 422-3731. **$79-$229, 21 day notice.** 58 Old Mill Rd. 3.6 mi s on Killington Rd, from jct SR 100/US 4, then just e. Int corridors. **Pets:** Other species. $25 daily fee/room. Designated rooms, service with restrictions, crate.
🆂🄰🅅🄴 🛢 ⊠ 🄯 🛢 🖵 🍴 ➔ ⊠

▲▲▲ ▼▼▼ Val Roc Motel 🄼 ❀
(802) 422-3881. **$60-$140, 14 day notice.** 8006 US 4. 5.9 mi e on US 4, from jct SR 100 N. Ext/int corridors. **Pets:** Other species. $5 daily fee/pet. Service with restrictions.
🆂🄰🅅🄴 🛢 ⊠ 🛢 🖵 ➔ ⊠

LUDLOW

▲▲▲ ▼▼▼ Timber Inn Motel 🄼
(802) 228-8666. **$69-$179, 14 day notice.** 112 Rt 103 S. On SR 103 S, 1 mi e. Ext corridors. **Pets:** Accepted.
🆂🄰🅅🄴 🛢 ⊠ 🛢 🖵 ➔ ⊠

MENDON

▼▼▼ Cortina Inn and Resort 🆂🄷 ❀
(802) 773-3333. **$119-$229.** 103 US Rt 4. Jct SR 100 N, 3 mi w. Int corridors. **Pets:** Large, other species. $10 daily fee/pet. Designated rooms, service with restrictions, supervision.
🄰🅂🄺 🛢 ⊠ 🄴 🛢 🖵 🍴 ➔ ⊠

▲▲▲ ▼▼▼ Econo Lodge-Killington Area 🆂🄷
(802) 773-6644. **$55-$120, 7 day notice.** 51 US 4. Jct US 7, 5.3 mi e. Int corridors. **Pets:** $10 one-time fee/room. Designated rooms, service with restrictions, supervision.
🆂🄰🅅🄴 🛢 ⊠ 🛢 🖵 ➔ ⊠

▲▲▲ ▼▼▼ Edelweiss Red Carpet Inn 🄼
(802) 775-5577. **$44-$125, 14 day notice.** 119 US Rt 4. Jct SR 100 N, 3 mi w. Ext corridors. **Pets:** Accepted.
🆂🄰🅅🄴 🛢 ⊠ 🛢 ➔ ⊠

▲▲▲ ▼▼▼ Mendon Mountainview Lodge 🆂🄷
(802) 773-4311. **$52-$209, 7 day notice.** 78 US 4. On US 4, 6 mi e of jct US 7. Int corridors. **Pets:** Medium, dogs only. $10 daily fee/room. Designated rooms, service with restrictions, crate.
🆂🄰🅅🄴 ⊠ 🛢 ➔ ⊠

MIDDLEBURY

▲▲▲ ▼▼▼▼ The Middlebury Inn 🆂🄷 ❀
(802) 388-4961. **$98-$395, 3 day notice.** 14 Court Square. On US 7; center. Ext/int corridors. **Pets:** Designated rooms, service with restrictions, crate.
🆂🄰🅅🄴 ⊠ 🄯 🄴 🛢 🖵 🍴

MONTPELIER

▲▲▲ ▼▼ Econo Lodge 🄼
(802) 223-5258. **$60-$78.** 101 Northfield St. Just s of jct US 302/SR 12. Ext corridors. **Pets:** $10 daily fee/room. Designated rooms, service with restrictions.
🆂🄰🅅🄴 🛢 ⊠ 🛢 🖵 🍴

NEWFANE

▽▽▽▽ **Four Columns Inn** 🄲🄸
(802) 365-7713. **$175-$400, 14 day notice.** 21 West St. Just w of SR 30; center. Int corridors. **Pets:** Dogs only. $25 daily fee/pet. Designated rooms, service with restrictions, crate.
⊠ 🍴 ⤳

NORTH HERO

🔺🔺🔺 ▽▽▽ **Shore Acres Inn** 🆂🅷
(802) 372-8722. **$100-$199, 14 day notice.** 237 Shore Acres Dr. 1 mi s on US 2. Ext/int corridors. **Pets:** Dogs only. $15 daily fee/pet. Supervision.
SAVE ⊠ 🖥 🍴 ⊠ 🐾

PERU

▽▽▽ **Johnny Seesaw's** 🄲🄸 🐾
(802) 824-5533. **$80-$180, 14 day notice.** 3574 Vt Rt 11. 2.1 mi e on SR 11, from jct SR 30 S. Ext/int corridors. **Pets:** Other species. $10 daily fee/pet.
🖥 🍴 ⤳ ⊠

PUTNEY

▽▽ **The Putney Inn** 🆂🅷 🐾
(802) 387-5517. **$98-$158.** 57 Putney Landing Rd. I-91, exit 4, just e. Ext corridors. **Pets:** Large. $10 daily fee/pet. Service with restrictions.
⊠ 🖥 🍴

RUTLAND

🔺🔺🔺 ▽▽▽▽ **Holiday Inn Rutland/Killington** 🅻🅷
(802) 775-1911. **$139-$299.** 476 US Rt 7 S. 2.4 mi s on US 7, from US 4 W; 0.4 mi n, US 7 from US 4 E. Int corridors. **Pets:** $10 daily fee/room. Service with restrictions, supervision.
SAVE 🆂🌀 ⊠ 🆖🅼 🌀 🖥 🖥 🍴 ⤳ ⊠

🔺🔺🔺 ▽▽▽ **Ramada Limited of Rutland** 🆂🅷
(802) 773-3361. **$99-$199.** 253 S Main St, US 7. 1.3 mi s on US 7, from US 4 W; 1.5 mi n on US 4 E, from US 4 E. Int corridors. **Pets:** Medium. $25 one-time fee/pet. Designated rooms, service with restrictions, supervision.
SAVE 🆂🌀 ⊠ 🖥 🖥 ⤳

▽▽▽▽ **Red Roof Inn Rutland-Killington** 🆂🅷
(802) 775-4303. **$69-$159, 14 day notice.** 401 US Hwy 7 S. On US 7/4. Int corridors. **Pets:** Medium. Service with restrictions, supervision.
ASK 🆂🌀 ⊠ 🆖 ⤳ ⊠

🔺🔺🔺 ▽▽ **Royal Motel** 🅼
(802) 773-9176. **$52-$109, 7 day notice.** 115 Woodstock Ave. Jct US 7, 0.5 mi e on US 4. Ext/int corridors. **Pets:** Other species. $10 daily fee/pet. No service.
SAVE 🆂🌀 ⊠ 🖥 ⤳

ST. ALBANS

▽▽▽▽ **Comfort Inn & Suites** 🆂🅷
(802) 524-3300. **$79-$189.** 813 Fairfax Rd. I-89, exit 19, just w, then just s on SR 104. Int corridors. **Pets:** Other species. $10 daily fee/room. Designated rooms, service with restrictions, supervision.
ASK 🆂🌀 ⊠ 🆖🅼 🖥 🖥 ⤳

🔺🔺🔺 ▽▽▽ **Econo Lodge** 🅼
(802) 524-5956. **$59-$109.** 287 S Main St. I-89, exit 19, 1 mi w to US 7, then 0.5 mi s. Ext/int corridors. **Pets:** Small. $10 daily fee/pet. Designated rooms, service with restrictions, supervision.
SAVE 🆂🌀 ⊠ 🖥 🖥

ST. JOHNSBURY

▽▽◇ **Fairbanks Inn** 🅼 🐾
(802) 748-5666. **$79-$279.** 401 Western Ave. I-91, exit 21, 1 mi e on US 2. Ext corridors. **Pets:** Dogs only. $5 daily fee/pet. Designated rooms, service with restrictions, supervision.
ASK 🆂🌀 ⊠ 🖥 🖥 ⤳

▽▽◇ **Holiday Motel & Annex** 🅼
(802) 748-8192. **$59-$139.** 222 Hastings St. Jct US 5 and Alternate Rt 5. Ext/int corridors. **Pets:** Medium, dogs only. $10 daily fee/pet. Designated rooms, service with restrictions, supervision.
ASK 🆂🌀 ⊠ 🖥 ⤳

SHAFTSBURY

▽▽◇ **Governor's Rock Motel** 🅼
(802) 442-4734. **$55-$85, 7 day notice.** 4325 Rt 7A. 3.3 mi n on Historic SR 7A, from jct SR 67. Ext corridors. **Pets:** Accepted.
ASK 🆂🌀 ⊠ 🖥

▽▽◇ **Serenity Motel** 🄲🄰
(802) 442-6490. **$55-$75.** 4379 Rt 7A. 3.3 mi n on Historic SR 7A, from jct SR 67. Ext corridors. **Pets:** Large, other species. Designated rooms, supervision.
⊠ 🖥 🖥

SOUTH BURLINGTON

▽▽◇ **Anchorage Inn** 🆂🅷
(802) 863-7000. **$59-$110.** 108 Dorset St. I-89, exit 14E, just e on US 2 to Dorset St, then 0.3 mi s. Int corridors. **Pets:** Dogs only. $50 deposit/room. Designated rooms, service with restrictions, supervision.
ASK 🆂🌀 ⊠ 🖥 🖥 ⤳

▽▽ **Best Western Windjammer Inn & Conference Center** 🆂🅷 🐾
(802) 863-1125. **$90-$200.** 1076 Williston Rd. I-89, exit 14E, 0.3 mi e on US 2. Int corridors. **Pets:** Other species. $5 daily fee/pet. Designated rooms, service with restrictions, supervision.
ASK 🆂🌀 ⊠ 🆖🅼 🌀 🆖 🖥 🖥 🍴 ⤳ ⊠

🔺🔺🔺 ▽▽▽▽ **Clarion Hotel and Suites** 🆂🅷 🐾
(802) 658-0250. **$115-$209.** 1117 Williston Rd. I-89, exit 14E, just e on US 2. Int corridors. **Pets:** $30 deposit/room. Designated rooms, service with restrictions, supervision.
SAVE 🆂🌀 ⊠ 🆖🅼 🌀 🆖 🖥 🖥 🍴 ⤳

▽▽◇ **Comfort Inn** 🆂🅷 🐾
(802) 865-3400. **$79-$185.** 1285 Williston Rd. I-89, exit 14E, 0.5 mi e on US 2. Int corridors. **Pets:** $10 daily fee/room. Service with restrictions.
ASK 🆂🌀 ⊠ 🆖🅼 🌀 🖥 🖥 ⤳

🔺🔺🔺 ▽▽▽▽ **Hawthorn Suites Hotel** 🆂🅷
(802) 860-1212. **$109-$239, 3 day notice.** 401 Dorset St. I-89, exit 14E, just e on US 2, then 0.8 mi s. Int corridors. **Pets:** Accepted.
SAVE 🆂🌀 ⊠ 🆖🅼 🆖 🖥 🖥 ⤳ ⊠

🔺🔺🔺 ▽▽▽▽ **Holiday Inn Burlington** 🅻🅷
(802) 863-6363. **$109-$189.** 1068 Williston Rd. I-89, exit 14E, just e on US 2. Int corridors. **Pets:** $20 one-time fee/room. Service with restrictions, supervision.
SAVE 🆂🌀 ⊠ 🆖🅼 🌀 🖥 🖥 🍴 ⤳

🔺🔺🔺 ▽▽▽ **MainStay Suites** 🆂🅷
(802) 846-1986. **$109-$209.** 1702 Shelburne Rd. I-89, exit 13 to US 7, then 1.5 mi s. Int corridors. **Pets:** Small. $25 one-time fee/room. Designated rooms, service with restrictions, crate.
SAVE 🆂🌀 ⊠ 🖥 ⤳

🔺🔺🔺 ▽▽▽ **Sheraton Burlington Hotel & Conference Center** 🅻🅷
(802) 865-6600. **$189-$249.** 870 Williston Rd. I-89, exit 14W, just w on US 2. Int corridors. **Pets:** Accepted.
SAVE 🆂🌀 ⊠ 🌀 🖥 🖥 🍴 ⤳ ⊠

▲▲▲ ▽▽▽▽ Smart Suites SH
(802) 860-9900. **$99-$189.** 1700 Shelburne Rd. I-89, exit 13 to US 7, then 1.5 mi s. Int corridors. **Pets:** Small. $25 one-time fee/room. Designated rooms, service with restrictions.
[SAVE] [S0] [✕] [📱] [💻]

SOUTH WOODSTOCK

▲▲▲ ▽▽▽▽ Kedron Valley Inn CI
(802) 457-1473. **$111-$329, 14 day notice.** Rt 106. Jct US 4, 5 mi s. Ext/int corridors. **Pets:** Accepted.
[SAVE] [✕] [📱] [💻] [🍴] [✕] [☎]

SPRINGFIELD

▽▽▽▽ The Hartness House CI
(802) 885-2115. **$99-$195, 7 day notice.** 30 Orchard St. 0.4 mi n on Summer St, bear left at old cemetery. Int corridors. **Pets:** Accepted.
[ASK] [✕] [📱] [🍴] [➡] [✕]

▽▽▽▽ Holiday Inn Express SH
(802) 885-4516. **$119-$179.** 818 Charlestown Rd. I-91, exit 7. Int corridors. **Pets:** Accepted.
[ASK] [S0] [✕] [6M] [✎] [📱] [💻] [🍴] [➡]

STOWE

▲▲▲ ▽▽▽▽ 1066 Ye Olde England Inne CI ✿
(802) 253-7558. **$119-$345, 15 day notice.** 433 Mountain Rd. 0.4 mi w on SR 108, from jct SR 100. Ext/int corridors. **Pets:** Other species. $10 daily fee/pet. Designated rooms, service with restrictions.
[SAVE] [S0] [✕] [✎] [📱] [🍴] [➡] [✕]

▲▲▲ ▽▽▽ Andersen Lodge-An Austrian Inn CI ✿
(802) 253-7336. **$85-$198, 14 day notice.** 3430 Mountain Rd. 3.5 mi w on SR 108, from jct SR 100. Int corridors. **Pets:** Dogs only. Service with restrictions, supervision.
[SAVE] [S0] [✕] [📱] [🍴] [➡] [✕]

▲▲▲ ▽▽▽ Commodores Inn LH
(802) 253-7131. **$98-$198.** 823 S Main St. Jct SR 108, 0.8 mi s on SR 100. Int corridors. **Pets:** Other species. $10 one-time fee/room.
[SAVE] [S0] [✕] [✎] [📱] [🍴] [➡] [✕]

▽▽▽▽ Edson Hill Manor CI
(802) 253-7371. **$99-$219, 15 day notice.** 1500 Edson Hill Rd. Jct SR 100, 3.5 mi w on SR 108, then 1.3 mi n. Ext/int corridors. **Pets:** Designated rooms, service with restrictions, supervision.
[✕] [🍴] [➡] [✕]

▲▲▲ ▽▽▽▽ Green Mountain Inn CI
(802) 253-7301. **$119-$379, 14 day notice.** 18 S Main St. Jct SR 108 on SR 100; center. Ext/int corridors. **Pets:** Accepted.
[SAVE] [S0] [✕] [📱] [💻] [🍴] [➡] [✕]

▲▲▲ ▽▽▽ Hob Knob Inn & Restaurant M ✿
(802) 253-8549. **$75-$235, 14 day notice.** 2364 Mountain Rd. Jct SR 100, 2.5 mi w on SR 108. Ext/int corridors. **Pets:** $15 daily fee/pet. Service with restrictions.
[SAVE] [✕] [📱] [💻] [🍴] [➡]

▲▲▲ ▽▽▽▽ Honeywood Country Lodge M
(802) 253-4124. **$79-$149, 15 day notice.** 4527 Mountain Rd. Jct SR 100, 4.5 mi w on SR 108. Ext corridors. **Pets:** Other species. $10 daily fee/pet. Designated rooms, service with restrictions, crate.
[SAVE] [S0] [✕] [📱] [💻] [✕]

▲▲▲ ▽▽ Innsbruck Inn at Stowe M
(802) 253-8582. **$74-$169, 15 day notice.** 4361 Mountain Rd. 4.5 mi w on SR 108, from jct SR 100. Ext/int corridors. **Pets:** Medium, dogs only. $20 daily fee/pet. Designated rooms, service with restrictions, supervision.
[SAVE] [✕] [📱] [💻] [➡] [✕]

▲▲▲ ▽▽▽▽ The Mountain Road Resort at Stowe M
(802) 253-4566. **$115-$260, 15 day notice.** 1007 Mountain Rd. 1 mi w on SR 108, from jct SR 100. Ext corridors. **Pets:** $25 one-time fee/pet.
[SAVE] [S0] [✕] [📱] [💻] [➡] [✕]

▲▲▲ ▽▽▽▽ Ten Acres Lodge CI
(802) 253-7638. **$120-$350, 14 day notice.** 14 Barrows Rd. Jct SR 100, 2.1 mi w on SR 108, then 0.5 mi s on Luce Hill Rd. Ext/int corridors. **Pets:** Accepted.
[SAVE] [S0] [✕] [➡] [✕]

▲▲▲ ▽▽▽▽ Topnotch at Stowe Resort & Spa LH ✿
(802) 253-8585. **$180-$525, 14 day notice.** 4000 Mountain Rd. 4.2 mi w on SR 108, from jct SR 100. Ext/int corridors. **Pets:** Other species. Designated rooms, service with restrictions, supervision.
[SAVE] [S0] [✕] [📱] [💻] [🍴] [➡] [✕]

WARREN

▲▲▲ ▽▽▽▽ PowderHound Inn & Condominiums CO ✿
(802) 496-5100. **$84-$144, 14 day notice.** 203 Powderhound Rd. On SR 100, 0.3 mi s of jct Sugarbush Access Rd. Ext corridors. **Pets:** Other species. $5 daily fee/pet.
[SAVE] [✕] [📱] [💻] [🍴] [➡] [✕]

WEST BRATTLEBORO

▽▽ Molly Stark Motel M
(802) 254-2440. **$45-$80.** 829 Marlboro Rd. I-91, exit 2, 3.3 mi w on SR 9. Ext corridors. **Pets:** Large, dogs only. $8 daily fee/pet. Service with restrictions, supervision.
[✕] [📱] [💻]

WEST DOVER

▲▲▲ ▽▽▽ The Gray Ghost Inn SH
(802) 464-2474. **$79-$137.** 290 Rt 100 N. 7.8 mi n on SR 100, from jct SR 9. Int corridors. **Pets:** Accepted.
[SAVE] [S0] [✕] [🍴] [✕] [✕] [☎]

▽▽ Red Oak Inn CI
(802) 464-8817. **$75-$189, 14 day notice.** 45 Rt 100. 5 mi n. Int corridors. **Pets:** Medium, dogs only. $30 one-time fee/room. Designated rooms, service with restrictions, supervision.
[ASK] [✕] [📱] [💻] [➡] [✕]

▲▲▲ ▽▽▽▽ Snow Goose Inn BB
(802) 464-3984. **$115-$395, 14 day notice.** 259 Rt 100. 7.5 mi n on SR 100, from jct SR 9. Int corridors. **Pets:** Accepted.
[SAVE] [S0] [✕] [📱] [💻]

WESTMORE

▲▲▲ ▽▽▽▽ WilloughVale Inn on Lake Willoughby CI
(802) 525-4123. **$85-$224, 14 day notice.** 793 VT Rt 5A. Just s on SR 5A, from jct SR 16. Ext/int corridors. **Pets:** Medium, dogs only. $20 daily fee/room. Designated rooms.
[SAVE] [S0] [✕] [📱] [💻] [🍴] [✕]

WHITE RIVER JUNCTION

▲▲▲ ▽▽▽ Best Western at the Junction SH
(802) 295-3015. **$89-$159.** 91 Ballardvale Dr. Jct I-89 and 91. Int corridors. **Pets:** Other species. $10 daily fee/pet. Designated rooms, service with restrictions, supervision.
[SAVE] [S0] [✕] [📱] [💻] [➡] [✕]

WILLIAMSTOWN

▽▽ Autumn Harvest Inn CI
(802) 433-1355. **$89-$159, 14 day notice.** 118 Clark Rd. I-89, exit 5, 2.1 mi e on SR 64; in Autumn Harvest Inn. Int corridors. **Pets:** Accepted.
[ASK] [S0] [✕] [🍴] [✕]

WILLISTON

▼▼▼ **TownePlace Suites by Marriott** SH
(802) 872-5900. **$86-$169.** 66 Zephyr Rd. I-89, exit 12, 1.1 mi n on SR 2A. Int corridors. **Pets:** Accepted.

A$K S✓ ✕ &M ☒ ▯ ◙ ➜ ✕

WOODSTOCK

AAA ▼ **Braeside Motel** M ❀
(802) 457-1366. **$68-$118, 15 day notice.** 432 US 4 E (Woodstock Rd). 1 mi e. Ext corridors. **Pets:** $10 daily fee/room. Designated rooms, service with restrictions, supervision.

SAVE ✕ ▯ ➜

AAA ▼▼▼ **The Winslow House** BB
(802) 457-1820. **$100-$175, 14 day notice.** 492 Woodstock Rd. 1.3 mi w on US 4. Int corridors. **Pets:** Accepted.

SAVE S✓ ✕ ▯

VIRGINIA

CITY INDEX

ABINGDON

▼▼▼▼ Quality Inn & Suites of Abingdon SH
(276) 676-9090. **$99-$129.** 930 E Main St. I-81, exit 19 (US 11), just w.
Int corridors. **Pets:** Other species. $30 one-time fee/room. Designated
rooms, service with restrictions.
[ASK] [S✿] [✕] [🚻] [🍴] [💻] [🏊]

ALTAVISTA

▼▼▼ Comfort Suites Hotel SH ❀
(434) 369-4000. **$81-$158, 7 day notice.** 1558 Main St. US 29 business route, at jct US 29. Int corridors. **Pets:** Other species. $10 one-time
fee/room. Designated rooms, service with restrictions.
[ASK] [S✿] [✕] [🚻] [💻] [🍴] [🏊]

APPOMATTOX

▼▼▼ Super 8 Motel M
(434) 352-2339. **$56-$66.** Rt 4, Box 100. US 460, just w of jct US 26.
Int corridors. **Pets:** Accepted.
[ASK] [S✿] [✕] [🚻] [💻]

BEDFORD

▼▼ Days Inn SH
(540) 586-8286. **$51-$68.** 921 Blue Ridge Ave. Jct US 221, 1.5 mi w,
on US 460. Ext corridors. **Pets:** Accepted.
[ASK] [S✿] [✕] [🚻] [💻] [🍴] [🏊]

BIG STONE GAP

▲▲▲ ▼ Country Inn Motel M
(276) 523-0374. **$50.** 627 Gilley Ave. US 23, 1 mi w on US 23 business
route and 58A. Ext corridors. **Pets:** Accepted.
[SAVE] [✕] [🚻]

BLACKSBURG

▼▼ Best Western Red Lion Inn SH
(540) 552-7770. **Call for rates.** 900 Plantation Rd. 1.7 mi w on SR 685;
jct US 460 Bypass and Prices Fork Rd. Ext corridors. **Pets:** Accepted.
[✕] [💻] [🏊]

▲▲▲ ▼▼▼ Comfort Inn SH
(540) 951-1500. **$60-$135, 7 day notice.** 3705 S Main St. 3.5 mi s on
US 460, jct US 460 Bypass. Int corridors. **Pets:** Other species. Service
with restrictions.
[SAVE] [S✿] [✕] [🚻] [💻] [🏊]

BRISTOL

▲▲▲ ▼ Econo Lodge M
(276) 466-2112. **$44-$350.** 912 Commonwealth Ave. I-81, exit 3, 1.5 mi
e. Ext corridors. **Pets:** Dogs only. $10 one-time fee/room. Designated
rooms, service with restrictions, supervision.
[SAVE] [S✿] [✕] [🌀] [🚻] [💻]

▼▼▼ Holiday Inn Hotel & Suites LH
(276) 466-4100. **$99.** 3005 Linden Dr. I-81, exit 7, just w. Int corridors.
Pets: Accepted.
[ASK] [S✿] [✕] [⚡M] [🐾] [🚻] [💻] [🍴] [🏊]

▲▲▲ ▼▼▼ La Quinta Inn Bristol SH
(276) 669-9353. **$68-$95.** 1014 Old Airport Rd. I-81, exit 7. Ext corridors. **Pets:** Small, other species. Service with restrictions, crate.
[SAVE] [✕] [⚡M] [🐾] [🚻] [💻] [🏊]

▼▼ Microtel Inn & Suites SH
(276) 669-8164. **$59-$64, 5 day notice.** 131 Bristol Rd E. I-81, exit 7
northbound, just w; exit southbound, just e. Int corridors. **Pets:** Small.
$10 one-time fee/pet. Designated rooms, service with restrictions, supervi-
sion.
[ASK] [S✿] [✕] [🚻] [💻] [🏊]

▼▼ Motel 6 SH
(276) 466-6060. **$52-$64.** 21561 Clear Creek Rd. I-81, exit 7, 0.3 mi w.
Int corridors. **Pets:** Accepted.
[✕] [⚡M] [🐾]

▼▼ Super 8 Motel SH
(276) 466-8800. **$44-$275.** 2139 Lee Hwy. I-81, exit 5, just s. Int corridors. **Pets:** Medium. $10 daily fee/pet. Designated rooms, service with
restrictions, supervision.
[ASK] [S✿] [✕] [🚻]

BUENA VISTA

▲▲▲ ▼ Buena Vista Motel M
(540) 261-2138. **$40-$70.** 447 E 29th St. I-81, exit 188A, 4.3 mi e on
US 60, 0.4 mi w of Blue Ridge Pkwy. Ext corridors. **Pets:** Accepted.
[SAVE] [S✿] [✕] [🚻] [💻]

BURKEVILLE

▲▲▲ ▼▼▼ Comfort Inn Burkeville SH
(434) 767-3750. **$75-$145.** 419 N Agnew St. On US 460, just e of jct
US 360. Int corridors. **Pets:** Small, other species. $20 one-time fee/room.
Service with restrictions, supervision.
[SAVE] [S✿] [✕] [🐾] [🚻] [💻] [🍴] [🏊]

CAPE CHARLES

Best Western Sunset Beach Resort SH
(757) 331-1776. **$64-$129.** 32246 Lankford Hwy. US 13, just n of the Chesapeake Bay Bridge Tunnel. Ext corridors. **Pets:** Other species. $10 daily fee/room. Designated rooms, service with restrictions.
[SAVE] [icons]

CHARLOTTESVILLE

Comfort Inn SH ❀
(434) 293-6188. **$65-$99.** 1807 Emmet St. Jct US 250 Bypass, just n on US 29. Int corridors. **Pets:** $10 daily fee/room. Designated rooms, service with restrictions, supervision.
[SAVE] [icons]

Days Inn University Area SH
(434) 293-9111. **$65-$99.** 1600 Emmet St. I-64, exit 118B (US 29), just n of jct US 250 Bypass. Ext corridors. **Pets:** $10 daily fee/pet. Service with restrictions, crate.
[ASK] [icons]

Doubletree Hotel Charlottesville SH
(434) 973-2121. **$79-$136.** 990 Hilton Heights Rd. I-64, exit 118B (US 29), 4 mi n of jct US 250 Bypass. Int corridors. **Pets:** Accepted.
[icons]

Econo Lodge-University M
(434) 296-2104. **$46-$160.** 400 Emmet St. Jct US 250 Bypass, 1 mi s on US 29 business route. Ext corridors. **Pets:** Medium, dogs only. $10 daily fee/pet. Designated rooms, service with restrictions, supervision.
[SAVE] [icons]

Holiday Inn-Monticello/Charlottesville LH ❀
(434) 977-5100. **$70-$90.** 1200 5th St SW. I-64, exit 120, just n on SR 631. Int corridors. **Pets:** Other species. $10 daily fee/pet. Service with restrictions, supervision.
[ASK] [icons]

Omni Charlottesville Hotel LH
(434) 971-5500. **$119-$179.** 235 W Main St. I-64, exit 120, 2.3 mi n on SR 631; downtown. Int corridors. **Pets:** Small, other species. $50 one-time fee/pet. Service with restrictions.
[SAVE] [icons]

Quality Inn-University Area SH
(434) 971-3746. **$65-$99.** 1600 Emmet St. US 29, just n of jct US 250 Bypass, just e on Holiday Dr. Ext corridors. **Pets:** $10 daily fee/pet. Service with restrictions, crate.
[ASK] [icons]

Red Roof Inn of Charlottesville SH
(434) 295-4333. **$74-$100.** 1309 W Main St. US 29 (Emmet St), 1 mi e on US 250 (University Ave). Int corridors. **Pets:** Accepted.
[icons]

Residence Inn by Marriott SH
(434) 923-0300. **$119-$159.** 1111 Millmont St. I-64, exit 118B (US 29), 2.5 mi n US 29/250 E, just s on Barracks Rd, then just se. Int corridors. **Pets:** $10 daily fee/pet, $200 one-time fee/room. Service with restrictions, supervision.
[SAVE] [icons]

Sleep Inn & Suites Monticello SH
(434) 244-9969. **$62-$98, 30 day notice.** 1185 5th St. I-64, exit 120, just n. Int corridors. **Pets:** $10 daily fee/pet. Service with restrictions, supervision.
[SAVE] [icons]

Super 8 Motel/Charlottesville SH
(434) 973-0888. **$49-$99.** 390 Greenbrier Dr. US 29, 1 mi n of US 250 Bypass. Int corridors. **Pets:** Accepted.
[SAVE] [icons]

CHRISTIANSBURG

Econo Lodge M
(540) 382-6161. **$45-$169.** 2430 Roanoke St. I-81, exit 118, just w on US 11/460. Ext corridors. **Pets:** Small. $10 daily fee/pet. Designated rooms, service with restrictions, supervision.
[SAVE] [icons]

Super 8 Motel-Christiansburg West SH
(540) 382-5813. **$57-$62, 14 day notice.** 55 Laurel St NE. I-81, exit 118, 1 mi w on US 11/460, then 3.5 mi nw on US 460 Bypass; jct SR 114. Int corridors. **Pets:** Accepted.
[icons]

CLARKSVILLE

Best Western On The Lake SH
(434) 374-5023. **$69-$114, 3 day notice.** 103 Second St. Just n of US 58. Int corridors. **Pets:** Other species. $100 deposit/pet, $10 daily fee/pet, $20 one-time fee/pet. Designated rooms, service with restrictions, supervision.
[ASK] [icons]

COLLINSVILLE

Knights Inn M
(276) 647-3716. **$60-$65.** 2357 Virginia Ave. Jct US 58, 3 mi n on US 220 business route. Ext corridors. **Pets:** Accepted.
[SAVE] [icons]

Quality Inn-Dutch Inn Hotel and Convention Center SH
(276) 647-3721. **$75-$85.** 2360 Virginia Ave. Jct US 58, 3 mi n on US 220 business route. Ext corridors. **Pets:** Medium, other species. $5 daily fee/pet. Service with restrictions.
[ASK] [icons]

COVINGTON

Best Western Mountain View SH
(540) 962-4951. **$88-$115.** 820 E Madison St. I-64, exit 16, just n. Ext corridors. **Pets:** Other species. $12 one-time fee/room. Service with restrictions, supervision.
[icons]

Comfort Inn M
(540) 962-2141. **$88-$101.** 203 Interstate Dr. I-64, exit 16, just sw. Int corridors. **Pets:** Large, other species. $10 one-time fee/room. Service with restrictions, supervision.
[ASK] [icons]

CULPEPER

Comfort Inn-Culpeper SH
(540) 825-4900. **$79-$129.** 890 Willis Ln. 2 mi s on US 29 business route; jct US 29, then just e. Ext corridors. **Pets:** Other species. $15 daily fee/pet. No service, crate.
[ASK] [icons]

DALEVILLE

Howard Johnson Express Inn SH ❀
(540) 992-1234. **$72.** 437 Roanoke Rd. I-81, exit 150B, just nw on US 220. Ext corridors. **Pets:** Medium. $15 one-time fee/pet. Service with restrictions, supervision.
[ASK] [icons]

DANVILLE

Comfort Inn & Suites SH
(434) 793-2000. **$74-$129.** 100 Tower Dr. US 58, just w of jct US 29 business route. Int corridors. **Pets:** Other species. $10 daily fee/room. Service with restrictions, crate.
[ASK] [icons]

◆◆ Innkeeper Danville North [M]
(434) 836-1700. **$52-$62, 3 day notice.** 1030 Piney Forest Rd. US 29 N, 2.4 mi n of US 58. Ext corridors. **Pets:** Accepted.
[A$K] [SD] ☒ ▣ 🏊

[AAA] ◆◆ Ramada Inn Stratford [SH] 🐾
(434) 793-2500. **$65-$116.** 2500 Riverside Dr. US 58, just e of jct US 29 business route. Ext corridors. **Pets:** $15 daily fee/room. Service with restrictions, supervision.
[SAVE] [SD] ☒ ♿M 👂 ♿ ▣ 💻 🍴 🏊

◆ Super 8 Motel [M]
(434) 799-5845. **$55-$65.** 2385 Riverside Dr. On US 58, just e of jct US 29 business route. Int corridors. **Pets:** Large, other species. $20 one-time fee/room. Service with restrictions.
[A$K] [SD] ☒ ▣

District Of Columbia Area

ALEXANDRIA

[AAA] ◆◆◆ Embassy Suites-Alexandria-Old Town [LH]
(703) 684-5900. **$139-$289.** 1900 Diagonal Rd. I-95/495, exit 176, 0.5 mi n on SR 241 N, then 0.5 mi e on SR 236. Int corridors. **Pets:** Medium. $25 daily fee/pet. Designated rooms, service with restrictions, crate.
[SAVE] ☒ 👂 ♿ ▣ 💻 🍴 🏊 🏋

◆◆ Hawthorn Suites LTD-Alexandria [SH]
(703) 370-1000. **$99-$179.** 420 N Van Dorn St. I-395, exit 3A, 0.3 mi e on SR 236 to S Van Dorn St, then 0.5 mi n. Int corridors. **Pets:** Accepted.
[A$K] [SD] ☒ 👂 ♿ ▣ 💻 🏊

◆◆◆ Hilton Alexandria Old Town [LH]
(703) 837-0440. **$139-$289.** 1767 King St. I-95/495, exit 176B, 0.5 mi n on SR 241, 0.5 mi e on SR 236, then just ne on Diagonal Rd. Int corridors. **Pets:** Accepted.
[A$K] ☒ 👂 ♿ 💻 🍴 🏊

[AAA] ◆◆◆ Holiday Inn Hotel & Suites-Historic District Alexandria [LH] 🐾
(703) 548-6300. **$109-$239.** 625 1st St. George Washington Memorial Pkwy; just e of jct 1st and Washington sts. Int corridors. **Pets:** Other species. $25 daily fee/room. Designated rooms, service with restrictions.
[SAVE] [SD] ☒ 👂 ♿ ▣ 💻 🍴 🏊 🏋

[AAA] ◆◆◆ Holiday Inn Select-Old Town [LH]
(703) 549-6080. **$209-$249.** 480 King St. On SR 7; between S Pitt and S Royal sts; just sw of City Hall. Int corridors. **Pets:** Accepted.
[SAVE] [SD] ☒ 👂 ♿ 💻 🍴 🏊 🏋

◆◆ Homestead Studio Suites Hotel-Alexandria [SH]
(703) 329-3399. **$110-$130.** 200 Blue Stone Rd. I-95/495, exit 174 (Eisenhower Ave Connector), just n to Eisenhower Ave, then 1.2 mi e. Int corridors. **Pets:** Accepted.
[A$K] [SD] ☒ ♿M 👂 ♿ ▣ 💻

◆◆ Red Roof Inn-Alexandria [M]
(703) 960-5200. **$70-$95.** 5975 Richmond Hwy. I-95/495, exit 177A, 0.5 mi s on US 1. Ext corridors. **Pets:** Large. Service with restrictions, crate.
☒ ♿M 👂 ♿ ▣

[AAA] ◆◆◆ Residence Inn by Marriott Alexandria-Old Town [LH]
(703) 548-5474. **$129-$339.** 1456 Duke St. I-95/495, exit 176, 0.5 mi n on SR 241, then 0.7 mi e on SR 236. Int corridors. **Pets:** Medium. $10 daily fee/room, $150 one-time fee/room. Service with restrictions, crate.
[SAVE] [SD] ☒ ♿M 👂 ♿ ▣ 💻 🏊

◆◆◆ Sheraton Pentagon South Hotel [LH]
(703) 740-8421. **$101-$170.** 4641 Kenmore Ave. I-395, exit 4, 0.8 mi s of jct SR 7. Int corridors. **Pets:** Accepted.
[A$K] [SD] ☒ 👂 ♿ ▣ 💻 🍴 🏊

[AAA] ◆◆◆ Sheraton Suites Alexandria [LH] 🐾
(703) 836-4700. **$109-$229.** 801 N St Asaph St. Just e of Washington St. Int corridors. **Pets:** Medium, dogs only. Designated rooms, service with restrictions, supervision.
[SAVE] [SD] ☒ 👂 ♿ ▣ 💻 🍴 🏊 🏋

[AAA] ◆◆◆ Washington Suites-Alexandria [SH]
(703) 370-9600. **$99-$209.** 100 S Reynolds St. I-395, exit 3A, 0.8 mi e on SR 236 E (Duke St), then just s. Int corridors. **Pets:** Medium. $10 daily fee/pet. Designated rooms, service with restrictions, crate.
[SAVE] [SD] ☒ ♿M 👂 ♿ ▣ 💻 🍴 🏊 🏋

ARLINGTON

[AAA] ◆◆ Best Western Washington Key Bridge [SH]
(703) 522-0400. **$89-$159.** 1850 N Fort Myer Dr. I-66, exit 73, just sw of Key Bridge. Int corridors. **Pets:** Accepted.
[SAVE] ☒ ▣ 💻 🏊

[AAA] ◆◆ Quality Hotel Courthouse Plaza [LH]
(703) 524-4000. **$109-$209.** 1200 N Courthouse Rd. 1.5 mi sw of Theodore Roosevelt Bridge on US 50. Ext/int corridors. **Pets:** Accepted.
[SAVE] [SD] ☒ 👂 ♿ ▣ 💻 🍴 🏊

◆◆ Quality Inn-Iwo Jima [SH]
(703) 524-5000. **$79-$159.** 1501 Arlington Blvd. 1 mi w of Theodore Roosevelt Bridge on US 50. Ext/int corridors. **Pets:** Medium, other species. $20 one-time fee/room. Designated rooms, service with restrictions, crate.
[A$K] [SD] ☒ ▣ 💻 🍴 🏊

[AAA] ◆◆◆ Residence Inn by Marriott-Pentagon City [LH]
(703) 413-6630. **$119-$249.** 550 Army Navy Dr. I-395, exit 8C, just 1 mi s of 14th St Bridge. Int corridors. **Pets:** Other species. $8 daily fee/room, $200 one-time fee/room.
[SAVE] [SD] ☒ ♿M 👂 ♿ ▣ 💻 🏊 🏋

◆◆◆◆ The Ritz-Carlton, Pentagon City [LH]
(703) 415-5000. **$299-$689.** 1250 S Hayes St. 1 mi s of 14th St Bridge. Int corridors. **Pets:** Accepted.
[A$K] [SD] ☒ ♿M 👂 ♿ ▣ 🍴 🏊 🏋

◆◆◆ Sheraton Crystal City Hotel [LH]
(703) 486-1111. **$85-$165.** 1800 Jefferson Davis Hwy. I-395, exit 8C, 1.4 mi s of 14th St Bridge on US 1; hotel entrance corner of Eads St. Int corridors. **Pets:** Accepted.
[A$K] [SD] ☒ 👂 ♿ ▣ 💻 🍴 🏊

[AAA] ◆◆◆ Sheraton National Hotel [LH]
(703) 521-1900. **$89-$279.** 900 S Orme St. I-395, exit 8A; jct SR 27 and 244, 1.3 mi s of 14th St Bridge. Int corridors. **Pets:** Accepted.
[SAVE] [SD] ☒ ▣ 💻 🍴 🏊

[AAA] ◆◆ The Virginian Suites [SH]
(703) 522-9600. **$89-$159.** 1500 Arlington Blvd. 1 mi w of Theodore Roosevelt Bridge, on US 50. Int corridors. **Pets:** Small. $150 deposit/pet, $10 daily fee/pet. Service with restrictions, crate.
[SAVE] [SD] ☒ ▣ 💻 🏊

CHANTILLY

AAA ▼▼▼ **AmeriSuites (Dulles Airport South/Chantilly) SH**
(703) 961-8160. **$159-$179.** 4994 Westone Plaza Dr. I-66, exit 53, 2 mi n on SR 28, just w on Westfields Blvd; 1.7 mi s of jct SR 28 and US 50. Int corridors. **Pets:** Accepted.

⬛ 🆂 ✖ 🖉 🖱 🛏 🖵 🏊

▼▼▼ **Holiday Inn Select Chantilly-Dulles Expo Center LH**
(703) 815-6060. **$99-$199.** 4335 Chantilly Shopping Center. I-66, exit 53, 3 mi n on SR 28, 1 mi s of jct US 50 and SR 28. Int corridors. **Pets:** Accepted.

⬛ 🆂 ✖ 🖐 🖉 🖱 🛏 🖵 ❌ 🏊

▼▼ **Homestead Studio Suites Hotel-Dulles/Chantilly M**
(703) 263-3361. **$96-$116.** 4504 Brookfield Corporate Dr. I-66, exit 53, 3 mi n on SR 28; jct SR 28 and 50, 1 mi s. Ext corridors. **Pets:** Accepted.

⬛ 🆂 ✖ 🖐 🖉 🖱 🛏 🖵

▼▼▼ **TownePlace Suites by Marriott-Chantilly SH** ❀
(703) 709-0453. **$84-$144.** 14036 Thunderbolt Pl. Jct SR 28, just e on US 50. Int corridors. **Pets:** Medium, other species. $75 one-time fee/pet. Designated rooms, service with restrictions, crate.

⬛ 🆂 ✖ 🖱 🛏 🖵 🏊

DUMFRIES

AAA ▼▼▼ **Quality Inn SH**
(703) 221-1141. **$69-$109.** 17133 Dumfries Rd. I-95, exit 152B, just w on SR 234 N. Ext/int corridors. **Pets:** Accepted.

⬛ 🆂 ✖ 🖉 🛏 🖵 🏊

FAIRFAX

AAA ▼▼▼ **Comfort Inn University Center SH** ❀
(703) 591-5900. **$69-$139.** 11180 Main St. I-66, exit 57A, 0.8 mi se on US 50, 0.5 mi nw of jct US 29. Int corridors. **Pets:** Other species. Service with restrictions.

⬛ 🆂 ✖ 🛏 🖵 ❌ 🏊 ✖

▼▼ **Homestead Studio Suites Hotel-Fair Oaks SH**
(703) 273-3444. **$85-$105.** 12104 Monument Dr. I-66, exit 57B, 0.8 mi w on US 50, 0.3 mi s on SR 620 (West Ox Rd), then just se. Ext corridors. **Pets:** Accepted.

⬛ 🆂 ✖ 🖐 🖉 🖱 🛏 🖵

▼▼ **Homestead Studio Suites Hotel-Falls Church/Merrifield SH**
(703) 204-0088. **$100-$120.** 8281 Willow Oaks Corporate Dr. I-495, exit 50A, just w on US 50 to Gallows Rd, then just s. Ext corridors. **Pets:** Accepted.

⬛ 🆂 ✖ 🖐 🖉 🛏 🖵

▼▼▼ **Residence Inn by Marriott-Fair Lakes SH**
(703) 266-4900. **$170-$209.** 12815 Fair Lakes Pkwy. I-66, exit 55 (Fairfax County Pkwy N), just w. Int corridors. **Pets:** Medium. $150 one-time fee/pet. Service with restrictions, supervision.

⬛ 🆂 ✖ 🖐 🖉 🖱 🛏 🖵 🏊 ✖

FALLS CHURCH

▼▼▼ **Fairfax-Merrifield Residence Inn by Marriott SH**
(703) 573-5200. **$149-$259.** 8125 Gatehouse Rd. I-495, exit 50A, just w to SR 640 N. Int corridors. **Pets:** Other species. $150 one-time fee/room. Service with restrictions, crate.

⬛ 🆂 ✖ 🖐 🖉 🖱 🛏 🖵 🏊 ✖

▼▼▼ **Homewood Suites by Hilton-Falls Church LH**
(703) 560-6644. **$109-$209.** 8130 Porter Rd. I-495, exit 50A, just w to SR 650; 0.4 mi n of SR 650. Int corridors. **Pets:** Medium. $100 one-time fee/room. Service with restrictions, crate.

⬛ 🆂 ✖ 🖐 🖉 🖱 🛏 🖵 🏊

▼▼▼ **TownePlace Suites by Marriott-Falls Church SH**
(703) 237-6172. **$89-$199.** 205 Hillwood Ave. I-495, exit 50B, 2.5 mi e on US 50, 0.6 mi n on Annandale Rd, then e. Int corridors. **Pets:** Accepted.

✖ 🖐 🖉 🛏 🖵 🏊

HERNDON

▼▼▼ **Hawthorn Suites SH**
(703) 437-5000. **$99-$185.** 467 Herndon Pkwy. SR 267 (Dulles Toll Rd), exit 11 (Fairfax County Pkwy). Int corridors. **Pets:** Medium. $100 deposit/room. Service with restrictions.

⬛ 🆂 ✖ 🛏 🖵 🏊 ✖

AAA ▼▼▼ **Hilton Washington Dulles Airport LH**
(703) 478-2900. **$67-$307.** 13869 Park Center Rd. SR 267 (Dulles Toll Rd), exit 9, 3 mi s on SR 28; in a business park. Int corridors. **Pets:** Accepted.

⬛ ✖ 🖉 🖐 🛏 🖵 ❌ 🏊 ✖

▼▼▼ **Homewood Suites by Hilton SH**
(703) 793-1700. **$109-$219.** 13460 Sunrise Valley Dr. SR 267 (Dulles Toll Rd), exit 10, 0.5 mi s on SR 657, then just w. Int corridors. **Pets:** Accepted.

⬛ 🆂 ✖ 🖐 🖉 🖱 🛏 🖵 🏊

▼▼▼ **Residence Inn by Marriott-Herndon/Reston SH**
(703) 435-0044. **$209-$229.** 315 Elden St. 0.5 mi e on SR 606. Int corridors. **Pets:** Accepted.

✖ 🖉 🛏 🖵 🏊 ✖

▼▼▼ **Staybridge Suites Dulles Airport SH** ❀
(703) 713-6800. **$205-$265.** 13700 Coppermine Rd. SR 267 (Dulles Toll Rd), exit 10, 0.7 mi s on Centreville Rd (SR 657), then 0.4 mi w. Ext corridors. **Pets:** Medium. $25 one-time fee/room. Service with restrictions, crate.

⬛ 🆂 ✖ 🖉 🖱 🛏 🖵 🏊 ✖

LEESBURG

▼▼▼ **Holiday Inn at Carradoc Hall SH**
(703) 771-9200. **$79-$99.** 1500 E Market St. 2 mi e on SR 7. Int corridors. **Pets:** Accepted.

⬛ 🆂 ✖ 🖐 🖱 🛏 🖵 ❌ 🏊

LORTON

▼▼▼ **Comfort Inn Gunston Corner SH** ❀
(703) 643-3100. **$89-$139.** 8180 Silverbrook Rd. I-95, exit 163, just w. Int corridors. **Pets:** $25 one-time fee/pet. Service with restrictions, supervision.

⬛ 🆂 ✖ 🖉 🖱 🛏 🖵 🏊 ✖

MANASSAS

AAA ▼▼▼ **Best Western Battlefield Inn SH** ❀
(703) 361-8000. **$89-$175.** 10820 Balls Ford Rd. I-66, exit 47A westbound; exit 47 eastbound, just s on SR 234, then just w. Ext corridors. **Pets:** Medium, dogs only. $10 daily fee/pet. Service with restrictions, supervision.

⬛ 🆂 ✖ 🖱 🛏 🖵 ❌ 🏊

AAA ▼▼▼ **Holiday Inn Manassas SH**
(703) 335-0000. **$59-$99.** 10800 Vandor Ln. I-66, exit 47 eastbound; exit 47B westbound, just n on SR 234, then just e. Int corridors. **Pets:** Accepted.

⬛ 🆂 ✖ 🖱 🛏 🖵 ❌ 🏊

▼▼ **Red Roof Inn-Manassas M**
(703) 335-9333. **$65-$90.** 10610 Automotive Dr. I-66, exit 47 eastbound; exit 47A westbound, just s on SR 234, then just e on Balls Ford Rd. Ext corridors. **Pets:** Accepted.

✖ 🖉 🖱 🛏

MCLEAN

ⒶⒶⒶ ▽▽▽ Best Western Tysons Westpark Hotel 🄻🄷
(703) 734-2800. **$79-$159.** 8401 Westpark Dr. I-495, exit 47A, 1.3 mi w on SR 7. Int corridors. **Pets:** Other species. Service with restrictions, crate.
(SAVE) 🆂🐾 ⊠ 🄶🄼 🕭 🄴 🎗 🖥 🖳 🍴 🏊 ⊠

ⒶⒶⒶ ▽▽▽▽ Holiday Inn Tysons Corner 🄻🄷
(703) 893-2100. **$229-$279.** 1960 Chain Bridge Rd. I-495, exit 46A, 0.5 mi s on SR 123, just nw on International Dr, then just sw on Greensboro Dr. Int corridors. **Pets:** Accepted.
(SAVE) 🆂🐾 ⊠ 🄶🄼 🕭 🄴 🖥 🖳 🍴 🏊 ⊠

ⒶⒶⒶ ▽▽▽▽ Staybridge Suites by Holiday Inn-McLean/ Tysons Corner 🅂🄷
(703) 448-5400. **$170-$230.** 6845 Old Dominion Dr. I-495, exit 46B, 2 mi n on SR 123, then 0.3 mi e on SR 309. Int corridors. **Pets:** Accepted.
(SAVE) 🆂🐾 ⊠ 🄶🄼 🕭 🄴 🖥 🖳 🏊

RESTON

▽▽▽▽ Homestead Studio Suites Hotel-Reston 🅂🄷
(703) 707-9700. **$100-$120.** 12190 Sunset Hills Rd. SR 267 (Dulles Toll Rd), exit 12 (Reston Pkwy), just n, then just w. Ext corridors. **Pets:** Accepted.
(ASK) 🆂🐾 ⊠ 🄴 🖥 🖳

SPRINGFIELD

▽▽▽ Comfort Inn Washington DC/Springfield 🅂🄷 🐾
(703) 922-9000. **$119-$129.** 6560 Loisdale Ct. I-95, exit 169A, just e on SR 644 E; jct I-395 and 495, 0.8 mi s. Int corridors. **Pets:** $25 deposit/ room. Service with restrictions.
(ASK) 🆂🐾 ⊠ 🕭 🄴 🖥 🖳

▽▽▽ Hampton Inn Washington DC/Springfield 🅂🄷 🐾
(703) 924-9444. **$134-$144.** 6550 Loisdale Ct. I-95, exit 169A, just e on SR 644 E; jct I-395 and 495, 0.8 mi s. Int corridors. **Pets:** $25 deposit/ room. Service with restrictions, supervision.
(ASK) 🆂🐾 ⊠ 🄶🄼 🕭 🄴 🖥 🖳 🏊

▽▽▽ Red Roof Inn Springfield 🅂🄷
(703) 644-5311. **$75-$90.** 6868 Springfield Blvd. I-95, exit 169B, just sw of SR 644; jct I-395 and 495, 0.8 mi s. Int corridors. **Pets:** Accepted.
⊠ 🄶🄼 🄴 🖥

▽▽▽ TownePlace Suites by Marriott 🅂🄷
(703) 569-8060. **$149-$199.** 6245 Brandon Ave. I-95, exit 169B, just nw of SR 644; jct I-395 and 495, 0.8 mi s. Int corridors. **Pets:** Other species. $75 one-time fee/room. Service with restrictions.
(ASK) 🆂🐾 ⊠ 🄶🄼 🕭 🄴 🖥 🖳 🏊

STERLING

ⒶⒶⒶ ▽▽▽ AmeriSuites (Dulles Airport North/Sterling) 🅂🄷
(703) 444-3909. **$79-$169.** 21481 Ridgetop Cir. 1.8 mi e on SR 7 from jct SR 28. Int corridors. **Pets:** Medium. $10 daily fee/pet. Service with restrictions, crate.
(SAVE) 🆂🐾 ⊠ 🕭 🖥 🖳 🏊

▽▽▽ Hampton Inn-Dulles/Cascades 🅂🄷
(703) 450-9595. **$69-$179.** 46331 McClellan Way. SR 28 N, 5 mi to exit 7E; SR 7 to Cascade Pkwy. Int corridors. **Pets:** Medium. $10 daily fee/pet. Designated rooms, service with restrictions, supervision.
(ASK) 🆂🐾 ⊠ 🄴 🖥 🖳 🏊 ⊠

▽▽▽▽ Hampton Inn Washington-Dulles Airport 🅂🄷
(703) 471-8300. **$59-$159.** 45440 Holiday Dr. SR 267 (Dulles Toll Rd), exit 9B, 1.8 mi n on SR 28, then just ne. Ext corridors. **Pets:** Accepted.
(ASK) 🆂🐾 ⊠ 🕭 🄴 🖥 🖳 🏊 ⊠

▽▽▽▽ Holiday Inn Washington Dulles International Airport 🅂🄷
(703) 471-7411. **$69-$179.** 1000 Sully Rd. SR 267 (Dulles Toll Rd), exit 9B, 1.8 mi n on SR 28. Ext/int corridors. **Pets:** Accepted.
(ASK) 🆂🐾 ⊠ 🕭 🄴 🖥 🖳 🍴 🏊 ⊠

▽▽▽▽ Homestead Studio Suites Hotel-Dulles/Sterling 🅂🄷
(703) 904-7575. **$96-$106.** 45350 Catalina Ct. SR 267 (Dulles Toll Rd), exit 9B, 0.8 mi n on SR 28, then just w on SR 606. Ext corridors. **Pets:** Accepted.
(ASK) 🆂🐾 ⊠ 🄴 🖥 🖳 ⊠

▽▽▽▽ TownePlace Suites by Marriott at Dulles Airport 🅂🄷
(703) 707-2017. **$69-$179.** 22744 Holiday Park Dr. SR 267 (Dulles Toll Rd), exit 9B, 1.8 mi n on SR 28, then just ne. Int corridors. **Pets:** Other species. $75 one-time fee/room.
(ASK) 🆂🐾 ⊠ 🕭 🄴 🖥 🖳 🏊

ⒶⒶⒶ ▽▽▽ TownePlace Suites by Marriott Sterling 🅂🄷
(703) 421-1090. **$59-$199.** 21123 Whitfield Pl. US 7 to Cascades Pkwy, 0.5 mi n to Palisades Pkwy, just e, then just s. Int corridors. **Pets:** Small. $10 daily fee/room, $100 one-time fee/room. Service with restrictions.
(SAVE) 🆂🐾 ⊠ 🄴 🖥 🖳 🏊

VIENNA

ⒶⒶⒶ ▽▽▽ Comfort Inn Tysons Corner 🄼
(703) 448-8020. **$129-$159.** 1587 Spring Hill Rd. I-495, exit 47A, 1.8 mi w on SR 7, then just s on Spring Hill Rd; just e of jct SR 267 (Dulles Toll Rd). Ext corridors. **Pets:** Accepted.
(SAVE) 🆂🐾 ⊠ 🖥 🖳 🏊

▽▽ Homestead Studio Suites Hotel-Tysons Corner 🅂🄷
(703) 356-6300. **$115-$135.** 8201 Old Courthouse Rd. I-495, exit 47A, 0.6 mi w on SR 7, then just s on Gallows Rd. Int corridors. **Pets:** Accepted.
(ASK) 🆂🐾 ⊠ 🄶🄼 🄴 🖥 🖳

▽▽▽ Residence Inn by Marriott-Tysons Corner 🅂🄷
(703) 893-0120. **$179-$299.** 8616 Westwood Center Dr. I-495, exit 47A, 1.9 mi w on SR 7, then just s. Ext corridors. **Pets:** Accepted.
(ASK) 🆂🐾 ⊠ 🖥 🖳 🏊 ⊠

▽▽▽ Residence Inn by Marriott Tysons Corner-Mall 🅂🄷
(703) 917-0800. **$119-$269.** 8400 Old Courthouse Rd. I-495, exit 46A, 1.1 mi s on SR 123; 0.3 mi s of jct SR 7 and 123. Int corridors. **Pets:** Accepted.
(ASK) 🆂🐾 ⊠ 🄶🄼 🕭 🄴 🖥 🖳 🏊

▽▽▽▽ Sheraton Premiere At Tysons Corner 🄻🄷 🐾
(703) 448-1234. **$219-$229.** 8661 Leesburg Pike. SR 7, just e of jct SR 267 (Dulles Toll Rd). Int corridors. **Pets:** Medium. Service with restrictions, crate.
(ASK) ⊠ 🕭 🄴 🖥 🖳 🍴 🏊 ⊠

WOODBRIDGE

ⒶⒶⒶ ▽▽▽ Quality Inn at Potomac Mills 🅂🄷
(703) 494-0300. **$60-$120.** 1109 Horner Rd. I-95, exit 161 southbound, 1.5 mi s on US 1, just n on SR 123, then just s; exit 160A northbound, 0.5 mi s on SR 123, then just s. Int corridors. **Pets:** Medium, other species. $25 daily fee/pet. Designated rooms, service with restrictions.
(SAVE) 🆂🐾 ⊠ 🕭 🖥 🖳 🏊

END AREA

DUBLIN

▼▼▼▼ **Comfort Inn-Dublin** SH ❀
(540) 674-1100. **$52-$75.** 4424 Cleburne Blvd. I-81, exit 98, just e. Int corridors. **Pets:** $10 daily fee/pet. Service with restrictions, supervision.
A$K S6 ✕ 🖉 🖥 🖳 ⚊

EMPORIA

AAA ▼▼▼▼ **Best Western Emporia** SH
(434) 634-3200. **$60-$85.** 1100 W Atlantic St. I-95, exit 11B, just w on US 58. Ext corridors. **Pets:** Other species. $10 daily fee/pet. Designated rooms, service with restrictions.
SAVE S6 ✕ 🖑 🖥 🖳 ⚊

AAA ▼▼ ▼ **Comfort Inn** SH
(434) 348-3282. **$52-$70.** 1411 Skippers Rd. I-95, exit 8, just e on US 301. Ext corridors. **Pets:** Accepted.
SAVE S6 ✕ 🖥 🖳 ⚊

AAA ▼▼▼▼ **Days Inn-Emporia** SH
(434) 634-9481. **$65-$85.** 921 W Atlantic St. I-95, exit 11B, just w on US 58. Ext corridors. **Pets:** Medium. $8 one-time fee/pet. Designated rooms, service with restrictions, crate.
SAVE S6 ✕ 🖥 ⚊

AAA ▼▼▼▼ **Hampton Inn** SH ❀
(434) 634-9200. **$64-$76.** 1207 W Atlantic St. I-95, exit 11B, just w on US 58. Ext corridors. **Pets:** Other species. Service with restrictions.
SAVE S6 ✕ 🖉 🖥 🖳 ⚊

AAA ▼▼ **Knights Inn** M
(434) 535-8535. **$40-$60.** 3173 Sussex Dr. I-95, exit 17, 0.5 mi s on US 301. Ext corridors. **Pets:** Accepted.
SAVE S6 ✕ 🖥 ⚊

FANCY GAP

AAA ▼▼▼▼ **Doe Run Lodge** SH
(276) 398-2212. **$99-$234, 7 day notice.** MM 189.2 on Blue Ridge Pkwy; 10 mi n from US 52 (parkway entrance). Ext corridors. **Pets:** Accepted.
SAVE ✕ 🖥 🖳 🍴 ⚊ ⊠

FARMVILLE

▼▼ **Super 8 Motel** M
(434) 392-8196. **$51-$105, 5 day notice.** 2012 S Main St. On US 15, just n of jct US 460. Int corridors. **Pets:** Accepted.
A$K S6 ✕ 🖥

FREDERICKSBURG

AAA ▼▼▼▼ **Best Western Central Plaza** M
(540) 786-7404. **$63-$77.** 3000 Plank Rd. I-95, exit 130B on SR 3. Ext corridors. **Pets:** Small, other species. $9 daily fee/pet. Designated rooms, service with restrictions, supervision.
SAVE S6 ✕ 🖑M 🖥 🖳 ⚊

AAA ▼▼▼▼ **Best Western Fredericksburg** SH
(540) 371-5050. **$67-$89, 15 day notice.** 2205 William St. I-95, exit 130A, 0.3 mi e on SR 3. Ext corridors. **Pets:** $9 daily fee/pet. Service with restrictions, supervision.
SAVE S6 ✕ 🖑M 🖥 🖳 ⚊

AAA ▼▼▼ **Dunning Mills Inn All Suites Hotel** SH
(540) 373-1256. **$69-$89.** 2305 C Jefferson Davis Hwy. I-95, exit 126, 3 mi n on US 1. Ext corridors. **Pets:** $200 deposit/room, $5 daily fee/pet. Service with restrictions.
SAVE S6 ✕ 🖥 🖳 ⚊

AAA ▼▼▼▼ **Hampton Inn** SH ❀
(540) 371-0330. **$77-$109.** 2310 William St. I-95, exit 130A on SR 3 E. Ext corridors. **Pets:** Other species. Designated rooms, service with restrictions, supervision.
SAVE S6 ✕ 🖥 🖳 ⚊

AAA ▼▼▼▼ **Holiday Inn-Fredericksburg North** SH
(540) 371-5550. **$80-$95.** 564 Warrenton Rd. I-95, exit 133, just nw on US 17. Ext corridors. **Pets:** Medium. Service with restrictions, supervision.
SAVE S6 ✕ 🖥 🖳 🍴 ⚊ ⊠

▼▼▼▼ **Holiday Inn Select Fredericksburg** LH
(540) 786-8321. **$99-$135.** 2801 Plank Rd. I-95, exit 130B on SR 3. Int corridors. **Pets:** Accepted.
A$K S6 ✕ 🖑M 🖉 🖑 🖥 🖳 🍴 ⚊

AAA ▼▼ **Howard Johnson Hotel** SH
(540) 898-1800. **$69-$109, 3 day notice.** 5327 Jefferson Davis Hwy. I-95, exit 126. Int corridors. **Pets:** Accepted.
SAVE S6 ✕ 🖑 🖥 🖳

AAA ▼▼ ▼ **Quality Inn Fredericksburg** SH
(540) 373-0000. **$57-$80.** 543 Warrenton Rd. I-95, exit 133, just n on US 17. Ext corridors. **Pets:** Medium, other species. $8 daily fee/pet. Service with restrictions.
SAVE S6 ✕ 🖳 🍴 ⚊

AAA ▼▼ ▼ **Ramada Inn South** SH
(540) 898-1102. **$39-$109.** 5324 Jefferson Davis Hwy. I-95, exit 126, just n on US 1. Ext/int corridors. **Pets:** $25 deposit/room. Designated rooms, service with restrictions, supervision.
SAVE S6 ✕ 🖥 🖳 🍴 ⚊ ⊠

FRONT ROYAL

AAA ▼▼ ▼ **Bluemont Inn** M
(540) 635-9447. **$47-$195.** 1525 N Shenandoah Ave. I-66, exit 6, 1.8 mi s on US 340/522. Ext corridors. **Pets:** Service with restrictions, supervision.
SAVE S6 ✕ 🖥

AAA ▼▼ **Budget Inn** M
(540) 635-2196. **$42-$75.** 1122 N Royal Ave. I-66, exit 6, 2.2 mi s on US 340/522 and SR 55. Ext corridors. **Pets:** Accepted.
SAVE S6 ✕ 🖥

AAA ▼▼ **Relax Inn** M
(540) 635-4101. **$50-$75.** 1801 Shenandoah Ave. I-66, exit 6, 1.5 mi s on US 340/522. Ext corridors. **Pets:** $5 daily fee/pet. Service with restrictions, supervision.
SAVE S6 ✕ 🖥 🖳 ⚊

AAA ▼▼▼▼ **Scottish Inn** M
(540) 636-6168. **$49-$79.** 533 S Royal Ave. I-66, exit 6, 3.8 mi s on US 340, jct SR 55. Ext corridors. **Pets:** $5 daily fee/room. Service with restrictions, supervision.
SAVE S6 ✕ 🖥 🖳

AAA ▼▼ **Twi-Lite Motel** M
(540) 635-4148. **$45-$89, 3 day notice.** 53 W 14th St. I-66, exit 6, 2.3 mi s on US 340/522. Ext corridors. **Pets:** Small. $5 deposit/pet. Designated rooms, service with restrictions, supervision.
SAVE ✕ 🖥 ⚊

GLADE SPRING

AAA ▼▼ ▼ **Swiss Inn Motel & Suites** M
(276) 429-5191. **$45-$65.** 33361 Lee Hwy. I-81, exit 29, just e. Ext corridors. **Pets:** Small, dogs only. $7 one-time fee/room. Service with restrictions, supervision.
SAVE S6 ✕ 🖥

GREENVILLE

◆◆ ▼▼▼ **Budget Host-Historic Hessian House** SH ❀
(540) 337-1231. **$40-$75, 3 day notice.** 3554 Lee Jackson Hwy. I-81, exit 213, 0.3 mi e. Ext corridors. **Pets:** Medium. $6 daily fee/pet. Designated rooms, service with restrictions.
SAVE SD ✕ ▯ ▭ ✕

GRUNDY

▼▼▼ **Comfort Inn** SH
(276) 935-5050. **$59-$135.** US 460 Main St. On US 460, 0.5 mi e. Int corridors. **Pets:** Medium. $20 one-time fee/room. Service with restrictions, supervision.
ASK SD ✕ ▤M ✑ ▨ ▯ ▭

HAMPTON ROADS AREA

CHESAPEAKE

◆◆ ▼▼▼ **Days Inn-Chesapeake** M
(757) 487-8861. **$45-$100, 7 day notice.** 1439 George Washington Hwy. I-64, exit 296, 2.5 mi n on US 17. Ext/int corridors. **Pets:** Small. $15 one-time fee/pet. Designated rooms, no service, supervision.
SAVE SD ✕ ▯ ▭

▼▼ **Red Roof Inn** M
(757) 523-0123. **$47-$74.** 724 Woodlake Dr. I-64, exit 289A, just n to Woodlake Dr, then just e. Ext corridors. **Pets:** Accepted.
✕ ▯

▼ **Super 8 Motel** M ❀
(757) 686-8888. **$52-$77, 3 day notice.** 3216 Churchland Blvd. I-664, exit 9B, 1 mi s on SR 17. Int corridors. **Pets:** Other species. $6 daily fee/room. Designated rooms, service with restrictions, crate.
ASK SD ✕ ▤M

▼▼▼ **TownePlace Suites By Marriott** SH
(757) 523-5004. **$69-$139.** 2000 Old Greenbrier Rd. I-64, exit 289A, just n on Greenbrier Pkwy. Int corridors. **Pets:** Accepted.
ASK SD ✕ ▤M ✑ ▨ ▯ ▭ ⇥

GLOUCESTER

▼▼▼ **Comfort Inn Gloucester** SH
(804) 695-1900. **$79-$109.** 6639 Forest Hill Ave. US 17, just s. Int corridors. **Pets:** Medium, dogs only. $10 daily fee/pet. Designated rooms, service with restrictions, crate.
ASK SD ✕ ▯ ▭ ⇥

HAMPTON

▼▼▼ **Candlewood Suites** SH
(757) 766-8976. **$59-$189.** 401 Butler Farm Rd. I-64, exit 261B (Hampton Roads Center Pkwy) eastbound; exit 262B (Magruder Blvd) westbound, then n. Int corridors. **Pets:** Accepted.
ASK SD ✕ ▤M ▨ ▯ ▭

▼▼▼ **Holiday Inn Hampton Hotel & Conference Center** LH
(757) 838-0200. **$59-$169.** 1815 W Mercury Blvd. I-64, exit 263B (Mercury Blvd) westbound; exit 263 eastbound. Ext/int corridors. **Pets:** Medium. $25 one-time fee/pet. Service with restrictions, supervision.
ASK SD ✕ ▤M ✑ ▨ ▯ ▭ 🍽 ⇥ ✕

◆◆ ▼▼▼▼ **La Quinta Inn Norfolk (Hampton)** SH
(757) 827-8680. **$70-$144.** 2138 W Mercury Blvd. I-64, exit 263 (Mercury Blvd), just s. Ext/int corridors. **Pets:** Accepted.
SAVE ✕ ▤M ✑ ▨ ▯ ▭ ⇥

◆◆ ▼▼▼ **Quality Inn & Suites Conference Center** SH
(757) 838-5011. **$90-$180.** 1809 W Mercury Blvd. I-64, exit 263B (Mercury Blvd), jct SR 58. Int corridors. **Pets:** $25 one-time fee/room. Designated rooms, service with restrictions, crate.
SAVE SD ✕ ▤M ✑ ▨ ▯ ▭ 🍽 ⇥

▼ **Super 8 Motel** M
(757) 723-2888. **$48-$85.** 1330 Thomas St. I-64, 265B westbound; exit 265C eastbound. Int corridors. **Pets:** Accepted.
ASK SD ✕ ▯ ▭

NEWPORT NEWS

▼▼▼ **Comfort Inn** SH
(757) 249-0200. **$109-$139.** 12330 Jefferson Ave. I-64, exit 255A, just s on Clarie Ln (mall parking lot). Int corridors. **Pets:** Other species. $10 daily fee/pet. Designated rooms, no service, supervision.
ASK SD ✕ ▤M ✑ ▯ ▭ ⇥

◆◆ ▼▼▼ **Days Inn** SH
(757) 874-0201. **$65-$85.** 14747 Warwick Blvd. I-64, exit 250A (SR 105/Ft Eustis Blvd S), 2.5 mi to US 60 E (Warwick Blvd). Ext corridors. **Pets:** Other species. $10 daily fee/pet. Service with restrictions, supervision.
SAVE SD ✕ ▯ ▭ ⇥

◆◆ ▼▼▼ **Days Inn-Oyster Point** SH
(757) 873-6700. **$85-$119, 3 day notice.** 11829 Fishing Point Dr. I-64, exit 255A, 2.5 mi s to Thimble Shoals Dr E, 1 blk to property. Int corridors. **Pets:** $15 daily fee/pet. Service with restrictions, crate.
SAVE SD ✕ ✑ ▯ ▭ ⇥

◆◆ ▼▼▼ **Host Inn** M
(757) 599-3303. **$50-$90.** 985 J Clyde Morris Blvd. I-64, exit 258B, 0.8 mi n. Ext corridors. **Pets:** Small, dogs only. $10 daily fee/pet. No service, supervision.
SAVE ✕ ▯ ⇥

NORFOLK

◆◆ ▼▼▼▼ **B & B @ Historic Page House Inn** BB
(757) 625-5033. **$140-$225, 7 day notice.** 323 Fairfax Ave. I-264, exit 9, 1.4 mi n on Waterside Dr to Olney Rd, just w to Mowbray Arch, then just s; in the Ghent historic district. Int corridors. **Pets:** Accepted.
SAVE SD ✕ ▯ ✕

◆◆ ▼▼▼ **Clarion Hotel James Madison** SH
(757) 622-6682. **$89-$139.** 345 Granby St. Jct Freemason St; downtown. Int corridors. **Pets:** $25 one-time fee/room. Service with restrictions, supervision.
SAVE SD ✕ ▨ ▯ ▭ 🍽

◆◆ ▼▼▼ **Quality Suites Lake Wright** SH
(757) 461-6251. **$109-$159, 3 day notice.** 6280 Northampton Blvd. I-64, exit 282, just w on US 13. Int corridors. **Pets:** Other species. $35 one-time fee/room. Service with restrictions, crate.
SAVE SD ✕ ▤M ▨ ▯ ▭ 🍽 ⇥

◆◆ ▼▼▼ **Radisson Hotel Norfolk** SH
(757) 627-5555. **$129-$166.** 700 Monticello Ave. Jct Brambleton Ave and St. Pauls Blvd; downtown. Int corridors. **Pets:** Small. $25 deposit/pet. Designated rooms, service with restrictions, crate.
SAVE SD ✕ ▤M ✑ ▨ ▯ ▭ 🍽 ⇥

▼▼▼ **Residence Inn by Marriott Norfolk Airport** SH
(757) 333-3000. **$79-$159.** 1590 N Military Hwy. I-64, exit 281B (Military Hwy). Int corridors. **Pets:** Accepted.
ASK SD ✕ ▤M ✑ ▯ ▭ ⇥ ✕

▼▼▼ **Sheraton Norfolk Waterside Hotel** LH
(757) 622-6664. **$79-$179, 3 day notice.** 777 Waterside Dr. I-264 to Waterside Dr; downtown. Int corridors. **Pets:** Accepted.
ASK SD ✕ ▤M ✑ ▨ ▯ ▭ 🍽 ⇥

⚠ ▼▼▼ Sleep Inn Lake Wright SH
(757) 461-1133. **$89-$139, 3 day notice.** 6280 Northampton Blvd. I-64, exit 282, just w on US 13. Int corridors. **Pets:** Other species. $25 one-time fee/room. Service with restrictions, crate.
[SAVE] 🛇 ⊗ &M 👜 🖵 🍴 🏊

PORTSMOUTH

⚠ ▼▼▼ Holiday Inn-Olde Towne Portsmouth SH
(757) 393-2573. **$99-$135.** 8 Crawford Pkwy. Just nw from High St. Int corridors. **Pets:** Accepted.
[SAVE] 🛇 ⊗ 👜 🖵 🍴 🏊

SUFFOLK

▼▼▼ Holiday Inn-Suffolk SH
(757) 934-2311. **$80.** 2864 Pruden Blvd. US 460 at jct US 58 Bypass. Ext corridors. **Pets:** Accepted.
[ASK] 🛇 ⊗ 🐾 👜 🖵 🍴 🏊

VIRGINIA BEACH

⚠ ▼▼▼ DoubleTree Hotel Virginia Beach SH ✿
(757) 422-8900. **$59-$229, 3 day notice.** 1900 Pavilion Dr. I-264, exit 22 (Birdneck Rd). Int corridors. **Pets:** Large, dogs only. $25 one-time fee/room. Designated rooms, service with restrictions, supervision.
[SAVE] 🛇 ⊗ 🐾 👜 🖵 🍴 🏊

⚠ ▼ Flagship Inn & Efficiencies M ✿
(757) 425-6422. **$59-$155.** 512 Atlantic Ave. I-264, 1 mi s of terminus; at Atlantic Ave and 6th St. Ext corridors. **Pets:** Large, other species. $125 one-time fee/room. Designated rooms, service with restrictions.
[SAVE] ⊗ 👜 🖵 🏊

⚠ ▼▼▼ La Quinta Inn Norfolk (Virginia Beach) SH
(757) 497-6620. **$75-$145.** 192 Newtown Rd. I-64, exit 284B to I-264 (Virginia Beach-Norfolk Expwy), exit Newtown Rd S. Int corridors. **Pets:** Other species. Service with restrictions, crate.
[SAVE] ⊗ &M 👜 🖵 🏊

⚠ ▼▼▼ Ramada Plaza Resort Oceanfront LH ✿
(757) 428-7025. **$80-$260, 3 day notice.** Atlantic Ave and 57th St. I-264, 2.2 mi n of terminus. Int corridors. **Pets:** Large, dogs only. $25 daily fee/pet. Designated rooms, service with restrictions, supervision.
[SAVE] 🛇 ⊗ &M 👜 🖵 🍴 🏊 ⊠

⚠ ▼▼ Red Roof Inn VA Beach (Norfolk Airport) M
(757) 460-6700. **$56-$176, 3 day notice.** 5745 Northampton Blvd. I-64, exit 282, 1 mi n on US 13 (Northampton Blvd). Ext corridors. **Pets:** Small, dogs only. $10 one-time fee/room. Designated rooms, no service, supervision.
[SAVE] 🛇 ⊗ 👜 🏊

▼▼ Red Roof Inn-Virginia Beach M
(757) 490-0225. **$46-$105.** 196 Ballard Ct. I-64/264, exit 284B (Newtown Rd). Ext corridors. **Pets:** Medium. Service with restrictions, supervision.
⊗ 👜 🏊

▼▼▼ Sheraton Oceanfront Hotel SH
(757) 425-9000. **$59-$179, 3 day notice.** 3501 Atlantic Ave. I-264, 1 mi n of terminus; jct 36th St. Int corridors. **Pets:** Dogs only. $75 deposit/room. Designated rooms, service with restrictions, supervision.
[ASK] 🛇 ⊗ &M 👜 🖵 🍴 🏊 ⊠

▼▼▼ TownePlace Suites By Marriott SH
(757) 490-9367. **$94-$180.** 5757 Cleveland St. I-64, exit 284B to I-264 (Virginia Beach-Norfolk Expwy), exit Newtown Rd N. Int corridors. **Pets:** Medium, other species. $75 one-time fee/room.
[ASK] ⊗ &M 👜 🖵 🏊

END AREA

HARRISONBURG

▼ Belle Meade Red Carpet Inn M
(540) 434-6704. **$50-$70, 4 day notice.** 3210 S Main St. I-81, exit 243, just nw. Ext corridors. **Pets:** $10 daily fee/pet. Service with restrictions, supervision.
[ASK] 🛇 ⊗ 👜 🏊

⚠ ▼▼▼ Comfort Inn SH
(540) 433-6066. **$79-$99.** 1440 E Market St. I-81, exit 247A, just e. Int corridors. **Pets:** Other species. Service with restrictions, supervision.
[SAVE] 🛇 ⊗ 🐾 👜 🖵 🏊

⚠ ▼▼▼ Days Inn Harrisonburg SH
(540) 433-9353. **$55-$170.** 1131 Forest Hill Rd. I-81, exit 245, just e. Int corridors. **Pets:** Dogs only. $10 daily fee/room. Designated rooms, service with restrictions, supervision.
[SAVE] 🛇 ⊗ 🐾 👜 🖵 🏊 ⊠

⚠ ▼▼ Four Points by Sheraton SH
(540) 433-2521. **$89-$139.** 1400 E Market St. I-81, exit 247A, just e on US 33. Int corridors. **Pets:** Accepted.
[SAVE] 🛇 ⊗ 🐾 &M 👜 🖵 🍴 🏊

⚠ ▼▼▼ Harrisonburg Econo Lodge M
(540) 433-2576. **$60-$150.** 1703 E Market St. I-81, exit 247A, 0.5 mi e on US 33. Ext/int corridors. **Pets:** Small, dogs only. Designated rooms, service with restrictions, supervision.
[SAVE] 🛇 ⊗ 👜 🖵 🏊

▼▼ Motel 6 Harrisonburg #1211 M
(540) 433-6939. **$43-$57.** 10 Linda Ln. I-81, exit 247A, just e on US 33. Ext corridors. **Pets:** Other species. No service, supervision.
🛇 ⊗ 👜 🏊

⚠ ▼▼ Ramada Inn SH
(540) 434-9981. **$55-$95.** 1 Pleasant Valley Rd. I-81, exit 243, just w, then just n on US 11. Ext corridors. **Pets:** Medium, dogs only. $10 one-time fee/room. Service with restrictions, supervision.
[SAVE] 🛇 ⊗ 🐾 👜 🖵 🏊

⚠ ▼▼ Super 8 Motel M
(540) 433-8888. **$39-$200.** 3330 S Main St. I-81, exit 243, just e, then just s on US 11. Int corridors. **Pets:** Small. $10 daily fee/pet. Designated rooms, no service, supervision.
[SAVE] 🛇 ⊗ 👜

⚠ ▼▼▼ The Village Inn SH ✿
(540) 434-7355. **$67-$74.** 4979 S Valley Pike. I-81, exit 240 southbound, 0.6 mi w on SR 257, then 1.5 mi n on US 11; exit 243 northbound, just w to US 11, then 1.7 mi s. Ext corridors. **Pets:** $7 daily fee/pet. Service with restrictions, supervision.
[SAVE] ⊗ 👜 🖵 🏊 ⊠

HILLSVILLE

⚠ ▼▼▼ Holiday Inn Express SH
(276) 728-2120. **$72-$185, 7 day notice.** 85 Airport Rd. I-77, exit 14, just w on US 58 and 221. Ext corridors. **Pets:** Small. $10 daily fee/pet. Designated rooms, service with restrictions, supervision.
[SAVE] 🛇 ⊗ &M 👜 🖵 🏊

♦ **Red Carpet Inn** [M]
(276) 728-9118. **$43-$131.** 2666 Old Galax Pike. I-77, exit 14, just n. Int corridors. **Pets:** Accepted.
[ASK] [SD] 🚭 🔌 📺

HOPEWELL

[AAA] ♦♦ **Candlewood Suites** [SH]
(804) 541-0200. **$69-$79.** 5113 Plaza Dr. I-295, exit 9B (SR 36), just w; adjacent to Oak Lawn Plaza. Int corridors. **Pets:** Accepted.
[SAVE] [SD] 🚭 ♿ 🔌 📺

[AAA] ♦♦ **Econo Lodge** [SH]
(804) 541-4849. **$69.** 4096 Oaklawn Blvd. I-295, exit 9A, just e. Int corridors. **Pets:** Small. Service with restrictions, supervision.
[SAVE] [SD] 🚭 [♿M] ♿ 🔌 📺

HOT SPRINGS

♦♦ **Roseloe Motel** [M]
(540) 839-5373. **$60-$80.** 590 US 220 N. 3 mi n. Ext corridors. **Pets:** $10 one-time fee/room. Service with restrictions, supervision.
🚭 🔌 📺

IRVINGTON

♦♦♦ **The Hope and Glory Inn** [BB]
(804) 438-6053. **$190-$350, 14 day notice.** 65 Tavern Rd. Just w of CR 200 on King Carter Dr. Ext/int corridors. **Pets:** Accepted.
[ASK] [SD] 🚭 🍴 🏋 [TV]

[AAA] ♦♦♦♦ **The Tides Inn** [SH] 🐾
(804) 438-5000. **$199-$375, 7 day notice.** 480 King Carter Dr. 0.3 mi w of CR 200. Ext/int corridors. **Pets:** Large. $30 one-time fee/room. Designated rooms, service with restrictions.
[SAVE] 🚭 [♿M] 🦻 🔌 📺 🍴 🏊 🏋

KESWICK

[AAA] ♦♦♦♦ **Keswick Hall at Monticello** [SH] 🐾
(434) 979-3440. **$295-$795, 3 day notice.** 701 Club Dr. I-64, exit 129, just n. Int corridors. **Pets:** $75 one-time fee/pet. Designated rooms, service with restrictions, supervision.
[SAVE] 🚭 [♿M] ♿ 🔌 🍴 🏊 🏋

KEYSVILLE

[AAA] ♦♦ **Sheldon's Motel** [SH]
(434) 736-8434. **$49-$75.** 1450 Four Locust Hwy. 1.3 mi n on US 15 and 360 business route. Ext corridors. **Pets:** Other species. Service with restrictions, supervision.
[SAVE] [SD] 🚭 🔌 🍴

LAWRENCEVILLE

♦♦♦ **Brunswick Mineral Springs B & B Circa 1785** [BB] 🐾
(434) 848-4010. **$85-$155, 5 day notice.** 14910 Western Mill Rd. 5 mi e on US 58, 1 mi s on SR 712, then just e. Int corridors. **Pets:** Large, dogs only. $25 one-time fee/pet. Service with restrictions, supervision.
[ASK] [SD] 🚭 🔌 📺

LEXINGTON

[AAA] ♦♦♦ **Best Western Inn at Hunt Ridge** [SH]
(540) 464-1500. **$69-$150.** 25 Willow Spring Rd. I-64, exit 55, just n on US 11 to SR 39; I-81, exit 191, 0.6 mi w. Int corridors. **Pets:** Other species. $25 one-time fee/room. Supervision.
[SAVE] [SD] 🚭 [♿M] 🦻 ♿ 🔌 📺 🍴 🏊

♦♦♦ **Comfort Inn-Virginia Horse Center** [SH]
(540) 463-7311. **$59-$150.** 62 Comfort Way. I-64, exit 55, just s on US 11; I-81, exit 191, 0.6 mi w. Int corridors. **Pets:** Medium, other species. $25 one-time fee/room. Designated rooms, service with restrictions, supervision.
[ASK] [SD] 🚭 🔌 📺 🏊

[AAA] ♦♦ **Days Inn Keydet General** [SH]
(540) 463-2143. **$55-$85, 3 day notice.** 325 W Midland Tr. I-81, exit 188B, 4.5 mi on US 60 W; I-64, exit 50, 5 mi e on US 60. Ext/int corridors. **Pets:** Other species. $10 daily fee/pet. Designated rooms, service with restrictions, supervision.
[SAVE] [SD] 🚭 🔌

[AAA] ♦♦ **Econo Lodge** [M]
(540) 463-7371. **$50-$150.** 65 Econo Ln. I-81, exit 191, just s on US 11. Ext corridors. **Pets:** Accepted.
[SAVE] [SD] 🚭 🔌 📺

[AAA] ♦♦♦ **Holiday Inn Express** [SH]
(540) 463-7351. **$55-$130.** 850 N Lee Hwy. I-64, exit 55, just s on US 11; I-81, exit 191, 1.6 mi w. Ext corridors. **Pets:** Other species. $25 one-time fee/room. Service with restrictions, supervision.
[SAVE] 🚭 🦻 🔌 📺

[AAA] ♦♦ **Howard Johnson Inn** [SH]
(540) 463-9181. **$65-$135.** 2836 N Lee Hwy. I-81, exit 195, just s on US 11. Int corridors. **Pets:** $5 daily fee/pet. No service, supervision.
[SAVE] [SD] 🚭 🦻 🔌 📺 🍴 🏊

♦♦ **Ramada Inn Lexington** [SH]
(540) 463-6400. **$90.** 2814 N Lee Hwy. I-81, exit 195, just sw on US 11. Int corridors. **Pets:** Accepted.
[ASK] [SD] 🚭 🦻 ♿ 🔌 📺 🏊

LURAY

[AAA] ♦♦♦ **Best Western Intown of Luray** [SH]
(540) 743-6511. **$65-$110.** 410 W Main St. 0.3 mi w on US 211 business route. Ext corridors. **Pets:** Other species. $20 daily fee/pet. Service with restrictions, supervision.
[SAVE] [SD] 🚭 🔌 📺 🍴 🏊

♦♦ **Days Inn-Luray** [SH]
(540) 743-4521. **$49-$109.** 138 Whispering Hill Rd. US 211 Bypass, 1.7 mi e of jct US 340. Ext corridors. **Pets:** Medium. $10 daily fee/pet. Designated rooms, service with restrictions, crate.
[ASK] [SD] 🚭 🍴 🏊

LYNCHBURG

[AAA] ♦♦ **Best Western Lynchburg** [M]
(434) 237-2986. **$69-$150.** 2815 Candlers Mountain Rd. Jct US 29 and 460. Ext corridors. **Pets:** Medium, other species. $25 one-time fee/room. Service with restrictions.
[SAVE] [SD] 🚭 🦻 🔌 📺 🏊

[AAA] ♦♦♦ **Comfort Inn** [SH] 🐾
(434) 847-9041. **$77-$80.** 3125 Albert Lankford Dr. US 29, exit 7, 2.5 mi s. Int corridors. **Pets:** Other species. $15 daily fee/room. Designated rooms, service with restrictions, supervision.
[SAVE] [SD] 🚭 🔌 📺 🏊

♦♦ **Days Inn** [SH]
(434) 847-8655. **$69-$89.** 3320 Candlers Mountain Rd. US 29, exit US 501, just e. Int corridors. **Pets:** Accepted.
[ASK] [SD] 🚭 🔌 📺 🍴 🏊 🏋

[AAA] ♦ **Econo Lodge** [M]
(434) 847-1045. **$60-$90, 3 day notice.** 2400 Stadium Rd. US 29, exit 4 southbound; exit 6 northbound, just w. Ext corridors. **Pets:** Medium, dogs only. $50 deposit/pet. Designated rooms, service with restrictions, supervision.
[SAVE] [SD] 🚭 🔌 📺

[AAA] ♦♦♦ **Holiday Inn Select** [SH]
(434) 528-2500. **$89.** 601 Main St. US 29 Expwy, exit 1 (Main St), just w; downtown. Int corridors. **Pets:** Accepted.
[SAVE] [SD] 🚭 ♿ 🔌 📺 🍴 🏊

MARION

◆◆ ▽▽ Best Western-Marion SH
(276) 783-3193. **$50-$75, 30 day notice.** 1424 N Main St. I-81, exit 47, 0.3 mi s on US 11. Ext corridors. **Pets:** Accepted.
SAVE 🔲 ✕ 🔲 🔲 🔲 🔲 🔲

MARTINSVILLE

▽▽ Best Lodge M
(276) 647-3941. **$38-$58, 30 day notice.** 1985 Virginia Ave. Jct US 58, 2.5 mi n on US 220 business route. Ext corridors. **Pets:** Accepted.
ASK 🔲 ✕ 🔲 🔲

◆◆ ▽▽▽ Best Western Martinsville Inn SH
(276) 632-5611. **$89-$119, 3 day notice.** US 220 Business Route S. Jct US 58, 2.3 mi n. Ext corridors. **Pets:** Accepted.
SAVE 🔲 ✕ 🔲 🔲 🔲 🔲

▽▽ Super 8 Motel M
(276) 666-8888. **$55-$65, 30 day notice.** 1044 N Memorial Blvd. Jct US 58, 1.5 mi n on US 220 business route. Int corridors. **Pets:** Accepted.
ASK 🔲 ✕ 🔲

MAX MEADOWS

◆◆ ▽▽▽ Comfort Inn SH
(276) 637-4281. **$59-$79.** 2594 E Lee Hwy. I-77/81, exit 80, just w. Int corridors. **Pets:** Accepted.
SAVE 🔲 ✕ 🔲 🔲 🔲 🔲 🔲 🔲

◆◆ ▽▽▽ Super 8 Motel SH
(276) 637-4141. **$50-$70.** 194 Ft Chiswell Rd. I-77/81, exit 80, just e. Ext corridors. **Pets:** Accepted.
SAVE ✕ 🔲 🔲 🔲

MIDDLETOWN

◆◆ ▽▽▽ Super 8 Motel M
(540) 868-1800. **$55-$165.** 2120 Relaince Rd. I-81, exit 302. Int corridors. **Pets:** Small. $10 daily fee/pet. Designated rooms, service with restrictions, supervision.
SAVE 🔲 ✕ 🔲 🔲

MINT SPRING

▽▽ Days Inn-Staunton M ❀
(540) 337-3031. **$49-$129.** 372 White Hill Rd. I-81, exit 217, just e on SR 654. Ext corridors. **Pets:** Other species. $8 daily fee/pet. Designated rooms, service with restrictions, supervision.
ASK 🔲 ✕ 🔲 🔲 🔲 🔲 🔲

▽ Red Carpet Inn M
(540) 337-2611. **Call for rates.** 210 White Hill Rd. I-81, exit 217, just w on SR 654. Ext corridors. **Pets:** Accepted.
✕ 🔲 🔲 🔲 🔲

MOUNT JACKSON

◆◆ ▽▽▽ Best Western-Shenandoah Valley SH ❀
(540) 477-2911. **$69-$110, 4 day notice.** 250 Conickville Rd. I-81, exit 273, just e. Ext corridors. **Pets:** Other species. $15 daily fee/pet. Designated rooms, service with restrictions, supervision.
SAVE 🔲 ✕ 🔲 🔲 🔲

▽▽▽ The Widow Kip's BB ❀
(540) 477-2400. **$90-$95, 7 day notice.** 355 Orchard Dr. I-81, exit 273, 1.5 mi s on US 11, just w on SR 263, then just sw on SR 698. Int corridors. **Pets:** Other species. $10 daily fee/pet. Designated rooms, service with restrictions, crate.
ASK 🔲 ✕ 🔲 🔲 🔲 🔲

NEW CHURCH

▽▽▽ The Garden & The Sea Inn CI ❀
(757) 824-0672. **$75-$205, 10 day notice.** 4188 Nelson Rd. US 13, 0.3 mi n, just w on CR 710 (Nelson Rd). Int corridors. **Pets:** Other species.
✕ 🔲 🔲 🔲 🔲

NEW MARKET

◆◆ ▽▽ Budget Inn M
(540) 740-3105. **$29-$79, 3 day notice.** 2192 Old Valley Pike. I-81, exit 264, 1 mi n on US 11. Ext corridors. **Pets:** Small. $5 one-time fee/pet. Designated rooms, no service, supervision.
SAVE 🔲 ✕ 🔲

◆◆ ▽▽ Days Inn SH
(540) 740-4100. **$45-$150.** 9360 George Collins Pkwy. I-81, exit 264, just w on US 211. Ext corridors. **Pets:** Large, other species. $500 daily fee/pet. Service with restrictions, crate.
SAVE 🔲 ✕ 🔲

NORTON

▽▽ Days Inn SH
(276) 679-5340. **$56-$76.** 375 Wharton Ln. Jct US 58 and 23. Int corridors. **Pets:** Small. $25 one-time fee/room. Service with restrictions, supervision.
ASK 🔲 ✕ 🔲 🔲 🔲 🔲 🔲

PETERSBURG

◆◆ ▽▽▽ Best Western-Steven Kent SH
(804) 733-0600. **$49-$80.** 12205 S Crater Rd. I-95, exit 45, jct US 301. Ext/int corridors. **Pets:** Accepted.
SAVE 🔲 ✕ 🔲 🔲 🔲 🔲 🔲 🔲 ✕

▽▽▽ Comfort Inn SH
(804) 732-2900. **$55-$120.** 11974 S Crater Rd. I-95, exit 45, n on US 301. Ext corridors. **Pets:** Medium. $10 daily fee/pet. Designated rooms, service with restrictions, supervision.
ASK 🔲 ✕ 🔲 🔲 🔲

◆◆ ▽▽▽ Days Inn SH
(804) 733-4400. **$50-$100.** 12208 S Crater Rd. I-95, exit 45, jct US 301. Ext corridors. **Pets:** Other species. $10 daily fee/pet. Service with restrictions, supervision.
SAVE 🔲 ✕ 🔲 🔲 🔲

◆◆ ▽▽▽ Econo Lodge-South SH
(804) 862-2717. **$50-$100.** 16905 Parkdale Rd. I-95, exit 41, just e. Ext corridors. **Pets:** Accepted.
SAVE 🔲 ✕ 🔲 🔲 🔲

◆◆ ▽▽▽ Quality Inn SH
(804) 733-1776. **$60-$105.** 405 E Washington St. I-95, exit 52 southbound; exit 50D northbound; I-85, exit 69; downtown. Ext corridors. **Pets:** Accepted.
SAVE 🔲 ✕ 🔲 🔲 🔲 🔲

PULASKI

▽▽ Days Inn SH
(540) 980-2230. **$50-$125.** 3063 Old Rt 100 Rd. I-81, exit 94, just e. Ext/int corridors. **Pets:** Accepted.
ASK 🔲 ✕ 🔲

RADFORD

△△△ ▼▼▼ Best Western Radford Inn **SH**
(540) 639-3000. **$71-$99.** 1501 Tyler Ave. I-81, exit 109, 2.7 mi nw on SR 177. Int corridors. **Pets:** Accepted.
SAVE SD X ⊟ ⬛ ▯▯ ≋ ⊠

RAPHINE

▼▼ Days Inn-Shenandoah Valley **M**
(540) 377-2604. **$54-$94.** 584 Oakland Cr. I-81, exit 205, just sw. Int corridors. **Pets:** Accepted.
ASK SD X ⊟ ≋

RICHMOND METROPOLITAN AREA

ASHLAND

▼▼ Days Inn Ashland **M**
(804) 798-4262. **$50-$90.** 806 England St. I-95, exit 92B, just w on SR 54. Ext corridors. **Pets:** Accepted.
ASK SD X ⊟ ≋

▼▼▼ The Henry Clay Inn **CI**
(804) 798-3100. **$90, 7 day notice.** 114 N Railroad Ave. I-95, exit 92, 1.5 mi w on SR 54, then n. Ext/int corridors. **Pets:** Accepted.
ASK SD X ⊟ ⬛

△△△ ▼▼▼ Quality Inn & Suites **SH**
(804) 798-4231. **$50-$100.** 810 England St. I-95, exit 92B, just w on SR 54. Ext/int corridors. **Pets:** Large. $15 daily fee/room. Service with restrictions, supervision.
SAVE SD X ⬛ ⊟ ⬛ ▯▯ ≋

CARMEL CHURCH

▼▼ Red Roof Inn **SH**
(804) 448-2828. **$49-$85.** 23500 Welcome Way Dr. I-95, exit 104 (SR 207), just w. Int corridors. **Pets:** Medium, other species. Designated rooms, service with restrictions, supervision.
ASK SD X ⬛ ⬛ ⊟ ⬛ ▯▯ ≋

CHESTER

△△△ ▼▼▼ Comfort Inn-Richmond/Chester **SH**
(804) 751-0000. **$59-$119.** 2100 W Hundred Rd. I-95, exit 61A, just e on SR 10. Int corridors. **Pets:** Other species. $20 one-time fee/room. Service with restrictions, supervision.
SAVE SD X ⬛ ⊟ ⬛ ▯▯ ≋

DOSWELL

△△△ ▼▼▼ Best Western-Kings Quarters **SH**
(804) 876-3321. **$34-$169, 3 day notice.** 16102 Theme Park Way. I-95, exit 98, just e on SR 30; at entrance to theme park. Ext corridors. **Pets:** Accepted.
SAVE SD X ⬛ ⊟ ⬛ ▯▯ ≋ ⊠

GLEN ALLEN

△△△ ▼▼▼ AmeriSuites (Richmond/Innsbrook) **SH**
(804) 747-9644. **$99-$159.** 4100 Cox Rd. I-64, exit 178B, 0.5 mi e to Dominion Blvd, then just n. Int corridors. **Pets:** Accepted.
SAVE SD X ⬛M ⬛ ⊟ ⬛ ≋

▼▼▼ Candlewood Suites Richmond-West **SH**
(804) 364-2000. **$89-$109, 7 day notice.** 4120 Brookriver Dr. I-64, exit 178, just w on W Broad St. Int corridors. **Pets:** Accepted.
ASK SD X ⬛M ⬛ ⬛ ⊟ ⬛

▼▼ Homestead Studio Suites
Hotel-Richmond/Innsbrook **M**
(804) 747-8898. **$59-$79.** 10961 W Broad St. I-64, exit 178B, just e on W Broad St, then just s on Cox Rd. Ext corridors. **Pets:** Medium, other species. $75 one-time fee/pet. Service with restrictions, supervision.
ASK SD X ⊟ ⬛

▼▼▼ Homewood Suites by Hilton Richmond West
End-Innsbrook **SH**
(804) 217-8000. **$109-$159.** 4100 Innslake Dr. I-64, exit 178B, just e on W Broad St to Cox Rd, then just n. Int corridors. **Pets:** Accepted.
ASK SD X ⬛M ⬛ ⬛ ⊟ ⬛ ≋

▼▼▼ Residence Inn by Marriott **SH**
(804) 762-9852. **$129-$169.** 3940 Westerre Pkwy. I-64, exit 180, n on Gaskins Rd to W Broad St. Int corridors. **Pets:** Other species. $75 one-time fee/room. Service with restrictions.
ASK SD X ⬛M ⬛ ⊟ ⬛ ≋ ⊠

▼▼▼ TownePlace Suites by Marriott **SH**
(804) 747-5253. **$59-$89.** 4231 Park Place Ct. I-64, exit 178B, just e on W Broad St to Cox Rd, then just n to Innslake Dr; in Innsbrook Corporate Center. Int corridors. **Pets:** Accepted.
ASK SD X ⬛M ⬛ ⊟ ⬛ ≋

RICHMOND

△△△ ▼▼▼ AmeriSuites (Richmond/Arboretum) **SH**
(804) 560-1566. **$104-$139.** 201 Arboretum Pl. Jct Powhite Pkwy (US 76) and Midlothian Tpke (US 60), just w. Int corridors. **Pets:** Medium. $10 daily fee/pet. Service with restrictions, supervision.
SAVE SD X ⬛M ⬛ ⬛ ⊟ ⬛ ≋

▼▼▼ Candlewood Suites **SH**
(804) 271-0016. **$84-$109.** 4301 Commerce Rd. I-95, exit 69, just n. Int corridors. **Pets:** Accepted.
ASK SD X ⬛M ⬛ ⊟ ⬛

△△△ ▼▼▼ Commonwealth Park Suites **SH**
(804) 343-7300. **$93-$123.** 901 Bank St. Jct 9th and Bank sts; across the green from the state capitol. Int corridors. **Pets:** Accepted.
SAVE SD X ⬛

▼▼ Days Inn-Richmond West **SH**
(804) 282-3300. **$49-$139.** 2100 Dickens Rd. I-64, exit 183B westbound; exit 183 eastbound, 0.3 mi e on W Broad St, just n. Int corridors. **Pets:** Accepted.
ASK SD X ⬛ ⊟ ⬛ ≋

△△△ ▼▼▼ Holiday Inn-Richmond North **SH**
(804) 266-8753. **$79-$139.** 801 E Parham Rd. I-95, exit 83B. Int corridors. **Pets:** Accepted.
SAVE SD X ⬛M ⬛ ⬛ ⊟ ⬛ ▯▯ ≋

▼▼▼ Homestead Studio Suites
Hotel-Richmond/Midlothian **SH**
(804) 272-1800. **$63-$83.** 241 Arboretum Pl. Jct Powhite Pkwy (US 76) and Midlothian Tpke (US 60), just w. Int corridors. **Pets:** Accepted.
ASK SD X ⬛M ⬛ ⬛ ⊟ ⬛

△△△ ▼▼▼ The Jefferson Hotel **LH**
(804) 788-8000. **$285-$335.** 101 W Franklin St. Franklin and Adams sts; center. Int corridors. **Pets:** Accepted.
SAVE SD X ⬛ ⬛ ⊟ ⬛ ▯▯ ≋

▼▼▼ Omni Richmond Hotel **LH**
(804) 344-7000. **$220-$240.** 100 S 12th St. I-95, exit 74A; I-195, exit Canal St. Int corridors. **Pets:** Accepted.
ASK X ⬛ ⊟ ⬛ ▯▯ ≋

AAA ▽▽▽▽ Quality Inn West End SH
(804) 346-0000. **$75-$99.** 8008 W Broad St. I-64, exit 183C westbound; exit 183 eastbound, 1.5 mi w. Int corridors. **Pets:** $10 daily fee/room, $25 one-time fee/room. Service with restrictions, supervision.
SAVE 🛇 ✕ 🛆 📶 🍽 🖵 ≈

▽▽▽▽ Radisson Hotel Historic Richmond SH
(804) 644-9871. **$89-$109, 3 day notice.** 301 W Franklin St. Franklin St at Madison. Int corridors. **Pets:** Accepted.
ASK 🛇 ✕ 🛆 📶 🍽 🖵 ≈

AAA ▽▽▽▽ Residence Inn by Marriott SH
(804) 285-8200. **$101-$129.** 2121 Dickens Rd. I-64, exit 183B, 0.3 mi e, then just n of US 60 (Broad St). Ext corridors. **Pets:** Accepted.
SAVE 🛇 ✕ 🛆ᴹ 🍳 📶 🍽 🖵 ≈ ✕

AAA ▽▽▽▽ Sheraton Richmond West LH
(804) 285-2000. **$81-$109.** 6624 W Broad St. I-64, exit 183 eastbound; exit 183B westbound. Int corridors. **Pets:** Accepted.
SAVE 🛇 ✕ 🛆ᴹ 🍳 🛆 📶 🍽 🖵 🍽 ≈ ✕

AAA ▽▽▽▽ Wyndham Richmond Airport SH
(804) 226-4300. **$89-$119.** 4700 S Laburnum Ave. I-64, exit 195, 0.5 mi s. Int corridors. **Pets:** Accepted.
SAVE ✕ 🛆 📶 🍽 🖵 🍽 ≈ ✕

SANDSTON

▽▽▽▽ Holiday Inn-Airport SH
(804) 222-6450. **$79-$169.** 5203 Williamsburg Rd. I-64, exit 195, 1.5 mi s to Williamsburg Rd, then just e. Ext/int corridors. **Pets:** Small, dogs only. $25 one-time fee/room. Designated rooms, service with restrictions, supervision.
ASK 🛇 ✕ 🛆 📶 🍽 🖵 🍽 ≈

AAA ▽ Microtel Inn & Suites SH
(804) 737-3322. **$59-$79.** 6000 Audubon Dr. I-64, exit 197A (Sandston-RIC Airport), just s. Int corridors. **Pets:** Medium, other species. $15 one-time fee/room. Service with restrictions, supervision.
SAVE 🛇 ✕ 🛆ᴹ 🍳 🛆 📶 🖵

▽ Motel 6-Richmond Airport #435 M
(804) 222-7600. **$40-$53.** 5704 Williamsburg Rd. I-64, exit 197A (Sandston-RIC Airport), just s to Williamsburg Rd, then just w. Ext corridors. **Pets:** Medium, other species. Service with restrictions, supervision.
🛇 ✕ 🛆 📶 ≈

END METROPOLITAN AREA

ROANOKE

AAA ▽▽▽▽ AmeriSuites (Roanoke/Valley View Mall) SH
(540) 366-4700. **$109-$179.** 5040 Valley View Blvd. I-581, exit 3E, just e, then just s via shopping center exit. Int corridors. **Pets:** Accepted.
SAVE ✕ 🛆ᴹ 🍳 🛆 📶 🖵 ≈

AAA ▽▽▽▽ Best Western Inn at Valley View SH
(540) 362-2400. **$59-$149.** 5050 Valley View Blvd. I-581, exit 3E, just e, then just s via shopping center exit. Int corridors. **Pets:** Large. $20 one-time fee/room. Service with restrictions, crate.
SAVE 🛇 ✕ 🛆 📶 🖵 ≈

AAA ▽▽▽▽ Clarion Hotel Roanoke Airport SH ❀
(540) 362-4500. **$70-$75.** 3315 Ordway Dr. I-581, exit 3W, just w to Ordway Dr, then 0.6 mi n via service road. Int corridors. **Pets:** Medium. $35 daily fee/room. Service with restrictions, supervision.
SAVE 🛇 ✕ 🍳 🛆 📶 🖵 ≈ ✕

▽▽ Days Inn SH
(540) 366-0341. **$54-$104.** 8118 Plantation Rd. I-81, exit 146, just e on SR 115. Ext/int corridors. **Pets:** Other species. $15 one-time fee/room. Service with restrictions, supervision.
ASK 🛇 ✕ 📶 🖵 ≈

AAA ▽▽▽▽ MainStay Suites Roanoke Airport SH
(540) 527-3030. **$79-$175.** 5080 Valley View Blvd. I-581, exit 3E, just n. Int corridors. **Pets:** Small, other species. $25 one-time fee/room. Service with restrictions, supervision.
SAVE 🛇 ✕ 📶 🖵

AAA ▽▽▽ Rodeway Inn-Civic Center SH
(540) 981-9341. **$38-$100.** 526 Orange Ave NE. I-581, exit 4E, jct US 400 and 11, just n. Ext corridors. **Pets:** Medium, dogs only. $10 daily fee/room. Designated rooms, service with restrictions.
SAVE 🛇 ✕ 🍳 📶 🖵

AAA ▽▽▽ Sleep Inn SH
(540) 772-1500. **$35-$99.** 4045 Electric Rd. I-581/US 220, exit Franklin Rd/Salem, 0.7 mi n on SR 419. Int corridors. **Pets:** $20 one-time fee/room. Service with restrictions.
SAVE 🛇 ✕ 📶 🖵

▽▽ Super 8 Motel SH
(540) 563-8888. **$50-$68.** 6616 Thirlane Rd. I-581, exit 25, s on SR 117 (Peters Creek Rd), then just w. Int corridors. **Pets:** Accepted.
ASK 🛇 ✕ 📶

ROCKY MOUNT

AAA ▽▽▽ Franklin Motel M
(540) 483-9962. **$45-$80.** 20281 Virgil H Goode Hwy. 6.5 mi n on US 220. Ext corridors. **Pets:** Very small, dogs only. $10 daily fee/pet. Designated rooms, service with restrictions, supervision.
SAVE 🛇 ✕ 📶

SALEM

AAA ▽▽ Blue Jay Budget Host Inn M ❀
(540) 380-2080. **$32-$80, 3 day notice.** 5399 W Main St. I-81, exit 132, just e, then 0.3 mi n on US 11/460. Ext corridors. **Pets:** Medium. $5 daily fee/pet, $5 one-time fee/pet. Designated rooms, service with restrictions, supervision.
SAVE 🛇 ✕ 📶 ≈

AAA ▽▽▽▽ Comfort Suites Inn at Ridgewood Farm SH
(540) 375-4800. **$59-$130.** 2898 Keagy Rd. I-81, exit 141, 4.7 mi s on SR 419, then just w. Int corridors. **Pets:** Large. $35 one-time fee/pet. Service with restrictions, supervision.
SAVE 🛇 ✕ 🛆 📶 🖵 ≈

AAA ▽▽▽ Econo Lodge-Roanoke/Salem M
(540) 389-0280. **$44-$91.** 301 Wildwood Rd. I-81, exit 137, just e on SR 112. Ext corridors. **Pets:** Accepted.
SAVE 🛇 ✕ 📶 🖵

AAA ▽▽▽▽ Quality Inn Roanoke/Salem SH
(540) 562-1912. **$51-$83, 7 day notice.** 179 Sheraton Dr. I-81, exit 141, 0.4 mi e on SR 419. Int corridors. **Pets:** Medium. $15 daily fee/pet. Designated rooms, service with restrictions, crate.
SAVE 🛇 ✕ 📶 🖵 ≈ ✕

SOUTH BOSTON

▼▼▼▼ Holiday Inn-Express SH
(434) 575-4000. **$90.** 1074 Bill Tuck Hwy. Just e on US 58, from jct US 501. Int corridors. **Pets:** Other species. $20 daily fee/pet. Service with restrictions, supervision.
[ASK] [S☉] [✕] [&M] [&] [🛏] [💻] [≋]

ⒶⒶⒶ ▼▼▼▼ Quality Inn Howard House SH
(434) 572-4311. **$72-$129.** 2001 Seymour Dr. Jct US 58, 501 and 360, 1 mi e on US 360. Ext corridors. **Pets:** Other species. $10 daily fee/room. Service with restrictions.
[SAVE] [S☉] [✕] [🛏] [💻] [▥] [≋]

SOUTH HILL

ⒶⒶⒶ ▼▼▼ Comfort Inn SH
(434) 447-2600. **$59-$79.** 918 E Atlantic St. I-85, exit 12B, just w. Ext corridors. **Pets:** Other species. $10 daily fee/room. Service with restrictions.
[SAVE] [S☉] [✕] [🛏]

▼▼▼ Super 8 Motel SH ☙
(434) 447-2313. **$53-$91.** 250 Thompson St. I-85, exit 12A, just n. Int corridors. **Pets:** Medium. $10 daily fee/pet. Service with restrictions, supervision.
[ASK] [S☉] [✕] [&M] [&] [🛏]

STAFFORD

ⒶⒶⒶ ▼▼▼▼ Days Inn Aquia-Quantico SH
(540) 659-0022. **$73-$89, 7 day notice.** 2868 Jefferson Davis Hwy. I-95, exit 143A, jct US 1 and SR 610. Ext corridors. **Pets:** Accepted.
[SAVE] [✕] [🛏] [💻] [▥] [≋]

STAUNTON

▼▼▼ Ashton Country House BB ☙
(540) 885-7819. **$95-$140, 7 day notice.** 1205 Middlebrook Ave. I-81, exit 220, 1 mi to SR 252 (Middlebrook Ave), then 0.3 mi n. Int corridors. **Pets:** Other species. $10 daily fee/room. Service with restrictions.
[ASK] [S☉] [✕] [🐾]

ⒶⒶⒶ ▼▼▼ Best Western Staunton Inn SH
(540) 885-1112. **$64-$130.** 92 Rowe Rd. I-81, exit 222, just e on US 250. Int corridors. **Pets:** Designated rooms, service with restrictions, supervision.
[SAVE] [S☉] [✕] [🐾] [🛏] [💻] [≋]

ⒶⒶⒶ ▼▼▼ Comfort Inn SH ☙
(540) 886-5000. **$69-$119.** 1302 Richmond Ave. I-81, exit 222, just w on US 250. Int corridors. **Pets:** $10 daily fee/room. Designated rooms, service with restrictions, supervision.
[SAVE] [S☉] [✕] [🐾] [🛏] [💻] [≋]

ⒶⒶⒶ ▼▼▼ Days Inn–Business Place SH
(540) 248-0888. **$49-$90.** 273-D Bells Ln. I-81, exit 225, just w. Ext corridors. **Pets:** Accepted.
[SAVE] [S☉] [✕] [&] [🛏] [💻] [≋]

ⒶⒶⒶ ▼▼▼ Econo Lodge Staunton M
(540) 885-5158. **$56-$86.** 1031 Richmond Ave. I-81, exit 222, 0.7 mi w on US 250. Ext/int corridors. **Pets:** $10 one-time fee/pet. Service with restrictions, supervision.
[SAVE] [S☉] [✕] [🛏] [💻]

ⒶⒶⒶ ▼▼▼ Holiday Inn Golf & Conference Center SH
(540) 248-6020. **$64-$200.** 152 Fairway Ln. I-81, exit 225, 0.3 mi w on SR 275 (Woodrow Wilson Pkwy). Int corridors. **Pets:** Small. $15 one-time fee/pet. Designated rooms, no service, supervision.
[SAVE] [S☉] [✕] [🐾] [🛏] [💻] [▥] [≋]

ⒶⒶⒶ ▼▼▼ Quality Inn-Conference Center SH
(540) 248-5111. **$55-$95.** 96 Baker Ln. I-81, exit 225, just e on SR 275 (Woodrow Wilson Pkwy). Ext corridors. **Pets:** Accepted.
[SAVE] [S☉] [✕] [🛏] [💻] [≋]

ⒶⒶⒶ ▼▼▼ Sleep Inn SH ☙
(540) 887-6500. **$64-$130.** 222 Jefferson Hwy. I-81, exit 222, just e on US 250. Int corridors. **Pets:** Service with restrictions, supervision.
[SAVE] [S☉] [✕] [&] [🛏] [💻]

ⒶⒶⒶ ▼▼▼ Super 8 Motel M
(540) 886-2888. **$45-$99, 3 day notice.** 1015 Richmond Rd. I-81, exit 222, 1.2 mi w on US 250. Int corridors. **Pets:** $10 daily fee/pet. Service with restrictions, supervision.
[SAVE] [S☉] [✕] [🛏]

STEPHENS CITY

ⒶⒶⒶ ▼▼▼▼ Comfort Inn-Stephens City SH
(540) 869-6500. **$69-$99.** 167 Town Run Ln. I-81, exit 307, just se. Int corridors. **Pets:** Other species. $10 daily fee/pet. Service with restrictions, supervision.
[SAVE] [S☉] [✕] [🐾] [🛏] [💻] [≋]

STONY CREEK

ⒶⒶⒶ ▼▼▼▼ Hampton Inn-Stony Creek SH
(434) 246-5500. **$79-$129.** 10476 Blue Star Hwy. I-95, exit 33, just sw. Int corridors. **Pets:** Large. $10 daily fee/pet. Service with restrictions, supervision.
[SAVE] [S☉] [✕] [&M] [🐾] [&] [🛏] [💻] [≋]

ⒶⒶⒶ ▼▼▼▼ Sleep Inn & Suites SH
(434) 246-5100. **$60-$109.** 11019 Blue Star Hwy. I-95, exit 33, 0.3 mi s on SR 301. Int corridors. **Pets:** Large. $10 daily fee/pet. Service with restrictions, supervision.
[SAVE] [S☉] [✕] [🐾] [🛏] [💻] [≋]

STRASBURG

ⒶⒶⒶ ▼▼▼▼ Hotel Strasburg CI ☙
(540) 465-9191. **$83-$105.** 213 Holliday St. I-81, exit 298, 2.2 mi s on US 11, then just s. Int corridors. **Pets:** Service with restrictions, crate.
[SAVE] [S☉] [✕] [▥]

TAPPAHANNOCK

▼▼▼ Super 8 Motel M
(804) 443-3888. **$56-$76.** 1800 Tappahannock Blvd. SR 17 and 360. Int corridors. **Pets:** Accepted.
[ASK] [S☉] [✕] [🛏]

THORNBURG

▼▼▼ Holiday Inn Express SH
(540) 582-1097. **$49-$169.** 6409 Dan Bell Ln. I-95, exit 118 (SR 606), just w. Ext corridors. **Pets:** Medium. $10 daily fee/room. Designated rooms, service with restrictions, supervision.
[ASK] [S☉] [✕] [&M] [&] [🛏] [💻] [≋]

TROUTVILLE

ⒶⒶⒶ ▼▼▼ Comfort Inn Troutville SH
(540) 992-5600. **$44-$99.** 2545 Lee Hwy S. I-81, exit 150A, just s on US 11. Int corridors. **Pets:** $20 one-time fee/room. Service with restrictions, crate.
[SAVE] [S☉] [✕] [🛏] [💻] [≋]

ⒶⒶⒶ ▼▼▼ Travelodge Roanoke North M
(540) 992-6700. **$40-$85.** 2619 Lee Hwy S. I-81, exit 150A, just e, then just s on US 11. Ext corridors. **Pets:** Accepted.
[SAVE] [S☉] [✕] [🛏] [💻] [≋] [✕]

VERONA

ⒶⒶⒶ ▼▼▼ Ramada Limited SH
(540) 248-8981. **$39-$125.** 70 Lodge Ln. I-81, exit 227, just w, then just n. Ext corridors. **Pets:** Medium. $10 daily fee/pet. Designated rooms, service with restrictions, supervision.
[SAVE] [S☉] [✕] [🐾] [🛏] [💻] [≋]

WARRENTON

Comfort Inn 🆂🅷
(540) 349-8900. **$69-$109.** 7379 Comfort Inn Dr. 1.5 mi n on US 15/29, on service road. Ext/int corridors. **Pets:** $10 daily fee/room. Service with restrictions, supervision.

Hampton Inn 🆂🅷
(540) 349-4200. **$89-$125.** 501 Blackwell Rd. 1 mi n on US 29 business route and US 211. Ext corridors. **Pets:** Small, dogs only. Service with restrictions, supervision.

Howard Johnson Inn-Warrenton Ⓜ
(540) 347-4141. **$70-$110.** 6 Broadview Ave. US 17/29 business route, jct US 211 W. Int corridors. **Pets:** Medium. $10 daily fee/pet. Designated rooms, service with restrictions, supervision.

WARSAW

Best Western Warsaw 🆂🅷
(804) 333-1700. **$77-$90.** 4522 Richmond Rd. US 360, just w of town. Int corridors. **Pets:** Small. $10 daily fee/pet. Service with restrictions, supervision.

WAYNESBORO

Days Inn Waynesboro Ⓜ
(540) 943-1101. **$49-$89.** 2060 Rosser Ave. I-64, exit 94, 0.5 mi n on US 340. Ext corridors. **Pets:** Other species. $10 daily fee/room. Service with restrictions.

Quality Inn Waynesboro 🆂🅷
(540) 942-1171. **$79-$109.** 640 W Broad St. I-64, exit 96, 3 mi w on SR 624, jct US 250 and 340. Ext/int corridors. **Pets:** Large. $10 daily fee/room. Service with restrictions, crate.

Super 8 Motel 🆂🅷
(540) 943-3888. **$60-$125, 3 day notice.** 2045 Rosser Ave. I-64, exit 94, n on US 340 to Lew DeWitt Blvd, then just w to Apple Tree Ln. Int corridors. **Pets:** Other species. $5 daily fee/pet. Service with restrictions, supervision.

WILLIAMSBURG, JAMESTOWN & YORKTOWN METROPOLITAN AREA

WILLIAMSBURG

Best Western Colonial Capitol Inn 🆂🅷
(757) 253-1222. **$59-$129, 3 day notice.** 111 Penniman Rd. Just n of jct US 60 and SR 5. Int corridors. **Pets:** Large. $10 one-time fee/room. Service with restrictions, crate.

Best Western Patrick Henry Inn 🆂🅷
(757) 229-9540. **$59-$179, 3 day notice.** 249 E York St NW. E on US 60 at jct SR 5 and 31; 1 blk from Colonial Williamsburg. Int corridors. **Pets:** Large. $15 one-time fee/room. Service with restrictions, crate.

Best Western Williamsburg Westpark Hotel 🆂🅷
(757) 229-1134. **$39-$109.** 1600 Richmond Rd. Jct US 60 (Richmond Rd) and SR 612 (Ironbound Rd). Ext/int corridors. **Pets:** $10 daily fee/room. Service with restrictions, crate.

Days Inn Colonial Downtown 🆂🅷
(757) 229-5060. **$35-$99.** 902 Richmond Rd. Just w of Colonial Williamsburg on US 60. Ext corridors. **Pets:** Small. $15 daily fee/pet. Service with restrictions, supervision.

Four Points by Sheraton Hotel & Suites Williamsburg Historic District 🆂🅷
(757) 229-4100. **$59-$169, 3 day notice.** 351 York St. US 60 E, 0.3 mi se of jct SR 5 and 31. Ext/int corridors. **Pets:** $10 one-time fee/pet. Designated rooms, service with restrictions, crate.

Holiday Inn Patriot 🆂🅷
(757) 565-2600. **$69-$149, 3 day notice.** 3032 Richmond Rd. I-64, exit 234 (SR 199 E) to US 60, 2.5 mi e. Int corridors. **Pets:** Accepted.

La Quinta Inn Williamsburg (Historic Area) 🆂🅷
(757) 253-1663. **$45-$135.** 119 Bypass Rd. US 60 Bypass Rd, 0.3 mi e of Richmond Rd. Ext corridors. **Pets:** Small. Service with restrictions, crate.

Motel Rochambeau Ⓜ
(757) 229-2851. **$26-$56.** 929 Capitol Landing Rd. I-64, exit 238, 1 mi e on SR 143, then just w on SR 5. Ext corridors. **Pets:** Accepted.

Quarterpath Inn Ⓜ
(757) 220-0960. **$39-$119, 3 day notice.** 620 York St. I-64, exit 242 (SR 199 W), 0.6 mi w to US 60 E, then just w. Ext corridors. **Pets:** Service with restrictions.

Ramada Inn 1776 🆂🅷 ☘
(757) 220-1776. **$49-$129.** 725 Bypass Rd. US 60 (Bypass Rd), 0.5 mi w of jct SR 132. Int corridors. **Pets:** Medium. Service with restrictions.

Ramada Inn & Suites 🆂🅷 ☘
(757) 565-2000. **$59-$109.** 5351 Richmond Rd. 3 mi w on US 60. Ext/int corridors. **Pets:** Small, other species. $15 daily fee/room. Designated rooms, service with restrictions, crate.

Residence Inn by Marriott Williamsburg 🆂🅷
(757) 941-2000. **$59-$359, 3 day notice.** 1648 Richmond Rd. US 60, just w of jct Bypass Rd. Int corridors. **Pets:** Other species. $75 one-time fee/room. Service with restrictions.

YORKTOWN

◆◆◆ Candlewood Suites-Yorktown 🆂🅷
(757) 952-1120. **$69-$109.** 329 Commonwealth Dr. I-64, exit 256B, just n, then just e. Int corridors. **Pets:** Accepted.

A$K S✆ ⊠ ᴸᴹ ⟨✦⟩ 🛢 🖳 ⤳

◆◆◆ TownePlace Suites by Marriott 🆂🅷
(757) 874-8884. **$125-$139.** 200 Cybemetics Way. I-64, exit 256B, e to Kiln Creek Pkwy. Int corridors. **Pets:** Other species. $75 one-time fee/room. Service with restrictions, crate.

SAVE S✆ ⊠ ᴸᴹ ⟨✦⟩ 🛢 🖳 ⤳

END METROPOLITAN AREA

WINCHESTER

◆◆◆ Best Western Lee-Jackson Motor Inn 🆂🅷
(540) 662-4154. **$59-$71.** 711 Millwood Ave. I-81, exit 313B, just nw on US 50/522/17. Ext corridors. **Pets:** Small. $5 daily fee/pet. Service with restrictions, supervision.

SAVE S✆ ⊠ 🛢 🖳 🍴 ⤳

◆◆◆ Days Inn 🆂🅷
(540) 667-1200. **$49-$75.** 2951 Valley Ave. I-81, exit 310, just w, then 1.8 mi n on US 11. Ext corridors. **Pets:** Other species. $5 daily fee/pet. Service with restrictions, supervision.

SAVE S✆ ⊠ 🛢 🍴 ⤳

◆ Mohawk Motel 🅼 🐾
(540) 667-1410. **$48-$53.** 2754 Northwestern Pike. I-81, exit 317, 3 mi s on SR 37, then 1.7 mi w on US 50. Ext corridors. **Pets:** Other species. $10 daily fee/pet. Designated rooms, service with restrictions, supervision.

A$K S✆ ⊠

◆◆ Quality Inn East 🆂🅷
(540) 667-2250. **$58-$73.** 603 Millwood Ave. I-81, exit 313 northbound; exit 313B southbound, 0.5 mi nw on US 50/522/17. Ext corridors. **Pets:** Accepted.

A$K S✆ ⊠ 🛢 🖳 ⤳

◆◆◆ Red Roof Inn 🆂🅷 🐾
(540) 667-5000. **$58-$79.** 991 Millwood Pike. I-81, exit 313 northbound; exit 313A southbound, just se on US 50/17. Ext corridors. **Pets:** Medium, other species. Service with restrictions, supervision.

SAVE S✆ ⊠ 🛢 🖳

◆◆◆ Super 8 Motel 🆂🅷
(540) 665-4450. **$49-$60.** 1077 Millwood Pike. I-81, exit 313 northbound; exit 313A southbound, 0.3 mi se on US 50/17. Int corridors. **Pets:** Accepted.

SAVE S✆ ⊠

◆◆ Tourist City Motel 🅼
(540) 662-9011. **$37-$42, 5 day notice.** 214 Millwood Ave. I-81, exit 313 northbound; exit 313B southbound, 1 mi nw on US 50/522. Ext corridors. **Pets:** Other species. $5 daily fee/pet. Designated rooms, no service, supervision.

SAVE S✆ ⊠ 🛢

◆◆◆ Travelodge of Winchester 🆂🅷
(540) 665-0685. **$82-$85.** 160 Front Royal Pike. I-81, exit 313 northbound; exit 313A southbound, just s on US 522. Int corridors. **Pets:** Medium, other species. $10 daily fee/pet. Service with restrictions, crate.

SAVE S✆ ⊠ ⟨✎⟩ 🛢 🖳 ⤳

WOODSTOCK

◆◆ Budget Host Inn 🅼
(540) 459-4086. **$45-$52.** 1290 S Main St. I-81, exit 283, 0.8 mi se on SR 42, then 0.6 mi s on US 11. Ext corridors. **Pets:** Other species. Service with restrictions, supervision.

SAVE S✆ ⊠ 🛢 ⤳

◆◆◆ Comfort Inn Shenandoah 🆂🅷
(540) 459-7600. **$74-$99.** 1011 Motel Dr. I-81, exit 283, just e. Int corridors. **Pets:** Other species. Service with restrictions, supervision.

SAVE S✆ ⊠ ⟨✦⟩ 🛢 🖳 ⤳

◆◆◆ Ramada Inn 🆂🅷
(540) 459-5000. **$59-$99.** 1130 Motel Dr. I-81, exit 283, just e on SR 42. Int corridors. **Pets:** Small. $10 daily fee/pet. Designated rooms, service with restrictions, supervision.

SAVE S✆ ⊠ 🛢 🖳 🍴 ⤳

WYTHEVILLE

◆◆◆ Best Western Wytheville Inn 🆂🅷
(276) 228-7300. **$50-$155, 3 day notice.** 355 Nye Rd. I-77, exit 41, just e. Int corridors. **Pets:** $6 daily fee/pet. Service with restrictions, supervision.

SAVE S✆ ⊠ 🛢 🖳 ⤳

◆◆ Budget Host Inn/Interstate Inn 🅼
(276) 228-8618. **$32-$150.** 705 Chapman Rd. I-77/81, exit 73, just w. Ext corridors. **Pets:** Small, other species. $5 daily fee/pet. Service with restrictions, supervision.

A$K S✆ ⊠ 🛢

◆◆ Days Inn 🆂🅷
(276) 228-5500. **$50-$70.** 150 Malin Dr. I-81, exit 73, just w. Ext corridors. **Pets:** Medium. $5 daily fee/pet. Service with restrictions, supervision.

A$K S✆ ⊠ ⟨✎⟩

◆◆◆ Econo Lodge 🅼
(276) 228-5517. **$39-$115.** 1160 E Main St. I-81, exit 73, 0.8 mi w. Ext corridors. **Pets:** Medium, dogs only. $10 daily fee/pet. Service with restrictions, supervision.

SAVE S✆ ⊠ ⟨✎⟩ 🛢 🖳

◆◆ Holiday Inn 🆂🅷
(276) 228-5483. **$75-$105.** 1800 E Main St. I-81, exit 73, just w. Ext/int corridors. **Pets:** Other species. Service with restrictions, supervision.

A$K S✆ ⊠ ⟨✎⟩ ⟨✦⟩ 🛢 🖳 🍴 ⤳

◆◆◆ Ramada Inn 🆂🅷
(276) 228-6000. **$59-$119.** 955 Peppers Ferry Rd. I-77, exit 41, just e. Ext corridors. **Pets:** Accepted.

SAVE S✆ ⊠ 🖳 🍴 ⤳

◆◆◆ Red Carpet Inn 🅼
(276) 228-5525. **$45-$130.** 280 Lithia Rd. I-77/81, exit 73, just w. Ext corridors. **Pets:** Very small. $10 deposit/pet. Designated rooms, service with restrictions, supervision.

SAVE S✆ ⊠ 🛢

◆ Super 8 Motel 🆂🅷
(276) 228-6620. **$53-$67.** 130 Nye Cir. I-77, exit 41, just e. Ext corridors. **Pets:** Large, other species. $10 one-time fee/room. Service with restrictions, supervision.

A$K S✆ ⊠

◆ Travelodge 🅼
(276) 228-3188. **$65-$120.** 140 Lithia Rd. I-77/81, exit 73, on US 11. Ext/int corridors. **Pets:** Other species. $15 daily fee/pet. Designated rooms, service with restrictions, supervision.

A$K S✆ ⊠ 🛢 🖳

WASHINGTON

ABERDEEN

▼▼▼ GuestHouse International Inn & Suites SH
(360) 537-7460. **$65-$200.** 701 E Heron St. Just e on US 12, cross street to Kansas St; downtown. Int corridors. **Pets:** Large, other species. $50 deposit/room, $10 daily fee/room. Service with restrictions, crate.

(ASK) (S🐾) (✕) (🎿) (♿) (🛗) (🛎️) (🏊)

▼▼ Olympic Inn M
(360) 533-4200. **$65-$85.** 616 W Heron St. 0.5 mi w; downtown. Ext corridors. **Pets:** Medium. $10 one-time fee/pet. Supervision.

(SAVE) (S🐾) (✕) (🛎️)

▼◆ Red Lion Inn Aberdeen SH
(360) 532-5210. **$69-$109.** 521 W Wishkah. 0.5 mi w on US 101 N. Ext corridors. **Pets:** Accepted.

(ASK) (S🐾) (✕) (🛗) (🎿) (🛎️) (🖥️)

AIRWAY HEIGHTS

▼◆ Microtel Inn & Suites SH
(509) 242-1200. **$44-$69.** 1215 S Garfield Rd. I-90, exit 277 to SR 2, 4 mi w. Int corridors. **Pets:** Accepted.

(ASK) (S🐾) (✕) (🎿) (♿) (🛎️) (🖥️)

ANACORTES

▲▲ ▼▼ Anaco Inn SH
(360) 293-8833. **$59-$119, 3 day notice.** 905 20th St. Just s of downtown. Ext/int corridors. **Pets:** Very small, other species. $20 one-time fee/pet. Designated rooms, service with restrictions, supervision.

(SAVE) (S🐾) (✕) (🛎️) (🖥️)

▲▲ ▼▼ Anacortes Inn M
(360) 293-3153. **$65-$85.** 3006 Commercial Ave. Just s of downtown. Ext corridors. **Pets:** Accepted.

(SAVE) (S🐾) (✕) (🛎️) (🖥️) (🏊)

▲▲ ▼▼ Cap Sante Inn M 🐾
(360) 293-0602. **$62-$85, 3 day notice.** 906 9th St. On 9th St, just e. Ext corridors. **Pets:** $10 daily fee/pet. Designated rooms, supervision.

(SAVE) (✕) (🛎️) (🐕)

▲▲ ▼▼▼ Fidalgo Country Inn SH 🐾
(360) 293-3494. **$79-$109.** 7645 SR 20. Jct Fidalgo Bay Rd. Ext/int corridors. **Pets:** Medium. $10 daily fee/pet. Designated rooms.

(SAVE) (S🐾) (✕) (♿) (🎿) (🛎️) (🖥️) (🏊)

▼ Islands Inn M
(360) 293-4644. **$69-$130.** 3401 Commercial Ave. Just s of downtown. Ext corridors. **Pets:** Dogs only. $5 daily fee/room. Supervision.

(✕) (🛎️) (🖥️) (🍴) (🏊)

BELLINGHAM

▲▲▲ ▼▼▼ Best Western Lakeway Inn SH 🌼
(360) 671-1011. **$79-$149.** 714 Lakeway Dr. I-5, exit 253 (Lakeway Dr), just se. Int corridors. **Pets:** Small. $10 daily fee/pet. Designated rooms, service with restrictions, supervision.

(SAVE) (S🐾) (✕) (🎿) (🛎️) (🖥️) (🍴) (🏊) (🐕)

▲▲▲ ▼▼▼ The Chrysalis Inn & Spa SH
(360) 756-1005. **$155-$199.** 804 10th St. I-5, exit 250, 1.3 mi nw on Old Fairhaven Pkwy, 0.6 mi n via 12th and 11th sts, just w on Taylor Ave, then just n. Int corridors. **Pets:** Small, dogs only. $50 one-time fee/pet. Designated rooms, service with restrictions, supervision.

(SAVE) (S🐾) (✕) (🛎️) (🖥️) (🍴)

▲▲▲ ▼▼▼ Fairhaven Village Inn SH 🐾
(360) 733-1311. **$109-$159.** 1200 10th St. I-5, exit 250, 1.5 mi w. Int corridors. **Pets:** $20 daily fee/pet. Service with restrictions, supervision.

(SAVE) (S🐾) (✕) (♿) (🎿) (🖥️) (🛎️) (🖥️)

▲▲▲ ▼▼▼ Holiday Inn Express-Bellingham SH
(360) 671-4800. **$89-$124.** 4160 Guide Meridian St. I-5, exit 256A, 0.7 mi e. Int corridors. **Pets:** Small, other species. $15 one-time fee/pet. Service with restrictions, supervision.

(SAVE) (S🐾) (✕) (♿) (🎿) (🖥️) (🛎️) (🖥️) (🏊)

▲▲▲ ▼▼▼ Hotel Bellwether SH
(360) 392-3100. **$107-$725, 3 day notice.** One Bellwether Way. I-5, exit 253 (Lakeway Dr), 0.9 mi nw via Lakeway Dr and E Holly St, just w on Bay St, 0.6 mi n on W Chestnut St, then just w. Int corridors. **Pets:** Other species. $65 one-time fee/room. Service with restrictions.

(SAVE) (S🐾) (✕) (🖥️) (🍴) (🐕)

▼▼ Motel 6-44 M
(360) 671-4494. **$45-$65.** 3701 Byron Ave. I-5, exit 252, just nw. Ext corridors. **Pets:** Other species. Service with restrictions, supervision.

(S🐾) (✕) (♿) (🏊)

◬ ▼▼▼▼ Quality Inn Baron Suites 🆂🅷 ❀
(360) 647-8000. **$94-$129.** 100 E Kellogg Rd. I-5, exit 256A, 1 mi ne via Guide Meridian St. Ext/int corridors. **Pets:** Medium. $25 one-time fee/room. Designated rooms, service with restrictions, supervision.
[SAVE] [S🔒] [✕] [🕭] [▮] [▭] [≈]

◬ ▼ Shangri-La Downtown Motel 🅼
(360) 733-7050. **$39-$59.** 611 E Holly St. I-5, exit 253 (Lakeway Dr), 0.3 mi nw. Ext corridors. **Pets:** Cats only. $6 one-time fee/pet. Designated rooms, service with restrictions, supervision.
[SAVE] [S🔒] [✕] [▮] [🎞]

◬ ▼▼ Travel House Inn 🆂🅷
(360) 671-4600. **$45-$89.** 3750 Meridian St. I-5, exit 256A, just w. Ext corridors. **Pets:** Other species. $6 daily fee/room. Designated rooms, service with restrictions, supervision.
[SAVE] [S🔒] [✕] [▮] [≈]

▼▼▼ Val-U Inn 🆂🅷
(360) 671-9600. **$60-$85.** 805 Lakeway Dr. I-5, exit 253 (Lakeway Dr), just ne. Int corridors. **Pets:** Large, dogs only. $5 daily fee/pet. Designated rooms, service with restrictions, supervision.
[ASK] [S🔒] [✕] [▮]

BLAINE

◬ ▼▼▼▼ ▼▼▼▼ Semiahmoo Resort 🆂🅷
(360) 318-2000. **$99-$409, 3 day notice.** 9565 Semiahmoo Pkwy. I-5, exit 270, 9.5 mi nw on Semiahmoo Spit. Int corridors. **Pets:** Accepted.
[SAVE] [S🔒] [✕] [🕭] [▮] [▭] [❙❙] [≈] [⊠]

BUCKLEY

◬ ▼▼▼ Mt View Inn 🆂🅷
(360) 829-1100. **$85-$95, 7 day notice.** 29405 SR 410 E. On SR 410 at SR 165. Int corridors. **Pets:** Small, dogs only. $20 one-time fee/pet. Designated rooms, service with restrictions, supervision.
[SAVE] [S🔒] [✕] [▮] [≈]

BURLINGTON

◬ ▼▼▼ Cocusa Motel 🆂🅷
(360) 757-6044. **$63-$95.** 370 W Rio Vista. I-5, exit 230, just e. Ext corridors. **Pets:** $10 one-time fee/room. Designated rooms, service with restrictions, supervision.
[SAVE] [✕] [👘] [▮] [▭] [≈]

CASHMERE

◬ ▼▼▼ Village Inn Motel 🅼
(509) 782-3522. **$49-$64.** 229 Cottage Ave. On Business Rt US 2 and 97; downtown. Ext corridors. **Pets:** Small, dogs only. $10 daily fee/pet. Designated rooms, no service, supervision.
[SAVE] [S🔒] [✕] [▮]

CASTLE ROCK

◬ ▼▼▼ Timberland Inn & Suites 🅼
(360) 274-6002. **$79-$149.** 1271 Mount St. Helens Way. I-5, exit 49, just ne. Ext corridors. **Pets:** Small. $10 daily fee/pet. Designated rooms, service with restrictions, supervision.
[SAVE] [S🔒] [✕] [▮] [▭]

CENTRALIA

▼ Motel 6–394 🅼
(360) 330-2057. **$35-$53.** 1310 Belmont Ave. I-5, exit 82, 0.6 mi nw. Ext corridors. **Pets:** Accepted.
[S🔒] [✕] [👘] [≈]

CHEHALIS

◬ ▼▼▼ Best Western Park Place Inn & Suites 🆂🅷
(360) 748-4040. **$77-$96, 7 day notice.** 201 SW Interstate Ave. I-5, exit 76, just se. Int corridors. **Pets:** Very small, dogs only. $10 daily fee/pet. Designated rooms, service with restrictions, crate.
[SAVE] [S🔒] [✕] [👘] [👘] [▮] [▭] [≈]

CHELAN

◬ ▼▼▼▼ Best Western Lakeside Lodge 🆂🅷
(509) 682-4396. **$89-$329, 7 day notice.** 2312 W Woodin Ave. West end of town. Ext corridors. **Pets:** Accepted.
[SAVE] [S🔒] [✕] [🕭] [👘] [▮] [▭] [≈] [⊠]

CHEWELAH

◬ ▼▼▼ Nordlig Motel 🅼
(509) 935-6704. **$56-$61.** W 101 Grant St. North edge of town on US 395. Ext corridors. **Pets:** Other species. $5 one-time fee/room. Supervision.
[SAVE] [S🔒] [✕] [▮]

CLE ELUM

◬ ▼ Cle Elum Travelers Inn 🅼
(509) 674-5535. **$40-$52.** 1001 E 1st St. I-90, exit 85, 1 mi w on SR 903. Ext/int corridors. **Pets:** Accepted.
[SAVE] [S🔒] [✕] [👘] [▮]

▼▼ Stewart Lodge 🅼
(509) 674-4548. **$48-$78.** 805 W 1st St. I-90, exit 84 eastbound, just n; exit westbound, 0.6 mi w. Ext corridors. **Pets:** Other species. $5 one-time fee/pet. Supervision.
[✕] [👘] [≈]

▼▼ Timber Lodge Inn 🅼
(509) 674-5966. **$60-$65.** 301 W 1st St. I-90, exit 84 eastbound, 1 mi ne; exit westbound, just w; downtown. Ext/int corridors. **Pets:** Accepted.
[ASK] [S🔒] [✕] [▮]

◬ ▼ Wind Blew Inn Motel 🅼
(509) 674-2294. **$50-$70.** 811 Hwy 970. I-90, exit 85, just w. Ext corridors. **Pets:** Accepted.
[SAVE] [✕] [👘] [▮] [▭]

COLFAX

◬ ▼▼▼▼ Best Western Wheatland Inn 🆂🅷
(509) 397-0397. **$69-$75.** 701 N Main. Downtown. Int corridors. **Pets:** Medium. $10 daily fee/pet. Service with restrictions, crate.
[SAVE] [S🔒] [✕] [👘] [🕭] [👘] [▮] [▭] [≈]

COLVILLE

◬ ▼▼▼▼ Colville Comfort Inn 🆂🅷
(509) 684-2010. **$62-$125.** 166 NE Canning Dr. 1.5 mi n on US 395. Int corridors. **Pets:** $50 deposit/room, $10 daily fee/room. Service with restrictions, supervision.
[SAVE] [S🔒] [✕] [👘] [🕭] [👘] [▮] [▭] [≈]

CONCRETE

◬ ▼▼▼▼ Ovenell's Heritage Inn B&B and Log Cabins 🅲🅰
(360) 853-8494. **$90-$120, 3 day notice.** 46276 Concrete Sauk Valley Rd. 0.5 mi w of downtown on SR 20, 3 mi se. Ext/int corridors. **Pets:** $10 daily fee/pet. Designated rooms, service with restrictions, supervision.
[SAVE] [S🔒] [✕] [▮] [▭] [⊠]

COUGAR

▼ Lone Fir Resort Ⓜ 🐾
(360) 238-5210. **$40-$85, 7 day notice.** 16806 Lewis River Rd. Center. Ext corridors. **Pets:** Large, other species. $10 one-time fee/pet. Designated rooms, service with restrictions, supervision.

ⒶⓈⓀ Ⓢⓓ ⓧ 🚪 💻 🏊 ⓧ ⓩ

COULEE DAM

⚫⚫ ▼ ◆ Coulee House Inn & Suites Ⓜ 🐾
(509) 633-1101. **$67-$133.** 110 Roosevelt Way. Just e of river bridge. Ext corridors. **Pets:** Other species. $15 daily fee/pet. Designated rooms, service with restrictions, supervision.

ⓈⒶⓋⒺ Ⓢⓓ ⓧ 🚪 💻 🏊

DAYTON

▼▼▼ The Weinhard Hotel 🅢🅗
(509) 382-4032. **$75-$150, 7 day notice.** 235 E Main St. Downtown. Int corridors. **Pets:** Dogs only. $20 one-time fee/pet. Supervision.

ⒶⓈⓀ ⓧ

EAST WENATCHEE

▼▼▼ Cedars Inn, East Wenatchee 🅢🅗
(509) 886-8000. **$77-$82.** 80 Ninth St NE. Just e of SR 28. Int corridors. **Pets:** Small. $10 daily fee/room. Designated rooms, service with restrictions, supervision.

ⒶⓈⓀ Ⓢⓓ ⓧ 🚪 🏊

EATONVILLE

⚫⚫ ▼▼ Mill Village Motel Ⓜ
(360) 832-3200. **$70-$90.** 210 Center St E. Downtown. Ext corridors. **Pets:** Small, other species. $10 one-time fee/room. Service with restrictions, supervision.

ⓈⒶⓋⒺ ⓧ 🖫 🚪 💻

ELLENSBURG

⚫⚫ ▼▼▼ Best Western Lincoln Inn & Suites 🅢🅗 🐾
(509) 925-4244. **$89-$159.** 211 W Umptanum Rd. I-90, exit 109, just n, then just w. Int corridors. **Pets:** Small, dogs only. $25 daily fee/pet. Designated rooms, service with restrictions, supervision.

ⓈⒶⓋⒺ Ⓢⓓ ⓧ 🖫Ⓜ 🐕 🖫 🚪 💻 🏊 ⓧ

▼▼▼ Ellensburg Comfort Inn 🅢🅗
(509) 925-7037. **Call for rates.** 1722 Canyon Rd. I-90, exit 109. Int corridors. **Pets:** Accepted.

ⓧ 🐕 🖫 🚪 💻 🏊

⚫⚫ ▼▼▼ Ellensburg Inn 🅢🅗 🐾
(509) 925-9801. **$62-$97.** 1700 Canyon Rd. I-90, exit 109, just n. Int corridors. **Pets:** $6 daily fee/pet. Designated rooms, service with restrictions, supervision.

ⓈⒶⓋⒺ Ⓢⓓ ⓧ 🚪 💻 🍴 🏊

⚫⚫ ▼▼▼ I-90 Inn Motel Ⓜ
(509) 925-9844. **$52-$70.** 1390 Dollar Way Rd. I-90, exit 106, just n. Ext corridors. **Pets:** Medium, dogs only. $10 one-time fee/room. Designated rooms, service with restrictions, supervision.

ⓈⒶⓋⒺ Ⓢⓓ ⓧ 🚪

▼▼ Nites Inn Ⓜ
(509) 962-9600. **$54-$59.** 1200 S Ruby. I-90, exit 109, 0.5 mi n. Ext corridors. **Pets:** Other species. $8 one-time fee/pet. Service with restrictions, supervision.

ⒶⓈⓀ Ⓢⓓ ⓧ 🚪 💻

ENUMCLAW

⚫⚫ ▼▼▼ Best Western Park Center 🅢🅗
(360) 825-4490. **$70-$80.** 1000 Griffin Ave. Downtown. Ext corridors. **Pets:** Medium. $10 daily fee/pet. Designated rooms, service with restrictions, supervision.

ⓈⒶⓋⒺ ⓧ 🚪 💻 🍴

EPHRATA

▼▼ Ephrata Travelodge Ⓜ
(509) 754-4651. **$50-$75.** 31 Basin St SW. On SR 28; downtown. Ext corridors. **Pets:** Accepted.

ⓧ 🚪 💻 🏊

FERNDALE

▼▼ Ferndale Super 8 🅢🅗
(360) 384-8881. **$56-$74.** 5788 Barrett Ave. I-5, exit 262, just ne. Int corridors. **Pets:** Accepted.

ⒶⓈⓀ Ⓢⓓ ⓧ 🖫Ⓜ 🐕 🚪 🏊

FORKS

⚫⚫ ▼▼▼ Forks Motel Ⓜ
(360) 374-6243. **$53-$96, 7 day notice.** 351 US 101 (Forks Ave S). Just s. Ext corridors. **Pets:** Small. $10 daily fee/pet. Service with restrictions.

ⓈⒶⓋⒺ ⓧ 🚪 🏊

▼▼ Manitou Lodge 🅑🅑 🐾
(360) 374-6295. **$95-$160, 14 day notice.** 813 Kilmer Rd. 7.7 mi sw on SR 110 (LaPush Rd), 0.7 mi w on Mora Rd, then 0.8 mi n. Ext/int corridors. **Pets:** Other species. $10 daily fee/room. Designated rooms, supervision.

ⓧ 🚪 💻 🐕 🖫 ⓩ

▼▼▼ Miller Tree Inn Bed & Breakfast 🅑🅑
(360) 374-6806. **$75-$180, 7 day notice.** 654 E Division St. 0.3 mi e of US 101 (S Forks Ave). Ext/int corridors. **Pets:** Other species. $10 daily fee/pet. Designated rooms, service with restrictions, crate.

ⓧ 🚪 💻 🐕 ⓩ

⚫⚫ ▼▼▼ Olympic Suites Inn Ⓜ
(360) 374-5400. **$54-$99.** 800 Olympic Dr. North end of town, just ne off US 101 (S Forks Ave). Ext corridors. **Pets:** Accepted.

ⓈⒶⓋⒺ ⓧ 🚪 💻 🐕

▼▼▼ Pacific Inn Motel Ⓜ 🐾
(360) 374-9400. **$53-$68.** 352 US 101 (S Forks Ave). Just s. Ext corridors. **Pets:** $10 daily fee/pet. Designated rooms, service with restrictions, crate.

ⒶⓈⓀ ⓧ 🚪 💻

FREELAND

▼▼▼ Harbour Inn Motel Ⓜ
(360) 331-6900. **$69-$86.** 1606 Main St. Just e of SR 525. Ext corridors. **Pets:** Accepted.

ⓧ 🚪 💻 🐕

ILWACO

⚫⚫ ▼ Heidi's Inn Ⓜ
(360) 642-2387. **$42-$80, 7 day notice.** 126 Spruce St. Downtown. Ext corridors. **Pets:** Small, dogs only. $5 one-time fee/pet. Designated rooms, service with restrictions, supervision.

ⓈⒶⓋⒺ ⓧ 🚪 🐕

KALALOCH

⚫⚫ ▼▼▼ Kalaloch Lodge 🅒🅐
(360) 962-2271. **$119-$273.** 157151 US 101. At MM 157. Ext/int corridors. **Pets:** Other species. $12.50 daily fee/pet. Designated rooms, service with restrictions, supervision.

ⓈⒶⓋⒺ ⓧ 🚪 💻 🍴 🐕 ⓩ

KALAMA

⚫⚫ ▼ Best Value Kalama River Inn Ⓜ
(360) 673-2855. **$39-$74.** 602 NE Frontage Rd. I-5, exit 30 northbound, 0.4 mi n; exit southbound, 0.4 mi s. Ext corridors. **Pets:** Medium. $5 daily fee/pet. Service with restrictions, crate.

ⓈⒶⓋⒺ Ⓢⓓ ⓧ 🚪

KELSO

AAA ▽▽▽▽ Best Western Aladdin SH
(360) 425-9660. **$59-$100.** 310 Long Ave. I-5, exit 39, 1.1 mi w via Allen St and W Main St, then just n on 5th Ave. Int corridors. **Pets:** Small, dogs only. $10 one-time fee/pet. Service with restrictions, supervision.
[SAVE] [S◯] ⊠ 🔲 💻 ⤳

▽▽▽▽ GuestHouse Inn & Suites SH
(360) 414-5953. **$75-$200.** 501 Three Rivers Dr. I-5, exit 39, 0.3 mi w on Allen St, then 0.3 mi s. Int corridors. **Pets:** Accepted.
[ASK] [S◯] ⊠ 🗒 ⌨ 🔲 💻 ⤳

▽▽▽ Motel 6–43 M
(360) 425-3229. **$42-$65.** 106 Minor Rd. I-5, exit 39, 0.3 mi ne. Ext corridors. **Pets:** Other species. Supervision.
[S◯] ⊠ ⌨ 🔲 ⤳

AAA ▽▽▽▽ Red Lion Hotel Kelso/Longview SH
(360) 636-4400. **$79-$99.** 510 Kelso Dr. I-5, exit 39, 0.3 mi se. Int corridors. **Pets:** Other species. $10 one-time fee/room. Designated rooms, service with restrictions, supervision.
[SAVE] [S◯] ⊠ 🗒 ⌨ 🔲 💻 🍴 ⤳

▽▽▽▽ Super 8 Motel SH 🐾
(360) 423-8880. **$52-$71.** 250 Kelso Dr. I-5, exit 39, just se. Int corridors. **Pets:** Medium, other species. $25 deposit/room, $15 one-time fee/room. Service with restrictions, supervision.
[ASK] [S◯] ⊠ [&M] ⌨ 🔲 ⤳

KENNEWICK

AAA ▽▽▽▽ Best Value Clearwater Inn SH
(509) 735-2242. **$68-$73.** 5616 W Clearwater Ave. US 395, 1.9 mi w. Int corridors. **Pets:** Accepted.
[SAVE] [S◯] ⊠ 🗒 ⌨ 🔲 💻

AAA ▽▽▽▽ Best Western Kennewick Inn SH
(509) 586-1332. **$79-$141.** 4001 W 27th Ave. I-82, exit 113 (US 395), 0.8 mi n. Int corridors. **Pets:** Large, other species. $10 one-time fee/room. Designated rooms, service with restrictions, supervision.
[SAVE] [S◯] ⊠ [&M] 🗒 ⌨ 🔲 💻 ⤳ ⊠

▽▽▽ Clover Island Inn SH
(509) 586-0541. **$79-$109.** 435 Clover Island Dr. US 395, exit Port of Kennewick, 1 mi e on Columbia Dr, then just n. Int corridors. **Pets:** Medium. $25 one-time fee/room. Service with restrictions, supervision.
[ASK] [S◯] ⊠ 🔲 💻 ⤳ ⊠

▽▽▽▽ Comfort Inn M
(509) 783-8396. **$69-$99.** 7801 W Quinault Ave. 0.5 mi s on Columbia Center Blvd from SR 240. Int corridors. **Pets:** Dogs only. $10 daily fee/pet. Service with restrictions, supervision.
[ASK] [S◯] ⊠ [&M] 🗒 ⌨ 🔲 💻 ⤳

AAA ▽▽▽ Days Inn Kennewick SH
(509) 735-9511. **$50-$85.** 2811 W 2nd Ave. Jct US 395 and Clearwater Ave, just s, just w. Ext/int corridors. **Pets:** Small, dogs only. $10 one-time fee/room. Designated rooms, service with restrictions, supervision.
[SAVE] [S◯] ⊠ 🔲 💻 ⤳

AAA ▽▽▽ Econo Lodge M
(509) 783-6191. **$75-$120.** 300 N Ely St #A. On US 395, jct Clearwater Ave. Ext corridors. **Pets:** Small, dogs only. $7 daily fee/pet. Designated rooms, service with restrictions, supervision.
[SAVE] [S◯] ⊠ 🔲 ⤳

▽▽▽ Kennewick Super 8 SH
(509) 736-6888. **$52-$71.** 626 Columbia Center Blvd. 1.1 mi s of SR 240. Int corridors. **Pets:** Other species. $10 one-time fee/room. Service with restrictions, supervision.
[ASK] ⊠ [&M] 🗒 ⌨ 🔲 ⤳

AAA ▽▽▽▽ La Quinta Inn & Suites Kennewick SH 🐾
(509) 736-3326. **$79-$139.** 4220 W 27th Pl. I-82, exit 113 (US 395), 0.8 mi n. Int corridors. **Pets:** Medium. Service with restrictions, supervision.
[SAVE] [S◯] ⊠ [&M] 🗒 ⌨ 🔲 💻 ⤳ ⊠

▽▽▽▽ Red Lion Hotel Columbia Center-Kennewick SH
(509) 783-0611. **$89.** 1101 N Columbia Center Blvd. SR 240, 0.5 mi s. Int corridors. **Pets:** Accepted.
[ASK] [S◯] ⊠ [&M] 🗒 ⌨ 🔲 💻 🍴 ⤳

AAA ▽▽▽ Travelodge Extended Stay SH
(509) 735-6385. **$59-$68.** 321 N Johnson St. US 395, just w on Clearwater Ave, just n. Int corridors. **Pets:** Medium, dogs only. $10 daily fee/room. Designated rooms, service with restrictions, supervision.
[SAVE] [S◯] ⊠ 🔲 💻 ⤳

LACEY

AAA ▽▽▽▽ Quality Inn & Suites SH
(360) 493-1991. **$55-$85.** 120 College St SE. I-5, exit 109, just sw. Int corridors. **Pets:** Small. $25 deposit/pet. Designated rooms, service with restrictions, crate.
[SAVE] [S◯] ⊠ 🗒 ⌨ 🔲 💻

LA CONNER

AAA ▽▽▽▽ La Conner Country Inn SH
(360) 466-3101. **$82-$135.** 107 S 2nd St. At 2nd and Morris sts; downtown. Ext/int corridors. **Pets:** $25 one-time fee/room. Designated rooms, service with restrictions, supervision.
[SAVE] [S◯] ⊠ ⌨ 🔲 💻 🍴 ✗

LANGLEY

▽▽▽▽ The Inn at Langley SH
(360) 221-3033. **$235-$260, 3 day notice.** 400 1st St. Center. Ext corridors. **Pets:** Accepted.
⊠ 🔲 💻 ✗

▽▽▽ Island Tyme Bed & Breakfast BB 🐾
(360) 221-5078. **$85-$140, 7 day notice.** 4940 S Bayview Rd. SR 525 at MM 15, just e on Marshview, 2.1 mi n. Int corridors. **Pets:** Dogs only. $10 daily fee/pet. Designated rooms, service with restrictions, supervision.
⊠ ✗

LEAVENWORTH

▽▽▽ Alpine Rivers Inn SH 🐾
(509) 548-8888. **$79, 7 day notice.** 1505 Alpensee St. East edge of town. Ext corridors. **Pets:** Large, dogs only. $10 one-time fee/pet. Designated rooms, service with restrictions, supervision.
⊠ 🔲 💻 ⤳

AAA ▽▽▽▽ Bavarian Ritz Hotel SH
(509) 548-5455. **$89-$199, 3 day notice.** 633 Front St. Center. Ext/int corridors. **Pets:** Dogs only. Supervision.
[SAVE] [S◯] ⊠ 🔲 💻

AAA ▽▽▽▽ Der Ritterhof Motor Inn SH
(509) 548-5845. **$86-$99, 3 day notice.** 190 US 2. 0.3 mi w. Ext corridors. **Pets:** Dogs only. $10 daily fee/pet. Service with restrictions, supervision.
[SAVE] ⊠ 🗒 🔲 💻 ⤳ ✗

▽▽▽ The Evergreen Inn M 🐾
(509) 548-5515. **$75-$135, 14 day notice.** 1117 Front St. US 2, just s. Ext corridors. **Pets:** $10 daily fee/room. Supervision.
[ASK] ⊠ 🔲 💻 ✗

▽▽▽ Howard Johnson Express Inn M
(509) 548-4326. **$59-$139, 14 day notice.** 405 W US 2. West end of town. Ext corridors. **Pets:** Accepted.
[ASK] [S◯] ⊠ 🔲 💻 ⤳

WWWW **Langston Inn & Suites** SH
(509) 548-7992. **$69-$119.** 185 US 2. 0.3 mi w. Ext corridors. **Pets:** Large, other species. $15 daily fee/pet. Designated rooms, service with restrictions, crate.

AASK SD X &M 🔊 🔌 🖥 💻 🏊 🗙

AAA WWW **Obertal Inn** M
(509) 548-5204. **$69-$139.** 922 Commercial St. Off US 2; center. Ext corridors. **Pets:** Accepted.

SAVE SD X 🖥 💻

WWW **River's Edge Lodge** M 🐾
(509) 548-7612. **$85-$125.** 8401 US 2. 3.5 mi e. Ext corridors. **Pets:** Other species. $10 one-time fee/room. Designated rooms, service with restrictions, supervision.

AASK SD X 🖥 💻 🏊

LIBERTY LAKE

WWWW **Comfort Inn Liberty Lake** SH
(509) 340-3333. **$51-$90.** 2327 N Madson Rd. I-90, exit 296, 1 mi e on Appleway, then just n. Int corridors. **Pets:** Accepted.

AASK SD X &M 🔊 🔌 🖥 💻 🏊 🗙

LONG BEACH

AAA WWW **Anchorage Cottages** CA
(360) 642-2351. **$65-$123, 7 day notice.** 2209 Boulevard N. Just w of SR 103. Ext corridors. **Pets:** Accepted.

SAVE X 🖥 💻 🗙 🗲

AAA WW **The Breakers** CO
(360) 642-4414. **$59-$119, 5 day notice.** 26th & SR 103. North end of downtown. Ext corridors. **Pets:** Accepted.

SAVE SD X 🖥 💻 🏊 🗙 🗙

AAA WWW **Edgewater Inn** SH
(360) 642-2311. **$74-$124, 3 day notice.** 409 Sid Snyder Dr. Just w of SR 103. Ext/int corridors. **Pets:** $10 daily fee/pet. Designated rooms, service with restrictions, supervision.

SAVE X 🔌 🖥 💻 🍴 🗙

AAA WW **Our Place at the Beach** SH
(360) 642-3793. **$45-$90.** 1309 South Blvd. Just w of SR 103 at south end of town. Ext corridors. **Pets:** Large, other species. $5 daily fee/pet. Service with restrictions, supervision.

SAVE SD X 🖥 💻 🗙 🗙

AAA WWW **Shaman Motel** SH
(360) 642-3714. **$54-$99, 7 day notice.** 115 3rd St SW. Downtown. Ext corridors. **Pets:** Accepted.

SAVE X 🖥 💻 🏊 🗙

AAA WWW **Super 8 Motel** SH 🐾
(360) 642-8988. **$59-$139, 5 day notice.** 500 Ocean Beach Blvd. On SR 103; downtown. Int corridors. **Pets:** Dogs only. $5 daily fee/pet. Service with restrictions, supervision.

SAVE SD X &M 🔊 🖥 💻 🗙

LONGVIEW

AAA WWW **Hudson Manor Inn** M
(360) 425-1100. **$48-$70.** 1616 Hudson St. Downtown. Ext corridors. **Pets:** Medium. $10 one-time fee/room. Service with restrictions.

SAVE X 🖥 💻

AAA WWW **Longview Travelodge** M
(360) 423-6460. **$49-$65.** 838 15th Ave. Downtown; opposite Medical Center. Ext corridors. **Pets:** Dogs only. $25 one-time fee/pet. Service with restrictions, supervision.

SAVE SD X 🖥 💻

WWWW **Ramada Limited Longview** SH
(360) 414-1000. **$54-$159.** 723 7th Ave. I-5, exit 36, 3 mi w on SR 432. Int corridors. **Pets:** Other species. $15 one-time fee/room. Designated rooms, service with restrictions, supervision.

AASK SD X &M 🔊 🔌 🖥 💻 🏊

AAA WW **The Townhouse Motel** M
(360) 423-7200. **$44-$57, 3 day notice.** 744 Washington Way. Downtown. Ext corridors. **Pets:** Large. $5 one-time fee/pet. No service, supervision.

SAVE SD X 🖥 💻 🏊

MOCLIPS

WW **Hi Tide Ocean Beach Resort** CO 🐾
(360) 276-4142. **$95-$190, 3 day notice.** 4890 Railroad Ave. SR 109, 0.8 mi nw on beach at 6th St and Railroad Ave. Ext corridors. **Pets:** Medium, dogs only. $12 daily fee/pet. No service, supervision.

AASK X 🖥 💻 🗙 🗲

AAA WWW **Ocean Crest Resort** SH
(360) 276-4465. **$39-$165, 7 day notice.** 4651 SR 109 N. South edge of town. Ext corridors. **Pets:** Accepted.

SAVE SD X 🔌 🖥 💻 🍴 🏊 🗙 🗙

MONTESANO

AAA WWW **Monte Square Motel** M 🐾
(360) 249-4424. **$59-$99.** 100 Brumfield Ave W. US 12, exit SR 107 (Montesano/Raymond), just nw. Ext corridors. **Pets:** Other species. $10 one-time fee/pet. Designated rooms, supervision.

SAVE SD X &M 🖥 💻

MORTON

AAA WWWW **The Seasons Motel** M
(360) 496-6835. **$70-$90.** 200 Westlake Ave. Jct SR 7 and US 12. Ext corridors. **Pets:** Small. $10 daily fee/pet. Service with restrictions, supervision.

SAVE X 🖥 💻

MOSES LAKE

WWWW **AmeriHost** SH
(509) 764-7500. **$75-$105.** 1157 N Stratford Rd. I-90, exit 179, 1 mi n to SR 17, 2.8 mi nw to Stratford exit, just n, then just e. Int corridors. **Pets:** Accepted.

AASK SD X &M 🔊 🔌 🖥 💻 🏊

AAA WWWW **Best Western Hallmark Inn** SH 🐾
(509) 765-9211. **$75-$106.** 3000 Marina Dr. I-90, exit 176, just nw. Int corridors. **Pets:** Medium. Service with restrictions, supervision.

SAVE SD X &M 🔊 🖥 💻 🍴 🏊 🗙

WWWW **Holiday Inn Express** SH
(509) 766-2000. **$72-$109.** 1745 E Kittleson. I-90, exit 179, just n. Int corridors. **Pets:** Accepted.

AASK SD X &M 🔌 🖥 💻 🏊

WWWW **Inn at Moses Lake** SH
(509) 766-7000. **$60-$85.** 1741 E Kittleson. I-90, exit 179, just n. Int corridors. **Pets:** Accepted.

AASK SD X 🖥

WWW **Moses Lake Super 8** SH
(509) 765-8886. **$60-$85, 10 day notice.** 449 Melva Ln. I-90, exit 176, just n. Int corridors. **Pets:** $15 deposit/room, $10 one-time fee/room. Service with restrictions, crate.

AASK SD X 🖥 💻

MOUNT VERNON

Best Western College Way Inn SH
(360) 424-4287. **$69-$91.** 300 W College Way. I-5, exit 227, just w. Ext corridors. **Pets:** Other species. $15 daily fee/room. Designated rooms, service with restrictions, supervision.
SAVE S/D X [icons]

Best Western CottonTree Inn & Convention Center SH
(360) 428-5678. **$79-$159.** 2300 Market St. I-5, exit 227, 0.3 mi e on College Way, then 0.5 mi n on Riverside Dr. Int corridors. **Pets:** Dogs only. $25 one-time fee/room. Designated rooms, service with restrictions, supervision.
SAVE X [icons]

Comfort Inn-Mount Vernon SH
(360) 428-7020. **$70-$90.** 1910 Freeway Dr. I-5, exit 227, just w on College Way, then just n. Ext corridors. **Pets:** Small. $10 one-time fee/pet. Designated rooms, service with restrictions, supervision.
SAVE S/D X [icons]

Tulip Inn M
(360) 428-5969. **$60-$80.** 2200 Freeway Dr. I-5, exit 227, just w on College Way, then just n. Ext corridors. **Pets:** Medium, other species. $10 daily fee/pet. Designated rooms, service with restrictions, supervision.
SAVE S/D X [icons]

OAK HARBOR

Acorn Motor Inn SH
(360) 675-6646. **$46-$98.** 31530 SR 20. On SR 20 at 300th Ave W (SE Barrington Dr). Int corridors. **Pets:** Other species. $10 daily fee/room. Designated rooms, service with restrictions, supervision.
SAVE S/D X [icons]

OCEAN PARK

Ocean Park Resort M
(360) 665-4585. **$89-$100, 10 day notice.** 25904 R St. Just e of SR 103; downtown. Ext corridors. **Pets:** Small, other species. $7 daily fee/pet. Designated rooms, service with restrictions, supervision.
SAVE X [icons]

OCEAN SHORES

The Grey Gull Resort CO
(360) 289-3381. **$120-$355, 3 day notice.** 651 Ocean Shores Blvd NW. Just s of Shores Mall. Ext corridors. **Pets:** Large, dogs only. $10 daily fee/pet. Designated rooms, service with restrictions, supervision.
SAVE S/D X [icons]

The Nautilus CO
(360) 289-2722. **$70-$150.** 835 Ocean Shores Blvd NW. North end of town. Ext corridors. **Pets:** Dogs only. $20 one-time fee/pet. Service with restrictions, supervision.
SAVE X [icons]

The Polynesian Condominium Resort CO
(360) 289-3361. **$99-$139.** 615 Ocean Shores Blvd NW. Just s of Shores Mall. Ext/int corridors. **Pets:** Other species. $15 daily fee/pet. Service with restrictions, supervision.
SAVE S/D X [icons]

OKANOGAN

Ponderosa Motor Lodge M
(509) 422-0400. **$47-$52.** 1034 S 2nd Ave. 0.3 mi n on SR 215 from jct SR 20. Ext corridors. **Pets:** Other species. Service with restrictions, crate.
SAVE S/D X [icons]

OLYMPIA

Ramada Inn Governor House SH
(360) 352-7700. **$140.** 621 S Capitol Way. I-5, exit 105 (City Center) northbound; exit 105A southbound, 0.4 mi w on 14th Ave, then 0.6 mi n; downtown. Int corridors. **Pets:** Large. $50 one-time fee/room. Service with restrictions, supervision.
SAVE S/D X [icons]

Red Lion Hotel Olympia SH
(360) 943-4000. **$99-$119.** 2300 Evergreen Park Dr SW. I-5, exit 104, 0.5 mi nw, via US 101 and Cooper Point Rd N exit. Int corridors. **Pets:** Medium, other species. $25 one-time fee/pet. Service with restrictions, supervision.
ASK S/D X [icons]

OLYMPIC NATIONAL PARK

Lake Crescent Lodge SH
(360) 928-3211. **$85-$211, 3 day notice.** 416 Lake Crescent Rd. 22 mi w of Port Angeles on US 101. Ext/int corridors. **Pets:** Large, other species. $12 daily fee/pet. Designated rooms, service with restrictions, supervision.
SAVE X [icons]

Log Cabin Resort CA
(360) 928-3325. **$53-$127, 7 day notice.** 3183 E Beach Rd. 3.3 mi nw of US 101 (MM 232). Ext corridors. **Pets:** Accepted.
X [icons]

OMAK

Motel Nicholas M
(509) 826-4611. **$46.** 527 E Grape Ave. 0.8 mi n on SR 215 business route; 0.3 mi w of US 97, on north exit to Omak. Ext corridors. **Pets:** Small, dogs only. $3 daily fee/pet. Service with restrictions, supervision.
SAVE S/D X [icons]

Omak Inn M
(509) 826-3822. **$67-$77.** 912 Koala Dr. On US 97, just n of Riverside Dr. Int corridors. **Pets:** Accepted.
SAVE S/D X [icons]

Rodeway Inn & Suites M
(509) 826-0400. **$44-$89.** 122 N Main St. Downtown. Ext corridors. **Pets:** Accepted.
ASK S/D X [icons]

OTHELLO

Best Western Lincoln Inn Othello SH
(509) 488-5671. **$69-$109.** 1020 E Cedar St. Just off Main St at 10th and Cedar sts. Int corridors. **Pets:** $10 daily fee/pet. Service with restrictions, supervision.
SAVE S/D X [icons]

PACIFIC BEACH

Sandpiper Beach Resort CO
(360) 276-4580. **$90-$95, 14 day notice.** 4159 SR 109. 1.8 mi s. Ext corridors. **Pets:** Other species. $10 daily fee/pet. Service with restrictions, supervision.
SAVE X [icons]

PACKWOOD

Inn of Packwood M
(360) 494-5500. **$65-$80.** 13032 US 12. Center. Ext corridors. **Pets:** $5 daily fee/pet. Designated rooms, service with restrictions, supervision.
ASK S/D X [icons]

PASCO

▼▼▼▼ AmeriSuites Pasco at TRAC 🆂🅷
(509) 543-7000. **$125-$139, 3 day notice.** 4525 Convention Pl. I-182, exit 9 (Rd 68), just n, then just e. Int corridors. **Pets:** Small, dogs only. $10 daily fee/pet. Designated rooms, service with restrictions, crate.

🅰️$🅺 🆂🅳 ✖ 🅼 ⟁ 🅸 🎬 ➿

▲▲▲ ▼ Budget Inn Ⓜ
(509) 546-2010. **$44.** 1520 N Oregon St. I-182, exit 14A (SR 395 S). Ext corridors. **Pets:** Medium. $5 daily fee/pet. Service with restrictions, supervision.

🆂🅰️🆅🅴 🆂🅳 ✖ 🅸 ➿

▼▼ Red Lion Hotel Pasco 🅻🅷
(509) 547-0701. **$109-$129, 5 day notice.** 2525 N 20th Ave. I-182, exit 12B, just n. Int corridors. **Pets:** Medium. Service with restrictions, supervision.

🅰️$🅺 🆂🅳 ✖ 🅼 ⟁ 🐾 🅸 🎬 🍽 ➿

▲▲▲ ▼▼ Sleep Inn 🆂🅷
(509) 545-9554. **$65-$105.** 9930 Bedford St. I-182, exit 7, just ne. Int corridors. **Pets:** $15 daily fee/room. Service with restrictions, supervision.
🆂🅰️🆅🅴 🆂🅳 ✖ 🅼 ⟁ 🐾 🅸 🎬 ➿

PORT ANGELES

▲▲▲ ▼ The Pond Motel Ⓜ
(360) 452-8422. **$40-$70, 3 day notice.** 1425 W US 101. 2 mi w. Ext corridors. **Pets:** Accepted.
🆂🅰️🆅🅴 ✖ 🅸 🎬 🅺 🈂️

▲▲▲ ▼▼ Portside Inn 🆂🅷 🐾
(360) 452-4015. **$49-$129, 3 day notice.** 1510 E Front St. Front St at Alder, on east side. Ext corridors. **Pets:** Medium. $25 deposit/room. Designated rooms, service with restrictions, crate.

🆂🅰️🆅🅴 🆂🅳 ✖ 🅸 🎬 ➿

▼▼▼▼ Red Lion Hotel Port Angeles 🆂🅷
(360) 452-9215. **$89-$159.** 221 N Lincoln St. On US 101 westbound; at ferry landing. Ext/int corridors. **Pets:** Accepted.
🅰️$🅺 🆂🅳 ✖ ⟁ 🐾 🅸 🎬 🍽 ➿

▲▲▲ ▼▼▼ Riviera Inn Ⓜ 🐾
(360) 417-3955. **$39-$139, 3 day notice.** 535 E Front St. On US 101 W; downtown. Ext corridors. **Pets:** Other species. Designated rooms, service with restrictions, supervision.
🆂🅰️🆅🅴 🆂🅳 ✖ 🅸 🅺

▼ Super 8 Motel Ⓜ
(360) 452-8401. **$65-$80, 7 day notice.** 2104 E 1st St. 1.8 mi e of downtown, just s of US 101. Int corridors. **Pets:** Other species. $15 deposit/room, $10 one-time fee/room. Designated rooms, service with restrictions, supervision.
🅰️$🅺 🆂🅳 ✖ 🅼 🅸

NEARBY OREGON
PORTLAND METROPOLITAN AREA

VANCOUVER

▲▲▲ ▼▼▼ Comfort Inn 🆂🅷
(360) 574-6000. **$59-$119.** 13207 NE 20th Ave. I-5, exit 7, just e; I-205, exit 36, just w. Int corridors. **Pets:** Large. $10 daily fee/room. Service with restrictions, supervision.
🆂🅰️🆅🅴 🆂🅳 ✖ ⟁ 🅸 🎬 ➿

▼▼ Ferryman's Inn 🆂🅷
(360) 574-2151. **Call for rates.** 7901 NE 6th Ave. I-5, exit 4, just nw. Ext/int corridors. **Pets:** Other species. $20 deposit/room, $5 daily fee/pet. Designated rooms, service with restrictions, supervision.
🆂🅳 ✖ 🅼 ⟁ 🅸 ➿

▼▼▼▼ Homewood Suites by Hilton 🆂🅷 🐾
(360) 750-1100. **$109-$139.** 701 SE Columbia Shores Blvd. SR 14, exit 1, just s. Ext/int corridors. **Pets:** Other species. $10 daily fee/pet, $25 one-time fee/pet.
🅰️$🅺 🆂🅳 ✖ 🐾 🅸 🎬 ➿ 🍴

▲▲▲ ▼▼▼▼ Quality Inn & Suites 🆂🅷
(360) 696-0516. **$69-$99.** 7001 NE Hwy 99. I-5, exit 4, 0.8 mi se. Int corridors. **Pets:** Other species. $10 daily fee/room. Service with restrictions, supervision.
🆂🅰️🆅🅴 🆂🅳 ✖ ⟁ 🅸 🎬 ➿

▼▼ Red Lion Hotel Vancouver @ the Quay 🆂🅷
(360) 694-8341. **$89-$109.** 100 Columbia St. 0.5 mi s on dock at foot of Columbia St. Int corridors. **Pets:** Accepted.
🅰️$🅺 🆂🅳 ✖ 🅼 ⟁ 🐾 🅸 🎬 🍽 ➿ 🍴

▼▼▼ Red Lion Inn At Salmon Creek 🆂🅷
(360) 566-1100. **$89.** 1500 NE 134th St. I-5, exit 7, just w; I-205, exit 36, 0.5 mi w. Int corridors. **Pets:** Small, other species. $25 one-time fee/room. Service with restrictions, crate.
🅰️$🅺 🆂🅳 ✖ 🅼 🐾 🅸 🎬 ➿

▼▼▼ Residence Inn Vancouver 🆂🅷
(360) 253-4800. **$99-$139.** 8005 NE Parkway Dr. I-205, exit 30 (SR 500 W), 0.5 mi w to Thurston Way, just n to NE Parkway Dr, then just w. Ext corridors. **Pets:** Other species. $75 one-time fee/room. Service with restrictions, crate.
🅰️$🅺 🆂🅳 ✖ 🅼 ⟁ 🅸 🎬 ➿ 🍴

▼▼ Sleep Inn 🆂🅷
(360) 254-0900. **Call for rates.** 9201 NE Vancouver Mall Dr. I-205, exit 30 (SR 500 W), 0.6 mi w to Thurston Way, just n to Vancouver Mall Dr, then 0.5 mi e; southeast edge of Westfield Shopping Center. Int corridors. **Pets:** Medium, dogs only. $100 deposit/room, $10 one-time fee/room. Service with restrictions, supervision.
🆂🅳 ✖ 🅼 ⟁ 🅸 🎬 ➿

▼▼▼▼ Staybridge Suites Vancouver-Portland 🆂🅷 🐾
(360) 891-8282. **$79-$169.** 7301 NE 41st St. I-205, exit 30 (SR 500 W), 1 mi w to NE Andresen Rd, just n to NE 40th St, just e to NE 72nd St, just n to NE 41st St, then just e. Int corridors. **Pets:** Other species. $50 deposit/pet, $10 daily fee/pet. Designated rooms, service with restrictions.
🅰️$🅺 🆂🅳 ✖ 🅼 ⟁ 🐾 🅸 🎬 ➿ 🍴

▲▲▲ ▼▼▼ Vancouver Days Inn 🆂🅷
(360) 256-7044. **$61-$119.** 221 NE Chkalov Dr. I-205, exit 28 (Mill Plain E), just ne. Ext corridors. **Pets:** Small, dogs only. $15 daily fee/pet. Designated rooms, service with restrictions, supervision.
🆂🅰️🆅🅴 🆂🅳 ✖ 🅸 🎬 ➿

END METROPOLITAN AREA

PORT TOWNSEND

ⒶⒶⒶ ▼▼▼▼ Bishop Victorian Hotel 🆂🅷
(360) 385-6122. **$99-$215, 3 day notice.** 714 Washington St. Corner of Washington and Quincy sts. Int corridors. **Pets:** Accepted.
〔SAVE〕 🆂🔥 ✕ 🍴 🖵 🎇

▼▼▼ Harborside Inn 🆂🅷
(360) 385-7909. **$70-$125.** 330 Benedict St. Just e of SR 20. Ext corridors. **Pets:** Medium, dogs only. $5 daily fee/pet. Service with restrictions, supervision.
〔ASK〕 ✕ 🎇 🍴 🖵 ➿ 🎇

ⒶⒶⒶ ▼▼ ◈ Palace Hotel 🆂🅷 🐾
(360) 385-0773. **$59-$289.** 1004 Water St. Downtown. Int corridors. **Pets:** Large, other species. $10 daily fee/pet. Designated rooms, service with restrictions, supervision.
〔SAVE〕 🆂🔥 ✕ 🍴 🖵 🎇

ⒶⒶⒶ ▼▼▼▼ The Swan Hotel 🅼
(360) 385-1718. **$80-$190, 3 day notice.** 216 Monroe St. Downtown. Ext corridors. **Pets:** Dogs only. $15 daily fee/pet. Designated rooms, supervision.
〔SAVE〕 🆂🔥 ✕ 🍴 🖵 🎇

PROSSER

▼▼▼ Best Western Prosser Inn 🆂🅷
(509) 786-7977. **$79-$109.** 225 Merlot Dr. I-82, exit 80, just s. Int corridors. **Pets:** Medium, dogs only. $10 daily fee/pet. Service with restrictions, supervision.
〔ASK〕 🆂🔥 ✕ 🕎 🍴 🖵 ➿

PULLMAN

ⒶⒶⒶ ▼▼▼▼ Hawthorn Inn & Suites 🆂🅷 🐾
(509) 332-0928. **$79-$89.** 928 NW Olsen St. 1.6 mi e on SR 270 from US 195. Int corridors. **Pets:** Medium. $15 one-time fee/room. Designated rooms, supervision.
〔SAVE〕 🆂🔥 ✕ 🕎 🎇 🕎 🍴 🖵 ➿ 🎇

ⒶⒶⒶ ▼▼▼▼ Holiday Inn Express Hotel & Suites 🆂🅷
(509) 334-4437. **$89-$94.** SE 1190 Bishop Blvd. Jct US 195 business route, 0.5 mi s, 1 mi e on SR 270. Int corridors. **Pets:** Accepted.
〔SAVE〕 🆂🔥 ✕ 🕎 🎇 🕎 🍴 🖵 ➿ 🎇

ⒶⒶⒶ ▼▼▼ Quality Inn Paradise Creek 🆂🅷
(509) 332-0500. **$115-$135, 3 day notice.** 1400 SE Bishop Blvd. Jct US 195 business route, just s, 1 mi e on SR 270. Int corridors. **Pets:** Accepted.
〔SAVE〕 🆂🔥 ✕ 🕎 🍴 🖵 ➿ 🎇

QUINAULT

ⒶⒶⒶ ▼▼▼ Lake Quinault Lodge 🆂🅷
(360) 288-2900. **$80-$187.** 345 S Shore Rd. 2 mi off US 101. Ext/int corridors. **Pets:** $10 daily fee/pet. Designated rooms, service with restrictions, supervision.
〔SAVE〕 ✕ 🖵 🍴 ➿ 🎇 🎇 🅩

QUINCY

▼▼ ▼ Traditional Inns 🅼
(509) 787-3525. **$61-$67.** 500 F St SW. West end of town on SR 28. Ext corridors. **Pets:** Very small, dogs only. $5 daily fee/room. Supervision.
〔ASK〕 🆂🔥 ✕ 🍴 🖵

REPUBLIC

ⒶⒶⒶ ▼▼ ◈ Prospector Inn 🆂🅷
(509) 775-3361. **$52-$105.** 979 S Clark Ave. Downtown. Int corridors. **Pets:** $10 daily fee/pet. Designated rooms, service with restrictions, supervision.
〔SAVE〕 🆂🔥 ✕ 🍴 🎇

RICHLAND

ⒶⒶⒶ ▼▼▼▼ Clarion Hotel & Conference Center 🆂🅷
(509) 946-4121. **$69-$89.** 1515 George Washington Way. I-182, exit 5B, 2.5 mi n. Int corridors. **Pets:** Medium. $10 daily fee/pet. Designated rooms, service with restrictions, supervision.
〔SAVE〕 🆂🔥 ✕ 🕎 🎇 🕎 🍴 🖵 🍴 ➿ 🎇

▼▼ Days Inn 🅼
(509) 943-4611. **$64.** 615 Jadwin Ave. I-182, exit 5B, 0.9 mi n; just w of SR 240 business route; downtown. Ext corridors. **Pets:** $10 daily fee/room. No service, supervision.
〔ASK〕 🆂🔥 ✕ 🍴 🖵 ➿

▼▼▼ Red Lion Hotel Richland Hanford House 🆂🅷
(509) 946-7611. **$89.** 802 George Washington Way. I-182, exit 5B, 1.3 mi n on SR 240 business route. Ext/int corridors. **Pets:** Large, other species. $30 deposit/room. Service with restrictions.
〔ASK〕 🆂🔥 ✕ 🕎 🎇 🕎 🍴 🖵 🍴 ➿ 🎇

▼▼▼▼ Shilo Inn Hotel Richland Conference Center 🆂🅷
(509) 946-4661. **$83-$143.** 50 Comstock St. I-182, exit 5B, 0.5 mi n. Ext corridors. **Pets:** Accepted.
〔ASK〕 🆂🔥 ✕ 🎇 🕎 🍴 🖵 🍴 ➿ 🎇

RIMROCK

▼ ◈ Game Ridge Motel 🅼
(509) 672-2212. **$65-$130, 7 day notice.** 27350 US Hwy 12. Downtown. Ext corridors. **Pets:** $10 daily fee/pet. Service with restrictions, supervision.
〔ASK〕 🆂🔥 ✕ 🍴 🖵 🎇 🎇 🅩

RITZVILLE

▼▼▼▼ Best Western Bronco Inn 🆂🅷
(509) 659-5000. **$64-$109.** 105 W Galbreath Way. I-90, exit 221, go over overpass, take second left. Int corridors. **Pets:** Other species. $10 daily fee/pet. Designated rooms, service with restrictions, supervision.
〔ASK〕 🆂🔥 ✕ 🍴 🖵 ➿

ⒶⒶⒶ ▼▼ ◈ Colwell Best Value Inn 🅼
(509) 659-1620. **$40-$59.** 501 W 1st Ave. I-90, exit 220, 0.9 mi n; downtown. Ext corridors. **Pets:** Medium. $4 daily fee/pet. Designated rooms, service with restrictions, supervision.
〔SAVE〕 🆂🔥 ✕ 🍴 🖵 ➿

ⒶⒶⒶ ▼▼ ◈ La Quinta Inn Ritzville 🆂🅷
(509) 659-1007. **$39-$79.** 1513 Smitty's Blvd. I-90, exit 221, just n. Int corridors. **Pets:** Medium, other species. Service with restrictions, supervision.
〔SAVE〕 🆂🔥 ✕ 🕎 🎇 🍴 🖵 ➿ 🎇

ⒶⒶⒶ ▼ Top Hat Motel 🅼 🐾
(509) 659-1100. **$42-$49.** 210 E 1st Ave. I-90, exit 221, 1 mi ne via Division St. Ext corridors. **Pets:** Small, dogs only. $4 one-time fee/room. Designated rooms, service with restrictions, supervision.
〔SAVE〕 🆂🔥 🍴

SAN JUAN ISLANDS AREA

DEER HARBOR

▼▼ Deer Harbor Inn 🅲🅸
(360) 376-4110. **$125-$325, 14 day notice.** 33 Inn Ln. 7 mi sw of ferry landing; 3.5 mi sw of Westsound. Ext/int corridors. **Pets:** Accepted.

EASTSOUND

▼▼ Outlook Inn on Orcas Island 🆂🅷
(360) 376-2200. **$54-$245, 7 day notice.** 171 Main St. In Eastsound; downtown. Ext/int corridors. **Pets:** Other species. $10 daily fee/pet. Designated rooms.

FRIDAY HARBOR

🄰🄰🄰 ▼▼▼ The Friday Harbor Inn 🆂🅷 🐾
(360) 378-4000. **$69-$199, 10 day notice.** 410 Spring St. In Friday Habor; 0.5 mi w of ferry dock. Ext corridors. **Pets:** Other species. $15 one-time fee/room. Designated rooms, service with restrictions, supervision.

🄰🄰🄰 ▼▼▼ Lakedale Resort 🆂🅷
(360) 378-2350. **$137-$279, 30 day notice.** 4313 Roche Harbor Rd. 4 mi n of Friday Harbor via Tucker Ave. Ext/int corridors. **Pets:** Accepted.

LOPEZ ISLAND

🄰🄰🄰 ▼▼ Lopez Islander 🆂🅷
(360) 468-2233. **$79-$190, 14 day notice.** 2864 Fisherman Bay Rd. From ferry landing, 4.8 mi s via Ferry Rd and Fisherman Bay Rd. Ext corridors. **Pets:** Medium, dogs only. $20 one-time fee/pet. Designated rooms, service with restrictions, supervision.

SEATTLE METROPOLITAN AREA

AUBURN

▼▼ Travelodge Suites 🆂🅷
(253) 833-7171. **$59-$99.** Nine 16th St NW. SR 167, exit 15th St NW, 0.8 mi e, then just n on A St NE. Int corridors. **Pets:** Other species. $10 daily fee/pet. Designated rooms, service with restrictions, supervision.

▼▼ Val U Inn 🆂🅷
(253) 735-9600. **$80-$129.** Nine 14th St NW. SR 167, exit 15th St NW, 0.8 mi e, just s on A St NE, then just w. Int corridors. **Pets:** Small, dogs only. $10 daily fee/pet. Designated rooms, service with restrictions, crate.

BAINBRIDGE ISLAND

🄰🄰🄰 ▼▼▼ Island Country Inn 🅼 🐾
(206) 842-6861. **$99-$119.** 920 Hildebrand Ln NE. 0.8 mi n of ferry dock on SR 305, just w on High School Rd, then just s. Ext corridors. **Pets:** Medium, other species. $10 daily fee/pet. Designated rooms, service with restrictions, crate.

BELLEVUE

🄰🄰🄰 ▼▼ ▼▼ Bellevue Club Hotel 🆂🅷
(425) 454-4424. **$175-$315.** 11200 SE 6th St. I-405, exit 12, 0.4 mi nw. Int corridors. **Pets:** Small, dogs only. $30 one-time fee/room. Designated rooms, service with restrictions, supervision.

🄰🄰🄰 ▼▼▼ Days Inn Bellevue 🆂🅷
(425) 643-6644. **$70-$97.** 3241 156th Ave SE. I-90, exit 11 westbound; exit 11A (156th Ave SE) eastbound, just ne. Ext corridors. **Pets:** Small. $25 one-time fee/pet. Service with restrictions, supervision.

▼▼▼▼ Embassy Suites Hotel Bellevue 🅻🅷
(425) 644-2500. **$89-$209.** 3225 158th Ave SE. I-90, exit 11 westbound; exit 11A (156th Ave SE) eastbound, just ne. Int corridors. **Pets:** Medium. $50 one-time fee/pet. Designated rooms, service with restrictions, supervision.

▼▼▼ Homestead Studio Suites Hotel-Bellevue/Factoria 🅼
(425) 865-8680. **$89-$99.** 3700 132nd Ave SE. I-90, exit 11A westbound; exit 10B eastbound, 0.5 mi se. Ext corridors. **Pets:** Other species. $75 one-time fee/pet. Service with restrictions, crate.

▼▼ Homestead Studio Suites Hotel-Redmond at Microsoft Headquarters Campus 🅼
(425) 885-6675. **$52-$66.** 15805 NE 28th St. I-405, exit 14 (SR 520), 3.3 mi e to 148th Ave NE (south exit), just e on 24th St, just ne on Bel-Red Rd, just n on 156th Ave, then just e. Ext corridors. **Pets:** Accepted.

🄰🄰🄰 ▼▼▼ La Residence Suite Hotel 🆂🅷
(425) 455-1475. **$105-$145.** 475 100th Ave SE. I-405, exit 13B, 0.9 mi w on NE 8th St, then just s. Int corridors. **Pets:** Accepted.

🄰🄰🄰 ▼▼▼▼ Larkspur Landing Bellevue/Seattle 🆂🅷
(425) 373-1212. **$79-$169.** 15805 SE 37th St. I-90, exit 11 westbound; exit 11A (150th Ave SE) eastbound, 0.9 mi se on south frontage road. Int corridors. **Pets:** Medium, other species. $10 daily fee/pet, $75 one-time fee/room. Service with restrictions.

🄰🄰🄰 ▼▼▼ Ramada Inn Bellevue Center 🆂🅷
(425) 455-1515. **$65-$109.** 818 112th Ave NE. I-405, exit 13B, 0.3 mi nw. Ext/int corridors. **Pets:** Small. $20 one-time fee/room. Service with restrictions.

▼▼▼ Red Lion Bellevue Inn 🆂🅷
(425) 455-5240. **$89-$159.** 11211 Main St. I-405, exit 12, 0.4 mi n on 114th St. Int corridors. **Pets:** Small. $25 daily fee/pet. Designated rooms, service with restrictions, supervision.

▼▼▼ The Residence Inn By Marriott, Bellevue-Redmond 🆂🅷 🐾
(425) 882-1222. **$199-$299.** 14455 NE 29th Pl. I-405, exit 14 (SR 520), 2.3 mi e to 148th Ave NE (north exit), then just nw. Ext corridors. **Pets:** Other species. $75 one-time fee/room. Supervision.

BOTHELL

▼▼▼▼ Residence Inn by Marriott Seattle NE SH
(425) 485-3030. **$139-$199.** 11920 NE 195th St. I-405, exit 24, 0.4 mi ne. Ext corridors. **Pets:** Accepted.
ASK SD ✕ ⟳ 🖥 🖵 ⊠

BREMERTON

▲▲ ▼▼▼ Flagship Inn SH
(360) 479-6566. **$65-$99.** 4320 Kitsap Way. 3.5 mi w of ferry terminal; SR 3, exit Kitsap Way, 0.5 mi e. Int corridors. **Pets:** Medium. $6 daily fee/pet. Supervision.
SAVE SD ✕ 🖥 🖵 ⇌

▲▲ ▼▼▼▼ Illahee Manor Bed & Breakfast BB
(360) 698-7555. **$115-$290, 10 day notice.** 6680 Illahee Rd NE. SR 3, exit East Bremerton, 4.9 mi se on Wheaton Way (SR 303), 1.2 mi e on McWilliams Rd, just n on East Rd, 0.3 mi e on 3rd St, then just n. Ext/int corridors. **Pets:** Accepted.
SAVE SD ✕ 🖥 🖵 🎛 ✍

▲▲ ▼▼▼ Midway Inn SH
(360) 479-2909. **$69-$99.** 2909 Wheaton Way. SR 303, 2 mi n. Int corridors. **Pets:** Very small. $100 deposit/room, $15 daily fee/room. Designated rooms, service with restrictions, supervision.
SAVE SD ✕ 🖥 🖵

▼▼ ▼▼ Super 8 Motel SH 🐾
(360) 377-8881. **$67-$77.** 5068 Kitsap Way. 4.2 mi w of ferry terminal; SR 3, exit Kitsap Way, just ne. Int corridors. **Pets:** Large, other species. $10 one-time fee/room. Service with restrictions, supervision.
ASK SD ✕ ♿

DUPONT

▼▼▼▼ GuestHouse Inn & Suites SH 🐾
(253) 912-8900. **$89-$155.** 1609 McNeil St. I-5, exit 118, 0.6 mi w. Int corridors. **Pets:** $50 deposit/room, $10 daily fee/pet. Designated rooms, service with restrictions, supervision.
ASK SD ✕ ♿ ⟳ 🖥 🖵 ⇌

EDMONDS

▲▲ ▼▼▼ Edmonds Harbor Inn & Suites SH 🐾
(425) 771-5021. **$99-$129.** 130 W Dayton St. Just s at Port of Edmonds. Ext/int corridors. **Pets:** $10 daily fee/room. Designated rooms, service with restrictions.
SAVE SD ✕ ⟳ 🖥 🖵

▲▲ ▼ K & E Motor Inn M
(425) 778-2181. **$44-$64.** 23921 Hwy 99. I-5, exit 177, 1.3 mi w, then just n of jct SR 99 and 104. Ext corridors. **Pets:** Small, other species. Designated rooms, service with restrictions, supervision.
SAVE SD ✕ 🖥

▲▲ ▼▼▼ Travelodge Seattle/Edmonds SH
(425) 771-8008. **$59-$109.** 23825 Hwy 99. I-5, exit 177, 1 mi w on SR 104, exit at SR 99 (Everett-Lynnwood), then just n. Ext corridors. **Pets:** Medium. $25 one-time fee/pet. Service with restrictions, supervision.
SAVE SD ✕ 🖥 🖵 ⇌

EVERETT

▲▲ ▼▼▼ Best Western Cascadia Inn SH
(425) 258-4141. **$59-$109.** 2800 Pacific Ave. I-5, exit 193 northbound; exit 194 southbound, just w. Int corridors. **Pets:** Medium, other species. $10 daily fee/room. Designated rooms, service with restrictions, crate.
SAVE SD ✕ ♿ 🖥 🖵 ⇌

▼▼ ▼▼ Days Inn SH
(425) 355-1570. **$59-$89.** 1602 SE Everett Mall Way. I-5, exit 189 northbound, 0.5 mi w on SR 527, then 0.5 mi s; exit southbound, 0.7 mi s. Ext corridors. **Pets:** Accepted.
ASK SD ✕ 🖥 🖵 ⇌

▲▲ ▼▼▼ Inn at Port Gardner SH 🐾
(425) 252-6779. **$79-$129.** 1700 W Marine View Dr. I-5, exit 193 northbound, 1.2 mi w on Pacific Ave, then 1.2 mi n; exit 194 southbound, 1.2 mi w on Everett Ave, then 1 mi n; in Everett Marina Village. Int corridors. **Pets:** Small. $25 deposit/pet. Service with restrictions, supervision.
SAVE SD ✕ 🖥 🖵

▼▼▼▼ Quality Inn Hotel & Conference Center SH
(425) 337-2900. **$89-$114.** 101 128th St SE. I-5, exit 186, just e. Int corridors. **Pets:** Accepted.
ASK SD ✕ ⟳ 🖥 🖵 🎛 ⇌

FEDERAL WAY

▲▲ ▼▼▼ Federal Way Comfort Inn SH
(253) 529-0101. **$59-$149.** 31622 Pacific Hwy S. I-5, exit 143, 0.5 mi w on 320th St, just n on 20th Ave, then just w on 316th Pl. Int corridors. **Pets:** Accepted.
SAVE SD ✕ ⟳ ♿ 🖥 🖵 ⇌ ⊠

▼▼ ▼▼ Federal Way Super 8 SH 🐾
(253) 838-8808. **$62-$72, 7 day notice.** 1688 S 348th St. I-5, exit 142B, just w. Int corridors. **Pets:** Small. $10 daily fee/room. Designated rooms, service with restrictions, supervision.
ASK SD ✕ 🖥

▲▲ ▼▼▼▼ La Quinta Inn & Suites SH
(253) 529-4000. **$74-$104.** 32124 25th Ave S. I-5, exit 143, just sw. Int corridors. **Pets:** Accepted.
SAVE ✕ 🖥 🖵 🎛 ⇌

▲▲ ▼▼▼▼ Quality Inn & Suites SH
(253) 835-4141. **$79-$99.** 1400 S 348th St. I-5, exit 142B, 0.5 mi w. Int corridors. **Pets:** Accepted.
SAVE ✕ ♿ ⟳ ♿ 🖥 🖵 ⇌

FIFE

▲▲ ▼▼▼ Best Western Emerald Queen Hotel &
          Casino SH
(253) 922-2000. **$69-$109.** 5700 Pacific Ave. I-5, exit 137, just ne. Int corridors. **Pets:** Medium. $35 one-time fee/room. Service with restrictions, crate.
SAVE SD ✕ ♿ ⟳ ♿ 🖥 🖵 🎛 ⇌

▼▼ Econo Lodge Inn & Suites SH
(253) 922-9520. **$52-$62.** 3100 Pacific Hwy E. I-5, exit 136B northbound; exit 136 southbound, just nw. Ext corridors. **Pets:** Accepted.
ASK SD ✕ 🖥 🖵 ⇌

▲▲ ▼▼▼ Quality Inn M
(253) 926-2301. **$65-$145.** 5601 Pacific Hwy E. I-5, exit 137, just e. Ext corridors. **Pets:** Small. $15 one-time fee/room. Designated rooms, service with restrictions, crate.
SAVE SD ✕ 🖥 🖵

▲▲ ▼▼▼ Ramada Limited M
(253) 926-1000. **$65-$105.** 3501 Pacific Hwy E. I-5, exit 136B northbound; exit 136 southbound, just ne. Ext corridors. **Pets:** Accepted.
SAVE SD ✕ 🖥 🖵

▲▲ ▼▼▼ Royal Coachman Inn SH
(253) 922-2500. **$52-$140.** 5805 Pacific Hwy E. I-5, exit 137, just ne. Ext corridors. **Pets:** Small. $10 daily fee/pet. Designated rooms, service with restrictions, supervision.
SAVE SD ✕ 🖥 🖵

GIG HARBOR

AAA ▼▼▼▼ **Best Western Wesley Inn** SH ☙
(253) 858-9690. **$119-$194.** 6575 Kimball Dr. SR 16, exit City Center, just e on Pioneer Way, then 0.3 mi s. Int corridors. **Pets:** $10 daily fee/pet. Designated rooms, service with restrictions, crate.
SAVE S◊ ☒ ᴸᴹ ☷ ☎ ☐ ≈

AAA ▼▼▼▼ **The Inn at Gig Harbor** SH ☙
(253) 858-1111. **$118-$129.** 3211 56th St NW. SR 16, exit Olympic Dr, just w, then 0.4 mi n. Int corridors. **Pets:** Medium. $25 one-time fee/room. Designated rooms, service with restrictions, supervision.
SAVE S◊ ☒ ᴸᴹ ☷ ☎ ☐ ⑪ ☒

ISSAQUAH

▼ **Motel 6-295** M
(425) 392-8405. **$55-$75.** 1885 15th PL NW. I-90, exit 15, 0.3 mi n on Renton Issaquah Rd, then just w on NW Sammamish Rd. Ext corridors. **Pets:** Accepted.
S◊ ☒ ☷ ☎ ≈

KENT

AAA ▼▼▼▼ **Comfort Inn Kent** SH
(253) 872-2211. **$69-$149.** 22311 84th Ave S. SR 167, exit 84th Ave S, just n. Int corridors. **Pets:** Medium. $10 one-time fee/pet. Designated rooms, supervision.
SAVE S◊ ☒ ☎ ☐ ≈

AAA ▼▼▼▼ **Kent-Ramada Inn** SH
(253) 520-6670. **$69-$99.** 25100 74th Ave S. I-5, exit 149, 2.5 mi se via Kent Des Moines Rd (SR 516) to 74th Ave. Int corridors. **Pets:** Small. $25 one-time fee/pet. Designated rooms, service with restrictions, supervision.
SAVE S◊ ☒ ᴸᴹ ☷ ☎ ☐ ≈ ☒

▼▼▼▼ **TownePlace Suites by Marriott-Seattle Southcenter** SH
(253) 796-6000. **$109-$119.** 18123 72nd Ave S. I-405, exit 1 (SR 181), 1.6 mi s on W Valley Hwy, just e on S 180th, then just s. Ext corridors. **Pets:** Accepted.
ASK ☒ ᴸᴹ ᴸᴹ ☷ ☎ ☐ ≈ ☒

▼▼▼▼ **Val U Inn** SH ☙
(253) 872-5525. **$60-$65.** 22420 84th Ave S. SR 167, exit 84th Ave S, then just n. Int corridors. **Pets:** Medium, dogs only. $10 daily fee/pet. Service with restrictions, supervision.
ASK S◊ ☒ ☷

KIRKLAND

AAA ▼▼▼ **Best Western Kirkland Inn** M
(425) 822-2300. **$77-$97, 7 day notice.** 12223 NE 116th St. I-405, exit 20A northbound; exit 20 southbound, just e; in Totem Lake area. Ext corridors. **Pets:** Medium. $50 one-time fee/room. Designated rooms, service with restrictions, crate.
SAVE S◊ ☒ ᴸᴹ ☷ ☎ ☐ ≈

▼▼▼▼ **La Quinta Inn Seattle (Bellevue/Kirkland)** SH
(425) 828-6585. **$104-$144.** 10530 NE Northup Way. I-405, exit 14 (SR 520) via 108th Ave exit, s on 108th Ave, then just w. Int corridors. **Pets:** Accepted.
ASK ☒ ᴸᴹ ☷ ☎ ☐ ≈

▼ **Motel 6-687** M
(425) 821-5618. **$55-$67.** 12010 120th Pl NE. I-405, exit 20B northbound; exit 20 southbound, just se. Ext corridors. **Pets:** Small, other species. Service with restrictions, supervision.
S◊ ☒ ᴸᴹ ☷ ≈

AAA ▼▼▼▼ **The Woodmark Hotel on Lake Washington** LH
(425) 822-3700. **$225-$1800.** 1200 Carillon Point. On Lake Washington Blvd, 1 mi n of SR 520. Int corridors. **Pets:** Accepted.
SAVE S◊ ☒ ᴸᴹ ☷ ☎ ⑪ ☒

LAKEWOOD

AAA ▼▼▼ **Best Value Inn** M ☙
(253) 589-8800. **$62-$85.** 4215 Sharondale St SW. I-5, exit 127 (S Tacoma Way), just w on SR 512, 0.8 m s on S Tacoma Way, then just w. Ext corridors. **Pets:** Other species. $20 one-time fee/pet. Designated rooms, service with restrictions, crate.
SAVE S◊ ☒ ᴸᴹ ☷ ☎

AAA ▼▼▼ **Best Western Lakewood Motor Inn** SH ☙
(253) 584-2212. **$70-$90, 3 day notice.** 6125 Motor Ave SW. I-5, exit 125, 2 mi nw via Bridgeport to Gravelly Lake Dr, then just left. Ext corridors. **Pets:** Small. $10 daily fee/room. Designated rooms, service with restrictions, crate.
SAVE S◊ ☒ ᴸᴹ ᴸᴹ ☷ ☎ ☐ ≈

AAA ▼▼▼ **Ramada Inn** SH ☙
(253) 588-5241. **$72-$99.** 9920 S Tacoma Way. I-5, exit 127 (S Tacoma Way), 0.3 mi nw. Ext corridors. **Pets:** Very small, dogs only. $50 one-time fee/pet. No service, crate.
SAVE S◊ ☒ ☎ ☐

LYNNWOOD

▼▼▼▼ **Embassy Suites Hotel Seattle North/Lynnwood** SH
(425) 775-2500. **$89-$179.** 20610 44th Ave W. I-5, exit 181A northbound, just se; exit 181 (SR 524 W) southbound, 0.5 w on 196th St SW, then 0.6 mi s. Int corridors. **Pets:** Medium. $50 one-time fee/room. Designated rooms, service with restrictions, crate.
ASK ☒ ᴸᴹ ᴸᴹ ☷ ☎ ☐ ⑪ ≈ ☒

AAA ▼▼▼▼ **La Quinta Inn Lynnwood** SH
(425) 775-7447. **$79-$99.** 4300 Alderwood Mall Blvd. I-5, exit 181A northbound, just w; exit 181 (SR 524 W) southbound, 0.5 mi w on 196th St SW, just s on 44th Ave SW, then just e. Int corridors. **Pets:** Small, dogs only. Service with restrictions, supervision.
SAVE ☒ ☷ ☎ ≈

▼▼▼▼ **The Residence Inn by Marriott-Seattle North** SH
(425) 771-1100. **$89-$209.** 18200 Alderwood Mall Pkwy. I-5, exit 183, just w on 164th St SW, then 1.5 mi se on 28th St W; just n of Alderwood Mall Shopping Center. Ext corridors. **Pets:** Medium. $75 one-time fee/room. Service with restrictions, supervision.
ASK S◊ ☒ ᴸᴹ ☷ ☎ ☐ ≈ ☒

MARYSVILLE

AAA ▼▼▼ **Village Inn & Suites** SH
(360) 659-0005. **$58-$71.** 235 Beach Ave. I-5, exit 199, just se. Int corridors. **Pets:** Small. $15 daily fee/pet. Service with restrictions, crate.
SAVE S◊ ☒ ☷ ☎

MONROE

AAA ▼▼▼▼ **Best Western Baron Inn** SH
(360) 794-3111. **$67-$139.** 19233 US 2. West end of town. Int corridors. **Pets:** $15 daily fee/pet. Service with restrictions, supervision.
SAVE S◊ ☒ ☷ ☎ ≈

MOUNTLAKE TERRACE

▼▼ ▼▼ **Studio 6 #6042** M
(425) 771-3139. **$53-$69.** 6017 244th St SW. I-5, exit 177, just ne. Ext corridors. **Pets:** Accepted.
S◊ ☒ ᴸᴹ ᴸᴹ ☷ ☎ ☐

MUKILTEO

▼▼▼ TownePlace Suites by Marriott-Mukilteo SH
(425) 551-5900. $59-$89. 8521 Mukilteo Speedway. Just se of jct 84th
St SW and SR 535 (Mukilteo Speedway). Ext corridors.
Pets: Accepted.

ASK S⊘ ✕ &M ⊘ ⦿ ⊟ ⊑ ⊸ ⊠

POULSBO

▲▲▲ ▼▼▼ Poulsbo Inn M
(360) 779-3921. $95-$125. 18680 SR 305. SR 3, 2.3 mi e. Ext corridors. Pets: Medium. $10 daily fee/pet. Designated rooms, service with
restrictions, supervision.

SAVE S⊘ ✕ &M ⦿ ⊟ ⊑ ⊸ ⊠

PUYALLUP

▲▲▲ ▼▼▼▼ Best Western Park Plaza SH ✿
(253) 848-1500. $119-$134. 620 S Hill Park Dr. SR 512, exit S Hill/
Eatonville, just w. Int corridors. Pets: Dogs only. $25 one-time fee/room.
Service with restrictions, supervision.

SAVE S⊘ ✕ &M ⊘ ⦿ ⊟ ⊑ ⊸

▼▼▼ Holiday Inn Express Hotel & Suites
Puyallup SH ✿
(253) 848-4900. $124-$129. 812 S Hill Park Dr. SR 512, exit S Hill/
Eatonville, just w. Int corridors. Pets: Dogs only. $25 one-time fee/room.
Service with restrictions, supervision.

ASK S⊘ ✕ ⊘ ⦿ ⊟ ⊑ ⊸

REDMOND

▲▲▲ ▼▼▼▼ Residence Inn by Marriott Redmond Town
Center ✿
(425) 497-9226. $199-$249. 7575 164th Ave NE. I-405, exit 14 (SR
520), 5 mi e to W Lake Sammamish Pkwy, just n to Leary Way, just e
to Bear Creek Pkwy, just s to 74th Ave, just w to 163rd Ave, then just
n; center. Int corridors. Pets: Medium, other species. $75 one-time fee/
room.

SAVE S⊘ ✕ ⦿ ⊟ ⊑ ⊸ ⊠

RENTON

▲▲▲ ▼ Best Value Inn SH
(425) 251-9591. $69-$79. 3700 E Valley Rd. SR 167, exit E Valley Rd,
just nw. Int corridors. Pets: $10 one-time fee/pet. Service with restrictions,
supervision.

SAVE S⊘ ✕ ⦿ ⊟ ⊑

▲▲▲ ▼▼ Econo Lodge M
(425) 228-2858. $59-$69. 4710 Lake Washington Blvd NE. I-405, exit
7, just ne. Ext corridors. Pets: Medium. $10 one-time fee/room. Service
with restrictions, supervision.

SAVE S⊘ ✕ ⦿ ⊟ ⊑ ⊸

▲▲▲ ▼▼▼▼ Holiday Inn Select Seattle-Renton SH
(425) 226-7700. $69-$89. One S Grady Way. I-405, exit 2 (SR 167/
Rainier Ave), jct SR 167 N. Int corridors. Pets: Medium. $50 deposit/
room. Designated rooms, service with restrictions, crate.

SAVE S⊘ ✕ ⊘ ⦿ ⊟ ⊑ ⊸

SEATAC

▲▲▲ ▼▼▼▼ Coast Gateway Hotel SH
(206) 248-8200. $77-$99. 18415 International Blvd. On SR 99. Int
corridors. Pets: Other species. $50 deposit/room. Designated rooms.

SAVE S⊘ ✕ &M ⊘ ⦿ ⊟ ⊑

▼▼▼▼ Doubletree Hotel Seattle Airport LH
(206) 246-8600. $74-$169. 18740 International Blvd. On SR 99. Int
corridors. Pets: Accepted.

✕ ⊘ ⦿ ⊟ ⊑ ⊨ ⊸

▲▲▲ ▼▼▼ Hilton Seattle Airport & Conference
Center LH
(206) 244-4800. $84-$189. 17620 International Blvd. On SR 99. Int
corridors. Pets: Accepted.

SAVE ✕ ⊘ ⦿ ⊟ ⊑ ⊑ ⊨ ⊸ ⊠

▼▼▼▼ Holiday Inn Express Hotel & Suites-Seattle Sea-Tac
Airport SH
(206) 824-3200. $84-$109. 19621 International Blvd. On SR 99. Int
corridors. Pets: Medium. $75 deposit/room, $50 one-time fee/room. Service with restrictions, supervision.

ASK S⊘ ✕ ⊟ ⊑

▲▲▲ ▼▼▼▼ Holiday Inn Seattle SeaTac International
Airport LH
(206) 248-1000. $99-$169. 17338 International Blvd. On SR 99. Int
corridors. Pets: Medium. $20 one-time fee/room. Designated rooms, serv-
ice with restrictions.

SAVE S⊘ ✕ &M ⊘ ⦿ ⊟ ⊑ ⊨ ⊸

▲▲▲ ▼▼▼▼ La Quinta Inn Seattle (Sea-Tac
International) SH
(206) 241-5211. $99-$134. 2824 S 188th St. On SR 99. Int corridors.
Pets: Accepted.

SAVE ✕ ⊘ ⦿ ⊑ ⊸

▼ Motel 6–1332 M
(206) 246-4101. $45-$59. 16500 International Blvd. On SR 99. Ext
corridors. Pets: Accepted.

S⊘ ✕ ⊘

▼ Motel 6–736 M
(206) 824-9902. $45-$59. 20651 Military Rd. I-5, exit 151, just se. Ext
corridors. Pets: Other species. Service with restrictions, supervision.

S⊘ ✕ ⊘ ⊘ ⦿ ⊸

▼ Motel 6–90 SH
(206) 241-1648. $45-$59. 18900 47th Ave S. I-5, exit 152, just sw. Int
corridors. Pets: Accepted.

S⊘ ✕ ⊘ ⊘ ⦿ ⊸

▼▼ Quality Inn Sea-Tac Airport SH
(206) 241-9292. $72-$82. 2900 S 192nd St. On SR 99. Int corridors.
Pets: Accepted.

ASK S⊘ ✕ ⦿ ⊑

▲▲▲ ▼▼▼▼ Radisson Hotel Seattle Airport SH ✿
(206) 244-6000. $69-$129. 17001 International Blvd. On SR 99. Int
corridors. Pets: Small. $25 one-time fee/pet. Designated rooms, service
with restrictions, supervision.

SAVE S⊘ ✕ ⊘ ⊑ ⊨ ⊸

▲▲▲ ▼▼▼▼ Red Lion Hotel Seattle Airport SH ✿
(206) 246-5535. $89-$149. 18220 International Blvd. On SR 99. Int
corridors. Pets: Designated rooms, service with restrictions.

SAVE S⊘ ✕ ⊘ ⦿ ⊟ ⊑ ⊨ ⊸ ⊠

▼▼ Red Roof Inn SH
(206) 248-0901. $58-$82. 16838 International Blvd. On SR 99. Int
corridors. Pets: Other species. Service with restrictions, supervision.

✕ ⦿

▼▼ Super 8 Motel Sea-Tac SH ✿
(206) 433-8188. $59-$79. 3100 S 192nd St. Just e of SR 99. Int
corridors. Pets: Other species. $25 deposit/room. Service with restrictions,
supervision.

ASK S⊘ ✕

SEATTLE

AAA ▼▼▼ ▼▼▼ **Alexis Hotel** LH ❖
(206) 624-4844. **$153-$287.** 1007 1st Ave. Corner of Madison St and 1st Ave. Int corridors. **Pets:** Large, other species. Service with restrictions, crate.
SAVE S⚡ ✕ 🖉 ♿ 🖥 🍴 ✕̶

AAA ▼▼▼ **Aurora Seafair Inn** M
(206) 524-3600. **$65-$95.** 9100 Aurora Ave N. I-5, exit 172, 1.5 mi w on N 85th St, then just n. Ext corridors. **Pets:** Accepted.
SAVE S⚡ ✕ 🖥

AAA ▼▼▼ **Best Western Evergreen Inn** SH
(206) 361-3700. **$92-$108.** 13700 Aurora Ave N. I-5, exit 175, 1.1 mi w on NE 145th St, then 0.3 mi s. Int corridors. **Pets:** Accepted.
SAVE S⚡ ✕ 🖥 🖥 ✕̶

AAA ▼▼▼ **Best Western Executive Inn/Seattle** SH
(206) 448-9444. **$129-$169.** 200 Taylor Ave N. I-5, exit 166, 1 mi w; near Seattle Center; just w of SR 99. Int corridors. **Pets:** Accepted.
SAVE S⚡ ✕ ♿M ♿ 🖥 🖥 🍴

▼▼▼ **Continental Plaza Inn** M
(206) 284-1900. **$54-$78.** 2500 Aurora Ave N. I-5, exit 167 (Mercer St), 2 mi nw; 2 mi n of downtown on SR 99 (Aurora Ave). Ext/int corridors. **Pets:** Accepted.
ASK S⚡ ✕ 🖥 🖥 ⇌

▼▼▼ **Crowne Plaza Seattle** LH
(206) 464-1980. **$198-$298.** 1113 6th Ave. Corner of 6th Ave and Seneca St. Int corridors. **Pets:** Other species. $50 one-time fee/room. Service with restrictions, supervision.
ASK S⚡ ✕ 🖉 🖥 🖥 🍴

▼▼▼ **The Edgewater** LH ❖
(206) 728-7000. **$225-$739.** 2411 Alaskan Way-Pier 67. On waterfront at Pier 67. Int corridors. **Pets:** Other species. Designated rooms, service with restrictions.
ASK S⚡ ✕ 🖉 🖥 🍴 ✕̶

▼▼ **Executive Pacific Plaza Hotel** SH ❖
(206) 623-3900. **$119-$129.** 400 Spring St. Between 4th and 5th aves. Int corridors. **Pets:** Small, dogs only. Designated rooms, service with restrictions, crate.
ASK S⚡ ✕ 🖉 🖥 🖥 ♴

AAA ▼◆▼◆▼ **The Fairmont Olympic Hotel** LH
(206) 621-1700. **$199-$365.** 411 University St. Corner of 4th Ave and University St. Int corridors. **Pets:** Accepted.
SAVE ✕ 🖉 🖥 ♿ 🖥 🖥 🍴 ⇌ ✕̶

▼▼▼▼ **Homewood Suites by Hilton-Seattle Downtown** SH ❖
(206) 281-9393. **$89-$189.** 206 Western Ave W. I-5, exit 167 (Mercer St), 0.3 mi w, 0.5 mi s on Fairview Ave, 1.2 mi w on Denny Way, then just n. Int corridors. **Pets:** Other species. $20 daily fee/room. Service with restrictions, supervision.
ASK S⚡ ✕ 🖥 🖥

AAA ▼▼▼ ▼▼▼ **Hotel Monaco** LH ❖
(206) 621-1770. **$219-$299.** 1101 4th Ave. Corner of 4th Ave and Spring St. Int corridors. **Pets:** Other species. Crate.
SAVE S⚡ ✕ 🖉 🖥 🖥 🍴 ✕̶

AAA ▼▼▼ ▼▼▼ **Hotel Vintage Park** LH ❖
(206) 624-8000. **$125-$233.** 1100 5th Ave. Corner of Spring St and 5th Ave. Int corridors. **Pets:** Service with restrictions.
SAVE S⚡ ✕ 🖉 🍴

AAA ▼▼▼▼ **La Quinta Inn & Suites Seattle Downtown** SH
(206) 624-6820. **$89-$159.** 2224 8th Ave. Corner of 8th Ave and Blanchard St. Int corridors. **Pets:** Accepted.
SAVE S⚡ ✕ 🖉 🖥 🖥 ✕̶

AAA ▼▼▼ **Ramada Inn Seattle University District North** SH ❖
(206) 365-0700. **$109-$129.** 2140 N Northgate Way. I-5, exit 173, just nw. Ext corridors. **Pets:** Other species. $10 daily fee/pet. Designated rooms, service with restrictions, crate.
SAVE S⚡ ✕ 🖉 🖥 🖥 ⇌

AAA ▼▼▼ ▼▼▼ **Red Lion Hotel on Fifth Avenue-Seattle** LH
(206) 971-8000. **$129-$179.** 1415 5th Ave. Between Pike and Union sts. Int corridors. **Pets:** Medium. $50 daily fee/room. Service with restrictions, supervision.
SAVE S⚡ ✕ 🖉 ♿ 🖥 🍴

▼▼▼ **Residence Inn Marriott Seattle Downtown/Lake Union** SH ❖
(206) 624-6000. **$109-$189.** 800 Fairview Ave. I-5, exit 167 (Mercer St), south end of Lake Union. Int corridors. **Pets:** Other species. $10 daily fee/pet. Service with restrictions.
ASK ✕ 🖉 🖥 🖥 ⇌ ✕̶

AAA ▼▼▼ ▼▼▼ **Sheraton Seattle Hotel & Towers** LH ❖
(206) 621-9000. **$159-$249.** 1400 6th Ave. Corner of 6th Ave and Pike St. Int corridors. **Pets:** Medium, dogs only. Designated rooms, service with restrictions, supervision.
SAVE S⚡ ✕ 🖉 ♿ 🖥 🖥 🍴 ⇌ ✕̶

AAA ▼▼▼ ▼▼▼ **Sorrento Hotel** SH ❖
(206) 622-6400. **$295-$2600.** 900 Madison St. I-5, exit Madison St, just e; at 9th Ave and Madison St. Int corridors. **Pets:** Other species. Service with restrictions, crate.
SAVE S⚡ ✕ 🖥 🍴 ✕̶

AAA ▼▼▼ **Travelodge by the Space Needle** SH
(206) 441-7878. **$99-$169.** 200 6th Ave N. I-5, exit 167 (Mercer St), just n on Fairview Ave, just w via Valley and Broad sts, just s on 5th Ave, then just e on John St. Int corridors. **Pets:** Large, dogs only. $10 daily fee/room. Service with restrictions, supervision.
SAVE S⚡ ✕ 🖉 🖥 🖥 ⇌

AAA ▼▼▼ **University Inn** SH 🐾
(206) 632-5055. **$105-$135.** 4140 Roosevelt Way NE. I-5, exit 169, 0.5 mi e, then just s. Int corridors. **Pets:** Medium, dogs only. $10 daily fee/pet. Designated rooms, service with restrictions, supervision.
SAVE S⚡ ✕ 🖉 🖥 🖥 🍴 ⇌

AAA ▼▼▼ **Vance Hotel** SH
(206) 441-4200. **$139-$159.** 620 Stewart St. Corner of 7th Ave and Stewart St. Int corridors. **Pets:** Other species. $25 one-time fee/room. Service with restrictions, crate.
SAVE S⚡ ✕ ♿M ♿ 🖥 🖥 🍴

AAA ▼▼▼ ▼▼▼ **The Westin Seattle** LH
(206) 728-1000. **$169-$189.** 1900 5th Ave. Corner of 5th Ave and Stewart St. Int corridors. **Pets:** Accepted.
SAVE ✕ ♿M 🖉 ♿ 🖥 🖥 🍴 ⇌

SILVERDALE

▼▼▼ **Cimarron Motel** SH
(360) 692-7777. **$79-$89.** 9734 NW Silverdale Way. Downtown. Int corridors. **Pets:** Small, dogs only. $10 one-time fee/room. Designated rooms, service with restrictions, supervision.
ASK S⚡ ✕ 🖥 🖥

▼▼▼ **Red Lion Silverdale Hotel** SH
(360) 698-1000. **$127.** 3073 NW Bucklin Hill Rd. On shoreline at north end of Dyes Inlet. Int corridors. **Pets:** Large, dogs only. $20 daily fee/room. Designated rooms, service with restrictions, crate.
ASK S⚡ ✕ 🖉 🖥 🖥 🍴 ⇌ ✕̶

SNOHOMISH

(AAA) ▽▽▽ Inn At Snohomish M
(360) 568-2208. **$65-$105.** 323 2nd St. East end of town. Ext corridors. **Pets:** $100 deposit/room. Crate.

[SAVE] [S] [X] [🛡] [💻]

TACOMA

(AAA) ▽▽▽▽ Howard Johnson Tacoma Inn SH
(253) 535-2880. **$89-$119.** 8726 S Hosmer St. I-5, exit 128 northbound, just se; exit 129 southbound, just e on 72nd St, then 1.2 mi s. Ext corridors. **Pets:** Accepted.

[SAVE] [S] [X] [✎] [🔥] [🛡] [💻] [🍽] [🏊] [X]

▽▽▽ La Quinta Inn & Suites Tacoma (Conference Center) SH
(253) 383-0146. **$109-$129.** 1425 E 27th St. I-5, exit 135 southbound; exit 134 northbound, just n. Int corridors. **Pets:** Other species. Service with restrictions, supervision.

[ASK] [X] [✎] [🛡] [💻] [🍽] [🏊]

(AAA) ▽▽▽▽ Sheraton Tacoma Hotel LH
(253) 572-3200. **$199-$219.** 1320 Broadway Plaza. I-5, exit 133 (City Center) to I-705 N, exit A St, left on 11th St, then left; downtown. Int corridors. **Pets:** Accepted.

[SAVE] [S] [X] [✎] [🛡] [💻] [🍽]

TUKWILA

(AAA) ▽▽▽▽ Comfort Suites Tukwila SH
(425) 227-7200. **$96-$131.** 7200 Fun Center Way. I-405, exit 1 (SR 181), just n on Interurban Ave, then just e. Int corridors. **Pets:** Medium. $15 daily fee/room. Designated rooms, service with restrictions, supervision.

[SAVE] [S] [X] [🔥M] [✎] [🔥] [🛡] [💻] [🏊] [X]

◈◈ Homestead Studio Suites Hotel-Sea-Tac Airport/Southcenter M
(425) 235-7160. **$55-$65.** 15635 W Valley Hwy. I-405, exit 1 (SR 181), just s. Ext corridors. **Pets:** $25 daily fee/room. Service with restrictions.

[ASK] [S] [X] [🔥M] [✎] [🔥] [🛡] [💻]

▽▽▽▽ Homewood Suites by Hilton SH
(206) 433-8000. **$119-$139.** 6955 Fort Dent Way. I-405, exit 1 (SR 181), just ne. Ext/int corridors. **Pets:** Small. $75 one-time fee/pet. Designated rooms, service with restrictions, supervision.

[ASK] [S] [X] [✎] [🛡] [💻] [🏊] [X]

▽▽▽ Ramada Limited Sea-Tac Airport SH
(206) 244-8800. **$79-$99.** 13900 Tukwila International Blvd. I-5, exit 158 southbound, 2 mi s; exit 154 (SR 158 W) northbound, just w; exit 99 N, 1 mi n. Int corridors. **Pets:** Small. $20 daily fee/pet. Service with restrictions, supervision.

[ASK] [S] [X] [🛡] [💻]

▽▽▽▽ Red Lion Hotel Seattle South SH
(206) 762-0300. **$72-$85.** 11244 Tukwila International Blvd. I-5, exit 158, 1 mi sw. Int corridors. **Pets:** Accepted.

[ASK] [S] [X] [🛡] [💻] [🍽] [🏊]

(AAA) ▽▽▽▽ Residence Inn by Marriott-Seattle South SH
(425) 226-5500. **$115-$145, 7 day notice.** 16201 W Valley Hwy. I-405, exit 1 (SR 181), just s. Ext corridors. **Pets:** Accepted.

[SAVE] [S] [X] [🔥M] [✎] [🔥] [🛡] [💻] [🏊] [X]

VASHON

▽▽ The Swallow's Nest Guest Cottages CA 🐾
(206) 463-2646. **$65-$250.** 6030 SW 248th St. From north end Ferry Landing, 7.8 mi s on Vashon Hwy; from south end (Tahlequah) Ferry Landing, 5.8 mi n on Vashon Hwy, 1.4 mi w on Quartermaster Dr, 1.5 mi s on Dockton Rd, 0.4 mi. Ext corridors. **Pets:** Other species. $10 daily fee/pet. Designated rooms, service with restrictions.

[X] [🛡] [💻] [🔥]

END METROPOLITAN AREA

SEDRO-WOOLLEY

(AAA) ▽▽▽ Three Rivers Inn SH
(360) 855-2626. **$59-$79.** 210 Ball St. On SR 20, just w of jct SR 9 N. Ext corridors. **Pets:** Medium. $10 one-time fee/pet. Service with restrictions, supervision.

[SAVE] [S] [X] [🔥M] [🛡] [💻] [🍽] [🏊]

SEQUIM

(AAA) ▽▽ Econo Lodge SH
(360) 683-7113. **$135-$270.** 801 E Washington St. US 101, exit Sequim Ave, 0.4 mi n, then 0.6 mi e; east end of downtown. Int corridors. **Pets:** Other species. $10 one-time fee/pet. Service with restrictions, supervision.

[SAVE] [S] [X] [✎] [🛡] [💻]

(AAA) ▽▽▽ Ramada Limited SH
(360) 683-1775. **$59-$199.** 1095 E Washington St. US 101, exit Sequim Ave, 0.4 mi n, then 0.9 mi e; east end of downtown. Int corridors. **Pets:** Very small, dogs only. $10 daily fee/pet. Designated rooms, service with restrictions, supervision.

[SAVE] [X] [🛡] [💻] [🏊]

(AAA) ▽▽▽ Sequim Bay Lodge SH
(360) 683-0691. **$65-$113, 7 day notice.** 268522 US 101. 3.2 mi se of town. Ext corridors. **Pets:** Accepted.

[SAVE] [S] [X] [✎] [🛡] [💻] [🏊]

(AAA) ▽▽▽ Sequim West Inn M
(360) 683-4144. **$69-$115.** 740 W Washington St. US 101, exit River Rd, 0.9 mi ne via River Rd and W Washington St. Ext corridors. **Pets:** Accepted.

[SAVE] [S] [X] [🛡] [💻]

SHELTON

▽▽ Super 8 Motel of Shelton SH
(360) 426-1654. **$55-$80.** 2943 Northview Cir. US 101, exit Wallace-Kneeland Blvd, just se. Int corridors. **Pets:** Dogs only. $30 daily fee/pet. Designated rooms, service with restrictions, supervision.

[S] [X] [🛡] [💻]

SKYKOMISH

(AAA) ▽▽ SkyRiver Inn M 🐾
(360) 677-2261. **$73-$110, 14 day notice.** 333 River Dr E. 16 mi w of Stevens Pass on US 2; south end of Skykomish River Bridge. Ext/int corridors. **Pets:** Other species. $5 daily fee/pet. Service with restrictions.

[SAVE] [X] [🛡] [💻]

SNOQUALMIE PASS

(AAA) ▽▽▽ Summit Lodge at Snoqualmie Pass SH
(425) 434-6300. **$109-$299, 3 day notice.** 603 SR 906. I-90, exit 52 eastbound, 0.3 mi e; exit 53 westbound, 0.3 mi w. Int corridors. **Pets:** Medium, dogs only. $25 one-time fee/pet. Service with restrictions, supervision.

[SAVE] [S] [X] [🛡] [💻] [🍽] [🏊]

SOAP LAKE

▼▼▼ Notaras Lodge Ⓜ
(509) 246-0462. **$65-$125.** 236 E Main Ave. Just w of SR 17. Ext corridors. **Pets:** Accepted.
⊠ 🖥 💻

SOUTH BEND

ⒶⒶⒶ ▼▼▼▼ The Russell House ⒷⒷ
(360) 875-6487. **$99-$250, 7 day notice.** 902 E Water St. 0.5 mi s on Harrison. Int corridors. **Pets:** Accepted.
ⓈⒶⓋⒺ 🆂 ⊠ 🅚

SPOKANE

ⒶⒶⒶ ▼▼▼ Apple Tree Inn Ⓜ
(509) 466-3020. **$49-$59.** 9508 N Division St. Jct US 2 and 395, just n. Ext/int corridors. **Pets:** Small, dogs only. $5 daily fee/pet. Designated rooms, supervision.
ⓈⒶⓋⒺ 🆂 ⊠ 🖥 🏊

▼▼▼ Best Western Trade Winds North Ⓜ ❀
(509) 326-5500. **$59-$129, 7 day notice.** 3033 N Division St. I-90, exit 281 (Division St), 2.3 mi n on US 2 and 395. Ext/int corridors. **Pets:** Large. $100 deposit/room. Designated rooms, service with restrictions, supervision.
🆂 ⊠ 🖥 💻 🏊

ⒶⒶⒶ ▼▼▼ Clinic Center Inn Ⓜ
(509) 747-6081. **$46-$50.** 702 S McClellan St. I-90, exit 281 (Division St) eastbound, just s to 5th Ave, just w to Browne St, just sw, then just s; exit westbound, just n to 2nd Ave, just w to Browne St, 0.5 mi s to 9th Ave, just e,. Ext corridors. **Pets:** $5 daily fee/pet.
ⓈⒶⓋⒺ 💻

▼▼▼ Comfort Inn North 🆂🅷
(509) 467-7111. **$47-$175.** 7111 N Division St. I-90, exit 281 (Division St), 4.6 mi n. Int corridors. **Pets:** Accepted.
🅰🆂🅺 🆂 ⊠ 💻 🏊 ⊠

ⒶⒶⒶ ▼▼▼▼▼ The Davenport Hotel 🅻🅷
(509) 455-8888. **$155-$1950.** 10 S Post St. Downtown. Int corridors. **Pets:** Accepted.
ⓈⒶⓋⒺ 🆂 ⊠ � 🅖 🖥 🍴 🏊 ⊠

▼▼▼ Doubletree Hotel Spokane City Center 🅻🅷
(509) 455-9600. **$99-$139.** 322 N Spokane Falls Ct. I-90, exit 281 (Division St), just n; downtown. Int corridors. **Pets:** Other species. $25 one-time fee/room. Service with restrictions, supervision.
🅰🆂🅺 ⊠ 🅖 🖥 💻 🍴 🏊

▼▼ Econo Lodge Ⓜ
(509) 747-2011. **$40-$89.** 120 W 3rd Ave. I-90, exit 281 (Division St), just n, then just w on 2nd Ave. Ext corridors. **Pets:** Small. $10 daily fee/pet. Service with restrictions, supervision.
🅰🆂🅺 🆂 ⊠ 🅖 🖥 💻 🏊

▼▼▼ Holiday Inn Spokane Airport 🆂🅷
(509) 838-1170. **$89-$129.** 1616 S Windsor Dr. I-90, exit 277 westbound; exit 277B eastbound, just w on US 2, then just s. Int corridors. **Pets:** Small. $50 deposit/room. Service with restrictions, crate.
🅰🆂🅺 🆂 ⊠ 🅖🅜 🅖 🖥 💻 🍴 🏊

▼▼ Howard Johnson Inn 🆂🅷
(509) 838-6630. **$55-$95.** 211 S Division St. I-90, exit 281 (Division St), just n. Int corridors. **Pets:** Small. $10 daily fee/pet. Designated rooms, service with restrictions, supervision.
🅰🆂🅺 🆂 ⊠ 🅖 🖥 💻

ⒶⒶⒶ ▼▼▼ Madison Inn 🆂🅷
(509) 474-4200. **$64-$69.** 15 W Rockwood Blvd. I-90, exit 281 (Division St) eastbound, just e to Cowley, 0.4 mi s, then just w; exit westbound, just n to 2nd Ave, just w to Browne St, 0.5 mi s to 9th Ave, then just e. Int corridors. **Pets:** Accepted.
ⓈⒶⓋⒺ 🆂 ⊠ 🅖🅜 🅖 🖥 💻

▼▼▼ Oxford Suites-Downtown Spokane 🆂🅷
(509) 353-9000. **$89-$159.** 115 W North River Dr. I-90, exit 281 (Division St), 1 mi n, then just n. Int corridors. **Pets:** Accepted.
🅰🆂🅺 🆂 ⊠ 🅖 🅖 🖥 💻 🏊 ⊠

▼▼▼ Quality Inn Oakwood 🆂🅷
(509) 467-4900. **$89-$119.** 7919 N Division St. I-90, exit 281 (Division St), 6.5 mi n. Int corridors. **Pets:** Medium, other species. $20 one-time fee/room. Designated rooms, service with restrictions, supervision.
🅰🆂🅺 🆂 ⊠ 🅖🅜 🅖 🖥 💻 🏊 ⊠

▼▼▼ Ramada Inn Airport 🆂🅷
(509) 838-5211. **$115-$125.** 8909 Airport Dr. I-90, exit 277B eastbound; exit 277 westbound, 3.4 mi n. Int corridors. **Pets:** Small, other species. $50 deposit/room. Service with restrictions, supervision.
🅰🆂🅺 🆂 ⊠ 🅖 🖥 💻 🍴 🏊 ⊠

ⒶⒶⒶ ▼▼▼ Ramada Limited Ⓜ
(509) 838-8504. **$70-$92.** 123 S Post St. I-90, exit 280B (Lincoln St), just n to 1st Ave W, just e to Post St, then just s. Ext corridors. **Pets:** $50 deposit/room. Service with restrictions, supervision.
ⓈⒶⓋⒺ 🆂 ⊠ 🅖 🖥 💻

▼▼▼ Ramada Limited Suites 🆂🅷
(509) 468-4201. **$79-$89.** 9601 N Newport Hwy. US 2 and 395, just n on US 2 (Newport Hwy). Int corridors. **Pets:** Small. $25 daily fee/pet. Service with restrictions, supervision.
🅰🆂🅺 🆂 ⊠ 🅖🅜 🅖 🖥 💻 🏊 ⊠

ⒶⒶⒶ ▼▼▼▼ Red Lion Hotel at the Park-Spokane 🅻🅷
(509) 326-8000. **$99-$149.** 303 W North River Dr. I-90, exit 281 (Division St), 1.5 mi n on US 195, then just w. Int corridors. **Pets:** Other species. Service with restrictions, crate.
ⓈⒶⓋⒺ 🆂 ⊠ 🅖 🅖 🖥 💻 🍴 🏊 ⊠

▼▼▼ Red Lion River Inn-Spokane 🆂🅷
(509) 326-5577. **$69-$85.** N 700 Division St. I-90, exit 281 (Division St), 0.8 mi n; downtown. Int corridors. **Pets:** Accepted.
🅰🆂🅺 🆂 ⊠ 🖥 💻 🍴 🏊 ⊠

ⒶⒶⒶ ▼▼ Shangri-La Motel Ⓜ ❀
(509) 747-2066. **$43-$48.** 2922 W Government Way. I-90, exit 277A eastbound; exit 277 westbound, Garden Springs Rd to Sunset Blvd, 1 mi e to Government Way, then just n to Hartson. Ext corridors. **Pets:** Dogs only. Service with restrictions, supervision.
ⓈⒶⓋⒺ 🆂 ⊠ 🖥 💻 🏊

▼▼ Shilo Inn Hotel 🆂🅷
(509) 535-9000. **$70-$110.** 923 E 3rd Ave. I-90, exit 281 (Division St), just n to E 3rd Ave, then 0.7 mi e. Int corridors. **Pets:** Accepted.
🅰🆂🅺 🆂 ⊠ 🅖🅜 🅖 🅖 🖥 💻 🍴 🏊 ⊠

▼▼ Super 8 West 🆂🅷 ❀
(509) 838-8800. **$69-$99.** 11102 W Westbow Blvd. I-90, exit 272 (Medical Lake), just s. Int corridors. **Pets:** Medium. $15 one-time fee/pet. Service with restrictions, supervision.
🅰🆂🅺 🆂 ⊠ 🅖🅜 🖥 💻 🏊

▼▼▼ Travelodge 🆂🅷 ❀
(509) 623-9727. **$70-$80.** W 33 Spokane Falls Blvd. I-90, exit 281 (Division St), 0.5 mi n, then just w. Int corridors. **Pets:** Large, other species. $10 one-time fee/room. Service with restrictions, crate.
🅰🆂🅺 🆂 ⊠ 🅖🅜 🅖 🖥 💻

ⒶⒶⒶ ▼▼▼ Travelodge Hotel 🆂🅷
(509) 838-1471. **$55-$80.** W 4301 Sunset Blvd. I-90, exit 277A eastbound, 1 mi n on Garden Springs Rd; exit 277 westbound, just n on Rustle St. Int corridors. **Pets:** Medium, dogs only. Designated rooms, service with restrictions, supervision.
ⓈⒶⓋⒺ 🆂 ⊠ 💻 🍴 🏊 ⊠

ⒶⒶⒶ ▼▼▼▼ WestCoast Ridpath Hotel 🅻🅷
(509) 838-2711. **$99-$129.** 515 W Sprague Ave. Downtown. Int corridors. **Pets:** Accepted.
ⓈⒶⓋⒺ 🆂 ⊠ 🅖 🅖 🖥 💻 🍴 🏊

SPOKANE VALLEY

Best Western Pheasant Hill SH
(509) 926-7432. **$69-$129.** 12415 E Mission. I-90, exit 289, just se. Int corridors. **Pets:** Small, dogs only. $10 daily fee/room. Designated rooms, service with restrictions, supervision.
[SAVE] [icons]

Broadway Inn & Suites SH
(509) 535-7185. **$49-$89.** 6309 E Broadway. I-90, exit 286, just w. Ext/int corridors. **Pets:** Other species. Service with restrictions, crate.
[SAVE] [icons]

Comfort Inn Valley SH
(509) 924-3838. **$60-$90.** 905 N Sullivan Rd. I-90, exit 291B, just s. Int corridors. **Pets:** Accepted.
[ASK] [icons]

Holiday Inn Express-Valley SH
(509) 927-7100. **$89-$189.** 9220 E Mission. I-90, exit 287, just s. Ext/int corridors. **Pets:** Dogs only. Designated rooms, service with restrictions, supervision.
[ASK] [icons]

La Quinta Inn & Suites Spokane (Spokane Valley) SH
(509) 893-0955. **$59-$109.** 3808 N Sullivan Rd. I-90, exit 291B, 1.3 mi n. Int corridors. **Pets:** Service with restrictions, supervision.
[SAVE] [icons]

Mirabeau Park Hotel and Convention Center SH
(509) 924-9000. **$69-$149.** 1100 N Sullivan Rd. I-90, exit 291B, just s. Int corridors. **Pets:** Other species. $25 deposit/room. Service with restrictions, supervision.
[SAVE] [icons]

Oxford Suites Spokane Valley SH
(509) 847-1000. **$95-$159.** 15015 E Indiana Ave. I-90, exit 291A eastbound; exit 291B westbound, just nw. Int corridors. **Pets:** Small. $10 daily fee/room. Service with restrictions, supervision.
[ASK] [icons]

Quality Inn Valley Suites SH
(509) 928-5218. **$69-$90.** 8923 E Mission. I-90, exit 287. Int corridors. **Pets:** Medium, dogs only. $50 deposit/pet. Designated rooms, service with restrictions, supervision.
[ASK] [icons]

Residence Inn by Marriott SH
(509) 892-9300. **$89-$169.** 15915 E Indiana. I-90, exit 291 westbound, just e; exit 291B eastbound, just n, then just e. Int corridors. **Pets:** Small, other species. $75 one-time fee/room. Designated rooms, supervision.
[ASK] [icons]

Super 8 Motel SH
(509) 928-4888. **$58-$93.** N 2020 Argonne Rd. I-90, exit 287, just n. Int corridors. **Pets:** Other species. $25 deposit/room. Designated rooms, service with restrictions, supervision.
[ASK] [icons]

STEVENSON

Dolce Skamania Lodge LH
(509) 427-7700. **$169-$369, 5 day notice.** 1131 SW Skamania Lodge Way. 1 mi w on SR 14, just n. Int corridors. **Pets:** Other species. $50 one-time fee/room. Designated rooms, supervision.
[ASK] [icons]

SULTAN

Dutch Cup Motel M
(360) 793-2215. **$57-$70, 7 day notice.** 918 Main St. Jct US 2 and Main St. Ext corridors. **Pets:** Medium, other species. $10 daily fee/room. Service with restrictions, supervision.
[SAVE] [icons]

SUNNYSIDE

Rodeway Inn SH
(509) 837-5781. **$89-$99.** 3209 Picard Pl. I-82, exit 69, just n. Int corridors. **Pets:** $10 daily fee/pet. Designated rooms, service with restrictions, supervision.
[ASK] [icons]

TOPPENISH

Best Western Lincoln Inn SH
(509) 865-7444. **$69-$129.** 515 S Elm St. I-82, exit 50, 3.1 mi e. Int corridors. **Pets:** Accepted.
[SAVE] [icons]

TUMWATER

Best Western Tumwater Inn SH
(360) 956-1235. **$70-$85.** 5188 Capitol Blvd. I-5, exit 102, just e. Int corridors. **Pets:** Other species. $10 daily fee/pet.
[SAVE] [icons]

Comfort Inn and Conference Center SH
(360) 352-0691. **$79-$95.** 1620 74th Ave SW. I-5, exit 101, just se. Int corridors. **Pets:** Other species. $10 daily fee/pet. Designated rooms, service with restrictions, crate.
[ASK] [icons]

GuestHouse Inn & Suites SH
(360) 943-5040. **$60-$130.** 1600 74th Ave SW. I-5, exit 101, just se. Int corridors. **Pets:** Accepted.
[ASK] [icons]

Motel 6—77 M
(360) 754-7320. **$43-$55.** 400 W Lee St. I-5, exit 102, just e on Trosper Rd, just s on Capital Blvd, then just w. Ext corridors. **Pets:** Accepted.
[icons]

TWISP

Idle-A-While Motel M
(509) 997-3222. **$51-$85, 4 day notice.** 505 N SR 20. Just n of town. Ext corridors. **Pets:** Dogs only. $5 daily fee/pet. Service with restrictions, supervision.
[ASK] [icons]

UNION GAP

Best Western Ahtanum Inn SH
(509) 248-9700. **$109-$139, 7 day notice.** 2408 Rudkin Rd. I-82, exit 36, just n. Int corridors. **Pets:** Accepted.
[ASK] [icons]

Quality Inn-Yakima Valley M
(509) 248-6924. **$69-$119.** 12 E Valley Mall Blvd. I-82, exit 36, just s. Ext corridors. **Pets:** Accepted.
[SAVE] [icons]

Super 8 Motel Yakima SH
(509) 248-8880. **$62-$80.** 2605 Rudkin Rd. I-82, exit 36, just s. Int corridors. **Pets:** Other species. $25 deposit/room. Service with restrictions, supervision.
[ASK] [icons]

WALLA WALLA

Best Western Walla Walla Suites Inn SH 🐾
(509) 525-4700. **$69-$119.** 7 E Oak St. US 12, exit 2nd Ave, just s. Int corridors. **Pets:** Dogs only. $10 daily fee/pet. Service with restrictions, supervision.

Budget Inn M
(509) 529-4410. **$55-$95.** 305 N 2nd Ave. US 12, exit 2nd Ave, 0.3 mi s. Ext corridors. **Pets:** Small. $5 daily fee/pet. Service with restrictions, supervision.

Holiday Inn Express SH
(509) 525-6200. **$75-$131.** 1433 W Pine St. US 12, exit Pendleton/Prescott. Int corridors. **Pets:** Large, other species. $10 daily fee/pet. Service with restrictions, supervision.

Howard Johnson Express Inn SH 🐾
(509) 529-4360. **$79-$119, 14 day notice.** 325 E Main St. US 12, exit 2nd Ave, 0.5 mi s, then just e. Ext/int corridors. **Pets:** Designated rooms, service with restrictions, supervision.

La Quinta Inn Walla Walla SH
(509) 525-2522. **$79-$119.** 520 N 2nd Ave. US 12, exit 2nd Ave, just s. Int corridors. **Pets:** Other species. Service with restrictions, supervision.

Walla Walla Super 8 SH 🐾
(509) 525-8800. **$66-$76.** 2315 Eastgate St N. US 12, exit Wilbur Ave, just s. Int corridors. **Pets:** Medium, other species. $15 deposit/room, $10 one-time fee/room. Designated rooms, service with restrictions, supervision.

Walla Walla Travelodge M
(509) 529-4940. **$55-$95.** 421 E Main St. US 12, exit 2nd Ave, 0.5 mi s, then just e. Ext/int corridors. **Pets:** Accepted.

WENATCHEE

Avenue Motel M
(509) 663-7161. **$50-$85.** 720 N Wenatchee Ave. On US 2 business loop; just nw of downtown. Ext/int corridors. **Pets:** Large, dogs only. $5 daily fee/room. Service with restrictions, supervision.

Coast Wenatchee Center Hotel LH
(509) 662-1234. **$89-$125, 3 day notice.** 201 N Wenatchee Ave. Downtown. Int corridors. **Pets:** $10 one-time fee/room. Service with restrictions, supervision.

Comfort Inn SH
(509) 662-1700. **$69-$110.** 815 N Wenatchee Ave. Downtown. Int corridors. **Pets:** Accepted.

Holiday Inn Express SH 🐾
(509) 663-6355. **$85-$99.** 1921 N Wenatchee Ave. Northwest side of town. Int corridors. **Pets:** Medium, other species. Designated rooms, service with restrictions, supervision.

La Quinta Inn & Suites Wenatchee SH 🐾
(509) 664-6565. **$79-$119.** 1905 N Wenatchee Ave. West end of town. Int corridors. **Pets:** Other species. Supervision.

Red Lion Hotel Wenatchee LH
(509) 663-0711. **$69-$99.** 1225 N Wenatchee Ave. Just nw of downtown. Int corridors. **Pets:** Accepted.

Super 8 SH
(509) 662-3443. **$79-$89.** 1401 N Miller St. 1.5 mi n on US 2. Int corridors. **Pets:** Medium. $10 daily fee/pet. Designated rooms, service with restrictions, supervision.

WESTPORT

CoHo Motel M
(360) 268-0111. **$53-$77, 3 day notice.** 2501 N Nyhus. Just e of boat basin. Ext corridors. **Pets:** Very small, other species. $10 daily fee/pet. Designated rooms, service with restrictions, supervision.

Windjammer Motel M
(360) 268-9351. **$45-$90.** 461 E Pacific Ave. Downtown. Ext corridors. **Pets:** Accepted.

WINTHROP

Best Western Cascade Inn M
(509) 996-3100. **$65-$179, 3 day notice.** 960 SR 20. 0.8 mi e. Ext corridors. **Pets:** Small, dogs only. $10 daily fee/pet. Designated rooms, service with restrictions, supervision.

River Run Inn M
(509) 996-2173. **$60-$125, 14 day notice.** 27 Rader Rd. 0.5 mi w on SR 20. Ext corridors. **Pets:** $10 daily fee/pet. Supervision.

Winthrop Inn M 🐾
(509) 996-2217. **$60-$95, 3 day notice.** 960 SR 20. 1 mi e. Int corridors. **Pets:** Dogs only. $7 daily fee/pet. Service with restrictions, supervision.

WOODLAND

Econo Lodge SH
(360) 225-6548. **$59-$74.** 1500 Atlantic Ave. I-5, exit 21, just ne. Ext corridors. **Pets:** Medium. $10 daily fee/pet. Service with restrictions, supervision.

Lewis River Inn M
(360) 225-6257. **$56-$76.** 1100 Lewis River Rd. I-5, exit 21, just e. Ext corridors. **Pets:** Large, other species. $6 daily fee/pet. Designated rooms, service with restrictions, supervision.

YAKIMA

Best Western Peppertree Yakima Inn SH
(509) 453-8898. **$74-$89.** 1614 N 1st St. I-82, exit 31, just s. Int corridors. **Pets:** Very small, dogs only. $10 one-time fee/room. Service with restrictions, supervision.

Cedars Inn and Suites M
(509) 452-8101. **$55-$65.** 1010 E A St. I-82, exit 33B eastbound; exit 33 westbound, just w to 9th St, just n to A St, then just e. Ext corridors. **Pets:** Accepted.

Clarion Hotel & Conference Center SH
(509) 248-7850. **$49-$109.** 1507 N 1st St. I-82, exit 31, 0.5 mi s. Int corridors. **Pets:** Small. $20 one-time fee/room. Service with restrictions, supervision.

(AAA) ▽▽▽ Comfort Suites SH
(509) 249-1900. **$89-$149.** 3702 Fruitvale Blvd. US 12, exit 40th Ave, just s. Int corridors. **Pets:** Small, dogs only. $10 daily fee/pet. Service with restrictions, supervision.
[SAVE] [S◇] [✕] [占M] [🖉] [🖧] [🖬] [💻] [⇌]

▽▽▽ Holiday Inn Express Yakima SH
(509) 249-1000. **$65-$89.** 1001 E A St. I-82, exit 33B eastbound; exit 33 westbound, just w to 9th St, just n to A St, then just e. Int corridors. **Pets:** Other species. $10 daily fee/pet. Service with restrictions, supervision.
[ASK] [S◇] [✕] [占M] [🖉] [🖧] [🖬] [💻] [⇌]

▽▽▽ Oxford Inn SH ❀
(509) 457-4444. **$65-$85.** 1603 E Yakima Ave. I-82, exit 33 westbound, just e; exit 33B eastbound. Int corridors. **Pets:** Small, dogs only. $25 one-time fee/room. Designated rooms, service with restrictions, supervision.
[ASK] [S◇] [✕] [占M] [🖉] [🖧] [🖬] [💻] [⇌] [✕]

▽▽▽ Oxford Suites SH
(509) 457-9000. **$95-$99.** 1701 E Yakima Ave. I-82, exit 33 westbound; exit 33B eastbound. Int corridors. **Pets:** Accepted.
[ASK] [S◇] [✕] [占M] [🖧] [🖬] [💻] [⇌] [✕]

(AAA) ▽▽▽ Ramada Limited M
(509) 453-0391. **$79-$109.** 818 N 1st St. I-82, exit 31, 1.2 mi s. Ext corridors. **Pets:** $10 daily fee/room. Supervision.
[SAVE] [S◇] [✕] [🖉] [🖧] [🖬] [💻] [⇌]

▽▽▽ Red Lion Hotel Yakima Center SH
(509) 248-5900. **$95-$125.** 607 E Yakima Ave. I-82, exit 33 westbound; exit 33B eastbound, 0.8 mi w. Ext/int corridors. **Pets:** Large. $5 daily fee/pet. Service with restrictions, crate.
[ASK] [S◇] [✕] [🖉] [🖧] [🖬] [💻] [🍴] [⇌]

▽▽▽ Red Lion Hotel Yakima Gateway SH
(509) 452-6511. **$95-$125.** 9 N 9th St. I-82, exit 33 westbound; exit 33B eastbound, just s. Int corridors. **Pets:** Large. $5 daily fee/pet. Service with restrictions, supervision.
[ASK] [S◇] [✕] [占M] [🖧] [🖬] [💻] [🍴] [⇌]

(AAA) ▽▽▽ Sun Country Inn M
(509) 248-5650. **$62-$76, 3 day notice.** 1700 N 1st St. I-82, exit 31, just s. Ext corridors. **Pets:** Large, other species. $5 daily fee/room. Service with restrictions, supervision.
[SAVE] [S◇] [✕] [🖧] [💻] [⇌]

ZILLAH

▽▽▽ Comfort Inn SH
(509) 829-3399. **$80-$161.** 911 Vintage Valley Pkwy. I-82, exit 52, just n. Int corridors. **Pets:** Other species. $10 daily fee/pet.
[ASK] [S◇] [✕] [🖉] [🖧] [🖬] [💻] [⇌]

WEST VIRGINIA

BARBOURSVILLE

▼▼▼ Comfort Inn by Choice Hotels SH
(304) 733-2122. **$70-$90.** 249 Mall Rd. I-64, exit 20, 0.4 mi n. Int corridors. **Pets:** Accepted.

BECKLEY

AAA ▼▼▼ Best Western Four Seasons Inn SH
(304) 252-0671. **$59-$104.** 1939 Harper Rd. I-64/77, exit 44, just e on SR 3. Ext/int corridors. **Pets:** Other species. $5 daily fee/pet. Service with restrictions.

▼▼▼ Comfort Inn SH 🐾
(304) 255-2161. **$55-$110.** 1909 Harper Rd. I-64/77, exit 44, 0.3 mi e on SR 3. Ext/int corridors. **Pets:** Other species. Service with restrictions, supervision.

AAA ▼▼▼ Country Inn & Suites By Carlson SH
(304) 252-5100. **$83-$160.** 2120 Harper Rd. I-64/77, exit 44, just w on SR 3. Int corridors. **Pets:** Small. $25 one-time fee/pet. Designated rooms, service with restrictions, supervision.

AAA ▼▼▼ Howard Johnson Express Inn SH
(304) 255-5900. **$70-$110.** 1907 Harper Rd. I-64/77, exit 44, 0.4 mi e on SR 3. Int corridors. **Pets:** Accepted.

AAA ▼▼ Microtel Inn SH
(304) 256-2000. **$49-$89.** 2130 Harper Rd. I-64/77, exit 44. Int corridors. **Pets:** Accepted.

▼▼▼ Park Inn & Suites SH
(304) 255-9091. **$49-$89.** 134 Harper Park Dr. I-64/77, exit 44, just w on SR 3. Int corridors. **Pets:** Accepted.

BLUEFIELD

▼▼▼ East River Mountain Inn SH
(304) 325-5421. **$62, 3 day notice.** 3175 E Cumberland Rd. I-77, exit 1, 3.8 mi nw via US 52/460, then 0.7 mi n on US 52. Ext corridors. **Pets:** Accepted.

AAA ▼▼▼ Econo Lodge M
(304) 327-8171. **$44-$135.** 3400 Cumberland Rd. I-77, exit 1, 3.8 mi nw via US 52/460, then 0.4 mi n on US 52. Ext corridors. **Pets:** Small, dogs only. $10 daily fee/room. Service with restrictions, supervision.

AAA ▼▼▼ Holiday Inn-On The Hill SH
(304) 325-6170. **$81-$99.** 3350 Big Laurel Hwy. I-77, exit 1, 3.8 mi nw via US 52/460. Int corridors. **Pets:** Service with restrictions.

BRIDGEPORT

AAA ▼▼▼ Holiday Inn Clarksburg-Bridgeport SH
(304) 842-5411. **$62-$85.** 100 Lodgeville Rd. I-79, exit 119, just e on US 50. Int corridors. **Pets:** Large, other species. Service with restrictions, crate.

▼▼▼ Knights Inn-Clarksburg M
(304) 842-7115. **$56-$85.** 1235 W Main St. I-79, exit 119, 0.3 mi e on US 50. Ext corridors. **Pets:** Other species. Service with restrictions.

▼▼▼ Sleep Inn SH
(304) 842-1919. **$65-$75.** 115 Tolley Dr. I-79, exit 119, just e on US 50. Int corridors. **Pets:** Other species. Supervision.

CHARLESTON

▼▼▼▼ Charleston Comfort Suites SH 🐾
(304) 925-1171. **$84-$150.** 107 Alex Ln. I-77, exit 95, just s on SR 61. Int corridors. **Pets:** Medium, other species. $50 one-time fee/room. Designated rooms.

▼▼▼▼ Country Inn & Suites By Carlson SH 🐾
(304) 925-4300. **$84-$119.** 105 Alex Ln. I-77, exit 95, just s on SR 61. Int corridors. **Pets:** Medium, other species. $50 one-time fee/pet. Designated rooms.

▼▼▼ Days Inn Charleston East M
(304) 925-1010. **$57-$63.** 6400 MacCorkle Ave. I-77, exit 95, just s on SR 61. Int corridors. **Pets:** Accepted.

▼▼▼▼ Holiday Inn Express Civic Center SH
(304) 345-0600. **$89-$139.** 100 Civic Center Dr. I-64, exit 58B eastbound; exit 58C westbound, just s; downtown. Int corridors. **Pets:** Small. $25 daily fee/room. Designated rooms, service with restrictions.

AAA ▼▼▼ Knights Inn-Charleston East M
(304) 925-0451. **$45-$58, 3 day notice.** 6401 MacCorkle Ave SE. I-77, exit 95, just s on SR 61. Ext corridors. **Pets:** Medium. $15 one-time fee/room. Service with restrictions.

▼▼▼ Red Roof Inn-Kanawha City M
(304) 925-6953. **$45-$53.** 6305 SE MacCorkle Ave. I-77, exit 95, just s on SR 61. Ext corridors. **Pets:** Medium. Service with restrictions, supervision.

CROSS LANES

AAA ▼▼▼ Comfort Inn West Charleston SH
(304) 776-8070. **$69-$89.** 102 Racer Dr. I-64, exit 47, just s. Int corridors. **Pets:** Accepted.

DAVIS

ΑΑΑ ▼▼▼▼ Deerfield Village Resort-Canaan Valley **CO**
(304) 866-4698. **$140-$275.** Cortland Ln. 7 mi s on SR 32. Ext corridors. **Pets:** Small. $50 one-time fee/pet. Supervision.
[SAVE] [X] [🔧] [💻] [🍴] [🏊] [X] [🐾]

ELKINS

ΑΑΑ ▼▼▼ Best Country Inn & Suites **M**
(304) 636-7711. **$58-$120, 3 day notice.** Route 219/250 S. 0.9 mi s of SR 219. Ext/int corridors. **Pets:** $5 one-time fee/room. Supervision.
[SAVE] [S6] [X] [🔧] [💻]

ΑΑΑ ▼▼▼▼ Cheat River Lodge & Inn **CA**
(304) 636-2301. **$68-$83, 30 day notice.** Rt 1, Box 115, Faulkner Rd. 4.8 mi e on US 33, then 1.5 mi ne. Ext corridors. **Pets:** Accepted.
[SAVE] [X] [🔧] [💻] [🍴] [X] [🐾]

▼▼▼ Econo Lodge **M**
(304) 636-5311. **$53-$85.** US 33 E. 1 mi e. Ext/int corridors. **Pets:** $5 one-time fee/room. Designated rooms, service with restrictions, supervision.
[ASK] [S6] [X] [🔧] [🐾]

▼▼▼ Elkins Days Inn **SH**
(304) 637-4667. **$70-$105.** 1200 Harrison Ave. 1 mi w on US 33/250/SR 92; downtown; in an office building. Int corridors. **Pets:** Large, other species. $5 daily fee/pet. Service with restrictions, crate.
[ASK] [S6] [X] [🔧M] [🔧] [💻] [🍴]

▼▼▼ Elkins Super 8 Motel **SH**
(304) 636-6500. **$55-$65.** 350 Beverly Pike. 0.8 mi s on SR 219. Int corridors. **Pets:** Service with restrictions, supervision.
[ASK] [S6] [X] [🔧]

FAIRMONT

ΑΑΑ ▼▼▼ Days Inn **SH**
(304) 366-5995. **$53-$70, 14 day notice.** 228 Middletown Rd. I-79, exit 132, just se on US 250, then just s. Ext corridors. **Pets:** Very small, dogs only. $10 one-time fee/pet. Designated rooms, service with restrictions, supervision.
[SAVE] [S6] [X] [🔧] [💻]

ΑΑΑ ▼▼▼▼ Holiday Inn Fairmont **SH**
(304) 366-5500. **$59-$99.** 930 E Grafton Rd. I-79, exit 137, just e. Int corridors. **Pets:** Designated rooms, service with restrictions, supervision.
[SAVE] [S6] [X] [🔧M] [🌀] [🐾] [🔧] [💻] [🍴] [🐾]

▼▼▼ Red Roof Inn **M**
(304) 366-6800. **$43-$60.** 50 Middletown Rd. I-79, exit 132, 0.3 mi s on US 250, just w, then just s. Ext corridors. **Pets:** Accepted.
[X] [🌀]

▼▼▼ Super 8 Motel **M**
(304) 363-1488. **$57-$79.** 2208 Pleasant Valley Rd. I-79, exit 133, just e. Int corridors. **Pets:** Accepted.
[ASK] [S6] [X] [🔧]

FROST

▼▼▼ The Inn at Mountain Quest **CI** ❁
(304) 799-7267. **$95-$140, 7 day notice.** Rt 92 Frost. On SR 92, 0.4 mi n. Ext corridors. **Pets:** Other species. $50 deposit/room. Service with restrictions, supervision.
[ASK] [S6] [X] [🍴] [X]

HARPERS FERRY

▼▼▼▼ Quality Inn & Conference Center **SH**
(304) 535-6302. **$70-$158.** 4328 William L Wilson Frwy. 0.2 mi w on US 340. Int corridors. **Pets:** Small. $10 daily fee/pet. Designated rooms, service with restrictions, supervision.
[ASK] [S6] [X] [🐾] [🔧] [💻] [🍴] [🐾] [X]

HUNTINGTON

▼▼▼ Red Roof Inn **SH**
(304) 733-3737. **$45-$65.** 5190 US Rt 60 E. I-64, exit 15, just s. Ext corridors. **Pets:** Accepted.
[X] [🔧]

HURRICANE

▼▼▼ Red Roof Inn **M**
(304) 757-6392. **$45-$55.** 500 Putnam Village Dr. I-64, exit 39, just n on SR 34, then just e. Ext corridors. **Pets:** Other species. Service with restrictions, supervision.
[X] [🐾] [🔧]

▼▼▼ Super 8 Motel-Hurricane **M**
(304) 562-3346. **$50.** 419 Hurricane Creek Rd. I-64, exit 34, just s. Ext corridors. **Pets:** $10 daily fee/room. Designated rooms, service with restrictions, crate.
[ASK] [S6] [X] [🔧] [🐾]

JANE LEW

ΑΑΑ ▼▼▼ Wilderness Plantation Inn **SH**
(304) 884-7806. **$60-$70.** Rt 7 Berlin Rd. I-79, exit 105, just e, then 0.3 mi s. Ext corridors. **Pets:** Accepted.
[SAVE] [X] [🐾] [🔧] [🐾]

KEYSER

ΑΑΑ ▼▼▼ Keyser Inn **SH**
(304) 788-0913. **$58-$65.** Rt 220 S. On US 220, 2.3 mi s. Int corridors. **Pets:** Medium. $30 one-time fee/room. Designated rooms, service with restrictions, supervision.
[SAVE] [S6] [X] [🔧] [💻]

LEWISBURG

ΑΑΑ ▼▼▼ Brier Inn **SH**
(304) 645-7722. **$59-$80.** 540 N Jefferson St. I-64, exit 169, just s on US 219. Ext corridors. **Pets:** Medium. $10 daily fee/pet. Designated rooms, service with restrictions, crate.
[SAVE] [S6] [X] [🐾] [🔧] [💻] [🍴] [🐾]

ΑΑΑ ▼▼▼ Days Inn **SH**
(304) 645-2345. **$55-$150, 3 day notice.** 635 N Jefferson St. I-64, exit 169, 0.3 mi n on US 219. Ext corridors. **Pets:** Small. $10 daily fee/pet. Service with restrictions, supervision.
[SAVE] [S6] [X] [🔧] [💻]

ΑΑΑ ▼▼▼ Rodeway Inn **M**
(304) 645-7070. **$30-$100.** 107 W Fair St. I-64, exit 169, 3.1 mi s on US 219, then just e. Ext corridors. **Pets:** Accepted.
[SAVE] [S6] [X] [🔧] [💻]

▼▼▼ Super 8 Motel **SH**
(304) 647-3188. **$57-$67, 30 day notice.** 550 N Jefferson St. I-64, exit 169, just s on US 219. Int corridors. **Pets:** Other species. $10 deposit/pet. Service with restrictions, supervision.
[ASK] [S6] [X] [🌀] [🔧]

MARTINSBURG

▼▼▼ Days Inn Martinsburg **SH**
(304) 263-1800. **$59-$69.** 209 Viking Way. I-81, exit 13, just e on W King St (CR 15). Ext/int corridors. **Pets:** Medium, dogs only. Service with restrictions, supervision.
[ASK] [S6] [X] [🔧] [💻]

ΑΑΑ ▼▼▼ Econo Lodge **M**
(304) 274-2181. **$60-$63.** 5595 Hammonds Mill Rd. I-81, exit 20, just e. Ext/int corridors. **Pets:** Other species. Service with restrictions, supervision.
[SAVE] [S6] [X] [💻]

Economy Inn M
(304) 267-2994. **$42-$60.** 1616 Winchester Ave (US 11 S). I-81, exit 12, 0.3 mi e on SR 45, then 0.3 mi s. Ext corridors. **Pets:** Very small. $5 deposit/pet. No service, supervision.

Knights Inn-Martinsburg M
(304) 267-2211. **$57-$75.** 1997 Edwin Miller Blvd. I-81, exit 16E, 0.4 mi e on SR 9. Ext corridors. **Pets:** Large, other species. $10 daily fee/pet. Designated rooms, service with restrictions.

Quality Inn of Martinsburg M
(304) 263-8811. **$69-$109, 7 day notice.** 94 McMillan Ct. I-81, exit 16E, just e. Ext/int corridors. **Pets:** Other species. $10 daily fee/pet. Service with restrictions, supervision.

Relax Inn M
(304) 263-0831. **$32-$59, 3 day notice.** 1022 Winchester Ave (US 11 N). I-81, exit 12, 0.3 mi e on SR 45, then just n. Ext corridors. **Pets:** Medium. $5 daily fee/pet. Service with restrictions, supervision.

Scottish Inns M
(304) 267-2935. **$40-$59.** 1024 Winchester Ave (US 11 N). I-81, exit 12, 0.3 mi e on SR 45, then just n. Ext corridors. **Pets:** Small. $10 daily fee/pet. Designated rooms, service with restrictions, supervision.

MINERALWELLS

Microtel Inn SH
(304) 489-3892. **$47-$61.** 104 Nickolette Rd. I-77, exit 170, just w. Int corridors. **Pets:** Accepted.

MORGANTOWN

Comfort Inn-Morgantown SH
(304) 296-9364. **$55-$125.** 225 Comfort Inn Dr. I-68, exit 1, 0.3 mi n on US 119. Int corridors. **Pets:** Accepted.

Friends Inn M
(304) 599-4850. **$65-$75.** 452 Country Club Rd. I-79, exit 155, s on US 19 to SR 705, then e on University Ave. Ext corridors. **Pets:** Medium. $20 deposit/pet, $5 daily fee/pet. Designated rooms, service with restrictions, supervision.

Ramada Inn and Conference Center SH
(304) 296-3431. **$70-$110.** 20 Scott Ave. I-68, exit 1, 0.3 mi n. Int corridors. **Pets:** Medium. Designated rooms, service with restrictions, supervision.

NITRO

Econo Lodge M
(304) 755-8341. **$56-$66.** 4115 1st Ave. I-64, exit 45, 0.8 mi e on SR 25. Ext corridors. **Pets:** Medium, dogs only. $10 daily fee/pet. Designated rooms, service with restrictions, supervision.

PARKERSBURG

Expressway Motor Inn M
(304) 485-1851. **$45-$56.** 6333 Emerson Ave. I-77, exit 179, 0.4 mi sw on SR 68. Ext corridors. **Pets:** Dogs only. $5 daily fee/pet. Service with restrictions, supervision.

Red Roof Inn M
(304) 485-1741. **$48-$63.** 3714 E 7th St. I-77, exit 176, just w on US 50. Ext corridors. **Pets:** Large, other species. Service with restrictions.

PHILIPPI

Philippi Lodging M
(304) 457-5888. **$53-$64.** Rt 4, Box 155. 2.5 mi s on US 250. Int corridors. **Pets:** Other species.

PRINCETON

Days Inn SH
(304) 425-8100. **$53-$78, 3 day notice.** 347 Meadowfield Ln. I-77, exit 9, 0.3 mi w on US 460, just s on Ambrose Ln, then just e. Ext corridors. **Pets:** Accepted.

Sleep Inn SH
(304) 431-2800. **$60-$150.** 1015 Oakvale Rd. I-77, exit 9, just w on US 460, then just n via service road. Int corridors. **Pets:** Medium, other species. Service with restrictions, supervision.

RIPLEY

Best Western McCoys Inn & Conference Center SH
(304) 372-9122. **$69-$89.** 701 W Main St. I-77, exit 138, just e. Ext/int corridors. **Pets:** Accepted.

Ripley Super 8 Motel M
(304) 372-8880. **$60-$70.** 102 Duke Dr. I-77, exit 138, just e on SR 33. Int corridors. **Pets:** Accepted.

SOUTH CHARLESTON

Ramada Plaza Hotel Charleston SH
(304) 744-4641. **$85-$94.** 400 2nd Ave. I-64, exit 56, just nw. Int corridors. **Pets:** Accepted.

STAR CITY

Econo Lodge-Coliseum SH
(304) 599-8181. **$59-$66.** 3506 Monongahela Blvd. I-79, exit 155, 1.4 mi s on US 119/SR 7. Ext corridors. **Pets:** Medium. Designated rooms, service with restrictions, supervision.

Holiday Inn Morgantown SH
(304) 599-1680. **$63-$129.** 1400 Saratoga Ave. I-79, exit 155, 1.7 mi s on US 119/SR 7. Ext corridors. **Pets:** Medium, other species. $10 one-time fee/room. Service with restrictions.

SUMMERSVILLE

Best Western Summersville Lake Motor Lodge SH
(304) 872-6900. **$60-$80.** 1203 S Broad St. US 19 and Broad St; 0.6 mi s of jct SR 39. Ext corridors. **Pets:** Small. $7 daily fee/pet. Designated rooms, service with restrictions, supervision.

Comfort Inn SH
(304) 872-6500. **$65-$150, 30 day notice.** 903 Industrial Dr N. US 19, 1.9 mi n of jct SR 39. Int corridors. **Pets:** Small, other species. $10 daily fee/pet. Designated rooms, no service.

Sleep Inn of Summersville SH

(304) 872-4500. **$50-$100, 30 day notice.** 701 Professional Park Dr. US 19, 1.7 mi n of jct SR 39. Int corridors. **Pets:** Small, other species. $10 daily fee/pet. Designated rooms, service with restrictions, supervision.

Super 8 Motel-Summersville SH

(304) 872-4888. **$54-$64.** 306 Merchants Walk. US 19, just n. Int corridors. **Pets:** Other species. $25 deposit/room. Service with restrictions, supervision.

TRIADELPHIA

Holiday Inn Express Wheeling East SH

(304) 547-1380. **$69-$129.** I-70, exit 11. Int corridors. **Pets:** Accepted.

WEIRTON

Holiday Inn SH

(304) 723-5522. **$99-$159.** 350 Three Springs Dr. 4.5 mi e on US 22, exit Three Springs Dr. Int corridors. **Pets:** Medium. $50 one-time fee/pet. Designated rooms, service with restrictions, supervision.

WESTON

Comfort Inn SH

(304) 269-7000. **$59-$109.** 2906 US 33 E. I-79, exit 99, just e. Ext corridors. **Pets:** Other species. $10 daily fee/room. Designated rooms, service with restrictions, supervision.

Weston Super 8 Motel SH

(304) 269-1086. **$56-$66.** 100 Market Place Mall, Suite 12. I-79, exit 99, just e. Int corridors. **Pets:** Accepted.

CITY INDEX

ABBOTSFORD

▼▼ Sleep Inn 🆂🅷 🐾
(715) 223-3337. **$70-$95.** 300 E Elderberry Rd. SR 29, exit 132 (SR 13), just se. Int corridors. **Pets:** Large, other species. $50 deposit/room, $15 daily fee/room. Designated rooms, service with restrictions, crate.

(A$K) 🆂🄳 ⊠ 🕖 🎞 🕮 📖 ➿ 🗶

ALGOMA

▼ Algoma Beach Motel 🆂🅷
(920) 487-2828. **$59-$159, 3 day notice.** 1500 Lake St. Jct SR 54, 0.4 mi s on SR 42. Ext/int corridors. **Pets:** Dogs only. $15 daily fee/pet. Designated rooms, service with restrictions, crate.

(A$K) 🆂🄳 ⊠ 🕮

▼ Scenic Shore Inn 🅼
(920) 487-3214. **$45-$63, 3 day notice.** 2221 Lake St. Jct SR 54, 0.8 mi s on SR 42. Ext corridors. **Pets:** Small, dogs only. Designated rooms, service with restrictions, supervision.

⊠ 🕮 📖 🗶

ANTIGO

▼▼ Super 8 Motel-Antigo 🆂🅷
(715) 623-4188. **$59-$69.** 535 Century Ave. On US 45 at jct SR 64 E. Int corridors. **Pets:** Dogs only. $15 daily fee/pet. Designated rooms, service with restrictions, supervision.

(A$K) 🆂🄳 ⊠ 🕖 🎞 🕮 📖 ➿ 🗶

APPLETON

⊕ ▼▼ Best Western Midway Hotel 🆂🅷
(920) 731-4141. **$89-$159.** 3033 W College Ave. US 41, exit 137 (SR 125), 0.5 mi e. Int corridors. **Pets:** Large. $10 daily fee/room. Designated rooms, service with restrictions, supervision.

(SAVE) 🆂🄳 ⊠ 🕖 🕮 📖 🍴 ➿ 🗶

▼▼ Budgetel Inn Appleton 🅼
(920) 734-6070. **$89-$199.** 3920 W College Ave. US 41, exit 137 (SR 125), just e. Ext/int corridors. **Pets:** Large. Service with restrictions, crate.

(A$K) 🆂🄳 ⊠ 🕮 📖 ➿

▼▼ Candlewood Suites 🆂🅷
(920) 739-8000. **$78-$165.** 4525 W College Ave. Just w of US 41. Int corridors. **Pets:** Dogs only. $75 one-time fee/pet. Designated rooms, service with restrictions.

(A$K) 🆂🄳 ⊠ 🎞 🕮 📖

▼▼▼ Comfort Suites Comfort Dome 🆂🅷
(920) 730-3800. **$100-$140.** 3809 W Wisconsin Ave. US 41, exit 138 (Wisconsin Ave), just e. Int corridors. **Pets:** Large, other species. Service with restrictions, crate.

(A$K) 🆂🄳 ⊠ 🕖 🕮 📖 ➿ 🗶

⊕ ▼▼▼ Country Inn & Suites By Carlson 🆂🅷
(920) 830-3240. **$75-$99.** 355 Fox River Dr. US 41, exit 137 (W SR 125), just nw. Int corridors. **Pets:** Accepted.

(SAVE) 🆂🄳 ⊠ 🎞 🕮 📖 ➿ 🗶

⊕ ▼ Exel Inn of Appleton 🅼
(920) 733-5551. **$43-$63.** 210 Westhill Blvd. US 41, exit 137 (SR 125), just e. Int corridors. **Pets:** Small, other species. Designated rooms, service with restrictions, supervision.

(SAVE) 🆂🄳 ⊠ 🕮 📖

⊕ ▼▼ Microtel Inn & Suites 🆂🅷
(920) 997-3121. **$45-$100.** 321 Metro Dr. US 41, exit 137 (W SR 125), just nw. Int corridors. **Pets:** Medium, other species. $10 daily fee/room. Designated rooms, service with restrictions, crate.

(SAVE) 🆂🄳 ⊠ 🎞 🕮 📖

▼▼▼ Residence Inn by Marriott 🆂🅷
(920) 954-0570. **$79-$169.** 310 Metro Dr. US 41, exit 137 (W SR 125), just nw on Mall Dr. Int corridors. **Pets:** Other species. $75 one-time fee/room.

(A$K) 🆂🄳 ⊠ 🕖 🎞 🕮 📖 ➿ 🗶

⊕ ▼▼▼ Woodfield Suites Appleton 🆂🅷
(920) 734-7777. **$45-$118.** 3730 W College Ave. US 41, exit 137 (SR 125), just e. Int corridors. **Pets:** Accepted.

(SAVE) 🆂🄳 ⊠ 🕮 📖 ➿ 🗶

ARCADIA

▼ RKD Motel 🅼
(608) 323-3338. **$50-$52.** 915 E Main St. On SR 95; 0.6 mi w of jct SR 93. Ext corridors. **Pets:** Other species. $6 daily fee/pet. Designated rooms, service with restrictions, supervision.

(A$K) 🆂🄳 ⊠ 🕮 📖

ASHLAND

⊕ ▼▼▼ AmericInn of Ashland 🆂🅷
(715) 682-9950. **$79-$199.** 3009 Lakeshore Dr E. On US 2, 2.1 mi e of jct SR 13 S. Int corridors. **Pets:** Accepted.

(SAVE) 🆂🄳 ⊠ 🎞 🕮 📖 ➿ 🗶

AAA WW Ashland Motel M
(715) 682-5503. **$45-$89.** 2300 W Lake Shore Dr. 1.8 mi w on US 2.
Ext corridors. **Pets:** Small. $5 daily fee/pet. Designated rooms, service with
restrictions, supervision.
[SAVE] [S] [X] [■]

WW Super 8 Motel SH
(715) 682-9377. **$59-$145.** 1610 W Lakeshore Dr. On US 2 at jct 16th
Ave. Int corridors. **Pets:** $25 one-time fee/room. Designated rooms, serv-
ice with restrictions, supervision.
[ASK] [S] [X] [&M] [⌀] [⌖] [■] [⊡] [≈]

BALDWIN

WWW AmericInn of Baldwin SH
(715) 684-5888. **$74-$154.** 500 Baldwin Plaza Dr. I-94, exit 19 (US 63),
just ne. Int corridors. **Pets:** Accepted.
[ASK] [S] [X] [⌖] [■] [⊡] [≈]

WW Super 8 Motel SH
(715) 684-2700. **$63-$78.** 2110 10th Ave. I-94, exit 19 (US 63), just se.
Int corridors. **Pets:** Medium, other species. Service with restrictions, supervision.
[ASK] [S] [X] [⌖] [■] [≈]

BARABOO

WWWW Park Plaza Baraboo SH
(608) 356-6422. **$76-$123.** 626 W Pine St. On US 12, 0.3 mi n of SR
33. Int corridors. **Pets:** Medium, other species. Designated rooms, service
with restrictions, supervision.
[ASK] [S] [X] [&M] [■] [⊡] [¶] [≈] [⊠]

BEAVER DAM

AAA WWW AmericInn Lodge & Suites SH
(920) 356-9000. **$77-$130.** 325 Seippel Blvd. US 151, exit 134 (CR
B/Industrial Dr). Int corridors. **Pets:** Medium. $10 daily fee/room. Desig-
nated rooms, service with restrictions.
[SAVE] [X] [⌖] [■] [⊡] [≈]

WW Super 8 Motel SH
(920) 887-8880. **$55-$77.** 711 Park Ave. US 151, exit 132 (SR 33), just
w. Int corridors. **Pets:** Large, other species. $50 deposit/pet. Designated
rooms, service with restrictions, supervision.
[ASK] [S] [X] [⌀]

BELOIT

AAA WWW Beloit Inn SH
(608) 362-5500. **$89-$139.** 500 Pleasant St. Downtown. Int corridors.
Pets: Medium. $50 deposit/room. Designated rooms, service with restric-
tions, supervision.
[SAVE] [S] [X] [⌖] [■] [⊡] [¶]

AAA WW Comfort Inn of Beloit SH
(608) 362-2666. **$59-$89.** 2786 Milwaukee Rd. I-90, exit 185A, just w at
jct I-43 and SR 81. Int corridors. **Pets:** Medium. $10 daily fee/room.
Service with restrictions, supervision.
[SAVE] [S] [X] [⌀] [■] [⊡] [≈]

AAA WW Econo Lodge M
(608) 364-4000. **$50-$80.** 2956 Milwaukee Rd. I-90, exit 185A, 0.3 mi
w. Ext/int corridors. **Pets:** Medium. $10 daily fee/room. Service with restric-
tions.
[SAVE] [S] [X] [⊡] [¶]

WW Super 8 Motel SH
(608) 365-8680. **$59-$79.** 3002 Milwaukee Rd. I-90, exit 185A, just sw
at jct I-43 and SR 81. Int corridors. **Pets:** Dogs only. $10 one-time
fee/room. Service with restrictions, supervision.
[ASK] [S] [X] [&M] [■]

BERLIN

AAA WWW Best Western Countryside M
(920) 361-4411. **$69-$129.** 227 Ripon Rd. On SR 49, at jct CR F. Int
corridors. **Pets:** Very small, dogs only. $10 daily fee/pet. Designated
rooms, service with restrictions, supervision.
[SAVE] [S] [X] [■] [⊡] [■]

BLACK RIVER FALLS

AAA WWW Best Western-Arrowhead Lodge &
  Suites SH ✿
(715) 284-9471. **$58-$97.** 600 Oasis Rd. I-94, exit 116, jct SR 54. Int
corridors. **Pets:** Large, other species. Service with restrictions, supervision.
[SAVE] [S] [X] [⌀] [⌖] [■] [⊡] [¶] [≈] [⊠]

AAA WW Days Inn SH
(715) 284-4333. **$74-$94.** 919 Hwy 54 E. I-94, exit 116, just w. Int
corridors. **Pets:** Accepted.
[SAVE] [S] [X] [⌖] [■] [⊡] [≈] [⊠]

BOSCOBEL

WW Sand's Motel M
(608) 375-4167. **$35-$61, 5 day notice.** Hwy 61 N. On US 61, 0.5 mi
nw. Ext/int corridors. **Pets:** Medium. $10 daily fee/pet. Service with restric-
tions, supervision.
[ASK] [S] [X]

BOULDER JUNCTION

WW White Birch Village VH
(715) 385-2182. **$700-$1600 (weekly) (no credit cards), 28 day
notice.** 8764 Hwy K. On CR K, 8 mi se. Ext corridors. **Pets:** Accepted.
[X] [■] [⊡] [⊠]

CADOTT

WW Countryside Motel M
(715) 289-4000. **$46-$90.** 545 Lavorata Rd. SR 29, exit 91 (SR 27),
just s. Int corridors. **Pets:** Small, dogs only. Designated rooms, service
with restrictions, supervision.
[X]

CAMERON

WW Viking Motel M
(715) 458-2111. **$55-$66.** 201 S 1st St. On US 8 and CR SS. Ext
corridors. **Pets:** Other species. Service with restrictions, supervision.
[S] [X] [⊡]

CAMP DOUGLAS

WW K & K Motel M
(608) 427-3100. **$60-$65.** 219 Hwy 12 & 16. I-90/94, exit 55, just s. Ext
corridors. **Pets:** Accepted.
[ASK] [S] [X] [■]

CHILTON

AAA WWW Best Western Stanton Inn SH
(920) 849-3600. **$75-$130, 3 day notice.** 1101 E Chestnut St. Jct US
151 and SR 32/57. Int corridors. **Pets:** Small. $50 deposit/room. Desig-
nated rooms, service with restrictions, supervision.
[SAVE] [X] [&M] [⌖] [■] [⊡] [≈]

CHIPPEWA FALLS

WW AmericInn of Chippewa Falls SH
(715) 723-5711. **$74-$139.** 11 W South Ave. 2 mi s on SR 124, access
via CR J. Int corridors. **Pets:** Medium, dogs only. Designated rooms,
service with restrictions, supervision.
[ASK] [S] [X] [⌀] [⌖] [■] [⊡] [≈] [⊠]

▼▼ Park Inn 🆂🅷
(715) 723-2281. **$89-$119.** 1009 W Park Ave. Jct SR 124 and CR J. Ext/int corridors. **Pets:** Accepted.
🄰🅂🄺 🆂🅕 ⊠ 🎗 🖥 💻 🍴 ⊸ ⊠

COLUMBUS

▼▼ Super 8 Motel-Columbus 🆂🅷
(920) 623-8800. **$62-$105.** 219 Industrial Dr. US 151, exit 118 (SR 16/60), just ne. Int corridors. **Pets:** $50 deposit/room, $10 one-time fee/room. Designated rooms, service with restrictions, supervision.
🄰🅂🄺 🆂🅕 ⊠ 🎗 🖥 💻 ⊸

CRIVITZ

▼ Shaffer Park Resort 🅼
(715) 854-2186. **$49-$77, 14 day notice.** N 7217 Shaffer Rd. 5 mi w on CR W. Ext corridors. **Pets:** Medium, dogs only. $6 daily fee/pet. Service with restrictions, supervision.
🖥 💻 🍴 ⊸ ⊠ 🕿

DE FOREST

▼▼▼ Holiday Inn Express 🆂🅷 🐾
(608) 846-8686. **$79-$119.** 7184 Morrisonville Rd. I-90/94, exit 126 (CR V), just e. Int corridors. **Pets:** Medium, other species. $20 one-time fee/room. Service with restrictions, crate.
🄰🅂🄺 🆂🅕 ⊠ 🎗 🎗 🖥 💻 ⊸

DE PERE

▼▼ Kress Inn 🆂🅷
(920) 403-5100. **$104-$139.** 300 Grant St. US 41, exit 163 (Main St), 1 mi e, then just s on 3rd St. Int corridors. **Pets:** Medium, dogs only. Supervision.
🄰🅂🄺 🆂🅕 ⊠ 🅲🅼 🎗 🖥 💻

DODGEVILLE

🄰🄰🄰 ▼▼▼ Best Western Quiet House & Suites 🆂🅷
(608) 935-7739. **$90-$160.** 1130 N Johns St. On US 18, just e of jct SR 23. Int corridors. **Pets:** Other species. $15 daily fee/pet. Designated rooms, supervision.
🆂🄰🆅🄴 🆂🅕 ⊠ 🎗 🎗 🖥 💻 ⊸

🄰🄰🄰 ▼ Pine Ridge Motel 🅼 🐾
(608) 935-3386. **$30-$65.** 405 CR YZ. On CR YZ, 0.5 mi e of jct SR 23. Ext corridors. **Pets:** Very small, dogs only. $10 one-time fee/pet. Designated rooms, service with restrictions, supervision.
🆂🄰🆅🄴 🆂🅕 ⊠ 🖥 💻

🄰🄰🄰 ▼▼ Super 8 Motel of Dodgeville 🆂🅷
(608) 935-3888. **$55-$90, 14 day notice.** 1308 Johns St. Just n of US 18. Int corridors. **Pets:** $50 deposit/room. Service with restrictions, supervision.
🆂🄰🆅🄴 🆂🅕 ⊠ 🎗 🖥

FISH CREEK

▼ Julie's Park Cafe & Motel 🅼 🐾
(920) 868-2999. **$41-$106, 10 day notice.** 4020 Hwy 42. On SR 42, 0.3 mi n. Ext corridors. **Pets:** $15 daily fee/pet. Supervision.
🄰🅂🄺 🆂🅕 ⊠ 🖥 🍴

GILLS ROCK

▼▼ Harbor House Inn 🅱🅱 🐾
(920) 854-5196. **$69-$199, 21 day notice.** 12666 SR 42. On SR 42; center. Ext/int corridors. **Pets:** $10 daily fee/pet. Service with restrictions, supervision.
⊠ 🖥 ⊠ 🕿

▼ Maple Grove Motel 🅼
(920) 854-2587. **$65-$85, 15 day notice.** 809 SR 42. On SR 42, 0.3 mi e, 1.5 mi w of car ferry. Ext corridors. **Pets:** Accepted.
⊠ 🖥 💻 🕿

STURGEON BAY

🄰🄰🄰 ▼ Super 8 Motel 🆂🅷 🐾
(920) 743-9211. **$51-$101.** 409 Green Bay Rd. 1 mi s on Business Rt SR 42/57. Int corridors. **Pets:** Large. $20 deposit/room, $5 daily fee/room. Designated rooms, service with restrictions, supervision.
🆂🄰🆅🄴 🆂🅕 ⊠ 🎗 🖥 ⊸

EAGLE RIVER

🄰🄰🄰 ▼▼ Best Western Derby Inn 🆂🅷
(715) 479-1600. **$70-$170.** 1800 Hwy 45 N. On US 45, 1 mi n. Int corridors. **Pets:** Small. $50 deposit/room. Designated rooms, service with restrictions, supervision.
🆂🄰🆅🄴 🆂🅕 ⊠ 🎗 🖥 💻 ⊸ ⊠

🄰🄰🄰 ▼▼ Days Inn 🆂🅷
(715) 479-5151. **$81-$102.** 844 Railroad St N. 0.5 mi n on US 45. Int corridors. **Pets:** Medium, other species. $10 daily fee/room. Designated rooms, service with restrictions, supervision.
🆂🄰🆅🄴 🆂🅕 ⊠ 🎗 🖥 💻 ⊸ ⊠

🄰🄰🄰 ▼ Traveler's Inn Motel 🅼
(715) 479-4403. **$48-$85.** 309 Wall St. Downtown. Ext/int corridors. **Pets:** Small, dogs only. $10 daily fee/pet. Designated rooms, service with restrictions, supervision.
🆂🄰🆅🄴 🆂🅕 ⊠ 🖥 💻

EAST TROY

▼▼▼ Country Inn & Suites 🆂🅷
(262) 642-2100. **$80-$135.** 2921 O'Leary Ln. I-43, exit 36, at jct SR 120. Int corridors. **Pets:** Accepted.
🄰🅂🄺 🆂🅕 ⊠ 🅲🅼 🎗 🖥 💻 ⊸

EAU CLAIRE

▼▼▼ AmericInn Motel & Suites 🆂🅷
(715) 874-4900. **$65-$145, 14 day notice.** 6200 Texaco Dr. I-94, exit 59, jct US 12. Int corridors. **Pets:** Dogs only. $10 one-time fee/pet. Service with restrictions, supervision.
🄰🅂🄺 🆂🅕 ⊠ 🎗 🖥 💻 ⊸ ⊠

▼▼▼ Best Western White House Inn 🆂🅷 🐾
(715) 832-8356. **$76-$130.** 1828 S Hastings Way. On US 53; 1.3 mi n of jct US 12. Int corridors. **Pets:** Designated rooms, service with restrictions.
🄰🅂🄺 🆂🅕 ⊠ 🎗 🖥 💻 ⊸ ⊠

▽▼ ◆ Comfort Inn 🆂🅷
(715) 833-9798. **$64-$89.** 3117 Craig Rd. I-94, exit 65, 1.3 mi n on SR 37; just s of jct US 12. Int corridors. **Pets:** Medium, dogs only. $10 one-time fee/pet. Service with restrictions, supervision.
🅰️$🅺 🆂🔟 ✖️ 🕌 🍴 🖳 🏊

▽▼ ▽▼ Days Inn-West 🆂🅷
(715) 874-5550. **$50-$130.** 6319 Truax Ln. I-94, exit 59, jct US 12. Int corridors. **Pets:** $25 deposit/room. Designated rooms, service with restrictions, crate.
🅰️$🅺 🆂🔟 ✖️ 🔧 🍴 🖳 🏊

▲▲▲ ▽▼ ▽▼ Econo Lodge 🆂🅷
(715) 833-8818. **$45-$125.** 4608 Royal Dr. I-94, exit 68, just n on SR 93, just w on Golf Rd, then just s. Int corridors. **Pets:** Medium, dogs only. Designated rooms, service with restrictions, supervision.
🆂🅰️🆅🅴 🆂🔟 ✖️ 🍴 🖳

▲▲▲ ▽▼ ▽▼ Exel Inn of Eau Claire 🆂🅷
(715) 834-3193. **$47-$67.** 2305 Craig Rd. I-94, exit 65, 1.3 mi n on SR 37; just w of jct US 12. Int corridors. **Pets:** Small, other species. Designated rooms, service with restrictions, supervision.
🆂🅰️🆅🅴 🆂🔟 ✖️ 🍴 🖳

▽▼ ◆ Grandstay Residential Suites 🆂🅷
(715) 834-1700. **$67-$129.** 5310 Prill Rd. I-94, exit 70, 0.8 mi n on US 53. Int corridors. **Pets:** Large, other species. $5 daily fee/pet. Designated rooms, service with restrictions, crate.
✖️ 🔧 🍴 🖳 🏊 ✖️

▽▼ ▽▼ Heartland Inn 🆂🅷
(715) 839-7100. **$76-$86.** 4075 Commonwealth Ave. I-94, exit 70, 0.8 mi n on US 53, just w on CR AA (Golf Rd), then just s. Int corridors. **Pets:** Small. $5 daily fee/room. Designated rooms, service with restrictions, supervision.
🅰️$🅺 🆂🔟 ✖️ 🔧 🍴 🖳

▽▼ ▽▼ Holiday Inn Campus Area 🆂🅷
(715) 835-2211. **$109-$129.** 2703 Craig Rd. I-94, exit 65, 1.3 mi n on SR 37; just w of jct US 12. Int corridors. **Pets:** $15 one-time fee/room. Designated rooms, service with restrictions, crate.
🅰️$🅺 🆂🔟 ✖️ 🍴 🔧 🖳 🍴 🏊 ✖️

▲▲▲ ▽▼ Maple Manor Motel Ⓜ️
(715) 834-2618. **$49.** 2507 S Hastings Way. I-94, exit 70, 3 mi n on US 53, exit US 12 (Clairemont Ave), then just se, follow signs for Storrs Ave. Ext corridors. **Pets:** Other species. Supervision.
🆂🅰️🆅🅴 🆂🔟 ✖️ 🔧 🖳 🍴

▽▼ ▽▼ Park Inn & Suites International 🆂🅷
(715) 838-9989. **$79-$139.** 3340 Mondovi Rd. I-94, exit 65, just n. Int corridors. **Pets:** Other species. $10 one-time fee/room. Designated rooms, service with restrictions, crate.
🅰️$🅺 🆂🔟 ✖️ 🍴 🔧 🍴 🖳 🏊 ✖️

▽▼ ▽▼ The Plaza Hotel & Suites 🅻🅷
(715) 834-3181. **$79-$200, 30 day notice.** 1202 W Clairemont Ave. I-94, exit 65, 1.3 mi n on SR 37; just w of jct US 12. Int corridors. **Pets:** $15 one-time fee/room. Designated rooms, service with restrictions, crate.
🅰️$🅺 🆂🔟 ✖️ 🕌 🍴 🔧 🍴 🖳 🍴 🏊 ✖️

▲▲▲ ▽▼ ▽▼ Ramada Inn Convention Center 🅻🅷
(715) 835-6121. **$79-$95.** 205 S Barstow St. S Barstow at Gibson sts; downtown. Int corridors. **Pets:** Accepted.
🆂🅰️🆅🅴 🆂🔟 ✖️ 🔧 🍴 🖳 🍴 🏊

EDGERTON

▽▼ ◆ Comfort Inn 🆂🅷
(608) 884-2118. **$58-$189.** 11102 Goede Rd. I-90, exit 163, just e. Int corridors. **Pets:** Accepted.
🅰️$🅺 🆂🔟 ✖️ 🍴 🔧 🍴 🖳

FITCHBURG

▲▲▲ ▽▼ ▽▼ Quality Inn & Suites 🆂🅷 🐾
(608) 274-7200. **$79-$139.** 2969 Cahill Main. US 12/18, exit 260 (Fish Hatchery/CR D), 1.5 mi s at jct CR PD. Int corridors. **Pets:** Large. $25 one-time fee/room. No service, crate.
🆂🅰️🆅🅴 🆂🔟 ✖️ 🍴 🔧 🍴 🖳 🏊 ✖️

FOND DU LAC

▽▼ ▽▼ Baymont Inn & Suites-Fond du Lac 🆂🅷
(920) 921-4000. **$62-$129.** 77 Holiday Ln. Sw of jct US 41 and 151. Int corridors. **Pets:** Other species. Service with restrictions.
🅰️$🅺 🆂🔟 ✖️ 🔧 🍴 🖳 🏊 ✖️

▽▼ ▽▼ Econo Lodge of Fond du Lac 🆂🅷
(920) 923-2020. **$69-$84.** 649 W Johnson St. On SR 23, 0.3 mi e of jct of US 41. Int corridors. **Pets:** Dogs only. Supervision.
🅰️$🅺 🆂🔟 ✖️ 🍴 🏊

▽▼ ▽▼ ▽▼ Holiday Inn 🆂🅷
(920) 923-1440. **$99-$225.** 625 W Rolling Meadows Dr. On US 151, just sw of jct US 41. Int corridors. **Pets:** Other species. $200 deposit/room. Designated rooms, service with restrictions, supervision.
🅰️$🅺 🆂🔟 ✖️ 🍴 🔧 🍴 🖳 🏊 ✖️

▲▲▲ ▽▼ ▽▼ Microtel Inn & Suites 🆂🅷
(920) 929-4000. **$44-$97.** 920 S Military Rd. Jct US 41 and 151. Int corridors. **Pets:** Medium, other species. $10 daily fee/room. Designated rooms, service with restrictions, crate.
🆂🅰️🆅🅴 🆂🔟 ✖️ 🍴 🔧 🍴 🖳 ✖️

▲▲▲ ▽▼ ▽▼ ▽▼ Ramada Plaza Hotel 🅻🅷
(920) 923-3000. **$69-$189.** 1 N Main St. Downtown. Int corridors. **Pets:** Small, dogs only. $20 daily fee/room. Designated rooms, service with restrictions, supervision.
🆂🅰️🆅🅴 🆂🔟 ✖️ 🔧 🍴 🖳 🍴 🏊 ✖️

▽▼ ▽▼ Super 8 Motel-FOND DU LAC 🆂🅷
(920) 922-1088. **$55-$110, 30 day notice.** 391 N Pioneer Rd. US 41, exit SR 23, just n on east frontage road (CR VV). Int corridors. **Pets:** Medium. $10 one-time fee/room. Designated rooms, service with restrictions, supervision.
✖️ 🍴 🔧

GREEN BAY

▲▲▲ ▽▼ ◆ AmericInn 🆂🅷
(920) 434-9790. **$70-$140.** 2032 Velp Ave. US 41, exit 170, 0.3 mi w. Int corridors. **Pets:** $10 daily fee/room. Designated rooms, service with restrictions, supervision.
🆂🅰️🆅🅴 🆂🔟 ✖️ 🍴 🔧 🍴 🖳

▲▲▲ ▽▼ ▽▼ Baymont Inn-Green Bay 🆂🅷
(920) 494-7887. **$76-$149.** 2840 S Oneida St. US 41, exit 164 (Oneida St), just e. Int corridors. **Pets:** Accepted.
🆂🅰️🆅🅴 🆂🔟 ✖️ 🔧 🍴 🖳

▲▲▲ ▽▼ Bay Motel Ⓜ️
(920) 494-3441. **$45-$65.** 1301 S Military Ave. US 41, exit 167 (Lombardi Ave), 0.4 mi e to Marlee, then 0.6 mi n. Ext corridors. **Pets:** Accepted.
🆂🅰️🆅🅴 ✖️ 🔧 🍴

▽▼ ▽▼ Comfort Inn by Choice Hotels 🆂🅷 🐾
(920) 498-2060. **$60-$160.** 2841 Ramada Way. US 41, exit 164 (Oneida St), just e. Int corridors. **Pets:** Small. $10 daily fee/room, $50 one-time fee/pet. Designated rooms, service with restrictions, supervision.
🅰️$🅺 🆂🔟 ✖️ 🕌 🍴 🔧 🖳

▲▲▲ ▽▼ ▽▼ ▽▼ Country Inn & Suites By Carlson 🆂🅷
(920) 336-6600. **$84-$154.** 2945 Allied St. US 41, exit 164 (Oneida St), just nw. Int corridors. **Pets:** Accepted.
🆂🅰️🆅🅴 🆂🔟 ✖️ 🍴 🔧 🖳 ✖️

Days Inn-Lambeau Field SH
(920) 498-8088. **$56-$109.** 1978 Holmgren Way. US 41, exit 167 (Lombardi Ave), 1.4 mi e, then just s. Int corridors. **Pets:** Other species. Service with restrictions, supervision.

Exel Inn of Green Bay SH
(920) 499-3599. **$46-$66.** 2870 Ramada Way. US 41, exit 164 (Oneida St), just e. Int corridors. **Pets:** Small. Supervision.

Holiday Inn City Centre LH
(920) 437-5900. **$89-$129.** 200 Main St. Downtown. Int corridors. **Pets:** Large. Designated rooms, service with restrictions, crate.

Residence Inn by Marriott SH
(920) 435-2222. **$159.** 335 W St Joseph St. SR 172, exit Riverside Dr, 1.1 mi n on SR 57, then just e. Ext corridors. **Pets:** $150 one-time fee/room. Service with restrictions.

Super 8 Motel SH
(920) 494-2042. **$61-$72.** 2868 S Oneida St. US 41, exit 164 (Oneida St), just e. Int corridors. **Pets:** Other species. $25 deposit/room. Supervision.

HAYWARD

AmericInn of Hayward SH
(715) 634-5140. **$66-$140.** 15601 US Hwy 63. On US 63, just n of jct SR 77. Int corridors. **Pets:** Medium. $6 daily fee/pet. Designated rooms, service with restrictions, supervision.

Best Western Northern Pine Inn SH ❖
(715) 634-4959. **$69-$119.** 9966 N Hwy 27. On SR 27 S, 1.7 mi s of jct US 63. Ext/int corridors. **Pets:** $10 daily fee/pet. Service with restrictions.

Comfort Suites SH
(715) 634-0700. **$70-$165.** 15586 CR B. On CR B, 0.5 mi s of jct SR 27. Int corridors. **Pets:** Accepted.

Ross' Teal Lake Lodge and Teal Wing Golf Club CA ❖
(715) 462-3631. **$140-$350, 21 day notice.** 12425 N Ross Rd. On SR 77, 20 mi ne of jct US 63. Int corridors. **Pets:** Other species. $5 daily fee/pet. Designated rooms, service with restrictions, supervision.

Super 8 Motel SH
(715) 634-2646. **$50.** 10444 N SR 27. On SR 27, 0.3 mi s of jct US 63. Ext/int corridors. **Pets:** Accepted.

HILLSBORO

Sleep Inn Hillsboro SH
(608) 489-3000. **$65-$125.** 1234 Water Ave. On SR 33, 1 mi e jct SR 80. Int corridors. **Pets:** Large. $50 deposit/pet, $50 one-time fee/pet. Designated rooms, service with restrictions, supervision.

HUDSON

Comfort Inn SH
(715) 386-6355. **$65-$89.** 811 Dominion Dr. I-94, exit 2 (CR F), 1 mi w on south frontage road (Crestview Dr). Int corridors. **Pets:** $50 deposit/room, $5 daily fee/room. Service with restrictions, supervision.

Super 8 Motel of Hudson SH
(715) 386-8800. **$72-$169.** 808 Dominion Dr. I-94, exit 2 (CR F), 1 mi w on south frontage road (Crestview Dr). Int corridors. **Pets:** Medium, dogs only. $5 one-time fee/pet. Designated rooms, service with restrictions, supervision.

HURLEY

Days Inn of Hurley SH
(715) 561-3500. **$74-$92.** 850 10th Ave N. Jct US 2 and 51; 0.4 mi s on US 51. Int corridors. **Pets:** Small, other species. $10 daily fee/room. Designated rooms, service with restrictions, supervision.

JANESVILLE

Baymont Inn & Suites-Janesville SH
(608) 758-4545. **$65-$95.** 616 Midland Rd. I-90, exit 175B (SR 11), just ne. Int corridors. **Pets:** Medium. $10 one-time fee/pet. Service with restrictions, crate.

Best Western Janesville SH ❖
(608) 756-4511. **$60-$80.** 3900 Milton Ave. I-90, exit 171A (SR 26), just e. Int corridors. **Pets:** Large, other species. $10 daily fee/pet. Service with restrictions, supervision.

Microtel Inn SH
(608) 752-3121. **$46-$66.** 3121 Wellington Pl. I-90, exit 171C (US 14), just se. Int corridors. **Pets:** Other species. $10.50 daily fee/room. Service with restrictions.

Select Inn SH
(608) 754-0251. **$45-$60.** 3520 Milton Ave. I-90, exit 171A (SR 26), just sw. Int corridors. **Pets:** Accepted.

JEFFERSON

Rodeway Inn M
(920) 674-4404. **$60-$89.** 1456 S Ryan Ave. On SR 26, 1.2 mi s of jct US 18. Int corridors. **Pets:** Accepted.

JOHNSON CREEK

Days Inn-Johnson Creek SH
(920) 699-8000. **$75-$90.** W4545 Linmar Ln. I-94, exit 267 (SR 26), just ne. Int corridors. **Pets:** $50 deposit/room. Service with restrictions, supervision.

KAUKAUNA

Settle Inn SH
(920) 766-0088. **$65-$145.** 1201 Maloney Rd. US 41, exit 148, just e. Int corridors. **Pets:** Medium. $15 daily fee/room. Designated rooms, service with restrictions, supervision.

KENOSHA

Country Inn & Suites By Carlson SH
(262) 857-3680. **$87-$135.** 7011 122nd Ave. I-94, exit 344 (SR 50), just nw. Int corridors. **Pets:** Accepted.

Holiday Inn Express-Harborside SH
(262) 658-3281. **$99-$255.** 5125 6th Ave. Just ne of jct SR 32 and 158; downtown. Int corridors. **Pets:** Accepted.

KEWAUNEE

▼▼▼ The Historic Karsten Inn SH
(920) 388-3800. **$69-$149, 3 day notice.** 122 Ellis St. Center. Int corridors. **Pets:** Small, dogs only. $25 one-time fee/room. Designated rooms, service with restrictions.
[A$K] [S⚬] [✕] [▇] [¶]

LA CROSSE

⚹⚹⚹ ▼▼▼ Best Western-Midway Hotel Riverfront
Resort SH
(608) 781-7000. **$79-$139.** 1835 Rose St. I-90, exit 3, 1 mi s on US 53. Int corridors. **Pets:** Small, dogs only. $50 deposit/room. Designated rooms, service with restrictions, supervision.
[SAVE] [S⚬] [✕] [⚆] [▇] [▆] [¶] [≈] [✕]

⚹⚹⚹ ▼▼▼ Days Inn Hotel & Conference Center SH ✿
(608) 783-1000. **$79-$94.** 101 Sky Harbour Dr. I-90, exit 2, just sw; on French Island. Int corridors. **Pets:** Small, dogs only. $10 daily fee/pet. Designated rooms, service with restrictions, supervision.
[SAVE] [S⚬] [✕] [▇] [▆] [¶] [≈]

⚹⚹⚹ ▼▼ Exel Inn of La Crosse SH
(608) 781-0400. **$43-$63.** 2150 Rose St. I-90, exit 3, 0.8 mi s on US 53. Int corridors. **Pets:** Small, other species. Designated rooms, service with restrictions, supervision.
[SAVE] [S⚬] [✕] [▇] [▆]

▼▼▼▼ Grandstay Residential Suites of La Crosse SH
(608) 796-1615. **$139.** 525 Front St N. I-90, exit 3; downtown. Int corridors. **Pets:** Medium. $100 one-time fee/pet. Designated rooms, service with restrictions.
[A$K] [S⚬] [✕] [⚆] [▇] [▆] [≈]

⚹⚹⚹ ▼ Guest House Motel SH
(608) 784-8840. **$60-$90, 3 day notice.** 810 S 4th St. 0.5 mi s on US 14, 61 and SR 33. Int corridors. **Pets:** Accepted.
[SAVE] [S⚬] [✕] [▇] [¶] [≈]

⚹⚹⚹ ▼▼▼ The Radisson Hotel La Crosse LH ✿
(608) 784-6680. **$149-$179.** 200 Harbourview Plaza. Just w of US 53; downtown. Int corridors. **Pets:** Small. $50 daily fee/room. Designated rooms, service with restrictions, crate.
[SAVE] [S⚬] [✕] [⚆] [▇] [▆] [¶] [≈] [✕]

LADYSMITH

▼▼▼ AmericInn Motel & Suites SH
(715) 532-6650. **$65-$129.** 800 W College Ave. On SR 27, 0.5 mi s of US 8. Int corridors. **Pets:** Medium, dogs only. $10 daily fee/pet. Designated rooms, service with restrictions, supervision.
[A$K] [✕] [⚆] [▇] [▆] [≈] [✕]

LAKE DELTON

▼▼ Lake Delton Travelodge SH
(608) 355-0700. **$49-$69.** E 10892 Fern Dell Rd. I-90/94, exit 92 (US 12), just s. Int corridors. **Pets:** Accepted.
[A$K] [S⚬] [✕] [⚆M] [⚆] [▆] [≈]

LAND O'LAKES

▼▼ Sunrise Lodge CA
(715) 547-3684. **$180-$200, 21 day notice.** 5894 W Shore Dr. 2 mi s on US 45, 2.8 mi e on CR E, then 1 mi n. Ext corridors. **Pets:** Other species. Service with restrictions, supervision.
[▇] [▆] [¶] [✕] [✕]

LUCK

⚹⚹⚹ ▼▼▼ Luck Country Inn SH
(715) 472-2000. **$50-$79.** 10 Robertson Rd. Jct SR 35 and 48. Int corridors. **Pets:** Small, dogs only. Service with restrictions, supervision.
[SAVE] [✕] [▇] [▆] [¶]

MADISON

▼▼▼▼ Baymont Inn & Suites-Madison West SH
(608) 831-7711. **$89-$139.** 8102 Excelsior Dr. US 12 and 14, exit 253 (Old Sauk Rd), just nw. Int corridors. **Pets:** Accepted.
[A$K] [S⚬] [✕] [⚆M] [⚆] [▇] [▆] [≈] [✕]

⚹⚹⚹ ▼▼▼ Best Western East Towne Suites SH
(608) 244-2020. **$89-$104, 7 day notice.** 4801 Annamark Dr. I-90/94, exit 135A, just sw on US 151. Int corridors. **Pets:** $20 deposit/room. Designated rooms, service with restrictions, supervision.
[SAVE] [S⚬] [✕] [⚇] [▇] [▆] [≈]

⚹⚹⚹ ▼▼▼ Best Western West Towne Suites SH
(608) 833-4200. **$59-$109.** 650 Grand Canyon Dr. US 12 and 14, exit 255 (Gammon Rd), just e on Odana Rd, then just sw. Int corridors. **Pets:** Medium. $25 deposit/pet. Designated rooms, service with restrictions, supervision.
[SAVE] [S⚬] [✕] [▇] [▆]

⚹⚹⚹ ▼▼▼▼ Clarion Suites Central SH ✿
(608) 284-1234. **$89-$199.** 2110 Rimrock Rd. US 12 and 18, exit 262 (Rimrock Rd), just nw. Int corridors. **Pets:** Dogs only. $25 daily fee/pet. Designated rooms, service with restrictions, supervision.
[SAVE] [S⚬] [✕] [⚆] [▇] [▆] [≈]

▼▼▼▼ Comfort Suites SH ✿
(608) 836-3033. **$99-$260.** 1253 John Q Hammons Dr. US 12 and 14, exit 252 (Greenway Blvd), just sw. Int corridors. **Pets:** Service with restrictions.
[A$K] [S⚬] [✕] [⚆] [▇] [▆] [≈] [✕]

⚹⚹⚹ ▼▼▼▼ Crowne Plaza Hotel and Resort LH ✿
(608) 244-4703. **$99-$209.** 4402 E Washington Ave. I-90/94, exit 135A, 0.4 mi w on US 151. Int corridors. **Pets:** Other species. $15 daily fee/pet. Designated rooms, service with restrictions.
[SAVE] [S⚬] [✕] [⚇] [▇] [▆] [¶] [≈] [✕]

⚹⚹⚹ ▼▼▼ Days Inn-Madison SH
(608) 223-1800. **$72-$135.** 4402 E Broadway Service Rd. US 12 and 18, exit 266 (US 51), just ne. Int corridors. **Pets:** Medium. $10 daily fee/pet. Service with restrictions, supervision.
[SAVE] [S⚬] [✕] [⚆] [▇] [▆] [≈]

⚹⚹⚹ ▼▼▼ Econo Lodge of Madison SH
(608) 241-4171. **$49-$99.** 4726 E Washington Ave. I-90/94, exit 135A (US 151), just w. Int corridors. **Pets:** Other species. $10 daily fee/room. Service with restrictions, supervision.
[SAVE] [S⚬] [✕] [⚇] [▇] [▆]

⚹⚹⚹ ▼▼▼ Exel Inn of Madison SH
(608) 241-3861. **$46-$76.** 4202 E Towne Blvd. I-90/94, exit 135A (US 151), 0.5 mi w. Int corridors. **Pets:** Small, other species. Designated rooms, service with restrictions, supervision.
[SAVE] [S⚬] [✕] [▇] [▆]

▼▼▼▼ GrandStay Residential Suites SH
(608) 241-2500. **$99-$109.** 5317 High Crossing Blvd. I-90/94, exit 135C (US 151), just e. Int corridors. **Pets:** Other species. $25 deposit/room. Service with restrictions, crate.
[A$K] [S⚬] [✕] [⚆M] [⚆] [▇] [▆] [≈] [✕]

⚹⚹⚹ ▼▼▼▼ Holiday Inn Express-Madison SH
(608) 255-7400. **$85-$115.** 722 John Nolen Dr. US 12 and 18, exit 263 (John Nolen Dr), just ne. Int corridors. **Pets:** Small, other species. Designated rooms, service with restrictions, supervision.
[SAVE] [S⚬] [✕] [⚆] [⚇] [▇] [▆] [≈]

⚹⚹⚹ ▼▼▼▼ Holiday Inn Madison East SH ✿
(608) 244-2481. **$79-$149.** 3841 E Washington Ave. I-90/94, exit 135A, 1 mi w on US 151. Int corridors. **Pets:** Large, other species. $15 daily fee/pet. Service with restrictions, supervision.
[SAVE] [S⚬] [✕] [⚆] [⚇] [▇] [▆] [¶] [≈] [✕]

Madison Wingate Inn SH
(608) 224-1500. **$79-$109.** 3510 Mill Pond Rd. I-90, exit 142B, just e on US 12 and 18, then w on south frontage road. Int corridors. **Pets:** Accepted.
[SAVE] [S6] [X] [icons] [icons] [icons] [icons]

Microtel Inn & Suites SH
(608) 242-9000. **$49-$69.** 2139 E Springs Dr. I-90/94, exit 135A, just s, then 0.5 mi e. Int corridors. **Pets:** Accepted.
[SAVE] [S6] [X] [icons] [icons]

Red Roof Inn-Madison #7052 M
(608) 241-1787. **$40-$75.** 4830 Hayes Rd. I-90/94, exit 135A, just sw on US 151. Ext corridors. **Pets:** Accepted.
[X] [icons] [icons]

Residence Inn by Marriott SH
(608) 244-5047. **$79-$159, 7 day notice.** 4862 Hayes Rd. I-90/94, exit 135A (US 151), just sw to Hayes Dr, then just ne. Int corridors. **Pets:** Other species. $75 one-time fee/room. Service with restrictions.
[ASK] [S6] [X] [icons] [icons] [icons] [icons] [icons] [icons]

Select Inn SH
(608) 249-1815. **$46-$88.** 4845 Hayes Rd. I-90/94, exit 135A, just sw on US 151. Int corridors. **Pets:** Other species. $25 deposit/pet, $5 daily fee/pet. Service with restrictions, supervision.
[SAVE] [S6] [X] [icons] [icons] [icons]

Staybridge Suites SH
(608) 241-2300. **$99-$129.** 3301 City View Dr. US 151, exit 98A, just e, then 0.5 mi s on High Crossing Blvd. Int corridors. **Pets:** Accepted.
[SAVE] [S6] [X] [icons] [icons] [icons] [icons] [icons] [icons]

Super 8 Motel SH
(608) 258-8882. **$59-$99.** 1602 W Beltline Hwy. US 12 and 18, exit 260B (CR D), just w on north frontage road. Int corridors. **Pets:** Accepted.
[SAVE] [S6] [X] [icons] [icons] [icons] [icons]

Woodfield Suites-Madison SH
(608) 245-0123. **$89-$109.** 5217 E Terrace Dr. US 151, exit 98B (American Pkwy), just sw. Int corridors. **Pets:** Medium. $50 deposit/room, $10 one-time fee/room. Designated rooms, service with restrictions, supervision.
[SAVE] [S6] [X] [GM] [icons] [icons] [icons] [icons] [icons]

MANITOWOC

Comfort Inn by Choice Hotels SH 🐾
(920) 683-0220. **$59-$109.** 2200 S 44th St. I-43, exit 149, just e. Int corridors. **Pets:** Other species. Service with restrictions, crate.
[ASK] [S6] [X] [icons] [icons]

Holiday Inn SH
(920) 682-6000. **$99-$149.** 4601 Calumet Ave. I-43, exit 149, just e. Int corridors. **Pets:** Accepted.
[ASK] [S6] [X] [icons] [icons] [icons] [icons] [icons] [icons]

MARSHFIELD

Holiday Inn & Conference Center SH
(715) 486-1500. **$69-$134.** 750 S Central Ave. Jct SR 13 and SR 97, 0.5 mi s on SR 13. Int corridors. **Pets:** Other species. Designated rooms.
[SAVE] [X] [GM] [icons] [icons] [icons] [icons] [icons] [icons]

Park Motel M
(715) 387-1741. **$39-$46, 3 day notice.** 1806 S Roddis Ave. 1 mi s on SR 13. Ext corridors. **Pets:** Medium. $5 one-time fee/pet. Service with restrictions, supervision.
[SAVE] [S6] [X] [icons]

MAUSTON

Country Inn By Carlson SH
(608) 847-5959. **$89-$99.** 1001 SR 82. I-90/94, exit 69, just ne. Int corridors. **Pets:** Other species. $5 daily fee/room. Service with restrictions, supervision.
[SAVE] [S6] [X] [icons] [icons] [icons]

Super 8 Motel M
(608) 847-2300. **$69-$89, 7 day notice.** 1001A Hwy 82 E. I-90/94, exit 69, just ne. Int corridors. **Pets:** Large, other species. $5 daily fee/pet. Service with restrictions, supervision.
[ASK] [S6] [X] [icons] [icons] [icons]

MENOMONIE

Country Inn & Suites SH
(715) 235-5664. **$99-$189, 3 day notice.** 320 Oak Ave. I-94, exit 41 (SR 25), just se. Int corridors. **Pets:** Dogs only. $15 daily fee/pet. Designated rooms, service with restrictions, supervision.
[SAVE] [S6] [X] [icons] [icons] [icons] [icons]

Menomonie Motel 6 #4109 SH
(715) 235-6901. **$42-$56.** 2100 Stout St. I-94, exit 41 (SR 25), just se. Int corridors. **Pets:** Medium. Service with restrictions, supervision.
[X] [icons]

Super 8 Motel-Menomonie SH
(715) 235-8889. **$49-$69.** 1622 N Broadway. I-94, exit 41 (SR 25), just s. Int corridors. **Pets:** Dogs only. $10 daily fee/room. Designated rooms, service with restrictions, supervision.
[ASK] [S6] [X] [icons] [icons]

MERRILL

AmericInn Lodge & Suites of Merrill SH 🐾
(715) 536-7979. **$79-$139.** 3300 E Main St. US 51, exit 208, 0.5 mi w on SR 64. Int corridors. **Pets:** Large, other species. $10 daily fee/pet. Designated rooms, service with restrictions, supervision.
[SAVE] [S6] [X] [icons] [icons] [icons] [icons]

Pine Ridge Inn SH
(715) 536-9526. **$45-$90.** 200 S Pine Ridge. I-39, exit 208, just w. Int corridors. **Pets:** Medium. $5 daily fee/pet. Service with restrictions, supervision.
[SAVE] [S6] [X] [icons] [icons] [icons]

Super 8 Motel SH
(715) 536-6880. **$66-$95.** 3209 E Main St. I-39, exit 208, 0.5 mi w on SR 64. Int corridors. **Pets:** Accepted.
[SAVE] [S6] [X] [GM] [icons] [icons] [icons] [icons] [icons]

MIDDLETON

Country Inn & Suites SH
(608) 831-6970. **$79-$179.** 2212 Deming Way. Just w of jct SR 14 and 12. Int corridors. **Pets:** $25 one-time fee/pet. Designated rooms, service with restrictions, supervision.
[SAVE] [S6] [X] [icons] [icons] [icons]

Marriott Madison West LH
(608) 831-2000. **$109-$179.** 1313 John Q Hammons Dr. US 12 and 14, exit 252 (Greenway Blvd), just w. Int corridors. **Pets:** Small, dogs only. Crate.
[SAVE] [X] [icons] [icons] [icons] [icons] [icons] [icons]

Staybridge Suites by Holiday Inn SH
(608) 664-5888. **$109-$159.** 7790 Elmwood Ave. US 12 and 14, exit 251 (University Ave), just nw. Int corridors. **Pets:** Accepted.
[SAVE] [S6] [X] [GM] [icons] [icons] [icons] [icons] [icons]

MILWAUKEE METROPOLITAN AREA

BROOKFIELD

(AAA) ▼▼▼▼ Baymont Inn & Suites Milwaukee-Brookfield SH
(262) 782-9100. **$60-$100.** 20391 W Bluemound Rd. I-94, exit 297, just e on US 18. Int corridors. **Pets:** Accepted.
[SAVE] [S🐾] [✕] [🐾] [🛏] [▦]

▼▼ Homestead Studio Suites Hotel-Milwaukee/Brookfield SH
(262) 782-9300. **$69-$84.** 325 N Brookfield Rd. I-94, exit 297, 1.1 mi e on US 18, then just e. Int corridors. **Pets:** Accepted.
[ASK] [S🐾] [✕] [🐾] [🛆] [🛏] [▦]

▼▼ TownePlace Suites by Marriott SH
(262) 784-8450. **$59-$119.** 600 N Calhoun Rd. I-94, exit 297 eastbound, 2.1 mi e on US 18; exit 301B westbound, 1.5 mi n on Moorland Rd, then 0.4 mi w on US 18. Int corridors. **Pets:** Accepted.
[ASK] [S🐾] [✕] [🛆] [🛏] [▦] [🛋]

DELAFIELD

(AAA) ▼▼▼ Baymont Inn & Suites Milwaukee-Delafield SH
(262) 646-8500. **$79-$119.** 2801 Hillside Dr. I-94, exit 287, just s on SR 83, then just e. Int corridors. **Pets:** Accepted.
[SAVE] [S🐾] [✕] [🅼] [🐾] [🛆] [🛏] [▦] [🛋]

GERMANTOWN

(AAA) ▼▼▼▼ Holiday Inn Express Milwaukee NW-Germantown SH
(262) 255-1100. **$99-$159.** W 177 N9675 Riversbend Ln. US 41 and 45, exit CR Q (County Line Rd), then just w. Int corridors. **Pets:** Accepted.
[SAVE] [S🐾] [✕] [🅼] [🛆] [🛏] [▦] [🛋] [🚫]

(AAA) ▼▼▼ Super 8 Motel-Germantown/Milwaukee SH
(262) 255-0880. **$69-$89.** N96 W17490 County Line Rd. US 41 and 45, exit CR Q (County Line Rd), then just w. Int corridors. **Pets:** $5 daily fee/pet. Service with restrictions, supervision.
[SAVE] [S🐾] [✕] [🛆] [🛏] [▦] [🛋]

GLENDALE

(AAA) ▼▼▼ Baymont Inn Milwaukee-Glendale SH
(414) 964-8484. **$64-$99.** 5110 N Port Washington Rd. I-43, exit 78A (Silver Spring Dr), 0.4 mi se. Int corridors. **Pets:** $25 deposit/room. Service with restrictions, crate.
[SAVE] [S🐾] [✕] [🛏] [▦]

(AAA) ▼▼▼ Exel Inn of Milwaukee Northeast SH
(414) 961-7272. **$61-$91.** 5485 N Port Washington Rd. I-43, exit 78A (Silver Spring Dr), just se. Int corridors. **Pets:** Small, other species. Designated rooms, service with restrictions, supervision.
[SAVE] [S🐾] [✕] [🛏] [▦]

▼▼▼ Residence Inn by Marriott SH
(414) 352-0070. **$149-$199.** 7275 N Port Washington Rd. I-43, exit 80 (Good Hope Rd), just e. Ext corridors. **Pets:** $75 one-time fee/room. Service with restrictions.
[ASK] [S🐾] [✕] [🐾] [🛆] [🛏] [▦] [🛋] [🚫]

(AAA) ▼▼▼ Woodfield Suites Milwaukee-Glendale SH
(414) 962-6767. **$110-$200.** 5423 N Port Washington Rd. I-43, exit 78A (Silver Spring Dr), just se. Int corridors. **Pets:** Medium, other species. $50 deposit/room, $10 daily fee/room. Service with restrictions, supervision.
[SAVE] [S🐾] [✕] [🅼] [🐾] [🛆] [🛏] [▦] [🛋] [🚫]

HARTFORD

▼▼ Super 8 Motel-Hartford SH
(262) 673-7431. **$59-$119, 3 day notice.** 1539 E Sumner St. On SR 60, 1.1 mi e of center. Int corridors. **Pets:** Medium. $50 deposit/pet, $10 daily fee/pet. Designated rooms, service with restrictions, supervision.
[ASK] [S🐾] [✕] [▦]

JACKSON

▼▼▼ Comfort Inn & Suites of Jackson SH
(262) 677-1133. **$69-$129.** W227 N16890 Tillie Lake Ct. Nw of jct US 45 and SR 60. Int corridors. **Pets:** Other species. $30 one-time fee/room. Service with restrictions, supervision.
[ASK] [S🐾] [✕] [🛆] [🛏] [▦] [🛋] [🚫]

MEQUON

(AAA) ▼▼▼▼ Best Western Quiet House & Suites SH
(262) 241-3677. **$86-$140.** 10330 N Port Washington Rd. I-43, exit 85 (Mequon Rd), just w on SR 167, then 1 mi s. Int corridors. **Pets:** Other species. $15 daily fee/pet. Designated rooms, service with restrictions, supervision.
[SAVE] [S🐾] [✕] [🅼] [🐾] [🛆] [🛏] [▦] [🛋]

(AAA) ▼▼▼ The Chalet Motel of Mequon M
(262) 241-4510. **$69-$159.** 10401 N Port Washington Rd. I-43, exit 85 (Mequon Rd), just w on SR 167, then 1 mi s. Ext corridors. **Pets:** Accepted.
[SAVE] [S🐾] [✕] [🛏] [▦] [🍴]

MILWAUKEE

(AAA) ▼▼▼▼ AmeriSuites Milwaukee/West SH
(414) 462-3500. **$84-$129.** 11777 W Silver Spring Dr. US 45, exit 46 (Silver Spring Dr), just w. Int corridors. **Pets:** Small. $10 one-time fee/room. Designated rooms, service with restrictions, supervision.
[SAVE] [S🐾] [✕] [🅼] [🐾] [🛏] [▦]

(AAA) ▼▼▼ Baymont Inn & Suites Milwaukee NW SH
(414) 535-1300. **$49-$87.** 5442 N Lovers Lane Rd. US 45, exit 46 (Silver Spring Dr), just se. Int corridors. **Pets:** Medium. $25 deposit/room. Designated rooms, service with restrictions, supervision.
[SAVE] [S🐾] [✕] [🐾] [🛏] [▦]

(AAA) ▼▼▼▼ Best Western Inn Towne Hotel SH ✿
(414) 224-8400. **$59-$119.** 710 N Old World 3rd St. Corner of Wisconsin Ave and N Old World 3rd St. Int corridors. **Pets:** Medium. $100 deposit/room. Designated rooms, service with restrictions.
[SAVE] [S🐾] [✕] [🛆] [🛏] [▦] [🍴]

▼▼▼ Hotel Metro-Milwaukee SH ✿
(414) 272-1937. **$169-$259.** 411 E Mason St. Corner of Mason and Milwaukee sts. Int corridors. **Pets:** Small. $25 daily fee/pet. Designated rooms, service with restrictions, supervision.
[✕] [🅼] [🐾] [🛆] [▦] [🍴]

OAK CREEK

(AAA) ▼▼▼ Baymont Inn & Suites Milwaukee-Airport SH
(414) 762-2266. **$55-$90.** 7141 S 13th St. I-94, exit 320 (Rawson Ave), just se. Int corridors. **Pets:** Small. Service with restrictions, supervision.
[SAVE] [S🐾] [✕] [🛏] [▦]

▼▼▼ Comfort Suites Milwaukee Airport SH
(414) 570-1111. **$89-$259, 30 day notice.** 6362 S 13th St. I-94, exit 319 (College Ave), just e on CR 22, then just s. Int corridors. **Pets:** Accepted.
[ASK] [S🐾] [✕] [🅼] [🐾] [🛆] [🛏] [▦] [🛋] [🚫]

Exel Inn of Milwaukee South SH
(414) 764-1776. **$42-$69.** 1201 W College Ave. I-94, exit 319 (College Ave), just e. Int corridors. **Pets:** Small, other species. Designated rooms, service with restrictions, supervision.

MainStay Suites Oak Creek SH
(414) 571-8800. **$69-$169.** 1001 W College Ave. I-94, exit 319 (College Ave), just e. Int corridors. **Pets:** Accepted.

Red Roof Inn-Milwaukee #7031 M
(414) 764-3500. **$43-$72.** 6360 S 13th St. I-94, exit 319 (College Ave), just e. Ext corridors. **Pets:** Accepted.

PORT WASHINGTON

Holiday Inn Harborview SH 🐾
(262) 284-9461. **$75-$149.** 135 E Grand Ave. On SR 43, waterfront of Lake Michigan; downtown. Int corridors. **Pets:** Medium, dogs only. $25 one-time fee/room. Designated rooms, service with restrictions, supervision.

WAUKESHA

Best Western Waukesha Grand SH
(262) 524-9300. **$75-$99.** 2840 N Grandview Blvd. I-94, exit 293, just s on CR T. Int corridors. **Pets:** Small, other species. Designated rooms, service with restrictions, supervision.

Select Inn SH
(262) 786-6015. **$45-$125.** 2510 Plaza Ct. I-94, exit 297, just w on CR JJ (Bluemound Rd). Int corridors. **Pets:** Medium. $25 deposit/room, $5 daily fee/room. Designated rooms, service with restrictions, supervision.

WAUWATOSA

Exel Inn of Milwaukee West SH
(414) 257-0140. **$53-$89.** 115 N Mayfair Rd. I-94, exit 304B, just n on SR 100. Int corridors. **Pets:** Small, other species. Designated rooms, service with restrictions, supervision.

END METROPOLITAN AREA

MINERAL POINT

Comfort Inn SH
(608) 987-4747. **$50-$95.** 1345 Business Park Rd. On US 151; 0.6 mi n of jct SR 23 and 39. Int corridors. **Pets:** Accepted.

MINOCQUA

AmericInn of Minocqua SH
(715) 356-3730. **$69-$179.** 700 Hwy 51. On US 51; downtown. Int corridors. **Pets:** Other species. $6 daily fee/room, $25 one-time fee/room. Designated rooms, service with restrictions, supervision.

Comfort Inn-Minocqua SH 🐾
(715) 358-2588. **$49-$99.** 8729 US 51 N. On US 51 at SR 70 W. Int corridors. **Pets:** Other species. $10 daily fee/room. Designated rooms, service with restrictions, supervision.

Lakeview Motor Lodge M
(715) 356-5208. **Call for rates.** 311 E Park Ave. North end of US 51 bridge; downtown. Ext/int corridors. **Pets:** Accepted.

Super 8 Motel M
(715) 356-9541. **$90-$100, 30 day notice.** 8730 Hwy 51 N. On US 51 at jct SR 70 W. Ext/int corridors. **Pets:** Accepted.

MONONA

AmericInn of Madison South/Monona SH 🐾
(608) 222-8601. **$79-$99.** 101 W Broadway. US 12 and 18, exit 265 (Monona Dr), just nw. Int corridors. **Pets:** Other species. $5 daily fee/room. Service with restrictions, crate.

MOSINEE

Comfort Inn SH
(715) 355-4449. **$63-$83.** 1510 County Hwy XX. I-39, exit 185 (US Business Rt 51), just se. Int corridors. **Pets:** Medium, dogs only. $15 daily fee/pet. Designated rooms, service with restrictions, supervision.

NEENAH

Holiday Inn Neenah Riverwalk SH
(920) 725-8441. **$93-$129.** 123 E Wisconsin Ave. US 41, exit 132 (Main St), 2 mi e; downtown. Int corridors. **Pets:** Accepted.

NEW LISBON

Edge O' the Wood Motel M
(608) 562-3705. **$35-$80.** W 7396 Frontage Rd. I-90/94, exit 61 (SR 80), just e. Ext corridors. **Pets:** Accepted.

Travelodge of New Lisbon SH
(608) 562-5141. **$55-$100.** 1700 E Bridge St. I-90/94, exit 61 (SR 80), just ne. Int corridors. **Pets:** Other species. $50 deposit/room. Designated rooms, service with restrictions, supervision.

NEW LONDON

AmericInn Lodge & Suites of New London SH
(920) 982-5700. **$69-$189.** 1404 N Shawano St. US 45, exit US 54, just n. Int corridors. **Pets:** Small. $10 one-time fee/pet. Designated rooms, service with restrictions, supervision.

RidgeMark Inns SH 🐾
(920) 982-5820. **$49-$115.** 1409 N Shawano St. US 45, exit US 54, just n. Int corridors. **Pets:** Dogs only. $8 daily fee/pet. Service with restrictions, supervision.

NEW RICHMOND

AmericInn Motel & Suites SH
(715) 246-3993. **$62-$139.** 1020 S Knowles Ave. Just s on SR 65. Int corridors. **Pets:** $25 deposit/room. Service with restrictions, supervision.

Super 8 Motel SH
(715) 246-7829. **$62-$99.** 1561 Dorset Ln. Just s on SR 65. Int corridors. **Pets:** Medium. $15 daily fee/pet. Service with restrictions, supervision.

ONALASKA

△△△ ▽▼▽▼ Baymont Inn & Suites LaCrosse-Onalaska SH
(608) 783-7191. **$75-$185.** 3300 Kinney Coulee Rd N. I-90, exit 5, just ne. Int corridors. **Pets:** $5 daily fee/pet. Designated rooms, service with restrictions, supervision.
SAVE SD X &M ⊘ & 🛏 🖳 ⌁

▽▼▽ Comfort Inn by Choice Hotels SH
(608) 781-7500. **$69-$144.** 1223 Crossing Meadows Dr. I-90, exit 4, just e on SR 157, then w on CR SS. Int corridors. **Pets:** Small, other species. Designated rooms, no service, supervision.
ASK SD X ⊘ 🛏 🖳 ⌁

▽▼▽▼ Holiday Inn Express SH
(608) 783-6555. **$89-$109.** 9409 Hwy 16. I-90, exit 5, 1 mi e. Int corridors. **Pets:** Designated rooms, service with restrictions, supervision.
ASK SD X & 🛏 🖳 ⌁ ⊠

▽▼▽ Microtel Inn SH
(608) 783-0833. **$54-$75.** 3240 N Kinney Coulee Rd. I-90, exit 5, just ne. Int corridors. **Pets:** Other species. $5 daily fee/room. Service with restrictions.
ASK SD X & 🛏

OSCEOLA

△△△ ▽▼▽ River Valley Inn SH
(715) 294-4060. **$65-$127.** 1030 Cascade St. Just n on SR 35. Int corridors. **Pets:** Small. $10 daily fee/pet. Designated rooms, service with restrictions, supervision.
SAVE SD X 🛏 🖳 ⌁

OSHKOSH

△△△ ▽▼▽ Baymont Inn Oshkosh SH
(920) 233-4190. **$59-$79.** 1950 Omro Rd. US 41, exit 119, jct SR 21. Int corridors. **Pets:** $25 deposit/pet. Service with restrictions, supervision.
SAVE SD X ⊘ 🛏 🖳

▽▼▽▼ Hawthorn Inn & Suites SH
(920) 303-1133. **$99-$299.** 3105 S Washburn St. US 41, exit 116 (SR 44), just w, then just s. Int corridors. **Pets:** Accepted.
ASK SD X &M & 🛏 🖳 ⫯ ⌁

▽▼▽▼ Holiday Inn Express Hotel & Suites SH 🐾
(920) 303-1300. **$104-$140.** 2251 Westowne Ave. US 41, exit 119, 0.4 mi sw of jct SR 21. Int corridors. **Pets:** Large, dogs only. Designated rooms, service with restrictions, crate.
ASK SD X &M & 🛏 🖳 ⌁ ⊠

△△△ ▽▼ Oshkosh Travelodge M
(920) 233-4300. **$38-$99.** 1015 S Washburn St. US 41, exit 117, just sw. Ext corridors. **Pets:** Other species. $10 daily fee/room. Service with restrictions, crate.
SAVE SD X 🛏 🖳 ⌁

PHILLIPS

▽▼▽ Super 8 Motel SH
(715) 339-2898. **$50.** 726 S Lake Ave. 0.6 mi s on SR 13. Int corridors. **Pets:** Accepted.
ASK SD X

PLATTEVILLE

△△△ ▽▼▽ Governor Dodge Hotel & Conference Center SH 🐾
(608) 348-2301. **$69-$89.** 300 Highway 151. Jct US 151 and SR 80, just w. Int corridors. **Pets:** Designated rooms, service with restrictions, supervision.
SAVE SD X 🛏 🖳 ⫯ ⌁

▽▼▽ Mound View Inn SH
(608) 348-9518. **$50-$65, 3 day notice.** 1755 E Hwy 151. On US 151; 2 mi n of jct SR 80/81 N. Int corridors. **Pets:** Medium. $20 deposit/pet. Service with restrictions, supervision.
⊠ ⊘ 🛏 ⊠

△△△ ▽▼▽ Super 8 Motel SH 🐾
(608) 348-8800. **$58-$90.** 100 Hwy 80/81 S. Jct US 151 and SR 80. Int corridors. **Pets:** Other species. $10 daily fee/pet. Service with restrictions, crate.
SAVE SD X 🛏 🖳 ⊠

PLEASANT PRAIRIE

△△△ ▽▼▽ Baymont Inn Kenosha-Pleasant Prairie SH
(262) 857-7911. **$53-$89.** 7540 118th Ave. I-94, exit 344 (SR 50), just e. Int corridors. **Pets:** Medium. $25 deposit/room. Service with restrictions, supervision.
SAVE SD X ⊘ 🛏 🖳

▽▼▽▼ Hawthorn Suites LTD Hotel SH
(262) 942-6000. **$79-$149.** 7887 94th Ave. I-94, exit 344 (SR 50), 1.5 mi e, then 0.3 mi s. Int corridors. **Pets:** Accepted.
ASK SD X &M ⊘ & 🛏 🖳 ⌁ ⊠

PORTAGE

▽▼▽▼ Super 8 Motel-Portage SH
(608) 742-8330. **$49-$59.** 3000 New Pinery. I-39, exit 92, just s. Int corridors. **Pets:** Dogs only. $10 daily fee/pet. Service with restrictions, supervision.
ASK SD X ⊘ 🛏 🖳

PRAIRIE DU CHIEN

△△△ ▽▼▽▼ Best Western Quiet House & Suites SH
(608) 326-4777. **$99-$189.** US 18 and SR 35. On US 18, 1.9 mi e of jct SR 27 N. Ext/int corridors. **Pets:** Medium. $15 daily fee/pet. Designated rooms, service with restrictions, supervision.
SAVE X 🛏 🖳 ⌁

△△△ ▽▼▽▼ Bridgeport Inn SH
(608) 326-6082. **$87-$129.** Hwy 18, 35 & 60 S. On US 18, 2.2 mi e of jct SR 27 N. Int corridors. **Pets:** Small. $15 daily fee/pet. Designated rooms, service with restrictions, supervision.
SAVE SD X 🛏 🖳 ⌁

△△△ ▽▼▽ Brisbois Motor Inn M
(608) 326-8404. **$64-$99.** 533 N Marquette Rd. On SR 35 N, 0.5 mi n of jct US 18/SR 35 S and 27 N. Ext/int corridors. **Pets:** Accepted.
SAVE SD X 🛏 🖳 ⌁

△△△ ▽▼▽ Super 8 Motel-Prairie Du Chien SH
(608) 326-8777. **$69-$109.** 1930 S Marquette Rd. On US 18, 1.9 mi e of jct SR 27 N. Ext/int corridors. **Pets:** Small. $15 daily fee/pet. Designated rooms, supervision.
SAVE X 🛏

RACINE

▽▼ Knights Inn M
(262) 886-6667. **$43-$99.** 1149 Oakes Rd. I-94, exit 333, 4 mi e on SR 20. Ext corridors. **Pets:** Accepted.
ASK SD X ⊘ 🛏 🖳

△△△ ▽▼▽▼ Microtel Inn & Suites SH
(262) 554-8855. **$64-$75, 14 day notice.** 5419 Durand Ave. On SR 11, 0.5 mi e of jct SR 31. Int corridors. **Pets:** Medium, other species. $10 deposit/pet. Designated rooms, service with restrictions, supervision.
SAVE SD X &M ⊘ & 🛏 🖳

▽▼▽▼ Racine Marriott Hotel LH
(262) 886-6100. **$156.** 7111 Washington Ave. I-94, exit 333, 4 mi e on SR 20. Int corridors. **Pets:** Accepted.
SD X ⊘ 🛏 🖳 ⫯ ⌁ ⊠

Super 8-Racine SH
(262) 884-0486. **$55-$160.** 1150 Oakes Rd. I-94, exit 333, 4 mi e on SR 20. Int corridors. **Pets:** Accepted.
[SAVE] [X] [✦] [🛏]

REEDSBURG

Copper Springs Motel M
(608) 524-4312. **$44-$68, 5 day notice.** E7278 Hwy 23 & 33. 2 mi e on SR 23 and 33. Ext corridors. **Pets:** Accepted.
[SAVE] [🛏] [💻]

RHINELANDER

AmericInn of Rhinelander SH
(715) 369-9600. **$57-$110.** 648 W Kemp St. On Business Rt US 8, 0.3 mi e of jct SR 47. Int corridors. **Pets:** Designated rooms, service with restrictions, crate.
[ASK] [S✦] [X] [🕖] [✦] [🛏] [💻] [🏊] [✕]

Best Western Claridge Motor Inn SH
(715) 362-7100. **$85-$150.** 70 N Stevens St. On SR 17; center. Int corridors. **Pets:** Medium, other species. $25 deposit/room, $10 daily fee/pet. Designated rooms, service with restrictions, supervision.
[SAVE] [S✦] [X] [🛏] [💻] [🍴] [🏊] [✕]

Comfort Inn SH ❀
(715) 369-1100. **$76-$106.** 1490 Lincoln St. On Business Rt US 8, 2.6 mi e of jct SR 47. Int corridors. **Pets:** Other species. $25 deposit/pet, $10 daily fee/pet. Designated rooms, service with restrictions, supervision.
[SAVE] [S✦] [X] [🛏] [💻] [🏊] [✕]

Holiday Acres Resort SH
(715) 369-1500. **$69-$289, 15 day notice.** 4060 S Shore Dr. 4.5 mi e on US business route 8, 2.3 mi n on W Lake George Rd. Ext/int corridors. **Pets:** Accepted.
[ASK] [S✦] [X] [🛏] [💻] [🍴] [🏊] [✕]

Holiday Inn Express SH
(715) 369-3600. **$74-$174.** 668 W Kemp St. On Business Rt US 8, just e of jct SR 47. Int corridors. **Pets:** Medium, other species. $25 one-time fee/room. Designated rooms, service with restrictions, supervision.
[SAVE] [S✦] [X] [✦M] [✦] [🛏] [💻] [🏊] [✕]

RICE LAKE

Currier's Lakeview Resort Motel M
(715) 234-7474. **$52-$97, 7 day notice.** 2010 E Sawyer St. Jct CR O, 1.5 mi n on CR SS, 1 mi e, then n on CR C. Ext/int corridors. **Pets:** Accepted.
[SAVE] [S✦] [X] [🛏] [💻] [✕]

Microtel Inn & Suites M
(715) 736-2010. **$45-$109.** 2771 Decker Dr. US 53, exit 140 (CR O), just ne. Int corridors. **Pets:** Medium, other species. $10 one-time fee/pet. Service with restrictions, supervision.
[SAVE] [S✦] [X] [✦] [🛏] [💻]

RICHLAND CENTER

Super 8 Motel-Richland Center SH
(608) 647-8988. **$63-$85.** 100 Foundry Dr. 0.9 mi e on US 14. Int corridors. **Pets:** Accepted.
[ASK] [S✦] [X] [🛏] [💻] [🏊] [✕]

RIVER FALLS

Super 8 Motel SH
(715) 425-8388. **$65-$129.** 1207 St. Croix St. On SR 65, 0.5 mi w jct SR 35. Int corridors. **Pets:** Accepted.
[ASK] [S✦] [X] [🛏] [💻] [🏊]

ST. GERMAIN

North Woods Rest Motel M
(715) 479-8770. **$52.** 8083 Hwy 70 E. On SR 70, 0.8 mi e. Ext corridors. **Pets:** Small, dogs only. $5 daily fee/pet. Service with restrictions, supervision.
[X] [🛏] [💻]

SHAWANO

Comfort Inn & Suites SH
(715) 524-9090. **$76-$126.** W7393 River Bend Rd. SR 29, exit 225, just n on SR 22. Int corridors. **Pets:** Accepted.
[SAVE] [S✦] [X] [✦M] [✦] [🛏] [💻] [🏊] [✕]

Super 8 Motel-Shawano SH
(715) 526-6688. **$55-$75.** 211 Waukechon St. 1.2 mi e on SR 29 business route; SR 29, exit 227, 1.8 mi n. then 1.1 mi w. Int corridors. **Pets:** Other species. $25 deposit/room. Service with restrictions, supervision.
[ASK] [S✦] [X] [🕖] [🛏] [💻]

SHEBOYGAN

AmericInn of Sheboygan SH
(920) 208-8130. **$78-$199.** 3664 S Taylor Dr. I-43, exit 123, just e. Int corridors. **Pets:** Accepted.
[ASK] [S✦] [X] [✦] [🛏] [💻] [🏊]

Baymont Inn Sheboygan SH
(920) 457-2321. **$69-$109.** 2932 Kohler Memorial Dr. I-43, exit 126, 1 mi e on SR 23. Int corridors. **Pets:** Accepted.
[SAVE] [S✦] [X] [✦] [🛏] [💻]

Comfort Inn-Sheboygan SH
(920) 457-7724. **$55-$95.** 4332 N 40th St. I-43, exit 128, 0.3 mi e on Business Rt 42. Int corridors. **Pets:** Other species. $10 daily fee/pet. Designated rooms, service with restrictions, supervision.
[ASK] [S✦] [X] [🕖] [🛏] [💻] [🏊]

Super 8 Motel-Sheboygan SH
(920) 458-8080. **$59-$79.** 3402 Wilgus Rd. I-43, exit 126, just ne. Int corridors. **Pets:** Dogs only. $10 one-time fee/room. Service with restrictions, supervision.
[ASK] [S✦] [X] [🛏] [💻]

SHELL LAKE

AmericInn of Shell Lake SH
(715) 468-4494. **$69-$199.** 315 Hwy 63 S. US 53, exit County Hwy B. Int corridors. **Pets:** $10 daily fee/room. Designated rooms, service with restrictions, supervision.
[ASK] [S✦] [X] [✦] [🛏] [💻] [🏊] [✕]

SIREN

The Lodge at Crooked Lake SH
(715) 349-2500. **$79-$119.** 24271 SR 35 N. On SR 35, 0.5 mi n of jct SR 70. Int corridors. **Pets:** $50 deposit/room. Service with restrictions, supervision.
[SAVE] [S✦] [X] [✦] [🛏] [💻] [🍴] [🏊] [✕]

Pine Wood Motel M
(715) 349-5225. **$45-$55.** 23862 Hwy 35 S. On SR 35, 0.3 mi s of jct SR 70 W and CR B E. Ext corridors. **Pets:** Medium, dogs only. No service, supervision.
[SAVE] [X] [🛏]

SPARTA

Best Nights Inn M
(608) 269-3066. **$39-$139.** 303 W Wisconsin St. I-90, exit 25 (SR 27), 0.5 mi n; exit 28 (SR 16), 1 mi w. Ext corridors. **Pets:** Medium, other species. $50 deposit/pet. Designated rooms, service with restrictions, crate.
[SAVE] [S✦] [X] [🛏] [💻] [🏊]

♦♦♦ **Best Western Sparta Trail Lodge** [SH]
(608) 269-2664. **$89-$159.** 4445 Theatre Rd. I-90, exit 28 (US 16), just w. Int corridors. **Pets:** $20 one-time fee/pet. Designated rooms, service with restrictions, supervision.
[A$K] [SD] 🚭 ♿M ♿ ■ ☕ 🍴 🏊 🏋

[AAA] ♦♦♦ **Country Inn By Carlson** [SH]
(608) 269-3110. **$78-$160.** 737 Avon Rd. I-90, exit 25 (SR 27), just n. Int corridors. **Pets:** Other species. $5 daily fee/pet. Service with restrictions, crate.
[SAVE] [SD] 🚭 ♿M ■ ☕ 🏊

♦♦ **Super 8 Sparta** [SH]
(608) 269-8489. **$75-$90, 30 day notice.** 716 Avon Rd. I-90, exit 25 (SR 27), just n. Int corridors. **Pets:** Accepted.
[A$K] [SD] 🚭 ■ ☕ 🏊

SPOONER

[AAA] ♦♦♦ **Best Western American Heritage Inn** [SH]
(715) 635-9770. **$84-$104.** 101 Maple St. On SR 70 at jct US 63, 1 mi w of US 53. Int corridors. **Pets:** Accepted.
[SAVE] [SD] 🚭 ☕ 🏊 🏋

[AAA] ♦♦ **Country House Motel & RV Park** [M] 🐾
(715) 635-8721. **$54-$99.** 717 S River St. On US 63, 0.5 mi s of jct SR 70. Ext/int corridors. **Pets:** Large, dogs only. $4 daily fee/pet. Designated rooms, service with restrictions, supervision.
[SAVE] 🚭 ♿M 👂 ♿ ■ ☕ 🏊

STEVENS POINT

[AAA] ♦♦♦ **Baymont Inn & Suites Stevens Point** [SH]
(715) 344-1900. **$54-$75.** 4917 Main St. I-39, exit 158B (US 10), just w. Int corridors. **Pets:** Small, other species. $50 deposit/room. Designated rooms, service with restrictions, supervision.
[SAVE] [SD] 🚭 👂 ■ ☕ 🏊

♦♦♦ **Country Inn & Suites By Carlson** [SH]
(715) 345-7000. **$99-$139.** 301 Division St N. I-39, exit 161, on US 51 business route, 0.6 mi s. Int corridors. **Pets:** Other species. $25 one-time fee/room. Designated rooms, supervision.
[A$K] [SD] 🚭 ♿ ■ ☕ 🏊

♦♦ **Fairfield Inn by Marriott** [SH]
(715) 342-9300. **$55-$90.** 5317 Hwy 10 E. I-39, exit 158 (US 10) at jct US 51. Int corridors. **Pets:** Large, other species. $50 one-time fee/room. Designated rooms, service with restrictions, supervision.
[A$K] [SD] 🚭 👂 ♿ ■ ☕ 🏊

♦ **Point Motel** [M]
(715) 344-8312. **$33-$70.** 209 Division St. I-39, exit 161 (US 51 business route), 0.7 mi s. Ext corridors. **Pets:** Accepted.
[A$K] [SD] 🚭 ■ ☕

STOUGHTON

[AAA] ♦♦ **Chose Family Inn** [SH]
(608) 873-0330. **$61-$72.** 1124 W Main St. On US 51 business route, just w of jct SR 138 S. Int corridors. **Pets:** Medium. $15 daily fee/pet. Designated rooms, service with restrictions, supervision.
[SAVE] [SD] 🚭 👂 ♿ ■ 🏊

STURTEVANT

[AAA] ♦♦ **Best Western Grandview Inn** [SH]
(262) 886-0385. **$59-$109.** 910 S Sylvania Ave. I-94, exit 333 (SR 20), just s on west frontage road. Int corridors. **Pets:** Accepted.
[SAVE] [SD] 🚭 ■ ☕ 🏊

[AAA] ♦♦ **Holiday Inn Express-Racine** [SH]
(262) 884-0200. **$69-$99.** 13339 Hospitality Ct. I-94, exit 333 (SR 20), just se. Int corridors. **Pets:** Small, other species. Designated rooms, service with restrictions, supervision.
[SAVE] [SD] 🚭 ♿M 👂 ♿ ■ ☕ 🏊

SUN PRAIRIE

[AAA] ♦ **McGovern's Motel & Suites** [M]
(608) 837-7321. **$58-$120.** 820 W Main St. On US 151, exit 101, 1.2 mi ne. Ext/int corridors. **Pets:** Dogs only. $5 daily fee/pet. Designated rooms, service with restrictions, supervision.
[SAVE] [SD] 🚭 ■ ☕ 🍴

SUPERIOR

[AAA] ♦♦ **Barkers Island Inn** [SH]
(715) 392-7152. **$69-$210.** 300 Marina Dr. Just ne of US 2/53; on Barkers Island. Int corridors. **Pets:** $50 deposit/pet, $10 daily fee/pet. Designated rooms, service with restrictions, supervision.
[SAVE] [SD] 🚭 ■ ☕ 🍴 🏊 🏋

♦♦♦ **Best Western Bay Walk Inn** [SH]
(715) 392-7600. **$59-$119.** 1405 Susquehanna Ave. Just e of US 2 on Belknap St. Int corridors. **Pets:** Accepted.
[A$K] [SD] 🚭 ■ ☕ 🏊 🏋

[AAA] ♦♦ **Best Western Bridgeview Motor Inn** [SH]
(715) 392-8174. **$49-$135.** 415 Hammond Ave. 0.8 mi n at south end of Blatnik Bridge. Int corridors. **Pets:** Accepted.
[SAVE] [SD] 🚭 ■ ☕ 🏊 🏋

[AAA] ♦♦ **Days Inn-Superior/Bayfront** [SH] 🐾
(715) 392-4783. **$59-$119.** 110 Harborview Pkwy. Just n of jct US 2/53. Int corridors. **Pets:** Dogs only. $25 deposit/room, $10 daily fee/pet. Designated rooms, service with restrictions, supervision.
[SAVE] [SD] 🚭 ♿ ■ ☕ 🍴 🏊 🏋

♦ **Stockade Motel** [M]
(715) 398-3585. **$45-$75.** 1616 E 2nd St. On US 2/53, 2.8 mi se. Ext corridors. **Pets:** Accepted.
🚭 ■ ☕

[AAA] ♦♦ **Superior Inn** [SH]
(715) 394-7706. **$85-$120.** 525 Hammond Ave. 0.8 mi n at south end of Blatnik Bridge. Int corridors. **Pets:** Other species. Service with restrictions, supervision.
[SAVE] [SD] 🚭 ■ ☕ 🏊

THORP

♦♦♦ **AmericInn Lodge & Suites** [SH]
(715) 669-5959. **$80-$141.** 203 1/2 W Hill St. US 29, exit 108 (SR 73), just nw. Int corridors. **Pets:** Accepted.
[A$K] 🚭 ♿ ■ ☕ 🏊 🏋

TOMAH

♦♦ **Comfort Inn by Choice Hotels** [SH]
(608) 372-6600. **$60-$129.** 305 Wittig Rd. I-94, exit 143 (SR 21), just w. Int corridors. **Pets:** Accepted.
[A$K] [SD] 🚭 👂 ■ ☕ 🏊

♦♦♦ **Cranberry Country Lodge** [SH]
(608) 374-2801. **$70-$200.** 319 Wittig Rd. I-94, exit 143 (SR 21), just w. Int corridors. **Pets:** Accepted.
[A$K] [SD] 🚭 ■ ☕ 🏊 🏋

♦♦ **Econo Lodge** [SH] 🐾
(608) 372-9100. **$59-$140.** 2005 N Superior Ave. I-94, exit 143 (SR 21), just w. Ext/int corridors. **Pets:** $5 daily fee/pet. Service with restrictions, supervision.
[A$K] [SD] 🚭 👂 ■ ☕ 🏊

♦♦♦ **Holiday Inn** [SH]
(608) 372-3211. **$80-$86.** 1017 E McCoy Blvd. I-94, exit 143 (SR 21), just e. Int corridors. **Pets:** Service with restrictions, supervision.
🚭 ■ ☕ 🍴 🏊 🏋

△△△ ▼▼ Lark Inn M
(608) 372-5981. **$59-$91.** 229 N Superior Ave. I-94, exit 143 (SR 21), 1.5 mi s on US 12; I-90, exit 41, 2 mi n on US 12. Ext/int corridors. **Pets:** $6 daily fee/pet. Service with restrictions, supervision.
[SAVE] [S☎] [✕] [📠] [💻]

▼▼ Super 8 Motel-Tomah SH
(608) 372-3901. **$48-$68.** 1008 E McCoy Blvd. I-94, exit 143 (SR 21), just e. Int corridors. **Pets:** Other species. $10 one-time fee/room. Designated rooms, service with restrictions, supervision.
[ASK] [S☎] [✕] [⅄] [📠] [💻]

TOMAHAWK

▼▼▼ Comfort Inn SH
(715) 453-8900. **$64-$94.** 1738 E Comfort Dr. US 51, exit 229. Int corridors. **Pets:** Accepted.
[ASK] [S☎] [✕] [⅄M] [⅄] [📠] [💻] [≈]

▼▼ Super 8 Motel-Tomahawk SH
(715) 453-5210. **$49-$85.** 108 W Mohawk Dr. On US 51 business route, 0.6 mi n of downtown. Int corridors. **Pets:** Accepted.
[ASK] [S☎] [⅄] [📠] [≈] [✕]

TWO RIVERS

▼▼ Lighthouse Inn on the Lake SH
(920) 793-4524. **$85-$115.** 1515 Memorial Dr. 0.3 mi s on SR 42. Int corridors. **Pets:** Accepted.
[ASK] [S☎] [✕] [📠] [💻] [⅃⅃] [≈] [✕]

△△△ ▼ Village Inn & Suites & RV Park M
(920) 794-8818. **$60-$90.** 3310 Memorial Dr. 2 mi s on SR 42. Ext/int corridors. **Pets:** Medium, other species. $10 one-time fee/pet. Designated rooms, service with restrictions, supervision.
[SAVE] [✕] [📠] [💻] [⅃⅃] [≈]

VERONA

▼▼ Super 8 Motel-Verona SH
(608) 848-7829. **$66-$81.** 131 Horizon Dr. US 18 and 151, exit 94 southbound; exit 89 northbound, just n. Int corridors. **Pets:** Accepted.
[ASK] [S☎] [✕] [📠] [≈] [✕]

WATERFORD

△△△ ▼▼▼ Baymont Inns & Suites-Waterford SH
(262) 534-4100. **$66-$150.** 750 Fox Ln. On SR 36, 1 mi s of jct SR 164. Int corridors. **Pets:** Other species. Service with restrictions, supervision.
[SAVE] [S☎] [✕] [⅄] [📠] [💻] [≈]

WATERTOWN

▼▼ Econo Lodge SH
(920) 261-9010. **$45-$130.** 700 E Main St. On SR 16 and 19. Int corridors. **Pets:** Accepted.
[ASK] [S☎] [✕] [📠]

▼▼▼ Holiday Inn Express SH
(920) 262-1910. **$72-$100.** 101 Aviation Way. On SR 26, 1.5 mi s of jct SR 19. Int corridors. **Pets:** $10 daily fee/pet. Designated rooms, service with restrictions, supervision.
[ASK] [S☎] [✕] [⅄] [📠] [💻] [≈] [✕]

▼▼ Super 8 Motel SH
(920) 261-1188. **$78-$93.** 1730 S Church St. On SR 26, 1.5 mi s of jct SR 19. Int corridors. **Pets:** $50 deposit/room. Service with restrictions, supervision.
[ASK] [S☎] [✕] [📠] [💻] [≈]

WAUPACA

△△△ ▼▼▼▼ Best Western Grand Seasons Hotel SH ❀
(715) 258-9212. **$159-$179.** 110 Grand Seasons Dr. Jct US 10 and SR 54. Int corridors. **Pets:** Medium. $50 deposit/room. Designated rooms, supervision.
[SAVE] [S☎] [✕] [⅄] [⅄] [📠] [💻] [≈] [✕]

△△△ ▼▼▼▼ Comfort Suites at Foxfire SH ❀
(715) 942-0500. **$79-$139.** 199 Foxfire Dr. SR 54, exit Foxfire Dr. Int corridors. **Pets:** Other species. $20 one-time fee/room. Designated rooms, service with restrictions.
[SAVE] [S☎] [✕] [📠] [💻] [⅃⅃] [≈] [✕]

WAUPUN

▼ Inn Town Motel M
(920) 324-4211. **$49-$70.** 27 S State St. US 151, exit 146 (SR 49), 1.3 mi w. Ext corridors. **Pets:** Small. $6 daily fee/pet. Service with restrictions, supervision.
[ASK] [S☎] [✕] [📠] [💻]

WAUSAU

△△△ ▼▼ Baymont Inn-Wausau SH
(715) 842-0421. **$60-$99.** 1910 Stewart Ave. I-39, exit 192, just e. Int corridors. **Pets:** Other species. $50 deposit/room. Designated rooms, service with restrictions, supervision.
[SAVE] [S☎] [✕] [⅄] [📠] [💻] [≈]

△△△ ▼▼ Best Western Midway Hotel SH
(715) 842-1616. **$85-$128.** 2901 Martin Ave. I-39, exit 190 (CR NN), 0.5 mi s. Int corridors. **Pets:** Accepted.
[SAVE] [S☎] [✕] [📠] [💻] [⅃⅃] [≈] [✕]

△△△ ▼▼▼ Days Inn-Wausau SH
(715) 355-5501. **$69-$79.** 4700 Rib Mountain Dr. I-39, exit 188, just e. Int corridors. **Pets:** Accepted.
[SAVE] [✕] [📠] [💻] [≈]

△△△ ▼▼▼ Exel Inn of Wausau M
(715) 842-0641. **$46-$66.** 116 S 17th Ave. I-39, exit 192, just e. Int corridors. **Pets:** Small, other species. Designated rooms, service with restrictions, supervision.
[SAVE] [S☎] [✕] [📠] [💻]

▼▼ Plaza Hotel & Suites SH
(715) 845-4341. **$79-$199.** 201 N 17th Ave. I-39, exit 193, just e. Int corridors. **Pets:** Accepted.
[ASK] [S☎] [✕] [⅄] [📠] [💻] [⅃⅃] [≈] [✕]

▼▼ Rib Mountain Inn SH
(715) 848-2802. **$62-$439, 3 day notice.** 2900 Rib Mountain Way. I-39, exit 190 (CR NN), 1 mi w. Ext/int corridors. **Pets:** Accepted.
[ASK] [📠] [💻] [✕]

△△△ ▼▼▼ Super 8 Motel SH
(715) 848-2888. **$59-$80, 7 day notice.** 2006 Stewart Ave W. I-39, exit 192, just e. Int corridors. **Pets:** Accepted.
[SAVE] [✕] [⅄] [⅄] [📠] [💻] [≈]

WAUTOMA

▼▼ AmericInn SH
(920) 787-5050. **$68-$128.** W7696 SR 21/73. On SR 21 and 73, 1.2 mi e. Int corridors. **Pets:** Dogs only. $10 one-time fee/room. Service with restrictions, supervision.
[ASK] [✕] [⅄M] [⅄] [📠] [💻] [≈]

▼▼ Super 8 Motel-Wautoma SH
(920) 787-4811. **$63-$79.** W7607 SR 21 and 73. On SR 21 and 73, 1.5 mi e. Int corridors. **Pets:** Other species. $25 deposit/room. Service with restrictions, supervision.
[ASK] [S☎] [✕] [📠] [≈]

WEST SALEM

▼▼▼▼ AmericInn SH
(608) 786-3340. **$71-$131.** 125 Buol Rd. I-90, exit 12, just sw on CR C. Int corridors. **Pets:** Accepted.

(A$K) (S🔥) (✕) (👓) (🛄) (💻) (🏊)

WHITEWATER

ⒶⒶⒶ ▼▼▼▼ AmeriHost Inn & Suites SH
(262) 472-9400. **$74-$84.** 1355 W Main St. On US 12, 0.5 mi w of jct SR 59 W. Int corridors. **Pets:** Other species. $10 daily fee/pet. Service with restrictions, supervision.

(SAVE) (S🔥) (✕) (&M) (🖉) (👓) (🛄) (💻) (🏊) (✕)

▼▼▼ Super 8 Motel SH
(262) 473-8818. **$39-$199.** 917 E Milwaukee St. On US 12, just e of jct SR 59 E. Int corridors. **Pets:** Accepted.

(A$K) (S🔥) (✕) (&M) (🛄)

WINDSOR

ⒶⒶⒶ ▼▼▼▼ Days Inn SH
(608) 846-7473. **$68-$130.** 6311 Rostad Cir. I-90/94, exit 131 (SR 19). Int corridors. **Pets:** Accepted.

(SAVE) (S🔥) (✕) (&M) (👓) (🛄) (💻) (🏊) (✕)

▼▼▼ Super 8 Motel-Windsor/North Madison SH
(608) 846-3971. **$48-$75.** 4506 Lake Cir. I-90/94, exit 131 (SR 19). Int corridors. **Pets:** Other species. $10 one-time fee/pet. Designated rooms, service with restrictions, supervision.

(A$K) (S🔥) (✕) (🛄) (💻)

WISCONSIN DELLS

ⒶⒶⒶ ▼▼▼ Baker's Sunset Bay Resort SH
(608) 254-8406. **$49-$150, 14 day notice.** 921 Canyon Rd. I-90/94, exit 92 (US 12), 0.5 mi w, right on E Adams St, right on Canyon Rd, then 0.8 mi on left. Ext/int corridors. **Pets:** $10 daily fee/room. Service with restrictions, crate.

(SAVE) (S🔥) (✕) (🛄) (💻) (🏊) (✕)

ⒶⒶⒶ ▼▼▼ Black Hawk Motel M 🐾
(608) 254-7770. **$35-$140, 3 day notice.** 720 Race St. I-90/94, exit 87 (SR 13), 2 mi e on SR 13, 16 and 23. Ext corridors. **Pets:** Small, other species. $5 daily fee/pet. Designated rooms, service with restrictions, crate.

(SAVE) (S🔥) (✕) (🛄) (💻) (🏊) (✕)

▼▼▼ Bridge View Motel M
(608) 254-6114. **$49-$99, 3 day notice.** 1020 River Rd. Just n of SR 13 (Broadway); center. Ext corridors. **Pets:** Small. $10 daily fee/pet. Designated rooms, service with restrictions, crate.

(A$K) (S🔥) (✕) (🛄) (🏊)

ⒶⒶⒶ ▼▼▼ Day's End Motel M
(608) 254-8171. **$34-$136, 3 day notice.** N 604 Hwy 12-16. I-90/94, exit 85 (US 12), 0.8 mi nw. Ext corridors. **Pets:** Other species. $7 daily fee/pet. Designated rooms, service with restrictions, crate.

(SAVE) (S🔥) (✕) (🛄) (💻) (🏊) (✕)

ⒶⒶⒶ ▼▼▼▼ Howard Johnson Hotel and Antiqua Bay Waterpark SH 🐾
(608) 254-8306. **$89-$170.** 655 Frontage Rd. I-90/94, exit 87 (SR 13), just e. Int corridors. **Pets:** Dogs only. $10 daily fee/pet. Designated rooms, no service, supervision.

(SAVE) (S🔥) (✕) (🖉) (🛄) (💻) (🍴) (🏊) (✕)

▼▼▼ Super 8 Motel-Wisconsin Dells SH
(608) 254-6464. **$56-$149.** 800 CR H. I-90/94, exit 87 (SR 13), just e. Int corridors. **Pets:** Other species. Designated rooms, service with restrictions, supervision.

(A$K) (✕) (🖉) (💻) (🏊) (✕)

WISCONSIN RAPIDS

ⒶⒶⒶ ▼▼▼ Best Western Rapids Motor Inn SH
(715) 423-3211. **$50-$82.** 911 Huntington Ave. 0.5 mi s on SR 13 of jct SR 54. Int corridors. **Pets:** Service with restrictions, supervision.

(SAVE) (S🔥) (✕) (🛄) (💻)

ⒶⒶⒶ ▼▼▼▼ Hotel Mead LH
(715) 423-1500. **$115-$184.** 451 E Grand Ave. Just e of downtown. Int corridors. **Pets:** Dogs only. $15 daily fee/room. Designated rooms, service with restrictions.

(SAVE) (S🔥) (✕) (🖉) (👓) (🛄) (💻) (🍴) (🏊) (✕)

▼▼▼ Super 8 Motel SH
(715) 423-8080. **$53-$73.** 3410 8th St S. 1.9 mi s on SR 13 of jct SR 54 W. Int corridors. **Pets:** Dogs only. $10 one-time fee/room. Service with restrictions, supervision.

(A$K) (S🔥) (✕) (🖉) (🛄) (💻)

WITTENBERG

▼▼▼▼ Comfort Inn & Wilderness Conference Center SH 🐾
(715) 253-3755. **$68-$90.** W17267 Red Oak Ln. US 29, exit 198, just se. Int corridors. **Pets:** Small, dogs only. $20 one-time fee/room. Designated rooms, service with restrictions, crate.

(A$K) (S🔥) (✕) (&M) (👓) (🛄) (💻) (🏊)

WYOMING

AFTON

♦♦♦ ▼▼ Hi Country Inn M
(307) 885-3856. **$95-$100, 5 day notice.** 689 S Washington St (US Hwy 89). On US 89, 0.8 mi s. Ext corridors. **Pets:** Accepted.

♦♦♦ ▼ Lazy B Motel M
(307) 885-3187. **$65-$75.** 219 Washington St (US Hwy 89). On US 89; center. Ext corridors. **Pets:** Other species. Service with restrictions, supervision.

▼ ▼ Mountain Inn M
(307) 885-3156. **$60-$80.** 83542 Hwy 89. On US 89, 1.5 mi s. Ext corridors. **Pets:** Accepted.

ALPINE

♦♦♦ ▼▼▼▼ Best Western Flying Saddle Lodge M
(307) 654-7561. **$69-$179.** 118878 Jct US 26 & 89. 0.5 mi e of jct US 26 and 89. Ext corridors. **Pets:** Other species. Service with restrictions, supervision.

BUFFALO

▼ Arrowhead Motel M
(307) 684-9453. **$35-$60.** 749 Fort St. Jct US 16/87/Business Loop I-25, 0.6 mi w. Ext corridors. **Pets:** Accepted.

♦♦♦ ▼▼▼ Big Horn Motel M ☙
(307) 684-7822. **$42-$75, 3 day notice.** 209 N Main St. On US 16; downtown. Ext corridors. **Pets:** Dogs only. $4 one-time fee/pet. Designated rooms, service with restrictions, supervision.

▼ Canyon Motel M ☙
(307) 684-2957. **$34-$60.** 997 Fort St. Jct US 16/87/Business Loop I-25, 0.9 mi w on US 16. Ext corridors. **Pets:** Other species. $3 daily fee/pet. Service with restrictions, supervision.

▼▼▼ Comfort Inn SH
(307) 684-9564. **$45-$130.** 65 Hwy 16 E. I-25, exit 299 (US 16), just e; I-90, exit 58, 1.3 mi w. Ext/int corridors. **Pets:** Medium. $5 daily fee/pet. Designated rooms, service with restrictions, supervision.

▼ Econo Lodge M
(307) 684-2219. **$49-$109.** 333 E Hart St. I-25, exit 299 (US 16), just w. Ext corridors. **Pets:** Small. $25 deposit/room, $5 daily fee/pet. Designated rooms, service with restrictions, supervision.

▼ Mountain View Cabins & Campground CA
(307) 684-2881. **$35-$100, 7 day notice.** 585 Fort St. Jct US 16/87/ Business Loop I-25, 0.4 mi w on US 16. Ext corridors. **Pets:** Small. Designated rooms, service with restrictions.

♦♦♦ ▼▼▼ Super 8 Motel of Buffalo SH
(307) 684-2531. **$59-$116.** 655 E Hart St. I-25, exit 299 (US 16), just w; I-90, exit 58, 1.3 mi w. Int corridors. **Pets:** Accepted.

♦♦♦ ▼▼ Wyoming Motel M
(307) 684-5505. **$27-$113.** 610 E Hart St. I-25, exit 299 (US 16), just w; I-90, exit 58, 1.3 mi w. Ext corridors. **Pets:** $5 one-time fee/room. Designated rooms, service with restrictions, supervision.

♦♦♦ ▼ ▼ Z-Bar Motel CA
(307) 684-5535. **$40-$69.** 626 Fort St. Jct US 16/87/Business Loop I-25, 0.5 mi w on US 16. Ext corridors. **Pets:** Other species. $4 daily fee/pet. Designated rooms, service with restrictions, supervision.

CASPER

▼▼ Days Inn Casper SH ☙
(307) 234-1159. **$75-$109.** 301 E 'E' St. I-25, exit 188A, just s. Int corridors. **Pets:** Medium, other species.

♦♦♦ ▼▼▼▼ Holiday Inn SH
(307) 235-2531. **$84-$109.** 300 W 'F' St. I-25, exit 188A, just e. Int corridors. **Pets:** Accepted.

♦♦♦ ▼▼▼ Parkway Plaza Hotel & Convention Centre SH
(307) 235-1777. **$86-$109.** 123 W 'E' St. I-25, exit 188A, just w. Ext/int corridors. **Pets:** Accepted.

♦♦♦ ▼▼▼ Quality Inn & Suites SH
(307) 266-2400. **$67-$109.** 821 N Poplar St. I-25, exit 188B, just e. Int corridors. **Pets:** Large, other species. $5 daily fee/room. Designated rooms, service with restrictions, supervision.

▼▼▼▼ Radisson Hotel Casper LH
(307) 266-6000. **$89-$94.** 800 N Poplar St. I-25, exit 188B, just e. Int corridors. **Pets:** Accepted.

♦♦♦ ▼ The Royal Inn M
(307) 234-3501. **$45-$55.** 440 E 'A' St. I-25, exit 188A (Center St), just s to 'A' St, then just e. Ext corridors. **Pets:** Medium. $4 daily fee/pet. Designated rooms, service with restrictions, supervision.

Skyler Inn SH
(307) 232-5100. **$68-$108.** 111 S Wilson St. I-25, exit 186, 0.5 mi s to Yellowstone Hwy, then 1 mi w, jct 1st St. Int corridors. **Pets:** Accepted.

Super 8 Motel SH
(307) 266-3480. **$65-$70, 30 day notice.** 3838 CY Ave. I-25, exit 188B, 1.7 mi w on S Poplar St (SR 220), then 1.8 mi n. Int corridors. **Pets:** Accepted.

CHEYENNE

Best Western Hitching Post Inn Resort & Conference Center SH
(307) 638-3301. **$89-$159.** 1700 W Lincolnway. I-25, exit 9, 0.8 mi e. Ext/int corridors. **Pets:** Accepted.

Comfort Inn of Cheyenne SH
(307) 638-7202. **$59-$99.** 2245 Etchepare Dr. I-25, exit 7, just w. Int corridors. **Pets:** Other species. $20 deposit/room. Service with restrictions.

Days Inn Cheyenne SH
(307) 778-8877. **$54-$160, 14 day notice.** 2360 W Lincolnway. I-25, exit 9, just e. Int corridors. **Pets:** Medium. $10 one-time fee/room. Designated rooms, service with restrictions, supervision.

Express Inn SH
(307) 632-7556. **$40-$70.** 2512 W Lincolnway. I-25, exit 9, just e. Int corridors. **Pets:** Accepted.

Fleetwood Motel M
(307) 638-8908. **$47-$59, 15 day notice.** 3800 E Lincolnway. I-80, exit 364, 1.2 mi n on N College Dr (SR 212), then just w on I-80/US 30 business loop. Ext corridors. **Pets:** Dogs only. $5 daily fee/pet. Service with restrictions, supervision.

Holiday Inn Cheyenne Dream in the West SH
(307) 638-4466. **$96-$100, 3 day notice.** 204 W Fox Farm Rd. I-80, exit 362, just s. Int corridors. **Pets:** Accepted.

La Quinta Inn Cheyenne SH
(307) 632-7117. **$75-$115.** 2410 W Lincolnway. I-25, exit 9, just e. Int corridors. **Pets:** Accepted.

Nagle Warren Mansion B & B BB
(307) 637-3333. **$118-$168, 3 day notice.** 222 E 17th St. I-80, exit 362, 1.2 mi n on I-25 business loop/US 85/87 business route, then just e; jct House St; downtown. Int corridors. **Pets:** Small. $20 daily fee/pet. Designated rooms, service with restrictions, supervision.

Oak Tree Inn SH
(307) 778-6620. **$65-$100.** 1625 Stillwater. 1.2 mi e of jct Dell Range Blvd and Yellowstone Rd, 0.4 mi s. Ext/int corridors. **Pets:** Small, other species. $5 daily fee/pet. Service with restrictions, crate.

The Plains Hotel SH
(307) 638-3311. **$59-$159.** 1600 Central Ave. I-80, exit 362, 1 mi n on I-180/I-25 business loop/US 85/87 business route, then just w on I-80 business loop/US 30; downtown. Int corridors. **Pets:** Accepted.

Porch Swing Bed & Breakfast BB
(307) 778-7182. **$85.** 502 E 24th St. I-80, exit 362, 1.8 mi n on I-25 business loop/US 85/87 business route, then just e; downtown. Int corridors. **Pets:** Large, other species. Service with restrictions, supervision.

Windy Hills Guest House BB
(307) 632-6423. **$99-$280, 15 day notice.** 393 Happy Jack Rd. I-25, exit 10B, 22 mi w on SR 210 (Happy Jack Rd), then 1 mi s on private gravel road. Ext corridors. **Pets:** Designated rooms, service with restrictions, crate.

CHUGWATER

Super 8 Motel-Chugwater SH
(307) 422-3248. **$52-$80.** 100 Buffalo Dr. I-25, exit 54, just ne. Int corridors. **Pets:** Medium, other species. $9.50 daily fee/pet. Designated rooms, no service, supervision.

CODY

Beartooth Inn of Cody SH
(307) 527-5505. **$59-$150.** 2513 Greybull Hwy. 1.5 mi e on US 14/16/20. Ext/int corridors. **Pets:** Medium, dogs only. Designated rooms, service with restrictions, supervision.

Best Western Sunset Motor Inn SH
(307) 587-4265. **$55-$155.** 1601 8th St. 0.8 mi w on US 14/16/20. Ext corridors. **Pets:** Medium, dogs only. $25 one-time fee/pet. Service with restrictions, supervision.

Big Bear Motel M
(307) 587-3117. **$44-$75.** 139 W Yellowstone Hwy. 2 mi w on US 14/16/20, from city center. Ext corridors. **Pets:** Other species. $50 deposit/pet. Designated rooms, supervision.

Cody Motor Lodge M
(307) 527-6291. **$49-$120.** 1455 Sheridan Ave. Just w on US 14/16/20 and SR 120. Int corridors. **Pets:** Other species. Designated rooms, service with restrictions, supervision.

Cody Super 8 Motel M
(307) 527-6214. **Call for rates.** 730 Yellowstone Rd. On US 14/16, 1 mi w of city center. Int corridors. **Pets:** Accepted.

Green Gables Inn M
(307) 587-6886. **$54-$108.** 1636 Central Ave. Just e on US 14/16/20 and SR 120. Ext corridors. **Pets:** Medium, dogs only. $25 deposit/room. Service with restrictions, supervision.

Skyline Motor Inn M
(307) 587-4201. **$38-$74.** 1919 17th St. 0.8 mi e on US 14/16/20 and SR 120. Ext corridors. **Pets:** Accepted.

Sunrise Motor Inn M
(307) 587-5566. **$39-$129.** 1407 8th St. 0.8 mi w on US 14/16/20. Ext corridors. **Pets:** Service with restrictions, supervision.

DOUGLAS

AAA **WWW** Best Western Douglas Inn & Conference Center **SH** 🐾
(307) 358-9790. **$76-$98.** 1450 Riverbend Dr. I-25, exit 140, 0.8 mi e. Int corridors. **Pets:** $15 one-time fee/room. Designated rooms, service with restrictions, supervision.
SAVE 🔊 ✕ 🔊M 🔊 🔊 🚪 💻 🍴 🚤 ✕

AAA **WWW** Holiday Inn Express Hotel & Suites **SH**
(307) 358-4500. **$79-$89.** 900 W Yellowstone Hwy. I-25, exit 140, 0.5 mi e. Int corridors. **Pets:** Medium. $20 daily fee/pet. Designated rooms, service with restrictions, supervision.
SAVE 🔊 ✕ 🔊M 🔊 🔊 🚪 💻 🚤

DUBOIS

WW Bald Mountain Inn **M**
(307) 455-2844. **$55-$110, 3 day notice.** 1349 W Ramshorn St. 1.6 mi w on US 26 and 287. Ext corridors. **Pets:** Dogs only. $7 daily fee/pet. Supervision.
ASK ✕ 🚪 💻 ✕ 🏎

AAA **WW** Branding Iron Inn **CA**
(307) 455-2893. **$40-$90.** 401 W Ramshorn St. 0.3 mi w on US 26 and 287. Ext corridors. **Pets:** Accepted.
SAVE 🔊 ✕ 🚪 💻 ✕

WWW Chinook Winds Mt. Lodge **M**
(307) 455-2987. **$45-$75.** 640 S First St. 0.8 mi e on US 26 and 287; center. Ext corridors. **Pets:** Other species. $5 daily fee/room. Designated rooms, service with restrictions, supervision.
ASK 🔊 ✕ 🚪 💻 ✕ 🏎

WW Riverside Inn & Campground **M**
(307) 455-2337. **$40-$49.** 5810 US Hwy 26. 3 mi e on US 26 and 287. Ext corridors. **Pets:** Medium, dogs only. $5 daily fee/pet. Designated rooms, supervision.
🔊 ✕ 🚪 💻 ✕ 🏎 🏎 🏎

AAA **WW** Stagecoach Motor Inn **SH** 🐾
(307) 455-2303. **$44-$78.** 103 Ramshorn St. On US 26 and 287; center. Ext corridors. **Pets:** Medium, dogs only. $20 daily fee/pet. Designated rooms, service with restrictions, supervision.
SAVE ✕ 🔊 🚪 💻 🚤 ✕ 🏎

EVANSTON

WWW Comfort Inn **SH**
(307) 789-7799. **$55-$105.** 1931 Harrison Dr. I-80, exit 3 (Harrison Dr). Int corridors. **Pets:** $10 daily fee/room. Designated rooms, service with restrictions, supervision.
ASK 🔊 ✕ 🔊 🚪 💻 🚤

AAA **WWW** Prairie Inn **M** 🐾
(307) 789-2920. **$50-$65.** 264 Bear River Dr. I-80, exit 6, 0.3 mi n. Ext/int corridors. **Pets:** Medium, other species. $5 daily fee/pet. Designated rooms, service with restrictions, supervision.
SAVE ✕ 🚪

EVANSVILLE

WWW Comfort Inn by Choice Hotels-Casper **SH**
(307) 235-3038. **$70-$90.** 480 Lathrop Rd. I-25, exit 185, just e. Int corridors. **Pets:** Accepted.
ASK 🔊 ✕ 🔊M 🔊 🔊 🚪 💻 🚤

WWWW Super 8 East Casper **SH** 🐾
(307) 237-8100. **$75-$169.** 269 Miracle Dr. I-25, exit 185, just e. Int corridors. **Pets:** Other species. Service with restrictions, supervision.
ASK 🔊 ✕ 🔊 🚪 💻 🚤

GILLETTE

AAA **WWWW** Best Western Tower West Lodge **SH**
(307) 686-2210. **$55-$169.** 109 N US Hwy 14-16. I-90, exit 124, just n. Int corridors. **Pets:** Accepted.
SAVE 🔊 ✕ 🔊 🚪 💻 🍴 🚤 ✕

WWW Clarion Western Plaza **SH**
(307) 686-3000. **$71-$160.** 2009 S Douglas Hwy 59. I-90, exit 126, just se. Ext/int corridors. **Pets:** Accepted.
ASK 🔊 ✕ 🔊 🚪 💻 🍴 🚤 ✕

WWW Comfort Inn & Suites of Gillette **SH**
(307) 685-2223. **$54-$209.** 1607 W 2nd Ave. I-90, exit 124, just ne. Int corridors. **Pets:** Small. $100 deposit/pet, $15 daily fee/pet, $15 one-time fee/pet. Designated rooms, service with restrictions, supervision.
ASK ✕ 🔊M 🔊 🚪 💻 🚤

WWW Holiday Inn Express Hotel & Suites **SH**
(307) 686-9576. **$89-$189.** 1908 Cliff Davis Dr. I-90, exit 126. Int corridors. **Pets:** Accepted.
ASK ✕ 🔊M 🔊 🔊 🚪 💻 🚤 ✕

GLENROCK

WWW All American Inn **M**
(307) 436-2772. **$35-$240, 3 day notice.** 500 W Aspen. I-25, exit 165, 2.2 mi n. Ext corridors. **Pets:** Accepted.
ASK 🔊 ✕ 🚪

GRAND TETON NATIONAL PARK

AAA **WWWW** Flagg Ranch Resort **LH**
(307) 543-2861. **$155-$170, 7 day notice.** US 89 and 191; 2 mi s of Yellowstone National Park south entrance; 5 mi n of Grand Teton National park north entrance. Ext corridors. **Pets:** Large, other species. $5 daily fee/pet. Service with restrictions, crate.
SAVE ✕ 🔊M 🔊 🔊 🚪 💻 🍴 ✕ 🏎 🏎

WWWW Jackson Lake Lodge **LH**
(307) 543-2811. **$128-$175, 7 day notice.** 5 mi nw of Moran at jct US 89 and 287. Ext/int corridors. **Pets:** Accepted.
✕ 🔊M 🔊 🔊 🚪 💻 🍴 🚤 ✕ 🏎 🏎

WWW Signal Mountain Lodge **SH**
(307) 543-2831. **$99-$265, 4 day notice.** Teton Park Rd, 2 mi s of US 89, 191 and 287. Ext corridors. **Pets:** Other species. $5 daily fee/room. Designated rooms, service with restrictions.
✕ 🚪 💻 🍴 ✕ 🏎 🏎

GREEN RIVER

AAA **WWW** Oak Tree Inn **SH**
(307) 875-3500. **$64-$79.** 1170 W Flaming Gorge Way. I-80, exit 89, just s. Ext/int corridors. **Pets:** Accepted.
SAVE 🔊 ✕ 🔊M 🔊 🔊 🚪 💻 🍴

GREYBULL

WWW A Maverik Motel **M**
(307) 765-4626. **$45-$65.** 625 N 6th St. On US 14/16/20, north end of town. Ext corridors. **Pets:** Accepted.
ASK 🔊 ✕ 🚪 💻 🏎

AAA **WW** Antler Motel **M**
(307) 765-4404. **$40-$60.** 1116 N 6th St. 0.8 mi w on US 14/16/20. Ext corridors. **Pets:** Small, dogs only. $10 one-time fee/pet. Designated rooms, supervision.
SAVE 🔊 ✕ 🚪 💻

AAA **WW** Yellowstone Motel **M**
(307) 765-4456. **$52-$79, 3 day notice.** 247 Greybull Ave. 0.4 mi e on US 14. Ext corridors. **Pets:** Small. Designated rooms, service with restrictions, supervision.
SAVE 🔊 ✕ 🚪 🚤

GUERNSEY

The Bunkhouse Motel M ❀
(307) 836-2356. **$50-$69.** 350 W Whalen. On US 26; center. Ext corridors. **Pets:** $10 daily fee/room. Designated rooms, service with restrictions, supervision.
SAVE ⊠ 🖥

JACKSON

49'er Inn and Suites (Quality Inn and Suites) SH
(307) 733-7550. **$62-$199, 14 day notice.** 330 W Pearl St. Just w and just s of town square. Ext/int corridors. **Pets:** Large. Service with restrictions, supervision.
SAVE 🖥 ⊠ 🖥 🖥 🖥 🖥 ⊠

Antler Inn SH
(307) 733-2535. **$82-$115, 14 day notice.** 43 W Pearl St. Just s of town square. Ext/int corridors. **Pets:** Dogs only. Service with restrictions, crate.
SAVE ⊠ 🖥 🖥

Cowboy Village Resort CA ❀
(307) 733-3121. **$70-$180.** 120 S Flat Creek Dr. 0.3 mi w on Broadway to Flat Creek Dr, just s; downtown. Ext corridors. **Pets:** Other species. Service with restrictions, supervision.
SAVE 🖥 ⊠ 🖥 🖥

Elk Country Inn M ❀
(307) 733-2364. **$60-$156, 14 day notice.** 480 W Pearl St. Just w, then just s of town square. Ext/int corridors. **Pets:** Other species. Designated rooms, supervision.
SAVE ⊠ 🖥 🖥 ⊠

Jackson Hole Lodge SH
(307) 733-2992. **$79-$124, 14 day notice.** 420 W Broadway. 0.3 mi w on US 26/89/191. Ext corridors. **Pets:** Medium. $50 deposit/room. Designated rooms, service with restrictions, supervision.
SAVE 🖥 ⊠ 🖥 🖥 🖥 ⊠

Painted Buffalo Inn SH
(307) 733-4340. **$70-$149.** 400 W Broadway. Just w of town square. Ext corridors. **Pets:** Other species. $10 one-time fee/room. No service, supervision.
SAVE 🖥 ⊠ 🖥 🖥 🖥

Snow King Resort LH
(307) 733-5200. **$140-$750.** 400 E Snow King Ave. Just se of town square. Ext/int corridors. **Pets:** Accepted.
SAVE 🖥 ⊠ 🖥 🖥 🖥 🖥 🖥 ⊠

LANDER

Budget Host Pronghorn Lodge SH
(307) 332-3940. **$48-$125, 14 day notice.** 150 E Main St. Just n of jct US 287 and SR 789. Ext corridors. **Pets:** Accepted.
SAVE 🖥 ⊠ 🖥 🖥 🖥 🖥 ⊠

Holiday Lodge M
(307) 332-2511. **$50-$55.** 210 McFarlane Dr. Just e of jct US 287 and SR 789. Ext corridors. **Pets:** $10 daily fee/pet. Designated rooms, service with restrictions, supervision.
SAVE ⊠ 🖥

Silver Spur Motel M
(307) 332-5189. **$39-$60.** 1240 W Main St. 1.5 mi n on US 287. Ext corridors. **Pets:** Accepted.
SAVE ⊠ 🖥 🖥 ⊠

LARAMIE

1st Inn Gold SH
(307) 742-3721. **$54-$70.** 421 Boswell. I-80, exit 313, just n on US 287. Ext/int corridors. **Pets:** Accepted.
ASK 🖥 ⊠ 🖥 ⊠

Days Inn SH
(307) 745-5678. **$60-$105.** 1368 McCue St. I-80, exit 310, just e. Int corridors. **Pets:** Small. $15 daily fee/pet. Designated rooms, supervision.
ASK 🖥 ⊠ 🖥 🖥 🖥 🖥 🖥 ⊠

Gas Lite Inn Motel M
(307) 742-6616. **$43-$66.** 960 N 3rd St. I-80, exit 313, 1.6 mi n on US 287; downtown. Ext corridors. **Pets:** Other species. $5 one-time fee/pet. Service with restrictions, supervision.
SAVE 🖥 ⊠ 🖥 ⊠

Howard Johnson Inn SH
(307) 742-8371. **$55-$112.** 1555 Snowy Range Rd. I-80, exit 311, just s. Ext corridors. **Pets:** Accepted.
SAVE 🖥 ⊠ 🖥 🖥 🖥 ⊠

Ramada Center Hotel SH
(307) 742-6611. **$84-$114, 14 day notice.** 2313 Soldier Springs Rd. I-80, exit 313, just s on US 287. Ext/int corridors. **Pets:** Medium. $10 one-time fee/pet. Designated rooms, service with restrictions, supervision.
ASK 🖥 ⊠ 🖥 🖥 🖥 🖥 ⊠

Sunset Inn M
(307) 742-3741. **$52-$75.** 1104 S 3rd St. I-80, exit 313, just n on US 287. Ext corridors. **Pets:** Small. Designated rooms, service with restrictions, supervision.
SAVE 🖥 ⊠ 🖥 ⊠

Travelodge Downtown M
(307) 742-6671. **$44-$74.** 165 N 3rd St. I-80, exit 313, 1 mi n on US 287; downtown. Ext corridors. **Pets:** $50 deposit/room. Designated rooms, service with restrictions, supervision.
SAVE 🖥 ⊠ 🖥 🖥

LUSK

Town House Motel, LLC M
(307) 334-2376. **$45-$90.** 525 S Main St. Just n of jct US 20/85. Ext corridors. **Pets:** Other species. $5 daily fee/pet. Designated rooms, service with restrictions.
ASK 🖥 ⊠ 🖥 🖥

NEWCASTLE

Auto Inn Motel M
(307) 746-2734. **$42-$69.** 2503 W Main St. West end of town on US 16. Ext corridors. **Pets:** $6 daily fee/pet. Designated rooms, no service, supervision.
SAVE 🖥 ⊠ 🖥

Pines Motel M ❀
(307) 746-4334. **$45-$100.** 248 E Wentworth St. Just e from jct US Business Rt 16; downtown. Ext corridors. **Pets:** Other species. $5 one-time fee/pet. Service with restrictions, supervision.
SAVE 🖥 ⊠ 🖥 🖥

Sage Motel M
(307) 746-2724. **$42-$60, 3 day notice.** 1227 S Summit Ave. 0.3 mi s of jct US 16 on US 85, just w. Ext corridors. **Pets:** Small, other species. $5 daily fee/pet. Designated rooms, service with restrictions, supervision.
SAVE 🖥 ⊠ 🖥 🖥

PAHASKA TEPEE

Elephant Head Lodge CA ❀
(307) 587-3980. **$105-$139, 30 day notice.** 1170 Yellowstone Hwy. 11.7 mi e of Yellowstone National Park East Gate on US 14/16/20. Ext corridors. **Pets:** Other species. Service with restrictions.
SAVE 🖥 ⊠ 🖥 🖥 🖥 ⊠ 🖥 🖥 🖥

PAINTER

▼ Hunter Peak Ranch 🆁🅰
(307) 587-3711. **$121-$158, 90 day notice.** 4027 Crandall Rd. SR 296, 5 mi s of US 212; 40 mi n of SR 120. Ext corridors. **Pets:** Medium, dogs only. $15 daily fee/pet. Designated rooms, no service, supervision.

❌ 🛏 🖥 🍴 ❌ 🎿 🎵 📶

PINEDALE

🔼🔼🔼 Best Western Pinedale Inn 🆂🅷
(307) 367-6869. **$69-$129, 30 day notice.** 850 W Pine St. 0.5 mi n on US 191. Int corridors. **Pets:** Dogs only. Designated rooms, service with restrictions, supervision.

🆂🅰🆅🅴 🆂🅾 ❌ 🛏 🖥 🏊

▼▼ Lakeside Lodge Resort & Marina 🆀🅰
(307) 367-2221. **$75-$139, 3 day notice.** 99 Forest Rd 111. 5 mi ne from US 191; on Fremont Lake. Ext corridors. **Pets:** Dogs only. Service with restrictions, supervision.

🅰🆂🅺 🆂🅾 ❌ 🛏 🖥 🍴 ❌ 🎿 📶

▼▼ The Lodge at Pinedale 🆂🅷
(307) 367-8800. **$65-$105.** 1054 W Pine St. 0.7 mi n on US 191. Int corridors. **Pets:** Accepted.

❌ 🛏 🏊

🔼🔼 Sun Dance Motel Ⓜ 🐾
(307) 367-4336. **$55-$140.** 148 E Pine St. US 191; city center. Ext corridors. **Pets:** Other species. $5 daily fee/pet. Designated rooms, service with restrictions, supervision.

🆂🅰🆅🅴 🆂🅾 ❌ 🛏 🖥 🎿

POWELL

▼▼ Kings Inn Ⓜ
(307) 754-5117. **$58-$76.** 777 E 2nd St. 0.3 mi e on US 14A. Ext corridors. **Pets:** Accepted.

🅰🆂🅺 🆂🅾 ❌ 🛏 🖥 🍴 🏊

RAWLINS

🔼🔼🔼 Best Western CottonTree Inn 🆂🅷
(307) 324-2737. **$89-$124.** 2221 W Spruce St. I-80, exit 211, just n. Ext/int corridors. **Pets:** Medium, other species. $10 daily fee/room. Designated rooms, service with restrictions, supervision.

🆂🅰🆅🅴 🆂🅾 ❌ 📶 🛏 🖥 🍴 🏊 ❌

🔼🔼🔼 The Lodge at Rawlins 🆂🅷
(307) 324-2783. **$55-$80.** 1801 E Cedar. I-80, exit 215, just w of jct US 287. Int corridors. **Pets:** Accepted.

🆂🅰🆅🅴 🆂🅾 ❌ 🛏 🖥 🍴 🏊

RIVERTON

▼▼ Days Inn 🆂🅷
(307) 856-9677. **$70-$100.** 909 W Main St. 0.5 mi nw on US 26. Ext corridors. **Pets:** Small. $5 daily fee/pet. No service, supervision.

🅰🆂🅺 🆂🅾 ❌ 🎿 🛏

🔼🔼🔼🔼 Holiday Inn Convention Center 🆂🅷 🐾
(307) 856-8100. **$49-$119, 3 day notice.** 900 E Sunset Dr. 0.8 mi ne on US 26/SR 789. Int corridors. **Pets:** $20 one-time fee/room. Designated rooms, service with restrictions, crate.

🆂🅰🆅🅴 🆂🅾 ❌ 🅼 🛏 🖥 🍴 🏊

▼ Paintbrush Motel Ⓜ 🐾
(307) 856-9238. **$46-$49.** 1550 N Federal Blvd. 1.3 mi ne on US 26/SR 789. Ext corridors. **Pets:** Dogs only. $5 daily fee/pet. Designated rooms, service with restrictions, supervision.

❌ 🛏

▼▼ Super 8 Motel 🆂🅷
(307) 857-2400. **$45-$75.** 1040 N Federal Blvd. 1 mi ne on US 26/SR 789. Int corridors. **Pets:** Other species. $5 daily fee/pet. Service with restrictions, supervision.

🅰🆂🅺 🆂🅾 ❌ 🛏

🔼🔼🔼 Thunderbird Motel Ⓜ
(307) 856-9201. **$44-$56.** 302 E Fremont. Just n of US 26; downtown. Ext corridors. **Pets:** Accepted.

🆂🅰🆅🅴 🆂🅾 ❌ 🛏

ROCK SPRINGS

🔼🔼🔼 Budget Host Inn Ⓜ
(307) 362-6673. **$49-$75.** 1004 Dewar Dr. I-80, exit 102 (Dewar Dr), 1.3 mi se. Ext corridors. **Pets:** $5 daily fee/pet. Service with restrictions, supervision.

🆂🅰🆅🅴 🆂🅾 ❌ 🛏

▼▼▼ Comfort Inn 🆂🅷
(307) 382-9490. **$69-$99.** 1670 Sunset Dr. I-80, exit 102 (Dewar Dr), 0.3 mi s, then just w. Ext corridors. **Pets:** Other species. $10 daily fee/pet. Designated rooms, service with restrictions, supervision.

🅰🆂🅺 🆂🅾 ❌ 🐕 🛏 🖥 🏊 ❌

▼▼▼ Econo Lodge 🆂🅷
(307) 382-4217. **$50-$95.** 1635 Elk St. I-80, exit 104 (Elk St), just n. Ext corridors. **Pets:** Accepted.

🅰🆂🅺 🆂🅾 ❌ 🛏 🖥 🏊

▼▼▼ Holiday Inn 🆂🅷
(307) 382-9200. **$80-$100.** 1675 Sunset Dr. I-80, exit 102 (Dewar Dr), 0.3 mi sw. Ext/int corridors. **Pets:** Large, other species. $10 one-time fee/room. Designated rooms, service with restrictions, supervision.

🅰🆂🅺 🆂🅾 ❌ 📶 🐕 🛏 🖥 🍴 🏊 ❌

▼▼▼ La Quinta Inn 🆂🅷
(307) 362-1770. **$70-$106.** 2717 Dewar Dr. I-80, exit 102 (Dewar Dr), just n. Int corridors. **Pets:** Accepted.

🅰🆂🅺 🆂🅾 ❌ 📶 🛏 🖥 🏊

▼ Motel 6–#395 Ⓜ
(307) 362-1850. **$43-$57.** 2615 Commercial Way. I-80, exit 102 (Dewar Dr), n to Foothills Blvd, then just e. Ext corridors. **Pets:** Other species. Service with restrictions, supervision.

🆂🅾 ❌ 🐕 🛏 🏊

🔼🔼🔼 Springs Motel Ⓜ
(307) 362-6683. **$42-$64.** 1525 9th St. I-80, exit 107, 0.3 mi w. Ext corridors. **Pets:** Accepted.

🆂🅰🆅🅴 ❌

SARATOGA

▼ Hacienda Motel Ⓜ
(307) 326-5751. **$56-$76.** 1500 S First St. 0.5 mi s on SR 130. Int corridors. **Pets:** $5 daily fee/pet. Designated rooms, service with restrictions, supervision.

🅰🆂🅺 🆂🅾 ❌ 🛏

SHERIDAN

🔼🔼🔼🔼 Best Western Sheridan Center 🆂🅷
(307) 674-7421. **$74-$129.** 612 N Main St. I-90, exit 20, 1.7 mi s. Ext/int corridors. **Pets:** Medium. $15 one-time fee/room. Designated rooms, service with restrictions, supervision.

🆂🅰🆅🅴 🆂🅾 ❌ 📶 🛏 🖥 🍴 🏊

🔼🔼🔼 Budget Host Inn Ⓜ
(307) 674-7496. **$50-$70.** 2007 N Main St. I-90, exit 20, 0.7 mi s; on I-90 business loop. Ext corridors. **Pets:** Accepted.

🆂🅰🆅🅴 ❌ 🛏 🖥

AAA ▼▼▼ **Holiday Inn Atrium & Convention Center** SH ❖
(307) 672-8931. **$99-$135.** 1809 Sugarland Dr. I-90, exit 25, 0.3 mi nw. Int corridors. **Pets:** $50 deposit/pet. Service with restrictions, supervision.
SAVE 50 ✕ 🐾 🖑 🖬 🖵 🍴 ⊷ ✕

▼ **Motel 6 #4227** SH
(307) 673-9500. **Call for rates.** 911 Sibley Cir. I-90, exit 23, just s. Int corridors. **Pets:** Accepted.
✕ 🖑ᴹ 🖑 ⊷

SUNDANCE

AAA ▼▼ **Best Western Inn at Sundance** SH
(307) 283-2800. **$58-$121, 30 day notice.** 2719 E Cleveland Ave. I-90, exit 189, just n, then just w on I-90 business loop. Int corridors. **Pets:** Large, other species. $10 daily fee/pet. Service with restrictions, supervision.
SAVE 50 ✕ 🖬 🖵 ⊷

AAA ▼ **Budget Host Arrowhead Motel** M
(307) 283-3307. **$39-$69.** 214 Cleveland Ave. I-90 business loop and US 14. Ext corridors. **Pets:** Dogs only. Designated rooms, service with restrictions, supervision.
SAVE ✕

AAA ▼▼ **Sundance Mountain Inn** M
(307) 283-3737. **$50-$83.** 26 SR 585. I-90, exit 187, 0.4 mi n. Ext corridors. **Pets:** Small. $25 deposit/room, $5 daily fee/pet. Designated rooms, service with restrictions, supervision.
SAVE 50 ✕ 🖬 🖵 ⊷

TETON VILLAGE

AAA ▼▼▼ **The Alpenhof Lodge** SH
(307) 733-3242. **$108-$539.** 3255 W Village Dr. Center. Int corridors. **Pets:** Accepted.
SAVE 50 ✕ 🖬 🍴 ⊷ ✕

▼▼ ▼▼ **Four Seasons Resort Jackson Hole** LH
(307) 732-5000. **$275-$4000, 30 day notice.** 7680 Granite Loop Rd. Located at the base of Jackson Hole Mountain Resort. Int corridors. **Pets:** Small, dogs only. Supervision.
✕ 🖑ᴹ 🐾 🖑 🖬 🖵 🍴 ⊷ ✕

THERMOPOLIS

▼▼ ▼▼ **Holiday Inn of the Waters** SH ❖
(307) 864-3131. **$81-$139.** 115 E Park St. In Hot Springs State Park. Ext/int corridors. **Pets:** Other species. Service with restrictions, supervision.
ASK ✕ 🐾 🖑 🖵 🍴 ⊷ ✕

TORRINGTON

AAA ▼▼▼ **Holiday Inn Express Hotel & Suites** SH
(307) 532-7600. **$60-$165.** 1700 E Valley Rd. US 85, e on US 26. Int corridors. **Pets:** $15 one-time fee/pet. Designated rooms, service with restrictions, supervision.
SAVE 50 ✕ 🖑ᴹ 🐾 🖑 🖬 🖵 ⊷ ✕

AAA ▼▼▼ **Kings Inn** SH ❖
(307) 532-4011. **$56-$67.** 1555 Main St. Just s of jct US 26/85. Int corridors. **Pets:** Other species. $5 daily fee/pet. Designated rooms, service with restrictions, supervision.
SAVE 50 ✕ 🖬 🖵 🍴 ⊷

▼ **Maverick Motel** M
(307) 532-4064. **$44-$48.** 4577 US Hwy 26/85. 1.7 mi w on US 26/85. Ext corridors. **Pets:** Accepted.
ASK 50 ✕ 🖬 🖵

UCROSS

AAA ▼▼▼▼ **The Ranch at Ucross** RA
(307) 737-2281. **$299.** 2673 US Hwy 14 E. Jct US 14/16, 0.5 mi w on US 14. Ext/int corridors. **Pets:** Dogs only. Supervision.
SAVE ✕ 🍴 ⊷ ✕ 🕮

WAPITI

AAA ▼▼▼ **Green Creek Inn** M
(307) 587-5004. **$40-$75.** 2908 Yellowstone Hwy. 2.8 mi w on US 14/16/20. Ext corridors. **Pets:** Other species. $10 daily fee/pet. Service with restrictions, supervision.
SAVE 50 ✕ 🗲

WHEATLAND

AAA ▼▼▼ **Best Western Torchlite Motor Inn** SH
(307) 322-4070. **$48-$89.** 1809 N 16th St. I-25, exit 78, just e; 1.5 mi n on US 87/I-25 business loop (16th St). Ext corridors. **Pets:** Other species. $5 daily fee/pet, $5 one-time fee/pet. Service with restrictions, supervision.
SAVE ✕ 🖬 🖵 ⊷ ✕

AAA ▼ **Vimbo's Motel** M
(307) 322-3842. **$42-$45.** 203 16th St. I-25, exit 78, just e; just n on US 87/I-25 business loop (16th St). Ext/int corridors. **Pets:** Other species. Designated rooms, service with restrictions, supervision.
SAVE ✕ 🖬 🍴

WILSON

▼▼ ▼▼ **Sassy Moose Inn of Jackson Hole** BB
(307) 733-1277. **Call for rates.** 3859 Miles Rd. 2 mi n on SR 390 from jct SR 22, just e on Tucker Ranch Rd, then just n. Int corridors. **Pets:** Accepted.
✕ 🐾 🗲

WORLAND

▼▼ ▼▼ **Days Inn** M
(307) 347-4251. **$65-$95.** 500 N 10th St. 0.5 mi n on US 20. Ext corridors. **Pets:** $10 one-time fee/room. Designated rooms, service with restrictions, supervision.
ASK 50 ✕ 🖬 🖵

Canada

ALBERTA

CITY INDEX

ATHABASCA

(AAA) ◆◆◆ Best Western Athabasca Inn SH
(780) 675-2294. $109-$139. 5211 41st Ave. 1 km s on Hwy 2. Int corridors. Pets: Other species. $10 one-time fee/room. Designated rooms, no service.
[SAVE] [S] [X] [fridge] [micro] [tv] [restaurant]

BANFF

◆◆◆ Banff Rocky Mountain Resort CO
(403) 762-5531. $155-$435, 3 day notice. 1029 Banff Ave. Banff Ave and Tunnel Mountain Rd; just s of Trans-Canada Hwy 1. Ext corridors. Pets: $15 daily fee/pet. Designated rooms, service with restrictions.
[ASK] [S] [X] [fridge] [micro] [restaurant] [pool] [X] [K]

(AAA) ◆◆◆ Best Western Siding 29 Lodge SH
(403) 762-5575. $95-$305. 453 Marten St. 1.3 km ne off Banff Ave. Int corridors. Pets: Other species. Supervision.
[SAVE] [S] [X] [fridge] [micro] [pool]

(AAA) ◆◆◆ Castle Mountain Chalets CA ❀
(403) 762-3868. $145-$335, 14 day notice. 32 km w on Trans-Canada Hwy 1, jct Castle, 1 km ne on Hwy 1A (Bow Valley Pkwy). Ext corridors. Pets: Medium. $25 daily fee/pet. Service with restrictions.
[SAVE] [X] [fridge] [micro] [pool] [X] [K] [Z]

(AAA) ◆◆◆ ◆◆◆ The Fairmont Banff Springs LH ❀
(403) 762-2211. $209-$649, 3 day notice. 405 Spray Ave. Just s on Banff Ave over the bridge, 0.5 km e. Int corridors. Pets: $40 daily fee/pet. Designated rooms, service with restrictions, supervision.
[SAVE] [X] [fridge] [micro] [micro] [tv] [restaurant] [pool] [X]

◆◆◆ Johnston Canyon Resort CA ❀
(403) 762-2971. $116-$279. Hwy 1A. 24 km nw on Hwy 1A (Bow Valley Pkwy). Ext corridors. Pets: Other species. $10 daily fee/pet. Supervision.
[X] [fridge] [micro] [restaurant] [X] [K] [Z]

(AAA) ◆◆◆ Red Carpet Inn M
(403) 762-4184. $79-$159. 425 Banff Ave. 1 km ne. Ext/int corridors. Pets: Other species. $10 daily fee/pet. Service with restrictions, supervision.
[SAVE] [X] [fridge] [micro]

BROOKS

(AAA) ◆◆◆ ◆◆◆ Best Western Brooks Inn SH
(403) 363-0080. $99-$149, 30 day notice. 115 Fifteenth Ave W. Just s off Trans-Canada Hwy 1. Ext/int corridors. Pets: Accepted.
[SAVE] [S] [X] [fridge] [micro] [micro] [pool] [X]

◆◆◆ The Douglas Country Inn BB
(403) 362-2873. $75. Hwy 873, 6.5 km n of jct Trans-Canada Hwy 1. Int corridors. Pets: Accepted.
[S] [X] [W] [Z]

◆◆◆ Heritage Inn SH
(403) 362-6666. $97. 1217 2nd St W. Hwy 873, 0.8 km s of jct Trans-Canada Hwy 1. Int corridors. Pets: $10 daily fee/room. Designated rooms, service with restrictions, supervision.
[ASK] [S] [X] [fridge] [micro] [tv] [X]

◆◆◆◆ Holiday Inn Express Hotel & Suites Brooks SH
(403) 362-7440. $125-$141. 1307 2nd St W. Trans-Canada Hwy 1, exit 2nd St W. Int corridors. Pets: Accepted.
[ASK] [S] [X] [micro] [fridge] [micro]

◆◆◆ Travelodge Brooks SH
(403) 362-8000. $91-$96. 1240 Cassils Rd E. Trans-Canada Hwy 1, 0.3 km sw on SR 542, exit E Brooks. Ext/int corridors. Pets: Accepted.
[ASK] [S] [X] [micro] [fridge] [micro]

CALGARY METROPOLITAN AREA

AIRDRIE

(AAA) ◆◆◆ Super 8 Motel-Airdrie SH ❀
(403) 948-4188. $70-$94, 3 day notice. 815 E Lake Blvd. Hwy 2, exit E Airdrie, 0.8 km e on Hwy 587 E, then 1.8 km s. Int corridors. Pets: Other species. $10 one-time fee/room. Service with restrictions, supervision.
[SAVE] [S] [X] [fridge] [micro]

CALGARY

(AAA) ◆◆◆ ◆◆◆ Best Western Hospitality Inn SH
(403) 278-5050. $169-$179. 135 Southland Dr SE. On Hwy 2A (MacLeod Tr); corner of Southland Dr. Int corridors. Pets: Accepted.
[SAVE] [S] [X] [fridge] [micro] [tv] [X]

(AAA) ◆◆◆ Best Western Village Park Inn SH
(403) 289-0241. $99-$189. 1804 Crowchild Tr NW. Just ne of jct Trans-Canada Hwy 1 and Crowchild Tr. Int corridors. Pets: Designated rooms, service with restrictions, supervision.
[SAVE] [S] [X] [micro] [fridge] [micro] [tv] [pool]

◆◆◆ Blackfoot Inn SH
(403) 252-2253. $99-$189, 3 day notice. 5940 Blackfoot Tr SE. At 58th Ave SE; access to property from 58th Ave only. Int corridors. Pets: Accepted.
[ASK] [S] [X] [fridge] [micro] [tv] [pool] [X]

(AAA) ◆◆◆ ◆◆◆ Calgary Marriott Hotel LH
(403) 266-7331. $113-$208. 110 9th Ave SE. Jct 9th Ave and Centre St; attached to Telus Convention Centre. Int corridors. Pets: Service with restrictions, crate.
[SAVE] [X] [micro] [fridge] [fridge] [micro] [tv] [pool] [X]

(AA) ▼▼▼▼ **Calgary Westways Guest House** 🅱🅱 ❀
(403) 229-1758. **$79-$139, 7 day notice.** 216 25th Ave SW. 1.7 km s
on Hwy 2A (MacLeod Tr S), 0.5 km w. Int corridors. **Pets:** Large, other
species. $8 daily fee/pet.
SAVE 🔳 ⊗

(AA) ▼▼ ▼ **Carriage House Inn** 🆂🅷
(403) 253-1101. **$89-$129, 3 day notice.** 9030 MacLeod Tr S. On Hwy
2A (MacLeod Tr); corner of 90th Ave SW. Int corridors. **Pets:** $10 daily
fee/pet. Designated rooms, service with restrictions, supervision.
SAVE ⊗ ⊟ ▣ ⊞ ‖ ⇘ ⊠

▼▼▼▼ **Coast Plaza Hotel & Conference Centre** 🅻🅷 ❀
(403) 248-8888. **$129-$189.** 1316 33rd St NE. Just s of jct 16th Ave
(Trans-Canada Hwy 1) and 36th St NE, just w on 12th Ave NE. Int
corridors. **Pets:** Other species. $15 daily fee/pet. Supervision.
A$K ⊗ ⊑ᴹ ⊡ ⊟ ▣ ⊞ ‖ ⇘ ⊠

▼▼▼▼ **Days Inn Calgary Airport** 🆂🅷
(403) 250-3297. **$100-$125.** 2799 Sunridge Way NE. Barlow Tr, just e
of Sunridge Way NE. Int corridors. **Pets:** Small, dogs only. $10 one-time
fee/pet. Designated rooms, service with restrictions, crate.
A$K 🔳 ⊗ ⊑ᴹ ⊟ ▣ ⇘ ⊠

(AA) ▼▼ ▼ **Days Inn Calgary South** 🆂🅷
(403) 243-5531. **$89-$179.** 3828 MacLeod Tr S. Corner of MacLeod Tr
and 38th Ave SE. Int corridors. **Pets:** Other species. $10 daily fee/pet.
Service with restrictions, crate.
SAVE 🔳 ⊗ ⊟ ▣ ⊞ ‖ ⇘ ⊠

▼▼▼▼ **Delta Bow Valley** 🅻🅷
(403) 266-1980. **$199-$289.** 209 4th Ave SE. 1st St SE and 4th Ave
SE. Int corridors. **Pets:** Accepted.
A$K 🔳 ⊗ ⊟ ▣ ‖ ⇘ ⊠

▼▼▼▼ **Delta Calgary Airport** 🅻🅷
(403) 291-2600. **$139-$249.** 2001 Airport Rd NE. At Calgary International Airport. Int corridors. **Pets:** Accepted.
A$K 🔳 ⊗ ⊟ ▣ ⊞ ‖ ⇘ ⊠

(AA) ▼▼ ▼ **Econo Lodge South** 🅼
(403) 252-4401. **$89-$189.** 7505 MacLeod Tr S. Corner of MacLeod Tr
and 75th Ave. Ext/int corridors. **Pets:** $10 daily fee/pet. Designated
rooms, service with restrictions, supervision.
SAVE 🔳 ⊗ ⊟ ▣ ⇘

(AA) ▼▼ **Elbow River Inn & Casino** 🆂🅷
(403) 269-6771. **$109-$159.** 1919 MacLeod Tr SE. Jct MacLeod Tr and
1st St SE. Int corridors. **Pets:** $15 daily fee/room. Service with restrictions,
supervision.
SAVE 🔳 ⊗ ‖

▼▼▼▼ **Executive Royal Inn North Calgary** 🆂🅷 ❀
(403) 291-2003. **$110-$150.** 2828 23rd St NE. 27th Ave NE and Barlow
Tr. Int corridors. **Pets:** Medium, other species. $20 one-time fee/room.
Service with restrictions.
A$K 🔳 ⊗ ⊑ᴹ ⊟ ▣ ‖ ⊠

▼▼ ▼▼ **The Fairmont Palliser** 🅻🅷
(403) 262-1234. **$129-$440.** 133 9th Ave SW. 9th Ave SW and 1st St
SW. Int corridors. **Pets:** Accepted.
A$K 🔳 ⊗ ▣ ‖ ⇘ ⊠

▼▼ ▼ **Glenmore Inn and Convention Centre** 🆂🅷
(403) 279-9611. **Call for rates.** 2720 Glenmore Tr SE. 3 km e of Hwy
2 (Deerfoot Tr), exit Glenmore Tr E; at Ogden Rd. Int corridors.
Pets: Accepted.
⊗ ⊟ ▣ ‖ ⊠

(AA) ▼▼▼▼ **Greenwood Inn Hotels** 🆂🅷
(403) 250-8855. **$99-$139.** 3515 26th St NE. From Barlow Tr N, just e
on 32nd Ave NE, then just n. Int corridors. **Pets:** Accepted.
SAVE 🔳 ⊡ ⊟ ▣ ⊞ ‖ ⊠

▼▼ ▼ **Hawthorn Hotel & Suites** 🅻🅷
(403) 263-0520. **$149-$199.** 618 5th Ave SW. Corner of 5th Ave SW
and 5th St SW. Int corridors. **Pets:** Accepted.
A$K ⊗ ⊗ ⊟ ▣ ⊞ ‖ ⇘ ⊠

(AA) ▼▼▼▼ **Holiday Inn Calgary-Airport** 🆂🅷
(403) 230-1999. **$99-$199.** 1250 McKinnon Dr NE. 1 km e of jct Hwy 2
(Deerfoot Tr) and 16th Ave NE (Trans-Canada Hwy 1). Int corridors.
Pets: Medium. $25 deposit/room. Designated rooms, service with restric-
tions, supervision.
SAVE 🔳 ⊗ ⊟ ▣ ⊞ ‖ ⇘

▼▼ ▼ **Holiday Inn Conference Centre Calgary**
   Downtown 🆂🅷
(403) 266-4611. **$129.** 119 12th Ave SW. At 1st St SW; centre. Int
corridors. **Pets:** Accepted.
A$K 🔳 ⊗ ⊑ᴹ ⊡ ⊟ ▣ ‖ ⇘

(AA) ▼▼▼▼ **Holiday Inn Express Calgary-University** 🆂🅷
(403) 289-6600. **$90-$158.** 2227 Banff Tr NW. 16th Ave (Trans-Canada
Hwy 1) and Banff Tr NW. Int corridors. **Pets:** Other species. Designated
rooms, service with restrictions, supervision.
SAVE 🔳 ⊗ ⊑ᴹ ⊟ ▣

(AA) ▼▼▼▼ **Holiday Inn Express Hotel & Suites Calgary**
   Downtown 🆂🅷
(403) 269-8262. **$99-$179.** 1020 8th Ave SW. 8th Ave at 10th St SW.
Int corridors. **Pets:** Small. $15 daily fee/room. Designated rooms, service
with restrictions, supervision.
SAVE 🔳 ⊗ ⊟ ▣

▼▼▼ **Holiday Inn Express Hotel & Suites**
   Calgary-South 🆂🅷
(403) 225-3000. **$149-$249.** 12025 Lake Fraser Dr SE (MacLeod Tr S).
Hwy 2 (Deerfoot Tr), exit Anderson Rd w, then just s on MacLeod Tr.
Int corridors. **Pets:** Accepted.
A$K ⊗ ⊟ ▣ ⇘ ⊠

(AA) ▼▼ ▼ **International Hotel of Calgary** 🅻🅷
(403) 265-9600. **$229-$259.** 220 4th Ave SW. Corner of 4th Ave and
2nd St SW. Int corridors. **Pets:** Accepted.
SAVE 🔳 ⊗ ▣ ‖ ⇘ ⊠

▼▼ ▼ **Marriott Residence Inn-Calgary Airport** 🆂🅷
(403) 735-3336. **$149-$219, 10 day notice.** 2622 39th Ave NE. Corner
of Barlow Tr and 39th Ave NE. Int corridors. **Pets:** Small, other species.
$100 one-time fee/room. Service with restrictions, crate.
A$K 🔳 ⊗ ⊑ᴹ ⊡ ⊟ ▣ ⇘ ⊠

(AA) ▼▼ ▼ **Quality Inn University** 🆂🅷
(403) 289-1973. **$79-$169, 3 day notice.** 2359 Banff Tr NW. Just n of
jct Trans-Canada Hwy 1 and Crowchild Tr. Ext/int corridors.
Pets: Medium, other species. $10 daily fee/pet. Designated rooms, service
with restrictions, crate.
SAVE 🔳 ⊗ ⊟ ▣ ‖ ⇘ ⊠

(AA) ▼▼▼▼ **Radisson Hotel Calgary Airport** 🆂🅷
(403) 291-4666. **$94-$135.** 2120 16th Ave NE. 0.5 km e of jct 16th Ave
NE (Trans-Canada Hwy 1) and Hwy 2 (Deerfoot Tr). Int corridors.
Pets: Dogs only. $10 daily fee/room. Designated rooms, service with restric-
tions, crate.
SAVE 🔳 ⊗ ⊑ᴹ ⊟ ▣ ‖ ⇘

▼▼▼▼ **Sandman Hotel Downtown Calgary** 🅻🅷
(403) 237-8626. **$109-$190.** 888 7th Ave SW. Corner of 7th Ave SW
and 8th St. Int corridors. **Pets:** Small. $10 daily fee/room. Designated
rooms, supervision.
A$K 🔳 ⊗ ⊟ ▣ ‖ ⇘

▼▼▼▼ **Sandman Hotel Suites & Spa Calgary Airport** 🆂🅷
(403) 219-2475. **$109-$169.** 25 Hopewell Way NE. Just n of jct Barlow
Tr and McKnight Blvd. Int corridors. **Pets:** Accepted.
A$K 🔳 ⊗ ⊟ ▣ ‖ ⇘ ⊠

Sheraton Cavalier Hotel LH ❖
(403) 291-0107. **$189-$269.** 2620 32nd Ave NE. Barlow Tr at 32nd Ave NE. Int corridors. **Pets:** Medium, dogs only. Designated rooms, service with restrictions, supervision.
ASK S✕ 🛏 🍴 ➰ ⊠

CAA **Sheraton Suites Calgary Eau Claire** LH ❖
(403) 266-7200. **$145-$235.** 255 Barclay Parade SW. At 3rd St SW and 2nd Ave SW. Int corridors. **Pets:** Large, dogs only. Designated rooms, service with restrictions, supervision.
SAVE S✕ 🛏 🖵 🍴 ➰ ⊠

CAA **Super 8 Motel Calgary Airport** SH
(403) 291-9888. **$65-$125.** 3030 Barlow Tr NE. Corner of 32nd Ave and Barlow Tr NE. Int corridors. **Pets:** Medium, dogs only. $10 daily fee/pet. Service with restrictions, supervision.
SAVE S✕ 🛏

CAA **Super 8 Motel-Motel Village** M
(403) 289-9211. **$59-$169.** 1904 Crowchild Tr NW. Just n of jct Trans-Canada Hwy 1 and Crowchild Tr. Ext corridors. **Pets:** Small, dogs only. $10 daily fee/pet. Service with restrictions, supervision.
SAVE S✕ 🛏 🖵 ➰

CAA **Travelodge Hotel Calgary Airport** SH
(403) 291-1260. **$95-$149.** 2750 Sunridge Blvd NE. Barlow Tr, then e. Int corridors. **Pets:** Other species. $100 deposit/room. Service with restrictions, crate.
SAVE S✕ 🛏 🖵 🍴 ➰

CAA **Travelodge Hotel Calgary Macleod Trail** SH
(403) 253-7070. **$89-$159.** 9206 MacLeod Tr S. On Hwy 2 (Deerfoot Tr) at 90th Ave SW. Int corridors. **Pets:** Medium. $15 one-time fee/room. Designated rooms, service with restrictions, supervision.
SAVE S✕ 🛏 🖵 🍴 ➰

CAA **The Westin Calgary** LH ❖
(403) 266-1611. **$99-$399.** 320 4th Ave SW. Corner of 4th Ave SW and 3rd St. Int corridors. **Pets:** Other species. Service with restrictions, crate.
SAVE S✕ ⌂M ⬚ 🛏 🖵 🍴 ➰ ⊠

Wingate Inn SH ❖
(403) 514-0099. **$135-$255.** 400 Midpark Way. Hwy 2A (MacLeod Tr), 0.5 km e on Sun Valley, 0.3 km n on Midpark Way, then just s. Int corridors. **Pets:** Other species. $25 daily fee/room. Service with restrictions, supervision.
ASK S✕ ⌂ 🛏 🖵 ➰ ⊠

COCHRANE

Best Western Harvest Country Inn SH
(403) 932-1410. **$89-$129.** 11 West Side Dr. Hwy 1A, 1 km sw on Hwy 22. Ext/int corridors. **Pets:** Small, other species. $7 daily fee/pet. Designated rooms, service with restrictions, supervision.
ASK S✕ 🛏 🖵

Bow River Inn M
(403) 932-7900. **$69-$109.** 3 West Side Dr. Hwy 1A, 1 km sw on Hwy 22. Ext corridors. **Pets:** Accepted.
ASK S✕ 🛏 🖵

Super 8 Motel-Cochrane SH
(403) 932-6355. **$100-$170.** 10 West Side Dr. Hwy 1A, 1 km sw on Hwy 22. Int corridors. **Pets:** Small, other species. $10 daily fee/pet. Designated rooms, service with restrictions, supervision.
ASK S✕ 🛏 🖵 ➰ ⊠

OKOTOKS

CAA **Best Western Okotoks Lodge** SH ❖
(403) 938-7400. **$119-$139.** 22 Southridge Dr. Hwy 2, exit 2A, 4 km s to Southridge Dr. Int corridors. **Pets:** Small. $5 daily fee/pet. Designated rooms, service with restrictions, supervision.
SAVE S✕ 🛏 🖵

STRATHMORE

CAA **Best Western Strathmore Inn** SH
(403) 934-5777. **$84-$179.** 550 Hwy 1. Trans-Canada Hwy 1, jct SR 817; centre. Int corridors. **Pets:** $10 one-time fee/room. Designated rooms, service with restrictions, supervision.
SAVE S✕ 🛏 🖵 ➰

Super 8 Motel M
(403) 934-1808. **$82-$151.** 450 Westlake Rd. Just n on SR 817. Ext/int corridors. **Pets:** Small. $10 daily fee/pet. Designated rooms, service with restrictions, supervision.
ASK S✕ 🛏 🖵

Travelodge Strathmore SH
(403) 901-0000. **$89-$109.** 350 Ridge Rd. Just n of Trans-Canada Hwy 1; at Ridge Rd. Int corridors. **Pets:** Other species. $10 daily fee/room. Designated rooms, service with restrictions, supervision.
ASK S✕ 🛏 🖵 ➰ ⊠

END METROPOLITAN AREA

CAMROSE

Norsemen Inn SH
(780) 672-9171. **$85-$179.** 6505 48th Ave. Hwy 13 (48th Ave) at 65th St; west end of town. Int corridors. **Pets:** Accepted.
ASK ✕ 🛏 🖵 🍴

The Travellers Inn M
(780) 672-3377. **$64-$99.** 6216 48th Ave. Hwy 13 E (48th Ave) at 62nd St. Ext corridors. **Pets:** Accepted.
ASK S✕ 🛏 🖵

CANMORE

CAA **Banff Boundary Lodge** CO
(403) 678-9555. **$99-$259, 3 day notice.** 1000 Harvie Heights Rd. Just e of Banff National Park east gate, parallel to Trans-Canada Hwy 1, exit Harvie Heights Rd. Ext corridors. **Pets:** Accepted.
SAVE S✕ 🛏 🖵 ⚞

CAA **Best Western Pocaterra Inn** SH
(403) 678-4334. **$99-$199.** 1725 Mountain Ave. 5.8 km e of Banff National Park east gate on Hwy 1A (Bow Valley Tr). Int corridors. **Pets:** Medium, other species. $15 one-time fee/room. Designated rooms, service with restrictions, supervision.
SAVE S✕ ⌂M 🛏 🖵 ➰ ⊠

CAA **Canadian Rockies Chalets** CO
(403) 678-3799. **$99-$269, 3 day notice.** 1206 Bow Valley Tr. 5.8 km e of Banff National Park east gate on Hwy 1A (Bow Valley Tr); Trans-Canada Hwy 1, exit Canmore. Ext corridors. **Pets:** Accepted.
SAVE S✕ 🛏 🖵 ⚞

CAA **Howard Johnson Canmore/Banff** SH
(403) 609-4656. **$59-$240.** 1402 Bow Valley Tr. 5.6 km e of Banff National Park east gate on Hwy 1A (Bow Valley Tr); Trans-Canada Hwy 1, exit Canmore. Int corridors. **Pets:** $15 one-time fee/pet. Designated rooms, service with restrictions.
SAVE S✕ 🛏 🖵 🍴 ➰

▼▼▼▼ **Mystic Springs Chalets & Hot Pools** CO
(403) 609-0333. **$159-$299, 5 day notice.** 140 Kananaskis Way. Trans-Canada Hwy 1, exit Three Sisters Pkwy; 3 km w to Kananaskis Way. Ext corridors. **Pets:** Medium. $15 daily fee/pet. Service with restrictions.
ASK Sō ☒ 目 ⬛ ⤳ ☒

CAA ▼▼▼ **Radisson Hotel & Conference Centre** SH ❀
(403) 678-3625. **$114-$269.** 511 Bow Valley Tr. Trans-Canada Hwy 1, exit Canmore; 6 km e of Banff National Park east gate on Hwy 1A (Bow Valley Tr). Ext/int corridors. **Pets:** $10 daily fee/pet. Service with restrictions, supervision.
SAVE Sō ☒ 目 ⬛ ⴹ ⤳ ☒

CAA ▼▼▼▼ **Residence Inn by Marriott** SH
(403) 678-3400. **$149-$279.** 91 Three Sisters Dr. Trans-Canada Hwy 1, exit Three Sisters Pkwy, then 4 km n. Int corridors. **Pets:** Accepted.
SAVE ☒ ⴹM ⴰ ⴳ 目 ⬛ ⤳ ☒

CAA ▼▼▼ **Rocky Mountain Ski Lodge** M
(403) 678-5445. **$65-$230.** 1711 Bow Valley Tr. Trans-Canada Hwy 1, exit Canmore; 4.8 km e of Banff National Park east gate on Hwy 1A (Bow Valley Tr). Ext corridors. **Pets:** Medium. $5 daily fee/room. Designated rooms, service with restrictions, supervision.
SAVE Sō ☒ 目 ⬛ ☒

CAA ▼▼▼ **Rundle Mountain Lodge** M ❀
(403) 678-5322. **$64-$135, 7 day notice.** 1723 Bow Valley Tr. Trans-Canada Hwy 1, exit Canmore; 4.8 km e of Banff National Park east gate on Hwy 1A (Bow Valley Tr). Ext corridors. **Pets:** Other species. $7 daily fee/pet. Service with restrictions, supervision.
SAVE ☒ 目 ⬛ ⤳

CAA ▼▼ **Rundle Ridge Chalets** CA ❀
(403) 678-5387. **$84-$215.** 1100 Harvie Heights Rd. Trans-Canada Hwy 1, exit Harvie Heights Rd; 1 km e of Banff National Park east gate. Ext corridors. **Pets:** $10 daily fee/pet. Designated rooms, service with restrictions, supervision.
SAVE ☒ 目 ☒ ⴸ ☎

CAA ▼▼ **The Stockade Log Cabins** CA
(403) 678-5212. **$78-$225.** 1050 Harvie Heights Rd. Trans-Canada Hwy 1, exit Harvie Heights Rd; 1 km e of Banff National Park east gate. Ext corridors. **Pets:** Accepted.
SAVE Sō ☒ 目 ⬛ ⴸ ☎

CAA ▼▼▼ **Windtower Lodge & Suites** CO
(403) 609-6600. **$89-$399, 3 day notice.** 160 Kananaskis Way. Trans-Canada Hwy 1, exit 1A (Bow Valley Tr), 1 km w, then n at Montane Dr. Int corridors. **Pets:** Accepted.
SAVE Sō ☒ 目 ⬛ ⴹ ⴰC

CLARESHOLM

▼▼ **Bluebird Motel** M ❀
(403) 625-3395. **$69-$80.** 5505 1st St W. 0.5 km n on Hwy 2. Ext corridors. **Pets:** Other species. Designated rooms, supervision.
ASK Sō ☒ 目 ⬛

DEAD MAN'S FLATS

CAA ▼ **Pigeon Mountain Motel** M
(403) 678-5756. **$75-$120, 4 day notice.** 250 1st Ave. On Trans-Canada Hwy 1. Ext corridors. **Pets:** Accepted.
SAVE Sō ☒ 目 ⬛ ⴰC

DRUMHELLER

CAA ▼▼▼ **Best Western Jurassic Inn** SH
(403) 823-7700. **$100-$130.** 1103 Hwy 9 S. Hwy 9, se access to town. Ext/int corridors. **Pets:** Accepted.
SAVE Sō ☒ 目 ⬛ ⴹ ⤳

CAA ▼▼▼▼ **Inn at Heartwood Manor** CI
(403) 823-6495. **$89-$260.** 320 N Railway Ave E. Just e of Hwy 9; downtown. Int corridors. **Pets:** Medium, other species. $10 daily fee/pet. Designated rooms, service with restrictions, crate.
SAVE Sō ☒ 目 ⬛

▼▼ **Super 8 Motel** M
(403) 823-8887. **$109-$149.** 600-680 2nd St SE. Off Hwy 9. Ext/int corridors. **Pets:** Accepted.
ASK Sō ☒ 目 ⬛ ⤳ ☒

EDMONTON METROPOLITAN AREA

EDMONTON

▼▼▼ **Alberta Place Suite Hotel** CO
(780) 423-1565. **$99-$149.** 10049 103rd St. Just s of Jasper Ave. Int corridors. **Pets:** Large. $10 daily fee/room. Designated rooms, supervision.
ASK Sō ☒ 目 ⬛ ⴹ ⤳

CAA ▼▼ **Argyll Plaza Hotel** SH ❀
(780) 438-5876. **$84-$129.** 9933 63rd Ave. 63rd Ave at 99th St. Int corridors. **Pets:** Medium. $5 daily fee/pet. Designated rooms, service with restrictions, supervision.
SAVE ☒ 目 ⬛ ⴹ

CAA ▼▼▼ **Best Western Cedar Park Inn** SH
(780) 434-7411. **$119-$169, 3 day notice.** 5116 Gateway Blvd. Hwy 2 (Gateway Blvd) at 51st Ave. Int corridors. **Pets:** Accepted.
SAVE Sō ☒ ⬛ ⴹ ⤳

CAA ▼▼▼▼ **Chateau Edmonton Hotel & Suites** LH ❀
(780) 465-7931. **$129-$349.** 7230 Argyll Rd. Hwy 2 (Gateway Blvd), 3.7 km e at 63rd Ave (turns into Argyll Rd); at 75th St. Int corridors. **Pets:** Large, other species. $25 one-time fee/room. Service with restrictions, supervision.
SAVE Sō ☒ 目 ⬛ ⴹ ⤳

CAA ▼▼▼ **Chateau Louis Hotel & Conference Centre** SH
(780) 452-7770. **$109-$199.** 11727 Kingsway. On Kingsway and 117th St. Int corridors. **Pets:** Accepted.
SAVE Sō ☒ ⴹM ⴰ ⴳ 目 ⬛ ⴹ

CAA ▼▼▼ **Comfort Inn West** SH
(780) 484-4415. **$90-$110.** 17610 100th Ave. At 176th St. Int corridors. **Pets:** $10 daily fee/pet. Service with restrictions, supervision.
SAVE Sō ☒ 目 ⬛ ⴹ

▼▼▼▼ **Crowne Plaza Edmonton-Chateau Lacombe** LH
(780) 428-6611. **$99-$159.** 10111 Bellamy Hill. Jct 101st St, MacDonald Dr and Bellamy Hill. Int corridors. **Pets:** Medium. Service with restrictions, supervision.
ASK Sō ☒ ⴹM ⬛ ⴹ

▼▼▼▼ **Delta Edmonton Centre Suite Hotel** LH
(780) 429-3900. **$105-$279.** 10222 102nd St. At 102nd St at 103rd Ave. Int corridors. **Pets:** Medium, other species. Designated rooms, service with restrictions.
☒ ⴰ ⴳ ⬛ ⴹ ☒

🆔 ▼▼▼ **Delta Edmonton South Hotel and Conference Centre** 🄻🄷
(780) 434-6415. **$111-$169.** 4404 Gateway Blvd. Jct Calgary Tr (Hwy 2) and Whitemud Dr. Int corridors. **Pets:** Accepted.
[SAVE] [X] [■] [■] [▮] [≈]

🆔 ▼▼ **Executive Royal Inn West Edmonton** 🅂🄷
(780) 484-6000. **$125-$232.** 10010 178th St. Corner of 178th St and 100th Ave. Int corridors. **Pets:** Accepted.
[SAVE] [S🄳] [X] [■] [■] [▮] [X]

🆔 ▼▼▼ **The Fairmont Hotel Macdonald** 🄻🄷
(780) 424-5181. **$169-$199.** 10065 100th St. Just s of Jasper Ave. Int corridors. **Pets:** Accepted.
[SAVE] [X] [&M] [■] [▮] [≈] [X]

🆔 ▼▼▼ **Greenwood Inn Hotels** 🅂🄷
(780) 431-1100. **$99-$139.** 4485 Gateway Blvd. Hwy 2 (Gateway Blvd), just n of Whitemud Dr. Int corridors. **Pets:** Accepted.
[SAVE] [X] [&M] [♪] [♿] [■] [■] [▮] [≈] [X]

🆔 ▼▼▼ **Holiday Inn Convention Centre (S.E. Edmonton)** 🅂🄷
(780) 468-5400. **$109.** 4520 76th Ave. Hwy 14, just s via 50th St exit, then just e. Int corridors. **Pets:** Small. $15 daily fee/room. Crate.
[SAVE] [S🄳] [X] [♪] [■] [■] [▮] [≈] [X]

🆔 ▼▼ **Holiday Inn Edmonton-The Palace** 🅂🄷
(780) 438-1222. **$96-$182.** 4235 Gateway Blvd. Just s of Whitemud Dr. Int corridors. **Pets:** $10 daily fee/room. Designated rooms, service with restrictions, supervision.
[SAVE] [S🄳] [X] [■] [■] [▮]

🆔 ▼▼▼ **Mayfield Inn & Suites at West Edmonton** 🄻🄷
(780) 484-0821. **$189.** 16615 109th Ave. 1.6 km n of jct Hwy 2 (Gateway Blvd) and 16A on Mayfield Rd. Int corridors. **Pets:** Accepted.
[SAVE] [S🄳] [X] [■] [■] [▮] [≈] [X]

▼▼▼ **The Met Hotel** 🅂🄷 🐾
(780) 465-8150. **$290-$350.** 10454 82nd Ave (Whyte Ave). Just e of 105th St. Int corridors. **Pets:** $25 one-time fee/pet. Designated rooms, supervision.
[ASK] [S🄳] [X] [■]

🆔 ▼▼ **Rosslyn Inn & Suites** 🅂🄷 🐾
(780) 476-6241. **$92-$139.** 13620 97 St. Hwy 16 (Yellowhead Hwy), 2 km n at 97th St. Int corridors. **Pets:** Medium. $10 daily fee/pet. Designated rooms, service with restrictions, crate.
[SAVE] [S🄳] [X] [■] [■] [▮]

🆔 ▼▼ **Super 8 Hotel** 🅂🄷
(780) 433-8688. **$89-$219.** 3610 Gateway Blvd. Jct 36th Ave. Int corridors. **Pets:** Accepted.
[SAVE] [S🄳] [X] [&M] [■] [■] [≈]

▼▼▼ **The Sutton Place Hotel, Edmonton** 🄻🄷
(780) 428-7111. **$152-$202.** 10235 101st St. 102nd Ave at 101st St. Int corridors. **Pets:** Small. $20 one-time fee/room. Designated rooms, service with restrictions, supervision.
[ASK] [S🄳] [X] [■] [■] [▮] [≈] [X]

🆔 ▼▼ **Travelodge Beverly Crest** 🅂🄷
(780) 474-0456. **$77-$97.** 3414 118th Ave. 8 km e of Capilano Dr, 1 km s from W Hwy 16 (Yellowhead Tr) on Victoria Tr exit. Int corridors. **Pets:** Medium. Designated rooms, service with restrictions, supervision.
[SAVE] [X] [■] [▮]

🆔 ▼▼ **Travelodge Edmonton South** 🅂🄷
(780) 436-9770. **$79-$115.** 10320 45th Ave S. Jct Calgary Tr (Hwy 2) and 45th Ave, just n of Whitemud Dr. Int corridors. **Pets:** $10 daily fee/room. Designated rooms, service with restrictions, supervision.
[SAVE] [S🄳] [X] [■] [■] [≈]

🆔 ▼▼▼ **Travelodge Edmonton West** 🅂🄷
(780) 483-6031. **$94-$119.** 18320 Stony Plain Rd. From Hwy 16, exit 184 St. Int corridors. **Pets:** Medium. $10 deposit/room. Designated rooms, service with restrictions, supervision.
[SAVE] [S🄳] [X] [■] [■] [▮] [≈] [X]

▼▼▼ **The Varscona Hotel** 🅂🄷
(780) 434-6111. **$225-$310.** 8208 106th St. Corner of 82nd Ave (Whyte Ave) and 106th St. Int corridors. **Pets:** Medium. $25 one-time fee/room. Designated rooms, service with restrictions, crate.
[ASK] [S🄳] [X] [■] [▮]

▼▼▼ **The Westin Edmonton** 🄻🄷 🐾
(780) 426-3636. **$289-$299.** 10135 100th St. 101st Ave at 100th St. Int corridors. **Pets:** Medium. Service with restrictions, supervision.
[ASK] [S🄳] [X] [♪] [■] [▮] [≈] [X]

🆔 ▼▼▼ **Wingate Inn Edmonton West** 🅂🄷
(780) 443-1000. **$108-$171.** 18220 100th Ave. 100th Ave at 182nd St. Int corridors. **Pets:** Large. $15 daily fee/pet. Service with restrictions, supervision.
[SAVE] [S🄳] [X] [&M] [■] [■] [≈] [X]

LEDUC

▼▼ **Edmonton International Airport-Super 8 Motel** 🅂🄷
(780) 986-8000. **$81-$101.** 8004 Sparrow Crescent. Hwy 2, exit N Business Section, 32 km s. Int corridors. **Pets:** Other species. $10 one-time fee/pet.
[X] [■] [■]

▼▼▼ **Executive Royal Inn Hotel & Conference Centre** 🅂🄷
(780) 986-1840. **$150.** 8450 Sparrow Dr. Hwy 2, 1 km e. Int corridors. **Pets:** $20 one-time fee/room. Service with restrictions, supervision.
[ASK] [S🄳] [X] [&M] [■] [■] [▮]

NISKU

🆔 ▼▼▼ **Holiday Inn Express Edmonton Int'l Airport** 🅂🄷
(780) 955-1000. **$99.** 1102 4th St. Hwy 2, exit Edmonton International Airport/Nisku Business Park (10th Ave), 0.8 km e. Int corridors. **Pets:** Accepted.
[SAVE] [S🄳] [X] [&M] [♪] [♿] [■] [■]

▼▼ **Nisku Inn & Conference Centre-Edmonton Airport** 🅂🄷
(780) 955-7744. **$139.** 1101 4th St. Hwy 2, exit Edmonton International Airport/Nisku Business Park (10th Ave), 0.5 km e. Int corridors. **Pets:** Other species. $20 daily fee/room. Service with restrictions, supervision.
[ASK] [X] [&M] [■] [■] [▮] [≈]

SHERWOOD PARK

🆔 ▼▼ **Franklin's Inn** 🅂🄷
(780) 467-1234. **$75-$135, 7 day notice.** 2016 Sherwood Dr. At Granada Blvd. Int corridors. **Pets:** $5 daily fee/pet. Designated rooms, service with restrictions, crate.
[SAVE] [X] [■] [■] [▮]

🆔 ▼▼ **Ramada Limited-Edmonton East/Sherwood Park** 🅂🄷
(780) 467-6727. **$116-$125.** 30 Broadway Blvd. Hwy 14, 1.5 km e on Baseline Rd, 0.4 km n on Broadmoor Blvd; Hwy 16, exit Broadmoor Blvd, 2.5 km s. Int corridors. **Pets:** Medium. $15 daily fee/pet. Designated rooms, service with restrictions, supervision.
[SAVE] [S🄳] [X] [&M] [■] [■]

ⓐ ▽▽ **Roadking Inns** 🅢🄷 🐾
(780) 464-1000. **$89-$99.** 26 Strathmoor Dr. Just sw of Hwy 16, exit Broadmoor Blvd. Int corridors. **Pets:** Other species. $200 deposit/room. Designated rooms, crate.
🅂🄰🅅🄴 🆂🄳 ☒ 🄷 🖵 🍴

SPRUCE GROVE

▽▽ **Royal Inn Express Hotel** 🅢🄷
(780) 962-6050. **$88-$94.** 20 Westgrove Dr. I-16A, just n. Int corridors. **Pets:** Small, dogs only. $10 daily fee/pet. Designated rooms, service with restrictions, supervision.
🄰🅂🄺 🆂🄳 ☒ 🄷 🖵

STONY PLAIN

▽▽▽▽ **Ramada Inn & Suites** 🅢🄷
(780) 963-0222. **$75-$129.** 3301 43rd Ave. Hwy 16A, exit Dunmore Rd, just s. Ext/int corridors. **Pets:** Other species. $4 daily fee/pet. Designated rooms, service with restrictions, crate.
🄰🅂🄺 🆂🄳 ☒ 🄷 🖵 🍴 🌫

▽▽ **Stony Convention Inn** 🅢🄷
(780) 963-3444. **$64-$81.** 4620 48th St. Hwy 16A, exit Stony Plain Rd, 0.8 km s on SR 779. Int corridors. **Pets:** Accepted.
🄰🅂🄺 🆂🄳 ☒ 🄷 🖵 🍴

END METROPOLITAN AREA

EDSON

▽▽▽ **Best Western High Road Inn** 🅢🄷
(780) 712-2378. **$109-$199.** 300 52nd St. On 2nd Ave; centre. Int corridors. **Pets:** Medium. $10 daily fee/pet. Designated rooms, supervision.
☒ 🄷 🖵 🍴 🌫 ⊠

ⓐ ▽▽▽ **Guest House Inn & Suites** Ⓜ
(780) 723-4486. **$84-$90.** 4411 4th Ave. 1 km e on Hwy 16. Ext/int corridors. **Pets:** Medium.
🅂🄰🅅🄴 🆂🄳 ☒ 🄷 🖵 🍴 ⊠

▽▽ **Super 8 Motel** 🅢🄷
(780) 723-2500. **$81-$94.** 4300 2nd Ave. 1.1 km e on Hwy 16. Int corridors. **Pets:** Small. $50 deposit/room, $10 daily fee/room. Designated rooms, service with restrictions, supervision.
☒ 🄷 🖵

FORT MACLEOD

▽ **Fort Motel** Ⓜ
(403) 553-3606. **$40-$55.** 451 Main St. Centre. Ext corridors. **Pets:** Accepted.
🄰🅂🄺 🆂🄳 ☒ 🄷 🖵

ⓐ ▽ **Sunset Motel** Ⓜ
(403) 553-4448. **$42-$62.** 104 Hwy 3W. 1 km w on Hwy 2 and 3. Ext corridors. **Pets:** Accepted.
🅂🄰🅅🄴 🆂🄳 ☒ 🄷 🖵

FORT MCMURRAY

ⓐ ▽▽ **Quality Hotel & Conference Centre Fort McMurray** 🅢🄷
(780) 791-7200. **$150-$270.** 424 Gregoire Dr. Hwy 63, 1 km e at Gregoire Dr. Int corridors. **Pets:** Medium, other species. $75 deposit/room. Designated rooms, service with restrictions, crate.
🅂🄰🅅🄴 🆂🄳 ☒ 🄷 🖵 🍴 🌫

▽▽ **Super 8 Motel** 🅢🄷
(780) 799-8450. **$99-$150.** 321 Sakitawaw Tr. Just w of Hwy 63, 5 km s. Int corridors. **Pets:** Accepted.
🄰🅂🄺 🆂🄳 ☒ 🄷 🖵 🍴

GRANDE PRAIRIE

ⓐ ▽▽▽▽ **AmeriHost Inn & Suites** 🅢🄷
(780) 831-2999. **$109-$275.** 11710 102nd St. 102nd St at 117th Ave. Int corridors. **Pets:** Accepted.
🅂🄰🅅🄴 🆂🄳 ☒ 🄷 🖵 🌫 ⊠

ⓐ ▽▽▽ **Best Western Grande Prairie Hotel & Suites** 🅢🄷
(780) 402-2378. **$99-$119.** 10745 117th Ave. Corner of Hwy 43 and 117th Ave. Int corridors. **Pets:** Large, other species. $20 one-time fee/ room. Service with restrictions, supervision.
🅂🄰🅅🄴 🆂🄳 ☒ 🎴 🄷 🖵 🍴 🌫

▽▽ **Quality Hotel & Conference Centre Grande Prairie** 🅢🄷
(780) 539-6000. **$90-$134.** 11201 100th Ave. 2.9 km w on Hwy 2. Int corridors. **Pets:** Accepted.
🄰🅂🄺 🆂🄳 ☒ 🄷 🖵 🍴

▽▽ **Service Plus Inns and Suites** 🅢🄷 🐾
(780) 538-3900. **$99-$250.** 10810 107th A Ave. 2.2 km w on Hwy 2, just n. Int corridors. **Pets:** $10 one-time fee/room. Designated rooms, service with restrictions, supervision.
🆂🄳 ☒ 🎴 🄷 🖵 🌫 ⊠

▽▽ **Stanford Inn** 🅢🄷 🐾
(780) 539-5678. **$72-$82.** 11401 100th Ave. 2.8 km w on Hwy 2. Ext/int corridors. **Pets:** Other species. $5 daily fee/pet. Service with restrictions, supervision.
🄰🅂🄺 🆂🄳 ☒ 🄷 🖵 🍴 ⊠

HIGH RIVER

▽▽ **Heritage Inn** 🅢🄷
(403) 652-3834. **$95-$97.** 1104 11th Ave SE. Trans-Canada Hwy 2, exit 23, 2 km w of Hwy 2. Int corridors. **Pets:** $10 daily fee/room. Service with restrictions, supervision.
🄰🅂🄺 🆂🄳 ☒ 🄷 🖵 🍴 🌫

▽▽▽ **Super 8 Motel** 🅢🄷
(403) 652-4448. **$100-$160.** 1601 13th Ave SE. Trans-Canada Hwy 2, exit High River, just w. Int corridors. **Pets:** Medium. $10 daily fee/pet. Designated rooms, service with restrictions, supervision.
🄰🅂🄺 🆂🄳 ☒ 🅶🄼 🎴 🄷 🖵 🌫 ⊠

HINTON

▽▽ **Best Western White Wolf Inn** 🅢🄷
(780) 865-7777. **$96-$170.** 828 Carmichael Ln. At west end of town; just off Hwy 16. Ext corridors. **Pets:** $10 daily fee/room. Designated rooms, service with restrictions, crate.
🄰🅂🄺 🆂🄳 ☒ 🄷 🖵 ⊠

▽▽▽ **Ramada Limited & Suites** 🅢🄷
(780) 865-2575. **$94-$149.** 500 Smith St. 6 km e on Hwy 16. Ext/int corridors. **Pets:** Accepted.
🄰🅂🄺 ☒ 🄷 🖵

▽▽ **Super 8 Motel** 🅢🄷
(780) 817-2228. **$87-$114.** 284 Smith St. 1.6 km e on Hwy 16. Int corridors. **Pets:** Accepted.
🄰🅂🄺 🆂🄳 ☒ 🅶🄼 🄷 🌫

JASPER

ⓐ ▽▽ **Amethyst Lodge** 🅢🄷
(780) 852-3394. **$65-$270.** 200 Connaught Dr. 0.5 km e. Ext/int corridors. **Pets:** Designated rooms, service with restrictions, supervision.
🅂🄰🅅🄴 🆂🄳 ☒ 🖵 🍴

▼▼▼▼ **The Fairmont Jasper Park Lodge** 🄻🄷 ❀
(780) 852-3301. **$199-$599, 3 day notice.** Lodge Rd. 4.8 km ne via Hwy 16; 3.2 km se off highway via Maligne Rd, follow signs for lodge. Ext corridors. **Pets:** Other species. $30 daily fee/pet. Supervision.

🅇 🄳 📧 🄷 📟 🍴 🏊 🅇 🄰

🄰🄰 ▼▼▼ **Jasper Inn Alpine Resort** 🅂🄷
(780) 852-4461. **$109-$425, 3 day notice.** 98 Geikie St. 1.2 km ne at Geikie and Bonhomme sts. Ext/int corridors. **Pets:** Other species. $10 one-time fee/room. Designated rooms, service with restrictions.

🅂🄰🅅🄴 🅂 🅇 🄷 📟 🍴 🏊 🅇 🄰

🄰🄰 ▼▼▼ **Lobstick Lodge** 🅂🄷
(780) 852-4431. **$75-$237.** 94 Geikie St. 1.2 km ne at Geikie and Juniper sts. Int corridors. **Pets:** Large, other species. Designated rooms, service with restrictions, supervision.

🅂🄰🅅🄴 🅂 🅇 🄷 📟 🍴 🅇 🄰

🄰🄰 ▼▼▼ **Marmot Lodge** 🄼
(780) 852-4471. **$70-$231.** 86 Connaught Dr. 1.6 km ne. Ext corridors. **Pets:** Accepted.

🅂🄰🅅🄴 🅂 🅇 🄷 📟 🍴 🏊

🄰🄰 ▼▼ **Patricia Lake Bungalows** 🄲🄰
(780) 852-3560. **$59-$250, 7 day notice.** Pyramid Lake Rd. 4.8 km nw via Pyramid Lake Rd. Ext corridors. **Pets:** Medium, dogs only. $10 daily fee/room. Designated rooms, service with restrictions, supervision.

🅇 🄷 📟 🅇 🄰 🅉

🄰🄰 ▼▼ **Pyramid Lake Resort** 🅂🄷
(780) 852-4900. **$125-$399, 7 day notice.** Pyramid Lake Rd. Jct Connaught Dr and Cedar St, 6 km nw via Pyramid Lake Rd. Ext corridors. **Pets:** Accepted.

🅂🄰🅅🄴 🅂 🅇 🄷 📟 🍴 🅇 🄰

🄰🄰 ▼▼▼ **The Sawridge Inn and Conference Centre** 🅂🄷 ❀
(780) 852-5111. **$115-$295, 5 day notice.** 82 Connaught Dr. 1.7 km e. Int corridors. **Pets:** Small, dogs only. $20 one-time fee/room. Designated rooms, supervision.

🅂🄰🅅🄴 🅂 🅇 🄼 🄷 📟 🍴 🏊 🅇

🄰🄰 ▼▼▼ **Sunwapta Falls Resort** 🄼 🐾
(780) 852-4852. **$79-$199.** Hwy 93. 55 km s on Icefields Pkwy (Hwy 93). Ext corridors. **Pets:** Large. $25 one-time fee/room. Service with restrictions, supervision.

🅂🄰🅅🄴 🅇 🄷 📟 🍴 🅇 🄰 🅉

KANANASKIS

▼▼▼▼ **Delta Lodge at Kananaskis** 🄻🄷
(403) 591-7711. **$129-$279, 3 day notice.** Kanasaskis Village. Trans-Canada Hwy 1, 23.5 km s on Hwy 40 (Kananaskis Tr), then 3 km on Kananaskis Village access road, follow signs. Int corridors. **Pets:** Accepted.

🄰🅂🄺 🅂 🅇 🄳 🄷 📟 🍴 🏊 🅇

LAKE LOUISE

🄰🄰 ▼▼▼▼ **The Fairmont Chateau Lake Louise** 🄻🄷
(403) 522-3511. **$199-$839, 3 day notice.** 111 Lake Louise Dr. 3 km up the hill from the village. Int corridors. **Pets:** Accepted.

🅂🄰🅅🄴 🅂 🅇 📟 🍴 🏊 🅇

▼▼▼ **Lake Louise Inn** 🅂🄷
(403) 522-3791. **Call for rates.** 210 Village Rd. Just w of 4-way stop. Ext/int corridors. **Pets:** Large. $100 deposit/room. Designated rooms, crate.

🅂 🅇 🄷 📟 🍴 🏊 🅇

LETHBRIDGE

▼▼▼ **Comfort Inn** 🅂🄷
(403) 320-8874. **$85-$110.** 3226 Fairway Plaza Rd S. Southeast end of city; Mayor Magrath Dr, exit n at Scenic Dr. Int corridors. **Pets:** Accepted.

🄰🅂🄺 🅂 🅇 🄷 📟 🏊

🄰🄰 ▼▼▼ **Days Inn Lethbridge** 🅂🄷
(403) 327-6000. **$79-$91.** 100 3rd Ave S. Corner of 3rd Ave and Scenic Dr; centre. Ext/int corridors. **Pets:** Designated rooms, service with restrictions, supervision.

🅂🄰🅅🄴 🅂 🅇 🄷 📟 🏊

▼▼▼ **Econo Lodge & Suites Lethbridge** 🄼
(403) 328-5591. **$58-$69, 7 day notice.** 1124 Mayor Magrath Dr S. Hwy 3, 4 or 5, exit Mayor Magrath Dr S. Ext corridors. **Pets:** Accepted.

🄰🅂🄺 🅂 🅇 🄷 📟 🏊

▼▼▼ **Holiday Inn Express Hotel & Suites Lethbridge** 🅂🄷
(403) 394-9292. **$84-$225.** 120 Stafford Dr S. Hwy 3, exit Stafford Dr, just s; downtown. Int corridors. **Pets:** Accepted.

🄰🅂🄺 🅂 🅇 🄷 📟 🏊 🅇

🄰🄰 ▼▼▼▼ **Lethbridge Lodge Hotel and Conference Centre** 🄻🄷
(403) 328-1123. **$110-$175.** 320 Scenic Dr. Scenic Dr at 4th Ave S; centre. Int corridors. **Pets:** $10 daily fee/pet. Service with restrictions, supervision.

🅂🄰🅅🄴 🅂 🅇 🄷 📟 🍴 🏊

▼▼▼ **Ramada Hotel & Suites** 🄻🄷
(403) 380-5050. **$145-$155, 14 day notice.** 2375 Mayor Magrath Dr S. 4.5 km se on Hwy 4 and 5, exit Mayor Magrath Dr S. Int corridors. **Pets:** Accepted.

🄰🅂🄺 🅂 🅇 🄷 📟 🍴 🏊 🅇

▼▼▼ **South Country Inn** 🅂🄷
(403) 380-6677. **$70-$125.** 2225 Mayor Magrath Dr. 4.5 km se on Hwy 4 and 5, exit Mayor Magrath Dr, then just w. Int corridors. **Pets:** Accepted.

🄰🅂🄺 🅂 🅇 🄷

🄰🄰 ▼▼ **Thriftlodge** 🄼
(403) 328-4436. **$50-$70.** 1142 Mayor Magrath Dr S. 4 km se on Hwy 4 and 5, exit Mayor Magrath Dr S. Ext corridors. **Pets:** Medium. $7 daily fee/pet. Designated rooms, service with restrictions, supervision.

🅂🄰🅅🄴 🅂 🅇 🄷 🏊

LLOYDMINSTER

▼▼▼ **Best Western Wayside Inn & Suites** 🅂🄷
(780) 875-4404. **$115-$127.** 5411 44th St. 0.8 km w on Hwy 16 from jct Hwy 17. Int corridors. **Pets:** Accepted.

🄰🅂🄺 🅂 🅇 🄷 📟 🍴 🏊

🄰🄰 ▼▼▼ **Tropical Inn** 🅂🄷
(780) 875-7000. **$92-$254.** 5621 44th St. Jct Hwy 16 and 17, 1 km w. Int corridors. **Pets:** Accepted.

🅂🄰🅅🄴 🅂 🅇 🄷 📟 🍴 🏊 🅇

MEDICINE HAT

▼▼▼ **Best Western Inn** 🅂🄷
(403) 527-3700. **$99-$249.** 722 Redcliff Dr. On Trans-Canada Hwy 1; 0.4 km w of jct Hwy 3, access 7th St SW. Ext/int corridors. **Pets:** Medium, other species. Designated rooms, service with restrictions, supervision.

🄰🅂🄺 🅂 🅇 🄼 🄷 📟 🏊 🅇

🄰🄰 ▼▼▼ **Imperial Inn** 🄼
(403) 527-8811. **$68-$84.** 3282 13th Ave SE. 3.6 km se; just n off Trans-Canada Hwy 1. Ext/int corridors. **Pets:** Other species. $100 deposit/room, $5 daily fee/room. Designated rooms, service with restrictions, supervision.

🅂🄰🅅🄴 🅂 🅇 🄷 📟 🍴 🏊 🅇

▼▼▼ **Medicine Hat Lodge Hotel Casino Convention Centre Health Spa & Indoor** 🕮
(403) 529-2222. **$101-$119.** 1051 Ross Glen Dr SE. East end approach to city on Trans-Canada Hwy 1, at jct Dunmore Rd. Int corridors. **Pets:** Other species. Designated rooms, service with restrictions.
[ASK] 🛏 ⊠ 🗎 💻 ⟨¶⟩ ⟰ ⊠

▼ **Ranchmen Motel** Ⓜ
(403) 527-2263. **$57-$67.** 535 16th St SW. Trans-Canada Hwy 1 at 16th St SW. Ext corridors. **Pets:** Small, dogs only. $5 daily fee/pet. Designated rooms, service with restrictions, supervision.
⊠ 🗎 💻

▼ ▼ **Super 8 Motel** 🕮
(403) 528-8888. **$73-$94.** 1280 Trans-Canada Way SE. Trans-Canada Way at 13 Ave SE; just n off Trans-Canada Hwy 1. Ext/int corridors. **Pets:** Other species. $5 daily fee/pet. Designated rooms, service with restrictions, crate.
[ASK] 🛏 ⊠ 🏵M 🗎 💻 ⟰

🅒 ▼▼▼ **Travelodge Hotel Medicine Hat** 🕮 🐾
(403) 527-2275. **$83-$125.** 1100 Redcliff Dr SW. 2.8 km sw on Trans-Canada Hwy 1 at jct Hwy 3. Ext/int corridors. **Pets:** Medium. $7 daily fee/pet. Designated rooms, service with restrictions, supervision.
[SAVE] 🛏 ⊠ 🗎 💻 ⟨¶⟩ ⟰ ⊠

PEACE RIVER

🅒 ▼▼▼ **Travellers Motor Hotel** Ⓜ
(780) 624-3621. **$64-$94.** 9510 100th St. Just s off Hwy 2 S, exit town centre. Ext/int corridors. **Pets:** Large, other species. $100 deposit/room. Designated rooms, service with restrictions, supervision.
[SAVE] 🛏 ⊠ 🗎 💻 ⟨¶⟩

PINCHER CREEK

▼▼ **Heritage Inn** 🕮
(403) 627-5000. **$90-$99.** 919 Waterton Ave (Hwy 6). SR 3, 4.7 km s on SR 6. Int corridors. **Pets:** $10 daily fee/room. Service with restrictions, supervision.
[ASK] 🛏 ⊠ 🗎 💻 ⟨¶⟩

RED DEER

🅒 ▼▼▼ **Capri Hotel Trade & Convention Centre** 🕮
(403) 346-2091. **$90-$175, 48 day notice.** 3310 50th Ave. 2 km s on Hwy 2A (Gaetz Ave). Int corridors. **Pets:** Small. Designated rooms, service with restrictions, crate.
[SAVE] 🛏 ⊠ 🗎 💻 ⟨¶⟩ ⟰ ⊠

🅒 ▼▼▼ **Holiday Inn 67 Street** 🕮 🐾
(403) 342-6567. **$90-$120.** 6500 67th St. 3.2 km nw, 0.8 km e of Hwy 2, exit 67th St. Int corridors. **Pets:** Small, other species. $15 daily fee/pet. Designated rooms, service with restrictions, supervision.
[SAVE] 🛏 ⊠ 🗎 💻 ⟨¶⟩ ⟰ ⊠

🅒 ▼▼▼ **Holiday Inn Express Red Deer** 🕮
(403) 343-2112. **$119-$149.** 2803 50th Ave. 1.8 km n e on Hwy 2A (Gaetz Ave). Int corridors. **Pets:** Medium, other species. $15 daily fee/room. Designated rooms, service with restrictions, supervision.
[SAVE] 🛏 ⊠ 🗎 💻 ⟰ ⊠

🅒 ▼▼▼ **Red Deer Lodge Hotel & Conference Centre** 🕮
(403) 346-8841. **$99-$159.** 4311 49th Ave. Corner of 43rd St and 49th Ave; centre. Int corridors. **Pets:** Medium, other species. $15 daily fee/room. Designated rooms, service with restrictions, supervision.
[SAVE] 🛏 ⊠ 🗎 💻 ⟨¶⟩ ⟰ ⊠

▼▼▼ **Sandman Hotel Red Deer** 🕮
(403) 343-7400. **$99-$109.** 2818 Gaetz Ave. 2 km n. Int corridors. **Pets:** Service with restrictions, supervision.
[ASK] 🛏 ⊠ 🏵M 🗎 💻 ⟨¶⟩ ⟰

🅒 ▼▼▼ **Service Plus Inns and Suites** 🕮
(403) 342-4445. **$94-$199.** 6853 66th St. 3.6 km nw, 0.5 km e of Hwy 2, exit 67th St. Int corridors. **Pets:** Small. $15 daily fee/room. Designated rooms, supervision.
[SAVE] 🛏 ⊠ 🗎 💻 ⟨¶⟩ ⟰ ⊠

▼▼ **Stanford Inn** 🕮
(403) 347-5551. **$80-$100.** 4707 Ross St. Hwy 2, exit Gaetz Ave to 49th St, just e. Int corridors. **Pets:** $10 daily fee/room. Designated rooms, service with restrictions, supervision.
[ASK] 🛏 ⊠ 🗎 💻 ⟨¶⟩

ROCKY MOUNTAIN HOUSE

🅒 ▼ **Chinook Inn** Ⓜ
(403) 845-2833. **$80-$90.** 5321 59th Ave. 1.3 km w on Hwy 11, then s. Int corridors. **Pets:** $10 daily fee/room. Designated rooms, supervision.
[SAVE] 🛏 ⊠ 🗎 💻

🅒 ▼▼ **Holiday Inn Express Rocky Mountain House** 🕮
(403) 845-2871. **$99-$109.** 4715 45th St. Just nw of jct 47th Ave and 45th St. Int corridors. **Pets:** $10 one-time fee/pet. Designated rooms, service with restrictions, supervision.
[SAVE] ⊠ 🗎 💻

▼▼▼ **Super 8 Motel** 🕮
(403) 846-0088. **$99-$159.** 4406 41st Ave. Just off Hwy 11 at east end of town. Int corridors. **Pets:** Medium. $10 daily fee/room. Designated rooms, supervision.
[ASK] 🛏 ⊠ 🗎 💻 ⟰ ⊠

TABER

▼▼▼ **Heritage Inn** 🕮
(403) 223-4424. **$76-$84.** 4830 46th Ave. 1 km e of jct Hwy 3 and 36 S, on Hwy 3. Int corridors. **Pets:** Accepted.
[ASK] 🛏 ⊠ 🗎 💻 ⟨¶⟩ ⊠

WATERTON PARK

🅒 ▼▼▼ **Bayshore Inn** Ⓜ
(403) 859-2211. **$95-$225, 3 day notice.** 111 Waterton Ave. Centre. Ext corridors. **Pets:** Accepted.
[SAVE] 🛏 ⊠ 🗎 💻 ⟨¶⟩ ⊠ 🄰

🅒 ▼▼▼ **Waterton Lakes Lodge** 🕮
(403) 859-2150. **$99-$245, 3 day notice.** 101 Clematis Ave. Centre. Ext/int corridors. **Pets:** Designated rooms, supervision.
[SAVE] ⊠ 🏵M 🄳 🗎 💻 ⟨¶⟩ ⟰ ⊠

WETASKIWIN

▼▼ **Best Western Wayside Inn** 🕮
(780) 352-6681. **$89-$99.** 4103 56 St. Just n of Hwy 13 W, on Hwy 2A. Int corridors. **Pets:** Small. $100 deposit/pet. Designated rooms, service with restrictions, crate.
[ASK] 🛏 ⊠ 💻 ⟨¶⟩

▼▼ **Super 8 Motel** 🕮
(780) 361-3808. **$89-$99.** 3820 56th St. On Hwy 2A, just s of jct Hwy 13 W. Ext/int corridors. **Pets:** Accepted.
[ASK] 🛏 ⊠ 🏵M

WHITECOURT

🅒 ▼▼ **Quality Inn** 🕮
(780) 778-5477. **$62-$78.** 5420 49th Ave. On Hwy 43, 0.5 km e of Hwy 32. Int corridors. **Pets:** Other species. Designated rooms.
[SAVE] 🛏 ⊠ 🗎 💻 ⟨¶⟩ ⊠

BRITISH COLUMBIA

100 MILE HOUSE

▼▼▼ 100 Mile House Super 8 **M**
(250) 395-8888. **$79-$88.** 989 Alder Ave. 1 km s on Hwy 97. Ext corridors. **Pets:** Accepted.
(ASK) (S6) (X) (📁) (💻)

▼▼ Ramada Limited **M**
(250) 395-2777. **$89-$98.** 917 Alder Rd. 1 km s on Hwy 97. Int corridors. **Pets:** Accepted.
(ASK) (S6) (X) (📁) (💻)

▼▼ Red Coach Inn **SH**
(250) 395-2266. **$65-$97.** 170 Cariboo Hwy N. On Hwy 97, on the north end of town. Ext/int corridors. **Pets:** Other species. $6 daily fee/room. Service with restrictions, supervision.
(ASK) (S6) (X) (⚙M) (📁) (💻) (🍴) (⤵)

108 MILE HOUSE

(CAA) ▼▼▼ 108 Resort & Conference Centre **SH**
(250) 791-5211. **$80-$120.** 4816 Telqua Dr. From Hwy 97, 1.6 km nw on access road, follow signs. Ext corridors. **Pets:** Small. $10 daily fee/pet. Designated rooms, service with restrictions, supervision.
(SAVE) (S6) (X) (⚙M) (📁) (💻) (🍴) (⤫)

ABBOTSFORD

▼▼▼ Coast Abbotsford Hotel & Suites **SH**
(604) 853-1880. **$94-$114, 14 day notice.** 2020 Sumas Way. Trans-Canada Hwy 1, exit 92 (Town Centre), just n on Hwy 11. Int corridors. **Pets:** Accepted.
(ASK) (S6) (X) (📁) (💻) (🍴) (⤵)

(CAA) ▼▼▼ Comfort Inn Abbotsford **SH**
(604) 859-6211. **$99-$129.** 2073 Clearbrook Rd. Trans-Canada Hwy 1, exit 87 (Clearbrook Rd). Ext/int corridors. **Pets:** Medium. $10 daily fee/pet. Service with restrictions, crate.
(SAVE) (S6) (X) (⚙M) (📁) (💻) (🍴) (⤵) (⤫)

▼▼▼ Ramada Inn & Conference Centre-Abbotsford **SH** ❀
(604) 870-1050. **$89-$109.** 36035 N Parallel Rd. Trans-Canada Hwy 1, exit 95 (Whatcom Rd). Int corridors. **Pets:** Medium, other species. $20 one-time fee/room. Designated rooms, service with restrictions, supervision.
(ASK) (S6) (X) (⚙M) (⚙) (📁) (💻) (🍴) (⤵) (⤫)

(CAA) ▼▼▼ Super 8 Motel Abbotsford **M**
(604) 853-1141. **$70-$120.** 1881 Sumas Way. Trans-Canada Hwy 1, exit 92 (Town Centre), just n on Hwy 11. Ext corridors. **Pets:** Accepted.
(SAVE) (S6) (X) (📁) (💻)

BLUE RIVER

▼▼ Glacier Mountain Lodge **M**
(250) 673-2393. **$79-$129.** 869 Shell Rd. On Hwy 5 (Yellowhead Hwy) at Shell Rd, follow signs. Int corridors. **Pets:** Accepted.
(ASK) (S6) (X) (📁)

▼▼▼ Mike Wiegele Helicopter Skiing **SH**
(250) 673-8381. **$85-$290, 3 day notice.** 1 Harrwood Dr. On Hwy 5 (Yellowhead Hwy) at Harrwood Dr, follow signs. Ext corridors. **Pets:** Accepted.
(ASK) (S6) (X) (📁) (💻) (⤫)

BOWEN ISLAND

▼▼ Wildwood Lane Cottages **CA**
(604) 947-2253. **$119-$175, 14 day notice.** 1291 Adams Rd. From ferry terminal, 5.6 km w on Grafton Rd, then 1 km n. Ext corridors. **Pets:** Accepted.
(ASK) (S6) (X) (📁) (💻) (⤫)

CACHE CREEK

(CAA) ▼▼ Bonaparte Motel **M**
(250) 457-9693. **$50-$100.** 1395 Hwy 97 N. 1 km n of jct Trans-Canada Hwy 1. Ext corridors. **Pets:** Other species. $10 one-time fee/pet. Designated rooms, no service, supervision.
(SAVE) (S6) (X) (📁) (⤵)

CAMPBELL RIVER

(CAA) ▼▼▼ Best Western Austrian Chalet **M**
(250) 923-4231. **$99-$179.** 462 S Island Hwy. 3.2 km s on Island Hwy 19A. Ext/int corridors. **Pets:** Medium, other species. $5 daily fee/pet. Service with restrictions, supervision.
(SAVE) (S6) (X) (📁) (💻) (⤵) (⤫) (⚙)

(CAA) ▼ Campbell River Lodge Fishing & Adventure Resort **M**
(250) 287-7446. **$64-$89, 3 day notice.** 1760 Island Hwy. On Island Hwy 19A, 2 km nw of downtown; just e from Hwy 19 and 28. Ext/int corridors. **Pets:** Accepted.
(SAVE) (S6) (X) (📁) (🍴) (⚙)

▼ Campbell River Super 8 **M**
(250) 286-6622. **$68-$90.** 340 S Island Hwy. 3 km s on Island Hwy 19A. Int corridors. **Pets:** Small, dogs only. $6 daily fee/pet. Designated rooms, no service, supervision.
(ASK) (S6) (X) (⚙M) (📁) (⤵)

(AA) ▽▽▽ Ramada Hotel & Suites **SH** 🐾
(250) 286-1131. **$109-$159.** 261 Island Hwy. On Island Hwy 19A, 2 km s. Int corridors. **Pets:** Small. $6 daily fee/pet. Designated rooms, service with restrictions, supervision.
SAVE S🐾 ⊠ 🛏 🖵 🍴 ⇨ 🎿

CHASE

▽▽▽ Chase Country Inn Motel **M**
(250) 679-3333. **$59-$95, 3 day notice.** 576 Coburn St. Trans-Canada Hwy 1 and Coburn St. Ext corridors. **Pets:** Small. $5 one-time fee/pet. Service with restrictions, supervision.
ASK S🐾 ⊠ 🛏 🖵 🍴

▽▽▽ Quaaout Resort & Conference Centre **SH**
(250) 679-3090. **$79-$180.** Trans-Canada Hwy 1, exit Squilax Bridge, 2.5 km w on Little Shuswap Rd. Int corridors. **Pets:** Other species. $10 daily fee/pet. Designated rooms.
S🐾 ⊠ 🖔M 🛏 🖵 🍴 ⇨ 🎿

CHILLIWACK

(AA) ▽▽▽ Best Western Rainbow Country Inn **SH**
(604) 795-3828. **$94-$130.** 43971 Industrial Way. Trans-Canada Hwy 1, exit 116 (Lickman Rd). Int corridors. **Pets:** Accepted.
SAVE S🐾 ⊠ 🛏 🖵 🍴 ⇨

(AA) ▽▽▽ Chilliwack Travelodge **SH**
(604) 792-4240. **$59-$87.** 45466 Yale Rd W. Trans-Canada Hwy 1, exit 119, just n. Int corridors. **Pets:** Medium. $5 daily fee/pet. Designated rooms, service with restrictions, supervision.
SAVE S🐾 ⊠ 🛏 🖵 🍴 ⇨

▽▽▽ Comfort Inn **M**
(604) 858-0636. **$90-$119.** 45405 Luckakuck Way. Trans-Canada Hwy 1, exit 119, s on Vedder Rd, then 1 km w. Int corridors. **Pets:** Medium, other species. $5 daily fee/room. Designated rooms, service with restrictions, crate.
ASK S🐾 ⊠ 🖔M 🖵

(AA) ▽▽▽ Rhombus Hotels & Resorts-Downtown
Chilliwack **SH**
(604) 795-4788. **$78-$130.** 45920 First Ave. Trans-Canada Hwy 1, exit 119, 3 km n on Yale Rd, then just w; downtown. Int corridors. **Pets:** Accepted.
SAVE S🐾 ⊠ 🖔M 🛏 🖵 🍴 ⇨

CHRISTINA LAKE

▽▽▽ New Horizon Motel **M**
(250) 447-9312. **$85-$145, 30 day notice.** 2037 Hwy 3. Just e. Ext corridors. **Pets:** Accepted.
⊠ 🛏 🖵 🎿

CLEARWATER

▽▽▽ Clearwater Lodge **SH**
(250) 674-3080. **$123-$145.** 331 Eden Rd. Jct Clearwater Valley Rd and Hwy 5 (Yellowhead Hwy). Ext/int corridors. **Pets:** Other species. $10 daily fee/room. Designated rooms, service with restrictions, supervision.
ASK S🐾 ⊠ 🖔M 🖼 🛏 🖵 🍴 ⇨ 🎿

(AA) ▽▽ Jasper Way Inn Motel on beautiful Dutch Lake **M**
(250) 674-3345. **$56-$95.** 57 E Old N Thompson Hwy. 1 km w on Old N Thompson Hwy, just off Hwy 5 (Yellowhead Hwy). Ext corridors. **Pets:** Accepted.
SAVE S🐾 ⊠ 🛏 🖵 🎿

COURTENAY

▽▽ The Coast Westerly Hotel **SH** 🐾
(250) 338-7741. **$129-$239.** 1590 Cliffe Ave. Corner of Cliffe Ave and Island Hwy 19A N. Int corridors. **Pets:** Large. $10 daily fee/pet. Service with restrictions, supervision.
ASK S🐾 ⊠ 🖔M 🛏 🖵 🍴 ⇨ 🎿

▽▽▽ Kingfisher Oceanside Resort & Spa **SH**
(250) 338-1323. **$125-$165, 7 day notice.** 4330 S Island Hwy. 5 km s on Hwy 19A S. Ext corridors. **Pets:** Accepted.
ASK S🐾 ⊠ 🖔M 🛏 🖵 🍴 ⇨ 🎿 🎾

(AA) ▽▽ Travelodge Courtenay **M**
(250) 334-4491. **$83-$128.** 2605 S Island Hwy (Cliffe Ave). 1.2 km s on Island Hwy 19A S. Ext corridors. **Pets:** Accepted.
SAVE S🐾 ⊠ 🛏 🖵 ⇨ 🎾

CRANBROOK

(AA) ▽▽▽▽ Delta St. Eugene Mission Resort **LH**
(250) 420-2000. **$129-$139.** 7731 Mission Rd. Hwy 3, exit Kimberley/Airport (Hwy 95A) to Mission Rd, 4.5 km n. Int corridors. **Pets:** Accepted.
SAVE S🐾 ⊠ 🛏 🖵 🍴 🎿

▽▽▽ Heritage Inn **SH**
(250) 489-4301. **$100-$105.** 803 Cranbrook St N. Hwy 3 and 95; centre. Int corridors. **Pets:** $10 daily fee/room. Designated rooms, service with restrictions, supervision.
ASK S🐾 ⊠ 🛏 🖵 🍴 ⇨

(AA) ▽▽▽ Model A Inn **M**
(250) 489-4600. **$80-$175.** 1908 Cranbrook St N. 2.5 km n on Hwy 3 and 95. Ext corridors. **Pets:** Accepted.
SAVE S🐾 ⊠ 🛏 🖵

(AA) ▽▽▽ Super 8 Motel **SH**
(250) 489-8028. **$90-$115.** 2370 Cranbrook St N. Just w of jct Hwy 93 and 95; corner of 30th Ave. Int corridors. **Pets:** Accepted.
SAVE S🐾 ⊠ 🖔M 🛏

CRESTON

▽▽ Downtowner Motor Inn **SH**
(250) 428-2238. **$45-$64.** 1218 Canyon St. Corner of 12th Ave N. Int corridors. **Pets:** $4 daily fee/pet.
⊠ 🛏

(AA) ▽▽▽ Skimmerhorn Inn **M**
(250) 428-4009. **$70-$90.** 2711 Hwy 3. On Hwy 3, 0.8 km e. Ext corridors. **Pets:** Accepted.
SAVE ⊠ 🛏 🖵 ⇨

(AA) ▽▽▽ Sunset Motel **M** 🐾
(250) 428-2229. **$64-$84.** 2705 Canyon St, Hwy 3 E. 1 km e on Hwy 3. Ext corridors. **Pets:** Small. $10 daily fee/pet. No service, supervision.
SAVE S🐾 ⊠ 🛏 🖵 ⇨

DAWSON CREEK

(AA) ▽▽▽ Dawson Creek Super 8 **SH** 🐾
(250) 782-8899. **$85-$150.** 1440 Alaska Ave. Just s of jct Hart Hwy 97 S and Alaska Hwy 97 N. Int corridors. **Pets:** Other species. $10 daily fee/pet. Designated rooms, service with restrictions, supervision.
SAVE S🐾 ⊠ 🛏 🖵

DUNCAN

(AA) ▽▽▽ Best Western Cowichan Valley Inn **SH**
(250) 748-2722. **$95-$135.** 6474 Trans-Canada Hwy 1. 3 km n. Int corridors. **Pets:** Large. Service with restrictions, supervision.
SAVE S🐾 ⊠ 🛏 🖵 🍴 ⇨

▽▽ Falcon Nest Motel **M**
(250) 748-8188. **$50-$67.** 5867 Trans-Canada Hwy 1. 1.5 km n. Ext corridors. **Pets:** Small. $7 daily fee/pet. Designated rooms, service with restrictions, supervision.
ASK S🐾 ⊠ 🛏 🖵 ⇨

▼▼▼ **Travelodge Silver Bridge Inn Duncan** SH
(250) 748-4311. **$99-$119.** 140 Trans-Canada Hwy 1. Just n of the
Silver Bridge. Ext corridors. **Pets:** Other species. $10 daily fee/pet. Designated rooms.
A$K S❻ ✕ ☰ ☲ ⟨↑⟩

ENDERBY

CAA ▼▼▼ **Howard Johnson Inn Fortunes Landing** SH
(250) 838-6825. **$79-$109.** 1510 George St. 1 km n on Hwy 97A. Ext
corridors. **Pets:** Other species. $5 daily fee/pet. Designated rooms, service
with restrictions, supervision.
SAVE S❻ ✕ ☰ ☲ ⟨↑⟩ ⤳

FERNIE

CAA ▼▼▼▼ **Best Western Fernie Mountain Lodge** SH
(250) 423-5500. **$97-$279.** 1622 7th Ave. Hwy 3, exit 7th Ave, on Hwy
3; east end of Fernie. Int corridors. **Pets:** Accepted.
SAVE S❻ ✕ ☰ ☲ ⟨↑⟩ ⤳

▼ **Fernie Log Inn** M
(250) 423-6222. **$65-$95.** 141 Commerce Rd. 1.8 km e on Hwy 3. Ext
corridors. **Pets:** Medium. $10 daily fee/pet. Crate.
A$K S❻ ✕ ☰ ☲ ⟨K⟩

CAA ▼▼▼▼ **Park Place Lodge** SH
(250) 423-6871. **$99-$229.** 742 Hwy 3. At 7th St. Int corridors.
Pets: Other species. Designated rooms, service with restrictions, supervision.
SAVE S❻ ✕ ☰ ☲ ⟨↑⟩ ⤳ ⟨✕⟩

CAA ▼▼▼▼ **Riverside Mountain Lodge** CO
(250) 423-5000. **$59-$159, 30 day notice.** 100 Riverside Way. Hwy 3,
2 km w. Ext/int corridors. **Pets:** Accepted.
SAVE S❻ ✕ ☰ ☲ ⟨↑⟩ ⤳ ⟨✕⟩

▼▼▼ **Super 8 Motel-Fernie** SH
(250) 423-6788. **$87-$99.** 2021 Hwy 3. 1.5 km w. Int corridors.
Pets: Accepted.
A$K S❻ ✕ ☰ ⟨✕⟩

FORT ST. JOHN

CAA ▼▼▼▼ **Quality Inn Northern Grand** LH
(250) 787-0521. **$109-$129.** 9830 100th Ave. Centre. Int corridors.
Pets: Large. $12 one-time fee/pet. Designated rooms.
SAVE S❻ ✕ ☰ ☲ ⟨↑⟩ ⟨✕⟩

▼▼ **Ramada Limited** SH
(250) 787-0779. **$105-$123.** 10103 98th Ave. Corner of 100th Ave;
centre of downtown. Int corridors. **Pets:** Small. $10 daily fee/room. Designated rooms, supervision.
A$K S❻ ✕ ⟨�'M⟩ ⟨↓⟩ ☰ ☲ ⟨↑⟩

▼▼▼ **Super 8 Motel-Fort St. John** SH ☙
(250) 785-7588. **$109-$275, 7 day notice.** 9500 Alaska Hwy. Just s on
Hwy 97 (Alaska Hwy). Int corridors. **Pets:** Large, other species. $25 daily
fee/pet. Service with restrictions, supervision.
A$K S❻ ✕ ⟨↑M⟩ ⟨↓⟩ ☰ ☲ ⟨↑⟩ ⤳ ⟨✕⟩

FORT STEELE

CAA ▼▼▼ **Bull River Guest Ranch** RA
(250) 429-3760. **$125-$145, 14 day notice.** Hwy 95, 21.9 km se of
town on Ft Steele-Wardner Rd, 12 km ne on gravel road, follow signs;
Hwy 3 W, 41 km e of Cranbrook, use Ft Steele Rd. Ext corridors.
Pets: Dogs only. Service with restrictions, supervision.
SAVE ✕ ☰ ☲ ⟨✕⟩ ⟨K⟩ ⟨W⟩ ⟨Z⟩

GIBSONS

CAA ▼▼▼ **Cedars Inn** M
(604) 886-3008. **$96-$136.** 895 Gibsons Way. Hwy 101 and Shaw Rd;
6 km n from ferry terminal. Ext/int corridors. **Pets:** $15 daily fee/pet.
Designated rooms, service with restrictions, crate.
SAVE S❻ ✕ ☰ ☲ ⟨↑⟩ ⤳ ⟨✕⟩

GOLD BRIDGE

▼▼▼ **Morrow Chalets** CA
(250) 238-2462. **$200, 30 day notice.** 8 km n from the Tyaughton Lake
turnoff, follow signs. Ext corridors. **Pets:** Other species. No service,
supervision.
A$K S❻ ✕ ☰ ⟨K⟩ ⟨W⟩

GOLDEN

CAA ▼▼▼▼ **Best Western Mountain View Inn** SH
(250) 344-2333. **$109-$189.** 1024 11th St N. On Trans-Canada Hwy 1,
south service road; 0.7 km w of jct Hwy 95 and Trans-Canada Hwy 1.
Int corridors. **Pets:** Accepted.
SAVE S❻ ✕ ☰ ☲ ⤳ ⟨✕⟩

▼ **Golden Gate Motel** M
(250) 344-2252. **$45-$70.** 1408 Golden View Rd. On Trans-Canada
Hwy 1, 1.5 km e of jct Hwy 95. Ext corridors. **Pets:** Small. $5 one-time
fee/pet. Designated rooms, service with restrictions.
A$K S❻ ✕ ☰

▼▼ **Golden Rim Motor Inn** M
(250) 344-2216. **$69-$110.** 1416 Golden View Rd. 1.5 km e on Trans-
Canada Hwy 1 from jct Hwy 95. Ext corridors. **Pets:** Small, dogs only.
$6 daily fee/pet. Designated rooms, service with restrictions, supervision.
A$K S❻ ✕ ☰ ☲ ⟨↑⟩ ⤳ ⟨✕⟩

CAA ▼▼▼▼ **Hillside Lodge & Chalets** CA
(250) 344-7281. **$108-$145, 5 day notice.** 1740 Seward Frontage Rd.
15 km w on Hwy 1, follow signs n off highway. Ext corridors.
Pets: Accepted.
SAVE ✕ ☰ ☲ ⟨✕⟩ ⟨K⟩ ⟨Z⟩

▼ **Quantum Leaps Lodge Ltd** SH
(250) 344-2114. **$80-$100, 30 day notice.** 2119 Blaeberry Rd. 17 km n
of town; from Hwy 1, exit Moberly Branch Rd, 2.1 km ne on Moberly
Branch Rd to Golden Donald Upper, 2.7 km e on Golden Donald
Upper, then 3.3 km ne. Ext corridors. **Pets:** Dogs only. $15 daily fee/pet.
Designated rooms, supervision.
A$K S❻ ✕ ☰ ☲ ⟨✕⟩ ⟨K⟩ ⟨W⟩ ⟨Z⟩

CAA ▼ **Rondo Motel** M
(250) 344-5295. **$60-$88.** 824 Park Dr. Jct Trans-Canada Hwy 1 and
95, 2 km s on 10th Ave, just w on Park Dr; downtown. Ext corridors.
Pets: Accepted.
SAVE S❻ ✕ ☰

GRAND FORKS

▼▼ **Ramada Limited** M
(250) 442-2127. **$89-$109.** 2729 Central Ave. West end of town on
Hwy 3. Ext corridors. **Pets:** Accepted.
A$K S❻ ✕ ☰ ☲ ⟨↑⟩ ⤳

CAA ▼ **Western Traveller Motel** M
(250) 442-5566. **$59-$129.** 1591 Central Ave. West end of town on
Hwy 3. Ext corridors. **Pets:** Small, dogs only. $7 daily fee/pet. Designated
rooms, service with restrictions, supervision.
SAVE S❻ ✕ ☰ ☲

GULF ISLANDS NATIONAL PARK RESERVE AREA

PENDER ISLAND

▼▼▼▼ Poets Cove Resort & Spa **SH**
(250) 629-2100. **$195-$345, 14 day notice.** 9801 Spalding Rd, South Pender Island. From Otter Bay Ferry Terminal, follow signs to South Pender Island 16 km s; Otter Bay Rd to Bidwell Harbour Rd to Canal Rd. Ext/int corridors. **Pets:** Small, other species. $25 daily fee/room. Designated rooms, service with restrictions, supervision.

[ASK] [S🐾] [✕] [👤M] [🔒] [💻] [🍴] [🏊] [✕]

QUADRA ISLAND

CAA ▼▼▼ Taku Resort **M**
(250) 285-3031. **$55-$265, 30 day notice.** 616 Taku Rd. From Campbell River ferry terminal, 6.6 km n on West Rd, then just e on Heriot Bay Rd, follow signs to Heriot Bay. Ext corridors. **Pets:** Accepted.

[SAVE] [✕] [🔒] [💻] [✕] [🐾]

SALTSPRING ISLAND

▼▼▼ Harbour House **SH**
(250) 537-5571. **$59-$295.** 121 Upper Ganges Rd. 1 km n on Lower Ganges Rd, then just e, towards Long Harbour ferry terminal. Ext/int corridors. **Pets:** Accepted.

[ASK] [S🐾] [✕] [👤M] [🔒] [💻] [🍴] [🐾]

▼▼▼ Seabreeze Inne **M**
(250) 537-4145. **$59-$185, 30 day notice.** 101 Bittancourt Rd. From Ganges township, 1 km s on Fulford-Ganges Rd. Ext corridors. **Pets:** Accepted.

[ASK] [S🐾] [✕] [🔒] [💻] [✕] [🐾]

END AREA

HARRISON HOT SPRINGS

CAA ▼▼▼▼ Harrison Hot Springs Resort & Spa **LH** 🐾
(604) 796-2244. **$134-$544, 3 day notice.** 100 Esplanade Ave. Just w. Int corridors. **Pets:** Medium, dogs only. $100 one-time fee/room. Designated rooms, service with restrictions, supervision.

[SAVE] [✕] [🔒] [💻] [🍴] [🐾] [✕]

HOPE

CAA ▼▼ Alpine Motel **M**
(604) 869-9931. **$65-$85.** 505 Old Hope-Princeton Way. Trans-Canada Hwy 1, exit 173 westbound; exit 170 eastbound, just n from lights. Ext corridors. **Pets:** Small. $100 deposit/room, $10 daily fee/room. No service, supervision.

[SAVE] [S🐾] [✕] [🔒] [💻]

CAA ▼ Best Continental Motel **M**
(604) 869-9726. **$55-$80.** 860 Fraser Ave. Trans-Canada Hwy 1, exit 170 to downtown; at Fort St. Ext corridors. **Pets:** Accepted.

[SAVE] [S🐾] [✕] [💻]

CAA ▼ Inn Towne Motel **M**
(604) 869-7276. **$65-$110.** 510 Trans-Canada Hwy. Trans-Canada Hwy 1, exit 170, 1 km n to downtown. Ext corridors. **Pets:** Accepted.

[SAVE] [✕] [🔒] [🐾]

CAA ▼▼ Quality Inn **M**
(604) 869-9951. **$70-$102.** 350 Old Hope-Princeton Way. Trans-Canada Hwy 1, exit 173 westbound; exit 170 eastbound, just n from lights. Int corridors. **Pets:** Small. Service with restrictions, supervision.

[SAVE] [S🐾] [✕] [👤M] [🔒] [💻] [🐾]

INVERMERE

CAA ▼▼▼ Best Western Invermere Inn **SH**
(250) 342-9246. **$89-$155.** 1310 7th Ave. 3 km w of Hwy 93 and 95 at Invermere exit; centre. Int corridors. **Pets:** Large. $10 daily fee/pet. Designated rooms, service with restrictions, supervision.

[SAVE] [S🐾] [✕] [🔒] [💻] [🍴]

KAMLOOPS

CAA ▼▼▼▼ Accent Inns **M** 🐾
(250) 374-8877. **$99-$149.** 1325 Columbia St W. Trans-Canada Hwy 1, exit 369 (Columbia St) eastbound at Notre Dame Dr; exit 370 (Summit Dr) westbound at Notre Dame Dr. Ext corridors. **Pets:** Other species. $10 daily fee/room. Service with restrictions, supervision.

[SAVE] [S🐾] [✕] [👤M] [🔒] [💻] [🐾] [✕]

▼▼ Best Value Super View Inn **M**
(250) 374-8100. **$65-$89.** 1200 Rogers Way. Trans-Canada Hwy 1, exit 368 (Hillside Ave), just s. Ext corridors. **Pets:** Medium. $5 daily fee/pet. Designated rooms, service with restrictions, supervision.

[ASK] [S🐾] [✕] [🔒] [💻] [🐾]

▼▼▼ Courtesy Motel **M**
(250) 372-8533. **$75-$89.** 1773 Trans-Canada Hwy E. 2.4 km e on Trans-Canada Hwy 1, south side of service access road. Ext corridors. **Pets:** Accepted.

[ASK] [S🐾] [✕] [🔒] [💻] [🐾]

▼▼▼ Days Inn **SH** 🐾
(250) 374-5911. **$109-$129.** 1285 Trans-Canada Hwy W. Trans-Canada Hwy 1, exit 368 (Hillside Ave), just s. Int corridors. **Pets:** Medium. $20 daily fee/pet. Designated rooms, service with restrictions, supervision.

[ASK] [✕] [🔒] [💻] [🍴] [🐾]

CAA ▼▼ Grandview Motel **M** 🐾
(250) 372-1312. **$55-$89.** 463 Grandview Terrace. Trans-Canada Hwy 1, exit 369 (Columbia St) eastbound, 2 km n; exit 370 (Summit Dr) westbound to Columbia St via City Centre. Ext corridors. **Pets:** Medium. $5 daily fee/pet. Designated rooms, service with restrictions, crate.

[SAVE] [S🐾] [✕] [🔒] [💻] [🐾]

▼▼ Hospitality Inn **M**
(250) 374-4164. **$55-$83.** 500 W Columbia St. Trans-Canada Hwy 1, exit 369 (Columbia St) eastbound, 2 km n; exit 370 (Summit Dr) westbound to Columbia St via City Centre. Ext corridors. **Pets:** Medium. $10 daily fee/pet. Designated rooms, service with restrictions.

[ASK] [S🐾] [✕] [🔒] [💻] [🍴] [🐾]

CAA ▼▼▼ Kamloops Super 8 Motel **M**
(250) 374-8688. **$62-$150.** 1521 Hugh Allan Dr. Trans-Canada Hwy 1, exit 367 (Pacific Way). Int corridors. **Pets:** Accepted.

[SAVE] [S🐾] [✕] [👤M]

CAA ▼▼▼ Ramada Inn-Kamloops **SH**
(250) 374-0358. **$69-$109.** 555 W Columbia St. Trans-Canada Hwy 1, exit 369 (Columbia St) eastbound, 2 km n; exit 370 (Summit Dr) westbound to Columbia St via City Centre. Int corridors. **Pets:** Medium. $10 daily fee/pet. Designated rooms, service with restrictions, supervision.

[SAVE] [S🐾] [✕] [🔒] [💻] [🍴] [🐾] [✕]

▼▼▼ **Ranchland Motel** **M**
(250) 828-8787. **$55-$71.** 2357 Trans-Canada Hwy E. 4.5 km e on Trans-Canada Hwy 1, exit River Rd, then just w along service access road. Ext corridors. **Pets:** Medium, dogs only. $8 daily fee/pet. Designated rooms, service with restrictions, supervision.

(ASK) (S$) (X) (🔋) (💻)

ⓒ ▼▼▼ **Scott's Inn & Restaurant** **M**
(250) 372-8221. **$59-$99.** 551 11th Ave. Trans-Canada Hwy 1, exit 369 (Columbia St) eastbound, 5 km n; exit City Centre westbound, 1.6 km s on Columbia St. Ext corridors. **Pets:** Medium. $10 daily fee/pet. Designated rooms, service with restrictions, supervision.

(SAVE) (S$) (X) (🔋) (💻) (🍴) (🏊)

KELOWNA

ⓒ ▼▼▼ **Accent Inns** **SH** 🐾
(250) 862-8888. **$99-$159.** 1140 Harvey Ave. Corner of Hwy 97 N (Harvey Ave) and Gordon Dr. Ext corridors. **Pets:** Medium. $10 daily fee/room. Designated rooms, service with restrictions, supervision.

(SAVE) (S$) (X) (⌚M) (🔋) (💻) (🍴) (🏊) (X)

ⓒ ▼▼▼▼ **Best Western Inn-Kelowna** **SH**
(250) 860-1212. **$115-$269.** 2402 Hwy 97 N. 1 km s of jct Hwy 33 and 97 N; corner of Leckie Rd. Ext/int corridors. **Pets:** Medium. $25 daily fee/pet. Designated rooms, service with restrictions, crate.

(SAVE) (S$) (X) (⌚) (🔋) (💻) (🍴) (🏊) (X)

ⓒ ▼▼▼ **Comfort Inn** **SH**
(250) 769-2355. **$89-$139.** 1655 Westgate Rd. Jct Hwy 97 (Harvey Ave) and Bartley Rd, s to Ross Rd. Int corridors. **Pets:** Medium, other species. $10 daily fee/pet. Designated rooms, service with restrictions, supervision.

(SAVE) (S$) (X) (🔋) (💻) (🏊)

▼▼▼ **The Grand Okanagan Lakefront Resort & Conference Centre** **LH** 🐾
(250) 763-4500. **$179-$539.** 1310 Water St. Hwy 97 (Harvey Ave), 1 km w. Int corridors. **Pets:** Other species. $10 daily fee/pet. Designated rooms, supervision.

(ASK) (S$) (X) (⌚M) (🔋) (💻) (🍴) (🏊) (X)

▼▼ **The Royal Anne Hotel** **SH**
(250) 763-2277. **$89-$189.** 348 Bernard St. Corner of Pandosy and Bernard St; downtown. Int corridors. **Pets:** Small. $10 daily fee/pet. Designated rooms, service with restrictions, supervision.

(ASK) (S$) (X) (💻)

▼▼ **Town & Country Motel** **M**
(250) 860-7121. **$83-$129.** 2629 Hwy 97 N. 0.5 km n on Hwy 97 N (Harvey Ave) from jct Hwy 33. Ext corridors. **Pets:** Accepted.

(ASK) (X) (⌚) (🔋) (💻) (🏊)

▼▼▼ **Vineyard Inn** **M** 🐾
(250) 860-5703. **$59-$159.** 2486 Hwy 97 N. Southwest corner of jct Hwy 97 (Harvey Ave) and 33. Ext corridors. **Pets:** Small, dogs only. $5 daily fee/pet. Service with restrictions, supervision.

(ASK) (S$) (X) (🔋) (💻) (🏊) (X)

KIMBERLEY

▼▼▼ **Mark Creek Lodge** **SH**
(250) 427-2266. **$89-$109.** 300 Wallinger Ave. Centre. Int corridors. **Pets:** $10 daily fee/pet. Designated rooms, service with restrictions, supervision.

(ASK) (S$) (X) (🔋) (💻) (🍴)

ⓒ ▼▼▼▼ **Trickle Creek Residence Inn by Marriott** **SH** 🐾
(250) 427-5175. **$137-$345.** 500 Stemwinder Dr. Hwy 95A, 3.1 km w on Ross St, follow signs for Alpine Village, then just e. Int corridors. **Pets:** Large. $75 one-time fee/pet. Service with restrictions, crate.

(SAVE) (X) (🌀) (⌚) (🔋) (💻) (🍴) (🏊) (X)

LOGAN LAKE

▼▼ **Logan Lake Lodge** **M** 🐾
(250) 523-9466. **$60-$65, 7 day notice.** 111 Chartrand Ave. Centre at Meadow Creek Rd and Chartrand Cresent. Int corridors. **Pets:** Other species. $15 one-time fee/room. Designated rooms, supervision.

(ASK) (S$) (X) (💻) (🍴) (🅰)

MADEIRA PARK

▼▼▼ **Sunshine Coast Resort** **CO** 🐾
(604) 883-9177. **$60-$145, 21 day notice.** 12695 Sunshine Coast (Hwy 101). Just n of Madeira Park Rd, follow signs. Ext/int corridors. **Pets:** $20 daily fee/pet. Designated rooms, supervision.

(X) (⌚M) (⌚) (🔋) (💻) (X) (🅰)

MANNING PARK

▼▼▼ **Manning Park Resort** **SH**
(250) 840-8822. **$74-$154, 30 day notice.** Hwy 3. Crowsnest Hwy 3; midway between Hope and Princeton. Ext/int corridors. **Pets:** Other species. $25 one-time fee/room. Designated rooms, service with restrictions, supervision.

(ASK) (S$) (X) (🔋) (💻) (🍴) (X) (🅰)

MCBRIDE

ⓒ ▼▼▼ **North Country Lodge** **M**
(250) 569-0001. **$65-$99.** 868 Frontage Rd N. Just w of village main exit, on Hwy 16 north service road. Ext corridors. **Pets:** Accepted.

(SAVE) (S$) (X) (🔋) (💻) (🍴)

MERRITT

ⓒ ▼▼▼▼ **Best Western Nicola Inn** **SH**
(250) 378-4253. **$79-$105.** 4025 Walters St. Hwy 5, exit 290, 1 km w. Ext corridors. **Pets:** $10 one-time fee/pet. No service, supervision.

(SAVE) (S$) (X) (🔋) (💻) (🍴) (🏊)

ⓒ ▼▼▼ **Merritt Motor Inn** **M**
(250) 378-9422. **$75-$105.** 3561 Voght St. Hwy 5, exit 290, just w. Ext corridors. **Pets:** Small. $9 deposit/pet. Designated rooms, service with restrictions, supervision.

(SAVE) (S$) (X) (🔋) (💻) (🍴)

▼▼ **Ramada Limited** **M**
(250) 378-3567. **$75-$100.** 3571 Voght St. Hwy 5, exit 290, just w. Ext corridors. **Pets:** Accepted.

(ASK) (S$) (X) (🔋) (💻) (🏊) (X)

NAKUSP

ⓒ ▼▼▼ **The Selkirk Inn** **SH**
(250) 265-3666. **$45-$79.** 210 W 6th Ave. Just n. Int corridors. **Pets:** Medium. $20 deposit/room, $8 daily fee/pet. Designated rooms, service with restrictions, supervision.

(SAVE) (X) (🔋) (💻)

NANAIMO

ⓒ ▼▼▼ **Best Western Northgate Inn** **SH** 🐾
(250) 390-2222. **$79-$129.** 6450 Metral Dr. Hwy 19A (Island Hwy), just w on Aulds Rd, then just s. Int corridors. **Pets:** $20 daily fee/pet. Designated rooms, service with restrictions, supervision.

(SAVE) (S$) (X) (🔋) (💻) (🍴) (X)

▼▼ **Days Inn Nanaimo Harbourview** **SH**
(250) 754-8171. **$109-$159.** 809 Island Hwy S. On Island Hwy 1, 2 km s. Int corridors. **Pets:** Small. $5 daily fee/pet. Designated rooms, service with restrictions, supervision.

(ASK) (S$) (X) (🔋) (💻) (🍴) (🏊)

ⓐ ▼▼▼ **Ramada Limited On Long Lake** 🆂🅷 ❖
(250) 758-1144. **$109-$169.** 4700 Island Hwy N. 5 km n on Hwy 19A (Island Hwy) from Departure Bay ferry terminal. Ext corridors. **Pets:** Other species. $20 one-time fee/pet. Supervision.

ⓐ ▼▼▼ **Travelodge Nanaimo** Ⓜ
(250) 754-6355. **$83-$106.** 96 Terminal Ave N. Jct Hwy 19A (Terminal Ave) and Island Hwy 1, access from either highway. Int corridors. **Pets:** Medium. $10 one-time fee/pet. Designated rooms, service with restrictions, supervision.

NANOOSE BAY

▼▼▼ **Fairwinds Schooner Cove Resort & Marina** 🆂🅷
(250) 468-7691. **$89-$159.** 3521 Dolphin Dr. Island Hwy 1, 8.5 km se, follow signs via Powderpoint Rd (becoming Fairwinds Dr). Int corridors. **Pets:** Medium, other species. $10 daily fee/pet. Designated rooms, service with restrictions, supervision.

NARAMATA

▼▼▼ **The Village Motel** Ⓜ
(250) 496-5535. **$59-$127, 14 day notice.** 244 Robinson Dr. 14 km n on Naramata Rd from Penticton. Ext corridors. **Pets:** Accepted.

NELSON

ⓐ ▼▼▼▼ **Best Western Baker Street Inn & Convention Centre** 🆂🅷
(250) 352-3525. **$109-$129.** 153 Baker St. Jct of Hwy 6 and 3A. Int corridors. **Pets:** Other species. Designated rooms, service with restrictions, supervision.

NEW DENVER

▼▼▼ **Sweet Dreams Guesthouse & Dining** 🅲🅸
(250) 358-2415. **$80-$95, 7 day notice.** 702 Eldorado St. 0.4 km w of Hwy 6 on Slocan Ave. Int corridors. **Pets:** Accepted.

PARKSVILLE

ⓐ ▼▼▼▼ **Bayside Oceanfront Inn** 🆂🅷
(250) 248-8333. **$99-$189.** 240 Dogwood St. Island Hwy 19, exit 51 (Parksville/Coombs), 2 km e, then 1 km n on Hwy 19A. Int corridors. **Pets:** Dogs only. $10 daily fee/pet. Designated rooms, service with restrictions, supervision.

▼▼ **Skylite Motel** Ⓜ ❖
(250) 248-4271. **$62-$129.** 459 E Island Hwy. Island Hwy 19, exit 46 (Parksville), 3.5 km n on Hwy 19A. Ext corridors. **Pets:** Other species. Service with restrictions, supervision.

ⓐ ▼▼▼▼ **Tigh-Na-Mara Seaside Spa Resort** 🅻🅷 ❖
(250) 248-2072. **$99-$229, 5 day notice.** 1155 Resort Dr. Island Hwy 19, exit 46 (Parksville), 2 km n on Hwy 19A. Ext corridors. **Pets:** Other species. $10 one-time fee/room. Designated rooms, service with restrictions, crate.

▼▼▼ **Travelodge Parksville** 🆂🅷
(250) 248-2232. **$99-$189.** 424 W Island Hwy. Island Hwy 19, exit 51 (Parksville/Coombs), 2 km e, then just n on Hwy 19A. Int corridors. **Pets:** Other species. $10 daily fee/pet. Designated rooms, service with restrictions, supervision.

ⓐ ▼▼▼ **V.I.P. Motel** Ⓜ ❖
(250) 248-3244. **$84-$129, 7 day notice.** 414 W Island Hwy. Island Hwy 19, exit 51 (Parksville/Coombs), 2 km e, then just n on Hwy 19A. Ext corridors. **Pets:** $20 deposit/pet. Service with restrictions, supervision.

PARSON

▼▼▼ **Timber Inn & Chalets** 🆂🅷
(250) 348-2228. **$65-$95, 30 day notice.** 3483 Hwy 95. Just off Hwy 95 in Parson; 34 km s of Golden. Ext/int corridors. **Pets:** Accepted.

PEMBERTON

ⓐ ▼▼▼▼ **Pemberton Valley Lodge** 🆂🅷 ❖
(604) 894-2000. **$169-$269.** 1490 Portage Rd. Just e on Hwy 99 from Pioneer Junction. Int corridors. **Pets:** Other species. $20 daily fee/room. Designated rooms, supervision.

PENTICTON

▼▼▼ **Best Western Inn at Penticton** 🆂🅷
(250) 493-0311. **$89-$127.** 3180 Skaha Lake Rd. 4 km s. Ext corridors. **Pets:** Accepted.

ⓐ ▼▼▼ **Days Inn Penticton** 🆂🅷 ❖
(250) 493-6616. **$79-$199.** 152 Riverside Dr. Hwy 97, just n. Ext/int corridors. **Pets:** Medium, dogs only. $10 daily fee/pet. Designated rooms, service with restrictions.

ⓐ ▼▼▼ **Golden Sands Resort Motel** 🅲🅾
(250) 492-4210. **$69-$295, 14 day notice.** 1028 Lakeshore Dr W. Riverside Dr and Lakeshore Dr W. Ext corridors. **Pets:** Very small, dogs only. $15 daily fee/pet. Designated rooms, service with restrictions, supervision.

ⓐ ▼▼▼▼ **Penticton Lakeside Resort, Convention Centre & Casino** 🅻🅷 ❖
(250) 493-8221. **$151-$259.** 21 Lakeshore Dr W. Main St at Lakeshore Dr W. Int corridors. **Pets:** Other species. $10 daily fee/room. Designated rooms, service with restrictions, supervision.

ⓐ ▼▼▼ **Penticton Slumber Lodge** Ⓜ
(250) 492-4008. **$78-$208, 14 day notice.** 274 Lakeshore Dr W. Corner of Lakeshore Dr and Winnipeg St; Hwy 97, n on Riverside, 1.5 km e. Ext corridors. **Pets:** Accepted.

▼▼ **Penticton Travelodge** 🆂🅷
(250) 492-0225. **$69-$199.** 950 Westminster Ave W. Hwy 97 (Eckhart Ave), just ne. Ext/int corridors. **Pets:** Accepted.

ⓐ ▼▼▼▼ **Ramada Inn & Suites** 🆂🅷 ❖
(250) 492-8926. **$89-$299.** 1050 Eckhardt Ave W. 1.2 km w on Hwy 97. Ext corridors. **Pets:** Other species. $10 daily fee/pet. Designated rooms, supervision.

ⓐ ▼▼▼ **Spanish Villa Resort** Ⓜ
(250) 492-2922. **$78-$208, 14 day notice.** 890 Lakeshore Dr W. Corner of Power St and Lakeshore Dr W. Ext corridors. **Pets:** Accepted.

▼▼▼ **Super 8 Motel Penticton** Ⓜ
(250) 492-3829. **$64-$116.** 1706 Main St. Jct Main St and Industrial. Ext/int corridors. **Pets:** Accepted.

▼▼ Waterfront Inn M
(250) 492-8228. **$65-$125, 30 day notice.** 3688 Parkview St. Hwy 97 to Channel Pkwy and Skaha Lake Rd, just ne to Lee Ave, then just s. Ext corridors. **Pets:** Accepted.
[ASK] [S⦵] [X] [🛏] [▭] [▭]

PORT ALBERNI

Ⓐ ▼▼▼ Best Western Barclay Hotel SH
(250) 724-7171. **$89-$149.** 4277 Stamp Ave. Johnston Rd (Hwy 4), just s on Gertrude St. Int corridors. **Pets:** Small, other species. $20 daily fee/room. Designated rooms, supervision.
[SAVE] [S⦵] [X] [🛏] [▭] [¶] [▭] [⨯]

▼▼▼ Coast Hospitality Inn SH
(250) 723-8111. **$120-$125.** 3835 Redford St. 3.2 km sw of jct Hwy 4 via City Centre/Port Alberni South Rt. Int corridors. **Pets:** Other species. $10 daily fee/pet. Designated rooms, service with restrictions, crate.
[X] [▭] [¶]

Ⓐ ▼ Riverside Motel M
(250) 724-9916. **$55-$93.** 5065 Roger St. Johnston Rd (Hwy 4), just s on Gertrude St, then just w. Ext corridors. **Pets:** Small. $10 daily fee/pet. Service with restrictions, supervision.
[SAVE] [S⦵] [X] [🛏] [▭] [⨯]

PORT HARDY

▼ Airport Inn SH ❦
(250) 949-9434. **$70-$105.** 4030 Byng Rd. Hwy 19, 5 km ne, follow signs. Int corridors. **Pets:** Other species.
[X] [🛏] [▭] [¶] [⨯]

▼▼ Glen Lyon Inn SH
(250) 949-7115. **$85-$130, 3 day notice.** 6435 Hardy Bay Rd. Hwy 19, 1.5 km n, follow signs. Ext corridors. **Pets:** Accepted.
[X] [🛏] [▭] [¶] [⨯]

Ⓐ ▼ Pioneer Inn M
(250) 949-7271. **$57-$112.** 8405 Byng Rd. Hwy 19, 1 km w, follow signs. Ext corridors. **Pets:** Medium, other species. $10 daily fee/pet. Designated rooms, service with restrictions, supervision.
[SAVE] [S⦵] [X] [🛏] [▭] [¶] [⨯]

POWELL RIVER

▼▼▼ Powell River Town Centre Hotel SH
(604) 485-3000. **$135-$165.** 4660 Joyce Ave. 0.8 km e on Duncan St (BC ferry terminal), then 1 km n. Int corridors. **Pets:** Accepted.
[ASK] [S⦵] [X] [L.M] [▭] [¶]

PRINCE GEORGE

Ⓐ ▼▼▼ P.G. Hi-Way Motel M
(250) 564-6869. **$55-$70.** 1737 20th Ave. Jct Hwy 97, 1.2 km e on Trans-Canada Hwy 16 (Yellowhead Hwy). Ext corridors. **Pets:** Very small. $10 daily fee/pet. Designated rooms, no service, supervision.
[SAVE] [S⦵] [X] [🛏] [▭]

PRINCE RUPERT

Ⓐ ▼ Aleeda Motel M
(250) 627-1367. **$60-$70.** 900 3rd Ave W. Corner of 3rd Ave W and 8th St. Int corridors. **Pets:** Accepted.
[SAVE] [S⦵] [X] [🛏] [▭] [⨯]

▼▼ Howard Johnson Highliner Plaza Hotel SH
(250) 624-9060. **$85-$125.** 815 1st Ave W. Corner of 1st Ave W and 7th St; downtown. Int corridors. **Pets:** Small. $10 daily fee/pet. Designated rooms, service with restrictions, supervision.
[ASK] [S⦵] [X] [🛏] [▭] [¶] [⨯]

PRINCETON

Ⓐ ▼▼▼ Best Western Princeton Inn M
(250) 295-3537. **$89-$119.** 169 Hwy 3. On Hwy 3. Ext corridors. **Pets:** Medium. $10 daily fee/pet. Designated rooms, service with restrictions, supervision.
[SAVE] [S⦵] [X] [🛏] [▭] [⤳]

Ⓐ ▼ Econo Lodge Princeton (Villager Inn) M
(250) 295-6996. **$79-$129.** 244 4th St. Just off Hwy 3. Ext corridors. **Pets:** Small. $10 one-time fee/pet. Designated rooms, service with restrictions, supervision.
[SAVE] [S⦵] [X] [🛏] [▭] [⤳]

QUALICUM BEACH

▼▼ Old Dutch Inn (By The Sea) SH
(250) 752-6914. **$69-$109.** 2690 Island Hwy W. Hwy 19, exit 60 (Qualicum Beach/Port Alberni), 4 km on Memorial Ave at jct Hwy 19A. Int corridors. **Pets:** Small, dogs only. $15 one-time fee/pet. Designated rooms, service with restrictions, supervision.
[ASK] [S⦵] [X] [🛏] [▭] [¶] [⤳] [⨯]

▼▼ Qualicum Heritage Inn SH
(250) 752-9262. **$89-$119.** 427 College Rd. Hwy 19, exit 60 (Qualicum Beach/Port Alberni), 4 km e on Memorial Ave, then 1 km s on Island Hwy 19A. Int corridors. **Pets:** Accepted.
[ASK] [S⦵] [X] [▭] [¶] [⨯]

QUESNEL

Ⓐ ▼▼ Talisman Inn M ❦
(250) 992-7247. **$65-$81.** 753 Front St. Hwy 97, 1 km n of Carson Ave. Int corridors. **Pets:** Other species. Designated rooms, service with restrictions, supervision.
[SAVE] [X] [🛏] [▭]

RADIUM HOT SPRINGS

▼ Chalet Europe M ❦
(250) 347-9305. **$79-$159, 7 day notice.** 5063 Madsen Rd. Hwy 93 and 95, just e, 1 km off Hwy 93 up the hill. Ext corridors. **Pets:** Dogs only. $10 deposit/room, $10 daily fee/room. Designated rooms, supervision.
[ASK] [S⦵] [X] [🛏] [▭] [⨯]

▼ Lido Motel M
(250) 347-9533. **$48-$75.** 4876 McKay St. Hwy 93 and 95 S, Stanley St W to Main St W, then s. Ext corridors. **Pets:** Other species. $5 daily fee/pet. Supervision.
[X] [🛏] [▭] [Ⓩ]

▼▼ Sunrise Suites Motel CO
(250) 347-0008. **$70-$175, 7 day notice.** 7369 Prospector Ave. Hwy 93 and 95, 0.7 km n on Hwy 95, just sw. Ext corridors. **Pets:** Accepted.
[X] [🛏] [▭] [⨯] [⨯]

▼ Sunset Motel M
(250) 347-0021. **$55-$120.** 4883 McKay St. Hwy 93 and 95 S, w to service road (Main St), just s. Ext corridors. **Pets:** Small, dogs only. $5 one-time fee/pet. Designated rooms, service with restrictions, supervision.
[S⦵] [X] [🛏] [▭] [Ⓩ]

REVELSTOKE

Ⓐ ▼▼▼ Best Western Wayside Inn SH
(250) 837-6161. **$89-$149.** 1901 LaForme Blvd. North side of Trans-Canada Hwy 1, at intersection nearest east end of Columbia River Bridge. Ext/int corridors. **Pets:** Accepted.
[SAVE] [S⦵] [X] [L.M] [🛏] [▭] [¶] [⤳]

Ⓐ ▼▼▼ The Coast Hillcrest Resort Hotel LH ❦
(250) 837-3322. **$110-$180.** 2100 Oak Dr. 4.3 km e on Trans-Canada Hwy 1, 0.9 km sw. Int corridors. **Pets:** Other species. $15 one-time fee/room. Designated rooms, service with restrictions, supervision.
[SAVE] [S⦵] [X] [🛏] [▭] [¶] [⨯]

(AA) 🔷🔷🔷 **Monashee Lodge** **M**
(250) 837-6778. **$45-$86.** 1601 3rd St W. South side of Trans-Canada Hwy 1, just e of Columbia River Bridge at Victoria Rd, then just se on Wright Ave. Ext corridors. **Pets:** Other species. $5 one-time fee/pet. Service with restrictions, supervision.
[SAVE] [✕] [📶] [📺]

(AA) 🔷🔷🔷 **The Regent Inn** **SH**
(250) 837-2107. **$119-$149.** 112 1st St E. 2 km s from Trans-Canada Hwy 1 at Victoria Rd; downtown. Int corridors. **Pets:** Accepted.
[SAVE] [S🐾] [✕] [❑] [✕]

(AA) 🔷 **Swiss Chalet Motel** **M**
(250) 837-4650. **$49-$82.** 1101 Victoria Rd. 1 km s from Trans-Canada Hwy 1. Ext corridors. **Pets:** Small, dogs only. $5 one-time fee/pet. Designated rooms, service with restrictions, supervision.
[SAVE] [✕] [📶] [📺]

ROSSLAND

🔷 **Thriftlodge Rossland** **M**
(250) 362-7364. **$64-$89, 3 day notice.** 1199 Nancy Green Hwy. 1 km w on Hwy 3B, jct Hwy 22. Ext corridors. **Pets:** Other species. $7 daily fee/room. Designated rooms, service with restrictions, supervision.
[ASK] [S🐾] [✕] [📶] [📺]

SALMON ARM

🔷🔷🔷 **Holiday Inn Express Hotel & Suites Salmon Arm** **SH**
(250) 832-7711. **$107-$125.** 1090 22nd St NE. 0.5 mi on Trans-Canada Hwy 1. Int corridors. **Pets:** Accepted.
[ASK] [S🐾] [✕] [🅜] [🗝] [📶] [📺] [🏊] [✕]

🔷 **Super 8 Motel** **SH**
(250) 832-8812. **$60-$150.** 2901 10th Ave NE. 1 km e on Trans-Canada Hwy 1. Int corridors. **Pets:** Accepted.
[S🐾] [✕] [🅜] [📶]

SECHELT

🔷🔷 **Driftwood Inn** **M**
(604) 885-5811. **$89-$169.** 5454 Trail Ave. Follow Sunshine Coast Hwy 101, just w of city centre. Ext/int corridors. **Pets:** $10 daily fee/pet. Service with restrictions, supervision.
[ASK] [S🐾] [✕] [📶] [📺] [❑] [🅐]

SICAMOUS

🔷🔷 **Sicamous Super 8 Motel** **SH**
(250) 836-4988. **$60-$130.** 1120 Riverside Ave. Trans-Canada Hwy 1, s on Hwy 97A, just w on Main St to traffic circle, then just s. Ext corridors. **Pets:** $7 daily fee/pet. No service, supervision.
[ASK] [S🐾] [✕] [🅜] [📶]

SILVERTON

🔷🔷 **William Hunter Cabins** **CA**
(250) 358-2844. **$85-$108, 10 day notice.** 303 Lake Ave. Centre. Ext corridors. **Pets:** Other species. No service, supervision.
[✕] [📶] [📺] [✕] [🅐]

SMITHERS

(AA) 🔷🔷🔷 **Aspen Motor Inn** **M**
(250) 847-4551. **$85-$95.** 4628 Yellowhead Hwy. 1.5 km w on Hwy 16 (Yellowhead Hwy). Ext corridors. **Pets:** Medium, other species. $7 daily fee/pet. Designated rooms, service with restrictions, supervision.
[SAVE] [S🐾] [✕] [📶] [📺] [❑] [🏊]

SQUAMISH

(AA) 🔷🔷🔷 **Sea To Sky Hotel** **SH**
(604) 898-4874. **$89-$159.** 40330 Tantalus Way. 4.5 km n on Hwy 99 at Garibaldi Way. Int corridors. **Pets:** Small. $15 daily fee/pet. Designated rooms, service with restrictions, supervision.
[SAVE] [S🐾] [✕] [📶] [📺] [❑] [✕]

SUMMERLAND

(AA) 🔷🔷🔷 **Summerland Motel** **M** 🐾
(250) 494-4444. **$69-$159, 7 day notice.** 2107 Tait St. 5 km s on Hwy 97. Ext corridors. **Pets:** $10 daily fee/pet. Designated rooms, service with restrictions, supervision.
[SAVE] [S🐾] [✕] [📶] [📺] [🏊]

SUN PEAKS

(AA) 🔷🔷🔷🔷 **Delta Sun Peaks Resort** **LH** 🐾
(250) 578-6000. **$99-$269, 7 day notice.** 3240 Village Way. Hwy 5, 31 km ne on Todd Mountain Rd, follow signs to village. Int corridors. **Pets:** Other species. $15 daily fee/pet. Designated rooms, service with restrictions.
[SAVE] [✕] [🅜] [📶] [📺] [❑] [🏊] [✕]

TERRACE

(AA) 🔷🔷🔷 **Best Western Terrace Inn** **SH**
(250) 635-0083. **$80-$115.** 4553 Greig Ave. Hwy 16, just e on Greig Ave, follow City Centre signs. Int corridors. **Pets:** Small, other species. $10 daily fee/pet. Supervision.
[SAVE] [S🐾] [✕] [📶] [📺] [❑]

(AA) 🔷🔷🔷 **Coast Inn of the West** **SH**
(250) 638-8141. **$75-$115.** 4620 Lakelse Ave. Hwy 16 to City Centre, 0.5 km e to Emerson, just n. Int corridors. **Pets:** Accepted.
[SAVE] [S🐾] [✕] [📺] [❑]

TOFINO

(AA) 🔷🔷🔷 **Best Western Tin Wis Resort Lodge** **SH**
(250) 725-4445. **$119-$199.** 1119 Pacific Rim Hwy. 3.5 km s on Hwy 4. Ext corridors. **Pets:** Accepted.
[SAVE] [S🐾] [✕] [🅜] [📶] [📺] [❑] [🅐]

(AA) 🔷🔷🔷 **Long Beach Lodge Resort** **SH** 🐾
(250) 725-2442. **$189-$529, 7 day notice.** 1441 Pacific Rim Hwy. 7.5 km s on Hwy 4. Int corridors. **Pets:** $50 one-time fee/room. Designated rooms, service with restrictions, crate.
[SAVE] [✕] [📶] [📺] [❑] [🅐]

(AA) 🔷🔷🔷🔷 **Wickaninnish Inn** **SH** 🐾
(250) 725-3100. **$220-$1500, 7 day notice.** Osprey Ln at Chesterman Beach. 4.3 km e on Hwy 4. Int corridors. **Pets:** Dogs only. $40 daily fee/pet. Designated rooms, service with restrictions, crate.
[SAVE] [✕] [🅜] [🗝] [📺] [❑] [✕] [🅐]

VALEMOUNT

(AA) 🔷🔷🔷 **Canoe Mountain Lodge** **SH**
(250) 566-9171. **$78-$125.** 1465 5th Ave. Just e of Hwy 5 (Yellowhead Hwy). Int corridors. **Pets:** Accepted.
[SAVE] [S🐾] [✕] [📶] [📺]

Ⓐ ▽▽▽ **Chalet Continental Motel** 🅜
(250) 566-9787. **$75-$130.** 1450 5th Ave. Just e, off Hwy 5 (Yellowhead Hwy). Ext corridors. **Pets:** Medium, dogs only. $10 daily fee/pet. Service with restrictions, supervision.
[SAVE] [S🐾] [✕] [🛏] [🖵] [🏊] [✕]

Ⓐ ▽▽▽▽ **Holiday Inn Hotel & Suites**
Valemount 🆂🅷 🐾
(250) 566-0086. **$85-$180, 7 day notice.** 1950 Hwy 5 S. 1.5 km s on Hwy 5 (Yellowhead Hwy). Int corridors. **Pets:** Medium, other species. $35 one-time fee/room. Designated rooms, service with restrictions, supervision.
[SAVE] [S🐾] [✕] [🅖🅜] [🎲] [🛗] [🛏] [🖵] [🍴] [🏊] [✕]

VANCOUVER METROPOLITAN AREA

ALDERGROVE

Ⓐ ▽▽▽▽ **Best Western Country Meadows** 🆂🅷
(604) 856-9880. **$79-$119.** 3070 264th St. Trans-Canada Hwy 1, exit 73 (264th St/Aldergrove), 5 km s on 264th St (Hwy 13). Int corridors. **Pets:** Small, dogs only. $10 daily fee/pet. Designated rooms, service with restrictions, supervision.
[SAVE] [S🐾] [✕] [🅖🅜] [🛏] [🖵] [🍴] [🏊]

BURNABY

Ⓐ ▽▽▽▽ **Accent Inns** 🅜
(604) 473-5000. **$109-$149.** 3777 Henning Dr. Trans-Canada Hwy 1, exit 28 (Grandview Hwy), just n on Boundary Rd. Ext corridors. **Pets:** Small, dogs only. $10 daily fee/room. Designated rooms, service with restrictions, supervision.
[SAVE] [S🐾] [✕] [🅖🅜] [🐾] [🛏] [🖵] [🍴] [✕]

Ⓐ ▽▽ **Best Western Kings Inn and Conference Centre** 🆂🅷 🐾
(604) 438-1383. **$76-$127.** 5411 Kingsway. Trans-Canada Hwy 1, exit 29 (Willingdon Ave S), 3 km s to Kingsway, then 2 km e. Ext corridors. **Pets:** Medium. $100 deposit/room, $10 daily fee/pet. Service with restrictions, supervision.
[SAVE] [✕] [🛏] [🖵] [🍴] [🏊]

Ⓐ ▽▽▽ ▽▽▽ **Hilton Vancouver Metrotown** 🅛🅗
(604) 438-1200. **$135-$229.** 6083 McKay Ave. Trans-Canada Hwy 1, exit 29 (Willingdon Ave S), 3 km S to Kingsway, then just e. Int corridors. **Pets:** Small, other species. $75 one-time fee/room. Service with restrictions, supervision.
[SAVE] [✕] [🅖🅜] [🎲] [🛏] [🖵] [🍴] [🏊]

Ⓐ ▽▽ **Lake City Motor Inn** 🅜
(604) 294-5331. **$79-$104.** 5415 Lougheed Hwy. Boundary Rd, 3 km e on Lougheed Hwy at Holdom Ave; entrance on north side of highway. Ext corridors. **Pets:** Accepted.
[ASK] [✕] [🛏] [🏊]

COQUITLAM

Ⓐ ▽▽▽ **Best Western Chelsea Inn** 🆂🅷
(604) 525-7777. **$109-$349.** 725 Brunette Ave. Trans-Canada Hwy 1, exit 40B (Brunette Ave N). Int corridors. **Pets:** Accepted.
[SAVE] [S🐾] [✕] [🅖🅜] [🛏] [🖵] [🍴] [🏊] [✕]

Ⓐ ▽▽▽▽ **Holiday Inn Vancouver-Coquitlam** 🆂🅷
(604) 931-4433. **$89-$159.** 631 Lougheed Hwy. Trans-Canada Hwy 1, exit 37 (Gaglardi Way) eastbound, 3.5 km e on Lougheed Hwy (Hwy 7); exit 44 (Coquitlam) westbound, then 3 km w on Lougheed Hwy (Hwy 7). Ext/int corridors. **Pets:** Other species. $30 one-time fee/pet. Designated rooms, service with restrictions, supervision.
[SAVE] [S🐾] [✕] [🅖🅜] [🛏] [🖵] [🍴] [🏊]

DELTA

▽▽▽▽ **River Run Cottages** 🅱🅱 🐾
(604) 946-7778. **$130-$210, 21 day notice.** 4551 River Rd W. Hwy 17, 2.5 km n on Ladner Trunk Rd (which becomes 47A St), then becomes River Rd W. Ext corridors. **Pets:** Dogs only. $20 daily fee/pet. Designated rooms, supervision.
[ASK] [S🐾] [✕] [🛏] [🖵] [K] [W] [Z]

LANGLEY

Ⓐ ▽▽ **Best Value Westward Inn** 🅜
(604) 534-9238. **$61-$77.** 19650 Fraser Hwy. Trans-Canada Hwy 1, exit 58 (200th St/Langley City), 5 km s on 200th St, 1 km w on Hwy 10, then just w. Ext corridors. **Pets:** Other species. $4 daily fee/room. Service with restrictions, supervision.
[SAVE] [S🐾] [✕] [🛏] [🖵]

Ⓐ ▽▽▽▽ **Best Western Langley Inn** 🆂🅷
(604) 530-9311. **$95-$119.** 5978 Glover Rd. Trans-Canada Hwy 1, exit 66 (232nd St), 6 km s, follow signs. Int corridors. **Pets:** Small, dogs only. $15 one-time fee/room. Service with restrictions, supervision.
[SAVE] [S🐾] [✕] [🛏] [🖵] [🍴] [🏊]

Ⓐ ▽▽▽▽ **Holiday Inn Express Hotel & Suites Langley** 🆂🅷
(604) 882-2000. **$107-$117.** 8750 204th St. Trans-Canada Hwy 1, exit 58 (200th St), just e on 88th Ave. Int corridors. **Pets:** Medium. $10 daily fee/pet. Designated rooms, service with restrictions, crate.
[SAVE] [S🐾] [✕] [🅖🅜] [🛏] [🖵] [🏊] [✕]

▽▽ **Sandman Hotel Langley** 🆂🅷 🐾
(604) 888-7263. **$119-$149.** 8855 202nd St. Trans-Canada Hwy 1, exit 58 (200th St), just e on 88th Ave. Int corridors. **Pets:** $10 daily fee/pet. Service with restrictions, supervision.
[ASK] [S🐾] [✕] [🛏] [🖵] [🍴]

▽▽ **Sleep Inn Langley** 🆂🅷
(604) 514-3111. **$80-$110.** 6722 Glover Rd. Trans-Canada Hwy 1, exit 66 (232nd St), 4 km s on Glover Rd, follow signs. Int corridors. **Pets:** Accepted.
[ASK] [S🐾] [✕]

Ⓐ ▽▽ **Travelodge-Langley City** 🅜
(604) 533-4431. **$69-$99.** 21653 Fraser Hwy. Trans-Canada Hwy 1, exit 66 (232nd St), 6 km s, 1 km se on Langley Bypass, then 1.5 km e to 216 St. Ext corridors. **Pets:** Medium. $10 daily fee/pet. Designated rooms, service with restrictions, supervision.
[SAVE] [S🐾] [✕] [🛏] [🖵]

MAPLE RIDGE

Ⓐ ▽▽ **Travelodge Maple Ridge** 🅜
(604) 467-1511. **$85-$99.** 21650 Lougheed Hwy. 2 km w on Lougheed Hwy (Hwy 7). Int corridors. **Pets:** Accepted.
[SAVE] [S🐾] [✕] [🛏] [🖵] [✕]

MISSION

Ⓐ ▽▽ **Best Western Mission City Lodge** 🆂🅷
(604) 820-5500. **$79-$122.** 32281 Lougheed Hwy. Just w of Hwy 11, corner of Lougheed Hwy (Hwy 7) and Hurd St. Int corridors. **Pets:** Medium. $10 daily fee/pet. Designated rooms, service with restrictions, supervision.
[SAVE] [S🐾] [✕] [🅖🅜] [🐾] [🛏] [🖵] [🍴] [🏊] [✕]

NORTH VANCOUVER

Ⓐ ▼▼▼▼ **Holiday Inn Hotel & Suites North Vancouver** 🄻🄷 ❀
(604) 985-3111. **$99-$179.** 700 Old Lillooet Rd. Trans-Canada Hwy 1, exit 22 (Mt Seymour Pkwy), follow signs. Int corridors. **Pets:** Medium, dogs only. $20 daily fee/pet. Supervision.
🅂🄰🅅🄴 🅂🖥 🗙 🖫🅼 🄶 🗐 🖵 🍴 🌊 🗙

▼ **Lionsgate Travelodge** 🄼
(604) 985-5311. **$89-$139.** 2060 Marine Dr. Trans-Canada Hwy 1, exit 14 (Capilano Rd), 1.5 km s; from n end of Lions Gate Bridge, just e on Marine Dr. Ext corridors. **Pets:** Medium. $50 deposit/room. Designated rooms, supervision.
🄰🅂🄺 🅂🖥 🗙 🖵 🌊

Ⓐ ▼▼▼ **Ramada Inn Vancouver North Shore** 🄼
(604) 987-4461. **$75-$131.** 1800 Capilano Rd. Trans-Canada Hwy 1, exit 14 (Capilano Rd), 1.5 km s; 1 km e on Marine Dr, then just n. Ext corridors. **Pets:** Small, dogs only. $100 deposit/pet. Designated rooms, service with restrictions, supervision.
🅂🄰🅅🄴 🗙 🖫🅼 🄶 🖵 🌊

RICHMOND

Ⓐ ▼▼▼ **Accent Inns** 🅂🄷 ❀
(604) 273-3311. **$99-$149.** 10551 St. Edwards Dr. Hwy 99, exit 39 (Bridgeport/Airport) northbound to St. Edwards Dr; exit 39A (Richmond/Airport) southbound. Ext corridors. **Pets:** Medium. $10 daily fee/room. Designated rooms, service with restrictions, crate.
🅂🄰🅅🄴 🅂🖥 🗙 🖫🅼 🄶 🗐 🖵 🍴

Ⓐ ▼▼ **Best Western Abercorn Inn** 🅂🄷
(604) 270-7576. **$79-$159.** 9260 Bridgeport Rd. Hwy 99, exit 39 (Bridgeport/Airport) northbound; exit 39A (Richmond/Airport) southbound. Int corridors. **Pets:** Medium, other species. $15 one-time fee/pet. Service with restrictions, crate.
🅂🄰🅅🄴 🅂🖥 🗙 🖫🅼 🗐 🖵 🍴

Ⓐ ▼▼ **Best Western Richmond Hotel & Convention Center** 🄻🄷 ❀
(604) 273-7878. **$89-$129.** 7551 Westminster Hwy. Corner of Minoru Rd and Westminster Hwy. Int corridors. **Pets:** Other species. $15 daily fee/room. Service with restrictions, supervision.
🅂🄰🅅🄴 🅂🖥 🗙 🖫🅼 🗐 🖵 🍴 🌊 🗙

Ⓐ ▼▼▼ **Comfort Inn Vancouver Airport** 🅂🄷
(604) 278-5161. **$84-$124.** 3031 #3 Rd. Hwy 99, exit 39 (Bridgeport/Airport) northbound; exit 39A (Richmond/Airport) southbound. Int corridors. **Pets:** Small. $10 daily fee/pet. Designated rooms, service with restrictions, crate.
🅂🄰🅅🄴 🅂🖥 🗙 🖵 🍴 🌊

Ⓐ ▼▼▼▼ **Delta Vancouver Airport** 🄻🄷
(604) 278-1241. **$149-$189.** 3500 Cessna Dr. Corner of Russ Baker Way and Cessna Dr; near the Moray Bridge. Int corridors. **Pets:** Accepted.
🅂🄰🅅🄴 🅂🖥 🗙 🖫🅼 🄶 🖵 🍴 🌊 🗙

Ⓐ ▼▼▼▼ **The Fairmont Vancouver Airport** 🄻🄷
(604) 207-5200. **$199-$289.** 3111 Grant McConachie Way. In Vancouver International Airport. Int corridors. **Pets:** Medium, other species. $25 daily fee/room. Service with restrictions, supervision.
🅂🄰🅅🄴 🅂🖥 🗙 🖫🅼 🄶 🖵 🍴 🌊 🗙

▼▼▼ **Holiday Inn Express Vancouver-Airport** 🅂🄷
(604) 273-8080. **$99-$159.** 9351 Bridgeport Rd. Hwy 99, exit 39 (Bridgeport/Airport) northbound; exit 39A (Richmond/Airport) southbound. Int corridors. **Pets:** Small. $10 daily fee/room. Designated rooms, service with restrictions.
🄰🅂🄺 🅂🖥 🗙 🖫🅼 🄶 🖵

Ⓐ ▼▼▼ **La Quinta Inn Vancouver Airport** 🅂🄷
(604) 276-2711. **$89-$189.** 8640 Alexandra Rd. N 3rd, just e on Alderbridge Way, just n on Kwantlen St. Int corridors. **Pets:** Accepted.
🅂🄰🅅🄴 🅂🖥 🗙 🖫🅼 🄶 🄶 🖵 🌊

Ⓐ ▼▼▼ **Park Plaza** 🅂🄷
(604) 278-9611. **$89-$129.** 10251 St Edwards Dr. Hwy 99, exit 39 (Bridgeport/Airport) northbound to St Edwards Dr; exit 39A (Richmond/Airport) southbound. Int corridors. **Pets:** Accepted.
🅂🄰🅅🄴 🅂🖥 🗙 🖫🅼 🄶 🖵 🍴 🌊 🗙

Ⓐ ▼▼▼ **Ramada Plaza** 🅂🄷
(604) 278-9611. **$89-$129.** 10251 St Edwards Dr. Hwy 99, exit 39 (Bridgeport/Airport) northbound to St Edwards Dr; exit 39A (Richmond/Airport) southbound. Int corridors. **Pets:** Accepted.
🄰🅂🄺 🅂🖥 🗙 🖫🅼 🄶 🗐 🖵 🍴 🌊 🗙

▼▼▼ **Sandman Hotel Vancouver Airport** 🅂🄷
(604) 303-8888. **$79-$159.** 3233 St. Edwards Dr. Hwy 99, exit 39 (Bridgeport/Airport) northbound to St. Edwards Dr; exit 39A (Richmond/Airport) southbound. Int corridors. **Pets:** Small, other species. $10 daily fee/pet. Designated rooms, service with restrictions, crate.
🄰🅂🄺 🅂🖥 🗙 🖫🅼 🗐 🖵 🍴 🌊

Ⓐ ▼▼▼▼ **Vancouver Airport Marriott** 🅂🄷
(604) 276-2112. **$119-$169.** 7571 Westminster Hwy. Corner of Minoru Rd and Westminster Hwy. Int corridors. **Pets:** Large, other species. $30 one-time fee/room. Service with restrictions, supervision.
🅂🄰🅅🄴 🗙 🖫🅼 🗐 🖵 🍴 🌊

SURREY

Ⓐ ▼▼▼ **Days Hotel-Surrey** 🅂🄷
(604) 588-9511. **$94-$125.** 9850 King George Hwy. Jct Fraser Hwy (Hwy 1A) and Hwy 99A (King George Hwy). Int corridors. **Pets:** Large, other species. $10 daily fee/room. Designated rooms, service with restrictions.
🅂🄰🅅🄴 🅂🖥 🗙 🖫🅼 🄶 🗐 🖵 🍴 🌊

▼▼▼ **Ramada Hotel & Suites Surrey/Guildford** 🅂🄷 ❀
(604) 930-4700. **$89-$139.** 10410 158th St. Trans-Canada Hwy 1, exit 50 (160th St), just w on 104th Ave. Int corridors. **Pets:** $10 daily fee/room. Supervision.
🄰🅂🄺 🅂🖥 🗙 🖫🅼 🄶 🗐 🖵 🍴 🌊

▼▼▼ **Ramada Limited Surrey-Langley** 🅂🄷 ❀
(604) 576-8388. **$95-$139.** 19225 Hwy 10. Trans-Canada Hwy 1, exit 58, 5 km s on 200th St, then 2 km w on Rt 10; corner of 192nd St and Rt 10. Int corridors. **Pets:** $10 daily fee/pet. Service with restrictions, supervision.
🄰🅂🄺 🅂🖥 🗙 🖫🅼 🄶 🗐 🖵 🍴 🌊

VANCOUVER

▼▼ **2400 Motel** 🄼
(604) 434-2464. **$55-$125.** 2400 Kingsway. 7.2 km se on Hwy 1A and 99A (Kingsway). Ext corridors. **Pets:** Other species. $5 daily fee/pet. Designated rooms, service with restrictions, crate.
🗙 🗐 🄺

Ⓐ ▼▼▼ **Best Western Chateau Granville** 🅂🄷
(604) 669-7070. **$139-$209.** 1100 Granville St. Between Davie and Helmcken sts. Int corridors. **Pets:** Medium. $25 one-time fee/pet. Designated rooms, service with restrictions, supervision.
🅂🄰🅅🄴 🅂🖥 🗙 🖫🅼 🄶 🖵 🍴

Ⓐ ▼▼▼ **Best Western Downtown Vancouver** 🅂🄷 ❀
(604) 669-9888. **$99-$219.** 718 Drake St. Corner of Drake and Granville sts. Int corridors. **Pets:** Small. $20 daily fee/pet. Designated rooms, service with restrictions, supervision.
🅂🄰🅅🄴 🅂🖥 🗙 🖫🅼 🄶 🖵 🗙

Best Western Sands SH
(604) 682-1831. **$129-$239.** 1755 Davie St. Between Bidwell and Denman sts. Int corridors. **Pets:** Large. $10 daily fee/pet. Designated rooms, service with restrictions, supervision.

Bosmans Hotel SH
(604) 682-3171. **$119-$129.** 1060 Howe St. Between Nelson and Helmcken sts. Int corridors. **Pets:** Designated rooms, service with restrictions, supervision.

Comfort Inn Downtown SH
(604) 605-4333. **$72-$229.** 654 Nelson St. Between Granville and Seymour sts. Int corridors. **Pets:** Large, other species. $25 one-time fee/room.

Crowne Plaza Vancouver-Hotel Georgia SH
(604) 682-5566. **$159-$239.** 801 W Georgia St. Between Howe and Hornby sts. Int corridors. **Pets:** Accepted.

Delta Vancouver Suites LH
(604) 689-8188. **$159-$269.** 550 W Hastings St. Between Seymour and Richards sts; entrance in alley way. Int corridors. **Pets:** Accepted.

The Fairmont Hotel Vancouver LH
(604) 684-3131. **$199-$379.** 900 W Georgia St. Corner of Burrard at W Georgia St; enter from Hornby St. Int corridors. **Pets:** Accepted.

The Fairmont Waterfront LH
(604) 691-1991. **$209-$349.** 900 Canada Place Way. Howe St at Cordova St. Int corridors. **Pets:** $25 daily fee/room. Service with restrictions, supervision.

Four Seasons Hotel Vancouver LH
(604) 689-9333. **$230-$1060.** 791 W Georgia St. Howe and W Georgia sts. Int corridors. **Pets:** Small. Designated rooms, service with restrictions, supervision.

The Georgian Court Hotel SH
(604) 682-5555. **$115-$260.** 773 Beatty St. Between Georgia and Robson sts. Int corridors. **Pets:** Accepted.

Granville Island Hotel SH
(604) 683-7373. **$150-$230.** 1253 Johnston St. Granville Island; below the bridge, follow signs. Int corridors. **Pets:** $25 daily fee/pet. Designated rooms, service with restrictions, supervision.

Holiday Inn Express Vancouver SH
(604) 254-1000. **$99-$315.** 2889 E Hastings St. Between Renfrew and Kaslo sts. Int corridors. **Pets:** Small. Service with restrictions, crate.

Holiday Inn Hotel & Suites Vancouver-Downtown LH
(604) 684-2151. **$109-$299.** 1110 Howe St. Between Helmcken and Davie sts. Int corridors. **Pets:** Other species. Service with restrictions, supervision.

Holiday Inn Vancouver-Centre (Broadway) SH
(604) 879-0511. **$169-$209.** 711 W Broadway. Between Heather and Willow sts. Int corridors. **Pets:** Other species. Designated rooms, service with restrictions, supervision.

Hotel Le Soleil SH
(604) 632-3000. **$165-$275.** 567 Hornby St. Between Dunsmuir and Pender sts. Int corridors. **Pets:** $75 one-time fee/room. Service with restrictions, crate.

Howard Johnson Hotel SH
(604) 688-8701. **$89-$229.** 1176 Granville St. Between Davie and Helmcken sts. Int corridors. **Pets:** Medium, other species. $20 daily fee/pet. Designated rooms, service with restrictions.

The London Guard Motel M
(604) 430-4646. **$49-$75.** 2227 Kingsway. 6.8 km se on Hwy 1A and 99A (Kingsway). Ext corridors. **Pets:** Accepted.

Metropolitan Hotel LH
(604) 687-1122. **$189-$399.** 645 Howe St. Between Georgia and Dunsmuir sts. Int corridors. **Pets:** Medium, other species. Service with restrictions, supervision.

Pacific Palisades Hotel LH
(604) 688-0461. **$130-$390.** 1277 Robson St. Between Jervis and Bute sts. Int corridors. **Pets:** Other species. Designated rooms, supervision.

Pan Pacific Vancouver LH
(604) 662-8111. **$390-$540.** 300-999 Canada Place. Motor entrance off Burrard St. Int corridors. **Pets:** Medium, other species. $30 deposit/pet. Service with restrictions, supervision.

Quality Hotel Downtown-The Inn at False Creek SH
(604) 682-0229. **$89-$209.** 1335 Howe St. Between Drake and Pacific sts. Int corridors. **Pets:** Medium. $20 daily fee/room. Designated rooms, service with restrictions, supervision.

Ramada Inn & Suites Downtown Vancouver SH
(604) 685-1111. **$99-$209.** 1221 Granville St. Between Davie and Drake sts. Int corridors. **Pets:** Other species. $20 daily fee/room. Service with restrictions, crate.

Renaissance Vancouver Hotel Harbourside LH
(604) 689-9211. **$129-$239.** 1133 W Hastings St. Between Bute and Thurlow sts. Int corridors. **Pets:** Accepted.

Residence Inn by Marriott Vancouver SH
(604) 688-1234. **$107-$233.** 1234 Hornby St. Between Drake and Davie sts. Int corridors. **Pets:** Accepted.

Sandman Hotel Downtown Vancouver SH
(604) 681-2211. **$119-$189.** 180 W Georgia St. Between Cambie and Beatty sts. Int corridors. **Pets:** Medium. $20 daily fee/pet. Designated rooms, service with restrictions, supervision.

Sheraton Vancouver Wall Centre Hotel LH
(604) 331-1000. **$165-$429.** 1088 Burrard St. Between Helmcken and Comox sts. Int corridors. **Pets:** Medium. $60 one-time fee/pet. Service with restrictions, supervision.

(CAA) ▽▽▽▽ **The Sutton Place Hotel** 🅛🅗 ❀
(604) 682-5511. **$185-$464, 3 day notice.** 845 Burrard St. Between Smythe and Robson sts. Int corridors. **Pets:** Other species. $150 one-time fee/room. Designated rooms, service with restrictions, supervision.
[SAVE] [S🐾] [✗] [&M] [🖉] [🖅] [¶] [⊇] [✗]

▽▽ **Sylvia Hotel** 🆂🅗
(604) 681-9321. **$80-$240.** 1154 Gilford St. Beach Ave and Gilford St; across from English Bay. Int corridors. **Pets:** Accepted.
[✗] [🖅] [¶] [🅐🅒]

(CAA) ▽▽▽▽ **Vancouver Marriott Pinnacle Downtown** 🅛🅗 ❀
(604) 684-1128. **$199-$339.** 1128 W Hastings St. Between Thurlow and Bute sts. Int corridors. **Pets:** $30 one-time fee/room. Supervision.
[SAVE] [S🐾] [✗] [&M] [🖅] [¶] [⊇] [✗]

(CAA) ▽▽▽ ▽▽▽ **The Westin Bayshore Resort & Marina** 🅛🅗 ❀
(604) 682-3377. **$170-$460.** 1601 Bayshore Dr. W Georgia and Cardero sts. Int corridors. **Pets:** Medium, dogs only. Service with restrictions, supervision.
[SAVE] [S🐾] [✗] [&M] [🖉] [🖅] [¶] [⊇] [✗]

(CAA) ▽▽▽ ▽▽▽ **The Westin Grand, Vancouver** 🅛🅗 ❀
(604) 602-1999. **$199-$429.** 433 Robson St. Between Homer and Richards sts. Int corridors. **Pets:** Medium. $50 one-time fee/room. Service with restrictions, supervision.
[SAVE] [S🐾] [✗] [&M] [🖅] [🖅] [¶] [⊇] [✗]

WHITE ROCK

(CAA) ▽▽▽▽ **Ocean Promenade Hotel** 🆂🅗 ❀
(604) 542-0102. **$139-$489.** 15611 Marine Dr. Hwy 99, exit 2B southbound; exit 2 (White Rock/8th Ave) northbound, 2 km w. Ext/int corridors. **Pets:** Medium, dogs only. $50 one-time fee/room. Designated rooms.
[SAVE] [S🐾] [✗] [🖅] [🖅]

END METROPOLITAN AREA

VERNON

(CAA) ▽▽ **Best Western Vernon Lodge & Conference Centre** 🆂🅗 ❀
(250) 545-3385. **$99-$170.** 3914 32nd St. 1.5 km n on Hwy 97 (32nd St). Int corridors. **Pets:** Medium. $10 daily fee/pet. Designated rooms, service with restrictions, supervision.
[SAVE] [S🐾] [✗] [&M] [🖅] [🖅] [¶] [⊇]

(CAA) ▽▽▽ **Best Western Villager Motor Inn** 🆂🅗
(250) 549-2224. **$73-$98.** 5121 26th St. 2.5 km n on 27th St. Ext/int corridors. **Pets:** Large, other species. $10 daily fee/pet. Crate.
[SAVE] [S🐾] [✗] [🖅] [🖅]

▽▽▽▽ **Holiday Inn Express Hotel & Suites Vernon** 🆂🅗
(250) 550-7777. **$104-$164.** 4716 34th St. Hwy 97 (32nd St) northbound at 48th Ave. Int corridors. **Pets:** Medium. $20 one-time fee/room. Designated rooms, service with restrictions, supervision.
[A$K] [S🐾] [✗] [🖅] [🖅] [⊇]

(CAA) ▽▽ **Schell Motel** 🅜
(250) 545-1351. **$55-$85.** 2810 35th St. Corner of 35th St and 30th Ave; centre. Ext corridors. **Pets:** Accepted.
[SAVE] [S🐾] [✗] [🖅] [🖅] [⊇]

(CAA) ▽▽▽ **Tiki Village Motor Inn** 🅜
(250) 503-5566. **$79-$155, 3 day notice.** 2408 34th St. Jct Hwy 97 (32nd St) and 6 (25th Ave), just w. Ext corridors. **Pets:** Accepted.
[SAVE] [S🐾] [✗] [🖅] [¶] [⊇] [✗]

▽▽▽ **Vernon Travelodge** 🆂🅗
(250) 545-2161. **$75-$115.** 3000 28th Ave. Hwy 97 (32nd St), just e on 28th Ave, near Polson Park. Ext corridors. **Pets:** Medium. $10 daily fee/pet. Designated rooms, service with restrictions, supervision.
[A$K] [S🐾] [✗] [🖅] [🖅] [⊇]

VICTORIA METROPOLITAN AREA

MALAHAT

▽▽ **Malahat Bungalows Motel** 🅜
(250) 478-3011. **$62-$150, 3 day notice.** Trans-Canada Hwy 1, 26 km n of Victoria. Ext corridors. **Pets:** Medium, other species. $10 daily fee/pet. Service with restrictions, supervision.
[✗] [🖅] [✗] [🅐🅒] [🖉]

SAANICHTON

(CAA) ▽▽▽ **Quality Inn Waddling Dog** 🆂🅗 ❀
(250) 652-1146. **$79-$139.** 2476 Mt Newton Crossroad. Corner of Hwy 17 and Mt Newton Crossroad. Int corridors. **Pets:** Dogs only. $10 daily fee/pet. Service with restrictions, supervision.
[SAVE] [S🐾] [✗] [🖅] [¶]

(CAA) ▽▽▽ **Super 8 Victoria/Saanichton** 🆂🅗
(250) 652-6888. **$74-$129.** 2477 Mt Newton Crossroad. Just e of Hwy 17. Int corridors. **Pets:** Medium, other species. $10 daily fee/pet. Designated rooms, service with restrictions, crate.
[SAVE] [S🐾] [✗] [&M] [🖅] [🖅]

SIDNEY

(CAA) ▽▽▽▽ **Best Western Emerald Isle Motor Inn** 🆂🅗 ❀
(250) 656-4441. **$119-$179.** 2306 Beacon Ave. Hwy 17, exit Sidney, just e. Int corridors. **Pets:** Other species. $20 one-time fee/pet. Designated rooms, service with restrictions, supervision.
[SAVE] [S🐾] [✗] [&M] [🖅] [🖅] [¶]

▽▽▽ **The Cedarwood Inn & Suites** 🆂🅗
(250) 656-5551. **$79-$245.** 9522 Lochside Dr. Hwy 17, just e on McTavish Rd, then 1.4 km n. Ext corridors. **Pets:** Medium. $15 daily fee/pet. Designated rooms, service with restrictions, crate.
[✗] [🖅] [🖅] [🅐🅒]

▽▽▽ **Shoal Harbour Inn & Latch Dining Room** 🆂🅗
(250) 656-6622. **$119-$339, 7 day notice.** 2328 Harbour Rd. Beacon Ave, 2 km n on Resthaven Dr, then 1 km e. Int corridors. **Pets:** Accepted.
[A$K] [S🐾] [✗] [&M] [🖅] [🖅] [🖅] [¶] [🅐🅒]

ⒸⒶ ♦♦♦ Victoria Airport Travelodge Sidney SH
(250) 656-1176. **$79-$200.** 2280 Beacon Ave. Just e of Hwy 17, exit Sidney. Int corridors. **Pets:** Accepted.
SAVE 🄢 ✕ 🄛 🄬 🛡 💻 🔁

SOOKE

♦♦ Ocean Wilderness Inn & Spa BB
(250) 646-2116. **$99-$175, 7 day notice.** 109 W Coast Rd. 14 km w on Hwy 14. Ext/int corridors. **Pets:** $15 daily fee/pet. Service with restrictions, supervision.
A$K 🄢 ✕ 🛡 🄴 🄿 🔁

ⒸⒶ ♦♦♦♦ Sooke Harbour House SH ❖
(250) 642-3421. **$250-$575, 14 day notice.** 1528 Whiffen Spit Rd. 2 km w on Hwy 14. Ext/int corridors. **Pets:** Other species. $30 daily fee/pet. Service with restrictions.
SAVE ✕ 🄛 🄬 🛡 💻 🍴 🄴 🄿

VICTORIA

ⒸⒶ ♦♦♦♦ Abigail's Hotel BB ❖
(250) 388-5363. **$199-$409, 14 day notice.** 906 McClure St. Blanshard St (Hwy 17), just e on Fairfield Rd, then just n on Vancouver St. Int corridors. **Pets:** Dogs only. $25 one-time fee/room. Designated rooms, service with restrictions, supervision.
SAVE ✕ 🛡 💻 🄴

ⒸⒶ ♦♦♦♦ Accent Inns SH ❖
(250) 475-7500. **$99-$159.** 3233 Maple St. 3 km n on Blanshard St (Hwy 17); corner of Blanchard St and Cloverdale Ave. Ext corridors. **Pets:** Small, other species. $10 daily fee/room. Designated rooms, service with restrictions, supervision.
SAVE 🄢 ✕ 🄛 🛡 💻 🍴

ⒸⒶ ♦♦♦♦ Admiral Inn M ❖
(250) 388-6267. **$89-$249.** 257 Belleville St. Corner of Belleville and Quebec sts. Ext corridors. **Pets:** Other species. $10 daily fee/room. Supervision.
SAVE 🄢 ✕ 🛡 💻

ⒸⒶ ♦♦♦ Blue Ridge Inns SH
(250) 388-4345. **$69-$149.** 3110 Douglas St. Between Finlayson St and Speed Ave. Ext corridors. **Pets:** Other species. $10 daily fee/room. Service with restrictions, supervision.
SAVE 🄢 ✕ 🛡 💻 🍴 🔁 🄴

♦♦♦♦ Chateau Victoria Hotel and Suites LH ❖
(250) 382-4221. **$82-$325.** 740 Burdett Ave. Between Douglas St and Fairfield Rd. Int corridors. **Pets:** Dogs only. $15 deposit/pet. Designated rooms, service with restrictions, crate.
✕ 🛡 💻 🍴 🔁

ⒸⒶ ♦♦♦♦ Comfort Inn & Suites SH
(250) 388-7861. **$79-$259.** 101 Island Hwy. Douglas St, 5 km w on Gorge Rd, then just s on Admirals Rd. Ext/int corridors. **Pets:** Dogs only. $10 daily fee/pet. Service with restrictions, supervision.
SAVE 🄢 ✕ 🛡 💻 🔁

ⒸⒶ ♦♦♦ Dashwood Seaside Manor BB
(250) 385-5517. **$95-$255, 14 day notice.** 1 Cook St. 1 km e of Douglas St on Dallas Rd. Int corridors. **Pets:** Accepted.
SAVE 🄢 ✕ 🛡 💻 🄴 🔁

ⒸⒶ ♦♦♦ Days Inn on the Harbour SH ❖
(250) 386-3451. **$99-$223.** 427 Belleville St. Entrance on Oswego at Quebec sts. Int corridors. **Pets:** $10 daily fee/room. Designated rooms, service with restrictions.
SAVE 🄢 ✕ 🛡 💻 🍴 🔁 🄴

ⒸⒶ ♦♦♦♦ Delta Victoria Ocean Pointe Resort & Spa LH ❖
(250) 360-2999. **$155-$310.** 45 Songhees Rd. Just w of Johnson St Bridge, Esquimalt at Tyee rds. Int corridors. **Pets:** Medium, dogs only. $25 one-time fee/room. Service with restrictions, crate.
SAVE 🄢 ✕ 🄛 🛡 💻 🍴 🔁 🄍

ⒸⒶ ♦♦♦♦ Executive House Hotel LH ❖
(250) 388-5111. **$85-$195.** 777 Douglas St. Between Blanshard and Douglas sts; downtown. Int corridors. **Pets:** Other species. $15 daily fee/pet.
SAVE 🄢 ✕ 🛡 💻 🍴 🄍 🄴

ⒸⒶ ♦♦♦♦ The Fairmont Empress LH
(250) 384-8111. **$179-$549.** 721 Government St. Between Belleville and Humboldt sts. Int corridors. **Pets:** Accepted.
SAVE ✕ 🄛 🄭 💻 🍴 🔁 🄍 🄴

ⒸⒶ ♦♦♦♦ Harbour Towers Hotel & Suites LH ❖
(250) 385-2405. **$99-$435.** 345 Quebec St. Between Oswego and Pendray sts. Int corridors. **Pets:** Medium. $15 daily fee/pet. Designated rooms, service with restrictions, supervision.
SAVE 🄢 ✕ 🄛 🄬 🛡 💻 🍴 🔁 🄍 🄴

ⒸⒶ ♦♦♦♦ Hotel Grand Pacific LH ❖
(250) 386-0450. **$119-$319.** 463 Belleville St. Belleville at Menzies St; downtown. Int corridors. **Pets:** Small. $60 one-time fee/room. Designated rooms, service with restrictions, crate.
SAVE 🄢 ✕ 🄛 🄭 💻 🍴 🔁 🄍

♦♦♦♦ Howard Johnson Hotel & Suites SH ❖
(250) 704-4656. **$109-$219.** 4670 Elk Lake Dr. Hwy 17, just w on Royal Oak Dr, then just n. Ext/int corridors. **Pets:** $15 daily fee/room. Designated rooms, service with restrictions, supervision.
A$K 🄢 ✕ 🄛 🄬 🛡 💻 🔁

ⒸⒶ ♦♦♦ Howard Johnson Hotel-City Centre LH ❖
(250) 382-2151. **$49-$169.** 310 Gorge Rd E. Douglas St, 1.4 km w. Int corridors. **Pets:** Medium, dogs only. $100 deposit/room. Designated rooms.
SAVE 🄢 ✕ 🛡 💻

ⒸⒶ ♦♦♦♦ The Magnolia Hotel & Spa SH ❖
(250) 381-0999. **$189-$349.** 623 Courtney St. Corner of Courtney and Gordon sts. Int corridors. **Pets:** Small. $60 one-time fee/room. Service with restrictions.
SAVE 🄢 ✕ 🄛 🛡 💻 🍴 🄍

ⒸⒶ ♦♦♦ Oxford Castle Inn SH
(250) 388-6431. **$78-$158.** 133 Gorge Rd E. Douglas St, 2 km w. Int corridors. **Pets:** Accepted.
SAVE 🄢 ✕ 🛡 💻 🔁 🄴

ⒸⒶ ♦♦♦♦ Ramada Huntingdon Hotel & Suites SH
(250) 381-3456. **$119-$229.** 330 Quebec St. Between Oswego and Pendray sts. Int corridors. **Pets:** Accepted.
SAVE ✕ 🛡 💻 🍴

ⒸⒶ ♦♦♦ Robin Hood Motel M
(250) 388-4302. **$51-$94.** 136 Gorge Rd E. Douglas St, 2.4 km w. Ext corridors. **Pets:** Dogs only. $5 daily fee/pet. Designated rooms, service with restrictions, supervision.
SAVE 🄢 ✕ 🛡 💻 🄴

[CAA] ◆◆◆ **Travelodge Victoria** [SH]
(250) 388-6611. **$65-$175.** 229 Gorge Rd E. Douglas St, 2 km w. Ext corridors. **Pets:** Medium, other species. $10 daily fee/pet. Designated rooms, service with restrictions.
[SAVE] [S/D] 🚭 ▣ ☕ 🍴 🏊

[CAA] ◆◆◆◆ **Victoria Marriott Inner Harbour** [LH]
(250) 381-8439. **$159-$479.** 728 Humboldt St. Between Blanshard and Douglas sts. Int corridors. **Pets:** Small, dogs only. $50 one-time fee/pet. Designated rooms, service with restrictions, crate.
[SAVE] [S/D] 🚭 ♿M ♿↗ ☕ 🍴 🏊 🎾

END METROPOLITAN AREA

WESTBANK

◆◆◆ **Holiday Inn Westbank** [SH]
(250) 768-8879. **$77-$155.** 2569 Dobbin Rd. Hwy 97 (Dobbin Rd) and Herbert Rd. Int corridors. **Pets:** $10 deposit/room. Designated rooms, service with restrictions, crate.
[ASK] [S/D] 🚭 ♿M ▣ ☕ 🍴 🏊

WHISTLER

[CAA] ◆◆◆ **Best Western Listel Whistler Hotel** [SH]
(604) 932-1133. **$99-$449.** 4121 Village Green. Hwy 99, just e on Village Gate Blvd, then follow Whistler Way. Int corridors. **Pets:** Medium. $15 daily fee/pet. Designated rooms, service with restrictions, supervision.
[SAVE] [S/D] 🚭 ▣ ☕ 🍴 🏊

◆◆◆ **Crystal Lodge** [SH] 🐾
(604) 932-2221. **$106-$1215, 30 day notice.** 4154 Village Green. Hwy 99, just e on Village Gate Blvd, then follow Whistler Way. Int corridors. **Pets:** Medium, dogs only. $20 daily fee/pet. Designated rooms, service with restrictions, supervision.
🚭 ♿M ♿↗ ▣ ☕ 🍴 🏊 🎾

[CAA] ◆◆◆ **Delta Whistler Village Suites** [SH]
(604) 905-3987. **$139-$1119, 30 day notice.** 4308 Main St. Hwy 99, just e on Village Gate Blvd, just n on Northlands Blvd, then just e. Int corridors. **Pets:** Accepted.
[SAVE] [S/D] 🚭 ♿M ▣ ☕ 🍴 🏊 🎾

[CAA] ◆◆ **Edgewater Lodge** [M] 🐾
(604) 932-0688. **$125-$320, 14 day notice.** 8030 Alpine Way. 4 km n of Whistler Village via Hwy 99, e on Alpine Way. Ext corridors. **Pets:** Dogs only. $20 one-time fee/pet. Designated rooms, service with restrictions, supervision.
[SAVE] [S/D] 🚭 🍴 [AC]

[CAA] ◆◆◆◆ **The Fairmont Chateau Whistler** [LH] 🐾
(604) 938-8000. **$165-$899, 30 day notice.** 4599 Chateau Blvd. Hwy 99, 1 km e on Lorimer Rd (Upper Village), then just w on Blackcomb Way. Int corridors. **Pets:** $30 daily fee/pet. Service with restrictions, supervision.
[SAVE] 🚭 ♿M ♿↗ ☕ 🍴 🏊 🎾

◆◆◆◆ **Four Seasons Resort Whistler** [LH] 🐾
(604) 935-3400. **$245-$690.** 4591 Blackcomb Way. Hwy 99, 1 km e on Lorimer Rd (Upper Village). Int corridors. **Pets:** Service with restrictions, supervision.
🚭 ♿M ☕ 🍴 🏊 🎾

◆◆◆ **Residence Inn by Marriott** [CO]
(604) 905-3400. **$159-$559, 30 day notice.** 4899 Painted Cliff Rd. Hwy 99, 1 km e on Lorimer Rd (Upper Village), just se on Blackcomb Way, then just w, follow road all the way to the end. Int corridors. **Pets:** Accepted.
[ASK] 🚭 ▣ ☕ 🏊 [AC]

[CAA] ◆◆◆ **Summit Lodge & Spa** [SH]
(604) 932-2778. **$139-$725, 30 day notice.** 4359 Main St. Hwy 99, just n on Village Gate Blvd, just w on Northlands Blvd. Int corridors. **Pets:** Accepted.
[SAVE] [S/D] 🚭 ▣ ☕ 🏊 🎾

◆◆◆ **Sundial Boutique Hotel** [SH]
(604) 932-2321. **$199-$949, 45 day notice.** 4340 Sundial Cir. Hwy 99, just e on Village Gate Blvd, then just s on Blackcomb Way. Int corridors. **Pets:** Accepted.
[ASK] [S/D] 🚭 ♿M ▣ ☕

[CAA] ◆◆ **Tantalus Resort Lodge** [CO] 🐾
(604) 932-4146. **$119-$799.** 4200 Whistler Way. Hwy 99, just e on Village Gate Blvd, then follow Whistler Way to the end. Int corridors. **Pets:** $15 one-time fee/pet. Designated rooms, service with restrictions, supervision.
[SAVE] [S/D] 🚭 ▣ ☕ 🏊 🎾 [AC]

WILLIAMS LAKE

◆◆ **Drummond Lodge Motel** [M] 🐾
(250) 392-5334. **$69-$114.** 1405 Cariboo Hwy. 1 km s on Hwy 97. Ext corridors. **Pets:** Medium, other species. $7 one-time fee/pet. Designated rooms, service with restrictions.
🚭 ▣ ☕

[CAA] ◆◆ **Williams Lake Super 8 Motel** [M]
(250) 398-8884. **$70-$81.** 1712 Broadway Ave S. 2 km s on Hwy 97. Int corridors. **Pets:** Other species. $7 daily fee/pet. Supervision.
[SAVE] [S/D] 🚭 ♿M ▣ ☕

MANITOBA

BRANDON

▼▼▼ Comfort Inn SH
(204) 727-6232. **$76-$96.** 925 Middleton Ave. Northside Trans-Canada Hwy 1 service road; between Hwy 10 N and 10 S, just e of McDonald's Restaurant. Int corridors. **Pets:** Other species. Designated rooms, service with restrictions, supervision.
[ASK] [S⌀] [✕] [&M] [🛏] [📶]

(AAA) ▼▼▼ Days Inn SH
(204) 727-3600. **$94-$104.** 2130 Currie Blvd. Jct Trans-Canada Hwy 1, 8 km s on Hwy 10 (Currie Blvd). Int corridors. **Pets:** Large. $10 daily fee/room. Designated rooms, service with restrictions, crate.
[SAVE] [S⌀] [✕] [🛏] [📶] [📶]

(AAA) ▼ Rodeway Inn Motel SH
(204) 728-7230. **$58-$63.** 300 18th St N. On Hwy 10 S, 3.2 km s of Trans-Canada Hwy 1. Ext/int corridors. **Pets:** Accepted.
[SAVE] [✕] [🛏] [📶]

▼▼ Royal Oak Inn & Suites SH
(204) 728-5775. **$84-$114.** 3130 Victoria Ave. 5 km s of Trans-Canada Hwy 1; 1.4 km w of jct Hwy 10 (18th St) and 1A (Victoria Ave). Int corridors. **Pets:** Accepted.
[ASK] [S⌀] [✕] [🛏] [📶] [🍴] [📶] [✕]

▼▼ Super 8 Motel Brandon SH 🐾
(204) 729-8024. **$87-$107.** 1570 Highland Ave. On Trans-Canada Hwy 1, south service road, just e of Hwy 10 (18th St). Int corridors. **Pets:** Other species. Designated rooms, service with restrictions, supervision.
[ASK] [S⌀] [✕] [&M] [🛏] [📶] [📶]

▼▼▼ Victoria Inn SH
(204) 725-1532. **$92-$110.** 3550 Victoria Ave. 5 km s of Trans-Canada Hwy 1; 1.8 km w of jct Hwy 10 (18th St) and 1A (Victoria Ave). Int corridors. **Pets:** $10 daily fee/room. No service.
[ASK] [✕] [🛏] [📶] [🍴] [📶] [✕]

CHURCHILL

▼▼ Polar Inn & Suites M
(204) 675-8878. **$135-$195.** 153 Kelsey Blvd. Centre. Int corridors. **Pets:** Service with restrictions, crate.
[ASK] [✕] [🛏] [📶] [Ⓚ]

▼▼ The Tundra Inn SH
(204) 675-8831. **$105-$195.** 34 Franklin St. Centre. Int corridors. **Pets:** Accepted.
[✕] [🛏] [📶] [Ⓚ]

DAUPHIN

▼ Canway Inn & Suites SH
(204) 638-5102. **$79.** 1601 Main St S. 2.4 km s on Hwy 5A and 10A (Main St). Ext/int corridors. **Pets:** Accepted.
[✕] [🛏] [📶] [🍴] [📶]

FLIN FLON

(AAA) ▼▼ Victoria Inn North SH
(204) 687-7555. **$75.** 160 Hwy 10A N. Jct Hwy 10 and 10A, 1 km nw (eastern approach to city). Int corridors. **Pets:** Accepted.
[SAVE] [✕] [🛏] [📶] [🍴] [📶]

HECLA

▼▼ Solmundson Gesta Hus BB
(204) 279-2088. **$55-$80.** On Hwy 8; in Hecla Village. Int corridors. **Pets:** Accepted.
[ASK] [S⌀] [✕] [✆]

NEEPAWA

▼▼▼ Bay Hill Inns & Suites M
(204) 476-8888. **$80-$85.** 160 Main St W. Hwy 16, just w of jct Rt 5. Int corridors. **Pets:** Accepted.
[ASK] [S⌀] [✕] [🛏] [🍴] [📶]

THE PAS

▼▼▼ Kikiwak Inn SH
(204) 623-1800. **Call for rates.** Hwy 10 N. On Hwy 10, 0.6 km n. Int corridors. **Pets:** Accepted.
[S⌀] [✕] [🛏] [📶] [🍴] [📶]

▼▼▼ Super 8 SH
(204) 623-1888. **$80-$110.** 1717 Gordon Ave. At southern approach to town. Int corridors. **Pets:** Accepted.
[✕] [🛏] [📶] [📶]

(AAA) ▼ Wescana Inn SH
(204) 623-5446. **$95.** 439 Fischer Ave. On Hwy 10, just s. Ext/int corridors. **Pets:** Designated rooms, service with restrictions, crate.
[SAVE] [S⌀] [✕] [🛏] [📶] [📶]

PORTAGE LA PRAIRIE

▼▼ Super 8 M
(204) 857-8883. **$74-$76, 7 day notice.** 1.5 km w on Trans-Canada Hwy 1A. Int corridors. **Pets:** Accepted.
[ASK] [S⌀] [✕] [🛏] [📶] [📶]

▼ Westgate Inn Motel M
(204) 239-5200. **$55-$69.** 1010 Saskatchewan Ave E. 1 km e on Trans-Canada Hwy 1A. Ext corridors. **Pets:** Other species. Designated rooms, service with restrictions.
[ASK] [S⌀] [✕] [🛏]

RUSSELL

▼▼ The Russell Inn Hotel & Conference Centre SH
(204) 773-2186. **$90-$96.** Hwy 16 Russell. 1.2 km se on Hwy 16 and 83. Ext/int corridors. **Pets:** Other species. Service with restrictions, supervision.
[ASK] [S⌀] [✕] [🛏] [📶] [🍴] [📶] [✕]

STEINBACH

▼▼ Days Inn SH
(204) 320-9200. **$76-$81.** 75 Hwy 12 N. Jct Trans-Canada Hwy 1 and 12, 20 km s. Int corridors. **Pets:** Other species. $10 one-time fee/room. Designated rooms, service with restrictions, crate.
[ASK] [S⌀] [✕] [&] [🛏] [📶] [📶]

THOMPSON

▼▼▼ Country Inn & Suites By Carlson SH 🐾
(204) 778-8879. **$108.** 70 Thompson Dr N. Just w of Hwy 6. Int corridors. **Pets:** $10 daily fee/pet. Designated rooms, service with restrictions, supervision.
[ASK] [S⌀] [✕] [🛏] [📶] [📶] [✕]

WINKLER

▼▼ Heartland Resort & Conference Centre SH
(204) 325-4381. **$89-$149.** 851 Main St N. Main St and Hwy 14; centre. Int corridors. **Pets:** Accepted.
[ASK] [S⌀] [✕] [&] [🛏] [📶] [🍴] [✕]

WINNIPEG METROPOLITAN AREA

WINNIPEG

Ⓒ ▼▼▼ **Canad Inns Polo Park** 🆂🅷
(204) 775-8791. **$119.** 1405 St. Matthews Ave. Just e of St James St. Int corridors. **Pets:** $25 one-time fee/room. Designated rooms, service with restrictions, crate.
〔SAVE〕 ⊠ 🐾 🖶 🖵 🍴 🏊 ⊠

Ⓒ ▼▼▼ **Carlton Inn** 🆂🅷
(204) 942-0881. **$83-$93.** 220 Carlton St. Just s off Metro Rt 85 (Portage Ave). Int corridors. **Pets:** Other species. Service with restrictions, supervision.
〔SAVE〕 🆂 ⊠ 🖶 🖵 🍴 🏊

▼▼▼ **Clarion Hotel & Suites** 🆂🅷
(204) 774-5110. **$139-$269.** 1445 Portage Ave. Jct Empress St. Int corridors. **Pets:** Accepted.
〔ASK〕 🆂 ⊠ 🖶 🖵 🍴 🏊 ⊠

▼▼ **Comfort Inn** 🆂🅷
(204) 783-5627. **$85-$106.** 1770 Sargent Ave. At Sargent Ave and King Edward St. Int corridors. **Pets:** Other species. $5 daily fee/room. Designated rooms, service with restrictions, supervision.
〔ASK〕 🆂 ⊠ 🅼 🖶 🖵

Ⓒ ▼▼ **Comfort Inn** 🆂🅷
(204) 269-7390. **$85-$125.** 3109 Pembina Hwy. Just n of jct Perimeter Hwy 100 and 75. Int corridors. **Pets:** Medium. $10 daily fee/room. Designated rooms, service with restrictions, supervision.
〔SAVE〕 🆂 ⊠ 🖶 🖵

▼▼▼ **Country Inn & Suites By Carlson** 🆂🅷 🐾
(204) 783-6900. **$99-$109.** 730 King Edward St. Just s of jct Wellington Ave. Int corridors. **Pets:** Medium. Service with restrictions, crate.
〔ASK〕 🆂 ⊠ 🅼 🖶 🖵

Ⓒ ▼▼▼ **Days Inn** 🆂🅷
(204) 586-8525. **$129-$139.** 550 McPhillips St. Just n of Logan Ave. Int corridors. **Pets:** Medium. $10 daily fee/pet. Designated rooms, service with restrictions, supervision.
〔SAVE〕 🆂 ⊠ 🖶 🖵 🍴 🏊 ⊠

Ⓒ ▼▼▼ **Delta Winnipeg** 🅻🅷
(204) 942-0551. **$89-$159.** 350 St. Mary Ave. At Hargrave St. Int corridors. **Pets:** Dogs only. $20 one-time fee/room. Designated rooms, service with restrictions, crate.
〔SAVE〕 ⊠ 🅼 🖶 🖵 🍴 🏊 ⊠

▼▼▼ **The Fairmont Winnipeg** 🅻🅷 🐾
(204) 957-1350. **$109-$359.** 2 Lombard Pl. Just e of corner Portage Ave and Main St. Int corridors. **Pets:** Large, other species. $25 daily fee/room.
〔ASK〕 🆂 ⊠ 🐾 🖶 🖵 🍴 🏊 ⊠

Ⓒ ▼▼▼ **Greenwood Inn** 🆂🅷
(204) 775-9889. **$99-$139.** 1715 Wellington Ave. Wellington Ave at Century St. Int corridors. **Pets:** Other species. Designated rooms, service with restrictions, supervision.
〔SAVE〕 ⊠ 🖶 🖵 🍴 🏊 ⊠

Ⓒ ▼▼▼ **Hilton Suites Winnipeg Airport** 🅻🅷
(204) 783-1700. **$139-$189.** 1800 Wellington Ave. At Berry St. Int corridors. **Pets:** Accepted.
〔SAVE〕 🆂 ⊠ 🅼 🖶 🖵 🍴 🏊 ⊠

Ⓒ ▼▼▼ **Holiday Inn Winnipeg-South** 🆂🅷
(204) 452-4747. **$120-$140.** 1330 Pembina Hwy. At McGillivray Blvd. Int corridors. **Pets:** Other species. Designated rooms, service with restrictions, supervision.
〔SAVE〕 🆂 ⊠ 🖶 🖵 🍴 🏊 ⊠

Ⓒ ▼▼▼ **Place Louis Riel All-Suite Hotel** 🅻🅷 🐾
(204) 947-6961. **$90-$150.** 190 Smith St. At St. Mary's Ave. Int corridors. **Pets:** Large, other species. $10 daily fee/room. Designated rooms, supervision.
〔SAVE〕 🆂 ⊠ 🅼 🖶 🖵 🍴 ⊠

▼▼▼ **Radisson Hotel Winnipeg Downtown** 🅻🅷
(204) 956-0410. **$92-$149.** 288 Portage Ave. At Smith St. Int corridors. **Pets:** Accepted.
〔ASK〕 🆂 ⊠ 🖶 🖵 🍴 🏊 ⊠

▼▼ **Ramada Marlborough Hotel** 🆂🅷
(204) 942-6411. **$120-$150.** 331 Smith St. Just n off Metro Rt 85 (Portage Ave). Int corridors. **Pets:** Accepted.
〔ASK〕 🆂 ⊠ 🖶 🖵 🍴 🏊 ⊠

Ⓒ ▼▼▼ **Sheraton Hotel** 🅻🅷
(204) 942-5300. **$89-$159.** 161 Donald St. At York Ave. Int corridors. **Pets:** Accepted.
〔SAVE〕 🆂 ⊠ 🖶 🖵 🍴 🏊 ⊠

▼▼▼ **Super 8** 🆂🅷 🐾
(204) 269-8888. **$98-$158.** 1714 Pembina Hwy. 1 km n of jct Bishop Grandin Blvd. Int corridors. **Pets:** Other species. $10 one-time fee/room. Service with restrictions, supervision.
〔ASK〕 🆂 ⊠ 🖶 🖵 🏊 ⊠

Ⓒ ▼▼ **Travelodge** 🆂🅷
(204) 255-6000. **$82-$96.** 20 Alpine Ave. Just e of jct Fermor Ave and St. Anne's Rd. Int corridors. **Pets:** Medium, other species. $6 daily fee/room. Designated rooms, service with restrictions, supervision.
〔SAVE〕 🆂 ⊠ 🖶 🖵 🍴 🏊 ⊠

▼▼ **Twin Pillars Bed & Breakfast** 🅱🅱
(204) 284-7590. **$60-$70.** 235 Oakwood Ave. 0.6 km e of Osborne St. Int corridors. **Pets:** Accepted.
〔ASK〕 ⊠

Ⓒ ▼▼ **Victoria Inn Hotel & Convention Centre** 🆂🅷
(204) 786-4801. **$99.** 1808 Wellington Ave. At Berry St. Int corridors. **Pets:** Large. $10 daily fee/pet. Designated rooms, service with restrictions, crate.
〔SAVE〕 🆂 ⊠ 🖶 🖵 🍴 🏊 ⊠

Ⓒ ▼▼ **Viscount Gort Hotel** 🆂🅷 🐾
(204) 775-0451. **$83-$119.** 1670 Portage Ave. Portage Ave at Rt 90. Int corridors. **Pets:** Other species. $10 daily fee/room. Designated rooms, service with restrictions, crate.
〔SAVE〕 ⊠ 🖶 🖵 🍴 🏊 ⊠

END METROPOLITAN AREA

NEW BRUNSWICK

BATHURST

▼▼ Comfort Inn SH
(506) 547-8000. $89-$129. 1170 St Peter's Ave. 3.4 km n on Rt 134 (St Peter's Ave). Int corridors. Pets: Accepted.
[ASK] [S🐾] [✕] [▣]

▼▼▼ Danny's Inn & Conference Centre SH
(506) 546-6621. $79-$88. Hwy 11, exit 310 (Vanier Blvd) northbound to Rt 134 (St Peter's Ave), 4 km n; exit 318 southbound to Rt 134 (St Peter's Ave), 3.8 km s. Ext/int corridors. Pets: Accepted.
[S🐾] [✕] [🛗] [▣] [⑪] [⛱] [✕]

▼▼ Lakeview Inn & Suites SH
(506) 548-4949. $90-$160. 777 St Peter's Ave. 3 km n on Rt 134 (St Peter's Ave). Int corridors. Pets: Accepted.
[ASK] [S🐾] [✕] [🛗] [🛗] [▣]

⊕ ▼▼ Le Chateau Bathurst SH
(506) 546-6691. $96-$110. 80 Main St. On Rt 134 (St Peter's Ave) and Rt 7; centre. Ext/int corridors. Pets: Large. $10 daily fee/room. Designated rooms, service with restrictions, supervision.
[SAVE] [✕] [▣] [⑪] [⛱] [✕]

BOUCTOUCHE

▼◆ Les Chalets Chebooktoosk CA
(506) 743-1999. $80-$185, 7 day notice. 23 Acadie St. 1 km e on Rt 134; centre. Ext corridors. Pets: Accepted.
[✕] [🛗] [▣] [♨]

CAMPBELLTON

▼▼ Comfort Inn SH
(506) 753-4121. $95-$130, 11 day notice. 111 Val D'amour Rd. Hwy 11, exit 415, 1 km e on Sugarloaf St W. Ext/int corridors. Pets: Accepted.
[ASK] [S🐾] [✕] [🛗] [▣]

⊕ ▼▼ Howard Johnson SH
(506) 753-4133. $115. 157 Water St. Hwy 134; in City Centre Complex. Int corridors. Pets: Accepted.
[SAVE] [✕] [🛗] [▣] [⑪]

CARAQUET

▼▼▼ Super 8 Motel SH
(506) 727-0888. $104-$142, 30 day notice. 9 Carrefour Ave. Just e of jct Hwy 11 and St Pierre Blvd E. Int corridors. Pets: $10 daily fee/room. Service with restrictions, supervision.
[ASK] [S🐾] [✕] [♿] [🅜] [♿] [🛗] [▣] [⛱] [✕]

CHANCE HARBOUR

⊕ ▼▼▼ The Mariner's Inn CI
(506) 659-2619. $109-$155, 3 day notice. 32 Mawhinney Cove Rd. Hwy 1, exit 96, 9 km s on Rt 790, 30 km w of Saint John. Int corridors. Pets: Small, dogs only. $15 daily fee/pet. Designated rooms, service with restrictions, supervision.
[SAVE] [✕] [🛗] [▣] [⑪]

COCAGNE

▼▼ Cocagne Motel M
(506) 576-6657. $55-$75. Hwy 11, exit 15, 1 km n on Rt 535. Ext corridors. Pets: Accepted.
[🛗] [♨]

DALHOUSIE

▼▼▼ Best Western Manoir Adelaide SH
(506) 684-5681. $109-$119. 385 Adelaide St. Centre. Int corridors. Pets: Accepted.
[ASK] [S🐾] [✕] [🛗] [▣] [⑪]

EDMUNDSTON

▼▼ Comfort Inn SH
(506) 739-8361. $82-$142. 5 Bateman Ave. Trans-Canada Hwy 2, exit 18 (Hebert Blvd). Int corridors. Pets: Service with restrictions, crate.
[ASK] [S🐾] [✕] [🛗] [▣]

▼▼▼ Days Inn Edmundston SH
(506) 263-0000. $99-$159. 10 rue Mathieu. 8 km e on Trans-Canada Hwy 2, exit 26. Int corridors. Pets: Designated rooms, service with restrictions, supervision.
[ASK] [S🐾] [✕] [🛗] [▣]

FREDERICTON

▼▼ Auberge Wandlyn Inn SH
(506) 462-4444. $109-$135. 958 Prospect St. Rt 8, exit 3 (Hanwell Rd) eastbound; exit 5 (Smythe St) westbound. Ext/int corridors. Pets: $300 deposit/room. Designated rooms, service with restrictions.
[ASK] [S🐾] [✕] [🛗] [▣] [⑪] [⛱]

▼▼ City Motel SH
(506) 450-9900. $75-$150. 1216 Regent St. Trans-Canada Hwy 2, exit 285A and B eastbound; exit 285B westbound, 3.3 km n on Rt 101 (Regent St). Int corridors. Pets: Designated rooms, service with restrictions, supervision.
[ASK] [S🐾] [✕] [⑪]

▼▼ Comfort Inn SH
(506) 453-0800. $90-$219. 797 Prospect St. Rt 8, exit 3 (Hanwell Rd) eastbound; exit 5 (Smythe St) westbound. Int corridors. Pets: Large. Designated rooms, service with restrictions, crate.
[ASK] [S🐾] [✕] [🛗] [▣]

▼▼▼ Delta Fredericton LH
(506) 457-7000. $244-$319, 30 day notice. 225 Woodstock Rd. 1.6 km n on Rt 102; downtown. Int corridors. Pets: Accepted.
[ASK] [S🐾] [✕] [🅜] [🛗] [▣] [⑪] [⛱] [✕]

▼▼ Holiday Inn Fredericton SH
(506) 363-5111. $129-$159. 35 Mactaquac Rd (Hwy 102). Trans-Canada Hwy 2, exit 258 eastbound, 11 km e; exit 294 westbound, 30 km w. Ext/int corridors. Pets: Accepted.
[ASK] [✕] [🅜] [🛗] [▣] [⑪] [⛱] [✕]

▼▼ Lakeview Inn & Suites-Fredericton SH
(506) 459-0035. $105-$134. 665 Prospect St. Rt 8, exit 3 (Hanwell Rd) eastbound; exit 5 (Smythe St) westbound. Int corridors. Pets: Small. $50 deposit/room. Designated rooms, service with restrictions, supervision.
[ASK] [S🐾] [✕] [🛗] [▣]

(CAA) ▽▽▽▽ **Lord Beaverbrook Hotel** 🏨
(506) 455-3371. **$129-$285.** 659 Queen St. Centre. Int corridors.
Pets: $15 one-time fee/room. Designated rooms, service with restrictions.
[SAVE] [S🐕] [✕] [📶] [🍽] [🏊] [✕]

▽▽▽▽ **Ramada Hotel Fredericton** 🅂🄷 ❀
(506) 460-5500. **$99-$149, 30 day notice.** 480 Riverside Dr. On Rt 105
at the north end of Princess Margaret Bridge. Int corridors. **Pets:** Designated rooms, service with restrictions, supervision.
[ASK] [S🐕] [✕] [📶] [📶] [🍽] [🏊] [✕]

GRAND FALLS

(CAA) ▽▽▽▽ **Auberge Pres-du-Lac Inn** 🅂🄷
(506) 473-1300. **$83-$120.** 10039 Rt 144. Trans-Canada Hwy 2, exit
75, just w. Ext/int corridors. **Pets:** Small. Designated rooms, service with
restrictions, supervision.
[SAVE] [S🐕] [✕] [📶] [🍽] [🏊] [✕]

▽▽▽ **Hilltop Motel & Restaurant** 🅂🄷
(506) 473-2684. **$60-$90.** 131 Madawaska Rd. Trans-Canada Hwy 2,
exit 75, 2.4 km se. Ext corridors. **Pets:** Small. Designated rooms, service
with restrictions, supervision.
[S🐕] [✕] [📶] [🍽]

MIRAMICHI

▽▽▽ **Comfort Inn** 🅂🄷
(506) 622-1215. **$89-$115, 7 day notice.** 201 Edward St. 1 km w on Rt
8. Int corridors. **Pets:** Medium. Designated rooms, service with restrictions,
supervision.
[ASK] [S🐕] [✕] [📶] [📶]

▽▽▽ **Lakeview Inn & Suites** 🅂🄷
(506) 627-1999. **$90-$109, 7 day notice.** 333 King George Hwy. 1.8
km w on Rt 8. Int corridors. **Pets:** Medium, other species. $50 deposit/
room. Designated rooms, service with restrictions, crate.
[ASK] [S🐕] [✕] [📶] [📶]

▽▽▽▽ **Rodd Miramichi River-A Rodd Signature Hotel** 🅂🄷
(506) 773-3111. **$101-$198.** 1809 Water St. Hwy 11, exit 120, 0.6 km e.
Int corridors. **Pets:** Accepted.
[ASK] [S🐕] [✕] [S.M] [♿] [📶] [📶] [🍽] [🏊]

MONCTON

(CAA) ▽▽▽ **Beacon Light Motel** Ⓜ
(506) 384-1734. **$75-$105.** 1062 Mountain Rd. Trans-Canada Hwy 2,
exit 454 (Mapleton Rd), 2.8 km to Rt 126 (Mountain Rd), then just s.
Ext/int corridors. **Pets:** Accepted.
[SAVE] [✕] [📶] [📶] [🍽] [🏊]

▽▽▽▽ **Best Western Moncton** 🅂🄷
(506) 388-0888. **$120-$137.** 300 Lewisville Rd. Trans-Canada Hwy 2,
exit 459A eastbound, s on Rt 115 to Lewisville Rd, then left; exit 467A
westbound, 8 km w on Hwy 15, exit 10. **Pets:** Accepted.
[ASK] [S🐕] [✕] [S.M] [♿] [📶] [📶] [🏊]

▽▽ **Colonial Inns** 🅂🄷
(506) 382-3395. **$90.** 42 Highfield St. 1 blk n of Main St; centre. Ext/int
corridors. **Pets:** Accepted.
[✕] [📶] [🍽] [🏊]

(CAA) ▽▽▽ **Comfort Inn** 🅂🄷
(506) 859-6868. **$85-$195.** 20 Maplewood Dr. Trans-Canada Hwy 2,
exit 459A onto Hwy 115 S, left on Rt 134 E (Lewisville Rd). Int
corridors. **Pets:** Medium. Service with restrictions, supervision.
[SAVE] [S🐕] [✕] [📶] [📶]

▽▽ **Comfort Inn** 🅂🄷
(506) 384-3175. **$85-$195.** 2495 Mountain Rd. Trans-Canada Hwy 2,
exit 450. Int corridors. **Pets:** Accepted.
[ASK] [S🐕] [✕] [📶] [📶]

▽▽ **Country Inn & Suites By Carlson** 🅂🄷
(506) 852-7000. **$130-$170.** 2475 Mountain Rd. Trans-Canada Hwy 2,
exit 450. Int corridors. **Pets:** Accepted.
[ASK] [S🐕] [✕] [📶] [📶]

(CAA) ▽▽▽▽ **Holiday Inn Express Hotel & Suites**
Moncton 🅂🄷 ❀
(506) 384-1050. **$150-$180.** 2515 Mountain Rd. Trans-Canada Hwy 2,
exit 450. Ext/int corridors. **Pets:** Medium. $100 deposit/room. Designated
rooms, service with restrictions, supervision.
[SAVE] [S🐕] [✕] [S.M] [🐾] [📶] [🍽] [🏊] [✕]

(CAA) ▽▽▽▽ **Howard Johnson Brunswick Plaza Hotel &**
Conference Centre 🏨
(506) 854-6340. **$89-$169.** 1005 Main St. Highfield and Main sts;
downtown. Int corridors. **Pets:** Accepted.
[SAVE] [S🐕] [✕] [📶] [🍽] [🏊]

▽▽▽ **Rodd Park House Inn** 🅂🄷
(506) 382-1664. **$78-$171.** 434 Main St. 1 km e on Rt 106. Ext/int
corridors. **Pets:** Accepted.
[ASK] [S🐕] [✕] [📶] [🍽] [🏊]

ROTHESAY

▽▽▽▽ **Shadow Lawn Inn** 🄲🄸
(506) 847-7539. **$119-$195, 3 day notice.** 3180 Rothesay Rd. Hwy 1,
exit 137B eastbound; exit 137A westbound, follow signs for Rothesay
Rd and Rt 100, 1.6 km left on Old Hampton Rd (Rt 100), then left. Int
corridors. **Pets:** Medium. $10 daily fee/pet. Service with restrictions, super-
vision.
[S🐕] [✕] [📶] [📶] [🍽]

SACKVILLE

▽▽▽ **Coastal Inn Sackville** 🅂🄷
(506) 536-0000. **$99-$115.** 15 Wright St. Trans-Canada Hwy 2, exit
504. Int corridors. **Pets:** Designated rooms, service with restrictions,
supervision.
[ASK] [S🐕] [✕]

(CAA) ▽▽▽▽ **Marshlands Inn** 🄲🄸
(506) 536-0170. **$84-$119.** 55 Bridge St. On Hwy 106; centre. Int
corridors. **Pets:** Accepted.
[SAVE] [✕] [🍽] [🐾]

ST. ANDREWS

(CAA) ▽▽▽▽ **The Fairmont Algonquin** 🏨 ❀
(506) 529-8823. **$89-$349, 3 day notice.** 184 Adolphus St. Off Hwy
127. Int corridors. **Pets:** Medium, other species. $25 daily fee/room. Des-
ignated rooms, service with restrictions, supervision.
[SAVE] [✕] [📶] [📶] [🍽] [🏊] [✕]

▽▽▽▽ **St. Andrews Cottages** 🄲🄰
(506) 529-8555. **$79-$139, 3 day notice.** 3907 Rt 127. On Hwy 127,
2.5 km n. Ext corridors. **Pets:** Accepted.
[✕] [📶] [🏊] [🐾]

(CAA) ▽▽▽▽ **The Windsor House of St. Andrews** 🄲🄸 ❀
(506) 529-3330. **$125-$300, 14 day notice.** 132 Water St. Centre. Int
corridors. **Pets:** Other species. Service with restrictions.
[SAVE] [S🐕] [✕] [🍽] [🐾]

ST. GEORGE

▽▽▽ **Lake Digdeguash Four Season Chalets** 🄲🄰
(506) 755-2737. **$695 (weekly) (no credit cards), 60 day notice.** Jct
Hwy 1, 9 km w on Rt 760 to entry road, 1.5 km e on gravel entry road.
Ext corridors. **Pets:** Accepted.
[📶] [✕] [🐾] [🐾] [🐾]

SAINT JOHN

◆ Colonial Inns SH
(506) 652-3000. **$97.** 175 City Rd. Adjacent to Hwy 1, exit 123. Ext/int corridors. **Pets:** Accepted.
[icons]

◆◆ Comfort Inn SH
(506) 674-1873. **$136-$159.** 1155 Fairville Blvd. Hwy 1, exit 117 westbound; exit 119 eastbound, turn left. Int corridors. **Pets:** Accepted.
[icons]

◆◆ Country Inn & Suites SH
(506) 635-0400. **$79-$139.** 1011 Fairville Blvd. Hwy 1, exit 119B eastbound, left on Catherwood Dr, left at lights; exit 119A westbound. Int corridors. **Pets:** $15 one-time fee/room. Service with restrictions, supervision.
[icons]

◆◆◆ Delta Brunswick LH
(506) 648-1981. **$135-$189.** 39 King St. Centre of downtown; in Brunswick Square Mall. Int corridors. **Pets:** Accepted.
[icons]

◆◆◆ Hilton Saint John LH
(506) 693-8484. **$119.** One Market Square. Hwy 1, exit 122 at Market Square. Int corridors. **Pets:** Accepted.
[icons]

CAA ◆◆◆◆ Holiday Inn Express Hotel & Suites SH
(506) 642-2622. **$109-$159.** 400 Main St/Chesley Dr. 1 km w on Hwy 1; north end Chesley Dr, exit 121; off Harbour Bridge. Int corridors. **Pets:** Accepted.
[icons]

CAA ◆◆◆ Inn on the Cove and Spa CI
(506) 672-7799. **$135-$250, 7 day notice.** 1371 Sand Cove Rd. Hwy 1, exit 119, right to Sand Cove Rd, then 2 km w. Int corridors. **Pets:** Accepted.
[icons]

◆ Regent Motel M
(506) 672-8273. **$55-$70, 3 day notice.** 2121 Ocean West Way. Hwy 1, exit 112 eastbound, 2.4 km e on Rt 100; exit 114 westbound onto exit 96W, 0.5 km w on Rt 100. Ext corridors. **Pets:** Accepted.
[icons]

ST-LEONARD

CAA ◆◆ Daigle's Motel SH
(506) 423-6351. **$78-$99.** 68 rue DuPont. Hwy 17, 1 km s of Trans-Canada Hwy 2, exit 58. Ext corridors. **Pets:** Small. $7 daily fee/pet. Designated rooms, service with restrictions, supervision.
[icons]

ST. STEPHEN

◆ St. Stephen Inn SH
(506) 466-1814. **$65-$99.** 99 King St. On Hwy 1; centre. Ext/int corridors. **Pets:** Accepted.
[icons]

SHEDIAC

◆◆ Gaudet Chalets & Motel M
(506) 533-8877. **$65-$119, 30 day notice.** 14 Belleview Heights. On Rt 133, 2.4 km w of Rt 15, exit 37. Ext corridors. **Pets:** Small, dogs only. $10 daily fee/pet. Designated rooms, service with restrictions, supervision.
[icons]

SUSSEX

◆ All Seasons Inn SH
(506) 433-2220. **$65-$100.** 1015 Main St. Hwy 1, exit 192 eastbound; exit 198 westbound, left towards Sussex Corner; centre. Ext corridors. **Pets:** Other species. $10 daily fee/pet. Service with restrictions, supervision.
[icons]

◆◆ Fairway Inn SH
(506) 433-3470. **$75-$125.** 216 Roachville Rd. Hwy 1, exit 193. Ext/int corridors. **Pets:** Small. $10 daily fee/room. Designated rooms, service with restrictions, supervision.
[icons]

◆◆ Pine Cone Motel M
(506) 433-3958. **$65-$75.** 12808 Rt 114. Hwy 1, exit 198, 2 km e on Hwy 114 towards Penobsquis. Ext corridors. **Pets:** Small, dogs only. Designated rooms, service with restrictions, supervision.
[icons]

WOODSTOCK

◆◆ Econo Lodge SH
(506) 328-8876. **$99-$124.** 168 Rt 555. Trans-Canada Hwy 2, exit 188 (Houlton Rd). Ext/int corridors. **Pets:** Accepted.
[icons]

◆◆ Howard Johnson Inn M
(506) 328-3315. **$89-$129.** Trans-Canada Hwy 2, exit 188 (Houlton Rd). Ext/int corridors. **Pets:** Small. $10 daily fee/pet. Designated rooms, service with restrictions, supervision.
[icons]

CAA ◆ Stiles Motel Hill View SH
(506) 328-6671. **$85-$105, 3 day notice.** 827 Main St. Trans-Canada Hwy 2, exit 185 eastbound, 2.5 km e; exit 188 (Houlton Rd) westbound, 5.5 km via Rt 555 and 103 (Main St). Ext corridors. **Pets:** Medium. Service with restrictions.
[icons]

YOUNGS COVE ROAD

CAA ◆ McCready's Motel M
(506) 362-2916. **$52-$60.** 10995 Rt 10. Trans-Canada Hwy 2, exit 365, just w. Ext corridors. **Pets:** Accepted.
[icons]

NEWFOUNDLAND AND LABRADOR

CHANNEL-PORT-AUX-BASQUES

◆◆◆ St. Christopher's Hotel 🆂🅷
(709) 695-7034. **$75-$100.** 146 Caribou Rd. Trans-Canada Hwy 1, exit Port Aux Basques (downtown), follow signs 2 km. Int corridors. **Pets:** Medium, other species. Designated rooms, service with restrictions, supervision.
🅰🆂🅺 🆂🅾 🗙 🔒 🖵 🍴

CLARENVILLE

◆◆ Restland Motel 🆂🅷
(709) 466-7636. **$74-$82.** 262 Memorial Dr. Centre. Ext/int corridors. **Pets:** Accepted.
🅰🆂🅺 🆂🅾 🗙 🔒 🍴 🅺

◆◆ St. Jude Hotel 🆂🅷
(709) 466-1717. **$92-$110.** On Trans-Canada Hwy 1; centre. Int corridors. **Pets:** Medium. Designated rooms, service with restrictions, supervision.
🅰🆂🅺 🆂🅾 🗙 🔒 🖵 🍴

CORNER BROOK

◆◆ Comfort Inn 🆂🅷
(709) 639-1980. **$102-$114.** 41 Maple Valley Rd. Trans-Canada Hwy 1, exit 5 eastbound; exit 6 westbound, via Confederation Ave. Int corridors. **Pets:** Other species. Service with restrictions, supervision.
🅰🆂🅺 🆂🅾 🗙 🍴

◆◆◆ Holiday Inn Corner Brook 🅻🅷
(709) 634-5381. **$100-$109.** 48 West St. Centre. Int corridors. **Pets:** Accepted.
🗙 🔒 🖵 🍴 🏊

◆◆ Mamateek Inn 🆂🅷
(709) 639-8901. **$99-$109, 30 day notice.** Maple Valley Rd. Trans-Canada Hwy 1, exit 5 eastbound; exit 6 westbound via Confederation Ave. Int corridors. **Pets:** Accepted.
🅰🆂🅺 🆂🅾 🗙 🍴

COW HEAD

◆◆ Shallow Bay Motel & Cabins 🆂🅷
(709) 243-2471. **$85-$105.** Hwy 430, 4 km w towards the ocean, follow signs. Ext/int corridors. **Pets:** Accepted.
🅰🆂🅺 🆂🅾 🗙 🔒 🖵 🍴 🏊 🅺

GANDER

◆◆ Albatross Hotel 🆂🅷
(709) 256-3956. **$88-$89.** On Trans-Canada Hwy 1. Ext/int corridors. **Pets:** Other species. Service with restrictions.
🗙 🔒 🖵 🍴

◆◆ Comfort Inn 🆂🅷
(709) 256-3535. **$129-$139.** 112 Trans-Canada Hwy 1. Centre. Ext/int corridors. **Pets:** Accepted.
🅰🆂🅺 🆂🅾 🗙 🔒 🖵 🍴

◆◆ Hotel Gander 🆂🅷
(709) 256-3931. **$85-$95.** 100 Trans-Canada Hwy 1. Centre. Int corridors. **Pets:** Accepted.
🆂🅾 🗙 🔒 🖵 🍴 🏊

◆◆ Sinbad's Hotel & Suites 🆂🅷
(709) 651-2678. **$86-$172, 30 day notice.** Bennett Dr. Centre. Ext corridors. **Pets:** Other species. Service with restrictions, supervision.
🅰🆂🅺 🆂🅾 🗙 🔒 🖵 🍴

GRAND FALLS-WINDSOR

◆◆ Mount Peyton Hotel 🆂🅷
(709) 489-2251. **$160-$250.** 214 Lincoln Rd. 1 km ne on Trans-Canada Hwy 1. Ext/int corridors. **Pets:** Accepted.
🅰🆂🅺 🆂🅾 🗙 🔒 🖵 🍴

L'ANSE AU CLAIR

◆◆ Northern Light Inn 🆂🅷
(709) 931-2332. **$75-$150.** Rt 510. On Rt 510; centre. Int corridors. **Pets:** Accepted.
🅰🆂🅺 🆂🅾 🗙 🔒 🍴

ST. JOHN'S

Ⓐ ◆◆ Best Western Travellers Inn 🆂🅷
(709) 722-5540. **$109-$159.** 199 Kenmount Rd. 4.8 km w on Trans-Canada Hwy 1. Ext/int corridors. **Pets:** Accepted.
🆂🅰🆅🅴 🆂🅾 🗙 🔒 🖵 🍴 🏊 🅺

◆◆◆ Delta St. John's Hotel and Conference Centre 🅻🅷
(709) 739-6404. **$145-$150.** 120 New Gower St. Centre. Int corridors. **Pets:** Accepted.
🅰🆂🅺 🗙 🖵 🍴 🏊 🗙

◆◆◆ The Fairmont Newfoundland 🅻🅷 🐾
(709) 726-4980. **$143-$287.** Cavendish Square. Centre. Int corridors. **Pets:** Small. $25 daily fee/room. Service with restrictions, crate.
🅰🆂🅺 🗙 🖵 🍴 🏊 🗙

◆◆◆ Holiday Inn St. John's-Govt Center 🅻🅷
(709) 722-0506. **$154-$172.** 180 Portugal Cove Rd. Trans-Canada Hwy 1, exit 47A, 1.4 km s. Ext/int corridors. **Pets:** Accepted.
🗙 🅻🅼 🛗 🔒 🍴 🏊

STEPHENVILLE

◆◆◆ Holiday Inn Stephenville 🆂🅷
(709) 643-6666. **$148-$158.** 44 Queen St. Centre. Int corridors. **Pets:** Accepted.
🅰🆂🅺 🆂🅾 🗙 🖵 🍴

NORTHWEST TERRITORIES

YELLOWKNIFE

▼▼▼ **Fraser Tower Suite Hotel** 🄻🄷
(867) 873-8700. **$139-$165.** 5303 52nd St. Corner of 52nd St and 53rd Ave. Int corridors. **Pets:** $10 daily fee/room. Service with restrictions.

Ⓐ$Ⓚ 🆂🄳 ⊠ 🖥 🖵 🄺

▼▼ **Yellowknife Super 8 Motel** 🄼 ❀
(867) 669-8888. **$129-$169.** 308 Old Airport Rd. 2 km s on Franklin, 1 km w; in Walmart Plaza. Int corridors. **Pets:** $25 one-time fee/room. Designated rooms, service with restrictions.

Ⓐ$Ⓚ 🆂🄳 ⊠ 🖥 🖵

NOVA SCOTIA

AMHERST

▼▼ Auberge Wandlyn Inn ⨁
(902) 667-3331. **$122.** Victoria St. Trans-Canada Hwy 104, exit 3, 1 km w. Ext/int corridors. **Pets:** Accepted.
Ⓐ⑨ⓧ🔧🖵🍴🌊

▼▼ Comfort Inn ⨁
(902) 667-0404. **$100-$145, 15 day notice.** 143 Albion St S. Trans-Canada Hwy 104, exit 4, 1.5 km n on Rt 2. Int corridors. **Pets:** Medium. Service with restrictions, supervision.
Ⓐ⑨ Ⓢ⑩ ⓧ 🖵

▼▼▼ Super 8 Motel ⨁
(902) 660-8888. **$109-$159.** 40 Lord Amherst Dr. Trans-Canada Hwy 104, exit 4. Int corridors. **Pets:** Accepted.
Ⓐ⑨ Ⓢ⑩ ⓧ 🄻Ⓜ 🔧 🖵 🌊

ANNAPOLIS ROYAL

▼▼ Annapolis Royal Inn Ⓜ
(902) 532-2323. **$89-$150.** 1 km w on Hwy 1. Ext corridors. **Pets:** Accepted.
Ⓐ⑨ Ⓢ⑩ ⓧ 🖵

▼▼ Champlain Motel Ⓜ
(902) 532-5473. **$105-$125.** RR 2. 4.2 km w on Hwy 1. Ext corridors. **Pets:** Accepted.
Ⓐ⑨ Ⓢ⑩ ⓧ 🔧 🖵 🌊

ANTIGONISH

ⒸⒶ ▼▼▼ Maritime Inn Antigonish ⨁
(902) 863-4001. **$103-$135.** 158 Main St. Centre. Ext/int corridors. **Pets:** Medium. Service with restrictions, crate.
ⓈⒶⓋⒺ ⓧ 🖵 🍴

AULD'S COVE

ⒸⒶ ▼▼▼ The Cove Motel & Restaurant Ⓜ
(902) 747-2700. **$107-$112.** 227 Auld's Cove. 1 km n off Trans-Canada Hwy 104; 3 km w of Canso Cswy. Ext corridors. **Pets:** Accepted.
Ⓢ⒜ⓥⒺ ⓧ 🖵 🍴 🅇

BADDECK

▼▼ The Ceilidh Country Lodge Ⓜ
(902) 295-3500. **$80-$150, 3 day notice.** 357 Shore Rd. Trans-Canada Hwy 105, exit 8, 1.6 km e on Rt 205 (Shore Rd). Ext/int corridors. **Pets:** Service with restrictions, supervision.
Ⓐ⑨ ⓧ 🔧 🖵

ⒸⒶ ▼▼▼ Inverary Resort ⨁
(902) 295-3500. **$100-$175, 3 day notice.** 368 Shore Rd. Trans-Canada Hwy 105, exit 8, 1.6 km on Rt 205 (Shore Rd). Ext/int corridors. **Pets:** Service with restrictions, supervision.
Ⓢ⒜ⓥⒺ Ⓢ⑩ ⓧ 🔧 🖵 🍴 🌊 🅇

▼▼▼ McIntyre's Housekeeping Cottages Ⓒ🅐
(902) 295-1133. **$68-$150, 4 day notice.** 8908 Hwy 105. Trans-Canada Hwy 105, 5 km w. Ext corridors. **Pets:** Other species. $7 daily fee/pet. Service with restrictions, crate.
ⓧ 🔧 🖵 🅇

ⒸⒶ ▼▼▼ Silver Dart Lodge & MacNeil House ⨁
(902) 295-2340. **$79-$165, 3 day notice.** 257 Hwy 205. Trans-Canada Hwy 105, exit 8, 1 km e on Rt 205 (Shore Rd). Ext/int corridors. **Pets:** Small. $15 daily fee/pet. Designated rooms, service with restrictions, crate.
Ⓢ⒜ⓥⒺ ⓧ 🔧 🖵 🍴 🌊 🅇

BRIDGETOWN

▼▼ Bridgetown Motor Inn ⨁
(902) 665-4403. **$72-$82.** 396 Granville St. Hwy 101, exit 20, 1 km w on Rt 1. Ext corridors. **Pets:** Accepted.
ⓧ 🍴 🌊

BRIDGEWATER

▼▼ Auberge Wandlyn Inn ⨁
(902) 543-7131. **$94-$170.** 50 North St. 1 km e on Hwy 325; Hwy 103, exit 12 to North St. Int corridors. **Pets:** Designated rooms, service with restrictions, supervision.
Ⓐ⑨ ⓧ 🔧 🖵 🍴 🌊

ⒸⒶ ▼▼▼ Bridgewater Inn ⨁
(902) 543-8171. **$74-$94.** 35 High St. Hwy 103, exit 13, just e. Int corridors. **Pets:** Service with restrictions.
Ⓢ⒜ⓥⒺ Ⓢ⑩ ⓧ 🖵 🍴 🌊

▼▼ Comfort Inn ⨁
(902) 543-1498. **$80-$160.** 49 North St. Hwy 103, exit 12, 1.7 km s on Rt 10. Int corridors. **Pets:** Other species. Service with restrictions.
Ⓐ⑨ Ⓢ⑩ ⓧ 🄻Ⓜ 🖵

CHESTER

▼▼ Windjammer Motel Ⓜ
(902) 275-3567. **$55-$75.** 4070 Rt 3. 1 km w. Ext corridors. **Pets:** Medium. Service with restrictions, supervision.
Ⓢ⑩ ⓧ 🔧

CHETICAMP

▼▼▼ Cabot Trail Sea & Golf Chalets Ⓒ🅐
(902) 224-1777. **$129-$169, 7 day notice.** 71 Fraser Doucet Ln. Centre. Ext corridors. **Pets:** Medium, dogs only. $15 daily fee/pet. Service with restrictions, crate.
ⓧ 🔧 🖵 🅇 🅩

▼▼ Laurie's Motor Inn ⨁
(902) 224-2400. **$85-$155, 3 day notice.** 15456 Laurie Rd. 1 km n, 7.2 km sw of West Gate Cape Breton Highlands National Park on Cabot Tr. Ext/int corridors. **Pets:** Large. Service with restrictions, crate.
Ⓐ⑨ Ⓢ⑩ ⓧ 🔧 🖵 🍴

ⒸⒶ ▼▼ Parkview Motel, Dining Room & Lounge Ⓜ 🐾
(902) 224-3232. **$79-$109, 7 day notice.** 16546 Cabot Tr. 7.2 km n at West Gate Cape Breton Highlands National Park. Ext corridors. **Pets:** Designated rooms, service with restrictions, supervision.
Ⓢ⒜ⓥⒺ ⓧ 🔧 🖵 🍴 🅩

CHURCH POINT

▼▼▼ Le Manoir Samson Inn **M**
(902) 769-2526. **$85-$125.** 1768 Rt 1. On Hwy 1; centre. Ext corridors. Pets: Accepted.
⟨ASK⟩ ⟨✕⟩ ⟨🛏⟩ ⟨🖥⟩ ⟨🐾⟩

DARTMOUTH

▼▼ Comfort Inn **SH** ✿
(902) 463-9900. **$119-$159.** 456 Windmill Rd. Hwy 111, exit Shannon Park. Int corridors. **Pets:** Designated rooms, service with restrictions, supervision.
⟨ASK⟩ ⟨S⟩ ⟨✕⟩ ⟨🖥⟩

▼▼ Country Inn & Suites By Carlson **SH** ✿
(902) 465-4000. **$95-$150.** 101 Yorkshire Ave Ext. Hwy 111, exit Princess Margaret Blvd. Int corridors. **Pets:** Medium. $50 deposit/room, $5 daily fee/pet. Designated rooms, service with restrictions, supervision.
⟨ASK⟩ ⟨S⟩ ⟨✕⟩ ⟨🛏⟩ ⟨🖥⟩

ⓐ ▼▼▼ Holiday Inn Halifax-Harbourview **LH**
(902) 463-1100. **$119-$189.** 99 Wyse Rd. Adjacent to Angus L MacDonald Bridge. Int corridors. **Pets:** $25 one-time fee/room. Designated rooms, service with restrictions, supervision.
⟨SAVE⟩ ⟨S⟩ ⟨✕⟩ ⟨🛏⟩ ⟨🖥⟩ ⟨🍽⟩ ⟨🏊⟩

ⓐ ▼▼▼ Park Place Hotel & Conference Centre Ramada Plaza **LH**
(902) 468-8888. **$104-$137.** 240 Brownlow Ave. From Murray Mackay Bridge, 1.2 km n on Hwy 111, exit 3 (Burnside Dr). Int corridors. **Pets:** Small. $50 deposit/room. Designated rooms, service with restrictions, supervision.
⟨SAVE⟩ ⟨S⟩ ⟨✕⟩ ⟨&M⟩ ⟨🖥⟩ ⟨🍽⟩ ⟨🏊⟩ ⟨✕⟩

ⓐ ▼▼ Quality Inn Halifax/Dartmouth **SH**
(902) 469-5850. **$100-$180.** 313 Prince Albert Rd. Hwy 111, exit 6A, 1 blk s. Int corridors. **Pets:** Medium. Designated rooms, service with restrictions, supervision.
⟨SAVE⟩ ⟨S⟩ ⟨✕⟩ ⟨🛏⟩ ⟨🖥⟩ ⟨🍽⟩

DIGBY

ⓐ ▼▼▼ Admiral Digby Inn **SH**
(902) 245-2531. **$70-$250.** 441 Shore Rd. Hwy 101, exit 26, 2.5 km n, follow St John Ferry signs, 5 km w on Victoria Rd, then 1 km e of ferry terminal. Ext corridors. **Pets:** Small. Service with restrictions, supervision.
⟨SAVE⟩ ⟨✕⟩ ⟨🛏⟩ ⟨🖥⟩ ⟨🍽⟩ ⟨🏊⟩

DINGWALL

▼▼ Markland Coastal Resort **CA**
(902) 383-2246. **Call for rates.** 802 Dingwall Rd. Follow signs marked "Resort" to end of winding road. Ext corridors. **Pets:** Accepted.
⟨✕⟩ ⟨🛏⟩ ⟨🖥⟩ ⟨🍽⟩ ⟨🏊⟩

HALIFAX

▼▼▼ Airport Hotel Halifax **SH**
(902) 873-3000. **$199, 21 day notice.** 60 Bell Blvd. Hwy 102, exit 6. Int corridors. **Pets:** Accepted.
⟨ASK⟩ ⟨S⟩ ⟨✕⟩ ⟨🛏⟩ ⟨🖥⟩ ⟨🍽⟩ ⟨🏊⟩ ⟨✕⟩

ⓐ ▼▼▼▼ Casino Nova Scotia Hotel **LH**
(902) 421-1700. **$109-$179.** 1919 Upper Water St. Adjacent to historic properties and Casino Nova Scotia. Int corridors. **Pets:** Designated rooms, service with restrictions, supervision.
⟨SAVE⟩ ⟨✕⟩ ⟨&M⟩ ⟨🐾⟩ ⟨🛏⟩ ⟨🖥⟩ ⟨🍽⟩ ⟨🏊⟩ ⟨✕⟩

▼ Chebucto Inn **SH**
(902) 453-4330. **$75-$145.** 6151 Lady Hammond Rd. Jct Hwy 111 and Rt 2 (Bedford Hwy), 0.7 km e. Ext corridors. **Pets:** Medium. $100 deposit/room. Designated rooms, service with restrictions, supervision.
⟨✕⟩ ⟨🍽⟩

ⓐ ▼▼▼ Citadel Halifax Hotel **LH**
(902) 422-1391. **$219-$299.** 1960 Brunswick St. Between Cogswell and Duke sts. Int corridors. **Pets:** Accepted.
⟨SAVE⟩ ⟨S⟩ ⟨✕⟩ ⟨🛏⟩ ⟨🖥⟩ ⟨🍽⟩ ⟨🏊⟩ ⟨✕⟩

ⓐ ▼▼▼ Delta Barrington **LH** ✿
(902) 429-7410. **$152-$212.** 1875 Barrington St. Between Cogswell and Duke sts. Int corridors. **Pets:** Medium, other species. Designated rooms, service with restrictions, supervision.
⟨SAVE⟩ ⟨S⟩ ⟨✕⟩ ⟨🖥⟩ ⟨🍽⟩ ⟨🏊⟩ ⟨✕⟩

ⓐ ▼▼▼ Delta Halifax **LH** ✿
(902) 425-6700. **$152-$212.** 1990 Barrington St. Corner of Cogswell and Barrington sts. Int corridors. **Pets:** Other species. Service with restrictions, supervision.
⟨SAVE⟩ ⟨S⟩ ⟨✕⟩ ⟨🖥⟩ ⟨🍽⟩ ⟨🏊⟩ ⟨✕⟩

ⓐ ▼▼▼ Econo Lodge & Suites **SH** ✿
(902) 443-0303. **$79-$169.** 560 Bedford Hwy. On Rt 2 (Bedford Hwy), 9.6 km w. Int corridors. **Pets:** $10 one-time fee/room. Designated rooms, service with restrictions, supervision.
⟨SAVE⟩ ⟨S⟩ ⟨✕⟩ ⟨&M⟩ ⟨🛏⟩ ⟨🖥⟩ ⟨🍽⟩ ⟨🏊⟩

▼▼ Esquire Motel **M**
(902) 835-3367. **$60-$90.** 771 Bedford Hwy. Hwy 102, exit 4A, 5.3 km e on Rt 2 (Bedford Hwy). Ext corridors. **Pets:** Service with restrictions, supervision.
⟨✕⟩ ⟨🛏⟩ ⟨🖥⟩ ⟨🏊⟩ ⟨🐾⟩

ⓐ ▼▼▼ Holiday Inn Express Halifax/Bedford **SH** ✿
(902) 445-1100. **$109-$129, 14 day notice.** 133 Kearney Lake Rd. Hwy 102, exit 2. Int corridors. **Pets:** Medium. $25 one-time fee/room. Designated rooms, service with restrictions, supervision.
⟨SAVE⟩ ⟨S⟩ ⟨✕⟩ ⟨&M⟩ ⟨🐾⟩ ⟨🛏⟩ ⟨🖥⟩ ⟨🏊⟩

ⓐ ▼▼▼ Holiday Inn Select Halifax-Centre **LH** ✿
(902) 423-1161. **$149-$209.** 1980 Robie St. Jct Quinpool St. Int corridors. **Pets:** Medium. Designated rooms, service with restrictions, crate.
⟨SAVE⟩ ⟨S⟩ ⟨✕⟩ ⟨🛏⟩ ⟨🖥⟩ ⟨🍽⟩ ⟨🏊⟩ ⟨✕⟩

▼▼▼ Lakeview Inn & Suites **SH** ✿
(902) 450-3020. **$145-$185.** 98 Chain Lake Dr. Hwy 102, exit 2A eastbound; Hwy 103, exit 2. Int corridors. **Pets:** Large. $100 deposit/pet. Designated rooms, service with restrictions, supervision.
⟨ASK⟩ ⟨S⟩ ⟨✕⟩ ⟨&M⟩ ⟨🛏⟩ ⟨🖥⟩ ⟨🏊⟩

ⓐ ▼▼▼▼ The Lord Nelson Hotel & Suites **LH** ✿
(902) 423-6331. **$169-$259.** 1515 S Park St. Corner of Park St and Spring Garden Rd; centre. Int corridors. **Pets:** Large, other species. Designated rooms, service with restrictions, supervision.
⟨SAVE⟩ ⟨S⟩ ⟨✕⟩ ⟨🛏⟩ ⟨🖥⟩ ⟨🍽⟩

ⓐ ▼▼▼▼ The Prince George Hotel **LH** ✿
(902) 425-1986. **$145-$225.** 1725 Market St. Between Prince and Carmichael sts. Int corridors. **Pets:** Other species. Service with restrictions.
⟨SAVE⟩ ⟨✕⟩ ⟨&M⟩ ⟨🖥⟩ ⟨🍽⟩ ⟨🏊⟩ ⟨✕⟩

▼▼ Residence Inn by Marriott **SH** ✿
(902) 422-0493. **$134-$249.** 1599 Grafton St. Corner of Sackville St. Int corridors. **Pets:** Large. $100 one-time fee/room. Service with restrictions.
⟨ASK⟩ ⟨S⟩ ⟨✕⟩ ⟨&M⟩ ⟨🐾⟩ ⟨🛏⟩ ⟨🖥⟩

▼ Travelers Motel **M**
(902) 835-3394. **$55-$82.** 773 Bedford Hwy. Hwy 102, exit 4A, 5.3 km e on Rt 2 (Bedford Hwy). Ext corridors. **Pets:** Accepted.
⟨S⟩ ⟨✕⟩ ⟨🛏⟩ ⟨🐾⟩

ⓐ ▼▼▼ The Westin Nova Scotian **LH**
(902) 421-1000. **$199-$275.** 1181 Hollis St. Between Barrington and Lower Water sts. Int corridors. **Pets:** Accepted.
⟨SAVE⟩ ⟨S⟩ ⟨✕⟩ ⟨&M⟩ ⟨🖥⟩ ⟨🍽⟩ ⟨🏊⟩ ⟨✕⟩

INGONISH BEACH

▼▼▼▼ Keltic Lodge 🏨
(902) 285-2880. **$129-$397, 3 day notice.** Middle Head Peninsula. Inside the Cape Breton Highlands National Park; off Cabot Tr main highway. Ext/int corridors. **Pets:** Other species. Designated rooms.

(A$K) ⊠ 🖥 💻 🍴 ➹ ⊠

KEMPTVILLE

▼▼▼▼ Trout Point Lodge 🄲
(902) 749-7629. **$222-$343, 21 day notice.** 289 Trout Point Rd. 11 km e on Rt 203, 3.5 km n on gravel entry road. Ext corridors. **Pets:** Accepted.

(A$K) 🌀 ⊠ 🍴 ⊠ 🐾 💤 🈯

KENTVILLE

(CAA) ▼ Allen's Motel Ⓜ
(902) 678-2683. **$60-$85.** 384 Park St. Hwy 101, exit 14, 3 km e on Rt 1. Ext corridors. **Pets:** Accepted.

(SAVE) 🌀 ⊠ 🈯 🈯

▼▼ Auberge Wandlyn Inn 🆂🅷
(902) 678-8311. **$112-$127.** 7270 Hwy 1. Hwy 101, exit 14. Ext/int corridors. **Pets:** Accepted.

(A$K) 🌀 ⊠ 🖥 💻 🍴 ➹

(CAA) ▼ Sun Valley Motel Ⓜ
(902) 678-7368. **$64-$80.** 905 Park St. Hwy 101, exit 14, 0.8 km e on Rt 1. Ext corridors. **Pets:** Accepted.

(SAVE) 🌀 ⊠ 🖥 💻 🈯 🈯

LISCOMB

▼▼▼▼ Liscombe Lodge 🆂🅷
(902) 779-2307. **$132, 3 day notice.** RR 1. On Hwy 7. Ext/int corridors. **Pets:** Accepted.

(A$K) ⊠ 🅼 🈯 🖥 💻 🍴 ➹ ⊠

LUNENBURG

(CAA) ▼▼▼▼ Boscawen Inn 🄲
(902) 634-3325. **$95-$205, 3 day notice.** 150 Cumberland St. Centre. Int corridors. **Pets:** Accepted.

(SAVE) ⊠ 🍴 🈯

▼▼ Homeport Motel & Inn Ⓜ
(902) 634-8234. **$75-$185.** 167 Victoria Rd. 1 km w on Rt 3. Ext corridors. **Pets:** Accepted.

(A$K) 🌀 ⊠ 🖥 💻

(CAA) ▼▼▼▼ Lunenburg Arms Hotel 🆂🅷 🐾
(902) 640-4040. **$89-$249, 14 day notice.** 94 Pelham St. Corner of Pelham and Duke sts; centre. Int corridors. **Pets:** Other species. Supervision.

(SAVE) ⊠ 🅼 🈯 💻 🍴

MAHONE BAY

▼▼▼▼ Bayview Pines Country Inn 🅱🅱
(902) 624-9970. **$90-$120, 3 day notice.** 678 Oakland Rd. Hwy 103, exit 10, 2 km w on Rt 3 to Kedy's Landing, 6 km e of Mahone Bay. Ext/int corridors. **Pets:** Small. Designated rooms, service with restrictions, supervision.

⊠ 🖥 💻 🈯 🈯

MAVILLETTE

▼▼▼ Cape View Motel & Cottages Ⓜ
(902) 645-2258. **$62-$84.** Rt 1, 32 km ne of Yarmouth; centre. Ext corridors. **Pets:** Service with restrictions, supervision.

🌀 ⊠ 🖥 🈯 🈯

MIDDLETON

▼▼ Mid-Valley Motel 🆂🅷
(902) 825-3433. **$80-$105.** 121 Main St. 1 km w on Rt 1; Hwy 101, exit 18. Ext corridors. **Pets:** Accepted.

⊠ 🖥 🍴 ➹

NEW GLASGOW

▼▼▼ Comfort Inn 🆂🅷
(902) 755-6450. **$99-$159.** 740 Westville Rd. On Hwy 289, just e of jct Trans-Canada Hwy 104, exit 23. Int corridors. **Pets:** Large. Service with restrictions, supervision.

(A$K) 🌀 ⊠ 🖥 💻

▼▼▼ Country Inn & Suites By Carlson 🆂🅷
(902) 928-1333. **$95-$155.** 700 Westville Rd. On Hwy 289, just e of jct Trans-Canada Hwy 104, exit 23. Int corridors. **Pets:** Accepted.

(A$K) 🌀 ⊠ 🖥 💻

NEW HARBOUR

▼▼▼▼ Lonely Rock Seaside Bungalows 🄲🄰
(902) 387-2668. **$100-$195, 14 day notice.** 150 New Harbour Rd. Rt 316, 0.7 km s. Ext corridors. **Pets:** Dogs only. No service, crate.

⊠ 🖥 💻 ⊠ 🈯 🈯

NORTH SYDNEY

(CAA) ▼▼▼ Clansman Motel 🆂🅷
(902) 794-7226. **$79-$125.** 9 Baird St. Hwy 125, exit 2, just e on King St. Ext/int corridors. **Pets:** Accepted.

(SAVE) 🌀 ⊠ 🖥 💻 🍴 ➹

PARRSBORO

▼▼ The Sunshine Inn Ⓜ
(902) 254-3135. **$84-$150.** 3.2 km n on Rt 2. Ext corridors. **Pets:** Accepted.

⊠ 🖥 ⊠ 🈯

PICTOU

▼▼ Willow House Inn 🅱🅱
(902) 485-5740. **$55-$120.** 11 Willow St. Corner of Willow and Church sts; centre. Int corridors. **Pets:** Accepted.

⊠ 🈯

PORT DUFFERIN

▼ Marquis of Dufferin Seaside Inn Ⓜ
(902) 654-2696. **$62-$76.** On Hwy 7. Ext corridors. **Pets:** Other species. $30 deposit/pet. Service with restrictions.

⊠ 🍴 ⊠ 🈯 🈯

PORT HASTINGS

▼▼ Econo Lodge MacPuffin Ⓜ
(902) 625-0621. **$79-$119.** 373 Hwy 4. 1.6 km n on Hwy 4; 1.6 km s of Canso Cswy. Ext corridors. **Pets:** Other species. Service with restrictions.

(A$K) 🌀 ⊠ 💻 🍴 ➹

(CAA) ▼ Howard Johnson Inn 🆂🅷
(902) 625-0460. **$74-$125.** E of Canso Cswy on Trans-Canada Hwy 105 rotary; entrance through north side of church. Ext/int corridors. **Pets:** Accepted.

(SAVE) 🌀 ⊠ 🖥 💻 🍴

PORT HAWKESBURY

(CAA) ▼▼▼ Maritime Inn Port Hawkesbury 🆂🅷
(902) 625-0320. **$94-$157.** 717 Reeves St. 6.4 km e of Canso Cswy on Hwy 4. Ext/int corridors. **Pets:** Accepted.

(SAVE) ⊠ 🖥 💻 🍴 ➹

SCOTSBURN

▼▼▼ Stoneham Lodge & Chalets 🅲🅰 ❀
(902) 485-3468. **$105-$150.** Rt 256, 12 km w of Pictou via Rt 376, last 2 km on gravel entry road. Ext corridors. **Pets:** Other species. Service with restrictions, supervision.

🆂 ⊠ 🛗 💻 ⊿ ⊠ 🐾

SHELBURNE

🅐🅐 ▼▼▼ MacKenzie's Motel & Cottages Ⓜ
(902) 875-2842. **$70-$90.** 260 Water St. Hwy 103, exit 26, 1.5 km e on Rt 3. Ext corridors. **Pets:** Very small, dogs only. Service with restrictions, supervision.

🆂 ⊠ 🛗 💻 ⊿

SMITHS COVE

▼▼▼ Hedley House Inn By The Sea Ⓜ
(902) 245-2500. **$69-$189.** RR 1. Hwy 101, exit 25 eastbound; exit 24 westbound. Ext corridors. **Pets:** Small. $20 daily fee/pet. Service with restrictions.

🆂 ⊠ 🛗 💻 ⊿ 🐾 ⊠

🅐🅐 ▼▼▼ Mountain Gap Inn 🆂🅷 ❀
(902) 245-5841. **$99-$155, 30 day notice.** 217 Hwy 1, Smiths Cove. Hwy 101, exit 25 eastbound; exit 24 westbound. Ext corridors. **Pets:** Other species. $10 one-time fee/pet. Supervision.

🆂 ⊠ 🛗 💻 ⊿ ⊿ ⊠

SYDNEY

🅐🅐 ▼▼▼▼ Cambridge Suites Hotel 🅛🅷
(902) 562-6500. **$159-$175.** 380 Esplanade. Hwy 4, 5 km e of jct Hwy 125, exit 6E; downtown. Int corridors. **Pets:** Accepted.

🆂 ⊠ 🛗 💻 ⊿

▼▼▼ Comfort Inn 🆂🅷
(902) 562-0200. **$99-$165.** 368 Kings Rd. Hwy 4, 3.5 km e of jct Hwy 125, exit 6E. Int corridors. **Pets:** Service with restrictions, supervision.

🅰🆂🅺 🆂 ⊠ 💻

🅐🅐 ▼▼▼▼ Days Inn Sydney 🆂🅷 ❀
(902) 539-6750. **$119.** 480 Kings Rd. Hwy 4, 2.8 km e of jct Hwy 125, exit 6E. Int corridors. **Pets:** Other species. Supervision.

🆂 🆂 ⊠ 🛗 💻 ⊿ ⊠

▼▼▼ Delta Sydney 🅛🅷
(902) 562-7500. **$189-$209.** 300 Esplanade. Hwy 4, 5.5 km e of jct Hwy 125, exit 6E; downtown. Int corridors. **Pets:** Accepted.

🅰🆂🅺 🆂 ⊠ 🛗 💻 ⊿ ⊿ ⊠

▼▼▼ Quality Inn Sydney 🆂🅷
(902) 539-8101. **$89-$195.** 560 Kings Rd. Hwy 4, 3.3 km e of jct Hwy 125. Int corridors. **Pets:** Accepted.

🅰🆂🅺 🆂 ⊠ ⊿ 💻 ⊿ ⊿

SYDNEY MINES

▼▼▼ Gowrie House Country Inn 🅒🅘
(902) 544-1050. **$99-$295, 3 day notice.** 840 Shore Rd. Hwy 105, exit 21E, 3 km n on Rt 305. Ext/int corridors. **Pets:** Small, other species. Service with restrictions, supervision.

⊠ 🛗 💻 ⊿

TRURO

▼▼▼ Comfort Inn 🆂🅷
(902) 893-0330. **$80-$165, 30 day notice.** 12 Meadow Dr. Trans-Canada Hwy 102, exit 14. Int corridors. **Pets:** Accepted.

🅰🆂🅺 🆂 ⊠ 💻

▼▼▼ Howard Johnson Hotel and Convention Centre 🆂🅷
(902) 895-1651. **$100.** 437 Prince St. Centre. Ext/int corridors. **Pets:** Accepted.

🅰🆂🅺 🆂 ⊠ 🛗 💻 ⊿ ⊿

🅐🅐 ▼▼▼ The Palliser Motel Ⓜ
(902) 893-8951. **$65-$79.** 103/104 Tidal Bore Rd. Trans-Canada Hwy 102, exit 14; Trans-Canada Hwy 104, exit 15, 3.2 km s. Ext corridors. **Pets:** Medium. Service with restrictions, supervision.

🆂 ⊠ ⊿ ⊿

▼▼▼ Super 8 Motel 🆂🅷
(902) 895-8884. **$99-$199.** 85 Treaty Tr. Hwy 102, exit 13A. Int corridors. **Pets:** Accepted.

🅰🆂🅺 🆂 ⊠ 🆖 ⊿ 🛗 💻 ⊿

WESTERN SHORE

🅐🅐 ▼▼▼▼ Oak Island Resort & Spa 🆂🅷
(902) 627-2600. **$89-$159.** 55 Vaughn Rd. Hwy 103, exit 9 or 10, follow signs on Rt 3, 10 km e of Mahone Bay. Int corridors. **Pets:** Accepted.

🆂 ⊠ 🆖 ⊿ 🛗 💻 ⊿ ⊿ ⊠

WHITE POINT

▼▼▼ White Point Beach Resort 🆂🅷
(902) 354-2711. **$100-$190, 3 day notice.** 75 White Point Rd 2. Hwy 103, exit 20A, 9 km w on Rt 3. Ext/int corridors. **Pets:** Designated rooms.

⊠ 🛗 💻 ⊿ ⊿ ⊠

YARMOUTH

🅐🅐 ▼▼▼ Best Western Mermaid Ⓜ
(902) 742-7821. **$79-$180.** 545 Main St. Corner of Main St and Starrs Rd. Ext corridors. **Pets:** Service with restrictions.

🆂 🆂 ⊠ 💻 ⊿ ⊿

▼▼▼ Capri Motel Ⓜ
(902) 742-7168. **$59-$150.** 8-12 Herbert St. Corner of Hebert and Main sts. Ext corridors. **Pets:** Service with restrictions.

🆂 ⊠ 🛗 💻

▼▼▼ Comfort Inn 🆂🅷
(902) 742-1119. **$80-$190.** 96 Starrs Rd. Jct Hwy 101 E and Hwy 3. Int corridors. **Pets:** Other species. Designated rooms, service with restrictions, crate.

🅰🆂🅺 🆂 ⊠ 💻

🅐🅐 ▼▼▼ Lakelawn Motel Ⓜ
(902) 742-3588. **$79-$99.** 641 Main St. 1 km n on Hwy 1. Ext/int corridors. **Pets:** Small. Designated rooms, service with restrictions, supervision.

🆂 ⊠ 🐾 ⊿

▼▼▼ Rodd Colony Harbour Inn 🆂🅷
(902) 742-9194. **$88-$143.** 6 Forest St. At ferry terminal. Int corridors. **Pets:** Accepted.

🅰🆂🅺 🆂 ⊠ 🛗 💻 🛗 🐾

▼▼▼ Rodd Grand Yarmouth-A Rodd Signature Hotel 🅛🅷
(902) 742-2446. **$125-$221.** 417 Main St. Near centre of downtown. Int corridors. **Pets:** Accepted.

🅰🆂🅺 🆂 ⊠ 🛗 💻 🛗 ⊿ ⊠

▼▼▼ Voyageur Motel Ⓜ
(902) 742-7157. **$69-$179.** 4.8 km ne on Hwy 1. Ext corridors. **Pets:** Accepted.

🅰🆂🅺 🆂 ⊠ 🛗 🐾

ONTARIO

CITY INDEX

AJAX

◆◆ Super 8 Motel-Ajax 🅂🄷
(905) 428-6884. **$94-$124.** 210 Westney Rd S. Jct Bayly St from Hwy 401, exit Westney Rd, 1 km s. Int corridors. **Pets:** Accepted.
(ASK) (S/D) (X) (⌂)

ARNPRIOR

◆ Country Squire Motel 🅼
(613) 623-6556. **$59-$89.** 111 Staye Court Dr. Hwy 17, exit White Lake Rd N. Ext corridors. **Pets:** Accepted.
(ASK) (S/D) (X) (🛏) (X)

AURORA

ⒶⒶ ◆◆ Howard Johnson Hotel Aurora 🅂🄷
(905) 727-1312. **$134-$162.** 15520 Yonge St. 0.5 km n of Wellington St. Int corridors. **Pets:** Accepted.
(SAVE) (S/D) (X) (🛏) (⌂) (🍴)

BANCROFT

ⒶⒶ ◆◆ Best Western Sword Motor Inn 🅼
(613) 332-2474. **$99-$144.** 146 Hastings St. On Hwy 62 N; centre. Ext/int corridors. **Pets:** Small. $25 deposit/pet. Designated rooms, service with restrictions, supervision.
(SAVE) (S/D) (X) (🛏) (⌂) (🍴) (🛏) (X)

BARRIE

◆◆ Comfort Inn 🅂🄷
(705) 722-3600. **$100-$145.** 75 Hart Dr. Hwy 400, exit 96A E (Dunlop St). Int corridors. **Pets:** Accepted.
(ASK) (S/D) (X) (🛏) (⌂)

◆◆ Days Inn Barrie 🅂🄷
(705) 733-8989. **$99-$140.** 60 Bryne Dr. Hwy 400, exit 94 (Essa Rd), just s, then just e. Int corridors. **Pets:** Other species. $10 daily fee/pet. Service with restrictions, supervision.
(ASK) (S/D) (X) (🛏) (⌂) (🛏)

ⒶⒶ ◆◆◆ Holiday Inn Barrie-Hotel & Conference Centre 🅂🄷
(705) 728-6191. **$139-$189.** 20 Fairview Rd. Hwy 400, exit 94 (Essa Rd), just e. Int corridors. **Pets:** Accepted.
(SAVE) (S/D) (X) (C/M) (🛏) (⌂) (🍴) (🛏) (X)

◆◆ Travelodge Barrie 🅂🄷
(705) 734-9500. **$109-$179.** 55 Hart Dr. Hwy 400, exit 96A E (Dunlop St). Int corridors. **Pets:** Accepted.
(ASK) (S/D) (X) (🛏) (⌂) (🍴) (🛏)

BARRY'S BAY

◆ Mountain View Motel 🅼
(613) 756-2757. **$60-$94, 7 day notice.** 18508 Hwy 60 E. On Hwy 60, 4 km e. Ext corridors. **Pets:** Accepted.
(X) (🛏) (⌂)

BAYFIELD

ⒶⒶ ◆◆ ◆◆ The Little Inn of Bayfield 🅲🄸 🐾
(519) 565-2611. **$175-$297, 3 day notice.** 26 Main St. Hwy 21, exit Main St, jct Catherine St. Int corridors. **Pets:** Medium. $25 one-time fee/room. Designated rooms, service with restrictions, supervision.
(SAVE) (X) (⌂) (🍴)

◆ The Martha Ritz House 🅲🄸
(519) 565-2325. **$120, 4 day notice.** 27 Main St. Hwy 21, exit Main St, jct Catherine St. Int corridors. **Pets:** Small, other species. $25 one-time fee/pet. Service with restrictions, supervision.
(🍴) (W) (🛏)

BELLEVILLE

ⒶⒶ ◆◆◆ Best Western Belleville 🅂🄷
(613) 969-1112. **$112-$135, 3 day notice.** 387 N Front St. Hwy 401, exit 543A, 0.5 km s on Hwy 62 (N Front St). Int corridors. **Pets:** Accepted.
(SAVE) (S/D) (X) (🛏) (⌂) (🛏)

◆◆ Comfort Inn 🅂🄷
(613) 966-7703. **$105-$118.** 200 N Park St. Hwy 401, exit 543A, 1 km s on Hwy 62 (N Front St). Int corridors. **Pets:** Accepted.
(ASK) (S/D) (X) (🛏) (⌂)

◆◆◆ Ramada Inn on the Bay 🅂🄷 🐾
(613) 968-3411. **$170-$205, 3 day notice.** 11 Bay Bridge Rd. Hwy 2, 0.5 km s. Int corridors. **Pets:** Designated rooms, service with restrictions, crate.
(ASK) (S/D) (X) (🛏) (⌂) (🍴) (🛏) (X)

BLIND RIVER

◆ Lakeview Inn 🅼
(705) 356-0800. **$74-$80, 3 day notice.** 143 Causley St (Hwy 17). On Hwy 17, just e of Hwy 557. Ext corridors. **Pets:** Small. Service with restrictions, supervision.
(ASK) (S/D) (X) (🛏) (🍴)

BRACEBRIDGE

ⒶⒶ ◆◆ Travelodge Bracebridge 🅼
(705) 645-2235. **$89-$169.** 320 Taylor Rd. Hwy 11, exit 189 (Hwy 42/Taylor Rd), 1 km w. Ext corridors. **Pets:** Medium. $10 one-time fee/pet. Service with restrictions, supervision.
(SAVE) (S/D) (X) (🛏) (⌂) (🛏) (X)

BRAMPTON

▼▼▼ Comfort Inn SH
(905) 452-0600. **$90-$129.** 5 Rutherford Rd S. Hwy 401, exit Hwy 410 N, 11 km to Hwy 7 E (Queen St), then 1 km w. Int corridors. **Pets:** Service with restrictions, supervision.
ASK SÒ X ⊟ ⊡ ⊒

▼▼ Motel 6 #1902 SH
(905) 451-3313. **$73-$85.** 160 Steelwell Rd. Hwy 410, exit Steeles Ave E, s on Tomken, then just w. Int corridors. **Pets:** Small, other species. Service with restrictions, supervision.
SÒ X

BRANTFORD

▼▼ Comfort Inn SH
(519) 753-3100. **$102-$139.** 58 King George Rd. Just s of jct Hwy 403 and 24. Int corridors. **Pets:** Other species. Designated rooms, service with restrictions, supervision.
ASK SÒ X ⊟ ⊡ ⊓

CAA ▼▼ Days Inn SH ❀
(519) 759-2700. **$98-$112.** 460 Fairview Dr. Hwy 403, exit Wayne Gretzky Pkwy, 0.8 km n. Int corridors. **Pets:** Other species. $15 one-time fee/room. Service with restrictions, crate.
SAVE SÒ X ⊟ ⊡ ⊓

▼▼▼ Holiday Inn Brantford SH
(519) 758-9999. **$89-$229.** 664 Colborne St. Hwy 403, exit Wayne Gretzky Pkwy, 2 km s to Colborne St, then just w. Int corridors. **Pets:** Accepted.
ASK SÒ X ⊟ ⊡ ⊓ ⇌

BRIGHTON

▼▼ Presquile Beach Motel M
(613) 475-1010. **$55-$99.** 243 Main St W. Hwy 401, exit 509, 4 km s on Hwy 30, then 2 km w on Hwy 2. Ext corridors. **Pets:** Other species. Crate.
X ⊟ ⊠

BROCKVILLE

CAA ▼▼▼ Best Western White House Motel M
(613) 345-1622. **$69-$119.** 1843 Hwy 2 E. Hwy 401, exit 698, 1.7 km s on N Augusta Rd, then 1.5 km e. Ext corridors. **Pets:** Very small. $10 daily fee/pet. Designated rooms, service with restrictions, supervision.
SAVE SÒ X ⊟ ⊡ ⊓ ⇌

▼▼ Comfort Inn SH ❀
(613) 345-0042. **$93-$129.** 7777 Kent Blvd. Hwy 401, exit 696, just nw. Int corridors. **Pets:** Other species. $5 daily fee/pet. Service with restrictions, crate.
ASK SÒ X ⊟ ⊡

BURLINGTON

CAA ▼◆▼ Burlington on the Lake Travelodge Hotel SH ❀
(905) 681-0762. **$149-$159.** 2020 Lakeshore Rd. Jct Brant. Int corridors. **Pets:** Other species. $10 daily fee/pet. Designated rooms, service with restrictions.
SAVE SÒ X ⊠ ⊟ ⊡ ⊓ ⇌ ⊠

CAA ▼▼ Comfort Inn SH ❀
(905) 639-1700. **$85-$145.** 3290 S Service Rd. QEW, exit Walker's Line Rd westbound, just s to Harvester Rd, then just w; exit Guelph Line Rd eastbound, just s to Harvester Rd, then just e. Int corridors. **Pets:** Other species. Designated rooms, service with restrictions, supervision.
SAVE SÒ X ⊟ ⊡

▼▼ Motel 6 Canada #1900 SH
(905) 331-1955. **$65-$81.** 4345 N Service Rd. QEW, exit Walker's Line Rd N to N Service Rd. Int corridors. **Pets:** Accepted.
SÒ X ⊠ ⊟

CAMBRIDGE

CAA ▼▼▼ Comfort Inn SH ❀
(519) 658-1100. **$112-$140.** 220 Holiday Inn Dr. Hwy 401, exit 282, just n to Groh Ave. Int corridors. **Pets:** Other species. Service with restrictions, supervision.
SAVE SÒ X ⊟ ⊡

CAA ▼▼▼▼ Langdon Hall Country House Hotel & Spa CI
(519) 740-2100. **$259-$329, 7 day notice.** RR 33. Hwy 401, exit 275 to Homer Watson Blvd (Fountain St), 1 km s to Blair Rd, then follow signs 1 km to Langdon Dr. Ext/int corridors. **Pets:** Accepted.
SAVE X ⊟ ⊡ ⊓ ⇌ ⊠

▼▼ Super 8 Motel-Cambridge SH
(519) 622-1070. **$65-$98.** 650 Hespeler Rd. Hwy 401, exit 282, 1 km n. Int corridors. **Pets:** Accepted.
SAVE SÒ X ⊟ ⊡ ⊓ ⇌

▼▼ Travelodge Cambridge SH
(519) 622-1180. **$80-$99.** 605 Hespeler Rd. Hwy 401, exit 282, 1 km s. Int corridors. **Pets:** Medium. Service with restrictions, supervision.
ASK SÒ X ⊟ ⊡ ⊓

CHAPLEAU

▼▼ Riverside Motel M
(705) 864-0440. **$68-$98.** 116 Cherry St. Corner of Grey and Cherry sts. Ext corridors. **Pets:** Accepted.
ASK SÒ X ⊟ ⊡ ⊠

CHATHAM

▼▼ Comfort Inn SH
(519) 352-5500. **$92-$104.** 1100 Richmond St. Hwy 401, exit 81 (Bloomfield Rd), 5 km n. Int corridors. **Pets:** Accepted.
ASK SÒ X ⊟ ⊡

▼▼ Travelodge Chatham M
(519) 436-1200. **$108-$117.** 555 Bloomfield Rd. Hwy 401, exit 81 (Bloomfield Rd), 5 km n. Int corridors. **Pets:** $25 deposit/room. Service with restrictions, supervision.
X ⊟ ⊡

CHATSWORTH

▼▼ Key Motel M
(519) 794-2350. **$60-$80.** 317051 Hwy 6/10. On Hwy 6 and 10. Ext/int corridors. **Pets:** Accepted.
X ⊟ ⇌ ⊠

COBOURG

CAA ▼▼▼ Best Western Cobourg Inn and Convention Centre SH ❀
(905) 372-2105. **$125-$150.** 930 Burnham St. Hwy 401, exit 472 (Burnham St S). Int corridors. **Pets:** Other species. Service with restrictions, supervision.
SAVE SÒ X ⊟ ⊡ ⊓ ⇌

CAA ▼▼ Comfort Inn SH
(905) 372-7007. **$99-$150.** 121 Densmore Rd. Hwy 401, exit 474, just se. Int corridors. **Pets:** Other species. Supervision.
SAVE SÒ X ⊟ ⊡

CORNWALL

CAA ▼▼▼ Best Western Parkway Inn & Conference Centre SH
(613) 932-0451. **$129-$199.** 1515 Vincent Massey Dr. Hwy 401, exit 789 (Brookdale Ave), 2.8 km s, then just w. Int corridors. **Pets:** Accepted.
SAVE SÒ X ⊡ ⊓ ⇌

ⒶⒶ ♦♦ Comfort Inn-Cornwall SH
(613) 937-0111. **$80-$250, 7 day notice.** 1625 Vincent Massey Dr. Hwy 401, exit 789 (Brookdale Ave), 2.8 km s, then 0.7 km w. Int corridors. **Pets:** $15 one-time fee/room. Designated rooms, service with restrictions, supervision.
🆂🅰🆅🄴 🆂🚭 ✕ 🔌 📺 🏊

ⒶⒶ ♦ Econo Lodge SH
(613) 936-1996. **$65-$88, 7 day notice.** 1142 Brookdale Ave. Hwy 401, exit 789 (Brookdale Ave), 3 km s. Ext/int corridors. **Pets:** Small. $15 daily fee/pet. Designated rooms, service with restrictions, supervision.
🆂🅰🆅🄴 ✕ 🔌

ⒶⒶ ♦♦♦ Ramada Inn & Conference Centre SH ☕
(613) 933-8000. **$89-$149.** 805 Brookdale Ave. Hwy 401, exit 789 (Brookdale Ave), 4 km s. Int corridors. **Pets:** Small. $10 daily fee/room. Designated rooms, crate.
🆂🅰🆅🄴 🆂🚭 ✕ 🔌 📺 🍽 🏊 🚭

DRYDEN

ⒶⒶ ♦♦♦ Best Western Motor Inn SH
(807) 223-3201. **$85-$99.** 349 Government St. On Hwy 17. Ext/int corridors. **Pets:** Designated rooms, service with restrictions, crate.
🆂🅰🆅🄴 🆂🚭 ✕ 🔌 📺 🍽 🏊 🚭

♦♦ Comfort Inn M ☕
(807) 223-3893. **$85-$105.** 522 Government St. On Hwy 17. Int corridors. **Pets:** Other species. Designated rooms, service with restrictions, supervision.
🅰🆂🅺 🆂🚭 ✕ 🔌 📺

ⒶⒶ ♦♦♦ Holiday Inn Express Dryden SH
(807) 223-3000. **$98-$129.** 585 Government St. On Hwy 17. Int corridors. **Pets:** Medium, other species. Designated rooms, service with restrictions, supervision.
🆂🅰🆅🄴 🆂🚭 ✕ 🔌 📺 🏊

ELLIOT LAKE

♦ Dunlop Lake Lodge SH
(705) 848-8090. **$65-$75.** 74 Dunlop Lake Rd. Hwy 17, 38.8 km n on Hwy 108, 0.8 km w, follow signs. Int corridors. **Pets:** Accepted.
🅰🆂🅺 🆂🚭 ✕ 🍽 🚭 🏌

FONTHILL

♦ Hipwell's Motel M
(905) 892-3588. **$52-$80.** 299 Regional Rd 20. 1.6 km w; centre. Ext corridors. **Pets:** $5 daily fee/pet. No service, supervision.
🅰🆂🅺 ✕ 🔌 🏊

FORT FRANCES

♦♦♦ Super 8 SH ☕
(807) 274-4945. **$89-$139.** 810 Kings Hwy. On Hwy 11. Int corridors. **Pets:** Other species. Designated rooms, service with restrictions, crate.
🅰🆂🅺 🆂🚭 ✕ 🔌 📺 🏊 🚭

GANANOQUE

ⒶⒶ ♦ Travelodge 1000 Islands M
(613) 382-4282. **$64-$199.** 555 King St E. Hwy 401, exit 647 eastbound; exit 648 westbound, 1.5 km w on Hwy 2 (King St). Ext corridors. **Pets:** Accepted.
🆂🅰🆅🄴 🆂🚭 ✕ 🍽 🏊

GRIMSBY

ⒶⒶ ♦♦♦ Super 8 Motel-Grimsby SH
(905) 309-8800. **$89-$139.** 11 Windward Dr. QEW, exit 74 (Casablanca N). Int corridors. **Pets:** Other species. $10 one-time fee/room. Service with restrictions.
🆂🅰🆅🄴 🆂🚭 ✕ 🔌 📺 🏊

GUELPH

ⒶⒶ ♦♦♦ Comfort Inn Guelph SH
(519) 763-1900. **$115-$145.** 480 Silvercreek Pkwy. Jct Hwy 6 and 7. Int corridors. **Pets:** Medium. Designated rooms, service with restrictions, supervision.
🆂🅰🆅🄴 🆂🚭 ✕ 🔌 📺

ⒶⒶ ♦♦♦♦ Holiday Inn Guelph LH
(519) 836-0231. **$135-$189.** 601 Scottsdale Dr. Jct Hwy 6 N and Stone Rd E, 8 km n of jct Hwy 401. Int corridors. **Pets:** Accepted.
🆂🅰🆅🄴 🆂🚭 ✕ 🔌 📺 🍽 🏊 🚭

ⒶⒶ ♦♦♦♦ Ramada Hotel & Conference Centre SH
(519) 836-1240. **$160-$195.** 716 Gordon St. Jct Gordon St and Stone Rd; 8 km n of Hwy 401 via Brock Rd. Int corridors. **Pets:** Other species. Designated rooms, service with restrictions, supervision.
🆂🅰🆅🄴 🆂🚭 ✕ 🔌 📺 🍽 🏊

HALIBURTON

♦ Lakeview Motel M
(705) 457-1027. **$85-$113, 5 day notice.** Jct Hwy 118, 2.5 km w on CR 121. Ext corridors. **Pets:** Medium. $8 daily fee/pet. Designated rooms, service with restrictions, supervision.
✕ 🔌 📺 🍽 🏊

HAMILTON

ⒶⒶ ♦♦♦ Knights Inn at Clappison Corners M ☕
(905) 689-6615. **$89-$119.** 15 Hwy 5 W. Jct Hwy 5 and 6. Ext/int corridors. **Pets:** $25 one-time fee/pet.
🆂🅰🆅🄴 🆂🚭 ✕ 🔌 📺 🏊

ⒶⒶ ♦♦♦♦ Sheraton Hamilton LH ☕
(905) 529-5515. **$109-$199.** 116 King St W. On Hwy 6 and 8 westbound; downtown. Int corridors. **Pets:** Other species. Supervision.
🆂🅰🆅🄴 ✕ 🅰🄼 🔌 📺 🍽 🏊 🚭

HANOVER

ⒶⒶ ♦♦♦ The Victorian Manor Bed & Breakfast BB
(519) 364-1117. **$80-$100.** 500 9th Ave. Just n of 10th St. Int corridors. **Pets:** Accepted.
🆂🅰🆅🄴 🆂🚭 ✕ 🇿

HAWKESBURY

♦♦ Best Western L'Heritage SH
(613) 632-5941. **$100-$105.** 1575 Tupper St. Jct Hwy 34, 3 km e on Hwy 17. Int corridors. **Pets:** Small. Designated rooms, service with restrictions, supervision.
🅰🆂🅺 🆂🚭 ✕ 🔌 📺 🍽

HUNTSVILLE

♦♦♦ Comfort Inn SH
(705) 789-1701. **$105-$167.** 86 King William St. Jct Hwy 60. Int corridors. **Pets:** Accepted.
🅰🆂🅺 🆂🚭 ✕ 🔌 📺

♦♦ Tulip Inn M ☕
(705) 789-4001. **$70-$145, 3 day notice.** 211 Arrowhead Park Rd. Hwy 11, exit 226 (Muskoka Rd 3), follow signs for Arrowhead Park. Ext corridors. **Pets:** Other species. Service with restrictions, crate.
🅰🆂🅺 ✕ 🔌 📺

INGERSOLL

♦♦♦ Travelodge Ingersoll SH
(519) 425-1100. **$95-$109.** 20 Samnah Crescent. Hwy 401, exit 216 (Culloden Rd). Int corridors. **Pets:** Accepted.
🅰🆂🅺 🆂🚭 ✕ 🔌 📺 🏊

JORDAN

(CAA) ▼▼▼ Best Western Beacon Harborside Resort & Conference Centre 🆂🅷
(905) 562-4155. **$89-$229.** 2793 Beacon Blvd. QEW, exit 57. Int corridors. **Pets:** Accepted.
🆂🅰🆅🅴 🆂❺ ✕ 🖵 ❙❘ ➘ ✗

KAPUSKASING

▼▼ Comfort Inn 🆂🅷
(705) 335-8583. **$99-$104, 14 day notice.** 172 Government Rd E. Hwy 11, corner of Brunelle Rd. Int corridors. **Pets:** Other species. $10 one-time fee/room. Designated rooms, service with restrictions, supervision.
🅰🆂🅺 🆂❺ ✕ 🛏 🖵

KENORA

▼▼▼ Best Western Lakeside Inn & Convention Centre 🆂🅷
(807) 468-5521. **$120-$299, 7 day notice.** 470 First Ave S. Centre. Int corridors. **Pets:** Small. Service with restrictions, supervision.
🅰🆂🅺 🆂❺ ✕ 🖵 ❙❘ ➘

▼▼ Comfort Inn Ⓜ
(807) 468-8845. **$90-$125.** 1230 Hwy 17 E. 1.5 km e. Int corridors. **Pets:** Accepted.
🅰🆂🅺 🆂❺ ✕ 🛏 🖵

▼▼ Days Inn 🆂🅷
(807) 468-2003. **$93-$102.** 920 Hwy 17 E. On Hwy 17, 1 km e. Ext/int corridors. **Pets:** Accepted.
🅰🆂🅺 🆂❺ ✕ 🛏 🖵 ❙❘ ➘ ✗

(CAA) ▼▼ Kenora Travelodge 🆂🅷
(807) 468-3155. **$90-$140.** 800 Hwy 17 E. 1 km e. Int corridors. **Pets:** Designated rooms, service with restrictions, crate.
🆂🅰🆅🅴 🆂❺ ✕ 🛏 🖵 ❙❘ ➘ ✗

KINGSTON

▼▼ Comfort Inn 🆂🅷
(613) 549-5550. **$99-$169.** 1454 Princess St. Hwy 401, exit 613 (Sydenham Rd), 4 km se. Int corridors. **Pets:** Medium. $10 daily fee/room. Designated rooms, service with restrictions, supervision.
🅰🆂🅺 🆂❺ ✕ 🛏 🖵

(CAA) ▼▼ Comfort Inn 🆂🅷
(613) 546-9500. **$99-$169.** 55 Warne Crescent. Hwy 401, exit 617 (Division St), 0.3 km s to Dalton Ave. Int corridors. **Pets:** Accepted.
🆂🅰🆅🅴 🆂❺ ✕ 🖵

(CAA) ▼ The Executive Motel Inn & Suites Ⓜ
(613) 549-1620. **$69-$125, 3 day notice.** 794 Hwy 2 E. Hwy 401, exit 623, 8 km s, then 2 km e. Ext corridors. **Pets:** Accepted.
🆂🅰🆅🅴 🆂❺ ✕ 🛏 🖵 ➘

(CAA) ▼▼ Howard Johnson Confederation Place Hotel 🆂🅷
(613) 549-6300. **$139-$239.** 237 Ontario St. Centre of downtown. Int corridors. **Pets:** Accepted.
🆂🅰🆅🅴 🆂❺ ✕ 🛏 🖵 ❙❘ ➘

(CAA) ▼▼ Peachtree Inn 🆂🅷
(613) 546-4411. **$95-$100.** 1187 Princess St. Hwy 401, exit 615 (Sir John A MacDonald Blvd), 4 km sw. Int corridors. **Pets:** Accepted.
🆂🅰🆅🅴 ✕ 🛏 🖵

KIRKLAND LAKE

▼▼ Comfort Inn 🆂🅷
(705) 567-4909. **$60-$155.** 455 Government Rd W. Rt 66, just w of centre. Int corridors. **Pets:** Other species. Designated rooms, service with restrictions, crate.
🅰🆂🅺 🆂❺ ✕ 🛏 🖵

KITCHENER

▼▼▼▼ Four Points by Sheraton Kitchener 🅻🅷
(519) 744-4141. **$89-$169.** 105 King St E. Corner of King and Benton sts; downtown. Int corridors. **Pets:** Medium, other species. $25 one-time fee/room. Service with restrictions, crate.
🅰🆂🅺 🆂❺ ✕ 🛏 🖵 ❙❘ ➘ ✗

(CAA) ▼▼▼▼ Holiday Inn Kitchener-Waterloo 🅻🅷
(519) 893-1211. **$89-$154.** 30 Fairway Rd S. Hwy 401, exit 278. 5.6 km w on Hwy 8, exit Weber St, then just e on King St. Int corridors. **Pets:** Accepted.
🆂🅰🆅🅴 🆂❺ ✕ 🛏 🖵 ❙❘ ➘ ✗

▼▼ The Howard Johnson Hotel 🆂🅷
(519) 893-1234. **$89-$109.** 1333 Weber St E. Hwy 401, exit 278, 6.4 km w on Hwy 8, exit Weber St W. Ext/int corridors. **Pets:** Small, dogs only. $15 daily fee/room. Designated rooms, service with restrictions, crate.
🅰🆂🅺 🆂❺ ✕ 🛏 🖵 ❙❘ ➘

▼▼ Mornington Crescent B&B 🅱🅱
(519) 743-4557. **$75-$120.** 11 Sunbridge Crescent. Hwy 86 N, exit University E, 1 km to Bridge St S, 0.5 km s to Bridal Tr, then just e. Int corridors. **Pets:** Other species. Supervision.
✕ 🛏 🖵 ➘ 🌀

(CAA) ▼▼▼▼ Radisson Hotel Kitchener 🆂🅷
(519) 894-9500. **$99-$149.** 2960 King St E. Hwy 401, exit 278, 6 km w on Hwy 8, exit Weber St. Int corridors. **Pets:** Other species. Service with restrictions, supervision.
🆂🅰🆅🅴 🆂❺ ✕ 🛏 🖵 ❙❘ ➘

LEAMINGTON

▼▼ Comfort Inn 🆂🅷
(519) 326-9071. **$75-$140.** 279 Erie St S. Just s of jct Talbot and Erie sts; on direct route to Point Pelee National Park. Int corridors. **Pets:** Accepted.
🅰🆂🅺 🆂❺ ✕ 🛏 🖵

(CAA) ▼▼▼ Ramada Limited Leamington 🆂🅷
(519) 325-0260. **$109-$189.** 201 Erie St N. 1 km n of Talbot St. Int corridors. **Pets:** Small. $10 daily fee/pet. Designated rooms, service with restrictions, supervision.
🆂🅰🆅🅴 🆂❺ ✕ 🔬 🛏 🖵 ➘ ✗

(CAA) ▼ Sun Parlor Motel Ⓜ
(519) 326-6131. **$58-$90, 7 day notice.** 135 Talbot St W. On Hwy 3, 1 km w of Erie St. Ext corridors. **Pets:** $10 one-time fee/room. Designated rooms, service with restrictions, supervision.
🆂🅰🆅🅴 🆂❺ ✕ 🛏

LISTOWEL

(CAA) ▼▼▼ Country Inn Motel Ⓜ
(519) 291-1580. **$99-$159.** RR 1 Hwy 23 N-8500 Rd 164. On Hwy 23 N, 3.5 km n of Main St. Ext/int corridors. **Pets:** Medium. Designated rooms, service with restrictions, supervision.
🆂🅰🆅🅴 🆂❺ ✕ 🛏 🖵 ✗

LONDON

▼▼▼ Airport Inn & Suites 🆂🅷
(519) 457-1200. **$101-$108.** 2230 Dundas St E. Hwy 401, exit Airport Rd, 7.7 km n; corner of Airport Rd and Dundas St E. Int corridors. **Pets:** Small. $15 daily fee/pet. Service with restrictions, supervision.
🅰🆂🅺 🆂❺ ✕ 🛏 🖵

(CAA) ▼▼▼ Best Western Lamplighter Inn & Conference Centre 🆂🅷
(519) 681-7151. **$129-$169.** 591 Wellington Rd S. 3.7 km n off Hwy 401, exit 186 (Wellington Rd). Int corridors. **Pets:** Accepted.
🆂🅰🆅🅴 🆂❺ ✕ 🛏 🖵 ❙❘ ➘ ✗

Ⓐ ▼▼ **Comfort Inn** 🆂🅷
(519) 685-9300. **$103-$133, 30 day notice.** 1156 Wellington Rd. Hwy 401, exit 186B (Wellington Rd), just n. Int corridors. **Pets:** Designated rooms, supervision.
[SAVE] [S⊘] [✕] [📶] [💻]

▼▼ **Days Inn London** 🆂🅷
(519) 681-1240. **$79-$99.** 1100 Wellington Rd S. Hwy 401, exit 186B (Wellington Rd), 1.5 km n. Int corridors. **Pets:** Large. Service with restrictions, crate.
[ASK] [S⊘] [✕] [📶] [💻] [🍽] [🏊]

Ⓐ ▼▼▼ **Delta London Armouries** 🅛🅗 🐾
(519) 679-6111. **$109-$169.** 325 Dundas St. On Hwy 2. Int corridors. **Pets:** Other species. Designated rooms, service with restrictions, crate.
[SAVE] [S⊘] [✕] [📶] [💻] [🍽] [🏊] [✕]

Ⓐ ▼▼▼ **Holiday Inn Hotel & Suites-London** 🆂🅷
(519) 680-0077. **$135-$155.** 864 Exeter Rd. Hwy 401, exit 186 (Wellington Rd) westbound; exit 186B eastbound. Int corridors. **Pets:** Service with restrictions, supervision.
[SAVE] [✕] [♿] [📶] [💻] [🍽] [🏊]

Ⓐ ▼▼▼ **London Executive Suites Hotel** 🆂🅷
(519) 679-3932. **$65-$109.** 362 Dundas St. Between Waterloo and Colborne sts. Int corridors. **Pets:** Large. $75 one-time fee/room. Service with restrictions, supervision.
[SAVE] [S⊘] [✕] [📶] [💻]

▼▼▼ **Marriott Residence Inn-London** 🆂🅷 🐾
(519) 433-7222. **$139-$199.** 383 Colborne St. Jct King St. Int corridors. **Pets:** Other species. $75 one-time fee/room. Service with restrictions, crate.
[ASK] [S⊘] [✕] [♿] [📶] [💻] [✕]

Ⓐ ▼▼▼ **Quality Suites** 🆂🅷
(519) 680-1024. **$109-$179.** 1120 Dearness Dr. Hwy 401, exit 186B (Wellington Rd), 1.6 km n. Int corridors. **Pets:** Other species. Service with restrictions, supervision.
[SAVE] [S⊘] [✕] [📶] [💻]

Ⓐ ▼▼▼ **StationPark All Suite Hotel** 🅛🅗
(519) 642-4444. **$132-$172.** 242 Pall Mall St. Hwy 401, exit 186B (Wellington Rd), 9 km n to Pall Mall St. Int corridors. **Pets:** Large. Designated rooms, service with restrictions.
[SAVE] [S⊘] [✕] [💻] [🍽] [✕]

MARATHON

Ⓐ ▼ **Peninsula Inn** 🅼
(807) 229-0651. **$85-$95, 3 day notice.** On Hwy 17, 2.4 km w of jct Hwy 626. Ext corridors. **Pets:** Small. Designated rooms, service with restrictions, supervision.
[SAVE] [✕] [📶] [🍽]

MASSEY

▼ **Mohawk Motel Canada** 🅼
(705) 865-2722. **$67-$85.** 335 Sable St. Centre. Ext/int corridors. **Pets:** Medium. $7 daily fee/pet. Designated rooms, service with restrictions, supervision.
[ASK] [✕] [📶] [💻]

MCKELLAR

Ⓐ ▼▼▼ ▼▼▼ **The Inn at Manitou** 🆂🅷
(705) 389-2171. **$540-$900, 30 day notice.** 81 The Inn Rd. Hwy 124, exit McKellar Centre Rd, 8 km s, follow signs. Ext corridors. **Pets:** Small, dogs only. Designated rooms, service with restrictions.
[SAVE] [✕] [📶] [🍽] [🏊] [✕]

MIDLAND

▼▼ **Comfort Inn** 🆂🅷
(705) 526-2090. **$109-$149.** 980 King St. Jct King St and Hwy 12. Int corridors. **Pets:** Accepted.
[ASK] [S⊘] [✕] [📶] [💻]

MINDEMOYA

Ⓐ ▼ **Mindemoya Motel** 🅼
(705) 377-4779. **$79-$107, 3 day notice.** 6375 Hwy 542. In Mindemoya; 1 km w of jct Hwy 551 and 542. Ext corridors. **Pets:** Small, dogs only. Designated rooms, service with restrictions, supervision.
[SAVE] [S⊘] [✕] [📶] [💻]

MISSISSAUGA

Ⓐ ▼▼▼ **Comfort Inn Airport West** 🆂🅷
(905) 624-6900. **$109-$144.** 1500 Matheson Blvd. Hwy 401, exit Dixie Rd, then s. Int corridors. **Pets:** Accepted.
[SAVE] [S⊘] [✕] [📶] [💻] [🍽]

Ⓐ ▼▼▼▼ **Comfort Inn & Suites Sheridan Park** 🆂🅷
(905) 823-8600. **$109-$189.** 2085 N Sheridan Way. QEW to Erin Mills Pkwy, n to N Sheridan Way, then w. Int corridors. **Pets:** Service with restrictions, supervision.
[SAVE] [S⊘] [✕] [♿M] [♿] [📶] [💻] [🏊]

Ⓐ ▼▼▼ **Comfort Inn Mississauga** 🆂🅷
(905) 858-8600. **$92-$98.** 2420 Surveyor Rd. Hwy 401, exit Erin Mills Pkwy, 2 km s. Int corridors. **Pets:** Accepted.
[SAVE] [S⊘] [✕] [📶] [💻]

Ⓐ ▼▼▼▼ **Delta Meadowvale Resort and Conference Centre** 🅛🅗
(905) 821-1981. **$99-$179.** 6750 Mississauga Rd. Hwy 401 W, exit 336 (Mississauga Rd), just s. Int corridors. **Pets:** Other species. Service with restrictions, supervision.
[SAVE] [S⊘] [✕] [📶] [💻] [🍽] [🏊] [✕]

Ⓐ ▼▼▼ **Delta Toronto Airport West** 🅛🅗
(905) 624-1144. **$278.** 5444 Dixie Rd. 1 km s of jct Hwy 401 and Dixie Rd. Int corridors. **Pets:** Medium. Service with restrictions, crate.
[SAVE] [S⊘] [✕] [📶] [💻] [🍽] [🏊] [✕]

Ⓐ ▼▼▼ **Hampton Inn & Suites Toronto Airport** 🆂🅷
(905) 671-4730. **$169-$189.** 3279 Caroga Dr. Hwy 401, exit Dixon Rd, 3.5 km w to Bresler Rd. Int corridors. **Pets:** Accepted.
[SAVE] [S⊘] [✕] [♿M] [♿] [📶] [💻] [🏊]

Ⓐ ▼▼▼ **Holiday Inn Toronto-West** 🆂🅷
(905) 890-5700. **$119-$155.** 100 Britannia Rd E. Hwy 401, exit Hwy 10 S (Hurontario St); jct Hwy 401 and 10. Int corridors. **Pets:** Medium, other species. Service with restrictions, crate.
[SAVE] [S⊘] [✕] [📶] [💻] [🍽] [🏊] [✕]

▼▼ **Motel 6 #1910** 🆂🅷
(905) 814-1664. **$71-$81.** 2935 Argentia Rd. Hwy 401, exit 333 (Winston Churchill Blvd), just s. Int corridors. **Pets:** Small, other species. Designated rooms, service with restrictions, supervision.
[S⊘] [✕] [♿M] [♿] [📶]

▼▼▼ **Novotel Hotel Mississauga** 🅛🅗
(905) 896-1000. **$209-$239.** 3670 Hurontario St. On Hwy 10 at Burnhamthorpe Rd; Hwy 401, exit Hwy 10 S (Hurontario St), 5 km. Int corridors. **Pets:** Medium. $15 daily fee/room. Designated rooms, service with restrictions, crate.
[ASK] [S⊘] [✕] [💻] [🍽] [🏊] [✕]

Ⓐ ▼▼ **Quality Hotel Airport** 🆂🅷 🐾
(905) 624-9500. **$84-$104.** 5599 Ambler Dr. Hwy 401, exit 346 (S Dixie Rd), w on Aerowood Dr, then just n. Int corridors. **Pets:** Other species. Designated rooms.
[SAVE] [S⊘] [✕] [📶] [💻] [🍽] [🏊]

ⓐ ▼▼▼ **Radisson Hotel Toronto-Mississauga** 🄻🄷
(905) 858-2424. **$109-$159.** 2501 Argentia Rd. Sw of Hwy 401 and Mississauga Rd; corner of Derry and Argentia rds. Int corridors. **Pets:** Accepted.
[SAVE] [S🄳] [✕] [🛏] [📺] [🍽] [🏊] [✕]

▼▼▼ **Residence Inn by Marriott** 🅂🄷
(905) 567-2577. **$159-$259.** 7005 Century Ave. Hwy 401, exit Erin Mills Pkwy/Mississauga Rd, s to Argentia Rd. Int corridors. **Pets:** Accepted.
[ASK] [S🄳] [✕] [🄻🄼] [🄴] [🛏] [📺] [🏊]

ⓐ ▼▼▼ **Sandalwood Suites Hotel Toronto Airport** 🅂🄷
(905) 238-9600. **$99-$209.** 5050 Orbitor Dr. Jct Eglinton Ave and Ren-forth Dr, 2.3 km w on Eglinton Ave. Int corridors. **Pets:** Medium. $10 daily fee/pet. Designated rooms, service with restrictions.
[SAVE] [S🄳] [✕] [🛏] [📺]

ⓐ ▼▼▼ ▼▼▼ **Sheraton Gateway Hotel In Toronto International Airport** 🄻🄷 ❧
(905) 672-7000. **$99-$339.** Box 3000, Toronto AMF. In Lester B. Pearson International Airport. Int corridors. **Pets:** Large. Service with restrictions, supervision.
[SAVE] [S🄳] [✕] [🄻🄼] [📺] [🍽] [🏊] [✕]

▼▼ ▼▼ **Studio 6 Mississauga #1908** 🄼
(905) 502-8897. **$91-$101.** 60 Brittannia Rd E. Hwy 401, exit Hwy 10 (Hurontario St). Int corridors. **Pets:** Accepted.
[S🄳] [✕] [🄴] [🛏] [📺]

MONETVILLE

▼▼ ▼▼ **Memquisit Lodge** 🄲🄰
(705) 898-2355. **Call for rates.** 506 Memquisit Rd. 20.8 km ne on west arm of Lake Nipissing, on Hwy 64 and Memquisit Lodge Rd; 36.8 km sw off Hwy 17, on Hwy 64. Ext corridors. **Pets:** Accepted.
[🛏] [📺] [🍽] [✕] [🄺] [🌂]

MORRISBURG

ⓐ ▼▼ ▼▼ **The McIntosh Country Inn & Conference Centre** 🅂🄷
(613) 543-3788. **$79-$159.** 12495 Hwy 2 E. Hwy 401, exit 750, 2 km s on Rt 31, then 1 km e. Int corridors. **Pets:** Large. $20 daily fee/pet. Designated rooms, service with restrictions, supervision.
[SAVE] [S🄳] [✕] [🛏] [📺] [🍽] [🏊] [✕]

NEWMARKET

▼▼ ▼▼ **Comfort Inn** 🅂🄷
(905) 895-3355. **$102-$128.** 1230 Journey's End Cir. Hwy 404, exit 51 (Davis Dr). Int corridors. **Pets:** Other species. Service with restrictions, supervision.
[ASK] [S🄳] [✕] [🛏] [📺]

NIAGARA FALLS METROPOLITAN AREA

FORT ERIE

ⓐ ▼▼ ▼▼ **Comfort Inn** 🅂🄷 ❧
(905) 871-8500. **$85-$130.** 1 Hospitality Dr. QEW, exit 2 (Berti St) westbound; exit 1B (Concession Rd S) eastbound. Int corridors. **Pets:** Other species. $10 daily fee/pet. Service with restrictions, supervision.
[SAVE] [S🄳] [✕] [🛏] [📺]

NIAGARA FALLS

ⓐ ▼▼ ▼▼ **Best Western Fallsview** 🅂🄷
(905) 356-0551. **$89-$299, 3 day notice.** 6289 Fallsview Blvd. Jct Niagara River Pkwy, just n on Murray St. Ext/int corridors. **Pets:** Large. $10 daily fee/pet. Supervision.
[SAVE] [S🄳] [✕] [📺] [🍽] [🏊] [✕]

▼▼ ▼▼ **Econo Lodge near the Falls** 🄼
(905) 358-6243. **$65-$205.** 6000 Stanley Ave. 1.3 km w on Hwy 20, just s. Ext/int corridors. **Pets:** Accepted.
[ASK] [S🄳] [✕] [🛏] [📺]

ⓐ ▼▼ ▼▼ **Flamingo Motor Inn** 🄼
(905) 356-4646. **$54-$179.** 7701 Lundy's Ln. QEW, exit Hwy 20, 3.4 km w. Ext corridors. **Pets:** Accepted.
[SAVE] [S🄳] [✕] [🛏] [🏊]

▼▼ **Hilltop Hotel** 🄼
(905) 374-7777. **$69-$200.** 4955 Clifton Hill. Just s of jct Victoria Ave. Int corridors. **Pets:** Accepted.
[ASK] [S🄳]

ⓐ ▼▼ **Niagara Parkway Court Motel** 🄼 ❧
(905) 295-3331. **$39-$199.** 3708 Main St. 2.5 km s of the falls on Niagara River Pkwy. Ext corridors. **Pets:** Medium. $10 daily fee/pet. Designated rooms, service with restrictions, supervision.
[SAVE] [S🄳] [✕] [🛏] [📺] [🌂]

ⓐ ▼▼ ▼▼ **Peninsula Inn & Resort** 🅂🄷
(905) 354-8812. **$59-$249.** 7373 Niagara Square Dr. QEW, exit McLeod Rd, just w. Int corridors. **Pets:** Accepted.
[SAVE] [✕] [🄻🄼] [🛏] [📺] [🍽] [🏊] [✕]

ⓐ ▼▼ ▼▼ ▼▼ **Sheraton Fallsview Hotel & Conference Centre** 🄻🄷
(905) 374-1077. **$99-$429.** 6755 Fallsview Blvd. Near Konica Minolta Tower. Int corridors. **Pets:** Accepted.
[SAVE] [S🄳] [✕] [🄻🄼] [🛏] [📺] [🍽] [🏊] [✕]

ⓐ ▼▼ ▼▼ **Sheraton on the Falls** 🄻🄷
(905) 374-4445. **$99-$999.** 5875 Falls Ave. Entrance to Rainbow Bridge on Hwy 20. Int corridors. **Pets:** Accepted.
[SAVE] [S🄳] [✕] [🛏] [📺] [🍽] [🏊]

ⓐ ▼▼ ▼▼ **Stanley Motor Inn** 🄼
(905) 358-9238. **$60-$150.** 6220 Stanley Ave. 2 blks from the falls; w of Skylon Tower. Ext/int corridors. **Pets:** Small, dogs only. $10 daily fee/pet. No service.
[SAVE] [✕] [🛏] [🏊] [🌂]

ⓐ ▼▼ **Thriftlodge Clifton Hill** 🄼
(905) 357-4330. **$59-$299.** 4945 Clifton Hill. Just s on jct Victoria Ave. Ext corridors. **Pets:** Medium. Service with restrictions, supervision.
[SAVE] [S🄳] [✕] [🛏] [📺]

NIAGARA-ON-THE-LAKE

▼▼ ▼▼ **Gate House Hotel** 🄲🄸
(905) 468-3263. **$145-$230, 7 day notice.** 142 Queen St. Jct Gate. Int corridors. **Pets:** Very small. Service with restrictions, supervision.
[🍽]

▼▼ ▼▼ **Harbour House Hotel** 🅂🄷 ❧
(905) 468-4683. **$275-$325, 10 day notice.** 85 Melville St. Jct Ricardo St. Int corridors. **Pets:** Medium, dogs only. $25 daily fee/room. Designated rooms, supervision.
[ASK] [S🄳] [✕] [📺]

(AA) ♦♦ ♦♦ **The Pillar & Post Inn Spa & Conference Centre** 🅲 ❧
(905) 468-2123. **$175-$365.** 48 John St. Just n on Hwy 55 (Mississauga St), just e; 13 mi from QEW. Ext/int corridors. **Pets:** Large. $35 one-time fee/room. Designated rooms, service with restrictions, supervision.
🆂🅰🆅🅴 ✕ 🍴 ⊷ ✕

(AA) ♦♦ ♦♦ **The Prince of Wales Hotel & Spa** 🆂🅷
(905) 468-3246. **$175-$365.** 6 Picton St. Jct Picton and King sts; 14.4 km e of jct QEW and Hwy 55, via Hwy 55. Ext/int corridors. **Pets:** Small, dogs only. $35 daily fee/pet. Designated rooms, service with restrictions, crate.
🆂🅰🆅🅴 ✕ 🅱 🍴 ⊷ ✕

(AA) ♦♦ ♦♦ **Queen's Landing Inn & Conference Resort** 🆂🅷
(905) 468-2195. **$175-$365.** 155 Byron St. Just n on King St, just e. Int corridors. **Pets:** Very small, dogs only. $100 daily fee/room. Service with restrictions.
🆂🅰🆅🅴 ✕ 🍴 ⊷ ✕

ST. CATHARINES

(AA) ♦♦ ♦♦ **Comfort Inn** 🆂🅷 ❧
(905) 687-8890. **$94-$149.** 2 Dunlop Dr. QEW, exit 46 (Lake St); between Lake and Geneva sts. Int corridors. **Pets:** Designated rooms, service with restrictions, supervision.
🆂🅰🆅🅴 🆂 ✕ 🅼 🅱 🖵 🍴

(AA) ♦♦ ♦♦ **Holiday Inn St. Catharines/Niagara** 🆂🅷
(905) 934-8000. **$129-$299.** 2 N Service Rd. QEW, exit 46 (Lake St), just e. Int corridors. **Pets:** $15 daily fee/pet. Designated rooms, service with restrictions, supervision.
🆂🅰🆅🅴 🆂 ✕ 🅱 🖵 🍴 ⊷ ✕

(AA) ♦♦ ♦♦ **Howard Johnson Hotel & Conference Centre** 🆂🅷 ❧
(905) 934-5400. **$79-$289.** 89 Meadowvale Dr. QEW, exit 46 (Lake St). Int corridors. **Pets:** $10 daily fee/room. Designated rooms, service with restrictions, supervision.
🆂🅰🆅🅴 🆂 ✕ 🅱 🖵 🍴 ⊷ ✕

(AA) ♦♦ ♦♦ **Quality Hotel Parkway Convention Centre** 🅻🅷
(905) 688-2324. **$89-$299.** 327 Ontario St. QEW, exit 47 (Ontario St), 0.8 km s. Int corridors. **Pets:** Service with restrictions, supervision.
🆂🅰🆅🅴 🆂 ✕ 🅱 🖵 🍴 ⊷ ✕

(AA) ♦♦ ♦ **The Travelodge St. Catharines** 🅼
(905) 688-1646. **$89-$129.** 420 Ontario St. QEW, exit 47 (Ontario St). Ext corridors. **Pets:** Small. $10 daily fee/room. Service with restrictions, crate.
🆂🅰🆅🅴 🆂 ✕ 🅱 🖵 🍴 ⊷

THOROLD

♦♦ ♦ **Four Points by Sheraton St. Catharines** 🅻🅷
(905) 984-8484. **$99-$199.** 3530 Schmon Pkwy. Hwy 406, exit St. David's Rd W. Int corridors. **Pets:** Other species. $10 daily fee/room. Designated rooms, service with restrictions, crate.
🅰🆂🅺 🆂 ✕ 🅲 🅱 🖵 🍴 ⊷ ✕

WELLAND

♦♦ ♦ **Comfort Inn** 🆂🅷
(905) 732-4811. **$85-$107.** 870 Niagara St. 2.5 km n. Int corridors. **Pets:** Other species. $10 daily fee/room. Designated rooms, service with restrictions, supervision.
🅰🆂🅺 ✕ 🅱 🖵

END METROPOLITAN AREA

NORTH BAY

(AA) ♦♦ ♦ **Best Western North Bay** 🆂🅷 ❧
(705) 474-5800. **$99-$199.** 700 Lakeshore Dr. Hwy 11, exit Lakeshore Dr, 4 km n on Hwy 11B. Int corridors. **Pets:** Other species. Service with restrictions, crate.
🆂🅰🆅🅴 🆂 ✕ 🅱 🖵 🍴 ⊷ ✕

(AA) ♦♦ ♦ **Clarion Resort Pinewood Park** 🆂🅷
(705) 472-0810. **$158-$185.** 201 Pinewood Park Dr. Hwy 11, exit Lakeshore Dr, immediately turn s on Pinewood Park Dr, then 0.7 km. Int corridors. **Pets:** Accepted.
🆂🅰🆅🅴 🆂 ✕ 🅱 🖵 🍴 ⊷ ✕

(AA) ♦♦ ♦ **Comfort Inn** 🆂🅷
(705) 494-9444. **$99-$129.** 676 Lakeshore Dr. Hwy 11B, exit Lakeshore Dr, 4 km n of jct Hwy 11. Int corridors. **Pets:** Accepted.
🆂🅰🆅🅴 🆂 ✕ 🅱 🖵

♦♦ ♦ **Comfort Inn-Airport** 🆂🅷
(705) 476-5400. **$87-$160.** 1200 O'Brien St. 3 km e on Hwy 11 and 17 Bypass at O'Brien St exit. Int corridors. **Pets:** Service with restrictions, supervision.
🅰🆂🅺 🆂 ✕ 🅱 🖵

♦♦ ♦ **Super 8** 🆂🅷
(705) 495-4551. **$87.** 570 Lakeshore Dr. Hwy 11, exit Lakeshore Dr, 4.5 km n on Hwy 11B. Int corridors. **Pets:** Accepted.
🅰🆂🅺 🆂 ✕ 🅲 🅱

♦♦ ♦ **Travelodge-Airport** 🆂🅷
(705) 495-1133. **$109-$149.** 1525 Seymour St. Jct Hwy 11, 17 and Seymour St. Int corridors. **Pets:** Accepted.
🅰🆂🅺 🆂 ✕ 🅱 🖵 ⊷

OAKVILLE

♦♦ ♦♦ **Holiday Inn Oakville-Centre** 🆂🅷 ❧
(905) 842-5000. **$135-$155.** 590 Argus Rd. QEW, exit Trafalgar Rd, then s. Int corridors. **Pets:** Designated rooms, service with restrictions, crate.
🅰🆂🅺 🆂 ✕ 🅱 🖵 🍴 ⊷ ✕

♦♦ ♦ **Quality Hotel & Suites-Oakville** 🆂🅷
(905) 847-6667. **$109-$139.** 754 Bronte Rd. QEW, exit 111 (Bronte Rd/Hwy 25), 0.4 km s. Int corridors. **Pets:** Accepted.
🅰🆂🅺 🆂 ✕ 🅱 🖵 🍴 ⊷ ✕

♦♦ ♦ **Ramada Inn and Convention Centre** 🆂🅷
(905) 845-7561. **$99-$159.** 360 Oakville Place Dr. QEW, exit Trafalgar Rd, just n. Int corridors. **Pets:** Accepted.
🅰🆂🅺 🆂 ✕ 🅱 🖵 🍴 ⊷ ✕

ORILLIA

♦♦ ♦ **Comfort Inn** 🆂🅷 ❧
(705) 327-7744. **$105-$133.** 75 Progress Dr (RR 1). Hwy 11 N, exit Hwy 12, s on Memorial Ave; corner of Progress Dr and Memorial Ave. Int corridors. **Pets:** $10 one-time fee/room. Designated rooms, supervision.
🅰🆂🅺 🆂 ✕ 🅱

(AA) ♦♦ ♦ **Econo Lodge** 🆂🅷
(705) 326-3554. **$79-$109.** 265 Memorial Ave. 0.5 km n of Hwy 12. Int corridors. **Pets:** Accepted.
🆂🅰🆅🅴 🆂 ✕ 🅱 🖵

OSHAWA

◆◆ Comfort Inn SH
(905) 434-5000. **$89-$149.** 605 Bloor St W. Hwy 401, exit 416 (Park Rd), s to Bloor St, then 0.8 km w. Int corridors. **Pets:** Accepted.
[A$K] [S/D] [X] [▯] [▣]

Ⓐ ◆◆◆ Holiday Inn Oshawa SH ❧
(905) 576-5101. **$119-$179.** 1011 Bloor St E. Hwy 401, exit 419 (Harmony Rd). Int corridors. **Pets:** Medium. $15 one-time fee/room. Designated rooms.
[SAVE] [S/D] [X] [▯] [▣] [¶] [≈] [⊠]

OTTAWA METROPOLITAN AREA

OTTAWA

Ⓐ ◆◆ Adam's Airport Inn SH
(613) 738-3838. **$94-$99.** 2721 Bank St. Jct Hunt Club Rd and Bank St, 1 km s. Int corridors. **Pets:** Accepted.
[SAVE] [X] [▯] [▣]

Ⓐ ◆◆ Aristocrat Suite Hotel SH
(613) 236-7500. **$119-$179.** 141 Cooper St. Between Elgin and Cartier sts. Int corridors. **Pets:** Accepted.
[SAVE] [S/D] [X] [▯] [▣] [¶] [⊠]

Ⓐ ◆◆ Best Western Barons Hotel & Conference Centre SH ❧
(613) 828-2741. **$117.** 3700 Richmond Rd. Hwy 417, exit 130, 2 km s. Int corridors. **Pets:** Large. $10 daily fee/room. Service with restrictions, supervision.
[SAVE] [S/D] [X] [⊡] [▯] [▣] [¶] [≈] [⊠]

◆◆◆ Bostonian Executive Suites SH
(613) 594-5757. **$159-$189.** 341 MacLaren St. Between Bank and O'Connor sts. Int corridors. **Pets:** Accepted.
[A$K] [S/D] [X] [▯] [▣]

Ⓐ ◆◆◆ Brookstreet Hotel LH
(613) 271-1800. **$139-$299.** 525 Legget Dr. Hwy 417, exit 138 (March Rd), 3.7 km n, just e on Solandt Dr to Legget Dr, then just n. Int corridors. **Pets:** Small. $250 deposit/pet. Designated rooms, service with restrictions, supervision.
[SAVE] [S/D] [X] [▣] [¶] [≈] [⊠]

Ⓐ ◆◆◆ Cartier Place Suite Hotel SH
(613) 236-5000. **$109-$229.** 180 Cooper St. Between Elgin and Cartier sts. Int corridors. **Pets:** Other species. $15 daily fee/room.
[SAVE] [S/D] [X] [▯] [▣] [¶] [≈] [⊠]

Ⓐ ◆◆ Comfort Inn SH
(613) 744-2900. **$100-$125.** 1252 Michael St. Hwy 417, exit 115 (St. Laurent Blvd), then ne. Int corridors. **Pets:** Accepted.
[SAVE] [S/D] [X] [▯] [▣]

Ⓐ ◆◆ Comfort Inn Ottawa West SH
(613) 592-2200. **$141-$151.** 222 Hearst Way. Hwy 417, exit 138 (Eagleson Rd), 0.6 km s, then 0.3 km w on Katimavik Rd. Int corridors. **Pets:** Other species. Service with restrictions, supervision.
[SAVE] [S/D] [X] [▯] [▣] [¶]

Ⓐ ◆◆ Days Inn-Downtown (Ottawa) SH
(613) 789-5555. **$109-$139.** 319 Rideau St. Between Nelson St and King Edward Ave. Ext/int corridors. **Pets:** Medium. Designated rooms, service with restrictions, supervision.
[SAVE] [S/D] [X] [▯] [▣] [¶]

◆◆ The Days Inn Ottawa West SH
(613) 726-1717. **$109-$129.** 350 Moodie Dr. Hwy 417, exit 134, 1.5 km s. Int corridors. **Pets:** $10 daily fee/room. Designated rooms, service with restrictions, supervision.
[X] [▯] [▣] [¶]

Ⓐ ◆◆◆ Delta Ottawa Hotel and Suites LH
(613) 238-6000. **$129-$199.** 361 Queen St. Corner of Lyon St. Int corridors. **Pets:** Other species. Designated rooms, service with restrictions, supervision.
[SAVE] [S/D] [X] [▯] [▣] [¶] [≈] [⊠]

Ⓐ ◆◆ Econo Lodge-Ottawa East M
(613) 745-1531. **$85-$99.** 2098 Montreal Rd. Hwy 417, exit 113, 2.5 km e on Hwy 174 to Montreal Rd W exit. Ext corridors. **Pets:** Large, other species. $5 daily fee/pet. Service with restrictions, crate.
[SAVE] [S/D] [X] [▯] [▣]

Ⓐ ◆◆◆◆ Fairmont Chateau Laurier LH
(613) 241-1414. **$189-$419.** 1 Rideau St. Just e of Parliament buildings. Int corridors. **Pets:** Accepted.
[SAVE] [S/D] [X] [⊠M] [▯] [▣] [¶] [≈] [⊠]

Ⓐ ◆◆◆ Holiday Inn Hotel & Suites LH
(613) 238-1331. **$135.** 111 Cooper St. Corner of Cartier St. Int corridors. **Pets:** Other species.
[SAVE] [X] [⊡] [▯] [▣] [¶]

Ⓐ ◆◆◆ Les Suites Hotel Ottawa LH ❧
(613) 232-2000. **$169-$209.** 130 Besserer St. Between Nicholas and Waller sts. Int corridors. **Pets:** $25 one-time fee/pet.
[SAVE] [S/D] [X] [⊠M] [▯] [▣] [¶] [≈] [⊠]

◆◆◆ Lord Elgin Hotel LH
(613) 235-3333. **$135-$175.** 100 Elgin St. Between Laurier Ave and Slater St. Int corridors. **Pets:** Accepted.
[A$K] [S/D] [X] [⊡] [▯] [▣] [¶] [≈] [⊠]

◆◆ The Mirada Inn M
(613) 741-1102. **$99-$110.** 545 Montreal Rd. Jct St. Laurent Blvd, just e. Ext/int corridors. **Pets:** Large. $50 deposit/room. Designated rooms, service with restrictions, supervision.
[A$K] [S/D] [X] [▯] [¶] [≈]

◆◆◆ Novotel Ottawa Hotel LH
(613) 230-3033. **$130-$145.** 33 Nicholas St. Corner of Daly Ave. Int corridors. **Pets:** Accepted.
[A$K] [S/D] [X] [▣] [¶] [≈] [⊠]

Ⓐ ◆◆◆ Ottawa Marriott LH
(613) 238-1122. **$119-$199, 7 day notice.** 100 Kent St. Corner of Queen St. Int corridors. **Pets:** Other species. Service with restrictions, crate.
[SAVE] [S/D] [X] [▯] [▣] [¶] [≈] [⊠]

Ⓐ ◆◆ Quality Hotel Ottawa, Downtown SH ❧
(613) 789-7511. **$134-$144.** 290 Rideau St. Corner of King Edward Ave. Int corridors. **Pets:** Medium. Designated rooms, service with restrictions, supervision.
[SAVE] [S/D] [X] [▯] [▣] [¶]

ⓒ ▼▼▼ **Radisson Hotel Ottawa Parliament**
Hill 🆂🅷 🐾
(613) 236-1133. **$129-$189.** 402 Queen St. Corner of Bay and Queen
sts. Int corridors. **Pets:** Medium, other species. Designated rooms, service
with restrictions, supervision.
🆂🅰🆅🅴 Ⓢ Ⓧ 🔒 💻 🍴

▼▼▼ **Residence Inn by Marriott** 🆂🅷
(613) 231-2020. **$139-$250.** 161 Laurier Ave W. Corner of Elgin St. Int
corridors. **Pets:** Accepted.
Ⓐ🆂🅺 Ⓢ Ⓧ 🔒 💻 🏊 ⓧ

▼▼ **Rideau Heights Motor Inn** Ⓜ
(613) 226-4152. **$89-$109.** 72 Rideau Heights Dr. Hwy 16 (Prince of
Wales Dr), 0.5 km n of Hunt Club Rd. Ext corridors. **Pets:** Small, other
species. $20 daily fee/pet. Designated rooms, service with restrictions,
supervision.
Ⓐ🆂🅺 Ⓢ Ⓧ 🔒 💻

ⓒ ▼▼▼ **Sheraton Ottawa Hotel** Ⓛ🅷
(613) 238-1500. **$129-$260.** 150 Albert St. Corner of O'Connor St. Int
corridors. **Pets:** Small. Designated rooms, service with restrictions, supervision.
🆂🅰🆅🅴 Ⓢ Ⓧ 🔒 💻 🍴 🏊

ⓒ ▼▼▼ **Southway Inn of Ottawa** 🆂🅷 🐾
(613) 737-0811. **$118-$138, 3 day notice.** 2431 Bank St. On Hwy 31,
corner of Hunt Club Rd. Int corridors. **Pets:** $25 daily fee/pet. Designated
rooms, service with restrictions, crate.
🆂🅰🆅🅴 Ⓢ Ⓧ 🔒 💻 🍴 🏊 ⓧ

ⓒ ▼▼▼ **Travelodge** 🆂🅷 🐾
(613) 745-1133. **$99-$149.** 1486 Innes Rd. Hwy 417, exit 112 (Innes
Rd), just e. Int corridors. **Pets:** Other species. Service with restrictions.
🆂🅰🆅🅴 Ⓢ Ⓧ 🔒 💻 🏊

ⓒ ▼▼▼ **Webb's Motel** Ⓜ
(613) 728-1881. **$95-$100.** 1705 Carling Ave. Hwy 417, exit 126, 0.5
km n on Maitland Ave, then 0.5 km e. Ext/int corridors. **Pets:** Accepted.
🆂🅰🆅🅴 Ⓧ 🔒

▼▼▼▼ **The Westin Ottawa** Ⓛ🅷 🐾
(613) 560-7000. **$159-$235.** 11 Colonel By Dr. Corner of Rideau St. Int
corridors. **Pets:** Small. Designated rooms, service with restrictions, supervision.
Ⓧ ⓩ Ⓖ 💻 🍴 🏊 ⓧ

END METROPOLITAN AREA

OWEN SOUND

ⓒ ▼▼ **Comfort Inn** 🆂🅷
(519) 371-5500. **$95-$145.** 955 9th Ave E. Jct Hwy 6, 10, 21 and 26.
Int corridors. **Pets:** Accepted.
🆂🅰🆅🅴 Ⓢ Ⓧ 🔒 💻

▼▼▼ **Days Inn Hotel and Convention Centre** 🆂🅷
(519) 376-1551. **$89-$169.** 950 6th St E. Jct Hwy 6 and 10. Int corridors. **Pets:** Accepted.
Ⓐ🆂🅺 Ⓢ Ⓧ 🔒 💻 🍴 🏊 ⓧ

▼▼ **Owen Sound Inn** 🆂🅷
(519) 371-3011. **$45-$150.** 485 9th Ave E. Jct Hwy 6, 10, 26 and 21;
follow Hwy 6 and 10 1 km s. Int corridors. **Pets:** Accepted.
Ⓐ🆂🅺 Ⓢ Ⓧ 🔒

▼▼ **Travelodge** 🆂🅷
(519) 371-9297. **$99-$130, 15 day notice.** 880 10th St E. Jct Hwy 6,
10, 21 and 26. Int corridors. **Pets:** Accepted.
Ⓐ🆂🅺 Ⓢ Ⓧ 🔒 💻

PARRY SOUND

▼▼ **Comfort Inn** 🆂🅷
(705) 746-6221. **$101-$164.** 120 Bowes St. Hwy 69, exit 224 (Bowes
St), just w. Int corridors. **Pets:** Other species. Designated rooms, service
with restrictions, supervision.
Ⓐ🆂🅺 Ⓢ Ⓧ 💻

▼▼ **Georgian Inn & Suites** 🆂🅷
(705) 746-5837. **$90-$179.** 48 Joseph St. Hwy 69, exit Parry Sound Dr,
2 km w. Ext/int corridors. **Pets:** Accepted.
Ⓐ🆂🅺 Ⓢ Ⓧ 🔒 💻 🍴 🏊 ⓧ

▼▼ **Log Cabin Inn** Ⓜ
(705) 746-7122. **$89-$150, 3 day notice.** RR 2 (Little Beaver Rd). Hwy
69, exit 220 (Hunter Dr), 1.9 km w on Oastler Park Dr, then 1.2 km s.
Ext corridors. **Pets:** Accepted.
Ⓧ 💻 🍴 ⓧ ⓚ

PEMBROKE

▼▼ **Best Western Pembroke Inn & Conference**
Centre 🆂🅷
(613) 735-0131. **$124-$199.** One International Dr. Jct Hwy 17 and 41.
Int corridors. **Pets:** Medium. $10 daily fee/pet. Designated rooms, service
with restrictions, supervision.
Ⓐ🆂🅺 Ⓢ Ⓧ 🔒 💻 🍴 🏊 ⓧ

▼▼ **Colonial Fireside Inn** Ⓜ
(613) 732-3623. **$63-$88.** 1350 Pembroke St W. Jct Hwy 17, 5 km n on
Forest Lea Rd, just e. Ext corridors. **Pets:** Small. $10 daily fee/pet.
Designated rooms, service with restrictions, supervision.
Ⓐ🆂🅺 Ⓢ Ⓧ 🔒 💻 🏊

▼▼ **Comfort Inn** 🆂🅷
(613) 735-1057. **$99-$169.** 959 Pembroke St E. 1.6 km e on Old Hwy
17. Int corridors. **Pets:** Large. Service with restrictions, supervision.
Ⓐ🆂🅺 Ⓢ Ⓧ 🔒 💻

PETERBOROUGH

▼▼ **King Bethune Guest House & Spa** 🅱🅱
(705) 743-4101. **$115-$275, 14 day notice.** 270 King St. From Charlotte and George St (clock tower), 1 blk s on George St to King St,
then just w. Int corridors. **Pets:** Other species. $10 daily fee/pet. Supervi-
sion.
Ⓧ 🔒 💻

ⓒ ▼▼▼ **Quality Inn** 🆂🅷
(705) 748-6801. **$115-$135.** 1074 Lansdowne St W. 3 km from jct Hwy
115 and Bypass. Int corridors. **Pets:** Accepted.
🆂🅰🆅🅴 Ⓢ Ⓧ 🔒 💻

▼▼ **Robyn's Motel** Ⓜ
(705) 745-3225. **Call for rates.** 1136 Hwy 7 E. On Hwy 7, 2.5 km e of
Television Rd. Ext corridors. **Pets:** Accepted.
Ⓧ 🔒

PICKERING

ⓒ ▼▼▼ **Comfort Inn** 🆂🅷
(905) 831-6200. **$85-$160.** 533 Kingston Rd. Hwy 401, exit 394 N
(White's Rd) to Hwy 2, 0.5 km w. Int corridors. **Pets:** Accepted.
🆂🅰🆅🅴 Ⓢ Ⓧ 🔒 💻

PLANTAGENET

▼▼ Motel de Champlain 2004 M
(613) 673-5220. **$80-$90, 5 day notice.** 5999 Hwy 17. Jct CR 9. Ext/int corridors. **Pets:** Accepted.
(ASK) (✕) (🛏) (🍴)

PORT HOPE

Ⓐ ▼▼ Comfort Inn SH
(905) 885-7000. **$105-$195.** Hwy 401 & 28. Hwy 401, exit 464, just n. Int corridors. **Pets:** Medium. Designated rooms, no service, supervision.
(SAVE) (Sᴅ) (✕) (🛏) (💻)

PROVIDENCE BAY

Ⓐ ▼ Huron Sands Motel M
(705) 377-4616. **$79-$89, 3 day notice.** 5216 Hwy 551. In Providence Bay; on Hwy 551, 27.2 km w of South Baymouth via 10th Side Rd, follow signs; centre. Ext corridors. **Pets:** Other species. Service with restrictions, supervision.
(SAVE) (✕) (🛏) (🍴) (☎)

RENFREW

Ⓐ ▼▼ The Renfrew Inn SH
(613) 432-8109. **$104-$129.** 760 Gibbons Rd. Hwy 17, exit O'Brien Rd. Int corridors. **Pets:** $10 daily fee/room. Service with restrictions, supervision.
(SAVE) (Sᴅ) (✕) (🛏) (💻) (🍴) (☎) (✕)

▼ The Rocky Mountain House M
(613) 432-5801. **$69-$89.** 409 Stewart St N. Jct Bruce St. Ext corridors. **Pets:** Accepted.
(ASK) (Sᴅ) (✕) (🛏) (💻) (🍴)

ROSSPORT

▼▼ The Willows Inn Bed & Breakfast BB
(807) 824-3389. **$85-$130, 7 day notice.** 1 Main St. Centre. Int corridors. **Pets:** Other species.
(✕) (🐾)

ST. THOMAS

Ⓐ ▼▼ Comfort Inn SH 🐾
(519) 633-4082. **$80-$105.** 100 Centennial Ave. 6.5 km e on Hwy 3. Int corridors. **Pets:** Small. $10 daily fee/pet. Designated rooms, crate.
(SAVE) (Sᴅ) (✕) (🛏) (💻)

SARNIA

Ⓐ ▼▼▼ Best Western Guildwood Inn SH
(519) 337-7577. **$125-$141.** 1400 Venetian Blvd. 1 km e of Bluewater Bridge. Ext/int corridors. **Pets:** Small. Service with restrictions, supervision.
(SAVE) (Sᴅ) (✕) (🛏) (💻) (🍴) (☎)

▼▼▼ Holiday Inn Sarnia SH
(519) 336-4130. **$105-$195.** 1498 Venetian Blvd. E of Bluewater Bridge. Int corridors. **Pets:** Accepted.
(✕) (🛏) (💻) (🍴) (☎) (✕)

SAULT STE. MARIE

Ⓐ ▼▼▼ Algoma's Water Tower Inn SH
(705) 949-8111. **$119-$179.** 360 Great Northern Rd. Jct Hwy 17 and Second Line. Int corridors. **Pets:** Large. Designated rooms, service with restrictions, supervision.
(SAVE) (Sᴅ) (✕) (📷) (🛏) (💻) (🍴) (☎) (✕)

▼ Ambassador Motel M
(705) 759-6199. **$64-$99.** 1275 Great Northern Rd. 6.4 km n on Hwy 17. Ext corridors. **Pets:** Accepted.
(✕) (🛏) (💻) (☎) (✕)

Ⓐ ▼ Bel-Air Motel M
(705) 945-7950. **$59-$99.** 398 Pim St. 2 km n on Hwy 17B. Ext corridors. **Pets:** $10 daily fee/pet. Designated rooms, service with restrictions.
(SAVE) (Sᴅ) (✕) (🛏)

Ⓐ ▼ Catalina Motel M
(705) 945-9260. **$88-$108.** 259 Great Northern Rd. 3.2 km n on Hwy 17B. Ext corridors. **Pets:** Accepted.
(SAVE) (Sᴅ) (✕) (🛏) (💻)

▼▼ Comfort Inn SH
(705) 759-8000. **$95-$139.** 333 Great Northern Rd. 3.6 km n on Hwy 17B. Ext/int corridors. **Pets:** Large. $5 one-time fee/room. Service with restrictions, supervision.
(ASK) (Sᴅ) (✕) (🛏) (💻)

▼▼ Glenview Cottages Ⓒ 🐾
(705) 759-3436. **$99-$140, 5 day notice.** 2611 Great Northern Rd. 9.6 km n on Hwy 17. Ext corridors. **Pets:** $5 daily fee/room. Designated rooms, service with restrictions, crate.
(ASK) (✕) (🛏) (💻) (☎) (✕)

Ⓐ ▼▼▼ Holiday Inn Sault Ste.
Marie-Waterfront SH 🐾
(705) 949-0611. **$115-$189.** 208 St. Marys River Dr. On the waterfront. Int corridors. **Pets:** Designated rooms, service with restrictions, supervision.
(SAVE) (Sᴅ) (✕) (🛏) (💻) (🍴) (☎) (✕)

▼ Holiday Motel M
(705) 759-8608. **$49-$74.** 435 Trunk Rd. Jct Hwy 17 and 17B, just e. Ext corridors. **Pets:** Medium. Designated rooms, no service, supervision.
(✕)

Ⓐ ▼ Northlander Motel M
(705) 254-6452. **$49-$85.** 243 Great Northern Rd. 3 km n on Hwy 17B. Ext corridors. **Pets:** $5 one-time fee/pet. Service with restrictions, supervision.
(SAVE) (Sᴅ) (✕) (🛏) (💻)

▼ Satelite Motel M
(705) 759-2897. **$50-$95.** 248 Great Northern Rd. 3 km n on Hwy 17B. Ext corridors. **Pets:** Medium, other species. $6 daily fee/room. Service with restrictions.
(✕) (🛏)

▼▼ Sleep Inn SH
(705) 253-7533. **$87-$121.** 727 Bay St. Between East and Church sts; downtown. Int corridors. **Pets:** Accepted.
(ASK) (Sᴅ) (✕) (🛏) (✕)

Ⓐ ▼▼ Travelodge SH
(705) 759-1400. **$109-$130.** 332 Bay St. Opposite Station Mall. Int corridors. **Pets:** Medium. Designated rooms, service with restrictions, supervision.
(SAVE) (Sᴅ) (✕) (🛏) (💻) (🍴)

SHARBOT LAKE

▼▼ Sharbot Lake Country Inn M
(613) 279-2198. **Call for rates.** 14152 Hwy 38. 3.5 km s of jct Hwy 7. Ext corridors. **Pets:** Accepted.
(✕) (🍴) (☎)

SIMCOE

▼▼ Comfort Inn SH
(519) 426-2611. **$86-$150.** 85 Queensway E. 0.5 km e on Hwy 3. Int corridors. **Pets:** Medium, other species. Service with restrictions, supervision.
(ASK) (Sᴅ) (✕) (🛏) (💻)

▼▼ **Travelodge Simcoe** 🆂🅷 ❀
(519) 426-4751. **$110.** 385 Queensway W (Hwy 3). 1 km w. Ext/int corridors. **Pets:** Large. $10 daily fee/pet. Service with restrictions, supervision.
🄰🅂🄺 🆂🄳 ⊠ 🔲 💻 ⇌ ⊠

SMITHS FALLS

▼▼ **Best Western Colonel By Inn** 🆂🅷
(613) 284-0001. **$77-$115.** 88 Lombard St. 1.2 km s on Hwy 15. Ext/int corridors. **Pets:** Accepted.
🄰🅂🄺 🆂🄳 ⊠ 💻 🍽 ⇌

▼ **Roger's Motel** 🄼
(613) 283-5200. **$55-$85.** 178 Lombard St. 1.6 km s on Hwy 15. Ext corridors. **Pets:** $10 daily fee/pet. Designated rooms, service with restrictions, supervision.
🄰🅂🄺 🆂🄳 ⊠ 🔲

STRATFORD

▼▼▼ **Arden Park Hotel** 🆂🅷
(519) 275-2936. **$94-$225.** 552 Ontario St. Jct Romeo St. Int corridors. **Pets:** Small. Designated rooms, service with restrictions, supervision.
⊠ 🔲 💻 🍽 ⇌

SUDBURY

🄲🄰🄰 ▼▼▼ **Best Western Downtown Sudbury Centre-Ville** 🆂🅷
(705) 673-7801. **$105.** 151 Larch St. Centre. Int corridors. **Pets:** Other species. $15 one-time fee/pet. Service with restrictions, supervision.
🆂🄰🆅🄴 🆂🄳 ⊠

▼▼ **Comfort Inn** 🆂🅷
(705) 522-1101. **$79-$156.** 2171 Regent St S. 5 km s on Hwy 46. Int corridors. **Pets:** Accepted.
🄰🅂🄺 🆂🄳 ⊠ 🔲 💻

▼▼ **Comfort Inn** 🆂🅷
(705) 560-4502. **$90-$175.** 440 Second Ave N. Kingsway at Second Ave. Int corridors. **Pets:** Other species. Designated rooms, service with restrictions, supervision.
🄰🅂🄺 🆂🄳 ⊠ 🅼 🔲 💻

🄲🄰🄰 ▼▼▼ **Quality Inn & Conference Centre** 🆂🅷
(705) 675-1273. **$85-$200.** 390 Elgin St S. Jct Hwy 55 and 80 (Paris St), 0.5 km s, just e. Int corridors. **Pets:** Designated rooms, service with restrictions, supervision.
🆂🄰🆅🄴 🆂🄳 ⊠ 🔲 💻 🍽 ⇌

▼▼ **Ramada Inn & Convention Centre** 🆂🅷
(705) 675-1123. **$99-$149.** 85 St. Anne Rd. Jct St. Anne Rd and Notre Dame Ave; downtown. Int corridors. **Pets:** Medium. $25 one-time fee/pet. Designated rooms, service with restrictions, supervision.
🄰🅂🄺 🆂🄳 ⊠ 🔲 💻 🍽 ⇌

🄲🄰🄰 ▼▼ **Travelodge Hotel Sudbury** 🆂🅷
(705) 522-1100. **$109-$159.** 1401 Paris St. 1.5 km n of jct Hwy 69 (Regent St). Int corridors. **Pets:** Other species. Designated rooms, service with restrictions, supervision.
🆂🄰🆅🄴 ⊠ 🔲 💻 🍽 ⇌

THESSALON

🄲🄰🄰 ▼ **Carolyn Beach Motor Inn** 🄼
(705) 842-3330. **$77-$105.** 1 Lakeside Dr. Just w on Hwy 17; jct Hwy 17B. Ext corridors. **Pets:** Medium. $10 daily fee/pet. Service with restrictions, supervision.
🆂🄰🆅🄴 ⊠ 🔲 💻 🍽 ⊠

THUNDER BAY

🄲🄰🄰 ▼▼ **Best Western Crossroads Motor Inn** 🆂🅷
(807) 577-4241. **$105-$150.** 655 W Arthur St. Jct Hwy 61, 17 and 11, just e. Int corridors. **Pets:** Accepted.
🆂🄰🆅🄴 🆂🄳 ⊠ 🔲 💻

🄲🄰🄰 ▼▼ **Best Western Nor'Wester Resort Hotel** 🆂🅷
(807) 473-9123. **$132-$249, 30 day notice.** 2080 Hwy 61. 9.2 km sw of jct Hwy 11, 17 and 61, exit Loch Lomond Rd. Int corridors. **Pets:** Dogs only. $50 deposit/pet. Designated rooms, service with restrictions, supervision.
🆂🄰🆅🄴 🆂🄳 ⊠ 🔲 💻 🍽 ⇌ ⊠

▼▼ **Comfort Inn** 🄼
(807) 475-3155. **$82-$129.** 660 W Arthur St. Jct Hwy 11, 17 and 61, just e. Int corridors. **Pets:** Accepted.
🄰🅂🄺 🆂🄳 ⊠ 🔲 💻

🄲🄰🄰 ▼▼ **Super 8 Motel** 🆂🅷
(807) 344-2612. **$78-$115.** 439 Memorial Ave. Jct Hwy 11, 17 and Harbour Expwy, 3 km e on Harbour Expwy, 2 km n. Int corridors. **Pets:** Other species. Designated rooms, supervision.
🆂🄰🆅🄴 🆂🄳 ⊠ 🔲

▼▼ **Victoria Inn** 🆂🅷
(807) 577-8481. **$90, 14 day notice.** 555 W Arthur St. 0.8 km e of jct Hwy 11B, 17B and 61 (western access to town). Int corridors. **Pets:** Medium, other species. Designated rooms, service with restrictions, supervision.
🄰🅂🄺 🆂🄳 ⊠ 🔲 💻 🍽 ⇌ ⊠

TILLSONBURG

🄲🄰🄰 ▼▼ **Super 8 Motel-Tillsonburg** 🆂🅷
(519) 842-7366. **$98-$108.** 92 Simcoe St. Hwy 19, just e. Int corridors. **Pets:** Other species. Service with restrictions, crate.
🆂🄰🆅🄴 🆂🄳 ⊠ 🔲 💻 🍽

TIMMINS

▼▼ **Comfort Inn** 🆂🅷
(705) 264-9474. **$105, 30 day notice.** 939 Algonquin Blvd E. Hwy 101, 0.5 km e of Hwy 655. Int corridors. **Pets:** Accepted.
🄰🅂🄺 🆂🄳 ⊠ 🔲

TORONTO METROPOLITAN AREA

MARKHAM

🄲🄰🄰 ▼▼▼ **Comfort Inn** 🆂🅷
(905) 477-6077. **$118-$128.** 8330 Woodbine Ave. Hwy 401, exit 375, 9 km n; Hwy 404, exit Hwy 7, just e, then s. Int corridors. **Pets:** Accepted.
🆂🄰🆅🄴 🆂🄳 ⊠ 🔲 💻 ⇌

🄲🄰🄰 ▼▼▼ **Holiday Inn Hotel & Suites Toronto-Markham** 🅻🅷
(905) 474-0444. **$119-$169.** 7095 Woodbine Ave. Just n of Steeles Ave. Int corridors. **Pets:** Accepted.
🆂🄰🆅🄴 🆂🄳 ⊠ 🔲 💻 🍽 ⇌ ⊠

▼▼▼ **Howard Johnson Hotel Toronto-Markham** 🆂🅷
(905) 479-5000. **$89-$159.** 555 Cochrane Dr. Hwy 404 N, exit Hwy 7E to E Valhalla Dr. Int corridors. **Pets:** Medium. $50 deposit/room. Designated rooms, service with restrictions, supervision.
🄰🅂🄺 🆂🄳 ⊠ 🔲 💻 🍽 ⇌ ⊠

🄲🄰🄰 ▼▼▼▼ **Radisson Hotel Toronto-Markham** 🅻🅷 ❀
(905) 477-2010. **$119-$149.** 50 E Valhalla Dr. Hwy 404, exit Hwy 7, then e. Int corridors. **Pets:** Medium, other species. $25 one-time fee/room. Service with restrictions, crate.
🆂🄰🆅🄴 🆂🄳 ⊠ 🔲 💻 🍽 ⇌ ⊠

▼▼▼ Residence Inn by Marriott SH
(905) 707-7933. $149-$229. 55 Minthorn Blvd. Directly s of jct Hwy 7
and Leslie St. Int corridors. Pets: Medium. $75 one-time fee/room. Serv-
ice with restrictions, crate.
ASK SD X ⛄ 🛏 🖵 🏊

▼▼▼ Staybridge Suites Toronto-Markham SH
(905) 771-9333. $139-$209, 6 day notice. 355 S Park Rd. Jct Hwy 404
and 7, w on Hwy 7, then e. Int corridors. Pets: Medium. $75 one-time
fee/room. Service with restrictions, supervision.
ASK SD X ⛄ 🛏 🖵 🏊

RICHMOND HILL

CAA ▼▼▼ Best Western Parkway Hotel Toronto
North SH
(905) 881-2600. $105-$139. 600 Hwy 7 E. Jct Hwy 401 and Don Valley
Pkwy, exit 375 via Don Valley Pkwy (Hwy 404), 8 km n to jct Hwy 7,
then 1 km w. Int corridors. Pets: Accepted.
SAVE SD X 🛏 🖵 🏊 ⊠

TORONTO

CAA ▼▼▼ Cambridge Suites Hotel LH
(416) 368-1990. $179-$199. 15 Richmond St E. Just e of Yonge St. Int
corridors. Pets: Accepted.
SAVE X ⛄ 🛏 🖵 🍴 ⊠

▼▼ Carlingview Airport Inn SH
(416) 675-3303. $89-$99, 30 day notice. 221 Carlingview Dr. QEW,
exit Hwy 427 N to Dixon Rd E, 1 km to Carlingview Dr, then just s.
Ext/int corridors. Pets: Other species. $15 daily fee/room. Designated
rooms, no service, supervision.
ASK SD X 🛏 🖵 🍴

▼▼▼ Cawthra Square Inn BB
(416) 966-0013. $119-$319, 14 day notice. 10 Cawthra Square.
Directly w of Jarvis St. Int corridors. Pets: Accepted.
ASK SD X

CAA ▼▼ Comfort Inn SH
(416) 736-4700. $69-$149. 66 Norfinch Dr. Hwy 400, exit Finch Ave E,
just n. Int corridors. Pets: Medium. $20 deposit/room. Designated rooms,
service with restrictions, supervision.
SAVE SD X 🛏 🖵 🍴

CAA ▼▼▼ Crowne Plaza Toronto Don Valley LH
(416) 449-4111. $149-$219. 1250 Eglinton Ave E. Don Valley Pkwy, exit
375 (Wynford Dr); jct Don Valley Pkwy and Eglinton Ave E. Int corridors. Pets: Accepted.
SAVE SD X ⛄ 🛏 🖵 🍴 ⊠

CAA ▼▼ Days Inn Toronto West Lakeshore SH
(416) 532-9900. $79-$159. 14 Roncesvalles Ave. Jct King and Queen
sts W and The Queensway. Int corridors. Pets: Small. $10 daily fee/pet.
Designated rooms, service with restrictions, crate.
SAVE SD X 🛏 🖵 🍴

CAA ▼▼▼ Delta Chelsea Hotel LH
(416) 595-1975. $140-$165. 33 Gerrard St W. W of Yonge St; just s of
College St. Int corridors. Pets: $50 deposit/room. Service with restrictions,
supervision.
SAVE X 🛏 🖵 🍴 🏊 ⊠

▼▼▼ Delta Toronto East LH
(416) 299-1500. $149-$199. 2035 Kennedy Rd. Just ne of jct Hwy 401
and Kennedy Rd, exit 379. Int corridors. Pets: Other species. $30 daily
fee/room. Designated rooms, service with restrictions, supervision.
X 🛏 🖵 🍴 🏊 ⊠

CAA ▼▼ Doubletree International Plaza Hotel Toronto
Airport LH
(416) 244-1711. $99-$258. 655 Dixon Rd. Jct Hwy 27 N, just w of jct
Hwy 401. Int corridors. Pets: Small. $20 one-time fee/pet. Service with
restrictions, crate.
SAVE SD X 🛏 🖵 🍴 🏊 ⊠

CAA ▼▼▼ The Fairmont Royal York LH
(416) 368-2511. $179-$329. 100 Front St W. QEW/Gardiner Expwy, exit
n on York or Bay sts; entrance on Wellington St. Int corridors.
Pets: Accepted.
SAVE SD X ⛄M 🛏 🖵 🍴 🏊 ⊠

CAA ▼▼▼ Four Seasons Hotel LH 🐾
(416) 964-0411. $355-$580. 21 Avenue Rd. Corner of Avenue Rd and
Cumberland Ave. Int corridors. Pets: Small.
SAVE X 🛏 🖵 🍴 🏊 ⊠

▼▼▼ Gloucester Square Inns of Toronto BB
(416) 966-0013. $119-$319, 14 day notice. 512-514 Jarvis St. Jct
Gloucester. Int corridors. Pets: Accepted.
ASK SD X

▼▼▼ Hilton Toronto LH
(416) 869-3456. $239-$394, 3 day notice. 145 Richmond St W. Jct
University Ave. Int corridors. Pets: Small. $25 one-time fee/room. Service
with restrictions, supervision.
ASK X ⛄ 🛏 🖵 🍴 🏊 ⊠

CAA ▼▼▼ Holiday Inn Toronto On King
(Downtown) LH 🐾
(416) 599-4000. $199-$289. 370 King St W. Between Spadina Ave and
Peter St. Int corridors. Pets: Other species. Designated rooms.
SAVE SD X ⛄ 🛏 🖵 🍴 🏊 ⊠

▼▼▼ Hotel Le Germain SH 🐾
(416) 345-9500. $225-$395. 30 Mercer St. Between John St and Blue
Jays Way. Int corridors. Pets: Dogs only. $30 daily fee/pet. Service with
restrictions, supervision.
⊠ 🍴

CAA ▼▼▼ InterContinental Toronto LH
(416) 960-5200. $225-$2000, 7 day notice. 220 Bloor St W. Just w of
Avenue Rd. Int corridors. Pets: Small. $35 one-time fee/room. Designated
rooms, service with restrictions.
SAVE SD X 🛏 🖵 🍴 🏊 ⊠

▼▼▼ Le Royal Meridien King Edward Hotel LH
(416) 863-3131. Call for rates. 37 King St E. Just e of Yonge St. Int
corridors. Pets: Accepted.
⊠ 🍴

▼▼▼ Metropolitan Hotel LH
(416) 977-5000. $229-$279. 108 Chestnut St. Just s of Dundas St. Int
corridors. Pets: Accepted.
ASK X 🛏 🖵 🏊 ⊠

▼▼▼ Montecassino Hotel & Suites SH
(416) 630-8100. $99-$399. 3710 Chesswood Dr. On Chesswood Dr at
Sheppard Ave. Int corridors. Pets: Small. $100 deposit/room. Designated
rooms, service with restrictions.
ASK SD X 🛏 🖵 🍴

CAA ▼▼▼ Novotel Toronto Centre LH 🐾
(416) 367-8900. $139-$229. 45 The Esplanade. Just ne of Gardiner
Expwy via Yonge St. Int corridors. Pets: Other species. Service with
restrictions.
SAVE SD X 🛏 🖵 🍴 🏊 ⊠

▼▼▼ Novotel Toronto North York LH 🐾
(416) 733-2929. $259-$279. 3 Park Home Ave. Hwy 401, exit Yonge St,
1 km n, then just w. Int corridors. Pets: Service with restrictions, crate.
ASK SD X 🛏 🖵 🍴 🏊

ⒸⒶⒶ ▼▼ ▼▼ **Quality Hotel & Suites Toronto Airport East** 🆂🅷
(416) 240-9090. **$69-$159.** 2180 Islington Ave. Hwy 401, exit 356. Int corridors. **Pets:** Accepted.
🆂🅰🆅🅴 🆂🐾 ⊠ 🛅 🖵 🍴

ⒸⒶⒶ ▼▼▼▼ **Quality Hotel Downtown** 🆂🅷
(416) 367-5555. **$110-$167.** 111 Lombard St. West side of Jarvis St; between Adelaide and Richmond sts; 1 km n off Gardiner Expwy at Jarvis St exit. Int corridors. **Pets:** Small. Designated rooms, service with restrictions, supervision.
🆂🅰🆅🅴 🆂🐾 ⊠ 🛅 🖵

ⒸⒶⒶ ▼▼▼▼ **Quality Hotel Midtown** 🆂🅷
(416) 968-0010. **$99-$199.** 280 Bloor St W. Just w of St. George. Int corridors. **Pets:** Accepted.
🆂🅰🆅🅴 🆂🐾 ⊠ 🛅 🖵 🍴

ⒸⒶⒶ ▼▼▼▼ **Quality Suites Toronto Airport** 🅻🅷
(416) 674-8442. **$166-$176.** 262 Carlingview Dr. 1 km w of jct Hwy 27 N and Dixon Rd. Int corridors. **Pets:** Other species. Designated rooms, service with restrictions, supervision.
🆂🅰🆅🅴 🆂🐾 ⊠ 🛅 🖵 🍴

ⒸⒶⒶ ▼▼▼▼ **Radisson Hotel Toronto East** 🅻🅷
(416) 493-7000. **$129-$169.** 55 Hallcrown Pl. Hwy 401, exit for Victoria Park N to Consumer's Rd, then w. Int corridors. **Pets:** Accepted.
🆂🅰🆅🅴 🆂🐾 ⊠ 🐾🄼 🅶 🛅 🖵 🍴 🔁

ⒸⒶⒶ ▼▼▼▼ **Radisson Suite Hotel Toronto Airport** 🅻🅷
(416) 242-7400. **$129-$189.** 640 Dixon Rd. Just e of jct Hwy 27; 0.3 km w of jct Hwy 401. Int corridors. **Pets:** Accepted.
🆂🅰🆅🅴 🆂🐾 ⊠ 🖵 🍴

ⒸⒶⒶ ▼▼▼▼ **Ramada Hotel Toronto Airport** 🅻🅷
(416) 621-2121. **$109-$129.** 2 Holiday Dr. Hwy 427, exit Holiday Dr southbound; exit Burnhamthorpe Rd northbound. Int corridors. **Pets:** Other species. $20 daily fee/pet. Designated rooms, service with restrictions, supervision.
🆂🅰🆅🅴 🆂🐾 ⊠ 🛅 🖵 🍴 🔁 🚫

ⒸⒶⒶ ▼▼▼ ▼▼ **Renaissance Toronto Airport Hotel** 🅻🅷
(416) 675-6100. **$229-$269.** 801 Dixon Rd. Jct Hwy 27 N and Dixon Rd. Int corridors. **Pets:** Small, dogs only. $50 deposit/room. Service with restrictions, supervision.
🆂🅰🆅🅴 🆂🐾 ⊠ 🐾🄼 📠 🅶 🛅 🖵 🍴 🔁

ⒸⒶⒶ ▼▼ ▼▼ ▼▼ **The Sheraton Centre Toronto Hotel** 🅻🅷 🐾
(416) 361-1000. **$320-$439.** 123 Queen St W. Opposite Toronto Civic Centre and City Hall. Int corridors. **Pets:** Medium, dogs only. Service with restrictions, supervision.
🆂🅰🆅🅴 🆂🐾 ⊠ 🐾🄼 🛅 🖵 🍴 🔁 🚫

▼▼ ▼▼ **SoHo Metropolitan Hotel** 🆂🅷
(416) 599-8800. **$280-$460.** 318 Wellington St W. Jct Blue Jays Way. Int corridors. **Pets:** Accepted.
🅰🆂🅺 ⊠ 🖵 🍴 🔁 🚫

ⒸⒶⒶ ▼▼ ▼▼ **The Sutton Place Hotel** 🅻🅷
(416) 924-9221. **$189-$500.** 955 Bay St. Jct Wellesley St. Int corridors. **Pets:** Small, other species. $150 deposit/pet. Crate.
🆂🅰🆅🅴 ⊠ 🛅 🖵 🍴 🔁 🚫

▼▼ ▼▼ **Toronto Airport Marriott Hotel** 🅻🅷
(416) 674-9400. **$109-$249.** 901 Dixon Rd. Corner of Dixon Rd and Carlingview Dr. Int corridors. **Pets:** $20 one-time fee/room. Service with restrictions, supervision.
🅰🆂🅺 ⊠ 🐾🄼 🛅 🖵 🍴 🔁 🚫

▼▼ ▼▼ **Toronto Marriott Downtown Eaton Centre** 🅻🅷
(416) 597-9200. **$169-$299.** 525 Bay St. Just s of Dundas St. Int corridors. **Pets:** Accepted.
🅰🆂🅺 ⊠ 🐾🄼 🛅 🖵 🍴 🔁 🚫

ⒸⒶⒶ ▼▼▼▼ **Travelodge Hotel and Conference Centre Toronto** 🅻🅷
(416) 636-4656. **$99-$169.** 2737 Keele St. Jct Hwy 401 and Keele St N. Int corridors. **Pets:** $25 one-time fee/room. Service with restrictions.
🆂🅰🆅🅴 🆂🐾 ⊠ 🛅 🖵 🍴 🔁 🚫

ⒸⒶⒶ ▼▼▼▼ **Travelodge Hotel Toronto Airport (Dixon Road)** 🆂🅷
(416) 674-2222. **$99-$160.** 925 Dixon Rd. Corner of Carlingview Dr and Dixon Rd. Int corridors. **Pets:** Designated rooms, supervision.
🆂🅰🆅🅴 🆂🐾 ⊠ 🛅 🖵 🍴 🔁 🚫

ⒸⒶⒶ ▼▼ ▼▼ **Travelodge Toronto East** 🆂🅷 🐾
(416) 299-9500. **$109-$149.** 20 Milner Business Ct. Jct Hwy 401 and Markham Rd, just n on Markham Rd. Int corridors. **Pets:** Other species.
🆂🅰🆅🅴 🆂🐾 ⊠ 🛅 🖵 🍴 🔁

ⒸⒶⒶ ▼▼ ▼▼ **Travelodge Toronto North (North York)** 🆂🅷
(416) 663-9500. **$99-$149.** 50 Norfinch Dr. Hwy 400, exit Finch Ave E. Int corridors. **Pets:** Small. $100 deposit/room. Designated rooms, no service, supervision.
🆂🅰🆅🅴 ⊠ 🛅 🖵 🔁

ⒸⒶⒶ ▼▼ ▼▼ **Windsor Arms** 🆂🅷
(416) 971-9666. **$295-$2000.** 18 St. Thomas St. Jct Bloor St. Int corridors. **Pets:** Accepted.
🆂🅰🆅🅴 🆂🐾 ⊠ 🍴 🔁 🚫

END METROPOLITAN AREA

TRENTON

ⒸⒶⒶ ▼▼ ▼▼ **Comfort Inn** 🆂🅷 🐾
(613) 965-6660. **$99-$139.** 68 Monogram Pl. Hwy 401, exit 526 (Glen Miller Rd S). Int corridors. **Pets:** Designated rooms, service with restrictions, supervision.
🆂🅰🆅🅴 🆂🐾 ⊠ 🐾🄼 🛅 🖵

▼▼ ▼▼ **Holiday Inn Trenton** 🆂🅷
(613) 394-4855. **$114-$160.** 99 Glen Miller Rd. Hwy 401, exit 526 (Glen Miller Rd S). Int corridors. **Pets:** $5 daily fee/pet. Designated rooms, service with restrictions, supervision.
🅰🆂🅺 🆂🐾 ⊠ 🛅 🖵 🍴 🔁 🚫

TWEED

▼▼ **Park Place Motel** 🅼
(613) 478-3134. **$64-$98.** 43 Victoria St. Hwy 37, 0.5 km s of centre. Ext corridors. **Pets:** Accepted.
🅰🆂🅺 ⊠ 🛅

WALLACEBURG

▼▼ ▼▼ **Super 8 Motel** 🆂🅷
(519) 627-0781. **$69-$99.** 76 McNaughton Ave. On Hwy 40 (McNaughton Ave), south side of town. Int corridors. **Pets:** Accepted.
⊠ 🛅

WASAGA BEACH

▼ Kingsbridge Inn M
(705) 429-6364. $45-$150. 268 Main St. Hwy 92, just n. Ext corridors.
Pets: Accepted.

⊠ 🛏 ▣ 🏊 ⊠ ☎

WATERLOO

▼▼ Comfort Inn SH
(519) 747-9400. $99-$159. 190 Weber St N. East side off Weber St,
0.3 km s of Hwy 86. Int corridors. Pets: Accepted.

A$K S📶 ⊠ 🛏 ▣ ⦙†⦙

▼▼▼ Les Diplomates B&B (Executive Guest House) BB
(519) 725-3184. $98-$156. 100 Blythwood Rd. Hwy 85 N, exit King St,
s to Columbia, w to Hazel St, then e. Ext/int corridors. Pets: $40
deposit/pet. Designated rooms, no service, supervision.

A$K S📶 ⊠ 🛏

CAA ▼▼▼ The Waterloo Inn & Conference Centre SH
(519) 884-0220. $135. 475 King St N. 3 km n on King St, jct Hwy 85.
Int corridors. Pets: Medium. $15 daily fee/pet. Designated rooms, service
with restrictions, supervision.

SAVE S📶 ⊠ 🛏 ▣ ⦙†⦙ 🏊 ⊠

WAWA

▼ Kinniwabi Pines Motel/Cottages M ❖
(705) 856-7302. $75-$89. 52 Hwy 17. Hwy 17, 5.3 km s of jct Hwy 101.
Ext corridors. Pets: $8 daily fee/pet. Service with restrictions, supervision.

⊠ 🛏 ▣ ⊠ 🐾

▼ Parkway Motel M ❖
(705) 856-7020. $65-$75. 938 Hwy 17. Hwy 17, 4 km s of jct Hwy 101.
Ext corridors. Pets: Other species. $5 one-time fee/pet. Service with
restrictions, supervision.

⊠ 🛏 ▣ 🐾

▼ Sportsman's Motel M
(705) 856-2272. $75. 45 Mission Rd. Hwy 101, 2.4 km e of jct Hwy 17.
Ext corridors. Pets: Small. $10 daily fee/room. Designated rooms, service
with restrictions, supervision.

⊠ 🛏 ▣ 🐾

CAA ▼ Wawa Northern Lights Motel & Chalets M ❖
(705) 856-1900. $79-$109. 237 Hwy 17. 8 km n of jct Hwy 101. Ext
corridors. Pets: Other species. Service with restrictions, supervision.

SAVE S📶 ⊠ 🛏 ▣ ⦙†⦙ 🐾

WHITBY

▼▼▼ Motel 6 #1907 SH
(905) 665-8883. $73-$91. 165 Consumers Dr. Hwy 401, exit 410 (Brock
St/Hwy 12), just ne. Int corridors. Pets: Other species. Service with
restrictions, supervision.

S📶 ⊠ 🐾 🛏

CAA ▼▼▼ Quality Suites SH
(905) 432-8800. $144-$199. 1700 Champlain Ave. Hwy 401, exit 412
(Thickson Rd), 0.5 km n to Champlain Ave, then 1 km e. Int corridors.
Pets: Service with restrictions.

SAVE S📶 ⊠ 🛏 ▣

WHITEFISH FALLS

CAA ▼▼▼ The Island Lodge CA
(705) 285-4343. $280, 30 day notice. In Whitefish Falls; parking and
dock, just w of Hwy 6 (phone for boat at Espanola or Little Current).
Ext corridors. Pets: Accepted.

SAVE 🛏 ▣ ⦙†⦙ ⊠ 🐾 ☎

WINDSOR

▼▼ Comfort Inn SH
(519) 966-7800. $99-$150. 2955 Dougall Ave. 5.3 km s on Hwy 3B, off
Hwy 401 via Detroit-Windsor Tunnel exit. Int corridors. Pets: Accepted.

A$K S📶 ⊠ 🛏 ▣

CAA ▼▼▼ Comfort Inn SH
(519) 972-1331. $96-$150, 7 day notice. 2765 Huron Church Rd. 0.8
km s of EC Row Expwy; west side of Huron Church Rd. Int corridors.
Pets: Small. $10 daily fee/pet. Service with restrictions, supervision.

S📶 ⊠ 🛏 ▣ ⦙†⦙

▼▼▼ Hampton Inn and Suites SH
(519) 972-0770. $129-$169. 1840 Huron Church Rd. 1.5 km n of EC
Row Expwy. Int corridors. Pets: Service with restrictions, supervision.

A$K S📶 ⊠ 🛏 ▣ 🏊

▼▼▼ Hilton Windsor LH
(519) 973-5555. $129-$199. 277 Riverside Dr W. 1 km w of Detroit-
Windsor Tunnel; 1 km e of Ambassador Bridge; downtown. Int corridors. Pets: Accepted.

A$K S📶 ⊠ ▣ ⦙†⦙ 🏊 ⊠

CAA ▼▼▼ Holiday Inn Select Windsor (Ambassador
Bridge) LH ❖
(519) 966-1200. $139-$159. 1855 Huron Church Rd. Jct Huron Church
and Malden rds; 1.5 km n of EC Row Expwy. Int corridors. Pets: Other
species. Service with restrictions.

SAVE S📶 ⊠ 🛏 ▣ ⦙†⦙ ⊠

CAA ▼▼▼ Quality Suites Windsor SH
(519) 977-9707. $129-$249. 250 Dougall Ave. Jct Dougall Ave and
Chatham St; downtown. Int corridors. Pets: Accepted.

SAVE S📶 ⊠ 🖳M 🛏 ▣ ⦙†⦙

CAA ▼▼▼ Radisson Riverfront Hotel LH
(519) 977-9777. $129-$199. 333 Riverside Dr W. 1 km w of Detroit-
Windsor Tunnel; 1 km e of Ambassador Bridge. Int corridors.
Pets: Small. Service with restrictions, crate.

SAVE S📶 ⊠ 🛏 ▣ ⦙†⦙ 🏊 ⊠

▼▼▼ Royal Marquis Hotel SH
(519) 966-1900. $100-$120, 7 day notice. 590 Grand Marais Rd E.
Just n of Devonshire Mall and EC Row Expwy. Int corridors.
Pets: Accepted.

⊠ 🛏 ⦙†⦙ 🏊 ⊠

CAA ▼▼▼ Travelodge Windsor Ambassador Bridge SH
(519) 972-1100. $85-$180. 2330 Huron Church Rd. N of EC Row
Expwy. Int corridors. Pets: Accepted.

SAVE S📶 ⊠ 🛏 ▣ 🏊 ⊠

WOODSTOCK

CAA ▼▼▼ Quality Hotel and Suites SH
(519) 537-5586. $124-$236. 580 Bruin Blvd. Hwy 401, exit 232, just n;
w of Hwy 59. Int corridors. Pets: Other species. Service with restrictions,
crate.

SAVE S📶 ⊠ 🛏 ▣ ⦙†⦙ 🏊 ⊠

▼▼ Super 8 Motel SH
(519) 421-4588. $86-$93. 560 Norwich Ave. Jct Hwy 401 and 59, exit
232, just n. Int corridors. Pets: Service with restrictions, supervision.

A$K S📶 ⊠ 🛏 ▣

WYOMING

CAA ▼▼ Country View Motel and RV Camping
Resort M
(519) 845-3394. $54-$89, 30 day notice. 4569 London Line. Hwy 402,
exit 25, 1 km s on Hwy 21 to Hwy 22, then just e. Ext corridors.
Pets: Accepted.

SAVE ⊠ 🛏 🏊 ⊠

PRINCE EDWARD ISLAND

CAVENDISH

◈◈ Bay Vista Motor Inn M
(902) 963-2225. **$51-$95, 3 day notice.** 9517 Cavendish Rd. Jct Rt 13, 4.8 km w on Rt 6. Ext corridors. **Pets:** Small. Service with restrictions, supervision.

◈◈ Cavendish Bosom Buddies Cottages CA
(902) 963-3449. **$80-$295, 14 day notice.** RR 1. Jct Rt 6 and 13, 0.6 km e on Rt 6. Ext corridors. **Pets:** Large. Designated rooms, service with restrictions, supervision.

◈◈ Cavendish Maples Cottages CA
(902) 963-2818. **$68-$270, 30 day notice.** Jct Rt 6 and 13, 2.5 km w on Rt 6. Ext corridors. **Pets:** Small. Service with restrictions, supervision.

CHARLOTTETOWN

◈◈ Best Western Charlottetown SH
(902) 892-2461. **$144-$195.** 238 Grafton St. Centre. Int corridors. **Pets:** Designated rooms.

◈◈ Comfort Inn SH
(902) 566-4424. **$103-$163.** 112 Trans-Canada Hwy 1. Trans-Canada Hwy 1, 4.5 km w. Int corridors. **Pets:** Other species. Service with restrictions, supervision.

◈◈ Delta Prince Edward LH ✿
(902) 566-2222. **$124-$207.** 18 Queen St. At Water and Queen sts. Int corridors. **Pets:** Medium, other species. $35 one-time fee/room. Service with restrictions, supervision.

◈◈ Econo Lodge M
(902) 368-1110. **$78-$189.** 20 Lower Malpeque Rd. Jct of Trans-Canada Hwy 1 and Lower Malpeque Rd, 4.5 km w. Ext/int corridors. **Pets:** Accepted.

◈◈ Holiday Inn Express Hotel & Suites Charlottetown SH ✿
(902) 892-1201. **$99-$166.** 200 Trans-Canada Hwy. On Trans-Canada Hwy 1, 4.8 km w. Int corridors. **Pets:** Other species. Service with restrictions, supervision.

◈◈ Quality Inn on the Hill SH
(902) 894-8572. **$109-$230.** 150 Euston St. Just e of University Ave. Int corridors. **Pets:** Medium. Designated rooms, service with restrictions, supervision.

◈◈ Rodd Charlottetown-A Rodd Signature Hotel SH
(902) 894-7371. **$103-$237.** 75 Kent St. Corner of Kent and Pownal sts. Int corridors. **Pets:** Accepted.

◈◈ Rodd Confederation Inn & Suites M
(902) 892-2481. **$72-$150.** Trans-Canada Hwy 1. On Trans-Canada Hwy 1, 4 km w. Ext/int corridors. **Pets:** Large. Designated rooms, service with restrictions, supervision.

◈◈ Rodd Royalty Inn SH
(902) 894-8566. **$90-$175.** Intersection Hwy 1 & 2. 4 km w on Trans-Canada Hwy 1. Ext/int corridors. **Pets:** Accepted.

CORNWALL

◈◈ Sunny King Motel M
(902) 566-2209. **$55-$116, 3 day notice.** On Hwy 1; centre. Ext corridors. **Pets:** Dogs only. Designated rooms, service with restrictions, supervision.

MAYFIELD

◈◈ Cavendish Gateway Resort by Clarion Collection M
(902) 963-2213. **$89-$175.** Rt 13. On Rt 13, 6 km w of Cavendish; centre. Ext/int corridors. **Pets:** Accepted.

MONTAGUE

◈◈ Rodd Marina Inn & Suites SH
(902) 838-4075. **$75-$157.** 115 Sackville St. Centre. Int corridors. **Pets:** Accepted.

NORTH RUSTICO

◈ St. Lawrence Motel M
(902) 963-2053. **$45-$149, 14 day notice.** On Gulf Shore Rd. Ext corridors. **Pets:** Accepted.

RICHMOND

◈◈ Caernarvon Cottages, B&B and Gardens CA
(902) 854-3418. **$80, 30 day notice.** 4697 Hwy 12, RR 1. Jct Hwy 2 and Rt 131, 10 km e. Ext/int corridors. **Pets:** Service with restrictions, supervision.

ROSENEATH

◈◈ Rodd Brudenell River-A Rodd Signature Resort LH
(902) 652-2332. **$120-$232, 3 day notice.** Jct Rt 4 and 3, 5.5 km e on Rt 3. Ext/int corridors. **Pets:** Accepted.

ST. PETERS

◈◈ Greenwich Gate Lodge M
(902) 961-3496. **$59-$129, 7 day notice.** Rt 2. Jct Rt 2 and 16; centre. Ext corridors. **Pets:** Dogs only. Service with restrictions, supervision.

SUMMERSIDE

◈◈ Econo Lodge SH
(902) 436-9100. **$80-$140.** 80 All Weather Hwy. Jct Hwy 1A and 2, 5 km w on Hwy 2. Int corridors. **Pets:** Accepted.

◈◈ Quality Inn Garden of the Gulf M
(902) 436-2295. **$89-$299.** 618 Water St. 1.6 km e on Hwy 11. Ext/int corridors. **Pets:** Designated rooms, service with restrictions, supervision.

WOODSTOCK

◈◈ Rodd Mill River Resort SH
(902) 859-3555. **$82-$198, 3 day notice.** Rt 180. On Rt 136, just e of jct Rt 2. Int corridors. **Pets:** Accepted.

QUEBEC

ALMA

▼▼▼ Comfort Inn SH
(418) 668-9221. **$82-$98.** 870 ave du Pont S. On Hwy 169; centre of town. Int corridors. **Pets:** Accepted.
ASK S X 🔒

▼▼ Hotel Motel Les Cascades M
(418) 662-6547. **$67-$87.** 140 ave du Pont N. On Hwy 169, just n of bridge; centre. Ext/int corridors. **Pets:** Small. No service, supervision.
ASK S X 🔒 🍴

BAIE-COMEAU

▼▼ Comfort Inn SH
(418) 589-8252. **$109-$128.** 745 boul Lafleche. On Rt 138. Int corridors. **Pets:** Service with restrictions, supervision.
ASK X 🔒 🖥

▼▼▼▼ Hotel Le Manoir SH ❀
(418) 296-3391. **$89-$179.** 8 ave Cabot. Rt 138, 4.4 km e, follow signs. Int corridors. **Pets:** Service with restrictions, crate.
ASK X 🖥 🍴 🔲

BAIE-ST-PAUL

▼▼ Hotel Baie-Saint-Paul SH
(418) 435-3683. **$59-$129, 3 day notice.** 911 boul Mgr-de-Laval. On Rt 138, 0.5 km e of Rt 362. Int corridors. **Pets:** Other species. $10 daily fee/room. Service with restrictions, supervision.
X 🔒 🖥 🍴 🔲

BERTHIERVILLE

▼▼ Days Inn Berthierville SH
(450) 836-1621. **$88-$165.** 760 rue Gadoury. Hwy 40, exit 144. Ext/int corridors. **Pets:** Small. Designated rooms, supervision.
ASK S X 🔒 🖥

CARLETON-SAINT-OMER

▼▼ Hostellerie Baie Bleue M
(418) 364-3355. **$70-$130.** 482 boul Perron. On Rt 132. Ext corridors. **Pets:** Accepted.
ASK S X 🔒 🖥 🍴 🔲 AC

CHICOUTIMI

▼▼ Comfort Inn SH
(418) 693-8686. **$90-$105.** 1595 boul Talbot. Jct Rt 170, 2.8 km n; in Chicoutimi sector. Int corridors. **Pets:** Small, other species. Service with restrictions, supervision.
ASK S X 🔒 🖥

▼▼ Hotel La Sagueneenne SH
(418) 545-8326. **$99-$129.** 250 des Sagueneens. Just w of jct Rt 175 (boul Talbot); in Saguenay sector. Int corridors. **Pets:** Medium. Designated rooms, service with restrictions, supervision.
ASK S X 🔒M 🔲 🔒 🖥 🍴 🔲 🔲

COWANSVILLE

▼▼ Days Inn-Cowansville SH
(450) 263-7331. **$70-$100.** 111 place Jean-Jacques Bertrand. Hwy 10, exit 68, 15.9 km s on Rt 139. Int corridors. **Pets:** Accepted.
ASK S X 🖥 🍴

DRUMMONDVILLE

(AA) ▼▼▼▼ Best Western Hotel Universel SH
(819) 478-4971. **$109-$259.** 915 rue Hains. Hwy 20, exit 177, 0.3 km s on boul St-Joseph, then just e. Int corridors. **Pets:** Accepted.
SAVE S X 🔒 🖥 🍴 🔲

▼▼▼ Comfort Inn SH
(819) 477-4000. **$94-$124.** 1055 rue Hains. Hwy 20, exit 177, 0.5 km s on boul St-Joseph, then just w. Int corridors. **Pets:** Large. Designated rooms, service with restrictions, supervision.
ASK S X 🔒 🖥

▼▼▼ Quality Suites SH
(819) 472-2700. **$109-$189.** 2125 rue Canadien. Hwy 20, exit 175, then just s. Int corridors. **Pets:** Very small. Designated rooms, service with restrictions, supervision.
ASK S X 🔒 🖥 🔲

GASPE

▼▼ Motel Adams M
(418) 368-2244. **$89-$109.** 20 rue Adams. Corner of rue Jacques Cartier; centre. Ext/int corridors. **Pets:** Very small. Service with restrictions, supervision.
X 🔒 🖥 🍴

GATINEAU

▼▼▼ Chateau Cartier Relais-Resort LH
(819) 778-0000. **$139-$299.** 1170 chemin Aylmer. On Hwy 148, 1 km w of Champlain Bridge; in Aylmer sector. Int corridors. **Pets:** Accepted.
ASK S X 🔒 🖥 🍴 🔲 🔲

(AA) ▼▼ Comfort Inn Gatineau SH
(819) 243-6010. **$100-$140.** 630 boul La Gappe. Hwy 50, exit 140, 2 km e. Int corridors. **Pets:** Other species. Designated rooms, supervision.
SAVE S X 🖥

(AA) ▼▼▼▼ Four Points by Sheraton & Conference Centre
Gatineau-Ottawa LH
(819) 778-6111. **$99.** 35 rue Laurier. Corner of rue Victoria, across from Canadian Museum of Civilization; in Hull sector. Int corridors. **Pets:** Large. Designated rooms, service with restrictions, supervision.
[SAVE] [S⬤] [✕] [🛏] [▣] [¶] [➳]

(AA) ▼▼▼▼ Holiday Inn Plaza La Chaudiere
Gatineau-Ottawa LH 🐾
(819) 778-3880. **$90-$112.** 2 rue Montcalm. 0.8 km w of Portage Bridge at Rt 148 and rue Montcalm; in Hull sector. Int corridors. **Pets:** Crate.
[SAVE] [S⬤] [✕] [🛏] [▣] [¶] [➳] [✕]

GRANBY

▼▼ ▼▼ Hotel Castel & Spa Comfort SH
(450) 378-9071. **$70-$125.** 901 rue Principale. On Rt 112, 1 km e of jct Rt 139; Hwy 10, exit 68. Int corridors. **Pets:** Accepted.
[ASK] [S⬤] [✕] [🛏] [▣] [¶] [➳] [✕]

LAC-BROME (KNOWLTON)

▼▼▼▼ Auberge Knowlton CI
(450) 242-6886. **$110-$120.** 286 chemin Knowlton Rd. Corner of Hwy 104 and Rt 243; centre. Int corridors. **Pets:** Accepted.
[✕] [¶] [𝒜𝒞]

LA MALBAIE

(AA) ▼▼▼▼ ▼▼▼▼ Fairmont Le Manoir Richelieu LH 🐾
(418) 665-3703. **$139-$189.** 181 rue Richelieu. On Rt 362, 4.1 km w of jct Rt 138. Int corridors. **Pets:** $25 daily fee/room. Designated rooms, service with restrictions, supervision.
[SAVE] [S⬤] [✕] [🛏] [▣] [¶] [➳] [✕]

LA POCATIERE

▼▼ ▼▼ Motel Le Pocatois M
(418) 856-1688. **$63-$90.** 235 Rt 132. Hwy 20, exit 439, 0.8 km s. Ext/int corridors. **Pets:** Small. Designated rooms, service with restrictions, supervision.
[✕] [🛏] [¶]

LENNOXVILLE

(AA) ▼▼ La Paysanne Motel M
(819) 569-5585. **$72-$82.** 42 rue Queen. On Rt 143. Ext/int corridors. **Pets:** Accepted.
[SAVE] [S⬤] [✕] [🛏] [¶] [➳]

L'ISLET

▼▼▼▼ Auberge La Paysanne CO
(418) 247-7276. **$70-$120.** 497 des Pionniers est. On Rt 132, 4.2 km e, jct Rt 285; centre. Ext corridors. **Pets:** Accepted.
[S⬤] [✕] [🛏] [▣] [¶] [𝒜𝒞]

LOUISEVILLE

▼▼▼▼ Gite du Carrefour et Maison historique J.L.L.
Hamelin BB
(819) 228-4932. **$75-$85 (no credit cards), 15 day notice.** 11 ave St-Laurent ouest. On Rt 138; Hwy 40, exit 174 westbound; exit 166 eastbound; centre. Int corridors. **Pets:** Accepted.
[✕] [𝒜𝒞] [𝒲] [⊘]

MARIA

▼▼▼▼ Hotel Honguedo SH
(418) 759-3488. **$84-$147.** 548 boul Perron. On Rt 132, in town centre. Ext/int corridors. **Pets:** Accepted.
[ASK] [S⬤] [✕] [🛏] [▣] [¶] [➳]

MATANE

(AA) ▼▼ Motel La Marina M
(418) 562-3234. **$52-$80.** 1032 ave du Phare ouest. On Rt 132. Ext corridors. **Pets:** Medium, dogs only. Designated rooms, service with restrictions, supervision.
[SAVE] [✕] [🛏] [▣] [➳] [𝒜𝒞]

MONTEBELLO

(AA) ▼▼▼▼ ▼▼▼▼ Fairmont Le Chateau Montebello LH 🐾
(819) 423-6341. **$189-$289, 3 day notice.** 392 rue Notre-Dame. On Rt 148. Int corridors. **Pets:** $35 daily fee/pet. Service with restrictions, crate.
[SAVE] [S⬤] [✕] [🛏] [▣] [¶] [➳] [✕]

MONTMAGNY

▼▼▼▼ Manoir des Erables CI
(418) 248-0100. **$89-$160, 10 day notice.** 220 boul Tache est (Rt 132). Hwy 20, exit 376, 2.2 km e on Rt 228, 1.5 km e. Ext/int corridors. **Pets:** Small, other species. $15 daily fee/pet. Designated rooms, service with restrictions, crate.
[✕] [▣] [¶] [➳] [✕]

MONTRÉAL METROPOLITAN AREA

BOUCHERVILLE

▼▼ ▼▼ Comfort Inn M
(450) 641-2880. **$115-$155.** 96 boul de Mortagne. Hwy 20, exit 92, just n. Int corridors. **Pets:** Very small. Designated rooms, service with restrictions, supervision.
[ASK] [S⬤] [✕] [▣]

BROSSARD

▼▼ ▼▼ Comfort Inn SH
(450) 678-9350. **$103-$113.** 7863 boul Taschereau. Rt 134, 1.5 km w of Hwy 10, exit boul Taschereau ouest. Int corridors. **Pets:** Accepted.
[ASK] [S⬤] [✕] [🛏]

DORVAL

(AA) ▼▼▼▼ Comfort Inn Dorval SH
(514) 636-3391. **$90-$140.** 340 ave Michel-Jasmin. Hwy 520, exit 2 eastbound; exit 1 westbound, 0.3 km along service road to ave Marshall, follow to ave Michel-Jasmin. Int corridors. **Pets:** Accepted.
[SAVE] [S⬤] [✕] [🛏] [▣]

(AA) ▼▼▼▼ Hampton Inn & Suites SH
(514) 633-8243. **$145-$185.** 1900 route Transcanadienne (Hwy 40). Hwy 40, exit 55, 0.8 km e of boul Sources on south side service road. Int corridors. **Pets:** Accepted.
[SAVE] [S⬤] [✕] [⬤M] [🛏] [▣] [➳]

(AA) ▼▼▼▼ Travelodge Dorval Airport SH
(514) 631-4537. **$106-$127.** 1010 chemin Herron. Hwy 20, exit 54 westbound, just s on boul Fenelon to ave Dumont, follow to chemin Herron; exit 56 eastbound, 1.7 km along service road. Int corridors. **Pets:** Other species. $40 deposit/room. Designated rooms, service with restrictions.
[SAVE] [S⬤] [✕] [🛏] [▣] [✕]

LAVAL

▼▼ ▼▼ Comfort Inn SH
(450) 686-0600. **$111-$126.** 2055 Autoroute des Laurentides. Hwy 15, exit 8, e on boul St-Martin, 0.7 km n on boul Le Corbusier, then w on boul Tessier. Int corridors. **Pets:** Small. Designated rooms, service with restrictions, supervision.
[ASK] [S⬤] [✕] [🛏] [¶]

▼▼ Econo Lodge SH
(450) 681-6411. **$89-$125.** 1981 boul Cure-Labelle. Hwy 15, exit 8 (boul St-Martin) northbound; exit 10 southbound, 2 km w on boul St-Martin ouest, then 0.5 km n. Ext/int corridors. **Pets:** Designated rooms, service with restrictions, supervision.
ASK SÔ ⊠ 🖬 🖭 ⮀

CAA ▼▼ Quality Suites Laval SH
(450) 686-6777. **$128-$149.** 2035 Autoroute des Laurentides. Hwy 15, exit 8, e on boul St-Martin, 0.7 km n on boul Le Corbusier, w on boul Tessier. Int corridors. **Pets:** Small. Designated rooms, service with restrictions, supervision.
SAVE SÔ ⊠ 🖬 🖭

LONGUEUIL

▼▼ Days Inn Longueuil SH
(450) 677-8911. **$82-$101, 3 day notice.** 2800 boul Marie-Victorin. Hwy 20/Rt 132, exit 15 eastbound, follow signs for boul Marie-Victorin est; exit 90 westbound from Pont-Tunnel Louis-Hippolyte-Lafontaine. Int corridors. **Pets:** Small. Service with restrictions.
ASK SÔ ⊠ 🖭 🍽

▼▼▼ Holiday Inn Montreal-Longueuil SH
(450) 646-8100. **$149-$179, 3 day notice.** 900 rue St-Charles est. Rt 132, exit 11. Int corridors. **Pets:** Small. $25 one-time fee/room. Designated rooms, service with restrictions, supervision.
ASK SÔ ⊠ 🖬 🖭 🍽 ⮀

MONTREAL

CAA ▼▼▼ Chateau Versailles Hotel SH 🐾
(514) 933-3611. **$205-$300.** 1659 rue Sherbrooke ouest. Corner rue St-Mathieu. Int corridors. **Pets:** $15 daily fee/pet. Designated rooms, service with restrictions, crate.
SAVE SÔ ⊠ 🖭

CAA ▼▼▼ Crowne Plaza Montreal-Metro Centre LH
(514) 842-8581. **$149-$229.** 505 Sherbrooke est. Between rue Berri and St-Hubert. Int corridors. **Pets:** Small. $25 one-time fee/room. Service with restrictions, supervision.
SAVE SÔ ⊠ 🖭 🍽 ⮀ ⊠

CAA ▼▼▼▼ Delta Montreal LH
(514) 286-1986. **$149-$289.** 475 ave President-Kennedy. Corner rue City Councillors. Int corridors. **Pets:** $30 one-time fee/room. Designated rooms, service with restrictions, crate.
SAVE SÔ ⊠ 🖬 🖭 🍽 ⮀ ⊠

CAA ▼▼▼▼ Fairmont The Queen Elizabeth LH
(514) 861-3511. **$139-$289.** 900 boul Rene-Levesque ouest. Between rue Universite and Mansfield. Int corridors. **Pets:** Medium. $25 daily fee/room. Service with restrictions, supervision.
SAVE ⊠ ⚷M 🖬 🖭 🍽 ⮀ ⊠

CAA ▼▼▼ Four Points by Sheraton Montreal
Centre-Ville LH
(514) 842-3961. **$149-$189.** 475 rue Sherbrooke ouest. Between rue Durocher and Aylmer. Int corridors. **Pets:** Accepted.
SAVE SÔ ⊠ 🖬 🖭 🍽 ⊠

CAA ▼▼▼▼ Hilton Montreal Bonaventure LH
(514) 878-2332. **$150-$300.** 900 rue de La Gauchetiere W, Ste 10750. Corner of Mansfield and de la Gauchetiere. Int corridors. **Pets:** Medium. Designated rooms, service with restrictions, supervision.
SAVE SÔ ⊠ 🖬 🖭 🍽 ⮀ ⊠

▼▼▼ Holiday Inn Montreal-Midtown LH
(514) 842-6111. **$119-$179.** 420 rue Sherbrooke ouest. Between rue Bleury and City Councillors. Int corridors. **Pets:** Accepted.
ASK SÔ ⊠ 🖬 🖭 🍽 ⮀ ⊠

▼▼▼ Hotel Gault SH
(514) 904-1616. **$199-$589.** 449 rue Ste-Helene. Just s of rue Notre-Dame. Int corridors. **Pets:** Other species. $8 daily fee/pet. Service with restrictions, crate.
⊠ 🖬 🖭

▼▼▼ Hotel Godin SH 🐾
(514) 843-6000. **$225-$450.** 10 rue Sherbrooke ouest. Corner of boul St-Laurent. Int corridors. **Pets:** $50 one-time fee/room. Service with restrictions, supervision.
ASK ⊠ 🖬 🖭 🍽

CAA ▼▼▼ Hotel La Tour Centre-Ville CO
(514) 866-8861. **$95-$139.** 400 boul Rene-Levesque ouest. Corner of rue de Bleury. Int corridors. **Pets:** Small. Service with restrictions, supervision.
SAVE SÔ ⊠ 🖬 🖭 🍽 ⮀ ⊠

▼▼▼ Hotel Le Germain SH 🐾
(514) 849-2050. **$230-$330.** 2050 rue Mansfield. Just n of ave President-Kennedy. Int corridors. **Pets:** $30 daily fee/room. Supervision.
⊠ 🖬 🖭 🍽

▼▼▼▼ Hotel Le St-James SH
(514) 841-3111. **$400-$675.** 355 rue St-Jacques ouest. Corner of rue St-Pierre. Int corridors. **Pets:** Accepted.
⊠ 🍽

CAA ▼▼▼▼ Hotel Maritime Plaza LH
(514) 932-1411. **$129-$400.** 1155 rue Guy. Corner of boul Rene-Levesque; centre. Int corridors. **Pets:** Accepted.
SAVE ⊠ 🖬 🖭 🍽 ⮀

▼▼▼ Hotel Omni Mont-Royal LH 🐾
(514) 284-1110. **$159-$329.** 1050 rue Sherbrooke ouest. Corner of rue Peel. Int corridors. **Pets:** Medium. $50 one-time fee/room. Service with restrictions, supervision.
ASK ⊠ 🕿 🖬 🖭 ⮀ ⊠

CAA ▼▼▼ Hotel Travelodge Montreal Centre SH
(514) 874-9090. **$109-$139.** 50 boul Rene-Levesque ouest. Between rue Clark and St-Urbain; in Chinatown. Int corridors. **Pets:** Small. $15 daily fee/pet. Service with restrictions, supervision.
SAVE SÔ ⊠ 🖬 🖭 🍽

CAA ▼▼▼▼ InterContinental Montreal LH
(514) 987-9900. **$159-$349.** 360 rue St-Antoine ouest. Corner of rue St-Pierre. Int corridors. **Pets:** Small. $35 one-time fee/pet. Service with restrictions, crate.
SAVE ⊠ 🖬 🖭 🍽 ⮀ ⊠

▼▼▼ La Presidence Appartements De Luxe CO 🐾
(514) 842-9988. **$149-$229.** 505 rue Sherbrooke est. Between rue Berri and St-Hubert. Int corridors. **Pets:** Small. $25 one-time fee/room. Service with restrictions, crate.
ASK SÔ ⊠ 🖭 🍽 ⮀ ⊠

CAA ▼▼▼▼ Le Centre Sheraton LH
(514) 878-2000. **$269-$299.** 1201 boul Rene-Levesque ouest. Between rue Drummond and Stanley. Int corridors. **Pets:** Accepted.
SAVE SÔ ⊠ ⚷ 🖬 🖭 🍽 ⮀ ⊠

CAA ▼▼▼▼ Le Meridien Versailles-Montreal SH 🐾
(514) 933-8111. **$169-$285.** 1808 rue Sherbrooke ouest. Corner of rue St-Mathieu. Int corridors. **Pets:** $15 daily fee/pet. Designated rooms, service with restrictions, crate.
SAVE SÔ ⊠ 🖬 🖭 🍽

CAA ▼▼▼▼ Le Saint-Sulpice Hotel Montreal SH 🐾
(514) 288-1000. **$169-$459.** 414 rue St-Sulpice. Just n of rue St-Paul. Int corridors. **Pets:** Medium, other species. $40 one-time fee/room. Service with restrictions, supervision.
SAVE ⊠ 🖬 🖭 🍽 ⊠

[CAA] ♦♦♦ **Le Square Phillips Hotel & Suites** [SH]
(514) 393-1193. **$130-$179.** 1193 Place Phillips. Between rue Ste-Catherine and boul Rene-Levesque. Int corridors. **Pets:** Designated rooms, service with restrictions, supervision.
[SAVE] [S/D] ⊠ ▣ ☕ 🍴 🏊

[CAA] ♦♦♦♦ **Loews Hotel Vogue** [LH] 🐾
(514) 285-5555. **$152-$428.** 1425 rue de la Montagne. Between rue Ste-Catherine and boul de Maisonneuve. Int corridors. **Pets:** Large, other species. Designated rooms.
[SAVE] [S/D] ⊠ ▣

[CAA] ♦♦♦ **Marriott Residence Inn-Montreal Downtown** [SH]
(514) 982-6064. **$145-$425.** 2045 rue Peel. Between rue Sherbrooke and boul de Maisonneuve. Int corridors. **Pets:** Medium. $250 one-time fee/room. Service with restrictions, crate.
[SAVE] [S/D] ⊠ ▣ ☕ 🏊

[CAA] ♦♦♦ **Novotel Montreal Centre** [LH] 🐾
(514) 861-6000. **$137-$175.** 1180 rue de la Montagne. Between rue Ste-Catherine and boul Rene-Levesque. Int corridors. **Pets:** Service with restrictions, supervision.
[SAVE] [S/D] ⊠ ☕ 🍴 ✂

[CAA] ♦♦ **Quality Hotel Downtown Montreal** [SH]
(514) 849-1413. **$99-$169.** 3440 ave du Parc. Between rue Sherbrooke and Milton. Int corridors. **Pets:** Accepted.
[SAVE] [S/D] ⊠ ▣ ☕ 🍴

[CAA] ♦♦♦ **Residence Inn by Marriott Montreal Westmount** [SH] 🐾
(514) 935-9224. **$115-$169.** 2170 ave Lincoln. Just e of rue Atwater. Int corridors. **Pets:** Medium. $105 one-time fee/pet. Service with restrictions, supervision.
[SAVE] [S/D] ⊠ ♿ ▣ ☕ 🏊

♦♦♦♦ **The Ritz-Carlton, Montreal** [LH] 🐾
(514) 842-4212. **$198-$268.** 1228 rue Sherbrooke ouest. Corner de la Montagne. Int corridors. **Pets:** Other species. $150 one-time fee/room. Service with restrictions, supervision.
[A$K] [S/D] ⊠ 🍴 ✂

♦♦♦♦ **Sofitel Montreal** [SH]
(514) 285-9000. **$180-$460.** 1155 rue Sherbrooke ouest. Corner of rue Stanley. Int corridors. **Pets:** Small, other species. $20 daily fee/pet. Service with restrictions, crate.
[A$K] [S/D] ⊠ ▣ 🍴 ✂

♦♦♦ **XIX siecle Hotel Montreal** [SH]
(514) 985-0019. **$145-$275.** 262 rue St-Jacques ouest. Between rue St-Jean and rue St-Pierre. Int corridors. **Pets:** Other species. $50 one-time fee/room. Service with restrictions, crate.
[A$K] [S/D] ⊠ ▣ 🍴

POINTE-CLAIRE

[CAA] ♦♦ **Comfort Inn** [SH]
(514) 697-6210. **$122-$155.** 700 boul St-Jean. Hwy 40, exit 52, 0.3 km s. Int corridors. **Pets:** Designated rooms, service with restrictions, supervision.
[SAVE] [S/D] ⊠ ▣ ☕

[CAA] ♦♦♦ **Quality Suites Montreal Aeroport, Pointe-Claire** [SH]
(514) 426-5060. **$122-$209.** 6300 Rt Transcanadienne. Hwy 40, exit 52 eastbound, south side service road; westbound, follow signs for boul St-Jean sud and Hwy 40 est to access south side service road. Int corridors. **Pets:** Accepted.
[SAVE] [S/D] ⊠ ♿ ▣ ☕ 🍴

ROSEMERE

♦♦♦ **Hotel Le Rivage** [SH]
(450) 437-2171. **$79-$249.** 125 boul LaBelle. Hwy 15, exit 19, 1.4 km e on Rt 344, then 0.5 km s. Int corridors. **Pets:** Accepted.
⊠ ▣ ☕ 🏊

ST-LAURENT

♦♦♦ **Holiday Inn Montreal-Airport** [SH]
(514) 739-3391. **$130.** 6500 Cote-de-Liesse. Hwy 520, exit 5 eastbound on south side service road; exit westbound to rue Ness, follow signs for rue Hickmore and Hwy 520 E. Ext/int corridors. **Pets:** Other species. Service with restrictions, supervision.
⊠ ♿ ▣ ☕ 🍴 🏊 ✂

[CAA] ♦♦♦ **Quality Hotel Dorval** [SH]
(514) 731-7821. **$176.** 7700 Cote-de-Liesse. Hwy 520, exit 4 eastbound on south side service road; exit Montee-de-Liesse westbound. Int corridors. **Pets:** Accepted.
[SAVE] ⊠ ▣ ☕ 🍴 🏊 ✂

[CAA] ♦♦♦ **Ramada Montreal Airport Hotel** [SH]
(514) 733-8818. **$129-$169, 3 day notice.** 7300 Cote-de-Liesse. Hwy 520, exit 4 eastbound on south side service road; exit Montee-de-Liesse westbound. Int corridors. **Pets:** Service with restrictions, supervision.
[SAVE] [S/D] ⊠ ▣ ☕ 🍴 🏊

END METROPOLITAN AREA

MONT-TREMBLANT

[CAA] ♦♦♦ **Le Grand Lodge Mont-Tremblant** [SH]
(819) 425-2734. **$100-$440, 8 day notice.** 2396 rue Labelle. Jct Hwy 117 and 327, 1.5 km s. Int corridors. **Pets:** Small. $25 daily fee/room. Designated rooms, service with restrictions, supervision.
[SAVE] ⊠ ▣ ☕ 🍴 🏊 ✂

NORTH HATLEY

[CAA] ♦♦♦♦ **Auberge Hatley** [CI]
(819) 842-2451. **$290-$590, 14 day notice.** 325 Virgin Hill Rd. Hwy 55, exit 29, 11 km e on Rt 108. Int corridors. **Pets:** $30 deposit/pet, $30 daily fee/pet. Service with restrictions, supervision.
[SAVE] ⊠ 🍴 🏊 ✂

PASPEBIAC

♦♦♦ **Auberge Du Parc Inn** [SH]
(418) 752-3355. **$79-$165.** 68 boul Gerard D Levesque ouest. On Rt 132; centre. Ext corridors. **Pets:** Accepted.
⊠ 🍴 🏊 ✂ [AC]

PERCE

♦ **Au Pic de l'Aurore** [CA]
(418) 782-2151. **$59-$145.** 1 Rt 132. 2 km e from village. Ext corridors. **Pets:** Medium. Service with restrictions, supervision.
⊠ ▣ ☕ [AC]

♦♦♦ **Hotel La Normandie** [SH]
(418) 782-2112. **$79-$239.** 221 Rt 132 ouest. Centre. Int corridors. **Pets:** Medium. $50 one-time fee/room. Designated rooms, service with restrictions, crate.
⊠ ▣ ☕ 🍴 [AC]

▼▼▼▼ Hotel/Motel Le Mirage 🅼
(418) 782-5151. **$69-$158, 7 day notice.** 288 Rt 132 ouest. On Rt 132.
Ext corridors. **Pets:** Small. Service with restrictions, supervision.

⊠ 🖥 �

▼▼▼ Hotel Motel Manoir de Perce 🆂🅷
(418) 782-2022. **$65-$168.** 212 Rt 132. Centre. Ext/int corridors.
Pets: Small. $25 daily fee/room. Service with restrictions, supervision.

🆂 ⊠ 🖥 🍴

PINE HILL

🅲🅰🅰 ▼▼▼ ▼▼▼ Hotel du Lac Carling 🅻🅷
(450) 533-9211. **$225-$250, 14 day notice.** 2255 Rt 327 nord. 5 km n.
Int corridors. **Pets:** Accepted.

🆂🅰🆅🅴 🆂 ⊠ 🖥 🖵 🍴 ➡ ⊠

PORTNEUF

▼▼ Hotel Le Portneuvois 🆂🅷
(418) 286-6400. **$75-$85.** 101 rue Simeon-Delisle. Hwy 40, exit 261,
then 0.5 km s on rue Provencher. Int corridors. **Pets:** Accepted.

⊠ 🖥 🖵

QUÉBEC METROPOLITAN AREA

BEAUPORT

▼▼ Comfort Inn 🆂🅷
(418) 666-1226. **$90-$145.** 240 boul Ste-Anne. Hwy 440, exit Francois-
de-Laval. Int corridors. **Pets:** No service, supervision.

🅰🆂🅺 🆂 ⊠ 🖥 🖵

▼▼ Gite du Vieux-Bourg 🅱🅱
(418) 661-0116. **$75-$105, 15 day notice.** 492 ave Royale. Hwy 440,
exit Francois-de-Laval, just n, then 0.5 km e. Int corridors. **Pets:** Small,
dogs only. Service with restrictions, supervision.

🅰🆂🅺 ⊠ ➡

BEAUPRE

🅲🅰🅰 ▼▼▼ Hotel Val des Neiges 🅻🅷
(418) 827-5711. **$99-$179.** 201 rue Val-des-Neiges. Just off Hwy 360.
Int corridors. **Pets:** Accepted.

🆂🅰🆅🅴 🆂 ⊠ 🖥 🖵 🍴 ➡ ⊠

L'ANCIENNE-LORETTE

▼▼ Comfort Inn 🆂🅷
(418) 872-5900. **$82-$145.** 1255 boul Duplessis. Jct boul Duplessis and
Wilfrid-Hamel (Hwy 138). Int corridors. **Pets:** Designated rooms, no service, supervision.

🅰🆂🅺 🆂 ⊠ 🖥 🖵

LEVIS

▼▼ Comfort Inn 🆂🅷
(418) 835-5605. **$92-$165.** 10 du Vallon est. Hwy 20, exit 325S eastbound; exit 325 westbound. Int corridors. **Pets:** Medium. Designated
rooms, service with restrictions, supervision.

🅰🆂🅺 🆂 ⊠ 🖥 🖵

▼▼ Hotel Motel Bernieres 🆂🅷 🐾
(418) 831-3119. **$75-$132.** 535 rue Arena. Hwy 20, exit 311, just sw; in
St-Nicolas sector. Ext/int corridors. **Pets:** Medium. Crate.

🅰🆂🅺 🆂 ⊠ 🖥 🖵 🍴

QUEBEC

▼▼ Appartements La Pergola 🅲🅾
(418) 681-1428. **$65-$120, 10 day notice.** 405 boul Rene-Levesque
ouest. Between aves Moncton and des Erables. Int corridors.
Pets: Accepted.

🅰🆂🅺 🆂 🖥 🖵

🅲🅰🅰 ▼▼▼ Delta Quebec 🅻🅷
(418) 647-1717. **$104-$299.** 690 boul Rene-Levesque est. Just w of
boul Honore-Mercier. Int corridors. **Pets:** Large, other species. Designated rooms, service with restrictions, supervision.

🆂🅰🆅🅴 🆂 ⊠ 🖥 🖵 🍴 ➡ ⊠

🅲🅰🅰 ▼▼▼ ▼▼▼ Hilton Quebec 🅻🅷
(418) 647-2411. **$119-$379.** 1100 boul Rene-Levesque est. Corner of
ave Honore-Mercier. Int corridors. **Pets:** Small. Designated rooms, service with restrictions, supervision.

🆂🅰🆅🅴 ⊠ 🖥 🖵 🍴 ➡ ⊠

🅲🅰🅰 ▼▼▼ Hotel Quality Suites Quebec 🆂🅷
(418) 622-4244. **$130-$185.** 1600 rue Bouvier. Hwy 40, exit 312N
(Pierre-Bertrand nord), 2 km w of jct Rt 358. Int corridors. **Pets:** Other
species. Supervision.

🆂🅰🆅🅴 🆂 ⊠ 🖥 🖵

🅲🅰🅰 ▼▼▼ L'Hotel du Vieux Quebec 🆂🅷 🐾
(418) 692-1850. **$99-$255.** 1190 rue St-Jean. Corner of rue de l'Hotel-
Dieu. Int corridors. **Pets:** Other species. Designated rooms, service with
restrictions.

🆂🅰🆅🅴 ⊠ 🖥 🍴

🅲🅰🅰 ▼▼▼ ▼▼▼ Loews Le Concorde 🅻🅷
(418) 647-2222. **$124-$295.** 1225 Cours du General-de-Montcalm. Corner of Grande Allee est. Int corridors. **Pets:** Accepted.

🆂🅰🆅🅴 🆂 ⊠ 🖥 🖵 🍴 ➡ ⊠

ST-FERREOL-LES-NEIGES

🅲🅰🅰 ▼▼ Chalets Montmorency Condominiums 🅲🅾 🐾
(418) 826-2600. **$89-$129.** 1768 ave Royale. On Hwy 360. Ext corridors. **Pets:** Dogs only. $25 daily fee/pet. No service, supervision.

🆂🅰🆅🅴 🆂 ⊠ 🖥 🖵 ➡ ⊠

▼▼ Chalets-Village Mont-Sainte-Anne 🅲🅰
(418) 826-3331. **$895-$9250 (weekly), 60 day notice.** 1815 boul Les
Neiges. On north side of Hwy 360; village center. Ext corridors.
Pets: Other species. $100 one-time fee/room. No service, supervision.

🖥 🖵 ⊠ 🅰🅺

STE-FOY

▼▼ Comfort Inn de l'Aeroport 🆂🅷
(418) 872-5038. **$82-$105.** 7320 boul Wilfrid-Hamel. Hwy 138, 1.5 km
w of boul Duplessis. Int corridors. **Pets:** Very small, other species. Designated rooms, service with restrictions, supervision.

🅰🆂🅺 🆂 ⊠ 🖥 🖵

▼▼▼ Hotel Clarion Quebec 🅻🅷
(418) 653-4901. **$95-$179.** 3125 boul Hochelaga. Hwy 73, exit 136
(Hochelaga ouest). Int corridors. **Pets:** Accepted.

🅰🆂🅺 🆂 ⊠ 🖥 🖵 🍴 ➡ ⊠

ⒶⒶ ▼▼ **Hotel Universel** 🅂🄷
(418) 653-5250. **$94-$144.** 2300 chemin Ste-Foy. Hwy 73, exit 137, 2.3 km e on chemin des Quatre-Bourgeois. Ext/int corridors. **Pets:** Designated rooms, service with restrictions, supervision.
〔SAVE〕 🆂 ⊠ 🍴 🖵 🍴 🏊

▼ **Motel Oncle Sam** 🄼
(418) 872-1488. **$49-$99.** 7025 boul Wilfrid-Hamel. On Hwy 138 at jct boul Duplessis. Ext corridors. **Pets:** Designated rooms, service with restrictions, supervision.
⊠ 🍴 🖵 🏊

END METROPOLITAN AREA

RIMOUSKI

▼▼ **Comfort Inn** 🅂🄷
(418) 724-2500. **$100-$140.** 455 boul St-Germain ouest. On Rt 132. Int corridors. **Pets:** Service with restrictions, supervision.
〔ASK〕 🆂 ⊠ 🍴 🖵

RIVIERE-DU-LOUP

▼▼ **Comfort Inn** 🅂🄷
(418) 867-4162. **$88-$170.** 85 boul Cartier. Hwy 20, exit 507, just sw; Hwy 185, exit 96 (Fraserville). Int corridors. **Pets:** Small. Designated rooms, service with restrictions.
〔ASK〕 🆂 ⊠ 🖵

ROBERVAL

ⒶⒶ ▼▼▼▼ **Hotel Chateau Roberval** 🄻🄷
(418) 275-7511. **$89-$139.** 1225 boul Marcotte. On Hwy 169; centre. Int corridors. **Pets:** Small. Service with restrictions, crate.
〔SAVE〕 ⊠ 🍴 🖵 🍴 🏊 ✕

ROUYN-NORANDA

▼▼ **Comfort Inn** 🅂🄷
(819) 797-1313. **$93-$116.** 1295 rue Lariviere. On Rt 117, 4 km s from town centre. Int corridors. **Pets:** Accepted.
〔ASK〕 ⊠ 🍴 🖵

▼ **Motel Mistral** 🄼
(819) 762-0884. **$90-$110.** 903 rue Lariviere. On Rt 117, 2 km s from town centre. Ext/int corridors. **Pets:** Accepted.
⊠ 🍴 🍴

ST-ANTOINE-DE-TILLY

▼▼▼▼ **Manoir de Tilly** 🄲🄸
(418) 886-2407. **$199-$340, 3 day notice.** 3854 chemin de Tilly. Jct Hwy 20, exit 291, 8.5 km n on Rt 273; centre. Int corridors. **Pets:** Accepted.
⊠ 🍴 ✕

ST-FAUSTIN-LAC-CARRE

▼▼ **Motel sur la Colline** 🄼
(819) 688-2102. **$70-$107, 15 day notice.** 357 Rt 117. On Rt 117, 4 km n of exit for city. Ext/int corridors. **Pets:** Medium. $15 daily fee/pet. Service with restrictions, supervision.
〔ASK〕 🆂 ⊠ 🍴 🖵 🏊

ST-FELICIEN

▼▼▼ **Hotel du Jardin** 🄻🄷
(418) 679-8422. **$95-$190.** 1400 boul du Jardin. On Hwy 167. Int corridors. **Pets:** Accepted.
〔ASK〕 ⊠ 🍴 🖵 🍴 🏊 ✕

ST-HONORE

▼ **Motel Jasper** 🄼
(418) 497-2322. **$62-$72.** 657 Rt 185. On Rt 185. Ext corridors. **Pets:** Accepted.
〔ASK〕 🆂 ⊠ 🍴

ST-HYACINTHE

▼▼▼▼ **Hotel des Seigneurs Saint-Hyacinthe** 🄻🄷
(450) 774-3810. **$160-$180.** 1200 rue Johnson. Hwy 20, exit 130S, just e on Gauvin St from boul Laframboise. Int corridors. **Pets:** Designated rooms, service with restrictions, crate.
〔ASK〕 🆂 ⊠ 🍴 🖵 🍴 🏊 ✕

ST-JEAN-PORT-JOLI

▼▼ **Auberge du Faubourg** 🄼
(418) 598-6455. **$89-$105, 10 day notice.** 280 ave de Gaspe ouest (Rt 132). 2.4 km w on Rt 132 from jct Rt 204; Hwy 20, exit 414. Ext corridors. **Pets:** Small, other species. $15 daily fee/pet. Service with restrictions, crate.
〔ASK〕 ⊠ 🍴 🖵 🍴 🏊 ✕ 🐾

ST-JEAN-SUR-RICHELIEU

▼▼ **Comfort Inn** 🅂🄷
(450) 359-4466. **$89-$149.** 700 rue Gadbois. Hwy 35, exit 9, e on rue Pierre-Caisse. Int corridors. **Pets:** Accepted.
〔ASK〕 🆂 ⊠ 🍴 🏊

▼▼ **Hotel Relais Gouverneur St-Jean-sur-Richelieu** 🅂🄷
(450) 348-7376. **$85-$89, 30 day notice.** 725 boul du Seminaire nord. Hwy 35, exit 7. Int corridors. **Pets:** Accepted.
〔ASK〕 ⊠ 🍴 🖵 🍴 🏊

ST-LIBOIRE

▼▼ **Econo Lodge** 🅂🄷
(450) 793-4444. **$83-$117.** 110 Rang Charlotte. Hwy 20, exit 147, just s. Int corridors. **Pets:** Accepted.
〔ASK〕 🆂 ⊠ 🍴 🖵 🍴 🏊

SALABERRY-DE-VALLEYFIELD

▼▼▼ **Hotel Plaza Valleyfield** 🄻🄷
(450) 373-1990. **$109-$114.** 40 ave du Centenaire. Corner of rue St-Laurent; centre. Int corridors. **Pets:** Accepted.
⊠ 🍴 🖵 🍴 🏊 ✕

SEPT-ILES

▼▼ **Comfort Inn** 🅂🄷
(418) 968-6005. **$99-$116.** 854 boul Laure. 4.5 km w on Rt 138. Int corridors. **Pets:** Small. Designated rooms, service with restrictions, supervision.
〔ASK〕 🆂 ⊠ 🍴

SHAWINIGAN

▼▼ **Auberge Escapade Inn** 🅂🄷
(819) 539-6911. **$73-$145.** 3383 rue Garnier. Hwy 55, exit 217, then 0.5 km n on Rt 351. Ext/int corridors. **Pets:** Small, dogs only. $7 daily fee/pet. Designated rooms, service with restrictions, supervision.
⊠ 🍴 🍴

ⒶⒶ ▼▼▼ **Auberge Gouverneur & Convention Center Shawinigan** 🅂🄷
(819) 537-6000. **$150-$175.** 1100 Promenade-du-St-Maurice. Hwy 55 N, exit 211, 4.4 km n on Hwy 153, follow signs. Int corridors. **Pets:** No service, supervision.
〔SAVE〕 🆂 ⊠ 🍴 🖵 🍴 🏊 ✕

(CAA) ▼▼▼▼ **Comfort Inn & Suites** SH
(819) 536-2000. **$89-$165, 30 day notice.** 500 boul du Capitaine. Hwy 55, exit 211, 4.4 km n on Hwy 153, then 2 km s on Rt 157. Int corridors. **Pets:** Designated rooms, no service, supervision.
SAVE S✪ ✕ 🛏 💻

SHAWINIGAN-SUD

▼ **Motel Safari** M
(819) 536-2664. **$85.** 4500 12ieme ave. Hwy 55, exit 211, 4.4 km n on Hwy 153, then 6.6 km s on Rt 157. Ext/int corridors. **Pets:** Accepted.
A$K S✪ ✕ 🛏 ✕

SHERBROOKE

▼▼ **Comfort Inn** SH
(819) 564-4400. **$86-$108.** 4295 boul Bourque. Hwy 410, exit 4, 1.5 km w on Rt 112. Ext/int corridors. **Pets:** Small. Designated rooms, service with restrictions, supervision.
A$K S✪ ✕

(CAA) ▼▼▼▼ **Delta Sherbrooke Hotel and Conference Centre** LH
(819) 822-1989. **$99-$149.** 2685 rue King ouest. Hwy 410, exit 4E, 1 km e on Rt 112. Int corridors. **Pets:** Accepted.
SAVE ✕ 🛏 💻 🍴 ➴ ✕

STE-ANNE-DES-MONTS

(CAA) ▼▼▼ **Motel Beaurivage** M
(418) 763-2291. **$55-$160.** 245 1ere Ave ouest. Just off Rt 132. Ext/int corridors. **Pets:** Accepted.
SAVE ✕ 🛏 💻 🍴 AC

STE-MARTHE

▼▼▼ **Auberge des Gallant** CI
(450) 459-4241. **$175-$295, 14 day notice.** 1171 chemin St-Henri. 8.5 km w on chemin St-Henri from Hwy 201. Int corridors. **Pets:** Accepted.
✕ 💻 🍴 ➴ ✕

THETFORD MINES

▼▼ **Comfort Inn** SH
(418) 338-0171. **$105-$115.** 123 boul Smith sud. On Rt 112. Int corridors. **Pets:** Other species. Service with restrictions, crate.
A$K S✪ ✕ 🛏

TROIS-RIVIERES

▼▼ **Comfort Inn** SH
(819) 371-3566. **$94-$100.** 6255 rue Corbeil. Hwy 55, exit 183 (boul Jean XXIII), 2 km n of Laviolette Bridge, then 0.5 km e. Int corridors. **Pets:** Designated rooms, supervision.
A$K S✪ ✕ 🛏 💻

(CAA) ▼▼▼ **Days Inn** SH
(819) 377-4444. **$80-$160.** 3155 boul St-Jean. Hwy 55, exit 183 (boul Jean XXIII), 0.5 km w, then 0.4 km n. Int corridors. **Pets:** $20 daily fee/pet. Service with restrictions, supervision.
SAVE S✪ ✕ 🛏 💻

▼▼▼ **Delta Trois-Rivieres Hotel and Conference Center** LH 🐾
(819) 376-1991. **$92.** 1620 rue Notre-Dame. Corner of rue St-Roch; centre. Int corridors. **Pets:** $30 one-time fee/room. Service with restrictions, supervision.
✕ 💻 🍴 ➴ ✕

▼▼▼ **Hotel Du Roy Trois-Rivieres** SH
(819) 379-3232. **$70-$95.** 3600 boul Royal. On Hwy 138, 2 km e of Pont Laviolette and jct Hwy 55. Ext/int corridors. **Pets:** Other species. $20 deposit/room. Designated rooms, service with restrictions, supervision.
A$K ✕ 🛏 💻 🍴 ➴

VAL-D'OR

(CAA) ▼▼▼ **Comfort Inn** SH
(819) 825-9360. **$89-$101.** 1665 3ieme ave. In town centre. Int corridors. **Pets:** Accepted.
SAVE S✪ ✕ 🛏 💻

▼▼▼ **Hotel Forestel** LH
(819) 825-5660. **$80-$100.** 1001 3 ieme Ave est. On Rt 117 N. Int corridors. **Pets:** Service with restrictions, supervision.
A$K S✪ ✕ 🛏 💻 🍴 ➴

▼▼▼ **Hotel-Motel Prelude** SH
(819) 825-0090. **$83-$89.** 1159 3ieme Ave. On Rt 117 N; in town centre,. Ext/int corridors. **Pets:** No service, supervision.
A$K S✪ ✕ 🛏 💻

▼▼▼ **Motel L'Escale Hotel Suite** SH
(819) 824-2711. **$90-$120.** 1100 rue L'Escale. In town centre. Ext/int corridors. **Pets:** Large, dogs only. Designated rooms, service with restrictions, supervision.
✕ 🛏 💻 🍴

SASKATCHEWAN

CARONPORT

▼▼ ▼▼ The Pilgrim Inn SH
(306) 756-5002. $77. Hwy 1 W. Jct Main Access; on Trans-Canada Hwy 1. Int corridors. Pets: Designated rooms, service with restrictions, supervision.
ASK SD X 🖅 🖵

ESTEVAN

CAA ▼▼▼▼ Perfect Inns & Suites SH
(306) 634-8585. $89-$99. 134 2nd Ave. Just n of jct Hwy 39 E and 2nd Ave. Int corridors. Pets: Accepted.
SAVE X 🖅 🖵

FOAM LAKE

▼▼ La Vista Motel M
(306) 272-3341. $60, 30 day notice. Jct Hwy 16 & 310. On Hwy 16. Int corridors. Pets: Accepted.
X 🖅 🖵

KINDERSLEY

CAA ▼▼ ▼▼ Best Western Westridge Inn SH
(306) 463-4687. $90, 7 day notice. 100 12 Ave NW. Jct of Hwy 7 and 21. Ext/int corridors. Pets: Medium. Service with restrictions, supervision.
SAVE SD X 🖅 🖵 🍽

MOOSE JAW

CAA ▼▼ Capone's Hideaway Motel M
(306) 692-6422. $63-$78. 1 Main St N. Jct Manitoba St E. Ext corridors. Pets: Dogs only. Designated rooms, supervision.
SAVE SD X 🖅 🖵

▼▼ ▼▼ Comfort Inn SH
(306) 692-2100. $92-$150. 155 Thatcher Dr W. Just w of jct Main St. Int corridors. Pets: Other species. $15 daily fee/pet. Designated rooms, service with restrictions, supervision.
ASK SD X 🖅 🖵

▼▼ ▼▼ Days Inn SH
(306) 691-5777. $100. 1720 Main St N. From jct Trans-Canada Hwy 1, just s. Int corridors. Pets: Medium. $10 daily fee/pet. Designated rooms, service with restrictions, supervision.
ASK SD X 🖅 🖵 🏊 X

▼▼ ▼▼ Heritage Inn SH
(306) 693-7550. $99-$100. 1590 Main St N. 1.5 km s of jct Trans-Canada Hwy 1 and 2; access from Hwy 2 via Thatcher Dr. Int corridors. Pets: Accepted.
ASK SD X 🖅 🖵 🍽 🏊

CAA ▼▼ ▼▼ Prairie Oasis Motel M
(306) 693-8888. $72-$75. 955 Thatcher Dr E. Just s of jct Trans-Canada Hwy 1 and Thatcher Dr E. Ext corridors. Pets: Service with restrictions, crate.
SAVE X 🖅 🖵 🏊 X

▼▼ ▼▼ Super 8 Motel-Moose Jaw M
(306) 692-8888. $72-$92. 1706 Main St N. 1.5 km s of jct Trans-Canada Hwy 1; access from Hwy 2 via Thatcher Dr. Int corridors. Pets: Other species. $15 one-time fee/room. Designated rooms, service with restrictions, supervision.
ASK SD X 🖅 🖅

NORTH BATTLEFORD

▼▼ Super 8 Motel SH
(306) 446-8888. $72-$78. 1006 Hwy 16 Bypass. 0.5 km nw of jct Hwy 16. Int corridors. Pets: $10 daily fee/room. Service with restrictions, supervision.
SD X 🖅

▼▼ ▼▼ Tropical Inn SH
(306) 446-4700. $90-$95. 1001 Hwy 16 Bypass. Corner of Battleford Rd and Hwy 16 Bypass. Int corridors. Pets: Accepted.
ASK X 🖅 🖵 🍽 🏊 X

PRINCE ALBERT

▼▼ ▼▼ Comfort Inn SH
(306) 763-4466. $90-$100. 3863 2nd Ave W. 2.3 km s at jct Hwy 2 and Marquis Rd. Int corridors. Pets: Other species. Service with restrictions, crate.
ASK SD X 🖅 🖵

▼▼ ▼▼ Super 8 SH
(306) 953-0088. $74-$79. 4444 2nd Ave W. Just s of jct Hwy 2 and Marquis Rd. Int corridors. Pets: Small. Designated rooms, service with restrictions, supervision.
ASK SD X

▼▼ ▼▼ Travelodge Prince Albert SH 🐾
(306) 764-6441. $68-$87. 3551 2nd Ave W. 2.2 km s at jct Hwy 2 and Marquis Rd. Ext/int corridors. Pets: Other species. Service with restrictions, supervision.
ASK SD X 🖅 🖵 🍽

REGINA

CAA ▼▼ ▼▼ Comfort Inn SH
(306) 789-5522. $91-$106. 3221 E Eastgate Dr. Trans-Canada Hwy 1, 2 km e of Ring Rd, at eastern approach to Regina. Int corridors. Pets: Accepted.
SAVE SD X 🖅 🖵

▼▼▼▼ Country Inn & Suites By Carlson SH
(306) 789-9117. $111-$124, 3 day notice. 3321 Eastgate Bay. Trans-Canada Hwy 1, 2 km e of Ring Rd, at eastern approach to city. Int corridors. Pets: Medium, other species. Designated rooms, service with restrictions, crate.
ASK SD X 🔊 🖅 🖵

▼▼ ▼▼ Days Inn SH
(306) 522-3297. $99-$135, 30 day notice. 3875 Eastgate Dr. Trans-Canada Hwy 1, exit Prince of Wales Dr, at eastern approach to city. Int corridors. Pets: Accepted.
ASK SD X 🖅 🖵 🏊

▼▼▼▼ Delta Regina LH
(306) 525-5255. $115. 1919 Saskatchewan Dr. At Rose St; centre. Int corridors. Pets: Other species. $35 one-time fee/room. Service with restrictions, supervision.
X 🖅 🖵 🍽 🏊 X

CAA ▼▼ ▼▼ Howard Johnson SH 🐾
(306) 584-8800. $120-$141. 4255 Albert St S. 1.25 km n of jct Trans-Canada Hwy 1 and Albert St (Hwy 6). Ext/int corridors. Pets: Service with restrictions, crate.
SAVE SD X 🖅 🖵 🍽 🏊

▼▼ ▼▼ ▼▼ Radisson Plaza Hotel Saskatchewan LH
(306) 522-7691. **$128-$148.** 2125 Victoria Ave. Victoria Ave at Scarth St; centre. Int corridors. **Pets:** $35 one-time fee/room. Designated rooms, service with restrictions, crate.
[SAVE] [X] [&M] [🖃] [💻] [¶] [⊠]

▼▼ ▼▼ Ramada Hotel & Convention Centre LH 🐾
(306) 569-1666. **$96-$190.** 1818 Victoria Ave. Victoria Ave and Broad St; centre of downtown. Int corridors. **Pets:** Other species. $12 one-time fee/pet. Service with restrictions, supervision.
[ASK] [🔊] [X] [🖃] [💻] [¶] [⊇] [⊠]

▼▼ ▼▼ ▼▼ Regina Inn Hotel & Conference Centre LH
(306) 525-6767. **$99-$109.** 1975 Broad St. Jct Victoria Ave; centre of downtown. Int corridors. **Pets:** $20 one-time fee/room. Designated rooms, service with restrictions, supervision.
[SAVE] [X] [🖃] [💻] [¶]

▼▼ ▼▼ ▼▼ Sandman Hotel Suites and Spa SH 🐾
(306) 757-2444. **$119-$199.** 1800 Victoria Ave E. Just e of jct Ring Rd. Int corridors. **Pets:** Other species. $10 daily fee/room. Supervision.
[ASK] [🔊] [X] [👁] [🖃] [💻] [¶] [⊇]

▼▼ ▼▼ ▼▼ Travelodge Regina East SH
(306) 565-0455. **$80-$109.** 1110 Victoria Ave E. Trans-Canada Hwy 1, just w of Ring Rd, at eastern approach to city. Int corridors. **Pets:** Accepted.
[SAVE] [🔊] [X] [🖃] [💻] [⊇]

SASKATOON

▼▼ ▼▼ ▼▼ Best Western Inn & Suites SH
(306) 244-5552. **$80-$125, 14 day notice.** 1715 Idylwyld Dr N. 2.6 km n on Hwy 11 (Idylwyld Dr). Ext/int corridors. **Pets:** Designated rooms, service with restrictions, supervision.
[SAVE] [🔊] [X] [🖃] [💻] [¶] [⊠]

▼▼ ▼▼ Colonial Square Motel & Suites SH 🐾
(306) 343-1676. **$79-$89.** 1301 8th St E. Just w of Cumberland St. Ext/int corridors. **Pets:** Small. $5 daily fee/room. Designated rooms, service with restrictions, supervision.
[SAVE] [🔊] [X] [🖃] [💻]

▼▼ ▼▼ Comfort Inn SH
(306) 934-1122. **$75-$135.** 2155 Northridge Dr. 3 km n; just ne of jct Hwy 11 (Idylwyld Dr) and Circle Dr. Int corridors. **Pets:** Medium, other species. Service with restrictions, supervision.
[SAVE] [🔊] [X] [&M] [🖃] [💻]

▼▼ ▼▼ Country Inn & Suites By Carlson SH
(306) 934-3900. **$88.** 617 Cynthia St. Just w of jct Hwy 11 (Idylwyld Dr) and Circle Dr. Int corridors. **Pets:** Accepted.
[ASK] [🔊] [X] [&M] [🖃] [💻]

▼▼ ▼▼ ▼▼ Delta Bessborough LH 🐾
(306) 244-5521. **$109-$199.** 601 Spadina Crescent E. At 21st St E; centre of downtown. Int corridors. **Pets:** Other species. Service with restrictions, crate.
[ASK] [🔊] [X] [🖃] [💻] [¶] [⊇] [⊠]

▼▼ ▼▼ Heritage Inn SH
(306) 665-8121. **$87-$89.** 102 Cardinal Crescent. Jct Circle and Airport drs. Int corridors. **Pets:** Accepted.
[ASK] [🔊] [X] [🖃] [💻] [¶] [⊇]

▼▼ ▼▼ ▼▼ Holiday Inn Express Hotel & Suites Saskatoon SH
(306) 384-8844. **$94-$159.** 315 Idylwyld Dr N. Jct 25th St W. Int corridors. **Pets:** Accepted.
[ASK] [🔊] [X] [&M] [🖃] [💻] [⊇]

▼▼ Quality Hotel SH
(306) 244-2311. **$99-$119.** 90 22nd St E. Just e of jct Hwy 11 (Idylwyld Dr), 1st and 22nd sts. Int corridors. **Pets:** Small, other species. $10 one-time fee/room. Designated rooms, service with restrictions, crate.
[ASK] [🔊] [X] [🖃] [💻] [¶] [⊇] [⊠]

▼▼ ▼▼ ▼▼ Radisson Hotel Saskatoon SH
(306) 665-3322. **$125-$160.** 405 20th St E. At 4th Ave S; centre. Int corridors. **Pets:** Accepted.
[SAVE] [🔊] [X] [&M] [🖃] [💻] [¶] [⊇] [⊠]

▼▼ ▼▼ Ramada Hotel & Golf Dome LH
(306) 665-6500. **$95, 3 day notice.** 806 Idylwyld Dr N. 4 km s of jct Circle Dr. Int corridors. **Pets:** Medium, other species. $10 daily fee/room. Designated rooms, service with restrictions, supervision.
[ASK] [🔊] [X] [🖃] [💻] [¶] [⊇]

▼▼ ▼▼ Sandman Hotel LH
(306) 477-4844. **$129-$139.** 310 Circle Dr W. Jct Ave C N. Int corridors. **Pets:** Accepted.
[ASK] [🔊] [X] [🖃] [💻] [¶] [⊇]

▼▼ ▼▼ ▼▼ Saskatoon Inn Hotel & Conference Centre LH
(306) 242-1440. **$115-$120.** 2002 Airport Dr. Jct Circle and Airport drs. Int corridors. **Pets:** Designated rooms, service with restrictions, supervision.
[SAVE] [🔊] [X] [🖃] [💻] [¶] [⊇]

▼▼ ▼▼ Saskatoon Travelodge Hotel SH
(306) 242-8881. **$109-$179.** 106 Circle Dr W. 3 km n, then just w of jct Hwy 11 (Idylwyld Dr). Int corridors. **Pets:** Accepted.
[SAVE] [🔊] [X] [🖃] [💻] [¶] [⊇] [⊠]

▼▼ ▼▼ ▼▼ Sheraton Cavalier SH
(306) 652-6770. **$135-$174.** 612 Spadina Crescent E. At 21st St E; centre of downtown. Int corridors. **Pets:** Accepted.
[ASK] [🔊] [X] [🖃] [¶] [⊇] [⊠]

▼▼ ▼▼ Super 8 SH
(306) 384-8989. **$85-$119.** 706 Circle Dr E. 2 km e of jct Hwy 11 (Idylwyld Dr). Ext/int corridors. **Pets:** Other species. $5 one-time fee/room. Service with restrictions, crate.
[ASK] [🔊] [X] [🖃] [💻]

▼▼ Thriftlodge M
(306) 244-2191. **$77-$99.** 1825 Idylwyld Dr N. Just s of Cirlce Dr N. Ext corridors. **Pets:** Small, dogs only. $5 daily fee/pet. Designated rooms, service with restrictions, supervision.
[SAVE] [🔊] [X] [🖃] [💻]

SHAUNAVON

▼▼ Hidden Hilten Motel M
(306) 297-4166. **$50-$70.** 352 5th St W. 0.5 km e from jct Hwy 13 and 37, just n. Ext corridors. **Pets:** No service, crate.
[ASK] [🔊] [X] [🖃] [💻]

SWIFT CURRENT

▼▼ Caravel Motel M
(306) 773-8385. **$42-$60.** 705 N Service Rd E. Just e of Central Ave. Ext corridors. **Pets:** Accepted.
[SAVE] [🔊] [X] [🖃] [💻]

▼▼ ▼▼ Comfort Inn SH
(306) 778-3994. **$90-$112.** 1510 S Service Rd E. Trans-Canada Hwy 1, just w of 22nd Ave NE. Int corridors. **Pets:** Large. Designated rooms, service with restrictions, supervision.
[ASK] [🔊] [X] [🖃] [💻]

▼▼ ▼▼ Rodeway Inn Motel SH
(306) 773-4664. **$52-$59.** 1200 S Service Rd E. Trans-Canada Hwy 1, just w of 22nd Ave NE. Ext/int corridors. **Pets:** Supervision.
[SAVE] [X] [🖃] [¶]

Ⓐ ◈ **Safari Motel** Ⓜ 🐾
(306) 773-4608. **$48-$60, 3 day notice.** 810 S Service Rd E. 1 km w of jct Hwy 1 and 4. Ext corridors. **Pets:** Designated rooms, supervision.
[SAVE] [S] [X] [⊟] [⊡]

◈◈ **Super 8 Motel** [SH]
(306) 778-6088. **$78-$94, 30 day notice.** 405 N Service Rd E. Just e of Central Ave. Int corridors. **Pets:** $5 daily fee/pet. Designated rooms, service with restrictions, supervision.
[ASK] [S] [X] [⊟] [⊡] [≈]

◈◈ **Swift Current Travelodge** Ⓜ
(306) 773-3101. **$75-$95.** Trans-Canada Hwy 1 E. Just e of Central Ave, on North Service Rd. Ext corridors. **Pets:** Accepted.
[ASK] [S] [X] [⊟] [⊡] [≈]

Ⓐ ◈ **Westwind Motel** Ⓜ
(306) 773-1441. **$52-$64.** 155 N Service Rd W. Trans-Canada Hwy 1, 0.5 km w of Central Ave. Ext corridors. **Pets:** Medium. Designated rooms, service with restrictions, supervision.
[SAVE] [S] [X] [⊟] [⊓] [≈]

WEYBURN

Ⓐ ◈◈ **Perfect Inns & Suites** Ⓜ
(306) 842-2691. **$57-$82.** 238 Sims Ave. 0.5 km w of jct Hwy 35 and 39. Ext/int corridors. **Pets:** $2 daily fee/room. Designated rooms, service with restrictions, supervision.
[SAVE] [X] [⊟] [⊡]

◈◈ **Weyburn Inn** [SH]
(306) 842-6543. **$80-$145.** 5 Government Rd. Centre. Ext/int corridors. **Pets:** Small. Designated rooms, service with restrictions.
[ASK] [S] [X] [⊟] [⊡] [⊓] [≈] [X]

YORKTON

◈◈◈ **Comfort Inn & Suites** [SH]
(306) 783-0333. **$74-$89.** 22 Dracup Ave. Just w of jct Hwy 9, 10 and 16 (Yellowhead Hwy). Int corridors. **Pets:** Medium, other species. $5 daily fee/room. Designated rooms, service with restrictions, supervision.
[ASK] [S] [X] [⊟] [⊡] [≈]

◈ **Howard Johnson Inn** [SH]
(306) 783-6581. **$68-$90.** 207 Broadway St E. Jct Hwy 9, 10 and 16 (Yellowhead Hwy). Ext/int corridors. **Pets:** Accepted.
[ASK] [S] [X] [⊟] [⊡] [⊓] [≈]

◈◈ **Travelodge Yorkton** [SH]
(306) 783-6571. **$109-$179.** 345 Broadway W. West end of town, just e of Agriplex (Hwy 10A). Ext/int corridors. **Pets:** Accepted.
[ASK] [S] [X] [⊟] [⊡] [⊓] [≈]

YUKON TERRITORY

DAWSON CITY

▼▼ Klondike Kates Cabins & Restaurant M
(867) 993-6527. $85-$135. 1103 3rd Ave & King St. Downtown.
Pets: Other species. $10 one-time fee/room. Service with restrictions,
supervision.
⊠ 🔌 💻 🐾

(AA) ▼▼▼ Westmark Inn Dawson City M
(867) 993-5542. $149. 5th St & Harper. At 5th and Harper sts; down-
town. Ext/int corridors. Pets: Accepted.
SAVE ⊠ 💻 🍴 🐾

HAINES JUNCTION

(AA) ▼▼▼ Alcan Motor Inn M
(867) 634-2371. $95-$130. Jct of Alaska and Haines hwys (1 and 3).
Ext corridors. Pets: Other species. $7.50 daily fee/pet. Designated rooms,
service with restrictions, supervision.
SAVE 🐾 ⊠ 🔌 💻

WHITEHORSE

(AA) ▼▼▼ High Country Inn SH ❀
(867) 667-4471. $99-$199, 3 day notice. 4051 4th Ave. 0.6 km e of
Main St. Int corridors. Pets: $15 daily fee/pet. Designated rooms, service
with restrictions, crate.
SAVE ⊠ 🔌 💻 🍴

(AA) ▼▼ The Town and Mountain Hotel SH
(867) 668-7644. $69-$89. 401 Main St. Downtown. Int corridors.
Pets: Other species. $10 daily fee/pet. Service with restrictions.
SAVE 🐾 ⊠ 🔌 💻 🍴 🐾

(AA) ▼▼▼ Westmark Whitehorse Hotel & Conference
Centre SH
(867) 393-9700. $129-$159. 201 Wood St. At 2nd Ave; centre. Int
corridors. Pets: Accepted.
SAVE ⊠ 🐾 🚭 🔌 💻 🍴 🐾

CAMPGROUNDS

United States
Canada

UNITED STATES

Alaska

ANCHORAGE — ANCHORAGE RV PARK (907) 338-7275. **2P $30-$39, XP $2.** 1200 N Muldoon Rd, 99506. SR 1, exit Muldoon Rd N, 0.5 mi nw.

Alabama

OZARK — OZARK TRAVEL PARK (334) 774-3219. **2P $26, XP $1.** 2414 N US 231, 36360. 3 mi n on US 231 N at MM 47.

PELHAM — BIRMINGHAM SOUTH CAMPGROUND. (205) 664-8832. **2P $30, XP $2.** 222 Hwy 33, 35124. I-65, exit 242, 0.5 mi w on CR 52, then 0.3 mi n.

Arizona

AMADO — DEANZA TRAILS RV RESORT. (520) 398-8628. **2P $23, XP $1-$2.** 2869 E Frontage Rd, 85645. I-19, exit 48, just e, then 1.6 mi s. (HC 65, Box 381, TUMACACORI, 85640).

APACHE JUNCTION — SUPERSTITION SUNRISE LUXURY RV RESORT. (480) 986-4524. **2P $35, XP $5. (no credit cards).** 702 S Meridian Rd, 85220. US 60, exit 193 (Signal Butte Rd), 0.4 mi n to Southern, 1 mi e, then 0.5 mi n.

BENSON — BUTTERFIELD RV RESORT. (520) 586-4400. **2P $20-$23, XP $2.** 251 S Ocotillo Ave, 85602. I-10, exit 304 (Ocotillo Ave), 0.6 mi s.

BENSON — COCHISE TERRACE RV RESORT. (520) 586-0600. **2P $15-$28, XP $2.** 1030 S Barrel Cactus Ridge, 85602. I-10, exit 302, 1 mi s on SR 90, then just w.

BENSON — PATO BLANCO LAKES RV PARK. (520) 586-8966. **2P $25-$32, XP $2.** 635 E Pearl St, 85602. I-10, exit 306, just s, 0.7 mi w on Frontage Rd, then 0.4 mi n on County Rd.

BENSON — SAN PEDRO TERRITORY MOBILE HOME & RV RESORT. (520) 586-9546. **2P $24, XP $2.** 1110 S Hwy 80, Box 1, 85602. I-10, exit 304 (Ocotillo Ave), 0.5 mi s, 1 mi e on 4th St, then 1.3 mi se.

CASA GRANDE — FIESTA GRANDE-RV RESORT (520) 836-7222. **2P $30, XP $2.** 1511 E Florence Blvd, 85222. I-10, exit 194, 2 mi w.

CASA GRANDE — PALM CREEK GOLF AND RV RESORT. (520) 421-7000. **2P $22-$39, XP $5.** 1110 N Henness Rd, 85222. I-10, exit 194, 1 mi w, then just n.

HUACHUCA CITY — TOMBSTONE TERRITORIES RV PARK (520) 457-2584. **2P $28-$29, XP $1.** 2111 E Hwy 82, 85616. Jct SR 90, 7.7 mi e on SR 82, between MM 59 and 60.

MESA — GOOD LIFE RV RESORT (480) 832-4990. **2P $20-$32, XP $3.** 3403 E Main St, 85213. US 60, exit 184 (Val Vista Dr), 2 mi n, then just w. Small pets allowed.

MESA — MESA SPIRIT RV RESORT (480) 832-1770. **2P $18-$45, XP $4.** 3020 E Main St, 85213. US 60, exit 184 (Val Vista Dr), 2 mi n to Main St, then 0.8 mi w.

MESA — VALLE DEL ORO RV RESORT. (480) 984-1146. **2P $18-$35, XP $5. (no credit cards).** 1452 S Ellsworth Rd, 85208. US 60, exit 191, just n. Small pets allowed.

PICACHO — PICACHO PEAK RV RESORT (520) 466-7841. **2P $23, XP $2.** 17065 E Peak Ln, 85241. I-10, exit 219, 1.3 mi s on frontage road. (PO Box 1100, RED ROCK, 85245).

SHOW LOW — VOYAGER AT JUNIPER RIDGE (928) 532-3456. **2P $25, XP $2.** 1993 Juniper Ridge Resort, 85901. Jct US 60, 7.3 mi n on SR 77 to White Mountain Lake Rd, then 3 mi e.

SIERRA VISTA — PUEBLO DEL SOL RV RESORT. (520) 378-0213. **2P $31, XP $5.** 3400 Resort Dr, 85650. Jct SR 90, 4 mi s on SR 92, just e on Canyon de Flores.

SUN CITY/SUN CITY WEST — PARADISE RV RESORT (623) 977-0344. **2P $25-$37, XP $2. (no credit cards).** 10950 W Union Hills Dr, 85373. Loop 101, 3.8 mi w. Small pets allowed.

TUCSON — BEAUDRY RV RESORT. (520) 239-1300. **2P $30-$58.** 5151 S Country Club, 85706. I-10, exit 264B (Palo Verde and Irvington), just n to Irvington, 0.5 mi w, then just s.

TUCSON — VOYAGER RV RESORT (520) 574-5000. **2P $26-$40, XP $2.** 8701 S Kolb Rd, 85706. I-10, exit 270, 0.7 mi s.

YUMA — BONITA MESA RV RESORT. (928) 342-2999. **2P $30, XP $2-$3. (no credit cards).** 9400 N Frontage Rd, 85365. I-8, exit 12 (Fortuna Rd), just n, then 1.6 mi w.

YUMA — COCOPAH RV & GOLF RESORT. (928) 343-9300. **2P $32, XP $2.** 6800 Strand Ave, 85364. I-8, exit Winterhaven/4th Ave, 0.5 mi s on 4th Ave, 2.4 mi w on 1st St, just s on Ave C, 1.4 mi w on Riverside, then 0.9 mi nw.

YUMA — SUN VISTA RV RESORT (928) 726-8920. **2P $34, XP $3.** 7201 E 32nd St (Business 8), 85365. I-8, exit 7 (Araby Rd), just s, then 0.5 mi e. Small pets allowed.

YUMA — WESTWIND RV & GOLF RESORT. (928) 342-2992. **2P $25-$35, XP $3.** 9797 E 32nd St, 85365. I-8, exit 12 (Fortuna Rd) on south side, 1 mi w. Small pets allowed.

California

AGUANGA — OUTDOOR RESORTS RANCHO CALIFORNIA. (951) 767-0848. **4P $49, XP $2.** 45525 Hwy 79 S, 92536. SR 371, just se.

BAKERSFIELD — BAKERSFIELD PALMS RV PARK (661) 366-6700. **2P $24-$26, XP $2.** 250 Fairfax Rd, 93307. SR 99, exit SR 58, 6 mi e, exit Fairfax Rd, then 0.5 mi n.

BIG BEAR LAKE — BIG BEAR SHORES RV RESORT & YACHT CLUB. (909) 866-4151. **6P $54-$120.** 40751 North Shore Ln, 92315. SR 18, 5 mi e of the dam on SR 38 (North Shore Dr), 1.2 mi se. (PO Box 1572).

BUELLTON — FLYING FLAGS RV PARK & CAMPGROUND 🅐🅐🅐
(805) 688-3716. **2P $19-$36, XP $3.** 180 Ave of the Flags, 93427. Just w
of US 101, exit SR 246.
🔜 ⨂

CASTAIC — VALENCIA TRAVEL VILLAGE 🅐🅐🅐 (661) 257-3333.
6P $43-$60, XP $2-$4. 27946 Henry Mayo Rd, 91384. I-5, exit SR 126, 1.3
mi w.
🄺 🔜 ⨂

CATHEDRAL CITY — OUTDOOR RESORTS/PALM SPRINGS.
(760) 324-4005. **6P $30-$65.** 69-411 Ramon Rd, 92234. I-10, exit Date
Palm Dr, 2.2 mi s, then 0.5 mi e.
🔜 ⨂

CHULA VISTA — CHULA VISTA RV RESORT. (619) 422-0111.
4P $42-$62, XP $3. 460 Sandpiper Way, 91910. I-5, exit J St/Marina Pkwy,
4 mi w, then 0.5 mi n. Small pets allowed.
🆂🅳 🄺 🔜 ⨂

CHULA VISTA — SAN DIEGO METRO KOA. (619) 427-3601.
2P $29-$79, XP $4. 111 N 2nd Ave, 91910. I-5, exit E St, 1 mi e to 2nd Ave,
then 1 mi n; I-805, exit E St, 1 mi w, then just n.
🔜 ⨂

COLOMA — COLOMA RESORT. (530) 621-2267. **2P $32-$34,
XP $4-$10.** 6921 Mt Murphy Rd, 95613. E off SR 49 on Mt. Murphy Rd; on
South Fork of the American River. (PO Box 516).
🔜 ⨂

DESERT HOT SPRINGS — SKY VALLEY RESORT. (760) 329-
2909. **2P $37-$38, XP $5.** 74-711 Dillon Rd, 92241. I-10, exit Palm Dr, 3.3
mi n, then 8.5 mi e.
🔜 ⨂

EL CENTRO — DESERT TRAILS RV PARK. (760) 352-7275.
2P $17-$32, XP $3. 225 Wake Ave, 92243. I-8, exit 4th St, just s, then just
e. Small pets allowed.
🄺 🔜 ⨂

EL CENTRO — SUNBEAM LAKE RV RESORT. (760) 352-7154.
2P $25-$30, XP $2. 1716 W Sunbeam Lake Dr, 92243. I-8, exit Drew Rd,
0.5 mi n, then 8 mi w of SR 86.
🄺 🔜 ⨂

FORTUNA — RIVERWALK RV PARK & CAMPGROUND. (707)
725-3359. **2P $30-$50, XP $3.** 2189 Riverwalk Dr, 95540. W of US 101,
exit Kenmar Rd.
🔜 ⨂

GARBERVILLE — BENBOW VALLEY RV RESORT & GOLF
COURSE. (707) 923-2777. **2P $30-$41, XP $3.** 7000 Benbow Dr, 95542.
US 101, exit Benbow Dr, 2 mi s.
🆂🅳 🄺 🔜 ⨂

HEMET — GOLDEN VILLAGE PALMS RV RESORT 🅐🅐🅐 (951) 925-
2518. **2P $35-$38, XP $10.** 3600 W Florida Ave, 92545. SR 79 N (San
Jacinto St), 3 mi w. Small pets allowed.
🔜 ⨂

INDIO — INDIAN WELLS RV PARK. (760) 347-0895. **2P $23-$36,
XP $3.** 47-340 Jefferson St, 92201. I-10, exit Jefferson St, 3 mi s.
🄺 🔜 ⨂

INDIO — OUTDOOR RESORTS-MOTORCOACH RESORT & SPA.
(760) 775-7255. **$40-$65.** 80-394 48th Ave, 92201. I-10, exit Jefferson St,
3.5 mi s, then just e.
🔜 ⨂

MORRO BAY — MORRO DUNES TRAVEL TRAILER PARK &
RESORT CAMPGROUND. (805) 772-2722. **2P $19-$27, XP $1.** 1700
Embarcadero, 93442. SR 1, exit SR 41, 0.5 mi w. Small pets allowed.

NEWPORT BEACH — NEWPORT DUNES WATERFRONT RV
RESORT. (949) 729-3863. **6P $35-$164.** 1131 Back Bay Dr, 92660. SR 73,
exit Jamboree Rd southbound, 3 mi s, then just n on SR 1; exit Bison Ave
northbound, just w to MacArthur Blvd, 2.5 mi s to SR 1, then 1.5 mi n.
🔜 ⨂

NILAND — FOUNTAIN OF YOUTH SPA. (760) 354-1340. **2P $25-
$40, XP $2-$5.** 10249 Coachella Canal Rd, 92257. 14 mi nw on SR 111,
then 2.3 mi ne on Hot Mineral Spa Rd.
⨂

ORANGE — ORANGELAND RECREATION VEHICLE PARK 🅐🅐🅐
(714) 633-0414. **8P $50-$65, XP $2.** 1600 W Struck Ave, 92867. SR 57,
exit Katella Ave, 0.5 mi e, then just s.
🔜 ⨂

PALOMAR MOUNTAIN — OAK KNOLL CAMPGROUND.
(760) 742-3437. **2P $25-$35, XP $3.** I-15, exit SR 76, 20 mi e, then just n
on CR S6. (PO Box 192, 92060).
🔜 ⨂

PAUMA VALLEY — RANCHO CORRIDO CAMPGROUND. (760)
742-3755. **2P $25-$75, XP $3-$9.** 14715 Hwy 76, 92061. I-15, exit SR 76,
10 mi e.
🔜 ⨂

PISMO BEACH — PACIFIC DUNES RANCH RV PARK. (805)
489-7787. **6P $25-$36, XP $5.** 1205 Silver Spur Pl, 93445. In Oceano; SR
1, exit 22nd St, 0.3 mi s, then 0.4 mi w. (1205 Silver Spur Pl, OCEANO).
🄺 ⨂

PISMO BEACH — PISMO COAST VILLAGE RV RESORT. (805)
773-1811. **6P $34-$47, XP $2.** 165 S Dolliver St, 93449. 0.5 mi s on SR 1.
🄺 🔜 ⨂

PLYMOUTH — FAR HORIZONS 49'ER VILLAGE 🅐🅐🅐 (209) 245-
6981. **4P $36-$56, XP $5.** 18265 Hwy 49, 95669. On SR 49, 0.3 mi s.
🔜 ⨂

SAN DIEGO — CAMPLAND ON THE BAY. (858) 581-4260. **4P $40-
$241, XP $4.** 2211 Pacific Beach Dr, 92109. I-5, exit Grand Ave northbound, 1 mi w to Olney, then 0.3 mi s; exit Balboa/Garnet southbound, s
on Mission Bay Dr to Grand Ave, then 1 mi w to Olney.
🆂🅳 🔜 ⨂

SAN DIMAS — EAST SHORE RV PARK 🅐🅐🅐 (909) 599-8355.
2P $34-$36, XP $2. 1440 Camper View Rd, 91773. I-10, exit Fairplex Dr,
1.5 mi n; in Frank G Bonelli Regional Park.
🆂🅳 🔜 ⨂

SAN JUAN BAUTISTA — BETABEL RV RESORT 🅐🅐🅐 (831)
623-2202. **2P $31-$35, XP $2.** 9664 Betabel Rd, 95045. US 101, exit Beta-
bel Rd, just w. Small pets allowed.
🆂🅳 🄺 🔜 ⨂

SHAVER LAKE — CAMP EDISON. (559) 841-3134. **2P $22-$24,
XP $2.** 42696 Tollhouse Rd, 93664. Just ne; lakeside. (PO Box 600).
🆂🅳 ⨂

TEMECULA — PECHANGA RV RESORT 🅐🅐🅐 (951) 303-2658.
$32-$37. 45000 Pechanga Pkwy, 92592. I-15, exit SR 79 S, 1 mi e, then
2 mi s.
🆂🅳 🄺 🔜 ⨂

TEMECULA — VAIL LAKE RESORT. (951) 303-0173. **4P $35-$40,
XP $3.** 38000 Hwy 79 S, 92592. I-15, exit SR 79 S, 9 mi se.
🔜 ⨂

TRINIDAD — EMERALD FOREST OF TRINIDAD 🅐🅐🅐 (707) 677-
3554. **2P $23-$36, XP $3.** 753 Patrick's Point Dr, 95570. US 101, exit
Patrick's Point Dr W. (PO Box 870).
⨂

WEAVERVILLE — TRINITY LAKE RESORTS AT PINEWOOD
COVE RV PARK & CAMPGROUND. (530) 286-2201. **2P $20-$28, XP $3-
$7.** 45110 State Hwy 3, 96091. 14 mi ne of town.
🆂🅳 🔜 ⨂

WILLITS — WILLITS-UKIAH KOA. (707) 459-6179. **2P $30-$160,
XP $3-$4.** 1600 Hwy 20, 95490. 1.5 mi w on SR 20 from jct US 101. (PO
Box 946).
🔜 ⨂

WINTERHAVEN — RIVER'S EDGE RV RESORT. (760) 572-5105.
2P $25, XP $2. 2299 Winterhaven Dr, 92283. I-8, exit first Winterhaven
eastbound; exit Winterhaven Dr westbound, 0.5 mi e on frontage road.
Small pets allowed.
🄺 🔜 ⨂

Colorado

FORT COLLINS — HERON LAKE RV PARK. (970) 484-9880. **2P $31-$48, XP $2.** 1910 N Taft Hill Rd, 80524. I-25, exit 269B, 6 mi w to Taft Hill, then 2.2 mi n.

GOLDEN — DAKOTA RIDGE RV PARK. (303) 279-1625. **2P $31-$35, XP $3.** 17800 W Colfax Ave, 80401. I-70, exit 262 (W Colfax Ave), 1.8 mi w on US 40.

LOVELAND — JOHNSON'S CORNER RV RETREAT. (970) 669-8400. **2P $25-$32, XP $3.** 3618 SE Frontage Rd, 80537. I-25, exit 254, 0.3 mi se; adjacent to the Great Colorado Marketplace. Small pets allowed.

Delaware

REHOBOTH BEACH — 3 SEASONS RV RESORT. (302) 227-2564. **2P $50-$65, XP $2-$5.** 727 Country Club Rd, 19971. 1.5 mi w of US 1, follow signs via Rd 273.

Florida

ARCADIA — TOBY'S RV RESORT (863) 494-1744. **2P $25-$35, XP $2.** 3550 NE Hwy 70, 34266. On SR 70, 2.7 mi e.

BRADENTON — ENCORE RV RESORT-SARASOTA NORTH. (941) 745-2600. **$25-$45.** 800 Kay Rd NE, 34212. I-75, exit 220 southbound; exit 220B northbound, 0.5 mi w on SR 64, then 0.8 mi n.

BRADENTON — HORSESHOE COVE RV RESORT. (941) 758-5335. **2P $26-$38, XP $3.** 5100 60th St E, 34203. I-75, exit 217 southbound; exit 217B northbound, 1.7 mi w on SR 70, then just n on Caruso Rd.

BUSHNELL — BLUEBERRY HILL RV PARK. (352) 793-4112. **2P $25, XP $2. (no credit cards).** 6233 CR 609, 33513. I-75, exit 314, just e on SR 48, then just s. Small pets allowed.

CHOKOLOSKEE — OUTDOOR RESORTS OF AMERICA OF CHOKOLOSKEE. (239) 695-2881. **4P $49-$69.** Hwy 29 S, 34138. Center. (PO Box 39).

CLERMONT — CLERBROOK RESORT. (352) 394-5513. **4P $18-$26, XP $5.** 20005 US 27, 34711. Florida Tpke, exit 285, 1.2 mi s. Small pets allowed.

CRYSTAL RIVER — ENCORE SUPERPARK CRYSTAL RIVER. (352) 795-3774. **2P $28-$37, XP $5.** 11419 W Fort Island Tr, 34429. Jct US 19, 4.5 mi w on SR 44 W.

CRYSTAL RIVER — ROCK CRUSHER CANYON RV PARK. (352) 795-3870. **2P $15-$45, XP $2.** 275 S Rock Crusher Rd, 34429. 1.5 mi s of SR 44.

CYPRESS GARDENS — HOLIDAY TRAVEL PARK. (863) 324-7400. **2P $21-$25, XP $2.** 7400 Cypress Gardens Blvd, 33884. On SR 540, 1.2 mi w of US 27. Small pets allowed.

DAVENPORT — DEER CREEK RV RESORT. (863) 424-3684. **2P $35-$40.** 42749 Hwy 27, 33837. I-4, exit 55, 1 mi se.

DAVENPORT — FORT SUMMIT KOA (863) 424-1880. **2P $29-$48, XP $4.** 2525 Frontage Rd, 33837. Jct US 27 and I-4, exit 55, on frontage road; behind Best Western.

DEBARY — HIGH BANKS MARINA & CAMP RESORT. (386) 668-4491. **2P $25-$30, XP $5.** 488 W High Banks Rd, 32713. 2.7 mi w of US 17-92.

DESTIN — DESTIN RV BEACH RESORT. (850) 837-3529. **2P $55-$69, XP $2.** 362 Miramar Beach Dr, 32550. 4.1 mi e of SR 293 (Mid-Bay Bridge), just s.

FORT MYERS BEACH — GULF WATERS RV RESORT (239) 437-5888. **2P $38-$54.** 11301 Summerlin Rd, 33931. 2.4 mi ne of jct Matanzas Pass Bridge, 0.8 mi ne on Pine Ridge Rd, just w.

FORT MYERS BEACH — INDIAN CREEK PARK RV RESORT (239) 466-6060. **2P $22-$45, XP $3.** 17340 San Carlos Blvd, 33931. 2.4 mi ne of jct Matanzas Pass Bridge.

JACKSONVILLE — FLAMINGO LAKE RV RESORT (904) 766-0672. **2P $29, XP $3.** 3640 Newcomb Rd, 32218. I-295, exit 32, just nw on SR 115. Small pets allowed.

JENNINGS — JENNINGS OUTDOOR RESORT CAMPGROUND. (386) 938-3321. **2P $20-$25, XP $2.** 2039 Hamilton Ave, 32053. I-75, exit 467, just w on SR 143.

JENSEN BEACH — NETTLES ISLAND. (772) 229-1300. **$34-$54.** 9803 S Ocean Dr, 34957. On SR A1A, 2.3 mi n of jct SR 732 (Jensen Beach Cswy); on S Hutchinson Island.

KENANSVILLE — LAKE MARIAN PARADISE RV PARK & MARINA. (407) 436-1464. **2P $26-$35, XP $3.** 901 Arnold Rd, 34739. Florida Tpke, exit 242, 4.6 mi s on US 192, then 31.7 mi on CR 523.

KISSIMMEE — OUTDOOR RESORTS AT ORLANDO. (863) 424-1259. **$30.** On US 192, 1 mi e of jct US 27; jct I-4, exit 64B, 6.3 mi w. (9000 W US 192, CLERMONT, 34711). Small pets allowed.

KISSIMMEE — TROPICAL PALMS RESORT (407) 396-4595. **$24-$49.** 2650 Holiday Tr, 34746. I-4, exit 64A, 1.5 mi e on US 192, 0.8 mi s.

LA BELLE — WHISPER CREEK RV RESORT. (863) 675-6888. **2P $25. (no credit cards).** 1980 Hickory Dr, 33935. On SR 29, 1.8 mi n of jct SR 80.

LAKE BUENA VISTA — DISNEY'S FORT WILDERNESS RESORT & CAMPGROUND (407) 939-2267. **2P $38-$89, XP $2.** 4510 N Fort Wilderness Tr, 32830. On US 192; in Walt Disney World. (PO Box 10,000).

LAKELAND — LAKELAND RV RESORT. (863) 687-6146. **2P $30-$34, XP $2.** 900 Old Combee Rd, 33805. I-4, exit 33 eastbound, 1 mi ne on SR 33, then just w; exit 38 westbound, 5 mi sw on SR 33, then just nw.

LAKELAND — SANLAN RANCH CAMPGROUND (863) 665-1726. **2P $20-$40, XP $3-$5.** 3929 US 98 S, 33813. I-4, exit 32, 8.7 mi s on US 98; just s of SR 570.

LEESBURG — HOLIDAY TRAVEL RESORT (352) 787-5151. **4P $28-$30, XP $3-$5.** 28229 CR 33, 34748. 3.5 mi s via US 27, 0.5 mi w.

MELBOURNE BEACH — OUTDOOR RESORTS MELBOURNE BEACH LUXURY RV RESORT. (321) 724-2600. **4P $30-$60, XP $3.** 214 Horizon Ln, 32951. 2.5 mi s.

MIMS — SEASONS IN THE SUN MOTOR COACH RESORT. (321) 385-0440. **2P $27-$35, XP $2-$3.** 2400 Seasons In The Sun Blvd, 32754. I-95, exit 223, just w.

NOKOMIS — ENCORE RESORT-SARASOTA SOUTH. (941) 488-9674. **2P $30-$50, XP $5.** 1070 Laurel Rd E, 34275. I-75, exit 195, 2.6 mi w.

OCALA — OCALA-SILVER SPRINGS KOA. (352) 237-2138. **2P $33-$70, XP $4-$7.** 3200 SW 38th Ave, 34474. I-75, exit 350, just w on SR 200, just n on SW 38th Ct, then 0.5 mi e.

OKEECHOBEE — OKEECHOBEE KOA RESORT & GOLF COURSE. (863) 763-0231. **2P $31-$146, XP $4-$7.** 4276 Hwy US 441 S, 34974. On US 98 and 441, 3 mi s of jct SR 70, 0.3 mi n of Lake Okeechobee and jct SR 78.

OLD TOWN — YELLOW JACKET CAMPGROUND. (352) 542-8365. **$20-$95, XP $6.** HC 1, Box 80, 32680. 10.7 mi s on SR 349, then 1.2 mi on dirt road.

ORMOND BEACH — ENCORE SUPERPARK-DAYTONA BEACH NORTH ⒶⒶⒶ (386) 672-3045. **2P $30-$40, XP $5.** 1701 N US 1, 32174. I-95, exit 273, 0.5 mi nw.

PANAMA CITY BEACH — EMERALD COAST RV BEACH RESORT ⒶⒶⒶ (850) 235-0924. **2P $36-$42, XP $3.** 1957 Allison Ave, 32407. US 98/98A and Allison Ave, 1.5 mi w of Hathaway Bridge.

PORT CHARLOTTE — ENCORE RV RESORT-PORT CHAR-LOTTE. (941) 624-4511. **2P $25-$40, XP $5.** 3737 El Jobean Rd, 33953. On SR 776, 4.6 mi w of jct US 41.

PORT CHARLOTTE — RIVERSIDE RV RESORT & CAMP-GROUND ⒶⒶⒶ (863) 993-2111. **4P $28-$42, XP $2.** 9770 SW CR 769, 34269. I-75, exit 170, 4.5 mi ne on CR 769 (Kings Hwy). (9770 SW CR 769, ARCADIA).

REDDICK — ENCORE RV PARK-OCALA. (352) 591-1723. **2P $25-$37, XP $5.** 16905 NW CR 225, 32686. I-75, exit 368, just w on CR 318, then 0.8 mi s.

RIVER RANCH — RIVER RANCH RV RESORT ⒶⒶⒶ (863) 692-1116. **4P $40-$50, XP $2.** 3400 River Ranch Blvd, 33867. 3.5 mi s of SR 60, 25 mi e of US 27, 23 mi w of Florida Tpke and US 441, just w of the Kissimmee River.

ROCKLEDGE — SPACE COAST RV RESORT. (321) 636-2873. **$30-$40, XP $3.** 820 Barnes Blvd, 32955. I-95, exit 195 (Fiske Blvd), 0.3 mi se, 2 mi w of US 1 on SR 502. Small pets allowed.

SARASOTA — SUN-N-FUN RV RESORT ⒶⒶⒶ (941) 371-2505. **$23-$57.** 7125 Fruitville Rd, 34240. I-75, exit 210, 1.2 mi e on SR 780.

SEBASTIAN — ENCORE RV PARK-VERO BEACH. (772) 589-7828. **2P $28-$38, XP $2-$4.** I-95, exit 156, just e on CR 512. (9455 108th Ave, VERO BEACH, 32967-3154).

SEBRING — BUTTONWOOD BAY RV RESORT ⒶⒶⒶ (863) 655-1122. **2P $23-$32, XP $3.** 10001 US 27 S, 33876. 1.5 mi s of SR 98. Small pets allowed.

SILVER SPRINGS — COLBY WOODS RV RESORT. (352) 625-1122. **2P $15-$24, XP $3-$5. (no credit cards).** 10313 E Hwy 40, 34488. On SR 40, 4.5 mi e of Silver Springs attraction.

SILVER SPRINGS — THE SPRINGS RV RESORT. (352) 236-5250. **2P $24, XP $3.** 2950 NE 52nd Ct, 34488. On SR 40, 0.5 mi w of Silver Springs attraction, 0.5 mi n.

ST. PETERSBURG — ST. PETERSBURG-MADEIRA BEACH RESORT KOA. (727) 392-2233. **2P $30-$85, XP $4-$7.** 5400 95th St N, 33708. Jct 38th Ave N, 1.4 mi n on Tyrone/Bay Pines Blvd (US Alternate Rt 19), 0.5 mi e.

SUMTERVILLE — SHADY BROOK GOLF & RV RESORT. (352) 568-2244. **2P $20-$25, XP $2.** 178 N US 301, 33585. I-75, exit 321, 2.5 mi e on CR 470, then 0.7 mi n. (PO Box 130).

TITUSVILLE — THE GREAT OUTDOORS RV & GOLF RESORT. (321) 269-5004. **2P $30-$50, XP $3.** 125 Plantation Dr, 32780. I-95, exit 215, 0.5 mi w on SR 50, 1.8 mi s on paved entrance road. Small pets allowed.

UMATILLA — OLDE MILL STREAM RV RESORT ⒶⒶⒶ (352) 669-3141. **2P $18-$27, XP $3.** 1000 N Central Ave, 32784. 0.8 mi n on SR 19. Small pets allowed.

Georgia

JEKYLL ISLAND — JEKYLL ISLAND CAMPGROUND. (912) 635-3021. **4P $19-$28, XP $4.** 1197 Riverview Dr, 31527. Jct Ben Fortson Pkwy/Riverview Dr, 4.5 mi n; on north end of island.

PINE MOUNTAIN — PINE MOUNTAIN CAMPGROUND. (706) 663-4329. **2P $19-$28, XP $2.** 8804 Hamilton Rd, 31822. I-185, exit 42, 8 mi s on US 27.

STONE MOUNTAIN — STONE MOUNTAIN PARK CAMP-GROUND. (770) 498-5710. **6P $22-$30, XP $2.** Stone Mountain Park, 30086. In Stone Mountain Memorial Park; on east side of Stone Mountain. (PO Box 778). Small pets allowed.

Idaho

CASCADE — ARROWHEAD R.V. PARK ON THE RIVER ⒶⒶⒶ (208) 382-4534. **$24-$26, XP $1.** 955 S Hwy 55, 83611. South end of town. (PO Box 337).

COEUR D'ALENE — BLACKWELL ISLAND RV RESORT. (208) 665-1300. **2P $26-$39, XP $2.** 800 S Marina Dr, 83814. I-90, exit 12, 1.5 mi s on US 95.

KAMIAH — LEWIS-CLARK RESORT RV PARK. (208) 935-2556. **$19, XP $1.** 1.5 mi e on US 12. (Rt 1, Box 17X, 83536).

PINEHURST — KELLOGG/SILVER VALLEY KOA. (208) 682-3612. **2P $22-$38, XP $3. (no credit cards).** 801 N Division St, 83850. I-90, exit 45, just s. (PO Box 949).

WHITE BIRD — SWIFTWATER RV PARK & STORE. (208) 839-2700. **2P $15-$23, XP $3.** HC 01, Box 24, 83554. Just n of Milepost 222, exit Hammer Creek Recreational area, 0.8 mi nw. (PO Box 150).

Illinois

LEE CENTER — O'CONNELL'S YOGI BEAR JELLYSTONE PARK ⒶⒶⒶ (815) 857-3860. **6P $42-$47, XP $10-$12.** 970 Greenwing Rd, 61310. I-39, exit 87 (US 30), 12.8 mi w to CR 1955 E, then 3.3 mi se, follow signs. (PO Box 200, AMBOY).

MILLBROOK — YOGI BEAR'S JELLYSTONE PARK CAMP RESORT ⒶⒶⒶ (630) 553-5172. **5P $47-$50, XP $4-$8.** 8574 Millbrook Rd, 60536. 1.5 mi n of jct SR 71. (PO Box 306). 🏊 ⊠

Indiana

CRAWFORDSVILLE — CRAWFORDSVILLE KOA. (765) 362-4190. **2P $23-$34, XP $3.** 1600 Lafayette Rd, 47933. I-74, exit 34, 2 mi s on US 231. 🏊 ⊠

FREMONT — YOGI BEAR'S JELLYSTONE PARK CAMP RESORT ⒶⒶⒶ (260) 833-1114. **5P $30-$48, XP $5-$7.** 140 Ln, 201 Barton Lake, 46737. I-69, exit 157 southbound; exit 154 northbound, 3 mi w on SR 120, then 0.5 mi n on CR 300 W; Toll Rd, exit 144 to SR 120. 🏊 ⊠

GRANGER — SOUTH BEND EAST KOA. (574) 277-1335. **2P $20-$45, XP $3-$4.** 50707 Princess Way, 46530. I-80/90, exit 83, 2.3 mi ne on SR 23. 🏊 ⊠

MONTICELLO — INDIANA BEACH CAMP RESORT. (574) 583-8306. **8P $18-$29, XP $3.** 5224 E Indiana Beach Rd, 47960. 0.5 mi w on US 24, 3.3 mi n on W Shafer Dr (6th St). ⊠

PIERCETON — YOGI BEAR'S JELLYSTONE PARK CAMP-RESORT. (574) 594-2124. **5P $33-$50, XP $5.** 1916 N 850 E, 46562. US 30, 4.3 mi n on SR 13, 1.3 mi e on CR 200. 🆂 🏊 ⊠

Louisiana

CARENCRO — BAYOU WILDERNESS RV RESORT. (337) 896-0598. **2P $26-$32.** 201 St Clair Rd, 70520. I-49, exit 2, 2.5 mi e on SR 98, then 1 mi n on Wilderness Tr. 🅺 🏊 ⊠

HAMMOND — NEW ORLEANS-HAMMOND KOA KAMP-GROUND. (985) 542-8094. **$25-$27, XP $3.** 14154 Club Deluxe Rd, 70403. I-12 to I-55 S, exit 28, 1 blk n, then 0.7 mi w. 🆂 🏊 ⊠

KINDER — COUSHATTA CASINO RV RESORT. (337) 738-1200. **$17-$22.** 777 Pow Wow Pkwy, 70648. N of jct US 190 and 165, 4.5 mi on US 165. (PO Box 1240). 🆂 🅺 🏊 ⊠

ROBERT — YOGI BEAR'S JELLYSTONE PARK CAMP-RESORT. (985) 542-1507. **5P $22-$43, XP $8-$10.** 46049 SR 445 N, 70455. I-12, exit 47, 3 mi n. (PO Box 519). ⊠

SCOTT — KOA KAMPGROUND OF LAFAYETTE. (337) 235-2739. **2P $30-$37, XP $3-$4.** 537 Apollo Rd, 70583. I-10, exit 97, 0.5 mi s. Small pets allowed. ⊠

SHREVEPORT — SHREVEPORT-BOSSIER KOA. (318) 687-1010. **2P $22-$32, XP $3.** 6510 W 70th St, 71129. I-20, exit 10 (Pines Rd), 0.7 mi s to W 70th St, then 1 mi w. 🏊 ⊠

SLIDELL — KOA-NEW ORLEANS-EAST. (985) 643-3850. **2P $25-$30, XP $3.** 56009 Hwy 433, 70461. I-10, exit 263, 0.8 mi e. 🏊 ⊠

VIDALIA — RIVER VIEW RV PARK ⒶⒶⒶ (318) 336-1400. **2P $20-$25, XP $2.** 100 River View Pkwy, 71373. From jct US 65/84, 0.7 mi s on SR 131. 🆂 🏊 ⊠

Massachusetts

BRIMFIELD — QUINEBAUG COVE CAMPGROUND. (413) 245-9525. **4P $25-$38, XP $6.** 49 E Brimfield-Holland Rd, 01010. I-84, exit 3B, 3.8 mi w on US 20, then 0.3 mi s. 🏊 ⊠

FOXBORO — NORMANDY FARMS CAMPGROUND. (508) 543-7600. **2P $32-$60, XP $6-$10.** 72 West St, 02035. I-495, exit 14A, 1 mi n on US 1, then 1.3 mi e on Thurston and West sts. 🏊 ⊠

OAKHAM — PINE ACRES FAMILY CAMPING RESORT. (508) 882-9509. **2P $22-$54, XP $5-$10.** 203 Bechan Rd, 01068. Jct SR 122, 2 mi sw on SR 148, then just s via Spencer Rd. 🏊 ⊠

SAVOY — SHADY PINES CAMPGROUND. (413) 743-2694. **2P $25-$27, XP $3-$8.** 547 Loop Rd, 01256. On SR 8A and 116, 3.1 mi se. 🏊 ⊠

Maryland

ABINGDON — BAR HARBOR RV PARK & MARINA ⒶⒶⒶ (410) 679-0880. **2P $35-$38, XP $2-$3.** 4228 Birch Ave, 21009. I-95, exit 80, 1.5 mi s on SR 543, 1.7 mi w on US 40, 0.7 mi s on Long Bar Harbor Rd, then 0.5 mi e on E Baker Ave. 🅺 🏊 ⊠

BERLIN — FRONTIER TOWN CAMPGROUND. (410) 641-0880. **2P $24-$59, XP $10-$5.** 8428 Stephen Decatur Hwy, 21811. Jct SR 50, 4 mi s on SR 611. (PO Box 691, OCEAN CITY, 21843). 🏊 ⊠

COLLEGE PARK — CHERRY HILL PARK ⒶⒶⒶ (301) 937-7116. **2P $34-$60, XP $4.** 9800 Cherry Hill Rd, 20740. I-95, exit 29B, 1 mi w on SR 212 (Powder Mill Rd), 1 mi s; I-495, exit 25, just s to Cherry Hill Rd, then 1 mi nw. 🆂 🏊 ⊠

FLINTSTONE — HIDDEN SPRINGS CAMPGROUND. (814) 767-9676, off season (301) 478-2282. **4P $23-$27, XP $2.** I-68, exit 50 to Rocky Gap State Park, 3.5 mi n on Pleasant Valley Rd. (PO Box 190, 21530). 🏊 ⊠

FREELAND — MORRIS MEADOWS RECREATION FARM. (410) 329-6636. **2P $21-$50, XP $5-$10.** 1523 Freeland Rd, 21053. I-83, exit 36 (SR 439), w to jct SR 45, 1 mi n, then 3 mi w, follow signs. 🏊 ⊠

WILLIAMSPORT — YOGI BEAR'S JELLYSTONE PARK CAMP RESORT HAGERSTOWN. (301) 223-7117. **2P $20-$47, XP $2-$6.** 16519 Lappans Rd, 21795. I-81, exit 1, 1.2 mi e on SR 68. 🆂 🏊 ⊠

Maine

CASCO — POINT SEBAGO RESORT. (207) 655-3821. **4P $23-$60, XP $5.** 261 Point Sebago Rd, 04015. Jct SR 121, 3.7 mi n on US 302, then 1 mi w, follow signs. ⊠

DAMARISCOTTA — LAKE PEMAQUID, INC. ⒶⒶⒶ (207) 563-5202. **4P $22-$42, XP $10.** Twin Cove Ln, 04543. 0.8 mi n on US 1 business route, 2 mi e on Biscay Rd, then 0.3 mi n on Egypt Rd. (PO Box 967). 🏊 ⊠

NORTH WATERFORD — PAPOOSE POND RESORT & CAMP-GROUND. (207) 583-4470. **6P $18-$60, XP $10.** 700 Norway Rd, 04088. 1.9 mi w on SR 118 from jct SR 37; 10 mi w on SR 118. ⊠

OLD ORCHARD BEACH — POWDER HORN FAMILY CAMP-ING RESORT. (207) 934-4733. **2P $24-$50, XP $3-$7.** 48 Cascade Rd, 04064. 1 mi w on SR 98; jct US 1, 1.8 mi e on SR 98. (PO Box 366A). 🏊 ⊠

OLD ORCHARD BEACH — WILD ACRES FAMILY CAMPING RESORT. (207) 934-2535. **2P $34-$55, XP $3-$8.** 179 Saco Ave, 04064. I-95 (Maine Tpke), exit 36, 3 mi e on I-195 and SR 5. 🏊 ⊠

SCARBOROUGH — BAYLEY'S CAMPING RESORT (207) 883-6043. **2P $25-$53, XP $5-$12.** 275 Pine Point Rd, 04074. Jct US 1, 2 mi e via SR 9 (Pine Point Rd), watch for sign.

WELLS — WELLS BEACH RESORT CAMPGROUND (207) 646-7570. **2P $37-$59, XP $7.** 1000 Post Rd (US 1), 04090. Jct SR 109 and 9, 1.3 mi s on US 1.

Michigan

BAY VIEW — PETOSKEY KOA RV & CABIN RESORT. (231) 347-0005. **2P $22-$169, XP $3.** 1800 N US 31, 49770. US 31, 1 mi n of SR 119. (1800 N US 31, PETOSKEY).

PORT HURON — PORT HURON KOA KAMPGROUND. (810) 987-4070. **2P $23-$60, XP $4.** 5111 Lapeer Rd, 48074. I-94, exit 262, 8 mi n on Wadhams Rd, then 0.3 mi e; I-69, exit 196, 0.5 mi n on Wadhams Rd, then 0.3 mi e.

Minnesota

CALEDONIA — DUNROMIN' PARK. (507) 724-2514. **$18-$40, XP $2-$4.** 12757 Dunromin Dr, 55921. 2.8 mi s on SR 76 S from jct SR 44, 0.5 mi e.

CASS LAKE — STONY POINT RESORT, TRAILER PARK CAMP-GROUNDS (218) 335-6311. **2P $19-$28, XP $2.** 5510 US 2 NW, 56633. On US 2, 2 mi e of jct SR 371. (PO Box 518).

COKATO — COKATO LAKE CAMPING & RV RESORT. (320) 286-5779. **2P $24-$38, XP $2-$3.** 2945 CR 4 SW, 55321. 2.8 mi n of jct SR 12.

DETROIT LAKES — FOREST HILLS GOLF & RV RESORT (218) 439-6033. **4P $26, XP $2.** 22931 185th St, 56501. 3.5 mi w on US 10.

HINCKLEY — GRAND CASINO HINCKLEY RV RESORT. (320) 384-4703. **$13-$18.** 711 Lady Luck Dr, 55037. I-35, exit 183, 1 mi e on SR 48. (Rt 3, Box 15).

PARK RAPIDS — BREEZE CAMPING & RV RESORT ON EAGLE LAKE. (218) 732-5888. **2P $28-$32, XP $3.** 25824 CR 89, 56470. 9 mi n on US 71 from jct SR 34.

PARK RAPIDS — VAGABOND VILLAGE CAMPGROUND. (218) 732-5234. **2P $30-$32, XP $3-$4. (no credit cards).** 23801 Green Pines Rd, 56470. 2 mi e on SR 34, 5.7 mi n on CR 4, just w on CR 40, then 0.5 mi w via signs.

PRIOR LAKE — DAKOTAH MEADOWS RV PARK AND CAMP-GROUND (952) 445-8800. **$20-$29.** 2341 Park Pl, 55372. Off CR 83.

RICHMOND — EL RANCHO MANANA (320) 597-2740. **5P $14-$39, XP $1-$2.** 27302 C Ranch Rd, 56368. 4 mi n on CR 9 from jct SR 23 and 24, 2 mi ne on Manana and Ranch rds; 9 mi s of jct I-94, exit 153, via CR 9.

STURGEON LAKE — TIMBERLINE CAMPGROUND. (218) 372-3272. **2P $22-$24, XP $6-$3.** 9152 Timberline Rd, 55783. I-35, exit 209, 2.3 mi w on CR 46 through business district, 0.8 mi n on access road, follow signs.

WALKER — SHORES OF LEECH LAKE CAMPGROUND & MARINA. (218) 547-1819. **$35, XP $5.** 6166 Morriss Point Rd, 56484. 2.8 mi nw on SR 371 and 200 from jct SR 34, 0.5 mi e on gravel road, follow signs.

Missouri

BRANSON — THE WILDERNESS AT SILVER DOLLAR CITY LOG CABINS AND RV'S. (417) 338-8189. **2P $26-$29, XP $2-$4.** 5125 SR 265, 65616. Jct SR 76, 0.5 mi s.

EUREKA — YOGI BEAR'S JELLYSTONE PARK CAMP-RESORT. (636) 938-5925. **2P $96-$40, XP $3.** 5300 Fox Creek Rd, 63069. I-44, exit 261, 0.5 mi w. (PO Box 626, 63025).

Mississippi

MERIDIAN — MERIDIAN EAST/TOOMSUBA KOA. (601) 632-1684. **2P $22-$49, XP $2-$3.** 3953 KOA Campground Rd, 39364. I-20/59, exit 165, 1.5 mi s, follow signs.

OCEAN SPRINGS — CAMP JOURNEY'S END. (228) 875-2100. **2P $19-$28, XP $2-$3.** 7501 Hwy 57, 39565. I-10, exit 57, 0.5 mi n.

Montana

MISSOULA — JELLYSTONE RV RESORT. (406) 543-9400. **2P $26-$30, XP $3-$4.** 9900 Jellystone Ave, 59808. I-90, exit 96 (west side entry), 0.9 mi n.

POLSON — POLSON/FLATHEAD LAKE KOA. (406) 883-2151. **2P $25-$60, XP $3-$5.** 200 Irvine Flats Rd, 59860. 1 mi n on US 93, 0.3 mi w.

WEST GLACIER — WEST GLACIER KOA. (406) 387-5341. **2P $22-$45, XP $4-$5.** 355 Halfmoon Flats Rd, 59936. 2.5 mi w on US 2, 1 mi s. (PO Box 215).

North Carolina

BOONE — KOA-BOONE. (828) 264-7250. **2P $24-$35, XP $2-$5.** 123 Harmony Mt Ln, 28607. Jct US 221 and 421, 3 mi n on SR 194, 1 mi w on CR 1326.

CANDLER — KOA ASHEVILLE WEST. (828) 665-7015. **2P $23-$39, XP $3-$5.** 309 Wiggins Rd, 28715. I-40, exit 37, just s, 0.5 mi w on US 19/23, then 0.3 mi n.

CASHIERS — SINGING WATERS CAMPING RESORT (828) 293-5872. **2P $21-$30, XP $2-$5.** Jct US 64, 10 mi n on SR 107, then 1 mi e. (1006 Trout Creek Rd, TUCKASEGEE, 28783). Small pets allowed.

CEDAR MOUNTAIN — BLACK FOREST CAMPING RESORT. (828) 884-2267. **2P $22-$28, XP $2-$4.** 100 Summer Rd, 28718. On US 276, 12.6 mi s of Brevard. (PO Box 709).

North Dakota

BISMARCK — BISMARCK KOA. (701) 222-2662. **2P $20-$32, XP $3.** 3720 Centennial Rd, 58503. I-94, exit 161 (Centennial Rd), 1 mi n.

Nebraska

NORTH PLATTE — HOLIDAY PARK (308) 534-2265. **2P $17-$28, XP $1-$2.** 601 Halligan Dr, 69101. I-80, exit 177, just n on US 83, then immediate right turn on frontage road (Halligan Dr), then 0.5 mi e.

New Hampshire

BARRINGTON — AYERS LAKE FARM CAMPGROUND ⒶⒶⒶ (603) 335-1110, off season (603) 332-5940. **4P $30-$37, XP $5-$7. (no credit cards).** 557 US 202, 03825. Spaulding Tpke, exit 13, 4.5 mi w.

BARRINGTON — BARRINGTON SHORES CAMPGROUND ⒶⒶⒶ (603) 664-9333. **5P $34-$40, XP $2-$10.** 70 Hall Rd, 03825. Jct SR 125 and US 4, 2.5 mi w on US 4, then 3 mi n.

CHICHESTER — HILLCREST CAMPGROUND. (603) 798-5124. **2P $26-$34, XP $8.** 78 Dover Rd, 03234. I-93, exit 15, 8 mi e on SR 4; jct SR 28 and 4, 2 mi w on SR 4.

FREEDOM — DANFORTH BAY CAMPING RESORT. (603) 539-2069. **4P $29-$45, XP $4-$6.** 196 Shawtown Rd, 0. Jct SR 25/153, 1 mi n on SR 153, 3 mi w on Ossipee Lake Rd. 196 Shawtown Rd.

HAMPTON FALLS — WAKEDA CAMPGROUND ⒶⒶⒶ (603) 772-5274. **5P $23-$55, XP $5.** 294 Exeter Rd (SR 88), 03844. SR 88, 3.8 mi w of jct US 1.

LACONIA — PAUGUS BAY CAMPGROUND. (603) 366-4757. **4P $25-$35, XP $6. (no credit cards).** 96 Hilliard Rd, 03246. 0.5 mi n of jct US 3 and SR 11B on US 3, then w. Small pets allowed.

MEREDITH — CLEARWATER CAMPGROUND ⒶⒶⒶ (603) 279-7761. **2P $20-$38, XP $1-$10.** 26 Campground Rd (SR 104), 03253. I-93, exit 23, 3 mi e.

MEREDITH — MEREDITH WOODS 4 SEASON CAMPING AREA ⒶⒶⒶ (603) 279-5449. **2P $26-$41, XP $1-$10.** 551 SR 104, 03253. I-93, exit 23, 3 mi e. (26 Campground Rd).

MILTON — MI-TE-JO LAKESIDE FAMILY CAMPGROUND ⒶⒶⒶ (603) 652-9022. **$29-$38, XP $8. (no credit cards).** 111 Mi-Te Jo Rd, 03851. SR 16, exit 17 northbound, 0.8 mi e on SR 75, 3.3 mi n on SR 125, then 1 mi e on Townhouse Rd; southbound, 3.3 mi on SR 125, 1 mi e on Townhouse Rd. (PO Box 830).

MOULTONBOROUGH — LONG ISLAND BRIDGE CAMP-GROUND. (603) 253-6053. **2P $21-$32, XP $5. (no credit cards).** 29 Long Island Rd, 03254. Jct US 3 and SR 25, 6.5 mi e on SR 25, then 6.5 mi s via Mooltonboro Neck Rd. (HC 62, Box 455, CENTER HARBOR, 03226). Small pets allowed.

NEW HAMPTON — TWIN TAMARACK FAMILY CAMPING & RV RESORT ⒶⒶⒶ (603) 279-4387. **$30-$34, XP $1-$8.** 41 Twin Tamarack Rd, 03256. I-93, exit 23, 2.5 mi e on SR 104.

RAYMOND — PINE ACRES FAMILY CAMPGROUND ⒶⒶⒶ (603) 895-2519. **5P $24-$51, XP $7-$12.** 74 Freetown Rd, 03077. On SR 107, just n of jct SR 102; SR 101, exit 5, 0.5 mi s.

SOUTH WEARE — COLD SPRINGS CAMP RESORT. (603) 529-2528. **2P $40-$44, XP $3-$7.** 62 Barnard Hill Rd, 03281. On jct SR 77/149, 1.5 mi se, 0.3 mi n on sign posted road; 10 mi nw of jct SR 114/101. (22 Wildlife Dr).

TAMWORTH — CHOCORUA CAMPING VILLAGE ⒶⒶⒶ (603) 323-8536. **2P $29-$49, XP $8.** 893 White Mountain Hwy, 03817. SR 16, 2.5 mi n of jct SR 25. (PO Box 484, CHOCORUA).

TWIN MOUNTAIN — TWIN MOUNTAIN KOA KAMPGROUND ⒶⒶⒶ (603) 846-5559. **2P $30-$40, XP $3-$10.** 372 SR 115, 03595. From jct US 302, 2.1 mi n on US 3, then 0.8 mi ne. (PO Box 148).

WOODSTOCK — BROKEN BRANCH KOA. (603) 745-8008. **2P $29-$37, XP $3-$8.** 1002 Eastside Rd (SR 175), 03293. I-93, exit 31, 2 mi s on SR 175, follow signs. (PO Box 6).

New Jersey

CAPE MAY COURT HOUSE — BIG TIMBER LAKE CAMPING RESORT ⒶⒶⒶ (609) 465-4456. **4P $35-$52, XP $3-$7.** 116 Swainton Goshen Rd, 08210. Garden State Pkwy, exit 13 southbound, 0.5 mi w on paved road, 1 mi s on US 9, then 1 mi w (CR 646). (PO Box 366).

CAPE MAY — BEACHCOMBER CAMPING RESORT. (609) 886-6035. **2P $23-$54, XP $3-$5.** 462 Seashore Rd, 08204. Garden State Pkwy, exit 4A (SR 47 N), w to 3rd traffic light, then 1 mi s; Railroad Ave and Seashore Rd.

CAPE MAY — CAPE ISLAND CAMPGROUND ⒶⒶⒶ (609) 884-5777. **4P $40-$50, XP $3-$5.** 709 Rt 9, 08204. Garden State Pkwy, exit 0 (US 9), 1.5 mi n on SR 109 and US 9.

CAPE MAY — HOLLY SHORES BEST HOLIDAY TRAV-L-PARK ⒶⒶⒶ (609) 886-1234. **2P $25-$44, XP $3-$5.** 491 US 9, 08204. Garden State Pkwy, exit 4A (SR 47 N) to 2nd traffic light, 1 mi s. Small pets allowed.

CAPE MAY — SEASHORE CAMPSITES INC ⒶⒶⒶ (609) 884-4010. **4P $24-$42, XP $5.** 720 Seashore Rd, 08204. Garden State Pkwy, exit 4A (SR 47 N), 1 mi n to CR 626, then 2.7 mi s.

OCEAN VIEW — OCEAN VIEW RESORT CAMPGROUND ⒶⒶⒶ (609) 624-1675. **4P $42-$56, XP $6.** 2555 Rt 9, 08230. US 9, 0.8 mi nw of Garden State Pkwy, exit 17 southbound; northbound, use service area turnaround. (PO Box 607).

New Mexico

ALBUQUERQUE — ALBUQUERQUE KOA-CENTRAL. (505) 296-2729. **2P $19-$55, XP $3-$5.** 12400 Skyline Rd NE, 87123. I-40, exit 166, just s, then left.

ALBUQUERQUE — AMERICAN RV PARK ⒶⒶⒶ (505) 831-3545. **2P $28-$40, XP $3.** 13500 Coronado Frwy SW, 87121. I-40, exit 149, just s, then w.

DEMING — A LITTLE VINEYARD RV PARK ⒶⒶⒶ (505) 546-3560. **2P $17-$19, XP $2.** 2901 E Pine St, 88030. I-10, exit 85, 1 mi w.

GALLUP — USA RV PARK ⒶⒶⒶ (505) 863-5021. **2P $25-$27, XP $2.** 2925 W Hwy 66, 87301. I-40, exit 16, 1 mi e.

LAS CRUCES — HACIENDA RV RESORT (505) 528-5800. **2P $28-$40, XP $2.** 740 Stern Dr, 88005. I-10, exit 140, just e. (PO Box 1479, MESILLA, 88046-1479).

RIO RANCHO — STAGECOACH STOP RV RESORT. (505) 867-1000. **2P $28-$36, XP $2-$3.** 3650 SR 528, 87144. I-25, exit 242, w to SR 528, then 0.5 mi s.

SILVER CITY — SILVER CITY KOA. (505) 388-3351. **4P $16-$35, XP $2-$3.** 11824 E Hwy 180, 88061. 4.9 mi e on US 180 and SR 90.

Nevada

BOULDER CITY — BOULDER OAKS RV RESORT. (702) 294-4425. **4P $30.** 1010 Industrial Rd, 89005. Just w of US 93.

LAS VEGAS — BOULDER LAKES RV RESORT (702) 435-1157. **2P $22-$25, XP $3.** 6201 Boulder Hwy, 89122. 1 mi e of I-515/SR 93 and 95, exit Russell Rd, 0.3 mi n at Desert Horizons Rd. Small pets allowed.

LAS VEGAS — OASIS LAS VEGAS RV RESORT. (702) 260-2020. **4P $28-$36, XP $1.** 2711 W Windmill Ln, 89123. I-15, exit 33 (Blue Diamond Rd), 0.5 mi e to Las Vegas Blvd, then 0.5 mi s. Small pets allowed.

MESQUITE — DESERT SKIES RV RESORT. (928) 347-6000. **2P $35, XP $3.** 350 E Hwy 91, 89024. I-15, exit 122, 1.5 mi ne via Hillside Dr. (PO Box 3780).

MINDEN — CARSON VALLEY RV RESORT. (775) 782-9711. **4P $22-$27, XP $6.** 1639 US 395 N, 89423. Center.

MINDEN — SILVER CITY RV RESORT. (775) 267-3359. **2P $20-$30, XP $2.** 3165 US 395, 89423. 6 mi s of Carson City; 3 mi s of jct US 50 W.

PAHRUMP — SEIBT DESERT RETREAT LUXURY RV PARK  (775) 751-1174. **4P $30-$180.** 301 W Leslie St, 89060. 10 mi n of SR 160 and 372, jct SR 160.

PAHRUMP — TERRIBLE'S LAKESIDE CASINO & RV RESORT. (775) 751-7770. **6P $20-$30, XP $2.** 5870 S Homestead Rd, 89048. SR 160, 3.5 mi s.

RENO — KOA AT THE RENO HILTON. (775) 789-2147. **2P $23-$69, XP $3-$5.** 2500 E 2nd St, 89595. US 395, exit Mill St, just e.

SPARKS — RIVERS EDGE RV PARK 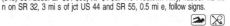 (775) 358-8533. **2P $25-$35, XP $2.** 1405 S Rock Blvd, 89431. I-80, exit Rock Blvd S; US 395, exit SR 66 (Mill St).

VERDI — GOLD RANCH CASINO & RV RESORT. (775) 345-8880. **4P $22-$42, XP $1.** 320 Gold Ranch Rd, 89439. I-80, exit 2. (PO Box 160).

ZEPHYR COVE — ZEPHYR COVE RESORT CAMPGROUND (775) 589-4907. **6P $26-$51, XP $6.** 760 Hwy 50, 89448. US 50, 4 mi n of state line. (PO Box 830).

New York

BATH — HICKORY HILL CAMPING RESORT ▲▲▲ (607) 776-4345. **2P $30-$39, XP $3.** 7531 Mitchellsville Rd, 14810. SR 17, exit 38, 1 mi n on SR 54, then at fork, 2 mi n on Haverling St.

DARIEN CENTER — SKYLINE RESORT. (585) 591-2021. **2P $26-$28, XP $2-$3.** 10933 Townline Rd, 14040. SR 77, 4 mi e on US 20, 1.3 mi s; SR 98, 3 mi w on US 20, 1.3 mi s.

DEWITTVILLE — CHAUTAUQUA HEIGHTS CAMPING RESORT CAMPGROUND. (716) 386-3804. **2P $24-$33, XP $2-$4.** 5652 Thumb Rd, 14728. I-86, exit 10 westbound, 5 mi on CR 430 W; I-90, exit 60 to Mayville, 2.4 mi on CR 430 E, just e.

GARDINER — YOGI BEAR'S JELLYSTONE PARK CAMP-RESORTS AT LAZY RIVER. (845) 255-5193. **4P $50-$55, XP $4-$10.** 50 Bevier Rd, 12525. 1.5 mi w on US 44 and SR 55, 0.8 mi se on Albany Post and Bevier rds, follow signs.

GARRATTSVILLE — YOGI BEAR'S JELLYSTONE PARK AT CRYSTAL LAKE. (607) 965-8265. **4P $35-$51, XP $5-$10.** 111 E Turtle Lake Rd, 13342. Jct SR 80, 6.2 mi s on CR 16, 0.7 mi n on CR 51, then 1.1 mi w on CR 17.

GREENFIELD PARK — YOGI BEAR'S JELLYSTONE PARK CAMP-RESORT AT BIRCHWOOD ACRES. (845) 434-4743. **4P $25-$53, XP $10-$12.** 85 Martinfeld Rd, 12789. Jct US 209 and SR 52, 8 mi w on SR 52, then 0.5 mi s. (PO Box 482, WOODRIDGE).

LAKE GEORGE — LAKE GEORGE ESCAPE. (518) 623-3207. **2P $19-$48, XP $6.** 175 E Schroon River Rd, 12845. I-87, exit 23, 0.4 mi e on Diamond Point Rd, then 0.8 mi n. (PO Box 431).

OLD FORGE — OLD FORGE CAMPING RESORT. (315) 369-6011. **2P $23-$145, XP $4.** 3347 SR 28, 13420. 1 mi n. (PO Box 51).

PLATTEKILL — NEWBURGH/NEW YORK CITY NORTH KOA ▲▲▲ (845) 564-2836. **2P $31-$55, XP $4-$6.** 119 Freetown Hwy, 12568. 1.5 mi n on SR 32, 3 mi s of jct US 44 and SR 55, 0.5 mi e, follow signs.

PULASKI — BRENNAN BEACH RV PARK ▲▲▲ (315) 298-2242. **2P $29-$39, XP $5.** 80 Brennan Beach, 13142. I-81, exit 36, 4 mi w on SR 13, 1 mi n on SR 3.

QUEENSBURY — LAKE GEORGE RV PARK. (518) 792-3775. **2P $37-$60, XP $6-$10.** I-87 (New York Thruway), exit 20, 0.5 mi n on US 9, then 0.4 mi e. (74 SR 149, LAKE GEORGE, 12845).

VERONA — THE VILLAGES AT TURNING STONE. (315) 361-7275. **4P $23-$39, XP $5.** 5065 SR 365, 13478. I-90, exit 33, 1.3 mi w. (PO Box 126).

Ohio

AURORA — JELLYSTONE PARK CAMP RESORT ▲▲▲ (330) 562-9100. **2P $25-$52, XP $2-$8.** 3392 SR 82, 44255. 4 mi e.

BROOKVILLE — DAYTON TALL TIMBERS RESORT KOA. (937) 833-3888. **2P $27-$125, XP $2-$10.** 7796 Wellbaum Rd, 45309. 0.5 mi n on SR 49; jct I-70, exit 24, 0.5 mi w on Pleasant Plain Rd, 0.3 mi s.

GENEVA-ON-THE-LAKE — INDIAN CREEK CAMPING & RESORT. (440) 466-8191. **2P $30-$39, XP $3-$5.** 4710 Lake Rd E, 44041. 2 mi e on SR 531.

SHELBY — **SHELBY/MANSFIELD KOA.** (419) 347-1392. **2P $26-$51, XP $4-$8.** 6787 Baker 47, 44875. 4 mi nw on SR 39, then 4.5 mi n, follow signs. 🏊 🎾

Oregon

ASHLAND — **HOWARD PRAIRIE LAKE RESORT** [AAA] (541) 482-1979. **2P $17, XP $5.** 3249 Hyatt Prairie Rd, 97520. I-5, exit 14, 0.7 mi e on SR 66, 17 mi e on Dead Indian Memorial Rd, then 3.4 mi s. (PO Box 4709, MEDFORD, 97501). 🎾

CANNON BEACH — **RV RESORT AT CANNON BEACH** [AAA] (503) 436-2231. **2P $26-$38, XP $3.** 345 Elk Creek Rd, 97110. US 101, exit Sunset Blvd. (PO Box 1037). 🚫⛺ 🏊 🎾

EUGENE — **PREMIER RV RESORT OF EUGENE.** (541) 686-3152. **2P $31-$40, XP $3.** 33022 Van Duyn Rd, 97408. I-5, exit 199, just e, then 0.4 mi s; n of Eugene at Coburg exit. 🚫⛺ 🏊 🎾

LEBANON — **PREMIER RV RESORT AT MALLARD CREEK GOLF COURSE.** (541) 259-0070. **2P $38, XP $3.** 31958 Bellinger Scale Rd, 97355. I-5, exit 228, 5.6 mi e on SR 34 (follow south and east truck route), 1.3 mi s on Denny School Rd, 2.2 mi e on Airport Dr, 4.6 mi s on US 20, 1.1 mi ne on Waterloo Rd, just e on Berlin Rd, then 0.4 mi n. 🚫⛺ 🎾

NEWPORT — **OUTDOOR RESORTS PACIFIC SHORES MOTORCOACH RESORT.** (541) 265-3750. **4P $40-$75, XP $5.** 6225 N Coast Hwy 101, 97365. On US 101, 3.4 mi n. 🚫⛺ 🏊 🎾

SALEM — **PHOENIX RV PARK.** (503) 581-2497. **2P $25-$28, XP $2.** 4130 Silverton Rd NE, 97305. I-5, exit 256, 0.3 mi e on Market, 1 mi n on Lancaster, then just e. 🚫⛺ 🎾

SALEM — **SALEM PREMIER RV RESORT.** (503) 364-7714. **2P $27-$32, XP $3.** 4700 Salem-Dallas Hwy 22, 97304. I-5, exit 260A (Salem Pkwy), follow signs to city center, 3 mi sw to Commercial St NE, 1.4 mi s to Marion St; 4.7 mi sw from the Marion St Bridge via SR 22; 4.3 mi e of jct SR 22 and 99 W. [SD] 🚫⛺ 🏊 🎾

SISTERS — **MOUNTAIN SHADOW RV PARK** [AAA] (541) 549-7275. **$27-$30, XP $3.** 540 Hwy 20 W, 97759. On US 20, 0.3 mi w. (PO Box 938). 🚫⛺ 🏊 🎾

SISTERS — **SISTERS/BEND KOA.** (541) 549-3021. **$20-$40, XP $2-$9.** 67667 Hwy 20 W, 97701. On US 20, 3.5 mi e. [SD] 🏊 🎾

WARM SPRINGS — **KAHNEETA HIGH DESERT RESORT & CASINO RV PARK.** (541) 553-1112. **3P $40, XP $8.** 6823 Hwy 8, 97761. 11 mi ne off US 26; on Warm Springs Indian Reservation. (PO Box 1240). 🚫⛺ 🏊 🎾

WARRENTON — **ASTORIA/WARRENTON/SEASIDE KOA** [AAA] (503) 861-2606. **2P $23-$165, XP $4-$5.** 1100 NW Ridge Rd, 97121. 4.6 mi nw of jct US 101, follow signs to Fort Stevens State Park. 🏊 🎾

WELCHES — **MT. HOOD VILLAGE VACATION COTTAGES & RV RESORT** [AAA] (503) 622-4011. **4P $30-$39, XP $10-$15.** 65000 E Hwy 26, 97067. On US 26, 2 mi w. 🏊 🎾

WILSONVILLE — **PHEASANT RIDGE RV RESORT** [AAA] (503) 682-7829. **2P $28-$35, XP $1.** 8275 SW Elligsen Rd, 97070. I-5, exit 286, just e. Small pets allowed. [SD] 🚫⛺ 🏊

Pennsylvania

BAKERSVILLE — **PIONEER PARK CAMPGROUND.** (814) 445-6348. **2P $19-$30, XP $2.** Just e on SR 31, 0.5 mi s via signs. (273 Trent Rd, SOMERSET, 15501). 🏊 🎾

BEDFORD — **FRIENDSHIP VILLAGE CAMPGROUND** [AAA] (814) 623-1677. **4P $24-$30, XP $2.** 348 Friendship Village Rd, 15522. 1.3 mi w on US 30 from jct US 220, 0.5 mi n via signs. 🏊 🎾

BELLEFONTE — **BELLEFONTE/STATE COLLEGE KOA** [AAA] (814) 355-7912. **2P $25-$45, XP $3-$6.** 2481 Jacksonville Rd, 16823. I-80, exit 161, 2.5 mi ne on SR 26. 🏊 🎾

BOWMANSVILLE — **LAKE IN WOOD CAMPGROUND.** (717) 445-5525. **2P $30-$48, XP $4-$7.** 576 Yellow Hill Rd, 17555. SR 23, 4.5 mi n on SR 625, 1 mi ne on Oaklyn Dr, then 1.5 mi e, follow signs. (576 Yellow Hill Rd, NARVON). 🏊 🎾

BUTLER — **SMITH GROVE CAMPGROUND** [AAA] (724) 285-3600. **4P $16-$20, XP $1-$5. (no credit cards).** 1085 Herman Rd, 16002. SR 8, e on SR 422 to Bonnie Brook Rd, follows signs s to Herman Rd, 2 mi w. 🏊 🎾

CLAY — **STARLITE CAMPING RESORT.** (717) 733-9655. **$34-$40, XP $2-$5.** 1500 Furnace Hill Rd, 17578. US 322, 1.1 mi n on Clay Rd, 2.4 mi ne, follow signs. (1500 Furnace Hill Rd, STEVENS). 🏊 🎾

COOKSBURG — **KALYUMET CAMPGROUND** [AAA] (814) 744-9622. **4P $20-$28, XP $4.** I-80, exit 62, 2 mi e on SR 68 E to light at Clarion Courthouse, go straight for 9.5 mi. (8630 Miola Rd, LUCINDA, 16235). Small pets allowed. 🏊 🎾

ELVERSON — **WARWICK WOODS FAMILY CAMPING RESORT** [AAA] (610) 286-9655. **2P $29-$40, XP $3-$6.** 401 Trythall Rd, 19520. I-76 (Pennsylvania Tpke), exit 298 eastbound, 1 mi s on SR 10, 7.5 mi e on SR 23 to sign at Trythall Rd; exit 312 westbound, 8.5 mi n on SR 100, 5 mi w on SR 23. (PO Box 280, ST. PETERS, 19470). 🏊 🎾

ERIE — **ERIE KOA KAMPGROUNDS.** (814) 476-7706. **2P $34-$75, XP $3-$6.** I-90, exit 18, 1.3 mi s on SR 832, then 0.8 mi e; I-79, exit 174, 1.5 mi w. (6645 West Rd, MCKEAN, 16426). 🏊 🎾

FARMINGTON — **BENNER'S MEADOW RUN CAMPING & CABINS.** (724) 329-4097. **2P $25-$32, XP $3-$8.** 315 Nelson Rd, 15437. 2.5 mi n of US 40, follow signs. Small pets allowed. 🏊 🎾

GARDNERS — **MOUNTAIN CREEK CAMPGROUND** [AAA] (717) 486-7681. **2P $23-$32, XP $5.** 349 Pine Grove Rd, 17324. 2 mi w of SR 34, follow signs. 🏊 🎾

GETTYSBURG — **DRUMMER BOY CAMPING RESORT** [AAA] (717) 334-3277. **$27-$40, XP $2-$5.** 1300 Hanover Rd, 17325. 2 mi e on SR 116 at US 15 Bypass, exit Hanover Rd. 🏊 🎾

GETTYSBURG — **GETTYSBURG CAMPGROUND** [AAA] (717) 334-3304. **2P $26-$35, XP $3-$5.** 2030 Fairfield Rd, 17325. 3 mi w on SR 116 W. 🏊 🎾

GETTYSBURG — **GETTYSBURG KOA KAMPGROUND** [AAA] (717) 642-5713. **2P $22-$45, XP $3-$6.** 20 Knox Rd, 17325. 3 mi w on US 30, 3 mi s on Knoxlyn Rd, follow signs. 🏊 🎾

GETTYSBURG — **GRANITE HILL CAMPGROUND** [AAA] (717) 642-8749. **2P $20-$31, XP $2-$8.** 3340 Fairfield Rd, 17325. 5.8 mi w on SR 116. [SD] 🏊 🎾

GETTYSBURG — ROUND TOP CAMPGROUND ⒶⒶⒶ (717) 334-9565. **$20-$38, XP $1-$4.** 180 Knight Rd, 17325. 3 mi s on SR 134 at US 15.

HARRISVILLE — KOZY REST KAMPGROUND ⒶⒶⒶ (724) 735-2417. **2P $20-$24, XP $2-$4.** 449 Campground Rd, 16038. Jct SR 8, 0.3 mi e on SR 58, 2 mi n on SR 4014.

HERSHEY — HERSHEY HIGHMEADOW CAMPGROUND. (717) 534-8999. **4P $26-$41, XP $4.** 1200 Matlack Rd, 17036. 0.5 mi n on SR 39 W from jct US 322 and 422. (PO Box 866, 17033).

HOLTWOOD — MUDDY RUN RECREATION PARK. (717) 284-5850. **6P $20, XP $3.** 172 Bethesda Church Rd W, 17532. 1.8 mi ne on SR 372.

JONESTOWN — JONESTOWN KOA. (717) 865-2526. **2P $26-$45, XP $2-$4.** 145 Old Rt 22, 17038. 2 mi e on US 22 from jct SR 72, 0.5 mi s; I-81, exit 90, 5 mi se; I-78, exit 6, 5 mi w, follow signs.

KNOX — WOLF'S CAMPING RESORT ⒶⒶⒶ (814) 797-1103. **2P $15-$21, XP $2-$4.** 308 Timberwolf Run, 16232. I-80, exit 53.

LANCASTER — OLD MILL STREAM CAMPGROUND. (717) 299-2314. **4P $29-$38, XP $3.** 2249 Lincoln Hwy E, 17602. 5 mi e on US 30.

LENHARTSVILLE — ROBIN HILL CAMPING RESORT. (610) 756-6117. **$32-$38, XP $1-$4.** 149 Robin Hill Rd, 19534. I-78, exit 40 (Krumsville) or exit 35 (Lenhartsville), follow signs for 3 mi.

LICKDALE — LICKDALE CAMPGROUND. (717) 865-6411. **4P $21-$27, XP $2.** 11 Lickdale Rd, 17038. I-81, exit 90, just e.

LIVERPOOL — FERRY BOAT CAMPSITES ⒶⒶⒶ (717) 444-3200. **2P $21-$35, XP $3.** 32 Ferry Ln, 17045. 2 mi s on US 11/15.

MANHEIM — PINCH POND FAMILY CAMPGROUND & RV PARK ⒶⒶⒶ (717) 665-7640. **2P $25-$37, XP $4-$7.** 3075 Pinch Rd, 17545. I-76 (Pennsylvania Tpke), exit 266, 1 mi s on SR 72, 0.5 mi w on Cider Press Rd, then 1 mi n.

MANSFIELD — BUCKTAIL CAMPING RESORT ⒶⒶⒶ (570) 662-2923. **4P $18-$44, XP $10-$7.** 1029 Mann Creek Rd, 16933. US 15, 2nd Mansfield exit, 0.3 mi e on US 6, then 1.5 mi n on Lambs Creek Rd.

MARSHALLS CREEK — OTTER LAKE CAMP RESORT. (570) 223-0123. **2P $32-$50, XP $3-$5.** I-80, exit 309, 3 mi n on US 209, just n on SR 402, then 7 mi w on Marshalls Creek Rd. (PO Box 850, 18335).

MEADVILLE — BROOKDALE FAMILY CAMPGROUND. (814) 789-3251. **2P $24-$32, XP $5.** 25164 State Hwy 27, 16335. On SR 27, 8 mi e.

MERCERSBURG — SAUNDEROSA PARK INC. (717) 328-2216. **4P $20-$30, XP $1.** 5909 Little Cove Rd, 17236. 4.8 mi w on SR 16, 2.5 mi s on SR 456.

MERCER — JUNCTION 19-80 CAMPGROUND. (724) 748-4174. **2P $18-$31, XP $3-$5. (no credit cards).** 1266 Old Mercer Rd, 16137. I-80, exit 15, 0.3 mi s on US 19, follow signs.

MERCER — MERCER-GROVE CITY KOA. (724) 748-3160. **2P $29-$65, XP $3-$4.** 1337 Butler Pike, 16137. I-79, exit 113, 3 mi n on SR 258, follow signs.

MERCER — ROCKY SPRINGS CAMPGROUND. (724) 662-4415. **2P $17-$24, XP $2. (no credit cards).** 84 Rocky Spring Rd, Rt 318, 16137. I-80, exit 15 westbound, 2 mi n on US 19 to Butler St (SR 318), then 4.5 mi w; exit eastbound, jct I-80 and exit 4A (SR 318), 6.5 mi ne.

MILL RUN — YOGI BEAR'S JELLYSTONE PARK CAMP RESORT. (724) 455-2929. **2P $23-$28, XP $4-$6.** 839 Mill Run Rd, 15464. Just s on SR 381. (PO Box 91).

NEW COLUMBIA — NITTANY MOUNTAIN CAMPGROUND ⒶⒶⒶ (570) 568-5541. **2P $23-$35, XP $3-$5.** 2751 Millers Bottom Rd, 17856. I-80, exit 210A, 0.5 mi s on US 15, 4.5 mi w on New Columbia Rd, then 0.4 mi nw.

NEW HOLLAND — SPRING GULCH RESORT ⒶⒶⒶ (717) 354-3100. **2P $26-$52, XP $2-$6.** 475 Lynch Rd, 17557. Jct SR 23 and 897, 4 mi s on SR 897.

NORTHUMBERLAND — YOGI-ON-THE-RIVER. (570) 473-8021. **4P $29-$41, XP $2-$4.** 213 Yogi Blvd, 17857. I-80, exit 224, 2 mi e on SR 54, 8 mi s on US 11; 2.5 mi on US 11.

PINE GROVE — PINE GROVE KOA AT TWIN GROVE PARK ⒶⒶⒶ (717) 865-4602. **2P $28-$36, XP $3-$10.** 1445 Suedburg Rd, 17963. I-81, exit 100, 5 mi w on SR 443.

PORTERSVILLE — BEAR RUN CAMPGROUND ⒶⒶⒶ (724) 368-3564. **2P $24-$29, XP $2-$6.** 184 Badger Hill Rd, 16051. I-79, exit 96, 0.8 mi n on SR 488.

PORTLAND — DRIFTSTONE ON THE DELAWARE ⒶⒶⒶ (570) 897-6859. **2P $30-$37, XP $3-$5.** 4 mi s from jct SR 611 and Portland Bridge. (2731 River Rd, MOUNT BETHEL, 18343).

QUARRYVILLE — YOGI BEAR'S JELLYSTONE PARK. (717) 786-3458. **2P $30-$44, XP $2-$10.** 340 Blackburn Rd, 17566. 2.7 mi s on US 222, 1.5 mi se, follow signs.

ROBESONIA — EAGLES PEAK CAMPGROUND ⒶⒶⒶ (610) 589-4800. **4P $33-$44, XP $2-$10.** 397 Eagles Peak Rd, 19551. 2.4 mi s on SR 419 from jct US 422, 2.3 mi e, follow signs.

ROSE POINT — COOPER'S LAKE. (724) 368-8710. **2P $14, XP $7.** 205 Currie Rd, 16057. I-79, exit 99, 0.8 mi w on US 422, then 1 mi n.

SANDY LAKE — GODDARD PARK VACATION LAND CAMPGROUND. (724) 253-4645. **2P $22-$28, XP $2-$3.** 867 Georgetown Rd, 16145. I-79, exit 130, 0.3 mi w on SR 358, then 3.5 mi n, follow signs.

SHARTLESVILLE — APPALACHIAN CAMPSITES. (610) 488-6319. **4P $27-$45, XP $3-$8.** 60 Motel Dr, 19554. I-78, exit 23, 0.5 mi w on service road (entrance just past motel). (PO Box 27).

SHARTLESVILLE — MOUNTAIN SPRINGS CAMPING RESORT INC & ARENA ⒶⒶⒶ (610) 488-6859. **4P $25-$29, XP $3-$5.** 3450 Mountain Rd, 19554. I-78, exit 23, 1 mi n. (PO Box 365).

SIGEL — CAMPERS' PARADISE CAMPGROUNDS, CABINS, BED & BREAKFAST & OUTPOST. (814) 752-2393. **$21-$28, XP $4.** 37 Steele Dr, 15860. On SR 949 N, 3 mi n of SR 36.

STRASBURG — WHITE OAK CAMPGROUND ⒶⒶⒶ (717) 687-6207. **4P $22-$28, XP $3.** 3156 White Oak Rd, 17566. 3.7 mi s of Centre Square on S Decatur St/May Post Office Rd, then 0.3 mi e. (PO Box 90, 17579).

UPPER BLACK EDDY — COLONIAL WOODS FAMILY CAMPING RESORT. (610) 847-5808. **$28-$34, XP $4-$6.** 545 Lonely Cottage Dr, 18972. 1.5 mi e on Marienstein Rd from jct SR 611, then 1 mi n, follow signs.

South Carolina

HILTON HEAD ISLAND — HILTON HEAD HARBOR RV RESORT & YACHT CLUB. (843) 681-3256. **4P $36-$46, XP $2.** 43 Jenkins Rd, 29926. 0.9 mi se of Intracoastal Waterway Bridge off US 278, 0.4 mi n, follow signs.

HILTON HEAD ISLAND — OUTDOOR RESORTS' MOTORCOACH RESORT ⟨AAA⟩ (843) 785-7699. **$41-$47.** 133 Arrow Rd, 29928. 5.6 mi e on Cross Island Pkwy (US 278 toll), then just w.

NORTH MYRTLE BEACH — MYRTLE BEACH RV RESORT. (843) 249-1484. **$20-$30. (no credit cards).** 5400 Little River Neck Rd, 29582. US 17, exit Cherry Grove, just w, then 3 mi ne.

South Dakota

CHAMBERLAIN — CEDAR SHORE CAMPGROUND ⟨AAA⟩ (605) 734-5273, off season (605) 734-6376. **$25-$27.** 1500 Shoreline Dr, 57365. I-90, exit 260, 2.5 mi e on US 16 and I-90 business loop, then 1 mi ne on Mickelson country road, follow signs. (PO Box 308, 57325).

HILL CITY — RAFTER J BAR RANCH CAMPGROUND ⟨AAA⟩ (605) 574-2527. **2P $20-$38, XP $3.** 12325 Rafter J Rd, 57745. 3.3 mi s on US 16 and 385 at SR 87/244. (PO Box 128).

INTERIOR — BADLANDS WHITE RIVER KOA ⟨AAA⟩ (605) 433-5337. **2P $18-$30, XP $3.** 20720 SD Hwy 44, 57750. On SR 44, 4 mi e from jct SR 377.

MITCHELL — RIVERSIDE KOA. (605) 996-1131. **2P $21-$29, XP $3.** 41244 SD Hwy 38, 57301. I-90, exit 335, 0.5 mi n, then 0.3 mi e.

NORTH SIOUX CITY — SIOUX CITY NORTH KOA. (605) 232-4519. **2P $22-$37, XP $3.** 601 Streeter Dr, 57049. I-29, exit 2 northbound, 1 mi n on west service road; exit 4 southbound, 1 mi s on west service road.

SIOUX FALLS — YOGI BEAR CAMP RESORT. (605) 332-2233. **2P $22-$29, XP $2.** 26014 478th Ave, 57005. I-90, exit 402, just n.

Tennessee

EAST RIDGE — BEST HOLIDAY TRAV-L-PARK/CHATTANOOGA. (706) 891-9766. **2P $26-$28, XP $2.** 1709 Mack Smith Rd, 37412. I-75, exit 1 southbound; exit 1B northbound, 0.3 mi w, then 1 mi s.

EAST RIDGE — SHIPP'S RV CENTER & CAMPGROUND. (423) 892-8275. **2P $16-$23, XP $2.** 6728 Ringgold Rd, 37412. I-75, exit 1, 0.3 mi e.

GATLINBURG — OUTDOOR RESORTS OF GATLINBURG. (865) 436-5861. **4P $28-$35, XP $2.** 11.5 mi e on US 321 N. (4229 Parkway E, 37738).

NASHVILLE — NASHVILLE JELLYSTONE PARK ⟨AAA⟩ (615) 889-4225. **2P $26-$42, XP $4.** 2572 Music Valley Dr, 37214. I-40, exit 215B (Briley Pkwy); exit 12B (McGavock Pike) off SR 155, 1 mi n, follow signs.

NASHVILLE — NASHVILLE KOA. (615) 889-0286. **2P $23-$140, XP $3-$7.** 2626 Music Valley Dr, 37214. I-40, exit 215B (Briley Pkwy), 5 mi n; exit 12B (McGavock Pike).

NASHVILLE — TWO RIVERS CAMPGROUND. (615) 883-8559. **2P $27-$37, XP $3.** 2616 Music Valley Dr, 37214. I-40, exit 215B (Briley Pkwy), 5 mi n, 0.3 mi w on McGavock Pike, then 1.5 mi n.

PIGEON FORGE — CLABOUGH'S CAMPGROUND. (865) 428-1951. **4P $21-$28, XP $2.** 405 Wear's Valley Rd, 37863. 0.7 mi w of jct US 441 at traffic light 3.

PIGEON FORGE — RIVEREDGE RV PARK. (865) 453-5813. **2P $24-$32, XP $4.** 4220 Huskey St, 37863. Just off US 441 at traffic light 10.

TELLICO PLAINS — KOA TELLICO PLAINS. (423) 253-2447. **2P $19-$50, XP $2-$3.** 7310 Hwy 360, 37385. I-75, exit 60, 25 mi s on SR 68, then 1.5 mi e on SR 165.

TOWNSEND — LITTLE RIVER VILLAGE CAMPGROUND ⟨AAA⟩ (865) 448-2241. **2P $14-$41, XP $2-$4.** 8533 State Hwy 73, 37882. On SR 73, 0.3 mi w of entrance to Great Smoky Mountain National Park.

Texas

ABILENE — KOA-ABILENE. (325) 672-3681. **2P $18-$35, XP $2-$3.** 4851 W Stamford St, 79603. I-20, exit 282 (Shirley Rd), 0.5 mi w of US 83-277, follow signs.

AMARILLO — AMARILLO RV RANCH ⟨AAA⟩ (806) 373-4962. **2P $20-$30, XP $2.** 1414 Sunrise Dr, 79104. I-40, exit 74 (Whitaker Rd), 0.3 mi w on north frontage road.

AMARILLO — FORT AMARILLO RV RESORT. (806) 331-1700. **2P $28-$32, XP $2.** 10101 Amarillo Blvd, 79124. I-40, exit 64 westbound, 0.3 mi n on Soncy to Amarillo Blvd, then 1 mi w; exit 62B eastbound, 0.7 mi e.

AUSTIN — AUSTIN LONE STAR RV RESORT. (512) 444-6322. **$30-$45.** 7009 I-35 S, 78744. I-35, exit 226B/227 (Slaughter/S Congress aves) southbound; exit 228/229 (Wm Cannon Dr) northbound, on northbound frontage road.

BEAUMONT — GULF COAST RV RESORT ⟨AAA⟩ (409) 842-2285. **2P $30, XP $3-$5.** 5175 Brooks Rd, 77705. I-10, exit 846 westbound; exit 845 eastbound, follow blue signs.

BOERNE — ALAMO FIESTA RV RESORT. (830) 249-4700. **2P $24-$27, XP $3.** 33000 IH-10 W, 78006. I-10, exit 543, 1 mi w on westbound access road. Small pets allowed.

DONNA — VICTORIA PALMS RESORT. (956) 464-7801. **2P $20-$30, XP $2.** 602 E Victoria Rd, 78537. Just s of jct US 83. Small pets allowed.

GOODLETT — OLD TOWNE COTTON GIN RV PARK. (940) 674-2477. **2P $18-$23, XP $3.** 230 Market St, 79252. US 287, 1 blk e; in town. (230 Market St, QUANAH).

KERRVILLE — GUADALUPE RIVER RV RESORT. (830) 367-5676. **2P $33-$38, XP $2-$5.** 2605 Junction Hwy, 78028. I-10, exit 505 (Harper Rd), 2.5 mi s, then 2.5 mi w on SR 27.

KERRVILLE — **KERRVILLE KOA.** (830) 895-1665. **2P $18-$25, XP $2.** 2400 Goat Creek Rd, 78028. I-10, exit 501, 1.5 mi s on FM 1338.

LA FERIA — **LA FERIA RV PARK.** (956) 797-1043. **2P $20-$29, XP $2. (no credit cards).** 300 E Expwy 83, 78559. 0.3 mi e of jct US 83 and FM 506, on south frontage road. Small pets allowed.

LUBBOCK — **LUBBOCK KOA.** (806) 762-8653. **2P $96-$19, XP $2.** 5502 CR 6300, 79416. 2.5 mi nw of Loop 289 on US 84.

LUBBOCK — **LUBBOCK RV PARK** ⒶⒶⒶ (806) 747-2366. **2P $20-$24, XP $2.** 4811 N I-27, 79403. I-27, exit 9, 2 mi n of Loop 289. (PO Box 597).

MERCEDES — **ENCORE MERCEDES.** (956) 565-2044. **2P $26, XP $5.** 8000 Paradise S, 78570. On Mile 2 W Rd, just n of US 83.

MONTGOMERY — **HAVENS LANDING RV RESORT** ⒶⒶⒶ (936) 582-1200. **2P $31, XP $3.** 19785 Hwy 105 W, 77356. I-45, exit 87, 13 mi w.

SAN ANTONIO — **ADMIRALTY RV RESORT** ⒶⒶⒶ (210) 647-7878. **2P $22-$50, XP $3.** 1485 N Ellison Dr, 78251. Jct Loop 1604 and SR 151, 1.3 mi nw on SR 151 to Military Dr, just w to Ellison Dr, then 0.7 mi n.

SAN ANTONIO — **ALAMO KOA KAMPGROUND.** (210) 224-9296. **2P $23-$31, XP $3.** 602 Gembler Rd, 78219. I-35, exit Coliseum, 0.5 mi s, then 0.8 mi e; I-10, exit WW White Rd, 0.3 mi n, then 1 mi w.

SAN ANTONIO — **BLAZING STAR LUXURY RV RESORT** ⒶⒶⒶ (210) 680-7827. **2P $32-$45, XP $4.** 1120 W Loop 1604 N, 78251. Just s of Military Hwy.

SAN BENITO — **FUN-N-SUN RV RESORT** ⒶⒶⒶ (956) 399-5125. **2P $26, XP $2.** 1400 Zillock Rd, 78586. 4 mi nw from US 83 and 77, exit Paso Real Rd, 0.3 mi s on access road to FM 509, then 0.5 mi s.

SOUTH PADRE ISLAND — **LONG ISLAND VILLAGE.** (956) 943-6449. **8P $40-$45, XP $2.** 900 S Garcia St, 78597. On SR 100, turn right before crossing causeway. (PO Box 695, PORT ISABEL, 78578).

UVALDE — **QUAIL SPRINGS RV PARK.** (830) 278-8182. **2P $23-$25, XP $6-$3.** 2727 E Main St, 78801. 2.2 mi e on US 90.

WICHITA FALLS — **WICHITA FALLS RV PARK** ⒶⒶⒶ (940) 723-1532. **2P $22-$25, XP $2.** 2944 Seymour Hwy (Business 277 S), 76301. I-44, exit 1A, 1.2 mi s.

Utah

BRYCE — **RUBY'S INN CAMPGROUND TRAILER PARK** ⒶⒶⒶ (435) 834-5301, off season (435) 834-5341. **2P $26-$29, XP $2.** 1230 S Hwy 63, 84764. On SR 63, 1 mi n of Bryce Canyon Park entrance. (PO Box 640022).

FRUIT HEIGHTS — **CHERRY HILL CAMPING RESORT** ⒶⒶⒶ (801) 451-5379. **2P $20-$32, XP $2.** 1325 S Main St, 84037. I-15 N, exit 326, 1.5 mi n via US 89 and 273, follow signs; I-15 S, exit 331, 2 mi se via 2nd N and Main sts, follow signs.

MOAB — **MOAB KOA CAMPGROUND** ⒶⒶⒶ (435) 259-6682. **2P $20-$60, XP $3.** 3225 S Hwy 191, 84532. 4 mi s; e off US 191.

MOAB — **MOAB VALLEY RV & CAMPARK.** (435) 259-4469. **2P $28, XP $5.** 1773 N Hwy 191, 84532. 2 mi n, just s of Colorado River Bridge. Small pets allowed.

RICHFIELD — **RICHFIELD KOA.** (435) 896-6674. **$25-$29, XP $2-$3.** 600 W 600 S, 84701. 6 blks w of US 89 (Main St); I-70, exit 40 southbound, 2.5 mi via Main St; exit 37 northbound, 1.5 mi via 1200 S and 400 W.

ST. GEORGE — **MCARTHUR'S TEMPLE VIEW RV RESORT** ⒶⒶⒶ (435) 673-6400. **2P $22-$35, XP $2.** 975 S Main St, 84770. I-15, exit 6 (Bluff St), 0.5 mi w, then just n. Small pets allowed.

ST. GEORGE — **REDLANDS RV PARK** ⒶⒶⒶ (435) 673-9700. **2P $17-$28, XP $2.** 650 W Telegraph, 84780. I-15, exit 10, 1 mi n of St. George, just e of off ramp. Small pets allowed.

ST. GEORGE — **SETTLERS RV PARK** ⒶⒶⒶ (435) 628-1624. **2P $24, XP $2.** 1333 E 100 South, 84790. E of I-15, exit 8, then right on River Rd. Small pets allowed.

VIRGIN — **ZION RIVER RESORT RV PARK & CAMPGROUND** ⒶⒶⒶ (435) 635-8594. **4P $38-$43, XP $3.** 730 E Hwy 9, 84779. I-15, exit 16 (SR 16), 22 mi ne. (PO Box 790219).

Virginia

BIG ISLAND — **WILDWOOD CAMPGROUND.** (434) 299-5228. **2P $20-$24, XP $2-$5.** SR 130, 1.3 mi e from jct Blue Ridge Pkwy, 14 mi w of SR 29. (6252 Elon Rd, MONROE, 24574).

CHARLOTTESVILLE — **CHARLOTTESVILLE KOA.** (434) 296-9881. **2P $22-$32, XP $2-$5.** 3825 Red Hill Rd, 22903. US 29 (s of I-64), 4.2 mi e on CR 708; SR 20, 1.4 mi w on CR 708.

CHERITON — **CHERRYSTONE FAMILY CAMPING RESORT** ⒶⒶⒶ (757) 331-3063. **2P $17-$51, XP $4.** 1511 Townfields Dr, 23316. 1.5 mi w on SR 680 from jct US 13. (PO Box 545).

DOSWELL — **PARAMOUNT KINGS DOMINION CAMPGROUND** ⒶⒶⒶ (804) 876-5355. **4P $29-$39, XP $8.** 10061 Kings Dominion Blvd, 23047. I-95, exit 98, 1 mi e on SR 30; adjacent to theme park.

FRONT ROYAL — **FRONT ROYAL/WASH DC WEST KOA.** (540) 635-2741. **2P $30-$68, XP $3-$5.** 585 KOA Dr, 22630. I-66, exit 6 or 13, entrance is 2 mi s of town on US 340 S. (PO Box 274).

HAYMARKET — **GREENVILLE FARM FAMILY CAMPGROUND.** (703) 754-7944. **2P $23-$29, XP $2-$4.** 14004 Shelter Ln, 20169. I-66, exit 40, 4 mi n on US 15, just se on SR 234, then 1.5 mi n on SR 601.

LURAY — **THE COUNTRY WAYE CAMPGROUND** ⒶⒶⒶ (540) 743-7222. **2P $22-$36, XP $3-$5.** 3402 Kimball Rd, 22835. Jct US 211, 2 mi n on US 340, then 0.3 mi e on SR 658.

LURAY — **YOGI BEAR'S JELLYSTONE PARK** ⒶⒶⒶ (540) 743-4002. **2P $30-$45, XP $3-$6.** 2250 Hwy 211 E, 22835. On US 211, 3 mi e. (PO Box 191).

MADISON — SHENANDOAH HILLS CAMPGROUND 🅰🅰🅰 (540) 948-4186. **2P $21-$35, XP $2-$5.** 110 Campground Ln, 22727. 2 mi s on US 29.

MARION — HUNGRY MOTHER CAMPGROUND. (276) 783-2046. **2P $20-$23, XP $2-$5. (no credit cards).** 2287 Park Blvd, 24354. I-81, exit 47, 1.3 mi sw on US 11, then 2.5 mi n on SR 16. (PO Box 106).

MEADOWS OF DAN — MEADOWS OF DAN CAMPGROUND 🅰🅰🅰 (276) 952-2292. **2P $18-$24, XP $1-$2.** 2182 JEB Stuart Hwy, 24120. US 58, just w of Blue Ridge Pkwy.

MINT SPRING — WALNUT HILLS CAMPGROUND. (540) 337-3920. **2P $25-$33, XP $3.** I-81, exit 217, 0.7 mi w to US 11, 1.5 mi s, then 1.2 mi e on SR 655. (484 Walnut Hills Rd, STAUNTON, 24401).

NATURAL BRIDGE — NATURAL BRIDGE KOA KAMP-GROUND 🅰🅰🅰 (540) 291-2770. **2P $20-$49, XP $2-$4.** 214 Kildeer Ln, 24578. I-81, exit 180 northbound; exit 180B southbound, just nw on US 11. (PO Box 148).

URBANNA — BETHPAGE CAMP RESORT. (804) 758-4349. **4P $29-$39, XP $2.** 679 Brown's Ln, 23175. 1 mi n of town on CR 602. (PO Box 178).

VIRGINIA BEACH — HOLIDAY TRAV-L-PARK 🅰🅰🅰 (757) 425-0249. **2P $18-$46, XP $5.** 1075 General Booth Blvd, 23451. I-264 terminus to Pacific Ave, 2.5 mi s.

VIRGINIA BEACH — OUTDOOR RESORTS/VIRGINIA BEACH. (757) 721-2020. **4P $40-$60, XP $7.** 3665 S Sandpiper Rd, 23456. I-264 terminus to Pacific Ave, 2 mi s to Rudee Inlet Bridge/General Booth Blvd, 5.6 mi s to Princess Anne Rd, 0.8 mi e to Sandbridge Rd, 5.5 mi e to Sandpiper Rd, then 3.5 mi s.

VIRGINIA BEACH — VIRGINIA BEACH KOA 🅰🅰🅰 (757) 428-1444. **6P $18-$46, XP $6.** 1240 General Booth Blvd, 23451. I-264 terminus to Pacific Ave and General Booth Blvd, 2 mi s.

Washington

BURLINGTON — BURLINGTON KOA. (360) 724-5511. **2P $23-$36, XP $3-$4.** 6397 N Green Rd, 98233. I-5, exit 232, 3.5 mi n on Old US 99.

CLARKSTON — GRANITE LAKE RV RESORT. (509) 751-1635. **4P $20-$31, XP $3.** 306 Granite Lake Dr, 99403. Just w of Snake River Bridge on US 12, just n on 5th St.

COULEE CITY — SUN LAKES PARK RESORT. (509) 632-5291. **4P $17-$27, XP $5.** 34228 Park Lake Rd NE, 99115. US 2, 4 mi s on SR 17.

EPHRATA — STARS AND STRIPES RV PARK & DRIVING RANGE. (509) 787-1062. **4P $18-$20, XP $2.** 5707 US 28 W, 98823. 5 mi w.

LYNDEN — LYNDEN KOA. (360) 354-4772. **2P $20-$57, XP $5.** 8717 Line Rd, 98264. 1.7 mi n of downtown on SR 539 (Guide Meridian Rd), 3 mi e on SR 546 (E Badger Rd), then 0.5 mi s.

MEAD — ALDERWOOD RV RESORT. (509) 467-5320. **2P $25-$37, XP $3.** 14007 N Newport Hwy, 99021. I-90, exit 281, 6 mi n, then 4 mi ne via US 2.

OAK HARBOR — NORTH WHIDBEY RV PARK. (360) 675-9597. **4P $25, XP $2.** 565 W Cornet Bay Rd, 98277. On SR 20, 1 mi s of Deception Pass Bridge, 8 mi n of Oak Harbor.

PORT ANGELES — PORT ANGELES/SEQUIM KOA. (360) 457-5916. **2P $20-$39, XP $2-$5.** 80 O'Brien Rd & US 101 E, 98362. 7 mi e on US 101; 8 mi w of Sequim on US 101, just e of US 101, MM 255.

SPOKANE VALLEY — SPOKANE KOA. (509) 924-4722. **2P $20, XP $2-$3.** I-90, exit 293, 1.5 mi n. (3025 N Barker Rd, OTIS ORCHARDS, 99027).

SPOKANE — YOGI BEAR'S CAMP RESORT. (509) 747-9415. **4P $25-$40, XP $5.** 7520 S Thomas Mallen Rd, 99004. I-90, exit 272, 2 mi s.

Wisconsin

BAGLEY — YOGI BEAR'S JELLYSTONE PARK CAMP RESORT. (608) 996-2201. **4P $20-$38, XP $6.** 11354 CR X, 53801. 1.3 mi n.

ELKHART LAKE — PLYMOUTH ROCK CAMPING RESORT. (920) 892-4252. **$28-$40.** N7271 Lando St, 53073. 3 mi s on SR 67, 4 mi n of Plymouth. (PO Box 445, 53020).

FORT ATKINSON — JELLYSTONE PARK OF FORT ATKINSON. (920) 568-4100. **4P $28-$34, XP $5-$9.** N 551 Wishing Well Dr, 53538. 5 mi s on SR 26 from jct US 12, 0.8 mi w on Koshkonong Lake Rd, then just s. Small pets allowed.

FREMONT — YOGI BEAR'S JELLYSTONE PARK CAMP RESORT. (920) 446-3420. **2P $18-$58, XP $10.** E 6506 Hwy 110, 54940. On SR 110 N, 1.5 mi w. (PO Box 497).

WARRENS — YOGI BEAR'S JELLYSTONE PARK CAMP RESORT. (608) 378-4977. **$20-$50, XP $3-$6.** 23694 CR EW, 54666. I-94, exit 135, 0.5 mi e.

WISCONSIN DELLS — YOGI BEAR'S JELLYSTONE PARK CAMP-RESORT 🅰🅰🅰 (608) 254-2568. **4P $17-$79, XP $4-$8.** I-90/94, exit 89 eastbound; exit 92 westbound, follow signs. (PO Box 510, 53965).

West Virginia

HARPERS FERRY — HARPERS FERRY/WASHINGTON D.C. NW KOA 🅰🅰🅰 (304) 535-6895. **2P $24-$45, XP $4-$5.** 343 Campground Rd, 25425. 1 mi sw on US 340 from Shenandoah River Bridge, 0.3 mi s, follow signs.

MILTON — FOX FIRE CAMPING RESORT. (304) 743-5622. **$24-$32, XP $3. (no credit cards).** US 60, 25541. I-64, exit 28, 0.3 mi s, then 2.7 mi w. (Rt 2, Box 655).

SUMMERSVILLE — MOUNTAIN LAKE CAMPGROUND 🅰🅰🅰 (304) 872-4220. **2P $14-$17, XP $1-$6.** Airport Rd, 26651. 1.5 mi s on US 19 from jct SR 39, 1.8 mi w. (PO Box 486).

CANADA

Alberta

CALGARY — PINE CREEK R.V. CAMPGROUND. (403) 256-3002. **2P $28-$30, XP $2.** 3.1 km s on Hwy 2A from Hwy 22X overpass. (PO Box 174, DE WINTON, T0L 0X0).

EDMONTON — GLOWING EMBERS TRAVEL CENTRE & RV PARK ⒸⒶⒶ (780) 962-8100. **4P $27-$30, XP $1.** 26309 Hwy 16A, T7X 5A6. 3 km w of city limits; 1.8 km sw from Devon exit (Hwy 60 S), follow signs. (26309 Hwy 16A, ACHESON).

HINTON — HINTON/JASPER KOA ⒸⒶⒶ (780) 865-5062, off season (403) 288-8351. **2P $20-$38, XP $3-$5.** Hwy 16, T9B 1X3. On Hwy 16, 4 km w. (4720 Vegas Rd NW, CALGARY, T3A 1W3).

OKOTOKS — COUNTRY LANE RV PARK. (403) 995-2330. **$32-$34.** E on Hwy 7 and 2A; jct Hwys 2, 7 and 2A. (PO Box 1530, T1S 1B4).

PINE LAKE — LEISURE CAMPGROUNDS. (403) 886-4705. **$22-$39.** On Hwy 42, 25 km e off Hwy 2. (PO Box 68, T0M 1S0).

SUNDRE — TALL TIMBER LEISURE PARK. (403) 638-3555. **2P $24-$30, XP $5.** 1 km e of Centre St on Main Ave E (Hwy 27 E). (PO Box 210, T0M 1X0).

British Columbia

ABBOTSFORD — ABBOTSFORD CAMP & RV PARK. (604) 855-3330. **2P $23-$28, XP $2.** 36114 Lower Sumas Mountain Rd, V3G 2J3. Trans-Canada Hwy 1, exit 95 (Whatcom Rd), just n to Lower Sumas Mountain Rd, follow signs.

BURNABY — BURNABY CARIBOO R.V. PARK ⒸⒶⒶ (604) 420-1722. **$30-$44, XP $3-$5.** 8765 Cariboo Pl, V3N 4T2. Trans-Canada Hwy 1, exit 37 (Cariboo Rd), follow signs.

CAMPBELL RIVER — RIPPLE ROCK RV PARK. (250) 287-7108. **2P $25-$33, XP $3.** 15011 Browns Bay Rd, V9H 1N9. Jct Hwy 19A, 28 and 19, 19 km n on Hwy 19, then 4.5 km e.

FAIRMONT HOT SPRINGS — FAIRMONT HOT SPRINGS RV PARK. (250) 345-6033. **$21-$47.** 1.6 km e off Hwy 93 and 95; adjacent to Fairmont Hot Springs Resort. (PO Box 10, V0B 1L0).

OLIVER — DESERT GEM RV RESORT ⒸⒶⒶ (250) 498-5544. **2P $17-$31, XP $2.** 34037 Hwy 97, V0H 1T0. 1 km s from 342nd Ave. (PO Box 400).

SURREY — PEACE ARCH RV PARK. (604) 594-7009. **$6-$28, XP $2.** 14601 40th Ave, V3S 0L2. Hwy 99, exit 10, follow signs.

VICTORIA — VICTORIA WEST KOA. (250) 478-3332. **2P $30-$32, XP $4-$6.** On Trans-Canada Hwy 1 (Malahat Dr), 25.6 km n of Victoria. (PO Box 103, MALAHAT, V0R 2L0).

WHISTLER — RIVERSIDE RV RESORT AND CAMPGROUND. (604) 905-5533. **2P $40-$45, XP $5.** 8018 Mons Rd, V0N 1B8. Hwy 99 (Upper Village), 1.5 km n. Small pets allowed.

New Brunswick

WOODSTOCK — YOGI BEAR'S JELLYSTONE PARK AT KOZY ACRES. (506) 328-6287. **5P $28-$36, XP $5-$6.** Trans-Canada Hwy 2, exit 191 (Beardsley Rd). (PO Box 9004, E7M 6B5).

Nova Scotia

BADDECK — BADDECK-CABOT TRAIL CAMPGROUND & GOOD SAM PARK ⒸⒶⒶ (902) 295-2288. **4P $22-$30, XP $3-$4.** 9584 Trans-Canada Hwy 105, B0E 1B0. 8 km w. (PO Box 417).

Ontario

AMHERSTBURG — YOGI BEAR JELLYSTONE PARK CAMP RESORTS. (519) 736-3201. **$34-$42, XP $2-$10.** 4610 County Rd 18, RR 1, N9V 2Y7. 4 km e on Pike Rd (Simco St).

BRADFORD — YOGI BEAR'S JELLYSTONE PARK & CAMP-RESORT ⒸⒶⒶ (905) 775-1377. **2P $32-$43, XP $6-$8.** 3666 Simcoe Rd 88, L3Z 2A4. Hwy 400, exit 64B, jct of Hwy 400 and Simcoe Rd 88. (RR 1, 3666 Simcoe Rd 88). Small pets allowed.

FOREST — OUR PONDEROSA FAMILY CAMPGROUND & GOLF RESORT. (519) 786-2031. **$25-$50.** 9338 W Ipperwash Rd, N0N 1J0. 3 km n on W Ipperwash Rd from jct CR 7. (RR 2).

KINCARDINE — FISHERMAN'S COVE TENT & TRAILER PARK LTD. (519) 395-2757. **2P $32-$38, XP $3-$4.** 13 Southline Ave, N2Z 2X5. Jct Hwy 21 and 9, 17.7 km e to Kinloss, then 3 km s; follow signs. (RR 4).

KITCHENER — BINGEMANS. (519) 744-1002. **6P $29-$40, XP $6.** 4250 Bingemans Centre Dr, N2B 3X7. 5.6 km on Hwy 7, 1.6 km e of jct Hwy 7 and Conestoga Pkwy (Hwy 86).

NIAGARA FALLS — CAMPARK RESORTS ⒸⒶⒶ (905) 358-3873. **2P $33-$48, XP $5.** 9387 Lundy's Ln, L2E 6S4. 6.3 km w of falls on Hwy 20.

NIAGARA FALLS — NIAGARA FALLS KOA KAMPGROUND. (905) 356-2267. **2P $33-$110, XP $4-$7.** 8625 Lundy's Ln, L2H 1H5. 5.6 km w on Hwy 20.

SAUBLE BEACH — CARSON'S CAMP LTD. (519) 422-1143. **2P $23-$35, XP $3-$7. (no credit cards).** 110 Southampton Pkwy, N0H 2G0. 1 km s on CR 13. (Rt 1).

SAUBLE BEACH — WOODLAND PARK. (519) 422-1161. **2P $25-$40, XP $2-$15.** 47 Sauble Falls Pkwy, RR 1, N0H 2G0. 1 km n on CR 13.

Québec

LEVIS — KOA-QUEBEC CITY. (418) 831-1813. **2P $21-$38, XP $2-$5.** 684 chemin Olivier, G7A 2N6. Hwy 20, exit 311, 1.5 km w, northside service road; in St-Nicolas sector.

ST-MATHIEU-DE-BELOEIL — CAMPING ALOUETTE ⒸⒶⒶ (450) 464-1661. **2P $25-$35, XP $2.** 3449 de l'Industrie, J3G 4S5. Hwy 20, exit 105; follow signs.

STE-SABINE — CAMPING CARAVELLE. (450) 293-7637. **2P $21-$28, XP $3. (no credit cards).** 180 Rang de la Gare, J0J 2B0. Jct Rt 104, 4.7 km s on Rt 235, then 0.8 km w on Rang de la Gare; 6 km s of Farnham.